PREFACE

This *Wisden*, the 131st edition, is the first to be produced since the publisher, John Wisden and Co., was taken over by J. Paul Getty. Mr Getty has become known for his generosity towards good cricketing causes. This, however, was a slightly different case since John Wisden is a business and, I am happy to say, a profitable one.

It is still being run as such. But Mr Getty said that his major objective was to continue and enhance the Almanack. And I am grateful for the support I have received towards that end from him, his son Mark, who is also a director, and my fellow-members of the new management committee. Mr Getty also said that he would maintain *Wisden's* traditional editorial independence and he has kept his word.

Thus the responsibility for the contents of the 1994 *Wisden* is, as ever, entirely that of the editor and I cannot blame the boss if something has gone horribly wrong. There was a gratifyingly warm response to the structural modifications introduced in last year's Almanack. There is one last major change contingent on that: the Births and Deaths have had to move closer to the front of the book, where they were in the early part of the century. This leaves the first and last sections of *Wisden* as essentially areas of opinion, with the facts in between. If you live in a lovely old house, it is always irritating, but sometimes necessary, to get the builders in; I believe the fabric is now sound enough, though there is always scope for improvements.

This *Wisden* contains a supplementary obituary. Since the Almanack began including an obituary in 1892, inevitably some important and interesting people have been missed – very often because they had drifted far enough away from the game for their deaths not to be reported.

The tireless work of Robert Brooke has enabled us to fill in a good many of the gaps. This supplement means that every England and Australian Test player (of those who have died since 1891) has now had a *Wisden* obituary and so have all the most significant figures from elsewhere. I hope this will help the game's scholars. I also hope cricket's less studious followers will be diverted by the only man given out twice for obstruction, a first-class cricketer who never got on the field, a John Major who did not become prime minister and many other characters.

The 1994 Almanack also contains a selection of the more remarkable and eccentric cricketing happenings of 1993 outside first-class cricket. Some people think *Wisden* has always reported such things. That is unfortunately not true, but I see no reason why it should not be true henceforth. *Wisden* remains, above all, a serious volume recording a serious game, but much of cricket's richness derives from its curiosities and its humour and it is proper that we should record them too.

I trust readers will find a number of other improvements that enhance the Almanack as well as continue it. My thanks go to all the contributors, who are listed as usual. My special thanks go to Harriet Monkhouse, the assistant editor, Christine Forrest, the production editor, Peter Bather and Mike Smith of our typesetters Spottiswoode Ballantyne, Gordon Burling, Bill Frindall, John Kitchin, Andrew Radd, Roy Smart and Marcus Williams, as well as to my colleagues on *The Guardian* and, above all, to Hilary and Laurie, my wife and son.

MATTHEW ENGEL

Newton St Margarets,
Herefordshire,
January 1994

LIST OF CONTRIBUTORS

Jack Arlidge
Chris Aspin
Jack Bailey
Philip Bailey
Jack Bannister
Greg Baum
Brian Bearshaw
Michael Berry
Edward Bevan
J. Watson Blair
Shaun Botterill
Dennis Bradley
Robert Brooke
Colin Bryden
John Callaghan
Ian Chappell
Charlie Chelliah
Mike Coward
Tony Cozier
John Cribbin
Jon Culley
Noah Davidson
Gareth A. Davies
Bill Day
Geoffrey Dean
Norman de Mesquita
Patrick Eagar
Ken Farmiloe
Brian Fell
Paton Fenton
James Ferguson
T. J. Finlayson
David Foot
Peter Foster
Bill Frindall

David Frith
Nigel Fuller
Simone Gambino
Andrew Gidley
Russell Grant
David Hallett
Maurice F. Hankey
David Hardy
Peter Hargreaves
Norman Harris
Peter Hayter
Murray Hedgcock
Simon Hewitt
Frank Heydenrych
Eric Hill
Philip Hoare
Grenville Holland
Gerald Howat
John Jameson
Martin Johnson
Peter Johnson
Abid Ali Kazi
John Kitchin
Peter Knight
Sri Krishnamurthi
Chris Lander
Ken Lawrence
Steve Lindsell
David Llewellyn
David Lloyd
Nick Lucy
John MacKinnon
Joe Mann
Vic Marks
Christopher Martin-Jenkins

R. Mohan
Brendan Monks
Chris Moore
Geoffrey Moorhouse
Graham Morris
Gerald Mortimer
David Munden
Patrick Murphy
Mike Neasom
Peter Nixon
Terry Power
Andrew Radd
Mark Ray
Amanda Ripley
Dicky Rutnagur
Carol Salmon
Wayne Satchell
Derek Scott
Jasmer Singh
Bill Smith
Patrick Smithers
Richard Streeton
Paul Sturgess
E. W. Swanton
John Thicknesse
Bob Thomas
Jan Traylen
Sudhir Vaidya
Gerry Vaidyasekera
Paul Weaver
Tim Wellock
Bruce Wilson
John Woodcock
Terry Yates-Round

Thanks are also accorded to the following for checking the scorecards of first-class matches: M. R. L. W. Ayers, L. Beaumont, G. R. Blackburn, Mrs C. Byatt, L. V. Chandler, W. Davies, A. E. Davis, B. T. Denning, J. C. Foley, G. S. Gordon, B. Hunt, V. H Isaacs, B. H. Jenkins, D. Kendix, A. C. Kingston, A. R. May, D. A. Oldam, S. W. Tacey, M. K. Walsh and R. D. Wilkinson.

The editor also acknowledges with gratitude assistance from the following: Graham Allen, David Armstrong, Clive Attenborough, Mike Averis, Peter Baxter, June Bayliss, Sir William Becher, Karena Birks, David Boardman, Dick Brittenden, Mark Campkin, Andrew Coad, James Colabavala, Andrew Collomosse, Geoffrey Copinger, Brian Croudy, John Featherstone, Cris Freddi, Ghulam Mustafa Khan, Stephen Green, Bridget Griffiths, Bob Harragan, Les Hatton, Brian Hilton, Clive Hitchcock, Lt-Col. K. Hitchcock, Derek Hodgson, Ken Ingman, David Jeater, Kate Jenkins, Patrick Keane, Frank Keating, Peter Knapp, Stephanie Lawrence, Alan Lee, Malcolm Lorimer, Steven Lynch, Colin Maynard, Allan Miller, Arthur Milton, Oscar Morse, Soren Nissen, Qasim E. Noorani, Charles Oliver, Francis Payne, S. S. Perera, S. Pervez Qaiser, Rex Roberts, Dan Ruparel, Ahmed Saidullah, Geoffrey Saulez, Karen Spink, Andrew Tupling, David Walsh, John Ward, Wendy Wimbush and Peter Wynne-Thomas.

The production of *Wisden* would not be possible without the support and co-operation of many other cricket officials, writers and lovers of the game. To them all, many thanks.

CONTENTS

Part Four: Overseas Cricket in 1992-93

Addresses of first-class and minor counties can now be found on pages 1252-3.

PART ONE: COMMENT

NOTES BY THE EDITOR

Shortly after lunch on the first day of the Edgbaston Test in 1993, Shane Warne was bowling leg-breaks to Alec Stewart, who had momentarily discarded both his helmet and his faded baseball cap in favour of a real, old-fashioned, three lions of England version. As he pushed forward, he looked the image of his father at the crease. Behind the stumps, there was Ian Healy wearing his baggy cap and air of ageless Australian aggression. And there was Warne, bowling beautifully with a method thought to have been relegated to the museum.

For a moment the years seemed to roll away. The detail of the cricket was suspended; the game was overtaken by the timelessness of the scene. It was summer in England and all was well. Then, of course, Stewart got out and everything became secondary to the fact that we were being licked again. Of England's national traumas, more later. In a number of respects cricket had a very good year in 1993. In England, India and Australia, crowds showed they would respond to the thrill of an exciting Test series, as well as to the gimcrack appeal of one-day cricket. Warne was the most talked-about player of the year and single-handedly did a huge amount to switch cricket back into a game where the batsman's fear is of mental torture rather than physical.

South Africa and Zimbabwe began to play more of a part in the comity of Test-playing nations. The women's World Cup was a success, and a success for England at that. And, cautiously, the game began to show signs of expansion round the world. It is best not to get over-excited about the prospects: soccer is not on the brink of being dethroned. Indeed, in some of cricket's heartlands, in the West Indies and the English cities, the game is under threat from simpler, cheaper pastimes: basketball on the one hand, computer games on the other. But when Malaysia talks of achieving Test status by the year 2020, it would be wise not to be too dismissive: things happen in that part of the world when they put their minds to it.

The year also saw the transformation of the International Cricket Council, newly independent of MCC and with its headquarters in a discreet little office on the other side of Lord's in what used to be the staff canteen. This, rather than the pavilion, is now the centre of power in world cricket. But it is the new secretary of MCC, Roger Knight, who gets the room with the view. From his office, the ICC chief executive, David Richards, can see about a square yard of the outfield.

In other respects, the new world order has brought changes, starting with the arrival of what they would prefer us not to call "neutral" umpires (all umpires are neutral, these are "third-country"), one in each Test for at least the next three years. This seems to me as essential a rite of passage for cricket as the change in ICC itself.

However, 1993 was also the year when the system of umpiring by video spread to engulf the Test-playing world. I may be in a minority; I remain utterly convinced that this is a disaster. Umpires can now call for help from a third official watching the TV replay on run-outs, stumpings and, sometimes, boundary decisions; indeed, they can hardly not do so. It is true that last year one or two players in Test matches may have been given in or out more

Notes by the Editor

accurately than would otherwise have been the case. What we also saw was very good umpires virtually giving up on their duties at square leg, knowing there was no point in even contemplating making a judgment: it could only get them into trouble; why take the risk? Remember that it was a couple of outrageously wrong decisions that led to the demand for this system, not a lot of marginal ones. We saw players starting to pressurise umpires if they did not call for a replay. And we saw increasing demands (sometimes on the field) for the system to be extended to close catches as well. The heart of the game, the finality of the umpire's verdict, is being eaten away.

Exeunt (almost) omnes

In another way, 1993 was an especially poignant year. In a full lifetime the diligent cricket-watcher might expect to watch four generations of players. Normally the change is imperceptible, as old soldiers fade away and new ones emerge. In 1993 one sensed the torch being passed from one generation of players to the next at frightening speed. Three of the greatest cricketers of our time, perhaps the three greatest, all announced their retirement: Ian Botham, David Gower and Viv Richards. The tributes begin on page 33. The magnificence of their best days will live for ever – and for that we should be grateful to the technology that brought us video umpiring (though in each case certain aspects of their game should perhaps be prefaced by the kind of warning they give when Superman jumps out of a window – Children: do not hit across the line like Viv, it's dangerous). It is always hard to imagine that a new generation will ever again produce players of such character.

Gower's retirement was accompanied by a particular sense of futility, because it was so unnecessary. As he proved in the closing weeks of the season, he was still a beautiful batsman; it would be too much to hope to see such an instinctive timer of a ball again. But I think the selectors were as right to ignore him for the 1993-94 winter tour as they were wrong 12 months earlier: with a new England captain, Mike Atherton, it was time to move on. And the bitter truth, as his financial advisers must have told him, is that Gower had to give up playing. The income available to him for writing about cricket (which he does adequately) and broadcasting (which he does tolerably well) was probably about four times as much as he could earn simply by playing (which he could still do sublimely).

In such a year, it is easy to overlook a lengthy list of other very, very good cricketers who have retired. Richards, Botham and Gower played for seven counties between them. Derek Randall was perhaps the last of the true local heroes – it was impossible to imagine him playing for anyone except Nottinghamshire. Yet his fame spread from Retford round the globe. On the 1982-83 Ashes tour, I met a man in a bar in a South Australian bush town. "That Randall," he said, "he bats like an octopus with piles." He did too, but he also brought a wonderful impish delight to all his cricket, his fielding most of all. Standing on the boundary in Palmerston North in 1983-84, he dived to his right and stuck out an arm to catch an extremely hard-hit shot. It would have been an amazing catch on its own. But in the same movement Randall switched the ball to his left hand and tossed it over his left shoulder. He might have been practising the trick all his life.

On the 1982-83 tour Chris Tavaré and Derek Pringle both became sort of folk-villains: Tavaré because of his slow play, Pringle because of his look of slightly gormless insouciance. They never quite shook off the reputations they won then, though in later years Tavaré would whack the off-spinners back over their heads far more often and Pringle's professionalism was good enough to keep him in the England team even under that stern judge, Graham Gooch. Either of them, had the wind blown slightly differently, might have been runners for the England captaincy, at least in 1988 when everyone had a crack. (Indeed, Pringle did do the job for a few hours at The Oval when Gooch was injured.) Tavaré, I think, might have found the limelight too blinding; Pringle's batting never flowered in county cricket as it did when he was such a commanding undergraduate at Cambridge and, anyway, he was far too lateral a thinker. Neil Foster has also retired: he was a very fine fast-medium bowler, though his body and (on occasion) his temperament rebelled against the demands placed on them. I shall miss too Kris Srikkanth, whose practice of opening Test matches as if he were Gilbert Jessop on speed finally laid to rest the idea that Indian batsmanship was inherently boring, and the New Zealander John Wright, not only for his batting, but for having the most beautiful manners of his generation. Most cricketers grunt when yet another ghastly hack introduces himself; when I first met Wright, years ago, he not only smiled, he stood up.

Goodness knows how they will all be replaced, though Pringle is another who will not be far away having, like Gower, given up the game prematurely for the apparent greater security and reasonable money of a cricket correspondent's job. Soon cricketers, the moment they have made a reputation, will go off and cash in on it by doing something else, in the way that Derby-winners are immediately sent to stud. When Richards and Botham met on the field in Championship matches, their presence did little to help the attendance. Put them on stage to banter with each other (a form of entertainment for which their gifts are less obvious), call it a roadshow, and the crowds flock in. The air is filled with the sound of ex-first-class players making a decent living from after-dinner speaking. The interest in hearing about cricket, as opposed to watching it, is enormous, which is one reason why the death of Brian Johnston in the first days of 1994 was felt so keenly.

The rewards at the top level of cricket may sound enticing. But how many Australian sportsmen are better-known than Allan Border? Greg Norman, perhaps. Last year 20 of them earned more money than Border, including a 16-year-old baseball pitcher, two golfers in their late 50s and a tennis player ranked outside the top 100. According to a survey in the Melbourne paper, the *Sunday Age*, Border earned $A848,000. That's not far off £400,000, but half of it came from book sales and a quarter from endorsements. It may beat working but Border, remember, is at the very top, and, according to the survey, it only just beats being a fairly obscure footballer playing in the French First Division.

Hats off

One can hardly expect every professional sportsman to be as well brought up as John Wright. But if cricketers do want to be better-paid they could work harder at justifying it. When actors take their bow at the end of a performance, they do not turn round and face the wings. It is hard to imagine anything more insulting to the paying public than a batsman who scores fifty or a hundred and waves his bat only at his team-mates. Since many modern cricketers are so anonymous, it might also be in their interests – as well as good manners – to take their helmets off as they do so. It should certainly be accepted etiquette that players remove their helmets before leaving the field, especially after a long innings, so spectators can see them as they applaud them in.

In return, spectators could start to behave better too. But cricket has some difficulty addressing the problems caused by drunks: Yorkshire's announcement that they would eject anyone who caused trouble by chanting was printed on a letterhead bearing the Tetley Bitter logo. And I suppose there may be someone, somewhere, who goes along with the notion that the ground is actually called Bass Headingley. The popularity of the dreary old Mexican Wave remains baffling, especially as its arrival seems to bear no relation to the state of the game. Why it should have started on the Sunday afternoon at Old Trafford when Warne and Mike Gatting were staging one of the most magnificent duels in modern Test cricket is completely bewildering.

The last days of Goochie and Ted

From that passage of play sprang all the events of the series: the removal of Gatting as a candidate for the England captaincy; the collapse of English morale and Australia's growing belief that, even without Craig McDermott, they were invulnerable; the selectors' desperate thrashing about; Gooch's loss of authority and his resignation, followed by Ted Dexter's resignation as chairman of selectors and the apotheosis, at The Oval, of a new, young and vigorous-looking captain in Atherton. The Ashes series of 1993 was extremely one-sided – all of them have been, one way or the other, for many years now – and the season was damp. But it was still entirely riveting. The grounds were full and both nations transfixed – in England by the extent of the horror, if nothing else. Before England's victory at The Oval, they had lost nine Tests out of ten. The summer ranked with the worst years of breast-beating and navel-contemplation: 1989, 1988, 1984, 1976 . . .

The 1993 series came immediately after a particularly unsuccessful tour of India and Sri Lanka – one well up with the worst of all time. Someone had to carry the can and both Dexter and Gooch did. The manager, Keith Fletcher, largely escaped criticism, even though the desperate sequence began when he took over from Micky Stewart, while Dexter and Gooch had each been in place since 1989, not without some success.

Fletcher had the sense to keep his head some distance below the parapet. Dexter, in contrast, stood there with a very English, if slightly batty, heroism as shot and shell flew about him. The people responsible for the absurdly overstated and doltishly brutal abuse in the tabloid press will have to answer to their consciences. My suspicion is that history will regard Dexter more kindly than either the newspapers or the Test match crowd who cheered his resignation. It might then be easier to put his four years in context with the amateurish shambles that preceded them.

Dexter set out to impose a logical system of international recognition for young players, leading up to the England team. He did bring in a more sensible selection system. This did not necessarily mean more sensible selections. But when you see Alan Knott spend an entire match at Abergavenny by the sightscreen with binoculars, to report on whether Colin Metson might be a better wicket-keeper than Jack Russell – something that would have been unthinkable before Dexter – you realise that not every development has been a negative one.

Though Dexter stoically took the blame for everything, he had made a conscious decision to apply a light touch and let the manager and captain take day-to-day control. His touch was almost certainly too light: when he wanted Gatting rather than Gower as captain in 1989 and was blocked by the chairman of the cricket committee, Ossie Wheatley, he should have screamed the place down, not taken it on the chin. I reckon he would have got his way. He should certainly have been more closely involved in 1993.

For a professional public relations man, he was also surprisingly inept at that part of the operation. In public, he kept silent when explanations were required, and kept talking (eventually saying something that was either daft or could be twisted to sound daft) when he should have shut up. In private, he failed – crucially – to win the support of the county chairmen.

They felt slighted when Dexter's system of an England committee, responsible for the best players in all age groups, was first foisted on them, as they saw it, by the TCCB executive. It was accompanied by a great deal of ill-considered propaganda from various sources about the counties being selfish and parochial and holding back the visionaries who wanted to make English cricket great again. Dexter had a powerful vision but he failed to let enough people see the picture. Part of his legacy will survive: regular A tours, the age-group squads, the system of identifying the best players at every level and giving them the best coaches and facilities. As far as selection is concerned, we now look like returning to a worse version of the old committee-room mess which could lead to the chairman, the manager, the captain and the other selectors all pulling against each other. In the short run, things can only get better than they were last summer. In the long run, I fear the worst.

Alphabet soup

When the hoi polloi rebelled against the omission of Gower from the Indian tour, the MCC committee fobbed them off with a working party under Lord Griffiths. In January 1994 Griffiths reported and proposed the abolition of the Cricket Council and the merger of the TCCB and NCA, sensible-sounding administrative simplications, but nothing to do with Gower and not of much interest to the hoi polloi. The Report said little about the confusion that exists where it matters most.

I am grateful to Ralph Dellor for explaining how the career of a cricketer in Berkshire might go. It starts in the Under-11s, where the team is run by the Berkshire Schools Cricket Association, the BSCA; it goes on to the Under-12s, run by the Berkshire Cricket Association, the BCA; for the Under-13s the two bodies run a joint team; then come the Under-14s (controlled by the BCA), the Under-15s (back to the BSCA) and the Under-16s (the BCA again). Clear? I thought not. At Under-19 there are three teams, because the Berkshire County Cricket Club, the BCCC, is also involved. That runs the Under-25 team and the senior team. But the BCA also has a senior team. And it runs the over-50s.

This may sound like boring administrative detail. The effect is ludicrous. And Berkshire is merely a microcosm of what occurs all over England; indeed, in the first-class counties, it can get more complicated. There are few enough gifted young cricketers; but when one gets identified, different organisations fight for his time like warring parents demanding custody and visiting rights. It is not unknown for different organisations to schedule fixtures involving the same boys on the same day. It is quite common for youngsters to get involved in so many different games run by so many squabbling bodies they find themselves fed up by mid-July.

Meanwhile, millions of other youngsters never even pick up a cricket bat. They cannot play in the streets because there is too much traffic and their parents are terrified of crime. Their schools have given up the game because it is too expensive, too complicated and too boring for 19 children out of 22 at any one time. Anyway, their summer terms are too short. Many school-teachers are also uncomfortable with anything to do with the unearthing of individual excellence.

There are many fine and dedicated people working with young cricketers, using both the traditional form of the game and more child-friendly versions like Kwik Cricket. One fears it can never be enough. The simplistic think England lose cricket matches solely because Boggins was picked instead of Snoggins. More subtle reasoners think it is because the counties are doing everything wrong. The roots of the problem run much deeper.

After Murray

The 1994 first-class season in England was the first given over to four-day cricket. By the end of it even the most conservative of cricket's constituencies, the county members, appeared to have accepted the principle of the change. Undoubtedly four-day cricket is better than three-day cricket *had become* on the dead wickets of modern England. There is no evidence yet that it is any better than three-day cricket once was. The orthodoxy of the moment is that players have to be allowed to build innings of Test-match length. One is now terrified to shout "Get on with it" to a boring blocker, in case this in some way inhibits the development of the poor darling. I believe that if the counties played less one-day cricket their players would be better able to develop classical technique and still entertain the public.

The other changes wrought by the Murray Report, which the counties were forced to accept en bloc, were, predictably, less successful. The 50-over Sunday League was a hopeless compromise between irreconcilable objectives – proper cricket and junk marketing – and was dumped after a season. At least a 40-over Sunday game does not go on too long. The idea of an all-knockout Benson and Hedges Cup was not wholly bad but it was imbecilic to schedule the opening round in April, leaving the knocked-out teams dismayed before they have had the chance to peel off the first layer of sweaters. That reform will be repealed before 1995.

One-day cricket is purely a revenue-raising exercise and it ought to be staged as late in the season as possible, when the players can cope with it. The main reason for staging it in April and May is to enable the selectors to assess "one-day form" before the one-day internationals in late May, as if that mattered a jot compared to getting the Test team right. In 1994 there are once again two Texaco Trophies, one against New Zealand and one against

South Africa. How can a trophy have any credibility if it is won twice in a season? In this particular case, I am astonished that the TCCB has never taken the chance to stage a couple of extra one-day games and make the Texaco a miniature World Series Cup. New Zealand v South Africa at Worcester or Canterbury or somewhere, during the period when the teams overlap, would be a nice little earner.

These twin-tour summers are always unsatisfactory. The South Africans – understandably after such a frantic re-introduction to world cricket – did not want a full series in 1994. But great Test cricket needs a full series to boil up, to get the public aware of the characters, for the drama, and all the subplots, to develop. The 1993 Ashes series was a glorious illustration. One hopes that, even with nine Test-playing countries, administrators are not going to lose sight of that.

After all these years

All being well, there will still be some wonderful moments when the South Africans finally arrive in England, 100 years after their first tour, and 29 after their last. Nothing in cricket has disgraced the game over the years so much as its relationship with South Africa. For two decades after the formal introduction of apartheid, administrators in the white countries did everything possible to avoid consideration of the ethical questions involved, although it was obvious at the time that South African cricket was rooted in a system that was fundamentally evil.

Even after Basil D'Oliveira's exclusion from South Africa they had to be dragged kicking and screaming towards the notion that the relationship must cease; it was the Home Secretary, James Callaghan, terrified that civil disorder would muck up a General Election, who forced the cancellation of the 1970 tour of England. For the next two decades of formal isolation, cricket's attitude was ineffectual and half-hearted. The culture of the game was such that no odium attached to the players who were so well-rewarded for going on the seven rebel tours though, in their own small and moral pygmyish way, they were acting as agents of apartheid.

That war has now been won. The future of South Africa remains clouded with all kinds of terrible possibilities but this summer it will be possible to welcome their cricketers without reservation. Since the collapse of the last rebel tour in 1990, when South African administrators ceased their equivocation about their real intentions and merged into the United Cricket Board, they have done an enormous amount for the good of the game. No country is doing more to spread cricket to its own people; if only Lord's worked as hard in the deprived areas of English cities. I am delighted to publish a piece about South African cricket in this year's *Wisden* (by E. W. Swanton) that has nothing to do with politics. And this summer we can look forward to seeing a team that will represent some of the very best of their country's national traditions: athleticism, spirit and skill.

It is thus bizarre that ICC, whose gallantry in the years of struggle over South Africa was not conspicuous, should now choose to start tinkering with cricket's records to withdraw first-class status from the rebel tours. I will be brief and try not to be boring. The arguments about whether the games should have been regarded as first-class at the time are so complex that, if taken into court, they could make the case of Jarndyce v Jarndyce look like summary justice. Since the written rules are unclear, they depend heavily on one's reading of the intentions of ICC in the 1960s, after South Africa had left the organisation, at a time when its administration (see Jack Bailey's article) and minute-taking were a mite casual.

Bailey, secretary of ICC when the rebel tours began, regarded the games as first-class. So did all statisticians. Had ICC expressed a different view at the time, fine. It did not. It is, however, simply unacceptable to legislate retroactively in an attempt to get in a kick at what is left of the old South Africa. It does not damage apartheid, which is dead; most of the players involved could not care a jot; the only damage is to cricket itself and to one of its most cherishable assets, its meticulously-crafted records.

After much anguish, I have decided that, in common with (I believe) all other serious record-keepers, *Wisden* cannot accept this decision, and our records thus remain unchanged. This is not intended in the least to offer a challenge to ICC's right to decide what is and is not first-class. Indeed, I hope one of the changes the new, more professional administration will bring about is greater central control of this matter. At the moment, there are huge gaps between what is acceptable in, for instance, England and South Africa, where the Boards prefer sentiment to rigour, and the much stricter regulations of Australia. What constitutes first-class cricket in Pakistan or Sri Lanka remains, to outsiders, one of life's mysteries.

However, ICC is as wrong to play around with the past records as are those researchers who will have us believe that Jack Hobbs did not really score 197 first-class centuries and W.G. 126. Let us get on with cricket's future. I still have hopes that ICC will be statesmanlike enough to amend its decision, maintaining its political position, if it wishes, but agreeing that, for statistical purposes at least, the games can be treated as if they were first-class. And I hope never again to have to think about this subject.

Spoofs and spies

There have, thank heaven, been some more pleasingly surreal moments in the past year. There was the story about Botham getting into trouble for not going into pubs enough – he was supposed to be doing promotion work for a brewery. Gooch, the man who did more than anyone to push Gower towards retirement, called for his return to the Test team the day before the Israelis and Palestinians signed their peace treaty. The *Yorkshire Post* ran an April Fool spoof about the formation of an alternative county club, to be led by Geoff Boycott. It fooled me: I have heard many more far-fetched stories in Yorkshire that have turned out to be true. And then there was the genuine revelation that the late spy Kim Philby kept the 1972 edition of *Wisden* in his Moscow flat. Did the old traitor particularly enjoy reading about the Empire shuddering as India won a Test in England for the first time? Or did he get nostalgic and regretful pleasure from reading the details of England's recapture of the Ashes?

Perhaps he would dwell, on those dull Moscow evenings, on the obituary of W. H. Copson, the Derbyshire and England fast bowler, who would never have come to cricket but for the General Strike; with the colliery closed, he took part in a game on the local recreation ground. I digress, but then old *Wisdens* get you that way, wherever you are in the world. I hope the 131st edition will work the same magic.

FIVE CRICKETERS OF THE YEAR

DAVID BOON

Two years ago, the pavilion at the ground in Launceston, Tasmania, was renamed "The David Boon Stand". Admittedly Launceston is Boon's adoring home town but, even so, having a grandstand named after you when you are only 31 years old and in the middle of a Test career is proof that you have become a living legend. Now, two years and hundreds of runs later, Boon is rivalling Allan Border as the most respected and admired cricketer in Australia. At big matches now, banners carry the simplest of messages: "Boonie" or, at their most verbose, "Boon – dead-set legend". His recently published autobiography is a best-seller and crowds have flocked to meet Boon at book-signings around the nation.

Boon had been Australia's leading batsman for some time before the 1993 Ashes tour, but it was his performances on that, his third, tour of England that elevated him to the stature of a diminutive but formidable national treasure. In ten Test innings in England in 1993 Boon made 555 runs at an average of 69.37. Importantly, he finally achieved an ambition by making his first Test century in England, an undefeated 164 at Lord's in the Second Test. This innings had followed a frustrating 93 in the First Test at Old Trafford, but Boon made up for that disappointment by following his Lord's century with another in the Third Test and another in the Fourth.

After the Ashes tour, Boon stood in fifth position on the list of all-time Test run-makers for Australia with 5,869 runs at 45.49 with 17 centuries. Against South Africa at the end of December he reached 1,241 Test runs in a calendar year, more than any Australian has scored except Bobby Simpson, and passed Neil Harvey's aggregate of 6,149 to lie behind only Border, Greg Chappell and Sir Donald Bradman in the all-time Australian Test scoring list. If we can judge a batsman by the company he keeps in the record books, Boon's reputation is assured.

DAVID CLARENCE BOON was born in Launceston on December 29 1960. His father Clarrie, who died three months before the tour began, was a respected sports administrator and a strong supporter of his son's career. His mother, Lesley, played hockey for Australia. Boon was educated at Launceston Grammar School where he excelled at cricket, Australian football and swimming. His cricket career gained impetus when the Lancashire professional Jack Simmons was coaching in Launceston and predicted the lad would play for Australia. Simmons was captaining Tasmania when Boon began his first-class career as a 17-year-old. Years later Boon formally recognised his debt to Simmons by naming his son after him. Boon's achievement in becoming a fine Test player from a state which at that stage was still to enter the Sheffield Shield is strong evidence of his singular determination.

Boon's efforts on his three tours to England tell the story of his career. In 1985 he seemed anchored to the crease by indecision against the spin of John Emburey, his seven somewhat embarrassing innings producing only 124 runs at 17.71. In 1989, he made a solid 442 runs at 55.25, yet he never quite gorged himself as Mark Taylor and Steve Waugh did. In 1993 Boon was the most assured batsman in the Australian team, feasting remorselessly on wayward England bowling.

The most striking features of Boon's batting in England in 1993 were his concentration and precise shot selection. It was as if he knew that every over England's bowlers would present him with a short ball to cut for four or a half volley to clip away to the mid-wicket rope. His method was to defend patiently against any reasonable delivery, then to despatch with minimal risk the inevitable bad ball. It was a simple but ruthlessly effective strategy. Boon now knows his strengths and weaknesses as well as Border knows his. Young batsmen like Slater, Hayden and Martyn talk of "the Bible according to Boon".

"I suppose the difference between my batting in 1989 and 1993 was that I converted 50s and 60s into hundreds in '93," Boon says. "I think my mental approach is different these days. I'm a lot harder now. Every innings really matters. My attitude has changed a lot in those four years. There's a definite progression there."

Off the field, Boon is a quiet character who does not waste words. However, he possesses a dry Australian wit and often reveals a mischievous glint in the eye. On the field, either at short leg where he is brilliant or at the batting crease, he is the rock on which Australia have built their recent good form. Border, one of his staunchest admirers, once said Boon had a heart to match that of Phar Lap, the great Australian racehorse. In Australian sport, there are few higher compliments. – Mark Ray.

IAN HEALY

Even though he is a wicket-keeper, Ian Healy is best described as a gloves-off cricketer. A proud and uncompromising professional, he plays for keeps. So forceful is his personality on point-duty that he elicits strong and mixed emotions from opponents, spectators and journalists alike. Indeed, at the start of the 1993 Ashes campaign, he was regarded as much for the strength of his resolve, his unremitting competitiveness and an extraordinarily high threshold of physical pain as he was for his talent as a player.

However, by the end of Australia's triumphant tour he had emerged as a wicket-keeper-batsman of outstanding ability, having established a particularly memorable collaboration with the leg-spinner Shane Warne. Poised and precise, he completed 26 dismissals (21 catches and five stumpings), a record in a Test series in England, and so upheld the wicket-keeping traditions of his native Queensland which numbers Don Tallon and Wally Grout among its finest sporting sons. His batting at No. 7 was neither as technically correct nor as aesthetically pleasing but its effectiveness was undeniable and his 296 runs were gathered at 59.20 – an average beyond the the reach of any of his opponents. His total included, at Old Trafford, his maiden first-class century.

No longer could it be said that Healy's words spoke louder than his actions. During a series which lifted to 53 his number of consecutive Test appearances, he elevated his performance level to the degree predicted by Greg Chappell five years before. Healy derived enormous satisfaction from his success, content that he had silenced those critics who primarily viewed him as a prickly combatant given to excessive and provocative appealing – best-known for his confrontation with Desmond Haynes in Barbados in 1990-91 and the dubious stumping of Brian Lara in Brisbane in 1992-93.

In commensurate numbers to Healy's critics are his admirers – some in high places. Indeed, he has enjoyed support among the influential since Chappell, in his last season as a selector in 1987-88, vigorously championed his cause. At the time Healy was understudy to his friend and practice partner Peter Anderson and unsure whether to give up keeping and turn his attention to batting. Having played his entire career alongside Rod Marsh, Chappell was acutely aware of the advantages offered by a permanent, dependable wicket-keeper-batsman. In their search for the ideal successor to Marsh the selectors had called on Wayne Phillips, considered Ray Phillips, looked momentarily at Roger Woolley and briefly revived Steve Rixon's career before turning to Tim Zoehrer and then Greg Dyer. Healy's selection for the rancorous 1988-89 tour to Pakistan after just six first-class matches generally was considered to be the most surprising since the choices of wrist-spinner John Watkins in 1972-73 and off-spinner Peter Taylor in 1986-87.

Healy's more ardent backers believed him to be a candidate to succeed the indefatigable Allan Border as Australian captain. (Barry Jarman, at the Headingley Test in 1968, is the only specialist wicket-keeper to have led Australia this century.) The fact that he skippered Australian XIs against the West Indians in 1991-92 and 1992-93 and in 1993 was entrusted with the captaincy of an official Australian team at the Hong Kong six-a-side tournament provided evidence that vice-captain Mark Taylor's elevation would not go unchallenged. And because Border has long sought respite from the incessant demands of leadership, Healy was captain of Queensland in 1992-93.

Born in Brisbane on April 30, 1964, IAN ANDREW HEALY moved to proud sporting country when his father, a bank manager, was transferred 600 kilometres north to the town of Biloela. It was 1972, the year Rod Marsh traded his iron gloves for silk gloves in England and along the way inspired Healy to start a career as a wicket-keeper. Young Healy was stimulated by the town's passion for all sports. He rode his bicycle everywhere to practise and compete at cricket, basketball, soccer, squash and rugby league. He became a cricket captain at the age of 11 and at a clinic conducted by the touring Sheffield Shield team met the Queensland wicket-keeper John Maclean and was allowed to examine his gloves. It is a memory he cherishes.

He played alongside adults throughout his adolescence, which probably contributed to his hard-headed and belligerent approach to all sport. When he returned with his family to the city, he was a self-contained, self-reliant 17-year-old who considered mental and physical toughness and raw competitiveness the most admirable qualities in a sportsperson. He still does.

Among his peers Healy is renowned for the fierceness of his loyalty and the thoroughness of his preparation. Interested in sports science and psychology since his days studying for a physical education diploma, he maintains comprehensive diaries analysing his own performance and those of his opponents. He is convinced that committing thoughts and impressions to paper makes him a calmer and more able professional.

Healy had a hand in the design of the new Australian team blazer paraded before an unsuspecting public at the start of the 1993-94 season. Once employed as a salesman in his in-laws' Brisbane fashion agency, Healy welcomed the arrival of what he described as an "honour blazer". That says it all, really. – Mike Coward.

MERV HUGHES

At the end of the Ashes season, the England captain who failed to regain them, and resigned his job as a result, looked back in an interview on it all: the good, the bad, the indigestible. In the course of it, Graham Gooch spoke of "dear old Merv Hughes". What? No matter that Gooch is eight years Hughes's senior. It is not the "old" that might send the moustaches twirling; it is the "dear old". Whoever spoke of "dear old Joel Garner" at the end of a series in which he had taken 31 wickets, or "dear old Dennis Lillee"?

Perhaps it is the action. When many of us saw Hughes for the first time down at Arundel in 1989 on that blazing sunny day, there was a mixture of mirth and disbelief: the mincing little steps leading to a stuttering run, the absurd stove-pipe trousers, the pre-bowl calisthenics, the whiskers, the silent-movie bad-guy theatrics. The action is not much different today, although it might tend a little more towards out-swing and the googly variation is not used quite so often. The eyes above the hooked nose still glare with the same passion. Insults fly, though if Gooch is to be believed not especially imaginative or distressing ones, just a couple of words. Sometimes, too, a childlike smile appears, all perhaps indicating the man behind the moustache: pretty straightforward, not too gaudy.

Now Hughes has been involved in two Ashes tours, and in each he has taken key wickets at key times. Last summer, in the absence of the one man thought to separate the two sides in strike-power, Craig McDermott, Hughes showed that in fact it was he who was the difference in the seam-bowling department. If Shane Warne bowled the ball which launched a thousand paragraphs, Merv Hughes ground out the overs which gave Australia a decent front-line assault.

In the course of the summer, Hughes took his 200th Test wicket and passed the Test tallies of two Australian fast bowlers, Geoff Lawson and Jeff Thomson, the second legendary and the first deeply respected. In doing this, Hughes had a strike-rate roughly the equal of Thomson's and rather better than Lawson's. Yet, until recently, it was unthinkable that he would be mentioned as being in the same class as those two. He has paid a price for his eccentricities, not least not being taken seriously.

MERVYN GREGORY HUGHES was born in rural Victoria on November 23, 1961, son of a schoolmaster. In Australian education, country schoolteachers often are itinerants, and Merv and his family travelled around before they settled in Werribee, south-west of Melbourne. There Hughes was preoccupied, like all good young Victorian boys, with Australian Rules football in the winter and cricket in the summer. He boasts that he is the only man to have played 96 games for Werribee First XVIII and taken 200 Test wickets. To get to Werribee from Melbourne, you must drive through Footscray, which has both a senior football team and a first-grade cricket club. It was there that Hughes naturally gravitated.

At Footscray, Hughes came under the influence of two men who had short and bitter Test careers: fast bowler Ron Gaunt, who played three Tests in one-match stands between 1957 and 1961, and Ken Eastwood, a left-handed opening bat, who played just one, disastrously, in 1970. At Sheffield Shield level, though, both were outstanding and at Grade level prodigious. Furthermore, they epitomised Footscray. This is a working-class area in Melbourne's western suburbs and the Footscray footballers and cricketers are known to themselves and to the rest of the city – one which has sharp social divides – as "Scraggers". If you are from outside Footscray, it is a jibe; if you are of Footscray, it is a boast. Merv Hughes was, is, always will be, a Scragger. In a way, the disappointments Gaunt and Eastwood felt have been reflected in Hughes's determination.

After Lillee and Thomson, there were always plenty of quicks off long runs around in Australia, sledging away and getting hit around the park bowling short on true wickets. Hughes ran – or minced – from the sight-screen, until wiser heads told him to cut his run. "It was simple enough," he said. "I was going to get the club fined for slow play." For the first time he learned that control was more important than sheer pace.

In the 1981-82 season Hughes made the Victorian side, and by 1985 he had been selected for Australia, playing one Test against Kapil Dev's touring Indians. He became almost, but not quite, a fixture. In 1989, Hughes came to England as the fourth seamer, behind Terry Alderman, Lawson and Carl Rackemann. An injury to Rackemann saw Hughes promoted, and he played all six Tests in a series dominated by Alderman. In the thrilling 1992-93 series against West Indies, Hughes took 20 wickets at 21.60, two more than McDermott and considerably cheaper. Yet he was still the second seamer when the party left for England, and had Bruce Reid been fit might have been the third.

The rest, as they say, is history. He took 31 wickets at 27.25, played an important innings of 38 at Edgbaston, dropped little and brilliantly helped run out Atherton at a crucial point of the Lord's Test. Recently married, he is now a sedate enough member of the side to have joined his captain in staying in the night the team went out at Leeds to celebrate the successful defence of the Ashes. Allan Border's eyes crinkle with affection when he sees "the Big Bloke" come into the bar. Hughes is one of Border's élite. He was, quite literally, exhausted by the end of the tour, but he could go back to Footscray as one proud Scragger. – Bruce Wilson.

SHANE WARNE

When Martin Crowe announced just before the 1993 Ashes series that Shane Warne was the best leg-spinner in the world, few alarm bells clanged in England. Such a declaration could be interpreted as an attempt to restore the confidence of Kiwi batsmen, notoriously vulnerable against spin, who had just been undermined by Warne. Moreover, no Australian wrist-spinner had made a significant impact in an English Test series since the days of Grimmett and O'Reilly between the wars. England, it was assumed, had to quell McDermott and Hughes to have a chance of retrieving the Ashes.

Such a complacent misconception was dispelled at Old Trafford by Warne's first delivery in Test cricket in England. It was bowled to Mike Gatting, an acknowledged master of spin. Warne does not indulge in low-risk "looseners" and that first ball was flicked vigorously out of the back of the hand. It set off on the line of Gatting's pads and then dipped in the air further towards the leg side until it was 18 inches adrift of the stumps; by this time Gatting was beginning to lose interest, until the ball bounced, turned and fizzed across his ample frame to clip the off bail. Gatting remained rooted at the crease for several seconds – in disbelief rather than dissent – before trudging off to the pavilion like a man betrayed. Now the Englishmen knew that Crowe's assessment was more than propaganda.

Throughout six Tests they could never master Warne. He bowled 439.5 overs in the series, took 34 wickets – surpassing Grimmett's 29 in the five Tests of 1930 – and also managed to concede under two runs per over, thereby flouting the tradition of profligate wrist-spinners buying their wickets. Some English batsmen were completely mesmerised; Robin Smith, England's "banker" in the middle order, was unable to detect any of his variations and had to be dropped. The admirable Gooch could obviously distinguish the googly from the leg-spinner, yet Warne still disposed of him five times in the series. Once Gooch carelessly clubbed a full toss to mid-on, but otherwise he was dismissed while playing the appropriate defensive stroke, the surest indication that Warne has a special talent.

Ominously for Test batsmen of the 1990s, Warne is not yet the complete wrist-spinner. His googly is not so penetrating or well-disguised as Mushtaq Ahmed's, which is one reason why he employs it so infrequently. His flipper is lethal if it is on target, but it often zooms down the leg side. But he is the most prodigious spinner of the ball of the last three decades, a gift which causes deceptive in-swing as well as excessive turn. He is also remarkably accurate, but if ever his control is threatened, he can regroup by bowling around the wicket to the right-handed batsman, thereby restricting him to just one scoring stroke, a risky sweep. Hence in the Ashes series his captain, Border, was able to use him as both shock and stock bowler.

Warne's success in 1993 was a triumph for the Australian selectors as well as his own resolve. They might easily have discarded him as a liability early in his career. SHANE KEITH WARNE, born in a smart bayside suburb of Melbourne on September 13, 1969, did not display many of the hallmarks of his predecessors – Grimmett, O'Reilly and Benaud – in his youth. Bleached blond hair, a stud in his ear plus a fondness for the good life, which caused his waistline to expand with alarming speed, and an aversion to discipline, which in 1990 led to his departure under a cloud from the Australian Cricket Academy in Adelaide, do not reflect the perfect credentials for the modern Australian Test cricketer. Yet the selectors trusted their judgment.

They pitched him into two Test matches against India in January 1992, after just four Sheffield Shield appearances, in which he had taken eight wickets. He had shown form on tour in Zimbabwe and against the West Indians. None the less, his state captain Simon O'Donnell expressed public reservations. Warne took one for 228 against the Indians and the gamble seemed to have backfired. Warne was then invited by Rod Marsh to return to the Academy, where he was coached by another reformed larrikin, Terry Jenner. Warne was now prepared to make the sort of sacrifices that impress Australians: he gave up beer, trained hard, lost 28 pounds and was rewarded by selection for the tour to Sri Lanka in August 1992.

In Colombo, having yielded 107 runs from 22 wicketless overs in the first innings of the opening Test, Warne took three for 11 from 5.1 overs in the second as Australia conjured a dramatic victory. His victims were only tailenders, but it was a start. That Border entrusted him with the ball at all at such a crucial moment did wonders for his confidence. His seven for 52 against West Indies at Melbourne in December 1992 was an isolated success in that series but confirmed his match-winning potential. But his efforts in New Zealand (17 wickets in three matches) and in last summer's Ashes series have established Warne as an integral cog, perhaps the integral cog, of the Australian team.

On a broader scale he has triggered a mini-renaissance in the art of wrist-spin bowling. In the summer of 1993 young village cricketers could be spied on the outfield, no longer seeking to emulate Curtly Ambrose or Merv Hughes, but attempting to ape the more subtle skills of Warne. For that we should all be grateful. – Vic Marks.

STEVE WATKIN

When the Cricketers' Association voted Steve Watkin as their player of the year at the end of the summer of 1993, they recognised his immense value and dedication to Glamorgan, who had enjoyed their most productive season for 24 years. The cricket fraternity appreciates a whole-hearted trier and there was enough evidence of Watkin's commitment and willingness to shoulder the burden of the attack by the 766.4 overs he sent down last season, a figure surpassed only by his county colleague Robert Croft and Peter Such of Essex, both slow bowlers. Watkin, with 92 victims, was also the country's leading wicket-taker.

His efforts were belatedly rewarded by the England selectors when they chose him, along with Devon Malcolm and Angus Fraser, in a revamped pace attack for the final Test against Australia. After taking two wickets in the first innings Watkin then set up England's first Test win in 11 matches, and their first against Australia in 19, by taking the first three Australian wickets in the second innings. He had Slater caught by Alec Stewart, trapped Boon leg before and then knocked back Taylor's leg stump. When fellow Glamorgan player Matthew Maynard caught Healy, the Australians were on their way to a 161-run defeat and Watkin, with match figures of six for 152, had vindicated his recall to Test cricket. His success compensated for the disappointment at being left out of the previous Test team at Edgbaston when, contrary to expectation, the pitch favoured the spinners. John Emburey was summoned to Birmingham while Watkin drove down the M5 to join his county colleagues in the Championship game against Warwickshire.

STEVEN LLEWELLYN WATKIN was born in Maesteg on September 15, 1964, brought up in Duffryn Rhondda and attended Cymmer Afan Comprehensive School, where there were limited opportunities for organised cricket. He played in only three competitive school matches but soon developed a natural aptitude for the game when he joined Maesteg Town Club and played for the first team at 15.

He was recommended to Tom Cartwright, who was then Glamorgan's Second XI coach, and was offered a two-year contract in 1986. Apart from learning how to grip the ball, Watkin says he has not changed his action since he "began bowling against my father on Porthcawl beach during the summer holidays". He is essentially an attacking bowler whose high arm action enables him to obtain bounce from unresponsive pitches, notably in Wales, while his unflagging determination is an inspiration to all his colleagues. He is also a thinker, and over the past two seasons has developed a subtle change of pace and an effective slower ball.

He made his first-class debut at Worcester in 1986 and gained a notable first victim when Graeme Hick struck a leading edge to mid-off. But he did not appear again until 1988 when he topped the county's bowling averages. He shared the new-ball attack with Greg Thomas that summer, but Thomas then left for Northamptonshire and since his departure Glamorgan have relied more and more on Watkin. It is unusual for fast bowlers to sustain form and fitness season after season but Watkin has kept going for long spells, summoning fresh energy often because there was no quick bowler to complement him from the other end. It was no secret that Glamorgan were searching for a fast bowler to replace Viv Richards as their overseas player, and Watkin warmly welcomes the arrival of the Barbadian Ottis Gibson.

Watkin was awarded his county cap at the end of a game at Old Trafford in 1989 when he took 13 wickets. Although Glamorgan ended bottom of the County Championship that season, Watkin claimed 94 victims at 25.09 and was the country's joint leading wicket-taker. His reward was selection for the England A team which toured Kenya and Zimbabwe in 1989-90, followed by successive A tours to Pakistan and Sri Lanka, and the West Indies. He achieved only moderate success, mainly because he did not bowl enough overs to get into any sort of rhythm, but in between the second and third tours the selectors recognised his effectiveness on English pitches and selected him for the First Test against West Indies at Headingley in June 1991.

He was initially chosen as cover for Derek Pringle but played instead when Chris Lewis was ill, and helped England gain their first home win against West Indies since 1969. After taking two wickets in the first innings, which included Desmond Haynes with his 14th ball in Test cricket, Watkin demolished the visitors' middle order in the second innings, dismissing Hooper, Richards and Logie for 11 runs. Any thoughts of a regular place in the team were quickly dispelled when he failed to take a wicket in the Second Test on a slow Lord's pitch, where West Indies scored 419. He returned to his county, wheeled down 728.5 first-class overs during the 1991 season and – as he has been for five successive years – was Glamorgan's leading wicket-taker.

Watkin's degree, gained in human movement studies, perhaps explains why he has missed only one game because of injury during his career. He has the ideal physique for a fast bowler, carrying no superfluous fat, while his great reserves of stamina enable him to soldier on while others tire.

Glamorgan's success last season owed much to Steve Watkin's prowess and exemplary attitude. A fierce competitor, yet unassuming and un-complaining, he plays cricket with dignity, control and goodwill, while his easy humour and cheerful temperament are qualities that have endeared him to his fellow players. – Edward Bevan

A full list of past Cricketers of the Year can be found on pages 262-3.

A WHOLE NEW WORLD

By JACK BAILEY

On February 2, 1993, what was almost certainly the most acrimonious and shambolic meeting in the history of ICC broke up amid signs of lasting anguish. The central debating point had been the venue for the next World Cup. So strongly had feelings run on all sides that a one-day meeting had gone on well into the night. The issue of the World Cup was finally resolved on the morning of the second day. It would be played in India, Pakistan and Sri Lanka – this in spite of a decision in favour of England at a previous ICC meeting.

The announcement of the World Cup decision was followed *sotto voce* – as an afterthought, almost – by a statement to the effect that David Richards, chief executive of the Australian Cricket Board, had been appointed chief executive of the International Cricket Council. He would take up his duties, at Lord's, five months later.

The meeting focused on the World Cup marked an alarming departure from the way business had been conducted within ICC from its foundation as the Imperial Cricket Conference in 1909. Since then, the name had changed to the International Cricket Conference and then to the International Cricket Council, and ICC had seen some contentious times. But that 1993 meeting was something different. It was the outward and visible sign, if one were needed, that the playing of cricket as a game, so long the chief preoccupation of those gathered round the tables of the MCC Committee room at Lord's, and pursued invariably with an attitude of quiet and civilised deference, had been overtaken.

The meeting had been prolonged, almost beyond endurance, by a series of legal quibbles concerning an interpretation of ICC rules. There were frequent adjournments so that India's two chief representatives (of the nine apparently present at various times) could seek the support of India's Lord Chief Justice for their contention that a simple majority of those voting was all that was necessary to determine the destination of the next World Cup.

This had been the case with the allocation of previous World Cups. By rule, the 19 Associate Members had one vote; the Test-playing countries, with two votes each, mustered 18 between them. But because this put the Associate Members in a position of strength, unwarranted in the eyes of Full Members, the voting had been changed. A "binding" resolution now required a simple majority of those present. But that would apply only if support were given by two-thirds of the Full Members, of whom at least one had to be a Foundation Member (England or Australia).

Complicated perhaps; but, since this rule change had been made with the backing of India and the other Full Members, not, one would have thought, questionable. The new voting system applied to all decisions categorised as "binding". From all accounts, the position of India and her supporters was to question that the World Cup vote should fall into the category of a "binding" decision. Here the mind boggles. If a decision as to where the World Cup would be staged, at a meeting called specifically to decide the issue, was not considered "binding", then what was?

Madhavrao Scindia, the President of the Indian Board and one-time Minister of Civil Aviation and Tourism, was supported by representatives

of Pakistan and Sri Lanka in a determined and prolonged attempt to win
the day. The intrusion of legalistic arguments into the game had already
become familiar to Sir Colin Cowdrey, chairman of the meeting. The
Pakistan tour of England, with its ball-tampering row and the swift
interventions by lawyers employed by Pakistan, had surely prepared him
and the MCC secretariat, or should have done. The obduracy of India and
others in the face of ICC's own lawyers must have come as a shock,
however, and the meeting degenerated. All that cricket used to stand for
was thrown out of the committee-room window.

Politicking and favour-seeking among member countries by those from
the sub-continent had apparently begun well before the meeting. Those
representing the Associate Members were aware that substantial funds
would be made available. India had supported Zimbabwe's elevation to full
membership; talk was rife of favours being called in.

After the ICC meeting, an unprecedented press conference was called by
the chief executive of the British Test and County Cricket Board, A. C.
Smith. Never one to volunteer information ("no comment but don't quote
me" has often been put forward as one of his more adventurous remarks),
Smith went to town. "We endured a fractious and unpleasant meeting beset
by procedural wrangling," he said. "There was no talk of anything like
cricket. It was, by a long way, the worst meeting I have ever attended." He
confirmed that although his board felt that a previous minute nominating
England as the next host country for the World Cup was still valid, they
had finally succumbed "in the best and wider interests of the world game".
Smith also confirmed that a price for his Board's compliance had been that
they would definitely host the World Cup after next, currently scheduled for
the English summer of 1998. As part of the deal, they also ensured that the
profits of the tournament supposed to be held in 1995 (which is actually
now scheduled for early 1996) would fund the new ICC secretariat.

For the Marylebone Cricket Club, the agreement to appoint Richards
was an outward manifestation of a notably unwelcome passage in their
history. They would no longer help to administer the international scene,
even peripherally. Their last remaining influence on the world stage of
cricket was officially at an end. It was a turn of events presaged by the
appointment in 1988 of a chairman, Cowdrey who, though nominated by
the President of MCC, was ostensibly, for the first time, an appointment of
ICC itself. What had happened since then had been a far cry from the
original idea when Francis Lacey, the secretary of MCC, came together in
conference with Australia and South Africa on June 15, 1909.

A memorandum was published in *The Times* a week later. There were two
parts to the memorandum. The first set out the regulations for Test matches
between the three member countries: England, Australia and South Africa.
Most of these regulations were still in existence in the 1980s. The other set
out a programme of matches between the three countries, including a
triangular contest in England in 1912. In general it was agreed that "every
team shall pay and receive a visit from each other country in every cycle of
four years".

Thus was a valuable "talking shop" opened. It was kept chiefly as a
conduit through which ideas could be passed and was run by the law-
makers, MCC. With few exceptions, thereafter, meetings kept to the
original intentions. Certainly, a framework of rules designed for recom-
mendations rather than decisions afforded precious little scope for it to be

[*MCC collection*   [*Patrick Eagar*

Sir Francis Lacey, first secretary of ICC, and David Richards, the first chief executive.

otherwise. In cases of emergency, member countries could be mobilised fairly swiftly, but throughout most of its long history ICC saw itself as a co-ordinator rather than a dictator. The conditions under which Test match cricket between two countries was played were left to them; the disciplining of players remained in the hands of individual boards. Positive changes remained few and far between. The *modus operandi* mirrored that of the Commonwealth of Nations. To all intents and purposes Lord's fulfilled the function of Buckingham Palace.

As Test cricket spread, so the founder members protected themselves with a power of veto, almost never used but there just in case. India, New Zealand and West Indies became members in 1926. The newly created Pakistan took its place in 1953. South Africa left the Commonwealth and ICC in 1961. In 1965 the rules were changed, the title International Cricket Conference was adopted and the first Associate Members, with strictly limited voting powers, were allowed inside, including, now that "Imperial" had been dropped, the United States.

Gradually, as governments throughout the world became more interested in sport, recognising the prestige it could bring, more and more countries applied for associate membership. The first World Cup brought an avalanche of them. MCC paid for all the administration and there were few barriers in the way of any country that could show that cricket was firmly established and organised. A loose-knit family was gradually formed: representation regarding the Laws could be made; Full Members were given the task of encouraging cricket in countries nearby. Other areas of common concern were tackled, but until the 1970s two issues above all others were kept strictly out of ICC's province: finance and politics. Without these two erratic and sometimes unpleasant strands of human existence to consider, ICC remained for a long time a benevolent but only mildly persuasive body. Goodwill prevailed.

Thus ICC was a source of guidance rather than a central bureaucracy. There were times when guidance had to be firm, but this applied in the main strictly to cricketing matters. The isolation of South Africa became the subject of a ruling only in the 1970s. For almost a decade after they left the Conference in 1961, their fellow founder members continued to visit them. These unofficial Test matches remained outside the province of the Conference and England and Australia saw that they remained so. Yet ICC, in conjunction with MCC, acted swiftly enough after the Bodyline controversy in the 1930s, came to an agreement about the spate of throwing that developed early in the 1960s and formed a united (if not successful) front against Kerry Packer and his rebel players in the 1970s. Throughout, undefined but pervading all contentious issues, was the same spirit of fair play that prevailed on the cricket field.

Often, ICC was the merest shadow of a co-ordinating, let along a ruling, body. At times Australia, for instance, wanted little part of a world governing organisation and would often make the point during the post-war years, sometimes by sending local representatives with limited powers to the annual meeting. The Anglo-Australian axis with its special position remained firmly against any thought of centralised power in the cricket world, although comparative newcomers such as Pakistan beavered away at achieving it.

For them, and for other emergent countries, a way to advancement lay through a homogenisation of world cricket. The dominance of England and Australia was all very well – but. The persistence of the Pakistani Board president Air Marshal Nur Khan led to the appointment of observers, forerunners of the Test match referees. They were powerless, but their appointment, even if only to view Test matches in Pakistan, was a small step in what Pakistan considered to be the right direction. Gradually, the days when Billy Griffith, secretary of ICC and MCC between 1962 and 1974, would issue brief communiqués to the press agencies at the end of a two-day meeting receded. Often in later years cricket writers were disappointed at the apparent lack of progress on the world front. But there was no short cut to decision-taking if even one of the Test-playing countries did not want there to be. Consequently, as secretary of ICC I found that the items of hard news to give to the press concerned either South Africa or the World Cup or Kerry Packer. So many other issues which were the subject of fierce, sometimes brilliant, debate could be frustrated by one or two dissidents who could not, by code of practice, be publicly named. Yet, by and large, cricket prospered.

It was inevitable, perhaps, that in the end there had to be a centralised administration employed by ICC itself. The appointment of Test match referees was a visible sign of an attempt to stamp the views of a central authority on cricket throughout the Test-playing world. Commercialism is snowballing. From 1994, at least one "neutral" umpire will stand in each Test match, a development abhorrent to the purists. Central control, with a chief executive answering to ICC sub-committees, and to the full panoply of countries probably more than once a year, was the almost certain outcome. Financial and political considerations will come high on the agenda. The welding together of many disparate points of view and aspirations will be a tough job. That 1993 World Cup meeting refers.

It is hard to imagine a combination better suited to deal with issues which confront them than the newly elected chairman, Clyde Walcott, and chief executive, Richards. Clyde's name as a cricketer puts him in a position of high regard, even from those for whom commercial and political gain is more important than the game itself. He is a modest man, a man of wit, with a strong sense of fair play and a shrewdness which underlies his genial exterior, and since he represents West Indies – strong in playing ability, less fortunate in terms of home-produced funds – he will see the point of view of the less well-off.

David Richards has not played first-class cricket, although he was a more than useful grade cricketer. He is a professional cricket administrator, tough, likeable and efficient. As secretary of the Victorian Cricket Association he played a pivotal role in the staging of the 1977 Centenary Test match in Melbourne and we hardened cricket administrators marvelled at the industry and ability he displayed in getting together former cricketers from all over the world. Since then, he has served with distinction as chief executive of the Australian board, having to come to terms early with the commercialisation of the game and the apparent lack of authority vested in the board itself after the deal had been struck with World Series Cricket. A fixture list dominated by one-day cricket was one outcome, the brash commercialism generated by the board "marketeers" who had previously acted on behalf of the Packer organisation was another. Whether or not PBL, the organisation responsible for marketing World Series Cricket for Kerry Packer, or the Australian board were calling the shots became a matter for conjecture, but Richards rode it all with equanimity and emerged not only unscathed but with a reputation sufficiently enhanced to hand him the number one job in cricket.

Still in his forties, Richards has the additional advantage of having come through a particularly hard school in which not too many words are minced before delivery. He also has positive views on the future and is backed by a cricket committee which includes Bob Cowper, a fellow Australian and formidable Test batsman who, as a banker in Monte Carlo, knows his way around the financial world.

Stationed at Lord's, but beholden to nothing and nobody other than his international role, Richards and his operation will be financed by a levy on World Cup income and membership fees from all members of ICC. "Victoria and Australia no longer claim my loyalties in a cricketing sense," he says. "It is a global sport and it will be a large part of my job to look at the year 2003 and make sure the game holds its place in global sports then." One move has been to form an off-shore company to deal with ICC's commercial activities. Richards sees a role for ICC in cricket at all levels and he is unashamedly in favour of all the recent innovations at Test match level: TV aids, referees, sponsorship of umpires, more stringent regulations. Aware of traditional values, he will not be bound by them.

Already many of the ties which bound his predecessors (in their joint roles) no longer apply to him. His empire seems bound to grow well beyond the two assistants now at his elbow. He will be a target for the media. He will need patience in dealing with strident politicians. He will need to be most things to all men, but never all things to anybody. One can only wish him, and cricket, well.

Jack Bailey was secretary of MCC, and therefore of ICC, from 1974 to 1987. He previously played for Oxford University and Essex. He is now a journalist, contributing mainly to The Times.

WHY WE BEAT THE POMS

By IAN CHAPPELL

Why do Australia beat England? In general, because Australia play an aggressive brand of cricket and, when the talent is there, they get in position to seek victory more often.

Notwithstanding that, Australia couldn't have lost the last three Ashes series even if they had bet heavily on the opposition. England played badly, often. In particular, the bowling was abysmal.

During the summer of 1993 I constantly heard the lament, "What is wrong with English cricket?" In part, the answer is the inability of people directing the English game to recognise the good that there is. For instance, one of the more common moans was "Where are all the England fast bowlers?" Answer: Devon Malcolm was playing for Derbyshire for the first five Tests. Or "What has happened to the old-fashioned English seamer?" Answer: Steve Watkin was playing for Glamorgan for the first five Tests. Or "Why were England 4-0 down after five Tests?" Answer: From the time of the second one-day international when, as captain, Graham Gooch froze like a rabbit caught in the headlights, it was obvious he wasn't the man to lead England to an Ashes victory.

England's ability to over-theorise and complicate the game of cricket is legendary. Ever since I became involved in Ashes battles, I've felt that Australia could rely on some assistance from the England selectors. In 1993 they ran truer to form than many of the players they picked. Their magnanimity gave Australia a four-game start before the penny dropped. They then promoted Mike Atherton to the captaincy and, in no time, England picked a reasonably well-balanced side with an attack that bore some semblance of hostility.

Atherton had one piece of good fortune which every captain needs to be successful. Angus Fraser chose the appropriate moment to return to full form and fitness. But even before that Atherton had displayed considerable cricket wisdom. He said at Edgbaston after only three days in the job: "Our most important task is to identify the talent to win games. Then we must be prepared to stick with them." He was as good as his word in helping to select the touring party for the Caribbean and in addition he cleverly used his new-found power to make important adjustments to the balance of the side.

Until the advent of Atherton, England's selections had often lacked rhyme or reason. A classic case was the predicament of 21-year-old Mark Lathwell in the one-day international series. At Lord's, Australia had an unbeatable 2-0 lead, so the selectors took the opportunity to play their talented 21-year-old, Damien Martyn. As he made mincemeat of the bowling on his way to a glorious half-century, an MCC member said to me, "How come you Australians always produce good young batsmen?" With Lathwell needlessly sitting in the pavilion watching his third match in a row, the answer wasn't difficult. "We play them," I replied.

Maybe Atherton doesn't need assistants like Keith Fletcher. The England cricket manager seems typical of a mentality that pervades county cricket – if it's difficult, take the easy way out. Fletcher's illogical call during the

Ashes series for groundsmen to help England by producing seaming pitches went as it should have done: unheeded. However, Fletcher's behaviour should have caught the attention of officials and received a reprimand.

Not only was the suggestion unfair, his reasoning was astray. This was proved at The Oval where a well-balanced side, capably led and playing good, aggressive cricket, beat Australia on one of the best cricket wickets I've seen in England. There was pace and bounce in Harry Brind's pitch (as usual) and it produced the best match of the series. If the counties followed the examples of Brind and Old Trafford's Peter Marron and, where possible, produced similar pitches, then England's good cricketers would benefit substantially at international level. Unfortunately, the county mentality is often similar to Fletcher's: pitches are prepared either to assist the home side or to blunt a strength in the opposition.

Fletcher incorrectly suggested that England is the only country where helping the home side with pitch preparation is not accepted practice. I haven't played on or seen any green-top fliers in the Caribbean, and my brother Greg has often said: "If you have to bat against four West Indies pace bowlers then the best place to do it is on their own turf."

And in more than thirty years of playing and watching cricket in Australia, I can honestly say that I've never seen a Test pitch that varies greatly from its behaviour during the Sheffield Shield season. In fact, one of the strengths of the Shield competition is that the players perform on pitches which are very close to Test standard. Under this system it's easy to identify the players who stand a chance at Test level, the ones who are capable of playing only first-class cricket and those who will soon return to club cricket.

When Australia hit rock bottom through the 1984-87 period, the standard of Sheffield Shield cricket was low. The problem was addressed because talented and gutsy young players were encouraged. Now it is a vibrant competition and an excellent breeding ground. England are on the right track with four-day first-class games, but it will take time for the benefits to accrue. I think they should go a step further and reduce the number of teams to make it more competitive, as there are players in the county structure who are not up to first-class standard. Any system that protects incompetence needs changing. If this means having a first and second division then that could be the way to accommodate part-time players who want to combine business and cricket.

These changes could be part of a package to convince the counties that they must put England's needs at the top of their list, rather than on a level with deciding which colour to paint the pavilion roof.

Any move to improve the structure should be aimed at increasing pride in playing for the national team. Encouragingly, since Atherton has become involved in the selection process, I detect a move back to the feeling that the England team is for English players. If this is the case it's good news: England was in danger of becoming a haven for career cricketers who were unsure of making it in their own country.

Lack of pride manifests itself in a number of ways and in England's case the most serious has been to capitulate in a Test when trouble loomed. Their players used to be the best in the world at extricating themselves from trouble. This generation needs to rediscover that urge. The inability to save Tests must also have something to do with technique and mental strength. In an age where we have more coaches than ever throughout the cricket world, I query how much good they are doing. I believe in good coaching, but I think players are better to have none (i.e. work it out for themselves) than to have bad coaching.

In Australia, I believe the Cricket Academy could be run more effectively by not removing the young players from their home environment. However, many of the players leaving the Academy are mentally tough and primed for first-class cricket. This is exactly what you would expect with Rod Marsh as head coach and there is no doubt it is having a positive effect on the depth of Australian first-class cricket.

Also, apart from a brief period when Australia, like other teams, were bluffed by West Indies into thinking that pace was the almighty weapon, there has been a broadbrush approach to bowling the opposition out. This includes having leg-spinners once again. In the period when they were forgotten in Australia, Bill "Tiger" O'Reilly was furious. But just as he did in his playing days, O'Reilly saved his most lethal delivery for the old enemy. "I can never forgive English cricket," he said, "for attempting to kill off leg-spin bowling." O'Reilly thought English captains had no idea how to handle leg-spinners.

This brings me in a roundabout way to uncovered pitches. This is often suggested as a recipe for helping English cricket. I say codswallop. Uncovered pitches at first-class level would encourage the expectancy of easy pickings for the bowlers. Leg-spinners are the antithesis of easy pickings.

Another suggestion is that there is too much one-day cricket. This is codswallop too. If young players are taught *properly* as they progress in the game, the smarter ones learn to adapt their thinking to all sorts of different pitches, bowlers and playing conditions.

Prior to the 1993-94 season, the Australian Cricket Board gave the selectors power to "rest a jaded or slightly injured player from one-day internationals, while still receiving full pay". This is recognition that Test cricket is the true measuring stick for a player's skill, but also acknowledges the contribution made by one-day cricket to the game's finances and spreading popularity. It could also be a solution to the vexing problem of the right balance in a touring team's itinerary.

The ACB's edict is an interesting development in the gradual evolution of the professional game, in places other than England. Like so many things, the English invented one-day cricket and other countries have improved on their system, leaving them languishing. There are some signs of modern thinking in the marketing of English cricket but it has taken an inordinate amount of time to occur. In the end, though, the marketing men need a strong England side. So does the whole of cricket.

Ian Chappell captained Australia in 30 Test matches between 1971 and 1975, 16 of them against England. He is now a broadcaster and journalist.

It is late on the Friday of the Lord's Test. The lone fielder is Graham Gooch, the England captain.

SUCCESS AT LAST

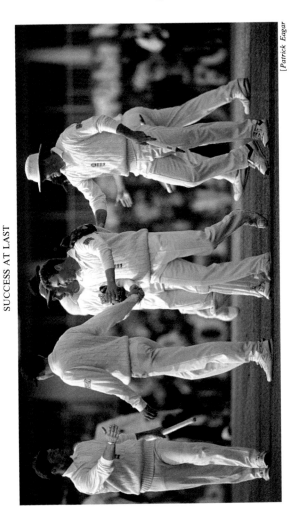

[*Patrick Eagar*

England's new captain Mike Atherton and his team-mates at the moment of triumph – England's win at The Oval, six and a half years and 18 Tests since their last victory over Australia.

THE BALL FROM HELL

[*Steve Lindsell, United Sports Picture Agency*]

Mike Gatting is astonished, Ian Healy delighted by Shane Warne's first ball of the series that turned from outside leg stump and set the pattern for the Ashes.

GOING OUT IN STYLE

[*Jan Traylen*

No one would have predicted that Viv Richards would walk out to play his last major innings, wearing navy blue and garish yellow, for Glamorgan, in a show-down for the Sunday League against Kent. Richards scored 46 not out and Glamorgan won their first trophy since 1969.

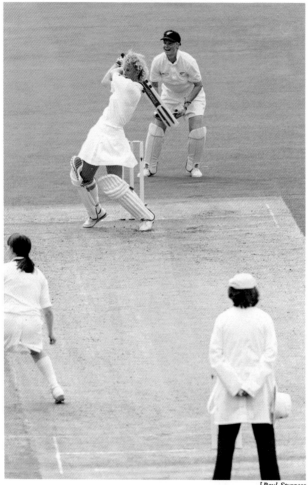

[*Paul Sturgess*

Jo Chamberlain, the star of the English women's team, hits out at Lord's on the way to England's 67-run win over New Zealand in the World Cup final.

AN ENGLISH SUMMER

[Patrick Eagar

Cricket at Ockley, Sussex, in 1993.

SUMMER ON THE VELD

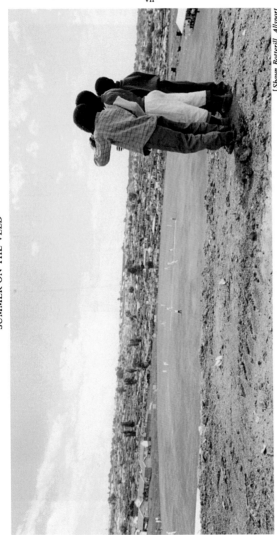

[*Shaun Botterill, Allsport*

Members of South Africa's most important cricketing audience watch the opening match of the England A tour in December 1993: against a Transvaal Invitation XI in the black township of Alexandra.

FIVE CRICKETERS OF THE YEAR

[*Patrick Eagar*

DAVID BOON

FIVE CRICKETERS OF THE YEAR

[*Bob Thomas*

IAN HEALY

FIVE CRICKETERS OF THE YEAR

[*Bob Thomas*

MERV HUGHES

FIVE CRICKETERS OF THE YEAR

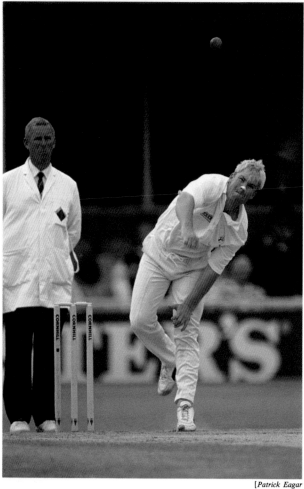

[*Patrick Eagar*

SHANE WARNE

FIVE CRICKETERS OF THE YEAR

[*David Munden*

STEVE WATKIN

THE GIANTS DEPART

1. BOTHAM AND RICHARDS

By JOHN WOODCOCK

With the retirement last season, within a few weeks of each other, of Ian Botham and Vivian Richards, first-class cricket lost two of the greatest of all its stars. Botham and Richards were good companions. Brought together by cricket, they became firm enough friends to spend a part of their winters going round the halls, exchanging banter with much the same abandon as they showed on the field. They had no particular talent for the stage, I think; but their prowess as cricketers deserves to be remembered for as long as the game is played.

Before Richards, Antigua had yet to be recognised as a nursery of prodigiously talented cricketers. That it now has a Test match ground and a quarter of a million tourists a year owes much to Richards. If Nelson put Antigua on the map by making it the base from which he sallied forth to do battle with the French in the Caribbean, Richards came to glamorise it by looking and batting as he did. He had the countenance to go with his style.

Richards first came to our notice in February 1974, when, playing for the Leeward Islands, he treated the bowling of Mike Denness's MCC side with dazzling disdain. A contract with Somerset soon followed, then the first of his 121 Test matches. Such was the impact he made and the conceit with which he played that when Clive Lloyd was looking for a way to counter the ascendancy of Lillee and Thomson in Australia in 1975-76 he sent Richards in first in the last two Test matches. Richards responded by making 30, 101, 50 and 98, and cutting a rare dash as he did so. In 1976 alone he scored 1,710 Test runs (just think of it!) at an average of 90, culminating in an innings of 291 against England at The Oval – and he was still only 24.

For most of the next two years Richards was lost to Test cricket while on the road with the Packer Circus. There was an intolerance, a belligerence about the way World Series Cricket was played which either hardened its adherents or flustered them. In the event, it confirmed Richards's supremacy. In a way, it made a man of him.

Ian Botham, meanwhile, was fast becoming the talk of English cricket. He was very strong, patently irrepressible and cheerfully insubordinate. By the time Richards joined Somerset in 1974, Botham, although almost four years his junior, was already on the staff there. They made a flamboyant, ultimately ungovernable pair. After a while Somerset hardly knew what had hit them. Botham played the first of his 102 Test matches against Australia at Trent Bridge in July 1977, when he was 21. By the end of his fourth he had taken five wickets in an innings three times, made the first of his 14 Test hundreds and run out his captain, Geoffrey Boycott, because he thought he was scoring too slowly if the match, against New Zealand at Christchurch, were to be won (which, eventually, it was). Within two years and one month Botham had scored 1,000 runs and taken 100 wickets in Test matches – no one has ever done that in a shorter time – and was well on the way to becoming a sporting legend.

Richards was a wonderful batsman. In saying that there has probably never been a more intimidating one, I have not forgotten "W.G.", who, like Richards, was known to unnerve umpires as well as bowlers and fielders, quite apart from his own partners. Antigua's first cricketer to make a name for himself was Danny Livingstone, who became the island's chief coach after a playing career with Hampshire. I once asked Livingstone whether there was a potential Richards born in Antigua every week or every year or perhaps every ten years. "Maybe every 50 years," came the reply.

It was not unusual for Richards to whip his first ball through mid-wicket for four, even when it was pitched precisely where the bowler had intended. He had the confidence which came of knowing that he was a symbol of West Indian cricketing dominance, the footwork with which the great natural batsmen are born, the power of lightning and bewildering reflexes. When he was in prime form the best bowlers were as helpless against him as all the rest.

After seeing Richards land a straight drive off Greg Matthews, Australia's off-beat off-spinner, a good 40 yards out of the Bourda Oval in Georgetown in 1991, I wondered whether he had ever made a bigger hit. Yes, he thought there was one against Sussex that beat it – another straight drive, this time off John Snow, which all but cleared the block of flats at the sea end of the county ground at Hove. His blazing, unbeaten 110 in 58 balls against England in Antigua in 1986 contained seven sixes, none slogged yet all bludgeoned. In terms of balls received it was comfortably the fastest Test hundred ever made.

Botham's broadsides were less calculated but every bit as spectacular. His deeds against Australia in three successive Test matches in 1981 – at Headingley, Edgbaston and Old Trafford – were miraculous. Three times, with the Ashes in the balance, he snatched victory from the jaws of defeat. If his 118 in the Fifth Test at Old Trafford was even more stupendous than his 149 in the Third at Headingley that is only because it was more measured – and he still went from 28, when Australia took a new ball, to 100 in not much over half an hour with Dennis Lillee doing his best to stop him. Of its kind it was arguably the finest innings ever played.

Not since Gilbert Jessop's 104 against Australia at The Oval in 1902 had such hitting been seen in a Test match. Jessop hit 17 fours off 76 balls; at Old Trafford Botham hit six sixes and 13 fours off 102 balls; at Headingley a six and 27 fours off 148 balls. To the man in the street Botham became an idol. He was as much of a sporting drawcard as Don Bradman had been, or Muhammad Ali. The bigger the occasion the better it suited him, except, to his chagrin, when it came to denying West Indies. In 38 innings Botham's highest score against them was 81, his average only 21. He took 61 West Indian wickets, however, including Richards's seven times.

Botham's 12 Tests as England's captain, from June 1980 to July 1981, were not among his happiest; but nine of them were against West Indies, and as Mike Brearley's counsellor-in-chief he had shown himself to be a good reader of the game. I suppose we should have known that it was asking too much of him to captain the side as well as doing so much else.

Only Allan Border, Greg Chappell and Richards have held more than Botham's 120 catches in Test cricket. The great majority of Botham's were taken at slip, where, contrary to accepted practice, he insisted upon standing only slightly crouched and with his hands on his thighs even when

[*Bob Thomas*

[*Graham Morris*

Botham and Richards in Antigua, as friends, in 1981 (top) and at Cardiff, as rivals for the last time, in 1993.

the ball was being delivered. Then there was the little matter of his 383 Test wickets. Not even Garfield Sobers had an all-round record much superior to Botham's.

Ian's bowling varied according to the state of his fitness. As a colt he was uninhibitedly aggressive and a brisk fast-medium. He came charging in off a longish run, taking wickets with a splendid out-swinger when he pitched the ball up and knocking back the bat when he dug it in. As time went by, wear and tear took their toll, though never of his enthusiasm. For his last five or six years he had to rely more on ingenuity then strength, and not least on make-believe; but even then something very often turned up, if only a catch to long leg off a long-hop. It is fashionable now, I am afraid, with short-pitched bowling so prevalent, for a bowler to station two long legs, and it was Botham who set the trend.

Even when he was merely ambling up to the wicket and bowling at the gentlest of paces, he did more than anyone to help England beat Australia at Sydney in the 1992 World Cup, taking four for 31 in his ten overs and then making 53 going in first. But his batteries were pretty nearly run down by then, and once the England selectors were no longer interested in him they went flat. Despite containing the last of his 38 first-class hundreds, for Durham against Worcestershire at Stockton, his final days were more melancholy than misty-eyed.

Armed with today's heavy bats, Botham and Richards hit the ball as hard and far as it can ever have been hit. At times when they were batting together, two or three balls might be seen floating like flotsam in the River Tone, which made it all the sadder when their years with Somerset ended not in the laughter which they liked to evoke but in mounting acrimony. The rights and wrongs of that dispute were too well-rehearsed at the time to need repetition here. Let it suffice to say that a parting of the ways was in Somerset's best interests.

Botham's brushes with authority, whether they concerned cricket or the law, in England or elsewhere, may have been evidence of a free spirit, but they were really no more excusable for that. Richards, for his part, had a temper to contend with, which was behind a swingeing two-year suspension, imposed in his late teens, from playing cricket in Antigua, and was another reason for his being held in fairly universal awe. It seemed to me that over the years the press generally exercised discretion in favour of both players, though I doubt very much whether they would subscribe to that view themselves.

To Botham the colour of a man's skin was of small account. To Richards it mattered much more; more, sometimes, than was helpful. Botham was quite without artifice. You got what you saw. Richards was proudly and defiantly black. The swagger with which he walked to the wicket, flashing that Rastafarian wristlet; the air with which he looked round the field, the conviction with which he twiddled his bat, the condescension with which from time to time he failed, were all a part of one of the supreme acts in the history of the game. He was stamped with "the image of a king". As he ruled, so too he raged, and so, in his tranquil moments, he responded to affection.

Viv was a hard cricketer, but a chivalrous, warm-hearted and unselfish one. In the years of his maturity his love of the game and still-unwavering determination inspired Glamorgan to a season to remember. Botham was just as fiercely competitive, just as chivalrous and chauvinistic, and just as contemptuous of averages. His marathon walks undertaken to raise funds for leukaemia have been magnificent, and reflect an abundantly generous spirit. He, too, "sounded forth the trumpet that shall never call retreat". They are two of the immortals, and it is an honour to salute them as such.

John Woodcock was cricket correspondent of The Times *from 1954 to 1987 and editor of* Wisden *from 1981 to 1986.*

2. DAVID GOWER

By MARTIN JOHNSON

In the spring of 1975, as was my custom in those days as cricket correspondent of the *Leicester Mercury*, I turned up to one of Leicestershire's pre-season training sessions to welcome back familiar faces and say hello to one or two unfamiliar ones. Sitting on a bench waiting to take part in a five-a-side football game was a blond, curly-headed young lad I had not seen before. "Hi there. David Gower," he responded to my introduction, and then, in reply to the inevitable follow-up of "what do you do?" he said: "I, um, bat."

In November 1993, when he announced his retirement from cricket at the age of 36, I thought to myself: "I, um, bat?" In retrospect, it was like Michelangelo saying that he dabbled in ceilings, or Mozart that he rattled off the odd tune. Gower's batting was the stuff of poetry, and enriched the lives of those who were privileged to watch him. Following, as it did, the summer retirements of Ian Botham and Viv Richards, his exit represented the completion of one of cricket's nastier hat-tricks, and cricket will be a poorer game for their passing.

However, what made Gower's departure the saddest of all is that, unlike the other two, he was some way short of his sell-by date. Furthermore, it is a matter more for anger than sadness that he was prematurely lost to the game by the fact that the England cricket team had come to regard genius with suspicion, and substituted the ethos that graft was now preferable to craft and perspiration to inspiration. If Beethoven had been employed by the Test and County Cricket Board, he would have been pensioned off with the reference: "It's all very well coming out with a concerto every now and again, but we'd have employed him for a good deal longer if the wretched boy had practised his scales more often."

Gower's 117 Test matches remain a record for England. But with more sympathetic handling, he might have played many more, and would probably have been adding to his total – not to mention adding to our own enjoyment – at least until his 40th birthday in April 1997. However, he ultimately became an anachronism in a joyless era of sprints and press-ups. Latterly, this failure to accommodate a class batsman and a true entertainer was a betrayal of cricket's essential romance, and one of the sadder legacies of an era in which the professional game found itself hijacked by marketing men in grey suits.

During the course of a career that spanned 19 summers, Gower collected a good many medals and gongs around the world, but the proudest possession on his mantelpiece at home is a trophy from a national newspaper that does not, on the face of it, mean very much, neither was it accompanied by any financial reward. It is a plaque inscribed with the words: "For Fun, Style and Excellence", which was a perfect way of summing up both his philosophy and his career. Cricket, even in the high-voltage atmosphere of modern Test matches, was never without fun while Gower was at the crease. Even those who claim he never made the fullest use of his talents would admit to an inimitable style, and you do not score 8,231 Test runs at an average of 44.25 without excelling at the game.

His first mentor at Leicester was Raymond Illingworth, a blunt York-shireman not much given to frivolity. Yet Illingworth recognised very early one of cricket's essential truisms. Change the man, and you change the cricketer. He had the occasional half-hearted stab, such as delivering a stern lecture over what he regarded as dress just the wrong side of acceptably casual during one away trip, whereupon Gower came down for breakfast next morning attired in full evening dress. Slightly suspicious, given the young Gower's already blossoming reputation as a *bon viveur*, Illingworth spluttered: "Bloody hell, Gower. Have you just come in?"

In a different context, the words "Gower's just come in" emptied bars in cricket grounds all around the world. Often they would be filled again soon enough, perhaps after one of those cameos in which Gower's entire career could be captured in a single over. A couple of sumptuous cover drives for four, a languid pull to the mid-wicket boundary, two leaden-footed air shots, and finally the seemingly careless snick to gully. However, he also played innings of prolonged genius and, occasionally, just to remind his detractors, he would get his head down and graft with every bit as single-minded a purpose as the England captain who finally gave up on him, Graham Gooch. He was rarely predictable. James Whitaker recalled batting with him in a county game at Old Trafford when the West Indian, Patrick Patterson, was bowling particularly quickly and Gower three times in an over almost gave his wicket away with rash shots. Junior man or not, Whitaker felt obliged to snort that it was not a benefit match, and such was the lack of reaction he wondered whether Gower had heard him. He had. In Patterson's next over Gower struck four magical boundaries, sauntered up the wicket, and with a deadpan delivery said: "Was that a bit better, then?"

Following Gower's dismissal after his second term as England captain in 1989, the new man, Gooch, was happier without him on that winter's tour to the West Indies. But it was in Australia the following winter that Gooch, who admired Gower as a player as much as anyone, formed the terminal view of his commitment. In the 1990-91 Adelaide Test he watched from the non-striker's end as Gower, wafting carelessly at the last ball before lunch, fell into an Australian trap so obvious that the ball was almost delivered by registered post. This followed an aerial prank during the match against Queensland at Carrara, when Gower and John Morris nipped out during play, hired a couple of Tiger Moths from the airfield across the road, and buzzed the ground. When the management found out, Gower and Morris were fined £1,000 each, a punishment some way out of proportion to the crime, and probably owing much to pique about Gower stealing the headlines from one of the few England victories on a miserable tour. From that point, Gooch never wavered from his view that Gower was a luxury item on tour, non-conducive to team discipline, which is why he helped make sure Gower was not picked for the 1992-93 tour to India despite his class performances (one of them an innings of stoical self-denial to save the

[*Patrick Eagar*

David Gower, aged 20, playing for MCC v Middlesex in 1977 and (inset) aged 35 in his last Test match, at The Oval 1992.

game at Headingley) in two of the final three Tests of the previous summer against Pakistan.

Gower was not selected against Australia the following summer, even when England were losing 4-0. And when, under the new captain Mike Atherton, he was left out of the tour to the West Indies, he decided that playing on for Hampshire was not sufficient motivation to resist offers of full-time media employment. He was comfortably the most treasured English cricketer of his generation, and possibly the most treasured ever. This puzzled even him (Gower at least recognised one or two of his more frustrating traits) but it may not have been unconnected to the Englishman's innate suspicion of perfection, plus his almost complete lack of ego.

His inherently lazy nature made him an indifferent captain, particularly at county level, where the fact that he was largely an instinctive player made it difficult for him to sympathise with and offer advice to individuals; and by his own admission he lost touch too often when away on Test duty. As a Test captain, he shone most brightly on the 1984-85 tour to India, where his bright, positive outlook rubbed off on the team in uncomfortable surroundings. Gower was tactically uninspiring, although he never wavered in his belief that Test players were good enough not to require the sergeant-majorish treatment that he latterly perceived from Gooch and the team manager, Micky Stewart.

When he started his career, he was a shy lad who liked the occasional glass of house wine. When he finished, he was an extrovert imbiber of vintage champagne. However, the reason he was loved, as well as admired, is that he finished with as few airs and graces as he had when he began – except in his batting, which was graceful to the last.

Martin Johnson has been cricket correspondent of The Independent *since the paper began in 1986. For 13 years before that he was cricket correspondent of the* Leicester Mercury. *He was co-author of* Gower: The Autobiography.

CAREER STATISTICS

I. T. BOTHAM

Born November 24, 1955

BATTING

	M	I	NO	R	HS	100s	Avge
First-class matches	402	617	46	19,399	228	38	33.97
Test matches	102	161	6	5,200	208	14	33.54
Limited-overs internationals	116	106	15	2,113	79	0	23.21

BOWLING

	R	W	BB	5W/i	10W/m	Avge	Ct
First-class matches	31,902	1,172	8-34	59	8	27.22	354
Test matches	10,878	383	8-34	27	4	28.40	120
Limited-overs internationals	4,139	145	4-31	0	0	28.54	36

Tests as captain – Played 12: lost 4, drew 8.

I. V. A. RICHARDS

Born March 7, 1952

BATTING

	M	I	NO	R	HS	100s	Avge
First-class matches	507	796	62	36,212	322	114	49.33
Test matches	121	182	12	8,540	291	24	50.23
Limited-overs internationals	187	167	24	6,721	189*	11	47.00

BOWLING

	R	W	BB	5W/i	10W/m	Avge	Ct/St
First-class matches	10,070	223	5-88	1	0	45.15	464/1
Test matches	1,964	32	2-17	0	0	61.37	122
Limited-overs internationals	4,228	118	6-41	2	0	35.83	101

Tests as captain – Played 50: won 27, lost 8, drew 15.

D. I. GOWER

Born April 1, 1957

BATTING

	M	I	NO	R	HS	100s	Avge
First-class matches	448	727	70	26,339	228	53	40.08
Test matches	117	204	18	8,231	215	18	44.25
Limited-overs internationals	114	111	8	3,170	158	7	30.77

BOWLING

	R	W	BB	5W/i	10W/m	Avge	Ct/St
First-class matches	227	4	3-47	0	0	56.75	280/1
Test matches	20	1	1-1	0	0	20.00	74
Limited-overs internationals	14	0	–	–	–	–	44

Tests as captain – Played 32: won 5, lost 18, drew 9.

[*David Frith collection*

England v South Africa: The Oval 1929. *Above:* Hammond stumped by Jock Cameron for 17. *Below:* Herbie Taylor on his way to 121. Ames is the wicket-keeper, Hammond and Woolley the fielders.

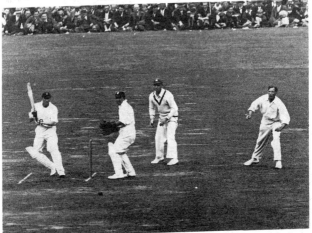

[*David Frith collection*

BEFORE THE INTERRUPTION

MEMORIES OF SOUTH AFRICA IN TEST CRICKET

By E. W. SWANTON

When I first saw a South African team in action, the one brought by H. G. Deane in 1929, their predecessors had been playing Test cricket of a sort for forty years. I put it this way because the nine English teams which had visited what became the Union of South Africa were well short of full Test strength. The very first visitors, led by C. Aubrey Smith (subsequently a star of stage and screen), thought they were engaged in a purely missionary exercise, and were amused that two of their games were posthumously rated as Tests and they accordingly as Test cricketers.

Before 1929 there had been three South African Test tours to England (one the Triangular Tournament of 1912) wherein seven out of the 11 games had ended in home victories, all but one by large margins. One batsman of world class had emerged, H. W. Taylor. South Africa's principal disadvantage was that they were strangers to turf pitches. On their own matting it was a different story, as the first MCC side of 1905-06, led by Pelham Warner, learned to their cost.

South Africa were always very much the juniors on the international scene but they had in that 1905-06 series made a substantial contribution to the evolution of cricket with the development of wrist-spin. Although an Englishman, Bosanquet, is credited with discovering the art, it was four South Africans, Schwarz, Faulkner, Vogler and White, who illustrated its effectiveness both in England and Australia.

Deane, nicknamed Nummy, led a young and popular side which was superb in the field and contained cricketers of notable achievement in the years prior to the Second World War: Mitchell and Siedle as batsmen; Morkel, Owen-Smith and Dalton as all-rounders; Vincent as a left-arm spinner, Bell, fastish, and, far from least, Cameron behind the stumps. Ten of them made hundreds, and although England won two Tests South Africa were ahead on first innings in the other three.

The most glamorous happening was the turnaround in the Headingley Test wherein the match was seemingly so nearly over after two days that Neville Cardus left the scene to pursue (so he subsequently reported) an affair of the heart somewhere out of London. Discovering from the evening papers that "Tuppy" Owen-Smith had made a hundred before lunch (the only South African ever to do so in a Test) and that it needed a characteristically brilliant effort by Frank Woolley to rescue England and finally bring them home, Cardus made haste to the National Liberal Club, composed what he described as one of his best reports and delivered it to the Fleet Street office of the *Manchester Guardian* as though hotfoot from the Leeds train. The great wordsmith was never inhibited by prosaic detail.

The MCC visit to South Africa in 1930-31 was notable in that something not too far removed from the best side that could have been sent was the third to be defeated (in the only completed Test); it was a foretaste of what was to come. On this tour the Cape Town Test was played on grass. By the next visit matting had everywhere given place to turf.

The 1935 South African side to England was a more sophisticated edition of that of 1929, yet still with an average age of only 27. They achieved at last the first Test victory on English soil, and at Lord's. It was the year when the square was infested with root-devouring leatherjackets. There were bare patches from which Xenophon Balaskas, the wrist-spinning Greek chemist, had the time of his life (nine for 103), and Cameron and Mitchell played innings of the strongest contrast but comparable value: 90 in one and threequarter hours in the first instance, a chanceless 164 not out in five and a half hours in the second. Patience personified, technique immaculate, Bruce Mitchell still heads the list of South African Test run-scorers; Jock Cameron, hugely popular, brilliant keeper and dangerous hitter, was dead of enteric fever before this year ended. I have a small memory which epitomised the attitude of this most likeable side: at Southend, match over, his side defeated, team bus waiting, deciding Fifth Test starting next day, "Herby" Wade signing, signing, until the last of a seemingly interminable line of autograph hunters had been satisfied.

The first of my four visits to South Africa took place in 1938-39 when for the first time MCC sent, under Walter Hammond, the strongest side available. They won by an innings the only Test decided, and were much too strong for most of the provinces. At first hand one could see the handicaps under which South African cricket laboured. Their recruiting grounds were confined to the small number of English-speaking schools. The Afrikaners had little liking for cricket, though as the series progressed I was joined for brief spells in the broadcasting box by an Afrikaans commentator. The Currie Cup, the provincial competition, did not function in seasons when overseas tourists were present. In six years in the 1930s South Africa had taken part in only two Test series, the one in England and – a poor arrangement – one at home directly following against Australia wherein a tired side, depressed by the loss of Cameron, were overwhelmed by Grimmett and O'Reilly.

For the 1938-39 series Alan Melville, who had proceeded from Michaelhouse, Natal to Oxford and captained in turn the University and Sussex, succeeded Wade in the captaincy. South Africa were strengthened also by the return from Oxford of the opening bat, Pieter van der Bijl. The broadcasting of cricket was a new thing in South Africa, and in the circumstances it gave the performer a perfect missionary opportunity. At first the SABC wanted to take only my BBC pieces, 30 minutes on Saturdays and holidays, 15 minutes in mid-week. We got off to a lucky start, for on Boxing Day 1938 Tom Goddard of Gloucestershire revived a somnolent session by doing the hat-trick – a commentator's dream and a rarity, for there have been only eight Test hat-tricks since. By the Third Test the time on the South African air had expanded to two hours.

South Africa found a strong fast-medium bowler in Gordon and a high-class medium-pacer in Langton, but England were never short of runs and were one up going into the Fifth Test at Durban, due to be played to a finish. As is now well-worn history, the game was washed out on the tenth afternoon with England at 654 for five, needing only 42 more for victory. The train taking them to the Cape to catch the Union Castle liner home left that evening and so that was that. The key to the highest-scoring Test match ever was a playing condition giving the groundsman liberty to roll twice between each day's play. On the third and seventh nights heavy rain was followed by dawn rollings, which under hot sun made a perfect fresh surface by the time play was resumed. (MCC, by the way, had banned air travel, which would have made an 11th day possible. The wisdom of this was illustrated to the captain and me – Hammond having abrogated the decree so far as he was concerned – when our aircraft had to make a forced landing at Mossel Bay.)

The South African tour to England of 1947 is recalled chiefly for the phenomenal scoring of Compton and Edrich in a summer of almost perpetual sunshine. Melville's side, average age 30 but containing only three others with Test experience, the evergreen Mitchell, Nourse and Viljoen, had to fulfil a programme of 34 matches on English rations – unfamiliarity with which proved their hardest trial. Melville, most elegant of batsmen, left for home a stone or two lighter and with a record that still stands: his 103 in the unfinished Test at Durban was followed eight years later by innings of 189 and 104 not out at Trent Bridge and 117 at Lord's. No one else has made four successive Test hundreds against England.

Having lost a golden chance of winning the First Test after leading on first innings by 325 runs, South Africa were beaten heavily thrice in succession. *Wisden* records that the tourists gave half their gates against Surrey and Lancashire to help restoration after war damage, yet took home a profit of £10,000.

A year later MCC, under F. G. Mann, took part in another conspicuously friendly and successful tour of South Africa. Whereas there was no English bowler fast enough to cause Godfrey Evans to stand back, for South Africa Cuan McCarthy's speed brought him 21 wickets in a well-fought series which England won by adventurous batting and superlative fielding. Although a recent election had put the Nationalists in power for the first time the only indication of a divided country was that the black sections of the crowds were palpably on England's side.

They were equally forthright when Australia visited South Africa in 1949-50. This series saw the advent of Hugh Tayfield, the off-spinner who was due to take many more Test wickets (170) than any other South African. In the Third Test at Durban he took seven for 23, Australia being bowled out on a turning wicket for 75. Although 236 runs ahead, Dudley Nourse, after a weekend's thought, decided against enforcing the follow-on. Thus reprieved, Australia bowled out South Africa in their second innings for 99, and set 336 to win, reached the target thanks to an epic 151 not out by the 21-year-old left-hander, Neil Harvey.

This result typified a fatal lack of self-confidence, as had the way they allowed England to wriggle out of their grasp at Trent Bridge in 1947. The inferiority complex at the heart of their cricket was not completely dissolved until the 1960s.

When, after an interval of 21 years, South Africa were again due on Australian soil in 1952-53, Louis Duffus, their foremost cricket-writer and historian, led the proposal that the tour should be called off because no good would be served by a further sequence of heavy defeats. Happily, this view did not prevail. South Africa found a determined leader in Jack Cheetham and, to the astonishment of all, won the Fifth Test by team effort rather than individual heroics, and so halved the rubber at 2-2. The fielding of the young South African side, which assisted Tayfield to a bag of 30 Test wickets, was said to be the finest seen in Australia.

In 1951 South Africa had won their second Test in England, and the combination of Cheetham and Viljoen as captain and manager respectively which had worked so well in Australia was repeated in 1955. They lost the first two Tests against an England side which had just brought home the Ashes but showed the moral strength to win the next two before losing at The Oval, which at this time was too conducive to spin.

The victory at Old Trafford, by three wickets with a few minutes to spare, had all the ingredients of a great match, including the moment when Paul Winslow, scorning safety in the last over before tea, reached his hundred with a six that pitched yards over the Stretford End sightscreen.

In the mid-1950s South Africa's stock stood high. At home in 1956-57 they again came from behind to square the rubber with England after being two down. But it was far from being a tour to make converts to cricket: it was conducted, almost without exception, slowly, solemnly, with little effort at enterprise by either side.

If that was a disappointment the tour to England in 1960 was a disaster. The political situation was beginning to come to a head and on the field South Africa contributed to their own destruction by sending a young bowler, Geoffrey Griffin, who had been no-balled for throwing at home, and was chosen for the Lord's Test despite having been called 17 times before on the tour. One way and another South African morale disintegrated. The first three Tests were lost, the crowds stayed away and the tour failed to make a profit.

After another battle of batting attrition in South Africa in 1964-65, South Africa came to England for the second half of the following summer. A new generation of players, headed by the tall, left-handed Graeme Pollock, gave their cricket a more enterprising and attractive face than it had ever shown before. In the only Test of three brought to a conclusion, at Trent Bridge, Pollock's 125, made out of 160 in just two and a quarter hours on a seaming, swingy day, invited comparisons with Frank Woolley; in other words it was in the highest possible class.

In their last conclusive gesture before the curtain came down South Africa won seven Tests and lost one in two successive visits by Australia. They now had two further cricketers of world class, in Barry Richards and Mike Procter. The exploits of these two for Hampshire and Gloucestershire respectively in the years ahead were constant reminders of high talent unfulfilled.

E. W. Swanton was on the staff of the Evening Standard *from 1927 to 1938 and began broadcasting in 1934. He was cricket correspondent of the* Daily Telegraph *from 1946 to 1975.*

COMPUTERISED SCORING

AN ENTHUSIAST'S VIEW

By KEN LAWRENCE

A laptop whizz-kid I most certainly am not; computer illiterate more accurately defines it, I suspect. And yet I champion the cause of computerised scoring, and do so moreover with total conviction. The twenty-first century approaches and cricket simply cannot languish in the eighteenth. To compile a scorebook with a quill pen might have a certain charm, but as far as first-class cricket is concerned computers do have advantages.

Let us be realistic: new technology allows us to watch Test matches being played all round the world, the pictures being bounced off a satellite somewhere in space. And television replays are now accepted as an aid to umpires in Test matches and one-day internationals. Why, therefore, not utilise new technology in the everyday scoring of our beautiful game?

I admit, readily, that the introduction of computerised scoring to county cricket in 1993 was a troubled one. Things did not always go right. The reasons have been well recorded: the late arrival of the laptops and thus a late start to the training of scorers; an intermittent "bug" in the system that brought problems; and there were broken promises, with the non-arrival of printers and the day's details each evening. Yet 1993 was far from the disaster some forecast. Despite everything, the scores from all major games did get to their intended destination – the Computer Newspaper Services headquarters in Howden, near Hull, and thence to the media.

CNS, which is a wholly owned subsidiary of the Press Association, endured its problems last summer, but it is worth noting that computerised scoring was successful enough for the Press Association to convert to a similar method for their whole sports results service in 1994. When the Test and County Cricket Board expressed disquiet at the progress, or lack of it, last summer, PA took a much tighter control of CNS. They guaranteed more money, set out to mend the broken promises and gave assurances (which this correspondent has no reason to doubt) that the system would satisfy all of cricket's requirements in its second summer.

Let us look more closely at the summer of 1993. There were stories of scorers not sleeping, or having nightmares. Those "victims" were never found. Tales of laptops being hurled from the box were entertaining – but untrue. Allegations that the scorers could not cope were nonsense. All of them had problems at some stage or other, but they conquered both the machine and their own doubts.

The intention was never to stop scorebooks from being kept as they were in the last century. An old traditionalist, I believe it is right and proper that they are maintained for posterity, as indeed they can be – either simultaneously with the machine or later from the computerised details. So, why the need for change at all, then? Well, the old method of getting details to the media was laborious: the information was man-handled several times – with each handling compounding the chances of a mistake. And the mistakes in cricket scoreboards were many. The new system eliminated these errors. Accurate scores for newspapers were therefore being flashed to media outlets via Howden within seconds rather than hours.

It is hoped that this faster service may encourage those newspapers which gave up cricket scoreboards to restore them, thus giving the game greater exposure. It is expected that editors will pay for camera-ready scoreboards (and other editorial for that matter) which can be dropped straight into sports pages without any work being necessary. Above all, cricket will have for the first time an official scoring system: accurate, efficient and money-raising.

There are, of course, cricketing spin-offs. A county coach will ultimately be able to glean a vast amount of information about his players – their weak shots, their strong ones, where a player is frequently caught – at the press of a key. For millions of facts apart from statistics will be recorded by the scorers. All are stored in a tiny "box" three inches high, 18 wide and 14 across.

Historians, yet men of a new age: that is the role of the 1994 scorers. And, to take liberties with Mr Grantland Rice, when the One Great Scorer comes to write against their names, it will be how well they moved the mouse as well as how they played the game. For computers are here to stay.

Ken Lawrence was formerly sports editor of the Daily Express *and* Sunday Express, *and Media Relations Manager for the TCCB in 1992 and 1993.*

A SCORER'S VIEW

By BILL FRINDALL

On the face of it, the introduction of the computer into the county scorebox was a logical development, perhaps even an inevitable one, utilising technology to improve the art of cricket scoring and construct a potentially valuable database. However, a change of this magnitude needed to be conceived with infinite care and planning. Three things should have been considered essential: a pilot scheme to locate and eradicate the experimental system's inevitable blips; a comprehensive training programme; and the maintenance of a back-up system in the form of a manual scorebook.

Lamentably, none of those three essentials was available to the 18 county scorers when they reported for duty last April. Fortunately for cricket's chroniclers, almost all did keep a traditional scorebook, mostly at their own expense. A few managed to work the computer with their left hand and score the traditional book with their right. The others either had an assistant to operate the computer or had to spend long hours after play writing up their books from the machine or their notes. No thought seems to have been spared for these devoted servants of the county game, many of them elderly and most of whom are paid little or nothing.

The strain of battling with an alien machine, one whose screen was barely visible in sunlight, and learning a system which was inadequately programmed for such eventualities as short runs, unusual dismissals (stumpings off wides and handled the ball) and umpires' changes of decision was considerable. Inexcusably, although printers were promised from the start of the season, none were ever received and so there was no easy access to the data which had been recorded. If an error was made, one scorer had to stop recording play and work laboriously back through the various combinations of key strokes while his colleague concentrated on the action in front of him. Small wonder that, before the end of September, three scorers had suffered heart attacks (all, happily, have recovered) and several others were close to exhaustion.

In checking the domestic first-class scores for this almanack, I maintain close contact with the scorers and could fill several pages with quotes from their correspondence to illustrate the frustration and despair which they suffered. The friendly atmosphere of the scorebox with its rich banter was totally destroyed. The only tangible product of this innovation was a vast increase in the number of scoring errors and differences in the two records of the same match, the last of which was not unravelled until two months after the season ended. This was a system conceived without sufficient planning and foisted upon the counties without due consideration for the welfare of those compelled to operate it. The fabric of our professional game is being whittled away by mindless opportunism.

One lesson should have been learnt from this chaos. Any mechanised system of scoring a cricket match *must* be supported by a manuscript record. Not only is this essential to fall back on when the machine (or its operator) breaks down, but it is vital to the continuity of cricket's archives. This record should be properly bound and not a file of loose print-outs.

Bill Frindall is chief statistician of Wisden *and has been BBC Test Match Special scorer since 1966.*

HOW THE WELSH WERE WON OVER

By EDWARD BEVAN

In 1993 Glamorgan had their best season since 1969 – their Championship year – and success on the field was matched by a bold recruiting drive, which increased membership from 3,600 to nearly 11,000, the second-largest among the counties, and boosted the club's income by £137,000. The scheme was organised in association with Andersen Consulting, who developed a strategy based on the idea that the club should be recognised as representative of the Welsh nation. In 1992, following years of regular defeats, public support had dwindled, there was no likely increase in membership and the club was being forced to sell assets.

The first decision was that, since Glamorgan are nomadic even in their home games, the cost of membership would be cut from £45 to £15. Office staff and players then embarked on a whistle-stop tour of Wales. The team, dressed in their new dark blue and yellow Sunday League strip, began the tour in Cardiff, carrying a huge daffodil and distributing leaflets in the city's shopping arcades. This exercise was repeated every day in different towns and augmented in the evenings by sports forums, coaching sessions and visits to local schools.

The club sent out mailshots explaining the new cut-price deal, placed coupons in Welsh newspapers, and had the players on TV and radio adverts. There was an immediate response, helped by a credit card hotline telephone number and freepost facility. When the season got under way it became clear that membership was cheap enough to be attractive to supporters of visiting counties, who could save on admission charges during a Championship game and the Sunday League fixture. There was immediate evidence of increased attendances; although it was impossible to tell which came first – the victories or the extra support – the Glamorgan players felt motivated and encouraged: "I am a much better player in front of five thousand than five hundred," said one, as temporary stands were hired for three home cup ties.

Paul Russell, a London Welshman and a partner in Andersen Consulting, worked tirelessly throughout the summer and was co-opted on to the county's executive committee. He became a familiar figure at home games, sitting at a desk near the entrance, enrolling new members almost as quickly as they passed through the turnstiles. Russell and Tony Dilloway, Glamorgan's commercial executive, were asked by the TCCB to prepare an interim report which was then circulated to all the other counties.

Plans for the 1994 season were drawn up last October, when a letter from Hugh Morris was sent to all members thanking them for their support and inviting them to renew their membership. The response was good enough to prompt the club to set a new target of 17,500, an ambitious figure but an attainable one, if last year's high marketing and playing standards are maintained.

SRI LANKA'S GREAT GAME

By CHRISTOPHER MARTIN-JENKINS

The really big cricket match in Colombo on March 13, 1993 attracted a crowd of 15,000. There was radio commentary all day long; most of the back-page space in Colombo's two newspapers was devoted to it. The build-up to the great event had been going on all week. President Premadasa (assassinated only a few weeks later) was there on the first day, not so much because he was a cricket enthusiast as because this was the place for a politician to be seen. The match was staged on Sri Lanka's most famous ground, where Test cricket was first played. But this was not a Test match: it was the annual game between two of Colombo's largest schools, Royal College and St Thomas's. The final day of three in the 114th match between the two clashed with the opening day of the Test between Sri Lanka and England and, though cricket followers in other lands may find it hard to believe, it completely put the Test into the shade.

Eton and Harrow at Lord's cannot, these days, hold a candle to what claims to be the oldest school fixture staged without interruption. Nowhere in the world is a school match accorded anything like the same attention. Tickets were more expensive, and in far greater demand, than those for a Test which ought to have been a rare treat for such a cricket-loving island, only the second Sri Lanka had ever played at home against England. In the circumstances it defies belief that the Sri Lankan Board should have allowed any other major event, let alone a Test, to clash with the "battle of the blues", although this is only the oldest and most important of many traditional encounters given extraordinary status at this climax of the school season. I was told that all five Sri Lankan radio channels were carrying cricket commentaries on March 13, only one of them on the Test.

Mike Atherton, who had played a match for England Schools before a crowd of 40,000 at the Khettarama Stadium a few years ago, had less than one-twentieth of that number to watch him open the innings for England at the Sinhalese Cricket Club. Crowds in Colombo are as excited by one-day internationals as they are elsewhere. But it is tradition that really matters. Royal and St Thomas's were modelled on the Victorian public schools of England and the game survives in a Henry Newbolt time-warp that is not only very charming but also ensures a steady stream of talented cricketers better prepared for tough, competitive two-innings cricket than their English counterparts.

Before the game began at the P. Saravanamuttu Stadium, the atmosphere was that of a university rag week, with bicycle parades of students carrying either the blue and gold colours of Royal (motto: *Disce aut Discede* – Learn or Leave) or the blue and black of St Thomas's (motto: *Esto Perpetua* – Let the School be forever). The atmosphere inside was pure carnival, reminding me of St John's, Antigua, when West Indies are winning a Test match. While the players, who all had to have been under 19 the previous September, went about their game with intense keenness, the social event whirled around them. A live band blasted out from the Mustang tent, where the most successful old boys of both schools mix merrily and the tipple is Scotch. Current pupils – and Royal has almost 7,000 boys ranging from six to 19 – yelled themselves hoarse from their designated "tents", actually tin-roofed, single-storey stands.

The batting was not obviously better than you would witness in a game between two leading English schools but the fielding was outstanding at times and a leg-spinner, Nalliah Rajan, took five for 77 – and would probably have had seven for 40 against, shall we say, Winchester. The appealing was often outrageous and so, alas, was the umpiring, but neither of those things is very different in English schools. What is completely different is the incredible interest the annual game generates. I like to think Royal v Thommies will still be the match to be at when Sri Lanka are playing their 50th home Test against England. It was not until the 1993 game had finished, indeed, that Sri Lankans began to notice that the Test had already started. The fact that Sri Lanka subsequently won it had much to do with the strength and prestige of their schools cricket.

Christopher Martin-Jenkins is cricket correspondent of the Daily Telegraph.

PART TWO: RECORDS

TEST CRICKETERS

FULL LIST FROM 1877 TO SEPTEMBER 19, 1993

These lists have been compiled on a home and abroad basis, appearances abroad being printed in *italics*.

Abbreviations. E: England. A: Australia. SA: South Africa. WI: West Indies. NZ: New Zealand. In: India. P: Pakistan. SL: Sri Lanka. Z: Zimbabwe.

All appearances are placed in this order of seniority. Hence, any England cricketer playing against Australia in England has that achievement recorded first and the remainder of his appearances at home (if any) set down before passing to matches abroad. The figures immediately following each name represent the total number of appearances in *all* Tests.

No Tests from the 1993-94 season have been included.

Where the season embraces two different years, the first year is given; i.e. 1876 indicates 1876-77.

ENGLAND

Number of Test cricketers: 565

Abel, R. 13: v A 1888 (3) 1896 (3) 1902 (2); *v A 1891 (3); v SA 1888 (2)*
Absolom, C. A. 1: *v A 1878*
Agnew, J. P. 3: v A 1985 (1); v WI 1984 (1); v SL 1984 (1)
Allen, D. A. 39: v A 1961 (4) 1964 (1); v SA 1960 (2); v WI 1963 (2) 1966 (1); v P 1962 (4); *v A 1962 (1) 1965 (4); v SA 1964 (4); v WI 1959 (5); v NZ 1965 (3); v In 1961 (5); v P 1961 (3)*
Allen, G. O. B. 25: v A 1930 (1) 1934 (2); v WI 1933 (1); v NZ 1931 (3); v In 1936 (3); *v A 1932 (5) 1936 (5); v WI 1947 (3); v NZ 1932 (2)*
Allom, M. J. C. 5: *v SA 1930 (1); v NZ 1929 (4)*
Allott, P. J. W. 13: v A 1981 (1) 1985 (4); v WI 1984 (3); v In 1982 (2); v SL 1984 (1); *v In 1981 (1); v SL 1981 (1)*
Ames, L. E. G. 47: v A 1934 (5) 1938 (2); v SA 1929 (1) 1935 (4); v WI 1933 (3); v NZ 1931 (3) 1937 (3); v In 1932 (1); *v A 1932 (5) 1936 (5); v SA 1938 (5); v WI 1929 (4) 1934 (4); v NZ 1932 (2)*
Amiss, D. L. 50: v A 1968 (1) 1975 (2) 1977 (2); v WI 1966 (1) 1973 (3) 1976 (1); v NZ 1973 (3); v In 1967 (2) 1971 (1) 1974 (3); v P 1967 (1) 1971 (3) 1974 (3); *v A 1974 (5) 1976 (1); v WI 1973 (5) v NZ 1974 (2); v In 1972 (3) 1976 (5); v P 1972 (3)*
Andrew, K. V. 2: v WI 1963 (1); *v A 1954 (1)*
Appleyard, R. 9: v A 1956 (1); v SA 1955 (1); v P 1954 (1); *v A 1954 (4); v NZ 1954 (2)*
Archer, A. G. 1: *v SA 1898*
Armitage, T. 2: *v A 1876 (2)*
Arnold, E. G. 10: v A 1905 (4); v SA 1907 (2); *v A 1903 (4)*
Arnold, G. G. 34: v A 1972 (3) 1975 (1); v WI 1973 (3); v NZ 1969 (1) 1973 (3); v In 1974 (2); v P 1967 (2) 1974 (3); *v A 1974 (4); v WI 1973 (3); v NZ 1974 (2); v In 1972 (4); v P 1972 (3)*
Arnold, J. 1: v NZ 1931
Astill, W. E. 9: *v SA 1927 (5); v WI 1929 (4)*
Atherton, M. A. 29: v A 1989 (2) 1993 (6); v WI 1991 (5); v NZ 1990 (3); v In 1990 (3); v P 1992 (3); *v A 1990 (5); v I 1992 (1); v SL 1992 (1)*
Athey, C. W. J. 23: v A 1980 (1); v WI 1988 (1); v NZ 1986 (3); v In 1986 (2); v P 1987 (4); *v A 1986 (5) 1987 (1); v WI 1980 (2); v NZ 1987 (3); v P 1987 (3)*
Attewell, W. 10: v A 1890 (1); *v A 1884 (5) 1887 (1) 1891 (3)*

Bailey, R. J. 4: v WI 1988 (1); *v WI 1989 (3)*
Bailey, T. E. 61: v A 1953 (5) 1956 (4); v SA 1951 (2) 1955 (5); v WI 1950 (2) 1957 (4); v NZ 1949 (4) 1958 (4); v P 1954 (3); *v A 1950 (4) 1954 (5) 1958 (5); v SA 1956 (5); v WI 1953 (5); v NZ 1950 (2) 1954 (2)*

Bairstow, D. L. 4: v A 1980 (1); v WI 1980 (1); v In 1979 (1); *v WI 1980 (1)*

Bakewell, A. H. 6: v SA 1935 (2); v WI 1933 (1); v NZ 1931 (2); *v In 1933 (1)*

Balderstone, J. C. 2: v WI 1976 (2)

Barber, R. W. 28: v A 1964 (1) 1968 (1); v SA 1960 (1) 1965 (3); v WI 1966 (2); v NZ 1965 (3); *v A 1965 (3); v SA 1964 (4); v In 1961 (5); v P 1961 (3)*

Barber, W. 2: v SA 1935 (2)

Barlow, G. D. 3: v A 1977 (1); *v In 1976 (2)*

Barlow, R. G. 17: v A 1882 (1) 1884 (3) 1886 (3); *v A 1881 (4) 1882 (4) 1886 (2)*

Barnes, S. F. 27: v A 1902 (1) 1909 (3) 1912 (3); v SA 1912 (3); *v A 1901 (3) 1907 (5) 1911 (5); v SA 1913 (4)*

Barnes, W. 21: v A 1880 (1) 1882 (1) 1884 (2) 1886 (2) 1888 (3) 1890 (2); *v A 1882 (4) 1884 (5) 1886 (1)*

Barnett, C. J. 20: v A 1938 (3) 1948 (1); v SA 1947 (3); v WI 1933 (1); v NZ 1937 (3); v In 1936 (1); *v A 1936 (5); v In 1933 (3)*

Barnett, K. J. 4: v A 1989 (3); v SL 1988 (1)

Barratt, F. 5: v SA 1929 (1); *v NZ 1929 (4)*

Barrington, K. F. 82: v A 1961 (5) 1964 (5) 1968 (3); v SA 1955 (2) 1960 (4) 1965 (3); v WI 1963 (5) 1966 (2); v NZ 1965 (2); v In 1959 (5) 1967 (3); v P 1962 (4) 1967 (3); *v A 1962 (5) 1965 (5); v SA 1964 (3); v WI 1959 (5) 1967 (5); v NZ 1962 (3); v In 1961 (5) 1963 (1); v P 1961 (2)*

Barton, V. A. 1: *v SA 1891*

Bates, W. 15: *v A 1881 (4) 1882 (4) 1884 (5) 1886 (2)*

Bean, G. 3: *v A 1891 (3)*

Bedser, A. V. 51: v A 1948 (5) 1953 (5); v SA 1947 (2) 1951 (5) 1955 (1); v WI 1950 (5); v NZ 1949 (2); v In 1946 (3) 1952 (4); v P 1954 (2); *v A 1946 (5) 1950 (5) 1954 (1); v SA 1948 (5); v NZ 1946 (1) 1950 (2)*

Benson, M. R. 1: v In 1986

Berry, R. 2: v WI 1950 (2)

Bicknell, M. P. 2: v A 1993 (2)

Binks, J. G. 2: *v In 1963 (2)*

Bird, M. C. 10: *v SA 1909 (5) 1913 (5)*

Birkenshaw, J. 5: *v WI 1973 (2); v In 1972 (2); v P 1972 (1)*

Blakey, R. J. 2: *v I 1992 (2)*

Bligh, Hon. I. F. W. 4: *v A 1882 (4)*

Blythe, C. 19: v A 1905 (1) 1909 (2); v SA 1907 (3); *v A 1901 (5) 1907 (1); v SA 1905 (5) 1909 (2)*

Board, J. H. 6: *v SA 1898 (2) 1905 (4)*

Bolus, J. B. 7: v WI 1963 (2); *v In 1963 (5)*

Booth, M. W. 2: *v SA 1913 (2)*

Bosanquet, B. J. T. 7: v A 1905 (3); *v A 1903 (4)*

Botham, I. T. 102: v A 1977 (2) 1980 (1) 1981 (6) 1985 (6) 1989 (3); v WI 1980 (5) 1984 (5) 1991 (1); v NZ 1978 (3) 1983 (4) 1986 (1); v In 1979 (4) 1982 (3); v P 1978 (3) 1982 (3) 1987 (5) 1992 (2); *v SL 1984 (1) 1991 (1); v A 1978 (6) 1979 (3) 1982 (5) 1986 (4); v WI 1980 (4) 1985 (5); v NZ 1977 (3) 1983 (3) 1991 (1); v In 1979 (1) 1981 (6); v P 1983 (1); v SL 1981 (1)*

Bowden, M. P. 2: *v SA 1888 (2)*

Bowes, W. E. 15: v A 1934 (3) 1938 (2); v SA 1935 (4); v WI 1939 (1); v In 1932 (1) 1946 (1); *v A 1932 (1); v NZ 1932 (1)*

Bowley, E. H. 5: v SA 1929 (2); *v NZ 1929 (3)*

Boycott, G. 108: v A 1964 (4) 1968 (3) 1972 (2) 1977 (1) 1980 (1) 1981 (6); v SA 1965 (2); v WI 1966 (4) 1969 (3) 1973 (3) 1980 (5); v NZ 1965 (2) 1969 (3) 1973 (3) 1978 (2); v In 1967 (2) 1971 (1) 1974 (1) 1979 (4); v P 1967 (1) 1971 (2); *v A 1965 (5) 1970 (5) 1978 (6) 1979 (3); v SA 1964 (5); v WI 1967 (5) 1973 (5) 1980 (4); v NZ 1965 (2) 1977 (3); v In 1979 (1) 1981 (4); v P 1977 (3)*

Bradley, W. M. 2: v A 1899 (2)

Braund, L. C. 23: v A 1902 (5); v SA 1907 (3); *v A 1901 (5) 1903 (5) 1907 (5)*

Brearley, J. M. 39: v A 1977 (5) 1981 (4); v WI 1976 (2); v NZ 1978 (3); v In 1979 (4); v P 1978 (3); *v A 1976 (1) 1978 (6) 1979 (3); v In 1976 (5) 1979 (1); v P 1977 (2)*

Brearley, W. 4: v A 1905 (2) 1909 (1); v SA 1912 (1)

Brennan, D. V. 2: v SA 1951 (2)

Briggs, John 33: v A 1886 (3) 1888 (3) 1893 (2) 1896 (1) 1899 (1); *v A 1884 (5) 1886 (2) 1887 (1) 1891 (3) 1894 (5) 1897 (5); v SA 1888 (2)*

Broad, B. C. 25: v A 1984 (2); v WI 1984 (4) 1988 (2); v P 1987 (4); v SL 1984 (1); *v A 1986 (5) 1987 (1); v NZ 1987 (3); v P 1987 (3)*

Brockwell, W. 7: v A 1893 (1) 1899 (1); *v A 1894 (5)*

Bromley-Davenport, H. R. 4: *v SA 1895 (3) 1898 (1)*

Brookes, D. 1: *v WI 1947*
Brown, A. 2: *v In 1961 (1); v P 1961 (1)*
Brown, D. J. 26: v A 1968 (4); v SA 1965 (2); v WI 1966 (1) 1969 (3); v NZ 1969 (1); v In 1967 (2): *v A 1965 (4); v WI 1967 (4); v NZ 1965 (2); v P 1968 (3)*
Brown, F. R. 22: v A 1953 (1); v SA 1951 (5); v WI 1950 (1); v NZ 1931 (2) 1937 (1) 1949 (2); v In 1932 (1); *v A 1950 (5); v NZ 1932 (2) 1950 (2)*
Brown, G. 7: v A 1921 (3); *v SA 1922 (4)*
Brown, J. T. 8: v A 1896 (2) 1899 (1); *v A 1894 (5)*
Buckenham, C. P. 4: *v SA 1909 (4)*
Butcher, A. R. 1: v In 1979
Butcher, R. O. 3: *v WI 1980 (3)*
Butler, H. J. 2: v SA 1947 (1); *v WI 1947 (1)*
Butt, H. R. 3: *v SA 1895 (3)*

Caddick, A. R. 4: v A 1993 (4)
Calthorpe, Hon. F. S. G. 4: *v WI 1929 (4)*
Capel, D. J. 15: v A 1989 (1); v WI 1988 (2); v P 1987 (1); *v A 1987 (1); v WI 1989 (4); v NZ 1987 (3); v P 1987 (3)*
Carr, A. W. 11: v A 1926 (4); v SA 1929 (2); *v SA 1922 (5)*
Carr, D. B. 2: *v In 1951 (2)*
Carr, D. W. 1: v A 1909
Cartwright, T. W. 5: v A 1964 (2); v SA 1965 (1); v NZ 1965 (1); *v SA 1964 (1)*
Chapman, A. P. F. 26: v A 1926 (4) 1930 (4); v SA 1924 (2); v WI 1928 (3); *v A 1924 (4) 1928 (4); v SA 1930 (5)*
Charlwood, H. R. J. 2: *v A 1876 (2)*
Chatterton, W. 1: *v SA 1891*
Childs, J. H. 2: v WI 1988 (2)
Christopherson, S. 1: v A 1884
Clark, E. W. 8: v A 1934 (2); v SA 1929 (1); v WI 1933 (2); *v In 1933 (3)*
Clay, J. C. 1: v SA 1935
Close, D. B. 22: v A 1961 (1); v SA 1955 (1); v WI 1957 (2) 1963 (5) 1966 (1) 1976 (3); v NZ 1949 (1); v In 1959 (1) 1967 (3); v P 1967 (3); *v A 1950 (1)*
Coldwell, L. J. 7: v A 1964 (2); v P 1962 (2); *v A 1962 (2); v NZ 1962 (1)*
Compton, D. C. S. 78: v A 1938 (4) 1948 (4) 1953 (5) 1956 (1); v SA 1947 (5) 1951 (4) 1955 (5); v WI 1939 (3) 1950 (1); v NZ 1937 (1) 1949 (4); v In 1946 (3) 1952 (2); v P 1954 (4); *v A 1946 (5) 1950 (4) 1954 (4); v SA 1948 (5) 1956 (5); v WI 1953 (5); v NZ 1946 (1) 1950 (2)*
Cook, C. 1: v SA 1947
Cook, G. 7: v In 1982 (3); *v A 1982 (3); v SL 1981 (1)*
Cook, N. G. B. 15: v A 1989 (3); v WI 1984 (3); v NZ 1983 (2); *v NZ 1983 (1); v P 1983 (3) 1987 (3)*
Cope, G. A. 3: *v P 1977 (3)*
Copson, W. H. 3: v SA 1947 (1); v WI 1939 (2)
Cornford, W. L. 4: *v NZ 1929 (4)*
Cottam, R. M. H. 4: *v In 1972 (2); v P 1968 (2)*
Coventry, Hon. C. J. 2: *v SA 1888 (2)*
Cowans, N. G. 19: v A 1985 (1); v WI 1984 (1); v NZ 1983 (4); *v A 1982 (4); v NZ 1983 (2); v In 1984 (5); v P 1983 (2)*
Cowdrey, C. S. 6: v WI 1988 (1); *v In 1984 (5)*
Cowdrey, M. C. 114: v A 1956 (5) 1961 (4) 1964 (3) 1968 (4); v SA 1955 (1) 1960 (5) 1965 (3); v WI 1957 (5) 1963 (2) 1966 (4); v NZ 1958 (4) 1965 (3); v In 1959 (5); v P 1962 (4) 1967 (2) 1971 (1); *v A 1954 (5) 1958 (5) 1962 (5) 1965 (4) 1970 (3) 1974 (5); v SA 1956 (5); v WI 1959 (5) 1967 (5); v NZ 1954 (2) 1958 (2) 1962 (3) 1965 (3) 1970 (1); v In 1963 (3); v P 1968 (3)*
Coxon, A. 1: v A 1948
Cranston, J. 1: v A 1890
Cranston, K. 8: v A 1948 (1); v SA 1947 (3); *v WI 1947 (4)*
Crapp, J. F. 7: v A 1948 (3); *v SA 1948 (4)*
Crawford, J. N. 12: v SA 1907 (2); *v A 1907 (5); v SA 1905 (5)*
Curtis, T. S. 5: v A 1989 (3); v WI 1988 (2)
Cuttell, W. R. 2: *v SA 1898 (2)*

Dawson, E. W. 5: *v SA 1927 (1); v NZ 1929 (4)*
Dean, H. 3: v A 1912 (2); v SA 1912 (1)

DeFreitas, P. A. J. 33: v A 1989 (1) 1993 (1); v WI 1988 (3) 1991 (5); v NZ 1990 (2); v P 1987 (1) 1992 (2); v SL 1991 (1); *v A 1986 (4) 1990 (3); v WI 1989 (2); v NZ 1987 (2) 1991 (3); v I 1992 (1); v P 1987 (2)*

Denness, M. H. 28: v A 1975 (1); v NZ 1969 (1); v In 1974 (3); v P 1974 (3); *v A 1974 (5); v WI 1973 (5); v NZ 1974 (2); v In 1972 (5); v P 1972 (3)*

Denton, D. 11: v A 1905 (1); *v SA 1905 (5) 1909 (5)*

Dewes, J. G. 5: v A 1948 (1); v WI 1950 (2); *v A 1950 (2)*

Dexter, E. R. 62: v A 1961 (5) 1964 (5) 1968 (2); v WI 1963 (5); v NZ 1958 (1) 1965 (2); v In 1959 (2); v P 1962 (5); *v A 1958 (2) 1962 (5); v SA 1964 (5); v WI 1959 (5); v NZ 1958 (2) 1962 (3); v In 1961 (5); v P 1961 (3)*

Dilley, G. R. 41: v A 1981 (3) 1989 (2); v WI 1980 (3) 1988 (4); v NZ 1983 (1) 1986 (2); v In 1986 (2); v P 1987 (4); *v A 1979 (2) 1986 (4) 1987 (1); v WI 1980 (4); v NZ 1987 (3); v In 1981 (4); v P 1983 (1) 1987 (1)*

Dipper, A. E. 1: v A 1921

Doggart, G. H. G. 2: v WI 1950 (2)

D'Oliveira, B. L. 44: v A 1968 (2) 1972 (5); v WI 1966 (4) 1969 (3); v NZ 1969 (1); v In 1967 (2) 1971 (3); v P 1967 (3) 1971 (3); *v A 1970 (6); v WI 1967 (5); v NZ 1970 (2); v P 1968 (3)*

Dollery, H. E. 4: v A 1948 (2); v SA 1947 (1); v WI 1950 (1)

Dolphin, A. 1: *v A 1920*

Douglas, J. W. H. T. 23: v A 1912 (1) 1921 (5); v SA 1924 (1); *v A 1911 (5) 1920 (5) 1924 (1); v SA 1913 (5)*

Downton, P. R. 30: v A 1981 (1) 1985 (6); v WI 1984 (5) 1988 (3); v In 1986 (1); v SL 1984 (1); *v WI 1980 (3) 1985 (5); v In 1984 (5)*

Druce, N. F. 5: *v A 1897 (5)*

Ducat, A. 1: v A 1921

Duckworth, G. 24: v A 1930 (5); v SA 1924 (1) 1929 (4) 1935 (1); v WI 1928 (1); v In 1936 (3); *v A 1928 (5); v SA 1930 (3); v NZ 1932 (1)*

Duleepsinhji, K. S. 12: v A 1930 (4); v SA 1929 (1); v NZ 1931 (3); *v NZ 1929 (4)*

Durston, F. J. 1: v A 1921

Edmonds, P. H. 51: v A 1975 (2) 1985 (5); v NZ 1978 (3) 1983 (2) 1986 (3); v In 1979 (4) 1982 (3) 1986 (2); v P 1978 (3) 1987 (5); *v A 1978 (1) 1986 (5); v WI 1985 (3); v NZ 1977 (3); v In 1984 (5); v P 1977 (2)*

Edrich, J. H. 77: v A 1964 (3) 1968 (5) 1972 (5) 1975 (4); v SA 1965 (1); v WI 1963 (3) 1966 (1) 1969 (3) 1976 (2); v NZ 1965 (1) 1969 (3); v In 1967 (2) 1971 (3) 1974 (3); v P 1971 (3) 1974 (3); *v A 1965 (5) 1970 (6) 1974 (4); v WI 1967 (5); v NZ 1965 (3) 1970 (2) 1974 (2); v In 1963 (2); v P 1968 (3)*

Edrich, W. J. 39: v A 1938 (4) 1948 (5) 1953 (3); v SA 1947 (4); v WI 1950 (2); v NZ 1949 (4); v In 1946 (1); v P 1954 (1); *v A 1946 (5) 1954 (4); v SA 1938 (5); v NZ 1946 (1)*

Elliott, H. 4: v WI 1928 (1); *v SA 1927 (1); v In 1933 (2)*

Ellison, R. M. 11: v A 1985 (2); v WI 1984 (1); v In 1986 (1); v SL 1984 (1); *v WI 1985 (3); v In 1984 (3)*

Emburey, J. E. 63: v A 1980 (1) 1981 (4) 1985 (6) 1989 (3) 1993 (1); v WI 1980 (3) 1988 (3); v NZ 1978 (1) 1986 (2); v In 1986 (3); v P 1987 (4); v SL 1988 (1); *v A 1978 (4) 1986 (5) 1987 (1); v WI 1980 (4) 1985 (4); v NZ 1987 (3); v In 1979 (1) 1981 (3) 1992 (1); v P 1987 (3); v SL 1981 (1) 1992 (1)*

Emmett, G. M. 1: v A 1948

Emmett, T. 7: *v A 1876 (2) 1878 (1) 1881 (4)*

Evans, A. J. 1: v A 1921

Evans, T. G. 91: v A 1948 (5) 1953 (5) 1956 (5); v SA 1947 (5) 1951 (3) 1955 (3); v WI 1950 (3) 1957 (5); v NZ 1949 (4) 1958 (5); v In 1946 (1) 1952 (4) 1959 (2); v P 1954 (4); *v A 1946 (4) 1950 (5) 1954 (4) 1958 (3); v SA 1948 (3) 1956 (5); v WI 1947 (4) 1953 (4); v NZ 1946 (1) 1950 (2) 1954 (2)*

Fagg, A. E. 5: v WI 1939 (1); v In 1936 (2); *v A 1936 (2)*

Fairbrother, N. H. 10: v NZ 1990 (3); v P 1987 (1); *v NZ 1987 (2); v I 1992 (2); v P 1987 (1); v SL 1992 (1)*

Fane, F. L. 14: *v A 1907 (4); v SA 1905 (5) 1909 (5)*

Farnes, K. 15: v A 1934 (2) 1938 (4); *v A 1936 (2); v WI 1934 (2)*

Farrimond, W. 4: v SA 1935 (1); *v SA 1930 (2); v WI 1934 (1)*

Fender, P. G. H. 13: v A 1921 (2); v SA 1924 (2) 1929 (1); *v A 1920 (3); v SA 1922 (5)*

Ferris, J. J. 1: *v SA 1891*

Fielder, A. 6: *v A 1903 (2) 1907 (4)*

Fishlock, L. B. 4: v In 1936 (2) 1946 (1); *v A 1946 (1)*

Flavell, J. A. 4: v A 1961 (2) 1964 (2)

Fletcher, K. W. R. 59: v A 1968 (1) 1972 (1) 1975 (2); v WI 1973 (3); v NZ 1969 (2) 1973 (3); v In 1971 (2) 1974 (3); v P 1974 (3); *v A 1970 (5) 1974 (5) 1976 (1); v WI 1973 (4); v NZ 1970 (1) 1974 (2); v In 1972 (5) 1976 (3) 1981 (6); v P 1968 (3) 1972 (3); v SL 1981 (1)*

Flowers, W. 8: v A 1893 (1); *v A 1884 (5) 1886 (2)*

Ford, F. G. J. 5: *v A 1894 (5)*

Foster, F. R. 11: v A 1912 (3); v SA 1912 (3); *v A 1911 (5)*

Foster, N. A. 29: v A 1985 (1) 1989 (3) 1993 (1); v WI 1984 (1) 1988 (2); v NZ 1983 (1) 1986 (1); v In 1986 (1); v P 1987 (5); v SL 1988 (1); *v A 1987 (1); v WI 1985 (3); v NZ 1983 (2); v In 1984 (2); v P 1983 (2) 1987 (2)*

Foster, R. E. 8: v SA 1907 (3); *v A 1903 (5)*

Fothergill, A. J. 2: *v SA 1888 (2)*

Fowler, G. 21: v WI 1984 (5); v NZ 1983 (2); v P 1982 (1); v SL 1984 (1); *v A 1982 (3); v NZ 1983 (2); v In 1984 (5); v P 1983 (2)*

Fraser, A. R. C. 12: v A 1989 (3) 1993 (1); v In 1990 (3); *v A 1990 (3); v WI 1989 (2)*

Freeman, A. P. 12: v SA 1929 (3); v WI 1928 (3); *v A 1924 (2); v SA 1927 (4)*

French, B. N. 16: v NZ 1986 (3); v In 1986 (2); v P 1987 (4); *v A 1987 (1); v NZ 1987 (3); v P 1987 (3)*

Fry, C. B. 26: v A 1899 (5) 1902 (3) 1905 (4) 1909 (3) 1912 (3); v SA 1907 (3) 1912 (3); *v SA 1895 (2)*

Gatting, M. W. 74: v A 1980 (1) 1981 (6) 1985 (6) 1989 (1) 1993 (2); v WI 1980 (4) 1984 (1) 1988 (2); v NZ 1983 (2) 1986 (3); v In 1986 (3); v P 1982 (3) 1987 (5); *v A 1986 (5) 1987 (1); v WI 1980 (1) 1985 (1); v NZ 1977 (1) 1983 (2) 1987 (3); v In 1981 (5) 1984 (5) 1992 (3); v P 1977 (1) 1983 (3) 1987 (3); v SL 1992 (1)*

Gay, L. H. 1: *v A 1894*

Geary, G. 14: v A 1926 (2) 1930 (1) 1934 (2); v SA 1924 (1) 1929 (1); *v A 1928 (4); v SA 1927 (2)*

Gibb, P. A. 8: v In 1946 (2); *v A 1946 (1); v SA 1938 (5)*

Gifford, N. 15: v A 1964 (2) 1972 (3); v NZ 1973 (2); v In 1971 (2); v P 1971 (2); *v In 1972 (2); v P 1972 (2)*

Gilligan, A. E. R. 11: v SA 1924 (4); *v A 1924 (5); v SA 1922 (2)*

Gilligan, A. H. H. 4: *v NZ 1929 (4)*

Gimblett, H. 3: v WI 1939 (1); v In 1936 (2)

Gladwin, C. 8: v SA 1947 (2); v NZ 1949 (1); *v SA 1948 (5)*

Goddard, T. W. 8: v A 1930 (1); v WI 1939 (2); v NZ 1937 (2); *v SA 1938 (3)*

Gooch, G. A. 107: v A 1975 (2) 1980 (1) 1981 (5) 1985 (6) 1989 (5) 1993 (6); v WI 1980 (5) 1988 (5) 1991 (5); v NZ 1978 (3) 1986 (3) 1990 (3); v In 1979 (1) 1986 (3) 1990 (3); v P 1978 (2) 1992 (5); v SL 1988 (1) 1991 (1); *v A 1978 (6) 1979 (2) 1990 (4); v WI 1980 (4) 1985 (5) 1989 (2); v NZ 1991 (3); v In 1979 (1) 1981 (6) 1992 (2); v P 1987 (3); v SL 1981 (1)*

Gover, A. R. 4: v NZ 1937 (2); v In 1936 (1) 1946 (1)

Gower, D. I. 117: v A 1980 (1) 1981 (5) 1985 (6) 1989 (6); v WI 1980 (1) 1984 (5) 1988 (4); v NZ 1978 (3) 1983 (4) 1986 (3); v In 1979 (4) 1982 (3) 1986 (2) 1990 (3); v P 1978 (3) 1982 (3) 1987 (5) 1992 (3); v SL 1984 (1); *v A 1978 (6) 1979 (3) 1982 (5) 1986 (5) 1990 (5); v WI 1980 (4) 1985 (5); v NZ 1983 (3); v In 1979 (1) 1981 (6) 1984 (5); v P 1983 (3); v SL 1981 (1)*

Grace, E. M. 1: v A 1880

Grace, G. F. 1: v A 1880

Grace, W. G. 22: v A 1880 (1) 1882 (1) 1884 (3) 1886 (3) 1888 (3) 1890 (2) 1893 (3) 1896 (3) 1899 (1); *v A 1891 (3)*

Graveney, T. W. 79: v A 1953 (5) 1956 (2) 1968 (5); v SA 1951 (1) 1955 (5); v WI 1957 (4) 1966 (4) 1969 (1); v NZ 1958 (4); v In 1952 (4) 1967 (3); v P 1954 (3) 1962 (4) 1967 (3); *v A 1954 (2) 1958 (5) 1962 (3); v WI 1953 (5) 1967 (5); v NZ 1954 (2) 1958 (2); v In 1951 (4); v P 1968 (3)*

Greenhough, T. 4: v SA 1960 (1); v In 1959 (3)

Greenwood, A. 2: *v A 1876 (2)*

Greig, A. W. 58: v A 1972 (5) 1975 (4) 1977 (5); v WI 1973 (3) 1976 (5); v NZ 1973 (3); v In 1974 (3); v P 1974 (3); *v A 1974 (6) 1976 (1); v WI 1973 (5); v NZ 1974 (2); v In 1972 (5) 1976 (5); v P 1972 (3)*

Greig, I. A. 2: v P 1982 (2)

Grieve, B. A. F. 2: *v SA 1888 (2)*

Griffith, S. C. 3: *v SA 1948 (2); v WI 1947 (1)*

Gunn, G. 15: v A 1909 (1); *v A 1907 (5) 1911 (5); v WI 1929 (4)*

Gunn, J. 6: v A 1905 (1); *v A 1901 (5)*
Gunn, W. 11: v A 1888 (2) 1890 (2) 1893 (3) 1896 (1) 1899 (1); *v A 1886 (2)*

Haig, N. E. 5: v A 1921 (1); *v WI 1929 (4)*
Haigh, S. 11: v A 1905 (2) 1909 (1) 1912 (1); *v SA 1898 (2) 1905 (5)*
Hallows, C. 2: v A 1921 (1); v WI 1928 (1)
Hammond, W. R. 85: v A 1930 (5) 1934 (5) 1938 (4); v SA 1929 (4) 1935 (5); v WI 1928 (3) 1933 (3) 1939 (3); v NZ 1931 (3) 1937 (3); v In 1932 (1) 1936 (2) 1946 (3); *v A 1928 (5) 1932 (5) 1936 (5) 1946 (4); v SA 1927 (5) 1930 (5) 1938 (5); v WI 1934 (4); v NZ 1932 (2) 1946 (1)*
Hampshire, J. H. 8: v A 1972 (1) 1975 (1); v WI 1969 (2); *v A 1970 (2); v NZ 1970 (2)*
Hardinge, H. T. W. 1: v A 1921
Hardstaff, J. 5: *v A 1907 (5)*
Hardstaff, J. jun. 23: v A 1938 (2) 1948 (1); v SA 1935 (1); v WI 1939 (3); v NZ 1937 (3); v In 1936 (2) 1946 (2); *v A 1936 (5) 1946 (1); v WI 1947 (3)*
Harris, Lord 4: v A 1880 (1) 1884 (2); *v A 1878 (1)*
Hartley, J. C. 2: *v SA 1905 (2)*
Hawke, Lord 5: *v SA 1895 (3) 1898 (2)*
Hayes, E. G. 5: v A 1909 (1); v SA 1912 (1); *v SA 1905 (3)*
Hayes, F. C. 9: v WI 1973 (3) 1976 (2); *v WI 1973 (4)*
Hayward, T. W. 35: v A 1896 (2) 1899 (5) 1902 (1) 1905 (5) 1909 (1); v SA 1907 (3); *v A 1897 (5) 1901 (5) 1903 (5); v SA 1895 (3)*
Hearne, A. 1: *v SA 1891*
Hearne, F. 2: *v SA 1888 (2)*
Hearne, G. G. 1: *v SA 1891*
Hearne, J. T. 12: v A 1896 (3) 1899 (3); *v A 1897 (5); v SA 1891 (1)*
Hearne, J. W. 24: v A 1912 (3) 1921 (1) 1926 (1); v SA 1912 (2) 1924 (3); *v A 1911 (5) 1920 (2) 1924 (4); v SA 1913 (3)*
Hemmings, E. E. 16: v A 1989 (1); v NZ 1990 (3); v In 1990 (3); v P 1982 (2); *v A 1982 (3) 1987 (1) 1990 (1); v NZ 1987 (1); v P 1987 (1)*
Hendren, E. H. 51: v A 1921 (2) 1926 (5) 1930 (2) 1934 (4); v SA 1924 (5) 1929 (4); v WI 1928 (1); *v A 1920 (5) 1924 (5) 1928 (5); v SA 1930 (5); v WI 1929 (4) 1934 (4)*
Hendrick, M. 30: v A 1977 (3) 1980 (1) 1981 (2); v WI 1976 (2) 1980 (2); v NZ 1978 (2); v In 1974 (3) 1979 (4); v P 1974 (2); *v A 1974 (2) 1978 (5); v NZ 1974 (1) 1977 (1)*
Heseltine, C. 2: *v SA 1895 (2)*
Hick, G. A. 18: v A 1993 (3); v WI 1991 (4); v P 1992 (4); *v NZ 1991 (3); v I 1992 (3); v SL 1992 (1)*
Higgs, K. 15: v A 1968 (1); v WI 1966 (5); v SA 1965 (1); v In 1967 (1); v P 1967 (3); *v A 1965 (1); v NZ 1965 (3)*
Hill, A. 2: *v A 1876 (2)*
Hill, A. J. L. 3: *v SA 1895 (3)*
Hilton, M. J. 4: v SA 1951 (1); v WI 1950 (1); *v In 1951 (2)*
Hirst, G. H. 24: v A 1899 (1) 1902 (4) 1905 (3) 1909 (4); v SA 1907 (3); *v A 1897 (4) 1903 (5)*
Hitch, J. W. 7: v A 1912 (1) 1921 (1); v SA 1912 (1); *v A 1911 (3) 1920 (1)*
Hobbs, J. B. 61: v A 1909 (3) 1912 (3) 1921 (1) 1926 (5) 1930 (5); v SA 1912 (3) 1924 (4) 1929 (1); v WI 1928 (2); *v A 1907 (4) 1911 (5) 1920 (5) 1924 (5) 1928 (5); v SA 1909 (5) 1913 (5)*
Hobbs, R. N. S. 7: v In 1967 (3); v P 1967 (1) 1971 (1); *v WI 1967 (1); v P 1968 (1)*
Hollies, W. E. 13: v A 1948 (1); v SA 1947 (3); v WI 1950 (2); v NZ 1949 (4); *v WI 1934 (3)*
Holmes, E. R. T. 5: v SA 1935 (1); *v WI 1934 (4)*
Holmes, P. 7: v A 1921 (1); v In 1932 (1); *v SA 1927 (5)*
Hone, L. 1: *v A 1878*
Hopwood, J. L. 2: v A 1934 (2)
Hornby, A. N. 3: v A 1882 (1) 1884 (1); *v A 1878 (1)*
Horton, M. J. 2: v In 1959 (2)
Howard, N. D. 4: *v In 1951 (4)*
Howell, H. 5: v A 1921 (1); v SA 1924 (1); *v A 1920 (3)*
Howorth, R. 5: v SA 1947 (1); *v WI 1947 (4)*
Humphries, J. 3: *v A 1907 (3)*
Hunter, J. 5: *v A 1884 (5)*
Hussain, N. 7: v A 1993 (4); *v WI 1989 (3)*
Hutchings, K. L. 7: v A 1909 (2); *v A 1907 (5)*
Hutton, L. 79: v A 1938 (3) 1948 (4) 1953 (5); v SA 1947 (5) 1951 (5); v WI 1939 (3) 1950 (3); v NZ 1937 (3) 1949 (4); v In 1946 (3) 1952 (4); v P 1954 (2); *v A 1946 (5) 1950 (5) 1954 (5); v SA 1938 (4) 1948 (5); v WI 1947 (2) 1953 (5); v NZ 1950 (2) 1954 (2)*
Hutton, R. A. 5: v In 1971 (3); v P 1971 (2)

Iddon, J. 5: v SA 1935 (1); *v WI 1934* (4)
Igglesden, A. P. 1: v A 1989
Ikin, J. T. 18: v SA 1951 (3) 1955 (1); v In 1946 (2) 1952 (2); *v A 1946* (5); *v NZ 1946* (1); *v WI 1947* (4)
Illingworth, R. 61: v A 1961 (2) 1968 (3) 1972 (5); v SA 1960 (4); v WI 1966 (2) 1969 (3) 1973 (3); v NZ 1958 (1) 1965 (1) 1969 (3) 1973 (3); v In 1959 (2) 1967 (3) 1971 (3); v P 1962 (1) 1967 (1) 1971 (3); *v A 1962* (2) *1970* (6); *v WI 1959* (5); *v NZ 1962* (3) *1970* (2)
Illingworth, R. K. 2: v WI 1991 (2)
Ilott, M. C. 3: v A 1993 (3)
Insole, D. J. 9: v A 1956 (1); v SA 1955 (1); v WI 1950 (1) 1957 (1); *v SA 1956* (5)

Jackman, R. D. 4: v P 1982 (2); *v WI 1980* (2)
Jackson, F. S. 20: v A 1893 (2) 1896 (3) 1899 (5) 1902 (5) 1905 (5)
Jackson, H. L. 2: v A 1961 (1); v NZ 1949 (1)
Jameson, J. A. 4: v In 1971 (2); *v WI 1973* (2)
Jardine, D. R. 22: v WI 1928 (2) 1933 (2); v NZ 1931 (3); v In 1932 (1); *v A 1928* (5) *1932* (5); *v NZ 1932* (1); *v In 1933* (3)
Jarvis, P. W. 9: v A 1989 (2); v WI 1988 (2); *v NZ 1987* (2); *v I 1992* (2), *v SL 1992* (1)
Jenkins, R. O. 9: v WI 1950 (2); v In 1952 (2); *v SA 1948* (5)
Jessop, G. L. 18: v A 1899 (1) 1902 (4) 1905 (1) 1909 (2); v SA 1907 (3) 1912 (2); *v A 1901* (5)
Jones, A. O. 12: v A 1899 (1) 1905 (2) 1909 (2); *v A 1901* (5) *1907* (2)
Jones, I. J. 15: v WI 1966 (2); *v A 1965* (4); *v WI 1967* (5); *v NZ 1965* (3); *v In 1963* (1)
Jupp, H. 2: *v A 1876* (2)
Jupp, V. W. C. 8: v A 1921 (2); v WI 1928 (2); *v SA 1922* (4)

Keeton, W. W. 2: v A 1934 (1); v WI 1939 (1)
Kennedy, A. S. 5: *v SA 1922* (5)
Kenyon, D. 8: v A 1953 (2); v SA 1955 (3); *v In 1951* (3)
Killick, E. T. 2: v SA 1929 (2)
Kilner, R. 9: v A 1926 (4); v SA 1924 (2); *v A 1924* (3)
King, J. H. 1: v A 1909
Kinneir, S. P. 1: *v A 1911*
Knight, A. E. 3: *v A 1903* (3)
Knight, B. R. 29: v A 1968 (2); v WI 1966 (1) 1969 (3); v NZ 1969 (2); v P 1962 (1); *v A 1962* (1) *1965* (2); *v NZ 1962* (3) *1965* (2); *v In 1961* (4) *1963* (5); *v P 1961* (2)
Knight, D. J. 2: v A 1921 (2)
Knott, A. P. E. 95: v A 1968 (5) 1972 (5) 1975 (4) 1977 (5) 1981 (2); v WI 1969 (3) 1973 (3) 1976 (5) 1980 (4); v NZ 1969 (3) 1973 (3); v In 1971 (3) 1974 (3); v P 1967 (2) 1971 (3) 1974 (3); *v A 1970* (6) *1974* (6) *1976* (1); *v WI 1967* (2) *1973* (5); *v NZ 1970* (1) *1974* (2); *v In 1972* (5) *1976* (5); *v P 1968* (3) *1972* (3)
Knox, N. A. 2: v SA 1907 (2)

Laker, J. C. 46: v A 1948 (3) 1953 (3) 1956 (5); v SA 1951 (2) 1955 (1); v WI 1950 (1) 1957 (4); v NZ 1949 (1) 1958 (4); v In 1952 (4); v P 1954 (1); *v A 1958* (4); *v SA 1956* (5); *v WI 1947* (4) *1953* (4)
Lamb, A. J. 79: v A 1985 (6) 1989 (1); v WI 1984 (5) 1988 (4) 1991 (4); v NZ 1983 (4) 1986 (1) 1990 (3); v In 1982 (3) 1986 (2) 1990 (3); v P 1982 (3) 1992 (2); v SL 1984 (1) 1988 (1); *v A 1982* (5) *1986* (5) *1990* (3); *v WI 1985* (5) *1989* (4); *v NZ 1983* (3) *1991* (3); *v In 1984* (5); *v P 1983* (3)
Langridge, James 8: v SA 1935 (1); v WI 1933 (2); v In 1936 (1) 1946 (1); *v In 1933* (3)
Larkins, W. 13: v A 1981 (1); v WI 1980 (3); *v A 1979* (1) *1990* (3); *v WI 1989* (4); *v In 1979* (1)
Larter, J. D. F. 10: v SA 1965 (2); v NZ 1965 (1); v P 1962 (1); *v NZ 1962* (3); *v In 1963* (3)
Larwood, H. 21: v A 1926 (2) 1930 (3); v SA 1929 (3); v WI 1928 (2); v NZ 1931 (1); *v A 1928* (5) *1932* (5)
Lathwell, M. N. 2: v A 1993 (2)
Lawrence, D. V. 5: v WI 1991 (2); v SL 1988 (1) 1991 (1); *v NZ 1991* (1)
Leadbeater, E. 2: *v In 1951* (2)
Lee, H. W. 1: *v SA 1930*
Lees, W. S. 5: *v SA 1905* (5)
Legge, G. B. 5: *v SA 1927* (1); *v NZ 1929* (4)
Leslie, C. F. H. 4: *v A 1882* (4)
Lever, J. K. 21: v A 1977 (3); v WI 1980 (1); v In 1979 (1) 1986 (1); *v A 1976* (1) *1978* (1) *1979* (1); *v NZ 1977* (1); *v In 1976* (5) *1979* (1) *1981* (2); *v P 1977* (3)

Lever, P. 17: v A 1972 (1) 1975 (1); v In 1971 (1); v P 1971 (3); *v A 1970 (5) 1974 (2); v NZ 1970 (2) 1974 (2)*
Leveson Gower, H. D. G. 3: *v SA 1909 (3)*
Levett, W. H. V. 1: *v In 1933*
Lewis, A. R. 9: v NZ 1973 (1); *v In 1972 (5); v P 1972 (3)*
Lewis, C. C. 20: v A 1993 (2); v WI 1991 (2); v NZ 1990 (1); v In 1990 (2); v P 1992 (5); v SL 1991 (1); *v A 1990 (1); v NZ 1991 (2); v I 1992 (3); v SL 1992 (1)*
Leyland, M. 41: v A 1930 (3) 1934 (5) 1938 (1); v SA 1929 (5) 1935 (4); v WI 1928 (1) 1933 (1); v In 1936 (2); *v A 1928 (1) 1932 (5) 1936 (5); v SA 1930 (5); v WI 1934 (3)*
Lilley, A. A. 35: v A 1896 (3) 1899 (4) 1902 (5) 1905 (5) 1909 (5); v SA 1907 (3); *v A 1901 (5) 1903 (5)*
Lillywhite, James jun. 2: *v A 1876 (2)*
Lloyd, D. 9: v In 1974 (2); v P 1974 (3); *v A 1974 (4)*
Lloyd, T. A. 1: v WI 1984
Loader, P. J. 13: v SA 1955 (1); v WI 1957 (2); v NZ 1958 (3); v P 1954 (1); *v A 1958 (2); v SA 1956 (4)*
Lock, G. A. R. 49: v A 1953 (2) 1956 (4) 1961 (3); v SA 1955 (3); v WI 1957 (3) 1963 (3); v NZ 1958 (5); v In 1952 (2); v P 1962 (3); *v A 1958 (4); v SA 1956 (1); v WI 1953 (5) 1967 (2); v NZ 1958 (2); v In 1961 (5); v P 1961 (2)*
Lockwood, W. H. 12: v A 1893 (2) 1899 (1) 1902 (4); *v A 1894 (5)*
Lohmann, G. A. 18: v A 1886 (3) 1888 (3) 1890 (2) 1896 (1); *v A 1886 (2) 1887 (1) 1891 (3); v SA 1895 (3)*
Lowson, F. A. 7: v SA 1951 (2) 1955 (1); *v In 1951 (4)*
Lucas, A. P. 5: v A 1880 (1) 1882 (1) 1884 (2); *v A 1878 (1)*
Luckhurst, B. W. 21: v A 1972 (4); v WI 1973 (2); v In 1971 (3); v P 1971 (3); *v A 1970 (5) 1974 (2); v NZ 1970 (2)*
Lyttelton, Hon. A. 4: v A 1880 (1) 1882 (1) 1884 (2)

Macaulay, G. G. 8: v A 1926 (1); v SA 1924 (1); v WI 1933 (2); *v SA 1922 (4)*
MacBryan, J. C. W. 1: v SA 1924
McCague, M. J. 2: v A 1993 (2)
McConnon, J. E. 2: v P 1954 (2)
McGahey, C. P. 2: *v A 1901 (2)*
MacGregor, G. 8: v A 1890 (2) 1893 (3); *v A 1891 (3)*
McIntyre, A. J. W. 3: v SA 1955 (1); v WI 1950 (1); *v A 1950 (1)*
MacKinnon, F. A. 1: *v A 1878*
MacLaren, A. C. 35: v A 1896 (2) 1899 (4) 1902 (5) 1905 (4) 1909 (5); *v A 1894 (5) 1897 (5) 1901 (5)*
McMaster, J. E. P. 1: *v SA 1888*
Makepeace, J. W. H. 4: *v A 1920 (4)*
Malcolm, D. E. 25: v A 1989 (1) v A 1993 (1); v WI 1991 (2); v NZ 1990 (3); v In 1990 (3); v P 1992 (3); *v A 1990 (5); v WI 1989 (4); v I 1992 (2); v SL 1992 (1)*
Mallender, N. A. 2: v P 1992 (2)
Mann, F. G. 7: v NZ 1949 (2); *v SA 1948 (5)*
Mann, F. T. 5: *v SA 1922 (5)*
Marks, V. J. 6: v NZ 1983 (1); v P 1982 (1); *v NZ 1983 (1); v P 1983 (3)*
Marriott, C. S. 1: v WI 1933
Martin, F. 2: v A 1890 (1); *v SA 1891 (1)*
Martin, J. W. 1: v SA 1947
Mason, J. R. 5: *v A 1897 (5)*
Matthews, A. D. G. 1: v NZ 1937
May, P. B. H. 66: v A 1953 (2) 1956 (5) 1961 (4); v SA 1951 (2) 1955 (5); v WI 1957 (5); v NZ 1958 (5); v In 1952 (4) 1959 (3); v P 1954 (4); *v A 1954 (5) 1958 (5); v SA 1956 (5); v WI 1953 (5) 1959 (3); v NZ 1954 (2) 1958 (2)*
Maynard, M. P. 3: v A 1993 (2); v WI 1988 (1)
Mead, C. P. 17: v A 1921 (2); *v A 1911 (4) 1928 (1); v SA 1913 (5) 1922 (5)*
Mead, W. 1: v A 1899
Midwinter, W. E. 4: *v A 1881 (4)*
Milburn, C. 9: v A 1968 (2); v WI 1966 (4); v In 1967 (1); v P 1967 (1); *v P 1968 (1)*
Miller, A. M. 1: *v SA 1895*
Miller, G. 34: v A 1977 (2); v WI 1976 (1) 1984 (2); v NZ 1978 (2); v In 1979 (3) 1982 (1); v P 1978 (3) 1982 (1); *v A 1978 (6) 1979 (1) 1982 (5); v WI 1980 (1); v NZ 1977 (3); v P 1977 (3)*

Milligan, F. W. 2: *v SA 1898 (2)*
Millman, G. 6: v P 1962 (2); *v In 1961 (2); v P 1961 (2)*
Milton, C. A. 6: v NZ 1958 (2); v In 1959 (2); *v A 1958 (2)*
Mitchell, A. 6: v SA 1935 (2); v In 1936 (1); *v In 1933 (3)*
Mitchell, F. 2: *v SA 1898 (2)*
Mitchell, T. B. 5: v A 1934 (2); v SA 1935 (1); *v A 1932 (1); v NZ 1932 (1)*
Mitchell-Innes, N. S. 1: v SA 1935
Mold, A. W. 3: *v A 1893 (3)*
Moon, L. J. 4: *v SA 1905 (4)*
Morley, F. 4: v A 1880 (1); *v A 1882 (3)*
Morris, H. 3: v WI 1991 (2); v SL 1991 (1)
Morris, J. E. 3: *v In 1990 (3)*
Mortimore, J. B. 9: v A 1964 (1); v In 1959 (2); *v A 1958 (1); v NZ 1958 (2); v In 1963 (3)*
Moss, A. E. 9: v A 1956 (1); v SA 1960 (2); v In 1959 (3); *v WI 1953 (1) 1959 (2)*
Moxon, M. D. 10: v A 1989 (2); v WI 1988 (2); v NZ 1986 (2); v P 1987 (1); *v A 1987 (1); v NZ 1987 (3)*
Munton, T. A. 2: v P 1992 (2)
Murdoch, W. L. 1: *v SA 1891*
Murray, J. T. 21: v A 1961 (5); v WI 1966 (1); v In 1967 (3); v P 1962 (3) 1967 (1); *v A 1962 (1); v SA 1964 (1); v NZ 1962 (1) 1965 (1); v In 1961 (3); v P 1961 (1)*

Newham, W. 1: *v A 1887*
Newport, P. J. 3: v A 1989 (1); v SL 1988 (1); *v A 1990 (1)*
Nichols, M. S. 14: v A 1930 (1); v SA 1935 (4); v WI 1933 (1) 1939 (1); *v NZ 1929 (4); v In 1933 (3)*

Oakman, A. S. M. 2: v A 1956 (2)
O'Brien, Sir T. C. 5: v A 1884 (1) 1888 (1); *v SA 1895 (3)*
O'Connor, J. 4: v SA 1929 (1); *v WI 1929 (3)*
Old, C. M. 46: v A 1975 (3) 1977 (2) 1980 (1) 1981 (2); v WI 1973 (1) 1976 (2) 1980 (1); v NZ 1973 (2) 1978 (1); v In 1974 (3); v P 1974 (3) 1978 (3); *v A 1974 (2) 1976 (1) 1978 (1); v WI 1973 (4) 1980 (1); v NZ 1974 (1) 1977 (2); v In 1972 (4) 1976 (4); v P 1972 (1) 1977 (1)*
Oldfield, N. 1: v WI 1939

Padgett, D. E. V. 2: v SA 1960 (2)
Paine, G. A. E. 4: *v WI 1934 (4)*
Palairet, L. C. H. 2: v A 1902 (2)
Palmer, C. H. 1: *v WI 1953*
Palmer, K. E. 1: *v SA 1964*
Parfitt, P. H. 37: v A 1964 (4) 1972 (3); v SA 1965 (2); v WI 1969 (1); v NZ 1965 (2); v P 1962 (5); *v A 1962 (2); v SA 1964 (5); v NZ 1962 (3) 1965 (3); v In 1961 (2) 1963 (3); v P 1961 (2)*
Parker, C. W. L. 1: v A 1921
Parker, P. W. G. 1: v A 1981
Parkhouse, W. G. A. 7: v WI 1950 (2); v In 1959 (2); *v A 1950 (2); v NZ 1950 (1)*
Parkin, C. H. 10: v A 1921 (4); v SA 1924 (1); *v A 1920 (5)*
Parks, J. H. 1: v NZ 1937
Parks, J. M. 46: v A 1964 (5); v SA 1960 (5) 1965 (3); v WI 1963 (4) 1966 (4); v NZ 1965 (3); v P 1954 (1); *v A 1965 (5); v SA 1964 (5); v WI 1959 (1) 1967 (3); v NZ 1965 (2); v In 1963 (5)*
Pataudi sen., Nawab of, 3: v A 1934 (1); *v A 1932 (2)*
Paynter, E. 20: v A 1938 (4); v WI 1939 (2); v NZ 1931 (1) 1937 (2); v In 1932 (1); *v A 1932 (3); v SA 1938 (5); v NZ 1932 (2)*
Peate, E. 9: v A 1882 (1) 1884 (3) 1886 (1); *v A 1881 (4)*
Peebles, I. A. R. 13: v A 1930 (2); v NZ 1931 (3); *v SA 1927 (4) 1930 (4)*
Peel, R. 20: v A 1888 (3) 1890 (1) 1893 (1) 1896 (1); *v A 1884 (5) 1887 (1) 1891 (3) 1894 (5)*
Penn, F. 1: v A 1880
Perks, R. T. D. 2: v WI 1939 (1); *v SA 1938 (1)*
Philipson, H. 5: *v A 1891 (1) 1894 (4)*
Pigott, A. C. S. 1: *v NZ 1983*
Pilling, R. 8: v A 1884 (1) 1886 (1) 1888 (1); *v A 1881 (4) 1887 (1)*
Place, W. 3: *v WI 1947 (3)*
Pocock, P. I. 25: v A 1968 (1); v WI 1976 (2) 1984 (2); v SL 1984 (1); *v WI 1967 (2) 1973 (4); v In 1972 (4) 1984 (5); v P 1968 (1) 1972 (3)*

Pollard, R. 4: v A 1948 (2); v In 1946 (1); *v NZ 1946 (1)*
Poole, C. J. 3: *v In 1951 (3)*
Pope, G. H. 1: v SA 1947
Pougher, A. D. 1: *v SA 1891*
Price, J. S. E. 15: v A 1964 (2) 1972 (1); v In 1971 (3); v P 1971 (1); *v SA 1964 (4); v In 1963 (4)*
Price, W. F. F. 1: v A 1938
Prideaux, R. M. 3: v A 1968 (1); *v P 1968 (2)*
Pringle, D. R. 30: v A 1989 (2); v WI 1984 (3) 1988 (4) 1991 (4); v NZ 1986 (1); v In 1982 (3) 1986 (3); v P 1982 (1) 1992 (3); v SL 1988 (1); *v A 1982 (3); v NZ 1991 (2)*
Pullar, G. 28: v A 1961 (5); v SA 1960 (3); v In 1959 (3); v P 1962 (2); *v A 1962 (4); v WI 1959 (5); v In 1961 (3); v P 1961 (3)*

Quaife, W. G. 7: v A 1899 (2); *v A 1901 (5)*

Radford, N. V. 3: v NZ 1986 (1); v In 1986 (1); *v NZ 1987 (1)*
Radley, C. T. 8: v NZ 1978 (3); v P 1978 (3); *v NZ 1977 (2)*
Ramprakash, M. R. 10: v A 1993 (1); v WI 1991 (5); v P 1992 (3); v SL 1991 (1)
Randall, D. W. 47: v A 1977 (5); v WI 1984 (1); v NZ 1983 (3); v In 1979 (3) 1982 (3); v P 1982 (3); *v A 1976 (1) 1978 (6) 1979 (2) 1982 (4); v NZ 1977 (3) 1983 (3); v In 1976 (4); v P 1977 (3) 1983 (3)*
Ranjitsinhji, K. S. 15: v A 1896 (2) 1899 (5) 1902 (3); *v A 1897 (5)*
Read, H. D. 1: v SA 1935
Read, J. M. 17: v A 1882 (1) 1890 (2) 1893 (1); *v A 1884 (5) 1886 (2) 1887 (1) 1891 (3); v SA 1888 (2)*
Read, W. W. 18: v A 1884 (2) 1886 (3) 1888 (3) 1890 (2) 1893 (2); *v A 1882 (4) 1887 (1); v SA 1891 (1)*
Reeve, D. A. 3: *v NZ 1991 (3)*
Relf, A. E. 13: v A 1909 (1); *v A 1903 (2); v SA 1905 (5) 1913 (5)*
Rhodes, H. J. 2: v In 1959 (2)
Rhodes, W. 58: v A 1899 (3) 1902 (5) 1905 (4) 1909 (4) 1912 (3) 1921 (1) 1926 (1); v SA 1912 (3); *v A 1903 (5) 1907 (5) 1911 (5) 1920 (5); v SA 1909 (5) 1913 (5); v WI 1929 (4)*
Richards, C. J. 8: v WI 1988 (2); v P 1987 (1); *v A 1986 (5)*
Richardson, D. W. 1: v WI 1957
Richardson, P. E. 34: v A 1956 (5); v WI 1957 (5) 1963 (1); v NZ 1958 (4); *v A 1958 (4); v SA 1956 (5); v NZ 1958 (2); v In 1961 (5); v P 1961 (3)*
Richardson, T. 14: v A 1893 (1) 1896 (3); *v A 1894 (5) 1897 (5)*
Richmond, T. L. 1: v A 1921
Ridgway, F. 5: *v In 1951 (5)*
Robertson, J. D. 11: v SA 1947 (1); v NZ 1949 (1); *v WI 1947 (4); v In 1951 (5)*
Robins, R. W. V. 19: v A 1930 (2); v SA 1929 (1) 1935 (3); v WI 1933 (2); v NZ 1931 (1) 1937 (3); v In 1932 (1) 1936 (2); *v A 1936 (4)*
Robinson, R. T. 29: v A 1985 (6) 1989 (1); v In 1986 (1); v P 1987 (5); v SL 1988 (1); *v A 1987 (1); v WI 1985 (4); v NZ 1987 (3); v In 1984 (5); v P 1987 (2)*
Roope, G. R. J. 21: v A 1975 (1) 1977 (2); v WI 1973 (1); v NZ 1973 (3) 1978 (1); v P 1978 (3); *v NZ 1977 (3); v In 1972 (2); v P 1972 (2) 1977 (3)*
Root, C. F. 3: v A 1926 (3)
Rose, B. C. 9: v WI 1980 (3); *v WI 1980 (1); v NZ 1977 (2); v P 1977 (3)*
Royle, V. P. F. A. 1: *v A 1878*
Rumsey, F. E. 5: v A 1964 (1); v NZ 1965 (3)
Russell, A. C. 10: v A 1921 (2); *v A 1920 (4); v SA 1922 (4)*
Russell, R. C. 31: v A 1989 (6); v WI 1991 (4); v NZ 1990 (3); v In 1990 (3); v P 1992 (3); v SL 1988 (1) 1991 (1); *v A 1990 (3); v WI 1989 (4); v NZ 1991 (3)*
Russell, W. E. 10: v SA 1965 (1); v WI 1966 (2); v P 1967 (1); *v A 1965 (1); v NZ 1965 (3); v In 1961 (1); v P 1961 (1)*

Salisbury, I. D. K. 4: v P 1992 (2); *v I 1992 (2)*
Sandham, A. 14: v A 1921 (1); v SA 1924 (2); *v A 1924 (2); v SA 1922 (5); v WI 1929 (4)*
Schultz, S. S. 1: *v A 1878*
Scotton, W. H. 15: v A 1884 (1) 1886 (3); *v A 1881 (4) 1884 (5) 1886 (2)*
Selby, J. 6: *v A 1876 (2) 1881 (4)*
Selvey, M. W. W. 3: v WI 1976 (2); *v In 1976 (1)*
Shackleton, D. 7: v SA 1951 (1); v WI 1950 (1) 1963 (4); *v In 1951 (1)*

Sharp, J. 3: v A 1909 (3)

Sharpe, J. W. 3: v A 1890 (1); *v A 1891* (2)

Sharpe, P. J. 12: v A 1964 (2); v WI 1963 (3) 1969 (3); v NZ 1969 (3); *v In 1963* (*1*)

Shaw, A. 7: v A 1880 (1); *v A 1876* (2) *1881* (4)

Sheppard, Rev. D. S. 22: v A 1956 (2); v WI 1950 (1) 1957 (2); v In 1952 (2); v P 1954 (2) 1962 (2); *v A 1950* (2) *1962* (5); *v NZ 1950* (*1*) *1963* (3)

Sherwin, M. 3: v A 1888 (1); *v A 1886* (2)

Shrewsbury, A. 23: v A 1884 (3) 1886 (3) 1890 (2) 1893 (3); *v A 1881* (4) *1884* (5) *1886* (2) *1887* (*1*)

Shuter, J. 1: v A 1888

Shuttleworth, K. 5: v P 1971 (1); *v A 1970* (2); *v NZ 1970* (2)

Sidebottom, A. 1: v A 1985

Simpson, R. T. 27: v A 1953 (3); v SA 1951 (3); v WI 1950 (3); v NZ 1949 (2); v In 1952 (2); v P 1954 (3); *v A 1950* (5) *1954* (*1*); *v SA 1948* (*1*); *v NZ 1950* (2) *1954* (2)

Simpson-Hayward, G. H. 5: *v SA 1909* (5)

Sims, J. M. 4: v SA 1935 (1); *v In 1936* (1); *v A 1936* (2)

Sinfield, R. A. 1: v A 1938

Slack, W. N. 3: v In 1986 (1); *v WI 1985* (2)

Smailes, T. F. 1: v In 1946

Small, G. C. 17: v A 1989 (1); v WI 1988 (1); v NZ 1986 (2) 1990 (3); *v A 1986* (2) *1990* (4); *v WI 1989* (4)

Smith, A. C. 6: *v A 1962* (4); *v NZ 1962* (2)

Smith, C. A. 1: *v SA 1888*

Smith, C. I. J. 5: v NZ 1937 (1); *v WI 1934* (4)

Smith, C. L. 8: v NZ 1983 (2); v In 1986 (1); *v NZ 1983* (2); *v P 1983* (3)

Smith, D. 2: v SA 1935 (2)

Smith, D. M. 2: *v WI 1985* (2)

Smith, D. R. 5: *v In 1961* (5)

Smith, D. V. 3: v WI 1957 (3)

Smith, E. J. 11: v A 1912 (3); v SA 1912 (3); *v A 1911* (4); *v SA 1913* (*1*)

Smith, H. 1: v WI 1928

Smith, M. J. K. 50: v A 1961 (1) 1972 (3); v SA 1960 (4) 1965 (3); v WI 1966 (1); v NZ 1958 (3) 1965 (3); v In 1959 (2); *v A 1965* (5); *v SA 1964* (5); *v WI 1959* (5); *v NZ 1965* (3); *v In 1961* (4) *1963* (5); *v P 1961* (3)

Smith, R. A. 45: v A 1989 (5) 1993 (5); v WI 1988 (2) 1991 (4); v NZ 1990 (3); v In 1990 (3); v P 1992 (5); v SL 1988 (1) 1991 (1); *v A 1990* (5); *v WI 1989* (4); *v NZ 1991* (3): *v I 1992* (3); *v SL 1992* (*1*)

Smith, T. P. B. 4: v In 1946 (1); *v A 1946* (2); *v NZ 1946* (*1*)

Smithson, G. A. 2: *v WI 1947* (2)

Snow, J. A. 49: v A 1968 (5) 1972 (5) 1975 (4); v SA 1965 (1); v WI 1966 (1) 1969 (3) 1973 (3) 1976 (3); v NZ 1965 (1) 1969 (2) 1973 (3); v In 1967 (3) 1971 (2); v P 1967 (1); *v A 1970* (6); *v WI 1967* (4); *v P 1968* (2)

Southerton, J. 2: *v A 1876* (2)

Spooner, R. H. 10: v A 1905 (2) 1909 (2) 1912 (3); v SA 1912 (3)

Spooner, R. T. 7: v SA 1955 (1); *v In 1951* (5); *v WI 1953* (*1*)

Stanyforth, R. T. 4: *v SA 1927* (4)

Staples, S. J. 3: *v SA 1927* (3)

Statham, J. B. 70: v A 1953 (1) 1956 (3) 1961 (4); v SA 1951 (2) 1955 (4) 1960 (5) 1965 (1); v WI 1957 (3) 1963 (2); v NZ 1958 (2); v In 1959 (3); v P 1954 (4) 1962 (3); *v A 1954* (5) *1958* (4) *1962* (5); *v SA 1956* (4); *v WI 1953* (4) *1959* (3); *v NZ 1950* (*1*) *1954* (2); *v In 1951* (5)

Steel, A. G. 13: v A 1880 (1) 1882 (1) 1884 (3) 1886 (3) 1888 (1); *v A 1882* (4)

Steele, D. S. 8: v A 1975 (3); v WI 1976 (5)

Stephenson, J. P. 1: v A 1989

Stevens, G. T. S. 10: v A 1926 (2); *v SA 1922* (*1*) *1927* (5); *v WI 1929* (2)

Stevenson, G. B. 2: *v WI 1980* (*1*); *v In 1979* (*1*)

Stewart, A. J. 32: v A 1993 (6); v WI 1991 (1); v NZ 1990 (3); v P 1992 (5); v SL 1991 (1); *v A 1990* (5); *v WI 1989* (4); *v NZ 1991* (3); *v I 1992* (3); *v SL 1992* (*1*)

Stewart, M. J. 8: v WI 1963 (4); v P 1962 (2); *v In 1963* (2)

Stoddart, A. E. 16: v A 1893 (3) 1896 (2); *v A 1887* (*1*) *1891* (3) *1894* (5) *1897* (2)

Storer, W. 6: v A 1899 (1); *v A 1897* (5)

Street, G. B. 1: *v SA 1922*

Strudwick, H. 28: v A 1921 (2) 1926 (5); v SA 1924 (1); *v A 1911* (*1*) *1920* (4) *1924* (5); *v SA 1909* (5) *1913* (5)

Studd, C. T. 5: v A 1882 (1); *v A 1882 (4)*
Studd, G. B. 4: *v A 1882 (4)*
Subba Row, R. 13: v A 1961 (5); v SA 1960 (4); v NZ 1958 (1); v In 1959 (1); *v WI 1959 (2)*
Such, P. M. 5: v A 1993 (5)
Sugg, F. H. 2: v A 1888 (2)
Sutcliffe, H. 54: v A 1926 (5) 1930 (4) 1934 (4); v SA 1924 (5) 1929 (5) 1935 (2); v WI 1928 (3)
    1933 (2); v NZ 1931 (2); v In 1932 (1); *v A 1924 (5) 1928 (4) 1932 (5); v SA 1927 (5); v NZ
    1932 (2)*
Swetman, R. 11: v In 1959 (3); *v A 1958 (2); v WI 1959 (4); v NZ 1958 (2)*

Tate, F. W. 1: v A 1902
Tate, M. W. 39: v A 1926 (5) 1930 (5); v SA 1924 (5) 1929 (5) 1935 (1); v WI 1928 (3); v NZ 1931
    (1); *v A 1924 (5) 1928 (5); v SA 1930 (5); v NZ 1932 (1)*
Tattersall, R. 16: v A 1953 (1); v SA 1951 (5); v P 1954 (1); *v A 1950 (2); v NZ 1950 (2); v In
    1951 (5)*
Tavaré, C. J. 31: v A 1981 (2) 1989 (1); v WI 1980 (2) 1984 (1); v NZ 1983 (4); v In 1982 (3); v P
    1982 (3); v SL 1984 (1); *v A 1982 (5); v NZ 1983 (2); v In 1981 (6); v SL 1981 (1)*
Taylor, J. P. 1: *v I 1992*
Taylor, K. 3: v A 1964 (1); v In 1959 (2)
Taylor, L. B. 2: v A 1985 (2)
Taylor, R. W. 57: v A 1981 (3); v NZ 1978 (3) 1983 (4); v In 1979 (3) 1982 (3); v P 1978 (3) 1982
    (3); *v A 1978 (6) 1979 (3) 1982 (5); v NZ 1970 (1) 1977 (3) 1983 (3); v In 1979 (1) 1981 (6);
    v P 1977 (3) 1983 (3); v SL 1981 (1)*
Tennyson, Hon. L. H. 9: v A 1921 (4); *v SA 1913 (5)*
Terry, V. P. 2: v WI 1984 (2)
Thomas, J. G. 5: v NZ 1986 (1); *v WI 1985 (4)*
Thompson, G. J. 6: v A 1909 (1); *v SA 1909 (5)*
Thomson, N. I. 5: *v SA 1964 (5)*
Thorpe, G. P. 3: v A 1993 (3)
Titmus, F. J. 53: v A 1962 (4) 1964 (5); v SA 1955 (2) 1965 (3); v WI 1963 (4) 1966 (3); v NZ 1965 (3); v P
    1962 (2) 1967 (2); *v A 1962 (5) 1965 (5) 1974 (4); v SA 1964 (5); v WI 1967 (2); v NZ 1962 (3);
    v In 1963 (5)*
Tolchard, R. W. 4: *v In 1976 (4)*
Townsend, C. L. 2: v A 1899 (2)
Townsend, D. C. H. 3: *v WI 1934 (3)*
Townsend, L. F. 4: *v WI 1929 (1); v In 1933 (3)*
Tremlett, M. F. 3: *v WI 1947 (3)*
Trott, A. E. 2: *v SA 1898 (2)*
Trueman, F. S. 67: v A 1953 (1) 1956 (2) 1961 (4) 1964 (4); v SA 1955 (1) 1960 (5); v WI 1957 (5)
    1963 (5); v NZ 1958 (5) 1965 (2); v In 1952 (4) 1959 (5); v P 1962 (4); *v A 1958 (3) 1962 (5);
    v WI 1953 (3) 1959 (5); v NZ 1958 (2) 1962 (2)*
Tufnell, N. C. 1: *v SA 1909*
Tufnell, P. C. R. 15: v A 1993 (2); v WI 1991 (1); v P 1992 (1); v SL 1991 (1); *v A 1990 (4); v NZ
    1991 (3); v I 1992 (2); v SL 1992 (1)*
Turnbull, M. J. 9: v WI 1933 (2); v In 1936 (1); *v SA 1930 (5); v NZ 1929 (1)*
Tyldesley, E. 14: v A 1921 (3) 1926 (1); v SA 1924 (1); v WI 1928 (3); *v A 1928 (1); v SA 1927 (5)*
Tyldesley, J. T. 31: v A 1899 (2) 1902 (5) 1905 (5) 1909 (4); v SA 1907 (3); *v A 1901 (5) 1903 (5);
    v SA 1898 (2)*
Tyldesley, R. K. 7: v A 1930 (2); v SA 1924 (4); *v A 1924 (1)*
Tylecote, E. F. S. 6: v A 1886 (2); *v A 1882 (4)*
Tyler, E. J. 1: *v SA 1895*
Tyson, F. H. 17: v A 1956 (1); v SA 1955 (2); v P 1954 (1); *v A 1954 (5) 1958 (2); v SA 1956 (2);
    v NZ 1954 (2) 1958 (2)*

Ulyett, G. 25: v A 1882 (1) 1884 (3) 1886 (3) 1888 (2) 1890 (1); *v A 1876 (2) 1878 (1) 1881 (4) 1884
    (5) 1887 (1); v SA 1888 (2)*
Underwood, D. L. 86: v A 1968 (4) 1972 (2) 1975 (4) 1977 (5); v WI 1966 (2) 1969 (2) 1973 (3)
    1976 (5) 1980 (1); v NZ 1969 (3) 1973 (1); v In 1971 (1) 1974 (3); v P 1967 (2) 1971 (1) 1974 (3);
    *v A 1970 (5) 1974 (5) 1976 (1) 1979 (3); v WI 1973 (4); v NZ 1970 (2) 1974 (2); v In 1972 (4) 1976
    (5) 1979 (1) 1981 (6); v P 1968 (3) 1972 (2); v SL 1981 (1)*

Valentine, B. H. 7: *v SA 1938 (5); v In 1933 (2)*

Verity, H. 40: v A 1934 (5) 1938 (4); v SA 1935 (4); v WI 1933 (2) 1939 (1); v NZ 1931 (2) 1937 (1); v In 1936 (3); *v A 1932 (4) 1936 (5); v In 1933 (5); v NZ 1932 (1); v In 1933 (3)*

Vernon, G. F. 1: *v A 1882*

Vine, J. 2: *v A 1911 (2)*

Voce, W. 27: v NZ 1931 (1) 1937 (1); v In 1932 (1) 1936 (1) 1946 (1); *v A 1932 (4) 1936 (5) 1946 (2); v SA 1930 (5); v WI 1929 (4); v NZ 1932 (2)*

Waddington, A. 2: *v A 1920 (2)*

Wainwright, E. 5: v A 1893 (1); *v A 1897 (4)*

Walker, P. M. 3: v SA 1960 (3)

Walters, C. F. 11: v A 1934 (5); v WI 1933 (3); *v In 1933 (3)*

Ward, A. 5: v WI 1976 (1); v NZ 1969 (3); v P 1971 (1)

Ward, A. 7: v A 1893 (2); *v A 1894 (5)*

Wardle, J. H. 28: v A 1953 (3) 1956 (1); v SA 1951 (2) 1955 (3); v WI 1950 (1) 1957 (1); v P 1954 (4); *v A 1954 (4); v SA 1956 (4); v WI 1947 (1) 1953 (2); v NZ 1954 (2)*

Warner, P. F. 15: v A 1909 (1) 1912 (1); v SA 1912 (1); *v A 1903 (5); v SA 1898 (2) 1905 (5)*

Warr, J. J. 2: *v A 1950 (2)*

Warren, A. R. 1: v A 1905

Washbrook, C. 37: v A 1948 (4) 1956 (3); v SA 1947 (5); v WI 1950 (2); v NZ 1937 (1) 1949 (2); v In 1946 (3); *v A 1946 (5) 1950 (5); v SA 1948 (5); v NZ 1946 (1) 1950 (1)*

Watkin, S. L. 3: v A 1993 (1); v WI 1991 (2)

Watkins, A. J. 15: v A 1948 (1); v NZ 1949 (1); v In 1952 (3); *v SA 1948 (5); v In 1951 (5)*

Watson, W. 23: v A 1953 (3) 1956 (2); v SA 1951 (5) 1955 (1); v NZ 1958 (2); v In 1952 (1); *v A 1958 (2); v WI 1953 (5); v NZ 1958 (2)*

Webbe, A. J. 1: *v A 1878*

Wellard, A. W. 2: v A 1938 (1); v NZ 1937 (1)

Wharton, A. 1: v NZ 1949

Whitaker, J. J. 1: *v A 1986*

White, D. W. 2: *v P 1961 (2)*

White, J. C. 15: v A 1921 (1) 1930 (1); v SA 1929 (3); v WI 1928 (1); *v A 1928 (5); v SA 1930 (4)*

Whysall, W. W. 4: v A 1930 (1); *v A 1924 (3)*

Wilkinson, L. L. 3: *v SA 1938 (3)*

Willey, P. 26: v A 1980 (1) 1981 (4) 1985 (1); v WI 1976 (2) 1980 (5); v NZ 1986 (1); v In 1979 (1); *v A 1979 (3); v WI 1980 (4) 1985 (2)*

Williams, N. F. 1: v In 1990

Willis, R. G. D. 90: v A 1977 (5) 1981 (6); v WI 1973 (1) 1976 (2) 1980 (4) 1984 (3); v NZ 1978 (3) 1983 (4); v In 1974 (1) 1979 (3) 1982 (3); v P 1974 (1) 1978 (3) 1982 (2); *v A 1970 (4) 1974 (5) 1976 (1) 1978 (6) 1979 (3) 1982 (5); v WI 1973 (3); v NZ 1970 (1) 1977 (3) 1983 (3); v In 1976 (5) 1981 (5); v P 1977 (3) 1983 (1); v SL 1981 (1)*

Wilson, C. E. M. 2: v SA 1898 (2)

Wilson, D. 6: *v NZ 1970 (1); v In 1963 (5)*

Wilson, E. R. 1: *v A 1920*

Wood, A. 4: v A 1938 (1); v WI 1939 (3)

Wood, B. 12: v A 1972 (1) 1975 (3); v WI 1976 (1); v P 1978 (1); *v NZ 1974 (2); v In 1972 (3); v P 1972 (1)*

Wood, G. E. C. 3: v SA 1924 (3)

Wood, H. 4: v A 1888 (1); *v SA 1888 (2) 1891 (1)*

Wood, R. 1: *v A 1886*

Woods S. M. J. 3: *v SA 1895 (3)*

Woolley, F. E. 64: v A 1909 (1) 1912 (3) 1921 (5) 1926 (5) 1930 (2) 1934 (1); v SA 1912 (3) 1924 (5) 1929 (3); v NZ 1931 (1); v In 1932 (1); *v A 1911 (5) 1920 (5) 1924 (5); v SA 1909 (5) 1913 (5) 1922 (5); v NZ 1929 (4)*

Woolmer, R. A. 19: v A 1975 (2) 1977 (5) 1981 (2); v WI 1976 (5) 1980 (2); *v A 1976 (1); v In 1976 (2)*

Worthington, T. S. 9: v In 1936 (3); *v A 1936 (3); v NZ 1929 (4)*

Wright, C. W. 3: *v SA 1895 (3)*

Wright, D. V. P. 34: v A 1938 (3) 1948 (1); v SA 1947 (4); v WI 1939 (3) 1950 (1); v NZ 1949 (1); v In 1946 (2); *v A 1946 (5) 1950 (5); v SA 1938 (3) 1948 (3); v NZ 1946 (1) 1950 (2)*

Wyatt, R. E. S. 40: v A 1930 (1) 1934 (4); v SA 1929 (2) 1935 (5); v WI 1933 (2); v In 1936 (1); *v A 1932 (5) 1936 (2); v SA 1927 (5) 1930 (5); v WI 1929 (2) 1934 (4); v NZ 1932 (2)*

Wynyard, E. G. 3: v A 1896 (1); *v SA 1905 (2)*

Yardley, N. W. D. 20: v A 1948 (5); v SA 1947 (5); v WI 1950 (3); *v A 1946 (5); v SA 1938 (1); v NZ 1946 (1)*
Young, H. I. 2: v A 1899 (2)
Young, J. A. 8: v A 1948 (3); v SA 1947 (1); v NZ 1949 (2); *v SA 1948 (2)*
Young, R. A. 2: *v A 1907 (2)*

AUSTRALIA

Number of Test cricketers: 357

a'Beckett, E. L. 4: v E 1928 (2); v SA 1931 (1); *v E 1930 (1)*
Alderman, T. M. 41: v E 1982 (1) 1990 (4); v WI 1981 (2) 1984 (3) 1988 (2); v NZ 1989 (1); v P 1981 (3) 1989 (2); v SL 1989 (2); *v E 1981 (6) 1989 (6); v WI 1983 (3) 1990 (1); v NZ 1981 (3) 1989 (1); v P 1982 (1)*
Alexander, G. 2: v E 1884 (1); *v E 1880 (1)*
Alexander, H. H. 1: v E 1932
Allan, F. E. 1: v E 1878
Allan, P. J. 1: v E 1965
Allen, R. C. 1: v E 1886
Andrews, T. J. E. 16: v E 1924 (3); *v E 1921 (5) 1926 (5); v SA 1921 (3)*
Angel, J. L.: v WI 1992
Archer, K. A. 5: v E 1950 (3); v WI 1951 (2)
Archer, R. G. 19: v E 1954 (4); v SA 1952 (1); *v E 1953 (3) 1956 (5); v WI 1954 (5); v P 1956 (1)*
Armstrong, W. W. 50: v E 1901 (4) 1903 (3) 1907 (5) 1911 (5) 1920 (5); v SA 1910 (5); *v E 1902 (5) 1905 (5) 1909 (5) 1921 (5); v SA 1902 (3)*

Badcock, C. L. 7: v E 1936 (3); *v E 1938 (4)*
Bannerman, A. C. 28: v E 1878 (1) 1881 (3) 1882 (4) 1884 (4) 1886 (1) 1887 (1) 1891 (3); *v E 1880 (1) 1882 (1) 1884 (3) 1888 (3) 1893 (3)*
Bannerman, C. 3: v E 1876 (2) 1878 (1)
Bardsley, W. 41: v E 1911 (4) 1920 (5) 1924 (3); v SA 1910 (5); *v E 1909 (5) 1912 (3) 1921 (5) 1926 (5); v SA 1912 (3) 1921 (3)*
Barnes, S. G. 13: v E 1946 (4); v In 1947 (3); *v E 1938 (1) 1948 (4); v NZ 1945 (1)*
Barnett, B. A. 4: *v E 1938 (4)*
Barrett, J. E. 2: *v E 1890 (2)*
Beard, G. R. 3: *v P 1979 (3)*
Benaud, J. 3: v P 1972 (2); *v WI 1972 (1)*
Benaud, R. 63: v E 1954 (5) 1958 (5) 1962 (5); v SA 1952 (4) 1963 (4); v WI 1951 (1) 1960 (5); *v E 1953 (3) 1956 (5) 1961 (4); v SA 1957 (5); v WI 1954 (5); v In 1956 (3) 1959 (5); v P 1956 (1) 1959 (3)*
Bennett, M. J. 3: v WI 1984 (2); *v E 1985 (1)*
Blackham, J. McC. 35: v E 1876 (2) 1878 (1) 1881 (4) 1882 (4) 1884 (2) 1886 (1) 1887 (1) 1891 (3) 1894 (1); *v E 1880 (1) 1882 (1) 1884 (3) 1886 (3) 1888 (3) 1890 (2) 1893 (3)*
Blackie, D. D. 3: v E 1928 (3)
Bonnor, G. J. 17: v E 1882 (4) 1884 (3); *v E 1880 (1) 1882 (1) 1884 (3) 1886 (2) 1888 (3)*
Boon, D. C. 80: v E 1986 (4) 1987 (1) 1990 (5); v WI 1984 (3) 1988 (5) 1992 (5); v NZ 1985 (3) 1987 (3) 1989 (1); v In 1985 (3) 1991 (5); v P 1989 (2); v SL 1987 (1) 1989 (2); *v E 1985 (4) 1989 (6) 1993 (6); v WI 1990 (5); v NZ 1985 (3) 1989 (1) 1992 (3); v In 1986 (3); v P 1988 (3); v SL 1992 (3)*
Booth, B. C. 29: v E 1962 (5) 1965 (5); v SA 1963 (4); v P 1964 (1); *v E 1961 (2) 1964 (5); v WI 1964 (5); v In 1964 (3); v P 1964 (1)*
Border, A. R. 147: v E 1978 (3) 1979 (3) 1982 (5) 1986 (5) 1987 (1) 1990 (5); v WI 1979 (3) 1981 (3) 1984 (5) 1988 (5) 1992 (5); v NZ 1980 (3) 1985 (3) 1987 (3) 1989 (1); v In 1980 (3) 1985 (3) 1991 (5); v P 1978 (2) 1981 (3) 1983 (5) 1989 (3); v SL 1987 (1) 1989 (2); *v E 1980 (1) 1981 (6) 1985 (6) 1989 (6) 1993 (6); v WI 1983 (3) 1990 (5); v NZ 1981 (3) 1985 (3) 1989 (1) 1992 (3); v In 1979 (6) 1986 (3); v P 1979 (2) 1982 (3) 1988 (3); v SL 1982 (1) 1992 (3)*
Boyle, H. F. 12: v E 1878 (1) 1881 (4) 1882 (1) 1884 (1); *v E 1880 (1) 1882 (1) 1884 (3)*
Bradman, D. G. 52: v E 1928 (4) 1932 (4) 1936 (5) 1946 (5); v SA 1931 (5); v WI 1930 (5); v In 1947 (5); *v E 1930 (5) 1934 (5) 1938 (4) 1948 (5)*

Bright, R. J. 25: v E 1979 (1); v WI 1979 (1); v NZ 1985 (1); v In 1985 (3); *v E 1977 (3) 1980 (1) 1981 (5); v NZ 1985 (2); v In 1986 (3); v P 1979 (3) 1982 (2)*

Bromley, E. H. 2: v E 1932 (1); *v E 1934 (1)*

Brown, W. A. 22: v E 1936 (2); v In 1947 (3); *v E 1934 (5) 1938 (4) 1948 (2); v SA 1935 (5); v NZ 1945 (1)*

Bruce, W. 14: v E 1884 (2) 1891 (3) 1894 (4); *v E 1886 (2) 1893 (3)*

Burge, P. J. P. 42: v E 1954 (1) 1958 (1) 1962 (3) 1965 (4); v SA 1963 (5); v WI 1960 (2); *v E 1956 (3) 1961 (5) 1964 (5); v SA 1957 (1); v WI 1954 (1); v In 1956 (3) 1959 (2) 1964 (3); v P 1959 (2) 1964 (1)*

Burke, J. W. 24: v E 1950 (2) 1954 (2) 1958 (5); v WI 1951 (1); *v E 1956 (5); v SA 1957 (5); v In 1956 (3); v P 1956 (1)*

Burn, K. E. 2: *v E 1890 (2)*

Burton, F. J. 2: v E 1886 (1) 1887 (1)

Callaway, S. T. 3: v E 1891 (2) 1894 (1)

Callen, I. W. 1: v In 1977

Campbell, G. D. 4: v P 1989 (1); v SL 1989 (1); *v E 1989 (1); v NZ 1989 (1)*

Carkeek, W. 6: *v E 1912 (3); v SA 1912 (3)*

Carlson, P. H. 2: v E 1978 (2)

Carter, H. 28: v E 1907 (5) 1911 (5) 1920 (2); v SA 1910 (5); *v E 1909 (5) 1921 (4); v SA 1921 (2)*

Chappell, G. S. 87: v E 1970 (5) 1974 (6) 1976 (1) 1979 (3) 1982 (5); v WI 1975 (6) 1979 (3) 1981 (3); v NZ 1973 (3) 1980 (3); v In 1980 (3); v P 1972 (3) 1976 (3) 1981 (3) 1983 (5); *v E 1972 (5) 1975 (4) 1977 (5) 1980 (1); v WI 1972 (5); v NZ 1973 (3) 1976 (2) 1981 (3); v P 1979 (3); v SL 1982 (1)*

Chappell, I. M. 75: v E 1965 (2) 1970 (6) 1974 (6) 1979 (2); v WI 1968 (5) 1975 (6) 1979 (1); v NZ 1973 (3); v In 1967 (4); v P 1964 (1) 1972 (3); *v E 1968 (5) 1972 (5) 1975 (4); v SA 1966 (5) 1969 (4); v WI 1972 (5); v NZ 1973 (3); v In 1969 (5)*

Chappell, T. M. 3: *v E 1981 (3)*

Charlton, P. C. 2: *v E 1890 (2)*

Chipperfield, A. G. 14: v E 1936 (3); *v E 1934 (5) 1938 (1); v SA 1935 (5)*

Clark, W. M. 10: v In 1977 (5); v P 1978 (1); *v WI 1977 (4)*

Colley, D. J. 3: *v E 1972 (3)*

Collins, H. L. 19: v E 1920 (5) 1924 (5); *v E 1921 (3) 1926 (3); v SA 1921 (3)*

Coningham, A. 1: v E 1894

Connolly, A. N. 29: v E 1965 (1) 1970 (1); v SA 1963 (3); v WI 1968 (5); v In 1967 (3); *v E 1968 (5); v SA 1969 (4); v In 1964 (2); 1969 (5)*

Cooper, B. B. 1: v E 1876

Cooper, W. H. 2: v E 1881 (1) 1884 (1)

Corling, G. E. 5: *v E 1964 (5)*

Cosier, G. J. 18: v E 1976 (1) 1978 (2); v WI 1975 (3); v In 1977 (4); v P 1976 (3); *v WI 1977 (3); v NZ 1976 (2)*

Cottam, W. J. 1: v E 1886

Cotter, A. 21: v E 1903 (2) 1907 (2) 1911 (4); v SA 1910 (5); *v E 1905 (3) 1909 (5)*

Coulthard, G. 1: v E 1881

Cowper, R. M. 27: v E 1965 (4); v In 1967 (4); v P 1964 (1); *v E 1964 (1) 1968 (4); v SA 1966 (5); v WI 1964 (5); v In 1964 (2); v P 1964 (1)*

Craig, I. D. 11: v SA 1952 (1); *v E 1956 (2); v SA 1957 (5); v In 1956 (2); v P 1956 (1)*

Crawford, W. P. A. 4: *v E 1956 (1); v In 1956 (3)*

Darling, J. 34: v E 1894 (5) 1897 (5) 1901 (3); *v E 1896 (3) 1899 (5) 1902 (5) 1905 (5); v SA 1902 (3)*

Darling, L. S. 12: v E 1932 (2) 1936 (1); *v E 1934 (4); v SA 1935 (5)*

Darling, W. M. 14: v E 1978 (4); v In 1977 (1); v P 1978 (1); *v WI 1977 (3); v In 1979 (5)*

Davidson, A. K. 44: v E 1954 (3) 1958 (5) 1962 (5); v WI 1960 (4); *v E 1953 (5) 1956 (2) 1961 (5); v SA 1957 (5); v In 1956 (1) 1959 (5); v P 1956 (1) 1959 (3)*

Davis, I. C. 15: v E 1976 (1); v NZ 1973 (3); v P 1976 (3); *v E 1977 (3); v NZ 1973 (3) 1976 (2)*

Davis, S. P. 1: *v NZ 1985*

De Courcy, J. H. 3: *v E 1953 (3)*

Dell, A. R. 2: v E 1970 (1); v NZ 1973 (1)

Dodemaide, A. I. C. 10: v E 1987 (1); v WI 1988 (1); v NZ 1987 (1); v SL 1987 (1); *v P 1988 (3); v SL 1992 (2)*

Donnan, H. 5: v E 1891 (2); *v E 1896 (3)*

Dooland, B. 3: v E 1946 (2); v In 1947 (1)

Duff, R. A. 22: v E 1901 (4) 1903 (5); *v E 1902 (5) 1905 (5)*; *v SA 1902 (3)*
Duncan, J. R. F. 1: v E 1970
Dyer, G. C. 6: v E 1986 (1) 1987 (1); v NZ 1987 (3); v SL 1987 (1)
Dymock, G. 21: v E 1974 (1) 1978 (3) 1979 (3); v WI 1979 (2); v NZ 1973 (1); v P 1978 (1); *v NZ 1973 (2); v In 1979 (5); v P 1979 (3)*
Dyson, J. 30: v E 1982 (5); v WI 1981 (2) 1984 (3); v NZ 1980 (3); v In 1977 (3) 1980 (3); *v E 1981 (5); v NZ 1981 (3); v P 1982 (3)*

Eady, C. J. 2: v E 1901 (1); *v E 1896 (1)*
Eastwood, K. H. 1: v E 1970
Ebeling, H. I. 1: *v E 1934*
Edwards, J. D. 3: *v E 1888 (3)*
Edwards, R. 20: v E 1974 (5); v P 1972 (2); *v E 1972 (4) 1975 (4); v WI 1972 (5)*
Edwards, W. J. 3: v E 1974 (3)
Emery, S. H. 4: *v E 1912 (2); v SA 1912 (2)*
Evans, E. 6: v E 1881 (2) 1882 (1) 1884 (1); *v E 1886 (2)*

Fairfax, A. G. 10: v E 1928 (1); v WI 1930 (5); *v E 1930 (4)*
Favell, L. E. 19: v E 1954 (4) 1958 (2); v WI 1960 (4); *v WI 1954 (2); v In 1959 (4); v P 1959 (3)*
Ferris, J. J. 8: v E 1886 (2) 1887 (1); *v E 1888 (3) 1890 (2)*
Fingleton, J. H. 18: v E 1932 (3) 1936 (5); v SA 1931 (1); *v E 1938 (4); v SA 1935 (5)*
Fleetwood-Smith, L. O'B. 10: v E 1936 (3); *v E 1938 (4); v SA 1935 (3)*
Francis, B. C. 3: *v E 1972 (3)*
Freeman, E. W. 11: v WI 1968 (4); v In 1967 (2); *v E 1968 (2); v SA 1969 (2); v In 1969 (1)*
Freer, F. W. 1: v E 1946

Gannon, J. B. 3: v In 1977 (3)
Garrett, T. W. 19: v E 1876 (2) 1878 (1) 1881 (3) 1882 (3) 1884 (3) 1886 (2) 1887 (1); *v E 1882 (1) 1886 (3)*
Gaunt, R. A. 3: v SA 1963 (1); *v E 1961 (1); v SA 1957 (1)*
Gehrs, D. R. A. 6: v E 1903 (1); v SA 1910 (4); *v E 1905 (1)*
Giffen, G. 31: v E 1881 (3) 1882 (4) 1884 (3) 1891 (3) 1894 (5); *v E 1882 (1) 1884 (3) 1886 (3) 1893 (3) 1896 (3)*
Giffen, W. F. 3: v E 1886 (1) 1891 (2)
Gilbert, D. R. 9: v NZ 1985 (3); v In 1985 (2); *v E 1985 (1); v NZ 1985 (1); v In 1986 (2)*
Gilmour, G. J. 15: v E 1976 (1); v WI 1975 (5); v NZ 1973 (2); v P 1976 (3); *v E 1975 (1); v NZ 1973 (1) 1976 (2)*
Gleeson, J. W. 29: v E 1970 (5); v WI 1968 (5); v In 1967 (4); *v E 1968 (5) 1972 (3); v SA 1969 (4); v In 1969 (3)*
Graham, H. 6: v E 1894 (2); *v E 1893 (3) 1896 (1)*
Gregory, D. W. 3: v E 1876 (2) 1878 (1)
Gregory, E. J. 1: v E 1876
Gregory, J. M. 24: v E 1920 (5) 1924 (5) 1928 (1); *v E 1921 (5) 1926 (5); v SA 1921 (3)*
Gregory, R. G. 2: v E 1936 (2)
Gregory, S. E. 58: v E 1891 (1) 1894 (5) 1897 (5) 1901 (5) 1903 (4) 1907 (2) 1911 (1); *v E 1890 (2) 1893 (3) 1896 (3) 1899 (5) 1902 (5) 1905 (3) 1909 (5) 1912 (3); v SA 1902 (3) 1912 (3)*
Grimmett, C. V. 37: v E 1924 (1) 1928 (5) 1932 (3); v SA 1931 (5); v WI 1930 (5); *v E 1926 (3) 1930 (5) 1934 (5); v SA 1935 (5)*
Groube, T. U. 1: *v E 1880*
Grout, A. T. W. 51: v E 1958 (5) 1962 (2) 1965 (5); v SA 1963 (5); v WI 1960 (5); *v E 1961 (5) 1964 (5); v SA 1957 (5); v WI 1964 (5); v In 1959 (4) 1964 (1); v P 1959 (3) 1964 (1)*
Guest, C. E. J. 1: v E 1962

Hamence, R. A. 3: v E 1946 (1); v In 1947 (2)
Hammond, J. R. 5: *v WI 1972 (5)*
Harry, J. 1: v E 1894
Hartigan, R. J. 2: v E 1907 (2)
Hartkopf, A. E. V. 1: v E 1924
Harvey, M. R. 1: v E 1946
Harvey, R. N. 79: v E 1950 (5) 1954 (5) 1958 (5) 1962 (5); v SA 1952 (5); v WI 1951 (5) 1960 (4); v In 1947 (2); *v E 1948 (2) 1953 (5) 1956 (5) 1961 (5); v SA 1949 (5) 1957 (4); v WI 1954 (5); v In 1956 (3) 1959 (5); v P 1956 (1) 1959 (3)*

Hassett, A. L. 43: v E 1946 (5) 1950 (5); v SA 1952 (5); v WI 1951 (4); v In 1947 (4); *v E 1938 (4) 1948 (5) 1953 (5); v SA 1949 (5); v NZ 1945 (1)*

Hawke, N. J. N. 27: v E 1962 (1) 1965 (4); v SA 1963 (4); v In 1967 (1); *v P 1964 (1); v E 1964 (5) 1968 (2); v SA 1966 (2); v WI 1964 (5); v In 1964 (1); v P 1964 (1)*

Hazlitt, G. R. 9: v E 1907 (2) 1911 (1); *v E 1912 (3); v SA 1912 (3)*

Healy, I. A. 53: v E 1990 (5); v WI 1988 (5) 1992 (5); v NZ 1989 (1); v I 1991 (5); v P 1989 (3); v SL 1989 (2); *v E 1989 (6) 1993 (6); v WI 1990 (5); v NZ 1989 (1) 1992 (3); v P 1988 (3); v SL 1992 (3)*

Hendry, H. S. T. L. 11: v E 1924 (1) 1928 (4); *v E 1921 (4); v SA 1921 (2)*

Hibbert, P. A. 1: v In 1977

Higgs, J. D. 22: v E 1978 (5) 1979 (1); v WI 1979 (1); v NZ 1980 (3); v In 1980 (2); *v WI 1977 (4); v In 1979 (6)*

Hilditch, A. M. J. 18: v E 1978 (1); v WI 1984 (2); v NZ 1985 (1); v P 1978 (2); *v E 1985 (6); v In 1979 (6)*

Hill, C. 49: v E 1897 (5) 1901 (5) 1903 (5) 1907 (5) 1911 (5); v SA 1910 (5); *v E 1896 (3) 1899 (3) 1902 (5) 1905 (5); v SA 1902 (3)*

Hill, J. C. 3: *v E 1953 (2); v WI 1954 (1)*

Hoare, D. E. 1: v WI 1960

Hodges, J. R. 2: v E 1876 (2)

Hogan, T. G. 7: v P 1983 (1); *v WI 1983 (5); v SL 1982 (1)*

Hogg, R. M. 38: v E 1978 (6) 1982 (3); v WI 1979 (2) 1984 (4); v NZ 1980 (2); v In 1980 (2); v P 1978 (2) 1983 (4); *v E 1981 (2); v WI 1983 (4); v In 1979 (6); v SL 1982 (1)*

Hohns, T. V. 7: v WI 1988 (2); *v E 1989 (5)*

Hole, G. B. 18: v E 1950 (1) 1954 (3); v SA 1952 (4); v WI 1951 (4); *v E 1953 (5)*

Holland, R. G. 11: v WI 1984 (3); v NZ 1985 (3); v In 1985 (1); *v E 1985 (4)*

Hookes, D. W. 23: v E 1976 (1) 1982 (5); v WI 1979 (1); v NZ 1985 (2); v In 1985 (2); *v E 1977 (5); v WI 1983 (5); v P 1979 (1); v SL 1982 (1)*

Hopkins, A. J. Y. 20: v E 1901 (2) 1903 (5); *v E 1902 (5) 1905 (3) 1909 (2); v SA 1902 (3)*

Horan, T. P. 15: v E 1876 (1) 1878 (1) 1881 (4) 1882 (4) 1884 (4); *v E 1882 (1)*

Hordern, H. V. 7: v E 1911 (5); v SA 1910 (2)

Hornibrook, P. M. 6: v E 1928 (1); *v E 1930 (5)*

Howell, W. P. 18: v E 1897 (3) 1901 (4) 1903 (5); *v E 1899 (5) 1902 (1); v SA 1902 (3)*

Hughes, K. J. 70: v E 1978 (6) 1979 (3) 1982 (5); v WI 1979 (3) 1981 (3) 1984 (4); v NZ 1980 (3); v In 1977 (2) 1980 (3); v P 1978 (2) 1981 (3) 1983 (5); *v E 1977 (1) 1980 (1) 1981 (6); v WI 1983 (5); v NZ 1981 (3); v In 1979 (6); v P 1979 (3) 1982 (3)*

Hughes, M. G. 51: v E 1986 (4) 1990 (4); v WI 1988 (4) 1992 (5); v NZ 1987 (1) 1989 (1); v In 1985 (1) 1991 (5); v P 1989 (3); v SL 1987 (1) 1989 (2); *v E 1989 (6) 1993 (6); v WI 1990 (5); v NZ 1992 (3)*

Hunt, W. A. 1: v SA 1931

Hurst, A. G. 12: v E 1978 (6); v NZ 1973 (1); v In 1977 (1); v P 1978 (2); *v In 1979 (2)*

Hurwood, A. 2: v WI 1930 (2)

Inverarity, R. J. 6: v WI 1968 (1); *v E 1968 (2) 1972 (3)*

Iredale, F. A. 14: v E 1894 (5) 1897 (4); *v E 1896 (5) 1899 (3)*

Ironmonger, H. 14: v E 1928 (2) 1932 (4); v SA 1931 (4); v WI 1930 (4)

Iverson, J. B. 5: v E 1950 (5)

Jackson, A. A. 8: v E 1928 (2); v WI 1930 (4); *v E 1930 (2)*

Jarman, B. N. 19: v E 1962 (3); v WI 1968 (4); v In 1967 (4); v P 1964 (1); *v E 1968 (4); v In 1959 (1) 1964 (2)*

Jarvis, A. H. 11: v E 1884 (3) 1894 (4); *v E 1886 (2) 1888 (2)*

Jenner, T. J. 9: v E 1970 (2) 1974 (2); v WI 1975 (1); *v WI 1972 (4)*

Jennings, C. B. 6: *v E 1912 (3); v SA 1912 (3)*

Johnson I. W. 45: v E 1946 (4) 1950 (5) 1954 (4); v SA 1952 (1); v WI 1951 (4); v In 1947 (4); *v E 1948 (4) 1956 (5); v SA 1949 (5); v WI 1954 (5); v NZ 1945 (1); v In 1956 (2); v P 1956 (1)*

Johnson, L. J. 1: v In 1947

Johnston W. A. 40: v E 1950 (5) 1954 (4); v SA 1952 (5); v WI 1951 (5); v In 1947 (4); *v E 1948 (5) 1953 (5); v SA 1949 (5); v WI 1954 (4)*

Jones, D. M. 52: v E 1986 (5) 1987 (1) 1990 (5); v WI 1988 (3); v NZ 1987 (3) 1989 (1); v I 1991 (5); v P 1989 (3); v SL 1987 (1) 1989 (2); *v E 1989 (6); v WI 1983 (2) 1990 (5); v NZ 1989 (1); v In 1986 (3); v P 1988 (3); v SL 1992 (3)*

Jones, E. 19: v E 1894 (1) 1897 (5) 1901 (2); *v E 1896 (3) 1899 (5) 1902 (2); v SA 1902 (1)*

Jones, S. P. 12: v E 1881 (2) 1884 (4) 1886 (1) 1887 (1); *v E 1882 (1) 1886 (3)*
Joslin, L. R. 1: v In 1967
Julian, B. P. 2: *v E 1993 (2)*

Kelleway, C. 26: v E 1911 (4) 1920 (5) 1924 (5) 1928 (1); v SA 1910 (5); *v E 1912 (3); v SA 1912 (3)*
Kelly, J. J. 36: v E 1897 (5) 1901 (5) 1903 (5); *v E 1896 (3) 1899 (5) 1902 (5) 1905 (5); v SA 1902 (3)*
Kelly, T. J. D. 2: v E 1876 (1) 1878 (1)
Kendall, T. 2: v E 1876 (2)
Kent, M. F. 3: *v E 1981 (3)*
Kerr, R. B. 2: v NZ 1985 (2)
Kippax, A. F. 22: v E 1924 (1) 1928 (5) 1932 (1); v SA 1931 (4); v WI 1930 (5); *v E 1930 (5) 1934 (1)*
Kline L. F. 13: v E 1958 (2); v WI 1960 (2); *v SA 1957 (5); v In 1959 (3); v P 1959 (1)*

Laird, B. M. 21: v E 1979 (2); v WI 1979 (3) 1981 (3); v P 1981 (3); *v E 1980 (1); v NZ 1981 (3); v P 1979 (3) 1982 (3)*
Langer, J. L. 5: v WI 1992 (2); *v NZ 1992 (3)*
Langley, G. R. A. 26: v E 1954 (2); v SA 1952 (3); v WI 1951 (5); *v E 1953 (4) 1956 (3); v WI 1954 (4); v In 1956 (2); v P 1956 (1)*
Laughlin, T. J. 3: v E 1978 (1); *v WI 1977 (2)*
Laver, F. 15: v E 1901 (1) 1903 (1); *v E 1899 (4) 1905 (5) 1909 (4)*
Lawry, W. M. 67: v E 1962 (5) 1965 (5) 1970 (5); v SA 1963 (5); v WI 1968 (5); v In 1967 (4); v P 1964 (1); *v E 1961 (5) 1964 (5) 1968 (4); v SA 1966 (5) 1969 (4); v WI 1964 (5); v In 1964 (3) 1969 (5); v P 1964 (1)*
Lawson, G. F. 46: v E 1982 (5) 1986 (1); v WI 1981 (1) 1984 (5) 1988 (1); v NZ 1980 (1) 1985 (2) 1989 (1); v P 1983 (5); v SL 1989 (1); *v E 1981 (3) 1985 (6) 1989 (6); v WI 1983 (5); v P 1982 (3)*
Lee, P. K. 2: v E 1932 (1); v SA 1931 (1)
Lillee, D. K. 70: v E 1970 (2) 1974 (6) 1976 (1) 1979 (3) 1982 (1); v WI 1975 (5) 1979 (3) 1981 (3); v NZ 1980 (3); v In 1980 (3); v P 1972 (3) 1976 (3) 1981 (3) 1983 (5); *v E 1972 (5) 1975 (4) 1980 (1) 1981 (6); v WI 1972 (1); v NZ 1976 (2) 1981 (3); v P 1979 (3); v SL 1982 (1)*
Lindwall, R. R. 61: v E 1946 (4) 1950 (5) 1954 (4) 1958 (2); v SA 1952 (4); v WI 1951 (5); v In 1947 (5); *v E 1948 (5) 1953 (5) 1956 (4); v SA 1949 (4); v WI 1954 (5); v NZ 1945 (1); v In 1956 (3) 1959 (2); v P 1956 (1) 1959 (2)*
Love, H. S. B. 1: v E 1932
Loxton, S. J. E. 12: v E 1950 (3); v In 1947 (1); *v E 1948 (3); v SA 1949 (5)*
Lyons, J. J. 14: v E 1886 (1) 1891 (3) 1894 (3) 1897 (1); *v E 1888 (1) 1890 (2) 1893 (3)*

McAlister, P. A. 8: v E 1903 (2) 1907 (4); *v E 1909 (2)*
Macartney, C. G. 35: v E 1907 (5) 1911 (1) 1920 (2); v SA 1910 (5); *v E 1909 (5) 1912 (3) 1921 (5) 1926 (5); v SA 1912 (3) 1921 (2)*
McCabe, S. J. 39: v E 1932 (5) 1936 (5); v SA 1931 (5); v WI 1930 (5); *v E 1930 (5) 1934 (5) 1938 (4); v SA 1935 (5)*
McCool, C. L. 14: v E 1946 (5); v In 1947 (3); *v SA 1949 (5) v NZ 1945 (1)*
McCormick, E. L. 12: v E 1936 (4); *v E 1938 (3); v SA 1935 (5)*
McCosker, R. B. 25: v E 1974 (3) 1976 (1) 1979 (2); v WI 1975 (4) 1979 (1); v P 1976 (3); *v E 1975 (4) 1977 (5); v NZ 1976 (2)*
McDermott, C. J. 49: v E 1986 (1) 1987 (1) 1990 (2); v WI 1984 (2) 1988 (2) 1992 (5); v NZ 1985 (2) 1987 (3) 1991 (5); v In 1985 (2) 1991 (5); v SL 1987 (1); *v E 1985 (6) 1993 (2); v WI 1990 (5); v NZ 1985 (2) 1992 (3); v In 1986 (2); v SL 1992 (3)*
McDonald, C. C. 47: v E 1954 (2) 1958 (5); v SA 1952 (5); v WI 1951 (1) 1960 (5); *v E 1956 (5) 1961 (3); v SA 1957 (5); v WI 1954 (5); v In 1956 (2) 1959 (5); v P 1956 (1) 1959 (3)*
McDonald, E. A. 11: v E 1920 (3); *v E 1921 (5); v SA 1921 (3)*
McDonnell, P. S. 19: v E 1881 (4) 1882 (3) 1884 (2) 1886 (2) 1887 (1); *v E 1880 (1) 1884 (3) 1888 (3)*
McIlwraith, J. 1: *v E 1886*
Mackay K. D. 37: v E 1958 (5) 1962 (5); v WI 1960 (5); *v E 1956 (3) 1961 (5); v SA 1957 (5); v In 1956 (3) 1959 (5); v P 1959 (3)*
McKenzie, G. D. 60: v E 1962 (5) 1965 (4) 1970 (3); v SA 1963 (5); v WI 1968 (5); v In 1967 (2); v P 1964 (1); *v E 1961 (3) 1964 (5) 1968 (5); v SA 1966 (5) 1969 (3); v WI 1964 (5); v In 1964 (3) 1969 (5); v P 1964 (1)*
McKibbin, T. R. 5: v E 1894 (1) 1897 (2); *v E 1896 (2)*
McLaren, J. W. 1: v E 1911

Maclean, J. A. 4: v E 1978 (4)
McLeod, C. E. 17: v E 1894 (1) 1897 (5) 1901 (2) 1903 (3); *v E 1899 (1) 1905 (5)*
McLeod, R. W. 6: v E 1891 (3); *v E 1893 (3)*
McShane, P. G. 3: v E 1884 (1) 1886 (1) 1887 (1)
Maddocks, L. V. 7: v E 1954 (3); *v E 1956 (2); v WI 1954 (1); v In 1956 (1)*
Maguire, J. N. 3: v P 1983 (1); *v WI 1983 (2)*
Mailey, A. A. 21: v E 1920 (5) 1924 (5); *v E 1921 (3) 1926 (5); v SA 1921 (3)*
Mallett, A. A. 38: v E 1970 (2) 1974 (5) 1979 (1); v WI 1968 (1) 1975 (6) 1979 (1); v NZ 1973 (3); v P 1972 (2); *v E 1968 (1) 1972 (2) 1975 (4) 1980 (1); v SA 1969 (1); v NZ 1973 (3); v In 1969 (5)*
Malone, M. F. 1: *v E 1977*
Mann, A. L. 4: v In 1977 (4)
Marr, A. P. 1: v E 1884
Marsh, G. R. 50: v E 1986 (5) 1987 (1) 1990 (5); v WI 1988 (5); v NZ 1987 (3); v In 1985 (3) 1991 (4); v P 1989 (2); v SL 1987 (1); *v E 1989 (6); v WI 1990 (5); v NZ 1985 (3) 1989 (1); v In 1986 (3); v P 1988 (3)*
Marsh, R. W. 96: v E 1970 (6) 1974 (6) 1976 (1) 1979 (3) 1982 (5); v WI 1975 (6) 1979 (3) 1981 (3); v NZ 1973 (3) 1980 (3); v In 1980 (3); v P 1972 (3) 1976 (3) 1981 (3) 1983 (5); *v E 1972 (5) 1975 (4) 1977 (5) 1980 (1) 1981 (6); v WI 1972 (5); v NZ 1973 (3) 1976 (2) 1981 (3); v P 1979 (3) 1982 (3)*
Martin, J. W. 8: v SA 1963 (1); v WI 1960 (3); *v SA 1966 (1); v In 1964 (2); v P 1964 (1)*
Martyn, D. R. 5: v WI 1992 (4); *v NZ 1992 (1)*
Massie, H. H. 9: v E 1881 (4) 1882 (3) 1884 (1); *v E 1882 (1)*
Massie, R. A. L. 6: v P 1972 (2); *v E 1972 (4)*
Matthews, C. D. 3: v E 1986 (2); v WI 1988 (1)
Matthews, G. R. J. 33: v E 1986 (4) 1990 (5); v WI 1984 (1) 1992 (2); v NZ 1985 (3); v In 1985 (3); v P 1983 (2); *v E 1985 (1); v WI 1983 (1) 1990 (2); v NZ 1985 (3); v In 1986 (3); v SL 1992 (3)*
Matthews, T. J. 8: v E 1911 (2); *v E 1912 (3); v SA 1912 (3)*
May, T. B. A. 13: v WI 1988 (3) 1992 (1); v NZ 1987 (1); *v E 1993 (5); v P 1988 (3)*
Mayne, E. R. 4: *v E 1912 (1); v SA 1912 (1) 1921 (2)*
Mayne, L. C. 6: v SA 1969 (2); *v WI 1964 (3); v In 1969 (1)*
Meckiff, I. 18: v E 1958 (4); v SA 1963 (1); v WI 1960 (2); *v SA 1957 (4); v In 1959 (5); v P 1959 (2)*
Meuleman, K. D. 1: *v NZ 1945*
Midwinter, W. E. 8: v E 1876 (2) 1882 (1) 1886 (2); *v E 1884 (3)*
Miller, K. R. 55: v E 1946 (5) 1950 (5) 1954 (4); v SA 1952 (4); v WI 1951 (5); v In 1947 (5); *v E 1948 (5) 1953 (5) 1956 (5); v SA 1949 (5); v WI 1954 (5); v NZ 1945 (1); v P 1956 (1)*
Minnett, R. B. 9: v E 1911 (5); *v E 1912 (1); v SA 1912 (3)*
Misson, F. M. 5: v WI 1960 (3); *v E 1961 (2)*
Moody, T. M. 8: v NZ 1989 (1); v I 1991 (1); v P 1989 (1); v SL 1989 (2); *v SL 1992 (3)*
Moroney, J. R. 7: v E 1950 (1); v WI 1951 (1); *v SA 1949 (5)*
Morris, A. R. 46: v E 1946 (5) 1950 (5) 1954 (4); v SA 1952 (5); v WI 1951 (5); v In 1947 (4); *v E 1948 (5) 1953 (5); v SA 1949 (5); v WI 1954 (4)*
Morris, S. 1: v E 1884
Moses, H. 6: v E 1886 (2) 1887 (1) 1891 (2) 1894 (1)
Moss, J. K. 1: v P 1978
Moule, W. H. 1: *v E 1880*
Murdoch, W. L. 18: v E 1876 (1) 1878 (1) 1881 (4) 1882 (4) 1884 (1); *v E 1880 (1) 1882 (1) 1884 (3) 1890 (2)*
Musgrove, H. 1: v E 1884

Nagel, L. E. 1: v E 1932
Nash, L. J. 2: v E 1936 (1); v SA 1931 (1)
Nitschke, H. C. 2: v SA 1931 (2)
Noble, M. A. 42: v E 1897 (4) 1901 (5) 1903 (5) 1907 (5); *v E 1899 (5) 1902 (5) 1905 (5) 1909 (5); v SA 1902 (3)*
Noblet, G. 3: v SA 1952 (1); v WI 1951 (1); *v SA 1949 (1)*
Nothling, O. E. 1: v E 1928

O'Brien, L. P. J. 5: v E 1932 (2) 1936 (1); *v SA 1935 (2)*
O'Connor, J. D. A. 4: v E 1907 (3); *v E 1909 (1)*
O'Donnell, S. P. 6: v NZ 1985 (1); *v E 1985 (5)*

Ogilvie, A. D. 5: v In 1977 (3); *v WI 1977* (2)
O'Keeffe, K. J. 24: v E 1970 (2) 1976 (1); v NZ 1973 (3); v P 1972 (2) 1976 (3); *v E 1977* (3); *v WI 1972* (5); *v NZ 1973* (3) *1976* (2)
Oldfield, W. A. 54: v E 1920 (3) 1924 (5) 1928 (5) 1932 (4) 1936 (5); v SA 1931 (5); v WI 1930 (5); *v E 1921* (1) *1926* (5) *1930* (5) *1934* (5); *v SA 1921* (1) *1935* (5)
O'Neill, N. C. 42: v E 1958 (5) 1962 (5); v SA 1963 (4); v WI 1960 (5); *v E 1961* (5) *1964* (4); *v WI 1964* (4); *v In 1959* (5) *1964* (2); *v P 1959* (5)
O'Reilly, W. J. 27: v E 1932 (5) 1936 (5); v SA 1931 (2); *v E 1934* (5) *1938* (4); *v SA 1935* (5); *v NZ 1945* (1)
Oxenham, R. K. 7: v E 1928 (3); v SA 1931 (1); v WI 1930 (3)

Palmer, G. E. 17: v E 1881 (4) 1882 (4) 1884 (2); *v E 1880* (1) *1884* (3) *1886* (3)
Park, R. L. 1: v E 1920
Pascoe, L. S. 14: v E 1979 (2); v WI 1979 (1) 1981 (1); v NZ 1980 (3); v In 1980 (3); *v E 1977* (3) *1980* (1)
Pellew, C. E. 10: v E 1920 (4); *v E 1921* (5); *v SA 1921* (1)
Phillips, W. B. 27: v WI 1984 (2); v NZ 1985 (3); v In 1985 (3); v P 1983 (5); *v E 1985* (6); *v WI 1983* (5); *v NZ 1985* (3)
Phillips, W. N. 1: v I 1991
Philpott, P. I. 8: v E 1965 (3); *v WI 1964* (5)
Ponsford, W. H. 29: v E 1924 (5) 1928 (2) 1932 (3); v SA 1931 (4); v WI 1930 (5); *v E 1926* (2) *1930* (4) *1934* (4)
Pope, R. J. 1: v E 1884

Rackemann, C. G. 12: v E 1982 (1) 1990 (1); v WI 1984 (1); v NZ 1989 (1); v P 1983 (2) 1989 (3); v SL 1989 (1); *v WI 1983* (1); *v NZ 1989* (1)
Ransford, V. S. 20: v E 1907 (5) 1911 (5); v SA 1910 (5); *v E 1909* (5)
Redpath, I. R. 66: v E 1965 (1) 1970 (6) 1974 (6); v SA 1963 (1); v WI 1968 (5) 1975 (6); v In 1967 (3); v P 1972 (3); *v E 1964* (5) *1968* (5); *v SA 1966* (5) *1969* (4); *v WI 1972* (5); *v NZ 1973* (3); *v In 1964* (2) *1969* (5); *v P 1964* (1)
Reedman, J. C. 1: v E 1894
Reid, B. A. 27: v E 1986 (5) 1990 (4); v WI 1992 (1); v NZ 1987 (2); v In 1985 (3) 1991 (2); *v E 1990* (2); *v NZ 1985* (3); *v In 1986* (2); *v P 1988* (3)
Reiffel, P. R. 7: v I 1991 (1); *v E 1993* (3); *v NZ 1992* (3)
Renneberg, D. A. 8: v In 1967 (3); *v SA 1966* (5)
Richardson, A. J. 9: v E 1924 (4); *v E 1926* (5)
Richardson, V. Y. 19: v E 1924 (3) 1928 (2) 1932 (5); *v E 1930* (4); *v SA 1935* (5)
Rigg, K. E. 8: v E 1936 (3); v SA 1931 (4); v WI 1930 (1)
Ring, D. T. 13: v SA 1952 (5); v WI 1951 (5); v In 1947 (1); *v E 1948* (1) *1953* (1)
Ritchie, G. M. 30: v E 1986 (4); v WI 1984 (1); v NZ 1985 (3); v In 1985 (2); *v E 1985* (6); *v WI 1983* (5); *v NZ 1985* (3); *v In 1986* (3); *v P 1982* (3)
Rixon, S. J. 13: v WI 1984 (3); v In 1977 (5); *v WI 1977* (5)
Robertson, W. R. 1: v E 1884
Robinson, R. D. 3: *v E 1977* (3)
Robinson, R. H. 1: v E 1936
Rorke, G. F. 4: v E 1958 (2); *v In 1959* (2)
Rutherford, J. W. 1: *v In 1956*
Ryder, J. 20: v E 1920 (5) 1924 (3) 1928 (5); *v E 1926* (4); *v SA 1921* (3)

Saggers, R. A. 6: *v E 1948* (1); *v SA 1949* (5)
Saunders, J. V. 14: v E 1901 (1) 1903 (1) 1907 (5); *v E 1902* (4); *v SA 1902* (2)
Scott, H. J. H. 8: v E 1884 (2); *v E 1884* (3) *1886* (3)
Sellers, R. H. D. 1: *v In 1964*
Serjeant, C. S. 12: v In 1977 (4); *v E 1977* (3); *v WI 1977* (5)
Sheahan, A. P. 31: v E 1970 (2); v WI 1968 (5); v NZ 1973 (2); v In 1967 (4); v P 1972 (2); *v E 1968* (5) *1972* (2); *v SA 1969* (4); *v In 1969* (5)
Shepherd, B. K. 9: v E 1962 (2); v SA 1963 (4); v P 1964 (1); *v WI 1964* (2)
Sievers, M. W. 3: v E 1936 (3)
Simpson, R. B. 62: v E 1958 (1) 1962 (5) 1965 (3); v SA 1963 (5); v WI 1960 (5); v In 1967 (3) 1977 (5); v P 1964 (1); *v E 1961* (5) *1964* (5); *v SA 1957* (5) *1966* (5); *v WI 1964* (5) *1977* (5); *v In 1964* (3); *v P 1964* (1)
Sincock, D. J. 3: v E 1965 (1); v P 1964 (1); *v WI 1964* (1)

Slater, K. N. 1: v E 1958
Slater, M. J. 6: *v E 1993 (6)*
Sleep, P. R. 14: v E 1986 (3) 1987 (1); v NZ 1987 (3); v P 1978 (1) 1989 (1); v SL 1989 (1); *v In 1979 (2); v P 1982 (1) 1988 (1)*
Slight, J. 1: *v E 1880*
Smith, D. B. M. 2: *v E 1912 (2)*
Smith, S. B. 3: *v WI 1983 (3)*
Spofforth, F. R. 18: v E 1876 (1) 1878 (1) 1881 (1) 1882 (4) 1884 (3) 1886 (1); *v E 1882 (1) 1884 (3) 1886 (3)*
Stackpole, K. R. 43: v E 1965 (2) 1970 (6); v WI 1968 (5); v NZ 1973 (3); v P 1972 (1); *v E 1972 (5); v SA 1966 (5) 1969 (4); v WI 1972 (4); v NZ 1973 (3); v In 1969 (5)*
Stevens, G. B. 4: *v In 1959 (2); v P 1959 (2)*

Taber, H. B. 16: v WI 1968 (1); *v E 1968 (1); v SA 1966 (5); 1969 (4); v In 1969 (5)*
Tallon, D. 21: v E 1946 (5) 1950 (5); v In 1947 (5); *v E 1948 (4) 1953 (1); v NZ 1945 (1)*
Taylor, J. M. 20: v E 1920 (5) 1924 (5); *v E 1921 (5) 1926 (3); v SA 1921 (2)*
Taylor, M. A. 46: v E 1990 (5); v WI 1988 (2) 1992 (4); v NZ 1989 (1); v I 1991 (5); v P 1989 (3); v SL 1989 (2); *v E 1989 (6) 1993 (6); v WI 1990 (5); v NZ 1989 (1) 1992 (3); v SL 1992 (3)*
Taylor, P. L. 13: v E 1986 (1) 1987 (1); v WI 1988 (2); v I 1991 (2); v P 1989 (2); v SL 1987 (1); *v WI 1990 (1); v NZ 1989 (1); v P 1988 (2)*
Thomas, G. 8: v E 1965 (3); *v WI 1964 (5)*
Thoms, G. R. 1: v WI 1951
Thomson, A. L. 4: v E 1970 (4)
Thomson, J. R. 51: v E 1974 (5) 1979 (1) 1982 (4); v WI 1975 (6) 1979 (1) 1981 (2); v In 1977 (5); v P 1972 (1) 1976 (1) 1981 (3); *v E 1975 (4) 1977 (5) 1985 (2); v WI 1977 (5); v NZ 1981 (3); v P 1982 (3)*
Thomson, N. F. D. 2: v E 1876 (2)
Thurlow, H. M. 1: v SA 1931
Toohey, P. M. 15: v E 1978 (5) 1979 (1); v WI 1979 (1); v In 1977 (5); *v WI 1977 (3)*
Toshack, E. R. H. 12: v E 1946 (5); v In 1947 (2); *v E 1948 (4); v NZ 1945 (1)*
Travers, J. P. F. 1: v E 1901
Tribe, G. E. 3: v E 1946 (3)
Trott, A. E. 3: v E 1894 (3)
Trott, G. H. S. 24: v E 1891 (3) 1894 (5) 1897 (5); *v E 1888 (3) 1890 (2) 1893 (3) 1896 (3)*
Trumble, H. 32: v E 1894 (1) 1897 (5) 1901 (5) 1903 (4); *v E 1890 (2) 1893 (3) 1896 (3) 1899 (5) 1902 (3); v SA 1902 (1)*
Trumble, J. W. 7: v E 1884 (4); *v E 1886 (3)*
Trumper, V. T. 48: v E 1901 (5) 1903 (5) 1907 (5) 1911 (5); v SA 1910 (5); *v E 1899 (5) 1902 (5) 1905 (5) 1909 (5); v SA 1902 (3)*
Turner, A. 14: v WI 1975 (6); v P 1976 (3); *v E 1975 (3); v NZ 1976 (2)*
Turner, C. T. B. 17: v E 1886 (2) 1887 (1) 1891 (3) 1894 (3); *v E 1888 (3) 1890 (2) 1893 (3)*

Veivers, T. R. 21: v E 1965 (4); v SA 1963 (3); v P 1964 (1); *v E 1964 (5); v SA 1966 (4); v In 1964 (3); v P 1964 (1)*
Veletta, M. R. J. 8: v E 1987 (1); v WI 1988 (2); v NZ 1987 (3); v P 1989 (1); v SL 1987 (1)

Waite, M. G. 2: *v E 1938 (2)*
Walker, M. H. N. 34: v E 1974 (6); 1976 (1); v WI 1975 (3); v NZ 1973 (1); v P 1972 (1) 1976 (2); *v E 1975 (4); 1977 (5); v WI 1972 (5); v NZ 1973 (3) 1976 (2)*
Wall, T. W. 18: v E 1928 (1) 1932 (4); v SA 1931 (3); v WI 1930 (1); *v E 1930 (5) 1934 (4)*
Walters, F. H. 1: v E 1884
Walters, K. D. 74: v E 1965 (5) 1970 (6) 1974 (6) 1976 (1); v WI 1968 (4); v NZ 1973 (3) 1980 (3); v In 1967 (2) 1980 (3); v P 1972 (1) 1976 (3); *v E 1968 (5) 1972 (4) 1975 (4) 1977 (5); v SA 1969 (4); v WI 1972 (5); v NZ 1973 (3) 1976 (2); v In 1969 (5)*
Ward, F. A. 4: v E 1936 (3); *v E 1938 (1)*
Warne, S. K. 17: v WI 1992 (4); v I 1991 (2); *v E 1993 (6); v NZ 1992 (3); v SL 1992 (2)*
Watkins, J. R. 1: v P 1972
Watson, G. D. 5: *v E 1972 (2); v SA 1966 (3)*
Watson, W. J. 4: v E 1954 (1); *v WI 1954 (3)*
Waugh, M. E. 27: v E 1990 (2); v WI 1992 (5); v I 1991 (4); *v E 1993 (6); v WI 1990 (5); v NZ 1992 (2); v SL 1992 (3)*

Waugh, S. R. 58: v E 1986 (5) 1987 (1) 1990 (3); v WI 1988 (5) 1992 (5); v NZ 1987 (3) 1989 (1);
    v In 1985 (2); v P 1989 (3); v SL 1987 (1) 1989 (2); *v E 1989 (6) 1993 (6); v WI 1990 (2); v NZ
    1985 (3) 1989 (1) 1992 (3); v In 1986 (3); v P 1988 (3)*
Wellham, D. M. 6: v E 1986 (1); v WI 1981 (1); v P 1981 (2); *v E 1981 (1) 1985 (1)*
Wessels, K. C. 24: v E 1982 (4); v WI 1984 (5); v NZ 1985 (1); v P 1983 (5); *v E 1985 (6); v WI
    1983 (2); v SL 1982 (1)*
Whatmore, D. F. 7: v P 1978 (2); *v In 1979 (5)*
Whitney, M. R. 12: v WI 1988 (1) 1992 (1); v NZ 1987 (1); v I 1991 (3); *v E 1981 (2); v WI
    1990 (2); v SL 1992 (2)*
Whitty, W. J. 14: v E 1911 (2); v SA 1910 (5); *v E 1909 (1) 1912 (3); v SA 1912 (3)*
Wiener, J. M. 6: v E 1979 (2); v WI 1979 (1); *v P 1979 (2)*
Wilson, J. W. 1: *v In 1956*
Wood, G. M. 59: v E 1978 (6) 1982 (1); v WI 1981 (3) 1984 (5) 1988 (3); v NZ 1980 (3); v In 1977
    (1) 1980 (3); v P 1978 (1) 1981 (3); *v E 1980 (1) 1981 (6) 1985 (5); v WI 1977 (5) 1983 (1); v NZ
    1981 (3); v In 1979 (2); v P 1982 (3) 1988 (3); v SL 1982 (1)*
Woodcock, A. J. 1: v NZ 1973
Woodfull, W. M. 35: v E 1928 (5) 1932 (5); v SA 1931 (5); v WI 1930 (5); *v E 1926 (5) 1930 (5)
    1934 (5)*
Woods, S. M. J. 3: *v E 1888 (3)*
Woolley, R. D. 2: *v WI 1983 (1); v SL 1982 (1)*
Worrall, J. 11: v E 1884 (1) 1887 (1) 1894 (1) 1897 (1); *v E 1888 (3) 1899 (4)*
Wright, K. J. 10: v E 1978 (2); v P 1978 (2); *v In 1979 (6)*

Yallop, G. N. 39: v E 1978 (6); v WI 1975 (3) 1984 (1); v In 1977 (1); v P 1978 (1) 1981 (1) 1983
    (5); *v E 1980 (1) 1981 (6); v WI 1977 (4); v In 1979 (6); v P 1979 (3); v SL 1982 (1)*
Yardley, B. 33: v E 1978 (4) 1982 (5); v WI 1981 (3); v In 1977 (1) 1980 (2); v P 1978 (1) 1981 (3);
    v WI 1977 (5); v NZ 1981 (3); v In 1979 (3); v P 1982 (2); v SL 1982 (1)

Zoehrer, T. J. 10: v E 1986 (4); *v NZ 1985 (3); v In 1986 (3)*

SOUTH AFRICA

Number of Test cricketers: 255

Adcock, N. A. T. 26: v E 1956 (5); v A 1957 (5); v NZ 1953 (5) 1961 (2); *v E 1955 (4) 1960 (5)*
Anderson, J. H. 1: v A 1902
Ashley, W. H. 1: v E 1888

Bacher, A. 12: v A 1966 (5) 1969 (4); *v E 1965 (3)*
Balaskas, X. C. 9: v E 1930 (2) 1938 (1); v A 1935 (3); *v E 1935 (1); v NZ 1931 (2)*
Barlow, E. J. 30: v E 1964 (5); v A 1966 (5) 1969 (4); v NZ 1961 (5); *v E 1965 (3); v A 1963 (5);
    v NZ 1963 (3)*
Baumgartner, H. V. 1: v E 1913
Beaumont, R. 5: v E 1913 (2); *v E 1912 (1); v A 1912 (2)*
Begbie, D. W. 5: v E 1948 (3); v A 1949 (2)
Bell, A. J. 16: v E 1930 (3); *v E 1929 (2) 1935 (3); v A 1931 (5); v NZ 1931 (2)*
Bisset, M. 3: v E 1898 (2) 1909 (1)
Bissett, G. F. 4: v E 1927 (4)
Blanckenberg, J. M. 18: v E 1913 (5) 1922 (5); v A 1921 (3); *v E 1924 (5)*
Bland, K. C. 21: v E 1964 (5); v A 1966 (1); v NZ 1961 (5); *v E 1965 (3); v A 1963 (4); v NZ
    1963 (3)*
Bock, E. G. 1: v A 1935
Bond, G. E. 1: v E 1938
Bosch, T. 1: *v WI 1991*
Botten, J. T. 3: *v E 1965 (3)*
Brann, W. H. 3: v E 1922 (3)
Briscoe, A. W. 2: v E 1938 (1); v A 1935 (1)
Bromfield, H. D. 9: v E 1964 (3); v NZ 1961 (5); *v E 1965 (1)*
Brown, L. S. 2: *v A 1931 (1); v NZ 1931 (1)*

Burger, C. G. de V. 2: v A 1957 (2)
Burke, S. F. 2: v E 1964 (1); v NZ 1961 (1)
Buys, I. D. 1: v E 1922

Cameron, H. B. 26: v E 1927 (5) 1930 (5); *v E 1929 (4) 1935 (5); v A 1931 (5); v NZ 1931 (2)*
Campbell, T. 5: v E 1909 (4); *v E 1912 (1)*
Carlstein, P. R. 8: v A 1957 (1); *v E 1960 (5); v A 1963 (2)*
Carter, C. P. 10: v E 1913 (2); v A 1921 (3); *v E 1912 (2) 1924 (3)*
Catterall, R. H. 24: v E 1922 (5) 1927 (5) 1930 (4); *v E 1924 (5) 1929 (5)*
Chapman, H. W. 2: v E 1913 (1); v A 1921 (1)
Cheetham, J. E. 24: v E 1948 (1); v A 1949 (3); v NZ 1953 (5); *v E 1951 (5) 1955 (3); v A 1952 (5); v NZ 1952 (2)*
Chevalier, G. A. 1: v A 1969
Christy, J. A. J. 10: v E 1930 (1); *v E 1929 (2); v A 1931 (5); v NZ 1931 (2)*
Chubb, G. W. A. 5: *v E 1951 (5)*
Cochran, J. A. K. 1: v E 1930
Coen, S. K. 2: v E 1927 (2)
Commaille, J. M. M. 12: v E 1909 (5) 1927 (2); *v E 1924 (5)*
Conyngham, D. P. 1: v E 1922
Cook, F. J. 1: v E 1895
Cook, S. J. 3: v I 1992 (2); *v SL 1993 (1)*
Cooper, A. H. C. 1: v E 1913
Cox, J. L. 3: v E 1913 (3)
Cripps, G. 1: v E 1891
Crisp, R. J. 9: v A 1935 (4); *v E 1935 (5)*
Cronje, W. J. 7: v I 1992 (3); *v WI 1991 (1); v SL 1993 (3)*
Cullinan, D. J. 4: v I 1992 (1); *v SL 1993 (3)*
Curnow, S. H. 7: v E 1930 (3); *v A 1931 (4)*

Dalton, E. L. 15: v E 1930 (1) 1938 (4); v A 1935 (1); *v E 1929 (1) 1935 (4); v A 1931 (2); v NZ 1931 (2)*
Davies, E. Q. 5: v E 1938 (3); v A 1935 (2)
Dawson, O. C. 9: v E 1948 (4); *v E 1947 (5)*
Deane, H. G. 17: v E 1927 (5) 1930 (2); *v E 1924 (5) 1929 (5)*
Dixon, C. D. 1: v E 1913
Donald, A. A. 8: v I 1992 (4); *v WI 1991 (1); v SL 1993 (3)*
Dower, R. R. 1: v E 1898
Draper, R. G. 2: v A 1949 (2)
Duckworth, C. A. R. 2: v E 1956 (2)
Dumbrill, R. 5: v A 1966 (2); *v E 1965 (3)*
Duminy, J. P. 3: v E 1927 (2); *v E 1929 (1)*
Dunell, O. R. 2: v E 1888 (2)
Du Preez, J. H. 2: v A 1966 (2)
Du Toit, J. F. 1: v E 1891
Dyer, D. V. 3: *v E 1947 (3)*

Eksteen, C. E. 1: *v SL 1993*
Elgie, M. K. 3: v NZ 1961 (3)
Endean, W. R. 28: v E 1956 (5); v A 1957 (5); v NZ 1953 (5); *v E 1951 (1) 1955 (5); v A 1952 (5); v NZ 1952 (2)*

Farrer, W. S. 6: v NZ 1961 (3); *v NZ 1963 (3)*
Faulkner, G. A. 25: v E 1905 (5) 1909 (5); *v E 1907 (3) 1912 (3) 1924 (1); v A 1910 (5) 1912 (3)*
Fellows-Smith, J. P. 4: *v E 1960 (4)*
Fichardt, C. G. 2: v E 1891 (1) 1895 (1)
Finlason, C. E. 1: v E 1888
Floquet, C. E. 1: v E 1909
Francis, H. H. 2: v E 1898 (2)
Francois, C. M. 5: v E 1922 (5)
Frank, C. N. 3: v A 1921 (3)
Frank, W. H. B. 1: v E 1895
Fuller, E. R. H. 7: v A 1957 (1); *v E 1955 (2); v A 1952 (2); v NZ 1952 (2)*
Fullerton, G. M. 7: v A 1949 (2); *v E 1947 (2) 1951 (3)*
Funston, K. J. 18: v E 1956 (3); v A 1957 (5); v NZ 1953 (3); *v A 1952 (5); v NZ 1952 (2)*

Gamsy, D. 2: v A 1969 (2)
Gleeson, R. A. 1: v E 1895
Glover, G. K. 1: v E 1895
Goddard, T. L. 41: v E 1956 (5) 1964 (5); v A 1957 (5) 1966 (5) 1969 (3); *v E 1955 (5) 1960 (5); v A 1963 (5); v NZ 1963 (3)*
Gordon, N. 5: v E 1938 (5)
Graham, R. 2: v E 1898 (2)
Grieveson, R. E. 2: v E 1938 (2)
Griffin, G. M. 2: *v E 1960 (2)*

Hall, A. E. 7: v E 1922 (4) 1927 (2) 1930 (1)
Hall, G. G. 1: v E 1964
Halliwell, E. A. 8: v E 1891 (1) 1895 (3) 1898 (1); v A 1902 (3)
Halse, C. G. 3: *v A 1963 (3)*
Hands, P. A. M. 7: v E 1913 (5); v A 1921 (1); *v E 1924 (1)*
Hands, R. H. M. 1: v E 1913
Hanley, M. A. 1: v E 1948
Harris, T. A. 3: v E 1948 (1); *v E 1947 (2)*
Hartigan, G. P. D. 5: v E 1913 (3); *v E 1912 (1); v A 1912 (1)*
Harvey, R. L. 2: v A 1935 (2)
Hathorn, C. M. H. 12: v E 1905 (5); v A 1902 (3); *v E 1907 (3); v A 1910 (1)*
Hearne, F. 4: v E 1891 (1) 1895 (3)
Hearne, G. A. L. 3: v E 1922 (2); *v E 1924 (1)*
Heine, P. S. 14: v E 1956 (5) 1964 (5); v A 1957 (4); v NZ 1961 (1); *v E 1955 (4)*
Henry, O. 3: v I 1992 (3)
Hime, C. F. W. 1: v E 1895
Hudson, A. C. 8: v I 1992 (4); *v WI 1991 (1); v SL 1993 (3)*
Hutchinson, P. 2: v E 1888 (2)

Ironside, D. E. J. 3: v NZ 1953 (3)
Irvine, B. L. 4: v A 1969 (4)

Johnson, C. L. 1: v E 1895

Keith, H. J. 8: v E 1956 (3); *v E 1955 (4); v A 1952 (1)*
Kempis, G. A. 1: v E 1888
Kirsten, P. N. 5: v I 1992 (4); *v WI 1991 (1)*
Kotze, J. J. 3: v A 1902 (2); *v E 1907 (1)*
Kuiper, A. P. 1: *v WI 1991*
Kuys, F. 1: v E 1898

Lance, H. R. 13: v A 1966 (5) 1969 (3); v NZ 1961 (2); *v E 1965 (3)*
Langton, A. B. C. 15: v E 1938 (5); v A 1935 (5); *v E 1935 (5)*
Lawrence, G. B. 5: v NZ 1961 (5)
Le Roux, F. le S. 1: v E 1913
Lewis, P. T. 1: v E 1913
Lindsay, D. T. 19: v E 1964 (3); v A 1966 (5) 1969 (2); *v E 1965 (3); v A 1963 (3); v NZ 1963 (3)*
Lindsay, J. D. 3: *v E 1947 (3)*
Lindsay, N. V. 1: v A 1921
Ling, W. V. S. 6: v E 1922 (3); v A 1921 (3)
Llewellyn, C. B. 15: v E 1895 (1) 1898 (1); v A 1902 (3); *v E 1912 (3); v A 1910 (5) 1912 (2)*
Lundie, E. B. 1: v E 1913

Macaulay, M. J. 1: v E 1964
McCarthy, C. N. 15: v E 1948 (5); v A 1949 (5); *v E 1951 (5)*
McGlew, D. J. 34: v E 1956 (1); v A 1957 (5); v NZ 1953 (5) 1961 (5); *v E 1951 (2) 1955 (5) 1960 (5); v A 1952 (4); v NZ 1952 (2)*
McKinnon, A. H. 8: v E 1964 (2); v A 1966 (2); v NZ 1961 (1); *v E 1960 (1) 1965 (2)*
McLean, R. A. 40: v E 1956 (5) 1964 (2); v A 1957 (4); v NZ 1953 (4) 1961 (5); *v E 1951 (3) 1955 (5) 1960 (5); v A 1952 (5); v NZ 1952 (2)*
McMillan, B. M. 6: v I 1992 (4); *v SL 1993 (2)*
McMillan, Q. 13: v E 1930 (5); *v E 1929 (2); v A 1931 (4); v NZ 1931 (2)*

Mann, N. B. F. 19: v E 1948 (5); v A 1949 (5); *v E 1947 (5) 1951 (4)*
Mansell, P. N. F. 13: *v E 1951 (2) 1955 (4); v A 1952 (5); v NZ 1952 (2)*
Markham, L. A. 1: v E 1948
Marx, W. F. E. 3: v A 1921 (3)
Matthews, C. R. 3: v I 1992 (3)
Meintjes, D. J. 2: v E 1922 (2)
Melle, M. G. 7: v A 1949 (2); *v E 1951 (1); v A 1952 (4)*
Melville, A. 11: v E 1938 (5) 1948 (1); *v E 1947 (5)*
Middleton, J. 6: v E 1895 (2) 1898 (2); v A 1902 (2)
Mills, C. 1: v E 1891
Milton, W. H. 3: v E 1888 (2) 1891 (1)
Mitchell, B. 42: v E 1930 (5) 1938 (5) 1948 (5); v A 1935 (5); *v E 1929 (5) 1935 (5) 1947 (5); v A 1931 (5) v NZ 1931 (2)*
Mitchell, F. 3: *v E 1912 (1); v A 1912 (2)*
Morkel, D. P. B. 16: v E 1927 (5); *v E 1929 (5); v A 1931 (5); v NZ 1931 (1)*
Murray, A. R. A. 10: v NZ 1953 (4); *v A 1952 (4); v NZ 1952 (2)*

Nel, J. D. 6: v A 1949 (5) 1957 (1)
Newberry, C. 4: v E 1913 (4)
Newson, E. S. 3: v E 1930 (1) 1938 (2)
Nicholson, F. 4: v A 1935 (4)
Nicolson, J. F. W. 3: v E 1927 (3)
Norton, N. O. 1: v E 1909
Nourse, A. D. 34: v E 1938 (5) 1948 (5); v A 1935 (5) 1949 (5); *v E 1935 (4) 1947 (5) 1951 (5)*
Nourse, A. W. 45: v E 1905 (5) 1909 (5) 1913 (5) 1922 (5); v A 1902 (3) 1921 (3); *v E 1907 (3) 1912 (3) 1924 (3); v A 1910 (5) 1912 (3)*
Nupen, E. P. 17: v E 1922 (4) 1927 (5) 1930 (3); v A 1921 (2) 1935 (1); *v E 1924 (2)*

Ochse, A. E. 2: v E 1888 (2)
Ochse, A. L. 3: v E 1927 (1); *v E 1929 (2)*
O'Linn, S. 7: v NZ 1961 (2); *v E 1960 (5)*
Owen-Smith, H. G. 5: *v E 1929 (5)*

Palm, A. W. 1: v E 1927
Parker, G. M. 2: *v E 1924 (2)*
Parkin, D. C. 1: v E 1891
Partridge, J. T. 11: v E 1964 (3); *v A 1963 (5); v NZ 1963 (3)*
Pearse, O. C. 3: *v A 1910 (3)*
Pegler, S. J. 16: v E 1909 (1); *v E 1912 (3) 1924 (5); v A 1910 (4) 1912 (3)*
Pithey, A. J. 17: v E 1956 (3) 1964 (5); *v E 1960 (2); v A 1963 (4); v NZ 1963 (3)*
Pithey, D. B. 8: v A 1966 (2); *v A 1963 (3); v NZ 1963 (3)*
Plimsoll, J. B. 1: *v E 1947*
Pollock, P. M. 28: v E 1964 (5); v A 1966 (5) 1969 (4); v NZ 1961 (3); *v E 1965 (3); v A 1963 (5); v NZ 1963 (3)*
Pollock, R. G. 23: v E 1964 (5); v A 1966 (5) 1969 (4); *v E 1965 (3); v A 1963 (5); v NZ 1963 (1)*
Poore, R. M. 3: v E 1895 (3)
Pothecary, J. E. 3: *v E 1960 (3)*
Powell, A. W. 1: v E 1898
Prince, C. F. H. 1: v E 1898
Pringle, M. W. 3: v I 1992 (2); *v WI 1991 (1)*
Procter, M. J. 7: v A 1966 (3) 1969 (4)
Promnitz, H. L. E. 2: v E 1927 (2)

Quinn, N. A. 12: v E 1930 (1); *v E 1929 (4); v A 1931 (5); v NZ 1931 (2)*

Reid, N. 1: v A 1921
Rhodes, J. N. 7: v I 1992 (4); *v SL 1993 (3)*
Richards, A. R. 1: v E 1895
Richards, B. A. 4: v A 1969 (4)
Richards, W. H. 1: v E 1888
Richardson, D. J. 8: v I 1992 (4); *v WI 1991 (1); v SL 1993 (3)*
Robertson, J. B. 3: v A 1935 (3)

Rose-Innes, A. 2: v E 1888 (2)
Routledge, T. W. 4: v E 1891 (1) 1895 (3)
Rowan, A. M. B. 15: v E 1948 (5); *v E 1947 (5) 1951 (5)*
Rowan, E. A. B. 26: v E 1938 (4) 1948 (4); v A 1935 (3); 1949 (5); *v E 1935 (5) 1951 (5)*
Rowe, G. A. 5: v E 1895 (2) 1898 (2); v A 1902 (1)
Rushmere, M. W. 1: *v WI 1991*

Samuelson, S. V. 1: v E 1909
Schultz, B. N. 5: v I 1992 (2); *v SL 1993 (3)*
Schwarz, R. O. 20: v E 1905 (5) 1909 (4); *v E 1907 (3) 1912 (1); v A 1910 (5) 1912 (2)*
Seccull, A. W. 1: v E 1895
Seymour, M. A. 7: v E 1964 (2); v A 1969 (1); *v A 1963 (4)*
Shalders, W. A. 12: v E 1898 (1) 1905 (5); v A 1902 (3); *v E 1907 (3)*
Shepstone, G. H. 2: v E 1895 (1) 1898 (1)
Sherwell, P. W. 13: v E 1905 (5); *v E 1907 (3); v A 1910 (5)*
Siedle, I. J. 18: v E 1927 (1) 1930 (5); v A 1935 (5); *v E 1929 (3) 1935 (4)*
Sinclair, J. H. 25: v E 1895 (3) 1898 (2) 1905 (5) 1909 (4); v A 1902 (3); *v E 1907 (3); v A 1910 (5)*
Smith, C. J. E. 3: v A 1902 (3)
Smith, F. W. 3: v E 1888 (2) 1895 (1)
Smith, V. I. 9: v A 1949 (3) 1957 (1); *v E 1947 (4) 1955 (1)*
Snell, R. P. 3: *v WI 1991 (1); v SL 1993 (2)*
Snooke, S. D. 1: *v E 1907*
Snooke, S. J. 26: v E 1905 (5) 1909 (5) 1922 (3); *v E 1907 (3) 1912 (3); v A 1910 (5) 1912 (2)*
Solomon, W. R. 1: v E 1898
Stewart, R. B. 1: v E 1888
Stricker, L. A. 13: v E 1909 (4); *v E 1912 (2); v A 1910 (5) 1912 (2)*
Susskind, M. J. 5: *v E 1924 (5)*
Symcox, P. L. 3: *v SL 1993 (3)*

Taberer, H. M. 1: v A 1902
Tancred, A. B. 2: v E 1888 (2)
Tancred, L. J. 14: v E 1905 (5) 1913 (1); v A 1902 (3); *v E 1907 (1) 1912 (2); v A 1912 (2)*
Tancred, V. M. 1: v E 1898
Tapscott, G. L. 1: v E 1913
Tapscott, L. E. 2: v E 1922 (2)
Tayfield, H. J. 37: v E 1956 (5); v A 1949 (5) 1957 (5); v NZ 1953 (5); *v E 1955 (5) 1960 (5); v A 1952 (5); v NZ 1952 (2)*
Taylor, A. I. 1: v E 1956
Taylor, D. 2: v E 1913 (2)
Taylor, H. W. 42: v E 1913 (5) 1922 (5) 1927 (5) 1930 (4); v A 1921 (3); *v E 1912 (3) 1924 (5) 1929 (3); v A 1912 (3) 1931 (5); v NZ 1931 (1)*
Theunissen, N. H. G. de J. 1: v E 1888
Thornton, P. G. 1: v A 1902
Tomlinson, D. S. 1: *v E 1935*
Traicos, A. J. 3: v A 1969 (3)
Trimborn, P. H. J. 4: v A 1966 (3) 1969 (1)
Tuckett, L. 9: v E 1948 (4); *v E 1947 (5)*
Tuckett, L. R. 1: v E 1913
Twentyman-Jones, P. S. 1: v A 1902

van der Bijl, P. G. V. 5: v E 1938 (5)
Van der Merwe, E. A. 2: v A 1935 (1); *v E 1929 (1)*
Van der Merwe, P. L. 15: v E 1964 (2); v A 1966 (5); *v E 1965 (3); v A 1963 (3); v NZ 1963 (2)*
Van Ryneveld, C. B. 19: v E 1956 (5); v A 1957 (4); v NZ 1953 (5); *v E 1951 (5)*
Varnals, G. D. 3: v E 1964 (3)
Viljoen, K. G. 27: v E 1930 (3) 1938 (4) 1948 (2); v A 1935 (4); *v E 1935 (4) 1947 (5); v A 1931 (4); v NZ 1931 (1)*
Vincent, C. L. 25: v E 1927 (5) 1930 (5); *v E 1929 (4) 1935 (4); v A 1931 (5); v NZ 1931 (2)*
Vintcent, C. H. 3: v E 1888 (2) 1891 (1)
Vogler, A. E. E. 15: v E 1905 (5) 1909 (5); *v E 1907 (3); v A 1910 (2)*

Wade, H. F. 10: v A 1935 (5); *v E 1935 (5)*
Wade, W. W. 11: v E 1938 (3) 1948 (5); v A 1949 (3)

Waite, J. H. B. 50: v E 1956 (5); 1964 (2); v A 1957 (5); v NZ 1953 (5) 1961 (5); *v E 1951 (4) 1955 (5) 1960 (5); v A 1952 (5) 1963 (4); v NZ 1952 (2) 1963 (3)*
Walter, K. A. 2: v NZ 1961 (2)
Ward, T. A. 23: v E 1913 (5) 1922 (5); v A 1921 (3); *v E 1912 (2) 1924 (5); v A 1912 (3)*
Watkins, J. C. 15: v E 1956 (2); v A 1949 (5); v NZ 1953 (3); *v A 1952 (5); v NZ 1952 (2)*
Wesley, C. 3: *v E 1960 (3)*
Wessels, K. C. 8: v I 1992 (4); *v WI 1991 (1); SL 1993 (3)*
Westcott, R. J. 5: v A 1957 (2); v NZ 1953 (3)
White, G. C. 17: v E 1905 (5) 1909 (4); *v E 1907 (3) 1912 (2); v A 1912 (3)*
Willoughby, J. T. I. 2: v E 1895 (2)
Wimble, C. S. 1: v E 1891
Winslow, P. L. 5: v A 1949 (2); *v E 1955 (3)*
Wynne, O. E. 6: v E 1948 (3); v A 1949 (3)

Zulch, J. W. 16: v E 1909 (5) 1913 (3); v A 1921 (3); *v A 1910 (5)*

WEST INDIES

Number of Test cricketers: 203

Achong, E. 6: v E 1929 (1) 1934 (2); *v E 1933 (3)*
Adams, J. C. 4: v SA 1991 (1); *v A 1992 (3)*
Alexander, F. C. M. 25: v E 1959 (5); v P 1957 (5); *v E 1957 (3); v A 1960 (5); v In 1958 (5); v P 1958 (3)*
Ali, Imtiaz 1: v In 1975
Ali, Inshan 12: v E 1973 (2); v A 1972 (3); v In 1970 (1); v P 1976 (1); v NZ 1971 (3); *v E 1973 (1); v A 1975 (1)*
Allan, D. W. 5: v A 1964 (1); v In 1961 (2); *v E 1966 (2)*
Allen, I. B. A. 2: *v E 1991 (2)*
Ambrose, C. E. L. 42: v E 1989 (3); v A 1990 (5); v SA 1991 (1); v In 1988 (4); v P 1987 (3) 1992 (3); *v E 1988 (5) 1991 (5); v A 1988 (5) 1992 (5); v P 1990 (3)*
Arthurton, K. L. T. 14: v SA 1991 (1); v In 1988 (4); v P 1992 (3); *v E 1988 (1); v A 1992 (5)*
Asgarali, N. 2: *v E 1957 (2)*
Atkinson, D. St E. 22: v E 1953 (4); v A 1954 (4); v P 1957 (1); *v E 1957 (2); v A 1951 (2); v NZ 1951 (1) 1955 (4); v In 1948 (4)*
Atkinson, E. St E. 8: v P 1957 (3); *v In 1958 (3); v P 1958 (2)*
Austin, R. A. 2: v A 1977 (2)

Bacchus, S. F. A. F. 19: v A 1977 (2); *v E 1980 (5); v A 1981 (2); v In 1978 (6); v P 1980 (4)*
Baichan, L. 3: *v A 1975 (1); v P 1974 (2)*
Baptiste, E. A. E. 10: v E 1989 (1); v A 1983 (3); *v E 1984 (5); v In 1983 (1)*
Barrett, A. G. 6: v E 1973 (2); v In 1970 (2); *v In 1974 (2)*
Barrow, I. 11: v E 1929 (1) 1934 (1); *v E 1933 (3) 1939 (1); v A 1930 (5)*
Bartlett, E. L. 5: *v E 1928 (1); v A 1930 (4)*
Benjamin, K. C. G. 2: v SA 1991 (1); *v A 1992 (1)*
Benjamin, W. K. M. 10: v In 1988 (1); v P 1987 (3) 1992 (2); *v E 1988 (3); v In 1987 (1)*
Best, C. A. 8: v E 1985 (3) 1989 (3); *v P 1990 (2)*
Betancourt, N. 1: v E 1929
Binns, A. P. 5: v A 1954 (1); v In 1952 (1); *v NZ 1955 (3)*
Birkett, L. S. 4: *v A 1930 (4)*
Bishop, I. R. 18: v E 1989 (4); v In 1988 (4); v P 1992 (2); *v A 1992 (5); v P 1990 (3)*
Boyce, K. D. 21: v E 1973 (4); v A 1972 (4); v In 1970 (1); *v E 1973 (3); v A 1975 (4); v In 1974 (3); v P 1974 (2)*
Browne, C. R. 4: v E 1929 (2); *v E 1928 (2)*
Butcher, B. F. 44: v E 1959 (2) 1967 (5); v A 1964 (3); *v E 1963 (5) 1966 (5) 1969 (3); v A 1968 (5); v NZ 1968 (3); v In 1958 (5) 1966 (3); v P 1958 (3)*
Butler, L. 1: v A 1954
Butts, C. G. 7: v NZ 1984 (1); *v NZ 1986 (1); v In 1987 (3); v P 1986 (2)*
Bynoe, M. R. 4: *v In 1966 (3); v P 1958 (1)*

Camacho, G. S. 11: v E 1967 (5); v In 1970 (2); *v E 1969 (2); v A 1968 (2)*
Cameron, F. J. 5: *v In 1948 (5)*
Cameron, J. H. 2: *v E 1939 (2)*
Carew, G. M. 4: v E 1934 (1) 1947 (2); *v In 1948 (1)*
Carew, M. C. 19: v E 1967 (1); v NZ 1971 (3); v In 1970 (3); *v E 1963 (2) 1966 (1) 1969 (1); v A 1968 (5); v NZ 1968 (3)*
Challenor, G. 3: *v E 1928 (3)*
Chang, H. S. 1: *v In 1978*
Christiani, C. M. 4: v E 1934 (4)
Christiani, R. J. 22: v E 1947 (4) 1953 (1); v In 1952 (2); *v E 1950 (4); v A 1951 (5); v NZ 1951 (1); v In 1948 (5)*
Clarke, C. B. 3: *v E 1939 (3)*
Clarke, S. T. 11: v A 1977 (1); *v In 1978 (5); v P 1980 (4)*
Constantine, L. N. 18: v E 1929 (3) 1934 (3); *v E 1928 (3) 1933 (1) 1939 (3); v A 1930 (5)*
Croft, C. E. H. 27: v E 1980 (4); v A 1977 (2); v P 1976 (5); *v E 1980 (3); v A 1979 (3) 1981 (3); v NZ 1979 (3); v P 1980 (4)*
Cummins, A. C. 3: *v P 1992 (2); v A 1992 (1)*

Da Costa, O. C. 5: v E 1929 (1) 1934 (1); *v E 1933 (3)*
Daniel, W. W. 10: v A 1983 (2); v In 1975 (1); *v E 1976 (4); v In 1983 (3)*
Davis, B. A. 4: v A 1964 (4)
Davis, C. A. 15: v A 1972 (2); v NZ 1971 (5); v In 1970 (4); *v E 1969 (3); v A 1968 (1)*
Davis, W. W. 15: v A 1983 (1); v NZ 1984 (2); v In 1982 (1); *v E 1984 (1); v In 1983 (6) 1987 (4)*
De Caires, F. I. 3: v E 1929 (3)
Depeiza, C. C. 5: v A 1954 (3); *v NZ 1955 (2)*
Dewdney, T. 9: v A 1954 (2); v P 1957 (3); *v E 1957 (1); v NZ 1955 (3)*
Dowe, U. G. 4: v A 1972 (1); v NZ 1971 (1); v In 1970 (2)
Dujon, P. J. L. 81: v E 1985 (4) 1989 (4); v A 1983 (2) 1990 (5); v NZ 1984 (4); v In 1982 (5) 1988 (4); v P 1987 (2); *v E 1984 (5) 1988 (5) 1991 (5); v A 1981 (3) 1984 (5) 1988 (5); v NZ 1986 (3); v In 1983 (6) 1987 (4); v P 1986 (3) 1990 (3)*

Edwards, R. M. 5: *v A 1968 (2); v NZ 1968 (3)*

Ferguson, W. 8: v E 1947 (4) 1953 (1); *v In 1948 (3)*
Fernandes, M. P. 2: v E 1929 (1); *v E 1928 (1)*
Findlay, T. M. 10: v A 1972 (1); v NZ 1971 (5); v In 1970 (2); *v E 1969 (2)*
Foster, M. L. C. 14: v E 1973 (1); v A 1972 (4) 1977 (1); v NZ 1971 (3); v In 1970 (2); v P 1976 (1); *v E 1969 (1) 1973 (1)*
Francis, G. N. 10: v E 1929 (1); *v E 1928 (3) 1933 (1); v A 1930 (5)*
Frederick, M. C. 1: v E 1953
Fredericks, R. C. 59: v E 1973 (5); v A 1972 (5); v NZ 1971 (5); v In 1970 (4) 1975 (4); v P 1976 (5); *v E 1969 (3) 1973 (3) 1976 (5); v A 1968 (4) 1975 (6); v NZ 1968 (3); v In 1974 (5); v P 1974 (2)*
Fuller, R. L. 1: v E 1934
Furlonge, H. A. 3: v A 1954 (1); *v NZ 1955 (2)*

Ganteaume, A. G. 1: v E 1947
Garner, J. 58: v E 1980 (4) 1985 (5); v A 1977 (2) 1983 (5); v NZ 1984 (4); v In 1982 (4); v P 1976 (5); *v E 1980 (5) 1984 (5); v A 1979 (3) 1981 (3) 1984 (5); v NZ 1979 (3) 1986 (2); v P 1980 (3)*
Gaskin, B. B. M. 2: v E 1947 (2)
Gibbs, G. L. R. 1: v A 1954
Gibbs, L. R. 79: v E 1967 (5) 1973 (5); v A 1964 (5) 1972 (5); v NZ 1971 (2); v In 1961 (5) 1970 (1); v P 1957 (4); *v E 1963 (5) 1966 (5) 1969 (3) 1973 (3); v A 1960 (3) 1968 (5) 1975 (6); v NZ 1968 (3); v In 1958 (1) 1966 (3) 1974 (5); v P 1958 (3) 1974 (2)*
Gilchrist, R. 13: v P 1957 (5); *v E 1957 (4); v In 1958 (4)*
Gladstone, G. 1: v E 1929
Goddard, J. D. C. 27: v E 1947 (4); *v E 1950 (4) 1957 (5); v A 1951 (4); v NZ 1951 (2) 1955 (3); v In 1948 (5)*
Gomes, H. A. 60: v E 1980 (4) 1985 (5); v A 1977 (2) 1983 (2); v NZ 1984 (4); v In 1982 (5); *v E 1976 (2) 1984 (5); v A 1981 (3) 1984 (5); v NZ 1986 (3); v In 1978 (6) 1983 (6); v P 1980 (4) 1986 (3)*

Gomez, G. E. 29: v E 1947 (4) 1953 (4); v In 1952 (4); *v E 1939 (2) 1950 (4); v A 1951 (5); v NZ 1951 (1); v In 1948 (5)*

Grant, G. C. 12: v E 1934 (4); *v E 1933 (3); v A 1930 (5)*

Grant, R. S. 7: v E 1934 (4); *v E 1939 (3)*

Gray, A. H. 5: *v NZ 1986 (2); v P 1986 (3)*

Greenidge, A. E. 6: v A 1977 (2); *v In 1978 (4)*

Greenidge, C. G. 108: v E 1980 (4) 1985 (5) 1989 (4); v A 1977 (2) 1983 (5) 1990 (5); v NZ 1984 (4); v In 1982 (5) 1988 (4); v P 1976 (5) 1987 (3); *v E 1976 (5) 1980 (5) 1984 (5) 1988 (4); v A 1975 (2) 1979 (3) 1981 (2) 1984 (5) 1988 (5); v NZ 1979 (3) 1986 (3); v In 1974 (5) 1983 (6) 1987 (3); v P 1986 (3) 1990 (3)*

Greenidge, G. A. 5: v A 1972 (3); v NZ 1971 (2)

Grell, M. G. 1: v E 1929

Griffith, C. C. 28: v E 1959 (1) 1967 (4); v A 1964 (5); *v E 1963 (5) 1966 (5); v A 1968 (3); v NZ 1968 (2); v In 1966 (3)*

Griffith, H. C. 13: v E 1929 (3); *v E 1928 (3) 1933 (2); v A 1930 (5)*

Guillen, S. C. 5: *v A 1951 (3); v NZ 1951 (2)*

Hall, W. W. 48: v E 1959 (5) 1967 (4); v A 1964 (5); v In 1961 (5); *v E 1963 (5) 1966 (5); v A 1960 (5) 1968 (2); v NZ 1968 (1); v In 1958 (5) 1966 (3); v P 1958 (3)*

Harper, R. A. 24: v E 1985 (2); v A 1983 (4); v NZ 1984 (1); *v E 1984 (5) 1988 (3); v A 1984 (2) 1988 (1); v In 1983 (2) 1987 (1); v P 1986 (3)*

Haynes, D. L. 111: v E 1980 (4) 1985 (5) 1989 (4); v A 1977 (2) 1983 (5) 1990 (5); v SA 1991 (1); v NZ 1984 (4); v In 1982 (5) 1988 (4); v P 1987 (3) 1992 (3); *v E 1980 (5) 1984 (5) 1988 (4) 1991 (5); v A 1979 (3) 1981 (3) 1984 (5) 1988 (5) 1992 (5); v NZ 1979 (3) 1986 (3); v In 1983 (6) 1987 (4); v P 1980 (4) 1986 (3) 1990 (3)*

Headley, G. A. 22: v E 1929 (4) 1934 (4) 1947 (1) 1953 (1); *v E 1933 (3) 1939 (3); v A 1930 (5); v In 1948 (1)*

Headley, R. G. A. 2: *v E 1973 (2)*

Hendriks, J. L. 20: v A 1964 (4); v In 1961 (1); *v E 1966 (3) 1969 (1); v A 1968 (5); v NZ 1968 (3); v In 1966 (3)*

Hoad, E. L. G. 4: v E 1929 (1); *v E 1928 (1) 1933 (2)*

Holder, V. A. 40: v E 1973 (1); v A 1972 (3) 1977 (3); v NZ 1971 (4); v In 1970 (3) 1975 (1); v P 1976 (1); *v E 1969 (3) 1973 (2) 1976 (4); v A 1975 (3); v In 1974 (4) 1978 (6); v P 1974 (2)*

Holding, M. A. 60: v E 1980 (4) 1985 (4); v A 1983 (3); v NZ 1984 (3); v In 1975 (4) 1982 (5); *v E 1976 (4) 1980 (5) 1984 (4); v A 1975 (5) 1979 (3) 1981 (3) 1984 (3); v NZ 1979 (3) 1986 (1); v In 1983 (6)*

Holford, D. A. J. 24: v E 1967 (4); v NZ 1971 (5); v In 1970 (1) 1975 (2); v P 1976 (1); *v E 1966 (5); v A 1968 (2); v NZ 1968 (3); v In 1966 (1)*

Holt, J. K. 17: v E 1953 (5); v A 1954 (5); *v In 1958 (5); v P 1958 (2)*

Hooper, C. L. 39: v E 1989 (3); v A 1990 (5); v P 1987 (3) 1992 (3); *v E 1988 (5) 1991 (5); v A 1988 (5) 1992 (4); v In 1987 (3); v P 1990 (3)*

Howard, A. B. 1: v NZ 1971

Hunte, C. C. 44: v E 1959 (5); v A 1964 (5); v In 1957 (5); *v E 1963 (5) 1966 (5); v A 1960 (5); v In 1958 (5) 1966 (3); v P 1958 (1)*

Hunte, E. A. C. 3: v E 1929 (3)

Hylton, L. G. 6: v E 1934 (4); *v E 1939 (2)*

Johnson, H. H. H. 3: v E 1947 (1); *v E 1950 (2)*

Johnson, T. F. 1: *v E 1939*

Jones, C. M. 4: v E 1929 (1) 1934 (3)

Jones, P. E. 9: v E 1947 (1); *v E 1950 (2); v A 1951 (1); v In 1948 (5)*

Julien, B. D. 24: v E 1973 (5); v In 1975 (4); v P 1976 (1); *v E 1973 (3) 1976 (2); v A 1975 (3); v In 1974 (4); v P 1974 (2)*

Jumadeen, R. R. 12: v A 1972 (1) 1977 (2); v NZ 1971 (1); v In 1975 (4); v P 1976 (1); *v E 1976 (1); v In 1978 (2)*

Kallicharran, A. I. 66: v E 1973 (5); v A 1972 (5) 1977 (5); v NZ 1971 (2); v In 1975 (4); v P 1976 (5); *v E 1973 (3) 1976 (3) 1980 (5); v A 1975 (6) 1979 (3); v NZ 1979 (3); v In 1974 (5) 1978 (6); v P 1974 (2) 1980 (4)*

Kanhai, R. B. 79: v E 1959 (5) 1967 (5) 1973 (5); v A 1964 (5) 1972 (5); v In 1961 (5) 1970 (5); v P 1957 (5); *v E 1957 (5) 1963 (5) 1966 (5) 1973 (3); v A 1960 (5) 1968 (5); v In 1958 (5) 1966 (3); v P 1958 (3)*

Kentish, E. S. M. 2: v E 1947 (1) 1953 (1)
King, C. L. 9: v P 1976 (1); *v E 1976 (3) 1980 (1); v A 1979 (1); v NZ 1979 (3)*
King, F. M. 14: v E 1953 (3); v A 1954 (4); v In 1952 (5); *v NZ 1955 (2)*
King, L. A. 2: v E 1967 (1); v In 1961 (1)

Lambert, C. B. 1: *v E 1991*
Lara, B. C. 10: v SA 1991 (1); v P 1992 (3); *v A 1992 (5); v P 1990 (1)*
Lashley, P. D. 4: *v E 1966 (2); v A 1960 (2)*
Legall, R. 4: v In 1952 (4)
Lewis, D. M. 3: v In 1970 (3)
Lloyd, C. H. 110: v E 1967 (5) 1973 (5) 1980 (4); v A 1972 (3) 1977 (2) 1983 (4); v NZ 1971 (2); v In 1970 (5) 1975 (4) 1982 (5); v P 1976 (5); *v E 1969 (3) 1973 (3) 1976 (5) 1980 (4) 1984 (5); v A 1968 (4) 1975 (6) 1979 (2) 1981 (3) 1984 (5); v NZ 1968 (3) 1979 (3); v In 1966 (3) 1974 (5) 1983 (6); v P 1974 (2) 1980 (4)*
Logie, A. L. 52: v E 1989 (3); v A 1983 (1) 1990 (5); v NZ 1984 (4); v In 1982 (5) 1988 (4); v P 1987 (2); *v E 1988 (5) 1991 (4); v A 1988 (5); v NZ 1986 (3); v In 1983 (3) 1987 (4); v P 1990 (3)*

McMorris, E. D. A. St J. 13: v E 1959 (4); v In 1961 (4); v P 1957 (1); *v E 1963 (2) 1966 (2)*
McWatt, C. A. 6: v E 1953 (5); v A 1954 (1)
Madray, I. S. 2: v P 1957 (2)
Marshall, M. D. 81: v E 1980 (1) 1985 (5) 1989 (2); v A 1983 (4) 1990 (5); v NZ 1984 (4); v In 1982 (5) 1988 (3); v P 1987 (2); *v E 1980 (4) 1984 (4) 1988 (5) 1991 (5); v A 1984 (5) 1988 (5); v NZ 1986 (3); v In 1978 (3) 1983 (6); v P 1980 (4) 1986 (3) 1990 (3)*
Marshall, N. E. 1: v A 1954
Marshall, R. E. 4: *v A 1951 (2); v NZ 1951 (2)*
Martin, F. R. 9: v E 1929 (1); *v E 1928 (3); v A 1930 (5)*
Martindale, E. A. 10: v E 1934 (4); *v E 1933 (3) 1939 (3)*
Mattis, E. H. 4: v E 1980 (4)
Mendonca, I. L. 2: v In 1961 (2)
Merry, C. A. 2: *v E 1933 (2)*
Miller, R. 1: v In 1952
Moodie, G. H. 1: v E 1934
Moseley, E. A. 2: v E 1989 (2)
Murray, D. A. 19: v E 1980 (4); *v A 1977 (3); v A 1981 (2); v In 1978 (6); v P 1980 (4)*
Murray, D. L. 62: v E 1967 (5) 1973 (5); v A 1972 (4) 1977 (2); v In 1975 (4); v P 1976 (5); *v E 1963 (3) 1973 (3) 1976 (5) 1980 (5); v A 1975 (4) 1979 (3); v NZ 1979 (3); v In 1974 (5); v P 1974 (2)*
Murray, J. R. 6: v P 1992 (3); *v A 1992 (3)*

Nanan, R. 1: *v P 1980*
Neblett, J. M. 1: v E 1934
Noreiga, J. M. 4: v In 1970 (4)
Nunes, R. K. 4: v E 1929 (1); *v E 1928 (3)*
Nurse, S. M. 29: v E 1959 (1) 1967 (5); v A 1964 (4); v In 1961 (1); *v E 1966 (5); v A 1960 (3) 1968 (5); v NZ 1968 (3); v In 1966 (2)*

Padmore, A. L. 2: v In 1975 (1); *v E 1976 (1)*
Pairaudeau, B. H. 13: v E 1953 (2); v In 1952 (5); *v E 1957 (2); v NZ 1955 (4)*
Parry, D. R. 12: v A 1977 (5); *v NZ 1979 (1); v In 1978 (6)*
Passailaigue, C. C. 1: v E 1929
Patterson, B. P. 28: v E 1985 (5) 1989 (1); v A 1990 (5); v SA 1991 (1); v P 1987 (1); *v E 1988 (2) 1991 (3); v A 1988 (4) 1992 (1); v In 1987 (4); v P 1986 (1)*
Payne, T. R. O. 1: v E 1985
Phillip, N. 9: v A 1977 (3); *v In 1978 (6)*
Pierre, L. R. 1: v E 1947

Rae, A. F. 15: v In 1952 (2); *v E 1950 (4); v A 1951 (3); v NZ 1951 (1); v In 1948 (5)*
Ramadhin, S. 43: v E 1953 (5) 1959 (4); v A 1954 (4); v In 1952 (4); *v E 1950 (4) 1957 (5); v A 1951 (5) 1960 (2); v NZ 1951 (2) 1955 (4); v In 1958 (2); v P 1958 (2)*
Richards, I. V. A. 121: v E 1980 (4) 1985 (5) 1989 (3); v A 1977 (2) 1983 (5) 1990 (5); v NZ 1984 (4); v In 1975 (4) 1982 (5) 1988 (4); v P 1976 (5) 1987 (2); *v E 1976 (4) 1980 (5) 1984 (5) 1988 (5) 1991 (5); v A 1975 (6) 1979 (3) 1981 (3) 1984 (5) 1988 (5); v NZ 1986 (3); v In 1974 (5) 1983 (6) 1987 (4); v P 1974 (2) 1980 (4) 1986 (3)*

Richardson, R. B. 71 : v E 1985 (5) 1989 (4); v A 1983 (5) 1990 (5); v SA 1991 (1); v NZ 1984 (4); v In 1988 (4); v P 1987 (3) 1992 (3); *v E 1988 (3) 1991 (5); v A 1984 (5) 1988 (5) 1992 (5); v NZ 1986 (3); v In 1983 (1) 1987 (4); v P 1986 (3) 1990 (3)*

Rickards, K. R. 2 : v E 1947 (1); *v A 1951 (1)*

Roach, C. A. 16 : v E 1929 (4) 1934 (1); *v E 1928 (3) 1933 (3); v A 1930 (5)*

Roberts, A. M. E. 47 : v E 1973 (1) 1980 (3); v A 1977 (2); v In 1975 (2) 1982 (5); v P 1976 (5); *v E 1976 (5) 1980 (3); v A 1975 (5) 1979 (3) 1981 (2); v NZ 1979 (2); v In 1974 (5) 1983 (2); v P 1974 (2)*

Roberts, A. T. 1 : *v NZ 1955*

Rodriguez, W. V. 5 : v E 1967 (1); v A 1964 (1); v In 1961 (2); *v E 1963 (1)*

Rowe, L. G. 30 : v E 1973 (5); v A 1972 (3); v NZ 1971 (4); v In 1975 (4); *v E 1976 (2); v A 1975 (6) 1979 (3); v NZ 1979 (3)*

St Hill, E. L. 2 : v E 1929 (2)

St Hill, W. H. 3 : v E 1929 (1); *v E 1928 (2)*

Scarlett, R. O. 3 : v E 1959 (3)

Scott, A. P. H. 1 : v In 1952

Scott, O. C. 8 : v E 1929 (1); *v E 1928 (2); v A 1930 (5)*

Sealey, B. J. 1 : *v E 1933*

Sealy, J. E. D. 11 : v E 1929 (2) 1934 (4); *v E 1939 (3); v A 1930 (2)*

Shepherd, J. N. 5 : v In 1970 (2); *v E 1969 (3)*

Shillingford, G. C. 7 : v NZ 1971 (2); v In 1970 (3); *v E 1969 (2)*

Shillingford, I. T. 4 : v A 1977 (1); v P 1976 (3)

Shivnarine, S. 8 : v A 1977 (3); *v In 1978 (5)*

Simmons, P. V. 16 : v SA 1991 (1); v P 1987 (1) 1992 (3); *v E 1991 (5); v A 1992 (5); v In 1987 (1)*

Singh, C. K. 2 : v E 1959 (2)

Small, J. A. 3 : v E 1929 (1); *v E 1928 (2)*

Small, M. A. 2 : v A 1983 (1); *v E 1984 (1)*

Smith, C. W. 5 : v In 1961 (1); *v A 1960 (4)*

Smith, O. G. 26 : v A 1954 (4); v P 1957 (5); *v E 1957 (5); v NZ 1955 (4); v In 1958 (5); v P 1958 (3)*

Sobers, G. S. 93 : v E 1953 (1) 1959 (5) 1967 (5) 1973 (4); v A 1954 (4) 1964 (5); v NZ 1971 (5); v In 1961 (5); 1970 (5); v P 1957 (5); *v E 1957 (5) 1963 (5) 1966 (5) 1969 (3) 1973 (3); v A 1960 (5) 1968 (5); v NZ 1955 (4) 1968 (3); v In 1958 (5) 1966 (3); v P 1958 (3)*

Solomon, J. S. 27 : v E 1959 (2); v A 1964 (4); v In 1961 (4); *v E 1963 (5); v A 1960 (5); v In 1958 (4); v P 1958 (3)*

Stayers, S. C. 4 : v In 1961 (4)

Stollmeyer, J. B. 32 : v E 1947 (2) 1953 (5); v A 1954 (2); v In 1952 (5); *v E 1939 (3) 1950 (4); v A 1951 (5); v NZ 1951 (2); v In 1948 (4)*

Stollmeyer, V. H. 1 : *v E 1939*

Taylor, J. 3 : v P 1957 (1); *v In 1958 (1); v P 1958 (1)*

Trim, J. 4 : v E 1947 (1); *v A 1951 (1); v In 1948 (2)*

Valentine, A. L. 36 : v E 1953 (3); v A 1954 (3); v In 1952 (5) 1961 (2); v P 1957 (1); *v E 1950 (4) 1957 (2); v A 1951 (5) 1960 (5); v NZ 1951 (2) 1955 (4)*

Valentine, V. A. 2 : *v E 1933 (2)*

Walcott, C. L. 44 : v E 1947 (4) 1953 (5) 1959 (2); v A 1954 (5); v In 1952 (5); v P 1957 (4); *v E 1950 (4) 1957 (5); v A 1951 (3); v NZ 1951 (2); v In 1948 (5)*

Walcott, L. A. 1 : v E 1929

Walsh, C. A. 59 : v E 1985 (1) 1989 (3); v A 1990 (5); v SA 1991 (1); v NZ 1984 (1); v In 1988 (4); v P 1987 (3) 1992 (3); *v E 1988 (5) 1991 (5); v A 1984 (5) 1988 (5) 1992 (5); v NZ 1986 (3); v In 1987 (1); v P 1986 (3) 1990 (3)*

Watson, C. 7 : v E 1959 (5); v In 1961 (1); *v A 1960 (1)*

Weekes, E. D. 48 : v E 1947 (4) 1953 (4); v A 1954 (5) v In 1952 (5); v P 1957 (5); *v E 1950 (4) 1957 (5); v A 1951 (5); v NZ 1951 (2) 1955 (4); v In 1948 (5)*

Weekes, K. H. 2 : *v E 1939 (2)*

White, W. A. 2 : v A 1964 (2)

Wight, C. V. 2 : v E 1929 (1); *v E 1928 (1)*

Wight, G. L. 1 : v In 1952

Wiles, C. A. 1 : *v E 1933*

Willett, E. T. 5 : v A 1972 (3); *v In 1974 (2)*

Williams, A. B. 7: v A 1977 (3); *v In 1978 (4)*
Williams, D. 3: v SA 1991 (1); *v A 1992 (2)*
Williams, E. A. V. 4: v E 1947 (3); *v E 1939 (1)*
Wishart, K. L. 1: v E 1934
Worrell, F. M. M. 51: v E 1947 (3) 1953 (4) 1959 (4); v A 1954 (4); v In 1952 (5) 1961 (5); *v E 1950 (4) 1957 (5) 1963 (5); v A 1951 (5) 1960 (5); v NZ 1951 (2)*

NEW ZEALAND

Number of Test cricketers: 183

Alabaster, J. C. 21: v E 1962 (2); v WI 1955 (1); v In 1967 (4); *v E 1958 (2); v SA 1961 (5); v WI 1971 (2); v In 1955 (4); v P 1955 (1)*
Allcott, C. F. W. 6: v E 1929 (2); v SA 1931 (1); *v E 1931 (3)*
Anderson, R. W. 9: v E 1977 (3); *v A 1978 (3); v P 1976 (3)*
Anderson, W. M. 1: v A 1945
Andrews, B. 2: *v A 1973 (2)*

Badcock, F. T. 7: v E 1929 (3) 1932 (2); v SA 1931 (2)
Barber, R. T. 1: v WI 1955
Bartlett, G. A. 10: v E 1965 (2); v In 1967 (2); v P 1964 (1); *v SA 1961 (5)*
Barton, P. T. 7: v E 1962 (3); *v SA 1961 (4)*
Beard, D. D. 4: v WI 1951 (2) 1955 (2)
Beck, J. E. F. 8: v WI 1955 (4); *v SA 1953 (4)*
Bell, W. 2: *v SA 1953 (2)*
Bilby, G. P. 2: v E 1965 (2)
Blain, T. E. 5: v A 1992 (2); *v E 1986 (1); v In 1988 (2)*
Blair, R. W. 19: v E 1954 (1) 1958 (2) 1962 (2); v SA 1952 (2) 1963 (3); v WI 1955 (2); *v E 1958 (3); v SA 1953 (4)*
Blunt, R. C. 9: v E 1929 (4); v SA 1931 (2); *v E 1931 (3)*
Bolton, B. A. 2: v E 1958 (2)
Boock, S. L. 30: v E 1977 (3) 1983 (2) 1987 (1); v WI 1979 (3) 1986 (2); v P 1978 (3) 1984 (2) 1988 (1); *v E 1978 (3); v A 1985 (1); v WI 1984 (3); v P 1984 (3); v SL 1983 (3)*
Bracewell, B. P. 6: v P 1978 (1) 1984 (1); *v E 1978 (3); v A 1980 (1)*
Bracewell, J. G. 41: v E 1987 (3); v A 1985 (2) 1989 (1); v WI 1986 (3); v In 1980 (1) 1989 (2); v P 1988 (2); *v E 1983 (4) 1986 (3) 1990 (3); v A 1980 (3) 1985 (2) 1987 (3); v WI 1984 (1); v In 1988 (3); v P 1984 (2); v SL 1983 (2) 1986 (1)*
Bradburn, G. E. 5: v SL 1990 (1); *v P 1990 (3); v SL 1992 (1)*
Bradburn, W. P. 2: v SA 1963 (2)
Brown, V. R. 2: *v A 1985 (2)*
Burgess, M. G. 50: v E 1970 (1) 1977 (3); v A 1973 (2) 1976 (2); v WI 1968 (2); v In 1967 (4) 1975 (3); v P 1972 (3) 1978 (3); *v E 1969 (2) 1973 (3) 1978 (3); v A 1980 (3); v WI 1971 (5); v In 1969 (3) 1976 (3); v P 1969 (3) 1976 (3)*
Burke, C. 1: v A 1945
Burtt, T. B. 10: v E 1946 (1) 1950 (2); v SA 1952 (1); v WI 1951 (2); *v E 1949 (4)*
Butterfield, L. A. 1: v A 1945

Cairns, B. L. 43: v E 1974 (1) 1977 (1) 1983 (3); v A 1976 (1) 1981 (3); v WI 1979 (3); v In 1975 (1) 1980 (3); v P 1978 (3) 1984 (3); *v E 1978 (3) 1983 (4); v A 1973 (1) 1980 (3) 1985 (1); v WI 1984 (2); v In 1976 (2); v P 1976 (2); v SL 1983 (2)*
Cairns, C. L. 7: v E 1991 (3); v A 1992 (2); v SL 1990 (1); *v A 1989 (1)*
Cameron, F. J. 19: v E 1962 (3); v SA 1963 (3); v P 1964 (3); *v E 1965 (2); v SA 1961 (5); v In 1964 (1); v P 1964 (2)*
Cave, H. B. 19: v E 1954 (2); v WI 1955 (3); *v E 1949 (4) 1958 (2); v In 1955 (5); v P 1955 (3)*
Chapple, M. E. 14: v E 1954 (1) 1965 (1); v SA 1952 (1) 1963 (3); v WI 1955 (1); *v SA 1953 (5) 1961 (2)*
Chatfield, E. J. 43: v E 1974 (1) 1977 (1) 1983 (3) 1987 (3); v A 1976 (2) 1981 (1) 1985 (3); v WI 1986 (3); v P 1984 (3) 1988 (2); v SL 1982 (2); *v E 1983 (3) 1986 (1); v A 1985 (2) 1987 (2); v WI 1984 (4); v In 1988 (3); v P 1984 (1); v SL 1983 (2) 1986 (1)*
Cleverley, D. C. 2: v SA 1931 (1); v A 1945 (1)
Collinge, R. O. 35: v E 1970 (2) 1974 (2) 1977 (3); v A 1973 (1); v In 1967 (2) 1975 (1); v P 1964 (3) 1972 (2); *v E 1965 (3) 1969 (1) 1973 (3) 1978 (1); v In 1964 (2) 1976 (1); v P 1964 (2) 1976 (2)*

Colquhoun, I. A. 2: v E 1954 (2)

Coney, J. V. 52: v E 1983 (3); v A 1973 (2) 1981 (3) 1985 (3); v WI 1979 (3) 1986 (3); v In 1980 (3); v P 1978 (3) 1984 (3); v SL 1982 (2); *v E 1983 (4) 1986 (3); v A 1973 (2) 1980 (2) 1985 (3); v WI 1984 (4); v P 1984 (3); v SL 1983 (3)*

Congdon, B. E. 61: v E 1965 (3) 1970 (2) 1974 (2) 1977 (3); v A 1973 (3) 1976 (2); v WI 1968 (3); v In 1967 (4) 1975 (3); v P 1964 (3) 1972 (3); *v E 1965 (3) 1969 (3) 1973 (3) 1978 (3); v A 1973 (3); v WI 1971 (5); v In 1964 (3) 1969 (3); v P 1964 (1) 1969 (3)*

Cowie, J. 9: v E 1946 (1); v A 1945 (1); *v E 1937 (3) 1949 (4)*

Cresswell G. F. 3: v E 1950 (2); *v E 1949 (1)*

Cromb, I. B. 5: v SA 1931 (2); *v E 1931 (3)*

Crowe, J. J. 39: v E 1983 (3) 1987 (2); v A 1989 (1); v WI 1986 (3); v P 1984 (3) 1988 (2); v SL 1982 (2); *v E 1983 (2) 1986 (3); v A 1985 (3) 1987 (3) 1989 (1); v WI 1984 (4); v P 1984 (3); v SL 1983 (3) 1986 (1)*

Crowe, M. D. 66: v E 1983 (3) 1987 (3) 1991 (3); v A 1981 (3) 1985 (3) 1992 (3); v WI 1986 (3); v In 1989 (3); v P 1984 (3) 1988 (2); v SL 1990 (2); *v E 1983 (4) 1986 (3) 1990 (3); v A 1985 (3) 1987 (3) 1989 (1); v WI 1984 (4); v P 1984 (3) 1990 (3); v SL 1983 (3) 1986 (1) 1992 (2); v Z 1992 (2)*

Cunis, R. S. 20: v E 1965 (3) 1970 (2); v SA 1963 (1); v WI 1968 (3); *v E 1969 (1); v WI 1971 (5); v In 1969 (3); v P 1969 (2)*

D'Arcy, J. W. 5: *v E 1958 (5)*

Dempster, C. S. 10: v E 1929 (4) 1932 (2); v SA 1931 (2); *v E 1931 (2)*

Dempster, E. W. 5: v SA 1952 (1); *v SA 1953 (4)*

Dick, A. E. 17: v E 1962 (3); v SA 1963 (3); v P 1964 (2); *v E 1965 (2); v SA 1961 (5); v P 1964 (3)*

Dickinson, G. R. 3: v E 1929 (2); v SA 1931 (1)

Donnelly, M. P. 7: *v E 1937 (3) 1949 (4)*

Doull, S. B. 1: *v Z 1992*

Dowling, G. T. 39: v E 1962 (3) 1970 (2); v In 1967 (4); v SA 1963 (1); v WI 1968 (3); v P 1964 (2); *v E 1965 (3) 1969 (3); v SA 1961 (4); v WI 1971 (2); v In 1964 (4) 1969 (3); v P 1964 (2) 1969 (3)*

Dunning, J. A. 4: v E 1932 (1); *v E 1937 (3)*

Edgar, B. A. 39: v E 1983 (3); v A 1981 (3) 1985 (3); v WI 1979 (3); v In 1980 (3); v P 1978 (3); v SL 1982 (2); *v E 1978 (3) 1983 (4) 1986 (3); v A 1980 (3) 1985 (3); v P 1984 (3)*

Edwards, G. N. 8: v E 1977 (1); v A 1976 (2); v In 1980 (3); *v E 1978 (2)*

Emery, R. W. G. 2: v WI 1951 (2)

Fisher, F. E. 1: v SA 1952

Foley, H. 1: v E 1929

Franklin, T. J. 21: v E 1987 (3); v A 1985 (1) 1989 (1); v In 1989 (3); v SL 1990 (3); *v E 1983 (1) 1990 (3); v In 1988 (3); v P 1990 (3)*

Freeman, D. L. 2: v E 1932 (2)

Gallichan, N. 1: *v E 1937*

Gedye, S. G. 4: v SA 1963 (3); v P 1964 (1)

Gillespie, S. R. 1: v A 1985

Gray, E. J. 10: *v E 1983 (2) 1986 (3); v A 1987 (1); v In 1988 (1); v P 1984 (2); v SL 1986 (1)*

Greatbatch, M. J. 26: v E 1987 (2) 1991 (1); v A 1989 (1) 1992 (3); v In 1989 (3); v P 1988 (1) 1992 (1); v SL 1990 (2); *v E 1990 (3); v A 1989 (1); v In 1988 (3); v P 1990 (3); v Z 1992 (2)*

Guillen, S. C. 3: v WI 1955 (3)

Guy, J. W. 12: v E 1958 (2); v WI 1955 (2); *v SA 1961 (2); v In 1955 (5); v P 1955 (1)*

Hadlee, D. R. 26: v E 1974 (2) 1977 (1); v A 1973 (3) 1976 (1); v In 1975 (3); v P 1972 (2); *v E 1969 (2) 1973 (3); v A 1973 (3); v In 1969 (3); v P 1969 (3)*

Hadlee, R. J. 86: v E 1977 (3) 1983 (3) 1987 (1); v A 1973 (2) 1976 (2) 1981 (3) 1985 (3) 1989 (1); v WI 1979 (3) 1986 (3); v In 1975 (2) 1980 (3) 1989 (3); v P 1972 (1) 1978 (3) 1984 (3) 1988 (2); v SL 1982 (2); *v E 1973 (1) 1978 (3) 1983 (4) 1986 (3) 1990 (3); v A 1973 (3) 1980 (3) 1985 (3) 1987 (3); v WI 1984 (4); v In 1976 (3) 1988 (3); v P 1976 (3); v SL 1983 (3) 1986 (1)*

Hadlee, W. A. 11: v E 1946 (1) 1950 (2); v A 1945 (1); *v E 1937 (3) 1949 (4)*

Harford, N. S. 8: *v E 1958 (4); v In 1955 (2); v P 1955 (2)*

Harford, R. I. 3: v In 1967 (3)

Harris, C. Z. 4: v A 1992 (1); v P 1992 (1); *v SL 1992 (2)*
Harris, P. G. Z. 9: v P 1964 (1); *v SA 1961 (5)*; *v In 1955 (1)*; *v P 1955 (2)*
Harris, R. M. 2: v E 1958 (2)
Hartland, B. R. 6: v E 1991 (3); v P 1992 (1); *v SL 1992 (2)*
Haslam, M. J. 2: *v Z 1992 (2)*
Hastings, B. F. 31: v E 1974 (2); v A 1973 (3); v WI 1968 (3); v In 1975 (1); v P 1972 (3); *v E 1969 (3) 1973 (3)*; *v A 1973 (3)*; *v WI 1971 (5)*; *v In 1969 (2)*; *v P 1969 (3)*
Hayes, J. A. 15: v E 1950 (2) 1954 (1); v WI 1951 (2); *v E 1958 (4)*; *v In 1955 (5)*; *v P 1955 (1)*
Henderson, M. 1: v E 1929
Horne, P. A. 4: v WI 1986 (1); *v A 1987 (1)*; *v P 1990 (1)*; *v SL 1986 (1)*
Hough, K. W. 2: v E 1958 (2)
Howarth, G. P. 47: v E 1974 (2) 1977 (3) 1983 (3); v A 1976 (2) 1981 (3); v WI 1979 (3); v In 1980 (3); v P 1978 (3) 1984 (3); v SL 1982 (2); *v E 1978 (3) 1983 (4)*; *v A 1980 (2)*; *v WI 1984 (4)*; *v In 1976 (2)*; *v P 1976 (3)*; *v SL 1983 (3)*
Howarth, H. J. 30: v E 1970 (2) 1974 (2); v A 1973 (3) 1976 (2); v In 1975 (2); v P 1972 (3); *v E 1969 (3) 1973 (2)*; *v WI 1971 (5)*; *v In 1969 (3)*; *v P 1969 (3)*

James, K. C. 11: v E 1929 (4) 1932 (2); v SA 1931 (2); *v E 1931 (3)*
Jarvis, T. W. 13: v E 1965 (1); v P 1972 (3); *v WI 1971 (4)*; *v In 1964 (2)*; *v P 1964 (3)*
Jones, A. H. 31: v E 1987 (1) 1991 (3); v A 1989 (1) 1992 (3); v In 1989 (3); v P 1988 (2) 1992 (1); v SL 1990 (3); *v E 1990 (3)*; *v A 1987 (3)*; *v In 1988 (3)*; *v SL 1986 (1) 1992 (2)*; *v Z 1992 (2)*

Kerr, J. L. 7: v E 1932 (1); *v E 1931 (2) 1937 (2)*
Kuggeleijn, C. M. 2: *v In 1988 (2)*

Latham, R. T. 4: v E 1991 (1); v P 1992 (1); *v Z 1992 (2)*
Lees, W. K. 21: v E 1977 (2); v A 1976 (1); v WI 1979 (3); v P 1978 (3); v SL 1982 (2); *v E 1983 (2)*; *v A 1980 (2)*; *v In 1976 (3)*; *v P 1976 (3)*
Leggat, I. B. 1: *v SA 1953*
Leggat, J. G. 9: v E 1954 (1); v SA 1952 (1); v WI 1951 (1) 1955 (1); *v In 1955 (3)*; *v P 1955 (2)*
Lissette, A. F. 2: v WI 1955 (2)
Lowry, T. C. 7: v E 1929 (4); *v E 1931 (3)*

MacGibbon, A. R. 26: v E 1950 (2) 1954 (2); v SA 1952 (1); v WI 1955 (3); *v E 1958 (5)*; *v SA 1953 (5)*; *v In 1955 (5)*; *v P 1955 (3)*
McEwan, P. E. 4: v WI 1979 (1); *v A 1980 (2)*; *v P 1984 (1)*
McGirr, H. M. 2: v E 1929 (2)
McGregor, S. N. 25: v E 1954 (2) 1958 (2); v SA 1963 (3); v WI 1955 (4); v P 1964 (2); *v SA 1961 (5)*; *v In 1955 (4)*; *v P 1955 (3)*
McLeod E. G. 1: v E 1929
McMahon T. G. 5: v WI 1955 (1); *v In 1955 (3)*; *v P 1955 (1)*
McRae, D. A. N. 1: v A 1945
Matheson, A. M. 2: v E 1929 (1); *v E 1931 (1)*
Meale, T. 2: *v E 1958 (2)*
Merritt, W. E. 6: v E 1929 (4); *v E 1931 (2)*
Meuli, E. M. 1: v SA 1952
Milburn, B. D. 3: v WI 1968 (3)
Miller, L. S. M. 13: v SA 1952 (2); v WI 1955 (3); *v E 1958 (4)*; *v SA 1953 (4)*
Mills, J. E. 7: v E 1929 (3) 1932 (1); *v E 1931 (3)*
Moir, A. M. 17: v E 1950 (2) 1954 (2) 1958 (2); v SA 1952 (1); v WI 1951 (2) 1955 (1); *v E 1958 (2)*; *v In 1955 (2)*; *v P 1955 (3)*
Moloney D. A. R. 3: *v E 1937 (3)*
Mooney, F. L. H. 14: v E 1950 (2); v SA 1952 (2); v WI 1951 (2); *v E 1949 (3)*; *v SA 1953 (5)*
Morgan, R. W. 20: v E 1965 (2) 1970 (2); v WI 1968 (1); v P 1964 (2); *v E 1965 (3)*; *v WI 1971 (3)*; *v In 1964 (4)*; *v P 1964 (3)*
Morrison, B. D. 1: v E 1962
Morrison, D. K. 29: v E 1987 (3) 1991 (3); v A 1989 (1) 1992 (3); v In 1989 (3); v P 1988 (1) 1992 (1); v SL 1990 (3); *v E 1990 (3)*; *v A 1987 (3) 1989 (1)*; *v In 1988 (1)*; *v P 1990 (3)*
Morrison, J. F. M. 17: v E 1974 (2); v A 1973 (3) 1981 (3); v In 1975 (3); *v A 1973 (3)*; *v In 1976 (1)*; *v P 1976 (2)*
Motz, R. C. 32: v E 1962 (2) 1965 (3); v SA 1963 (3); v WI 1968 (3); v In 1967 (4); v P 1964 (3); *v E 1965 (3) 1969 (3)*; *v SA 1961 (5)*; *v In 1964 (3)*; *v P 1964 (1)*
Murray, B. A. G. 13: v E 1970 (1); v In 1967 (4); *v E 1969 (2)*; *v In 1969 (3)*; *v P 1969 (3)*

Nash, D. J. 2: *v SL 1992 (1); v Z 1992 (1)*
Newman J. 3: v E 1932 (2); v SA 1931 (1)

O'Sullivan, D. R. 11: v In 1975 (1); v P 1972 (1); *v A 1973 (3); v In 1976 (3); v P 1976 (3)*
Overton, G. W. F. 3: *v SA 1953 (3)*
Owens, M. B. 5: v A 1992 (2); v P 1992 (1); *v SL 1992 (2)*

Page, M. L. 14: v E 1929 (4) 1932 (2); v SA 1931 (2); *v E 1931 (3) 1937 (3)*
Parker, J. M. 36: v E 1974 (2) 1977 (3); v A 1973 (3) 1976 (2); v WI 1979 (3); v In 1975 (3); v P 1972 (1) 1978 (2); *v E 1973 (3) 1978 (2); v A 1973 (3) 1980 (3); v In 1976 (3); v P 1976 (3)*
Parker, N. M. 3: *v In 1976 (2); v P 1976 (1)*
Parore, A. C. 8: v E 1991 (1); v A 1992 (1); v P 1992 (1); *v E 1990 (1); v SL 1992 (2); v Z 1992 (2)*
Patel, D. N. 22: v E 1991 (3); v A 1992 (3); v WI 1986 (3); v P 1988 (1) 1992 (1); v SL 1990 (2); *v A 1987 (3) 1989 (1); v P 1990 (3); v Z 1992 (2)*
Petherick, P. J. 6: v A 1976 (1); *v In 1976 (3); v P 1976 (2)*
Petrie, E. C. 14: v E 1958 (2) 1965 (3); *v E 1958 (5); v In 1955 (2); v P 1955 (2)*
Playle, W. R. 8: v E 1962 (3); *v E 1958 (5)*
Pollard, V. 32: v E 1965 (3) 1970 (1); v WI 1968 (3); v In 1967 (4); v P 1972 (1); *v E 1965 (3) 1969 (3) 1973 (3); v In 1964 (4) 1969 (1); v P 1964 (3) 1969 (3)*
Poore, M. B. 14: v E 1954 (1); v SA 1952 (1); *v SA 1953 (5); v In 1955 (4); v P 1955 (3)*
Priest, M. W. 1: *v E 1990*
Pringle, C. 7: v E 1991 (1); v SL 1990 (2); *v P 1990 (3); v SL 1992 (1)*
Puna, N. 3: v E 1965 (3)

Rabone, G. O. 12: v E 1954 (2); v SA 1952 (1); v WI 1951 (2); *v E 1949 (4); v SA 1953 (3)*
Redmond, R. E. 1: v P 1972
Reid, J. F. 19: v A 1985 (3); v In 1980 (3); v P 1978 (1) 1984 (3); *v A 1985 (3); v P 1984 (3); v SL 1983 (3)*
Reid, J. R. 58: v E 1950 (2) 1954 (2) 1958 (2) 1962 (3); v SA 1952 (2) 1963 (3); v WI 1951 (2) 1955 (4); v P 1964 (3); *v E 1949 (2) 1958 (5) 1965 (3); v SA 1953 (5) 1961 (5); v In 1955 (5) 1964 (4); v P 1955 (3) 1964 (3)*
Roberts, A. D. G. 7: v In 1975 (2); *v In 1976 (3); v P 1976 (2)*
Roberts, A. W. 5: v E 1929 (1); v SA 1931 (2); *v E 1937 (2)*
Robertson, G. K. 1: v A 1985
Rowe, C. G. 1: v A 1945
Rutherford, K. R. 38: v E 1987 (2) 1991 (2); v A 1985 (3) 1989 (1) 1992 (3); v WI 1986 (2); v In 1989 (3); v P 1992 (1); v SL 1990 (3); *v E 1986 (1) 1990 (2); v A 1987 (1); v WI 1984 (4); v In 1988 (2); v P 1990 (3); v SL 1986 (1) 1992 (2); v Z 1992 (2)*

Scott, R. H. 1: v E 1946
Scott, V. J. 10: v E 1946 (1) 1950 (2); v A 1945 (1); v WI 1951 (2); *v E 1949 (4)*
Shrimpton, M. J. F. 10: v E 1962 (2) 1965 (3) 1970 (2); v SA 1963 (1); *v A 1973 (2)*
Sinclair, B. W. 21: v E 1962 (3) 1965 (3); v SA 1963 (3); v In 1967 (2); v P 1964 (2); *v E 1965 (3); v In 1964 (2); v P 1964 (3)*
Sinclair, I. M. 2: v WI 1955 (2)
Smith, F. B. 4: v E 1946 (1); v WI 1951 (1); *v E 1949 (2)*
Smith, H. D. 1: v E 1932
Smith, I. D. S. 63: v E 1983 (3) 1987 (3) 1991 (2); v A 1981 (3) 1985 (3) 1989 (1); v WI 1986 (3); v In 1980 (3) 1989 (3); v P 1984 (3) 1988 (2); v SL 1990 (3); *v E 1983 (2) 1986 (2) 1990 (2); v A 1980 (1) 1985 (3) 1987 (3) 1989 (1); v WI 1984 (4); v In 1988 (3); v P 1984 (3) 1990 (3); v SL 1983 (3) 1986 (1)*
Snedden, C. A. 1: v E 1946
Snedden, M. C. 25: v E 1983 (1) 1987 (2); v A 1981 (3) 1989 (1); v WI 1986 (1); v In 1980 (3) 1989 (3); v SL 1982 (2); *v E 1983 (1) 1990 (3); v A 1985 (1) 1987 (1) 1989 (1); v In 1988 (1); v SL 1986 (1)*
Sparling, J. T. 11: v E 1958 (2) 1962 (1); v SA 1963 (2); *v E 1958 (3); v SA 1961 (3)*
Stirling, D. A. 6: *v E 1986 (2); v WI 1984 (1); v P 1984 (3)*
Su'a, M. L. 9: v E 1991 (2); v A 1992 (2); v P 1992 (1); *v SL 1992 (2); v Z 1992 (2)*
Sutcliffe, B. 42: v E 1946 (1) 1950 (2) 1954 (2) 1958 (2); v SA 1952 (2); v WI 1951 (2) 1955 (2); *v E 1949 (4) 1958 (4) 1965 (1); v SA 1953 (5); v In 1955 (5) 1964 (4); v P 1955 (3) 1964 (3)*

Taylor, B. R. 30: v E 1965 (1); v WI 1968 (3); v In 1967 (3); v P 1972 (3); *v E 1965 (2) 1969 (2)*
    1973 (3); v WI 1971 (4); v In 1964 (3) 1969 (2); v P 1964 (3) 1969 (1)
Taylor, D. D. 3: v E 1946 (1); v WI 1955 (2)
Thomson, K. 2: v In 1967 (2)
Thomson, S. A. 4: v E 1991 (1); v In 1989 (1); v SL 1990 (2)
Tindill, E. W. T. 5: v E 1946 (1); v A 1945 (1); *v E 1937 (3)*
Troup, G. B. 15: v A 1981 (2) 1985 (2); v WI 1979 (3); v In 1980 (2); v P 1978 (2); *v A 1980 (2);*
    v WI 1984 (1); v In 1976 (1)
Truscott, P. B. 1: v P 1964
Turner, G. M. 41: v E 1970 (2) 1974 (2); v A 1973 (3) 1976 (2); v WI 1968 (3); v In 1975 (3); v P
    1972 (3); v SL 1982 (2); *v E 1969 (2) 1973 (3); v A 1973 (2); v WI 1971 (5); v In 1969 (3) 1976*
    (3); v P 1969 (1) 1976 (2)

Vance, R. H. 4: v E 1987 (1); v P 1988 (2); *v A 1989 (1)*
Vaughan, J. T. C. 1: *v SL 1992*
Vivian, G. E. 5: *v WI 1971 (4); v In 1964 (1)*
Vivian, H. G. 7: v E 1932 (1); v SA 1931 (1); *v E 1931 (2) 1937 (3)*

Wadsworth, K. J. 33: v E 1970 (2) 1974 (2); v A 1973 (3); v In 1975 (3); v P 1972 (3); *v E 1969 (3)*
    1973 (3); v A 1973 (3); v WI 1971 (5); v In 1969 (3); v P 1969 (3)
Wallace, W. M. 13: v E 1946 (1) 1950 (2); v A 1945 (1); v SA 1952 (2); *v E 1937 (3) 1949 (4)*
Ward, J. T. 8: v SA 1963 (1); v In 1967 (1); v P 1964 (1); *v E 1965 (1); v In 1964 (4)*
Watson, W. 14: v E 1991 (1); v A 1992 (2); v SL 1990 (3); *v E 1986 (2); v A 1989 (1); v P 1990 (3);*
    v Z 1992 (2)
Watt, L. 1: v E 1954
Webb, M. G. 3: v E 1970 (1); v A 1973 (1); *v WI 1971 (1)*
Webb, P. N. 2: v WI 1979 (2)
Weir, G. L. 11: v E 1929 (3) 1932 (2); v SA 1931 (2); *v E 1931 (3) 1937 (1)*
White, D. J. 2: *v P 1990 (2)*
Whitelaw, P. E. 2: v E 1932 (2)
Wright, J. G. 82: v E 1977 (3) 1983 (3) 1987 (3) 1991 (3); v A 1981 (3) 1985 (2) 1989 (1) 1992 (3);
    v WI 1979 (3) 1986 (3); v In 1980 (3) 1989 (3); v P 1978 (3) 1984 (3) 1988 (2); v SL 1982 (2)
    1990 (3); *v E 1978 (2) 1983 (3) 1986 (3) 1990 (3); v A 1980 (3) 1985 (3) 1987 (3) 1989 (1); v WI*
    1984 (4); v In 1988 (3); v P 1984 (3); v SL 1983 (3) 1992 (2)

Yuile, B. W. 17: v E 1962 (2); v WI 1968 (3); v In 1967 (1); v P 1964 (3); *v E 1965 (1); v In 1964 (3)*
    1969 (1); v P 1964 (1) 1969 (2)

INDIA

Number of Test cricketers: 199

Abid Ali, S. 29: v E 1972 (4); v A 1969 (1); v WI 1974 (2); v NZ 1969 (3); *v E 1971 (3) 1974 (3);*
    v A 1967 (4); v WI 1970 (5); v NZ 1967 (4)
Adhikari, H. R. 21: v E 1951 (3); v A 1956 (2); v WI 1948 (5) 1958 (1); v P 1952 (2); *v E 1952 (3);*
    v A 1947 (5)
Amarnath, L. 24: v E 1933 (3) 1951 (3); v WI 1948 (5); v P 1952 (5); *v E 1946 (3); v A 1947 (5)*
Amarnath, M. 69: v E 1976 (2) 1984 (5); v A 1986 (1) 1979 (1) 1986 (3); v WI 1978 (2) 1983 (3)
    1987 (3); v NZ 1976 (3); v P 1983 (2) 1986 (5); v SL 1986 (2); *v E 1979 (2) 1986 (2); v A 1977 (5)*
    1985 (3); v WI 1975 (4) 1982 (5); v NZ 1975 (3); v P 1978 (3) 1982 (6) 1984 (2); v SL 1985 (2)
Amarnath, S. 10: v WI 1976 (2); v NZ 1975 (3); v P 1978 (3)
Amar Singh 7: v E 1933 (3); *v E 1932 (1) 1936 (3)*
Amir Elahi 1: *v A 1947*
Amre, P. K. 11: v E 1992 (3); v Z 1992 (1); *v SA 1992 (4); v SL 1993 (3)*
Ankola, S. A. 1: *v P 1989*
Apte, A. L. 1: *v E 1959*
Apte, M. L. 7: v P 1952 (2); *v WI 1952 (5)*
Arshad Ayub 13: v WI 1987 (4); v NZ 1988 (3); *v WI 1988 (4); v P 1989 (2)*
Arun, B. 2: v SL 1986 (2)

Arun Lal 16: v WI 1987 (4); v NZ 1988 (3); v P 1986 (1); v SL 1982 (1); *v WI 1988 (4); v P 1982 (3)*

Azad, K. 7: v E 1981 (3); v WI 1983 (2); v P 1983 (1); *v NZ 1980 (1)*

Azharuddin, M. 58: v E 1984 (3) 1992 (3); v A 1986 (3); v WI 1987 (3); v NZ 1988 (3); v P 1986 (5); v SL 1986 (1) 1990 (1); v Z 1992 (1); *v E 1986 (3) 1990 (3); v A 1985 (3) 1991 (5); v SA 1992 (4); v WI 1988 (3); v NZ 1989 (3); v P 1989 (4); v SL 1985 (3) 1993 (3); v Z 1992 (1)*

Baig, A. A. 10: v A 1959 (3); v WI 1966 (2); v P 1960 (3); *v E 1959 (2)*

Banerjee, S. A. 1: v WI 1948

Banerjee, S. N. 1: v WI 1948

Banerjee, S. T. 1: *v A 1991*

Baqa Jilani, M. 1: *v E 1936*

Bedi, B. S. 67: v E 1972 (5) 1976 (5); v A 1969 (5); v WI 1966 (2) 1974 (4) 1978 (3); v NZ 1969 (3) 1976 (3); *v E 1967 (3) 1971 (3) 1974 (3) 1979 (3); v A 1967 (2) 1977 (5); v WI 1970 (5) 1975 (4); v NZ 1967 (4) 1975 (2); v P 1978 (3)*

Bhandari, P. 3: v A 1956 (1); v NZ 1955 (1); *v P 1954 (1)*

Bhat, A. R. 2: v WI 1983 (1); v P 1983 (1)

Binny, R. M. H. 27: v E 1979 (1); v WI 1983 (6); v P 1979 (6) 1983 (2) 1986 (3); *v E 1986 (3); v A 1980 (1) 1985 (2); v NZ 1980 (1); v P 1984 (1); v SL 1985 (1)*

Borde, C. G. 55: v E 1961 (5) 1963 (5); v A 1959 (5) 1964 (3) 1969 (1); v WI 1958 (4) 1966 (3); v NZ 1964 (4); v P 1960 (5); *v E 1959 (4) 1967 (3); v A 1967 (4); v WI 1961 (5); v NZ 1967 (4)*

Chandrasekhar, B. S. 58: v E 1963 (4) 1972 (5) 1976 (5); v A 1964 (2); v WI 1966 (3) 1974 (4) 1978 (4); v NZ 1964 (2) 1976 (3); *v E 1967 (3) 1971 (3) 1974 (2) 1979 (1); v A 1967 (2) 1977 (5); v WI 1975 (4); v NZ 1975 (3); v P 1978 (3)*

Chauhan, C. P. S. 40: v E 1972 (2); v A 1969 (1) 1979 (6); v WI 1978 (6); v NZ 1969 (3); v P 1979 (6); *v E 1979 (4); v A 1977 (4) 1980 (3); v NZ 1980 (3); v P 1978 (3)*

Chauhan, R. K. 7: v E 1992 (3); v Z 1992 (1); *v SL 1993 (3)*

Chowdhury, N. R. 2: v E 1951 (1); v WI 1948 (1)

Colah, S. H. M. 2: v E 1933 (1); *v E 1932 (1)*

Contractor, N. J. 31: v E 1961 (5); v A 1956 (1) 1959 (5); v WI 1958 (4); v NZ 1955 (4); v P 1960 (5); *v E 1959 (4); v WI 1961 (2)*

Dani, H. T. 1: v P 1952

Desai, R. B. 28: v E 1961 (4) 1963 (2); v A 1959 (3); v WI 1958 (1); v NZ 1964 (3); v P 1960 (5); *v E 1959 (5); v A 1967 (1); v WI 1961 (3); v NZ 1967 (1)*

Dilawar Hussain 3: v E 1933 (2); *v E 1936 (1)*

Divecha, R. V. 5: v E 1951 (2); v P 1952 (1); *v E 1952 (2)*

Doshi, D. R. 33: v E 1979 (1) 1981 (6); v A 1979 (6); v P 1979 (6) 1983 (1); v SL 1982 (1); *v E 1982 (3); v A 1980 (3); v NZ 1980 (2); v P 1982 (4)*

Durani, S. A. 29: v E 1961 (5) 1963 (5) 1972 (3); v A 1959 (1) 1964 (3); v WI 1966 (1); v NZ 1964 (3); *v WI 1961 (5) 1970 (3)*

Engineer, F. M. 46: v E 1961 (4) 1972 (5); v A 1969 (5); v WI 1966 (1) 1974 (5); v NZ 1964 (4) 1969 (2); *v E 1967 (3) 1971 (3) 1974 (3); v A 1967 (4); v WI 1961 (3); v NZ 1967 (4)*

Gadkari, C. V. 6: *v WI 1952 (3); v P 1954 (3)*

Gaekwad, A. D. 40: v E 1976 (4) 1984 (3); v WI 1974 (3) 1978 (5) 1983 (6); v NZ 1976 (3); v P 1983 (3); *v E 1979 (2); v A 1977 (1); v WI 1975 (3) 1982 (5); v P 1984 (2)*

Gaekwad, D. K. 11: v WI 1958 (1); v P 1952 (2) 1960 (1); *v E 1952 (1) 1959 (4); v WI 1952 (2)*

Gaekwad, H. G. 1: v P 1952

Gandotra, A. 2: v A 1969 (1); v NZ 1969 (1)

Gavaskar, S. M. 125: v E 1972 (5) 1976 (5) 1979 (1) 1981 (6) 1984 (5); v A 1979 (6) 1986 (3); v WI 1974 (2) 1978 (6) 1983 (6); v NZ 1976 (3); v P 1979 (6) 1983 (3) 1986 (4); v SL 1982 (1) 1986 (3); *v E 1971 (3) 1974 (3) 1979 (4) 1982 (3) 1986 (3); v A 1977 (5) 1980 (3) 1985 (3); v WI 1970 (4) 1975 (4) 1982 (5); v NZ 1975 (3) 1980 (3); v P 1978 (3) 1982 (6) 1984 (2); v SL 1985 (3)*

Ghavri, K. D. 39: v E 1976 (3) 1979 (1); v A 1979 (6); v WI 1974 (3) 1978 (6); v NZ 1976 (2); v P 1979 (6); *v E 1979 (4); v A 1977 (3) 1980 (3); v NZ 1980 (1); v P 1978 (1)*

Ghorpade, J. M. 8: v A 1956 (1); v WI 1958 (1); v NZ 1955 (1); *v E 1959 (3); v WI 1952 (2)*

Ghulam Ahmed 22: v E 1951 (2); v A 1956 (2); v WI 1948 (3) 1958 (2); v NZ 1955 (1); v P 1952 (4); *v E 1952 (4); v P 1954 (4)*

Gopalan, M. J. 1: v E 1933

Gopinath, C. D. 8: v E 1951 (3); v A 1959 (1); v P 1952 (1); *v E 1952 (1); v P 1954* (2)
Guard, G. M. 2: v A 1959 (1); v WI 1958 (1)
Guha, S. 4: v A 1969 (3); *v E 1967 (1)*
Gul Mahomed 8: v P 1952 (2); *v E 1946 (1); v A 1947* (5)
Gupte, B. P. 3: v E 1963 (1); v NZ 1964 (1); v P 1960 (1)
Gupte, S. P. 36: v E 1951 (1) 1961 (2); v A 1956 (3); v WI 1958 (5); v NZ 1955 (3); v P 1952 (2)
    1960 (3); *v E 1959 (5); v WI 1952 (5); v P 1954* (5)
Gursharan Singh 1: *v NZ 1989*

Hafeez, A. 3: *v E 1946 (3)*
Hanumant Singh 14: v E 1963 (2); v A 1964 (3); v WI 1966 (2); v NZ 1964 (4) 1969 (1); *v E
    1967* (2)
Hardikar, M. S. 2: v WI 1958 (2)
Hazare, V. S. 30: v E 1951 (5); v WI 1948 (5); v P 1952 (3); *v E 1946 (3) 1952 (4); v A 1947 (5);
    v WI 1952* (5)
Hindlekar, D. D. 4: *v E 1936 (1) 1946* (3)
Hirwani, N. D. 14: v WI 1987 (1); v NZ 1988 (3); v SL 1990 (1); *v E 1990 (3); v WI 1988 (3);
    v NZ 1989* (3)

Ibrahim, K. C. 4: v WI 1948 (4)
Indrajitsinhji, K. S. 4: v A 1964 (3); v NZ 1969 (1)
Irani, J. K. 2: *v A 1947* (2)

Jadeja, A. D. 3: *v SA 1992* (3)
Jahangir Khan, M. 4: *v E 1932 (1) 1936* (3)
Jai, L. P. 1: v E 1933
Jaisimha, M. L. 39: v E 1961 (5) 1963 (5); v A 1959 (1) 1964 (3); v WI 1966 (2); v NZ 1964 (4)
    1969 (1); v P 1960 (4); *v E 1959 (1); v A 1967 (2); v WI 1961 (4) 1970 (3); v NZ 1967* (4)
Jamshedji, R. J. 1: v E 1933
Jayantilal, K. 1: *v WI 1970*
Joshi, P. G. 12: v E 1951 (2); v A 1959 (1); v WI 1958 (1); v P 1952 (1) 1960 (1); *v E 1959 (3); v WI
    1952* (3)

Kambli, V. G. 7: v E 1992 (3); v Z 1992 (1); *v SL 1993* (3)
Kanitkar, H. S. 2: v WI 1974 (2)
Kapil Dev 127: v E 1979 (1) 1981 (6) 1984 (4) 1992 (3); v A 1979 (6) 1986 (3); v WI 1978 (6) 1983
    (6) 1987 (4); v NZ 1988 (3); v P 1979 (6) 1983 (3) 1986 (5); v SL 1982 (1) 1986 (3) 1990 (1); v Z
    1992 (1); *v E 1979 (4) 1982 (3) 1986 (3) 1990 (3); v A 1980 (3) 1985 (3) 1991 (5); v SA 1992 (4);
    v WI 1982 (5) 1988 (4); v NZ 1980 (3) 1989 (3); v P 1978 (3) 1982 (6) 1984 (2) 1989 (4); v SL
    1985 (3) 1993 (3); v Z 1992 (1)*
Kardar, A. H. (*see* Hafeez)
Kenny, R. B. 5: v A 1959 (4); v WI 1958 (1)
Kirmani, S. M. H. 88: v E 1976 (5) 1979 (1) 1981 (6) 1984 (5); v A 1979 (6); v WI 1978 (6) 1983
    (6); v NZ 1976 (3); v P 1979 (6) 1983 (3); v SL 1982 (1); *v E 1982 (3); v A 1977 (5) 1980 (3) 1985
    (3); v WI 1975 (4) 1982 (5); v NZ 1975 (3) 1980 (3); v P 1978 (3) 1982 (6) 1984* (2)
Kischenchand, G. 5: v P 1952 (1); *v A 1947* (4)
Kripal Singh, A. G. 14: v E 1961 (3) 1963 (2); v A 1956 (2) 1964 (1); v WI 1958 (1); v NZ 1955
    (4); *v E 1959 (1)*
Krishnamurthy, P. 5: *v WI 1970* (5)
Kulkarni, R. R. 3: v A 1986 (1); v P 1986 (2)
Kulkarni, U. N. 4: *v A 1967 (3); v NZ 1967 (1)*
Kumar, V. V. 2: v E 1961 (1); v P 1960 (1)
Kumble, A. 13: v E 1992 (3); v Z 1992 (1); *v E 1990 (1); v SA 1992 (4); v SL 1993 (3); v Z 1992 (1)*
Kunderan, B. K. 18: v E 1961 (1) 1963 (5); v A 1959 (3); v WI 1966 (2); v NZ 1964 (1); v P 1960
    (2); *v E 1967 (2); v WI 1961* (2)

Lall Singh 1: *v E 1932*
Lamba, R. 4: v WI 1987 (1); v SL 1986 (3)

Madan Lal 39: v E 1976 (2) 1981 (6); v WI 1974 (2) 1983 (3); v NZ 1976 (1); v P 1983 (3); v SL
    1982 (1); *v E 1974 (2) 1982 (3) 1986 (1); v A 1977 (2); v WI 1975 (4) 1982 (2); v NZ 1975 (3); v P
    1982 (3) 1984 (1)*
Maka, E. S. 2: v P 1952 (1); *v WI 1952 (1)*

Malhotra, A. 7: v E 1981 (2) 1984 (1); v WI 1983 (3); *v E 1982 (1)*

Maninder Singh 35: v A 1986 (3); v WI 1983 (4) 1987 (3); v P 1986 (4); v SL 1986 (3); v Z 1992 (1); *v E 1986 (3); v WI 1982 (3); v P 1982 (1984 (1) 1989 (3); v SL 1985 (2)*

Manjrekar, S. V. 26: v WI 1987 (1); v SL 1990 (1); *v E 1990 (3); v A 1991 (5); v SA 1992 (4); v WI 1988 (4); v NZ 1989 (3); v P 1989 (4); v Z 1992 (1)*

Manjrekar, V. L. 55: v E 1951 (2) 1961 (5) 1963 (4); v A 1956 (3) 1964 (3); v WI 1958 (4); v NZ 1955 (5) 1964 (1); v P 1952 (3) 1960 (5); *v E 1952 (4) 1959 (2); v WI 1952 (4) 1961 (5); v P 1954 (5)*

Mankad, A. V. 22: v E 1976 (1); v A 1969 (5); v WI 1974 (1); v NZ 1969 (2) 1976 (3); *v E 1971 (3) 1974 (1); v A 1977 (3); v WI 1970 (3)*

Mankad, V. 44: v E 1951 (5); v A 1956 (3); v WI 1948 (5) 1958 (2); v NZ 1955 (4); v P 1952 (4); *v E 1946 (3) 1952 (3); v A 1947 (5); v WI 1952 (5); v P 1954 (5)*

Mansur Ali Khan (*see* Pataudi)

Mantri, M. K. 4: v E 1951 (1); *v E 1952 (2); v P 1954 (1)*

Meherhomji, K. R. 1: *v E 1936*

Mehra, V. L. 8: v E 1961 (1) 1963 (2); v NZ 1955 (2); *v WI 1961 (3)*

Merchant, V. M. 10: v E 1933 (3) 1951 (1); *v E 1936 (3) 1946 (3)*

Milkha Singh, A. G. 4: v E 1961 (1); v A 1959 (1); v P 1960 (2)

Modi, R. S. 10: v E 1951 (1); v WI 1948 (5); v P 1952 (1); *v E 1946 (3)*

More, K. S. 49: v E 1992 (3); v A 1986 (2); v WI 1987 (3); v NZ 1988 (3); v P 1986 (5); v SL 1986 (3) 1990 (1); *v E 1986 (3) 1990 (3); v A 1991 (3); v SA 1992 (4); v WI 1988 (4); v NZ 1989 (3); v P 1989 (4); v SL 1993 (3); v Z 1992 (1)*

Muddiah, V. M. 2: v A 1959 (1); v P 1960 (1)

Mushtaq Ali, S. 11: v E 1933 (2) 1951 (1); v WI 1948 (1); *v E 1936 (3) 1946 (2)*

Nadkarni, R. G. 41: v E 1961 (1) 1963 (5); v A 1959 (5) 1964 (3); v WI 1958 (1) 1966 (1); v NZ 1955 (1) 1964 (4); v P 1960 (4); *v E 1959 (4); v A 1967 (3); v WI 1961 (5); v NZ 1967 (4)*

Naik, S. S. 3: v WI 1974 (2); *v E 1974 (1)*

Naoomal Jeoomal 3: v E 1933 (2); *v E 1932 (1)*

Narasimha Rao, M. V. 4: v A 1979 (2); v WI 1978 (2)

Navle, J. G. 2: v E 1933 (1); *v E 1932 (1)*

Nayak, S. V. 2: *v E 1982 (2)*

Nayudu, C. K. 7: v E 1933 (3); *v E 1932 (1) 1936 (3)*

Nayudu, C. S. 11: v E 1933 (2) 1951 (1); *v E 1936 (2) 1946 (2); v A 1947 (4)*

Nazir Ali, S. 2: v E 1933 (1); *v E 1932 (1)*

Nissar, Mahomed 6: v E 1933 (2); *v E 1932 (1) 1936 (3)*

Nyalchand, S. 1: v P 1952

Pai, A. M. 1: v NZ 1969

Palia, P. E. 2: *v E 1932 (1) 1936 (1)*

Pandit, C. S. 5: v A 1986 (2); *v E 1986 (1); v A 1991 (2)*

Parkar, G. A. 1: *v E 1982*

Parkar, R. D. 2: v E 1972 (2)

Parsana, D. D. 2: v WI 1978 (2)

Patankar, C. T. 1: v NZ 1955

Pataudi sen., Nawab of, 3: *v E 1946 (3)*

Pataudi jun., Nawab of (now Mansur Ali Khan) 46: v E 1961 (3) 1963 (5) 1972 (3); v A 1964 (3) 1969 (5); v WI 1966 (3) 1974 (4); v NZ 1964 (4) 1969 (3); *v E 1967 (3); v A 1967 (3); v WI 1961 (3); v NZ 1967 (3)*

Patel, B. P. 21: v E 1976 (5); v WI 1974 (3); v NZ 1976 (3); *v E 1974 (2); v A 1977 (2); v WI 1975 (3); v NZ 1975 (3)*

Patel, J. M. 7: v A 1956 (2) 1959 (3); v NZ 1955 (1); *v P 1954 (1)*

Patel, R. 1: v NZ 1988

Patiala, Yuvraj of, 1: v E 1933

Patil, S. M. 29: v E 1979 (1) 1981 (4) 1984 (2); v WI 1983 (2); v P 1979 (2) 1983 (3); v SL 1982 (1); *v E 1982 (2); v A 1980 (3); v NZ 1980 (3); v P 1982 (4) 1984 (2)*

Patil, S. R. 1: v NZ 1955

Phadkar, D. G. 31: v E 1951 (4); v A 1956 (1); v WI 1948 (4) 1958 (4); v NZ 1955 (4); v P 1952 (2); *v E 1952 (4); v A 1947 (4); v WI 1952 (4); v P 1954 (3)*

Prabhakar, M. 30: v E 1984 (2) 1992 (3); v SL 1990 (1); v Z 1992 (1); *v E 1990 (3); v A 1991 (5); v SA 1992 (4); v NZ 1989 (3); v P 1989 (4); v SL 1993 (3); v Z 1992 (1)*

Prasanna, E. A. S. 49: v E 1961 (1) 1972 (3) 1976 (4); v A 1969 (5); v WI 1966 (1) 1974 (5); v NZ 1969 (3); *v E 1967 (3) 1974 (2); v A 1967 (4) 1977 (4); v WI 1961 (1) 1970 (3) 1975 (1); v NZ 1967 (4) 1975 (3); v P 1978 (2)*

Punjabi, P. H. 5: *v P 1954 (5)*

Rai Singh, K. 1: *v A 1947*
Rajinder Pal 1: v E 1963
Rajindernath, V. 1: v P 1952
Rajput, L. S. 2: *v SL 1985 (2)*
Raju, S. L. V. 14: v E 1992 (3); v SL 1990 (1); *v A 1991 (4); v SA 1992 (2); v NZ 1989 (2); v SL 1993 (1); v Z 1992 (1)*
Raman, W. V. 8: v WI 1987 (1); v NZ 1988 (1); *v SA 1992 (1); v WI 1988 (1); v NZ 1989 (3); v Z 1992 (1)*
Ramaswami, C. 2: *v E 1936 (2)*
Ramchand, G. S. 33: v A 1956 (3) 1959 (5); v WI 1958 (3); v NZ 1955 (5); v P 1952 (3); *v E 1952 (4); v WI 1952 (5); v P 1954 (5)*
Ramji, L. 1: v E 1933
Rangachary, C. R. 4: v WI 1948 (2); *v A 1947 (2)*
Rangnekar, K. M. 3: *v A 1947 (3)*
Ranjane, V. B. 7: v E 1961 (3) 1963 (1); v A 1964 (1); v WI 1958 (1); *v WI 1961 (1)*
Razdan, V. 2: *v P 1989 (2)*
Reddy, B. 4: *v E 1979 (4)*
Rege, M. R. 1: v WI 1948
Roy, A. 4: v A 1969 (2); v NZ 1969 (2)
Roy, Pankaj 43: v E 1951 (5); v A 1956 (3) 1959 (5); v WI 1958 (5); v NZ 1955 (3); v P 1952 (3) 1960 (1); *v E 1952 (4) 1959 (5); v WI 1952 (4); v P 1954 (5)*
Roy, Pranab 2: v E 1981 (2)

Sandhu, B. S. 8: v WI 1983 (1); *v WI 1982 (4); v P 1982 (3)*
Sardesai, D. N. 30: v E 1961 (1) 1963 (5) 1972 (1); v A 1964 (3) 1969 (1); v WI 1966 (2); v NZ 1964 (3); *v E 1967 (1) 1971 (3); v A 1967 (2); v WI 1961 (3) 1970 (5)*
Sarwate, C. T. 9: v E 1951 (1); v WI 1948 (2); *v E 1946 (1); v A 1947 (5)*
Saxena, R. C. 1: *v E 1967*
Sekar, T. A. P. 2: *v P 1982 (2)*
Sen, P. 14: v E 1951 (2); v WI 1948 (5); v P 1952 (2); *v E 1952 (2); v A 1947 (3)*
Sengupta, A. K. 1: v WI 1958
Sharma, Ajay 1: v WI 1987
Sharma, Chetan 23: v E 1984 (3); v A 1986 (2); v WI 1987 (3); v SL 1986 (2); *v E 1986 (2); v A 1985 (2); v WI 1988 (4); v P 1984 (2); v SL 1985 (3)*
Sharma, Gopal 5: v E 1984 (1); v P 1986 (2); v SL 1990 (1); *v SL 1985 (1)*
Sharma, P. 5: v E 1976 (2); v WI 1974 (2); *v WI 1975 (1)*
Sharma, Sanjeev 2: v NZ 1988 (1); *v E 1990 (1)*
Shastri, R. J. 80: v E 1981 (6) 1984 (5); v A 1986 (3); v WI 1983 (6) 1987 (4); v NZ 1988 (3); v P 1983 (2) 1986 (5); v SL 1986 (3) 1990 (1); *v E 1982 (3) 1986 (3) 1990 (3); v A 1985 (3) 1991 (3); v SA 1992 (3); v WI 1982 (5) 1988 (4); v NZ 1980 (3); v P 1982 (2) 1984 (2) 1989 (4); v SL 1985 (3); v Z 1992 (1)*
Shinde, S. G. 7: v E 1951 (3); v WI 1948 (1); *v E 1946 (1) 1952 (2)*
Shodhan, R. H. 3: v P 1952 (1); *v WI 1952 (2)*
Shukla, R. C. 1: v SL 1982
Sidhu, N. S. 27: v E 1992 (3); v WI 1983 (2); v NZ 1988 (3); v Z 1992 (1); *v E 1990 (3); v A 1991 (3); v WI 1988 (4); v NZ 1989 (1); v P 1989 (4); v SL 1993 (3)*
Sivaramakrishnan, L. 9: v E 1984 (5); *v A 1985 (2); v WI 1982 (1); v SL 1985 (1)*
Sohoni, S. W. 4: v E 1951 (1); *v E 1946 (2); v A 1947 (1)*
Solkar, E. D. 27: v E 1972 (5) 1976 (1); v A 1969 (4); v WI 1974 (4); v NZ 1969 (1); *v E 1971 (3) 1974 (3); v WI 1970 (5) 1975 (1)*
Sood, M. M. 1: v A 1959
Srikkanth, K. 43: v E 1981 (4) 1984 (2); v A 1986 (3); v WI 1987 (4); v NZ 1988 (3); v P 1986 (5); v SL 1986 (3); *v E 1986 (3); v A 1985 (3) 1991 (4); v P 1982 (2) 1989 (4); v SL 1985 (3)*
Srinath, J. 11: *v A 1991 (5); v SA 1992 (3); v SL 1993 (2); v Z 1992 (1)*
Srinivasan, T. E. 1: *v NZ 1980*
Subramanya, V. 9: v WI 1966 (2); v NZ 1964 (1); *v E 1967 (2); v A 1967 (2); v NZ 1967 (2)*
Sunderram, G. 2: v NZ 1955 (2)

Surendranath, R. 11: v A 1959 (2); v WI 1958 (2); v P 1960 (2); *v E 1959 (5)*
Surti, R. F. 26: v E 1963 (1); v A 1964 (2) 1969 (1); v WI 1966 (2); v NZ 1964 (1) 1969 (2); v P 1960 (2); *v E 1967 (2); v A 1967 (4); v WI 1961 (5); v NZ 1967 (4)*
Swamy, V. N. 1: v NZ 1955

Tamhane, N. S. 21: v A 1956 (3) 1959 (1); v WI 1958 (4); v NZ 1955 (4); v P 1960 (2); *v E 1959 (2); v P 1954 (5)*
Tarapore, K. K. 1: v WI 1948
Tendulkar, S. R. 28: v E 1992 (3); v SL 1990 (1); v Z 1992 (1); *v E 1990 (3); v A 1991 (5); v SA 1992 (4); v NZ 1989 (3); v P 1989 (4); v SL 1993 (3); v Z 1992 (1)*

Umrigar, P. R. 59: v E 1951 (5) 1961 (4); v A 1956 (3) 1959 (3); v WI 1948 (1) 1958 (5); v NZ 1955 (5); v P 1952 (5) 1960 (5); *v E 1952 (4) 1959 (4); v WI 1952 (5) 1961 (5); v P 1954 (5)*

Vengsarkar, D. B. 116: v E 1976 (1) 1979 (1) 1981 (6) 1984 (5); v A 1979 (6) 1986 (2); v WI 1978 (6) 1983 (5) 1987 (3); v NZ 1988 (3); v P 1979 (5) 1983 (1) 1986 (5); v SL 1982 (1) 1986 (3) 1990 (1); *v E 1979 (4) 1982 (3) 1986 (3) 1990 (3); v A 1977 (5) 1980 (3) 1985 (3) 1991 (5); v WI 1975 (2) 1982 (5) 1988 (4); v NZ 1975 (3) 1980 (3) 1989 (2); v P 1978 (3) 1982 (6) 1984 (2); v SL 1985 (3)*
Venkataraghavan, S. 57: v E 1972 (2) 1976 (1); v A 1969 (5) 1979 (3); v WI 1966 (2) 1974 (2) 1978 (6); v NZ 1964 (4) 1969 (2) 1976 (3); v P 1983 (2); *v E 1967 (1) 1971 (3) 1974 (2) 1979 (4); v A 1977 (1); v WI 1970 (5) 1975 (3) 1982 (5); v NZ 1975 (1)*
Venkataramana, M. 1: *v WI 1988*
Viswanath, G. R. 91: v E 1972 (5) 1976 (5) 1979 (1) 1981 (6); v A 1969 (4) 1979 (6); v WI 1974 (5) 1978 (6); v NZ 1976 (3); v P 1979 (6); v SL 1982 (1); *v E 1971 (3) 1974 (3) 1979 (4) 1982 (3); v A 1977 (5) 1980 (3); v WI 1970 (3) 1975 (4); v NZ 1975 (3) 1980 (3); v P 1978 (3) 1982 (6)*
Viswanath, S. 3: *v SL 1985 (3)*
Vizianagram, Maharaj Kumar of, Sir Vijay A. 3: *v E 1936 (3)*

Wadekar, A. L. 37: v E 1972 (5); v A 1969 (5); v WI 1966 (2); v NZ 1969 (3); *v E 1967 (3) 1971 (3) 1974 (3); v A 1967 (4); v WI 1970 (5); v NZ 1967 (4)*
Wassan, A. S. 4: *v E 1990 (1); v NZ 1989 (3)*
Wazir Ali, S. 7: v E 1933 (3); *v E 1932 (1) 1936 (3)*

Yadav, N. S. 35: v E 1979 (1) 1981 (1) 1984 (4); v A 1979 (5) 1986 (3); v WI 1983 (3); v P 1979 (5) 1986 (4); v SL 1986 (2); *v A 1980 (2) 1985 (3); v NZ 1980 (1); v P 1984 (1)*
Yadav, V. S. 1: v Z 1992
Yajurvindra Singh 4: v E 1976 (2); v A 1979 (1); *v E 1979 (1)*
Yashpal Sharma 37: v E 1979 (1) 1981 (2); v A 1979 (6); v WI 1983 (1); v P 1979 (6) 1983 (3); v SL 1982 (1); *v E 1979 (3) 1982 (3); v A 1980 (3); v WI 1982 (5); v NZ 1980 (1); v P 1982 (2)*
Yograj Singh 1: *v NZ 1980*

Note: Hafeez, on going later to Oxford University, took his correct name, Kardar.

PAKISTAN

Number of Test cricketers: 129

Aamer Malik 13: v E 1987 (2); v A 1988 (1); v WI 1990 (1); v In 1989 (4); *v A 1989 (2); v WI 1987 (1); v NZ 1988 (2)*
Aamir Nazir 1: *v WI 1992*
Aamir Sohail 8: *v E 1992 (5); v WI 1992 (2); v NZ 1992 (1)*
Abdul Kadir 4: v A 1964 (1); *v A 1964 (1); v NZ 1964 (2)*
Abdul Qadir 67: v E 1977 (3) 1983 (3) 1987 (3); v A 1982 (3) 1988 (3); v WI 1980 (2) 1986 (3) 1990 (2); v NZ 1984 (3) 1990 (2); v In 1982 (5) 1984 (1) 1989 (4); v SL 1985 (3); *v E 1982 (3) 1987 (4); v A 1983 (5); v WI 1987 (3); v NZ 1984 (2) 1988 (2); v In 1979 (3) 1986 (3); v SL 1985 (2)*
Afaq Hussain 2: v E 1961 (1); *v A 1964 (1)*
Aftab Baloch 2: v WI 1974 (1); v NZ 1969 (1)
Aftab Gul 6: v E 1968 (2); v NZ 1969 (1); *v E 1971 (3)*
Agha Saadat Ali 1: v NZ 1955
Agha Zahid 1: v WI 1974
Akram Raza 3: v WI 1990 (1); v In 1989 (1); v SL 1991 (1)

Alim-ud-Din 25: v E 1961 (2); v A 1956 (1) 1959 (1); v WI 1958 (1); v NZ 1955 (3); v In 1954 (5); *v E 1954 (3) 1962 (3); v WI 1957 (5); v In 1960 (1)*

Amir Elahi 5: *v In 1952 (5)*

Anil Dalpat 9: v E 1983 (3); v NZ 1984 (3); *v NZ 1984 (3)*

Anwar Hussain 4: *v In 1952 (4)*

Anwar Khan 1: *v NZ 1978*

Aqib Javed 14: v NZ 1990 (3); v SL 1991 (3); *v E 1992 (5); v A 1989 (1); v NZ 1988 (1) 1992 (3)*

Arif Butt 3: *v A 1964 (1); v NZ 1964 (2)*

Ashraf Ali 8: v E 1987 (3); v In 1984 (2); v SL 1981 (2) 1985 (1)

Asif Iqbal 58: v E 1968 (3) 1972 (3); v A 1964 (1); v WI 1974 (2); v NZ 1964 (3) 1969 (3) 1976 (3); v In 1978 (3); *v E 1967 (3) 1971 (3) 1974 (3); v A 1964 (1) 1972 (3) 1976 (3) 1978 (2); v WI 1976 (5); v NZ 1964 (3) 1972 (3) 1978 (2); v In 1979 (6)*

Asif Masood 16: v E 1968 (2) 1972 (1); v WI 1974 (2); v NZ 1969 (1); *v E 1971 (3) 1974 (3); v A 1972 (3) 1976 (3)*

Asif Mujtaba 12: v E 1987 (1); v WI 1986 (2); *v E 1992 (5); v WI 1992 (3); v NZ 1992 (1)*

Ata-ur-Rehman 4: *v E 1992 (1); v WI 1992 (3)*

Azeem Hafeez 18: v E 1983 (2); v NZ 1984 (3); v In 1984 (2); *v A 1983 (5); v NZ 1984 (3); v In 1983 (3)*

Azhar Khan 1: v A 1979

Azmat Rana 1: v A 1979

Basit Ali 3: *v WI 1992 (3)*

Burki, J. 25: v E 1961 (3); v A 1964 (1); v NZ 1964 (3) 1969 (1); *v E 1962 (5) 1967 (3); v A 1964 (1); v NZ 1964 (3); v In 1960 (5)*

D'Souza, A. 6: v E 1961 (2); v WI 1958 (1); *v E 1962 (3)*

Ehtesham-ud-Din 5: v A 1979 (1); *v E 1982 (1); v In 1979 (3)*

Farooq Hamid 1: *v A 1964*

Farrukh Zaman 1: v NZ 1976

Fazal Mahmood 34: v E 1961 (1); v A 1956 (1) 1959 (2); v WI 1958 (3); v NZ 1955 (2); v In 1954 (4); *v E 1954 (4) 1962 (2); v WI 1957 (5); v In 1952 (5) 1960 (5)*

Ghazali, M. E. Z. 2: *v E 1954 (2)*

Ghulam Abbas 1: *v E 1967*

Gul Mahomed 1: v A 1956

Hanif Mohammad 55: v E 1961 (3) 1968 (3); v A 1956 (1) 1959 (3) 1964 (1); v WI 1958 (1); v NZ 1955 (3) 1964 (3) 1969 (1); v In 1954 (5); *v E 1954 (4) 1962 (5) 1967 (3); v A 1964 (1); v WI 1957 (5); v NZ 1964 (3); v In 1952 (5) 1960 (5)*

Haroon Rashid 23: v E 1977 (3); v A 1979 (2) 1982 (3); v In 1982 (1); v SL 1981 (2); *v E 1978 (3) 1982 (1); v A 1976 (1) 1978 (1); v WI 1976 (5); v NZ 1978 (1)*

Haseeb Ahsan 12: v E 1961 (2); v A 1959 (1); v WI 1958 (1); *v WI 1957 (3); v In 1960 (5)*

Ibadulla, K. 4: v A 1964 (1); *v E 1967 (2); v NZ 1964 (1)*

Ijaz Ahmed 19: v E 1987 (3); v A 1988 (3); v WI 1990 (3); *v E 1987 (4); v A 1989 (3); v WI 1987 (2); v In 1986 (1)*

Ijaz Butt 8: v A 1959 (2); v WI 1958 (3); *v E 1962 (3)*

Ijaz Faqih 5: v WI 1980 (1); *v A 1981 (1); v WI 1987 (2); v In 1986 (1)*

Imran Khan 88: v A 1979 (2) 1982 (3); v WI 1980 (4) 1986 (3) 1990 (3); v NZ 1976 (3); v In 1978 (3) 1982 (6) 1989 (4); v SL 1981 (1) 1985 (3) 1991 (3); *v E 1971 (1) 1974 (3) 1982 (3) 1987 (5); v A 1976 (3) 1978 (2) 1981 (3) 1983 (2) 1989 (3); v WI 1976 (5) 1987 (3); v NZ 1978 (2) 1988 (2); v In 1979 (5) 1986 (5); v SL 1985 (3)*

Imtiaz Ahmed 41: v E 1961 (3); v A 1956 (1) 1959 (3); v WI 1958 (3); v NZ 1955 (3); v In 1954 (5); *v E 1954 (4) 1962 (4); v WI 1957 (5); v In 1952 (5) 1960 (5)*

Intikhab Alam 47: v E 1961 (2) 1968 (3) 1972 (3); v A 1959 (1) 1964 (1); v WI 1974 (2); v NZ 1964 (3) 1969 (3) 1976 (3); *v E 1962 (3) 1967 (3) 1971 (3) 1974 (3); v A 1964 (1) 1972 (3); v WI 1976 (1); v NZ 1964 (3) 1972 (3); v In 1960 (3)*

Inzamam-ul-Haq 8: *v E 1992 (4); v WI 1992 (3); v NZ 1992 (1)*

Iqbal Qasim 50: v E 1977 (3) 1987 (3); v A 1979 (3) 1982 (3) 1988 (3); v WI 1980 (4); v NZ 1984 (3); v In 1978 (3) 1982 (2); v SL 1981 (3); *v E 1978 (3) 1982 (3); v A 1976 (3) 1981 (2); v WI 1976 (2); v NZ 1984 (1); v In 1979 (6) 1983 (1) 1986 (3)*

Israr Ali 4: v A 1959 (2); *v In 1952 (2)*

Jalal-ud-Din 6: v A 1982 (1); v In 1982 (2) 1984 (2); v SL 1985 (1)

Javed Akhtar 1: *v E 1962*

Javed Miandad 121: v E 1977 (3) 1987 (3); v A 1979 (3) 1982 (3) 1988 (3); v WI 1980 (4) 1986 (3) 1990 (2); v NZ 1976 (3) 1984 (3) 1990 (3); v In 1978 (3) 1982 (6) 1984 (2) 1989 (4); v SL 1981 (3) 1985 (3) 1991 (3); *v E 1978 (3) 1982 (3) 1987 (5) 1992 (5); v A 1976 (3) 1978 (2) 1981 (3) 1983 (5) 1989 (3); v WI 1976 (1) 1987 (3) 1992 (3); v NZ 1978 (3) 1984 (3) 1988 (2) 1992 (1); v In 1979 (6) 1983 (3) 1986 (4); v SL 1985 (3)*

Kardar, A. H. 23: v A 1956 (1); v NZ 1955 (3); v In 1954 (5); *v E 1954 (4); v WI 1957 (5); v In 1952 (5)*

Khalid Hassan 1: *v E 1954*

Khalid Wazir 2: *v E 1954 (2)*

Khan Mohammad 13: v A 1956 (1); v NZ 1955 (3); v In 1954 (4); *v E 1954 (2); v WI 1957 (2); v In 1952 (1)*

Liaqat Ali 5: v E 1977 (2); v WI 1974 (1); *v E 1978 (2)*

Mahmood Hussain 27: v E 1961 (1); v WI 1958 (3); v NZ 1955 (1); v In 1954 (5); *v E 1954 (2) 1962 (3); v WI 1957 (3); v In 1952 (4) 1960 (5)*

Majid Khan 63: v E 1968 (3) 1972 (3); v A 1964 (1) 1979 (3); v WI 1974 (2) 1980 (4); v NZ 1964 (3) 1976 (3); v In 1978 (3) 1982 (1); v SL 1981 (1); *v E 1967 (3) 1971 (2) 1974 (3) 1982 (1); v A 1972 (3) 1976 (3) 1978 (2) 1981 (3); v WI 1976 (5); v NZ 1972 (3) 1978 (2); v In 1979 (6)*

Mansoor Akhtar 19: v A 1982 (3); v WI 1980 (2); v In 1982 (3); v SL 1981 (1); *v E 1982 (3) 1987 (5); v A 1981 (1) 1989 (1)*

Manzoor Elahi 4: v NZ 1984 (1); v In 1984 (1); *v In 1986 (2)*

Maqsood Ahmed 16: v NZ 1955 (2); v In 1954 (5); *v E 1954 (4); v In 1952 (5)*

Masood Anwar 1: v WI 1990

Mathias, Wallis 21: v E 1961 (1); v A 1956 (1) 1959 (2); v WI 1958 (3); v NZ 1955 (1); *v E 1962 (3); v WI 1957 (5); v In 1960 (5)*

Miran Bux 2: v In 1954 (2)

Mohammad Aslam 1: *v E 1954*

Mohammad Farooq 7: v NZ 1964 (3); *v E 1962 (2); v In 1960 (2)*

Mohammad Ilyas 10: v E 1968 (2); v NZ 1964 (3); *v E 1967 (1); v A 1964 (1); v NZ 1964 (3)*

Mohammad Munaf 4: v E 1961 (2); v A 1959 (2)

Mohammad Nazir 14: v E 1972 (1); v WI 1980 (1); v NZ 1969 (3); *v A 1983 (3); v In 1983 (3)*

Mohsin Kamal 7: v E 1983 (1); v SL 1985 (1); *v E 1987 (4); v SL 1985 (1)*

Mohsin Khan 48: v E 1977 (1) 1983 (3); v A 1982 (3); v WI 1986 (3); v In 1982 (6) 1984 (2); v SL 1981 (2) 1985 (2); *v E 1978 (3) 1982 (3); v A 1978 (1) 1981 (2) 1983 (5); v NZ 1978 (1) 1984 (3); v SL 1985 (3)*

Moin Khan 11: v WI 1990 (2); v SL 1991 (1); *v E 1992 (4); v WI 1992 (2)*

Mudassar Nazar 76: v E 1977 (3) 1983 (1) 1987 (3); v A 1979 (3) 1982 (3) 1988 (3); v WI 1986 (2); v NZ 1984 (3); v In 1978 (2) 1982 (6) 1984 (2); v SL 1981 (1) 1985 (3); *v E 1978 (3) 1982 (3) 1987 (5); v A 1976 (1) 1978 (1) 1981 (1) 1983 (5); v WI 1987 (3); v NZ 1978 (1) 1984 (3) 1988 (2); v In 1979 (5) 1983 (3); v SL 1985 (3)*

Mufasir-ul-Haq 1: *v NZ 1964*

Munir Malik 3: v A 1959 (1); *v E 1962 (2)*

Mushtaq Ahmed 10: v WI 1990 (2); *v E 1992 (5); v A 1989 (1); v WI 1992 (1); v NZ 1992 (1)*

Mushtaq Mohammad 57: v E 1961 (1) 1968 (3) 1972 (3); v WI 1958 (1) 1974 (2); v NZ 1969 (2) 1976 (3); v In 1978 (3); *v E 1962 (5) 1967 (3) 1971 (3) 1974 (3); v A 1972 (3) 1976 (3) 1978 (2); v WI 1976 (5); v NZ 1972 (2) 1978 (3); v In 1960 (5)*

Nadeem Abbasi 3: v In 1989 (3)

Nadeem Ghauri 1: *v A 1989*

Nadeem Khan 1: *v WI 1992*

Nasim-ul-Ghani 29: v E 1961 (2); v A 1959 (2) 1964 (1); v WI 1958 (3); *v E 1962 (5) 1967 (2); v A 1964 (1) 1972 (1); v WI 1957 (5); v NZ 1964 (3); v In 1960 (4)*

Naushad Ali 6: v NZ 1964 (3); *v NZ 1964 (3)*

Naved Anjum 2: v NZ 1990 (1); v In 1989 (1)

Nazar Mohammad 5: *v In 1952 (5)*

Nazir Junior (*see* Mohammad Nazir)

Niaz Ahmed 2: v E 1968 (1); *v E 1967 (1)*

Pervez Sajjad 19: v E 1968 (1) 1972 (2); v A 1964 (1); v NZ 1964 (3) 1969 (3); *v E 1971 (3); v NZ 1964 (3) 1972 (3)*

Qasim Omar 26: v E 1983 (3); v WI 1986 (3); v NZ 1984 (3); v In 1984 (2); v SL 1985 (3); *v A 1983 (5); v NZ 1984 (3); v In 1983 (1); v SL 1985 (3)*

Ramiz Raja 48: v E 1983 (2) 1987 (3); v A 1988 (3); v WI 1986 (3) 1990 (2); v NZ 1990 (3); v In 1989 (4); v SL 1985 (1) 1991 (3); *v E 1987 (2) 1992 (5); v A 1989 (2); v WI 1987 (3) 1992 (3); v NZ 1992 (1); v In 1986 (5); v SL 1985 (3)*

Rashid Khan 4: v SL 1981 (2); *v A 1983 (1); v NZ 1984 (1)*

Rashid Latif 3: *v E 1992 (1); v WI 1992 (1); v NZ 1992 (1)*

Rehman, S. F. 1: *v WI 1957*

Rizwan-uz-Zaman 11: v WI 1986 (1); v SL 1981 (2); *v A 1981 (1); v NZ 1988 (2); v In 1986 (5)*

Sadiq Mohammad 41: v E 1972 (3) 1977 (2); v WI 1974 (1) 1980 (3); v NZ 1969 (3) 1976 (3); v In 1978 (1); *v E 1971 (3) 1974 (3) 1978 (3); v A 1972 (3) 1976 (2); v WI 1976 (5); v NZ 1972 (3); v In 1979 (3)*

Saeed Ahmed 41: v E 1961 (3) 1968 (3); v A 1959 (3) 1964 (1); v WI 1958 (3); v NZ 1964 (3); *v E 1962 (5) 1967 (3) 1971 (1); v A 1964 (1) 1972 (2); v WI 1957 (5); v NZ 1964 (3); v In 1960 (5)*

Saeed Anwar 1: v WI 1990

Salah-ud-Din 5: v E 1968 (1); v NZ 1964 (3) 1969 (1)

Saleem Jaffer 14: v E 1987 (1); v A 1988 (2); v WI 1986 (1); v NZ 1990 (2); v In 1989 (1); v SL 1991 (2); *v E 1987 (1); v NZ 1988 (2); v In 1986 (2)*

Salim Altaf 21: v E 1972 (3); v NZ 1969 (2); v In 1978 (1); *v E 1967 (2) 1971 (2); v A 1972 (3) 1976 (2); v WI 1976 (3); v NZ 1972 (3)*

Salim Malik 72: v E 1983 (3) 1987 (3); v A 1988 (3); v WI 1986 (1) 1990 (3); v NZ 1984 (3) 1990 (3); v In 1982 (6) 1984 (2) 1989 (4); v SL 1981 (2) 1985 (3) 1991 (3); *v E 1987 (5) 1992 (5); v A 1983 (3) 1989 (1); v WI 1987 (3); v NZ 1984 (3) 1988 (2) 1992 (1); v In 1983 (2) 1986 (5); v SL 1985 (3)*

Salim Yousuf 32: v A 1988 (3); v WI 1986 (3) 1990 (1); v NZ 1990 (3); v In 1989 (1); v SL 1981 (1) 1985 (2); *v E 1987 (5); v A 1989 (3); v WI 1987 (3); v NZ 1988 (2); v In 1986 (5)*

Sarfraz Nawaz 55: v E 1968 (1) 1972 (2) 1977 (2) 1983 (3); v A 1979 (3); v WI 1974 (2) 1980 (2); v NZ 1976 (3); v In 1978 (3) 1982 (6); *v E 1974 (3) 1978 (2) 1982 (1); v A 1972 (2) 1976 (2) 1978 (2) 1981 (3) 1983 (3); v WI 1976 (4); v NZ 1972 (3) 1978 (3)*

Shafiq Ahmed 6: v E 1977 (3); v WI 1980 (2); *v E 1974 (1)*

Shafqat Rana 5: v E 1968 (3); v A 1964 (1); v NZ 1969 (2)

Shahid Israr 1: v NZ 1976

Shahid Mahboob 1: v In 1989

Shahid Mahmood 1: *v E 1962*

Shahid Saeed 1: v In 1989

Shakeel Ahmed 1: *v WI 1992*

Sharpe, D. 3: v A 1959 (3)

Shoaib Mohammad 39: v E 1983 (1) 1987 (1); v A 1988 (3); v WI 1990 (3); v NZ 1984 (1) 1990 (3); v In 1989 (4); v SL 1985 (1) 1991 (3); *v E 1987 (4) 1992 (1); v A 1989 (3); v WI 1987 (3); v NZ 1984 (1) 1988 (2); v In 1983 (2) 1986 (3)*

Shuja-ud-Din 19: v E 1961 (2); v A 1959 (3); v WI 1958 (3); v NZ 1955 (3); v In 1954 (5); *v E 1954 (3)*

Sikander Bakht 26: v E 1977 (2); v WI 1980 (1); v NZ 1976 (1); v In 1978 (2) 1982 (1); *v E 1978 (3) 1982 (2); v A 1978 (2) 1981 (3); v WI 1976 (1); v NZ 1978 (3); v In 1979 (5)*

Tahir Naqqash 15: v A 1982 (3); v In 1982 (2); v SL 1981 (3); *v E 1982 (2); v A 1983 (1); v NZ 1984 (1); v In 1983 (3)*

Talat Ali 10: v E 1972 (3); *v E 1978 (2); v A 1972 (1); v NZ 1972 (1) 1978 (3)*

Taslim Arif 6: v A 1979 (3); v WI 1980 (2); *v In 1979 (1)*

Tauseef Ahmed 33: v E 1983 (2) 1987 (2); v A 1979 (3) 1988 (3); v WI 1986 (3); v NZ 1984 (1) 1990 (2); v In 1984 (1); v SL 1981 (3) 1985 (1); *v E 1987 (2); v A 1989 (3); v NZ 1988 (1); v In 1986 (4); v SL 1985 (2)*

Waqar Hassan 21: v A 1956 (1) 1959 (1); v WI 1958 (1); v NZ 1955 (3); v In 1954 (5); *v E 1954 (4); v WI 1957 (1); v In 1952 (5)*

Waqar Younis 23: v WI 1990 (3); v NZ 1990 (3); v In 1989 (2); v SL 1991 (3); *v E 1992 (5); v A 1989 (3); v WI 1992 (3); v NZ 1992 (1)*

Wasim Akram 48: v E 1987 (2); v WI 1986 (2) 1990 (3); v NZ 1990 (2); v In 1989 (4); v SL 1985 (3) 1991 (3); *v E 1987 (5) 1992 (4); v A 1989 (3); v WI 1987 (3) 1992 (3); v NZ 1984 (2) 1992 (1); v In 1986 (5); v SL 1985 (3)*

Wasim Bari 81: v E 1968 (3) 1972 (3) 1977 (3); v A 1982 (3); v WI 1974 (2) 1980 (2); v NZ 1969 (3) 1976 (2); v In 1978 (3) 1982 (6); *v E 1967 (3) 1971 (3) 1974 (3) 1978 (3) 1982 (3); v A 1972 (3) 1976 (3) 1978 (2) 1981 (3) 1983 (5); v WI 1976 (5); v NZ 1972 (3) 1978 (3); v In 1979 (6) 1983 (3)*

Wasim Raja 57: v E 1972 (1) 1977 (3) 1983 (3); v A 1979 (3); v WI 1974 (2) 1980 (4); v NZ 1976 (1) 1984 (1); v In 1982 (1) 1984 (1); v SL 1981 (3); *v E 1974 (2) 1978 (3) 1982 (1); v A 1978 (1) 1981 (3) 1983 (2); v WI 1976 (5); v NZ 1972 (3) 1978 (3) 1984 (2); v In 1979 (6) 1983 (3)*

Wazir Mohammad 20: v A 1956 (1) 1959 (1); v WI 1958 (3); v NZ 1955 (2); v In 1954 (5); *v E 1954 (2); v WI 1957 (5); v In 1952 (1)*

Younis Ahmed 4: v NZ 1969 (2); *v In 1986 (2)*

Zaheer Abbas 78: v E 1972 (2) 1983 (3); v A 1979 (2) 1982 (3); v WI 1974 (2) 1980 (3); v NZ 1969 (1) 1976 (3) 1984 (3); v In 1978 (3) 1982 (6) 1984 (2); v SL 1981 (1) 1985 (2); *v E 1971 (3) 1974 (3) 1982 (3); v A 1972 (3) 1976 (3) 1978 (2) 1981 (2) 1983 (5); v WI 1976 (3); v NZ 1972 (3) 1978 (2) 1984 (2); v In 1979 (5) 1983 (3)*

Zahid Fazal 6: v WI 1990 (3); v SL 1991 (3)

Zakir Khan 2: v In 1989 (1); *v SL 1985 (1)*

Zulfiqar Ahmed 9: v A 1956 (1); v NZ 1955 (3); *v E 1954 (2); v In 1952 (3)*

Zulqarnain 3: *v SL 1985 (3)*

SRI LANKA

Number of Test cricketers: 59

Ahangama, F. S. 3: v In 1985 (3)

Amalean, K. N. 2: v P 1985 (1); *v A 1987 (1)*

Amerasinghe, A. M. J. G. 2: v NZ 1983 (2)

Anurasiri, S. D. 13: v A 1992 (3); v NZ 1986 (1) 1992 (2); v P 1985 (2); *v E 1991 (1); v In 1986 (1); v P 1991 (3)*

Atapattu, M. S. 2: v A 1992 (1); *v In 1990 (1)*

Dassanayake, P. B. 3: v SA 1993 (3)

de Alwis, R. G. 11: v A 1982 (1); v NZ 1983 (3); v P 1985 (2); *v A 1987 (1); v NZ 1982 (1); v In 1986 (3)*

de Mel, A. L. F. 17: v E 1981 (1); v A 1982 (1); v In 1985 (3); v P 1985 (3); *v E 1984 (1); v In 1982 (1) 1986 (1); v P 1981 (3) 1985 (3)*

de Silva, A. M. 3: v E 1992 (1); v In 1993 (2)

de Silva, D. S. 12: v E 1981 (1); v A 1982 (1); v NZ 1983 (3); *v E 1984 (1); v NZ 1982 (2); v In 1982 (1); v P 1981 (3)*

de Silva, E. A. R. 10: v In 1985 (1); v P 1985 (1); *v A 1989 (2); v NZ 1990 (3); v In 1986 (3)*

de Silva, G. R. A. 4: v E 1981 (1); *v In 1982 (1); v P 1981 (2)*

de Silva, P. A. 37: v E 1992 (1); v A 1992 (3); v SA 1993 (3); v NZ 1992 (2); v In 1985 (3) 1993 (3); v P 1985 (3); *v E 1984 (1) 1988 (1) 1991 (1); v A 1987 (1) 1989 (2); v NZ 1990 (3); v In 1986 (3) 1990 (1); v P 1985 (3) 1991 (3)*

Dharmasena, H. D. P. K. 2: v SA 1993 (2)

Dias, R. L. 20: v E 1981 (1); v A 1982 (1); v NZ 1983 (2) 1986 (1); v In 1985 (3); v P 1985 (1); *v E 1984 (1); v In 1982 (1) 1986 (3); v P 1981 (3) 1985 (3)*

Fernando, E. R. N. S. 5: v A 1982 (1); v NZ 1983 (2); *v NZ 1982 (2)*

Goonatillake, H. M. 5: v E 1981 (1); *v In 1982 (1); v P 1981 (3)*

Gunasekera, Y. 2: *v NZ 1982 (2)*

Guneratne, R. P. W. 1: v A 1982

Gurusinha, A. P. 27: v E 1992 (1); v A 1992 (3); v SA 1993 (1); v NZ 1986 (1) 1992 (2); v In 1993 (3); v P 1985 (2); *v E 1991 (1); v A 1989 (2); v NZ 1990 (3); v In 1986 (3) 1990 (1); v P 1985 (1) 1991 (3)*

Hathurusinghe, U. C. 18 : v E 1992 (1); v A 1992 (3); v SA 1993 (3); v NZ 1992 (2); v In 1993 (3); *v E 1991 (1); v NZ 1990 (2); v P 1991 (3)*

Jayasekera, R. S. A. 1 : *v P 1981*
Jayasuriya S. T. 12 : v E 1992 (1); v A 1992 (2); v SA 1993 (2); v In 1993 (1); *v E 1991 (1); v NZ 1990 (2); v P 1991 (3)*
Jeganathan, S. 2 : *v NZ 1982 (2)*
John, V. B. 6 : v NZ 1983 (3); *v E 1984 (1); v NZ 1982 (2)*
Jurangpathy, B. R. 2 : v In 1985 (1); *v In 1986 (1)*

Kalpage, R. S. 2 : v SA 1993 (1); v In 1993 (1)
Kaluperuma, L. W. 2 : v E 1981 (1); *v P 1981 (1)*
Kaluperuma, S. M. S. 4 : v NZ 1983 (3); *v A 1987 (1)*
Kaluwitharana, R. S. 3 : v A 1992 (2); v In 1993 (1)
Kuruppu, D. S. B. P. 4 : v NZ 1986 (1); *v E 1988 (1) 1991 (1); v A 1987 (1)*
Kuruppuarachchi, A. K. 2 : v NZ 1986 (1); v P 1985 (1)

Labrooy, G. F. 9 : *v E 1988 (1); v A 1987 (1) 1989 (2); v NZ 1990 (3); v In 1986 (1) 1990 (1)*
Liyanage, D. K. 7 : v A 1992 (2); v SA 1993 (1); v NZ 1992 (2); v In 1993 (2)

Madugalle, R. S. 21 : v E 1981 (1); v A 1982 (1); v NZ 1983 (3) 1986 (1); v In 1985 (3); *v E 1984 (1) 1988 (1); v A 1987 (1); v NZ 1982 (2); v In 1982 (1); v P 1981 (3) 1985 (3)*
Madurasinghe, A. W. R. 3 : v A 1992 (1); *v E 1988 (1); v In 1990 (1)*
Mahanama, R. S. 23 : v E 1992 (1); v A 1992 (3); v SA 1993 (3); v NZ 1986 (1) 1992 (2); v In 1993 (3); v P 1985 (2); *v E 1991 (1); v A 1987 (1) 1989 (2); v NZ 1990 (3); v In 1990 (1); v P 1991 (2)*
Mendis, L. R. D. 24 : v E 1981 (1); v A 1982 (1); v NZ 1983 (3) 1986 (1); v In 1985 (3); v P 1985 (3); *v E 1984 (1) 1988 (1); v In 1982 (1) 1986 (3); v P 1981 (3) 1985 (3)*
Muralitharan, M. 9 : v E 1992 (1); v A 1992 (2); v SA 1993 (3); v NZ 1992 (1); v In 1993 (2)

Ramanayake, C. P. H. 18 : v E 1992 (1); v A 1992 (3); v SA 1993 (3); v NZ 1992 (1); v In 1993 (1); *v E 1988 (1) 1991 (1); v A 1987 (1) 1989 (2); v NZ 1990 (3); v P 1991 (2)*
Ranasinghe, A. N. 2 : *v In 1982 (1); v P 1981 (1)*
Ranatunga, A. 45 : v E 1981 (1) 1992 (1); v A 1982 (1) 1992 (3); v SA 1993 (3); v NZ 1983 (3) 1986 (1) 1992 (2); v In 1985 (3) 1993 (3); v P 1985 (3); *v E 1984 (1) 1988 (1); v A 1987 (1) 1989 (2); v NZ 1990 (3); v In 1982 (1) 1986 (3) 1990 (1); v P 1981 (2) 1985 (3) 1991 (3)*
Ranatunga, D. 2 : *v A 1989 (2)*
Ratnayake, R. J. 23 : v A 1982 (1); v NZ 1983 (1) 1986 (1); v In 1985 (3); v P 1985 (1); *v E 1991 (1); v A 1989 (1); v NZ 1982 (2) 1990 (3); v In 1986 (2) 1990 (1); v P 1985 (3) 1991 (3)*
Ratnayeke, J. R. 22 : v NZ 1983 (2) 1986 (1); v P 1985 (3); *v E 1984 (1) 1988 (1); v A 1987 (1) 1989 (2); v NZ 1982 (2); v In 1982 (1) 1986 (3); v P 1981 (2) 1985 (3)*

Samarasekera, M. A. R. 4 : *v E 1988 (1); v A 1989 (1); v In 1990 (1); v P 1991 (1)*
Senanayake, C. P. 3 : *v NZ 1990 (3)*
Silva, S. A. R. 9 : v In 1985 (3); v P 1985 (1); *v E 1984 (1) 1988 (1); v NZ 1982 (1); v P 1985 (2)*

Tillekeratne, H. P. 19 : v E 1992 (1); v A 1992 (1); v SA 1993 (3); v NZ 1992 (2); v In 1993 (3); *v E 1991 (1); v A 1989 (1); v NZ 1990 (3); v In 1990 (1); v P 1991 (3)*

Warnapura, B. 4 : v E 1981 (1); *v In 1982 (1); v P 1981 (2)*
Warnaweera, K. P. J. 9 : v E 1992 (1); v NZ 1992 (2); v In 1993 (3); v P 1985 (1); *v NZ 1990 (1); v In 1990 (1)*
Weerasinghe, C. D. U. S. 1 : v In 1985
Wettimuny, M. D. 2 : *v NZ 1982 (2)*
Wettimuny, S. 23 : v E 1981 (1); v A 1982 (1); v NZ 1983 (3); v In 1985 (3); v P 1985 (3); *v E 1984 (1); v NZ 1982 (2); v In 1986 (3); v P 1981 (3) 1985 (3)*
Wickremasinghe, A. G. D. 3 : v NZ 1992 (2); *v A 1989 (1)*
Wickremasinghe, G. P. 8 : v A 1992 (1); v SA 1993 (2); v In 1993 (2); *v P 1991 (3)*
Wijegunawardene, K. I. W. 2 : *v E 1991 (1); v P 1991 (1)*
Wijesuriya, R. G. C. E. 4 : *v P 1981 (1) 1985 (3)*
Wijetunge, P. K. 1 : v SA 1993

ZIMBABWE

Number of Test cricketers: 15

Arnott, K. J. 4: v NZ 1992 (2); v I 1992 (1); *v I 1992 (I)*
Brain, D. H. 2: v NZ 1992 (1); *v I 1992 (I)*
Brandes, E. A. 3: v NZ 1992 (1); v I 1992 (1); *v I 1992 (I)*
Briant, G. A. 1: *v I 1992*
Burmester, M. G. 3: v NZ 1992 (2); v I 1992 (1)
Campbell, A. D. R. 4: v NZ 1992 (2); v I 1992 (1); *v I 1992 (I)*
Crocker, G. J. 3: v NZ 1992 (2); v I 1992 (1)
Flower, A. 4: v NZ 1992 (2); v I 1992 (1); *v I 1992 (I)*
Flower, G. W. 4: v NZ 1992 (2); v I 1992 (1); *v I 1992 (I)*
Houghton, D. L. 4: v NZ 1992 (2); v I 1992 (1); *v I 1992 (I)*
Jarvis, M. P. 2: v NZ 1992 (1); v I 1992 (1)
Pycroft, A. J. 3: v NZ 1992 (2); v I 1992 (1)
Ranchod, U. 1: *v I 1992*
Shah, A. H. 2: v NZ 1992 (1); *v 1992 (I)*
Traicos, A. J. 4: v NZ 1992 (2); v I 1992 (1); *v I 1992 (I)*

TWO COUNTRIES

Fourteen cricketers have appeared for two countries in Test matches, namely:

Amir Elahi, *India and Pakistan.*
J. J. Ferris, *Australia and England.*
S. C. Guillen, *West Indies and NZ.*
Gul Mahomed, *India and Pakistan.*
F. Hearne, *England and South Africa.*
A. H. Kardar, *India and Pakistan.*
W. E. Midwinter, *England and Australia.*

F. Mitchell, *England and South Africa.*
W. L. Murdoch, *Australia and England.*
Nawab of Pataudi, sen., *England and India.*
A. J. Traicos, *South Africa and Zimbabwe.*
A. E. Trott, *Australia and England.*
K. C. Wessels, *Australia and South Africa.*
S. M. J. Woods, *Australia and England.*

ENGLAND v REST OF THE WORLD

In 1970, owing to the cancellation of the South African tour to England, a series of matches was arranged, with the trappings of a full Test series, between England and the Rest of the World. It was played for the Guinness Trophy.

The following were awarded England caps for playing against the Rest of the World in that series, although the five matches played are now generally considered not to have rated as full Tests: D. L. Amiss (1), G. Boycott (2), D. J. Brown (2), M. C. Cowdrey (4), M. H. Denness (1), B. L. D'Oliveira (4), J. H. Edrich (2), K. W. R. Fletcher (4), A. W. Greig (3), R. Illingworth (5), A. Jones (1), A. P. E. Knott (5), P. Lever (1), B. W. Luckhurst (5), C. M. Old (2), P. J. Sharpe (1), K. Shuttleworth (1), J. A. Snow (5), D. L. Underwood (3), A. Ward (1), D. Wilson (2).

The following players represented the Rest of the World: E. J. Barlow (5), F. M. Engineer (2), L. R. Gibbs (4), Intikhab Alam (5), R. B. Kanhai (5), C. H. Lloyd (5), G. D. McKenzie (3), D. L. Murray (3), Mushtaq Mohammad (2), P. M. Pollock (1), R. G. Pollock (5), M. J. Procter (5), B. A. Richards (5), G. S. Sobers (5).

LIMITED-OVERS INTERNATIONAL CRICKETERS

The following players have appeared in limited-overs internationals but had not represented their countries in Test matches by the end of the 1993 season:

England

D. G. Cork, I. J. Gould, G. W. Humpage, T. E. Jesty, J. D. Love, M. A. Lynch, S. J. Rhodes, M. J. Smith, C. M. Wells.

Australia

G. A. Bishop, S. F. Graf, M. L. Hayden, R. J. McCurdy, K. H. MacLeay, G. D. Porter, J. D. Siddons, G. S. Trimble, A. K. Zesers.

South Africa

D. J. Callaghan, P. S. de Villiers, C. E. B. Rice, T. G. Shaw, E. L. R. Stewart, C. J. P. G. van Zyl, M. Yachad.

West Indies

R. S. Gabriel, R. C. Haynes, M. R. Pydanna, P. A. Wallace.

New Zealand

B. R. Blair, P. G. Coman, B. G. Hadlee, R. T. Hart, G. R. Larsen†, B. J. McKechnie, E. B. McSweeney, J. P. Millmow, R. G. Petrie, R. B. Reid, S. J. Roberts, L. W. Stott, R. J. Webb, J. Wilson, B. A. Young.

India

G. Bose, V. B. Chandrasekhar, S. C. Ganguly, R. S. Ghai, S. P. Mukherjee, Randhir Singh, R. P. Singh, R. R. Singh, Sudhakar Rao.

Pakistan

Aamer Hameed, Arshad Khan, Arshad Pervez, Ghulam Ali, Haafiz Shahid, Hasan Jamil, Iqbal Sikandar, Mansoor Rana, Maqsood Rana, Masood Iqbal, Moin-ul-Atiq, Naeem Ahmed, Naseer Malik, Parvez Mir, Saadat Ali, Sajid Ali, Sajjad Akbar, Salim Pervez, Shakil Khan, Sohail Fazal, Tanvir Mehdi, Wasim Haider, Zahid Ahmed.

Sri Lanka

D. L. S. de Silva, G. N. de Silva, E. R. Fernando, T. L. Fernando, F. R. M. Goonatillake, P. D. Heyn, S. A. Jayasinghe, S. H. U. Karnain, A. R. M. Opatha, S. P. Pasqual, K. G. Perera, H. S. M. Pieris, S. K. Ranasinghe, N. Ranatunga, N. L. K. Ratnayake, A. P. B. Tennekoon, M. H. Tissera, D. M. Vonhagt, S. R. de S. Wettimuny.

Zimbabwe

R. D. Brown, I. P. Butchart, K. M. Curran, M. H. Dekker, K. G. Duers, E. A. Essop-Adam, C. N. Evans, D. A. G. Fletcher, J. G. Heron, V. R. Hogg, W. R. James, M. A. Meman, G. A. Paterson, S. G. Peall, G. E. Peckover, P. W. E. Rawson, A. C. Waller.

† *G. R. Larsen has appeared for New Zealand in 35 limited-overs internationals without making his Test debut.*

CRICKET RECORDS

Amended by BILL FRINDALL to end of the 1993 season in England
(Including the Indian and South African tours of Sri Lanka of July–September 1993.)

Unless stated to be of a minor character, all records apply only to first-class cricket including some performances in the distant past which have always been recognised as of exceptional merit.

* Denotes not out or an unbroken partnership.

(A), (SA), (WI), (NZ), (I), (P), (SL) or (Z) indicates either the nationality of the player, or the country in which the record was made.

FIRST-CLASS RECORDS

BATTING RECORDS

BOWLING RECORDS

ALL-ROUND RECORDS

WICKET-KEEPING RECORDS

FIELDING RECORDS

TEAM RECORDS

TEST MATCH RECORDS

BATTING RECORDS

BOWLING RECORDS

ALL-ROUND RECORDS

WICKET-KEEPING RECORDS

FIELDING RECORDS

TEAM RECORDS

CAPTAINCY

UMPIRING

TEST SERIES

LIMITED-OVERS INTERNATIONAL RECORDS

MISCELLANEOUS

UMPIRES

FIRST-CLASS RECORDS

BATTING RECORDS

HIGHEST INDIVIDUAL SCORES

499	Hanif Mohammad	Karachi v Bahawalpur at Karachi	1958-59
452*	D. G. Bradman	NSW v Queensland at Sydney	1929-30
443*	B. B. Nimbalkar	Maharashtra v Kathiawar at Poona	1948-49
437	W. H. Ponsford	Victoria v Queensland at Melbourne	1927-28
429	W. H. Ponsford	Victoria v Tasmania at Melbourne.	1922-23
428	Aftab Baloch	Sind v Baluchistan at Karachi	1973-74
424	A. C. MacLaren	Lancashire v Somerset at Taunton	1895
405*	G. A. Hick	Worcestershire v Somerset at Taunton	1988
385	B. Sutcliffe	Otago v Canterbury at Christchurch	1952-53
383	C. W. Gregory	NSW v Queensland at Brisbane	1906-07
377	S. V. Manjrekar	Bombay v Hyderabad at Bombay.	1990-91
369	D. G. Bradman	South Australia v Tasmania at Adelaide	1935-36
366	N. H. Fairbrother	Lancashire v Surrey at The Oval	1990
365*	C. Hill	South Australia v NSW at Adelaide	1900-01
365*	G. S. Sobers	West Indies v Pakistan at Kingston	1957-58
364	L. Hutton	England v Australia at The Oval	1938
359*	V. M. Merchant	Bombay v Maharashtra at Bombay	1943-44
359	R. B. Simpson	NSW v Queensland at Brisbane	1963-64
357*	R. Abel	Surrey v Somerset at The Oval	1899
357	D. G. Bradman	South Australia v Victoria at Melbourne	1935-36
356	B. A. Richards	South Australia v Western Australia at Perth	1970-71
355*	G. R. Marsh	Western Australia v South Australia at Perth	1989-90
355	B. Sutcliffe	Otago v Auckland at Dunedin	1949-50
352	W. H. Ponsford	Victoria v NSW at Melbourne	1926-27
350	Rashid Israr	Habib Bank v National Bank at Lahore	1976-77
345	C. G. Macartney	Australians v Nottinghamshire at Nottingham	1921
344*	G. A. Headley	Jamaica v Lord Tennyson's XI at Kingston	1931-32
344	W. G. Grace	MCC v Kent at Canterbury	1876
343*	P. A. Perrin	Essex v Derbyshire at Chesterfield	1904
341	G. H. Hirst	Yorkshire v Leicestershire at Leicester	1905
340*	D. G. Bradman	NSW v Victoria at Sydney	1928-29
340	S. M. Gavaskar	Bombay v Bengal at Bombay	1981-82

338*	R. C. Blunt	Otago v Canterbury at Christchurch	1931-32
338	W. W. Read	Surrey v Oxford University at The Oval	1888
337*	Pervez Akhtar	Railways v Dera Ismail Khan at Lahore	1964-65
337†	Hanif Mohammad	Pakistan v West Indies at Bridgetown	1957-58
336*	W. R. Hammond	England v New Zealand at Auckland	1932-33
336	W. H. Ponsford	Victoria v South Australia at Melbourne	1927-28
334	D. G. Bradman	Australia v England at Leeds	1930
333	K. S. Duleepsinhji	Sussex v Northamptonshire at Hove	1930
333	G. A. Gooch	England v India at Lord's	1990
332	W. H. Ashdown	Kent v Essex at Brentwood	1934
331*	J. D. Robertson	Middlesex v Worcestershire at Worcester	1949
325*	H. L. Hendry	Victoria v New Zealanders at Melbourne	1925-26
325	A. Sandham	England v West Indies at Kingston	1929-30
325	C. L. Badcock	South Australia v Victoria at Adelaide	1935-36
324	J. B. Stollmeyer	Trinidad v British Guiana at Port-of-Spain	1946-47
324	Waheed Mirza	Karachi Whites v Quetta at Karachi	1976-77
323	A. L. Wadekar	Bombay v Mysore at Bombay	1966-67
322	E. Paynter	Lancashire v Sussex at Hove	1937
322	I. V. A. Richards	Somerset v Warwickshire at Taunton	1985
321	W. L. Murdoch	NSW v Victoria at Sydney	1881-82
320	R. Lamba	North Zone v West Zone at Bhilai	1987-88
319	Gul Mahomed	Baroda v Holkar at Baroda	1946-47
318*	W. G. Grace	Gloucestershire v Yorkshire at Cheltenham	1876
317	W. R. Hammond	Gloucestershire v Nottinghamshire at Gloucester . . .	1936
317	K. R. Rutherford	New Zealanders v D. B. Close's XI at Scarborough .	1986
316*	J. B. Hobbs	Surrey v Middlesex at Lord's	1926
316*	V. S. Hazare	Maharashtra v Baroda at Poona	1939-40
316	R. H. Moore	Hampshire v Warwickshire at Bournemouth	1937
315*	T. W. Hayward	Surrey v Lancashire at The Oval	1898
315	P. Holmes	Yorkshire v Middlesex at Lord's	1925
315*	A. F. Kippax	NSW v Queensland at Sydney	1927-28
314*	C. L. Walcott	Barbados v Trinidad at Port-of-Spain	1945-46
313*	S. J. Cook	Somerset v Glamorgan at Cardiff	1990
313	H. Sutcliffe	Yorkshire v Essex at Leyton	1932
313	W. V. Raman	Tamil Nadu v Goa at Panjim	1988-89
312*	W. W. Keeton	Nottinghamshire v Middlesex at The Oval‡	1939
312*	J. M. Brearley	MCC Under-25 v North Zone at Peshawar	1966-67
311*	G. M. Turner	Worcestershire v Warwickshire at Worcester	1982
311	J. T. Brown	Yorkshire v Sussex at Sheffield	1897
311	R. B. Simpson	Australia v England at Manchester	1964
311	Javed Miandad	Karachi Whites v National Bank at Karachi	1974-75
310*	J. H. Edrich	England v New Zealand at Leeds	1965
310	H. Gimblett	Somerset v Essex at Eastbourne	1948
309	V. S. Hazare	The Rest v Hindus at Bombay	1943-44
308*	F. M. M. Worrell	Barbados v Trinidad at Bridgetown	1943-44
307	M. C. Cowdrey	MCC v South Australia at Adelaide	1962-63
307	R. M. Cowper	Australia v England at Melbourne	1965-66
306*	A. Ducat	Surrey v Oxford University at The Oval	1919
306*	E. A. B. Rowan	Transvaal v Natal at Johannesburg	1939-40
306*	D. W. Hookes	South Australia v Tasmania at Adelaide	1986-87
305*	F. E. Woolley	MCC v Tasmania at Hobart	1911-12
305*	F. R. Foster	Warwickshire v Worcestershire at Dudley	1914
305*	W. H. Ashdown	Kent v Derbyshire at Dover	1935
304*	A. W. Nourse	Natal v Transvaal at Johannesburg	1919-20
304*	P. H. Tarilton	Barbados v Trinidad at Bridgetown	1919-20
304*	E. D. Weekes	West Indians v Cambridge University at Cambridge	1950
304	R. M. Poore	Hampshire v Somerset at Taunton	1899
304	D. G. Bradman	Australia v England at Leeds	1934
303*	W. W. Armstrong	Australians v Somerset at Bath	1905
303*	Mushtaq Mohammad	Karachi Blues v Karachi University at Karachi	1967-68
303*	Abdul Azeem	Hyderabad v Tamil Nadu at Hyderabad	1986-87
302*	P. Holmes	Yorkshire v Hampshire at Portsmouth	1920

302*	W. R. Hammond	Gloucestershire v Glamorgan at Bristol	1934
302*	Arjan Kripal Singh	Tamil Nadu v Goa at Panjim	1988-89
302	W. R. Hammond	Gloucestershire v Glamorgan at Newport	1939
302	L. G. Rowe	West Indies v England at Bridgetown	1973-74
301*	E. H. Hendren	Middlesex v Worcestershire at Dudley	1933
301	W. G. Grace	Gloucestershire v Sussex at Bristol	1896
300*	V. T. Trumper	Australians v Sussex at Hove	1899
300*	F. B. Watson	Lancashire v Surrey at Manchester	1928
300*	Imtiaz Ahmed	PM's XI v Commonwealth XI at Bombay	1950-51
300	J. T. Brown	Yorkshire v Derbyshire at Chesterfield	1898
300	D. C. S. Compton	MCC v N. E. Transvaal at Benoni	1948-49
300	R. Subba Row	Northamptonshire v Surrey at The Oval	1958

† *Hanif Mohammad batted for 16 hours 10 minutes – the longest innings in first-class cricket.*
‡ *Played at The Oval because Lord's was required for Eton v Harrow.*
Note: W. V. Raman (313) and Arjan Kripal Singh (302*) provide the only instance of two
triple-hundreds in the same innings.

HIGHEST SCORE FOR EACH FIRST-CLASS COUNTY

Derbyshire	274	G. Davidson v Lancashire at Manchester	1896
Durham	159	P. W. G. Parker v Warwickshire at Darlington . . .	1993
Essex	343*	P. A. Perrin v Derbyshire at Chesterfield	1904
Glamorgan	287*	D. E. Davies v Gloucestershire at Newport	1939
Gloucestershire	318*	W. G. Grace v Yorkshire at Cheltenham	1876
Hampshire	316	R. H. Moore v Warwickshire at Bournemouth . . .	1937
Kent	332	W. H. Ashdown v Essex at Brentwood	1934
Lancashire	424	A. C. MacLaren v Somerset at Taunton	1895
Leicestershire	252*	S. Coe v Northamptonshire at Leicester	1914
Middlesex	331*	J. D. Robertson v Worcestershire at Worcester . . .	1949
Northamptonshire	300	R. Subba Row v Surrey at The Oval	1958
Nottinghamshire	312*	W. W. Keeton v Middlesex at The Oval†	1939
Somerset	322	I. V. A. Richards v Warwickshire at Taunton . . .	1985
Surrey	357*	R. Abel v Somerset at The Oval	1899
Sussex	333	K. S. Duleepsinhji v Northamptonshire at Hove . .	1930
Warwickshire	305*	F. R. Foster v Worcestershire at Dudley	1914
Worcestershire	405*	G. A. Hick v Somerset at Taunton	1988
Yorkshire	341	G. H. Hirst v Leicestershire at Leicester	1905

† *Played at The Oval because Lord's was required for Eton v Harrow.*

HIGHEST SCORE AGAINST EACH FIRST-CLASS COUNTY

Derbyshire	343*	P. A. Perrin (Essex) at Chesterfield	1904
Durham	247	C. C. Lewis (Nottinghamshire) at Chester-le-Street	1993
Essex	332	W. H. Ashdown (Kent) at Brentwood	1934
Glamorgan	313*	S. J. Cook (Somerset) at Cardiff	1990
Gloucestershire	296	A. O. Jones (Nottinghamshire) at Nottingham . . .	1903
Hampshire	302*	P. Holmes (Yorkshire) at Portsmouth	1920
Kent	344	W. G. Grace (MCC) at Canterbury	1876
Lancashire	315*	T. W. Hayward (Surrey) at The Oval	1898
Leicestershire	341	G. H. Hirst (Yorkshire) at Leicester	1905
Middlesex	316*	J. B. Hobbs (Surrey) at Lord's	1926
Northamptonshire	333	K. S. Duleepsinhji (Sussex) at Hove	1930
Nottinghamshire	345	C. G. Macartney (Australians) at Nottingham . . .	1921
Somerset	424	A. C. MacLaren (Lancashire) at Taunton	1895
Surrey	366	N. H. Fairbrother (Lancashire) at The Oval	1990
Sussex	322	E. Paynter (Lancashire) at Hove	1937
Warwickshire	322	I. V. A. Richards (Somerset) at Taunton	1985
Worcestershire	331*	J. D. B. Robertson (Middlesex) at Worcester . . .	1949
Yorkshire	318*	W. G. Grace (Gloucestershire) at Cheltenham . . .	1876

DOUBLE-HUNDRED ON DEBUT

227	T. Marsden	Sheffield & Leicester v Nottingham at Sheffield ..	1826
207	N. F. Callaway	New South Wales v Queensland at Sydney	1914-15
240	W. F. E. Marx	Transvaal v Griqualand West at Johannesburg ...	1920-21
200*	A. Maynard	Trinidad v MCC at Port-of-Spain.............	1934-35
232*	S. J. E. Loxton	Victoria v Queensland at Melbourne	1946-47
215*	G. H. G. Doggart	Cambridge University v Lancashire at Cambridge ..	1948
202	J. Hallebone	Victoria v Tasmania at Melbourne.............	1951-52
230	G. R. Viswanath	Mysore v Andhra at Vijayawada	1967-68

TWO SEPARATE HUNDREDS ON DEBUT

148 and 111	A. R. Morris	New South Wales v Queensland at Sydney ..	1940-41
152 and 102*	N. J. Contractor	Gujarat v Baroda at Baroda	1952-53
132* and 110	Aamer Malik	Lahore "A" v Railways at Lahore	1979-80

Notes: J. S. Solomon, British Guiana, scored a hundred in each of his first three innings in first-class cricket: 114* v Jamaica; 108 v Barbados in 1956-57; 121 v Pakistanis in 1957-58.

R. Watson-Smith, Border, scored 310 runs before he was dismissed in first-class cricket, including not-out centuries in his first two innings: 183* v Orange Free State and 125* v Griqualand West in 1969-70.

G. R. Viswanath and D. M. Wellham alone have scored a hundred on their debut in both first-class cricket and Test cricket. Viswanath scored 230 for Mysore v Andhra in 1967-68 and 137 for India v Australia in 1969-70. Wellham scored 100 for New South Wales v Victoria in 1980-81 and 103 for Australia v England in 1981.

HUNDRED ON DEBUT IN BRITAIN

(The following list does not include instances of players who have previously appeared in first-class cricket outside the British Isles or who performed the feat before 1965. Full lists of earlier instances are in *Wisdens* prior to 1984.)

108	D. R. Shepherd	Gloucestershire v Oxford University at Oxford.....	1965
110*	A. J. Harvey-Walker	Derbyshire v Oxford University at Burton upon Trent	†1971
173	J. Whitehouse	Warwickshire v Oxford University at Oxford	1971
106	J. B. Turner	Minor Counties v Pakistanis at Jesmond..........	1974
112	J. A. Claughton	Oxford University v Gloucestershire at Oxford.....	†1976
100*	A. W. Lilley	Essex v Nottinghamshire at Nottingham.........	†1978
146*	J. S. Johnson	Minor Counties v Indians at Wellington	1979
110	N. R. Taylor	Kent v Sri Lankans at Canterbury..............	1979
146*	D. G. Aslett	Kent v Hampshire at Bournemouth	1981
116	M. D. Moxon	Yorkshire v Essex at Leeds.....................	†1981
100	D. A. Banks	Worcestershire v Oxford University at Oxford ...	1983
122	A. A. Metcalfe	Yorkshire v Nottinghamshire at Bradford	1983
117*	K. T. Medlycott	} Surrey v Cambridge University at Banstead	‡1984
101*	N. J. Falkner		
106	A. C. Storie	Northamptonshire v Hampshire at Northampton ...	†1985
102	M. P. Maynard	Glamorgan v Sussex at Swansea	1985
117*	R. J. Bartlett	Somerset v Oxford University at Oxford	1986
100*	P. D. Bowler	Leicestershire v Hampshire at Leicester	1986
145	I. L. Philip	Scotland v Ireland at Glasgow	1986
114*	P. D. Atkins	Surrey v Cambridge University at The Oval.......	1988
100	B. M. W. Patterson	Scotland v Ireland at Dumfries................	1988
116*	J. J. B. Lewis	Essex v Surrey at The Oval....................	1990
117	J. D. Glendenen	Durham v Oxford University at Oxford	1992
109	J. R. Wileman	Nottinghamshire v Cambridge U. at Nottingham ..	1992
123	A. J. Hollioake	Surrey v Derbyshire at Ilkeston	†1993

† *In his second innings.*
‡ *The only instance in England of two players performing the feat in the same match.*

TWO DOUBLE-HUNDREDS IN A MATCH

| A. E. Fagg........ | 244 | 202* | Kent v Essex at Colchester .... | 1938 |

TRIPLE-HUNDRED AND HUNDRED IN A MATCH

| G. A. Gooch ...... | 333 | 123 | England v India at Lord's .... | 1990 |

DOUBLE-HUNDRED AND HUNDRED IN A MATCH

C. B. Fry	125	229	Sussex v Surrey at Hove	1900
W. W. Armstrong..	157*	245	Victoria v South Australia at Melbourne.	1920-21
H. T. W. Hardinge .	207	102*	Kent v Surrey at Blackheath	1921
C. P. Mead	113	224	Hampshire v Sussex at Horsham	1921
K. S. Duleepsinhji .	115	246	Sussex v Kent at Hastings	1929
D. G. Bradman	124	225	Woodfull's XI v Ryder's XI at Sydney ...	1929-30
B. Sutcliffe	243	100*	New Zealanders v Essex at Southend ...	1949
M. R. Hallam	210*	157	Leicestershire v Glamorgan at Leicester .	1959
M. R. Hallam	203*	143*	Leicestershire v Sussex at Worthing ...	1961
Hanumant Singh ...	109	213*	Rajasthan v Bombay at Bombay	1966-67
Salah-ud-Din	256	102*	Karachi v East Pakistan at Karachi	1968-69
K. D. Walters	242	103	Australia v West Indies at Sydney......	1968-69
S. M. Gavaskar	124	220	India v West Indies at Port-of-Spain....	1970-71
L. G. Rowe	214	100*	West Indies v New Zealand at Kingston .	1971-72
G. S. Chappell	247*	133	Australia v New Zealand at Wellington .	1973-74
L. Baichan	216*	102	Berbice v Demerara at Georgetown	1973-74
Zaheer Abbas	216*	156*	Gloucestershire v Surrey at The Oval ...	1976
Zaheer Abbas	230*	104*	Gloucestershire v Kent at Canterbury...	1976
Zaheer Abbas	205*	108*	Gloucestershire v Sussex at Cheltenham .	1977
Saadat Ali	141	222	Income Tax v Multan at Multan	1977-78
Talat Ali	214*	104	PIA v Punjab at Lahore	1978-79
Shafiq Ahmad	129	217*	National Bank v MCB at Karachi	1978-79
D. W. Randall	209	146	Notts. v Middlesex at Nottingham	1979
Zaheer Abbas	215*	150*	Gloucestershire v Somerset at Bath	1981
Qasim Omar	210*	110	MCB v Lahore at Lahore	1982-83
A. I. Kallicharran .	200*	117*	Warwicks. v Northants at Birmingham .	1984
Rizwan-uz-Zaman..	139	217*	PIA v PACO at Lahore	1989-90
G. A. Hick	252*	100*	Worcs. v Glamorgan at Abergavenny ...	1990
N. R. Taylor	204	142	Kent v Surrey at Canterbury	1990
N. R. Taylor	111	203*	Kent v Sussex at Hove	1991
W. V. Raman	226	120	Tamil Nadu v Haryana at Faridabad ..	1991-92
A. J. Lamb	209	107	Northants v Warwicks. at Northampton	1992

TWO SEPARATE HUNDREDS IN A MATCH

Eight times: Zaheer Abbas.

Seven times: W. R. Hammond.

Six times: J. B. Hobbs, G. M. Turner.

Five times: C. B. Fry.

Four times: D. G. Bradman, G. S. Chappell, J. H. Edrich, L. B. Fishlock, G. A. Gooch, T. W. Graveney, C. G. Greenidge, H. T. W. Hardinge, E. H. Hendren, Javed Miandad, G. L. Jessop, P. A. Perrin, B. Sutcliffe, H. Sutcliffe.

Three times: Agha Zahid, L. E. G. Ames, G. Boycott, I. M. Chappell, D. C. S. Compton, S. J. Cook, M. C. Cowdrey, D. Denton, K. S. Duleepsinhji, R. E. Foster, R. C. Fredericks, S. M. Gavaskar, W. G. Grace, G. Gunn, M. R. Hallam, Hanif Mohammad, M. J. Harris, T. W. Hayward, V. S. Hazare, D. W. Hookes, L. Hutton, A. Jones, P. N. Kirsten, R. B. McCosker, P. B. H. May, C. P. Mead, H. Morris, Rizwan-uz-Zaman, R. T. Robinson, A. C. Russell, Sadiq Mohammad, J. T. Tyldesley, K. C. Wessels.

Twice: Ali Zia, D. L. Amiss, C. W. J. Athey, L. Baichan, Basit Ali, D. C. Boon, A. R. Border, B. J. T. Bosanquet, R. J. Boyd-Moss, A. R. Butcher, M. D. Crowe, C. C. Dacre, G. M. Emmett, A. E. Fagg, L. E. Favell, H. Gimblett, C. Hallows, R. A. Hamence, A. L. Hassett, G. A. Headley, G. A. Hick, D. M. Jones, A. I. Kallicharran, J. H. King, A. F. Kippax, A. J. Lamb, J. G. Langridge, H. W. Lee, E. Lester, C. B. Llewellyn, C. G. Macartney, M. P. Maynard, C. A. Milton, A. R. Morris, P. H. Parfitt, Nawab of Pataudi jun., E. Paynter, C. Pinch, R. G. Pollock, R. M. Prideaux, Qasim Omar, W. Rhodes, B. A. Richards, I. V. A. Richards, Pankaj Roy, Salim Malik, James Seymour, Shafiq Ahmad, R. B. Simpson, C. L. Smith, G. S. Sobers, M. A. Taylor, N. R. Taylor, E. Tyldesley, C. L. Walcott, W. W. Whysall, G. N. Yallop.

Notes: W. Lambert scored 107 and 157 for Sussex v Epsom at Lord's in 1817 and it was not until W. G. Grace made 130 and 102* for South of the Thames v North of the Thames at Canterbury in 1868 that the feat was repeated.

Zaheer Abbas (Gloucestershire) set a unique record in 1976 by twice scoring a double hundred and a hundred in the same match without being dismissed: 216* and 156* v Surrey at The Oval and 230* and 104* v Kent at Canterbury. In 1977 he achieved this feat for a third time, scoring 205* and 108* v Sussex at Cheltenham, and in 1981 for a fourth time, scoring 215* and 150* v Somerset at Bath.

C. J. B. Wood, 107* and 117* for Leicestershire v Yorkshire at Bradford in 1911, and S. J. Cook, 120* and 131* for Somerset v Nottinghamshire at Nottingham in 1989, are alone in carrying their bats and scoring hundreds in each innings.

FOUR HUNDREDS OR MORE IN SUCCESSION

Six in succession: C. B. Fry 1901; D. G. Bradman 1938-39; M. J. Procter 1970-71.

Five in succession: E. D. Weekes 1955-56.

Four in succession: C. W. J. Athey 1987; M. Azharuddin 1984-85; M. G. Bevan 1990-91; A. R. Border 1985; D. G. Bradman 1931-32, 1948-49; D. C. S. Compton 1946-47; N. J. Contractor 1957-58; S. J. Cook 1989; K. S. Duleepsinhji 1931; C. B. Fry 1911; C. G. Greenidge 1986; W. R. Hammond 1936-37, 1945-46; H. T. W. Hardinge 1913; T. W. Hayward 1906; J. B. Hobbs 1920, 1925; D. W. Hookes 1976-77; P. N. Kirsten 1976-77; J. G. Langridge 1949; C. G. Macartney 1921; K. S. McEwan 1977; P. B. H. May 1956-57; V. M. Merchant 1941-42; A. Mitchell 1933; Nawab of Pataudi sen. 1931; L. G. Rowe 1971-72; Pankaj Roy 1962-63; Rizwan-uz-Zaman 1989-90; Sadiq Mohammad 1976; Saeed Ahmed 1961-62; M. V. Sridhar 1990-91, 1991-92; H. Sutcliffe 1931, 1939; E. Tyldesley 1926; W. W. Whysall 1930; F. E. Woolley 1929; Zaheer Abbas 1970-71, 1982-83.

Notes: T. W. Hayward (Surrey v Nottinghamshire and Leicestershire) and D. W. Hookes (South Australia v Queensland and New South Wales) are the only players listed above to score two hundreds in two successive matches. Hayward scored his in six days, June 4-9, 1906.

The most fifties in consecutive innings is ten – by E. Tyldesley in 1926 and by D. G. Bradman in the 1947-48 and 1948 seasons.

MOST HUNDREDS IN A SEASON

Eighteen: D. C. S. Compton in 1947. These included six hundreds against the South Africans. His aggregate for the season was 3,816, also a record.

Sixteen: J. B. Hobbs in 1925, when aged 42. It was during this season that he exceeded the number of hundreds obtained in first-class cricket by W. G. Grace.

Fifteen: W. R. Hammond 1938.

Fourteen: H. Sutcliffe 1932.

Thirteen: G. Boycott 1971, D. G. Bradman 1938, C. B. Fry 1901, W. R. Hammond 1933 and 1937, T. W. Hayward 1906, E. H. Hendren 1923, 1927 and 1928, C. P. Mead 1928, H. Sutcliffe 1928 and 1931.

Since 1969 (excluding G. Boycott – above)

Twelve: G. A. Gooch 1990.

Eleven: S. J. Cook 1991, Zaheer Abbas 1976.

Ten: G. A. Hick 1988, H. Morris 1990, G. M. Turner 1970, Zaheer Abbas 1981.

MOST HUNDREDS IN A CAREER

(35 or more)

		100s	Total Inns	100th 100 Season	Inns	400+	300+	200+
1	J. B. Hobbs	197	1,315	1923	821	0	1	16
2	E. H. Hendren	170	1,300	1928-29	740	0	1	22
3	W. R. Hammond	167	1,005	1935	679	0	4	36
4	C. P. Mead	153	1,340	1927	892	0	0	13
5	G. Boycott	151	1,014	1977	645	0	0	10
6	H. Sutcliffe	149	1,088	1932	700	0	1	17
7	F. E. Woolley	145	1,532	1929	1,031	0	1	9
8	L. Hutton	129	814	1951	619	0	1	11
9	W. G. Grace	126	1,493	1895	1,113	0	3	13
10	D. C. S. Compton	123	839	1952	552	0	1	9
11	T. W. Graveney	122	1,223	1964	940	0	0	7
12	D. G. Bradman	117	338	1947-48	295	1	6	37
13	**I. V. A. Richards**	**114**	**796**	**1988-89**	**658**	**0**	**1**	**10**
14	Zaheer Abbas	108	768	1982-83	658	0	0	10
15	A. Sandham	107	1,000	1935	871	0	1	11
	M. C. Cowdrey	107	1,130	1973	1,035	0	1	3
17	**G. A. Gooch**	**106**	**859**	**1992-93**	**820**	**0**	**1**	**9**
18	T. W. Hayward	104	1,138	1913	1,076	0	1	8
19	J. H. Edrich	103	979	1977	945	0	1	4
	G. M. Turner	103	792	1982	779	0	1	10
	E. Tyldesley	102	961	1934	919	0	0	7
21	L. E. G. Ames	102	951	1950	915	0	0	9
	D. L. Amiss	102	1,139	1986	1,081	0	0	3

E. H. Hendren, D. G. Bradman and I. V. A. Richards scored their 100th hundreds in Australia, G. A. Gooch scored his in India. His record includes his century in South Africa in 1981-82, which is no longer accepted by ICC. Zaheer Abbas scored his in Pakistan. Zaheer Abbas and G. Boycott did so in Test matches.

Most double-hundreds scored by batsmen not included in the above list:

Sixteen: C. B. Fry.
Fourteen: C. G. Greenidge, K. S. Ranjitsinhji.
Thirteen: W. H. Ponsford (including two 400s and two 300s), J. T. Tyldesley.
Twelve: P. Holmes, Javed Miandad, R. B. Simpson.
Eleven: J. W. Hearne, V. M. Merchant.
Ten: S. M. Gavaskar, J. Hardstaff, jun., V. S. Hazare, A. Shrewsbury, R. T. Simpson.

J. W. Hearne	96	K. F. Barrington	76	D. Denton	69
C. B. Fry	94	**M. W. Gatting**	**76**	M. J. K. Smith	69
C. G. Greenidge	92	J. G. Langridge	76	R. E. Marshall	68
A. I. Kallicharran	87	C. Washbrook	76	R. N. Harvey	67
W. J. Edrich	86	H. T. W. Hardinge	75	P. Holmes	67
G. S. Sobers	86	R. Abel	74	J. D. Robertson	67
J. T. Tyldesley	86	G. S. Chappell	74	**A. R. Border**	**66**
P. B. H. May	85	D. Kenyon	74	P. A. Perrin	66
R. E. S. Wyatt	85	K. S. McEwan	74	R. G. Pollock	64
A. J. Lamb	**84**	Majid Khan	73	R. T. Simpson	64
J. Hardstaff, jun.	83	**G. A. Hick**	**72**	**M. D. Crowe**	**63**
R. B. Kanhai	83	Mushtaq Mohammad	72	K. W. R. Fletcher	63
S. M. Gavaskar	81	J. O'Connor	72	G. Gunn	62
Javed Miandad	**80**	W. G. Quaife	72	V. S. Hazare	60
M. Leyland	80	K. S. Ranjitsinhji	72	G. H. Hirst	60
B. A. Richards	80	D. Brookes	71	R. B. Simpson	60
C. H. Lloyd	79	A. C. Russell	71	P. F. Warner	60

I. M. Chappell 59	E. G. Hayes 48

I. M. Chappell 59
S. J. Cook **59**
A. L. Hassett 59
A. Shrewsbury 59
J. G. Wright **59**
A. E. Fagg 58
P. H. Parfitt 58
W. Rhodes 58
L. B. Fishlock 56
A. Jones 56
W. Larkins **56**
C. A. Milton 56
C. Hallows 55
Hanif Mohammad 55
D. B. Vengsarkar 55
W. Watson 55
D. L. Haynes **54**
D. J. Insole 54
W. W. Keeton 54
K. C. Wessels **54**
W. Bardsley 53
B. F. Davison 53
A. E. Dipper 53
D. I. Gower **53**
G. L. Jessop 53
James Seymour 53
Shafiq Ahmad 53
E. H. Bowley 52
D. B. Close 52
A. Ducat 52
D. W. Randall **52**
D. C. Boon **51**
E. R. Dexter 51
J. M. Parks 51
W. W. Whysall 51
G. Cox, jun. 50
H. E. Dollery 50
K. S. Duleepsinhji ... 50
H. Gimblett 50
W. M. Lawry 50
Sadiq Mohammad 50
F. B. Watson 50
B. C. Broad **49**
P. N. Kirsten **49**
C. G. Macartney 49
R. T. Robinson **49**
M. J. Stewart 49
K. G. Suttle 49
P. R. Umrigar 49
W. M. Woodfull 49
C. J. Barnett 48
W. Gunn 48

E. G. Hayes 48
B. W. Luckhurst 48
M. J. Procter 48
C. E. B. Rice **48**
C. J. Tavaré **48**
C. W. J. Athey **47**
A. C. MacLaren 47
P. W. G. Parker **47**
W. H. Ponsford 47
C. L. Smith 47
A. R. Butcher 46
J. Iddon 46
A. R. Morris 46
C. T. Radley 46
Younis Ahmed 46
W. W. Armstrong 45
Asif Iqbal 45
M. R. Benson **45**
L. G. Berry 45
J. M. Brearley 45
A. W. Carr 45
C. Hill 45
N. C. O'Neill 45
E. Paynter 45
Rev. D. S. Sheppard . . 45
K. D. Walters 45
H. H. I. Gibbons 44
V. M. Merchant 44
A. Mitchell 44
P. E. Richardson 44
B. Sutcliffe 44
G. R. Viswanath 44
P. Willey 44
E. J. Barlow 43
K. J. Barnett **43**
B. L. D'Oliveira 43
J. H. Hampshire 43
A. F. Kippax 43
J. W. H. Makepeace . 43
M. E. Waugh **43**
James Langridge 42
Mudassar Nazar **42**
H. W. Parks 42
T. F. Shepherd 42
V. T. Trumper 42
M. J. Harris 41
G. D. Mendis **41**
K. R. Miller 41
A. D. Nourse 41
J. H. Parks 41
R. M. Prideaux 41
G. Pullar 41

W. E. Russell 41
R. C. Fredericks 40
J. Gunn 40
M. J. Smith 40
C. L. Walcott 40
D. M. Young 40
Arshad Pervez **39**
W. H. Ashdown 39
J. B. Bolus 39
W. A. Brown 39
R. J. Gregory 39
W. R. D. Payton 39
J. R. Reid 39
R. A. Smith **39**
F. M. M. Worrell . . . 39
I. T. Botham **38**
F. L. Bowley 38
P. J. Burge 38
J. F. Crapp 38
D. Lloyd 38
V. L. Manjrekar 38
A. W. Nourse 38
N. Oldfield 38
Rev. J. H. Parsons . . . 38
W. W. Read 38
J. Sharp 38
N. R. Taylor **38**
L. J. Todd 38
J. Arnold 37
G. Brown 37
G. Cook 37
G. M. Emmett 37
H. W. Lee 37
M. A. Noble 37
B. P. Patel 37
H. S. Squires 37
R. T. Virgin 37
C. J. B. Wood 37
N. F. Armstrong 36
G. Fowler **36**
H. Morris **36**
E. Oldroyd 36
W. Place 36
A. L. Wadekar 36
E. D. Weekes 36
C. S. Dempster 35
D. R. Jardine 35
T. E. Jesty 35
D. M. Jones **35**
B. H. Valentine 35
G. M. Wood 35

Bold type denotes those who played in 1992-93 and 1993 seasons.

3,000 RUNS IN A SEASON

	Season	I	NO	R	HS	100s	Avge
D. C. S. Compton	1947	50	8	3,816	246	18	90.85
W. J. Edrich	1947	52	8	3,539	267*	12	80.43
T. W. Hayward	1906	61	8	3,518	219	13	66.37
L. Hutton	1949	56	6	3,429	269*	12	68.58
F. E. Woolley........	1928	59	4	3,352	198	12	60.94

	Season	I	NO	R	HS	100s	Avge
H. Sutcliffe	1932	52	7	3,336	313	14	74.13
W. R. Hammond	1933	54	5	3,323	264	13	67.81
E. H. Hendren	1928	54	7	3,311	209*	13	70.44
R. Abel	1901	68	8	3,309	247	7	55.15
W. R. Hammond	1937	55	5	3,252	217	13	65.04
M. J. K. Smith	1959	67	11	3,245	200*	8	57.94
E. H. Hendren	1933	65	9	3,186	301*	11	56.89
C. P. Mead	1921	52	6	3,179	280*	10	69.10
T. W. Hayward	1904	63	5	3,170	203	11	54.65
K. S. Ranjitsinhji....	1899	58	8	3,159	197	8	63.18
C. B. Fry	1901	43	3	3,147	244	13	78.67
K. S. Ranjitsinhji....	1900	40	5	3,065	275	11	87.57
L. E. G. Ames	1933	57	5	3,058	295	9	58.80
J. T. Tyldesley	1901	60	5	3,041	221	9	55.29
C. P. Mead	1928	50	10	3,027	180	13	75.67
J. B. Hobbs	1925	48	5	3,024	266*	16	70.32
E. Tyldesley	1928	48	10	3,024	242	10	79.57
W. E. Alley	1961	64	11	3,019	221*	11	56.96
W. R. Hammond	1938	42	2	3,011	271	15	75.27
E. H. Hendren	1923	51	12	3,010	200*	13	77.17
H. Sutcliffe	1931	42	11	3,006	230	13	96.96
J. H. Parks	1937	63	4	3,003	168	11	50.89
H. Sutcliffe	1928	44	5	3,002	228	13	76.97

Notes: W. G. Grace scored 2,739 runs in 1871 – the first batsman to reach 2,000 runs in a season. He made ten hundreds and twice exceeded 200, with an average of 78.25 in all first-class matches. At the time, the over consisted of four balls.

The highest aggregate in a season since the reduction of County Championship matches in 1969 is 2,755 by S. J. Cook (42 innings) in 1991.

2,000 RUNS IN A SEASON

Since Reduction of Championship Matches in 1969

Five times: G. A. Gooch 2,746 (1990), 2,559 (1984), 2,324 (1988), 2,208 (1985), 2,023 (1993).

Three times: D. L. Amiss 2,239 (1984), 2,110 (1976), 2,030 (1978); S. J. Cook 2,755 (1991), 2,608 (1990), 2,241 (1989); M. W. Gatting 2,257 (1984), 2,057 (1991), 2,000 (1992); G. A. Hick 2,713 (1988), 2,347 (1990), 2,004 (1986); G. M. Turner 2,416 (1973), 2,379 (1970), 2,101 (1981).

Twice: G. Boycott 2,503 (1971), 2,051 (1970); J. H. Edrich 2,238 (1969), 2,031 (1971); A. I. Kallicharran 2,301 (1984), 2,120 (1982); Zaheer Abbas 2,554 (1976), 2,306 (1981).

Once: M. Azharuddin 2,016 (1991); J. B. Bolus 2,143 (1970); P. D. Bowler 2,044 (1992); B. C. Broad 2,226 (1990); A. R. Butcher 2,116 (1990); C. G. Greenidge 2,035 (1986); M. J. Harris 2,238 (1971); D. L. Haynes 2,346 (1990); Javed Miandad 2,083 (1981); A. J. Lamb 2,049 (1981); K. S. McEwan 2,176 (1990); Majid Khan 2,074 (1972); A. A. Metcalfe 2,047 (1990); H. Morris 2,276 (1990); D. W. Randall 2,151 (1985); I. V. A. Richards 2,161 (1977); R. T. Robinson 2,032 (1984); M. A. Roseberry 2,044 (1992); C. L. Smith 2,000 (1985); R. T. Virgin 2,223 (1970); D. M. Ward 2,072 (1990); M. E. Waugh 2,072 (1990).

1,000 RUNS IN A SEASON MOST TIMES

(Includes Overseas Tours and Seasons)

28 times: W. G. Grace 2,000 (6); F. E. Woolley 3,000 (1), 2,000 (12).

27 times: M. C. Cowdrey 2,000 (2); C. P. Mead 3,000 (2), 2,000 (9).

26 times: G. Boycott 2,000 (3); J. B. Hobbs 3,000 (1), 2,000 (16).

25 times: E. H. Hendren 3,000 (3), 2,000 (12).

24 times: D. L. Amiss 2,000 (3); W. G. Quaife 2,000 (1); H. Sutcliffe 3,000 (3), 2,000 (12).

23 times: A. Jones.

22 times: T. W. Graveney 2,000 (7); W. R. Hammond 3,000 (3), 2,000 (9).

21 times: D. Denton 2,000 (5); J. H. Edrich 2,000 (6); W. Rhodes 2,000 (2).

20 times: D. B. Close; K. W. R. Fletcher; G. Gunn; T. W. Hayward 3,000 (2), 2,000 (8); James Langridge 2,000 (1); J. M. Parks 2,000 (3); A. Sandham 2,000 (8); M. J. K. Smith 3,000 (1), 2,000 (5); C. Washbrook 2,000 (2).

19 times: J. W. Hearne 2,000 (4); G. H. Hirst 2,000 (3); D. Kenyon 2,000 (7); E. Tyldesley 3,000 (1), 2,000 (5); J. T. Tyldesley 3,000 (1), 2,000 (4).

18 times: L. G. Berry 2,000 (1); G. A. Gooch 2,000 (5); H. T. W. Hardinge 2,000 (5); R. E. Marshall 2,000 (6); P. A. Perrin; G. M. Turner 2,000 (5); R. E. S. Wyatt 2,000 (5).

17 times: L. E. G. Ames 3,000 (1), 2,000 (5); T. E. Bailey 2,000 (1); D. Brookes 2,000 (6); D. C. S. Compton 3,000 (1), 2,000 (5); C. G. Greenidge 2,000 (1); L. Hutton 3,000 (1), 2,000 (8); J. G. Langridge 2,000 (11); M. Leyland 2,000 (3); I. V. A. Richards 2,000 (1); K. G. Suttle 2,000 (1), Zaheer Abbas 2,000 (2).

16 times: D. G. Bradman 2,000 (4); D. E. Davies 2,000 (1); M. W. Gatting 2,000 (3); E. G. Hayes 2,000 (2); C. A. Milton 2,000 (1); J. O'Connor 2,000 (4); C. T. Radley; James Seymour 2,000 (1); C. J. Tavaré.

15 times: G. Barker; K. F. Barrington 2,000 (3); E. H. Bowley 2,000 (4); M. H. Denness; A. E. Dipper 2,000 (5); H. E. Dollery 2,000 (2); W. J. Edrich 3,000 (1), 2,000 (8); J. H. Hampshire; P. Holmes 2,000 (7); Mushtaq Mohammad; R. B. Nicholls 2,000 (1); P. H. Parfitt 2,000 (3); W. G. A. Parkhouse 2,000 (1); B. A. Richards 2,000 (1); J. D. Robertson 2,000 (9); G. S. Sobers; M. J. Stewart 2,000 (1).

Notes: F. E. Woolley reached 1,000 runs in 28 consecutive seasons (1907-1938). C. P. Mead did so 27 seasons in succession (1906-1936).

Outside England, 1,000 runs in a season has been reached most times by D. G. Bradman (in 12 seasons in Australia).

Three batsmen have scored 1,000 runs in a season in each of four different countries: G. S. Sobers in West Indies, England, India and Australia; M. C. Cowdrey and G. Boycott in England, South Africa, West Indies and Australia.

HIGHEST AGGREGATES OUTSIDE ENGLAND

	Season	I	NO	R	HS	100s	Avge
In Australia							
D. G. Bradman	1928-29	24	6	1,690	340*	7	93.88
In South Africa							
J. R. Reid...........	1961-62	30	2	1,915	203	7	68.39
In West Indies							
E. H. Hendren	1929-30	18	5	1,765	254*	6	135.76
In New Zealand							
M. D. Crowe	1986-87	21	3	1,676	175*	8	93.11
In India							
C. G. Borde	1964-65	28	3	1,604	168	6	64.16
In Pakistan							
Saadat Ali	1983-84	27	1	1,649	208	4	63.42
In Sri Lanka							
P. A. de Silva	1992-93	22	1	1,308	231	3	62.28
In Zimbabwe							
D. L. Houghton	1989-90	9	1	701	202	3	87.62

Note: In more than one country, the following aggregates of over 2,000 runs have been recorded:

	Season	I	NO	R	HS	100s	Avge
M. Amarnath (P/I/WI)	1982-83	34	6	2,234	207	9	79.78
J. R. Reid (SA/A/NZ).	1961-62	40	2	2,188	203	7	57.57
S. M. Gavaskar (I/P) .	1978-79	30	6	2,121	205	10	88.37
R. B. Simpson (I/P/A/WI)	1964-65	34	4	2,063	201	8	68.76

LEADING BATSMEN IN AN ENGLISH SEASON

(Qualification: 8 innings)

Season	Leading scorer	Runs	Avge	Top of averages	Runs	Avge
1946	D. C. S. Compton ...	2,403	61.61	W. R. Hammond ...	1,783	84.90
1947	D. C. S. Compton ...	3,816	90.85	D. C. S. Compton ...	3,816	90.85
1948	L. Hutton	2,654	64.73	D. G. Bradman	2,428	89.92
1949	L. Hutton	3,429	68.58	J. Hardstaff	2,251	72.61
1950	R. T. Simpson	2,576	62.82	E. Weekes	2,310	79.65
1951	J. D. Robertson	2,917	68.79	P. B. H. May	2,339	68.79
1952	L. Hutton	2,567	61.11	D. S. Sheppard	2,262	64.62
1953	W. J. Edrich	2,557	47.35	W. A. Johnston	102	102.00†
1954	D. Kenyon	2,636	51.68	D. C. S. Compton ...	1,524	58.61
1955	D. J. Insole	2,427	42.57	D. J. McGlew	1,871	58.46
1956	T. W. Graveney	2,397	49.93	K. Mackay	1,103	52.52
1957	T. W. Graveney	2,361	49.18	P. B. H. May	2,347	61.76
1958	P. B. H. May	2,231	63.74	P. B. H. May	2,231	63.74
1959	M. J. K. Smith	3,245	57.94	V. L. Manjrekar	755	68.63
1960	M. J. K. Smith	2,551	45.55	R. Subba Row	1,503	55.66
1961	W. E. Alley	3,019	56.96	W. M. Lawry	2,019	61.18
1962	J. H. Edrich	2,482	51.70	R. T. Simpson	867	54.18
1963	J. B. Bolus	2,190	41.32	G. S. Sobers	1,333	47.60
1964	T. W. Graveney	2,385	54.20	K. F. Barrington....	1,872	62.40
1965	J. H. Edrich	2,319	62.67	M. C. Cowdrey.....	2,093	63.42
1966	A. R. Lewis	2,198	41.47	G. S. Sobers	1,349	61.31
1967	C. A. Milton	2,089	46.42	K. F. Barrington....	2,059	68.63
1968	B. A. Richards	2,395	47.90	G. Boycott.........	1,487	64.65
1969	J. H. Edrich	2,238	69.93	J. H. Edrich	2,238	69.93
1970	G. M. Turner	2,379	61.00	G. S. Sobers	1,742	75.73
1971	G. Boycott.........	2,503	100.12	G. Boycott.........	2,503	100.12
1972	Majid Khan	2,074	61.00	G. Boycott.........	1,230	72.35
1973	G. M. Turner	2,416	67.11	G. M. Turner	2,416	67.11
1974	R. T. Virgin	1,936	56.94	C. H. Lloyd........	1,458	63.39
1975	G. Boycott.........	1,915	73.65	R. B. Kanhai	1,073	82.53
1976	Zaheer Abbas	2,554	75.11	Zaheer Abbas	2,554	75.11
1977	I. V. A. Richards ...	2,161	65.48	R. P. Baker	215	71.66‡
1978	D. L. Amiss	2,030	53.42	C. E. B. Rice	1,871	66.82
1979	K. C. Wessels	1,800	52.94	G. Boycott.........	1,538	102.53
1980	P. N. Kirsten	1,895	63.16	A. J. Lamb	1,797	66.55
1981	Zaheer Abbas	2,306	88.69	Zaheer Abbas	2,306	88.69
1982	A. I. Kallicharran...	2,120	66.25	G. M. Turner	1,171	90.07
1983	K. S. McEwan	2,176	64.00	I. V. A. Richards ...	1,204	75.25
1984	G. A. Gooch........	2,559	67.34	C. G. Greenidge....	1,069	82.23
1985	G. A. Gooch........	2,208	71.22	I. V. A. Richards ...	1,836	76.50
1986	C. G. Greenidge.....	2,035	67.83	J. G. Bracewell	386	77.20§
1987	G. A. Hick	1,879	52.19	M. D. Crowe.......	1,627	67.79
1988	G. A. Hick	2,713	77.51	R. A. Harper.......	622	77.75
1989	S. J. Cook	2,241	60.56	D. M. Jones	1,510	88.82
1990	G. A. Gooch........	2,746	101.70	G. A. Gooch........	2,746	101.70
1991	S. J. Cook	2,755	81.02	C. L. Hooper.......	1,501	93.81
1992	{ P. D. Bowler	2,044	65.93	Salim Malik	1,184	78.93
	{ M. A. Roseberry	2,044	56.77			
1993	G. A. Gooch........	2,023	63.21	G. Yates	367	91.75‖

† *Johnston had 17 innings with 16 not outs, highest score 28*.*
‡ *Baker had 12 innings with 9 not outs, highest score 77*.*
§ *Bracewell had 11 innings with 6 not outs, highest score 110.*
‖ *Yates had 10 innings with 6 not outs, highest score 134*.*

Note: The highest average recorded in an English season was 115.66 (2,429 runs, 26 innings) by D. G. Bradman in 1938.

25,000 RUNS IN A CAREER

Dates in italics denote the first half of an overseas season; i.e. *1945* denotes the 1945-46 season.

		Career	R	I	NO	HS	100s	Avge
1	J. B. Hobbs	1905-34	61,237	1,315	106	316*	197	50.65
2	F. E. Woolley	1906-38	58,969	1,532	85	305*	145	40.75
3	E. H. Hendren	1907-38	57,611	1,300	166	301*	170	50.80
4	C. P. Mead	1905-36	55,061	1,340	185	280*	153	47.67
5	W. G. Grace	1865-1908	54,896	1,493	105	344	126	39.55
6	W. R. Hammond	1920-51	50,551	1,005	104	336*	167	56.10
7	H. Sutcliffe	1919-45	50,138	1,088	123	313	149	51.95
8	G. Boycott	1962-86	48,426	1,014	162	261*	151	56.83
9	T. W. Graveney	1948-*71*	47,793	1,223	159	258	122	44.91
10	T. W. Hayward	1893-1914	43,551	1,138	96	315*	104	41.79
11	D. L. Amiss	1960-87	43,423	1,139	126	262*	102	42.86
12	M. C. Cowdrey	1950-76	42,719	1,130	134	307	107	42.89
13	A. Sandham	1911-*37*	41,284	1,000	79	325	107	44.82
14	L. Hutton	1934-60	40,140	814	91	364	129	55.51
15	M. J. K. Smith	1951-75	39,832	1,091	139	204	69	41.84
16	W. Rhodes	1898-1930	39,802	1,528	237	267*	58	30.83
17	J. H. Edrich	1956-78	39,790	979	104	310*	103	45.47
18	R. E. S. Wyatt	1923-57	39,405	1,141	157	232	85	40.04
19	D. C. S. Compton	1936-64	38,942	839	88	300	123	51.85
20	E. Tyldesley	1909-36	38,874	961	106	256*	102	45.46
21	G. A. Gooch	1973-93	38,427	859	70	333	106	48.70
22	J. T. Tyldesley	1895-1923	37,897	994	62	295*	86	40.66
23	K. W. R. Fletcher	1962-88	37,665	1,167	170	228*	63	37.77
24	C. G. Greenidge	1970-92	37,354	889	75	273*	92	45.88
25	J. W. Hearne	1909-36	37,252	1,025	116	285*	96	40.98
26	L. E. G. Ames	1926-51	37,248	951	95	295	102	43.51
27	D. Kenyon	1946-67	37,002	1,159	59	259	74	33.63
28	W. J. Edrich	1934-58	36,965	964	92	267*	86	42.39
29	J. M. Parks	1949-76	36,673	1,227	172	205*	51	34.76
30	D. Denton	1894-1920	36,479	1,163	70	221	69	33.37
31	G. H. Hirst	1891-1929	36,323	1,215	151	341	60	34.13
32	I. V. A. Richards	1971-93	36,212	796	62	322	114	49.33
33	A. Jones	1957-83	36,049	1,168	72	204*	56	32.89
34	W. Quaife	1894-1928	36,012	1,203	185	255*	72	35.37
35	R. E. Marshall	*1945*-72	35,725	1,053	59	228*	68	35.94
36	G. Gunn	1902-32	35,208	1,061	82	220	62	35.96
37	D. B. Close	1949-86	34,994	1,225	173	198	52	33.26
38	Zaheer Abbas	*1965*-86	34,843	768	92	274	108	51.54
39	J. G. Langridge	1928-55	34,380	984	66	250*	76	37.45
40	G. M. Turner	*1964*-82	34,346	792	101	311*	103	49.70
41	C. Washbrook	1933-64	34,101	906	107	251*	76	42.67
42	M. Leyland	1920-48	33,660	932	101	263	80	40.50
43	H. T. W. Hardinge	1902-33	33,519	1,021	103	263*	75	36.51
44	R. Abel	1881-1904	33,124	1,007	73	357*	74	35.46
45	A. I. Kallicharran	*1966*-90	32,650	834	86	243*	87	43.64
46	C. A. Milton	1948-74	32,150	1,078	125	170	56	33.73
47	J. D. Robertson	1937-59	31,914	897	46	331*	67	37.50
48	J. Hardstaff, jun.	1930-55	31,847	812	94	266	83	44.35
49	James Langridge	1924-53	31,716	1,058	157	167	42	35.20
50	K. F. Barrington	1953-68	31,714	831	136	256	76	45.63
51	C. H. Lloyd	*1963*-86	31,232	730	96	242*	79	49.26
52	Mushtaq Mohammad	*1956*-85	31,091	843	104	303*	72	42.07
53	C. B. Fry	1892-*1921*	30,886	658	43	258*	94	50.22
54	D. Brookes	1934-59	30,874	925	70	257	71	36.10

		Career	*R*	*I*	*NO*	*HS*	*100s*	*Avge*
55	P. Holmes	1913-35	30,573	810	84	315*	67	42.11
56	R. T. Simpson	1944-63	30,546	852	55	259	64	38.32
57 {	L. G. Berry	1924-51	30,225	1,056	57	232	45	30.25
	K. G. Suttle	1949-71	30,225	1,064	92	204*	49	31.09
59	**A. J. Lamb**	**1972-93**	**30,223**	**722**	**103**	**294**	**84**	**48.82**
60	**M. W. Gatting**	**1975-93**	**30,114**	**713**	**113**	**258**	**76**	**50.19**
61	P. A. Perrin	1896-1928	29,709	918	91	343*	66	35.92
62	P. F. Warner	1894-1929	29,028	875	75	244	60	36.28
63	R. B. Kanhai	1954-81	28,774	669	82	256	83	49.01
64	J. O'Connor	1921-39	28,764	903	79	248	72	34.90
65	T. E. Bailey	1945-67	28,641	1,072	215	205	28	33.42
66	**Javed Miandad**	*1973-92*	**28,504**	**626**	**95**	**311**	**80**	**53.67**
67	**D. W. Randall**	**1972-93**	**28,456**	**827**	**81**	**237**	**52**	**38.14**
68	E. H. Bowley	1912-34	28,378	859	47	283	52	34.94
69	B. A. Richards	*1964-82*	28,358	576	58	356	80	54.74
70	G. S. Sobers	*1952-74*	28,315	609	93	365*	86	54.87
71	A. E. Dipper	1908-32	28,075	865	69	252*	53	35.27
72	D. G. Bradman	*1927-48*	28,067	338	43	452*	117	95.14
73	J. H. Hampshire	1961-84	28,059	924	112	183*	43	34.55
74	P. B. H. May	1948-63	27,592	618	77	285*	85	51.00
75	B. F. Davison	*1967-87*	27,453	766	79	189	53	39.96
76	Majid Khan	*1961-84*	27,444	700	62	241	73	43.01
77	A. C. Russell	1908-30	27,358	717	59	273	71	41.57
78	E. G. Hayes	1896-1926	27,318	896	48	276	48	32.21
79	A. E. Fagg	1932-57	27,291	803	46	269*	58	36.05
80	James Seymour	1900-26	27,237	911	62	218*	53	32.08
81	P. H. Parfitt	1956-*73*	26,924	845	104	200*	58	36.33
82	G. L. Jessop	1894-1914	26,698	855	37	286	53	32.63
83	K. S. McEwan	*1972-91*	26,628	705	67	218	74	41.73
84	D. E. Davies	1924-54	26,564	1,032	80	287*	32	27.90
85	A. Shrewsbury	1875-1902	26,505	813	90	267	59	36.65
86	M. J. Stewart	1954-72	26,492	898	93	227*	49	32.90
87	C. T. Radley	1964-87	26,441	880	134	200	46	35.44
88	**D. I. Gower**	**1975-93**	**26,339**	**727**	**70**	**228**	**53**	**40.08**
89	**C. E. B. Rice**	*1969-92*	**26,262**	**764**	**123**	**246**	**48**	**40.97**
90	Younis Ahmed	*1961-86*	26,073	762	118	221*	46	40.48
91	P. E. Richardson	1949-65	26,055	794	41	185	44	34.60
92	M. H. Denness	1959-80	25,886	838	65	195	33	33.48
93	S. M. Gavaskar	*1966-87*	25,834	563	61	340	81	51.46
94	J. W. H. Makepeace	1906-30	25,799	778	66	203	43	36.23
95	W. Gunn	1880-1904	25,691	850	72	273	48	33.02
96	W. Watson	1939-64	25,670	753	109	257	55	39.86
97	G. Brown	1908-33	25,649	1,012	52	232*	37	26.71
98	G. M. Emmett	1936-59	25,602	865	50	188	37	31.41
99	J. B. Bolus	1956-75	25,598	833	81	202*	39	34.03
100	W. E. Russell	1956-72	25,525	796	64	193	41	34.87
101	**W. Larkins**	**1972-93**	**25,429**	**792**	**51**	**252**	**56**	**34.31**
102	C. J. Barnett	1927-53	25,389	821	45	259	48	32.71
103	L. B. Fishlock	1931-52	25,376	699	54	253	56	39.34
104	D. J. Insole	1947-63	25,241	743	72	219*	54	37.61
105	J. M. Brearley	1961-83	25,185	768	102	312*	45	37.81
106	J. Vine	1896-1922	25,171	920	79	202	34	29.92
107	R. M. Prideaux	1958-74	25,136	808	75	202*	41	34.29
108	J. H. King	1895-1925	25,122	988	69	227*	34	27.33
109	**J. G. Wright**	*1975-92*	**25,073**	**636**	**44**	**192**	**59**	**42.35**

Bold type denotes those who played in 1992-93 and 1993 seasons.

Note: Some works of reference provide career figures which differ from those in this list, owing to the exclusion or inclusion of matches recognised or not recognised as first-class by *Wisden.*

Current Players with 20,000 Runs

	Career	R	I	NO	HS	100s	Avge
C. J. Tavaré	1974-93	24,906	717	75	219	48	38.79
A. R. Border........	1976-93	24,770	570	89	205	66	51.49
D. L. Haynes	1976-93	22,727	552	65	255*	54	46.66
C. W. J. Athey......	1976-93	21,729	669	67	184	47	36.09
G. D. Mendis.......	1974-93	21,436	643	61	209*	41	36.83
B. C. Broad	1979-93	21,396	593	38	227*	49	38.55
R. T. Robinson	1978-93	21,361	574	75	220*	49	42.80
G. A. Hick	1983-93	21,106	407	44	405*	72	58.14
K. C. Wessels.......	1973-93	20,172	435	37	254	54	50.68

CAREER AVERAGE OVER 50

(Qualification: 10,000 runs)

Avge		Career	I	NO	R	HS	100s
95.14	D. G. Bradman	1927-48	338	43	28,067	452*	117
71.22	V. M. Merchant	1929-51	229	43	13,248	359*	44
65.18	W. H. Ponsford	1920-34	235	23	13,819	437	47
64.99	W. M. Woodfull	1921-34	245	39	13,388	284	49
58.24	A. L. Hassett	1932-53	322	32	16,890	232	59
58.19	V. S. Hazare	1934-66	365	45	18,621	316*	60
58.14	**G. A. Hick**	**1983-93**	**407**	**44**	**21,106**	**405***	**72**
57.22	A. F. Kippax	1918-35	256	33	12,762	315*	43
57.02	**M. D. Crowe**	**1979-92**	**367**	**55**	**17,791**	**299**	**63**
56.83	G. Boycott	1962-86	1,014	162	48,426	261*	151
56.80	**M. E. Waugh**	**1985-93**	**270**	**41**	**13,008**	**229***	**43**
56.55	C. L. Walcott	1941-63	238	29	11,820	314*	40
56.37	K. S. Ranjitsinhji	1893-1920	500	62	24,692	285*	72
56.22	R. B. Simpson	1952-77	436	62	21,029	359	60
56.10	W. R. Hammond	1920-51	1,005	104	50,551	336*	167
55.51	L. Hutton	1934-60	814	91	40,140	364	129
55.34	E. D. Weekes	1944-64	241	24	12,010	304*	36
54.87	G. S. Sobers	1952-74	609	93	28,315	365*	86
54.74	B. A. Richards	1964-82	576	58	28,358	356	80
54.67	R. G. Pollock	1960-86	437	54	20,940	274	64
54.24	F. M. M. Worrell	1941-64	326	49	15,025	308*	39
53.78	R. M. Cowper	1959-69	228	31	10,595	307	26
53.67	**Javed Miandad**	**1973-92**	**626**	**95**	**28,504**	**311**	**80**
53.67	A. R. Morris	1940-63	250	15	12,614	290	12
52.86	D. B. Vengsarkar	1975-91	390	52	17,868	284	55
52.36	**M. Azharuddin**	**1981-92**	**219**	**25**	**10,158**	**226**	**34**
52.32	Hanif Mohammad	1951-75	371	45	17,059	499	55
52.27	P. R. Umrigar	1944-67	350	41	16,154	252*	49
52.20	G. S. Chappell	1966-83	542	72	24,535	247*	74
51.95	H. Sutcliffe	1919-45	1,088	123	50,138	313	149
51.85	D. C. S. Compton	1936-64	839	88	38,942	300	123
51.54	Zaheer Abbas	1965-86	768	92	34,843	274	108
51.53	A. D. Nourse	1931-52	269	27	12,472	260*	41
51.49	**A. R. Border**	**1976-93**	**570**	**89**	**24,770**	**205**	**66**
51.46	S. M. Gavaskar	1966-87	563	61	25,834	340	81
51.44	W. A. Brown	1932-49	284	15	13,838	265*	39
51.00	P. B. H. May	1948-63	618	77	27,592	285*	85

Avge		Career	I	NO	R	HS	100s
50.95	N. C. O'Neill	1955-67	306	34	13,859	284	45
50.93	R. N. Harvey	1946-62	461	35	21,699	231*	67
50.90	W. M. Lawry	1955-71	417	49	18,734	266	50
50.90	A. V. Mankad	1963-82	326	71	12,980	265	31
50.80	E. H. Hendren	1907-38	1,300	166	57,611	301*	170
50.68	**K. C. Wessels**	**1973-92**	**435**	**37**	**20,172**	**254**	**54**
50.65	J. B. Hobbs	1905-34	1,315	106	61,237	316*	197
50.40	**D. M. Jones**	**1981-93**	**278**	**30**	**12,500**	**248**	**35**
50.33	**S. J. Cook**	**1972-92**	**449**	**53**	**19,931**	**313***	**59**
50.22	C. B. Fry	1892-1921	658	43	30,886	258*	94
50.19	**M. W. Gatting**	**1975-93**	**713**	**113**	**30,114**	**258**	**76**
50.01	Shafiq Ahmad	1967-90	449	58	19,555	217*	53

Bold type denotes those who played Test cricket in 1992-93 and 1993 seasons or Sri Lanka v India and South Africa in 1993-94.

FASTEST FIFTIES

Minutes

11	C. I. J. Smith (66)	Middlesex v Gloucestershire at Bristol	1938
14	S. J. Pegler (50)	South Africans v Tasmania at Launceston	1910-11
14	F. T. Mann (53)	Middlesex v Nottinghamshire at Lord's	1921
14	H. B. Cameron (56)	Transvaal v Orange Free State at Johannesburg. . . .	1934-35
14	C. I. J. Smith (52)	Middlesex v Kent at Maidstone	1935

Note: The following fast fifties were scored in contrived circumstances when runs were given from full tosses and long hops to expedite a declaration: C. C. Inman (8 minutes), Leicestershire v Nottinghamshire at Nottingham, 1965; G. Chapple (10 minutes), Lancashire v Glamorgan at Manchester, 1993; T. M. Moody (11 minutes), Warwickshire v Glamorgan at Swansea, 1990; A. J. Stewart (14 minutes), Surrey v Kent at Dartford, 1986; M. P. Maynard (14 minutes), Glamorgan v Yorkshire at Cardiff, 1987.

FASTEST HUNDREDS

Minutes

35	P. G. H. Fender (113*)	Surrey v Northamptonshire at Northampton . . .	1920
40	G. L. Jessop (101)	Gloucestershire v Yorkshire at Harrogate	1897
40	Ahsan-ul-Haq (100*)	Muslims v Sikhs at Lahore	1923-24
42	G. L. Jessop (191)	Gentlemen of South v Players of South at Hastings	1907
43	A. H. Hornby (106)	Lancashire v Somerset at Manchester	1905
43	D. W. Hookes (107)	South Australia v Victoria at Adelaide.	1982-83
44	R. N. S. Hobbs (100)	Essex v Australians at Chelmsford	1975

Notes: The fastest recorded authentic hundred in terms of balls received was scored off 34 balls by D. W. Hookes (above).

Research of the scorebook has shown that P. G. H. Fender scored his hundred from between 40 and 46 balls. He contributed 113 to an unfinished sixth-wicket partnership of 171 in 42 minutes with H. A. Peach.

E. B. Alletson (Nottinghamshire) scored 189 out of 227 runs in 90 minutes against Sussex at Hove in 1911. It has been estimated that his last 139 runs took 37 minutes.

The following fast hundreds were scored in contrived circumstances when runs were given from full tosses and long hops to expedite a declaration: G. Chapple (21 minutes), Lancashire v Glamorgan at Manchester, 1993; T. M. Moody (26 minutes), Warwickshire v Glamorgan at Swansea, 1990; S. J. O'Shaughnessy (35 minutes), Lancashire v Leicestershire at Manchester, 1983; C. M. Old (37 minutes), Yorkshire v Warwickshire at Birmingham, 1977; N. F. M. Popplewell (41 minutes), Somerset v Gloucestershire at Bath, 1983.

FASTEST DOUBLE-HUNDREDS

Minutes
113	R. J. Shastri (200*)	Bombay v Baroda at Bombay...............	1984-85
120	G. L. Jessop (286)	Gloucestershire v Sussex at Hove...........	1903
120	C. H. Lloyd (201*)	West Indians v Glamorgan at Swansea......	1976
130	G. L. Jessop (234)	Gloucestershire v Somerset at Bristol........	1905
131	V. T. Trumper (293)	Australians v Canterbury at Christchurch.....	1913-14

FASTEST TRIPLE-HUNDREDS

Minutes
181	D. C. S. Compton (300)	MCC v N. E. Transvaal at Benoni..........	1948-49
205	F. E. Woolley (305*)	MCC v Tasmania at Hobart................	1911-12
205	C. G. Macartney (345)	Australians v Nottinghamshire at Nottingham.	1921
213	D. G. Bradman (369)	South Australia v Tasmania at Adelaide......	1935-36

300 RUNS IN ONE DAY

345	C. G. Macartney	Australians v Nottinghamshire at Nottingham........	1921
334	W. H. Ponsford	Victoria v New South Wales at Melbourne............	1926-27
333	K. S. Duleepsinhji	Sussex v Northamptonshire at Hove	1930
331*	J. D. Robertson	Middlesex v Worcestershire at Worcester	1949
325*	B. A. Richards	S. Australia v W. Australia at Perth	1970-71
322†	E. Paynter	Lancashire v Sussex at Hove	1937
322	I. V. A. Richards	Somerset v Warwickshire at Taunton	1985
318	C. W. Gregory	New South Wales v Queensland at Brisbane..........	1906-07
317	K. R. Rutherford	New Zealanders v D. B. Close's XI at Scarborough....	1986
316†	R. H. Moore	Hampshire v Warwickshire at Bournemouth	1937
315*	R. C. Blunt	Otago v Canterbury at Christchurch	1931-32
312*	J. M. Brearley	MCC Under 25 v North Zone at Peshawar	1966-67
311*	G. M. Turner	Worcestershire v Warwickshire at Worcester	1982
311*	N. H. Fairbrother	Lancashire v Surrey at The Oval	1990
309*	D. G. Bradman	Australia v England at Leeds	1930
307*	W. H. Ashdown	Kent v Essex at Brentwood....................	1934
306*	A. Ducat	Surrey v Oxford University at The Oval	1919
305*	F. R. Foster	Warwickshire v Worcestershire at Dudley..........	1914

† *E. Paynter's 322 and R. H. Moore's 316 were scored on the same day: July 28, 1937.*

1,000 RUNS IN MAY

	Runs	*Avge*
W. G. Grace, May 9 to May 30, 1895 (22 days):		
13, 103, 18, 25, 288, 52, 257, 73*, 18, 169	1,016	112.88
Grace was within two months of completing his 47th year.		
W. R. Hammond, May 7 to May 31, 1927 (25 days):		
27, 135, 108, 128, 17, 11, 99, 187, 4, 30, 83, 7, 192, 14	1,042	74.42
Hammond scored his 1,000th run on May 28, thus equalling Grace's record of 22 days.		
C. Hallows, May 5 to May 31, 1928 (27 days):		
100, 101, 51*, 123, 101*, 22, 74, 104, 58, 34*, 232	1,000	125.00

1,000 RUNS IN APRIL AND MAY

	Runs	*Avge*
T. W. Hayward, April 16 to May 31, 1900:		
120*, 55, 108, 131*, 55, 193, 120, 5, 6, 3, 40, 146, 92...........	1,074	97.63
D. G. Bradman, April 30 to May 31, 1930:		
236, 185*, 78, 9, 48*, 66, 4, 44, 252*, 32, 47*	1,001	143.00
On April 30 Bradman was 75 not out.		

D. G. Bradman, April 30 to May 31, 1938:

258, 58, 137, 278, 2, 143, 145*, 5, 30*	1,056	150.85

    Bradman scored 258 on April 30, and his 1,000th run on May 27.

W. J. Edrich, April 30 to May 31, 1938:

104, 37, 115, 63, 20*, 182, 71, 31, 53*, 45, 15, 245, 0, 9, 20*	1,010	84.16

    Edrich was 21 not out on April 30. All his runs were scored at
Lord's.

G. M. Turner, April 24 to May 31, 1973:

41, 151*, 143, 85, 7, 8, 17*, 81, 13, 53, 44, 153*, 3, 2, 66*, 30, 10*, 111	1,018	78.30

G. A. Hick, April 17 to May 29, 1988:

61, 37, 212, 86, 14, 405*, 8, 11, 6, 7, 172.	1,019	101.90

    Hick scored a record 410 runs in April, and his 1,000th run on
May 28.

1,000 RUNS IN TWO SEPARATE MONTHS

Only four batsmen, C. B. Fry, K. S. Ranjitsinhji, H. Sutcliffe and L. Hutton, have scored over
1,000 runs in each of two months in the same season. L. Hutton, by scoring 1,294 in June 1949,
made more runs in a single month than anyone else. He also made 1,050 in August 1949.

MOST RUNS SCORED OFF ONE OVER

(All instances refer to six-ball overs)

36	G. S. Sobers	off M. A. Nash, Nottinghamshire v Glamorgan at Swansea (six sixes)	1968
36	R. J. Shastri	off Tilak Raj, Bombay v Baroda at Bombay (six sixes) . . .	1984-85
34	E. B. Alletson	off E. H. Killick, Sussex v Sussex at Hove (46604446; including two no-balls)	1911
34	F. C. Hayes	off M. A. Nash, Lancashire v Glamorgan at Swansea (646666)	1977
32	I. T. Botham	off I. R. Snook, England XI v Central Districts at Palmerston North (466666)	1983-84
32	P. W. G. Parker	off A. I. Kallicharran, Sussex v Warwickshire at Birmingham (466664)	1982
32	I. R. Redpath	off N. Rosendorff, Australians v Orange Free State at Bloemfontein (666644)	1969-70
32	C. C. Smart	off G. Hill, Glamorgan v Hampshire at Cardiff (664664) .	1935

Notes: The following instances have been excluded from the above table because of the bowlers'
compliance: 34 – M. P. Maynard off S. A. Marsh, Glamorgan v Kent at Swansea, 1992;
34 – G. Chapple off P. A. Cottey, Lancashire v Glamorgan at Manchester, 1993; 32 –
C. C. Inman off N. W. Hill, Leicestershire v Nottinghamshire at Nottingham, 1965; 32 – T. E.
Jesty off R. J. Boyd-Moss, Hampshire v Northamptonshire at Southampton, 1984; 32 –
G. Chapple off P. A. Cottey, Lancashire v Glamorgan at Manchester, 1983. Chapple's 34 and
32 came off successive overs from Cottey.

    The greatest number of runs scored off an eight-ball over is 34 (40446664) by R. M. Edwards
off M. C. Carew, Governor-General's XI v West Indians at Auckland, 1968-69.

    In a Shell Trophy match against Canterbury at Christchurch in 1989-90, R. H. Vance
(Wellington), acting on the instructions of his captain, deliberately conceded 77 runs in an over
of full tosses which contained 17 no-balls and, owing to the umpire's miscalculation, only five
legitimate deliveries.

MOST SIXES IN AN INNINGS

15	J. R. Reid (296)	Wellington v N. Districts at Wellington	1962-63
14	Shakti Singh (128)	Himachal Pradesh v Haryana at Dharmsala ...	1990-91
13	Majid Khan (147*)	Pakistanis v Glamorgan at Swansea	1967
13	C. G. Greenidge (273*)	D. H. Robins' XI v Pakistanis at Eastbourne ..	1974
13	C. G. Greenidge (259)	Hampshire v Sussex at Southampton	1975
13	G. W. Humpage (254)	Warwickshire v Lancashire at Southport	1982
13	R. J. Shastri (200*)	Bombay v Baroda at Bombay	1984-85
12	Gulfraz Khan (207)	Railways v Universities at Lahore	1976-77
12	I. T. Botham (138*)	Somerset v Warwickshire at Birmingham	1985
12	R. A. Harper (234)	Northamptonshire v Gloucestershire at Northampton	1986
12	D. M. Jones (248)	Australians v Warwickshire at Birmingham	1989
12	D. N. Patel (204)	Auckland v Northern Districts at Auckland ...	1991-92
12	W. V. Raman (206)	Tamil Nadu v Kerala at Madras	1991-92
11	C. K. Nayudu (153)	Hindus v MCC at Bombay	1926-27
11	C. J. Barnett (194)	Gloucestershire v Somerset at Bath	1934
11	R. Benaud (135)	Australians v T. N. Pearce's XI at Scarborough	1953
11	R. Bora (126)	Assam v Tripura at Gauhati	1987-88
11	G. A. Hick (405*)	Worcestershire v Somerset at Taunton	1988

Note: W. J. Stewart (Warwickshire) hit 17 sixes in the match v Lancashire, at Blackpool, 1959: ten in his first innings of 155 and seven in his second innings of 125.

MOST SIXES IN A SEASON

80	I. T. Botham	1985		57	A. W. Wellard	1938
66	A. W. Wellard	1935		51	A. W. Wellard	1933
57	A. W. Wellard	1936				

MOST BOUNDARIES IN AN INNINGS

	4s/6s			
68	68/–	P. A. Perrin (343*)	Essex v Derbyshire at Chesterfield	1904
64	64/–	Hanif Mohammad (499)	Karachi v Bahawalpur at Karachi	1958-59
63	62/1	A. C. MacLaren (424)	Lancashire v Somerset at Taunton	1895
57	52/5	J. H. Edrich (310*)	England v New Zealand at Leeds	1965
55	55/–	C. W. Gregory (383)	NSW v Queensland at Brisbane	1906-07
55	53/2	G. R. Marsh (355*)	W. Australia v S. Australia at Perth	1989-90
54	53/1	G. H. Hirst (341)	Yorkshire v Leicestershire at Leicester	1905
54	51/2†	S. V. Manjrekar (377)	Bombay v Hyderabad at Bombay	1990-91
53	53/–	A. W. Nourse (304*)	Natal v Transvaal at Johannesburg	1919-20
53	45/8	K. R. Rutherford (317)	New Zealanders v D. B. Close's XI at Scarborough	1986
52	47/5	N. H. Fairbrother (366)	Lancashire v Surrey at The Oval	1990
51	47/4	C. G. Macartney (345)	Australians v Notts. at Nottingham	1921
51	50/1	B. B. Nimbalkar (443*)	Maharashtra v Kathiawar at Poona	1948-49
50	46/4	D. G. Bradman (369)	S. Australia v Tasmania at Adelaide ..	1935-36
50	47/–‡	A. Ducat (306*)	Surrey v Oxford U. at The Oval	1919
50	35/15	J. R. Reid (296)	Wellington v N. Districts at Wellington	1962-63
50	42/8	I. V. A. Richards (322)	Somerset v Warwickshire at Taunton .	1985

† Plus one five.
‡ Plus three fives.

HIGHEST PARTNERSHIPS

577	V. S. Hazare (288) and Gul Mohomed (319), fourth wicket, Baroda v Holkar at Baroda	1946-47
574*	F. M. M. Worrell (255*) and C. L. Walcott (314*), fourth wicket, Barbados v Trinidad at Port-of-Spain	1945-46
561	Waheed Mirza (324) and Mansoor Akhtar (224*), first wicket, Karachi Whites v Quetta at Karachi	1976-77
555	P. Holmes (224*) and H. Sutcliffe (313), first wicket, Yorkshire v Essex at Leyton	1932
554	J. T. Brown (300) and J. Tunnicliffe (243), first wicket, Yorkshire v Derbyshire at Chesterfield	1898
502*	F. M. M. Worrell (308*) and J. D. C. Goddard (218*), fourth wicket, Barbados v Trinidad at Bridgetown	1943-44
490	E. H. Bowley (283) and J. G. Langridge (195), first wicket, Sussex v Middlesex at Hove	1933
487*	G. A. Headley (344*) and C. C. Passailaigue (261*), sixth wicket, Jamaica v Lord Tennyson's XI at Kingston	1931-32
475	Zahir Alam (257) and L. S. Rajput (239), second wicket, Assam v Tripura at Gauhati	1991-92
470	A. I. Kallicharran (230*) and G. W. Humpage (254), fourth wicket, Warwickshire v Lancashire at Southport	1982

HIGHEST PARTNERSHIPS FOR EACH WICKET

The following lists include all stands above 400; otherwise the top ten for each wicket.

First Wicket

561	Waheed Mirza and Mansoor Akhtar, Karachi Whites v Quetta at Karachi	1976-77
555	P. Holmes and H. Sutcliffe, Yorkshire v Essex at Leyton	1932
554	J. T. Brown and J. Tunnicliffe, Yorkshire v Derbyshire at Chesterfield	1898
490	E. H. Bowley and J. G. Langridge, Sussex v Middlesex at Hove	1933
456	E. R. Mayne and W. H. Ponsford, Victoria v Queensland at Melbourne	1923-24
451*	S. Desai and R. M. H. Binny, Karnataka v Kerala at Chikmagalur	1977-78
431	M. R. J. Veletta and G. R. Marsh, Western Australia v South Australia at Perth	1989-90
428	J. B Hobbs and A. Sandham, Surrey v Oxford University at The Oval	1926
424	I. J. Siedle and J. F. W. Nicolson, Natal v Orange Free State at Bloemfontein	1926-27
421	S. M. Gavaskar and G. A. Parkar, Bombay v Bengal at Bombay	1981-82
418	Kamal Najamuddin and Khalid Alvi, Karachi v Railways at Karachi	1980-81
413	V. Mankad and Pankaj Roy, India v New Zealand at Madras	1955-56
405	C. P. S. Chauhan and M. S. Gupte, Maharashtra v Vidarbha at Poona	1972-73

Second Wicket

475	Zahir Alam and L. S. Rajput, Assam v Tripura at Gauhati	1991-92
465*	J. A. Jameson and R. B. Kanhai, Warwicks. v Gloucestershire at Birmingham	1974
455	K. V. Bhandarkar and B. B. Nimbalkar, Maharashtra v Kathiawar at Poona	1948-49
451	W. H. Ponsford and D. G. Bradman, Australia v England at The Oval	1934
446	C. C. Hunte and G. S. Sobers, West Indies v Pakistan at Kingston	1957-58
429*	J. G. Dewes and G. H. G. Doggart, Cambridge U. v Essex at Cambridge	1949
426	Arshad Pervez and Mohsin Khan, Habib Bank v Income Tax at Lahore	1977-78
415	A. D. Jadeja and S. V. Manjrekar, Indians v Bowl XI at Springs	1992-93
403	G. A. Gooch and P. J. Prichard, Essex v Leicestershire at Chelmsford	1990
398	A. Shrewsbury and W. Gunn, Nottinghamshire v Sussex at Nottingham	1890

Third Wicket

467	A. H. Jones and M. D. Crowe, New Zealand v Sri Lanka at Wellington ..	1990-91
456	Khalid Irtiza and Aslam Ali, United Bank v Multan at Karachi	1975-76
451	Mudassar Nazar and Javed Miandad, Pakistan v India at Hyderabad	1982-83
445	P. E. Whitelaw and W. N. Carson, Auckland v Otago at Dunedin	1936-37
434	J. B. Stollmeyer and G. E. Gomez, Trinidad v British Guiana at Port-of-Spain	1946-47
424*	W. J. Edrich and D. C. S. Compton, Middlesex v Somerset at Lord's	1948
413	D. J. Bicknell and D. M. Ward, Surrey v Kent at Canterbury	1990
410	R. S. Modi and L. Amarnath, India in England v The Rest at Calcutta ...	1946-47
405	A. D. Jadeja and A. S. Kaypee, Haryana v Services at Faridabad	1991-92
399	R. T. Simpson and D. C. S. Compton, MCC v N. E. Transvaal at Benoni.	1948-49

Fourth Wicket

577	V. S. Hazare and Gul Mahomed, Baroda v Holkar at Baroda	1946-47
574*	C. L. Walcott and F. M. M. Worrell, Barbados v Trinidad at Port-of-Spain	1945-46
502*	F. M. M. Worrell and J. D. C. Goddard, Barbados v Trinidad at Bridgetown	1943-44
470	A. I. Kallicharran and G. W. Humpage, Warwicks. v Lancs. at Southport .	1982
462*	D. W. Hookes and B. B. Phillips, South Australia v Tasmania at Adelaide	1986-87
448	R. Abel and T. W. Hayward, Surrey v Yorkshire at The Oval	1899
425*	A. Dale and I. V. A. Richards, Glamorgan v Middlesex at Cardiff	1993
424	I. S. Lee and S. O. Quin, Victoria v Tasmania at Melbourne	1933-34
411	P. B. H. May and M. C. Cowdrey, England v West Indies at Birmingham.	1957
410	G. Abraham and P. Balan Pandit, Kerala v Andhra at Palghat	1959-60
402	W. Watson and T. W. Graveney, MCC v British Guiana at Georgetown .	1953-54
402	R. B. Kanhai and K. Ibadulla, Warwicks. v Notts. at Nottingham	1968

Note: The partnership between A. Dale and I. V. A. Richards includes 13 runs for no-balls under TCCB playing conditions. Under the Laws of Cricket, only five runs would have resulted from six no-balls bowled in this partnership.

Fifth Wicket

464*	M. E. Waugh and S. R. Waugh, New South Wales v Western Australia at Perth	1990-91
405	S. G. Barnes and D. G. Bradman, Australia v England at Sydney	1946-47
397	W. Bardsley and C. Kelleway, New South Wales v South Australia at Sydney	1920-21
393	E. G. Arnold and W. B. Burns, Worcestershire v Warwickshire at Birmingham	1909
360	U. M. Merchant and M. N. Raiji, Bombay v Hyderabad at Bombay	1947-48
355	Altaf Shah and Tariq Bashir, HBFC v Multan at Multan	1976-77
355	A. J. Lamb and J. J. Strydom, OFS v Eastern Province at Bloemfontein ..	1987-88
347	D. Brookes and D. W. Barrick, Northamptonshire v Essex at Northampton	1952
344	M. C. Cowdrey and T. W. Graveney, MCC v South Australia at Adelaide .	1962-63
343	R. I. Maddocks and J. Hallebone, Victoria v Tasmania at Melbourne	1951-52

Note: The Waugh twins achieved the first instance of brothers each scoring a double-hundred in the same first-class innings. Their partnership includes 20 runs for no-balls under ACB playing conditions. Under the Laws of Cricket, only seven runs would have resulted from ten no-balls bowled in this partnership.

Sixth Wicket

487*	G. A. Headley and C. C. Passailaigue, Jamaica v Lord Tennyson's XI at Kingston	1931-32
428	W. W. Armstrong and M. A. Noble, Australians v Sussex at Hove	1902
411	R. M. Poore and E. G. Wynyard, Hampshire v Somerset at Taunton	1899
376	R. Subba Row and A. Lightfoot, Northamptonshire v Surrey at The Oval .	1958
371	V. M. Merchant and R. S. Modi, Bombay v Maharashtra at Bombay	1943-44
356	W. V. Raman and A. Kripal Singh, Tamil Nadu v Goa at Panjim	1988-89
353	Salah-ud-Din and Zaheer Abbas, Karachi v East Pakistan at Karachi......	1968-69
346	J. H. W. Fingleton and D. G. Bradman, Australia v England at Melbourne	1936-37
332	N. G. Marks and G. Thomas, New South Wales v South Australia at Sydney	1958-59
323	E. H. Hendren and J. W. H. T. Douglas, MCC v Victoria at Melbourne ..	1920-21

Seventh Wicket

347	D. St E. Atkinson and C. C. Depeiza, West Indies v Australia at Bridgetown	1954-55
344	K. S. Ranjitsinhji and W. Newham, Sussex v Essex at Leyton	1902
340	K. J. Key and H. Philipson, Oxford University v Middlesex at Chiswick Park	1887
336	F. C. W. Newman and C. R. N. Maxwell, Sir J. Cahn's XI v Leicestershire at Nottingham	1935
335	C. W. Andrews and E. C. Bensted, Queensland v New South Wales at Sydney	1934-35
325	G. Brown and C. H. Abercrombie, Hampshire v Essex at Leyton	1913
323	E. H. Hendren and L. F. Townsend, MCC v Barbados at Bridgetown	1929-30
308	Waqar Hassan and Imtiaz Ahmed, Pakistan v New Zealand at Lahore	1955-56
301	C. C. Lewis and B. N. French, Nottinghamshire v Durham at Chester-le-Street	1993
299	B. Mitchell and A. Melville, Transvaal v Griqualand West at Kimberley	1946-47

Eighth Wicket

433	V. T. Trumper and A. Sims, A. Sims' Aust. XI v Canterbury at Christchurch	1913-14
292	R. Peel and Lord Hawke, Yorkshire v Warwickshire at Birmingham	1896
270	V. T. Trumper and E. P. Barbour, New South Wales v Victoria at Sydney	1912-13
263	D. R. Wilcox and R. M. Taylor, Essex v Warwickshire at Southend	1946
255	E. A. V. Williams and E. A. Martindale, Barbados v Trinidad at Bridgetown	1935-36
246	L. E. G. Ames and G. O. B. Allen, England v New Zealand at Lord's	1931
243	R. J. Hartigan and G. Hill, Australia v England at Adelaide	1907-08
242*	T. J. Zoehrer and K. H. MacLeay, W. Australia v New South Wales at Perth	1990-91
240	Gulfraz Khan and Raja Sarfraz, Railways v Universities at Lahore	1976-77
239	W. R. Hammond and A. E. Wilson, Gloucestershire v Lancashire at Bristol	1938

Ninth Wicket

283	J. Chapman and A. Warren, Derbyshire v Warwickshire at Blackwell	1910
251	J. W. H. T. Douglas and S. N. Hare, Essex v Derbyshire at Leyton	1921
245	V. S. Hazare and N. D. Nagarwalla, Maharashtra v Baroda at Poona	1939-40
244*	Arshad Ayub and M. V. Ramanamurthy, Hyderabad v Bihar at Hyderabad	1986-87
239	H. B. Cave and I. B. Leggat, Central Districts v Otago at Dunedin	1952-53
232	C. Hill and E. Walkley, South Australia v New South Wales at Adelaide	1900-01
231	P. Sen and J. Mitter, Bengal v Bihar at Jamshedpur	1950-51
230	D. A. Livingstone and A. T. Castell, Hampshire v Surrey at Southampton	1962
226	C. Kelleway and W. A. Oldfield, New South Wales v Victoria at Melbourne	1925-26
225	W. W. Armstrong and E. A. Windsor, Australian XI v The Rest at Sydney	1907-08

Tenth Wicket

307	A. F. Kippax and J. E. H. Hooker, New South Wales v Victoria at Melbourne	1928-29
249	C. T. Sarwate and S. N. Banerjee, Indians v Surrey at The Oval	1946
235	F. E. Woolley and A. Fielder, Kent v Worcestershire at Stourbridge	1909
233	Ajay Sharma and Maninder Singh, Delhi v Bombay at Bombay	1991-92
230	R. W. Nicholls and W. Roche, Middlesex v Kent at Lord's	1899
228	R. Illingworth and K. Higgs, Leicestershire v Northamptonshire at Leicester	1977
218	F. H. Vigar and T. P. B. Smith, Essex v Derbyshire at Chesterfield	1947
211	M. Ellis and T. J. Hastings, Victoria v South Australia at Melbourne	1902-03
196*	Nadim Yousuf and Maqsood Kundi, MCB v National Bank at Lahore	1981-82
192	H. A. W. Bowell and W. H. Livsey, Hampshire v Worcs. at Bournemouth	1921

UNUSUAL DISMISSALS

Handled the Ball

J. Grundy	MCC v Kent at Lord's	1857
G. Bennett	Kent v Sussex at Hove	1872
W. H. Scotton	Smokers v Non-Smokers at East Melbourne	1886-87
C. W. Wright	Nottinghamshire v Gloucestershire at Bristol	1893
E. Jones	South Australia v Victoria at Melbourne	1894-95
A. W. Nourse	South Africans v Sussex at Hove	1907
E. T. Benson	MCC v Auckland at Auckland	1929-30
A. W. Gilbertson	Otago v Auckland at Auckland	1952-53
W. R. Endean	South Africa v England at Cape Town	1956-57
P. J. Burge	Queensland v New South Wales at Sydney	1958-59
Dildar Awan	Services v Lahore at Lahore	1959-60
M. Mehra	Railways v Delhi at Delhi	1959-60
Mahmood-ul-Hasan	Karachi University v Railways-Quetta at Karachi	1960-61
Ali Raza	Karachi Greens v Hyderabad at Karachi	1961-62
Mohammad Yusuf	Rawalpindi v Peshawar at Peshawar	1962-63
A. Rees	Glamorgan v Middlesex at Lord's	1965
Pervez Akhtar	Multan v Karachi Greens at Sahiwal	1971-72
Javed Mirza	Railways v Punjab at Lahore	1972-73
R. G. Pollock	Eastern Province v Western Province at Cape Town	1973-74
C. I. Dey	Northern Transvaal v Orange Free State at Bloemfontein	1973-74
Nasir Valika	Karachi Whites v National Bank at Karachi	1974-75
Haji Yousuf	National Bank v Railways at Lahore	1974-75
Masood-ul-Hasan	PIA v National Bank B at Lyallpur	1975-76
D. K. Pearse	Natal v Western Province at Cape Town	1978-79
A. M. J. Hilditch	Australia v Pakistan at Perth	1978-79
Musleh-ud-Din	Railways v Lahore at Lahore	1979-80
Jalal-ud-Din	IDBP v Habib Bank at Bahawalpur	1981-82
Mohsin Khan	Pakistan v Australia at Karachi	1982-83
D. L. Haynes	West Indies v India at Bombay	1983-84
K. Azad	Delhi v Punjab at Amritsar	1983-84
Athar A. Khan	Allied Bank v HBFC at Sialkot	1983-84
A. N. Pandya	Saurashtra v Baroda at Baroda	1984-85
G. L. Linton	Barbados v Windward Islands at Bridgetown	1985-86
R. B. Gartrell	Tasmania v Victoria at Melbourne	1986-87
R. Nayyar	Himachal Pradesh v Punjab at Una	1988-89
R. Weerawardene	Moratuwa v Nomads SC at Colombo	1988-89
A. M. Kane	Vidarbha v Railways at Nagpur	1989-90
P. Bali	Jammu and Kashmir v Services at Delhi	1991-92
M. J. Davis	Northern Transvaal B v OFS B at Bloemfontein	1991-92
J. T. C. Vaughan	Emerging Players v England XI at Hamilton	1991-92
G. A. Gooch	England v Australia at Manchester	1993

Obstructing the Field

C. A. Absolom	Cambridge University v Surrey at The Oval	1868
T. Straw	Worcestershire v Warwickshire at Worcester	1899
T. Straw	Worcestershire v Warwickshire at Birmingham	1901
J. P. Whiteside	Leicestershire v Lancashire at Leicester	1901
L. Hutton	England v South Africa at The Oval	1951
J. A. Hayes	Canterbury v Central Districts at Christchurch	1954-55
D. D. Deshpande	Madhya Pradesh v Uttar Pradesh at Benares	1956-57
K. Ibadulla	Warwickshire v Hampshire at Coventry	1963
Qaiser Khan	Dera Ismail Khan v Railways at Lahore	1964-65
Ijaz Ahmed	Lahore Greens v Lahore Blues at Lahore	1973-74
Qasim Feroze	Bahawalpur v Universities at Lahore	1974-75
T. Quirk	Northern Transvaal v Border at East London	1978-79
Mahmood Rashid	United Bank v Muslim Commercial Bank at Bahawalpur	1981-82
Arshad Ali	Sukkur v Quetta at Quetta	1983-84
H. R. Wasu	Vidarbha v Rajasthan at Akola	1984-85
Khalid Javed	Railways v Lahore at Lahore	1985-86
C. Binduhewa	Singha SC v Sinhalese SC at Colombo	1990-91

Hit the Ball Twice

H. E. Bull	MCC v Oxford University at Lord's	1864
H. R. J. Charlwood	Sussex v Surrey at Hove	1872
R. G. Barlow	North v South at Lord's	1878
P. S. Wimble	Transvaal v Griqualand West at Kimberley	1892-93
G. B. Nicholls	Somerset v Gloucestershire at Bristol	1896
A. A. Lilley	Warwickshire v Yorkshire at Birmingham	1897
J. H. King	Leicestershire v Surrey at The Oval	1906
A. P. Binns	Jamaica v British Guiana at Georgetown	1956-57
K. Bhavanna	Andhra v Mysore at Guntur	1963-64
Zaheer Abbas	PIA A v Karachi Blues at Karachi	1969-70
Anwar Miandad	IDBP v United Bank at Lahore	1979-80
Anwar Iqbal	Hyderabad v Sukkur at Hyderabad	1983-84
Iqtidar Ali	Allied Bank v Muslim Commercial Bank at Lahore	1983-84
Aziz Malik	Lahore Division v Faisalabad at Sialkot	1984-85
Javed Mohammad	Multan v Karachi Whites at Sahiwal	1986-87
Shahid Pervez	Jammu and Kashmir v Punjab at Srinigar	1986-87

BOWLING RECORDS

TEN WICKETS IN AN INNINGS

	O	M	R		
E. Hinkly (Kent)				v England at Lord's	1848
*J. Wisden (North)				v South at Lord's	1850
V. E. Walker (England)	43	17	74	v Surrey at The Oval	1859
V. E. Walker (Middlesex)	44.2	5	104	v Lancashire at Manchester	1865
G. Wootton (All England)	31.3	9	54	v Yorkshire at Sheffield	1865
W. Hickton (Lancashire)	36.2	19	46	v Hampshire at Manchester	1870
S. E. Butler (Oxford)	24.1	11	38	v Cambridge at Lord's	1871
James Lillywhite (South)	60.2	22	129	v North at Canterbury	1872
A. Shaw (MCC)	36.2	8	73	v North at Lord's	1874
E. Barratt (Players)	29	11	43	v Australians at The Oval	1878
G. Giffen (Australian XI)	26	10	66	v The Rest at Sydney	1883-84
W. G. Grace (MCC)	36.2	17	49	v Oxford University at Oxford	1886
G. Burton (Middlesex)	52.3	25	59	v Surrey at The Oval	1888
†A. E. Moss (Canterbury)	21.3	10	28	v Wellington at Christchurch	1889-90
S. M. J. Woods (Cambridge U.)	31	6	69	v Thornton's XI at Cambridge	1890
T. Richardson (Surrey)	15.3	3	45	v Essex at The Oval	1894
H. Pickett (Essex)	27	11	32	v Leicestershire at Leyton	1895
E. J. Tyler (Somerset)	34.3	15	49	v Surrey at Taunton	1895
W. P. Howell (Australians)	23.2	14	28	v Surrey at The Oval	1899
C. H. G. Bland (Sussex)	25.2	10	48	v Kent at Tonbridge	1899
J. Briggs (Lancashire)	28.5	7	55	v Worcestershire at Manchester	1900
A. E. Trott (Middlesex)	14.2	5	42	v Somerset at Taunton	1900
F. Hinds (A. B. St Hill's XI)	19.1	6	36	v Trinidad at Port-of-Spain	1900-01
A. Fielder (Players)	24.5	1	90	v Gentlemen at Lord's	1906
E. G. Dennett (Gloucestershire)	19.4	7	40	v Essex at Bristol	1906
A. E. E. Vogler (E. Province)	12	2	26	v Griqualand W. at Johannesburg	1906-07
C. Blythe (Kent)	16	7	30	v Northants at Northampton	1907
A. Drake (Yorkshire)	8.5	0	35	v Somerset at Weston-s-Mare	1914
W. Bestwick (Derbyshire)	19	2	40	v Glamorgan at Cardiff	1921
A. A. Mailey (Australians)	28.4	5	66	v Gloucestershire at Cheltenham	1921
C. W. L. Parker (Glos.)	40.3	13	79	v Somerset at Bristol	1921
T. Rushby (Surrey)	17.5	4	43	v Somerset at Taunton	1921
J. C. White (Somerset)	42.2	11	76	v Worcestershire at Worcester	1921
G. C. Collins (Kent)	19.3	4	65	v Nottinghamshire at Dover	1922
H. Howell (Warwickshire)	25.1	5	51	v Yorkshire at Birmingham	1923

	O	M	R		
A. S. Kennedy (Players)	22.4	10	37	v Gentlemen at The Oval	1927
G. O. B. Allen (Middlesex)	25.3	10	40	v Lancashire at Lord's	1929
A. P. Freeman (Kent)	42	9	131	v Lancashire at Maidstone	1929
G. Geary (Leicestershire)	16.2	8	18	v Glamorgan at Pontypridd	1929
C. V. Grimmett (Australians) . . .	22.3	8	37	v Yorkshire at Sheffield	1930
A. P. Freeman (Kent)	30.4	8	53	v Essex at Southend	1930
H. Verity (Yorkshire)	18.4	6	36	v Warwickshire at Leeds	1931
A. P. Freeman (Kent)	36.1	9	79	v Lancashire at Manchester	1931
V. W. C. Jupp (Northants)	39	6	127	v Kent at Tunbridge Wells	1932
H. Verity (Yorkshire)	19.4	16	10	v Nottinghamshire at Leeds	1932
T. W. Wall (South Australia) . . .	12.4	2	36	v New South Wales at Sydney . . .	1932-33
T. B. Mitchell (Derbyshire)	19.1	4	64	v Leicestershire at Leicester	1935
J. Mercer (Glamorgan)	26	10	51	v Worcestershire at Worcester . . .	1936
T. W. J. Goddard (Glos.)	28.4	4	113	v Worcestershire at Cheltenham .	1937
T. F. Smailes (Yorkshire)	17.1	5	47	v Derbyshire at Sheffield	1939
E. A. Watts (Surrey)	24.1	8	67	v Warwickshire at Birmingham . .	1939
*W. E. Hollies (Warwickshire) . .	20.4	4	49	v Notts. at Birmingham	1946
J. M. Sims (East)	18.4	2	90	v West at Kingston	1948
T. E. Bailey (Essex)	39.4	9	90	v Lancashire at Clacton	1949
J. K. Graveney (Glos.)	18.4	2	66	v Derbyshire at Chesterfield	1949
R. Berry (Lancashire)	36.2	9	102	v Worcestershire at Blackpool . . .	1953
S. P. Gupte (President's XI)	24.2	7	78	v Combined XI at Bombay	1954-55
J. C. Laker (Surrey)	46	18	88	v Australians at The Oval	1956
J. C. Laker (England)	51.2	23	53	v Australia at Manchester	1956
G. A. R. Lock (Surrey)	29.1	18	54	v Kent at Blackheath	1956
K. Smales (Nottinghamshire) . . .	41.3	20	66	v Gloucestershire at Stroud	1956
P. M. Chatterjee (Bengal)	19	11	20	v Assam at Jorhat	1956-57
J. D. Bannister (Warwickshire) .	23.3	11	41	v Comb. Services at Birmingham	1959
A. J. G. Pearson (Cambridge U.)	30.3	8	78	v Leics. at Loughborough	1961
N. I. Thomson (Sussex)	34.2	19	49	v Warwickshire at Worthing	1964
P. J. Allan (Queensland)	15.6	3	61	v Victoria at Melbourne	1965-66
I. J. Brayshaw (W. Australia) . . .	17.6	4	44	v Victoria at Perth	1967-68
Shahid Mahmood (Karachi					
Whites)	25	5	58	v Khairpur at Karachi	1969-70
E. E. Hemmings					
(International XI)	49.3	14	175	v West Indies XI at Kingston . . .	1982-83
P. Sunderam (Rajasthan)	22	5	78	v Vidarbha at Jodhpur	1985-86
S. T. Jefferies (W. Province)	22.5	7	59	v Orange Free State at Cape Town	1987-88
Imran Adil (Bahawalpur)	22.5	3	92	v Faisalabad at Faisalabad	1989-90
G. P. Wickremasinghe					
(Sinhalese SC)	19.2	5	41	v Kalutara at Colombo (SSC) . . .	1991-92

* J. Wisden and W. E. Hollies achieved the feat without the direct assistance of a fielder. Wisden's ten were all bowled; Hollies bowled seven and had three lbw.

† On debut in first-class cricket.

Note: The following instances were achieved in 12-a-side matches:

E. M. Grace (MCC)	32.2	7	69	v Gents of Kent at Canterbury . . .	1862
W. G. Grace (MCC)	46.1	15	92	v Kent at Canterbury	1873

OUTSTANDING ANALYSES

	O	M	R	W		
H. Verity (Yorkshire)	19.4	16	10	10	v Nottinghamshire at Leeds	1932
G. Elliott (Victoria)	19	17	2	9	v Tasmania at Launceston	1857-58
Ahad Khan (Railways)	6.3	4	7	9	v Dera Ismail Khan at Lahore . . .	1964-65
J. C. Laker (England)	14	12	2	8	v The Rest at Bradford	1950
D. Shackleton (Hampshire) . . .	11.1	7	4	8	v Somerset at Weston-s-Mare . . .	1955
E. Peate (Yorkshire)	16	11	5	8	v Surrey at Holbeck	1883

		O	M	R	W		
F. R. Spofforth (Australians)	.	8.3	6	3	7	v England XI at Birmingham	1884
W. A. Henderson (N.E. Transvaal)	. . . .	9.3	7	4	7	v Orange Free State at Bloemfontein	1937-38
Rajinder Goel (Haryana)	. . . . .	7	4	4	7	v Jammu and Kashmir at Chandigarh	1977-78
V. I. Smith (South Africans)	.	4.5	3	1	6	v Derbyshire at Derby	1947
S. Cosstick (Victoria)	. . . .	21.1	20	1	6	v Tasmania at Melbourne	1868-69
Israr Ali (Bahawalpur)	. . . .	11	10	1	6	v Dacca U. at Bahawalpur	1957-58
A. D. Pougher (MCC)	. . . .	3	3	0	5	v Australians at Lord's	1896
G. R. Cox (Sussex)	. . . .	6	6	0	5	v Somerset at Weston-s-Mare	1921
R. K. Tyldesley (Lancashire)	.	5	5	0	5	v Leicestershire at Manchester . . .	1924
P. T. Mills (Gloucestershire)	.	6.4	6	0	5	v Somerset at Bristol	1928

MOST WICKETS IN A MATCH

19-90	J. C. Laker	England v Australia at Manchester	1956
17-48	C. Blythe	Kent v Northamptonshire at Northampton	1907
17-50	C. T. B. Turner	Australians v England XI at Hastings	1888
17-54	W. P. Howell	Australians v Western Province at Cape Town . . .	1902-03
17-56	C. W. L. Parker	Gloucestershire v Essex at Gloucester	1925
17-67	A. P. Freeman	Kent v Sussex at Hove	1922
17-89	W. G. Grace	Gloucestershire v Nottinghamshire at Cheltenham.	1877
17-89	F. C. L. Matthews	Nottinghamshire v Northants at Nottingham	1923
17-91	H. Dean	Lancashire v Yorkshire at Liverpool	1913
17-91	H. Verity	Yorkshire v Essex at Leyton	1933
17-92	A. P. Freeman	Kent v Warwickshire at Folkestone	1932
17-103	W. Mycroft	Derbyshire v Hampshire at Southampton	1876
17-106	G. R. Cox	Sussex v Warwickshire at Horsham	1926
17-106	T. W. J. Goddard	Gloucestershire v Kent at Bristol	1939
17-119	W. Mead	Essex v Hampshire at Southampton	1895
17-137	W. Brearley	Lancashire v Somerset at Manchester	1905
17-159	S. F. Barnes	England v South Africa at Johannesburg	1913-14
17-201	G. Giffen	South Australia v Victoria at Adelaide	1885-86
17-212	J. C. Clay	Glamorgan v Worcestershire at Swansea	1937

Notes: H. A. Arkwright took 18 wickets for 96 runs in a 12-a-side match for Gentlemen of MCC v Gentlemen of Kent at Canterbury in 1861.

W. Mead took 17 wickets for 205 runs for Essex v Australians at Leyton in 1893, the year before Essex were raised to first-class status.

F. P. Fenner took 17 wickets for Cambridge Town Club v University of Cambridge at Cambridge in 1844.

SIXTEEN OR MORE WICKETS IN A DAY

17-48	C. Blythe	Kent v Northamptonshire at Northampton	1907
17-91	H. Verity	Yorkshire v Essex at Leyton	1933
17-106	T. W. J. Goddard	Gloucestershire v Kent at Bristol	1939
16-38	T. Emmett	Yorkshire v Cambridgeshire at Hunslet	1869
16-52	J. Southerton	South v North at Lord's	1875
16-69	T. G. Wass	Nottinghamshire v Lancashire at Liverpool	1906
16-38	A. E. E. Vogler	E. Province v Griqualand West at Johannesburg . .	1906-07
16-103	T. G. Wass	Nottinghamshire v Essex at Nottingham	1908
16-83	J. C. White	Somerset v Worcestershire at Bath	1919

FOUR WICKETS WITH CONSECUTIVE BALLS

J. Wells	Kent v Sussex at Brighton	1862
G. Ulyett	Lord Harris's XI v New South Wales at Sydney	1878-79
G. Nash	Lancashire v Somerset at Manchester	1882
J. B. Hide	Sussex v MCC and Ground at Lord's.................	1890
F. J. Shacklock	Nottinghamshire v Somerset at Nottingham	1893
A. D. Downes	Otago v Auckland at Dunedin.......................	1893-94
F. Martin	MCC and Ground v Derbyshire at Lord's	1895
A. W. Mold	Lancashire v Nottinghamshire at Nottingham	1895
W. Brearley†	Lancashire v Somerset at Manchester................	1905
S. Haigh	MCC v Army XI at Pretoria	1905-06
A. E. Trott‡	Middlesex v Somerset at Lord's.....................	1907
F. A. Tarrant	Middlesex v Gloucestershire at Bristol	1907
A. Drake	Yorkshire v Derbyshire at Chesterfield	1914
S. G. Smith	Northamptonshire v Warwickshire at Birmingham	1914
H. A. Peach	Surrey v Sussex at The Oval	1924
A. F. Borland	Natal v Griqualand West at Kimberley	1926-27
J. E. H. Hooker†	New South Wales v Victoria at Sydney	1928-29
R. K. Tyldesley†	Lancashire v Derbyshire at Derby	1929
R. J. Crisp	Western Province v Griqualand West at Johannesburg ...	1931-32
R. J. Crisp	Western Province v Natal at Durban	1933-34
A. R. Gover	Surrey v Worcestershire at Worcester.................	1935
W. H. Copson	Derbyshire v Warwickshire at Derby	1937
W. A. Henderson	N.E. Transvaal v Orange Free State at Bloemfontein....	1937-38
F. Ridgway	Kent v Derbyshire at Folkestone	1951
A. K. Walker§	Nottinghamshire v Leicestershire at Leicester	1956
S. N. Mohol	President's XI v Combined XI at Poona	1965-66
P. I. Pocock	Surrey v Sussex at Eastbourne	1972
S. S. Saini†	Delhi v Himachal Pradesh at Delhi	1988-89
D. Dias	W. Province (Suburbs) v Central Province at Colombo ..	1990-91

† *Not all in the same innings.*

‡ *Trott achieved another hat-trick in the same innings of this, his benefit match.*

§ *Walker dismissed Firth with the last ball of the first innings and Lester, Tompkin and Smithson with the first three balls of the second innings, a feat without parallel.*

Notes : In their match with England at The Oval in 1863, Surrey lost four wickets in the course of a four-ball over from G. Bennett.

Sussex lost five wickets in the course of the final (six-ball) over of their match with Surrey at Eastbourne in 1972. P. I. Pocock, who had taken three wickets in his previous over, captured four more, taking in all seven wickets with 11 balls, a feat unique in first-class matches. (The eighth wicket fell to a run-out.)

HAT-TRICKS

Double Hat-Trick

Besides Trott's performance, which is given in the preceding section, the following instances are recorded of players having performed the hat-trick twice in the same match, Rao doing so in the same innings.

A. Shaw	Nottinghamshire v Gloucestershire at Nottingham	1884
T. J. Matthews	Australia v South Africa at Manchester	1912
C. W. L. Parker	Gloucestershire v Middlesex at Bristol	1924
R. O. Jenkins	Worcestershire v Surrey at Worcester	1949
J. S. Rao	Services v Northern Punjab at Amritsar	1963-64
Amin Lakhani	Combined XI v Indians at Multan	1978-79

Five Wickets with Six Consecutive Balls

W. H. Copson	Derbyshire v Warwickshire at Derby	1937
W. A. Henderson	N.E. Transvaal v Orange Free State at Bloemfontein....	1937-38
P. I. Pocock	Surrey v Sussex at Eastbourne	1972

Most Hat-Tricks

Seven times: D. V. P. Wright.
Six times: T. W. J. Goddard, C. W. L. Parker.
Five times: S. Haigh, V. W. C. Jupp, A. E. G. Rhodes, F. A. Tarrant.
Four times: R. G. Barlow, J. T. Hearne, J. C. Laker, G. A. R. Lock, G. G. Macaulay, T. J. Matthews, M. J. Procter, T. Richardson, F. R. Spofforth, F. S. Trueman.
Three times: W. M. Bradley, H. J. Butler, S. T. Clarke, W. H. Copson, R. J. Crisp, J. W. H. T. Douglas, J. A. Flavell, A. P. Freeman, G. Giffen, K. Higgs, A. Hill, W. A. Humphreys, R. D. Jackman, R. O. Jenkins, A. S. Kennedy, W. H. Lockwood, E. A. McDonald, T. L. Pritchard, J. S. Rao, A. Shaw, J. B. Statham, M. W. Tate, H. Trumble, D. Wilson, G. A. Wilson.
Twice (current players only): E. E. Hemmings, M. D. Marshall, P. A. Smith, C. J. van Heerden.

250 WICKETS IN A SEASON

	Season	O	M	R	W	Avge
A. P. Freeman	1928	1,976.1	423	5,489	304	18.05
A. P. Freeman	1933	2,039	651	4,549	298	15.26
T. Richardson	1895‡	1,690.1	463	4,170	290	14.37
C. T. B. Turner**	1888†	2,427.2	1,127	3,307	283	11.68
A. P. Freeman	1931	1,618	360	4,307	276	15.60
A. P. Freeman	1930	1,914.3	472	4,632	275	16.84
T. Richardson	1897‡	1,603.4	495	3,945	273	14.45
A. P. Freeman	1929	1,670.5	381	4,879	267	18.27
W. Rhodes............	1900	1,553	455	3,606	261	13.81
J. T. Hearne	1896	2,003.1	818	3,670	257	14.28
A. P. Freeman	1932	1,565.5	404	4,149	253	16.39
W. Rhodes............	1901	1,565	505	3,797	251	15.12

† Indicates 4-ball overs; ‡ 5-ball overs.
*** Exclusive of matches not reckoned as first-class.*

Notes: In four consecutive seasons (1928-31), A. P. Freeman took 1,122 wickets, and in eight consecutive seasons (1928-35), 2,090 wickets. In each of these eight seasons he took over 200 wickets.

T. Richardson took 1,005 wickets in four consecutive seasons (1894-97).

In 1896, J. T. Hearne took his 100th wicket as early as June 12. In 1931, C. W. L. Parker did the same and A. P. Freeman obtained his 100th wicket a day later.

LEADING BOWLERS IN AN ENGLISH SEASON

(Qualification: 10 wickets in 10 innings)

Season	Leading wicket-taker	Wkts	Avge	Top of averages	Wkts	Avge
1946	W. E. Hollies........	184	15.60	A. Booth...........	111	11.61
1947	T. W. J. Goddard	238	17.30	J. C. Clay..........	65	16.44
1948	J. E. Walsh	174	19.56	J. C. Clay..........	41	14.17
1949	R. O. Jenkins	183	21.19	T. W. J. Goddard ...	160	19.18
1950	R. Tattersall	193	13.59	R. Tattersall	193	13.59
1951	R. Appleyard	200	14.14	R. Appleyard	200	14.14
1952	J. H. Wardle	177	19.54	F. S. Trueman	61	13.78
1953	B. Dooland..........	172	16.58	C. J. Knott........	38	13.71
1954	B. Dooland..........	196	15.48	J. B. Statham	92	14.13
1955	G. A. R. Lock	216	14.49	R. Appleyard	85	13.01
1956	D. J. Shepherd.......	177	15.36	G. A. R. Lock	155	12.46
1957	G. A. R. Lock	212	12.02	G. A. R. Lock	212	12.02
1958	G. A. R. Lock	170	12.08	H. L. Jackson......	143	10.99

Season	Leading wicket-taker	Wkts	Avge	Top of averages	Wkts	Avge
1959	D. Shackleton	148	21.55	J. B. Statham	139	15.01
1960	F. S. Trueman	175	13.98	J. B. Statham	135	12.31
1961	J. A. Flavell	171	17.79	J. A. Flavell	171	17.79
1962	D. Shackleton	172	20.15	C. Cook	58	17.13
1963	D. Shackleton	146	16.75	C. C. Griffith	119	12.83
1964	D. Shackleton	142	20.40	J. A. Standen	64	13.00
1965	D. Shackleton	144	16.08	H. J. Rhodes	119	11.04
1966	D. L. Underwood	157	13.80	D. L. Underwood ...	157	13.80
1967	T. W. Cartwright......	147	15.52	D. L. Underwood ...	136	12.39
1968	R. Illingworth	131	14.36	O. S. Wheatley.....	82	12.95
1969	R. M. H. Cottam.....	109	21.04	A. Ward	69	14.82
1970	D. J. Shepherd.......	106	19.16	Majid Khan	11	18.81
1971	L. R. Gibbs	131	18.89	G. G. Arnold	83	17.12
1972	{ T. W. Cartwright...... { B. Stead	98 98	18.64 20.38	I. M. Chappell	10	10.60
1973	B. S. Bedi	105	17.94	T. W. Cartwright....	89	15.84
1974	A. M. E. Roberts	119	13.62	A. M. E. Roberts....	119	13.62
1975	P. G. Lee	112	18.45	A. M. E. Roberts....	57	15.80
1976	G. A. Cope	93	24.13	M. A. Holding	55	14.38
1977	M. J. Procter	109	18.04	R. A. Woolmer	19	15.21
1978	D. L. Underwood	110	14.49	D. L. Underwood ...	110	14.49
1979	{ D. L. Underwood .... { J. K. Lever..........	106 106	14.85 17.30	J. Garner	55	13.83
1980	R. D. Jackman	121	15.40	J. Garner	49	13.93
1981	R. J. Hadlee	105	14.89	R. J. Hadlee........	105	14.89
1982	M. D. Marshall	134	15.73	R. J. Hadlee........	61	14.57
1983	{ J. K. Lever......... { D. L. Underwood	106 106	16.28 19.28	Imran Khan	12	7.16
1984	R. J. Hadlee	117	14.05	R. J. Hadlee........	117	14.05
1985	N. V. Radford	101	24.68	R. M. Ellison	65	17.20
1986	C. A. Walsh........	118	18.17	M. D. Marshall	100	15.08
1987	N. V. Radford	109	20.81	R. J. Hadlee.......	97	12.64
1988	F. D. Stephenson......	125	18.31	M. D. Marshall	42	13.16
1989	{ D. R. Pringle .... { S. L. Watkin	94 94	18.64 25.09	T. M. Alderman....	70	15.64
1990	N. A. Foster	94	26.61	I. R. Bishop	59	19.05
1991	Waqar Younis	113	14.65	Waqar Younis	113	14.65
1992	C. A. Walsh.........	92	15.96	C. A. Walsh........	92	15.96
1993	S. L. Watkin	92	22.80	Wasim Akram	59	19.27

100 WICKETS IN A SEASON

Since Reduction of Championship Matches in 1969

Five times: D. L. Underwood 110 (1978), 106 (1979), 106 (1983), 102 (1971), 101 (1969).

Four times: J. K. Lever 116 (1984), 106 (1978), 106 (1979), 106 (1983).

Twice: B. S. Bedi 112 (1974), 105 (1973); T. W. Cartwright 108 (1969), 104 (1971); N. A. Foster 109 (1986), 102 (1991); N. Gifford 105 (1970), 104 (1983); R. J. Hadlee 117 (1984), 105 (1981); P. G. Lee 112 (1975), 101 (1973); M. D. Marshall 134 (1982), 100 (1986); M. J. Procter 109 (1977), 108 (1969); N. V. Radford 109 (1987), 101 (1985); F. J. Titmus 105 (1970), 104 (1971).

Once: J. P. Agnew 101 (1987); I. T. Botham 100 (1978); K. E. Cooper 101 (1988); R. M. H. Cottam 109 (1969); D. R. Doshi 101 (1980); J. E. Emburey 103 (1983); L. R. Gibbs 131 (1971); R. N. S. Hobbs 102 (1970); Intikhab Alam 104 (1971); R. D. Jackman 121 (1980); A. M. E. Roberts 119 (1974); P. J. Sainsbury 107 (1971); Sarfraz Nawaz 101 (1975); M. W. W. Selvey 101 (1978); D. J. Shepherd 106 (1970); F. D. Stephenson 125 (1988); C. A. Walsh 118 (1986); Waqar Younis 113 (1991); D. Wilson 102 (1969).

100 WICKETS IN A SEASON MOST TIMES

(Includes Overseas Tours and Seasons)

23 times: W. Rhodes 200 wkts (3).

20 times: D. Shackleton (In successive seasons – 1949 to 1968 inclusive).

17 times: A. P. Freeman 300 wkts (1), 200 wkts (7).

16 times: T. W. J. Goddard 200 wkts (4), C. W. L. Parker 200 wkts (5), R. T. D. Perks, F. J. Titmus.

15 times: J. T. Hearne 200 wkts (3), G. H. Hirst 200 wkts (1), A. S. Kennedy 200 wkts (1).

14 times: C. Blythe 200 wkts (1), W. E. Hollies, G. A. R. Lock 200 wkts (2), M. W. Tate 200 wkts (3), J. C White.

13 times: J. B. Statham.

12 times: J. Briggs, E. G. Dennett 200 wkts (1), C. Gladwin, D. J. Shepherd, N. I. Thomson, F. S. Trueman.

11 times: A. V. Bedser, G. Geary, S. Haigh, J. C. Laker, M. S. Nichols, A. E. Relf.

10 times: W. Attewell, W. G. Grace, R. Illingworth, H. L. Jackson, V. W. C. Jupp, G. G. Macaulay 200 wkts (1), W. Mead, T. B. Mitchell, T. Richardson 200 wkts (3), J. Southerton 200 wkts (1), R. K. Tyldesley, D. L. Underwood, J. H. Wardle, T. G. Wass, D. V. P. Wright.

9 times: W. E. Astill, T. E. Bailey, W. E. Bowes, C. Cook, R. Howorth, J. Mercer, A. W. Mold 200 wkts (2), J. A. Newman, C. F. Root 200 wkts (1), A. Shaw 200 wkts (1), H. Verity 200 wkts (3).

8 times: T. W. Cartwright, H. Dean, J. A. Flavell, A. R. Gover 200 wkts (2), H. Larwood, G. A. Lohmann 200 wkts (3), R. Peel, J. M. Sims, F. A. Tarrant, R. Tattersall, G. J. Thompson, G. E. Tribe, A. W. Wellard, F. E. Woolley, J. A. Young.

100 WICKETS IN A SEASON OUTSIDE ENGLAND

W		Season	Country	R	Avge
116	M. W. Tate	1926-27	India/Ceylon	1,599	13.78
107	Ijaz Faqih	1985-86	Pakistan	1,719	16.06
106	C. T. B. Turner	1887-88	Australia	1,441	13.59
106	R. Benaud	1957-58	South Africa	2,056	19.39
104	S. F. Barnes	1913-14	South Africa	1,117	10.74
104	Sajjad Akbar	1989-90	Pakistan	2,328	22.38
103	Abdul Qadir	1982-83	Pakistan	2,367	22.98

1,500 WICKETS IN A CAREER

Dates in italics denote the first half of an overseas season; i.e. *1970* denotes the 1970-71 season.

		Career	W	R	Avge
1	W. Rhodes	1898-1930	4,187	69,993	16.71
2	A. P. Freeman	1914-36	3,776	69,577	18.42
3	C. W. L. Parker	1903-35	3,278	63,817	19.46
4	J. T. Hearne	1888-1923	3,061	54,352	17.75
5	T. W. J. Goddard	1922-52	2,979	59,116	19.84
6	W. G. Grace	1865-1908	2,876	51,545	17.92
7	A. S. Kennedy	1907-36	2,874	61,034	21.23
8	D. Shackleton	1948-69	2,857	53,303	18.65
9	G. A. R. Lock	1946-*70*	2,844	54,709	19.23
10	F. J. Titmus	1949-82	2,830	63,313	22.37
11	M. W. Tate	1912-37	2,784	50,571	18.16
12	G. H. Hirst	1891-1929	2,739	51,282	18.72
13	C. Blythe	1899-1914	2,506	42,136	16.81

		Career	W	R	Avge
14	D. L. Underwood	1963-87	2,465	49,993	20.28
15	W. E. Astill	1906-39	2,431	57,783	23.76
16	J. C. White	1909-37	2,356	43,759	18.57
17	W. E. Hollies..........	1932-57	2,323	48,656	20.94
18	F. S. Trueman	1949-69	2,304	42,154	18.29
19	J. B. Statham..........	1950-68	2,260	36,999	16.37
20	R. T. D. Perks	1930-55	2,233	53,770	24.07
21	J. Briggs.............	1879-1900	2,221	35,431	15.95
22	D. J. Shepherd	1950-72	2,218	47,302	21.32
23	E. G. Dennett	1903-26	2,147	42,571	19.82
24	T. Richardson	1892-1905	2,104	38,794	18.43
25	T. E. Bailey	1945-67	2,082	48,170	23.13
26	R. Illingworth	1951-83	2,072	42,023	20.28
27	{ N. Gifford	1960-88	2,068	48,731	23.56
	{ F. E. Woolley	1906-38	2,068	41,066	19.85
29	G. Geary	1912-38	2,063	41,339	20.03
30	D. V. P. Wright	1932-57	2,056	49,307	23.98
31	J. A. Newman	1906-30	2,032	51,111	25.15
32	†A. Shaw	1864-97	2,027	24,580	12.12
33	S. Haigh.............	1895-1913	2,012	32,091	15.94
34	H. Verity	1930-39	1,956	29,146	14.90
35	W. Attewell	1881-1900	1,951	29,896	15.32
36	J. C. Laker	1946-*64*	1,944	35,791	18.41
37	A. V. Bedser	1939-60	1,924	39,279	20.41
38	W. Mead	1892-1913	1,916	36,388	18.99
39	A. E. Relf	1900-21	1,897	39,724	20.94
40	P. G. H. Fender	1910-36	1,894	47,458	25.05
41	J. W. H. T. Douglas.....	1901-30	1,893	44,159	23.32
42	J. H. Wardle	1946-*67*	1,846	35,027	18.97
43	G. R. Cox	1895-1928	1,843	42,136	22.86
44	G. A. Lohmann	1884-97	1,841	25,295	13.73
45	J. W. Hearne	1909-36	1,839	44,926	24.42
46	G. G. Macaulay	1920-35	1,837	32,440	17.65
47	M. S. Nichols	1924-39	1,833	39,666	21.63
48	J. B. Mortimore	1950-75	1,807	41,904	23.18
49	C. Cook	1946-64	1,782	36,578	20.52
50	R. Peel	1882-99	1,752	28,442	16.23
51	H. L. Jackson	1947-63	1,733	30,101	17.36
52	J. K. Lever	1967-89	1,722	41,772	24.25
53	T. P. B. Smith	1929-52	1,697	45,059	26.55
54	J. Southerton	1854-79	1,681	24,290	14.44
55	A. E. Trott...........	*1892-1911*	1,674	35,317	21.09
56	A. W. Mold	1889-1901	1,673	26,010	15.54
57	T. G. Wass	1896-1920	1,666	34,092	20.46
58	V. W. C. Jupp.........	1909-38	1,658	38,166	23.01
59	C. Gladwin	1939-58	1,653	30,265	18.30
60	W. E. Bowes	1928-47	1,639	27,470	16.76
61	A. W. Wellard........	1927-50	1,614	39,302	24.35
62	P. I. Pocock	1964-86	1,607	42,648	26.53
63	N. I. Thomson........	1952-72	1,597	32,867	20.58
64	{ J. Mercer	1919-47	1,591	37,210	23.38
	{ G. J. Thompson	1897-1922	1,591	30,058	18.89
66	J. M. Sims	1929-53	1,581	39,401	24.92
67	**M. D. Marshall ....**	***1977-93***	**1,580**	**29,821**	**18.87**
68	{ T. Emmett	1866-88	1,571	21,314	13.56
	{ Intikhab Alam..........	*1957-82*	1,571	43,474	27.67
70	B. S. Bedi	*1961-81*	1,560	33,843	21.69
71	W. Voce..............	1927-52	1,558	35,961	23.08
72	A. R. Gover	1928-48	1,555	36,753	23.63

		Career	W	R	Avge
73	{ T. W. Cartwright	1952-77	1,536	29,357	19.11
	{ K. Higgs	1958-86	1,536	36,267	23.61
75	James Langridge	1924-53	1,530	34,524	22.56
76	J. A. Flavell.............	1949-67	1,529	32,847	21.48
77	{ C. F. Root	1910-33	1,512	31,933	21.11
	{ F. A. Tarrant..........	*1898-1936*	1,512	26,450	17.49
79	R. K. Tyldesley	1919-35	1,509	25,980	17.21

Bold type denotes player who appeared in 1992-93 and 1993 seasons.

  † *The figures for A. Shaw exclude one wicket for which no analysis is available.*

Note: Some works of reference provide career figures which differ from those in this list, owing to the exclusion or inclusion of matches recognised or not recognised as first-class by *Wisden*.

Current Players with 1,000 Wickets

	Career	W	R	Avge
E. E. Hemmings	1966-93	1,467	43,002	29.31
J. E. Emburey	1973-93	1,444	37,442	25.92
I. T. Botham	1974-93	1,172	31,902	27.22
P. Carrick.............	1970-93	1,081	32,237	29.82
C. A. Walsh	*1981*-93	1,078	24,509	22.73

ALL-ROUND RECORDS

HUNDRED AND TEN WICKETS IN AN INNINGS

V. E. Walker, England v Surrey at The Oval; 20*, 108, ten for 74, and four for 17. 1859
W. G. Grace, MCC v Oxford University at Oxford; 104, two for 60, and ten for 49. 1886

Note: E. M. Grace, for MCC v Gentlemen of Kent in a 12-a-side match at Canterbury in 1862, scored 192* and took five for 77 and ten for 69.

TWO HUNDRED RUNS AND SIXTEEN WICKETS

G. Giffen, South Australia v Victoria at Adelaide; 271, nine for 96, and seven for 70. 1891-92

HUNDRED IN EACH INNINGS AND FIVE WICKETS TWICE

G. H. Hirst, Yorkshire v Somerset at Bath; 111, 117*, six for 70, and five for 45. 1906

HUNDRED IN EACH INNINGS AND TEN WICKETS

B. J. T. Bosanquet, Middlesex v Sussex at Lord's; 103, 100*, three for 75, and
  eight for 53 1905
F. D. Stephenson, Nottinghamshire v Yorkshire at Nottingham; 111, 117, four for
  105, and seven for 117 1988

HUNDRED AND HAT-TRICK

G. Giffen, Australians v Lancashire at Manchester; 13, 113, and six for 55 including hat-trick 1884

W. E. Roller, Surrey v Sussex at The Oval; 204, four for 28 including hat-trick, and two for 16. (Unique instance of 200 and hat-trick.) 1885

W. B. Burns, Worcestershire v Gloucestershire at Worcester; 102*, three for 56 including hat-trick, and two for 21 1913

V. W. C. Jupp, Sussex v Essex at Colchester; 102, six for 61 including hat-trick, and six for 78 1921

R. E. S. Wyatt, MCC v Ceylon at Colombo; 124 and five for 39 including hat-trick. 1926-27

L. N. Constantine, West Indians v Northamptonshire at Northampton; seven for 45 including hat-trick, 107 (five 6s), and six for 67 1928

D. E. Davies, Glamorgan v Leicestershire at Leicester; 139, four for 27, and three for 31 including hat-trick 1937

V. M. Merchant, Dr C. R. Pereira's XI v Sir Homi Mehta's XI at Bombay; 1, 142, three for 31 including hat-trick, and no wicket for 17 1946-47

M. J. Procter, Gloucestershire v Essex at Westcliff-on-Sea; 51, 102, three for 43, and five for 30 including hat-trick (all lbw) 1972

M. J. Procter, Gloucestershire v Leicestershire at Bristol; 122, no wkt for 32, and seven for 26 including hat-trick 1979

Note: W. G. Grace, for MCC v Kent in a 12-a-side match at Canterbury in 1874, scored 123 and took five for 82 and six for 47 including a hat-trick.

SEASON DOUBLES

2,000 Runs and 200 Wickets

1906   G. H. Hirst   2,385 runs and 208 wickets

3,000 Runs and 100 Wickets

1937   J. H. Parks   3,003 runs and 101 wickets

2,000 Runs and 100 Wickets

	Season	R	W		Season	R	W
W. G. Grace	1873	2,139	106	F. E. Woolley	1914	2,272	125
W. G. Grace	1876	2,622	129	J. W. Hearne	1920	2,148	142
C. L. Townsend ...	1899	2,440	101	V. W. C. Jupp	1921	2,169	121
G. L. Jessop	1900	2,210	104	F. E. Woolley	1921	2,101	167
G. H. Hirst	1904	2,501	132	F. E. Woolley	1922	2,022	163
G. H. Hirst	1905	2,266	110	F. E. Woolley	1923	2,091	101
W. Rhodes	1909	2,094	141	L. F. Townsend ...	1933	2,268	100
W. Rhodes	1911	2,261	117	D. E. Davies	1937	2,012	103
F. A. Tarrant	1911	2,030	111	James Langridge ...	1937	2,082	101
J. W. Hearne	1913	2,036	124	T. E Bailey	1959	2,011	100
J. W. Hearne	1914	2,116	123				

1,000 Runs and 200 Wickets

	Season	R	W		Season	R	W
A. E. Trott	1899	1,175	239	M. W. Tate	1923	1,168	219
A. E. Trott	1900	1,337	211	M. W. Tate	1924	1,419	205
A. S. Kennedy	1922	1,129	205	M. W. Tate	1925	1,290	228

1,000 Runs and 100 Wickets

Sixteen times: W. Rhodes.

Fourteen times: G. H. Hirst.

Ten times: V. W. C. Jupp.

Nine times: W. E. Astill.

Eight times: T. E. Bailey, W. G. Grace, M. S. Nichols, A. E. Relf, F. A. Tarrant, M. W. Tate†, F. J. Titmus, F. E. Woolley.

Seven times: G. E. Tribe.

Six times: P. G. H. Fender, R. Illingworth, James Langridge.

Five times: J. W. H. T. Douglas, J. W. Hearne, A. S. Kennedy, J. A. Newman.

Four times: E. G. Arnold, J. Gunn, R. Kilner, B. R. Knight.

Three times: W. W. Armstrong (Australians), L. C. Braund, G. Giffen (Australians), N. E. Haig, R. Howorth, C. B. Llewellyn, J. B. Mortimore, Ray Smith, S. G. Smith, L. F. Townsend, A. W. Wellard.

† *M. W. Tate also scored 1,193 runs and took 116 wickets for MCC in first-class matches on the 1926-27 MCC tour of India and Ceylon.*

Note: R. J. Hadlee (1984) and F. D. Stephenson (1988) are the only players to perform the feat since the reduction of County Championship matches. A complete list of those performing the feat before then will be found on p. 202 of the 1982 *Wisden*.

Wicket-Keepers' Double

	Season	R	D
L. E. G. Ames	1928	1,919	122
L. E. G. Ames	1929	1,795	128
L. E. G. Ames	1932	2,482	104
J. T. Murray	1957	1,025	104

20,000 RUNS AND 2,000 WICKETS IN A CAREER

	Career	R	Avge	W	Avge	'Doubles'
W. E. Astill........	1906-39	22,731	22.55	2,431	23.76	9
T. E. Bailey........	1945-67	28,641	33.42	2,082	23.13	8
W. G. Grace........	1865-1908	54,896	39.55	2,876	17.92	8
G. H. Hirst	1891-1929	36,323	34.13	2,739	18.72	14
R. Illingworth	1951-83	24,134	28.06	2,072	20.28	6
W. Rhodes	1898-1930	39,802	30.83	4,187	16.71	16
M. W. Tate	1912-37	21,717	25.01	2,784	18.16	8
F. J. Titmus	1949-82	21,588	23.11	2,830	22.37	8
F. E. Woolley	1906-38	58,969	40.75	2,068	19.85	8

WICKET-KEEPING RECORDS

MOST DISMISSALS IN AN INNINGS

9 (8ct, 1st)	Tahir Rashid	Habib Bank v PACO at Gujranwala	1992-93
8 (all ct)	A. T. W. Grout	Queensland v Western Australia at Brisbane	1959-60
8 (all ct)†	D. E. East	Essex v Somerset at Taunton	1985
8 (all ct)	S. A. Marsh‡	Kent v Middlesex at Lord's....................	1991
8 (6ct, 2st)	T. J. Zoehrer	Australians v Surrey at The Oval	1993
7 (4ct, 3st)	E. J. Smith	Warwickshire v Derbyshire at Birmingham	1926
7 (6ct, 1st)	W. Farrimond	Lancashire v Kent at Manchester	1930
7 (all ct)	W. F. F. Price	Middlesex v Yorkshire at Lord's................	1937
7 (3ct, 4st)	D. Tallon	Queensland v Victoria at Brisbane.............	1938-39
7 (all ct)	R. A. Saggers	New South Wales v Combined XI at Brisbane....	1940-41
7 (1ct, 6st)	H. Yarnold	Worcestershire v Scotland at Dundee...........	1951
7 (4ct, 3st)	J. Brown	Scotland v Ireland at Dublin...................	1957

7 (6ct, 1st)	N. Kirsten	Border v Rhodesia at East London	1959-60
7 (all ct)	M. S. Smith	Natal v Border at East London	1959-60
7 (all ct)	K. V. Andrew	Northamptonshire v Lancashire at Manchester	1962
7 (all ct)	A. Long	Surrey v Sussex at Hove	1964
7 (all ct)	R. M. Schofield	Central Districts v Wellington at Wellington	1964-65
7 (all ct)	R. W. Taylor	Derbyshire v Glamorgan at Derby	1966
7 (6ct, 1st)	H. B. Taber	New South Wales v South Australia at Adelaide	1968-69
7 (6ct, 1st)	E. W. Jones	Glamorgan v Cambridge University at Cambridge.	1970
7 (6ct, 1st)	S. Benjamin	Central Zone v North Zone at Bombay	1973-74
7 (all ct)	R. W. Taylor	Derbyshire v Yorkshire at Chesterfield	1975
7 (6ct, 1st)	Shahid Israr	Karachi Whites v Quetta at Karachi	1976-77
7 (4ct, 3st)	Wasim Bari	PIA v Sind at Lahore	1977-78
7 (all ct)	J. A. Maclean	Queensland v Victoria at Melbourne	1977-78
7 (5ct, 2st)	Taslim Arif	National Bank v Punjab at Lahore	1978-79
7 (all ct)	Wasim Bari	Pakistan v New Zealand at Auckland	1978-79
7 (all ct)	R. W. Taylor	England v India at Bombay	1979-80
7 (all ct)	D. L. Bairstow	Yorkshire v Derbyshire at Scarborough	1982
7 (6ct, 1st)	R. B. Phillips	Queensland v New Zealanders at Bundaberg	1982-83
7 (3ct, 4st)	Masood Iqbal	Habib Bank v Lahore at Lahore	1982-83
7 (3ct, 4st)	Arif-ud-Din	United Bank v PACO at Sahiwal	1983-84
7 (6ct, 1st)	R. J. East	OFS v Western Province B at Cape Town	1984-85
7 (all ct)	B. A. Young	Northern Districts v Canterbury at Christchurch	1986-87
7 (all ct)	D. J. Richardson	Eastern Province v OFS at Bloemfontein	1988-89
7 (6ct, 1st)	Dildar Malik	Multan v Faisalabad at Sahiwal	1988-89
7 (all ct)	W. K. Hegg	Lancashire v Derbyshire at Chesterfield	1989
7 (all ct)	Imran Zia	Bahawalpur v Faisalabad at Faisalabad	1989-90
7 (all ct)	I. D. S. Smith	New Zealand v Sri Lanka at Hamilton	1990-91
7 (all ct)	J. F. Holyman	Tasmania v Western Australia at Hobart	1990-91
7 (all ct)	P. J. L. Radley	OFS v Western Province at Cape Town	1990-91
7 (all ct)	C. P. Metson	Glamorgan v Derbyshire at Chesterfield	1991

† *The first eight wickets to fall.*   ‡ *S. A. Marsh also scored 108*.*

WICKET-KEEPERS' HAT-TRICKS

W. H. Brain, Gloucestershire v Somerset at Cheltenham, 1893 – three stumpings off successive balls from C. L. Townsend.

G. O. Dawkes, Derbyshire v Worcestershire at Kidderminster, 1958 – three catches off successive balls from H. L. Jackson.

R. C. Russell, Gloucestershire v Surrey at The Oval, 1986 – three catches off successive balls from C. A. Walsh and D. V. Lawrence (2).

MOST DISMISSALS IN A MATCH

12 (8ct, 4st)	E. Pooley	Surrey v Sussex at The Oval	1868
12 (9ct, 3st)	D. Tallon	Queensland v New South Wales at Sydney	1938-39
12 (9ct, 3st)	H. B. Taber	New South Wales v South Australia at Adelaide.	1968-69
11 (all ct)	A. Long	Surrey v Sussex at Hove	1964
11 (all ct)	R. W. Marsh	Western Australia v Victoria at Perth	1975-76
11 (all ct)	D. L. Bairstow	Yorkshire v Derbyshire at Scarborough	1982
11 (all ct)	W. K. Hegg	Lancashire v Derbyshire at Chesterfield	1989
11 (all ct)	A. J. Stewart	Surrey v Leicestershire at Leicester	1989
11 (all ct)	T. J. Nielsen	South Australia v Western Australia at Perth	1990-91
10 (5ct, 5st)	H. Phillips	Sussex v Surrey at The Oval	1872
10 (2ct, 8st)	E. Pooley	Surrey v Kent at The Oval	1878
10 (9ct, 1st)	T. W. Oates	Nottinghamshire v Middlesex at Nottingham	1906
10 (1ct, 9st)	F. H. Huish	Kent v Surrey at The Oval	1911
10 (9ct, 1st)	J. C. Hubble	Kent v Gloucestershire at Cheltenham	1923
10 (8ct, 2st)	H. Elliott	Derbyshire v Lancashire at Manchester	1935
10 (7ct, 3st)	P. Corrall	Leicestershire v Sussex at Hove	1936

10 (9ct, 1st)	R. A. Saggers	New South Wales v Combined XI at Brisbane .	1940-41
10 (all ct)	A. E. Wilson	Gloucestershire v Hampshire at Portsmouth ...	1953
10 (7ct, 3st)	B. N. Jarman	South Australia v New South Wales at Adelaide.	1961-62
10 (all ct)	L. A. Johnson	Northamptonshire v Sussex at Worthing	1963
10 (all ct)	R. W. Taylor	Derbyshire v Hampshire at Chesterfield	1963
10 (8ct, 2st)	L. A. Johnson	Northamptonshire v Warwickshire at Birmingham	1965
10 (9ct, 1st)	R. C. Jordon	Victoria v South Australia at Melbourne	1970-71
10 (all ct)	R. W. Marsh†	Western Australia v South Australia at Perth ..	1976-77
10 (6ct, 4st)	Taslim Arif	National Bank v Punjab at Lahore	1978-79
10 (9ct, 1st)	Arif-ud-Din	United Bank v Karachi B at Karachi..........	1978-79
10 (all ct)	R. W. Taylor	England v India at Bombay	1979-80
10 (all ct)	R. J. Parks	Hampshire v Derbyshire at Portsmouth	1981
10 (9ct, 1st)	A. Ghosh	Bihar v Assam at Bhagalpur	1981-82
10 (8ct, 2st)	Z. Parkar	Bombay v Maharashtra at Bombay............	1981-82
10 (all ct)	R. V. Jennings	Transvaal v Arosa Sri Lankans at Johannesburg	1982-83
10 (9ct, 1st)	Kamal Najamuddin	Karachi v Lahore at Multan	1982-83
10 (all ct)	D. A. Murray	West Indies XI v South Africa at Port Elizabeth.	1983-84
10 (7ct, 3st)	Azhar Abbas	Bahawalpur v Lahore City Greens at Bahawalpur	1983-84
10 (all ct)	B. N. French	Nottinghamshire v Oxford University at Oxford.	1984
10 (8ct, 2st)	R. J. Ryall	Western Province v Transvaal at Cape Town ..	1984-85
10 (all ct)	S. J. Rixon	Australian XI v South Africa at Johannesburg .	1985-86
10 (8ct, 2st)	Anil Dalpat	Karachi v United Bank at Lahore............	1985-86
10 (all ct)	R. V. Jennings	Transvaal v Northern Transvaal at Verwoerdburg	1986-87
10 (all ct)	S. J. Rixon	Australian XI v South Africa at Johannesburg .	1986-87
10 (all ct)	R. V. Jennings	Transvaal v Orange Free State at Johannesburg	1986-87
10 (9ct, 1st)	C. J. Richards	Surrey v Sussex at Guildford	1987
10 (all ct)	C. W. Scott	Nottinghamshire v Derbyshire at Derby	1988
10 (all ct)	D. J. Richardson	Eastern Province v OFS at Bloemfontein	1988-89
10 (all ct)	A. N. Aymes	Hampshire v Oxford University at Oxford	1989
10 (all ct)	L. R. Fernando	Moratuwa v Panadura at Moratuwa	1989-90
10 (all ct)	Imran Zia	Bahawalpur v Faisalabad at Faisalabad	1989-90
10 (9ct, 1st)	D. J. Richardson	Eastern Province v N. Transvaal at Verwoerdburg	1989-90

† *R. W. Marsh also scored 104.*

MOST DISMISSALS IN A SEASON

128 (79ct, 49st)	L. E. G. Ames	Kent.................	1929
122 (70ct, 52st)	L. E. G. Ames	Kent.................	1928
110 (63ct, 47st)	H. Yarnold	Worcestershire.............	1949
107 (77ct, 30st)	G. Duckworth	Lancashire...............	1928
107 (96ct, 11st)	J. G. Binks	Yorkshire................	1960
104 (40ct, 64st)	L. E. G. Ames	Kent.................	1932
104 (82ct, 22st)	J. T. Murray	Middlesex.............	1957
102 (69ct, 33st)	F. H. Huish	Kent.................	1913
102 (95ct, 7st)	J. T. Murray	Middlesex.............	1960
101 (62ct, 39st)	F. H. Huish	Kent.................	1911
101 (85ct, 16st)	R. Booth	Worcestershire.............	1960
100 (91ct, 9st)	R. Booth	Worcestershire.............	1964

MOST DISMISSALS IN A CAREER

Dates in italics denote the first half of an overseas season; i.e. *1914* denotes the 1914-15 season.

		Career	M	Ct	St	Total
1	R. W. Taylor...........	1960-88	639	1,473	176	1,649
2	J. T. Murray...........	1952-75	635	1,270	257	1,527
3	H. Strudwick..........	1902-27	675	1,242	255	1,497
4	A. P. E. Knott	1964-85	511	1,211	133	1,344

		Career	M	Ct	St	Total
5	F. H. Huish	1895-1914	497	933	377	1,310
6	B. Taylor	1949-73	572	1,083	211	1,294
7	D. Hunter	1889-1909	548	906	347	1,253
8	H. R. Butt	1890-1912	550	953	275	1,228
9	J. H. Board	1891-*1914*	525	852	355	1,207
10	H. Elliott	1920-47	532	904	302	1,206
11	J. M. Parks	1949-76	739	1,088	93	1,181
12	R. Booth	1951-70	468	948	178	1,126
13	L. E. G. Ames	1926-51	593	703	418	1,121
14	D. L. Bairstow	1970-90	459	961	138	1,099
15	G. Duckworth	1923-47	504	753	343	1,096
16	H. W. Stephenson	1948-64	462	748	334	1,082
17	J. G. Binks	1955-75	502	895	176	1,071
18	T. G. Evans	1939-69	465	816	250	1,066
19	A. Long	1960-80	452	922	124	1,046
20	G. O. Dawkes	1937-61	482	895	148	1,043
21	R. W. Tolchard	1965-83	483	912	125	1,037
22	W. L. Cornford	1921-47	496	675	342	1,017

Current Players with 500 Dismissals

	Career	M	Ct	St	Total
B. N. French	1976-93	357	812	100	912
R. C. Russell	1981-93	274	626	92	718
R. J. Parks	1980-93	256	642	72	714
R. V. Jennings	*1973-92*	159	567	54	621
S. J. Rhodes	1981-93	231	544	69	613

FIELDING RECORDS

(Excluding wicket-keepers)

MOST CATCHES IN AN INNINGS

7	M. J. Stewart	Surrey v Northamptonshire at Northampton	1957
7	A. S. Brown	Gloucestershire v Nottinghamshire at Nottingham	1966

MOST CATCHES IN A MATCH

10	W. R. Hammond†	Gloucestershire v Surrey at Cheltenham	1928
8	W. B. Burns	Worcestershire v Yorkshire at Bradford	1907
8	F. G. Travers	Europeans v Parsees at Bombay	1923-24
8	A. H. Bakewell	Northamptonshire v Essex at Leyton	1928
8	W. R. Hammond	Gloucestershire v Worcestershire at Cheltenham	1932
8	K. J. Grieves	Lancashire v Sussex at Manchester	1951
8	C. A. Milton	Gloucestershire v Sussex at Hove	1952
8	G. A. R. Lock	Surrey v Warwickshire at The Oval	1957
8	J. M. Prodger	Kent v Gloucestershire at Cheltenham	1961
8	P. M. Walker	Glamorgan v Derbyshire at Swansea	1970
8	Masood Anwar	Rawalpindi v Lahore Division at Rawalpindi	1983-84

† *Hammond also scored a hundred in each innings.*

MOST CATCHES IN A SEASON

78	W. R. Hammond	1928		65	D. W. Richardson	1961
77	M. J. Stewart	1957		64	K. F. Barrington	1957
73	P. M. Walker	1961		64	G. A. R. Lock	1957
71	P. J. Sharpe	1962		63	J. Tunnicliffe	1896
70	J. Tunnicliffe	1901		63	J. Tunnicliffe	1904
69	J. G. Langridge	1955		63	K. J. Grieves	1950
69	P. M. Walker	1960		63	C. A. Milton	1956
66	J. Tunnicliffe	1895		61	J. V. Wilson	1955
65	W. R. Hammond	1925		61	M. J. Stewart	1958
65	P. M. Walker	1959				

Note: The most catches by a fielder since the reduction of County Championship matches in 1969 is 49 by C. J. Tavaré in 1978.

MOST CATCHES IN A CAREER

Dates in italics denote the first half of an overseas season; i.e. *1970* denotes the 1970-71 season.

1,018	F. E. Woolley (1906-38)		784	J. G. Langridge (1928-55)
887	W. G. Grace (1865-1908)		764	W. Rhodes (1898-1930)
830	G. A. R. Lock (1946-*70*)		758	C. A. Milton (1948-74)
819	W. R. Hammond (1920-51)		754	E. H. Hendren (1907-38)
813	D. B. Close (1949-86)			

Most Catches by Current Players

495	G. A. Gooch (1973-93)		418	C. J. Tavaré (1974-93)
464	I. V. A. Richards (*1971*-93)		399	C. E. B. Rice (*1969*-92)
423	J. E. Emburey (1973-93)		395	M. W. Gatting (1975-93)

TEAM RECORDS

HIGHEST TOTALS

1,107	Victoria v New South Wales at Melbourne	1926-27
1,059	Victoria v Tasmania at Melbourne	1922-23
951-7 dec.	Sind v Baluchistan at Karachi	1973-74
918	New South Wales v South Australia at Sydney	1900-01
912-8 dec.	Holkar v Mysore at Indore	1945-46
912-6 dec.†	Tamil Nadu v Goa at Panjim	1988-89
910-6 dec.	Railways v Dera Ismail Khan at Lahore	1964-65
903-7 dec.	England v Australia at The Oval	1938
887	Yorkshire v Warwickshire at Birmingham	1896
868†	North Zone v West Zone at Bhilai	1987-88
863	Lancashire v Surrey at The Oval	1990
855-6 dec.†	Bombay v Hyderabad at Bombay	1990-91
849	England v West Indies at Kingston	1929-30
843	Australians v Oxford and Cambridge Universities Past and Present at Portsmouth	1893

† *Tamil Nadu's total of 912-6 dec. included 52 penalty runs from their opponents' failure to meet the required bowling rate by 13 overs. North Zone's total of 868 included 68 penalty runs (17 overs) and Bombay's total of 855-6 dec. included 48 penalty runs (four overs).*

HIGHEST FOR EACH FIRST-CLASS COUNTY

Derbyshire	645	v Hampshire at Derby	1898
Durham	521-9 dec.	v Glamorgan at Cardiff	1992
Essex	761-6 dec.	v Leicestershire at Chelmsford	1990
Glamorgan	587-8 dec.	v Derbyshire at Cardiff	1951
Gloucestershire	653-6 dec.	v Glamorgan at Bristol	1928
Hampshire	672-7 dec.	v Somerset at Taunton	1899
Kent	803-4 dec.	v Essex at Brentwood	1934
Lancashire	863	v Surrey at The Oval	1990
Leicestershire	701-4 dec.	v Worcestershire at Worcester	1906
Middlesex	642-3 dec.	v Hampshire at Southampton	1923
Northamptonshire	636-6 dec.	v Essex at Chelmsford	1990
Nottinghamshire	739-7 dec.	v Leicestershire at Nottingham	1903
Somerset	675-9 dec.	v Hampshire at Bath	1924
Surrey	811	v Somerset at The Oval	1899
Sussex	705-8 dec.	v Surrey at Hastings	1902
Warwickshire	657-6 dec.	v Hampshire at Birmingham	1899
Worcestershire	633	v Warwickshire at Worcester	1906
Yorkshire	887	v Warwickshire at Birmingham	1896

HIGHEST AGAINST EACH FIRST-CLASS COUNTY

Derbyshire	662	by Yorkshire at Chesterfield	1898
Durham	629	by Nottinghamshire at Chester-le-Street	1993
Essex	803-4 dec.	by Kent at Brentwood	1934
Glamorgan	653-6 dec.	by Gloucestershire at Bristol	1928
Gloucestershire	774-7 dec.	by Australians at Bristol	1948
Hampshire	742	by Surrey at The Oval	1909
Kent	676	by Australians at Canterbury	1921
Lancashire	707-9 dec.	by Surrey at The Oval	1990
Leicestershire	761-6 dec.	by Essex at Chelmsford	1990
Middlesex	665	by West Indians at Lord's	1939
Northamptonshire	670-9 dec.	by Sussex at Hove	1921
Nottinghamshire	706-4 dec.	by Surrey at Nottingham	1947
Somerset	811	by Surrey at The Oval	1899
Surrey	863	by Lancashire at The Oval	1990
Sussex	726	by Nottinghamshire at Nottingham	1895
Warwickshire	887	by Yorkshire at Birmingham	1896
Worcestershire	701-4 dec.	by Leicestershire at Worcester	1906
Yorkshire	630	by Somerset at Leeds	1901

LOWEST TOTALS

12	Oxford University v MCC and Ground at Oxford	†1877
12	Northamptonshire v Gloucestershire at Gloucester	1907
13	Auckland v Canterbury at Auckland	1877-78
13	Nottinghamshire v Yorkshire at Nottingham	1901
14	Surrey v Essex at Chelmsford	1983
15	MCC v Surrey at Lord's	1839
15	Victoria v MCC at Melbourne	†1903-04
15	Northamptonshire v Yorkshire at Northampton	†1908
15	Hampshire v Warwickshire at Birmingham	1922
	(Following on, Hampshire scored 521 and won by 155 runs.)	
16	MCC and Ground v Surrey at Lord's	1872
16	Derbyshire v Nottinghamshire at Nottingham	1879
16	Surrey v Nottinghamshire at The Oval	1880
16	Warwickshire v Kent at Tonbridge	1913
16	Trinidad v Barbados at Bridgetown	1942-43
16	Border v Natal at East London (first innings)	1959-60
17	Gentlemen of Kent v Gentlemen of England at Lord's	1850
17	Gloucestershire v Australians at Cheltenham	1896

18	The Bs v England at Lord's	1831
18	Kent v Sussex at Gravesend	†1867
18	Tasmania v Victoria at Melbourne	1868-69
18	Australians v MCC and Ground at Lord's	†1896
18	Border v Natal at East London (second innings)	1959-60
19	Sussex v Surrey at Godalming	1830
19	Sussex v Nottinghamshire at Hove	†1873
19	MCC and Ground v Australians at Lord's	1878
19	Wellington v Nelson at Nelson	1885-86

† *Signifies that one man was absent.*

Note: At Lord's in 1810, The Bs, with one man absent, were dismissed by England for 6.

LOWEST TOTAL IN A MATCH

34	(16 and 18) Border v Natal at East London	1959-60
42	(27 and 15) Northamptonshire v Yorkshire at Northampton	1908

Note: Northamptonshire batted one man short in each innings.

LOWEST FOR EACH FIRST-CLASS COUNTY

Derbyshire	16	v Nottinghamshire at Nottingham	1879
Durham	83	v Lancashire at Manchester	1993
Essex	30	v Yorkshire at Leyton	1901
Glamorgan	22	v Lancashire at Liverpool	1924
Gloucestershire	17	v Australians at Cheltenham	1896
Hampshire	15	v Warwickshire at Birmingham	1922
Kent	18	v Sussex at Gravesend	1867
Lancashire	25	v Derbyshire at Manchester	1871
Leicestershire	25	v Kent at Leicester	1912
Middlesex	20	v MCC at Lord's	1864
Northamptonshire	12	v Gloucestershire at Gloucester	1907
Nottinghamshire	13	v Yorkshire at Nottingham	1901
Somerset	25	v Gloucestershire at Bristol	1947
Surrey	14	v Essex at Chelmsford	1983
Sussex	19	v Nottinghamshire at Hove	1873
Warwickshire	16	v Kent at Tonbridge	1913
Worcestershire	24	v Yorkshire at Huddersfield	1903
Yorkshire	23	v Hampshire at Middlesbrough	1965

LOWEST AGAINST EACH FIRST-CLASS COUNTY

Derbyshire	23	by Hampshire at Burton upon Trent	1958
Durham	86	by Oxford University at Oxford	1993
Essex	14	by Surrey at Chelmsford	1983
Glamorgan	33	by Leicestershire at Ebbw Vale	1965
Gloucestershire	12	by Northamptonshire at Gloucester	1907
Hampshire	23	by Yorkshire at Middlesbrough	1965
Kent	16	by Warwickshire at Tonbridge	1913
Lancashire	22	by Glamorgan at Liverpool	1924
Leicestershire	24	by Oxford University at Oxford	1985
Middlesex	31	by Gloucestershire at Bristol	1924
Northamptonshire	33	by Lancashire at Northampton	1977
Nottinghamshire {	16	by Derbyshire at Nottingham	1879
	16	by Surrey at The Oval	1880
Somerset	22	by Gloucestershire at Bristol	1920
Surrey	16	by MCC at Lord's	1872
Sussex	18	by Kent at Gravesend	1867
Warwickshire	15	by Hampshire at Birmingham	1922
Worcestershire	30	by Hampshire at Worcester	1903
Yorkshire	13	by Nottinghamshire at Nottingham	1901

HIGHEST MATCH AGGREGATES

2,376 for 37 wickets	Maharashtra v Bombay at Poona......................	1948-49
2,078 for 40 wickets	Bombay v Holkar at Bombay.........................	1944-45
1,981 for 35 wickets	England v South Africa at Durban....................	1938-39
1,929 for 39 wickets	New South Wales v South Australia at Sydney	1925-26
1,911 for 34 wickets	New South Wales v Victoria at Sydney...............	1908-09
1,905 for 40 wickets	Otago v Wellington at Dunedin	1923-24

In Britain

1,808 for 20 wickets	Sussex v Essex at Hove.............................	1993
1,723 for 31 wickets	England v Australia at Leeds	1948
1,650 for 19 wickets	Surrey v Lancashire at The Oval	1990
1,641 for 16 wickets	Glamorgan v Worcestershire at Abergavenny..........	1990
1,614 for 30 wickets	England v India at Manchester	1990
1,603 for 28 wickets	England v India at Lord's...........................	1990
1,601 for 29 wickets	England v Australia at Lord's	1930
1,578 for 37 wickets	Sussex v Kent at Hove	1991
1,570 for 29 wickets	Essex v Kent at Chelmsford	1988
1,531 for 31 wickets	Kent v Essex at Maidstone..........................	1993
1,530 for 19 wickets	Essex v Leicestershire at Chelmsford................	1990
1,509 for 36 wickets	Somerset v Worcestershire at Taunton	1990
1,507 for 28 wickets	England v West Indies at The Oval	1976
1,502 for 28 wickets	MCC v New Zealanders at Lord's....................	1927

LOWEST AGGREGATE IN A COMPLETED MATCH

105 for 31 wickets	MCC v Australians at Lord's	1878

Note: The lowest aggregate since 1900 is 158 for 22 wickets, Surrey v Worcestershire at The Oval, 1954.

HIGHEST FOURTH-INNINGS TOTALS

(Unless otherwise stated, the side making the runs won the match.)

654-5	England v South Africa at Durban................................	1938-39
	(After being set 696 to win. The match was left drawn on the tenth day.)	
604	Maharashtra v Bombay at Poona	1948-49
	(After being set 959 to win.)	
576-8	Trinidad v Barbados at Port-of-Spain	1945-46
	(After being set 672 to win. Match drawn on fifth day.)	
572	New South Wales v South Australia at Sydney.....................	1907-08
	(After being set 593 to win.)	
529-9	Combined XI v South Africans at Perth	1963-64
	(After being set 579 to win. Match drawn on fourth day.)	
518	Victoria v Queensland at Brisbane	1926-27
	(After being set 753 to win.)	
507-7	Cambridge University v MCC and Ground at Lord's	1896
506-6	South Australia v Queensland at Adelaide..........................	1991-92
502-6	Middlesex v Nottinghamshire at Nottingham	1925
	(Game won by an unfinished stand of 271; a county record.)	
502-8	Players v Gentlemen at Lord's	1900
500-7	South African Universities v Western Province at Stellenbosch	1978-79

LARGEST VICTORIES

Largest Innings Victories

Inns and 851 runs:	Railways (910-6 dec.) v Dera Ismail Khan (Lahore)	1964-65
Inns and 666 runs:	Victoria (1,059) v Tasmania (Melbourne)	1922-23
Inns and 656 runs:	Victoria (1,107) v New South Wales (Melbourne)	1926-27
Inns and 605 runs:	New South Wales (918) v South Australia (Sydney)	1900-01
Inns and 579 runs:	England (903-7 dec.) v Australia (The Oval)	1938
Inns and 575 runs:	Sind (951-7 dec.) v Baluchistan (Karachi)	1973-74
Inns and 527 runs:	New South Wales (713) v South Australia (Adelaide)	1908-09
Inns and 517 runs:	Australians (675) v Nottinghamshire (Nottingham)	1921

Largest Victories by Runs Margin

685 runs:	New South Wales (235 and 761-8 dec.) v Queensland (Sydney)	1929-30
675 runs:	England (521 and 342-8 dec.) v Australia (Brisbane)	1928-29
638 runs:	New South Wales (304 and 770) v South Australia (Adelaide)	1920-21
625 runs:	Sargodha (376 and 416) v Lahore Municipal Corporation (Faisalabad)	1978-79
609 runs:	Muslim Commercial Bank (575 and 282-0 dec.) v WAPDA (Lahore)	1977-78
573 runs:	Sinhalese SC (395-7 dec. and 350-2 dec.) v Sebastianites C and AC (63 and 109) at Colombo	1990-91
571 runs:	Victoria (304 and 649) v South Australia (Adelaide)	1926-27
562 runs:	Australia (701 and 327) v England (The Oval)	1934

Victory Without Losing a Wicket

Lancashire (166-0 dec. and 66-0) beat Leicestershire by ten wickets (Manchester)	1956
Karachi A (277-0 dec.) beat Sind A by an innings and 77 runs (Karachi)	1957-58
Railways (236-0 dec. and 16-0) beat Jammu and Kashmir by ten wickets (Srinagar)	1960-61
Karnataka (451-0 dec.) beat Kerala by an innings and 186 runs (Chikmagalur)	1977-78

TIED MATCHES IN FIRST-CLASS CRICKET

Since 1948 a tie has been recognised only when the scores are level with all the wickets down in the fourth innings.

The following are the instances since then:

D. G. Bradman's XI v A. L. Hassett's XI at Melbourne	1948-49
Hampshire v Kent at Southampton	1950
Sussex v Warwickshire at Hove	1952
Essex v Lancashire at Brentwood	1952
Northamptonshire v Middlesex at Peterborough	1953
Yorkshire v Leicestershire at Huddersfield	1954
Sussex v Hampshire at Eastbourne	1955
Victoria v New South Wales at Melbourne	1956-57
T. N. Pearce's XI v New Zealanders at Scarborough	1958
Essex v Gloucestershire at Leyton	1959
Australia v West Indies (First Test) at Brisbane	1960-61
Bahawalpur v Lahore B at Bahawalpur	1961-62
Hampshire v Middlesex at Portsmouth	1967
England XI v England Under-25 XI at Scarborough	1968
Yorkshire v Middlesex at Bradford	1973
Sussex v Essex at Hove	1974
South Australia v Queensland at Adelaide	1976-77
Central Districts v England XI at New Plymouth	1977-78
Victoria v New Zealanders at Melbourne	1982-83
Muslim Commercial Bank v Railways at Sialkot	1983-84
Sussex v Kent at Hastings	1984
Northamptonshire v Kent at Northampton	1984

Eastern Province B v Boland at Albany SC, Port Elizabeth   1985-86
Natal B v Eastern Province B at Pietermaritzburg   1985-86
India v Australia (First Test) at Madras   1986-87
Gloucestershire v Derbyshire at Bristol   1987
Bahawalpur v Peshawar at Bahawalpur   1988-89
Wellington v Canterbury at Wellington   1988-89
Sussex v Kent at Hove   1991
Nottinghamshire v Worcestershire at Nottingham   1993
    Sussex (436) scored the highest total to tie a first-class match.

MATCHES BEGUN AND FINISHED ON FIRST DAY

Since 1900. A fuller list may be found in the Wisden of 1981 and preceding editions.

Yorkshire v Worcestershire at Bradford, May 7   1900
MCC and Ground v London County at Lord's, May 20   1903
Transvaal v Orange Free State at Johannesburg, December 30   1906
Middlesex v Gentlemen of Philadelphia at Lord's, July 20   1908
Gloucestershire v Middlesex at Bristol, August 26   1909
Eastern Province v Orange Free State at Port Elizabeth, December 26   1912
Kent v Sussex at Tonbridge, June 21   1919
Lancashire v Somerset at Manchester, May 21   1925
Madras v Mysore at Madras, November 4   1934
Ireland v New Zealanders at Dublin, September 11   1937
Derbyshire v Somerset at Chesterfield, June 11   1947
Lancashire v Sussex at Manchester, July 12   1950
Surrey v Warwickshire at The Oval, May 16   1953
Somerset v Lancashire at Bath, June 6 (H. F. T. Buse's benefit)   1953
Kent v Worcestershire at Tunbridge Wells, June 15   1960

TEST MATCH RECORDS

Note: This section covers all Tests up to September 19, 1993.

BATTING RECORDS

HIGHEST INDIVIDUAL INNINGS

365*	G. S. Sobers	West Indies v Pakistan at Kingston	1957-58
364	L. Hutton	England v Australia at The Oval	1938
337	Hanif Mohammad	Pakistan v West Indies at Bridgetown	1957-58
336*	W. R. Hammond	England v New Zealand at Auckland	1932-33
334	D. G. Bradman	Australia v England at Leeds.............	1930
333	G. A. Gooch	England v India at Lord's	1990
325	A. Sandham	England v West Indies at Kingston	1929-30
311	R. B. Simpson	Australia v England at Manchester	1964
310*	J. H. Edrich	England v New Zealand at Leeds	1965
307	R. M. Cowper	Australia v England at Melbourne	1965-66
304	D. G. Bradman	Australia v England at Leeds............	1934
302	L. G. Rowe	West Indies v England at Bridgetown	1973-74
299*	D. G. Bradman	Australia v South Africa at Adelaide	1931-32
299	M. D. Crowe	New Zealand v Sri Lanka at Wellington ..	1990-91
291	I. V. A. Richards.....	West Indies v England at The Oval	1976
287	R. E. Foster	England v Australia at Sydney	1903-04
285*	P. B. H. May	England v West Indies at Birmingham	1957
280*	Javed Miandad	Pakistan v India at Hyderabad	1982-83
278	D. C. S. Compton	England v Pakistan at Nottingham	1954
277	B. C. Lara	West Indies v Australia at Sydney	1992-93
274	R. G. Pollock	South Africa v Australia at Durban	1969-70
274	Zaheer Abbas	Pakistan v England at Birmingham	1971
271	Javed Miandad	Pakistan v New Zealand at Auckland	1988-89
270*	G. A. Headley	West Indies v England at Kingston	1934-35
270	D. G. Bradman	Australia v England at Melbourne	1936-37
268	G. N. Yallop	Australia v Pakistan at Melbourne	1983-84
267	P. A. de Silva	Sri Lanka v New Zealand at Wellington ..	1990-91
266	W. H. Ponsford	Australia v England at The Oval	1934
262*	D. L. Amiss	England v West Indies at Kingston	1973-74
261	F. M. M. Worrell	West Indies v England at Nottingham	1950
260	C. C. Hunte	West Indies v Pakistan at Kingston	1957-58
260	Javed Miandad	Pakistan v England at The Oval	1987
259	G. M. Turner........	New Zealand v West Indies at Georgetown .	1971-72
258	T. W. Graveney......	England v West Indies at Nottingham	1957
258	S. M. Nurse	West Indies v New Zealand at Christchurch ..	1968-69
256	R. B. Kanhai	West Indies v India at Calcutta	1958-59
256	K. F. Barrington	England v Australia at Manchester	1964
255*	D. J. McGlew	South Africa v New Zealand at Wellington ...	1952-53
254	D. G. Bradman	Australia v England at Lord's	1930
251	W. R. Hammond	England v Australia at Sydney	1928-29
250	K. D. Walters	Australia v New Zealand at Christchurch ..	1976-77
250	S. F. A. F. Bacchus ..	West Indies v India at Kanpur	1978-79

The highest individual innings for India and Zimbabwe are:

236*	S. M. Gavaskar	India v West Indies at Madras	1983-84
121	D. L. Houghton	Zimbabwe v India at Harare.............	1992-93

HUNDRED ON TEST DEBUT

C. Bannerman (165*)	Australia v England at Melbourne	1876-77
W. G. Grace (152)	England v Australia at The Oval.............	1880
H. Graham (107).	Australia v England at Lord's	1893
†K. S. Ranjitsinhji (154*)...	England v Australia at Manchester	1896

†P. F. Warner (132*)	England v South Africa at Johannesburg	1898-99
†R. A. Duff (104)	Australia v England at Melbourne	1901-02
R. E. Foster (287)	England v Australia at Sydney.	1903-04
G. Gunn (119).	England v Australia at Sydney.	1907-08
†R. J. Hartigan (116)	Australia v England at Adelaide	1907-08
†H. L. Collins (104)	Australia v England at Sydney.	1920-21
W. H. Ponsford (110)	Australia v England at Sydney.	1924-25
A. A. Jackson (164)	Australia v England at Adelaide	1928-29
†G. A. Headley (176)	West Indies v England at Bridgetown	1929-30
J. E. Mills (117)	New Zealand v England at Wellington.	1929-30
Nawab of Pataudi sen. (102)	England v Australia at Sydney.	1932-33
B. H. Valentine (136)	England v India at Bombay	1933-34
†L. Amarnath (118)	India v England at Bombay	1933-34
†P. A. Gibb (106)	England v South Africa at Johannesburg	1938-39
S. C. Griffith (140)	England v West Indies at Port-of-Spain	1947-48
A. G. Ganteaume (112)	West Indies v England at Port-of-Spain	1947-48
†J. W. Burke (101*)	Australia v England at Adelaide	1950-51
P. B. H. May (138)	England v South Africa at Leeds.	1951
R. H. Shodhan (110).	India v Pakistan at Calcutta	1952-53
B. H. Pairaudeau (115). . . .	West Indies v India at Port-of-Spain	1952-53
†O. G. Smith (104)	West Indies v Australia at Kingston	1954-55
A. G. Kripal Singh (100*) .	India v New Zealand at Hyderabad	1955-56
C. C. Hunte (142)	West Indies v Pakistan at Bridgetown	1957-58
C. A. Milton (104*)	England v New Zealand at Leeds	1958
†A. A. Baig (112)	India v England at Manchester	1959
Hanumant Singh (105)	India v England at Delhi	1963-64
Khalid Ibadulla (166)	Pakistan v Australia at Karachi	1964-65
B. R. Taylor (105)	New Zealand v India at Calcutta	1964-65
K. D. Walters (155)	Australia v England at Brisbane	1965-66
J. H. Hampshire (107)	England v West Indies at Lord's	1969
†G. R. Viswanath (137)	India v Australia at Kanpur	1969-70
G. S. Chappell (108)	Australia v England at Perth	1970-71
‡L. G. Rowe (214, 100*) . . .	West Indies v New Zealand at Kingston	1971-72
A. I. Kallicharran (100*) . .	West Indies v New Zealand at Georgetown	1971-72
R. E. Redmond (107)	New Zealand v Pakistan at Auckland	1972-73
†F. C. Hayes (106*)	England v West Indies at The Oval	1973
†C. G. Greenidge (107)	West Indies v India at Bangalore	1974-75
†L. Baichan (105*)	West Indies v Pakistan at Lahore	1974-75
G. J. Cosier (109)	Australia v West Indies at Melbourne	1975-76
S. Amarnath (124).	India v New Zealand at Auckland	1975-76
Javed Miandad (163)	Pakistan v New Zealand at Lahore	1976-77
†A. B. Williams (100).	West Indies v Australia at Georgetown	1977-78
†D. M. Wellham (103)	Australia v England at The Oval	1981
†Salim Malik (100*)	Pakistan v Sri Lanka at Karachi	1981-82
K. C. Wessels (162)	Australia v England at Brisbane	1982-83
W. B. Phillips (159)	Australia v Pakistan at Perth.	1983-84
§M. Azharuddin (110)	India v England at Calcutta	1984-85
D. S. B. P. Kuruppu (201*)	Sri Lanka v New Zealand at Colombo (CCC) . .	1986-87
†M. J. Greatbatch (107*) . . .	New Zealand v England at Auckland	1987-88
M. E. Waugh (138)	Australia v England at Adelaide	1990-91
A. C. Hudson (163)	South Africa v West Indies at Bridgetown	1991-92
R. S. Kaluwitharana (132*)	Sri Lanka v Australia at Colombo (SSC)	1992-93
D. L. Houghton (121)	Zimbabwe v India at Harare	1992-93
P. K. Amre (103)	India v South Africa at Durban	1992-93
†G. P. Thorpe (114*)	England v Australia at Nottingham	1993

† *In his second innings of the match.*
‡ *L. G. Rowe is the only batsman to score a hundred in each innings on debut.*
§ *M. Azharuddin is the only batsman to score hundreds in each of his first three Tests.*

Note: L. Amarnath and S. Amarnath provide the only instance of a father and son scoring a hundred on debut.

300 RUNS IN FIRST TEST

314	L. G. Rowe (214, 100*)	West Indies v New Zealand at Kingston	1971-72
306	R. E. Foster (287, 19)	England v Australia at Sydney	1903-04

TWO SEPARATE HUNDREDS IN A TEST

Three times: S. M. Gavaskar v West Indies (1970-71), v Pakistan (1978-79), v West Indies (1978-79).

Twice in one series: C. L. Walcott v Australia (1954-55).

Twice: H. Sutcliffe v Australia (1924-25), v South Africa (1929); G. A. Headley v England (1929-30 and 1939); G. S. Chappell v New Zealand (1973-74), v West Indies (1975-76); ‡A. R. Border v Pakistan (1979-80), v New Zealand (1985-86).

Once: W. Bardsley v England (1909); A. C. Russell v South Africa (1922-23); W. R. Hammond v Australia (1928-29); E. Paynter v South Africa (1938-39); D. C. S. Compton v Australia (1946-47); A. R. Morris v England (1946-47); A. Melville v England (1947); B. Mitchell v England (1947); D. G. Bradman v India (1947-48); V. S. Hazare v Australia (1947-48); E. D. Weekes v India (1948-49); J. Moroney v South Africa (1949-50); G. S. Sobers v Pakistan (1957-58); R. B. Kanhai v Australia (1960-61); Hanif Mohammad v England (1961-62); R. B. Simpson v Pakistan (1964-65); K. D. Walters v West Indies (1968-69); †L. G. Rowe v New Zealand (1971-72); I. M. Chappell v New Zealand (1973-74); G. M. Turner v Australia (1973-74); C. G. Greenidge v England (1976); G. P. Howarth v England (1977-78); L. R. D. Mendis v India (1982-83); Javed Miandad v New Zealand (1984-85); D. M. Jones v Pakistan (1989-90); G. A. Gooch v India (1990); A. H. Jones v Sri Lanka (1990-91); A. P. Gurusinha v New Zealand (1990-91).

† *L. G. Rowe's two hundreds were on his Test debut.*

‡ *A. R. Border scored 150* and 153 against Pakistan to become the first batsman to score 150 in each innings of a Test match.*

TRIPLE-HUNDRED AND HUNDRED IN SAME TEST

†G. A. Gooch (England)   333 and 123 v India at Lord's 1990

† *G. A. Gooch became the first to score a hundred and a triple-hundred in the same first-class match.*

DOUBLE-HUNDRED AND HUNDRED IN SAME TEST

K. D. Walters (Australia)	242 and 103 v West Indies at Sydney	1968-69
S. M. Gavaskar (India)	124 and 220 v West Indies at Port-of-Spain	1970-71
†L. G. Rowe (West Indies)	214 and 100* v New Zealand at Kingston	1971-72
G. S. Chappell (Australia)	247* and 133 v New Zealand at Wellington	1973-74

† *On Test debut.*

MOST RUNS IN A SERIES

	T	I	NO	R	HS	100s	Avge		
D. G. Bradman ...	5	7	0	974	334	4	139.14	A v E	1930
W. R. Hammond .	5	9	1	905	251	4	113.12	E v A	1928-29
M. A. Taylor	6	11	1	839	219	2	83.90	A v E	1989
R. N. Harvey	5	9	0	834	205	4	92.66	A v SA	1952-53
I. V. A. Richards .	4	7	0	829	291	3	118.42	WI v E	1976
C. L. Walcott	5	10	0	827	155	5	82.70	WI v A	1954-55

	T	I	NO	R	HS	100s	Avge		
G. S. Sobers	5	8	2	824	365*	3	137.33	WI v P	1957-58
D. G. Bradman ...	5	9	0	810	270	3	90.00	A v E	1936-37
D. G. Bradman ...	5	5	1	806	299*	4	201.50	A v SA	1931-32
E. D. Weekes	5	7	0	779	194	4	111.28	WI v I	1948-49
†S. M. Gavaskar ..	4	8	3	774	220	4	154.80	I v WI	1970-71
Mudassar Nazar ..	6	8	2	761	231	4	126.83	P v I	1982-83
D. G. Bradman ...	5	8	0	758	304	2	94.75	A v E	1934
D. C. S. Compton .	5	8	0	753	208	4	94.12	E v SA	1947
‡G. A. Gooch	3	6	0	752	333	3	125.33	E v I	1990

† *Gavaskar's aggregate was achieved in his first Test series.*

‡ *G. A. Gooch is alone in scoring 1,000 runs in Test cricket during an English season with 1,058 runs in eleven innings against New Zealand and India in 1990.*

1,000 TEST RUNS IN A CALENDAR YEAR

	T	I	NO	R	HS	100s	Avge	Year
I. V. A. Richards (WI)	11	19	0	1,710	291	7	90.00	1976
S. M. Gavaskar (I)	18	27	1	1,555	221	5	59.80	1979
G. R. Viswanath (I)	17	26	3	1,388	179	5	60.34	1979
R. B. Simpson (A)	14	26	3	1,381	311	3	60.04	1964
D. L. Amiss (E)	13	22	2	1,379	262*	5	68.95	1974
S. M. Gavaskar (I)	18	32	4	1,310	236*	5	46.78	1983
G. A. Gooch (E)	9	17	1	1,264	333	4	79.00	1990
M. A. Taylor (A)	11	20	1	1,219	219	4	64.15	1989†
G. S. Sobers (WI)	7	12	3	1,193	365*	5	132.55	1958
D. B. Vengsarkar (I)	18	27	4	1,174	146*	5	51.04	1979
K. J. Hughes (A)	15	28	4	1,163	130*	2	48.45	1979
D. C. S. Compton (E)	9	15	1	1,159	208	6	82.78	1947
C. G. Greenidge (WI)	14	22	4	1,149	223	4	63.83	1984
A. R. Border (A)	11	20	3	1,099	196	4	64.64	1985
D. M. Jones (A)	11	18	3	1,099	216	4	73.26	1989
I. T. Botham (E)	14	22	0	1,095	208	3	49.77	1982
K. W. R. Fletcher (E)	13	22	4	1,090	178	2	60.55	1973
M. Amarnath (I)	14	24	1	1,077	120	4	46.82	1983
A. R. Border (A)	14	27	3	1,073	162	3	44.70	1979
C. Hill (A)	12	21	2	1,061	142	2	55.84	1902
D. I. Gower (E)	14	25	2	1,061	114	1	46.13	1982
D. I. Gower (E)	14	25	1	1,059	136	2	44.12	1986
W. M. Lawry (A)	14	27	2	1,056	157	2	42.24	1964
S. M. Gavaskar (I)	9	15	2	1,044	205	4	80.30	1978
G. A. Gooch (E)	9	17	1	1,040	174	3	65.00	1991
K. F. Barrington (E)	12	22	2	1,039	132*	3	51.95	1963
E. R. Dexter (E)	11	15	1	1,038	205	2	74.14	1962
K. F. Barrington (E)	10	17	4	1,032	172	4	79.38	1961
Mohsin Khan (P)	10	17	3	1,029	200	4	73.50	1982
D. G. Bradman (A)	8	13	4	1,025	201	5	113.88	1948
S. M. Gavaskar (I)	11	20	1	1,024	156	4	53.89	1976
A. R. Border (A)	11	19	3	1,000	140	5	62.50	1986

† *The year of his debut.*

Notes: The earliest date for completing 1,000 runs is May 3 by M. Amarnath in 1983.

D. G. Bradman (A) scored 1,005 runs in five consecutive Tests, all against England, in 1936-37 and 1938: 13, 270, 26, 212, 169, 51, 144*, 18, 102*.

MOST RUNS IN A CAREER

(Qualification: 2,000 runs)

ENGLAND

		T	I	NO	R	HS	100s	Avge
1	**G. A. Gooch**	**107**	**195**	**6**	**8,293**	**333**	**19**	**43.87**
2	D. I. Gower	117	204	18	8,231	215	18	44.25
3	G. Boycott	108	193	23	8,114	246*	22	47.72
4	M. C. Cowdrey	114	188	15	7,624	182	22	44.06
5	W. R. Hammond	85	140	16	7,249	336*	22	58.45
6	L. Hutton	79	138	15	6,971	364	19	56.67
7	K. F. Barrington	82	131	15	6,806	256	20	58.67
8	D. C. S. Compton	78	131	15	5,807	278	17	50.06
9	J. B. Hobbs	61	102	7	5,410	211	15	56.94
10	I. T. Botham	102	161	6	5,200	208	14	33.54
11	J. H. Edrich	77	127	9	5,138	310*	12	43.54
12	T. W. Graveney	79	123	13	4,882	258	11	44.38
13	A. J. Lamb	79	139	10	4,656	142	14	36.09
14	H. Sutcliffe	54	84	9	4,555	194	16	60.73
15	P. B. H. May	66	106	9	4,537	285*	13	46.77
16	E. R. Dexter	62	102	8	4,502	205	9	47.89
17	A. P. E. Knott	95	149	15	4,389	135	5	32.75
18	**M. W. Gatting**	**74**	**129**	**14**	**4,227**	**207**	**9**	**36.75**
19	D. L. Amiss	50	88	10	3,612	262*	11	46.30
20	A. W. Greig	58	93	4	3,599	148	8	40.43
21	E. H. Hendren	51	83	9	3,525	205*	7	47.63
22	F. E. Woolley	64	98	7	3,283	154	5	36.07
23	K. W. R. Fletcher	59	96	14	3,272	216	7	39.90
24	**R. A. Smith**	**45**	**84**	**14**	**3,237**	**148***	**8**	**46.24**
25	M. Leyland	41	65	5	2,764	187	9	46.06
26	C. Washbrook	37	66	6	2,569	195	6	42.81
27	B. L. D'Oliveira	44	70	8	2,484	158	5	40.06
28	D. W. Randall	47	79	5	2,470	174	7	33.37
29	W. J. Edrich	39	63	2	2,440	219	6	40.00
30	T. G. Evans	91	133	14	2,439	104	2	20.49
31	L. E. G. Ames	47	72	12	2,434	149	8	40.56
32	W. Rhodes	58	98	21	2,325	179	2	30.19
33	T. E. Bailey	61	91	14	2,290	134*	1	29.74
34	M. J. K. Smith	50	78	6	2,278	121	3	31.63
35	**A. J. Stewart**	**32**	**60**	**4**	**2,083**	**190**	**4**	**37.19**
36	P. E. Richardson	34	56	1	2,061	126	5	37.47

AUSTRALIA

		T	I	NO	R	HS	100s	Avge
1	**A. R. Border**	**147**	**252**	**43**	**10,695**	**205**	**26**	**51.17**
2	G. S. Chappell	87	151	19	7,110	247*	24	53.86
3	D. G. Bradman	52	80	10	6,996	334	29	99.94
4	R. N. Harvey	79	137	10	6,149	205	21	48.41
5	**D. C. Boon**	**80**	**145**	**16**	**5,869**	**200**	**17**	**45.49**
6	K. D. Walters	74	125	14	5,357	250	15	48.26
7	I. M. Chappell	75	136	10	5,345	196	14	42.42
8	W. M. Lawry	67	123	12	5,234	210	13	47.15
9	R. B. Simpson	62	111	7	4,869	311	10	46.81
10	I. R. Redpath	66	120	11	4,737	171	8	43.45
11	K. J. Hughes	70	124	6	4,415	213	9	37.41
12	R. W. Marsh	96	150	13	3,633	132	3	26.51
13	**D. M. Jones**	**52**	**89**	**11**	**3,631**	**216**	**11**	**46.55**
14	M. A. Taylor	46	84	5	3,588	219	10	45.41

		T	I	NO	R	HS	100s	Avge
15	A. R. Morris	46	79	3	3,533	206	12	46.48
16	C. Hill	49	89	2	3,412	191	7	39.21
17	G. M. Wood	59	112	6	3,374	172	9	31.83
18	V. T. Trumper	48	89	8	3,163	214*	8	39.04
19	C. C. McDonald	47	83	4	3,107	170	5	39.32
20	A. L. Hassett	43	69	3	3,073	198*	10	46.56
21	K. R. Miller	55	87	7	2,958	147	7	36.97
22	**S. R. Waugh**	**58**	**89**	**15**	**2,919**	**177***	**5**	**39.44**
23	W. W. Armstrong	50	84	10	2,863	159*	6	38.68
24	R. G. Marsh	50	93	7	2,854	138	4	33.18
25	K. R. Stackpole	43	80	5	2,807	207	7	37.42
26	N. C. O'Neill	42	69	8	2,779	181	6	45.55
27	G. N. Yallop	39	70	3	2,756	268	8	41.13
28	S. J. McCabe	39	62	5	2,748	232	6	48.21
29	W. Bardsley	41	66	5	2,469	193*	6	40.47
30	W. M. Woodfull	35	54	4	2,300	161	7	46.00
31	P. J. Burge	42	68	8	2,290	181	4	38.16
32	S. E. Gregory	58	100	7	2,282	201	4	24.53
33	R. Benaud	63	97	7	2,201	122	3	24.45
34	C. G. Macartney	35	55	4	2,131	170	7	41.78
35	W. H. Ponsford	29	48	4	2,122	266	7	48.22
36	R. M. Cowper	27	46	2	2,061	307	5	46.84

SOUTH AFRICA

		T	I	NO	R	HS	100s	Avge
1	B. Mitchell	42	80	9	3,471	189*	8	48.88
2	A. D. Nourse	34	62	7	2,960	231	9	53.81
3	H. W. Taylor	42	76	4	2,936	176	7	40.77
4 {	E. J. Barlow	30	57	2	2,516	201	6	45.74
{	T. L. Goddard	41	78	5	2,516	112	1	34.46
6	D. J. McGlew	34	64	6	2,440	255*	7	42.06
7	J. H. B. Waite	50	86	7	2,405	134	4	30.44
8	R. G. Pollock	23	41	4	2,256	274	7	60.97
9	A. W. Nourse	45	83	8	2,234	111	1	29.78
10	R. A. McLean	40	73	3	2,120	142	5	30.28

K. C. Wessels has scored 2,377 runs in 32 Tests: 1,761 (average 42.95) in 24 Tests for Australia, and 616 (average 44.00) in 8 Tests for South Africa.

WEST INDIES

		T	I	NO	R	HS	100s	Avge
1	I. V. A. Richards.....	121	182	12	8,540	291	24	50.23
2	G. S. Sobers	93	160	21	8,032	365*	26	57.78
3	C. G. Greenidge	108	185	16	7,558	226	19	44.72
4	C. H. Lloyd	110	175	14	7,515	242*	19	46.67
5	**D. L. Haynes**	**111**	**194**	**24**	**7,250**	**184**	**18**	**42.64**
6	R. B. Kanhai	79	137	6	6,227	256	15	47.53
7	**R. B. Richardson**	**71**	**122**	**10**	**5,231**	**194**	**15**	**46.70**
8	E. D. Weekes	48	81	5	4,455	207	15	58.61
9	A. I. Kallicharran	66	109	10	4,399	187	12	44.43
10	R. C. Fredericks	59	109	7	4,334	169	8	42.49
11	F. M. M. Worrell	51	87	9	3,860	261	9	49.48
12	C. L. Walcott........	44	74	7	3,798	220	15	56.68
13	P. J. L. Dujon	81	115	11	3,322	139	5	31.94
14	C. C. Hunte	44	78	6	3,245	260	8	45.06
15	H. A. Gomes	60	91	11	3,171	143	9	39.63
16	B. F. Butcher	44	78	6	3,104	209*	7	43.11

		T	I	NO	R	HS	100s	Avge
17	S. M. Nurse	29	54	1	2,523	258	6	47.60
18	A. L. Logie.........	52	78	9	2,470	130	2	35.79
19	G. A. Headley	22	40	4	2,190	270*	10	60.83
20	J. B. Stollmeyer	32	56	5	2,159	160	4	42.33
21	L. G. Rowe	30	49	2	2,047	302	7	43.55

NEW ZEALAND

		T	I	NO	R	HS	100s	Avge
1	**J. G. Wright**	**82**	**148**	**7**	**5,334**	**185**	**12**	**37.82**
2	**M. D. Crowe**	**66**	**112**	**10**	**4,777**	**299**	**15**	**46.83**
3	B. E. Congdon	61	114	7	3,448	176	7	32.22
4	J. R. Reid...........	58	108	5	3,428	142	6	33.28
5	R. J. Hadlee..........	86	134	19	3,124	151*	2	27.16
6	G. M. Turner	41	73	6	2,991	259	7	44.64
7	B. Sutcliffe	42	76	8	2,727	230*	5	40.10
8	M. G. Burgess	50	92	6	2,684	119*	5	31.20
9	J. V. Coney	52	85	14	2,668	174*	3	37.57
10	G. P. Howarth.......	47	83	5	2,531	147	6	32.44
11	G. T. Dowling	39	77	3	2,306	239	3	31.16
12	**A. H. Jones**	**31**	**58**	**7**	**2,276**	**186**	**6**	**44.62**

INDIA

		T	I	NO	R	HS	100s	Avge
1	S. M. Gavaskar	125	214	16	10,122	236*	34	51.12
2	D. B. Vengsarkar.....	116	185	22	6,868	166	17	42.13
3	G. R. Viswanath	91	155	10	6,080	222	14	41.93
4	**Kapil Dev**	**127**	**180**	**14**	**5,131**	**163**	**8**	**30.90**
5	M. Amarnath........	69	113	10	4,378	138	11	42.50
6	**R. J. Shastri**	**80**	**121**	**14**	**3,830**	**206**	**11**	**35.79**
7	**M. Azharuddin**	**58**	**84**	**3**	**3,650**	**199**	**12**	**45.06**
8	P. R. Umrigar	59	94	8	3,631	223	12	42.22
9	V. L. Manjrekar	55	92	10	3,208	189*	7	39.12
10	C. G. Borde	55	97	11	3,061	177*	5	35.59
11	Nawab of Pataudi jun.	46	83	3	2,793	203*	6	34.91
12	S. M. H. Kirmani ...	88	124	22	2,759	102	2	27.04
13	F. M. Engineer	46	87	3	2,611	121	2	31.08
14	Pankaj Roy	43	79	4	2,442	173	5	32.56
15	V. S. Hazare	30	52	6	2,192	164*	7	47.65
16	A. L. Wadekar.......	37	71	3	2,113	143	1	31.07
17	V. Mankad..........	44	72	5	2,109	231	5	31.47
18	C. P. S. Chauhan....	40	68	2	2,084	97	0	31.57
19	K. Srikkanth	43	72	3	2,062	123	2	29.88
20	M. L. Jaisimha	39	71	4	2,056	129	3	30.68
21	D. N. Sardesai.......	30	55	4	2,001	212	5	39.23

PAKISTAN

		T	I	NO	R	HS	100s	Avge
1	**Javed Miandad**	**121**	**184**	**21**	**8,689**	**280***	**23**	**53.30**
2	Zaheer Abbas........	78	124	11	5,062	274	12	44.79
3	Mudassar Nazar	76	116	8	4,114	231	10	38.09
4	Majid Khan	63	106	5	3,931	167	8	38.92
5	Hanif Mohammad	55	97	8	3,915	337	12	43.98
6	Imran Khan..........	88	126	25	3,807	136	6	37.69

		T	I	NO	R	HS	100s	Avge
7	**Salim Malik**	**72**	**103**	**18**	**3,757**	**165**	**10**	**44.20**
8	Mushtaq Mohammad .	57	100	7	3,643	201	10	39.17
9	Asif Iqbal..............	58	99	7	3,575	175	11	38.85
10	Saeed Ahmed........	41	78	4	2,991	172	5	40.41
11	Wasim Raja	57	92	14	2,821	125	4	36.16
12	Mohsin Khan........	48	79	6	2,709	200	7	37.10
13	Sadiq Mohammad	41	74	2	2,579	166	5	35.81
14	Shoaib Mohammad ...	39	58	6	2,443	203*	7	46.98
15	**Ramiz Raja**	**48**	**78**	**5**	**2,243**	**122**	**2**	**30.72**
16	Imtiaz Ahmed	41	72	1	2,079	209	3	29.28

SRI LANKA

		T	I	NO	R	HS	100s	Avge
1	**A. Ranatunga**	**45**	**75**	**4**	**2,582**	**135***	**4**	**36.36**
2	**P. A. de Silva**	**37**	**62**	**2**	**2,478**	**267**	**6**	**41.30**

ZIMBABWE: The highest aggregate is 341, average 68.20, by **A. Flower** in 4 Tests.

Bold type denotes those who played Test cricket in 1992-93 and 1993 seasons or Sri Lanka v India and South Africa in 1993-94.

HIGHEST CAREER AVERAGES

(Qualification: 20 innings)

Avge		T	I	NO	R	HS	100s
99.94	D. G. Bradman (A) ...	52	80	10	6,996	334	29
60.97	R. G. Pollock (SA)	23	41	4	2,256	274	7
60.83	G. A. Headley (WI)	22	40	4	2,190	270*	10
60.73	H. Sutcliffe (E)	54	84	9	4,555	194	16
59.23	E. Paynter (E)...........	20	31	5	1,540	243	4
58.67	K. F. Barrington (E)	82	131	15	6,806	256	20
58.61	E. D. Weekes (WI)........	48	81	5	4,455	207	15
58.45	W. R. Hammond (E)	85	140	16	7,249	336*	22
57.78	G. S. Sobers (WI).......	93	160	21	8,032	365*	26
56.94	J. B. Hobbs (E)...........	61	102	7	5,410	211	15
56.68	C. L. Walcott (WI)........	44	74	7	3,798	220	15
56.67	L. Hutton (E)	79	138	15	6,971	364	19
55.00	E. Tyldesley (E)	14	20	2	990	122	3
54.20	C. A. Davis (WI)	15	29	5	1,301	183	4
53.86	G. S. Chappell (A)	87	151	19	7,110	247*	24
53.81	A. D. Nourse (SA)	34	62	7	2,960	231	9
53.30	**Javed Miandad (P)**	**121**	**184**	**21**	**8,689**	**280***	**23**
51.62	J. Ryder (A)	20	32	5	1,394	201*	3
51.17	**A. R. Border (A)**	**147**	**252**	**43**	**10,695**	**205**	**26**
51.12	S. M. Gavaskar (I)	125	214	16	10,122	236*	34
50.23	I. V. A. Richards (WI).....	121	182	12	8,540	291	24
50.06	D. C. S. Compton (E)	78	131	15	5,807	278	17

Bold type denotes those who played Test cricket in 1992-93 and 1993 seasons.

MOST HUNDREDS

	Total	200+	Inns	E	A	SA	WI	NZ	I	P	SL	Z
S. M. Gavaskar (I)	34	4	214	4	8	–	13	2	–	5	2	–
D. G. Bradman (A)	29	12	80	19	–	4	2	–	4	–	–	–
A. R. Border (A)	**26**	**2**	**252**	**8**	**–**	**–**	**3**	**4**	**4**	**6**	**1**	**–**
G. S. Sobers (WI)	26	2	160	10	4	–	–	1	8	3	–	–
G. S. Chappell (A)	24	4	151	9	–	5	3	1	6	0	–	–
I. V. A. Richards (WI)	24	3	182	8	5	–	–	1	8	2	–	–
Javed Miandad (P)	**23**	**6**	**184**	**2**	**6**	**–**	**2**	**7**	**5**	**–**	**1**	**–**
G. Boycott (E)	22	1	193	–	7	1	5	2	4	3	–	–
M. C. Cowdrey (E)	22	0	188	–	5	3	6	2	3	3	–	–
W. R. Hammond (E)	22	7	140	–	9	6	1	4	2	–	–	–
R. N. Harvey (A)	21	2	137	6	–	8	3	–	4	0	–	–
K. F. Barrington (E)	20	1	131	–	5	2	3	3	3	4	–	–
G. A. Gooch (E)	**19**	**1**	**195**	**–**	**4**	**–**	**5**	**3**	**5**	**1**	**1**	**–**
C. G. Greenidge (WI)	19	4	185	7	4	–	–	2	5	1	–	–
L. Hutton (E)	19	4	138	–	5	4	5	3	2	–	–	–
C. H. Lloyd (WI)	19	1	175	5	6	–	–	0	7	1	–	–
D. I. Gower (E)	18	2	204	–	9	–	1	4	2	2	0	–
D. L. Haynes (WI)	**18**	**0**	**194**	**5**	**5**	**0**	**–**	**3**	**2**	**3**	**–**	**–**
D. C. S. Compton (E)	17	2	131	–	5	7	2	2	0	–	–	–
D. C. Boon (A)	**17**	**1**	**145**	**6**	**–**	**–**	**3**	**2**	**6**	**0**	**0**	**–**
D. B. Vengsarkar (I)	17	0	185	5	2	–	6	0	–	2	2	–
H. Sutcliffe (E)	16	0	84	–	8	6	0	2	0	–	–	–
M. D. Crowe (NZ)	**15**	**3**	**112**	**3**	**3**	**–**	**3**	**–**	**1**	**2**	**2**	**1**
J. B. Hobbs (E)	15	1	102	–	12	2	1	–	–	–	–	–
R. B. Kanhai (WI)	15	2	137	5	5	–	–	–	4	1	–	–
R. B. Richardson (WI)	**15**	**0**	**122**	**4**	**8**	**0**	**–**	**1**	**2**	**0**	**–**	**–**
C. L. Walcott (WI)	15	1	74	4	–	–	–	1	4	1	–	–
K. D. Walters (A)	15	2	125	4	–	0	6	3	1	1	–	–
E. D. Weekes (WI)	15	2	81	3	1	–	–	3	7	1	–	–

The most double-hundreds by batsmen not qualifying for the above list is four by Zaheer Abbas (12 hundreds for Pakistan) and three by R. B. Simpson (10 hundreds for Australia).

Bold type denotes those who played Test cricket in 1992-93 and 1993 seasons. Dashes indicate that a player did not play against the country concerned.

CARRYING BAT THROUGH TEST INNINGS

(Figures in brackets show side's total)

A. B. Tancred	26*	(47)	South Africa v England at Cape Town	1888-89
J. E. Barrett	67*	(176)	Australia v England at Lord's	1890
R. Abel	132*	(307)	England v Australia at Sydney	1891-92
P. F. Warner	132*	(237)	England v South Africa at Johannesburg	1898-99
W. W. Armstrong	159*	(309)	Australia v South Africa at Johannesburg	1902-03
J. W. Zulch	43*	(103)	South Africa v England at Cape Town	1909-10
W. Bardsley	193*	(383)	Australia v England at Lord's	1926
W. M. Woodfull	30*	(66)‡	Australia v England at Brisbane	1928-29
W. M. Woodfull	73*	(193)†	Australia v England at Adelaide	1932-33
W. A. Brown	206*	(422)	Australia v England at Lord's	1938
L. Hutton	202*	(344)	England v West Indies at The Oval	1950
L. Hutton	156*	(272)	England v Australia at Adelaide	1950-51
Nazar Mohammad	124*	(331)	Pakistan v India at Lucknow	1952-53
F. M. M. Worrell	191*	(372)	West Indies v England at Nottingham	1957
T. L. Goddard	56*	(99)	South Africa v Australia at Cape Town	1957-58

D. J. McGlew	127* (292)	South Africa v New Zealand at Durban	1961-62
C. C. Hunte	60* (131)	West Indies v Australia at Port-of-Spain	1964-65
G. M. Turner	43* (131)	New Zealand v England at Lord's	1969
W. M. Lawry	49* (107)	Australia v India at Delhi	1969-70
W. M. Lawry	60* (116)†	Australia v England at Sydney	1970-71
G. M. Turner	223* (386)	New Zealand v West Indies at Kingston	1971-72
I. R. Redpath	159* (346)	Australia v New Zealand at Auckland	1973-74
G. Boycott	99* (215)	England v Australia at Perth	1979-80
S. M. Gavaskar	127* (286)	India v Pakistan at Faisalabad	1982-83
Mudassar Nazar	152* (323)	Pakistan v India at Lahore	1982-83
S. Wettimuny	63* (144)	Sri Lanka v New Zealand at Christchurch	1982-83
D. C. Boon	58* (103)	Australia v New Zealand at Auckland	1985-86
D. L. Haynes	88* (211)	West Indies v Pakistan at Karachi	1986-87
G. A. Gooch	154* (252)	England v West Indies at Leeds	1991
D. L. Haynes	75* (176)	West Indies v England at The Oval	1991
A. J. Stewart	69* (175)	England v Pakistan at Lord's	1992
D. L. Haynes	143* (382)	West Indies v Pakistan at Port-of-Spain	1992-93

† *One man absent.*   ‡ *Two men absent.*

Notes: G. M. Turner (223*) holds the record for the highest score by a player carrying his bat through a Test innings. He is also the youngest player to do so, being 22 years 63 days old when he first achieved the feat (1969).

G. A. Gooch (61.11%) holds the record for the highest percentage of a side's total by anyone carrying his bat throughout a Test innings.

Nazar Mohammad and Mudassar Nazar provide the only instance of a father and son carrying their bat through a Test innings.

D. L. Haynes, who is alone in achieving this feat on three occasions, also opened the batting and was last man out in each innings for West Indies v New Zealand at Dunedin, 1979-80.

FASTEST FIFTIES

Minutes

28	J. T. Brown	England v Australia at Melbourne	1894-95
29	S. A. Durani	India v England at Kanpur	1963-64
30	E. A. V. Williams	West Indies v England at Bridgetown	1947-48
30	B. R. Taylor	New Zealand v West Indies at Auckland	1968-69
33	C. A. Roach	West Indies v England at The Oval	1933
34	C. R. Browne	West Indies v England at Georgetown	1929-30

The fastest fifties in terms of balls received (where recorded) are:

Balls

30	Kapil Dev	India v Pakistan at Karachi (2nd Test)	1982-83
32	I. V. A. Richards	West Indies v India at Kingston	1982-83
32	I. T. Botham	England v New Zealand at The Oval	1986
33	R. C. Fredericks	West Indies v Australia at Perth	1975-76
33	Kapil Dev	India v Pakistan at Karachi	1978-79
33	Kapil Dev	India v England at Manchester	1982
33	A. J. Lamb	England v New Zealand at Auckland	1991-92

FASTEST HUNDREDS

Minutes

70	J. M. Gregory	Australia v South Africa at Johannesburg	1921-22
75	G. L. Jessop	England v Australia at The Oval	1902
78	R. Benaud	Australia v West Indies at Kingston	1954-55
80	J. H. Sinclair	South Africa v Australia at Cape Town	1902-03
81	I. V. A. Richards	West Indies v England at St John's	1985-86
86	B. R. Taylor	New Zealand v West Indies at Auckland	1968-69

The fastest hundreds in terms of balls received (where recorded) are:

Balls

56	I. V. A. Richards ..	West Indies v England at St John's	1985-86
67	J. M. Gregory	Australia v South Africa at Johannesburg	1921-22
71	R. C. Fredericks ...	West Indies v Australia at Perth.............	1975-76
74	Kapil Dev	India v Sri Lanka at Kanpur	1986-87
76	G. L. Jessop	England v Australia at The Oval	1902
77	Majid Khan........	Pakistan v New Zealand at Karachi	1976-77

FASTEST DOUBLE-HUNDREDS

Minutes

214	D. G. Bradman....	Australia v England at Leeds	1930
223	S. J. McCabe	Australia v England at Nottingham	1938
226	V. T. Trumper	Australia v South Africa at Adelaide	1910-11
234	D. G. Bradman	Australia v England at Lord's	1930
240	W. R. Hammond ..	England v New Zealand at Auckland	1932-33
241	S. E. Gregory	Australia v England at Sydney	1894-95
245	D. C. S. Compton..	England v Pakistan at Nottingham...........	1954

The fastest double-hundreds in terms of balls received (where recorded) are:

Balls

220	I. T. Botham	England v India at The Oval...............	1982
232	C. G. Greenidge ...	West Indies v England at Lord's.............	1984
240	C. H. Lloyd	West Indies v India at Bombay.............	1974-75
241	Zaheer Abbas	Pakistan v India at Lahore	1982-83
242	D. G. Bradman	Australia v England at The Oval	1934
242	I. V. A. Richards ..	West Indies v Australia at Melbourne	1984-85

FASTEST TRIPLE-HUNDREDS

Minutes

288	W. R. Hammond ..	England v New Zealand at Auckland	1932-33
336	D. G. Bradman....	Australia v England at Leeds	1930

MOST RUNS IN A DAY BY A BATSMAN

309	D. G. Bradman	Australia v England at Leeds	1930
295	W. R. Hammond......	England v New Zealand at Auckland	1932-33
273	D. C. S. Compton	England v Pakistan at Nottingham...........	1954
271	D. G. Bradman	Australia v England at Leeds	1934

SLOWEST INDIVIDUAL BATTING

2* in 81 minutes	P. C. R. Tufnell, England v India at Bombay	1992-93
3* in 100 minutes	J. T. Murray, England v Australia at Sydney	1962-63
5 in 102 minutes	Nawab of Pataudi jun., India v England at Bombay	1972-73
7 in 123 minutes	G. Miller, England v Australia at Melbourne	1978-79
9 in 125 minutes	T. W. Jarvis, New Zealand v India at Madras	1964-65
10* in 133 minutes	T. G. Evans, England v Australia at Adelaide	1946-47
16* in 147 minutes	D. B. Vengsarkar, India v Pakistan at Kanpur	1979-80
17* in 166 minutes	G. M. Ritchie, Australia v India at Sydney	1985-86
18 in 194 minutes	W. R. Playle, New Zealand v England at Leeds	1958
19 in 217 minutes	M. D. Crowe, New Zealand v Sri Lanka at Moratuwa ...	1983-84
25 in 242 minutes	D. K. Morrison, New Zealand v Pakistan at Faisalabad ..	1990-91

28* in 250 minutes	J. W. Burke, Australia v England at Brisbane............	1958-59
31 in 264 minutes	K. D. Mackay, Australia v England at Lord's...........	1956
34* in 271 minutes	Younis Ahmed, Pakistan v India at Ahmedabad	1986-87
35 in 332 minutes	C. J. Tavaré, England v India at Madras	1981-82
55 in 336 minutes	B. A. Edgar, New Zealand v Australia at Wellington ...	1981-82
57 in 346 minutes	G. S. Camacho, West Indies v England at Bridgetown ...	1967-68
58 in 367 minutes	Ijaz Butt, Pakistan v Australia at Karachi..............	1959-60
60 in 390 minutes	D. N. Sardesai, India v West Indies at Bridgetown	1961-62
62 in 408 minutes	Ramiz Raja, Pakistan v West Indies at Karachi.........	1986-87
68 in 458 minutes	T. E. Bailey, England v Australia at Brisbane..........	1958-59
99 in 505 minutes	M. L. Jaisimha, India v Pakistan at Kanpur	1960-61
105 in 575 minutes	D. J. McGlew, South Africa v Australia at Durban	1957-58
114 in 591 minutes	Mudassar Nazar, Pakistan v England at Lahore	1977-78
120* in 609 minutes	J. J. Crowe, New Zealand v Sri Lanka, Colombo (CCC) .	1986-87
146* in 655 minutes	M. J. Greatbatch, New Zealand v Australia at Perth.....	1989-90
163 in 720 minutes	Shoaib Mohammad, Pakistan v New Zealand at Wellington	1988-89
201* in 777 minutes	D. S. B. P. Kuruppu, Sri Lanka v New Zealand at Colombo (CCC)	1986-87
337 in 970 minutes	Hanif Mohammad, Pakistan v West Indies at Bridgetown.	1957-58

SLOWEST HUNDREDS

557 minutes	Mudassar Nazar, Pakistan v England at Lahore	1977-78
545 minutes	D. J. McGlew, South Africa v Australia at Durban	1957-58
516 minutes	J. J. Crowe, New Zealand v Sri Lanka, Colombo (CCC)	1986-87
500 minutes	S. V. Manjrekar, India v Zimbabwe at Harare	1992-93
488 minutes	P. E. Richardson, England v South Africa at Johannesburg	1956-57

Notes: The slowest hundred for any Test in England is 458 minutes (329 balls) by K. W. R. Fletcher, England v Pakistan, The Oval, 1974.

The slowest double-hundred in a Test was scored in 777 minutes (548 balls) by D. S. B. P. Kuruppu for Sri Lanka v New Zealand at Colombo (CCC), 1986-87, on his debut. It is also the slowest-ever first-class double-hundred.

HIGHEST PARTNERSHIPS FOR EACH WICKET

413 for 1st	V. Mankad (231)/Pankaj Roy (173)........	I v NZ	Madras	1955-56
451 for 2nd	W. H. Ponsford (266)/D. G. Bradman (244).	A v E	The Oval	1934
467 for 3rd	A. H. Jones (186)/M. D. Crowe (299)	NZ v SL	Wellington	1990-91
411 for 4th	P. B. H. May (285*)/M. C. Cowdrey (154)..	E v WI	Birmingham	1957
405 for 5th	S. G. Barnes (234)/D. G. Bradman (234) ...	A v E	Sydney	1946-47
346 for 6th	J. H. W. Fingleton (136)/D. G. Bradman (270)	A v E	Melbourne	1936-37
347 for 7th	D. St E. Atkinson (219)/C. C. Depeiza (122)	WI v A	Bridgetown	1954-55
246 for 8th	L. E. G. Ames (137)/G. O. B. Allen (122) .	E v NZ	Lord's	1931
190 for 9th	Asif Iqbal (146)/Intikhab Alam (51)	P v E	The Oval	1967
151 for 10th	B. F. Hastings (110)/R. O. Collinge (68*)...	NZ v P	Auckland	1972-73

PARTNERSHIPS OF 300 AND OVER

467 for 3rd	A. H. Jones (186)/M. D. Crowe (299)	NZ v SL	Wellington	1990-91
451 for 2nd	W. H. Ponsford (266)/D. G. Bradman (244) ...	A v E	The Oval	1934
451 for 3rd	Mudassar Nazar (231)/Javed Miandad (280*) ..	P v I	Hyderabad	1982-83
446 for 2nd	C. C. Hunte (260)/G. S. Sobers (365*)........	WI v P	Kingston	1957-58
413 for 1st	V. Mankad (231)/Pankaj Roy (173)	I v NZ	Madras	1955-56
411 for 4th	P. B. H. May (285*)/M. C. Cowdrey (154) ...	E v WI	Birmingham	1957
405 for 5th	S. G. Barnes (234)/D. G. Bradman (234)	A v E	Sydney	1946-47
399 for 4th	G. S. Sobers (226)/F. M. M. Worrell (197*) ...	WI v E	Bridgetown	1959-60

397	for 3rd	Qasim Omar (206)/Javed Miandad (203*)	P v SL	Faisalabad	1985-86
388	for 4th	W. H. Ponsford (181)/D. G. Bradman (304)	A v E	Leeds	1934
387	for 1st	G. M. Turner (259)/T. W. Jarvis (182)	NZ v WI	Georgetown	1971-72
382	for 2nd	L. Hutton (364)/M. Leyland (187)	E v A	The Oval	1938
382	for 1st	W. M. Lawry (210)/R. B. Simpson (201)	A v WI	Bridgetown	1964-65
370	for 3rd	W. J. Edrich (189)/D. C. S. Compton (208)	E v SA	Lord's	1947
369	for 2nd	J. H. Edrich (310*)/K. F. Barrington (163)	E v NZ	Leeds	1965
359	for 1st	L. Hutton (158)/C. Washbrook (195)	E v SA	Johannesburg	1948-49
351	for 2nd	G. A. Gooch (196)/D. I. Gower (157)	E v A	The Oval	1985
350	for 4th	Mushtaq Mohammad (201)/Asif Iqbal (175)	P v NZ	Dunedin	1972-73
347	for 7th	D. St E. Atkinson (219)/C. C. Depeiza (122)	WI v A	Bridgetown	1954-55
346	for 6th	J. H. Fingleton (136)/D. G. Bradman (270)	A v E	Melbourne	1936-37
344*	for 2nd	S. M. Gavaskar (182*)/D. B. Vengsarkar (157*)	I v WI	Calcutta	1978-79
341	for 3rd	E. J. Barlow (201)/R. G. Pollock (175)	SA v A	Adelaide	1963-64
338	for 3rd	E. D. Weekes (206)/F. M. M. Worrell (167)	WI v E	Port-of-Spain	1953-54
336	for 4th	W. M. Lawry (151)/K. D. Walters (242)	A v WI	Sydney	1968-69
332*	for 5th	A. R. Border (200*)/S. R. Waugh (157*)	A v E	Leeds	1993
331	for 2nd	R. T. Robinson (148)/D. I. Gower (215)	E v A	Birmingham	1985
329	for 1st	G. R. Marsh (138)/M. A. Taylor (219)	A v E	Nottingham	1989
323	for 1st	J. B. Hobbs (178)/W. Rhodes (179)	E v A	Melbourne	1911-12
322	for 4th	Javed Miandad (153*)/Salim Malik (165)	P v E	Birmingham	1992
319	for 3rd	A. Melville (189)/A. D. Nourse (149)	SA v E	Nottingham	1947
316†	for 3rd	G. R. Viswanath (222)/Yashpal Sharma (140)	I v E	Madras	1981-82
308	for 7th	Waqar Hassan (189)/Imtiaz Ahmed (209)	P v NZ	Lahore	1955-56
308	for 3rd	R. B. Richardson (154)/I. V. A. Richards (178)	WI v A	St John's	1983-84
308	for 3rd	G. A. Gooch (333)/A. J. Lamb (139)	E v I	Lord's	1990
303	for 3rd	I. V. A. Richards (232)/A. I. Kallicharran (97)	WI v E	Nottingham	1976
301	for 3rd	A. R. Morris (182)/D. G. Bradman (173*)	A v E	Leeds	1948

† *415 runs were scored for this wicket in two separate partnerships: D. B. Vengsarkar retired hurt when he and Viswanath had added 99 runs.*

BOWLING RECORDS

MOST WICKETS IN AN INNINGS

10-53	J. C. Laker	England v Australia at Manchester	1956
9-28	G. A. Lohmann	England v South Africa at Johannesburg	1895-96
9-37	J. C. Laker	England v Australia at Manchester	1956
9-52	R. J. Hadlee	New Zealand v Australia at Brisbane	1985-86
9-56	Abdul Qadir	Pakistan v England at Lahore	1987-88
9-69	J. M. Patel	India v Australia at Kanpur	1959-60
9-83	Kapil Dev	India v West Indies at Ahmedabad	1983-84
9-86	Sarfraz Nawaz	Pakistan v Australia at Melbourne	1978-79
9-95	J. M. Noreiga	West Indies v India at Port-of-Spain	1970-71
9-102	S. P. Gupte	India v West Indies at Kanpur	1958-59
9-103	S. F. Barnes	England v South Africa at Johannesburg	1913-14
9-113	H. J. Tayfield	South Africa v England at Johannesburg	1956-57
9-121	A. A. Mailey	Australia v England at Melbourne	1920-21
8-7	G. A. Lohmann	England v South Africa at Port Elizabeth	1895-96
8-11	J. Briggs	England v South Africa at Cape Town	1888-89
8-29	S. F. Barnes	England v South Africa at The Oval	1912
8-29	C. E. H. Croft	West Indies v Pakistan at Port-of-Spain	1976-77
8-31	F. Laver	Australia v England at Manchester	1909
8-31	F. S. Trueman	England v India at Manchester	1952
8-34	I. T. Botham	England v Pakistan at Lord's	1978
8-35	G. A. Lohmann	England v Australia at Sydney	1886-87
8-38	L. R. Gibbs	West Indies v India at Bridgetown	1961-62
8-43†	A. E. Trott	Australia v England at Adelaide	1894-95
8-43	H. Verity	England v Australia at Lord's	1934

8-43	R. G. D. Willis	England v Australia at Leeds	1981
8-45	C. E. L. Ambrose . .	West Indies v England at Bridgetown	1989-90
8-51	D. L. Underwood . .	England v Pakistan at Lord's	1974
8-52	V. Mankad	India v Pakistan at Delhi	1952-53
8-53	G. B. Lawrence	South Africa v New Zealand at Johannesburg .	1961-62
8-53†	R. A. L. Massie . . .	Australia v England at Lord's	1972
8-55	V. Mankad	India v England at Madras	1951-52
8-56	S. F. Barnes	England v South Africa at Johannesburg	1913-14
8-58	G. A. Lohmann	England v Australia at Sydney	1891-92
8-58	Imran Khan	Pakistan v Sri Lanka at Lahore	1981-82
8-59	C. Blythe	England v South Africa at Leeds	1907
8-59	A. A. Mallett	Australia v Pakistan at Adelaide	1972-73
8-60	Imran Khan	Pakistan v India at Karachi	1982-83
8-61†	N. D. Hirwani	India v West Indies at Madras	1987-88
8-65	H. Trumble	Australia v England at The Oval	1902
8-68	W. Rhodes	England v Australia at Melbourne	1903-04
8-69	H. J. Tayfield	South Africa v England at Durban	1956-57
8-69	Sikander Bakht	Pakistan v India at Delhi	1979-80
8-70	S. J. Snooke	South Africa v England at Johannesburg	1905-06
8-71	G. D. McKenzie . . .	Australia v West Indies at Melbourne	1968-69
8-72	S. Venkataraghavan	India v New Zealand at Delhi	1964-65
8-75†	N. D. Hirwani	India v West Indies at Madras	1987-88
8-76	E. A. S. Prasanna . .	India v New Zealand at Auckland	1975-76
8-79	B. S. Chandrasekhar	India v England at Delhi	1972-73
8-81	L. C. Braund	England v Australia at Melbourne	1903-04
8-83	J. R. Ratnayeke	Sri Lanka v Pakistan at Sialkot	1985-86
8-84†	R. A. L. Massie	Australia v England at Lord's	1972
8-85	Kapil Dev	India v Pakistan at Lahore	1982-83
8-86	A. W. Greig	England v West Indies at Port-of-Spain	1973-74
8-87	M. G. Hughes	Australia v West Indies at Perth	1988-89
8-92	M. A. Holding	West Indies v England at The Oval	1976
8-94	T. Richardson	England v Australia at Sydney	1897-98
8-97	C. J. McDermott . . .	Australia v England at Perth	1990-91
8-103	I. T. Botham	England v West Indies at Lord's	1984
8-104†	A. L. Valentine	West Indies v England at Manchester	1950
8-106	Kapil Dev	India v Australia at Adelaide	1985-86
8-107	B. J. T. Bosanquet .	England v Australia at Nottingham	1905
8-107	N. A. Foster	England v Pakistan at Leeds	1987
8-112	G. F. Lawson	Australia v West Indies at Adelaide	1984-85
8-126	J. C. White	England v Australia at Adelaide	1928-29
8-141	C. J. McDermott . . .	Australia v England at Manchester	1985
8-143	M. H. N. Walker . .	Australia v England at Melbourne	1974-75

† *On Test debut.*

OUTSTANDING ANALYSES

	O	*M*	*R*	*W*		
J. C. Laker (E)	51.2	23	53	10	v Australia at Manchester	1956
G. A. Lohmann (E)	14.2	6	28	9	v South Africa at Johannesburg .	1895-96
J. C. Laker (E)	16.4	4	37	9	v Australia at Manchester	1956
G. A. Lohmann (E)	9.4	5	7	8	v South Africa at Port Elizabeth	1895-96
J. Briggs (E)	14.2	5	11	8	v South Africa at Cape Town . .	1888-89
J. Briggs (E)	19.1	11	17	7	v South Africa at Cape Town . .	1888-89
M. A. Noble (A)	7.4	2	17	7	v England at Melbourne	1901-02
W. Rhodes (E)	11	3	17	7	v Australia at Birmingham	1902
A. E. R. Gilligan (E)	6.3	4	7	6	v South Africa at Birmingham . .	1924
S. Haigh (E)	11.4	6	11	6	v South Africa at Cape Town . .	1898-99
D. L. Underwood (E)	11.6	7	12	6	v New Zealand at Christchurch.	1970-71
S. L. V. Raju (I)	17.5	13	12	6	v Sri Lanka at Chandigarh	1990-91

	O	M	R	W		
H. J. Tayfield (SA)	14	7	13	6	v New Zealand at Johannesburg.	1953-54
C. T. B. Turner (A)	18	11	15	6	v England at Sydney..........	1886-87
M. H. N. Walker (A)	16	8	15	6	v Pakistan at Sydney	1972-73
E. R. H. Toshack (A)	2.3	1	2	5	v India at Brisbane...........	1947-48
H. Ironmonger (A)	7.2	5	6	5	v South Africa at Melbourne ...	1931-32
Pervez Sajjad (P)	12	8	5	4	v New Zealand at Rawalpindi.	1964-65
K. Higgs (E)	9	7	5	4	v New Zealand at Christchurch.	1965-66
P. H. Edmonds (E)	8	6	6	4	v Pakistan at Lord's	1978
J. C. White (E)	6.3	2	7	4	v Australia at Brisbane........	1928-29
J. H. Wardle (E)	5	2	7	4	v Australia at Manchester	1953
R. Appleyard (E)	6	3	7	4	v New Zealand at Auckland ...	1954-55
R. Benaud (A)	3.4	3	0	3	v India at Delhi	1959-60

MOST WICKETS IN A MATCH

19-90	J. C. Laker	England v Australia at Manchester	1956
17-159	S. F. Barnes	England v South Africa at Johannesburg	1913-14
16-136†	N. D. Hirwani....	India v West Indies at Madras	1987-88
16-137†	R. A. L. Massie ..	Australia v England at Lord's	1972
15-28	J. Briggs	England v South Africa at Cape Town	1888-89
15-45	G. A. Lohmann...	England v South Africa at Port Elizabeth ...	1895-96
15-99	C. Blythe	England v South Africa at Leeds	1907
15-104	H. Verity	England v Australia at Lord's	1934
15-123	R. J. Hadlee	New Zealand v Australia at Brisbane	1985-86
15-124	W. Rhodes	England v Australia at Melbourne.........	1903-04
14-90	F. R. Spofforth ..	Australia v England at The Oval	1882
14-99	A. V. Bedser	England v Australia at Nottingham	1953
14-102	W. Bates	England v Australia at Melbourne.........	1882-83
14-116	Imran Khan......	Pakistan v Sri Lanka at Lahore	1981-82
14-124	J. M. Patel	India v Australia at Kanpur..............	1959-60
14-144	S. F. Barnes	England v South Africa at Durban	1913-14
14-149	M. A. Holding....	West Indies v England at The Oval	1976
14-199	C. V. Grimmett...	Australia v South Africa at Adelaide	1931-32

† *On Test debut.*

Notes: The best for South Africa is 13-165 by H. J. Tayfield against Australia at Melbourne, 1952-53. The best for Sri Lanka is 9-125 by R. J. Ratnayake against India at Colombo (PSS), 1985-86. The best for Zimbabwe is 5-86 by A. J. Traicos against India at Harare, 1992-93.

MOST WICKETS IN A SERIES

	T	R	W	*Avge*		
S. F. Barnes	4	536	49	10.93	England v South Africa.	1913-14
J. C. Laker	5	442	46	9.60	England v Australia....	1956
C. V. Grimmett	5	642	44	14.59	Australia v South Africa	1935-36
T. M. Alderman	6	893	42	21.26	Australia v England....	1981
R. M. Hogg	6	527	41	12.85	Australia v England....	1978-79
T. M. Alderman	6	712	41	17.36	Australia v England....	1989
Imran Khan	6	558	40	13.95	Pakistan v India	1982-83
A. V. Bedser	5	682	39	17.48	England v Australia....	1953
D. K. Lillee	6	870	39	22.30	Australia v England....	1981
M. W. Tate	5	881	38	23.18	England v Australia....	1924-25
W. J. Whitty	5	632	37	17.08	Australia v South Africa	1910-11
H. J. Tayfield	5	636	37	17.18	South Africa v England.	1956-57
A. E. E. Vogler	5	783	36	21.75	South Africa v England.	1909-10
A. A. Mailey	5	946	36	26.27	Australia v England....	1920-21
G. A. Lohmann	3	203	35	5.80	England v South Africa.	1895-96
B. S. Chandrasekhar ..	5	662	35	18.91	India v England	1972-73
M. D. Marshall	5	443	35	12.65	West Indies v England .	1988

MOST WICKETS IN A CAREER

(Qualification: 100 wickets)

ENGLAND

		T	Balls	R	W	Avge	5W/i	10W/m
1	I. T. Botham	102	21,815	10,878	383	28.40	27	4
2	R. G. D. Willis	90	17,357	8,190	325	25.20	16	—
3	F. S. Trueman	67	15,178	6,625	307	21.57	17	3
4	D. L. Underwood	86	21,862	7,674	297	25.83	17	6
5	J. B. Statham	70	16,056	6,261	252	24.84	9	1
6	A. V. Bedser	51	15,918	5,876	236	24.89	15	5
7	J. A. Snow	49	12,021	5,387	202	26.66	8	1
8	J. C. Laker	46	12,027	4,101	193	21.24	9	3
9	S. F. Barnes	27	7,873	3,106	189	16.43	24	7
10	G. A. R. Lock	49	13,147	4,451	174	25.58	9	3
11	M. W. Tate	39	12,523	4,055	155	26.16	7	1
12	F. J. Titmus	53	15,118	4,931	153	32.22	7	—
13	**J. E. Emburey**	**63**	**15,211**	**5,564**	**147**	**37.85**	**6**	**—**
14	H. Verity	40	11,173	3,510	144	24.37	5	2
15	C. M. Old	46	8,858	4,020	143	28.11	4	—
16	A. W. Greig	58	9,802	4,541	141	32.20	6	2
17	G. R. Dilley	41	8,192	4,107	138	29.76	6	—
18	T. E. Bailey	61	9,712	3,856	132	29.21	5	1
19	W. Rhodes	58	8,231	3,425	127	26.96	6	1
20	P. H. Edmonds	51	12,028	4,273	125	34.18	2	—
21 {	D. A. Allen	39	11,297	3,779	122	30.97	4	—
	R. Illingworth	61	11,934	3,807	122	31.20	3	—
23	J. Briggs	33	5,332	2,095	118	17.75	9	4
24	G. G. Arnold	34	7,650	3,254	115	28.29	6	—
25	G. A. Lohmann	18	3,821	1,205	112	10.75	9	5
26	D. V. P. Wright	34	8,135	4,224	108	39.11	6	1
27	J. H. Wardle	28	6,597	2,080	102	20.39	5	1
28	R. Peel	20	5,216	1,715	101	16.98	5	1
29	C. Blythe	19	4,546	1,863	100	18.63	9	4

AUSTRALIA

		T	Balls	R	W	Avge	5W/i	10W/m
1	D. K. Lillee	70	18,467	8,493	355	23.92	23	7
2	R. Benaud	63	19,108	6,704	248	27.03	16	1
3	G. D. McKenzie	60	17,681	7,328	246	29.78	16	3
4	R. R. Lindwall	61	13,650	5,251	228	23.03	12	—
5	C. V. Grimmett	37	14,513	5,231	216	24.21	21	7
6	**M. G. Hughes**	**51**	**11,865**	**5,780**	**208**	**27.78**	**7**	**1**
7	J. R. Thomson	51	10,535	5,601	200	28.00	8	—
8	**C. J. McDermott**	**49**	**11,141**	**5,738**	**198**	**28.97**	**9**	**2**
9	A. K. Davidson	44	11,587	3,819	186	20.53	14	2
10	G. F. Lawson	46	11,118	5,501	180	30.56	11	2
11 {	K. R. Miller	55	10,461	3,906	170	22.97	7	1
	T. M. Alderman	41	10,181	4,616	170	27.15	14	1
13	W. A. Johnston	40	11,048	3,826	160	23.91	7	—
14	W. J. O'Reilly	27	10,024	3,254	144	22.59	11	3
15	H. Trumble	32	8,099	3,072	141	21.78	9	3

		T	Balls	R	W	Avge	5W/i	10W/m
16	M. H. N. Walker	34	10,094	3,792	138	27.47	6	—
17	A. A. Mallett	38	9,990	3,940	132	29.84	6	1
18	B. Yardley	33	8,909	3,986	126	31.63	6	1
19	R. M. Hogg	38	7,633	3,503	123	28.47	6	2
20	M. A. Noble	42	7,159	3,025	121	25.00	9	2
21	**B. A. Reid**	**27**	**6,244**	**2,784**	**113**	**24.63**	**5**	**2**
22	I. W. Johnson	45	8,780	3,182	109	29.19	3	—
23	G. Giffen	31	6,457	2,791	103	27.09	7	1
24	A. N. Connolly	29	7,818	2,981	102	29.22	4	—
25	C. T. B. Turner	17	5,179	1,670	101	16.53	11	2

SOUTH AFRICA

		T	Balls	R	W	Avge	5W/i	10W/m
1	H. J. Tayfield	37	13,568	4,405	170	25.91	14	2
2	T. L. Goddard	41	11,736	3,226	123	26.22	5	—
3	P. M. Pollock	28	6,522	2,806	116	24.18	9	1
4	N. A. T. Adcock	26	6,391	2,195	104	21.10	5	—

WEST INDIES

		T	Balls	R	W	Avge	5W/i	10W/m
1	M. D. Marshall	81	17,584	7,876	376	20.94	22	4
2	L. R. Gibbs	79	27,115	8,989	309	29.09	18	2
3	J. Garner	58	13,169	5,433	259	20.97	7	—
4	M. A. Holding	60	12,680	5,898	249	23.68	13	2
5	G. S. Sobers	93	21,599	7,999	235	34.03	6	—
6 {	A. M. E. Roberts.....	47	11,136	5,174	202	25.61	11	2
{	**C. A. Walsh**	**59**	**11,652**	**5,118**	**202**	**25.33**	**5**	**1**
8	W. W. Hall	48	10,421	5,066	192	26.38	9	1
9	**C. E. L. Ambrose**	**42**	**10,353**	**4,070**	**190**	**21.42**	**9**	**2**
10	S. Ramadhin	43	13,939	4,579	158	28.98	10	1
11	A. L. Valentine	36	12,953	4,215	139	30.32	8	2
12	C. E. H. Croft	27	6,165	2,913	125	23.30	3	—
13	V. A. Holder	40	9,095	3,627	109	33.27	3	—

NEW ZEALAND

		T	Balls	R	W	Avge	5W/i	10W/m
1	R. J. Hadlee	86	21,918	9,611	431	22.29	36	9
2	B. L. Cairns	43	10,628	4,280	130	32.92	6	1
3	E. J. Chatfield	43	10,360	3,958	123	32.17	3	1
4	R. O. Collinge	35	7,689	3,392	116	29.24	3	—
5	B. R. Taylor	30	6,334	2,953	111	26.60	4	—
6	**D. K. Morrison**	**29**	**6,089**	**3,382**	**103**	**32.83**	**8**	—
7	J. G. Bracewell	41	8,403	3,653	102	35.81	4	1
8	R. C. Motz	32	7,034	3,148	100	31.48	5	—

INDIA

		T	Balls	R	W	Avge	5W/i	10W/m
1	**Kapil Dev**	**127**	**27,250**	**12,619**	**425**	**29.69**	**23**	**2**
2	B. S. Bedi	67	21,364	7,637	266	28.71	14	1
3	B. S. Chandrasekhar . .	58	15,963	7,199	242	29.74	16	2
4	E. A. S. Prasanna	49	14,353	5,742	189	30.38	10	2
5	V. Mankad	44	14,686	5,236	162	32.32	8	2
6	S. Venkataraghavan . .	57	14,877	5,634	156	36.11	3	1
7	**R. J. Shastri**	**80**	**15,751**	**6,185**	**151**	**40.96**	**2**	—
8	S. P. Gupte	36	11,284	4,403	149	29.55	12	1
9	D. R. Doshi	33	9,322	3,502	114	30.71	6	—
10	K. D. Ghavri	39	7,042	3,656	109	33.54	4	—
11	N. S. Yadav	35	8,349	3,580	102	35.09	3	—

PAKISTAN

		T	Balls	R	W	Avge	5W/i	10W/m
1	Imran Khan	88	19,458	8,258	362	22.81	23	6
2	Abdul Qadir	67	17,126	7,742	236	32.80	15	5
3	**Wasim Akram**	**48**	**10,616**	**4,569**	**186**	**24.56**	**12**	**2**
4	Sarfraz Nawaz	55	13,927	5,798	177	32.75	4	1
5	Iqbal Qasim	50	13,019	4,807	171	28.11	8	2
6	Fazal Mahmood	34	9,834	3,434	139	24.70	13	4
7	Intikhab Alam	47	10,474	4,494	125	35.95	5	2
8	**Waqar Younis**	**23**	**4,587**	**2,373**	**121**	**19.61**	**12**	**2**

SRI LANKA: The highest aggregate is 73 wickets, average 35.10, by **R. J. Ratnayake** in 23 Tests.

ZIMBABWE: The highest aggregate is 14 wickets, average 40.14, by **A. J. Traicos** in 4 Tests. He also took 4 wickets, average 51.75, in 3 Tests for South Africa.

Bold type denotes those who played Test cricket in 1992-93 and 1993 seasons or Sri Lanka v India and South Africa in 1993-94.

WICKET WITH FIRST BALL IN TEST CRICKET

	Batsman dismissed			
A. Coningham	A. C. MacLaren	A v E	Melbourne	1894-95
W. M. Bradley	F. Laver	E v A	Manchester	1899
E. G. Arnold	V. T. Trumper	E v A	Sydney	1903-04
G. G. Macaulay	G. A. L. Hearne	A v SA	Cape Town	1922-23
M. W. Tate	M. J. Susskind	E v SA	Birmingham	1924
M. Henderson	E. W. Dawson	NZ v E	Christchurch	1929-30
H. D. Smith	E. Paynter	NZ v E	Christchurch	1932-33
T. F. Johnson	W. W. Keeton	WI v E	The Oval	1939
R. Howorth	D. V. Dyer	E v SA	The Oval	1947
Intikhab Alam	C. C. McDonald	P v A	Karachi	1959-60
R. K. Illingworth	P. V. Simmons	E v WI	Nottingham	1991

HAT-TRICKS

F. R. Spofforth	Australia v England at Melbourne	1878-79
W. Bates	England v Australia at Melbourne	1882-83
J. Briggs..........	England v Australia at Sydney	1891-92
G. A. Lohmann ...	England v South Africa at Port Elizabeth	1895-96
J. T. Hearne	England v Australia at Leeds	1899
H. Trumble	Australia v England at Melbourne	1901-02
H. Trumble	Australia v England at Melbourne	1903-04
T. J. Matthews† ⎫ T. J. Matthews ... ⎬	Australia v South Africa at Manchester	1912
M. J. C. Allom‡ ...	England v New Zealand at Christchurch	1929-30
T. W. J. Goddard ..	England v South Africa at Johannesburg	1938-39
P. J. Loader.......	England v West Indies at Leeds	1957
L. F. Kline	Australia v South Africa at Cape Town	1957-58
W. W. Hall	West Indies v Pakistan at Lahore	1958-59
G. M. Griffin	South Africa v England at Lord's	1960
L. R. Gibbs.......	West Indies v Australia at Adelaide	1960-61
P. J. Petherick‡ ...	New Zealand v Pakistan at Lahore	1976-77
C. A. Walsh§	West Indies v Australia at Brisbane	1988-89
M. G. Hughes§	Australia v West Indies at Perth	1988-89

† T. J. Matthews did the hat-trick in each innings of the same match.
‡ On Test debut.
§ Not all in the same innings.

FOUR WICKETS IN FIVE BALLS

M. J. C. Allom	England v New Zealand at Christchurch	1929-30
	On debut, in his eighth over: W-WWW	
C. M. Old	England v Pakistan at Birmingham	1978
	Sequence interrupted by a no-ball: WW-WW	
Wasim Akram.....	Pakistan v West Indies at Lahore (*WW-WW*)........	1990-91

MOST BALLS BOWLED IN A TEST

S. Ramadhin (West Indies) sent down 774 balls in 129 overs against England at Birmingham, 1957. It was the most delivered by any bowler in a Test, beating H. Verity's 766 for England against South Africa at Durban, 1938-39. In this match Ramadhin also bowled the most balls (588) in any single first-class innings, including Tests.

It should be noted that six balls were bowled to the over in the Australia v England Test series of 1928-29 and 1932-33, when the eight-ball over was otherwise in force in Australia.

ALL-ROUND RECORDS

100 RUNS AND FIVE WICKETS IN AN INNINGS

England

A. W. Greig	148	6-164	v West Indies	Bridgetown	1973-74
I. T. Botham	103	5-73	v New Zealand	Christchurch	1977-78
I. T. Botham	108	8-34	v Pakistan	Lord's	1978
I. T. Botham	114	6-58 7-48 }	v India	Bombay	1979-80
I. T. Botham	149*	6-95	v Australia	Leeds	1981
I. T. Botham	138	5-59	v New Zealand	Wellington	1983-84

Australia

C. Kelleway	114	5-33	v South Africa	Manchester	1912
J. M. Gregory	100	7-69	v England	Melbourne	1920-21
K. R. Miller	109	6-107	v West Indies	Kingston	1954-55
R. Benaud	100	5-84	v South Africa	Johannesburg	1957-58

South Africa
J. H. Sinclair	106	6-26	v England	Cape Town	1898-99
G. A. Faulkner	123	5-120	v England	Johannesburg	1909-10

West Indies
D. St E. Atkinson	219	5-56	v Australia	Bridgetown	1954-55
O. G. Smith	100	5-90	v India	Delhi	1958-59
G. S. Sobers	104	5-63	v India	Kingston	1961-62
G. S. Sobers	174	5-41	v England	Leeds	1966

New Zealand
B. R. Taylor†	105	5-86	v India	Calcutta	1964-65

India
V. Mankad	184	5-196	v England	Lord's	1952
P. R. Umrigar	172*	5-107	v West Indies	Port-of-Spain	1961-62

Pakistan
Mushtaq Mohammad	201	5-49	v New Zealand	Dunedin	1972-73
Mushtaq Mohammad	121	5-28	v West Indies	Port-of-Spain	1976-77
Imran Khan	117	6-98 ⎱ 5-82 ⎰	v India	Faisalabad	1982-83
Wasim Akram	123	5-100	v Australia	Adelaide	1989-90

  † *On debut.*

100 RUNS AND FIVE DISMISSALS IN AN INNINGS

D. T. Lindsay	182	6ct	SA v A	Johannesburg	1966-67
I. D. S. Smith	113*	4ct, 1st	NZ v E	Auckland	1983-84
S. A. R. Silva	111	5ct	SL v I	Colombo (PSS)	1985-86

100 RUNS AND TEN WICKETS IN A TEST

A. K. Davidson	44 80	5-135 ⎱ 6-87 ⎰	A v WI	Brisbane..........	1960-61
I. T. Botham	114	6-58 ⎱ 7-48 ⎰	E v I	Bombay	1979-80
Imran Khan	117	6-98 ⎱ 5-82 ⎰	P v I	Faisalabad	1982-83

1,000 RUNS AND 100 WICKETS IN A CAREER

	Tests	Runs	Wkts	Tests for Double
England				
T. E. Bailey.............	61	2,290	132	47
†I. T. Botham	102	5,200	383	21
J. E. Emburey	**63**	**1,705**	**147**	**46**
A. W. Greig	58	3,599	141	37
R. Illingworth	61	1,836	122	47
W. Rhodes.............	58	2,325	127	44
M. W. Tate	39	1,198	155	33
F. J. Titmus	53	1,449	153	40
Australia				
R. Benaud	63	2,201	248	32
A. K. Davidson	44	1,328	186	34
G. Giffen...............	31	1,238	103	30
I. W. Johnson	45	1,000	109	45
R. R. Lindwall	61	1,502	228	38
K. R. Miller	55	2,958	170	33
M. A. Noble	42	1,997	121	27

	Tests	Runs	Wkts	Tests for Double
South Africa				
T. L. Goddard	41	2,516	123	36
West Indies				
M. D. Marshall	81	1,810	376	49
†G. S. Sobers	93	8,032	235	48
New Zealand				
J. G. Bracewell	41	1,001	102	41
R. J. Hadlee	86	3,124	431	28
India				
Kapil Dev	**127**	**5,131**	**425**	**25**
V. Mankad	44	2,109	162	23
R. J. Shastri	**80**	**3,830**	**151**	**44**
Pakistan				
Abdul Qadir	67	1,029	236	62
Imran Khan	88	3,807	362	30
Intikhab Alam	47	1,493	125	41
Sarfraz Nawaz	55	1,045	177	55
Wasim Akram	**48**	**1,057**	**186**	**45**

Bold type denotes those who played Test cricket in 1992-93 and 1993 seasons or Sri Lanka v India and South Africa in 1993-94.

† I. T. Botham (120 catches) and G. S. Sobers (109) are the only players to have achieved the treble of 1,000 runs, 100 wickets and 100 catches.

WICKET-KEEPING RECORDS

Most Dismissals in an Innings

7 (all ct)	Wasim Bari	Pakistan v New Zealand at Auckland ...	1978-79
7 (all ct)	R. W. Taylor......	England v India at Bombay............	1979-80
7 (all ct)	I. D. S. Smith	New Zealand v Sri Lanka at Hamilton ..	1990-91
6 (all ct)	A. T. W. Grout....	Australia v South Africa at Johannesburg	1957-58
6 (all ct)	D. T. Lindsay	South Africa v Australia at Johannesburg	1966-67
6 (all ct)	J. T. Murray	England v India at Lord's	1967
6 (5ct, 1st)	S. M. H. Kirmani..	India v New Zealand at Christchurch ...	1975-76
6 (all ct)	R. W. Marsh	Australia v England at Brisbane	1982-83
6 (all ct)	S. A. R. Silva	Sri Lanka v India at Colombo (SSC) ...	1985-86
6 (all ct)	R. C. Russell	England v Australia at Melbourne	1990-91

Note: The most stumpings in an innings is 5 by K. S. More for India v West Indies at Madras in 1987-88.

Most Dismissals in a Test

10 (all ct)	R. W. Taylor......	England v India at Bombay............	1979-80
9 (8ct, 1st)	G. R. A. Langley ..	Australia v England at Lord's	1956
9 (all ct)	D. A. Murray	West Indies v Australia at Melbourne ...	1981-82
9 (all ct)	R. W. Marsh	Australia v England at Brisbane	1982-83
9 (all ct)	S. A. R. Silva	Sri Lanka v India at Colombo (SSC)	1985-86
9 (8ct, 1st)	S. A. R. Silva	Sri Lanka v India at Colombo (PSS)	1985-86
9 (all ct)	D. J. Richardson...	South Africa v India at Port Elizabeth ...	1992-93
8 (all ct)	J. J. Kelly	Australia v England at Sydney	1901-02

8 (6ct, 2st)	L. E. G. Ames	England v West Indies at The Oval	1933
8 (all ct)	G. R. A. Langley ..	Australia v West Indies at Kingston.....	1954-55
8 (6ct, 2st)	A. T. W. Grout....	Australia v Pakistan at Lahore	1959-60
8 (all ct)	A. T. W. Grout....	Australia v England at Lord's	1961
8 (all ct)	J. M. Parks	England v New Zealand at Christchurch .	1965-66
8 (all ct)	D. T. Lindsay	South Africa v Australia at Johannesburg	1966-67
8 (7ct, 1st)	H. B. Taber.......	Australia v South Africa at Johannesburg	1966-67
8 (all ct)	Wasim Bari	Pakistan v England at Leeds...........	1971
8 (all ct)	R. W. Marsh......	Australia v West Indies at Melbourne ...	1975-76
8 (all ct)	R. W. Marsh......	Australia v New Zealand at Christchurch .	1976-77
8 (7ct, 1st)	R. W. Marsh......	Australia v India at Sydney	1980-81
8 (all ct)	W. K. Lees	New Zealand v Sri Lanka at Wellington .	1982-83
8 (all ct)	R. W. Marsh......	Australia v England at Adelaide	1982-83
8 (all ct)	I. D. S. Smith	New Zealand v Sri Lanka at Hamilton ..	1990-91
8 (6ct, 2st)	I. A. Healy	Australia v West Indies at Adelaide	1992-93
8 (all ct)	J. R. Murray	West Indies v Australia at Perth	1992-93
8 (all ct)	D. J. Richardson...	South Africa v Sri Lanka at Colombo (SSC)	1993-94

Notes: S. A. R. Silva made 18 dismissals in two successive Tests.
   The most stumpings in a match is 6 by K. S. More for India v West Indies at Madras in 1987-88.

Most Dismissals in a Series

(Played in 5 Tests unless otherwise stated)

28 (all ct)	R. W. Marsh......	Australia v England	1982-83
26 (23ct, 3st)	J. H. B. Waite	South Africa v New Zealand...........	1961-62
26 (all ct)	R. W. Marsh......	Australia v West Indies (6 Tests)	1975-76
26 (21ct, 5st)	I. A. Healy	Australia v England (6 Tests)	1993
24 (22ct, 2st)	D. L. Murray	West Indies v England	1963
24 (all ct)	D. T. Lindsay	South Africa v Australia	1966-67
24 (21ct, 3st)	A. P. E. Knott	England v Australia (6 Tests)	1970-71
24 (all ct)	I. A. Healy	Australia v England	1990-91
23 (16ct, 7st)	J. H. B. Waite	South Africa v New Zealand...........	1953-54
23 (22ct, 1st)	F. C. M. Alexander.	West Indies v England	1959-60
23 (20ct, 3st)	A. T. W. Grout....	Australia v West Indies	1960-61
23 (21ct, 2st)	A. E. Dick........	New Zealand v South Africa	1961-62
23 (21ct, 2st)	R. W. Marsh......	Australia v England	1972
23 (22ct, 1st)	A. P. E. Knott	England v Australia (6 Tests)	1974-75
23 (all ct)	R. W. Marsh......	Australia v England (6 Tests)	1981
23 (all ct)	P. J. L. Dujon	West Indies v Australia	1990-91
23 (19ct, 4st)	I. A. Healy	Australia v West Indies	1992-93
22 (all ct)	S. J. Rixon	Australia v India.....................	1977-78
22 (21ct, 1st)	S. A. R. Silva	Sri Lanka v India (3 Tests)	1985-86
21 (15ct, 6st)	H. Strudwick	England v South Africa	1913-14
21 (13ct, 8st)	R. A. Saggers	Australia v South Africa	1949-50
21 (16ct, 5st)	G. R. A. Langley .	Australia v West Indies	1951-52
21 (20ct, 1st)	A. T. W. Grout....	Australia v England	1961
21 (all ct)	R. W. Marsh......	Australia v Pakistan	1983-84
20 (16ct, 4st)	D. Tallon	Australia v England	1946-47
20 (16ct, 4st)	G. R. A. Langley .	Australia v West Indies (4 Tests)	1954-55
20 (18ct, 2st)	T. G. Evans	England v South Africa	1956-57
20 (17ct, 3st)	A. T. W. Grout....	Australia v England	1958-59
20 (19ct, 1st)	H. B. Taber......	Australia v South Africa	1966-67
20 (18ct, 2st)	R. W. Taylor.....	England v Australia (6 Tests)	1978-79
20 (19ct, 1st)	P. J. L. Dujon	West Indies v Australia	1983-84
20 (19ct, 1st)	P. R. Downton	England v Australia (6 Tests)	1985
20 (all ct)	P. J. L. Dujon	West Indies v England	1988

Most Dismissals in a Career

		T	Ct	St	Total
1	R. W. Marsh (Australia)	96	343	12	355
2	P. J. L. Dujon (West Indies)	81	267	5	272
3	A. P. E. Knott (England)	95	250	19	269
4	Wasim Bari (Pakistan)	81	201	27	228
5	T. G. Evans (England)	91	173	46	219
6	S. M. H. Kirmani (India)	88	160	38	198
7	D. L. Murray (West Indies)	62	181	8	189
8	A. T. W. Grout (Australia)	51	163	24	187
9	**I. A. Healy (Australia)**	**53**	**167**	**12**	**179**
10	I. D. S. Smith (New Zealand)	63	168	8	176
11	R. W. Taylor (England)	57	167	7	174
12	J. H. B. Waite (South Africa)	50	124	17	141
13	**K. S. More (India)**	**49**	**110**	**20**	**130**
	W. A. Oldfield (Australia)	54	78	52	130
15	J. M. Parks (England)	46	103	11	114
16	Salim Yousuf (Pakistan)	32	91	13	104

Notes: The records for P. J. L. Dujon and J. M. Parks each include two catches taken when not keeping wicket in two and three Tests respectively.

The most dismissals for other countries are Sri Lanka 34 (S. A. R. Silva 33ct, 1st in 9 Tests) and Zimbabwe 9 (**A. Flower** 7ct, 2st in 4 Tests).

Bold type denotes those who played Test cricket in 1992-93 and 1993 seasons or Sri Lanka v India and South Africa in 1993-94.

FIELDING RECORDS

(Excluding wicket-keepers)

Most Catches in an Innings

5	V. Y. Richardson	Australia v South Africa at Durban	1935-36
5	Yajurvindra Singh	India v England at Bangalore	1976-77
5	M. Azharuddin	India v Pakistan at Karachi	1989-90
5	K. Srikkanth	India v Australia at Perth	1991-92

Most Catches in a Test

7	G. S. Chappell	Australia v England at Perth	1974-75
7	Yajurvindra Singh	India v England at Bangalore	1976-77
7	H. P. Tillekeratne	Sri Lanka v New Zealand at Colombo (SSC) . . .	1992-93
6	A. Shrewsbury	England v Australia at Sydney	1887-88
6	A. E. E. Vogler	South Africa v England at Durban	1909-10
6	F. E. Woolley	England v Australia at Sydney	1911-12
6	J. M. Gregory	Australia v England at Sydney	1920-21
6	B. Mitchell	South Africa v Australia at Melbourne	1931-32
6	V. Y. Richardson	Australia v South Africa at Durban	1935-36
6	R. N. Harvey	Australia v England at Sydney	1962-63
6	M. C. Cowdrey	England v West Indies at Lord's	1963
6	E. D. Solkar	India v West Indies at Port-of-Spain	1970-71
6	G. S. Sobers	West Indies v England at Lord's	1973
6	I. M. Chappell	Australia v New Zealand at Adelaide	1973-74
6	A. W. Greig	England v Pakistan at Leeds	1974
6	D. F. Whatmore	Australia v India at Kanpur	1979-80
6	A. J. Lamb	England v New Zealand at Lord's	1983
6	R. B. Richardson	West Indies v South Africa at Bridgetown	1991-92
6	G. A. Hick	England v Pakistan at Leeds	1992

Most Catches in a Series

15	J. M. Gregory	Australia v England	1920-21
14	G. S. Chappell	Australia v England (6 Tests)	1974-75
13	R. B. Simpson	Australia v South Africa	1957-58
13	R. B. Simpson	Australia v West Indies	1960-61

Most Catches in a Career

A. R. Border (Australia)	**148 in 147 matches**
G. S. Chappell (Australia)	122 in 87 matches
I. V. A. Richards (West Indies)	122 in 121 matches
I. T. Botham (England)	120 in 102 matches
M. C. Cowdrey (England)	120 in 114 matches
R. B. Simpson (Australia)	110 in 62 matches
W. R. Hammond (England)	110 in 85 matches
G. S. Sobers (West Indies)	109 in 93 matches
S. M. Gavaskar (India)	108 in 125 matches
I. M. Chappell (Australia)	105 in 75 matches

Bold type denotes player who played Test cricket in 1992-93 and 1993 seasons.

TEAM RECORDS

HIGHEST INNINGS TOTALS

903-7 dec.	England v Australia at The Oval	1938
849	England v West Indies at Kingston	1929-30
790-3 dec.	West Indies v Pakistan at Kingston	1957-58
758-8 dec.	Australia v West Indies at Kingston	1954-55
729-6 dec.	Australia v England at Lord's	1930
708	Pakistan v England at The Oval	1987
701	Australia v England at The Oval	1934
699-5	Pakistan v India at Lahore	1989-90
695	Australia v England at The Oval	1930
687-8 dec.	West Indies v England at The Oval	1976
681-8 dec.	West Indies v England at Port-of-Spain	1953-54
676-7	India v Sri Lanka at Kanpur	1986-87
674-6	Pakistan v India at Faisalabad	1984-85
674	Australia v India at Adelaide	1947-48
671-4	New Zealand v Sri Lanka at Wellington	1990-91
668	Australia v West Indies at Bridgetown	1954-55
659-8 dec.	Australia v England at Sydney	1946-47
658-8 dec.	England v Australia at Nottingham	1938
657-8 dec.	Pakistan v West Indies at Bridgetown	1957-58
656-8 dec.	Australia v England at Manchester	1964
654-5	England v South Africa at Durban	1938-39
653-4 dec.	England v India at Lord's	1990
653-4 dec.	Australia v England at Leeds	1993
652-7 dec.	England v India at Madras	1984-85
652-8 dec.	West Indies v England at Lord's	1973
652	Pakistan v India at Faisalabad	1982-83
650-6 dec.	Australia v West Indies at Bridgetown	1964-65

The highest innings for the countries not mentioned above are:

622-9 dec.	South Africa v Australia at Durban	1969-70
547-8 dec.	Sri Lanka v Australia at Colombo (SSC)	1992-93
456	Zimbabwe v India at Harare	1992-93

HIGHEST FOURTH-INNINGS TOTALS

To win

406-4	India (needing 403) v West Indies at Port-of-Spain	1975-76
404-3	Australia (needing 404) v England at Leeds	1948
362-7	Australia (needing 359) v West Indies at Georgetown	1977-78
348-5	West Indies (needing 345) v New Zealand at Auckland	1968-69
344-1	West Indies (needing 342) v England at Lord's.....................	1984

To tie

347	India v Australia at Madras...................................	1986-87

To draw

654-5	England (needing 696 to win) v South Africa at Durban.............	1938-39
429-8	India (needing 438 to win) v England at The Oval.................	1979
423-7	South Africa (needing 451 to win) v England at The Oval	1947
408-5	West Indies (needing 836 to win) v England at Kingston	1929-30

To lose

445	India (lost by 47 runs) v Australia at Adelaide	1977-78
440	New Zealand (lost by 38 runs) v England at Nottingham..............	1973
417	England (lost by 45 runs) v Australia at Melbourne	1976-77
411	England (lost by 193 runs) v Australia at Sydney.....................	1924-25

MOST RUNS IN A DAY (BOTH SIDES)

588	England (398-6), India (190-0) at Manchester (2nd day)	1936
522	England (503-2), South Africa (19-0) at Lord's (2nd day)	1924
508	England (221-2), South Africa (287-6) at The Oval (3rd day)	1935

MOST RUNS IN A DAY (ONE SIDE)

503	England (503-2) v South Africa at Lord's (2nd day)	1924
494	Australia (494-6) v South Africa at Sydney (1st day)...................	1910-11
475	Australia (475-2) v England at The Oval (1st day)....................	1934
471	England (471-8) v India at The Oval (1st day).......................	1936
458	Australia (458-3) v England at Leeds (1st day).......................	1930
455	Australia (455-1) v England at Leeds (2nd day)	1934

MOST WICKETS IN A DAY

27	England (18-3 to 53 out and 62) v Australia (60) at Lord's (2nd day)	1888
25	Australia (112 and 48-5) v England (61) at Melbourne (1st day)	1901-02

HIGHEST MATCH AGGREGATES

Runs	Wkts			Days played
1,981	35	South Africa v England at Durban....................	1938-39	10†
1,815	34	West Indies v England at Kingston	1929-30	9‡
1,764	39	Australia v West Indies at Adelaide	1968-69	5
1,753	40	Australia v England at Adelaide	1920-21	6

				Days
Runs	*Wkts*			*played*
1,723	31	England v Australia at Leeds	1948	5
1,661	36	West Indies v Australia at Bridgetown	1954-55	6

† *No play on one day.*   ‡ *No play on two days.*

LOWEST INNINGS TOTALS

26	New Zealand v England at Auckland	1954-55
30	South Africa v England at Port Elizabeth	1895-96
30	South Africa v England at Birmingham	1924
35	South Africa v England at Cape Town	1898-99
36	Australia v England at Birmingham	1902
36	South Africa v Australia at Melbourne	1931-32
42	Australia v England at Sydney	1887-88
42	New Zealand v Australia at Wellington	1945-46
42†	India v England at Lord's	1974
43	South Africa v England at Cape Town	1888-89
44	Australia v England at The Oval	1896
45	England v Australia at Sydney	1886-87
45	South Africa v Australia at Melbourne	1931-32
47	South Africa v England at Cape Town	1888-89
47	New Zealand v England at Lord's	1958

The lowest innings for the countries not mentioned above are:

53	West Indies v Pakistan at Faisalabad	1986-87
62	Pakistan v Australia at Perth	1981-82
82	Sri Lanka v India at Chandigarh	1990-91
137	Zimbabwe v New Zealand at Harare	1992-93

† *Batted one man short.*

FEWEST RUNS IN A FULL DAY'S PLAY

95   At Karachi, October 11, 1956. Australia 80 all out; Pakistan 15 for two (first day, 5½ hours).

104 At Karachi, December 8, 1959. Pakistan 0 for no wicket to 104 for five v Australia (fourth day, 5½ hours).

106 At Brisbane, December 9, 1958. England 92 for two to 198 all out v Australia (fourth day, 5 hours). *England were dismissed five minutes before the close of play, leaving no time for Australia to start their second innings.*

112 At Karachi, October 15, 1956. Australia 138 for six to 187 all out; Pakistan 63 for one (fourth day, 5½ hours).

115 At Karachi, September 19, 1988. Australia 116 for seven to 165 all out and 66 for five following on v Pakistan (fourth day, 5½ hours).

117 At Madras, October 19, 1956. India 117 for five v Australia (first day, 5½ hours).

117 At Colombo (SSC), March 21, 1984. New Zealand 6 for no wicket to 123 for four (fifth day, 5 hours, 47 minutes).

In England

151 At Lord's, August 26, 1978. England 175 for two to 289 all out; New Zealand 37 for seven (third day, 6 hours).

159 At Leeds, July 10, 1971. Pakistan 208 for four to 350 all out; England 17 for one (third day, 6 hours).

LOWEST MATCH AGGREGATES

(For a completed match)

				Days
Runs	*Wkts*			*played*
234	29	Australia v South Africa at Melbourne	1931-32	3†
291	40	England v Australia at Lord's	1888	2

Runs	Wkts			Days played
295	28	New Zealand v Australia at Wellington................	1945-46	2
309	29	West Indies v England at Bridgetown	1934-35	3
323	30	England v Australia at Manchester....................	1888	2

† *No play on one day.*

YOUNGEST TEST PLAYERS

Years	Days			
15	124	Mushtaq Mohammad.....	Pakistan v West Indies at Lahore	1958-59
16	189	Aqib Javed	Pakistan v New Zealand at Wellington	1988-89
16	205	S. R. Tendulkar	India v Pakistan at Karachi	1989-90
16	221	Aftab Baloch	Pakistan v New Zealand at Dacca	1969-70
16	248	Nasim-ul-Ghani	Pakistan v West Indies at Bridgetown .	1957-58
16	352	Khalid Hassan	Pakistan v England at Nottingham ...	1954
17	5	Zahid Fazal............	Pakistan v West Indies at Karachi	1990-91
17	69	Ata-ur-Rehman	Pakistan v England at Birmingham ...	1992
17	118	L. Sivaramakrishnan	India v West Indies at St John's......	1982-83
17	122	J. E. D. Sealy	West Indies v England at Bridgetown .	1929-30
17	189	C. D. U. S. Weerasinghe..	Sri Lanka v India at Colombo (PSS) ..	1985-86
17	193	Maninder Singh	India v Pakistan at Karachi	1982-83
17	239	I. D. Craig	Australia v South Africa at Melbourne.	1952-53
17	245	G. S. Sobers	West Indies v England at Kingston ...	1953-54
17	265	V. L. Mehra	India v New Zealand at Bombay	1955-56
17	300	Hanif Mohammad	Pakistan v India at Delhi	1952-53
17	341	Intikhab Alam	Pakistan v Australia at Karachi	1959-60
17	364	Waqar Younis..........	Pakistan v India at Karachi	1989-90

Note: The youngest Test players for countries not mentioned above are: England – D. B. Close, 18 years 149 days, v New Zealand at Manchester, 1949; New Zealand – D. L. Freeman, 18 years 197 days, v England at Christchurch, 1932-33; South Africa – A. E. Ochse, 19 years 1 day, v England at Port Elizabeth, 1888-89; Zimbabwe – A. D. R. Campbell, 20 years 25 days, v India at Harare, 1992-93.

OLDEST PLAYERS ON TEST DEBUT

Years	Days			
49	119	J. Southerton.....	England v Australia at Melbourne	1876-77
47	284	Miran Bux.......	Pakistan v India at Lahore	1954-55
46	253	D. D. Blackie	Australia v England at Sydney	1928-29
46	237	H. Ironmonger ...	Australia v England at Brisbane	1928-29
42	242	N. Betancourt	West Indies v England at Port-of-Spain .	1929-30
41	337	E. R. Wilson.....	England v Australia at Sydney	1920-21
41	27	R. J. D. Jamshedji	India v England at Bombay...........	1933-34
40	345	C. A. Wiles	West Indies v England at Manchester ..	1933
40	295	O. Henry........	South Africa v India at Durban	1992-93
40	216	S. P. Kinneir	England v Australia at Sydney	1911-12
40	110	H. W. Lee.......	England v South Africa at Johannesburg	1930-31
40	56	G. W. A. Chubb ..	South Africa v England at Nottingham .	1951
40	37	C. Ramaswami	India v England at Manchester........	1936

Note: The oldest Test player on debut for New Zealand was H. M. McGirr, 38 years 101 days, v England at Auckland, 1929-30; for Sri Lanka, D. S. de Silva, 39 years 251 days, v England at Colombo (PSS), 1981-82; for Zimbabwe, M. P. Jarvis, 36 years 317 days, v India at Harare, 1992-93. A. J. Traicos was 45 years 154 days old when he made his debut for Zimbabwe (v India at Harare, 1992-93) having played 3 Tests for South Africa in 1969-70.

OLDEST TEST PLAYERS

(Age on final day of their last Test match)

Years	Days			
52	165	W. Rhodes..........	England v West Indies at Kingston ...	1929-30
50	327	H. Ironmonger	Australia v England at Sydney	1932-33
50	320	W. G. Grace	England v Australia at Nottingham ...	1899
50	303	G. Gunn	England v West Indies at Kingston ...	1929-30
49	139	J. Southerton	England v Australia at Melbourne	1876-77
47	302	Miran Bux	Pakistan v India at Peshawar	1954-55
47	249	J. B. Hobbs	England v Australia at The Oval	1930
47	87	F. E. Woolley	England v Australia at The Oval	1934
46	309	D. D. Blackie	Australia v England at Adelaide	1928-29
46	206	A. W. Nourse	South Africa v England at The Oval ..	1924
46	202	H. Strudwick	England v Australia at The Oval	1926
46	41	E. H. Hendren	England v West Indies at Kingston ...	1934-35
45	304	A. J. Traicos	Zimbabwe v India at Delhi..........	1992-93
45	245	G. O. B. Allen	England v West Indies at Kingston ...	1947-48
45	215	P. Holmes	England v India at Lord's	1932
45	140	D. B. Close	England v West Indies at Manchester .	1976

MOST TEST APPEARANCES

147	**A. R. Border (Australia)**		114	M. C. Cowdrey (England)
127	**Kapil Dev (India)**		**111**	**D. L. Haynes (West Indies)**
125	S. M. Gavaskar (India)		110	C. H. Lloyd (West Indies)
121	**Javed Miandad (Pakistan)**		108	G. Boycott (England)
121	I. V. A. Richards (West Indies)		108	C. G. Greenidge (West Indies)
117	D. I. Gower (England)		**107**	**G. A. Gooch (England)**
116	D. B. Vengsarkar (India)		102	I. T. Botham (England)

The most appearances for New Zealand is 86 by R. J. Hadlee, for South Africa 50 by J. H. B. Waite, for Sri Lanka 45 by **A. Ranatunga** and for Zimbabwe 4 by **K. J. Arnott, A. D. R. Campbell, A. Flower, G. W. Flower, D. L. Houghton** and **A. J. Traicos.**

Bold type denotes those who played Test cricket in 1992-93 or 1993 seasons or Sri Lanka v India and South Africa in 1993-94.

MOST CONSECUTIVE TEST APPEARANCES

144*	A. R. Border (Australia)	March 1979 to August 1993
106	S. M. Gavaskar (India)	January 1975 to February 1987
87	G. R. Viswanath (India)	March 1971 to February 1983
85	G. S. Sobers (West Indies)......	April 1955 to April 1972
72	D. L. Haynes (West Indies)	December 1979 to June 1988
71	I. M. Chappell (Australia)	January 1966 to February 1976
66	Kapil Dev (India)..............	October 1978 to December 1984
65	I. T. Botham (England)	February 1978 to March 1984
65	A. P. E. Knott (England).......	March 1971 to August 1977

* Sequence still in progress.

The most consecutive Test appearances for the countries not mentioned above are:

58†	J. R. Reid (New Zealand)	July 1949 to July 1965
53	Javed Miandad (Pakistan)	December 1977 to January 1984
45†	A. W. Nourse (South Africa)	October 1902 to August 1924
26	A. Ranatunga (Sri Lanka)	April 1983 to March 1991

The most for Zimbabwe is 4 (as above).

† *Indicates complete Test career.*

CAPTAINCY

MOST TESTS AS CAPTAIN

	P	W	L	D		P	W	L	D
A. R. Border (A)	84	28	20	35*	**G. A. Gooch (E)**	34	10	12	12
C. H. Lloyd (WI)	74	36	12	26	**Javed Miandad (P)**	34	14	6	14
I. V. A. Richards (WI)	50	27	8	15	Kapil Dev (I)	34	4	7	22*
G. S. Chappell (A)	48	21	13	14	J. R. Reid (NZ)	34	3	18	13
Imran Khan (P)	48	14	8	26	D. I. Gower (E)	32	5	18	9
S. M. Gavaskar (I)	47	9	8	30	J. M. Brearley (E)	31	18	4	9
P. B. H. May (E)	41	20	10	11	R. Illingworth (E)	31	12	5	14
Nawab of Pataudi jun. (I)	40	9	19	12	I. M. Chappell (A)	30	15	5	10
R. B. Simpson (A)	39	12	12	15	E. R. Dexter (E)	30	9	7	14
G. S. Sobers (WI)	39	9	10	20	G. P. Howarth (NZ)	30	11	7	12

* *One match tied.*

Most Tests as captain of countries not mentioned above:

	P	W	L	D
H. W. Taylor (SA)	18	1	10	7
L. R. D. Mendis (SL)	19	2	8	9
D. L. Houghton (Z)	4	0	2	2

Notes: A. R. Border has captained Australia in 84 consecutive Tests.

W. W. Armstrong (Australia) captained his country in the most Tests without being defeated: ten matches with eight wins and two draws.

I. T. Botham (England) captained his country in the most Tests without ever winning: 12 matches with eight draws and four defeats.

Bold type denotes those who were captains in 1992-93 and 1993 seasons or Sri Lanka v India and South Africa in 1993-94.

UMPIRING

MOST TEST MATCHES

		First Test	Last Test
55	H. D. Bird (England)	1973	1993
48	F. Chester (England)	1924	1955
42	C. S. Elliott (England)	1957	1974
36	D. J. Constant (England)	1971	1988
33	J. S. Buller (England)	1956	1969
33	A. R. Crafter (Australia)	1978-79	1991-92
32	R. W. Crockett (Australia)	1901-02	1924-25
31	D. Sang Hue (West Indies)	1961-62	1980-81

Note: H. D. Bird's total includes three Tests in Zimbabwe and three Tests in West Indies in 1992-93. C. S. Elliott's total includes one Test in New Zealand in 1970-71.

SUMMARY OF ALL TEST MATCHES

To September 19, 1993

	Opponents	Tests				Won by						Tied	Drawn
			E	A	SA	WI	NZ	I	P	SL	Z		
England	v Australia	280	89	108	–	–	–	–	–	–	–	–	83
	v South Africa	102	46	–	18	–	–	–	–	–	–	–	38
	v West Indies	104	24	–	–	43	–	–	–	–	–	–	37
	v New Zealand	72	33	–	–	–	4	–	–	–	–	–	35
	v India	81	31	–	–	–	–	14	–	–	–	–	36
	v Pakistan	52	14	–	–	–	–	–	7	–	–	–	31
	v Sri Lanka	5	3	–	–	–	–	–	–	1	–	–	1
Australia	v South Africa	53	–	29	11	–	–	–	–	–	–	–	13
	v West Indies	77	–	30	–	26	–	–	–	–	–	1	20
	v New Zealand	29	–	11	–	–	7	–	–	–	–	–	11
	v India	50	–	24	–	–	–	8	–	–	–	1	17
	v Pakistan	34	–	12	–	–	–	–	9	–	–	–	13
	v Sri Lanka	7	–	4	–	–	–	–	–	0	–	–	3
South Africa	v West Indies	1	–	–	0	1	–	–	–	–	–	–	–
	v New Zealand	17	–	–	9	–	2	–	–	–	–	–	6
	v India	4	–	–	1	–	–	0	–	–	–	–	3
	v Sri Lanka	3	–	–	1	–	–	–	–	0	–	–	2
West Indies	v New Zealand	24	–	–	–	8	4	–	–	–	–	–	12
	v India	62	–	–	–	26	–	6	–	–	–	–	30
	v Pakistan	31	–	–	–	12	–	–	7	–	–	–	12
New Zealand	v India	31	–	–	–	–	6	12	–	–	–	–	13
	v Pakistan	33	–	–	–	–	3	–	14	–	–	–	16
	v Sri Lanka	11	–	–	–	–	4	–	–	1	–	–	6
	v Zimbabwe	2	–	–	–	–	1	–	–	–	0	–	1
India	v Pakistan	44	–	–	–	–	–	4	7	–	–	–	33
	v Sri Lanka	11	–	–	–	–	–	4	–	1	–	–	6
	v Zimbabwe	2	–	–	–	–	–	1	–	–	0	–	1
Pakistan	v Sri Lanka	12	–	–	–	–	–	–	6	1	–	–	5
		1,234	240	218	40	116	31	49	50	4	0	2	484

	Tests	Won	Lost	Drawn	Tied	Toss Won
England	696	240	195	261	–	345
Australia	530	218	150	160	2	268
South Africa	180	40	78	62	–	85
West Indies	299	116	71	111	1	154
New Zealand	219	31	88	100	–	109
India	285	49	96	139	1	142
Pakistan	206	50	46	110	–	104
Sri Lanka	49	4	22	23	–	26
Zimbabwe	4	0	2	2	–	1

ENGLAND v AUSTRALIA

		Captains					
Season	England		Australia	T	E	A	D
1876-77	James Lillywhite		D. W. Gregory	2	1	1	0
1878-79	Lord Harris		D. W. Gregory	1	0	1	0
1880	Lord Harris		W. L. Murdoch	1	1	0	0
1881-82	A. Shaw		W. L. Murdoch	4	0	2	2
1882	A. N. Hornby		W. L. Murdoch	1	0	1	0

THE ASHES

		Captains						
Season	England		Australia	T	E	A	D	Held by
1882-83	Hon. Ivo Bligh		W. L. Murdoch	4*	2	2	0	E
1884	Lord Harris[1]		W. L. Murdoch	3	1	0	2	E
1884-85	A. Shrewsbury		T. P. Horan[2]	5	3	2	0	E
1886	A. G. Steel		H. J. H. Scott	3	3	0	0	E

	Captains						
Season	England	Australia	T	E	A	D	Held by
1886-87	A. Shrewsbury	P. S. McDonnell	2	2	0	0	E
1887-88	W. W. Read	P. S. McDonnell	1	1	0	0	E
1888	W. G. Grace[3]	P. S. McDonnell	3	2	1	0	E
1890†	W. G. Grace	W. L. Murdoch	2	2	0	0	E
1891-92	W. G. Grace	J. McC. Blackham	3	1	2	0	A
1893	W. G. Grace[4]	J. McC. Blackham	3	1	0	2	E
1894-95	A. E. Stoddart	G. Giffen[5]	5	3	2	0	E
1896	W. G. Grace	G. H. S. Trott	3	2	1	0	E
1897-98	A. E. Stoddart[6]	G. H. S. Trott	5	1	4	0	A
1899	A. C. MacLaren[7]	J. Darling	5	0	1	4	A
1901-02	A. C. MacLaren	J. Darling[8]	5	1	4	0	A
1902	A. C. MacLaren	J. Darling	5	1	2	2	A
1903-04	P. F. Warner	M. A. Noble	5	3	2	0	E
1905	Hon. F. S. Jackson	J. Darling	5	2	0	3	E
1907-08	A. O. Jones[9]	M. A. Noble	5	1	4	0	A
1909	A. C. MacLaren	M. A. Noble	5	1	2	2	A
1911-12	J. W. H. T. Douglas	C. Hill	5	4	1	0	E
1912	C. B. Fry	S. E. Gregory	3	1	0	2	E
1920-21	J. W. H. T. Douglas	W. W. Armstrong	5	0	5	0	A
1921	Hon. L. H. Tennyson[10]	W. W. Armstrong	5	0	3	2	A
1924-25	A. E. R. Gilligan	H. L. Collins	5	1	4	0	A
1926	A. W. Carr[11]	H. L. Collins[12]	5	1	0	4	E
1928-29	A. P. F. Chapman[13]	J. Ryder	5	4	1	0	E
1930	A. P. F. Chapman[14]	W. M. Woodfull	5	1	2	2	A
1932-33	D. R. Jardine	W. M. Woodfull	5	4	1	0	E
1934	R. E. S. Wyatt[15]	W. M. Woodfull	5	1	2	2	A
1936-37	G. O. B. Allen	D. G. Bradman	5	2	3	0	A
1938†	W. R. Hammond	D. G. Bradman	4	1	1	2	A
1946-47	W. R. Hammond[16]	D. G. Bradman	5	0	3	2	A
1948	N. W. D. Yardley	D. G. Bradman	5	0	4	1	A
1950-51	F. R. Brown	A. L. Hassett	5	1	4	0	A
1953	L. Hutton	A. L. Hassett	5	1	0	4	E
1954-55	L. Hutton	I. W. Johnson[17]	5	3	1	1	E
1956	P. B. H. May	I. W. Johnson	5	2	1	2	E
1958-59	P. B. H. May	R. Benaud	5	0	4	1	A
1961	P. B. H. May[18]	R. Benaud[19]	5	1	2	2	A
1962-63	E. R. Dexter	R. Benaud	5	1	1	3	A
1964	E. R. Dexter	R. B. Simpson	5	0	1	4	A
1965-66	M. J. K. Smith	R. B. Simpson[20]	5	1	1	3	A
1968	M. C. Cowdrey[21]	W. M. Lawry[22]	5	1	1	3	A
1970-71†	R. Illingworth	W. M. Lawry[23]	6	2	0	4	E
1972	R. Illingworth	I. M. Chappell	5	2	2	1	E
1974-75	M. H. Denness[24]	I. M. Chappell	6	1	4	1	A
1975	A. W. Greig[25]	I. M. Chappell	4	0	1	3	A
1976-77‡	A. W. Greig	G. S. Chappell	1	0	1	0	—
1977	J. M. Brearley	G. S. Chappell	5	3	0	2	E
1978-79	J. M. Brearley	G. N. Yallop	6	5	1	0	E
1979-80‡	J. M. Brearley	G. S. Chappell	3	0	3	0	—
1980‡	I. T. Botham	G. S. Chappell	1	0	0	1	—
1981	J. M. Brearley[26]	K. J. Hughes	6	3	1	2	E
1982-83	R. G. D. Willis	G. S. Chappell	5	1	2	2	A
1985	D. I. Gower	A. R. Border	6	3	1	2	E
1986-87	M. W. Gatting	A. R. Border	5	2	1	2	E
1987-88‡	M. W. Gatting	A. R. Border	1	0	0	1	—
1989	D. I. Gower	A. R. Border	6	0	4	2	A
1990-91	G. A. Gooch[27]	A. R. Border	5	0	3	2	A
1993	G. A. Gooch[28]	A. R. Border	6	1	4	0	A

	In Australia		145	51	70	24	
	In England		135	38	38	59	
	Totals		280	89	108	83	

* *The Ashes were awarded in 1882-83 after a series of three matches which England won 2-1.
A fourth unofficial match was played, each innings being played on a different pitch, and this was
won by Australia.*

† *The matches at Manchester in 1890 and 1938 and at Melbourne (Third Test) in 1970-71 were
abandoned without a ball being bowled and are excluded.*

‡ *The Ashes were not at stake in these series.*

Notes: The following deputised for the official touring captain or were appointed by the home authority for only a minor proportion of the series:

[1]A. N. Hornby (First). [2]W. L. Murdoch (First), H. H. Massie (Third), J. McC. Blackham (Fourth). [3]A. G. Steel (First). [4]A. E. Stoddart (First). [5]J. McC. Blackham (First). [6]A. C. MacLaren (First, Second and Fifth). [7]W. G. Grace (First). [8]H. Trumble (Fourth and Fifth). [9]F. L. Fane (First, Second and Third). [10]J. W. H. T. Douglas (First and Second). [11]A. P. F. Chapman (Fifth). [12]W. Bardsley (Third and Fourth). [13]J. C. White (Fifth). [14]R. E. S. Wyatt (Fifth). [15]C. F. Walters (First). [16]N. W. D. Yardley (Fifth). [17]A. R. Morris (Second). [18]M. C. Cowdrey (First and Second). [19]R. N. Harvey (Second). [20]B. C. Booth (First and Third). [21]T. W. Graveney (Fourth). [22]B. N. Jarman (Fourth). [23]I. M. Chappell (Seventh). [24]J. H. Edrich (Fourth). [25]M. H. Denness (First). [26]I. T. Botham (First and Second). [27]A. J. Lamb (First). [28]M. A. Atherton (Fifth and Sixth).

HIGHEST INNINGS TOTALS

For England in England: 903-7 dec. at The Oval	1938
in Australia: 636 at Sydney	1928-29
For Australia in England: 729-6 dec. at Lord's	1930
in Australia: 659-8 dec. at Sydney	1946-47

LOWEST INNINGS TOTALS

For England in England: 52 at The Oval	1948
in Australia: 45 at Sydney	1886-87
For Australia in England: 36 at Birmingham	1902
in Australia: 42 at Sydney	1887-88

INDIVIDUAL HUNDREDS

For England (199)

R. Abel (1)
132*‡ Sydney 1891-92

L. E. G. Ames (1)
120 Lord's 1934

M. A. Atherton (1)
105 Sydney 1990-91

R. W. Barber (1)
185 Sydney 1965-66

W. Barnes (1)
134 Adelaide 1884-85

C. J. Barnett (2)
129 Adelaide 1936-37
126 Nottingham . 1938

K. F. Barrington (5)
132* Adelaide 1962-63
101 Sydney 1962-63
256 Manchester.. 1964

102 Adelaide 1965-66
115 Melbourne .. 1965-66

I. T. Botham (4)
119* Melbourne .. 1979-80
149* Leeds 1981
118 Manchester .. 1981
138 Brisbane 1986-87

G. Boycott (7)
113 The Oval.... 1964
142* Sydney 1970-71
119* Adelaide 1970-71
107 Nottingham . 1977
191 Leeds 1977
128* Lord's 1980
137 The Oval.... 1981

L. C. Braund (2)
103* Adelaide 1901-02
102 Sydney 1903-04

J. Briggs (1)
121 Melbourne .. 1884-85

B. C. Broad (4)
162 Perth....... 1986-87
116 Adelaide 1986-87
112 Melbourne .. 1986-87
139 Sydney 1987-88

J. T. Brown (1)
140 Melbourne .. 1894-95

A. P. F. Chapman (1)
121 Lord's 1930

D. C. S. Compton (5)
102† Nottingham . 1938
147
103* } Adelaide 1946-47
184 Nottingham . 1948
145* Manchester. 1948

M. C. Cowdrey (5)
102 Melbourne .. 1954-55
100* Sydney 1958-59
113 Melbourne .. 1962-63
104 Melbourne .. 1965-66
104 Birmingham . 1968

M. H. Denness (1)
188 Melbourne .. 1974-75

E. R. Dexter (2)
180 Birmingham . 1961
174 Manchester .. 1964

B. L. D'Oliveira (2)
158 The Oval 1968
117 Melbourne .. 1970-71

K. S. Duleepsinhji (1)
173† Lord's 1930

J. H. Edrich (7)
120† Lord's 1964
109 Melbourne .. 1965-66
103 Sydney 1965-66
164 The Oval 1968
115* Perth 1970-71
130 Adelaide 1970-71
175 Sydney 1975

W. J. Edrich (2)
119 Sydney 1946-47
111 Leeds 1948

K. W. R. Fletcher (1)
146 Melbourne .. 1974-75

R. E. Foster (1)
287† Sydney 1903-04

C. B. Fry (1)
144 The Oval 1905

M. W. Gatting (3)
160 Manchester .. 1985
100* Birmingham . 1985
100 Adelaide 1986-87

G. A. Gooch (4)
196 The Oval 1985
117 Adelaide 1990-91
133 Manchester .. 1993
120 Nottingham .. 1993

D. I. Gower (9)
102 Perth 1978-79
114 Adelaide 1982-83
166 Nottingham .. 1985
215 Birmingham . 1985
157 The Oval 1985
136 Perth 1986-87
106 Lord's 1989
100 Melbourne .. 1990-91
123 Sydney 1990-91

W. G. Grace (2)
152† The Oval 1880
170 The Oval 1886

T. W. Graveney (1)
111 Sydney 1954-55

A. W. Greig (1)
110 Brisbane 1974-75

G. Gunn (2)
119† Sydney 1907-08
122* Sydney 1907-08

W. Gunn (1)
102* Manchester .. 1893

W. R. Hammond (9)
251 Sydney 1928-29
200 Melbourne .. 1928-29
119* ⎫ Adelaide .. 1928-29
177 ⎭
113 Leeds 1930
112 Sydney 1932-33
101 Sydney 1932-33
231* Sydney 1936-37
240 Lord's 1938

J. Hardstaff jun. (1)
169* The Oval 1938

T. W. Hayward (2)
130 Manchester .. 1899
137 The Oval 1899

J. W. Hearne (1)
114 Melbourne .. 1911-12

E. H. Hendren (3)
127* Lord's 1926
169 Brisbane 1928-29
132 Manchester .. 1934

J. B. Hobbs (12)
126* Melbourne .. 1911-12
187 Adelaide 1911-12
178 Melbourne .. 1911-12
107 Lord's 1912
122 Melbourne .. 1920-21
123 Adelaide 1920-21
115 Sydney 1924-25
154 Melbourne .. 1924-25
119 Adelaide 1924-25
119 Lord's 1926
100 The Oval 1926
142 Melbourne .. 1928-29

K. L. Hutchings (1)
126 Melbourne .. 1907-08

L. Hutton (5)
100† Nottingham .. 1938
364 The Oval 1938
122* Sydney 1946-47
156*† Adelaide 1950-51
145 Lord's 1953

Hon. F. S. Jackson (5)
103 The Oval 1893
118 The Oval 1899
128 Manchester .. 1902
144* Leeds 1905
113 Manchester .. 1905

G. L. Jessop (1)
104 The Oval 1902

A. P. E. Knott (2)
106* Adelaide 1974-75
135 Nottingham .. 1977

A. J. Lamb (1)
125 Leeds 1989

M. Leyland (7)
137† Melbourne .. 1928-29
109 Lord's 1934
153 Manchester .. 1934
110 The Oval 1934
126 Brisbane 1936-37
111* Melbourne .. 1936-37
187 The Oval 1938

B. W. Luckhurst (2)
131 Perth 1970-71
109 Melbourne .. 1970-71

A. C. MacLaren (5)
120 Melbourne .. 1894-95
109 Sydney 1897-98
124 Adelaide 1897-98
116 Sydney 1901-02
140 Nottingham . 1905

J. W. H. Makepeace (1)
117 Melbourne .. 1920-21

P. B. H. May (3)
104 Sydney 1954-55
101 Leeds 1956
101 Melbourne .. 1958-59

C. P. Mead (1)
182* The Oval 1921

Nawab of Pataudi sen. (1)
102† Sydney 1932-33

E. Paynter (1)
216* Nottingham . 1938

D. W. Randall (3)
174† Melbourne .. 1976-77
150 Sydney 1978-79
115 Perth 1982-83

K. S. Ranjitsinhji (2)
154*† Manchester .. 1896
175 Sydney 1897-98

W. W. Read (1)
117 The Oval 1884

W. Rhodes (1)
179 Melbourne .. 1911-12

C. J. Richards (1)
133 Perth 1986-87

P. E. Richardson (1)
104 Manchester .. 1956

R. T. Robinson (2)
175† Leeds 1985
148 Birmingham . 1985

A. C. Russell (3)
135* Adelaide 1920-21
101 Manchester .. 1921
102* The Oval 1921

R. C. Russell (1)
128* Manchester .. 1989

J. Sharp (1)
105 The Oval 1909

Rev. D. S. Sheppard (2)
113 Manchester .. 1956
113 Melbourne .. 1962-63

A. Shrewsbury (3)
105* Melbourne .. 1884-85
164 Lord's 1886
106 Lord's 1893

R. T. Simpson (1)
156* Melbourne .. 1950-51

R. A. Smith (2)
143 Manchester .. 1989
101 Nottingham .. 1989

A. G. Steel (2)
135* Sydney 1882-83
148 Lord's 1884

A. E. Stoddart (2)
134	Adelaide	1891-92
173	The Oval....	1894-95

R. Subba Row (2)
112†	Birmingham .	1961
137	The Oval....	1961

H. Sutcliffe (8)
115†	Sydney	1924-25
176	} Melbourne ..	1924-25
127		
143	Melbourne ..	1924-25
161	The Oval....	1926

135	Melbourne ..	1928-29
161	The Oval....	1930
194	Sydney	1932-33

G. P. Thorpe (1)
114*†	Nottingham .	1993

J. T. Tyldesley (3)
138	Birmingham .	1902
100	Leeds	1905
112*	The Oval....	1905

G. Ulyett (1)
149	Melbourne ..	1881-82

A. Ward (1)
117	Sydney	1894-95

C. Washbrook (2)
112	Melbourne ..	1946-47
143	Leeds	1948

W. Watson (1)
109†	Lord's	1953

F. E. Woolley (2)
133*	Sydney	1911-12
123	Sydney	1924-25

R. A. Woolmer (3)
149	The Oval....	1975
120	Lord's	1977
137	Manchester..	1977

† *Signifies hundred on first appearance in England–Australia Tests.*
‡ *Carried his bat.*
Note: In consecutive innings in 1928-29, W. R. Hammond scored 251 at Sydney, 200 and 32 at Melbourne, and 119* and 177 at Adelaide.

For Australia (224)

W. W. Armstrong (4)
133*	Melbourne ..	1907-08
158	Sydney	1920-21
121	Adelaide	1920-21
123*	Melbourne ..	1920-21

C. L. Badcock (1)
118	Melbourne ..	1936-37

C. Bannerman (1)
165*†	Melbourne ..	1876-77

W. Bardsley (3)
136	} The Oval....	1909
130		
193*‡	Lord's	1926

S. G. Barnes (2)
234	Sydney	1946-47
141	Lord's	1948

G. J. Bonnor (1)
128	Sydney	1884-85

D. C. Boon (6)
103	Adelaide	1986-87
184*	Sydney	1987-88
121	Adelaide	1990-91
164*	Lord's	1993
101	Nottingham .	1993
107	Leeds	1993

B. C. Booth (2)
112	Brisbane	1962-63
103	Melbourne ..	1962-63

A. R. Border (8)
115	Perth.......	1979-80
123*	Manchester..	1981
106*	The Oval....	1981
196	Lord's	1985
146*	Manchester..	1985
125	Perth.......	1986-87
100*	Adelaide	1986-87
200*	Leeds	1993

D. G. Bradman (19)
112	Melbourne ..	1928-29
123	Melbourne ..	1928-29

131	Nottingham .	1930
254	Lord's	1930
334	Leeds	1930
232	The Oval....	1930
103*	Melbourne ..	1932-33
304	Leeds	1934
244	The Oval....	1934
270	Melbourne ..	1936-37
212	Adelaide	1936-37
169	Melbourne ..	1936-37
144*	Nottingham .	1938
102*	Lord's	1938
103	Leeds	1938
187	Brisbane	1946-47
234	Sydney	1946-47
138	Nottingham .	1948
173*	Leeds	1948

W. A. Brown (3)
105	Lord's	1934
133	Nottingham .	1938
206*‡	Lord's	1938

P. J. Burge (4)
181	The Oval....	1961
103	Sydney	1962-63
160	Leeds	1964
120	Melbourne ..	1965-66

J. W. Burke (1)
101*†	Adelaide	1950-51

G. S. Chappell (9)
108†	Perth.......	1970-71
131	Lord's	1972
113	The Oval....	1972
144	Sydney	1974-75
102	Melbourne ..	1974-75
112	Manchester..	1977
114	Melbourne ..	1979-80
115	Perth.......	1982-83
115	Adelaide	1982-83

I. M. Chappell (4)
111	Melbourne ..	1970-71

104	Adelaide	1970-71
118	The Oval....	1972
192	The Oval....	1975

H. L. Collins (3)
104†	Sydney	1920-21
162	Adelaide	1920-21
114	Sydney	1924-25

R. M. Cowper (1)
307	Melbourne ..	1965-66

J. Darling (3)
101	Sydney	1897-98
178	Adelaide	1897-98
160	Sydney	1897-98

R. A. Duff (2)
104†	Melbourne ..	1901-02
146	The Oval....	1905

J. Dyson (1)
102	Leeds	1981

R. Edwards (2)
170*	Nottingham .	1972
115	Perth.......	1974-75

J. H. Fingleton (2)
100	Brisbane	1936-37
136	Melbourne ..	1936-37

G. Giffen (1)
161	Sydney	1894-95

H. Graham (2)
107†	Lord's	1893
105	Sydney	1894-95

J. M. Gregory (1)
100	Melbourne ..	1920-21

S. E. Gregory (4)
201	Sydney	1894-95
103	Lord's	1896
117	The Oval....	1899
112	Adelaide	1903-04

R. J. Hartigan (1)
116†	Adelaide	1907-08

R. N. Harvey (6)		
112†	Leeds	1948
122	Manchester..	1953
162	Brisbane ..	1954-55
167	Melbourne ..	1958-59
114	Birmingham .	1961
154	Adelaide	1962-63
A. L. Hassett (4)		
128	Brisbane ..	1946-47
137	Nottingham .	1948
115	Nottingham .	1953
104	Lord's	1953
I. A. Healy (1)		
102*	Manchester..	1993
H. S. T. L. Hendry (1)		
112	Sydney	1928-29
A. M. J. Hilditch (1)		
119	Leeds	1985
C. Hill (4)		
188	Melbourne ..	1897-98
135	Lord's	1899
119	Sheffield ...	1902
160	Adelaide	1907-08
T. P. Horan (1)		
124	Melbourne ..	1881-82
K. J. Hughes (3)		
129	Brisbane ..	1978-79
117	Lord's	1980
137	Sydney	1982-83
F. A. Iredale (2)		
140	Adelaide	1894-95
108	Manchester..	1896
A. A. Jackson (1)		
164†	Adelaide	1928-29
D. M. Jones (3)		
184*	Sydney	1986-87
157	Birmingham .	1989
122	The Oval....	1989
C. Kelleway (1)		
147	Adelaide	1920-21
A. F. Kippax (1)		
100	Melbourne ..	1928-29
W. M. Lawry (7)		
130	Lord's	1961
102	Manchester..	1961
106	Manchester..	1964
166	Brisbane ..	1965-66
119	Adelaide	1965-66
108	Melbourne ..	1965-66
135	The Oval....	1968
R. R. Lindwall (1)		
100	Melbourne ..	1946-47
J. J. Lyons (1)		
134	Sydney	1891-92
C. G. Macartney (5)		
170	Sydney	1920-21
115	Leeds	1921
133*	Lord's	1926
151	Leeds	1926
109	Manchester..	1926

S. J. McCabe (4)		
187*	Sydney	1932-33
137	Manchester..	1934
112	Melbourne ..	1936-37
232	Nottingham .	1938
C. L. McCool (1)		
104*	Melbourne ..	1946-47
R. B. McCosker (2)		
127	The Oval ...	1975
107	Nottingham .	1977
C. C. McDonald (2)		
170	Adelaide ...	1958-59
133	Melbourne ..	1958-59
P. S. McDonnell (3)		
147	Sydney	1881-82
103	The Oval....	1884
124	Adelaide ...	1884-85
C. E. McLeod (1)		
112	Melbourne ..	1897-98
G. R. Marsh (2)		
110†	Brisbane ..	1986-87
138	Nottingham .	1989
R. W. Marsh (1)		
110*	Manchester..	1976-77
G. R. J. Matthews (1)		
128	Sydney	1990-91
K. R. Miller (3)		
141*	Adelaide	1946-47
145*	Sydney	1950-51
109	Lord's	1953
A. R. Morris (8)		
155	Melbourne ..	1946-47
122	} Adelaide ..	1946-47
124*		
105	Lord's	1948
182	Leeds	1948
196	The Oval	1948
206	Adelaide	1950-51
153	Brisbane	1954-55
W. L. Murdoch (2)		
153*	Sydney	1880
211	The Oval....	1884
M. A. Noble (1)		
133	Sydney	1903-04
N. C. O'Neill (2)		
117	The Oval....	1961
100	Adelaide	1962-63
C. E. Pellew (2)		
116	Melbourne ..	1920-21
104	Adelaide	1920-21
W. H. Ponsford (5)		
110†	Sydney	1924-25
128	Melbourne ..	1924-25
110	The Oval....	1930
181	Leeds	1934
266	The Oval....	1934
V. S. Ransford (1)		
143*	Lord's	1909

I. R. Redpath (2)		
171	Perth.......	1970-71
105	Sydney	1974-75
A. J. Richardson (1)		
100	Leeds	1926
V. Y. Richardson (1)		
138	Melbourne ..	1924-25
G. M. Ritchie (1)		
146	Nottingham .	1985
J. Ryder (2)		
201*	Adelaide	1924-25
112	Melbourne ..	1928-29
H. J. H. Scott (1)		
102	The Oval....	1884
R. B. Simpson (2)		
311	Manchester..	1964
225	Adelaide	1965-66
M. J. Slater (1)		
152	Lord's	1993
K. R. Stackpole (3)		
207	Brisbane ..	1970-71
136	Adelaide	1970-71
114	Nottingham .	1972
J. M. Taylor (1)		
108	Sydney	1924-25
M. A. Taylor (4)		
136†	Leeds	1989
219	Nottingham .	1989
124	Manchester..	1993
111	Lord's	1993
G. H. S. Trott (1)		
143	Lord's	1896
V. T. Trumper (6)		
135*	Lord's	1899
104	Manchester..	1902
185*	Sydney	1903-04
113	Adelaide	1903-04
166	Sydney	1907-08
113	Sydney	1911-12
K. D. Walters (4)		
155†	Brisbane ..	1965-66
115	Melbourne ..	1965-66
112	Brisbane ..	1970-71
103	Perth......	1974-75
M. E. Waugh (2)		
138†	Adelaide	1990-91
137	Birmingham .	1993
S. R. Waugh (3)		
177*	Leeds	1989
152*	Lord's	1989
157*	Leeds	1993
D. M. Wellham (1)		
103†	The Oval....	1981
K. C. Wessels (1)		
162†	Brisbane	1982-83
G. M. Wood (3)		
100	Melbourne ..	1978-79
112	Lord's	1980
172	Nottingham .	1985

W. M. Woodfull (6)					**G. N. Yallop** (3)		
141	Leeds	1926	107	Melbourne .. 1928-29	102†	Brisbane	1978-79
117	Manchester..	1926	102	Melbourne .. 1928-29	121	Sydney	1978-79
111	Sydney	1928-29	155	Lord's 1930	114	Manchester ..	1981

† *Signifies hundred on first appearance in England–Australia Tests.*

‡ *Carried his bat.*

Notes: D. G. Bradman's scores in 1930 were 8 and 131 at Nottingham, 254 and 1 at Lord's, 334 at Leeds, 14 at Manchester, and 232 at The Oval.

D. G. Bradman scored a hundred in eight successive Tests against England in which he batted – three in 1936-37, three in 1938 and two in 1946-47. He was injured and unable to bat at The Oval in 1938.

W. H. Ponsford and K. D. Walters each hit hundreds in their first two Tests.

C. Bannerman and H. Graham each scored their maiden hundred in first-class cricket in their first Test.

No right-handed batsman has obtained two hundreds for Australia in a Test match against England, and no left-handed batsman for England against Australia.

H. Sutcliffe, in his first two games for England, scored 59 and 115 at Sydney and 176 and 127 at Melbourne in 1924-25. In the latter match, which lasted into the seventh day, he was on the field throughout except for 86 minutes, namely 27 hours and 52 minutes.

C. Hill made 98 and 97 at Adelaide in 1901-02, and F. E. Woolley 95 and 93 at Lord's in 1921.

H. Sutcliffe in 1924-25, C. G. Macartney in 1926 and A. R. Morris in 1946-47 made three hundreds in consecutive innings.

J. B. Hobbs and H. Sutcliffe shared 11 first-wicket three-figure partnerships.

L. Hutton and C. Washbrook twice made three-figure stands in each innings, at Adelaide in 1946-47 and at Leeds in 1948.

H. Sutcliffe, during his highest score of 194, v Australia in 1932-33, took part in three stands each exceeding 100, viz. 112 with R. E. S. Wyatt for the first wicket, 188 with W. R. Hammond for the second wicket, and 123 with the Nawab of Pataudi sen. for the third wicket. In 1903-04 R. E. Foster, in his historic innings of 287, added 192 for the fifth wicket with L. C. Braund, 115 for the ninth with A. E. Relf, and 130 for the tenth with W. Rhodes.

When L. Hutton scored 364 at The Oval in 1938 he added 382 for the second wicket with M. Leyland, 135 for the third wicket with W. R. Hammond and 215 for the sixth wicket with J. Hardstaff jun.

D. C. S. Compton and A. R. Morris at Adelaide in 1946-47 provided the first instance of a player on each side hitting two separate hundreds in a Test match.

G. S. and I. M. Chappell at The Oval in 1972 provide the first instance in Test matches of brothers each scoring hundreds in the same innings.

RECORD PARTNERSHIPS FOR EACH WICKET

For England

323 for 1st	J. B. Hobbs and W. Rhodes at Melbourne	1911-12
382 for 2nd†	L. Hutton and M. Leyland at The Oval	1938
262 for 3rd	W. R. Hammond and D. R. Jardine at Adelaide	1928-29
222 for 4th	W. R. Hammond and E. Paynter at Lord's	1938
206 for 5th	E. Paynter and D. C. S. Compton at Nottingham	1938
215 for 6th {	L. Hutton and J. Hardstaff jun. at The Oval	1938
	G. Boycott and A. P. E. Knott at Nottingham	1977
143 for 7th	F. E. Woolley and J. Vine at Sydney	1911-12
124 for 8th	E. H. Hendren and H. Larwood at Brisbane	1928-29
151 for 9th	W. H. Scotton and W. W. Read at The Oval	1884
130 for 10th†	R. E. Foster and W. Rhodes at Sydney	1903-04

For Australia

329 for 1st	G. R. Marsh and M. A. Taylor at Nottingham.............	1989
451 for 2nd†	W. H. Ponsford and D. G. Bradman at The Oval	1934
276 for 3rd	D. G. Bradman and A. L. Hassett at Brisbane	1946-47
388 for 4th†	W. H. Ponsford and D. G. Bradman at Leeds	1934
405 for 5th†‡	S. G. Barnes and D. G. Bradman at Sydney	1946-47
346 for 6th†	J. H. Fingleton and D. G. Bradman at Melbourne	1936-37

165 for 7th	C. Hill and H. Trumble at Melbourne	1897-98
243 for 8th†	R. J. Hartigan and C. Hill at Adelaide	1907-08
154 for 9th†	S. E. Gregory and J. McC. Blackham at Sydney	1894-95
127 for 10th†	J. M. Taylor and A. A. Mailey at Sydney	1924-25

† *Denotes record partnership against all countries.*
‡ *Record fifth-wicket partnership in first-class cricket.*

MOST RUNS IN A SERIES

England in England	732 (average 81.33)	D. I. Gower	1985
England in Australia	905 (average 113.12)	W. R. Hammond	1928-29
Australia in England	974 (average 139.14)	D. G. Bradman	1930
Australia in Australia	810 (average 90.00)	D. G. Bradman	1936-37

TEN WICKETS OR MORE IN A MATCH

For England (36)

13-163 (6-42, 7-121)	S. F. Barnes, Melbourne	1901-02
14-102 (7-28, 7-74)	W. Bates, Melbourne	1882-83
10-105 (5-46, 5-59)	A. V. Bedser, Melbourne	1950-51
14-99 (7-55, 7-44)	A. V. Bedser, Nottingham	1953
11-102 (6-44, 5-58)	C. Blythe, Birmingham	1909
11-176 (6-78, 5-98)	I. T. Botham, Perth	1979-80
10-253 (6-125, 4-128)	I. T. Botham, The Oval	1981
11-74 (5-29, 6-45)	J. Briggs, Lord's	1886
12-136 (6-49, 6-87)	J. Briggs, Adelaide	1891-92
10-148 (5-34, 5-114)	J. Briggs, The Oval	1893
10-104 (6-77, 4-27)†	R. M. Ellison, Birmingham	1985
10-179 (5-102, 5-77)†	K. Farnes, Nottingham	1934
10-60 (6-41, 4-19)	J. T. Hearne, The Oval	1896
11-113 (5-58, 6-55)	J. C. Laker, Leeds	1956
19-90 (9-37, 10-53)	J. C. Laker, Manchester	1956
10-124 (5-96, 5-28)	H. Larwood, Sydney	1932-33
11-76 (6-48, 5-28)	W. H. Lockwood, Manchester	1902
12-104 (7-36, 5-68)	G. A. Lohmann, The Oval	1886
10-87 (8-35, 2-52)	G. A. Lohmann, Sydney	1886-87
10-142 (8-58, 2-84)	G. A. Lohmann, Sydney	1891-92
12-102 (6-50, 6-52)†	F. Martin, The Oval	1890
11-68 (7-31, 4-37)	R. Peel, Manchester	1888
15-124 (7-56, 8-68)	W. Rhodes, Melbourne	1903-04
10-156 (5-49, 5-107)†	T. Richardson, Manchester	1893
11-173 (6-39, 5-134)	T. Richardson, Lord's	1896
13-244 (7-168, 6-76)	T. Richardson, Manchester	1896
10-204 (8-94, 2-110)	T. Richardson, Sydney	1897-98
11-228 (6-130, 5-98)†	M. W. Tate, Sydney	1924-25
11-88 (5-58, 6-30)	F. S. Trueman, Leeds	1961
10-130 (4-45, 6-85)	F. H. Tyson, Sydney	1954-55
10-82 (4-37, 6-45)	D. L. Underwood, Leeds	1972
11-215 (7-113, 4-102)	D. L. Underwood, Adelaide	1974-75
15-104 (7-61, 8-43)	H. Verity, Lord's	1934
10-57 (6-41, 4-16)	W. Voce, Brisbane	1936-37
13-256 (5-130, 8-126)	J. C. White, Adelaide	1928-29
10-49 (5-29, 5-20)	F. E. Woolley, The Oval	1912

For Australia (38)

10-151 (5-107, 5-44)	T. M. Alderman, Leeds..........................	1989
10-239 (4-129, 6-110)	L. O'B. Fleetwood-Smith, Adelaide.............	1936-37
10-160 (4-88, 6-72)	G. Giffen, Sydney..............................	1891-92
11-82 (5-45, 6-37)†	C. V. Grimmett, Sydney........................	1924-25
10-201 (5-107, 5-94)	C. V. Grimmett, Nottingham....................	1930
10-122 (5-65, 5-57)	R. M. Hogg, Perth.............................	1978-79
10-66 (5-30, 5-36)	R. M. Hogg, Melbourne.........................	1978-79
12-175 (5-85, 7-90)†	H. V. Hordern, Sydney.........................	1911-12
10-161 (5-95, 5-66)	H. V. Hordern, Sydney.........................	1911-12
10-164 (7-88, 3-76)	E. Jones, Lord's...............................	1899
11-134 (6-47, 5-87)	G. F. Lawson, Brisbane........................	1982-83
10-181 (5-58, 5-123)	D. K. Lillee, The Oval.........................	1972
11-165 (6-26, 5-139)	D. K. Lillee, Melbourne........................	1976-77
11-138 (6-60, 5-78)	D. K. Lillee, Melbourne........................	1979-80
11-159 (7-89, 4-70)	D. K. Lillee, The Oval.........................	1981
11-85 (7-58, 4-27)	C. G. Macartney, Leeds........................	1909
11-157 (8-97, 3-60)	C. J. McDermott, Perth........................	1990-91
10-302 (5-160, 5-142)	A. A. Mailey, Adelaide.........................	1920-21
13-236 (4-115, 9-121)	A. A. Mailey, Melbourne.......................	1920-21
16-137 (8-84, 8-53)†	R. A. L. Massie, Lord's........................	1972
10-152 (5-72, 5-80)	K. R. Miller, Lord's...........................	1956
13-77 (7-17, 6-60)	M. A. Noble, Melbourne........................	1901-02
11-103 (5-51, 6-52)	M. A. Noble, Sheffield.........................	1902
10-129 (5-63, 5-66)	W. J. O'Reilly, Melbourne......................	1932-33
11-129 (4-75, 7-54)	W. J. O'Reilly, Nottingham.....................	1934
10-122 (5-66, 5-56)	W. J. O'Reilly, Leeds..........................	1938
11-165 (7-68, 4-97)	G. E. Palmer, Sydney..........................	1881-82
10-126 (7-65, 3-61)	G. E. Palmer, Melbourne.......................	1882-83
13-148 (6-97, 7-51)	B. A. Reid, Melbourne.........................	1990-91
13-110 (6-48, 7-62)	F. R. Spofforth, Melbourne.....................	1878-79
14-90 (7-46, 7-44)	F. R. Spofforth, The Oval......................	1882
11-117 (4-73, 7-44)	F. R. Spofforth, Sydney........................	1882-83
10-144 (4-54, 6-90)	F. R. Spofforth, Sydney........................	1884-85
12-89 (6-59, 6-30)	H. Trumble, The Oval..........................	1896
10-128 (4-75, 6-53)	H. Trumble, Manchester........................	1902
12-173 (8-65, 4-108)	H. Trumble, The Oval..........................	1902
12-87 (5-44, 7-43)	C. T. B. Turner, Sydney........................	1887-88
10-63 (5-27, 5-36)	C. T. B. Turner, Lord's........................	1888

† *Signifies ten wickets or more on first appearance in England–Australia Tests.*

Note: J. Briggs, J. C. Laker, T. Richardson in 1896, R. M. Hogg, A. A. Mailey, H. Trumble and C. T. B. Turner took ten wickets or more in successive Tests. J. Briggs was omitted, however, from the England team for the first Test match in 1893.

MOST WICKETS IN A SERIES

England in England........	46 (average 9.60)	J. C. Laker............	1956
England in Australia.......	38 (average 23.18)	M. W. Tate...........	1924-25
Australia in England.......	42 (average 21.26)	T. M. Alderman (6 Tests)	1981
Australia in Australia......	41 (average 12.85)	R. M. Hogg (6 Tests)...	1978-79

WICKET-KEEPING – MOST DISMISSALS

	M	*Ct*	*St*	*Total*
†R. W. Marsh (Australia)	42	141	7	148
A. P. E. Knott (England).......	34	97	8	105
†W. A. Oldfield (Australia)	38	59	31	90
A. A. Lilley (England)	32	65	19	84
A. T. W. Grout (Australia)	22	69	7	76
T. G. Evans (England)	31	63	12	75

† *The number of catches by R. W. Marsh (141) and stumpings by W. A. Oldfield (31) are respective records in England–Australia Tests.*

SCORERS OF OVER 2,000 RUNS

	T		I		NO		R		HS		Avge
D. G. Bradman	37	..	63	..	7	..	5,028	..	334	..	89.78
J. B. Hobbs	41	..	71	..	4	..	3,636	..	187	..	54.26
A. R. Border	47	..	82	..	19	..	3,548	..	200*	..	56.31
D. I. Gower	42	..	77	..	4	..	3,269	..	215	..	44.78
G. Boycott	38	..	71	..	9	..	2,945	..	191	..	47.50
W. R. Hammond	33	..	58	..	3	..	2,852	..	251	..	51.85
H. Sutcliffe	27	..	46	..	5	..	2,741	..	194	..	66.85
C. Hill	41	..	76	..	1	..	2,660	..	188	..	35.46
J. H. Edrich	32	..	57	..	3	..	2,644	..	175	..	48.96
G. S. Chappell	35	..	65	..	8	..	2,619	..	144	..	45.94
M. C. Cowdrey	43	..	75	..	4	..	2,433	..	113	..	34.26
L. Hutton	27	..	49	..	6	..	2,428	..	364	..	56.46
R. N. Harvey	37	..	68	..	5	..	2,416	..	167	..	38.34
G. A. Gooch	37	..	69	..	0	..	2,387	..	196	..	34.59
V. T. Trumper	40	..	74	..	5	..	2,263	..	185*	..	32.79
W. M. Lawry	29	..	51	..	5	..	2,233	..	166	..	48.54
S. E. Gregory	52	..	92	..	7	..	2,193	..	201	..	25.80
W. W. Armstrong	42	..	71	..	9	..	2,172	..	158	..	35.03
I. M. Chappell	30	..	56	..	4	..	2,138	..	192	..	41.11
K. F. Barrington	23	..	39	..	6	..	2,111	..	256	..	63.96
A. R. Morris	24	..	43	..	2	..	2,080	..	206	..	50.73

BOWLERS WITH 100 WICKETS

	T		Balls		R		W		5W/i		Avge
D. K. Lillee	29	..	8,516	..	3,507	..	167	..	11	..	21.00
I. T. Botham	36	..	8,479	..	4,093	..	148	..	9	..	27.65
H. Trumble	31	..	7,895	..	2,945	..	141	..	9	..	20.88
R. G. D. Willis	35	..	7,294	..	3,346	..	128	..	7	..	26.14
M. A. Noble	39	..	6,845	..	2,860	..	115	..	9	..	24.86
R. R. Lindwall	29	..	6,728	..	2,559	..	114	..	6	..	22.44
W. Rhodes	41	..	5,791	..	2,616	..	109	..	6	..	24.00
S. F. Barnes	20	..	5,749	..	2,288	..	106	..	12	..	21.58
C. V. Grimmett	22	..	9,224	..	3,439	..	106	..	11	..	32.44
D. L. Underwood	29	..	8,000	..	2,770	..	105	..	4	..	26.38
A. V. Bedser	21	..	7,065	..	2,859	..	104	..	7	..	27.49
G. Giffen	31	..	6,457	..	2,791	..	103	..	7	..	27.09
W. J. O'Reilly	19	..	7,864	..	2,587	..	102	..	8	..	25.36
R. Peel	20	..	5,216	..	1,715	..	101	..	5	..	16.98
C. T. B. Turner	17	..	5,195	..	1,670	..	101	..	11	..	16.53
T. M. Alderman	17	..	4,717	..	2,117	..	100	..	11	..	21.17
J. R. Thomson	21	..	4,951	..	2,418	..	100	..	5	..	24.18

RESULTS ON EACH GROUND

In England

THE OVAL (31)

England (14)   1880, 1886, 1888, 1890, 1893, 1896, 1902, 1912, 1926, 1938, 1953, 1968, 1985, 1993.

Australia (5)   1882, 1930, 1934, 1948, 1972.

Drawn (12)   1884, 1899, 1905, 1909, 1921, 1956, 1961, 1964, 1975, 1977, 1981, 1989.

MANCHESTER (26)

England (7)   1886, 1888, 1905, 1956, 1972, 1977, 1981.

Australia (6)   1896, 1902, 1961, 1968, 1989, 1993.

Drawn (13)   1884, 1893, 1899, 1909, 1912, 1921, 1926, 1930, 1934, 1948, 1953, 1964, 1985.

The scheduled matches in 1890 and 1938 were abandoned without a ball bowled and are excluded.

LORD'S (30)

England (5)	1884, 1886, 1890, 1896, 1934.
Australia (12)	1888, 1899, 1909, 1921, 1930, 1948, 1956, 1961, 1972, 1985, 1989, 1993.
Drawn (13)	1893, 1902, 1905, 1912, 1926, 1938, 1953, 1964, 1968, 1975, 1977, 1980, 1981.

NOTTINGHAM (17)

England (3)	1905, 1930, 1977.
Australia (5)	1921, 1934, 1948, 1981, 1989.
Drawn (9)	1899, 1926, 1938, 1953, 1956, 1964, 1972, 1985, 1993.

LEEDS (21)

England (6)	1956, 1961, 1972, 1977, 1981, 1985.
Australia (7)	1909, 1921, 1938, 1948, 1964, 1989, 1993.
Drawn (8)	1899, 1905, 1926, 1930, 1934, 1953, 1968, 1975.

BIRMINGHAM (9)

England (3)	1909, 1981, 1985.
Australia (2)	1975, 1993.
Drawn (4)	1902, 1961, 1968, 1989.

SHEFFIELD (1)

Australia (1)	1902.

In Australia

MELBOURNE (49)

England (18)	*1876, 1882, 1884(2), 1894(2), 1903, 1907, 1911(2), 1924, 1928, 1950, 1954, 1962, 1974, 1982, 1986.*
Australia (24)	*1876, 1878, 1882, 1891, 1897(2), 1901(2), 1903, 1907, 1920(2), 1924, 1928, 1932, 1936(2), 1950, 1958(2), 1976, 1978, 1979, 1990.*
Drawn (7)	*1881(2), 1946, 1965(2), 1970, 1974.*

One scheduled match in 1970-71 was abandoned without a ball bowled and is excluded.

SYDNEY (49)

England (20)	*1882, 1886(2), 1887, 1894, 1897, 1901, 1903(2), 1911, 1928, 1932(2), 1936, 1954, 1965, 1970(2), 1978(2).*
Australia (23)	*1881(2), 1882, 1884(2), 1891, 1894, 1897, 1901, 1907(2), 1911, 1920(2), 1924(2), 1946(2), 1950, 1962, 1974, 1979, 1986.*
Drawn (6)	*1954, 1958, 1962, 1982, 1987, 1990.*

ADELAIDE (25)

England (7)	*1884, 1891, 1911, 1928, 1932, 1954, 1978.*
Australia (13)	*1894, 1897, 1901, 1903, 1907, 1920, 1924, 1936, 1950, 1958, 1965, 1974, 1982.*
Drawn (5)	*1946, 1962, 1970, 1986, 1990.*

BRISBANE Exhibition Ground (1)

England (1)	*1928.*

BRISBANE Woolloongabba (14)

England (4)	*1932, 1936, 1978, 1986.*
Australia (7)	*1946, 1950, 1954, 1958, 1974, 1982, 1990.*
Drawn (3)	*1962, 1965, 1970.*

PERTH (7)

England (1)	*1978.*
Australia (3)	*1974, 1979, 1990.*
Drawn (3)	*1970, 1982, 1986.*

For Tests in Australia the first year of the season is given in italics; i.e. *1876* denotes the 1876-77 season.

ENGLAND v SOUTH AFRICA

Captains

Season	England	South Africa	T	E	SA	D
1888-89	C. A. Smith[1]	O. R. Dunell[2]	2	2	0	0
1891-92	W. W. Read	W. H. Milton	1	1	0	0
1895-96	Lord Hawke[3]	E. A. Halliwell[4]	3	3	0	0
1898-99	Lord Hawke	M. Bisset	2	2	0	0
1905-06	P. F. Warner	P. W. Sherwell	5	1	4	0
1907	R. E. Foster	P. W. Sherwell	3	1	0	2
1909-10	H. D. G. Leveson Gower[5]	S. J. Snooke	5	2	3	0
1912	C. B. Fry	F. Mitchell[6]	3	3	0	0
1913-14	J. W. H. T. Douglas	H. W. Taylor	5	4	0	1
1922-23	F. T. Mann	H. W. Taylor	5	2	1	2
1924	A. E. R. Gilligan[7]	H. W. Taylor	5	3	0	2
1927-28	R. T. Stanyforth[8]	H. G. Deane	5	2	2	1
1929	J. C. White[9]	H. G. Deane	5	2	0	3
1930-31	A. P. F. Chapman	H. G. Deane[10]	5	0	1	4
1935	R. E. S. Wyatt	H. F. Wade	5	0	1	4
1938-39	W. R. Hammond	A. Melville	5	1	0	4
1947	N. W. D. Yardley	A. Melville	5	3	0	2
1948-49	F. G. Mann	A. D. Nourse	5	2	0	3
1951	F. R. Brown	A. D. Nourse	5	3	1	1
1955	P. B. H. May	J. E. Cheetham[11]	5	3	2	0
1956-57	P. B. H. May	C. B. van Ryneveld[12]	5	2	2	1
1960	M. C. Cowdrey	D. J. McGlew	5	3	0	2
1964-65	M. J. K. Smith	T. L. Goddard	5	1	0	4
1965	M. J. K. Smith	P. L. van der Merwe	3	0	1	2
	In South Africa		58	25	13	20
	In England		44	21	5	18
	Totals		102	46	18	38

Notes: The following deputised for the official touring captain or were appointed by the home authority for only a minor proportion of the series:

[1]M. P. Bowden (Second). [2]W. H. Milton (Second). [3]Sir T. C. O'Brien (First). [4]A. R. Richards (Third). [5]F. L. Fane (Fourth and Fifth). [6]L. J. Tancred (Second and Third). [7]J. W. H. T. Douglas (Fourth). [8]G. T. S. Stevens (Fifth). [9]A. W. Carr (Fourth and Fifth). [10]E. P. Nupen (First), H. B. Cameron (Fourth and Fifth). [11]D. J. McGlew (Third and Fourth). [12]D. J. McGlew (Second).

HIGHEST INNINGS TOTALS

For England in England:	554-8 dec. at Lord's	1947
in South Africa:	654-5 at Durban	1938-39
For South Africa in England:	538 at Leeds	1951
in South Africa:	530 at Durban	1938-39

LOWEST INNINGS TOTALS

For England in England: 76 at Leeds 1907
in South Africa: 92 at Cape Town 1898-99

For South Africa in England: 30 at Birmingham 1924
in South Africa: 30 at Port Elizabeth 1895-96

INDIVIDUAL HUNDREDS

For England (87)

R. Abel (1)
120   Cape Town . . 1888-89
L. E. G. Ames (2)
148*   The Oval   1935
115   Cape Town . . 1938-39
K. F. Barrington (2)
148*   Durban 1964-65
121   Johannesburg 1964-65
G. Boycott (1)
117   Pt Elizabeth . 1964-65
L. C. Braund (1)
104†   Lord's   1907
D. C. S. Compton (7)
163†   Nottingham .   1947
208   Lord's   1947
115   Manchester . .   1947
113   The Oval   1947
114   Johannesburg 1948-49
112   Nottingham .   1951
158   Manchester . .   1955
M. C. Cowdrey (3)
101   Cape Town . . 1956-57
155   The Oval   1960
105   Nottingham .   1965
D. Denton (1)
104   Johannesburg 1909-10
E. R. Dexter (1)
172   Johannesburg 1964-65
J. W. H. T. Douglas (1)
119†   Durban 1913-14
W. J. Edrich (3)
219   Durban 1938-39
189   Lord's   1947
191   Manchester . .   1947
F. L. Fane (1)
143   Johannesburg 1905-06
C. B. Fry (1)
129   The Oval   1907
P. A. Gibb (2)
106†   Johannesburg 1938-39
120   Durban 1938-39
W. R. Hammond (6)
138*   Birmingham .   1929
101*   The Oval   1929
136*   Durban 1930-31

181   Cape Town . . 1938-39
120   Durban 1938-39
140   Durban 1938-39
T. W. Hayward (1)
122   Johannesburg 1895-96
E. H. Hendren (2)
132   Leeds   1924
142   The Oval   1924
A. J. L. Hill (1)
124   Cape Town . . 1895-96
J. B. Hobbs (2)
187   Cape Town . . 1909-10
211   Lord's   1924
L. Hutton (4)
100   Leeds   1947
158   Johannesburg 1948-49
123   Johannesburg 1948-49
100   Leeds   1951
D. J. Insole (1)
110*   Durban 1956-57
M. Leyland (2)
102   Lord's   1929
161   The Oval   1935
F. G. Mann (1)
136*   Pt Elizabeth . 1948-49
P. B. H. May (3)
138†   Leeds   1951
112   Lord's   1955
117   Manchester . .   1955
C. P. Mead (3)
102   Johannesburg 1913-14
117   Pt Elizabeth . 1913-14
181   Durban 1922-23
P. H. Parfitt (1)
122*   Johannesburg 1964-65
J. M. Parks (1)
108*   Durban 1964-65
E. Paynter (3)
117 ⎫
100 ⎬†Johannesburg 1938-39
243 ⎭ Durban 1938-39
G. Pullar (1)
175   The Oval   1960
W. Rhodes (1)
152   Johannesburg 1913-14

P. E. Richardson (1)
117†   Johannesburg 1956-57
R. W. V. Robins (1)
108   Manchester . .   1935
A. C. Russell (2)
140 ⎫
111 ⎬ Durban 1922-23
R. T. Simpson (1)
137   Nottingham .   1951
M. J. K. Smith (1)
121   Cape Town . . 1964-65
R. H. Spooner (1)
119†   Lord's   1912
H. Sutcliffe (6)
122   Lord's   1924
102   Johannesburg 1927-28
114   Birmingham .   1929
100   Lord's   1929
104 ⎫
109* ⎬ The Oval   1929
M. W. Tate (1)
100*   Lord's   1929
E. Tyldesley (2)
122   Johannesburg 1927-28
100   Durban 1927-28
J. T. Tyldesley (1)
112   Cape Town . . 1898-99
B. H. Valentine (1)
112   Cape Town . . 1938-39
P. F. Warner (1)
132*†‡Johannesburg 1898-99
C. Washbrook (1)
195   Johannesburg 1948-49
A. J. Watkins (1)
111   Johannesburg 1948-49
H. Wood (1)
134*   Cape Town . . 1891-92
F. E. Woolley (3)
115*   Johannesburg 1922-23
134*   Lord's   1924
154   Manchester . .   1929
R. E. S. Wyatt (2)
113   Manchester . .   1929
149   Nottingham .   1935

For South Africa (58)

E. J. Barlow (1)			**P. W. Sherwell** (1)		
138	Cape Town	1964-65	189	} Nottingham	1947	115	Lord's	1907
K. C. Bland (2)			104*			**I. J. Siedle** (1)		
144*	Johannesburg	1964-65	117	Lord's	1947	141	Cape Town	1930-31
127	The Oval	1965	**B. Mitchell** (7)			**J. H. Sinclair** (1)		
R. H. Catterall (3)			123	Cape Town	1930-31	106	Cape Town	1898-99
120	Birmingham	1924	164*	Lord's	1935	**H. W. Taylor** (7)		
120	Lord's	1924	128	The Oval	1935	109	Durban	1913-14
119	Durban	1927-28	109	Durban	1938-39	176	Johannesburg	1922-23
E. L. Dalton (2)			120	} The Oval	1947	101	Johannesburg	1922-23
117	The Oval	1935	189*			102	Durban	1922-23
102	Johannesburg	1938-39	120	Cape Town	1948-49	101	Johannesburg	1927-28
W. R. Endean (1)			**A. D. Nourse** (7)			121	The Oval	1929
116*	Leeds	1955	120	Cape Town	1938-39	117	Cape Town	1930-31
G. A. Faulkner (1)			103	Durban	1938-39	**P. G. V. van der Bijl** (1)		
123	Johannesburg	1909-10	149	Nottingham	1947	125	Durban	1938-39
T. L. Goddard (1)			115	Manchester	1947	**K. G. Viljoen** (1)		
112	Johannesburg	1964-65	112	Cape Town	1948-49	124	Manchester	1935
C. M. H. Hathorn (1)			129*	Johannesburg	1948-49	**W. W. Wade** (1)		
102	Johannesburg	1905-06	208	Nottingham	1951	125	Pt Elizabeth	1948-49
D. J. McGlew (2)			**H. G. Owen-Smith** (1)			**J. H. B. Waite** (1)		
104*	Manchester	1955	129	Leeds	1929	113	Manchester	1955
133	Leeds	1955	**A. J. Pithey** (1)			**G. C. White** (2)		
R. A. McLean (3)			154	Cape Town	1964-65	147	Johannesburg	1905-06
142	Lord's	1955	**R. G. Pollock** (2)			118	Durban	1909-10
100	Durban	1956-57	137	Pt Elizabeth	1964-65	**P. L. Winslow** (1)		
109	Manchester	1960	125	Nottingham	1965	108	Manchester	1955
A. Melville (4)			**E. A. B. Rowan** (2)					
103	Durban	1938-39	156*	Johannesburg	1948-49			
			236	Leeds	1951			

† Signifies hundred on first appearance in England–South Africa Tests. The highest scores on debut in this series for South Africa are (in South Africa) 93* by A. W. Nourse at Johannesburg in 1905-06 and (in England) 90 by P. N. F. Mansell at Leeds in 1951.

‡ P. F. Warner carried his bat through the second innings.

A. Melville's four hundreds were made in successive Test innings.

H. Wood scored the only hundred of his career in a Test match.

RECORD PARTNERSHIP FOR EACH WICKET

For England

359	for 1st†	L. Hutton and C. Washbrook at Johannesburg	1948-49
280	for 2nd	P. A. Gibb and W. J. Edrich at Durban	1938-39
370	for 3rd†	W. J. Edrich and D. C. S. Compton at Lord's	1947
197	for 4th	W. R. Hammond and L. E. G. Ames at Cape Town	1938-39
237	for 5th	D. C. S. Compton and N. W. D. Yardley at Nottingham	1947
206*	for 6th	K. F. Barrington and J. M. Parks at Durban	1964-65
115	for 7th	M. C. Bird and J. W. H. T. Douglas at Durban	1913-14
154	for 8th	C. W. Wright and H. R. Bromley-Davenport at Johannesburg	1895-96
71	for 9th	H. Wood and J. T. Hearne at Cape Town	1891-92
92	for 10th	A. C. Russell and A. E. R. Gilligan at Durban	1922-23

For South Africa

260	for 1st†	I. J. Siedle and B. Mitchell at Cape Town	1930-31
198	for 2nd†	E. A. B. Rowan and C. B. van Ryneveld at Leeds	1951
319	for 3rd	A. Melville and A. D. Nourse at Nottingham	1947
214	for 4th†	H. W. Taylor and H. G. Deane at The Oval	1929
157	for 5th†	A. J. Pithey and J. H. B. Waite at Johannesburg	1964-65
171	for 6th	J. H. B. Waite and P. L. Winslow at Manchester	1955
123	for 7th	H. G. Deane and E. P. Nupen at Durban	1927-28

109* for 8th	B. Mitchell and L. Tuckett at The Oval		1947
137 for 9th†	E. L. Dalton and A. B. C. Langton at The Oval		1935
103 for 10th†	H. G. Owen-Smith and A. J. Bell at Leeds		1929

† *Denotes record partnership against all countries.*

MOST RUNS IN A SERIES

England in England	753 (average 94.12)	D. C. S. Compton	1947
England in South Africa	653 (average 81.62)	E. Paynter	1938-39
South Africa in England	621 (average 69.00)	A. D. Nourse	1947
South Africa in South Africa	582 (average 64.66)	H. W. Taylor	1922-23

TEN WICKETS OR MORE IN A MATCH

For England (23)

11-110 (5-25, 6-85)†	S. F. Barnes, Lord's	1912
10-115 (6-52, 4-63)	S. F. Barnes, Leeds	1912
13-57 (5-28, 8-29)	S. F. Barnes, The Oval	1912
10-105 (5-57, 5-48)	S. F. Barnes, Durban	1913-14
17-159 (8-56, 9-103)	S. F. Barnes, Johannesburg	1913-14
14-144 (7-56, 7-88)	S. F. Barnes, Durban	1913-14
12-112 (7-58, 5-54)	A. V. Bedser, Manchester	1951
11-118 (6-68, 5-50)	C. Blythe, Cape Town	1905-06
15-99 (8-59, 7-40)	C. Blythe, Leeds	1907
10-104 (7-46, 3-58)	C. Blythe, Cape Town	1909-10
15-28 (7-17, 8-11)	J. Briggs, Cape Town	1888-89
13-91 (6-54, 7-37)†	J. J. Ferris, Cape Town	1891-92
10-207 (7-115, 3-92)	A. P. Freeman, Leeds	1929
12-171 (7-71, 5-100)	A. P. Freeman, Manchester	1929
12-130 (7-70, 5-60)	G. Geary, Johannesburg	1927-28
11-90 (6-7, 5-83)	A. E. R. Gilligan, Birmingham	1924
10-119 (4-64, 6-55)	J. C. Laker, The Oval	1951
15-45 (7-38, 8-7)†	G. A. Lohmann, Port Elizabeth	1895-96
12-71 (9-28, 3-43)	G. A. Lohmann, Johannesburg	1895-96
11-97 (6-63, 5-34)	J. B. Statham, Lord's	1960
12-101 (7-52, 5-49)	R. Tattersall, Lord's	1951
12-89 (5-53, 7-36)	J. H. Wardle, Cape Town	1956-57
10-175 (5-95, 5-80)	D. V. P. Wright, Lord's	1947

For South Africa (6)

11-112 (4-49, 7-63)†	A. E. Hall, Cape Town	1922-23
11-150 (5-63, 6-87)	E. P. Nupen, Johannesburg	1930-31
10-87 (5-53, 5-34)	P. M. Pollock, Nottingham	1965
12-127 (4-57, 8-70)	S. J. Snooke, Johannesburg	1905-06
13-192 (4-79, 9-113)	H. J. Tayfield, Johannesburg	1956-57
12-181 (5-87, 7-94)	A. E. E. Vogler, Johannesburg	1909-10

† *Signifies ten wickets or more on first appearance in England–South Africa Tests.*

Note: S. F. Barnes took ten wickets or more in his first five Tests v South Africa and in six of his seven Tests v South Africa. A. P. Freeman and G. A. Lohmann took ten wickets or more in successive matches.

MOST WICKETS IN A SERIES

England in England	34 (average 8.29)	S. F. Barnes	1912
England in South Africa	49 (average 10.93)	S. F. Barnes	1913-14
South Africa in England	26 (average 21.84)	H. J. Tayfield	1955
South Africa in England	26 (average 22.57)	N. A. T. Adcock	1960
South Africa in South Africa	37 (average 17.18)	H. J. Tayfield	1956-57

ENGLAND v WEST INDIES

	Captains					
Season	*England*	*West Indies*	*T*	*E*	*WI*	*D*
1928	A. P. F. Chapman	R. K. Nunes	3	3	0	0
1929-30	Hon. F. S. G. Calthorpe	E. L. G. Hoad[1]	4	1	1	2
1933	D. R. Jardine[2]	G. C. Grant	3	2	0	1
1934-35	R. E. S. Wyatt	G. C. Grant	4	1	2	1
1939	W. R. Hammond	R. S. Grant	3	1	0	2
1947-48	G. O. B. Allen[3]	J. D. C. Goddard[4]	4	0	2	2
1950	N. W. D. Yardley[5]	J. D. C. Goddard	4	1	3	0
1953-54	L. Hutton	J. B. Stollmeyer	5	2	2	1
1957	P. B. H. May	J. D. C. Goddard	5	3	0	2
1959-60	P. B. H. May[6]	F. C. M. Alexander	5	1	0	4

THE WISDEN TROPHY

	Captains						
Season	*England*	*West Indies*	*T*	*E*	*WI*	*D*	*Held by*
1963	E. R. Dexter	F. M. M. Worrell	5	1	3	1	WI
1966	M. C. Cowdrey[7]	G. S. Sobers	5	1	3	1	WI
1967-68	M. C. Cowdrey	G. S. Sobers	5	1	0	4	E
1969	R. Illingworth	G. S. Sobers	3	2	0	1	E
1973	R. Illingworth	R. B. Kanhai	3	0	2	1	WI
1973-74	M. H. Denness	R. B. Kanhai	5	1	1	3	WI
1976	A. W. Greig	C. H. Lloyd	5	0	3	2	WI
1980	I. T. Botham	C. H. Lloyd[8]	5	0	1	4	WI
1980-81†	I. T. Botham	C. H. Lloyd	4	0	2	2	WI
1984	D. I. Gower	C. H. Lloyd	5	0	5	0	WI
1985-86	D. I. Gower	I. V. A. Richards	5	0	5	0	WI
1988	J. E. Emburey[9]	I. V. A. Richards	5	0	4	1	WI
1989-90‡	G. A. Gooch[10]	I. V. A. Richards[11]	4	1	2	1	WI
1991	G. A. Gooch	I. V. A. Richards	5	2	2	1	WI

In England	....	59	16	26	17
In West Indies	....	45	8	17	20
Totals	....	104	24	43	37

† *The Second Test, at Georgetown, was cancelled owing to political pressure and is excluded.*
‡ *The Second Test, at Georgetown, was abandoned without a ball being bowled and is excluded.*

Notes: The following deputised for the official touring captain or were appointed by the home authority for only a minor proportion of the series:
[1]N. Betancourt (Second), M. P. Fernandes (Third), R. K. Nunes (Fourth). [2]R. E. S. Wyatt (Third). [3]K. Cranston (First). [4]G. A. Headley (First), G. E. Gomez (Second). [5]F. R. Brown (Fourth). [6]M. C. Cowdrey (Fourth and Fifth). [7]M. J. K. Smith (First), D. B. Close (Fifth). [8]I. V. A. Richards (Fifth). [9]M. W. Gatting (First), C. S. Cowdrey (Fourth), G. A. Gooch (Fifth). [10]A. J. Lamb (Fourth and Fifth). [11]D. L. Haynes (Third).

HIGHEST INNINGS TOTALS

For England in England: 619-6 dec. at Nottingham 1957
          in West Indies: 849 at Kingston 1929-30

For West Indies in England: 687-8 dec. at The Oval 1976
          in West Indies: 681-8 dec. at Port-of-Spain 1953-54

LOWEST INNINGS TOTALS

For England in England: 71 at Manchester 1976
in West Indies: 103 at Kingston 1934-35

For West Indies in England: 86 at The Oval 1957
in West Indies: 102 at Bridgetown 1934-35

INDIVIDUAL HUNDREDS

For England (88)

L. E. G. Ames (3)
105   Port-of-Spain 1929-30
149   Kingston 1929-30
126   Kingston 1934-35
D. L. Amiss (4)
174   Port-of-Spain 1973-74
262*   Kingston 1973-74
118   Georgetown . 1973-74
203   The Oval 1976
A. H. Bakewell (1)
107†   The Oval 1933
K. F. Barrington (3)
128†   Bridgetown . . 1959-60
121   Port-of-Spain 1959-60
143   Port-of-Spain 1967-68
G. Boycott (5)
116   Georgetown . . 1967-68
128   Manchester . . 1969
106   Lord's 1969
112   Port-of-Spain 1973-74
104*   St John's 1980-81
D. C. S. Compton (2)
120†   Lord's 1939
133   Port-of-Spain 1953-54
M. C. Cowdrey (6)
154†   Birmingham . 1957
152   Lord's 1957
114   Kingston 1959-60
119   Port-of-Spain 1959-60
101   Kingston 1967-68
148   Port-of-Spain 1967-68
E. R. Dexter (2)
136*† Bridgetown . . 1959-60
110   Georgetown . . 1959-60
J. H. Edrich (1)
146   Bridgetown . . 1967-68
T. G. Evans (1)
104   Manchester . . 1950
K. W. R. Fletcher (1)
129*   Bridgetown . . 1973-74
G. Fowler (1)
106   Lord's 1984
G. A. Gooch (5)
123   Lord's 1980
116   Bridgetown . . 1980-81

153   Kingston 1980-81
146   Nottingham . . 1988
154*‡ Leeds 1991
D. I. Gower (1)
154*   Kingston 1980-81
T. W. Graveney (5)
258   Nottingham . . 1957
164   The Oval 1957
109   Nottingham . . 1966
165   The Oval 1966
118   Port-of-Spain 1967-68
A. W. Greig (3)
148   Bridgetown . . 1973-74
121   Georgetown . . 1973-74
116   Leeds 1976
S. C. Griffith (1)
140†   Port-of-Spain 1947-48
W. R. Hammond (1)
138   The Oval 1939
J. H. Hampshire (1)
107†   Lord's 1969
F. C. Hayes (1)
106*† The Oval 1973
E. H. Hendren (2)
205*   Port-of-Spain 1929-30
123   Georgetown . . 1929-30
J. B. Hobbs (1)
159   The Oval 1928
L. Hutton (5)
196†   Lord's 1939
165*   The Oval 1939
202*‡ The Oval 1950
169   Georgetown . . 1953-54
205   Kingston 1953-54
R. Illingworth (1)
113   Lord's 1969
D. R. Jardine (1)
127   Manchester . . 1933
A. P. E. Knott (1)
116   Leeds 1976
A. J. Lamb (6)
110   Lord's 1984
100   Leeds 1984

100*   Manchester . . 1984
113   Lord's 1988
132   Kingston 1989-90
119   Bridgetown . . 1989-90
P. B. H. May (3)
135   Port-of-Spain 1953-54
285*   Birmingham . 1957
104   Nottingham . . 1957
C. Milburn (1)
126*   Lord's 1966
J. T. Murray (1)
112†   The Oval 1966
J. M. Parks (1)
101*† Port-of-Spain 1959-60
W. Place (1)
107   Kingston 1947-48
P. E. Richardson (2)
126   Nottingham . . 1957
107   The Oval 1957
J. D. Robertson (1)
133   Port-of-Spain 1947-48
A. Sandham (2)
152†   Bridgetown . . 1929-30
325   Kingston 1929-30
M. J. K. Smith (1)
108   Port-of-Spain 1959-60
R. A. Smith (2)
148*   Lord's 1991
109   The Oval 1991
D. S. Steele (1)
106†   Nottingham . . 1976
R. Subba Row (1)
100†   Georgetown . . 1959-60
E. Tyldesley (1)
122†   Lord's 1928
C. Washbrook (2)
114†   Lord's 1950
102   Nottingham . . 1950
W. Watson (1)
116†   Kingston 1953-54
P. Willey (2)
100*   The Oval 1980
102*   St John's 1980-81

For West Indies (99)

I. Barrow (1)
105   Manchester . .   1933

C. A. Best (1)
164   Bridgetown . .   1989-90

B. F. Butcher (2)
133   Lord's   1963
209* Nottingham .   1966

G. M. Carew (1)
107   Port-of-Spain   1947-48

C. A. Davis (1)
103   Lord's   1969

P. J. L. Dujon (1)
101   Manchester . .   1984

R. C. Fredericks (3)
150   Birmingham .   1973
138   Lord's   1976
109   Leeds   1976

A. G. Ganteaume (1)
112† Port-of-Spain   1947-48

H. A. Gomes (2)
143   Birmingham .   1984
104* Leeds   1984

C. G. Greenidge (7)
134 ⎫
101 ⎬ Manchester . .   1976
115   Leeds   1976
214* Lord's   1984
223   Manchester . .   1984
103   Lord's   1988
149   St John's   1989-90

D. L. Haynes (5)
184   Lord's   1980
125   The Oval   1984
131   St John's   1985-86
109   Bridgetown . .   1989-90
167   St John's   1989-90

G. A. Headley (8)
176† Bridgetown . .   1929-30
114 ⎫
112 ⎬ Georgetown .   1929-30
223   Kingston   1929-30
169* Manchester . .   1933
270* Kingston   1934-35

106 ⎫
107 ⎬ Lord's   1939

D. A. J. Holford (1)
105* Lord's   1966

J. K. Holt (1)
166   Bridgetown . .   1953-54

C. L. Hooper (1)
111   Lord's   1991

C. C. Hunte (3)
182   Manchester . .   1963
108* The Oval   1963
135   Manchester . .   1966

B. D. Julien (1)
121   Lord's   1973

A. I. Kallicharran (2)
158   Port-of-Spain   1973-74
119   Bridgetown . .   1973-74

R. B. Kanhai (5)
110   Port-of-Spain   1959-60
104   The Oval   1966
153   Port-of-Spain   1967-68
150   Georgetown .   1967-68
157   Lord's   1973

C. H. Lloyd (5)
118† Port-of-Spain   1967-68
113* Bridgetown . .   1967-68
132   The Oval   1973
101   Manchester . .   1980
100   Bridgetown . .   1980-81

S. M. Nurse (2)
137   Leeds   1966
136   Port-of-Spain   1967-68

A. F. Rae (2)
106   Lord's   1950
109   The Oval   1950

I. V. A. Richards (8)
232† Nottingham .   1976
135   Manchester .   1976
291   The Oval   1976
145   Lord's   1980
182* Bridgetown . .   1980-81
114   St John's   1980-81
117   Birmingham .   1984
110* St John's   1985-86

R. B. Richardson (4)
102   Port-of-Spain   1985-86
160   Bridgetown . .   1985-86
104   Birmingham .   1991
121   The Oval . . .   1991

C. A. Roach (2)
122   Bridgetown . .   1929-30
209   Georgetown .   1929-30

L. G. Rowe (3)
120   Kingston   1973-74
302   Bridgetown . .   1973-74
123   Port-of-Spain   1973-74

O. G. Smith (2)
161† Birmingham .   1957
168   Nottingham .   1957

G. S. Sobers (10)
226   Bridgetown . .   1959-60
147   Kingston   1959-60
145   Georgetown .   1959-60
102   Leeds   1963
161   Manchester . .   1966
163* Lord's   1966
174   Leeds   1966
113* Kingston   1967-68
152   Georgetown .   1967-68
150* Lord's   1973

C. L. Walcott (4)
168* Lord's   1950
220   Bridgetown . .   1953-54
124   Port-of-Spain   1953-54
116   Kingston   1953-54

E. D. Weekes (3)
141   Kingston   1947-48
129   Nottingham .   1950
206   Port-of-Spain   1953-54

K. H. Weekes (1)
137   The Oval   1939

F. M. M. Worrell (6)
131* Georgetown .   1947-48
261   Nottingham .   1950
138   The Oval   1950
167   Port-of-Spain   1953-54
191*‡ Nottingham .   1957
197* Georgetown .   1959-60

† *Signifies hundred on first appearance in England–West Indies Tests. S. C. Griffith provides the only instance for England of a player hitting his maiden century in first-class cricket in his first Test.*
‡ *Carried his bat.*

RECORD PARTNERSHIPS FOR EACH WICKET

For England

212	for 1st	C. Washbrook and R. T. Simpson at Nottingham	1950
266	for 2nd	P. E. Richardson and T. W. Graveney at Nottingham	1957
264	for 3rd	L. Hutton and W. R. Hammond at The Oval	1939
411	for 4th†	P. B. H. May and M. C. Cowdrey at Birmingham	1957

130*	for 5th	C. Milburn and T. W. Graveney at Lord's	1966
163	for 6th	A. W. Greig and A. P. E. Knott at Bridgetown	1973-74
197	for 7th†	M. J. K. Smith and J. M. Parks at Port-of-Spain	1959-60
217	for 8th	T. W. Graveney and J. T. Murray at The Oval	1966
109	for 9th	G. A. R. Lock and P. I. Pocock at Georgetown	1967-68
128	for 10th	K. Higgs and J. A. Snow at The Oval	1966

For West Indies

298	for 1st†	C. G. Greenidge and D. L. Haynes at St John's.............	1989-90
287*	for 2nd	C. G. Greenidge and H. A. Gomes at Lord's	1984
338	for 3rd†	E. D. Weekes and F. M. M. Worrell at Port-of-Spain	1953-54
399	for 4th†	G. S. Sobers and F. M. M. Worrell at Bridgetown	1959-60
265	for 5th†	S. M. Nurse and G. S. Sobers at Leeds	1966
274*	for 6th†	G. S. Sobers and D. A. J. Holford at Lord's	1966
155*	for 7th‡	G. S. Sobers and B. D. Julien at Lord's	1973
99	for 8th	C. A. McWatt and J. K. Holt at Georgetown	1953-54
150	for 9th	E. A. E. Baptiste and M. A. Holding at Birmingham	1984
67*	for 10th	M. A. Holding and C. E. H. Croft at St John's	1980-81

† *Denotes record partnership against all countries.*

‡ *231 runs were added for this wicket in two separate partnerships: G. S. Sobers retired ill and was replaced by K. D. Boyce when 155 had been added.*

TEN WICKETS OR MORE IN A MATCH

For England (11)

11-98 (7-44, 4-54)	T. E. Bailey, Lord's	1957
10-93 (5-54, 5-39)	A. P. Freeman, Manchester...........................	1928
13-156 (8-86, 5-70)	A. W. Greig, Port-of-Spain	1973-74
11-48 (5-28, 6-20)	G. A. R. Lock, The Oval.............................	1957
10-137 (4-60, 6-77)	D. E. Malcolm, Port-of-Spain	1989-90
11-96 (5-37, 6-59)†	C. S. Marriott, The Oval	1933
10-142 (4-82, 6-60)	J. A. Snow, Georgetown	1967-68
10-195 (5-105, 5-90)†	G. T. S. Stevens, Bridgetown	1929-30
11-152 (6-100, 5-52)	F. S. Trueman, Lord's...............................	1963
12-119 (5-75, 7-44)	F. S. Trueman, Birmingham	1963
11-149 (4-79, 7-70)	W. Voce, Port-of-Spain	1929-30

For West Indies (12)

10-127 (2-82, 8-45)	C. E. L. Ambrose, Bridgetown	1989-90
11-147 (5-70, 6-77)†	K. D. Boyce, The Oval	1973
11-229 (5-137, 6-92)	W. Ferguson, Port-of-Spain	1947-48
11-157 (5-59, 6-98)†	L. R. Gibbs, Manchester	1963
10-106 (5-37, 5-69)	L. R. Gibbs, Manchester	1966
14-149 (8-92, 6-57)	M. A. Holding, The Oval	1976
10-96 (5-41, 5-55)†	H. H. H. Johnson, Kingston	1947-48
10-92 (6-32, 4-60)	M. D. Marshall, Lord's..............................	1988
11-152 (5-66, 6-86)	S. Ramadhin, Lord's................................	1950
10-123 (5-60, 5-63)	A. M. E. Roberts, Lord's	1976
11-204 (8-104, 3-100)†	A. L. Valentine, Manchester	1950
10-160 (4-121, 6-39)	A. L. Valentine, The Oval	1950

† *Signifies ten wickets or more on first appearance in England–West Indies Tests.*

Note: F. S. Trueman took ten wickets or more in successive matches.

ENGLAND v NEW ZEALAND

		Captains				
Season	England	New Zealand	T	E	NZ	D
1929-30	A. H. H. Gilligan	T. C. Lowry	4	1	0	3
1931	D. R. Jardine	T. C. Lowry	3	1	0	2
1932-33	D. R. Jardine[1]	M. L. Page	2	0	0	2
1937	R. W. V. Robins	M. L. Page	3	1	0	2
1946-47	W. R. Hammond	W. A. Hadlee	1	0	0	1
1949	F. G. Mann[2]	W. A. Hadlee	4	0	0	4
1950-51	F. R. Brown	W. A. Hadlee	2	1	0	1
1954-55	L. Hutton	G. O. Rabone	2	2	0	0
1958	P. B. H. May	J. R. Reid	5	4	0	1
1958-59	P. B. H. May	J. R. Reid	2	1	0	1
1962-63	E. R. Dexter	J. R. Reid	3	3	0	0
1965	M. J. K. Smith	J. R. Reid	3	3	0	0
1965-66	M. J. K. Smith	B. W. Sinclair[3]	3	0	0	3
1969	R. Illingworth	G. T. Dowling	3	2	0	1
1970-71	R. Illingworth	G. T. Dowling	2	1	0	1
1973	R. Illingworth	B. E. Congdon	3	2	0	1
1974-75	M. H. Denness	B. E. Congdon	2	1	0	1
1977-78	G. Boycott	M. G. Burgess	3	1	1	1
1978	J. M. Brearley	M. G. Burgess	3	3	0	0
1983	R. G. D. Willis	G. P. Howarth	4	3	1	0
1983-84	R. G. D. Willis	G. P. Howarth	3	0	1	2
1986	M. W. Gatting	J. V. Coney	3	0	1	2
1987-88	M. W. Gatting	J. J. Crowe[4]	3	0	0	3
1990	G. A. Gooch	J. G. Wright	3	1	0	2
1991-92	G. A. Gooch	M. D. Crowe	3	2	0	1
	In New Zealand		35	13	2	20
	In England		37	20	2	15
	Totals.........................		72	33	4	35

Notes: The following deputised for the official touring captain or were appointed by the home authority for only a minor proportion of the series:

[1]R. E. S. Wyatt (Second). [2]F. R. Brown (Third and Fourth). [3]M. E. Chapple (First). [4]J. G. Wright (Third).

HIGHEST INNINGS TOTALS

For England in England: 546-4 dec. at Leeds............................	1965
in New Zealand: 593-6 dec. at Auckland	1974-75
For New Zealand in England: 551-9 dec. at Lord's....................	1973
in New Zealand: 537 at Wellington	1983-84

LOWEST INNINGS TOTALS

For England in England: 158 at Birmingham	1990
in New Zealand: 64 at Wellington	1977-78
For New Zealand in England: 47 at Lord's............................	1958
in New Zealand: 26 at Auckland	1954-55

INDIVIDUAL HUNDREDS

For England (75)

G. O. B. Allen (1)
122† Lord's 1931

L. E. G. Ames (2)
137† Lord's 1931
103 Christchurch. 1932-33

D. L. Amiss (2)
138*† Nottingham . 1973
164* Christchurch. 1974-75

M. A. Atherton (1)
151† Nottingham . 1990

T. E. Bailey (1)
134* Christchurch. 1950-51

K. F. Barrington (3)
126† Auckland . . . 1962-63
137 Birmingham . 1965
163 Leeds 1965

I. T. Botham (3)
103 Christchurch. 1977-78
103 Nottingham . 1983
138 Wellington . . 1983-84

E. H. Bowley (1)
109 Auckland . . . 1929-30

G. Boycott (2)
115 Leeds 1973
131 Nottingham . 1978

B. C. Broad (1)
114† Christchurch. 1987-88

D. C. S. Compton (2)
114 Leeds 1949
116 Lord's 1949

M. C. Cowdrey (2)
128* Wellington . . 1962-63
119 Lord's 1965

M. H. Denness (1)
181 Auckland . . . 1974-75

E. R. Dexter (1)
141 Christchurch. 1958-59

B. L. D'Oliveira (1)
100 Christchurch. 1970-71

K. S. Duleepsinhji (2)
117 Auckland . . . 1929-30
109 The Oval. . . . 1931

J. H. Edrich (3)
310*† Leeds 1965
115 Lord's 1969
155 Nottingham . 1969

W. J. Edrich (1)
100 The Oval. . . . 1949

K. W. R. Fletcher (2)
178 Lord's 1973
216 Auckland . . . 1974-75

G. Fowler (1)
105† The Oval. . . . 1983

M. W. Gatting (1)
121 The Oval. . . . 1986

G. A. Gooch (3)
183 Lord's 1986
154 Birmingham . 1990
114 Auckland . . . 1991-92

D. I. Gower (4)
111† The Oval. . . . 1978
112* Leeds 1983
108 Lord's 1983
131 The Oval. . . . 1986

A. W. Greig (1)
139† Nottingham . 1973

W. R. Hammond (4)
100* The Oval. . . . 1931
227 Christchurch. 1932-33
336* Auckland . . . 1932-33
140 Lord's 1937

J. Hardstaff jun. (2)
114† Lord's 1937
103 The Oval. . . . 1937

L. Hutton (3)
100 Manchester. . 1937
101 Leeds 1949
206 The Oval. . . . 1949

B. R. Knight (1)
125† Auckland . . . 1962-63

A. P. E. Knott (1)
101 Auckland . . . 1970-71

A. J. Lamb (3)
102*† The Oval. . . . 1983
137* Nottingham . 1983
142 Wellington . . 1991-92

G. B. Legge (1)
196 Auckland . . . 1929-30

P. B. H. May (3)
113* Leeds 1958
101 Manchester. . 1958
124* Auckland . . . 1958-59

C. A. Milton (1)
104*† Leeds 1958

P. H. Parfitt (1)
131*† Auckland . . . 1962-63

C. T. Radley (1)
158 Auckland . . . 1977-78

D. W. Randall (2)
164 Wellington . . 1983-84
104 Auckland . . . 1983-84

P. E. Richardson (1)
100† Birmingham . 1958

J. D. Robertson (1)
121† Lord's 1949

P. J. Sharpe (1)
111 Nottingham . 1969

R. T. Simpson (1)
103† Manchester. . 1949

A. J. Stewart (2)
148 Christchurch. 1991-92
107 Wellington . . 1991-92

H. Sutcliffe (2)
117† The Oval. . . . 1931
109* Manchester. . 1931

C. J. Tavaré (1)
109† The Oval. . . . 1983

C. Washbrook (1)
103* The Oval. . . . 1949

For New Zealand (36)

J. G. Bracewell (1)
110 Nottingham . 1986

M. G. Burgess (2)
104 Auckland . . . 1970-71
105 Lord's 1973

J. V. Coney (1)
174* Wellington . . 1983-84

B. E. Congdon (3)
104 Christchurch. 1965-66
176 Nottingham . 1973
175 Lord's 1973

J. J. Crowe (1)
128 Auckland . . . 1983-84

M. D. Crowe (3)
100 Wellington . . 1983-84
106 Lord's 1986
143 Wellington . . 1987-88

C. S. Dempster (2)
136 Wellington . . 1929-30
120 Lord's 1931

M. P. Donnelly (1)
206 Lord's 1949

T. J. Franklin (1)
101 Lord's 1990

M. J. Greatbatch (1)
107*† Auckland . . . 1987-88

W. A. Hadlee (1)
116 Christchurch. 1946-47

G. P. Howarth (3)
122 ⎫
102 ⎬ Auckland . . . 1977-78
123 Lord's 1978

A. H. Jones (1)
143 Wellington . . 1991-92

J. E. Mills (1)	**J. R. Reid** (1)	**B. Sutcliffe** (2)
117† Wellington .. 1929-30	100 Christchurch. 1962-63	101 Manchester.. 1949
M. L. Page (1)	**K. R. Rutherford** (1)	116 Christchurch. 1950-51
104 Lord's 1931	107* Wellington .. 1987-88	**J. G. Wright** (4)
J. M. Parker (1)	**B. W. Sinclair** (1)	130 Auckland ... 1983-84
121 Auckland ... 1974-75	114 Auckland ... 1965-66	119 The Oval.... 1986
V. Pollard (2)	**I. D. S. Smith** (1)	103 Auckland ... 1987-88
116 Nottingham .. 1973	113* Auckland ... 1983-84	116 Wellington .. 1991-92
105* Lord's 1973		

† *Signifies hundred on first appearance in England–New Zealand Tests.*

RECORD PARTNERSHIPS FOR EACH WICKET

For England

223	for 1st	G. Fowler and C. J. Tavaré at The Oval	1983
369	for 2nd	J. H. Edrich and K. F. Barrington at Leeds...................	1965
245	for 3rd	W. R. Hammond and J. Hardstaff jun. at Lord's..............	1937
266	for 4th	M. H. Denness and K. W. R. Fletcher at Auckland	1974-75
242	for 5th	W. R. Hammond and L. E. G. Ames at Christchurch	1932-33
240	for 6th†	P. H. Parfitt and B. R. Knight at Auckland	1962-63
149	for 7th	A. P. E. Knott and P. Lever at Auckland	1970-71
246	for 8th†	L. E. G. Ames and G. O. B. Allen at Lord's	1931
163*	for 9th†	M. C. Cowdrey and A. C. Smith at Wellington	1962-63
59	for 10th	A. P. E. Knott and N. Gifford at Nottingham...............	1973

For New Zealand

276	for 1st	C. S. Dempster and J. E. Mills at Wellington	1929-30
241	for 2nd†	J. G. Wright and A. H. Jones at Wellington	1991-92
210	for 3rd	B. A. Edgar and M. D. Crowe at Lord's....................	1986
155	for 4th	M. D. Crowe and M. J. Greatbatch at Wellington	1987-88
177	for 5th	B. E. Congdon and V. Pollard at Nottingham	1973
134	for 6th	K. R. Rutherford and J. G. Bracewell at Wellington	1987-88
117	for 7th	D. N. Patel and C. L. Cairns at Christchurch	1991-92
104	for 8th	D. A. R. Moloney and A. W. Roberts at Lord's	1937
118	for 9th	J. V. Coney and B. L. Cairns at Wellington	1983-84
57	for 10th	F. L. H. Mooney and J. Cowie at Leeds...................	1949

† *Denotes record partnership against all countries.*

TEN WICKETS OR MORE IN A MATCH

For England (8)

11-140 (6-101, 5-39)	I. T. Botham, Lord's.....................	1978
10-149 (5-98, 5-51)	A. W. Greig, Auckland	1974-75
11-65 (4-14, 7-51)	G. A. R. Lock, Leeds...................	1958
11-84 (5-31, 6-53)	G. A. R. Lock, Christchurch	1958-59
11-147 (4-100, 7-47)†	P. C. R. Tufnell, Christchurch	1991-92
11-70 (4-38, 7-32)†	D. L. Underwood, Lord's...............	1969
12-101 (6-41, 6-60)	D. L. Underwood, The Oval	1969
12-97 (6-12, 6-85)	D. L. Underwood, Christchurch	1970-71

For New Zealand (4)

10-144 (7-74, 3-70)	B. L. Cairns, Leeds....................	1983
10-140 (4-73, 6-67)	J. Cowie, Manchester...................	1937
10-100 (4-74, 6-26)	R. J. Hadlee, Wellington	1977-78
10-140 (6-80, 4-60)	R. J. Hadlee, Nottingham	1986

† *Signifies ten wickets or more on first appearance in England–New Zealand Tests.*
Note: D. L. Underwood took 12 wickets in successive matches against New Zealand in 1969 and 1970-71.

HAT-TRICK AND FOUR WICKETS IN FIVE BALLS

M. J. C. Allom, in his first Test match, v New Zealand at Christchurch in 1929-30, dismissed C. S. Dempster, T. C. Lowry, K. C. James, and F. T. Badcock to take four wickets in five balls (w-www).

ENGLAND v INDIA

Season	England	India	T	E	I	D
		Captains				
1932	D. R. Jardine	C. K. Nayudu	1	1	0	0
1933-34	D. R. Jardine	C. K. Nayudu	3	2	0	1
1936	G. O. B. Allen	Maharaj of Vizianagram	3	2	0	1
1946	W. R. Hammond	Nawab of Pataudi sen.	3	1	0	2
1951-52	N. D. Howard[1]	V. S. Hazare	5	1	1	3
1952	L. Hutton	V. S. Hazare	4	3	0	1
1959	P. B. H. May[2]	D. K. Gaekwad[3]	5	5	0	0
1961-62	E. R. Dexter	N. J. Contractor	5	0	2	3
1963-64	M. J. K. Smith	Nawab of Pataudi jun.	5	0	0	5
1967	D. B. Close	Nawab of Pataudi jun.	3	3	0	0
1971	R. Illingworth	A. L. Wadekar	3	0	1	2
1972-73	A. R. Lewis	A. L. Wadekar	5	1	2	2
1974	M. H. Denness	A. L. Wadekar	3	3	0	0
1976-77	A. W. Greig	B. S. Bedi	5	3	1	1
1979	J. M. Brearley	S. Venkataraghavan	4	1	0	3
1979-80	J. M. Brearley	G. R. Viswanath	1	1	0	0
1981-82	K. W. R. Fletcher	S. M. Gavaskar	6	0	1	5
1982	R. G. D. Willis	S. M. Gavaskar	3	1	0	2
1984-85	D. I. Gower	S. M. Gavaskar	5	2	1	2
1986	M. W. Gatting[4]	Kapil Dev	3	0	2	1
1990	G. A. Gooch	M. Azharuddin	3	1	0	2
1992-93	G. A. Gooch[5]	M. Azharuddin	3	0	3	0
	In England		38	21	3	14
	In India		43	10	11	22
	Totals		81	31	14	36

Notes: The 1932 Indian touring team was captained by the Maharaj of Porbandar but he did not play in the Test match.

The following deputised for the official touring captain or were appointed by the home authority for only a minor proportion of the series: [1]D. B. Carr (Fifth). [2]M. C. Cowdrey (Fourth and Fifth). [3]Pankaj Roy (Second). [4]D. I. Gower (First). [5]A. J. Stewart (Second).

HIGHEST INNINGS TOTALS

For England in England: 653-4 dec. at Lord's	1990
in India: 652-7 dec. at Madras	1984-85
For India in England: 606-9 dec. at The Oval	1990
in India: 591 at Bombay	1992-93

LOWEST INNINGS TOTALS

For England in England: 101 at The Oval	1971
in India: 102 at Bombay	1981-82
For India in England: 42 at Lord's	1974
in India: 83 at Madras	1976-77

INDIVIDUAL HUNDREDS

For England (72)

D. L. Amiss (2)
188   Lord's   1974
179   Delhi.   1976-77

M. A. Atherton (1)
131   Manchester. .   1990

K. F. Barrington (3)
151*   Bombay   1961-62
172   Kanpur   1961-62
113*   Delhi.   1961-62

I. T. Botham (5)
137   Leeds   1979
114   Bombay . .   1979-80
142   Kanpur   1981-82
128   Manchester .   1982
208   The Oval. . . .   1982

G. Boycott (4)
246*†   Leeds   1967
155   Birmingham .   1979
125   The Oval. . . .   1979
105   Delhi   1981-82

M. C. Cowdrey (3)
160   Leeds   1959
107   Calcutta   1963-64
151   Delhi   1963-64

M. H. Denness (2)
118   Lord's   1974
100   Birmingham .   1974

E. R. Dexter (1)
126*   Kanpur   1961-62

B. L. D'Oliveira (1)
109†   Leeds   1967

J. H. Edrich (1)
100*   Manchester . .   1974

T. G. Evans (1)
104   Lord's   1952

K. W. R. Fletcher (2)
113   Bombay   1972-73
123*   Manchester. .   1974

G. Fowler (1)
201   Madras   1984-85

M. W. Gatting (3)
136   Bombay   1984-85
207   Madras   1984-85
183*   Birmingham .   1986

G. A. Gooch (5)
127   Madras   1981-82
114   Lord's   1986
333 }
123 } Lord's   1990
116   Manchester. .   1990

D. I. Gower (2)
200*†   Birmingham .   1979
157*   The Oval . . .   1990

T. W. Graveney (2)
175†   Bombay   1951-52
151   Lord's   1967

A. W. Greig (3)
148   Bombay   1972-73
106   Lord's   1974
103   Calcutta   1976-77

W. R. Hammond (2)
167   Manchester. .   1936
217   The Oval. . . .   1936

J. Hardstaff jun. (1)
205*   Lord's   1946

G. A. Hick (1)
178   Bombay   1992-93

L. Hutton (2)
150   Lord's   1952
104   Manchester. .   1952

R. Illingworth (1)
107   Manchester. .   1971

B. R. Knight (1)
127   Kanpur   1963-64

A. J. Lamb (3)
107   The Oval. . . .   1982

139   Lord's   1990
109   Manchester. .   1990

A. R. Lewis (1)
125   Kanpur   1972-73

C. C. Lewis (1)
117   Madras   1992-93

D. Lloyd (1)
214*   Birmingham .   1974

B. W. Luckhurst (1)
101   Manchester. .   1971

P. B. H. May (1)
106   Nottingham .   1959

P. H. Parfitt (1)
121   Kanpur   1963-64

G. Pullar (2)
131   Manchester. .   1959
119   Kanpur   1961-62

D. W. Randall (1)
126   Lord's   1982

R. T. Robinson (1)
160   Delhi.   1984-85

D. S. Sheppard (1)
119   The Oval . . .   1952

M. J. K. Smith (1)
100†   Manchester . .   1959

R. A. Smith (2)
100*†   Lord's   1990
121*   Manchester . .   1990

C. J. Tavaré (1)
149   Delhi.   1981-82

B. H. Valentine (1)
136†   Bombay   1933-34

C. F. Walters (1)
102   Madras   1933-34

A. J. Watkins (1)
137*†   Delhi.   1951-52

T. S. Worthington (1)
128   The Oval. . . .   1936

For India (60)

L. Amarnath (1)
118†   Bombay   1933-34

M. Azharuddin (6)
110†   Calcutta   1984-85
105   Madras   1984-85
122   Kanpur   1984-85
121   Lord's   1990
179   Manchester. .   1990
182   Calcutta   1992-93

A. A. Baig (1)
112†   Manchester. .   1959

F. M. Engineer (1)
121   Bombay   1972-73

S. M. Gavaskar (4)
101   Manchester. .   1974

108   Bombay   1976-77
221   The Oval. . . .   1979
172   Bangalore . . .   1981-82

Hanumant Singh (1)
105†   Delhi.   1963-64

V. S. Hazare (2)
164*   Delhi.   1951-52
155   Bombay   1951-52

M. L. Jaisimha (2)
127   Delhi.   1961-62
129   Calcutta   1963-64

V. G. Kambli (1)
224   Bombay   1992-93

Kapil Dev (2)
116   Kanpur   1981-82
110   The Oval . . .   1990

S. M. H. Kirmani (1)
102   Bombay   1984-85

B. K. Kunderan (2)
192   Madras   1963-64
100   Delhi.   1963-64

V. L. Manjrekar (3)
133   Leeds   1952
189*   Delhi.   1961-62
108   Madras   1963-64

V. Mankad (1)
184   Lord's   1952

V. M. Merchant (3)
114   Manchester. .   1936
128   The Oval . . .   1946
154   Delhi.   1951-52

Mushtaq Ali (1)			**R. J. Shastri** (4)			**D. B. Vengsarkar** (5)	
112	Manchester..	1936	142	Bombay	1984-85	103	Lord's	1979
R. G. Nadkarni (1)			111	Calcutta	1984-85	157	Lord's	1982
122*	Kanpur.....	1963-64	100	Lord's	1990	137	Kanpur ...	1984-85
Nawab of Pataudi jun. (3)			187	The Oval ...	1990	126*	Lord's	1986
103	Madras	1961-62	**N. S. Sidhu** (1)			102*	Leeds	1986
203*	Delhi.......	1963-64	106	Madras	1992-93	**G. R. Viswanath** (4)		
148	Leeds	1967	**S. R. Tendulkar** (2)			113	Bombay ...	1972-73
S. M. Patil (1)			119*	Manchester..	1990	113	Lord's	1979
129*	Manchester..	1982	165	Madras	1992-93	107	Delhi.......	1981-82
D. G. Phadkar (1)			**P. R. Umrigar** (3)			222	Madras	1981-82
115	Calcutta	1951-52	130*	Madras	1951-52	**Yashpal Sharma** (1)		
Pankaj Roy (2)			118	Manchester..	1959	140	Madras	1981-82
140	Bombay	1951-52	147*	Kanpur	1961-62			
111	Madras	1951-52						

† Signifies hundred on first appearance in England–India Tests.

Notes: G. A. Gooch's match aggregate of 456 (333 and 123) for England at Lord's in 1990 is the record in Test matches and provides the only instance of a batsman scoring a triple-hundred and a hundred in the same first-class match. His 333 is the highest innings in any match at Lord's.

M. Azharuddin scored hundreds in each of his first three Tests.

RECORD PARTNERSHIPS FOR EACH WICKET

For England

225 for 1st	G. A. Gooch and M. A. Atherton at Manchester	1990
241 for 2nd	G. Fowler and M. W. Gatting at Madras	1984-85
308 for 3rd	G. A. Gooch and A. J. Lamb at Lord's	1990
266 for 4th	W. R. Hammond and T. S. Worthington at The Oval.........	1936
254 for 5th†	K. W. R. Fletcher and A. W. Greig at Bombay.............	1972-73
171 for 6th	I. T. Botham and R. W. Taylor at Bombay	1979-80
125 for 7th	D. W. Randall and P. H. Edmonds at Lord's...............	1982
168 for 8th	R. Illingworth and P. Lever at Manchester	1971
83 for 9th	K. W. R. Fletcher and N. Gifford at Madras.................	1972-73
70 for 10th	P. J. W. Allott and R. G. D. Willis at Lord's...............	1982

For India

213 for 1st	S. M. Gavaskar and C. P. S. Chauhan at The Oval	1979
192 for 2nd	F. M. Engineer and A. L. Wadekar at Bombay	1972-73
316 for 3rd†‡	G. R. Viswanath and Yashpal Sharma at Madras	1981-82
222 for 4th†	V. S. Hazare and V. L. Manjrekar at Leeds	1952
214 for 5th†	M. Azharuddin and R. J. Shastri at Calcutta	1984-85
130 for 6th	S. M. H. Kirmani and Kapil Dev at The Oval	1982
235 for 7th†	R. J. Shastri and S. M. H. Kirmani at Bombay	1984-85
128 for 8th	R. J. Shastri and S. M. H. Kirmani at Delhi	1981-82
104 for 9th	R. J. Shastri and Madan Lal at Delhi	1981-82
51 for 10th	{ R. G. Nadkarni and B. S. Chandrasekhar at Calcutta	1963-64
	{ S. M. H. Kirmani and Chetan Sharma at Madras.............	1984-85

† Denotes record partnership against all countries.

‡ 415 runs were added between the fall of the 2nd and 3rd wickets: D. B. Vengsarkar retired hurt when he and Viswanath had added 99 runs.

TEN WICKETS OR MORE IN A MATCH

For England (7)

10-78 (5-35, 5-43)†	G. O. B. Allen, Lord's	1936
11-145 (7-49, 4-96)†	A. V. Bedser, Lord's	1946
11-93 (4-41, 7-52)	A. V. Bedser, Manchester	1946
13-106 (6-58, 7-48)	I. T. Botham, Bombay	1979-80
11-163 (6-104, 5-59)†	N. A. Foster, Madras	1984-85
10-70 (7-46, 3-24)†	J. K. Lever, Delhi	1976-77
11-153 (7-49, 4-104)	H. Verity, Madras	1933-34

For India (4)

10-177 (6-105, 4-72)	S. A. Durani, Madras	1961-62
12-108 (8-55, 4-53)	V. Mankad, Madras	1951-52
10-188 (4-130, 6-58)	Chetan Sharma, Birmingham	1986
12-181 (6-64, 6-117)†	L. Sivaramakrishnan, Bombay	1984-85

† *Signifies ten wickets or more on first appearance in England–India Tests.*

Note: A. V. Bedser took 11 wickets in a match in each of the first two Tests of his career.

ENGLAND v PAKISTAN

		Captains				
Season	England	Pakistan	T	E	P	D
1954	L. Hutton[1]	A. H. Kardar	4	1	1	2
1961-62	E. R. Dexter	Imtiaz Ahmed	3	1	0	2
1962	E. R. Dexter[2]	Javed Burki	5	4	0	1
1967	D. B. Close	Hanif Mohammad	3	2	0	1
1968-69	M. C. Cowdrey	Saeed Ahmed	3	0	0	3
1971	R. Illingworth	Intikhab Alam	3	1	0	2
1972-73	A. R. Lewis	Majid Khan	3	0	0	3
1974	M. H. Denness	Intikhab Alam	3	0	0	3
1977-78	J. M. Brearley[3]	Wasim Bari	3	0	0	3
1978	J. M. Brearley	Wasim Bari	3	2	0	1
1982	R. G. D. Willis[4]	Imran Khan	3	2	1	0
1983-84	R. G. D. Willis[5]	Zaheer Abbas	3	0	1	2
1987	M. W. Gatting	Imran Khan	5	0	1	4
1987-88	M. W. Gatting	Javed Miandad	3	0	1	2
1992	G. A. Gooch	Javed Miandad	5	1	2	2
	In England		34	13	5	16
	In Pakistan		18	1	2	15
	Totals		52	14	7	31

Notes: The following deputised for the official touring captain or were appointed by the home authority for only a minor proportion of the series:
[1]D. S. Sheppard (Second and Third). [2]M. C. Cowdrey (Third). [3]G. Boycott (Third). [4]D. I. Gower (Second). [5]D. I. Gower (Second and Third).

HIGHEST INNINGS TOTALS

For England in England: 558-6 dec. at Nottingham		1954
in Pakistan: 546-8 dec. at Faisalabad		1983-84
For Pakistan in England: 708 at The Oval		1987
in Pakistan: 569-9 dec. at Hyderabad		1972-73

LOWEST INNINGS TOTALS

For England in England: 130 at The Oval 1954
           in Pakistan: 130 at Lahore 1987-88

For Pakistan in England: 87 at Lord's 1954
           in Pakistan: 191 at Faisalabad 1987-88

INDIVIDUAL HUNDREDS

For England (44)

D. L. Amiss (3)
112   Lahore 1972-73
158   Hyderabad .. 1972-73
183   The Oval.... 1974
C. W. J. Athey (1)
123   Lord's 1987
K. F. Barrington (4)
139† Lahore 1961-62
148   Lord's 1967
109* Nottingham . 1967
142   The Oval.... 1967
I. T. Botham (2)
100† Birmingham . 1978
108   Lord's 1978
G. Boycott (3)
121* Lord's 1971
112   Leeds 1971
100* Hyderabad .. 1977-78
B. C. Broad (1)
116   Faisalabad .. 1987-88
D. C. S. Compton (1)
278   Nottingham . 1954
M. C. Cowdrey (3)
159† Birmingham . 1962

182   The Oval.... 1962
100   Lahore 1968-69
E. R. Dexter (2)
205   Karachi 1961-62
172   The Oval.... 1962
B. L. D'Oliveira (1)
114* Dacca 1968-69
K. W. R. Fletcher (1)
122   The Oval.... 1974
M. W. Gatting (2)
124   Birmingham . 1987
150* The Oval.... 1987
G. A. Gooch (1)
135   Leeds 1992
D. I. Gower (2)
152   Faisalabad .. 1983-84
173* Lahore 1983-84
T. W. Graveney (3)
153   Lord's 1962
114   Nottingham . 1962
105   Karachi 1968-69
A. P. E. Knott (1)
116   Birmingham . 1971

B. W. Luckhurst (1)
108*† Birmingham . 1971
C. Milburn (1)
139   Karachi 1968-69
P. H. Parfitt (4)
111   Karachi 1961-62
101* Birmingham . 1962
119   Leeds 1962
101* Nottingham . 1962
G. Pullar (1)
165   Dacca 1961-62
C. T. Radley (1)
106† Birmingham . 1978
D. W. Randall (1)
105   Birmingham . 1982
R. T. Robinson (1)
166† Manchester .. 1987
R. T. Simpson (1)
101   Nottingham . 1954
R. A. Smith (1)
127† Birmingham . 1992
A. J. Stewart (1)
190† Birmingham . 1992

For Pakistan (33)

Aamir Sohail (1)
205   Manchester.. 1992
Alim-ud-Din (1)
109   Karachi 1961-62
Asif Iqbal (3)
146   The Oval.... 1967
104* Birmingham . 1971
102   Lahore 1972-73
Hanif Mohammad (3)
111 ⎫
104 ⎬ Dacca 1961-62
187* Lord's 1967
Haroon Rashid (2)
122† Lahore 1977-78
108   Hyderabad .. 1977-78
Imran Khan (1)
118   The Oval.... 1987

Intikhab Alam (1)
138   Hyderabad .. 1972-73
Javed Burki (3)
138† Lahore 1961-62
140   Dacca 1961-62
101   Lord's 1962
Javed Miandad (2)
260   The Oval.... 1987
153* Birmingham . 1992
Mohsin Khan (2)
200   Lord's 1982
104   Lahore 1983-84
Mudassar Nazar (3)
114† Lahore 1977-88
124   Birmingham . 1987
120   Lahore 1987-88

Mushtaq Mohammad (3)
100* Nottingham . 1962
100   Birmingham . 1971
157   Hyderabad .. 1972-73
Nasim-ul-Ghani (1)
101   Lord's 1962
Sadiq Mohammad (1)
119   Lahore 1972-73
Salim Malik (3)
116   Faisalabad .. 1983-84
102   The Oval.... 1987
165   Birmingham . 1992
Wasim Raja (1)
112   Faisalabad .. 1983-84
Zaheer Abbas (2)
274† Birmingham . 1971
240   The Oval.... 1974

† *Signifies hundred on first appearance in England–Pakistan Tests.*

Note: Three batsmen – Majid Khan, Mushtaq Mohammad and D. L. Amiss – were dismissed for 99 at Karachi, 1972-73: the only instance in Test matches.

RECORD PARTNERSHIPS FOR EACH WICKET

For England

198	for 1st	G. Pullar and R. W. Barber at Dacca	1961-62
248	for 2nd	M. C. Cowdrey and E. R. Dexter at The Oval	1962
227	for 3rd	A. J. Stewart and R. A. Smith at Birmingham	1992
188	for 4th	E. R. Dexter and P. H. Parfitt at Karachi	1961-62
192	for 5th	D. C. S. Compton and T. E. Bailey at Nottingham	1954
153*	for 6th	P. H. Parfitt and D. A. Allen at Birmingham	1962
167	for 7th	D. I. Gower and V. J. Marks at Faisalabad	1983-84
99	for 8th	P. H. Parfitt and D. A. Allen at Leeds	1962
76	for 9th	T. W. Graveney and F. S. Trueman at Lord's	1962
79	for 10th	R. W. Taylor and R. G. D. Willis at Birmingham	1982

For Pakistan

173	for 1st	Mohsin Khan and Shoaib Mohammad at Lahore	1983-84
291	for 2nd†	Zaheer Abbas and Mushtaq Mohammad at Birmingham	1971
180	for 3rd	Mudassar Nazar and Haroon Rashid at Lahore	1977-78
322	for 4th	Javed Miandad and Salim Malik at Birmingham	1992
197	for 5th	Javed Burki and Nasim-ul-Ghani at Lord's	1962
145	for 6th	Mushtaq Mohammad and Intikhab Alam at Hyderabad	1972-73
89	for 7th	Ijaz Ahmed and Salim Yousuf at The Oval	1987
130	for 8th†	Hanif Mohammad and Asif Iqbal at Lord's	1967
190	for 9th†	Asif Iqbal and Intikhab Alam at The Oval	1967
62	for 10th	Sarfraz Nawaz and Asif Masood at Leeds	1974

† *Denotes record partnership against all countries.*

TEN WICKETS OR MORE IN A MATCH

For England (2)

11-83 (6-65, 5-18)†	N. G. B. Cook, Karachi	1983-84
13-71 (5-20, 8-51)	D. L. Underwood, Lord's	1974

For Pakistan (6)

10-194 (5-84, 5-110)	Abdul Qadir, Lahore	1983-84
13-101 (9-56, 4-45)	Abdul Qadir, Lahore	1987-88
10-186 (5-88, 5-98)	Abdul Qadir, Karachi	1987-88
10-211 (7-96, 3-115)	Abdul Qadir, The Oval	1987
12-99 (6-53, 6-46)	Fazal Mahmood, The Oval	1954
10-77 (3-37, 7-40)	Imran Khan, Leeds	1987

† *Signifies ten wickets or more on first appearance in England–Pakistan Tests.*

FOUR WICKETS IN FIVE BALLS

C. M. Old, v Pakistan at Birmingham in 1978, dismissed Wasim Raja, Wasim Bari, Iqbal Qasim and Sikander Bakht to take four wickets in five balls (ww-ww).

ENGLAND v SRI LANKA

Captains

Season	England	Sri Lanka	T	E	SL	D
1981-82	K. W. R. Fletcher	B. Warnapura	1	1	0	0
1984	D. I. Gower	L. R. D. Mendis	1	0	0	1
1988	G. A. Gooch	R. S. Madugalle	1	1	0	0
1991	G. A. Gooch	P. A. de Silva	1	1	0	0
1992-93	A. J. Stewart	A. Ranatunga	1	0	1	0
	In England		3	2	0	1
	In Sri Lanka		2	1	1	0
	Totals.........................		5	3	1	1

HIGHEST INNINGS TOTALS

For England in England: 429 at Lord's.................................... 1988
in Sri Lanka: 380 at Colombo (SSC)......................... 1992-93

For Sri Lanka in England: 491-7 dec. at Lord's............................ 1984
in Sri Lanka: 469 at Colombo (SSC) 1992-93

LOWEST INNINGS TOTALS

For England in England: 282 at Lord's.................................... 1991
in Sri Lanka: 223 at Colombo (PSS)......................... 1981-82

For Sri Lanka in England: 194 at Lord's 1988
in Sri Lanka: 175 at Colombo (PSS) 1981-82

INDIVIDUAL HUNDREDS

For England (4)

G. A. Gooch (1)	**R. A. Smith** (1)	
174　Lord's	1991	128　Colombo (SSC) 1992-93
A. J. Lamb (1)	**A. J. Stewart** (1)	
107†　Lord's	1984	113*†　Lord's ...... 　1991

For Sri Lanka (3)

L. R. D. Mendis (1)	**S. A. R. Silva** (1)	**S. Wettimuny** (1)	
111　Lord's	1984	102*†　Lord's 1984	190　Lord's 1984

† *Signifies hundred on first appearance in England–Sri Lanka Tests.*

BEST BOWLING

Best bowling in an innings for England: 7-70 by P. A. J. DeFreitas at Lord's ... 1991
for Sri Lanka: 5-69 by R. J. Ratnayake at Lord's 1991

RECORD PARTNERSHIPS FOR EACH WICKET

For England

78 for 1st	G. A. Gooch and H. Morris at Lord's	1991
139 for 2nd	G. A. Gooch and A. J. Stewart at Lord's	1991
112 for 3rd	R. A. Smith and G. A. Hick at Colombo (SSC)	1992-93
122 for 4th	R. A. Smith and A. J. Stewart at Colombo (SSC)...........	1992-93

40 for 5th	A. J. Stewart and I. T. Botham at Lord's	1991
87 for 6th	A. J. Lamb and R. M. Ellison at Lord's	1984
63 for 7th	A. J. Stewart and R. C. Russell at Lord's	1991
20 for 8th	J. E. Emburey and P. W. Jarvis at Colombo (SSC)	1992-93
37 for 9th	P. J. Newport and N. A. Foster at Lord's	1988
40 for 10th	J. E. Emburey and D. E. Malcolm at Colombo (SSC)	1992-93

For Sri Lanka

99 for 1st	R. S. Mahanama and U. C. Hathurusinghe at Colombo (SSC) .	1992-93
83 for 2nd	B. Warnapura and R. L. Dias at Colombo (PSS)	1981-82
101 for 3rd	S. Wettimuny and R. L. Dias at Lord's	1984
148 for 4th	S. Wettimuny and A. Ranatunga at Lord's	1984
150 for 5th†	S. Wettimuny and L. R. D. Mendis at Lord's	1984
138 for 6th†	S. A. R. Silva and L. R. D. Mendis at Lord's	1984
74 for 7th	U. C. Hathurusinghe and R. J. Ratnayake at Lord's	1991
29 for 8th	R. J. Ratnayake and C. P. H. Ramanayake at Lord's	1991
83 for 9th†	H. P. Tillekeratne and M. Muralitharan at Colombo (SSC) ...	1992-93
64 for 10th†	J. R. Ratnayeke and G. F. Labrooy at Lord's	1988

† *Denotes record partnership against all countries.*

AUSTRALIA v SOUTH AFRICA

	Captains					
Season	*Australia*	*South Africa*	*T*	*A*	*SA*	*D*
1902-03S	J. Darling	H. M. Taberer[1]	3	2	0	1
1910-11A	C. Hill	P. W. Sherwell	5	4	1	0
1912E	S. E. Gregory	F. Mitchell[2]	3	2	0	1
1921-22S	H. L. Collins	H. W. Taylor	3	1	0	2
1931-32A	W. M. Woodfull	H. B. Cameron	5	5	0	0
1935-36S	V. Y. Richardson	H. F. Wade	5	4	0	1
1949-50S	A. L. Hassett	A. D. Nourse	5	4	0	1
1952-53A	A. L. Hassett	J. E. Cheetham	5	2	2	1
1957-58S	I. D. Craig	C. B. van Ryneveld[3]	5	3	0	2
1963-64A	R. B. Simpson[4]	T. L. Goddard	5	1	1	3
1966-67S	R. B. Simpson	P. L. van der Merwe	5	1	3	1
1969-70S	W. M. Lawry	A. Bacher	4	0	4	0
	In South Africa..................		30	15	7	8
	In Australia....................		20	12	4	4
	In England		3	2	0	1
	Totals........................		53	29	11	13

S Played in South Africa.   A Played in Australia.   E Played in England.

Notes: The following deputised for the official touring captain or were appointed by the home authority for only a minor proportion of the series:
[1]J. H. Anderson (Second), E. A. Halliwell (Third). [2]L. J. Tancred (Third). [3]D. J. McGlew (First). [4]R. Benaud (First).

HIGHEST INNINGS TOTALS

For Australia in Australia: 578 at Melbourne............................	1910-11
in South Africa: 549-7 dec. at Port Elizabeth	1949-50
For South Africa in Australia: 595 at Adelaide	1963-64
in South Africa: 622-9 dec. at Durban	1969-70

LOWEST INNINGS TOTALS

For Australia in Australia: 153 at Melbourne   1931-32
           in South Africa: 75 at Durban   1949-50

For South Africa in Australia: 36† at Melbourne   1931-32
             in South Africa: 85 at Johannesburg   1902-03

† *Scored 45 in the second innings giving the smallest aggregate of 81 (12 extras) in Test cricket.*

INDIVIDUAL HUNDREDS

For Australia (55)

W. W. Armstrong (2)
159*‡ Johannesburg 1902-03
132   Melbourne . . 1910-11
W. Bardsley (3)
132† Sydney 1910-11
121   Manchester . .   1912
164   Lord's   1912
R. Benaud (2)
122   Johannesburg 1957-58
100   Johannesburg 1957-58
B. C. Booth (2)
169† Brisbane 1963-64
102* Sydney 1963-64
D. G. Bradman (4)
226† Brisbane 1931-32
112   Sydney 1931-32
167   Melbourne . . 1931-32
299* Adelaide 1931-32
W. A. Brown (1)
121   Cape Town . . 1935-36
J. W. Burke (1)
189   Cape Town 1957-58
A. G. Chipperfield (1)
109† Durban 1935-36
H. L. Collins (1)
203   Johannesburg 1921-22
J. H. Fingleton (3)
112   Cape Town . . 1935-36

108   Johannesburg 1935-36
118   Durban 1935-36
J. M. Gregory (1)
119   Johannesburg 1921-22
R. N. Harvey (8)
178   Cape Town . . 1949-50
151* Durban 1949-50
100   Johannesburg 1949-50
116   Pt Elizabeth . 1949-50
109   Brisbane 1952-53
190   Sydney 1952-53
116   Adelaide 1952-53
205   Melbourne . . 1952-53
A. L. Hassett (3)
112† Johannesburg 1949-50
167   Pt Elizabeth . 1949-50
163   Adelaide 1952-53
C. Hill (3)
142† Johannesburg 1902-03
191   Sydney 1910-11
100   Melbourne . . 1910-11
C. Kelleway (1)
114   Manchester . .   1912
102   Lord's   1912
W. M. Lawry (1)
157   Melbourne . . 1963-64
S. J. E. Loxton (1)
101† Johannesburg 1949-50

C. G. Macartney (2)
137   Sydney 1910-11
116   Durban 1921-22
S. J. McCabe (2)
149   Durban 1935-36
189* Johannesburg 1935-36
C. C. McDonald (1)
154   Adelaide 1952-53
J. Moroney (2)
118   ⎫
101* ⎬ Johannesburg 1949-50
A. R. Morris (2)
111   Johannesburg 1949-50
157   Pt Elizabeth . 1949-50
K. E. Rigg (1)
127† Sydney 1931-32
J. Ryder (1)
142   Cape Town . . 1921-22
R. B. Simpson (1)
153   Cape Town . . 1966-67
K. R. Stackpole (1)
134   Cape Town . . 1966-67
V. T. Trumper (2)
159   Melbourne . . 1910-11
214* Adelaide 1910-11
W. M. Woodfull (1)
161   Melbourne . . 1931-32

For South Africa (36)

E. J. Barlow (5)
114† Brisbane 1963-64
109   Melbourne . . 1963-64
201   Adelaide 1963-64
127   Cape Town . . 1969-70
110   Johannesburg 1969-70
K. C. Bland (1)
126   Sydney 1963-64
W. R. Endean (1)
162* Melbourne . . 1952-53
G. A. Faulkner (3)
204   Melbourne . . 1910-11
115   Adelaide 1910-11
122* Manchester . .   1912
C. N. Frank (1)
152   Johannesburg 1921-22
B. L. Irvine (1)
102   Pt Elizabeth . 1969-70

D. T. Lindsay (3)
182   Johannesburg 1966-67
137   Durban 1966-67
131   Johannesburg 1966-67
D. J. McGlew (2)
108   Johannesburg 1957-58
105   Durban 1957-58
A. D. Nourse (2)
231   Johannesburg 1935-36
114   Cape Town . . 1949-50
A. W. Nourse (1)
111   Johannesburg 1921-22
R. G. Pollock (5)
122   Sydney 1963-64
175   Adelaide 1963-64
209   Cape Town . . 1966-67
105   Pt Elizabeth . 1966-67
274   Durban 1969-70

B. A. Richards (2)
140   Durban 1969-70
126   Pt Elizabeth . 1969-70
E. A. B. Rowan (1)
143   Durban 1949-50
J. H. Sinclair (2)
101   Johannesburg 1902-03
104   Cape Town . . 1902-03
S. J. Snooke (1)
103   Adelaide 1910-11
K. G. Viljoen (1)
111   Melbourne . . 1931-32
J. H. B. Waite (2)
115   Johannesburg 1957-58
134   Durban 1957-58
J. W. Zulch (2)
105   Adelaide 1910-11
150   Sydney 1910-11

† *Signifies hundred on first appearance in Australia–South Africa Tests.*
‡ *Carried his bat.*

RECORD PARTNERSHIPS FOR EACH WICKET

For Australia

233 for 1st	J. H. Fingleton and W. A. Brown at Cape Town	1935-36
275 for 2nd	C. C. McDonald and A. L. Hassett at Adelaide	1952-53
242 for 3rd	C. Kelleway and W. Bardsley at Lord's	1912
168 for 4th	R. N. Harvey and K. R. Miller at Sydney	1952-53
143 for 5th	W. W. Armstrong and V. T. Trumper at Melbourne	1910-11
107 for 6th	C. Kelleway and V. S. Ransford at Melbourne	1910-11
160 for 7th	R. Benaud and G. D. McKenzie at Sydney	1963-64
83 for 8th	A. G. Chipperfield and C. V. Grimmett at Durban	1935-36
78 for 9th	{ D. G. Bradman and W. J. O'Reilly at Adelaide	1931-32
	{ K. D. Mackay and I. Meckiff at Johannesburg	1957-58
82 for 10th	V. S. Ransford and W. J. Whitty at Melbourne	1910-11

For South Africa

176 for 1st	D. J. McGlew and T. L. Goddard at Johannesburg	1957-58
173 for 2nd	L. J. Tancred and C. B. Llewellyn at Johannesburg	1902-03
341 for 3rd†	E. J. Barlow and R. G. Pollock at Adelaide	1963-64
206 for 4th	C. N. Frank and A. W. Nourse at Johannesburg	1921-22
129 for 5th	J. H. B. Waite and W. R. Endean at Johannesburg	1957-58
200 for 6th†	R. G. Pollock and H. R. Lance at Durban	1969-70
221 for 7th	D. T. Lindsay and P. L. van der Merwe at Johannesburg	1966-67
124 for 8th†	A. W. Nourse and E. A. Halliwell at Johannesburg	1902-03
85 for 9th	R. G. Pollock and P. M. Pollock at Cape Town	1966-67
53 for 10th	L. A. Stricker and S. J. Pegler at Adelaide	1910-11

† *Denotes record partnership against all countries.*

TEN WICKETS OR MORE IN A MATCH

For Australia (5)

14-199 (7-116, 7-83)	C. V. Grimmett, Adelaide	1931-32
10-88 (5-32, 5-56)	C. V. Grimmett, Cape Town	1935-36
10-110 (3-70, 7-40)	C. V. Grimmett, Johannesburg	1935-36
13-173 (7-100, 6-73)	C. V. Grimmett, Durban	1935-36
11-24 (5-6, 6-18)	H. Ironmonger, Melbourne	1931-32

For South Africa (2)

10-116 (5-43, 5-73)	C. B. Llewellyn, Johannesburg	1902-03
13-165 (6-84, 7-81)	H. J. Tayfield, Melbourne	1952-53

Note: C. V. Grimmett took ten wickets or more in three consecutive matches in 1935-36.

AUSTRALIA v WEST INDIES

Captains

Season	Australia	West Indies	T	A	WI	T	D
1930-31A	W. M. Woodfull	G. C. Grant	5	4	1	0	0
1951-52A	A. L. Hassett[1]	J. D. C. Goddard[2]	5	4	1	0	0
1954-55W	I. W. Johnson	D. St E. Atkinson[3]	5	3	0	0	2
1960-61A	R. Benaud	F. M. M. Worrell	5	2	1	1	1

THE FRANK WORRELL TROPHY

Season	Australia		West Indies	T	A	WI	T	D	Held by
		Captains							
1964-65*W*	R. B. Simpson		G. S. Sobers	5	1	2	0	2	WI
1968-69*A*	W. M. Lawry		G. S. Sobers	5	3	1	0	1	A
1972-73*W*	I. M. Chappell		R. B. Kanhai	5	2	0	0	3	A
1975-76*A*	G. S. Chappell		C. H. Lloyd	6	5	1	0	0	A
1977-78*W*	R. B. Simpson		A. I. Kallicharran[4]	5	1	3	0	1	WI
1979-80*A*	G. S. Chappell		C. H. Lloyd[5]	3	0	2	0	1	WI
1981-82*A*	G. S. Chappell		C. H. Lloyd	3	1	1	0	1	WI
1983-84*W*	K. J. Hughes		C. H. Lloyd[6]	5	0	3	0	2	WI
1984-85*A*	A. R. Border[7]		C. H. Lloyd	5	1	3	0	1	WI
1988-89*A*	A. R. Border		I. V. A. Richards	5	1	3	0	1	WI
1990-91*W*	A. R. Border		I. V. A. Richards	5	1	2	0	2	WI
1992-93*A*	A. R. Border		R. B. Richardson	5	1	2	0	2	WI
	In Australia			47	22	16	1	8	
	In West Indies			30	8	10	0	12	
	Totals			77	30	26	1	20	

A Played in Australia. W Played in West Indies.

Notes: The following deputised for the official touring captain or were appointed by the home authority for only a minor proportion of the series:
[1]A. R. Morris (Third). [2]J. B. Stollmeyer (Fifth). [3]J. B. Stollmeyer (Second and Third). [4]C. H. Lloyd (First and Second). [5]D. L. Murray (First). [6]I. V. A. Richards (Second). [7]K. J. Hughes (First and Second).

HIGHEST INNINGS TOTALS

For Australia in Australia: 619 at Sydney 1968-69
in West Indies: 758-8 dec. at Kingston 1954-55

For West Indies in Australia: 616 at Adelaide 1968-69
in West Indies: 573 at Bridgetown 1964-65

LOWEST INNINGS TOTALS

For Australia in Australia: 76 at Perth 1984-85
in West Indies: 90 at Port-of-Spain 1977-78

For West Indies in Australia: 78 at Sydney 1951-52
in West Indies: 109 at Georgetown 1972-73

INDIVIDUAL HUNDREDS

For Australia (74)

R. G. Archer (1)
128 Kingston 1954-55
R. Benaud (1)
121 Kingston 1954-55
D. C. Boon (3)
149 Sydney 1988-89
109* Kingston . . . 1990-91
111 Brisbane 1992-93
B. C. Booth (1)
117 Port-of-Spain 1964-65
A. R. Border (3)
126 Adelaide 1981-82
100* Port-of-Spain 1983-84
110 Melbourne . . 1992-93

D. G. Bradman (2)
223 Brisbane 1930-31
152 Melbourne . . 1930-31
G. S. Chappell (5)
106 Bridgetown . . 1972-73
123 ⎫
109* ⎬ ‡Brisbane . . 1975-76
182* Sydney 1975-76
124 Brisbane 1979-80
I. M. Chappell (5)
117† Brisbane 1968-69
165 Melbourne . . 1968-69
106* Bridgetown . . 1972-73

109 Georgetown . 1972-73
156 Perth 1975-76
G. J. Cosier (1)
109† Melbourne . . 1975-76
R. M. Cowper (2)
143 Port-of-Spain 1964-65
102 Bridgetown . . 1964-65
J. Dyson (1)
127*† Sydney 1981-82
R. N. Harvey (3)
133 Kingston 1954-55
133 Port-of-Spain 1954-55
204 Kingston 1954-55

A. L. Hassett (2)
132 Sydney 1951-52
102 Melbourne ... 1951-52

A. M. J. Hilditch (1)
113† Melbourne ... 1984-85

K. J. Hughes (2)
130*† Brisbane 1979-80
100* Melbourne ... 1981-82

D. M. Jones (1)
216 Adelaide 1988-89

A. F. Kippax (1)
146† Adelaide 1930-31

W. M. Lawry (4)
210 Bridgetown .. 1964-65
105 Brisbane 1968-69
205 Melbourne .. 1968-69
151 Sydney 1968-69

R. R. Lindwall (1)
118 Bridgetown .. 1954-55

R. B. McCosker (1)
109* Melbourne .. 1975-76

C. C. McDonald (2)
110 Port-of-Spain 1954-55
127 Kingston 1954-55

K. R. Miller (4)
129 Sydney 1951-52
147 Kingston.... 1954-55
137 Bridgetown... 1954-55
109 Kingston.... 1954-55

A. R. Morris (1)
111 Port-of-Spain 1954-55

N. C. O'Neill (1)
181† Brisbane 1960-61

W. B. Phillips (1)
120 Bridgetown .. 1983-84

W. H. Ponsford (2)
183 Sydney 1930-31
109 Brisbane 1930-31

I. R. Redpath (4)
132 Sydney 1968-69
102 Melbourne .. 1975-76
103 Adelaide 1975-76
101 Melbourne .. 1975-76

C. S. Serjeant (1)
124 Georgetown . 1977-78

R. B. Simpson (1)
201 Bridgetown .. 1964-65

K. R. Stackpole (1)
142 Kingston.... 1972-73

M. A. Taylor (1)
144 St John's.... 1990-91

P. M. Toohey (1)
122 Kingston.... 1977-78

A. Turner (1)
136 Adelaide 1975-76

K. D. Walters (6)
118 Sydney 1968-69
110 Adelaide 1968-69
242 ⎫Sydney 1968-69
103 ⎭
102* Bridgetown . 1972-73
112 Port-of-Spain 1972-73

M. E. Waugh (2)
139* St John's.... 1990-91
112 Melbourne .. 1992-93

S. R. Waugh (1)
100 Sydney 1992-93

K. C. Wessels (1)
173 Sydney 1984-85

G. M. Wood (2)
126 Georgetown . 1977-78
111 Perth........ 1988-89

For West Indies (77)

F. C. M. Alexander (1)
108 Sydney 1960-61

K. L. T. Arthurton (1)
157* Brisbane 1992-93

D. St E. Atkinson (1)
219 Bridgetown .. 1954-55

B. F. Butcher (3)
117 Port-of-Spain 1964-65
101 Sydney 1968-69
118 Adelaide 1968-69

C. C. Depeiza (1)
122 Bridgetown .. 1954-55

P. J. L. Dujon (2)
130 Port-of-Spain 1983-84
139 Perth....... 1984-85

M. L. C. Foster (1)
125† Kingston.... 1972-73

R. C. Fredericks (1)
169 Perth....... 1975-76

H. A. Gomes (6)
101† Georgetown . 1977-78
115 Kingston.... 1977-78
126 Sydney 1981-82
124* Adelaide 1981-82
127 Perth....... 1984-85
120* Adelaide 1984-85

C. G. Greenidge (4)
120* Georgetown . 1983-84
127 Kingston.... 1983-84
104 Adelaide 1988-89
226 Bridgetown .. 1990-91

D. L. Haynes (5)
103* Georgetown . 1983-84
145 Bridgetown .. 1983-84
100 Perth....... 1988-89
143 Sydney 1988-89
111 Georgetown . 1990-91

G. A. Headley (2)
102* Brisbane 1930-31
105 Sydney 1930-31

C. C. Hunte (1)
110 Melbourne .. 1960-61

A. I. Kallicharran (4)
101 Brisbane 1975-76
127 Port-of-Spain 1977-78
126 Kingston.... 1977-78
106 Adelaide 1979-80

R. B. Kanhai (5)
117 ⎫Adelaide ... 1960-61
115 ⎭
129 Bridgetown .. 1964-65
121 Port-of-Spain 1964-65
105 Bridgetown .. 1972-73

B. C. Lara (1)
277 Sydney 1992-93

C. H. Lloyd (6)
129† Brisbane 1968-69
178 Georgetown . 1972-73
149 Perth....... 1975-76
102 Melbourne .. 1975-76
121 Adelaide 1979-80
114 Brisbane 1984-85

F. R. Martin (1)
123* Sydney 1930-31

S. M. Nurse (2)
201 Bridgetown .. 1964-65
137 Sydney 1968-69

I. V. A. Richards (5)
101 Adelaide 1975-76
140 Brisbane 1979-80
178 St John's.... 1983-84
208 Melbourne .. 1984-85
146 Perth....... 1988-89

R. B. Richardson (8)
131* Bridgetown .. 1983-84
154 St John's.... 1983-84
138 Brisbane 1984-85
122 Melbourne .. 1988-89
106 Adelaide 1988-89
104* Kingston.... 1990-91
182 Georgetown . 1990-91
109 Sydney 1992-93

L. G. Rowe (1)
107 Brisbane 1975-76

P. V. Simmons (1)
110 Melbourne .. 1992-93

O. G. Smith (1)
104† Kingston.... 1954-55

G. S. Sobers (4)
132 Brisbane 1960-61
168 Sydney 1960-61
110 Adelaide 1968-69
113 Sydney 1968-69

J. B. Stollmeyer (1)	155 } Kingston 1954-55	**F. M. M. Worrell** (1)
104 Sydney 1951-52	110 }	108 Melbourne .. 1951-52
C. L. Walcott (5)	**E. D. Weekes** (1)	
108 Kingston.... 1954-55	139 Port-of-Spain 1954-55	
126 } Port-of-Spain 1954-55	**A. B. Williams** (1)	
110 }	100† Georgetown . 1977-78	

† *Signifies hundred on first appearance in Australia–West Indies Tests.*

‡ *G. S. Chappell is the only player to score hundreds in both innings of his first Test as captain.*

Note: F. C. M. Alexander and C. C. Depeiza scored the only hundreds of their careers in a Test match.

RECORD PARTNERSHIPS FOR EACH WICKET

For Australia

382 for 1st†	W. M. Lawry and R. B. Simpson at Bridgetown..............	1964-65
298 for 2nd	W. M. Lawry and I. M. Chappell at Melbourne..............	1968-69
295 for 3rd†	C. C. McDonald and R. N. Harvey at Kingston	1954-55
336 for 4th	W. M. Lawry and K. D. Walters at Sydney	1968-69
220 for 5th	K. R. Miller and R. G. Archer at Kingston	1954-55
206 for 6th	K. R. Miller and R. G. Archer at Kingston	1954-55
134 for 7th	A. K. Davidson and R. Benaud at Brisbane	1960-61
137 for 8th	R. Benaud and I. W. Johnson at Kingston	1954-55
114 for 9th	D. M. Jones and M. G. Hughes at Adelaide	1988-89
97 for 10th	T. G. Hogan and R. M. Hogg at Georgetown................	1983-84

For West Indies

250* for 1st	C. G. Greenidge and D. L. Haynes at Georgetown	1983-84
297 for 2nd	D. L. Haynes and R. B. Richardson at Georgetown	1990-91
308 for 3rd	R. B. Richardson and I. V. A. Richards at St John's	1983-84
198 for 4th	L. G. Rowe and A. I. Kallicharran at Brisbane	1975-76
210 for 5th	R. B. Kanhai and M. L. C. Foster at Kingston	1972-73
165 for 6th	R. B. Kanhai and D. L. Murray at Bridgetown	1972-73
347 for 7th†‡	D. St E. Atkinson and C. C. Depeiza at Bridgetown	1954-55
87 for 8th	P. J. L. Dujon and C. E. L. Ambrose at Port-of-Spain	1990-91
122 for 9th	D. A. J. Holford and J. L. Hendriks at Adelaide	1968-69
56 for 10th	J. Garner and C. E. H. Croft at Brisbane	1979-80

† *Denotes record partnership against all countries.*

‡ *Record seventh-wicket partnership in first-class cricket.*

TEN WICKETS OR MORE IN A MATCH

For Australia (11)

11-96 (7-46, 4-50)	A. R. Border, Sydney.....................	1988-89
11-222 (5-135, 6-87)†	A. K. Davidson, Brisbane.................	1960-61
11-183 (7-87, 4-96)†	C. V. Grimmett, Adelaide................	1930-31
10-115 (6-72, 4-43)	N. J. N. Hawke, Georgetown.............	1964-65
10-144 (6-54, 4-90)	R. G. Holland, Sydney..................	1984-85
13-217 (5-130, 8-87)	M. G. Hughes, Perth....................	1988-89
11-79 (7-23, 4-56)	H. Ironmonger, Melbourne...............	1930-31
11-181 (8-112, 3-69)	G. F. Lawson, Adelaide..................	1984-85
10-127 (7-83, 3-44)	D. K. Lillee, Melbourne.................	1981-82
10-159 (8-71, 2-88)	G. D. McKenzie, Melbourne..............	1968-69
10-185 (3-87, 7-98)	B. Yardley, Sydney.....................	1981-82

For West Indies (4)

10-120 (6-74, 4-46)	C. E. L. Ambrose, Adelaide..............	1992-93
10-113 (7-55, 3-58)	G. E. Gomez, Sydney...................	1951-52
11-107 (5-45, 6-62)	M. A. Holding, Melbourne...............	1981-82
10-107 (5-69, 5-38)	M. D. Marshall, Adelaide	1984-85

† *Signifies ten wickets or more on first appearance in Australia–West Indies Tests.*

AUSTRALIA v NEW ZEALAND

	Captains					
Season	Australia	New Zealand	T	A	NZ	D
1945-46N	W. A. Brown	W. A. Hadlee	1	1	0	0
1973-74A	I. M. Chappell	B. E. Congdon	3	2	0	1
1973-74N	I. M. Chappell	B. E. Congdon	3	1	1	1
1976-77N	G. S. Chappell	G. M. Turner	2	1	0	1
1980-81A	G. S. Chappell	G. P. Howarth[1]	3	2	0	1
1981-82N	G. S. Chappell	G. P. Howarth	3	1	1	1

TRANS-TASMAN TROPHY

	Captains						
Season	Australia	New Zealand	T	A	NZ	D	Held by
1985-86A	A. R. Border	J. V. Coney	3	1	2	0	NZ
1985-86N	A. R. Border	J. V. Coney	3	0	1	2	NZ
1987-88A	A. R. Border	J. J. Crowe	3	1	0	2	A
1989-90A	A. R. Border	J. G. Wright	1	1	0	0	A
1989-90N	A. R. Border	J. G. Wright	1	0	1	0	NZ
1992-93N	A. R. Border	M. D. Crowe	3	1	1	1	NZ

	T	A	NZ	D
In Australia	13	6	2	5
In New Zealand	16	5	5	6
Totals	29	11	7	11

A Played in Australia. N Played in New Zealand.

Note: The following deputised for the official touring captain: [1]M. G. Burgess (Second).

HIGHEST INNINGS TOTALS

For Australia in Australia: 521-9 dec. at Perth	1989-90
in New Zealand: 552 at Christchurch	1976-77
For New Zealand in Australia: 553-7 dec. at Brisbane	1985-86
in New Zealand: 484 at Wellington	1973-74

LOWEST INNINGS TOTALS

For Australia in Australia: 162 at Sydney	1973-74
in New Zealand: 103 at Auckland	1985-86
For New Zealand in Australia: 121 at Perth	1980-81
in New Zealand: 42 at Wellington	1945-46

INDIVIDUAL HUNDREDS

For Australia (23)

D. C. Boon (2)
143   Brisbane 1987-88
200   Perth 1989-90

A. R. Border (4)
152* Brisbane 1985-86
140 ⎫
114* ⎬ Christchurch. 1985-86
205   Adelaide 1987-88

G. S. Chappell (3)
247* ⎫
133 ⎬ Wellington .. 1973-74
176   Christchurch. 1981-82

I. M. Chappell (2)
145 ⎫
121 ⎬ Wellington .. 1973-74

G. J. Gilmour (1)
101   Christchurch. 1976-77

G. R. Marsh (1)
118   Auckland ... 1985-86

R. W. Marsh (1)
132   Adelaide 1973-74

G. R. J. Matthews (2)
115† Brisbane 1985-86
130   Wellington .. 1985-86

I. R. Redpath (1)
159*‡ Auckland ... 1973-74

K. R. Stackpole (1)
122† Melbourne .. 1973-74

K. D. Walters (3)
104* Auckland ... 1973-74
250   Christchurch. 1976-77
107   Melbourne .. 1980-81

G. M. Wood (2)
111† Brisbane 1980-81
100   Auckland ... 1981-82

For New Zealand (18)

J. V. Coney (1)	**M. J. Greatbatch** (1)	**J. F. Reid** (1)
101* Wellington .. 1985-86	146*† Perth 1989-90	108† Brisbane 1985-86
B. E. Congdon (2)	**B. F. Hastings** (1)	**K. R. Rutherford** (1)
132 Wellington .. 1973-74	101 Wellington .. 1973-74	102 Christchurch. 1992-93
107* Christchurch. 1976-77	**A. H. Jones** (1)	**G. M. Turner** (2)
M. D. Crowe (3)	150 Adelaide 1987-88	101 ⎫
188 Brisbane 1985-86	**J. F. M. Morrison** (1)	110* ⎬ Christchurch. 1973-74
137 Christchurch. 1985-86	117 Sydney 1973-74	**J. G. Wright** (2)
137 Adelaide 1987-88	**J. M. Parker** (1)	141 Christchurch. 1981-82
B. A. Edgar (1)	108 Sydney 1973-74	117* Wellington .. 1989-90
161 Auckland ... 1981-82		

† *Signifies hundred on first appearance in Australia–New Zealand Tests.*
‡ *Carried his bat.*

Notes: G. S. and I. M. Chappell at Wellington in 1973-74 provide the only instance in Test matches of brothers both scoring a hundred in each innings and in the same Test.

RECORD PARTNERSHIPS FOR EACH WICKET

For Australia

106 for 1st	B. M. Laird and G. M. Wood at Auckland	1981-82
168 for 2nd	G. R. Marsh and W. B. Phillips at Auckland................	1985-86
264 for 3rd	I. M. Chappell and G. S. Chappell at Wellington	1973-74
116 for 4th	A. R. Border and S. R. Waugh at Adelaide	1987-88
213 for 5th	G. M. Ritchie and G. R. J. Matthews at Wellington	1985-86
197 for 6th	A. R. Border and G. R. J. Matthews at Brisbane	1985-86
217 for 7th†	K. D. Walters and G. J. Gilmour at Christchurch	1976-77
93 for 8th	G. J. Gilmour and K. J. O'Keeffe at Auckland	1976-77
61 for 9th	A. I. C. Dodemaide and C. J. McDermott at Melbourne ...	1987-88
60 for 10th	K. D. Walters and J. D. Higgs at Melbourne	1980-81

For New Zealand

111 for 1st	M. J. Greatbatch and J. G. Wright at Wellington	1992-93
128* for 2nd	J. G. Wright and A. H. Jones at Wellington	1989-90
224 for 3rd	J. F. Reid and M. D. Crowe at Brisbane	1985-86
229 for 4th†	B. E. Congdon and B. F. Hastings at Wellington	1973-74
88 for 5th	J. V. Coney and M. G. Burgess at Perth	1980-81
109 for 6th	K. R. Rutherford and J. V. Coney at Wellington	1985-86
132* for 7th	J. V. Coney and R. J. Hadlee at Wellington..............	1985-86
88* for 8th	M. J. Greatbatch and M. C. Snedden at Perth............	1989-90
73 for 9th	H. J. Howarth and D. R. Hadlee at Christchurch	1976-77
124 for 10th	J. G. Bracewell and S. L. Boock at Sydney................	1985-86

† *Denotes record partnership against all countries.*

TEN WICKETS OR MORE IN A MATCH

For Australia (2)

10-174 (6-106, 4-68)	R. G. Holland, Sydney	1985-86
11-123 (5-51, 6-72)	D. K. Lillee, Auckland	1976-77

For New Zealand (4)

10-106 (4-74, 6-32)	J. G. Bracewell, Auckland	1985-86
15-123 (9-52, 6-71)	R. J. Hadlee, Brisbane	1985-86
11-155 (5-65, 6-90)	R. J. Hadlee, Perth	1985-86
10-176 (5-109, 5-67)	R. J. Hadlee, Melbourne	1987-88

AUSTRALIA v INDIA

Captains

Season	Australia	India	T	A	I	T	D
1947-48*A*	D. G. Bradman	L. Amarnath	5	4	0	0	1
1956-57*I*	I. W. Johnson[1]	P. R. Umrigar	3	2	0	0	1
1959-60*I*	R. Benaud	G. S. Ramchand	5	2	1	0	2
1964-65*I*	R. B. Simpson	Nawab of Pataudi jun.	3	1	1	0	1
1967-68*A*	R. B. Simpson[2]	Nawab of Pataudi jun.[3]	4	4	0	0	0
1969-70*I*	W. M. Lawry	Nawab of Pataudi jun.	5	3	1	0	1
1977-78*A*	R. B. Simpson	B. S. Bedi	5	3	2	0	0
1979-80*I*	K. J. Hughes	S. M. Gavaskar	6	0	2	0	4
1980-81*A*	G. S. Chappell	S. M. Gavaskar	3	1	1	0	1
1985-86*A*	A. R. Border	Kapil Dev	3	0	0	0	3
1986-87*I*	A. R. Border	Kapil Dev	3	0	0	1	2
1991-92*A*	A. R. Border	M. Azharuddin	5	4	0	0	1
	In Australia		25	16	3	0	6
	In India		25	8	5	1	11
	Totals		50	24	8	1	17

A Played in Australia. I Played in India.

Notes: The following deputised for the official touring captain or were appointed by the home authority for only a minor proportion of the series:
[1]R. R. Lindwall (Second). [2]W. M. Lawry (Third and Fourth). [3]C. G. Borde (First).

HIGHEST INNINGS TOTALS

For Australia in Australia: 674 at Adelaide 1947-48
      in India: 574-7 dec. at Madras 1986-87

For India in Australia: 600-4 dec. at Sydney 1985-86
     in India: 517-5 dec. at Bombay 1986-87

LOWEST INNINGS TOTALS

For Australia in Australia: 83 at Melbourne 1980-81
      in India: 105 at Kanpur 1959-60

For India in Australia: 58 at Brisbane 1947-48
     in India: 135 at Delhi 1959-60

INDIVIDUAL HUNDREDS

For Australia (51)

S. G. Barnes (1)
112 Adelaide 1947-48
D. C. Boon (6)
123† Adelaide 1985-86
131 Sydney 1985-86
122 Madras 1986-87
129* Sydney 1991-92
135 Adelaide 1991-92
107 Perth....... 1991-92
A. R. Border (4)
162† Madras 1979-80
124 Melbourne .. 1980-81
163 Melbourne .. 1985-86
106 Madras 1986-87

D. G. Bradman (4)
185† Brisbane ... 1947-48
132 ⎫
127* ⎬ Melbourne .. 1947-48
201 Adelaide 1947-48
J. W. Burke (1)
161 Bombay 1956-57
G. S. Chappell (1)
204† Sydney 1980-81
I. M. Chappell (2)
151 Melbourne .. 1967-68
138 Delhi....... 1969-70
R. M. Cowper (2)
108 Adelaide 1967-68
165 Sydney 1967-68

L. E. Favell (1)
101 Madras 1959-60
R. N. Harvey (4)
153 Melbourne .. 1947-48
140 Bombay 1956-57
114 Delhi....... 1959-60
102 Bombay 1959-60
A. L. Hassett (1)
198* Adelaide 1947-48
K. J. Hughes (2)
100 Madras 1979-80
213 Adelaide 1980-81
D. M. Jones (2)
210† Madras 1986-87
150* Perth....... 1991-92

W. M. Lawry (1)			N. C. O'Neill (2)			K. R. Stackpole (1)		
100	Melbourne	1967-68	163	Bombay	1959-60	103†	Bombay	1969-70
A. L. Mann (1)			113	Calcutta	1959-60	M. A. Taylor (1)		
105	Perth	1977-78	G. M. Ritchie (1)			100	Adelaide	1991-92
G. R. Marsh (1)			128†	Adelaide	1985-86	K. D. Walters (1)		
101	Bombay	1986-87	A. P. Sheahan (1)			102	Madras	1969-70
G. R. J. Matthews (1)			114	Kanpur	1969-70	G. M. Wood (1)		
100*	Melbourne	1985-86	R. B. Simpson (4)			125	Adelaide	1980-81
T. M. Moody (1)			103	Adelaide	1967-68	G. N. Yallop (2)		
101†	Perth	1991-92	109	Melbourne	1967-68	121†	Adelaide	1977-78
A. R. Morris (1)			176	Perth	1977-78	167	Calcutta	1979-80
100*	Melbourne	1947-48	100	Adelaide	1977-78			

For India (35)

M. Amarnath (2)			M. L. Jaisimha (1)			R. J. Shastri (2)		
100	Perth	1977-78	101	Brisbane	1967-68	121*	Bombay	1986-87
138	Sydney	1985-86	Kapil Dev (1)			206	Sydney	1991-92
M. Azharuddin (1)			119	Madras	1986-87	K. Srikkanth (1)		
106	Adelaide	1991-92	S. M. H. Kirmani (1)			116	Sydney	1985-86
N. J. Contractor (1)			101*	Bombay	1979-80	S. R. Tendulkar (2)		
108	Bombay	1959-60	V. Mankad (2)			148*	Sydney	1991-92
S. M. Gavaskar (8)			116	Melbourne	1947-48	114	Perth	1991-92
113†	Brisbane	1977-78	111	Melbourne	1947-48	D. B. Vengsarkar (2)		
127	Perth	1977-78	Nawab of Pataudi jun. (1)			112	Bangalore	1979-80
118	Melbourne	1977-78	128*†	Madras	1964-65	164*	Bombay	1986-87
115	Delhi	1979-80	S. M. Patil (1)			G. R. Viswanath (4)		
123	Bombay	1979-80	174	Adelaide	1980-81	137†	Kanpur	1969-70
166*	Adelaide	1985-86	D. G. Phadkar (1)			161*	Bangalore	1979-80
172	Sydney	1985-86	123	Adelaide	1947-48	131	Delhi	1979-80
103	Bombay	1986-87	G. S. Ramchand (1)			114	Melbourne	1980-81
V. S. Hazare (2)			109	Bombay	1956-57	Yashpal Sharma (1)		
116 ⎫ Adelaide		1947-48				100*	Delhi	1979-80
145 ⎭								

† *Signifies hundred on first appearance in Australia–India Tests.*

RECORD PARTNERSHIPS FOR EACH WICKET

For Australia

217	for 1st	D. C. Boon and G. R. Marsh at Sydney	1985-86
236	for 2nd	S. G. Barnes and D. G. Bradman at Adelaide	1947-48
222	for 3rd	A. R. Border and K. J. Hughes at Madras	1979-80
178	for 4th	D. M. Jones and A. R. Border at Madras	1986-87
223*	for 5th	A. R. Morris and D. G. Bradman at Melbourne	1947-48
151	for 6th	T. R. Veivers and B. N. Jarman at Bombay	1964-65
66	for 7th	G. R. J. Matthews and R. J. Bright at Melbourne	1985-86
73	for 8th	T. R. Veivers and G. D. McKenzie at Madras	1964-65
87	for 9th	I. W. Johnson and W. P. A. Crawford at Madras	1956-57
77	for 10th	A. R. Border and D. R. Gilbert at Melbourne	1985-86

For India

192	for 1st	S. M. Gavaskar and C. P. S. Chauhan at Bombay	1979-80
224	for 2nd	S. M. Gavaskar and M. Amarnath at Sydney	1985-86
159	for 3rd	S. M. Gavaskar and G. R. Viswanath at Delhi	1979-80
159	for 4th	D. B. Vengsarkar and G. R. Viswanath at Bangalore	1979-80
196	for 5th	R. J. Shastri and S. R. Tendulkar at Sydney	1991-92
298*	for 6th†	D. B. Vengsarkar and R. J. Shastri at Bombay	1986-87
132	for 7th	V. S. Hazare and H. R. Adhikari at Adelaide	1947-48
127	for 8th	S. M. H. Kirmani and K. D. Ghavri at Bombay	1979-80
81	for 9th	S. R. Tendulkar and K. S. More at Perth	1991-92
94	for 10th	S. M. Gavaskar and N. S. Yadav at Adelaide	1985-86

† *Denotes record partnership against all countries.*

TEN WICKETS OR MORE IN A MATCH

For Australia (11)

11-105 (6-52, 5-53)	R. Benaud, Calcutta	1956-57
12-124 (5-31, 7-93)	A. K. Davidson, Kanpur	1959-60
12-166 (5-99, 7-67)	G. Dymock, Kanpur	1979-80
10-168 (5-76, 5-92)	C. J. McDermott, Adelaide	1991-92
10-91 (6-58, 4-33)†	G. D. McKenzie, Madras	1964-65
10-151 (7-66, 3-85)	G. D. McKenzie, Melbourne	1967-68
10-144 (5-91, 5-53)	A. A. Mallett, Madras	1969-70
10-249 (5-103, 5-146)	G. R. J. Matthews, Madras	1986-87
12-126 (6-66, 6-60)	B. A. Reid, Melbourne	1991-92
11-31 (5-2, 6-29)†	E. R. H. Toshack, Brisbane	1947-48
11-95 (4-68, 7-27)	M. R. Whitney, Perth	1991-92

For India (6)

10-194 (5-89, 5-105)	B. S. Bedi, Perth	1977-78
12-104 (6-52, 6-52)	B. S. Chandrasekhar, Melbourne	1977-78
10-130 (7-49, 3-81)	Ghulam Ahmed, Calcutta	1956-57
11-122 (5-31, 6-91)	R. G. Nadkarni, Madras	1964-65
14-124 (9-69, 5-55)	J. M. Patel, Kanpur	1959-60
10-174 (4-100, 6-74)	E. A. S. Prasanna, Madras	1969-70

† *Signifies ten wickets or more on first appearance in Australia–India Tests.*

AUSTRALIA v PAKISTAN

Captains

Season	Australia	Pakistan	T	A	P	D
1956-57 *P*	I. W. Johnson	A. H. Kardar	1	0	1	0
1959-60 *P*	R. Benaud	Fazal Mahmood[1]	3	2	0	1
1964-65 *P*	R. B. Simpson	Hanif Mohammad	1	0	0	1
1964-65 *A*	R. B. Simpson	Hanif Mohammad	1	0	0	1
1972-73 *A*	I. M. Chappell	Intikhab Alam	3	3	0	0
1976-77 *A*	G. S. Chappell	Mushtaq Mohammad	3	1	1	1
1978-79 *A*	G. N. Yallop[2]	Mushtaq Mohammad	2	1	1	0
1979-80 *P*	G. S. Chappell	Javed Miandad	3	0	1	2
1981-82 *A*	G. S. Chappell	Javed Miandad	3	2	1	0
1982-83 *P*	K. J. Hughes	Imran Khan	3	0	3	0
1983-84 *A*	K. J. Hughes	Imran Khan[3]	5	2	0	3
1988-89 *P*	A. R. Border	Javed Miandad	3	0	1	2
1989-90 *A*	A. R. Border	Imran Khan	3	1	0	2
	In Pakistan		14	2	6	6
	In Australia		20	10	3	7
	Totals		34	12	9	13

A Played in Australia. P Played in Pakistan.

Notes: The following deputised for the official touring captain or were appointed by the home authority for only a minor proportion of the series:
[1]Imtiaz Ahmed (Second). [2]K. J. Hughes (Second). [3]Zaheer Abbas (First, Second and Third).

HIGHEST INNINGS TOTALS

For Australia in Australia: 585 at Adelaide		1972-73
in Pakistan: 617 at Faisalabad		1979-80
For Pakistan in Australia: 624 at Adelaide		1983-84
in Pakistan: 501-6 dec. at Faisalabad		1982-83

LOWEST INNINGS TOTALS

For Australia in Australia: 125 at Melbourne...................... 1981-82
     in Pakistan: 80 at Karachi 1956-57

For Pakistan in Australia: 62 at Perth 1981-82
     in Pakistan: 134 at Dacca 1959-60

INDIVIDUAL HUNDREDS

For Australia (37)

J. Benaud (1)	**I. C. Davis** (1)	**G. M. Ritchie** (1)
142 Melbourne .. 1972-73	105† Adelaide 1976-77	106* Faisalabad .. 1982-83
A. R. Border (6)	**K. J. Hughes** (2)	**A. P. Sheahan** (1)
105† Melbourne .. 1978-79	106 Perth....... 1981-82	127 Melbourne .. 1972-73
150*⎱Lahore 1979-80	106 Adelaide 1983-84	**R. B. Simpson** (2)
153 ⎰	**D. M. Jones** (2)	153⎱†Karachi 1964-65
118 Brisbane 1983-84	116⎱Adelaide 1989-90	115⎰
117* Adelaide 1983-84	121*⎰	**M. A. Taylor** (2)
113* Faisalabad .. 1988-89	**R. B. McCosker** (1)	101† Melbourne .. 1989-90
G. S. Chappell (6)	105 Melbourne.. 1976-77	101* Sydney 1989-90
116* Melbourne .. 1972-73	**R. W. Marsh** (1)	**K. D. Walters** (1)
121 Melbourne .. 1976-77	118† Adelaide 1972-73	107 Adelaide 1976-77
235 Faisalabad .. 1979-80	**N. C. O'Neill** (1)	**K. C. Wessels** (1)
201 Brisbane 1981-82	134 Lahore...... 1959-60	179 Adelaide 1983-84
150* Brisbane 1983-84	**W. B. Phillips** (1)	**G. M. Wood** (1)
182 Sydney 1983-84	159† Perth....... 1983-84	100 Melbourne .. 1981-82
I. M. Chappell (1)	**I. R. Redpath** (1)	**G. N. Yallop** (3)
196 Adelaide 1972-73	135 Melbourne.. 1972-73	172 Faisalabad .. 1979-80
G. J. Cosier (1)		141 Perth 1983-84
168 Melbourne . 1976-77		268 Melbourne .. 1983-84

For Pakistan (31)

Asif Iqbal (3)	131 Adelaide 1983-84	**Mushtaq Mohammad** (1)
152* Adelaide 1976-77	211 Karachi 1988-89	121 Sydney 1972-73
120 Sydney 1976-77	107 Faisalabad .. 1988-89	**Qasim Omar** (1)
134* Perth....... 1978-79	**Khalid Ibadulla** (1)	113 Adelaide 1983-84
Hanif Mohammad (2)	166† Karachi 1964-65	**Sadiq Mohammad** (2)
101* Karachi 1959-60	**Majid Khan** (3)	137 Melbourne .. 1972-73
104 Melbourne .. 1964-65	158 Melbourne .. 1972-73	105 Melbourne .. 1976-77
Ijaz Ahmed (2)	108 Melbourne .. 1978-79	**Saeed Ahmed** (1)
122 Faisalabad .. 1988-89	110* Lahore 1979-80	166 Lahore 1959-60
121 Melbourne .. 1989-90	**Mansoor Akhtar** (1)	**Taslim Arif** (1)
Imran Khan (1)	111 Faisalabad .. 1982-83	210* Faisalabad .. 1979-80
136 Adelaide 1989-90	**Mohsin Khan** (3)	**Wasim Akram** (1)
Javed Miandad (6)	135 Lahore 1982-83	123 Adelaide 1989-90
129* Perth....... 1978-79	149 Adelaide 1983-84	**Zaheer Abbas** (2)
106* Faisalabad .. 1979-80	152 Melbourne .. 1983-84	101 Adelaide 1976-77
138 Lahore 1982-83		126 Faisalabad .. 1982-83

† *Signifies hundred on first appearance in Australia–Pakistan Tests.*

RECORD PARTNERSHIPS FOR EACH WICKET

For Australia

134 for 1st	I. C. Davis and A. Turner at Melbourne	1976-77
259 for 2nd	W. B. Phillips and G. N. Yallop at Perth	1983-84
203 for 3rd	G. N. Yallop and K. J. Hughes at Melbourne	1983-84
217 for 4th	G. S. Chappell and G. N. Yallop at Faisalabad	1979-80
171 for 5th	{ G. S. Chappell and G. J. Cosier at Melbourne	1976-77
	{ A. R. Border and G. S. Chappell at Brisbane	1983-84
139 for 6th	R. M. Cowper and T. R. Veivers at Melbourne	1964-65
185 for 7th	G. N. Yallop and G. R. J. Matthews at Melbourne	1983-84
117 for 8th	G. J. Cosier and K. J. O'Keeffe at Melbourne	1976-77
83 for 9th	J. R. Watkins and R. A. L. Massie at Sydney	1972-73
52 for 10th	{ D. K. Lillee and M. H. N. Walker at Sydney	1976-77
	{ G. F. Lawson and T. M. Alderman at Lahore	1982-83

For Pakistan

249 for 1st†	Khalid Ibadulla and Abdul Kadir at Karachi	1964-65
233 for 2nd	Mohsin Khan and Qasim Omar at Adelaide	1983-84
223* for 3rd	Taslim Arif and Javed Miandad at Faisalabad	1979-80
155 for 4th	Mansoor Akhtar and Zaheer Abbas at Faisalabad	1982-83
186 for 5th	Javed Miandad and Salim Malik at Adelaide	1983-84
191 for 6th	Imran Khan and Wasim Akram at Adelaide	1989-90
104 for 7th	Intikhab Alam and Wasim Bari at Adelaide	1972-73
111 for 8th	Majid Khan and Imran Khan at Lahore	1979-80
56 for 9th	Intikhab Alam and Afaq Hussain at Melbourne	1964-65
87 for 10th	Asif Iqbal and Iqbal Qasim at Adelaide	1976-77

† *Denotes record partnership against all countries.*

TEN WICKETS OR MORE IN A MATCH

For Australia (3)

10-111 (7-87, 3-24)†	R. J. Bright, Karachi	1979-80
10-135 (6-82, 4-53)	D. K. Lillee, Melbourne	1976-77
11-118 (5-32, 6-86)†	C. G. Rackemann, Perth	1983-84

For Pakistan (6)

11-218 (4-76, 7-142)	Abdul Qadir, Faisalabad	1982-83
13-114 (6-34, 7-80)†	Fazal Mahmood, Karachi	1956-57
12-165 (6-102, 6-63)	Imran Khan, Sydney	1976-77
11-118 (4-69, 7-49)	Iqbal Qasim, Karachi	1979-80
11-125 (2-39, 9-86)	Sarfraz Nawaz, Melbourne	1978-79
11-160 (6-62, 5-98)†	Wasim Akram, Melbourne	1989-90

† *Signifies ten wickets or more on first appearance in Australia–Pakistan Tests.*

AUSTRALIA v SRI LANKA

		Captains				
Season	Australia	Sri Lanka	T	A	SL	D
1982-83S	G. S. Chappell	L. R. D. Mendis	1	1	0	0
1987-88A	A. R. Border	R. S. Madugalle	1	1	0	0
1989-90A	A. R. Border	A. Ranatunga	2	1	0	1
1992-93S	A. R. Border	A. Ranatunga	3	1	0	2
	In Australia		3	2	0	1
	In Sri Lanka		4	2	0	2
	Totals		7	4	0	3

A Played in Australia. S Played in Sri Lanka.

INNINGS TOTALS

Highest innings total for Australia: 514-4 dec. at Kandy 1982-83
for Sri Lanka: 547-8 dec. at Colombo (SSC) 1992-93

Lowest innings total for Australia: 224 at Hobart 1989-90
for Sri Lanka: 153 at Perth 1987-88

INDIVIDUAL HUNDREDS

For Australia (10)

A. R. Border (1)
106   Moratuwa ... 1992-93
D. W. Hookes (1)
143*† Kandy 1982-83
D. M. Jones (3)
102† Perth 1987-88

118* Hobart 1989-90
100* Colombo (KS) 1992-93
T. M. Moody (1)
106† Brisbane 1989-90
M. A. Taylor (2)
164† Brisbane 1989-90
108   Hobart 1989-90

S. R. Waugh (1)
134* Hobart 1989-90
K. C. Wessels (1)
141† Kandy 1982-83

For Sri Lanka (4)

P. A. de Silva (1)
167   Brisbane 1989-90
A. P. Gurusinha (1)
137   Colombo (SSC) 1992-93

A. Ranatunga (1)
127   Colombo (SSC) 1992-93
R. S. Kaluwitharana (1)
132*† Colombo (SSC) 1992-93

† *Signifies hundred on first appearance in Australia–Sri Lanka Tests.*

BEST BOWLING

Best bowling in an innings for Australia: 5-66 by T. G. Hogan at Kandy 1982-83
for Sri Lanka: 6-66 by R. J. Ratnayake at Hobart ... 1989-90

RECORD PARTNERSHIPS FOR EACH WICKET

For Australia

120	for 1st	G. R. Marsh and D. C. Boon at Perth	1987-88
170	for 2nd	K. C. Wessels and G. N. Yallop at Kandy	1982-83
158	for 3rd	T. M. Moody and A. R. Border at Brisbane	1989-90
163	for 4th	M. A. Taylor and A. R. Border at Hobart	1989-90
155*	for 5th	D. W. Hookes and A. R. Border at Kandy	1982-83
260*	for 6th	D. M. Jones and S. R. Waugh at Hobart	1989-90
129	for 7th	G. R. J. Matthews and I. A. Healy at Moratuwa	1992-93
56	for 8th	G. R. J. Matthews and C. J. McDermott at Colombo (SSC)	1992-93
45	for 9th	I. A. Healy and S. K. Warne at Colombo (SSC)	1992-93
49	for 10th	I. A. Healy and M. R. Whitney at Colombo (SSC)	1992-93

For Sri Lanka

110	for 1st	R. S. Mahanama and U. C. Hathurusinghe at Colombo (KS) ...	1992-93
92	for 2nd	R. S. Mahanama and A. P. Gurusinha at Colombo (SSC)	1992-93
107	for 3rd	U. C. Hathurusinghe and P. A. de Silva at Colombo (KS)	1992-93
		R. S. Mahanama and P. A. de Silva at Moratuwa	1992-93
230	for 4th	A. P. Gurusinha and A. Ranatunga at Colombo (SSC)	1992-93
116	for 5th	H. P. Tillekeratne and A. Ranatunga at Moratuwa	1992-93
96	for 6th	A. Ranatunga and R. S. Kaluwitharana at Colombo (SSC)	1992-93
144	for 7th†	P. A. de Silva and J. R. Ratnayeke at Brisbane	1989-90
33	for 8th	A. Ranatunga and C. P. H. Ramanayake at Perth	1987-88
44*	for 9th	R. S. Kaluwitharana and A. W. R. Madurasinghe at Colombo (SSC)	1992-93
27	for 10th	P. A. de Silva and C. P. H. Ramanayake at Brisbane	1989-90

† *Denotes record partnership against all countries.*

SOUTH AFRICA v WEST INDIES

Season	South Africa	*Captains* West Indies	T	SA	WI	D
1991-92 *W*	K. C. Wessels	R. B. Richardson	1	0	1	0

W Played in West Indies.

HIGHEST INNINGS TOTALS

For South Africa: 345 at Bridgetown 1991-92

For West Indies: 283 at Bridgetown 1991-92

INDIVIDUAL HUNDREDS

For South Africa (1)

A. C. Hudson (1)

163†   Bridgetown .. 1991-92

Highest score for West Indies: 79* by J. C. Adams.

† *Signifies hundred on first appearance in South Africa–West Indies Tests.*

HIGHEST PARTNERSHIPS

For South Africa

125 for 2nd   A. C. Hudson and K. C. Wessels at Bridgetown.............. 1991-92

For West Indies

99 for 1st   D. L. Haynes and P. V. Simmons at Bridgetown 1991-92

BEST MATCH BOWLING ANALYSES

For South Africa

8-158 (4-84, 4-74)   R. P. Snell, Bridgetown 1991-92

For West Indies

8-81 (2-47, 6-34)   C. E. L. Ambrose, Bridgetown 1991-92

SOUTH AFRICA v NEW ZEALAND

Season	South Africa	*Captains* New Zealand	T	SA	NZ	D
1931-32 *N*	H. B. Cameron	M. L. Page	2	2	0	0
1952-53 *N*	J. E. Cheetham	W. M. Wallace	2	1	0	1
1953-54 *S*	J. E. Cheetham	G. O. Rabone[1]	5	4	0	1
1961-62 *S*	D. J. McGlew	J. R. Reid	5	2	2	1
1963-64 *N*	T. L. Goddard	J. R. Reid	3	0	0	3
	In New Zealand		7	3	0	4
	In South Africa...............		10	6	2	2
	Totals........................		17	9	2	6

N Played in New Zealand. S Played in South Africa.

Note: The following deputised for the official touring captain:

[1]B. Sutcliffe (Fourth and Fifth).

HIGHEST INNINGS TOTALS

For South Africa in South Africa: 464 at Johannesburg 1961-62
        in New Zealand: 524-8 at Wellington 1952-53

For New Zealand in South Africa: 505 at Cape Town 1953-54
        in New Zealand: 364 at Wellington 1931-32

LOWEST INNINGS TOTALS

For South Africa in South Africa: 148 at Johannesburg 1953-54
        in New Zealand: 223 at Dunedin 1963-64

For New Zealand in South Africa: 79 at Johannesburg 1953-54
        in New Zealand: 138 at Dunedin 1963-64

INDIVIDUAL HUNDREDS

For South Africa (11)

X. C. Balaskas (1)
122* Wellington . . 1931-32
J. A. J. Christy (1)
103† Christchurch . 1931-32
W. R. Endean (1)
116   Auckland . . . 1952-53
D. J. McGlew (3)
255*† Wellington . . 1952-53

127*‡ Durban 1961-62
120   Johannesburg 1961-62
R. A. McLean (2)
101   Durban 1953-54
113   Cape Town . 1961-62
B. Mitchell (1)
113† Christchurch . 1931-32

A. R. A. Murray (1)
109† Wellington . . 1952-53
J. H. B. Waite (1)
101   Johannesburg 1961-62

For New Zealand (7)

P. T. Barton (1)
109   Pt Elizabeth . 1961-62
P. G. Z. Harris (1)
101   Cape Town . 1961-62
G. O. Rabone (1)
107   Durban 1953-54

J. R. Reid (2)
135   Cape Town . 1953-54
142   Johannesburg 1961-62
B. W. Sinclair (1)
138   Auckland . . . 1963-64

H. G. Vivian (1)
100† Wellington . . 1931-32

   † *Signifies hundred on first appearance in South Africa–New Zealand Tests.*
   ‡ *Carried his bat.*

RECORD PARTNERSHIPS FOR EACH WICKET

For South Africa

196 for 1st	J. A. J. Christy and B. Mitchell at Christchurch	. . . .	1931-32
76 for 2nd	J. A. J. Christy and H. B. Cameron at Wellington	. . . .	1931-32
112 for 3rd	D. J. McGlew and R. A. McLean at Johannesburg	. . . .	1961-62
135 for 4th	K. J. Funston and R. A. McLean at Durban	. . . .	1953-54
130 for 5th	W. R. Endean and J. E. Cheetham at Auckland	. . . .	1952-53
83 for 6th	K. C. Bland and D. T. Lindsay at Auckland	. . . .	1963-64
246 for 7th†	D. J. McGlew and A. R. A. Murray at Wellington	. . . .	1952-53
95 for 8th	J. E. Cheetham and H. J. Tayfield at Cape Town	. . . .	1953-54
60 for 9th	P. M. Pollock and N. A. T. Adcock at Port Elizabeth	. . . .	1961-62
47 for 10th	D. J. McGlew and H. D. Bromfield at Port Elizabeth	. . . .	1961-62

For New Zealand

126	for 1st	G. O. Rabone and M. E. Chapple at Cape Town	1953-54
51	for 2nd	W. P. Bradburn and B. W. Sinclair at Dunedin	1963-64
94	for 3rd	M. B. Poore and B. Sutcliffe at Cape Town	1953-54
171	for 4th	B. W. Sinclair and S. N. McGregor at Auckland	1963-64
174	for 5th	J. R. Reid and J. E. F. Beck at Cape Town	1953-54
100	for 6th	H. G. Vivian and F. T. Badcock at Wellington	1931-32
84	for 7th	J. R. Reid and G. A. Bartlett at Johannesburg	1961-62
73	for 8th	P. G. Z. Harris and G. A. Bartlett at Durban	1961-62
69	for 9th	C. F. W. Allcott and I. B. Cromb at Wellington	1931-32
49*	for 10th	A. E. Dick and F. J. Cameron at Cape Town	1961-62

† *Denotes record partnership against all countries.*

TEN WICKETS OR MORE IN A MATCH

For South Africa (1)

11-196 (6-128, 5-68)†	S. F. Burke, Cape Town	1961-62

† *Signifies ten wickets or more on first appearance in South Africa–New Zealand Tests.*

Note: The best match figures by a New Zealand bowler are 8-180 (4-61, 4-119), J. C. Alabaster at Cape Town, 1961-62.

SOUTH AFRICA v INDIA

		Captains					
Season	South Africa		India	T	SA	I	D
1992-93S	K. C. Wessels		M. Azharuddin	4	1	0	3

S Played in South Africa.

HIGHEST INNINGS TOTALS

For South Africa: 360-9 dec. at Cape Town	1992-93

For India: 277 at Durban	1992-93

INDIVIDUAL HUNDREDS

For South Africa (2)

W. J. Cronje (1)	**K. C. Wessels** (1)
135 Port Elizabeth 1992-93	118† Durban 1992-93

For India (3)

P. K. Amre (1)	**Kapil Dev** (1)	**S. R. Tendulkar** (1)
103† Durban 1992-93	129 Port Elizabeth 1992-93	111 Johannesburg 1992-93

† *Signifies hundred on first appearance in South Africa–India Tests.*

HUNDRED PARTNERSHIPS

For South Africa

117 for 2nd   A. C. Hudson and W. J. Cronje at Port Elizabeth 1992-93

For India

101 for 8th   P. K. Amre and K. S. More at Durban 1992-93

TEN WICKETS OR MORE IN A MATCH

For South Africa (1)

12-139 (5-55, 7-84)   A. A. Donald at Port Elizabeth 1992-93

Note: The best match figures by an Indian bowler are 8-113 (2-60, 6-53), A. Kumble at Johannesburg, 1992-93.

SOUTH AFRICA v SRI LANKA

		Captains				
Season	South Africa		Sri Lanka	T	SA	SL	D
1993-94*SL*	K. C. Wessels		A. Ranatunga	3	1	0	2

SL Played in Sri Lanka.

HIGHEST INNINGS TOTALS

For South Africa: 495 at Colombo (SSC) 1993-94

For Sri Lanka: 331 at Moratuwa 1993-94

INDIVIDUAL HUNDREDS

For South Africa (3)

W. J. Cronje (1)	**D. J. Cullinan** (1)	**J. N. Rhodes** (1)
122 Colombo (SSC) 1993-94	102 Colombo (PSS) 1993-94	101*† Moratuwa ... 1993-94

For Sri Lanka (1)

A. Ranatunga (1)
131†   Moratuwa ... 1993-94

† *Signifies hundred on first appearance in South Africa–Sri Lanka Tests.*

HUNDRED PARTNERSHIPS

For South Africa

137 for 1st	K. C. Wessels and A. C. Hudson at Colombo (SSC)	1993-94
122 for 6th	D. J. Cullinan and D. J. Richardson at Colombo (PSS).......	1993-94
105 for 3rd	W. J. Cronje and D. J. Cullinan at Colombo (SSC)	1993-94
104 for 1st	K. C. Wessels and A. C. Hudson at Moratuwa..............	1993-94

For Sri Lanka

121 for 5th	P. A. de Silva and A. Ranatunga at Moratuwa..............	1993-94
103 for 6th	A. Ranatunga and H. P. Tillekeratne at Moratuwa	1993-94
101 for 4th	P. A. de Silva and A. Ranatunga at Colombo (PSS)..........	1993-94

BEST MATCH BOWLING ANALYSES

For South Africa

9-106 (5-48, 4-58)	B. N. Schultz, Colombo (SSC).........................	1993-94

For Sri Lanka

6-152 (5-104, 1-48)	M. Muralitharan, Moratuwa	1993-94

WEST INDIES v NEW ZEALAND

Captains

Season	West Indies	New Zealand	T	WI	NZ	D
1951-52*N*	J. D. C. Goddard	B. Sutcliffe	2	1	0	1
1955-56*N*	D. St E. Atkinson	J. R. Reid[1]	4	3	1	0
1968-69*N*	G. S. Sobers	G. T. Dowling	3	1	1	1
1971-72*W*	G. S. Sobers	G. T. Dowling[2]	5	0	0	5
1979-80*N*	C. H. Lloyd	G. P. Howarth	3	0	1	2
1984-85*W*	I. V. A. Richards	G. P. Howarth	4	2	0	2
1986-87*N*	I. V. A. Richards	J. V. Coney	3	1	1	1
	In New Zealand		15	6	4	5
	In West Indies		9	2	0	7
	Totals..........................		24	8	4	12

N Played in New Zealand. W Played in West Indies.

Notes: The following deputised for the official touring captain or were appointed by the home authority for only a minor proportion of the series:
[1]H. B. Cave (First). [2]B. E. Congdon (Third, Fourth and Fifth).

HIGHEST INNINGS TOTALS

For West Indies in West Indies: 564-8 at Bridgetown......................		1971-72
in New Zealand: 546-6 dec. at Auckland		1951-52
For New Zealand in West Indies: 543-3 dec. at Georgetown		1971-72
in New Zealand: 460 at Christchurch		1979-80

LOWEST INNINGS TOTALS

For West Indies in West Indies: 133 at Bridgetown 1971-72
in New Zealand: 77 at Auckland 1955-56

For New Zealand in West Indies: 94 at Bridgetown 1984-85
in New Zealand: 74 at Dunedin 1955-56

INDIVIDUAL HUNDREDS

By West Indies (25)

M. C. Carew (1)
109† Auckland ... 1968-69
C. A. Davis (1)
183 Bridgetown .. 1971-72
R. C. Fredericks (1)
163 Kingston 1971-72
C. G. Greenidge (2)
100 Port-of-Spain 1984-85
213 Auckland ... 1986-87
D. L. Haynes (3)
105† Dunedin 1979-80
122 Christchurch. 1979-80
121 Wellington .. 1986-87
A. I. Kallicharran (2)
100*† Georgetown . 1971-72

101 Port-of-Spain 1971-72
C. L. King (1)
100* Christchurch. 1979-80
S. M. Nurse (2)
168† Auckland ... 1968-69
258 Christchurch. 1968-69
I. V. A. Richards (1)
105 Bridgetown .. 1984-85
R. B. Richardson (1)
185 Georgetown . 1984-85
L. G. Rowe (3)
214 ⎱†Kingston ... 1971-72
100* ⎰
100 Christchurch. 1979-80

G. S. Sobers (1)
142 Bridgetown .. 1971-72
J. B. Stollmeyer (1)
152 Auckland ... 1951-52
C. L. Walcott (1)
115 Auckland ... 1951-52
E. D. Weekes (3)
123 Dunedin 1955-56
103 Christchurch. 1955-56
156 Wellington .. 1955-56
F. M. M. Worrell (1)
100 Auckland ... 1951-52

By New Zealand (17)

M. G. Burgess (1)
101 Kingston 1971-72
B. E. Congdon (2)
166* Port-of-Spain 1971-72
126 Bridgetown .. 1971-72
J. J. Crowe (1)
112 Kingston 1984-85
M. D. Crowe (3)
188 Georgetown . 1984-85
119 Wellington .. 1986-87

104 Auckland ... 1986-87
B. A. Edgar (1)
127 Auckland ... 1979-80
R. J. Hadlee (1)
103 Christchurch. 1979-80
B. F. Hastings (2)
117* Christchurch. 1968-69
105 Bridgetown .. 1971-72
G. P. Howarth (1)
147 Christchurch. 1979-80

T. W. Jarvis (1)
182 Georgetown . 1971-72
B. R. Taylor (1)
124† Auckland ... 1968-69
G. M. Turner (2)
223*‡ Kingston.... 1971-72
259 Georgetown . 1971-72
J. G. Wright (1)
138 Wellington .. 1986-87

† *Signifies hundred on first appearance in West Indies–New Zealand Tests.*
‡ *Carried his bat.*

Notes: E. D. Weekes in 1955-56 made three hundreds in consecutive innings.
L. G. Rowe and A. I. Kallicharran each scored hundreds in their first two innings in Test cricket, Rowe being the only batsman to do so in his first match.

RECORD PARTNERSHIPS FOR EACH WICKET

For West Indies

225 for 1st	C. G. Greenidge and D. L. Haynes at Christchurch..........	1979-80
269 for 2nd	R. C. Fredericks and L. G. Rowe at Kingston	1971-72
185 for 3rd	C. G. Greenidge and R. B. Richardson at Port-of-Spain	1984-85
162 for 4th ⎰	E. D. Weekes and O. G. Smith at Dunedin	1955-56
⎱	C. G. Greenidge and A. I. Kallicharran at Christchurch.....	1979-80
189 for 5th	F. M. M. Worrell and C. L. Walcott at Auckland	1951-52
254 for 6th	C. A. Davis and G. S. Sobers at Bridgetown	1971-72
143 for 7th	D. St E. Atkinson and J. D. C. Goddard at Christchurch	1955-56
83 for 8th	I. V. A. Richards and M. D. Marshall at Bridgetown	1984-85
70 for 9th	M. D. Marshall and J. Garner at Bridgetown	1984-85
31 for 10th	T. M. Findlay and G. C. Shillingford at Bridgetown	1971-72

For New Zealand

387	for 1st†	G. M. Turner and T. W. Jarvis at Georgetown	1971-72
210	for 2nd	G. P. Howarth and J. J. Crowe at Kingston	1984-85
241	for 3rd	J. G. Wright and M. D. Crowe at Wellington	1986-87
175	for 4th	B. E. Congdon and B. F. Hastings at Bridgetown	1971-72
142	for 5th	M. D. Crowe and J. V. Coney at Georgetown	1984-85
220	for 6th	G. M. Turner and K. J. Wadsworth at Kingston	1971-72
143	for 7th	M. D. Crowe and I. D. S. Smith at Georgetown	1984-85
136	for 8th†	B. E. Congdon and R. S. Cunis at Port-of-Spain	1971-72
62*	for 9th	V. Pollard and R. S. Cunis at Auckland	1968-69
41	for 10th	B. E. Congdon and J. C. Alabaster at Port-of-Spain	1971-72

† *Denotes record partnership against all countries.*

TEN WICKETS OR MORE IN A MATCH

For West Indies (1)

11-120 (4-40, 7-80)	M. D. Marshall, Bridgetown	1984-85

For New Zealand (3)

10-124 (4-51, 6-73)†	E. J. Chatfield, Port-of-Spain	1984-85
11-102 (5-34, 6-68)†	R. J. Hadlee, Dunedin	1979-80
10-166 (4-71, 6-95)	G. B. Troup, Auckland	1979-80

† *Signifies ten wickets or more on first appearance in West Indies–New Zealand Tests.*

WEST INDIES v INDIA

Captains

Season	West Indies	India	T	WI	I	D
1948-49*I*	J. D. C. Goddard	L. Amarnath	5	1	0	4
1952-53*W*	J. B. Stollmeyer	V. S. Hazare	5	1	0	4
1958-59*I*	F. C. M. Alexander	Ghulam Ahmed[1]	5	3	0	2
1961-62*W*	F. M. M. Worrell	N. J. Contractor[2]	5	5	0	0
1966-67*I*	G. S. Sobers	Nawab of Pataudi jun.	3	2	0	1
1970-71*W*	G. S. Sobers	A. L. Wadekar	5	0	1	4
1974-75*I*	C. H. Lloyd	Nawab of Pataudi jun.[3]	5	3	2	0
1975-76*W*	C. H. Lloyd	B. S. Bedi	4	2	1	1
1978-79*I*	A. I. Kallicharran	S. M. Gavaskar	6	0	1	5
1982-83*W*	C. H. Lloyd	Kapil Dev	5	2	0	3
1983-84*I*	C. H. Lloyd	Kapil Dev	6	3	0	3
1987-88*I*	I. V. A. Richards	D. B. Vengsarkar[4]	4	1	1	2
1988-89*W*	I. V. A. Richards	D. B. Vengsarkar	4	3	0	1
	In India		34	13	4	17
	In West Indies		28	13	2	13
	Totals.		62	26	6	30

I Played in India. W Played in West Indies.

Notes: The following deputised for the official touring captain or were appointed by the home authority for only a minor proportion of the series:
[1]P. R. Umrigar (First), V. Mankad (Fourth), H. R. Adhikari (Fifth). [2]Nawab of Pataudi jun. (Third, Fourth and Fifth). [3]S. Venkataraghavan (Second). [4]R. J. Shastri (Fourth).

HIGHEST INNINGS TOTALS

For West Indies in West Indies: 631-8 dec. at Kingston 1961-62
           in India: 644-8 dec. at Delhi 1958-59

For India in West Indies: 469-7 at Port-of-Spain 1982-83
         in India: 644-7 dec. at Kanpur 1978-79

LOWEST INNINGS TOTALS

For West Indies in West Indies: 214 at Port-of-Spain 1970-71
           in India: 127 at Delhi 1987-88

For India in West Indies: 97† at Kingston 1975-76
         in India: 75 at Delhi 1987-88

     † *Five men absent hurt. The lowest with 11 men batting is 98 at Port-of-Spain, 1961-62.*

INDIVIDUAL HUNDREDS

For West Indies (76)

S. F. A. F. Bacchus (1)
250   Kanpur   1978-79
B. F. Butcher (2)
103   Calcutta 1958-59
142   Madras 1958-59
R. J. Christiani (1)
107†   Delhi 1948-49
C. A. Davis (2)
125*   Georgetown . 1970-71
105   Port-of-Spain 1970-71
P. J. L. Dujon (1)
110   St John's . . . 1982-83
R. C. Fredericks (2)
100   Calcutta 1974-75
104   Bombay 1974-75
H. A. Gomes (1)
123   Port-of-Spain 1982-83
G. E. Gomez (1)
101†   Delhi 1948-49
C. G. Greenidge (5)
107†   Bangalore . . . 1974-75
154*   St John's 1982-83
194   Kanpur 1983-84
141   Calcutta 1987-88
117   Bridgetown . 1988-89
D. L. Haynes (2)
136   St John's 1982-83
112*   Bridgetown . 1988-89
J. K. Holt (1)
123   Delhi 1958-59
C. L. Hooper (1)
100*   Calcutta 1987-88
C. C. Hunte (1)
101   Bombay . . . 1966-67

A. I. Kallicharran (3)
124†   Bangalore . . . 1974-75
103*   Port-of-Spain 1975-76
187   Bombay . . . 1978-79
R. B. Kanhai (4)
256   Calcutta 1958-59
138   Kingston . . . 1961-62
139   Port-of-Spain 1961-62
158*   Kingston . . . 1970-71
C. H. Lloyd (7)
163   Bangalore . . . 1974-75
242*   Bombay . . . 1974-75
102   Bridgetown . 1975-76
143   Port-of-Spain 1982-83
106   St John's . . . 1982-83
103   Delhi 1983-84
161*   Calcutta 1983-84
A. L. Logie (2)
130   Bridgetown . 1982-83
101   Calcutta 1987-88
E. D. A. McMorris (1)
125†   Kingston . . . 1961-62
B. H. Pairaudeau (1)
115†   Port-of-Spain 1952-53
A. F. Rae (2)
104   Bombay 1948-49
109   Madras 1948-49
I. V. A. Richards (8)
192*   Delhi 1974-75
142   Bridgetown . 1975-76
130   Port-of-Spain 1975-76
177   Port-of-Spain 1975-76
109   Georgetown . 1982-83
120   Bombay . . . 1983-84
109*   Delhi 1987-88
110   Kingston . . . 1988-89

R. B. Richardson (2)
194   Georgetown . 1988-89
156   Kingston . . . 1988-89
O. G. Smith (1)
100   Delhi 1958-59
G. S. Sobers (8)
142*† Bombay 1958-59
198   Kanpur 1958-59
106*   Calcutta 1958-59
153   Kingston . . . 1961-62
104   Kingston . . . 1961-62
108*   Georgetown . 1970-71
178*   Bridgetown . 1970-71
132   Port-of-Spain 1970-71
J. S. Solomon (1)
100*   Delhi 1958-59
J. B. Stollmeyer (2)
160   Madras 1948-49
104*   Port-of-Spain 1952-53
C. L. Walcott (4)
152†   Delhi 1948-49
108   Calcutta 1948-49
125   Georgetown . 1952-53
118   Kingston . . . 1952-53
E. D. Weekes (7)
128†   Delhi 1948-49
194   Bombay 1948-49
162   } Calcutta 1948-49
101
207   Port-of-Spain 1952-53
161   Port-of-Spain 1952-53
109   Kingston . . . 1952-53
A. B. Williams (1)
111   Calcutta 1978-79
F. M. M. Worrell (1)
237   Kingston . . . 1952-53

For India (55)

H. R. Adhikari (1)		120	Delhi	1978-79
114*† Delhi 1948-49		147*	Georgetown .	1982-83
M. Amarnath (3)		121	Delhi	1983-84
101* Kanpur 1978-79		236*	Madras	1983-84
117 Port-of-Spain 1982-83		**V. S. Hazare** (2)		
116 St John's 1982-83		134*	Bombay	1948-49
M. L. Apte (1)		122	Bombay	1948-49
163* Port-of-Spain 1952-53		**Kapil Dev** (3)		
C. G. Borde (3)		126*	Delhi	1978-79
109 Delhi 1958-59		100*	Port-of-Spain	1982-83
121 Bombay 1966-67		109	Madras	1987-88
125 Madras 1966-67		**S. V. Manjrekar** (1)		
S. A. Durani (1)		108	Bridgetown .	1988-89
104 Port-of-Spain 1961-62		**V. L. Manjrekar** (1)		
F. M. Engineer (1)		118	Kingston ...	1952-53
109 Madras 1966-67		**R. S. Modi** (1)		
A. D. Gaekwad (1)		112	Bombay	1948-49
102 Kanpur 1978-79		**Mushtaq Ali** (1)		
S. M. Gavaskar (13)		106†	Calcutta	1948-49
116 Georgetown . 1970-71		**B. P. Patel** (1)		
117* Bridgetown . 1970-71		115*	Port-of-Spain	1975-76
124 ⎫ Port-of-Spain 1970-71		**Pankaj Roy** (1)		
220 ⎭		150	Kingston ...	1952-53
156 Port-of-Spain 1975-76		**D. N. Sardesai** (3)		
102 Port-of-Spain 1975-76		212	Kingston ...	1970-71
205 Bombay 1978-79		112	Port-of-Spain	1970-71
107 ⎫ Calcutta 1978-79		150	Bridgetown .	1970-71
182* ⎭				

R. J. Shastri (2)		
102 St John's	1982-83
107 Bridgetown .	1988-89
N. S. Sidhu (1)		
116 Kingston ...	1988-89
E. D. Solkar (1)		
102 Bombay	1974-75
P. R. Umrigar (3)		
130 Port-of-Spain	1952-53
117 Kingston ...	1952-53
172* Port-of-Spain	1961-62
D. B. Vengsarkar (6)		
157* Calcutta	1978-79
109 Delhi	1978-79
159 Delhi	1983-84
100 Bombay	1983-84
102 Delhi	1987-88
102* Calcutta	1987-88
G. R. Viswanath (4)		
139 Calcutta	1974-75
112 Port-of-Spain	1975-76
124 Madras	1978-79
179 Kanpur	1978-79

† *Signifies hundred on first appearance in West Indies–India Tests.*

RECORD PARTNERSHIPS FOR EACH WICKET

For West Indies

296	for 1st	C. G. Greenidge and D. L. Haynes at St John's	1982-83
255	for 2nd	E. D. A. McMorris and R. B. Kanhai at Bridgetown	1961-62
220	for 3rd	I. V. A. Richards and A. I. Kallicharran at Bridgetown	1975-76
267	for 4th	C. L. Walcott and G. E. Gomez at Delhi	1948-49
219	for 5th	E. D. Weekes and B. H. Pairaudeau at Port-of-Spain	1952-53
250	for 6th	C. H. Lloyd and D. L. Murray at Bombay	1974-75
130	for 7th	C. G. Greenidge and M. D. Marshall at Kanpur	1983-84
124	for 8th†	I. V. A. Richards and K. D. Boyce at Delhi	1974-75
161	for 9th†	C. H. Lloyd and A. M. E. Roberts at Calcutta	1983-84
98*	for 10th	F. M. M. Worrell and W. W. Hall at Port-of-Spain	1961-62

For India

153	for 1st	S. M. Gavaskar and C. P. S. Chauhan at Bombay	1978-79
344*	for 2nd†	S. M. Gavaskar and D. B. Vengsarkar at Calcutta	1978-79
159	for 3rd	M. Amarnath and G. R. Viswanath at Port-of-Spain	1975-76
172	for 4th	G. R. Viswanath and A. D. Gaekwad at Kanpur	1978-79
204	for 5th	S. M. Gavaskar and B. P. Patel at Port-of-Spain	1975-76
170	for 6th	S. M. Gavaskar and R. J. Shastri at Madras	1983-84
186	for 7th	D. N. Sardesai and E. D. Solkar at Bridgetown	1970-71
107	for 8th	Yashpal Sharma and B. S. Sandhu at Kingston	1982-83
143*	for 9th	S. M. Gavaskar and S. M. H. Kirmani at Madras	1983-84
62	for 10th	D. N. Sardesai and B. S. Bedi at Bridgetown	1970-71

† *Denotes record partnership against all countries.*

TEN WICKETS OR MORE IN A MATCH

For West Indies (4)

11-126 (6-50, 5-76)	W. W. Hall, Kanpur	1958-59
11-89 (5-34, 6-55)	M. D. Marshall, Port-of-Spain............	1988-89
12-121 (7-64, 5-57)	A. M. E. Roberts, Madras	1974-75
10-101 (6-62, 4-39)	C. A. Walsh, Kingston...................	1988-89

For India (4)

11-235 (7-157, 4-78)†	B. S. Chandrasekhar, Bombay...............	1966-67
10-223 (9-102, 1-121)	S. P. Gupte, Kanpur	1958-59
16-136 (8-61, 8-75)†	N. D. Hirwani, Madras	1987-88
10-135 (1-52, 9-83)	Kapil Dev, Ahmedabad	1983-84

† *Signifies ten wickets or more on first appearance in West Indies–India Tests.*

WEST INDIES v PAKISTAN

	Captains					
Season	*West Indies*	*Pakistan*	*T*	*WI*	*P*	*D*
1957-58*W*	F. C. M. Alexander	A. H. Kardar	5	3	1	1
1958-59*P*	F. C. M. Alexander	Fazal Mahmood	3	1	2	0
1974-75*P*	C. H. Lloyd	Intikhab Alam	2	0	0	2
1976-77*W*	C. H. Lloyd	Mushtaq Mohammad	5	2	1	2
1980-81*P*	C. H. Lloyd	Javed Miandad	4	1	0	3
1986-87*P*	I. V. A. Richards	Imran Khan	3	1	1	1
1987-88*W*	I. V. A. Richards[1]	Imran Khan	3	1	1	1
1990-91*P*	D. L. Haynes	Imran Khan	3	1	1	1
1992-93*W*	R. B. Richardson	Wasim Akram	3	2	0	1
	In West Indies		16	8	3	5
	In Pakistan		15	4	4	7
	Totals.........................		31	12	7	12

P Played in Pakistan. W Played in West Indies.

Note: The following was appointed by the home authority for only a minor proportion of the series:
[1]C. G. Greenidge (First).

HIGHEST INNINGS TOTALS

For West Indies in West Indies: 790-3 dec. at Kingston.....................	1957-58
in Pakistan: 493 at Karachi	1974-75
For Pakistan in West Indies: 657-8 dec. at Bridgetown.....................	1957-58
in Pakistan: 406-8 dec. at Karachi	1974-75

LOWEST INNINGS TOTALS

For West Indies in West Indies: 127 at Port-of-Spain	1992-93
in Pakistan: 53 at Faisalabad	1986-87
For Pakistan in West Indies: 106 at Bridgetown	1957-58
in Pakistan: 77 at Lahore	1986-87

INDIVIDUAL HUNDREDS
For West Indies (24)

L. Baichan (1)			**C. L. Hooper** (2)			**I. V. A. Richards** (3)		
105*†	Lahore	1974-75	134	Lahore	1990-91	120*	Multan	1980-81
P. J. L. Dujon (1)			178*	St John's	1992-93	123	Port-of-Spain	1987-88
106*	Port-of-Spain	1987-88	**C. C. Hunte** (3)			**I. T. Shillingford** (1)		
R. C. Fredericks (1)			142†	Bridgetown	1957-58	120	Georgetown	1976-77
120	Port-of-Spain	1976-77	260	Kingston	1957-58	**G. S. Sobers** (3)		
C. G. Greenidge (1)			114	Georgetown	1957-58	365*	Kingston	1957-58
100	Kingston	1976-77	**B. D. Julien** (1)			125	⎫ Georgetown	1957-58
D. L. Haynes (3)			101	Karachi	1974-75	109*	⎭	
117	Karachi	1990-91	**A. I. Kallicharran** (1)			**C. L. Walcott** (1)		
143*‡	Port-of-Spain	1992-93	115	Karachi	1974-75	145	Georgetown	1957-58
125	Bridgetown	1992-93	**R. B. Kanhai** (1)			**E. D. Weekes** (1)		
			217	Lahore	1958-59	197†	Bridgetown	1957-58
			C. H. Lloyd (1)					
			157	Bridgetown	1976-77			

For Pakistan (18)

Asif Iqbal (1)			**Javed Miandad** (2)			**Saeed Ahmed** (1)		
135	Kingston	1976-77	114	Georgetown	1987-88	150	Georgetown	1957-58
Hanif Mohammad (2)			102	Port-of-Spain	1987-88	**Salim Malik** (1)		
337†	Bridgetown	1957-58	**Majid Khan** (2)			102	Karachi	1990-91
103	Karachi	1958-59	100	Karachi	1974-75	**Wasim Raja** (2)		
Imtiaz Ahmed (1)			167	Georgetown	1976-77	107*	Karachi	1974-75
122	Kingston	1957-58	**Mushtaq Mohammad** (2)			117*	Bridgetown	1976-77
Imran Khan (1)			123	Lahore	1974-75	**Wazir Mohammad** (2)		
123	Lahore	1980-81	121	Port-of-Spain	1976-77	106	Kingston	1957-58
Inzamam-ul-Haq (1)						189	Port-of-Spain	1957-58
123	St John's	1992-93						

† *Signifies hundred on first appearance in West Indies–Pakistan Tests.*
‡ *Carried his bat.*

RECORD PARTNERSHIPS FOR EACH WICKET
For West Indies

182	for 1st	R. C. Fredericks and C. G. Greenidge at Kingston		1976-77
446	for 2nd†	C. C. Hunte and G. S. Sobers at Kingston		1957-58
169	for 3rd	D. L. Haynes and B. C. Lara at Port-of-Spain		1992-93
188*	for 4th	G. S. Sobers and C. L. Walcott at Kingston		1957-58
185	for 5th	E. D. Weekes and O. G. Smith at Bridgetown		1957-58
151	for 6th	C. H. Lloyd and D. L. Murray at Bridgetown		1976-77
70	for 7th	C. H. Lloyd and J. Garner at Bridgetown		1976-77
60	for 8th	C. L. Hooper and A. C. Cummins at St John's		1992-93
61*	for 9th	P. J. L. Dujon and W. K. M. Benjamin at Bridgetown		1987-88
106	for 10th†	C. L. Hooper and C. A. Walsh at St John's		1992-93

For Pakistan

159	for 1st[1]	Majid Khan and Zaheer Abbas at Georgetown		1976-77
178	for 2nd	Hanif Mohammad and Saeed Ahmed at Karachi		1958-59
169	for 3rd	Saeed Ahmed and Wazir Mohammad at Port-of-Spain		1957-58
174	for 4th	Shoaib Mohammad and Salim Malik at Karachi		1990-91
88	for 5th	Basit Ali and Inzamam-ul-Haq at St John's		1992-93
166	for 6th	Wazir Mohammad and A. H. Kardar at Kingston		1957-58
128	for 7th[2]	Wasim Raja and Wasim Bari at Karachi		1974-75

94 for 8th	Salim Malik and Salim Yousuf at Port-of-Spain	1987-88
96 for 9th	Inzamam-ul-Haq and Nadeem Khan at St John's	1992-93
133 for 10th†	Wasim Raja and Wasim Bari at Bridgetown	1976-77

† *Denotes record partnership against all countries.*

[1] *219 runs were added for this wicket in two separate partnerships: Sadiq Mohammad retired hurt and was replaced by Zaheer Abbas when 60 had been added. The highest partnership by two opening batsmen is 152 by Hanif Mohammad and Imtiaz Ahmed at Bridgetown, 1957-58.*

[2] *Although the seventh wicket added 168 runs against West Indies at Lahore in 1980-81, this comprised two partnerships with Imran Khan adding 72* with Abdul Qadir (retired hurt) and a further 96 with Sarfraz Nawaz.*

TEN WICKETS OR MORE IN A MATCH

For Pakistan (2)

| 12-100 (6-34, 6-66) | Fazal Mahmood, Dacca .... | 1958-59 |
| 11-121 (7-80, 4-41) | Imran Khan, Georgetown .... | 1987-88 |

Note: The best match figures by a West Indian bowler are 9-95 (8-29, 1-66) by C. E. H. Croft at Port-of-Spain, 1976-77.

NEW ZEALAND v INDIA

Season	New Zealand	Captains	India	T	NZ	I	D
1955-56 *I*	H. B. Cave		P. R. Umrigar[1]	5	0	2	3
1964-65 *I*	J. R. Reid		Nawab of Pataudi jun.	4	0	1	3
1967-68 *N*	G. T. Dowling[2]		Nawab of Pataudi jun.	4	1	3	0
1969-70 *I*	G. T. Dowling		Nawab of Pataudi jun.	3	1	1	1
1975-76 *N*	G. M. Turner		B. S. Bedi[3]	3	1	1	1
1976-77 *I*	G. M. Turner		B. S. Bedi	3	0	2	1
1980-81 *N*	G. P. Howarth		S. M. Gavaskar	3	1	0	2
1988-89 *I*	J. G. Wright		D. B. Vengsarkar	3	1	2	0
1989-90 *N*	J. G. Wright		M. Azharuddin	3	1	0	2
	In India			18	2	8	8
	In New Zealand			13	4	4	5
	Totals........................			31	6	12	13

I Played in India. N Played in New Zealand.

Notes: The following deputised for the official touring captain or were appointed by the home authority for a minor proportion of the series:

[1]Ghulam Ahmed (First). [2]B. W. Sinclair (First). [3]S. M. Gavaskar (First).

HIGHEST INNINGS TOTALS

| For New Zealand in New Zealand: 502 at Christchurch .... | 1967-68 |
| in India: 462-9 dec. at Calcutta .... | 1964-65 |

| For India in New Zealand: 482 at Auckland .... | 1989-90 |
| in India: 537-3 dec. at Madras .... | 1955-56 |

LOWEST INNINGS TOTALS

| For New Zealand in New Zealand: 100 at Wellington .... | 1980-81 |
| in India: 124 at Hyderabad .... | 1988-89 |

| For India in New Zealand: 81 at Wellington .... | 1975-76 |
| in India: 88 at Bombay .... | 1964-65 |

INDIVIDUAL HUNDREDS

For New Zealand (21)

M. D. Crowe (1)
113   Auckland ... 1989-90
G. T. Dowling (3)
120   Bombay 1964-65
143   Dunedin ... 1967-68
239   Christchurch. 1967-68
J. W. Guy (1)
102† Hyderabad .. 1955-56
G. P. Howarth (1)
137* Wellington .. 1980-81
A. H. Jones (1)
170* Auckland ... 1989-90

J. M. Parker (1)
104   Bombay 1976-77
J. F. Reid (1)
123* Christchurch. 1980-81
J. R. Reid (2)
119* Delhi 1955-56
120   Calcutta 1955-56
I. D. S. Smith (1)
173   Auckland ... 1989-90
B. Sutcliffe (3)
137*† Hyderabad .. 1955-56

230* Delhi....... 1955-56
151* Calcutta 1964-65
B. R. Taylor (1)
105† Calcutta 1964-65
G. M. Turner (2)
117   Christchurch. 1975-76
113   Kanpur...... 1976-77
J. G. Wright (3)
110   Auckland ... 1980-81
185   Christchurch. 1989-90
113* Napier 1989-90

For India (22)

S. Amarnath (1)
124† Auckland ... 1975-76
M. Azharuddin (1)
192   Auckland ... 1989-90
C. G. Borde (1)
109   Bombay 1964-65
S. M. Gavaskar (2)
116† Auckland ... 1975-76
119   Bombay 1976-77
A. G. Kripal Singh (1)
100*† Hyderabad .. 1955-56
V. L. Manjrekar (3)
118† Hyderabad .. 1955-56

177   Delhi....... 1955-56
102* Madras 1964-65
V. Mankad (2)
223   Bombay 1955-56
231   Madras 1955-56
Nawab of Pataudi jun. (2)
153   Calcutta 1964-65
113   Delhi....... 1964-65
G. S. Ramchand (1)
106* Calcutta 1955-56
Pankaj Roy (2)
100   Calcutta 1955-56
173   Madras 1955-56

D. N. Sardesai (2)
200* Bombay 1964-65
106   Delhi....... 1964-65
N. S. Sidhu (1)
116† Bangalore ... 1988-89
P. R. Umrigar (1)
223† Hyderabad .. 1955-56
G. R. Viswanath (1)
103* Kanpur 1976-77
A. L. Wadekar (1)
143   Wellington .. 1967-68

† *Signifies hundred on first appearance in New Zealand–India Tests. B. R. Taylor provides the only instance for New Zealand of a player scoring his maiden hundred in first-class cricket in his first Test.*

RECORD PARTNERSHIPS FOR EACH WICKET

For New Zealand

149	for 1st	T. J. Franklin and J. G. Wright at Napier....................	1989-90
155	for 2nd	G. T. Dowling and B. E. Congdon at Dunedin	1967-68
222*	for 3rd	B. Sutcliffe and J. R. Reid at Delhi	1955-56
125	for 4th	J. G. Wright and M. J. Greatbatch at Christchurch	1989-90
119	for 5th	G. T. Dowling and K. Thomson at Christchurch	1967-68
87	for 6th	J. W. Guy and A. R. MacGibbon at Hyderabad	1955-56
163	for 7th	B. Sutcliffe and B. R. Taylor at Calcutta	1964-65
103	for 8th	R. J. Hadlee and I. D. S. Smith at Auckland	1989-90
136	for 9th†	I. D. S. Smith and M. C. Snedden at Auckland	1989-90
61	for 10th	J. T. Ward and R. O. Collinge at Madras	1964-65

For India

413	for 1st†	V. Mankad and Pankaj Roy at Madras	1955-56
204	for 2nd	S. M. Gavaskar and S. Amarnath at Auckland	1975-76
238	for 3rd	P. R. Umrigar and V. L. Manjrekar at Hyderabad	1955-56
171	for 4th	P. R. Umrigar and A. G. Kripal Singh at Hyderabad ...	1955-56
127	for 5th	V. L. Manjrekar and G. S. Ramchand at Delhi	1955-56
193*	for 6th	D. N. Sardesai and Hanumant Singh at Bombay	1964-65
128	for 7th	S. R. Tendulkar and K. S. More at Napier.............	1989-90
143	for 8th†	R. G. Nadkarni and F. M. Engineer at Madras.........	1964-65
105	for 9th	{ S. M. H. Kirmani and B. S. Bedi at Bombay.............	1976-77
		{ S. M. H. Kirmani and N. S. Yadav at Auckland.........	1980-81
57	for 10th	R. B. Desai and B. S. Bedi at Dunedin	1967-68

† *Denotes record partnership against all countries.*

TEN WICKETS OR MORE IN A MATCH

For New Zealand (2)

11-58 (4-35, 7-23)	R. J. Hadlee, Wellington	1975-76
10-88 (6-49, 4-39)	R. J. Hadlee, Bombay	1988-89

For India (2)

11-140 (3-64, 8-76)	E. A. S. Prasanna, Auckland.......................	1975-76
12-152 (8-72, 4-80)	S. Venkataraghavan, Delhi	1964-65

NEW ZEALAND v PAKISTAN

Season	New Zealand		Pakistan	T	NZ	P	D
		Captains					
1955-56P	H. B. Cave		A. H. Kardar	3	0	2	1
1964-65N	J. R. Reid		Hanif Mohammad	3	0	0	3
1964-65P	J. R. Reid		Hanif Mohammad	3	0	2	1
1969-70P	G. T. Dowling		Intikhab Alam	3	1	0	2
1972-73N	B. E. Congdon		Intikhab Alam	3	0	1	2
1976-77P	G. M. Turner[1]		Mushtaq Mohammad	3	0	2	1
1978-79N	M. G. Burgess		Mushtaq Mohammad	3	0	1	2
1984-85P	J. V. Coney		Zaheer Abbas	3	0	2	1
1984-85N	G. P. Howarth		Javed Miandad	3	2	0	1
1988-89N†	J. G. Wright		Imran Khan	2	0	0	2
1990-91P	M. D. Crowe		Javed Miandad	3	0	3	0
1992-93N	K. R. Rutherford		Javed Miandad	1	0	1	0
	In Pakistan			18	1	11	6
	In New Zealand			15	2	3	10
	Totals...........................			33	3	14	16

N Played in New Zealand. P Played in Pakistan.
† *The First Test at Dunedin was abandoned without a ball being bowled and is excluded.*

Note: The following deputised for the official touring captain:
[1]J. M. Parker (Third).

HIGHEST INNINGS TOTALS

For New Zealand in New Zealand 492 at Wellington.....................		1984-85
in Pakistan: 482-6 dec. at Lahore		1964-65
For Pakistan in New Zealand: 616-5 dec. at Auckland.....................		1988-89
in Pakistan: 565-9 dec. at Karachi		1976-77

LOWEST INNINGS TOTALS

For New Zealand in New Zealand: 93 at Hamilton		1992-93
in Pakistan: 70 at Dacca		1955-56
For Pakistan in New Zealand: 169 at Auckland		1984-85
in Pakistan: 102 at Faisalabad		1990-91

INDIVIDUAL HUNDREDS

For New Zealand (19)

M. G. Burgess (2)
119* Dacca 1969-70
111   Lahore 1976-77
J. V. Coney (1)
111* Dunedin 1984-85
M. D. Crowe (2)
174   Wellington .. 1988-89
108* Lahore 1990-91
B. A. Edgar (1)
129† Christchurch. 1978-79
M. J. Greatbatch (1)
133   Hamilton .. 1992-93

B. F. Hastings (1)
110   Auckland ... 1972-73
G. P. Howarth (1)
114   Napier 1978-79
W. K. Lees (1)
152   Karachi 1976-77
S. N. McGregor (1)
111   Lahore 1955-56
R. E. Redmond (1)
107† Auckland ... 1972-73
J. F. Reid (3)
106   Hyderabad .. 1984-85

148   Wellington .. 1984-85
158* Auckland ... 1984-85
J. R. Reid (1)
128   Karachi 1964-65
B. W. Sinclair (1)
130   Lahore 1964-65
G. M. Turner (1)
110† Dacca 1969-70
J. G. Wright (1)
107   Karachi 1984-85

For Pakistan (33)

Asif Iqbal (3)
175   Dunedin 1972-73
166   Lahore 1976-77
104   Napier 1978-79
Hanif Mohammad (3)
103   Dacca 1955-56
100* Christchurch. 1964-65
203* Lahore 1964-65
Imtiaz Ahmed (1)
209   Lahore 1955-56
Javed Miandad (7)
163† Lahore 1976-77
206   Karachi 1976-77
160* Christchurch. 1978-79
104   ⎫ Hyderabad .. 1984-85
103* ⎭

118   Wellington .. 1988-89
271   Auckland ... 1988-89
Majid Khan (3)
110   Auckland ... 1972-73
112   Karachi 1976-77
119* Napier 1978-79
Mohammad Ilyas (1)
126   Karachi 1964-65
Mudassar Nazar (1)
106   Hyderabad .. 1984-85
Mushtaq Mohammad (3)
201   Dunedin 1972-73
101   Hyderabad .. 1976-77
107   Karachi 1976-77

Sadiq Mohammad (2)
166   Wellington .. 1972-73
103* Hyderabad .. 1976-77
Saeed Ahmed (1)
172   Karachi 1964-65
Salim Malik (1)
119* Karachi 1984-85
Shoaib Mohammad (5)
163   Wellington .. 1988-89
112   Auckland ... 1988-89
203* Karachi 1990-91
105   Lahore 1990-91
142   Faisalabad .. 1990-91
Waqar Hassan (1)
189   Lahore 1955-56
Zaheer Abbas (1)
135   Auckland ... 1978-79

† *Signifies hundred on first appearance in New Zealand–Pakistan Tests.*

Notes: Mushtaq and Sadiq Mohammad, at Hyderabad in 1976-77, provide the fourth instance in Test matches, after the Chappells (thrice), of brothers each scoring hundreds in the same innings.

Shoaib Mohammad scored his first four hundreds in this series in successive innings.

RECORD PARTNERSHIPS FOR EACH WICKET

For New Zealand

159 for 1st	R. E. Redmond and G. M. Turner at Auckland	1972-73
195 for 2nd	J. G. Wright and G. P. Howarth at Napier.................	1978-79
178 for 3rd	B. W. Sinclair and J. R. Reid at Lahore	1964-65
128 for 4th	B. F. Hastings and M. G. Burgess at Wellington	1972-73
183 for 5th†	M. G. Burgess and R. W. Anderson at Lahore	1976-77
145 for 6th	J. F. Reid and R. J. Hadlee at Wellington	1984-85
186 for 7th†	W. K. Lees and R. J. Hadlee at Karachi.................	1976-77
100 for 8th	B. W. Yuile and D. R. Hadlee at Karachi................	1969-70
96 for 9th	M. G. Burgess and R. S. Cunis at Dacca.................	1969-70
151 for 10th†	B. F. Hastings and R. O. Collinge at Auckland	1972-73

For Pakistan

172 for 1st	Ramiz Raja and Shoaib Mohammad at Karachi.............	1990-91
114 for 2nd	Mohammad Ilyas and Saeed Ahmed at Rawalpindi	1964-65
248 for 3rd	Shoaib Mohammad and Javed Miandad at Auckland.........	1988-89
350 for 4th†	Mushtaq Mohammad and Asif Iqbal at Dunedin	1972-73

281 for 5th†	Javed Miandad and Asif Iqbal at Lahore	1976-77
217 for 6th†	Hanif Mohammad and Majid Khan at Lahore	1964-65
308 for 7th†	Waqar Hassan and Imtiaz Ahmed at Lahore	1955-56
89 for 8th	Anil Dalpat and Iqbal Qasim at Karachi	1984-85
52 for 9th	Intikhab Alam and Arif Butt at Auckland	1964-65
65 for 10th	Salah-ud-Din and Mohammad Farooq at Rawalpindi	1964-65

† *Denotes record partnership against all countries.*

TEN WICKETS OR MORE IN A MATCH

For New Zealand (1)

11-152 (7-52, 4-100)	C. Pringle, Faisalabad	1990-91

For Pakistan (6)

10-182 (5-91, 5-91)	Intikhab Alam, Dacca	1969-70
11-130 (7-52, 4-78)	Intikhab Alam, Dunedin	1972-73
10-106 (3-20, 7-86)	Waqar Younis, Lahore	1990-91
12-130 (7-76, 5-54)	Waqar Younis, Faisalabad	1990-91
10-128 (5-56, 5-72)	Wasim Akram, Dunedin	1984-85
11-79 (5-37, 6-42)†	Zulfiqar Ahmed, Karachi	1955-56

† *Signifies ten wickets or more on first appearance in New Zealand–Pakistan Tests.*

Note: Waqar Younis's performances were in successive matches.

NEW ZEALAND v SRI LANKA

	Captains					
Season	New Zealand	Sri Lanka	T	NZ	SL	D
1982-83N	G. P. Howarth	D. S. de Silva	2	2	0	0
1983-84S	G. P. Howarth	L. R. D. Mendis	3	2	0	1
1986-87S†	J. J. Crowe	L. R. D. Mendis	1	0	0	1
1990-91N	M. D. Crowe[1]	A. Ranatunga	3	0	0	3
1992-93S	M. D. Crowe	A. Ranatunga	2	0	1	1
	In New Zealand		5	2	0	3
	In Sri Lanka		6	2	1	3
	Totals		11	4	1	6

N Played in New Zealand. S Played in Sri Lanka.

† *The Second and Third Tests were cancelled owing to civil disturbances.*

Note: The following was appointed by the home authority for only a minor proportion of the series:

[1]I. D. S. Smith (Third).

HIGHEST INNINGS TOTALS

For New Zealand in New Zealand: 671-4 at Wellington	1990-91
in Sri Lanka: 459 at Colombo (CCC)	1983-84
For Sri Lanka in New Zealand: 497 at Wellington	1990-91
in Sri Lanka: 397-9 dec. at Colombo (CCC)	1986-87

LOWEST INNINGS TOTALS

For New Zealand in New Zealand: 174 at Wellington	1990-91
in Sri Lanka: 102 at Colombo (SSC)	1992-93
For Sri Lanka in New Zealand: 93 at Wellington	1982-83
in Sri Lanka: 97 at Kandy	1983-84

INDIVIDUAL HUNDREDS

For New Zealand (10)

J. J. Crowe (1)
120* Colombo (CCC) 1986-87

M. D. Crowe (2)
299 Wellington .. 1990-91
107 Colombo (SSC) 1992-93

R. J. Hadlee (1)
151* Colombo (CCC) 1986-87

A. H. Jones (3)
186 Wellington .. 1990-91
122 } Hamilton ... 1990-91
100* }

J. F. Reid (1)
180 Colombo (CCC) 1983-84

K. R. Rutherford (1)
105 Moratuwa ... 1992-93

J. G. Wright (1)
101 Hamilton ... 1990-91

For Sri Lanka (8)

P. A. de Silva (2)
267† Wellington .. 1990-91
123 Auckland ... 1990-91

R. L. Dias (1)
108† Colombo (SSC) 1983-84

A. P. Gurusinha (2)
119 } Hamilton ... 1990-91
102 }

D. S. B. P. Kuruppu (1)
201*† Colombo (CCC) 1986-87

R. S. Mahanama (2)
153 Moratuwa ... 1992-93
109 Colombo (SSC) 1992-93

† *Signifies hundred on first appearance in New Zealand–Sri Lanka Tests.*

Note: A. P. Gurusinha and A. H. Jones at Hamilton in 1990-91 provided the second instance of a player on each side hitting two separate hundreds in a Test match.

RECORD PARTNERSHIPS FOR EACH WICKET

For New Zealand

161 for 1st	T. J. Franklin and J. G. Wright at Hamilton	1990-91
76 for 2nd	J. G. Wright and A. H. Jones at Auckland	1990-91
467 for 3rd†‡	A. H. Jones and M. D. Crowe at Wellington	1990-91
82 for 4th	J. F. Reid and S. L. Boock at Colombo (CCC)	1983-84
151 for 5th	K. R. Rutherford and C. Z. Harris at Moratuwa	1992-93
246* for 6th†	J. J. Crowe and R. J. Hadlee at Colombo (CCC)	1986-87
30 for 7th {	R. J. Hadlee and I. D. S. Smith at Kandy	1983-84
{	R. J. Hadlee and J. J. Crowe at Kandy	1983-84
79 for 8th	J. V. Coney and W. K. Lees at Christchurch	1983-84
42 for 9th	W. K. Lees and M. C. Snedden at Christchurch	1982-83
52 for 10th	W. K. Lees and E. J. Chatfield at Christchurch	1982-83

For Sri Lanka

102 for 1st	R. S. Mahanama and U. C. Hathurusinghe at Colombo (SSC)	1992-93
137 for 2nd	R. S. Mahanama and A. P. Gurusinha at Moratuwa	1992-93
159* for 3rd†¹	S. Wettimuny and R. L. Dias at Colombo (SSC)	1983-84
178 for 4th	P. A. de Silva and A. Ranatunga at Wellington	1990-91
130 for 5th	R. S. Madugalle and D. S. de Silva at Wellington	1982-83
109* for 6th²	R. S. Madugalle and A. Ranatunga at Colombo (CCC)	1983-84
55 for 7th	A. P. Gurusinha and A. Ranatunga at Hamilton	1990-91
69 for 8th	H. P. Tillekeratne and S. D. Anurasiri at Colombo (SSC)	1992-93
31 for 9th {	G. F. Labrooy and R. J. Ratnayake at Auckland	1990-91
{	S. T. Jayasuriya and R. J. Ratnayake at Auckland	1990-91
60 for 10th	V. B. John and M. J. G. Amerasinghe at Kandy	1983-84

† *Denotes record partnership against all countries.*

‡ *Record third-wicket partnership in first-class cricket.*

¹ *163 runs were added for this wicket in two separate partnerships: S. Wettimuny retired hurt and was replaced by L. R. D. Mendis when 159 had been added.*

² *119 runs were added for this wicket in two separate partnerships: R. S. Madugalle retired hurt and was replaced by D. S. de Silva when 109 had been added.*

TEN WICKETS OR MORE IN A MATCH

For New Zealand (1)

10-102 (5-73, 5-29)   R. J. Hadlee, Colombo (CCC) 1983-84

Note: The best match figures by a Sri Lankan bowler are 8-159 (5-86, 3-73), V. B. John at Kandy, 1983-84.

NEW ZEALAND v ZIMBABWE

Season	New Zealand	Captains Zimbabwe	T	NZ	Z	D
1992-93Z	M. D. Crowe	D. L. Houghton	2	1	0	1

Z Played in Zimbabwe.

HIGHEST INNINGS TOTALS

For New Zealand: 335 at Harare 1992-93

For Zimbabwe: 283-9 dec. at Harare 1992-93

INDIVIDUAL HUNDREDS

For New Zealand (2)

M. D. Crowe (1)   **R. T. Latham** (1)
140   Harare ..... 1992-93 │ 119† Bulawayo ... 1992-93

For Zimbabwe (1)

K. J. Arnott (1)
101*† Bulawayo ... 1992-93

† *Signifies hundred on first appearance in New Zealand–Zimbabwe Tests.*

HUNDRED PARTNERSHIPS

For New Zealand

168 for 4th	M. D. Crowe and K. R. Rutherford at Harare	1992-93
130 for 5th	K. R. Rutherford and D. N. Patel at Harare	1992-93
127 for 2nd	R. T. Latham and A. H. Jones at Bulawayo	1992-93
116 for 1st	M. J. Greatbatch and R. T. Latham at Bulawayo	1992-93
102 for 1st	M. J. Greatbatch and R. T. Latham at Bulawayo	1992-93

For Zimbabwe

107 for 2nd†	K. J. Arnott and A. D. R. Campbell at Harare	1992-93
105* for 2nd	K. J. Arnott and A. D. R. Campbell at Bulawayo	1992-93

† *Denotes record partnership against all countries.*

BEST MATCH BOWLING ANALYSES

For New Zealand

8-131 (2-81, 6-50) D. N. Patel, Harare 1992-93

For Zimbabwe

4-101 (3-49, 1-52) D. H. Brain, Harare 1992-93

INDIA v PAKISTAN

Season	India		Pakistan	T	I	P	D
		Captains					
1952-53*I*	L. Amarnath		A. H. Kardar	5	2	1	2
1954-55*P*	V. Mankad		A. H. Kardar	5	0	0	5
1960-61*I*	N. J. Contractor		Fazal Mahmood	5	0	0	5
1978-79*P*	B. S. Bedi		Mushtaq Mohammad	3	0	2	1
1979-80*I*	S. M. Gavaskar[1]		Asif Iqbal	6	2	0	4
1982-83*P*	S. M. Gavaskar		Imran Khan	6	0	3	3
1983-84*I*	Kapil Dev		Zaheer Abbas	3	0	0	3
1984-85*P*	S. M. Gavaskar		Zaheer Abbas	2	0	0	2
1986-87*I*	Kapil Dev		Imran Khan	5	0	1	4
1989-90*I*	K. Srikkanth		Imran Khan	4	0	0	4
	In India			24	4	2	18
	In Pakistan			20	0	5	15
	Totals			44	4	7	33

I Played in India.   P Played in Pakistan.

Note: The following was appointed by the home authority for only a minor proportion of the series:

[1]G. R. Viswanath (Sixth).

HIGHEST INNINGS TOTALS

For India in India: 539-9 dec. at Madras 1960-61
    in Pakistan: 509 at Lahore 1989-90

For Pakistan in India: 487-9 dec. at Madras 1986-87
    in Pakistan: 699-5 at Lahore 1989-90

LOWEST INNINGS TOTALS

For India in India: 106 at Lucknow 1952-53
    in Pakistan: 145 at Karachi 1954-55

For Pakistan in India: 116 at Bangalore 1986-87
    in Pakistan: 158 at Dacca 1954-55

INDIVIDUAL HUNDREDS

For India (31)

M. Amarnath (4)
109* Lahore 1982-83
120   Lahore 1982-83
103* Karachi 1982-83
101* Lahore 1984-85
M. Azharuddin (3)
141   Calcutta 1986-87
110   Jaipur 1986-87
109   Faisalabad . . 1989-90
C. G. Borde (1)
177* Madras 1960-61
A. D. Gaekwad (1)
201   Jullundur . . . 1983-84
S. M. Gavaskar (5)
111 ⎱
137 ⎰ Karachi 1978-79

166   Madras 1979-80
127*‡ Faisalabad . . 1982-83
103* Bangalore . . . 1983-84
V. S. Hazare (1)
146* Bombay 1952-53
S. V. Manjrekar (2)
113*† Karachi 1989-90
218   Lahore 1989-90
S. M. Patil (1)
127   Faisalabad . . 1984-85
R. J. Shastri (3)
128   Karachi 1982-83
139   Faisalabad . . 1984-85
125   Jaipur 1986-87
R. H. Shodhan (1)
110† Calcutta 1952-53

K. Srikkanth (1)
123   Madras 1986-87
P. R. Umrigar (5)
102   Bombay 1952-53
108   Peshawar . . . 1954-55
115   Kanpur 1960-61
117   Madras 1960-61
112   Delhi 1960-61
D. B. Vengsarkar (2)
146* Delhi 1979-80
109   Ahmedabad . . 1986-87
G. R. Viswanath (1)
145† Faisalabad . . 1978-79

For Pakistan (41)

Aamer Malik (2)
117   Faisalabad . . 1989-90
113   Lahore 1989-90
Alim-ud-Din (1)
103* Karachi 1954-55
Asif Iqbal (1)
104† Faisalabad . . 1978-79
Hanif Mohammad (2)
142   Bahawalpur . . 1954-55
160   Bombay 1960-61
Ijaz Faqih (1)
105† Ahmedabad . 1986-87
Imtiaz Ahmed (1)
135   Madras 1960-61
Imran Khan (3)
117   Faisalabad . . 1982-83
135* Madras 1986-87
109* Karachi 1989-90
Javed Miandad (5)
154*† Faisalabad . . 1978-79
100   Karachi 1978-79

126   Faisalabad . . 1982-83
280* Hyderabad . . 1982-83
145   Lahore 1989-90
Mohsin Khan (1)
101*† Lahore 1982-83
Mudassar Nazar (6)
126   Bangalore . . . 1979-80
119   Karachi 1982-83
231   Hyderabad . . 1982-83
152*‡ Lahore 1982-83
152   Karachi 1982-83
199   Faisalabad . . 1984-85
Mushtaq Mohammad (1)
101   Delhi 1960-61
Nazar Mohammad (1)
124*‡ Lucknow 1952-53
Qasim Omar (1)
210   Faisalabad . . 1984-85
Ramiz Raja (1)
114   Jaipur 1986-87

Saeed Ahmed (2)
121† Bombay 1960-61
103   Madras 1960-61
Salim Malik (3)
107   Faisalabad . . 1982-83
102* Faisalabad . . 1984-85
102* Karachi 1989-90
Shoaib Mohammad (2)
101   Madras 1986-87
203* Lahore 1989-90
Wasim Raja (1)
125   Jullundur . . . 1983-84
Zaheer Abbas (6)
176† Faisalabad . . 1978-79
235* Lahore 1978-79
215   Lahore 1982-83
186   Karachi 1982-83
168   Faisalabad . . 1982-83
168* Lahore 1984-85

† Signifies hundred on first appearance in India–Pakistan Tests.
‡ Carried his bat.

RECORD PARTNERSHIPS FOR EACH WICKET

For India

200 for 1st	S. M. Gavaskar and K. Srikkanth at Madras	1986-87
135 for 2nd	N. S. Sidhu and S. V. Manjrekar at Karachi.	1989-90
190 for 3rd	M. Amarnath and Yashpal Sharma at Lahore.	1982-83
186 for 4th	S. V. Manjrekar and R. J. Shastri at Lahore.	1989-90
200 for 5th	S. M. Patil and R. J. Shastri at Faisalabad	1984-85
143 for 6th	M. Azharuddin and Kapil Dev at Calcutta	1986-87
155 for 7th	R. M. H. Binny and Madan Lal at Bangalore	1983-84
122 for 8th	S. M. H. Kirmani and Madan Lal at Faisalabad	1982-83
149 for 9th†	P. G. Joshi and R. B. Desai at Bombay	1960-61
109 for 10th†	H. R. Adhikari and Ghulam Ahmed at Delhi.	1952-53

For Pakistan

162 for 1st	Hanif Mohammad and Imtiaz Ahmed at Madras	1960-61
250 for 2nd	Mudassar Nazar and Qasim Omar at Faisalabad............	1984-85
451 for 3rd†	Mudassar Nazar and Javed Miandad at Hyderabad..........	1982-83
287 for 4th	Javed Miandad and Zaheer Abbas at Faisalabad............	1982-83
213 for 5th	Zaheer Abbas and Mudassar Nazar at Karachi	1982-83
207 for 6th	Salim Malik and Imran Khan at Faisalabad................	1982-83
154 for 7th	Imran Khan and Ijaz Faqih at Ahmedabad................	1986-87
112 for 8th	Imran Khan and Wasim Akram at Madras	1986-87
60 for 9th	Wasim Bari and Iqbal Qasim at Bangalore................	1979-80
104 for 10th	Zulfiqar Ahmed and Amir Elahi at Madras	1952-53

† *Denotes record partnership against all countries.*

TEN WICKETS OR MORE IN A MATCH

For India (3)

11-146 (4-90, 7-56)	Kapil Dev, Madras	1979-80
10-126 (7-27, 3-99)	Maninder Singh, Bangalore	1986-87
13-131 (8-52, 5-79)†	V. Mankad, Delhi......................................	1952-53

For Pakistan (5)

12-94 (5-52, 7-42)	Fazal Mahmood, Lucknow...............................	1952-53
11-79 (3-19, 8-60)	Imran Khan, Karachi	1982-83
11-180 (6-98, 5-82)	Imran Khan, Faisalabad	1982-83
10-175 (4-135, 6-40)	Iqbal Qasim, Bombay	1979-80
11-190 (8-69, 3-121)	Sikander Bakht, Delhi	1979-80

† *Signifies ten wickets or more on first appearance in India–Pakistan Tests.*

INDIA v SRI LANKA

	Captains					
Season	India	Sri Lanka	T	I	SL	D
1982-83*I*	S. M. Gavaskar	B. Warnapura	1	0	0	1
1985-86*S*	Kapil Dev	L. R. D. Mendis	3	0	1	2
1986-87*I*	Kapil Dev	L. R. D. Mendis	3	2	0	1
1990-91*I*	M. Azharuddin	A. Ranatunga	1	1	0	0
1993-94*S*	M. Azharuddin	A. Ranatunga	3	1	0	2
	In India		5	3	0	2
	In Sri Lanka		6	1	1	4
	Totals..................		11	4	1	6

I Played in India. S Played in Sri Lanka.

HIGHEST INNINGS TOTALS

For India in India: 676-7 at Kanpur.....................		1986-87
in Sri Lanka: 446 at Colombo (PSS)		1993-94
For Sri Lanka in India: 420 at Kanpur.....................		1986-87
in Sri Lanka: 385 at Colombo (PSS)		1985-86

LOWEST INNINGS TOTALS

For India in India: 288 at Chandigarh		1990-91
in Sri Lanka: 198 at Colombo (PSS)		1985-86
For Sri Lanka in India: 82 at Chandigarh		1990-91
in Sri Lanka: 198 at Kandy		1985-86

INDIVIDUAL HUNDREDS

For India (13)

M. Amarnath (2)	**V. G. Kambli** (2)	**N. S. Sidhu** (1)
116* Kandy..... 1985-86	125 Colombo (SSC) 1993-94	104 Colombo (SSC) 1993-94
131 Nagpur..... 1986-87	120 Colombo (PSS) 1993-94	**S. R. Tendulkar** (1)
M. Azharuddin (1)	**Kapil Dev** (1)	104* Colombo (SSC) 1993-94
199 Kanpur..... 1986-87	163 Kanpur..... 1986-87	**D. B. Vengsarkar** (2)
S. M. Gavaskar (2)	**S. M. Patil** (1)	153 Nagpur..... 1986-87
155† Madras..... 1982-83	114*† Madras..... 1982-83	166 Cuttack..... 1986-87
176 Kanpur..... 1986-87		

For Sri Lanka (9)

P. A. de Silva (1)	**R. S. Mahanama** (1)	**A. Ranatunga** (1)
148 Colombo (PSS) 1993-94	151 Colombo (PSS) 1993-94	111 Colombo
R. L. Dias (1)	**L. R. D. Mendis** (3)	(SSC)..... 1985-86
106 Kandy...... 1985-86	105 ⎫ †Madras..... 1982-83	**S. A. R. Silva** (1)
R. S. Madugalle (1)	105 ⎬	111 Colombo
103 Colombo	124 Kandy...... 1985-86	(PSS)..... 1985-86
(SSC)..... 1985-86		

† Signifies hundred on first appearance in India–Sri Lanka Tests.

RECORD PARTNERSHIPS FOR EACH WICKET

For India

171	for 1st	M. Prabhakar and N. S. Sidhu at Colombo (SSC)...........	1993-94
173	for 2nd	S. M. Gavaskar and D. B. Vengsarkar at Madras...........	1982-83
173	for 3rd	M. Amarnath and D. B. Vengsarkar at Nagpur...........	1986-87
163	for 4th	S. M. Gavaskar and M. Azharuddin at Kanpur...........	1986-87
78	for 5th	M. Amarnath and M. Azharuddin at Kandy...........	1985-86
272	for 6th	M. Azharuddin and Kapil Dev at Kanpur...........	1986-87
78*	for 7th	S. M. Patil and Madan Lal at Madras...........	1982-83
70	for 8th	Kapil Dev and L. Sivaramakrishnan at Colombo (PSS)...........	1985-86
28	for 9th	Kapil Dev and R. K. Chauhan at Colombo (PSS)...........	1993-94
29	for 10th	Kapil Dev and Chetan Sharma at Colombo (PSS)...........	1985-86

For Sri Lanka

159	for 1st†	S. Wettimuny and J. R. Ratnayeke at Kanpur...........	1986-87
95	for 2nd	S. A. R. Silva and R. S. Madugalle at Colombo (PSS)...........	1985-86
153	for 3rd	R. L. Dias and L. R. D. Mendis at Madras...........	1982-83
216	for 4th	R. L. Dias and L. R. D. Mendis at Kandy...........	1985-86
144	for 5th	R. S. Madugalle and A. Ranatunga at Colombo (SSC)...........	1985-86
89	for 6th	L. R. D. Mendis and A. N. Ranasinghe at Madras...........	1982-83
77	for 7th	R. S. Madugalle and D. S. de Silva at Madras...........	1982-83
40*	for 8th	P. A. de Silva and A. L. F. de Mel at Kandy...........	1985-86
60	for 9th	H. P. Tillekeratne and A. W. R. Madurasinghe at Chandigarh.	1990-91
44	for 10th	R. J. Ratnayake and E. A. R. de Silva at Nagpur...........	1986-87

† Denotes record partnership against all countries.

TEN WICKETS OR MORE IN A MATCH

For India (1)

10-107 (3-56, 7-51)	Maninder Singh, Nagpur...........................	1986-87

Note: The best match figures by a Sri Lankan bowler are 9-125 (4-76, 5-49) by R. J. Ratnayake against India at Colombo (PSS), 1985-86.

INDIA v ZIMBABWE

Captains

Season	India	Zimbabwe	T	I	Z	D
1992-93Z	M. Azharuddin	D. L. Houghton	1	0	0	1
1992-93I	M. Azharuddin	D. L. Houghton	1	1	0	0
	In India...........................		1	1	0	0
	In Zimbabwe		1	0	0	1
	Totals...........................		2	1	0	1

I Played in India.   Z Played in Zimbabwe.

HIGHEST INNINGS TOTALS

For India: 536-7 dec. at Delhi 1992-93

For Zimbabwe: 456 at Harare 1992-93

INDIVIDUAL HUNDREDS

For India (2)

V. G. Kambli (1)	**S. V. Manjrekar** (1)
227† Delhi....... 1992-93	104† Harare 1992-93

For Zimbabwe (2)

A. Flower (1)	**D. L. Houghton** (1)
115 Delhi....... 1992-93	121† Harare 1992-93

† *Signifies hundred on first appearance in India–Zimbabwe Tests.*

HUNDRED PARTNERSHIPS

For India

137 for 3rd	V. G. Kambli and S. R. Tendulkar at Delhi	1992-93
107 for 2nd	N. S. Sidhu and V. G. Kambli at Delhi.....................	1992-93
107 for 4th	V. G. Kambli and M. Azharuddin at Delhi..................	1992-93

For Zimbabwe

192 for 4th†	G. W. Flower and A. Flower at Delhi	1992-93
165 for 6th†	D. L. Houghton and A. Flower at Harare	1992-93
100 for 1st†	K. J. Arnott and G. W. Flower at Harare	1992-93

† *Denotes record partnership against all countries.*

BEST MATCH BOWLING ANALYSES

For India

8-160 (3-90, 5-70)   A. Kumble, Delhi.................................... 1992-93

For Zimbabwe

5-86 (5-86)   A. J. Traicos, Harare 1992-93

PAKISTAN v SRI LANKA

		Captains				
Season	*Pakistan*	*Sri Lanka*	*T*	*P*	*SL*	*D*
1981-82*P*	Javed Miandad	B. Warnapura[1]	3	2	0	1
1985-86*P*	Javed Miandad	L. R. D. Mendis	3	2	0	1
1985-86*S*	Imran Khan	L. R. D. Mendis	3	1	1	1
1991-92*P*	Imran Khan	P. A. de Silva	3	1	0	2
	In Pakistan		9	5	0	4
	In Sri Lanka		3	1	1	1
	Totals...............		12	6	1	5

P Played in Pakistan.   S Played in Sri Lanka.

Note: The following deputised for the official touring captain:
[1]L. R. D. Mendis (Second).

HIGHEST INNINGS TOTALS

For Pakistan in Pakistan: 555-3 at Faisalabad 1985-86
     in Sri Lanka: 318 at Colombo (PSS)................... 1985-86

For Sri Lanka in Pakistan: 479 at Faisalabad 1985-86
     in Sri Lanka: 323-3 at Colombo (PSS) 1985-86

LOWEST INNINGS TOTALS

For Pakistan in Pakistan: 221 at Faisalabad 1991-92
     in Sri Lanka: 132 at Colombo (CCC)................ 1985-86

For Sri Lanka in Pakistan: 149 at Karachi 1981-82
     in Sri Lanka: 101 at Kandy 1985-86

INDIVIDUAL HUNDREDS

For Pakistan (8)

Haroon Rashid (1)
153† Karachi 1981-82
Javed Miandad (1)
203* Faisalabad .. 1985-86
Mohsin Khan (1)
129 Lahore 1981-82
Qasim Omar (1)
206† Faisalabad .. 1985-86

Ramiz Raja (1)
122 Colombo
 (PSS)....... 1985-86
Salim Malik (2)
100*† Karachi 1981-82
101 Sialkot 1991-92
Zaheer Abbas (1)
134† Lahore 1981-82

For Sri Lanka (6)

P. A. de Silva (2)
122† Faisalabad .. 1985-86
105 Karachi 1985-86
R. L. Dias (1)
109 Lahore 1981-82
A. P. Gurusinha (1)
116* Colombo
 (PSS)....... 1985-86

A. Ranatunga (1)
135* Colombo
 (PSS)....... 1985-86
S. Wettimuny (1)
157 Faisalabad .. 1981-82

† *Signifies hundred on first appearance in Pakistan–Sri Lanka Tests.*

RECORD PARTNERSHIPS FOR EACH WICKET

For Pakistan

128 for 1st	Ramiz Raja and Shoaib Mohammad at Sialkot...............	1991-92
151 for 2nd	Mohsin Khan and Majid Khan at Lahore...................	1981-82
397 for 3rd	Qasim Omar and Javed Miandad at Faisalabad.............	1985-86
162 for 4th	Salim Malik and Javed Miandad at Karachi...............	1981-82
132 for 5th	Salim Malik and Imran Khan at Sialkot.................	1991-92
100 for 6th	Zaheer Abbas and Imran Khan at Lahore.................	1981-82
104 for 7th	Haroon Rashid and Tahir Naqqash at Karachi............	1981-82
29 for 8th	{ Ashraf Ali and Iqbal Qasim at Faisalabad............	1981-82
	Salim Yousuf and Abdul Qadir at Sialkot............	1985-86
	Salim Yousuf and Abdul Qadir at Karachi............	1985-86
127 for 9th	Haroon Rashid and Rashid Khan at Karachi.............	1981-82
48 for 10th	Rashid Khan and Tauseef Ahmed at Faisalabad	1981-82

For Sri Lanka

81 for 1st	R. S. Mahanama and U. C. Hathurusinghe at Faisalabad......	1991-92
217 for 2nd†	S. Wettimuny and R. L. Dias at Faisalabad..............	1981-82
85 for 3rd	S. Wettimuny and R. L. Dias at Faisalabad.............	1985-86
240* for 4th†	A. P. Gurusinha and A. Ranatunga at Colombo (PSS).....	1985-86
58 for 5th	R. L. Dias and L. R. D. Mendis at Lahore..............	1981-82
121 for 6th	A. Ranatunga and P. A. de Silva at Faisalabad..........	1985-86
66 for 7th	P. A. de Silva and J. R. Ratnayake at Faisalabad........	1985-86
61 for 8th†	R. S. Madugalle and D. S. de Silva at Faisalabad........	1981-82
52 for 9th	P. A. de Silva and R. J. Ratnayake at Faisalabad........	1985-86
36 for 10th	R. J. Ratnayake and R. G. C. E. Wijesuriya at Faisalabad.....	1985-86

† Denotes record partnership against all countries.

TEN WICKETS OR MORE IN A MATCH

For Pakistan (1)

14-116 (8-58, 6-58)	Imran Khan, Lahore	1981-82

Note: The best match figures by a Sri Lankan bowler are 9-162 (4-103, 5-59), D. S. de Silva at Faisalabad, 1981-82.

TEST MATCH GROUNDS

In Chronological Sequence

	City and Ground	First Test Match		Tests
1.	Melbourne, Melbourne Cricket Ground	March 15, 1877	A v E	85
2.	London, Kennington Oval	September 6, 1880	E v A	76
3.	Sydney, Sydney Cricket Ground (No. 1)	February 17, 1882	A v E	79
4.	Manchester, Old Trafford	July 11, 1884	E v A	60
5.	London, Lord's	July 21, 1884	E v A	90
6.	Adelaide, Adelaide Oval	December 12, 1884	A v E	51
7.	Port Elizabeth, St George's Park	March 12, 1889	SA v E	13
8.	Cape Town, Newlands	March 25, 1889	SA v E	25
9.	Johannesburg, Old Wanderers	March 2, 1896	SA v E	22
	Now the site of Johannesburg Railway Station.			
10.	Nottingham, Trent Bridge	June 1, 1899	E v A	41
11.	Leeds, Headingley	June 29, 1899	E v A	55
12.	Birmingham, Edgbaston	May 29, 1902	E v A	30

	City and Ground	*First Test Match*		*Tests*
13.	Sheffield, Bramall Lane	July 3, 1902	E v A	1
	Sheffield United Football Club have built a stand over the cricket pitch.			
14.	Durban, Lord's	January 21, 1910	SA v E	4
	Ground destroyed and built on.			
15.	Durban, Kingsmead	January 18, 1923	SA v E	20
16.	Brisbane, Exhibition Ground	November 30, 1928	A v E	2
	No longer used for cricket.			
17.	Christchurch, Lancaster Park	January 10, 1930	NZ v E	31
18.	Bridgetown, Kensington Oval	January 11, 1930	WI v E	29
19.	Wellington, Basin Reserve	January 24, 1930	NZ v E	28
20.	Port-of-Spain, Queen's Park Oval	February 1, 1930	WI v E	42
21.	Auckland, Eden Park	February 17, 1930	NZ v E	35
22.	Georgetown, Bourda	February 21, 1930	WI v E	22
23.	Kingston, Sabina Park	April 3, 1930	WI v E	29
24.	Brisbane, Woolloongabba	November 27, 1931	A v SA	35
25.	Bombay, Gymkhana Ground	December 15, 1933	I v E	1
	No longer used for first-class cricket.			
26.	Calcutta, Eden Gardens	January 5, 1934	I v E	27
27.	Madras, Chepauk (Chidambaram Stadium)	February 10, 1934	I v E	21
28.	Delhi, Feroz Shah Kotla	November 10, 1948	I v WI	23
29.	Bombay, Brabourne Stadium	December 9, 1948	I v WI	17
	Rarely used for first-class cricket.			
30.	Johannesburg, Ellis Park	December 27, 1948	SA v E	6
	Mainly a rugby stadium, no longer used for cricket.			
31.	Kanpur, Green Park (Modi Stadium)	January 12, 1952	I v E	16
32.	Lucknow, University Ground	October 25, 1952	I v P	1
	Ground destroyed, now partly under a river bed.			
33.	Dacca, Dacca Stadium	January 1, 1955	P v I	7
	Ceased staging Tests after East Pakistan seceded and became Bangladesh.			
34.	Bahawalpur, Dring (now Bahawal) Stadium	January 15, 1955	P v I	1
	Still used for first-class cricket.			
35.	Lahore, Lawrence Gardens (Bagh-i-Jinnah)	January 29, 1955	P v I	3
	Still used for club and occasional first-class matches.			
36.	Peshawar, Services Club Ground	February 13, 1955	P v I	1
	Superseded by new stadium.			
37.	Karachi, National Stadium	February 26, 1955	P v I	30
38.	Dunedin, Carisbrook	March 11, 1955	NZ v E	8
39.	Hyderabad, Fateh Maidan (Lal Bahadur Stadium)	November 19, 1955	I v NZ	3
40.	Madras, Corporation Stadium	January 6, 1956	I v NZ	9
	Superseded by rebuilt Chepauk Stadium.			
41.	Johannesburg, New Wanderers	December 24, 1956	SA v E	12
42.	Lahore, Gaddafi Stadium	November 21, 1959	P v A	25
43.	Rawalpindi, Pindi Club Ground	March 27, 1965	P v NZ	1
	Superseded by new stadium.			
44.	Nagpur, Vidarbha C.A. Ground	October 3, 1969	I v NZ	3
45.	Perth, Western Australian C.A. Ground	December 11, 1970	A v E	20
46.	Hyderabad, Niaz Stadium	March 16, 1973	P v E	5
47.	Bangalore, Karnataka State C.A. Ground (Chinnaswamy Stadium)	November 22, 1974	I v WI	9
48.	Bombay, Wankhede Stadium	January 23, 1975	I v WI	14
49.	Faisalabad, Iqbal Stadium	October 16, 1978	P v I	16
50.	Napier, McLean Park	February 16, 1979	NZ v P	1
51.	Multan, Ibn-e-Qasim Bagh Stadium	December 30, 1980	P v WI	1
52.	St John's (Antigua), Recreation Ground	March 27, 1981	WI v E	7
53.	Colombo, P. Saravanamuttu Stadium	February 17, 1982	SL v E	5
54.	Kandy, Asgiriya Stadium	April 22, 1983	SL v A	5
55.	Jullundur, Burlton Park	September 24, 1983	I v P	1
56.	Ahmedabad, Gujarat Stadium	November 12, 1983	I v WI	2

City and Ground	First Test Match		Tests
57. Colombo, Sinhalese Sports Club Ground	March 16, 1984	SL v NZ	8
58. Colombo, Colombo Cricket Club Ground	March 24, 1984	SL v NZ	2
59. Sialkot, Jinnah Stadium	October 27, 1985	P v SL	3
60. Cuttack, Barabati Stadium	January 4, 1987	I v SL	1
61. Jaipur, Sawai Mansingh Stadium	February 21, 1987	I v P	1
62. Hobart, Bellerive Oval	December 16, 1989	A v SL	1
63. Chandigarh, Sector 16 Stadium	November 23, 1990	I v SL	1
64. Hamilton, Trust Bank (Seddon) Park	February 22, 1991	NZ v SL	2
65. Gujranwala, Municipal Stadium	December 20, 1991	P v SL	1
66. Colombo, Khettarama Stadium	August 28, 1992	SL v A	1
67. Moratuwa, Tyronne Fernando Stadium	September 8, 1992	SL v A	3
68. Harare, Harare Sports Club	October 18, 1992	Z v I	2
69. Bulawayo, Bulawayo Athletic Club	November 1, 1992	Z v NZ	1

FAMILIES IN TEST CRICKET

FATHERS AND SONS

England

M. C. Cowdrey (114 Tests, 1954-55–1974-75) and C. S. Cowdrey (6 Tests, 1984-85–1988).

J. Hardstaff (5 Tests, 1907-08) and J. Hardstaff jun. (23 Tests, 1935–1948).

L. Hutton (79 Tests, 1937–1954-55) and R. A. Hutton (5 Tests, 1971).

F. T. Mann (5 Tests, 1922-23) and F. G. Mann (7 Tests, 1948-49–1949).

J. H. Parks (1 Test, 1937) and J. M. Parks (46 Tests, 1954–1967-68).

M. J. Stewart (8 Tests, 1962–1963-64) and A. J. Stewart (32 Tests, 1989-90–1993).

F. W. Tate (1 Test, 1902) and M. W. Tate (39 Tests, 1924–1935).

C. L. Townsend (2 Tests, 1899) and D. C. H. Townsend (3 Tests, 1934-35).

Australia

E. J. Gregory (1 Test, 1876-77) and S. E. Gregory (58 Tests, 1890–1912).

South Africa

F. Hearne (4 Tests, 1891-92–1895-96) and G. A. L. Hearne (3 Tests, 1922-23–1924).
F. Hearne also played 2 Tests for England in 1888-89.

J. D. Lindsay (3 Tests, 1947) and D. T. Lindsay (19 Tests, 1963-64–1969-70).

A. W. Nourse (45 Tests, 1902-03–1924) and A. D. Nourse (34 Tests, 1935–1951).

L. R. Tuckett (1 Test, 1913-14) and L. Tuckett (9 Tests, 1947–1948-49).

West Indies

G. A. Headley (22 Tests, 1929-30–1953-54) and R. G. A. Headley (2 Tests, 1973).

O. C. Scott (8 Tests, 1928–1930-31) and A. P. H. Scott (1 Test, 1952-53).

New Zealand

W. M. Anderson (1 Test, 1945-46) and R. W. Anderson (9 Tests, 1976-77–1978).

W. P. Bradburn (2 Tests, 1963-64) and G. E. Bradburn (4 Tests, 1990-91).

B. L. Cairns (43 Tests, 1973-74–1985-86) and C. L. Cairns (7 Tests, 1989-90–1992-93).

W. A. Hadlee (11 Tests, 1937–1950-51) and D. R. Hadlee (26 Tests, 1969–1977-78); Sir R. J. Hadlee (86 Tests, 1972-73–1990).

P. G. Z. Harris (9 Tests, 1955-56–1964-65) and C. Z. Harris (4 Tests, 1992-93).

H. G. Vivian (7 Tests, 1931–1937) and G. E. Vivian (5 Tests, 1964-65–1971-72).

India

L. Amarnath (24 Tests, 1933-34–1952-53) and M. Amarnath (69 Tests, 1969-70–1987-88); S. Amarnath (10 Tests, 1975-76–1978-79).

D. K. Gaekwad (11 Tests, 1952–1960-61) and A. D. Gaekwad (40 Tests, 1974-75–1984-85).

Nawab of Pataudi (Iftikhar Ali Khan) (3 Tests, 1946) and Nawab of Pataudi (Mansur Ali Khan) (46 Tests, 1961-62–1974-75).
Nawab of Pataudi sen. also played 3 Tests for England, 1932-33–1934.

V. L. Manjrekar (55 Tests, 1951-52–1964-65) and S. V. Manjrekar (26 Tests, 1987-88–1992-93).
V. Mankad (44 Tests, 1946–1958-59) and A. V. Mankad (22 Tests, 1969-70–1977-78).
Pankaj Roy (43 Tests, 1951-52–1960-61) and Pranab Roy (2 Tests, 1981-82).

India and Pakistan
M. Jahangir Khan (4 Tests, 1932–1936) and Majid Khan (63 Tests, 1964-65–1982-83).
S. Wazir Ali (7 Tests, 1932–1936) and Khalid Wazir (2 Tests, 1954).

Pakistan
Hanif Mohammad (55 Tests, 1954–1969-70) and Shoaib Mohammad (39 Tests, 1983-84–1992).
Nazar Mohammad (5 Tests, 1952-53) and Mudassar Nazar (76 Tests, 1976-77–1988-89).

GRANDFATHERS AND GRANDSONS

Australia
V. Y. Richardson (19 Tests, 1924-25–1935-36) and G. S. Chappell (87 Tests, 1970-71–1983-84);
   I. M. Chappell (75 Tests, 1964-65–1979-80); T. M. Chappell (3 Tests, 1981).

GREAT-GRANDFATHER AND GREAT-GRANDSON

Australia
W. H. Cooper (2 Tests, 1881-82 and 1884-85) and A. P. Sheahan (31 Tests, 1967-68–1973-74).

BROTHERS IN SAME TEST TEAM

England
E. M., G. F. and W. G. Grace: 1 Test, 1880.
C. T. and G. B. Studd: 4 Tests, 1882-83.
A. and G. G. Hearne: 1 Test, 1891-92.
   F. Hearne, their brother, played in this match for South Africa.
D. W. and P. E. Richardson: 1 Test, 1957.

Australia
E. J. and D. W. Gregory: 1 Test, 1876-77.
C. and A. C. Bannerman: 1 Test, 1878-79.
G. and W. F. Giffen: 2 Tests, 1891-92.
G. H. S. and A. E. Trott: 3 Tests, 1894-95.
I. M. and G. S. Chappell: 43 Tests, 1970-71–1979-80.
S. R. and M. E. Waugh: 15 Tests, 1990-91–1993 – the first instance of twins appearing together.

South Africa
S. J. and S. D. Snooke: 1 Test, 1907.
D. and H. W. Taylor: 2 Tests, 1913-14.
R. H. M. and P. A. M. Hands: 1 Test, 1913-14.
E. A. B. and A. M. B. Rowan: 9 Tests, 1948-49–1951.
P. M. and R. G. Pollock: 23 Tests, 1963-64–1969-70.
A. J. and D. B. Pithey: 5 Tests, 1963-64.

West Indies
G. C. and R. S. Grant: 4 Tests, 1934-35.
J. B. and V. H. Stollmeyer: 1 Test, 1939.
D. St E. and E. St E. Atkinson: 1 Test, 1957-58.

New Zealand
J. J. and M. D. Crowe: 34 Tests, 1983–1989-90.
D. R. and R. J. Hadlee: 10 Tests, 1973–1977-78.
H. J. and G. P. Howarth: 4 Tests, 1974-75–1976-77.
J. M. and N. M. Parker: 3 Tests, 1976-77.
B. P. and J. G. Bracewell: 1 Test, 1980-81.

India

S. Wazir Ali and S. Nazir Ali: 2 Tests, 1932–1933-34.
L. Ramji and Amar Singh: 1 Test, 1933-34.
C. K. and C. S. Nayudu: 4 Tests, 1933-34–1936.
A. G. Kripal Singh and A. G. Milkha Singh: 1 Test, 1961-62.
S. and M. Amarnath: 8 Tests, 1975-76–1978-79.

Pakistan

Wazir and Hanif Mohammad: 18 Tests, 1952-53–1959-60.
Wazir and Mushtaq Mohammad: 1 Test, 1958-59.
Hanif and Mushtaq Mohammad: 19 Tests, 1960-61–1969-70.
Hanif, Mushtaq and Sadiq Mohammad: 1 Test, 1969-70.
Mushtaq and Sadiq Mohammad: 26 Tests, 1969-70–1978-79.
Wasim and Ramiz Raja: 2 Tests, 1983-84.

Sri Lanka

A. and D. Ranatunga: 2 Tests, 1989-90.
M. D. and S. Wettimuny: 2 Tests, 1982-83.

Zimbabwe

A. and G. W. Flower: 4 Tests, 1992-93.

LIMITED-OVERS INTERNATIONAL RECORDS

Note: Limited-overs international matches do not have first-class status.

SUMMARY OF ALL LIMITED-OVERS INTERNATIONALS

To October 27, 1993

	Opponents	Matches	Won by												Tied	NR
			E	A	I	NZ	P	SA	SL	WI	Z	B	C	EA		
England	Australia	55	25	28	–	–	–	–	–	–	–	–	–	–	1	1
	India	29	16	–	13	–	–	–	–	–	–	–	–	–	–	–
	New Zealand	40	20	–	–	17	–	–	–	–	–	–	–	–	–	3
	Pakistan	36	23	–	–	–	12	–	–	–	–	–	–	–	–	1
	South Africa	2	2	–	–	–	–	0	–	–	–	–	–	–	–	–
	Sri Lanka	11	8	–	–	–	–	–	3	–	–	–	–	–	–	–
	West Indies	43	18	–	–	–	–	–	–	23	–	–	–	–	–	2
	Zimbabwe	1	0	–	–	–	–	–	–	–	1	–	–	–	–	–
	Canada	1	1	–	–	–	–	–	–	–	–	–	0	–	–	–
	East Africa	1	1	–	–	–	–	–	–	–	–	–	–	0	–	–
Australia	India	40	–	24	13	–	–	–	–	–	–	–	–	–	–	3
	New Zealand	55	–	37	–	16	–	–	–	–	–	–	–	–	–	2
	Pakistan	38	–	18	–	–	17	–	–	–	–	–	–	–	1	2
	South Africa	1	–	0	–	–	–	1	–	–	–	–	–	–	–	–
	Sri Lanka	24	–	17	–	–	–	–	5	–	–	–	–	–	–	2
	West Indies	69	–	26	–	–	–	–	–	41	–	–	–	–	1	1
	Zimbabwe	5	–	4	–	–	–	–	–	–	1	–	–	–	–	–
	Bangladesh	1	–	1	–	–	–	–	–	–	–	0	–	–	–	–
	Canada	1	–	1	–	–	–	–	–	–	–	–	0	–	–	–
India	New Zealand	29	–	–	16	13	–	–	–	–	–	–	–	–	–	–
	Pakistan	38	–	–	12	–	24	–	–	–	–	–	–	–	–	2
	South Africa	11	–	–	4	–	–	7	–	–	–	–	–	–	–	–
	Sri Lanka	29	–	–	18	–	–	–	9	–	–	–	–	–	–	2
	West Indies	40	–	–	10	–	–	–	–	29	–	–	–	–	1	–
	Zimbabwe	9	–	–	9	–	–	–	–	–	0	–	–	–	–	–
	Bangladesh	2	–	–	2	–	–	–	–	–	–	0	–	–	–	–
	East Africa	1	–	–	1	–	–	–	–	–	–	–	–	0	–	–
New Zealand	Pakistan	28	–	–	–	13	14	–	–	–	–	–	–	–	–	1
	South Africa	1	–	–	–	1	–	0	–	–	–	–	–	–	–	–
	Sri Lanka	26	–	–	–	19	–	–	6	–	–	–	–	–	–	1
	West Indies	14	–	–	–	2	–	–	–	11	–	–	–	–	–	1
	Zimbabwe	5	–	–	–	5	–	–	–	–	0	–	–	–	–	–
	Bangladesh	1	–	–	–	1	–	–	–	–	–	0	–	–	–	–
	East Africa	1	–	–	–	1	–	–	–	–	–	–	–	0	–	–
Pakistan	South Africa	4	–	–	–	–	3	1	–	–	–	–	–	–	–	–
	Sri Lanka	38	–	–	–	–	30	–	7	–	–	–	–	–	–	1
	West Indies	70	–	–	–	–	20	–	–	48	–	–	–	–	2	–
	Zimbabwe	3	–	–	–	–	3	–	–	–	0	–	–	–	–	–
	Bangladesh	2	–	–	–	–	2	–	–	–	–	0	–	–	–	–
	Canada	1	–	–	–	–	1	–	–	–	–	–	0	–	–	–
South Africa	Sri Lanka	4	–	–	–	–	–	1	2	–	–	–	–	–	–	1
	West Indies	7	–	–	–	–	–	3	–	4	–	–	–	–	–	–
	Zimbabwe	1	–	–	–	–	–	1	–	–	0	–	–	–	–	–
Sri Lanka	West Indies	12	–	–	–	–	–	–	1	11	–	–	–	–	–	–
	Zimbabwe	2	–	–	–	–	–	–	2	–	0	–	–	–	–	–
	Bangladesh	3	–	–	–	–	–	–	3	–	–	0	–	–	–	–
West Indies	Zimbabwe	3	–	–	–	–	–	–	–	3	0	–	–	–	–	–
		838	114	156	98	88	126	14	38	170	2	0	0	0	6	26

	Matches	Won	Lost	Tied	No Result	% Won (excl. NR)
West Indies	258	170	80	4	4	66.92
Australia	289	156	119	3	11	56.11
England	219	114	97	1	7	53.77
Pakistan	258	126	122	3	7	50.19
South Africa	31	14	16	–	1	46.66
New Zealand	200	88	104	–	8	45.83
India	228	98	122	1	7	44.34
Sri Lanka	149	38	104	–	7	26.76
Zimbabwe	29	2	27	–	–	6.89
Bangladesh	9	0	9	0	0	0
Canada	3	0	3	0	0	0
East Africa	3	0	3	0	0	0

MOST RUNS

	M	I	NO	R	HS	100s	Avge
D. L. Haynes (West Indies)	225	224	28	8,194	152*	16	41.80
Javed Miandad (Pakistan)	222	211	40	7,233	119*	8	42.29
I. V. A. Richards (West Indies)	187	167	24	6,721	189*	11	47.00
A. R. Border (Australia)	255	237	36	6,171	127*	3	30.70
D. M. Jones (Australia)	150	147	25	5,599	145	7	45.89
R. B. Richardson (West Indies)	185	178	23	5,306	122	5	34.23
C. G. Greenidge (West Indies)	128	127	13	5,134	133*	11	45.03
Ramiz Raja (Pakistan)	159	158	11	4,915	119*	8	33.43
D. C. Boon (Australia)	142	138	10	4,524	122	5	35.34
M. D. Crowe (New Zealand)	133	132	18	4,412	105*	3	38.70
G. R. Marsh (Australia)	117	115	6	4,357	126*	9	39.97
Salim Malik (Pakistan)	170	158	19	4,335	102	5	31.18
G. A. Gooch (England)	120	117	6	4,206	142	8	37.89
M. Azharuddin (India)	157	144	27	4,114	108*	3	35.16
K. Srikkanth (India)	146	145	4	4,092	123	4	29.02
A. J. Lamb (England)	122	118	16	4,010	118	4	39.31

Leading aggregates for other countries are:

A. Ranatunga (Sri Lanka)	124	117	21	3,201	88*	0	33.34
K. C. Wessels (South Africa)	31	31	2	1,134	90	0	39.10
D. L. Houghton (Zimbabwe)	29	28	0	835	142	1	29.82

Note: K. C. Wessels also scored 1,740 runs for Australia.

HIGHEST INDIVIDUAL SCORE FOR EACH COUNTRY

189*	I. V. A. Richards	West Indies v England at Manchester	1984
175*	Kapil Dev	India v Zimbabwe at Tunbridge Wells	1983
171*	G. M. Turner	New Zealand v East Africa at Birmingham	1975
167*	R. A. Smith	England v Australia at Birmingham	1993
145	D. M. Jones	Australia v England at Brisbane	1990-91
142	D. L. Houghton	Zimbabwe v New Zealand at Hyderabad (India) . .	1987-88
126*	Shoaib Mohammad	Pakistan v New Zealand at Wellington	1988-89
121	R. L. Dias	Sri Lanka v India at Bangalore	1982-83
108	A. C. Hudson	South Africa v India at Bloemfontein	1992-93

MOST HUNDREDS

Total		E	A	SA	WI	NZ	I	P	SL	Z
16	D. L. Haynes (West Indies)	1	6	0	–	2	2	4	1	0
11	C. G. Greenidge (West Indies) . .	0	1	–	3	3	2	1	1
11	I. V. A. Richards (West Indies)..	3	3	–	1	3	0	1	0
9	G. R. Marsh (Australia)	1	–	0	2	2	3	1	0	0
8	G. A. Gooch (England)	–	4	0	1	1	1	1	0	0
8	Javed Miandad (Pakistan)	1	0	1	1	0	3	–	2	0
8	Ramiz Raja (Pakistan)	1	0	0	1	3	0	–	3	0
7	D. I. Gower (England)	–	2	–	0	3	0	1	1	–
7	D. M. Jones (Australia)	3	–	0	0	2	0	1	1	0
7	Zaheer Abbas (Pakistan)	0	2	–	0	1	3	–	1	0

HIGHEST PARTNERSHIP FOR EACH WICKET

212	for 1st	G. R. Marsh and D. C. Boon	A v I	Jaipur	1986-87
221	for 2nd	C. G. Greenidge and I. V. A. Richards	WI v I	Jamshedpur	1983-84
224*	for 3rd	D. M. Jones and A. R. Border	A v SL	Adelaide	1984-85
173	for 4th	D. M. Jones and S. R. Waugh	A v P	Perth	1986-87
152	for 5th	I. V. A. Richards and C. H. Lloyd	I v SL	Brisbane	1984-85
154	for 6th	R. B. Richardson and P. J. L. Dujon	WI v P	Sharjah	1991-92
115	for 7th	P. J. L. Dujon and M. D. Marshall	WI v P	Gujranwala	1986-87
117	for 8th	D. L. Houghton and I. P. Butchart	Z v NZ	Hyderabad (India)	1987-88
126*	for 9th	Kapil Dev and S. M. H. Kirmani	I v Z	Tunbridge Wells	1983
106*	for 10th	I. V. A. Richards and M. A. Holding	WI v E	Manchester	1984

MOST WICKETS

	M	Balls	R	W	BB	4W/i	Avge
Kapil Dev (India)	208	10,512	6,511	243	5-43	4	26.79
Wasim Akram (Pakistan)	153	7,837	4,995	215	5-16	12	23.23
Imran Khan (Pakistan)	175	7,461	4,845	182	6-14	4	26.62
R. J. Hadlee (New Zealand) . . .	115	6,182	3,407	158	5-25	6	21.56
M. D. Marshall (West Indies)..	136	7,175	4,233	157	4-18	6	26.96
C. J. McDermott (Australia)...	104	5,647	3,862	155	5-44	5	24.91
J. Garner (West Indies)	98	5,330	2,752	146	5-31	5	18.84
I. T. Botham (England)	116	6,271	4,139	145	4-31	3	28.54
M. A. Holding (West Indies) ..	102	5,473	3,034	142	5-26	6	21.36
S. R. Waugh (Australia)	147	5,985	4,448	141	4-33	2	31.54
E. J. Chatfield (New Zealand)..	114	6,065	3,618	140	5-34	4	25.84
C. E. L. Ambrose (West Indies)	91	4,956	2,852	139	5-17	8	20.51
Abdul Qadir (Pakistan)	102	4,996	3,375	131	5-44	6	25.76
R. J. Shastri (India)	150	6,613	4,650	129	5-15	3	36.04
Waqar Younis (Pakistan)	74	3,637	2,526	127	6-26	11	19.88
C. A. Walsh (West Indies)	111	5,991	3,849	124	5-1	6	31.04
M. Prabhakar (India).	94	4,630	3,164	119	4-19	4	26.58
I. V. A. Richards (West Indies)	187	5,644	4,228	118	6-41	3	35.83
M. C. Snedden (New Zealand) .	93	4,525	3,237	114	4-34	1	28.39
Mudassar Nazar (Pakistan). . . .	122	4,855	3,431	111	5-28	2	30.90
S. P. O'Donnell (Australia) . . .	87	4,350	3,102	108	5-13	6	28.72
D. K. Lillee (Australia)	63	3,593	2,145	103	5-34	6	20.82

Leading aggregates for other countries are:

	M	Balls	R	W	BB	4W/i	Avge
J. R. Ratnayeke (Sri Lanka) . . .	78	3,573	2,866	85	4-23	1	33.71
A. A. Donald (South Africa) . . .	30	1,660	1,056	45	5-29	1	23.46
E. A. Brandes (Zimbabwe)	19	992	816	26	4-21	1	31.38

BEST BOWLING FOR EACH COUNTRY

7-37	Aqib Javed	Pakistan v India at Sharjah	1991-92
7-51	W. W. Davis	West Indies v Australia at Leeds	1983
6-14	G. J. Gilmour	Australia v England at Leeds	1975
6-29	S. T. Jayasuriya	Sri Lanka v England at Moratuwa	1992-93
5-15	R. J. Shastri	India v Australia at Perth	1991-92
5-20	V. J. Marks	England v New Zealand at Wellington	1983-84
5-23	R. O. Collinge	New Zealand v India at Christchurch	1975-76
5-29	A. A. Donald	South Africa v India at Calcutta	1991-92
4-21	E. A. Brandes	Zimbabwe v England at Albury	1991-92

HAT-TRICKS

Jalal-ud-Din	Pakistan v Australia at Hyderabad	1982-83
B. A. Reid	Australia v New Zealand at Sydney	1985-86
Chetan Sharma	India v New Zealand at Nagpur	1987-88
Wasim Akram	Pakistan v West Indies at Sharjah	1989-90
Wasim Akram	Pakistan v Australia at Sharjah	1989-90
Kapil Dev	India v Sri Lanka at Calcutta	1990-91
Aqib Javed	Pakistan v India at Sharjah	1991-92

MOST DISMISSALS IN AN INNINGS

5 (all ct)	R. W. Marsh	Australia v England at Leeds	1981
5 (all ct)	R. G. de Alwis	Sri Lanka v Australia at Colombo (PSS)	1982-83
5 (all ct)	S. M. H. Kirmani	India v Zimbabwe at Leicester	1983
5 (3ct, 2st)	S. Viswanath	India v England at Sydney	1984-85
5 (3ct, 2st)	K. S. More	India v New Zealand at Sharjah	1987-88
5 (all ct)	H. P. Tillekeratne	Sri Lanka v Pakistan at Sharjah	1990-91

MOST DISMISSALS IN A CAREER

	M	Ct	St	Total
P. J. L. Dujon (West Indies)	169	183	21	204
R. W. Marsh (Australia)	92	120	4	124
I. A. Healy (Australia)	91	105	12	117
Salim Yousuf (Pakistan)	86	81	22	103
K. S. More (India)	94	63	27	90
I. D. S. Smith (New Zealand)	98	81	5	86
Wasim Bari (Pakistan)	51	52	10	62

MOST CATCHES IN AN INNINGS

(Excluding wicket-keepers)

4	Salim Malik	Pakistan v New Zealand at Sialkot	1984-85
4	S. M. Gavaskar	India v Pakistan at Sharjah	1984-85
4	R. B. Richardson	West Indies v England at Birmingham	1991
4	K. C. Wessels	South Africa v West Indies at Kingston	1991-92
4	M. A. Taylor	Australia v West Indies at Sydney	1992-93
4	C. L. Hooper	West Indies v Pakistan at Durban	1992-93

Note: While fielding as substitute, J. G. Bracewell held 4 catches for New Zealand v Australia at Adelaide, 1980-81.

MOST CATCHES IN A CAREER

	M	Ct		M	Ct
A. R. Border (A)	255	118	Kapil Dev (I)	208	65
I. V. A. Richards (WI)	187	101	R. B. Richardson (WI)	185	65
Javed Miandad (P)	222	68	M. D. Crowe (NZ)	133	64

ALL-ROUND
1,000 Runs and 100 Wickets

	M	R	W
I. T. Botham (England)..........	116	2,113	145
R. J. Hadlee (New Zealand).......	115	1,751	158
Imran Khan (Pakistan)...........	175	3,709	182
Kapil Dev (India)	208	3,672	243
Mudassar Nazar (Pakistan).......	122	2,653	111
S. P. O'Donnell (Australia).......	87	1,242	108
M. Prabhakar (India)...........	94	1,010	119
I. V. A. Richards (West Indies)....	187	6,721	118
R. J. Shastri (India).............	150	3,108	129
Wasim Akram (Pakistan).........	153	1,327	215
S. R. Waugh (Australia)	147	2,916	141

1,000 Runs and 100 Dismissals

	M	R	D
P. J. L. Dujon (West Indies)	169	1,945	204
R. W. Marsh (Australia)..........	92	1,225	124

TEAM RECORDS
HIGHEST INNINGS TOTALS

363-7	(55 overs)	England v Pakistan at Nottingham.................	1992
360-4	(50 overs)	West Indies v Sri Lanka at Karachi..............	1987-88
338-4	(50 overs)	New Zealand v Bangladesh at Sharjah.............	1989-90
338-5	(60 overs)	Pakistan v Sri Lanka at Swansea	1983
334-4	(60 overs)	England v India at Lord's	1975
333-8	(45 overs)	West Indies v India at Jamshedpur	1983-84
333-9	(60 overs)	England v Sri Lanka at Taunton.................	1983
332-3	(50 overs)	Australia v Sri Lanka at Sharjah...............	1989-90
330-6	(60 overs)	Pakistan v Sri Lanka at Nottingham	1975

Highest totals by other countries are:

313-7	(49.2 overs)	Sri Lanka v Zimbabwe at New Plymouth	1991-92
312-4	(50 overs)	Zimbabwe v Sri Lanka at New Plymouth	1991-92
299-4	(40 overs)	India v Sri Lanka at Bombay	1986-87
288-2	(46.4 overs)	South Africa v India at Delhi	1991-92

HIGHEST TOTALS BATTING SECOND
Winning

313-7	(49.2 overs)	Sri Lanka v Zimbabwe at New Plymouth	1991-92
298-6	(54.5 overs)	New Zealand v England at Leeds.................	1990
297-6	(48.5 overs)	New Zealand v England at Adelaide	1982-83

Losing

289-7	(40 overs)	Sri Lanka v India at Bombay	1986-87
288-9	(60 overs)	Sri Lanka v Pakistan at Swansea	1983
288-8	(50 overs)	Sri Lanka v Pakistan at Adelaide	1989-90

HIGHEST MATCH AGGREGATES

626-14	(120 overs)	Pakistan v Sri Lanka at Swansea	1983
625-11	(99.2 overs)	Sri Lanka v Zimbabwe at New Plymouth	1991-92
619-19	(118 overs)	England v Sri Lanka at Taunton.................	1983
604-9	(120 overs)	Australia v Sri Lanka at The Oval	1975
603-11	(100 overs)	Pakistan v Sri Lanka at Adelaide	1989-90

LOWEST INNINGS TOTALS

43	(19.5 overs)	Pakistan v West Indies at Cape Town	1992-93
45	(40.3 overs)	Canada v England at Manchester....................	1979
55	(28.3 overs)	Sri Lanka v West Indies at Sharjah	1986-87
63	(25.5 overs)	India v Australia at Sydney........................	1980-81
64	(35.5 overs)	New Zealand v Pakistan at Sharjah	1985-86
70	(25.2 overs)	Australia v England at Birmingham	1977
70	(26.3 overs)	Australia v New Zealand at Adelaide	1985-86

Note: This section does not take into account those matches in which the number of overs was reduced.

Lowest totals by other countries are:

87	(29.3 overs)	West Indies v Australia at Sydney	1992-93
93	(36.2 overs)	England v Australia at Leeds	1975
134	(46.1 overs)	Zimbabwe v England at Albury	1991-92
152	(43.4 overs)	South Africa v West Indies at Port-of-Spain	1991-92

LARGEST VICTORIES

232 runs	Australia (323-2 in 50 overs) v Sri Lanka (91 in 35.5 overs) at Adelaide.. 1984-85
206 runs	New Zealand (276-7 in 50 overs) v Australia (70 in 26.3 overs) at Adelaide.. 1985-86
202 runs	England (334-4 in 60 overs) v India (132-3 in 60 overs) at Lord's 1975

By ten wickets: There have been nine instances of victory by ten wickets.

TIED MATCHES

West Indies 222-5 (50 overs) v Australia 222-9 (50 overs) at Melbourne........	1983-84
England 226-5 (55 overs) v Australia 226-8 (55 overs) at Nottingham..........	1989
West Indies 186-5 (39 overs) v Pakistan 186-9 (39 overs) at Lahore	1991-92
India 126 (47.4 overs) v West Indies 126 (41 overs) at Perth	1991-92
Australia 228-7 (50 overs) v Pakistan 228-9 (50 overs) at Hobart	1992-93
Pakistan 244-6 (50 overs) v West Indies 244-5 (50 overs) at Georgetown	1992-93

MOST APPEARANCES

(175 or more)

	Total	E	A	SA	WI	NZ	I	P	SL	Z	C	B
A. R. Border (A).......	255	43	–	1	61	48	38	34	23	5	1	1
D. L. Haynes (WI).....	225	31	64	7	–	13	40	59	9	2	–	–
Javed Miandad (P).....	222	26	35	3	62	23	34	–	34	3	1	1
Kapil Dev (I)	208	23	40	11	39	25	–	32	28	8	–	2
I. V. A. Richards (WI)..	187	36	54	–	–	12	31	41	11	2	–	–
R. B. Richardson (WI)..	185	27	45	7	–	11	29	56	9	1	–	–
Imran Khan (P)	175	20	29	1	49	12	29	–	32	1	1	1

Most appearances for other countries:

	Total	E	A	SA	WI	NZ	I	P	SL	Z	C	B
J. G. Wright (NZ)	149	30	42	–	11	–	21	18	24	2	–	1
A. Ranatunga (SL)	124	9	20	4	8	22	25	32	–	2	–	2
A. J. Lamb (E)	122	–	23	1	26	28	15	22	6	1	–	–
K. C. Wessels (SA).....	31	2	1	–	7	1	11	4	4	1	–	–
D. L. Houghton (Z)	29	1	5	1	3	5	9	3	2	–	–	–

Note: K. C. Wessels also appeared 54 times for Australia.

WORLD CUP RECORDS 1975-1992

RESULTS SUMMARY

	Played	Won	Lost	No Result
England	34	23	10	1
West Indies	32	22	9	1
Australia.........	30	17	13	0
Pakistan	31	17	13	1
New Zealand	29	16	13	0
India	29	14	14	1
South Africa	9	5	4	0
Sri Lanka	26	4	20	2
Zimbabwe	20	2	18	0
Canada	3	0	3	0
East Africa.......	3	0	3	0

WORLD CUP FINALS

1975	WEST INDIES (291-8) beat Australia (274) by 17 runs	Lord's
1979	WEST INDIES (286-9) beat England (194) by 92 runs	Lord's
1983	INDIA (183) beat West Indies (140) by 43 runs	Lord's
1987-88	AUSTRALIA (253-5) beat England (246-8) by seven runs	Calcutta
1991-92	PAKISTAN (249-6) beat England (227) by 22 runs	Melbourne

BATTING RECORDS

Most Runs

	M	I	NO	R	HS	100s	Avge
Javed Miandad (P)	28	27	4	1,029	103	1	44.73
I. V. A. Richards (WI)....	23	21	4	1,013	181	3	59.58
G. A. Gooch (E).........	21	21	1	897	115	1	44.85
M. D. Crowe (NZ)	21	21	5	880	100*	1	55.00
D. L. Haynes (WI)	25	25	2	854	105	1	37.13
D. C. Boon (A)..........	16	16	1	815	100	2	54.33

Highest Score

181   I. V. A. Richards   WI v SL   Karachi   1987-88

Hundred Before Lunch

101   A. Turner   A v SL   The Oval   1975

Most Hundreds

3   I. V. A. Richards (WI), Ramiz Raja (P)

Highest Partnership for Each Wicket

182	for 1st	R. B. McCosker and A. Turner	A v SL	The Oval	1975
176	for 2nd	D. L. Amiss and K. W. R. Fletcher	E v I	Lord's	1975
195*	for 3rd	C. G. Greenidge and H. A. Gomes	WI v Z	Worcester	1983
149	for 4th	R. B. Kanhai and C. H. Lloyd	WI v A	Lord's	1975
145*	for 5th	A. Flower and A. C. Waller	Z v SL	New Plymouth	1991-92
144	for 6th	Imran Khan and Shahid Mahboob	P v SL	Leeds	1983
75*	for 7th	D. A. G. Fletcher and I. P. Butchart	Z v A	Nottingham	1983
117	for 8th	D. L. Houghton and I. P. Butchart	Z v NZ	Hyderabad (India)	1987-88
126*	for 9th	Kapil Dev and S. M. H. Kirmani	I v Z	Tunbridge Wells	1983
71	for 10th	A. M. E. Roberts and J. Garner	WI v I	Manchester	1983

BOWLING RECORDS

Most Wickets

	Balls	R	W	BB	4W/i	Avge
Imran Khan (P)	1,017	655	34	4-37	2	19.26
I. T. Botham (E)..........	1,332	862	30	4-31	1	28.73
Kapil Dev (I)	1,422	892	28	5-43	1	31.85
A. M. E. Roberts (WI)	1,021	552	26	3-32	0	21.23
C. J. McDermott (A).......	876	587	26	5-44	2	22.57
Wasim Akram (P)	918	633	25	4-32	1	25.32

Best Bowling

7-51   W. W. Davis   WI v A   Leeds   1983

Hat-trick

Chetan Sharma   I v NZ   Nagpur   1987-88

Most Economical Bowling

12-8-6-1   B. S. Bedi   I v EA   Leeds   1975

Most Expensive Bowling

12-1-105-2   M. C. Snedden   NZ v E   The Oval   1983

WICKET-KEEPING RECORDS

Most Dismissals

Wasim Bari (P)	22	(18 ct, 4 st)
P. J. L. Dujon (WI)	20	(19 ct, 1 st)
R. W. Marsh (A)..........	18	(17 ct, 1 st)
K. S. More (I)	18	(12 ct, 6 st)
D. L. Murray (WI)	16	(16 ct)
D. J. Richardson (SA)	15	(14 ct, 1 st)

Most Dismissals in an Innings

5 (5 ct)   S. M. H. Kirmani   I v Z   Leicester   1983

FIELDING RECORDS

Most Catches

C. H. Lloyd (WI)	12		I. T. Botham (E)	10
Kapil Dev (I)	12		A. R. Border (A)	10
D. L. Haynes (WI)	12			

Most Catches in an Innings

3	C. H. Lloyd	WI v SL	Manchester	1975
3	D. A. Reeve	E v P	Adelaide	1991-92
3	Ijaz Ahmed	P v A	Perth	1991-92
3	A. R. Border	A v Z	Hobart	1991-92

MOST APPEARANCES

28   Imran Khan (P), Javed Miandad (P)
26   Kapil Dev (I)
25   A. R. Border (A), D. L. Haynes (WI)

TEAM RECORDS

Highest Total	360-4	West Indies v Sri Lanka	Karachi	1987-88
– **Batting Second**	313-7	Sri Lanka v Zimbabwe	New Plymouth	1991-92
Lowest Total	45	Canada v England	Manchester	1979
Highest Aggregate	626	Pakistan v Sri Lanka	Swansea	1983
Largest Victories	10 wkts	India beat East Africa	Leeds	1975
	10 wkts	West Indies beat Zimbabwe	Birmingham	1983
	10 wkts	West Indies beat Pakistan	Melbourne	1991-92
	202 runs	England beat India	Lord's	1975
Narrowest Victories	1 wkt	West Indies beat Pakistan	Birmingham	1975
	1 wkt	Pakistan beat West Indies	Lahore	1987-88
	1 run	Australia beat India	Madras	1987-88
	1 run	Australia beat India	Brisbane	1991-92

CAPTAINCY

LIMITED-OVERS INTERNATIONAL CAPTAINS

England

G. A. Gooch 50; M. W. Gatting 37; R. G. D. Willis 29; J. M. Brearley 25; D. I. Gower 24; M. H. Denness 12; I. T. Botham 9; A. J. Stewart 6; K. W. R. Fletcher 5; J. E. Emburey 4; A. J. Lamb 4; D. B. Close 3; R. Illingworth 3; G. Boycott 2; N. Gifford 2; A. W. Greig 2; J. H. Edrich 1; A. P. E. Knott 1.

Australia

A. R. Border 160; G. S. Chappell 49; K. J. Hughes 49; I. M. Chappell 11; M. A. Taylor 7; G. R. Marsh 4; G. N. Yallop 4; R. B. Simpson 2; R. J. Bright 1; D. W. Hookes 1; W. M. Lawry 1.

South Africa

K. C. Wessels 28; C. E. B. Rice 3.

West Indies

I. V. A. Richards 108; C. H. Lloyd 81; R. B. Richardson 48; C. G. Greenidge 8; D. L. Haynes 5; M. A. Holding 2; R. B. Kanhai 2; D. L. Murray 2; P. J. L. Dujon 1; A. I. Kallicharran 1.

New Zealand

G. P. Howarth 60; M. D. Crowe 44; J. G. Wright 31; J. V. Coney 25; J. J. Crowe 16; M. G. Burgess 8; B. E. Congdon 7; G. M. Turner 7; A. H. Jones 2.

India

Kapil Dev 74; M. Azharuddin 59; S. M. Gavaskar 37; D. B. Vengsarkar 18; K. Srikkanth 13; R. J. Shastri 11; S. Venkataraghavan 7; B. S. Bedi 4; A. L. Wadekar 2; M. Amarnath 1; S. M. H. Kirmani 1; G. R. Viswanath 1.

Pakistan

Imran Khan 139; Javed Miandad 62; Wasim Akram 16; Zaheer Abbas 13; Asif Iqbal 6; Abdul Qadir 5; Wasim Bari 5; Mushtaq Mohammad 4; Intikhab Alam 3; Majid Khan 2; Ramiz Raja 1; Salim Malik 1; Sarfraz Nawaz 1.

Sri Lanka

L. R. D. Mendis 61; A. Ranatunga 48; P. A. de Silva 13; R. S. Madugalle 13; B. Warnapura 8; A. P. B. Tennekoon 4; D. S. de Silva 1; J. R. Ratnayeke 1.

Zimbabwe

D. L. Houghton 17; D. A. G. Fletcher 6; A. J. Traicos 6.

Others

Gazi Ashraf (Bangladesh) 7; B. M. Mauricette (Canada) 3; Harilal R. Shah (East Africa) 3; Minhaz-ul-Abedin (Bangladesh) 2.

MISCELLANEOUS

LARGE ATTENDANCES

Test Series

943,000	Australia v England (5 Tests)	1936-37
In England		
549,650	England v Australia (5 Tests)	1953

Test Match

†350,534	Australia v England, Melbourne (Third Test)	1936-37
325,000+	India v England, Calcutta (Second Test)	1972-73
In England		
158,000+	England v Australia, Leeds (Fourth Test)	1948
137,915	England v Australia, Lord's (Second Test)	1953

Test Match Day

90,800	Australia v West Indies, Melbourne (Fifth Test, 2nd day)	1960-61

Other First-Class Matches in England

80,000+	Surrey v Yorkshire, The Oval (3 days)	1906
78,792	Yorkshire v Lancashire, Leeds (3 days)	1904
76,617	Lancashire v Yorkshire, Manchester (3 days)	1926

Limited-Overs International

‡90,000	India v Pakistan, Calcutta..........................	1986-87
‡90,000	India v South Africa, Calcutta......................	1991-92
87,182	England v Pakistan, Melbourne (World Cup final)	1991-92
86,133	Australia v West Indies, Melbourne	1983-84

  † *Although no official figures are available, the attendance at the Fourth Test between India and England at Calcutta, 1981-82, was thought to have exceeded this figure.*

  ‡ *No official attendance figures were issued for these games, but 90,000 seats were believed to be occupied. Press reports which gave much higher figures included security guards, food vendors etc., as well as paying spectators.*

LORD'S CRICKET GROUND

Lord's and the MCC were founded in 1787. The Club has enjoyed an uninterrupted career since that date, but there have been three grounds known as Lord's. The first (1787-1810) was situated where Dorset Square now is; the second (1809-13), at North Bank, had to be abandoned owing to the cutting of the Regent's Canal; and the third, opened in 1814, is the present one at St John's Wood. It was not until 1866 that the freehold of Lord's was secured by the MCC. The present pavilion was erected in 1890 at a cost of £21,000.

HIGHEST INDIVIDUAL SCORES MADE AT LORD'S

333	G. A. Gooch	England v India	1990
316*	J. B. Hobbs	Surrey v Middlesex	1926
315*	P. Holmes	Yorkshire v Middlesex	1925
281*	W. H. Ponsford.....	Australians v MCC	1934
278	W. Ward	MCC v Norfolk (with E. H. Budd, T. Vigne and F. Ladbroke)	1820
278	D. G. Bradman.....	Australians v MCC	1938
277*	E. H. Hendren	Middlesex v Kent	1922

Note: The longest innings in a first-class match at Lord's was played by S. Wettimuny (636 minutes, 190 runs) for Sri Lanka v England, 1984.

HIGHEST TOTALS AT LORD'S

First-Class Matches

729-6 dec.	Australia v England	1930
665	West Indians v Middlesex	1939
653-4 dec.	England v India	1990
652-8 dec.	West Indies v England	1973
629	England v India	1974
612-8 dec.	Middlesex v Nottinghamshire	1921
610-5 dec.	Australians v Gentlemen	1948
609-8 dec.	Cambridge University v MCC and Ground...........	1913
608-7 dec.	Middlesex v Hampshire	1919
607	MCC and Ground v Cambridge University..............	1902

Minor Match

| 735-9 dec. | MCC and Ground v Wiltshire .... | 1888 |

BIGGEST HIT AT LORD'S

The only known instance of a batsman hitting a ball over the present pavilion at Lord's occurred when A. E. Trott, appearing for MCC against Australians on July 31, August 1, 2, 1899, drove M. A. Noble so far and high that the ball struck a chimney pot and fell behind the building.

HIGHEST SCORE IN A MINOR COUNTY MATCH

323* F. E. Lacey   Hampshire v Norfolk at Southampton   1887

HIGHEST SCORES IN MINOR COUNTIES CHAMPIONSHIP

282	E. Garnett	Berkshire v Wiltshire at Reading	1908
254	H. E. Morgan	Glamorgan v Monmouthshire at Cardiff	1901
253*	G. J. Whittaker	Surrey II v Gloucestershire II at The Oval	1950
253	A. Booth	Lancashire II v Lincolnshire at Grimsby	1950
252	J. A. Deed	Kent II v Surrey II at The Oval (on debut)	1924

HIGHEST SCORE FOR ENGLISH PUBLIC SCHOOL

278   J. L. Guise   Winchester v Eton at Eton   1921

HIGHEST SCORES IN OTHER MATCHES

628*	A. E. J. Collins, Clark's House v North Town at Clifton College.
	(A Junior House match. His innings of 6 hours 50 minutes was spread over four afternoons.) 1899
566	C. J. Eady, Break-o'-Day v Wellington at Hobart 1901-02
515	D. R. Havewalla, B.B. and C.I. Rly v St Xavier's at Bombay 1933-34
506*	J. C. Sharp, Melbourne GS v Geelong College at Melbourne 1914-15
502*	Chaman Lal, Mehandra Coll., Patiala v Government Coll., Rupar at Patiala 1956-57
485	A. E. Stoddart, Hampstead v Stoics at Hampstead 1886
475*	Mohammad Iqbal, Muslim Model HS v Islamia HS, Sialkot at Lahore 1958-59
466*	G. T. S. Stevens, Beta v Lambda (University College School House match) at Neasden 1919
459	J. A. Prout, Wesley College v Geelong College at Geelong 1908-09

HIGHEST PARTNERSHIP IN MINOR CRICKET

664* for 3rd   V. G. Kambli and S. R. Tendulkar, Sharadashram Vidyamandir
                    School v St Xavier's High School at Bombay 1987-88

RECORD HIT

The Rev. W. Fellows, while at practice on the Christ Church ground at Oxford in 1856, drove a ball bowled by Charles Rogers 175 yards from hit to pitch.

THROWING THE CRICKET BALL

140 yards 2 feet, Robert Percival, on the Durham Sands, Co. Durham Racecourse   c1882
140 yards 9 inches, Ross Mackenzie, at Toronto 1872

Notes: W. F. Forbes, on March 16, 1876, threw 132 yards at the Eton College sports. He was then 18 years of age.

Onochie Onuorah, on June 5, 1987, threw a 4½oz ball 100 yards 1 foot 8½ inches (91.94 metres) at The Abbey School, Westgate, sports. He was then 13 years of age.

William Yardley, while a boy at Rugby, threw 100 yards with his right hand and 78 yards with his left.

Charles Arnold, of Cambridge, once threw 112 yards with the wind and 108 against.

W. H. Game, at The Oval in 1875, threw the ball 111 yards and then back the same distance. W. G. Grace threw 109 yards one way and back 105, and George Millyard 108 with the wind and 103 against. At The Oval in 1868, W. G. Grace made three successive throws of 116, 117 and 118 yards, and then threw back over 100 yards. D. G. Foster (Warwickshire) threw 133 yards, and in 1930 he made a Danish record with 120.1 metres – about 130 yards.

DATES OF FORMATION OF COUNTY CLUBS NOW FIRST-CLASS

County	First known county organisation	Present Club Original date	Reorganisation, if substantial
Derbyshire	November 4, 1870	November 4, 1870	—
Durham	January 24, 1874	May 10, 1882	March, 1991
Essex	By May, 1790	January 14, 1876	—
Glamorgan	August 5, 1861	July 6, 1888	—
Gloucestershire	November 3, 1863	1871	—
Hampshire	April 3, 1849	August 12, 1863	July, 1879
Kent	August 6, 1842	March 1, 1859	December 6, 1870
Lancashire	January 12, 1864	January 12, 1864	—
Leicestershire	By August, 1820	March 25, 1879	—
Middlesex	December 15, 1863	February 2, 1864	—
Northamptonshire	1820†	July 31, 1878	—
Nottinghamshire	March/April, 1841	March/April, 1841	December 11, 1866
Somerset	October 15, 1864	August 18, 1875	—
Surrey	August 22, 1845	August 22, 1845	—
Sussex	June 16, 1836	March 1, 1839	August, 1857
Warwickshire	May, 1826	1882	—
Worcestershire	1844	March 5, 1865	—
Yorkshire	March 7, 1861	January 8, 1863	December 10, 1891

† *Town club.*

DATES OF FORMATION OF CLUBS IN THE CURRENT MINOR COUNTIES CHAMPIONSHIP

County	First known county organisation	Present Club
Bedfordshire	May, 1847	November 3, 1899
Berkshire	By May, 1841	March 17, 1895
Buckinghamshire	November, 1864	January 15, 1891
Cambridgeshire	March 13, 1844	June 6, 1891
Cheshire	1819	September 29, 1908
Cornwall	1813	November 12, 1894
Cumberland	January 2, 1884	April 10, 1948
Devon	1824	November 26, 1899
Dorset	1862 *or* 1871	February 5, 1896
Herefordshire	July 13, 1836	January 9, 1991
Hertfordshire	1838	March 8, 1876
Lincolnshire	1853	September 28, 1906
Norfolk	January 11, 1827	October 14, 1876
Northumberland	1834	December, 1895
Oxfordshire	1787	December 14, 1921
Shropshire	1819 or 1829	June 28, 1956
Staffordshire	November 24, 1871	November 24, 1871
Suffolk	July 27, 1864	August, 1932
Wiltshire	February 24, 1881	January, 1893

CONSTITUTION OF COUNTY CHAMPIONSHIP

There are references in the sporting press to a champion county as early as 1825, but the list is not continuous and in some years only two counties contested the title. The earliest reference in any cricket publication is from 1864, and at this time there were eight leading counties who have come to be regarded as first-class from that date – Cambridgeshire,

Hampshire, Kent, Middlesex, Nottinghamshire, Surrey, Sussex and Yorkshire. The newly formed Lancashire club began playing inter-county matches in 1865, Gloucestershire in 1870 and Derbyshire in 1871, and they are therefore regarded as first-class from these respective dates. Cambridgeshire dropped out after 1871, Hampshire, who had not played inter-county matches in certain seasons, after 1885, and Derbyshire after 1887. Somerset, who had played matches against the first-class counties since 1879, were regarded as first-class from 1882 to 1885, and were admitted formally to the Championship in 1891. In 1894, Derbyshire, Essex, Leicestershire and Warwickshire were granted first-class status, but did not compete in the Championship until 1895 when Hampshire returned. Worcestershire, Northamptonshire and Glamorgan were admitted to the Championship in 1899, 1905 and 1921 respectively and are regarded as first-class from these dates. An invitation in 1921 to Buckinghamshire to enter the Championship was declined, owing to the lack of necessary playing facilities, and an application by Devon in 1948 was unsuccessful. Durham were admitted to the Championship in 1992 and were granted first-class status prior to their pre-season tour of Zimbabwe.

MOST COUNTY CHAMPIONSHIP APPEARANCES

763	W. Rhodes	Yorkshire	1898-1930
707	F. E. Woolley	Kent	1906-38
665	C. P. Mead	Hampshire	1906-36

MOST CONSECUTIVE COUNTY CHAMPIONSHIP APPEARANCES

423	K. G. Suttle	Sussex	1954-69
412	J. G. Binks	Yorkshire	1955-69
399	J. Vine	Sussex	1899-1914
344	E. H. Killick	Sussex	1898-1912
326	C. N. Woolley	Northamptonshire	1913-31
305	A. H. Dyson	Glamorgan	1930-47
301	B. Taylor	Essex	1961-72

Notes: J. Vine made 417 consecutive appearances for Sussex in all first-class matches between July 1900 and September 1914.

J. G. Binks did not miss a Championship match for Yorkshire between making his debut in June 1955 and retiring at the end of the 1969 season.

UMPIRES

MOST COUNTY CHAMPIONSHIP APPEARANCES

569	T. W. Spencer	1950-1980
533	F. Chester	1922-1955
516	H. G. Baldwin	1932-1962
457	A. Skelding	1931-1958
457	P. B. Wight	1966-1993

MOST SEASONS ON FIRST-CLASS LIST

31	T. W. Spencer	1950-1980
28	F. Chester	1922-1955
28	P. B. Wight	1966-1993
27	J. Moss	1899-1929
26	W. A. J. West	1896-1925
25	H. G. Baldwin	1932-1962
25	D. J. Constant	1969-1993
25	A. Jepson	1960-1984
25	J. G. Langridge	1956-1980

WISDEN'S CRICKETERS OF THE YEAR, 1889-1994

| 1889 | *Six Great Bowlers of the Year:* J. Briggs, J. J. Ferris, G. A. Lohmann, R. Peel, C. T. B. Turner, S. M. J. Woods. |

1889   *Six Great Bowlers of the Year:* J. Briggs, J. J. Ferris, G. A. Lohmann, R. Peel, C. T. B. Turner, S. M. J. Woods.

1890   *Nine Great Batsmen of the Year:* R. Abel, W. Barnes, W. Gunn, L. Hall, R. Henderson, J. M. Read, A. Shrewsbury, F. H. Sugg, A. Ward.

1891   *Five Great Wicket-Keepers:* J. McC. Blackham, G. MacGregor, R. Pilling, M. Sherwin, H. Wood.

1892   *Five Great Bowlers:* W. Attewell, J. T. Hearne, F. Martin, A. W. Mold, J. W. Sharpe.

1893   *Five Batsmen of the Year:* H. T. Hewett, L. C. H. Palairet, W. W. Read, S. W. Scott, A. E. Stoddart.

1894   *Five All-Round Cricketers:* G. Giffen, A. Hearne, F. S. Jackson, G. H. S. Trott, E. Wainwright.

1895   *Five Young Batsmen of the Season:* W. Brockwell, J. T. Brown, C. B. Fry, T. W. Hayward, A. C. MacLaren.

1896   W. G. Grace.

1897   *Five Cricketers of the Season:* S. E. Gregory, A. A. Lilley, K. S. Ranjitsinhji, T. Richardson, H. Trumble.

1898   *Five Cricketers of the Year:* F. G. Bull, W. R. Cuttell, N. F. Druce, G. L. Jessop, J. R. Mason.

1899   *Five Great Players of the Season:* W. H. Lockwood, W. Rhodes, W. Storer, C. L. Townsend, A. E. Trott.

1900   *Five Cricketers of the Season:* J. Darling, C. Hill, A. O. Jones, M. A. Noble, Major R. M. Poore.

1901   *Mr R. E. Foster and Four Yorkshiremen:* R. E. Foster, S. Haigh, G. H. Hirst, T. L. Taylor, J. Tunnicliffe.

1902   L. C. Braund, C. P. McGahey, F. Mitchell, W. G. Quaife, J. T. Tyldesley.

1903   W. W. Armstrong, C. J. Burnup, J. Iremonger, J. J. Kelly, V. T. Trumper.

1904   C. Blythe, J. Gunn, A. E. Knight, W. Mead, P. F. Warner.

1905   B. J. T. Bosanquet, E. A. Halliwell, J. Hallows, P. A. Perrin, R. H. Spooner.

1906   D. Denton, W. S. Lees, G. J. Thompson, J. Vine, L. G. Wright.

1907   J. N. Crawford, A. Fielder, E. G. Hayes, K. L. Hutchings, N. A. Knox.

1908   A. W. Hallam, R. O. Schwarz, F. A. Tarrant, A. E. E. Vogler, T. G. Wass.

1909   *Lord Hawke and Four Cricketers of the Year:* W. Brearley, Lord Hawke, J. B. Hobbs, A. Marshal, J. T. Newstead.

1910   W. Bardsley, S. F. Barnes, D. W. Carr, A. P. Day, V. S. Ransford.

1911   H. K. Foster, A. Hartley, C. B. Llewellyn, W. C. Smith, F. E. Woolley.

1912   *Five Members of the MCC's Team in Australia:* F. R. Foster, J. W. Hearne, S. P. Kinneir, C. P. Mead, H. Strudwick.

1913   John Wisden: Personal Recollections.

1914   M. W. Booth, G. Gunn, J. W. Hitch, A. E. Relf, Hon. L. H. Tennyson.

1915   J. W. H. T. Douglas, P. G. H. Fender, H. T. W. Hardinge, D. J. Knight, S. G. Smith.

1916-17 No portraits appeared.

1918   *School Bowlers of the Year:* H. L. Calder, J. E. D'E. Firth, C. H. Gibson, G. A. Rotherham, G. T. S. Stevens.

1919   *Five Public School Cricketers of the Year:* P. W. Adams, A. P. F. Chapman, A. C. Gore, L. P. Hedges, N. E. Partridge.

1920   *Five Batsmen of the Year:* A. Ducat, E. H. Hendren, P. Holmes, H. Sutcliffe, E. Tyldesley.

1921   P. F. Warner.

1922   H. Ashton, J. L. Bryan, J. M. Gregory, C. G. Macartney, E. A. McDonald.

1923   A. W. Carr, A. P. Freeman, C. W. L. Parker, A. C. Russell, A. Sandham.

1924   *Five Bowlers of the Year:* A. E. R. Gilligan, R. Kilner, G. G. Macaulay, C. H. Parkin, M. W. Tate.

1925   R. H. Catterall, J. C. W. MacBryan, H. W. Taylor, R. K. Tyldesley, W. W. Whysall.

1926   J. B. Hobbs.

1927   G. Geary, H. Larwood, J. Mercer, W. A. Oldfield, W. M. Woodfull.

1928   R. C. Blunt, C. Hallows, W. R. Hammond, D. R. Jardine, V. W. C. Jupp.

1929   L. E. G. Ames, G. Duckworth, M. Leyland, S. J. Staples, J. C. White.

1930	E. H. Bowley, K. S. Duleepsinhji, H. G. O. Owen-Smith, R. W. V. Robins, R. E. S. Wyatt.
1931	D. G. Bradman, C. V. Grimmett, B. H. Lyon, I. A. R. Peebles, M. J. Turnbull.
1932	W. E. Bowes, C. S. Dempster, James Langridge, Nawab of Pataudi sen., H. Verity.
1933	W. E. Astill, F. R. Brown, A. S. Kennedy, C. K. Nayudu, W. Voce.
1934	A. H. Bakewell, G. A. Headley, M. S. Nichols, L. F. Townsend, C. F. Walters.
1935	S. J. McCabe, W. J. O'Reilly, G. A. E. Paine, W. H. Ponsford, C. I. J. Smith.
1936	H. B. Cameron, E. R. T. Holmes, B. Mitchell, D. Smith, A. W. Wellard.
1937	C. J. Barnett, W. H. Copson, A. R. Gover, V. M. Merchant, T. S. Worthington.
1938	T. W. J. Goddard, J. Hardstaff jun., L. Hutton, J. H. Parks, E. Paynter.
1939	H. T. Bartlett, W. A. Brown, D. C. S. Compton, K. Farnes, A. Wood.
1940	L. N. Constantine, W. J. Edrich, W. W. Keeton, A. B. Sellers, D. V. P. Wright.
1941-46	No portraits appeared.
1947	A. V. Bedser, L. B. Fishlock, V. (M. H.) Mankad, T. P. B. Smith, C. Washbrook.
1948	M. P. Donnelly, A. Melville, A. D. Nourse, J. D. Robertson, N. W. D. Yardley.
1949	A. L. Hassett, W. A. Johnston, R. R. Lindwall, A. R. Morris, D. Tallon.
1950	T. E. Bailey, R. O. Jenkins, J. G. Langridge, R. T. Simpson, B. Sutcliffe.
1951	T. G. Evans, S. Ramadhin, A. L. Valentine, E. D. Weekes, F. M. M. Worrell.
1952	R. Appleyard, H. E. Dollery, J. C. Laker, P. B. H. May, E. A. B. Rowan.
1953	H. Gimblett, T. W. Graveney, D. S. Sheppard, W. S. Surridge, F. S. Trueman.
1954	R. N. Harvey, G. A. R. Lock, K. R. Miller, J. H. Wardle, W. Watson.
1955	B. Dooland, Fazal Mahmood, W. E. Hollies, J. B. Statham, G. E. Tribe.
1956	M. C. Cowdrey, D. J. Insole, D. J. McGlew, H. J. Tayfield, F. H. Tyson.
1957	D. Brookes, J. W. Burke, M. J. Hilton, G. R. A. Langley, P. E. Richardson.
1958	P. J. Loader, A. J. W. McIntyre, O. G. Smith, M. J. Stewart, C. L. Walcott.
1959	H. L. Jackson, R. E. Marshall, C. A. Milton, J. R. Reid, D. Shackleton.
1960	K. F. Barrington, D. B. Carr, R. Illingworth, G. Pullar, M. J. K. Smith.
1961	N. A. T. Adcock, E. R. Dexter, R. A. McLean, R. Subba Row, J. V. Wilson.
1962	W. E. Alley, R. Benaud, A. K. Davidson, W. M. Lawry, N. C. O'Neill.
1963	D. Kenyon, Mushtaq Mohammad, P. H. Parfitt, P. J. Sharpe, F. J. Titmus.
1964	D. B. Close, C. C. Griffith, C. C. Hunte, R. B. Kanhai, G. S. Sobers.
1965	G. Boycott, P. J. P. Burge, J. A. Flavell, G. D. McKenzie, R. B. Simpson.
1966	K. C. Bland, J. H. Edrich, R. C. Motz, P. M. Pollock, R. G. Pollock.
1967	R. W. Barber, B. L. D'Oliveira, C. Milburn, J. T. Murray, S. M. Nurse.
1968	Asif Iqbal, Hanif Mohammad, K. Higgs, J. M. Parks, Nawab of Pataudi jun.
1969	J. G. Binks, D. M. Green, B. A. Richards, D. L. Underwood, O. S. Wheatley.
1970	B. F. Butcher, A. P. E. Knott, Majid Khan, M. J. Procter, D. J. Shepherd.
1971	J. D. Bond, C. H. Lloyd, B. W. Luckhurst, G. M. Turner, R. T. Virgin.
1972	G. G. Arnold, B. S. Chandrasekhar, L. R. Gibbs, B. Taylor, Zaheer Abbas.
1973	G. S. Chappell, D. K. Lillee, R. A. L. Massie, J. A. Snow, K. R. Stackpole.
1974	K. D. Boyce, B. E. Congdon, K. W. R. Fletcher, R. C. Fredericks, P. J. Sainsbury.
1975	D. L. Amiss, M. H. Denness, N. Gifford, A. W. Greig, A. M. E. Roberts.
1976	I. M. Chappell, P. G. Lee, R. B. McCosker, D. S. Steele, R. A. Woolmer.
1977	J. M. Brearley, C. G. Greenidge, M. A. Holding, I. V. A. Richards, R. W. Taylor.
1978	I. T. Botham, M. Hendrick, A. Jones, K. S. McEwan, R. G. D. Willis.
1979	D. I. Gower, J. K. Lever, C. M. Old, C. T. Radley, J. N. Shepherd.
1980	J. Garner, S. M. Gavaskar, G. A. Gooch, D. W. Randall, B. C. Rose.
1981	K. J. Hughes, R. D. Jackman, A. J. Lamb, C. E. B. Rice, V. A. P. van der Bijl.
1982	T. M. Alderman, A. R. Border, R. J. Hadlee, Javed Miandad, R. W. Marsh.
1983	Imran Khan, T. E. Jesty, A. I. Kallicharran, Kapil Dev, M. D. Marshall.
1984	M. Amarnath, J. V. Coney, J. E. Emburey, M. W. Gatting, C. L. Smith.
1985	M. D. Crowe, H. A. Gomes, G. W. Humpage, J. Simmons, S. Wettimuny.
1986	P. Bainbridge, R. M. Ellison, C. J. McDermott, N. V. Radford, R. T. Robinson.
1987	J. H. Childs, G. A. Hick, D. B. Vengsarkar, C. A. Walsh, J. J. Whitaker.
1988	J. P. Agnew, N. A. Foster, D. P. Hughes, P. M. Roebuck, Salim Malik.
1989	K. J. Barnett, P. J. L. Dujon, P. A. Neale, F. D. Stephenson, S. R. Waugh.
1990	S. J. Cook, D. M. Jones, R. C. Russell, R. A. Smith, M. A. Taylor.
1991	M. A. Atherton, M. Azharuddin, A. R. Butcher, D. L. Haynes, M. E. Waugh.
1992	C. E. L. Ambrose, P. A. J. DeFreitas, A. A. Donald, R. B. Richardson, Waqar Younis.
1993	N. E. Briers, M. D. Moxon, I. D. K. Salisbury, A. J. Stewart, Wasim Akram.
1994	D. C. Boon, I. A. Healy, M. G. Hughes, S. K. Warne, S. L. Watkin.

BIRTHS AND DEATHS OF CRICKETERS

The qualifications for inclusion are as follows:

1. All players who have appeared in a Test match or a one-day international for a Test-match playing country.

2. English county players who have appeared in 50 or more first-class matches during their careers and, if dead, were still living ten years ago.

3. Players who appeared in 15 or more first-class matches in the 1993 English season.

4. English county captains, county caps and captains of Oxford and Cambridge Universities who, if dead, were still living ten years ago.

5. All players chosen as *Wisden* Cricketers of the Year, including the Public Schoolboys chosen for the 1918 and 1919 Almanacks. Cricketers of the Year are identified by the italic notation *CY* and year of appearance. A list of the Cricketers of the Year from 1889 to 1993 appears on pages 262-263.

6. Players or personalities not otherwise qualified who are thought to be of sufficient interest to merit inclusion.

Key to abbreviations and symbols

CUCC – Cambridge University, OUCC – Oxford University.

Australian states: NSW – New South Wales, Qld – Queensland, S. Aust. – South Australia, Tas. – Tasmania, Vic. – Victoria, W. Aust. – Western Australia.

Indian teams: Guj. – Gujarat, H'bad – Hyderabad, Ind. Rlwys – Indian Railways, Ind. Serv. – Indian Services, J/K – Jammu and Kashmir, Karn. – Karnataka (Mysore to 1972-73), M. Pradesh – Madhya Pradesh (Central India [C. Ind.] to 1939-40, Holkar to 1954-55, Madhya Bharat to 1956-57), M'tra – Maharashtra, Naw. – Nawanagar, Raja. – Rajasthan, S'tra – Saurashtra (West India [W. Ind.] to 1945-46, Kathiawar to 1949-50), S. Punjab – Southern Punjab (Patiala to 1958-59, Punjab since 1968-69), TC – Travancore-Cochin (Kerala since 1956-57), TN – Tamil Nadu (Madras to 1959-60), U. Pradesh – Uttar Pradesh (United Provinces [U. Prov.] to 1948-49), Vidarbha (CP & Berar to 1949-50, Madhya Pradesh to 1956-57).

New Zealand provinces: Auck. – Auckland, Cant. – Canterbury, C. Dist. – Central Districts, N. Dist. – Northern Districts, Wgtn – Wellington.

Pakistani teams: ADBP – Agricultural Development Bank of Pakistan, B'pur – Bahawalpur, HBFC – House Building Finance Corporation, HBL – Habib Bank Ltd, IDBP – Industrial Development Bank of Pakistan, Kar. – Karachi, MCB – Muslim Commercial Bank, NBP – National Bank of Pakistan, NWFP – North-West Frontier Province, PACO – Pakistan Automobile Corporation, Pak. Rlwys – Pakistan Railways, Pak. Us – Pakistan Universities, PIA – Pakistan International Airlines, PNSC – Pakistan National Shipping Corporation, PWD – Public Works Department, R'pindi – Rawalpindi, UBL – United Bank Ltd, WAPDA – Water and Power Development Authority.

South African provinces: E. Prov. – Eastern Province, E. Tvl – Eastern Transvaal, Griq. W. – Griqualand West, N. Tvl – Northern Transvaal, NE Tvl – North-Eastern Transvaal, OFS – Orange Free State, Rhod. – Rhodesia, Tvl – Transvaal, W. Prov. – Western Province.

Sri Lankan teams: Ant. – Antonians, BRC – Burgher Recreation Club, CCC – Colombo Cricket Club, Mor. – Moratuwa Sports Club, NCC – Nondescripts Cricket Club, Pan. – Panadura Sports Club, SLAF – Air Force, SSC – Sinhalese Sports Club, TU – Tamil Union Cricket and Athletic Club, Under-23 – Board Under-23 XI.

West Indies islands: B'dos – Barbados, BG – British Guiana (Guyana since 1966), Comb. Is. – Combined Islands, Jam. – Jamaica, T/T – Trinidad & Tobago.

* *Denotes Test player.* ** *Denotes appeared for two countries. There is a list of Test players country by country from page 53.*
† *Denotes also played for team under its previous name.*

Aamer Hameed (Pak. Us, Lahore, Punjab & OUCC) b Oct. 18, 1954

*Aamer Malik (ADBP, PIA & Multan) b Jan. 3, 1963

*Aamir Nazir (Pak.) b Jan. 2, 1971

*Aamir Sohail (HBL & Sargodha) b Sept. 14, 1966

Abberley, R. N. (Warwicks.) b April 22, 1944

*a'Beckett, E. L. (Vic.) b Aug. 11, 1907, d June 2, 1989

*Abdul Kadir (Kar. & NBP) b May 10, 1944

*Abdul Qadir (HBL, Lahore & Punjab) b Sept. 15, 1955

*Abel, R. (Surrey; CY 1890) b Nov. 30, 1857, d Dec. 10, 1936

Abell, Sir G. E. B. (OUCC, Worcs. & N. Ind.) b June 22, 1904, d Jan. 11, 1989

*Abid Ali, S. (H'bad) b Sept. 9, 1941

Abrahams, J. (Lancs.) b July 21, 1952

*Absolom, C. A. (CUCC & Kent) b June 7, 1846, d July 30, 1889

Acfield D. L. (CUCC & Essex) b July 24, 1947

*Achong, E. (T/T) b Feb. 16, 1904, d Aug. 29, 1986

Ackerman, H. M. (Border, NE Tvl, Northants, Natal & W. Prov.) b April 28, 1947

A'Court, D. G. (Glos.) b July 27, 1937

Adam, Sir Ronald, 2nd Bt (Pres. MCC 1946-47) b Oct. 30, 1885, d Dec. 26, 1982

Adams, C. J. (Derbys.) b May 6, 1970

*Adams, J. C. (Jam.) b Jan. 9, 1968

Adams, P. W. (Cheltenham & Sussex; CY 1919) b 1900, d Feb. 28, 1962

*Adcock, N. A. T. (Tvl & Natal; CY 1961) b March 8, 1931

*Adhikari, H. R. (Guj., Baroda & Ind. Serv.) b July 31, 1919

*Afaq Hussain (Kar., Pak. Us, PIA & PWD) b Dec. 31, 1939

Afford, J. A. (Notts.) b May 12, 1964

*Aftab Baloch (PWD, Kar., Sind, NBP & PIA) b April 1, 1953

*Aftab Gul (Punjab U., Pak. Us & Lahore) b March 31, 1946

*Agha Saadat Ali (Pak. Us, Punjab, B'pur & Lahore) b June 21, 1929

*Agha Zahid (Pak. Us, Punjab, Lahore & HBL) b Jan. 7, 1953

Agnew, J. P. (Leics; CY 1988) b April 4, 1960

Ahangama, F. S. (SSC) b Sept. 14, 1959

Aird, R. (CUCC & Hants; Sec. MCC 1953-62, Pres. MCC 1968-69) b May 4, 1902, d Aug. 16, 1986

Aislabie, B. (Surrey, Hants, Kent & Sussex; Sec. MCC 1822-42) b Jan. 14, 1774, d June 2, 1842

Aitchison, Rev. J. K. (Scotland) b May 26, 1920

*Akram Raza (Sargodha & HBL) b Nov. 22, 1964

*Alabaster, J. C. (Otago) b July 11, 1930

Alcock, C. W. (Sec. Surrey CCC 1872-1907, Editor Cricket 1882-1907) b Dec. 2, 1842, d Feb. 26, 1907

Alderman, A. E. (Derbys.) b Oct. 30, 1907, d June 4, 1990

*Alderman, T. M. (W. Aust., Kent & Glos.; CY 1982) b June 12, 1956

Aldridge, K. J. (Worcs & Tas.) b March 13, 1935

Alexander of Tunis, 1st Lord (Pres. MCC 1955-56) b Dec. 10, 1891, d June 16, 1969

*Alexander, F. C. M. (CUCC & Jam.) b Nov. 2, 1928

*Alexander, G. (Vic.) b April 22, 1851, d Nov. 6, 1930

*Alexander, H. H. (Vic.) b June 9, 1905, d April 15, 1993

Alikhan, R. I. (Sussex, PIA & Surrey) b Dec. 28, 1962

*Alim-ud-Din (Rajputana, Guj., Sind, B'pur, Kar. & PWD) b Dec. 15, 1930

*Allan, D. W. (B'dos) b Nov. 5, 1937

*Allan, F. E. (Vic.) b Dec. 2, 1849, d Feb. 9, 1917

Allan, J. M. (OUCC, Kent, Warwicks. & Scotland) b April 2, 1932

*Allan, P. J. (Qld) b Dec. 31, 1935

*Allcott, C. F. W. (Auck.) b Oct. 7, 1896, d Nov. 19, 1973

Allen, A. W. (CUCC & Northants) b Dec. 22, 1912

*Allen, D. A. (Glos.) b Oct. 29, 1935

*Allen, Sir G. O. B. (CUCC & Middx; Pres. MCC 1963-64; special portrait 1987) b July 31, 1902, d Nov. 29, 1989

*Allen, I. B. A. (Windwards) b Oct. 6, 1965

Allen, M. H. J. (Northants & Derbys.) b Jan. 7, 1933

*Allen, R. C. (NSW) b July 2, 1858, d May 2, 1952

Alletson, E. B. (Notts.) b March 6, 1884, d July 5, 1963

Alley, W. E. (NSW & Som.; CY 1962) b Feb. 3, 1919

Alleyne, H. L. (B'dos, Worcs., Natal & Kent) b Feb. 28, 1957

Alleyne, M. W. (Glos.) b May 23, 1968

*Allom, M. J. C. (CUCC & Surrey; Pres. MCC 1969-70) b March 23, 1906

Allott, P. J. W. (Lancs. & Wgtn) b Sept. 14, 1956

Altham, H. S. (OUCC, Surrey & Hants; Pres. MCC 1959-60) b Nov. 30, 1888, d March 11, 1965

*Amalean, K. N. (SL) b April 7, 1965

*Amarnath, Lala (N. Ind., S. Punjab, Guj., Patiala, U. Pradesh & Ind. Rlwys) b Sept. 11, 1911

*Amarnath, M. (Punjab & Delhi; *CY 1984*) b Sept. 24, 1950

*Amarnath, S. (Punjab & Delhi) b Dec. 30, 1948

*Amar Singh, L. (Patiala, W. Ind. & Naw.) b Dec. 4, 1910, d May 20, 1940

*Ambrose, C. E. L. (Leewards & Northants; *CY 1992*) b Sept. 21, 1963

*Amerasinghe, A. M. J. G. (Nomads) b Feb. 2, 1954

*Ames, L. E. G. (Kent; *CY 1929*) b Dec. 3, 1905, d Feb. 26, 1990

**Amir Elahi (Baroda, N. Ind., S. Punjab & B'pur) b Sept. 1, 1908, d Dec. 28, 1980

*Amiss, D. L. (Warwicks.; *CY 1975*) b April 7, 1943

*Amre, P. K. (Ind. Rlwys & Raja.) b Aug. 14, 1968

Anderson, I. S. (Derbys. & Boland) b April 24, 1960

*Anderson, J. H. (W. Prov.) b April 26, 1874, d March 11, 1926

*Anderson, R. W. (Cant., N. Dist., Otago & C. Dist.) b Oct. 2, 1948

*Anderson, W. McD. (Otago, C. Dist. & Cant.) b Oct. 8, 1919, d Dec. 21, 1979

Andrew, C. R. (CUCC) b Feb. 18, 1963

*Andrew, K. V. (Northants) b Dec. 15, 1929

Andrew, S. J. W. (Hants & Essex) b Jan. 27, 1966

*Andrews, B. (Cant., C. Dist. & Otago) b April 4, 1945

*Andrews, T. J. E. (NSW) b Aug. 26, 1890, d Jan. 28, 1970

Andrews, W. H. R. (Som.) b April 14, 1908, d Jan. 9, 1989

*Angel, J. (W. Aust.) b April 22, 1968

Angell, F. L. (Som.) b June 29, 1922

Anil Dalpat (Kar. & PIA) b Sept. 20, 1963

*Ankola, S. A. (M'tra & Bombay) b March 1, 1968

*Anurasiri, S. D. (Pan.) b Feb. 25, 1966

*Anwar Hussain (N. Ind., Bombay, Sind & Kar.) b July 16, 1920

*Anwar Khan (Kar., Sind & NBP) b Dec. 24, 1955

*Appleyard, R. (Yorks.; *CY 1952*) b June 27, 1924

*Apte, A. L. (Ind. Us, Bombay & Raja.) b Oct. 24, 1934

*Apte, M. L. (Bombay & Bengal) b Oct. 5, 1932

*Aqib Javed (PACO & Hants) b Aug. 5, 1972

*Archer, A. G. (Worcs.) b Dec. 6, 1871, d July 15, 1935

*Archer, K. A. (Qld) b Jan. 17, 1928

*Archer, R. G. (Qld) b Oct. 25, 1933

*Arif Butt (Lahore & Pak. Rlwys) b May 17, 1944

Arlott, John (Writer & Broadcaster) b Feb. 25, 1914, d Dec. 14, 1991

*Armitage, T. (Yorks.) b April 25, 1848, d Sept. 21, 1922

Armstrong, N. F. (Leics.) b Dec. 22, 1892, d Jan. 19, 1990

Armstrong, T. R. (Derbys.) b Oct. 13, 1909

*Armstrong, W. W. (Vic.; *CY 1903*) b May 22, 1879, d July 13, 1947

Arnold, A. P. (Cant. & Northants) b Oct. 16, 1926

*Arnold, E. G. (Worcs.) b Nov. 7, 1876, d Oct. 25, 1942

*Arnold, G. G. (Surrey & Sussex; *CY 1972*) b Sept. 3, 1944

*Arnold, J. (Hants) b Nov. 30, 1907, d April 4, 1984

*Arnott, K. J. (Zimb.) b March 8, 1961

*Arshad Ayub (H'bad) b Aug. 2, 1958

Arshad Khan (Peshawar) b March 22, 1971

Arshad Pervez (Sargodha, Lahore, Pak. Us, Servis Ind., HBL & Punjab) b Oct. 1, 1952

*Arthurton, K. L. T. (Leewards) b Feb. 21, 1965

*Arun, B. (TN) b Dec. 14, 1962

*Arun Lal (Delhi & Bengal) b Aug. 1, 1955

*Asgarali, N. (T/T) b Dec. 28, 1920

Ashdown, W. H. (Kent) b Dec. 27, 1898, d Sept. 15, 1979

*Ashley, W. H. (W. Prov.) b Feb. 10, 1862, d July 14, 1930

*Ashraf Ali (Lahore, Income Tax, Pak Us, Pak Rlwys & UBL) b April 22, 1958

Ashton, C. T. (CUCC & Essex) b Feb. 19, 1901, d Oct. 31, 1942

Ashton, G. (CUCC & Worcs.) b Sept. 27, 1896, d Feb. 6, 1981

Ashton, Sir H. (CUCC & Essex; *CY 1922*; Pres. MCC 1960-61) b Feb. 13, 1898, d June 17,1979

Asif Din, M. (Warwicks.) b Sept. 21, 1960

*Asif Iqbal (H'bad, Kar., Kent, PIA & NBP; *CY 1968*) b June 6, 1943

*Asif Masood (Lahore, Punjab U. & PIA) b Jan. 23, 1946

*Asif Mujtaba (Kar. & PIA) b Nov. 4, 1967

Aslett, D. G. (Kent) b Feb. 12, 1958

Aspinall, R. (Yorks.) b Nov. 27, 1918

*Astill, W. E. (Leics.; *CY 1933*) b March 1, 1888, d Feb. 10, 1948

*Atapattu, M. S. (SSC) b Nov. 22, 1972

*Ata-ur-Rehman (Lahore & PACO) b March 28, 1975

*Atherton, M. A. (CUCC & Lancs.; *CY 1991*) b March 23, 1968

*Athey, C. W. J. (Yorks., Glos. & Sussex) b Sept. 27, 1957

Atkinson, C. R. M. (Som.) b July 23, 1931, d June 25, 1991

*Atkinson, D. St E. (B'dos & T/T) b Aug. 9, 1926

*Atkinson, E. St E. (B'dos) b Nov. 6, 1927

Atkinson, G. (Som. & Lancs.) b March 29, 1938

Atkinson, J. C. M. (Som. & CUCC) b July 10, 1968

Atkinson, T. (Notts.) b Sept. 27, 1930, d Sept. 2, 1990

*Attewell, W. (Notts.; *CY 1892*) b June 12, 1861, d June 11, 1927

Austin, Sir H. B. G. (B'dos) b July 15, 1877, d July 27, 1943

Austin, I. D. (Lancs.) b May 30, 1966

*Austin, R. A. (Jam.) b Sept. 5, 1954

Avery, A. V. (Essex) b Dec. 19, 1914

Aworth, C. J. (CUCC & Surrey) b Feb. 19, 1953

Ayling, J. R. (Hants) b June 13, 1967

Aylward, J. (Hants & All-England) b 1741, d Dec. 27, 1827

Aymes, A. N. (Hants) b June 4, 1964

*Azad, K. (Delhi) b Jan. 2, 1959

*Azeem Hafeez (Kar., Allied Bank & PIA) b July 29, 1963

*Azhar Khan (Lahore, Punjab, Pak. Us., PIA & HBL) b Sept. 7, 1955

*Azharuddin, M. (H'bad & Derbys.; *CY 1991*) b Feb. 8, 1963

*Azmat Rana (B'pur, PIA, Punjab, Lahore & MCB) b Nov. 3, 1951

Babington, A. M. (Sussex & Glos.) b July 22, 1963

*Bacchus, S. F. A. F. (Guyana, W. Prov. & Border) b Jan. 31, 1954

*Bacher, Dr A. (Tvl) b May 24, 1942

*Badcock, C. L. (Tas. & S. Aust.) b April 10, 1914, d Dec. 13, 1982

*Badcock, F. T. (Wgtn & Otago) b Aug. 9, 1895, d Sept. 19, 1982

*Baichan, L. (Guyana) b May 12, 1946

*Baig, A. A. (H'bad, OUCC & Som.) b March 19, 1939

Bailey, Sir D. T. L. (Glos.) b Aug. 5, 1918

Bailey, J. (Hants) b April 6, 1908, d Feb. 9, 1988

Bailey, J. A. (Essex & OUCC; Sec. MCC 1974-87) b June 22, 1930

*Bailey, R. J. (Northants) b Oct. 28, 1963

*Bailey, T. E. (Essex & CUCC; *CY 1950*) b Dec. 3, 1923

Baillie, A. W. (Sec. MCC 1858-63) b June 22, 1830, d May 10, 1867

Bainbridge, P. (Glos. & Durham; *CY 1986*) b April 16, 1958

*Bairstow, D. L. (Yorks. & Griq. W.) b Sept. 1, 1951

Baker, R. P. (Surrey) b April 9, 1954

*Bakewell, A. H. (Northants; *CY 1934*) b Nov. 2, 1908, d Jan. 23, 1983

Bakker, P. J. (Hants) b Aug. 19, 1957

*Balaskas, X. C. (Griq. W., Border, W. Prov., Tvl & NE Tvl) b Oct. 15, 1910

*Balderstone, J. C. (Yorks. & Leics.) b Nov. 16, 1940

Baldry, D. O. (Middx & Hants) b Dec. 26, 1931

*Banerjee, S. A. (Bengal & Bihar) b Nov. 1, 1919, d. Sept. 14, 1992

*Banerjee, S. N. (Bengal, Naw., Bihar & M. Pradesh) b Oct. 3, 1911, d Oct. 14, 1980

*Banerjee, S. T. (Bihar) b Feb. 13, 1969

*Bannerman, A. C. (NSW) b March 22, 1854, d Sept. 19, 1924

*Bannerman, Charles (NSW) b July 23, 1851, d Aug. 20, 1930

Bannister, J. D. (Warwicks.) b Aug. 23, 1930

*Baptiste, E. A. E. (Kent, Leewards, Northants & E. Prov.) b March 12, 1960

*Baqa Jilani, M. (N. Ind.) b July 20, 1911, d July 2, 1941

Barber, A. T. (OUCC & Yorks.) b June 17, 1905, d March 10, 1985

*Barber, R. T. (Wgtn & C. Dist.) b June 23, 1925

*Barber, R. W. (Lancs., CUCC & Warwicks.; *CY 1967*) b Sept. 26, 1935

*Barber, W. (Yorks.) b April 18, 1901, d Sept. 10, 1968

Barclay, J. R. T. (Sussex & OFS) b Jan. 22, 1954

*Bardsley, W. (NSW; *CY 1910*) b Dec. 7, 1882, d Jan. 20, 1954

Baring, A. E. G. (Hants) b Jan. 21, 1910, d Aug. 29, 1986

Barker, G. (Essex) b July 6, 1931

Barling, H. T. (Surrey) b Sept. 1, 1906, d Jan. 2, 1993

*Barlow, E. J. (Tvl, E. Prov., W. Prov., Derbys. & Boland) b Aug. 12, 1940

*Barlow, G. D. (Middx) b March 26, 1950

*Barlow, R. G. (Lancs.) b May 28, 1851, d July 31, 1919

Barnard, H. M. (Hants) b July 18, 1933

Barnes, A. R. (Sec. Aust. Cricket Board 1960-81) b Sept. 12, 1916, d March 14, 1989

*Barnes, S. F. (Warwicks. & Lancs.; *CY 1910*) b April 19, 1873, d Dec. 26, 1967

*Barnes, S. G. (NSW) b June 5, 1916, d Dec. 16, 1973

*Barnes, W. (Notts.; *CY 1890*) b May 27, 1852, d March 24, 1899

Barnett, A. A. (Middx & Lancs.) b Sept. 11, 1970

*Barnett, B. A. (Vic.) b March 23, 1908, d June 29, 1979

*Barnett, C. J. (Glos.; *CY 1937*) b July 3, 1910, d May 28, 1993

*Barnett, K. J. (Derbys. & Boland; *CY 1989*) b July 17, 1960

Barnwell, C. J. P. (Som.) b June 23, 1914

Baroda, Maharaja of (Manager, Ind. in Eng., 1959) b April 2, 1930, d Sept. 1, 1988

*Barratt, F. (Notts.) b April 12, 1894, d Jan. 29, 1917

Barratt, R. J. (Leics.) b May 3, 1942

*Barrett, A. G. (Jam.) b April 5, 1942

Barrett, B. J. (Auck., C. Dist., Worcs. & N. Dist.) b Nov. 16, 1966

*Barrett, J. E. (Vic.) b Oct. 15, 1866, d Feb. 6, 1916

Barrick, D. W. (Northants) b April 28, 1926

*Barrington, K. F. (Surrey; *CY 1960*) b Nov. 24, 1930, d March 14, 1981

Barron, W. (Lancs. & Northants) b Oct. 26, 1917

*Barrow, I. (Jam.) b Jan. 6, 1911, d April 2, 1979

*Bartlett, E. L. (B'dos) b March 18, 1906, d Dec. 21, 1976

*Bartlett, G. A. (C. Dist. & Cant.) b Feb. 3, 1941

Bartlett, H. T. (CUCC, Surrey & Sussex; *CY 1939*) b Oct. 7, 1914, d June 26, 1988

Bartlett, R. J. (Som.) b Oct. 8, 1966

Bartley, T. J. (Umpire) b March 19, 1908, d April 2, 1964

Barton, M. R. (OUCC & Surrey) b Oct. 14, 1914

*Barton, P. T. (Wgtn) b Oct. 9, 1935

*Barton, V. A. (Kent & Hants) b Oct. 6, 1867, d March 23, 1906

Barwick, S. R. (Glam.) b Sept. 6, 1960

Base, S. J. (W. Prov., Glam., Derbys., Boland & Border) b Jan. 2, 1960

*Basit Ali (Kar. & UBL) b Dec. 13, 1970

Bates, D. L. (Sussex) b May 10, 1933

*Bates, W. (Yorks.) b Nov. 19, 1855, d Jan. 8, 1900

Batty, J. D. (Yorks.) b May 15, 1971

*Baumgartner, H. V. (OFS & Tvl) b Nov. 17, 1883, d April 8, 1938

Baxter, A. D. (Devon, Lancs., Middx & Scotland) b Jan. 20, 1910, d Jan. 28, 1986

*Bean, G. (Notts & Sussex) b March 7, 1864, d March 16, 1923

Bear, M. J. (Essex & Cant.) b Feb. 23, 1934

*Beard, D. D. (C. Dist. & N. Dist.) b Jan. 14, 1920, d July 15, 1982

*Beard, G. R. (NSW) b Aug. 19, 1950

Beauclerk, Lord Frederick (Middx, Surrey & MCC) b May 8, 1773, d April 22, 1850

Beaufort, 10th Duke of (Pres. MCC 1952-53) b April 4, 1900, d Feb. 5, 1984

*Beaumont, R. (Tvl) b Feb. 4, 1884, d May 25, 1958

*Beck, J. E. F. (Wgtn) b Aug. 1, 1934

*Bedi, B. S. (N. Punjab, Delhi & Northants) b Sept. 25, 1946

*Bedser, A. V. (Surrey; *CY 1947*) b July 4, 1918

Bedser, E. A. (Surrey) b July 4, 1918

Beet, G. (Derbys.; Umpire) b April 24, 1886, d Dec. 13, 1946

*Begbie, D. W. (Tvl) b Dec. 12, 1914

Beldham, W. (Hambledon & Surrey) b Feb. 5, 1766, d Feb. 20, 1862

*Bell, A. J. (W. Prov. & Rhod.) b April 15, 1906, d Aug. 2, 1985

Bell, R. V. (Middx & Sussex) b Jan. 7, 1931, d Oct. 26, 1989

*Bell, W. (Cant.) b Sept. 5, 1931

Bellamy, B. W. (Northants) b April 22, 1891, d Dec. 20, 1985

*Benaud, J. (NSW) b May 11, 1944

*Benaud, R. (NSW; *CY 1962*) b Oct. 6, 1930

Benjamin, J. E. (Warwicks. & Surrey) b Feb. 2, 1961

*Benjamin, K. C. G. (Leewards & Worcs.) b April 8, 1967

*Benjamin, W. K. M. (Leewards & Leics.) b Dec. 31, 1964

Bennett, D. (Middx) b Dec. 18, 1933

*Bennett, M. J. (NSW) b Oct. 16, 1956

Bennett, N. H. (Surrey) b Sept. 23, 1912

Bennett, R. (Lancs.) b June 16, 1940

Benson, J. D. R. (Leics.) b March 1, 1967

*Benson, M. R. (Kent) b July 6, 1958

Bernard, J. R. (CUCC & Glos.) b Dec. 7, 1938

Berry, L. G. (Leics.) b April 28, 1906, d Feb. 5, 1985

*Berry, R. (Lancs., Worcs. & Derbys.) b Jan. 29, 1926

*Best, C. A. (B'dos) b May 14, 1959

*Betancourt, N. (T/T) b June 4, 1887, d Oct. 12, 1947

Bhalekar, R. B. (M'tra) b Feb. 17, 1952

*Bhandari, P. (Delhi & Bengal) b Nov. 27, 1935

*Bhat, A. R. (Karn.) b April 16, 1958

Bick, D. A. (Middx) b Feb. 22, 1936, d Jan. 13, 1992

Bicknell, D. J. (Surrey) b June 24, 1967

*Bicknell, M. P. (Surrey) b Jan. 14, 1969

Biddulph, K. D. (Som.) b May 29, 1932

Bilby, G. P. (Wgtn) b May 7, 1941

*Binks, J. G. (Yorks.; *CY 1969*) b Oct. 5, 1935

*Binns, A. P. (Jam.) b July 24, 1929

*Binny, R. M. H. (Karn.) b July 19, 1955

Birch, J. D. (Notts.) b June 18, 1955

Bird, H. D. (Yorks. & Leics.; Umpire) b April 19, 1933

*Bird, M. C. (Lancs. & Surrey) b March 25, 1888, d Dec. 9, 1933

Bird, R. E. (Worcs.) b April 4, 1915, d Feb. 20, 1985

Birkenshaw, J. (Yorks., Leics. & Worcs.) b Nov. 13, 1940

*Birkett, L. S. (B'dos, BG & T/T) b April 14, 1904

Birrell, H. B. (E. Prov., Rhod. & OUCC) b Dec. 1, 1927

Bishop, G. A. (S. Aust.) b Feb. 25, 1960
*Bishop, I. R. (T/T & Derbys.) b Oct. 24, 1967
*Bisset, Sir Murray (W. Prov.) b April 14, 1876, d Oct. 24, 1931
*Bissett, G. F. (Griq. W., W. Prov. & Tvl) b Nov. 5, 1905, d Nov. 14, 1965
Bissex, M. (Glos.) b Sept. 28, 1944
*Blackham, J. McC. (Vic.; *CY 1891*) b May 11, 1854, d Dec. 28, 1932
*Blackie, D. D. (Vic.) b April 5, 1882, d April 18, 1955
*Blackledge, J. F. (Lancs.) b April 15, 1928
Blain, T. E. (C. Dist.) b Feb. 17, 1962
Blair, B. R. (Otago) b Dec. 27, 1957
*Blair, R. W. (Wgtn & C. Dist.) b June 23, 1932
Blake, D. E. (Hants) b April 27, 1925
Blake, Rev. P. D. S. (OUCC & Sussex) b May 23, 1927
Blakey, R. J. (Yorks.) b Jan. 15, 1967
*Blanckenberg, J. M. (W. Prov. & Natal) b Dec. 31, 1893, 'presumed dead'
*Bland, K. C. (Rhod., E. Prov. & OFS; *CY 1966*) b April 5, 1938
Blenkiron, W. (Warwicks.) b July 21, 1942
Bligh, Hon. Ivo (*see* 8th Earl of Darnley)
Blundell, Sir E. D. (CUCC & NZ) b May 29, 1907, d Sept. 24, 1984
*Blunt, R. C. (Cant. & Otago; *CY 1928*) b Nov. 3, 1900, d June 22, 1966
*Blythe, C. (Kent; *CY 1904*) b May 30, 1879, d Nov. 8, 1917
*Board, J. H. (Glos.) b Feb. 23, 1867, d April 16, 1924
*Bock, E. G. (Griq. W., Tvl & W. Prov.) b Sept. 17, 1908, d Sept. 5, 1961
Bodkin, P. E. (CUCC) b Sept. 15, 1924
*Bolton, B. A. (Cant. & Wgtn) b May 31, 1935
*Bolus, J. B. (Yorks., Notts. & Derbys.) b Jan. 31, 1934
*Bond, G. E. (W. Prov.) b April 5, 1909, d Aug. 27, 1965
Bond, J. D. (Lancs. & Notts.; *CY 1971*) b May 6, 1932
*Bonnor, G. J. (Vic. & NSW) b Feb. 25, 1855, d June 27, 1912
*Boock, S. L. (Otago & Cant.) b Sept. 20, 1951
*Boon, D. C. (Tas.; *CY 1993*) b Dec. 29, 1960
Boon, T. J. (Leics.) b Nov. 1, 1961
*Booth, B. C. (NSW) b Oct. 19, 1933
Booth, B. J. (Lancs. & Leics.) b Dec. 3, 1935
*Booth, M. W. (Yorks.; *CY 1914*) b Dec. 10, 1886, d July 1, 1916
Booth, P. (Leics.) b Nov. 2, 1952
Booth, P. A. (Yorks. & Warwicks.) b Sept. 5, 1965
Booth, R. (Yorks. & Worcs.) b Oct. 1, 1926

*Borde, C. G. (Baroda & M'tra) b July 21, 1934
*Border, A. R. (NSW, Glos, Qld & Essex; *CY 1982*) b July 27, 1955
Bore, M. K. (Yorks. & Notts.) b June 2, 1947
Borrington, A. J. (Derbys.) b Dec. 8, 1948
*Bosanquet, B. J. T. (OUCC & Middx; *CY 1905*) b Oct. 13, 1877, d Oct. 12, 1936
*Bosch T. (N. Tvl) b March 14, 1966
Bose, G. (Bengal) b May 20, 1947
Boshier, B. S. (Leics.) b March 6, 1932
*Botham, I. T. (Som., Worcs., Durham & Qld; *CY 1978*) b Nov. 24, 1955
*Botten, J. T. (NE Tvl & N. Tvl) b June 21, 1938
Boucher, J. C. (Ireland) b Dec. 22, 1910
Bourne, W. A. (B'dos & Warwicks.) b Nov. 15, 1952
*Bowden, M. P. (Surrey & Tvl) b Nov. 1, 1865, d Feb. 19, 1892
*Bowes, W. E. (Yorks.; *CY 1932*) b July 25, 1908, d Sept. 5, 1987
Bowler, P. D. (Leics., Tas. & Derbys.) b July 30, 1963
*Bowley, E. H. (Sussex & Auck.; *CY 1930*) b June 6, 1890, d July 9, 1974
Bowley, F. L. (Worcs.) b Nov. 9, 1873, d May 31, 1943
Box, T. (Sussex) b Feb. 7, 1808, d July 12, 1876
*Boyce, K. D. (B'dos & Essex; *CY 1974*) b Oct. 11, 1943
*Boycott, G. (Yorks. & N. Tvl; *CY 1965*) b Oct. 21, 1940
Boyd-Moss, R. J. (CUCC & Northants) b Dec. 16, 1959
Boyes, G. S. (Hants) b March 31, 1899, d Feb. 11, 1973
*Boyle, H. F. (Vic.) b Dec. 10, 1847, d Nov. 21, 1907
*Bracewell, B. P. (C. Dist., Otago & N. Dist.) b Sept. 14, 1959
*Bracewell, J. G. (Otago & Auck.) b April 15, 1958
*Bradburn, G. E. (N. Dist.) b May 26, 1966
*Bradburn, W. P. (N. Dist.) b Nov. 24, 1938
*Bradley, W. M. (Kent) b Jan. 2, 1875, d June 19, 1944
*Bradman, Sir D. G. (NSW & S. Aust.; *CY 1931*) b Aug. 27, 1908
Bradshaw, J. C. (Leics.) b Jan. 25, 1902, d Nov. 8, 1984
Brain, B. M. (Worcs. & Glos.) b Sept. 13, 1940
*Brain, D. H. (Zimb.) b Oct. 4, 1964
Bramall, Field-Marshal The Lord (Pres. MCC 1988-89) b Dec. 18, 1923
*Brandes, E. A. (Zimb.) b March 5, 1963
*Brann, W. H. (E. Prov.) b April 4, 1899, d Sept. 22, 1953
Brassington, A. J. (Glos.) b Aug. 9, 1954

*Braund, L. C. (Surrey & Som.; *CY 1902*) b Oct. 18, 1875, d Dec. 23, 1955

Bray, C. (Essex) b April 6, 1898, d Sept. 12, 1993

Brayshaw, I. J. (W. Aust.) b Jan. 14, 1942

Brazier, A. F. (Surrey & Kent) b Dec. 7, 1924

Breakwell, D. (Northants & Som.) b July 2, 1948

*Brearley, J. M. (CUCC & Middx; *CY 1977*) b April 28, 1942

*Brearley, W. (Lancs.; *CY 1909*) b March 11, 1876, d Jan. 13, 1937

*Brennan, D. V. (Yorks.) b Feb. 10, 1920, d Jan. 9, 1985

Briant, G. A. (Zimb.) b April 11, 1969

Bridge, W. B. (Warwicks.) b May 29, 1938

Bridger, Rev. J. R. (Hants) b April 8, 1920, d July 14, 1986

Brierley, T. L. (Glam., Lancs. & Canada) b June 15, 1910, d Jan. 7, 1989

Briers, N. E. (Leics.; *CY 1993*) b Jan. 15, 1955

*Briggs, John (Lancs.; *CY 1889*) b Oct. 3, 1862, d Jan. 11, 1902

*Bright, R. J. (Vic.) b July 13, 1954

*Briscoe, A. W. (Tvl) b Feb. 6, 1911, d April 22, 1941

*Broad, B. C. (Glos. & Notts.) b Sept. 29, 1957

Broadbent, R. G. (Worcs.) b June 21, 1924, d April 26, 1993

Brocklehurst, B. G. (Som.) b Feb. 18, 1922

*Brockwell, W. (Kimberley & Surrey; *CY 1895*) b Jan. 21, 1865, d June 30, 1935

Broderick, V. (Northants) b Aug. 17, 1920

Brodhurst, A. H. (CUCC & Glos.) b July 21, 1916

Bromfield, H. D. (W. Prov.) b June 26, 1932

*Bromley, E. H. (W. Aust. & Vic.) b Sept. 2, 1912, d Feb. 1, 1967

*Bromley-Davenport, H. R. (CUCC, Bombay Eur. & Middx) b Aug. 18, 1870, d May 23, 1954

*Brookes, D. (Northants; *CY 1957*) b Oct. 29, 1915

Brookes, W. H. (Editor of *Wisden* 1936-39) b Dec. 5, 1894, d May 28, 1955

Brooks, R. A. (OUCC & Som.) b June 14, 1943

*Brown, A. (Kent) b Oct. 17, 1935

Brown, A. D. (Surrey) b Feb. 11, 1970

Brown, A. S. (Glos.) b June 24, 1936

*Brown, D. J. (Warwicks.) b Jan. 30, 1942

Brown, D. W. J. (Glos.) b Feb. 26, 1942

*Brown, F. R. (CUCC, Surrey & Northants; *CY 1933*; Pres. MCC 1971-72) b Dec. 16, 1910, d July 24, 1991

*Brown, G. (Hants) b Oct. 6, 1887, d Dec. 3, 1964

Brown, J. (Scotland) b Sept. 24, 1931

*Brown, J. T. (Yorks.; *CY 1895*) b Aug. 20, 1869, d Nov. 4, 1904

Brown, K. R. (Middx) b March 18, 1963

*Brown, L. S. (Tvl, NE Tvl & Rhod.) b Nov. 24, 1910, d Sept. 1, 1983

Brown, R. D. (Zimb.) b March 11, 1951

Brown, S. J. E. (Northants & Durham) b June 29, 1969

Brown, S. M. (Middx) b Dec. 8, 1917, d Dec. 28, 1987

*Brown, V. R. (Cant. & Auck.) b Nov. 3, 1959

*Brown, W. A. (NSW & Qld; *CY 1939*) b July 31, 1912

Brown, W. C. (Northants) b Nov. 13, 1900, d Jan. 20, 1986

*Browne, C. R. (B'dos & BG) b Oct. 8, 1890, d Jan. 12, 1964

Bruce, Hon. C. N. (3rd Lord Aberdare) (OUCC & Middx) b Aug. 2, 1885, d Oct. 4, 1957

*Bruce, W. (Vic.) b May 22, 1864, d Aug. 3, 1925

Bryan, G. J. (Kent) b Dec. 29, 1902, d April 4, 1991

Bryan, J. L. (CUCC & Kent; *CY 1922*) b May 26, 1896, d April 23, 1985

Bryan, R. T. (Kent) b July 30, 1898, d July 27, 1970

*Buckenham, C. P. (Essex) b Jan. 16, 1876, d Feb. 23, 1937

Buckingham, J. (Warwicks.) b Jan. 21, 1903, d Jan. 25, 1987

Budd, E. H. (Middx & All-England) b Feb. 23, 1785, d March 29, 1875

Budd, W. L. (Hants) b Oct. 25, 1913, d Aug. 23, 1986

Bull, F. G. (Essex; *CY 1898*) b April 2, 1875, d Sept. 16, 1910

Buller, J. S. (Yorks. & Worcs.; Umpire) b Aug. 23, 1909, d Aug. 7, 1970

Burden, M. D. (Hants) b Oct. 4, 1930, d Nov. 9, 1987

*Burge, P. J. P. (Qld; *CY 1965*) b May 17, 1932

*Burger, C. G. de V. (Natal) b July 12, 1935

Burgess, G. I. (Som.) b May 5, 1943

*Burgess, M. G. (Auck.) b July 17, 1944

*Burke, C. (Auck.) b March 22, 1914

*Burke, J. W. (NSW; *CY 1957*) b June 12, 1930, d Feb. 2, 1979

Burke, S. F. (NE Tvl & OFS) b March 11, 1934

Burki, Javed (Pak. Us, OUCC, Punjab, Lahore, Kar., R'pindi & NWFP) b May 8, 1938

*Burmester, M. G. (Zimb.) b Jan. 24, 1968

*Burn, E. J. K. (K. E.) (Tas.) b Sept. 17, 1862, d July 20, 1956

Burnet, J. R. (Yorks.) b Oct. 11, 1918

Burns, N. D. (Essex, W. Prov. & Som.) b Sept. 19, 1965

Burnup, C. J. (CUCC & Kent; *CY 1903*) b Nov. 21, 1875, d April 5, 1960

Burrough, H. D. (Som.) b Feb. 6, 1909

*Burton, F. J. (Vic. & NSW) b Nov. 2, 1865, d Aug. 25, 1929

*Burtt, T. B. (Cant.) b Jan. 22, 1915, d May 24, 1988

Buse, H. F. T. (Som.) b Aug. 5, 1910, d Feb. 23, 1992

Bushby, M. H. (CUCC) b July 29, 1931

Buss, A. (Sussex) b Sept. 1, 1939

Buss, M. A. (Sussex & OFS) b Jan. 24, 1944

Buswell, J. E. (Northants) b July 3, 1909

Butchart, I. P. (Zimb.) b May 9, 1967

*Butcher, A. R. (Surrey & Glam.; *CY 1991*) b Jan. 7, 1954

*Butcher, B. F. (Guyana; *CY 1970*) b Sept. 3, 1933

Butcher, I. P. (Leics. & Glos.) b July 1, 1962

*Butcher, R. O. (Middx, B'dos & Tas.) b Oct. 14, 1953

*Butler, H. J. (Notts.) b March 12, 1913, d July 17, 1991

*Butler, L. S. (T/T) b Feb. 9, 1929

*Butt, H. R. (Sussex) b Dec. 27, 1865, d Dec. 21, 1928

*Butterfield, L. A. (Cant.) b Aug. 29, 1913

Butts, C. G. (Guyana) b July 8, 1957

Buxton, I. R. (Derbys.) b April 17, 1938

*Buys, I. D. (W. Prov.) b Feb. 3, 1895, dead

Byas, D. (Yorks.) b Aug. 26, 1963

*Bynoe, M. R. (B'dos) b Feb. 23, 1941

Caccia, Lord (Pres. MCC 1973-74) b Dec. 21, 1905, d Oct. 31, 1990

*Caddick, A. R. (Som.) b Nov. 21, 1968

Caesar, Julius (Surrey & All-England) b March 25, 1830, d March 6, 1878

Caffyn, W. (Surrey & NSW) b Feb. 2, 1828, d Aug. 28, 1919

Caine, C. Stewart (Editor of *Wisden* 1926-33) b Oct. 28, 1861, d April 15, 1933

*Cairns, B. L. (C. Dist., Otago & N. Dist.) b Oct. 10, 1949

*Cairns, C. L. (N. Dist., Notts. & Cant.) b June 13, 1970

Calder, H. L. (Cranleigh; *CY 1918*) b 1900

Callaghan, D. J. (E. Prov.) b Feb. 1, 1965

*Callaway, S. T. (NSW & Cant.) b Feb. 6, 1868, d Nov. 25, 1923

*Callen, I. W. (Vic. & Boland) b May 2, 1955

*Calthorpe, Hon. F. S. Gough- (CUCC, Sussex & Warwicks.) b May 27, 1892, d Nov. 19, 1935

*Camacho, G. S. (Guyana) b Oct. 15, 1945

*Cameron, F. J. (Jam.) b June 22, 1923

*Cameron, F. J. (Otago) b June 1, 1932

*Cameron, H. B. (Tvl, E. Prov. & W. Prov.; *CY 1936*) b July 5, 1905, d Nov. 2, 1935

*Cameron, J. H. (CUCC, Jam. & Som.) b April 8, 1914

*Campbell, A. D. R. (Zimb.) b Sept. 23, 1972

*Campbell, G. D. (Tas.) b March 10, 1964

*Campbell, T. (Tvl) b Feb. 9, 1882, d Oct. 5, 1924

Cannings, V. H. D. (Warwicks. & Hants) b April 3, 1919

*Capel, D. J. (Northants & E. Prov.) b Feb. 6, 1963

Caple, R. G. (Middx & Hants) b Dec. 8, 1939

Cardus, Sir Neville (Cricket Writer) b April 3, 1888, d Feb. 27, 1975

*Carew, G. McD. (B'dos) b June 4, 1910, d Dec. 9, 1974

*Carew, M. C. (T/T) b Sept. 15, 1937

*Carkeek, W. (Vic.) b Oct. 17, 1878, d Feb. 20, 1937

*Carlson, P. H. (Qld) b Aug. 8, 1951

*Carlstein, P. R. (OFS, Tvl, Natal & Rhod.) b Oct. 28, 1938

Carpenter, D. (Glos.) b Sept. 12, 1935

Carpenter, R. (Cambs. & Utd England XI) b Nov. 18, 1830, d July 13, 1901

*Carr, A. W. (Notts.; *CY 1923*) b May 21, 1893, d Feb. 7, 1963

*Carr, D. B. (OUCC & Derbys.; *CY 1960*; Sec. TCCB 1974-86) b Dec. 28, 1926

*Carr, D. W. (Kent; *CY 1910*) b March 17, 1872, d March 23, 1950

Carr, J. D. (OUCC & Middx) b June 15, 1963

Carrick, P. (Yorks. & E. Prov.) b July 16, 1952

Carrington, E. (Derbys.) b March 25, 1914

Carse, J. A. (Rhod., W. Prov., E. Prov. & Northants) b Dec. 13, 1958

*Carter, C. P. (Natal & Tvl) b April 23, 1881, d Nov. 8, 1952

*Carter, H. (NSW) b Halifax, Yorks. March 15, 1878, d June 8, 1948

Carter, R. G. (Warwicks.) b April 14, 1933

Carter, R. G. M. (Worcs.) b July 11, 1937

Carter, R. M. (Northants & Cant.) b May 25, 1960

Cartwright, H. (Derbys.) b May 12, 1951

*Cartwright, T. W. (Warwicks., Som. & Glam.) b July 22, 1935

Carty, R. A. (Hants) b July 28, 1922, d March 31, 1984

Cass, G. R. (Essex, Worcs. & Tas.) b April 23, 1940

Castell, A. T. (Hants) b Aug. 6, 1943

Castle, F. (Som.) b April 9, 1909

Catt, A. W. (Kent & W. Prov.) b Oct. 2, 1933

*Catterall, R. H. (Tvl, Rhod., Natal & OFS; *CY 1925*) b July 10, 1900, d Jan. 2, 1961

*Cave, H. B. (Wgtn & C. Dist.) b Oct. 10, 1922, d Sept. 15, 1989

Chalk, F. G. H. (OUCC & Kent) b Sept. 7, 1910, d Feb. 17, 1943

*Challenor, G. (B'dos) b June 28, 1888, d July 30, 1947

Chamberlain, W. R. F. (Northants; Chairman TCCB) b April 13, 1925

*Chandrasekhar, B. S. (†Karn.; *CY 1972*) b May 17, 1945

Chandrasekhar, V. B. (TN) b Aug. 21, 1961

*Chang, H. S. (Jam.) b July 22, 1952

*Chapman, A. P. F. (Uppingham, OUCC & Kent; *CY 1919*) b Sept. 3, 1900, d Sept. 16, 1961

*Chapman, H. W. (Natal) b June 30, 1890, d Dec. 1, 1941

*Chappell, G. S. (S. Aust., Som. & Qld; *CY 1973*) b Aug. 7, 1948

*Chappell, I. M. (S. Aust. & Lancs.; *CY 1976*) b Sept. 26, 1943

*Chappell, T. M. (S. Aust., W. Aust. & NSW) b Oct. 21, 1952

*Chapple, M. E. (Cant. & C. Dist.) b July 25, 1930, d July 31, 1985

*Charlton, P. C. (NSW) b April 9, 1867, d Sept. 30, 1954

*Charlwood, H. R. J. (Sussex) b Dec. 19, 1846, d June 6, 1888

*Chatfield, E. J. (Wgtn) b July 3, 1950

*Chatterton, W. (Derbys.) b Dec. 27, 1861, d March 19, 1913

*Chauhan, C. P. S. (M'tra & Delhi) b July 21, 1947

*Chauhan, R. K. (M. Pradesh) b Dec. 19, 1966

Cheatle, R. G. L. (Sussex & Surrey) b July 31, 1953

*Cheetham, J. E. (W. Prov.) b May 26, 1920, d Aug. 21, 1980

Chester, F. (Worcs.; Umpire) b Jan. 20, 1895, d April 8, 1957

Chesterton, G. H. (OUCC & Worcs.) b July 15, 1922

*Chevalier, G. A. (W. Prov.) b March 9, 1937

*Childs, J. H. (Glos. & Essex; *CY 1987*) b Aug. 15, 1951

*Chipperfield, A. G. (NSW) b Nov. 17, 1905, d July 29, 1987

Chisholm, R. H. E. (Scotland) b May 22, 1927

*Chowdhury, N. R. (Bihar & Bengal) b May 23, 1923, d Dec. 14, 1979

*Christiani, C. M. (BG) b Oct. 28, 1913, d April 4, 1938

*Christiani, R. J. (BG) b July 19, 1920

*Christopherson, S. (Kent; Pres. MCC 1939-45) b Nov. 11, 1861, d April 6, 1949

*Christy, J. A. J. (Tvl & Qld) b Dec. 12, 1904, d Feb. 1, 1971

*Chubb, G. W. A. (Border & Tvl) b April 12, 1911, d Aug. 28, 1982

Clark, D. G. (Kent; Pres. MCC 1977-78) b Jan. 27, 1919

Clark, E. A. (Middx) b April 15, 1937

*Clark, E. W. (Northants) b Aug. 9, 1902, d April 28, 1982

Clark, L. S. (Essex) b March 6, 1914

*Clark, W. M. (W. Aust.) b Sept. 19, 1953

*Clarke, Dr C. B. (B'dos, Northants & Essex) b April 7, 1918, d Oct. 14, 1993

*Clarke, S. T. (B'dos, Surrey, Tvl, OFS & N. Tvl) b Dec. 11, 1954

Clarke, William (Notts.; founded All-England XI & Trent Bridge ground) b Dec. 24, 1798, d Aug. 25, 1856

Clarkson, A. (Yorks. & Som.) b Sept. 5, 1939

Claughton, J. A. (OUCC & Warwicks.) b Sept. 17, 1956

*Clay, J. C. (Glam.) b March 18, 1898, d Aug. 12, 1973

Clay, J. D. (Notts.) b Oct. 15, 1924

Clayton, G. (Lancs. & Som.) b Feb. 3, 1938

Clements, S. M. (OUCC) b April 19, 1956

*Cleverley, D. C. (Auck.) b Dec. 23, 1909

Clift, Patrick B. (Rhod., Leics. & Natal) b July 14, 1953

Clift, Philip B. (Glam.) b Sept. 3, 1918

Clinton, G. S. (Kent, Surrey & Zimb.-Rhod.) b May 5, 1953

*Close, D. B. (Yorks. & Som.; *CY 1964*) b Feb. 24, 1931

Cobb, R. A. (Leics. & Natal) b May 18, 1961

Cobham, 10th Visct (Hon. C. J. Lyttelton) (Worcs.; Pres. MCC 1954) b Aug. 8, 1909, d March 20, 1977

*Cochrane, J. A. K. (Tvl & Griq. W.) b July 15, 1909, d June 15, 1987

Cock, D. F. (Essex) b Oct. 22, 1914, d Sept. 26, 1992

*Coen, S. K. (OFS, W. Prov., Tvl & Border) b Oct. 14, 1902, d Jan. 28, 1967

*Colah, S. M. H. (Bombay, W. Ind. & Naw.) b Sept. 22, 1902, d Sept. 11, 1950

Colchin, Robert ("Long Robin") (Kent & All-England) b Nov. 1713, d April 1750

*Coldwell, L. J. (Worcs.) b Jan. 10, 1933

*Colley, D. J. (NSW) b March 15, 1947

Collin, T. (Warwicks.) b April 7, 1911

*Collinge, R. O. (C. Dist., Wgtn & N. Dist.) b April 2, 1946

*Collins, H. L. (NSW) b Jan. 21, 1889, d May 28, 1959

Collins, R. (Lancs.) b March 10, 1934

*Colquhoun, I. A. (C. Dist.) b June 8, 1924

Coman, P. G. (Cant.) b April 13, 1943

*Commaille, J. M. M. (W. Prov., Natal, OFS & Griq. W.) b Feb. 21, 1883, d July 27, 1956

*Compton, D. C. S. (Middx & Holkar; *CY 1939*) b May 23, 1918

Compton, L. H. (Middx) b Sept. 12, 1912, d Dec. 27, 1984

*Coney, J. V. (Wgtn; *CY 1984*) b June 21, 1952

*Congdon, B. E. (C. Dist., Wgtn, Otago & Cant.; *CY 1974*) b Feb. 11, 1938

*Coningham, A. (NSW & Qld) b July 14, 1863, d June 13, 1939

*Connolly, A. N. (Vic. & Middx) b June 29, 1939

Connor, C. A. (Hants) b March 24, 1961

Constable, B. (Surrey) b Feb. 19, 1921

*Constant, D. J. (Kent & Leics.; Umpire) b Nov. 9, 1941

*Constantine, Lord L. N. (T/T & B'dos; *CY 1940*) b Sept. 21, 1902, d July 1, 1971

Constantine, L. S. (T/T) b May 25, 1874, d Jan. 5, 1942

*Contractor, N. J. (Guj. & Ind. Rlwys) b March 7, 1934

*Conyngham, D. P. (Natal, Tvl & W. Prov.) b May 10, 1897, d July 7, 1979

*Cook, C. (Glos.) b Aug. 23, 1921

*Cook, F. J. (E. Prov.) b 1870, dead

*Cook, G. (Northants & E. Prov.) b Oct. 9, 1951

*Cook, N. G. B. (Leics. & Northants) b June 17, 1956

*Cook, S. J. (Tvl & Som.; *CY 1990*) b July 31, 1953

Cook, T. E. (Sussex) b Feb. 5, 1901, d Jan. 15, 1950

*Cooper, A. H. C. (Tvl) b Sept 2, 1893, d July 18, 1963

*Cooper, B. B. (Middx, Kent & Vic.) b March 15, 1844, d Aug. 7, 1914

Cooper, F. S. Ashley- (Cricket Historian) b March 17, 1877, d Jan. 31, 1932

Cooper, G. C. (Sussex) b Sept. 2, 1936

Cooper, H. P. (Yorks. & N. Tvl) b April 17, 1949

Cooper, K. E. (Notts.) b Dec. 27, 1957

*Cooper, W. H. (Vic.) b Sept. 11, 1849, d April 5, 1939

*Cope, G. A. (Yorks.) b Feb. 23, 1947

*Copson, W. H. (Derbys.; *CY 1937*) b April 27, 1908, d Sept. 14, 1971

Cordle, A. E. (Glam.) b Sept. 21, 1940

Cork, D. G. (Derbys.) b Aug. 7, 1971

*Corling, G. E. (NSW) b July 13, 1941

Cornford, J. H. (Sussex) b Dec. 9, 1911, d June 17, 1985

*Cornford, W. L. (Sussex) b Dec. 25, 1900, d Feb. 6, 1964

Corrall, P. (Leics.) b July 16, 1906

Corran, A. J. (OUCC & Notts.) b Nov. 25, 1936

*Cosier, G. J. (Vic., S. Aust. & Qld) b April 25,1953

*Cottam, J. T. (NSW) b Sept. 5, 1867, d Jan. 30, 1897

*Cottam, R. M. H. (Hants & Northants) b Oct. 16, 1944

*Cotter, A. (NSW) b Dec. 3, 1884, d Oct. 31, 1917

Cottey, P. A. (Glam. & E. Tvl) b June 2, 1966

Cotton, J. (Notts. & Leics.) b Nov. 7, 1940

Cottrell, G. A. (CUCC) b March 23, 1945

*Coulthard, G. (Vic.) b Aug. 1, 1856, d Oct. 22, 1883

*Coventry, Hon. C. J. (Worcs.) b Feb. 26, 1867, d June 2, 1929

Coverdale, S. P. (CUCC, Yorks., & Northants) b Nov. 20, 1954

Cowan, M. J. (Yorks.) b June 10, 1933

*Cowans, N. G. (Middx) b April 17, 1961

*Cowdrey, C. S. (Kent & Glam.) b Oct. 20, 1957

Cowdrey, G. R. (Kent) b June 27, 1964

*Cowdrey, Sir M. C. (OUCC & Kent; *CY 1956*; Pres. MCC 1986-87) b Dec. 24, 1932

*Cowie, J. (Auck.) b March 30, 1912

Cowley, N. G. (Hants & Glam.) b March 1, 1953

*Cowper, R. M. (Vic. & W. Aust.) b Oct. 5, 1940

Cox, A. L. (Northants) b July 22, 1907, d Nov. 1986

Cox, G., jun. (Sussex) b Aug. 23, 1911, d March 30, 1985

Cox, G. R. (Sussex) b Nov. 29, 1873, d March 24, 1949

*Cox, J. L. (Natal) b June 28, 1886, d July 4, 1971

*Coxon, A. (Yorks.) b Jan. 18, 1916

Craig, E. J. (CUCC & Lancs.) b March 26, 1942

*Craig, I. D. (NSW) b June 12, 1935

Cranfield, L. M. (Glos.) b Aug. 29, 1909, d Nov. 18, 1993

Cranmer, P. (Warwicks.) b Sept. 10, 1914

*Cranston, J. (Glos.) b Jan. 9, 1859, d Dec. 10, 1904

*Cranston, K. (Lancs.) b Oct. 20, 1917

*Crapp, J. F. (Glos.) b Oct. 14, 1912, d Feb. 15, 1981

*Crawford, J. N. (Surrey, S. Aust., Wgtn & Otago; *CY 1907*) b Dec. 1, 1886, d May 2, 1963

*Crawford, P. (NSW) b Aug. 3, 1933

Crawley, A. M. (OUCC & Kent; Pres. MCC 1972-73) b April 10, 1908, d Nov. 3, 1993

Crawley, J. P. (Lancs. & CUCC) b Sept. 21, 1971

Crawley, M. A. (OUCC, Lancs. & Notts.) b Dec. 16, 1967

Cray, S. J. (Essex) b May 29, 1921

*Cresswell, G. F. (Wgtn & C. Dist.) b March 22, 1915, d Jan. 10, 1966

*Cripps, G. (W. Prov.) b Oct. 19, 1865, d July 27, 1943

*Crisp, R. J. (Rhod., W. Prov. & Worcs.) b May 28, 1911

*Crocker, G. J. (Zimb.) b May 16, 1962

*Croft, C. E. H. (Guyana & Lancs.) b March 15, 1953

Croft, R. D. B. (Glam.) b May 25, 1970

*Cromb, I. B. (Cant.) b June 25, 1905, d March 6, 1984

*Cronje, W. J. (OFS) b Sept. 25, 1969

Crookes, N. S. (Natal) b Nov. 15, 1935

Cross, G. F. (Leics.) b Nov. 15, 1943

*Crowe, J. J. (S. Aust. & Auck.) b Sept. 14, 1958

*Crowe, M. D. (Auck., C. Dist., Som. & Wgtn; *CY 1985*) b Sept. 22, 1962

Crump, B. S. (Northants) b April 25, 1938

Crush, E. (Kent) b April 25, 1917

*Cullinan, D. J. (Border, W. Prov. & Tvl) b March 4, 1967

Cumbes, J. (Lancs., Surrey, Worcs. & Warwicks.) b May 4, 1944

*Cummins, A. C. (B'dos & Durham) b May 7, 1966

*Cunis, R. S. (Auck. & N. Dist.) b Jan. 5, 1941

*Curnow, S. H. (Tvl) b Dec. 16, 1907, d July 28, 1986

Curran, K. M. (Glos., Zimb, Natal & Northants) b Sept. 7, 1959

*Curtis, T. S. (Worcs. & CUCC) b Jan. 15, 1960

Cuthbertson, G. B. (Middx, Sussex & Northants) b March 23, 1901, d August 9, 1993

Cutmore, J. A. (Essex) b Dec. 28, 1898, d Nov. 30, 1985

*Cuttell, W. R. (Lancs.; *CY 1898*) b Sept. 13, 1864, d Dec. 9, 1929

*Da Costa, O. C. (Jam.) b Sept. 11, 1907, d Oct. 1, 1936

Dacre, C. C. (Auck. & Glos.) b May 15, 1899, d Nov. 2, 1975

Daft, Richard (Notts. & All-England) b Nov. 2, 1835, d July 18, 1900

Dakin, G. F. (E. Prov.) b Aug. 13, 1935

Dale, A. (Glam.) b Oct. 24, 1968

*Dalton, E. L. (Natal) b Dec. 2, 1906, d June 3, 1981

Dani, H. T. (M'tra & Ind. Serv.) b May 24, 1933

*Daniel, W. W. (B'dos, Middx & W. Aust.) b Jan. 16, 1956

*D'Arcy, J. W. (Cant., Wgtn & Otago) b April 23, 1936

Dare, R. (Hants) b Nov. 26, 1921

*Darling, J. S. (S. Aust.; *CY 1900*) b Nov. 21, 1870, d Jan. 2, 1946

*Darling, L. S. (Vic.) b Aug. 14, 1909, d June 24, 1992

*Darling, W. M. (S. Aust.) b May 1, 1957

*Darnley, 8th Earl of (Hon. Ivo Bligh) (CUCC & Kent; Pres. MCC 1900) b March 13, 1859, d April 10, 1927

*Dassanayake, P. B. (Colts & Under-23) b July 11, 1970

Davey, J. (Glos.) b Sept. 4, 1944

*Davidson, A. K. (NSW; *CY 1962*) b June 14, 1929

Davies, Dai (Glam.) b Aug. 26, 1896, d July 16, 1976

Davies, Emrys (Glam.) b June 27, 1904, d Nov. 10, 1975

*Davies, E. Q. (E. Prov., Tvl & NE Tvl) b Aug. 26, 1909, d Nov. 11, 1976

Davies, H. D. (Glam.) b July 23, 1932

Davies, H. G. (Glam.) b April 23, 1912, d Sept. 4, 1993

Davies, J. G. W. (CUCC & Kent; Pres. MCC 1985-86) b Sept. 10, 1911, d Nov. 5, 1992

Davies, M. (Glam. & Glos.) b April 18, 1969

Davies, T. (Glam.) b Oct. 25, 1960

*Davis, B. A. (T/T & Glam.) b May 2, 1940

*Davis, C. A. (T/T) b Jan. 1, 1944

Davis, E. (Northants) b March 8, 1922

*Davis, I. C. (NSW & Qld) b June 25, 1953

Davis, M. R. (Som.) b Feb. 26, 1962

Davis, P. C. (Northants) b May 24, 1915

Davis, R. C. (Glam.) b Jan. 1, 1946

Davis, R. P. (Kent) b March 18, 1966

*Davis, S. P. (Vic.) b Nov. 8, 1959

*Davis, W. W. (Windwards, Glam., Tas., Northants & Wgtn) b Sept. 18, 1958

Davison, B. F. (Rhod., Leics, Tas. & Glos.) b Dec. 21, 1946

Davison, I. J. (Notts.) b Oct. 4, 1937

Dawkes, G. O. (Leics. & Derbys.) b July 19, 1920

*Dawson, E. W. (CUCC & Leics.) b Feb. 13, 1904, d June 4, 1979

*Dawson, O. C. (Natal & Border) b Sept. 1, 1919

Day, A. P. (Kent; *CY 1910*) b April 10, 1885, d Jan. 22, 1969

*de Alwis, R. G. (SSC) b Feb. 15, 1959

*Dean, H. (Lancs.) b Aug. 13, 1884, d March 12, 1957

*Deane, H. G. (Natal & Tvl) b July 21, 1895, d Oct. 21, 1939

*De Caires, F. I. (BG) b May 12, 1909, d Feb. 2, 1959

*De Courcy, J. H. (NSW) b April 18, 1927

*DeFreitas, P. A. J. (Leics. & Lancs.; *CY 1992*) b Feb. 18, 1966

Dekker, M. H. (Zimb.) b Dec. 5, 1969

Delisle, G. P. S. (OUCC & Middx) b Dec. 25, 1934

*Dell, A. R. (Qld) b Aug. 6, 1947

*de Mel, A. L. F. (SL) b May 9, 1959

*Dempster, C. S. (Wgtn, Leics., Scotland & Warwicks.; *CY 1932*) b Nov. 15, 1903, d Feb. 14, 1974

*Dempster, E. W. (Wgtn) b Jan. 25, 1925

*Denness, M. H. (Scotland, Kent & Essex; *CY 1975*) b Dec. 1, 1940

Dennett, E. G. (Glos.) b April 27, 1880, d Sept. 14, 1937

Denning, P. W. (Som.) b Dec. 16, 1949

Dennis, F. (Yorks.) b June 11, 1907

Dennis, S. J. (Yorks., OFS & Glam.) b Oct. 18, 1960

*Denton, D. (Yorks.; *CY 1906*) b July 4, 1874, d Feb. 16, 1950

Deodhar, D. B. (M'tra) b Jan. 14, 1892, d Aug. 24, 1993

*Depeiza, C. C. (B'dos) b Oct. 10, 1927

Derrick, J. (Glam.) b Jan. 15, 1963

*Desai, R. B. (Bombay) b June 20, 1939

De Saram, F. C. (OUCC & Ceylon) b Sept. 5, 1912, d April 11, 1983

*de Silva, A. M. (CCC) b Dec. 3, 1963

de Silva, D. L. S. (SL) b Nov. 17, 1956, d April 12, 1980

*de Silva, D. S. (SL) b June 11, 1942

*de Silva, E. A. R. (NCC) b March 28, 1956

de Silva, G. N. (SL) b March 12, 1955

*de Silva, G. R. A. (SL) b Dec. 12, 1952

*de Silva, P. A. (NCC) b Oct. 17, 1965

de Smidt, R. W. (W. Prov., longest-lived known first-class cricketer) b Nov. 24, 1883, d Aug. 3, 1986

Devereux, L. N. (Middx, Worcs. & Glam.) b Oct. 20, 1931

de Villiers, P. S. (N. Tvl & Kent) b Oct. 13, 1964

Dewdney, C. T. (Jam.) b Oct. 23, 1933

*Dewes, J. G. (CUCC & Middx) b Oct. 11, 1926

Dews, G. (Worcs.) b June 5, 1921

*Dexter, E. R. (CUCC & Sussex; *CY 1961*) b May 15, 1935

*Dharmasena, H. D. P. K. (TU & Ant.) b April 24, 1971

*Dias, R. L. (CCC) b Oct. 18, 1952

Dibbs, A. H. A. (Pres. MCC 1983-84) b Dec. 9, 1918, d Nov. 28, 1985

*Dick, A. E. (Otago & Wgtn) b Oct. 10, 1936

*Dickinson, G. R. (Otago) b March 11, 1903, d March 17, 1978

*Dilley, G. R. (Kent, Natal & Worcs.) b May 18, 1959

Diment, R. A. (Glos. & Leics.) b Feb. 9, 1927

*Dipper, A. E. (Glos.) b Nov. 9, 1885, d Nov. 7, 1945

*Divecha, R. V. (Bombay, OUCC, Northants, Vidarbha & S'tra) b Oct. 18, 1927

Diver, A. J. D. (Cambs., Middx, Notts. & All-England) b June 6, 1824, d March 25, 1876

Dixon, A. L. (Kent) b Nov. 27, 1933

*Dixon, C. D. (Tvl) b Feb. 12, 1891, d Sept. 9, 1969

Dodds, T. C. (Essex) b May 29, 1919

*Dodemaide, A. I. C. (Vic. & Sussex) b Oct. 5, 1963

*Doggart, G. H. G. (CUCC & Sussex; Pres. MCC 1981-82) b July 18, 1925

*D'Oliveira, B. L. (Worcs.; *CY 1967*) b Oct. 4, 1931

D'Oliveira, D. B. (Worcs.) b Oct. 19, 1960

*Dollery, H. E. (Warwicks. & Wgtn; *CY 1952*) b Oct. 14, 1914, d Jan. 20, 1987

Dollery, K. R. (Qld, Auck., Tas. & Warwicks.) b Dec. 9, 1924

*Dolphin, A. (Yorks.) b Dec. 24, 1885, d Oct. 23, 1942

*Donald, A. A. (OFS & Warwicks.; *CY 1992*) b Oct. 20, 1966

Donelan, B. T. P. (Sussex) b Jan. 3, 1968

*Donnan, H. (NSW) b Nov. 12, 1864, d Aug. 13, 1956

*Donnelly, M. P. (Wgtn, Cant., Middx, Warwicks. & OUCC; *CY 1948*) b Oct. 17, 1917

*Dooland, B. (S. Aust. & Notts.; *CY 1955*) b Nov. 1, 1923, d Sept. 8, 1980

Dorrinton, W. (Kent & All-England) b April 29, 1809, d Nov. 8, 1848

Dorset, 3rd Duke of (Kent) b March 24, 1745, d July 19, 1799

*Doshi, D. R. (Bengal, Notts., Warwicks. & S'tra) b Dec. 22, 1947

*Douglas, J. W. H. T. (Essex; *CY 1915*) b Sept. 3, 1882, d Dec. 19, 1930

Doull, S. B. (N. Dist.) b Aug. 6, 1969

Dowding, A. L. (OUCC) b April 4, 1929

Dowe, U. G. (Jam.) b March 29, 1949

*Dower, R. R. (E. Prov.) b June 4, 1876, d Sept. 15, 1964

*Dowling, G. T. (Cant.) b March 4, 1937

*Downton, P. R. (Kent & Middx) b April 4, 1957

*Draper, R. G. (E. Prov. & Griq. W.) b Dec. 24, 1926

Dredge, C. H. (Som.) b Aug. 4, 1954

*Druce, N. F. (CUCC & Surrey; *CY 1898*) b Jan. 1, 1875, d Oct. 27, 1954

Drybrough, C. D. (OUCC & Middx) b Aug. 31, 1938

*D'Souza, A. (Kar., Peshawar & PIA) b Jan. 17, 1939

*Ducat, A. (Surrey; *CY 1920*) b Feb. 16, 1886, d July 23, 1942

*Duckworth, C. A. R. (Natal & Rhod.) b March 22, 1933

*Duckworth, G. (Lancs.; *CY 1929*) b May 9, 1901, d Jan. 5, 1966

Dudleston, B. (Leics., Glos. & Rhod.) b July 16, 1945

Duers, K. G. (Zimb.) b June 30, 1960

*Duff, R. A. (NSW) b Aug. 17, 1878, d Dec. 13, 1911

*Dujon, P. J. L. (Jam.; *CY 1989*) b May 28, 1956

*Duleepsinhji, K. S. (CUCC & Sussex; *CY 1930*) b June 13, 1905, d Dec. 5, 1959

*Dumbrill, R. (Natal & Tvl) b Nov. 19, 1938

*Duminy, J. P. (OUCC, W. Prov. & Tvl) b Dec. 16, 1897, d Jan. 31, 1980

*Duncan, J. R. F. (Qld & Vic.) b March 25, 1944

*Dunell, O. R. (E. Prov.) b July 15, 1856, d Oct. 21, 1929

*Dunning, J. A. (Otago & OUCC) b Feb. 6, 1903, d June 24, 1971

*Du Preez, J. H. (Rhod. & Zimb.) b Nov. 14, 1942

*Durani, S. A. (S'tra, Guj. & Raja.) b Dec. 11, 1934

Durose, A. J. (Northants) b Oct. 10, 1944

*Durston, F. J. (Middx) b July 11, 1893, d April 8, 1965

*Du Toit, J. F. (SA) b April 5, 1868, d July 10, 1909

Dye, J. C. J. (Kent, Northants & E. Prov.) b July 24, 1942

Dyer, D. D. (Natal & Tvl) b Dec. 3, 1946

*Dyer, D. V. (Natal) b May 2, 1914, d June 18, 1990

*Dyer, G. C. (NSW) b March 16, 1959

Dyer, R. I. H. B. (Warwicks.) b Dec. 22, 1958

*Dymock, G. (Qld) b July 21, 1945

*Dyson, A. H. (Glam.) b July 10, 1905, d June 7, 1978

Dyson, J. (Lancs.) b July 8, 1934

*Dyson, John (NSW) b June 11, 1954

*Eady, C. J. (Tas.) b Oct. 29, 1870, d Dec. 20, 1945

*Eagar, E. D. R. (OUCC, Glos. & Hants) b Dec. 8, 1917, d Sept. 13, 1977

Eagar, M. A. (OUCC & Glos.) b March 20, 1934

Eaglestone, J. T. (Middx & Glam.) b July 24, 1923

Ealham, A. G. E. (Kent) b Aug. 30, 1944

Ealham, M. A. (Kent) b Aug. 27, 1969

East, D. E. (Essex) b July 27, 1959

East, R. E. (Essex) b June 20, 1947

Eastman, G. F. (Essex) b April 7, 1903, d March 15, 1991

Eastman, L. C. (Essex & Otago) b June 3, 1897, d April 17, 1941

*Eastwood, K. H. (Vic.) b Nov. 23, 1935

*Ebeling, H. I. (Vic.) b Jan. 1, 1905, d Jan. 12, 1980

Eckersley, P. T. (Lancs.) b July 2, 1904, d Aug. 13, 1940

*Edgar, B. A. (Wgtn) b Nov. 23, 1956

Edinburgh, HRH Duke of (Pres. MCC 1948-49, 1974-75) b June 10, 1921

Edmeades, B. E. A. (Essex) b Sept. 17, 1941

*Edmonds, P. H. (CUCC, Middx & E. Prov.) b March 8, 1951

Edmonds, R. B. (Warwicks.) b March 2, 1941

Edrich, B. R. (Kent & Glam.) b Aug. 18, 1922

Edrich, E. H. (Lancs.) b March 27, 1914, d July 9, 1993

Edrich, G. A. (Lancs.) b July 13, 1918

*Edrich, J. H. (Surrey; *CY 1966*) b June 21, 1937

*Edrich, W. J. (Middx; *CY 1940*) b March 26, 1916, d April 24, 1986

Edwards, G. N. (C. Dist.) b May 27, 1955

*Edwards, J. D. (Vic.) b June 12, 1862, d July 31, 1911

Edwards, M. J. (CUCC & Surrey) b March 1, 1940

*Edwards, R. (W. Aust. & NSW) b Dec. 1, 1942

*Edwards, R. M. (B'dos) b June 3, 1940

*Edwards, W. J. (W. Aust.) b Dec. 23, 1949

Eele, P. J. (Som.) b Jan. 27, 1935

Eggar, J. D. (OUCC, Hants & Derbys.) b Dec. 1, 1916, d May 3, 1983

*Ehtesham-ud-Din (Lahore, Punjab, PIA, NBP & UBL) b Sept. 4, 1950

Eksteen, C. E. (Tvl) b Dec. 2, 1966

*Elgie, M. K. (Natal) b March 6, 1933

Elliott, C. S. (Derbys.) b April 24, 1912

*Elliott, H. (Derbys.) b Nov. 2, 1891, d Feb. 2, 1976

Ellis, G. P. (Glam.) b May 24, 1950

Ellis, R. G. P. (OUCC & Middx) b Oct. 20 1960

*Ellison, R. M. (Kent & Tas.; *CY 1986*) b Sept. 21, 1959

Elms, R. B. (Kent & Hants) b April 5, 1949

*Emburey, J. E. (Middx & W. Prov.; *CY 1984*) b Aug. 20, 1952

*Emery, R. W. G. (Auck. & Cant.) b March 28, 1915, d Dec. 18, 1982

*Emery, S. H. (NSW) b Oct. 16, 1885, d Jan. 7, 1967

*Emmett, G. M. (Glos.) b Dec. 2, 1912, d Dec. 18, 1976

*Emmett, T. (Yorks.) b Sept. 3, 1841, d June 30, 1904

*Endean, W. R. (Tvl) b May 31, 1924

*Engineer, F. M. (Bombay & Lancs.) b Feb. 25, 1938

Essop-Adam, E. A. (Zimb.) b Nov. 16, 1968

*Evans, A. J. (OUCC, Hants & Kent) b May 1, 1889, d Sept. 18, 1960

Evans, C. N. (Zimb.) b Nov. 29, 1969

Evans, D. G. L. (Glam.; Umpire) b July 27, 1933, d March 25, 1990

*Evans, E. (NSW) b March 6, 1849, d July 2, 1921

Evans, G. (OUCC, Glam. & Leics.) b Aug. 13, 1915

Evans, J. B. (Glam.) b Nov. 9, 1936

Evans, K. P. (Notts.) b Sept. 10, 1963

*Evans, T. G. (Kent; *CY 1951*) b Aug. 18, 1920

Every, T. (Glam.) b Dec. 19, 1909, d Jan. 20, 1990

Eyre, T. J. P. (Derbys.) b Oct. 17, 1939

Faber, M. J. J. (OUCC & Sussex) b Aug. 15, 1950, d Dec. 10, 1991

*Fagg, A. E. (Kent) b June 18, 1915, d Sept. 13, 1977

Fairbairn, A. (Middx) b Jan. 25, 1923

Fairbrother, N. H. (Lancs.) b Sept. 9, 1963

*Fairfax, A. G. (NSW) b June 16, 1906, d May 17, 1955

Fairservice, C. (Kent & Middx) b Aug. 21, 1909

*Fane, F. L. (OUCC & Essex) b April 27, 1875, d Nov. 27, 1960

Fantham, W. E. (Warwicks.) b May 14, 1918

*Farnes, K. (CUCC & Essex; *CY 1939*) b July 8, 1911, d Oct. 20, 1941

*Farooq Hamid (Lahore & PIA) b March 3, 1945

*Farrer, W. S. (Border) b Dec. 8, 1936

*Farrimond, W. (Lancs.) b May 23, 1903, d Nov. 14, 1979

Farrukh Zaman (Peshawar, NWFP, Punjab & MCB) b April 2, 1956

*Faulkner, G. A. (Tvl) b Dec. 17, 1881, d Sept. 10, 1930

*Favell, L. E. (S. Aust.) b Oct. 6, 1929, d June 14, 1987

*Fazal Mahmood (N. Ind., Punjab & Lahore; *CY 1955*) b Feb. 18, 1927

Fearnley, C. D. (Worcs.) b April 12, 1940

Featherstone, N. G. (Tvl, N. Tvl, Middx & Glam.) b Aug. 20, 1949

'Felix', N. (Wanostrocht) (Kent, Surrey & All-England) b Oct. 4, 1804, d Sept. 3, 1876

*Fellows-Smith, J. P. (OUCC, Tvl & Northants) b Feb. 3, 1932

Feltham, M. A. (Surrey & Middx) b June 26, 1963

Felton, N. A. (Som. & Northants) b Oct. 24, 1960

*Fender, P. G. H. (Sussex & Surrey; *CY 1915*) b Aug. 22, 1892, d June 15, 1985

Ferguson, W. (T/T) b Dec. 14, 1917, d Feb. 23, 1961

*Fernandes, M. P. (BG) b Aug. 12, 1897, d May 8, 1981

Fernando, E. R. (SL) b Feb. 22, 1944

*Fernando, E. R. N. S. (SLAF) b Dec. 19, 1955

Fernando, T. L. (Colts) b Dec. 27, 1962

Ferreira, A. M. (N. Tvl & Warwicks.) b April 13, 1955

Ferris, G. J. F. (Leics. & Leewards) b Oct. 18, 1964

**Ferris, J. J. (NSW, Glos. & S. Aust.; *CY 1889*) b May 21, 1867, d Nov. 21, 1900

*Fichardt, C. G. (OFS) b March 20, 1870, d May 30, 1923

Fiddling, K. (Yorks. & Northants) b Oct. 13, 1917, d June 19, 1992

*Fielder, A. (Kent; *CY 1907*) b July 19, 1877, d Aug. 30, 1949

Findlay, T. M. (Comb. Is. & Windwards) b Oct. 19, 1943

Findlay, W. (OUCC & Lancs.; Sec. Surrey CCC, Sec. MCC 1926-36) b June 22, 1880, d June 19, 1953

*Fingleton, J. H. (NSW) b April 28, 1908, d Nov. 22, 1981

*Finlason, C. E. (Tvl & Griq. W.) b Feb. 19, 1860, d July 31, 1917

Finney, R. J. (Derbys.) b Aug. 2, 1960

Firth, Rev. Canon J. D'E. E. (Winchester, OUCC & Notts.; *CY 1918*) b Jan. 21, 1900, d Sept. 21, 1957

Fisher, F. E. (Wgtn & C. Dist.) b July 28, 1924

Fisher, P. B. (OUCC, Middx & Worcs.) b Dec. 19, 1954

*Fishlock, L. B. (Surrey; *CY 1947*) b Jan. 2, 1907, d June 26, 1986

Fitton, J. D. (Lancs.) b Aug. 24, 1965

Fitzgerald, R. A. (CUCC & Middx; Sec. MCC 1863-76) b Oct. 1, 1834, d Oct. 28, 1881

*Flavell, J. A. (Worcs.; *CY 1965*) b May 15, 1929

*Fleetwood-Smith, L. O'B. (Vic.) b March 30, 1908, d March 16, 1971

Fleming, M. V. (Kent) b Dec. 12, 1964

Fletcher, D. A. G. (Rhod. & Zimb.) b Sept. 27, 1948

Fletcher, D. G. W. (Surrey) b July 6, 1924

*Fletcher, K. W. R. (Essex; *CY 1974*) b May 20, 1944

Fletcher, S. D. (Yorks. & Lancs.) b June 8, 1964

*Floquet, C. E. (Tvl) b Nov. 3, 1884, d Nov. 22, 1963

*Flower, A. (Zimb.) b April 28, 1968

*Flower, G. W. (Zimb.) b Dec. 20, 1970

*Flowers, W. (Notts.) b Dec. 7, 1856, d Nov. 1, 1926

Foat, J. C. (Glos.) b Nov. 21, 1952

*Foley, H. (Wgtn) b Jan. 28, 1906, d Oct. 16, 1948

Folland, N. A. (Som.) b Sept. 17, 1963

Folley, I. (Lancs. & Derbys.) b Jan. 9, 1963, d Aug. 30, 1993

Foord, C. W. (Yorks.) b June 11, 1924

Forbes, C. (Notts.) b Aug. 9, 1936

*Ford, F. G. J. (CUCC & Middx) b Dec. 14, 1866, d Feb. 7, 1940

Ford, N. M. (OUCC, Derbys. & Middx) b Nov. 18, 1906

Fordham, A. (Northants) b Nov. 9, 1964

Foreman, D. J. (W. Prov. & Sussex) b Feb. 1, 1933

*Foster, F. R. (Warwicks.; *CY 1912*) b Jan. 31, 1889, d May 3, 1958

Foster, G. N. (OUCC, Worcs. & Kent) b Oct. 16, 1884, d Aug. 11, 1971

Foster, H. K. (OUCC & Worcs.; *CY 1911*) b Oct. 30, 1873, d June 23, 1950

Foster, M. K. (Worcs.) b Jan. 1, 1889, d Dec. 3, 1940

*Foster, M. L. C. (Jam.) b May 9, 1943

*Foster, N. A. (Essex & Tvl; *CY 1988*) b May 6, 1962

Foster, P. G. (Kent) b Oct. 9, 1916

*Foster, R. E. (OUCC & Worcs.; *CY 1901*) b April 16, 1878, d May 13, 1914

*Fothergill, A. J. (Som.) b Aug. 26, 1854, d Aug. 1, 1932

Fotheringham, H. R. (Natal & Tvl) b April 4, 1953

*Fowler, G. (Lancs. & Durham) b April 20, 1957

Fowler, W. P. (Derbys., N. Dist. & Auck.) b March 13, 1959

*Francis, B. C. (NSW & Essex) b Feb. 18, 1948

Francis, D. A. (Glam.) b Nov. 29, 1953

*Francis, G. N. (B'dos) b Dec. 7, 1897, d Jan. 12, 1942

*Francis, H. H. (Glos. & W. Prov.) b May 26, 1868, d Jan. 7, 1936

Francke, F. M. (SL & Qld) b March 29, 1941

*Francois, C. M. (Griq. W.) b June 20, 1897, d May 26, 1944

*Frank, C. N. (Tvl) b Jan. 27, 1891, d Dec. 26, 1961

*Frank, W. H. B. (SA) b Nov. 23, 1872, d Feb. 16, 1945

Franklin, H. W. F. (OUCC, Surrey & Essex) b June 30, 1901, d May 25, 1985

*Franklin, T. J. (Auck.) b March 18, 1962

*Fraser, A. R. C. (Middx) b Aug. 8, 1965

*Frederick, M. C. (B'dos, Derbys. & Jam.) b May 6, 1927

*Fredericks, R. C. (†Guyana & Glam.; *CY 1974*) b Nov. 11, 1942

*Freeman, A. P. (Kent; *CY 1923*) b May 17, 1888, d Jan. 28, 1965

*Freeman, D. L. (Wgtn) b Sept. 8, 1914

*Freeman, E. W. (S. Aust.) b July 13, 1944

*Freer, F. W. (Vic.) b Dec. 4, 1915

*French, B. N. (Notts.) b Aug. 13, 1959

Frost, G. (Notts.) b Jan. 15, 1947

Frost, M. (Surrey & Glam.) b Oct. 21, 1962

Fry, C. A. (OUCC, Hants & Northants) b Jan. 14, 1940

*Fry, C. B. (OUCC, Sussex & Hants; *CY 1895*) b April 25, 1872, d Sept. 7, 1956

*Fuller, E. R. H. (W. Prov.) b Aug. 2, 1931

*Fuller, R. L. (Jam.) b Jan. 30, 1913, d May 3, 1987

*Fullerton, G. M. (Tvl) b Dec. 8, 1922

Funston, G. K. (NE Tvl & Griq. W.) b Nov. 21, 1948

*Funston, K. J. (NE Tvl, OFS & Tvl) b Dec. 3, 1925

*Furlonge, H. A. (T/T) b June 19, 1934

Gabriel, R. S. (T/T) b June 5, 1952

*Gadkari, C. V. (M'tra & Ind. Serv.) b Feb. 3, 1928

*Gaekwad, A. D. (Baroda) b Sept. 23, 1952

*Gaekwad, D. K. (Baroda) b Oct. 27, 1928

*Gaekwad, H. G. (†M. Pradesh) b Aug. 29, 1923

Gale, R. A. (Middx) b Dec. 10, 1933

Gallian, J. E. R. (Lancs. & OUCC) b June 25, 1971

*Gallichan, N. (Wgtn) b June 3, 1906, d March 25, 1969

*Gamsy, D. (Natal) b Feb. 17, 1940

*Gandotra, A. (Delhi & Bengal) b Nov. 24, 1948

Ganguly, S. C. (Bengal) b July 8, 1966

*Gannon, J. B. (W. Aust.) b Feb. 8, 1947

*Ganteaume, A. G. (T/T) b Jan. 22, 1921

Gard, T. (Som.) b June 2, 1957

Gardner, L. R. (Leics.) b Feb. 23, 1934

Garland-Wells, H. M. (OUCC & Surrey) b Nov. 14, 1907, d May 28, 1993

Garlick, R. G. (Lancs. & Northants) b April 11, 1917, d May 16, 1988

*Garner, J. (B'dos, Som. & S. Aust.; *CY 1980*) b Dec. 16, 1952

Garnham, M. A. (Glos., Leics. & Essex) b Aug. 20, 1960

Garrett, T. W. (NSW) b July 26, 1858, d Aug. 6, 1943

*Gaskin, B. B. MacG. (BG) b March 21, 1908, d May 1, 1979

*Gatting, M. W. (Middx; *CY 1984*) b June 6, 1957

*Gaunt, R. A. (W. Aust. & Vic.) b Feb. 26, 1934

*Gavaskar, S. M. (Bombay & Som.; *CY 1980*) b July 10, 1949

*Gay, L. H. (CUCC, Hants & Som.) b March 24, 1871, d Nov. 1, 1949

Geary, A. C. T. (Surrey) b Sept. 11, 1900, d Jan. 23, 1989

*Geary, G. (Leics.; *CY 1927*) b July 9, 1893, d March 6, 1981

Gedye, S. G. (Auck.) b May 2, 1929

*Gehrs, D. R. A. (S. Aust.) b Nov. 29, 1880, d June 25, 1953

Ghai, R. S. (Punjab) b June 12, 1960

*Ghavri, K. D. (S'tra & Bombay) b Feb. 28, 1951

*Ghazali, M. E. Z. (M'tra & Pak. Serv.) b June 15, 1924

*Ghorpade, J. M. (Baroda) b Oct. 2, 1930, d March 29, 1978

*Ghulam Abbas (Kar., NBP & PIA) b May 1, 1947

*Ghulam Ahmed (H'bad) b July 4, 1922

Ghulam Ali (Kar. & PACO) b Sept. 8, 1966

*Gibb, P. A. (CUCC, Scotland, Yorks. & Essex) b July 11, 1913, d Dec. 7, 1977

Gibbons, H. H. (Worcs.) b Oct. 10, 1904, d Feb. 16, 1973

*Gibbs, G. L. (BG) b Dec. 27, 1925, d Feb. 21, 1979

*Gibbs, L. R. (†Guyana, S. Aust. & Warwicks.; *CY 1972*) b Sept. 29, 1934

Gibbs, P. J. K. (OUCC & Derbys.) b Aug. 17, 1944

Gibson, C. H. (Eton, CUCC & Sussex; *CY 1918*) b Aug. 23, 1900, d Dec. 31, 1976

Gibson, D. (Surrey) b May 1, 1936

Giddins, E. S. H. (Sussex), b July 20, 1971

*Giffen, G. (S. Aust.; *CY 1894*) b March 27, 1859, d Nov. 29, 1927

*Giffen, W. F. (S. Aust.) b Sept. 20, 1861, d June 29, 1949

*Gifford, N. (Worcs. & Warwicks.; *CY 1975*) b March 30, 1940

*Gilbert, D. R. (NSW, Tas. & Glos.) b Dec. 29, 1960

*Gilchrist, R. (Jam. & H'bad) b June 28, 1934

Giles, R. J. (Notts.) b Oct. 17, 1919

Gilhouley, K. (Yorks. & Notts.) b Aug. 8, 1934

Gill, A. (Notts.) b Aug. 4, 1940

*Gillespie, S. R. (Auck.) b March 2, 1957

Gilliat, R. M. C. (OUCC & Hants) b May 20, 1944

*Gilligan, A. E. R. (CUCC, Surrey & Sussex; *CY 1924*; Pres. MCC 1967-68) b Dec. 23, 1894, d Sept. 5, 1976

*Gilligan, A. H. H. (Sussex) b June 29, 1896, d May 5, 1978

Gilligan, F. W. (OUCC & Essex) b Sept. 20, 1893, d May 4, 1960

*Gilmour, G. J. (NSW) b June 26, 1951

*Gimblett, H. (Som.; *CY 1953*) b Oct. 19, 1914, d March 30, 1978

Gladstone, G. (*see* Marais, G. G.)

Gladwin, Chris (Essex & Derbys.) b May 10, 1962

*Gladwin, Cliff (Derbys.) b April 3, 1916, d April 10, 1988

*Gleeson, J. W. (NSW & E. Prov.) b March 14, 1938

*Gleeson, R. A. (E. Prov.) b Dec. 6, 1873, d Sept. 27, 1919

Glendenen, J. D. (Durham) b June 20, 1965

*Glover, G. K. (Kimberley & Griq. W.) b May 13, 1870, d Nov. 15, 1938

Glover, T. R. (OUCC) b Nov. 26, 1951

Goddard, G. F. (Scotland) b May 19, 1938

*Goddard, J. D. C. (B'dos) b April 21, 1919, d Aug. 26, 1987

*Goddard, T. L. (Natal & NE Tvl) b Aug. 1, 1931

*Goddard, T. W. J. (Glos.; *CY 1938*) b Oct. 1, 1900, d May 22, 1966

Goel, R. (Patiala & Haryana) b Sept. 29, 1942

Goldsmith, S. C. (Kent & Derbys.) b Dec. 19, 1964

Goldstein, F. S. (OUCC, Northants, Tvl & W. Prov.) b Oct. 14, 1944

*Gomes, H. A. (T/T & Middx; *CY 1985*) b July 13, 1953

*Gomez, G. E. (T/T) b Oct. 10, 1919

*Gooch, G. A. (Essex & W. Prov.; *CY 1980*) b July 23, 1953

Goodway, C. C. (Warwicks.) b July 10, 1909, d May 22, 1991

Goodwin, K. (Lancs.) b June 25, 1938

Goodwin, T. J. (Leics.) b Jan. 22, 1929

Goonatillake, F. R. M. de S. (SL) b. Aug. 15, 1951

*Goonatillake, H. M. (SL) b Aug. 16, 1952

Goonesena, G. (Ceylon, Notts., CUCC & NSW) b Feb. 16, 1931

*Gopalan, M. J. (Madras) b June 6, 1909

*Gopinath, C. D. (Madras) b March 1, 1930

*Gordon, N. (Tvl) b Aug. 6, 1911

Gore, A. C. (Eton & Army; *CY 1919*) b May 14, 1900, d June 7, 1990

Gough, D. (Yorks.) b Sept. 18, 1970

Gould, I. J. (Middx, Auck. & Sussex) b Aug. 19, 1957

*Gover, A. R. (Surrey; *CY 1937*) b Feb. 29, 1908

*Gower, D. I. (Leics. & Hants; *CY 1979*) b April 1, 1957

Gowrie, 1st Lord (Pres. MCC 1948-49) b July 6, 1872, d May 2, 1955

Grace, Dr Alfred b May 17, 1840, d May 24, 1916

Grace, Dr Alfred H. (Glos.) b March 10, 1866, d Sept. 16, 1929

Grace, C. B. (Clifton) b March 1882, d June 6, 1938

*Grace, Dr E. M. (Glos.) b Nov. 28, 1841, d May 20, 1911

Grace, Dr Edgar M. (MCC) (son of E. M. Grace) b Oct. 6, 1886, d Nov. 24, 1974

*Grace, G. F. (Glos.) b Dec. 13, 1850, d Sept. 22, 1880

Grace, Dr Henry (Glos.) b Jan. 31, 1833, d Nov. 15, 1895

Grace, Dr H. M. (father of W. G., E. M. and G. F.) b Feb. 21, 1808, d Dec. 23, 1871

Grace, Mrs H. M. (mother of W. G., E. M. and G. F.) b July 18, 1812, d July 25, 1884

*Grace, Dr W. G. (Glos.; *CY 1896*) b July 18, 1848, d Oct. 23, 1915

Grace, W. G., jun. (CUCC & Glos.) b July 6, 1874, d March 2, 1905

Graf, S. F. (Vic., W. Aust. & Hants) b May 19, 1957

*Graham, H. (Vic. & Otago) b Nov. 22, 1870, d Feb. 7, 1911

Graham, J. N. (Kent) b May 8, 1943

*Graham, R. (W. Prov.) b Sept. 16, 1877, d April 21, 1946

*Grant, G. C. (CUCC, T/T & Rhod.) b May 9, 1907, d Oct. 26, 1978

*Grant, R. S. (CUCC & T/T) b Dec. 15, 1909, d Oct. 18, 1977

Graveney, D. A. (Glos., Som. & Durham) b Jan. 2, 1953

Graveney, J. K. (Glos.) b Dec. 16, 1924

*Graveney, T. W. (Glos., Worcs. & Qld; *CY 1953*) b June 16, 1927

Graves, P. J. (Sussex & OFS) b May 19, 1946

*Gray, A. H. (T/T & Surrey) b May 23, 1963

*Gray, E. J. (Wgtn) b Nov. 18, 1954

Gray, J. R. (Hants) b May 19, 1926

Greasley, D. G. (Northants) b Jan. 20, 1926

*Greatbatch, M. J. (C. Dist.) b Dec. 11, 1963

Green, A. M. (Sussex & OFS) b May 28, 1960

Green, D. J. (Derbys. & CUCC) b Dec. 18, 1935

Green, D. M. (OUCC, Lancs. & Glos.; *CY 1969*) b Nov. 10, 1939

*Greenhough, T. (Lancs.) b Nov. 9, 1931

*Greenidge, A. E. (B'dos) b Aug. 20, 1956

*Greenidge, C. G. (Hants & B'dos; *CY 1977*) b May 1, 1951

*Greenidge, G. A. (B'dos & Sussex) b May 26, 1948

Greensmith, W. T. (Essex) b Aug. 16, 1930

*Greenwood, A. (Yorks.) b Aug. 20, 1847, d Feb. 12, 1889

Greenwood, P. (Lancs.) b Sept. 11, 1924

Greetham, C. (Som.) b Aug. 28, 1936

*Gregory, David W. (NSW; first Australian captain) b April 15, 1845, d Aug. 4, 1919

*Gregory, E. J. (NSW) b May 29, 1839, d April 22, 1899

*Gregory, J. M. (NSW; *CY 1922*) b Aug. 14, 1895, d Aug. 7, 1973

*Gregory, R. G. (Vic.) b Feb. 28, 1916, d June 10, 1942

*Gregory, S. E. (NSW; *CY 1897*) b April 14, 1870, d August 1, 1929

*Greig, A. W. (Border, E. Prov. & Sussex; *CY 1975*) b Oct. 6, 1946

*Greig, I. A. (CUCC, Border, Sussex & Surrey) b Dec. 8, 1955

*Grell, M. G. (T/T) b Dec. 18, 1899, d Jan. 11, 1976

*Grieve, B. A. F. (Eng.) b May 28, 1864, d Nov. 19, 1917

Grieves, K. J. (NSW & Lancs.) b Aug. 27, 1925, d Jan. 3, 1992

*Grieveson, R. E. (Tvl) b Aug. 24, 1909

*Griffin, G. M. (Natal & Rhod.) b June 12, 1939

*Griffith, C. C. (B'dos; *CY 1964*) b Dec. 14, 1938

Griffith, G. ("Ben") (Surrey & Utd England XI) b Dec. 20, 1833, d May 3, 1879

*Griffith, H. C. (B'dos) b Dec. 1, 1893, d March 18, 1980

Griffith, K. (Worcs.) b Jan. 17, 1950

Griffith, M. G. (CUCC & Sussex) b Nov. 25, 1943

*Griffith, S. C. (CUCC, Surrey & Sussex; Sec. MCC 1962-74; Pres. MCC 1979-80) b June 16, 1914, d April 7, 1993

Griffiths, B. J. (Northants) b June 13, 1949

Griffiths, Rt Hon. The Lord (W. H.) (CUCC & Glam.; Pres. MCC 1990-91) b Sept. 26, 1923

*Grimmett, C. V. (Wgtn, Vic. & S. Aust.; *CY 1931*) b Dec. 25, 1891, d May 2, 1980

Grimshaw, N. (Northants) b May 5, 1911

*Groube, T. U. (Vic.) b Sept. 2, 1857, d Aug. 5, 1927

*Grout, A. T. W. (Qld) b March 30, 1927, d Nov. 9, 1968

Grover, J. N. (OUCC) b Oct. 15, 1915, d Dec. 17, 1990

Groves, M. G. M. (OUCC, Som. & W. Prov.) b Jan. 14, 1943

Grundy, J. (Notts. & Utd England XI) b March 5, 1824, d Nov. 24, 1873

*Guard, G. M. (Bombay & Guj.) b Dec. 12, 1925, d March 13, 1978

*Guest, C. E. J. (Vic. & W. Aust.) b Oct. 7, 1937

*Guha, S. (Bengal) b Jan. 31, 1946

**Guillen, S. C. (T/T & Cant.) b Sept. 24, 1924

Guise, J. L. (OUCC & Middx) b Nov. 25, 1903, d June 29, 1991

**Gul Mahomed (N. Ind., Baroda, H'bad, Punjab & Lahore) b Oct. 15, 1921, d May 8, 1992

*Gunasekera, Y. (SL) b Nov. 8, 1957

*Guneratne, R. P. W. (Nomads) b Jan. 26, 1962

*Gunn, G. (Notts.; *CY 1914*) b June 13, 1879, d June 29, 1958

Gunn, G. V. (Notts.) b June 21, 1905, d Oct. 14, 1957

*Gunn, J. (Notts.; *CY 1904*) b July 19, 1876, d Aug. 21, 1963

Gunn, T. (Sussex) b Sept. 27, 1935

*Gunn, William (Notts.; *CY 1890*) b Dec. 4, 1858, d Jan. 29, 1921

*Gupte, B. P. (Bombay, Bengal & Ind. Rlwys) b Aug. 30, 1934

*Gupte, S. P. (Bombay, Bengal, Raja. & T/T) b Dec. 11, 1929

*Gursharan Singh (Punjab) b March 8, 1963

*Gurusinha, A. P. (SSC & NCC) b Sept. 16, 1966

*Guy, J. W. (C. Dist., Wgtn, Northants, Cant., Otago & N. Dist.) b Aug. 29, 1934

Haafiz Shahid (WAPDA) b May 10, 1963

Hacker, P. J. (Notts., Derbys. & OFS) b July 16, 1952

Hadlee, B. G. (Cant.) b Dec. 14, 1941

*Hadlee, D. R. (Cant.) b Jan. 6, 1948

*Hadlee, Sir R. J. (Cant., Notts. & Tas.; *CY 1982*) b July 3, 1951

*Hadlee, W. A. (Cant. & Otago) b June 4, 1915

Hafeez, A. (*see* Kardar)

*Haig, N. E. (Middx) b Dec. 12, 1887, d Oct. 27, 1966

*Haigh, S. (Yorks.; *CY 1901*) b March 19, 1871, d Feb. 27, 1921

Halfyard, D. J. (Kent & Notts.) b April 3, 1931

*Hall, A. E. (Tvl & Lancs.) b Jan. 23, 1896, d Jan. 1, 1964

*Hall, G. G. (NE Tvl & E. Prov.) b May 24, 1938, d June 26, 1987

Hall, I. W. (Derbys.) b Dec. 27, 1939

Hall, J. W. (Sussex) b March 30, 1968

Hall, Louis (Yorks.; *CY 1890*) b Nov. 1, 1852, d Nov. 19, 1915

Hall, T. A. (Derbys. & Som.) b Aug. 19, 1930, d April 21, 1984

*Hall, W. W. (B'dos, T/T & Qld) b Sept. 12, 1937

Hallam, A. W. (Lancs. & Notts.; *CY 1908*) b Nov. 12, 1869, d July 24, 1940

Hallam, M. R. (Leics.) b Sept. 10, 1931

*Halliwell, E. A. (Tvl & Middx; *CY 1905*) b Sept. 7, 1864, d Oct. 2, 1919

*Hallows, C. (Lancs.; *CY 1928*) b April 4, 1895, d Nov. 10, 1972

Hallows, J. (Lancs.; *CY 1905*) b Nov. 14, 1873, d May 20, 1910

Halse, C. G. (Natal) b Feb. 28, 1935

*Hamence, R. A. (S. Aust.) b Nov. 25, 1915

Hamer, A. (Yorks. & Derbys.) b Dec. 8, 1916, d Nov. 3, 1993

Hammond, H. E. (Sussex) b Nov. 7, 1907, d June 16, 1985

*Hammond, J. R. (S. Aust.) b April 19, 1950

*Hammond, W. R. (Glos.; *CY 1928*) b June 19, 1903, d July 1, 1965

Hampshire, J. H. (Yorks., Derbys. & Tas.; Umpire) b Feb. 10, 1941

Hancock, T. H. C. (Glos.) b April 20, 1972

*Hands, P. A. M. (W. Prov.) b March 18, 1890, d April 27, 1951

*Hands, R. H. M. (W. Prov.) b July 26, 1888, d April 20, 1918

*Hanif Mohammad (B'pur, Kar. & PIA; *CY 1968*) b Dec. 21, 1934

*Hanley, M. A. (Border & W. Prov.) b Nov. 10, 1918

Hanley, R. W. (E. Prov., OFS, Tvl & Northants) b Jan. 29, 1952

*Hanumant Singh (M. Pradesh & Raja.) b March 29, 1939

Harbord, W. E. (Yorks. & OUCC) b Dec. 15, 1908, d July 28, 1992

Harden, R. J. (Som. & C. Dist.) b Aug. 16, 1965

Hardie, B. R. (Scotland & Essex) b Jan. 14, 1950

Hardikar, M. S. (Bombay) b Feb. 8, 1936

*Hardinge, H. T. W. (Kent; *CY 1915*) b Feb. 25, 1886, d May 8, 1965

*Hardstaff, J. (Notts.) b Nov. 9, 1882, d April 2, 1947

*Hardstaff, J., jun. (Notts. & Auck.; *CY 1938*) b July 3, 1911, d Jan. 1, 1990

Hardy, J. J. E. (Hants, Som., W. Prov. & Glos.) b Oct. 2, 1960

Harfield, L. (Hants) b Aug. 16, 1905, d Nov. 19, 1985

*Harford, N. S. (C. Dist. & Auck.) b Aug. 30, 1930, d March 30, 1981

*Harford, R. I. (Auck.) b May 30, 1936

Harman, R. (Surrey) b Dec. 28, 1941

*Haroon Rashid (Kar., Sind, NBP, PIA & UBL) b March 25, 1953

*Harper, R. A. (Guyana & Northants) b March 17, 1963

*Harris, 4th Lord (OUCC & Kent; Pres. MCC 1895) b Feb. 3, 1851, d March 24, 1932

*Harris, C. Z. (Cant.) b Nov. 20, 1969

Harris, David (Hants & All-England) b 1755, d May 19, 1803

Harris, M. J. (Middx, Notts., E. Prov. & Wgtn) b May 25, 1944

*Harris, P. G. Z. (Cant.) b July 18, 1927, d Dec. 1, 1991

*Harris, R. M. (Auck.) b July 27, 1933

*Harris, T. A. (Griq. W. & Tvl) b Aug. 27, 1916, d March 7, 1993

Harrison, L. (Hants) b June 8, 1922

*Harry, J. (Vic.) b Aug. 1, 1857, d Oct. 27, 1919

Hart, G. E. (Middx) b Jan. 13, 1902, d April 11, 1987

Hart, R. T. (C. Dist. & Wgtn) b Nov. 7, 1961

*Hartigan, G. P. D. (Border) b Dec. 30, 1884, d Jan. 7, 1955

*Hartigan, R. J. (NSW & Qld) b Dec. 12, 1879, d June 7, 1958

*Hartkopf, A. E. V. (Vic.) b Dec. 28, 1889, d May 20, 1968

*Hartland, B. R. (Cant.) b Oct. 22, 1966

Hartley, A. (Lancs.; *CY 1911*) b April 11, 1879, d Oct. 9, 1918

*Hartley, J. C. (OUCC & Sussex) b Nov. 15, 1874, d March 8, 1963

Hartley, P. J. (Warwicks. & Yorks.) b April 18, 1960

Hartley, S. N. (Yorks. & OFS) b March 18, 1956

Harvey, J. F. (Derbys.) b Sept. 27, 1939

*Harvey, M. R. (Vic.) b April 29, 1918

Harvey, P. F. (Notts.) b Jan. 15, 1923

*Harvey, R. L. (Natal) b Sept. 14, 1911

*Harvey, R. N. (Vic. & NSW; *CY 1954*) b Oct. 8, 1928

Harvey-Walker, A. J. (Derbys.) b July 21, 1944

Hasan Jamil (Kalat, Kar., Pak. Us & PIA) b July 25, 1952

*Haseeb Ahsan (Peshawar, Pak. Us, Kar. & PIA) b July 15, 1939

*Haslam, M. J. (Auck.) b Sept. 26, 1972

Hassan, B. (Notts.) b March 24, 1944

*Hassett, A. L. (Vic.; *CY 1949*) b Aug. 28, 1913, d June 16, 1993

Hastings, B. F. (Wgtn., C. Dist. & Cant.) b March 23, 1940

*Hathorn, C. M. H. (Tvl) b April 7, 1878, d May 17, 1920

Hathurusinghe, U. C. (TU) b Sept. 13, 1968

*Hawke, 7th Lord (CUCC & Yorks.; *CY 1909*; Pres. MCC 1914-18) b Aug. 16, 1860, d Oct. 10, 1938

*Hawke, N. J. N. (W. Aust., S. Aust. & Tas.) b June 27, 1939

Hawker, Sir Cyril (Essex; Pres. MCC 1970-71) b July 21, 1900, d Feb. 22, 1991

Hawkins, D. G. (Glos.) b May 18, 1935

Hayden, M. L. (Qld) b Oct. 29, 1971

*Hayes, E. G. (Surrey & Leics.; *CY 1907*) b Nov. 6, 1876, d Dec. 2, 1953

*Hayes, F. C. (Lancs.) b Dec. 6, 1946

*Hayes, J. A. (Auck. & Cant.) b Jan. 11, 1927

Hayes, K. A. (OUCC & Lancs.) b Sept. 26, 1962

Haygarth, A. (Sussex; Historian) b Aug. 4, 1825, d May 1, 1903

Hayhurst, A. N. (Lancs. & Som.) b Nov. 23, 1962

*Haynes, D. L. (B'dos & Middx; *CY 1991*) b Feb. 15, 1956

Haynes, R. C. (Jam.) b Nov. 11, 1964

Hayman, M. D. (S. Aust., Leics. & N. Tvl) b April 22, 1961

Hayward, T. (Cambs. & All-England) b March 21, 1835, d July 21, 1876

*Hayward, T. W. (Surrey; *CY 1895*) b March 29, 1871, d July 19, 1939

Haywood, P. R. (Leics.) b March 30, 1947

*Hazare, V. S. (M'tra, C. Ind. & Baroda) b March 11, 1915

Hazell, H. L. (Som.) b Sept. 30, 1909, d March 31, 1990

Hazlerigg, Lord, formerly Hon. A. G. (CUCC & Leics.) b Feb. 24, 1910

*Hazlitt, G. R. (Vic. & NSW) b Sept. 4, 1888, d Oct. 30, 1915

Headley, D. W. (Middx & Kent) b Jan. 27, 1970

*Headley, G. A. (Jam.; *CY 1934*) b May 30, 1909, d Nov. 30, 1983

*Headley, R. G. A. (Worcs. & Jam.) b May 29, 1939

*Healy, I. A. (Qld; *CY 1993*) b April 30, 1964

Hearn, P. (Kent) b Nov. 18, 1925

*Hearne, Alec (Kent; *CY 1894*) b July 22, 1863, d May 16, 1952

**Hearne, Frank (Kent & W. Prov.) b Nov. 23, 1858, d July 14, 1949

*Hearne, G. A. L. (W. Prov.) b March 27, 1888, d Nov. 13, 1978

*Hearne, George G. (Kent) b July 7, 1856, d Feb. 13, 1932

*Hearne, J. T. (Middx; *CY 1892*) b May 3, 1867, d April 17, 1944

*Hearne, J. W. (Middx; *CY 1912*) b Feb. 11, 1891, d Sept. 14, 1965

Hearne, Thos. (Middx) b Sept. 4, 1826, d May 13, 1900

Hearne, Thos., jun. (Lord's Ground Superintendent) b Dec. 29, 1849, d Jan. 29, 1910

Heath, G. E. M. (Hants) b Feb. 20, 1913

Heath, M. (Hants) b March 9, 1934

Hedges, B. (Glam.) b Nov. 10, 1927

Hedges, L. P. (Tonbridge, OUCC, Kent & Glos.; *CY 1919*) b July 13, 1900, d Jan. 12, 1933

Hegg, W. K. (Lancs.) b Feb. 23, 1968

*Heine, P. S. (NE Tvl, OFS & Tvl) b June 28, 1928

*Hemmings, E. E. (Warwicks., Notts. & Sussex) b Feb. 20, 1949

Hemsley, E. J. O. (Worcs.) b Sept. 1, 1943

*Henderson, M. (Wgtn) b Aug. 2, 1895, d June 17, 1970

Henderson, R. (Surrey; *CY 1890*) b March 30, 1865, d Jan. 29, 1931

Henderson, S. P. (CUCC, Worcs. & Glam.) b Sept. 24, 1958

*Hendren, E. H. (Middx; *CY 1920*) b Feb. 5, 1889, d Oct. 4, 1962

*Hendrick, M. (Derbys. & Notts.; *CY 1978*) b Oct. 22, 1948

*Hendriks, J. L. (Jam.) b Dec. 21, 1933

*Hendry, H. S. T. L. (NSW & Vic.) b May 24, 1895, d Dec. 16, 1988

*Henry, O. (W. Prov., Boland, OFS & Scotland) b Jan. 23, 1952

Hepworth, P. N. (Leics.) b May 4, 1967

Herman, O. W. (Hants) b Sept. 18, 1907, d June 24, 1987

Herman, R. S. (Middx, Border, Griq. W. & Hants) b Nov. 30, 1946

Heron, J. G. (Zimb.) b Nov. 8, 1948

*Heseltine, C. (Hants) b Nov. 26, 1869, d June 13, 1944

Hever, N. G. (Middx & Glam.) b Dec. 17, 1924, d Sept. 11, 1987

Hewett, H. T. (OUCC & Som.; *CY 1893*) b May 25, 1864, d March 4, 1921

Heyhoe-Flint, Rachael (England Women) b June 11, 1939

Heyn, P. D. (SL) b June 26, 1945

*Hibbert, P. A. (Vic.) b July 23, 1952

*Hick, G. A. (Worcs., Zimb., N. Dist. & Qld; *CY 1987*) b May 23, 1966

*Higgs, J. D. (Vic.) b July 11, 1950

*Higgs, K. (Lancs. & Leics.; *CY 1968*) b Jan. 14, 1937

Hignell, A. J. (CUCC & Glos.) b Sept. 4, 1955

*Hilditch, A. M. J. (NSW & S. Aust.) b May 20, 1956

Hill, Alan (Derbys. & OFS) b June 29, 1950

*Hill, Allen (Yorks.) b Nov. 14, 1843, d Aug. 29, 1910

*Hill, A. J. L. (CUCC & Hants) b July 26, 1871, d Sept. 6, 1950

*Hill, C. (S. Aust.; *CY 1900*) b March 18, 1877, d Sept. 5, 1945

Hill, E. (Som.) b July 9, 1923

Hill, G. (Hants) b April 15, 1913

*Hill, J. C. (Vic.) b June 25, 1923, d Aug. 11, 1974

Hill, L. W. (Glam.) b April 14, 1942

Hill, M. (Notts., Derbys & Som.) b Sept. 14, 1935

Hill, N. W. (Notts.) b Aug. 22, 1935

Hill, W. A. (Warwicks.) b April 27, 1910

Hills, R. W. (Kent) b Jan. 8, 1951

Hill-Wood, C. K. (OUCC & Derbys.) b June 5, 1907, d Sept. 21, 1988

Hilton, C. (Lancs. & Essex) b Sept. 26, 1937

Hilton, J. (Lancs. & Som.) b Dec. 29, 1930

*Hilton, M. J. (Lancs.; *CY 1957*) b Aug. 2, 1928, d July 8, 1990

*Hime, C. F. W. (Natal) b Oct. 24, 1869, d Dec. 6, 1940

*Hindlekar, D. D. (Bombay) b Jan. 1, 1909, d March 30, 1949

Hinks, S. G. (Kent & Glos.) b Oct. 12, 1960

*Hirst, G. H. (Yorks.; *CY 1901*) b Sept. 7, 1871, d May 10, 1954

*Hirwani, N. D. (M. Pradesh) b Oct. 18, 1968

*Hitch, J. W. (Surrey; *CY 1914*) b May 7, 1886, d July 7, 1965

Hitchcock, R. E. (Cant. & Warwicks.) b Nov. 28, 1929

*Hoad, E. L. G. (B'dos) b Jan. 29, 1896, d March 5, 1986

*Hoare, D. E. (W. Aust.) b Oct. 19, 1934

*Hobbs, Sir J. B. (Surrey; *CY 1909, special portrait 1926*) b Dec. 16, 1882, d Dec. 21, 1963

*Hobbs, R. N. S. (Essex & Glam.) b May 8, 1942

*Hodges, J. R. (Vic.) b Aug. 11, 1855, death unknown

Hodgkinson, G. F. (Derbys.) b Feb. 19, 1914, d Jan. 7, 1987

Hodgson, A. (Northants) b Oct. 27, 1951

Hodgson, G. D. (Glos.) b Oct. 22, 1966

Hofmeyr, M. B. (OUCC & NE Tvl) b Dec. 9, 1925

*Hogan, T. G. (W. Aust.) b Sept. 23, 1956

*Hogg, R. M. (S. Aust.) b March 5, 1951

Hogg, W. (Lancs. & Warwicks.) b July 12, 1955

*Hohns, T. V. (Qld) b Jan. 23, 1954

Holder, J. W. (Hants; Umpire) b March 19, 1945

*Holder, V. A. (B'dos, Worcs. & OFS) b Oct. 8, 1945

*Holding, M. A. (Jam., Lancs., Derbys., Tas. & Cant.; *CY 1977*) b Feb. 16, 1954

*Hole, G. B. (NSW & S. Aust.) b Jan. 6, 1931, d Feb. 14, 1990

*Holford, D. A. J. (B'dos & T/T) b April 16, 1940

*Holland, R. G. (NSW & Wgtn) b Oct. 19, 1946

*Hollies, W. E. (Warwicks.; *CY 1955*) b June 5, 1912, d April 16, 1981

Hollingdale, R. A. (Sussex) b March 6, 1906, d Aug. 1989

Holmes, Gp Capt. A. J. (Sussex) b June 30, 1899, d May 21, 1950

*Holmes, E. R. T. (OUCC & Surrey; *CY 1936*) b Aug. 21, 1905, d Aug. 16, 1960

Holmes, G. C. (Glam.) b Sept. 16, 1958

*Holmes, P. (Yorks.; *CY 1920*) b Nov. 25, 1886, d Sept. 3, 1971

Holt, A. G. (Hants) b April 8, 1911

*Holt, J. K., jun. (Jam.) b Aug. 12, 1923

Home of the Hirsel, Lord (Middx; Pres. MCC 1966-67) b July 2, 1903

*Hone, L. (MCC) b Jan. 30, 1853, d Dec. 31, 1896

Hooker, R. W. (Middx) b Feb. 22, 1935

*Hookes, D. W. (S. Aust.) b May 3, 1955

*Hooper, C. L. (Guyana & Kent) b Dec. 15, 1966

*Hopkins, A. J. Y. (NSW) b May 3, 1874, d April 25, 1931

Hopkins, J. A. (Glam. & E. Prov.) b June 16, 1953

Hopkins, V. (Glos.) b Jan. 21, 1911, d Aug. 6, 1984

Hopwood, J. L. (Lancs.) b Oct. 30, 1903, d June 15, 1985

*Horan, T. P. (Vic.) b March 8, 1854, d April 16, 1916

*Hordern, H. V. (NSW & Philadelphia) b Feb. 10, 1884, d June 17, 1938

*Hornby, A. N. (Lancs.) b Feb. 10, 1847, d Dec. 17, 1925

*Horne, P. A. (Auck.) b Jan. 21, 1960

Horner, N. F. (Yorks. & Warwicks.) b May 10, 1926

*Hornibrook, P. M. (Qld) b July 27, 1899, d Aug. 25, 1976

Horton, H. (Worcs. & Hants) b April 18, 1923

Horton, J. (Worcs.) b Aug. 12, 1916

*Horton, M. J. (Worcs. & N. Dist.) b April 21, 1934

Hossell, J. J. (Warwicks.) b May 25, 1914

Hough, K. W. (Auck.) b Oct. 24, 1928

*Houghton, D. L. (Zimb.) b June 23, 1957

Howard, A. B. (B'dos) b Aug. 27, 1946

Howard, A. R. (Glam.) b Dec. 11, 1909, d March, 1993

Howard, B. J. (Lancs.) b May 21, 1926

Howard, N. K. (Lancs.) b June 29, 1941

*Howard, N. D. (Lancs.) b May 18, 1925, d May 31, 1979

Howard, Major R. (Lancs.; MCC Team Manager) b April 17, 1890, d Sept. 10, 1967

*Howarth, G. P. (Auck., Surrey & N. Dist.) b March 29, 1951

*Howarth, H. J. (Auck.) b Dec. 25, 1943

*Howell, H. (Warwicks.) b Nov. 29, 1890, d July 9, 1932

*Howell, W. P. (NSW) b Dec. 29, 1869, d July 14, 1940

Howland, C. B. (CUCC, Sussex & Kent) b Feb. 6, 1936

*Howorth, R. (Worcs.) b April 26, 1909, d April 2, 1980

Hudson, A. C. (Natal) b March 17, 1966

Hughes, D. P. (Lancs. & Tas.; CY 1988) b May 13, 1947

*Hughes, K. J. (W. Aust. & Natal; CY 1981) b Jan. 26, 1954

*Hughes, M. G. (Vic. & Essex; CY 1993) b Nov. 23, 1961

Hughes, S. P. (Middx, N. Tvl & Durham) b Dec. 20, 1959

Huish, F. H. (Kent) b Nov. 15, 1869, d March 16, 1957

Hulme, J. H. A. (Middx) b Aug. 26, 1904, d Sept. 26, 1991

Human, J. H. (CUCC & Middx) b Jan. 13, 1912, d July 22, 1991

Humpage, G. W. (Warwicks. & OFS; CY 1985) b April 24, 1954

Humphries, D. J. (Leics. & Worcs.) b Aug. 6, 1953

*Humphries, J. (Derbys.) b May 19, 1876, d May 7, 1946

Hunt, A. V. (Scotland & Bermuda) b Oct. 1, 1910

*Hunt, W. A. (NSW) b Aug. 26, 1908, d Dec. 30, 1983

*Hunte, C. C. (B'dos; CY 1964) b May 9, 1932

*Hunte, E. A. C. (T/T) b Oct. 3, 1905, d June 26, 1967

Hunter, David (Yorks.) b Feb. 23, 1860, d Jan. 11, 1927

*Hunter, Joseph (Yorks.) b Aug. 3, 1855, d Jan. 4, 1891

Hurd, A. (CUCC & Essex) b Sept. 7, 1937

*Hurst, A. G. (Vic.) b July 15, 1950

Hurst, R. J. (Middx) b Dec. 29, 1933

Hurwood, A. (Qld) b June 17, 1902, d Sept. 26, 1982

*Hussain, M. Dilawar (C. Ind. & U. Prov.) b March 19, 1907, d Aug. 26, 1967

*Hussain, N. (Essex) b March 28, 1968

*Hutchings, K. L. (Kent; CY 1907) b Dec. 7, 1882, d Sept. 3, 1916

Hutchinson, J. M. (Derbys.) (oldest known living county cricketer) b Nov. 29, 1896

*Hutchinson, P. (SA) b Jan. 26, 1862, d Sept. 30, 1925

*Hutton, Sir Leonard (Yorks.; CY 1938) b June 23, 1916, d Sept. 6, 1990

*Hutton, R. A. (CUCC, Yorks. & Tvl) b Sept. 6, 1942

*Hylton, L. G. (Jam.) b March 29, 1905, d May 17, 1955

*Ibadulla, K. (Punjab, Warwicks., Tas. & Otago) b Dec. 20, 1935

*Ibrahim, K. C. (Bombay) b Jan. 26, 1919

*Iddon, J. (Lancs.) b Jan. 8, 1902, d April 17, 1946

*Igglesden, A. P. (Kent & W. Prov.) b Oct. 8, 1964

*Ijaz Ahmed (Gujranwala, PACO & HBL) b Sept. 20, 1968

*Ijaz Butt (Pak. Us, Punjab, Lahore, R'pindi & Multan) b March 10, 1938

*Ijaz Faqih (Kar., Sind, PWD & MCB) b March 24, 1956

*Ikin, J. T. (Lancs.) b March 7, 1918, d Sept. 15, 1984

*Illingworth, R. (Yorks. & Leics.; CY 1960) b June 8, 1932

*Illingworth, R. K. (Worcs. & Natal) b Aug. 23, 1963

*Ilott, M. C. (Essex) b Aug. 27, 1970

*Imran Khan (Lahore, Dawood, Worcs., OUCC, PIA, Sussex & NSW; CY 1983) b Nov. 25, 1952

*Imtiaz Ahmed (N. Ind., Comb. Us, NWFP, Pak. Serv., Peshawar & PAF) b Jan. 5, 1928

*Imtiaz Ali (T/T) b July 28, 1954

Inchmore, J. D. (Worcs. & N. Tvl) b Feb. 22, 1949

*Indrajitsinhji, K. S. (S'tra & Delhi) b June 15, 1937

Ingle, R. A. (Som.) b Nov. 5, 1903, d Dec. 19, 1992

Ingleby-Mackenzie, A. C. D. (Hants) b Sept. 15, 1933

Inman, C. C. (Ceylon & Leics.) b Jan. 29, 1936

*Inshan Ali (T/T) b Sept. 25, 1949

*Insole, D. J. (CUCC & Essex; *CY 1956*) b April 18, 1926

*Intikhab Alam (Kar., PIA, Surrey, PWD, Sind & Punjab) b Dec. 28, 1941

*Inverarity, R. J. (W. Aust. & S. Aust.) b Jan. 31, 1944

*Inzamam-ul-Haq (Multan & UBL) b March 3, 1970

*Iqbal Qasim (Kar., Sind & NBP) b Aug. 6, 1953

Iqbal Sikandar (Karachi & PIA) b Dec. 19, 1958

*Irani, J. K. (Sind) b Aug. 18, 1923, d Feb. 25, 1982

*Iredale, F. A. (NSW) b June 19, 1867, d April 15, 1926

*Iremonger, J. (Notts.; *CY 1903*) b March 5, 1876, d March 25, 1956

*Ironmonger, H. (Qld & Vic.) b April 7, 1882, d June 1, 1971

*Ironside, D. E. J. (Tvl) b May 2, 1925

*Irvine, B. L. (W. Prov., Natal, Essex & Tvl) b March 9, 1944

*Israr Ali (S. Punjab, B'pur & Multan) b May 1, 1927

*Iverson, J. B. (Vic.) b July 27, 1915, d Oct. 24, 1973

*Jackman, R. D. (Surrey, W. Prov. & Rhod.; *CY 1981*) b Aug. 13, 1945

*Jackson, A. A. (NSW) b Sept. 5, 1909, d Feb. 16, 1933

Jackson, A. B. (Derbys.) b Aug. 21, 1933

Jackson, Sir A. H. M. (Derbys.) b Nov. 9, 1899, d Oct. 11, 1983

*Jackson, Rt Hon. Sir F. S. (CUCC & Yorks.; *CY 1894*; Pres. MCC 1921) b Nov. 21, 1870, d March 9, 1947

Jackson, G. R. (Derbys.) b June 23, 1896, d Feb. 21, 1966

*Jackson, H. L. (Derbys.; *CY 1959*) b April 5, 1921

Jackson, John (Notts. & All-England) b May 21, 1833, d Nov. 4, 1901

Jackson, P. F. (Worcs.) b May 11, 1911

Jacques, T. A. (Yorks.) b Feb. 19, 1905

*Jadeja, A. D. (Haryana) b Feb. 1, 1971

*Jahangir Khan (N. Ind. & CUCC) b Feb. 1, 1910, d July 23, 1988

*Jai, L. P. (Bombay) b April 1, 1902, d Jan. 29, 1968

*Jaisimha, M. L. (H'bad) b March 3, 1939

Jakeman, F. (Yorks. & Northants) b Jan. 10, 1920, d May 18, 1986

*Jalal-ud-Din (PWD, Kar., IDBP & Allied Bank) b June 12, 1959

*James, A. E. (Sussex) b Aug. 7, 1924

James, C. L. R. (Writer) b Jan. 4, 1901, d May 31, 1989

*James, K. C. (Wgtn & Northants) b March 12, 1904, d Aug. 21, 1976

James, K. D. (Middx, Hants & Wgtn) b March 18, 1961

James, R. M. (CUCC & Wgtn) b Oct. 2, 1934

James, S. P. (Glam. & CUCC) b Sept. 7, 1967

James, W. R. (Zimb.) b Aug. 27, 1965

*Jameson, J. A. (Warwicks.) b June 30, 1941

*Jamshedji, R. J. D. (Bombay) b Nov. 18, 1892, d April 5, 1976

*Jardine, D. R. (OUCC & Surrey; *CY 1928*) b Oct. 23, 1900, d June 18, 1958

*Jarman, B. N. (S. Aust.) b Feb. 17, 1936

Jarrett, D. W. (OUCC & CUCC) b April 19, 1952

*Jarvis, A. H. (S. Aust.) b Oct. 19, 1860, d Nov. 15, 1933

Jarvis, K. B. S. (Kent & Glos.) b April 23, 1953

*Jarvis, M. P. (Zimb.) b Dec. 6, 1955

Jarvis, P. W. (Yorks.) b June 29, 1965

*Jarvis, T. W. (Auck. & Cant.) b July 29, 1944

*Javed Akhtar (R'pindi & Pak. Serv.) b Nov. 21, 1940

*Javed Miandad (Kar., Sind, Sussex, HBL & Glam.; *CY 1982*) b June 12, 1957

*Jayantilal, K. (H'bad) b Jan. 13, 1948

*Jayasekera, R. S. A. (SL) b Dec. 7, 1957

Jayasinghe, S. (Ceylon & Leics.) b Jan. 19, 1931

Jayasinghe, S. A. (SL) b July 15, 1955

*Jayasuriya, S. T. (CCC) b June 30, 1969

Jean-Jacques, M. (Derbys.) b July 2, 1960

Jefferies, S. T. (W. Prov., Derbys., Lancs. & Hants) b Dec. 8, 1959

Jefferson, R. I. (CUCC & Surrey) b Aug. 15, 1941

*Jeganathan, S. (SL) b July 11, 1951

*Jenkins, R. O. (Worcs.; *CY 1950*) b Nov. 24, 1918

Jenkins, V. G. J. (OUCC & Glam.) b Nov. 2, 1911

*Jenner, T. J. (W. Aust. & S. Aust.) b Sept. 8, 1944

*Jennings, C. B. (S. Aust.) b June 5, 1884, d June 20, 1950

Jennings, K. F. (Som.) b Oct. 5, 1953

Jennings, R. V. (Tvl & N. Tvl) b Aug. 9, 1954

Jepson, A. (Notts.) b July 12, 1915

*Jessop, G. L. (CUCC & Glos.; *CY 1898*) b May 19, 1874, d May 11, 1955

Jesty, T. E. (Hants., Border, Griq. W., Cant., Surrey & Lancs.; *CY 1983*) b June 2, 1948

*John, V. B. (SL) b May 27, 1960

Johnson, C. (Yorks.) b Sept. 5, 1947

*Johnson, C. L. (Tvl) b 1871, d May 31, 1908

Johnson, G. W. (Kent & Tvl) b Nov. 8, 1946

*Johnson, H. H. H. (Jam.) b July 17, 1910, d June 24, 1987

Johnson, H. L. (Derbys.) b Nov. 8, 1927

*Johnson, I. W. (Vic.) b Dec. 8, 1918

Johnson, L. A. (Northants) b Aug. 12, 1936

*Johnson, L. J. (Qld) b March 18, 1919, d April 20, 1977

Johnson, P. (Notts.) b April 24, 1965

Johnson, P. D. (CUCC & Notts.) b Nov. 12, 1949

*Johnson, T. F. (T/T) b Jan. 10, 1917, d April 5, 1985

Johnston, Brian A. (Broadcaster) b June 24, 1912, d Jan. 5, 1994

*Johnston, W. A. (Vic.; *CY 1949*) b Feb. 26, 1922

Jones, A. (Glam., W. Aust., N. Tvl & Natal; *CY 1978*) b Nov. 4, 1938

Jones, A. A. (Sussex, Som., Middx, Glam., N. Tvl & OFS) b Dec. 9, 1947

*Jones, A. H. (Wgtn) b May 9, 1959

Jones, A. L. (Glam.) b June 1, 1957

Jones, A. N. (Sussex, Border & Som.) b July 22, 1961

*Jones, A. O. (Notts. & CUCC; *CY 1900*) b Aug. 16, 1872, d Dec. 21, 1914

Jones, B. J. R. (Worcs.) b Nov. 2, 1955

*Jones, C. M. (C. E. L.) (BG) b Nov. 3, 1902, d Dec. 10, 1959

*Jones, D. M. (Vic. & Durham; *CY 1990*) b March 24, 1961

*Jones, Ernest (S. Aust. & W. Aust.) b Sept. 30, 1869, d Nov. 23, 1943

Jones, E. C. (Glam.) b Dec. 14, 1912, d April 14, 1989

Jones, E. W. (Glam.) b June 25, 1942

*Jones, I. J. (Glam.) b Dec. 10, 1941

Jones, K. V. (Middx) b March 28, 1942

*Jones, P. E. (T/T) b June 6, 1917, d Nov. 20, 1991

Jones, P. H. (Kent) b June 19, 1935

*Jones, S. P. (NSW, Qld & Auck.) b Aug. 1, 1861, d July 14, 1951

Jones, W. E. (Glam.) b Oct. 31, 1916

Jordan, J. M. (Lancs.) b Feb. 7, 1932

Jorden, A. M. (CUCC & Essex) b Jan. 28, 1947

Jordon, R. C. (Vic.) b Feb. 17, 1937

*Joshi, P. G. (M'tra) b Oct. 27, 1926, d Jan. 8, 1987

Joshi, U. C. (S'tra, Ind. Rlwys, Guj. & Sussex) b Dec. 23, 1944

*Joslin, L. R. (Vic.) b Dec. 13, 1947

Jowett, D. C. P. R. (OUCC) b Jan. 24, 1931

Judd, A. K. (CUCC & Hants) b Jan. 1, 1904, d Feb. 15, 1988

Judge, P. F. (Middx, Glam. & Bengal) b May 23, 1916, d March 4, 1992

*Julian, B. P. (W. Aust.) b Aug. 10, 1970

Julian, R. (Leics.) b Aug. 23, 1936

*Julien, B. D. (T/T & Kent) b March 13, 1950

*Jumadeen, R. R. (T/T) b April 12, 1948

*Jupp, H. (Surrey) b Nov. 19, 1841, d April 8, 1889

*Jupp, V. W. C. (Sussex & Northants; *CY 1928*) b March 27, 1891, d July 9, 1960

*Jurangpathy, B. R. (CCC) b June 25, 1967

*Kallicharran, A. I. (Guyana, Warwicks., Qld, Tvl & OFS; *CY 1983*) b March 21, 1949

Kalpage, R. S. (NCC) b Feb. 19, 1970

*Kaluperuma, L. W. (SL) b May 25, 1949

*Kaluperuma, S. M. S. (SL) b Oct. 22, 1961

*Kaluwitharana, R. S. (SL) b Nov. 24, 1969

*Kambli, V. G. (Bombay) b Jan. 18, 1972

*Kanhai, R. B. (†Guyana, T/T, W. Aust., Warwicks. & Tas.; *CY 1964*) b Dec. 26, 1935

*Kanitkar, H. S. (M'tra) b Dec. 8, 1942

*Kapil Dev (Haryana, Northants & Worcs.; *CY 1983*) b Jan. 6, 1959

**Kardar, A. H. (formerly Abdul Hafeez) (N. Ind., OUCC, Warwicks. & Pak. Serv.) b Jan. 17, 1925

Karnain, S. H. U. (NCC & Moors) b Aug. 11, 1962

*Keeton, W. W. (Notts.; *CY 1940*) b April 30, 1905, d Oct. 10, 1980

Keighley, W. G. (OUCC & Yorks.) b Jan. 10, 1925

*Keith, H. J. (Natal) b Oct. 25, 1927

Kelleher, H. R. A. (Surrey & Northants) b March 3, 1929

Kellett, S. A. (Yorks.) b Oct. 16, 1967

*Kelleway, C. (NSW) b April 25, 1886, d Nov. 16, 1944

Kelly, J. (Notts.) b Sept. 15, 1930

*Kelly, J. J. (NSW; *CY 1903*) b May 10, 1867, d Aug. 14, 1938

*Kelly, T. J. D. (Vic.) b May 3, 1844, d July 20, 1893

*Kempis, G. A. (Natal) b Aug. 4, 1865, d May 19, 1890

*Kendall, T. (Vic. & Tas.) b Aug. 24, 1851, d Aug. 17, 1924

Kennedy, A. (Lancs.) b Nov. 4, 1949

*Kennedy, A. S. (Hants; *CY 1933*) b Jan. 24, 1891, d Nov. 15, 1959

*Kenny, R. B. (Bombay & Bengal) b Sept. 29, 1930, d Nov. 21, 1985

*Kent, M. F. (Qld) b Nov. 23, 1953

*Kentish, E. S. M. (Jam. & OUCC) b Nov. 21, 1916

*Kenyon, D. (Worcs.; *CY 1963*) b May 15, 1924

*Kerr, J. L. (Cant.) b Dec. 28, 1910

Kerr, K. J. (Tvl & Warwicks.) b Sept. 11, 1961

*Kerr, R. B. (Qld) b June 16, 1961

Kerslake, R. C. (CUCC & Som.) b Dec. 26, 1942

Kettle, M. K. (Northants) b March 18, 1944

*Khalid Hassan (Punjab & Lahore) b July 14, 1937

*Khalid Wazir (Pak.) b April 27, 1936

*Khan Mohammad (N. Ind., Pak. Us, Som., B'pur, Sind, Kar. & Lahore) b Jan. 1, 1928

Khanna, S. C. (Delhi) b June 3, 1956

Kidd, E. L. (CUCC & Middx) b Oct. 18, 1889, d July 2, 1984

Kilborn, M. J. (OUCC) b Sept. 20, 1962

*Killick, Rev. E. T. (CUCC & Middx) b May 9, 1907, d May 18, 1953

Kilner, Norman (Yorks. & Warwicks.) b July 21, 1895, d April 28, 1979

*Kilner, Roy (Yorks.; *CY 1924*) b Oct. 17, 1890, d April 5, 1928

Kimpton, R. C. M. (OUCC & Worcs.) b Sept. 21, 1916

*King, C. L. (B'dos, Glam., Worcs. & Natal) b June 11, 1951

*King, F. McD. (B'dos) b Dec. 14, 1926, d Dec. 23, 1990

King, I. M. (Warwicks. & Essex) b Nov. 10, 1931

King, J. B. (Philadelphia) b Oct. 19, 1873, d Oct. 17, 1965

*King, J. H. (Leics.) b April 16, 1871, d Nov. 18, 1946

*King, L. A. (Jam. & Bengal) b Feb. 27, 1939

Kingsley, Sir P. G. T. (OUCC) b May 26, 1908

*Kinnear, S. P. (Warwicks.; *CY 1912*) b May 13, 1871, d Oct. 16, 1928

*Kippax, A. F. (NSW) b May 25, 1897, d Sept. 4, 1972

Kirby, D. (CUCC & Leics.) b Jan. 18, 1939

*Kirmani, S. M. H. (†Karn.) b Dec. 29, 1949

*Kirsten, P. N. (W. Prov., Sussex, Derbys. & Border) b May 14, 1955

*Kischenchand, G. (W. Ind., Guj. & Baroda) b April 14, 1925

Kitchen, M. J. (Som.; Umpire) b Aug. 1, 1940

*Kline, L. F. (Vic.) b Sept. 29, 1934

*Knight, A. E. (Leics.; *CY 1904*) b Oct. 8, 1872, d April 25, 1946

*Knight, B. R. (Essex & Leics.) b Feb. 18, 1938

*Knight, D. J. (OUCC & Surrey; *CY 1915*) b May 12, 1894, d Jan. 5, 1960

Knight, R. D. V. (CUCC, Surrey, Glos. & Sussex) b Sept. 6, 1946

Knight, W. H. (Editor of *Wisden* 1870-79) b Nov. 29, 1812, d Aug. 16, 1879

*Knott, A. P. E. (Kent & Tas.; *CY 1970*) b April 9, 1946

Knott, C. H. (OUCC & Kent) b March 20, 1901, d June 18, 1988

Knott, C. J. (Hants) b Nov. 26, 1914

Knowles, J. (Notts.) b March 25, 1910

Knox, G. K. (Lancs.) b April 22, 1937

*Knox, N. A. (Surrey; *CY 1907*) b Oct. 10, 1884, d March 3, 1935

Kortright, C. J. (Essex) b Jan. 9, 1871, d Dec. 12, 1952

*Kotze, J. J. (Tvl & W. Prov.) b Aug. 7, 1879, d July 7, 1931

Krikken, K. M. (Derbys.) b April 9, 1969

*Kripal Singh, A. G. (Madras & H'bad) b Aug. 6, 1933, d July 23, 1987

*Krishnamurthy, P. (H'bad) b July 12, 1947

*Kuggeleijn, C. M. (N. Dist.) b May 10, 1956

*Kuiper, A. P. (W. Prov. & Derbys.) b Aug. 24, 1959

*Kulkarni, R. R. (Bombay) b Sept. 25, 1962

*Kulkarni, U. N. (Bombay) b March 7, 1942

*Kumar, V. V. (†TN) b June 22, 1935

Kumble, A. (Karn.) b Oct. 17, 1970

*Kunderan, B. K. (Ind. Rlwys & Mysore) b Oct. 2, 1939

*Kuruppu, D. S. B. P. (BRC) b Jan. 5, 1962

*Kuruppuarachchi, A. K. (NCC) b Nov. 1, 1964

*Kuys, F. (W. Prov.) b March 21, 1870, d Sept. 12, 1953

Kynaston, R. (Middx; Sec. MCC 1846-58) b Nov. 5, 1805, d June 21, 1874

*Labrooy, G. F. (CCC) b June 7, 1964

Lacey, Sir F. E. (CUCC & Hants; Sec MCC 1898-1926) b Oct. 19, 1859, d May 26, 1946

*Laird, B. M. (W. Aust.) b Nov. 21, 1950

*Laker, J. C. (Surrey, Auck. & Essex; *CY 1952*) b Feb. 9, 1922, d April 23, 1986

*Lall Singh (S. Punjab) b Dec. 16, 1909, d Nov. 19, 1985

*Lamb, A. J. (W. Prov., Northants & OFS; *CY 1981*) b June 20, 1954

Lamb, T. M. (OUCC, Middx & Northants) b March 24, 1953

*Lamba, R. (Delhi) b Jan. 2, 1958

*Lambert, C. B. (Guyana) b Feb. 2, 1962

Lambert, G. E. E. (Glos. & Som.) b May 11, 1918, d Oct. 31, 1991

*Lambert, R. H. (Ireland) b July 18, 1874, d March 24, 1956

Lambert, Wm (Surrey) b 1779, d April 19, 1851

Lampitt, S. R. (Worcs.) b July 29, 1966

*Lance, H. R. (NE Tvl & Tvl) b June 6, 1940

*Langer, J. L. (W. Aust.) b Nov. 21, 1970

Langford, B. A. (Som.) b Dec. 17, 1935

*Langley, G. R. A. (S. Aust.; *CY 1957*) b Sept. 14, 1919

*Langridge, James (Sussex; *CY 1932*) b July 10, 1906, d Sept. 10, 1966

Langridge, J. G. (John) (Sussex; *CY 1950*) b Feb. 10, 1910

Langridge, R. J. (Sussex) b April 13, 1939

*Langton, A. B. C. (Tvl) b March 2, 1912, d Nov. 27, 1942

*Lara, B. C. (T/T) b May 2, 1969
*Larkins, W. (Northants, E. Prov. & Durham) b Nov. 22, 1953
Larsen, G. R. (Wgtn) b Sept. 27, 1962
*Larter, J. D. F. (Northants) b April 24, 1940
*Larwood, H. (Notts.; *CY 1927*) b Nov. 14, 1904
*Lashley, P. D. (B'dos) b Feb. 11, 1937
Latchman, H. C. [A. H.] (Middx & Notts.) b July 26, 1943
*Latham, R. T. (Cant.) b June 12, 1961
*Lathwell, M. N. (Som.) b Dec. 26, 1971
*Laughlin, T. J. (Vic.) b Jan. 30, 1951
*Laver, F. (Vic.) b Dec. 7, 1869, d Sept. 24, 1919
*Lawrence, D. V. (Glos.) b Jan. 28, 1964
*Lawrence, G. B. (Rhod. & Natal) b March 31, 1932
Lawrence, J. (Som.) b March 29, 1914, d Dec. 10, 1988
*Lawry, W. M. (Vic.; *CY 1962*) b Feb. 11, 1937
Lawson, G. F. (NSW & Lancs.) b Dec. 7, 1957
Leadbeater, B. (Yorks.) b Aug. 14, 1943
*Leadbeater, E. (Yorks. & Warwicks.) b Aug. 15, 1927
*Leary, S. E. (Kent) b April 30, 1933, d Aug. 21, 1988
Lee, C. (Yorks. & Derbys.) b March 17, 1924
Lee, F. S. (Middx & Som.; Umpire) b July 24, 1905, d March 30, 1982
*Lee, H. W. (Middx) b Oct. 26, 1890, d April 21, 1981
Lee, J. W. (Middx & Som.) b Feb. 1, 1904, d June 20, 1944
Lee, P. G. (Northants & Lancs.; *CY 1976*) b Aug. 27, 1945
*Lee, P. K. (S. Aust.) b Sept. 14, 1904, d Aug. 9, 1980
Lees, W. K. (Otago) b March 19, 1952
*Lees, W. S. (Surrey; *CY 1906*) b Dec. 25, 1875, d Sept. 10, 1924
Leese, Sir Oliver, Bt (Pres. MCC 1965-66) b Oct. 27, 1894, d Jan. 20, 1978
Lefebvre, R. P. (Holland, Som., Cant. & Glam.) b Feb. 7, 1963
*Legall, R. A. (B'dos & T/T) b Dec. 1, 1925
Legard, E. (Warwicks.) b Aug. 23, 1935
*Leggat, I. B. (C. Dist.) b June 7, 1930
*Leggat, J. G. (Cant.) b May 27, 1926, d March 8, 1973
*Legge, G. B. (OUCC & Kent) b Jan. 26, 1903, d Nov. 21, 1940
Lenham, L. J. (Sussex) b May 24, 1936
Lenham, N. J. (Sussex) b Dec. 17, 1965
*le Roux, F. L. (Tvl & E. Prov.) b Feb. 5, 1882, d Sept. 22, 1963
le Roux, G. S. (W. Prov. & Sussex) b Sept. 4, 1955

*Leslie, C. F. H. (OUCC & Middx) b Dec. 8, 1861, d Feb. 12, 1921
Lester, E. (Yorks.) b Feb. 18, 1923
Lester, G. (Leics.) b Dec. 27, 1915
Lester, Dr J. A. (Philadelphia) b Aug. 1, 1871, d Sept. 3, 1969
Lethbridge, C. (Warwicks.) b June 23, 1961
*Lever, J. K. (Essex & Natal; *CY 1979*) b Feb. 24, 1949
*Lever, P. (Lancs. & Tas.) b Sept. 17, 1940
*Leveson Gower, Sir H. D. G. (OUCC & Surrey) b May 8, 1873, d Feb. 1, 1954
*Levett, W. H. V. (Kent) b Jan. 25, 1908
Lewington, P. J. (Warwicks.) b Jan. 30, 1950
*Lewis, A. R. (CUCC & Glam.) b July 6, 1938
Lewis, C. (Kent) b July 27, 1908, d April 26, 1993
*Lewis, C. C. (Leics. & Notts.) b Feb. 14, 1968
*Lewis, D. M. (Jam.) b Feb. 21, 1946
Lewis, E. J. (Glam. & Sussex) b Jan. 31, 1942
*Lewis, P. T. (W. Prov.) b Oct. 2, 1884, d Jan. 30, 1976
Lewis, R. V. (Hants) b Aug. 6, 1947
*Leyland, M. (Yorks.; *CY 1929*) b July 20, 1900, d Jan. 1, 1967
*Liaqat Ali (Kar., Sind, HBL & PIA) b May 21, 1955
Lightfoot, A. (Northants) b Jan. 8, 1936
*Lillee, D. K. (W. Aust., Tas. & Northants; *CY 1973*) b July 18, 1949
*Lilley, A. A. (Warwicks.; *CY 1897*) b Nov. 28, 1866, d Nov. 17, 1929
Lilley, A. W. (Essex) b May 8, 1959
Lilley, B. (Notts.) b Feb. 11, 1895, d Aug. 4, 1950
Lillywhite, Fred (Sussex; Editor of *Lillywhite's Guide to Cricketers*) b July 23, 1829, d Sept. 15, 1866
Lillywhite, F. W. ("William") (Sussex) b June 13, 1792, d Aug. 21, 1854
*Lillywhite, James, jun. (Sussex) b Feb. 23, 1842, d Oct. 25, 1929
*Lindsay, D. T. (NE Tvl, N. Tvl & Tvl) b Sept 4, 1939
*Lindsay, J. D. (Tvl & NE Tvl) b Sept. 8, 1909, d Aug. 31, 1990
*Lindsay, N. V. (Tvl & OFS) b July 30, 1886, d Feb. 2, 1976
*Lindwall, R. R. (NSW & Qld; *CY 1949*) b Oct. 3, 1921
*Ling, W. V. S. (Griq. W. & E. Prov.) b Oct. 3, 1891, d Sept. 26, 1960
*Lissette, A. F. (Auck. & N. Dist.) b Nov. 6, 1919, d Jan. 24, 1973
Lister, J. (Yorks. & Worcs.) b May 14, 1930, d Jan. 28, 1991
Lister, W. H. L. (Lancs.) b Oct. 7, 1911

Livingston, L. (NSW & Northants) b May 3, 1920

Livingstone, D. A. (Hants) b Sept. 21, 1933, d Sept. 8, 1988

*Liyanage, D. K. (Colts) b June 6, 1972

*Llewellyn, C. B. (Natal & Hants; *CY 1911*) b Sept. 26, 1876, d June 7, 1964

Llewellyn, M. J. (Glam.) b Nov. 27, 1953

Llong, N. J. (Kent) b Feb. 11, 1969

Lloyd, B. J. (Glam.) b Sept. 6, 1953

*Lloyd, C. H. (†Guyana & Lancs.; *CY 1971*) b Aug. 31, 1944

*Lloyd, D. (Lancs.) b March 18, 1947

Lloyd, G. D. (Lancs.) b July 1, 1969

*Lloyd, T. A. (Warwicks. & OFS) b Nov. 5, 1956

Lloyds, J. W. (Som., OFS & Glos.) b Nov. 17, 1954

*Loader, P. J. (Surrey and W. Aust.; *CY 1958*) b Oct. 25, 1929

Lobb, B. (Warwicks. & Som.) b Jan. 11, 1931

*Lock, G. A. R. (Surrey, Leics. & W. Aust.; *CY 1954*) b July 5, 1929

Lockwood, Ephraim (Yorks.) b April 4, 1845, d Dec. 19, 1921

*Lockwood, W. H. (Notts. & Surrey; *CY 1899*) b March 25, 1868, d April 26, 1932

Lockyer, T. (Surrey & All-England) b Nov. 1, 1826, d Dec. 22, 1869

Logan, J. D. (SA) b June 24, 1880, d Jan. 3, 1960

*Logie, A. L. (T/T) b Sept. 28, 1960

*Lohmann, G. A. (Surrey, W. Prov. & Tvl; *CY 1889*) b June 2, 1865, d Dec. 1, 1901

Lomax, J. G. (Lancs. & Som.) b May 5, 1925, d May 21, 1992

Long, A. (Surrey & Sussex) b Dec. 18, 1940

Lord, G. J. (Warwicks. & Worcs.) b April 25, 1961

Lord, Thomas (Middx; founder of Lord's) b Nov. 23, 1755, d Jan. 13, 1832

*Love, H. S. B. (NSW & Vic.) b Aug. 10, 1895, d July 22, 1969

Love, J. D. (Yorks.) b April 22, 1955

Lovell, G. B. T. (OUCC) b July 11, 1966

*Lowry, T. C. (Wgtn, CUCC & Som.) b Feb. 17, 1898, d July 20, 1976

*Lowson, F. A. (Yorks.) b July 1, 1925, d Sept. 8, 1984

*Loxton, S. J. E. (Vic.) b March 29, 1921

Loye, M. B. (Northants) b Sept. 27, 1972

*Lucas, A. P. (CUCC, Surrey, Middx & Essex) b Feb. 20, 1857, d Oct. 12, 1923

*Luckhurst, B. W. (Kent; *CY 1971*) b Feb. 5, 1939

Lumb, R. G. (Yorks.) b Feb. 27, 1950

*Lundie, E. B. (E. Prov., W. Prov. & Tvl) b March 15, 1888, d Sept. 12, 1917

Lynch, M. A. (Surrey & Guyana) b May 21, 1958

Lyon, B. H. (OUCC & Glos.; *CY 1931*) b Jan. 19, 1902, d June 22, 1970

Lyon, J. (Lancs.) b May 17, 1951

Lyon, M. D. (CUCC & Som.) b April 22, 1898, d Feb. 17, 1964

*Lyons, J. J. (S. Aust.) b May 21, 1863, d July 21, 1927

Lyons, K. J. (Glam.) b Dec. 18, 1946

*Lyttelton, Rt Hon. Alfred (CUCC & Middx; Pres. MCC 1898) b Feb. 7, 1857, d July 5, 1913

Lyttelton, Rev. Hon. C. F. (CUCC & Worcs.) b Jan. 26, 1887, d Oct. 3, 1931

Lyttelton, Hon. C. G. (CUCC) b Oct. 27, 1842, d June 9, 1922

Lyttelton, Hon. C. J. (*see* 10th Visct Cobham)

*McAlister, P. A. (Vic.) b July 11, 1869, d May 10, 1938

*Macartney, C. G. (NSW & Otago; *CY 1922*) b June 27, 1886, d Sept. 9, 1958

*Macaulay, G. G. (Yorks.; *CY 1924*) b Dec. 7, 1897, d Dec. 13, 1940

*Macaulay, M. J. (Tvl, W. Prov., OFS, NE Tvl & E. Prov.) b April 19, 1939

*MacBryan, J. C. W. (CUCC & Som.; *CY 1925*) b July 22, 1892, d July 14, 1983

*McCabe, S. J. (NSW; *CY 1935*) b July 16, 1910, d Aug. 25, 1968

*McCague, M. J. (Kent & W. Aust.) b May 24, 1969

McCanlis, M. A. (OUCC, Surrey & Glos.) b June 17, 1906, d Sept. 27, 1991

*McCarthy, C. N. (Natal & CUCC) b March 24, 1929

McConnon, J. E. (Glam.) b June 21, 1922

*McCool, C. L. (NSW, Qld & Som.) b Dec. 9, 1915, d April 5, 1986

McCorkell, N. T. (Hants) b March 23, 1912

*McCormick, E. L. (Vic.) b May 16, 1906, d June 28, 1991

*McCosker, R. B. (NSW; *CY 1976*) b Dec. 11, 1946

McCurdy, R. J. (Vic., Derbys., S. Aust., E. Prov. & Natal) b Dec. 30, 1959

*McDermott, C. J. (Qld; *CY 1986*) b April 14, 1965

*McDonald, C. C. (Vic.) b Nov. 17, 1928

*McDonald, E. A. (Tas., Vic. & Lancs.; *CY 1922*) b Jan. 6, 1891, d July 22, 1937

*McDonnell, P. S. (Vic., NSW & Qld) b Nov. 13, 1858, d Sept. 24, 1896

McEvoy, M. S. A. (Essex & Worcs.) b Jan. 25, 1956

McEwan, K. S. (E. Prov., W. Prov., Essex & W. Aust; *CY 1978*) b July 16, 1952

*McEwan, P. E. (Cant.) b Dec. 19, 1953

McEwan, S. M. (Worcs. & Durham) b May 5, 1962

McFarlane, L. L. (Northants, Lancs. & Glam.) b Aug. 19, 1952

*McGahey, C. P. (Essex; *CY 1902*) b Feb. 12, 1871, d Jan. 10, 1935
*MacGibbon, A. R. (Cant.) b Aug. 28, 1924
*McGirr, H. M. (Wgtn) b Nov. 5, 1891, d April 14, 1964
*McGlew, D. J. (Natal; *CY 1956*) b March 11, 1929
*MacGregor, G. (CUCC & Middx; *CY 1891*) b Aug. 31, 1869, d Aug. 20, 1919
*McGregor, S. N. (Otago) b Dec. 18, 1931
McHugh, F. P. (Yorks. & Glos.) b Nov. 15, 1925
*McIlwraith, J. (Vic.) b Sept. 7, 1857, d July 5, 1938
Macindoe, D. H. (OUCC) b Sept. 1, 1917, d March 3, 1986
*McIntyre, A. J. W. (Surrey; *CY 1958*) b May 14, 1918
*Mackay, K. D. (Qld) b Oct. 24, 1925, d June 13, 1982
McKechnie, B. J. (Otago) b Nov. 6, 1953
*McKenzie, G. D. (W. Aust. & Leics.; *CY 1965*) b June 24, 1941
*McKibbin, T. R. (NSW) b Dec. 10, 1870, d Dec. 15, 1939
*McKinnon, A. H. (E. Prov. & Tvl) b Aug. 20, 1932, d Dec. 2, 1983
*MacKinnon, F. A. (CUCC & Kent) b April 9, 1848, d Feb. 27, 1947
*MacLaren, A. C. (Lancs.; *CY 1895*) b Dec. 1, 1871, d Nov. 17, 1944
*McLaren, J. W. (Qld) b Dec. 24, 1887, d Nov. 17, 1921
*Maclean, J. A. (Qld) b April 27, 1946
Maclean, J. F. (Worcs. & Glos.) b March 1, 1901, d March 9, 1986
*McLean, R. A. (Natal; *CY 1961*) b July 9, 1930
MacLeay, K. H. (W. Aust. & Som.) b April 2, 1959
*McLeod, C. E. (Vic.) b Oct. 24, 1869, d Nov. 26, 1918
*McLeod, E. G. (Auck. & Wgtn) b Oct. 14, 1900, d Sept. 14, 1989
*McLeod, R. W. (Vic.) b Jan. 19, 1868, d June 14, 1907
McMahon, J. W. (Surrey & Som.) b Dec. 28, 1919
*McMahon, T. G. (Wgtn) b Nov. 8, 1929
*McMaster, J. E. P. (Eng.) b March 16, 1861, d June 7, 1929
*McMillan, B. M. (Tvl, W. Prov. & Warwicks.) b Dec. 22, 1963
*McMillan, Q. (Tvl) b June 23, 1904, d July 3, 1948
*McMorris, E. D. A. (Jam.) b April 4, 1935
*McRae, D. A. N. (Cant.) b Dec. 25, 1912
*McShane, P. G. (Vic.) b 1857, d Dec. 11, 1903
McSweeney, E. B. (C. Dist. & Wgtn) b March 8, 1957

McVicker, N. M. (Warwicks. & Leics.) b Nov. 4, 1940
*McWatt, C. A. (BG) b Feb. 1, 1922
*Madan Lal (Punjab & Delhi) b March 20, 1951
*Maddocks, L. V. (Vic. & Tas.) b May 24, 1926
*Madray, I. S. (BG) b July 2, 1934
*Madugalle, R. S. (NCC) b April 22, 1959
*Madurasinghe, A. W. R. (Kurunegala) b Jan. 30, 1961
*Maguire, J. N. (Qld, E. Prov. & Leics.) b Sept. 15, 1956
*Mahanama, R. S. (CCC) b May 31, 1966
Maher, B. J. M. (Derbys.) b Feb. 11, 1958
*Mahmood Hussain (Pak. Us, Punjab, Kar., E. Pak. & NTB) b April 2, 1932, d Dec. 25, 1991
*Mailey, A. A. (NSW) b Jan. 3, 1886, d Dec. 31, 1967
*Majid Khan (Lahore, Pak. Us, CUCC, Glam., PIA, Qld & Punjab; *CY 1970*) b Sept. 28, 1946
*Maka, E. S. (Bombay) b March 5, 1922
*Makepeace, J. W. H. (Lancs.) b Aug. 22, 1881, d Dec. 19, 1952
*Malcolm, D. E. (Derbys.) b Feb. 22, 1963
*Malhotra, A. (Haryana & Bengal) b Jan. 26, 1957
*Mallender, N. A. (Northants, Otago & Som.) b Aug. 13, 1961
*Mallett, A. A. (S. Aust.) b July 13, 1945
Mallett, A. W. H. (OUCC & Kent) b Aug. 29, 1924
*Malone, M. F. (W. Aust. & Lancs.) b Oct. 9, 1950
Malone, S. J. (Essex, Hants & Glam.) b Oct. 19, 1953
*Maninder Singh (Delhi) b June 13, 1965
*Manjrekar, S. V. (Bombay) b July 12, 1965
*Manjrekar, V. L. (Bombay, Bengal, Andhra, U. Pradesh, Raja. & M'tra) b Sept. 26, 1931, d Oct. 18, 1983
*Mankad, A. V. (Bombay) b Oct. 12, 1946
*Mankad, V. (M. H.) (W. Ind., Naw., M'tra, Guj., Bengal, Bombay & Raja.; *CY 1947*) b April 12, 1917, d Aug. 21, 1978
*Mann, A. L. (W. Aust.) b Nov. 8, 1945
*Mann, F. G. (CUCC & Middx; Pres. MCC 1984-85) b Sept. 6, 1917
*Mann, F. T. (CUCC & Middx) b March 3, 1888, d Oct. 6, 1964
Mann, J. P. (Middx) b June 13, 1919
*Mann, N. B. F. (Natal & E. Prov.) b Dec. 28, 1920, d July 31, 1952
Manning, J. S. (S. Aust. & Northants) b June 11, 1924, d May 5, 1988
*Mansell, P. N. F. (Rhod.) b March 16, 1920
*Mansoor Akhtar (Kar., UBL & Sind) b Dec. 25, 1956
Mansoor Rana (ADBP & Lahore) b Dec. 27, 1962
Mansur Ali Khan (*see* Pataudi, Mansur Ali, Nawab of)

*Mantri, M. K. (Bombay & M'tra) b Sept. 1, 1921

*Manzoor Elahi (Multan, Pak. Rlwys & IDBP) b April 15, 1963

*Maqsood Ahmed (S. Punjab, R'pindi & Kar.) b March 26, 1925

Maqsood Rana (Lahore) b Aug. 1, 1972

*Marais, G. G. ("G. Gladstone") (Jam.) b Jan. 14, 1901, d May 19, 1978

Marie, G. V. (OUCC) b Feb. 17, 1945

Markham, L. A. (Natal) b Sept. 12, 1924

Marks, V. J. (OUCC, Som. & W. Aust.) b June 25, 1955

Marlar, R. G. (CUCC & Sussex) b Jan. 2, 1931

Marner, P. T. (Lancs. & Leics.) b March 31, 1936

*Marr, A. P. (NSW) b March 28, 1862, d March 15, 1940

Marriott, C. S. (CUCC, Lancs. & Kent) b Sept. 14, 1895, d Oct. 13, 1966

Marsden, Tom (Eng.) b 1805, d Feb. 27, 1843

Marsh, F. E. (Derbys.) b July 7, 1920

Marsh, G. R. (W. Aust.) b Dec. 31, 1958

*Marsh, R. W. (W. Aust.; *CY 1982*) b Nov. 4, 1947

Marsh, S. A. (Kent) b Jan. 27, 1961

Marshal, Alan (Qld & Surrey; *CY 1909*) b June 12, 1883, d July 23, 1915

Marshall, J. M. A. (Warwicks.) b Oct. 26, 1916

*Marshall, M. D. (B'dos & Hants; *CY 1983*) b April 18, 1958

*Marshall, N. E. (B'dos & T/T) b Feb. 27, 1924

*Marshall, R. E. (B'dos & Hants; *CY 1959*) b April 25, 1930, d Oct. 27, 1992

Martin, E. J. (Notts.) b Aug. 17, 1925

*Martin, F. (Kent; *CY 1892*) b Oct. 12, 1861, d Dec. 13, 1921

*Martin, F. R. (Jam.) b Oct. 12, 1893, d Nov. 23, 1967

Martin, J. D. (OUCC & Som.) b Dec. 23, 1941

*Martin, J. W. (NSW & S. Aust.) b July 28, 1931, d July 16, 1992

*Martin, J. W. (Kent) b Feb. 16, 1917, d Jan. 4, 1987

Martin, P. J. (Lancs.) b Nov. 15, 1968

Martin, S. H. (Worcs., Natal & Rhod.) b Jan. 11, 1909, d Feb. 1988

Martindale, D. J. R. (Notts.) b Dec 13, 1963

*Martindale, E. A. (B'dos) b Nov. 25, 1909, d March 17, 1972

*Martyn, D. R. (W. Aust.) b Oct. 21, 1971

Maru, R. J. (Middx & Hants) b Oct. 28, 1962

*Marx, W. F. E. (Tvl) b July 4, 1895, d June 2, 1974

*Mason, J. R. (Kent; *CY 1898*) b March 26, 1874, d Oct. 15, 1958

*Masood Anwar (UBL & Multan) b Dec. 12, 1967

Masood Iqbal (Lahore, Punjab U., Pak. Us & HBL) b April 17, 1952

*Massie, H. H. (NSW) b April 11, 1854, d Oct. 12, 1938

*Massie, R. A. L. (W. Aust.; *CY 1973*) b April 14, 1947

*Matheson, A. M. (Auck.) b Feb. 27, 1906, d Dec. 31, 1985

Mathias, Wallis (Sind, Kar. & NBP) b Feb. 4, 1935

*Matthews, A. D. G. (Northants & Glam.) b May 3, 1904, d July 29, 1977

*Matthews, C. D. (W. Aust. & Lancs.) b Sept. 22, 1962

*Matthews, C. R. (W. Prov.) b Feb. 15, 1965

Matthews, C. S. (Notts.) b Oct. 17, 1931, d March 15, 1990

*Matthews, G. R. J. (NSW) b Dec. 15, 1959

*Matthews, T. J. (Vic.) b April 3, 1884, d Oct. 14, 1943

Mattis, E. H. (Jam.) b April 11, 1957

*May, P. B. H. (CUCC & Surrey; *CY 1952*; Pres. MCC 1980-81) b Dec. 31, 1929

*May, T. B. A. (S. Aust.) b Jan. 26, 1962

Mayer, J. H. (Warwicks.) b March 2, 1902, d Sept. 6, 1981

Mayes, R. (Kent) b Oct. 7, 1921

Maynard, C. (Warwicks. & Lancs.) b April 8, 1958

*Maynard, M. P. (Glam. & N. Dist.) b March 21, 1966

*Mayne, E. R. (S. Aust. & Vic.) b July 2, 1882, d Oct. 26, 1961

*Mayne, L. C. (W. Aust.) b Jan. 23, 1942

*Mead, C. P. (Hants; *CY 1912*) b March 9, 1887, d March 26, 1958

*Mead, W. (Essex; *CY 1904*) b March 25, 1868, d March 18, 1954

Meads, E. A. (Notts.) b Aug. 17, 1916

*Meale, T. (Wgtn) b Nov. 11, 1928

*Meckiff, I. (Vic.) b Jan. 6, 1935

Medlycott, K. T. (Surrey & N. Tvl) b May 12, 1965

*Meher-Homji, K. R. (W. Ind. & Bombay) b Aug. 9, 1911, d Feb. 10, 1982

Mehra, V. L. (E. Punjab, Ind. Rlwys & Delhi) b March 12, 1938

*Meintjes, D. J. (Tvl) b June 9, 1890, d July 17, 1979

*Melle, M. G. (Tvl & W. Prov.) b June 3, 1930

Melluish, M. E. L. (CUCC & Middx; Pres. MCC 1991-92) b June 13, 1932

*Melville, A. (OUCC, Sussex, Natal & Tvl; *CY 1948*) b May 19, 1910, d April 18, 1983

Mence, M. D. (Warwicks. & Glos.) b April 13, 1944

Mendis, G. D. (Sussex & Lancs.) b April 20, 1955

*Mendis, L. R. D. (SSC) b Aug. 25, 1952

*Mendonca, I. L. (BG) b July 13, 1934

Mercer, J. (Sussex, Glam. & Northants; *CY 1927*) b April 22, 1895, d Aug. 31, 1987

*Merchant, V. M. (Bombay; *CY 1937*) b Oct. 12, 1911, d Oct. 27, 1987

Merrick, T. A. (Leewards, Warwicks. & Kent) b June 10, 1963

*Merritt, W. E. (Cant. & Northants) b Aug. 18, 1908, d June 9, 1977

*Merry, C. A. (T/T) b Jan. 20, 1911, d April 19, 1964

Metcalfe, A. A. (Yorks. & OFS) b Dec. 25, 1963

Metson, C. P. (Middx & Glam.) b July 2, 1963

Meuleman, K. D. (Vic. & W. Aust.) b Sept. 5, 1923

*Meuli, E. M. (C. Dist.) b Feb. 20, 1926

Meyer, B. J. (Glos.; Umpire) b Aug. 21, 1932

*Meyer, R. J. O. (CUCC, Som. & W. Ind.) b March 15, 1905, d March 9, 1991

Mian Mohammad Saaed (N. Ind. Patiala & S. Punjab; Pak.'s first captain) b Aug. 31, 1910, d Aug. 23, 1979

*Middleton, J. (W. Prov.) b Sept. 30, 1865, d Dec. 23, 1913

Middleton, T. C. (Hants) b Feb. 1, 1964

**Midwinter, W. E. (Vic. & Glos.) b June 19, 1851, d Dec. 3, 1890

*Milburn, B. D. (Otago) b Nov. 24, 1943

*Milburn, C. (Northants & W. Aust.; *CY 1967*) b Oct. 23, 1941, d Feb. 28, 1990

*Milkha Singh, A. G. (Madras) b Dec. 31, 1941

Miller, A. J. T. (OUCC & Middx) b May 30, 1963

*Miller, A. M. (Eng.) b Oct. 19, 1869, d June 26, 1959

*Miller, G. (Derbys., Natal & Essex) b Sept. 8, 1952

*Miller, K. R. (Vic., NSW & Notts.; *CY 1954*) b Nov. 28, 1919

*Miller, L. S. M. (C. Dist. & Wgtn) b March 31, 1923

Miller, R. (Warwicks.) b Jan. 6, 1941

*Miller, R. C. (Jam.) b Dec. 24, 1924

*Milligan, F. W. (Yorks.) b March 19, 1870, d March 31, 1900

*Millman, G. (Notts.) b Oct. 2, 1934

Millmow, J. P. (Wgtn) b Sept. 22, 1967

Millns, D. J. (Notts. & Leics.) b Feb. 27, 1965

*Mills, C. H. (Surrey, Kimberley & W. Prov.) b Nov. 26, 1867, d July 26, 1948

*Mills, J. E. (Auck.) b Sept. 3, 1905, d Dec. 11, 1972

Mills, J. M. (CUCC & Warwicks.) b July 27, 1921

Mills, J. P. C. (CUCC & Northants) b Dec. 6, 1958

Milner, J. (Essex) b Aug. 22, 1937

*Milton, C. A. (Glos.; *CY 1959*) b March 10, 1928

*Milton, W. H. (W. Prov.) b Dec. 3, 1854, d March 6, 1930

*Minnett, R. B. (NSW) b June 13, 1888, d Oct. 21, 1955

"Minshull", John (scorer of first recorded century) b *circa* 1741, d Oct. 1793

*Miran Bux (Pak. Serv., Punjab & R'pindi) b April 20, 1907, d Feb. 8, 1991

*Misson, F. M. (NSW) b Nov. 19, 1938

*Mitchell, A. (Yorks.) b Sept. 13, 1902, d Dec. 25, 1976

*Mitchell, B. (Tvl; *CY 1936*) b Jan. 8, 1909

Mitchell, C. G. (Som.) b Jan. 27, 1929

**Mitchell, F. (CUCC, Yorks. & Tvl; *CY 1902*) b Aug. 13, 1872, d Oct. 11, 1935

*Mitchell, T. B. (Derbys.) b Sept. 4, 1902

*Mitchell-Innes, N. S. (OUCC & Som.) b Sept. 7, 1914

*Modi, R. S. (Bombay) b Nov. 11, 1924

*Mohammad Aslam (N. Ind. & Pak. Rlwys) b Jan. 5, 1920

*Mohammad Farooq (Kar.) b April 8, 1938

*Mohammad Ilyas (Lahore & PIA) b March 19, 1946

*Mohammad Munaf (Sind, E. Pak., Kar. & PIA) b Nov. 2, 1935

*Mohammad Nazir (Pak. Rlwys) b March 8, 1946

*Mohsin Kamal (Lahore, Allied Bank & PNSC) b June 16, 1963

*Mohsin Khan (Pak. Rlwys, Kar., Sind, Pak. Us & HBL) b March 15, 1955

*Moin Khan (Karachi & PIA) b Sept. 23, 1971

Moin-ul-Atiq (UBL, Karachi & HBL) b Aug. 5, 1964

*Moir, A. McK. (Otago) b July 17, 1919

Moir, D. G. (Derbys. & Scotland) b April 13, 1957

*Mold, A. W. (Lancs.; *CY 1892*) b May 27, 1863, d April 29, 1921

Moles, A. J. (Warwicks. & Griq. W.) b Feb. 12, 1961

*Moloney, D. A. R. (Wgtn, Otago & Cant.) b Aug. 11, 1910, d July 15, 1942

Monckton of Brenchley, 1st Lord (Pres. MCC 1956-57) b Jan. 17, 1891, d Jan. 9, 1965

Mongia, N. R. (Baroda) b Dec. 19, 1969

Monkhouse, G. (Surrey) b April 26, 1954

*Moodie, G. H. (Jam.) b Nov. 25, 1915

*Moody, T. M. (W. Aust., Warwicks. & Worcs.) b Oct. 2, 1965

*Moon, L. J. (CUCC & Middx) b Feb. 9, 1878, d Nov. 23, 1916

*Mooney, F. L. H. (Wgtn) b May 26, 1921

Moore, D. N. (OUCC & Glos.) b Sept. 26, 1910

Moore, H. I. (Notts.) b Feb. 28, 1941

Moore, R. H. (Hants) b Nov. 14, 1913

Moores, P. (Worcs., Sussex & OFS) b Dec. 18, 1962

*More, K. S. (Baroda) b Sept. 4, 1962

Morgan, D. C. (Derbys.) b Feb. 26, 1929

Morgan, M. (Notts.) b May 21, 1936

*Morgan, R. W. (Auck.) b Feb. 12, 1941

*Morkel, D. P. B. (W. Prov.) b Jan. 25, 1906, d Oct. 6, 1980

*Morley, F. (Notts.) b Dec. 16, 1850, d Sept. 28, 1884

Morley, J. D. (Sussex) b Oct. 20, 1950

Moroney, J. (NSW) b July 24, 1917

*Morris, A. R. (NSW; *CY 1949*) b Jan. 19, 1922

*Morris, H. (Glam.) b Oct. 5, 1963

Morris, H. M. (CUCC & Essex) b April 16, 1898, d Nov. 18, 1984

*Morris, J. E. (Derbys. & Griq. W.) b April 1, 1964

Morris, R. E. (OUCC) b June 8, 1967

*Morris, S. (Vic.) b June 22, 1855, d Sept. 20, 1931

*Morrison, B. D. (Wgtn) b Dec. 17, 1933

*Morrison, D. K. (Auck. & Lancs.) b Feb. 3, 1966

*Morrison, J. F. M. (C. Dist. & Wgtn) b Aug. 27, 1947

Mortensen, O. H. (Denmark & Derbys.) b Jan. 29, 1958

*Mortimore, J. B. (Glos.) b May 14, 1933

Mortlock, W. (Surrey & Utd Eng. XI) b July 18, 1832, d Jan. 23, 1884

*Moseley, E. A. (B'dos, Glam., E. Prov. & N. Tvl) b Jan. 5, 1958

Moseley, H. R. (B'dos & Som.) b May 28, 1948

Moses, H. (NSW) b Feb. 13, 1858, d Dec. 7, 1938

*Moss, A. E. (Middx) b Nov. 14, 1930

Moss, J. K. (Vic.) b June 29, 1947

*Motz, R. C. (Cant.; *CY 1966*) b Jan. 12, 1940

Moulding, R. P. (OUCC & Middx) b Jan. 3, 1958

*Moule, W. H. (Vic.) b Jan. 31, 1858, d Aug. 24, 1939

*Moxon, M. D. (Yorks. & Griq. W.; *CY 1993*) b May 4, 1960

Mudassar Nazar (Lahore, Punjab, Pak. Us, HBL, PIA & UBL) b April 6, 1956

*Muddiah, V. M. (Mysore & Ind. Serv.) b June 8, 1929

Mukherjee, S. P. (Bengal) b Oct. 5, 1964

Mullally, A. D. (W. Aust., Hants & Leics.) b July 12, 1969

Munden, V. S. (Leics.) b Jan. 2, 1928

*Munir Malik (Punjab, R'pindi, Pak. Serv. & Kar.) b July 10, 1934

*Munton, T. A. (Warwicks.) b July 30, 1965

*Muralitharan, M. (TU) b April 17, 1972

**Murdoch, W. L. (NSW & Sussex) b Oct. 18, 1854, d Feb. 18, 1911

Murphy, A. J. (Lancs. & Surrey) b Aug. 6, 1962

*Murray, A. R. A. (E. Prov.) b April 30, 1922

*Murray, B. A. G. (Wgtn) b Sept. 18, 1940

*Murray, D. A. (B'dos) b Sept. 29, 1950

*Murray, D. L. (T/T, CUCC, Notts. & Warwicks.) b May 20, 1943

*Murray, J. R. (Windwards) b Jan. 20, 1968

*Murray, J. T. (Middx; *CY 1967*) b April 1, 1935

Murray-Willis, P. E. (Worcs. & Northants) b July 14, 1910

Murrell, H. R. (Kent & Middx) b Nov. 19, 1879, d Aug. 15, 1952

Murrills, T. J. (CUCC) b Dec. 22, 1953

*Musgrove, H. (Vic.) b Nov. 27, 1860, d Nov. 2, 1931

*Mushtaq Ahmed (UBL, Multan & Som.) b June 28, 1970

*Mushtaq Ali, S. (C. Ind., Guj., †M. Pradesh & U. Pradesh) b Dec. 17, 1914

*Mushtaq Mohammad (Kar., Northants & PIA; *CY 1963*) b Nov. 22, 1943

Mynn, Alfred (Kent & All-Eng.) b Jan. 19, 1807, d Oct. 31, 1861

*Nadkarni, R. G. (M'tra & Bombay) b April 4, 1932

*Nadeem Abbasi (R'pindi) b April 15, 1964

*Nadeem Ghauri (HBL) b Oct 12, 1962

*Nadeem Khan (Kar. & NBP) b Dec. 10, 1969

Naeem Ahmed (Kar., Pak. Us, NBP, UBL & PIA) b Sept. 20, 1952

Naeem Ahmed (Sargodha) b April 14, 1971

*Nagel, L. E. (Vic.) b March 6, 1905, d Nov. 23, 1971

*Naik, S. S. (Bombay) b Feb. 21, 1945

*Nanan, R. (T/T) b May 29, 1953

*Naoomal Jaoomal, M. (N. Ind. & Sind) b April 17, 1904, d July 18, 1980

*Narasimha Rao, M. V. (H'bad) b Aug. 11, 1954

Naseer Malik (Khairpair & NBP) b Feb. 1, 1950

*Nash, D. J. (N. Dist. & Otago) b Nov. 20, 1971

*Nash, L. J. (Tas. & Vic.) b May 2, 1910, d July 24, 1986

Nash, M. A. (Glam.) b May 9, 1945

*Nasim-ul-Ghani (Kar., Pak. Us, Dacca, E. Pak., PWD & NBP) b May 14, 1941

*Naushad Ali (Kar., E. Pak., R'pindi, Peshawar, NWFP, Punjab & Pak. Serv.) b Oct. 1, 1943

*Naved Anjum (Lahore, UBL & HBL) b July 27, 1963

*Navle, J. G. (Rajputna, C. Ind., Holkar & Gwalior) b Dec. 7, 1902, d Sept. 7, 1979

Nayak, S. V. (Bombay) b Oct. 20, 1954

*Nayudu, Col. C. K. (C. Ind., Andhra, U. Pradesh & Holkar; *CY 1933*) b Oct. 31, 1895, d Nov. 14, 1967

*Nayudu, C. S. (C. Ind., Holkar, Baroda, Bengal, Andhra & U. Pradesh) b April 18, 1914

*Nazar Mohammad (N. Ind. & Punjab) b March 5, 1921

*Nazir Ali, S. (S. Punjab & Sussex) b June 8, 1906, d Feb. 18, 1975

Neale, P. A. (Worcs.; *CY 1989*) b June 5, 1954

*Neblett, J. M. (B'dos & BG) b Nov. 13, 1901, d March 28, 1959

Needham, A. (Surrey & Middx) b March 23, 1957

*Nel, J. D. (W. Prov.) b July 10, 1928

Nevell, W. T. (Middx, Surrey & Northants) b June 13, 1916

*Newberry, C. (Tvl) b 1889, d Aug. 1, 1916

Newell, M. (Notts.) b Feb. 25, 1965

*Newham, W. (Sussex) b Dec 12, 1860, d June 26, 1944

Newland, Richard (Sussex) b *circa* 1718, d May 29, 1791

*Newman, Sir J. (Wgtn & Cant.) b July 3, 1902

Newman, J. A. (Hants & Cant.) b Nov. 12, 1884, d Dec. 21, 1973

Newman, P. G. (Derbys.) b Jan. 10, 1959

*Newport, P. J. (Worcs., Boland & N. Tvl) b Oct. 11, 1962

*Newson, E. S. (Tvl & Rhod.) b Dec. 2, 1910, d April 24, 1988

Newstead, J. T. (Yorks.; *CY 1909*) b Sept. 8, 1877, d March 25, 1952

*Niaz Ahmed (Dacca, PWD, E. Pak. & Pak. Rlwys) b Nov. 11, 1945

Nicholas, M. C. J. (Hants) b Sept. 29, 1957

Nicholls, D. (Kent) b Dec. 8, 1943

Nicholls, R. B. (Glos.) b Dec. 4, 1933

*Nichols, M. S. (Essex; *CY 1934*) b Oct. 6, 1900, d Jan. 26, 1961

Nicholson, A. G. (Yorks.) b June 25, 1938, d Nov. 4, 1985

*Nicholson, F. (OFS) b Sept. 17, 1909, d July 30, 1982

*Nicolson, J. F. W. (Natal & OUCC) b July 19, 1899, d Dec. 13, 1935

*Nissar, Mahomed (Patiala, S. Punjab & U. Pradesh) b Aug. 1, 1910, d March 11, 1963

*Nitschke, H. C. (S. Aust.) b April 14, 1905, d Sept. 29, 1982

Nixon, P. A. (Leics.) b Oct. 21, 1970

*Noble, M. A. (NSW; *CY 1900*) b Jan. 28, 1873, d June 22, 1940

*Noblet, G. (S. Aust.) b Sept. 14, 1916

*Noreiga, J. M. (T/T) b April 15, 1936

Norfolk, 16th Duke of (Pres. MCC 1957-58) b May 30, 1908, d Jan. 31, 1975

Norman, M. E. J. C. (Northants & Leics.) b Jan. 19, 1933

*Norton, N. O. (W. Prov. & Border) b May 11, 1881, d June 27, 1968

*Nothling, O. E. (NSW & Qld) b Aug. 1, 1900, d Sept. 26, 1965

*Nourse, A. D. ("Dudley") (Natal; *CY 1948*) b Nov. 12, 1910, d Aug. 14, 1981

*Nourse, A. W. ("Dave") (Natal, Tvl & W. Prov.) b Jan. 26, 1878, d July 8, 1948

Nugent, 1st Lord (Pres. MCC 1962-63) b Aug. 11, 1895, d April 27, 1973

*Nunes, R. K. (Jam.) b June 7, 1894, d July 22, 1958

*Nupen, E. P. (Tvl) b Jan. 1, 1902, d Jan. 29, 1977

*Nurse, S. M. (B'dos; *CY 1967*) b Nov. 10, 1933

Nutter, A. E. (Lancs. & Northants) b June 28, 1913

*Nyalchand, S. (W. Ind., Kathiawar, Guj. & S'tra) b Sept. 14, 1919

Nye, J. K. (Sussex) b May 23, 1914

Nyren, John (Hants) b Dec. 15, 1764, d June 28, 1837

Nyren, Richard (Hants & Sussex) b 1734, d April 25, 1797

Oakes, C. (Sussex) b Aug. 10, 1912

Oakes, J. (Sussex) b March 3, 1916

*Oakman, A. S. M. (Sussex) b April 20, 1930

Oates, T. W. (Notts.) b Aug. 9, 1875, d June 18, 1949

Oates, W. F. (Yorks. & Derbys.) b June 11, 1929

O'Brien, F. P. (Cant. & Northants) b Feb. 11, 1911, d Oct. 22, 1991

*O'Brien, L. P. J. (Vic.) b July 2, 1907

*O'Brien, Sir T. C. (OUCC & Middx) b Nov. 5, 1861, d Dec. 9, 1948

*Ochse, A. E. (Tvl) b March 11, 1870, d April 11, 1918

*Ochse, A. L. (E. Prov.) b Oct. 11, 1899, d May 6, 1949

*O'Connor, J. (Essex) b Nov. 6, 1897, d Feb. 22, 1977

*O'Connor, J. D. A. (NSW & S. Aust.) b Sept. 9, 1875, d Aug. 23, 1941

*O'Donnell, S. P. (Vic.) b Jan. 26, 1963

*Ogilvie, A. D. (Qld) b June 3, 1951

O'Gorman, T. J. G. (Derbys.) b May 15, 1967

*O'Keeffe, K. J. (NSW & Som.) b Nov. 25, 1949

*Old, C. M. (Yorks., Warwicks. & N. Tvl; CY 1979) b Dec. 22, 1948

*Oldfield, N. (Lancs. & Northants) b April 30, 1911

*Oldfield, W. A. (NSW; CY 1927) b Sept. 9, 1894, d Aug. 10, 1976

Oldham, S. (Yorks. & Derbys.) b July 26, 1948

Oldroyd, E. (Yorks.) b Oct. 1, 1888, d Dec. 27, 1964

*O'Linn, S. (Kent, W. Prov. & Tvl) b May 5, 1927

Oliver, P. R. (Warwicks.) b May 9, 1956

*O'Neill, N. C. (NSW; CY 1962) b Feb. 19, 1937

Ontong, R. C. (Border, Tvl, N. Tvl & Glam.) b Sept. 9, 1955

Opatha, A. R. M. (SL) b Aug. 5, 1947

Ord, J. S. (Warwicks.) b July 12, 1912

*O'Reilly, W. J. (NSW; CY 1935) b Dec. 20, 1905, d Oct. 6, 1992

O'Riordan, A. J. (Ireland) b July 20, 1940

Ormrod, J. A. (Worcs. & Lancs.) b Dec. 22, 1942

O'Shaughnessy, S. J. (Lancs. & Worcs.) b Sept. 9, 1961

Oslear, D. O. (Umpire) b March 3, 1929

Ostler, D. P. (Warwicks.) b July 15, 1970

*O'Sullivan, D. R. (C. Dist. & Hants) b Nov. 16, 1944

Outschoorn, L. (Worcs.) b Sept. 26, 1918

*Overton, G. W. F. (Otago) b June 8, 1919, d. Sept. 7, 1993

Owens, M. B. (Cant.) b Nov. 11, 1969

*Owen-Smith, H. G. O. (W. Prov., OUCC & Middx; CY 1930) b Feb. 18, 1909, d Feb. 28, 1990

Owen-Thomas, D. R. (CUCC & Surrey) b Sept. 20, 1948

*Oxenham, R. K. (Qld) b July 28, 1891, d Aug. 16, 1939

*Padgett, D. E. V. (Yorks.) b July 20, 1934

Padmore, A. L. (B'dos) b Dec. 17, 1946

Page, H. A. (Tvl & Essex) b July 3, 1962

Page, J. C. T. (Kent) b May 20, 1930, d Dec. 14, 1990

Page, M. H. (Derbys.) b June 17, 1941

*Page, M. L. (Cant.) b May 8, 1902, d Feb. 13, 1987

*Pai, A. M. (Bombay) b April 28, 1945

*Paine, G. A. E. (Middx & Warwicks.; CY 1935) b June 11, 1908, d March 30, 1978

*Pairaudeau, B. H. (BG & N. Dist.) b April 14, 1931

*Palairet, L. C. H. (OUCC & Som.; CY 1893) b May 27, 1870, d March 27, 1933

Palairet, R. C. N. (OUCC & Som.; Joint-Manager MCC in Australia 1932-33) b June 25, 1871, d Feb. 11, 1955

*Palm, A. W. (W. Prov.) b June 8, 1901, d Aug. 17, 1966

*Palmer, C. H. (Worcs. & Leics.; Pres. MCC 1978-79) b May 15, 1919

*Palmer, G. E. (Vic. & Tas.) b Feb. 22, 1860, d Aug. 22, 1910

Palmer, G. V. (Som.) b Nov. 1, 1965

*Palmer, K. E. (Som.; Umpire) b April 22, 1937

Palmer, R. (Som.) b July 12, 1942

*Pandit, C. S. (Bombay) b Sept. 30, 1961

Pardon, Charles Frederick (Editor of Wisden 1887-90) b March 28, 1850, d April 18, 1890

Pardon, Sydney H. (Editor of Wisden 1891-1925) b Sept. 23, 1855, d Nov. 20, 1925

*Parfitt, P. H. (Middx; CY 1963) b Dec. 8, 1936

Paris, C. G. A. (Hants; Pres. MCC 1975-76) b Aug. 20, 1911

Parish, R. J. (Aust. Administrator) b May 7, 1916

*Park, R. L. (Vic.) b July 30, 1892, d Jan. 23, 1947

*Parkar, G. A. (Bombay) b Oct. 24, 1955

*Parkar, R. D. (Bombay) b Oct. 31, 1946

Parkar, Z. (Bombay) b Nov. 22, 1957

*Parker, C. W. L. (Glos.; CY 1923) b Oct. 14, 1882, d July 11, 1959

*Parker, G. M. (SA) b May 27, 1899, d May 1, 1969

Parker, G. W. (CUCC & Glos.) b Feb. 11, 1912

Parker, J. F. (Surrey) b April 23, 1913, d Jan. 27, 1983

*Parker, J. M. (N. Dist. & Worcs.) b Feb. 21, 1951

Parker, J. P. (Hants) b Nov. 29, 1902, d Aug. 9, 1984

*Parker, N. M. (Otago & Cant.) b Aug. 28, 1948

*Parker, P. W. G. (CUCC, Sussex, Natal & Durham) b Jan. 15, 1956

Parkhouse, W. G. A. (Glam.) b Oct. 12, 1925

*Parkin, C. H. (Yorks. & Lancs.; CY 1924) b Feb. 18, 1886, d June 15, 1943

*Parkin, D. C. (E. Prov., Tvl & Griq. W.) b Feb. 18, 1870, d March 20, 1936

Parks, H. W. (Sussex) b July 18, 1906, d May 7, 1984

*Parks, J. H. (Sussex & Cant.; CY 1938) b May 12, 1903, d Nov. 21, 1980

*Parks, J. M. (Sussex & Som.; CY 1968) b Oct. 21, 1931

Parks, R. J. (Hants & Kent) b June 15, 1959

*Parore, A. C. (Auck.) b Jan. 23, 1971

Parr, F. D. (Lancs.) b June 1, 1928

Parr, George (Notts. & All-England) b May 22, 1826, d June 23, 1891

*Parry, D. R. (Comb. Is. & Leewards) b Dec. 22, 1954

Births and Deaths of Cricketers

*Parsana, D. D. (S'tra, Ind. Rlwys & Guj.) b Dec. 2, 1947

Parsons, A. B. D. (CUCC & Surrey) b Sept. 20, 1933

Parsons, A. E. W. (Auck. & Sussex) b Jan. 9, 1949

Parsons, G. J. (Leics., Warwicks., Boland, Griq. W. & OFS) b Oct. 17, 1959

Parsons, Canon J. H. (Warwicks.) b May 30, 1890, d Feb. 2, 1981

*Partridge, J. T. (Rhod.) b Dec. 9, 1932, d June 7, 1988

Partridge, N. E. (Malvern, CUCC & Warwicks.; *CY 1919*) b Aug. 10, 1900, d March 10, 1982

Partridge, R. J. (Northants) b Feb. 11, 1912

Parvez Mir (R'pindi, Lahore, Punjab, Pak. Us, Derbys., HBL & Glam.) b Sept. 24, 1953

*Pascoe, L. S. (NSW) b Feb. 13, 1950

Pasqual, S. P. (SL) b Oct. 15, 1961

*Passailaigue, C. C. (Jam.) b Aug. 1902, d Jan. 7, 1972

*Patankar, C. T. (Bombay) b Nov. 24, 1930

**Pataudi, Iftikhar Ali, Nawab of (OUCC, Worcs., Patiala, N. Ind. & S. Punjab; *CY 1932*) b March 16, 1910, d Jan. 5, 1952

*Pataudi, Mansur Ali, Nawab of (Sussex, OUCC, Delhi & H'bad; *CY 1968*) b Jan. 5, 1941

Patel, A. (S'tra) b March 6, 1957

*Patel, B. P. (Karn.) b Nov. 24, 1952

*Patel, D. N. (Worcs. & Auck.) b Oct. 25, 1958

*Patel, J. M. (Guj.) b Nov. 26, 1924, d Dec. 12, 1992

*Patel, R. (Baroda) b June 1, 1964

Pathmanathan, G. (OUCC, CUCC & SL) b Jan. 23, 1954

*Patiala, Maharaja of (N. Ind., Patiala & S. Punjab) b Jan. 17, 1913, d June 17, 1974

*Patil, S. M. (Bombay & M. Pradesh) b Aug. 18, 1956

*Patil, S. R. (M'tra) b Oct. 10, 1933

*Patterson, B. P. (Jam., Tas. & Lancs.) b Sept. 15, 1961

Pauline, D. B. (Surrey & Glam.) b Dec. 15, 1960

Pawson, A. G. (OUCC & Worcs.) b May 30, 1888, d Feb. 25, 1986

Pawson, H. A. (OUCC & Kent) b Aug. 22, 1921

Payn, L. W. (Natal) b May 6, 1915, d May 2, 1992

Payne, T. R. O. (B'dos) b Feb. 13, 1957

*Paynter, E. (Lancs.; *CY 1938*) b Nov. 5, 1901, d Feb. 5, 1979

Payton, W. R. D. (Notts.) b Feb. 13, 1882, d May 2, 1943

Peall, S. G. (Zimb.) b Sept. 2, 1970

Pearce, G. (Sussex) b Oct. 27, 1908, d June 16, 1986

Pearce, T. N. (Essex) b Nov. 3, 1905

*Pearse, C. O. C. (Natal) b Oct. 10, 1884, d May 7, 1953

Pearson, D. B. (Worcs.) b March 29, 1937

*Peate, E. (Yorks.) b March 2, 1856, d March 11, 1900

Peck, I. G. (CUCC & Northants) b Oct. 18, 1957

*Peebles, I. A. R. (OUCC, Middx & Scotland; *CY 1931*) b Jan. 20, 1908, d Feb. 28, 1980

*Peel, R. (Yorks.; *CY 1889*) b Feb. 12, 1857, d Aug. 12, 1941

*Pegler, S. J. (Tvl) b July 28, 1888, d Sept. 10, 1972

*Pellew, C. E. (S. Aust.) b Sept. 21, 1893, d May 9, 1981

Penn, C. (Kent) b June 19, 1963

*Penn, F. (Kent) b March 7, 1851, d Dec. 26, 1916

Penney, T. L. (Boland & Warwicks.) b June 11, 1968

Pepper, C. G. (NSW & Aust. Serv.; Umpire) b Sept. 15, 1918, d March 24, 1993

Perera, K. G. (Mor.) b May 22, 1964

Perkins, C. G. (Northants) b June 4, 1911

Perkins, H. (CUCC & Cambs.; Sec. MCC 1876-97) b Dec. 10, 1832, d May 6, 1916

*Perks, R. T. D. (Worcs.) b Oct. 4, 1911, d Nov. 22, 1977

*Perrin, P. A. (Essex; *CY 1905*) b May 26, 1876, d Nov. 20, 1945

Perryman, S. P. (Warwicks. & Worcs.) b Oct. 22, 1955

*Pervez Sajjad (Lahore, PIA & Kar.) b Aug. 30, 1942

*Petherick, P. J. (Otago & Wgtn) b Sept. 25, 1942

*Petrie, E. C. (Auck. & N. Dist.) b May 22, 1927

Petrie, R. G. (Cant.) b Aug. 23, 1967

*Phadkar, D. G. (M'tra, Bombay, Bengal & Ind. Rlwys) b Dec. 10, 1925, d March 17, 1985

Phebey, A. H. (Kent) b Oct. 1, 1924

Phelan, P. J. (Essex) b Feb. 9, 1938

*Philipson, H. (OUCC & Middx) b June 8, 1866, d Dec. 4, 1935

Phillip, N. (Comb. Is., Windwards & Essex) b June 12, 1948

Phillips, R. B. (NSW & Qld) b May 23, 1954

*Phillips, W. B. (S. Aust.) b March 1, 1958

*Phillips, W. N. (Vic.) b Nov. 7, 1962

Phillipson, C. P. (Sussex) b Feb. 10, 1952

Phillipson, W. E. (Lancs.) b Dec. 3, 1910, d Aug. 24, 1991

*Philpott, P. I. (NSW) b Nov. 21, 1934

Piachaud, J. D. (OUCC, Hants & Ceylon) b March 1, 1937

Pick, R. A. (Notts. & Wgtn) b Nov. 19, 1963

Pickles, C. S. (Yorks.) b Jan. 30, 1966

Pickles, L. (Som.) b Sept. 17, 1932

Pienaar, R. F. (Tvl, W. Prov., N. Tvl & Kent) b July 17, 1961

Pieris, H. S. M. (SL) b Feb. 16, 1946

*Pierre, L. R. (T/T) b June 5, 1921, d April 14, 1989

Pierson, A. R. K. (Warwicks. & Leics.) b July 21, 1963

*Pigott, A. C. S. (Sussex & Wgtn) b June 4, 1958

Pilch, Fuller (Norfolk & Kent) b March 17, 1804, d May 1, 1870

Pilling, H. (Lancs.) b Feb. 23, 1943

*Pilling, R. (Lancs.; *CY 1891*) b July 5, 1855, d March 28, 1891

Piper, K. J. (Warwicks.) b Dec. 18, 1969

*Pithey, A. J. (Rhod. & W. Prov.) b July 17, 1933

*Pithey, D. B. (Rhod., OUCC, Northants, W. Prov., Natal & Tvl) b Oct. 4, 1936

Pitman, R. W. C. (Hants) b Feb. 21, 1933

*Place, W. (Lancs.) b Dec 7, 1914

Platt, R. K. (Yorks. & Northants) b Dec. 21, 1932

*Playle, W. R. (Auck. & W. Aust.) b Dec. 1, 1938

Pleass, J. E. (Glam.) b May 21, 1923

*Plimsoll, J. B. (W. Prov. & Natal) b Oct. 27, 1917

Pocock, N. E. J. (Hants) b Dec. 15, 1951

*Pocock, P. I. (Surrey & N. Tvl) b Sept. 24, 1946

Pollard, P. R. (Notts.) b Sept. 24, 1968

*Pollard, R. (Lancs.) b June 19, 1912, d Dec. 16, 1985

*Pollard, V. (C. Dist. & Cant.) b Burnley Sept. 7, 1945

Pollock, A. J. (CUCC) b April 19, 1962

*Pollock, P. M. (E. Prov.; *CY 1966*) b June 30, 1941

*Pollock, R. G. (E. Prov. & Tvl; *CY 1966*) b Feb. 27, 1944

*Ponsford, W. H. (Vic.; *CY 1935*) b Oct. 19, 1900, d April 6, 1991

Pont, K. R. (Essex) b Jan. 16, 1953

*Poole, C. J. (Notts.) b March 13, 1921

Pooley, E. (Surrey & first England tour) b Feb. 13, 1838, d July 18, 1907

*Poore, M. B. (Cant.) b June 1, 1930

*Poore, Brig-Gen. R. M. (Hants & SA; *CY 1900*) b March 20, 1866, d July 14, 1938

Pope, A. V. (Derbys.) b Aug. 15, 1909

*Pope, G. H. (Derbys.) b Jan. 27, 1911, d Oct. 29, 1993

*Pope, R. J. (NSW) b Feb. 18, 1864, d July 27, 1952

Popplewell, N. F. M. (CUCC & Som.) b Aug. 8, 1957

Portal of Hungerford, 1st Lord (Pres. MCC 1958-59) b May 21, 1893, d April 22, 1971

Porter, A. (Glam.) b March 25, 1914

Porter, G. D. (W. Aust.) b March 18, 1955

Pothecary, A. E. (Hants) b March 1, 1906, d May 21, 1991

*Pothecary, J. E. (W. Prov.) b Dec. 6, 1933

Potter, G. (Sussex) b Oct. 26, 1931

Potter, L. (Kent, Griq. W., Leics. & OFS) b Nov. 7, 1962

*Pougher, A. D. (Leics.) b April 19, 1865, d May 20, 1926

Pountain, F. R. (Sussex) b April 23, 1941

*Powell, A. W. (Griq. W.) b July 18, 1873, d Sept. 11, 1948

*Prabhakar, M. (Delhi) b April 15, 1963

*Prasanna, E. A. S. (†Karn.) b May 22, 1940

Pratt, R. L. (Leics.) b Nov. 15, 1938

Pressdee, J. S. (Glam. & NE Tvl) b June 19, 1933

Preston, Hubert (Editor of *Wisden* 1944-51) b Dec. 16, 1868, d Aug. 6, 1960

Preston, K. C. (Essex) b Aug. 22, 1925

Preston, Norman (Editor of *Wisden* 1952-80) b March 18, 1903, d March 6, 1980

Pretlove, J. F. (CUCC & Kent) b Nov. 23, 1932

Price, D. G. (CUCC) b Feb. 7, 1965

Price, E. J. (Lancs. & Essex) b Oct. 27, 1918

*Price, J. S. E. (Middx) b July 22, 1937

*Price, W. F. F. (Middx) b April 25, 1902, d Jan. 13, 1969

Prichard, P. J. (Essex) b Jan. 7, 1965

*Prideaux, R. M. (CUCC, Kent, Northants, Sussex & OFS) b July 31, 1939

Pridgeon, A. P. (Worcs.) b Feb. 22, 1954

*Priest, M. W. (Cant.) b Aug. 12, 1961

*Prince, C. F. H. (W. Prov., Border & E. Prov.) b Sept. 11, 1874, d March 5, 1948

*Pringle, C. (Auck.) b Jan. 26, 1968

*Pringle, D. R. (CUCC & Essex) b Sept. 18, 1958

*Pringle, M. W. (W. Prov.) b June 22, 1966

Pritchard, T. L. (Wgtn, Warwicks. & Kent) b March 10, 1917

*Procter, M. J. (Glos., Natal, W. Prov., Rhod. & OFS; *CY 1970*) b Sept. 15, 1946

Prodger, J. M. (Kent) b Sept. 1, 1939

*Promnitz, H. L. E. (Border, Griq. W. & OFS) b Feb. 23, 1904, d Sept. 7, 1983

Prouton, R. O. (Hants) b March 1, 1926

Pugh, C. T. M. (Glos.) b March 13, 1937

Pullan, D. A. (Notts.) b May 1, 1904

*Pullar, G. (Lancs. & Glos.; *CY 1960*) b Aug. 1, 1935

*Puna, N. (N. Dist.) b Oct. 28, 1929

*Punjabi, P. H. (Sind & Guj.) b Sept. 20, 1921

*Pycroft, A. J. (Zimb.) b June 6, 1956

Pydanna, M. R. (Guyana), b Jan. 27, 1950

*Qasim Omar (Kar. & MCB) b Feb. 9, 1957

Quaife, B. W. (Warwicks. & Worcs.) b Nov. 24, 1899, d Nov. 28, 1984

*Quaife, William (W. G.) (Warwicks. & Griq. W.; *CY 1902*) b March 17, 1872, d Oct. 13, 1951

*Quinn, N. A. (Griq. W. & Tvl) b Feb. 21, 1908, d Aug. 5, 1934

*Rabone, G. O. (Wgtn & Auck.) b Nov. 6, 1921

*Rackemann, C. G. (Qld) b June 3, 1960

*Radford, N. V. (Lancs., Tvl & Worcs.; *CY 1986*) b June 7, 1957

*Radley, C. T. (Middx; *CY 1979*) b May 13, 1944

*Rae, A. F. (Jam.) b Sept. 30, 1922

Raees Mohammad (Kar.) b Dec. 24, 1932

*Rai Singh, K. (S. Punjab & Ind. Serv.) b Feb. 24, 1922

Rait Kerr, Col. R. S. (Sec. MCC 1936-52) b April 13, 1891, d April 2, 1961

Rajadurai, B. E. A. (SSC) b Aug. 24, 1965

*Rajindernath, V. (N. Ind., U. Prov., S. Punjab, Bihar & E. Punjab) b Jan. 7, 1928, d Nov. 22, 1989

*Rajinder Pal (Delhi, S. Punjab & Punjab) b Nov. 18, 1937

*Rajput, L. S. (Bombay) b Dec. 18, 1961

*Raju, S. L. V. (H'bad) b July 9, 1969

Ralph, L. H. R. (Essex) b May 22, 1920

*Ramadhin, S. (T/T & Lancs.; *CY 1951*) b May 1, 1929

*Raman, W. V. (TN) b May 23, 1965

*Ramanayake, C. P. H. (TU) b Jan. 8, 1965

*Ramaswami, C. (Madras) b June 18, 1896

*Ramchand, G. S. (Sind, Bombay & Raj.) b July 26, 1927

*Ramiz Raja (Lahore, Allied Bank & PNSC) b July 14, 1962

*Ramji, L. (W. Ind.) b 1900, d Dec. 20, 1948

*Ramprakash, M. R. (Middx) b Sept. 5, 1969

Ramsamooj, D. (T/T & Northants) b July 5, 1932

*Ranasinghe, A. N. (BRC) b Oct. 13, 1956

Ranasinghe, S. K. (SL) b July 4, 1962

*Ranatunga, A. (SSC) b Dec. 1, 1963

*Ranatunga, D. (SSC) b Oct. 12, 1962

Ranatunga, N. (Colts) b Jan. 22, 1966

*Ranchod, U. (Zimb.) b May 17, 1969

*Randall, D. W. (Notts.; *CY 1980*) b Feb. 24, 1951

Randhir Singh (Orissa & Bihar) b Aug. 16, 1957

*Rangachari, C. R. (Madras) b April 14, 1916, d Oct. 9, 1993

*Rangnekar, K. M. (M'tra, Bombay & †M. Pradesh) b June 27, 1917, d Oct. 11, 1984

*Ranjane, V. B. (M'tra & Ind. Rlwys) b July 22, 1937

*Ranjitsinhji, K. S., afterwards H. H. the Jam Sahib of Nawanagar (CUCC & Sussex; *CY 1897*) b Sept. 10, 1872, d April 2, 1933

*Ransford, V. S. (Vic.; *CY 1910*) b March 20, 1885, d March 19, 1958

Ransom, V. J. (Hants & Surrey) b March 17, 1918

*Rashid Khan (PWD, Kar. & PIA) b Dec. 15, 1959

*Rashid Latif (Kar. & UBL) b Oct. 14, 1968

Ratcliffe, J. D. (Warwicks.) b June 19, 1969

Ratcliffe, R. M. (Lancs.) b Oct. 29, 1951

Ratnayake, N. L. K. (SSC) b Nov. 22, 1968

*Ratnayake, R. J. (NCC) b Jan. 2, 1964

*Ratnayeke, J. R. (NCC) b May 2, 1960

Rawson, P. W. E. (Zimb. & Natal) b May 25, 1957

Rayment, A. W. H. (Hants) b May 29, 1928

*Razdan, V. (Delhi) b Aug. 25, 1969

*Read, H. D. (Surrey & Essex) b Jan. 28, 1910

*Read, J. M. (Surrey; *CY 1890*) b Feb. 9, 1859, d Feb. 17, 1929

*Read, W. W. (Surrey; *CY 1893*) b Nov. 23, 1855, d Jan. 6, 1907

*Reddy, B. (TN) b Nov. 12, 1954

*Redmond, R. E. (Wgtn & Auck.) b Dec. 29, 1944

*Redpath, I. R. (Vic.) b May 11, 1941

Reed, B. L. (Hants) b Sept. 17, 1937

*Reedman, J. C. (S. Aust.) b Oct. 9, 1865, d March 25, 1924

Rees, A. (Glam.) b Feb. 17, 1938

*Reeve, D. A. (Sussex & Warwicks.) b April 2, 1963

Reeves, W. (Essex; Umpire) b Jan. 22, 1875, d March 22, 1944

Rege, M. R. (M'tra) b March 18, 1924

*Rehman, S. F. (Punjab, Pak. Us & Lahore) b June 11, 1935

*Reid, B. A. (W. Aust.) b March 14, 1963

*Reid, J. F. (Auck.) b March 3, 1956

*Reid, J. R. (Wgtn & Otago; *CY 1959*) b June 3, 1928

*Reid, N. (W. Prov.) b Dec. 26, 1890, d June 6, 1947

Reid, R. B. (Wgtn & Auck.) b Dec. 3, 1958

Reidy, B. W. (Lancs.) b Sept. 18, 1953

*Reiffel, P. R. (Vic.) b April 19, 1966

*Relf, A. E. (Sussex & Auck.; *CY 1914*) b June 26, 1874, d March 26, 1937

*Renneburg, D. A. (NSW) b Sept. 23, 1942

Revill, A. C. (Derbys. & Leics.) b March 27, 1923

Reynolds, B. L. (Northants) b June 10, 1932

Rhodes, A. E. G. (Derbys.) b Oct. 10, 1916, d Oct. 18, 1983

*Rhodes, H. J. (Derbys.) b July 22, 1936

*Rhodes, J. N. (Natal) b July 26, 1969

Rhodes, S. D. (Notts.) b March 24, 1910, d Jan. 7, 1989

Rhodes, S. J. (Yorks. & Worcs.) b June 17, 1964

*Rhodes, W. (Yorks.; *CY 1899*) b Oct. 29, 1877, d July 8, 1973

Rice, C. E. B. (Tvl & Notts.; *CY 1981*) b July 23, 1949

Rice, J. M. (Hants) b Oct. 23, 1949

*Richards, A. R. (W. Prov.) b 1868, d Jan. 9, 1904

*Richards, B. A. (Natal, Glos., Hants & S. Aust.; *CY 1969*) b July 21, 1945

*Richards, C. J. (Surrey & OFS) b Aug. 10, 1958

Richards, D. L. (Chief Exec. ICC 1993-) b July 28, 1946

Richards, G. (Glam.) b Nov. 29, 1951

*Richards, I. V. A. (Comb. Is., Leewards, Som., Qld & Glam.; *CY 1977*) b March 7, 1952

*Richards, W. H. M. (SA) b Aug. 1862, d Jan. 4, 1903

*Richardson, A. J. (S. Aust.) b July 24, 1888, d Dec. 23, 1973

*Richardson, D. J. (E. Prov. & N. Tvl) b Sept. 16, 1959

*Richardson, D. W. (Worcs.) b Nov. 3, 1934

Richardson, G. W. (Derbys.) b April 26, 1938

*Richardson, P. E. (Worcs. & Kent; *CY 1957*) b July 4, 1931

*Richardson, R. B. (Leewards & Yorks.; *CY 1992*) b Jan. 12, 1962

*Richardson, T. (Surrey & Som.; *CY 1897*) b Aug. 11, 1870, d July 2, 1912

*Richardson, V. Y. (S. Aust.) b Sept. 7, 1894, d Oct. 29, 1969

*Richmond, T. L. (Notts.) b June 23, 1890, d Dec. 29, 1957

*Rickards, K. R. (Jam. & Essex) b Aug. 23, 1923

Riddington, A. (Leics.) b Dec. 22, 1911

*Ridgway, F. (Kent) b Aug. 10, 1923

*Rigg, K. E. (Vic.) b May 21, 1906

Riley, H. (Leics.) b Oct. 3, 1902, d Jan. 24, 1989

*Ring, D. T. (Vic.) b Oct. 14, 1918

Ripley, D. (Northants) b Sept. 13, 1966

Rist, F. H. (Essex) b March 30, 1914

*Ritchie, G. M. (Qld) b Jan. 23, 1960

*Rixon, S. J. (NSW) b Feb. 25, 1954

*Rizwan-uz-Zaman (Kar. & PIA) b Sept. 4, 1962

*Roach, C. A. (T/T) b March 13, 1904, d April 16, 1988

*Roberts, A. D. G. (N. Dist.) b May 6, 1947, d Oct. 26, 1989

*Roberts, A. M. E. (Comb. Is., Leewards, Hants, NSW & Leics.; *CY 1975*) b Jan. 29, 1951

*Roberts, A. T. (Windwards) b Sept. 18, 1937

*Roberts, A. W. (Cant. & Otago) b Aug. 20, 1909, d May 13, 1978

Roberts, B. (Tvl & Derbys.) b May 30, 1962

Roberts, The Hon. Sir Denys (Pres. MCC 1989-90) b Jan. 19, 1923

Roberts, S. J. (Cant.) b March 22, 1965

Roberts, W. B. (Lancs. & Victory Tests) b Sept. 27, 1914, d Aug. 24, 1951

*Robertson, G. K. (C. Dist.) b July 15, 1960

*Robertson, J. B. (W. Prov.) b June 5, 1906, d July 5, 1985

*Robertson, J. D. (Middx; *CY 1948*) b Feb. 22, 1917

*Robertson, W. R. (Vic.) b Oct. 6, 1861, d June 24, 1938

Robertson-Glasgow, R. C. (OUCC & Som.; Writer) b July 15, 1901, d March 4, 1965

Robins, D. H. (Warwicks.) b June 26, 1914

Robins, R. V. C. (Middx) b March 13, 1935

*Robins, R. W. V. (CUCC & Middx; *CY 1930*) b June 3, 1906, d Dec. 12, 1968

Robinson, A. L. (Yorks.) b Aug. 17, 1946

Robinson, Emmott (Yorks.) b Nov. 16, 1883, d Nov. 17, 1969

Robinson, Ellis P. (Yorks. & Som.) b Aug. 10, 1911

Robinson, H. B. (OUCC & Canada) b March 3, 1919

Robinson, M. (Glam., Warwicks., H'bad & Madras) b July 16, 1921

Robinson, M. A. (Northants & Yorks.) b Nov. 23, 1966

Robinson, P. E. (Yorks. & Leics.) b Aug. 3, 1963

Robinson, P. J. (Worcs. & Som.) b Feb. 9, 1943

*Robinson, R. D. (Vic.) b June 8, 1946

*Robinson, R. H. (NSW, S. Aust. & Otago) b March 26, 1914, d Aug. 10, 1965

*Robinson, R. T. (Notts.; *CY 1986*) b Nov. 21, 1958

Robson, E. (Som.) b May 1, 1870, d May 23, 1924

Rochford, P. (Glos.) b Aug. 27, 1928, d June 18, 1992

*Rodriguez, W. V. (T/T) b June 25, 1934

Roe, B. (Som.) b Jan. 27, 1939

Roebuck, P. M. (CUCC & Som.; *CY 1988*) b March 6, 1956

Rogers, N. H. (Hants) b March 9, 1918

Romaines, P. W. (Northants, Glos. & Griq. W.) b Dec. 25, 1955

*Roope, G. R. J. (Surrey & Griq. W.) b July 12, 1946

*Root, C. F. (Derbys. & Worcs.) b April 16, 1890, d Jan. 20, 1954

*Rorke, G. F. (NSW) b June 27, 1938

*Rose, B. C. (Som.; *CY 1980*) b June 4, 1950

Rose, G. D. (Middx & Som.) b April 12, 1964

Roseberry, M. A. (Middx) b Nov. 28, 1966

*Rose-Innes, A. (Kimberley & Tvl) b Feb. 16, 1868, d Nov. 22, 1946

Ross, C. J. (Wgtn & OUCC) b June 24, 1954

Rotherham, G. A. (Rugby, CUCC, War-wicks. & Wgtn; *CY 1918*) b May 28, 1899, d Jan. 31, 1985

Rouse, S. J. (Warwicks.) b Jan. 20, 1949

Routledge, R. (Middx) b June 12, 1920

*Routledge, T. W. (W. Prov. & Tvl) b April 18, 1867, d May 9, 1927

*Rowan, A. M. B. (Tvl) b Feb. 7, 1921

*Rowan, E. A. B. (Tvl; *CY 1952*) b July 20, 1909, d April 30, 1993

*Rowe, C. G. (Wgtn & C. Dist.) b June 30, 1915

Rowe, C. J. C. (Kent & Glam.) b Nov. 11, 1951

Rowe, E. J. (Notts.) b July 21, 1920, d Dec. 17, 1989

*Rowe, G. A. (W. Prov.) b June 15, 1874, d Jan. 8, 1950

*Rowe, L. G. (Jam. & Derbys.) b Jan. 8, 1949

*Roy, A. (Bengal) b June 5, 1945

*Roy, Pankaj (Bengal) b May 31, 1928

*Roy, Pranab (Bengal) b Feb. 10, 1957

*Royle, Rev. V. P. F. A. (OUCC & Lancs.) b Jan. 29, 1854, d May 21, 1929

*Rumsey, F. E. (Worcs., Som. & Derbys.) b Dec. 4, 1935

*Rushmere, M. W. (E. Prov.) b Jan. 7, 1965

*Russell, A. C. [C. A. G.] (Essex; *CY 1923*) b Oct. 7, 1887, d March 23, 1961

*Russell, P. E. (Derbys.) b May 9, 1944

*Russell, R. C. (Glos.; *CY 1990*) b Aug. 15, 1963

*Russell, S. E. (Middx & Glos.) b Oct. 4, 1937

*Russell, W. E. (Middx) b July 3, 1936

Russom, N. (CUCC & Som.) b Dec. 3, 1958

Rutherford, I. A. (Worcs. & Otago) b June 30, 1957

*Rutherford, J. W. (W. Aust.) b Sept. 25, 1929

*Rutherford, K. R. (Otago) b Oct. 26, 1965

Ryan, M. (Yorks.) b June 23, 1933

*Ryder, J. (Vic.) b Aug. 8, 1889, d April 3, 1977

Saadat Ali (Lahore, UBL & HBFC) b Feb. 6, 1955

*Sadiq Mohammad (Kar., PIA, Tas., Essex, Glos. & UBL) b May 3, 1945

*Saeed Ahmed (Punjab, Pak. Us, Lahore, PIA, Kar., PWD & Sind) b Oct. 1, 1937

*Saeed Anwar (UBL & ADBP) b Sept. 6, 1968

*Saggers, R. A. (NSW) b May 15, 1917, d March 1987

Sainsbury, G. E. (Essex & Glos.) b Jan. 17, 1958

Sainsbury, P. J. (Hants; *CY 1974*) b June 13, 1934

*St Hill, E. L. (T/T) b March 9, 1904, d May 21, 1957

*St Hill, W. H. (T/T) b July 6, 1893, d 1957

Sajid Ali (Kar. & NBP) b July 1, 1963

Sajjad Akbar (PNSC & Sargodha) b March 1, 1961

*Salah-ud-Din (Kar., PIA & Pak. Us) b Feb. 14, 1947

Sale, R., jun. (OUCC, Warwicks. & Derbys.) b Oct. 4, 1919, d Feb. 3, 1987

*Saleem Altaf (Lahore & PIA) b April 19, 1944

*Saleem Jaffer (Kar. & UBL) b Nov. 19, 1962

*Salim Malik (Lahore, HBL & Essex; *CY 1988*) b April 16, 1963

Salim Pervez (NBP) b Sept. 9, 1947

*Salim Yousuf (Sind, Kar., IDBP, Allied Bank & Customs) b Dec. 7, 1959

*Salisbury, I. D. K. (Sussex; *CY 1993*) b Jan. 21, 1970

Samaranayake, A. D. A. (SL) b Feb. 25, 1962

*Samarasekera, M. A. R. (CCC) b Aug. 5, 1961

Sampson, H. (Yorks. & All-England) b March 13, 1813, d March 29, 1885

*Samuelson, S. V. (Natal) b Nov. 21, 1883, d Nov. 18, 1958

*Sandham, A. (Surrey; *CY 1923*) b July 6, 1890, d April 20, 1982

*Sandhu, B. S. (Bombay) b Aug. 3, 1956

*Sardesai, D. N. (Bombay) b Aug. 8, 1940

*Sarfraz Nawaz (Lahore, Punjab, Northants, Pak. Rlwys & UBL) b Dec. 1, 1948

*Sarwate, C. T. (CP & B, M'tra, Bombay & †M. Pradesh) b June 22, 1920

*Saunders, J. V. (Vic. & Wgtn) b Feb. 3, 1876, d Dec. 21, 1927

Savage, J. S. (Leics. & Lancs.) b March 3, 1929

Savage, R. Le Q. (OUCC & Warwicks.) b Dec. 10, 1955

Savill, L. A. (Essex) b June 30, 1935

Saville, G. J. (Essex) b Feb. 5, 1944

Saxelby, K. (Notts.) b Feb. 23, 1959

*Saxena, R. C. (Delhi & Bihar) b Sept. 20, 1944

Sayer, D. M. (OUCC & Kent) b Sept. 19, 1936

*Scarlett, R. O. (Jam.) b Aug. 15, 1934

*Schultz, B. N. (E. Prov.) b Aug. 26, 1970

*Schultz, S. S. (CUCC & Lancs.) b Aug. 29, 1857, d Dec. 18, 1937

*Schwarz, R. O. (Middx & Natal; *CY 1908*) b May 4, 1875, d Nov. 18, 1918

*Scott, A. P. H. (Jam.) b July 29, 1934

Scott, Christopher J. (Lancs.) b Sept. 16, 1959

Scott, Colin J. (Glos.) b May 1, 1919, d Nov. 22, 1992

Scott, C. W. (Notts. & Durham) b Jan. 23, 1964

*Scott, H. J. H. (Vic.) b Dec. 26, 1858, d Sept. 23, 1910

Scott, M. E. (Northants) b May 8, 1936

*Scott, O. C. (Jam.) b Aug. 25, 1893, d June 16, 1961

*Scott, R. H. (Cant.) b March 6, 1917

Scott, R. J. (Hants & Glos.) b Nov. 2, 1963

*Scott, S. W. (Middx; *CY 1893*) b March 24, 1854, d Dec. 8, 1933

*Scott, V. J. (Auck.) b July 31, 1916, d Aug. 2, 1980

*Scotton, W. H. (Notts.) b Jan. 15, 1856, d July 9, 1893

Sealey, B. J. (T/T) b Aug. 12, 1899, d Sept. 12, 1963

*Sealy, J. E. D. (B'dos & T/T) b Sept. 11, 1912, d Jan. 3, 1982

Seamer, J. W. (Som. & OUCC) b June 23, 1913

Seccull, A. W. (Kimberley, W. Prov. & Tvl) b Sept. 14, 1868, d July 20, 1945

*Sekar, T. A. P. (TN) b March 28, 1955

*Selby, J. (Notts.) b July 1, 1849, d March 11, 1894

Sellers, A. B. (Yorks.; *CY 1940*) b March 5, 1907, d Feb. 20, 1981

*Sellers, R. H. D. (S. Aust.) b Aug. 20, 1940

*Selvey, M. W. W. (CUCC, Surrey, Middx, Glam. & OFS) b April 25, 1948

*Sen, P. (Bengal) b May 31, 1926, d Jan. 27, 1970

*Sen Gupta, A. K. (Ind. Serv.) b Aug. 3, 1939

*Senanayake, C. P. (CCC) b Dec. 19, 1962

*Serjeant, C. S. (W. Aust.) b Nov. 1, 1951

Seymour, James (Kent) b Oct. 25, 1879, d Sept. 30, 1930

*Seymour, M. A. (W. Prov.) b June 5, 1936

*Shackleton, D. (Hants.; *CY 1959*) b Aug. 12, 1924

*Shafiq Ahmad (Lahore, Punjab, NBP & UBL) b March 28, 1949

*Shafqat Rana (Lahore & PIA) b Aug. 10, 1943

*Shah, A. H. (Zimb.) b Aug. 7, 1959

*Shahid Israr (Kar. & Sind) b March 1, 1950

*Shahid Mahboob (Karachi, Quetta & PACO) b Aug. 25, 1962

*Shahid Mahmood (Kar., Pak. Us & PWD) b March 17, 1939

Shahid, N. (Essex) b April 23, 1969

*Shahid Saeed (HBFC) b Jan. 6, 1966

*Shakeel Ahmed (B'pur & HBL) b Nov. 12, 1971

Shakil Khan (WAPDA & HBL) b May 28, 1968

*Shalders, W. A. (Griq. W. & Tvl) b Feb. 12, 1880, d March 18, 1917

*Sharma, Ajay (Delhi) b April 3, 1964

*Sharma, Chetan (Haryana) b Jan. 3, 1966

*Sharma, Gopal (U. Pradesh) b Aug. 3, 1960

*Sharma, P. (Raja.) b Jan. 5, 1948

Sharma, R. (Derbys.) b June 27, 1962

Sharma, Sanjeev (Delhi) b Aug. 25, 1965

Sharp, G. (Northants) b March 12, 1950

Sharp, H. P. H. (Middx; Middx scorer) b Oct. 6, 1917

*Sharp, J. (Lancs.) b Feb. 15, 1878, d Jan. 28, 1938

Sharp, K. (Yorks. & Griq. W.) b April 6, 1959

*Sharpe, D. (Punjab, Pak. Rlwys, Lahore & S. Aust.) b Aug. 3, 1937

*Sharpe, J. W. (Surrey & Notts.; *CY 1892*) b Dec. 9, 1866, d June 19, 1936

*Sharpe, P. J. (Yorks. & Derbys.; *CY 1963*) b Dec. 27, 1936

*Shastri, R. J. (Bombay & Glam.) b May 27, 1962

Shaw, Alfred (Notts. & Sussex) b Aug. 29, 1842, d Jan. 16, 1907

Shaw, C. (Yorks.) b Feb. 17, 1964

Shaw, T. G. (E. Prov.) b July 5, 1959

*Sheahan, A. P. (Vic.) b Sept. 30, 1946

Sheffield, J. R. (Essex & Wgtn) b Nov. 19, 1906

*Shepherd, B. K. (W. Aust.) b April 23, 1937

Shepherd, D. J. (Glam.; *CY 1970*) b Aug. 12, 1927

Shepherd, D. R. (Glos.; Umpire) b Dec. 27, 1940

*Shepherd, J. N. (B'dos, Kent, Rhod. & Glos.; *CY 1979*) b Nov. 9, 1943

Shepherd, T. F. (Surrey) b Dec. 5, 1889, d Feb. 13, 1957

*Sheppard, Rt Rev. D. S. (Bishop of Liverpool) (CUCC & Sussex; *CY 1953*) b March 6, 1929

*Shepstone, G. H. (Tvl) b April 8, 1876, d July 3, 1940

*Sherwell, P. W. (Tvl) b Aug. 17, 1880, d April 17, 1948

*Sherwin, M. (Notts.; *CY 1891*) b Feb. 26, 1851, d July 3, 1910

*Shillingford, G. C. (Comb. Is. & Windwards) b Sept. 25, 1944

*Shillingford, I. T. (Comb. Is. & Windwards) b April 18, 1944

*Shinde, S. G. (Baroda, M'tra & Bombay) b Aug. 18, 1923, d June 22, 1955

Shine, K. J. (Hants) b Feb. 22, 1969

Shirreff, A. C. (CUCC, Hants, Kent & Som.) b Feb. 12, 1919

*Shivnarine, S. (Guyana) b May 13, 1952

*Shoaib Mohammad (Kar. & PIA) b Jan. 8, 1961

*Shodhan, R. H. (Guj. & Baroda) b Oct. 18, 1928

*Shrewsbury, Arthur (Notts.; *CY 1890*) b April 11, 1856, d May 19, 1903

*Shrimpton, M. J. F. (C. Dist. & N. Dist.) b June 23, 1940

*Shuja-ud-Din, Col. (N. Ind., Pak. Us, Pak. Serv., B'pur & R'pindi) b April 10, 1930

*Shukla, R. C. (Bihar & Delhi) b Feb. 4, 1948

*Shuter, J. (Kent & Surrey) b Feb. 9, 1855, d July 5, 1920

*Shuttleworth, K. (Lancs. & Leics.) b Nov. 13, 1944

Siddons, J. D. (Vic. & S. Aust.) b April 25, 1964

*Sidebottom, A. (Yorks. & OFS) b April 1, 1954

*Sidhu, N. S. (Punjab) b Oct. 20, 1963

*Siedle, I. J. (Natal) b Jan. 11, 1903, d Aug. 24, 1982

*Sievers, M. W. (Vic.) b April 13, 1912, d May 10, 1968

*Sikander Bakht (PWD, PIA, Sind, Kar. & UBL) b Aug. 25, 1957

Silk, D. R. W. (CUCC & Som.; Pres. MCC 1992–) b Oct. 8, 1931

*Silva, S. A. R. (NCC) b Dec. 12, 1960

Simmons, J. (Lancs. & Tas.; *CY 1985*) b March 28, 1941

Simmons, P. V. (T/T) b April 18, 1963

*Simpson, R. B. (NSW & W. Aust.; *CY 1965*) b Feb. 3, 1936

*Simpson, R. T. (Notts. & Sind; *CY 1950*) b Feb. 27, 1920

*Simpson-Hayward, G. H. (Worcs.) b June 7, 1875, d Oct. 2, 1936

Sims, Sir Arthur (Cant.) b July 22, 1877, d April 27, 1969

*Sims, J. M. (Middx) b May 13, 1903, d April 27, 1973

*Sinclair, B. W. (Wgtn) b Oct. 23, 1936

*Sinclair, I. McK. (Cant.) b June 1, 1933

*Sinclair, J. H. (Tvl) b Oct. 16, 1876, d Feb. 23, 1913

*Sincock, D. J. (S. Aust.) b Feb. 1, 1942

*Sinfield, R. A. (Glos.) b Dec. 24, 1900, d March 17, 1988

*Singh, Charan K. (T/T) b 1938

Singh, "Robin" [R. R.] (TN) b Sept. 14, 1963

Singh, R. P. (U. Pradesh) b Jan. 6, 1963

Singh, Swaranjit (CUCC, Warwicks., E. Punjab & Bengal) b July 18, 1931

Singleton, A. P. (OUCC, Worcs. & Rhod.) b Aug. 5, 1914

*Sivaramakrishnan, L. (TN) b Dec. 31, 1965

*Skelding, A. (Leics.; Umpire) b Sept. 5, 1886, d April 17, 1960

Skinner, D. A. (Derbys.) b March 22, 1920

Skinner, L. E. (Surrey & Guyana) b Sept. 7, 1950

*Slack, W. N. (Middx & Windwards) b Dec. 12, 1954, d Jan. 15, 1989

Slade, D. N. F. (Worcs.) b Aug. 24, 1940

Slade, W. D. (Glam.) b Sept. 27, 1941

*Slater, K. N. (W. Aust.) b March 12, 1935

*Slater, M. J. (NSW) b Feb. 21, 1970

*Sleep, P. R. (S. Aust.) b May 4, 1957

*Slight, J. (Vic.) b Oct. 20, 1855, d Dec. 9, 1930

Slocombe, P. A. (Som.) b Sept. 6, 1954

*Smailes, T. F. (Yorks.) b March 27, 1910, d Dec. 1, 1970

Smales, K. (Yorks. & Notts.) b Sept. 15, 1927

*Small, G. C. (Warwicks. & S. Aust.) b Oct. 18, 1961

Small, John, sen. (Hants & All-England) b April 19, 1737, d Dec. 31, 1826

*Small, J. A. (T/T) b Nov. 3, 1892, d April 26, 1958

*Small, M. A. (B'dos) b Feb. 12, 1964

Smedley, M. J. (Notts.) b Oct. 28, 1941

*Smith, A. C. (OUCC & Warwicks.; Chief Exec. TCCB 1987–) b Oct. 25, 1936

Smith, B. F. (Leics.) b April 3, 1972

*Smith, Sir C. Aubrey (OUCC, Sussex & Tvl) b July 21, 1863, d Dec. 20, 1948

*Smith, C. I. J. (Middx; *CY 1935*) b Aug. 25, 1906, d Feb. 9, 1979

*Smith, C. J. E. (Tvl) b Dec. 25, 1872, d March 27, 1947

*Smith, C. L. (Natal, Glam. & Hants; *CY 1984*) b Oct. 15, 1958

Smith, C. S. (CUCC & Lancs.) b Oct. 1, 1932

*Smith, C. W. (B'dos) b July 29, 1933

*Smith, Denis (Derbys.; *CY 1936*) b Jan. 24, 1907, d Sept. 12, 1979

*Smith, D. B. M. (Vic.) b Sept. 14, 1884, d July 29, 1963

Smith, D. H. K. (Derbys. & OFS) b June 29, 1940

*Smith, D. M. (Surrey, Worcs. & Sussex) b Jan. 9, 1956

*Smith, D. R. (Glos.) b Oct. 5, 1934

*Smith, D. V. (Sussex) b June 14, 1923

Smith, Edwin (Derbys.) b Jan. 2, 1934

*Smith, E. J. (Warwicks.) b Feb. 6, 1886, d Aug. 31, 1979

*Smith, F. B. (Cant.) b March 13, 1922

*Smith, F. W. (Tvl) No details of birth or death known

Smith, G. (Kent) b Nov. 30, 1925

Smith, G. J. (Essex) b April 2, 1935

*Smith, Harry (Glos.) b May 21, 1890, d Nov. 12, 1937

*Smith, H. D. (Otago & Cant.) b Jan. 8, 1913, d Jan. 25, 1986

Smith, I. (Glam. & Durham) b March 11, 1967

*Smith, I. D. S. (C. Dist. & Auck.) b Feb. 28, 1957

*Smith, K. D. (Warwicks.) b July 9, 1956

Smith, M. J. (Middx) b Jan. 4, 1942

*Smith, M. J. K. (OUCC, Leics. & Warwicks.; *CY 1960*) b June 30, 1933

Smith, N. (Yorks. & Essex) b April 1, 1949

Smith, N. M. K. (Warwicks.) b July 27, 1967

*Smith, O. G. (Jam.; *CY 1958*) b May 5, 1933, d Sept. 9, 1959

Smith, P. A. (Warwicks.) b April 5, 1964

Smith, Ray (Essex) b Aug. 10, 1914

Smith, Roy (Som.) b April 14, 1930

*Smith, R. A. (Natal & Hants; *CY 1990*) b Sept. 13, 1963

Smith, R. C. (Leics.) b Aug. 3, 1935

*Smith, S. B. (NSW & Tvl) b Oct. 18, 1961

Smith, S. G. (T/T, Northants & Auck.; *CY 1915*) b Jan. 15, 1881, d Oct. 25, 1963

*Smith, T. P. B. (Essex; *CY 1947*) b Oct. 30, 1908, d Aug. 4, 1967

Smith, V. I. (Natal) b Feb. 23, 1925

Smith, W. A. (Surrey) b Sept. 15, 1937

Smith, W. C. (Surrey; *CY 1911*) b Oct. 4, 1877, d July 16, 1946

*Smithson, G. A. (Yorks. & Leics.) b Nov. 1, 1926, d Sept. 6, 1970

*Snedden, C. A. (Auck.) b Jan. 7, 1918, d May 19, 1993

*Snedden, M. C. (Auck.) b Nov. 23, 1958

*Snell, R. P. (Tvl & Som.) b Sept. 12, 1968

Snellgrove, K. L. (Lancs.) b Nov. 12, 1941

*Snooke, S. D. (W. Prov. & Tvl) b Nov. 11, 1878, d April 4, 1959

*Snooke, S. J. (Border, W. Prov. & Tvl) b Feb. 1, 1881, d Aug. 14, 1966

*Snow, J. A. (Sussex; *CY 1973*) b Oct. 13, 1941

Snowden, W. (CUCC) b Sept. 27, 1952

*Sobers, Sir G. S. (B'dos, S. Aust. & Notts.; *CY 1964*) b July 28, 1936

Sohail Fazal (Lahore) b Nov. 11, 1967

*Sohoni, S. W. (M'tra, Baroda & Bombay) b March 5, 1918, d May 19, 1993

Solanky, J. W. (E. Africa & Glam.) b June 30, 1942

*Solkar, E. D. (Bombay & Sussex) b March 18, 1948

*Solomon, J. S. (BG) b Aug. 26, 1930

*Solomon, W. R. T. (Tvl & E. Prov.) b April 23, 1872, d July 12, 1964

*Sood, M. M. (Delhi) b July 6, 1939

Southern, J. W. (Hants) b Sept. 2, 1952

*Southerton, James (Surrey, Hants & Sussex) b Nov. 16, 1827, d June 16, 1880

Southerton, S. J. (Editor of *Wisden* 1934-35) b July 7, 1874, d March 12, 1935

*Sparling, J. T. (Auck.) b July 24, 1938

Speak, N. J. (Lancs.) b Nov. 21, 1966

Speight, M. P. (Sussex & Wgtn) b Oct. 24, 1967

Spencer, C. T. (Leics.) b Aug. 18, 1931

Spencer, J. (CUCC & Sussex) b Oct. 6, 1949

Spencer, T. W. (Kent) b March 22, 1914

Sperry, J. (Leics.) b March 19, 1910

*Spofforth, F. R. (NSW & Vic.) b Sept. 9, 1853, d June 4, 1926

*Spooner, R. H. (Lancs.; *CY 1905*) b Oct. 21, 1880, d Oct. 2, 1961

*Spooner, R. T. (Warwicks.) b Dec. 30, 1919

Springall, J. D. (Notts.) b Sept. 19, 1932

*Srikkanth, K. (TN) b Dec. 21, 1959

*Srinath, J. (Karn.) b Aug. 31, 1969

*Srinivasan, T. E. (TN) b Oct. 26, 1950

*Stackpole, K. R. (Vic.; *CY 1973*) b July 10, 1940

Standen, J. A. (Worcs.) b May 30, 1935

Standing, D. K. (Sussex) b Oct. 21, 1963

Stanworth, J. (Lancs.) b Sept. 30, 1960

*Stanyforth, Lt-Col. R. T. (Yorks.) b May 30, 1892, d Feb. 20, 1964

*Staples, S. J. (Notts.; *CY 1929*) b Sept. 18, 1892, d June 4, 1950

Starkie, S. (Northants) b April 4, 1926

*Statham, J. B. (Lancs.; *CY 1955*) b June 17, 1930

Stayers, S. C. (†Guyana & Bombay) b June 9, 1937

*Steel, A. G. (CUCC & Lancs.; Pres. MCC 1902) b Sept. 24, 1858, d June 15, 1914

*Steele, D. S. (Northants & Derbys.; *CY 1976*) b Sept. 29, 1941

Steele, J. F. (Leics., Natal & Glam.) b July 23, 1946

Stemp, R. D. (Worcs. & Yorks.) b Dec. 11, 1967

Stephens, E. J. (Glos.) b March 23, 1909, d April 3, 1983

Stephenson, F. D. (B'dos, Glos., Tas., Notts., Sussex & OFS; *CY 1989*) b April 8, 1959

Stephenson, G. R. (Derbys. & Hants) b Nov. 19, 1942

Stephenson, H. H. (Surrey & All-England) b May 3, 1832, d Dec. 17, 1896

Stephenson, H. W. (Som.) b July 18, 1920

*Stephenson, J. P. (Essex & Boland) b March 14, 1965

Stephenson, Lt-Col. J. R. (Sec. MCC 1987-93) b Feb. 25, 1931

Stevens, Edward ("Lumpy") (Hants) b *circa* 1735, d Sept. 7, 1819

*Stevens, G. B. (S. Aust.) b Feb. 29, 1932

*Stevens, G. T. S. (UCS, OUCC & Middx; *CY 1918*) b Jan. 7, 1901, d Sept. 19, 1970

*Stevenson, G. B. (Yorks. & Northants) b Dec. 16, 1955

Stevenson, K. (Derbys. & Hants) b Oct. 6, 1950

Stevenson, M. H. (CUCC & Derbys.) b June 13, 1927

*Stewart, A. J. (Surrey; *CY 1993*) b April 8, 1963

Stewart, E. L. R. (Natal) b July 30, 1969

*Stewart, M. J. (Surrey; *CY 1958*) b Sept. 16, 1932

*Stewart, R. B. (SA) b Sept. 3, 1856, d Sept. 12, 1913

Stewart, R. W. (Glos. & Middx) b Feb. 28, 1945

Stewart, W. J. (Warwicks. & Northants) b Oct. 31, 1934

*Stirling, D. A. (C. Dist.) b Oct. 5, 1961

Stocks, F. W. (Notts.) b Nov. 6, 1917

*Stoddart, A. E. (Middx; *CY 1893*) b March 11, 1863, d April 3, 1915

*Stollmeyer, J. B. (T/T) b April 11, 1921, d Sept. 10, 1989

*Stollmeyer, V. H. (T/T) b Jan. 24, 1916

*Storer, W. (Derbys.; *CY 1899*) b Jan. 25, 1867, d Feb. 28, 1912

Storey, S. J. (Surrey & Sussex) b Jan. 6, 1941

Stott, L. W. (Auck.) b Dec. 8, 1946

Stott, W. B. (Yorks.) b July 18, 1934

Stovold, A. W. (Glos. & OFS) b March 19, 1953

*Street, G. B. (Sussex) b Dec. 6, 1889, d April 24, 1924

*Stricker, L. A. (Tvl) b May 26, 1884, d Feb. 5, 1960

Stringer, P. M. (Yorks. & Leics.) b Feb. 23, 1943

*Strudwick, H. (Surrey; *CY 1912*) b Jan. 28, 1880, d Feb. 14, 1970

*Studd, C. T. (CUCC & Middx) b Dec. 2, 1860, d July 16, 1931

*Studd, G. B. (CUCC & Middx) b Oct. 20, 1859, d Feb. 13, 1945

Studd, Sir Peter M. (CUCC) b Sept. 15, 1916

Sturt, M. O. C. (Middx) b Sept. 12, 1940

*Su'a, M. L. (N. Dist. & Auck.) b Nov. 7, 1966

*Subba Row, R. (CUCC, Surrey & Northants; *CY 1961*) b Jan. 29, 1932

Subramanya, V. (Mysore) b July 16, 1936

*Such, P. M. (Notts., Leics. & Essex) b June 12, 1964

Sudhakar Rao, R. (Karn.) b Aug. 8, 1952

Sueter, T. (Hants & Surrey) b *circa* 1749, d Feb. 17, 1827

*Sugg, F. H. (Yorks., Derbys. & Lancs.; *CY 1890*) b Jan. 11, 1862, d May 29, 1933

Sullivan, J. (Lancs.) b Feb. 5, 1945

Sully, H. (Som. & Northants) b Nov. 1, 1939

*Sunderram, G. R. (Bombay & Raja.) b March 29, 1930

Sunnucks, P. R. (Kent) b June 22, 1916

*Surendranath, R. (Ind. Serv.) b Jan. 4, 1937

Surridge, W. S. (Surrey; *CY 1953*) b Sept. 3, 1917, d April 13, 1992

*Surti, R. F. (Guj., Raja. & Qld) b May 25, 1936

*Susskind, M. J. (CUCC, Middx & Tvl) b June 8, 1891, d July 9, 1957

*Sutcliffe, B. (Auck., Otago & N. Dist.; *CY 1950*) b Nov. 17, 1923

*Sutcliffe, H. (Yorks.; *CY 1920*) b Nov. 24, 1894, d Jan. 22, 1978

Sutcliffe, S. P. (OUCC & Warwicks.) b May 22, 1960

Sutcliffe, W. H. H. (Yorks.) b Oct. 10, 1926

Suttle, K. G. (Sussex) b Aug. 25, 1928

Swallow, I. G. (Yorks. & Som.) b Dec. 18, 1962

*Swamy, V. N. (Ind. Serv.) b May 23, 1924, d May 1, 1983

Swanton, E. W. (Middx; Writer) b Feb. 11, 1907

Swarbrook, F. W. (Derbys., Griq. W. & OFS) b Dec. 17, 1950

Swart, P. D. (Rhod., W. Prov., Glam. & Boland) b April 27, 1946

*Swetman, R. (Surrey, Notts & Glos.) b Oct. 25, 1933

Sydenham, D. A. D. (Surrey) b April 6, 1934

Symcox, P. L. (Natal) b April 14, 1960

Symington, S. J. (Leics.) b Sept. 16, 1926

*Taber, H. B. (NSW) b April 29, 1940

*Taberer, H. M. (OUCC & Natal) b Oct. 7, 1870, d June 5, 1932

*Tahir Naqqash (Servis Ind., MCB, Punjab & Lahore) b July 6, 1959

Tait, A. (Northants & Glos.) b Dec. 27, 1953

*Talat Ali (Lahore, PIA & UBL) b May 29, 1950

*Tallon, D. (Qld; *CY 1949*) b Feb. 17, 1916, d Sept. 7, 1984

*Tamhane, N. S. (Bombay) b Aug. 4, 1931

*Tancred, A. B. (Kimberley, Griq. W. & Tvl) b Aug. 20, 1865, d Nov. 23, 1911

*Tancred, L. J. (Tvl) b Oct. 7, 1876, d July 28, 1934

*Tancred, V. M. (Tvl) b July 7, 1875, d June 3, 1904

Tanvir Mehdi (Lahore & UBL) b Nov. 7, 1972

*Tapscott, G. L. (Griq. W.) b Nov. 7, 1889, d Dec. 13, 1940

*Tapscott, L. E. (Griq. W.) b March 18, 1894, d July 7, 1934

*Tarapore, K. K. (Bombay) b Dec. 17, 1910, d June 15, 1986

Tarrant, F. A. (Vic., Middx & Patiala; *CY 1908*) b Dec. 11, 1880, d Jan. 29, 1951

Tarrant, George F. (Cambs. & All-England) b Dec. 7, 1838, d July 2, 1870

*Taslim Arif (Kar., Sind & NBP) b May 1, 1954

*Tate, F. W. (Sussex) b July 24, 1867, d Feb. 24, 1943

*Tate, M. W. (Sussex; *CY 1924*) b May 30, 1895, d May 18, 1956

*Tattersall, R. (Lancs.) b Aug. 17, 1922

*Tauseef Ahmed (PWD, UBL & Kar.) b May 10, 1958

*Tavaré, C. J. (OUCC, Kent & Som.) b Oct. 27, 1954

*Tayfield, H. J. (Natal, Rhod. & Tvl; *CY 1956*) b Jan. 30, 1929

*Taylor, A. I. (Tvl) b July 25, 1925

Taylor, B. (Essex; *CY 1972*) b June 19, 1932

*Taylor, B. R. (Cant. & Wgtn) b July 12, 1943

Taylor, C. W. (Middx) b Aug. 12, 1966

*Taylor, D. D. (Auck. & Warwicks.) b March 2, 1923, d Dec. 5, 1980

Taylor, D. J. S. (Surrey, Som. & Griq. W.) b Nov. 12, 1942

Taylor, G. R. (Hants) b Nov. 25, 1909, d Oct. 31, 1986

*Taylor, H. W. (Natal, Tvl & W. Prov.; *CY 1925*) b May 5, 1889, d Feb. 8, 1973

*Taylor, J. M. (NSW) b Oct. 10, 1895, d May 12, 1971

Taylor, J. O. (T/T) b Jan. 3, 1932

Taylor, J. P. (Derbys. & Northants) b Aug. 8, 1964

Taylor, K. (Yorks. & Auck.) b Aug. 21, 1935

Taylor, K. A. (Warwicks.) b Sept. 29, 1916

*Taylor, L. B. (Leics. & Natal) b Oct. 25, 1953

*Taylor, M. A. (NSW; *CY 1990*) b Oct 27, 1964

Taylor, M. N. S. (Notts. & Hants) b Nov. 12, 1942

Taylor, N. R. (Kent) b July 21, 1959

*Taylor, P. L. (NSW & Qld) b Aug. 22, 1956

Taylor, R. M. (Essex) b Nov. 30, 1909, d Jan. 1984

*Taylor, R. W. (Derbys.; *CY 1977*) b July 17, 1941

*Taylor, T. L. (CUCC & Yorks.; *CY 1901*) b May 25, 1878, d March 16, 1960

Taylor, W. (Notts.) b Jan. 24, 1947

Tedstone, G. A. (Warwicks. & Glos.) b Jan. 19, 1961

*Tendulkar, S. R. (Bombay & Yorks.) b April 24, 1973

Tennekoon, A. P. B. (SL) b Oct. 29, 1946

*Tennyson, 3rd Lord (Hon. L. H.) (Hants; *CY 1914*) b Nov. 7, 1889, d June 6, 1951

*Terry, V. P. (Hants) b Jan. 14, 1959

Theunissen, N. H. (W. Prov.) b May 4, 1867, d Nov. 9, 1929

Thomas, D. J. (Surrey, N. Tvl & Glos.) b June 30, 1959

*Thomas, G. (NSW) b March 21, 1938

Thomas, J. G. (Glam., Border, E. Prov. & Northants) b Aug. 12, 1960

Thompson, A. W. (Middx) b April 17, 1916

*Thompson, G. J. (Northants; *CY 1906*) b Oct. 27, 1877, d March 3, 1943

Thompson, J. R. (CUCC & Warwicks.) b May 10, 1918

Thompson, R. G. (Warwicks.) b Sept. 26, 1932

*Thoms, G. R. (Vic.) b March 22, 1927

*Thomson, A. L. (Vic.) b Dec. 2, 1945

*Thomson, J. R. (NSW, Qld & Middx) b Aug. 16, 1950

*Thomson, K. (Cant.) b Feb. 26, 1941

*Thomson, N. F. D. (NSW) b May 29, 1839, d Sept. 2, 1896

*Thomson, N. I. (Sussex) b Jan. 23, 1929

*Thomson, S. A. (N. Dist.) b Jan. 27, 1969

Thorne, D. A. (Warwicks & OUCC) b Dec. 12, 1964

Thornton, C. I. (CUCC, Kent & Middx) b March 20, 1850, d Dec. 10, 1929

*Thornton, P. G. (Yorks., Middx & SA) b Dec. 24, 1867, d Jan. 31, 1939

*Thorpe, G. P. (Surrey) b Aug. 1, 1969

*Thurlow, H. M. (Qld) b Jan. 10, 1903, d Dec. 3, 1975

*Tillekeratne, H. P. (NCC) b July 14, 1967

Tilly, H. W. (Middx) b May 25, 1932

*Timms, B. S. V. (Hants & Warwicks.) b Dec. 17, 1940

*Timms, J. E. (Northants) b Nov. 3, 1906, d May 18, 1980

Timms, W. W. (Northants) b Sept. 28, 1902, d Sept. 30, 1986

Tindall, M. (CUCC & Middx) b March 31, 1914

Tindall, R. A. E. (Surrey) b Sept. 23, 1935

*Tindill, E. W. T. (Wgtn) b Dec. 18, 1910

Tissera, M. H. (SL) b March 23, 1939

*Titmus, F. J. (Middx, Surrey & OFS; *CY 1963*) b Nov. 24, 1932

Todd, L. J. (Kent) b June 19, 1907, d Aug. 20, 1967

Todd, P. A. (Notts. & Glam.) b March 12, 1953

Tolchard, J. G. (Leics.) b March 17, 1944

*Tolchard, R. W. (Leics.) b June 15, 1946

Tolley, C. M. (Worcs.) b Dec. 30, 1967

Tomlins, K. P. (Middx & Glos.) b Oct. 23, 1957

*Tomlinson, D. S. (Rhod. & Border) b Sept. 4, 1910, d July 11, 1993

Tompkin, M. (Leics.) b Feb. 17, 1919, d Sept. 27, 1956

Toogood, G. J. (OUCC) b Nov. 19, 1961

*Toohey, P. M. (NSW) b April 20, 1954

Tooley, C. D. M. (OUCC) b April 19, 1964

Topley, T. D. (Surrey, Essex & Griq. W.) b Feb. 25, 1964

Tordoff, G. G. (CUCC & Som.) b Dec. 6, 1929

*Toshack, E. R. H. (NSW) b Dec. 15, 1914

Townsend, A. (Warwicks.) b Aug. 26, 1921

Townsend, A. F. (Derbys.) b March 29, 1912

*Townsend, C. L. (Glos.; *CY 1899*) b Nov. 7, 1876, d Oct. 17, 1958

*Townsend, D. C. H. (OUCC) b April 20, 1912

*Townsend, L. F. (Derbys. & Auck.; *CY 1934*) b June 8, 1903, d Feb. 17, 1993

**Traicos, A. J. (Rhod. & Zimb.) b May 17, 1947

*Travers, J. P. F. (S. Aust.) b Jan. 10, 1871, d Sept. 15, 1942

*Tremlett, M. F. (Som. & C. Dist.) b July 5, 1923, d July 30, 1984

Tremlett, T. M. (Hants) b July 26, 1956

*Tribe, G. E. (Vic. & Northants; *CY 1955*) b Oct. 4, 1920

*Trim, J. (BG) b Jan. 24, 1915, d Nov. 12, 1960

Trimble, G. S. (Qld) b Jan. 1, 1963

*Trimborn, P. H. J. (Natal) b May 18, 1940

**Trott, A. E. (Vic., Middx & Hawkes Bay; *CY 1899*) b Feb. 6, 1873, d July 30, 1914

*Trott, G. H. S. (Vic.; *CY 1894*) b Aug. 5, 1866, d Nov. 10, 1917

*Troup, G. B. (Auck.) b Oct. 3, 1952

*Trueman, F. S. (Yorks.; *CY 1953*) b Feb. 6, 1931

*Trumble, H. (Vic.; *CY 1897*) b May 12, 1867, d Aug. 14, 1938

*Trumble, J. W. (Vic.) b Sept. 16, 1863, d Aug. 17, 1944

Trump, H. R. J. (Som.) b Oct. 11, 1968

*Trumper, V. T. (NSW; *CY 1903*) b Nov. 2, 1877, d June 28, 1915

Truscott, P. B. (Wgtn) b Aug. 14, 1941

*Tuckett, L. (OFS) b Feb. 6, 1919

*Tuckett, L. R. (Natal & OFS) b April 19, 1885, d April 8, 1963

*Tufnell, N. C. (CUCC & Surrey) b June 13, 1887, d Aug. 3, 1951

*Tufnell, P. C. R. (Middx) b April 29, 1966

Tuke, Sir Anthony (Pres. MCC 1982-83) b Aug. 22, 1920

Tunnicliffe, C. J. (Derbys.) b Aug. 11, 1951

Tunnicliffe, H. T. (Notts.) b March 4, 1950

*Tunnicliffe, J. (Yorks.; *CY 1901*) b Aug. 26, 1866, d July 11, 1948

*Turnbull, M. J. (CUCC & Glam.; *CY 1931*) b March 16, 1906, d Aug. 5, 1944

*Turner, A. (NSW) b July 23, 1950

*Turner, C. T. B. (NSW; *CY 1889*) b Nov. 16, 1862, d Jan. 1, 1944

Turner, D. R. (Hants & W. Prov.) b Feb. 5, 1949

Turner, F. M. (Leics.) b Aug. 8, 1934

Turner, G. J. (W. Prov., N. Tvl & OUCC) b Aug. 5, 1964

*Turner, G. M. (Otago, N. Dist. & Worcs.; *CY 1971*) b May 26, 1947

Turner, R. J. (CUCC & Som.) b Nov. 25, 1967

Turner, S. (Essex & Natal) b July 18, 1943

*Twentyman-Jones, P. S. (W. Prov.) b Sept. 13, 1876, d March 8, 1954

Twining, R. H. (OUCC & Middx; Pres. MCC 1964-65) b Nov. 3, 1889, d Jan. 3, 1979

Twose, R. G. (Warwicks. & N. Dist.) b April 17, 1968

*Tyldesley, E. (Lancs.; *CY 1920*) b Feb. 5, 1889, d May 5, 1962

*Tyldesley, J. T. (Lancs.; *CY 1902*) b Nov. 22, 1873, d Nov. 27, 1930

*Tyldesley, R. K. (Lancs.; *CY 1925*) b March 11, 1897, d Sept. 17, 1943

*Tylecote, E. F. S. (OUCC & Kent) b June 23, 1849, d March 15, 1938

*Tyler, E. J. (Som.) b Oct. 13, 1864, d Jan. 25, 1917

*Tyson, F. H. (Northants; *CY 1956*) b June 6, 1930

Udal, S. D. (Hants) b March 18, 1969

Ufton, D. G. (Kent) b May 31, 1928

*Ulyett, G. (Yorks.) b Oct. 21, 1851, d June 18, 1898

*Umrigar, P. R. (Bombay & Guj.) b March 28, 1926

*Underwood, D. L. (Kent; *CY 1969*) b June 8, 1945

Unwin, F. St G. (Essex) b April 23, 1911, d Oct. 4, 1990

*Valentine, A. L. (Jam.; *CY 1951*) b April 29, 1930

*Valentine, B. H. (CUCC & Kent) b Jan. 17, 1908, d Feb. 2, 1983

*Valentine, V. A. (Jam.) b April 4, 1908, d July 6, 1972

*Vance, R. H. (Wgtn) b March 31, 1955

*van der Bijl, P. G. (W. Prov. & OUCC) b Oct. 21, 1907, d Feb. 16, 1973

van der Bijl, V. A. P. (Natal, Middx & Tvl; *CY 1981*) b March 19, 1948

Van der Gucht, P. I. (Glos. & Bengal) b Nov. 2, 1911, d Dec. 15, 1993

*Van der Merwe, E. A. (Tvl) b Nov. 9, 1904, d Feb. 28, 1971

*Van der Merwe, P. L. (W. Prov. & E. Prov.) b March 14, 1937

Vandrau, M. J. (Tvl & Derbys.) b July 22, 1969

van Geloven, J. (Yorks. & Leics.) b Jan. 4, 1934

*Van Ryneveld, C. B. (W. Prov. & OUCC) b March 19, 1928

van Zyl, C. J. P. G. (OFS & Glam.) b Oct. 1, 1961

Varachia, R. (First Pres. SA Cricket Union) b Oct. 12, 1915, d Dec. 11, 1981

Varey, D. W. (CUCC & Lancs.) b Oct. 15, 1961

*Varnals, G. D. (E. Prov., Tvl & Natal) b July 24, 1935

*Vaughan, J. T. C. (Auck.) b Aug. 30, 1967

Vaulkhard, P. (Notts. & Derbys.) b Sept. 15, 1911

*Veivers, T. R. (Qld) b April 6, 1937

*Veletta, M. R. J. (W. Aust.) b Oct. 30, 1963

*Vengsarkar, D. B. (Bombay; *CY 1987*) b April 6, 1956

*Venkataraghavan, S. (†TN & Derbys.) b April 21, 1946

*Venkataramana, M. (TN) b April 24, 1966

*Vernon, G. F. (Middx) b June 20, 1856, d Aug. 10, 1902

Vigar, F. H. (Essex) b July 7, 1917

*Viljoen, K. G. (Griq. W., OFS & Tvl) b May 14, 1910, d Jan. 21, 1974

*Vincent, C. L. (Tvl) b Feb. 16, 1902, d Aug. 24, 1968

*Vine, J. (Sussex; *CY 1906*) b May 15, 1875, d April 25, 1946

*Vintcent, C. H. (Tvl & Griq. W.) b Sept. 2, 1866, d Sept. 28, 1943

Virgin, R. T. (Som., Northants & W. Prov.; *CY 1971*) b Aug. 26, 1939

*Viswanath, G. R. (†Karn.) b Feb. 12, 1949

*Viswanath, S. (Karn.) b Nov. 29, 1962

*Vivian, G. E. (Auck.) b Feb. 28, 1946

*Vivian, H. G. (Auck.) b Nov. 4, 1912, d Aug. 12, 1983

*Vizianagram, Maharaj Kumar of, Sir Vijay A. (U. Prov.) b Dec. 28, 1905, d Dec. 2, 1965

*Voce, W. (Notts.; *CY 1933*) b Aug. 8, 1909, d June 6, 1984

*Vogler, A. E. E. (Middx, Natal, Tvl & E. Prov.; *CY 1908*) b Nov. 28, 1876, d Aug. 9, 1946

Vonhagt, D. M. (Moors) b March 31, 1965

*Waddington, A. (Yorks.) b Feb. 4, 1893, d Oct. 28, 1959

Waddington, J. E. (Griq. W.) b Dec. 30, 1918, d Nov. 24, 1985

*Wade, H. F. (Natal) b Sept. 14, 1905, d Nov. 22, 1980

Wade, T. H. (Essex) b Nov. 24, 1910, d July 25, 1987

*Wade, W. W. (Natal) b June 18, 1914

*Wadekar, A. L. (Bombay) b April 1, 1941

*Wadsworth, K. J. (C. Dist. & Cant.) b Nov. 30, 1946, d Aug. 19, 1976

*Wainwright, E. (Yorks.; *CY 1894*) b April 8, 1865, d Oct. 28, 1919

*Waite, J. H. B. (E. Prov. & Tvl) b Jan. 19, 1930

*Waite, M. G. (S. Aust.) b Jan. 7, 1911, d Dec. 16, 1985

*Walcott, C. L. (B'dos & BG; *CY 1958*) b Jan. 17, 1926

*Walcott, L. A. (B'dos) b Jan. 18, 1894, d Feb. 27, 1984

Walden, F. I. (Northants; Umpire) b March 1, 1888, d May 3, 1949

Walford, M. M. (OUCC & Som.) b Nov. 27, 1915

Walker, A. (Northants) b July 7, 1962

Walker, A. K. (NSW & Notts.) b Oct. 4, 1925

Walker, C. (Yorks. & Hants) b June 27, 1919, d Dec. 3, 1992

Walker, I. D. (Middx) b Jan. 8, 1844, d July 6, 1898

*Walker, M. H. N. (Vic.) b Sept. 12, 1948

*Walker, P. M. (Glam., Tvl & W. Prov.) b Feb. 17, 1936

Walker, V. E. (Middx) b April 20, 1837, d Jan. 3, 1906

Walker, W. (Notts.) b Nov. 24, 1892, d Dec. 3, 1991

*Wall, T. W. (S. Aust.) b May 13, 1904, d March 25, 1981

Wallace, P. A. (B'dos) b Aug. 2, 1970

*Wallace, W. M. (Auck.) b Dec. 19, 1916

Waller, A. C. (Zimb.) b Sept. 25, 1959

Waller, C. E. (Surrey & Sussex) b Oct. 3, 1948

*Walsh, C. A. (Jam. & Glos.; *CY 1987*) b Oct. 30, 1962

Walsh, J. E. (NSW & Leics.) b Dec. 4, 1912, d May 20, 1980

*Walter, K. A. (Tvl) b Nov. 5, 1939

*Walters, C. F. (Glam. & Worcs.; *CY 1934*) b Aug. 28, 1905, d Dec. 23, 1992

*Walters, F. H. (Vic. & NSW) b Feb. 9, 1860, d June 1, 1922

Walters, J. (Derbys.) b Aug. 7, 1949

*Walters, K. D. (NSW) b Dec. 21, 1945

Walton, A. C. (OUCC & Middx) b Sept. 26, 1933

*Waqar Hassan (Pak. Us, Punjab, Pak. Serv. & Kar.) b Sept. 12, 1932

*Waqar Younis (Multan, UBL & Surrey; *CY 1992*) b Nov. 16, 1971

*Ward, Alan (Derbys., Leics. & Border) b Aug. 10, 1947

*Ward, Albert (Yorks. & Lancs.; *CY 1890*) b Nov. 21, 1865, d Jan. 6, 1939

Ward, B. (Essex) b Feb. 28, 1944

Ward, D. (Glam.) b Aug. 30, 1934

Ward, D. M. (Surrey) b Feb. 10, 1961

*Ward, F. A. (S. Aust.) b Feb. 23, 1909, d March 25, 1974

*Ward, J. T. (Cant.) b March 11, 1937

*Ward, T. A. (Tvl) b Aug. 2, 1887, d Feb. 16, 1936

Ward, T. R. (Kent) b Jan. 18, 1968

Ward, William (MCC & Hants) b July 24, 1787, d June 30, 1849

*Wardle, J. H. (Yorks.; *CY 1954*) b Jan. 8, 1923, d July 23, 1985

*Warnapura, B. (SL) b March 1, 1953

*Warnaweera, K. P. J. (Galle) b Nov. 23, 1960

Warne, F. B. (Worcs., Vic. & Tvl) b Oct. 3, 1906

*Warne, S. K. (Vic.; *CY 1993*) b Sept. 13, 1969

Warner, A. E. (Worcs. & Derbys.) b May 12, 1959

*Warner, Sir P. F. (OUCC & Middx; *CY 1904, special portrait 1921*; Pres. MCC 1950-51) b Oct. 2, 1873, d Jan. 30, 1963

*Warr, J. J. (CUCC & Middx; Pres. MCC 1987-88) b July 16, 1927

*Warren, A. R. (Derbys.) b April 2, 1875, d Sept. 3, 1951

*Washbrook, C. (Lancs.; *CY 1947*) b Dec. 6, 1914

*Wasim Akram (Lahore, PACO, PNSC, PIA & Lancs.; *CY 1993*) b June 3, 1966

*Wasim Bari (Kar., PIA & Sind) b March 23, 1948

Wasim Haider (Faisalabad & PIA) b June 6, 1967

*Wasim Raja (Lahore, Sargodha, Pak. Us, PIA, Punjab & NBP) b July 3, 1952

Wass, T. G. (Notts.; *CY 1908*) b Dec. 26, 1873, d Oct. 27, 1953

*Wassan, A. S. (Delhi) b March 23, 1968

Wassell, A. (Hants) b April 15, 1940

*Watkin, S. L. (Glam.; *CY 1993*) b Sept. 15, 1964

*Watkins, A. J. (Glam.) b April 21, 1922

*Watkins, J. C. (Natal) b April 10, 1923

*Watkins, J. R. (NSW) b April 16, 1943

Watkinson, M. (Lancs.) b Aug. 1, 1961

*Watson, C. (Jam. & Delhi) b July 1, 1938

Watson, F. B. (Lancs.) b Sept. 17, 1898, d Feb. 1, 1976

*Watson, G. D. (Vic., W. Aust. & NSW) b March 8, 1945

Watson, G. G. (NSW, W. Aust. & Worcs.) b Jan. 29, 1955

*Watson, W. (Yorks. & Leics.; *CY 1954*) b March 7, 1920

*Watson, W. (Auck.) b Aug. 31, 1965

*Watson, W. J. (NSW) b Jan. 31, 1931

Watson, W. K. (Border, N. Tvl, E. Prov. & Notts.) b May 21, 1955

*Watt, L. (Otago) b Sept. 17, 1924

Watts, H. E. (CUCC & Som.) b March 4, 1922, d Dec. 27, 1993

Watts, P. D. (Northants & Notts.) b March 31, 1938

Watts, P. J. (Northants) b June 16, 1940

*Waugh, M. E. (NSW & Essex; *CY 1991*) b June 2, 1965

*Waugh, S. R. (NSW & Som.; *CY 1989*) b June 2, 1965

*Wazir Ali, S. (C. Ind., S. Punjab & Patiala) b Sept. 15, 1903, d June 17, 1950

*Wazir Mohammad (B'pur & Kar.) b Dec. 22, 1929

*Webb, M. G. (Otago & Cant.) b June 22, 1947

*Webb, P. N. (Auck.) b July 14, 1957

Webb, R. J. (Otago) b Sept. 15, 1952

Webb, R. T. (Sussex) b July 11, 1922

*Webbe, A. J. (OUCC & Middx) b Jan. 16, 1855, d Feb. 19, 1941

Webster, J. (CUCC & Northants) b Oct. 28, 1917

Webster, Dr R. V. (Warwicks. & Otago) b June 10, 1939

Webster, W. H. (CUCC & Middx; Pres. MCC 1976-77) b Feb. 22, 1910, d June 19, 1986

*Weekes, E. D. (B'dos; *CY 1951*) b Feb. 26, 1925

*Weekes, K. H. (Jam.) b Jan. 24, 1912

Weekes, P. N. (Middx) b July 8, 1969

Weeks, R. T. (Warwicks.) b April 30, 1930

*Weerasinghe, C. D. U. S. (TU) b March 1, 1968

*Weir, G. L. (Auck.) b June 2, 1908

*Wellard, A. W. (Som.; *CY 1936*) b April 8, 1902, d Dec. 31, 1980

*Wellham, D. M. (NSW, Tas. & Qld) b March 13, 1959

Wellings, E. M. (OUCC & Surrey) b April 6, 1909, d Sept. 10, 1992

Wells, A. P. (Sussex & Border) b Oct. 2, 1961

Wells, B. D. (Glos. & Notts.) b July 27, 1930

Wells, C. M. (Sussex, Border & W. Prov.) b March 3, 1960

Wells, V. J. (Kent & Leics.) b Aug. 6, 1965

Wenman, E. G. (Kent & England) b Aug. 18, 1803, d Dec. 31, 1879

*Wensley, A. F. (Sussex) b May 23, 1898, d June 17, 1970

*Wesley, C. (Natal) b Sept. 5, 1937

**Wessels, K. C. (OFS, W. Prov., N. Tvl, Sussex, Qld & E. Prov.) b Sept. 14, 1957

West, G. H. (Editor of *Wisden* 1880-86) b 1851, d Oct. 6, 1896

*Westcott, R. J. (W. Prov.) b Sept. 19, 1927

Weston, M. J. (Worcs.) b April 8, 1959

*Wettimuny, M. D. (SL) b June 11, 1951

*Wettimuny, S. (SL; *CY 1985*) b Aug. 12, 1956

Wettimuny, S. R. de S. (SL) b Feb. 7, 1949

*Wharton, A. (Lancs. & Leics.) b April 30, 1923, d Aug. 26, 1993

*Whatmore, D. F. (Vic.) b March 16, 1954

Wheatley, K. J. (Hants) b Jan. 20, 1946

Wheatley, O. S. (CUCC, Warwicks. & Glam.; *CY 1969*) b May 28, 1935

Whitaker, Haddon (Editor of *Wisden* 1940-43) b Aug. 30, 1908, d Jan. 5, 1982

*Whitaker, J. J. (Leics.; *CY 1987*) b May 5, 1962

Whitcombe, P. A. (OUCC & Middx) b April 23, 1923

White, A. F. T. (CUCC, Warwicks. & Worcs.) b Sept. 5, 1915, d March 16, 1993

White, C. (Vic. & Yorks.) b Dec. 16, 1969

*White, D. J. (N. Dist.) b June 26, 1961

*White, D. W. (Hants & Glam.) b Dec. 14, 1935

White, E. C. S. (NSW) b July 14, 1913

*White, G. C. (Tvl) b Feb. 5, 1882, d Oct. 17, 1918

*White, J. C. (Som.; *CY 1929*) b Feb. 19, 1891, d May 2, 1961

White, Hon. L. R. (5th Lord Annaly) (Middx & Victory Test) b March 15, 1927, d Sept. 30, 1990

White, R. A. (Middx & Notts.; Umpire) b Oct. 6, 1936

White, R. C. (CUCC, Glos. & Tvl) b Jan. 29, 1941

*White, W. A. (B'dos) b Nov. 20, 1938

Whitehouse, J. P. (Yorks. & Worcs.) b Sept. 3, 1925

Whitehouse, J. (Warwicks.) b April 8, 1949

*Whitelaw, P. E. (Auck.) b Feb. 10, 1910, d Aug. 28, 1988

Whitfield, B. J. (Natal) b March 14, 1959

Whitfield, E. W. (Surrey & Northants) b May 31, 1911

Whiting, N. H. (Worcs.) b Oct. 2, 1920

Whitington, R. S. (S. Aust. & Victory Tests; Writer) b June 30, 1912, d March 13, 1984

*Whitney, M. R. (NSW & Glos.) b Feb. 24, 1959

Whittaker, G. J. (Surrey) b May 29, 1916

Whitticase, P. (Leics.) b March 15, 1965

Whittingham, N. B. (Notts.) b Oct. 22, 1940

*Whitty, W. J. (S. Aust.) b Aug. 15, 1886, d Jan. 30, 1974

*Whysall, W. W. (Notts.; *CY 1925*) b Oct. 31, 1887, d Nov. 11, 1930

*Wickremasinghe, A. G. D. (NCC) b Dec. 27, 1965

*Wickremasinghe, G. P. (BRC & SSC) b Aug. 14, 1971

*Wiener, J. M. (Vic.) b May 1, 1955

*Wight, C. V. (BG) b July 28, 1902, d Oct. 4, 1969

*Wight, G. L. (BG) b May 28, 1929

Wight, P. B. (BG, Som., & Cant.) b June 25, 1930

*Wijegunawardene, K. I. W. (CCC) b Nov. 23, 1964

*Wijesuriya, R. G. C. E. (Mor.) b Feb. 18, 1960

*Wijetunge, P. K. (SSC) b Aug. 6, 1971

Wild, D. J. (Northants) b Nov. 28, 1962

*Wiles, C. A. (B'dos & T/T) b Aug. 11, 1892, d Nov. 4, 1957

Wilkins, A. H. (Glam., Glos. & N. Tvl) b Aug. 22, 1953

Wilkins, C. P. (Derbys., Border, E. Prov. & Natal) b July 31, 1944

*Wilkinson, L. L. (Lancs.) b Nov. 5, 1916

Wilkinson, P. A. (Notts.) b Aug. 23, 1951

Willatt, G. L. (CUCC, Notts. & Derbys.) b May 7, 1918

*Willett, E. T. (Comb. Is. & Leewards) b May 1, 1953

Willett, M. D. (Surrey) b April 21, 1933

*Willey, P. (Northants, E. Prov. & Leics.) b Dec. 6, 1949

*Williams, A. B. (Jam.) b Nov. 21, 1949

Williams, C. C. P. (Lord Williams of Elvet) (OUCC & Essex) b Feb. 9, 1933

*Williams, D. (T/T) b Nov. 4, 1963

Williams, D. L. (Glam.) b Nov. 20, 1946

*Williams, E. A. V. (B'dos) b April 10, 1914

*Williams, N. F. (Middx, Windwards & Tas.) b July 2, 1962

Williams, R. G. (Northants) b Aug. 10, 1957

*Williams, R. J. (Natal) b April 12, 1912, d May 14, 1984

Williamson, J. G. (Northants) b April 4, 1936

*Willis, R. G. D. (Surrey, Warwicks. & N. Tvl; *CY 1978*) b May 30, 1949

*Willoughby, J. T. (SA) b Nov. 7, 1874, d *circa* 1955

Willsher, E. (Kent & All-England) b Nov. 22, 1828, d Oct. 7, 1885

Wilmot, K. (Warwicks.) b April 3, 1911

Wilson, A. (Lancs.) b April 24, 1921

Wilson, A. E. (Middx & Glos.) b May 18, 1910

*Wilson, Rev. C. E. M. (CUCC & Yorks.) b May 15, 1875, d Feb. 8, 1944

*Wilson, D. (Yorks. & MCC) b Aug. 7, 1937

*Wilson, E. R. (CUCC & Yorks.) b March 25, 1879, d July 21, 1957

Wilson, J. V. (Yorks.; *CY 1961*) b Jan. 17, 1921

Wilson, J. W. (Otago) b Oct. 24, 1973

*Wilson, J. W. (Vic. & S. Aust.) b Aug. 20, 1921, d Oct. 13, 1985

Wilson, P. H. L. (Surrey, Som. & N. Tvl) b Aug. 17, 1958

Wilson, R. C. (Kent) b Feb. 18, 1928

*Wimble, C. S. (Tvl) b Jan. 9, 1864, d Jan. 28, 1930

Windows, A. R. (Glos. & CUCC) b Sept. 25, 1942

Winfield, H. M. (Notts.) b June 13, 1933

Wingfield Digby, Rev. A. R. (OUCC) b July 25, 1950

Winn, C. E. (OUCC & Sussex) b Nov. 13, 1926

*Winslow, P. L. (Sussex, Tvl & Rhod.) b May 21, 1929

Wisden, John (Sussex; founder John Wisden and Co. and *Wisden's Cricketers' Almanack*) b Sept. 5, 1826, d April 5, 1884

*Wishart, K. L. (BG) b Nov. 28, 1908, d Oct. 18, 1972

Wolton, A. V. G. (Warwicks.) b June 12, 1919, d Sept. 9, 1990

*Wood, A. (Yorks.; *CY 1939*) b Aug. 25, 1898, d April 1, 1973

*Wood, B. (Yorks., Lancs., Derbys. & E. Prov.) b Dec. 26, 1942

Wood, C. J. B. (Leics.) b Nov. 21, 1875, d June 5, 1960

Wood, D. J. (Sussex) b May 19, 1914, d March 12, 1989

*Wood, G. E. C. (CUCC & Kent) b Aug. 22, 1893, d March 18, 1971

*Wood, G. M. (W. Aust.) b Nov. 6, 1956

*Wood, H. (Kent & Surrey; *CY 1891*) b Dec. 14, 1854, d April 30, 1919

*Wood, R. (Lancs. & Vic.) b March 7, 1860, d Jan. 6, 1915

*Woodcock, A. J. (S. Aust.) b Feb. 27, 1948

Woodcock, John C. (Editor of *Wisden* 1981-86) b Aug. 7, 1926

*Woodfull, W. M. (Vic.; *CY 1927*) b Aug. 22, 1897, d Aug. 11, 1965

Woodhead, F. G. (Notts.) b Oct. 30, 1912, d May 24, 1991

Woodhouse, G. E. S. (Som.) b Feb. 15, 1924, d Jan. 19, 1988

**Woods, S. M. J. (CUCC & Som.; *CY 1889*) b April 13, 1867, d April 30, 1931

Wookey, S. M. (CUCC & OUCC) b Sept. 2, 1954

Wooler, C. R. D. (Leics. & Rhod.) b June 30, 1930

Wooller, W. (CUCC & Glam.) b Nov. 20, 1912

Woolley, C. N. (Glos. & Northants) b May 5, 1886, d Nov. 3, 1962

*Woolley, F. E. (Kent; *CY 1911*) b May 27, 1887, d Oct. 18, 1978

*Woolley, R. D. (Tas.) b Sept. 16, 1954

*Woolmer, R. A. (Kent, Natal & W. Prov.; *CY 1976*) b May 14, 1948

*Worrall, J. (Vic.) b May 12, 1863, d Nov. 17, 1937

*Worrell, Sir F. M. M. (B'dos & Jam.; *CY 1951*) b Aug. 1, 1924, d March 13, 1967

Worsley, D. R. (OUCC & Lancs.) b July 18, 1941

Worsley, Sir W. A. 4th Bt (Yorks.; Pres. MCC 1961-62) b April 5, 1890, d Dec. 4, 1973

*Worthington, T. S. (Derbys.; *CY 1937*) b Aug. 21, 1905, d Aug. 31, 1973

Wright, A. (Warwicks.) b Aug. 25, 1941

Wright, A. J. (Glos.) b July 27, 1962

*Wright, C. W. (CUCC & Notts.) b May 27, 1863, d Jan. 10, 1936

*Wright, D. V. P. (Kent; *CY 1940*) b Aug. 21, 1914

Wright, Graeme A. (Editor of *Wisden* 1987-92) b April 23, 1943

*Wright, J. G. (N. Dist., Derbys., Cant. & Auck.) b July 5, 1954

*Wright, K. J. (W. Aust. & S. Aust.) b Dec. 27, 1953

Wright, L. G. (Derbys.; *CY 1906*) b June 15, 1862, d Jan. 11, 1953

Wyatt, J. G. (Som.) b June 19, 1963

*Wyatt, R. E. S. (Warwicks. & Worcs.; *CY 1930*) b May 2, 1901

*Wynne, O. E. (Tvl & W. Prov.) b June 1, 1919, d July 13, 1975

*Wynyard, E. G. (Hants) b April 1, 1861, d Oct. 30, 1936

Yachad, M. (N. Tvl & Tvl) b Nov. 17, 1960

*Yadav, N. S. (H'bad) b Jan. 26, 1957

*Yadav, V. S. (Haryana) b March 14, 1967

*Yajurvindra Singh (M'tra & S'tra) b Aug. 1, 1952

*Yallop, G. N. (Vic.) b Oct. 7, 1952

*Yardley, B. (W. Aust.) b Sept. 5, 1947

*Yardley, N. W. D. (CUCC & Yorks.; *CY 1948*) b March 19, 1915, d Oct. 4, 1989

Yardley, T. J. (Worcs. & Northants) b Oct. 27, 1946

Yarnold, H. (Worcs.) b July 6, 1917, d Aug. 13, 1974

*Yashpal Sharma (Punjab) b Aug. 11, 1954

Yawar Saeed (Som. & Punjab) b Jan. 22, 1935

*Yograj Singh (Haryana & Punjab) b March 25, 1958

*Young, B. A. (N. Dist.) b Nov. 3, 1964

Young, D. M. (Worcs. & Glos.) b April 15, 1924, d June 18, 1993

*Young, H. I. (Essex) b Feb. 5, 1876, d Dec. 12, 1964

Young, J. A. (Middx) b Oct. 14, 1912, d Feb. 5, 1993

*Young, R. A. (CUCC & Sussex) b Sept. 16, 1885, d July 1, 1968

*Younis Ahmed (Lahore, Kar., Surrey, PIA, S. Aust., Worcs. & Glam.) b Oct. 20, 1947

*Yuile, B. W. (C. Dist.) b Oct. 29, 1941

*Zaheer Abbas (Kar., Glos., PWD, Dawood Indust., Sind & PIA; *CY 1972*) b July 24, 1947

Zahid Ahmed (PIA & Peshawar) b Nov. 15, 1961

*Zahid Fazal (PACO & PIA) b Nov. 10, 1973

*Zakir Khan (Sind, Peshawar & ADBP) b April 3, 1963

Zesers, A. K. (S. Aust.) b March 11, 1967

*Zoehrer, T. J. (W. Aust.) b Sept. 25, 1961

*Zulch, J. W. (Tvl) b Jan. 2, 1886, d May 19, 1924

*Zulfiqar Ahmed (B'pur & PIA) b Nov. 22, 1926

*Zulqarnain (Pak. Rlwys, Lahore & HBFC) b May 25, 1962

PART THREE: ENGLISH CRICKET IN 1993

FEATURES OF 1993

Double-Hundreds (8)

R. J. Bailey	200	Northamptonshire v Sussex at Hove.
A. R. Border	200*	Australia v England (Fourth Test) at Leeds.
A. Dale	214*	Glamorgan v Middlesex at Cardiff.
C. L. Hooper	236*	Kent v Glamorgan at Canterbury.
C. C. Lewis	247	Nottinghamshire v Durham at Chester-le-Street.
J. E. Morris	229	Derbyshire v Gloucestershire at Cheltenham.
P. J. Prichard	225*	Essex v Sussex at Hove.
I. V. A. Richards	224*	Glamorgan v Middlesex at Cardiff.

Hundred on First-Class Debut

A. J. Hollioake 123   Surrey v Derbyshire at Ilkeston.

Three Hundreds in Successive Innings

D. C. Boon (Australians) ....   112, 107 and 120.

Hundred in Each Innings of a Match

D. C. Boon	108	106	Australians v Worcestershire at Worcester.
N. A. Folland	101	108*	Somerset v Sussex at Taunton.
G. A. Gooch	109	114	Essex v Hampshire at Chelmsford.
H. Morris	102	133	Glamorgan v Nottinghamshire at Swansea.
P. J. Prichard	104	106	Essex v Kent at Maidstone.
R. T. Robinson	119	139*	Nottinghamshire v Glamorgan at Swansea.

Fastest Authentic Hundreds

P. Johnson .... 73 balls (105 minutes) Nottinghamshire v Glamorgan at Swansea.
M. P. Maynard ..... 73 balls (93 minutes) Glamorgan v Australians at Neath.

In contrived circumstances, G. Chapple (Lancashire) scored 100 off 27 balls in 21 minutes against Glamorgan at Manchester.

Hundred Before Lunch

M. P. Maynard	132	Glamorgan v Australians at Neath (2nd day).
M. J. Slater	111*	Australians v Combined Universities at Oxford (1st day).
R. A. Smith	107*	Hampshire v Australians at Southampton (2nd day).

First to 1,000 Runs

H. Morris (Glamorgan) on July 1.

2,000 Runs

G. A. Gooch (Essex and England) on September 20.

Carrying Bat Through Completed Innings

C. W. J. Athey ...   72*†   Sussex (174) v Derbyshire at Derby.
K. J. Barnett ..... 108*   Derbyshire (214) v Glamorgan at Derby.
K. J. Barnett .....   73*†   Derbyshire (183) v Sussex at Derby.

   † *In the same match.*

Unusual Dismissal – Handled the Ball

G. A. Gooch ....   England v Australia at Manchester (First Test).

First-Wicket Partnership of 100 in Each Innings

127 179 G. D. Mendis/S. P. Titchard, Lancashire v Sussex at Manchester.
135 143 N. J. Lenham/C. W. J. Athey, Sussex v Durham at Durham.
291 150 P. R. Pollard/W. A. Dessaur, Nottinghamshire v Derbyshire at Nottingham.
162 109 A. J. Moles/J. D. Ratcliffe, Warwickshire v Somerset at Birmingham.

Other Notable Partnerships

First Wicket
291   P. R. Pollard/W. A. Dessaur, Nottinghamshire v Derbyshire at Nottingham.
279   B. C. Broad/G. D. Hodgson, Gloucestershire v Hampshire at Bristol.
260   M. A. Taylor/M. J. Slater, Australia v England (Second Test) at Lord's.

Second Wicket
313   J. W. Hall/C. M. Wells, Sussex v Cambridge University at Hove.
299   D. J. Bicknell/G. P. Thorpe, Surrey v Worcestershire at Worcester.
281   N. A. Felton/R. J. Bailey, Northamptonshire v Sussex at Hove.
278   P. N. Hepworth/V. J. Wells, Leicestershire v Glamorgan at Leicester.
275   P. D. Bowler/C. J. Adams, Derbyshire v Nottinghamshire at Nottingham.
262   T. S. Curtis/G. R. Haynes, Worcestershire v Kent at Worcester.

Third Wicket
321   M. W. Gatting/M. R. Ramprakash, Middlesex v Yorkshire at Scarborough.
262   J. E. Emburey/M. W. Gatting, Middlesex v Glamorgan at Cardiff.

Fourth Wicket
425*†   A. Dale/I. V. A. Richards, Glamorgan v Middlesex at Cardiff.
290   Salim Malik/N. Hussain, Essex v Derbyshire at Chelmsford.

Fifth Wicket
332*   A. R. Border/S. R. Waugh, Australia v England (Fourth Test) at Leeds.
302*†   J. E. Morris/D. G. Cork, Derbyshire v Gloucestershire at Cheltenham.
Fifth wicket added 346 in all; Cork retired hurt after 302.

Sixth Wicket
241   M. P. Speight/P. Moores, Sussex v Nottinghamshire at Eastbourne.

Seventh Wicket
301†   C. C. Lewis/B. N. French, Nottinghamshire v Durham at Chester-le-Street.

   * *Unbroken partnership.*   † *County record for that wicket.*

Twelve or More Wickets in a Match

M. C. J. Ball	14-169	Gloucestershire v Somerset at Taunton.
S. Bastien	12-105	Glamorgan v Essex at Cardiff.
A. R. Caddick	12-120	Somerset v Lancashire at Taunton.
P. A. J. DeFreitas	12-131	Lancashire v Somerset at Taunton.
J. E. Emburey	12-115	Middlesex v Hampshire at Lord's.
E. E. Hemmings	12-58	Sussex v Leicestershire at Horsham.
Mushtaq Ahmed	12-175	Somerset v Sussex at Taunton.
M. M. Patel	12-182	Kent v Lancashire at Lytham.
M. A. Robinson	12-124	Yorkshire v Northamptonshire at Harrogate.
Wasim Akram	12-125	Lancashire v Yorkshire at Manchester.

Eight or More Wickets in an Innings

M. C. J. Ball	8-46	Gloucestershire v Somerset at Taunton.
A. R. Caddick	9-32	Somerset v Lancashire at Taunton.
J. E. Emburey	8-40	Middlesex v Hampshire at Lord's.
M. A. Robinson	9-37	Yorkshire v Northamptonshire at Harrogate.
P. C. R. Tufnell	8-29	Middlesex v Glamorgan at Cardiff.
Wasim Akram	8-68	Lancashire v Yorkshire at Manchester.

Hat-Trick

W. J. Holdsworth ... Australians v Derbyshire at Derby.

100 Wickets

No bowler took 100 wickets. The highest aggregate was 92 by S. L. Watkin (Glamorgan and England).

Eleven Bowlers in an Innings

Gloucestershire v Sussex (128-0) at Hove.

Nine Wicket-Keeping Dismissals in a Match

W. K. Hegg	8 ct, 1st .	Lancashire v Yorkshire at Manchester.
C. P. Metson	9 ct	Glamorgan v Worcestershire at Worcester.
A. J. Stewart	9 ct	Surrey v Glamorgan at The Oval.
T. J. Zoehrer	7 ct, 2st .	Australians v Surrey at The Oval.

Six or More Wicket-Keeping Dismissals in an Innings

C. P. Metson	6 ct	Glamorgan v Worcestershire at Worcester.
A. J. Stewart	6 ct	Surrey v Glamorgan at The Oval.
T. J. Zoehrer	6 ct, 2st .	Australians v Surrey at The Oval.

No Byes Conceded in Total of 500 or More

A. J. Stewart . . . . . England v Australia (Second Test) (632-4 dec.) at Lord's.
P. A. Nixon. . . . . . Leicestershire v Middlesex (551-5 dec.) at Lord's.
C. P. Metson . . . . . Glamorgan v Kent (524-6 dec.) at Canterbury.
R. C. Russell . . . . Gloucestershire v Derbyshire (521) at Cheltenham.
A. N. Aymes . . . . . Hampshire v Gloucestershire (501-7 dec.) at Bristol.
K. M. Krikken . . . Derbyshire v Nottinghamshire (500-8 dec.) at Nottingham.

Highest Innings Totals

653-4 dec. . . . . Australia v England (Fourth Test) at Leeds.
632-4 dec. . . . . Australia v England (Second Test) at Lord's.
629 . . . . Nottinghamshire v Durham at Chester-le-Street.
591 . . . . Sussex v Essex at Hove.
584 . . . . Middlesex v Glamorgan at Cardiff.
568-7 dec. . . . . Worcestershire v Kent at Worcester.
562-3 dec. . . . . Glamorgan v Middlesex at Cardiff.
560 . . . . Worcestershire v Derbyshire at Kidderminster.
560 . . . . Nottinghamshire v Lancashire at Manchester.
559 . . . . Hampshire v Surrey at The Oval.
558 . . . . Somerset v Sussex at Taunton.
551-5 dec. . . . . Middlesex v Leicestershire at Lord's.
524-6 dec. . . . . Kent v Glamorgan at Canterbury.
521 . . . . Derbyshire v Gloucestershire at Cheltenham.
515-9 dec. . . . . Durham v Lancashire at Manchester.
501-7 dec. . . . . Gloucestershire v Hampshire at Bristol.
500-6 dec. . . . . Somerset v Hampshire at Southampton.
500-8 dec. . . . . Nottinghamshire v Derbyshire at Nottingham.

Highest Fourth-Innings Total

412-3 . . . . Essex v Sussex at Hove (set 411).

Match Aggregates of 1,400 Runs

Runs-Wkts
†1,808-20 . . . . Sussex v Essex at Hove.
 1,531-31 . . . . Kent v Essex at Maidstone.
 1,497-38 . . . . Derbyshire v Lancashire at Derby.
 1,457-35 . . . . Hampshire v Sussex at Portsmouth.
 1,448-36 . . . . Somerset v Sussex at Taunton.

 † *Record first-class match aggregate in Britain.*

Tied Match

Worcestershire (203, 325-8 dec.) v Nottinghamshire (233, 295) at Nottingham.

Victory after Following On

Nottinghamshire (242, 330-9 dec.) beat Kent (394, 104) at Nottingham.

Lowest Innings Totals

68	Nottinghamshire v Surrey at The Oval.
68	Middlesex v Worcestershire at Worcester.
72	Lancashire v Somerset at Taunton.
72	Leicestershire (second innings) v Sussex at Horsham.
83	Durham v Lancashire at Manchester.
83	Zimbabweans v Kent at Canterbury.
86	Oxford University v Durham at Oxford.
88	Warwickshire v Surrey at Birmingham.
88	Hampshire v Middlesex at Lord's.
89	Derbyshire v Middlesex at Lord's.
89	Durham v Northamptonshire at Northampton.
90	Worcestershire v Australians at Worcester.
95	Gloucestershire v Middlesex at Bristol.
97	Leicestershire (first innings) v Sussex at Horsham.
97	Northamptonshire v Yorkshire at Harrogate.
99	Oxford University v Glamorgan at Oxford.

Fifty Extras in an Innings

	b	l-b	w	n-b	
70	12	11	3	44	Nottinghamshire v Durham at Chester-le-Street.
59	13	14	0	32	Durham v Lancashire at Manchester.
59	5	21	1	32	Surrey v Durham at The Oval.
58	2	17	1	38	Sussex v Nottinghamshire at Eastbourne.
56	2	18	0	36	Sussex v Somerset at Taunton.
55	3	18	2	32	Durham v Warwickshire at Darlington.
53	4	2	2	45	Hampshire v Australians at Southampton.
53	9	7	1	36	Glamorgan v Warwickshire at Cardiff.
53	6	20	4	23	Somerset v Derbyshire at Derby.
53	5	14	0	34	Worcestershire (second innings) v Surrey at Worcester.
50	0	18	0	32	Gloucestershire v Derbyshire at Cheltenham.
50	9	12	1	28	Worcestershire (first innings) v Surrey at Worcester.

Under TCCB regulations, two extras were scored for every no-ball bowled. Any runs scored off the bat were credited to the batsman, while byes and leg-byes were counted as no-balls, in accordance with Law 24.9, in addition to the initial penalty.

Career Aggregate Milestones†

35,000 runs	I. V. A. Richards.
30,000 runs	M. W. Gatting, A. J. Lamb.
25,000 runs	W. Larkins.
20,000 runs	G. A. Hick.
10,000 runs	M. A. Atherton, K. M. Curran, M. D. Marshall§, T. M. Moody, P. J. Prichard, R. B. Richardson.
1,000 wickets	C. A. Walsh.

† *Achieved since September 1992.*
§ *Completed 10,000 runs and 1,000 wickets double.*

FIRST-CLASS AVERAGES, 1993

BATTING

(Qualification: 8 innings)

* Signifies not out. † *Denotes a left-handed batsman.*

		M	I	NO	R	HS	100s	50s	Avge
1	G. Yates (*Lancs.*)	7	10	6	367	134*	1	1	91.75
2	D. C. Boon (*Australians*)	14	23	4	1,437	164*	9	2	75.63
3	M. E. Waugh (*Australians*)	16	25	6	1,361	178	4	9	71.63
4	D. R. Martyn (*Australians*)	12	15	3	838	138*	4	3	69.83
5	S. R. Waugh (*Australians*)	16	21	8	875	157*	3	2	67.30
6	K. J. Barnett (*Derbys.*)	16	24	5	1,223	168	5	5	64.36
7	C. W. J. Athey (*Sussex*)	17	30	5	1,600	137	5	9	64.00
8	G. A. Gooch (*Essex*)	19	35	3	2,023	159*	6	14	63.21
9	C. L. Hooper (*Kent*)	16	24	2	1,304	236*	3	6	59.27
10	†M. L. Hayden (*Australians*)	13	21	1	1,150	151*	3	7	57.50
11	A. P. Wells (*Sussex*)	18	27	2	1,432	144	6	5	57.28
12	M. W. Gatting (*Middx*)	16	24	4	1,132	182	3	6	56.60
13	G. A. Hick (*Worcs.*)	18	30	2	1,522	187	4	7	54.35
14	T. S. Curtis (*Worcs.*)	19	32	3	1,553	127	5	8	53.55
15	N. Hussain (*Essex*)	20	35	5	1,604	152	7	7	53.46
16	M. J. Slater (*Australians*)	17	28	4	1,275	152	4	8	53.12
17	J. E. Morris (*Derbys.*)	18	29	1	1,461	229	5	6	52.17
18	J. E. Emburey (*Middx*)	17	21	7	730	123	2	5	52.14
19	R. J. Bailey (*Northants*)	18	30	5	1,282	200	2	9	51.28
20	M. A. Ealham (*Kent*)	12	16	3	666	85	0	8	51.23
21	†P. R. Pollard (*Notts.*)	19	32	3	1,463	180	3	9	50.44
22	M. P. Speight (*Sussex*)	13	22	1	1,009	184	3	5	48.04
23	J. P. Crawley (*CUCC & Lancs.*)	20	34	3	1,474	187*	3	8	47.54
24	I. V. A. Richards (*Glam.*)	17	32	6	1,235	224*	2	7	47.50
25	V. P. Terry (*Hants*)	19	33	2	1,469	174	4	7	47.38
26	J. D. Carr (*Middx*)	17	24	6	848	192*	2	3	47.11
27	R. A. Smith (*Hants*)	17	29	2	1,253	191	4	4	46.40
28	†A. R. Border (*Australians*)	16	21	3	823	200*	1	4	45.72
29	A. D. Brown (*Surrey*)	19	34	3	1,382	150*	3	4	44.58
30	M. P. Maynard (*Glam.*)	19	32	1	1,378	145	3	7	44.45
31	R. T. Robinson (*Notts.*)	18	30	4	1,152	139*	3	7	44.30
32	M. A. Atherton (*Lancs.*)	19	32	1	1,364	137	3	9	44.00
33	J. E. R. Gallian (*OUCC & Lancs.*)	11	19	3	702	141*	2	3	43.87
34	C. L. Cairns (*Notts.*)	15	23	1	962	93	0	9	43.72
35	A. S. Rollins (*Derbys.*)	7	13	4	392	85	0	2	43.55
36	†M. R. Benson (*Kent*)	15	23	2	913	107	3	6	43.47
37	P. D. Bowler (*Derbys.*)	17	29	3	1,123	153*	2	7	43.19
38	G. D. Hodgson (*Glos.*)	14	27	2	1,079	166	2	7	43.16
39	†D. J. Bicknell (*Surrey*)	19	35	2	1,418	190	4	8	42.96
40	†N. J. Llong (*Kent*)	18	27	5	943	116*	2	6	42.86
41	G. Chapple (*Lancs.*)	8	13	7	256	109*	1	0	42.66
42	M. D. Moxon (*Yorks.*)	19	33	2	1,317	171*	1	9	42.48
43	P. Johnson (*Notts.*)	16	27	1	1,099	187	5	3	42.26
44	†M. A. Taylor (*Australians*)	15	25	2	972	124	3	4	42.26
45	†D. I. Gower (*Hants*)	16	28	1	1,136	153	4	5	42.07
46	A. J. Stewart (*Surrey*)	16	28	1	1,094	127	2	8	40.51
47	A. J. Lamb (*Northants*)	18	28	1	1,092	172	2	6	40.44
48	K. R. Brown (*Middx*)	18	24	6	725	88*	0	4	40.27
49	†H. Morris (*Glam.*)	19	35	2	1,326	134*	5	6	40.18
50	P. J. Prichard (*Essex*)	19	36	3	1,319	225*	4	7	39.96

		M	I	NO	R	HS	100s	50s	Avge
51	A. Dale (*Glam.*)	20	38	1	1,472	214*	3	7	39.78
52	D. L. Haynes (*Middx.*)	15	24	4	793	115	2	4	39.65
53	A. J. Moles (*Warwicks.*)	19	34	3	1,228	117	2	8	39.61
54	A. N. Aymes (*Hants*)	19	29	11	709	107*	1	5	39.38
55	K. Greenfield (*Sussex*)	8	12	3	353	100	1	3	39.22
56	A. J. Hollioake (*Surrey*)	5	9	0	352	123	1	2	39.11
57	M. Watkinson (*Lancs.*)	19	30	4	1,016	107	2	4	39.07
58	R. J. Harden (*Somerset*)	18	32	3	1,133	132	3	4	39.06
59	W. Larkins (*Durham*)	17	30	3	1,045	151	3	5	38.70
60	M. R. Ramprakash (*Middx*)	17	24	1	883	140	2	5	38.39
61	I. A. Healy (*Australians*)	16	20	7	499	102*	1	3	38.38
62	P. Bainbridge (*Durham*)	19	32	2	1,150	150*	2	7	38.33
63	M. B. Loye (*Northants*)	18	28	3	956	153*	2	4	38.24
64	N. J. Lenham (*Sussex*)	12	22	1	799	149	2	5	38.04
65	G. D. Lloyd (*Lancs.*)	18	31	2	1,095	116	2	5	37.75
66	A. Fordham (*Northants*)	17	29	1	1,052	193	3	5	37.57
67	J. J. B. Lewis (*Essex*)	13	24	4	736	136*	1	5	36.80
68	M. C. J. Nicholas (*Hants*)	18	29	4	918	95	0	6	36.72
69	Salim Malik (*Essex*)	15	27	2	917	132	2	3	36.68
70	†N. A. Felton (*Northants*)	18	30	2	1,026	109	2	7	36.64
71	†D. M. Smith (*Sussex*)	15	23	1	802	150	1	4	36.45
72	D. A. Reeve (*Warwicks.*)	17	28	7	765	87*	0	5	36.42
73	R. Q. Cake (*CUCC*)	11	19	6	472	108	1	3	36.30
74	†G. P. Thorpe (*Surrey*)	17	31	2	1,043	171	3	5	35.96
75	N. J. Speak (*Lancs.*)	21	35	2	1,185	122	1	8	35.90
76	P. A. Cottey (*Glam.*)	19	34	5	1,039	105	2	8	35.82
77	†D. Byas (*Yorks.*)	19	33	3	1,073	156	1	9	35.76
78	R. R. Montgomerie (*OUCC & Northants*)	8	14	1	462	109	1	3	35.53
79	G. B. T. Lovell (*OUCC*)	8	13	2	389	114	1	1	35.36
80	S. J. Rhodes (*Worcs.*)	18	27	3	848	101	2	2	35.33
81	R. B. Richardson (*Yorks.*)	14	23	1	759	112	1	6	34.50
82	C. White (*Yorks.*)	19	32	6	896	146	1	4	34.46
83	M. V. Fleming (*Kent*)	18	28	4	826	100	1	6	34.41
84	T. L. Penney (*Warwicks.*)	17	29	6	788	135*	1	4	34.26
85	J. J. Whitaker (*Leics.*)	18	28	1	925	126	1	4	34.25
86	†B. C. Broad (*Glos.*)	18	34	0	1,161	131	2	7	34.14
87	D. P. Ostler (*Warwicks.*)	19	34	3	1,052	174	1	6	33.93
88	D. R. Pringle (*Essex*)	14	22	4	610	76	0	3	33.88
89	J. P. Stephenson (*Essex*)	17	32	2	1,011	122	2	4	33.70
90	M. N. Lathwell (*Somerset*)	17	31	1	1,009	132	2	4	33.63
91	S. A. Kellett (*Yorks.*)	5	9	0	301	85	0	4	33.44
92	†N. H. Fairbrother (*Lancs.*)	18	31	4	901	110	1	6	33.37
93	M. G. Hughes (*Australians*)	14	12	3	299	71	0	2	33.22
94	†R. C. Russell (*Glos.*)	19	33	7	863	99*	0	5	33.19
95	T. J. Boon (*Leics.*)	18	29	1	921	110	2	5	32.89
96	W. A. Dessaur (*Notts.*)	7	10	0	325	104	1	2	32.50
97	Asif Din (*Warwicks.*)	6	9	0	291	66	0	3	32.33
98	G. D. Mendis (*Lancs.*)	18	34	0	1,099	106	1	7	32.32
99	†N. A. Folland (*Somerset*)	17	30	3	872	108*	2	4	32.29
100	K. M. Curran (*Northants*)	16	23	4	612	91	0	5	32.21
101	†W. P. C. Weston (*Worcs.*)	13	21	2	610	113	2	1	32.10
102	C. C. Lewis (*Notts.*)	15	24	2	705	247	1	2	32.04
103	G. D. Rose (*Somerset*)	17	29	2	865	138	2	2	32.03
104	P. J. Newport (*Worcs.*)	17	26	6	630	79*	0	0	31.50
105	T. R. Ward (*Kent*)	19	30	1	903	141	2	3	31.13
106	M. A. Roseberry (*Middx*)	16	26	4	685	185	1	2	31.13
107	A. A. Metcalfe (*Yorks.*)	10	16	1	467	133*	1	3	31.13
108	M. W. Alleyne (*Glos.*)	18	34	2	994	142*	3	2	31.06
109	†M. Saxelby (*Notts.*)	12	18	0	558	77	0	5	31.00
110	C. M. Gupte (*OUCC*)	9	16	3	397	61	0	1	30.53
111	A. N. Hayhurst (*Somerset*)	14	23	1	669	169	2	1	30.40

		M	I	NO	R	HS	100s	50s	Avge
112	†D. L. Hemp (*Glam.*)	10	19	2	508	90*	0	5	29.88
113	P. W. G. Parker (*Durham*)	19	32	1	924	159	3	3	29.80
114	G. F. Archer (*Notts.*)	6	9	2	208	59*	0	1	29.71
115	G. R. Haynes (*Worcs.*)	9	13	0	383	158	1	2	29.46
116	J. D. Ratcliffe (*Warwicks.*)	19	34	0	999	101	1	6	29.38
117	V. J. Wells (*Leics.*)	15	23	2	602	167	1	1	28.66
118	R. J. Blakey (*Yorks.*)	19	32	2	859	95	0	5	28.63
119 {	P. J. Martin (*Lancs.*)	16	21	7	399	43	0	0	28.50
	J. A. North (*Sussex*)	7	11	3	228	114	1	1	28.50
121	T. J. G. O'Gorman (*Derbys.*)	14	21	3	511	130*	1	2	28.38
122	F. D. Stephenson (*Sussex*)	14	21	2	538	90	0	3	28.31
123	N. R. Taylor (*Kent*)	16	26	2	679	86	0	4	28.29
124	S. P. James (*Glam.*)	16	30	1	819	138*	1	4	28.24
125	C. J. Adams (*Derbys.*)	18	30	0	843	175	1	7	28.10
126	D. W. Randall (*Notts.*)	5	10	0	280	98	0	2	28.00
127 {	M. A. Garnham (*Essex*)	17	29	4	694	106	1	3	27.76
	†K. D. James (*Hants*)	17	29	4	694	71	0	4	27.76
129	D. M. Ward (*Surrey*)	13	22	1	580	151*	1	3	27.61
130	†S. Hutton (*Durham*)	10	17	0	469	73	0	2	27.58
131	D. G. Cork (*Derbys.*)	16	24	2	606	104	1	4	27.54
132	P. N. Hepworth (*Leics.*)	8	13	1	328	129	1	1	27.33
133	†M. A. Butcher (*Surrey*)	6	11	3	218	66*	0	1	27.25
134	N. E. Briers (*Leics.*)	12	19	1	487	79	0	3	27.05
135	L. Potter (*Leics.*)	12	17	2	404	103*	1	1	26.93
136	T. H. C. Hancock (*Glos.*)	16	29	2	723	76	0	4	26.77
137	S. A. Marsh (*Kent*)	19	27	2	667	111	1	4	26.68
138 {	A. W. Smith (*Surrey*)	14	23	2	560	68	0	3	26.66
	P. J. Hartley (*Yorks.*)	13	21	6	400	102	1	1	26.66
140	R. D. B. Croft (*Glam.*)	20	34	7	718	107	1	1	26.59
141	R. S. M. Morris (*Hants*)	8	14	0	372	92	0	2	26.57
142	†G. Fowler (*Durham*)	14	24	0	633	138	1	3	26.37
143	H. R. J. Trump (*Somerset*)	8	11	8	79	22*	0	0	26.33
144	C. J. Tavaré (*Somerset*)	13	25	1	628	141*	1	2	26.16
145	N. A. Foster (*Essex*)	8	12	3	235	37	0	0	26.11
146 {	I. T. Botham (*Durham*)	10	17	1	416	101	1	3	26.00
	J. W. Hall (*Sussex*)	9	16	1	390	114	1	1	26.00
148	T. C. Middleton (*Hants*)	12	22	0	571	90	0	5	25.95
149	G. I. Macmillan (*OUCC*)	9	14	1	336	63	0	3	25.84
150	B. P. Julian (*Australians*)	13	17	6	284	66	0	2	25.81
151	J. A. Daley (*Durham*)	13	22	0	563	79	0	3	25.59
152	D. P. Fulton (*Kent*)	7	13	1	307	75	0	2	25.58
153	P. Moores (*Sussex*)	19	27	4	583	85*	0	2	25.34
154	†G. J. Parsons (*Leics.*)	18	23	7	405	59	0	1	25.31
155	D. A. Leatherdale (*Worcs.*)	11	16	2	354	119*	1	2	25.28
156	R. K. Illingworth (*Worcs.*)	18	24	8	401	58	0	1	25.06
157	N. A. Mallender (*Somerset*)	13	16	6	250	46	0	0	25.00
158	I. Fletcher (*Somerset*)	7	10	1	223	65*	0	1	24.77
159	M. A. Lynch (*Surrey*)	15	28	1	666	90	0	3	24.66
160	†Wasim Akram (*Lancs.*)	13	21	0	516	117	1	1	24.57
161 {	S. P. Titchard (*Lancs.*)	5	10	0	237	87	0	2	23.70
	†A. C. H. Seymour (*Worcs.*)	7	11	1	237	54*	0	1	23.70
163	M. P. Bicknell (*Surrey*)	12	19	2	398	57	0	2	23.41
164	H. S. Malik (*OUCC*)	9	13	3	234	64*	0	1	23.40
165	P. J. Berry (*Durham*)	9	14	4	232	46	0	0	23.20
166	K. P. Evans (*Notts.*)	10	14	4	231	56	0	1	23.10
167 {	M. J. Weston (*Worcs.*)	7	13	1	277	59	0	2	23.08
	M. E. D. Jarrett (*CUCC*)	8	13	1	277	51	0	1	23.08
169	†N. D. Burns (*Somerset*)	13	23	2	479	102*	1	2	22.80
170	†P. A. Nixon (*Leics.*)	19	28	6	501	113*	1	3	22.77
171	G. R. Cowdrey (*Kent*)	12	21	0	478	139	1	1	22.76
172	C. L. Keey (*OUCC*)	10	16	1	341	111	1	1	22.73

		M	I	NO	R	HS	100s	50s	Avge
173	A. P. Grayson (*Yorks.*)	10	17	0	386	64	0	2	22.70
174	†N. V. Knight (*Essex*)	7	13	0	295	94	0	3	22.69
175	†R. M. F. Cox (*Hants*)	6	10	1	204	63	0	2	22.66
176	W. K. Hegg (*Lancs.*)	21	34	9	566	69*	0	2	22.64
177	P. R. Reiffel (*Australians*)	13	9	1	181	52	0	1	22.62
178	W. K. M. Benjamin (*Leics.*)	9	13	0	294	83	0	2	22.61
179	N. Shahid (*Essex*)	7	13	1	270	69*	0	2	22.50
180	C. M. Tolley (*Worcs.*)	18	24	7	381	78	0	2	22.41
181	S. K. Warne (*Australians*)	16	15	4	246	47	0	0	22.36
182	D. Ripley (*Northants*)	18	24	6	398	62*	0	3	22.11
183	A. J. Murphy (*Surrey*)	11	14	10	88	24*	0	0	22.00
184	R. I. Dawson (*Glos.*)	9	17	1	350	58	0	1	21.87
185	{ I. D. K. Salisbury (*Sussex*)	16	23	5	390	63*	0	2	21.66
	R. J. Turner (*Somerset*)	6	10	1	195	70	0	1	21.66
187	D. W. Headley (*Kent*)	14	20	7	281	36	0	0	21.61
188	D. B. D'Oliveira (*Worcs.*)	15	24	0	513	94	0	3	21.37
189	†S. G. Hinks (*Glos.*)	12	24	1	482	68	0	3	20.95
190	A. C. Cummins (*Durham*)	16	26	2	502	70	0	4	20.91
191	†G. M. Charlesworth (*CUCC*)	10	15	3	250	49	0	0	20.83
192	D. A. Graveney (*Durham*)	19	28	14	289	32	0	0	20.64
193	S. D. Udal (*Hants*)	19	27	2	509	79*	0	2	20.36
194	P. E. Robinson (*Leics.*)	18	29	3	526	71	0	3	20.23
195	{ B. N. French (*Notts.*)	17	24	3	420	123	1	1	20.00
	G. W. Mike (*Notts.*)	8	13	1	240	50	0	1	20.00
	C. A. Connor (*Hants*)	10	11	1	200	59	0	1	20.00
198	Mushtaq Ahmed (*Somerset*)	16	25	0	498	90	0	3	19.92
199	R. P. Lefebvre (*Glam.*)	19	28	3	484	50	0	1	19.36
200	M. J. Vandrau (*Derbys.*)	15	23	2	404	58	0	2	19.23
201	M. A. Feltham (*Middx*)	16	19	4	288	73	0	1	19.20
202	M. A. Crawley (*Notts.*)	10	18	2	306	81	0	1	19.12
203	S. R. Lampitt (*Worcs.*)	16	25	2	438	68*	0	2	19.04
204	P. D. Atkins (*Surrey*)	7	12	0	228	62	0	1	19.00
205	R. I. Alikhan (*Surrey*)	4	8	0	149	41	0	0	18.62
206	F. A. Griffith (*Derbys.*)	11	14	0	257	56	0	2	18.35
207	A. E. Warner (*Derbys.*)	12	14	1	238	95*	0	1	18.30
208	M. Keech (*Middx*)	5	10	1	164	35	0	0	18.22
209	†P. A. Booth (*Warwicks.*)	7	11	3	144	49*	0	0	18.00
210	†R. J. Scott (*Glos.*)	5	10	0	179	51	0	1	17.90
211	{ M. D. Marshall (*Hants*)	13	16	2	250	75*	0	1	17.85
	J. Wood (*Durham*)	9	17	3	250	63*	0	1	17.85
213	N. M. K. Smith (*Warwicks.*)	18	26	2	420	51*	0	1	17.50
214	D. J. Capel (*Northants*)	5	8	2	102	54	0	1	17.00
215	A. J. Wright (*Glos.*)	11	21	2	322	75	0	1	16.94
216	P. A. Smith (*Warwicks.*)	10	15	0	253	55	0	1	16.86
217	K. A. Parsons (*Somerset*)	5	9	1	134	63	0	1	16.75
218	P. A. J. DeFreitas (*Lancs.*)	21	31	3	465	51	0	1	16.60
219	R. W. Sladdin (*Derbys.*)	9	11	3	131	51*	0	1	16.37
220	C. W. Scott (*Durham*)	14	24	3	343	64	0	2	16.33
221	K. M. Krikken (*Derbys.*)	13	18	4	227	40	0	0	16.21
222	G. W. Jones (*CUCC*)	10	16	1	241	45*	0	0	16.06
223	I. Smith (*Durham*)	6	12	0	192	39	0	0	16.00
224	P. W. Jarvis (*Yorks.*)	9	14	1	207	76	0	1	15.92
225	N. M. Kendrick (*Surrey*)	12	20	5	237	41	0	0	15.80
226	R. D. Stemp (*Yorks.*)	16	23	6	265	37	0	0	15.58
227	R. S. Yeabsley (*OUCC*)	10	13	4	138	36	0	0	15.33
228	R. M. Wight (*Glos.*)	7	11	1	152	54	0	1	15.20
229	†C. E. L. Ambrose (*Northants*)	13	15	2	197	38	0	0	15.15
230	G. J. Kersey (*Surrey*)	12	20	2	272	38*	0	0	15.11
231	C. A. Walsh (*Glos.*)	14	21	3	266	57	0	1	14.77
232	C. P. Metson (*Glam.*)	20	31	8	338	25*	0	0	14.69
233	B. F. Smith (*Leics.*)	11	18	0	263	84	0	1	14.61

		M	I	NO	R	HS	100s	50s	Avge
234	A. R. Caddick (*Somerset*)	16	26	4	318	35*	0	0	14.45
235	T. J. Zoehrer (*Australians & President's XI*)	9	9	1	115	38	0	0	14.37
236	M. C. J. Ball (*Glos.*)	4	8	0	113	71	0	1	14.12
237	T. D. Topley (*Essex*)	8	12	1	155	33	0	0	14.09
238	K. J. Piper (*Warwicks.*)	10	14	1	183	52	0	1	14.07
239 {	†M. C. Ilott (*Essex*)	18	25	5	280	51	0	2	14.00
	A. R. K. Pierson (*Leics.*)	18	23	6	238	58	0	1	14.00
241	A. C. S. Pigott (*Sussex*)	12	13	2	153	52	0	1	13.90
242	†A. L. Penberthy (*Northants*)	9	14	2	164	54*	0	1	13.66
243	†R. A. Pick (*Notts.*)	13	12	4	109	22	0	0	13.62
244	C. W. J. Lyons (*OUCC*)	9	12	4	108	28	0	0	13.50
245	N. F. Williams (*Middx*)	14	12	1	146	44	0	0	13.27
246	J. D. Batty (*Yorks.*)	15	19	2	221	50	0	1	13.00
247	S. L. Watkin (*Glam.*)	19	24	8	204	31	0	0	12.75
248	Waqar Younis (*Surrey*)	13	18	1	214	28	0	0	12.58
249	J. Boiling (*Surrey*)	9	13	5	100	28	0	0	12.50
250	†R. G. Twose (*Warwicks.*)	11	18	0	224	37	0	0	12.44
251	M. G. Field-Buss (*Notts.*)	10	14	6	99	20*	0	0	12.37
252	M. Davies (*Glos.*)	14	23	5	220	44*	0	0	12.22
253	D. Gough (*Yorks.*)	16	24	3	248	39	0	0	11.80
254	†D. J. Millns (*Leics.*)	7	8	3	59	24	0	0	11.80
255	N. V. Radford (*Worcs.*)	13	14	5	106	29	0	0	11.77
256	R. P. Davis (*Kent*)	14	16	2	164	42	0	0	11.71
257	J. P. Arscott (*CUCC*)	10	12	3	105	22*	0	0	11.66
258	†K. E. Cooper (*Glos.*)	14	25	6	218	52	0	1	11.47
259	A. R. Whittall (*CUCC*)	10	9	2	80	40	0	0	11.42
260	†J. H. Childs (*Essex*)	17	19	11	89	23	0	0	11.12
261	A. R. C. Fraser (*Middx*)	18	17	2	162	29	0	0	10.80
262	P. C. R. Tufnell (*Middx*)	18	18	6	128	30*	0	0	10.66
263	K. C. G. Benjamin (*Worcs.*)	11	11	3	85	26	0	0	10.62
264	R. M. Pearson (*CUCC*)	10	10	1	94	31	0	0	10.44
265	P. M. Such (*Essex*)	20	27	5	228	54	0	1	10.36
266	C. M. Pitcher (*CUCC*)	9	8	2	61	27*	0	0	10.16
267	D. E. Malcolm (*Derbys.*)	11	14	7	69	19	0	0	9.85
268	A. P. van Troost (*Somerset*)	14	17	6	108	35	0	0	9.81
269	A. A. Barnett (*Lancs.*)	19	23	7	157	38	0	0	9.81
270	G. C. Small (*Warwicks.*)	13	19	4	147	39	0	0	9.80
271	M. Burns (*Warwicks.*)	6	10	0	96	22	0	0	9.60
272	N. J. Haste (*CUCC*)	10	9	1	76	36	0	0	9.50
273	†J. P. Taylor (*Northants*)	19	22	11	100	21	0	0	9.09
274	A. M. Smith (*Glos.*)	7	11	1	87	33	0	0	8.70
275	M. J. McCague (*Kent*)	9	11	3	69	22*	0	0	8.62
276	M. A. V. Bell (*Warwicks.*)	9	12	5	60	22*	0	0	8.57
277	A. A. Donald (*Warwicks.*)	10	12	4	68	19	0	0	8.50
278	J. I. D. Kerr (*Somerset*)	7	11	3	67	19*	0	0	8.37
279	A. D. Mullally (*Leics.*)	17	20	4	132	26	0	0	8.25
280	S. J. E. Brown (*Durham*)	16	24	5	152	31	0	0	8.00
281	A. R. Roberts (*Northants*)	10	16	1	119	19*	0	0	7.93
282	O. H. Mortensen (*Derbys.*)	10	14	5	70	29	0	0	7.77
283	T. B. A. May (*Australians*)	17	9	5	31	15	0	0	7.75
284 {	S. J. W. Andrew (*Essex*)	11	14	4	75	18	0	0	7.50
	S. R. Barwick (*Glam.*)	12	11	3	60	23*	0	0	7.50
286	S. J. Base (*Derbys.*)	14	19	0	139	27	0	0	7.31
287	J. E. Benjamin (*Surrey*)	17	26	7	128	23	0	0	6.73
288	†A. M. Babington (*Glos.*)	7	9	3	40	23	0	0	6.66
289	A. R. Fothergill (*Durham*)	5	8	0	53	29	0	0	6.62
290	T. A. Munton (*Warwicks.*)	13	13	5	51	18	0	0	6.37
291	J. P. Carroll (*CUCC*)	8	12	1	69	21	0	0	6.27
292	N. G. B. Cook (*Northants*)	8	9	1	50	18	0	0	6.25
293	S. P. Hughes (*Durham*)	6	8	2	37	30	0	0	6.16

		M	I	NO	R	HS	100s	50s	Avge
294	K. J. Shine (*Hants*)	13	14	5	54	12	0	0	6.00
295	D. P. J. Flint (*Hants*)	10	13	5	47	14*	0	0	5.87
296	J. A. Afford (*Notts.*)	14	17	8	50	11	0	0	5.55
297	A. P. Igglesden (*Kent*)	13	13	7	32	10	0	0	5.33
298	E. E. Hemmings (*Sussex*)	15	20	4	78	17*	0	0	4.87
299	M. A. Robinson (*Yorks.*)	17	22	10	53	16*	0	0	4.41
300	M. P. W. Jeh (*OUCC*)	10	10	4	26	9	0	0	4.33
301	R. H. Macdonald (*OUCC*)	10	8	2	22	11	0	0	3.66
302	E. S. H. Giddins (*Sussex*)	15	19	8	12	4	0	0	1.09

BOWLING

(Qualification: 10 wickets in 10 innings)

† *Denotes a left-arm bowler.*

		O	M	R	W	BB	5W/i	Avge
1	†Wasim Akram (*Lancs.*)	409.2	93	1,137	59	8-68	5	19.27
2	K. M. Curran (*Northants*)	458	123	1,293	67	7-47	3	19.29
3	J. E. Emburey (*Middx*)	719.4	226	1,401	71	8-40	2	19.73
4	A. P. Igglesden (*Kent*)	438.5	111	1,068	54	6-58	3	19.77
5	M. P. Bicknell (*Surrey*)	502.2	137	1,341	67	6-43	6	20.01
6	C. E. L. Ambrose (*Northants*)	543.4	150	1,207	59	6-49	2	20.45
7	C. White (*Yorks.*)	130	36	310	15	3-9	0	20.66
8	Mushtaq Ahmed (*Somerset*)	694.3	212	1,773	85	7-91	8	20.85
9	W. K. M. Benjamin (*Leics.*)	281.3	81	702	32	7-83	3	21.93
10	A. E. Warner (*Derbys.*)	322.5	76	900	41	5-27	3	21.95
11	S. K. Warne (*Australians*)	765.5	281	1,698	75	5-61	2	22.64
12	Waqar Younis (*Surrey*)	449.4	89	1,407	62	6-42	4	22.69
13	A. R. C. Fraser (*Middx*)	532.4	131	1,388	61	7-40	2	22.75
14	S. L. Watkin (*Glam.*)	766.4	173	2,098	92	5-71	2	22.80
15	C. L. Cairns (*Notts.*)	411.5	74	1,242	53	6-70	3	23.43
16	C. A. Walsh (*Glos.*)	528.1	119	1,516	64	5-59	3	23.68
17	†P. C. R. Tufnell (*Middx*)	688.5	189	1,529	64	8-29	3	23.89
18	D. A. Reeve (*Warwicks.*)	284.1	108	528	22	3-38	0	24.00
19	N. A. Mallender (*Somerset*)	329.5	102	772	32	5-49	1	24.12
20	P. J. Newport (*Worcs.*)	546.5	135	1,454	60	6-63	1	24.23
21	†A. D. Mullally (*Leics.*)	528.1	141	1,506	62	7-72	2	24.29
22	E. E. Hemmings (*Sussex*)	683.2	208	1,541	63	7-31	2	24.46
23	K. C. G. Benjamin (*Worcs.*)	283.5	42	911	37	6-70	2	24.62
24	G. J. Parsons (*Leics.*)	490.1	151	1,111	45	3-23	0	24.68
25	M. N. Bowen (*Northants*)	147.5	30	554	22	4-124	0	25.18
26	G. D. Rose (*Somerset*)	324.3	62	1,090	43	6-83	3	25.34
27	P. Bainbridge (*Durham*)	333.1	76	1,021	40	5-53	2	25.52
28	†R. K. Illingworth (*Worcs.*)	645	219	1,404	55	6-28	1	25.52
29	†J. P. Taylor (*Northants*)	646.5	191	1,789	69	6-82	2	25.92
30	†M. A. V. Bell (*Warwicks.*)	212.1	52	649	25	7-48	3	25.96
31	†K. D. James (*Hants*)	323.2	83	942	36	4-33	0	26.16
32	K. E. Cooper (*Glos.*)	502.4	149	1,233	47	5-83	1	26.23
33	K. P. Evans (*Notts.*)	265.3	69	660	25	6-67	1	26.40
34	D. Gough (*Yorks.*)	507.3	115	1,517	57	7-42	3	26.61
35	A. R. Caddick (*Somerset*)	541	115	1,678	63	9-32	5	26.63
36	M. G. Field-Buss (*Notts.*)	307.3	112	748	28	6-42	1	26.71
37	T. B. A. May (*Australians*)	562.5	156	1,429	53	5-89	1	26.96
38	J. I. D. Kerr (*Somerset*)	109.1	15	405	15	3-47	0	27.00
39	A. A. Donald (*Warwicks.*)	268.1	59	811	30	7-98	2	27.03
40	P. W. Jarvis (*Yorks.*)	267.4	62	705	26	4-51	0	27.11
41	M. W. Alleyne (*Glos.*)	246.3	50	707	26	3-25	0	27.19

		O	M	R	W	BB	5W/i	Avge
42	T. A. Munton (*Warwicks.*)	334.3	112	740	27	7-41	1	27.40
43	R. G. Twose (*Warwicks.*)	102.2	16	302	11	4-85	0	27.45
44	M. A. Robinson (*Yorks.*)	514	131	1,346	49	9-37	3	27.46
45	P. J. Hartley (*Yorks.*)	351.4	91	1,027	37	5-51	1	27.75
46	J. E. Benjamin (*Surrey*)	625.2	154	1,783	64	6-19	2	27.85
47	†J. H. Childs (*Essex*)	709	207	1,729	62	6-37	3	27.88
48	F. D. Stephenson (*Sussex*)	397	77	1,155	41	5-55	1	28.17
49	P. M. Such (*Essex*)	812	197	2,148	76	6-67	7	28.26
50	D. W. Headley (*Kent*)	439.4	106	1,191	42	7-79	2	28.35
51	†C. M. Tolley (*Worcs.*)	442.5	115	1,194	42	5-55	1	28.42
52	M. J. McCague (*Kent*)	298.1	67	888	31	5-33	2	28.64
53 {	N. F. Williams (*Middx*)	372	65	1,131	39	6-61	1	29.00
	A. L. Penberthy (*Northants*)	171	43	522	18	5-37	1	29.00
55	†J. A. Afford (*Notts.*)	720.5	225	1,659	57	5-64	3	29.10
56	M. A. Ealham (*Kent*)	281.2	56	917	31	5-14	2	29.58
57	M. G. Hughes (*Australians*)	470.2	113	1,420	48	5-92	1	29.58
58	D. G. Cork (*Derbys.*)	396.5	85	1,102	37	4-90	0	29.78
59	G. C. Small (*Warwicks.*)	251.4	71	629	21	4-39	0	29.95
60	S. J. Base (*Derbys.*)	310.1	69	1,080	36	5-59	3	30.00
61	P. R. Reiffel (*Australians*)	375.4	85	1,113	37	6-71	2	30.08
62	S. Bastien (*Glam.*)	167.3	27	573	19	6-52	2	30.15
63	S. D. Udal (*Hants*)	763.2	183	2,232	74	6-141	5	30.16
64	†R. D. Stemp (*Yorks.*)	540	188	1,207	40	6-92	2	30.17
65	J. P. Stephenson (*Essex*)	265.5	52	908	30	5-31	1	30.26
66	A. C. Cummins (*Durham*)	504.3	95	1,614	53	6-115	3	30.45
67	D. B. Pennett (*Notts.*)	172	34	520	17	5-36	1	30.58
68	O. H. Mortensen (*Derbys.*)	255	66	643	21	5-55	1	30.61
69	N. V. Radford (*Worcs.*)	269.5	46	1,012	33	6-49	1	30.66
70	M. D. Marshall (*Hants*)	345.3	102	859	28	5-62	1	30.67
71	D. E. Malcolm (*Derbys.*)	336.5	57	1,262	41	6-57	2	30.78
72	†R. P. Davis (*Kent*)	479.4	141	1,118	36	7-127	2	31.05
73	A. R. K. Pierson (*Leics.*)	528.5	141	1,371	44	6-87	4	31.15
74	M. A. Feltham (*Middx*)	327.4	88	905	29	4-48	0	31.20
75	S. R. Lampitt (*Worcs.*)	333	62	1,062	34	3-9	0	31.23
76	P. J. Martin (*Lancs.*)	406.5	105	1,188	38	5-35	1	31.26
77	R. P. Lefebvre (*Glam.*)	619.1	177	1,379	44	4-70	0	31.34
78	†M. M. Patel (*Kent*)	199.5	52	533	17	7-75	2	31.35
79	†L. Potter (*Leics.*)	352.1	123	758	24	5-45	1	31.58
80	M. V. Fleming (*Kent*)	422	103	1,086	34	4-31	0	31.94
81	A. J. Murphy (*Surrey*)	333.4	79	1,043	32	5-58	1	32.59
82	P. A. J. DeFreitas (*Lancs.*)	651.4	130	1,970	60	7-76	4	32.83
83 {	Salim Malik (*Essex*)	255.1	41	792	24	5-67	1	33.00
	†P. A. Booth (*Warwicks.*)	174.5	49	396	12	2-16	0	33.00
85	†N. M. Kendrick (*Surrey*)	368	113	960	29	7-115	1	33.10
86	N. M. K. Smith (*Warwicks.*)	588.1	151	1,593	48	6-122	3	33.18
87	†M. C. Ilott (*Essex*)	640.4	130	1,962	59	7-85	2	33.25
88	S. J. W. Andrew (*Essex*)	281.4	55	934	28	7-47	2	33.35
89	A. P. van Troost (*Somerset*)	282	49	1,036	31	5-47	1	33.41
90	A. Dale (*Glam.*)	393.1	81	1,238	37	6-18	1	33.45
91	R. J. Bailey (*Northants*)	244.3	69	612	18	5-54	1	34.00
92	J. D. Batty (*Yorks.*)	383.2	97	1,065	31	5-36	1	34.35
93	†D. A. Graveney (*Durham*)	579.1	187	1,306	38	5-78	1	34.36
94	†D. P. J. Flint (*Hants*)	388.2	95	1,066	31	5-32	1	34.38
95	R. D. B. Croft (*Glam.*)	850.5	265	2,158	61	5-112	2	35.37
96	R. H. Macdonald (*OUCC*)	250	66	710	20	5-20	1	35.50
97	D. R. Pringle (*Essex*)	378.5	98	1,041	29	4-33	0	35.89
98	P. A. Smith (*Warwicks.*)	130.5	18	505	14	4-35	0	36.07
99	W. J. Holdsworth (*Australians*)	204.5	32	833	23	5-117	1	36.21
100	I. D. K. Salisbury (*Sussex*)	616.3	132	2,007	54	5-81	2	37.16
101	R. S. Yeabsley (*OUCC*)	237.1	53	762	20	3-30	0	38.10
102	†M. Davies (*Glos.*)	515.1	141	1,412	37	5-57	2	38.16

		O	M	R	W	BB	5W/i	Avge
103	M. Watkinson (*Lancs.*)	662.5	146	1,950	51	5-12	1	38.23
104	C. C. Lewis (*Notts.*)	561.1	122	1,619	42	4-34	0	38.54
105	C. L. Hooper (*Kent*)	545	126	1,281	33	4-35	0	38.81
106	P. W. Trimby (*OUCC*)	143.2	31	469	12	3-72	0	39.08
107	V. J. Wells (*Leics.*)	241.4	66	705	18	2-5	0	39.16
108	†S. J. E. Brown (*Durham*)	509	78	1,861	47	7-70	3	39.59
109	I. T. Botham (*Durham*)	185.5	46	516	13	4-11	0	39.69
110	†B. P. Julian (*Australians*)	318.5	58	1,158	29	5-63	1	39.93
111	A. R. Roberts (*Northants*)	289.5	75	760	19	3-51	0	40.00
112	G. W. Mike (*Notts.*)	205	42	708	17	5-65	1	41.64
113	T. D. Topley (*Essex*)	181.5	41	627	15	3-15	0	41.80
114	F. A. Griffith (*Derbys.*)	170.5	29	593	14	3-32	0	42.35
115	†A. A. Barnett (*Lancs.*)	713.2	177	2,005	47	5-36	3	42.65
116	R. A. Pick (*Notts.*)	346	78	1,070	25	5-53	1	42.80
117	P. J. Berry (*Durham*)	200.1	33	648	15	3-39	0	43.20
118	G. Yates (*Lancs.*)	233	46	692	16	5-108	1	43.25
119	†R. W. Sladdin (*Derbys.*)	326.5	96	1,017	23	3-30	0	44.21
120	J. Wood (*Durham*)	192	26	735	16	4-106	0	45.93
121	G. Chapple (*Lancs.*)	155	34	507	11	3-50	0	46.09
122	M. P. W. Jeh (*OUCC*)	297	48	1,140	24	5-63	1	47.50
123	A. C. S. Pigott (*Sussex*)	282.3	43	1,001	21	4-51	0	47.66
124	S. R. Barwick (*Glam.*)	506.4	208	1,016	21	3-26	0	48.38
125	R. M. Pearson (*CUCC*)	335.3	68	1,020	21	3-61	0	48.57
126	A. M. Babington (*Glos.*)	219.2	49	634	13	3-51	0	48.76
127	K. J. Shine (*Hants*)	296.1	57	1,172	24	6-62	2	48.83
128	C. M. Pitcher (*CUCC*)	203.1	35	698	14	3-50	0	49.85
129	C. A. Connor (*Hants*)	261.4	65	803	16	4-77	0	50.18
130	A. R. Whittall (*CUCC*)	309.3	63	969	19	3-79	0	51.00
131	E. S. H. Giddins (*Sussex*)	379	55	1,490	29	5-120	1	51.37
132	J. E. R. Gallian (*OUCC & Lancs.*)	195	43	585	11	3-52	0	53.18
133	G. M. Charlesworth (*CUCC*)	229.5	52	645	12	3-33	0	53.75
134	†A. M. Smith (*Glos.*)	205.2	36	672	12	3-59	0	56.00
135	M. J. Vandrau (*Derbys.*)	288.4	62	937	16	2-8	0	58.56
136	N. A. Foster (*Essex*)	250.3	60	723	12	5-58	1	60.25
137	G. A. Hick (*Worcs.*)	203.4	59	603	10	2-15	0	60.30
138	J. Boiling (*Surrey*)	221.1	59	669	11	5-100	1	60.81
139	N. J. Haste (*CUCC*)	225	43	715	10	2-44	0	71.50

The following bowlers took ten wickets but bowled in fewer than ten innings:

	O	M	R	W	BB	5W/i	Avge
N. G. Cowans (*Middx*)	81	16	234	16	4-43	0	14.62
D. J. Capel (*Northants*)	117.4	37	252	12	3-15	0	21.00
D. J. Millns (*Leics.*)	184.3	51	584	25	5-21	2	23.36
T. J. Zoehrer (*Australians*)	126.1	33	335	14	3-16	0	23.92
M. C. J. Ball (*Glos.*)	157.3	35	439	18	8-46	2	24.38
C. Penn (*Kent*)	142	39	296	12	4-12	0	24.66
S. D. Thomas (*Glam.*)	141.3	21	556	20	5-76	1	27.80
M. A. Butcher (*Surrey*)	134	24	436	15	4-51	0	29.06
H. R. J. Trump (*Somerset*)	237.4	79	589	15	4-74	0	39.26

INDIVIDUAL SCORES OF 100 AND OVER

There were 276 three-figure innings in 199 first-class matches in 1993, 29 fewer than in 1992 when 234 matches were played. Of these, eight were double-hundreds, compared with 14 in 1992. The list includes 198 hundreds hit in the County Championship, 32 by the Australian touring team, two by the Zimbabwean touring team and 44 in other first-class games.

* Signifies not out.

D. C. Boon (9)
108 ⎫
106 ⎬ Australians v Worcs., Worcester
123 Australians v Leics., Leicester
164* Australia v England, Lord's
146 Australians v Hants, Southampton
101 Australia v England, Nottingham
112 Australians v Durham, Durham University
107 Australia v England, Leeds
120 Australians v Glam., Neath

N. Hussain (7)
118 Essex v England A, Chelmsford
111 Essex v Cambridge U., Cambridge
152 Essex v Derbys., Chelmsford
107* Essex v Warwicks., Ilford
103 Essex v Leics., Southend
118 Essex v Sussex, Hove
102 Essex v Hants, Chelmsford

G. A. Gooch (6)
105 Essex v Cambridge U., Cambridge
133 England v Australia, Manchester
120 England v Australia, Nottingham
159* Essex v Worcs., Chelmsford
109 ⎫
114 ⎬ Essex v Hants, Chelmsford

A. P. Wells (6)
120 Sussex v Glam., Cardiff
130 Sussex v Warwicks., Birmingham
144 Sussex v Somerset, Taunton
133 Sussex v Worcs., Hove
106 Sussex v Essex, Hove
123 Sussex v Yorks., Scarborough

C. W. J. Athey (5)
101 Sussex v Lancs., Manchester
107 Sussex v Cambridge U., Hove
137 Sussex v Somerset, Taunton
118* Sussex v Durham, Durham University
112 Sussex v Yorks., Scarborough

K. J. Barnett (5)
108* Derbys. v Glam., Derby
130* Derbys. v Essex, Chelmsford
161 Derbys. v Lancs., Derby
168 Derbys. v Worcs., Kidderminster
114 Derbys. v Australians, Derby

T. S. Curtis (5)
113 Worcs. v Notts., Nottingham
100* Worcs. v Oxford U., Worcester
116* Worcs. v Durham, Stockton-on-Tees
107 Worcs. v Sussex, Hove
127 Worcs. v Kent, Worcester

P. Johnson (5)
100 Notts. v Hants, Nottingham
112* Notts. v Glam., Swansea
187 Notts. v Lancs., Manchester
101 Notts. v Yorks., Nottingham
130 Notts. v Durham, Chester-le-Street

H. Morris (5)
109* Glam. v Oxford U., Oxford
100 Glam. v Derbys., Derby
134* Glam. v Yorks., Middlesbrough
102 ⎫
133 ⎬ Glam. v Notts., Swansea

J. E. Morris (5)
136 Derbys. v Cambridge U., Cambridge
151 Derbys. v Lancs., Derby
104 Derbys. v Sussex, Derby
229 Derbys. v Glos., Cheltenham
127 Derbys. v Surrey, Ilkeston

D. J. Bicknell (4)
190 Surrey v Sussex, Hove
119 Surrey v Kent, Canterbury
130 Surrey v Worcs., Worcester
122 Surrey v Hants, The Oval

D. I. Gower (4)
153 Hants v Notts., Nottingham
117 Hants v Lancs., Southampton
113 Hants v Sussex, Portsmouth
134 Hants v Essex, Chelmsford

G. A. Hick (4)
187 Worcs. v Australians, Worcester
104* Worcs. v Leics., Worcester
173 Worcs. v Derbys., Kidderminster
182 Worcs. v Surrey, Worcester

D. R. Martyn (4)
136 Australians v Sussex, Hove
116 Australians v Warwicks., Birmingham
138* Australians v Combined Universities, Oxford
105* Australians v Kent, Canterbury

P. J. Prichard (4)
123   Essex v Somerset, Chelmsford
104 ⎫
106 ⎬ Essex v Kent, Maidstone
225*   Essex v Sussex, Hove

M. J. Slater (4)
122   Australians v Somerset, Taunton
152   Australia v England, Lord's
111   Australians v Combined
       Universities, Oxford
133*   Australians v Derbys., Derby

R. A. Smith (4)
101   Hants v Derbys., Derby
191   Hants v Australians, Southampton
131   Hants v Warwicks., Southampton
127   Hants v Surrey, The Oval

V. P. Terry (4)
117   Hants v Oxford U., Oxford
111   Hants v Durham, Stockton-on-Tees
143*   Hants v Lancs., Southampton
174   Hants v Glam., Swansea

M. E. Waugh (4)
178   Australians v Surrey, The Oval
152*   Australians v Glam., Neath
137   Australia v England, Birmingham
108   Australians v Essex, Chelmsford

M. W. Alleyne (3)
104   Glos. v Durham, Bristol
142*   Glos. v Lancs., Cheltenham
104   Glos. v Essex, Bristol

M. A. Atherton (3)
107   Lancs. v Oxford U., Oxford
137   Lancs. v Durham, Manchester
137   Lancs. v Derbys., Derby

M. R. Benson (3)
107   Kent v Middx, Lord's
107   Kent v Warwicks., Canterbury
103   Kent v Glos., Tunbridge Wells

A. D. Brown (3)
150*   Surrey v Durham, The Oval
141   Surrey v Kent, Canterbury
138   Surrey v Zimbabweans, The Oval

J. P. Crawley (3)
187*   Cambridge U. v Sussex, Hove
109   Lancs. v Australians, Manchester
103   Lancs. v Northants, Manchester

A. Dale (3)
100   Glam. v Yorks., Middlesbrough
214*   Glam. v Middx, Cardiff
124   Glam. v Worcs., Worcester

A. Fordham (3)
193   Northants v Worcs., Northampton
109   Northants v Hants, Northampton
160   Northants v Essex, Northampton

M. W. Gatting (3)
173   Middx v Glam., Cardiff
121   Middx v Leics., Lord's
182   Middx v Yorks., Scarborough

R. J. Harden (3)
121   Somerset v Kent, Taunton
132   Somerset v Surrey, The Oval
100   Somerset v Durham, Hartlepool

M. L. Hayden (3)
115   Australians v Hants, Southampton
151*   Australians v Durham, Durham
       University
111   Australians v Essex, Chelmsford

C. L. Hooper (3)
142   Kent v Essex, Maidstone
166*   Kent v Lancs., Lytham
236*   Kent v Glam., Canterbury

W. Larkins (3)
151   Durham v Australians, Durham
       University
106   Durham v Sussex, Durham
       University
113*   Durham v Warwicks., Darlington

M. P. Maynard (3)
110*   Glam. v Oxford U., Oxford
145   Glam. v Derbys., Derby
132   Glam. v Australians, Neath

P. W. G. Parker (3)
123   Durham v Lancs., Manchester
109   Durham v Middx, Gateshead Fell
159   Durham v Warwicks., Darlington

P. R. Pollard (3)
104*   Notts. v Cambridge U., Cambridge
117   Notts. v Sussex, Eastbourne
180   Notts. v Derbys., Nottingham

R. T. Robinson (3)
112 ⎫ Notts. v Middx, Lord's
119 ⎬
139* ⎭ Notts. v Glam., Swansea

M. P. Speight (3)
184   Sussex v Notts., Eastbourne
121   Sussex v Hants, Portsmouth
114   Sussex v Glos., Hove

M. A. Taylor (3)
124   Australia v England, Manchester
111   Australia v England, Lord's
122   Australians v Lancs., Manchester

G. P. Thorpe (3)
104   Surrey v Glam., The Oval
114*   England v Australia, Nottingham
171   Surrey v Worcs., Worcester

S. R. Waugh (3)
124   Australians v Sussex, Hove
157*   Australia v England, Leeds
123   Australians v Kent, Canterbury

R. J. Bailey (2)
200   Northants v Sussex, Hove
103   Northants v Derbys., Derby

P. Bainbridge (2)
150*   Durham v Essex, Chelmsford
103*   Durham v Yorks., Leeds

T. J. Boon (2)
105   Leics. v Durham, Leicester
110   Leics. v Northants, Northampton

P. D. Bowler (2)
143   Derbys. v Surrey, Ilkeston
153*   Derbys. v Notts., Nottingham

B. C. Broad (2)
131   Glos. v Hants, Bristol
120   Glos. v Derbys., Cheltenham

J. D. Carr (2)
108*   Middx v Kent, Lord's
192*   Middx v Warwicks., Birmingham

P. A. Cottey (2)
100*   Glam. v Notts., Swansea
105   Glam. v Leics., Leicester

J. E. Emburey (2)
123   Middx v Glam., Cardiff
120   Middx v Northants, Lord's

N. A. Felton (2)
109   Northants v Sussex, Hove
105   Northants v Leics., Northampton

N. A. Folland (2)
101 ⎫
108* ⎬ Somerset v Sussex, Taunton

J. E. R. Gallian (2)
141*   Oxford U. v Notts., Oxford
115   Oxford U. v Cambridge U., Lord's

A. N. Hayhurst (2)
169   Somerset v Derbys., Derby
117   Somerset v Glos., Taunton

D. L. Haynes (2)
115   Middx v Somerset, Bath
112   Middx v Surrey, Lord's

G. D. Hodgson (2)
166   Glos. v Hants, Bristol
126   Glos. v Glam., Abergavenny

A. J. Lamb (2)
172   Northants v Somerset, Luton
162   Northants v Leics., Northampton

M. N. Lathwell (2)
132   Somerset v Essex, Chelmsford
109   Somerset v Derbys., Derby

N. J. Lenham (2)
149   Sussex v Essex, Hove
105   Sussex v Glos., Hove

N. J. Llong (2)
116*   Kent v Cambridge U., Cambridge
108   Kent v Middx, Lord's

G. D. Lloyd (2)
100*   Lancs. v Oxford U., Oxford
116   Lancs. v Yorks., Leeds

M. B. Loye (2)
105   Northants v Glos., Northampton
153*   Northants v Kent, Canterbury

A. J. Moles (2)
113   Warwicks. v Yorks., Birmingham
117   Warwicks. v Glos., Birmingham

M. R. Ramprakash (2)
140   Middx v Yorks., Scarborough
117*   Middx v Lancs., Lord's

S. J. Rhodes (2)
100*   Worcs. v Kent, Worcester
101   Worcs. v Warwicks., Birmingham

I. V. A. Richards (2)
109*   Glam. v Oxford U., Oxford
224*   Glam. v Middx, Cardiff

G. D. Rose (2)
138   Somerset v Sussex, Taunton
124   Somerset v Glos., Taunton

Salim Malik (2)
132   Essex v Derbys., Chelmsford
121   Essex v Notts., Nottingham

J. P. Stephenson (2)
113*   Essex v Notts., Nottingham
122   Essex v Sussex, Hove

A. J. Stewart (2)
109   Surrey v Leics., Leicester
127   Surrey v Sussex, Hove

T. R. Ward (2)
141   Kent v Surrey, Canterbury
137   Kent v Glam., Canterbury

M. Watkinson (2)
107   Lancs. v Surrey, The Oval
102   Lancs. v Notts., Manchester

W. P. C. Weston (2)
113   Worcs. v Oxford U., Worcester
109   Worcs. v Derbys., Kidderminster

The following each played one three-figure innings:

C. J. Adams, 175, Derbys. v Notts., Nottingham; K. J. Arnott, 111*, Zimbabweans v President's XI, Scarborough; K. L. T. Arthurton, 103, President's XI v Zimbabweans, Scarborough; A. N. Aymes, 107*, Hants v Sussex, Portsmouth.

J. D. R. Benson, 153, Leics. v Glos., Leicester; A. R. Border, 200*, Australia v England, Leeds; I. T. Botham, 101, Durham v Worcs., Stockton-on-Tees; N. D. Burns, 102*, Somerset v Hants, Southampton; D. Byas, 156, Yorks. v Essex, Chelmsford.

R. Q. Cake, 108, Combined Universities v Australians, Oxford; G. Chapple, 109*, Lancs. v Glam., Manchester; D. G. Cork, 104, Derbys. v Glos., Cheltenham; G. R. Cowdrey, 139, Kent v Northants, Canterbury; R. D. B. Croft, 107, Glam. v Cambridge U., Cambridge.

W. A. Dessaur, 104, Notts. v Derbys., Nottingham.

N. H. Fairbrother, 110, Lancs. v Northants, Manchester; M. V. Fleming, 100, Kent v Essex, Maidstone; G. W. Flower, 130, Zimbabweans v President's XI, Scarborough; G. Fowler, 138, Durham v Yorks., Leeds; B. N. French, 123, Notts. v Durham, Chester-le-Street.

M. A. Garnham, 106, Essex v Durham, Chelmsford; K. Greenfield, 107, Sussex v Essex, Hove.

J. W. Hall, 114, Sussex v Cambridge U., Hove; P. J. Hartley, 102, Yorks. v Glos., Sheffield; G. R. Haynes, 158, Worcs. v Kent, Worcester; I. A. Healy, 102*, Australia v England, Manchester; P. N. Hepworth, 129, Leics. v Glam., Leicester; A. J. Hollioake, 123, Surrey v Derbys., Ilkeston.

S. P. James, 138*, Glam. v Lancs., Manchester.

C. L. Keey, 111, Oxford U. v Northants, Oxford.

D. A. Leatherdale, 119*, Worcs. v Essex, Chelmsford; C. C. Lewis, 247, Notts. v Durham, Chester-le-Street; J. J. B. Lewis, 136*, Essex v Notts., Nottingham; G. B. T. Lovell, 114, Oxford U. v Cambridge U., Lord's.

S. A. Marsh, 111, Kent v Zimbabweans, Canterbury; G. D. Mendis, 106, Lancs. v Cambridge U., Cambridge; A. A. Metcalfe, 133*, Yorks. v Cambridge U., Cambridge; R. R. Montgomerie, 109, Oxford U. v Worcs., Worcester; M. D. Moxon, 171*, Yorks. v Kent, Leeds.

P. A. Nixon, 113*, Leics. v Lancs., Leicester; J. A. North, 114, Sussex v Essex, Hove.

T. J. G. O'Gorman, 130*, Derbys. v Cambridge U., Cambridge; D. P. Ostler, 174, Warwicks. v Essex, Ilford.

T. L. Penney, 135*, Warwicks. v Hants, Southampton; L. Potter, 103*, Leics. v Cambridge U., Cambridge.

J. D. Ratcliffe, 101, Warwicks. v Sussex, Birmingham; M. P. Rea, 115, Ireland v Scotland, Eglinton; R. B. Richardson, 112, Yorks. v Warwicks., Birmingham; M. A. Roseberry, 185, Middx v Leics., Lord's.

P. R. Sleep, 151, President's XI v Zimbabweans, Scarborough; D. M. Smith, 150, Sussex v Hants, Portsmouth; N. J. Speak, 122, Lancs. v Worcs., Worcester.

C. J. Tavaré, 141*, Somerset v Glam., Taunton.

D. M. Ward, 151*, Surrey v Kent, Canterbury; Wasim Akram, 117, Lancs. v Derbys., Derby; C. M. Wells, 185, Sussex v Cambridge U., Hove; V. J. Wells, 167, Leics. v Glam., Leicester; J. J. Whitaker, 126, Leics. v Yorks., Leicester; C. White, 146, Yorks. v Durham, Leeds.

G. Yates, 134*, Lancs. v Northants, Manchester.

TEN WICKETS IN A MATCH

There were 28 instances of bowlers taking ten or more wickets in a match in first-class cricket in 1993, three more than in 1992. The list includes 27 in the County Championship and one in another first-class match. Two of the instances occurred in the same match, when P. A. J. DeFreitas took 12 wickets for Lancashire and A. R. Caddick 12 for Somerset at Taunton.

A. R. Caddick (3)

10-92, Somerset v Hants, Southampton; 12-120, Somerset v Lancs., Taunton; 10-129, Somerset v Glam., Taunton.

Mushtaq Ahmed (3)

10-145, Somerset v Worcs., Worcester; 12-175, Somerset v Sussex, Taunton; 10-95, Somerset v Kent, Taunton.

P. M. Such (3)
11-124, Essex v England A, Chelmsford; 10-146, Essex v Leics., Southend; 10-160, Essex v Hants, Chelmsford.
M. P. Bicknell (2)
11-108, Surrey v Sussex, Hove; 11-192, Surrey v Worcs., Worcester.
S. D. Udal (2)
10-171, Hants v Notts., Nottingham; 10-192, Hants v Warwicks., Southampton.

The following each took ten wickets in a match on one occasion:

M. C. J. Ball, 14-169, Glos. v Somerset, Taunton; S. Bastien, 12-105, Glam. v Essex, Cardiff.
M. Davies, 10-141, Glos. v Northants, Northampton; R. P. Davis, 10-198, Kent v Notts., Nottingham; P. A. J. DeFreitas, 12-131, Lancs. v Somerset, Taunton; A. A. Donald, 10-129, Warwicks. v Yorks., Birmingham.
J. E. Emburey, 12-115, Middx v Hants, Lord's.
D. Gough, 10-96, Yorks. v Somerset, Taunton.
E. E. Hemmings, 12-58, Sussex v Leics., Horsham.
A. P. Igglesden, 10-125, Kent v Durham, Darlington.
A. D. Mullally, 10-170, Leics. v Glos., Leicester.
M. M. Patel, 12-182, Kent v Lancs., Lytham.
M. A. Robinson, 12-124, Yorks. v Northants, Harrogate.
A. E. Warner, 10-120, Derbys. v Glos., Cheltenham; Wasim Akram, 12-125, Lancs. v Yorks., Manchester.

FIELDING IN 1993

(Qualification: 20 dismissals)

63	R. C. Russell (56 ct, 7 st)		31	C. W. Scott (27 ct, 4 st)
61	S. A. Marsh (57 ct, 4 st)		28	M. A. Lynch
58	W. K. Hegg (49 ct, 9 st)		27	K. M. Krikken (22 ct, 5 st)
56	D. Ripley (52 ct, 4 st)		26	P. R. Pollard
54	C. P. Metson (50 ct, 4 st)		25	M. A. Taylor
53	*I. A. Healy (42 ct, 11 st)		24	G. A. Hick
48	P. A. Nixon (42 ct, 6 st)		24	W. Larkins
47	S. J. Rhodes (40 ct, 7 st)		24	C. W. J. Lyons (22 ct, 2 st)
46	R. J. Blakey (41 ct, 5 st)		22	C. L. Hooper
45	B. N. French (40 ct, 5 st)		22	M. P. Maynard
44	K. R. Brown (38 ct, 6 st)		22	D. A. Reeve
44	P. Moores (39 ct, 5 st)		22	C. J. Tavaré
41	N. D. Burns (37 ct, 4 st)		21	D. Byas
39	A. N. Aymes (34 ct, 5 st)		21	S. R. Lampitt
39	J. D. Carr		21	P. E. Robinson
39	M. A. Garnham (34 ct, 5 st)		21	*T. J. Zoehrer (17 ct, 4 st)
37	G. J. Kersey (34 ct, 3 st)		20	D. P. Ostler
36	†A. J. Stewart (34 ct, 2 st)		20	J. P. Stephenson
33	R. J. Harden		20	A. P. Wells

* *I. A. Healy and T. J. Zoehrer played together for the Australians against Warwickshire, Kent and Essex and shared wicket-keeping duties. Zoehrer took one catch off his own bowling against Kent and one in the field against Essex.*

† *A. J. Stewart took one catch in the field.*

THE AUSTRALIANS IN ENGLAND, 1993

Australia's third overwhelming Ashes victory in succession was as well merited as its predecessors in a series that ended Graham Gooch's reign as England captain and Ted Dexter's as chairman of the England committee. The course of the series – Allan Border leading his team to victory at Old Trafford, Lord's, Headingley and Edgbaston before The Oval brought England the consolation of their first win in 19 Tests against Australia – stemmed even more than usual from confidence. In England's case, it was the lack of it, following a tour of India and Sri Lanka on which they lost all four Tests and five one-day internationals out of eight. It was no surprise, then, that when Mike Atherton, taking over the captaincy from Gooch, led England to a big win at The Oval in his second match in charge, the change of fortune aroused relief as much as joy.

The significance of the victory, by 161 runs, was impossible to judge. To take the pessimistic view, there was no doubt that in a series containing an unacceptable number of umpiring errors all but one of the wrong decisions at The Oval favoured England, among them the one that lowered the curtain on Border's final innings in a Test on English soil. Conversely, however, England's bowling and fielding showed such vast improvement on the previous Tests that it was possible they were passing a watershed. If so, much of the credit was due to Angus Fraser, the 28-year-old Middlesex seamer who, after missing 24 Tests through his injury at Melbourne in 1990-91, fortuitously came into the side when Martin Bicknell failed a fitness test the day before, and returned match figures of eight for 131. The win, completed in the second of the final 15 overs, ended a sequence of nine defeats and a draw since the Headingley Test of 1992, when Pakistan were beaten by six wickets.

Annoying as it was for Australia to stumble at the final hurdle, defeat did no more than tarnish a fine all-round performance, in which a bowler even more exceptional than Fraser, 23-year-old leg-spinner Shane Warne, played the starring role. Arriving in England after a well-fought series against West Indies in the southern summer, the tourists were into their stride with wins against Worcestershire and Somerset in their first two three-day games, took the Texaco Trophy 3-0, and were in control of the Cornhill series from the moment they won the First Test at Old Trafford, by 179 runs. Such was their confidence that when Craig McDermott, their best fast bowler, was forced to fly home for treatment to a twisted bowel with four Tests still to play, it was decided not to send for a replacement. Merv Hughes, who took over McDermott's role as spearhead, shouldered the extra burden with a will that at times came close to heroism, though it was clearly a factor in England's Oval win; Hughes was visibly flagging in the final month. The management's refusal to reinforce the team was an effective means of assuring the remaining players that Border and the coach, Bob Simpson, had full faith in them to do the job. Two new caps, Michael Slater and Brendon Julian, both 23, were among the 13 called on for the Test series; Damien Martyn and Matthew Hayden, both 21, played in the one-day internationals; while Wayne Holdsworth, the New South Wales fast bowler, and Tim Zoehrer, the reserve wicket-keeper, took no part in either series. Zoehrer's main contribution was to top the tour bowling averages with his leg-breaks. It was a tribute to the immensely strong batting at Border's command that neither Martyn, who averaged 69.83, nor the left-handed Hayden, who scored 1,150 runs at 57.50, could force his way into the Test team.

Although Warne had two startling analyses to his credit in his 11 previous Tests, seven for 52 against West Indies and four for eight against New Zealand, his reputation before the tour was more that of a beach-boy than a budding Test-winner. His shock of dyed blond hair, earring and blobs of white sun-block on the tip of his nose and lower lip lent his appearance a deceptive air of amiability, which an expression of wide-eyed innocence enhanced. However, his incessant niggling of umpires and truculent questioning of unfavourable decisions made it obvious that the sunny exterior hid a graceless streak, which stopped him earning the unqualified respect of his opponents. In his hitherto unexplored method of attack, founded on ferociously spun leg-breaks, as often as not angled a foot or more outside the leg stump from round the wicket, he left no doubt that Australia had uncovered not only a match-winner of singular inventiveness but a cricketer crowds would flock to see.

Thanks to TV, Warne's first ball in Ashes cricket, which bowled Mike Gatting at Old Trafford, may become the most famous ever bowled. It was flighted down the line of middle and leg, the fierceness of the spin causing it to swerve almost a foot in its last split-seconds in the air, so that it pitched six inches outside the leg stump. From there, it spun viciously past Gatting's half-formed forward stroke to hit the off stump within two inches of the top. Had Gatting been in half an hour longer, or ever faced Warne before, he might have got a pad to it. As it was the ball was unplayable and, by impressing the bowler's capabilities on England, it had a profound impact on the series. Of Warne's subsequent 33 wickets, only two came from deliveries that appeared to turn as far – 18 inches or more – and in each case the spin was accentuated by the ball being delivered round the wicket. Gooch was the victim on both occasions, caught at slip for 120 in the second innings of the Third Test, and bowled behind his legs for 48 in the second innings of the Fifth. Nothing better illustrated England's problems than the fact that one of the most experienced batsmen in the world could be bowled in such a way when all he was attempting was to block the ball's progress with his pads.

Warne bowled half as many overs again as any other bowler, without showing signs of tiring even in his frequent two-hour spells. Of leg-spinners, only Arthur Mailey, with 36 in 1920-21 (in five Tests) has taken more wickets in an Ashes series than Warne's 34.

Several of his team-mates had a big hand in Australia's win and nobody more than David Boon, who scored 555 runs at No. 3, and Hughes, who in the first four Tests took 25 wickets compared with 23 by Warne. Ian Healy made 26 dismissals behind the stumps, a record for any series in England, and played several vital innings. The Waugh twins, sharing 966 runs, and Tim May and Paul Reiffel, who took 21 and 19 wickets with off-spin and fast-medium seam respectively, also made important contributions. There was little doubt, though, that the main difference between the teams was Warne. He was considerably helped by the perversity of the England selectors, who waited until two Tests had been lost before introducing a left-hander, 23-year-old Graham Thorpe of Surrey, previously uncapped, as a possible antidote. He scored 114 not out in the second innings of his maiden Test, adding 150 with Gooch when England were in danger of losing at Trent Bridge, though the circumstances of the innings compelled an open verdict: for much of the partnership Hughes was off the field nursing a strained groin, while twice when Thorpe was in the 50s he almost fell to Warne, picking the wrong ball to attack. Irrespective of Thorpe's good showing, however – in three Tests he averaged 46.00 and was dismissed only once by Warne – the absence of a left-hander at Old Trafford made it abundantly clear that the panel either under-rated Warne or had failed to notice his lack of success against the West Indian left-handers in Australia. Brian Lara, Keith Arthurton and Jimmy Adams headed the tourists' Test averages, and on Warne's four appearances, Arthurton, once, was the only one of them he brought to book.

A number of factors combined in England's failure, not least that, by wasting two gilt-edged chances of victory in the one-day series, they went into the Test series with eight consecutive defeats behind them. By flying in the face of Warne's revealing record against left-handers, however, not to mention basic cricket sense, the selectors – Dexter, Gooch, team manager Keith Fletcher, and Dennis Amiss – gratuitously aggravated England's problems. It was essential not to lose at Old Trafford, with the tourists in possession of the Ashes, and Lord's – England's bogey ground against Australia – following a fortnight later. Thorpe was the obvious candidate as a left-hander in the First Test. He had batted serviceably in the Texaco Trophy and had a look at Warne, who missed those games, when Surrey played the Australians a week before the Test. But because of his class and experience and his good record against Australia – nine hundreds – there was also a case for David Gower, despite his habitual lack of runs in county cricket. (Ironically, having been ignored, as he had been with disastrous and far-reaching consequences on the tour of India, Gower scored 153 for Hampshire on the first day of the Tests, only to crack a rib by falling on a ball while fielding, which ruled him out of contention for Lord's.) Hugh Morris, who had made two hundreds and three fifties in ten innings opening for Glamorgan, was another possible candidate.

Regrettably, as so often during Gooch's captaincy, the selectors were the only ones in step. At Old Trafford they paraded six right-handed batsmen followed by the (right-handed) all-rounder Chris Lewis and a four-man (right-handed) tail. Then, after Hughes and Warne, with eight for 151 and eight for 137 respectively, had bowled Australia to victory, they picked the same six specialists for Lord's. When a ten-man Australian team (McDermott never took the field) won by an innings, having lost only four wickets in the match, the question became not whether resignations would be forced upon the chairman and the captain but when. In the event, Gooch bowed out at Headingley, when Australia made certain of the Ashes, and Dexter at Edgbaston, a few hours before they took a 4-0 lead. It was little consolation that the downfall of both men could be traced to Gower's omission from the tour of India, since when nothing had gone right for English cricket.

Gooch had already made it clear that he would not be touring the West Indies the following winter. But at the start of the season, Atherton was only third favourite to succeed him. The confusion over Alec Stewart's role in the team – batsman or wicket-keeper? – worked against his candidacy. There was a growing feeling that Gatting might be installed as a stop-gap.

But after Lord's he lost his place in the side just as Atherton was looking increasingly secure. Thus that one ball from Warne may have decided far more than was apparent at the time.

But for that and another freakish dismissal in the First Test, Gooch's on the final afternoon, when he ended a flawless 133 by cuffing a looping deflection off Hughes away from the stumps to be out "handled the ball", England might have got away from Old Trafford unbeaten; Australia won with only 58 balls to spare. It would have been an escape neither the selectors nor the team deserved, however. Not only had the former discounted Warne, they failed to grasp that, because of England's low spirits and lack of penetrative bowling, the priority should have been to make Australia sweat blood for victory by selecting seven batsmen. The team had put on two feeble batting displays in which each of the specialists had a hand in his dismissal in one innings or the other. Gooch subsequently criticised the attitude of certain players, implying defeatism (nobody was named, but Lord's was the last Test of the summer for Lewis and Philip Tufnell). However, Gooch himself appeared to have earned a large measure of blame, through going on to the defensive at a time in Australia's second innings when two wickets would have evened up the game. Two days after this crushing defeat, Gooch's appointment as captain, initially for the first three Tests, was extended to cover the series, which suggested only one plausible explanation, that Dexter was attempting to create an illusion of stability. In the event, 24 players appeared in the series, Warne and May dislodging even the steadfast Robin Smith before The Oval. Gooch, Atherton and Stewart, who kept wicket, were the only ever-presents, though Peter Such, the Essex off-spinner, played everywhere but Headingley, where the attack comprised four seamers.

At Lord's, any slight chance England might have had of gaining a toehold on the series disappeared. In what turned out to be his penultimate first-class match before being forced into retirement by his weak left knee, Neil Foster replaced Phillip DeFreitas from the team beaten at Old Trafford. But when Australia won the toss in easy batting conditions, and Mark Taylor and Slater, the openers, rattled up 101 by lunch, 212 by tea, and 260 before Slater fell for 152 an hour and five minutes from the close, the only question Border had to answer was how long to bat before the declaration. In the event he called a halt at 11.45 a.m. on the third day, when nearly 13 hours had brought 632 for four at all but 100 runs a session. England were demoralised. Although Atherton held an end for more than four hours, making 80, a score of 193 for nine off 90 overs by the close represented England's most supine piece of batting since Bob Willis's team were demolished for 82 and 93 by New Zealand at Christchurch in 1983-84.

There was stronger resistance in the follow-on, which lasted nine hours and ten minutes. But when Atherton was run out for 99, slipping on the turn when Gatting sent him back on what would have been a safe third run had they taken the first two more quickly, and Gatting was the victim of a badly judged lbw decision half an hour into the final day, Australia never looked like being stopped. Two Tests later, at Headingley, they won by an even bigger margin, an innings and 148 runs compared with an innings and 62 at Lord's. But it was the flat pitch at Lord's that exposed more emphatically the gulf between the teams. In conditions favouring the bat, the England attack was putty in the hands of the Australians, while their own batsmen were always on edge against Warne and Hughes, especially when Gooch failed, as he did twice at Lord's.

The simple fact was that until The Oval, where Devon Malcolm and Steve Watkin, as well as Fraser, were making their first appearance of the series, Australia's batting was much too good for England's bowling. The tourists had an ideal balance – two quick-footed strokeplayers, Slater and Mark Waugh, two left-handed accumulators, Taylor and Border, a rocklike No. 3 in Boon (until a double failure at The Oval, his average batting time was three and a half hours), and in Steve Waugh and wicket-keeper Healy a No. 6 and No. 7 capable of attacking or defending as the position of the game required. Between them the Australians scored ten hundreds in the Tests and shared 13 three-figure stands, the highest an unbroken 332 between Border and Steve Waugh at Headingley, which has been bettered only once for the fifth wicket in Test history.

And from June 7, when Boon took over at the top, they dominated the national averages, eventually occupying the first four places (statistical freaks apart). Taylor had a modest series compared to 1989, when he amassed 839 at 83.90. For England, though, only Gooch, with 673, and Atherton, with 553, scored more than his 428, one of six Australian aggregates above 400. During Gooch's 79 in the second innings at The Oval, he became England's highest scorer, overtaking Gower's 8,231 when he reached 18. But Gooch and Thorpe made the only three hundreds, there were only five three-figure stands, and the longest Australia had to wait to take a wicket was three hours 40 minutes at Trent Bridge, when Gooch and Thorpe put on 150 for the sixth wicket in the second innings. Statistically, the gulf between the teams was overwhelming, Australia's average stand being 51.28, England's 30.86.

In Border's ninth year of captaincy, his single-minded pursuit of victory showed no sign of weakening, while his batting contained a quality – absolute determination not to make a present of his wicket – that was echoed among England's batsmen only by his opposing captains, Gooch and Atherton. By scoring 433 runs at 54.12 in the Tests, the fourth time in four full tours of England he had averaged more than 50 in a series, he lifted his aggregate in Anglo-Australian Tests to 3,548, third behind Bradman (5,028) and Hobbs (3,636).

That he will be remembered in England with respect rather than affection stemmed from his condoning, not infrequently his participation in, the sledging of opponents and umpires during play, in open violation of the International Cricket Council's code of conduct. By insisting on a panel of eight, the Test and County Cricket Board are much to blame for the deterioration in the standard of England's Test umpiring – not since 1989 has an umpire been helped to get the feel of a series by being appointed for successive Tests. But Border, who usually fielded within earshot of his bowlers, may also have contributed indirectly to the more obvious misjudgments of lbws and bat-pad catches, estimated by some at more than a dozen in the series, by failing to stamp out the questioning of decisions that sapped the umpires' confidence.

Despite all of that, and the promise of England's win at The Oval, the figures of the last three series were conclusive – England 1, Australia 11, drawn 5. Nobody could question that Border was the man Australia had to thank for that. – John Thicknesse.

AUSTRALIAN TOURING PARTY

A. R. Border (Queensland) (*captain*), M. A. Taylor (New South Wales) (*vice-captain*), D. C. Boon (Tasmania), M. L. Hayden (Queensland), I. A. Healy (Queensland), W. J. Holdsworth (New South Wales), M. G. Hughes (Victoria), B. P. Julian (Western Australia), C. J. McDermott (Queensland), D. R. Martyn (Western Australia), T. B. A. May (South Australia), P. R. Reiffel (Victoria), M. J. Slater (New South Wales), S. K. Warne (Victoria), M. E. Waugh (New South Wales), S. R. Waugh (New South Wales), T. J. Zoehrer (Western Australia).

C. J. McDermott returned to Australia after an abdominal operation during the Second Test at Lord's.

Manager: D. J. Rundle. *Coach:* R. B. Simpson.

AUSTRALIAN TOUR RESULTS

Test matches – Played 6: Won 4, Lost 1, Drawn 1.
First-class matches – Played 21: Won 10, Lost 2, Drawn 9.
Wins – England (4), Worcestershire, Somerset, Surrey, Leicestershire, Combined Universities, Kent.
Losses – England, Lancashire.
Draws – England, Sussex, Warwickshire, Gloucestershire, Hampshire, Derbyshire, Durham, Glamorgan, Essex.
One-day internationals – Played 3: Won 3.
Other non first-class matches – Played 6: Won 5, Lost 1. *Wins* – England Amateur XI, Lavinia, Duchess of Norfolk's XI, Middlesex, Minor Counties, Ireland. *Loss* – Northamptonshire.

TEST MATCH AVERAGES

ENGLAND – BATTING

	M	I	NO	R	HS	100s	Avge	Ct/St
G. A. Gooch	6	12	0	673	133	2	56.08	2
M. A. Atherton	6	12	0	553	99	0	46.08	1
G. P. Thorpe	3	6	1	230	114*	1	46.00	5
G. A. Hick	3	6	0	256	80	0	42.66	0
A. J. Stewart	6	12	0	378	78	0	31.50	14/2
N. Hussain	4	8	2	184	71	0	30.66	2
R. A. Smith	5	10	0	283	86	0	28.30	2
M. W. Gatting	2	4	0	91	59	0	22.75	2
M. N. Lathwell	2	4	0	78	33	0	19.50	0
A. R. Caddick	4	8	1	101	25	0	14.42	2
C. C. Lewis	2	4	0	52	43	0	13.00	1
M. P. Maynard	2	4	0	39	20	0	9.75	2
P. M. Such	5	9	3	56	14*	0	9.33	2
M. C. Ilott	3	5	1	28	15	0	7.00	0
M. P. Bicknell	2	4	0	26	14	0	6.50	0
P. C. R. Tufnell	2	4	2	3	2*	0	1.50	1

Played in two Tests: M. J. McCague 9, 0, 11 (1 ct). Played in one Test: P. A. J. DeFreitas 5, 7 (1 ct); J. E. Emburey 55*, 37; N. A. Foster 16, 20; A. R. C. Fraser 28, 13 (1 ct); D. E. Malcolm 0*, 0*; M. R. Ramprakash 6, 64 (2 ct); S. L. Watkin 13, 4 (1 ct).

* *Signifies not out.*

BOWLING

	O	M	R	W	BB	5W/i	Avge
A. R. C. Fraser	45.5	9	131	8	5-87	1	16.37
S. L. Watkin	53	13	152	6	4-65	0	25.33
D. E. Malcolm.....	46	8	170	6	3-84	0	28.33
P. M. Such........	239.5	64	541	16	6-67	1	33.81
M. C. Ilott	129	28	412	8	3-108	0	51.50
P. C. R. Tufnell....	104	12	319	5	2-78	0	63.80
A. R. Caddick	153	28	488	5	3-32	0	97.60

Also bowled: M. P. Bicknell 87–17–263–4; P. A. J. DeFreitas 47–9–126–2; J. E. Emburey 57–13–150–3; N. A. Foster 30–4–94–0; G. A. Gooch 25–6–66–0; G. A. Hick 25–7–52–0; C. C. Lewis 58–7–238–2; M. J. McCague 79.3–13–294–4; G. P. Thorpe 6–1–14–0.

AUSTRALIA – BATTING

	M	I	NO	R	HS	100s	Avge	Ct/St
S. R. Waugh	6	9	4	416	157*	1	83.20	5
D. C. Boon	6	10	2	555	164*	3	69.37	5
M. E. Waugh	6	10	1	550	137	1	61.11	9
I. A. Healy	6	7	2	296	102*	1	59.20	21/5
A. R. Border	6	9	1	433	200*	1	54.12	8
M. A. Taylor....	6	10	0	428	124	2	42.80	11
M. J. Slater	6	10	0	416	152	1	41.60	2
S. K. Warne	6	5	2	113	37	0	37.66	4
M. G. Hughes	6	5	0	76	38	0	15.20	0
T. B. A. May	5	4	2	23	15	0	11.50	2

Played in three Tests: P. R. Reiffel 20, 0, 42 (1 ct). Played in two Tests: B. P. Julian 0, 5, 56* (2 ct); C. J. McDermott 8.

* Signifies not out.

BOWLING

	O	M	R	W	BB	5W/i	Avge
P. R. Reiffel	140.4	31	396	19	6-71	2	20.84
S. K. Warne	439.5	178	877	34	5-82	1	25.79
M. G. Hughes....	296.2	78	845	31	5-92	1	27.25
T. B. A. May	278	90	592	21	5-89	1	28.19
B. P. Julian	82	16	291	5	2-30	0	58.20

Also bowled: A. R. Border 27–11–35–1; C. J. McDermott 48–11–126–0; M. E. Waugh 56–17–161–1; S. R. Waugh 32–9–82–2.

AUSTRALIAN TOUR AVERAGES – FIRST-CLASS MATCHES

BATTING

	M	I	NO	R	HS	100s	Avge	Ct/St
D. C. Boon	14	23	4	1,437	164*	9	75.63	10
M. E. Waugh ...	16	25	6	1,361	178	4	71.63	18
D. R. Martyn ...	12	15	3	838	138*	4	69.83	9/1
S. R. Waugh ...	16	21	8	875	157*	3	67.30	7
M. L. Hayden ...	13	21	1	1,150	151*	3	57.50	9
M. J. Slater	17	28	4	1,275	152	4	53.12	6

	M	I	NO	R	HS	100s	Avge	Ct/St
A. R. Border	16	21	3	823	200*	1	45.72	15
M. A. Taylor	15	25	2	972	124	3	42.26	25
I. A. Healy	16	20	7	499	102*	1	38.38	42/11
M. G. Hughes...	14	12	3	299	71	0	33.22	3
B. P. Julian	13	17	6	284	66	0	25.81	7
P. R. Reiffel	13	9	1	181	52	0	22.62	3
S. K. Warne	16	15	4	246	47	0	22.36	8
T. J. Zoehrer....	8	9	1	115	38	0	14.37	17/4
T. B. A. May ...	17	9	5	31	15	0	7.75	5

Played in nine matches: W. J. Holdsworth 0, 5, 12 (2 ct). Played in six matches: C. J. McDermott 23, 8, 11 (3 ct).

* *Signifies not out.*

BOWLING

	O	M	R	W	BB	5W/i	Avge
T. J. Zoehrer	87.2	21	250	12	3-16	0	20.83
S. K. Warne	765.5	281	1,698	75	5-61	2	22.64
T. B. A. May	562.5	156	1,429	53	5-89	1	26.96
M. G. Hughes	470.2	113	1,420	48	5-92	1	29.58
P. R. Reiffel	375.4	85	1,113	37	6-71	2	30.08
S. R. Waugh	73.1	19	229	7	2-9	0	32.71
W. J. Holdsworth....	204.5	32	833	23	5-117	1	36.21
B. P. Julian	318.5	58	1,158	29	5-63	1	39.93
M. E. Waugh	121.1	28	403	6	3-26	0	67.16
C. J. McDermott	143	26	449	6	2-36	0	74.83

Also bowled: A. R. Border 65–17–177–3; M. L. Hayden 8.4–1–31–1; D. R. Martyn 8–2–21–0; M. A. Taylor 9–0–31–1.

Note: Matches in this section which were not first-class are signified by a dagger.

†ENGLAND AMATEUR XI v AUSTRALIANS

At Radlett, April 30. Australians won by 94 runs. Toss: Australians.

The tourists' first match was staged in the small Hertfordshire town that was once the home of England captain Douglas Jardine. Hayden batted solidly until the penultimate over and hit four sixes and nine fours, while all his partners gained useful practice. But the most spectacular innings came from the Amateurs' opener, Steve Dean of Staffordshire, who took the attack to McDermott and Holdsworth right from the start and hit 48 from 44 balls. When he departed, one of five catches for wicket-keeper Zoehrer, no one else could hope to maintain such momentum.

Australians

M. J. Slater c Evans b Van Lint 41	M. E. Waugh not out 1
M. L. Hayden c Van Lint b Hackett ...151	L-b 13, w 5, n-b 4 22
*M. A. Taylor c Dean b Hackett 53	
D. C. Boon not out 24	1/92 2/211 3/283 (3 wkts, 55 overs) 292

D. R. Martyn, †T. J. Zoehrer, S. K. Warne, C. J. McDermott, B. P. Julian and W. J. Holdsworth did not bat.

Bowling: Arnold 11–2–51–0; Roshier 11–1–62–0; Hackett 10–0–74–2; Van Lint 11–0–49–1; Evans 11–2–40–0; Sharma 1–0–3–0.

England Amateur XI

S. J. Dean c Zoehrer b Holdsworth	....	48	R. A. Evans not out	 12
†S. N. V. Waterton c Zoehrer b Julian	..	8	K. A. Arnold c Holdsworth b Warne	. 5
*M. J. Roberts b Holdsworth	....	17	N. P. Hackett b Warne	 1
I. W. E. Stokes c Zoehrer b Holdsworth		1	L-b 5, w 18, n-b 18	 41
R. Sharma c Zoehrer b Julian	......	11		
M. Hussain c Zoehrer b McDermott	...	39	1/60 2/82 3/99	(45.2 overs) 198
P. G. Roshier c and b Julian	......	12	4/102 5/125 6/149	
A. T. Van Lint c Taylor b McDermott	.	3	7/166 8/183 9/192	

Bowling: McDermott 10-0-35-2; Holdsworth 8-3-28-3; Julian 11-2-60-3; Warne 9.2-1-41-2; Martyn 6-0-23-0; Taylor 1-0-6-0.

Umpires: B. Dudleston and J. H. Hampshire.

†LAVINIA, DUCHESS OF NORFOLK'S XI v AUSTRALIANS

At Arundel, May 2. Australians won by seven runs. Toss: Australians.

A huge crowd – the gates were shut on more than 16,000 spectators – had more or less forgotten the possibility of the Australians losing when Parker changed the tone of the game. He had been batting 40 overs for 63, but with 22 needed from the last over he suddenly hit a six and two fours. Two balls remained, with eight runs required, but Holdsworth trapped him with the first. Most of the crowd were preoccupied with Botham, however, and the cool response of Ted Dexter, chairman of the selectors, during a radio interview could not dampen speculation that he might be recalled for an Ashes series one last time. Botham took two for 29, and when he bowled Border the Australians were 68 for five at the mid-point of their innings. Steve Waugh, with support from Healy, halted the rush. Kent's new recruit Headley collected five wickets, as did Mark Waugh when the tourists took the field. Again the biggest cheer came for Botham, who hit six and four from consecutive balls – but Waugh bowled him for 13.

Australians

M. J. Slater b Graveney	 13	P. R. Reiffel b Headley	 9
D. C. Boon c Parks b Headley	 14	S. K. Warne b Headley	 0
M. E. Waugh b Headley	 6		
D. R. Martyn c Garner b Botham	 5	L-b 5, w 7	 12
*A. R. Border b Botham	 18		
S. R. Waugh b Garner	 59	1/20 2/27 3/40	(9 wkts, 50 overs) 203
†I. A. Healy not out	 47	4/42 5/68 6/150	
B. P. Julian c Cowdrey b Headley	 20	7/188 8/203 9/203	

W. J. Holdsworth did not bat.

Bowling: Garner 10-2-32-1; Headley 10-1-51-5; Graveney 10-2-32-1; Botham 10-1-29-2; Fleming 7-0-32-0; Greig 3-0-22-0.

Lavinia, Duchess of Norfolk's XI

T. R. Ward run out	 33	D. W. Headley c M. E. Waugh b Julian 16	
G. Fowler c Healy b Julian	 11	J. Garner b Julian	 8
*P. W. G. Parker lbw b Holdsworth	.. 77	D. A. Graveney not out	 5
G. R. Cowdrey c S. R. Waugh			
b M. E. Waugh	. 0	L-b 12, w 12, n-b 2	 26
M. V. Fleming c Healy b M. E. Waugh	0		
I. T. Botham b M. E. Waugh	... 13	1/38 2/66 3/66	(49.5 overs) 196
I. A. Greig c Healy b M. E. Waugh	... 6	4/66 5/87 6/112	
†R. J. Parks c Healy b M. E. Waugh	.. 1	7/114 8/162 9/176	

Bowling: Holdsworth 9.5-1-42-1; Julian 10-0-49-3; Reiffel 10-0-35-0; Warne 10-1-26-0; M. E. Waugh 10-2-32-5.

Umpires: G. I. Burgess and D. J. Constant.

†MIDDLESEX v AUSTRALIANS

At Lord's, May 3. Australians won by 69 runs. Toss: Australians.

A crowd approaching 10,000 turned out to watch a game in which the cricket seemed to take second place to clashes of temperament. Not that the players directed their hostility towards the opposing team; the first display of temper occurred when Gatting kept a disgruntled Fraser out of the Middlesex attack until the 20th over. Fraser's first four overs cost 35 runs and his obvious annoyance when taken off led to a severe finger-wagging from his captain. But Gatting was even less pleased later in the day when he was run out – sent back, quite justifiably, by Roseberry. Still seething, he put his hand through a glass panel in the dressing-room door and was taken to hospital for stitches. The injury ruled him out of the one-day internationals. His opposite number, Border, also expressed his frustration when bowled by a full toss from Fraser, swiping at the stumps with his bat. As for the game, the Australians had few difficulties. Though they lost Taylor and Slater by the 14th over, Hayden reached 122 and struck two sixes and 12 fours. After Middlesex lost three wickets for 14 only Roseberry held up the Australians, batting 41 overs for his 47.

Australians

M. A. Taylor b Feltham	7	†T. J. Zoehrer not out	7
M. L. Hayden c Roseberry b Fraser	122		
M. J. Slater run out	1	L-b 7, w 6	13
D. R. Martyn run out	66		
*A. R. Border b Fraser	8	1/23 2/28 3/167 (5 wkts, 55 overs)	243
S. R. Waugh not out	19	4/187 5/226	

P. R. Reiffel, T. B. A. May, C. J. McDermott and W. J. Holdsworth did not bat.

Bowling: Feltham 8-4-19-1; Cowans 11-0-36-0; Emburey 11-4-37-0; Fraser 11-0-76-2; Weekes 7-1-31-0; Keech 7-0-37-0.

Middlesex

M. Keech b McDermott	0	J. E. Emburey b Martyn	10
M. A. Roseberry c Taylor b Martyn	47	A. R. C. Fraser not out	0
M. R. Ramprakash lbw b McDermott	0	N. G. Cowans c Zoehrer b Holdsworth	0
J. D. Carr c Zoehrer b Reiffel	3		
*M. W. Gatting run out	32	L-b 6, w 9, n-b 14	29
P. N. Weekes c Zoehrer b Martyn	12		
†K. R. Brown c Holdsworth b McDermott	24	1/5 2/5 3/14 (48.1 overs)	174
		4/74 5/103 6/140	
M. A. Feltham b Reiffel	17	7/145 8/169 9/173	

Bowling: McDermott 11-2-51-3; Reiffel 8-3-23-2; Holdsworth 7.1-0-22-1; May 11-2-31-0; Martyn 11-1-41-3.

Umpires: V. A. Holder and R. A. White.

WORCESTERSHIRE v AUSTRALIANS

At Worcester, May 5, 6, 7. Australians won by five wickets. Toss: Australians.

Steve Waugh hit Illingworth's penultimate ball for six over extra cover to win a contest of baffling fluctuations. The first four sessions saw 21 wickets fall for 373 runs, while the next five produced 724 runs for only eight. Considering Worcestershire followed on 172 adrift, after losing nine wickets for 59, it was remarkable that Curtis was able to set a target of 287 from 55 overs. Worcestershire's recovery owed everything to Hick's 187, including 132 in boundaries. He reached his 69th century, on the fifth anniversary of his 405 against Somerset, off 136 balls and won hands down his first confrontation with Warne, off whom he scored 96 from 77 balls. However, Warne appeared entirely unruffled by the experience and close observation suggested his main concern was to give Hick as little idea as possible of his tricks and variations. Curtis helped Hick add 168 in 40 overs and later Seymour and Lampitt shared 121. On the first day Boon had galvanised the Australians with a four-hour century, but his second hundred of the game came off just 97 balls as he and Hayden set up the platform for victory.

Close of play: First day, Worcestershire 14-1 (W. P. C. Weston 9*, G. A. Hick 1*); Second day, Worcestershire 311-3 (G. A. Hick 161*, A. C. H. Seymour 12*).

Australians

M. L. Hayden c Lampitt b Tolley	3	– (2) c Hick b Newport	96
*M. A. Taylor c Rhodes b Illingworth	39	– (1) c Lampitt b Radford	40
D. C. Boon lbw b Radford	108	– st Rhodes b Illingworth	106
M. E. Waugh c Curtis b Tolley	7	– run out	15
D. R. Martyn c Lampitt b Illingworth	25	– c Newport b Illingworth	3
S. R. Waugh not out	49	– not out	12
†I. A. Healy c Hick b Newport	6	– not out	1
B. P. Julian c Weston b Newport	9		
P. R. Reiffel b Lampitt	5		
S. K. Warne b Lampitt	3		
W. J. Holdsworth c Weston b Newport	0		
L-b 5, w 1, n-b 2	8	L-b 4, w 8, n-b 2	14

1/3 2/104 3/124 4/170 5/194   262   1/71 2/252 3/262   (5 wkts) 287
6/212 7/248 8/253 9/261   4/273 5/275

Bowling: *First Innings*—Newport 22.5-6-59-3; Tolley 16-5-36-2; Radford 15-5-53-1; Lampitt 16-3-47-2; Illingworth 15-2-52-2; Weston 2-0-10-0. *Second Innings*—Newport 15-1-58-1; Tolley 9-2-40-0; Radford 7-1-56-1; Illingworth 12.5-1-70-2; Hick 6-0-33-0; Lampitt 5-0-26-0.

Worcestershire

*T. S. Curtis lbw b Julian	1	– lbw b Julian	67
W. P. C. Weston c Martyn b Julian	17	– c Taylor b Holdsworth	16
G. A. Hick c Taylor b Reiffel	5	– lbw b Holdsworth	187
D. B. D'Oliveira c Healy b Holdsworth	13	– b Warne	27
A. C. H. Seymour c Healy b Julian	6	– not out	54
S. R. Lampitt lbw b Reiffel	4	– not out	68
†S. J. Rhodes c Healy b Reiffel	0		
R. K. Illingworth c Taylor b Holdsworth	12		
P. J. Newport run out	7		
N. V. Radford c Healy b Holdsworth	4		
C. M. Tolley not out	0		
B 1, l-b 5, w 3, n-b 12	21	L-b 10, w 1, n-b 28	39

1/1 2/31 3/35 4/47 5/55   90   1/21 2/189 3/252   (4 wkts dec.) 458
6/59 7/59 8/68 9/82   4/337

Bowling: *First Innings*—Holdsworth 7.5-3-15-3; Julian 13-6-31-3; Reiffel 10-5-21-3; M. E. Waugh 3-0-17-0. *Second Innings*—Holdsworth 23-3-96-2; Reiffel 26-7-68-0; Julian 19-1-96-1; Warne 23-6-122-1; M. E. Waugh 15.1-2-59-0; Martyn 2-1-7-0.

Umpires: B. J. Meyer and R. Palmer.

SOMERSET v AUSTRALIANS

At Taunton, May 8, 9, 10. Australians won by 35 runs. Toss: Australians. First-class debut: J. I. D. Kerr.

The Australians scored at a brisk 4.75 an over on a true pitch on the opening day. Slater led the way in a delightful three-hour century, containing 20 fours, and Border and Mark Waugh stepped up the pace. Rain ended play early, and Somerset's innings finally began at 3.15 p.m. the next day, in misty weather on a pitch freshened by its lengthy covering. McDermott took two early wickets – Lathwell lasted three balls – but Hayhurst and Tavaré steadied Somerset with 117 in 33 overs. Two declarations preceded Somerset's determined attempt to score 321 in 84 overs. A fighting innings by Hayhurst kept them on course and at 216 for three after 59 overs the target was in view. But then Warne bowled Hayhurst round his legs. Despite the efforts of Folland and the tail the Australian spinners finished them off, with nearly seven overs left. Attention was diverted from the game during the chase when an Australian television microphone picked up a forthright exchange between Border and McDermott, who had conceded three no-balls in his first over, after being asked to switch ends.

Close of play: First day, Australians 431; Second day, Somerset 151-4 (A. N. Hayhurst 49*, N. D. Burns 7*).

Australians

M. J. Slater c Lathwell b Kerr	122	– (2) not out	12
M. A. Taylor c Lathwell b van Troost	0	– (1) not out	18
D. C. Boon c Parsons b Kerr	27		
*A. R. Border c Burns b van Troost	54		
M. E. Waugh c Lathwell b van Troost	68		
S. R. Waugh c Burns b Caddick	38		
†T. J. Zoehrer b van Troost	22		
M. G. Hughes c Harden b Trump	36		
T. B. A. May not out	4		
S. K. Warne st Burns b Trump	11		
C. J. McDermott c Folland b Kerr	23		
B 4, l-b 8, n-b 14	26	B 1, l-b 1, n-b 8	10

1/0 2/64 3/187 4/245 5/305   431   (no wkt dec.) 40
6/332 7/381 8/385 9/396

Bowling: *First Innings*—Caddick 22–1–90–1; van Troost 18–2–89–4; Kerr 12.4–2–77–3; Hayhurst 14–4–50–0; Trump 22–3–101–2; Lathwell 2–0–12–0. *Second Innings*—Caddick 6–1–14–0; van Troost 5–1–16–0; Kerr 0.3–0–8–0.

Somerset

A. N. Hayhurst not out	49	– b Warne	89
M. N. Lathwell c Zoehrer b McDermott	0	– c Zoehrer b Hughes	15
R. J. Harden c Border b McDermott	7	– c Boon b May	34
*C. J. Tavaré c and b May	62	– c Taylor b Warne	31
N. A. Folland lbw b Warne	1	– st Zoehrer b Warne	32
†N. D. Burns not out	7	– run out	6
K. A. Parsons (did not bat)		– c McDermott b May	1
J. I. D. Kerr (did not bat)		– c Hughes b May	12
A. R. Caddick (did not bat)		– c McDermott b May	13
A. P. van Troost (did not bat)		– c S. R. Waugh b Warne	8
H. R. J. Trump (did not bat)		– not out	0
L-b 7, n-b 18	25	B 17, l-b 9, n-b 18	44

1/1 2/19 3/136 4/137   (4 wkts dec.) 151   1/37 2/135 3/187 4/216 5/231   285
6/245 7/253 8/274 9/284

Bowling: *First Innings*—McDermott 10–2–36–2; Hughes 15–3–63–0; M. E. Waugh 6–0–17–0; May 10–2–23–1; Warne 6–3–5–1. *Second Innings*—McDermott 14–0–72–0; Hughes 11–2–32–1; M. E. Waugh 1–0–3–0; May 23.3–5–75–4; Warne 28–6–77–4.

Umpires: K. E. Palmer and D. R. Shepherd.

SUSSEX v AUSTRALIANS

At Hove, May 13, 14, 15. Drawn. Toss: Sussex. County debut: C. W. J. Athey.

Batsmen on both sides made the most of another flat Hove pitch. Sussex's early progress was slow but Athey determinedly saw off the opening attack in his first game for his third county. Greenfield and Alan Wells moved up a gear, though Wells spent more than an hour in the 70s before falling for 93. After a rapid 59 from Salisbury Sussex reached a healthy 353. The crowd were then treated to some dazzling strokeplay from the two youngsters contending for an opener's place in the Australian team, Slater and Hayden, before Martyn scored a splendid 136, keeping the tempo up to four an over. Martyn added 205 with Waugh, who hit some superb cover drives, and both accelerated gracefully to centuries on the third morning. The tourists declared 137 ahead, but rain after tea the previous day meant they had 48 overs to bowl Sussex out. Although May found some slow turn, Sussex were never in danger. Border went to the press box to make peace with the media after rounding on a local TV reporter who had asked for an interview before the match.

Close of play: First day, Sussex 353; Second day, Australians 306-3 (D. R. Martyn 78*, S. R. Waugh 41*).

Sussex

N. J. Lenham c Healy b McDermott	11	– b May	19
C. W. J. Athey c Hayden b Julian	33	– c Martyn b May	27
K. Greenfield c Border b Julian	55	– st Healy b May	3
*A. P. Wells c Martyn b McDermott	93		
M. P. Speight lbw b Julian	0	– (4) c Healy b Reiffel	0
C. M. Wells c Hayden b Hughes	6	– (5) not out	4
†P. Moores c Healy b Hughes	22	– (6) not out	5
I. D. K. Salisbury c Reiffel b Julian	59		
A. C. S. Pigott c Reiffel b Julian	5		
A. N. Jones b Waugh	20		
E. S. H. Giddins not out	0		
B 4, l-b 12, w 3, n-b 30	49	B 6, l-b 10, n-b 18	34

1/22 2/76 3/209 4/209 5/220   353   1/60 2/75   (4 wkts) 92
6/244 7/295 8/322 9/350   3/78 4/78

Bowling: *First Innings*—McDermott 23-3-89-2; Hughes 16-3-58-2; Reiffel 21-2-58-0; Julian 22-5-63-5; May 17-3-53-0; Waugh 2.1-0-16-1. *Second Innings*—McDermott 5-1-16-0; Julian 5-0-13-0; Hughes 10-3-19-0; May 14-6-19-3; Reiffel 5-1-9-1.

Australians

M. J. Slater b Giddins	73	B. P. Julian not out	16
M. L. Hayden st Moores b Salisbury	66		
D. R. Martyn c Giddins b C. M. Wells	136	B 1, l-b 7, w 2, n-b 8	18
*A. R. Border run out	33		
S. R. Waugh st Moores b C. M. Wells	124	1/115 2/174 3/237 (5 wkts dec.) 490
†I. A. Healy not out	24	4/442 5/451	

T. B. A. May, M. G. Hughes, C. J. McDermott and P. R. Reiffel did not bat.

Bowling: Jones 18-1-90-0; Giddins 21-3-95-1; Pigott 25-4-73-0; Salisbury 33-1-116-1; C. M. Wells 18-0-67-2; Athey 8-0-41-0.

Umpires: H. D. Bird and M. J. Kitchen.

†NORTHAMPTONSHIRE v AUSTRALIANS

At Northampton, May 16. Northamptonshire won on scoring-rate. Toss: Northamptonshire.

A batsman's match ended in a hollow victory for Northamptonshire. The Australians, chasing a revised target of 264 in 53 overs after a shower, were left stranded 11 runs short of 194, the total required to exceed Northamptonshire's scoring-rate in the 39 overs possible before the weather intervened for the final time. Having lost only two wickets, and with Taylor well established, they were in a very strong position. Fordham shone for the county, hitting nine fours in a fluent innings, and his partnership of 136 in 28 overs with Bailey provided Lamb with a platform from which to launch a furious assault, 37 runs in 28 balls. But the Australians looked to be pacing their reply to perfection, with Mark Waugh's polished strokeplay bringing him a six and eight fours in 86 deliveries.

Northamptonshire

A. Fordham lbw b McDermott	101
N. A. Felton c M. E. Waugh b Reiffel	32
R. J. Bailey not out	82
*A. J. Lamb not out	37
L-b 12, w 5, n-b 4	21

1/67 2/203   (2 wkts, 55 overs) 273

M. B. Loye, D. J. Capel, A. L. Penberthy, †D. Ripley, J. P. Taylor, A. Walker and N. G. B. Cook did not bat.

Bowling: McDermott 11-1-48-1; Hughes 9-0-52-0; S. R. Waugh 4-0-20-0; Reiffel 10-1-35-1; May 11-0-49-0; Border 7-0-40-0; M. E. Waugh 3-0-17-0.

Australians

M. A. Taylor not out 89
M. E. Waugh b Cook 74
D. C. Boon st Ripley b Bailey 12
*A. R. Border not out 3
　　　　B 3, l-b 1, w 1 5

1/144 2/171　　　(2 wkts, 39 overs) 183

S. R. Waugh, D. R. Martyn, †I. A. Healy, T. B. A. May, M. G. Hughes, P. R. Reiffel and
C. J. McDermott did not bat.

Bowling: Taylor 7–0–26–0; Walker 5–0–17–0; Penberthy 6–0–32–0; Capel 5–0–35–0;
Cook 8–0–34–1; Bailey 8–1–35–1.

Umpires: J. H. Harris and A. A. Jones.

†ENGLAND v AUSTRALIA

First Texaco Trophy Match

At Manchester, May 19. Australia won by four runs. Toss: England. International debuts:
A. R. Caddick, G. P. Thorpe; M. L. Hayden.
　The first serious contest of the tour ended in a tense finish and a win for Australia off the
penultimate ball. England had needed seven from the final over but the last pair could
manage only two before finishing up at the same end. Australia's victory was founded on
the bowling of McDermott, who found form far above anything he had shown in the
preliminaries, and Steve Waugh, whose shrewd changes of pace in the closing stages upset
England's calculations. Taylor and Mark Waugh dominated the morning session but
Australia lost ground to four catches in quick succession at square leg. England began
raggedly themselves but recovered with a stand of 127 between Hick and Fairbrother. An
intelligent innings by Thorpe in difficult circumstances was not quite enough. Cork,
Lathwell and Ramprakash (brought in as cover for Fairbrother) were the England squad
members left out of the team; Australia had unexpectedly played Hayden ahead of Martyn.
Ted Dexter, the chairman of England's selectors, was obliged to watch the game from a
hospital bed after back surgery.
　Man of the Match: C. J. McDermott.　　*Attendance:* 20,613; *receipts* £461,400.

Australia

M. L. Hayden c Stewart b Lewis 29
M. A. Taylor c Fairbrother b Illingworth 79
M. E. Waugh c Fairbrother b Jarvis . . . 56
D. C. Boon c Fairbrother b Illingworth . 2
*A. R. Border c Lewis b Illingworth . . . 4
S. R. Waugh c and b Lewis 27
†I. A. Healy c Thorpe b Caddick 20
M. G. Hughes b Lewis 20
P. R. Reiffel run out 2

C. J. McDermott not out 3
T. B. A. May not out 1
　　　　B 1, l-b 8, w 2, n-b 4 15

1/60 (1) 2/168 (3)　　　(9 wkts, 55 overs) 258
3/171 (4) 4/178 (2)
5/186 (5) 6/219 (7)
7/237 (6) 8/254 (9)
9/255 (8)

Bowling: Caddick 11–1–50–1; Pringle 10–3–36–0; Lewis 11–1–54–3; Jarvis 11–0–55–1;
Illingworth 11–0–48–3; Hick 1–0–6–0.

England

*G. A. Gooch c M. E. Waugh
　　　　　　　　b McDermott . 4
†A. J. Stewart b Hughes 22
R. A. Smith c and b McDermott 9
G. A. Hick b Reiffel 85
N. H. Fairbrother c Reiffel
　　　　　　　　b S. R. Waugh . 59
G. P. Thorpe c Taylor b McDermott . . . 31
C. C. Lewis run out 4
D. R. Pringle c Taylor b S. R. Waugh . 6

R. K. Illingworth run out 12
P. W. Jarvis c Reiffel b S. R. Waugh . . 2
A. R. Caddick not out 1
　　　　L-b 8, w 9, n-b 2 19

1/11 (1) 2/38 (2)　　　(54.5 overs) 254
3/44 (3) 4/171 (5)
5/194 (4) 6/211 (7)
7/227 (8) 8/240 (6)
9/247 (10) 10/254 (9)

Bowling: McDermott 11–2–38–3; Hughes 9.5–1–40–1; May 11–2–40–0; Reiffel 11–0–63–1; M. E. Waugh 2–0–12–0; S. R. Waugh 10–0–53–3.

Umpires: B. J. Meyer and D. R. Shepherd.
Referee: Mansur Ali Khan, formerly Nawab of Pataudi (India).

†ENGLAND v AUSTRALIA

Second Texaco Trophy Match

At Birmingham, May 21. Australia won by six wickets. Toss: Australia.

Australia won the game and thus the series despite being totally overwhelmed by one of the greatest innings ever seen in limited-overs cricket. Smith scored 167 not out, the highest score for England in a one-day international, and the fifth-highest in all. England, forced to bat on a damp morning, struggled in the early stages. But Smith, theoretically out of form, was always aggressive in intent and after lunch he became simply ferocious – he moved from 100 to 150 in 20 balls and scored 76 from his last 30; McDermott was the only bowler to escape the carnage. Smith hit 17 fours and three sixes in 163 balls. It was an innings of physical strength allied to magnificent technique and was still the talk of the ground when the Australians batted. It dawned only slowly on the fielders and spectators that such a performance might not be enough. England's all-seam attack looked inadequate and the fielding ragged. The bowlers made no headway against a stand of 168 between Mark Waugh, who matched Smith in inventiveness if not power, and Border. Australia eased to victory with nine balls remaining.

Man of the Match: R. A. Smith.   *Attendance*: 18,279; *receipts* £390,500.

England

*G. A. Gooch c Healy b McDermott	. .	17
†A. J. Stewart b McDermott	. . . .	0
R. A. Smith not out	. . . .	167
G. A. Hick c Healy b Reiffel	. . . .	2
N. H. Fairbrother c Taylor b S. R. Waugh		23
G. P. Thorpe c Border b McDermott	. .	36

C. C. Lewis not out 13

B 2, l-b 4, w 2, n-b 11 19

1/3 (2) 2/40 (1)   (5 wkts, 55 overs) 277
3/55 (4) 4/105 (5)
5/247 (6)

D. R. Pringle, D. G. Cork, P. W. Jarvis and A. R. Caddick did not bat.

Bowling: McDermott 11–1–29–3; Hughes 11–2–51–0; Reiffel 11–1–70–1; May 11–0–45–0; S. R. Waugh 8–0–55–1; M. E. Waugh 3–0–21–0.

Australia

M. A. Taylor b Lewis	. . . .	26
M. L. Hayden b Jarvis	. . . .	14
M. E. Waugh c Fairbrother b Lewis	. . .	113
D. C. Boon c Stewart b Pringle	. . . . . .	21
*A. R. Border not out	. . . .	86

S. R. Waugh not out 6

L-b 5, w 3, n-b 6 14

1/28 (2) 2/55 (1)   (4 wkts, 53.3 overs) 280
3/95 (4) 4/263 (3)

†I. A. Healy, M. G. Hughes, C. J. McDermott, P. R. Reiffel and T. B. A. May did not bat.

Bowling: Caddick 11–1–43–0; Jarvis 10–1–51–1; Lewis 10.3–0–61–2; Pringle 11–0–63–1; Cork 11–1–57–0.

Umpires: M. J. Kitchen and K. E. Palmer. Referee: Mansur Ali Khan (India).

†ENGLAND v AUSTRALIA

Third Texaco Trophy Match

At Lord's, May 23. Australia won by 19 runs. Toss: England. International debut: B. P. Julian.

England slumped to their seventh successive defeat in a one-day international after apparently being in complete control. Chasing 231, they were 96 without loss and 159 for three. The collapse was partly engineered by the young left-arm fast bowler Julian, who after a rocky start tore through England's middle order, and partly through thoroughly poor batting. Though Gooch made 42, he was sufficiently worried about his form to announce that he would play for the Essex Second XI later in the week for the first time in 19 years. There was some surprise that England, with the series lost, did not give 21-year-old Lathwell an opportunity. Batting conditions were most difficult early on and Australia, without Border, struggled to put a score together; only Martyn looked in real touch. The day was enlivened by one great one-handed catch – taken by Hayden, leaping backwards in the deep, and worthy of a more distinguished victim than Jarvis – and by the Band of the Coldstream Guards playing "Happy Birthday" to Denis Compton on his 75th. The great man stood on a balcony and raised a glass, grinning.

Man of the Match: B. P. Julian.   *Attendance*: 26,099; *receipts* £718,200.

Men of the Series: England – R. A. Smith; Australia – C. J. McDermott.

Australia

M. L. Hayden c Stewart b Caddick	4	†I. A. Healy not out		12
*M. A. Taylor c Stewart b Reeve	57	L-b 4, w 6, n-b 2		11
M. E. Waugh c Stewart b Caddick	14			
D. C. Boon b Illingworth	73	1/12 (1) 2/31 (3) (5 wkts, 55 overs)		230
D. R. Martyn not out	9	3/139 (2) 4/193 (4)		
S. R. Waugh c Gooch b Caddick	8	5/208 (6)		

B. P. Julian, M. G. Hughes, C. J. McDermott and T. B. A. May did not bat.

Bowling: Jarvis 11–1–51–0; Caddick 11–3–39–3; Cork 9–2–24–0; Illingworth 10–0–46–1; Reeve 11–1–50–1; Hick 3–0–17–0.

England

*G. A. Gooch c Hughes b May	42	P. W. Jarvis c Hayden b McDermott		3
†A. J. Stewart c M. E. Waugh b Julian	74	A. R. Caddick not out		2
R. A. Smith st Healy b May	6	L-b 6, w 8, n-b 1		15
G. A. Hick b Julian	7			
N. H. Fairbrother c Boon b Julian	18	1/96 (1) 2/115 (3) (53.1 overs)		211
G. P. Thorpe c Healy b S. R. Waugh	22	3/129 (4) 4/159 (5)		
D. A. Reeve run out	2	5/160 (2) 6/169 (7)		
D. G. Cork b Hughes	11	7/195 (8) 8/201 (6)		
R. K. Illingworth c Healy b Hughes	9	9/208 (10) 10/211 (9)		

Bowling: McDermott 10–1–35–1; Hughes 10.1–0–41–2; Julian 11–1–50–3; May 11–1–36–2; S. R. Waugh 11–0–43–1.

Umpires: H. D. Bird and R. Palmer. Referee: Mansur Ali Khan (India).

SURREY v AUSTRALIANS

At The Oval, May 25, 26, 27. Australians won by 174 runs. Toss: Surrey.

Surrey were completely outplayed by the touring team and a particularly fine leg-side catch off Warne, to dismiss Thorpe, sparked their final collapse for 144 after they had been set to chase 319 in 84 overs. On the first day, Mark Waugh scored an awesome century, his 40th in first-class cricket. He reached 100 in 123 balls and then tore into a Surrey attack missing both Waqar Younis and Martin Bicknell. Fifty-one balls and half a dozen sixes later he had transformed the day and hit a total of 108 in boundaries. He was halted after three hours by Thorpe, who returned a career-best four for 40 with his unregarded seamers. Surrey had little to offer with the bat in their first innings, only Kendrick emerging with much credit. But it was Murphy who saved the follow-on: six runs were needed and he got them with one rustic shot off Warne. Zoehrer became the second Australian, after A. T. W. Grout, to claim eight victims in an innings, with six catches and two stumpings in Surrey's second innings, though it was no longer a world record as Tahir Rashid of Habib Bank had caught eight and stumped one six months earlier.

Close of play: First day, Surrey 19-0 (D. J. Bicknell 7*, M. A. Lynch 8*); Second day, Australians 152-2 (M. A. Taylor 67*).

Australians

M. L. Hayden c Kersey b Butcher	36	– (2) b Kendrick	33
M. J. Slater c Lynch b Benjamin	5	– (1) c Lynch b Murphy	50
M. A. Taylor c Brown b Benjamin	7	– c Bicknell b Murphy	80
M. E. Waugh lbw b Thorpe	178		
D. R. Martyn c Brown b Kendrick	84		
†T. J. Zoehrer c sub b Thorpe	1	– (4) c Thorpe b Murphy	4
*A. R. Border c and b Kendrick	28		
B. P. Julian c Lynch b Thorpe	27	– (5) not out	0
P. R. Reiffel c Lynch b Thorpe	0		
S. K. Warne not out	6		
L-b 5, w 1	6	L-b 4	4

1/17 2/35 3/67 4/304 5/306   (9 wkts dec.) 378   1/44 2/152   (4 wkts dec.) 171
6/329 7/362 8/363 9/378   3/171 4/171

W. J. Holdsworth did not bat.

Bowling: *First Innings*—Benjamin 9-4-19-2; Murphy 20-1-66-0; Butcher 16-2-73-1; Kendrick 25-6-90-2; Boiling 12-1-85-0; Thorpe 13.3-4-40-4. *Second Innings*—Murphy 17.4-0-48-3; Thorpe 8-1-41-0; Kendrick 19-4-60-1; Boiling 4-1-18-0.

Surrey

D. J. Bicknell c Waugh b Holdsworth	15	– c Zoehrer b Julian	8
*M. A. Lynch b Warne	48	– c Zoehrer b Reiffel	22
G. P. Thorpe c Warne b Julian	3	– c Zoehrer b Warne	23
A. D. Brown c Border b Reiffel	35	– c Border b Reiffel	1
D. M. Ward c Martyn b Reiffel	9	– c Zoehrer b Holdsworth	28
M. A. Butcher lbw b Warne	4	– (7) st Zoehrer b Warne	10
†G. J. Kersey lbw b Warne	1	– (6) c Zoehrer b Julian	17
N. M. Kendrick c Taylor b Waugh	41	– c Zoehrer b Julian	5
J. Boiling run out	19	– not out	5
J. E. Benjamin c Zoehrer b Holdsworth	4	– st Zoehrer b Warne	2
A. J. Murphy not out	24	– c Holdsworth b Warne	5
B 2, l-b 14, w 8, n-b 4	28	B 2, l-b 4, w 2, n-b 10	18

1/31 2/37 3/120 4/122 5/127   231   1/8 2/42 3/45 4/73 5/99   144
6/135 7/135 8/196 9/201   6/116 7/130 8/131 9/138

Bowling: *First Innings*—Holdsworth 17-2-81-2; Julian 15-4-31-1; Warne 23.5-8-68-3; Reiffel 10-3-22-2; Waugh 5-2-13-1. *Second Innings*—Julian 12-4-30-3; Holdsworth 10-2-43-1; Reiffel 11-0-27-2; Warne 19.1-6-38-4.

Umpires: V. A. Holder and N. T. Plews.

LEICESTERSHIRE v AUSTRALIANS

At Leicester, May 29, 30, 31. Australians won by 97 runs. Toss: Australians.

The tourists might have wished for a more even contest in their last match before the First Test. Left-armer Mullally, born in England but formerly with Western Australia and Victoria, gave away only 12 runs in his opening nine overs and removed Hayden with an out-swinger. However, he conceded 14 in one over to Slater when he went around the wicket. This seemed to act as a springboard for Slater, who reached 91 in the first innings and added 50 in the second, securing his Test place at Hayden's expense. Together with Boon, completing an almost effortless third century of the tour, Slater put on 214 in four hours. Showers restricted the second day to 66 overs, but there was time enough for Hughes to confirm his fitness, and for May to press his own Test claims, as Leicestershire surrendered six wickets for 66. The county then agreed to declare 155 behind, and the Australians set them a target of 244 in 72 overs. The spinners were the dominant figures again: Warne took his 100th first-class wicket in his 32nd match; May finished the innings with three in five balls for the tourists' fourth win in five first-class matches.

Close of play: First day, Australians 323-3 (A. R. Border 42*, S. R. Waugh 44*); Second day, Leicestershire 168-7 (P. N. Hepworth 37*, G. J. Parsons 3*).

Australians

M. L. Hayden c Nixon b Mullally	2	– c Hepworth b Pierson	15
M. J. Slater c and b Wells	91	– (3) not out	50
D. C. Boon c Parsons b Wells	123		
*A. R. Border not out	42		
S. R. Waugh not out	44		
†I. A. Healy (did not bat)		– (2) c Mullally b Parsons	4
B. P. Julian (did not bat)		– (4) c Robinson b Pierson	5
S. K. Warne (did not bat)		– (5) st Nixon b Wells	6
M. G. Hughes (did not bat)		– (6) not out	5
B 6, l-b 3, w 8, n-b 4	21	L-b 3	3

1/2 2/216 3/227   (3 wkts dec.) 323   1/9 2/54   (4 wkts dec.) 88
                                              3/62 4/70

T. B. A. May and C. J. McDermott did not bat.

Bowling: *First Innings*—Mullally 26–5–65–1; Parsons 28–6–64–0; Wells 25–7–70–2; Pierson 23–6–82–0; Hepworth 5–0–33–0. *Second Innings*—Parsons 9–3–12–1; Wells 5–0–28–1; Pierson 7.5–0–45–2.

Leicestershire

T. J. Boon lbw b May	32	– lbw b McDermott	11
*N. E. Briers b Julian	24	– c Boon b McDermott	12
J. J. Whitaker c Slater b May	18	– c McDermott b Julian	18
P. E. Robinson c Healy b Warne	11	– b Warne	31
B. F. Smith b Warne	0	– lbw b Warne	31
P. N. Hepworth not out	37	– run out	2
V. J. Wells c Healy b May	17	– b Warne	9
†P. A. Nixon c Hayden b Warne	5	– c Waugh b May	21
G. J. Parsons not out	3	– b May	5
A. D. Mullally (did not bat)		– c Julian b May	0
A. R. K. Pierson (did not bat)		– not out	0
B 2, l-b 8, w 1, n-b 10	21	N-b 6	6

1/59 2/83 3/104 4/104 5/104   (7 wkts dec.) 168   1/19 2/26 3/56 4/84 5/92   146
6/136 7/149   6/111 7/128 8/146 9/146

Bowling: *First Innings*—McDermott 11–1–27–0; Hughes 9–2–19–0; May 24–7–62–3; Julian 10–2–19–1; Warne 12–5–31–3. *Second Innings*—McDermott 14–4–38–2; Hughes 8–1–21–0; Julian 6–0–21–1; May 13.3–3–39–3; Warne 13–7–27–3.

Umpires: B. Leadbeater and G. Sharp.

ENGLAND v AUSTRALIA

First Cornhill Test

At Manchester, June 3, 4, 5, 6, 7. Australia won by 179 runs. Toss: England. Test debuts: A. R. Caddick, P. M. Such; B. P. Julian, M. J. Slater.

An enthralling match of splendid individual achievements was won by Australia with 9.4 overs to spare. A rarity among modern Tests in England, it was shaped by slow bowling and finally decided by leg-spin. Warne, the 23-year-old Victorian, returned match figures of eight for 137, the best in England by an Australian leg-spinner since W. J. O'Reilly took ten for 122 at Leeds in 1938. One particular delivery from Warne set the tone for the series. His first ball in an Ashes contest pitched outside leg stump and hit the top of Gatting's off stump. Gatting looked understandably bewildered as he dragged himself off the field. Thereafter only Gooch played Warne with conviction: never, perhaps, has one delivery cast so long a shadow over a game, or a series. Warne also produced a stunning catch at backward square leg to dismiss Caddick in the tense final stages as England tried to salvage a draw. He was rightly named Man of the Match.

No time was lost in the Test but a succession of wet days beforehand had hampered the preparations of the groundstaff. The soft pitch was not planned but it allowed the spinners to hold unexpected sway on the first two days, and improved the cricket. It ought to have given England the advantage since they fielded two spinners to Australia's one. There was more confusion, though, about England's seam attack. Alan Igglesden was prevented from adding to his solitary cap when he sustained a groin strain in the indoor school the day before the game. DeFreitas was summoned from Lancashire's match and then picked ahead of Ilott, who had been in the original 12. DeFreitas did little to justify his selection.

Such, however, found himself bowling before Thursday lunchtime and shared the first day's honours with Taylor – who made another impressive start to an Ashes series – and Slater. The opening pair, both from the New South Wales town of Wagga Wagga, began with a stand of 128 but then Australia lost three wickets for 11 in the final hour, including Steve Waugh, who was bowled off stump trying to drive – a classic off-spinner's dismissal. On the second day, Such moved on to take six for 67 and his cool and control compared favourably with the palpable lack of confidence shown by Tufnell.

With Australia out for 289 and Gooch and Atherton resuming their sequence of reassuring opening partnerships England briefly looked like a team ready to compete for the Ashes. Then Atherton was out, Warne came on for the 28th over, bowled what became known as The Ball from Hell and the series really began. Gatting's departure was followed by that of Smith, caught at slip, and Gooch, who hit a full-toss to mid-on. By the close England had eight down and Keith Fletcher, the England manager, was saying he had never seen a Test pitch in England turn so much.

The third day began with another flurry of wickets. Such came on to bowl the ninth over of the Australian innings and took his fifth ball had Taylor lbw, sweeping. But Boon then batted with his customary pragmatism while Mark Waugh unleashed a series of glittering strokes. The cricket was more attritional after Waugh was out but Australia were just as sure-footed as The Ball from Hell. Steve Waugh and Healy batted England out of the match with an unbroken stand of 180 in 164 minutes. Healy became the first Australian to make his maiden first-class century in a Test since H. Graham, exactly a hundred years earlier, at Lord's. England looked depressingly pallid in the field during this partnership. With the pitch drying out and the spinners negated by the lack of bounce, there was little attempt to wrest the initiative.

The declaration came at 3 p.m. and England were left to score 512 in a day and a half. Gooch and Atherton again batted securely, with the captain notably authoritative. Then Gatting played with freedom until he was bowled off his pads from the last ball of the day by the indefatigable Hughes, a due reward for his willingness to vary his line and length. Gooch was understandably more circumspect on the final morning and – although Smith was tormented and then bowled by Warne – he reached his 18th Test hundred and England had the chance of a draw. Yet half an hour after lunch Gooch became the fifth cricketer, and the first Englishman, to be dismissed "handled the ball" in a Test as he instinctively flicked out with a glove at a ball dropping on to his stumps. Umpire Bird had no hesitation in giving Gooch out, with the moral victory, if not the wicket, going to Hughes for extracting extra bounce on an increasingly lifeless pitch.

Although the first ten English batsmen all batted for at least half an hour in the second innings, none could match the technical skill and authority of Gooch. For a time Caddick and Such threatened an unlikely stalemate but brilliant catches by Warne and Border completed their downfall. The Australians embarked on some typically committed celebrations. – *Patrick Murphy*.

Man of the Match: S. K. Warne.   *Attendance:* 55,788; *receipts* £812,100.

Close of play: First day, Australia 242-5 (A. R. Border 9*, I. A. Healy 6*); Second day, England 202-8 (A. R. Caddick 6*, P. M. Such 9*); Third day, Australia 231-3 (D. C. Boon 85*, A. R. Border 29*); Fourth day, England 133-2 (G. A. Gooch 82*).

Australia

M. A. Taylor c and b Such	124	– (2) lbw b Such	9
M. J. Slater c Stewart b DeFreitas	58	– (1) c Caddick b Such	27
D. C. Boon c Lewis b Such	21	– c Gatting b DeFreitas	93
M. E. Waugh c and b Tufnell	6	– b Tufnell	64
*A. R. Border st Stewart b Such	17	– c and b Caddick	31
S. R. Waugh b Such	3	– not out	78
†I. A. Healy c Such b Tufnell	12	– not out	102
B. P. Julian c Gatting b Such	0		
M. G. Hughes c DeFreitas b Such	2		
S. K. Warne not out	15		
C. J. McDermott run out	8		
B 8, l-b 8, n-b 7	23	B 6, l-b 14, w 8	28

1/128 (2) 2/183 (3) 3/221 (4) 4/225 (1)   289   1/23 (2) 2/46 (1)   (5 wkts dec.) 432
5/232 (6) 6/260 (5) 7/264 (8)   3/155 (4) 4/234 (5)
8/266 (9) 9/267 (10) 10/289 (11)   5/252 (3)

Bowling: *First Innings*—Caddick 15–4–38–0; DeFreitas 23–8–46–1; Lewis 13–2–44–0; Such 33.3–9–67–6; Tufnell 28–5–78–2. *Second Innings*—Caddick 20–3–79–1; DeFreitas 24–1–80–1; Such 31–6–78–2; Tufnell 37–4–112–1; Hick 9–1–20–0; Lewis 9–0–43–0.

England

*G. A. Gooch c Julian b Warne	65	– handled the ball	133
M. A. Atherton c Healy b Hughes	19	– c Taylor b Warne	25
M. W. Gatting b Warne	4	– b Hughes	23
R. A. Smith c Taylor b Warne	4	– b Warne	18
G. A. Hick c Border b Hughes	34	– c Healy b Hughes	22
†A. J. Stewart b Julian	27	– c Healy b Warne	11
C. C. Lewis c Boon b Hughes	9	– c Taylor b Warne	43
P. A. J. DeFreitas lbw b Julian	5	– lbw b Julian	7
A. R. Caddick c Healy b Warne	7	– c Warne b Hughes	25
P. M. Such not out	14	– c Border b Hughes	9
P. C. R. Tufnell c Healy b Hughes	1	– not out	0
B 6, l-b 10, n-b 5	21	L-b 11, w 1, n-b 4	16

1/71 (2) 2/80 (3) 3/84 (4) 4/123 (1)   210   1/73 (2) 2/133 (3) 3/171 (4)   332
5/148 (5) 6/168 (7) 7/178 (8)   4/223 (1) 5/230 (5) 6/238 (6)
8/183 (6) 9/203 (9) 10/210 (11)   7/260 (8) 8/299 (7)
                                 9/331 (9) 10/332 (10)

Bowling: *First Innings*—McDermott 18–2–50–0; Hughes 20.5–5–59–4; Julian 11–2–30–2; Warne 24–10–51–4; Border 1–0–4–0. *Second Innings*—McDermott 30–9–76–0; Hughes 27.2–4–92–4; Warne 49–26–86–4; Julian 14–1–67–1.

Umpires: H. D. Bird and K. E. Palmer. Referee: Mansur Ali Khan (India).

WARWICKSHIRE v AUSTRALIANS

At Birmingham, June 9, 10, 11. Drawn. Toss: Australians.

Rain, which disrupted the first two days and washed out the third, robbed the tourists of any chance of their fifth victory of the ten they needed to win the jackpot of £50,000 in the Tetley Bitter Challenge. On the first day Slater passed fifty for the seventh time in ten first-class innings in England, while Border returned to form, scoring 66. Next day Martyn advanced to his second hundred of the tour before Border declared. Another player anxious to recover his form was Warwickshire's South African pace bowler, Donald, who had taken only eight wickets for 322 in four Championship games. But he was heavily punished for 67 from ten overs. Moles top-scored with 49 as Warwickshire struggled to 184 for eight against May and the tourists' second-string seamers. The wicket-keeper, Zoehrer, removed his pads to take the wicket of Penney in his first over of the summer.

Close of play: First day, Australians 263-4 (D. R. Martyn 86*, T. J. Zoehrer 3*); Second day, Warwickshire 184-8 (G. C. Small 7*, A. A. Donald 5*).

Australians

M. L. Hayden lbw b Munton	10	I. A. Healy not out	1
M. J. Slater c Twose b Reeve	64		
M. E. Waugh b Small	8	B 1, l-b 15, w 1, n-b 10	27
D. R. Martyn c Donald b Smith	116		
*A. R. Border b Smith	66	1/36 2/53 3/108 (7 wkts dec.) 317	
†T. J. Zoehrer c Twose b Smith	20	4/255 5/285	
B. P. Julian c Ostler b Reeve	5	6/293 7/317	

P. R. Reiffel, T. B. A. May and W. J. Holdsworth did not bat.

Bowling: Donald 10–0–67–0; Small 13–3–40–1; Munton 20–4–57–1; Reeve 23–5–55–2; Smith 15.5–4–55–3; Twose 8–3–27–0.

Warwickshire

A. J. Moles c Border b Reiffel	49	G. C. Small not out	7
J. D. Ratcliffe c Zoehrer b Holdsworth	2	A. A. Donald not out	5
R. G. Twose c Waugh b Julian	29		
D. P. Ostler b May	5	B 8, l-b 11, w 1, n-b 26	46
*D. A. Reeve c Slater b May	23		
T. L. Penney lbw b Zoehrer	11	1/12 2/84 3/107 (8 wkts) 184	
†M. Burns run out	7	4/125 5/149 6/162	
N. M. K. Smith c Healy b May	0	7/162 8/162	

T. A. Munton did not bat.

Bowling: Holdsworth 9–0–34–1; Reiffel 14–8–30–1; Julian 11–2–40–1; May 23.3–5–58–3; Zoehrer 4–3–3–1.

Umpires: J. C. Balderstone and G. I. Burgess.

GLOUCESTERSHIRE v AUSTRALIANS

At Bristol, June 12, 13, 14. Drawn. Toss: Australians.

The biggest crowds at Nevil Road for some years enjoyed a relaxed couple of days, enhanced by a barrage of boundaries by Hughes into the sponsors' tents and on to the ice-cream van. The final day was then washed out with Australia well-placed for victory. At the start, Broad renewed local speculation about a possible Test recall with a competent 80. However, Hughes and Warne quickly worked through the other batsmen though McDermott, as in the Test, failed to take a wicket. The Australians then rattled up 400 in less than 90 overs with only ten batsmen: Healy had cracked his thumb in the field. Gloucestershire's attack was limited and even Walsh lacked his usual zest, but de la Pena's four wickets, the best return of his short career, were a bonus.

Close of play: First day, Gloucestershire 183-7 (R. C. Russell 8*, A. M. Smith 0*); Second day, Australians 400.

Gloucestershire

B. C. Broad c Hayden b Warne	80	A. M. Smith b Hughes	3
G. D. Hodgson lbw b Hughes	16	J. M. de la Pena b Hughes	0
M. W. Alleyne c Healy b Hughes	2	C. A. Walsh not out	4
T. H. C. Hancock c Hayden b Warne	37		
*A. J. Wright c Taylor b Warne	23	B 3, l-b 8, n-b 6	17
R. I. Dawson b Warne	1		
†R. C. Russell c Martyn b Warne	26	1/57 2/59 3/134 4/171 5/172	211
R. C. Williams b May	2	6/173 7/182 8/204 9/204	

Bowling: McDermott 18–4–45–0; Hughes 15–5–27–4; S. R. Waugh 5–0–24–0; Warne 28–9–61–5; M. E. Waugh 5–0–19–0; May 14–5–24–1.

Australians

M. L. Hayden c Hodgson b Walsh	57	C. J. McDermott b Alleyne	11
*M. A. Taylor lbw b de la Pena	12	T. B. A. May lbw b Alleyne	4
D. C. Boon c Smith b de la Pena	70	†I. A. Healy absent injured	
M. E. Waugh c Wright b Walsh	66		
D. R. Martyn c Williams b de la Pena	51	L-b 10, n-b 35	45
S. R. Waugh c Hodgson b de la Pena	21		—
M. G. Hughes not out	46		400
S. K. Warne c Russell b Williams	17		

1/28 2/149 3/170 4/270 5/311
6/319 7/357 8/370 9/400

Bowling: Walsh 15–2–50–2; de la Pena 20–2–77–4; Williams 24–2–115–1; Smith 19–1–85–0; Alleyne 8.2–0–55–2; Hancock 2–1–8–0.

Umpires: N. T. Plews and G. A. Stickley.

ENGLAND v AUSTRALIA

Second Cornhill Test

At Lord's, June 17, 18, 19, 20, 21. Australia won by an innings and 62 runs. Toss: Australia.

England's lamentable record against Australia at Lord's – their last win was in 1934 – continued as the tourists romped to an innings victory. Of more immediate concern, this was England's seventh consecutive Test defeat, prompting a national outcry on a scale more familiar in football. For Australia the match offered reassuring confirmation of the stamina and resourcefulness of a bowling attack deprived of McDermott. He was rushed to hospital on the second day for an operation on a twisted bowel, which was to rule him out of the rest of the series.

Even before the game began there were signs of desperation in the England camp. After the defeat at Old Trafford Gooch, who had originally been appointed to lead the side for the first three Tests, was, perversely, entrusted with the captaincy for the rest of the series. Yet a throwaway remark by Gooch that he would stand down if performances did not improve only added to the disarray in the dressing-room. By the end of the third day, when another defeat was well-nigh inevitable, speculation about his position was rife. In the end he stayed on.

The England selectors resisted wholesale changes after the First Test, merely replacing DeFreitas with 31-year-old Foster, who thus played in his first Test for four years. He became the fourth South African "rebel" to be rehabilitated, after Gatting, Emburey and Jarvis, and his selection was designed to bring more aggression to the English attack. But on a docile pitch at Foster's least favourite Test ground his recall was not a success. Indeed, he played only one more county game before retiring. Australia replaced Julian with the off-spinner May, a more fruitful decision.

Border won the toss and settled back for a day and a half to watch his batsmen expertly dissect the English attack. But for an aberration by Mark Waugh against Tufnell on 99, the first four Australian batsmen would have completed centuries. Taylor was anonymously effective, Boon was remorseless in the pursuit and achievement of his elusive first Test hundred on English soil, but Slater, in his second Test, was captivating. After an uncertain start against Caddick, his innings of 152, punctuated by a series of immaculate straight drives and 18 fours, dominated the first day. His impromptu jig of delight when he reached his hundred was followed by a beaming smile and a kiss bestowed on the Australian badge on his helmet. This exuberant display of joy enchanted a capacity crowd as much as his fleet-footed strokeplay. It was nearly five hours before he became England's first wicket; by then Australia had 260.

Mark Waugh and then Border sustained the demolition of England's attack with such certainty that, when a ball eventually beat the bat, there was a spontaneous, if somewhat desperate, round of applause from the stands. By 11.45 on the third morning Border was able to declare at 632 for four. For England, Such, though wicketless, had been the most impressive bowler.

On such a bland surface a draw should have been within England's capabilities, but May and Warne conjured more turn than the English spinners and Hughes, refusing to be daunted by the sluggishness of the pitch or the absence of McDermott – Mark Waugh shared the new ball – was not to be denied. Gooch and Gatting were dismissed in unfamiliar and humiliating ways; Gooch was caught at long leg, hooking, while Gatting, supposedly the master of spin, was bowled through the gate by a perfectly flighted off-break. But the most notable dismissal was that of Smith, who became the first victim in an English Test of trial by television. Smith came down the wicket to May, the ball turned down the leg side and Healy whipped off the bails. Umpire Kitchen signalled to the third umpire, Chris Balderstone, at the top of the pavilion and, after 69 seconds, three TV replays and a brief walkie-talkie conversation, raised his finger.

Only Atherton, who batted 253 minutes for 80, had a clear idea of how to blunt the Australian attack as England were bundled out for 205. Atherton was also the cornerstone of England's second innings, remaining for another 242 minutes until a moment of masochistic madness. After Gooch had succumbed to a perfect Warne leg-break, Atherton and a subdued Gatting had added 104 to offer England hope of scrambling a draw. Atherton had reached 97, batting more fluently than in the first innings, when he clipped a ball to mid-wicket off Border. Both batsmen were swayed by the impending landmark as they debated a third run. Atherton set off, stalled and then slipped as Hughes hurled the ball from the boundary; he was agonisingly stranded as Healy removed the bails. If he had been on seven or 87 a third run would not have been contemplated.

Despite resistance from Hick and Stewart on the fifth day England were unable to recover from this self-inflicted wound. The Australian spinners, who shared 15 wickets in the match, patiently removed the middle order. Warne then took the last two wickets in consecutive balls by bowling Such and Tufnell around their legs, a suitably humiliating end for England. For the Australians there was enough time to spruce themselves up before meeting the Queen who, optimistically, had maintained the tradition of visiting Lord's at tea-time on the Monday, even though, with Sunday play, it was now the final day. – Vic Marks.

Man of the Match: M. J. Slater.   *Attendance:* 110,802; *receipts* £2,092,400.

Close of play: First day, Australia 292-2 (D. C. Boon 11*, M. E. Waugh 6*); Second day, Australia 592-4 (D. C. Boon 138*, S. R. Waugh 0*); Third day, England 193-9 (A. R. Caddick 11*, P. C. R. Tufnell 0*); Fourth day, England 237-3 (M. W. Gatting 58*, G. A. Hick 30*).

Australia

M. A. Taylor st Stewart b Tufnell	.....	111	S. R. Waugh not out	 13
M. J. Slater c sub (B. F. Smith)				
b Lewis		.152	L-b 1, w 1, n-b 14	 16
D. C. Boon not out	....	164		
M. E. Waugh b Tufnell	....	99	1/260 (2) 2/277 (1)	(4 wkts dec.) 632
*A. R. Border b Lewis	....	77	3/452 (4) 4/591 (5)	

†I. A. Healy, M. G. Hughes, S. K. Warne, T. B. A. May and C. J. McDermott did not bat.

Bowling: Caddick 38–5–120–0; Foster 30–4–94–0; Such 36–6–90–0; Tufnell 39–3–129–2; Lewis 36–5–151–2; Gooch 9–1–26–0; Hick 8–3–21–0.

England

*G. A. Gooch c May b Hughes	 12	– c Healy b Warne	 29
M. A. Atherton b Warne	 80	– run out	 99
M. W. Gatting b May	 5	– lbw b Warne	 59
R. A. Smith st Healy b May	 22	– c sub (M. L. Hayden) b May	... 5
G. A. Hick c Healy b Hughes	 20	– c Taylor b May	 64
†A. J. Stewart b Hughes	 3	– lbw b May	 62
C. C. Lewis lbw b Warne	 0	– st Healy b May	 0
N. A. Foster c Border b Warne	 16	– c M. E. Waugh b Border	 20
A. R. Caddick c Healy b Hughes	 21	– not out	 0
P. M. Such c Taylor b Warne	 7	– b Warne	 4
P. C. R. Tufnell not out	 2	– b Warne	 0
L-b 8, n-b 9	 17	B 10, l-b 13	 23

1/33 (1) 2/50 (3) 3/84 (4) 4/123 (5) 205	1/71 (1) 2/175 (2) 3/180 (4) 365
5/131 (6) 6/132 (7) 7/167 (8)	4/244 (3) 5/304 (5) 6/312 (7)
8/174 (2) 9/189 (10) 10/205 (9)	7/361 (6) 8/361 (8)
	9/365 (10) 10/365 (11)

Bowling: *First Innings*—Hughes 20–5–52–4; M. E. Waugh 6–1–16–0; S. R. Waugh 4–1–5–0; May 31–12–64–2; Warne 35–12–57–4; Border 3–1–3–0. *Second Innings*—Hughes 31–9–75–0; M. E. Waugh 17–4–55–0; May 51–23–81–4; S. R. Waugh 2–0–13–0; Warne 48.5–17–102–4; Border 16–9–16–1.

Umpires: M. J. Kitchen and D. R. Shepherd. Referee: Mansur Ali Khan (India).

COMBINED UNIVERSITIES v AUSTRALIANS

At Oxford, June 23, 24, 25. Australians won by 166 runs. Toss: Combined Universities. First-class debut: S. F. Shephard.

Slater scored 111, his third century of the summer, out of 188 without loss in the first session – the first Australian tourist to reach 100 before lunch on the opening day of a match since R. M. Cowper in 1964, against T. N. Pearce's XI. When he fell just after the interval, Martyn took over, with an unbeaten 138 out of 200 before the declaration at tea. But next day the headlines were stolen by the maiden century of the Cambridge fresher Russell Cake, playing only because John Crawley was at his graduation ceremony. He hit 19 fours in 237 balls and claimed he could read Warne. Only Hick and Gooch had previously taken first-class hundreds off the Australians. After Gallian declared behind, Taylor set the Universities 324 at an unlikely four an over; Zoehrer, who handed his gloves to Martyn and bowled his leg-breaks ahead of May's off-spin, finished them off with three wickets. This was the first true Combined Universities team to meet a touring party; formerly only students of Oxford and Cambridge were eligible.

Close of play: First day, Combined Universities 107-2 (R. Q. Cake 33*, G. B. T. Lovell 7*); Second day, Australians 178-4 (M. E. Waugh 64*, S. K. Warne 15*).

Australians

M. L. Hayden c Windows b Gallian	98	– (2) c Montgomerie b Macdonald	18
M. J. Slater c Gallian b Pearson	111	– (7) not out	3
D. R. Martyn not out	138		
B. P. Julian b Hallett	1	– (5) c Wileman b Macdonald	18
†T. J. Zoehrer c and b Hallett	4	– (4) c Montgomerie b Macdonald	0
S. K. Warne lbw b Hallett	5	– c Montgomerie b Snape	47
M. E. Waugh not out	29	– (3) b Snape	84
*M. A. Taylor (did not bat)	–	(1) c Shephard b Macdonald	57
B 2	2	L-b 4, w 2	6

1/189 2/260 3/261 4/271 5/283   (5 wkts dec.) 388   1/31 2/107 3/107   (6 wkts dec.) 233
                                                  4/153 5/208 6/233

P. R. Reiffel, T. B. A. May and W. J. Holdsworth did not bat.

Bowling: *First Innings*—Hallett 19–1–85–3; Macdonald 11–1–68–0; Gallian 13–0–62–1; Pearson 20–1–107–1; Snape 11–1–64–0. *Second Innings*—Hallett 7–1–26–0; Macdonald 23–1–80–4; Pearson 5–0–37–0; Gallian 7–0–37–0; Snape 8.5–1–49–2.

Combined Universities

R. R. Montgomerie st Martyn b Warne	52	– b Julian	4
*J. E. R. Gallian lbw b Holdsworth	1	– c Waugh b Julian	16
R. Q. Cake c Julian b Warne	108	– c Waugh b Reiffel	16
G. B. T. Lovell st Zoehrer b Warne	20	– retired hurt	4
J. N. Snape c Waugh b Holdsworth	18	– lbw b Julian	0
M. G. N. Windows b Reiffel	36	– c Julian b Zoehrer	44
J. R. Wileman not out	10	– c Taylor b Warne	48
†S. F. Shephard c Waugh b Julian	5	– lbw b Warne	0
J. C. Hallett (did not bat)	–	not out	6
R. M. Pearson (did not bat)	–	c Taylor b Zoehrer	1
R. H. Macdonald (did not bat)	–	c Waugh b Zoehrer	4
B 7, l-b 12, w 1, n-b 28	48	B 4, n-b 10	14

1/15 2/94 3/154 4/207 5/249   (7 wkts dec.) 298   1/25 2/26 3/30 4/63 5/138   157
6/285 7/298   6/145 7/146 8/151 9/157

In the second innings G. B. T. Lovell retired hurt at 30-2.

THE AUSTRALIAN TOURING PARTY

[*Patrick Eagar*

Back row: E. L. Alcott (*physiotherapist*), S. K. Warne, M. E. Waugh, P. R. Reiffel, M. G. Hughes, B. P. Julian, C. J. McDermott, M. L. Hayden, M. J. Slater, D. R. Martyn, W. J. Holdsworth, M. K. Walsh (*scorer*). *Front row:* T. J. Zoehrer, T. B. A. May, R. B. Simpson (*coach*), M. A. Taylor (*vice-captain*), D. J. Rundle (*manager*), A. R. Border (*captain*), D. C. Boon, S. R. Waugh, I. A. Healy.

THE ENGLAND TEAM FOR THE EDGBASTON TEST

[*Patrick Eagar*

Back row: P. M. Such, N. Hussain, M. P. Bicknell, M. C. Ilott, M. P. Maynard, G. P. Thorpe. *Front row*: J. E. Emburey,
A. J. Stewart, M. A. Atherton (*captain*), G. A. Gooch, R. A. Smith.

Bowling: *First Innings*—Holdsworth 21–5–52–2; Julian 16.5–2–67–1; Reiffel 15–5–43–1; Zoehrer 17–4–53–0; Warne 22–7–45–3; Waugh 5–2–19–0. *Second Innings*—Holdsworth 6–0–19–0; Julian 12–1–57–3; Reiffel 9–1–30–1; Warne 12–6–21–2; Zoehrer 11.3–7–16–3; Taylor 3–0–10–0.

Umpires: D. J. Constant and R. Julian.

HAMPSHIRE v AUSTRALIANS

At Southampton, June 26, 27, 28. Drawn. Toss: Australians.

Three days of unbroken sunshine saw batsmen thrive in front of large crowds. Boon delighted them on the first day with a pugnacious 146, his fifth century of the trip, but the second day belonged to Smith. On the day the England selectors were meeting, with his place in question, he hit 191 off as many balls. Admittedly, Warne was not there to haunt him, but Smith struck 32 fours and four sixes and outscored Middleton by four to one as they shared 233 in 44 overs. He advanced from 32 to 139 on Sunday morning. Nicholas declared 19 behind and the Australians responded with a rapid 271 for seven. Hayden finally added a first-class hundred to his two in the early one-day games and Hughes enlivened the final morning with a brutal unbeaten 61 – seven sixes and two fours in 50 balls. Hampshire were set 291 in 64 overs. Terry and Middleton raised their hopes with 167 in 41 overs but, when Smith went first ball and three more wickets quickly followed, Gower had to bat for the draw.

Close of play: First day, Hampshire 73-2 (T. C. Middleton 16*, R. A. Smith 32*); Second day, Australians 113-3 (M. L. Hayden 59*, D. R. Martyn 6*).

Australians

M. L. Hayden c Nicholas b Shine	85 – c Smith b Connor	115
M. A. Taylor c Maru b Udal	49 – (7) c Aymes b Udal	24
D. C. Boon c Aymes b Maru	146 – (9) not out	0
S. R. Waugh c Middleton b Udal	6 – (3) b Connor	0
*A. R. Border c and b James	41 – (6) c Maru b Connor	3
D. R. Martyn c Middleton b James	6 – (5) b Connor	13
†I. A. Healy lbw b James	3 – (2) lbw b James	16
B. P. Julian not out	26 – (4) c Aymes b Udal	28
P. R. Reiffel not out	8	
M. G. Hughes (did not bat)	– (8) not out	61
L-b 15, n-b 8	23	L-b 3, n-b 8	11

1/91 2/225 3/240 4/319 5/327 (7 wkts dec.) 393 1/37 2/40 3/96 (7 wkts dec.) 271
6/345 7/359 4/122 5/132
  6/187 7/268

T. B. A. May did not bat.

Bowling: *First Innings*—Shine 16–2–81–1; Connor 16–0–55–0; Udal 24–4–123–2; Maru 15–1–62–1; James 17–2–57–3. *Second Innings*—Shine 2.4–0–8–0; Connor 19–3–77–4; James 11.2–3–32–1; Maru 15–3–57–0; Udal 17–3–94–2.

Hampshire

V. P. Terry lbw b Hughes	2 – (2) run out	82
T. C. Middleton c Hayden b Hughes	53 – (1) c Taylor b Hughes	78
D. I. Gower c Martyn b Hughes	8 – not out	23
R. A. Smith c Hughes b May	191 – c Healy b Hughes	0
*M. C. J. Nicholas b May	19 – b Border	12
K. D. James not out	31 – st Healy b May	1
†A. N. Aymes not out	17 – (8) not out	8
S. D. Udal (did not bat)	– (7) lbw b May	0
B 4, l-b 2, w 2, n-b 45	53	B 3, l-b 3, n-b 10	16

1/2 2/28 3/261 4/317 5/322 (5 wkts dec.) 374 1/167 2/178 3/178 (6 wkts) 220
  4/199 5/200 6/200

R. J. Maru, C. A. Connor and K. J. Shine did not bat.

Bowling: *First Innings*—Hughes 18–2–60–3; Julian 19–1–95–0; May 15–2–63–2; Reiffel 15–1–76–0; Waugh 6–1–29–0; Border 7–0–45–0. *Second Innings*—Hughes 14–3–47–2; Julian 7–1–16–0; Reiffel 10–1–45–0; May 18–4–57–2; Border 15–3–49–1.

Umpires: R. A. White and P. Willey
(A. R. Bundy and T. E. Jesty deputised for R. A. White on 2nd day).

ENGLAND v AUSTRALIA

Third Cornhill Test

At Nottingham, July 1, 2, 3, 5, 6. Drawn. Toss: England. Test debuts: M. C. Ilott, M. N. Lathwell, M. J. McCague, G. P. Thorpe.

Rarely before can a draw have been welcomed with such rapture in England, for, after seven consecutive Test defeats, this was not only a moral victory but a victory for morale. After three days, another Australian win looked almost certain. That evening, however, Australia were severely censured by the referee, Clive Lloyd, for their deportment on the field after complaints from both umpires. To what extent that influenced the change that overtook the match is problematic. Australian coach Bob Simpson said not at all: if his players were more subdued after the rest day it was just that England gave them nothing to become excited about.

What could be quantified were inspiring centuries from the patriarch Gooch and the initiate Thorpe, the first England player since F. C. Hayes in 1973 to score a century on Test debut. By Tuesday evening, it was England who felt cheated out of victory. But this was a very different England team. At last recognising the stability they had sought for the stagnation it had become, England dropped Gatting, Hick, Foster, Lewis and Tufnell and brought into the squad Igglesden, McCague, Bicknell, Hussain, Thorpe and Lathwell to go along with the uncapped Ilott, left out at Old Trafford and Lord's – seven men, with a total experience of four Tests, none gained in the previous three years.

The selection of McCague to bowl with the New Zealand emigré Caddick provoked a storm in both hemispheres, for although he was born in Ulster, he grew up in Port Hedland in Australia's dusty north-west, graduated from the Australian Cricket Academy, and played Sheffield Shield cricket and high-class Australian Rules football. But when he was made twelfth man for the 1991-92 Shield final, he became disillusioned with Western Australia. He had already joined Kent, where his Irish birth conveniently made him an English player, and now an England player – a rat joining a sinking ship, said a Sydney newspaper.

His Kent partner Igglesden again had to withdraw through injury, and Bicknell was omitted. That left an attack whose total exposure to Test cricket was the four games Caddick and Such had played between them in this series, but a seven-man batting line-up, with Gooch dropping down to No. 5 so that the 21-year-old Lathwell could open, even though the Gooch-Atherton partnership had been just about England's only success of the first two Tests. Australia brought in Julian for the homeward-bound McDermott.

The pitch was predicted to be a spitting, seaming monster, but neither captain could see it and Gooch had no hesitation in batting first. The early portents were familiar. Smith, relieved to have escaped the purge and elevated to No. 3, made a roistering 86 from 113 balls until Julian, seeking only to stop a powerful drive, caught and bowled him with one outflung hand. Hussain, in his first Test for three years, batted elegantly for a maiden fifty, but Hughes and Warne were too good for the others and England were out early on Friday for 321. Hughes, now Australia's premier bowler, took five wickets in an innings for the first time against England.

McCague immediately entered into the affections of uncertain Englishmen by making the first breach in Australia's innings. But Boon and Mark Waugh ran up their third century partnership in successive Tests, 123 at more than five an over, until the brilliant and enigmatic Waugh again threw away a century, swiping at Such for McCague to take a catch in the outfield. Boon proceeded serenely and smoothly to another century; the elusive was now becoming a habit. Australia faltered slightly, but Border, batting laboriously at No. 8 because of illness, and Warne stretched the lead to 52.

Then came the acrimony. Atherton stood his ground after a low catch by Healy. While the Australians clustered around Atherton, Barrie Meyer seemed to waver for a moment before giving him out. Warne cast a spell over Lathwell and deceived Smith with a beautiful leg-break. That left England 122 for four at the close and in familiar waters. However, on Monday, it took a chastened Australia more than an hour to remove the night-watchman Caddick, who had now batted nearly seven and a half hours in the series, and almost another four to claim the next wicket. Gooch repaid Australia's aggression with 11 boundaries in the first session, and though he was less cavalier later, he achieved his 19th Test century, his 11th as captain and his 8,000th Test run. It was a masterful innings, and yet he could scarcely bring himself to make one celebratory flourish of his bat, for all the statistics would ring hollow if England were to lose another match. Hughes, desperately seeking to get rid of him, bent his back into an especially fast bouncer, strained a groin muscle and was out of the Test match.

Warne eventually turned out Gooch, but Thorpe remained and early on Tuesday reached his century with his patent whipped hook. The Surrey left-hander had batted with a poker-faced stoicism that enabled him to rise above the suspicion that, after four England A tours, he was not good enough for Test level, and the indignation of the public that he was not Gower. He was, at least, verifiably English.

Thorpe and Hussain had put on 113 when Gooch felt able to indulge himself in the rare luxury of a declaration, leaving Australia 371 to win in 77 overs. Slater went before lunch, charging impetuously at Such, and the Australian batsmen suddenly seemed mortal and susceptible to pressure. Australia lost five wickets in a feverish middle session – more than they had lost in the entire second Test – as Caddick began, without notice, to swing the ball disconcertingly. It was 115 for six at tea but Australia need not have feared. Julian, seemingly oblivious to the gravity of Australia's position, stroked his way to 47 and then hoisted Such's arm ball into the stands at long-on to go to his maiden Test fifty. Steve Waugh also rose to Australia's two hours of need. The ball grew soft, the pitch remained firm, the bowlers became tired and, in the finish, Australia averted disaster comfortably.

Before the match, there had been another rash of reports that Gooch would resign his commission if England lost. Asked to verify them afterwards, he answered: "We didn't lose, did we?" In a more emotional man, those words might have caught in his throat; it had been nearly a year since the last Test when he was able to utter them. – Greg Baum.

Man of the Match: G. P. Thorpe. *Attendance:* 48,824; *receipts* £828,100.

Close of play: First day, England 276-6 (N. Hussain 50*, A. R. Caddick 10*); Second day, Australia 262-5 (D. C. Boon 88*, B. P. Julian 5*); Third day, England 122-4 (G. A. Gooch 12*, A. R. Caddick 0*); Fourth day, England 362-6 (G. P. Thorpe 88*, N. Hussain 16*).

England

M. N. Lathwell c Healy b Hughes	20	– lbw b Warne	33
M. A. Atherton c Boon b Warne	11	– c Healy b Hughes	9
R. A. Smith c and b Julian	86	– c Healy b Warne	50
†A. J. Stewart c M. E. Waugh b Warne	25	– lbw b Hughes	6
*G. A. Gooch c Border b Hughes	38	– c Taylor b Warne	120
G. P. Thorpe c S. R. Waugh b Hughes	6	– (7) not out	114
N. Hussain c Boon b Warne	71	– (8) not out	47
A. R. Caddick lbw b Hughes	15	– (6) c Boon b Julian	12
M. J. McCague c M. E. Waugh b Hughes	9		
M. C. Ilott c Taylor b May	6		
P. M. Such not out	0		
B 5, l-b 23, w 4, n-b 2	34	B 11, l-b 11, n-b 9	31
	321	(6 wkts dec.)	**422**

1/28 (1) 2/63 (2) 3/153 (4) 4/159 (3)   321   1/11 (2) 2/100 (3)   (6 wkts dec.) 422
5/174 (6) 6/220 (5) 7/290 (8)   3/109 (1) 4/117 (4)
8/304 (9) 9/321 (7) 10/321 (10)   5/159 (6) 6/309 (5)

Bowling: *First Innings*—Hughes 31-7-92-5; Julian 24-3-84-1; Warne 40-17-74-3; May 14.4-7-31-1; S. R. Waugh 8-4-12-0; M. E. Waugh 1-1-0-0. *Second Innings*—Hughes 22-8-41-2; Julian 33-10-110-1; May 38-6-112-0; Warne 50-21-108-3; S. R. Waugh 1-0-3-0; Border 5-0-11-0; M. E. Waugh 6-3-15-0.

Australia

M. J. Slater lbw b Caddick	40	– (2) b Such	26
M. A. Taylor c Stewart b McCague	28	– (1) c Atherton b Such	28
D. C. Boon b McCague	101	– c Stewart b Caddick	18
M. E. Waugh c McCague b Such	70	– b Caddick	1
S. R. Waugh c Stewart b McCague	13	– (6) not out	47
†I. A. Healy c Thorpe b Ilott	9	– (7) lbw b Ilott	5
B. P. Julian c Stewart b Ilott	5	– (8) not out	56
*A. R. Border c Smith b Such	38	– (5) c Thorpe b Caddick	2
M. G. Hughes b Ilott	17		
S. K. Warne not out	35		
T. B. A. May lbw b McCague	1		
B 4, l-b 8, w 4	16	B 5, l-b 5, w 4, n-b 5	19

1/55 (2) 2/74 (1) 3/197 (4) 4/239 (5)   373   1/46 (2) 2/74 (1)   (6 wkts) 202
5/250 (6) 6/262 (7) 7/284 (3)   3/75 (4) 4/81 (5)
8/311 (9) 9/356 (8) 10/373 (11)   5/93 (3) 6/115 (7)

Bowling: *First Innings*—McCague 32.3–5–121–4; Ilott 34–8–108–3; Such 20–7–51–2; Caddick 22–5–81–1. *Second Innings*—McCague 19–6–58–0; Ilott 18–5–44–1; Such 23–6–58–2; Caddick 16–6–32–3.

Umpires: B. J. Meyer and R. Palmer. Referee: C. H. Lloyd (West Indies).

†MINOR COUNTIES v AUSTRALIANS

At Stone, July 8. Australians won by 58 runs. Toss: Minor Counties.

A crowd of 3,000 saw the Australians bowled out for the first time in eight one-day matches. The tourists were 37 for three – two of the wickets having gone to the former Derbyshire player Newman – after 11 overs, and Taylor took 37 overs to score 53; some late hitting from Julian and Reiffel, 50 not out from 57 balls, boosted their total. Dean, who had gone after Holdsworth's bowling in the Australians' opening game with the England Amateurs, lasted only three balls this time. Cockbain pulled the Minor Counties round from 47 for four, with the highest score of the match, but had little support. Reiffel took five wickets and the match award.

Australians

M. L. Hayden c Humphries b Newman	19	P. R. Reiffel not out	50
M. J. Slater lbw b Newman	1	S. K. Warne c Dean b Smith	8
D. R. Martyn c Humphries b Donohue	14	W. J. Holdsworth c Derrick b Smith	5
S. R. Waugh b Evans	22	L-b 8, w 3	11
*M. A. Taylor c Cockbain b Newman	53		
I. A. Healy c Dean b Evans	16	1/1 2/31 3/37 (54.3 overs) 230
†T. J. Zoehrer c Humphries b Derrick	0	4/77 5/97 6/98
B. P. Julian b Smith	31	7/138 8/199 9/219

Bowling: Newman 10–1–49–3; Donohue 11–0–43–1; Evans 11–1–48–2; Derrick 11–1–41–1; Smith 10.3–0–36–3; Adams 1–0–5–0.

Minor Counties

S. J. Dean b Holdsworth	4	R. A. Evans st Zoehrer b Taylor	5
N. R. Gaywood c Zoehrer b Reiffel	14	K. Donohue lbw b Reiffel	0
N. J. Adams c Zoehrer b Holdsworth	11	A. Smith not out	0
*I. Cockbain c Zoehrer b Reiffel	70		
M. R. Davies c Zoehrer b Reiffel	0	B 5, l-b 10, w 3, n-b 4	22
J. Derrick st Zoehrer b Warne	16		
†M. I. Humphries c Waugh b Holdsworth	21	1/4 2/23 3/47 (48.3 overs) 172
		4/47 5/104 6/141
P. G. Newman lbw b Reiffel	9	7/157 8/170 9/170

Bowling: Holdsworth 11–3–44–3; Reiffel 9.3–3–28–5; Martyn 4–0–33–0; Julian 11–2–23–0; Warne 11–5–22–1; Taylor 2–1–7–1.

Umpires: D. J. Halfyard and S. Kuhlmann.

†IRELAND v AUSTRALIANS

At Castle Avenue, Dublin, July 10. Australians won by 272 runs. Toss: Ireland.

The Australians massacred the Irish bowling and then hurried out their batting for 89. Hayden scored an unbeaten 133 but the most spectacular performance came from Border, who smashed 111 from 54 balls, including eight sixes and ten fours. In one over from the off-spinner Dunlop he hit five successive sixes followed by an anticlimactic two. He put on 153 in 15 overs with Hayden. Holdsworth and Reiffel had reduced Ireland to 52 for five after 23 overs, when the tourists' multi-talented wicket-keeper, Zoehrer, handed the gloves to Healy and finished off the innings with his leg-breaks.

Australians

M. J. Slater b Curry	....	56
M. L. Hayden not out	....	133
M. E. Waugh c Curry b Harrison	.....	26
*A. R. Border c McCrum b Moore	....	111
B 4, l-b 5, n-b 26	....	35

1/155 2/208 3/361   (3 wkts dec.) 361

D. R. Martyn, †T. J. Zoehrer, I. A. Healy, B. P. Julian, P. R. Reiffel, W. J. Holdsworth and T. B. A. May did not bat.

Bowling: McCrum 8-1-46-0; Moore 9.4-0-66-1; Benson 4-0-25-0; Lewis 3-0-36-0; Curry 12-0-75-1; Harrison 12-0-72-1; Dunlop 1-0-32-0.

Ireland

J. D. R. Benson c Julian b Holdsworth	. 1		†R. B. Millar c Holdsworth b Zoehrer	.. 9
M. P. Rea lbw b Holdsworth	 11		P. McCrum not out	 2
*S. J. S. Warke c Zoehrer b Holdsworth	4		E. R. Moore c Healy b Zoehrer	 0
D. A. Lewis b Reiffel	 14			
G. D. Harrison b Zoehrer	 15		B 6, l-b 4, w 1, n-b 6	 17
D. J. Curry c Zoehrer b Reiffel	 0			—
A. R. Dunlop c Waugh b Hayden	 2		1/2 2/19 3/22 4/39 5/41	89
N. G. Doak c Healy b Slater	 14		6/59 7/65 8/85 9/88	

Bowling: Holdsworth 6-2-13-3; Julian 5-1-7-0; May 6-1-14-0; Reiffel 6-1-10-2; Zoehrer 10-4-23-3; Hayden 4-1-5-1; Slater 5-1-7-1.

Umpires: W. B. Arlow and L. P. Hogan.

DERBYSHIRE v AUSTRALIANS

At Derby, July 13, 14, 15. Drawn. Toss: Australians.

Only four sessions were possible but an aggregate of 573 runs from 118 overs accurately reflected some woefully inaccurate bowling from both teams. Cork, riding high after his Benson and Hedges final triumph, hit nine fours in his fifty and Barnett scored his third century in consecutive matches. But Holdsworth, who had conceded 113 in 20 overs on the first day, took four for nought in eight balls, dismissing Griffith, Vandrau and Krikken for the first hat-trick by an Australian tourist in England since T. J. Matthews, who did it twice in the 1912 Triangular Test against South Africa at Old Trafford. Slater batted brilliantly, taking full advantage of the erratic Base and Malcolm to score 133 in 149 balls, striking 19 fours and a six. When 116, he became the first of his party to complete 1,000 runs; he added 107 between lunch and tea and his unbroken partnership of 179 with Mark Waugh came at seven an over.

Close of play: First day, Derbyshire 244-5 (K. J. Barnett 78*, F. A. Griffith 35*); Second day, Australians 268-1 (M. J. Slater 133*, M. E. Waugh 60*).

Derbyshire

*K. J. Barnett c Zoehrer b Reiffel	114	†K. M. Krikken c Zoehrer	
P. D. Bowler c Zoehrer b Reiffel	 30	b Holdsworth .	1
J. E. Morris c Warne b Julian	 2	S. J. Base c Zoehrer b Holdsworth	 7
C. J. Adams c Hayden b Reiffel	 4	D. E. Malcolm not out	 0
T. J. G. O'Gorman c M. E. Waugh			
b Reiffel .	6		
D. G. Cork c Martyn b Holdsworth	.. 56	L-b 14, n-b 30	 44
F. A. Griffith b Holdsworth	 41		
M. J. Vandrau c M. E. Waugh		1/71 2/74 3/91 4/103 5/201	305
b Holdsworth .	0	6/296 7/296 8/296 9/304	

Bowling: Holdsworth 22–3–117–5; Julian 19–3–71–1; Reiffel 21–3–82–4; Warne 10–5–20–0; S. R. Waugh 2–1–1–0.

Australians

M. L. Hayden c Vandrau b Cork	 40
M. J. Slater not out	133
M. E. Waugh not out	 60
L-b 3, w 1, n-b 31	 35

1/89   (1 wkt) 268

D. R. Martyn, *A. R. Border, S. R. Waugh, †T. J. Zoehrer, S. K. Warne, B. P. Julian, P. R. Reiffel and W. J. Holdsworth did not bat.

Bowling: Malcolm 12–0–85–0; Cork 12–0–55–1; Base 10–1–85–0; Vandrau 7–1–27–0; Adams 3–0–13–0.

Umpires: J. H. Harris and A. A. Jones.

DURHAM v AUSTRALIANS

At Durham University, July 17, 18, 19. Drawn. Toss: Durham.

Durham enforced the follow-on for the first time as a first-class county when they dismissed the tourists for 221. It was the only match in which the Australians followed on all summer. Left-arm seamer Brown went into the game with 13 wickets at 46.15, but rediscovered his in-swinger to collect a career-best seven for 70. His performance was matched by Larkins, who struck a magnificent 151, his best for Durham, with all but 31 runs coming in boundaries: 27 fours and two sixes. At their lowest point the tourists were 113 for seven on the second day, when Durham performed with more zest than for a long time. That morning a Sunday newspaper had revealed that Botham was playing his last first-class game. He said he wanted to bow out against his greatest adversaries, but showed little appetite in his bowling on the final rain-affected day, when, with 3,000 in the ground, play began at 2.30 p.m. and Hayden and Boon helped themselves to easy runs. Botham was given one last chance to make his mark; he kept wicket for the final over without pads or gloves.

Close of play: First day, Durham 385-8 dec.; Second day, Australians 62-1 (M. L. Hayden 33*, D. C. Boon 24*).

Durham

G. Fowler c Healy b Julian	 41	†C. W. Scott c and b May	 5
W. Larkins c Taylor b Holdsworth	151	P. J. Berry not out	 24
P. W. G. Parker c Martyn b Julian	... 2	L-b 4, w 1, n-b 6	 11
S. Hutton c Boon b Reiffel	 47		
P. Bainbridge c Border b Holdsworth	.. 3	1/91 2/95 3/232	(8 wkts dec.) 385
I. T. Botham c Julian b Waugh	 32	4/246 5/249 6/296	
A. C. Cummins c Healy b Hayden	 69	7/317 8/385	

*D. A. Graveney and S. J. E. Brown did not bat.

Bowling: Holdsworth 18–1–118–2; Julian 20–5–62–2; Reiffel 21–7–50–1; Waugh 14–3–50–1; May 16–4–63–1; Hayden 7.4–1–24–1; Martyn 6–1–14–0.

Australians

M. A. Taylor b Cummins	10	– (2) c Graveney b Cummins	1
M. L. Hayden c Scott b Brown	7	– (1) not out	151
D. C. Boon c Parker b Brown	27	– c Larkins b Berry	112
S. R. Waugh c Scott b Brown	19	– (5) not out	6
D. R. Martyn c Larkins b Brown	0		
*A. R. Border run out	17		
†I. A. Healy not out	70		
B. P. Julian b Graveney	6		
P. R. Reiffel c Scott b Brown	39		
T. B. A. May lbw b Brown	0		
W. J. Holdsworth c and b Brown	5	– (4) c Parker b Berry	12
B 4, l-b 7, n-b 10	21	B 3, l-b 3, w 3, n-b 4	13

1/8 2/38 3/66 4/66 5/83   221   1/10 2/235 3/251   (3 wkts dec.) 295
6/101 7/113 8/213 9/213

Bowling: First Innings—Cummins 18–4–62–1; Brown 22.4–1–70–7; Botham 6–2–21–0; Graveney 10–6–18–1; Bainbridge 5–0–27–0; Berry 4–0–12–0. *Second Innings*—Cummins 11–3–25–1; Brown 11–3–39–0; Bainbridge 11–1–51–0; Berry 14–1–91–2; Graveney 3–2–6–0; Botham 11–2–45–0; Parker 5–0–32–0.

Umpires: J. H. Hampshire and D. O. Oslear.

ENGLAND v AUSTRALIA

Fourth Cornhill Test

At Leeds, July 22, 23, 24, 25, 26. Australia won by an innings and 148 runs. Toss: Australia. Test debut: M. P. Bicknell.

England lost the Ashes and, within minutes, their captain too when Graham Gooch honoured his promise to resign. In his final, most unwanted, press conference he explained haltingly: "It is the best way forward . . . the team might benefit from fresh ideas, a fresh approach, someone else to look up to." His departure was inevitable. This was his 34th Test in charge and, though ten of those ended in victory, this was England's eighth defeat in their last nine. It was by far the most comprehensive and, six weeks earlier, Gooch had said he would go if there was no improvement.

Ironic, though, that it should all end so meekly at Headingley where, in the two previous summers, Gooch had made defiant, match-winning centuries against West Indies and Pakistan. But this was not the Headingley he knew and loved, the pitch which traditionally transforms the tidy English seam bowler into a monster. To Gooch's unconcealed disgust, that had been dug up after bad reports from umpires Ken Palmer and Mervyn Kitchen the year before. The Test and County Cricket Board denied that they had ordered the excavation but Yorkshire, fearful that another pitch scandal would cost them their place on the Test rota, felt obliged to do it anyway. The new strip, laid in 1988 and used for only one first-class match – in which Essex, without Gooch, lost to Yorkshire by an innings – was an unknown quantity and called for some shrewd guesswork from the captains.

Gooch guessed wrong. Having named an unchanged squad, apart from Igglesden, who was unfit again, England left out off-spinner Such, gave a Test debut to Surrey's Martin Bicknell and went into the match with four pace bowlers who had a combined experience of five Tests. By the end of the first hour – traditionally the bewitching hour at Headingley – it was clear that they were ill-equipped. Through an innings lasting nearly 14 dismaying hours, Bicknell, who trapped Taylor leg before with only his 17th delivery, was the pick of the attack. But that is not saying much. England had an unforeseen problem when, on the second day, McCague went off with an injury later diagnosed as a stress fracture of the back. Their bowling, however, was shorter and shoddier than at any time in the series; long before they adjusted their sights they had been, literally, cut out of the match.

Slater glided to 67 before he got too audacious and played across the line at Ilott. Boon, the rock on which so many Australian innings had been balanced, gratefully took everything on offer. His five-hour 107 was his third century in successive Tests and took his average to 100.80 for the series. It was the second morning before Ilott got him leg before, the only wicket to fall on Gooch's 40th birthday. By then he had shared one punishing stand of 106 with Mark Waugh – their fourth century partnership of the series – and another cold-blooded affair of 105 with Border. The Australian captain's first double-hundred in England was always intended to be psychologically brutal. He was not building an unassailable total so much as grinding down the will to resist. In the course of an innings lasting 569 minutes he equalled Sobers's total of 26 Test centuries – only Gavaskar and Bradman have more – and shared an unbroken stand of 332 with Steve Waugh. This was the Waugh of 1989 when, it seemed, England were destined never to get him out. The pickings, it has to be said, were just as easy. Nearly half his 157 came from boundaries, hit with wrists of flexible steel. Only S. G. Barnes and Bradman had exceeded their partnership for the fifth wicket in Tests – against England in Sydney, 1946-47. Border's declaration came on the third morning when he drove his 200th run and carried on running, fists pummelling the air, into the pavilion.

England simply shrank in awe from a total of 653 for four – the highest ever made at Leeds, but Australia's second over 600 in successive visits. When Lathwell chased Hughes's third ball into Healy's gloves, the pattern was set, the sense of futility rampant. Significantly it was Reiffel, the closest thing the Australians had to an English seamer, who did the damage. He began the series third in line behind McDermott, who departed, and Julian, now injured. Yet he took five for 65 in the first innings and always looked quicker and better able to move the ball than the England quartet. Only Atherton and Gooch, with a fourth-wicket stand of 108, challenged the supremacy of the Australians, as well as the doubtful wisdom of dropping Gooch into the middle order. Atherton was widely believed – rightly so, it transpired a few days later – to be batting for the captaincy. He spoiled a solid half-century by shouldering arms to an in-ducker from Reiffel. But he returned next day, when England followed on 453 behind, to get another 63 and make it a long weekend by spending more than seven hours at the crease.

This time he fell to a stumping decision so hairline that even the TV umpire, Barrie Leadbeater, lingered over his verdict. Then Gooch was stumped, leaving only a few formalities to be completed on the final day. Stewart, formerly the favourite for the captaincy, aimed for an electioneering hundred but fell 22 short. Hughes took some punishment from him but became the seventh Australian to reach 200 Test wickets when he got Caddick. At 2.22 p.m. it was Border, fittingly, who accepted the skier from Ilott which gave him victory, the Ashes, the series and the unwelcome distinction of costing his "old mate" Gooch his job. The crowd at the end was very subdued. But as in other recent Tests at Leeds and elsewhere, the chanting and swearing from the lager-drinkers through the game, especially on the Western Terrace, caused great offence to other spectators. – Peter Johnson.

Man of the Match: A. R. Border. *Attendance:* 70,450; *receipts* £1,018,900.

Close of play: First day, Australians 307-3 (D. C. Boon 102*, A. R. Border 38*); Second day, Australians 613-4 (A. R. Border 175*, S. R. Waugh 144*); Third day, England 195-7 (A. R. Caddick 9*, M. P. Bicknell 7*); Fourth day, England 237-4 (A. J. Stewart 59*, G. P. Thorpe 10*).

Australia

M. J. Slater b Ilott	67	S. R. Waugh not out	157
M. A. Taylor lbw b Bicknell	27	B 8, l-b 22, w 4, n-b 9	43
D. C. Boon lbw b Ilott	107		
M. E. Waugh b Ilott	52	1/86 (2) 2/110 (1)	(4 wkts dec.) 653
*A. R. Border not out	200	3/216 (4) 4/321 (3)	

†I. A. Healy, P. R. Reiffel, M. G. Hughes, S. K. Warne and T. B. A. May did not bat.

Bowling: McCague 28-2-115-0; Ilott 51-11-161-3; Caddick 42-5-138-0; Bicknell 50-8-155-1; Gooch 16-5-40-0; Thorpe 6-1-14-0.

England

M. N. Lathwell c Healy b Hughes	0	– b May	25
M. A. Atherton b Reiffel	55	– st Healy b May	63
R. A. Smith c and b May	23	– lbw b Reiffel	35
†A. J. Stewart c Slater b Reiffel	5	– c M. E. Waugh b Reiffel	78
*G. A. Gooch lbw b Reiffel	59	– st Healy b May	26
G. P. Thorpe c Healy b Reiffel	0	– c Taylor b Reiffel	13
N. Hussain b Reiffel	15	– not out	18
A. R. Caddick c M. E. Waugh b Hughes	9	– lbw b Hughes	12
M. P. Bicknell b Border b Hughes	12	– lbw b Hughes	0
M. J. McCague c Taylor b Warne	0	– b Hughes	11
M. C. Ilott not out	0	– c Border b May	4
B 2, l-b 3, n-b 17	22	B 5, l-b 3, w 1, n-b 11	20
	200		**305**

1/0 (1) 2/43 (3) 3/50 (4) 4/158 (2)   1/60 (1) 2/131 (2) 3/149 (3)
5/158 (6) 6/169 (5) 7/184 (7)   4/202 (5) 5/256 (6) 6/263 (4)
8/195 (8) 9/200 (10) 10/200 (9)   7/279 (8) 8/279 (9)
     9/295 (10) 10/305 (11)

Bowling: *First Innings*—Hughes 15.5-3-47-3; Reiffel 26-6-65-5; May 15-3-33-1; Warne 23-9-43-1; M. E. Waugh 3-0-7-0. *Second Innings*—Hughes 30-10-79-3; Reiffel 28-8-87-3; Warne 40-16-63-0; May 27-6-65-4; M. E. Waugh 2-1-3-0.

Umpires: H. D. Bird and N. T. Plews. Referee: C. H. Lloyd (West Indies).

LANCASHIRE v AUSTRALIANS

At Manchester, July 28, 29, 30. Lancashire won by five wickets. Toss: Australians.

Though they were in the midst of an appalling run of county form, Lancashire achieved only their second win over the Australians since the First World War – the other was in 1972. This was due mainly to a magnificent century from 21-year-old Crawley, the former Cambridge University captain. He opened the innings after Lancashire had been set a generous 227 in 61 overs and batted for three hours with style and a maturity beyond his years to steer Lancashire towards a victory which came with four balls to spare, when acting-captain Watkinson hit May for six. It was the Australians' first first-class defeat of the summer. Taylor, who had started the Ashes series with 124 on this ground eight weeks earlier, hit his third century of the tour and shared hundred stands with Hayden and Martyn on the opening day. But everything that afternoon was eclipsed by a Lancastrian who was not playing: Atherton, who was proclaimed the successor to Gooch as England captain.

Close of play: First day, Australians 282-3 (D. R. Martyn 70*, M. E. Waugh 4*); Second day, Australians 54-2 (M. L. Hayden 28*, T. J. Zoehrer 3*).

Australians

*M. A. Taylor c DeFreitas b Barnett	122	– (9) not out	7
M. L. Hayden lbw b Martin	61	– lbw b Watkinson	79
D. R. Martyn not out	70	– (6) st Hegg b Barnett	38
M. J. Slater lbw b Martin	20	– (1) c Hegg b DeFreitas	3
M. E. Waugh not out	4	– b Barnett	21
S. R. Waugh (did not bat)		– (3) b Martin	17
†T. J. Zoehrer (did not bat)		– (4) c Watkinson b DeFreitas	9
S. K. Warne (did not bat)		– (7) b Barnett	3
M. G. Hughes (did not bat)		– (8) b Barnett	4
T. B. A. May (did not bat)		– not out	0
L-b 1, n-b 4	5	L-b 1, n-b 12	13
	(3 wkts dec.) 282		**(8 wkts dec.) 194**

1/117 2/243 3/275   1/7 2/47 3/65
   4/104 5/160 6/169
   7/187 8/188

W. J. Holdsworth did not bat.

Bowling: *First Innings*—DeFreitas 17-2-41-0; Martin 20-5-63-2; Watkinson 14-1-68-0; Barnett 20-1-87-1; Gallian 9-0-22-0. *Second Innings*—DeFreitas 14-4-46-2; Martin 12-2-36-1; Barnett 24-5-83-4; Watkinson 8-1-28-1.

Lancashire

G. D. Mendis b Warne	29	– c Taylor b Warne	24
J. P. Crawley run out	14	– c Slater b May	109
S. P. Titchard c Taylor b Hughes	2	– run out	11
N. J. Speak c and b Warne	48	– not out	39
G. D. Lloyd b Hughes	44	– run out	6
J. E. R. Gallian not out	42	– c Hayden b May	0
*M. Watkinson c May b Holdsworth	15	– not out	14
P. A. J. DeFreitas c Holdsworth b Warne	1		
†W. K. Hegg not out	26		
B 14, l-b 1, w 4, n-b 10	29	B 15, l-b 4, n-b 6	25

1/24 2/34 3/77 4/144 5/161	(7 wkts dec.) 250	1/81 2/134 3/196 (5 wkts) 228
6/185 7/186		4/206 5/211

P. J. Martin and A. A. Barnett did not bat.

Bowling: *First Innings*—Holdsworth 12–0–58–1; Hughes 13–5–32–2; Warne 32.4–12–54–3; May 15–2–48–0; Zoehrer 8–2–26–0; Taylor 5–0–17–0. *Second Innings*—Hughes 6–1–20–0; Holdsworth 2–0–11–0; M. E. Waugh 2–0–13–0; May 25.2–3–99–2; Warne 24–7–61–1; S. R. Waugh 1–0–5–0.

Umpires: B. Dudleston and M. K. Reed.

GLAMORGAN v AUSTRALIANS

At Neath, July 31, August 1, 2. Drawn. Toss: Australians. First-class debuts: B. S. Phelps, J. R. A. Williams.

Glamorgan's supporters had been demanding a chance for their heroes – persistently ignored by the England selectors – to tackle Australia, and here they had the ideal opportunity to show what they could do. There was plenty to enthuse a large and appreciative crowd, starting with centuries from Boon and Mark Waugh, who hit four successive sixes off the debutant Phelps. Then came Maynard's superb 132 scored before lunch on the second morning. Maynard reached his century from only 73 balls, equalling the fastest hundred of the season against serious bowling and, apart from adopted Pakistanis, became the first Glamorgan player to score a century against the Australians since J. S. Pressdee at Cardiff in 1961. He hit 25 fours and a five. The two captains adopted a positive approach throughout and Border's declaration left Glamorgan to score 287 in a minimum of 64 overs. They were never in contention after losing their openers for eight runs. Despite useful contributions from the middle order Glamorgan required another 118 runs when a second bout of rain caused an early finish with eight overs remaining. However, the spectators were happy: Maynard and Watkin, who missed this match, were both named in the squad for the Fifth Test.

Close of play: First day, Glamorgan 37-2 (A. Dale 15*); Second day, Australians 146-4 (P. R. Reiffel 37*, M. G. Hughes 25*).

Australians

M. J. Slater c and b Thomas	72	– c and b Croft	43
D. C. Boon c Cottey b Bastien	120	– (9) not out	2
M. E. Waugh not out	152	– (8) not out	2
D. R. Martyn b Phelps	38	– (2) c Metson b Thomas	15
†I. A. Healy c Morris b Dale	5	– (3) c Croft b Thomas	4
*A. R. Border not out	14	– (7) b Dale	23
P. R. Reiffel (did not bat)		– (4) c and b Thomas	52
S. K. Warne (did not bat)		– (5) run out	18
M. G. Hughes (did not bat)		– (6) b Dale	71
B 2, l-b 7, n-b 4	13	L-b 5	5

1/158 2/215 3/328 4/355	(4 wkts dec.) 414	1/37 2/45 3/65 (7 wkts dec.) 235
		4/100 5/176
		6/213 7/232

T. B. A. May and W. J. Holdsworth did not bat.

Bowling: *First Innings*—Thomas 20–2–93–1; Bastien 17–0–70–1; Croft 21–2–71–0; Dale 20–3–66–1; Phelps 23–3–105–1. *Second Innings*—Thomas 18–2–95–3; Bastien 10–0–31–0; Dale 9–0–41–2; Croft 12–2–46–1; Phelps 3–0–17–0.

Glamorgan

J. R. A. Williams c Healy b Hughes	0	– c Boon b Hughes 6
*H. Morris c Healy b Hughes.	18	– c Boon b Holdsworth 2
A. Dale c Healy b Holdsworth	25	– c Healy b Warne 31
M. P. Maynard lbw b Waugh	132	– b Holdsworth 36
P. A. Cottey b Warne	68	– c Martyn b Border 38
D. L. Hemp b Warne	40	– b Warne 16
R. D. B. Croft lbw b Warne	17	– not out 11
†C. P. Metson not out	22	– not out 7
S. D. Thomas st Healy b Warne	9	
B 2, l-b 9, w 1, n-b 20	32	B 1, l-b 12, w 1, n-b 8 ... 22

1/4 2/37 3/78 4/254 5/274   (8 wkts dec.) 363   1/8 2/8 3/92   (6 wkts) 169
6/318 7/337 8/363   4/96 5/132 6/158

B. S. Phelps and S. Bastien did not bat.

Bowling: *First Innings*—Hughes 13–2–67–2; Holdsworth 22–5–91–1; Reiffel 8–0–58–0; Waugh 15–4–56–1; Warne 26.2–6–67–4; Border 5–1–13–0. *Second Innings*—Hughes 7–1–23–1; Holdsworth 12–2–43–2; Reiffel 10–1–34–0; Warne 17–3–44–2; Border 5–2–12–1.

Umpires: A. G. T. Whitehead and P. B. Wight.

ENGLAND v AUSTRALIA

Fifth Cornhill Test

At Birmingham, August 5, 6, 7, 8, 9. Australia won by eight wickets. Toss: England.

England stumbled from one crisis to another as the post-mortem raged over Gooch's failure to wrest the Ashes from Australia. They began the Fifth Test hopefully, as Atherton became his country's 71st captain and the fifth from Lancashire. But England were vanquished by another huge margin. Their downfall was overshadowed by Ted Dexter's resignation as chairman of the selectors, six months before his five-year term officially ended; the announcement was greeted with applause around the ground.

Lathwell and Caddick were both dropped, while McCague's back ruled him out. So Malcolm and Watkin were summoned, along with Maynard, for his first Test since his debut against West Indies in 1988 and subsequent ban for touring South Africa. Then, 48 hours before the match and 17 days before his 41st birthday, Emburey was recalled, as an afterthought, when team manager Keith Fletcher realised the truth of warnings about a bare pitch likely to suit the spinners. Just to add spice Russell, a casualty of the selectors' batsman/wicket-keeper policy, dashed up as stand-by for Stewart, who was nursing "very tender bruised ribs". But with Stewart pronounced fit he was sent away again, as were Watkin and Malcolm. Australia were unchanged.

Atherton's initial strategy must have been to win the toss, bat first and score at least 450. The first two he pulled off, the last was wishful thinking. Atherton himself played with a calming assurance that suggested he would enjoy the mantle of captaincy. His 72, occupying 192 minutes, was England's biggest contribution in either innings and set the kind of example which had been Gooch's trademark, until he was scuttled by a shooter from Reiffel, leaving England 156 for five. Their unexpected rescuer was Emburey, perhaps Test cricket's most effective No. 8. He frayed Australian tempers for 160 minutes as he chiselled out 116 priceless runs with Thorpe, Bicknell, Such and Ilott. His unbeaten 55 demonstrated a burning desire to survive and a variety of improvised strokes hinting at a DIY batting kit rather than the MCC coaching manual.

However, when Ilott became Reiffel's sixth wicket on the second morning Atherton may have been regretting the decision to go for Emburey's bowling. England were left with the new-ball pairing of Bicknell and Ilott (joint Test record: eight for 468) and two off-spinners, one of whom thought his Test days were over. By the end of the day Australia were 258 for five, 18 runs behind. England were virtually out of the contest and heartily fed up with the Waugh twins. It could have been very different had Stewart stumped Steve Waugh off his second ball, from Such, when Australia were 80 for four. Reprieved, Steve united with his brother as never before in 13 Tests, adding 153 for the fifth wicket. It said much for the calibre of Mark Waugh's strokeplay that he batted with such fluency and dominance after

Australia's most jittery start to date. He picked the ball off his toes and exhibited the strength in his wrists with a stream of whippy leg-side shots. His 137, including 18 fours, was Australia's tenth Test century of the summer, equalling the Ashes record and eclipsing the eight shared by Bradman's "Invincibles" in 1948.

Atherton shuffled his bowlers well, no easy task with such limited resources, and placed his field shrewdly. Nor was he shy of consulting Gooch and Stewart, his chief rival for the captaincy. Gooch responded with a warm hug when Mark Waugh was finally dismissed on Friday evening, lured into a trap at backward square leg which he and his successor had planned minutely. But on Saturday an exasperated England lost their grip in the face of rampant lower-order batting, led by Healy, and began to match earlier Australian dissent. When umpire Shepherd ignored raucous appeals for a bat-pad catch against Hughes, Thorpe was so peeved he chucked the ball to the ground in a sulk, while Stewart had already raced down the pitch to congratulate Such. Thorpe was officially rebuked by Fletcher and referee Clive Lloyd "noted" Stewart's reactions. Atherton, without condoning these antics, felt that they stemmed from the team's new-found enthusiasm.

England entered the fourth day at 89 for one, trailing by 43. Gooch was still there but his early departure, bowled round his legs by Warne, must have sent more jitters through the dressing-room. Baffled by May's flight and sharp turn, Maynard looked as though he was batting in quicksand, and lasted just 24 balls in two innings. There was a glimmer of hope that the Australians might face a tricky run-chase, with the tenacious Thorpe and Emburey holding the fort on 216 for six at tea. Thorpe resisted the spinners without apparent stress for nearly four hours. But once Emburey – whose six hours of batting in the match represented far better value than his three wickets – was prised out the Australians sensed another runaway win. At 5.27 p.m. the innings ended in bizarre fashion, with Ilott bowled off his backside. England had been spun dry by May and Warne, who split the wickets evenly between them.

Australia did suffer a couple of hiccups on Monday morning, losing both openers on 12. But Mark Waugh played with such freedom and panache against Such and Emburey that they seemed to be bowling on a different pitch to the Australians and Waugh and Boon extended their run of century partnerships to five in five Tests. By two o'clock Australia were 4-0 up, after their 12th success in 18 Tests against England, and looking to make it 5-0 for the second time in Ashes history. Atherton had endured the same losing fate as his seven predecessors, Gower, Gatting, Emburey, Cowdrey, Gooch, Lamb and Stewart; Willis was the last England captain to win his first Test. The press conference was, by then, distracted by Dexter's resignation, announced during the final morning. The young captain adopted a diplomatic air before a battery of cameras, microphones, arc lights and tape recorders, when grilled as to whether he thought it perverse that Dexter had not informed him beforehand. He preferred to look to the future, promising "to identify young players, with two things, talent and temperament, and then show faith in them". – Chris Lander.

Man of the Match: M. E. Waugh.   *Attendance:* 63,000; *receipts* £1,040,000.

Close of play: First day, England 276-9 (J. E. Emburey 55*, M. C. Ilott 3*); Second day, Australia 258-5 (S. R. Waugh 57*, I. A. Healy 12*); Third day, England 89-1 (G. A. Gooch 44*, R. A. Smith 7*); Fourth day, Australia 9-0 (M. J. Slater 7*, M. A. Taylor 2*).

England

G. A. Gooch c Taylor b Reiffel	8	– b Warne	48
*M. A. Atherton b Reiffel	72	– c Border b Warne	28
R. A. Smith b M. E. Waugh	21	– lbw b Warne	19
M. P. Maynard c S. R. Waugh b May	0	– c Healy b May	10
†A. J. Stewart c and b Warne	45	– lbw b Warne	5
G. P. Thorpe c Healy b May	37	– st Healy b Warne	60
N. Hussain b Reiffel	3	– c S. R. Waugh b May	0
J. E. Emburey not out	55	– c Healy b May	37
M. P. Bicknell c M. E. Waugh b Reiffel	14	– c S. R. Waugh b May	0
P. M. Such b Reiffel	1	– not out	7
M. C. Ilott c Healy b Reiffel	3	– b May	15
B 4, l-b 6, n-b 7	17	B 11, l-b 9, n-b 2	22

1/17 (1) 2/71 (3) 3/76 (4) 4/156 (5)   276
5/156 (2) 6/160 (7) 7/215 (6)
8/262 (9) 9/264 (10) 10/276 (11)

1/60 (2) 2/104 (3) 3/115 (4)   251
4/115 (1) 5/124 (5) 6/125 (7)
7/229 (8) 8/229 (9)
9/229 (6) 10/251 (11)

Bowling: *First Innings*—Hughes 19-4-53-0; Reiffel 22.5-3-71-6; M. E. Waugh 15-5-43-1; S. R. Waugh 5-2-4-0; May 19-9-32-2; Warne 21-7-63-1. *Second Innings*—Hughes 18-7-24-0; Reiffel 11-2-30-0; May 48.2-15-89-5; Warne 49-23-82-5; Border 2-1-1-0; M. E. Waugh 5-2-5-0.

Australia

M. A. Taylor run out	19	– (2) c Thorpe b Such 4
M. J. Slater c Smith b Such	22	– (1) c Thorpe b Emburey 8
D. C. Boon lbw b Emburey	0	– not out 38
M. E. Waugh c Thorpe b Ilott	137	– not out 62
*A. R. Border c Hussain b Such	3	
S. R. Waugh c Stewart b Bicknell	59	
†I. A. Healy c Stewart b Bicknell	80	
M. G. Hughes b Bicknell	38	
P. R. Reiffel b Such	20	
S. K. Warne c Stewart b Emburey	10	
T. B. A. May not out	3	
B 7, l-b 8, n-b 2	17	B 3, l-b 5 8

1/34 (2) 2/39 (3) 3/69 (1) 4/80 (5)   **408**   1/12 (2) 2/12 (1)   (2 wkts) **120**
5/233 (4) 6/263 (6) 7/370 (7)
8/379 (8) 9/398 (10) 10/408 (9)

Bowling: *First Innings*—Bicknell 34-9-99-3; Ilott 24-4-85-1; Such 52.5-18-90-3; Emburey 39-9-119-2. *Second Innings*—Bicknell 3-0-9-0; Such 20.3-4-58-1; Emburey 18-4-31-1; Ilott 2-0-14-0.

Umpires: J. H. Hampshire and D. R. Shepherd. Referee: C. H. Lloyd (West Indies).

KENT v AUSTRALIANS

At Canterbury, August 11, 12, 13. Australians won by 89 runs. Toss: Australians.

The Australians achieved a comfortable victory, surprisingly their first over a county since the end of May. Kent collapsed after tea on the final afternoon, losing their last five wickets for only 18 runs. Zoehrer and Taylor were the unlikely match-winners; Davis was Taylor's first first-class victim. Earlier, Hayden had made history, as the first Australian to score 1,000 runs on tour without playing in a Test. Another disregarded batsman, Martyn, scored his fourth hundred of the summer, after Steve Waugh reached his third. Kent declared on the last morning – allowing two more improbables, Julian and Warne used as openers, to score enough to set a target of 312 in 87 overs. Kent looked well placed before Cowdrey's run-out began their demise.

Close of play: First day, Australians 296-3 (S. R. Waugh 111*, D. R. Martyn 58*); Second day, Kent 114-2 (D. P. Fulton 40*, S. A. Marsh 16*).

Australians

*M. A. Taylor c Cowdrey b Ellison	78	
M. J. Slater c Fulton b Ealham	7	
M. L. Hayden c Igglesden b Ellison	31	
S. R. Waugh b Igglesden	123	
D. R. Martyn not out	105	
I. A. Healy not out	33	
B. P. Julian (did not bat)		– (1) not out 15
S. K. Warne (did not bat)		– (2) not out 17
L-b 3, w 1, n-b 10	14	L-b 2 2

1/22 2/90 3/151 4/315   (4 wkts dec.) **391**   (no wkt dec.) **34**

†T. J. Zoehrer, T. B. A. May and W. J. Holdsworth did not bat.

Bowling: *First Innings*—Igglesden 22-4-59-1; Ealham 25-1-103-1; Ellison 30-6-97-2; Davis 35-12-96-0; Patel 10-1-33-0. *Second Innings*—Davis 5-0-22-0; Patel 4-1-10-0.

Kent

D. P. Fulton not out	40	– c Zoehrer b Holdsworth	4
G. R. Cowdrey lbw b Warne	25	– (5) run out	51
N. J. Llong c Taylor b Waugh	15	– (4) lbw b Waugh	0
†S. A. Marsh not out	16	– (6) lbw b May	14
*M. R. Benson (did not bat)		– (2) c Warne b Waugh	14
T. R. Ward (did not bat)		– (3) c Taylor b Warne	69
M. A. Ealham (did not bat)		– lbw b May	34
R. M. Ellison (did not bat)		– c and b Zoehrer	1
R. P. Davis (did not bat)		– b Taylor	6
M. M. Patel (did not bat)		– st Healy b Zoehrer	2
A. P. Igglesden (did not bat)		– not out	0
L-b 3, w 1, n-b 14	18	L-b 12, w 1, n-b 14	27

1/71 2/90   (2 wkts dec.) 114   1/21 2/27 3/29 4/158 5/168   222
                                                              6/204 7/211 8/211 9/220

Bowling: First Innings—Holdsworth 7-2-20-0; Julian 9-2-41-0; Warne 9-1-30-1; Waugh 6-3-13-1; Hayden 1-0-7-0. *Second Innings*—Holdsworth 16-4-35-1; Julian 8-1-49-0; Waugh 5-2-9-2; Warne 20-6-50-1; May 14-2-39-2; Zoehrer 9.2-1-24-2; Taylor 1-0-4-1.

Umpires: P. Adams and J. W. Holder.

ESSEX v AUSTRALIANS

At Chelmsford, August 14, 15, 16. Drawn. Toss: Australians.

An entertaining match, which attracted nearly 20,000 spectators over three days, ended with Essex's last-wicket pair surviving the final eight deliveries to earn a share of the honours. Left a target of 308 in 72 overs, Gooch and the more subdued Knight inspired hopes of a home victory with an opening stand of 121 in 30 overs. Essex were still in the game at 245, with seven wickets and nearly nine overs remaining, but they then lost six for 32 in their quest for victory. Mark Waugh, with an effortless 108 from 133 balls – 76 runs coming in boundaries – and Hayden, who struck 18 fours and two sixes, put the Essex bowlers to the sword on the opening day after Hayden's rival, Slater, made the first half of what turned out to be a pair. Gooch and Hussain batted positively in reply, as did Julian when Border juggled the order and sent him in to open in the second innings, which yielded Such and Pringle four wickets each.

Close of play: First day, Essex 51-1 (G. A. Gooch 29*, P. J. Prichard 17*); Second day, Australians 119-5 (T. J. Zoehrer 4*, I. A. Healy 1*).

Australians

M. J. Slater lbw b Pringle	0	– (2) c Salim Malik b Ilott	0
M. L. Hayden c Such b Pringle	111	– (8) c Gooch b Such	36
D. C. Boon st Garnham b Childs	15	– b Childs	26
M. E. Waugh b Salim Malik	108	– (9) c Lewis b Pringle	9
*A. R. Border c Pringle b Childs	57	– (10) c Knight b Pringle	12
†I. A. Healy c Hussain b Childs	32	– (7) c Ilott b Such	4
T. J. Zoehrer not out	17	– (6) c Knight b Such	38
B. P. Julian not out	1	– (1) b Pringle	66
P. R. Reiffel (did not bat)		– (4) lbw b Such	15
M. G. Hughes (did not bat)		– (5) lbw b Pringle	0
T. B. A. May (did not bat)		– not out	0
L-b 6, n-b 10	16	L-b 2, n-b 10	12

1/3 2/81 3/198 4/291   (6 wkts dec.) 357   1/1 2/98 3/98 4/99 5/115   218
5/325 6/347   6/127 7/175 8/196 9/218

Bowling: First Innings—Ilott 19-2-52-0; Pringle 14-1-48-2; Gooch 6-2-14-0; Such 16-2-102-0; Childs 23-4-86-3; Salim Malik 12-0-49-1. *Second Innings*—Ilott 9-1-47-1; Pringle 19-4-65-4; Childs 17-6-52-1; Such 14.1-3-52-4.

Essex

*G. A. Gooch c and b Julian	61	– c Hughes b May	73
N. V. Knight c Healy b Reiffel	1	– c Hayden b Zoehrer	87
P. J. Prichard b Reiffel	21	– b May	1
Salim Malik c Border b May	17	– lbw b Zoehrer	39
N. Hussain c Slater b May	57	– c Zoehrer b Waugh	32
J. J. B. Lewis lbw b Zoehrer	8	– (8) not out	1
†M. A. Garnham run out	17	– run out	12
D. R. Pringle c Healy b Zoehrer	9	– (6) b Waugh	1
M. C. Ilott st Healy b Zoehrer	24	– c sub b Zoehrer	1
P. M. Such c Healy b May	15	– (11) not out	0
J. H. Childs not out	11	– (10) st Healy b Waugh	0
B 4, l-b 9, n-b 14	27	B 10, l-b 14, n-b 6	30

1/10 2/74 3/96 4/122 5/153	268	1/121 2/124 3/198 (9 wkts) 277
6/198 7/205 8/211 9/240		4/245 5/249 6/275
		7/275 8/277 9/277

Bowling: *First Innings*—Hughes 10–1–55–0; Reiffel 14–5–32–2; May 29–10–71–3; Julian 8–2–40–1; Zoehrer 21.3–3–57–3. *Second Innings*—Hughes 9–1–32–0; Reiffel 15–4–32–0; May 13–3–44–2; Julian 5–0–25–0; Border 6–0–23–0; Zoehrer 16–1–71–3; Waugh 8–1–26–3.

Umpires: J. D. Bond and M. J. Harris.

ENGLAND v AUSTRALIA

Sixth Cornhill Test

At The Oval, August 19, 20, 21, 22, 23. England won by 161 runs. Toss: England.

To general astonishment, England reversed the form of the summer, outplayed Australia and won the final Test deservedly and decisively. The result came more than six and a half years or – as one paper recorded – 2,430 days, 11 hours and 49 minutes after England's last win over Australia, at Melbourne in December 1986. It brought about a halt, at least temporarily, in the mood of national teeth-gnashing that had accompanied England's previous failures. For Australia, who had enjoyed a triumphal progress round the British Isles with only trivial setbacks, the defeat came hours before they flew home; it was like having the perfect holiday and then being nabbed by customs.

The win was a particular triumph for the England captain Mike Atherton, in his second game in charge; he was immediately named as captain for the winter tour to the West Indies. It was a cause for quieter satisfaction for Ted Dexter, the much-vilified chairman of selectors who had announced his resignation two weeks earlier. This was the last team for which he was responsible.

It was a greatly changed team too, but if England finally found the right combination there was as much accident as design and, at last, a bit of luck. Smith was dropped, for the first time, after 45 Tests, along with Ilott and Embury. Back into the squad came Hick, Tufnell and Malcolm. But the selectors took what might have been a gamble by naming Fraser, whose brief but brilliant Test career had been halted two and a half years earlier by a serious hip injury, as cover for Martin Bicknell, who had a dodgy knee. The evidence that Fraser was back to his best was based on only a couple of games but when Bicknell did pull out he had to play. It was a turning point. The combination of Fraser, Malcolm and Watkin (who made it into the final 11 this time, while Tufnell did not) on a pacy wicket transformed England. None had played a game before in the series; they shared the 20 wickets between them.

England had to make a fifth change less than an hour before the start when Thorpe was hit on the hand by a net bowler, broke his thumb and fainted; Ramprakash was summoned from Lord's. The short notice meant it had to be someone playing nearby; had Middlesex been at Swansea or Darlington, someone else might have got the chance. As it was, Ramprakash – in his tenth Test – finally passed thirty and began to add a little achievement to his unquestioned promise.

The next bit of English luck came when Atherton won the toss. England made their familiar good start, racing to 143 for one. Australia were again unchanged, except that they were two weeks further along a hard tour and even someone as great-hearted as Hughes was beginning to show signs of weariness. The batsmen were right on top all day but, in familiar English fashion, they got themselves out, often for no good reason – Hick, in particular, was blazing away and hit a regal six to reach 80 two balls before being caught at third man off a thoroughly ill-judged cut.

In the field, Australia seemed more intent on getting mad than getting even and the verbal battle appeared to reach new heights, or depths: the managers were called in for a quieter word by the referee, Clive Lloyd, after the first day. Next morning, England were all out for 380 and the consensus was that they had scored a hundred too few. But that assumed England's attack would live up to past form. Instead, Malcolm's speed, Watkin's resilience and Fraser's relentlessness completely transformed their prospects. The wicket was hard enough to favour strokeplay and to ensure that class bowlers could always make a batsman uncomfortable. England fielded tightly, with the young men darting everywhere and Gooch loyally putting on the short-leg helmet. Australia crumpled to 196 for eight. But then England could not finish them off and the last two wickets took the score past 300.

Australia could have got back in the game but, once again, the top three England batsmen tore into some jaded bowling and by the middle of Saturday afternoon England, at 157 for one, already looked fireproof. The runs included an off-driven four off Reiffel by Gooch which took his score to 21 and his total of Test runs to 8,235, more than David Gower and every other England player. The applause was unstinting, though the moment had a bittersweet touch: Gower might have scored many more if Gooch, as captain, had let him play.

The innings meandered later and England's prospects were hindered on the fourth day by the loss of two hours' play to the weather – only 41 minutes had been lost throughout the series while Australia had been on top. But the presence of the seventh specialist batsman, Ramprakash, enabled England to take the lead to 390 before they were bowled out to save Atherton having to decide whether to risk a declaration.

The rain effectively ruled out the remote chance of an Australian win. Could England do it? Again the luck was with them. The weather improved and umpire Meyer gave them two successive decisions that might have gone the other way: replays showed that Slater was given out caught off his armguard, and the first-ball lbw decision against Boon was not a certain one. Then Taylor played on and it was 30 for three. There was a stand between Mark Waugh and Border, who was caught behind – another decision that was not universally approved – straight after lunch and left an English cricket field for what was presumed to be the last time without once looking up. Mark Waugh and Healy were both out hooking and, though Steve Waugh dug in with Hughes, Malcolm was getting ready for another burst. His first ball back had Waugh leg before.

At 5.18 p.m. England won. The heroes of the hour were English but the heroes of the summer were Australian: it was Border who was presented with a replica of the Ashes. What England had won, at the very last minute, was some self-respect. – Matthew Engel.

Man of the Match: A. R. C. Fraser.   *Attendance:* 70,650; receipts £1,242,400.

Men of the Series: England – G. A. Gooch; Australia – S. K. Warne.

Close of play: First day, England 353-7 (A. R. C. Fraser 15*, S. L. Watkin 8*); Second day, Australia 239-8 (I. A. Healy 39*, S. K. Warne 14*); Third day, England 210-5 (A. J. Stewart 14*, M. R. Ramprakash 12*); Fourth day, Australia 1-0 (M. J. Slater 1*, M. A. Taylor 0*).

England

G. A. Gooch c Border b S. R. Waugh	56	– c Healy b Warne	79
*M. A. Atherton lbw b S. R. Waugh	50	– c Warne b Reiffel	42
G. A. Hick c Warne b May	80	– c Boon b May	36
M. P. Maynard b Warne	20	– c Reiffel b Hughes	9
N. Hussain c Taylor b Warne	30	– c M. E. Waugh b Hughes	0
†A. J. Stewart c Healy b Hughes	76	– c M. E. Waugh b Reiffel	35
M. R. Ramprakash c Healy b Hughes	6	– c Slater b Hughes	64
A. R. C. Fraser b Reiffel	28	– c Healy b Reiffel	13
S. L. Watkin c S. R. Waugh b Reiffel	13	– lbw b Warne	4
P. M. Such c M. E. Waugh b Hughes	4	– lbw b Warne	10
D. E. Malcolm not out	0	– not out	0
L-b 7, w 1, n-b 9	17	B 5, l-b 12, w 1, n-b 3	21

1/88 (1) 2/143 (2) 3/177 (4) 4/231 (3)   380   1/77 (2) 2/157 (3) 3/180 (4)   313
5/253 (5) 6/272 (7) 7/339 (6)   4/180 (5) 5/186 (1) 6/254 (6)
8/363 (9) 9/374 (10) 10/380 (8)   7/276 (8) 8/283 (9)
                                                                              9/313 (10) 10/313 (7)

Bowling: *First Innings*—Hughes 30–7–121–3; Reiffel 28.5–4–88–2; S. R. Waugh 12–2–45–2; Warne 20–5–70–2; M. E. Waugh 1–0–17–0; May 10–3–32–1. *Second Innings*—Hughes 31.2–9–110–3; Reiffel 24–8–55–3; Warne 40–15–78–3; May 24–6–53–1.

Australia

M. A. Taylor c Hussain b Malcolm	70	– (2) b Watkin	8
M. J. Slater c Gooch b Malcolm	4	– (1) c Stewart b Watkin	12
D. C. Boon c Gooch b Malcolm	13	– lbw b Watkin	0
M. E. Waugh c Stewart b Fraser	10	– c Ramprakash b Malcolm	49
*A. R. Border c Stewart b Fraser	48	– c Stewart b Malcolm	17
S. R. Waugh b Fraser	20	– lbw b Malcolm	26
†I. A. Healy not out	83	– c Maynard b Watkin	5
M. G. Hughes c Ramprakash b Watkin	7	– c Watkin b Fraser	12
P. R. Reiffel c Maynard b Watkin	0	– c and b Fraser	42
S. K. Warne c Stewart b Fraser	16	– lbw b Fraser	37
T. B. A. May c Stewart b Fraser	15	– not out	4
B 5, l-b 6, w 2, n-b 4	17	B 2, l-b 6, w 2, n-b 7	17
	303		**229**

1/9 (2) 2/30 (3) 3/53 (4) 4/132 (1)   303
5/164 (6) 6/181 (5) 7/196 (8)
8/196 (9) 9/248 (10) 10/303 (11)

1/23 (1) 2/23 (3) 3/30 (2)   229
4/92 (5) 5/95 (4) 6/106 (7)
7/142 (6) 8/143 (8)
9/217 (9) 10/229 (10)

Bowling: *First Innings*—Malcolm 26–5–86–3; Watkin 28–4–87–2; Fraser 26.4–4–87–5; Such 14–4–32–0. *Second Innings*—Malcolm 20–3–84–3; Watkin 25–9–65–4; Fraser 19.1–5–44–3; Such 9–4–17–0; Hick 8–3–11–0.

Umpires: M. J. Kitchen and B. J. Meyer. Referee: C. H. Lloyd (West Indies).

THE ASHES

"In affectionate remembrance of English cricket which died at The Oval, 29th August, 1882. Deeply lamented by a large circle of sorrowing friends and acquaintances, R.I.P. N.B. The body will be cremated and the Ashes taken to Australia."

Australia's first victory on English soil over the full strength of England, on August 29, 1882, inspired a young London journalist, Reginald Shirley Brooks, to write this mock "obituary". It appeared in the *Sporting Times*.

Before England's defeat at The Oval, by 7 runs, arrangements had already been made for the Hon. Ivo Bligh, afterwards Lord Darnley, to lead a team to Australia. Three weeks later they set out, now with the popular objective of recovering the Ashes. In the event, Australia won the First Test by nine wickets, but with England winning the next two it became generally accepted that they brought back the Ashes.

It was long accepted that the real Ashes – a small urn believed to contain the ashes of a bail used in the third match – were presented to Bligh by a group of Melbourne women. At the time of the 1982 centenary of The Oval Test match, however, evidence was produced which suggested that these ashes were the remains of a ball and that they were given to the England captain by Sir William Clarke, the presentation taking place before the Test matches in Australia in 1883. The certain origin of the Ashes, therefore, is the subject of some dispute.

After Lord Darnley's death in 1927, the urn was given to MCC by Lord Darnley's Australian-born widow, Florence. It can be seen in the cricket museum at Lord's, together with a red and gold velvet bag, made specially for it, and the scorecard of the 1882 match.

THE ZIMBABWEANS IN ENGLAND, 1993

Almost unnoticed by the press or public, the Zimbabweans made their fourth tour of England and their first since gaining Test status without playing any major fixtures. Several players were already in the country, playing for English league teams, including Andy Flower, the new captain. He took over from David Houghton, who had led the country in the years leading up to their successful application for full membership of ICC as well as during their first Tests in 1992-93. Houghton toured, but the veteran off-spinner John Traicos was missing and the attack looked weak in his absence; the batting, especially that of Flower and his brother Grant, was more substantial, but collapsed alarmingly in their final match against Kent.

ZIMBABWEAN TOURING PARTY

A. Flower (*captain*), K. J. Arnott, D. H. Brain, E. A. Brandes, G. A. Briant, A. D. R. Campbell, G. W. Flower, D. L. Houghton, S. G. Peall, U. Ranchod, J. A. Rennie, D. J. Rowett, H. H. Streak, G. J. Whittal.
Manager: V. R. Hogg.

ZIMBABWEAN TOUR RESULTS

First-class matches – Played 3: Lost 1, Drawn 2. *Loss* – Kent. *Draws* – President's XI, Surrey.
Non first-class matches – Played 4: Won 2, Lost 1, No result 1. *Wins* – League Cricket Conference, President's XI. *Loss* – Glamorgan. *No result* – Warwickshire.

Note: Matches in this section which were not first-class are signified by a dagger.

†LEAGUE CRICKET CONFERENCE v ZIMBABWEANS

At Haslingden, August 27. Zimbabweans won by eight wickets. Toss: League Cricket Conference.

Two substantial stands, first by the Flower brothers and then by Campbell and Houghton, saw the Zimbabweans home with more than five overs to spare. The Conference owed much to former Australian Test player Sleep, like Andy Flower a professional in the Central Lancashire League. He dismissed both Flowers with his leg-spin and, earlier, added 111 with Minor Counties captain Cockbain for the third wicket. Another Australian, Fleming of Victoria, ensured that the tourists would have a total over 200 to chase.

League Cricket Conference

S. J. Dean c Houghton b Brain	12	†J. Macauley run out	4
G. I. Foley b Brain	19	R. Ellwood not out	4
P. R. Sleep b Peall	71		
I. Cockbain c Arnott b Brandes	36	B 4, l-b 8, w 6, n-b 4	22
D. Smith c Arnott b Rennie	6		
*N. J. Heaton b Brandes	0	1/33 2/44 3/155 (8 wkts, 55 overs) 231
R. G. Hignett c Brain b Rennie	22	4/163 5/163 6/174
D. W. Fleming not out	35	7/201 8/209

N. D. Peel did not bat.

Bowling: Brandes 11-2-40-2; Brain 10-1-37-2; Streak 11-1-36-0; Peall 11-3-39-1; G. W. Flower 3-1-15-0; Rennie 9-0-52-2.

Zimbabweans

*†A. Flower c Macauley b Sleep	75
G. W. Flower c and b Sleep	51
A. D. R. Campbell not out	42
D. L. Houghton not out	56
L-b 3, w 1, n-b 4	8

1/121 2/136   (2 wkts, 49.3 overs) 232

G. A. Briant, K. J. Arnott, H. H. Streak, E. A. Brandes, J. A. Rennie, S. G. Peall and D. H. Brain did not bat.

Bowling: Fleming 9.3-0-44-0; Peel 10-1-37-0; Sleep 11-2-40-2; Hignett 7-0-48-0; Ellwood 11-1-46-0; Smith 1-0-14-0.

Umpires: J. Collier and D. Murray.

†PRESIDENT'S XI v ZIMBABWEANS

At Scarborough, August 30. Zimbabweans won by virtue of their faster scoring-rate in the first 15 overs of their innings. Toss: Zimbabweans.

The two teams finished with identical totals but the Zimbabweans took the match by scoring 55 in their first 15 overs, nine more than the President's XI. Captain Andy Flower and Campbell added 202 in 134 minutes for the second wicket and both scored centuries. Then Campbell was dismissed by Blewett, and Flower and Briant were both run out in the 45th over. Their opponents had suffered a similar mini-collapse at 216 when Brandes removed Arthurton and Zoehrer with consecutive deliveries and Jones fell for 101 – in as many balls – in the next over, caught off Brain.

President's XI

G. S. Blewett b Peall	42	R. A. Harper lbw b Brandes	6
P. V. Simmons c A. Flower b Brandes	4	†D. S. Berry not out	6
*D. M. Jones c Streak b Brain	101	B 2, l-b 6, w 5, n-b 8	21
K. L. T. Arthurton b Brandes	52		
T. J. Zoehrer lbw b Brandes	0	1/15 2/103 3/216 (6 wkts, 50 overs) 256
P. R. Sleep not out	24	4/216 5/216 6/231	

Mudassar Nazar, J. Angel and D. K. Morrison did not bat.

Bowling: Brandes 10-1-32-4; Brain 10-3-38-1; Streak 10-1-70-0; Peall 10-0-51-1; Rennie 9-0-48-0; G. W. Flower 1-0-9-0.

Zimbabweans

*†A. Flower run out	101	H. H. Streak not out	1
G. W. Flower c Berry b Angel	1	E. A. Brandes not out	4
A. D. R. Campbell c Sleep b Blewett	102	L-b 12, w 6	18
G. A. Briant run out	0		
G. J. Whittal c Harper b Morrison	22	1/3 2/205 3/215 (6 wkts, 50 overs) 256
K. J. Arnott run out	7	4/216 5/251 6/252	

J. A. Rennie, S. G. Peall and D. H. Brain did not bat.

Bowling: Morrison 10-0-56-1; Angel 5.3-0-22-1; Simmons 10-0-38-0; Mudassar Nazar 8.3-0-55-0; Harper 10-0-42-0; Sleep 3-0-16-0; Blewett 3-0-15-1.

Umpires: J. H. Hampshire and B. Leadbeater.

PRESIDENT'S XI v ZIMBABWEANS

At Scarborough, September 1, 2, 3. Drawn. Toss: Zimbabweans.

Faced with a first-innings deficit of 300, the Zimbabweans devoted the final day to survival in a manner some way removed from Festival tradition. Though they finished still 21 behind they lost only two wickets, after Arnott and Grant Flower spent well over four hours accumulating 207. Flower's century was his first in first-class matches and he hit 20 fours. He also scored fifty on the first day before being bowled by West Indian off-spinner Harper, who finished with six for 71. The Zimbabwean attack struggled against a world-class batting line-up. Arthurton hit 14 fours and three sixes in his hundred, but even he was overshadowed by Australian Peter Sleep. By now all too familiar to the tourists, Sleep scored a century in his only first-class innings of the season for the second year running; he had taken 182 off the Pakistanis in a similar fixture in 1992. He added 191 with Arthurton and 124 with Harper after the President's XI were in slight difficulties at 116 for four.

Close of play: First day, President's XI 120-4 (K. L. T. Arthurton 9*, P. R. Sleep 3*); Second day, Zimbabweans 17-0 (K. J. Arnott 4*, G. W. Flower 10*).

Zimbabweans

K. J. Arnott c Adams b Mudassar Nazar	18	– not out	111
G. W. Flower b Harper	53	– c Simmons b Adams	130
A. D. R. Campbell b Harper	0		
D. L. Houghton lbw b Harper	36		
*†A. Flower b Morrison	1		
G. J. Whittal b Harper	1	– (3) c Berry b Adams	20
H. H. Streak c and b Harper	6	– (4) not out	4
E. A. Brandes c Simmons b Harper	0		
S. G. Peall b Zoehrer	20		
D. H. Brain c Mudassar Nazar b Zoehrer	8		
U. Ranchod not out	12		
L-b 5	5	B 6, l-b 5, w 1, n-b 2	14

1/31 2/32 3/82 4/85 5/88   160   1/207 2/262   (2 wkts) 279
6/102 7/106 8/125 9/147

Bowling: *First Innings*—Morrison 17–7–36–1; Simmons 13–9–10–0; Harper 34–9–71–6; Mudassar Nazar 6–5–9–1; Zoehrer 11.5–3–29–2. *Second Innings*—Morrison 16–3–55–0; Simmons 5–2–10–0; Zoehrer 27–9–56–0; Harper 13–5–27–0; Adams 26–10–66–2; Mudassar Nazar 7–1–21–0; Sleep 5–1–17–0; Lambert 3–0–11–0; Arthurton 6–5–5–0.

President's XI

P. V. Simmons c A. Flower b Streak	46	†D. S. Berry c A. Flower b Peall	4
C. B. Lambert lbw b Brandes	9	Mudassar Nazar not out	2
*D. M. Jones c A. Flower b Streak	32	B 5, l-b 16, n-b 1	22
K. L. T. Arthurton c Ranchod b Peall	103		
J. C. Adams st A. Flower b Peall	15	1/35 2/84 3/101	(7 wkts dec.) 460
P. R. Sleep lbw b Brandes	151	4/116 5/307	
R. A. Harper not out	76	6/431 7/446	

T. J. Zoehrer and D. K. Morrison did not bat.

Bowling: Brandes 22–1–108–1; Brain 16–2–56–0; Streak 23–5–87–3; Peall 28–6–109–3; Ranchod 14–3–48–0; G. W. Flower 5–1–31–0.

Umpires: J. H. Hampshire and B. Leadbeater.

†GLAMORGAN v ZIMBABWEANS

At Christ College, Brecon, September 5. Glamorgan won by 53 runs. Toss: Zimbabweans.

The tourists, without their captain, Andy Flower, and other Zimbabweans with playing commitments in the English leagues, failed to come to terms with a slow pitch. James, a coach in Zimbabwe during the winter, top-scored with 77 for Glamorgan. Campbell, the Zimbabweans' left-handed opening batsman, struck 43 before being run out, while Brandes and acting-captain Arnott provided some late entertainment with some hard hitting.

Glamorgan

S. P. James run out	77	R. P. Lefebvre b Brandes	0
*H. Morris b Brandes	7	†A. D. Shaw not out	6
A. Dale c and b Ranchod	33	L-b 8, w 12, n-b 14	34
M. P. Maynard st Briant b Ranchod	0		
P. A. Cottey b Ranchod	12	1/12 2/97 3/98	(8 wkts, 55 overs) 221
D. L. Hemp c Peall b Brandes	39	4/124 5/190 6/213	
R. D. B. Croft c Arnott b Streak	13	7/213 8/221	

S. L. Watkin and S. R. Barwick did not bat.

Bowling: Brandes 11–0–55–3; Streak 11–0–37–1; Rowett 7–0–34–0; Ranchod 11–3–34–3; Rennie 4–1–19–0; Peall 11–0–34–0.

Zimbabweans

G. W. Flower c Shaw b Lefebvre	4	J. A. Rennie run out	9
A. D. R. Campbell run out	43	U. Ranchod c Barwick b Dale	13
†G. A. Briant lbw b Lefebvre	12	D. J. Rowett not out	5
G. J. Whittal c Lefebvre b Barwick	0	L-b 8, w 7, n-b 4	19
*K. J. Arnott c Hemp b Dale	26		
H. H. Streak c James b Watkin	7	1/23 2/48 3/52	(51.2 overs) 168
E. A. Brandes c Lefebvre b Barwick	23	4/85 5/93 6/128	
S. G. Peall run out	9	7/128 8/139 9/160	

Bowling: Watkin 11–2–35–1; Lefebvre 9–4–18–2; Croft 11–3–25–0; Barwick 10–1–23–2; Dale 10.2–0–59–2.

Umpires: J. W. Holder and G. Sharp.

†WARWICKSHIRE v ZIMBABWEANS

At Birmingham, September 7. No result. Toss: Zimbabweans.

Rain ended play during the 29th over of Warwickshire's innings; another eight balls had to be bowled for a result to stand, from which the county would have needed another six runs to satisfy a retrospective "target" of 115 in 30 overs. The abrupt finish deprived Penney of the chance to shine against his native country after a solid start from Moles and Burns, the wicket-keeper promoted to open. For the Zimbabweans, Grant Flower and Whittal made fifties, but most of the middle order fell to the medium-pace of Welch.

Zimbabweans

G. W. Flower st Burns b Giles	54	S. G. Peall c Moles b Bell	0
*†A. Flower c Penney b Brown	21	D. H. Brain not out	11
A. D. R. Campbell b Welch	11		
D. L. Houghton b Welch	3	L-b 11, w 6, n-b 2	19
G. A. Briant c Moles b Welch	20		
G. J. Whittal not out	52	1/45 2/84 3/99	(8 wkts, 55 overs) 209
H. H. Streak c Moles b Ratcliffe	9	4/101 5/134 6/161	
E. A. Brandes b Bell	9	7/184 8/184	

U. Ranchod did not bat.

Bowling: Brown 10–0–57–1; Smith 8–0–27–0; Bell 8–0–43–2; Welch 11–1–28–3; Giles 11–3–16–1; Ratcliffe 7–0–27–1.

Warwickshire

*A. J. Moles c A. Flower b Streak	39
†M. Burns not out	48
J. D. Ratcliffe c A. Flower b Brandes	19
T. L. Penney not out	0
L-b 2, w 1	3

1/80 2/109   (2 wkts, 28.4 overs) 109

D. P. Ostler, P. A. Smith, Asif Din, D. R. Brown, M. A. V. Bell, A. F. Giles and G. Welch did not bat.

Bowling: Brandes 6.4–3–11–1; G. W. Flower 1–0–5–0; Ranchod 6–0–16–0; Brain 4–1–28–0; Streak 5–1–22–1; Peall 6–1–25–0.

Umpires: H. D. Bird and D. R. Shepherd.

SURREY v ZIMBABWEANS

At The Oval, September 8, 9, 10. Drawn. Toss: Zimbabweans. First-class debut: D. J. Rowett.

Thorpe, leading Surrey for the first time, had to declare twice to set up a run-chase in a rain-interrupted match. The Zimbabweans were in with a chance of reaching 273 in 59 overs while Andy Flower and Campbell were in. With ten overs remaining, 88 were needed with six wickets standing, but two wickets in an over gave the advantage to Surrey and the game petered out. In the first innings Brown made his third hundred of the season, and his quickest, reaching three figures in just 90 balls, with two sixes and 20 fours in all, against some uninspired bowling – though Brain looked more impressive second time around.

Close of play: First day, Surrey 304-7 (M. A. Butcher 15*, G. J. Kersey 10*); Second day, Surrey 114-6 (A. D. Brown 4*, A. W. Smith 3*).

Surrey

D. J. Bicknell c A. Flower b Brandes	5	– c A. Flower b Brandes	7
R. I. Alikhan lbw b Rowett	38	– lbw b Brain	10
A. W. Smith c Houghton b Peall	60	– (8) c Rowett b Peall	9
*G. P. Thorpe b Streak	3	– c A. Flower b Peall	37
A. D. Brown b Peall	138	– (7) c Brain b Brandes	20
D. M. Ward c Rowett b Peall	9	– (3) b Brain	4
A. J. Hollioake c and b G. W. Flower	10	– (5) run out	8
M. A. Butcher not out	15	– (6) run out	1
†G. J. Kersey not out	10	– st A. Flower b Peall	23
J. Boiling (did not bat)		– not out	7
A. J. Murphy (did not bat)		– not out	16
B 4, l-b 8, n-b 4	16	B 2, l-b 3, w 1, n-b 4	10

1/24 2/61 3/64 4/229 5/261 (7 wkts dec.) 304 1/16 2/21 3/22 (9 wkts dec.) 189
6/274 7/278 4/91 5/107 6/110
7/132 8/136 9/171

Bowling: *First Innings*—Brandes 12–0–46–1; Brain 6–1–38–0; Streak 11–2–59–1; Rowett 9–3–28–1; Peall 21–3–86–3; G. W. Flower 11–2–35–1. *Second Innings*—Brandes 13–1–60–2; Brain 7–2–12–2; Streak 6–1–13–0; Rowett 2–0–20–0; Peall 20–4–46–3; G. W. Flower 10–2–31–0.

Zimbabweans

G. J. Whittal b Hollioake	7	– (6) c Bicknell b Butcher	11
G. W. Flower c Butcher b Murphy	0	– b Butcher	14
A. D. R. Campbell c Kersey b Murphy	8	– c Hollioake b Butcher	31
D. L. Houghton lbw b Alikhan	23	– c Kersey b Murphy	23
*†A. Flower run out	11	– (1) c Brown b Murphy	82
G. A. Briant lbw b Butcher	54	– (5) c Bicknell b Butcher	5
H. H. Streak c Thorpe b Murphy	12	– (8) not out	4
E. A. Brandes c Kersey b Murphy	9		
S. G. Peall b Murphy	33	– (7) not out	4
D. H. Brain not out	26		
D. J. Rowett not out	8		
B 6, l-b 10, w 2, n-b 12	30	L-b 2	2

1/4 2/14 3/30 4/59 5/59 (9 wkts dec.) 221 1/36 2/128 3/129 (6 wkts) 196
6/104 7/134 8/161 9/197 4/168 5/188 6/188

Bowling: *First Innings*—Murphy 21–7–58–5; Butcher 10–2–24–1; Hollioake 11–0–37–1; Boiling 14–1–51–0; Alikhan 3–0–15–1; Smith 4–1–20–0. *Second Innings*—Murphy 16–2–69–2; Butcher 15–1–51–4; Boiling 11–3–48–0; Smith 9–4–21–0; Hollioake 2–0–5–0.

Umpires: B. Dudleston and P. Willey.

KENT v ZIMBABWEANS

At Canterbury, September 11, 12, 13. Kent won by 196 runs. Toss: Kent. First-class debut: S. C. Willis.

The Zimbabweans were swept aside by impressive seam bowling from Ealham and Spencer. Set 280 to win after lengthy interruptions by rain forced reciprocal declarations, they were bowled out inside 28 overs. Spencer claimed the first four wickets as they reached 35 and Ealham completed the job. In a 34-ball spell he achieved career-best figures of five for 14. It might have ended even sooner but for Brain, who threw his bat for 31. Kent made a shaky start – Ward, the non-striker, was run out off the first ball of the match, and their top five were out with only 36 on the board. But Marsh and Spencer put on 166 in 39 overs for the seventh wicket. Marsh reached his first hundred of the season; Spencer scored his maiden fifty. Both hit two sixes.

Close of play: First day, Kent 125-6 (S. A. Marsh 34*, D. J. Spencer 24*); Second day, Zimbabweans 53-1 (G. W. Flower 18*, A. D. R. Campbell 26*).

Kent

D. P. Fulton c Briant b Brain	10	– b Brandes	32
T. R. Ward run out	0	– not out	36
G. R. Cowdrey b Rennie	10		
N. J. Llong c Brandes b Brain	2		
M. V. Fleming lbw b Brain	4		
*S. A. Marsh c Brandes b Ranchod	111		
M. A. Ealham c Briant b Brain	28		
D. J. Spencer c Rowett b Ranchod	75		
D. W. Headley c Briant b Brain	7		
†S. C. Willis not out	0		
M. M. Patel c Peall b Brain	0		
B 8, l-b 8, w 1	17		

1/1 2/11 3/19 4/23 5/36   264   1/68   (1 wkt dec.) 68
6/82 7/248 8/263 9/264

Bowling: *First Innings*—Brain 20.4-6-48-6; Brandes 18-5-65-0; Streak 13-3-28-0; Rennie 10-3-40-1; Peall 6-0-30-0; Rowett 6-3-19-0; Ranchod 3-0-18-2. *Second Innings*—Brain 4-1-15-0; Brandes 8-0-33-1; Rennie 5-1-20-0.

Zimbabweans

G. W. Flower not out	18	– c and b Spencer	9
S. G. Peall run out	0	– (5) c Willis b Spencer	7
A. D. R. Campbell not out	26	– (2) c Fleming b Spencer	4
G. J. Whittal (did not bat)		– (3) b Spencer	9
†G. A. Briant (did not bat)		– (4) b Ealham	15
H. H. Streak (did not bat)		– c Willis b Fleming	3
*E. A. Brandes (did not bat)		– b Ealham	0
J. A. Rennie (did not bat)		– lbw b Ealham	0
D. H. Brain (did not bat)		– b Ealham	31
U. Ranchod (did not bat)		– c Patel b Ealham	2
D. J. Rowett (did not bat)		– not out	0
B 4, l-b 4, w 1	9	L-b 3	3

1/4   (1 wkt dec.) 53   1/7 2/22 3/23 4/35 5/47   83
6/47 7/49 8/57 9/75

Bowling: *First Innings*—Spencer 7-4-20-0; Headley 8-2-15-0; Fleming 2-0-10-0. *Second Innings*—Spencer 11-1-46-4; Headley 8-5-6-0; Ealham 5.4-3-14-5; Fleming 3-1-14-1.

Umpires: J. C. Balderstone and T. E. Jesty.

BRITANNIC ASSURANCE
COUNTY CHAMPIONSHIP, 1993

The 1993 County Championship, the first consisting entirely of four-day matches, turned into a procession long before it could develop into a race. Middlesex became joint leaders in early June after a two-day win over Derbyshire; on June 28 they became outright leaders. After that, they were never headed and hardly so much as threatened.

From the middle of June to the end of August they won eight of their nine matches, mostly by large margins; in the other, against Yorkshire at Scarborough, they were denied by the last-wicket pair. This sequence concluded when they crushed Essex, the 1992 champions, inside two days at Colchester, the ground where Essex were accustomed to polishing off the opposition on their own way to the Championship.

Middlesex's triumph, their seventh (including a tie) in the past 18 seasons, was achieved despite the comparatively indifferent form of their leading batsmen and the absence of a settled pace attack. However, the spin attack of John Emburey and Phil Tufnell was superior to anyone else's and a succession of other players produced match-winning performances when required.

On the Bank Holiday Monday, August 30, when Northamptonshire failed to win their game against Leicestershire, Middlesex officially became champions, the earliest winners since Essex in 1979. Their final margin, 36 points, was less than Essex achieved in 1992. However, it would have been considerably greater but for an extraordinary turnaround in the final match at Worcester when Middlesex were bowled out for 68 on the first morning, equalling the lowest score of the season. They lost by an innings in two

BRITANNIC ASSURANCE CHAMPIONSHIP

Win = 16 points; Tie = 8 points	Played	Won	Lost	Tied	Drawn	Bonus points Batting	Bowling	Points
1 – Middlesex (11)	17	11	1	0	5	37	59	272
2 – Worcestershire (17)	17	9	4	1	3	32	52	236
3 – Glamorgan (14)	17	9	5	0	3	32	55	231
4 – Northamptonshire (3)	17	8	4	0	5	35	59	222
5 – Somerset (9)	17	8	7	0	2	26	59	213
6 – Surrey (13)	17	6	6	0	5	40	60	196
7 – Nottinghamshire (4)	17	6	3	1	7	34	56	194
8 – Kent (2)	17	6	4	0	7	40	54	190
9 – Leicestershire (8)	17	6	5	0	6	23	61	180
10 – Sussex (7)	17	5	7	0	5	42	54	176
11 – Essex (1)	17	4	6	0	7	44	55	163
12 – Yorkshire (16)	17	5	4	0	8	21	56	157
13 ⎰ Hampshire (15)	17	4	5	0	8	39	47	150
⎱ Lancashire (12)	17	4	8	0	5	38	48	150
15 – Derbyshire (5)	17	4	7	0	6	33	50	147
16 – Warwickshire (6)	17	4	8	0	5	24	49	137
17 – Gloucestershire (10)	17	3	10	0	4	24	56	128
18 – Durham (18)	17	2	10	0	5	29	52	113

1992 positions are shown in brackets.

days. It was not merely their first defeat, it was the first time they had been behind on first innings (except for a declaration) since the opening game of the season, which they won.

Worcestershire's victory, their fifth in a row, put them into second place, after they had finished second-bottom in 1992. This leap of 15 places is the greatest in the history of the Championship. The Worcestershire pitches came top of the table of marks awarded by umpires, and their groundsman, Roy McLaren, won the TCCB Groundsman of the Year award. Middlesex, however, finished bottom of this table, which can be found on page 384.

Glamorgan, Middlesex's closest challengers for most of the season, faded into third after losing their final match to Kent. However, this represented not merely their best performance since they were runners-up in 1970 but only their third top-ten finish in the 23 seasons since then. Glamorgan's hopes of making a wonderful season even better were effectively wrecked when they met Middlesex at Cardiff at the beginning of July. Both teams passed 500 on the first innings and Viv Richards and Adrian Dale both scored double-centuries. In the second innings, though, Glamorgan suddenly crumpled to Tufnell, who took eight for 29. Northamptonshire, who achieved five of their eight wins with a day to spare, came fourth; they might have run Middlesex closer had they managed to win an away game before September.

The most unexpected decline came from Essex, who began the season as favourites to secure a hat-trick of titles but slumped so badly that after the Middlesex defeat they were actually third-bottom. They recovered to finish 11th, still one of their three worst performances in the past two decades and a particularly worrying one since the state of their attack suggested the county, after a decade and a half of success, might be reaching the end of an era.

Durham, in their second year in the competition, again won only two matches and finished last, though they were not quite so far behind everyone else as in 1992. It was September before they finally settled behind Gloucestershire, who did not win until the Cheltenham Festival in August.

In a damp summer, the four-day Championship did not wholly succeed in avoiding contrived finishes and joke bowling, as the 21-minute century by Glen Chapple for Lancashire against Glamorgan proved most conclusively. However, 105 of the 153 Championship matches produced a positive result (including the tie between Nottinghamshire and Worcestershire) compared to 104 out of the scheduled 198 in 1992. Indeed, about a fifth of all matches still finished inside three days – six of them in two days, thus ensuring that the amount of cricket available to county members dwindled even further than the TCCB intended when they framed the fixture list.

Under TCCB playing conditions, two extras were scored for every no-ball bowled whether scored off or not. Any runs scored off the bat were credited to the batsman, while byes and leg-byes were counted as no-balls, in accordance with Law 24.9, in addition to the initial penalty.

Pre-season betting (William Hill): 11-4 Essex; 11-2 MIDDLESEX; 8-1 Lancashire, Northamptonshire and Worcestershire; 10-1 Kent; 11-1 Nottinghamshire; 12-1 Hampshire; 14-1 Surrey and Warwickshire; 18-1 Somerset; 22-1 Derbyshire; 33-1 Yorkshire; 40-1 Sussex; 50-1 Gloucestershire and Leicestershire; 66-1 Glamorgan; 125-1 Durham.

Leaders: from May 10 Surrey; May 24 Nottinghamshire; May 31 Somerset; June 7 Glamorgan and Middlesex; June 28 onwards Middlesex. Middlesex became champions on August 30.

Bottom place: from May 10 Hampshire; May 31 Hampshire and Leicestershire; June 7 Durham and Gloucestershire; June 14 Gloucestershire; July 19 Durham; July 26 Gloucestershire; August 16 Durham; August 23 Gloucestershire; September 3 onwards Durham.

Prize money

First (Middlesex)	£46,000
Second (Worcestershire)	£23,000
Third (Glamorgan)	£13,250
Fourth (Northamptonshire)	£6,750
Fifth (Somerset)	£3,375
Winner of each match	£250
County of the Month	£1,000
Player of the Month	£300

Scoring of Points

(*a*) For a win, 16 points plus any points scored in the first innings.

(*b*) In a tie, each side scores eight points, plus any points scored in the first innings.

(*c*) If the scores are equal in a drawn match, the side batting in the fourth innings scores eight points, plus any points scored in the first innings.

(*d*) First-innings points (awarded only for performances in the first 120 overs of each first innings and retained whatever the result of the match).

(i) A maximum of four batting points to be available: 200 to 249 runs – 1 point; 250 to 299 runs – 2 points; 300 to 349 – 3 points; 350 runs or over – 4 points.

(ii) A maximum of four bowling points to be available: 3 or 4 wickets taken – 1 point; 5 or 6 wickets taken – 2 points; 7 or 8 wickets taken – 3 points; 9 or 10 wickets taken – 4 points.

(*e*) If play starts when less than eight hours' playing time remains and a one-innings match is played, no first-innings points shall be scored. The side winning on the one innings scores 12 points.

(*f*) A county which is adjudged to have prepared a pitch unsuitable for first-class cricket shall be liable to have 25 points deducted.

(*g*) The side which has the highest aggregate of points shall be the Champion County. Should any sides in the Championship table be equal on points the side with most wins will have priority.

CHAMPION COUNTY SINCE 1864

Note: The earliest county champions were decided usually by the fewest matches lost, but in 1888 an unofficial points system was introduced. In 1890, the Championship was constituted officially. From 1977 to 1983 it was sponsored by Schweppes, and since 1984 by Britannic Assurance.

1864	Surrey	1901	Yorkshire	1952	Surrey
1865	Nottinghamshire	1902	Yorkshire	1953	Surrey
1866	Middlesex	1903	Middlesex	1954	Surrey
1867	Yorkshire	1904	Lancashire	1955	Surrey
1868	Nottinghamshire	1905	Yorkshire	1956	Surrey
1869	{ Nottinghamshire / Yorkshire	1906	Kent	1957	Surrey
		1907	Nottinghamshire	1958	Surrey
1870	Yorkshire	1908	Yorkshire	1959	Yorkshire
1871	Nottinghamshire	1909	Kent	1960	Yorkshire
1872	Nottinghamshire	1910	Kent	1961	Hampshire
1873	{ Gloucestershire / Nottinghamshire	1911	Warwickshire	1962	Yorkshire
		1912	Yorkshire	1963	Yorkshire
1874	Gloucestershire	1913	Kent	1964	Worcestershire
1875	Nottinghamshire	1914	Surrey	1965	Worcestershire
1876	Gloucestershire	1919	Yorkshire	1966	Yorkshire
1877	Gloucestershire	1920	Middlesex	1967	Yorkshire
1878	Undecided	1921	Middlesex	1968	Yorkshire
1879	{ Nottinghamshire / Lancashire	1922	Yorkshire	1969	Glamorgan
		1923	Yorkshire	1970	Kent
1880	Nottinghamshire	1924	Yorkshire	1971	Surrey
1881	Lancashire	1925	Yorkshire	1972	Warwickshire
1882	{ Nottinghamshire / Lancashire	1926	Lancashire	1973	Hampshire
		1927	Lancashire	1974	Worcestershire
1883	Nottinghamshire	1928	Lancashire	1975	Leicestershire
1884	Nottinghamshire	1929	Nottinghamshire	1976	Middlesex
1885	Nottinghamshire	1930	Lancashire	1977	{ Middlesex / Kent
1886	Nottinghamshire	1931	Yorkshire		
1887	Surrey	1932	Yorkshire	1978	Kent
1888	Surrey	1933	Yorkshire	1979	Essex
1889	{ Surrey / Lancashire / Nottinghamshire	1934	Lancashire	1980	Middlesex
		1935	Yorkshire	1981	Nottinghamshire
		1936	Derbyshire	1982	Middlesex
1890	Surrey	1937	Yorkshire	1983	Essex
1891	Surrey	1938	Yorkshire	1984	Essex
1892	Surrey	1939	Yorkshire	1985	Middlesex
1893	Yorkshire	1946	Yorkshire	1986	Essex
1894	Surrey	1947	Middlesex	1987	Nottinghamshire
1895	Surrey	1948	Glamorgan	1988	Worcestershire
1896	Yorkshire	1949	{ Middlesex / Yorkshire	1989	Worcestershire
1897	Lancashire			1990	Middlesex
1898	Yorkshire	1950	{ Lancashire / Surrey	1991	Essex
1899	Surrey			1992	Essex
1900	Yorkshire	1951	Warwickshire	1993	Middlesex

Notes: The title has been won outright as follows: Yorkshire 31 times, Surrey 18, Nottinghamshire 14, Middlesex 11, Lancashire 8, Essex 6, Kent 6, Worcestershire 5, Gloucestershire 3, Warwickshire 3, Glamorgan 2, Hampshire 2, Derbyshire 1, Leicestershire 1.

Eight times the title has been shared as follows: Nottinghamshire 5, Lancashire 4, Middlesex 2, Surrey 2, Yorkshire 2, Gloucestershire 1, Kent 1.

The earliest date the Championship has been won in any season since it was expanded in 1895 was August 12, 1910, by Kent.

Wooden Spoons: Since the major expansion of the Championship from nine teams to 14 in 1895, the counties have finished outright bottom as follows: Derbyshire, Northamptonshire and Somerset 11, Glamorgan and Nottinghamshire 8; Leicestershire 7; Gloucestershire, Sussex and Worcestershire 6; Hampshire 5; Warwickshire 3; Durham 2; Essex, Kent and Yorkshire 1. Lancashire, Middlesex and Surrey have never finished bottom. Leicestershire have also shared bottom place twice, once with Hampshire and once with Somerset.

BRITANNIC ASSURANCE CHAMPIONSHIP STATISTICS FOR 1993

County	For			Against		
	Runs	Wickets	Avge	Runs	Wickets	Avge
Derbyshire	7,506	249	30.14	7,807	219	35.64
Durham	7,270	278	26.15	8,157	210	38.84
Essex	8,822	256	34.46	9,468	274	34.55
Glamorgan	8,789	269	32.67	8,819	273	32.30
Gloucestershire	7,959	299	26.61	8,045	248	32.43
Hampshire	7,942	244	32.54	7,272	211	34.46
Kent	8,159	238	34.28	8,108	275	29.48
Lancashire	8,551	268	31.90	8,504	243	34.99
Leicestershire	6,267	236	26.55	6,631	239	27.74
Middlesex	6,930	191	36.28	6,729	282	23.86
Northamptonshire ..	7,474	236	31.66	7,332	282	26.00
Nottinghamshire	8,214	239	34.36	8,793	272	32.32
Somerset	7,440	263	28.28	6,890	277	24.87
Surrey	8,316	265	31.38	7,699	274	28.09
Sussex	8,574	239	35.87	8,875	245	36.22
Warwickshire	7,148	270	26.47	6,461	207	31.21
Worcestershire	7,786	240	32.44	7,503	264	28.42
Yorkshire	7,149	254	28.14	7,203	239	30.13
	140,296	4,534	30.94	140,296	4,534	30.94

COUNTY CHAMPIONSHIP – MATCH RESULTS, 1864-1993

County	Years of Play	Played	Won	Lost	Tied	Drawn
Derbyshire	1871-87; 1895-1993	2,173	537	787	1	848
Durham	1992-1993	39	4	20	0	15
Essex	1895-1993	2,136	611	613	5	907
Glamorgan	1921-1993	1,670	365	568	0	737
Gloucestershire ..	1870-1993	2,410	708	893	2	807
Hampshire	1864-85; 1895-1993	2,245	585	770	4	886
Kent	1864-1993	2,533	916	761	5	851
Lancashire	1865-1993	2,611	965	540	3	1,103
Leicestershire	1895-1993	2,103	457	781	1	864
Middlesex.......	1864-1993	2,313	861	583	5	864
Northamptonshire	1905-1993	1,870	450	657	3	760
Nottinghamshire ..	1864-1993	2,442	743	639	1	1,059
Somerset........	1882-85; 1891-1993	2,143	500	867	3	773
Surrey	1864-1993	2,690	1,061	593	4	1,032
Sussex	1864-1993	2,582	717	887	6	972
Warwickshire....	1895-1993	2,117	556	623	1	937
Worcestershire ...	1899-1993	2,057	511	715	2	829
Yorkshire	1864-1993	2,711	1,207	457	2	1,045
Cambridgeshire ..	1864-69; 1871	19	8	8	0	3
		19,432	11,762	11,762	24	7,646

Notes: Matches abandoned without a ball bowled are wholly excluded.

Counties participated in the years shown, except that there were no matches in the years 1915-18 and 1940-45; Hampshire did not play inter-county matches in 1868-69, 1871-74 and 1879; Worcestershire did not take part in the Championship in 1919.

OVERS BOWLED AND RUNS SCORED IN THE BRITANNIC ASSURANCE CHAMPIONSHIP, 1993

County	Over-rate per hour	Run-rate/ 100 balls
Derbyshire (15)	18.99	54.77
Durham (18)	18.70	48.81
Essex (11)	18.72	52.34
Glamorgan (3)	20.00	55.85
Gloucestershire (17)	18.78	44.29
Hampshire (13)	18.60	44.32
Kent (8)	19.10	51.68
Lancashire (13)	18.52	54.44
Leicestershire (9)	18.64	42.48
Middlesex (1)	18.97	49.27
Northamptonshire (4)	18.93	49.37
Nottinghamshire (7)	18.56	50.51
Somerset (5)	18.98	47.73
Surrey (6)	18.58	49.14
Sussex (10)	18.84	50.58
Warwickshire (16)	18.54	42.28
Worcestershire (2)	18.83	45.75
Yorkshire (12)	18.51	46.53
1993 average rate	18.82	48.90

1993 Championship positions are shown in brackets.

SUMMARY OF RESULTS, 1993

	Derbyshire	Durham	Essex	Glamorgan	Gloucestershire	Hampshire	Kent	Lancashire	Leicestershire	Middlesex	Northamptonshire	Nottinghamshire	Somerset	Surrey	Sussex	Warwickshire	Worcestershire	Yorkshire
Derbyshire	—	*D*	*D*	**L**	W	**D**	*L*	*L*	**L**	*D*	**L**	*L*	**L**	**W**	**W**	*W*	*L*	**D**
Durham	**D**	—	*W*	**L**	*D*	**D**	**D**	*L*	*L*	**L**	*D*	**L**	*L*	**L**	*L*	**L**	**W**	*L*	**D**
Essex	**D**	**L**	—	*L*	*D*	**D**	*D*	*D*	**L**	**L**	*L*	*D*	**W**	*D*	**W**	*W*	*W*	**L**
Glamorgan	*W*	**W**	**W**	—	**W**	**L**	*L*	*W*	**D**	*L*	**D**	*L*	**D**	*L*	**D**	*W*	**W**	*W*
Gloucestershire	**L**	**D**	**D**	*L*	—	**L**	*L*	*W*	**L**	*L*	**L**	**D**	*W*	*L*	**L**	*W*	**L**	**D**
Hampshire	*D*	*D*	*D*	**W**	**W**	—	**D**	*D*	**D**	*L*	*W*	*W*	**L**	*D*	*L*	**L**	**D**	**L**
Kent	**W**	**W**	**D**	*W*	**W**	**D**	—	*W*	*W*	**D**	*D*	**L**	**L**	*D*	*D*	**L**	*L*	**D**
Lancashire	*W*	**W**	**D**	*L*	*L*	**D**	*L*	—	**L**	*D*	**D**	**L**	*L*	*W*	**W**	**D**	*L*	**L**
Leicestershire	**D**	*W*	*W*	**D**	*W*	**D**	*L*	**W**	—	*L*	*D*	**L**	*W*	**L**	*L*	*D*	**D**	*W*
Middlesex	*W*	**D**	*W*	*W*	**W**	*W*	**D**	*W*	**D**	—	**W**	*D*	**W**	**W**	**W**	*W*	*L*	**D**
Northamptonshire	*W*	**W**	**W**	*D*	**W**	*L*	*D*	**D**	*D*	*L*	—	**W**	**W**	**W**	*D*	*L*	**W**	*L*
Nottinghamshire	**D**	*W*	**D**	*W*	*D*	**L**	**W**	*W*	*W*	**D**	*L*	—	**D**	*L*	**D**	**D**	*T*	**W**
Somerset	*W*	**W**	*L*	**W**	*L*	**W**	*W*	**W**	**L**	*L*	*L*	**D**	—	**W**	**W**	*D*	*L*	**L**
Surrey	*L*	**W**	*D*	**D**	**W**	*D*	*D*	*L*	**W**	*L*	**W**	**L**	*L*	—	**W**	*W*	**W**	*D*
Sussex	*L*	**W**	*L*	*L*	**W**	**W**	*D*	*L*	**W**	*D*	**D**	*L*	*L*	**L**	—	*D*	**W**	**D**
Warwickshire	**L**	*L*	*L*	*L*	**L**	*W*	**W**	*D*	*D*	**L**	**W**	*D*	**D**	*L*	**D**	—	**L**	**W**
Worcestershire	**W**	**W**	*L*	**L**	*W*	**D**	*W*	**W**	*D*	**W**	*L*	**T**	*W*	**W**	*W*	**L**	—	*D*
Yorkshire	*D*	**D**	*W*	**L**	*D*	**W**	*D*	**W**	*L*	**D**	*W*	**L**	*W*	*D*	**D**	*L*	**D**	—

Home games in bold, away games in italics. W = Won, L = Lost, T = Tied, D = Drawn.

COUNTY CHAMPIONSHIP – FINAL POSITIONS, 1890-1993

	Derbyshire	Essex	Glamorgan	Gloucestershire	Hampshire	Kent	Lancashire	Leicestershire	Middlesex	Northamptonshire	Nottinghamshire	Somerset	Surrey	Sussex	Warwickshire	Worcestershire	Yorkshire
1890	—	—	—	6	—	3	2	—	7	—	5	—	1	8	—	—	3
1891	—	—	—	9	—	5	2	—	3	—	4	5	1	7	—	—	8
1892	—	—	—	7	—	7	4	—	5	—	2	3	1	9	—	—	6
1893	—	—	—	9	—	4	2	—	3	—	6	8	5	7	—	—	1
1894	—	—	—	9	—	4	4	—	3	—	7	6	1	8	—	—	2
1895	5	9	—	4	10	14	2	12	6	—	12	8	1	11	6	—	3
1896	7	5	—	10	8	9	2	13	3	—	6	11	4	14	12	—	1
1897	14	3	—	5	9	12	1	13	8	—	10	11	2	6	7	—	4
1898	9	5	—	3	12	7	6	13	2	—	8	13	4	9	9	—	1
1899	15	6	—	9	10	8	4	13	2	—	10	13	1	5	7	12	3
1900	13	10	—	7	15	3	2	14	7	—	5	11	7	3	6	12	1
1901	15	10	—	14	7	7	3	12	12	—	9	12	4	2	6	9	1
1902	10	13	—	14	15	7	5	11	12	—	3	7	4	2	6	9	1
1903	12	8	—	13	14	8	4	14	1	—	5	10	11	2	7	6	3
1904	10	14	—	9	15	3	1	7	4	—	5	12	11	6	7	13	2
1905	14	12	—	8	16	6	2	5	11	13	10	15	4	3	7	8	1
1906	16	7	—	9	8	1	4	15	11	11	5	11	3	10	6	14	2
1907	16	7	—	10	12	8	6	11	5	15	1	14	4	13	9	2	2
1908	14	11	—	10	9	2	7	13	4	15	8	16	3	5	12	6	1
1909	15	14	—	16	8	1	2	13	6	17	10	11	5	4	12	8	3
1910	15	11	—	12	6	1	4	10	3	9	5	16	2	7	14	13	8
1911	14	6	—	12	11	2	4	15	3	10	8	16	5	13	1	9	7
1912	12	15	—	11	6	3	4	13	5	2	8	14	7	10	9	16	1
1913	13	15	—	9	10	1	8	14	6	4	5	16	3	7	11	12	2
1914	12	8	—	16	5	3	11	13	2	9	10	15	1	6	7	14	4
1919	9	14	—	8	7	2	5	9	13	12	3	5	4	11	15	—	1
1920	16	9	—	8	11	5	2	13	1	14	7	10	3	6	12	15	4
1921	12	15	17	7	6	4	5	11	1	13	8	10	2	9	16	14	3
1922	11	8	16	13	6	4	5	14	7	15	2	10	3	9	12	17	1
1923	10	13	16	11	7	5	3	14	8	17	2	9	4	6	12	15	1
1924	17	15	13	6	12	5	4	11	2	16	6	8	3	10	9	14	1
1925	14	7	17	10	9	5	3	12	6	11	4	15	2	13	8	16	1
1926	11	9	8	15	7	3	1	13	6	16	4	14	5	10	12	17	2
1927	5	8	15	12	13	4	1	7	9	16	2	14	6	10	11	17	3
1928	10	16	15	5	12	2	1	9	8	13	3	14	6	7	11	17	4
1929	7	12	17	4	11	8	2	9	6	13	1	15	10	4	14	16	2
1930	9	6	11	2	13	5	1	12	16	17	4	13	8	7	15	10	3
1931	7	10	15	2	12	3	6	16	11	17	5	13	8	4	9	14	1
1932	10	14	15	13	8	3	6	12	10	16	4	7	5	2	9	17	1
1933	6	4	16	10	14	3	5	17	12	13	8	11	9	2	7	15	1
1934	3	8	13	7	14	5	1	12	10	17	9	15	11	2	4	16	5
1935	2	9	13	15	16	10	4	6	3	17	5	14	11	7	8	12	1
1936	1	9	16	4	10	8	11	15	2	17	5	7	6	14	13	12	3
1937	3	6	7	4	14	12	9	16	2	17	10	13	8	5	11	15	1
1938	5	6	16	10	14	9	4	15	2	17	12	7	3	8	13	11	1
1939	9	4	13	3	15	5	6	17	2	16	12	14	8	10	11	7	1
1946	15	8	6	5	10	6	3	11	2	16	13	4	11	17	14	8	1
1947	5	11	9	2	16	4	3	14	1	17	11	11	6	9	15	7	7
1948	6	13	1	8	9	15	5	11	3	17	14	12	2	16	7	10	4
1949	15	9	8	7	16	13	11	17	1	6	11	9	5	13	4	3	1

	Derbyshire	Durham	Essex	Glamorgan	Gloucestershire	Hampshire	Kent	Lancashire	Leicestershire	Middlesex	Northamptonshire	Nottinghamshire	Somerset	Surrey	Sussex	Warwickshire	Worcestershire	Yorkshire
1950	5	—	17	11	7	12	9	1	16	14	10	15	7	1	13	4	6	3
1951	11	—	8	5	12	9	16	3	15	7	13	17	14	6	10	1	4	2
1952	4	—	10	7	9	12	15	3	6	5	8	16	17	1	13	10	14	2
1953	6	—	12	10	6	14	16	3	3	5	11	8	17	1	2	9	15	12
1954	3	—	15	4	13	14	11	10	16	7	7	5	17	1	9	6	11	2
1955	8	—	14	16	12	3	13	9	6	5	7	11	17	1	4	9	15	2
1956	12	—	11	13	3	6	16	2	17	5	4	8	15	1	9	14	9	7
1957	4	—	5	9	12	13	14	6	17	7	2	15	8	1	9	11	16	3
1958	5	—	6	15	14	2	8	7	12	10	4	17	3	1	13	16	9	11
1959	7	—	9	6	2	8	13	5	16	10	11	17	12	3	15	4	14	1
1960	5	—	6	11	8	12	10	2	17	3	9	16	14	7	4	15	13	1
1961	7	—	6	14	5	1	11	13	9	3	16	17	10	15	8	12	4	2
1962	7	—	9	14	4	10	11	16	17	13	8	15	6	5	12	3	2	1
1963	17	—	12	2	8	10	13	15	16	6	7	9	3	11	4	4	14	5
1964	12	—	10	11	17	3	7	14	16	6	3	15	8	4	9	2	1	5
1965	9	—	15	3	10	12	5	13	14	6	2	17	7	8	16	11	1	4
1966	9	—	16	14	15	11	4	12	8	12	5	17	3	7	10	6	2	1
1967	6	—	15	14	17	12	2	11	2	7	9	15	8	4	13	10	5	1
1968	8	—	14	3	16	5	2	6	9	10	13	4	12	15	17	11	7	1
1969	16	—	6	1	2	5	10	15	14	11	9	8	17	3	7	4	12	13
1970	7	—	12	2	17	10	1	3	15	16	14	11	13	5	9	7	6	4
1971	17	—	10	16	8	9	4	3	5	6	14	12	7	1	11	2	15	13
1972	17	—	5	13	3	9	2	15	6	8	4	14	11	12	16	1	7	10
1973	16	—	8	11	5	1	4	12	9	13	3	17	10	2	15	7	6	14
1974	17	—	12	16	14	2	10	8	4	6	3	15	5	7	13	9	1	11
1975	15	—	7	9	16	3	5	4	1	11	8	13	12	6	17	14	10	2
1976	15	—	6	17	3	12	14	16	4	1	2	13	7	9	10	5	11	8
1977	7	—	6	14	3	11	1	16	5	1	9	17	4	14	8	10	13	12
1978	14	—	2	13	10	8	1	12	6	3	17	7	5	16	9	11	15	4
1979	16	—	1	17	10	2	5	13	6	14	11	9	8	3	4	15	2	7
1980	9	—	8	13	7	17	16	15	10	1	12	3	5	2	4	14	11	6
1981	12	—	5	14	13	7	9	16	8	4	15	1	3	6	2	17	11	10
1982	11	—	7	16	15	3	13	12	2	1	9	4	6	5	8	17	14	10
1983	9	—	1	15	12	3	7	12	4	2	6	14	10	8	11	5	16	17
1984	12	—	1	13	17	15	5	16	4	3	11	2	7	8	6	9	10	14
1985	13	—	4	12	3	2	9	14	16	1	10	8	17	6	7	15	5	11
1986	11	—	1	17	2	6	8	15	7	12	9	4	16	3	14	12	5	10
1987	6	—	12	13	10	5	14	2	3	16	7	1	11	4	17	15	9	8
1988	14	—	3	17	10	15	2	9	8	7	12	5	11	4	16	6	1	13
1989	6	—	2	17	9	6	15	4	13	3	5	11	14	12	10	8	1	16
1990	12	—	2	8	13	3	16	6	7	1	11	13	15	9	7	2	6	14
1991	3	—	1	12	13	9	6	8	16	15	10	4	17	5	11	2	6	14
1992	5	18	11	3	17	15	5	2	12	8	11	3	4	9	13	7	6	10
1993	15	18	11	3	17	13	8	13	9	1	4	7	5	6	10	16	2	12

Note: From 1969 onwards, positions have been given in accordance with the Championship regulations which state that "Should *any* sides in the table be equal on points the side with most wins will have priority".

TCCB COUNTY PITCHES TABLE OF MERIT

First-Class Matches

		Points	Matches	Average in 1993	Average in 1992
1	Worcestershire (18)	98	10	4.90	4.09
2	Gloucestershire (5)	88	9	4.89	4.75
	Nottinghamshire (4)	88	9	4.89	4.85
4	Sussex (3)	97	10	4.85	4.86
5	Hampshire (12)	87	9	4.83	4.50
6	Derbyshire (9)	84	9	4.67	4.58
	Surrey (16)	112	12	4.67	4.25
8	Durham (7)	93	10	4.65	4.63
	Kent (17)	93	10	4.65	4.18
10	Lancashire (1)	102	11	4.64	5.13
11	Leicestershire (9)	92	10	4.60	4.58
12	Somerset (13)	82	9	4.56	4.46
13	Glamorgan (14)	88	10	4.40	4.42
14	Northamptonshire (6)	77	9	4.28	4.67
15	Essex (2)	94	11	4.27	4.92
16	Yorkshire (14)	83	10	4.15	4.42
17	Warwickshire (7)	90	11	4.09	4.67
18	Middlesex (11)	86	11	3.91	4.53
	Oxford University	77	8	4.81	5.00
	Cambridge University	78	9	4.33	4.00

One-Day Matches

		Points	Matches	Average in 1993	Average in 1992
1	Lancashire (1)	96	10	4.80	5.10
2	Derbyshire (12)	86	9	4.78	4.58
3	Nottinghamshire (2)	94	10	4.70	5.07
4	Gloucestershire (17)	103	11	4.68	4.69
5	Sussex (7)	112	12	4.67	4.77
6	Kent (18)	93	10	4.65	4.27
7	Hampshire (9)	82	9	4.56	4.63
8	Middlesex (5)	118	13	4.54	4.83
9	Surrey (3)	98	11	4.45	5.04
10	Glamorgan (11)	114	13	4.38	4.59
11	Yorkshire (16)	96	11	4.36	4.42
12	Durham (14)	84	10	4.20	4.50
	Worcestershire (13)	84	10	4.20	4.55
14	Northamptonshire (8)	97	12	4.04	4.75
15	Essex (6)	80	10	4.00	4.79
16	Leicestershire (10)	103	13	3.96	4.62
	Warwickshire (4)	95	12	3.96	4.96
18	Somerset (14)	76	10	3.80	4.50
	Oxford University	0	0	—	4.00
	Cambridge University	0	0	—	4.00

In both tables 1992 positions are shown in brackets. Each umpire in a game marks the pitch on the following scale of merit: 6 – very good; 5 – good; 4 – above average; 3 – below average; 2 – poor; 1 – unfit.

The tables, provided by the TCCB, cover all major matches, including Tests etc., played on grounds under the county's jurisdiction. Middlesex pitches at Lord's are the responsibility of MCC.

We're only out
for fair play.

We hope that we can help
maintain standards of fair play
in cricket.

We'll keep working to do
exactly the same in electricity.

National Grid
MAKING ELECTRICITY WORK

THE NATIONAL GRID COMPANY plc. NATIONAL GRID HOUSE. KIRBY CORNER ROAD. COVENTRY CV4 8JY

DERBYSHIRE

President: C. S. Elliott
Chairman: M. A. Horton
Chairman, Cricket Committee: B. Holling
Secretary/General Manager: R. G. Taylor
Captain: K. J. Barnett
Coach: 1993 – P. E. Russell
　　　　1994 – A. Hill
Head Groundsman: S. Birks
Scorer: S. W. Tacey

The exciting and emotional victory over Lancashire in the Benson and Hedges Cup final made Derbyshire's season memorable. With only three other entries on their honours board – the Championship in 1936, the NatWest Trophy in 1981 and the Refuge Assurance League in 1990 – Derbyshire do not mount the rostrum often enough to take it for granted. They won the trophy without their overseas player Ian Bishop, who was injured while playing for West Indies against Pakistan and forced to rest for a year with a stress fracture in his back. Bishop appeared in one Benson and Hedges match, against Middlesex, and his enforced absence was in Kim Barnett's mind when he described the final at Lord's as the greatest day in his 11 years as captain. Lancashire, the overwhelming favourites, were outfielded by Derbyshire, who do not outfield anyone that often, as well as battered by Dominic Cork's unbeaten 92.

While attaining one of their playing peaks, Derbyshire were involved in a financial crisis serious enough to threaten the club's existence. In May, chief executive Bob Lark and administrative secretary Hiren Bakhda were made redundant and commercial manager Ian Davies was dismissed. The decision was described as necessary to cut costs and it was subsequently revealed that the bank overdraft had gone over £400,000. At successive annual meetings members had expressed alarm about rising administrative costs and their fears had been given substance. Honorary treasurer Jim Crowther resigned and, in September, so did the chairman Chris Middleton.

Middleton's eight years in the position were marked by great enthusiasm and a willingness to speak loudly on Derbyshire's behalf. The fact that this alienated officials at Lord's caused no offence in Derbyshire but it was ironic that he was, very publicly, calling for Ted Dexter's resignation as chairman of selectors immediately before he felt obliged to go himself. In addition, the ground development on which Derbyshire had based their hopes of financial salvation gave every sign of foundering. Two committee members, Vic Brownett and Mike Horton, administered the club until a new secretary, Reg Taylor, was appointed in September. The annual loss, at £120,999, was a record.

Although the players were able to distance themselves from financial worries, a problem arose in the dressing-room when, in August, John Morris asked to be relieved of the vice-captaincy. At the end of the season, he tried to secure his release from a contract that had a year to run and, after initial resistance, Derbyshire succumbed and let him go. Morris will be much missed, because his batting was often glorious. His 229 against Gloucestershire at Cheltenham, during which he shared a county record fifth-wicket stand, an unbroken 302 with Cork, was majestic and his 151 against Lancashire at Derby was pointing towards a famous victory until Wasim Akram snuffed it out in a spell of six for 11. Derbyshire sent the ball used by Lancashire in the fourth innings to the TCCB, who said there was nothing wrong with it. But the incident lent an extra edge to the Benson and Hedges final a fortnight later.

Barnett, Morris and Peter Bowler carried the batting. Barnett completed 1,000 runs for the 11th consecutive season, a Derbyshire record, and had the highest average of any front-line England-qualified batsman in first-class cricket, the first Derbyshire player to occupy that position. Already their longest-serving captain, Barnett overtook Donald Carr's record of matches in charge when he led Derbyshire for the 228th time, against Hampshire in May. Bowler could not match his feats of 1992 but remained central to the construction of an innings. He prospered in one-day cricket, beating two of Barnett's records with 768 Sunday runs and 1,003 in the three limited-overs competitions. The middle order disappointed. Chris Adams, so powerful in one-day games, was often in too much of a hurry in the Championship and Tim O'Gorman had a lean season. Cork, capped during the season, scored his maiden century at Cheltenham but there were few consistent contributors otherwise until Adrian Rollins earned a place.

Derbyshire's hectic batting style meant they were either scoring heavily or collapsing, quickly in both cases. Victories and defeats were all by wide margins and, too often, they played themselves into trouble on the first day. "Drive carefully" would be a good rule for 1994. Allan Warner, playing better than ever, was the best of the bowlers. Having failed to take five wickets in an innings since 1985, Warner did it twice at Cheltenham and again the next time he bowled, against Surrey at Ilkeston. Devon Malcolm began the season well and it was surprising that he did not regain his England place until the final Test. Simon Base, recovered from the previous year's back operation, mixed excellent days with very poor ones: like Cork, who played in two one-day internationals, Base found the thread of consistency elusive. At the end of the season he left the club to concentrate on cricket in South Africa. Ole Mortensen had to overcome a knee operation and wicket-keeper Karl Krikken twice suffered finger injuries, causing a temporary loss of rhythm behind the stumps.

However, the hope that Bishop would return in 1994 combined with the signing from Lancashire of Phil DeFreitas, who will probably bat higher up the order for Derbyshire, gave room for optimism about the fast bowling. Spin remains a problem. Matthew Vandrau and Richard Sladdin seldom made much impact in 1993 and the feeling persists that Derbyshire have yet to come to terms with the four-day game – they dropped ten places from fifth in 1992. At the end of the season, Philip Russell emigrated to South Africa to take up an appointment as coach and groundsman at Kingsmead, Durban. As Derbyshire coach since 1977, Russell played an important part in rebuilding the team after the upheaval of 1983, when Barry Wood resigned as captain. Russell's association with the county goes back to his debut in 1965 and he was succeeded by another former Derbyshire player, Alan Hill. Although officially in charge of cricket development, Hill had to spend four months of the 1993 season as acting-secretary. Derbyshire need stability, on and off the field. – Gerald Mortimer.

DERBYSHIRE 1993

[Bill Smith]

Back row: P. R. Whitaker, T. J. G. O'Gorman, T. A. Tweats, A. W. Richardson, F. A. Griffith, D. J. Lovell. *Middle row*: S. W. Tacey (*scorer*), A. E. Warner, K. M. Krikken, D. G. Cork, S. J. Base, A. S. Rollins, C. J. Adams, R. W. Sladdin, R. J. Lark (*chief executive*), *Front row*: B. J. M. Maher (*Second XI captain*), P. D. Bowler, P. E. Russell (*coach*), K. J. Barnett (*captain*), J. E. Morris, O. H. Mortensen, D. E. Malcolm. *Insets*: I. G. S. Steer, I. R. Bishop.

DERBYSHIRE RESULTS

All first-class matches – Played 19: Won 4, Lost 7, Drawn 8.

County Championship matches – Played 17: Won 4, Lost 7, Drawn 6.

Bonus points – Batting 33, Bowling 50.

*Competition placings – Britannic Assurance County Championship, 15th;
NatWest Bank Trophy, 2nd round; Benson and Hedges Cup, winners;
AXA Equity & Law League, 11th.*

BRITANNIC ASSURANCE CHAMPIONSHIP AVERAGES

BATTING

	Birthplace	M	I	NO	R	HS	Avge
‡K. J. Barnett	Stoke-on-Trent	14	22	5	1,067	168	62.76
‡J. E. Morris	Crewe	16	27	1	1,323	229	50.88
A. S. Rollins	Barking	7	13	4	392	85	43.55
‡P. D. Bowler	Plymouth	15	26	2	1,005	153*	41.87
I. G. S. Steer	Birmingham	4	7	2	157	67	31.40
‡C. J. Adams	Whitwell	16	27	0	818	175	30.29
‡D. G. Cork	Newcastle-under-Lyme	13	20	2	427	104	23.72
‡T. J. G. O'Gorman . .	Woking	12	19	2	375	86	22.05
M. J. Vandrau	Epsom	14	22	2	404	58	20.20
‡A. E. Warner	Birmingham	11	14	1	238	95*	18.30
‡K. M. Krikken	Bolton	11	17	4	226	40	17.38
R. W. Sladdin	Halifax	8	11	3	131	51*	16.37
F. A. Griffith	Whipps Cross, London	9	12	0	191	56	15.91
‡D. E. Malcolm	Kingston, Jamaica	9	11	4	69	19	9.85
‡O. H. Mortensen . . .	Vejle, Denmark	10	14	5	70	29	7.77
‡S. J. Base	Maidstone	12	18	0	132	27	7.33
‡B. J. M. Maher	Hillingdon	5	5	1	22	17	5.50

Also batted: A. W. Richardson (*Derby*) (1 match) 9, 0.

* *Signifies not out.*   ‡ *Denotes county cap.*

The following played a total of 12 three-figure innings for Derbyshire in County
Championship matches – K. J. Barnett 4, J. E. Morris 4, P. D. Bowler 2, C. J. Adams 1,
D. G. Cork 1.

BOWLING

	O	M	R	W	BB	5W/i	Avge
A. E. Warner	298.5	61	875	41	5-27	3	21.34
S. J. Base	286.1	64	972	34	5-59	3	28.58
D. E. Malcolm	278.5	49	1,007	35	6-57	2	28.77
O. H. Mortensen	255	66	643	21	5-55	1	30.61
D. G. Cork	326.3	67	931	30	4-90	0	31.03
F. A. Griffith	147.1	22	546	12	3-32	0	45.50
R. W. Sladdin	272.5	70	941	18	3-30	0	52.27
M. J. Vandrau	281.4	61	910	16	2-8	0	56.87

Also bowled: C. J. Adams 100.2–7–469–5; K. J. Barnett 33–9–78–2; P. D. Bowler
18–8–37–0; A. W. Richardson 22–5–74–0; I. G. S. Steer 9–2–34–3.

Wicket-keepers: K. M. Krikken 20 ct, 4 st; B. J. M. Maher 9 ct; A. S. Rollins 3 ct, 1 st;
P. D. Bowler 2 ct.

Leading Fielder: C. J. Adams 16.

At Cambridge, April 14, 15, 16. DERBYSHIRE drew with CAMBRIDGE UNIVERSITY.

At Birmingham, May 6, 7, 8. DERBYSHIRE beat WARWICKSHIRE by an innings and 72 runs.

DERBYSHIRE v GLAMORGAN

At Derby, May 13, 14, 15, 17. Glamorgan won by 191 runs. Glamorgan 23 pts, Derbyshire 6 pts. Toss: Derbyshire.

Glamorgan were in charge throughout and took complete control on the third day. Only Barnett's unbeaten century, the second time he had carried his bat in five Championship matches, delayed their deserved victory. Derbyshire's morale was further deflated when they learned that Bishop, injured playing for West Indies against Pakistan, had a stress fracture of the back. In Glamorgan's first innings Richards stirred memories scoring 86 but, thanks to Bowler, their lead was kept down to 37. Glamorgan then pressed ahead at four an over. Morris and Maynard, who shared a partnership of 155 in 37 overs, both scored centuries; if Morris, who hit 17 fours, was impressive, there was a touch of magic to Maynard, who hit 20 fours in 188 balls and looked a player of the highest quality. Derbyshire were set 406, more than they had ever scored in a fourth innings, and were swept away by excellent seam bowling from Watkin as Barnett looked in vain for a partner. The Derbyshire wicket-keeper, Krikken, cracked a knuckle batting; Bowler and, briefly, Adams deputised behind the stumps.

Close of play: First day, Derbyshire 58-1 (P. D. Bowler 34*, J. E. Morris 8*); Second day, Derbyshire 278-9 (D. G. Cork 34*); Third day, Derbyshire 14-0 (K. J. Barnett 9*, P. D. Bowler 5*).

Glamorgan

S. P. James lbw b Warner	34	– lbw b Warner	24
*H. Morris c sub b Cork	37	– c Cork b Base	100
A. Dale c Bowler b Base	33	– c Bowler b Warner	2
M. P. Maynard b Base	15	– b Cork	145
I. V. A. Richards c O'Gorman b Malcolm	86	– c Morris b Adams	3
R. D. B. Croft c Barnett b Base	25	– lbw b Cork	22
R. P. Lefebvre lbw b Base	0	– lbw b Cork	0
P. A. Cottey c Base b Warner	15	– (9) b Griffith	25
†C. P. Metson lbw b Griffith	14	– (8) not out	25
S. L. Watkin b Griffith	31		
S. Bastien not out	14		
B 5, l-b 8, w 1, n-b 2	16	B 5, l-b 7, w 2, n-b 8	22

1/52 2/103 3/113 4/126 5/158   320   1/53 2/65 3/220   (8 wkts dec.) 368
6/166 7/212 8/262 9/272   4/245 5/305 6/305
                                           7/318 8/368

Bonus points – Glamorgan 3, Derbyshire 4.

Bowling: *First Innings*—Malcolm 23-4-101-1; Cork 17-3-50-1; Griffith 17.4-5-76-2; Warner 19-4-27-2; Base 15-4-53-4. *Second Innings*—Malcolm 22-3-98-0; Warner 16-3-55-2; Cork 17-4-53-3; Griffith 13.5-1-46-1; Base 12-2-51-1; Adams 11-0-53-1.

Derbyshire

*K. J. Barnett b Bastien	13 – not out	108
P. D. Bowler c Richards b Lefebvre	96 – c Metson b Watkin	6
J. E. Morris lbw b Dale	51 – c Metson b Watkin	2
C. J. Adams b Dale	24 – c Richards b Bastien	5
T. J. G. O'Gorman c sub b Dale	14 – c Metson b Watkin	0
F. A. Griffith c Richards b Lefebvre	4 – c and b Lefebvre	10
†K. M. Krikken c Metson b Watkin	29 – c Dale b Lefebvre	5
D. G. Cork not out	38 – c Lefebvre b Watkin	17
A. E. Warner b Croft	6 – c and b Croft	24
S. J. Base c Metson b Watkin	0 – c James b Watkin	22
D. E. Malcolm lbw b Lefebvre	1 – c Watkin b Bastien	9
L-b 7	7	L-b 6	6

1/21 2/137 3/169 4/187 5/201   283   1/18 2/22 3/35 4/38 5/68   214
6/208 7/270 8/277 9/278   6/86 7/114 8/164 9/205

Bonus points – Derbyshire 2, Glamorgan 4.

Bowling: *First Innings*—Watkin 22–2–87–2; Bastien 16–1–61–1; Lefebvre 20–3–59–3; Dale 18–2–63–3; Croft 2–0–6–1. *Second Innings*—Watkin 20–2–71–5; Lefebvre 19–5–47–2; Dale 4–1–17–0; Bastien 13–3–40–2; Croft 17–7–33–1.

Umpires: D. J. Constant and N. T. Plews.

At Chelmsford, May 20, 21, 22, 24. DERBYSHIRE drew with ESSEX.

DERBYSHIRE v HAMPSHIRE

At Derby, May 27, 28, 29, 31. Drawn. Derbyshire 8 pts, Hampshire 4 pts. Toss: Derbyshire.

The first day was lost to rain and there was a further delay of 75 minutes on the second, before Barnett won the toss. It was his 228th first-class match as Derbyshire captain, passing the record set by D. B. Carr. Hampshire were indebted to a solid contribution from Middleton, who rebuilt the first innings after Warner, again the pick of Derbyshire's attack, took three early wickets. Barnett and Bowler began soundly; Derbyshire's top five all passed 50, for only the fourth time in their history and the first in the Championship since 1933. Barnett prolonged the innings for 70 minutes on the final morning, taking the lead to 146, but his hopes of dismissing Hampshire a second time proved wildly optimistic. After an attractive 52 by Gower, Smith joined Terry in a partnership of 177. For Smith, fresh from a spectacular one-day international innings, it was his first century of the summer in first-class cricket.

Close of play: First day, No play; Second day, Hampshire 192-7 (A. N. Aymes 1*); Third day, Derbyshire 287-3 (C. J. Adams 41*, T. J. G. O'Gorman 31*).

Hampshire

V. P. Terry c Adams b Warner	4 – lbw b Barnett	96
T. C. Middleton c Maher b Cork	90 – c Bowler b Warner	9
D. I. Gower c and b Warner	5 – c and b Vandrau	52
R. A. Smith c Cork b Warner	9 – lbw b Barnett	101
K. D. James c Cork b Griffith	37 – not out	0
*M. C. J. Nicholas c Morris b Cork	15		
M. D. Marshall lbw b Warner	5		
†A. N. Aymes c Maher b Malcolm	15 – (6) not out	0
S. D. Udal c Bowler b Cork	0		
M. Jean-Jacques not out	11		
C. A. Connor b Malcolm	20		
B 1, l-b 15, w 4, n-b 12	32	B 8, l-b 14, n-b 10	32

1/19 2/29 3/45 4/147 5/183   243   1/20 2/98   (4 wkts dec.) 290
6/184 7/192 8/197 9/216   3/275 4/290

Bonus points – Hampshire 1, Derbyshire 4.

Bowling: *First Innings*—Malcolm 18-2-45-2; Warner 30-10-52-4; Cork 27-7-39-3; Griffith 15-0-38-1; Adams 7-0-28-0; Vandrau 10-3-25-0. *Second Innings*—Malcolm 11-3-54-0; Warner 8-1-32-1; Cork 10-1-34-0; Griffith 7-0-35-0; Vandrau 22-7-73-1; Barnett 17-7-40-2.

Derbyshire

*K. J. Barnett b Marshall	58	M. J. Vandrau not out	10
P. D. Bowler c Udal b James	79	D. G. Cork not out	25
J. E. Morris run out	61	B 2, l-b 8, n-b 12	22
C. J. Adams c Gower b Udal	65		
T. J. G. O'Gorman c Connor b Udal	55	1/129 2/204 3/222 (7 wkts dec.) 389	
A. E. Warner c Marshall b Jean-Jacques	0	4/334 5/340	
F. A. Griffith lbw b Jean-Jacques	14	6/344 7/357	

†B. J. M. Maher and D. E. Malcolm did not bat.

Bonus points – Derbyshire 4, Hampshire 3.

Bowling: Marshall 17-2-69-1; Connor 5-0-25-0; James 24-2-90-1; Jean-Jacques 24-5-117-2; Udal 36-14-78-2.

Umpires: B. Dudleston and R. Palmer.

At Lord's, June 3, 4. DERBYSHIRE lost to MIDDLESEX by ten wickets.

DERBYSHIRE v YORKSHIRE

At Chesterfield, June 10, 11, 12, 14. Drawn. Derbyshire 2 pts.

Rain ruined the only Championship match of the season at Queen's Park, another blow to Derbyshire's ailing finances. Play was possible only on the first day and even then was limited to 72 overs. Malcolm bowled well in two long spells and Yorkshire would have been in deeper trouble had all the slip catches been held. Cork missed the game with knee trouble but was awarded his county cap before the start.

Close of play: First day, Yorkshire 154-6 (P. W. Jarvis 15*, P. J. Hartley 0*); Second day, No play; Third day, No play.

Yorkshire

*M. D. Moxon c Base b Malcolm	39	P. W. Jarvis not out	15
A. A. Metcalfe lbw b Malcolm	21	P. J. Hartley not out	0
R. B. Richardson c Bowler b Mortensen	14	L-b 5, w 1, n-b 2	8
D. Byas c Maher b Malcolm	28		
†R. J. Blakey c Adams b Malcolm	10	1/40 2/65 3/91 (6 wkts) 154	
C. White c and b Base	19	4/119 5/120 6/154	

R. D. Stemp, J. D. Batty and M. A. Robinson did not bat.

Bonus points – Derbyshire 2.

Bowling: Malcolm 24-8-57-4; Warner 16-4-38-0; Base 17-8-32-1; Mortensen 15-6-22-1.

Derbyshire

*K. J. Barnett, P. D. Bowler, J. E. Morris, C. J. Adams, T. J. G. O'Gorman, M. J. Vandrau, †B. J. M. Maher, A. E. Warner, D. E. Malcolm, O. H. Mortensen and S. J. Base.

Umpires: A. A. Jones and P. B. Wight.

At Canterbury, June 17, 18, 19. DERBYSHIRE lost to KENT by nine wickets.

DERBYSHIRE v LANCASHIRE

At Derby, June 24, 25, 26, 28. Lancashire won by 111 runs. Lancashire 21 pts, Derbyshire 8 pts. Toss: Derbyshire.

No Derbyshire match had ever produced so many runs, the aggregate 1,497 passing the 1,391 between Derbyshire and Essex at Chesterfield in 1904, but the conclusion was startling. On the final afternoon, when Morris was 151 and his team 243 for two, Wasim Akram took six for 11 in 49 deliveries. Although the umpires inspected the ball regularly, Derbyshire were sufficiently concerned about its condition to send it to the TCCB. No action was judged necessary at Lord's but the incident, with its suggestion of tampering, raised the temperature for the Benson and Hedges Cup final a fortnight later. Cork was ordered out of the attack in Lancashire's first innings, for running down the pitch, while Atherton and Wasim scored accomplished centuries. Barnett responded with a fine 161 and then Lancashire's declaration set Derbyshire 379 in 86 overs. While Morris was batting with rare brilliance – he hit 23 fours and a six in 176 balls – they had a chance. But when he became Wasim's first victim of the match, the end was unexpectedly near.

Close of play: First day, Lancashire 433-7 (Wasim Akram 91*, W. K. Hegg 1*); Second day, Derbyshire 318-3 (K. J. Barnett 155*, T. J. G. O'Gorman 6*); Third day, Lancashire 270-8 (M. Watkinson 7*, P. J. Martin 9*).

Lancashire

G. D. Mendis c Adams b Cork	40	– c Cork b Malcolm	4
M. A. Atherton c Bowler b Mortensen	137	– c Maher b Malcolm	28
N. J. Speak b Malcolm	74	– c Morris b Malcolm	8
*N. H. Fairbrother c Griffith b Malcolm	2	– c Mortensen b Griffith	59
G. D. Lloyd b Vandrau	22	– lbw b Mortensen	80
Wasim Akram c Maher b Malcolm	117	– c and b Vandrau	42
P. A. J. DeFreitas c Adams b Griffith	28	– lbw b Mortensen	3
M. Watkinson c Maher b Malcolm	17	– (9) not out	35
†W. K. Hegg lbw b Malcolm	13	– (8) b Mortensen	7
P. J. Martin c Maher b Griffith	1	– not out	36
A. A. Barnett not out	3		
B 5, l-b 9, w 5, n-b 4	23	B 13, l-b 10, n-b 2	25

1/62 2/180 3/194 4/254 5/316   477   1/4 2/44 3/59   (8 wkts dec.) 327
6/370 7/422 8/454 9/459   4/171 5/235 6/244
    7/247 8/255

Bonus points – Lancashire 4, Derbyshire 4 (Score at 120 overs: 467-9).

Bowling: *First Innings*—Malcolm 25.2–3–98–5; Mortensen 25–6–82–1; Cork 11.3–1–37–1; Griffith 22–2–102–2; Vandrau 30.3–7–119–1; Adams 8–0–25–0. *Second Innings*—Malcolm 14–2–42–3; Cork 16–3–78–0; Griffith 9–2–48–1; Vandrau 18–3–78–1; Mortensen 21–1–58–3.

Derbyshire

*K. J. Barnett run out	161	– (5) lbw b Wasim Akram	0
P. D. Bowler b DeFreitas	32	– (1) c Mendis b Watkinson	25
J. E. Morris c Hegg b Watkinson	21	– (2) c Hegg b Wasim Akram	151
C. J. Adams c and b Watkinson	74	– lbw b Wasim Akram	13
T. J. G. O'Gorman b Martin	27	– (3) c Lloyd b Watkinson	35
F. A. Griffith c Hegg b DeFreitas	27	– (7) c DeFreitas b Watkinson	0
M. J. Vandrau c Hegg b DeFreitas	12	– (8) lbw b Wasim Akram	0
D. G. Cork c Lloyd b DeFreitas	0	– (6) c Hegg b Wasim Akram	3
†B. J. M. Maher c Hegg b DeFreitas	17	– not out	1
D. E. Malcolm b Martin	19	– b Watkinson	11
O. H. Mortensen not out	2	– b Wasim Akram	0
B 8, l-b 8, n-b 18	34	B 4, l-b 4, w 2, n-b 18	28

1/88 2/137 3/304 4/340 5/376   426   1/71 2/216 3/243 4/243 5/249   267
6/376 7/376 8/391 9/412   6/250 7/255 8/256 9/267

Bonus points – Derbyshire 4, Lancashire 1 (Score at 120 overs: 372-4).

Bowling: *First Innings*—Wasim Akram 17–4–83–0; DeFreitas 23–3–109–5; Martin 20.3–1–64–2; Barnett 39–14–79–0; Watkinson 37–7–75–2. *Second Innings*—DeFreitas 15–2–49–0; Wasim Akram 18.1–5–45–6; Martin 6–0–34–0; Watkinson 23–6–72–4; Barnett 12–3–59–0.

Umpires: V. A. Holder and G. Sharp.

At Kidderminster, July 1, 2, 3, 5. DERBYSHIRE lost to WORCESTERSHIRE by nine wickets.

At Derby, July 13, 14, 15. DERBYSHIRE drew with AUSTRALIANS (See Australian tour section).

DERBYSHIRE v SUSSEX

At Derby, July 22, 23, 24. Derbyshire won by 195 runs. Derbyshire 20 pts, Sussex 4 pts. Toss: Sussex.

The heavy rain that curtailed the Australian match left the pitch green but, although there was some movement, the fall of 19 wickets on the first day was largely the result of bad batting; Barnett, a rare exception, carried his bat for the third time in 11 months. Derbyshire, relieved to be only ten behind on first innings, then proceeded to bat a great deal better. Barnett had to drop down the order after a rib injury prevented him from fielding, but Bowler and Morris put on 177 for the first wicket and Adams reached 95 not out at the end of the second day, though he missed a hundred through a poor shot off Pigott, Sussex's most consistent bowler. Chasing 370, Sussex were 66 for five before a 93-run partnership between Athey and Moores, who broke a pavilion window hooking Malcolm for six. But Malcolm swept him away, the first of five wickets for four in 18 balls, as he returned his best figures for Derbyshire to ensure victory in three days. Athey was left on 72 not out. This was the first time since C. H. Bull and H. H. I. Gibbons, playing for Worcestershire against Lancashire in 1935, that two separate players have carried their bat in the same game. The last time two players on different sides performed the feat was in 1933 at The Oval, when A. Sandham carried his bat for Surrey and G. Brown did so for Hampshire.

Close of play: First day, Sussex 187-9 (F. D. Stephenson 55*, E. S. H. Giddins 0*); Second day, Derbyshire 350-6 (C. J. Adams 95*).

Derbyshire

*K. J. Barnett not out	73	– (6) b Hemmings ... 29
P. D. Bowler c Moores b Giddins	7	– (1) c Moores b Giddins ... 87
J. E. Morris b Moores b Stephenson	10	– (2) b Pigott ... 104
C. J. Adams c Athey b Stephenson	3	– (3) c Giddins b Pigott ... 96
T. J. G. O'Gorman b Stephenson	5	– (4) b North ... 3
D. G. Cork c Athey b Pigott	5	– (5) b Hemmings ... 11
†K. M. Krikken b Giddins	6	– run out ... 17
A. E. Warner lbw b North	20	– b Hemmings ... 16
S. J. Base b Pigott	27	– c Hall b Pigott ... 0
D. E. Malcolm lbw b Pigott	0	– c Hall b Hemmings ... 10
O. H. Mortensen c Athey b Giddins	3	– not out ... 1
B 1, l-b 17, w 4, n-b 2	24	B 1, l-b 3, w 1 ... 5

1/11 2/51 3/57 4/73 5/82   183   1/177 2/220 3/227 4/253 5/322   379
6/95 7/125 8/168 9/176   6/350 7/357 8/361 9/374

Bonus points – Sussex 4.

Bowling: *First Innings*—Stephenson 12–3–31–3; Giddins 18.2–1–60–3; North 8–2–29–1; Pigott 15–3–45–3. *Second Innings*—Stephenson 16–2–61–0; Giddins 20–1–85–1; North 15–1–65–1; Pigott 23–3–99–3; Hemmings 35.5–10–65–4.

Sussex

C. W. J. Athey c Krikken b Warner	12	– not out	72
J. W. Hall c Adams b Cork	2	– b Warner	2
D. M. Smith lbw b Cork	5	– b Warner	0
*A. P. Wells c Mortensen b Base	40	– b Malcolm	11
M. P. Speight c Base b Malcolm	27	– c Krikken b Cork	19
J. A. North c Adams b Base	2	– c Base b Cork	2
†P. Moores lbw b Base	27	– c Warner b Malcolm	41
F. D. Stephenson not out	57	– c Cork b Malcolm	0
A. C. S. Pigott c Mortensen b Base	7	– c Cork b Malcolm	0
E. E. Hemmings lbw b Base	1	– c Base b Malcolm	4
E. S. H. Giddins c Adams b Cork	4	– b Malcolm	0
L-b 7, n-b 2	9	L-b 13, w 2, n-b 8	23

1/3 2/21 3/23 4/92 5/94   193   1/2 2/6 3/17 4/58 5/66   174
6/95 7/156 8/168 9/174   6/159 7/164 8/164 9/174

Bonus points – Derbyshire 4.

Bowling: *First Innings*—Cork 13–3–31–3; Warner 9-2-26–1; Base 19–5–59–5; Malcolm 8–1–47–1; Mortensen 8–0–23–0. *Second Innings*—Malcolm 16.3–3–57–6; Warner 15–7–39–2; Cork 11–4–16–2; Mortensen 17–10–19–0; Base 11–3–30–0.

Umpires: M. J. Kitchen and B. J. Meyer.

At Cheltenham, July 29, 30, 31, August 2. DERBYSHIRE beat GLOUCESTERSHIRE by seven wickets.

At Durham University, August 5, 6, 7, 9. DERBYSHIRE drew with DURHAM.

DERBYSHIRE v SOMERSET

At Derby, August 12, 13, 14. Somerset won by an innings and 97 runs. Somerset 23 pts, Derbyshire 2 pts. Toss: Somerset.

Derbyshire effectively lost the game on the first day when Caddick and Mallender made excellent use of helpful conditions, each taking five for 49; with Barnett injured, the flimsiness of Derbyshire's batting was exposed. They were all out in 38 overs, and it could have been swifter: Adams was twice put down at slip by Harden. Hayhurst and Lathwell pressed home Somerset's advantage, taking a lead of 91 before the first wicket fell; Hayhurst maintained his concentration into the third day before Harden declared with a lead of 318. Derbyshire were unable to apply themselves to building a long innings, scoring at four an over but losing wickets regularly. The only redeeming feature was the batting of Rollins. Somerset's first victory over Derbyshire since 1975 was emphatic, with a day to spare. Afterwards Morris asked Derbyshire to relieve him of the vice-captaincy, a move that reflected tensions inside the dressing-room.

Close of play: First day, Somerset 79-0 (A. N. Hayhurst 28*, M. N. Lathwell 33*); Second day, Somerset 391-7 (A. N. Hayhurst 165*).

Derbyshire

P. D. Bowler c Burns b Caddick	0	– lbw b Mallender	4
*J. E. Morris c Burns b Caddick	11	– c Harden b Caddick	37
C. J. Adams b Mallender	50	– lbw b Mallender	0
A. S. Rollins lbw b Mallender	2	– c Harden b Mushtaq Ahmed	85
I. G. S. Steer c Burns b Caddick	5	– c Mushtaq Ahmed b Caddick	11
D. G. Cork b Mallender	11	– c Mushtaq Ahmed b Payne	7
M. J. Vandrau c Harden b Mallender	30	– c Lathwell b Mushtaq Ahmed	41
†K. M. Krikken c Burns b Mallender	5	– not out	20
S. J. Base b Caddick	3	– st Burns b Mushtaq Ahmed	4
A. W. Richardson b Caddick	0	– c Payne b Mushtaq Ahmed	0
O. H. Mortensen not out	0	– c Mushtaq Ahmed b Caddick	0
L-b 5, n-b 4	9	L-b 3, w 1, n-b 8	12
	135		**221**

1/0 2/23 3/30 4/41 5/81   1/27 2/27 3/72 4/98 5/137
6/106 7/115 8/124 9/126   6/163 7/204 8/218 9/220

Bonus points – Somerset 4.

Bowling: *First Innings*—Caddick 16–5–49–5; Mallender 16–3–49–5; Rose 4–2–19–0; Mushtaq Ahmed 2–0–13–0. *Second Innings*—Caddick 15.5–3–57–3; Mallender 11–0–46–2; Rose 10–0–53–0; Mushtaq Ahmed 11–2–28–4; Payne 6–1–34–1.

Somerset

A. N. Hayhurst run out	169	A. Payne not out	22
M. N. Lathwell b Cork	109	A. R. Caddick c Vandrau b Cork	24
*R. J. Harden c Krikken b Cork	0		
N. A. Folland lbw b Cork	33	B 6, l-b 20, w 4, n-b 23	53
I. Fletcher c Krikken b Base	8		
†N. D. Burns lbw b Base	7	1/226 2/226 3/296	(9 wkts dec.) 453
G. D. Rose run out	0	4/325 5/339 6/339	
Mushtaq Ahmed c Krikken b Vandrau	28	7/391 8/398 9/453	

N. A. Mallender did not bat.

Bonus points – Somerset 3, Derbyshire 2 (Score at 120 overs: 339-5).

Bowling: Mortensen 32–9–79–0; Base 35–7–116–2; Richardson 22–5–74–0; Cork 32.5–7–90–4; Vandrau 22–5–49–1; Adams 5–0–19–0.

Umpires: P. B. Wight and P. Willey.

DERBYSHIRE v SURREY

At Ilkeston, August 19, 20, 21. Derbyshire won by six wickets. Derbyshire 24 pts, Surrey 4 pts. Toss: Derbyshire. First-class debut: A. J. Hollioake.

Warner, who had not taken five wickets in an innings for eight years until he did it twice at Cheltenham in July, returned after injury to perform the feat for the third time in succession. In the first innings, Surrey never settled, their highest score being 68 from Smith. Then Bowler, leading Derbyshire for the first time, ended 13 months without a first-class century, while Morris, in his fifth century of the season, hit 92 in boundaries (two sixes and 20 fours). Their stand of 192 prepared the way for Derbyshire's highest total against Surrey, passing the 386 at Derby in 1904. At 150 for six, Surrey appeared to be heading for an innings defeat, but the Australian-born debutant Adam Holliooake scored an attractive century, striking three sixes and 17 fours in 178 balls, the first to do so against Derbyshire since A. C. L. Payne, for MCC in 1905. But Derbyshire won on the third day after claiming the extra half-hour.

Close of play: First day, Derbyshire 106-0 (P. D. Bowler 39*, J. E. Morris 62*); Second day, Surrey 30-1 (D. J. Bicknell 17*).

Surrey

D. J. Bicknell lbw b Cork	0	– b Cork	32
P. D. Atkins lbw b Mortensen	10	– lbw b Cork	12
D. M. Ward lbw b Mortensen	2	– (6) c Adams b Steer	5
*M. A. Lynch b Warner	38	– (3) lbw b Steer	58
A. D. Brown lbw b Warner	23	– (4) c Bowler b Steer	20
A. W. Smith c Krikken b Vandrau	68	– (5) lbw b Mortensen	14
A. J. Hollioake c Krikken b Warner	13	– c and b Warner	123
†G. J. Kersey c Krikken b Warner	16	– c Bowler b Sladdin	33
Waqar Younis c and b Vandrau	6	– c Mortensen b Vandrau	19
J. E. Benjamin not out	6	– c Krikken b Warner	0
A. J. Murphy lbw b Warner	8	– not out	1
B 2, l-b 4, w 1, n-b 8	15	B 1, l-b 6, n-b 8	15

1/0 2/7 3/16 4/58 5/93   205 1/30 2/69 3/110 4/131 5/143 332
6/111 7/177 8/189 9/189   6/150 7/288 8/327 9/331

Bonus points – Surrey 1, Derbyshire 4.

Bowling: *First Innings*—Cork 16–6–27–1; Mortensen 14–6–34–2; Warner 21.4–5–57–5; Adams 2–1–6–0; Sladdin 12–7–30–0; Vandrau 8–0–34–2; Steer 3–1–11–0. *Second Innings*—Warner 22.4–5–73–2; Cork 27–4–80–2; Mortensen 13–3–42–1; Steer 6–1–23–3; Sladdin 22–5–66–1; Vandrau 11–1–41–1.

Derbyshire

*P. D. Bowler lbw b Waqar Younis	143	– c Hollioake b Murphy	45
J. E. Morris lbw b Hollioake	127	– c Kersey b Murphy	35
C. J. Adams lbw b Waqar Younis	42	– b Murphy	15
A. S. Rollins lbw b Benjamin	18	– c Lynch b Benjamin	0
I. G. S. Steer b Murphy	36	– not out	1
D. G. Cork b Waqar Younis	5		
M. J. Vandrau lbw b Waqar Younis	2	– (6) not out	0
†K. M. Krikken not out	13		
A. E. Warner c Smith b Hollioake	25		
R. W. Sladdin run out	0		
L-b 17, n-b 10	27	L-b 4	4

1/192 2/255 3/289 4/382 5/390 (9 wkts dec.) 438 1/79 2/88 (4 wkts) 100
6/394 7/403 8/430 9/438   3/99 4/99

O. H. Mortensen did not bat.

Bonus points – Derbyshire 4, Surrey 3 (Score at 120 overs: 415–7).

Bowling: *First Innings*—Waqar Younis 27–3–97–4; Benjamin 40–10–111–1; Murphy 23–1–115–1; Hollioake 23.3–3–75–2; Smith 9–1–23–0; Lynch 1–1–0–0. *Second Innings*—Waqar Younis 3–0–28–0; Benjamin 10.5–1–30–1; Murphy 8–1–38–3.

Umpires: R. Julian and D. O. Oslear.

At Nottingham, August 26, 27, 28, 30. DERBYSHIRE drew with NOTTINGHAMSHIRE.

DERBYSHIRE v NORTHAMPTONSHIRE

At Derby, September 9, 10, 11. Northamptonshire won by an innings and 46 runs. Northamptonshire 24 pts, Derbyshire 2 pts. Toss: Northamptonshire.

 Northamptonshire brushed aside a poor all-round performance from Derbyshire to maintain their challenge for second place in the Championship, a campaign which might have been stronger had this not been their first away win of the season. Only the weather prolonged the match – which was completed in the equivalent of five sessions – into the third day. Against bowlers maintaining a full length, Derbyshire gave no hint of permanence in a first innings that occupied only 35 overs and Northamptonshire duly exploited the situation. Fordham and Bailey secured the lead with a partnership of 136, Bailey going on to his second century of the summer. Although Ambrose left the field with a groin strain during his eighth over on the first day, he bowled magnificently to destroy Derbyshire's second innings. Only Rollins and Vandrau batted with any conviction. Derbyshire's last four home games had all finished in three days, with two wins and two defeats.

Close of play: First day, Northamptonshire 3-0 (A. Fordham 2*, N. A. Felton 1*); Second day, Northamptonshire 196-3 (R. J. Bailey 75*, A. J. Lamb 1*).

Derbyshire

P. D. Bowler c Lamb b Taylor	0	– c Ripley b Ambrose	26
J. E. Morris c Fordham b Ambrose	0	– lbw b Ambrose	22
C. J. Adams lbw b Ambrose	1	– c Ripley b Bowen	1
A. S. Rollins c Ripley b Bowen	19	– not out	44
*K. J. Barnett lbw b Bowen	53	– lbw b Ambrose	0
D. G. Cork lbw b Curran	21	– b Ambrose	0
M. J. Vandrau c Ripley b Curran	0	– b Taylor	58
†K. M. Krikken lbw b Curran	22	– b Ambrose	4
A. E. Warner c Felton b Bowen	2	– b Taylor	5
S. J. Base b Curran	0	– c Loye b Ambrose	7
O. H. Mortensen not out	3	– c Warren b Bowen	19
L-b 3, w 1, n-b 2	6	L-b 5, w 2, n-b 2	9

1/1 2/2 3/6 4/52 5/95   127   1/34 2/53 3/53 4/55 5/57   195
6/99 7/101 8/104 9/108   6/141 7/150 8/161 9/172

Bonus points – Northamptonshire 4.

Bowling: *First Innings*—Ambrose 7.4–3–9–2; Taylor 8–1–32–1; Curran 10.2–2–35–4; Bowen 9–1–48–3. *Second Innings*—Ambrose 18–4–49–6; Taylor 12–2–51–2; Curran 7–2–38–0; Bowen 10.5–0–52–2.

Northamptonshire

A. Fordham c Bowler b Adams	71	K. M. Curran not out	58
N. A. Felton lbw b Warner	15		
R. J. Bailey lbw b Warner	103	L-b 8, w 3, n-b 20	31
M. B. Loye c Barnett b Adams	15		
*A. J. Lamb lbw b Mortensen	38	1/26 2/162 3/194 (5 wkts dec.) 368	
R. J. Warren not out	37	4/255 5/282	

†D. Ripley, C. E. L. Ambrose, M. N. Bowen and J. P. Taylor did not bat.

Bonus points – Northamptonshire 4, Derbyshire 2.

Bowling: Cork 12–2–58–0; Warner 24–3–87–2; Base 19–2–63–0; Mortensen 19–3–55–1; Adams 16–0–88–2; Vandrau 3–1–9–0.

Umpires: B. Leadbeater and D. R. Shepherd.

At Leicester, September 16, 17, 18, 20. DERBYSHIRE drew with LEICESTERSHIRE.

DURHAM

Patrons: Sir Donald Bradman and A. W. Austin
President: I. D. Caller
Chairman: J. D. Robson
Director of Cricket: G. Cook
Chief Executive: G. A. Wright
Captain: 1993 – D. A. Graveney
        1994 – P. Bainbridge
Head Groundsman: T. Flintoft
Scorer: B. Hunt

In their second season of first-class cricket, it seemed that every time Durham were edging up the ladder to success, a huge snake was waiting to take them back to base. Five innings defeats exposed their limited resources and they duly retained the Championship's wooden spoon.

Significant progress was made, however, following the sudden retirement of Ian Botham. Even the Durham chairman, Don Robson, did not know of Botham's plans to quit until they were reported in a Sunday newspaper the day before he bowed out, with an unbecoming, flippant performance in the match against the Australians. Botham scored a magnificent century at Stockton against his old Worcestershire team-mates, at a time when the England No. 7 slot was clearly vacant. But Durham still suffered their fifth defeat in eight games – the other three were rain-affected draws – and lost their next, at The Oval, inside two days. That turned out to be Botham's last Championship match. When he retired they were next to bottom of the Sunday League and had gone out of the one-day knockouts as soon as they met first-class opposition.

Botham said he would continue to play on Sundays as long as there was a chance of winning prize money. In the event, it was mutually agreed that one farewell was enough. But the tourist match did mark a bit of a turning point. Durham had played magnificently on the first two days of this game and were the only team all summer to make the Australians follow on. The next game produced their first Championship win in almost 14 months – against an admittedly depleted Essex – and Durham won their last six Sunday League games to finish seventh.

Second-season syndrome afflicted some of the youngsters, notably Paul Henderson, who was called the Young Botham when he made a sensational debut the previous season. He was never in good enough form to make the first team, and after two seasons left-hander Darren Blenkiron was still awaiting his first-class debut. John Glendenen, the first player to score a first-class century for Durham, was released at the end of the season, along with Mark Briers, who failed to bring the necessary consistency to his all-round talents, especially his leg-spin bowling. But two teenage pace bowlers, Steven Lugsden and Melvyn Betts, made one appearance each and showed great promise, while batsmen Jimmy Daley and Stewart Hutton made excellent progress.

Only two players, Wayne Larkins and Phil Bainbridge, averaged over 30 with the bat, and they were also the only two to top 1,000 runs. At 39,

Larkins's eye remained as sharp as ever, as he proved by holding 24 catches, mostly at slip. There were times when he took the opposition apart with astonishingly destructive strokeplay. Paul Parker, in what always seemed likely to be his final season, scored three memorable centuries, but Graeme Fowler proved a disappointment on his arrival from Lancashire until he ran into some late-season form. Parker has now taken a job teaching at Tonbridge School but has offered to play in the holidays if required. In the close season Durham reduced the necessity for this by signing the high-quality batsman they wanted, John Morris from Derbyshire, and two batsmen with county experience: Mark Saxelby from Nottinghamshire and Jonathan Longley from Kent.

Bainbridge often hauled Durham out of trouble with the bat and, in an outstanding season, he was also the only bowler to average under 30, taking 40 wickets with his medium pace at 25.52. He was rewarded with the captaincy for 1994. Anderson Cummins, the 27-year-old West Indian pace bowler, took time to adjust to English conditions and also endured more than his share of dropped catches. But he proved a whole-hearted performer, who was prepared to defy a groin injury which plagued him for much of the season. He improved his career-best figures twice in a week, setting up the victory against Essex with his first five-wicket haul, then taking six for 115 against Sussex. He finished with 53 wickets at 30.45 and was retained as Durham's overseas player in 1994 even though Dean Jones, their Australian batsman of the previous year, was keen to return.

At the age of 40, the captain, David Graveney, worked hard at his fitness, bowled better than in the previous season, held many excellent catches, and was undefeated in 14 of his 27 Championship innings. While his left-arm spin rarely threatened to bowl sides out, his excellent control meant that in just under 580 overs he conceded runs at fewer than two and a quarter an over. While some would argue that his leadership lacked aggression, he always maintained his dignity and achieved a remarkable rapport with the supporters, many of whom were saddened by his treatment at the end of the season. Graveney himself had known for some time that he was to be replaced as captain, but the board ignored his wish that this should be made public, falling back on the excuse that any decision would have to be ratified by the AGM. Graveney deserved better treatment than this, but he agreed to play on and said he was much more optimistic about Durham's future than he had been 12 months earlier.

Before the season began, Durham had parted company with their chief executive, Mike Gear, and the club muddled through the season with Geoff Cook, the director of cricket, and other members of the administrative staff bearing the brunt of extra responsibility. Alan Wright began work as Gear's successor on November 1. Wright was best known locally as the presenter of the morning programme on BBC Radio Cleveland. The chairman talked about the focus of the chief executive's job changing and, since Wright had also run a public relations company, it was assumed that he was to concentrate on the PR and marketing side.

The initial impetus of Durham's entry into first-class cricket has not been lost. Despite failure on the field, Botham's departure and bad weather, membership remained above 6,000 and on fine Sundays the grounds were again full. New sponsors were still coming in, particularly for the new stadium being built at Chester-le-Street: business is due to start at the Riverside Ground in August with the first Second XI matches. – Tim Wellock.

400

DURHAM 1993

[Durham CCC]

Back row: P. W. Henderson, S. J. E. Brown, I. Smith, G. Wigham, J. Wood, S. M. McEwan, P. J. Berry, M. P. Briers. Middle row: D. M. Cox, C. W. Scott, R. M. S. Weston, A. R. Fothergill, S. Hutton, J. D. Glendenen, J. P. Searle, J. A. Daley, D. A. Blenkiron. Front row: G. Fowler, P. Bainbridge, I. T. Botham, D. A. Graveney (captain), W. G. Parker, W. Larkins, S. P. Hughes.

DURHAM RESULTS

All first-class matches – Played 19: Won 2, Lost 10, Drawn 7.

County Championship matches – Played 17: Won 2, Lost 10, Drawn 5.

Bonus points – Batting 29, Bowling 52.

Competition placings – Britannic Assurance County Championship, 18th;
NatWest Bank Trophy, 2nd round; Benson and Hedges Cup, 1st round;
AXA Equity & Law League, 7th.

BRITANNIC ASSURANCE CHAMPIONSHIP AVERAGES

BATTING

	Birthplace	*M*	*I*	*NO*	*R*	*HS*	*Avge*
P. Bainbridge	*Stoke-on-Trent*	17	29	2	1,116	150*	41.33
W. Larkins	*Roxton*	15	27	3	837	113*	34.87
P. W. G. Parker ...	*Bulawayo, S. Rhodesia*	17	29	1	866	159	30.92
S. Hutton	*Stockton-on-Tees*	9	16	0	422	73	26.37
J. A. Daley	*Sunderland*	12	20	0	521	79	26.05
G. Fowler	*Accrington*	12	21	0	540	138	25.71
I. T. Botham	*Heswall*	9	16	1	384	101	25.60
D. A. Graveney	*Bristol*	17	27	14	276	32	21.23
A. C. Cummins§ ...	*Packer's Valley, Barbados*	15	25	2	433	70	18.82
J. Wood............	*Wakefield*	8	15	2	235	63*	18.07
C. W. Scott	*Thorpe-on-the-Hill*	12	21	3	320	64	17.77
P. J. Berry	*Saltburn*	7	11	2	136	46	15.11
I. Smith	*Shotley Bridge*	5	10	0	143	39	14.30
J. D. Glendenen ...	*Middlesbrough*	4	6	1	41	18	8.20
S. J. E. Brown	*Cleadon*	14	23	4	150	31	7.89
A. R. Fothergill ...	*Newcastle-upon-Tyne*	5	8	0	53	29	6.62
S. P. Hughes	*Kingston-upon-Thames*	6	8	2	37	30	6.16

Also batted: M. M. Betts (*Sacriston*) (1 match) 0*, 4; M. P. Briers (*Loughborough*) (1 match) 1, 1; S. Lugsden (*Gateshead*) (1 match) 5*.

* *Signifies not out.* § *Overseas player.* *Durham have awarded all playing staff county caps.*

The following played a total of nine three-figure innings for Durham in County Championship matches – P. W. G. Parker 3, P. Bainbridge 2, W. Larkins 2, I. T. Botham 1, G. Fowler 1.

BOWLING

	O	*M*	*R*	*W*	*BB*	*5W/i*	*Avge*
P. Bainbridge.........	306.2	74	909	38	5-53	2	23.92
A. C. Cummins	475.3	89	1,527	51	6-115	3	29.94
I. T. Botham	168.5	42	450	13	4-11	0	34.61
D. A. Graveney.......	531.1	163	1,233	33	5-78	1	37.36
P. J. Berry	154.1	28	474	11	3-39	0	43.09
S. J. E. Brown	450.2	71	1,687	37	5-78	2	45.59
J. Wood	176	25	687	13	4-106	0	52.84

Also bowled: M. M. Betts 6-1-19-1; M. P. Briers 19-3-69-0; S. P. Hughes 211.3-61-552-8; S. Hutton 2-1-1-0; W. Larkins 4-0-18-0; S. Lugsden 26-2-85-2; P. W. G. Parker 16-3-38-0; I. Smith 24-6-74-1.

Wicket-keepers: C. W. Scott 24 ct, 2 st; A. R. Fothergill 6 ct, 2 st.

Leading Fielder: W. Larkins 21.

At Oxford, April 14, 15, 16. DURHAM drew with OXFORD UNIVERSITY.

At Manchester, May 6, 7, 8, 10. DURHAM lost to LANCASHIRE by six wickets.

DURHAM v HAMPSHIRE

At Stockton-on-Tees, May 13, 14, 15, 17. Drawn. Hampshire 2 pts, Durham 1 pt. Toss: Durham. Championship debut: A. C. Cummins.

Rain reduced the match to three sessions – two on the opening day and one on the third. What little cricket was played hardly set the pulse racing. Put in on a slow, seaming wicket, Hampshire openers Middleton and Terry batted with suitable care in an opening stand of 134. Gower brightened the gloom on the third day, punctuating diligent defence against the turning ball with 11 sweetly struck boundaries in his 64. Terry, meanwhile, ground his way to his second hundred in successive first-class innings, remaining 373 minutes, before the match subsided into a watery grave.

Close of play: First day, Hampshire 192-1 (V. P. Terry 82*, D. I. Gower 32*); Second day, No play; Third day, Hampshire 289-3 (M. C. J. Nicholas 31*, R. A. Smith 4*).

Hampshire

T. C. Middleton c Parker b Bainbridge.	65	R. A. Smith not out 4
V. P. Terry c Botham b Berry	111	B 3, l-b 5, w 2, n-b 4 14
D. I. Gower c Fowler b Graveney	64	—
*M. C. J. Nicholas not out	31	1/134 2/230 3/273 (3 wkts) 289

J. R. Ayling, M. D. Marshall, †A. N. Aymes, S. D. Udal, M. Jean-Jacques and C. A. Connor did not bat.

Bonus points – Hampshire 2, Durham 1.

Bowling: Cummins 15–2–48–0; Hughes 28–10–64–0; Botham 20–4–61–0; Bainbridge 20–4–66–1; Graveney 16–5–24–1; Berry 14–5–18–1.

Durham

G. Fowler, W. Larkins, P. W. G. Parker, P. Bainbridge, J. A. Daley, I. T. Botham, P. J. Berry, A. C. Cummins, †A. R. Fothergill, *D. A. Graveney and S. P. Hughes.

Umpires: V. A. Holder and B. J. Meyer.

At Bristol, May 20, 21, 22, 24. DURHAM drew with GLOUCESTERSHIRE.

DURHAM v KENT

At Darlington, May 27, 28, 29. Kent won by an innings and 22 runs. Kent 23 pts, Durham 4 pts. Toss: Kent.

Durham's batsmen were unable to cope with the swing of Igglesden, who had match figures of ten for 125. In the first innings the rest of the Kent attack looked ordinary, but in the second McCague regained his rhythm to take five for 33. Durham's hopes of recovery were thwarted on the second day by Davis, the night-watchman, and Fleming. Although Cummins often beat the bat three times an over, Davis survived three and a half hours for 42. In contrast, Fleming plundered 70 off 65 balls to give Kent a first-innings lead of 157. Durham slumped to 51 for five on the third day before 19-year-old Daley marshalled some resistance, playing several attractive strokes in his 39. But on a pitch which the umpires marked as "above average", Durham were beaten with a day and a half to spare. It was the first time they had lost a first-class match by an innings.

Close of play: First day, Kent 93-2 (N. R. Taylor 19*, R. P. Davis 2*); Second day, Durham 28-2 (W. Larkins 8*, P. Bainbridge 9*).

Durham

W. Larkins c Marsh b Fleming	54	– lbw b McCague	14
J. D. Glendenen c Marsh b Igglesden	1	– c Davis b McCague	0
P. W. G. Parker b Headley	10	– lbw b Igglesden	8
P. Bainbridge lbw b Igglesden	34	– c Hooper b Igglesden	13
J. A. Daley b Igglesden	0	– b McCague	39
I. T. Botham c Fleming b Igglesden	4	– lbw b McCague	7
A. C. Cummins c Marsh b Igglesden	2	– c Hooper b Fleming	19
J. Wood c Marsh b McCague	21	– c Marsh b Igglesden	5
†A. R. Fothergill c Hooper b Igglesden	2	– c Davis b McCague	10
*D. A. Graveney not out	11	– not out	7
S. J. E. Brown b McCague	0	– b Igglesden	0
L-b 20, w 1	21	L-b 12, w 1	13
	160		**135**

1/15 2/30 3/110 4/110 5/112   160   1/1 2/18 3/38 4/38 5/51   135
6/116 7/125 8/143 9/160   6/107 7/116 8/118 9/134

Bonus points – Kent 4.

Bowling: *First Innings*—McCague 14.1–3–43–2; Igglesden 31–6–58–6; Headley 21–10–32–1; Fleming 8–5–7–1. *Second Innings*—McCague 18–6–33–5; Igglesden 24–4–67–4; Headley 8–3–20–0; Fleming 5–3–3–1.

Kent

T. R. Ward lbw b Botham	26	D. W. Headley not out	23
*M. R. Benson b Cummins	25	M. J. McCague b Bainbridge	0
N. R. Taylor lbw b Botham	36	A. P. Igglesden b Botham	7
R. P. Davis c Fothergill b Brown	42		
C. L. Hooper c Larkins b Cummins	19	B 5, l-b 14, w 3, n-b 19	41
N. J. Llong c Glendenen b Wood	27		
M. V. Fleming c Botham b Bainbridge	70	1/53 2/75 3/130 4/161 5/207	**317**
†S. A. Marsh lbw b Wood	5	6/215 7/238 8/300 9/302	

Bonus points – Kent 3, Durham 4.

Bowling: Cummins 29–9–76–2; Brown 27–9–71–1; Wood 17–2–75–2; Botham 19.3–3–52–3; Bainbridge 5–1–15–2; Graveney 2–0–9–0.

Umpires: J. C. Balderstone and R. A. White.

At Leicester, June 3, 4, 5. DURHAM lost to LEICESTERSHIRE by an innings and five runs.

DURHAM v MIDDLESEX

At Gateshead Fell, June 10, 11, 12, 14. Drawn. Durham 1 pt, Middlesex 4 pts. Toss: Middlesex.

Play began at 1.50 p.m. on the first day, the second was washed out and, with only 85 minutes' play possible on the third, Middlesex forfeited their first innings in an effort to contrive a result. But the fourth day also fell foul of the weather. Parker, the Durham vice-captain, displayed the fighting spirit which had typified his efforts for the county when he rescued them with his second century of the season – first from 27 for three, and again when three wickets fell for one run later in the day. Williams exploited the damp conditions on the opening day with some impressive seam bowling.

Close of play: First day, Durham 175-7 (P. W. G. Parker 85*, J. Wood 0*); Second day, No play; Third day, Durham 11-0 (I. T. Botham 1*, W. Larkins 5*).

Durham

I. T. Botham c Emburey b Fraser	0	– not out	1
W. Larkins c Carr b Williams	4	– not out	5
P. W. G. Parker b Feltham	109		
J. A. Daley c Carr b Williams	10		
P. Bainbridge c Sims b Williams	40		
J. D. Glendenen c Feltham b Tufnell	1		
A. C. Cummins lbw b Williams	0		
†C. W. Scott c Gatting b Feltham	15		
J. Wood b Fraser	27		
*D. A. Graveney not out	0		
S. J. E. Brown c Brown b Feltham	1		
B 2, l-b 4, w 3, n-b 18	27	L-b 5	5

1/1 2/7 3/27 4/123 5/124   234   (no wkt) 11
6/124 7/159 8/229 9/233

Bonus points – Durham 1, Middlesex 4.

Bowling: *First Innings*—Williams 23–2–73–4; Fraser 24–5–69–2; Feltham 16.2–6–31–3; Emburey 8–1–28–0; Gatting 4–0–10–0; Tufnell 15–7–17–1. *Second Innings*—Fraser 1.2–0–5–0; Feltham 1–0–1–0.

Middlesex

Middlesex forfeited their first innings.

D. L. Haynes, *M. W. Gatting, M. R. Ramprakash, J. D. Carr, †K. R. Brown, R. J. Sims, M. A. Feltham, J. E. Emburey, A. R. C. Fraser, N. F. Williams and P. C. R. Tufnell.

Umpires: B. Leadbeater and P. Willey.

At Colwyn Bay, June 17, 18, 19, 21. DURHAM lost to GLAMORGAN by 113 runs.

DURHAM v WORCESTERSHIRE

At Stockton-on-Tees, June 24, 25, 26, 28. Worcestershire won by three wickets. Worcestershire 22 pts, Durham 4 pts. Toss: Durham.

Worcestershire triumphed, but not before Botham made his presence felt against his former county. Though Graveney chose to bat on a good pitch, only Bainbridge, with 69, reached 20; Benjamin exploited mistakes rather than anything else to take five for 65. Botham then took three wickets as Worcestershire slipped to 139 for seven, before Lampitt and Newport staged a recovery with a stand of 104. But the biggest stand of the game came when Parker was out in the second innings, having batted superbly, and Durham looked doomed at 143 for five. A sixth-wicket partnership of 152, a county record, was fashioned by Botham and Cummins, with a career-best 70. Botham mixed a rare discipline with his usual aggression in scoring 101 off 150 balls, with 18 fours. It was his 38th first-class century, his second for Durham and, so it later proved, the last before retirement. Needing 266 to win, Worcestershire were again tottering at 196 for seven. But Curtis, their captain, saw them home, batting seven and a half hours for 116 not out. Felled by a Cummins bouncer on 91, he finished a memorable match wearing Botham's helmet over his bandaged head. Umpire Dudleston could sympathise; he had left the field for an hour on the first day after his head intercepted a throw from the Worcestershire wicket-keeper.

Close of play: First day, Worcestershire 115-5 (G. A. Hick 59*, S. R. Lampitt 1*); Second day, Durham 177-5 (I. T. Botham 52*, A. C. Cummins 7*); Third day, Worcestershire 123-2 (T. S. Curtis 48*, D. B. D'Oliveira 6*).

Durham

I. T. Botham b Benjamin	8	– (6) c Rhodes b Hick 101
J. D. Glendenen c Curtis b Tolley	18	– lbw b Benjamin 10
P. W. G. Parker c Newport b Benjamin	1	– (1) lbw b Newport 63
S. Hutton c Lampitt b Benjamin	11	– (3) lbw b Benjamin 14
P. Bainbridge lbw b Illingworth	69	– c Rhodes b Newport 0
J. A. Daley lbw b Lampitt	0	– (4) c D'Oliveira b Newport 21
A. C. Cummins c Hick b Newport	15	– c Rhodes b Illingworth 70
P. J. Berry c Rhodes b Benjamin	16	– c Hick b Illingworth 1
†C. W. Scott lbw b Benjamin	13	– not out 28
*D. A. Graveney not out	6	– b Benjamin 16
S. J. E. Brown b Illingworth	4	– run out 2
B 2, l-b 14, n-b 10	26	B 12, l-b 9, n-b 8 29
	—	—
	187	355

1/10 2/20 3/34 4/60 5/68   187   1/41 2/69 3/102 4/102 5/143   355
6/108 7/152 8/168 9/176   6/295 7/303 8/306 9/342

Bonus points – Worcestershire 4.

Bowling: *First Innings*—Benjamin 25-4-65-5; Tolley 14-2-44-1; Lampitt 10-2-26-1; Newport 12-8-10-1; Illingworth 9-3-19-2; Haynes 3-1-7-0. *Second Innings*—Benjamin 24-1-80-3; Newport 24.2-5-75-3; Lampitt 22-4-102-0; Illingworth 22-8-44-2; Haynes 3-1-7-0; Hick 8-2-26-1.

Worcestershire

*T. S. Curtis lbw b Brown	6	– not out 116
W. P. C. Weston c Scott b Cummins	13	– b Bainbridge 26
G. A. Hick c Scott b Botham	69	– lbw b Cummins 32
D. B. D'Oliveira lbw b Brown	10	– lbw b Botham 6
G. R. Haynes c Botham b Brown	7	– c Scott b Botham 4
R. K. Illingworth c Cummins b Botham	1	
S. R. Lampitt b Bainbridge	58	– (6) c Parker b Graveney 9
†S. J. Rhodes lbw b Botham	0	– (7) c Botham b Cummins 16
P. J. Newport b Cummins	51	– (8) b Cummins 5
C. M. Tolley not out	11	– (9) not out 26
K. C. G. Benjamin b Bainbridge	7	
B 10, l-b 13, w 5, n-b 16	44	B 8, l-b 10, n-b 8 26
	—	—
	277	(7 wkts) 266

1/15 2/39 3/81 4/97 5/114   277   1/60 2/108 3/126 4/130 (7 wkts) 266
6/139 7/139 8/243 9/267   5/161 6/190 7/196

Bonus points – Worcestershire 2, Durham 4.

Bowling: *First Innings*—Cummins 24-3-75-2; Brown 25-3-98-3; Botham 31-10-55-3; Graveney 11-4-18-0; Bainbridge 3.4-1-8-2. *Second Innings*—Cummins 29-4-80-3; Brown 15-1-40-0; Graveney 53-31-53-1; Bainbridge 5-1-23-1; Botham 20-6-44-2; Berry 1-0-8-0.

Umpires: J. D. Bond and B. Dudleston (G. Cook deputised for B. Dudleston on 1st day).

At The Oval, July 1, 2. DURHAM lost to SURREY by an innings and 205 runs.

At Durham University, July 17, 18, 19. DURHAM drew with AUSTRALIANS (See Australian tour section).

At Chelmsford, July 22, 23, 24, 26. DURHAM beat ESSEX by 146 runs.

DURHAM v SUSSEX

At Durham University, July 29, 30, 31, August 2. Sussex won by 267 runs. Sussex 24 pts, Durham 6 pts. Toss: Durham.

Durham began this match one point ahead of Sussex but wasted their chance to pull away. Having asked for more grass to be left on the pitch to assist the seamers, they put the visitors in and bowled badly. Cummins was the exception, improving his career-best figures for the second time in a week, to six for 115. Sussex's total of 440 looked vulnerable while Larkins, at his most destructive, was assembling a glorious 88-ball century, with 17 fours and two sixes. But Durham collapsed to the medium-pace of Lenham, who took four for 13. A century from Athey then enabled Sussex to build a lead of 477 before declaring. Athey shared century stands with Lenham, Speight – who hit 66 off 42 balls – and Wells. With Stephenson producing the most hostile bowling of the match, Durham never looked like getting near their daunting target.

Close of play: First day, Sussex 334-6 (F. D. Stephenson 59*, I. D. K. Salisbury 20*); Second day, Durham 279-7 (A. C. Cummins 24*, D. A. Graveney 9*); Third day, Durham 26-2 (W. Larkins 18*, S. P. Hughes 0*).

Sussex

N. J. Lenham c Scott b Brown	88	– b Graveney	78
C. W. J. Athey c Smith b Cummins	36	– not out	118
D. M. Smith lbw b Cummins	38		
*A. P. Wells c Scott b Cummins	0	– not out	67
M. P. Speight st Scott b Graveney	51	– (3) st Scott b Bainbridge	66
†P. Moores c Scott b Cummins	9		
F. D. Stephenson c Larkins b Cummins	90		
I. D. K. Salisbury c Hutton b Cummins	22		
A. C. S. Pigott c Parker b Graveney	52		
E. E. Hemmings not out	8		
E. S. H. Giddins c Hutton b Hughes	1		
B 7, l-b 12, w 8, n-b 18	45	L-b 14, w 7, n-b 12	33

1/135 2/139 3/139 4/220 5/237   **440**   1/143 2/243   (2 wkts dec.) **362**
6/270 7/344 8/395 9/439

Bonus points – Sussex 4, Durham 3 (Score at 120 overs: 365-7).

Bowling: *First Innings*—Cummins 36–9–115–6; Brown 25–4–101–1; Hughes 29.3–6–91–1; Bainbridge 16–3–47–0; Graveney 24–7–48–2; Smith 6–1–19–0. *Second Innings*—Cummins 11–1–48–0; Brown 14–1–87–0; Hughes 16–3–47–0; Bainbridge 19–1–80–1; Graveney 12–1–57–1; Smith 4–0–29–0.

Durham

G. Fowler c Stephenson b Pigott	4	– c Salisbury b Stephenson	0
W. Larkins c Pigott b Lenham	106	– c Moores b Stephenson	22
P. W. G. Parker lbw b Lenham	65	– lbw b Stephenson	8
S. Hutton b Salisbury	41	– (5) c Speight b Salisbury	27
P. Bainbridge c Moores b Lenham	0	– (6) c Wells b Salisbury	42
I. Smith c Wells b Salisbury	6	– (7) c Moores b Stephenson	22
†C. W. Scott b Lenham	2	– (9) c Moores b Salisbury	4
A. C. Cummins not out	35	– lbw b Stephenson	18
*D. A. Graveney c Athey b Giddins	32	– (10) not out	29
S. J. E. Brown c Salisbury b Giddins	9	– (11) st Moores b Salisbury	18
S. P. Hughes lbw b Giddins	2	– (4) c Hemmings b Giddins	2
B 2, l-b 11, n-b 10	23	L-b 8, n-b 10	18

1/4 2/181 3/194 4/194 5/203   **325**   1/8 2/26 3/31 4/41 5/84   **210**
6/206 7/262 8/309 9/321   6/131 7/135 8/155 9/159

Bonus points – Durham 3, Sussex 4.

Bowling: *First Innings*—Pigott 14–1–53–1; Giddins 14.4–2–71–3; Stephenson 11–0–48–0; Salisbury 27–8–89–2; Hemmings 15–4–38–0; Lenham 15–9–13–4. *Second Innings*—Stephenson 18–5–55–5; Giddins 15–5–57–1; Lenham 7–2–17–0; Salisbury 19.2–5–63–4; Pigott 4–0–10–0.

Umpires: J. W. Holder and V. A. Holder.

DURHAM v DERBYSHIRE

At Durham University, August 5, 6, 7, 9. Drawn. Durham 6 pts, Derbyshire 7 pts. Toss: Derbyshire. First-class debuts: S. Lugsden; I. G. S. Steer.

In a match ruined by rain, Derbyshire's lesser-known players seized their chances in the absence of injured colleagues, and Durham's 17-year-old debutant, pace bowler Steven Lugsden, also caught the eye. After the first day was washed out, Rollins and Sladdin scored their maiden half-centuries for Derbyshire, while Mortensen showed unexpected batting talents – hitting two sixes – in a last-wicket stand of 66 with Sladdin. Mortensen then wrecked Durham's reply after they had reached 205 for three, taking four for five in 11 balls. Six Durham batsmen were lbw, all given out by umpire White. With rain preventing play until 2.30 p.m. on the last day there was no chance of a result, but there was at least the opportunity for the Derbyshire newcomer Gary Steer to make up for his second-ball nought in the first innings with 37 not out and for Lugsden to take his first two wickets.

Close of play: First day, No play; Second day, Durham 7-0 (G. Fowler 4*, W. Larkins 3*); Third day, Derbyshire 66-2 (J. E. Morris 41*, A. S. Rollins 15*).

Derbyshire

P. D. Bowler c Larkins b Brown	17	– c Graveney b Cummins	5
*J. E. Morris c Cummins b Bainbridge	45	– c Hutton b Cummins	83
C. J. Adams c Fowler b Brown	0	– c and b Brown	5
A. S. Rollins c Graveney b Brown	52	– c Scott b Lugsden	35
I. G. S. Steer c Graveney b Bainbridge	0	– not out	37
M. J. Vandrau lbw b Graveney	8	– b Lugsden	11
F. A. Griffith c Scott b Cummins	56		
†K. M. Krikken c Bainbridge b Brown	10	– (7) not out	4
S. J. Base c Berry b Graveney	26		
R. W. Sladdin not out	51		
O. H. Mortensen c Larkins b Berry	29		
L-b 5, w 1, n-b 22	28	L-b 2	2

1/55 2/55 3/99 4/99   322   1/22 2/33 3/115   (5 wkts) 182
5/110 6/192 7/214 8/218 9/256   4/148 5/164

Bonus points – Derbyshire 3, Durham 4.

Bowling: *First Innings*—Cummins 24–3–107–1; Brown 25–8–68–4; Lugsden 14–1–42–0; Bainbridge 13–4–43–2; Graveney 22–9–53–2; Berry 3.1–1–4–1. *Second Innings*—Cummins 17–5–44–2; Brown 11–3–40–1; Graveney 7–1–24–0; Lugsden 12–1–43–2; Berry 15–7–26–0; Parker 2–0–2–0; Hutton 2–1–1–0.

Durham

G. Fowler c Krikken b Sladdin	54	*D. A. Graveney c Rollins b Base	3
W. Larkins lbw b Mortensen	21	S. J. E. Brown lbw b Vandrau	31
P. W. G. Parker lbw b Base	3	S. Lugsden not out	5
S. Hutton c Base b Mortensen	57		
P. Bainbridge c and b Base	78	L-b 3, n-b 40	43
A. C. Cummins lbw b Mortensen	4		
P. J. Berry lbw b Mortensen	0	1/45 2/71 3/79 4/205 5/209	299
†C. W. Scott lbw b Mortensen	0	6/213 7/213 8/231 9/260	

Bonus points – Durham 2, Derbyshire 4.

Bowling: Mortensen 18–2–55–5; Base 16–1–98–3; Griffith 7.4–3–16–0; Sladdin 22.2–7–65–1; Vandrau 10–0–40–1; Adams 9–2–22–0.

Umpires: H. D. Bird and R. A. White.

At Northampton, August 12, 13, 14. DURHAM lost to NORTHAMPTONSHIRE by an innings and 48 runs.

DURHAM v WARWICKSHIRE

At Darlington, August 19, 20, 21, 23. Durham won by nine wickets. Durham 23 pts, Warwickshire 5 pts. Toss: Warwickshire.

Durham's win came on the same ground as their last home Championship victory, against Somerset almost 15 months previously, and in similar fashion. Then Larkins led the run-chase with 92 and this time he made 113 not out as Durham beat depleted opposition with 4.3 overs to spare. The game had been drifting towards a draw until Cummins took three wickets in three overs with the new ball on the final morning. Even then Durham looked like being frustrated by Penney, who held out for ten overs batting with a dislocated shoulder. On a pitch where the scoring-rate had been under three an over, a target of 240 off 68 overs looked testing enough even before 16 overs were lost to rain. But Larkins and Fowler put on 202 before Parker, who batted seven and a half hours in the first innings for 159 – his own highest Championship score, and the highest yet for Durham – came in to finish the job.

Close of play: First day, Durham 14-0 (G. Fowler 4*, W. Larkins 1*); Second day, Durham 312-7 (P. W. G. Parker 122*, D. A. Graveney 6*); Third day, Warwickshire 226-5 (P. A. Smith 30*, N. M. K. Smith 17*).

Warwickshire

*A. J. Moles c Larkins b Cummins	42	– c Scott b Cummins	0
J. D. Ratcliffe c Larkins b Brown	24	– lbw b Graveney	29
D. P. Ostler b Cummins	16	– c Daley b Brown	85
T. L. Penney c Scott b Hughes	41	– (11) not out	9
Asif Din c Scott b Hughes	10	– (4) c Scott b Brown	25
R. G. Twose c Parker b Bainbridge	19	– (5) c Parker b Graveney	23
P. A. Smith lbw b Brown	55	– (6) lbw b Cummins	49
N. M. K. Smith c Graveney b Brown	34	– (7) c Scott b Brown	46
†K. J. Piper b Brown	4	– c Scott b Cummins	22
A. F. Giles not out	11	– (8) c Larkins b Cummins	2
M. A. V. Bell c Scott b Brown	2	– (10) c Bainbridge b Cummins	1
B 4, l-b 12, w 1, n-b 6	23	B 2, l-b 16, w 4, n-b 14	36
	281		**327**

1/43 2/84 3/93 4/118 5/164
6/195 7/243 8/251 9/275

1/0 2/68 3/142 4/151 5/200
6/276 7/281 8/295 9/309

Bonus points – Warwickshire 2, Durham 4.

Bowling: *First Innings*—Cummins 19-3-41-2; Hughes 22-6-60-2; Brown 21-2-78-5; Graveney 17-10-28-0; Bainbridge 23-9-58-1. *Second Innings*—Cummins 29.4-6-83-5; Hughes 25-9-46-0; Brown 28-2-102-3; Bainbridge 12-3-29-0; Graveney 26-9-49-2.

Durham

G. Fowler lbw b P. A. Smith	6	– c Ostler b Giles	72
W. Larkins lbw b P. A. Smith	2	– not out	113
P. W. G. Parker c Asif Din b Twose	159	– not out	29
S. Hutton lbw b Twose	18		
P. Bainbridge c Ratcliffe b P. A. Smith	5		
J. A. Daley c Asif Din b Moles	79		
†C. W. Scott lbw b Bell	6		
A. C. Cummins c sub b Twose	17		
*D. A. Graveney b Bell	7		
S. J. E. Brown c Asif Din b Twose	12		
S. P. Hughes not out	3		
B 3, l-b 18, w 2, n-b 32	55	B 6, l-b 11, w 2, n-b 10	29
	369	(1 wkt)	**243**

1/17 2/34 3/70 4/79 5/264
6/272 7/304 8/326 9/344

1/202

Bonus points – Durham 3, Warwickshire 3 (Score at 120 overs: 331-8).

Bowling: *First Innings*—Bell 31–9–96–2; P. A. Smith 26–6–69–3; Twose 34–4–85–4; N. M. K. Smith 25–10–51–0; Giles 11–1–37–0; Moles 5–1–10–1. *Second Innings*—Bell 1–3–48–0; P. A. Smith 11–1–57–0; Twose 10–2–46–0; N. M. K. Smith 11.3–1–48–0; Giles 4–0–27–1.

Umpires: G. I. Burgess and J. H. Hampshire.

At Leeds, August 26, 27, 28, 30. DURHAM drew with YORKSHIRE.

DURHAM v NOTTINGHAMSHIRE

At Chester-le-Street, August 31, September 1, 2. Nottinghamshire won by an innings and 157 runs. Nottinghamshire 24 pts, Durham 5 pts. Toss: Nottinghamshire.

Durham's fifth innings defeat of the season was completed on the third day when they subsided woefully against the bowling of Pennett, whose five for 36 was the third career-best performance of the match by a Nottinghamshire player. The most spectacular came from Lewis, who stroked the ball to all parts of the small ground to make 247, and shared a stand of 301 – the ninth-highest for the seventh wicket ever – with French, who made his own best score, 123. Johnson had led the remarkable recovery from four for two in the second over in pugnacious style; Nottinghamshire scored 508 runs on the second day against increasingly wayward bowling and slipshod fielding. Lewis continued the punishment on the third morning before being last out, caught on the cover boundary after hitting 35 fours and two sixes off 371 balls. It was the highest innings of the season, and Nottinghamshire's 629 the biggest Championship total.

Close of play: First day, Durham 308; Second day, Nottinghamshire 508-6 (C. C. Lewis 197*, B. N. French 74*).

Durham

G. Fowler b Pennett	10	– c French b Pick 38
W. Larkins lbw b Pennett	62	– lbw b Pennett 23
P. W. G. Parker c Robinson b Mike	6	– c Johnson b Pennett 7
S. Hutton c Mike b Pennett	13	– b Pennett 0
P. Bainbridge lbw b Lewis	45	– c Dessaur b Pennett.......... 0
J. A. Daley c Johnson b Mike	9	– c French b Pennett 44
A. C. Cummins c French b Mike	23	– c French b Pick 4
J. Wood not out	63	– c Dessaur b Pick 2
*D. A. Graveney lbw b Lewis	20	– (10) not out 15
†A. R. Fothergill c Lewis b Pick	5	– (9) lbw b Pick 0
S. J. E. Brown c Johnson b Hindson	21	– c Pollard b Pick 9
B 3, l-b 8, n-b 20	31	B 2, l-b 9, w 3, n-b 8 22

1/21 2/41 3/104 4/111 5/143   308   1/50 2/70 3/70 4/70 5/92   164
5/181 7/191 8/219 9/259   6/102 7/104 8/122 9/144

Bonus points – Durham 3, Nottinghamshire 4.

Bowling: *First Innings*—Lewis 25–9–44–2; Pennett 24–3–73–3; Pick 23–8–66–1; Mike 21–3–90–3; Hindson 10.5–2–24–1. *Second Innings*—Lewis 2–0–7–0; Pennett 16–5–36–5; Mike 14–1–57–0; Pick 17–5–53–5.

Nottinghamshire

P. R. Pollard lbw b Cummins	17	J. E. Hindson c Parker b Bainbridge... 1
W. A. Dessaur b Cummins	0	R. A. Pick b Brown.............. 5
M. Saxelby run out	0	D. B. Pennett not out 10
P. Johnson c Daley b Bainbridge	130	
*R. T. Robinson c Daley b Bainbridge	5	B 12, l-b 11, w 3, n-b 44 70
C. C. Lewis c sub b Cummins	247	
G. W. Mike c Larkins b Cummins	21	1/3 2/4 3/49 4/71 5/249 629
†B. N. French c Fothergill b Brown	123	6/302 7/603 8/604 9/609

Bonus points – Nottinghamshire 4, Durham 2 (Score at 120 overs: 569-6).

Bowling: Cummins 29.1–0–137–4; Wood 26–1–148–0; Brown 31–3–161–2; Bainbridge 35–5–132–3; Larkins 4–0–18–0; Parker 7–3–10–0.

Umpires: J. D. Bond and P. Willey.

DURHAM v SOMERSET

At Hartlepool, September 16, 17, 18, 20. Somerset won by five wickets. Somerset 24 pts, Durham 4 pts. Toss: Durham. First-class debut: M. M. Betts.

Durham began the final match of the season hoping for a victory to lift them off the foot of the table. After the first day's washout they made a promising start, reducing Somerset to 107 for four. But then two bowlers were injured and a third – 18-year-old fast bowler Melvyn Betts, who had bowled Lathwell in his third over of first-class cricket – went down with flu. With Durham's attack thus handicapped, Somerset's acting-captain Harden took advantage with a patient century. Then Caddick extracted far more life from the pitch that the Durham bowlers, in a superb opening spell of 13 overs which brought him five for 44. Despite a high-class 73 by Daley, Durham failed by nine runs to avoid the follow-on. They reached the relative prosperity of 217 for five in their second innings before Rose took four for ten in 18 balls, leaving Somerset to score 101 in 39 overs. With rain threatening, they sped home in the 22nd over, sacrificing wickets on the way.

Close of play: First day, No play; Second day, Somerset 273-5 (R. J. Harden 82*, G. D. Rose 42*); Third day, Durham 84-2 (P. W. G. Parker 34*, S. J. E. Brown 0*).

Somerset

A. N. Hayhurst st Fothergill b Bainbridge	37	– c Graveney b Cummins	4
M. N. Lathwell b Betts	30	– c Fothergill b Brown	24
N. A. Folland c Fowler b Bainbridge	28	– b Bainbridge	9
*R. J. Harden c Brown b Graveney	100	– b Bainbridge	28
I. Fletcher c and b Graveney	2	– c Larkins b Bainbridge	11
†R. J. Turner b Cummins	34	– (7) not out	0
G. D. Rose c Larkins b Cummins	83	– (6) not out	6
Mushtaq Ahmed run out	0		
N. A. Mallender c Fothergill b Cummins	5		
A. R. Caddick st Fothergill b Graveney	6		
A. P. van Troost not out	0		
B 6, l-b 8, w 1, n-b 12	27	B 4, w 1, n-b 14	19

1/50 2/99 3/102 4/107 5/207   352   1/28 2/32 3/64   (5 wkts) 101
6/312 7/312 8/331 9/348   4/89 5/94

Bonus points – Somerset 4, Durham 4.

Bowling: *First Innings*—Cummins 22.3-3-58-3; Brown 28-1-120-0; Betts 6-1-19-1; Graveney 47-12-105-3; Bainbridge 9-4-10-2; Parker 7-0-26-0. *Second Innings*—Cummins 9-2-40-1; Brown 6-0-25-1; Bainbridge 4.2-1-31-3; Graveney 2-1-1-0.

Durham

G. Fowler c Turner b Caddick	14	– c Lathwell b Mushtaq Ahmed	19
W. Larkins c Mushtaq Ahmed b Caddick	4	– lbw b Rose	17
P. W. G. Parker c Rose b Caddick	0	– c Turner b Mushtaq Ahmed	47
S. Hutton c Turner b Mallender	4	– (5) c Rose b Mushtaq Ahmed	32
J. A. Daley b Mushtaq Ahmed	73	– (7) lbw b Rose	24
P. Bainbridge c Mushtaq Ahmed b Caddick	0	– c Hayhurst b Rose	51
A. C. Cummins c Turner b Caddick	4	– (8) c Harden b Rose	22
†A. R. Fothergill c Hayhurst b Mallender	29	– (9) lbw b Rose	0
*D. A. Graveney c Turner b van Troost	13	– (10) not out	8
S. J. E. Brown c Turner b Caddick	9	– (4) c Rose b Mushtaq Ahmed	0
M. M. Betts not out	0	– c Turner b Caddick	4
B 2, l-b 5, w 1, n-b 36	44	B 10, l-b 1, w 1, n-b 22	34

1/5 2/5 3/14 4/48 5/48   194   1/20 2/80 3/84 4/116 5/145   258
6/66 7/127 8/147 9/190   6/217 7/232 8/232 9/247

Bonus points – Somerset 4.

Bowling: *First Innings*—Caddick 19.2-4-73-6; Mallender 11-4-24-2; Mushtaq Ahmed 14-5-32-1; van Troost 6-0-58-1. *Second Innings*—Caddick 23-6-63-1; Rose 13-1-46-5; Mallender 10-1-39-0; Mushtaq Ahmed 26-10-63-4; van Troost 7-0-36-0.

Umpires: B. Leadbeater and N. T. Plews.

ESSEX

President: T. N. Pearce
Chairman: D. L. Acfield
Chairman, Cricket Committee: G. J. Saville
Secretary/General Manager: P. J. Edwards
Captain: G. A. Gooch
Head Groundsman: S. Kerrison
Scorer: C. F. Driver

Catastrophic might be too strong a word but Graham Gooch and his Essex players would be the first to admit that 1993 was a summer of immense disappointment and unfulfilled promise. The campaign began with many commentators predicting that, after 14 years of success, Essex would do even better following the introduction of a full four-day Championship programme. In the event, Essex were never in the hunt for a third successive title, touching third from bottom in the last week in August and finishing 11th. They came 12th in the Sunday League and succumbed as soon as they met first-class opponents in both knockouts. Test cricket played a prominent part: six players were picked for England, up to four of them at the same time. However, Essex had overcome similar problems in the past and the fear at the end of 1993 was that the good times were finally over.

Neil Foster's retirement through injury with two months of the season left was a particularly hard blow. But the biggest problem was a collective loss of form. Too many people failed to live up to expectations, from the moment they suffered a crushing 239-run defeat in the opening Championship match against Yorkshire at Chelmsford. This was especially true among the seam bowlers. The left-arm Mark Ilott was easily the leading wicket-taker with 51, and reached the Test team, but even he failed to develop the variations in his bowling that everyone expected when, as a teenager, he looked such a promising successor to John Lever.

Meanwhile, Derek Pringle, Don Topley, Steve Andrew and Foster managed only 84 wickets between them in a combined total of 40 first-class matches for Essex – not a strike-rate that wins titles. Opposing bowlers of the same type often looked more menacing, proved more penetrating and appeared to have a greater appetite for battle. Indeed, John Stephenson, whose bowling depends on the fact that his little out-swingers are not as innocuous as they look, took more wickets than any of them. Pringle, at 35, appeared to have lost much of his enthusiasm and, in the winter, followed Foster into retirement, becoming cricket correspondent of the Independent on Sunday. Topley and Andrew were keen enough but rarely had much effect. Andrew's 28 wickets included two "seven-fors", against Lancashire and Glamorgan, but otherwise his form was indifferent. For the first time since Hugh Page's unhappy season in 1987, Essex decided to sign a bowler as their overseas player: the Australian paceman Michael Kasprowicz.

Although Essex failed to impress as a cohesive force, several players will look back on 1993 with a measure of personal satisfaction. As well as Ilott, off-spinner Peter Such won his first England cap and Nasser Hussain returned to the Test team after more than three years. It is impossible to find fresh words to describe the massive contribution Gooch continued to make as a batsman. He was 40 in July but his consistency, concentration and skill – not to mention dedication – still made him a national treasure. Only four times in 19 matches for Essex and England did he fail to score at least one half-century; it was late August before he missed out in the Championship. He was the only batsman in the country to reach 2,000 runs for the season, scoring 2,023 in all, and collected six hundreds and 14 fifties.

Yet it was Hussain's vast improvement which was the most heartening feature. In 1993 he discovered how to make bowlers work for his wicket rather than gifting it with a loose shot. His greater mental toughness, allied to far better judgment in the selection of strokes, brought him seven centuries and 1,604 runs at an average of 53.46. Paul Prichard's four centuries included a double-hundred and two hundreds in a match (a feat Gooch achieved for the fourth time in the final game against Hampshire) but other batsmen too often struggled for fluency and form. Stephenson reserved his best efforts for the Sunday League in which he aggregated 663 runs. But he only just managed to top 1,000 in first-class cricket. Salim Malik was right out of touch on his return to the county.

Of the younger generation, Jonathan Lewis could feel reasonably satisfied with 736 runs at 36.80, but Nick Knight and Nadeem Shahid failed to make much of their admittedly limited opportunities. But one youngster who seemed certain to break through sooner rather than later was Robert Rollins. An injury to Mike Garnham provided the England Under-19 wicket-keeper with his chance towards the end of the season and he impressed everyone. The spinners, Such and John Childs, who was awarded a benefit in 1994, were easily the county's most successful wicket-takers. Such's final haul of 76 was by far the best of his career to date and included six for 67 on his Test debut against Australia at Old Trafford. That represented one of seven occasions he captured five or more in an innings. Childs's guile and persistence were rewarded with 62 wickets. But with very little penetration coming from elsewhere to supplement the spinners, Essex seldom looked like bowling sides out.

That brings us back to Foster. In June he was ecstatic at collecting his 29th Test cap, his Lord's appearance following a gap of four years during which he was banned for touring South Africa. Deep despair arrived the following month with the announcement that he had played his last game for club and country; he played just once after the Test. A succession of knee operations over the years – nine in all – finally took their toll and he heeded advice to retire. He bowed out with 908 wickets and 4,343 runs – and the knowledge that he contributed as much as anyone towards Essex's years of success. On the two occasions Foster took 100 wickets in a season, the county won the Championship; had he steered clear of injury – the early part of his career was beset with back problems – he would have made even more impact. Pringle was another important figure: his relaxed demeanour belied the fact that he was a better bowler than many people thought. He was probably a better batsman than he himself thought, and with more self-belief might have been a great all-rounder.

Essex's profits declined both because of reduced sponsorship at four-day games, as the club had predicted all along, and the disappointments on the field. There was squeezing room only in the ground for all three days of the Australian game at Chelmsford. But it was hard to envisage too many more great days like that until a new generation of fast bowlers comes along. – Nigel Fuller.

413

ESSEX 1993

[Bill Smith]

Back row: R. J. Rollins, D. W. Ayres, J. J. B. Lewis, M. Diwan, D. D. J. Robinson, J. P. Stephenson, L. Tennant, G. A. Khan. *Middle row*: M. C. Ilott, J. W. S. Davis (*physiotherapist*), N. Shahid, P. M. Such, A. G. J. Fraser, S. J. W. Andrew, D. J. P. Boden. D. M. Cousins, N. Hussain, N. V. Knight, A. R. Butcher (*Second XI captain/coach*). *Front row*: M. A. Garnham, J. H. Childs, D. R. Pringle, G. A. Gooch (*captain*), P. J. Prichard, N. A. Foster, T. D. Topley.

ESSEX RESULTS

All first-class matches – Played 20: Won 5, Lost 6, Drawn 9.

County Championship matches – Played 17: Won 4, Lost 6, Drawn 7.

Bonus points – Batting 44, Bowling 55.

*Competition placings – Britannic Assurance County Championship, 11th;
NatWest Bank Trophy, 2nd round; Benson and Hedges Cup, 1st round;
AXA Equity & Law League, 12th.*

BRITANNIC ASSURANCE CHAMPIONSHIP AVERAGES

BATTING

	Birthplace	M	I	NO	R	HS	Avge
‡G. A. Gooch	Leytonstone	10	18	2	991	159*	61.9
‡N. Hussain	Madras, India	13	23	3	1,102	152	55.1
‡P. J. Prichard	Billericay	17	32	3	1,237	225*	42.6
J. J. B. Lewis	Isleworth	11	20	2	706	136*	39.2
‡D. R. Pringle	Nairobi, Kenya	12	19	4	575	76	38.3
‡Salim Malik§	Lahore, Pakistan	14	25	2	861	132	37.4
‡J. P. Stephenson	Stebbing	16	30	2	944	122	33.7
‡M. A. Garnham	Johannesburg, SA	14	24	4	637	106	31.8
D. D. J. Robinson . .	Braintree	2	4	0	112	67	28.0
N. Shahid	Karachi, Pakistan	6	11	1	258	69*	25.8
‡N. A. Foster	Colchester	6	8	2	136	37	22.6
‡M. C. Ilott	Watford	13	17	4	195	51	15.0
N. V. Knight	Watford	4	8	0	102	36	12.7
‡T. D. Topley	Canterbury	6	9	0	101	33	11.2
‡J. H. Childs	Plymouth	14	15	8	76	23	10.8
‡P. M. Such	Helensburgh	12	14	1	131	54	10.0
S. J. W. Andrew	London	10	13	4	74	18	8.2
R. J. Rollins	Plaistow	3	4	1	14	7	4.6

Also batted: D. J. P. Boden (*Eccleshall*) (2 matches) 0, 5; D. M. Cousins (*Cambridge*)
(1 match) 0*, 0; B. J. Hyam (*Romford*) (1 match) 1, 0.

* *Signifies not out.*   ‡ *Denotes county cap.*   § *Overseas player.*

The following played a total of 18 three-figure innings for Essex in County Championship
matches – N. Hussain 5, P. J. Prichard 4, G. A. Gooch 3, Salim Malik 2, J. P. Stephenson
2, M. A. Garnham 1, J. J. B. Lewis 1.

BOWLING

	O	M	R	W	BB	5W/i	Avge
M. C. Ilott	452.4	95	1,349	48	7-85	2	28.1
P. M. Such	478.1	110	1,284	44	5-66	4	29.1
J. H. Childs	608.3	175	1,466	49	6-37	3	29.9
J. P. Stephenson	257.5	51	866	28	5-31	2	30.9
Salim Malik	243.1	41	743	23	5-67	1	32.3
S. J. W. Andrew	255.4	46	886	25	7-47	2	35.4
D. R. Pringle	311.5	79	863	22	4-33	0	39.2
T. D. Topley	153.1	31	560	12	2-46	0	46.6
N. A. Foster	196.3	50	559	11	5-58	1	50.8

Also bowled: D. J. P. Boden 40-3-216-3; D. M. Cousins 27-4-109-1; G. A. Gooch
5-1-30-0; N. Hussain 10.3-0-108-1; P. J. Prichard 6-0-77-1; N. Shahid 7-1-22-0.

Wicket-keepers: M. A. Garnham 31 ct, 4 st; R. J. Rollins 3 ct, 3 st.

Leading Fielders: J. P. Stephenson 20, P. J. Prichard 15.

ESSEX v ENGLAND A

At Chelmsford, April 22, 23, 24, 25. Toss: England A. Essex won by nine wickets.

Career-best match figures of 11 for 124 from off-spinner Such enabled champions Essex to confirm their class against pretenders to full England status. The selectors added Salisbury and Taylor, who had been with the senior squad in India and Sri Lanka, and Crawley, the Cambridge captain, to the A team which toured Australia. However, Such's variety proved too much for many of his younger opponents, although Lathwell emerged from the match with his reputation enhanced, showing judgment and patience in both innings. Gooch just failed to record what was either his 100th or 101st first-class century – the question was in dispute – when he became the first of three wickets in four balls for Taylor. Caddick, who twice had the Essex captain dropped, and Cork had little luck during lively spells; and neither could disturb the smooth progress of Hussain, whose hundred spanned 319 minutes. Lloyd's belligerent 95 helped England A avoid an innings defeat after Gooch made them follow on, but, despite rain delaying the final day's play, Essex won with more than 21 overs to spare.

Close of play: First day, Essex 306-7 (N. Hussain 76*, M. C. Ilott 18*); Second day, England A 137-8 (D. G. Cork 18*, I. D. K. Salisbury 4*); Third day, England A 217-6 (G. D. Lloyd 64*, D. G. Cork 7*).

Essex

*G. A. Gooch c Russell b Taylor	88	– not out		32
J. P. Stephenson c Caddick b Salisbury	38	– c Caddick b Salisbury		29
J. J. B. Lewis c Russell b Cork	16	– not out		5
N. Hussain lbw b Cork	118			
N. V. Knight b Taylor	0			
†M. A. Garnham lbw b Taylor	0			
D. R. Pringle run out	25			
T. D. Topley lbw b Taylor	10			
M. C. Ilott b Caddick	32			
P. M. Such b Cork	26			
J. H. Childs not out	1			
B 14, l-b 11, w 1, n-b 14	40	L-b 1, n-b 8		9

1/89 2/158 3/180 4/180 5/180   **394** 1/50   (1 wkt) **75**
6/235 7/263 8/330 9/393

Bowling: *First Innings*—Caddick 35-5-99-1; Taylor 36-9-94-4; Cork 33.2-10-78-3; Thorpe 2-0-10-0; Salisbury 31-10-83-1. *Second Innings*—Caddick 6-1-19-0; Taylor 7-1-41-0; Salisbury 4.4-0-14-1.

England A

M. N. Lathwell c Lewis b Ilott	30	– c Childs b Stephenson		84
M. A. Roseberry c Knight b Ilott	0	– b Such		6
*M. D. Moxon c Knight b Childs	26	– lbw b Such		40
G. P. Thorpe lbw b Such	26	– b Stephenson		0
G. D. Lloyd c Gooch b Childs	6	– c Knight b Pringle		95
J. P. Crawley b Such	15	– b Such		0
†R. C. Russell b Such	0	– b Such		11
D. G. Cork lbw b Such	52	– c Lewis b Such		15
A. R. Caddick b Childs	3	– c Lewis b Such		0
I. D. K. Salisbury b Such	6	– not out		12
J. P. Taylor not out	0	– b Childs		21
L-b 2, n-b 8	10	B 1, l-b 6, w 1, n-b 2		10

1/2 2/41 3/72 4/88 5/108   **174** 1/26 2/135 3/135 4/145 5/145   **294**
6/110 7/113 8/116 9/143   6/207 7/243 8/259 9/260

Bowling: *First Innings*—Pringle 13-6-17-0; Ilott 19-2-59-2; Topley 6-1-23-0; Childs 16-3-47-3; Such 13.5-6-26-5. *Second Innings*—Pringle 21-8-48-1; Ilott 12-2-43-0; Such 32-8-98-6; Topley 5-0-17-0; Childs 13.3-4-39-1; Stephenson 8-1-42-2.

Umpires: B. Leadbeater and K. E. Palmer.

At Cambridge, May 1, 2, 3. ESSEX drew with CAMBRIDGE UNIVERSITY.

ESSEX v YORKSHIRE

At Chelmsford, May 6, 7, 8, 10. Yorkshire won by 239 runs. Yorkshire 24 pts, Essex 6 pts. Toss: Yorkshire.

A career-best 156 from Byas, with 23 fours and three sixes, underpinned Yorkshire's substantial total. The Essex reply was disappointing, apart from an enterprising fifty by Garnham, and they only just avoided the follow-on. Their hopes rose when Yorkshire's second innings got off to a disastrous start, as Ilott removed three batsmen with only five on the board. But half-centuries from Byas, who played another classy innings, Grayson and Blakey enabled Yorkshire to recover. Essex finally faced a huge target of 455. Gooch and Stephenson inspired faint hope with an opening stand of 91 but early on the final day Jarvis, acting-captain because Moxon's wife had just given birth, turned the tide firmly in Yorkshire's favour. He dismissed Gooch, Salim Malik and Hussain in 15 balls. Ilott was left once again to Garnham to give the champions' response respectability; he was last out for a second fifty.

Close of play: First day, Yorkshire 353-8 (D. Gough 0*); Second day, Yorkshire 11-3 (D. Byas 4*, R. D. Stemp 4*); Third day, Essex 98-1 (G. A. Gooch 46*, M. C. Ilott 1*).

Yorkshire

S. A. Kellett c Garnham b Such	52	– c Stephenson b Ilott	0
A. A. Metcalfe lbw b Foster	5	– c Garnham b Ilott	0
D. Byas c Hussain b Salim Malik	156	– c Ilott b Salim Malik	50
C. White c Gooch b Foster	31	– c Garnham b Ilott	1
†R. J. Blakey c Garnham b Pringle	46	– (6) st Garnham b Such	74
A. P. Grayson b Ilott	30	– (7) lbw b Such	55
*P. W. Jarvis c Garnham b Ilott	1	– (8) lbw b Childs	21
D. Gough c Foster b Such	39	– (9) c Stephenson b Such	0
J. D. Batty c Pringle b Ilott	4	– (10) run out	25
R. D. Stemp b Ilott	5	– (5) lbw b Childs	37
M. A. Robinson not out	0	– not out	16
B 4, l-b 12, w 6, n-b 6	28	B 4, l-b 20, n-b 4	28
	397		**307**

1/11 2/137 3/217 4/297 5/342
6/348 7/349 8/353 9/359

1/0 2/1 3/5 4/83 5/102
6/237 7/256 8/256 9/270

Bonus points – Yorkshire 4, Essex 4 (Score at 120 overs: 381-9).

Bowling: *First Innings*—Foster 24–4–94–2; Ilott 25–6–79–4; Pringle 18–8–32–1; Stephenson 5–1–25–0; Childs 20–3–57–0; Such 23.3–3–55–2; Salim Malik 11–0–39–1. *Second Innings*—Foster 13–8–21–0; Ilott 21.4–2–67–3; Salim Malik 5–0–25–1; Such 27–8–73–3; Childs 21–4–76–2; Pringle 6–1–21–0.

Essex

*G. A. Gooch c Gough b Robinson	38	– b Jarvis	50
J. P. Stephenson c Stemp b Gough	32	– lbw b Robinson	40
P. J. Prichard b Jarvis	12	– (8) b White	7
Salim Malik b Jarvis	4	– c and b Jarvis	0
N. Hussain lbw b White	9	– c Batty b Jarvis	13
†M. A. Garnham run out	53	– c Blakey b Jarvis	58
D. R. Pringle c and b Batty	39	– c Byas b White	7
N. A. Foster c White b Batty	18	– (9) lbw b White	5
M. C. Ilott not out	11	– (3) lbw b Robinson	1
P. M. Such lbw b Gough	6	– b Robinson	0
J. H. Childs c Blakey b Gough	0	– not out	12
B 4, l-b 10, n-b 14	28	L-b 10, w 2, n-b 10	22
	250		**215**

1/52 2/94 3/98 4/98 5/129
6/207 7/218 8/238 9/250

1/91 2/105 3/105 4/121 5/121
6/144 7/159 8/159 9/179

Bonus points – Essex 2, Yorkshire 4.

Bowling: *First Innings*—Jarvis 19-3-64-2; Gough 14.2-1-53-3; Robinson 17-5-34-1; Stemp 9-2-27-0; White 5-1-15-1; Batty 14-3-43-2. *Second Innings*—Jarvis 20.4-2-76-4; Gough 11-1-52-0; Robinson 19-5-45-3; Batty 5-0-21-0; White 7-3-9-3; Stemp 1-0-2-0.

Umpires: A. A. Jones and B. Leadbeater.

At The Oval, May 13, 14, 15, 17. ESSEX drew with SURREY.

ESSEX v DERBYSHIRE

At Chelmsford, May 20, 21, 22, 24. Drawn. Essex 8 pts, Derbyshire 3 pts. Toss: Essex. County debut: M. J. Vandrau.

On a ground where they had lost their five previous Championship matches by an innings, Derbyshire easily saved the match despite following on 268 behind late on the third day. As the pitch became easier, Barnett batted with fine resolution throughout the final day to score his first century against Essex, which gave him hundreds against every county but Durham. He hit 14 boundaries. After the first day's play had been lost to the weather, Hussain and Salim Malik had shared a stand of 290 in 71 overs. Hussain's 152 spanned 225 balls and contained 21 fours and a six; Malik took 33 balls and 35 minutes to open his account before going on to amass 132, including 13 fours and four sixes. When Derbyshire replied, Foster struck in each of his first two overs. Only Adams and Griffith performed with any degree of confidence, whereas the next day Derbyshire lost only one wicket, the night-watchman Sladdin for a career-best 42.

Close of play: First day, No play; Second day, Essex 421-5 (M. A. Garnham 20*, N. A. Foster 9*); Third day, Derbyshire 5-0 (K. J. Barnett 1*, R. W. Sladdin 0*).

Essex

*P. J. Prichard c O'Gorman b Warner	33	T. D. Topley c Bowler b Warner		0
J. P. Stephenson b Sladdin	43			
J. J. B. Lewis c Bowler b Vandrau	8	B 10, l-b 8, n-b 8		26
Salim Malik c Maher b Griffith	132			
N. Hussain c Maher b Malcolm	152	1/55 2/89 3/93	(7 wkts dec.)	471
†M. A. Garnham not out	40	4/383 5/397		
N. A. Foster c Griffith b Sladdin	37	6/464 7/471		

M. C. Ilott, P. M. Such and J. H. Childs did not bat.

Bonus points – Essex 4, Derbyshire 2 (Score at 120 overs: 461-5).

Bowling: Malcolm 19-4-63-1; Warner 20-4-81-2; Adams 12-1-66-0; Griffith 13-2-43-1; Sladdin 34-11-121-2; Vandrau 24-9-79-1.

Derbyshire

*K. J. Barnett lbw b Foster	2	– not out		130
P. D. Bowler lbw b Foster	5	– (3) not out		71
J. E. Morris c Garnham b Ilott	24			
C. J. Adams c Salim Malik b Such	54			
T. J. G. O'Gorman st Garnham b Childs	17			
F. A. Griffith b Ilott	53			
M. J. Vandrau c Such b Topley	21			
†B. J. M. Maher lbw b Ilott	0			
A. E. Warner c and b Salim Malik	3			
R. W. Sladdin c Lewis b Salim Malik	10	– (2) c sub b Salim Malik		42
D. E. Malcolm not out	1			
B 4, l-b 7, n-b 2	13	L-b 7, w 1, n-b 2		10

1/2 2/11 3/72 4/86 5/123	203	1/98 (1 wkt) 253
6/178 7/178 8/183 9/195		

Bonus points – Derbyshire 1, Essex 4.

Bowling: *First Innings*—Foster 13–6–16–2; Ilott 23–7–49–3; Childs 26–12–26–1; Topley 5–0–17–1; Such 17–2–51–1; Salim Malik 16.4–5–33–2. *Second Innings*—Foster 17–4–47–0; Ilott 11–5–37–0; Childs 28–19–24–0; Such 19–5–44–0; Salim Malik 23–8–56–1; Topley 5–0–17–0; Stephenson 6–0–21–0.

Umpires: J. H. Hampshire and P. Willey.

ESSEX v SOMERSET

At Chelmsford, June 3, 4, 5. Essex won by seven wickets. Essex 22 pts, Somerset 5 pts. Toss: Essex.

Even Lathwell's magnificent 132, his highest score for Somerset, could not prevent Essex claiming their first Championship victory of the summer with over a day to spare. Lathwell's innings ended when he was caught on the boundary seeking his third six in an over from Topley. In all he batted just over four hours, facing 201 balls, and contributed 67 per cent of a total of 197. Mushtaq Ahmed had rescued Somerset on the opening day after they had struggled on a green pitch in overcast conditions. As the sun came out, Prichard took full advantage and guided Essex to a useful first-innings lead, while Foster's fire and accuracy soon spelled trouble for Somerset – apart from Lathwell – when they went in again. Left needing a modest 135 for victory, Essex overcame the early loss of Prichard to reach their target with ease.

Close of play: First day, Essex 73-1 (P. J. Prichard 30*, J. J. B. Lewis 9*); Second day, Somerset 88-6 (M. N. Lathwell 46*, N. A. Mallender 8*).

Somerset

A. N. Hayhurst c Garnham b Foster	6	– run out	3
M. N. Lathwell lbw b Topley	48	– c Andrew b Topley	132
R. J. Harden c Garnham b Andrew	10	– c Topley b Foster	4
*C. J. Tavaré c Garnham b Andrew	0	– c Pringle b Topley	5
N. A. Folland c Garnham b Foster	4	– c Hussain b Foster	9
†N. D. Burns c Garnham b Pringle	8	– b Foster	4
G. D. Rose c Prichard b Andrew	7	– lbw b Foster	0
Mushtaq Ahmed c Salim Malik b Childs	71	– (9) c Stephenson b Childs	0
N. A. Mallender b Stephenson b Topley	12	– (8) lbw b Foster	13
J. I. D. Kerr not out	19	– not out	8
A. P. van Troost b Pringle	1	– c Pringle b Salim Malik	4
B 4, w 2, n-b 10	16	B 4, l-b 3, n-b 8	15
	202		197

1/18 2/47 3/53 4/80 5/80 6/96 7/98 8/144 9/193

1/14 2/36 3/49 4/60 5/70 6/72 7/110 8/123 9/192

Bonus points – Somerset 1, Essex 4.

Bowling: *First Innings*—Foster 19–4–40–2; Pringle 20.1–8–29–2; Andrew 20–9–48–3; Topley 14–3–46–2; Stephenson 3–1–22–0; Childs 6–1–13–1. *Second Innings*—Foster 29–8–58–5; Andrew 12–3–31–0; Topley 14–4–50–2; Childs 9–2–23–1; Pringle 5–1–22–0; Salim Malik 1.5–0–6–1.

Essex

*P. J. Prichard c Lathwell b Mushtaq Ahmed	123	– c Hayhurst b Kerr	5
J. P. Stephenson c Kerr b Rose	32	– c Burns b Rose	17
J. J. B. Lewis c Tavaré b Rose	10	– c Burns b Hayhurst	50
Salim Malik b Mallender	0	– not out	49
N. Hussain c Tavaré b Mallender	2	– not out	1
†M. A. Garnham c Tavaré b Kerr	12		
D. R. Pringle c and b Kerr	54		
N. A. Foster c Folland b Kerr	15		
T. D. Topley lbw b Mushtaq Ahmed	0		
S. J. W. Andrew b Mallender	4		
J. H. Childs not out	2		
L-b 7, w 2, n-b 2	11	B 2, l-b 8, n-b 4	14
	265	(3 wkts)	136

1/52 2/75 3/82 4/94 5/117 6/235 7/251 8/256 9/259

1/7 2/67 3/131

Bonus points – Essex 2, Somerset 4.

Bowling: *First Innings*—Mallender 15.1–4–36–3; van Troost 12–1–38–0; Rose 19–4–55–2; Kerr 17–2–47–3; Mushtaq Ahmed 25–6–60–2; Hayhurst 8–3–22–0. *Second Innings*—Mallender 10–4–27–0; Kerr 8–3–14–1; Rose 9–2–24–1; Mushtaq Ahmed 14–5–31–0; van Troost 5–1–12–0; Lathwell 4–2–3–0; Hayhurst 3–0–13–1; Tavaré 1–0–2–0.

Umpires: V. A. Holder and A. G. T. Whitehead.

At Manchester, June 10, 11, 12, 14. ESSEX drew with LANCASHIRE.

At Nottingham, June 17, 18, 19, 21. ESSEX drew with NOTTINGHAMSHIRE.

ESSEX v WARWICKSHIRE

At Ilford, June 24, 25, 26, 28. Essex won by three wickets. Essex 22 pts, Warwickshire 5 pts. Toss: Warwickshire.

Victory was achieved with 17 of the final 20 overs remaining, although Essex made hard work of it after Gooch and Stephenson had opened with a century stand. The result could have been quite different had the visitors accepted catches offered by Stephenson, when 40, and Salim Malik, put down with only a single to his name. They were also handicapped by the breakdown of Small in his second spell. Ostler, with 24 fours in his 174, provided the backbone of Warwickshire's first innings, while Hussain collected his fourth first-class century of the season, striking 16 fours and a six, before Essex declared 64 adrift. Malik, with his best-ever figures in the Championship, and Stephenson unhinged Warwickshire when they batted again after they had reached 111 with only one wicket down. Two wickets fell at that score to enhance the ancient superstition.

Close of play: First day, Warwickshire 355-5 (T. L. Penney 32*, T. A. Munton 0*); Second day, Essex 271-3 (Salim Malik 53*, N. Hussain 42*); Third day, Warwickshire 206.

Warwickshire

A. J. Moles c and b Ilott	17	– c Garnham b Salim Malik	55
J. D. Ratcliffe c Garnham b Stephenson	80	– c Stephenson b Salim Malik	36
D. P. Ostler c Stephenson b Ilott	174	– c Pringle b Salim Malik	43
P. A. Smith lbw b Stephenson	6	– lbw b Salim Malik	0
*D. A. Reeve c Garnham b Pringle	19	– lbw b Stephenson	19
T. L. Penney lbw b Such	50	– lbw b Stephenson	4
T. A. Munton c Garnham b Ilott	5	– (11) lbw b Stephenson	0
†P. C. L. Holloway lbw b Such	12	– (7) lbw b Stephenson	0
N. M. K. Smith c Stephenson b Childs	33	– (8) c and b Stephenson	16
G. C. Small b Salim Malik	18	– (9) c Garnham b Salim Malik	7
A. A. Donald not out	0	– (10) not out	7
B 2, l-b 18, n-b 14	34	B 4, l-b 7, n-b 8	19

1/31 2/158 3/186 4/234 5/355   448   1/75 2/111 3/111 4/156 5/162   206
6/381 7/381 8/403 9/442   6/163 7/174 8/195 9/201

Bonus points – Warwickshire 4, Essex 2 (Score at 120 overs: 370-5).

Bowling: *First Innings*—Foster 15–3–37–0; Ilott 23–4–64–3; Such 28–3–95–2; Childs 37.1–9–82–1; Salim Malik 17–2–70–1; Pringle 10–3–36–1; Stephenson 16–5–44–2. *Second Innings*—Foster 3–0–6–0; Ilott 4–0–19–0; Such 13–1–44–0; Childs 14–5–28–0; Salim Malik 26–5–67–5; Stephenson 12.2–4–31–5.

Essex

*G. A. Gooch b N. M. K. Smith	71	– lbw b N. M. K. Smith	63
J. P. Stephenson c Holloway b Munton	15	– c Holloway b Small	64
P. J. Prichard c Ratcliffe b P. A. Smith	68	– c Ratcliffe b P. A. Smith	30
Salim Malik c Donald b Reeve	90	– b Munton	35
N. Hussain not out	107	– c P. A. Smith b N. M. K. Smith	12
†M. A. Garnham not out	4	– lbw b Munton	11
D. R. Pringle (did not bat)	–	– not out	14
N. A. Foster (did not bat)	–	– c Penney b P. A. Smith	8
M. C. Ilott (did not bat)	–	– not out	0
L-b 13, n-b 16	29	B 5, l-b 14, w 1, n-b 16	36

1/51 2/131 3/186 4/349   (4 wkts dec.) 384   1/114 2/173 3/187 4/204 (7 wkts) 273
                                                    5/239 6/254 7/267

P. M. Such and J. H. Childs did not bat.

Bonus points – Essex 4, Warwickshire 1.

Bowling: *First Innings*—Donald 17-4-57-0; Small 17-4-34-0; Munton 26-13-54-1; N. M. K. Smith 28-2-126-1; Reeve 13-1-47-1; P. A. Smith 10-3-53-1. *Second Innings*—Donald 21-2-56-0; Small 7.4-2-16-1; Munton 25-3-80-2; N. M. K. Smith 12.2-3-42-2; Reeve 9-2-33-0; P. A. Smith 10-3-27-2.

Umpires: A. A. Jones and G. A. Stickley.

At Maidstone, July 1, 2, 3, 5. ESSEX drew with KENT.

ESSEX v LEICESTERSHIRE

At Southend, July 15, 16, 17, 19. Leicestershire won by 77 runs. Leicestershire 23 pts, Essex 4 pts. Toss: Essex.

Set 288 on the third evening, Essex never mounted a serious threat and Pierson spun them to defeat on the stroke of tea next day. The pitch was greener than usual but did not behave as badly as the efforts of many batsmen suggested. The application of Boon, Robinson and Nixon gave Leicestershire a healthy first-innings total of 321 while Gooch and Hussain dominated the reply for Essex. Hussain's magnificent innings, his fifth century of the summer, contained 16 fours. Such, with his second five-wicket haul of the match, and Childs provided the spin which undermined Leicestershire on the third day. But it was to no avail and only Prichard and Pringle provided much resistance. It was Leicestershire's fourth Championship win out of five.

Close of play: First day, Leicestershire 203-5 (P. E. Robinson 51*, P. A. Nixon 11*); Second day, Essex 190-9 (N. Hussain 78*, J. H. Childs 2*); Third day, Essex 42-2 (P. J. Prichard 9*, P. M. Such 0*).

Leicestershire

T. J. Boon c Prichard b Childs	70	– c and b Childs	18
*N. E. Briers c Prichard b Childs	42	– b Childs	28
J. J. Whitaker c Such b Salim Malik	4	– c Gooch b Such	26
J. D. R. Benson lbw b Childs	11	– c Pringle b Such	41
P. E. Robinson lbw b Pringle	71	– b Such	21
L. Potter b Such	3	– c Prichard b Childs	11
†P. A. Nixon lbw b Such	56	– c Stephenson b Such	0
W. K. M. Benjamin c Stephenson b Such	35	– b Childs	44
G. J. Parsons not out	11	– not out	3
A. R. K. Pierson c Stephenson b Such	2	– lbw b Such	0
A. D. Mullally c Gooch b Such	0	– b Childs	0
L-b 8, n-b 8	16	B 2, l-b 3, n-b 2	7

1/109 2/116 3/123 4/158 5/165   321   1/38 2/65 3/83 4/127 5/140   199
6/262 7/298 8/311 9/319   6/142 7/196 8/197 9/198

Bonus points – Leicestershire 3, Essex 3 (Score at 120 overs: 301-7).

Bowling: *First Innings*—Ilott 18–5–54–0; Pringle 15–3–24–1; Andrew 3–0–6–0; Stephenson 3–0–11–0; Such 32.2–6–66–5; Childs 43–8–106–3; Salim Malik 16–4–46–1. *Second Innings*—Ilott 4–0–19–0; Pringle 13–5–24–0; Childs 23.5–6–64–5; Such 27–7–80–5; Salim Malik 3–0–7–0.

Essex

*G. A. Gooch b Benjamin	51	– b Benjamin	25
J. P. Stephenson c Nixon b Mullally	5	– c Benson b Pierson	8
P. J. Prichard c Nixon b Benjamin	0	– lbw b Parsons	60
Salim Malik c Nixon b Mullally	20	– (5) lbw b Pierson	19
N. Hussain c Benjamin b Pierson	103	– (6) b Benjamin	16
†M. A. Garnham lbw b Benjamin	0	– (7) b Parsons	10
D. R. Pringle b Parsons	12	– (8) not out	57
M. C. Ilott b Parsons	0	– (9) c Benson b Pierson	0
P. M. Such c Nixon b Mullally	5	– (4) lbw b Benjamin	2
S. J. W. Andrew b Mullally	2	– c Robinson b Pierson	0
J. H. Childs not out	18	– b Pierson	6
B 1, l-b 9, w 5, n-b 2	17	B 2, l-b 3, n-b 2	7

1/16 2/19 3/48 4/98 5/102   233   1/30 2/37 3/45 4/82 5/115   210
6/134 7/134 8/159 9/183   6/135 7/150 8/161 9/165

Bonus points – Essex 1, Leicestershire 4.

Bowling: *First Innings*—Benjamin 21–5–58–3; Mullally 24–7–62–4; Potter 15–4–36–0; Parsons 20–6–56–2; Pierson 1.5–0–11–1. *Second Innings*—Benjamin 22–3–54–3; Mullally 9–2–38–0; Pierson 22.4–4–78–5; Potter 5–2–17–0; Parsons 8–2–18–2.

Umpires: J. W. Holder and G. A. Stickley.

ESSEX v DURHAM

At Chelmsford, July 22, 23, 24, 26. Durham won by 146 runs. Durham 24 pts, Essex 7 pts. Toss: Durham.

Durham celebrated their first first-class victory since they beat Somerset on June 4, 1992, after Essex lost their last six wickets for only 16 runs. The fire and accuracy of Cummins and Brown, who shared 16 wickets, were the key factors in the defeat of the reigning champions. Durham's first-innings total of 483 was built around Bainbridge's maiden century for the county. His unbeaten 150 contained 18 fours, and the last three wickets helped him to add 161. Garnham's hundred anchored the Essex reply before he became one of Brown's five victims in a lively performance. With the pitch wearing, both counties found run-gathering more difficult second time around, but the batsmen did not help their cause with a succession of poor strokes. Graveney's declaration set Essex 301 in 63 overs, but Cummins finished them off by taking five wickets in an innings for the first time. The match was Durham's first since Botham's retirement. On the final day, Foster announced that he was retiring at once, adding to the feeling in Essex that an era of success might be ending.

Close of play: First day, Durham 364-8 (P. Bainbridge 87*, D. A. Graveney 0*); Second day, Essex 246-5 (M. A. Garnham 42*, D. R. Pringle 19*); Third day, Durham 84-2 (G. Fowler 26*, S. Hutton 7*).

Durham

G. Fowler c Salim Malik b Andrew	23	– c Prichard b Childs	29
W. Larkins c Salim Malik b Childs	80	– c Stephenson b Such	20
P. W. G. Parker lbw b Pringle	22	– c Stephenson b Such	13
S. Hutton c Knight b Childs	31	– lbw b Such	31
P. Bainbridge not out	150	– b Childs	36
I. Smith c Topley b Salim Malik	39	– c Knight b Childs	4
A. C. Cummins lbw b Childs	5	– c Lewis b Childs	10
†C. W. Scott b Childs	33	– c Garnham b Such	1
P. J. Berry c Knight b Childs	9	– not out	20
*D. A. Graveney c Pringle b Such	32	– not out	6
S. J. E. Brown c Lewis b Salim Malik	19		
B 4, l-b 12, n-b 24	40	B 15, l-b 10, n-b 4	29

1/67 2/140 3/158 4/191 5/258	483	1/46 2/66 3/92 (8 wkts dec.) 199
6/266 7/322 8/362 9/423		4/149 5/157 6/157
		7/159 8/175

Bonus points – Durham 4, Essex 3 (Score at 120 overs: 375-8).

Bowling: *First Innings*—Pringle 25–7–88–1; Andrew 13–1–35–1; Topley 19–4–100–0; Stephenson 13–6–33–0; Childs 48–11–99–5; Such 17–2–69–1; Salim Malik 11.3–0–43–2. *Second Innings*—Pringle 8–3–13–0; Topley 9–3–18–0; Stephenson 10–3–27–0; Such 30.2–11–61–4; Childs 22–5–55–4.

Essex

*P. J. Prichard b Brown	67	– c and b Cummins	2
J. P. Stephenson c Smith b Brown	0	– c Scott b Brown	13
N. V. Knight c Scott b Cummins	10	– (5) b Cummins	36
Salim Malik b Smith b Brown	40	– b Graveney	30
J. J. B. Lewis b Berry	32	– (3) c Hutton b Brown	10
†M. A. Garnham c Cummins b Brown	106	– b Cummins	42
D. R. Pringle b Berry	57	– lbw b Brown	0
T. D. Topley c Larkins b Brown	22	– c Hutton b Graveney	2
P. M. Such lbw b Cummins	1	– lbw b Cummins	0
S. J. W. Andrew c Scott b Cummins	6	– c Larkins b Cummins	0
J. H. Childs not out	0	– not out	1
B 5, l-b 6, w 4, n-b 26	41	B 8, l-b 4, w 2, n-b 4	18

1/11 2/56 3/133 4/148 5/211	382	1/2 2/17 3/30 4/68 5/138	154
6/298 7/367 8/374 9/382		6/143 7/149 8/149 9/149

Bonus points – Essex 4, Durham 4 (Score at 120 overs: 382-9).

Bowling: *First Innings*—Cummins 30.1–2–102–3; Brown 31–10–111–5; Bainbridge 8–2–11–0; Graveney 22–6–50–0; Berry 29–3–97–2. *Second Innings*—Cummins 14.4–5–32–5; Brown 15–5–40–3; Berry 14–2–47–0; Graveney 13–7–23–2.

Umpires: D. R. Shepherd and P. B. Wight.

ESSEX v WORCESTERSHIRE

At Chelmsford, July 29, 30, 31, August 2. Essex won by four wickets. Essex 22 pts, Worcestershire 7 pts. Toss: Worcestershire.

A masterful unbeaten century from Gooch steered Essex to victory with more than five overs to spare. Just over half his 159 came in boundaries – 18 fours and two sixes – most of them during a second-wicket stand of 164 in 52 overs with Prichard. Leatherdale's first century of the season gave Worcestershire's first-innings total a formidable look but he departed first ball in the second as Childs made his presence felt with six wickets. Curtis underlined his consistency with two half-centuries, while Such stole the batting honours in Essex's first innings – reaching the first fifty of his career with a six.

Close of play: First day, Worcestershire 274-8 (D. A. Leatherdale 75*, R. K. Illingworth 17*); Second day, Essex 217-6 (M. A. Garnham 29*, M. C. Ilott 8*); Third day, Worcestershire 198-7 (P. J. Newport 10*, C. M. Tolley 6*).

Worcestershire

*T. S. Curtis c Garnham b Such	65	– lbw b Childs	82
M. J. Weston c Prichard b Such	30	– c Pringle b Such	27
G. A. Hick c Garnham b Ilott	33	– c Hussain b Such	1
D. B. D'Oliveira c Gooch b Such	6	– b Childs	10
D. A. Leatherdale not out	119	– c Prichard b Childs	0
S. R. Lampitt c Such b Andrew	14	– lbw b Childs	0
†S. J. Rhodes c Garnham b Andrew	10	– lbw b Ilott	46
P. J. Newport c Hussain b Andrew	0	– b Such	11
C. M. Tolley c Hussain b Such	10	– not out	9
R. K. Illingworth c Garnham b Salim Malik	58	– c Garnham b Childs	1
N. V. Radford lbw b Stephenson	14	– c Prichard b Childs	2
B 4, l-b 1, w 1, n-b 14	20	B 8, l-b 3, n-b 8	19

1/76 2/130 3/144 4/145 5/168   379   1/69 2/77 3/100 4/100 5/102   208
6/187 7/187 8/220 9/362   6/182 7/186 8/201 9/206

Bonus points – Worcestershire 3, Essex 3 (Score at 120 overs: 305-8).

Bowling: *First Innings*—Ilott 19-5-36-1; Andrew 24-5-79-3; Stephenson 8.3-2-34-1; Pringle 18-2-46-0; Such 36-9-92-4; Childs 23-9-53-0; Salim Malik 12-1-34-1. *Second Innings*—Ilott 14-3-44-1; Andrew 2-0-22-0; Such 33-12-58-3; Stephenson 9-2-18-0; Childs 25-11-37-6; Salim Malik 6-0-18-0.

Essex

*G. A. Gooch c Hick b Lampitt	31	– not out	159
J. P. Stephenson c sub b Lampitt	44	– c Newport b Tolley	5
P. J. Prichard b Hick	28	– b Illingworth	64
Salim Malik b Illingworth	1	– c Rhodes b D'Oliveira	19
N. Hussain c and b Tolley	65	– lbw b Illingworth	4
†M. A. Garnham c Rhodes b Tolley	30	– lbw b D'Oliveira	16
D. R. Pringle b Lampitt	7	– b D'Oliveira	11
M. C. Ilott c Leatherdale b Illingworth	11	– not out	0
P. M. Such b Hick	54		
S. J. W. Andrew run out	18		
J. H. Childs not out	4		
B 1, l-b 11	12	L-b 7, w 1	8

1/69 2/80 3/89 4/143 5/187   305   1/24 2/188 3/215   (6 wkts) 286
6/202 7/218 8/236 9/291   4/227 5/264 6/278

Bonus points – Essex 3, Worcestershire 4.

Bowling: *First Innings*—Newport 4-1-14-0; Tolley 27-7-86-2; Lampitt 19-3-43-3; Illingworth 35-16-54-2; Radford 5-0-25-0; Hick 18.1-5-58-2; D'Oliveira 4-2-6-0; Curtis 1-0-7-0. *Second Innings*—Newport 8-0-32-0; Tolley 7-1-12-1; Lampitt 5-0-17-0; Hick 27-4-97-0; Illingworth 32.5-4-85-2; D'Oliveira 12-0-36-3.

Umpires: R. Palmer and R. A. White.

At Northampton, August 5, 6, 7. ESSEX lost to NORTHAMPTONSHIRE by eight wickets.

At Chelmsford, August 14, 15, 16. ESSEX drew with AUSTRALIANS (See Australian tour section).

At Bristol, August 19, 20, 21, 23. ESSEX drew with GLOUCESTERSHIRE.

ESSEX v MIDDLESEX

At Colchester, August 26, 27. Middlesex won by seven wickets. Middlesex 20 pts, Essex 4 pts. Toss: Essex. Championship debut: D. J. P. Boden.

As so often in recent years, Colchester Week proved crucial in settling the destination of the County Championship, but this time Essex were the hapless victims. They were crushed inside two days, which made it all but a mathematical certainty that Middlesex would be champions. Formal confirmation was delayed until the Monday, August 30, when Northamptonshire failed to beat Leicestershire, but that still made Middlesex the earliest champions in 14 years. For Essex, their hopes of retaining the title long dead, the worst aspect was the loss of two days, Bank Holiday cricket which cost them an estimated £15,000 in receipts. Despite the clatter of wickets, the umpires gave no thought to reporting the pitch; after three low-scoring innings, dominated by the seam bowlers, Gatting showed what could be done by scoring a robust unbeaten 76 with 11 fours and a six to win the match. Fraser and Cowans quickly despatched the Essex first innings but Ilott, with six for 42, bowled Middlesex out before the end of the first day and restricted their lead to 19. With Gooch falling cheaply for the second time – this was the first Championship match of the season in which he had failed to reach 50 – Essex were soon in trouble once more. Only Hussain, who resisted for two and a half hours, and Garnham prevented an utter rout before Gatting led the charge for victory.

Close of play: First day, Middlesex 167.

Essex

*G. A. Gooch c Brown b Cowans	15	– c Brown b Cowans	4
J. P. Stephenson c Brown b Fraser	4	– c Cowans b Emburey	10
P. J. Prichard c Emburey b Cowans	0	– lbw b Cowans	5
Salim Malik c Ramprakash b Fraser	36	– b Fraser	1
N. Hussain c Emburey b Fraser	40	– c Brown b Tufnell	73
†M. A. Garnham lbw b Cowans	0	– lbw b Cowans	23
T. D. Topley c Carr b Cowans	33	– st Brown b Emburey	6
M. C. Ilott b Fraser	5	– c Ramprakash b Emburey	5
D. J. P. Boden c Tufnell b Emburey	0	– c Ramprakash b Fraser	5
P. M. Such run out	3	– not out	4
J. H. Childs not out	0	– b Fraser	1
L-b 6, n-b 6	12	L-b 12, n-b 4	16
	148		**153**

1/17 2/19 3/23 4/104 5/105   1/11 2/17 3/20 4/60 5/123
6/105 7/122 8/127 9/144   6/129 7/140 8/141 9/151

Bonus points – Middlesex 4.

Bowling: *First Innings*—Fraser 16-8-19-4; Cowans 13.1-4-43-4; Feltham 16-3-43-0; Tufnell 8-3-12-0; Emburey 11-2-51-1. *Second Innings*—Fraser 14.1-7-27-3; Cowans 15-5-26-3; Feltham 3-1-13-0; Tufnell 21-9-39-1; Emburey 23-8-36-3.

Middlesex

D. L. Haynes lbw b Ilott	19	– lbw b Stephenson	3
M. A. Roseberry b Boden	4		
*M. W. Gatting b Ilott	31	– not out	76
M. R. Ramprakash lbw b Ilott	0	– lbw b Topley	35
J. D. Carr c Hussain b Stephenson	45	– not out	2
†K. R. Brown lbw b Stephenson	33		
J. E. Emburey b Ilott	9		
M. A. Feltham lbw b Ilott	3	– (2) c and b Stephenson	17
A. R. C. Fraser not out	9		
P. C. R. Tufnell c Salim Malik b Ilott	4		
N. G. Cowans c Prichard b Stephenson	0		
B 1, l-b 1, n-b 8	10	L-b 2	2
	167	(3 wkts)	**135**

1/4 2/46 3/46 4/55 5/133   1/5 2/20 3/113
6/144 7/151 8/162 9/166

Bonus points – Essex 4.

Bowling: *First Innings*—Ilott 13–2–42–6; Boden 5–0–36–1; Topley 6–2–18–0; Stephenson 11–0–42–3; Such 6–0–27–0. *Second Innings*—Ilott 6–0–36–0; Stephenson 9–1–27–2; Childs 5–0–23–0; Topley 5.1–1–20–1; Such 5–0–27–0.

Umpires: B. Dudleston and N. T. Plews.

At Hove, August 31, September 1, 2, 3. ESSEX beat SUSSEX by seven wickets.

At Cardiff, September 9, 10, 11, 13. ESSEX lost to GLAMORGAN by 22 runs.

ESSEX v HAMPSHIRE

At Chelmsford, September 16, 17, 18, 20. Drawn. Essex 6 pts, Hampshire 7 pts. Toss: Hampshire. First-class debut: J. N. B. Bovill.

Only two overs were possible in the final hour before rain arrived with Hampshire pressing for victory as Essex stumbled in their pursuit of 320 in 71 overs. Earlier, Gooch completed his second century of the match, the fourth time he had achieved this feat; he also became the only batsman to reach 2,000 runs for the season. During the course of his two innings, Gooch struck six sixes and 22 fours. Hussain made his seventh hundred of the summer, while Gower lit up Hampshire's innings with the 53rd of his career and his third in six matches, which took him to 1,000 runs for the 13th time. It spanned 194 balls and brought him 12 fours and four sixes, all scored with the nonchalant timing that has always been his trademark. The innings was given poignancy by speculation – confirmed two months later – that Gower would retire before the next season. Such's off-spin earned five wickets in each innings, underlining the value of accuracy and taking his total for the season in all forms of cricket past 100.

Close of play: First day, Hampshire 211-3 (D. I. Gower 95*, M. C. J. Nicholas 2*); Second day, Essex 48-3 (N. Hussain 20*); Third day, Hampshire 150-2 (K. D. James 41*, D. I. Gower 3*).

Hampshire

T. C. Middleton c Rollins b Childs	41	– (2) c Shahid b Such 16
V. P. Terry lbw b Ilott	17	– (1) b Ilott 87
K. D. James c Shahid b Childs	41	– c Prichard b Childs 54
D. I. Gower st Rollins b Such	134	– b Such 25
*M. C. J. Nicholas c Lewis b Such	48	– c Prichard b Such 11
R. M. F. Cox st Rollins b Childs	19	– b Such 2
†A. N. Aymes c Shahid b Such	4	– not out 15
S. D. Udal b Such	17	– c Prichard b Such 5
J. N. B. Bovill not out	3	– (10) not out 0
K. J. Shine c Shahid b Such	0	– (9) c Rollins b Ilott 6
D. P. J. Flint c Prichard b Childs	0	
L-b 11, n-b 12	23	B 3, l-b 4, n-b 12 19

1/45 2/84 3/198 4/287 5/310	347	1/33 2/134 3/182 (8 wkts dec.) 240
6/326 7/326 8/344 9/344		4/202 5/210 6/212
		7/233 8/240

Bonus points – Hampshire 3, Essex 4.

Bowling: *First Innings*—Ilott 19–1–86–1; Andrew 10–0–44–0; Such 48–13–89–5; Childs 31.3–6–89–4; Stephenson 5–1–13–0; Shahid 5–1–15–0. *Second Innings*—Ilott 10–5–18–2; Andrew 17–2–56–0; Childs 21–5–79–1; Such 27–5–71–5; Stephenson 1–0–9–0.

Essex

P. J. Prichard c Aymes b Bovill	4	– c Nicholas b Bovill	2
J. P. Stephenson lbw b Bovill	5	– c Gower b Udal	43
J. J. B. Lewis c Aymes b Udal	13	– (5) not out	10
N. Hussain c Middleton b James	102	– c Terry b Udal	5
N. Shahid lbw b Udal	3	– (6) c and b Flint	10
*G. A. Gooch lbw b Udal	109	– (3) c James b Udal	114
†R. J. Rollins lbw b James	0	– not out	6
M. C. Ilott c Gower b Udal	8		
P. M. Such c Aymes b James	4		
S. J. W. Andrew not out	5		
J. H. Childs run out	0		
B 2, l-b 6, w 1, n-b 6	15	L-b 2, n-b 4	6

1/8 2/13 3/48 4/52 5/191   268   1/5 2/132 3/167   (5 wkts) 196
6/191 7/213 8/230 9/268   4/168 5/183

Bonus points – Essex 2, Hampshire 4.

Bowling: *First Innings*—Shine 12–1–41–0; Bovill 13–5–32–2; Flint 22–3–57–0; Udal 21.1–4–77–4; James 18–5–53–3. *Second Innings*—Shine 6–1–32–0; Bovill 7–3–16–1; Flint 20.2–2–60–1; Udal 17–3–70–3; James 4–0–16–0.

Umpires: J. H. Hampshire and G. Sharp.

THE CHAMPIONS

The dates on which the County Championship has been settled since 1979 are as follows:

			Final margin
1979	Essex	August 21	77 pts
1980	Middlesex	September 2	13 pts
1981	Nottinghamshire	September 14	2 pts
1982	Middlesex	September 11	39 pts
1983	Essex	September 13	16 pts
1984	Essex	September 11	14 pts
1985	Middlesex	September 17	18 pts
1986	Essex	September 10	28 pts
1987	Nottinghamshire	September 14	4 pts
1988	Worcestershire	September 16	1 pt
1989	Worcestershire	August 31	6 pts
1990	Middlesex	September 20	31 pts
1991	Essex	September 19	13 pts
1992	Essex	September 3	41 pts
1993	Middlesex	August 30	36 pts

COUNTY BENEFITS AWARDED FOR 1994

Derbyshire	O. H. Mortensen.	Northamptonshire	D. J. Capel.
Essex	J. H. Childs.	Nottinghamshire	Nottinghamshire CCC.
Glamorgan	H. Morris.	Somerset	N. A. Mallender.
Gloucestershire	R. C. Russell.	Surrey	A. J. Stewart.
Hampshire	V. P. Terry.	Warwickshire	Asif Din.
Leicestershire	G. J. Parsons and L. Spence (head groundsman).	Worcestershire	T. S. Curtis.
Middlesex	N. F. Williams.	Yorkshire	P. Carrick (testimonial).

No benefit was awarded by Durham, Kent, Lancashire or Sussex.

GLAMORGAN

Patron: HRH The Prince of Wales
President: W. Wooller
Chairman: F. D. Morgan
Chairman, Cricket Committee: H. D. Davies
Secretary: G. R. Stone
Cricket Secretary: M. J. Fatkin
Captain: H. Morris
Director of Coaching: A. Jones
Grounds Supervisor: L. A. Smith
Scorer: B. T. Denning

Glamorgan staged a remarkable resurgence in 1993 when, under Hugh Morris's imaginative captaincy, they gained their first trophy since winning the County Championship 24 years before. Their AXA Equity & Law Sunday League triumph was achieved against Kent, the runners-up, in front of a capacity crowd at Canterbury, many of whom had travelled from Wales to witness a memorable and emotional occasion. They finished third in the Championship with nine wins, their highest position since 1970 by far, and also qualified for the semi-final of the NatWest Trophy.

Their success took almost everyone by surprise. Many people had been aware for some time that the Glamorgan team was more talented than the results suggested. Except for the acquisition of Roland Lefebvre from Somerset, who made a big difference in the one-day games, there was no significant change in the personnel that had had yet another indifferent season in 1992. However, several of the young players reached maturity at the same time and once the team acquired the habit of winning, which had been missing from Glamorgan cricket for a long time, they became addicted.

Above all, their success was a collective effort. Five batsmen scored over 1,000 first-class runs, Steve Watkin was well supported by the other bowlers and Glamorgan's outstanding fielding – especially on Sundays – characterised their self-belief and will to win. Their remarkable Sunday League record of 14 successive games without defeat, a competition record, began on June 6 against Yorkshire at Middlesbrough after they had lost their opening two games and had the other rained off at Taunton. On the following Sunday, Surrey were beaten by ten wickets, and that was the first of 12 consecutive wins. There was one further washout before the trophy was clinched on the final Sunday of the season. Their triumph atoned for the disappointment of losing against Sussex at Hove in the semi-final of the NatWest Trophy. Sussex, needing 221 to win, stumbled to 110 for six after 44 overs but Glamorgan were denied a Lord's final – which Viv Richards, above all, wanted so much – by a superb unbeaten century from Alan Wells.

Glamorgan's successful Championship season was based on a positive approach of scoring at more than three runs an over and allowing their bowlers enough time to dismiss the opposition. They won three of the opening five games and challenged Middlesex at the top of the table until they lost an extraordinary match against the leaders at Cardiff at the start of July. The two sides totalled 1,146 runs in the first innings before

Glamorgan collapsed spectacularly to 109 all out; Middlesex won by ten wickets and extended their lead at the top to 30 points. From then until the end of the season Glamorgan performed consistently and would have finished second had Worcestershire not gained an unexpected win over Middlesex in the final Championship game.

Consistency was also the hallmark of Glamorgan's batting and appropriately Richards, in his final season, topped the club averages and achieved his ambition of helping his adopted county win a title. His enthusiasm inspired the younger players and bred confidence within the team. Morris scored 1,326 first-class runs, created a new Glamorgan Sunday League record, and led by example. His captaincy, which included meticulous pre-season preparation and regular team discussions, was an important factor.

Stephen James, who had forged a successful opening partnership with Morris the previous year, had a disappointing Championship season despite contributing significantly on Sundays. However, Adrian Dale, who scored 1,472 runs including a career-best 214 not out against Middlesex, played splendidly, his emerging talent rewarded with selection for the England A team to tour South Africa. Matthew Maynard, who scored a memorable century from only 73 balls against the Australians, had another productive year and was selected for the final two Test matches and the West Indies tour. Tony Cottey became the fifth Glamorgan batsman to pass 1,000 runs, in the final match with Kent, while David Hemp, a young left-hander of considerable promise, struck five half-centuries, including a particularly valuable one which enabled Glamorgan to beat Worcestershire in the final over.

Glamorgan's attack again relied on Steve Watkin, who responded magnificently. The country's leading wicket-taker with 92 victims from 766.4 overs, he fully justified his recall to the England team with six wickets in their win at The Oval, and deserved the accolade of becoming one of the *Wisden* Five Cricketers of the Year. Lefebvre also contributed much to Glamorgan's success. He conceded only four runs from his opening eight overs in the NatWest quarter-final tie against Worcestershire, played match-winning innings in the Championship games against Worcestershire and Warwickshire and held some outstanding catches in the deep. Darren Thomas, the 18-year-old seamer, had limited opportunities but 20 wickets in four games earned him selection for the England Under-19 team and a tour to Sri Lanka during the winter. Robert Croft, the only specialist spinner in the team, had a busy summer, bowling more than 850 overs including 96, a Glamorgan record, during the game against Hampshire at Swansea. His 61 wickets and 718 runs ensured him a second England A tour in three years and further development could gain him a senior cap. The selection of seven Glamorgan players on three winter tours reflected their success, but there was again disappointment at wicket-keeper Colin Metson's omission from any representative side.

The successful membership drive, described elsewhere in *Wisden*, created an atmosphere of enthusiasm that was conducive to success. The club's coaching structure, backed by ASW Holdings, the main sponsors, promoted continuity, with young players graduating through the ranks to the first team. Glamorgan could look forward optimistically to 1994. With Ottis Gibson, a highly recommended young Barbadian fast bowler, replacing Richards as their overseas signing, they expected to have a potent new-ball attack as part of a well-balanced team, capable of challenging for their first Championship since 1969. – Edward Bevan.

GLAMORGAN 1993

[Bill Smith]

Back row: G. P. Butcher, A. J. Jones, J. Bishop, A. D. Shaw, G. H. J. Rees, S. Purdie, E. P. M. Holland, O. T. Parkin, S. D. Thomas, A. J. Dalton. *Middle row:* D. Conway (*physiotherapist*), B. T. Denning (*First XI scorer*), S. P. James, R. P. Lefebvre, S. Bastien, D. L. Hemp, A. Dale, P. A. Cottey, G. R. Stone (*secretary*), G. N. Lewis (*Second XI scorer*). *Front row:* A. Jones (*senior coach*), M. Frost, C. P. Metson, I. V. A. Richards, M. P. Maynard, H. Morris (*captain*), S. R. Barwick, S. L. Watkin, R. D. B. Croft, J. F. Steele (*assistant coach*).

GLAMORGAN RESULTS

All first-class matches – Played 20: Won 9, Lost 5, Drawn 6.

County Championship matches – Played 17: Won 9, Lost 5, Drawn 3.

Bonus points – Batting 32, Bowling 55.

*Competition placings – Britannic Assurance County Championship, 3rd;
NatWest Bank Trophy, s-f; Benson and Hedges Cup, 1st round;
AXA Equity & Law League, winners.*

BRITANNIC ASSURANCE CHAMPIONSHIP AVERAGES

BATTING

	Birthplace	M	I	NO	R	HS	Avge
‡M. P. Maynard	Oldham	14	24	0	1,041	145	43.37
‡I. V. A. Richards§ ..	St John's, Antigua	16	31	5	1,126	224*	43.30
‡A. Dale	Germiston, SA	17	33	1	1,303	214*	40.71
‡H. Morris	Cardiff	16	31	1	1,146	134*	38.20
‡P. A. Cottey	Swansea	16	29	4	855	105	34.20
D. L. Hemp	Bermuda	8	15	2	400	90*	30.76
‡S. P. James	Lydney	14	26	1	726	138*	29.04
‡R. D. B. Croft	Morriston	17	29	5	532	60	22.16
‡M. Frost	Barking	2	4	3	19	7	19.00
‡R. P. Lefebvre	Rotterdam, Netherlands	17	25	2	426	50	18.52
S. D. Thomas	Morriston	3	6	4	37	16*	18.50
‡C. P. Metson	Goff's Oak	17	26	4	269	25*	12.22
‡S. L. Watkin	Maesteg	16	20	6	161	31	11.50
‡S. R. Barwick	Neath	10	11	3	60	23*	7.50
S. Bastien	Stepney	4	5	5	23	14*	–

* *Signifies not out.*   ‡ *Denotes county cap.*   § *Overseas player.*

The following played a total of 12 three-figure innings for Glamorgan in County Championship matches – H. Morris 4, A. Dale 3, P. A. Cottey 2, S. P. James 1, M. P. Maynard 1, I. V. A. Richards 1.

BOWLING

	O	M	R	W	BB	5W/i	Avge
S. D. Thomas	103.3	17	368	16	5-76	1	23.00
S. L. Watkin	669.4	144	1,866	81	5-71	2	23.03
S. Bastien	140.3	27	472	18	6-52	2	26.22
R. P. Lefebvre	578.1	160	1,304	41	4-70	0	31.80
A. Dale	341.1	70	1,071	31	6-18	1	34.54
R. D. B. Croft	750.5	224	1,947	54	5-112	2	36.05
S. R. Barwick	455	192	920	15	3-28	0	61.33

Also bowled: P. A. Cottey 7–0–123–0; M. Frost 58.1–11–180–7; M. P. Maynard 6–0–110–1; I. V. A. Richards 84–18–235–4.

Wicket-keeper: C. P. Metson 47 ct, 4 st.

Leading Fielders: S. P. James 16, I. V. A. Richards 16.

At Oxford, April 21, 22, 23. GLAMORGAN drew with OXFORD UNIVERSITY.

GLAMORGAN v SUSSEX

At Cardiff, April 29, 30, May 1, 2. Glamorgan won by 274 runs. Glamorgan 21 pts, Sussex 6 pts. Toss: Glamorgan. County debut: E. E. Hemmings.

Glamorgan achieved their first Championship win over Sussex since 1978 when the visitors capitulated after lunch on the final day, losing their last seven wickets for 49 runs. Glamorgan gained a lead of 22 in the first innings, in which 44-year-old Hemmings took four on his debut for Sussex, his third county. But the Glamorgan batsmen attacked with relish at the second attempt. James and Dale put on 124 for the second wicket, and Maynard struck a brisk fifty, reaching 10,000 runs for Glamorgan when 30, before Cottey and Croft plundered a tired attack, adding 71 in their last seven overs. Sussex, set 385 to win in 102 overs, lost their openers cheaply. Much depended on their captain, Wells, who had scored 120 in the first innings, but when he departed before lunch, quickly followed by Smith, Sussex were in trouble. Smith had batted two and a quarter hours for 19 before falling to Barwick, whose accurate off-cutters cost only seven runs from 21 overs. Watkin then removed the middle order, taking three wickets in seven balls, while Croft disposed of the tail.

Close of play: First day, Sussex 13-0 (N. J. Lenham 10*, J. W. Hall 3*); Second day, Sussex 275-6 (I. D. K. Salisbury 0*, F. D. Stephenson 10*); Third day, Glamorgan 362-5 (P. A. Cottey 68*, R. D. B. Croft 44*).

Glamorgan

S. P. James lbw b Hemmings	78	– b Hemmings	61
*H. Morris c Moores b Hemmings	45	– c Pigott b Stephenson	18
A. Dale lbw b Salisbury	0	– c Moores b Salisbury	81
M. P. Maynard c Moores b Hemmings	37	– c and b Stephenson	52
I. V. A. Richards c Giddins b Hemmings	8	– c Smith b Salisbury	17
P. A. Cottey c Hall b Lenham	22	– not out	68
R. D. B. Croft c Lenham b Stephenson	60	– not out	44
R. P. Lefebvre c Moores b Stephenson	9		
†C. P. Metson lbw b Salisbury	7		
S. L. Watkin c Hall b Pigott	29		
S. R. Barwick not out	23		
B 4, l-b 5, n-b 4	13	B 4, l-b 8, w 1, n-b 8	21
	331	(5 wkts dec.)	**362**

1/110 2/113 3/151 4/175 5/176
6/236 7/250 8/261 9/281

1/25 2/149 3/209 (5 wkts dec.) 362
4/237 5/251

Bonus points – Glamorgan 3, Sussex 4.

Bowling: *First Innings*—Stephenson 16-1-63-2; Giddins 16-2-75-0; Pigott 6.1-1-18-1; Hemmings 30-6-69-4; Salisbury 32-7-93-2; Lenham 1-0-4-1. *Second Innings*—Stephenson 17-7-27-2; Giddins 12-2-70-0; Hemmings 24-4-91-1; Salisbury 28-6-93-2; Pigott 10-1-36-0; Lenham 5-0-33-0.

Sussex

N. J. Lenham lbw b Lefebvre	10	– c Metson b Lefebvre	3
J. W. Hall lbw b Dale	40	– b Barwick	11
D. M. Smith c Maynard b Dale	39	– c and b Barwick	19
*A. P. Wells b Watkin	120	– c Richards b Croft	19
M. P. Speight c James b Barwick	23	– b Watkin	21
†P. Moores c Lefebvre b Watkin	29	– lbw b Watkin	4
I. D. K. Salisbury lbw b Watkin	6	– (8) lbw b Croft	6
F. D. Stephenson run out	34	– (7) c Maynard b Watkin	4
A. C. S. Pigott c Metson b Watkin	4	– b Croft	7
E. E. Hemmings c Metson b Watkin	0	– b Croft	6
E. S. H. Giddins not out	0	– not out	1
L-b 4	4	B 1, l-b 6, n-b 2	9
	309		**110**

1/13 2/65 3/159 4/210 5/262
6/265 7/292 8/296 9/309

1/3 2/25 3/55 4/61 5/82
6/83 7/88 8/92 9/107

Bonus points – Sussex 2, Glamorgan 2 (Score at 120 overs: 266-6).

Bowling: *First Innings*—Watkin 29–6–87–5; Barwick 35–11–71–1; Lefebvre 20–8–38–1; Croft 36–13–88–0; Dale 12–5–21–2. *Second Innings*—Watkin 14–5–26–3; Lefebvre 7–3–11–1; Barwick 21–16–7–2; Croft 19.5–6–55–4; Dale 1–0–4–0.

Umpires: J. H. Harris and N. T. Plews.

At Cambridge, May 5, 6, 7. GLAMORGAN drew with CAMBRIDGE UNIVERSITY.

At Derby, May 13, 14, 15, 17. GLAMORGAN beat DERBYSHIRE by 191 runs.

GLAMORGAN v NORTHAMPTONSHIRE

At Swansea, May 20, 21, 22, 24. Drawn. Glamorgan 4 pts, Northamptonshire 5 pts. Toss: Northamptonshire.

A downpour after lunch on the final day saved Glamorgan from their first Championship defeat of the season. Northamptonshire, pursuing a modest 161 with a day to get them, had reached 103 with nine wickets and 64 overs remaining before the rain, which had already disrupted play on Saturday, caused the game to be abandoned. Glamorgan, put in on a seaming pitch, were undone in the first innings by the medium-pacer Penberthy, who took a career-best five for 37. The only resistance was a defiant half-century from Richards. Penberthy later confirmed his all-round ability with an undefeated 54, which enabled Northamptonshire to gain a 52-run lead. The top order succumbed to Ambrose in Glamorgan's second innings and, although the tailenders made significant contributions, they were unable to leave their opponents a serious target.

Close of play: First day, Northamptonshire 133-5 (K. M. Curran 20*, A. L. Penberthy 4*); Second day, Glamorgan 130-6 (R. P. Lefebvre 1*, C. P. Metson 0*); Third day, Glamorgan 212.

Glamorgan

S. P. James b Penberthy	28	– lbw b Curran	8
*H. Morris lbw b Taylor	7	– c and b Ambrose	61
A. Dale b Penberthy	20	– b Ambrose	9
I. V. A. Richards c Bailey b Curran	64	– c sub b Ambrose	4
D. L. Hemp b Penberthy	0	– b Taylor	10
R. D. B. Croft b Penberthy	2	– b Ambrose	23
R. P. Lefebvre c Felton b Penberthy	12	– c Cook b Penberthy	15
†C. P. Metson lbw b Curran	5	– c Bailey b Penberthy	25
S. L. Watkin lbw b Curran	9	– lbw b Curran	8
S. R. Barwick b Ambrose	7	– not out	14
M. Frost not out	5	– c Ripley b Curran	7
L-b 3, w 3	6	B 5, l-b 13, w 2, n-b 8	28

1/20 2/53 3/60 4/60 5/66   165   1/15 2/32 3/44 4/73 5/115   212
6/103 7/122 8/134 9/147   6/130 7/175 8/190 9/190

Bonus points – Northamptonshire 4.

Bowling: *First Innings*—Ambrose 18–5–47–1; Taylor 9–1–33–1; Curran 14.2–2–45–3; Penberthy 10–1–37–5. *Second Innings*—Ambrose 27–7–61–4; Taylor 20–7–36–1; Curran 20–7–44–3; Penberthy 18–3–53–2; Bailey 1–1–0–0.

Northamptonshire

A. Fordham c Richards b Watkin	6	– not out	56
N. A. Felton c Metson b Watkin	6	– c James b Croft	27
R. J. Bailey c Metson b Lefebvre	47	– not out	12
*A. J. Lamb c Metson b Frost	45		
M. B. Loye b Frost	2		
K. M. Curran b Watkin	23		
A. L. Penberthy not out	54		
†D. Ripley c James b Croft	14		
C. E. L. Ambrose c Morris b Croft	1		
J. P. Taylor c James b Watkin	11		
N. G. B. Cook lbw b Frost	1		
L-b 5, n-b 2	7	L-b 4, n-b 4	8

1/8 2/13 3/72 4/104 5/115   217   1/80   (1 wkt) 103
6/152 7/179 8/183 9/208

Bonus points – Northamptonshire 1, Glamorgan 4.

Bowling: *First Innings*—Watkin 27–4–79–4; Frost 14.1–4–25–3; Barwick 22–15–26–0; Lefebvre 18–3–47–1; Dale 5–2–13–0; Croft 17–9–22–2. *Second Innings*—Watkin 8–0–32–0; Lefebvre 6–1–9–0; Frost 5–1–15–0; Barwick 9–4–15–0; Dale 4–0–11–0; Croft 6–1–17–1.

Umpires: J. D. Bond and R. A. White.

At Taunton, May 27, 28, 29, 31. GLAMORGAN lost to SOMERSET by 84 runs.

At Middlesbrough, June 3, 4, 5, 7. GLAMORGAN beat YORKSHIRE by 121 runs.

At The Oval, June 10, 11, 12, 14. GLAMORGAN drew with SURREY.

GLAMORGAN v DURHAM

At Colwyn Bay, June 17, 18, 19, 21. Glamorgan won by 113 runs. Glamorgan 22 pts, Durham 6 pts. Toss: Glamorgan.

Glamorgan gained their fourth Championship win of the season with more than two hours to spare after Durham had been set 401 in an hour and a day. The declaration was set up by Maynard, striking four sixes and ten fours from 109 balls, including 18 off an over from Botham. Botham, who had recorded his best figures for Durham in Glamorgan's first innings, then hit a belligerent 50 as Durham chased an improbable victory. They lost two wickets on Saturday night but, after Botham's dismissal, Bainbridge and Daley frustrated Glamorgan with a partnership of 60 in 27 overs. Cummins also scored a quick half-century but, once he was out, three wickets fell for only four runs, two of them to the country's leading wicket-taker, Watkin, who had made the initial breakthrough by removing Botham.

Close of play: First day, Durham 5–0 (I. T. Botham 2*, W. Larkins 3*); Second day, Durham 263; Third day, Durham 62–2 (I. T. Botham 26*, J. Wood 0*).

Glamorgan

S. P. James c Scott b Brown	10	– b Graveney	32
*H. Morris b Graveney	52	– c Scott b Berry	33
A. Dale c Berry b Wood	60	– c Bainbridge b Cummins	85
M. P. Maynard lbw b Botham	46	– lbw b Wood	98
I. V. A. Richards b Berry	34	– not out	62
P. A. Cottey b Berry	7	– lbw b Cummins	5
R. D. B. Croft c Scott b Botham	36	– c Wood b Bainbridge	2
R. P. Lefebvre c Daley b Berry	12	– c Brown b Cummins	2
†C. P. Metson c Wood b Botham	13	– not out	10
S. L. Watkin not out	1		
S. R. Barwick lbw b Botham	2		
L-b 4, w 1, n-b 22	27	B 9, l-b 7, n-b 18	34

1/17 2/127 3/160 4/223 5/223　　　　　300　　1/73 2/73 3/229　　(7 wkts dec.) 363
6/236 7/262 8/293 9/298　　　　　　　　　　　　4/294 5/304
　　　　　　　　　　　　　　　　　　　　　　　6/323 7/332

Bonus points – Glamorgan 3, Durham 4.

Bowling: *First Innings*—Cummins 24.5–5–75–0; Brown 17–1–59–1; Wood 12–1–47–1; Graveney 26–5–65–1; Botham 6.5–2–11–4; Berry 16–3–39–3. *Second Innings*—Cummins 17.2–6–48–3; Brown 6–1–25–0; Berry 29–3–112–1; Graveney 20–5–64–1; Botham 4–0–27–0; Wood 7–1–37–1; Bainbridge 6–0–34–1.

Durham

I. T. Botham c and b Lefebvre	14	– c Cottey b Watkin	50
W. Larkins c Maynard b Dale	77	– c Richards b Lefebvre	5
P. W. G. Parker lbw b Lefebvre	0	– lbw b Croft	30
J. A. Daley b Lefebvre	2	– (5) c Metson b Lefebvre	17
P. Bainbridge c James b Croft	71	– (6) c James b Croft	62
P. J. Berry c Barwick b Croft	46	– (7) c James b Barwick	10
A. C. Cummins c and b Croft	0	– (8) c Maynard b Watkin	56
†C. W. Scott c Richards b Croft	18	– (9) not out	20
J. Wood c Metson b Watkin	8	– (4) b Watkin	9
*D. A. Graveney b Dale	11	– lbw b Watkin	0
S. J. E. Brown not out	0	– c Barwick b Lefebvre	14
B 2, l-b 14	16	L-b 6, n-b 8	14

1/19 2/19 3/30 4/159 5/184　　　　　263　　1/12 2/60 3/96 4/97 5/157　　287
6/186 7/212 8/233 9/255　　　　　　　　　　6/217 7/252 8/254 9/256

Bonus points – Durham 2, Glamorgan 3 (Score at 120 overs: 251-8).

In the second innings P. J. Berry, when 2, retired hurt at 167 and resumed at 217.

Bowling: *First Innings*—Watkin 24–7–54–1; Barwick 28–12–54–0; Lefebvre 24–7–55–3; Croft 42–11–70–4; Dale 10.5–3–14–2. *Second Innings*—Watkin 23–4–93–4; Lefebvre 22.2–7–50–3; Barwick 22–12–28–1; Croft 21–7–40–2; Dale 10–1–52–0; Richards 4–1–18–0.

Umpires: R. Julian and A. G. T. Whitehead.

GLAMORGAN v NOTTINGHAMSHIRE

At Swansea, June 24, 25, 26, 28. Nottinghamshire won by eight wickets. Nottinghamshire 23 pts, Glamorgan 7 pts. Toss: Glamorgan.

Glamorgan suffered their first home defeat of the season as Nottinghamshire chased 336 in what become 91 overs on a placid St Helen's pitch which offered no assistance to the bowlers over the four days. Both captains, Morris and Robinson, scored a century in each innings, but it was Robinson who guided his team to victory with 8.4 overs to spare. Morris was dismissed only four runs short of winning the race to 1,000 runs for the season – earlier Watkin had become the first bowler to reach 50 wickets – but Cottey led the way to the declaration with an unbeaten century. Pollard and Robinson laid the foundation of

Nottinghamshire's win with a second-wicket partnership of 121 before Johnson struck the season's fastest century to date, from only 73 deliveries. Robinson was dropped at deep square leg on 87 but, with so many wickets and overs in hand, it would have made little difference to the outcome had Cottey held on to a difficult chance.

Close of play: First day, Glamorgan 304-8 (C. P. Metson 1*, S. L. Watkin 0*); Second day, Nottinghamshire 308-8 (B. N. French 27*, M. G. Field-Buss 4*); Third day, Glamorgan 291-5 (P. A. Cottey 56*, R. D. B. Croft 2*).

Glamorgan

S. P. James c Archer b Cairns	9	– c Pollard b Cairns 0
*H. Morris st French b Field-Buss	102	– b Field-Buss 133
A. Dale c and b Evans	92	– c Pollard b Field-Buss 51
M. P. Maynard lbw b Evans	49	– run out 33
I. V. A. Richards c Pollard b Evans	11	– c Pick b Field-Buss 4
P. A. Cottey c Pollard b Afford	0	– not out 100
R. D. B. Croft b Cairns	14	– not out 17
R. P. Lefebvre c Robinson b Cairns	10	
†C. P. Metson c French b Pick	16	
S. L. Watkin not out	8	
S. R. Barwick b Cairns	0	
B 5, l-b 9, w 2, n-b 2	18	L-b 12, n-b 2 14

1/28 2/190 3/258 4/277 5/277   329   1/4 2/129 3/191   (5 wkts dec.) 352
6/277 7/300 8/303 9/328   4/204 5/285

Bonus points – Glamorgan 3, Nottinghamshire 4 (Score at 120 overs: 328-9).

Bowling: *First Innings*—Cairns 23.3-6-66-4; Pick 19-2-63-1; Evans 22-6-48-3; Afford 36-11-92-1; Field-Buss 20-5-46-1. *Second Innings*—Cairns 14-2-58-1; Pick 15.5-2-71-0; Afford 25-4-86-0; Field-Buss 33-8-82-3; Evans 9-0-43-0.

Nottinghamshire

P. R. Pollard c Dale b Croft	27	– b Croft 72
M. Saxelby st Metson b Croft	14	– c Metson b Watkin 9
*R. T. Robinson b Croft	119	– not out 139
P. Johnson c James b Lefebvre	70	– not out 112
G. F. Archer c Morris b Croft	10	
C. L. Cairns c James b Watkin	24	
K. P. Evans c James b Barwick	7	
†B. N. French c Metson b Watkin	47	
R. A. Pick c Watkin b Croft	0	
M. G. Field-Buss b Watkin	16	
J. A. Afford not out	0	
B 4, l-b 6, n-b 2	12	L-b 6 6

1/40 2/41 3/135 4/161 5/218   346   1/19 2/140   (2 wkts) 338
6/250 7/285 8/291 9/337

Bonus points – Nottinghamshire 3, Glamorgan 4 (Score at 120 overs: 344-9).

Bowling: *First Innings*—Watkin 23.2-4-72-3; Lefebvre 20-2-59-1; Barwick 27-12-58-1; Croft 37-8-112-5; Dale 3-0-14-0; Richards 10-5-21-0. *Second Innings*—Watkin 14-1-55-1; Lefebvre 9-1-35-0; Croft 29-4-97-1; Barwick 14-3-55-0; Richards 11-3-49-0; Dale 5.2-0-41-0.

Umpires: J. H. Harris and D. O. Oslear.

GLAMORGAN v MIDDLESEX

At Cardiff, July 1, 2, 3, 5. Middlesex won by ten wickets. Middlesex 20 pts, Glamorgan 3 pts. Toss: Glamorgan.

The clash between the top two teams in the Championship was dominated by batting titans for three and a half days – then Glamorgan's batsmen collapsed dramatically to

Tufnell, giving him career-best figures of eight for 29. Their ten-wicket defeat was a most unlikely result, especially as the first two innings had produced 1,146 runs. After Morris who became the first player to 1,000 runs in the season, and Maynard went cheaply, Dale and Richards, the rising talent and the fading hero, shared a stand of 425, a new Glamorgan record for any wicket, easily outstripping the 330 by openers A. Jones and R. C. Fredericks against Northamptonshire at Swansea in 1972. It was the seventh-highest fourth-wicket stand in the history of first-class cricket. Dale scored his maiden double-century, also passing 1,000 runs, and Richards his first for Glamorgan. Middlesex's batsmen also prospered on the placid pitch, night-watchman Emburey making his sixth hundred and putting on 262 with Gatting, and Middlesex batted on for a first-innings lead of 22 before Glamorgan began their second innings at 12.10 p.m. on the last day. A draw looked certain. Tufnell came on in the eighth over and with his fifth ball bowled James to begin an astonishing collapse; Glamorgan slumped from 25 for one at lunch to 104 for eight at tea. Richards was caught first ball. Nine wickets fell for only 60 runs – the last five in ten overs – which left Middlesex the simple task of scoring 88 from 33 overs. Haynes and Roseberry cruised to victory from 19.4 as Glamorgan's spinners failed to exploit the wearing pitch which had caused such panic within their own ranks.

Close of play: First day, Glamorgan 319-3 (A. Dale 108*, I. V. A. Richards 97*); Second day, Middlesex 129-1 (M. A. Roseberry 54*, J. E. Emburey 0*); Third day, Middlesex 477-5 (J. D. Carr 9*, K. R. Brown 23*).

Glamorgan

S. P. James c Carr b Tufnell	42	– b Tufnell	11
*H. Morris c Brown b Williams	27	– c Brown b Tufnell	14
A. Dale not out	214	– lbw b Tufnell	14
M. P. Maynard c Gatting b Feltham	14	– c Carr b Tufnell	32
I. V. A. Richards not out	224	– c Carr b Tufnell	0
P. A. Cottey (did not bat)		– run out	15
R. D. B. Croft (did not bat)		– not out	2
†C. P. Metson (did not bat)		– c Gatting b Tufnell	0
R. P. Lefebvre (did not bat)		– b Tufnell	0
S. L. Watkin (did not bat)		– c Carr b Tufnell	0
S. R. Barwick (did not bat)		– c Carr b Emburey	1
B 4, l-b 13, w 1, n-b 23	41	B 6, l-b 4, n-b 10	20

1/50 2/86 3/137   (3 wkts dec.) 562   1/25 2/49 3/62 4/62 5/95   109
                                                6/102 7/102 8/104 9/104

Bonus points – Glamorgan 3, Middlesex 1 (Score at 120 overs: 349-3).

Bowling: *First Innings*—Williams 26-5-85-1; Fraser 33-3-127-0; Feltham 27-4-117-1; Emburey 35-5-102-0; Tufnell 45-8-114-1. *Second Innings*—Fraser 3-2-2-0; Williams 3-0-16-0; Emburey 23.2-6-52-1; Tufnell 23-8-29-8.

Middlesex

D. L. Haynes lbw b Watkin	73	– not out	50
M. A. Roseberry c Cottey b Watkin	58	– not out	31
J. E. Emburey b Dale	123		
*M. W. Gatting b Lefebvre	173		
M. R. Ramprakash c Morris b Dale	4		
J. D. Carr c Croft b Watkin	18		
†K. R. Brown not out	88		
M. A. Feltham lbw b Watkin	0		
N. F. Williams b Croft	21		
A. R. C. Fraser c Dale b Croft	5		
P. C. R. Tufnell c and b Croft	5		
B 9, l-b 5, n-b 2	16	B 4, l-b 3	7

1/122 2/135 3/397 4/441 5/441   584   (no wkt) 88
6/493 7/493 8/561 9/575

Bonus points – Middlesex 3 (Score at 120 overs: 307-2).

Bowling: *First Innings*—Watkin 31–4–87–4; Lefebvre 30–8–72–1; Barwick 44–14–131–0; Croft 54–9–174–3; Dale 22–6–55–2; Richards 13–1–51–0. *Second Innings*—Watkin 2–0–7–0; Barwick 3–0–9–0; Croft 8.4–2–45–0; Richards 6–0–20–0.

Umpires: J. C. Balderstone and V. A. Holder.

At Manchester, July 15, 16, 17, 19. GLAMORGAN beat LANCASHIRE by seven wickets.

At Worcester, July 22, 23, 24, 26. GLAMORGAN beat WORCESTERSHIRE by one wicket.

At Neath, July 31, August 1, 2. GLAMORGAN drew with AUSTRALIANS (See Australian tour section).

GLAMORGAN v WARWICKSHIRE

At Cardiff, August 5, 6, 7. Glamorgan won by two wickets. Glamorgan 21 pts, Warwickshire 4 pts. Toss: Glamorgan.

Morris's disciplined half-century guided Glamorgan to their seventh Championship win on an unpredictable pitch, reported to Lord's after 17 wickets fell on the opening day. There was plenty of help for the quicker bowlers and Dale picked up a career-best six for 18 after Thomas made early inroads. Glamorgan gained a 111-run lead on first innings. After Warwickshire had batted more resolutely second time round, thanks in part to Asif Din, in his first Championship innings of the season, Glamorgan required 138 to win. At lunch they had slumped to 91 for six and when Morris departed they were still 22 runs short. Hemp, stricken by tonsillitis, lasted for only two runs, but Lefebvre denied himself any liberties, staying in for an hour and threequarters to see Glamorgan home before tea on the third day. Harry Brind, the TCCB's inspector of pitches, examined the surface on the second day and pronounced that, though there was too much grass on it before the game began, it was by no means unplayable.

Close of play: First day, Glamorgan 194-7 (R. D. B. Croft 40*, D. L. Hemp 0*); Second day, Warwickshire 248.

Warwickshire

A. J. Moles c Metson b Thomas	2	– c Watkin b Thomas 0
J. D. Ratcliffe b Dale	25	– c Richards b Dale 68
D. P. Ostler c Metson b Thomas	5	– c Metson b Thomas 9
T. L. Penney lbw b Thomas	3	– b Lefebvre 13
Asif Din c Morris b Thomas	35	– (6) b Dale 66
*D. A. Reeve c Metson b Dale	31	– (5) c sub b Watkin 57
P. A. Smith c Croft b Dale	4	– c sub b Thomas 3
†K. J. Piper c Watkin b Dale	0	– lbw b Lefebvre 16
P. A. Booth c Morris b Dale	0	– c Dale b Watkin 1
G. C. Small c James b Dale	8	– not out 6
M. A. V. Bell not out	4	– b Watkin 0
L-b 2, n-b 6	8	B 1, l-b 4, w 4 9
	125	**248**

1/4 2/14 3/20 4/52 5/71   125   1/1 2/15 3/41 4/136 5/174   248
6/71 7/77 8/103 9/118   6/190 7/220 8/235 9/247

Bonus points – Glamorgan 4.

In the first innings Asif Din, when 19, retired hurt at 60 and resumed at 77.

Bowling: *First Innings*—Thomas 16–5–49–4; Lefebvre 13–3–30–0; Dale 13.3–3–18–6; Watkin 8–0–26–0. *Second Innings*—Watkin 25.4–1–64–3; Thomas 17–2–57–3; Lefebvre 24–8–52–2; Dale 25–5–59–2; Croft 4–1–11–0.

Glamorgan

S. P. James lbw b Small	0	– c Small b Smith	10
*H. Morris c Ostler b Bell	18	– c and b Booth	54
A. Dale c Piper b Bell	30	– c Piper b Small	0
I. V. A. Richards lbw b Bell	26	– c Booth b Smith	8
P. A. Cottey c Booth b Smith	8	– c Booth b Smith	1
R. D. B. Croft c Penney b Smith	54	– c Reeve b Booth	18
†C. P. Metson c Ratcliffe b Smith	8	– c Piper b Smith	3
R. P. Lefebvre b Bell	40	– not out	15
D. L. Hemp retired ill	0	– c Ostler b Bell	2
S. D. Thomas c Ratcliffe b Bell	5	– not out	2
S. L. Watkin not out	2		
B 9, l-b 7, w 1, n-b 36	53	B 7, l-b 3, w 1, n-b 14	25

1/0 2/48 3/73 4/91 5/99   236   1/37 2/38 3/51 4/53   (8 wkts) 138
6/111 7/194 8/228 9/236   5/81 6/91 7/116 8/123

Bonus points – Glamorgan 1, Warwickshire 4.

In the first innings D. L. Hemp retired ill at 194-7.

Bowling: *First Innings*—Small 14–0–53–1; Bell 23–2–86–5; Reeve 16–8–22–0; Smith 12.5–0–59–3. *Second Innings*: Small 21–4–43–2; Bell 8.5–2–34–0; Smith 10–2–35–4; Reeve 1–1–0–0; Booth 14–5–16–2.

Umpires: G. I. Burgess and G. Sharp.

At Leicester, August 12, 13, 14, 16. GLAMORGAN drew with LEICESTERSHIRE.

GLAMORGAN v HAMPSHIRE

At Swansea, August 19, 20, 21, 23. Hampshire won by 98 runs. Hampshire 23 pts, Glamorgan 4 pts. Toss: Hampshire.

Hampshire were always in control after Terry's 174 laid the foundation of a substantial first-innings total. Glamorgan avoided the follow-on but Hampshire capitalised on a 129-run lead to set a target of 326 from 76 overs. Croft, who had sent down 62 overs in Hampshire's first innings and 96 in all, broke B. L. Muncer's county record of 90.5 bowled against Sussex on the same ground in 1948 and claimed nine of the 14 wickets to fall. But when Glamorgan batted they struggled on a turning pitch against his fellow off-spinner, Udal, who took seven wickets in the game, and the swing and seam of Marshall, who took eight. Marshall's spell of three for no runs in 13 deliveries on the third day effectively ended Glamorgan's hopes of overtaking Middlesex at the top of the table; defeat left them 58 points adrift with three games left. The only batsmen to threaten were Morris and the young left-hander Hemp, who scored 63 to follow up his career-best 84 not out against Hampshire in 1992.

Close of play: First day, Hampshire 338-8 (M. D. Marshall 13*); Second day, Glamorgan 217-5 (D. L. Hemp 10*, R. D. B. Croft 23*); Third day, Hampshire 150-3 (D. I. Gower 35*, R. M. F. Cox 31*).

Hampshire

R. A. Smith b Barwick	29	– c Hemp b Croft	48
V. P. Terry run out	174	– c Lefebvre b Croft	32
D. I. Gower c Cottey b Croft	6	– b Croft	56
*M. C. J. Nicholas c Lefebvre b Croft	31	– c Cottey b Croft	1
R. M. F. Cox lbw b Lefebvre	21	– not out	48
K. D. James c Dale b Croft	7	– not out	7
†A. N. Aymes lbw b Lefebvre	55		
M. D. Marshall not out	75		
S. D. Udal c Cottey b Croft	0		
K. J. Shine c sub b Croft	12		
D. P. J. Flint c Metson b Lefebvre	5		
B 1, l-b 1	2	L-b 2, w 2	4

1/66 2/79 3/163 4/210 5/227   417   1/67 2/84   (4 wkts dec.) 196
6/320 7/334 8/338 9/402   3/89 4/186

Bonus points – Hampshire 3, Glamorgan 2 (Score at 120 overs: 320-5).

Bowling: *First Innings*—Thomas 19–3–78–0; Lefebvre 29.5–6–74–3; Barwick 43–12–93–1; Croft 62–16–157–5; Richards 5–0–13–0. *Second Innings*—Thomas 3–0–24–0; Lefebvre 2–0–5–0; Croft 34–9–74–4; Dale 10–1–32–0; Barwick 23–7–59–0.

Glamorgan

S. P. James b Flint	80	– lbw b Flint 19
*H. Morris c Nicholas b Shine	8	– c Cox b Udal 60
A. Dale lbw b Marshall	5	– c Gower b Udal 36
I. V. A. Richards b Flint	67	– (6) c Aymes b Marshall 1
P. A. Cottey c Smith b Udal	6	– (4) st Aymes b Flint 0
D. L. Hemp c Aymes b Marshall	24	– (5) c Flint b Udal 63
R. D. B. Croft c Udal b Marshall	23	– b Marshall 2
†C. P. Metson lbw b Marshall	3	– lbw b Marshall 0
R. P. Lefebvre c and b Marshall	19	– lbw b Udal 18
S. D. Thomas not out	16	– c Gower b Udal 0
S. R. Barwick b Udal	11	– not out 0
L-b 7, w 1, n-b 18	26	L-b 12, w 2, n-b 14 28
	288	**227**

1/12 2/19 3/157 4/180 5/180
6/225 7/231 8/238 9/259

1/50 2/110 3/111 4/171 5/174
6/180 7/192 8/216 9/218

Bonus points – Glamorgan 2, Hampshire 4.

Bowling: *First Innings*—Shine 9–2–35–1; Marshall 23–8–62–5; James 8–2–32–0; Udal 38–9–109–2; Flint 20–9–43–2. *Second Innings*—Shine 9–2–35–0; Marshall 15–6–31–3; Flint 17–4–74–2; Udal 24.1–6–75–5.

Umpires: J. W. Holder and P. B. Wight.

GLAMORGAN v GLOUCESTERSHIRE

At Abergavenny, August 26, 27, 28, 30. Glamorgan won by 82 runs. Glamorgan 22 pts, Gloucestershire 4 pts. Toss: Glamorgan.

Glamorgan gained their eighth Championship win of the season shortly after lunch on the final day. The match got off to a rattling start, with a third-wicket partnership of 187, scored at six runs an over, between Maynard and Richards. But Glamorgan lost their last eight wickets for 84 and at the end of the first day Glamorgan's seamers had Gloucestershire at 84 for seven, 59 short of the follow-on. To the relief of the local club, who feared a popular fixture might end in two days, Broad and Davies added 53 for the eighth wicket and Davies, playing against his old county, stayed until the danger was past. Glamorgan's second effort left Gloucestershire requiring 432 to win in a day and a half. Hodgson gave them a glimmer of hope with a disciplined innings, but when he was out the middle order subsided, losing five wickets for only one run, three of them to Croft. Walsh swung merrily, striking four sixes in a 52-ball 57, before Watkin removed him and Cooper to take his season's tally to 86 wickets.

Close of play: First day, Gloucestershire 84-7 (B. C. Broad 52*); Second day, Glamorgan 258-6 (C. P. Metson 4*, R. P. Lefebvre 0*); Third day, Gloucestershire 208-3 (G. D. Hodgson 107*, M. Davies 0*).

Glamorgan

S. P. James c Hinks b Walsh	0	– lbw b Walsh 1
A. Dale c Alleyne b Walsh	9	– c Russell b Walsh 10
*M. P. Maynard c Russell b Hancock	93	– st Russell b Davies 95
I. V. A. Richards c Russell b Hancock	95	– absent injured
P. A. Cottey c Ball b Hancock	4	– (4) c Ball b Cooper 63
D. L. Hemp b Walsh	18	– (5) c Russell b Alleyne 52
R. D. B. Croft lbw b Ball	16	– (6) c Ball b Hancock 21
†C. P. Metson c Ball b Cooper	1	– (7) not out 18
R. P. Lefebvre c Broad b Davies	25	– (8) c Russell b Walsh 17
S. L. Watkin not out	6	– (9) lbw b Cooper 1
S. R. Barwick c Hinks b Walsh	0	– (10) c Ball b Cooper 0
B 4, l-b 5, n-b 16	25	L-b 14, n-b 5 19
	292	**297**

1/0 2/21 3/208 4/214 5/217
6/246 7/249 8/282 9/292

1/4 2/21 3/129 4/221 5/253
6/257 7/286 8/293 9/297

Bonus points – Glamorgan 2, Gloucestershire 4.

Bowling: *First Innings*—Walsh 14.1–3–71–4; Cooper 14–1–51–1; Alleyne 14–3–54–0; Davies 11–2–54–1; Ball 17–5–43–1; Hancock 4–0–10–3. *Second Innings*—Walsh 25–6–83–3; Cooper 25.2–8–66–3; Alleyne 8–3–14–1; Hancock 8–1–35–1; Davies 17–3–57–1; Ball 8–1–28–0.

Gloucestershire

B. C. Broad st Metson b Croft	72	– c Metson b Watkin	33
G. D. Hodgson lbw b Lefebvre	0	– b Dale	126
R. I. Dawson lbw b Dale	5	– c Hemp b Croft	46
S. G. Hinks lbw b Watkin	2	– c Metson b Watkin	19
M. W. Alleyne b Watkin	1	– (6) b Dale	0
T. H. C. Hancock b Barwick	3	– (7) c sub b Croft	1
†R. C. Russell c Richards b Watkin	15	– (8) c Cottey b Croft	0
M. C. J. Ball c Richards b Lefebvre	3	– (9) c sub b Croft	0
M. Davies not out	4	– (5) not out	41
*C. A. Walsh c Dale b Croft	5	– c Metson b Watkin	57
K. E. Cooper b Croft	5	– b Watkin	19
L-b 3	3	L-b 6, w 1	7

1/2 2/30 3/33 4/41 5/51   158   1/85 2/171 3/208 4/241 5/241   349
6/77 7/84 8/137 9/151   6/242 7/242 8/242 9/325

Bonus points – Glamorgan 4.

Bowling: *First Innings*—Watkin 21–4–60–3; Lefebvre 6–1–20–2; Dale 9–3–14–1; Croft 17.4–9–35–3; Barwick 12–4–26–1. *Second Innings*—Watkin 35.3–10–106–4; Barwick 30–11–56–0; Croft 51–22–115–4; Dale 22–6–66–2.

Umpires: K. E. Palmer and G. A. Stickley.

At Brecon, September 5. GLAMORGAN beat ZIMBABWEANS by 53 runs (See Zimbabwean tour section).

GLAMORGAN v ESSEX

At Cardiff, September 9, 10, 11, 13. Glamorgan won by 22 runs. Glamorgan 20 pts, Essex 4 pts. Toss: Essex. First-class debut: B. J. Hyam.

Rain curtailed the first two days to 32 overs after which the seamers on both teams exploited a green pitch: Andrew, with seven for 69, dismissed Glamorgan cheaply in the first innings but Bastien responded with a career-best six for 52, restricting Essex to a 17-run lead. After another delayed start on the final day and some generous offerings from Essex's occasional bowlers, Morris set them 201 in a minimum of 60 overs. Essex were soon in trouble at 27 for three, all taken by Bastien in a 19-ball spell, and had slumped to 80 for six by tea. Lewis and Ilott raised their hopes, adding 53, before the return of Bastien and Watkin ensured Glamorgan's ninth Championship victory of the season, in Richards's final home game for the county. Bastien, in only his third Championship game of the season, took 12 for 105. It was Glamorgan's most successful year since 1970, when they finished second and also won nine matches.

Close of play: First day, No play; Second day, Glamorgan 134-6 (C. P. Metson 6*, R. D. B. Croft 0*); Third day, Glamorgan 64-3 (I. V. A. Richards 19*, C. P. Metson 1*).

Glamorgan

A. Dale c Knight b Andrew	3	– c Gooch b Stephenson	18
*H. Morris b Andrew	30	– c Hyam b Ilott	4
M. P. Maynard c Ilott b Stephenson	28	– c Hyam b Andrew	10
I. V. A. Richards c Lewis b Andrew	30	– c and b Hussain	29
P. A. Cottey c Knight b Stephenson	6	– (6) not out	44
†C. P. Metson lbw b Andrew	11	– (5) c Knight b Prichard	4
D. L. Hemp b Andrew	2	– not out	90
R. D. B. Croft run out	8		
R. P. Lefebvre c Shahid b Andrew	16		
S. L. Watkin lbw b Andrew	0		
S. Bastien not out	1		
B 6, l-b 5, w 3, n-b 20	34	L-b 5, w 1, n-b 12	18

1/19 2/75 3/109 4/125 5/125   169   1/11 2/30 3/61   (5 wkts dec.) 217
6/131 7/147 8/150 9/150   4/74 5/82

Bonus points – Essex 4.

Bowling: *First Innings*—Ilott 14–5–47–0; Andrew 18–3–69–7; Stephenson 11–4–42–2. *Second Innings*—Ilott 6–0–28–1; Andrew 6–2–26–1; Stephenson 3–0–6–1; Hussain 6.2–0–75–1; Prichard 6–0–77–1.

Essex

P. J. Prichard c Metson b Bastien	8	– lbw b Bastien	21
J. P. Stephenson b Watkin	12	– c Richards b Bastien	0
J. J. B. Lewis c Metson b Lefebvre	29	– b Bastien	54
N. Hussain b Bastien	51	– c Metson b Bastien	0
*G. A. Gooch b Bastien	23	– run out	14
N. Shahid c Morris b Watkin	32	– lbw b Bastien	1
N. V. Knight b Bastien	0	– b Croft	14
M. C. Ilott c Metson b Watkin	1	– b Watkin	43
†B. J. Hyam b Bastien	1	– c Cottey b Bastien	0
P. M. Such b Bastien	7	– b Croft	19
S. J. W. Andrew not out	16	– not out	0
L-b 2, n-b 4	6	B 4, l-b 7, w 1	12

1/15 2/29 3/92 4/106 5/155   186   1/10 2/27 3/27 4/64 5/65   178
6/155 7/158 8/163 9/163   6/80 7/133 8/133 9/174

Bonus points – Glamorgan 4.

Bowling: *First Innings*—Watkin 22–5–49–3; Bastien 25.5–8–52–6; Lefebvre 17–5–37–1; Dale 13–3–46–0. *Second Innings*—Watkin 21–2–60–1; Bastien 17–5–53–6; Lefebvre 8–0–17–0; Dale 5–1–22–0; Croft 8.5–3–15–2.

Umpires: M. J. Kitchen and R. Palmer.

At Canterbury, September 16, 17, 18, 20. GLAMORGAN lost to KENT by 236 runs.

GLOUCESTERSHIRE

Patron: HRH The Princess of Wales
President: D. N. Perry
Chairman: R. W. Rossiter
Secretary: P. G. M. August
Captain: 1993 – A. J. Wright
        1994 – C. A. Walsh
Coach: A. W. Stovold
Assistant Coach: P. W. Romaines
Head Groundsman: D. Bridle
Scorer: B. H. Jenkins

Not for the first time in the county's history, the Gothic chapel at the College ground in Cheltenham looked benevolently on Gloucestershire. Ecclesiastical support was more eagerly embraced than usual in 1993. Gloucestershire were on the bottom of the table and it was already August when they won at last in the Championship.

Victory was achieved efficiently against a surprisingly ordinary Lancashire side and never has a Cheltenham tonic been more timely. The county had been increasingly bruised by cynicism, some of it justified, and insensitive taunts. Tony Wright, the captain, had a month earlier asked to be relieved of his responsibilities. His batting had suffered painfully; now he wanted to try to play his way back into form and confidence as just another member of the team.

It did not work for him in the short term and he will be glad to start afresh in 1994. But Gloucestershire did improve, albeit modestly, in technique and resolve. They completed the season with three wins and might even have had three in a row if the Essex match in Bristol had found some momentum on the last day. They had at least avoided the ignominy of finishing below the hapless Durham.

Courtney Walsh took over the leadership temporarily from Wright and, after a few weeks of apparent uncertainty, it was announced – to relief all round – that he would be signing a new contract, and with it accepting the captaincy. He had done the job at home in Jamaica. The early evidence at Gloucestershire was of commendable enthusiasm, some unstinting bowling and an intelligent regard for flexible tactics. Walsh may have taken fewer wickets than in the previous season but at times he was marvellously rhythmic. It was a constant regret that there was not more formidable support.

Jack Russell, too, accepted a new contract and was named as Walsh's vice-captain. The two had already forged an easy and productive partnership. The comic disparity in physique should not imply any differences in attitudes. They could not always disguise completely their embarrassment at some of the county's more ignoble performances, and worked hard in tandem to introduce a more competitive streak and tougher mental outlook. Russell's wicket-keeping remained unfailingly tidy, without ostentation. If he saw the summer's Test selections as an illogical snub, he kept his thoughts to himself. At the same time, his self-imposed rigours and single-minded striving for perfection made his eventual recall, for the West Indies party, all the more welcome. He continued to work, and succeed, with his batting. The peculiarity of his stance showed no signs of disappearing but he produced opportune innings of immense grit.

Chris Broad's return was something of a disappointment and he passed his 1,000 runs with not too much to spare. Bill Athey had gone and there was not a great deal of reliable experience in the batting: and often the early order appeared disturbingly fragile. Dean Hodgson was the only other batsman to reach 1,000 runs. Once again, Mark Alleyne lacked consistency and was, for all his obvious skills, unfulfilled as a batsman. With three hundreds, at times admirably composed, he still failed to score 1,000. For much of the summer, the club's lack of backbone was far too easily revealed. Although Tim Hancock again gave grounds for mid-order optimism, Richard Scott, previously with Hampshire, mostly waited in vain. He, like the left-arm seamer, Martin Gerrard, was released at the end of the season.

The bowling leaned too demandingly on the silky Walsh. Kevin Cooper brought some old-campaigner's experience with him, was just short of 50 wickets and celebrated, yes, at Cheltenham, with a maiden half-century. In the previous match there, against Derbyshire, Gloucestershire chose not to include a single slow bowler, and one off-spinner, Martyn Ball, must have feared that he would not be given a run at all. But his chance came in the closing matches when he went down to Taunton and won the game virtually on his own, taking a career-best eight for 46 in the second innings, and 14 for 169 in the match. There must have been a case for playing him earlier, although Gloucestershire clearly wanted a good look at Marcus Wight.

The left-arm slow bowler, Mark Davies, who had arrived quite successfully by way of Glamorgan the previous season, made less impact and took fewer wickets in 1993. He had some problems with his action and lost accuracy. There were matches when the county's attack had a thoroughly unbalanced appearance, without challenge or penetration. David Lawrence maintained the remedial programme on his ravaged knee-cap; he cheered 3,000 spectators by getting through half a dozen overs, at something approaching full pace, in a benefit match during the Cheltenham festival. Never was one so conscious of a crowd holding its collective breath. Lawrence originally hoped to play a few Second XI games and maybe one in the Sunday League. He decided to go to Australia instead to test the knee at some kind of competitive level. His absence from the Gloucestershire side was again felt acutely. One appreciated increasingly what his presence and enthusiasm had meant.

There were few memorable moments for the county to cherish in the one-day competitions; indeed the Benson and Hedges Cup came and went for Gloucestershire before the end of April. The glimpses of late-season vitality should not obscure the long, gloomy weeks that came first, when the county seemed to be drifting. The future remains inconclusive. Robert Dawson can perhaps find a permanent place as Hancock has now done; Robert Cunliffe could be pressing along with Matthew Windows for more opportunities than have yet come their way. Useful teenage talent is being nurtured, and one or two real discoveries may emerge in 1994. The need is painfully urgent. – David Foot.

GLOUCESTERSHIRE 1993

[*Bill Smith*]

Back row: M. C. J. Ball, A. M. Smith, M. Davies, R. I. Dawson, T. H. C. Hancock, R. C. J. Williams. *Middle row:* B. H. Jenkins (*scorer*), R. C. Williams, S. G. Hinks, M. J. Gerrard, J. M. de la Pena, A. M. Babington, R. M. Wight, R. Horrell. *Front row:* G. D. Hodgson, M. W. Alleyne, A. W. Stovold (*coach*), P. G. M. August (*secretary*), A. J. Wright (*captain*), R. W. Rossiter (*chairman*), B. C. Broad, K. E. Cooper, R. J. Scott. *Insets:* C. A. Walsh, D. V. Lawrence, R. J. Cunliffe, M. G. N. Windows, R. C. Russell.

GLOUCESTERSHIRE RESULTS

All first-class matches – Played 18: Won 3, Lost 10, Drawn 5.

County Championship matches – Played 17: Won 3, Lost 10, Drawn 4.

Bonus points – Batting 24, Bowling 56.

Competition placings – Britannic Assurance County Championship, 17th;
NatWest Bank Trophy, 2nd round; Benson and Hedges Cup, preliminary round;
AXA Equity & Law League, 13th.

BRITANNIC ASSURANCE CHAMPIONSHIP AVERAGES

BATTING

	Birthplace	M	I	NO	R	HS	Avge
‡G. D. Hodgson	Carlisle	13	26	2	1,063	166	44.29
‡R. C. Russell......	Stroud	17	30	2	826	99*	35.91
‡B. C. Broad........	Bristol	17	33	0	1,081	131	32.75
‡M. W. Alleyne.....	Tottenham	17	33	2	992	142*	32.00
R. C. Williams	Camberwell	3	6	3	90	38	30.00
T. H. C. Hancock .	Reading	15	28	2	686	76	26.38
R. I. Dawson	Exmouth	8	16	1	349	58	23.26
S. G. Hinks........	Northfleet	12	24	1	482	68	20.95
R. J. Scott	Bournemouth	5	10	0	179	51	17.90
‡A. J. Wright	Stevenage	10	20	2	299	75	16.61
R. M. Wight	London	7	11	1	152	54	15.20
‡C. A. Walsh§	Kingston, Jamaica	13	20	2	262	57	14.55
M. C. J. Ball......	Bristol	4	8	0	113	71	14.12
M. Davies	Neath	14	23	5	220	44*	12.22
K. E. Cooper	Hucknall	14	25	6	218	52	11.47
A. M. Smith	Dewsbury, Yorkshire	6	10	1	84	33	9.33
A. M. Babington ...	London	7	9	3	40	23	6.66
M. J. Gerrard	Southmead, Bristol	3	5	2	20	9	6.66

Also batted: J. M. de la Pena (*London*) (1 match) 7*; M. G. N. Windows (*Bristol*)
(1 match) 21, 37.

* *Signifies not out.* ‡ *Denotes county cap.* § *Overseas player.*

The following played a total of seven three-figure innings for Gloucestershire in County
Championship matches – M. W. Alleyne 3, B. C. Broad 2, G. D. Hodgson 2.

BOWLING

	O	M	R	W	BB	5W/i	Avge
C. A. Walsh..........	513.1	117	1,466	62	5-59	3	23.64
M. C. J. Ball	157.3	35	439	18	8-46	2	24.38
K. E. Cooper	502.4	149	1,233	47	5-83	1	26.23
M. W. Alleyne	238.1	50	652	24	3-25	0	27.16
M. Davies	515.1	141	1,412	37	5-57	2	38.16
A. M. Babington	219.2	49	634	13	3-51	0	48.76
A. M. Smith	186.2	35	587	12	3-59	0	48.91

Also bowled: B. C. Broad 1–0–1–0; R. I. Dawson 1–0–2–0; J. M. de la Pena 1–0–1–0;
M. J. Gerrard 89.1–16–298–8; T. H. C. Hancock 42–11–128–6; S. G. Hinks 1–0–2–0; R. C.
Russell 1.5–0–15–0; R. J. Scott 60–14–157–2; R. M. Wight 181.2–47–478–9; R. C. Williams
66–13–247–5; M. G. N. Windows 1–0–3–0.

Wicket-keeper: R. C. Russell 53 ct, 7 st.

Leading Fielder: M. C. J. Ball 13.

GLOUCESTERSHIRE v MIDDLESEX

At Bristol, April 29, 30, May 1, 2. Middlesex won by four wickets. Middlesex 20 pts, Gloucestershire 6 pts. Toss: Gloucestershire. County debut: M. A. Feltham.

A first-innings lead of 119 runs counted for nothing as Gloucestershire were tumbled out, lacking resolve or technical wisdom against the turn and bounce of Emburey and Tufnell, for a negligible 95 in fewer than 54 overs. Some of the Middlesex batting also carried the wary, edgy characteristics of early season. Ramprakash was a notable exception. His second innings of 75, partly in the company of Gatting, gave the match a touch of calibre that for much of the time it clearly lacked, though it was left to Brown and Feltham, on his first appearance for Middlesex, to hit the winning runs. Although Walsh was not yet back from the West Indies and Lawrence was sadly absent, his recovery from his knee-cap injury once more in question, it was not the bowlers who let Gloucestershire down. The experienced Cooper, like Broad no longer wanted by Nottinghamshire, took seven wickets on his Championship debut for Gloucestershire, while the left-arm Gerrard and Smith both found some effective swing, and Russell's seven catches proved he was as agile as ever.

Close of play: First day, Gloucestershire 261-8 (M. Davies 2*, K. E. Cooper 0*); Second day, Middlesex 180; Third day, Middlesex 141-5 (M. R. Ramprakash 68*, K. R. Brown 0*).

Gloucestershire

B. C. Broad lbw b Feltham	58	– c Emburey b Tufnell	15
S. G. Hinks c Ramprakash b Keech	25	– c Carr b Feltham	7
R. J. Scott c Brown b Fraser	24	– c Ramprakash b Fraser	12
M. W. Alleyne c Carr b Feltham	25	– c Brown b Tufnell	31
*A. J. Wright b Keech	35	– c Brown b Emburey	1
T. H. C. Hancock c Gatting b Taylor	24	– c Brown b Emburey	9
†R. C. Russell c Carr b Fraser	22	– c Emburey b Tufnell	0
A. M. Smith c Ramprakash b Fraser	27	– c Gatting b Tufnell	0
M. Davies not out	18	– lbw b Emburey	2
K. E. Cooper c Carr b Fraser	13	– c Gatting b Emburey	4
M. J. Gerrard c Fraser b Feltham	9	– not out	5
B 3, l-b 7, w 9	19	B 2, l-b 7	9

1/78 2/107 3/121 4/152 5/204   299   1/12 2/39 3/45 4/58 5/72   95
6/204 7/240 8/261 9/275   6/73 7/75 8/86 9/86

Bonus points – Gloucestershire 2, Middlesex 4 (Score at 120 overs: 278-9).

Bowling: *First Innings*—Fraser 30-10-76-4; Taylor 30-7-93-1; Emburey 10-4-9-0; Feltham 34.5-13-68-3; Keech 16-7-28-2; Tufnell 10-6-15-0. *Second Innings*—Fraser 10-2-30-1; Feltham 10-6-8-1; Tufnell 20-10-33-4; Emburey 13.2-6-15-4.

Middlesex

M. Keech c Russell b Smith	35	– c Russell b Cooper	2
M. A. Roseberry lbw b Smith	32	– c Wright b Cooper	7
*M. W. Gatting b Gerrard	2	– lbw b Smith	45
M. R. Ramprakash b Gerrard	35	– c Russell b Cooper	75
J. D. Carr c Russell b Gerrard	6	– c Russell b Smith	12
†K. R. Brown lbw b Gerrard	15	– (7) not out	38
M. A. Feltham c Scott b Gerrard	5	– (8) not out	24
J. E. Emburey not out	4		
A. R. C. Fraser c Alleyne b Cooper	3		
C. W. Taylor b Cooper	0	– (6) c Russell b Smith	0
P. C. R. Tufnell c Russell b Cooper	0		
L-b 10, w 4, n-b 4	18	L-b 7, w 2, n-b 4	13

1/67 2/76 3/142 4/147 5/162   180   1/2 2/11 3/114   (6 wkts) 216
6/170 7/174 8/178 9/180   4/140 5/140 6/156

Bonus points – Gloucestershire 4.

Bowling: *First Innings*—Cooper 22-9-33-4; Gerrard 25-4-50-4; Smith 17-5-49-2; Davies 3-0-13-0; Scott 12-3-19-0; Hancock 6-4-6-0. *Second Innings*—Cooper 22-7-53-3; Gerrard 13.3-3-39-0; Smith 22-5-59-3; Scott 4-1-13-0; Davies 17-2-45-0.

Umpires: V. A. Holder and G. Sharp.

At Northampton, May 6, 7, 8, 10. GLOUCESTERSHIRE lost to NORTHAMPTON-SHIRE by five wickets.

GLOUCESTERSHIRE v DURHAM

At Bristol, May 20, 21, 22, 24. Drawn. Gloucestershire 5 pts, Durham 5 pts. Toss: Durham.

In the end Gloucestershire were left to score 268 in 50 overs, a demanding target, though Durham argued they did not have a fully fit attack. A match which had not offered many shafts of excitement after a first-day washout then drifted predictably to its close. In their first innings Durham had relied on a seventh-wicket stand of 93 between Scott and Cummins, the Barbadian fast bowler, parading application in his maiden fifty. In turn, Gloucestershire responded with a century of calm composure from Alleyne, who gave hopes of a more productive summer to match his undeniable technique. The home county declared 93 runs behind but was always going to be too slow for these two nondescript sides to generate real interest. Botham, despite a ricked neck, did his best to adjust the pattern with a lively second-innings 73 from 78 balls, before being stumped as he tried to hit Davies over the pavilion clock.

Close of play: First day, No play; Second day, Durham 292-8 (A. C. Cummins 57*, J. Wood 7*); Third day, Gloucestershire 227-6 (R. C. Russell 10*, R. M. Wight 2*).

Durham

G. Fowler c Russell b Walsh	0	– c Wight b Smith	11
W. Larkins c Wight b Smith	29	– c Alleyne b Walsh	13
P. W. G. Parker c Russell b Walsh	13		
P. Bainbridge b Alleyne	29	– (3) c Alleyne b Walsh	6
J. A. Daley b Alleyne	39	– (4) c Wight b Smith	37
I. T. Botham lbw b Walsh	21	– (5) st Russell b Davies	73
†C. W. Scott c Hodgson b Smith	64	– (6) b Scott	8
A. C. Cummins b Davies	62	– (7) c Russell b Scott	1
P. J. Berry run out	10	– (8) not out	5
J. Wood st Russell b Davies	17	– (9) not out	2
*D. A. Graveney not out	11		
L-b 5, n-b 20	25	B 4, l-b 4, n-b 10	18
	320	(7 wkts dec.)	**174**

1/2 2/41 3/70 4/116 5/137 6/165 7/258 8/282 9/301

1/13 2/24 3/47 4/76 5/78 6/146 7/172

Bonus points – Durham 3, Gloucestershire 4.

In the second innings I. T. Botham, when 12, retired hurt at 65 and resumed at 78.

Bowling: *First Innings*—Walsh 20-7-54-3; Smith 28-4-109-2; Scott 12-4-25-0; Hancock 3-0-15-0; Davies 24.1-8-32-2; Alleyne 20-3-48-2; Wight 10-2-32-0. *Second Innings*—Walsh 16-2-43-2; Smith 14-1-45-2; Scott 12-3-48-2; Davies 7-0-30-1.

Gloucestershire

B. C. Broad b Cummins	23	– c Bainbridge b Graveney	26
G. D. Hodgson c Parker b Berry	5	– c Bainbridge b Berry	11
R. J. Scott b Cummins	13	– lbw b Cummins	49
M. W. Alleyne c Larkins b Bainbridge	104	– c and b Graveney	9
*A. J. Wright c Botham b Graveney	18	– not out	28
T. H. C. Hancock c Scott b Cummins	23	– not out	29
†R. C. Russell not out	10		
R. M. Wight not out	2		
B 2, l-b 9, w 2, n-b 16	29	B 2, l-b 2, n-b 12	16
	(6 wkts dec.) **227**	(4 wkts)	**168**

1/33 2/33 3/85 4/132 5/213 6/215

1/41 2/53 3/70 4/116

A. M. Smith, M. Davies and C. A. Walsh did not bat.

Bonus points – Gloucestershire 1, Durham 2.

Bowling: *First Innings*—Cummins 17–5–43–3; Wood 16–2–54–0; Berry 6–1–34–1; Graveney 22–5–54–1; Botham 8–2–23–0; Bainbridge 6.4–3–8–1. *Second Innings*—Cummins 9–2–45–1; Wood 4–1–18–0; Graveney 19–3–57–2; Berry 15–0–44–1.

Umpires: G. I. Burgess and D. O. Oslear.

GLOUCESTERSHIRE v WORCESTERSHIRE

At King's School, Gloucester, May 27, 28, 29, 31. Worcestershire won by an innings and five runs. Worcestershire 21 pts, Gloucestershire 4 pts. Toss: Worcestershire.

The Gloucester Festival, threatened when the TCCB ruled that the Wagon Works pitch was unfit, was saved when the school authorities offered Archdeacon Meadow, an evocative ground that offered memories of the Gloucestershire spin bowling tradition from the start. However, this was thoroughly disconcerting for the home county who, after the first day had been washed out, were put in on a pitch that was wet at one end and offered bounce and turn reminiscent of the days of uncovered wickets. Illingworth, brought on within the first half-hour, took six for 28, his best in the Championship, as Gloucestershire were bowled out for 101. Worcestershire took the lead through Curtis and Hick with only one man out. Walsh broke through and the last eight wickets went down for only 67. But Benjamin bowled sharply in the second innings, Worcestershire held on to their close catches and Gloucestershire were again tumbled out cheaply.

Close of play: First day, No play; Second day, Worcestershire 120-1 (T. S. Curtis 60*, G. A. Hick 34*); Third day, Gloucestershire 50-5 (A. J. Wright 4*, R. C. Russell 1*).

Gloucestershire

B. C. Broad c Leatherdale b Illingworth	5	– lbw b Benjamin	14
G. D. Hodgson c Curtis b Illingworth	9	– lbw b Tolley	2
R. J. Scott c Lampitt b Hick	13	– b Benjamin	5
M. W. Alleyne c Lampitt b Illingworth	2	– c Tolley b Benjamin	7
*A. J. Wright c Leatherdale b Illingworth	0	– b Illingworth	9
T. H. C. Hancock c Illingworth b Hick	32	– c Curtis b Benjamin	9
†R. C. Russell c Hick b Benjamin	9	– lbw b Illingworth	32
A. M. Smith lbw b Illingworth	9	– c Leatherdale b Illingworth	0
M. Davies lbw b Benjamin	2	– c Lampitt b Newport	0
C. A. Walsh st Rhodes b Illingworth	5	– b Newport	4
K. E. Cooper not out	1	– not out	15
B 2, l-b 5, w 1, n-b 6	14	B 3, l-b 10, w 2, n-b 4	19

1/15 2/26 3/30 4/30 5/55   101   1/3 2/12 3/26 4/37 5/49   116
6/78 7/83 8/93 9/100   6/81 7/81 8/92 9/96

Bonus points – Worcestershire 4.

Bowling: *First Innings*—Benjamin 16–7–32–2; Tolley 3–0–8–0; Illingworth 18.4–6–28–6; Newport 9–3–11–0; Hick 6–3–15–2. *Second Innings*—Benjamin 18–5–35–4; Tolley 13–6–14–1; Illingworth 13.2–2–34–3; Newport 11–5–20–2.

Worcestershire

*T. S. Curtis c Wright b Walsh	68	R. K. Illingworth lbw b Walsh	4
W. P. C. Weston c and b Davies	17	C. M. Tolley c Alleyne b Walsh	3
G. A. Hick c Hodgson b Davies	68	K. C. G. Benjamin not out	5
D. A. Leatherdale c Alleyne b Cooper	8		
A. C. H. Seymour b Smith	4	B 2, l-b 9, w 2, n-b 6	19
S. R. Lampitt c Russell b Cooper	2		
†S. J. Rhodes b Walsh	24	1/42 2/137 3/155 4/164 5/169	222
P. J. Newport b Walsh	0	6/186 7/193 8/199 9/207	

Bonus points – Worcestershire 1, Gloucestershire 4.

Bowling: Walsh 31.3–10–62–5; Cooper 24–11–26–2; Davies 32–7–74–2; Smith 19–4–42–1; Alleyne 3–1–7–0.

Umpires: M. J. Kitchen and P. B. Wight.

At Tunbridge Wells, June 3, 4, 5, 7. GLOUCESTERSHIRE lost to KENT by an innings and 69 runs.

At Bristol, June 12, 13, 14. GLOUCESTERSHIRE drew with AUSTRALIANS (See Australian tour section).

At Sheffield, June 17, 18, 19, 21. GLOUCESTERSHIRE drew with YORKSHIRE.

At Leicester, June 24, 25, 26, 28. GLOUCESTERSHIRE lost to LEICESTERSHIRE by five wickets.

GLOUCESTERSHIRE v HAMPSHIRE

At Bristol, July 1, 2, 3, 5. Hampshire won by one wicket. Hampshire 20 pts, Gloucestershire 6 pts. Toss: Gloucestershire. First-class debut: D. P. J. Flint.

As the match progressed, the Nevil Road wicket befriended the spinners – and Hampshire's were the more effective. The match had started with an opening stand of 279 between Broad and Hodgson, Gloucestershire's highest for any wicket at Bristol, and Wright was able to declare when the team passed 500. But in the second innings, they collapsed for a miserable 102. Darren Flint, a left-arm spinner from Basingstoke making his first-class debut, was their undoing: he had a spell of four for four and finished with five wickets; off-spinner Udal took three of the others. Nicholas had been so confident in their ability that he had given them the new ball. That left Hampshire, who had declared 108 behind on first innings, 211 in 64 overs to win. With only 78 wanted off the last 20 and three men out, Hampshire looked certain winners but wickets then fell steadily and the asking-rate rose to eight an over. However, Hampshire kept attacking and, with four wanted and two balls left, Connor drove Davies for a straight six.

Close of play: First day, Gloucestershire 342-2 (G. D. Hodgson 156*, M. W. Alleyne 18*); Second day, Hampshire 141-2 (R. S. M. Morris 54*, S. D. Udal 0*); Third day, Gloucestershire 14-0 (B. C. Broad 7*, G. D. Hodgson 7*).

Gloucestershire

B. C. Broad c Morris b Udal	131	– c Terry b Marshall	15
G. D. Hodgson c Middleton b James	166	– lbw b Connor	10
S. G. Hinks b Flint b Connor	12	– c Terry b Udal	11
M. W. Alleyne b James	38	– c Gower b Udal	19
*A. J. Wright c Aymes b Flint	25	– c Aymes b Udal	6
†R. C. Russell c Middleton b Connor	42	– c Udal b Flint	13
R. M. Wight c James b Flint	14	– st Aymes b Flint	4
R. C. Williams not out	26	– not out	6
M. Davies not out	10	– c Terry b Flint	0
M. J. Gerrard (did not bat)		– b Flint	0
A. M. Babington (did not bat)		– c Nicholas b Flint	0
L-b 7, n-b 30	37	N-b 8	8

1/279 2/304 3/365 4/374 5/439   (7 wkts dec.) 501   1/23 2/27 3/63 4/63 5/72   102
6/459 7/459   6/81 7/86 8/90 9/90

Bonus points – Gloucestershire 4, Hampshire 1 (Score at 120 overs: 373-3).

Bowling: *First Innings*—Marshall 33-10-81-0; Connor 44.1-13-143-2; James 25-7-60-2; Udal 30-7-98-1; Flint 39-9-112-2. *Second Innings*—Udal 12-4-25-3; Flint 13-3-32-5; Connor 8-1-26-1; Marshall 8-3-19-1.

Hampshire

R. S. M. Morris c Wight b Gerrard	92	– (2) c Alleyne b Babington	8
T. C. Middleton c Wight b Williams	12	– (1) lbw b Davies	6
D. I. Gower c Russell b Gerrard	61	– b Gerrard	44
S. D. Udal c Wright b Davies	16	– (9) b Wight	10
V. P. Terry c Alleyne b Wight	17	– (4) c Russell b Davies	43
*M. C. J. Nicholas c Hodgson b Alleyne	83	– (5) c Davies b Wight	37
K. D. James not out	69	– (6) c Wight b Davies	6
†A. N. Aymes not out	17	– run out	17
M. D. Marshall (did not bat)		– (7) c Gerrard b Davies	16
C. A. Connor (did not bat)		– not out	11
D. P. J. Flint (did not bat)		– not out	1
B 2, l-b 3, w 1, n-b 20	26	B 1, l-b 8, w 1, n-b 4	14

1/39 2/141 3/182 4/216　　　(6 wkts dec.) 393　　1/15 2/15 3/85　　(9 wkts) 213
5/225 6/356　　　　　　　　　　　　　　　　　　4/138 5/154 6/155
　　　　　　　　　　　　　　　　　　　　　　　7/178 8/198 9/205

Bonus points – Hampshire 3, Gloucestershire 2 (Score at 120 overs: 308-5).

Bowling: *First Innings*—Gerrard 20–6–36–2; Babington 24–7–77–0; Wight 33.4–9–86–1; Williams 12–4–43–1; Davies 54–16–116–1; Alleyne 14–3–30–1. *Second Innings*—Babington 11–2–30–1; Gerrard 8–3–22–1; Davies 22.5–6–82–4; Wight 18–3–58–2; Williams 4–2–12–0.

Umpires: H. D. Bird and P. B. Wight.

At Guildford, July 15, 16, 17. GLOUCESTERSHIRE lost to SURREY by an innings and 66 runs.

GLOUCESTERSHIRE v DERBYSHIRE

At Cheltenham, July 29, 30, 31, August 2. Derbyshire won by seven wickets. Derbyshire 24 pts, Gloucestershire 4 pts. Toss: Gloucestershire.

A match with two totals above 500 went Derbyshire's way because of a terrible first-innings collapse by Gloucestershire. Despite the loss of 30 overs on the opening day Derbyshire raced to 408 for five before the close with Cork scoring his maiden Championship hundred, though a hamstring injury meant he needed a runner to reach three figures and was unable to bowl later. The most fluent and entertaining batting came from Morris, with 32 fours and three sixes in his first double-century; he figured in a Derbyshire fifth-wicket record of 302 before Cork retired. It was a formidable recovery after they had been 58 for four. Little had gone Gloucestershire's way in 1993 and here they were bowled out in 30.3 overs, 382 behind. Malcolm bowled with impressive pace, though he was eventually upstaged by Warner, who equalled his best analysis, five for 27, after nine years, and took ten in a match for the first time – despite a groin strain. Following on, however, Gloucestershire showed much more fibre, even given an injury-ridden attack. Broad, batting down the order, produced a welcome hundred and they fell only one short of Derbyshire's first innings: Russell, with a timely reminder to the England selectors, was stranded on 99. But Derbyshire had little difficulty knocking off 139 by lunch on the last day.

Close of play: First day, Derbyshire 408-5 (M. J. Vandrau 15*, K. M. Krikken 3*); Second day, Gloucestershire 136-2 (G. D. Hodgson 64*, B. C. Broad 0*); Third day, Derbyshire 42-2 (J. E. Morris 11*, C. J. Adams 21*).

Derbyshire

*K. J. Barnett c Dawson b Walsh	18		
P. D. Bowler c Hinks b Gerrard	20	– (1) c Dawson b Walsh	2
J. E. Morris lbw b Hancock	229	– (2) not out	71
C. J. Adams c Russell b Walsh	0	– c Russell b Walsh	33
T. J. G. O'Gorman c Broad b Walsh	0	– not out	22
D. G. Cork c Hinks b Alleyne	104		
M. J. Vandrau b Walsh	57		
†K. M. Krikken c Russell b Alleyne	40		
A. E. Warner c Hancock b Cooper	19		
S. J. Base b Cooper	0	– (3) c Hodgson b Walsh	2
D. E. Malcolm not out	1		
L-b 6, w 5, n-b 22	33	B 1, l-b 2, n-b 6	9

1/46 2/46 3/58 4/58 5/404   521   1/6 2/8 3/83   (3 wkts) 139
6/472 7/484 8/513 9/516

Bonus points – Derbyshire 4, Gloucestershire 4.

In the first innings D. G. Cork, when 100, retired hurt at 360 and resumed at 472.

Bowling: *First Innings*—Walsh 30.1–10–95–4; Gerrard 19–0–125–1; Cooper 28–4–119–2; Smith 18–0–108–0; Alleyne 11–2–55–2; Hancock 4–0–13–1. *Second Innings*—Walsh 14–1–52–3; Cooper 8–1–40–0; Smith 3–0–18–0; Gerrard 3.4–0–26–0.

Gloucestershire

G. D. Hodgson b Base	25	– c Morris b Malcolm	64
S. G. Hinks lbw b Warner	15	– c sub b Warner	16
R. I. Dawson c Krikken b Malcolm	11	– b Malcolm	46
B. C. Broad c Krikken b Malcolm	0	– c sub b Warner	120
M. W. Alleyne c Base b Malcolm	0	– b Warner	46
T. H. C. Hancock c Krikken b Malcolm	19	– c O'Gorman b Vandrau	56
†R. C. Russell c Krikken b Warner	25	– not out	99
*C. A. Walsh lbw b Warner	9	– c Krikken b Malcolm	5
A. M. Smith b Warner	1	– c Krikken b Warner	4
K. E. Cooper c sub b Warner	0	– b Warner	12
M. J. Gerrard not out	4	– c Krikken b Adams	2
L-b 5, w 1, n-b 24	30	L-b 18, n-b 32	50

1/40 2/59 3/61 4/61 5/89   139   1/20 2/123 3/136 4/207 5/322   520
6/90 7/116 8/128 9/128   6/436 7/461 8/482 9/502

Bonus points – Derbyshire 4.

Bowling: *First Innings*—Malcolm 15–0–77–4; Warner 7.3–1–27–5; Base 8–2–30–1. *Second Innings*—Base 20.5–9–94–0; Warner 29–3–93–5; Vandrau 29–7–91–1; Adams 6.4–0–44–1; Barnett 16–2–38–0; Malcolm 30–4–140–3; Bowler 7–5–2–0.

Umpires: J. C. Balderstone and J. H. Harris.

GLOUCESTERSHIRE v LANCASHIRE

At Cheltenham, August 5, 6, 7. Gloucestershire won by nine wickets. Gloucestershire 24 pts, Lancashire 5 pts. Toss: Lancashire.

Growing fears in the West Country that Gloucestershire would go through the summer without a Championship win were efficiently stifled at the expense of a jaded, nondescript Lancashire. At the start, Lancashire's batting – especially that of Mendis – was painfully laboured; in their second innings, they lost six wickets by the 23rd over. Both times the injured Fairbrother and Hegg did their best to keep the game open, but Gloucestershire never looked like a bottom-of-the-table team. Walsh, as if inspired by the sudden call to captaincy, bowled quite brilliantly – to the marked discomfiture of a succession of Lancashire batsmen – and Alleyne's unbeaten 142 in the first innings was invaluable. On the second day he was circumspect, but next morning he blazed away with Cooper, who recorded his maiden fifty – after 17 years – as Gloucestershire headed towards 450. More than the acquisition of 24 points with a day to spare, the victory was a psychological break-through for a county whose exuberance and confidence had been so patently lacking.

Close of play: First day, Lancashire 294; Second day, Gloucestershire 315-7 (M. W. Alleyne 69*, C. A. Walsh 8*).

Lancashire

G. D. Mendis b Walsh	81	– c Russell b Walsh	15
J. P. Crawley lbw b Davies	30	– c Russell b Walsh	2
N. J. Speak run out	21	– c Dawson b Cooper	7
G. D. Lloyd c Russell b Babington	5	– c Broad b Walsh	1
*N. H. Fairbrother c Russell b Walsh	40	– (7) c Dawson b Babington	38
Wasim Akram c Russell b Cooper	17	– (5) c Walsh b Babington	25
P. A. J. DeFreitas c Hinks b Cooper	9	– (6) c Dawson b Alleyne	12
†W. K. Hegg c Russell b Babington	59	– c Broad b Babington	49
I. D. Austin c Russell b Davies	1	– b Walsh	10
P. J. Martin b Davies	11	– not out	5
A. A. Barnett not out	5	– c Dawson b Walsh	9
L-b 3, n-b 12	15	B 2, l-b 4, n-b 10	16

1/70 2/101 3/120 4/190 5/195   294   1/5 2/16 3/17 4/44 5/67   213
6/216 7/232 8/233 9/259   6/69 7/137 8/161 9/187

Bonus points – Lancashire 2, Gloucestershire 4.

Bowling: *First Innings*—Walsh 24-4-68-2; Cooper 25-8-41-2; Babington 23.3-5-67-2; Davies 29-9-85-3; Alleyne 8-0-30-0. *Second Innings*—Walsh 19.2-2-83-5; Cooper 9-3-19-1; Alleyne 6-2-22-1; Babington 15-4-51-3; Davies 7-3-24-0; Hancock 2-1-8-0.

Gloucestershire

G. D. Hodgson c Hegg b Barnett	38	– not out	28
S. G. Hinks c Lloyd b DeFreitas	64	– c Lloyd b Martin	15
R. I. Dawson c Hegg b DeFreitas	13	– not out	7
B. C. Broad c Fairbrother b DeFreitas	0		
M. W. Alleyne not out	142		
T. H. C. Hancock c Crawley b Wasim Akram	59		
†R. C. Russell b Barnett	22		
M. Davies c Hegg b Wasim Akram	1		
*C. A. Walsh c Mendis b DeFreitas	12		
K. E. Cooper c DeFreitas b Austin	52		
A. M. Babington c Hegg b DeFreitas	0		
B 4, l-b 11, w 2, n-b 30	47	L-b 3, w 1, n-b 4	8

1/76 2/116 3/120 4/131 5/238   450   1/40   (1 wkt) 58
6/293 7/306 8/337 9/442

Bonus points – Gloucestershire 4, Lancashire 3 (Score at 120 overs: 389-8).

Bowling: *First Innings*—Wasim Akram 32-6-92-2; DeFreitas 33.3-7-104-5; Austin 18-0-66-1; Martin 21-1-75-0; Barnett 29-4-98-2. *Second Innings*—DeFreitas 5-0-24-0; Wasim Akram 2-0-6-0; Martin 5-1-12-1; Austin 1.2-0-13-0.

Umpires: B. Dudleston and M. J. Kitchen.

At Birmingham, August 12, 13, 14, 16. GLOUCESTERSHIRE beat WARWICKSHIRE by five wickets.

GLOUCESTERSHIRE v ESSEX

At Bristol, August 19, 20, 21, 23. Drawn. Gloucestershire 7 pts, Essex 5 pts. Toss: Gloucestershire.

Improving Gloucestershire had sensed that here might be their third win in a row but the notion was dashed by Essex's caution on the last day. Essex, with Gooch and Hussain at the Test, were completely inhibited by a target of 325 on a pitch that did not encourage strokeplay. Despite the solidity of the uncapped Robinson and Lewis, they never really lifted the tempo and, in the end, Prichard and Garnham played out a draw. This was not the Essex of Championship grandeur. They might have followed on had not their acting-captain Prichard, who was suffering from a viral infection, left his hotel bed to make a crucial 46 at No. 8. It was a frustrating conclusion for Gloucestershire, for whom Alleyne, with a conscientious hundred supported by Hancock, had ensured a first-innings recovery from 91 for four, while Cooper, Walsh and Babington bowled well to dismiss Essex for 216 on the second day.

Close of play: First day, Gloucestershire 320; Second day, Gloucestershire 32-1 (B. C. Broad 14*, R. I. Dawson 3*); Third day, Gloucestershire 220.

Gloucestershire

B. C. Broad lbw b Ilott	24	c Pringle b Childs	18
G. D. Hodgson c Robinson b Pringle	20	lbw b Childs	7
R. I. Dawson lbw b Pringle	18	c Shahid b Ilott	41
S. G. Hinks c Garnham b Pringle	18	lbw b Childs	3
M. W. Alleyne c Knight b Pringle	104	c Topley b Salim Malik	27
T. H. C. Hancock lbw b Salim Malik	52	b Ilott	0
†R. C. Russell c Garnham b Ilott	14	c Childs b Topley	65
M. Davies c Childs b Topley	20	c Knight b Ilott	0
*C. A. Walsh c sub b Childs	4	c Garnham b Topley	27
K. E. Cooper c Garnham b Topley	17	run out	6
A. M. Babington not out	0	not out	0
B 3, l-b 4, w 3, n-b 20	29	B 5, l-b 6, w 1, n-b 14	26

1/34 2/65 3/80 4/91 5/193   320   1/28 2/37 3/46 4/102 5/103   220
6/220 7/282 8/290 9/320   6/120 7/132 8/203 9/220

Bonus points – Gloucestershire 3, Essex 4.

Bowling: *First Innings*—Ilott 30-6-79-2; Pringle 26-6-90-4; Topley 19.1-3-77-2; Childs 16-5-32-1; Salim Malik 16-4-36-1. *Second Innings*—Ilott 29-10-38-3; Topley 23.5-6-71-2; Childs 30-9-62-3; Salim Malik 15-1-38-1.

Essex

D. D. J. Robinson c Hinks b Walsh	6	c Dawson b Walsh	67
N. V. Knight c Hinks b Cooper	0	st Russell b Davies	30
J. J. B. Lewis b Cooper	46	c Dawson b Cooper	56
Salim Malik lbw b Alleyne	25	b Cooper	23
N. Shahid b Babington	45	c Russell b Walsh	12
†M. A. Garnham b Cooper	1	not out	17
D. R. Pringle c Russell b Babington	14		
*P. J. Prichard not out	46	(7) not out	21
T. D. Topley c Hinks b Walsh	11		
M. C. Ilott c Russell b Walsh	0		
J. H. Childs b Babington	4		
L-b 6, n-b 12	18	B 7, l-b 3, w 2, n-b 2	14

1/0 2/10 3/61 4/100 5/102   216   1/64 2/140 3/173   (5 wkts) 240
6/143 7/148 8/202 9/202   4/180 5/203

Bonus points – Essex 1, Gloucestershire 4.

Bowling: *First Innings*—Walsh 21–6–57–3; Cooper 22–8–30–3; Babington 19.5–5–71–3; Alleyne 16–7–19–1; Davies 8–5–21–0; Hancock 2–1–12–0. *Second Innings*—Walsh 24–7–51–2; Cooper 20–5–48–2; Babington 18–2–70–0; Davies 23–9–34–1; Alleyne 12–0–27–0.

Umpires: J. D. Bond and R. A. White.

At Abergavenny, August 26, 27, 28, 30. GLOUCESTERSHIRE lost to GLAMORGAN by 82 runs.

At Taunton, August 31, September 1, 2, 3. GLOUCESTERSHIRE beat SOMERSET by 22 runs.

GLOUCESTERSHIRE v NOTTINGHAMSHIRE

At Bristol, September 9, 10, 11, 13. Drawn. Gloucestershire 5 pts, Nottinghamshire 6 pts. Toss: Nottinghamshire.

The visitors' last hopes of finishing runners-up to Middlesex disappeared with this match. Cairns had returned from New Zealand specially, having flown home on compassionate leave after the death of his sister. But Walsh gave Nottinghamshire little chance after his batsmen had been fed with 173 runs in an hour, a statistic that meant little except to Ball and Dawson, who were able to make career-best scores. The target was 259 in 46 overs, which was never on. Play had been cut by about half on both the first two days and the match never took shape. Gloucestershire supporters were reassured by the news that Walsh would be returning as captain in 1994, with Russell as his deputy. Appositely, the pair put on 86, the best and liveliest stand of the first innings. Some of Nottinghamshire's best batting came on the third day from Saxelby, who had recently scored an unbeaten 238 for their Second XI on the same ground.

Close of play: First day, Gloucestershire 132-5 (M. W. Alleyne 27*, R. C. Russell 3*); Second day, Nottinghamshire 15-0 (P. R. Pollard 7*, W. A. Dessaur 6*); Third day, Gloucestershire 59-2 (M. C. J. Ball 4*, R. I. Dawson 5*).

Gloucestershire

B. C. Broad b Lewis	21	– b Cairns	24
G. D. Hodgson b Pick	13	– b Bates	22
R. I. Dawson b Pick	30	– (4) c Johnson b Pollard	58
S. G. Hinks c French b Cairns	8	– (5) not out	25
M. W. Alleyne b Cairns	49	– (6) not out	22
T. H. C. Hancock c French b Lewis	11		
†R. C. Russell not out	69		
M. C. J. Ball c French b Cairns	0	– (3) c Pick b Pollard	71
*C. A. Walsh c French b Bates	35		
K. E. Cooper b Lewis	5		
B 5, l-b 8, w 1, n-b 22	36	B 1, l-b 1, n-b 8	10

1/26 2/50 3/63 4/105 5/122 (9 wkts dec.) 277 1/50 2/50 (4 wkts dec.) 232
6/181 7/183 8/269 9/277 3/180 4/181

A. M. Babington did not bat.

Bonus points – Gloucestershire 2, Nottinghamshire 4.

Bowling: *First Innings*—Cairns 23–6–47–3; Lewis 31.1–6–87–3; Pennett 23–5–55–0; Pick 30–11–67–2; Bates 5–2–8–1. *Second Innings*—Lewis 6–0–18–0; Pennett 3–0–18–0; Pick 3–1–6–0; Cairns 5–1–10–1; Bates 10–3–19–1; Dessaur 11–0–80–0; Pollard 6–0–79–2.

Nottinghamshire

P. R. Pollard c Ball b Walsh	49	– c Walsh b Babington	29
W. A. Dessaur lbw b Cooper	11	– c and b Ball	11
M. Saxelby c Russell b Walsh	59	– c sub b Ball	37
P. Johnson c Dawson b Walsh	18	– c Hinks b Walsh	23
*R. T. Robinson lbw b Cooper	46	– c and b Ball	4
C. L. Cairns c Russell b Walsh	7	– not out	35
C. C. Lewis c Russell b Cooper	12	– c Ball b Cooper	6
†B. N. French c Walsh b Alleyne	8	– not out	4
R. T. Bates not out	18		
R. A. Pick not out	12		
B 2, l-b 5, n-b 4	11	B 1, l-b 5	6

1/38 2/117 3/132 4/145 5/153   (8 wkts dec.) 251   1/38 2/53 3/94   (6 wkts) 155
6/175 7/198 8/227   4/104 5/114 6/141

D. B. Pennett did not bat.

Bonus points – Nottinghamshire 2, Gloucestershire 3.

Bowling: *First Innings*—Walsh 28.5–5–76–4; Cooper 23–7–50–3; Babington 16–2–47–0; Alleyne 15–0–50–1; Ball 8–2–15–0; Hancock 2–0–6–0. *Second Innings*—Walsh 11.3–4–26–1; Cooper 10–1–39–1; Babington 6–0–28–1; Ball 13–0–56–3.

Umpires: R. Julian and N. T. Plews.

At Hove, September 16, 17, 18, 20. GLOUCESTERSHIRE lost to SUSSEX by ten wickets.

HAMPSHIRE

President: W. J. Weld
Chairman: D. Rich
Chairman, Cricket Committee: J. R. Gray
Chief Executive: A. F. Baker
Captain: M. C. J. Nicholas
Coach: T. M. Tremlett
Head Groundsman: N. Gray
Scorer: V. H Isaacs

Hampshire began their season on Thursday, April 29 – little more than 24 hours later, people already suspected it was going to be a tough five months. By then, Somerset had hammered their way to 500 for six and ripped the heart out of Hampshire's reply. They were five for five, before Mark Nicholas ensured that they trailed by only 344 on first innings. Hampshire were invited to try to do better but before the close of the third day had been beaten by an innings and 148 runs.

Unfortunately, first impressions were not false. The message of that bleak beginning was all too clear; the cutting edge of Hampshire's cricket had finally been blunted by the passage of time. Somerset's fast bowler Andrew Caddick had found life and bounce in an apparently benign Northlands Road pitch which defeated Hampshire's batsmen; before him Malcolm Marshall had been unable to extract any venom at all. That is not to pin responsibility for Hampshire's modest summer on the shoulders of the man who had been one of the world's most proficient destroyers of class batting for so long. But when a side's major strike weapon finishes a season with 28 wickets in 13 matches, then it is not difficult to find reasons for failure, particularly as Hampshire had admitted for years that the back-up for Marshall was not good enough.

Thus Nicholas's dream of adding the Championship to the four trophies that had garnished his years as captain was not going to come true in 1993 – and this time there was to be no compensatory one-day success. Only the NatWest Trophy offered a chance of giving the season some lustre; and the promise was only brief and crushed on possibly Hampshire's most numbing day all summer. Staffordshire were nonchalantly hurdled on the back of a classically proficient century by Robin Smith, who scored another against Sussex at Hove in the second round. But although Paul Terry supported him in a partnership of 126 for the second wicket, a target of 249 was always modest and in the end looked derisory: David Smith and Bill Athey ground the bowling into submission with a partnership of 248 to inflict a nine-wicket defeat, Hampshire's heaviest in the 60-overs competition.

By that time Hampshire had won Championship matches at Trent Bridge, Northampton and Bristol to offer hope of a recovery. But after Cardigan Connor's six off the penultimate ball at Bristol on July 5 scrambled Hampshire breathlessly to a one-wicket victory (only the sixth in their history), they won just one more four-day game. That was at Swansea in late August, where Marshall discovered the sparkle of old and his lone five-wicket innings of the summer helped them to a 98-run victory over

Glamorgan. The attack in 1994 may depend on two bowlers released by other counties: Winston Benjamin, late of Leicestershire, the new overseas player, and Norman Cowans from Middlesex, who swapped counties with Kevin Shine.

Amid the disappointment at the overall performance, the sadness at Marshall's departure and at Jon Ayling's final acceptance of the dreadful truth that his reconstructed knee would never withstand the hammering of day-in, day-out cricket, there were compensations. Possibly the greatest was the sudden blossoming of Adrian Aymes as a genuine wicket-keeper-batsman. His keeping was again solid rather than sensational, but his batting took on a new dimension. Previously he had looked a dependable but unadventurous technician with a limited range of shots; suddenly he gave his ambition full rein, revealed unsuspected fluency and was rewarded with a maiden century against Sussex.

The other principal pluses were amongst the young players: Shaun Udal, after some early season stutters as he worked the benefits of coaching suggestions from England's Lilleshall think-tank out of his system, again finished the leading wicket-taker and bowling work-horse. He wheeled his way through 763.2 overs – almost twice as many as anyone else – enjoyed his first two ten-wicket matches against Nottinghamshire and Warwickshire and finished with 74, a more than useful 509 runs as a lower-order batsman and a distinct air of disillusion when overlooked for the England A tour of South Africa. At the same time, left-arm spinner Darren Flint was given his chance and responded by taking 31 wickets, thus consigning Ian Turner to the job-search brigade.

Even on the batting front there were some bright spots. Paul Terry played with much of the self-belief which earned him a brief sortie with England nine years earlier, especially during a magnificent 174 at Swansea. Robin Smith was Robin Smith: although he struggled in the Tests against Shane Warne's leg-spin, he batted with international authority for Hampshire, his season crowned by 191 against the Warne-less Australians.

And then there was David Gower, tantalising as ever: initially he was diffident, then came a lovely hundred at Trent Bridge, injury, more diffidence, then a late-season flourish which brought centuries off Lancashire, Sussex and Essex. It was too late to prise open England's door. In November Gower decided that his appetite could not survive another summer's Championship stodge with little chance of Test match piquancy. The club had, in any case, refused to let him go on the West Indies tour as a journalist if that meant returning late for the new season. Within the club, some were content to see him go. The spectators will miss him.

Nicholas also had a good summer with the bat; he did not score 1,000 runs for the county, a mark reached only by Terry and Gower, but much of the old authority returned and, on occasions, his was the bat that averted utter disaster. Otherwise, the batting disappointed; Middleton never recovered from the nightmare of his England A tour of Australia; Sean Morris, Julian Wood and Rupert Cox had their chances without providing the evidence to suggest that they can bridge the gap between second team and county cricket. Wood lost his opportunity with Hampshire, joining Turner as surplus to future needs. In the Gower-less future, it will be crucial for Morris and Cox to prove the leap is within their scope; otherwise Hampshire may face some more lean seasons. – Mike Neasom.

458

HAMPSHIRE 1993

[Bill Smith]

Back row: T. C. Middleton, J. R. Wood, J. N. B. Bovill, K. J. Shine, D. P. J. Flint, J. S. Laney, R. M. F. Cox. *Middle row*: R. J. Maru, R. E. Hayward (*assistant coach*), A. N. Aymes, R. S. M. Morris, S. D. Udal, I. J. Turner, J. R. Ayling, M. Jean-Jacques, K. D. James, M. J. Thursfield, T. M. Tremlett (*coach*). *Front row*: J. R. Byrne, R. A. Smith, V. P. Terry, M. C. J. Nicholas (*captain*), M. D. Marshall, D. I. Gower, C. A. Connor, M. Garaway.

HAMPSHIRE RESULTS

All first-class matches – Played 19: Won 4, Lost 5, Drawn 10.

County Championship matches – Played 17: Won 4, Lost 5, Drawn 8.

Bonus points – Batting 39, Bowling 47.

Competition placings – Britannic Assurance County Championship, 13th equal;
NatWest Bank Trophy, 2nd round; Benson and Hedges Cup, q-f;
AXA Equity & Law League, 15th.

BRITANNIC ASSURANCE CHAMPIONSHIP AVERAGES

BATTING

	Birthplace	*M*	*I*	*NO*	*R*	*HS*	*Avge*
‡R. A. Smith	*Durban, SA*	10	15	1	761	131	54.35
‡V. P. Terry	*Osnabruck, W. Germany*	17	29	2	1,257	174	46.55
‡D. I. Gower	*Tunbridge Wells*	15	26	0	1,105	153	42.50
‡A. N. Aymes	*Southampton*	17	26	9	682	107*	40.11
‡M. C. J. Nicholas...	*London*	16	26	4	825	95	37.50
‡K. D. James	*Lambeth*	15	26	3	630	71	27.39
R. S. M. Morris ...	*Great Horwood*	8	14	0	372	92	26.57
R. M. F. Cox	*Guildford*	6	10	1	204	63	22.66
‡S. D. Udal.........	*Farnborough, Hants*	17	25	2	503	79*	21.86
‡T. C. Middleton ...	*Winchester*	10	18	0	377	90	20.94
‡C. A. Connor	*The Valley, Anguilla*	9	11	1	200	59	20.00
M. J. Thursfield ...	*South Shields*	2	4	2	36	36*	18.00
‡M. D. Marshall§...	*St Michael, Barbados*	13	16	2	250	75*	17.85
‡J. R. Ayling	*Portsmouth*	3	4	0	62	21	15.50
D. P. J. Flint	*Basingstoke*	10	13	5	47	14*	5.87
K. J. Shine	*Bracknell*	11	13	5	47	12	5.87
I. J. Turner	*Denmead*	3	4	1	12	8	4.00

Also batted: J. N. B. Bovill (*High Wycombe*) (1 match) 3*, 0*; M. Jean-Jacques (*Soufrière, Dominica*) (3 matches) 11*, 10; J. R. Wood (*Winchester*) (1 match) 25.

* *Signifies not out.*   ‡ *Denotes county cap.*   § *Overseas player.*

The following played a total of 11 three-figure innings for Hampshire in County Championship matches – D. I. Gower 4, R. A. Smith 3, V. P. Terry 3, A. N. Aymes 1.

BOWLING

	O	*M*	*R*	*W*	*BB*	*5W/i*	*Avge*
K. D. James	276	73	806	31	4-33	0	26.00
S. D. Udal	678.3	167	1,889	65	6-141	5	29.06
M. D. Marshall	345.3	102	859	28	5-62	1	30.67
D. P. J. Flint	388.2	95	1,066	31	5-32	1	34.38
K. J. Shine..........	256.3	49	1,016	22	6-62	2	46.18
C. A. Connor........	226.4	62	671	12	3-81	0	55.91

Also bowled: J. R. Ayling 33–6–138–3; J. N. B. Bovill 20–8–48–3; M. Jean-Jacques 25.3–5–120–2; T. C. Middleton 0.2–0–4–0; R. S. M. Morris 0.4–0–1–0; M. C. J. Nicholas 1–0–4–0; R. A. Smith 1–0–2–0; M. J. Thursfield 43–13–143–5; I. J. Turner 76.4–20–265–5.

Wicket-keeper: A. N. Aymes 29 ct, 4 st.

Leading Fielder: V. P. Terry 15.

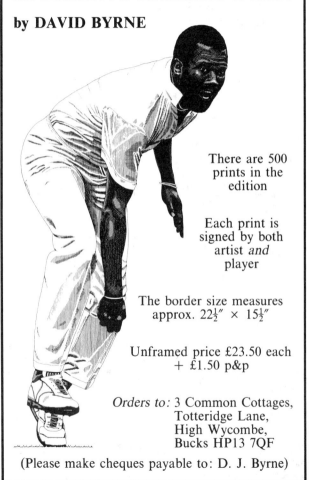

HAMPSHIRE v SOMERSET

At Southampton, April 29, 30, May 1. Somerset won by an innings and 148 runs. Somerset 24 pts, Hampshire 2 pts. Toss: Somerset.

Two young men on the brink of selection for England made the opening match one of misery for Hampshire. Lathwell displayed nonchalant fluency in a superb 99 and Somerset built a massive total of 500 for six, Folland adding 81 to an unbeaten 82 in his only previous Championship match and Burns scoring an unbeaten century. On a pitch that appeared hopelessly bland a game of declarations seemed inevitable. Then Caddick, finding life and movement that had utterly eluded Marshall, took four wickets for three runs in 17 balls, while Gower played a loose shot at Mallender, leaving Hampshire on five for five. Although Nicholas battled gamely, the follow-on was inevitable. Caddick, who had taken a career-best six for 48, claimed another four wickets in the second innings. He wrapped up Hampshire's tail with three in four balls, earning Somerset victory with a day to spare – the first result of the Championship season.

Close of play: First day, Somerset 343-5 (N. D. Burns 8*, G. D. Rose 7*); Second day, Hampshire 140-8 (M. C. J. Nicholas 69*, C. A. Connor 9*).

Somerset

A. N. Hayhurst c Terry b Connor	23	G. D. Rose c Shine b Udal	64
M. N. Lathwell c Middleton b Udal	99	A. R. Caddick not out	2
R. J. Harden b Marshall	97	B 1, l-b 8, n-b 8	17
*C. J. Tavaré c Morris b Connor	15		
N. A. Folland c Terry b Connor	81		(6 wkts dec.) 500
†N. D. Burns not out	102	1/70 2/169 3/205	
		4/310 5/330 6/489	

N. A. Mallender, H. R. J. Trump and A. P. van Troost did not bat.

Bonus points – Somerset 4, Hampshire 2 (Score at 120 overs: 352-5).

Bowling: Marshall 30-8-67-1; Connor 36-12-81-3; Shine 20-1-101-0; Turner 30-6-120-0; Udal 34-6-118-2; Nicholas 1-0-4-0.

Hampshire

V. P. Terry lbw b Caddick	2	c Lathwell b Rose	10
T. C. Middleton c Lathwell b Caddick	0	c Trump	7
R. S. M. Morris c Harden b Caddick	0	c Harden b Trump	37
D. I. Gower c Folland b Mallender	3	c and b Hayhurst	14
*M. C. J. Nicholas c Rose b Caddick	76	b Caddick	47
M. D. Marshall lbw b Caddick	0	c Folland b Rose	8
†A. N. Aymes b Mallender	33	lbw b Caddick	26
S. D. Udal c Tavaré b Trump	16	c Folland b Trump	39
I. J. Turner lbw b Rose	0	lbw b Caddick	0
C. A. Connor c Harden b Caddick	12	b Caddick	0
K. J. Shine not out	6	not out	2
L-b 4, n-b 4	8	L-b 4, n-b 2	6
	156		**196**

1/2 2/2 3/5 4/5 5/5   156   1/12 2/26 3/45 4/112 5/123   196
6/66 7/113 8/114 9/145   6/141 7/190 8/190 9/190

Bonus points – Somerset 4.

Bowling: *First Innings*—Mallender 21-12-15-2; Caddick 25-10-48-6; van Troost 9.3-4-24-0; Rose 15.3-4-31-1; Trump 13-3-29-1; Hayhurst 2-0-5-0. *Second Innings*—Caddick 22-5-44-4; Rose 16-3-37-2; Trump 30.3-13-59-3; Hayhurst 13-7-21-1; Mallender 8-4-17-0; Lathwell 4-0-14-0.

Umpires: A. A. Jones and G. A. Stickley.

At Oxford, May 5, 6, 7. HAMPSHIRE drew with OXFORD UNIVERSITY.

Hampshire in 1993

At Stockton-on-Tees, May 13, 14, 15, 17. HAMPSHIRE drew with DURHAM.

HAMPSHIRE v YORKSHIRE

At Southampton, May 20, 21, 22, 24. Yorkshire won by six wickets. Yorkshire 20 pts, Hampshire 7 pts. Toss: Yorkshire. First-class debuts: M. J. Foster, C. E. W. Silverwood.

Rain claimed the opening day, and when play started Hampshire struggled to score freely on a slow pitch. Yorkshire newcomer Michael Foster removed Terry in his first over and Marshall in the first of his second spell, and Nicholas retired after being struck on the finger by Robinson. Only spirited late resistance enabled Hampshire to earn their third batting point. However, all-rounders Ayling and James bowled the home county to a lead of 59 before Hampshire made a wretched start to the second innings. James, with support from Ayling and Marshall, pulled them round from 73 for four, allowing Nicholas to set a generous challenge of 222 in 42 overs. Moxon and Metcalfe scored only ten from the eight overs before tea but 57 from the four immediately afterwards – 30 off Shine, 27 off James – and Byas took 53 from 33 balls as Yorkshire galloped home with 7.4 overs to spare.

Close of play: First day, No play; Second day, Hampshire 247-6 (A. N. Aymes 30*, S. D. Udal 39*); Third day, Hampshire 18-0 (T. C. Middleton 10*, V. P. Terry 8*).

Hampshire

V. P. Terry lbw b Foster	24	– (2) c Blakey b Gough	8
T. C. Middleton b Stemp	46	– (1) lbw b Robinson	11
D. I. Gower run out	28	– lbw b Gough	1
*M. C. J. Nicholas retired hurt	28	– (9) not out	3
K. D. James c Blakey b Gough	0	– (4) c Byas b Gough	51
J. R. Ayling c Moxon b Stemp	21	– (5) c and b Silverwood	21
M. D. Marshall c Stemp b Foster	4	– (6) c Blakey b Stemp	34
†A. N. Aymes not out	50	– (7) lbw b Gough	0
S. D. Udal c and b Foster	39	– (8) st Blakey b Stemp	11
C. A. Connor c Blakey b Stemp	37	– c Blakey b Gough	2
L-b 8, w 4, n-b 18	30	B 4, l-b 1, w 3, n-b 12	20

1/39 2/91 3/138 4/145 5/176   (8 wkts dec.) 307
6/180 7/248 8/307

1/22 2/24 3/24   (9 wkts dec.) 162
4/73 5/146 6/146
7/146 8/157 9/162

K. J. Shine did not bat.

Bonus points – Hampshire 3, Yorkshire 3.

In the first innings M. C. J. Nicholas retired hurt at 161.

Bowling: *First Innings*—Robinson 26-8-49-0; Gough 23-4-90-1; Silverwood 14-2-56-0; Foster 15.3-3-39-3; White 5-2-13-0; Stemp 25.2-10-52-3. *Second Innings*—Robinson 17-6-30-1; Gough 17.3-3-50-5; Foster 2-0-11-0; Stemp 22-9-47-2; Silverwood 6-1-19-1.

Yorkshire

*M. D. Moxon c Connor b Ayling	75	– c Middleton b Udal	61
A. A. Metcalfe c sub b Ayling	42	– c Shine b James	25
R. B. Richardson c sub b Marshall	9	– lbw b Udal	35
D. Byas b Marshall	2	– not out	53
†R. J. Blakey c Connor b James	43	– c Aymes b Marshall	21
C. White c Ayling b Connor	10	– not out	6
D. Gough b James	19		
M. J. Foster c Aymes b Ayling	6		
R. D. Stemp not out	18		
M. A. Robinson lbw b James	0		
C. E. W. Silverwood lbw b James	0		
B 1, l-b 16, w 1, n-b 6	24	L-b 1, n-b 22	23

1/81 2/98 3/100 4/175 5/199   248
6/207 7/222 8/234 9/242

1/72 2/138 3/138 4/201   (4 wkts) 224

Bonus points – Yorkshire 1, Hampshire 4.

Bowling: *First Innings*—Marshall 18–8–35–2; Connor 15–5–37–1; Shine 12–3–41–0; Udal 3–0–17–0; Ayling 17–2–68–3; James 12.4–3–33–4. *Second Innings*—Marshall 10–1–44–1; Connor 7–3–34–0; Shine 2–0–30–0; James 4–0–36–1; Ayling 5–0–38–0; Udal 6–1–37–2; Middleton 0.2–0–4–0.

Umpires: R. Julian and A. G. T. Whitehead.

At Derby, May 27, 28, 29, 31. HAMPSHIRE drew with DERBYSHIRE.

At Nottingham, June 3, 4, 5, 7. HAMPSHIRE beat NOTTINGHAMSHIRE by 169 runs.

HAMPSHIRE v KENT

At Basingstoke, June 10, 11, 12, 14. Drawn. Hampshire 5 pts, Kent 5 pts. Toss: Kent.

Persistent rain claimed the third and fourth days to reduce a potentially interesting match to futility. What play there was gave supporters a chance to see the West Indian Hooper at his elegant best, stroking 69 from 78 balls with 11 fours and two sixes. He was cut off in full flow when brilliantly run out by his former Test colleague Marshall off his own bowling. On a slow pitch, Hampshire's reply was laboured, though Nicholas confirmed his early-season form and Udal batted with some enterprise until Hampshire accepted an offer of bad light. The weather never allowed him to resume.

Close of play: First day, Hampshire 20-0 (T. C. Middleton 3*, R. S. M. Morris 11*); Second day, Hampshire 232-7 (A. N. Aymes 18*, S. D. Udal 27*); Third day, No play.

Kent

T. R. Ward b Marshall	16	R. P. Davis lbw b James	2
*M. R. Benson b Marshall	1	C. Penn c Marshall b Udal	16
N. R. Taylor c Nicholas b Udal	57	M. M. Patel lbw b Marshall	4
C. L. Hooper run out	69		
N. J. Llong c Morris b Udal	41	L-b 6, w 2, n-b 20	28
M. V. Fleming c Turner b Udal	8		
†S. A. Marsh c Aymes b James	12	1/15 2/36 3/156 4/172 5/203	275
R. M. Ellison not out	21	6/232 7/232 8/241 9/270	

Bonus points – Kent 2, Hampshire 4.

Bowling: Marshall 21.3–5–67–3; Shine 17–3–63–0; James 19–4–69–2; Turner 3–0–27–0; Udal 30–16–43–4.

Hampshire

T. C. Middleton c Marsh b Fleming	10	M. D. Marshall lbw b Fleming	0
R. S. M. Morris lbw b Fleming	24	S. D. Udal not out	27
R. A. Smith run out	12		
V. P. Terry c Hooper b Penn	46	B 4, l-b 3, w 2, n-b 2	11
*M. C. J. Nicholas b Davis	73		
K. D. James c Penn b Davis	11	1/43 2/54 3/60 4/140	(7 wkts) 232
†A. N. Aymes not out	18	5/175 6/188 7/189	

I. J. Turner and K. J. Shine did not bat.

Bonus points – Hampshire 1, Kent 3.

Bowling: Penn 22–9–32–1; Ellison 18–8–27–0; Hooper 22–6–37–0; Patel 1–0–4–0; Fleming 28–8–82–3; Davis 16–5–43–2.

Umpires: J. H. Harris and D. O. Oslear.

At Northampton, June 17, 18, 19, 21. HAMPSHIRE beat NORTHAMPTONSHIRE by seven wickets.

At Southampton, June 26, 27, 28. HAMPSHIRE drew with AUSTRALIANS (See Australian tour section).

At Bristol, July 1, 2, 3, 5. HAMPSHIRE beat GLOUCESTERSHIRE by one wicket.

HAMPSHIRE v WORCESTERSHIRE

At Portsmouth, July 15, 16, 17, 19. Drawn. Hampshire 6 pts, Worcestershire 5 pts. Toss: Hampshire.

The weather won hands down, reducing the first day by 85 overs, the second by 53 and then, after a mercifully sunny Saturday, washing out the fourth completely. Hampshire's innings was dominated by a forceful 91 from Smith, until he became one of Benjamin's three victims in seven balls on the second evening. But next morning Aymes and Udal steered Hampshire towards maximum batting points as they added 114 for the eighth wicket. Marshall showed much of his old fire in removing Worcestershire's openers for 42 but the home bowlers were checked by a defiant 94 from D'Oliveira.

Close of play: First day, Hampshire 65-2 (D. I. Gower 33*, R. A. Smith 4*); Second day, Hampshire 222-7 (A. N. Aymes 3*, S. D. Udal 0*); Third day, Worcestershire 206-5 (S. J. Rhodes 25*, P. J. Newport 2*).

Hampshire

V. P. Terry c Rhodes b Tolley	9	S. D. Udal b Tolley	66
R. S. M. Morris c Hick b Newport	14	C. A. Connor b Tolley	0
D. I. Gower c Lampitt b Benjamin	38	D. P. J. Flint not out	14
R. A. Smith lbw b Benjamin	91	B 4, l-b 5, w 4, n-b 6	19
*M. C. J. Nicholas b Radford	27		
K. D. James c Weston b Benjamin	27		(9 wkts dec.) 355
†A. N. Aymes not out	50	1/16 2/44 3/75	
M. D. Marshall c Hick b Benjamin	0	4/144 5/215 6/220	
		7/220 8/334 9/334	

Bonus points – Hampshire 3, Worcestershire 4.

Bowling: Benjamin 32–5–99–4; Tolley 25–6–80–3; Newport 29–6–80–1; Radford 12–2–34–1; Illingworth 12–3–27–0; Lampitt 6–1–23–0; Hick 2–0–3–0.

Worcestershire

*T. S. Curtis c Aymes b Marshall	10	P. J. Newport not out	2
W. P. C. Weston c Aymes b Marshall	1		
G. A. Hick c Aymes b Flint	52	B 4, l-b 9, w 1, n-b 4	18
D. B. D'Oliveira c Morris b Marshall	94		
S. R. Lampitt b Udal	4	1/7 2/42 3/125	(5 wkts) 206
†S. J. Rhodes not out	25	4/134 5/203	

C. M. Tolley, R. K. Illingworth, N. V. Radford and K. C. G. Benjamin did not bat.

Bonus points – Worcestershire 1, Hampshire 2.

Bowling: Marshall 21–8–37–3; Connor 10–4–35–0; James 11–4–21–0; Flint 16–2–42–1; Udal 16–1–58–1.

Umpires: D. J. Constant and P. Willey.

At Lord's, July 22, 23, 24. HAMPSHIRE lost to MIDDLESEX by nine wickets.

HAMPSHIRE v WARWICKSHIRE

At Southampton, July 29, 30, 31, August 2. Warwickshire won by 80 runs. Warwickshire 20 pts, Hampshire 6 pts. Toss: Warwickshire.

The fragility of Hampshire's batting was exposed again as they went down to defeat. Only Nicholas offered genuine resistance as Bell claimed five wickets in an innings for the first time, on a pitch better suited to the spinners, who collected 26 wickets in the match.

Udal took ten for the second time in 1993, hustling out Warwickshire for only 190 in the first innings with his partner Flint. Then an aggressive century from Smith, who was dropped before scoring but went on to hit 16 fours and three sixes, sharing a sixth-wicket stand of 151 with Aymes, gave Hampshire a healthy first-innings lead of 104. But a lively fifty from Ostler and an unbeaten century from Penney enabled Warwickshire to set a target of 289 in what became 81 overs. Bell, with support from Neil Smith's off-spin, bowled them out with 11.3 overs to spare.

Close of play: First day, Warwickshire 190; Second day, Hampshire 294; Third day, Warwickshire 330-8 (T. L. Penney 98*).

Warwickshire

A. J. Moles c Aymes b Udal	36	st Aymes b Flint	26
J. D. Ratcliffe c Aymes b Thursfield	0	b Flint	28
D. P. Ostler c Morris b James	41	lbw b Udal	55
T. L. Penney b Marshall	8	not out	135
*D. A. Reeve c and b Udal	42	c Aymes b Flint	13
P. A. Smith c Gower b Flint	17	c Aymes b Udal	20
N. M. K. Smith c Morris b Flint	2	(8) c Terry b Flint	47
†K. J. Piper c and b Udal	1	(7) lbw b Udal	13
P. A. Booth not out	23	c Smith b Udal	9
G. C. Small c Nicholas b Flint	7	st Aymes b Udal	19
M. A. V. Bell c Morris b Udal	7	c Morris b Udal	5
L-b 4, n-b 2	6	B 3, l-b 16, w 1, n-b 2	22
	190		**392**

1/4 2/77 3/77 4/101 5/145   1/48 2/67 3/136 4/170 5/215
6/152 7/153 8/162 9/179   6/239 7/317 8/330 9/384

Bonus points – Hampshire 4.

Bowling: *First Innings*—Marshall 19-4-57-1; Thursfield 10-3-27-1; Udal 27.4-8-51-4; James 7-0-17-1; Flint 12-4-34-3. *Second Innings*—Marshall 25-7-50-0; Thursfield 8-0-38-0; Udal 48.4-9-141-6; Flint 41-8-131-4; James 7-4-13-0.

Hampshire

R. S. M. Morris lbw b Small	7	(2) c Piper b Bell	3
V. P. Terry c Small b Booth	36	(1) c Small b Bell	10
R. A. Smith b Reeve	131	c Piper b Bell	22
D. I. Gower b N. M. K. Smith	3	lbw b N. M. K. Smith	37
*M. C. J. Nicholas c Piper b Booth	4	c Reeve b N. M. K. Smith	63
K. D. James c Piper b N. M. K. Smith	5	c Ostler b N. M. K. Smith	13
†A. N. Aymes lbw b Reeve	74	c Ratcliffe b N. M. K. Smith	22
M. D. Marshall c Piper b Bell	12	c Penney b Booth	32
S. D. Udal c and b Bell	7	c Piper b Bell	1
M. J. Thursfield not out	0	c Penney b Bell	0
D. P. J. Flint c and b Bell	4	not out	0
B 6, w 1, n-b 4	11	B 1, l-b 4	5
	294		**208**

1/14 2/73 3/88 4/97 5/106   1/12 2/31 3/44 4/86 5/106
6/257 7/264 8/289 9/290   6/166 7/205 8/208 9/208

Bonus points – Hampshire 2, Warwickshire 4.

Bowling: *First Innings*—Small 11-2-32-1; Reeve 21-5-43-2; N. M. K. Smith 40-7-85-2; Bell 16-5-47-3; Booth 23-4-81-2. *Second Innings*—Small 4-0-15-0; Bell 17.3-6-43-5; N. M. K. Smith 33-9-93-4; Booth 15-4-52-1.

Umpires: J. D. Bond and R. Julian.

HAMPSHIRE v LANCASHIRE

At Southampton, August 12, 13, 14, 16. Drawn. Hampshire 6 pts, Lancashire 7 pts. Toss: Hampshire.

Lancashire's lack of ambition robbed the crowd of a potentially exciting climax. Set to score 237 in a minimum of 51 overs, they showed little interest, especially after a burst of three wickets in 12 deliveries from Udal, and abandoned the pretence of a chase when 99 short with five overs remaining. Earlier, England's new captain, Atherton, watched from the slips as Gower made his bid to play in the Oval Test with his second century of the season, containing 15 fours and a six. After a flowing 81 on the first day, he applied himself for 45 minutes next morning to reach three figures. But when the squad was announced on Monday, not only was Gower ignored, his team-mate Smith had been dropped. Smith's house-guest Atherton had broken the news to him over breakfast. Meanwhile, Lancashire looked in some trouble at 136 for four, but Fairbrother, Watkinson and DeFreitas – the last two sharing 132 for the seventh wicket – saw them to a 22-run lead. The home team's second innings was built round a fluent century by Terry, the first Hampshire batsman to reach 1,000 runs for the summer.

Close of play: First day, Hampshire 233-4 (D. I. Gower 81*, S. D. Udal 0*); Second day, Lancashire 145-4 (G. Yates 5*, N. H. Fairbrother 4*); Third day, Hampshire 77-2 (V. P. Terry 32*, S. D. Udal 0*).

Hampshire

V. P. Terry b Barnett	57	– not out 143
T. C. Middleton c Hegg b Martin	28	– b DeFreitas 0
R. A. Smith b DeFreitas	38	– c Atherton b Barnett 34
D. I. Gower c Speak b Watkinson	117	– (5) c Atherton b DeFreitas 1
*M. C. J. Nicholas b Barnett	21	– (6) lbw b DeFreitas 36
S. D. Udal lbw b DeFreitas	8	– (4) c Barnett b DeFreitas 2
K. D. James c Hegg b Martin	21	– c Speak b Watkinson 4
†A. N. Aymes not out	33	– not out 11
M. D. Marshall lbw b Watkinson	6	
K. J. Shine c Crawley b Watkinson	0	
D. P. J. Flint lbw b Watkinson	8	
B 5, l-b 12, n-b 10	27	B 16, l-b 8, w 1, n-b 2 ... 27
	364	**(6 wkts dec.) 258**

1/65 2/102 3/149 4/219 5/242   364   1/0 2/72 3/83   (6 wkts dec.) 258
6/302 7/318 8/332 9/332   4/85 5/183 6/195

Bonus points – Hampshire 4, Lancashire 4 (Score at 120 overs: 351-9).

Bowling: *First Innings*—DeFreitas 24–7–49–2; Martin 25–8–65–2; Watkinson 40.3–11–104–4; Barnett 23–5–95–2; Yates 14–2–34–0. *Second Innings*—DeFreitas 16–2–50–4; Watkinson 23–2–74–1; Barnett 19–4–74–1; Yates 15–3–36–0.

Lancashire

G. D. Mendis c and b Shine	58	– c Middleton b Udal 23
J. P. Crawley c Terry b Shine	4	– c Terry b Udal 23
M. A. Atherton lbw b Udal	56	– b Udal 4
N. J. Speak c Smith b Flint	2	– not out 26
G. Yates b Flint	32	
*N. H. Fairbrother c Smith b Udal	47	– (5) not out 47
M. Watkinson c Gower b Udal	81	
P. A. J. DeFreitas c Aymes b Flint	51	
†W. K. Hegg b Udal	12	
P. J. Martin c Terry b Udal	8	
A. A. Barnett not out	0	
B 2, l-b 9, w 2, n-b 22	35	B 9, l-b 4, n-b 2 ... 15
	386	**(3 wkts) 138**

1/8 2/121 3/136 4/136 5/199   386   1/51 2/58 3/59   (3 wkts) 138
6/234 7/366 8/366 9/379

Bonus points – Lancashire 3, Hampshire 2 (Score at 120 overs: 346-6).

Bowling: *First Innings:* Marshall 14–2–44–0; Shine 19–5–64–2; Flint 51–17–116–3; Udal 47.5–8–131–5; James 3–0–20–0. *Second Innings*—Marshall 6–2–10–0; Shine 4–0–11–0; Udal 21–3–68–3; Flint 19–9–34–0; Smith 1–0–2–0.

Umpires: D. J. Constant and V. A. Holder.

At Swansea, August 19, 20, 21, 23. HAMPSHIRE beat GLAMORGAN by 98 runs.

HAMPSHIRE v SUSSEX

At Portsmouth, August 26, 27, 28, 30. Sussex won by 57 runs. Sussex 24 pts, Hampshire 5 pts. Toss: Sussex.

Hampshire were challenged to score 409 in 94 overs for their first first-class victory on home soil in 15 months – and looked like achieving it while Robin Smith and Terry were opening with 70 in 19 overs. But both fell to Salisbury and the impetus was lost; a late flourish by Udal (a career-best 79 not out) and Marshall, which added 71 in 12 overs, came too late. Salisbury finished with five wickets to add to his unbeaten 63. Though Sussex began the game by losing both openers for five runs, on a fast, true pitch the two teams totalled 1,457, the highest aggregate in a Hampshire Championship match. David Smith and the brisker Speight dominated Sussex's first innings with a fourth-wicket partnership of 214 in 62 overs. Then Gower scored his third hundred of the summer, taking Hampshire within four runs of saving the follow-on, and wicket-keeper Aymes batted on for a maiden century to restrict the deficit to 90. Wells saw Sussex's lead past 400 before declaring; in the end his caution was vindicated.

Close of play: First day, Sussex 375-4 (D. M. Smith 142*, P. Moores 36*); Second day, Hampshire 287-6 (A. N. Aymes 79*, D. P. J. Flint 0*); Third day, Sussex 272-6 (I. D. K. Salisbury 48*, D. M. Smith 23*).

Sussex

N. J. Lenham c Gower b Shine	2	– (2) lbw b James	28
C. W. J. Athey c Aymes b Marshall	2	– (1) lbw b James	74
D. M. Smith b Shine	150	– (8) c Flint b James	23
*A. P. Wells c Cox b Udal	42	– c Cox b Flint	57
M. P. Speight c and b Udal	121	– c Smith b Flint	13
†P. Moores not out	48	– (3) b Udal	7
F. D. Stephenson lbw b James	23	– (6) c Aymes b Flint	6
I. D. K. Salisbury c Aymes b James	12	– (7) not out	63
E. E. Hemmings c Flint b James	3		
E. S. H. Giddins lbw b James	0		
A. C. S. Pigott absent		– (9) not out	21
L-b 18, n-b 18	36	B 4, l-b 4, w 2, n-b 16	26

1/3 2/5 3/94 4/308 5/388   439   1/41 2/87 3/151   (7 wkts dec.) 318
6/434 7/434 8/438 9/439   4/166 5/176
                                     6/213 7/272

Bonus points – Sussex 4, Hampshire 2 (Score at 120 overs: 402-5).

In the first innings F. D. Stephenson, when 23, retired hurt at 416 and resumed at 434-6.

Bowling: *First Innings*—Marshall 33–10–73–1; Shine 21–2–104–2; James 16.3–3–55–4; Udal 41–12–102–2; Flint 20–3–87–0. *Second Innings*—Shine 15–3–74–0; James 24–6–67–3; Udal 30–4–96–1; Flint 23–0–73–3.

Hampshire

R. A. Smith c Smith b Stephenson	12	– c sub b Salisbury	98
V. P. Terry lbw b Hemmings	11	– lbw b Salisbury	20
K. D. James c Moores b Giddins	14	– lbw b Stephenson	45
D. I. Gower c Wells b Hemmings	113	– c Moores b Giddins	37
*M. C. J. Nicholas c and b Salisbury	35	– b Giddins	0
R. M. F. Cox b Hemmings	6	– (9) b Pigott	3
†A. N. Aymes not out	107	– c Athey b Stephenson	2
D. P. J. Flint c sub b Pigott	4	– (11) c Athey b Salisbury	10
M. D. Marshall retired hurt	11	– c Wells b Salisbury	35
S. D. Udal c Athey b Stephenson	12	– (8) not out	79
K. J. Shine c Moores b Pigott	4	– (10) c Athey b Salisbury	0
L-b 4, n-b 16	20	B 5, l-b 10, w 3, n-b 4	22

1/14 2/26 3/67 4/131 5/148   349   1/70 2/137 3/198 4/198 5/201   351
6/286 7/301 8/344 9/349   6/213 7/227 8/298 9/306

Bonus points – Hampshire 3, Sussex 4.

In the first innings M. D. Marshall retired hurt at 330.

Bowling: *First Innings*—Stephenson 14–1–48–2; Giddins 23–0–86–1; Hemmings 32–15–74–3; Salisbury 13–1–65–1; Lenham 9–2–28–0; Athey 5–1–14–0; Pigott 9.2–0–30–2. *Second Innings*—Stephenson 19–5–59–3; Giddins 18–5–73–2; Pigott 16–3–86–0; Salisbury 24.1–4–95–5; Athey 6–2–23–0.

Umpires: A. A. Jones and D. R. Shepherd.

At The Oval, August 31, September 1, 2, 3. HAMPSHIRE drew with SURREY.

HAMPSHIRE v LEICESTERSHIRE

At Southampton, September 9, 10, 11, 13. Drawn. Leicestershire 4 pts. Toss: Hampshire.

The weather ensured a soggy and frustrating end to Hampshire's home programme – and to Marshall's Championship career. Hampshire's first innings, delayed and twice interrupted by rain, was destroyed inside 60 overs by Millns's pace and movement. He claimed five for 21, the first three in the space of 12 balls for one run. Leicestershire closed the first day on eight for one, Marshall having trapped Hepworth lbw with the final ball. It proved to be his last wicket for the county – though he later had Whitaker caught behind off a no-ball. The morning of the second day was spent mopping up after torrential rain, and there were two more breaks for drizzle before storms washed out the rest of the match.

Close of play: First day, Leicestershire 8–1 (T. J. Boon 5*); Second day, Leicestershire 85–1 (T. J. Boon 31*, J. J. Whitaker 33*); Third day, No play.

Hampshire

R. A. Smith c Wells b Millns	5	S. D. Udal c Nixon b Mullally	12
V. P. Terry c Wells b Millns	4	K. J. Shine not out	7
K. D. James b Millns	22	D. P. J. Flint c Millns b Parsons	1
D. I. Gower c Whitaker b Millns	4		
*M. C. J. Nicholas c Wells b Mullally	8	N-b 4	4
R. M. F. Cox c Nixon b Wells	21		
†A. N. Aymes lbw b Wells	23	1/9 2/12 3/18 4/32 5/65	115
M. D. Marshall c Wells b Millns	4	6/79 7/85 8/103 9/107	

Bonus points – Leicestershire 4.

Bowling: Millns 16–8–21–5; Mullally 12–4–31–2; Parsons 13.1–8–13–1; Wells 14–4–36–2; Pierson 4–0–14–0.

Leicestershire

T. J. Boon not out	31
P. N. Hepworth lbw b Marshall	0
*J. J. Whitaker not out	33
L-b 2, w 1, n-b 18	21

1/8 (1 wkt) 85

V. J. Wells, P. E. Robinson, †P. A. Nixon, G. J. Parsons, A. R. K. Pierson, D. J. Millns, M. T. Brimson and A. D. Mullally did not bat.

Bowling: Marshall 9–1–31–1; Shine 10–1–48–0; James 3.5–1–3–0; Udal 2–1–1–0.

Umpires: J. H. Harris and K. E. Palmer.

At Chelmsford, September 16, 17, 18, 20. HAMPSHIRE drew with ESSEX.

KENT

Patron: HRH The Duke of Kent
President: D. E. Beney
Chairman: D. S. Kemp
Chairman, Cricket Committee: D. G. Ufton
Secretary: S. T. W. Anderson
Captain: M. R. Benson
Cricket Administrator: Ms D. F. Potter
Coach: D. H. Foster
Head Groundsman: B. A. Fitch
Scorer: J. Foley

Kent's hopes of lifting their first major honour for 15 years depended on the outcome of their final Sunday League game against Glamorgan on the penultimate day of the season, which drew a capacity crowd to Canterbury. Many facets of the revised format had been criticised by administrators, players and public, but the atmosphere on that pleasant mid-September day was magnificent. Sadly for Kent, it was Glamorgan who were to take over the players' balcony to celebrate. Once again, Kent had to experience the disappointment of coming second, as they had done twice the year before, losing at Lord's in the final of the Benson and Hedges Cup and then finishing runners-up in the Championship.

Interest in the B and H in 1993 was short-lived, as Glamorgan triumphed comprehensively on a cool April day, but even after that there were still optimistic noises about Kent's Championship chances. Three wins out of four in late May and early June put them in third place, but they failed to sustain any kind of momentum and fell away to finish eighth. Kent found the bowler they needed to give balance to the seam attack when they picked up Dean Headley from Middlesex. A TCCB ruling delayed his competitive debut until early May but he soon confirmed both his ability and his anxiety to prove himself, taking career-best figures of seven for 79 in the innings victory over Gloucestershire at Tunbridge Wells.

Headley was seen as the ideal support for Alan Igglesden and Martin McCague. Both were chosen by England but also had their seasons ruined first by hamstring trouble and then by back injuries. Igglesden never actually did appear in the Test team and McCague had to withdraw after two promising matches. Soon after his Gloucestershire triumph, Headley was also struck down by ankle ligament damage. Kent had another useful bowler, like McCague brought over by their coach Daryl Foster from Western Australia, but able to play because of a British birth qualification: Duncan Spencer, originally from Burnley. Spencer bowled one exceptionally rapid spell against Surrey at Canterbury but he had ankle problems. The combined effect was that Kent were rarely able to play anything like their full attack.

There was even greater disappointment in the top-order batting. Only Carl Hooper passed 1,000 runs in the Championship – on his way to 2,258 in all competitions. He finished the season with the first double-century of his career, 236 not out against Glamorgan. Mark Benson started the season in excellent form but he too was affected by injury after being struck on the knee at Worcester. He missed the final month and needed an operation to put things right. Trevor Ward, Neil Taylor and – especially – Graham Cowdrey (until he hit a century at Northampton, having been given out and called back by Dickie Bird) all fell short of their best form and were left out to accommodate youngsters like Nigel Llong, David Fulton and Jonathan Longley.

Llong started with hundreds against Cambridge University and Middlesex, then found himself omitted when Hooper returned. However, he maintained his form, regained his place and, like Headley, was given his county cap – a fitting reward for his best season since he made his first-class debut in 1990. Fulton also looked a good prospect and made two Championship half-centuries at Northampton. Longley, however, was released and signed for Durham.

Mark Ealham maintained his reputation as a useful man in difficult situations with both bat and ball, as did Matthew Fleming, who played some of the most thrilling Sunday innings of the season. Both men were important in the Sunday League success. Kent were never out of the top two in this competition, and were unbeaten between June 20 and the final showdown at Canterbury. Hooper was nearly always at the centre of things. He scored 854 runs, passing 50 nine times and, week after week, his bowling was almost unhittable. Although the make-up of their opening attack varied, Kent were very good at containing teams in the first 15 overs and then, just as they were looking to accelerate, the batsmen found themselves facing Hooper.

The three last Sunday wins all came under the captaincy of Steve Marsh, who took charge while Benson was injured and also led the team to two Championship victories, including the final one against Glamorgan when he opted not to enforce the follow-on. He kept wicket well and had 61 first-class victims. The left-arm spinner Richard Davis had a disappointing season, however, eventually losing his place to Min Patel, who returned to fitness after a serious knee injury. Patel made the most of his chance and took a career-best seven for 75 against Lancashire at Lytham. Although Davis was offered a new one-year contract for 1994, he chose instead to move to Warwickshire.

The season ended on a sad note when the much-liked chairman Bill Sale died suddenly, aged 60. He was succeeded by a former president, David Kemp. The matches at Kent's only remaining out-grounds, Tunbridge Wells and Maidstone, were great successes, blessed with good weather and crowds to match. The new four-day format meant that Canterbury Week was fragmented, but 13 days' cricket was staged there in late July and early August – including the Australian match – and again the club were mostly lucky in dodging the rain. Kent spectators are still anxious to watch a successful team and there is reason for optimism that in 1994 they can be 16th time lucky. – Andrew Gidley.

KENT 1993

[Bill Smith]

Back row: J. I. Longley, N. J. Llong, D. P. Fulton, T. N. Wren, D. J. Spencer, M. M. Patel, S. C. Willis. Middle row: J. C. Foley (scorer), A. G. E. Ealham (director of youth coaching), M. A. Ealham, R. P. Davis, M. J. McCague, D. W. Headley, M. V. Fleming, D. H. Foster (coach), M. J. Walker, F. Errington (physiotherapist). Front row: T. R. Ward, C. Penn, N. R. Taylor, S. A. Marsh, M. R. Benson (captain), R. M. Ellison, G. R. Cowdrey, A. P. Igglesden. Inset: C. L. Hooper.

KENT RESULTS

All first-class matches – Played 20: Won 8, Lost 5, Drawn 7.

County Championship matches – Played 17: Won 6, Lost 4, Drawn 7.

Bonus points – Batting 40, Bowling 54.

Competition placings – Britannic Assurance County Championship, 8th;
NatWest Bank Trophy, 2nd round; Benson and Hedges Cup, preliminary round;
AXA Equity & Law League, 2nd.

BRITANNIC ASSURANCE CHAMPIONSHIP AVERAGES

BATTING

	Birthplace	*M*	*I*	*NO*	*R*	*HS*	*Avge*
‡C. L. Hooper§	*Georgetown, Guyana*	16	24	2	1,304	236*	59.27
‡M. A. Ealham	*Willesborough*	10	14	3	604	85	54.90
‡M. R. Benson	*Shoreham*	14	22	2	899	107	44.95
‡N. J. Llong	*Ashford, Kent*	15	23	4	810	108	42.63
‡M. V. Fleming	*Macclesfield*	16	26	4	805	100	36.59
‡T. R. Ward	*Farningham*	16	26	0	781	141	30.03
‡N. R. Taylor.......	*Orpington*	15	25	2	645	86	28.04
D. P. Fulton	*Lewisham*	5	9	0	221	75	24.55
‡G. R. Cowdrey	*Farnborough, Kent*	9	17	0	379	139	22.29
‡S. A. Marsh	*Westminster*	16	23	1	469	63	21.31
‡D. W. Headley	*Stourbridge*	12	18	6	248	36	20.66
‡C. Penn...........	*Dover*	3	4	0	63	23	15.75
‡R. P. Davis	*Margate*	12	15	2	158	42	12.15
‡M. J. McCague.....	*Larne, N. Ireland*	7	8	3	49	22*	9.80
M. M. Patel	*Bombay, India*	5	5	3	12	4	6.00
‡A. P. Igglesden	*Farnborough, Kent*	11	12	6	32	10	5.33

Also batted: ‡R. M. Ellison (*Willesborough*) (2 matches) 68, 2, 21*; J. I. Longley (*New Brunswick, USA*) (1 match) 47, 3; R. J. Parks (*Cuckfield*) (1 match) 13*; D. J. Spencer (*Burnley*) (1 match) 4.

* *Signifies not out.*   ‡ *Denotes county cap.*   § *Overseas player.*

The following played a total of 11 three-figure innings for Kent in County Championship matches – M. R. Benson 3, C. L. Hooper 3, T. R. Ward 2, G. R. Cowdrey 1, M. V. Fleming 1, N. J. Llong 1.

BOWLING

	O	*M*	*R*	*W*	*BB*	*5W/i*	*Avge*
A. P. Igglesden	393	101	968	50	6-58	3	19.36
M. J. McCague	218.4	54	594	27	5-33	2	22.00
D. W. Headley	405.4	94	1,125	41	7-79	2	27.43
M. M. Patel	185.5	50	490	17	7-75	2	28.82
R. P. Davis	404.4	114	946	30	7-127	1	31.53
M. A. Ealham	250.4	52	800	25	5-66	1	32.00
M. V. Fleming	401	94	1,043	32	4-31	0	32.59
C. L. Hooper	545	126	1,281	33	4-35	0	38.81

Also bowled: R. M. Ellison 21–13–72–2; N. J. Llong 33.2–6–96–1; C. Penn 117–29–263–8; D. J. Spencer 24–3–94–0.

Wicket-keepers: S. A. Marsh 52 ct, 3 st; R. J. Parks 4 ct.

Leading Fielder: C. L. Hooper 22.

At Cambridge, April 21, 22, 23. KENT beat CAMBRIDGE UNIVERSITY by an innings and 34 runs.

At Lord's, May 6, 7, 8, 10. KENT drew with MIDDLESEX.

KENT v WARWICKSHIRE

At Canterbury, May 13, 14, 15, 17. Warwickshire won by 110 runs. Warwickshire 22 pts, Kent 3 pts. Toss: Warwickshire. First-class debut: A. F. Giles.

Off-spinner Neil Smith proved to be Warwickshire's match-winner in a marathon spell on the final afternoon, making full use of a responsive pitch to achieve a career-best. He was further rewarded with his county cap. Kent were set 342 to win with the whole of the last day available and reached lunch on 104 for one, but Taylor's departure signalled the start of their demise. Benson stayed to complete his second hundred in successive Championship matches: it spanned four hours before he was eighth out. Reeve had chosen to bat, but his side struggled, scoring at just over two runs an over. Then Munton accounted for seven of Kent's batsmen before the last pair, McCague and Igglesden, added 28 to save the follow-on. Ashley Giles, a left-arm spinner who was rushed from the Second XI game at Maidstone when Donald was sidelined with a muscle strain, batted confidently in both Warwickshire innings, and his bowling revealed potential.

Close of play: First day, Warwickshire 257-7 (D. A. Reeve 22*, G. C. Small 1*); Second day, Warwickshire 9-0 (A. J. Moles 8*, R. G. Twose 1*); Third day, Warwickshire 213.

Warwickshire

A. J. Moles c Marsh b Davis	65	– run out			50
R. G. Twose c Davis b Hooper	24	– c Marsh b Headley			2
J. D. Ratcliffe c Taylor b Headley	25	– lbw b Fleming			13
D. P. Ostler c Cowdrey b Davis	47	– lbw b Fleming			24
T. L. Penney c Marsh b McCague	57	– c Marsh b Headley			6
*D. A. Reeve c Marsh b Davis	44	– not out			72
†M. Burns lbw b McCague	0	– b Davis			4
N. M. K. Smith c Marsh b McCague	2	– lbw b Igglesden			7
G. C. Small b Igglesden	4	– lbw b Igglesden			0
A. F. Giles b Hooper	23	– lbw b Hooper			17
T. A. Munton not out	0	– b Fleming			14
B 3, l-b 9, n-b 2	14	L-b 2, n-b 2			4

1/64 2/109 3/122 4/207 5/241   305   1/14 2/67 3/68 4/82 5/103   213
6/241 7/255 8/260 9/305   6/108 7/125 8/127 9/184

Bonus points – Warwickshire 2, Kent 3 (Score at 120 overs: 260-7).

Bowling: *First Innings*—Igglesden 23-6-43-1; McCague 25-5-62-3; Headley 22-8-50-1; Hooper 18.2-2-49-2; Davis 32-9-54-3; Fleming 19-3-35-0. *Second Innings*—Igglesden 20-8-35-2; Headley 25-4-59-2; Fleming 20.2-5-44-3; Davis 32-11-54-1; Hooper 9-2-19-1.

Kent

T. R. Ward c Smith b Small	8	– b Smith	34
*M. R. Benson c Burns b Reeve	12	– c Reeve b Smith	107
N. R. Taylor c Burns b Munton	23	– lbw b Smith	30
C. L. Hooper c Penney b Munton	75	– st Burns b Smith	2
G. R. Cowdrey c Burns b Munton	2	– c Ostler b Giles	1
M. V. Fleming lbw b Munton	21	– b Munton	18
†S. A. Marsh c Reeve b Munton	0	– c Reeve b Small	14
D. W. Headley c Burns b Munton	3	– b Smith	5
R. P. Davis c Ostler b Munton	0	– lbw b Reeve	1
M. J. McCague not out	22	– not out	7
A. P. Igglesden c Reeve b Giles	3	– c Ostler b Smith	0
L-b 6, n-b 2	8	B 4, l-b 6, n-b 2	12

1/10 2/38 3/78 4/84 5/116   177   1/65 2/123 3/125 4/130 5/160   231
6/122 7/132 8/142 9/149   6/190 7/219 8/222 9/222

Bonus points – Warwickshire 4.

Bowling: *First Innings*—Small 12–5–12–1; Munton 22–5–41–7; Giles 12.3–3–33–1; Smith 13–3–61–0; Reeve 15–9–23–1; Twose 1–0–1–0. *Second Innings*—Small 11–4–24–1; Munton 19–8–28–1; Smith 46.1–11–122–6; Reeve 13–5–16–1; Giles 14–2–31–1.

Umpires: B. Dudleston and G. Sharp.

At Nottingham, May 20, 21, 22, 24. KENT lost to NOTTINGHAMSHIRE by 74 runs.

At Darlington, May 27, 28, 29. KENT beat DURHAM by an innings and 22 runs.

KENT v GLOUCESTERSHIRE

At Tunbridge Wells, June 3, 4, 5, 7. Kent won by an innings and 69 runs. Kent 22 pts, Gloucestershire 3 pts. Toss: Kent.

Kent completed their second innings victory – and Gloucestershire's second innings defeat – in successive matches just before lunch on the final day. Gloucestershire subsided first to Fleming's medium-pace, which earned him a career-best four for 31, and then to an impressive late burst from McCague. On the first day, McCague had been forced out of the attack by hamstring trouble and a century stand from Broad and Hodgson gave Gloucestershire their best start of the season so far. But the other batsmen surrendered to Headley, who took seven wickets for the first time. Benson and Hooper then put Kent firmly in control, adding 206 for the second wicket. The later batsmen built on this and Ealham added 70 for the ninth wicket with Headley, whose all-round contribution demonstrated the talent that had persuaded Kent to sign him.

Close of play: First day, Gloucestershire 221-5 (T. H. C. Hancock 17*, R. C. Russell 6*); Second day, Kent 285-5 (N. R. Taylor 22*, R. P. Davis 1*); Third day, Gloucestershire 104-3 (M. W. Alleyne 39*, T. H. C. Hancock 10*).

Gloucestershire

B. C. Broad c Marsh b Ealham	64	– b Hooper	15
G. D. Hodgson c Hooper b Headley	75	– lbw b Hooper	34
*A. J. Wright b Hooper	20	– c Hooper b Davis	2
M. W. Alleyne c Davis b Headley	22	– c Davis b Fleming	43
T. H. C. Hancock c Marsh b Headley	17	– c Llong b Fleming	27
R. J. Scott lbw b Headley	0	– c Marsh b Fleming	1
†R. C. Russell not out	16	– c Hooper b McCague	12
A. M. Smith c Davis b Headley	1	– c Marsh b McCague	1
C. A. Walsh b Headley	2	– c Davis b McCague	1
M. Davies lbw b Headley	0	– c Hooper b Fleming	6
K. E. Cooper b Fleming	5	– not out	10
B 3, l-b 9, w 3, n-b 6	21	L-b 5, w 3, n-b 2	10

1/117 2/157 3/195 4/208 5/210   243   1/48 2/51 3/59 4/116 5/122   162
6/223 7/225 8/234 9/234   6/129 7/130 8/136 9/143

Bonus points – Gloucestershire 1, Kent 2 (Score at 120 overs: 225-6).

Bowling: *First Innings*—McCague 3.1–0–9–0; Headley 39–11–79–7; Ealham 28–12–58–1; Davis 17–8–17–0; Hooper 11.5–4–8–1; Fleming 28.5–9–60–1. *Second Innings*—Headley 6–0–21–0; Ealham 6–2–12–0; Davis 23–8–47–1; Hooper 21–9–27–2; Llong 3–1–4–0; McCague 11.2–4–15–3; Fleming 11.2–31–4.

Kent

T. R. Ward c Russell b Cooper	20	M. A. Ealham c Hodgson b Cooper	55
*M. R. Benson run out	103	D. W. Headley not out	30
C. L. Hooper b Smith	96	M. J. McCague c Davies b Alleyne	4
N. J. Llong c Davies b Cooper	4		
N. R. Taylor b Cooper	32	L-b 9, w 3, n-b 8	20
M. V. Fleming c Russell b Davies	22		
R. P. Davis b Davies	34	1/27 2/233 3/234 4/242 5/278	474
†S. A. Marsh c Walsh b Davies	54	6/299 7/371 8/398 9/468	

Bonus points – Kent 4, Gloucestershire 2 (Score at 120 overs: 358-6).

Bowling: Walsh 31–7–87–0; Cooper 39–10–108–4; Smith 27–6–71–1; Davies 32–7–109–3; Scott 11–1–24–0; Alleyne 15.5–0–59–1; Hancock 2–0–7–0.

Umpires: B. J. Meyer and P. Willey.

At Basingstoke, June 10, 11, 12, 14. KENT drew with HAMPSHIRE.

KENT v DERBYSHIRE

At Canterbury, June 17, 18, 19. Kent won by nine wickets. Kent 23 pts, Derbyshire 4 pts. Toss: Derbyshire.

Kent needed less than half an hour to complete an emphatic victory on the third morning, after claiming the extra half-hour the previous evening. They were held up by Warner, who counter-attacked gamely and was finally stranded five short of his maiden century after adding 87 runs in 20 overs with Vandrau. Derbyshire's first innings had collapsed after lunch on the opening day, with Igglesden and McCague sharing nine wickets and showing the aggressive form that had taken both to the brink of Test cricket. Kent recovered from a disastrous start, when both openers went for nought, through some impressive middle-order batting, especially from Llong.

Close of play: First day, Kent 194-3 (N. R. Taylor 55*, N. J. Llong 83*); Second day, Derbyshire 228-9 (A. E. Warner 94*, O. H. Mortensen 2*).

Derbyshire

*K. J. Barnett c Hooper b Igglesden	4	– c Fleming b Igglesden	17
P. D. Bowler c Marsh b McCague	38	– c Marsh b Igglesden	9
J. E. Morris c Llong b Ealham	57	– run out	24
C. J. Adams c Marsh b Igglesden	2	– lbw b Igglesden	5
T. J. G. O'Gorman c Fleming b McCague	5	– c Igglesden b Fleming	12
M. J. Vandrau lbw b McCague	0	– b Fleming	30
†B. J. M. Maher c Hooper b Igglesden	2	– lbw b McCague	2
A. E. Warner b McCague	1	– not out	95
S. J. Base c Hooper b Igglesden	8	– c McCague b Igglesden	7
R. W. Sladdin not out	1	– c Llong b Davis	9
O. H. Mortensen b McCague	1	– c Marsh b McCague	2
B 10, l-b 4, n-b 2	16	B 4, l-b 5, n-b 8	17

1/5 2/89 3/96 4/108 5/112   135   1/21 2/42 3/54 4/69 5/70   229
6/119 7/119 8/128 9/134   6/74 7/161 8/192 9/216

Bonus points – Kent 4.

Bowling: *First Innings*—McCague 13.3–4–34–5; Igglesden 16–6–26–4; Fleming 6–0–27–0; Ealham 9–1–30–1; Hooper 2–0–4–0. *Second Innings*—McCague 19.4–3–87–2; Igglesden 19–4–51–4; Fleming 11–3–28–2; Ealham 7–3–28–0; Davis 9–3–14–1; Hooper 5–2–12–0.

Kent

T. R. Ward c Barnett b Warner	0	– lbw b Mortensen	12
*M. R. Benson lbw b Mortensen	0	– not out	5
N. R. Taylor b Sladdin	73	– not out	8
C. L. Hooper lbw b Base	34		
N. J. Llong c Adams b Mortensen	84		
M. V. Fleming c Morris b Base	53		
†S. A. Marsh c Warner b Base	51		
M. A. Ealham c Vandrau b Base	9		
R. P. Davis c O'Gorman b Base	5		
M. J. McCague c Morris b Sladdin	1		
A. P. Igglesden not out	0		
B 2, l-b 7, n-b 22	31		

1/0 2/0 3/60 4/201 5/240   341   1/16   (1 wkt) 25
6/316 7/332 8/335 9/338

Bonus points – Kent 3, Derbyshire 4.

Bowling: *First Innings*—Warner 20–4–57–1; Mortensen 20–5–48–2; Base 23.5–3–93–5; Sladdin 29–5–114–2; Adams 7–2–19–0; Vandrau 4–3–1–0. *Second Innings*—Mortensen 2–0–3–1; Adams 1.4–0–22–0.

Umpires: K. E. Palmer and N. T. Plews.

At Leeds, June 24, 25, 26, 28. KENT drew with YORKSHIRE.

KENT v ESSEX

At Maidstone, July 1, 2, 3, 5. Drawn. Kent 6 pts, Essex 6 pts. Toss: Kent. First-class debuts: D. J. Spencer; D. M. Cousins, D. D. J. Robinson. Championship debut: R. J. Rollins. County debut: R. J. Parks.

The most surprising thing about this match was that a definite result was almost achieved on a pitch that had produced more than 1,500 runs – and it could have gone either way. Set 341 in 82 overs after a sporting declaration from Benson, Essex looked on course for victory when they needed 92 off the last 20 overs, but a mid-innings collapse – four wickets for seven runs – left the last pair to block five overs. Prichard completed two hundreds in a Championship match for the first time – his first coming from just 96 balls. Stephenson also produced a valuable all-round performance for Essex, six wickets and 85 runs in the match, while, for Kent, Fleming and Hooper both scored centuries. In the end, Essex's batting inexperience told against them: Test calls and injuries had deprived them of six senior players. In addition to the first-class debutants, Essex called up Robert Rollins to play his first Championship match on the very morning his brother Adrian was starting his first-class debut for Derbyshire. Kent included 34-year-old Parks, the former Hampshire wicket-keeper, having signed him on a special registration to replace the injured Marsh.

Close of play: First day, Kent 304-5 (M. V. Fleming 39*, M. A. Ealham 17*); Second day, Essex 257-4 (D. J. Robinson 14*, R. J. Rollins 0*); Third day, Kent 230-3 (C. L. Hooper 108*, N. J. Llong 20*).

Kent

T. R. Ward c Robinson b Stephenson	30	– c Garnham b Pringle	18
*M. R. Benson run out	96	– c Lewis b Cousins	71
N. R. Taylor lbw b Stephenson	4	– c Pringle b Andrew	7
C. L. Hooper c Lewis b Stephenson	11	– c Prichard b Stephenson	142
N. J. Llong lbw b Childs	89	– not out	52
M. V. Fleming lbw b Childs	100	– not out	33
M. A. Ealham c Stephenson b Pringle	32		
D. W. Headley b Stephenson	26		
D. J. Spencer lbw b Stephenson	4		
R. P. Davis not out	12		
†R. J. Parks not out	13		
B 6, l-b 4, w 2, n-b 16	28	L-b 4, n-b 8	12

1/53 2/67 3/79 4/237 5/248   (9 wkts dec.) 445   1/29 2/40   (4 wkts dec.) 335
6/368 7/416 8/416 9/420   3/153 4/277

Bonus points – Kent 4, Essex 2 (Score at 120 overs: 358-5).

Bowling: *First Innings*—Andrew 28-4-98-0; Pringle 33-7-102-1; Stephenson 38-4-111-5; Cousins 19-4-58-0; Childs 25-10-59-2; Shahid 2-0-7-0. *Second Innings*—Andrew 25-3-114-1; Pringle 12-3-31-1; Childs 4-0-36-0; Stephenson 19-2-99-1; Cousins 8-0-51-1.

Essex

*P. J. Prichard c Davis b Fleming	104	– c and b Headley	106
J. P. Stephenson c Llong b Headley	2	– c Llong b Headley	83
J. J. B. Lewis c Parks b Headley	67	– b Headley	14
N. Shahid c and b Headley	60	– (5) c Ealham b Fleming	13
D. D. J. Robinson b Hooper	27	– (6) run out	12
R. J. Rollins c Parks b Fleming	7	– (8) c Llong b Davis	1
†M. A. Garnham c Parks b Ealham	66	– not out	14
D. R. Pringle c Llong b Fleming	76	– (4) c Parks b Davis	48
S. J. W. Andrew b Ealham	12	– lbw b Hooper	0
D. M. Cousins not out	0	– b Hooper	0
J. H. Childs (did not bat)	–	– not out	1
L-b 17, w 2	19	L-b 13, n-b 6	19

1/4 2/133 3/240 4/257 5/276   (9 wkts dec.) 440   1/185 2/209 3/216   (9 wkts) 311
6/282 7/408 8/438 9/440   4/247 5/278 6/298
                                        7/303 8/305 9/305

Bonus points – Essex 4, Kent 2 (Score at 120 overs: 382-6).

Bowling: *First Innings*—Spencer 17-2-62-0; Headley 22-3-61-3; Ealham 24-5-76-2; Fleming 21.2-4-63-3; Davis 21-4-69-0; Hooper 25-3-81-1; Llong 2-0-11-0. *Second Innings*—Spencer 7-1-32-0; Headley 22-5-75-3; Hooper 17-4-48-2; Fleming 9-1-36-1; Ealham 13-0-56-0; Davis 14-1-51-2.

Umpires: D. J. Constant and R. Julian.

At Arundel, July 15, 16, 17, 19. KENT drew with SUSSEX.

At Taunton, July 22, 23, 24. KENT lost to SOMERSET by seven wickets.

KENT v LEICESTERSHIRE

At Canterbury, July 29, 30, 31, August 2. Kent won by three wickets. Kent 22 pts, Leicestershire 5 pts. Toss: Leicestershire.

Kent completed an exciting win, which seemed most unlikely at lunch on the last day. They needed 225, but had collapsed to 86 for five. Benson, however, took up the challenge and was still there at 5.15 p.m. after batting for nearly five and a half hours with support from Taylor and Ealham, both making their second major contribution of the match. In the first innings Kent had struggled against some hostile bowling from Benjamin – just released by Leicestershire – until Ealham's 59 helped add 94 for the ninth wicket with Headley. Their efforts brought about a useful 42-run lead. On the first day the former Kent player Wells was only 19 away from a maiden century in his first Championship appearance since mid-June.

Close of play: First day, Kent 28-2 (T. R. Ward 14*, N. R. Taylor 4*); Second day, Leicestershire 35-1 (N. E. Briers 9*, J. J. Whitaker 20*); Third day, Kent 2-0 (T. R. Ward 2*, M. R. Benson 0*).

Leicestershire

T. J. Boon c Marsh b Headley	72	– c Llong b Headley		0
*N. E. Briers b Ealham	5	– c Hooper b Ealham		37
J. J. Whitaker c Taylor b Ealham	20	– b Hooper		69
V. J. Wells lbw b Headley	81	– c Hooper b Fleming		17
P. E. Robinson c Marsh b Headley	4	– run out		53
L. Potter c Marsh b Fleming	26	– c Marsh b Fleming		37
†P. A. Nixon c Marsh b Fleming	8	– lbw b Fleming		1
W. K. M. Benjamin b Ealham	7	– c sub b Hooper		7
G. J. Parsons lbw b Ealham	7	– not out		19
A. R. K. Pierson b Fleming	7	– c Ward b Hooper		15
A. D. Mullally not out	8	– b Hooper		0
L-b 2, w 1, n-b 8	11	B 4, l-b 5, n-b 2		11

1/16 2/61 3/130 4/138 5/197   249   1/0 2/91 3/126 4/144 5/222   266
6/220 7/234 8/234 9/234   6/223 7/230 8/231 9/266

Bonus points – Leicestershire 1, Kent 4.

Bowling: *First Innings*—Headley 26–2–68–3; Ealham 19–5–40–4; Fleming 27.4–4–74–3; Hooper 14–3–36–0; Davis 11–2–29–0. *Second Innings*—Headley 12–3–31–1; Ealham 24–8–60–1; Hooper 34.4–13–55–4; Fleming 26–7–48–3; Davis 17–4–45–0; Llong 5–1–18–0.

Kent

T. R. Ward c Nixon b Mullally	15	– b Benjamin		10
*M. R. Benson b Benjamin	4	– not out		71
R. P. Davis c Boon b Mullally	2			
N. R. Taylor lbw b Benjamin	86	– (7) c Robinson b Wells		42
C. L. Hooper lbw b Parsons	13	– (3) lbw b Parsons		4
N. J. Llong not out	35	– (4) c Benjamin b Pierson		8
G. R. Cowdrey lbw b Benjamin	1	– (5) c Potter b Parsons		8
M. V. Fleming c Nixon b Benjamin	4	– (6) c Potter b Mullally		16
†S. A. Marsh b Benjamin	5	– (8) b Mullally		4
M. A. Ealham b Wells	59	– (9) not out		21
D. W. Headley c Nixon b Mullally	28			
B 11, l-b 8, n-b 18	37	B 11, l-b 4, n-b 10		25

1/13 2/16 3/35 4/80 5/159   291   1/23 2/32 3/45 4/54   (7 wkts) 225
6/165 7/171 8/182 9/276   5/74 6/154 7/190

Bonus points – Kent 2, Leicestershire 4.

In the first innings N. J. Llong, when 23, retired hurt at 165 and resumed at 276.

Bowling: *First Innings*—Benjamin 22-8-46-5; Mullally 29.2-6-80-3; Parsons 18-6-43-1; Wells 13-0-43-1; Pierson 16-3-41-0; Potter 7-3-19-0. *Second Innings*—Mullally 14-1-56-2; Benjamin 22-6-45-1; Parsons 19-9-20-2; Pierson 18-6-55-1; Potter 7.4-1-18-0; Wells 6-1-16-1.

Umpires: M. J. Kitchen and N. T. Plews.

KENT v SURREY

At Canterbury, August 5, 6, 7, 9. Drawn. Kent 5 pts, Surrey 8 pts. Toss: Surrey. Championship debut: D. P. Fulton.

Rain proved the eventual winner in a match that produced 1,236 runs in three innings. Kent were due to chase 303 for victory but the match was abandoned before they could begin their reply. Of the four centuries in the match, Bicknell's provided an impressive anchor: he reached three figures in almost six hours and 290 balls, contrasting sharply with Brown, who took 152 balls and half that time – a leisurely innings for him. For Kent, the newcomer David Fulton lasted only seven deliveries, but Trevor Ward scored his first century of the summer – off 131 balls – adding 150 with Benson and 148 in 33 overs with Hooper. Ealham's impressive form continued, pushing Kent towards a three-run lead, before David Ward, hitting 20 fours and two sixes, shared century partnerships with Bicknell and Brown in Surrey's second innings.

Close of play: First day, Surrey 333-3 (D. J. Bicknell 119*, A. D. Brown 110*); Second day, Kent 266-2 (T. R. Ward 122*, C. L. Hooper 55*); Third day, Surrey 136-1 (D. J. Bicknell 53*, D. M. Ward 69*).

Surrey

D. J. Bicknell lbw b Penn	119	– c Fulton b Patel	81
P. D. Atkins c Fulton b Ealham	6	– c Fulton b Penn	5
D. M. Ward c Marsh b Penn	61	– not out	151
*M. A. Lynch c Ward b Hooper	24	– hit wkt b Hooper	2
A. D. Brown b Penn	141	– not out	45
A. W. Smith b Penn	21		
†G. J. Kersey c Ward b Ealham	31		
N. M. Kendrick c Hooper b Ealham	32		
Waqar Younis c and b Hooper	11		
J. E. Benjamin c Ward b Ealham	0		
A. J. Murphy not out	0		
B 4, l-b 10, n-b 4	18	B 4, l-b 9, n-b 8	21
	464	(3 wkts dec.)	**305**

1/18 2/109 3/146 4/334 5/382 6/387 7/453 8/460 9/460

1/17 2/194 3/201

Bonus points – Surrey 4, Kent 1 (Score at 120 overs: 361-4).

Bowling: *First Innings*—Penn 43-7-121-4; Ealham 30-3-100-4; Fleming 34-8-81-0; Patel 19-3-63-0; Hooper 33-7-73-2; Llong 3-0-12-0. *Second Innings*—Penn 12-0-37-1; Ealham 5-0-33-0; Hooper 31-6-106-1; Patel 31-7-108-1; Fleming 6-1-8-0.

Kent

D. P. Fulton c Kersey b Benjamin	0	M. A. Ealham c and b Kendrick	54
*M. R. Benson b Benjamin	61	C. Penn c Brown b Kendrick	23
T. R. Ward c Kersey b Benjamin	141	M. M. Patel not out	3
C. L. Hooper lbw b Benjamin	81		
N. R. Taylor b Waqar Younis	30	B 9, l-b 15, w 1, n-b 18	43
N. J. Llong b Benjamin	0		
M. V. Fleming c Bicknell b Murphy	0	1/3 2/153 3/301 4/316 5/318	**467**
†S. A. Marsh c Murphy b Kendrick	31	6/333 7/351 8/407 9/450	

Bonus points – Kent 4, Surrey 4 (Score at 120 overs: 450-9).

Bowling: Waqar Younis 25-2-98-1; Benjamin 31-9-114-5; Murphy 40-9-118-1; Kendrick 23.2-4-81-3; Smith 4-1-32-0.

Umpires: V. A. Holder and A. A. Jones.

At Canterbury, August 11, 12, 13. KENT lost to AUSTRALIANS by 89 runs (See Australian tour section).

At Worcester, August 19, 20, 21, 23. KENT lost to WORCESTERSHIRE by an innings and 130 runs.

At Lytham, August 26, 27, 28, 30. KENT beat LANCASHIRE by 159 runs.

KENT v NORTHAMPTONSHIRE

At Canterbury, August 31, September 1, 2, 3. Drawn. Kent 6 pts, Northamptonshire 4 pts. Toss: Kent.

Umpire Bird was involved in an unusual incident just before the close of the opening day: he called back Cowdrey after originally giving him out, caught behind off Ambrose, then deciding that the ball had come off his forearm. Cowdrey resumed his innings and next morning, after another escape when he was caught off an Ambrose no-ball, reached his first hundred of the season, adding 153 in 26 overs with Ealham. Cowdrey hit 17 fours and four sixes, while Ealham made 64 in boundaries. Northamptonshire looked in real danger, 86 short of the follow-on, until Ambrose joined Loye, helping him to reach a career-best 153 not out including 21 fours. By the evening Fulton had completed his second fifty of the match – and in first-class cricket – before Marsh set Northamptonshire a target of 314 off a minimum of 89 overs. They were never likely to reach it and struggled against Hooper. Kent were set for a sixth Championship win before the rain came.

Close of play: First day, Kent 302-6 (G. R. Cowdrey 65*, M. A. Ealham 0*); Second day, Northamptonshire 177-5 (M. B. Loye 71*, D. Ripley 28*); Third day, Kent 115-2 (D. P. Fulton 51*, N. J. Llong 33*).

Kent

D. P. Fulton lbw b Bowen	75	– c Fordham b Roberts	52
J. I. Longley lbw b Bowen	47	– c Felton b Taylor	3
G. R. Cowdrey b Bailey	139	– st Ripley b Bailey	25
C. L. Hooper c and b Bailey	34		
N. J. Llong c Ripley b Roberts	0	– (4) not out	54
M. V. Fleming b Bailey	23	– (5) not out	26
*†S. A. Marsh c Ripley b Ambrose	47		
M. A. Ealham c Taylor b Bowen	76		
D. W. Headley not out	14		
M. M. Patel c Ripley b Bowen	0		
A. P. Igglesden c Loye b Taylor	10		
B 1, l-b 3, n-b 10	14	B 1, l-b 2, n-b 2	5

1/116 2/137 3/190 4/191 5/216   479   1/8 2/57 3/118   (3 wkts dec.) 165
6/302 7/455 8/455 9/456

Bonus points – Kent 3, Northamptonshire 2 (Score at 120 overs: 341-6).

Bowling: *First Innings*—Ambrose 27-8-55-1; Taylor 26.4-8-80-1; Bowen 29-4-124-4; Bailey 30-6-108-3; Roberts 28-5-108-1. *Second Innings*—Ambrose 15-3-31-0; Taylor 10-6-12-1; Bailey 18-2-49-1; Bowen 13-6-45-0; Roberts 8.4-0-25-1.

Northamptonshire

A. Fordham c Fulton b Hooper	39	– c Fulton b Hooper	27
N. A. Felton c Fulton b Ealham	8	– c Marsh b Headley	4
R. J. Bailey c Longley b Ealham	4	– c Fulton b Hooper	21
M. B. Loye not out	153	– b Igglesden	42
*A. J. Lamb c Longley b Igglesden	4	– st Marsh b Patel	13
R. J. Warren c Fulton b Hooper	3	– c Patel b Hooper	7
†D. Ripley c Marsh b Ealham	54	– not out	7
A. R. Roberts lbw b Ealham	0	– c Fleming b Hooper	11
M. N. Bowen run out	5	– not out	2
C. E. L. Ambrose b Fleming	38		
J. P. Taylor b Ealham	0		
B 5, l-b 12, n-b 6	23	N-b 6	6

1/22 2/26 3/95 4/104 5/115	**331**	1/16 2/47 3/72 4/87	(7 wkts) **140**
6/238 7/238 8/244 9/330		5/108 6/127 7/138	

Bonus points – Northamptonshire 2, Kent 3 (Score at 120 overs: 250-8).

Bowling: *First Innings*—Igglesden 29–7–69–1; Ealham 25.4–6–66–5; Patel 27–11–44–0; Fleming 15–5–46–1; Hooper 40–13–89–2. *Second Innings*—Igglesden 14–5–33–1; Headley 7–2–25–1; Ealham 4–1–16–0; Hooper 17–2–35–4; Patel 14.5–4–31–1.

Umpires: H. D. Bird and R. A. White.

At Canterbury, September 11, 12, 13. KENT beat ZIMBABWEANS by 196 runs (See Zimbabwean tour section).

KENT v GLAMORGAN

At Canterbury, September 16, 17, 18, 20. Kent won by 236 runs. Kent 24 pts, Glamorgan 2 pts. Toss: Glamorgan.

Glamorgan arrived hoping to cement second place in the Championship, but had to settle for third after a heavy defeat. After a first-day washout Kent recovered from losing two wickets in Watkin's first over to complete their highest total of the season, with Ward and Hooper sharing a stand of 229 in 50 overs – Kent's best partnership of 1993. Ward dominated the attack from the start, scoring 137 off 157 balls with three sixes and 23 fours. Next morning Hooper completed a maiden double-century, hitting three sixes and 21 fours in 397 minutes and 330 balls, before Marsh declared. Without Maynard, who was resting a neck injury, Glamorgan also started badly but, with only Cottey surviving long, they staged no recovery and were all out just after tea. Despite leading by 380 runs Kent did not enforce the follow-on. While their bowlers had a breather, Fleming made an unbeaten 81, out of 95, in 20 overs and by the evening Glamorgan were batting again. Marsh had set them 476 to win, but they lost Dale and Morris before the close. Richards delighted the small crowd with two sixes and 14 fours in his final innings, 83 in 61 balls, and Cottey became the fifth Glamorgan player to pass 1,000 first-class runs in the season. But victory for Kent was inevitable, though it was little compensation for the defeat in the more frantic atmosphere of the Sunday League decider the previous day.

Close of play: First day, No play; Second day, Kent 395-3 (C. L. Hooper 187*, N. J. Llong 61*); Third day, Glamorgan 7-2 (C. P. Metson 0*, P. A. Cottey 1*).

Kent

D. P. Fulton b Watkin	0	– b Dale	1
T. R. Ward c sub b Bastien	137		
G. R. Cowdrey c Hemp b Watkin	0	– st Metson b Croft	9
C. L. Hooper not out	236		
N. J. Llong c sub b Lefebvre	62		
M. V. Fleming c Metson b Lefebvre	0	– (2) not out	81
*†S. A. Marsh c Croft b Bastien	21		
M. A. Ealham not out	50		
D. W. Headley (did not bat)	–	– (4) not out	4
L-b 13, w 1, n-b 4	18		

1/0 2/0 3/229 4/400   (6 wkts dec.) 524   1/23 2/78   (2 wkts dec.) 95
5/402 6/447

M. M. Patel and A. P. Igglesden did not bat.

Bonus points – Kent 4, Glamorgan 2.

Bowling: *First Innings*—Watkin 26.3–2–126–2; Bastien 30–5–115–2; Lefebvre 35–3–106–2; Croft 18–1–91–0; Dale 8–0–73–0. *Second Innings*—Bastien 4–1–30–0; Dale 10–1–43–1; Croft 4–1–15–1; Richards 2–0–7–0.

Glamorgan

A. Dale c Ward b Igglesden	0	– b Igglesden	2
*H. Morris b Headley	1	– c Marsh b Headley	0
P. A. Cottey b Headley	79	– (4) c Headley b Patel	53
I. V. A. Richards c Marsh b Ealham	17	– (5) c Fulton b Hooper	83
D. L. Hemp c and b Ealham	13	– (6) b Patel	12
R. D. B. Croft c Headley b Ealham	0	– (7) c Marsh b Headley	0
†C. P. Metson c Ward b Headley	5	– (3) lbw b Headley	14
R. P. Lefebvre c Llong b Patel	4	– (9) b Igglesden	49
S. L. Watkin c Headley b Igglesden	13	– (10) c Fleming b Igglesden	9
S. Bastien not out	5	– (11) not out	3
M. P. Maynard absent injured	–	– (8) c Marsh b Headley	14
L-b 1, n-b 6	7	B 6, l-b 6, n-b 2	14

1/0 2/6 3/66 4/84 5/88   144   1/4 2/4 3/25 4/131 5/162   239
6/119 7/126 8/126 9/144   6/162 7/162 8/186 9/212

Bonus points – Kent 4.

Bowling: *First Innings*—Igglesden 9–2–27–2; Headley 15–6–29–3; Fleming 10–1–41–0; Ealham 9–1–31–3; Patel 3–0–15–1. *Second Innings*—Igglesden 12.2–3–45–3; Headley 16–2–97–4; Hooper 6–0–26–1; Ealham 2–0–16–0; Patel 8–1–43–2.

Umpires: D. J. Constant and G. A. Stickley.

LANCASHIRE

Patron: HM The Queen
President: K. Cranston
Chairman: R. Bennett
Chief Executive: J. M. Bower
Cricket Secretary: Miss R. B. FitzGibbon
Captain: 1993 – N. H. Fairbrother
　　　　　1994 – M. Watkinson
Manager: 1993 – D. P. Hughes
Coach: D. Lloyd
Head Groundsman: P. Marron
Scorer: W. Davies

Another miserable season for Lancashire, in which they lost seven of the last ten Championship matches, ended with the departure of David Hughes, the manager, and the resignation of the captain, Neil Fairbrother. After winning four of the first seven games to hold third place in the table, Lancashire failed to win again and slipped to finish joint 13th, their lowest position since 1986. The batting was inconsistent, although there were regularly ten players in the side who had scored first-class centuries; the bowling lacked balance and was too often denied by the opposition's middle order. Only Hampshire had fewer bowling bonus points.

Fairbrother's decision was clearly the right one. Since he took over from Hughes midway through the 1991 season little had gone right for him or his team. After Lancashire surprisingly lost the Benson and Hedges Cup final to Derbyshire, the captaincy became a burden and team spirit consequently suffered. A change of leadership was essential and, in appointing Mike Watkinson, Lancashire might just prove to have made an inspired choice similar to that of Hughes in 1987.

Hughes suffered the fate of his predecessor Alan Ormrod the previous year. Both carried the can, in the manner of a football manager, for the failure of the team in a club with vociferous and impatient supporters. David Lloyd, brought in to back up Hughes a year earlier, survived and was given a more prominent role for 1994, but without the title of manager.

At the end of June everything had seemed set fair. Lancashire were in the Cup final and lying third in the Championship and fifth in the Sunday League. Things began to go wrong from the first two days of July when they allowed Leicestershire to wriggle free from 215 for seven to 455 all out. They lost that game by an innings in three days, and a week later lost the final. Eight days after that, Lancashire lost to Glamorgan, the eventual champions, in the Sunday League, and although they were not to drop below seventh place, they were never again in a position to challenge for the title. In the Championship Lancashire went from disaster to disaster, the Leicestershire defeat being the first of seven in eight games, several by wide margins. Their inability to ram home an advantage was again shown at Lytham where Kent were allowed to escape from 123 for five in their second innings, only 58 ahead, to reach 427 for eight and win easily.

The one distraction, and that was the result of a generous declaration, came when Lancashire beat the Australians, the only county to do so in a first-class match. This was only their second win over them since 1912, the other having come in 1972.

Watkinson, one of the most whole-hearted cricketers Lancashire can ever have had, was the outstanding player of the season. He topped 1,000 runs in first-class cricket for the first time and also took 51 wickets to become the first since Peter Marner in 1962 to accomplish the mini-double of 1,000 runs and 50 wickets. He took nearly all his wickets with off-breaks and bowled medium-pace only occasionally.

Wasim Akram was regularly available, played in 13 of the 17 Championship matches and headed the national averages with 59 wickets at 19.27 runs each. But although Wasim and Phillip DeFreitas should have been able to form one of the best opening attacks in the country, DeFreitas had a depressing season – his 49 wickets costing 32.20 runs each – and he and the club became increasingly frustrated with each other. At the end of the season he moved to Derbyshire. Lancashire persevered with pace bowler Peter Martin and left-arm spinner Alex Barnett, but they failed to make the progress expected of them.

Graham Lloyd and Nick Speak both scored more than 1,000 runs, but neither was as convincing as the previous season when they both averaged over 50. Lloyd's average dropped to 37.75, Speak's to 35.90. It must have been an especially disappointing season for Lloyd, who returned from Australia with England A to start the season in high style, scoring centuries against Oxford University and Yorkshire and 95 for England A against Essex. By the end of the fourth Championship match he had scored over 700 runs. The rest of the season produced fewer than 400, a frustrating period in which he was dropped for a time and then fined £100 for exchanging words with a spectator.

Fairbrother did not score a century until the final match and failed to reach 1,000. Like DeFreitas he slipped out of England contention. Mike Atherton, on the other hand, moved ever upwards. He scored 1,364 runs and his appointment as England captain provided a rare moment of pride and delight for Lancastrians in the latter part of the season. This came before Fairbrother's resignation, and Atherton made it clear that he did not want both jobs. John Crawley, who followed Atherton's path on to the full-time staff from Manchester Grammar School and the Cambridge captaincy, maintained his progress and was chosen for the England A tour to South Africa. So was the off-spinner Dexter Fitton.

Further signs of great promise came from the Yorkshire-born pace bowler Glen Chapple, whose season will be mostly recalled for what will always be regarded as the dubious distinction of scoring a century in 21 minutes against helpful Glamorgan bowling. Gehan Mendis was released despite scoring 1,000 runs for the seventh time in eight seasons at Old Trafford. David Hughes's sad farewell ends a career at the club which stretched back to 1965, when he first played for Lancashire Club and Ground, and was marked by five years of captaincy in which Lancashire won three major trophies. That seems now like a distant golden age. – Brian Bearshaw.

LANCASHIRE 1993

[*Bill Smith*]

Back row: J. S. Savage (*chief scout*), G. Chapple, S. D. Fletcher, J. M. Fielding, G. Yates, S. P. Titchard, M. A. Sharp, P. J. Martin, R. C. Irani, N. A. Derbyshire, J. D. Fitton, M. E. Harvey, A. A. Barnett. *Front row*: L. Brown (*physiotherapist*), G. D. Mendis, J. Stanworth, I. D. Austin, M. Watkinson, P. A. J. Defreitas, N. H. Fairbrother (*captain*), M. A. Atherton, W. K. Hegg, N. J. Speak, G. D. Lloyd. D. P. Hughes (*manager*), D. Lloyd (*coach*). *Insets*: Wasim Akram, G. J. Cordingley, J. E. R. Gallian, J. P. Crawley.

LANCASHIRE RESULTS

All first-class matches – Played 21: Won 5, Lost 9, Drawn 7.

County Championship matches – Played 17: Won 4, Lost 8, Drawn 5.

Bonus points – Batting 38, Bowling 48.

Competition placings – Britannic Assurance County Championship, 13th equal;
NatWest Bank Trophy, 1st round; Benson and Hedges Cup, finalists;
AXA Equity & Law League, 6th.

BRITANNIC ASSURANCE CHAMPIONSHIP AVERAGES

BATTING

	Birthplace	*M*	*I*	*NO*	*R*	*HS*	*Avge*
G. Yates	*Ashton-under-Lyne*	7	10	6	367	134*	91.75
G. Chapple	*Skipton*	6	11	6	239	109*	47.80
‡M. Watkinson	*Westhoughton*	15	24	2	936	107	42.54
‡M. A. Atherton	*Manchester*	10	16	0	557	137	34.81
‡N. H. Fairbrother . .	*Warrington*	16	28	3	855	110	34.20
J. P. Crawley	*Maldon*	9	15	0	508	103	33.86
‡N. J. Speak	*Manchester*	17	29	1	931	122	33.25
S. P. Titchard	*Warrington*	4	8	0	224	87	28.00
‡G. D. Mendis	*Colombo, Ceylon*	14	27	0	875	94	32.40
‡G. D. Lloyd	*Accrington*	13	22	1	574	80	27.33
P. J. Martin	*Accrington*	12	17	5	310	43	25.83
‡Wasim Akram§	*Lahore, Pakistan*	13	21	0	516	117	24.57
‡W. K. Hegg	*Whitefield*	17	28	6	488	69*	22.18
‡P. A. J. DeFreitas . .	*Scotts Head, Dominica*	16	25	3	426	51	19.36
R. C. Irani	*Leigh*	2	4	0	44	44	11.00
A. A. Barnett	*Malaga, Spain*	15	20	6	146	38	10.42

Also batted: ‡I. D. Austin (*Haslingden*) (1 match) 1, 10.

* *Signifies not out.*   ‡ *Denotes county cap.*   § *Overseas player.*

The following played a total of ten three-figure innings for Lancashire in County Championship matches – M. A. Atherton 2, M. Watkinson 2, G. Chapple 1, J. P. Crawley 1, N. H. Fairbrother 1, N. J. Speak 1, Wasim Akram 1, G. Yates 1.

BOWLING

	O	*M*	*R*	*W*	*BB*	*5W/i*	*Avge*
Wasim Akram	409.2	93	1,137	59	8-68	5	19.27
P. A. J. DeFreitas	511.4	100	1,578	49	7-76	4	32.20
M. Watkinson	550.1	126	1,621	44	5-12	1	36.84
P. J. Martin	314.5	74	966	26	4-63	0	37.15
G. Yates . . . .:. . . .	233	46	692	16	5-108	1	43.25
G. Chapple	127	25	445	10	3-50	0	44.50
A. A. Barnett	568.2	141	1,618	35	5-36	2	46.22

Also bowled: I. D. Austin 19.2-0-79-1; R. C. Irani 1-0-6-0.

Wicket-keeper: W. K. Hegg 45 ct, 7 st.

Leading Fielder: P. A. J. DeFreitas 13.

At Oxford, April 17, 19, 20. LANCASHIRE drew with OXFORD UNIVERSITY.

At Leeds, April 29, 30, May 1, 3. LANCASHIRE lost to YORKSHIRE by 116 runs (Non-Championship fixture).

LANCASHIRE v DURHAM

At Manchester, May 6, 7, 8, 10. Lancashire won by six wickets. Lancashire 21 pts, Durham 8 pts. Toss: Durham.

A game that looked to be heading for a certain draw was turned on its head by the Lancashire spinners, Barnett and Watkinson. Durham, 52 for one at lunch on the final day, which they intended to bat out, showed too much hesitancy and too little self-belief. They lost their remaining wickets for 31 runs in 20.1 overs on a pitch taking spin but far from unplayable. It was their first first-class total under 100; in the first innings they had scored their second over 500. This included a stand of 169 for the third wicket between Parker and Bainbridge. Only Lancashire's last-wicket pair saved the follow-on. Parker's carefully constructed century was the 45th of his career, and Atherton scored his fourth in five Championship matches extending back into 1992. Over the first three days, the pitch offered help to the seam bowlers, but on the last afternoon Barnett claimed the best return of his career. Although Lancashire lurched in mid-innings, Fairbrother and Watkinson saw them comfortably home with 7.3 overs left.

Close of play: First day, Durham 330-2 (P. W. G. Parker 85*, P. Bainbridge 79*); Second day, Lancashire 118-2 (M. A. Atherton 56*, N. H. Fairbrother 13*); Third day, Durham 34-0 (G. Fowler 9*, W. Larkins 15*).

Durham

G. Fowler c Hegg b DeFreitas	49	– st Hegg b Barnett	28
W. Larkins lbw b Chapple	76	– c sub b Barnett	19
P. W. G. Parker c Atherton b Watkinson	123	– c Atherton b Barnett	0
P. Bainbridge c Lloyd b Martin	79	– c Hegg b Watkinson	3
J. A. Daley c Martin b Watkinson	50	– b Watkinson	0
I. T. Botham c Watkinson b Chapple	3	– (8) c Fairbrother b Barnett	5
M. P. Briers c Hegg b Watkinson	1	– (6) lbw b Barnett	1
†C. W. Scott c DeFreitas b Chapple	26	– (7) lbw b Watkinson	3
J. Wood c Speak b Martin	28	– (10) st Hegg b Watkinson	7
*D. A. Graveney not out	21	– (9) not out	1
S. J. E. Brown not out	0	– c Atherton b Watkinson	0
B 13, l-b 14, n-b 32	59	B 4, n-b 12	16

1/143 2/161 3/330 4/395 5/404   (9 wkts dec.) 515   1/46 2/52 3/59 4/62 5/63   83
6/413 7/432 8/476 9/497   6/63 7/70 8/76 9/83

Bonus points – Durham 4, Lancashire 1 (Score at 120 overs: 402-4).

Bowling: *First Innings*—DeFreitas 34-3-118-1; Martin 29-9-83-2; Chapple 29-6-97-3; Barnett 37-9-65-0; Watkinson 40-12-125-3. *Second Innings*—DeFreitas 11-4-18-0; Martin 4-1-13-0; Barnett 19-7-36-5; Chapple 2-2-0-0; Watkinson 10.1-5-12-5.

Lancashire

G. D. Mendis c Fowler b Wood	1	– lbw b Graveney	9
M. A. Atherton c Fowler b Wood	137	– c and b Graveney	30
N. J. Speak c Daley b Graveney	43		
*N. H. Fairbrother c Larkins b Wood	43	– not out	36
G. D. Lloyd c Fowler b Graveney	45	– (3) b Brown	47
†W. K. Hegg c Briers b Botham	27	– (5) c Botham b Graveney	0
M. Watkinson b Wood	31	– (6) not out	30
P. A. J. DeFreitas lbw b Brown	0		
P. J. Martin lbw b Graveney	15		
G. Chapple not out	37		
A. A. Barnett b Graveney	38		
B 4, l-b 11, w 2, n-b 8	25	L-b 2, w 3	5

1/2 2/89 3/160 4/221 5/298   **442**   1/21 2/86 3/94 4/95   **(4 wkts) 157**
6/333 7/334 8/358 9/360

Bonus points – Lancashire 4, Durham 4 (Score at 120 overs: 373-9).

Bowling: *First Innings*—Wood 35-7-106-4; Brown 29-8-104-1; Botham 18-4-32-1; Bainbridge 5-1-13-0; Graveney 42-7-131-4; Briers 13-3-41-0. *Second Innings*—Brown 10-0-36-1; Bainbridge 3-1-2-0; Graveney 16-1-66-3; Briers 6-0-28-0; Botham 3.3-0-23-0.

Umpires: N. T. Plews and A. G. T. Whitehead.

At Taunton, May 13, 14. LANCASHIRE lost to SOMERSET by 15 runs.

At Cambridge, May 19, 20, 21. LANCASHIRE drew with CAMBRIDGE UNIVERSITY.

LANCASHIRE v WARWICKSHIRE

At Liverpool, May 27, 28, 29, 31. Drawn. Lancashire 2 pts, Warwickshire 3 pts. Toss: Warwickshire.

After the first two days and 80 overs of the third had been lost to rain, all but nine overs' play was possible on the final day. Lancashire were force-fed with runs in the morning session, when 195 were scored in the hour before lunch. They then faced one ball after the interval before declaring. Following a forfeiture of innings by both sides, Warwickshire were left with what turned out to be 72 overs in which to score 280. Spinners Barnett and Watkinson took advantage of a helpful pitch to reduce them to 87 for six in the 42nd over. But Reeve and Smith, in a partnership of 71, held out long enough.

Close of play: First day, No play; Second day, No play; Third day, Lancashire 65-2 (G. D. Mendis 25*, N. H. Fairbrother 33*).

Lancashire

G. D. Mendis c Penney b Moles	49	†W. K. Hegg not out	69
M. A. Atherton lbw b Small	1	P. J. Martin not out	33
N. J. Speak b Small	4	L-b 4	4
*N. H. Fairbrother b Twose	33		
G. D. Lloyd c Donald b Ratcliffe	41	1/8 2/12 3/66 (7 wkts dec.) 279	
M. Watkinson c Ratcliffe b Moles	0	4/130 5/130	
P. A. J. DeFreitas c Ostler b Moles	45	6/131 7/200	

Wasim Akram and A. A. Barnett did not bat.

Bonus points – Lancashire 2, Warwickshire 3.

Bowling: Donald 6-3-11-0; Small 8-3-24-2; Munton 11-4-24-0; Reeve 7-6-2-0; Smith 2-0-10-0; Twose 3-0-9-1; Ratcliffe 10-1-82-1; Moles 9-1-87-3; Ostler 3-0-13-0; Penney 2.1-0-13-0.

Lancashire forfeited their second innings.

Warwickshire

Warwickshire forfeited their first innings.

A. J. Moles b Barnett	34	N. M. K. Smith c sub b Watkinson	37
J. D. Ratcliffe lbw b DeFreitas	1	G. C. Small not out	0
R. G. Twose st Hegg b Watkinson	17	B 2, l-b 6, n-b 4	12
D. P. Ostler c Speak b Barnett	8		
T. L. Penney c sub b Watkinson	17	1/11 2/47 3/61 (7 wkts)	171
*D. A. Reeve not out	45	4/70 5/86	
†M. Burns c sub b Barnett	0	6/87 7/158	

A. A. Donald and T. A. Munton did not bat.

Bowling: DeFreitas 10–2–21–1; Martin 7–3–12–0; Barnett 27.5–9–48–3; Watkinson 27–6–82–3.

Umpires: D. J. Constant and J. H. Harris.

At The Oval, June 3, 4, 5, 7. LANCASHIRE beat SURREY by 96 runs.

LANCASHIRE v ESSEX

At Manchester, June 10, 11, 12, 14. Drawn. Lancashire 5 pts, Essex 7 pts. Toss: Lancashire.
 The second and fourth days of this game were lost to rain. Lancashire batted boldly on a true, bouncy pitch on the first day: the backbone of their innings came from a third-wicket stand of 141 between Speak, who often looked vulnerable against the short-pitched delivery, and Fairbrother, who hit Such for four sixes after being dropped in the off-spinner's first over. While Andrew returned career-best figures, Foster produced a succession of errors from the batsmen without taking a wicket and, in his frustration, kicked two stumps out of the ground at the end of his 18th over, an action for which Essex fined him £250. Essex declared 17 runs behind and Lancashire had advanced their lead to 146 on a pitch taking an increasing amount of spin by the end of the third day.
 Close of play: First day, Essex 37–1 (G. A. Gooch 23*, M. A. Garnham 1*); Second day, No play; Third day, Lancashire 129–3 (N. H. Fairbrother 41*, G. D. Lloyd 20*).

Lancashire

G. D. Mendis c Stephenson b Ilott	1	– b Salim Malik	28
M. A. Atherton c Salim Malik b Andrew	39	– c Gooch b Such	26
N. J. Speak c Garnham b Andrew	99	– c Hussain b Such	1
*N. H. Fairbrother c Such b Andrew	63	– not out	41
G. D. Lloyd lbw b Andrew	0	– not out	20
Wasim Akram b Andrew	6		
M. Watkinson c Hussain b Ilott	27		
P. A. J. DeFreitas lbw b Andrew	43		
†W. K. Hegg lbw b Ilott	4		
P. J. Martin c Gooch b Andrew	15		
A. A. Barnett not out	0		
B 3, l-b 13, w 2, n-b 6	24	B 4, l-b 5, n-b 4	13

1/1 2/60 3/201 4/203 5/226   321   1/44 2/48 3/96   (3 wkts) 129
6/241 7/274 8/292 9/320

Bonus points – Lancashire 3, Essex 4.

Bowling: *First Innings*—Foster 19–2–77–0; Ilott 24–3–79–3; Pringle 16–3–55–0; Andrew 15.1–2–47–7; Such 8–0–41–0; Salim Malik 3–0–6–0. *Second Innings*—Foster 8–2–26–0; Ilott 7–0–41–0; Such 17–10–20–2; Salim Malik 11–4–33–1.

Essex

*G. A. Gooch lbw b Barnett	66	P. J. Prichard lbw b Martin	12
J. P. Stephenson lbw b DeFreitas	4	N. A. Foster not out	29
†M. A. Garnham lbw b Barnett	45	L-b 10, w 1, n-b 30	41
Salim Malik c Hegg b Watkinson	6		
N. Hussain st Hegg b Barnett	36	1/24 2/117 3/140 (6 wkts. dec.)	304
D. R. Pringle not out	65	4/142 5/216 6/237	

M. C. Ilott, P. M. Such and S. J. W. Andrew did not bat.

Bonus points – Essex 3, Lancashire 2.

Bowling: Wasim Akram 15-2-46-0; DeFreitas 16-0-75-1; Martin 15-3-61-1; Barnett 26-6-78-3; Watkinson 6.3-1-34-1.

Umpires: J. D. Bond and B. J. Meyer.

LANCASHIRE v SUSSEX

At Manchester, June 17, 18, 19, 21. Lancashire won by four wickets. Lancashire 21 pts, Sussex 7 pts. Toss: Sussex.

Lancashire turned a first-innings deficit of 123 into a comfortable win with 17.4 overs to spare. Sussex passed 400 with Athey scoring his first century for them and Moores steadying the second half of an innings in which off-spinner Yates, making his first appearance of the season, took five wickets for the first time. Lancashire failed to build on a solid start and Sussex then patiently extended their advantage to 325, with Greenfield resisting for nearly four and a half hours and Wells, batting late because of illness, propelling Sussex into what looked like a winning advantage. But Mendis and Titchard supplied the platform for victory by becoming the first Lancashire openers in 30 years to share a century stand in both innings of a Championship match. Off-spinners Hemmings and Donelan were unable to take full advantage of the helpful pitch, on which 28 of the 36 wickets fell to spin.

Close of play: First day, Sussex 314-7 (P. Moores 37*, B. T. P. Donelan 12*); Second day, Sussex 23-1 (J. W. Hall 6*); Third day, Lancashire 17-0 (G. D. Mendis 12*, S. P. Titchard 5*).

Sussex

C. W. J. Athey c and b Yates	101	– c Fairbrother b Barnett	15
J. W. Hall b Wasim Akram	53	– c Speak b Yates	34
D. M. Smith c Barnett b Yates	15	– (9) c DeFreitas b Martin	1
*A. P. Wells b Yates	0	– (8) b Barnett	53
K. Greenfield run out	0	– (3) not out	60
J. A. North lbw b Yates	23	– (4) c DeFreitas b Yates	0
F. D. Stephenson c Wasim Akram b Yates	36	– (5) c Fairbrother b Barnett	1
†P. Moores not out	85	– (6) b Barnett	4
B. T. P. Donelan c Hegg b Wasim Akram	41	– (7) c Speak b Yates	2
A. N. Jones c Hegg b Wasim Akram	0	– lbw b Martin	5
E. E. Hemmings c DeFreitas b Wasim Akram	0	– c Speak b Barnett	5
B 9, l-b 12, n-b 28	49	L-b 10, n-b 12	22

1/147 2/172 3/176 4/178 5/218	403	1/23 2/77 3/81 4/82 5/90	202
6/251 7/280 8/403 9/403		6/95 7/186 8/187 9/197	

Bonus points – Sussex 3, Lancashire 3 (Score at 120 overs: 334-7).

Bowling: *First Innings*—Wasim Akram 27.1-8-55-4; Martin 18-7-41-0; DeFreitas 23-8-67-0; Barnett 34-6-111-0; Yates 40-8-108-5. *Second Innings*—DeFreitas 16-4-27-0; Yates 27-6-90-3; Barnett 37.5-13-65-5; Martin 6-1-10-2.

Lancashire

G. D. Mendis c Hall b Donelan	63	– lbw b Hemmings	85
S. P. Titchard c Athey b Donelan	57	– b Donelan	87
N. J. Speak c North b Hemmings	3	– c sub b Donelan	59
*N. H. Fairbrother c Wells b Hemmings	0	– b Hemmings	37
G. D. Lloyd b Donelan	47	– b Hemmings	7
Wasim Akram c Greenfield b Hemmings	37	– (7) lbw b Donelan	7
P. A. J. DeFreitas c Wells b Hemmings	10	– (6) not out	8
†W. K. Hegg not out	10	– not out	3
G. Yates c North b Donelan	14		
P. J. Martin lbw b Stephenson	7		
A. A. Barnett lbw b Donelan	4		
B 5, l-b 1, n-b 22	28	B 13, l-b 2, n-b 18	33

1/127 2/138 3/138 4/138 5/215   280   1/179 2/201 3/296   (6 wkts) 326
6/236 7/241 8/266 9/273   4/307 5/312 6/322

Bonus points – Lancashire 2, Sussex 4.

Bowling: *First Innings*—Stephenson 9-1-26-1; Jones 7-0-35-0; North 3-0-15-0; Hemmings 23-4-86-4; Donelan 21.3-0-112-5. *Second Innings*—Stephenson 13-2-35-0; Hemmings 38.2-10-100-2; Donelan 35-3-157-4; Jones 5-0-19-0.

Umpires: G. I. Burgess and B. Leadbeater.

At Derby, June 24, 25, 26, 28. LANCASHIRE beat DERBYSHIRE by 111 runs.

At Leicester, July 1, 2, 3. LANCASHIRE lost to LEICESTERSHIRE by an innings and 58 runs.

LANCASHIRE v GLAMORGAN

At Manchester, July 15, 16, 17, 19. Glamorgan won by seven wickets. Glamorgan 23 pts, Lancashire 5 pts. Toss: Lancashire.

Glamorgan maintained their Championship challenge, easily reaching a contrived target of 243. However, it is the contrivance that will be remembered, and not kindly. After the fourth morning – like the whole of the first day – was washed out, Glamorgan declared behind, Lancashire put in their tailenders and Maynard and Cottey bowled, or presented, 12 overs in half an hour, which produced 235 runs. In that time 19-year-old Glen Chapple, who had never scored a fifty, hit first-class cricket's fastest century, which took 21 minutes and 27 balls with ten fours and nine sixes. It is not recognised as a record by *Wisden* because of the connivance of the bowlers and, indeed, the fielders; Richards even tried to kick the ball over the boundary. In one over from Cottey, Chapple hit 34 (664666) and the innings in total produced 31 fours, ten sixes and 20 no-balls, many deliberate. The no-balls, in particular, left the computerised scoring system struggling to keep up. The timing of Chapple's century was confirmed because play was, by chance, being recorded on video. When normal cricket was resumed, Glamorgan had to bat without James, who had broken his thumb scoring his first century of the season. However, Dale took his place as opener and steered Glamorgan to within 31 of victory.

Close of play: First day, No play; Second day, Lancashire 310-9 (G. Chapple 24*, A. A. Barnett 3*); Third day, Glamorgan 303-5 (S. P. James 138*, R. D. B. Croft 33*).

Lancashire

M. A. Atherton b Barwick	63			
J. P. Crawley c James b Watkin	9			
N. J. Speak b Croft	13			
G. D. Lloyd c James b Watkin	19			
*N. H. Fairbrother b Croft	34			
M. Watkinson c Metson b Lefebvre	49			
P. A. J. DeFreitas c Watkin b Barwick	40			
†W. K. Hegg st Metson b Richards	12			
G. Yates c Cottey b Croft	37	– (3) not out	94
G. Chapple not out	24	– (1) not out	109
A. A. Barnett c Metson b Watkin	3	– (2) b Maynard	4
B 3, l-b 3, w 1	7	B 4, w 4, n-b 20	28

1/19 2/52 3/83 4/122 5/174   310   1/9   (1 wkt dec.) 235
6/215 7/240 8/258 9/292

Bonus points – Lancashire 3, Glamorgan 4.

Bowling: *First Innings*—Watkin 23.5–5–69–3; Lefebvre 22–9–38–1; Dale 5–0–13–0; Croft 33–9–101–3; Barwick 21–8–53–2; Richards 12–1–30–1. *Second Innings*—Maynard 6–0–110–1; Cottey 6–0–121–0.

Glamorgan

S. P. James not out	138			
*H. Morris b Watkinson	39	– (1) lbw b Barnett	24
A. Dale b Watkinson	2	– (2) c Fairbrother b DeFreitas	95
M. P. Maynard b Yates	5	– (3) b DeFreitas	55
I. V. A. Richards c Hegg b Watkinson	1	– (4) not out	44
P. A. Cottey lbw b DeFreitas	67	– (5) not out	8
R. D. B. Croft not out	33			
B 4, l-b 11, w 1, n-b 2	18	B 9, l-b 6, n-b 2	17

1/95 2/111 3/118 4/121 5/240   (5 wkts dec.) 303   1/26 2/157 3/212   (3 wkts) 243

R. P. Lefebvre, †C. P. Metson, S. L. Watkin and S. R. Barwick did not bat.

Bonus points – Glamorgan 3, Lancashire 2.

Bowling: *First Innings*—DeFreitas 17–6–31–1; Chapple 7–1–22–0; Barnett 21–2–76–0; Watkinson 25–2–97–3; Yates 17–2–62–1. *Second Innings*—Chapple 1–0–13–0; DeFreitas 16.1–2–65–2; Watkinson 12–0–54–0; Barnett 14–2–57–1; Yates 9–0–39–0.

Umpires: B. Leadbeater and B. J. Meyer.

LANCASHIRE v NOTTINGHAMSHIRE

At Manchester, July 22, 23, 24, 26. Nottinghamshire won by an innings and three runs. Nottinghamshire 24 pts, Lancashire 4 pts. Toss: Lancashire.

A career-best innings by Johnson led Nottinghamshire to their highest-ever total against Lancashire, who went down to their third consecutive Championship defeat. From a slow start, in which his first 50 took 139 balls, Johnson accelerated to reach 187 in 306 balls and 381 minutes, with 22 fours and two sixes. He and Lewis, who scored 83 in 112 balls, shared in a sixth-wicket stand of 178 to help Nottinghamshire to a first-innings lead of 265. Watkinson, Lancashire's acting-captain, played determinedly throughout. He was their top scorer in both innings, scoring the fifth century of his career on the first day, and also the leading bowler, with his off-breaks. But despite his efforts Lancashire, 99 for two when play started at 2 p.m. on the final day, lost their remaining wickets in two and threequarter hours. Cairns finished with match figures of nine for 88, his first-innings analysis of six for 70 exactly matching his best for the county, in the equivalent fixture the previous year.

Close of play: First day, Lancashire 289-9 (P. J. Martin 13*, A. A. Barnett 9*); Second day, Nottinghamshire 244-4 (P. Johnson 54*, C. L. Cairns 26*); Third day, Lancashire 99-2 (J. P. Crawley 52*, N. J. Speak 5*).

Lancashire

G. D. Mendis c Saxelby b Cairns	32	– (2) lbw b Cairns	10
J. P. Crawley c Saxelby b Cairns	28	– (1) c Robinson b Afford	56
S. P. Titchard b Cairns	27	– lbw b Afford	16
N. J. Speak b Afford	2	– c French b Field-Buss	20
G. D. Lloyd c French b Cairns	9	– b Field-Buss	6
*M. Watkinson b Afford	102	– lbw b Afford	64
P. A. J. DeFreitas c Crawley b Lewis	3	– c Robinson b Afford	22
†W. K. Hegg b Cairns	17	– not out	31
G. Chapple lbw b Field-Buss	19	– (10) b Cairns	1
P. J. Martin not out	18	– (9) st French b Field-Buss	3
A. A. Barnett b Cairns	10	– b Cairns	0
B 9, l-b 1, n-b 18	28	B 14, l-b 7, w 2, n-b 10	33
	295		**262**

1/53 2/76 3/87 4/100 5/125   295
6/132 7/217 8/255 9/268

1/24 2/49 3/103 4/118 5/143   262
6/218 7/221 8/238 9/262

Bonus points – Lancashire 2, Nottinghamshire 4.

Bowling: *First Innings*—Lewis 29–5–105–1; Cairns 27–9–70–6; Evans 6–1–23–0; Afford 33–13–65–2; Field-Buss 8–2–22–1. *Second Innings*—Cairns 11–2–18–3; Evans 7–2–23–0; Lewis 6–3–11–0; Afford 39–10–84–4; Field-Buss 38–18–105–3.

Nottinghamshire

P. R. Pollard lbw b Watkinson	65	†B. N. French st Hegg b Watkinson	40
M. Saxelby c and b Watkinson	41	M. G. Field-Buss not out	4
*R. T. Robinson c Crawley b Watkinson	13	J. A. Afford b Chapple	8
P. Johnson lbw b Chapple	187		
M. A. Crawley c Hegg b DeFreitas	24	B 24, l-b 10, n-b 10	44
C. L. Cairns c Hegg b Martin	51		
C. C. Lewis c Hegg b Martin	83	1/108 2/121 3/146 4/199 5/290	560
K. P. Evans lbw b Martin	0	6/468 7/468 8/523 9/543	

Bonus points – Nottinghamshire 4, Lancashire 2 (Score at 120 overs: 362-5).

Bowling: DeFreitas 25–4–81–1; Martin 32–6–105–3; Chapple 20.5–4–83–2; Barnett 45–13–140–0; Watkinson 40–10–117–4.

Umpires: G. Sharp and R. A. White.

At Manchester, July 28, 29, 30. LANCASHIRE beat AUSTRALIANS by five wickets (See Australian tour section).

At Cheltenham, August 5, 6, 7. LANCASHIRE lost to GLOUCESTERSHIRE by nine wickets.

At Southampton, August 12, 13, 14, 16. LANCASHIRE drew with HAMPSHIRE.

LANCASHIRE v YORKSHIRE

At Manchester, August 19, 20, 21, 23. Yorkshire won by 19 runs. Yorkshire 21 pts, Lancashire 4 pts. Toss: Lancashire. First-class debut: M. P. Vaughan.

Despite Wasim Akram's match-return of 12 for 125, the best of his career, Lancashire lost their fourth first-class Roses match out of five. But they gave Yorkshire a fright, falling only 20 short of what would have been a record 334 to win against their old rivals. The Manchester-born 18-year-old Michael Vaughan (the first Lancashire-born player to appear for Yorkshire in 73 years) survived five partners in scoring 64 on his debut before becoming one of Wasim's eight first-innings wickets. After surrendering a first-innings lead of 75 and being frustrated for the second time by Yorkshire's ninth-wicket pair, Lancashire fought back to leave themselves needing 197 with eight wickets standing on the final day. The initiative fluctuated as Lancashire's middle-order batsmen all made worthwhile contributions but Yorkshire, with Robinson taking six of the first seven wickets, held their nerve to win at Old Trafford for the first time since 1978. The only survivor from that match, Carrick, who had been recalled for another attempt at completing the double of 10,000 runs and 1,000 wickets for Yorkshire, finished 20 runs short.

Close of play: First day, Lancashire 72-3 (G. D. Mendis 38*, N. H. Fairbrother 4*); Second day, Yorkshire 187-3 (D. Byas 49*, R. J. Blakey 35*); Third day, Lancashire 137-2 (J. P. Crawley 68*, N. J. Speak 33*).

Yorkshire

*M. D. Moxon c Hegg b Wasim Akram	26	– c DeFreitas b Martin	16
M. P. Vaughan c Hegg b Wasim Akram	64	– c Hegg b DeFreitas	28
R. B. Richardson lbw b Wasim Akram	1	– st Hegg b Watkinson	50
D. Byas c Hegg b Wasim Akram	2	– b Wasim Akram	73
†R. J. Blakey c Hegg b Martin	2	– c Crawley b Wasim Akram	37
C. White c Hegg b Martin	9	– c Hegg b DeFreitas	3
A. P. Grayson b Wasim Akram	64	– b DeFreitas	3
P. J. Hartley lbw b Wasim Akram	1	– (10) not out	13
P. Carrick c DeFreitas b Wasim Akram	15	– (8) c Fairbrother b Wasim Akram	0
D. Gough not out	29	– (9) c Hegg b Martin	23
M. A. Robinson b Wasim Akram	0	– b Wasim Akram	0
B 4, l-b 7, n-b 18	29	B 1, l-b 3, n-b 8	12

1/53 2/61 3/71 4/76 5/98   242   1/23 2/73 3/123 4/194 5/216   258
6/134 7/138 8/162 9/236   6/218 7/220 8/220 9/257

Bonus points – Yorkshire 1, Lancashire 4.

Bowling: *First Innings*—Wasim Akram 23-4-68-8; DeFreitas 20-2-76-0; Martin 21-9-60-2; Chapple 7-1-17-0; Watkinson 4-1-10-0. *Second Innings*—Wasim Akram 29.4-8-57-4; Martin 16-4-43-2; DeFreitas 22-4-55-3; Watkinson 20-6-71-1; Chapple 5-0-22-0; Irani 1-0-6-0.

Lancashire

G. D. Mendis lbw b Hartley	55	– c Byas b Robinson	26
J. P. Crawley c Blakey b Robinson	26	– lbw b Robinson	80
R. C. Irani c Moxon b Gough	0	– c Richardson b Robinson	0
N. J. Speak lbw b Gough	0	– c Blakey b Robinson	40
*N. H. Fairbrother b Hartley	26	– b Carrick	22
M. Watkinson st Blakey b Carrick	7	– b Robinson	27
Wasim Akram b Hartley	0	– b Robinson	39
P. A. J. DeFreitas not out	10	– c White b Hartley	27
†W. K. Hegg lbw b Hartley	9	– c Blakey b Hartley	7
P. J. Martin b Gough	18	– not out	13
G. Chapple b Gough	0	– lbw b Gough	4
L-b 6, w 2, n-b 8	16	B 4, l-b 8, w 1, n-b 16	29

1/48 2/67 3/67 4/115 5/125   167   1/60 2/60 3/153 4/164 5/200   314
6/126 7/126 8/137 9/163   6/235 7/264 8/294 9/307

Bonus points – Yorkshire 4.

Bowling: *First Innings*—Hartley 16-5-62-4; Gough 12.1-3-46-4; Robinson 11-2-37-1; Carrick 13-7-16-1. *Second Innings*—Gough 25.5-4-101-1; Robinson 33-14-62-6; Hartley 10-1-50-2; Carrick 30-11-54-1; Vaughan 4-0-19-0; White 6-1-16-0.

Umpires: H. D. Bird and K. E. Palmer.

LANCASHIRE v KENT

At Lytham, August 26, 27, 28, 30. Kent won by 159 runs. Kent 21 pts, Lancashire 6 pts. Toss: Kent.

Outstanding performances from Hooper and Patel enabled Kent to turn a first-innings deficit of 65 into a handsome victory. Kent, 58 for five early on the first day, were revived by a career-best innings from Ealham, who shared in a century partnership with Marsh. Another fine innings from Crawley, backed up by Fairbrother, with only his third half-century of the summer, carried Lancashire into the lead. Their position looked even stronger when the top half of Kent's innings again faltered so badly that, at 123 for five, they were only 58 ahead. But Hooper's highest innings yet for the county, 166 not out, made over nearly six hours with excellent support from Ealham, allowed Kent to set Lancashire a victory target of 363 in 91 overs. Only Mendis showed any resolution. The slow left-armer Patel, recently recovered from a serious knee injury, returned career-best figures of seven for 75 and 12 for 182 overall. On the opening day, spectators were surprised to discover that the new paint on the seats had not quite dried, with unfortunate consequences for their dry cleaning bills.

Close of play: First day, Lancashire 38-1 (J. P. Crawley 19*, G. Yates 14*); Second day, Kent 9-0 (D. P. Fulton 4*, T. R. Ward 1*); Third day, Kent 389-7 (C. L. Hooper 147*, D. W. Headley 8*).

Kent

D. P. Fulton lbw b Watkinson	25	– c Crawley b Yates	40
T. R. Ward c Hegg b Wasim Akram	1	– lbw b Watkinson	1
N. J. Llong b Wasim Akram	0	– b Wasim Akram	40
C. L. Hooper c Mendis b Barnett	12	– not out	166
N. R. Taylor st Hegg b Barnett	11	– lbw b Wasim Akram	4
G. R. Cowdrey lbw b Wasim Akram	38	– lbw b Wasim Akram	8
*†S. A. Marsh lbw b DeFreitas	63	– run out	39
M. A. Ealham c Fairbrother b Watkinson	85	– c and b Yates	79
D. W. Headley b Wasim Akram	1	– b Watkinson	24
M. M. Patel not out	2	– not out	3
A. P. Igglesden c Irani b Wasim Akram	7		
B 5, l-b 3, n-b 10	18	B 4, l-b 1, n-b 18	23
	263	(8 wkts dec.)	**427**

1/7 2/7 3/42 4/42 5/58
6/116 7/216 8/248 9/252

1/9 2/71 3/99
4/111 5/123 6/210
7/366 8/415

Bonus points – Kent 2, Lancashire 4.

Bowling: *First Innings*—Wasim Akram 21.4–4–69–5; DeFreitas 23–7–46–1; Watkinson 31–7–89–2; Barnett 18–3–40–2; Yates 4–2–11–0. *Second Innings*—Wasim Akram 21–5–55–3; DeFreitas 16–2–57–0; Watkinson 30–4–127–2; Yates 37–5–108–2; Barnett 19–4–75–0.

Lancashire

G. D. Mendis c Fulton b Igglesden	1	– c Headley b Patel	94
J. P. Crawley lbw b Patel	78	– c Hooper b Headley	6
G. Yates b Headley	19	– (10) not out	10
N. J. Speak b Patel	23	– (3) lbw b Igglesden	2
*N. H. Fairbrother c Patel b Hooper	75	– (4) c Ward b Patel	22
R. C. Irani c Marsh b Patel	44	– (5) c Headley b Hooper	0
M. Watkinson c Marsh b Patel	2	– (6) c Cowdrey b Patel	14
Wasim Akram b Patel	17	– st Marsh b Patel	10
P. A. J. DeFreitas not out	37	– (7) c Ward b Patel	5
†W. K. Hegg b Hooper	4	– (9) b Patel	8
A. A. Barnett c Marsh b Igglesden	10	– c Headley b Patel	31
B 6, l-b 10, n-b 2	18	L-b 1	1
	328		**203**

1/6 2/57 3/120 4/133 5/237
6/246 7/269 8/299 9/299

1/10 2/23 3/71 4/74 5/114
6/126 7/136 8/150 9/169

Bonus points – Lancashire 2, Kent 3 (Score at 120 overs: 282-8).

Bowling: *First Innings*—Igglesden 19–5–58–2; Headley 17–4–54–1; Hooper 45–13–93–2; Patel 52–15–107–5. *Second Innings*—Igglesden 7–0–27–1; Headley 6–0–22–1; Hooper 30–6–74–1; Patel 30–9–75–7; Llong 1–0–4–0.

Umpires: J. D. Bond and P. Willey.

At Worcester, August 31, September 1, 2, 3. LANCASHIRE lost to WORCESTERSHIRE by one wicket.

At Lord's, September 9, 10, 11, 13. LANCASHIRE drew with MIDDLESEX.

LANCASHIRE v NORTHAMPTONSHIRE

At Manchester, September 16, 17, 18, 20. Drawn. Lancashire 6 pts, Northamptonshire 5 pts. Toss: Lancashire.

Fairbrother's first century at Old Trafford for six years – only his second anywhere since early July 1991 – helped Lancashire recover from 30 for three in a first innings in which Taylor recorded his best bowling figures of the season, six for 82. After Wasim Akram's fifth five-wicket return of the summer in 13 Championship games, Northamptonshire were all out 37 behind, and centuries from Crawley and Yates, who batted over six hours for his second as a night-watchman, enabled Lancashire to set a target of 430 in 109 overs. But on a rain-interrupted fourth day fewer than 42 overs were possible, denying Northamptonshire their receding opportunity of finishing second instead of fourth in the Championship. By then Lancashire were distracted by events off the field; David Hughes had resigned as manager on the Saturday, and Fairbrother quit the captaincy within weeks.

Close of play: First day, Lancashire 277-8 (M. Watkinson 67*, G. Yates 3*); Second day, Lancashire 86-3 (J. P. Crawley 40*, G. Yates 9*); Third day, Northamptonshire 15-1 (N. A. Felton 4*, A. R. Roberts 3*).

Lancashire

M. A. Atherton lbw b Ambrose	10	– c Ripley b Ambrose	4
J. P. Crawley lbw b Ambrose	0	– c and b Roberts	103
N. J. Speak b Taylor	14	– run out	27
*N. H. Fairbrother c Felton b Taylor	110	– b Curran	4
G. D. Lloyd b Ambrose	38	– (6) lbw b Curran	7
M. Watkinson c Fordham b Taylor	67	– (7) b Roberts	45
Wasim Akram b Taylor	0	– (8) b Taylor	30
P. A. J. DeFreitas b Taylor	2	– (9) st Ripley b Bailey	24
†W. K. Hegg c Warren b Ambrose	19	– (10) not out	3
G. Yates not out	3	– (5) not out	134
A. A. Barnett b Taylor	0		
B 4, l-b 7, w 1, n-b 2	14	B 2, l-b 3, n-b 6	11

1/5 2/22 3/30 4/122 5/212   277   1/4 2/56 3/61   (8 wkts. dec.) 392
6/212 7/214 8/265 9/277   4/204 5/220 6/294
                                                 7/343 8/385

Bonus points – Lancashire 2, Northamptonshire 4.

Bowling: *First Innings*—Ambrose 25–4–86–4; Taylor 18.5–4–82–6; Curran 6–0–17–0; Roberts 23–10–56–0; Bailey 11–3–25–0. *Second Innings*—Ambrose 27–2–77–1; Taylor 25–8–70–1; Roberts 36–3–124–2; Curran 24–7–72–2; Bailey 14–1–44–1.

Northamptonshire

A. Fordham c Hegg b Wasim Akram	0	– c Lloyd b Wasim Akram	6
N. A. Felton c Barnett b DeFreitas	46	– not out	72
R. J. Bailey c Hegg b Wasim Akram	55	– (4) not out	71
M. B. Loye lbw b Wasim Akram	0		
*A. J. Lamb c Speak b Yates	67		
R. J. Warren lbw b DeFreitas	6		
K. M. Curran c Fairbrother b Barnett	23		
†D. Ripley c Speak b Wasim Akram	1		
A. R. Roberts lbw b Barnett	10	– (3) c Watkinson b Wasim Akram	3
C. E. L. Ambrose b Wasim Akram	1		
J. P. Taylor not out	1		
L-b 6, n-b 24	30	B 2, l-b 5, n-b 2	9

1/0 2/104 3/104 4/122 5/140   240   1/10 2/16   (2 wkts) 161
6/197 7/210 8/231 9/236

Bonus points – Northamptonshire 1, Lancashire 4.

Bowling: *First Innings*—Wasim Akram 17–3–63–5; DeFreitas 14–5–39–2; Watkinson 16–1–42–0; Yates 12–6–27–1; Barnett 16.2–2–63–2. *Second Innings*—Wasim Akram 11–1–31–2; DeFreitas 10–4–21–0; Barnett 17.3–3–83–0; Watkinson 8–2–10–0; Yates 2–0–9–0.

Umpires: J. C. Balderstone and P. B. Wight.

YOUNG CRICKETER OF THE YEAR

(*Elected by the Cricket Writers' Club*)

1950	R. Tattersall	1973	M. Hendrick
1951	P. B. H. May	1974	P. H. Edmonds
1952	F. S. Trueman	1975	A. Kennedy
1953	M. C. Cowdrey	1976	G. Miller
1954	P. J. Loader	1977	I. T. Botham
1955	K. F. Barrington	1978	D. I. Gower
1956	B. Taylor	1979	P. W. G. Parker
1957	M. J. Stewart	1980	G. R. Dilley
1958	A. C. D. Ingleby-Mackenzie	1981	M. W. Gatting
1959	G. Pullar	1982	N. G. Cowans
1960	D. A. Allen	1983	N. A. Foster
1961	P. H. Parfitt	1984	R. J. Bailey
1962	P. J. Sharpe	1985	D. V. Lawrence
1963	G. Boycott	1986 {	A. A. Metcalfe
1964	J. M. Brearley		J. J. Whitaker
1965	A. P. E. Knott	1987	R. J. Blakey
1966	D. L. Underwood	1988	M. P. Maynard
1967	A. W. Greig	1989	N. Hussain
1968	R. M. H. Cottam	1990	M. A. Atherton
1969	A. Ward	1991	M. R. Ramprakash
1970	C. M. Old	1992	I. D. K. Salisbury
1971	J. Whitehouse	1993	M. N. Lathwell
1972	D. R. Owen-Thomas		

An additional award, in memory of Norman Preston, Editor of *Wisden* from 1951 to 1980, was made to C. W. J. Athey in 1980.

LEICESTERSHIRE

President: B. A. F. Smith
Chairman: J. M. Josephs
Chairman, Cricket Committee: P. R. Haywood
Chief Executive: A. O. Norman
Captain: N. E. Briers
Cricket Manager: J. Birkenshaw
Head Groundsman: L. Spence
Scorer: G. R. Blackburn

Leicestershire's history reached a turning-point on September 15, 1993, when Mike Turner dramatically resigned. It really was the end of an era. Turner, a leg-spin bowler of modest achievement who rose to be chief executive of his only county, had given 42 years of unbroken service, 33 of them in the club's main managerial role, the majority in a position that gave him something close to dictatorship of the club's affairs.

The announcement that Turner was leaving, a year before the expiry of his contract, brought to the surface a power struggle that had been gathering momentum for some years. Never a man with much faith in committees, Turner's management style had not been to everyone's taste; and after Bill Bentley, the club president, died in 1986 and Charles Palmer had relinquished the chairmanship, his position had been slowly eroded. The appointment of a cricket manager in 1990, a move which, ostensibly at any rate, Turner fully supported, led to problems as recruitment and selection were traditionally part of his sphere of influence; and his relations with both Bobby Simpson and his successor Jack Birkenshaw were difficult.

By the end of the summer, Turner learned that a majority of the committee were against offering him a new deal when his five-year contract expired and he resigned, without concealing his sense of betrayal. He cited "disagreements over management procedures" as his reason for leaving and made it clear in an emotional farewell from the pavilion balcony during the last home match that the decision was not of his choosing.

A financial settlement was agreed and peace of a sort declared when Turner was made a life vice-president and re-engaged to act as a consultant in ground development. But it was difficult to avoid the verdict that one of cricket's most accomplished administrators had been unceremoniously dumped by a committee who appeared to pay only reluctant lip service to his colossal achievements. Turner had been the catalyst for all Leicestershire's successes in his time, on the field and round Grace Road, and even his detractors could not really quarrel with his record.

It was not a pleasant season. At the end of July, the decision to replace Winston Benjamin as the overseas player with his West Indian team-mate Phil Simmons brought a public expression of dismay from Benjamin, who felt he had been treated shabbily. Already unhappy about the quality of Grace Road pitches, Benjamin had a final fling when he took out his frustration on the Kent batsmen; after that he found his motivation irreparably damaged and appeared in only one more Championship match. He has now signed for Hampshire. Laurie Potter also departed at the end of the year, having decided not to seek a new contract, as did Justin Benson, who was not offered one. A threat that Alan Mullally might also leave receded when the Australian-raised, England-qualified, left-arm seamer ended a pay dispute by signing a three-year deal.

Mullally's 62 wickets at 24.29 brought him into contention for winter tour selection but, with David Millns absent until August because of an Achilles tendon injury sustained on the preceding winter's England A tour, Leicestershire's attack lacked a cutting edge. Neither the robust all-round contribution of their player of the year, Gordon Parsons, nor the promise of off-spinner Adrian Pierson was adequate compensation. In addition to claiming 45 first-class wickets, Parsons was both leading batsman and bowler in the Sunday League. Pitches tended to be prepared with the spinners in mind and this led to the blunting of the quicker bowlers' pace and the undermining of some batsmen's confidence.

No batsman reached 1,000 first-class runs, and captain Nigel Briers's season ended abruptly when he ruptured an Achilles tendon in the first week of August. That provided James Whitaker with an opportunity to captain the side, which seemed to have a beneficial effect on his batting. His century against Yorkshire in September was his first for almost two years. Tim Boon was the only batsman to score more than one century. Ben Smith has still to advance his status after starting with promise two summers ago and more than a quarter of Vince Wells's 602 runs came in one innings.

Although they won four matches in five during June and July, Leicestershire were ill-equipped to mount a sustained Championship bid. A run in the Benson and Hedges Cup raised hopes of a second consecutive one-day final but Lancashire won by a wide margin in the semi-final at Grace Road and the club's NatWest Trophy ambitions ended in the second round. Four of the first five Sunday League matches were won but a run of nine defeats in the next ten was interrupted only when the match against Surrey at Grace Road in July was embarrassingly abandoned because of an unfit pitch.

The arrival of Simmons should bolster the batting, in limited-overs as well as four-day matches, and his seam bowling could be a valuable support to Millns and Mullally, a potent new-ball combination when both are fit. Matthew Brimson, a left-arm spinner from Durham University who made his debut in 1993, is regarded as having much potential. – Jon Culley.

LEICESTERSHIRE 1993

Back row: N. S. de Silva, P. A. Nixon, A. F. Haye, S. Atkinson, A. D. Mullally, A. R. K. Pierson, J. M. Dakin, M. T. Brimson, D. L. Maddy. *Middle row:* R. Stenner (*physiotherapist*), B. F. Smith, R. A. Cobb, V. J. Wells, L. Potter, D. J. Millns, P. E. Robinson, J. D. R. Benson, P. N. Hepworth, G. R. Blackburn (*scorer*). *Front row:* P. Whiticase, T. J. Boon, J. M. Benson, J. Birkenshaw (*manager*), B. A. F. Smith (*president*), N. E. Briers (*captain*), F. M. Turner (*chief executive*), J. J. Whitaker, G. J. Parsons.

[*Bill Smith*]

LEICESTERSHIRE RESULTS

All first-class matches – Played 19; Won 6, Lost 6, Drawn 7.

County Championship matches – Played 17; Won 6, Lost 5, Drawn 6.

Bonus points – Batting 23, Bowling 61.

Competition placings – Britannic Assurance County Championship, 9th;
NatWest Bank Trophy, 2nd round; Benson and Hedges Cup, s-f;
AXA Equity & Law League, 14th.

BRITANNIC ASSURANCE CHAMPIONSHIP AVERAGES

BATTING

	Birthplace	M	I	NO	R	HS	Avge
J. D. R. Benson	Dublin, Ireland	5	6	0	232	153	38.66
‡J. J. Whitaker......	Skipton	17	26	1	889	126	35.56
‡T. J. Boon	Doncaster	17	27	1	878	110	33.76
V. J. Wells	Dartford	13	20	2	575	167	31.94
‡N. E. Briers	Leicester	11	17	1	451	79	28.18
P. N. Hepworth	Ackworth	6	10	0	271	129	27.10
P. A. Nixon	Carlisle	17	25	6	475	113*	25.00
‡G. J. Parsons	Slough	16	20	6	338	49*	24.14
‡W. K. M. Benjamin§	St John's, Antigua	9	13	0	294	83	22.61
‡L. Potter	Bexleyheath	11	16	1	301	62	20.06
P. E. Robinson	Keighley	16	26	3	451	71	19.60
B. F. Smith	Corby	9	15	0	215	84	14.33
A. R. K. Pierson ...	Enfield	16	21	5	223	58	13.93
‡D. J. Millns	Clipstone	7	8	3	59	24	11.80
‡A. D. Mullally	Southend-on-Sea	15	18	4	125	26	8.92

Also batted: M. T. Brimson (*Plumstead*) (2 matches) 0.

* *Signifies not out.*   ‡ *Denotes county cap.*   § *Overseas player.*

The following played a total of seven three-figure innings for Leicestershire in County Championship matches – T. J. Boon 2, J. D. R. Benson 1, P. N. Hepworth 1, P. A. Nixon 1, V. J. Wells 1, J. J. Whitaker 1.

BOWLING

	O	M	R	W	BB	5W/i	Avge
W. K. M. Benjamin ...	281.3	81	702	32	7-83	3	21.93
A. D. Mullally	473.1	123	1,371	59	7-72	2	23.23
D. J. Millns	184.3	51	584	25	5-21	2	23.36
G. J. Parsons	432.1	134	976	40	3-23	0	24.40
A. R. K. Pierson	466	125	1,160	41	6-87	4	28.29
L. Potter	322.3	111	707	22	5-45	1	32.13
V. J. Wells	204.4	57	595	14	2-5	0	42.50

Also bowled: T. J. Boon 8-1-38-0; M. T. Brimson 20-3-66-2; P. N. Hepworth 16-2-55-1; P. E. Robinson 13.3-1-78-1; B. F. Smith 6-2-8-0.

Wicket-keeper: P. A. Nixon 39 ct, 4 st.

Leading Fielder: P. E. Robinson 20.

LEICESTERSHIRE v SURREY

At Leicester, April 29, 30, May 1, 2. Surrey won by 89 runs. Surrey 21 pts, Leicestershire 6 pts. Toss: Surrey. County debuts: A. R. K. Pierson; G. J. Kersey.

Leicestershire, chasing 306 from 94 overs, looked reasonably placed at tea on the last day with two wickets down and 136 wanted, but the Surrey seamers claimed the last eight wickets for 43. Leicestershire's two quickest bowlers were absent, Benjamin with West Indies and Millns nursing his Achilles tendon. Consolation came from Pierson, newly arrived from Warwickshire. The tall off-spinner bowled with a teasing loop and found turn from the start, compiling match figures of nine for 181. The first three wickets went to slow bowling, with both openers stumped; Brown apart, Surrey struggled to build on Darren Bicknell's fifty. Briers made barely a false stroke in organising a Leicestershire recovery from 98 for five next day, to achieve a ten-run first-innings lead. But a four-and-a-half-hour century from Stewart regained the advantage for Surrey. Boon then seemed to be heading for his hundred and a home win, until he became frustrated by a defensive field and Leicestershire fell apart.

Close of play: First day, Leicestershire 18-1 (N. E. Briers 9*, A. R. K. Pierson 0*); Second day, Surrey 5-0 (D. J. Bicknell 5*, A. J. Stewart 0*); Third day, Surrey 299-9 (G. J. Kersey 25*, A. J. Murphy 4*).

Surrey

D. J. Bicknell st Nixon b Potter	50	– c Whitaker b Pierson	41
*A. J. Stewart st Nixon b Pierson	27	– c Robinson b Pierson	109
G. P. Thorpe c Nixon b Potter	23	– run out	21
M. A. Lynch c Robinson b Mullally	23	– b Pierson	20
D. M. Ward c Nixon b Mullally	12	– st Nixon b Potter	15
A. D. Brown c Potter b Pierson	49	– c Wells b Potter	21
†G. J. Kersey lbw b Pierson	11	– not out	38
M. P. Bicknell c Potter b Parsons	20	– c Boon b Pierson	14
N. M. Kendrick c Robinson b Pierson	7	– lbw b Potter	4
J. E. Benjamin c Potter b Parsons	12	– b Pierson	8
A. J. Murphy not out	3	– b Mullally	7
B 1, l-b 1, n-b 6	8	B 5, l-b 11, w 1	17
	245		**315**

1/70 2/104 3/111 4/134 5/149   1/68 2/120 3/160 4/207 5/237
6/194 7/203 8/216 9/238   6/249 7/274 8/285 9/294

Bonus points – Surrey 1, Leicestershire 4.

Bowling: *First Innings*—Mullally 25–8–70–2; Parsons 12.2–4–37–2; Wells 13–5–19–0; Pierson 32–7–57–4; Potter 26–10–60–2. *Second Innings*—Mullally 24–10–49–1; Parsons 10–4–22–0; Pierson 50–15–124–5; Potter 46–17–79–3; Wells 7–2–25–0.

Leicestershire

T. J. Boon c Thorpe b Murphy	3	– c Kersey b Murphy	91
*N. E. Briers lbw b Benjamin	79	– c Lynch b M. P. Bicknell	11
A. R. K. Pierson b Benjamin	0	– (10) c Kersey b M. P. Bicknell	1
J. J. Whitaker c and b M. P. Bicknell	9	– (3) lbw b Benjamin	42
P. E. Robinson c Kendrick b Thorpe	6	– (4) b Murphy	24
B. F. Smith c Thorpe b Murphy	5	– (5) c Murphy b M. P. Bicknell	9
L. Potter c Lynch b Kendrick	21	– (6) c and b M. P. Bicknell	4
V. J. Wells c Brown b Murphy	47	– (7) not out	16
†P. A. Nixon c Kersey b Kendrick	7	– (8) c Kersey b Murphy	6
G. J. Parsons not out	29	– (9) lbw b Benjamin	0
A. D. Mullally c Ward b Benjamin	8	– c M. P. Bicknell b Benjamin	1
B 1, l-b 10, w 1, n-b 29	41	B 1, l-b 3, w 1, n-b 6	11
	255		**216**

1/12 2/25 3/46 4/57 5/98   1/29 2/138 3/173 4/178 5/190
6/150 7/183 8/191 9/236   6/190 7/207 8/212 9/215

Bonus points – Leicestershire 2, Surrey 4.

Bowling: *First Innings*—M. P. Bicknell 19-4-46-1; Benjamin 30.5-4-86-3; Murphy 26-10-55-3; Thorpe 10-3-29-1; Kendrick 20-11-28-2. *Second Innings*—M. P. Bicknell 26-9-53-4; Benjamin 21.1-3-63-3; Murphy 25-10-56-3; Kendrick 15-4-40-0.

Umpires: J. D. Bond and A. G. T. Whitehead.

LEICESTERSHIRE v NOTTINGHAMSHIRE

At Leicester, May 6, 7, 8, 10. Nottinghamshire won by eight wickets. Nottinghamshire 22 pts, Leicestershire 5 pts. Toss: Leicestershire.

A groin injury cost Lewis the chance to play against his old county but Nottinghamshire's bowlers were still able to instigate two collapses and claim victory early on the final day. Mistrust of a slow Leicestershire's approach: Briers stayed four and a quarter hours for 53 but, as in the previous match, the Leicestershire lower order crumpled, eight wickets falling for 86. After Randall was out first ball, Robinson led Nottinghamshire towards the lead, but Potter disrupted things by claiming five wickets in an innings with his left-arm spin for the first time in a career which began in 1981. Whitaker, who passed 50 for the first time in 11 months, then held Leicestershire in check for a while, but the spinners Field-Buss and Afford removed the last five batsmen for 15 and Nottinghamshire were left with more than a day to score 143.

Close of play: First day, Leicestershire 219; Second day, Nottinghamshire 280; Third day, Nottinghamshire 46-1 (P. R. Pollard 13*, R. T. Robinson 6*).

Leicestershire

T. J. Boon c Pollard b Afford	46	– c Crawley b Cairns	9
*N. E. Briers run out	53	– c French b Pennett	1
J. J. Whitaker c Crawley b Cairns	11	– b Field-Buss	93
P. E. Robinson c French b Pennett	17	– b Pick	3
B. F. Smith c Cairns	0	– c Afford b Cairns	41
L. Potter c Pollard b Pennett	32	– lbw b Afford	4
V. J. Wells st French b Field-Buss	1	– c Robinson b Field-Buss	28
†P. A. Nixon c Crawley b Afford	11	– c Pollard b Field-Buss	2
G. J. Parsons run out	7	– c Randall b Afford	0
A. R. K. Pierson c French b Cairns	1	– lbw b Afford	9
A. D. Mullally not out	11	– not out	0
L-b 19, n-b 10	29	B 1, l-b 8, n-b 4	13

1/70 2/89 3/133 4/134 5/156 219 1/2 2/26 3/48 4/118 5/130 203
6/158 7/195 8/197 9/199   6/188 7/193 8/194 9/198

Bonus points – Leicestershire 1, Nottinghamshire 4.

Bowling: *First Innings*—Pick 18-5-44-0; Cairns 21.2-3-50-3; Pennett 25-10-42-2; Afford 29-13-44-2; Field-Buss 13-6-20-1. *Second Innings*—Cairns 14-3-32-2; Pennett 14-2-39-1; Pick 12-3-42-1; Afford 22.3-8-53-3; Field-Buss 16-7-28-3.

Nottinghamshire

P. R. Pollard c Whitaker b Potter	28	– not out	51
D. W. Randall c Robinson b Mullally	0	– c Robinson b Pierson	20
*R. T. Robinson c Pierson b Potter	70	– c Mullally b Potter	18
M. A. Crawley c Robinson b Mullally	0	– not out	38
G. F. Archer lbw b Parsons	48		
C. L. Cairns c Potter b Parsons	28		
†B. N. French c Parsons b Potter	54		
R. A. Pick c Wells b Potter	12		
M. G. Field-Buss c Robinson b Parsons	12		
D. B. Pennett lbw b Potter	0		
J. A. Afford not out	5		
B 10, l-b 7, n-b 6	23	B 7, l-b 8, w 1	16

1/1 2/99 3/108 4/112 5/167 280 1/39 2/70 (2 wkts) 143
6/198 7/233 8/266 9/267

Bonus points – Nottinghamshire 2, Leicestershire 4.

Bowling: *First Innings*—Mullally 24–5–65–2; Parsons 24–7–61–3; Wells 7–2–32–0; Pierson 25–9–60–0; Potter 32–17–45–5. *Second Innings*—Mullally 6–1–8–0; Parsons 9–3–17–0; Pierson 22–4–61–1; Potter 20.1–6–39–1; Smith 2–0–3–0.

Umpires: D. O. Oslear and G. A. Stickley.

At Cambridge, May 15, 16, 17. LEICESTERSHIRE drew with CAMBRIDGE UNIVERSITY.

At Horsham, May 20, 21, 22. LEICESTERSHIRE lost to SUSSEX by an innings and 102 runs.

At Leicester, May 29, 30, 31. LEICESTERSHIRE lost to AUSTRALIANS by 97 runs (See Australian tour section).

LEICESTERSHIRE v DURHAM

At Leicester, June 3, 4, 5. Leicestershire won by an innings and five runs. Leicestershire 23 pts, Durham 3 pts. Toss: Leicestershire.

After losing their first three Championship matches Leicestershire secured victory this time with a day to spare. The match mixed explosive passages with interminably dull ones. On the first day Durham plodded along at less than two runs an over on a damp, seaming pitch, Parker's 39 lasting three hours 43 minutes; Benjamin bowled 13 maidens in 19 overs. In improving conditions, Boon spent almost five hours constructing his first century since May 1992, but Leicestershire seemed destined for a modest total until Benjamin savaged Durham's attack, by then deprived of the injured Cummins, for 83. Even after Daley caught Benjamin off a fierce square cut, the last pair, Mullally and Parsons, put on 34. Botham, opening as stand-in for Larkins, who had been hit by Benjamin, struck a violent 65 in 80 balls before Benjamin bowled him with an in-swinging yorker, and Parker offered dashing accompaniment. But later only Daley could delay Leicestershire.

Close of play: First day, Leicestershire 11-0 (T. J. Boon 4*, N. E. Briers 3*); Second day, Leicestershire 330-8 (W. K. M. Benjamin 81*, G. J. Parsons 19*).

Durham

P. W. G. Parker c Mullally b Parsons	39	– (2) c Briers b Wells	58
W. Larkins retired hurt	4	– (8) c Boon b Potter	15
I. Smith c Robinson b Benjamin	4	– c Robinson b Benjamin	8
P. Bainbridge c Benjamin b Potter	22	– b Mullally	8
J. A. Daley c Benjamin b Potter	37	– c Nixon b Parsons	32
I. T. Botham c Nixon b Potter	24	– (1) b Benjamin	65
A. C. Cummins c Potter b Mullally	8	– lbw b Mullally	0
P. J. Berry c Nixon b Potter	10	– (6) c Robinson b Potter	9
†A. R. Fothergill b Mullally	2	– b Parsons	5
*D. A. Graveney c Benjamin b Mullally	4	– b Parsons	0
S. J. E. Brown not out	0	– not out	0
L-b 4, n-b 2	6	L-b 3, w 1, n-b 2	6

1/9 2/45 3/95 4/133 5/138   160   1/95 2/111 3/142 4/142 5/171   206
6/154 7/156 8/160 9/160   6/174 7/201 8/201 9/201

Bonus points – Leicestershire 4.

In the first innings W. Larkins retired hurt at 5.

Bowling: *First Innings*—Benjamin 19–13–24–1; Mullally 18.4–10–25–3; Parsons 16–6–29–1; Wells 15–5–32–0; Potter 23–7–46–4. *Second Innings*—Benjamin 13–0–50–2; Mullally 16–7–45–2; Parsons 10–2–30–3; Potter 20–7–53–2; Wells 7–2–25–1.

Leicestershire

T. J. Boon c and b Berry	105	W. K. M. Benjamin c Daley b Brown	83
*N. E. Briers c Botham b Brown	18	G. J. Parsons not out	27
J. J. Whitaker lbw b Graveney	46	A. D. Mullally c Bainbridge b Brown	26
P. E. Robinson c Fothergill b Cummins	5		
B. F. Smith b Cummins	4	B 8, l-b 3, n-b 12	23
L. Potter c Fothergill b Bainbridge	30		
V. J. Wells c Daley b Bainbridge	1	1/50 2/126 3/131 4/143 5/211	371
†P. A. Nixon b Bainbridge	3	6/220 7/223 8/248 9/337	

Bonus points – Leicestershire 3, Durham 3 (Score at 120 overs: 331-8).

Bowling: Cummins 19-2-58-2; Brown 31.2-3-102-3; Botham 18-8-27-0; Graveney 33-8-74-1; Berry 12-3-45-1; Bainbridge 17-4-54-3.

Umpires: A. A. Jones and R. Palmer.

At Worcester, June 10, 11, 12, 14. LEICESTERSHIRE drew with WORCESTERSHIRE.

LEICESTERSHIRE v GLOUCESTERSHIRE

At Leicester, June 24, 25, 26, 28. Leicestershire won by five wickets. Leicestershire 24 pts, Gloucestershire 3 pts. Toss: Gloucestershire.

Leicestershire's second Championship win was achieved with only four balls to spare after Gloucestershire put up stiffer resistance than expected. Mullally found plenty of edges to return a career-best seven for 72 on the first day, but Hodgson saved face on a docile pitch with a workmanlike 79, supported by a maiden fifty for the county by Wight, before Walsh and Cooper smashed 54 in eight overs. However, against an attack weakened by a hamstring injury to Cooper, Leicestershire compiled their largest total since May 1990, dominated by Benson, who hit a career-best 153 in his first Championship innings of the season. Gloucestershire resumed 209 adrift, but Hodgson dug in again for four and three-quarter hours, and though Gloucestershire started the last day only 11 runs on they kept Leicestershire in the field until tea and set them 168 from 34 overs. Walsh bowled a magnificent 16 overs unchanged, but his rhythm was disturbed when Wright asked him to change ends to bowl the last over: a high full toss provided four byes and Robinson steered the winning single.

Close of play: First day, Leicestershire 85-1 (T. J. Boon 41*, J. J. Whitaker 27*); Second day, Leicestershire 433-7 (J. D. R. Benson 153*, G. J. Parsons 12*); Third day, Gloucestershire 220-4 (A. J. Wright 7*, R. C. Russell 24*).

Gloucestershire

B. C. Broad c Nixon b Mullally	15	– b Pierson	56
G. D. Hodgson c Nixon b Mullally	79	– c Benjamin b Pierson	89
M. W. Alleyne b Benjamin b Mullally	12	– c Robinson b Pierson	2
T. H. C. Hancock c Benson b Mullally	2	– c Benson b Potter	33
*A. J. Wright lbw b Parsons	0	– c and b Pierson	28
†R. C. Russell c Potter b Mullally	0	– c Nixon b Mullally	64
R. M. Wight c Benson b Parsons	54	– b Pierson	2
R. C. Williams lbw b Mullally	0	– c Benson b Mullally	38
M. Davies c Benjamin b Parsons	4	– c Nixon b Mullally	26
C. A. Walsh not out	40	– lbw b Parsons	10
K. E. Cooper c Potter b Mullally	25	– not out	0
L-b 12, w 2	14	B 10, l-b 14, w 2, n-b 2	28

1/28 2/46 3/54 4/71 5/80	245	1/91 2/101 3/186 4/188 5/283	376
6/165 7/165 8/180 9/191		6/291 7/294 8/361 9/370	

Bonus points – Gloucestershire 1, Leicestershire 4.

Bowling: *First Innings*—Benjamin 16-1-49-0; Mullally 23.4-6-72-7; Parsons 20-5-59-3; Pierson 6-0-21-0; Potter 10-4-32-0. *Second Innings*—Benjamin 26-6-58-0; Mullally 31-6-98-3; Parsons 30.4-9-72-1; Pierson 50-18-72-5; Potter 29-11-52-1.

Leicestershire

T. J. Boon c Cooper b Wight	85	– lbw b Davies	15
*N. E. Briers lbw b Cooper	4	– c Wight b Davies	47
J. J. Whitaker c Russell b Walsh	41	– c Wright b Walsh	20
J. D. R. Benson b Walsh	153	– lbw b Walsh	8
P. E. Robinson b Walsh	5	– (6) not out	29
L. Potter st Russell b Davies	62		
W. K. M. Benjamin c Russell b Williams	35	– (5) b Davies	13
†P. A. Nixon b Williams	9	– (7) not out	17
G. J. Parsons lbw b Williams	16		
A. R. K. Pierson not out	4		
A. D. Mullally c Russell b Walsh	5		
B 3, l-b 13, w 1, n-b 18	35	B 8, l-b 7, n-b 4	19

1/12 2/103 3/207 4/221 5/344   **454**   1/37 2/86 3/96   (5 wkts) **168**
6/391 7/413 8/442 9/449   4/104 5/114

Bonus points – Leicestershire 4, Gloucestershire 2 (Score at 120 overs: 357-5).

Bowling: *First Innings*—Walsh 34–12–70–4; Cooper 22.1–7–56–1; Williams 33–7–101–3; Wight 34–9–85–1; Davies 30–7–119–1; Alleyne 3–1–7–0. *Second Innings*—Walsh 16.2–3–55–2; Williams 5–0–32–0; Davies 12–0–66–3.

Umpires: J. C. Balderstone and A. G. T. Whitehead.

LEICESTERSHIRE v LANCASHIRE

At Leicester, July 1, 2, 3. Leicestershire won by an innings and 58 runs. Leicestershire 23 pts, Lancashire 4 pts. Toss: Leicestershire.

A handsome victory over third-placed Lancashire, with more than a day to spare, continued the turnaround in Leicestershire's Championship form since losing their first three matches. Leicestershire lost their grip only briefly, on the first day, when four mid-innings wickets fell for one run. But Nixon and Pierson both achieved their highest scores to ensure that the efforts of Boon and Briers, who provided their county's first century opening partnership of the summer, were not wasted. The last three wickets added 240. Aside from Speak in the first innings and Lloyd in the second, Lancashire's batting was feeble even while the pitch was at its most benign on the second afternoon. Fairbrother succumbed without scoring twice, the second time attempting to sweep a full-pitched first ball from the off-spinner, Pierson – a dreadful shot but symptomatic of a general malaise. Benjamin's destruction of Lancashire's first attempt earned him Championship-best figures of seven for 83; Pierson wrapped up the follow-on on a deteriorating pitch with six wickets, his best return since joining Leicestershire.

Close of play: First day, Leicestershire 287-8 (P. A. Nixon 35*); Second day, Lancashire 148-7 (M. Watkinson 28*, W. K. Hegg 8*).

Leicestershire

T. J. Boon c Lloyd b Chapple	85	G. J. Parsons lbw b Watkinson	33
*N. E. Briers lbw b DeFreitas	58	A. R. K. Pierson c Wasim Akram	
J. J. Whitaker c Hegg b DeFreitas	15	b Watkinson	58
J. D. R. Benson c Titchard b Barnett	17	A. D. Mullally c Barnett b Chapple	23
P. E. Robinson b Barnett	22		
L. Potter lbw b Watkinson	0	B 17, l-b 3, w 3, n-b 8	31
W. K. M. Benjamin c Watkinson			
b Barnett	0	1/132 2/160 3/170 4/214 5/215	**455**
†P. A. Nixon not out	113	6/215 7/215 8/287 9/406	

Bonus points – Leicestershire 3, Lancashire 3 (Score at 120 overs: 300-8).

Bowling: DeFreitas 30–6–70–2; Wasim Akram 24–6–47–0; Watkinson 48–18–119–3; Chapple 25.3–0–101–2; Barnett 41–11–98–3.

Lancashire

J. D. Mendis c Robinson b Benjamin	6	– c Benjamin b Pierson 26
P. Titchard c Nixon b Benjamin	11	– b Pierson 14
J. J. Speak lbw b Parsons	64	– st Nixon b Potter 7
N. H. Fairbrother b Benjamin	0	– lbw b Pierson 0
G. D. Lloyd c Nixon b Benjamin	0	– lbw b Parsons 75
Wasim Akram c Benjamin b Pierson	24	– b Potter 2
*A. J. DeFreitas lbw b Parsons	1	– c Robinson b Pierson 0
M. Watkinson c Boon b Benjamin	43	– b Pierson 10
†W. K. Hegg c Nixon b Benjamin	25	– c Nixon b Parsons 28
G. Chapple not out	16	– not out 8
A. A. Barnett lbw b Benjamin	1	– c Briers b Pierson 9
B 4, l-b 5, w 2, n-b 2	13	B 4, l-b 10 14
	204	**193**

1/6 2/45 3/45 4/45 5/103
1/33 2/42 3/42 4/48 5/52
1/104 7/129 8/175 9/184
6/59 7/87 8/162 9/178

Bonus points – Lancashire 1, Leicestershire 4.

Bowling: *First Innings*—Benjamin 23.3–3–83–7; Mullally 14–2–58–0; Pierson 11–5–12–1; Parsons 18–6–42–2. *Second Innings*—Benjamin 5–3–10–0; Mullally 5–0–14–0; Parsons 10–2–33–2; Potter 21–10–35–2; Pierson 19.3–3–87–6.

Umpires: J. H. Hampshire and N. T. Plews.

At Southend, July 15, 16, 17, 19. LEICESTERSHIRE beat ESSEX by 77 runs.

LEICESTERSHIRE v WARWICKSHIRE

At Leicester, July 22, 23, 24, 26. Drawn. Leicestershire 4 pts, Warwickshire 6 pts. Toss: Leicestershire.

Worsening weather permitted only 58 overs on the second day, 35.2 on the third and a mere 22 balls on the fourth. Perhaps mindful of a damp patch on the wicket at the pavilion end, Warwickshire's batsmen seemed excessively guarded as they occupied most of an uninterrupted first day. Ostler's fifty was a modest highlight, though Pierson, bowling creditably against his old county, helped ensure that no one offered him prolonged support. A stop-start second day kept Donald fresh enough to derail Leicestershire's reply at 54 for six, in his last Championship match before joining South Africa's tour of Sri Lanka. But though Warwickshire's spinners made the ball bite during the two hours possible on the third afternoon, Nixon applied himself steadfastly to save the follow-on.

Close of play: First day, Leicestershire 6-1 (T. J. Boon 6*, A. R. K. Pierson 0*); Second day, Leicestershire 103-6 (L. Potter 24*, P. A. Nixon 15*); Third day, Leicestershire 188.

Warwickshire

A. J. Moles lbw b Mullally	20	– not out 6
J. D. Ratcliffe c Benson b Pierson	14	– lbw b Benjamin 2
D. P. Ostler lbw b Benjamin	51	– not out 1
T. L. Penney c Benjamin b Pierson	17	
D. A. Reeve c Benson b Mullally	31	
P. A. Smith c Mullally b Pierson	47	
N. M. K. Smith lbw b Mullally	0	
†K. J. Piper run out	52	
P. A. Booth not out	17	
A. A. Donald b Parsons	0	
M. A. V. Bell c Benjamin b Potter	0	
B 6, l-b 8, w 1, n-b 20	35	L-b 2 2
	284	**(1 wkt) 11**

1/44 2/60 3/96 4/138 5/191
1/9
6/191 7/231 8/278 9/283

Bonus points – Warwickshire 2, Leicestershire 4.

Bowling: *First Innings*—Benjamin 20–5–60–1; Mullally 21–6–64–3; Pierson 29–6–86–3; Potter 16.4–5–31–1; Parsons 18–9–29–1. *Second Innings*—Benjamin 2–1–4–1; Mullally 1.4–0–5–0.

Leicestershire

T. J. Boon lbw b Reeve	7	W. K. M. Benjamin c Reeve b Booth	1
*N. E. Briers b Donald	0	G. J. Parsons lbw b Donald	18
A. R. K. Pierson c Donald b Reeve	22	A. D. Mullally b Donald	2
J. J. Whitaker c Piper b Donald	10		
J. D. R. Benson c Piper b Donald	2	B 3, l-b 13, w 4, n-b 6	26
P. E. Robinson b Donald	8		
L. Potter c Ostler b N. M. K. Smith	28	1/5 2/7 3/32 4/34 5/52	188
†P. A. Nixon not out	64	6/54 7/117 8/122 9/172	

Bonus points – Warwickshire 4.

Bowling: Donald 25.2–9–57–6; N. M. K. Smith 27–6–54–1; Reeve 20–12–20–2; Bell 8–3–13–0; Booth 15–3–28–1.

Umpires: V. A. Holder and A. G. T. Whitehead.

At Canterbury, July 29, 30, 31, August 2. LEICESTERSHIRE lost to KENT by three wickets.

At Lord's, August 5, 6, 7. LEICESTERSHIRE lost to MIDDLESEX by an innings and 184 runs.

LEICESTERSHIRE v GLAMORGAN

At Leicester, August 12, 13, 14, 16. Drawn. Leicestershire 3 pts, Glamorgan 8 pts. Toss: Glamorgan. First-class debut: M. T. Brimson.

Although most of the first day was washed out, Glamorgan's failure to close the gap on Middlesex ultimately owed more to a partnership only 11 short of Leicestershire's second-wicket record. Unflappable application earned Hepworth in his first Championship match of 1993 – a career-best 129 and Wells a maiden century as they added 278 over five hours and 40 minutes. During the 11.1 overs bowled on the first day Millns, making his first home appearance of the season, removed both Glamorgan openers. But his lack of fitness told later, and without Benjamin (released) and Mullally (injured) Leicestershire could not exploit a greenish wicket. A brilliant 82 in 87 balls from Maynard, followed by a prosaic partnership of 161 between Cottey and Hemp, put Glamorgan in control, though the stand ended when both fell in quick succession to the left-arm spin of newcomer Matthew Brimson. Leicestershire were five for three in reply until Whitaker, the acting-captain, dug in for almost five hours. Barwick, helped by the low bounce, conceded only 28 runs in 27 overs. Watkin dismissed Boon quickly as Leicestershire followed on but the pitch eased and Hepworth and Wells denied Glamorgan another wicket until 4.35 p.m. on the final afternoon.

Close of play: First day, Glamorgan 28-2 (A. Dale 2*, M. P. Maynard 14*); Second day, Leicestershire 4-2 (P. N. Hepworth 2*, J. J. Whitaker 0*); Third day, Leicestershire 50-1 (P. N. Hepworth 22*, V. J. Wells 20*).

Glamorgan

S. P. James c Nixon b Millns	8	R. P. Lefebvre c Wells b Parsons	24
*H. Morris c Robinson b Millns	3	S. L. Watkin not out	7
A. Dale c and b Wells	22		
M. P. Maynard c Millns b Wells	82	B 1, l-b 7, w 1, n-b 4	13
P. A. Cottey b Brimson	105		
D. L. Hemp c Parsons b Brimson	62	1/10 2/12 3/104	(8 wkts dec.) 351
R. D. B. Croft lbw b Hepworth	7	4/129 5/290 6/291	
†C. P. Metson not out	18	7/299 8/340	

S. R. Barwick did not bat.

Bonus points – Glamorgan 4, Leicestershire 3.

Bowling: Millns 24–5–92–2; Parsons 27–4–74–1; Wells 12–2–39–2; Brimson 20–3–66–2; Pierson 16–3–55–0; Hepworth 7–1–17–1.

Leicestershire

T. J. Boon c Cottey b Watkin	1	– c Morris b Watkin	7
P. N. Hepworth c Croft b Watkin	3	– c Morris b Dale	129
†P. A. Nixon b Barwick	1	– (6) not out	2
*J. J. Whitaker c Cottey b Watkin	75		
V. J. Wells c Dale b Barwick	20	– (3) c Lefebvre b Croft	167
P. E. Robinson lbw b Dale	7	– (5) not out	7
B. F. Smith lbw b Watkin	22	– (4) b Dale	1
G. J. Parsons c Cottey b Barwick	36		
A. R. K. Pierson not out	6		
D. J. Millns c Watkin b Croft	1		
M. T. Brimson c Metson b Croft	0		
B 3, l-b 1, n-b 2	6	L-b 2	2

1/2 2/3 3/5 4/44 5/64   178   1/8 2/286 3/300   (4 wkts dec.) 315
6/92 7/160 8/177 9/178   4/306

Bonus points – Glamorgan 4.

Bowling: *First Innings*—Watkin 23–8–49–4; Lefebvre 18–7–35–0; Barwick 27–17–28–3; Dale 13–6–24–1; Croft 18.4–6–38–2. *Second Innings*—Watkin 20–6–52–1; Lefebvre 16–4–33–0; Barwick 25–11–51–0; Dale 26.3–3–90–2; Croft 33–12–85–1; Cottey 1–0–2–0.

Umpires: H. D. Bird and B. Dudleston.

At Weston-super-Mare, August 19, 20, 21. LEICESTERSHIRE beat SOMERSET by an innings and 15 runs.

At Northampton, August 26, 27, 28, 30. LEICESTERSHIRE drew with NORTHAMPTONSHIRE.

LEICESTERSHIRE v YORKSHIRE

At Leicester, August 31, September 1, 2, 3. Leicestershire won by 74 runs. Leicestershire 20 pts, Yorkshire 5 pts. Toss: Yorkshire.

Whitaker's first century for almost two years inspired Leicestershire's sixth Championship success. On a wicket with more pace and bounce than usual at Grace Road, Yorkshire dismissed Leicestershire by 3.30 p.m. on the opening day before achieving a useful first-innings lead of 44. Mullally earned his county cap with five wickets but Byas played what looked a decisive role in holding Yorkshire together. Then Whitaker, whose form had improved markedly since an injury to Briers had caused his elevation to acting-captain, hit 126 before becoming Vaughan's first first-class victim. Leicestershire were indebted to Parsons and Wells, batting at No. 9 with a painful knee, for extending their lead to 227. Yorkshire had more than five sessions to make the runs but the final seven overs of the third day cost them three wickets: Hepworth at extra cover brilliantly caught a full-blooded drive from White and Millns induced two slip catches. Mullally claimed the last three for four runs in 23 balls on the final morning, improving his match analysis to nine for 108.

Close of play: First day, Yorkshire 130-5 (D. Byas 43*, A. P. Grayson 9*); Second day, Leicestershire 190-5 (J. J. Whitaker 111*, G. J. Parsons 19*); Third day, Yorkshire 139-7 (R. D. Stemp 4*).

Leicestershire

T. J. Boon c Blakey b Robinson	14	– c Byas b Gough	20
P. N. Hepworth c Blakey b Hartley	3	– c Blakey b Hartley	3
*J. J. Whitaker c Blakey b Robinson	4	– b Vaughan	126
V. J. Wells c Blakey b White	20	– (9) c Gough b Hartley	35
P. E. Robinson b Stemp	25	– (4) c Kellett b Stemp	7
B. F. Smith lbw b Gough	6	– (5) c Kellett b Stemp	4
†P. A. Nixon b Hartley	18	– (6) b Stemp	8
G. J. Parsons c White b Gough	4	– (7) c Byas b Gough	36
A. R. K. Pierson not out	32	– (8) b Gough	5
D. J. Millns c White b Hartley	5	– lbw b Robinson	4
A. D. Mullally c Moxon b Gough	7	– not out	0
B 4, l-b 6, n-b 10	20	L-b 3, w 2, n-b 18	23

1/7 2/14 3/37 4/64 5/81   158 1/13 2/52 3/75 4/97 5/135 271
6/87 7/94 8/135 9/141   6/215 7/222 8/231 9/271

Bonus points – Yorkshire 4.

Bowling: *First Innings*—Hartley 17–4–53–3; Gough 15.4–2–44–3; Robinson 17–6–31–2; White 5–2–20–1; Stemp 1–1–0–1. *Second Innings*—Hartley 19.1–1–49–2; Gough 22–3–88–3; Robinson 23–4–71–1; Stemp 31–19–33–3; Grayson 4–3–4–0; Vaughan 9–4–23–1.

Yorkshire

*M. D. Moxon c Millns b Mullally	30	– lbw b Millns	42
M. P. Vaughan b Mullally	13	– c Whitaker b Mullally	13
D. Byas b Pierson	62	– lbw b Pierson	12
C. White c Boon b Mullally	0	– c Hepworth b Millns	44
S. A. Kellett c Nixon b Mullally	4	– c Nixon b Parsons	11
†R. J. Blakey c Parsons b Pierson	28	– c Parsons b Millns	7
A. P. Grayson c Nixon b Millns	31	– c Parsons b Millns	1
P. J. Hartley b Millns	0	– (9) not out	9
D. Gough not out	6	– (10) b Mullally	5
R. D. Stemp b Mullally	21	– (8) c Nixon b Mullally	4
M. A. Robinson b Parsons	2	– b Mullally	0
L-b 1, w 2, n-b 2	5	L-b 3, w 2	5

1/28 2/55 3/55 4/63 5/108   202 1/45 2/63 3/89 4/119 5/132 153
6/167 7/168 8/173 9/195   6/134 7/139 8/139 9/153

Bonus points – Yorkshire 1, Leicestershire 4.

Bowling: *First Innings*—Millns 17–3–54–2; Mullally 26–5–67–5; Parsons 18.4–4–44–1; Wells 5–3–10–0; Pierson 13–3–25–2; Hepworth 1–0–1–0. *Second Innings*—Mullally 21.5–8–41–4; Pierson 25–10–38–1; Parsons 17–3–34–1; Millns 18–7–37–4.

Umpires: B. Dudleston and R. Julian.

At Southampton, September 9, 10, 11, 13. LEICESTERSHIRE drew with HAMPSHIRE.

LEICESTERSHIRE v DERBYSHIRE

At Leicester, September 16, 17, 18, 20. Drawn. Leicestershire 4 pts, Derbyshire 2 pts. Toss Leicestershire.

The surprise resignation of Leicestershire's chief executive, Mike Turner, after 33 years in charge, distracted attention from the cricket, but there was not much of that anyway The first two days were washed out and attempts to contrive a result came to nothing on the final afternoon. The contest meandered fairly aimlessly after its belated start. However Steer's maiden fifty for Derbyshire and Hepworth's 50 in Leicestershire's reply were more meaningful than the 94 runs fed to Barnett on the last morning, when Robinson bowled 13.3 overs for 78 runs and took his third wicket in ten years. Barnett's declaration left the home side 51 overs to chase 261 on a pitch aiding bowlers with its movement and uneven bounce. The rain almost certainly spared Leicestershire defeat.

Close of play: First day, No play; Second day, No play; Third day, Leicestershire 128-4 (P. E. Robinson 11*).

Derbyshire

*K. J. Barnett c Wells b Mullally	4	– not out	94
M. J. Vandrau b Mullally	18	– lbw b Robinson	29
T. J. G. O'Gorman c Whitaker b Parsons	11	– not out	45
A. S. Rollins c Boon b Wells	37		
I. G. S. Steer c Parsons b Pierson	67		
D. G. Cork c Nixon b Parsons	13		
F. A. Griffith c Wells b Mullally	5		
†K. M. Krikken c Pierson b Parsons	12		
A. E. Warner lbw b Millns	14		
S. J. Base c Parsons b Millns	11		
O. H. Mortensen not out	3		
B 2, l-b 13, w 3	18	L-b 1, w 2, n-b 4	7

1/10 2/23 3/59 4/91 5/116   213   1/69   (1 wkt dec.) 175
6/125 7/172 8/196 9/198

Bonus points – Derbyshire 1, Leicestershire 4.

Bowling: First Innings—Millns 16.3-2-57-2; Mullally 19-3-62-3; Parsons 14-2-35-3; Wells 9-4-24-1; Pierson 8-1-20-1. *Second Innings*—Wells 7-2-22-0; Pierson 10-7-8-0; Smith 4-2-5-0; Hepworth 6-1-23-0; Robinson 13.3-1-78-1; Boon 8-1-38-0.

Leicestershire

T. J. Boon lbw b Base	7	– c Cork b Mortensen	0
P. N. Hepworth lbw b Base	50	– b Mortensen	16
*J. J. Whitaker b Base	18	– b Warner	13
V. J. Wells lbw b Base	25	– not out	18
P. E. Robinson not out	11	– c Griffith b Warner	1
B. F. Smith (did not bat)		– c O'Gorman b Mortensen	13
†P. A. Nixon (did not bat)		– not out	0
N-b 17	17		

1/41 2/76 3/87 4/128   (4 wkts dec.) 128   1/0 2/29 3/29   (5 wkts) 61
                                                          4/30 5/57

G. J. Parsons, A. R. K. Pierson, D. J. Millns and A. D. Mullally did not bat.

Bonus point – Derbyshire 1.

Bowling: First Innings—Mortensen 11-4-38-0; Warner 5-0-19-0; Base 12-2-35-4; Griffith 6-0-36-0. *Second Innings*—Mortensen 9-1-26-3; Warner 9-1-35-2.

Umpires: J. W. Holder and B. J. Meyer.

MIDDLESEX

Patron: HRH The Duke of Edinburgh
President: D. C. S. Compton
Chairman-Designate: R. V. C. Robins
Chairman, Cricket Committee: R. A. Gale
Secretary: J. Hardstaff
Captain: M. W. Gatting
Coach: D. Bennett
Scorer: 1993 – H. P. H. Sharp
       1994 – M. J. Smith

If ever confirmation was needed of the cricketing adage that bowlers win matches, Middlesex's 1993 Championship success provided it. They won the title without a single batsman scoring 1,000 Championship runs. There were, of course, several reasons for that. It was a 17-match season and nobody went to the crease more than 24 times. Since two matches were won by an innings, three by ten wickets and two by nine wickets, opportunities for the batsmen were limited.

It was the bowlers, especially the spinners, who won the title, and John Emburey in particular had a year to remember. He took 68 wickets at 18.39 apiece and scored 638 runs at an average of 49.07 in his unique and (for the opposition bowlers) frustrating style. Yet it was not just the number of runs he scored, but the state of the game on so many occasions when he scored them. Against Sussex, against Surrey in both innings, against Glamorgan at Cardiff and back at Lord's against Hampshire and Northamptonshire, Emburey and Keith Brown put together partnerships which, on each occasion, turned a none-too-promising position into a match-winning total. Victory was gained in all five of those matches.

For Brown, there was, at last, justification in the selection policy of including him as wicket-keeper principally for his run-scoring potential. Had the Championship been closer, his shortcomings behind the stumps might have been crucial. A missed stumping in the 100th over cost a bowling point against Nottinghamshire and a dropped catch at Scarborough probably made the difference between a draw and a win. Paul Farbrace continued to keep well for the Second XI and also scored heavily in helping them to win their own Championship title, but was not considered for first-team duty. It is generally agreed that there are few better wicket-keepers than Colin Metson, but Bob Gale, chairman of the cricket committee, was significantly non-committal when asked if Metson had he been retained rather than Paul Downton in 1987, would have been playing for the first team. He just said: "It is all about balance."

As far as the Middlesex bowling was concerned, its balance was the envy of the circuit. In Emburey and Philip Tufnell, they still had the best pair of spinners in the county game, more than compensating for any shortcomings in the pace attack. The return to form of Angus Fraser in the latter part of the season was certainly a bonus, but the support seam bowling was not really of Championship-winning calibre. All the bowlers had their moments and the return of Norman Cowans for the games against Northamptonshire at Lord's and Essex at Colchester proved fortuitous. In all four innings, he took vital early wickets which undermined the opposition's confidence even before the spinners entered the attack. But he was released after 14 years with the county at the end of the season and joined Hampshire. Neil Williams, as ever, looked as fast and as dangerous as any of the bowlers, but his appearances were restricted by injury and he did not appear in the last three matches. Mark Feltham proved to be a useful acquisition from Surrey following the departure of Dean Headley and, although his figures with both bat and ball were not exciting, he was an important cog in the machine.

Desmond Haynes had his least productive season for Middlesex and his decline was an important factor in the unsuccessful defence of the Sunday League title – odd, because it might have been thought that Middlesex would have been better suited by the longer, 50-overs format. Three successive victories were achieved in late July to early August, but at no other time could Middlesex win consecutive Sunday games; mainly they failed to score enough runs. In both of the knockout competitions, Middlesex played poorly, losing interest at their first attempt in each competition. The performance at Canterbury in the NatWest Trophy was particularly disappointing.

But the County Championship is the title that all the players still regard as the most rewarding. It represented the eighth title (three Championships, two NatWest Trophies, two Benson and Hedges Cups and one Sunday League) during Gatting's 11-year tenure of office, but the appointment of John Carr as vice-captain indicated that Gatting expected his captaincy to end sooner rather than later. Carr acquitted himself well when suddenly forced to lead the side – after Gatting had put his arm through a dressing-room door during a one-day game with the Australians – and he responded particularly well with the bat. The rest of his season was not as productive as he would have liked, while Mark Ramprakash, in contrast, did not really find form until the latter part of the season.

But somebody always turned up with some runs or wickets to compensate for any loss of form by his colleagues, which was the secret of Middlesex's success. It was very much a team effort, though one drawback was the limited number of opportunities to introduce new, young blood to the side. Eleven players made 13 or more Championship appearances and the average age of those players at the end of the season was 31. Life may have begun at 40 for John Emburey, but if the Middlesex success story is to have future chapters, that average must surely be drastically reduced. – Norman de Mesquita.

MIDDLESEX 1993

[*Bill Smith*]

Back row: A. Habib, R. J. Sims, T. A. Radford, K. P. Dutch, P. Farbrace, M. A. Roseberry, M. Keech. *Middle row*: H. P. H. Sharp (*scorer*), S. Shephard (*physiotherapist*), D. Bennett (*coach*), M. A. Feltham, J. C. Harrison, C. W. Taylor, R. L. Johnson, M. R. Ramprakash, P. N. Weekes, J. C. Pooley, I. J. Gould (*Second XI coach*), A. Jones (*Second XI scorer*). *Front row*: A. R. C. Fraser, P. C. R. Tufnell, N. F. Williams, J. D. Carr, M. W. Gatting (*captain*), J. E. Emburey, N. G. Cowans, K. R. Brown. *Insets*: D. L. Haynes, R. J. Ballinger, D. A. Walker, B. C. Usher.

MIDDLESEX RESULTS

All first-class matches – Played 18 : Won 11, Lost 1, Drawn 6.

County Championship matches – Played 17 : Won 11, Lost 1, Drawn 5.

Bonus points – Batting 37, Bowling 59.

Competition placings – Britannic Assurance County Championship, winners ;
NatWest Bank Trophy, 1st round ; Benson and Hedges Cup, 1st round ;
AXA Equity & Law League, 8th.

BRITANNIC ASSURANCE CHAMPIONSHIP AVERAGES

BATTING

	Birthplace	*M*	*I*	*NO*	*R*	*HS*	*Avge*
‡M. W. Gatting	*Kingsbury*	13	19	4	981	182	65.40
‡J. E. Emburey......	*Peckham*	16	19	6	638	123	49.07
‡P. N. Weekes	*Hackney*	3	4	1	144	47	48.00
‡J. D. Carr	*St John's Wood*	17	24	6	848	192*	47.11
‡K. R. Brown	*Edmonton*	17	22	5	714	88*	42.00
‡D. L. Haynes§	*Holders Hill, Barbados*	15	24	4	793	115	39.65
‡M. R. Ramprakash .	*Bushey*	16	22	1	813	140	38.71
‡M. A. Roseberry...	*Houghton-le-Spring*	15	24	4	679	185	33.95
M. A. Feltham	*St John's Wood*	16	19	4	288	73	19.20
M. Keech	*Hampstead*	4	8	0	137	35	17.12
‡N. F. Williams	*Hope Well, St Vincent*	13	11	1	140	44	14.00
‡P. C. R. Tufnell	*Barnet*	15	13	4	113	30*	12.55
‡A. R. C. Fraser	*Billinge*	16	14	2	106	29	8.83
N. G. Cowans	*Enfield St Mary, Jamaica*	5	4	1	9	7	3.00

Also batted: R. L. Johnson (*Chertsey*) (1 match) 4, 4; J. C. Pooley (*Hammersmith*) (1 match) 33, 7; R. J. Sims (*Hillingdon*) (2 matches) 0; C. W. Taylor (*Banbury*) (1 match) 0, 0. K. P. Dutch (*Harrow*) (1 match) did not bat.

* *Signifies not out.*   ‡ *Denotes county cap.*   § *Overseas player.*

The following played a total of 12 three-figure innings for Middlesex in County Championship matches – M. W. Gatting 3, J. D. Carr 2, J. E. Emburey 2, D. L. Haynes 2, M. R. Ramprakash 2, M. A. Roseberry 1.

BOWLING

	O	*M*	*R*	*W*	*BB*	*5W/i*	*Avge*
N. G. Cowans	69	15	202	15	4-43	0	13.46
J. E. Emburey	662.4	213	1,251	68	8-40	2	18.39
P. C. R. Tufnell	583.5	176	1,210	59	8-29	3	20.50
A. R. C. Fraser	472.5	121	1,219	50	7-40	1	24.38
N. F. Williams	361	61	1,097	39	6-61	1	28.12
M. A. Feltham	327.4	88	905	29	4-48	0	31.20

Also bowled: J. D. Carr 10.5-0-73-4; K. P. Dutch 5-1-18-0; M. W. Gatting 4-0-10-0; D. L. Haynes 7-1-61-1; R. L. Johnson 16-5-58-1; M. Keech 50-16-109-5; M. R. Ramprakash 8.4-1-39-1; C. W. Taylor 30-7-93-1; P. N. Weekes 34-6-95-1.

Wicket-keeper: K. R. Brown 37 ct, 6 st.

Leading Fielders: J. D. Carr 39, J. E. Emburey 18, M. R. Ramprakash 15.

At Cambridge, April 24. COMBINED UNIVERSITIES v MIDDLESEX. Abandoned.

At Bristol, April 29, 30, May 1, 2. MIDDLESEX beat GLOUCESTERSHIRE by four wickets.

At Lord's, May 3. MIDDLESEX lost to AUSTRALIANS by 69 runs (See Australian tour section).

MIDDLESEX v KENT

At Lord's, May 6, 7, 8, 10. Drawn. Middlesex 7 pts, Kent 6 pts. Toss: Kent.

A damp, sluggish pitch made scoring difficult and Kent's first innings of 265 occupied nearly 107 overs, more than half bowled by the spinners, Emburey and Tufnell. In reply, Middlesex did a little better. Carr, acting-captain for Gatting, who was still nursing his arm after an argument with a dressing-room door during the Australian match, scored an admirable unbeaten century to give his side a first-innings lead of 46. Llong, in the Kent team only because of Hooper's late return from the West Indies, scored his maiden Championship century in the second innings and Benson his 43rd first-class hundred as they shared a stand of 203 in 57 overs for the second wicket. But Benson delayed his declaration too long on the final morning. Though Carr played another unbeaten innings, Middlesex made no serious attempt to chase what they saw as an unreasonable target of 347 in 90 overs. The most diverting moment came when Ramprakash complained that he was having difficulty sighting the ball because of the red sweater worn by a lady watching above the sightscreen at the Nursery End; she had to borrow a white cardigan.

Close of play: First day, Middlesex 16-0 (M. A. Roseberry 6*, M. Keech 6*); Second day, Middlesex 291-9 (J. D. Carr 100*, P. C. R. Tufnell 0*); Third day, Kent 335-5 (M. V. Fleming 53*, N. R. Taylor 7*).

Kent

T. R. Ward c and b Feltham	10	– b Williams	9
*M. R. Benson b Tufnell	57	– c Fraser b Emburey	107
N. R. Taylor c Roseberry b Feltham	42	– (7) c Brown b Williams	13
N. J. Llong c Brown b Williams	18	– (3) c Brown b Emburey	108
G. R. Cowdrey b Tufnell	1	– (4) b Feltham	28
M. V. Fleming c Carr b Williams	57	– (5) run out	62
†S. A. Marsh lbw b Tufnell	24	– (6) c Roseberry b Fraser	7
R. P. Davis c Emburey b Williams	2	– not out	24
C. Penn b Emburey	22	– b Williams	2
M. J. McCague st Brown b Tufnell	5	– not out	9
A. P. Igglesden not out	0		
B 3, l-b 12, n-b 12	27	L-b 15, n-b 8	23

1/24 2/109 3/119 4/121 5/186   265   1/20 2/223 3/254   (8 wkts dec.) 392
6/199 7/207 8/250 9/260   4/301 5/323 6/345
                                       7/365 8/377

Bonus points – Kent 2, Middlesex 4.

Bowling: *First Innings*—Feltham 16–5–49–2; Fraser 15–5–24–0; Emburey 30–9–60–1; Williams 13–2–33–3; Tufnell 26.4–9–64–4; Keech 6–1–20–0. *Second Innings*—Feltham 17–1–73–1; Fraser 25–5–76–1; Williams 21–4–53–3; Tufnell 15–2–65–0; Emburey 32–5–110–2.

Middlesex

M. A. Roseberry run out	38	– c Benson b McCague	32
M. Keech b Igglesden	31	– c Marsh b Igglesden	18
M. R. Ramprakash c Marsh b Davis	34	– b McCague	55
*J. D. Carr not out	108	– not out	70
J. C. Pooley b Penn	33	– lbw b Davis	7
†K. R. Brown b Igglesden	3	– b Davis	13
M. A. Feltham lbw b Igglesden	22	– not out	18
J. E. Emburey lbw b Igglesden	0		
N. F. Williams c Ward b Davis	14		
A. R. C. Fraser lbw b Igglesden	0		
P. C. R. Tufnell c McCague b Igglesden	10		
L-b 3, w 1, n-b 14	18	B 7, l-b 5, n-b 6	18

1/61 2/96 3/121 4/190 5/200   311   1/23 2/67 3/150   (5 wkts) 231
6/249 7/249 8/284 9/285   4/165 5/195

Bonus points – Middlesex 3, Kent 4 (Score at 120 overs: 306-9).

Bowling: *First Innings*—McCague 22-7-62-0; Igglesden 29-7-81-5; Penn 24-9-45-2; Fleming 15-3-45-0; Davis 28-8-67-2; Llong 5-0-8-0. *Second Innings*—Igglesden 19-6-48-1; McCague 25-7-65-2; Penn 16-4-28-0; Fleming 2-2-9-0; Davis 19-1-63-2; Llong 2-0-6-0.

Umpires: J. H. Harris and M. J. Kitchen.

MIDDLESEX v NOTTINGHAMSHIRE

At Lord's, May 13, 14, 15, 17. Drawn. Middlesex 5 pts, Nottinghamshire 6 pts. Toss: Middlesex.

Another over-watered pitch restricted strokeplay and Middlesex spent most of the first day making 281, with the courage of Roseberry the highlight of the innings. He retired on two with a broken finger in the sixth over of the day, having suffered a blow from Cairns. But he returned at the fall of the sixth wicket, against the wishes of the team physio-therapist, added 117 with Feltham, and was 79 not out when the innings ended. Notting-hamshire's reply, based round a hundred by Robinson, spread from a rain-affected second day until lunch on the third, when they conceded a lead of 15. The Middlesex second innings was a laborious affair, and though Haynes and Emburey enabled Carr to declare, the final day was dreadful, with Nottinghamshire refusing to chase a more than reasonable target of 282 in more than 80 overs.

Close of play: First day, Nottinghamshire 4-0 (P. R. Pollard 4*, D. W. Randall 0*); Second day, Nottinghamshire 196-3 (P. Johnson 3*, M. A. Crawley 3*); Third day, Middlesex 219-8 (J. E. Emburey 33*, P. C. R. Tufnell 2*).

Middlesex

D. L. Haynes lbw b Cairns	11	– lbw b Cairns	98
M. A. Roseberry not out	79	– (7) b Afford	0
M. R. Ramprakash c Robinson b Cairns	39	– c Robinson b Afford	3
*J. D. Carr b Pick	38	– lbw b Pick	3
M. Keech b Cairns	9	– (2) lbw b Pick	32
†K. R. Brown c French b Afford	14	– (5) c Lewis b Afford	11
M. A. Feltham lbw b Crawley	73		
J. E. Emburey c French b Mike	0	– (6) b Pick	54
N. F. Williams lbw b Lewis	2	– (8) lbw b Cairns	6
A. R. C. Fraser b Cairns	0	– (9) lbw b Afford	16
P. C. R. Tufnell c Randall b Cairns	4	– (10) not out	18
B 4, l-b 4, n-b 4	12	B 4, l-b 13, n-b 8	25

1/13 2/97 3/99 4/117 5/143   281   1/78 2/81 3/92   (9 wkts dec.) 266
6/144 7/261 8/270 9/277   4/131 5/163 6/164
                                     7/171 8/204 9/266

Bonus points – Middlesex 2, Nottinghamshire 4.

In the first innings M. A. Roseberry, when 2, retired hurt at 13-1 and resumed at 144.

Bowling: *First Innings*—Lewis 23–13–37–1; Cairns 22.3–4–68–5; Mike 20–5–56–1; Pick 17–6–55–1; Afford 14–4–25–1; Crawley 9–2–32–1. *Second Innings*—Lewis 19–1–42–0; Cairns 22–3–76–2; Mike 4–0–19–0; Afford 22–8–59–4; Pick 12.2–1–53–3.

Nottinghamshire

P. R. Pollard c Carr b Emburey	70	– (2) c Keech b Tufnell	10
D. W. Randall lbw b Fraser	1	– (1) c Brown b Fraser	24
*R. T. Robinson c Tufnell b Emburey	112	– c Keech b Emburey	69
P. Johnson c Brown b Fraser	11	– c sub b Emburey	52
M. A. Crawley c Emburey b Tufnell	14	– b Tufnell	13
C. L. Cairns b Emburey	8	– c sub b Emburey	20
C. C. Lewis c Keech b Tufnell	28	– not out	17
G. W. Mike lbw b Tufnell	2	– not out	11
†B. N. French b Tufnell	2		
R. A. Pick not out	6		
J. A. Afford lbw b Tufnell	0		
B 1, l-b 9, n-b 2	12	B 4, l-b 13, w 1, n-b 13	31

1/14 2/184 3/187 4/206 5/220   266   1/42 2/42 3/158   (6 wkts) 247
6/238 7/247 8/251 9/266   4/182 5/194 6/228

Bonus points – Nottinghamshire 2, Middlesex 3 (Score at 120 overs: 261-8).

Bowling: *First Innings*—Williams 18–2–54–0; Fraser 23–8–52–2; Feltham 4.1–0–9–0; Embury 32.5–11–55–3; Tufnell 40.4–9–77–5; Keech 6–1–9–0. *Second Innings*—Williams 9–1–40–0; Fraser 13–5–15–1; Embury 26–5–83–3; Tufnell 28–3–87–2; Keech 3–1–5–0.

Umpires: R. Julian and P. Willey.

At Oxford, May 19, 20, 21. MIDDLESEX drew with OXFORD UNIVERSITY.

MIDDLESEX v SUSSEX

At Lord's, May 27, 28, 29, 31. Middlesex won by an innings and 35 runs. Middlesex 23 pts, Sussex 2 pts. Toss: Sussex.

Damp and dreary weather made Alan Wells regret his decision to bat. Williams had all the Sussex batsmen in trouble, and his six for 61 was mainly responsible for a disappointing total of 161; the innings was over by tea. Friday was a better day, particularly for Haynes and Gatting, both of whom reached 70 as Middlesex built up a first-innings lead of 178. Brown, who had been struggling to score the runs which would justify his inclusion as batsman-keeper, finally came good with 66 in two and a half hours while Emburey proved his all-round form with his second successive first-class half-century. In spite of a stubborn fifty from Athey, his first in the Championship for his new county, Sussex only just took the match into the final day, losing their last five wickets in the first 45 minutes of Monday morning. It was Middlesex's first innings win since they beat Sussex in September 1990 to seal the Championship.

Close of play: First day, Middlesex 20-0 (D. L. Haynes 12*, M. A. Roseberry 7*); Second day, Middlesex 258-5 (K. R. Brown 39*, J. E. Emburey 29*); Third day, Sussex 120-5 (C. W. J. Athey 55*, P. Moores 0*).

Sussex

N. J. Lenham c Carr b Williams	4	– lbw b Williams	3
C. W. J. Athey c Carr b Cowans	30	– st Brown b Tufnell	55
D. M. Smith b Embury	19	– b Embury	31
*A. P. Wells b Embury	5	– b Embury	0
M. P. Speight c and b Williams	10	– c Roseberry b Tufnell	15
C. M. Wells c Brown b Williams	3	– c Embury b Tufnell	0
†P. Moores c Embury b Williams	0	– c Gatting b Embury	2
F. D. Stephenson c Carr b Cowans	60	– b Tufnell	8
I. D. K. Salisbury c Brown b Williams	2	– not out	7
E. E. Hemmings not out	17	– b Embury	0
E. S. H. Giddins b Williams	1	– lbw b Tufnell	0
L-b 2, n-b 8	10	B 3, l-b 9, n-b 10	22

1/6 2/53 3/53 4/60 5/71   161   1/7 2/78 3/82 4/113 5/119   143
6/71 7/80 8/106 9/158   6/124 7/132 8/132 9/134

Bonus points – Middlesex 4.

Bowling: *First Innings*—Williams 19–2–61–6; Fraser 13–1–40–0; Cowans 7–1–17–2; Embury 23–9–37–2; Tufnell 1–0–4–0. *Second Innings*—Fraser 5–0–13–0; Williams 9–2–24–1; Embury 37–17–46–4; Cowans 3–2–1–0; Tufnell 29.2–12–47–5.

Middlesex

D. L. Haynes c and b C. M. Wells	73	A. R. C. Fraser c Smith b Salisbury	13
M. A. Roseberry c Moores b Stephenson	11	P. C. R. Tufnell run out	0
*M. W. Gatting b Salisbury	70	N. G. Cowans lbw b Stephenson	0
M. R. Ramprakash lbw b Salisbury	1		
J. D. Carr c Athey b C. M. Wells	19		
†K. R. Brown b Salisbury	66	B 10, l-b 10, w 1, n-b 2	23
J. E. Embury not out	62		
N. F. Williams c Stephenson		1/33 2/148 3/153 4/178 5/194	339
b Hemmings	1	6/301 7/304 8/333 9/334	

Bonus points – Middlesex 3, Sussex 2 (Score at 120 overs: 301-6).

Bowling: Stephenson 28.4–4–63–2; Giddins 22–4–60–0; C. M. Wells 15–4–36–2; Salisbury 47–14–104–4; Hemmings 28–9–56–1; Lenham 1–1–0–0.

Umpires: D. O. Oslear and G. A. Stickley.

MIDDLESEX v DERBYSHIRE

At Lord's, June 3, 4. Middlesex won by ten wickets. Middlesex 20 pts, Derbyshire 4 pts. Toss: Derbyshire.

Middlesex moved to the top of the Championship table with a two-day win over Derbyshire that was notable for the contributions made by so many bowlers. In Derbyshire's first innings, Fraser at last showed a return to his old self; he had valuable support from Feltham, who had his best return for his new county. While the top five batsmen all reached double figures (two of them only just) the tail was non-existent and the last five wickets fell for only 21 runs. Middlesex's first-innings lead was a slender 25, thanks to some excellent spin from both Vandrau and Sladdin, but it was a combination of speed and spin which saw Derbyshire dismissed for 89 in their second innings. Middlesex needed 65 for victory. They claimed the extra half-hour on Friday evening but only one delivery of it was required; Haynes hit it for six.

Close of play: First day, Middlesex 72-2 (J. D. Carr 13*, J. E. Embury 11*).

Derbyshire

*K. J. Barnett c Brown b Feltham	33	– c Weekes b Fraser	3
J. E. Morris b Fraser	10	– c Haynes b Williams	12
T. J. G. O'Gorman c Emburey b Cowans	10	– c Carr b Emburey	20
C. J. Adams lbw b Fraser	53	– c Brown b Williams	0
D. G. Cork lbw b Feltham	38	– c and b Emburey	8
F. A. Griffith c Brown b Feltham	0	– lbw b Williams	1
M. J. Vandrau lbw b Feltham	8	– c Feltham b Williams	20
†K. M. Krikken c Weekes b Emburey	3	– c Emburey b Fraser	12
S. J. Base c Roseberry b Williams	0	– c Brown b Fraser	0
R. W. Sladdin c Carr b Fraser	1	– c Carr b Emburey	0
D. E. Malcolm not out	7	– not out	9
L-b 3, n-b 2	5	B 2, l-b 2	4

1/24 2/49 3/85 4/128 5/131   168   1/7 2/19 3/21 4/44 5/45   89
6/147 7/160 8/160 9/160   6/47 7/64 8/66 9/67

Bonus points – Middlesex 4.

Bowling: *First Innings*—Williams 14–1–38–1; Fraser 16.3–3–39–3; Cowans 6–0–35–1; Feltham 13–1–48–4; Emburey 6–2–5–1. *Second Innings*—Williams 13.1–2–36–4; Fraser 14–1–33–3; Feltham 3–2–2–0; Emburey 14–6–14–3.

Middlesex

D. L. Haynes c Adams b Cork	25	– not out	33
M. A. Roseberry st Krikken b Vandrau	12		
M. R. Ramprakash c Morris b Malcolm	11		
*J. D. Carr c Adams b Malcolm	20	– (2) not out	27
J. E. Emburey c Adams b Base	28		
P. N. Weekes st Krikken b Vandrau	43		
†K. R. Brown c Barnett b Cork	10		
M. A. Feltham c and b Sladdin	22		
N. F. Williams c O'Gorman b Sladdin	5		
A. R. C. Fraser c O'Gorman b Sladdin	0		
N. G. Cowans not out	2		
B 4, l-b 11	15	L-b 8	8

1/39 2/57 3/91 4/97 5/151   193   (no wkt) 68
6/177 7/185 8/187 9/190

Bonus points – Derbyshire 4.

In the first innings M. A. Roseberry, when 11, retired hurt at 37 and resumed at 177.

Bowling: *First Innings*—Malcolm 21–2–54–2; Cork 21–4–48–2; Griffith 7–1–14–0; Base 13–5–24–1; Sladdin 11.1–3–30–3; Vandrau 6–1–18–2. *Second Innings*—Malcolm 6–2–18–0; Base 2–0–11–0; Sladdin 4–0–25–0; Vandrau 0.1–0–6–0.

Umpires: J. D. Bond and D. R. Shepherd.

At Gateshead Fell, June 10, 11, 12, 14. MIDDLESEX drew with DURHAM.

At Bath, June 17, 18, 19, 21. MIDDLESEX beat SOMERSET by five wickets.

MIDDLESEX v SURREY

At Lord's, June 24, 25, 26, 28. Middlesex won by four wickets. Middlesex 23 pts, Surrey 7 pts. Toss: Surrey.

Surrey were up against it from the sixth over of the match, when Williams took two wickets, but in the end Middlesex scored only a very nervous victory, secured by two of their middle-order batsmen, Brown and Emburey. They put on 94 for the seventh wicket in the first innings to help Middlesex to a lead of just eight. Then, when their team needed 218 for victory and fell to 120 for six, they made the rest of the runs without being parted. There was only one other Middlesex score of consequence: Haynes hit his second century in successive innings. The variety of their attack, however, was a major advantage. Darren Bicknell was Surrey's top scorer in both innings. In the second, he was one of four victims for Williams in 22 balls as the last eight wickets went down for 72.

Close of play: First day, Middlesex 5-0 (D. L. Haynes 0*, M. A. Roseberry 5*); Second day, Middlesex 330; Third day, Middlesex 29-1 (M. A. Roseberry 7*, M. W. Gatting 11*).

Surrey

D. J. Bicknell c Fraser b Emburey	72	– lbw b Williams	77
M. A. Lynch b Williams	1	– c Tufnell b Fraser	0
G. P. Thorpe c Ramprakash b Williams	0	– c Emburey b Feltham	24
*†A. J. Stewart st Brown b Tufnell	33	– c Gatting b Emburey	58
A. D. Brown b Emburey	67	– b Tufnell	1
A. W. Smith c and b Feltham	20	– c Brown b Williams	22
M. P. Bicknell c Ramprakash b Feltham	32	– c Roseberry b Tufnell	22
N. M. Kendrick c Gatting b Tufnell	20	– lbw b Williams	0
Waqar Younis c Williams b Emburey	28	– c Haynes b Williams	0
J. Boiling run out	5	– c Gatting b Emburey	9
J. E. Benjamin not out	1	– not out	0
L-b 9, n-b 34	43	L-b 2, n-b 10	12
	322		**225**

1/4 2/4 3/78 4/172 5/201 6/253 7/256 8/309 9/315

1/1 2/54 3/153 4/162 5/192 6/203 7/205 8/205 9/225

Bonus points – Surrey 3, Middlesex 4.

Bowling: *First Innings*—Fraser 24–5–94–0; Williams 17–2–76–2; Feltham 10–2–41–2; Emburey 26.2–12–48–3; Tufnell 23–7–54–2. *Second Innings*—Fraser 14–3–41–1; Williams 21–4–73–4; Emburey 34.1–14–50–2; Feltham 6–2–20–1; Tufnell 21–7–39–2.

Middlesex

D. L. Haynes c Lynch b Boiling	112	– b M. P. Bicknell	11
M. A. Roseberry lbw b Benjamin	23	– b Waqar Younis	20
*M. W. Gatting b Benjamin	0	– c Stewart b Waqar Younis	16
M. R. Ramprakash c Lynch b Boiling	6	– c M. P. Bicknell b Boiling	31
J. D. Carr c Stewart b Benjamin	0	– c Thorpe b Benjamin	1
†K. R. Brown c M. P. Bicknell b Boiling	80	– not out	79
M. A. Feltham c D. J. Bicknell b Kendrick	7	– lbw b Waqar Younis	6
J. E. Emburey not out	65	– not out	36
N. F. Williams c D. J. Bicknell b Boiling	0		
A. R. C. Fraser c Boiling b Kendrick	5		
P. C. R. Tufnell lbw b Boiling	0		
B 9, l-b 16, w 1, n-b 6	32	B 6, l-b 5, w 4, n-b 4	19
	330	(6 wkts)	**219**

1/66 2/66 3/73 4/74 5/183 6/200 7/294 8/294 9/329

1/15 2/48 3/57 4/58 5/98 6/120

Bonus points – Middlesex 3, Surrey 4.

Bowling: *First Innings*—Waqar Younis 22–4–68–0; M. P. Bicknell 21–10–28–0; Boiling 28–3–100–5; Benjamin 19–4–43–3; Kendrick 23–4–66–2. *Second Innings*—Waqar Younis 24–3–70–3; M. P. Bicknell 11–4–34–1; Benjamin 16.4–4–41–1; Boiling 14–2–37–1; Kendrick 10–4–15–0; Smith 4–0–11–0.

Umpires: H. D. Bird and N. T. Plews.

At Cardiff, July 1, 2, 3, 5. MIDDLESEX beat GLAMORGAN by ten wickets.

At Birmingham, July 15, 16, 17, 19. MIDDLESEX beat WARWICKSHIRE by nine wickets.

MIDDLESEX v HAMPSHIRE

At Lord's, July 22, 23, 24. Middlesex won by nine wickets. Middlesex 23 pts, Hampshire 6 pts. Toss: Hampshire.

A month away from his 41st birthday, Emburey recorded his best figures in 20 years of cricket to transform what had been an even contest. Beginning the second innings only 30 behind, Hampshire were routed for 88, with Emburey, getting bounce and turn from the Pavilion End, taking eight for 40; Tufnell helped by securing the vital wickets of Gower and Terry. Gower had dominated the opening day, scoring 91 and stroking 12 fours with his familiar grace just as England, who had again ignored him, were setting out towards another defeat in the Headingley Test. Gower's shot selection was perfect until he hit across a full-length ball from Fraser and became one of four batsmen in the innings to play on. He put on 139 with the much slower Morris and Thursfield did well in his first innings in first-class cricket. Gatting, less forceful than usual, dominated the Middlesex batting and it needed some big hitting from the tail to put them in front. To everyone's surprise, however, they needed only 59 for victory and despite two hours of rain Gatting took the extra half-hour and wrapped up the game on the third day.

Close of play: First day, Hampshire 275-8 (M. J. Thursfield 32*, C. A. Connor 27*); Second day, Middlesex 231-8 (N. F. Williams 12*, A. R. C. Fraser 5*).

Hampshire

R. M. F. Cox c Brown b Williams	4	– b Emburey	17
R. S. M. Morris lbw b Feltham	54	– c Roseberry b Emburey	4
D. I. Gower b Fraser	91	– lbw b Tufnell	5
V. P. Terry b Williams	7	– b Tufnell	13
*M. C. J. Nicholas b Emburey	8	– c Roseberry b Emburey	15
K. D. James b Emburey	13	– c and b Emburey	0
†A. N. Aymes c Carr b Tufnell	7	– c Gatting b Emburey	0
S. D. Udal c Carr b Emburey	7	– c Haynes b Emburey	25
M. J. Thursfield not out	36	– c and b Emburey	0
C. A. Connor b Tufnell	27	– b Emburey	8
D. P. J. Flint lbw b Emburey	0	– not out	0
B 2, l-b 6, n-b 18	26	L-b 1	1
	280		**88**

1/7 2/146 3/156 4/176 5/178   280   1/14 2/21 3/31 4/41 5/44   88
6/197 7/197 8/216 9/275   6/44 7/63 8/65 9/83

Bonus points – Hampshire 2, Middlesex 4.

Bowling: *First Innings*—Fraser 20-4-42-1; Williams 26-6-80-2; Feltham 17-7-46-1; Emburey 39.5-13-75-4; Tufnell 16-7-29-2. *Second Innings*—Feltham 3-1-3-0; Fraser 2-1-2-0; Emburey 28.2-9-40-8; Tufnell 28-11-42-2.

Middlesex

D. L. Haynes c Terry b Udal	22	– not out	41
M. A. Roseberry c Flint b Thursfield	5	– lbw b Udal	14
*M. W. Gatting lbw b Flint	84	– not out	4
M. R. Ramprakash b Udal	0		
J. D. Carr lbw b James	15		
†K. R. Brown c Morris b Thursfield	45		
J. E. Emburey c Aymes b Thursfield	29		
M. A. Feltham c Aymes b Connor	0		
N. F. Williams c Flint b Connor	44		
A. R. C. Fraser c Terry b Thursfield	29		
P. C. R. Tufnell not out	17		
B 1, l-b 17, n-b 2	20		
	310		**59**

1/14 2/74 3/76 4/109 5/166   310   1/51   (1 wkt) 59
6/201 7/202 8/216 9/262

Bonus points – Middlesex 3, Hampshire 4.

Bowling: *First Innings*—Connor 25.3–8–70–2; Thursfield 25–10–78–4; James 15–7–25–1; Flint 22–5–47–1; Udal 29–8–72–2. *Second Innings*—Udal 6–0–36–1; Flint 3–0–16–0; Connor 2–1–6–0; Morris 0.4–0–1–0.

Umpires: G. I. Burgess and J. H. Hampshire.

MIDDLESEX v LEICESTERSHIRE

At Lord's, August 5, 6, 7. Middlesex won by an innings and 184 runs. Middlesex 24 pts, Leicestershire 1 pt. Toss: Middlesex. First-class debut: K. P. Dutch.

Middlesex won their ninth Championship match out of 12 and their sixth in succession without any difficulty whatever. For the first time all season they gained maximum batting points, after a stand of 230 in 63 overs between Gatting and Roseberry. Gatting's 75th first-class century was his first against Leicestershire, leaving only Durham unscathed; Roseberry's 185 was his highest score. Leicestershire did not start batting until midway through the second afternoon and were quickly in trouble against Fraser. His seven for 40 was his career-best and marked a return to top form after his long battle against the hip trouble that threatened to end his career. He bowled 17 overs unchanged with all his old snap and aggression. In contrast, Millns, playing his first match of the season after being injured when close to a Test place in 1992, had looked as forlorn as his team-mates. Following on 437 behind, Leicestershire lost their captain Briers with an Achilles tendon injury which was to end his season. His team's torment ended at 4.30 on the third day.

Close of play: First day, Middlesex 352-2 (M. A. Roseberry 175*, M. R. Ramprakash 26*); Second day, Leicestershire 44-1 (N. E. Briers 20*, J. J. Whitaker 22*).

Middlesex

D. L. Haynes lbw b Parsons	20	M. A. Feltham not out	32
M. A. Roseberry c Benjamin b Millns	185		
*M. W. Gatting c Whitaker b Pierson	121	L-b 10, n-b 2	12
M. R. Ramprakash b Potter	83		
J. D. Carr not out	74	1/56 2/286 3/372	(5 wkts dec.) 551
†K. R. Brown c Nixon b Wells	24	4/470 5/507	

K. P. Dutch, N. F. Williams, A. R. C. Fraser and P. C. R. Tufnell did not bat.

Bonus points – Middlesex 4, Leicestershire 1 (Score at 120 overs: 372-3).

Bowling: Benjamin 22–6–48–0; Millns 26–6–108–1; Parsons 32–6–79–1; Wells 26.4–5–113–1; Potter 30–4–111–1; Pierson 27–5–82–1.

Leicestershire

T. J. Boon c Ramprakash b Fraser	9	– lbw b Feltham	2
*N. E. Briers c Carr b Fraser	18	– retired hurt	33
J. J. Whitaker b Fraser	6	– c Tufnell b Feltham	42
V. J. Wells lbw b Feltham	30	– c Dutch b Williams	7
P. E. Robinson c Carr b Fraser	14	– c Carr b Tufnell	21
L. Potter c Brown b Fraser	2	– b Feltham	19
†P. A. Nixon c Dutch b Fraser	5	– run out	32
W. K. M. Benjamin c Ramprakash b Fraser	5	– (9) c Haynes b Ramprakash	63
G. J. Parsons lbw b Feltham	14	– (8) b Tufnell	0
A. R. K. Pierson b Feltham	1	– lbw b Fraser	3
D. J. Millns not out	0	– not out	8
L-b 2, n-b 8	10	L-b 6, w 1, n-b 16	23
	114		**253**

1/17 2/27 3/36 4/80 5/88   1/2 2/90 3/104 4/132 5/169
6/88 7/94 8/113 9/113   6/173 7/185 8/198 9/253

Bonus points – Middlesex 4.

In the second innings N. E. Briers retired hurt at 80.

Bowling: *First Innings*—Williams 10–1–48–0; Fraser 17–4–40–7; Feltham 7.2–1–24–3. *Second Innings*—Feltham 15–3–40–3; Fraser 21–6–56–1; Tufnell 27–8–57–2; Dutch 5–1–18–0; Williams 16–2–54–1; Ramprakash 3.4–0–22–1.

Umpires: J. D. Bond and B. Leadbeater.

At Scarborough, August 12, 13, 14, 16. MIDDLESEX drew with YORKSHIRE.

MIDDLESEX v NORTHAMPTONSHIRE

At Lord's, August 19, 20, 21. Middlesex won by ten wickets. Middlesex 23 pts, Northamptonshire 3 pts. Toss: Middlesex.

Middlesex crushed the one team who looked as though they might overhaul them in the Championship table, with their third successive three-day home win. Embury had another magnificent game, which began when he joined Brown at 161 for five. They more than doubled the total, Emburey scoring his second century of the season on his 41st birthday – it was only his second at Lord's, the other also having come off Northamptonshire, 11 years earlier. Cowans, playing his first Championship match since early June, took two early wickets and Northamptonshire were bowled out 21 short of avoiding the follow-on, with Bailey, who had been dropped three times, stranded on 95. Second time round, they did even worse. Middlesex's bowling was again vigorous and confident but they were helped by some self-destructive batting, typified by Curran's decision to charge Tufnell first ball; he was stumped and completed a pair. Emburey demolished the tail for match figures of seven for 89. Middlesex only needed an over to score the 11 they required to win but their regal progress was interrupted when Roseberry was forced to retire with a bruised forearm.

Close of play: First day, Middlesex 295-5 (K. R. Brown 64*, J. E. Emburey 78*); Second day, Northamptonshire 174-7 (R. J. Bailey 74*, C. E. L. Ambrose 7*).

Middlesex

D. L. Haynes c Ripley b Taylor	20	– not out	9
M. A. Roseberry lbw b Curran	13	– retired hurt	0
*M. W. Gatting c Fordham b Ambrose	28	– not out	0
J. D. Carr c Fordham b Roberts	33		
P. N. Weekes b Curran	47		
†K. R. Brown c Ripley b Curran	72		
J. E. Emburey c Ripley b Ambrose	120		
M. A. Feltham lbw b Curran	8		
N. F. Williams c Loye b Taylor	1		
P. C. R. Tufnell not out	30		
N. G. Cowans b Ambrose	7		
B 1, l-b 13, w 1, n-b 8	23	L-b 2	2
1/23 2/47 3/75 4/131 5/161	**402**	(no wkt)	**11**
6/324 7/336 8/339 9/392			

Bonus points – Middlesex 3, Northamptonshire 2 (Score at 120 overs: 322-5).

In the second innings M. A. Roseberry retired hurt at 2.

Bowling: *First Innings*—Ambrose 30-9-69-3; Taylor 27-8-69-2; Curran 30-8-82-4; Cook 20-3-65-0; Roberts 23-4-69-1; Bailey 10-1-34-0. *Second Innings*—Taylor 1-0-9-0.

Northamptonshire

A. Fordham lbw b Cowans	4	– b Cowans	4
N. A. Felton c Brown b Cowans	0	– lbw b Cowans	15
R. J. Bailey not out	95	– c Carr b Emburey	29
*A. J. Lamb lbw b Feltham	15	– run out	39
M. B. Loye b Tufnell	41	– c Carr b Tufnell	35
K. M. Curran c Roseberry b Tufnell	0	– st Brown b Tufnell	0
†D. Ripley run out	10	– c Carr b Emburey	8
A. R. Roberts c Roseberry b Emburey	3	– c Roseberry b Tufnell	12
C. E. L. Ambrose lbw b Emburey	19	– c Carr b Emburey	16
N. G. B. Cook c Tufnell b Emburey	16	– b Emburey	3
J. P. Taylor c Haynes b Cowans	0	– not out	8
B 8, l-b 10, w 1, n-b 10	29	L-b 9, n-b 2	11
1/1 2/12 3/34 4/122 5/122	**232**	1/4 2/41 3/53 4/130 5/130	**180**
6/137 7/160 8/192 9/222		6/131 7/144 8/168 9/171	

Bonus points – Northamptonshire 1, Middlesex 4.

Bowling: *First Innings*—Williams 4–2–5–0; Cowans 15.5–2–43–3; Emburey 31–10–51–3; Feltham 15–3–30–1; Tufnell 33–7–70–2; Weekes 6–2–15–0. *Second Innings*—Cowans 9–1–37–2; Feltham 8–3–21–0; Emburey 21.3–8–38–4; Tufnell 14–3–56–3; Weekes 5–0–19–0.

Umpires: D. J. Constant and A. G. T. Whitehead.

At Colchester, August 26, 27. MIDDLESEX beat ESSEX by seven wickets.

MIDDLESEX v LANCASHIRE

At Lord's, September 9, 10, 11, 13. Drawn. Middlesex 3 pts, Lancashire 3 pts. Toss: Middlesex.

Heavy rain and its aftermath deprived Middlesex of the opportunity to end their home programme in the grand manner; play was possible on only the first and third days. At least Middlesex supporters were able to applaud Gatting as he received the Championship trophy on the first day and see some evidence that he was still one of the best attacking batsmen in the game. After a blank second day, only 68 overs were possible on the third, but that was enough for Ramprakash to complete his second century in three Championship matches.

Close of play: First day, Middlesex 136–2 (M. W. Gatting 54*, M. R. Ramprakash 27*); Second day, No play; Third day, Middlesex 328–7 (M. R. Ramprakash 117*, A. R. C. Fraser 3*).

Middlesex

D. L. Haynes lbw b Watkinson	12	M. A. Feltham c Hegg b Barnett	3
M. A. Roseberry c Yates b Watkinson	25	A. R. C. Fraser not out	3
*M. W. Gatting c Lloyd b DeFreitas	73	B 3, l-b 6, w 7, n-b 18	34
M. R. Ramprakash not out	117		
J. D. Carr lbw b Barnett	8	1/31 2/57 3/188 (7 wkts)	328
†K. R. Brown c Lloyd b Barnett	21	4/210 5/244	
J. E. Emburey c DeFreitas b Yates	46	6/299 7/310	

P. C. R. Tufnell and N. G. Cowans did not bat.

Bonus points – Middlesex 3, Lancashire 3.

Bowling: Wasim Akram 18–5–56–0; DeFreitas 24–5–74–1; Watkinson 17–3–49–2; Yates 30–5–86–1; Barnett 24–8–54–3.

Lancashire

J. P. Crawley, M. A. Atherton, N. J. Speak, *N. H. Fairbrother, G. D. Lloyd, Wasim Akram, M. Watkinson, P. A. J. DeFreitas, †W. K. Hegg, G. Yates and A. A. Barnett.

Umpires: J. W. Holder and A. A. Jones.

At Worcester, September 16, 17. MIDDLESEX lost to WORCESTERSHIRE by an innings and 36 runs.

NORTHAMPTONSHIRE

Patron: The Earl of Dalkeith
President: W. R. F. Chamberlain
Chairman: L. A. Wilson
Chairman, Cricket Committee: R. Wills
Chief Executive: S. P. Coverdale
Captain: A. J. Lamb
Director of Cricket: P. A. Neale
Coach: R. M. Carter
Cricket Development Officer: B. L. Reynolds
Head Groundsman: R. R. Bailey
Scorer: A. C. Kingston

So high were expectations following Northamptonshire's strong finish to the previous season, culminating in their NatWest Trophy triumph, that the failure to win any of the major competitions in 1993 inevitably came as a disappointment to players, officials and supporters alike. It was, however, a very satisfactory year in most respects, and certainly one to hearten the newly appointed director of cricket, Phil Neale. Settling quickly and with quiet authority into his first managerial role, the former Worcestershire captain watched and listened intently throughout the campaign, and undoubtedly learned much about his new charges.

He saw the side remain in contention for the elusive first Championship title until the end of August, before they eventually finished fourth – just one place lower than in 1992 – with eight victories. They were unluckily denied another, over Glamorgan at Swansea in May, when rain intervened with 58 runs needed, nine wickets in hand and two sessions remaining. In one-day cricket Northamptonshire came fifth in the Sunday League, reached the semi-finals of the Benson and Hedges Cup, and overcame Lancashire and Essex in defence of the 60-overs trophy before going out with a substandard performance against Sussex.

The NatWest win at Chelmsford on July 7 was, perhaps, the high-water mark of the season. It featured a magnificent, decisive innings from Allan Lamb who, free from Test calls for only the second summer since making his England debut in 1982, was able to devote all his energies to Northamptonshire's cause and led the team purposefully from first game to last. Supporting him that day was Malachy Loye, and the blossoming of the 20-year-old Northampton-born batsman was, in the opinion of Neale and many other close observers, the year's most gratifying aspect.

Loye began with two promising innings to brighten a heavy defeat at Edgbaston in the opening Championship fixture, followed up with a maiden first-class century against Gloucestershire in his home town, and only narrowly missed completing 1,000 runs in his first full season. A career-best 153 not out at Canterbury early in September sealed a place for him on the England A tour to South Africa, and he subsequently topped the Cricketers' Association poll to find their outstanding young cricketer of 1993 before also being named as the county's player of the year. At least as important as the statistics and awards was the manner in which he made his runs; his confident, assertive strokeplay was frequently a joy to watch, and never more so than during a memorable 122 against Somerset at Luton – Northamptonshire's only Sunday League hundred of the season.

In all competitions, Rob Bailey proved the most solidly consistent batsman, and he enjoyed a successful benefit year on and off the field. Lamb, Fordham – although generally below his fluent best – and the hard-working Felton all shone on occasions, but the absence from the middle order of David Capel, whose left arm was broken by Malcolm Marshall on June 17, was keenly felt. Capel, for so long the pivotal all-rounder, was initially replaced by Tony Penberthy, but the young Cornishman did not play to his potential and, thereafter, balancing the side was a major problem. This was compounded by David Ripley's inability to get going with the bat. His keeping, though, was tidy for the most part, and at the end of the year he saw off another challenger when Wayne Noon, his deputy for five years, left the club to join Nottinghamshire. The long-serving but injury-prone seamer Alan Walker also departed, not awarded a new contract after 11 seasons on the staff, and joined Durham.

Kevin Curran lacked the patience to score runs regularly at No. 6, but with the ball he produced many telling spells and captured 67 wickets to finish second in the national first-class averages. Indeed, it was the seam bowlers who did most to keep Northamptonshire in the Championship race, with Curran, Curtly Ambrose and Paul Taylor between them claiming 187 wickets at 21.87 in the 17-match programme. The pitches prepared at Northampton gave them every assistance; six of the eight wins were achieved at the County Ground, three of them with a full day to spare. There was also an encouraging advance from Mark Bowen, who made the most of the opportunities granted him in the latter part of the season when some of his colleagues, faced with the additional workload imposed by Capel's injury, began to show signs of fatigue.

Such a heavy reliance on the quicker bowlers was not good news for the spinners and it was in this department that Northamptonshire were most conspicuously found wanting. In stark contrast to the fruitful efforts of the trio of seamers, the three slow men – Bailey, Nick Cook and Andy Roberts – collectively managed only 39 Championship wickets at 42.71. Cook and Roberts, in particular, were starved of bowling for much of the summer, and it was hardly surprising that, when needed to perform in the final run-in, they were unable to settle into a rhythm. Bailey broke some stubborn partnerships with his off-breaks but rarely looked like running through a side. This deficiency may have been addressed at the end of the season with the signing of another Northampton-born player: left-arm spinner Andrew Cottam – son of Bob, the county's former opening bowler – who was released by Somerset, where his father is manager.

If Loye's progress represented the greatest single cause for optimism in 1993, then that of another home-grown batsman, Russell Warren, was a further good omen. Although without a substantial innings in his five Championship appearances, Warren played well in the Sunday League and revealed a mature temperament in some testing limited-overs situations. All-rounder Kevin Innes, chosen for England's Under-19 tour of Sri Lanka, may be the next local player to make the step up and, with Neale keen to stress the importance of fostering the talent to emerge within Northamptonshire's own boundaries, the club is offering a strong and welcome incentive to all young cricketers in the county. If they respond, the future will be bright. – *Andrew Radd*.

NORTHAMPTONSHIRE 1993

[*Bill Smith*]

Back row: J. N. Snape, J. G. Hughes, R. J. Warren, J. Tomlinson, N. A. Stanley, A. L. Penberthy, K. J. Innes. *Middle row:* R. Norman (*physiotherapist*), W. M. Noon, M. B. Loye, K. M. Curran, A. Fordham, M. N. Bowen, N. A. Felton, A. R. Roberts, R. M. Carter (*coach*). *Front row:* A. Walker, D. J. Capel, R. J. Bailey, A. J. Lamb (*captain*), P. A. Neale (*director of cricket*), N. G. B. Cook, D. Ripley. *Insets:* C. E. L. Ambrose, R. R. Montgomerie.

NORTHAMPTONSHIRE RESULTS

All first-class matches – Played 18: Won 8, Lost 4, Drawn 6.

County Championship matches – Played 17: Won 8, Lost 4, Drawn 5.

Bonus points – Batting 35, Bowling 59.

Competition placings – Britannic Assurance County Championship, 4th;
NatWest Bank Trophy, q-f; Benson and Hedges Cup, s-f;
AXA Equity & Law League, 5th.

BRITANNIC ASSURANCE CHAMPIONSHIP AVERAGES

BATTING

	Birthplace	M	I	NO	R	HS	Avge
‡R. J. Bailey	Biddulph	17	29	5	1,191	200	49.62
‡A. J. Lamb	Langebaanweg, SA	17	27	1	1,046	172	40.23
‡A. Fordham	Bedford	16	28	1	1,024	193	37.92
‡N. A. Felton	Guildford	17	29	2	1,010	109	37.40
M. B. Loye	Northampton	17	26	1	879	153*	35.16
‡K. M. Curran	Rusape, S. Rhodesia	16	23	4	612	91	32.21
M. N. Bowen	Redcar	5	6	2	72	23*	18.00
‡D. J. Capel	Northampton	5	8	2	102	54	17.00
A. L. Penberthy	Troon	8	12	2	161	54*	16.10
‡D. Ripley	Leeds	17	22	4	286	54	15.88
‡C. E. L. Ambrose§ . .	Swetes Village, Antigua	13	15	2	197	38	15.15
R. J. Warren	Northampton	5	6	1	56	37*	11.20
A. R. Roberts	Kettering	9	15	1	116	19*	8.28
‡J. P. Taylor	Ashby-de-la-Zouch	17	20	10	79	14*	7.90
‡N. G. B. Cook	Leicester	7	8	1	48	18	6.85

Also batted: R. R. Montgomerie (*Rugby*) (1 match) 35.

* *Signifies not out.*   ‡ *Denotes county cap.*   § *Overseas player.*

The following played a total of 11 three-figure innings for Northamptonshire in County Championship matches – A. Fordham 3, R. J. Bailey 2, N. A. Felton 2, A. J. Lamb 2, M. B. Loye 2.

BOWLING

	O	M	R	W	BB	5W/i	Avge
K. M. Curran	458	123	1,293	67	7-47	3	19.29
C. E. L. Ambrose	543.4	150	1,207	59	6-49	2	20.45
D. J. Capel	117.4	37	252	12	3-15	0	21.00
M. N. Bowen	147.5	30	554	22	4-124	0	25.18
J. P. Taylor	573.5	169	1,590	61	6-82	2	26.06
A. L. Penberthy	151	38	462	16	5-37	1	28.87
R. J. Bailey	238.3	68	590	18	5-54	1	32.77
A. R. Roberts	258.4	64	705	16	3-51	0	44.06

Also bowled: N. G. B. Cook 175.5–60–371–5; M. B. Loye 0.1–0–1–0.

Wicket-keeper: D. Ripley 50 ct, 3 st.

Leading Fielders: M. B. Loye 18, N. A. Felton 16, R. J. Bailey 15.

At Cambridge, April 25. COMBINED UNIVERSITIES v NORTHAMPTONSHIRE.
Abandoned.

At Birmingham, April 29, 30, May 1, 2. NORTHAMPTONSHIRE lost to WARWICK-
SHIRE by 197 runs.

NORTHAMPTONSHIRE v GLOUCESTERSHIRE

At Northampton, May 6, 7, 8, 10. Northamptonshire won by five wickets. Northamptonshire 21 pts, Gloucestershire 3 pts. Toss: Gloucestershire. Championship debut: R. M.
Wight.

After dominating a low-key contest virtually throughout, Northamptonshire wobbled and
almost fell on the final afternoon against the left-arm spin of Davies, who claimed ten
wickets in a match for the first time. It took them three hours to score 110 for victory;
Bailey, badly out of touch, faced 70 deliveries for his ten not out. The highlight for
Northamptonshire was a maiden first-class century from 20-year-old Loye, which secured a
lead of 186 after Curran, with four for nine in 27 balls after lunch on the first day, and
Capel had dismissed Gloucestershire cheaply. Loye, who batted four hours and hit 11 fours,
showed excellent judgment and application on a slow pitch, while Curran lent restrained but
invaluable support. Gloucestershire produced a more determined display in their second
innings, typified by a 56-over vigil from Russell, and carried the game into a fourth day.
But despite Davies's intelligent exploitation of helpful conditions Northamptonshire inched
home.

Close of play: First day, Northamptonshire 105-4 (M. B. Loye 16*, D. J. Capel 0*);
Second day, Gloucestershire 56-2 (R. J. Scott 33*, M. W. Alleyne 11*); Third day,
Gloucestershire 281-7 (R. C. Russell 35*, A. M. Smith 30*).

Gloucestershire

B. C. Broad c Ripley b Curran	13	– lbw b Taylor	4
S. G. Hinks c Ripley b Taylor	10	– c Loye b Taylor	8
R. J. Scott b Taylor	11	– c Capel b Curran	51
M. W. Alleyne b Capel	4	– lbw b Cook	30
*A. J. Wright c Ripley b Curran	28	– lbw b Taylor	75
T. H. C. Hancock c Bailey b Curran	4	– c Bailey b Curran	39
†R. C. Russell c Cook b Capel	2	– not out	40
R. M. Wight lbw b Curran	4	– c Ripley b Capel	4
A. M. Smith not out	8	– b Capel	33
M. Davies c Lamb b Curran	3	– c Bailey b Curran	5
K. E. Cooper b Capel	15	– c Ripley b Capel	0
L-b 5	5	B 3, l-b 2, w 1	6

1/23 2/23 3/32 4/55 5/67   107   1/6 2/21 3/84 4/103 5/185   295
6/70 7/80 8/80 9/90   6/216 7/221 8/287 9/294

Bonus points – Northamptonshire 4.

Bowling: *First Innings*—Taylor 14–8–22–2; Curran 15–6–38–5; Capel 11.3–5–15–3; Cook
7–3–16–0; Roberts 2–0–11–0. *Second Innings*—Taylor 32–9–61–3; Curran 27–8–71–3;
Roberts 21–9–45–0; Capel 32.1–13–56–3; Cook 29–10–49–1; Bailey 2–1–8–0.

Northamptonshire

A. Fordham lbw b Cooper	54	– c Alleyne b Davies	17
N. A. Felton lbw b Davies	25	– b Davies	45
R. J. Bailey b Davies	0	– not out	10
*A. J. Lamb c Davies b Smith	8	– lbw b Davies	14
M. B. Loye c Cooper b Davies	105	– c Broad b Davies	8
D. J. Capel c Russell b Alleyne	16	– c Wright b Davies	0
K. M. Curran lbw b Cooper	53	– not out	9
†D. Ripley b Davies	2		
A. R. Roberts c Wright b Wight	11		
J. P. Taylor c Russell b Davies	9		
N. G. B. Cook not out	1		
L-b 5, n-b 4	9	W 1, n-b 6	7

1/58 2/62 3/82 4/99 5/193   293   1/51 2/65 3/85   (5 wkts) 110
6/231 7/245 8/263 9/286   4/95 5/98

Bonus points – Northamptonshire 1, Gloucestershire 3 (Score at 120 overs: 246-7).

Bowling: *First Innings*—Cooper 24.1–15–26–2; Smith 27–5–56–1; Scott 9–2–28–0; Davies 37–10–84–5; Wight 39–13–85–1; Alleyne 5–1–9–1. *Second Innings*—Cooper 16–6–23–0; Smith 11.2–5–30–0; Davies 19–2–57–5.

Umpires: J. H. Hampshire and J. W. Holder.

At Oxford, May 15, 17, 18. NORTHAMPTONSHIRE drew with OXFORD UNIVERSITY.

At Northampton, May 16. NORTHAMPTONSHIRE beat AUSTRALIANS on scoring-rate (See Australian tour section).

At Swansea, May 20, 21, 22, 24. NORTHAMPTONSHIRE drew with GLAMORGAN.

NORTHAMPTONSHIRE v WORCESTERSHIRE

At Northampton, June 3, 4, 5, 7. Northamptonshire won by six wickets. Northamptonshire 23 pts, Worcestershire 1 pt. Toss: Worcestershire.

A gallant fightback by Worcestershire ultimately counted for nothing; Northamptonshire, left to score 108 for victory in 24 overs, reached their target when Bailey hit Illingworth for six over long-on with three balls remaining. There appeared to be no way back for Worcestershire on the second evening. Having suffered at the hands of Fordham, who scored 193 in eight hours with a six and 25 fours, they subsided to 68 for eight after Taylor took three wickets in eight deliveries. The resistance began with Newport and Tolley adding 108 in 30 overs. Although forced to follow on 263 behind, the visitors batted tenaciously, and the last pair, Illingworth and Newport, who was batting with a runner, frustrated Northamptonshire for a further 22 overs. It was not until the first over after tea that Bailey bowled Newport – his fourth victim in a career-best return – before finally settling the issue with his bat.

Close of play: First day, Northamptonshire 252-2 (A. Fordham 125*, A. J. Lamb 5*); Second day, Worcestershire 157-8 (P. J. Newport 46*, C. M. Tolley 47*); Third day, Worcestershire 199-5 (G. R. Haynes 49*, S. J. Rhodes 7*).

Northamptonshire

A. Fordham c Haynes b Illingworth	193	– run out	7
N. A. Felton c Lampitt b Haynes	59	– b Benjamin	11
R. J. Bailey b Benjamin	40	– not out	35
*A. J. Lamb c Benjamin b Illingworth	64	– b Benjamin	20
M. B. Loye b Haynes	6	– run out	18
D. J. Capel st Rhodes b Illingworth	54	– not out	7
K. M. Curran not out	38		
†D. Ripley not out	2		
B 3, l-b 13, w 6, n-b 16	38	B 5, l-b 3, w 2, n-b 2	12

1/152 2/243 3/379 4/386   (6 wkts dec.) 494   1/13 2/27 3/66 4/87   (4 wkts) 110
5/397 6/479

C. E. L. Ambrose, J. P. Taylor and N. G. B. Cook did not bat.

Bonus points – Northamptonshire 3 (Score at 120 overs: 330-2).

Bowling: *First Innings*—Benjamin 30–4–103–1; Tolley 18–4–60–0; Newport 30–7–91–0; Lampitt 31–5–110–0; Illingworth 31–6–63–3; Haynes 18–3–51–2. *Second Innings*—Benjamin 12–0–54–2; Tolley 1–0–5–0; Illingworth 10.3–0–43–0.

Worcestershire

*T. S. Curtis c Ripley b Ambrose	6	– c Felton b Taylor	74
W. P. C. Weston c Loye b Taylor	6	– b Ambrose	6
A. C. H. Seymour lbw b Capel	20	– c Ripley b Ambrose	25
D. A. Leatherdale b Taylor	1	– b Bailey	5
G. R. Haynes lbw b Taylor	0	– b Capel	70
S. R. Lampitt c Capel	7	– c Ripley b Curran	9
†S. J. Rhodes c Ripley b Capel	11	– lbw b Bailey	72
P. J. Newport not out	79	– (11) b Bailey	29
R. K. Illingworth c Ripley b Curran	5	– not out	21
C. M. Tolley c Bailey b Curran	60	– (8) c Felton b Taylor	12
K. C. G. Benjamin c Ripley b Taylor	26	– (10) lbw b Bailey	10
B 1, l-b 7, n-b 2	10	B 15, l-b 1, w 1, n-b 10	37

1/8 2/18 3/20 4/20 5/37   231   1/25 2/88 3/101 4/146 5/190   370
6/42 7/61 8/68 9/176   6/255 7/278 8/309 9/326

Bonus points – Worcestershire 1, Northamptonshire 4.

Bowling: *First Innings*—Ambrose 21–8–38–1; Taylor 17.4–4–64–4; Capel 15–4–44–3; Curran 12–0–60–2; Cook 5–0–17–0. *Second Innings*—Ambrose 35–5–84–2; Capel 20–4–41–1; Cook 34–20–33–0; Taylor 31–7–77–2; Curran 23–5–59–1; Bailey 17.4–7–50–4.

Umpires: D. O. Oslear and N. T. Plews.

At Hove, June 10, 11, 12, 14. NORTHAMPTONSHIRE drew with SUSSEX.

NORTHAMPTONSHIRE v HAMPSHIRE

At Northampton, June 17, 18, 19, 21. Hampshire won by seven wickets. Hampshire 21 pts, Northamptonshire 4 pts. Toss: Hampshire.

Hampshire coasted to victory 25 minutes before lunch on the fourth day, efficiently completing the job begun by Shine and Marshall on the first morning. Shine made significant inroads, dismissing Fordham, Felton and Lamb in a hostile 18-ball burst, while Marshall put Capel out of action by breaking his left forearm. Hampshire were also made to struggle, with Ambrose claiming his first five-wicket haul in the Championship since September 1990, but Udal – dropped in the slips before scoring – guided them to a position of strength, 122 runs ahead. Northamptonshire hit back strongly, Fordham and Felton clearing the arrears, before James made the critical breakthrough with a spell of three for none in 14 deliveries on the third morning. Fordham battled on, hitting ten fours in a patient six-hour stay, and Curran, riding his luck, counter-attacked boldly. However, Hampshire were left needing 182 with time no object. Despite the early loss of Middleton, they were always in control.

Close of play: First day, Hampshire 113-4 (M. C. J. Nicholas 24*, J. R. Wood 9*); Second day, Northamptonshire 142-1 (A. Fordham 63*, N. G. B. Cook 0*); Third day, Hampshire 91-1 (R. S. M. Morris 41*, K. D. James 43*).

Northamptonshire

A. Fordham lbw b Shine	3	– lbw b Connor	109
N. A. Felton c Aymes b Shine	10	– c Morris b Udal	64
R. J. Bailey c and b Shine	59	– (4) c Middleton b James	4
*A. J. Lamb b Shine	6	– (5) c Nicholas b James	0
M. B. Loye c James b Marshall	1	– (6) lbw b James	0
D. J. Capel retired hurt	18	– absent injured	
K. M. Curran b Marshall	0	– b Shine	71
†D. Ripley not out	9	– b Marshall	5
C. E. L. Ambrose c Aymes b Shine	2	– b Shine	19
J. P. Taylor c Morris b Marshall	1	– not out	9
N. G. B. Cook b Shine	0	– (3) b Marshall	1
L-b 5, w 1, n-b 10	16	L-b 17, n-b 4	21

1/3 2/28 3/36 4/37 5/109   125   1/141 2/145 3/170 4/174 5/174   303
6/113 7/118 8/124 9/125   6/239 7/252 8/286 9/303

Bonus points – Hampshire 4.

In the first innings D. J. Capel retired hurt at 109-4.

Bowling: *First Innings*—Marshall 13-5-29-3; Shine 14-1-62-6; Connor 7-3-13-0; James 8-5-9-0; Udal 2-0-7-0. *Second Innings*—Marshall 30-12-53-2; Shine 21.4-5-74-2; Connor 17-1-51-1; James 19-8-40-3; Udal 32-7-68-1.

Hampshire

T. C. Middleton b Curran	9	– b Ambrose	4
R. S. M. Morris c Ripley b Ambrose	31	– c Ripley b Ambrose	41
K. D. James c Loye b Ambrose	22	– run out	71
V. P. Terry lbw b Taylor	7	– lbw b James	58
*M. C. J. Nicholas c Bailey b Ambrose	24	– not out	5
J. R. Wood c sub b Curran	25		
†A. N. Aymes c Lamb b Bailey	31		
M. D. Marshall lbw b Taylor	8		
S. D. Udal b Ambrose	44		
C. A. Connor lbw b Ambrose	24		
K. J. Shine not out	0		
B 2, l-b 16, n-b 4	22	L-b 3	3

1/24 2/55 3/72 4/99 5/130   247   1/16 2/98 3/160   (3 wkts) 182
6/132 7/145 8/195 9/244

Bonus points – Hampshire 1, Northamptonshire 4.

Bowling: *First Innings*—Ambrose 33.5-7-76-5; Taylor 21-7-49-2; Curran 27-8-62-2; Cook 21-7-33-0; Bailey 9-6-9-1. *Second Innings*—Ambrose 19-7-28-2; Curran 9-2-31-0; Taylor 10-2-32-0; Cook 19-5-57-0; Bailey 17-8-30-0; Loye 0.1-0-1-0.

Umpires: J. W. Holder and R. Palmer.

NORTHAMPTONSHIRE v SOMERSET

At Luton, June 24, 25, 26. Northamptonshire won by an innings and five runs. Northamptonshire 24 pts, Somerset 2 pts. Toss: Northamptonshire. Championship debut: K. A. Parsons.

Lamb's 50th century for Northamptonshire paved the way for an emphatic victory with five sessions remaining. Lamb, who batted five and a half hours at his imperious best, striking three sixes and 23 fours, completely subdued an attack buoyant after early successes. It was his first century against Somerset, leaving only Durham to complete his county set. His partnership with Curran – which began with Northamptonshire in trouble at 107 for four – realised 212 in 60 overs. Rose and Caddick polished off the tail on the second morning, but Somerset promptly handed back the initiative with an irresolute and careless batting display, their last eight wickets falling for 65 in 20 overs. They fared little better in the follow-on despite another forthright innings from Tavaré and a promising one from the debutant Keith Parsons. Northamptonshire might have sealed their win inside two days; in the event, it took them just 110 minutes on the third, after Mallender had provided a late flourish with 46 off 32 balls, including two big sixes off the leg-spinner, Roberts.

Close of play: First day, Northamptonshire 363-6 (A. L. Penberthy 8*, D. Ripley 8*); Second day, Somerset 110-5 (K. A. Parsons 36*, G. D. Rose 2*).

Northamptonshire

A. Fordham c Burns b Mallender	. . . . .	0
N. A. Felton c Trump b Caddick	. . . . .	7
R. J. Bailey c Mushtaq Ahmed b Rose	. .	22
*A. J. Lamb c Lathwell b Caddick	. . . .	172
M. B. Loye c Tavaré b Caddick	. . . . .	28
K. M. Curran c Trump b Rose	. . . . .	91
A. L. Penberthy c Burns b Caddick	. . . .	14
†D. Ripley c Harden b Rose	. . . . .	12

A. R. Roberts c Tavaré b Rose	. . . . . .	0
C. E. L. Ambrose not out	. . . .	6
J. P. Taylor c Folland b Rose	. . . .	3
L-b 11, n-b 16		27
1/0 2/33 3/37 4/107 5/319		382
6/350 7/373 8/373 9/382		

Bonus points – Northamptonshire 4, Somerset 2 (Score at 120 overs: 372-6).

D. Ripley, when 12, retired hurt at 372 and resumed at 382.

Bowling: Mallender 21–9–41–1; Caddick 32–12–91–4; Rose 24–2–96–5; Mushtaq Ahmed 23–5–75–0; Trump 28–9–68–0.

Somerset

	First Innings		Second Innings	
M. N. Lathwell c Penberthy b Taylor	. . . .	4	– b Ambrose	0
N. A. Folland c Fordham b Penberthy	. . . .	34	– run out	13
R. J. Harden b Taylor	. . . .	29	– lbw b Ambrose	4
*C. J. Tavaré c Fordham b Penberthy	. . . . . .	48	– c Roberts b Curran	39
K. A. Parsons b Ambrose	. . . .	4	– c Felton b Ambrose	43
†N. D. Burns c Loye b Ambrose	. . . .	14	– c Felton b Taylor	14
G. D. Rose lbw b Curran	. . . .	25	– lbw b Ambrose	12
Mushtaq Ahmed c Fordham b Curran	. . . . . .	0	– c Taylor b Penberthy	19
A. R. Caddick c Lamb b Curran	. . . .	0	– lbw b Curran	46
N. A. Mallender c Ambrose b Penberthy	. . . .	3	– c Penberthy b Roberts	46
H. R. J. Trump not out	. . . .	5	– not out	1
L-b 5, n-b 2		7	B 1, l-b 7, w 1	9
1/5 2/47 3/96 4/101 5/103		161	1/12 2/16 3/44 4/65 5/103	216
6/131 7/132 8/136 9/151			6/128 7/141 8/157 9/180	

Bonus points – Northamptonshire 4.

Bowling: *First Innings*—Ambrose 17–5–64–2; Taylor 13–5–38–2; Curran 8.4–1–32–3; Penberthy 12–3–22–3. *Second Innings*—Ambrose 19–6–36–4; Taylor 16–6–46–1; Curran 12–5–32–2; Penberthy 12–2–49–1; Roberts 10–3–44–1; Bailey 1–0–1–0.

Umpires: J. H. Hampshire and K. E. Palmer.

NORTHAMPTONSHIRE v NOTTINGHAMSHIRE

At Northampton, July 1, 2, 3. Northamptonshire won by 171 runs. Northamptonshire 21 pts, Nottinghamshire 4 pts. Toss: Nottinghamshire.

Nottinghamshire, despite a determined career-best 77 by Saxelby, succumbed with a day to spare. They were bowled out after being set an unlikely target of 405 on a pitch offering substantial help to Northamptonshire's spinners, Bailey, who took five wickets in an or the first time, and Roberts. The relaid strip was the principal talking-point once 17 wickets had fallen on the first day. The umpires, worried by its variable bounce, called in TCCB inspector Harry Brind, who decided against recommending the 25-point penalty. In any case, by the time Brind arrived Northamptonshire were well on the way to a substantial second-innings total. On the eventful first day Bailey had adopted a positive approach, hitting 11 fours while making 63 out of 76 for the second wicket, while Robinson grafted for two and a half hours to keep his side in contention.

Close of play: First day, Nottinghamshire 162-7 (K. P. Evans 27*, B. N. French 6*); Second day, Northamptonshire 363-8 (A. R. Roberts 18*, C. E. L. Ambrose 0*).

Northamptonshire

A. Fordham c Saxelby b Cairns	4	c and b Cairns	19
N. A. Felton b Cairns	20	c and b Cairns	65
R. J. Bailey c Evans b Lewis	63	c Johnson b Cairns	39
*A. J. Lamb c Lewis b Pennett	21	lbw b Lewis	12
M. B. Loye c French b Cairns	10	b Lewis	58
K. M. Curran b French b Lewis	19	(7) c Cairns b Pennett	68
A. L. Penberthy c Afford b Evans	7	(6) c Saxelby b Lewis	6
†D. Ripley c Archer b Lewis	3	c Archer b Afford	43
A. R. Roberts c Saxelby b Lewis	13	not out	19
C. E. L. Ambrose run out	25	b Evans	0
J. P. Taylor not out	14	b Cairns	0
B 5, l-b 5, w 1, n-b 2	13	B 9, l-b 13, w 1, n-b 12	35

1/5 2/81 3/106 4/118 5/123   212   1/42 2/135 3/136 4/163 5/195   364
6/149 7/151 8/158 9/185   6/252 7/322 8/343 9/363

Bonus points – Northamptonshire 1, Nottinghamshire 4.

Bowling: *First Innings*—Lewis 18.1-2-58-4; Cairns 14.1-1-58-3; Evans 16-4-44-1; Pennett 9-2-42-1. *Second Innings*—Lewis 21-2-82-2; Evans 19.5-48-1; Cairns 19.1-2-54-5; Pennett 14-2-74-1; Afford 33-11-84-1.

Nottinghamshire

P. R. Pollard c Lamb b Taylor	0	c Ripley b Roberts	40
M. Saxelby c Ripley b Ambrose	0	st Ripley b Bailey	77
*R. T. Robinson c Felton b Curran	51	b Taylor	4
P. Johnson c and b Curran	23	c Loye b Bailey	10
G. F. Archer c Bailey b Taylor	2	b Ambrose	14
C. L. Cairns c Ambrose b Penberthy	25	b Roberts	13
C. C. Lewis c Lamb b Curran	19	c sub b Bailey	8
K. P. Evans c Ripley b Ambrose	35	not out	34
†B. N. French c Felton b Curran	8	lbw b Bailey	3
D. B. Pennett not out	0	lbw b Roberts	1
J. A. Afford lbw b Curran	0	c Loye b Bailey	11
B 1, l-b 7, w 1	9	B 5, l-b 5, n-b 8	18

1/1 2/1 3/32 4/37 5/80   172   1/82 2/89 3/117 4/150 5/170   233
6/117 7/141 8/172 9/172   6/172 7/185 8/209 9/214

Bonus points – Northamptonshire 4.

Bowling: *First Innings*—Ambrose 17-3-53-2; Taylor 11-4-44-2; Curran 13.3-2-32-5; Penberthy 6-2-28-1; Bailey 5-3-5-0; Roberts 3-1-2-0. *Second Innings*—Ambrose 16-6-24-1; Taylor 12-3-32-1; Penberthy 5-1-16-0; Curran 10-3-27-0; Bailey 27.5-9-54-5; Roberts 27-5-70-3.

Umpires: A. A. Jones and D. R. Shepherd.

At Harrogate, July 15, 16, 17, 19. NORTHAMPTONSHIRE lost to YORKSHIRE by four wickets.

NORTHAMPTONSHIRE v SURREY

At Northampton, July 22, 23, 24, 26. Northamptonshire won by 304 runs. Northamptonshire 21 pts, Surrey 4 pts. Toss: Surrey.

Surrey, second in the table at the start of the match, suffered a severe setback at the hands of Northamptonshire, two places below them, in the 100th Championship contest between the two counties. The visitors lost their last eight wickets for 48 on the fourth day, succumbing half an hour after lunch; Curran and Taylor encountered serious resistance only from Lynch, who stayed 25 overs for 15. Northamptonshire led by 49 on first innings, and consolidated through Fordham and Bailey who added 133 in 35 overs. The game really came to life on the rain-shortened third day, when Lamb took on the Surrey bowlers in thrilling fashion. He hit 18 boundaries — including four in an over off Murphy — in 93 balls. Wickets fell rapidly in the quest for quick runs, but Surrey were left a daunting target of 413; they lost Bicknell and Ward before Saturday's close, and Monday morning turned into a sorry procession.

Close of play: First day, Surrey 79-4 (D. M. Ward 35*, A. W. Smith 14*); Second day, Northamptonshire 166-2 (A. Fordham 54*, A. J. Lamb 18*); Third day, Surrey 60-2 (P. D. Atkins 21*, G. J. Kersey 2*).

Northamptonshire

A. Fordham lbw b Waqar Younis	18	– c Ward b Murphy	87
N. A. Felton lbw b Murphy	66	– c Kersey b Benjamin	3
R. J. Bailey c Smith b Benjamin	4	– c Lynch b Butcher	86
*A. J. Lamb c Bicknell b Butcher	15	– lbw b Waqar Younis	88
M. B. Loye lbw b Butcher	16	– run out	42
K. M. Curran run out	41	– b Waqar Younis	16
A. L. Penberthy c Lynch b Smith	32	– run out	21
†D. Ripley lbw b Murphy	0	– c Kersey b Butcher	4
A. R. Roberts c Atkins b Butcher	10	– b Butcher	0
C. E. L. Ambrose c Lynch b Smith	15	– c Murphy b Smith	6
J. P. Taylor not out	2	– not out	2
B 2, l-b 2, w 1, n-b 14	19	B 1, l-b 7	8

1/36 2/43 3/97 4/123 5/175   238   1/12 2/145 3/269 4/279 5/303   363
6/177 7/177 8/197 9/227   6/339 7/349 8/349 9/356

Bonus points – Northamptonshire 1, Surrey 4.

Bowling: *First Innings*—Waqar Younis 20–4–58–1; Benjamin 17–3–55–1; Murphy 19–4–63–2; Butcher 13–4–51–3; Smith 5–2–7–2. *Second Innings*—Waqar Younis 21–4–74–2; Benjamin 22–5–58–1; Murphy 26–7–94–1; Butcher 18–5–73–3; Smith 10–0–56–1.

Surrey

D. J. Bicknell c Lamb b Taylor	6	– lbw b Taylor	5
P. D. Atkins c Ripley b Ambrose	4	– c Loye b Taylor	21
D. M. Ward b Ambrose	40	– lbw b Curran	32
*M. A. Lynch b Taylor	11	– (5) lbw b Curran	15
A. D. Brown b Taylor	4	– (6) c Bailey b Curran	4
A. W. Smith lbw b Roberts	40	– (7) lbw b Taylor	8
M. A. Butcher not out	42	– (8) c Ripley b Taylor	1
†G. J. Kersey c Taylor b Bailey	8	– (4) c Ripley b Curran	16
Waqar Younis c Curran b Taylor	6	– c and b Taylor	0
J. E. Benjamin lbw b Ambrose	1	– c Felton b Ambrose	0
A. J. Murphy c Ripley b Ambrose	1	– not out	2
B 9, l-b 17	26	B 1, l-b 1	2

1/9 2/11 3/37 4/45 5/85   189   1/11 2/44 3/60 4/70 5/78   108
6/147 7/162 8/174 9/179   6/89 7/92 8/103 9/104

Bonus points – Northamptonshire 4.

Bowling: *First Innings*—Ambrose 26.3–12–40–4; Taylor 23–9–51–4; Curran 10–3–34–0; Penberthy 14–6–22–0; Roberts 7–3–10–1; Bailey 2–0–6–1. *Second Innings*—Ambrose 19–11–22–1; Taylor 19.4–7–45–5; Penberthy 8–4–13–0; Curran 12–7–11–4; Roberts 2–0–7–0; Bailey 1–0–8–0.

Umpires: J. C. Balderstone and R. Julian.

NORTHAMPTONSHIRE v ESSEX

At Northampton, August 5, 6, 7. Northamptonshire won by eight wickets. Northamptonshire 24 pts, Essex 6 pts. Toss: Northamptonshire.

Fordham's diligence and another efficient performance by Northamptonshire's seam bowlers condemned Essex, weakened by Test calls, to defeat with four sessions to spare. Stephenson and Prichard batted with great fluency on the first morning, adding 135 in 31 overs and casting doubt on Lamb's decision to bowl first. But Essex failed to build properly on this foundation and Northamptonshire were able to secure an 84-run advantage, thanks to Fordham, who hit 20 fours and a six and was ninth out after occupying the crease for 112 overs. Essex then collapsed to Ambrose and Taylor, and at 60 for six – effectively seven after Stephenson was struck on the right hand by Ambrose – they still needed 24 to avoid losing by an innings. Gallant batting by Shahid, and a late flourish from Childs, averted that but Northamptonshire completed their sixth win of the season just before tea.

Close of play: First day, Northamptonshire 25–1 (A. Fordham 12*, D. Ripley 0*); Second day, Essex 18–1 (J. P. Stephenson 8*).

Essex

N. V. Knight c Ripley b Ambrose	2	– c Loye b Ambrose	10
J. P. Stephenson c Lamb b Taylor	95	– retired hurt	11
*P. J. Prichard c Ripley b Taylor	61	– c Penberthy b Ambrose	0
Salim Malik c Lamb b Penberthy	14	– c Bailey b Taylor	3
J. J. B. Lewis c Ripley b Ambrose	6	– c Ripley b Taylor	7
N. Shahid c Ripley b Penberthy	5	– not out	69
†M. A. Garnham lbw b Taylor	34	– c Ripley b Curran	2
D. R. Pringle b Ambrose	28	– lbw b Curran	4
T. D. Topley c Ripley b Curran	22	– c Ripley b Ambrose	5
S. J. W. Andrew not out	6	– c Penberthy b Taylor	5
J. H. Childs c Felton b Ambrose	4	– c Fordham b Curran	23
L-b 7, n-b 2	9	B 2, l-b 3, w 2	7
	286		**146**

1/2 2/137 3/155 4/166 5/173
6/202 7/223 8/276 9/276

1/18 2/18 3/23 4/31 5/46
6/60 7/104 8/115 9/146

Bonus points – Essex 2, Northamptonshire 4.

In the second innings J. P. Stephenson retired hurt at 25.

Bowling: *First Innings*—Ambrose 22.2–7–35–4; Taylor 23–2–82–3; Curran 25–8–58–1; Penberthy 21–5–96–2; Bailey 2–0–8–0. *Second Innings*—Ambrose 20–8–39–3; Taylor 18–4–53–3; Curran 6.5–1–22–3; Penberthy 8–1–27–0.

Northamptonshire

A. Fordham lbw b Topley	160	– lbw b Pringle	8
N. A. Felton c Shahid b Topley	7	– not out	18
†D. Ripley b Stephenson	22		
R. J. Bailey lbw b Stephenson	14	– (3) c Salim Malik b Andrew	29
*A. J. Lamb c Andrew b Childs	52	– (4) not out	4
M. B. Loye st Garnham b Childs	21		
R. J. Warren lbw b Childs	0		
K. M. Curran c Andrew b Pringle	36		
A. L. Penberthy c Stephenson b Pringle	0		
C. E. L. Ambrose not out	21		
J. P. Taylor b Pringle	0		
L-b 9, n-b 28	37	L-b 1, n-b 4	5
	370	(2 wkts)	**64**

1/23 2/66 3/104 4/180 5/244
6/250 7/317 8/317 9/369

1/10 2/58

Bonus points – Northamptonshire 4, Essex 4.

Bowling: *First Innings*—Andrew 21–1–91–0; Pringle 30.5–8–71–3; Topley 24–4–92–2; Stephenson 19–3–55–2; Childs 18–3–52–3. *Second Innings*—Pringle 8–2–23–1; Topley 9–1–34–0; Andrew 1.3–1–6–1.

Umpires: B. J. Meyer and D. O. Oslear.

NORTHAMPTONSHIRE v DURHAM

At Northampton, August 12, 13, 14. Northamptonshire won by an innings and 48 runs. Northamptonshire 23 pts, Durham 4 pts. Toss: Northamptonshire.

Northamptonshire's run of home success continued in their 2,000th first-class match, with their 482nd win: Durham capitulated abjectly on the third afternoon. Facing a deficit of 137, they were dismissed in 43.3 overs. Only Bainbridge demonstrated the required application, for two hours, after an equally determined 142-minute stay in the first innings. Taylor and Bowen did the early damage, aided by Parker, who ran himself out attempting a sharp single to cover, and the tail was no match for Ambrose. Durham had also struggled on the opening day when their hesitant progress was interrupted by a thunderstorm which docked 71 overs. Northamptonshire's reply was built around a fourth-wicket stand of 168 in 47 overs between Lamb and Loye, both dropped before reaching 50. Graveney eventually dismissed them with successive deliveries, returning his best figures for Durham, but Ripley and Bowen batted sensibly to extend the lead, and Northamptonshire pressed home their advantage.

Close of play: First day, Durham 120–5 (P. Bainbridge 24*, I. Smith 4*); Second day, Northamptonshire 226–3 (A. J. Lamb 62*, M. B. Loye 65*).

Durham

G. Fowler c Loye b Taylor	1	– lbw b Taylor	10
W. Larkins c Loye b Bowen	41	– lbw b Bowen	5
P. W. G. Parker c sub b Ambrose	24	– run out	0
S. Hutton lbw b Taylor	8	– c Ripley b Ambrose	14
P. Bainbridge lbw b Bailey	68	– c Ripley b Bowen	40
S. P. Hughes b Curran	0	(11) c Curran b Ambrose	0
I. Smith c and b Curran	26	– (6) c Ripley b Taylor	7
A. C. Cummins lbw b Bowen	6	– (7) b Bowen	6
†C. W. Scott c Warren b Curran	9	– (8) c Loye b Ambrose	3
*D. A. Graveney not out	9	– (9) not out	0
S. J. E. Brown b Curran	1	– (10) b Ambrose	0
B 1, l-b 12, n-b 6	19	B 1, l-b 1, n-b 2	4

1/5 2/66 3/79 4/102 5/115   210   1/15 2/16 3/16 4/51 5/69   89
6/165 7/178 8/200 9/200   6/78 7/87 8/89 9/89

Bonus points – Durham 1, Northamptonshire 4.

Bowling: *First Innings*—Ambrose 21–8–43–1; Taylor 19–4–60–2; Curran 15.2–3–53–4; Bowen 12–2–34–2; Bailey 4–1–7–1. *Second Innings*—Ambrose 12.3–4–24–4; Taylor 12–4–18–2; Bowen 14–4–32–3; Bailey 1–1–0–0; Curran 4–1–13–0.

Northamptonshire

R. R. Montgomerie c Parker b Graveney	35	M. N. Bowen not out	23
N. A. Felton c Larkins b Bainbridge	30	C. E. L. Ambrose c Cummins b Hughes	18
R. J. Bailey c Larkins b Hughes	18	J. P. Taylor c Parker b Graveney	0
*A. J. Lamb c Fowler b Graveney	70		
M. B. Loye c Larkins b Graveney	80	B 13, l-b 8, w 4, n-b 14	39
R. J. Warren c Smith b Hughes	3		
K. M. Curran c Brown b Graveney	4	1/60 2/80 3/94 4/262 5/262	347
†D. Ripley lbw b Cummins	27	6/266 7/275 8/320 9/346	

Bonus points – Northamptonshire 3, Durham 3 (Score at 120 overs: 336-8).

Bowling: Cummins 28–7–89–1; Hughes 24–10–48–3; Brown 14–2–74–0; Graveney 43.1–18–78–5; Bainbridge 18–7–37–1.

Umpires: J. H. Harris and G. A. Stickley.

At Lord's, August 19, 20, 21. NORTHAMPTONSHIRE lost to MIDDLESEX by ten wickets.

NORTHAMPTONSHIRE v LEICESTERSHIRE

At Northampton, August 26, 27, 28, 30. Drawn. Northamptonshire 8 pts, Leicestershire 6 pts. Toss: Northamptonshire.

Needing a victory to keep alive their faint hopes of overhauling Middlesex – who beat Essex inside two days – for the Championship title, Northamptonshire were frustrated by Smith. He defied their attack on a wearing pitch for 78 overs, well supported by the lower order, after Leicestershire had followed on 160 behind with nine and a half hours left. Hepworth set the tone, resisting for four hours before Taylor removed him on the last morning. At 179 for five Northamptonshire glimpsed a way through, but Nixon kept Smith company for 26 overs and Parsons for a further 27. By the time Smith's 259-minute vigil ended Leicestershire were safe, 167 ahead. Northamptonshire had established a strong position as Lamb batted for nearly five hours to hit his sixth century against Leicestershire with 20 fours and a six, and overshadowed Felton's more workmanlike effort. Boon became the only visiting batsman to score a hundred at Northampton in 1993, but Curran and Roberts worked through the rest.

Close of play: First day, Northamptonshire 335-6 (A. J. Lamb 75*, A. R. Roberts 0*); Second day, Leicestershire 173-2 (T. J. Boon 84*, V. J. Wells 22*); Third day, Leicestershire 136-3 (P. N. Hepworth 38*, P. E. Robinson 27*).

Northamptonshire

A. Fordham c Smith b Mullally	21	M. N. Bowen c Robinson b Pierson	22
N. A. Felton c Whitaker b Mullally	105	C. E. L. Ambrose c Boon b Mullally	10
R. J. Bailey lbw b Wells	59	J. P. Taylor not out	0
M. B. Loye lbw b Parsons	7		
*A. J. Lamb b Mullally	162	B 3, l-b 9, w 1, n-b 10	23
K. M. Curran lbw b Parsons	47		
†D. Ripley b Pierson	6	1/71 2/182 3/197 4/212 5/306	467
A. R. Roberts lbw b Millns	5	6/327 7/355 8/445 9/458	

Bonus points – Northamptonshire 4, Leicestershire 3 (Score at 120 overs: 363-7).

Bowling: Mullally 29.2-5-111-4; Millns 27-4-104-1; Parsons 31-11-62-2; Wells 26-4-70-1; Pierson 33-8-94-2; Hepworth 2-0-14-0.

Leicestershire

T. J. Boon c Lamb b Bowen	110	– b Roberts	37
P. N. Hepworth c Bowen b Bowen	13	– b Taylor	42
*J. J. Whitaker c Loye b Taylor	44	– b Roberts	21
V. J. Wells b Curran	50	– c Lamb b Bowen	1
P. E. Robinson lbw b Curran	13	– c Taylor b Bailey	54
B. F. Smith c Bailey b Curran	6	– lbw b Roberts	84
†P. A. Nixon c Bailey b Roberts	16	– run out	17
G. J. Parsons b Roberts	5	– c Ripley b Curran	31
A. R. K. Pierson not out	10	– not out	19
D. J. Millns c Bowen b Roberts	13	– not out	4
A. D. Mullally b Ambrose	9		
B 8, l-b 7, w 1, n-b 2	18	B 13, l-b 14, w 1, n-b 6	34
1/24 2/105 3/209 4/239 5/246	307	1/53 2/97 3/98 (8 wkts dec.)	344
6/249 7/262 8/267 9/288		4/143 5/179 6/220	
		7/285 8/327	

Bonus points – Leicestershire 3, Northamptonshire 4.

Bowling: *First Innings*—Ambrose 23.5-3-60-1; Taylor 18-6-57-1; Curran 16-6-35-3; Bowen 17-3-57-2; Roberts 24-6-51-3; Bailey 19-7-32-0. *Second Innings*—Ambrose 26-5-57-0; Taylor 28-12-40-1; Curran 16-5-48-1; Bowen 16-6-43-1; Roberts 44-15-83-3; Bailey 27-8-46-1.

Umpires: G. I. Burgess and P. B. Wight.

At Canterbury, August 31, September 1, 2, 3. NORTHAMPTONSHIRE drew with KENT.

At Derby, September 9, 10, 11. NORTHAMPTONSHIRE beat DERBYSHIRE by an innings and 46 runs.

At Manchester, September 16, 17, 18, 20. NORTHAMPTONSHIRE drew with LANCASHIRE.

RUNS SCORED ON EACH GROUND, 1993

This table shows the average runs per wicket in the County Championship on all grounds which staged two or more Championship games in 1993.

	Matches	Runs	Wkts	Avge
Hove	5	5,313	117	45.41
Portsmouth	2	2,018	51	39.57
Durham University	2	2,140	57	37.54
Scarborough	2	1,597	43	37.14
Cheltenham	2	2,334	64	36.47
Manchester	7	7,421	207	35.85
Swansea	3	3,190	92	34.67
Nottingham	8	7,581	221	34.30
Leeds	2	2,273	67	33.93
Chelmsford	6	6,343	198	32.04
Canterbury	6	6,040	189	31.96
Derby	6	6,032	191	31.58
Southampton	5	4,223	137	30.82
Bristol	5	4,799	157	30.57
Cardiff	4	3,952	131	30.17
The Oval	8	7,206	239	30.15
Darlington	2	1,832	61	30.03
Worcester	7	6,162	214	28.79
Lord's	9	7,324	257	28.50
Birmingham	9	7,216	262	27.54
Northampton	8	7,376	268	27.52
Leicester	9	7,396	270	27.39
Taunton	6	5,634	226	24.93

NOTTINGHAMSHIRE

President: C. F. Ward
Chairman: M. A. Youdell
Chairman, Cricket Committee: A. Wheelhouse
General Manager/Secretary: B. Robson
Captain: R. T. Robinson
Team Manager: 1993 – M. Hendrick
Head Groundsman: R. Allsopp
Scorer: 1993 – L. Beaumont
1994 – G. Stringfellow

Nottinghamshire knew, when they decided to release three experienced players – Eddie Hemmings, Chris Broad and Kevin Cooper – at the end of 1992 and concentrate on youth, that there could be short-term drawbacks as well as long-term gains. In fact, they ended with a season not dissimilar to the previous one, but once again felt something had to be done. This time the team manager, Mike Hendrick, appointed only 18 months earlier, was sacked. The club said his style of man-management had failed to get the best out of the players.

In the Championship Nottinghamshire finished seventh, three positions down. They led briefly in late May after they beat Kent, having been forced to follow on. Thereafter, as in 1992, they were almost always in the top half but never put together the sequence of victories that might have made them realistic challengers even for place money. In one-day cricket they had another dismal year, going out early – to Somerset both times – in the two knockouts and having a disastrous time and finishing next to bottom for the second year running in the Sunday League. It remains quite mysterious why a county which won the competition with such panache in 1991 should subsequently have won only seven games out of 34.

This time, though, Nottinghamshire were not completely outplayed that often and were usually competing up to the end. However, when they did get in a promising position, they failed to exploit it. It was possible to extract more optimism from the performances in the County Championship. The bowlers in particular adapted well to four-day cricket and the total of 56 bowling points showed that they rarely allowed teams to bat longer than a day. Consequently, when the batsmen did score runs the bowlers could usually convert the advantage into a winning position, as they did against Lancashire, Yorkshire and Durham. The win over Yorkshire gave the team immense pleasure because it was achieved with what was effectively a two-man attack owing to injuries to Chris Cairns, Michael Field-Buss and, late on, Kevin Evans.

In general, Nottinghamshire played best against the best teams. They could, and indeed should, have defeated the eventual champions Middlesex, they tied with the runners-up Worcestershire and beat Glamorgan, Leicestershire and Kent. They were pushing hard to beat Somerset before the weather stopped them and lost narrowly to Surrey after being bowled out for a miserable 68 and stung into a fightback.

Among the individual successes were the opener Paul Pollard and left-arm spinner Andy Afford, who responded well to the extra responsibility

caused by the absence of Broad and Hemmings. Afford, in particular
found that a secure place in the team gave him more confidence. The
biggest improvement, though, came from the New Zealand all-rounder
Cairns, who upheld the tradition of successful overseas players at Trent
Bridge, scoring 962 runs at an average of 43.72 and taking 53 wickets at
23.43. He also showed immense character by returning for the last two
matches having had to go home after the tragic death of his sister. There
were those who doubted Nottinghamshire's wisdom in allowing Franklyn
Stephenson to leave in 1991 after four successful seasons to accommodate
Cairns. He not merely justified captain Tim Robinson's assertion that he
would develop into the county's most consistent batsman, he became a
more accurate bowler without sacrificing any of his pace. Cairns has
decided to take a rest after New Zealand's short tour of England in 1994
and his replacement, the West Indian batsman Jimmy Adams, has a very
hard act to follow.

Of the other front-line bowlers, Evans, who had become such a
dependable all-rounder, had injury trouble, Andy Pick came back to fitness
but lost his form and David Pennett struggled for a time before finishing
well. The biggest problem was Chris Lewis, who took a long time to
recover from the shock of losing his England place. It was September
before he really produced his best form and that was with the bat: a
remarkable, career-best, 247 against Durham, when he was suffering from
flu.

Among the specialist batsmen, Robinson had an indifferent season by his
high standards, while Mark Crawley and Graeme Archer were both
hampered by ankle injuries and unable to develop the promise they showed
in 1992. That gave Wayne Dessaur an opportunity and, like Archer a year
earlier, he took it; though he scored a century as an opener against
Derbyshire he seemed more comfortable batting at No. 3.

Yet again, Paul Johnson's sparkling strokeplay was the most attractive
feature of Nottinghamshire's batting and he hit five Championship
centuries. However, despite the previous year's clear-out it was evident
that the dressing-room was still not an entirely happy place: Johnson
resigned the vice-captaincy early in the season and then prevaricated over a
new contract. However, he signed, for three years, immediately Hendrick
was sacked.

Even so, with Broad gone, Derek Randall retired and Mark Saxelby
reluctantly allowed to go to Durham in search of a regular first-team place,
a team that once seemed to have ample batting was suddenly in danger of
looking very thin. With a little encouragement, Randall might have agreed
to play on but he finally left the game he had adorned, with Nottinghamshire desperate to find a young batsman of similar quality even if they
could never find one who would occupy such a place in the hearts of the
supporters.

The club continued to defend Robinson's captaincy against accusations of
negative tactics and lack of communication and once again found a
different culprit. But Nottinghamshire began 1994 reviewing their entire
management structure and thinking that the long-term gains they were
seeking may still lie a little further into the future. – Nick Lucy.

543

[Bill Smith]

NOTTINGHAMSHIRE 1993

Back row: G. F. Archer, D. B. Pennett, S. Bramhall, R. J. Chapman, R. T. Bates, J. E. Hindson, S. A. Sylvester, M. P. Dowman.
Middle row: M. G. Field-Buss, P. R. Pollard, G. W. Mike, C. C. Lewis, C. L. Cairns, M. A. Crawley, M. Saxelby, W. A. Dessaur.
Front row: J. A. Afford, K. P. Evans, D. W. Randall, M. A. Youdell (chairman), R. T. Robinson (captain), R. A. Pick, M. Newell.
P. Johnson, B. N. French, R. A. Pick, M. Newell.
M. Hendrick (manager),

NOTTINGHAMSHIRE RESULTS

All first-class matches – Played 19: Won 6, Lost 4, Tied 1, Drawn 8.

County Championship matches – Played 17: Won 6, Lost 3, Tied 1, Drawn 7.

Bonus points – Batting 34, Bowling 56.

Competition placings – Britannic Assurance County Championship, 7th;
NatWest Bank Trophy, 2nd round; Benson and Hedges Cup, 1st round;
AXA Equity & Law League, 17th.

BRITANNIC ASSURANCE CHAMPIONSHIP AVERAGES

BATTING

	Birthplace	*M*	*I*	*NO*	*R*	*HS*	*Avge*
‡P. R. Pollard	*Nottingham*	17	29	1	1,273	180	45.46
‡P. Johnson	*Newark*	15	25	1	1,089	187	45.37
‡C. L. Cairns§	*Picton, New Zealand*	15	23	1	962	93	43.72
‡R. T. Robinson	*Sutton-in-Ashfield*	17	29	4	1,092	139*	43.68
W. A. Dessaur	*Nottingham*	6	9	0	325	104	36.11
C. C. Lewis	*Georgetown, Guyana*	12	18	2	577	247	36.06
G. F. Archer	*Carlisle*	4	6	1	163	59*	32.60
M. Saxelby	*Worksop*	10	15	0	464	73	30.93
‡D. W. Randall	*Retford*	5	10	0	280	98	28.00
‡K. P. Evans	*Calverton*	8	12	3	206	56	22.88
M. A. Crawley	*Newton-le-Willows*	9	16	2	306	81	21.85
G. W. Mike	*Nottingham*	7	12	1	237	50	21.54
‡B. N. French	*Warsop*	17	24	3	420	123	20.00
R. T. Bates	*Stamford*	4	4	2	37	18*	18.50
‡R. A. Pick	*Nottingham*	11	12	4	109	22	13.62
M. G. Field-Buss . . .	*Mtarfa, Malta*	9	13	5	79	16	9.87
‡J. A. Afford	*Crowland*	13	17	8	50	11	5.55
D. B. Pennett	*Leeds*	6	4	2	11	10*	5.50

Also batted: J. E. Hindson (*Huddersfield*) (2 matches) 1.

* *Signifies not out.* ‡ *Denotes county cap.* § *Overseas player.*

The following played a total of 13 three-figure innings for Nottinghamshire in County Championship matches – P. Johnson 5, R. T. Robinson 3, P. R. Pollard 2, W. A. Dessaur 1, B. N. French 1, C. C. Lewis 1.

BOWLING

	O	*M*	*R*	*W*	*BB*	*5W/i*	*Avge*
C. L. Cairns	411.5	74	1,242	53	6-70	3	23.43
M. G. Field-Buss	305.3	111	747	28	6-42	1	26.67
J. A. Afford	718.5	223	1,659	57	5-64	3	29.10
K. P. Evans	238.3	57	623	21	6-67	1	29.66
D. B. Pennett	166	33	506	16	5-36	1	31.62
C. C. Lewis	467.2	110	1,280	36	4-34	0	35.55
R. A. Pick	312	73	956	25	5-53	1	38.24
G. W. Mike	200	40	698	17	5-65	1	41.05

Also bowled: G. F. Archer 6.3–0–72–0; R. T. Bates 83–27–215–5; M. A. Crawley 27–6–72–1; W. A. Dessaur 17–2–94–0; J. E. Hindson 39.5–10–114–1; P. R. Pollard 14–0–135–2.

Wicket-keepers: B. N. French 40 ct, 5 st; P. R. Pollard 1 ct.

Leading Fielder: P. R. Pollard 24.

NOTTINGHAMSHIRE v WORCESTERSHIRE

At Nottingham, April 29, 30, May 1, 2. Tied. Nottinghamshire 13 pts, Worcestershire 13 pts. Toss: Worcestershire. First-class debut: A. Wylie.

The season began with Nottinghamshire's first-ever tie in first-class cricket and Worcestershire's first since 1939. Pick, suffering from a badly bruised foot, missed the third day's play, on which he became the father of a son. He returned to be at the centre of the drama. He was beaten by Seymour's accurate throw from the square-leg boundary and just failed to complete the second run that would have given Nottinghamshire victory off the last available ball. The last pair had needed five when Newport began the final over. Earlier, 20-year-old Alex Wylie had shown plenty of raw pace though he collected only one wicket, when French fell on his stumps trying to hook and bruised his shoulder. He was unable to keep wicket and Pollard took over. Both sides found runs easier to get in the second innings: Curtis watchfully steered Worcestershire towards a declaration, batting two minutes short of six hours for his 113 and then setting a target of 296 in 87 overs. Randall began his final season with a flourish, and timed the ball exquisitely in the early stages. But both he and Nottinghamshire lost their way later and Newport bowled Worcestershire back into the contest to set up the finale.

Close of play: First day, Nottinghamshire 6-0 (D. W. Randall 2*, P. R. Pollard 4*); Second day, Worcestershire 28-0 (T. S. Curtis 13*, W. P. C. Weston 15*); Third day, Worcestershire 288-6 (S. J. Rhodes 18*).

Worcestershire

*T. S. Curtis b Pick	43	– c Cairns b Field-Buss	113
W. P. C. Weston c Lewis b Afford	38	– c sub b Mike	49
G. A. Hick c Pollard b Pick	1	– c sub b Mike	8
D. B. D'Oliveira b Pick	1	– c Pollard b Mike	5
A. C. H. Seymour c Pick b Afford	32	– c sub b Afford	49
S. R. Lampitt lbw b Cairns	0	– lbw b Lewis	33
†S. J. Rhodes b Cairns	10	– c Field-Buss b Mike	26
R. K. Illingworth b Lewis	30	– c Randall b Mike	11
P. J. Newport c Randall b Afford	0	– (10) not out	4
N. V. Radford not out	12	– (9) not out	12
A. Wylie c Crawley b Lewis	0		
B 6, l-b 13, w 7, n-b 10	36	B 7, l-b 6, w 2	15
	203	(8 wkts dec.)	**325**

1/76 2/83 3/97 4/98 5/98 6/115 7/187 8/187 9/203

1/104 2/112 3/122 4/226 5/242 6/288 7/300 8/313

Bonus points – Worcestershire 1, Nottinghamshire 4.

Bowling: *First Innings*—Lewis 22-7-27-2; Pick 16-8-28-3; Afford 26-11-43-3; Cairns 17-3-53-2; Mike 16-5-25-0; Field-Buss 7-4-8-0. *Second Innings*—Lewis 34-13-69-1; Cairns 15-2-49-0; Afford 36-10-67-1; Field-Buss 22-6-60-1; Mike 24-5-65-5; Crawley 2-0-2-0.

Nottinghamshire

D. W. Randall c Hick b Lampitt	13	– c D'Oliveira b Newport	98
P. R. Pollard c Illingworth b Lampitt	18	– b Newport	22
*R. T. Robinson b Illingworth	17	– c Curtis b Newport	2
M. A. Crawley c sub b Lampitt	13	– lbw b Newport	39
C. L. Cairns c Lampitt b Newport	40	– c D'Oliveira b Newport	68
C. C. Lewis b Illingworth	13	– lbw b Radford	26
G. W. Mike lbw b Newport	47	– b Lampitt	1
†B. N. French lbw b Wylie	28	– b Newport	5
R. A. Pick lbw b Newport	2	– run out	22
M. G. Field-Buss not out	2	– lbw b Lampitt	4
J. A. Afford b Radford	2	– not out	4
B 5, l-b 15, w 16, n-b 2	38	L-b 1, w 1, n-b 2	4
	233		**295**

1/39 2/40 3/54 4/83 5/129 6/129 7/207 8/216 9/231

1/63 2/65 3/155 4/170 5/226 6/237 7/242 8/285 9/290

Bonus points – Nottinghamshire 1, Worcestershire 4.

Bowling: *First Innings*—Wylie 17–3–50–1; Newport 24–7–50–3; Lampitt 17–5–33–3; Illingworth 26–13–39–2; Hick 9–3–25–0; Radford 4.3–1–8–1; D'Oliveira 1–0–8–0. *Second Innings*—Wylie 5–0–23–0; Radford 11–2–56–1; Lampitt 22–3–85–2; Newport 22–3–63–6; Illingworth 27–5–67–0.

Umpires: B. J. Meyer and P. B. Wight.

At Leicester, May 6, 7, 8, 10. NOTTINGHAMSHIRE beat LEICESTERSHIRE by eight wickets.

At Lord's, May 13, 14, 15, 17. NOTTINGHAMSHIRE drew with MIDDLESEX.

NOTTINGHAMSHIRE v KENT

At Nottingham, May 20, 21, 22, 24. Nottinghamshire won by 74 runs. Nottinghamshire 20 pts, Kent 8 pts. Toss: Kent.

In a remarkable turnaround of fortunes, Nottinghamshire won after following on, their first such victory since 1863, and reached the top of the Championship table. A lively burst of three for ten from Igglesden had reduced them to 30 for three and put Kent in firm control after a solid batting display, enlivened by Fleming's 62-ball 76. But Nottinghamshire's bold approach second time round on a wearing pitch set up an improbable success. Randall, Pollard and Johnson carried the attack to the Kent spinners and all made half-centuries. Kent were left with a tricky target of 179 in 36 overs, but after Ward set off with a blistering 33 from 20 balls they slumped to 68 for five and never recovered. Field-Buss claimed career-best figures of six for 42 and was ably assisted by his fellow-spinner Afford, who snapped up the other four victims as Nottinghamshire won with more than five overs to spare.

Close of play: First day, Kent 110-2 (M. R. Benson 67*, C. L. Hooper 20*); Second day, Kent 394; Third day, Nottinghamshire 68-0 (P. R. Pollard 23*, D. W. Randall 40*).

Kent

T. R. Ward c French b Field-Buss	16	– c French b Field-Buss	33
*M. R. Benson c French b Pick	73	– (5) lbw b Afford	11
N. R. Taylor lbw b Afford	1	– lbw b Field-Buss	8
C. L. Hooper st French b Afford	37	– c Pollard b Afford	0
G. R. Cowdrey c Crawley b Field-Buss	18	– (6) c Pollard b Field-Buss	40
M. V. Fleming c Randall b Mike	76	– (2) c Pollard b Afford	2
†S. A. Marsh c Pollard b Afford	27	– b Field-Buss	1
R. M. Ellison c Mike b Afford	68	– b Field-Buss	2
D. W. Headley b Afford	36	– c Robinson b Afford	3
R. P. Davis c Johnson b Mike	15	– lbw b Field-Buss	2
A. P. Igglesden not out	2	– not out	0
B 2, l-b 17, w 2, n-b 4	25	N-b 2	2

1/73 2/82 3/134 4/138 5/230　394　1/35 2/35 3/36 4/46 5/68　104
6/243 7/284 8/362 9/391　　　　6/85 7/91 8/100 9/104

Bonus points – Kent 4, Nottinghamshire 3 (Score at 120 overs: 386-8).

Bowling: *First Innings*—Cairns 18–4–61–0; Pick 21–3–79–1; Mike 20–5–71–2; Field-Buss 33–12–85–2; Afford 30.2–8–79–5. *Second Innings*—Cairns 2–0–27–0; Afford 14.2–3–35–4; Field-Buss 14–5–42–6.

Nottinghamshire

P. R. Pollard lbw b Igglesden	8	– lbw b Davis	50
D. W. Randall c Benson b Igglesden	10	– c Cowdrey b Davis	73
*R. T. Robinson lbw b Igglesden	0	– st Marsh b Hooper	37
P. Johnson c Cowdrey b Headley	9	– lbw b Davis	54
M. A. Crawley c Ward b Davis	81	– c Benson b Hooper	12
C. L. Cairns c Marsh b Ellison	93	– c Taylor b Davis	34
G. W. Mike c Cowdrey b Davis	2	– c Marsh b Davis	29
†B. N. French c Marsh b Ellison	1	– not out	14
R. A. Pick not out	11	– c and b Davis	0
M. G. Field-Buss c Ward b Davis	4	– c Ellison b Davis	3
J. A. Afford lbw b Headley	0	– not out	2
B 6, l-b 12, w 5	23	B 6, l-b 13, w 1, n-b 2	22

1/15 2/15 3/30 4/30 5/220   242   1/130 2/133 3/215   (9 wkts dec.) 330
6/224 7/225 8/225 9/241   4/234 5/247 6/299
    7/317 8/317 9/325

Bonus points – Nottinghamshire 1, Kent 4.

Bowling: *First Innings*—Igglesden 14–4–49–3; Headley 16.2–4–32–2; Davis 28–10–71–3; Hooper 13–2–27–0; Ellison 10–4–30–2; Fleming 5–0–15–0. *Second Innings*—Igglesden 9–1–29–0; Headley 10–4–20–0; Ellison 3–1–15–0; Davis 40–8–127–7; Fleming 2–0–4–0; Hooper 37–4–116–2.

Umpires: V. A. Holder and P. B. Wight.

At Oxford, May 29, 31, June 1. NOTTINGHAMSHIRE lost to OXFORD UNIVERSITY by seven wickets.

NOTTINGHAMSHIRE v HAMPSHIRE

At Nottingham, June 3, 4, 5, 7. Hampshire won by 169 runs. Hampshire 23 pts, Nottinghamshire 5 pts. Toss: Hampshire.

Hampshire began the game with a below-strength side and later lost Jean-Jacques with a dislocated finger. But they pulled off their first Championship win in 16 matches, having been lifted by a marvellous century from Gower – the 50th of his first-class career. On the opening day of the match (and, presumably by coincidence, the Ashes series) he prompted fresh calls for his return to the England team by batting masterfully for five hours and hitting 19 fours on a wicket already helping the spinners. From then on, Nottinghamshire were on the back foot, despite a fortnight hundred from Johnson and two fine fifties from the rapidly improving Cairns. Nottinghamshire faced 324 on the final day and there was no escape: off-spinner Udal, who had apparently ironed out problems with his delivery after a coaching session with Ray Illingworth, took five for 74, and ten in the match for the first time.

Close of play: First day, Hampshire 297-6 (A. N. Aymes 46*, S. D. Udal 14*); Second day, Nottinghamshire 275-9 (R. A. Pick 4*); Third day, Hampshire 256-9 (K. J. Shine 0*).

Hampshire

T. C. Middleton c Pollard b Cairns	0	– c Crawley b Field-Buss	23
R. S. M. Morris c Randall b Cairns	15	– c Field-Buss b Mike	42
D. I. Gower lbw b Field-Buss	153	– c French b Field-Buss	0
*V. P. Terry lbw b Afford	26	– run out	94
K. D. James c Cairns b Field-Buss	25	– c Crawley b Pick	21
J. R. Ayling b Field-Buss	4	– b Pick	16
†A. N. Aymes c Pollard b Afford	62	– run out	1
S. D. Udal c French b Pick	27	– c Field-Buss b Afford	23
M. Jean-Jacques c Afford b Field-Buss	10		
I. J. Turner not out	4	– (9) run out	8
K. J. Shine b Afford	10	– (10) not out	0
B 10, l-b 8, w 1	19	B 4, l-b 17, w 1, n-b 6	28

1/0 2/35 3/113 4/177 5/184	355	1/33 2/33 3/165 (9 wkts dec.) 256
6/252 7/322 8/331 9/337		4/193 5/211 6/212
		7/229 8/256 9/256

Bonus points – Hampshire 3, Nottinghamshire 3 (Score at 120 overs: 324-7).

Bowling: *First Innings*—Cairns 28-6-77-2; Pick 18-5-51-1; Mike 11-0-57-0; Afford 41.3-15-78-3; Field-Buss 36-13-66-4; Crawley 3-0-8-0. *Second Innings*—Cairns 12-2-26-0; Pick 18.3-4-37-2; Afford 41.1-14-92-1; Field-Buss 23.3-10-51-2; Crawley 2-0-12-0; Mike 4-1-17-1.

Nottinghamshire

D. W. Randall c Gower b James	40	– (2) c Aymes b Shine	1
P. R. Pollard c Morris b Turner	14	– (1) b Shine	15
*R. T. Robinson run out	4	– b Udal	3
P. Johnson c Terry b Udal	100	– c Middleton b Udal	2
M. A. Crawley c Middleton b Udal	6	– (6) c and b Turner	27
C. L. Cairns b Udal	81	– (5) c Ayling b Turner	64
G. W. Mike c Morris b James	21	– c Middleton b Udal	0
†B. N. French lbw b Udal	0	– c James b Udal	0
R. A. Pick not out	10	– c Ayling b Turner	11
M. G. Field-Buss c Morris b Udal	1	– c Middleton b Udal	14
J. A. Afford b Turner	7	– not out	2
B 3, l-b 1	4	B 1, l-b 7, w 1	9

1/37 2/53 3/61 4/85 5/235	288	1/4 2/9 3/11 4/27 5/75	154
6/270 7/270 8/271 9/275		6/92 7/92 8/119 9/152

Bonus points – Nottinghamshire 2, Hampshire 4.

Bowling: *First Innings*—Jean-Jacques 1.3-0-3-0; Shine 8-1-38-0; Turner 28-11-67-2; James 14-2-51-2; Udal 25-6-97-5; Ayling 7-2-28-0. *Second Innings*—Shine 11-6-17-2; Ayling 4-2-4-0; Udal 22-3-74-5; Turner 15.4-3-51-3.

Umpires: J. C. Balderstone and B. Leadbeater.

At Cambridge, June 12, 13, 14. NOTTINGHAMSHIRE drew with CAMBRIDGE UNIVERSITY.

NOTTINGHAMSHIRE v ESSEX

At Nottingham, June 17, 18, 19, 21. Drawn. Nottinghamshire 5 pts, Essex 5 pts. Toss: Essex.

After Stephenson and Prichard had given Essex a flying start, Pakistan batsman Salim Malik steered them to a commanding total with 121 in four hours. He was supported by Ilott, who had rushed up from Lord's after being omitted by England, came in as nightwatchman and made a maiden fifty. Cairns also produced a polished innings, and shared a rousing fifth-wicket stand of 144 with Archer before Nottinghamshire declared 71 runs behind. Lewis and Stephenson helped themselves to unbeaten centuries on the final morning, 128 coming off 14.3 helpful overs from Pollard and Archer. Set a target of 332 in what became 77 overs, Nottinghamshire made a steady enough start. But Pringle swung the ball around in an afternoon spell that brought him four victims and left the home side hanging on for a draw. Robinson held out for 38 overs, batting with an injured wrist.

Close of play: First day, Essex 330-4 (Salim Malik 91*, M. C. Ilott 1*); Second day, Nottinghamshire 174-2 (R. T. Robinson 44*, P. Johnson 21*); Third day, Essex 106-1 (J. P. Stephenson 51*, J. J. B. Lewis 46*).

Essex

*P. J. Prichard c Pollard b Cairns	58	– c Archer b Cairns	8
J. P. Stephenson c Afford b Cairns	97	– not out	113
J. J. B. Lewis c French b Evans	35	– not out	136
Salim Malik c Robinson b Evans	121		
N. Hussain b Cairns	30		
M. C. Ilott not out	50		
N. Shahid c French b Evans	8		
†M. A. Garnham b Field-Buss	8		
D. R. Pringle c Pollard b Cairns	17		
B 4, l-b 9, w 3, n-b 10	26	B 1, l-b 2	3

1/146 2/171 3/245 4/322 5/374   (8 wkts dec.) 450   1/18   (1 wkt dec.) 260
6/400 7/415 8/450

S. J. W. Andrew and J. H. Childs did not bat.

Bonus points – Essex 4, Nottinghamshire 2 (Score at 120 overs: 387-5).

Bowling: *First Innings*—Cairns 30.2–4–88–4; Pick 22–2–95–0; Evans 36–7–102–3; Afford 31–11–72–0; Field-Buss 18–3–80–1. *Second Innings*—Cairns 8–2–19–1; Pick 12–1–30–0; Evans 14–4–33–0; Afford 19–8–42–0; Field-Buss 6–4–5–0; Pollard 8–0–56–0; Archer 6.3–0–72–0.

Nottinghamshire

P. R. Pollard c Shahid b Andrew	37	– c Ilott b Childs	29
M. Saxelby b Ilott	57	– c Garnham b Ilott	38
*R. T. Robinson c Hussain b Childs	59	– (6) not out	30
P. Johnson c Pringle b Childs	45	– b Pringle	21
C. L. Cairns st Garnham b Stephenson	80	– b Childs	0
G. F. Archer not out	59	– (3) c Ilott b Pringle	30
†B. N. French lbw b Stephenson	0	– lbw b Pringle	6
K. P. Evans not out	1	– lbw b Pringle	4
R. A. Pick (did not bat)		– lbw b Salim Malik	18
M. G. Field-Buss (did not bat)		– not out	0
B 11, l-b 11, w 1, n-b 18	41	B 4, l-b 2, w 1, n-b 14	21

1/88 2/124 3/211 4/218   (6 wkts dec.) 379   1/70 2/75 3/122   (8 wkts) 197
5/362 6/362   4/125 5/125 6/133
                                               7/143 8/184

J. A. Afford did not bat.

Bonus points – Nottinghamshire 3, Essex 1 (Score at 120 overs: 308-4).

Bowling: *First Innings*—Ilott 27–4–60–1; Andrew 29–5–75–1; Pringle 18–3–50–0; Childs 37–9–90–2; Salim Malik 12–1–39–0; Stephenson 14–3–43–2. *Second Innings*—Ilott 20–3–54–1; Andrew 11–5–39–0; Childs 24–7–50–2; Pringle 13.5–4–33–4; Salim Malik 8–3–15–1.

Umpires: H. D. Bird and B. Dudleston.

At Swansea, June 24, 25, 26, 28. NOTTINGHAMSHIRE beat GLAMORGAN by eight wickets.

At Northampton, July 1, 2, 3. NOTTINGHAMSHIRE lost to NORTHAMPTONSHIRE by 171 runs.

NOTTINGHAMSHIRE v SOMERSET

At Nottingham, July 15, 16, 17, 19. Drawn. Nottinghamshire 5 pts, Somerset 2 pts. Toss: Nottinghamshire.

A game badly disrupted by the weather, with the first day washed out, ended with Nottinghamshire pressing hard for victory, only for the rain to have the final say. Pick took four Somerset wickets in the first innings, providing a rare moment of encouragement for him in a frustrating season. And after left-handers Pollard and Saxelby had shared a stand of 138 to set up a declaration 41 runs behind, Somerset again ran into trouble. With Lewis firing away, it took a defiant innings from Harden, battling for 220 minutes and hitting 12 fours, to frustrate Nottinghamshire. Harden accepted an offer to go off for bad light when he was one short of a well-deserved century; play never resumed.

Close of play: First day, No play; Second day, Somerset 181-7 (Mushtaq Ahmed 13*, A. R. Caddick 5*); Third day, Somerset 13-2 (A. R. Caddick 0*, R. J. Harden 0*).

Somerset

M. N. Lathwell b Pick	29	– c and b Cairns	9
N. A. Folland hit wkt b Cairns	57	– c French b Lewis	2
R. J. Harden c Pollard b Afford	16	– (4) not out	99
*C. J. Tavaré c Evans b Cairns	17	– (5) b Lewis	29
K. A. Parsons lbw b Pick	14	– (6) c French b Lewis	1
†N. D. Burns lbw b Evans	16	– (7) c sub b Lewis	8
G. D. Rose c Evans b Lewis	2	– (8) not out	26
Mushtaq Ahmed c Afford b Pick	50		
A. R. Caddick c French b Lewis	19	– (3) lbw b Cairns	8
N. A. Mallender c Evans b Pick	4		
H. R. J. Trump not out	4		
B 1, l-b 1, w 7, n-b 4	13	L-b 1, n-b 12	13

1/50 2/102 3/112 4/131 5/149   241   1/13 2/13 3/27   (6 wkts) 195
6/157 7/161 8/219 9/236   4/100 5/112 6/132

Bonus points – Somerset 1, Nottinghamshire 4.

Bowling: *First Innings*—Lewis 27–5–79–2; Cairns 17–2–63–2; Pick 19.2–5–43–4; Evans 15–4–42–1; Afford 5–1–12–1. *Second Innings*—Lewis 18–4–54–4; Cairns 17–3–53–2; Evans 12–0–24–0; Pick 9–0–42–0; Afford 10–2–21–0.

Nottinghamshire

P. R. Pollard st Burns b Trump	91	*R. T. Robinson not out	2
M. Saxelby c Caddick b Trump	71	L-b 6	6
M. A. Crawley not out	22		
P. Johnson lbw b Mushtaq Ahmed	8	1/138 2/183 3/192	(3 wkts dec.) 200

C. L. Cairns, C. C. Lewis, K. P. Evans, †B. N. French, R. A. Pick and J. A. Afford did not bat.

Bonus points – Nottinghamshire 1, Somerset 1.

Bowling: Caddick 13–2–39–0; Mallender 19–5–49–0; Mushtaq Ahmed 14–1–44–1; Rose 6–0–27–0; Trump 15.5–4–35–2.

Umpires: R. Julian and M. J. Kitchen.

At Manchester, July 22, 23, 24, 26. NOTTINGHAMSHIRE beat LANCASHIRE by an innings and three runs.

At The Oval, July 29, 30, 31. NOTTINGHAMSHIRE lost to SURREY by three wickets.

NOTTINGHAMSHIRE v YORKSHIRE

At Nottingham, August 5, 6, 7, 9. Nottinghamshire won by 115 runs. Nottinghamshire 23 pts, Yorkshire 5 pts. Toss: Nottinghamshire.

Nottinghamshire gained a remarkable win, given that they were reduced to three front-line bowlers when Field-Buss broke his arm, struck by Gough, in Nottinghamshire's first innings and Cairns aggravated an ankle injury when Yorkshire replied. However, Cairns had already boosted his county by scoring 92, including two sixes and ten fours, partnering first Dessaur, in his second Championship game, and later Evans. It was Evans who then took up the role of strike bowler, claiming a career-best six for 67 to give Nottinghamshire a lead of 76. Johnson, with his fourth hundred of the season, and Dessaur strengthened their grip on the game, adding 145 for the fourth wicket, and Yorkshire were left with a stiff target of 336 in just over a day. Although Evans briefly joined the casualty list, with a strained hamstring, and White mounted defiant resistance for the second time in the match, assisted by Batty's first Championship 50, Afford spun Nottinghamshire to victory. Last man Robinson gave him his 50th first-class wicket of the season.

Close of play: First day, Yorkshire 33-0 (M. D. Moxon 24*, A. P. Grayson 7*); Second day, Nottinghamshire 2-1 (M. Saxelby 1*, B. N. French 1*); Third day, Yorkshire 10-1 (A. P. Grayson 2*, R. D. Stemp 3*).

Nottinghamshire

P. R. Pollard lbw b Hartley	8	– b Stemp	0
M. Saxelby b Robinson	18	– b Hartley	7
W. A. Dessaur c Blakey b Stemp	62	– (4) lbw b Batty	49
P. Johnson b Gough	4	– (5) c Batty b Stemp	101
*R. T. Robinson b Batty	19	– (6) b Stemp	22
C. L. Cairns run out	92	– (7) b Stemp	44
C. C. Lewis lbw b Stemp	11	– (8) c Blakey b Stemp	3
K. P. Evans b Gough	40	– (9) lbw b Batty	15
†B. N. French b Stemp	13	– (3) b Hartley	12
M. G. Field-Buss b Gough	12	– absent injured	
J. A. Afford not out	1	– (10) not out	2
L-b 15, n-b 21	36	L-b 2, n-b 2	4
	316		259

1/8 2/41 3/52 4/100 5/201   316   1/1 2/19 3/20 4/165 5/186   259
6/225 7/256 8/274 9/301   6/206 7/216 8/239 9/259

Bonus points – Nottinghamshire 3, Yorkshire 4.

Bowling: *First Innings*—Hartley 15-1-89-1; Gough 20.2-4-52-3; Robinson 18-6-51-1; Stemp 25-4-68-3; Batty 10-1-41-1. *Second Innings*—Gough 19-7-44-0; Stemp 39.5-14-89-5; Hartley 14-6-36-2; Robinson 11-2-44-0; Batty 18-4-44-2.

Yorkshire

*M. D. Moxon c Pollard b Afford	41	– b Lewis	3
A. P. Grayson c French b Evans	22	– c Evans b Lewis	14
R. B. Richardson c Lewis b Evans	38	– (4) c Evans b Afford	5
D. Byas c Afford b Evans	0	– (5) c Pollard b Afford	0
†R. J. Blakey c French b Afford	41	– (6) c Pollard b Afford	22
C. White not out	46	– (7) not out	74
P. J. Hartley c sub b Evans	21	– (8) c Lewis b Evans	6
D. Gough lbw b Lewis	3	– (9) b Evans	3
R. D. Stemp c French b Lewis	1	– (3) c Evans b Lewis	12
J. D. Batty c Robinson b Evans	7	– c Robinson b Afford	50
M. A. Robinson b Evans	0	– b Afford	4
L-b 4, n-b 16	20	B 2, l-b 7, n-b 18	27
	240		220

1/63 2/69 3/69 4/141 5/159   240   1/4 2/29 3/36 4/36 5/48   220
6/198 7/207 8/223 9/240   6/74 7/97 8/101 9/206

Bonus points – Yorkshire 1, Nottinghamshire 4.

Bowling: *First Innings*—Cairns 4–1–6–0; Evans 33–10–67–6; Lewis 31–9–69–2; Afford 50–18–94–2. *Second Innings*—Lewis 24–3–84–3; Evans 16–4–39–2; Afford 31.2–9–77–5; Dessaur 2–0–11–0.

Umpires: D. J. Constant and J. W. Holder.

At Eastbourne, August 12, 13, 14, 16. NOTTINGHAMSHIRE drew with SUSSEX.

NOTTINGHAMSHIRE v DERBYSHIRE

At Nottingham, August 26, 27, 28, 30. Drawn. Nottinghamshire 6 pts, Derbyshire 5 pts. Toss: Nottinghamshire.

Pollard and Dessaur set the tone for a run-scoring feast with a stand of 291, Nottinghamshire's highest opening partnership against Derbyshire, beating the 230 compiled by Broad and Crawley at Derby a year earlier. It was also the best opening stand for Nottinghamshire for 44 years and the fourth highest in the club's history. Pollard hit a career-best 180 in 321 minutes, with 27 fours, while Dessaur registered a more sedate maiden Championship hundred in six hours. Two Derbyshire batsmen then cashed in themselves on the easy surface. Bowler and Adams put on 275 in 71 overs; Adams struck 25 fours and two sixes in 175, his highest score, while Bowler batted more than seven hours for his unbeaten 153 until Barnett declared 97 behind. This was the signal for Pollard and Dessaur to get to work again, putting on another 150, the eighth instance in Nottinghamshire's history of a century opening partnership in each innings. The game briefly changed character when Pennett took three wickets in nine balls, at the start of Derbyshire's second innings, spoiling their hopes of making 339 in 67 overs for victory. But on such a pitch Barnett and Rollins had little trouble in guiding them to a draw. In the process, Barnett overtook D. Morgan's total of 17,482 runs for Derbyshire, thus becoming the county's second-highest run-scorer with only D. Smith's 20,516 ahead of him.

Close of play: First day, Nottinghamshire 320-3 (R. T. Robinson 10*, P. Johnson 9*); Second day, Derbyshire 155-1 (P. D. Bowler 57*, C. J. Adams 76*); Third day, Nottinghamshire 81-0 (P. R. Pollard 32*, W. A. Dessaur 49*).

Nottinghamshire

P. R. Pollard c Adams b Sladdin	180	– c Krikken b Sladdin	91
W. A. Dessaur b Griffith	104	– st Krikken b Vandrau	82
M. A. Crawley c Adams b Base	4	– (5) b Sladdin	9
*R. T. Robinson c Rollins b Base	78	– not out	18
P. Johnson c Adams b Cork	31	– (3) c Morris b Sladdin	19
C. C. Lewis c Cork b Vandrau	42	– not out	16
G. W. Mike c Cork b Sladdin	20		
†B. N. French c Krikken b Vandrau	5		
R. T. Bates not out	9		
L-b 4, w 3, n-b 20	27	B 3, l-b 3	6

1/291 2/300 3/306 4/381 5/442   (8 wkts dec.) 500   1/150 2/185   (4 wkts dec.) 241
6/482 7/488 8/500   3/202 4/222

J. E. Hindson and D. B. Pennett did not bat.

Bonus points – Nottinghamshire 4, Derbyshire 1 (Score at 120 overs: 354-3).

Bowling: *First Innings*—Cork 27–5–97–1; Base 24–6–77–2; Griffith 20–5–60–1; Vandrau 30–6–81–2; Sladdin 39.2–15–126–2; Bowler 11–3–35–0; Adams 6–1–20–0. *Second Innings*—Cork 10–2–24–0; Base 8–2–24–0; Vandrau 26–2–104–1; Sladdin 24–4–83–3.

Derbyshire

P. D. Bowler not out 153	– b Pennett	6
J. E. Morris c Mike b Lewis 13	– b Pennett	12
C. J. Adams b Bates 175	– c Pollard b Pennett	1
A. S. Rollins lbw b Mike 5	– not out	46
M. J. Vandrau lbw b Mike 3		
D. G. Cork c French b Lewis 27		
F. A. Griffith b Lewis 1		
†K. M. Krikken not out 2		
*K. J. Barnett (did not bat)	– (5) not out	55
B 1, l-b 12, w 1, n-b 10 24	L-b 1, w 4, n-b 4	9

1/37 2/312 3/329 4/333   (6 wkts dec.) 403   1/15 2/18 3/21   (3 wkts) 129
5/377 6/387

R. W. Sladdin and S. J. Base did not bat.

Bonus points – Derbyshire 4, Nottinghamshire 2.

Bowling: *First Innings*—Lewis 27–5–91–3; Mike 23–6–87–2; Pennett 14–1–57–0; Hindson 15–2–67–0; Bates 24–7–70–1; Crawley 11–4–18–0. *Second Innings*—Lewis 11–1–43–0; Pennett 13–3–29–3; Bates 14–7–28–0; Mike 4–2–2–0; Hindson 14–6–23–0; Dessaur 4–2–3–0.

Umpires: V. A. Holder and R. Palmer.

At Chester-le-Street, August 31, September 1, 2. NOTTINGHAMSHIRE beat DURHAM by an innings and 157 runs.

At Bristol, September 9, 10, 11, 13. NOTTINGHAMSHIRE drew with GLOUCESTER-SHIRE.

NOTTINGHAMSHIRE v WARWICKSHIRE

At Nottingham, September 16, 17, 18, 20. Drawn. Toss: Nottinghamshire.

The season ended on a damp and dismal note for both counties, heavy rain washing out all but 50 overs on the third day. Trent Bridge had been flooded for most of the previous week, prompting a visit from the fire brigade to pump out water. Although the sun shone for most of Friday and Saturday, the damage had been done, and when the match did eventually start, the players were running around gingerly. There was, however, sufficient time for Ratcliffe to suffer a double misfortune. He was run out backing up when Moles's drive was deflected on to the stumps at the non-striker's end, leaving him one short of 1,000 first-class runs for the season.

Close of play: First day, No play; Second day, No play; Third day, Warwickshire 172-2 (A. J. Moles 54*, T. L. Penney 46*).

Warwickshire

A. J. Moles not out 54	
J. D. Ratcliffe run out 26	
D. P. Ostler c Pick b Cairns 19	
T. L. Penney not out 46	
L-b 2, w 1, n-b 24 27	

1/39 2/82   (2 wkts) 172

*D. A. Reeve, Asif Din, N. M. K. Smith, †K. J. Piper, G. C. Small, M. A. V. Bell and T. A. Munton did not bat.

Bowling: Lewis 14–6–22–0; Pick 9–1–31–0; Pennett 11–0–41–0; Cairns 11–1–58–1; Bates 5–2–18–0.

Nottinghamshire

P. R. Pollard, W. A. Dessaur, M. Saxelby, P. Johnson, *R. T. Robinson, C. L. Cairns, C. C. Lewis, †B. N. French, R. T. Bates, R. A. Pick and D. B. Pennett.

Umpires: B. Dudleston and A. A. Jones.

SOMERSET

President: J. Luff
Chairman: R. Parsons
Chairman, Cricket Committee: B. C. Rose
Chief Executive: P. W. Anderson
Captain: 1993 – C. J. Tavaré
       1994 – A. N. Hayhurst
Director of Cricket: R. M. H. Cottam
Coach: P. J. Robinson
Head Groundsman: P. Frost
Scorer: D. A. Oldam

A fascinating season, full of compelling cricket and reverberating with high and low points, brought Somerset no honours but many new friends, besides adding something to their old reputation for unpredictability.

Winning three of the first four Championship matches, including a fantastic Lancashire game, over in two days, and only just losing the fourth to Worcestershire, gave Somerset an excellent start. Although that challenge faltered when the internationals began and Andrew Caddick and Mark Lathwell were called up by England, fifth position and eight victories (both the best since 1981) out of 17 matches constituted the highest percentage of success since 1892. Somerset won the toss only four times, but claimed victory in all four of those games, two of them by an innings. They also lost two matches by an innings.

In the Sunday League Somerset came bottom for the first time, an almost inexplicably dire performance, except that after their early defeats, mostly caused by bad batting, the players lost heart and the club then used the competition for experiments. But there were good performances in the knockouts, which brought a home Benson and Hedges quarter-final – lost to Derbyshire on a bowl-out – and an excellent victory over Surrey to reach the last four in the NatWest. But a below-par effort against Warwickshire brought a fourth one-day semi-final defeat in five years on one of several poor Taunton one-day pitches. In contrast, Taunton's Championship pitches were excellent.

The player of the year, at the heart of much of Somerset's success, was unmistakably Mushtaq Ahmed. His beautiful leg-breaks brought 85 first-class wickets at 20.85, his lively batting produced some valuable innings and his fielding was good as well. But it was his huge and obvious enthusiasm for the team which so endeared him to the supporters.

One other newcomer excelled. Nick Folland, with a distinguished Devon record behind him, proved a cultured and dedicated left-hand batsman, who adapted well to the first-class game. Often opening the innings, he averaged over 33 in the Championship in his first full year at the age of 29. If he too often got out in the twenties, two centuries in one match and a Sunday century offered hope of further improvement. Richard Harden was the only batsman to reach 1,000 runs for Somerset. After a poor start he produced several vital innings, besides taking 33 catches, mostly at slip or close in for Mushtaq.

Lathwell began superbly but after being summoned to the one-day internationals (and, to general disgust, not getting a game) he only occasionally produced his best, although his 132 out of 197 all out against Essex was described as "awesome". Caddick had a similar experience. In his first three Championship games, all of which Somerset won, he took 32 wickets for 341 runs, but his last seven brought him only 24 for 627; after appearing for England – he played four Test matches – he found wickets much more elusive. Even so, he was selected for the West Indies and Lathwell, after two Tests, for the England A tour of South Africa.

Andy Hayhurst started the season well but suffered injury and loss of form before returning with two vital centuries while, by his own standards, captain Chris Tavaré, in his last season before retiring, had a poor season that nevertheless included one match-winning century against Glamorgan.

Tavaré's five years with the county, four as captain, had been rewarding ones. He will be kindly remembered as a splendid contributor to the team and a dignified upholder of cricket's best traditions. It was January before Somerset were able to name a successor. They had hopes of signing either John Morris from Derbyshire or James Whitaker from Leicestershire as captain but, in the end, settled on Hayhurst ahead of two other internal candidates, Harden and Folland.

No other specialist batsman made an indelible mark although Ian Fletcher, unluckily injured during a fine innings (his first of the season) and Keith Parsons showed some promise. As the only authentic all-rounder Graham Rose, who played every Championship match, had an excellent year, with 865 first-class runs and 43 wickets and a string of good one-day efforts, while the youngsters Jason Kerr and Andrew Payne showed glimpses of ability. Neil Mallender, despite missing most of May through injury, was his usual reliable self, with 32 wickets at 24.12, while Andre van Troost, whose very sharp pace occasionally conjured a wicket in unpromising circumstances, was still erratic and expensive at times. Off-spinner Harvey Trump, given fewer chances than most had hoped, still applied himself well, but Andrew Cottam, the slow left-armer, left at the end of the season for Northamptonshire. Wicket-keeper Neil Burns adapted well to the wiles of Mushtaq for much of the season but, in an attempt to gain batting solidity, was later replaced by Rob Turner, who took over capably for the last five matches. In September Piran Holloway was signed from Warwickshire.

Gates were generally good, a successful drive brought 1,000 new members, and strong local efforts for the two festivals at Bath and Weston-super-Mare made them safe for at least one more season, despite only one Championship match and one Sunday League game being allotted to each. Helped by the profits from the well-attended Ashes series, the club announced a huge surplus of £332,033, which included £120,000 raised by the Centenary Fund.

Among the many pleasant memories of the season was one which should have erased any bitter thoughts remaining from the 1986 crisis, when Viv Richards and Joel Garner were sacked and Ian Botham resigned. The county offered – and happily the offer was accepted – honorary life membership to all three, and also to Roy Kerslake, the former chairman who supported them. – Eric Hill.

SOMERSET 1993

[Bill Smith]

Back row: I. Fletcher, A. Payne, G. W. White, P. R. Clifford, K. A. Parsons, N. A. Folland, H. R. J. Trump, A. C. Cottam. Middle row: P. J. Robinson (coach), J. I. D. Kerr, K. J. Parsons, A. P. van Troost, J. C. Hallett, R. J. Turner, N. A. Mallender. Front row: M. N. Lathwell, A. R. Caddick, N. D. Burns, C. J. Tavaré (captain), R. Parsons (chairman), R. M. H. Cottam (director of cricket), R. J. Harden, G. D. Rose, A. N. Hayhurst. Insets: Mushtaq Ahmed, M. E. Trescothick.

SOMERSET RESULTS

All first-class matches – Played 18: Won 8, Lost 8, Drawn 2.

County Championship matches – Played 17: Won 8, Lost 7, Drawn 2.

Bonus points – Batting 26, Bowling 59.

Competition placings – Britannic Assurance County Championship, 5th;
NatWest Bank Trophy, s-f; Benson and Hedges Cup, q-f;
AXA Equity & Law League, 18th.

BRITANNIC ASSURANCE CHAMPIONSHIP AVERAGES

BATTING

	Birthplace	M	I	NO	R	HS	Avge
‡R. J. Harden	Bridgwater	17	30	3	1,092	132	40.44
‡M. N. Lathwell	Bletchley	13	23	1	802	132	36.45
N. A. Folland	Bristol	16	28	1	839	108*	33.56
‡G. D. Rose	Tottenham	17	29	2	865	138	32.03
H. R. J. Trump	Taunton	7	10	7	79	22*	26.33
‡A. N. Hayhurst	Manchester	13	21	0	531	169	25.28
‡N. A. Mallender	Kirk Sandall	13	16	6	250	46	25.00
I. Fletcher	Sawbridgeworth	7	10	1	223	65*	24.77
‡C. J. Tavaré	Orpington	12	23	1	535	141*	24.31
‡N. D. Burns	Chelmsford	12	21	1	466	102*	23.30
R. J. Turner	Malvern	6	10	1	195	70	21.66
‡Mushtaq Ahmed§	Sahiwal, Pakistan	16	25	0	498	90	19.92
K. A. Parsons	Taunton	4	8	1	133	63	19.00
‡A. R. Caddick	Christchurch, N. Zealand	10	15	3	201	35*	16.75
A. P. van Troost	Schiedam, Netherlands	13	16	6	100	35	10.00
J. I. D. Kerr	Bolton	6	10	3	55	19*	7.85
M. E. Trescothick	Keynsham	3	6	0	14	6	2.33

Also batted: A. Payne (*Rossendale*) (2 matches) 17, 22*.

* *Signifies not out.*   ‡ *Denotes county cap.*   § *Overseas player.*

The following played a total of 13 three-figure innings for Somerset in County Championship matches – R. J. Harden 3, N. A. Folland 2, A. N. Hayhurst 2, M. N. Lathwell 2, G. D. Rose 2, N. D. Burns 1, C. J. Tavaré 1.

BOWLING

	O	M	R	W	BB	5W/i	Avge
A. R. Caddick	319	79	968	56	9-32	5	17.28
Mushtaq Ahmed	694.3	212	1,773	85	7-91	8	20.85
N. A. Mallender	329.5	102	772	32	5-49	1	24.12
G. D. Rose	324.3	62	1,090	43	6-83	2	25.34
J. I. D. Kerr	96	13	320	12	3-47	0	26.66
A. P. van Troost	259	46	931	27	5-47	1	34.48
H. R. J. Trump	215.4	76	488	13	4-74	0	37.53

Also bowled: R. J. Harden 0.3-0-0-0; A. N. Hayhurst 44-15-118-3; M. N. Lathwell 23-8-61-1; K. A. Parsons 1-0-14-0; A. Payne 18.2-4-62-4; C. J. Tavaré 1-0-2-0.

Wicket-keepers: N. D. Burns 35 ct, 3 st; R. J. Turner 12 ct, 3 st.

Leading Fielders: R. J. Harden 32, C. J. Tavaré 22, M. N. Lathwell 16.

At Southampton, April 29, 30, May 1. SOMERSET beat HAMPSHIRE by an innings and 148 runs.

At Taunton, May 8, 9, 10. SOMERSET lost to AUSTRALIANS by 35 runs (See Australian tour section).

SOMERSET v LANCASHIRE

At Taunton, May 13, 14. Somerset won by 15 runs. Somerset 20 pts, Lancashire 5 pts. Toss: Somerset. First-class debut: M. E. Trescothick. Championship debut: Mushtaq Ahmed.

A remarkable game, full of rapid changes of emphasis, ended at 5.30 p.m. on the second day, during which 26 wickets fell on a greenish pitch of fair pace. The ball swung throughout and Caddick improved his career-best match and innings figures for the second consecutive Championship game; both he and DeFreitas took 12 wickets. A third bowler, van Troost, played an unexpectedly decisive role with the bat. On the first morning DeFreitas reduced Somerset to 12 for three before Lathwell led a partial recovery with the highest innings of the match; Folland helped him in the largest stand – 79 in 23 overs generously spiced with fortune. Lancashire seemed to have built the base for a handsome lead before Somerset broke through, but the home batting then slumped again. DeFreitas and Wasim had them at 72 for nine before van Troost scored an extraordinary 35 in 28 balls and extended Lancashire's target to 88. But in the final twist Mushtaq Ahmed and Caddick shared the new ball, all the catches were taken and Lancashire collapsed to 16 for six. Only Watkinson gave them a chance of reaching their goal, before Caddick took his figures to nine for 32 and 12 for 120 in the match.

Close of play: First day, Lancashire 142-4 (N. J. Speak 48*, Wasim Akram 4*).

Somerset

M. N. Lathwell c Atherton b DeFreitas	71	– c Hegg b Wasim Akram	5
M. E. Trescothick lbw b DeFreitas	1	– c Hegg b DeFreitas	3
R. J. Harden c Hegg b DeFreitas	0	– b DeFreitas	18
*C. J. Tavaré c sub b DeFreitas	3	– c Atherton b DeFreitas	3
N. A. Folland c Atherton b Martin	26	– c Atherton b Wasim Akram	6
†N. D. Burns b DeFreitas	10	– b Wasim Akram	3
G. D. Rose b DeFreitas	8	– lbw b Wasim Akram	13
A. R. Caddick c Hegg b Wasim Akram	22	– lbw b DeFreitas	9
Mushtaq Ahmed lbw b DeFreitas	24	– lbw b DeFreitas	4
H. R. J. Trump c Hegg b Wasim Akram	0	– not out	3
A. P. van Troost not out	9	– c DeFreitas b Martin	35
B 1, l-b 8, w 2, n-b 10	21	L-b 2, n-b 10	12

1/4 2/4 3/12 4/91 5/127   **195**   1/9 2/9 3/16 4/31 5/41   **114**
6/140 7/145 8/181 9/181   6/49 7/66 8/66 9/72

Bonus points – Lancashire 4.

Bowling: *First Innings*—Wasim Akram 15-1-45-2; DeFreitas 17.3-4-76-7; Martin 11-1-35-1; Watkinson 4-1-13-0; Barnett 8-3-17-0. *Second Innings*—DeFreitas 17-2-55-5; Wasim Akram 18-5-42-4; Martin 1.2-0-15-1.

Lancashire

G. D. Mendis b Mushtaq Ahmed	37	– c Harden b Caddick 0
M. A. Atherton lbw b Rose	21	– c Tavaré b Caddick 0
N. J. Speak b Rose	58	– lbw b Mushtaq Ahmed 1
G. D. Lloyd c Burns b Caddick	16	– lbw b Caddick 5
†W. K. Hegg c Tavaré b Mushtaq Ahmed	5	– c Harden b Caddick 0
Wasim Akram c Folland b Mushtaq Ahmed	39	– c and b Caddick 11
*N. H. Fairbrother b Rose	0	– c Burns b Caddick 5
M. Watkinson c Burns b Caddick	21	– b Caddick 39
P. A. J. DeFreitas c Folland b Mushtaq Ahmed	6	– c Folland b Caddick 0
P. J. Martin not out	6	– lbw b Caddick 5
A. A. Barnett lbw b Caddick	0	– not out 5
L-b 10, w 1, n-b 2	13	L-b 1 1

1/50 2/76 3/117 4/130 5/153   222   1/0 2/1 3/1 4/1 5/8   72
6/153 7/204 8/208 9/220   6/16 7/39 8/39 9/65

Bonus points – Lancashire 1, Somerset 4.

Bowling: *First Innings*—Caddick 23.2–4–88–3; van Troost 8–2–24–0; Rose 13–2–60–3; Mushtaq Ahmed 14–2–40–4. *Second Innings*—Caddick 11.1–2–32–9; Mushtaq Ahmed 11–3–39–1.

Umpires: J. C. Balderstone and R. Palmer.

At Worcester, May 20, 21, 22, 24. SOMERSET lost to WORCESTERSHIRE by two wickets.

SOMERSET v GLAMORGAN

At Taunton, May 27, 28, 29, 31. Somerset won by 84 runs. Somerset 20 pts, Glamorgan 6 pts. Toss: Glamorgan.

A memorable innings by Lathwell on a very green pitch exactly matched the margin of the victory which carried Somerset to the top of the Championship table. While his partners struggled on the first morning he scored 84 out of 105, hitting 11 fours from 117 balls. As the pitch eased, Glamorgan moved to a promising lead of 33 with only three wickets down, but Somerset captured the last seven for only 34 more. Their batsmen then buckled down well, Tavaré leading the way with an unbeaten 141 – his 48th first-class century, made in the dogged, unruffled fashion that made him famous – and Rose helping to add 85 in 41 overs. The equation for Glamorgan was 300 in what became 79 overs. A brisk start was ended when Caddick bowled James; next he deflected the ball on to the stumps, running out Morris. Dale and Richards, adding 48 in 17 overs, gave Glamorgan some hope and even after Richards was torpedoed by a shooter, the battle continued in gripping style. Caddick, just named in England's party for the First Test, had the last word, taking ten wickets for the third time in three Championship matches.

Close of play: First day, Glamorgan 134-2 (A. Dale 14*, M. P. Maynard 25*); Second day, Somerset 124-3 (C. J. Tavaré 33*, N. A. Folland 6*); Third day, Somerset 289-5 (C. J. Tavaré 108*, G. D. Rose 33*).

Somerset

A. N. Hayhurst c Metson b Watkin	0	– c Metson b Frost	6
M. N. Lathwell c Metson b Watkin	84	– b Watkin	40
R. J. Harden b Lefebvre	2	– b Lefebvre	35
*C. J. Tavaré lbw b Lefebvre	3	– not out	141
N. A. Folland run out	21	– c Croft b Frost	35
†N. D. Burns c Maynard b Frost	6	– c Lefebvre b Dale	22
G. D. Rose c Maynard b Lefebvre	12	– lbw b Watkin	33
Mushtaq Ahmed c Morris b Frost	8	– run out	9
A. R. Caddick not out	35	– not out	30
J. I. D. Kerr b Watkin	3		
A. P. van Troost c Maynard b Watkin	9		
L-b 2	2	B 4, l-b 11	15

1/6 2/19 3/55 4/105 5/110	185	1/32 2/69 3/108 (7 wkts dec.) 366
6/129 7/129 8/147 9/161		4/171 5/205
		6/290 7/304

Bonus points – Glamorgan 4.

Bowling: *First Innings*—Watkin 20.2–8–45–4; Frost 13–1–45–2; Lefebvre 23–4–50–3; Dale 11–0–42–0; Croft 1–0–1–0. *Second Innings*—Watkin 34–8–71–2; Lefebvre 36–14–63–1; Frost 26–5–95–2; Croft 49.1–25–88–0; Dale 15–5–30–1; Richards 5–2–4–0.

Glamorgan

S. P. James c Rose b van Troost	35	– b Caddick	12
*H. Morris c Tavaré b van Troost	53	– run out	20
A. Dale c Burns b Kerr	47	– lbw b Mushtaq Ahmed	42
M. P. Maynard c Tavaré b Caddick	25	– lbw b Caddick	8
I. V. A. Richards c Harden b Kerr	56	– b Caddick	30
P. A. Cottey c Tavaré b Mushtaq Ahmed	9	– c Burns b Kerr	19
R. D. B. Croft c Burns b Caddick	9	– b Caddick	28
R. P. Lefebvre c Harden b Caddick	0	– c Harden b Mushtaq Ahmed	22
†C. P. Metson c Lathwell b Caddick	6	– lbw b Caddick	0
S. L. Watkin c Hayhurst b Mushtaq Ahmed	0	– c Lathwell b Caddick	12
M. Frost not out	2	– not out	5
B 4, l-b 3, w 1, n-b 2	10	B 1, l-b 13, w 1, n-b 2	17

1/74 2/99 3/136 4/218 5/235	252	1/43 2/47 3/64 4/112 5/135	215
6/235 7/244 8/245 9/250		6/164 7/179 8/179 9/197

Bonus points – Glamorgan 2, Somerset 4.

Bowling: *First Innings*—Caddick 23–4–63–4; Kerr 16–2–56–2; Mushtaq Ahmed 29.5–11–62–2; Rose 11–2–34–0; van Troost 12–2–30–2. *Second Innings*—Caddick 22.4–6–66–6; Rose 4–0–13–0; Mushtaq Ahmed 29–9–89–2; van Troost 4–1–12–0; Kerr 7–2–21–1.

Umpires: D. R. Shepherd and P. Willey.

At Chelmsford, June 3, 4, 5. SOMERSET lost to ESSEX by seven wickets.

SOMERSET v MIDDLESEX

At Bath, June 17, 18, 19, 21. Middlesex won by five wickets. Middlesex 22 pts, Somerset 5 pts. Toss: Middlesex.

Middlesex won with an over to spare, having been set 258 to win on a slow pitch. This followed an incident that ranks as bizarre even by modern standards of pre-declaration County Championship goings-on. Somerset's last man van Troost hit a slow long hop from the acting Middlesex captain Carr straight to Haynes on the boundary. Carr shouted "Drop it," because he had already agreed with the Somerset captain Tavaré what the victory target would be. Haynes, however, caught it. And, though there was no audible appeal, umpire Meyer ruled that van Troost was out. The match had begun with its highest stand, 120 between the experimental Somerset openers Folland and Fletcher. After rain on the second day, Carr batted patiently with Ramprakash to enable Middlesex to declare behind and then fed Somerset cheap runs. After taking the catch, Haynes dominated the batting, accelerating after a slow start, hitting nine fours and two sixes and seeing Middlesex to a victory they would probably have achieved even if they had adhered to the agreed formula.

Close of play: First day, Somerset 267-6 (N. A. Mallender 2*, J. I. D. Kerr 0*); Second day, Middlesex 24-2 (M. R. Ramprakash 6*, J. D. Carr 0*); Third day, Somerset 37-0 (N. D. Burns 19*, N. A. Folland 16*).

Somerset

N. A. Folland c Sims b Williams	54	– (2) st Brown b Weekes 23
I. Fletcher retired hurt		– absent injured
R. J. Harden b Feltham	16	– c Brown b Carr 24
*C. J. Tavaré lbw b Feltham	47	– (5) c Carr b Keech 43
A. N. Hayhurst c Brown b Fraser	17	– absent injured
†N. D. Burns b Keech	30	– (1) c Keech b Haynes 79
G. D. Rose c Carr b Fraser	30	– (4) c Haynes b Keech 38
Mushtaq Ahmed lbw b Williams	0	– (6) c sub b Carr 18
N. A. Mallender not out	30	– (7) c Ramprakash b Carr 0
J. I. D. Kerr c Carr b Williams	0	– (8) not out 4
A. P. van Troost c Haynes b Williams	4	– (9) c Haynes b Carr 0
B 3, l-b 12, w 1, n-b 9	25	B 4, l-b 4, w 3 11

1/120 2/150 3/202 4/231 5/264   318   1/54 2/108 3/150 4/208   240
6/264 7/269 8/296 9/318   5/236 6/236 7/240 8/240

Bonus points – Somerset 2, Middlesex 3 (Score at 120 overs: 282-7).

In the first innings I. Fletcher retired hurt at 131; G. D. Rose, when 16, retired hurt at 261 and resumed at 269.

Bowling: *First Innings*—Williams 28.1–4–71–4; Fraser 33–5–93–2; Feltham 28–7–48–2; Emburey 21–5–45–0; Keech 12–5–17–1; Weekes 9–2–29–0. *Second Innings*—Fraser 4–0–18–0; Williams 3–1–7–0; Emburey 11–8–11–0; Weekes 14–2–32–1; Carr 10.5–0–73–4; Haynes 7–1–61–1; Keech 7–1–30–2.

Middlesex

D. L. Haynes c Burns b Mallender	13	– c Burns b van Troost 115
M. Keech c Burns b van Troost	5	– lbw b Rose 5
M. R. Ramprakash c Burns b Kerr	70	– c Burns b Kerr 48
*J. D. Carr c sub b Kerr	49	– lbw b Mushtaq Ahmed 6
R. J. Sims lbw b Kerr	0	
†K. R. Brown lbw b Rose	40	– not out 38
P. N. Weekes not out	45	– (5) c Tavaré b Rose 9
M. A. Feltham c and b Mushtaq Ahmed	32	
J. E. Emburey c Burns b Rose	1	– (7) not out 6
N. F. Williams not out	15	
B 9, l-b 4, w 2, n-b 16	31	L-b 23, n-b 8 31

1/16 2/24 3/126 4/126 5/187   (8 wkts dec.) 301   1/12 2/107 3/122   (5 wkts) 258
6/195 7/267 8/268   4/151 5/248

A. R. C. Fraser did not bat.

Bonus points – Middlesex 3, Somerset 3.

Bowling: *First Innings*—Mallender 19–2–48–1; van Troost 21.3–8–50–1; Rose 18–4–48–2; Mushtaq Ahmed 26–7–70–1; Kerr 16–1–51–3; Hayhurst 3–0–21–0. *Second Innings*—Mallender 14–1–32–0; van Troost 9–2–37–1; Rose 12–4–36–2; Kerr 7–0–29–1; Mushtaq Ahmed 27–5–101–1.

Umpires: B. J. Meyer and G. Sharp.

At Luton, June 24, 25, 26. SOMERSET lost to NORTHAMPTONSHIRE by an innings and five runs.

SOMERSET v SUSSEX

At Taunton, July 1, 2, 3, 5. Somerset won by 120 runs. Somerset 21 pts, Sussex 5 pts. Toss: Sussex.

Two of Somerset's newer recruits inspired victory. Folland, who had stepped up after 12 seasons with Devon, made his maiden century and followed it up with another in the second innings; Mushtaq Ahmed, the Pakistani leg-spinner, took 12 for 175, a remarkable effort as a blow to his bowling hand, late in his lively first-innings 90, reduced him to five overs on the second day. On another grassy pitch Somerset recovered splendidly through a 112-run stand between Folland and Parsons, who hit ten fours in a maiden fifty. Burns, Rose and, especially, Mushtaq shone in taking Somerset past 500. Athey, with his third hundred in successive matches, and Wells responded in kind, but van Troost and Mushtaq suddenly swept away the last five wickets for 11 runs. Folland's second excellent century then set up a target of 350 in 86 overs. Mushtaq, who bowled throughout the innings, took two early wickets, but Athey and Wells ground out 94 in 36 overs the match seemed dead. However, van Troost made the vital breakthrough and Mushtaq steadily mopped up.

Close of play: First day, Somerset 418-6 (G. D. Rose 86*, Mushtaq Ahmed 38*); Second day, Sussex 204-2 (C. W. J. Athey 99*, A. P. Wells 18*); Third day, Somerset 132-2 (N. A. Folland 63*, C. J. Tavaré 22*).

Somerset

N. A. Folland c Greenfield b Hemmings	101	– not out	108
M. E. Trescothick b Giddins	6	– c Greenfield b Hemmings	0
R. J. Harden b Salisbury	24	– c Smith b Salisbury	31
*C. J. Tavaré lbw b Salisbury	0	– b Giddins	57
K. A. Parsons lbw b Salisbury	63	– (6) lbw b Hemmings	0
†N. D. Burns c Wells b Hemmings	73	– (7) c and b Hemmings	3
G. D. Rose c sub b Giddins	138	– (5) c Stephenson b Hemmings	9
Mushtaq Ahmed b Giddins	90		
N. A. Mallender c Athey b Giddins	6		
H. R. J. Trump not out	22		
A. P. van Troost b Giddins	2		
B 5, l-b 15, w 1, n-b 12	33	L-b 6, n-b 12	18

1/33 2/90 3/92 4/204 5/210   558   1/1 2/76 3/188   (6 wkts dec.) 226
6/343 7/492 8/500 9/549   4/209 5/216 6/226

Bonus points – Somerset 4, Sussex 2 (Score at 120 overs: 468-6).

Bowling: *First Innings*—Stephenson 22–4–87–0; Jones 27–1–108–0; Giddins 27.5–4–120–5; Salisbury 32–7–128–3; Hemmings 32–10–92–2; Athey 1–0–3–0. *Second Innings*—Hemmings 32.4–7–67–4; Jones 4–2–13–0; Salisbury 14–1–80–1; Giddins 14–2–60–1.

Sussex

C. W. J. Athey c Rose b Mushtaq Ahmed	137	– c Trescothick b van Troost	93
J. W. Hall c Tavaré b Rose	29	– lbw b Mushtaq Ahmed	4
D. M. Smith lbw b Trump	39	– c and b Mushtaq Ahmed	0
*A. P. Wells c Burns b van Troost	144	– c Harden b Mushtaq Ahmed	37
K. Greenfield c Tavaré b Mushtaq Ahmed	4	– c Trescothick b van Troost	7
F. D. Stephenson c Parsons b Mushtaq Ahmed	19	– st Burns b Mushtaq Ahmed	13
†P. Moores c Burns b Mushtaq Ahmed	22	– b Mallender	6
I. D. K. Salisbury c Tavaré b Mushtaq Ahmed	6	– lbw b Mushtaq Ahmed	0
A. N. Jones b van Troost	0	– c Burns b Mushtaq Ahmed	4
E. S. H. Giddins not out	0	– (11) not out	0
E. E. Hemmings b van Troost	0	– (10) c Burns b Mushtaq Ahmed	9
B 1, l-b 4, w 1, n-b 28	34	B 2, l-b 18, n-b 36	56

1/62 2/171 3/284 4/334 5/368   435   1/22 2/48 3/142 4/171 5/188   229
6/424 7/430 8/435 9/435   6/214 7/214 8/220 9/220

Bonus points – Sussex 3, Somerset 1 (Score at 120 overs: 336-4).

Bowling: *First Innings*—Mallender 19–5–47–0; Rose 17–3–51–1; Mushtaq Ahmed 40–13–84–5; van Troost 19–1–86–3; Trump 56–16–162–1. *Second Innings*—Mallender 8–3–20–1; Mushtaq Ahmed 40.5–16–91–7; van Troost 18–1–73–2; Trump 15–7–25–0.

Umpires: J. H. Harris and J. W. Holder.

At Nottingham, July 15, 16, 17, 19. SOMERSET drew with NOTTINGHAMSHIRE.

SOMERSET v KENT

At Taunton, July 22, 23, 24. Somerset won by seven wickets. Somerset 21 pts, Kent 4 pts. Toss: Somerset.

Fifteen wickets fell before the first tea interval, most of them to the new ball on a firm, grassy pitch. Kent collapsed to 50 for five, though Llong, dropped on two, went on to an unbeaten fifty which made the total a more respectable 144. Then Somerset slumped to 34 for five. Their recovery was the work of Harden, who batted for four hours and was last out for a well-deserved century, including 14 fours. Rose helped him to add 78, then Harden's intelligent farming of the strike brought a valuable 64 from a last-wicket stand with van Troost. When Kent resumed, Ward attacked brilliantly, striking 95 from 91 balls with one six and 17 fours, and Fleming hit out again. But Mushtaq Ahmed, who finished with his third ten-wicket haul of the season, and Mallender, with seven for 75 in the match, gradually worked through their innings. Folland and Harden advanced steadily towards a target of 135, and Somerset won their fourth victory in four Championship matches at Taunton in 1993 after 90 minutes of the third day.

Close of play: First day, Somerset 138-8 (R. J. Harden 72*); Second day, Somerset 55-1 (N. A. Folland 37*).

Kent

T. R. Ward c Burns b van Troost	4	– c Folland b Mushtaq Ahmed	95
*M. R. Benson c Harden b Rose	8	– c Harden b Mallender	10
N. R. Taylor c Folland b Mallender	1	– c Folland b Mushtaq Ahmed	3
C. L. Hooper c Tavaré b Mallender	0	– c and b Mushtaq Ahmed	7
N. J. Llong not out	56	– c Rose b Mushtaq Ahmed	17
G. R. Cowdrey c Harden b Rose	6	– b Mushtaq Ahmed	8
M. V. Fleming lbw b Mushtaq Ahmed	30	– c Tavaré b Mallender	32
†S. A. Marsh b Mushtaq Ahmed	0	– c Burns b Mallender	9
M. A. Ealham c Burns b Mallender	15	– c Harden b Mushtaq Ahmed	0
D. W. Headley c Parsons b Mushtaq Ahmed	1	– (11) not out	1
R. P. Davis lbw b Mushtaq Ahmed	6	– (10) lbw b Mallender	11
B 4, l-b 3, n-b 10	17	N-b 8	8
	144		201

1/5 2/8 3/8 4/28 5/50 6/96 7/98 8/125 9/128

1/23 2/69 3/89 4/134 5/148 6/152 7/177 8/186 9/190

Bonus points – Somerset 4.

Bowling: *First Innings*—Mallender 15–4–42–3; van Troost 12–4–14–1; Rose 9–2–26–2; Mushtaq Ahmed 17.2–7–55–4. *Second Innings*—Mallender 15–6–33–4; van Troost 9–2–44–0; Rose 3–0–42–0; Mushtaq Ahmed 19–6–40–6; Kerr 6–1–28–0; Parsons 1–0–14–0.

Somerset

A. N. Hayhurst lbw b Ealham	5	– c Llong b Hooper	14
N. A. Folland c Marsh b Headley	8	– c Marsh b Davis	58
R. J. Harden c Ealham b Headley	121	– not out	41
*C. J. Tavaré b Ealham	0	– c Ward b Llong	8
K. A. Parsons c Hooper b Headley	4	– not out	4
†N. D. Burns c Marsh b Headley	5		
G. D. Rose c Hooper b Davis	36		
Mushtaq Ahmed c Benson b Davis	1		
J. I. D. Kerr b Headley	7		
N. A. Mallender lbw b Ealham	4		
A. P. van Troost not out	13		
B 4, l-b 1, n-b 2	7	B 4, l-b 4, n-b 2	10

1/13 2/17 3/17 4/28 5/34   211   1/55 2/97 3/120   (3 wkts) 135
6/112 7/114 8/138 9/147

Bonus points – Somerset 1, Kent 4.

Bowling: First Innings—Headley 21.2–3–70–5; Ealham 15–1–49–3; Hooper 22–3–51–0; Fleming 5–1–9–0; Davis 13–6–27–2. *Second Innings*—Headley 8–1–34–0; Ealham 3–0–26–0; Hooper 14–8–17–1; Davis 15–3–44–1; Llong 5.2–3–6–1.

Umpires: J. D. Bond and B. Dudleston.

SOMERSET v YORKSHIRE

At Taunton, July 29, 30, 31, August 2. Yorkshire won by 48 runs. Yorkshire 21 pts, Somerset 5 pts. Toss: Yorkshire.

A dry pitch which rewarded good cricket made for a highly interesting match. After a second-wicket stand of 70 between Richardson and Grayson, Yorkshire lost four wickets for two runs before White led them to 244. Somerset's innings followed a similar course; after an opening stand of 65, they collapsed to 117 for six, to be revived by Rose and Mallender. Mushtaq Ahmed then took the new ball and bowled throughout Yorkshire's second innings; he might have had Richardson caught when four but the West Indian captain profited from his escape to steer his side to 161 for four, sharing the highest stand of the match – 98 in 39 overs – with Blakey, but the last seven wickets perished for 48 runs. Somerset needed 219 and had four sessions to get them, but were thwarted by the lively Gough, who started with three for no runs in 13 deliveries. Rose and Burns, and later Mushtaq, tried to rally the innings from 56 for five, but Gough's final burst – three wickets in an over – earned him career-best figures and ended the match 40 minutes into the final day.

Close of play: First day, Somerset 45-0 (A. N. Hayhurst 15*, M. N. Lathwell 28*); Second day, Yorkshire 101-3 (R. B. Richardson 28*, R. J. Blakey 15*); Third day, Somerset 142-6 (G. D. Rose 33*, Mushtaq Ahmed 24*).

Yorkshire

*M. D. Moxon c Burns b Caddick	8	– b Mushtaq Ahmed	11
A. P. Grayson b Mushtaq Ahmed	37	– lbw b Mushtaq Ahmed	24
R. B. Richardson c Harden b van Troost	45	– (4) c Tavaré b Caddick	68
D. Byas c Lathwell b Mushtaq Ahmed	0	– (3) b Mushtaq Ahmed	20
†R. J. Blakey c Hayhurst b Rose	2	– c Harden b Mushtaq Ahmed	36
C. White not out	74	– c Burns b Mallender	23
P. J. Hartley c Burns b van Troost	26	– c Tavaré b Mushtaq Ahmed	2
D. Gough c van Troost b Rose	11	– b Caddick	3
R. D. Stemp b Rose	0	– c Hayhurst b Mushtaq Ahmed	12
J. D. Batty c Burns b Rose	7	– c Burns b Mallender	0
M. A. Robinson c Tavaré b Caddick	12	– not out	0
B 1, l-b 3, n-b 18	22	B 1, l-b 7, n-b 2	10

1/27 2/97 3/97 4/97 5/99   244   1/25 2/44 3/63 4/161 5/167   209
6/168 7/192 8/192 9/202   6/181 7/188 8/209 9/209

Bonus points – Yorkshire 1, Somerset 4.

Bowling: *First Innings*—Caddick 19–4–65–2; Mallender 11–3–29–0; Rose 14–5–33–4; Mushtaq Ahmed 31–12–68–2; van Troost 10–2–45–2. *Second Innings*—Caddick 25–6–80–2; Mushtaq Ahmed 39.3–10–86–6; Mallender 9–6–8–2; Lathwell 1–1–0–0; Rose 5–0–27–0.

Somerset

A. N. Hayhurst run out	30	– b Batty	27
M. N. Lathwell c Byas b Batty	31	– b Gough	5
N. A. Folland c Grayson b Stemp	29	– c Blakey b Gough	0
R. J. Harden b Gough	13	– lbw b Gough	5
*C. J. Tavaré c Blakey b Batty	0	– b Batty	11
†N. D. Burns b Batty	2	– c Blakey b Gough	27
G. D. Rose lbw b Hartley	41	– c Blakey b Gough	43
Mushtaq Ahmed c Moxon b Batty	14	– c Stemp b Hartley	41
A. R. Caddick b Gough	20	– b Gough	0
N. A. Mallender not out	36	– b Gough	0
A. P. van Troost b Gough	8	– not out	0
B 2, l-b 1, n-b 8	11	B 2, l-b 7, n-b 2	11

1/65 2/65 3/90 4/93 5/103   235   1/16 2/16 3/22 4/51 5/56   170
6/117 7/136 8/165 9/220   6/107 7/168 8/168 9/168

Bonus points – Somerset 1, Yorkshire 4.

Bowling: *First Innings*—Hartley 10–2–29–1; Gough 17.4–4–54–3; Robinson 12–3–36–0; Stemp 17–7–33–1; Batty 26–7–80–4. *Second Innings*—Hartley 11.2–4–19–1; Gough 21–7–42–7; Stemp 19–10–24–0; Robinson 3–1–4–0; Batty 28–10–72–2.

Umpires: J. H. Hampshire and K. E. Palmer.

At Derby, August 12, 13, 14. SOMERSET beat DERBYSHIRE by an innings and 97 runs.

SOMERSET v LEICESTERSHIRE

At Weston-super-Mare, August 19, 20, 21. Leicestershire won by an innings and 15 runs. Leicestershire 23 pts, Somerset 4 pts. Toss: Leicestershire.

A seam bowlers' pitch, grassy and uneven, had claimed 15 wickets for 188 runs shortly after tea on the first day. After Somerset were bowled out inside 44 overs and their main strike bowler, Caddick, broke down, Rose made the initial breakthrough, but a beautifully crafted innings by acting-captain Whitaker, who struck 17 fours, gave Leicestershire control. While Mushtaq Ahmed wheeled away willingly but unluckily, Nixon accompanied Whitaker in a match-winning stand of 141 and Parsons and Millns added a lively 59 in 11 overs for the last wicket. Somerset's second-innings defiance came mostly after Leicestershire claimed the extra half-hour on the second day, when the last pair, Rose and Mallender, began a battling stand which lasted 14 overs into the third day. Millns ended with match figures of eight for 111 before Leicestershire completed their third innings victory of the season.

Close of play: First day, Leicestershire 139-5 (J. J. Whitaker 35*, P. A. Nixon 35*); Second day, Somerset 151-9 (G. D. Rose 16*, N. A. Mallender 8*).

Somerset

A. N. Hayhurst c Nixon b Wells	5	– c Smith b Mullally	13
M. N. Lathwell c Robinson b Parsons	15	– lbw b Millns	1
N. A. Folland c Robinson b Wells	4	– c Millns b Parsons	12
*R. J. Harden c Millns b Mullally	21	– c Nixon b Millns	38
I. Fletcher b Millns	9	– b Millns	24
M. E. Trescothick c Nixon b Mullally	4	– c Nixon b Mullally	0
G. D. Rose c Nixon b Millns	7	– c Millns b Mullally	40
†R. J. Turner lbw b Parsons	11	– c Nixon b Millns	1
Mushtaq Ahmed c Parsons b Millns	11	– lbw b Millns	5
A. R. Caddick b Parsons	4	– b Mullally	6
N. A. Mallender not out	0	– not out	25
B 4, l-b 4, w 1, n-b 12	21	B 17, l-b 1, w 1, n-b 9	28

1/25 2/25 3/33 4/55 5/63   112   1/9 2/15 3/49 4/98 5/99   193
6/80 7/82 8/98 9/107   6/99 7/103 8/109 9/116

Bonus points – Leicestershire 4.

Bowling: *First Innings*—Mullally 12–4–43–2; Millns 15–7–33–3; Parsons 11.2–7–23–3; Wells 5–3–5–2. *Second Innings*—Mullally 20.4–5–63–4; Millns 25–9–78–5; Parsons 11–4–17–1; Pierson 11–6–10–0; Wells 7–5–7–0.

Leicestershire

T. J. Boon c Mushtaq Ahmed b Rose	20	G. J. Parsons not out	49
P. N. Hepworth c and b Rose	12	A. R. K. Pierson b Mushtaq Ahmed	15
*J. J. Whitaker b Hayhurst	92	A. D. Mullally c Turner b Mallender	2
V. J. Wells c Trescothick b Rose	1	D. J. Millns lbw b Rose	24
P. E. Robinson c Trescothick b Rose	2	B 4, l-b 12, w 2, n-b 12	30
B. F. Smith c Folland b Mushtaq Ahmed	12		
†P. A. Nixon lbw b Rose	61		

1/28 2/39 3/49 4/51 5/76   320
6/217 7/231 8/254 9/261

Bonus points – Leicestershire 3, Somerset 4.

Bowling: Caddick 2–0–8–0; Mallender 28–10–78–1; Rose 26–4–83–6; Mushtaq Ahmed 49–14–115–2; Hayhurst 12–5–20–1; Lathwell 2–2–0–0.

Umpires: N. T. Plews and D. R. Shepherd.

At The Oval, August 26, 27, 28, 30. SOMERSET beat SURREY by 281 runs.

SOMERSET v GLOUCESTERSHIRE

At Taunton, August 31, September 1, 2, 3. Gloucestershire won by 22 runs. Gloucestershire 20 pts, Somerset 6 pts. Toss: Gloucestershire.

This entertaining contest ended half-way through the fourth day, the spinners having taken 30 of the wickets on a bare, dry pitch. Off-spinner Ball improved on his career-best figures in both innings, ending with 14 for 169, the best return of the season, while Mushtaq Ahmed took nine for 190. Gloucestershire lost both openers in the first eight balls of the match, but from 81 for five were rescued by Hancock and acting-captain Russell, who added 143 in 36 overs, the highest stand of the game. After a century stand between Harden and Hayhurst Somerset slipped to 178 for five, but the patient Hayhurst, who batted for seven and a half hours, and the more vigorous Rose, who hit two sixes and 18 fours, both scored centuries to give Somerset a lead of 126. Broad and Hinks knocked off the deficit before van Troost broke through, and the Somerset spinners carried on the work until the last pair, Davies and Babington, swung 37 in seven overs. Those runs proved crucial. Chasing only 138, Somerset never recovered from the loss of three wickets in the first two overs, despite the determination of Rose and Turner, who stayed together for 21 overs on the wearing pitch. It was a sad end for Somerset's captain, Tavaré, who had announced that this would be his last first-class match.

Close of play: First day, Somerset 79-1 (A. N. Hayhurst 32*, R. J. Harden 37*); Second day, Somerset 350-8 (G. D. Rose 102*, H. R. J. Trump 1*); Third day, Somerset 18-3 (M. N. Lathwell 9*, C. J. Tavaré 5*).

Gloucestershire

B. C. Broad c Turner b van Troost	4	– c Harden b van Troost 58
S. G. Hinks c Harden b Rose	0	– st Turner b Trump 68
R. I. Dawson c Turner b Mushtaq Ahmed	31	– c Harden b Trump 5
M. W. Alleyne b Mushtaq Ahmed	24	– c Lathwell b van Troost 4
T. H. C. Hancock c Rose b van Troost	76	– c Tavaré b Mushtaq Ahmed 32
A. J. Wright c Trump b Mushtaq Ahmed	0	– c Mushtaq Ahmed b Trump 15
*†R. C. Russell c Harden b Trump	65	– b Mushtaq Ahmed 7
M. Davies c Lathwell b Mushtaq Ahmed	3	– not out 15
M. C. J. Ball lbw b Trump	11	– c and b Mushtaq Ahmed 6
K. E. Cooper not out	2	– c Trump b Mushtaq Ahmed 1
A. M. Babington c Trump b Mushtaq Ahmed	1	– c Mushtaq Ahmed b Trump 23
B 10, l-b 7, n-b 22	39	B 6, l-b 11, n-b 12 29
	256	**263**

1/6 2/14 3/54 4/81 5/81 6/224 7/242 8/246 9/255   1/128 2/136 3/139 4/147 5/186 6/207 7/214 8/220 9/226

Bonus points – Gloucestershire 2, Somerset 4.

Bowling: *First Innings*—van Troost 15-1-68-2; Rose 13-4-29-1; Mushtaq Ahmed 24.2-5-81-5; Trump 17-6-36-2; Kerr 5-0-25-0. *Second Innings*—van Troost 12-1-46-2; Mushtaq Ahmed 37-10-109-4; Rose 3-0-13-0; Trump 40.2-18-74-4; Lathwell 1-0-4-0.

Somerset

A. N. Hayhurst c Hancock b Cooper	117	– c Ball b Cooper 4
M. N. Lathwell lbw b Cooper	7	– b Ball 12
R. J. Harden lbw b Ball	70	– lbw b Ball 0
*C. J. Tavaré c Russell b Alleyne	11	– (5) b Ball 9
I. Fletcher lbw b Ball	0	– (6) c and b Ball 18
†R. J. Turner c Wright b Ball	10	– (7) lbw b Ball 22
G. D. Rose c Cooper b Ball	124	– (8) b Davies 24
Mushtaq Ahmed c Cooper b Ball	16	– (9) c Hancock b Ball 16
J. I. D. Kerr c Ball b Hancock	4	– (10) c Alleyne b Ball 2
H. R. J. Trump not out	10	– (4) c Dawson b Ball 0
A. P. van Troost st Russell b Ball	0	– not out 0
L-b 6, w 1, n-b 6	13	B 2, l-b 4, n-b 2 8
	382	**115**

1/21 2/138 3/155 4/160 5/178 6/306 7/334 8/340 9/382   1/4 2/5 3/5 4/25 5/42 6/47 7/90 8/102 9/114

Bonus points – Somerset 2, Gloucestershire 2 (Score at 120 overs: 276-5).

Bowling: *First Innings*—Cooper 29-8-77-2; Babington 16-5-42-0; Davies 36-13-90-0; Alleyne 19-5-41-1; Ball 54.1-14-123-6; Hancock 6-4-3-1. *Second Innings*—Cooper 12-2-34-1; Ball 25.2-8-46-8; Davies 5-0-12-1; Babington 9-2-17-0.

Umpires: A. A. Jones and D. O. Oslear.
(K. E. Palmer deputised for D. O. Oslear on the 4th day).

At Birmingham, September 9, 10, 11, 13. SOMERSET drew with WARWICKSHIRE.

At Hartlepool, September 16, 17, 18, 20. SOMERSET beat DURHAM by five wickets.

568

SURREY

Patron: HM The Queen
President: 1993 – Sir John Stocker
Chairman: D. H. Newton
Chairman, Cricket Committee: A. Long
Chief Executive: G. A. Woodman
Captain: A. J. Stewart
Coach: 1993 – G. G. Arnold
　　　　1994 – G. S. Clinton
Director of Cricket: M. J. Edwards
Head Groundsman: H. T. Brind
Scorer: M. R. L. W. Ayers

Another season of broken promise and unfulfilled potential demonstrated the difficulty of translating ability into something tangible, such as the County Championship. Surrey were never out of the top six in the title fight, but many felt they should have finished, if not as champions, then certainly in the top three. Surrey did come third, their highest ever, in the Sunday League. But this is not what the club regards as important. Three defeats in a row in August wiped out all hope of challenging Middlesex for the Championship and the weather ensured a finish in a damp, depressing sixth place – a big improvement on the previous summer's 13th but, for Surrey, unsatisfactory all the same.

The fault lay with the batting. There was an appalling propensity for dramatic match-losing collapses. The infamous Benson and Hedges Cup tie against Lancashire was a warning of what was to come. A record stand of 212 had taken Surrey to within 25 runs of victory with more than five overs remaining, and nine wickets left. Those nine wickets fell for 18 runs. That was a pattern the batsmen were unable to break in the Championship. Only two batsmen, Darren Bicknell and Alistair Brown, scored more than 1,000 Championship runs. Captain Alec Stewart and Graham Thorpe reached four figures in all first-class matches, but Monte Lynch and David Ward had poor seasons by their usual high standards, both averaging under 30. Brown's performance was commendable in his first full season, though the stern tradition at The Oval of keeping county caps a little out of reach prevented him receiving a reward that would have encouraged him. Many felt he should have scored a lot more, but he still made three very good hundreds – all of them slower than those of 1992 – and he displayed a degree more wisdom at the crease.

Martin Bicknell deservedly topped the Surrey bowling and finished fifth nationally with 67 wickets – four of them at Test level, after winning two caps against Australia. A knee injury, ultimately necessitating surgery, brought his season to a premature close just before the Oval Test. But Bicknell was just one of three Surrey strike bowlers. Between them Waqar Younis, Joey Benjamin and Bicknell accounted for 187 wickets in the County Championship and each was responsible for bowling the county to victory at various stages of the season. Their performance only served to highlight the poverty of the batting. Benjamin sent down some 200 more overs than Bicknell and 160-odd more than Waqar. He took a career-best six for 19 against Nottinghamshire and his overall effort was not in vain. He was awarded his cap, quite rightly. The greener pitches at The Oval delighted Stewart but they gave the spinners little opportunity to get among the wickets. In the Nottinghamshire match Neil Kendrick took seven second-innings wickets but managed a total of only 29 in 12 first-class matches, while poor James Boiling, given only seven county games, just scraped into double figures.

The season was not without successes. Three Surrey players, Stewart, Thorpe and Martin Bicknell, played in the Fourth and Fifth Tests of the Ashes series – the last time the county had three men in the same England side was in 1972-73, when Graham Roope, Geoff Arnold and Pat Pocock appeared in the Fifth Test against India in Bombay. Thorpe, who along with Stewart also played in the one-day internationals, made an unbeaten century in the second innings of his maiden Test at Trent Bridge as well as hitting a fifty at Edgbaston. He missed the final Test at The Oval only because he suffered a broken thumb during nets before the start, the offending bowler being a member of Thorpe's own Farnham club.

There was also the emergence of Mark Butcher, Adam Hol64ioake and Andy Smith, products of the excellent Surrey youth scheme. They all showed promise, Hol64ioake's maiden first-class century on his debut against Derbyshire revealing some powerful strokeplay coupled with a mature approach. He and Butcher batted particularly well together and the latter's unbeaten maiden half-century in the final match of the season was just reward. Smith, son of W. A. (Bill), who played in the sixties, was another fine prospect, precocious yet patient. Here were three musketeers who could develop into big shots. The signing of Graham Kersey from Kent as wicket-keeper revealed a tidy, unfussy wicket-keeper of ability and agility, who could allow Stewart a permanent break from the stumper's job.

Before the season Glyn Woodman was appointed chief executive. Thereafter there were more goings than comings, most dramatically the departure of coach Geoff Arnold in confused circumstances; some reports said he had been fired, which the club denied. However, Surrey made it clear they wanted more of a strategist in future. Grahame Clinton was then promoted to coach, but he will have to work under a new Director of Cricket, 53-year-old Mike Edwards, the Surrey player of the 1960s and 1970s, who has been out of the first-class game for almost two decades. This appointment did not appear to end the discontent Stewart felt after Arnold's departure and he left on England's Caribbean tour without signalling his readiness to carry on as captain.

There was also surprise, and some protests, when chief steward Maurice Cook and the visitors' dressing-room attendant Ted Woodley went. There were suggestions that the county would be dispensing with their regular stewards and employing outside contractors in future. New brooms may sweep clean but there is a danger of scrubbing bare: Surrey's stewards have long had a reputation for being courteous and helpful. There were three departures among the players: Rehan Alikhan retired, while Paul Atkins and Ian Ward were released. At the end of the season the club became incorporated as an "industrial and provident society" with the committee retaining executive powers. Woodman said members' rights would be safeguarded. – David Llewellyn.

SURREY 1993

[Bill Smith]

Back row: A. W. Smith, M. A. Butcher, D. J. M. Kelleher, A. J. Hollioake, J. Boiling, I. J. Ward, M. R. Bainbridge, G. J. Kersey. Middle row: M. R. L. W. Ayers (scorer), N. F. Sargeant, A. D. Brown, A. J. Murphy, R. I. Alikhan, J. E. Benjamin, N. M. Kendrick, J. Deary (physiotherapist). Front row: P. D. Atkins, D. J. Bicknell, D. M. Ward, A. J. Stewart (captain), M. A. Lynch, M. P. Bicknell, G. P. Thorpe, G. G. Arnold (county coach). Insets: G. S. Clinton (assistant coach), Waqar Younis.

SURREY RESULTS

All first-class matches – Played 19: Won 6, Lost 7, Drawn 6.

County Championship matches – Played 17: Won 6, Lost 6, Drawn 5.

Bonus points – Batting 40, Bowling 60.

Competition placings – Britannic Assurance County Championship, 6th;
NatWest Bank Trophy, q-f; Benson and Hedges Cup, 1st round;
AXA Equity & Law League, 3rd.

BRITANNIC ASSURANCE CHAMPIONSHIP AVERAGES

BATTING

	Birthplace	M	I	NO	R	HS	Avge
A. J. Stewart	Merton	10	16	1	716	127	47.73
D. J. Bicknell	Guildford	17	31	2	1,383	190	47.68
A. D. Brown	Beckenham	17	30	3	1,188	150*	44.00
A. J. Hollioake	Melbourne, Australia	4	7	0	304	123	43.42
G. P. Thorpe	Farnham	11	19	1	721	171	40.05
M. A. Butcher	Croydon	4	7	2	181	66*	36.20
D. M. Ward	Croydon	11	18	1	530	151*	31.17
M. P. Bicknell	Guildford	10	15	2	372	28	28.61
A. W. Smith	Sutton	13	21	2	491	68	25.84
M. A. Lynch	Georgetown, B. Guiana	14	26	1	596	90	23.84
P. D. Atkins	Aylesbury	7	12	0	228	62	19.00
R. I. Alikhan	Westminster	3	6	0	101	41	16.83
G. J. Kersey	Plumstead	10	16	1	221	38*	14.73
N. M. Kendrick	Bromley	11	18	5	191	39*	14.69
A. J. Murphy	Manchester	9	11	8	43	17*	14.33
Waqar Younis§	Vehari, Pakistan	13	18	1	214	28	12.58
J. Boiling	New Delhi, India	7	10	3	69	28	9.85
J. E. Benjamin	Christ Church, St Kitts	16	24	7	122	23	7.17

* Signifies not out.   ‡ Denotes county cap.   § Overseas player.

The following played a total of 12 three-figure innings for Surrey in County Championship matches – D. J. Bicknell 4, A. D. Brown 2, A. J. Stewart 2, G. P. Thorpe 2, A. J. Hollioake 1, D. M. Ward 1.

BOWLING

	O	M	R	W	BB	5W/i	Avge
M. P. Bicknell	415.2	120	1,078	63	6-43	6	17.11
Waqar Younis	449.4	89	1,407	62	6-42	4	22.69
J. E. Benjamin	616.2	150	1,764	62	6-19	2	28.45
N. M. Kendrick	324	103	810	26	7-115	1	31.15
A. J. Murphy	259	69	802	22	3-38	0	36.45
Boiling	180.1	55	467	11	5-100	1	42.45

Also bowled: D. J. Bicknell 1–0–21–0; A. D. Brown 1–0–6–0; M. A. Butcher 43–19–288–9; A. J. Hollioake 89.3–17–263–4; M. A. Lynch 1–1–0–0; A. W. Smith 10–0–346–5; G. P. Thorpe 48–9–165–3.

Wicket-keepers: G. J. Kersey 30 ct, 3 st; A. J. Stewart 19 ct.

Leading Fielders: M. A. Lynch 24, A. D. Brown 15.

At Leicester, April 29, 30, May 1, 2. SURREY beat LEICESTERSHIRE by 89 runs.

At Hove, May 6, 7, 8. SURREY beat SUSSEX by ten wickets.

SURREY v ESSEX

At The Oval, May 13, 14, 15, 17. Drawn. Surrey 6 pts, Essex 8 pts. Toss: Surrey.

A strange, often desperately dull match ended with a frenetic run-chase followed by thunderstorm which washed away Surrey's hopes of scoring an unlikely 242 in 34 overs. B the time they lost their first wicket, they had reached 56 in the sixth over, well ahead of th seven an over required. Despite worsening light, Surrey maintained the momentum an when they were forced off the field by rain needed less than a run a ball. On the secon day, Such had driven a no-ball from Benjamin over long-on for six – thought to be th second of Such's career and certainly the first time any bowler had conceded eight under th new regulation awarding a two-run penalty on top of runs scored. Another Essex bowle Ilott, pressed his claims for an England place in more conventional fashion, with a caree best seven for 85. The Essex batsmen, however, plodded through more than two sessions o the final day for 115.

Close of play: First day, Essex 317-6 (J. J. B. Lewis 51*, D. R. Pringle 9*); Second day Surrey 133-3 (G. P. Thorpe 39*, D. M. Ward 9*); Third day, Essex 38-3 (Salim Malik 16 N. Hussain 7*).

Essex

*G. A. Gooch c Kersey b Waqar Younis	79	– c Kersey b M. P. Bicknell
J. P. Stephenson lbw b M. P. Bicknell	16	– run out
P. J. Prichard c Kersey b Thorpe	26	– c Kersey b Benjamin
Salim Malik c Waqar Younis b Benjamin	41	– c Kersey b M. P. Bicknell	1
N. Hussain lbw b Thorpe	41	– c Lynch b Benjamin	5
J. J. B. Lewis c Kersey b Waqar Younis	56	– c Lynch b Benjamin	2
†M. A. Garnham st Kersey b Kendrick	33	– b Kendrick	1
D. R. Pringle not out	52	– c Lynch b Kendrick	1
N. A. Foster c Kersey b Benjamin	19	– not out	1
M. C. Ilott b Waqar Younis	5	– b Waqar Younis	
P. M. Such c Brown b M. P. Bicknell	25	– lbw b Waqar Younis	1
B 1, l-b 8, n-b 16	25	L-b 12, n-b 2	
	418		15

1/46 2/118 3/162 4/190 5/231   418   1/0 2/7 3/24 4/41 5/110   15
6/302 7/329 8/372 9/379   6/111 7/141 8/142 9/153

Bonus points – Essex 4, Surrey 3 (Score at 120 overs: 350-7).

Bowling: *First Innings*—Waqar Younis 34–9–117–3; M. P. Bicknell 38.3–10–98–2 Benjamin 35–5–111–2; Kendrick 19–13–30–1; Thorpe 13–1–53–2. *Second Innings*—Waqa Younis 25.2–7–43–2; M. P. Bicknell 25–11–46–2; Benjamin 24–10–33–3; Thorpe 7–3–8–0 Kendrick 4–2–11–2.

Surrey

D. J. Bicknell c Salim Malik b Ilott	23	– c Salim Malik b Such	3
*A. J. Stewart c Such b Ilott	48	– (5) not out	1
G. P. Thorpe lbw b Ilott	89	– (6) not out	
M. A. Lynch run out	8	– c Garnham b Pringle	3
D. M. Ward c Garnham b Ilott	27	– (3) c Lewis b Pringle	5
A. D. Brown c Hussain b Such	46	– (2) c Stephenson b Ilott	3
†G. J. Kersey c Lewis b Ilott	2		
M. P. Bicknell b Ilott	34		
N. M. Kendrick c Ilott b Salim Malik	20		
Waqar Younis not out	27		
J. E. Benjamin lbw b Ilott	0		
L-b 6	6	L-b 6	
	330	(4 wkts)	178

1/50 2/87 3/109 4/158 5/238   330   1/56 2/85 3/150 4/169   (4 wkts) 178
6/249 7/256 8/297 9/330

Bonus points – Surrey 3, Essex 4.

Bowling: *First Innings*—Foster 30–8–91–0; Pringle 14–2–59–0; Such 29–8–57–1; Ilott 31.4–8–85–7; Gooch 4–1–25–0; Salim Malik 4–2–7–1. *Second Innings*—Foster 6.3–1–46–0; Ilott 7–0–46–1; Such 6–0–66–1; Pringle 2–0–14–2.

Umpires: G. I. Burgess and J. W. Holder.

At The Oval, May 25, 26, 27. SURREY lost to AUSTRALIANS by 174 runs (See Australian tour section).

SURREY v LANCASHIRE

At The Oval, June 3, 4, 5, 7. Lancashire won by 96 runs. Lancashire 24 pts, Surrey 6 pts. Toss: Surrey. First-class debut: A. W. Smith.

The match came to life when Waqar Younis unleashed his pace and swing but he lost out on the final day to his Test partner Wasim Akram. A dozen balls in Lancashire's second innings were enough for Waqar to rediscover his yorker, and he snapped up Speak, Fairbrother, Mendis and Lloyd in those 12 deliveries for one run. Surrey had to score 399 for victory, which was steep but not impossible; Darren Bicknell and Lynch, opening for Alikhan, who had sprained his foot, reached 114 on the third day and Thorpe and Brown advanced the score to 225. But after Brown holed out just before lunch, only debutant Andrew Smith (son of 1960s Surrey player W. A.) showed any fight. In the end the Surrey batting was too brittle and Wasim too good: the last six wickets fell for six runs, with Wasim taking four in 15 balls. Only fifty from Martin Bicknell in the first innings had enabled Surrey to avoid the follow-on, after Watkinson had steadied Lancashire, reaching the fourth century of his career, but his third against Surrey, with a six off Benjamin.

Close of play: First day, Surrey 4-0 (D. J. Bicknell 2*, R. I. Alikhan 2*); Second day, Lancashire 24-1 (G. D. Mendis 11*, P. J. Martin 8*); Third day, Surrey 114-0 (D. J. Bicknell 51*, M. A. Lynch 55*).

Lancashire

G. D. Mendis lbw b M. P. Bicknell	9	– b Waqar Younis	68
S. P. Titchard c Kersey b M. P. Bicknell	7	– c Kersey b Benjamin	5
N. J. Speak c Kersey b Benjamin	73	– (4) lbw b Waqar Younis	69
*N. H. Fairbrother c M. P. Bicknell b Waqar Younis	9	– (5) b Waqar Younis	0
G. D. Lloyd c Smith b Benjamin	79	– (6) lbw b Waqar Younis	5
Wasim Akram b Benjamin	60	– (7) c Brown b Benjamin	11
M. Watkinson c and b Benjamin	107	– (8) c sub b Smith	28
†W. K. Hegg lbw b M. P. Bicknell	2	– (9) c Kersey b Benjamin	0
P. J. Martin c M. P. Bicknell b Waqar Younis	24	– (3) c D. J. Bicknell b M. P. Bicknell	43
G. Chapple c Alikhan b Smith	5	– not out	16
A. A. Barnett not out	2	– c Lynch b Waqar Younis	12
B 6, l-b 4, w 3, n-b 2	15	B 1, l-b 4, n-b 4	9
	392		**266**

1/10 2/19 3/44 4/163 5/188   392   1/12 2/93 3/191 4/191 5/192   266
5/298 7/301 8/346 9/371   6/197 7/232 8/232 9/238

Bonus points – Lancashire 4, Surrey 4.

Bowling: *First Innings*—Waqar Younis 22–4–85–2; M. P. Bicknell 30–3–92–3; Benjamin 26.1–5–96–4; Kendrick 12–3–49–0; Thorpe 10–1–47–0; Smith 3–0–13–1. *Second Innings*—Waqar Younis 23–6–52–5; M. P. Bicknell 18–3–65–1; Benjamin 19–3–64–3; Kendrick 10–2–36–0; Smith 11–1–44–1.

Surrey

D. J. Bicknell c Hegg b Martin	9	– lbw b Wasim Akram ... 5⊓
R. I. Alikhan lbw b Chapple	14	– (7) lbw b Wasim Akram ...
G. P. Thorpe c Hegg b Martin	6	– b Wasim Akram ... 5
*M. A. Lynch c Lloyd b Chapple	32	– (2) c Hegg b Barnett 6˙
A. D. Brown lbw b Wasim Akram	46	– (4) c Speak b Watkinson 4
A. W. Smith b Martin	14	– (5) b Barnett 4
†G. J. Kersey lbw b Wasim Akram	27	– (6) lbw b Wasim Akram 1⊓
M. P. Bicknell c Watkinson b Chapple	57	– not out. 7
N. M. Kendrick lbw b Wasim Akram	2	– lbw b Wasim Akram ... 0
Waqar Younis c and b Martin	22	– b Wasim Akram ... 0
J. E. Benjamin not out	4	– c Wasim Akram b Barnett ... 0
L-b 5, w 2, n-b 20	27	B 12, l-b 5, n-b 2 ... 1⊓

1/17 2/23 3/56 4/63 5/115   260   1/124 2/142 3/225 4/236 5/296   30
6/123 7/200 8/202 9/251   6/296 7/301 8/301 9/301

Bonus points – Surrey 2, Lancashire 4.

Bowling: First Innings—Wasim Akram 24–8–65–3; Martin 24–7–63–4; Watkinson 24–7–54–0; Chapple 15.4–5–50–3; Barnett 10–3–23–0. *Second Innings*—Wasim Akram 28–10–49–6; Martin 18–4–54–0; Chapple 14–6–40–0; Barnett 30.5–7–84–3; Watkinson 21–4–58–1.

Umpires: R. Julian and G. A. Stickley.

SURREY v GLAMORGAN

At The Oval, June 10, 11, 12, 14. Drawn. Surrey 6 pts, Glamorgan 4 pts. Toss: Glamorgan.
Waqar Younis showed he had returned to the ranks of the unplayable with his second successive five-wicket haul, helped by Stewart, who took six catches in an innings for the third time. But rain ruined Surrey's hopes of joining Glamorgan and Middlesex at the head of the Championship table. Glamorgan had the worst of it from the first innings, when Thorpe scored his first hundred of the season and Maynard broke his left thumb catching Lynch. Waqar's fire then reduced them to 24 for five, though they were saved from the follow-on by Cottey and Lefebvre. In Surrey's second innings, there were two century stands before the declaration came on the third evening, giving Glamorgan 427 to chase. Surrey took three wickets before the close but on the final day they faced only 17.1 overs in four spells during which Stewart took his ninth catch. Richards finished unbeaten on 44 from 46 balls and left the field to a standing ovation in what was presumed to be his last appearance at The Oval.

Close of play: First day, Surrey 233-6 (G. P. Thorpe 90*, M. P. Bicknell 7*); Second day, Surrey 39-0 (D. J. Bicknell 16*, M. A. Lynch 23*); Third day, Glamorgan 16-3 (I. V. A. Richards 1*, P. A. Cottey 4*).

Surrey

D. J. Bicknell b Dale	11	– c James b Croft ... 8⊓
M. A. Lynch c Maynard b Bastien	22	– c Metson b Watkin 2⊓
G. P. Thorpe c Metson b Lefebvre	104	– b Croft 14
*†A. J. Stewart c James b Dale	75	– c Morris b Watkin 2
A. D. Brown c Dale b Watkin	16	– c Morris b Watkin 2
D. M. Ward b Watkin	0	– b Croft 2
A. W. Smith b Lefebvre	7	– not out. 5⊓
M. P. Bicknell lbw b Croft	29	– not out. 5⊓
Waqar Younis c sub b Lefebvre	3	
J. E. Benjamin c Dale b Lefebvre	5	
A. J. Murphy not out	2	
L-b 6, w 2	8	B 5, l-b 9, w 1, n-b 2 ... 1⊓

1/30 2/45 3/181 4/211 5/213   282   1/47 2/66 3/184   (6 wkts dec.) 31⊓
6/220 7/265 8/273 9/275   4/184 5/189 6/189

Bonus points – Surrey 2, Glamorgan 4.

Bowling: *First Innings*—Watkin 27–10–60–2; Bastien 18–2–68–1; Lefebvre 30.5–7–70–4; Dale 12–1–52–2; Croft 11–3–26–1. *Second Innings*—Watkin 21–3–63–3; Lefebvre 18–6–50–0; Croft 33–5–94–3; Bastien 16.4–2–53–0; Dale 11–1–36–0.

Glamorgan

S. P. James c Stewart b Waqar Younis	5	– c Stewart b M. P. Bicknell	2
*H. Morris c Lynch b M. P. Bicknell	5	– c Stewart b Waqar Younis	7
A. Dale c Stewart b Waqar Younis	2	– c Ward b M. P. Bicknell	2
I. V. A. Richards c Ward b M. P. Bicknell	1	– not out	44
P. A. Cottey c Stewart b Waqar Younis	70	– c Stewart b Waqar Younis	23
R. D. B. Croft c Brown b Waqar Younis	5	– not out	14
R. P. Lefebvre c Stewart b Waqar Younis	48		
†C. P. Metson c Stewart b Benjamin	25		
S. L. Watkin c Stewart b Benjamin	2		
S. Bastien not out	0		
M. P. Maynard absent injured			
L-b 3	3	L-b 1	1

1/10 2/10 3/13 4/13 5/24   166   1/7 2/11 3/11 4/64   (4 wkts) 93
6/104 7/160 8/164 9/166

Bonus points – Surrey 4.

Bowling: *First Innings*—Waqar Younis 14–4–60–5; M. P. Bicknell 16–5–30–2; Benjamin 10.5–3–24–2; Murphy 10–3–49–0. *Second Innings*—Waqar Younis 10–2–32–2; M. P. Bicknell 13–3–44–2; Thorpe 4–0–13–0; Smith 1–0–3–0.

Umpires: J. H. Hampshire and R. Palmer.

At Birmingham, June 17, 18. SURREY beat WARWICKSHIRE by eight wickets.

At Lord's, June 24, 25, 26, 28. SURREY lost to MIDDLESEX by four wickets.

SURREY v DURHAM

At The Oval, July 1, 2. Surrey won by an innings and 205 runs. Surrey 24 pts, Durham 4 pts. Toss: Durham.

The margin of victory emphasised the gap between the two sides; Surrey needed less than half the prescribed playing time to move into second place in the Championship after declaring at their first-day 473. Brown made a chanceless, unbeaten 150 at a run a ball, slow by his standards but littered with sparkling strokeplay. Next day, Martin Bicknell's disappointment was Surrey's good fortune. Left out of the squad for the Trent Bridge Test, he bowled beautifully for eight wickets in the match. Waqar Younis could not be kept out of the action. In the first innings he sent two Durham players, Glendenen and Graveney, off for X-rays on elbow and foot; neither was able to bat second time around. Waqar had claimed seven wickets when he limped off with cramp, allowing Durham's last pair, Scott and Hughes, to turn a disastrous 29 for seven into a face-saving 120. The visitors' only other consolation was Bainbridge's five-wicket haul, the first by any Durham bowler in any competition in 1993.

Close of play: First day, Surrey 473-9 (A. D. Brown 150*, A. J. Murphy 17*).

Surrey

D. J. Bicknell b Wood	71	Waqar Younis c Graveney b Bainbridge	7
P. D. Atkins lbw b Cummins	62	J. E. Benjamin b Bainbridge	0
D. M. Ward lbw b Bainbridge	86	A. J. Murphy not out	17
*M. A. Lynch c Scott b Cummins	5	B 5, l-b 21, w 1, n-b 32	59
A. D. Brown not out	150		
A. W. Smith lbw b Bainbridge	6	1/165 2/169 3/191	(9 wkts dec.) 473
†G. J. Kersey c Botham b Hughes	9	4/367 5/381 6/420	
M. P. Bicknell b Bainbridge	1	7/425 8/439 9/439	

Bonus points – Surrey 4, Durham 4.

Bowling: Cummins 22–4–83–2; Wood 14–3–74–1; Hughes 27–9–87–1; Botham 20–3–95–0; Graveney 3–0–18–0; Bainbridge 24–1–90–5.

Durham

G. Fowler c Murphy b M. P. Bicknell	28	– c Kersey b M. P. Bicknell	2
J. D. Glendenen retired hurt	11	– absent injured	
P. W. G. Parker c Smith b M. P. Bicknell	4	– (2) b Waqar Younis	4
J. A. Daley c Brown b Murphy	8	– c Smith b Waqar Younis	0
P. Bainbridge c M. P. Bicknell b Waqar Younis	25	– (3) b Waqar Younis	1
I. T. Botham c Atkins b Murphy	4	– (5) c Benjamin b M. P. Bicknell	4
A. C. Cummins not out	43	– (6) c M. P. Bicknell b Waqar Younis	5
J. Wood c Waqar Younis b M. P. Bicknell	7	– (7) c Brown b M. P. Bicknell	9
†C. W. Scott lbw b Waqar Younis	0	– (8) not out	58
*D. A. Graveney lbw b Waqar Younis	0	– absent injured	
S. P. Hughes b M. P. Bicknell	0	– (9) lbw b M. P. Bicknell	30
L-b 12, n-b 6	18	L-b 3, n-b 4	7

1/43 2/50 3/77 4/81 5/115	148	1/5 2/7 3/7 4/11	120
6/136 7/147 8/147 9/148		5/16 6/20 7/29 8/120	

Bonus points – Surrey 4.

In the first innings J. D. Glendenen retired hurt at 21.

Bowling: *First Innings*—Waqar Younis 11–4–41–3; M. P. Bicknell 11.5–2–44–4; Benjamin 7–1–28–0; Murphy 5–0–23–2. *Second Innings*—Waqar Younis 5–0–21–4; M. P. Bicknell 8.4–2–26–4; Benjamin 9–1–27–0; Murphy 9–2–23–0; Smith 5–2–20–0.

Umpires: K. E. Palmer and R. A. White.

SURREY v GLOUCESTERSHIRE

At Guildford, July 15, 16, 17. Surrey won by an innings and 66 runs. Surrey 24 pts, Gloucestershire 4 pts. Toss: Surrey.

An embarrassingly one-sided match was an inauspicious start to Walsh's reign as Gloucestershire captain, following the resignation of Wright a week earlier. Martin Bicknell became the third bowler after Watkin and Warne to pass 50 wickets for the season, on his home club ground, and duly earned his England call-up. When Bicknell was not taking wickets Waqar Younis was. Once again Surrey cocked a snook at the four-day format by winning inside three days, despite rain on all three which cost some 65 overs. Lynch, who had not reached double figures for a month, rediscovered his touch in a classy 90 and Thorpe emphasised his international status with a composed half-century during Surrey's only innings. On the first day, Stewart, the incumbent England wicket-keeper, claimed his 250th first-class catch (not all behind the stumps) for Surrey, watched from the pavilion by Russell – the man he displaced in the Test team.

Close of play: First day, Surrey 24-0 (D. J. Bicknell 10*, P. D. Atkins 10*); Second day, Surrey 321-7 (A. W. Smith 26*, Waqar Younis 11*).

Gloucestershire

B. C. Broad lbw b M. P. Bicknell	1	– b Waqar Younis	2
G. D. Hodgson lbw b Waqar Younis	3	– c Thorpe b Boiling	60
S. G. Hinks c Brown b Waqar Younis	45	– c Lynch b Waqar Younis	6
M. W. Alleyne c Stewart b Waqar Younis	14	– b M. P. Bicknell	28
A. J. Wright c Stewart b Benjamin	3	– c Lynch b Boiling	2
†R. C. Russell b M. P. Bicknell	12	– hit wkt b Waqar Younis	42
R. M. Wight lbw b Waqar Younis	22	– c Stewart b M. P. Bicknell	0
R. C. Williams not out	18	– lbw b M. P. Bicknell	2
M. Davies c D. J. Bicknell b M. P. Bicknell	0	– c Waqar Younis b M. P. Bicknell	0
*C. A. Walsh b Waqar Younis	21	– not out	3
K. E. Cooper b Waqar Younis	6	– b M. P. Bicknell	1
L-b 4, n-b 4	8	B 1, l-b 1, w 4, n-b 10	16

1/3 2/5 3/29 4/36 5/61   153   1/10 2/28 3/90 4/97 5/128   162
6/96 7/107 8/108 9/143   6/138 7/140 8/156 9/160

Bonus points – Surrey 4.

Bowling: *First Innings*—Waqar Younis 18.3–5–42–6; M. P. Bicknell 20–7–54–3; Benjamin 13–4–49–1; Thorpe 1–0–4–0. *Second Innings*—Waqar Younis 16–4–44–3; M. P. Bicknell 16.5–6–41–5; Benjamin 11–0–51–0; Boiling 13–4–24–2; Smith 1–1–0–0.

Surrey

D. J. Bicknell run out	10	Waqar Younis c Hodgson b Walsh	18
P. D. Atkins b Cooper	41	J. Boiling c Russell b Walsh	2
G. P. Thorpe c Russell b Williams	57	J. E. Benjamin c Wight b Alleyne	22
*†A. J. Stewart b Walsh	0		
M. A. Lynch b Alleyne	90	B 8, l-b 2, w 2, n-b 27	39
A. D. Brown lbw b Alleyne	39		
A. W. Smith not out	46	1/25 2/99 3/100 4/158 5/249	381
M. P. Bicknell c Wright b Wight	17	6/263 7/295 8/332 9/340	

Bonus points – Surrey 4, Gloucestershire 4.

Bowling: Walsh 36–10–90–3; Cooper 36–10–99–1; Williams 12–0–59–1; Davies 8–3–42–0; Alleyne 16.5–3–52–3; Wight 9–3–29–1.

Umpires: G. Sharp and D. R. Shepherd.

At Northampton, July 22, 23, 24, 26. SURREY lost to NORTHAMPTONSHIRE by 304 runs.

SURREY v NOTTINGHAMSHIRE

At The Oval, July 29, 30, 31. Surrey won by three wickets. Surrey 21 pts, Nottinghamshire 4 pts. Toss: Surrey.

Surrey hardly missed the injured Waqar Younis and Martin Bicknell, who had taken 101 of their Championship wickets to date. In their absence, Benjamin and Kendrick stepped up to record career-best figures. Nottinghamshire wilted woefully before Benjamin in their first innings. No one was bowled out for less than their 68 all season and it was the county's worst since they were bundled out for 65 by Kent in 1988. The Oval wicket had been shorn of anything green and was expected to suit spin – as Afford's five wickets on the first day proved – but there seemed to be something in it for everyone. Kendrick's slow left-armers earned seven wickets as Nottinghamshire followed on, though Pollard, Cairns and Evans all played substantial innings to set Surrey 147. The batsmen ran into trouble as Lewis had Smith, Brown and Stewart in quick succession but Surrey's lower order saw them safely home. Five of their six victories had been completed inside three days and they had won their last three home matches, using only eight days out of 12.

Close of play: First day, Nottinghamshire 29-3 (P. R. Pollard 12*, R. T. Robinson 11*); Second day, Nottinghamshire 263-6 (C. L. Cairns 55*, K. P. Evans 36*).

Surrey

D. J. Bicknell lbw b Evans	41	– lbw b Cairns 0
P. D. Atkins c French b Afford	39	– b Lewis 8
G. P. Thorpe c French b Lewis	32	– c Lewis b Afford 39
M. A. Lynch c Pollard b Afford	15	– c Field-Buss b Afford 32
A. D. Brown c French b Afford	60	– c French b Lewis 20
A. W. Smith lbw b Afford	10	– b Lewis 12
*†A. J. Stewart c French b Evans	2	– b Lewis 14
N. M. Kendrick lbw b Evans	0	– not out 5
J. Boiling lbw b Afford	0	– not out 2
J. E. Benjamin c Cairns b Evans	2	
A. J. Murphy not out	4	
B 9, l-b 10, n-b 4	23	B 4, l-b 9, n-b 2 15

1/59 2/117 3/123 4/149 5/173   228   1/0 2/27 3/90 4/100   (7 wkts) 147
6/186 7/186 8/187 9/212   5/123 6/136 7/141

Bonus points – Surrey 1, Nottinghamshire 4.

Bowling: *First Innings*—Cairns 11-2-44-0; Lewis 18-5-36-1; Evans 17-4-51-4; Afford 29.5-8-64-5; Field-Buss 9-7-14-0. *Second Innings*—Cairns 5-0-11-1; Afford 22-5-51-2; Lewis 12-3-34-4; Field-Buss 9-1-33-0; Evans 2-1-5-0.

Nottinghamshire

P. R. Pollard c Lynch b Benjamin	12	– c Smith b Kendrick 97
M. Saxelby c Brown b Murphy	0	– run out 36
M. A. Crawley lbw b Benjamin	0	– (5) c Brown b Kendrick 4
P. Johnson c Stewart b Kendrick	5	– c Boiling b Benjamin 7
*R. T. Robinson c Stewart b Benjamin	24	– (3) lbw b Murphy 26
C. L. Cairns lbw b Benjamin	0	– c Lynch b Kendrick 56
C. C. Lewis lbw b Benjamin	13	– c Lynch b Kendrick 1
K. P. Evans c Bicknell b Murphy	0	– c Lynch b Kendrick 56
†B. N. French b Benjamin	0	– c Brown b Kendrick 15
M. G. Field-Buss not out	5	– not out 2
J. A. Afford c Stewart b Kendrick	3	– b Kendrick 2
B 4, l-b 1, w 1	6	B 1, l-b 1, n-b 2 4

1/0 2/1 3/10 4/30 5/30   68   1/87 2/139 3/149 4/168 5/175   306
6/54 7/55 8/59 9/59   6/203 7/264 8/297 9/304

Bonus points – Surrey 4.

Bowling: *First Innings*—Benjamin 13-7-19-6; Murphy 12-6-22-2; Boiling 4-3-4-0; Kendrick 7-2-11-2; Smith 2-0-7-0. *Second Innings*—Benjamin 31-13-73-1; Murphy 11-3-32-1; Boiling 29-13-44-0; Smith 7-0-40-0; Kendrick 39.1-11-115-7.

Umpires: B. Leadbeater and B. J. Meyer.

At Canterbury, August 5, 6, 7, 9. SURREY drew with KENT.

At Worcester, August 12, 13, 14, 16. SURREY lost to WORCESTERSHIRE by 65 runs.

At Ilkeston, August 19, 20, 21. SURREY lost to DERBYSHIRE by six wickets.

SURREY v SOMERSET

At The Oval, August 26, 27, 28, 30. Somerset won by 281 runs. Somerset 22 pts, Surrey 4 pts. Toss: Surrey.

A third successive defeat was the result of another failure by Surrey's batting. Only a sturdy unbeaten 39 from Kendrick saved the follow-on with van Troost taking his first five-wicket haul of the summer. But, on a good cricket wicket, Harden was able to build a second-innings century and put on 151 with Turner. Benjamin was once again the pick of Surrey's bowling, but he had little support. With Waqar Younis looking exhausted there was nothing to stop Somerset setting an imposing, and ultimately impossible, target of 421. Play throughout seemed unconscionably slow, particularly during Somerset's first innings, though their batsmen argued that this was a fine example of innings-building in the four-day game. Both sides were hampered by injuries to key batsmen: Stewart missed the second innings with a bad neck, while Folland suffered a back spasm. He bravely reappeared at nine down in the first innings, but Harden's efforts spared him further agony.

Close of play: First day, Somerset 275-9 (N. A. Folland 6*, N. A. Mallender 32*); Second day, Somerset 101-3 (R. J. Harden 45*, R. J. Turner 10*); Third day, Surrey 36-1 (R. I. Alikhan 9*, A. W. Smith 14*).

Somerset

A. N. Hayhurst lbw b Hollioake	17	– lbw b Benjamin 6
M. N. Lathwell c Bicknell b Benjamin	12	– c Stewart b Benjamin 6
N. A. Folland not out	6	
*R. J. Harden c Kersey b Waqar Younis	32	– (3) c Brown b Kendrick 132
I. Fletcher c Kersey b Butcher	63	– (4) c Butcher b Waqar Younis . . 23
†R. J. Turner b Waqar Younis	30	– (5) c Kersey b Benjamin 70
G. D. Rose c Kendrick b Waqar Younis	6	– (6) c and b Holliooake. 27
Mushtaq Ahmed c Brown b Benjamin	23	– (7) c Butcher b Benjamin 6
N. A. Mallender not out	32	– (8) not out 34
H. R. J. Trump b Kendrick	19	– (9) not out 15
A. P. van Troost b Kendrick	5	
B 3, l-b 12, w 3, n-b 12	30	B 1, l-b 8, n-b 16 25

1/32 2/49 3/94 4/166 5/184   (9 wkts dec.) 275   1/7 2/14 3/75   (7 wkts dec.) 344
6/187 7/220 8/247 9/255   4/226 5/262
                                                  6/270 7/304

Bonus points – Somerset 2, Surrey 4.

In the first innings N. A. Folland, when 0, retired hurt at 33 and resumed at 255.

Bowling: First Innings—Waqar Younis 24-5-73-3; Benjamin 30-7-80-2; Butcher 18-3-45-1; Holliooake 24-6-49-1; Kendrick 7-2-13-2. *Second Innings*—Benjamin 29-6-79-4; Waqar Younis 28-6-85-1; Holliooake 18-3-63-1; Butcher 14-1-35-0; Kendrick 37-15-50-1; Smith 5-1-23-0.

Surrey

R. I. Alikhan c Lathwell b van Troost	0	– (2) lbw b Mallender 9
D. J. Bicknell c Turner b van Troost.	0	– (1) c and b van Troost. 2
A. W. Smith b Rose	12	– c sub b van Troost 15
*A. J. Stewart c Turner b van Troost	34	– absent injured
A. D. Brown c sub b van Troost	45	– (4) b Mallender. 21
A. J. Holliooake c Harden b van Troost	2	– (5) c Lathwell b Mushtaq Ahmed 3
M. A. Butcher c Harden b Mushtaq Ahmed	0	– (6) c Harden b Mushtaq Ahmed. 37
†G. J. Kersey c Lathwell b Mushtaq Ahmed	10	– (7) c Lathwell b Rose 6
N. M. Kendrick not out	39	– (8) c Harden b van Troost 0
Waqar Younis c and b Mallender	27	– st Turner b Mushtaq Ahmed 15
J. E. Benjamin b Mallender	5	– (10) not out 0
B 7, l-b 5, w 1, n-b 12	25	L-b 18, w 1, n-b 12 31

1/0 2/1 3/29 4/86 5/94   199   1/2 2/36 3/64 4/64 5/93   139
6/99 7/105 8/134 9/193   6/124 7/124 8/133 9/139

Bonus points – Somerset 4.

Bowling: *First Innings*—van Troost 18–4–47–5; Mallender 14.4–5–35–2; Rose 11–0–44–1; Hayhurst 3–0–16–0; Mushtaq Ahmed 21–6–45–2. *Second Innings*—van Troost 14–6–40–3; Mallender 12–4–27–2; Rose 10–6–18–1; Mushtaq Ahmed 10.2–1–36–3.

Umpires: D. J. Constant and D. O. Oslear.

SURREY v HAMPSHIRE

At The Oval, August 31, September 1, 2, 3. Drawn. Surrey 5 pts, Hampshire 7 pts. Toss: Surrey.

Surrey's collapse to the new ball on the second morning meant that they missed out on a possible run feast as Hampshire proved by passing their highest score against Surrey for the second year running. Shine's pace brought him the last five wickets, which fell for 53. A fourth consecutive defeat hung over The Oval until the talented Hollioake, in only his sixth first-class innings, made 70 to follow his maiden hundred against Derbyshire. Two opposing openers, Darren Bicknell and Robin Smith, both reached their fourth centuries of the season. Bicknell had given Surrey the early advantage. Then came Smith's tour de force. He dominated the first-wicket stand with Terry so completely that he scored 127 out of 170 while Terry reached 28. Later, his captain Nicholas fell a frustrating five runs short of his first first-class hundred since June 1991, but night-watchman Connor made an enterprising career-best.

Close of play: First day, Surrey 327-5 (D. J. Bicknell 122*, M. A. Butcher 12*); Second day, Hampshire 297-3 (K. D. James 40*, C. A. Connor 0*); Third day, Surrey 36-0 (D. J. Bicknell 21*, R. I. Alikhan 8*).

Surrey

D. J. Bicknell c Terry b Shine	122	– c Aymes b Connor	50
R. I. Alikhan c Cox b James	41	– lbw b James	36
A. W. Smith b Shine	25	– c Nicholas b Flint	26
*M. A. Lynch lbw b James	32	– c Udal b James	1
A. D. Brown c and b Udal	62	– c Gower b Flint	54
A. J. Hollioake b Connor	8	– b Flint	70
M. A. Butcher c Aymes b Shine	33	– lbw b Flint	2
†G. J. Kersey c Aymes b Shine	3	– b Shine	4
N. M. Kendrick c Aymes b Shine	7	– retired hurt	2
J. Boiling c Terry b Shine	6	– not out	2
J. E. Benjamin not out	10	– not out	8
B 3, l-b 10, n-b 18	31	B 5, l-b 3, w 2, n-b 16	26
	380	(8 wkts)	**281**

1/63 2/104 3/193 4/290 5/301 6/327 7/341 8/355 9/369   380

1/89 2/114 3/116 4/136 5/208 6/216 7/267 8/271   (8 wkts) 281

Bonus points – Surrey 3, Hampshire 3 (Score at 120 overs: 341-7).

In the second innings N. M. Kendrick retired hurt at 269.

Bowling: *First Innings*—Shine 25.5–3–97–6; Connor 36–6–121–1; James 20–8–49–2; Udal 36–13–56–1; Flint 12–1–44–0. *Second Innings*—Shine 20–9–49–1; Connor 14–5–29–1; Udal 41–14–84–0; James 13–2–47–2; Flint 38–16–64–4.

Hampshire

R. A. Smith b Kendrick	127	†A. N. Aymes c Butcher b Benjamin	9
V. P. Terry c Kersey b Butcher	91	S. D. Udal st Kersey b Kendrick	10
K. D. James st Kersey b Kendrick	44	K. J. Shine b Benjamin	0
D. I. Gower b Boiling	13	D. P. J. Flint not out	0
C. A. Connor lbw b Boiling	59	B 1, l-b 7, w 2, n-b 38	48
*M. C. J. Nicholas c Hollioake b Benjamin	95		
R. M. F. Cox c Lynch b Butcher	63		**559**

1/170 2/263 3/296 4/301 5/380 6/512 7/546 8/559 9/559   559

Bonus points – Hampshire 4, Surrey 2 (Score at 120 overs: 402-5).

Bowling: Benjamin 34–6–104–3; Butcher 28–6–81–2; Hollioake 24–5–76–0; Kendrick 33.3–8–94–3; Boiling 40.1–9–129–2; Smith 13–1–67–0.

Umpires: M. J. Kitchen and A. G. T. Whitehead.

At The Oval, September 8, 9, 10. SURREY drew with ZIMBABWEANS (See Zimbabwean tour section).

SURREY v YORKSHIRE

At The Oval, September 16, 17, 18, 20. Drawn. Surrey 4 pts, Yorkshire 3 pts. Toss: Yorkshire.

The loss of the first two days left little to play for. At the start of the fourth day the teams planned to contrive a run-chase but, as the rain continued, it was decided to play on for bonus points. The unrelenting weather forbade even this. Carrick, sent in to make the 20 runs he needed for the double of 10,000 first-class runs for Yorkshire to go with his 1,018 wickets, was thus left a tantalising six short. He achieved the mark in all first-class games on his previous visit to The Oval, in 1992. Spectators were left with memories of half-centuries from Thorpe and Stewart and a 135-run stand between two likely stars of the future, Hollioake and Butcher, who reached a maiden fifty. The most notable event, however, was the arrival of a member of the groundstaff with bucket, spade and besom to deal with some wasps which had congregated at the Vauxhall End.

Close of play: First day, No play; Second day, No play; Third day, Yorkshire 30-0 (P. Carrick 14*, D. Byas 8*).

Surrey

D. J. Bicknell lbw b Hartley	25	A. J. Hollioake c Grayson b Gough	85
D. M. Ward lbw b Gough	0	M. A. Butcher not out	66
G. P. Thorpe b Batty	60	L-b 9, w 1, n-b 18	28
*†A. J. Stewart c Moxon b Hartley	58		
A. D. Brown lbw b Robinson	26	1/4 2/51 3/121 4/174 (7 wkts dec.)	359
A. W. Smith lbw b Gough	11	5/195 6/224 7/359	

J. Boiling, Waqar Younis and A. J. Murphy did not bat.

Bonus points – Surrey 4, Yorkshire 3.

Bowling: Hartley 18–2–78–2; Gough 19.2–4–70–3; Robinson 21–3–81–1; Batty 25–6–83–1; Carrick 17–6–38–0.

Yorkshire

P. Carrick not out	14
D. Byas not out	8
N-b 8	8

(no wkt) 30

*M. D. Moxon, A. P. Grayson, R. B. Richardson, C. White, †R. J. Blakey, P. J. Hartley, D. Gough, J. D. Batty and M. A. Robinson did not bat.

Bowling: Murphy 2–2–0–0; Butcher 2–0–3–0; Brown 1–0–6–0; Bicknell 1–0–21–0.

Umpires: J. H. Harris and R. Palmer.

SUSSEX

President: The Duke of Richmond and Gordon
Chairman: A. M. Caffyn
Secretary: N. Bett
Captain: A. P. Wells
Manager: N. Gifford
Coach: C. E. Waller
Head Groundsman: P. Eaton
Scorer: L. V. Chandler

Although a trophy again eluded Sussex in 1993, they could hardly have come closer. And once they had recovered from the disappointment of losing the epic NatWest trophy final to Warwickshire off the final ball – having made the highest total ever in the final, 321 – they were still able to find good cause for optimism as they approached 1994.

In the Championship, they finished tenth, a drop of three places, but this represented quite a comeback. At the end of July they were second-bottom in the table with only one victory but they won four of the last seven; in the other three they dominated two drawn games, against Yorkshire and Nottinghamshire, and lost to Essex on a Hove pitch that produced the highest aggregate of runs ever in a match in England and, without declarations, might not have produced a result in a fortnight.

In the Sunday League, a competition in which Sussex started superbly but finished terribly in 1992, they sustained their early-season form and finished fourth. Captain Alan Wells and cricket manager Norman Gifford were both delighted at the form of the closing weeks. "We looked so confident and played really top cricket," said Wells.

At the end of his second season in charge Wells was named vice-captain of the England A party to tour South Africa. But many Sussex followers felt he was unlucky not to have been better rewarded for his consistency. In the NatWest semi-final against Glamorgan he played one of the finest one-day innings seen for a long time; in first-class cricket, he finished 11th in the national averages with 1,432 runs, average 57.28, and also enjoyed an excellent season in the Sunday League, with 738 runs.

Not everyone had been enthusiastic about the decision to strengthen the team by signing two highly experienced players, Bill Athey and Eddie Hemmings, both now at their third county. But, at 35, Athey scored over 1,600 first-class runs. The veteran off-spinner Hemmings, meanwhile, at 44 the oldest player on the county circuit, took 63 wickets and formed a new and occasionally lethal combination with Ian Salisbury, the leg-spinner. Salisbury was handicapped by a shoulder injury and loss of form before he regained enough confidence to be included in the England tour party to the West Indies. When signing Hemmings, Sussex said they hoped he would assist the development of fellow off-spinner Bradleigh Donelan, nearly 20 years younger, but Donelan played in only three Championship matches, compared with 16 in 1992, and was not re-engaged after five years with the club.

Batting inconsistencies affected Sussex's early Championship showing and, apart from Wells and Athey, the aggressive Martin Speight was the only batsman to reach 1,000 runs. Speight's thrilling half-century in the NatWest final underlined his exciting if not always disciplined talent. Neil Lenham came back strongly after a loss of form early in the season. Indeed, there was such competition for a place in the top order that Jamie Hall was restricted to only eight Championship games, having played in all but two in 1992, when he was capped.

Franklyn Stephenson led the way among Sussex's pace bowlers with 41 Championship wickets, while the tall and promising Ed Giddins gained valuable experience opening the attack with him. In August Danny Law, another bowler of genuine pace, made his Championship debut against Worcestershire and he later impressed observers when he played for England Under-19 against West Indies.

At the end of the season it was announced "with great regret" that Tony Pigott was not being offered a fresh contract after 16 years with the club. There have been few players more dedicated than "Lester" to Sussex's cause and although management felt he could not last another season he disagreed, as did Surrey, who took him on. Pigott shrugged off a serious back operation early in his career to win his only Test cap in New Zealand in 1983-84, and battled through with enormous determination after being diagnosed as a diabetic. In July Adrian Jones was forced to announce his retirement on his 32nd birthday with an ankle injury. Jones returned to the club in 1991 after four years at Somerset and was leading wicket-taker in his first season back. He was then cruelly hit by injury and claimed only 13 more victims in the next two years.

However, in their place, Sussex signed the 28-year-old England fast bowler Paul Jarvis from Yorkshire on a three-year contract. Jarvis chose Sussex after reportedly speaking to eight of the 12 counties that expressed an interest. He mentioned the club's "happy atmosphere" as one of the factors in his decision. The team still has to gel together but Sussex believe they are getting together the players who will enable them to begin winning trophies again. – Jack Arlidge.

584

SUSSEX 1993

[*Bill Smith*]

Back row: B. T. P. Donelan, C. C. Remy, J. A. North, K. Newell, S. Humphries, M. T. E. Peirce, J. W. Dean. *Middle row*: L. V. Chandler (*First XI scorer*), C. P. Cale (*assistant coach*), E. E. Hemmings, C. W. J. Athey, M. P. Speight, I. D. K. Salisbury, E. S. H. Giddins, J. W. Hall, K. Greenfield, I. C. C. Waring (*assistant coach*), S. Bennett (*physiotherapist*), F. T. Ketley (*Second XI scorer*). *Front row*: C. E. Waller (*coach*), P. Moores, A. N. Jones, C. M. Wells, N. J. Gifford (*cricket manager*), A. P. Wells (*captain*), A. C. S. Pigott, D. M. Smith, N. J. Lenham. *Inset*: F. D. Stephenson.

SUSSEX RESULTS

All first-class matches – Played 19: Won 5, Lost 7, Drawn 7.

County Championship matches – Played 17: Won 5, Lost 7, Drawn 5.

Bonus points – Batting 42, Bowling 54.

Competition placings – Britannic Assurance County Championship, 10th;
NatWest Bank Trophy, finalists; Benson and Hedges Cup, q-f;
AXA Equity & Law League, 4th.

BRITANNIC ASSURANCE CHAMPIONSHIP AVERAGES

BATTING

	Birthplace	*M*	*I*	*NO*	*R*	*HS*	*Avge*
‡C. W. J. Athey	*Middlesbrough*	15	26	5	1,432	137	68.19
‡A. P. Wells	*Newhaven*	17	26	2	1,339	144	55.79
‡M. P. Speight	*Walsall*	12	20	1	1,009	184	53.10
K. Greenfield	*Brighton*	7	10	3	295	107	42.14
‡N. J. Lenham	*Worthing*	11	20	1	769	149	40.47
‡D. M. Smith	*Balham*	15	23	1	802	150	36.45
‡F. D. Stephenson§ . .	*St James, Barbados*	14	21	2	538	90	28.31
‡P. Moores	*Macclesfield*	17	23	2	523	85*	24.90
‡I. D. K. Salisbury . . .	*Northampton*	13	19	4	303	63*	20.20
J. A. North	*Slindon*	6	10	2	158	114	19.75
‡J. W. Hall	*Chichester*	8	14	0	275	53	19.64
‡A. C. S. Pigott	*London*	10	12	2	148	52	14.80
‡E. E. Hemmings	*Leamington Spa*	15	20	4	78	17*	4.87
‡A. N. Jones	*Woking*	4	5	1	19	10*	4.75
E. S. H. Giddins	*Eastbourne*	14	18	7	12	4	1.09

Also batted: B. T. P. Donelan (*Park Royal, London*) (3 matches) 41, 2, 36*; D. R. Law (*London*) (2 matches) 0, 11; C. C. Remy (*Castries, St Lucia*) (3 matches) 39, 17, 0; ‡C. M. Wells (*Newhaven*) (1 match) 3, 0.

* *Signifies not out.*   ‡ *Denotes county cap.*   § *Overseas player.*

The following played a total of 18 three-figure innings for Sussex in County Championship matches – A. P. Wells 6, C. W. J. Athey 4, M. P. Speight 3, N. J. Lenham 2, K. Greenfield 1, J. A. North 1, D. M. Smith 1.

BOWLING

	O	*M*	*R*	*W*	*BB*	*5W/i*	*Avge*
E. E. Hemmings	683.2	208	1,541	63	7-31	2	24.46
F. D. Stephenson	397	77	1,155	41	5-55	1	28.17
I. D. K. Salisbury	519.5	113	1,736	49	5-81	2	35.42
A. C. S. Pigott	229.3	32	844	20	4-51	0	42.20
E. S. H. Giddins	358	52	1,395	28	5-120	1	49.82

Also bowled: C. W. J. Athey 39–7–154–2; B. T. P. Donelan 94.3–8–450–9; K. Greenfield 39–7–136–5; A. N. Jones 66–7–283–2; D. R. Law 43.4–7–155–4; N. J. Lenham 93–23–255–9; J. A. North 88–11–357–7; C. C. Remy 11–2–66–0; C. M. Wells 15–4–36–2.

Wicket-keeper: P. Moores 38 ct, 3 st.

Leading Fielders: A. P. Wells 20, C. W. J. Athey 16, D. M. Smith 15.

At Cardiff, April 29, 30, May 1, 2. SUSSEX lost to GLAMORGAN by 274 runs.

SUSSEX v SURREY

At Hove, May 6, 7, 8. Surrey won by ten wickets. Surrey 24 pts, Sussex 3 pts. Toss: Sussex.
   The Bicknell brothers led Surrey to a handsome victory on the third evening – one with a career-best score, the other with ten wickets in a match for the first time. Darren Bicknell, who was on the field throughout, spent almost nine hours at the crease, spread over three days, and gave the bowlers no hope at all until just before the end. Stewart had accompanied him in a stand of 240 in 68 overs with a harder-hitting innings of 127. Together, they exposed some sub-standard Sussex bowling. Earlier, Martin Bicknell had ripped through their batting, finding movement both off the seam and in the air and hustling Sussex out for 213. Second time round, Smith offered most resistance, but when he was dismissed the Sussex challenge evaporated. Bicknell again found life from a surface which seemed bland to most bowlers: his match return was 11 for 108.
   Close of play: First day, Surrey 37-0 (D. J. Bicknell 8*, M. A. Lynch 29*); Second day, Surrey 392-6 (D. J. Bicknell 154*, N. M. Kendrick 14*).

Sussex

N. J. Lenham c Thorpe b M. P. Bicknell	0	– lbw b M. P. Bicknell	6
J. W. Hall lbw b M. P. Bicknell	12	– lbw b Murphy	19
D. M. Smith b Benjamin	32	– c Brown b Boiling	74
*A. P. Wells b Kendrick	26	– lbw b Benjamin	26
M. P. Speight c Kendrick b M. P. Bicknell	25	– b Murphy	8
†P. Moores c Stewart b M. P. Bicknell	24	– c Lynch b Murphy	19
F. D. Stephenson lbw b Benjamin	20	– b M. P. Bicknell	33
I. D. K. Salisbury lbw b Benjamin	43	– c Murphy b M. P. Bicknell	32
A. C. S. Pigott c Stewart b M. P. Bicknell	11	– b M. P. Bicknell	1
E. E. Hemmings c Lynch b M. P. Bicknell	2	– c Benjamin b M. P. Bicknell	1
E. S. H. Giddins not out	0	– not out	0
B 4, l-b 6, n-b 8	18	L-b 14, n-b 10	24

1/0 2/25 3/72 4/72 5/108   213
6/133 7/152 8/196 9/200

1/24 2/28 3/88 4/118 5/155   243
6/170 7/228 8/235 9/241

Bonus points – Sussex 1, Surrey 4.

   Bowling: *First Innings*—M. P. Bicknell 25–11–43–6; Benjamin 22.1–7–64–3; Murphy 23–6–61–0; Kendrick 15–5–33–1; Boiling 9–8–2–0. *Second Innings*—M. P. Bicknell 16.5–2–65–5; Benjamin 17–7–51–1; Kendrick 13–3–24–0; Murphy 20–5–53–3; Boiling 12–5–36–1.

Surrey

D. J. Bicknell lbw b Hemmings	190	– not out	1
M. A. Lynch lbw b Stephenson	46	– not out	0
G. P. Thorpe lbw b Hemmings	1		
*†A. J. Stewart lbw b Hemmings	127		
D. M. Ward lbw b Salisbury	8		
A. D. Brown c Moores b Stephenson	24		
M. P. Bicknell b Stephenson	0		
N. M. Kendrick run out	20		
J. Boiling c Moores b Giddins	7		
J. E. Benjamin c Stephenson b Hemmings	9		
A. J. Murphy not out	0		
L-b 16, n-b 8	24		

1/77 2/82 3/322 4/339 5/371   456
6/371 7/407 8/440 9/455

(no wkt) 1

Bonus points – Surrey 4, Sussex 2 (Score at 120 overs: 388-6).

Bowling: *First Innings*—Stephenson 36–10–98–3; Giddins 15–2–66–1; Hemmings 46.1–19–87–4; Pigott 16–1–66–0; Salisbury 24–4–92–1; Lenham 8–0–31–0. *Second Innings*—Giddins 0.3–0–1–0.

Umpires: G. Sharp and P. B. Wight.

At Hove, May 13, 14, 15. SUSSEX drew with AUSTRALIANS (See Australian tour section).

SUSSEX v LEICESTERSHIRE

At Horsham, May 20, 21, 22. Sussex won by an innings and 102 runs. Sussex 22 pts, Leicestershire 4 pts. Toss: Sussex.

A game that began a day late was over by 3.25 p.m. on the third day, after veteran off-spinner Hemmings bowled Leicestershire to their third consecutive Championship defeat with match figures of 12 for 58. Though the ground had taken a terrific soaking on the first day, the pitch was firm and dry, and Leicestershire's cricket manager Jack Birkenshaw had no complaints. Hemmings made the most of the rough outside off stump; woeful Leicestershire batting and some outstanding close catching did the rest. After Sussex had made 271, with 78 from Wells, Stephenson removed both openers on Friday evening, and next morning Leicestershire lost seven wickets for 40. Following on, they did even worse. At 40 for nine they were in danger of beating their own record for the lowest score against Sussex on the ground, 51 in 1924, but last-wicket pair Nixon and Mullally added 32 before Hemmings picked up his 11th wicket in less than four hours' play. Disappointing crowds and poor commercial support increased fears that Sussex might soon scrap their annual visit to the north of the county.

Close of play: First day, No play; Second day, Leicestershire 57-3 (P. E. Robinson 9*, A. R. K. Pierson 11*).

Sussex

N. J. Lenham c Nixon b Benjamin	15	A. N. Jones not out	10
C. W. J. Athey c Nixon b Wells	35	E. E. Hemmings c Nixon b Mullally	9
D. M. Smith lbw b Pierson	20	E. S. H. Giddins b Benjamin	0
*A. P. Wells b Mullally	78		
M. P. Speight lbw b Mullally	26	B 4, l-b 15, n-b 2	21
†P. Moores c Potter b Wells	13		—
F. D. Stephenson c Robinson b Pierson	33	1/20 2/68 3/84 4/148 5/182	271
I. D. K. Salisbury c Nixon b Benjamin	11	6/213 7/243 8/255 9/270	

Bonus points – Sussex 2, Leicestershire 4.

Bowling: Benjamin 20–10–46–3; Mullally 22–6–71–3; Pierson 16–2–49–2; Wells 16–4–52–2; Potter 14–3–34–0.

Leicestershire

T. J. Boon c Speight b Stephenson	12	(3) b Giddins	2
*N. E. Briers c Wells b Stephenson	17	c Wells b Stephenson	0
J. J. Whitaker c Speight b Hemmings	3	(4) c Smith b Hemmings	6
P. E. Robinson c Wells b Stephenson	16	(5) c Salisbury b Giddins	5
A. R. K. Pierson c Moores b Stephenson	13	(10) c and b Hemmings	0
B. F. Smith c Smith b Hemmings	1	c Moores b Hemmings	7
L. Potter not out	13	(1) lbw b Hemmings	9
V. J. Wells c Speight b Hemmings	8	(7) lbw b Hemmings	2
†P. A. Nixon c Smith b Hemmings	0	(8) not out	18
A. D. Mullally st Moores b Salisbury	2	(11) b Hemmings	21
W. K. M. Benjamin st Moores b Hemmings	1	(9) c and b Hemmings	0
B 6, l-b 3, n-b 2	11	B 1, l-b 1	2

1/16 2/27 3/33 4/61 5/62	97	1/1 2/10 3/17 4/18 5/30	72
6/68 7/87 8/87 9/96		6/30 7/36 8/40 9/40	

Bonus points – Sussex 4.

Bowling: *First Innings*—Stephenson 14–2–45–4; Giddins 3–1–6–0; Hemmings 16.2–7–27–5; Salisbury 6–2–10–1. *Second Innings*—Stephenson 4–1–8–1; Giddins 15–7–19–2; Jones 2–2–0–0; Salisbury 4–1–12–0; Hemmings 14.1–7–31–7.

Umpires: J. C. Balderstone and D. J. Constant.

At Lord's, May 27, 28, 29, 31. SUSSEX lost to MIDDLESEX by an innings and 35 runs.

At Birmingham, June 3, 4, 5, 7. SUSSEX drew with WARWICKSHIRE.

SUSSEX v NORTHAMPTONSHIRE

At Hove, June 10, 11, 12, 14. Drawn. Sussex 2 pts, Northamptonshire 4 pts. Toss: Northamptonshire.

A fixture which normally provides an exciting contest was beaten by the weather. Only 110 overs were possible over the first two days, and none at all on the third and fourth, when the ground was virtually under water with streams flowing gently towards the Gilligan Stand. The only memory to savour was a marvellous double-hundred from Bailey on the opening day. An exhilarating exhibition of shots on either side of the wicket brought him his hundred, off only 107 balls, and he moved to 150 in 35 more. He holed out on reaching 200, with 28 fours and two sixes, and Felton advanced to a well-deserved century after playing the sheet-anchor role in a stand of 281. Lamb and Loye raced on next day before the rains returned and Sussex could slink away.

Close of play: First day, Northamptonshire 335-2 (N. A. Felton 108*, A. J. Lamb 10*); Second day, Northamptonshire 447-6 (K. M. Curran 11*, A. L. Penberthy 3*); Third day, No play.

Northamptonshire

A. Fordham c Moores b Jones	4	K. M. Curran not out	11
N. A. Felton c Moores b Jones	109	A. L. Penberthy not out	3
R. J. Bailey c Donelan b Pigott	200	L-b 12, w 5, n-b 2	19
*A. J. Lamb c Moores b Giddins	60		
M. B. Loye c Wells b Stephenson	35	1/17 2/298 3/336 4/407	(6 wkts) 447
D. J. Capel c Moores b Giddins	6	5/429 6/430	

N. G. B. Cook, †D. Ripley and J. P. Taylor did not bat.

Bonus points – Northamptonshire 4, Sussex 2.

Bowling: Stephenson 29–3–91–1; Jones 21–2–108–2; Giddins 19–0–96–2; Pigott 23–7–77–1; Donelan 12–2–51–0; Athey 6–0–12–0.

Sussex

C. W. J. Athey, J. W. Hall, D. M. Smith, *A. P. Wells, K. Greenfield, †P. Moores, F. D. Stephenson, B. T. P. Donelan, A. C. S. Pigott, A. N. Jones and E. S. H. Giddins.

Umpires: D. J. Constant and B. Dudleston.

At Manchester, June 17, 18, 19, 21. SUSSEX lost to LANCASHIRE by four wickets.

SUSSEX v CAMBRIDGE UNIVERSITY

At Hove, June 26, 27, 28. Drawn. Toss: Sussex. First-class debuts: S. Humphries, D. R. Law, N. C. Phillips.

Sussex introduced three youngsters but it was an old hand, Colin Wells, who starred for the county. Wells, Sussex's beneficiary, scored his first century for nearly three seasons, adding 313 with Hall, who scored his first of the season, before Sussex declared.

Cambridge, warming up for the Varsity match, found batting just as comfortable and Crawley celebrated a degree in history by hitting a career-best 187 off 304 balls, with a six and 26 fours. Of the three debutants, all Sussex-bred, Danny Law, a 17-year-old from Worthing, bowled quickly without success, Shaun Humphries from Horsham kept wicket tidily, but it was the 19-year-old off-spinner, Nicky Phillips from Hastings, who had most to remember: he took three for 39 after acting-captain Athey made 107 and set Cambridge 284 in 63 overs. However, Jones batted almost three hours for 45 and Cambridge were in no real danger of defeat.

Close of play: First day, Cambridge University 32-0 (J. P. Crawley 26*, G. W. Jones 5*); Second day, Sussex 37-1 (C. W. J. Athey 19*).

Sussex

*C. W. J. Athey c Arscott b Pitcher	1	– (2) c Pitcher b Whittall	107
J. W. Hall c Charlesworth b Haste	114	– (6) not out	1
C. M. Wells c Pitcher b Haste	185		
P. Moores not out	15	– (1) b Whittall	18
C. C. Remy not out	15	– (3) lbw b Pitcher	14
J. A. North (did not bat)		– (4) not out	70
I. D. K. Salisbury (did not bat)		– (5) c Pitcher b Whittall	10
B 4, l-b 6, w 6, n-b 4	20	B 6, l-b 5, n-b 2	13

1/3 2/316 3/327   (3 wkts dec.) 350   1/37 2/60 3/205   (4 wkts dec.) 233
4/221

D. R. Law, A. C. S. Pigott, †S. Humphries and N. C. Phillips did not bat.

Bowling: First Innings—Pitcher 15-4-42-1; Haste 21-1-82-2; Jenkins 12-0-64-0; Charlesworth 11-1-53-0; Whittall 23-3-99-0. *Second Innings*—Pitcher 12-4-44-1; Haste 14-3-69-0; Charlesworth 6-1-17-0; Whittall 20-2-79-3; Jenkins 4-1-13-0.

Cambridge University

*J. P. Crawley not out	187	– c Humphries b Law	20
G. W. Jones c Humphries b Remy	28	– not out	45
M. E. D. Jarrett c Moores b Remy	0	– c Salisbury b Phillips	18
R. Q. Cake c Hall b Salisbury	57	– b Phillips	6
G. M. Charlesworth c and b Pigott	3	– b Salisbury	14
J. P. Carroll not out	16	– c Remy b Phillips	0
†J. P. Arscott (did not bat)		– not out	6
L-b 5, n-b 4	9	L-b 6	6

1/101 2/103 3/238 4/250   (4 wkts dec.) 300   1/27 2/64 3/75   (5 wkts) 115
4/100 5/102

N. J. Haste, C. M. Pitcher, R. H. J. Jenkins and A. R. Whittall did not bat.

Bowling: First Innings—Pigott 20-6-63-1; Law 13-3-41-0; Salisbury 15-4-31-1; Remy 13-5-37-2; Phillips 21-3-64-0; North 16-3-56-0; Athey 1-0-3-0. *Second Innings*—Pigott 8-2-21-0; Law 7-2-20-1; Phillips 22-10-39-3; Salisbury 13-4-27-1; Moores 1-1-0-0; Athey 2-0-2-0.

Umpires: D. R. Shepherd and P. B. Wight.

At Taunton, July 1, 2, 3, 5. SUSSEX lost to SOMERSET by 120 runs.

SUSSEX v KENT

At Arundel, July 15, 16, 17, 19. Drawn. Sussex 2 pts, Kent 5 pts. Toss: Kent.

Rain again ruined Sussex's annual visit to the Castle ground with the first two days badly affected and the fourth day totally lost. What play there was saw Kent in dominant form. On a dampish wicket, their seamers Igglesden and McCague profited from some poor batting to dismiss Sussex for 168. The only resistance came from Moores, with a determined

33, and Salisbury, who strengthened his all-round credentials with an undefeated 34. Kent had the sun on their backs when they batted on the third day and, after losing both openers cheaply, scored quickly. The recovery was led by Taylor and Hooper, who hit a flamboyant 65, including some fine drives and pulls off Salisbury and Hemmings. Hoping to make a game of it, Benson declared after securing one batting point but the weather frustrated his intentions.

Close of play: First day, Sussex 59-4 (D. M. Smith 2*, J. A. North 0*); Second day, Sussex 157-7 (I. D. K. Salisbury 28*, A. C. S. Pigott 13*); Third day, Sussex 59-1 (C. W. J. Athey 34*, I. D. K. Salisbury 5*).

Sussex

C. W. J. Athey c Llong b McCague	24	– not out	34
J. W. Hall b Igglesden	4	– c Marsh b Davis	19
D. M. Smith lbw b Fleming	16		
*A. P. Wells c Hooper b Fleming	9		
K. Greenfield c Marsh b Fleming	10		
J. A. North c Cowdrey b McCague	0		
†P. Moores c Llong b Hooper	33		
I. D. K. Salisbury not out	34	– (3) not out	5
A. C. S. Pigott c Marsh b McCague	13		
E. E. Hemmings c Marsh b McCague	1		
E. S. H. Giddins c Marsh b Igglesden	4		
B 7, l-b 11, w 2	20	L-b 1	1

1/33 2/33 3/47 4/59 5/61   168   1/52   (1 wkt) 59
6/105 7/111 8/157 9/163

Bonus points – Kent 4.

Bowling: *First Innings*—Igglesden 23.4–11–41–2; McCague 21–6–55–4; Fleming 15–7–32–3; Hooper 10–2–21–1; Davis 1–0–1–0. *Second Innings*—Igglesden 4–0–17–0; McCague 4–2–9–0; Hooper 13–4–24–0; Davis 12–5–8–1.

Kent

T. R. Ward b Pigott	4	M. V. Fleming not out ... 2
*M. R. Benson c Moores b Pigott	1	
N. R. Taylor not out	74	B 1, l-b 6 ... 7
C. L. Hooper c Moores b Pigott	65	
N. J. Llong c Moores b Hemmings	0	1/5 2/8 3/80 4/103 (5 wkts dec.) 200
G. R. Cowdrey c Hemmings b Giddins	47	5/194

†S. A. Marsh, R. P. Davis, M. J. McCague and A. P. Igglesden did not bat.

Bonus points – Kent 1, Sussex 2.

Bowling: Giddins 15–6–30–1; Pigott 16–4–43–3; Salisbury 11–1–50–0; Hemmings 25–6–70–1.

Umpires: R. Palmer and A. G. T. Whitehead.

At Derby, July 22, 23, 24. SUSSEX lost to DERBYSHIRE by 195 runs.

At Durham University, July 29, 30, 31, August 2. SUSSEX beat DURHAM by 267 runs.

SUSSEX v WORCESTERSHIRE

At Hove, August 5, 6, 7, 9. Sussex won by nine wickets. Sussex 24 pts, Worcestershire 4 pts. Toss: Worcestershire. Championship debut: D. R. Law.

Sussex enjoyed a comfortable victory after Worcestershire batted poorly on a good pitch. Curtis made 107 out of 253, a disappointing first-innings total given that he and Martin Weston had shared 104 for the first wicket. But Hemmings and Salisbury tore the heart out of their middle order, and there were two wickets on Championship debut for Law. When Sussex batted, Wells led from the front with 133. Athey and Smith offered solid support before Speight hit a rapid 72. That was enough to set up a first-innings lead of 171 and once North's medium-pace had accounted for Worcestershire's top three the visitors were struggling. Hemmings and Salisbury made good use of a pitch now taking some spin and, although Newport offered solid resistance, Sussex were left with 86 overs to score 167. Rain held them up for 23 overs before Speight bludgeoned 71 from 40 balls in 49 minutes, including four sixes.

Close of play: First day, Sussex 65-1 (C. W. J. Athey 30*, D. M. Smith 5*); Second day, Sussex 412-6 (A. P. Wells 128*, I. D. K. Salisbury 18*); Third day, Worcestershire 293-8 (P. J. Newport 64*).

Worcestershire

*T. S. Curtis c and b Lenham	107	– b North		28
M. J. Weston c Hemmings b North	51	– c Smith b North		59
G. A. Hick b Hemmings	11	– c Moores b North		21
D. B. D'Oliveira c and b Hemmings	15	– c Smith b Hemmings		17
D. A. Leatherdale c Wells b Salisbury	24	– b Hemmings		18
S. R. Lampitt not out	19	– c Smith b Hemmings		18
†S. J. Rhodes lbw b Lenham	8	– c Moores b Salisbury		32
P. J. Newport lbw b Salisbury	6	– b Giddins		65
C. M. Tolley lbw b Salisbury	0	– c Moores b Giddins		21
R. K. Illingworth c Salisbury b Law	4	– not out		24
K. C. G. Benjamin c Speight b Law	0	– c Wells b Salisbury		9
B 1, l-b 3, w 4	8	B 14, l-b 9, n-b 2		25

1/104 2/134 3/167 4/215 5/215   253   1/65 2/111 3/116 4/142 5/167   337
6/234 7/245 8/245 9/252   6/174 7/243 8/293 9/300

Bonus points – Worcestershire 2, Sussex 4.

Bowling: First Innings—Giddins 14-1-66-0; Law 10.4-2-38-2; Lenham 23-7-50-2; North 11-1-46-1; Hemmings 14-4-23-2; Salisbury 12-5-26-3. *Second Innings*—Giddins 13-0-69-2; Law 14-3-38-0; North 17-7-32-3; Lenham 10-1-26-0; Salisbury 26.2-6-88-2; Hemmings 43-15-61-3.

Sussex

N. J. Lenham c Hick b Tolley	20	– c Illingworth b Weston		55
C. W. J. Athey b Lampitt	81	– not out		32
D. M. Smith c Rhodes b Weston	58			
*A. P. Wells c Rhodes b Newport	133			
M. P. Speight c Curtis b Tolley	72	– (3) not out		71
J. A. North c Leatherdale b Newport	3			
†P. Moores c Rhodes b Hick	8			
I. D. K. Salisbury c Illingworth b Tolley	22			
D. R. Law b Newport	0			
E. E. Hemmings b Tolley	0			
E. S. H. Giddins not out	0			
B 4, l-b 18, w 1, n-b 4	27	B 2, l-b 7		9

1/47 2/164 3/213 4/340 5/343   424   1/79   (1 wkt) 167
6/366 7/420 8/420 9/424

Bonus points – Sussex 4, Worcestershire 2 (Score at 120 overs: 360-5).

Bowling: First Innings—Benjamin 18-3-65-0; Tolley 36.5-9-90-4; Newport 31-7-83-3; Illingworth 17-5-49-0; Lampitt 17-3-48-1; Hick 12-4-39-1; Weston 8-4-15-1; D'Oliveira 2-0-13-0. *Second Innings*—Newport 7-0-31-0; Tolley 12-6-19-0; Illingworth 7-3-15-0; Lampitt 10-3-28-0; Weston 6-1-36-1; Hick 4.3-0-29-0.

Umpires: G. A. Stickley and P. B. Wight.

SUSSEX v NOTTINGHAMSHIRE

At Eastbourne, August 12, 13, 14, 16. Drawn. Sussex 8 pts, Nottinghamshire 4 pts. Toss: Sussex. Championship debut: R. T. Bates.

Having gone ten weeks without a Championship win, Sussex narrowly failed to record their third in a row after Nottinghamshire responded gallantly to a challenge to score 430 in what became 105 overs on a turning pitch. Stephenson quickly separated the openers and Robinson was dropped when the score was 11, but he survived to add 77 with Pollard, who made a superb 117. Hemmings, against the county that released him a year earlier, and Salisbury sent down nearly 79 overs and picked up five wickets but determined middle-order resistance ensured a draw. The abiding memory of this game, though, was a marvellous 184 from Speight, his highest score, with strokeplay that bettered anything seen on the Saffrons for many years. He drove, pulled, cut and improvised as he led Sussex from 141 for five to 424. Robinson led Nottinghamshire's reply with a gritty 69 but it needed 50 from Mike to save the follow-on. After that, Lenham and Athey opened with a stand of 145 and Stephenson and Wells hit out boldly, effectively batting Nottinghamshire out of the game.

Close of play: First day, Sussex 170-5 (M. P. Speight 44*, P. Moores 10*); Second day, Nottinghamshire 141-4 (C. L. Cairns 9*, C. C. Lewis 4*); Third day, Sussex 268-3 (A. P. Wells 29*, F. D. Stephenson 42*).

Sussex

N. J. Lenham c French b Afford	29	st French b Afford	71
C. W. J. Athey run out	31	c French b Afford	75
D. M. Smith run out	3		
*A. P. Wells c French b Afford	19	c Pollard b Mike	34
M. P. Speight c Cairns b Afford	184	(3) c Johnson b Afford	30
J. A. North c Robinson b Mike	7	not out	4
†P. Moores c Bates b Lewis	78		
F. D. Stephenson c and b Bates	13	(5) b Mike	46
I. D. K. Salisbury b Bates	0		
A. C. S. Pigott not out	1		
E. E. Hemmings b Afford	1		
B 2, l-b 17, w 1, n-b 38	58	B 6, l-b 6, w 1, n-b 10	23
	424	(5 wkts dec.)	**283**

1/49 2/66 3/87 4/115 5/141
6/382 7/418 8/422 9/422

1/145 2/186 3/199 (5 wkts dec.) 283
4/274 5/283

Bonus points – Sussex 4, Nottinghamshire 2 (Score at 120 overs: 362-5).

Bowling: *First Innings*—Lewis 30–6–114–1; Evans 14.3–5–31–0; Mike 26.3–3–105–1; Afford 48.5–14–112–4; Bates 17–6–43–2. *Second Innings*—Lewis 19–2–67–0; Mike 12.3–4–47–2; Afford 29–4–128–3; Bates 8–0–29–0.

Nottinghamshire

P. R. Pollard c Athey b Lenham	26	c Moores b Hemmings	117
W. A. Dessaur c Moores b Stephenson	5	b Stephenson	1
*R. T. Robinson c Pigott b North	69	lbw b Hemmings	32
P. Johnson c Wells b Hemmings	25	c Salisbury b Athey	22
C. L. Cairns c Salisbury b Pigott	42	c Hemmings b Salisbury	57
C. C. Lewis b Salisbury	7	c Smith b Athey	25
K. P. Evans c Lenham b Stephenson	14	(9) not out	0
G. W. Mike c Wells b Pigott	50	(7) c Wells b Salisbury	27
R. T. Bates c Smith b Pigott	0	(8) lbw b Salisbury	10
†B. N. French c Moores b Pigott	27	not out	5
J. A. Afford not out	1		
B 4, l-b 6, n-b 2	12	B 4, l-b 6, n-b 2	12
	278	(8 wkts)	**308**

1/15 2/47 3/128 4/130 5/149
6/184 7/203 8/217 9/265

1/7 2/84 3/147 4/233 (8 wkts) 308
5/247 6/278 7/299 8/301

Bonus points – Nottinghamshire 2, Sussex 4.

Bowling: *First Innings*—Stephenson 17–7–43–2; Pigott 18–2–51–4; Hemmings 20–6–58–1; Lenham 3–0–15–1; Salisbury 23–5–86–1; North 4–0–15–1. *Second Innings*—Stephenson 9–1–18–1; North 7–0–16–0; Hemmings 42.5–6–97–2; Salisbury 36–6–127–3; Athey 10–1–40–2.

Umpires: G. Sharp and A. G. T. Whitehead.

At Portsmouth, August 26, 27, 28, 30. SUSSEX beat HAMPSHIRE by 57 runs.

SUSSEX v ESSEX

At Hove, August 31, September 1, 2, 3. Essex won by seven wickets. Essex 21 pts, Sussex 5 pts. Toss: Sussex.

Hove groundsman Peter Eaton produced a wicket for batsmen to gorge themselves on; there was criticism from Sussex members that it was too good. But they sat back and enjoyed some superb batting as only 20 wickets fell for 1,808 runs in four days. It was an aggregate record for a first-class match in England and Sussex's first-innings 591 was their highest score for 55 years. On the final day Essex made 411 for victory with eight of their 92 overs remaining, and had little difficulty in doing so. There were seven centuries and two more Sussex players reached the 90s. There was little surprise at Wells's fifth hundred of the season but spectators were delighted at the less expected centuries by North and Greenfield. The highest score came from Prichard, whose undefeated 225 included 35 fours and underpinned Essex's 493 in reply to 591 from Sussex. Lenham fell one short of 150 after he and Athey opened Sussex's second innings with a stand of 228 and even Sussex must have been uneasy when he declared on the final morning. Prichard went early this time, but Stephenson and Hussain both hit centuries as they added 215 in 51 overs. Although they fell in successive overs from Greenfield, Gooch and Salim Malik steered Essex to victory, which Gooch sealed with a six. Chasing the ball unsuccessfully round the field was not the ideal preparation for Sussex's NatWest final the next day.

Close of play: First day, Sussex 392-4 (M. P. Speight 75*, J. A. North 5*); Second day, Essex 256-3 (P. J. Prichard 123*, M. C. Ilott 1*); Third day, Sussex 228-2 (N. J. Lenham 121*).

Sussex

N. J. Lenham c Lewis b Boden 52	– c Hussain b Salim Malik	149
C. W. J. Athey c Lewis b Boden 26	– c sub b Salim Malik	96
K. Greenfield b Ilott 107	– (4) not out	50
*A. P. Wells c Rollins b Childs 106		
M. P. Speight c Gooch b Ilott 95		
J. A. North c Prichard b Stephenson........114	– (5) not out	3
†P. Moores c Stephenson b Ilott........... 1		
I. D. K. Salisbury st Rollins b Childs 6		
B. T. P. Donelan not out.................. 36		
A. C. S. Pigott c Salim Malik b Stephenson 18		
E. S. H. Giddins b Ilott................... 0	– (3) c Stephenson b Ilott	0
B 1, l-b 6, w 6, n-b 14 30	B 6, w 2, n-b 6	14

1/73 2/80 3/263 4/371 5/438	591	1/228 2/228 3/296 (3 wkts dec.) 312
6/444 7/461 8/569 9/591		

Bonus points – Sussex 4, Essex 1 (Score at 120 overs: 436-4).

Bowling: *First Innings*—Ilott 38.3–11–119–4; Boden 25–3–118–2; Stephenson 33–8–111–2; Childs 34–12–104–2; Such 26–4–87–0; Salim Malik 7–0–37–0; Gooch 1–0–5–0. *Second Innings*—Ilott 7.5–0–23–1; Boden 10–0–62–0; Childs 17–4–47–0; Such 3–1–11–0; Stephenson 9–1–42–0; Salim Malik 18.1–1–88–2; Hussain 4.1–0–33–0.

Essex

P. J. Prichard not out	225	– lbw b Giddins	24
J. P. Stephenson c Wells b Pigott	9	– c Salisbury b Greenfield	122
J. J. B. Lewis c Salisbury b Lenham	43		
Salim Malik b Giddins	73	– not out	63
M. C. Ilott b Salisbury	51		
N. Hussain not out	70	– (3) c Athey b Greenfield	118
*G. A. Gooch (did not bat)		– (5) not out	74
B 4, l-b 4, w 2, n-b 12	22	B 3, l-b 3, w 3, n-b 2	11

1/21 2/120 3/254 4/342 (4 wkts dec.) 493 1/46 2/261 3/269 (3 wkts) 412

†R. J. Rollins, J. H. Childs, D. J. P. Boden and P. M. Such did not bat.

Bonus points – Essex 4, Sussex 1.

Bowling: *First Innings*—Pigott 23–0–127–1; Giddins 21.4–2–99–1; North 10–0–52–0; Donelan 14–2–64–0; Lenham 7–1–27–1; Salisbury 24–2–94–1; Athey 5–2–22–0. *Second Innings*—Giddins 10–0–37–1; Pigott 12–2–43–0; Salisbury 23–4–102–0; Donelan 12–1–66–0; Athey 3–0–31–0; North 13–0–87–0; Greenfield 11–0–40–2.

Umpires: G. I. Burgess and J. H. Harris.

At Scarborough, September 9, 10, 11, 13. SUSSEX drew with YORKSHIRE.

SUSSEX v GLOUCESTERSHIRE

At Hove, September 16, 17, 18, 20. Sussex won by ten wickets. Sussex 24 pts, Gloucestershire 7 pts. Toss: Gloucestershire.

Sussex ended the season with their fourth Championship victory in seven matches, during which time they rose from 17th to tenth in the table. They completed a ten-wicket triumph with 59 overs to spare. After the first morning was lost to rain Broad and Hinks put on 98 for Gloucestershire's first wicket. But the batting subsided in the face of accurate spin from Hemmings and Salisbury, who celebrated his selection for the West Indies tour with five for 81 – even though he did not bowl before tea. In reply, Lenham and Speight continued their fine end-of-season form with centuries: Lenham mixed controlled aggression with some courageous defence, particularly against the hostile Walsh, while Speight hit an entertaining 114, including 14 fours and two sixes. They enabled Sussex to take a lead of 51, after which Hemmings and Salisbury combined again to take seven wickets. When Stephenson took the last two wickets in three balls on the final morning Sussex needed just 127 to win. Walsh gave all his players a bowl but the only batsman to depart was Lenham, who retired hurt with a damaged ankle.

Close of play: First day, Gloucestershire 172-4 (M. W. Alleyne 9*, T. H. C. Hancock 6*); Second day, Sussex 202-4 (M. P. Speight 11*, I. D. K. Salisbury 5*); Third day, Gloucestershire 177-8 (R. C. Russell 28*, K. E. Cooper 2*).

Gloucestershire

B. C. Broad b Salisbury	45	– b Hemmings	26
S. G. Hinks b Salisbury	66	– c Moores b Hemmings	16
R. I. Dawson c Wells b Salisbury	1	– c Moores b Hemmings	24
M. G. N. Windows c Speight b Salisbury	21	– lbw b Law	37
M. W. Alleyne b Salisbury	18	– c Speight b Salisbury	0
T. H. C. Hancock c Smith b Hemmings	34	– c Moores b Salisbury	5
†R. C. Russell not out	49	– c Moores b Stephenson	28
M. C. J. Ball b Hemmings	18	– c and b Salisbury	4
K. E. Cooper c Remy b Law	2	– (10) not out	2
*C. A. Walsh b Stephenson	12	– (9) c Wells b Salisbury	10
A. M. Babington c Moores b Stephenson	0	– c Speight b Stephenson	0
B 4, l-b 6, w 4, n-b 24	38	B 7, l-b 4, n-b 18	29

1/98 2/104 3/146 4/157 5/198 304 1/33 2/78 3/83 4/102 5/116 177
6/236 7/277 8/285 9/304 6/150 7/155 8/169 9/177

Bonus points – Gloucestershire 3, Sussex 4.

Bowling: *First Innings*—Law 15–1–72–1; Stephenson 19.5–3–56–3; Remy 5–1–22–0; Hemmings 31–15–52–1; Lenham 4–0–11–0; Salisbury 34–7–81–5. *Second Innings*—Stephenson 7.3–2–14–2; Hemmings 29–11–46–3; Salisbury 28–4–99–4; Law 4–1–7–1.

Sussex

N. J. Lenham lbw b Babington	105 – retired hurt		24
C. W. J. Athey lbw b Walsh	9 – not out		57
D. M. Smith c Broad b Alleyne	35 – not out		34
*A. P. Wells c Cooper b Walsh	29		
M. P. Speight c Hinks b Alleyne	114		
I. D. K. Salisbury c Ball b Cooper	13		
C. C. Remy c Russell b Cooper	0		
†P. Moores c Russell b Cooper	24		
F. D. Stephenson c Russell b Cooper	4		
D. R. Law b Alleyne	11		
E. E. Hemmings not out	1		
L-b 8, n-b 2	10	L-b 2, w 1, n-b 10	13

1/25 2/93 3/155 4/190 5/229   355   (no wkt) 128
6/229 7/291 8/303 9/346

Bonus points – Sussex 4, Gloucestershire 4.

In the second innings N. J. Lenham retired hurt at 38.

Bowling: *First Innings*—Walsh 21–1–72–2; Cooper 26–6–93–4; Ball 23–3–96–0; Babington 16–4–42–1; Alleyne 9.3–2–33–3; Hancock 2–0–11–0. *Second Innings*—Walsh 7–1–23–0; Cooper 6–1–19–0; Ball 9–2–32–0; Babington 5–0–18–0; Alleyne 5–1–9–0; Broad 1–0–1–0; Hinks 1–0–2–0; Russell 1.5–0–15–0; Hancock 1–0–2–0; Windows 1–0–3–0; Dawson 1–0–2–0.

Umpires: K. E. Palmer and P. Willey.

COUNTY CAPS AWARDED IN 1993

Derbyshire	D. G. Cork.
Essex	M. C. Ilott.
Glamorgan	R. P. Lefebvre.
Kent	D. W. Headley, N. J. Llong.
Leicestershire	A. D. Mullally.
Middlesex	P. N. Weekes.
Nottinghamshire ...	C. L. Cairns.
Somerset	Mushtaq Ahmed.
Surrey	J. E. Benjamin.
Sussex	C. W. J. Athey, E. E. Hemmings.
Warwickshire	N. M. K. Smith.
Worcestershire	C. M. Tolley.
Yorkshire	D. Gough, R. B. Richardson, C. White.

No caps were awarded by Gloucestershire, Hampshire, Lancashire or Northamptonshire. Durham give caps to all their playing staff.

WARWICKSHIRE

President: The Earl of Aylesford
Chairman: M. J. K. Smith
Chairman, Cricket Committee: D. L. Amiss
Chief Executive: D. M. W. Heath
Captain: D. A. Reeve
Director of Coaching: R. A. Woolmer
Head Groundsman: 1993 – A. Atkinson
Scorer: A. E. Davis

Warwickshire's magnificent last-ball win against Sussex in the NatWest Trophy final redeemed an otherwise poor season, in which they fell from sixth to 16th place in the Championship, from eighth to tenth in the Sunday League, and failed to survive their first Benson and Hedges match.

The winning hit at Lord's by Roger Twose, off the only ball he faced, accomplished a unique double: both knockout finals were won by sides which, on the day, did not have an overseas cricketer. It was also only the second time in the 22 years of two knockout competitions when both went to Midlands teams – 1989 was the other.

The match was a triumph for the new club captain, Dermot Reeve, who could easily have won his third Man of the Match award in as many finals. The win epitomised his rare combination of all-round talent and innovative approach – qualities which inspired his ordinary-looking side to overcome injuries to key bowlers, as well as the loss of Allan Donald, on tour with South Africa, after the quarter-final. Typical of the team's resilience in the face of the highest total ever scored in a final were the performances of Asif Din and Paul Smith, two experienced players who were still not sure of their place in the side. Both scored over 500 runs in one-day cricket, with Asif Din's season resurrected in the last six weeks by the NatWest campaign.

Smith had a largely disappointing year in four-day cricket after failing to win a place in early games. His modest bowling record – 14 Championship wickets at 34.57 apiece – was part of a startling decline in the effectiveness of a pace attack which, in previous years, had been the county's main strength. With Donald missing the last seven weeks of the season, and injuries to Munton and Small limiting their contributions, Warwickshire won only four of their 17 four-day games, and only one after Donald's departure. Donald, Munton and Small took 75 wickets from a combined 32 Championship games, compared with 146 from 53 games in 1992. With the batsmen unable to compensate with big scores, on pitches too variable to be considered satisfactory for four-day cricket, a string of poor results was predictable.

The two bright spots on the bowling front were provided by off-spinner Neil Smith, who found greater opportunities in four-day cricket, and left-arm pace bowler Michael Bell. Smith bowled 562.2 overs in the Championship, almost twice as many as anyone else, and was the leading wicket-taker, with 44. The 26-year-old Bell, a late entry into first-class cricket, had a purple patch of 22 wickets in three games from late July to mid-August. By no means fast, he was nevertheless lively, and moved the ball enough to suggest a bright future. Reeve managed to top the bowling averages, but injury limited him to under 300 overs, which may explain his preference for the all-rounder Manoj Prabhakar instead of David Boon as Donald's temporary overseas stand-in in 1994, when South Africa are touring.

The figures of the top six batsmen – no one averaged as much as 40 – made a strong case for a quality player who could be expected to contribute 1,500 runs or more but would also help the progress of young batsmen like Dominic Ostler, Jason Ratcliffe and Trevor Penney. It seems that chairman Mike Smith, cricket chairman Dennis Amiss and director of coaching Bob Woolmer wanted Boon, but they supported the principle of giving the captain the final say. It is still difficult to avoid the conclusion that the Indian all-rounder would duplicate talent already available, like Reeve, Paul Smith and Twose, with one of the latter pair the likeliest to drop out.

Only Andy Moles and Ostler managed to pass 1,000 first-class runs, although Ratcliffe emulated A. C. Smith in 1961 and found himself stranded on 999. To add insult to injury, he was run out in his final innings, backing up at the non-striker's end. He and Moles shared five of only eight century partnerships for Warwickshire and an aggregate of five individual hundreds was the lowest number by any side. While Ostler had an adequate season, he needs to convert more of his fifties into big hundreds if he is to play cricket at a higher level. Penney scored nearly 800 runs before a dislocated shoulder forced him to miss most of the last month of the season, while Twose is not the first young player to follow a successful season with a poor one: he played in only nine Championship games. Wicket-keeper Keith Piper suffered again with hand injuries and could play only ten games. His vulnerability was worrying; if, as is likely, it was caused by technical faults, they could be remedied.

The standard of Edgbaston pitches was partly responsible for the fact that only one of nine home games went the full distance, and only one other lasted until mid-afternoon on the final day. In particular, the strip prepared for the Middlesex match could hardly have been prepared better for the visitors. The ball turned from the start of the game, and the 15 wickets obtained by Emburey and Tufnell emphasised the gulf in class of spin between the two sides. The pitches received poor marks from the captains and umpires, and attracted attention from Lord's, although there was never a question of penalties being imposed. Amid some mutual disenchantment, groundsman Andy Atkinson resigned; he left immediately after the Test match in early August to take up a post at Newlands in Cape Town.

The exclusively four-day format exposes those sides with limited bowling resources. Without Donald in 1994, much depends upon the fitness of Munton and Small and the form of Prabhakar. Only if they do well, and at least one batsman has an outstanding season, can Warwickshire hope to do better in the Championship. Administratively, the club also had problems, following the announcement in midwinter that David Heath, the chief executive for seven years, would retire early because of ill-health. – Jack Bannister.

WARWICKSHIRE 1993

[Bill Smith

Back row: C. E. Mulraine, M. F. Robinson, D. R. Brown, M. A. V. Bell, A. F. Giles, G. Welch, P. C. L. Holloway. *Middle row:* K. J. Piper, M. Burns, T. L. Penney, P. A. Booth, J. D. Ratcliffe, N. M. K. Smith, W. G. Khan, R. G. Twose, S. Rouse (*assistant coach*), S. J. Nottingham (*physiotherapist*). *Front row:* R. N. Abberley (*coach, youth cricket organiser*), G. C. Small, A. J. Moles, R. A. Woolmer (*director of cricket*), D. A. Reeve (*captain*), M. J. K. Smith (*chairman*), T. A. Munton, A. A. Donald, P. A. Smith, Asif Din, D. P. Ostler.

WARWICKSHIRE RESULTS

All first-class matches – Played 19; Won 4, Lost 8, Drawn 7.

County Championship matches – Played 17; Won 4, Lost 8, Drawn 5.

Bonus points – Batting 24, Bowling 49.

*Competition placings – Britannic Assurance County Championship, 16th;
NatWest Bank Trophy, winners; Benson and Hedges Cup, 1st round;
AXA Equity & Law League, 10th.*

BRITANNIC ASSURANCE CHAMPIONSHIP AVERAGES

BATTING

	Birthplace	M	I	NO	R	HS	Avge
‡A. J. Moles	Solihull	17	32	5	1,100	117	37.93
‡D. A. Reeve	Kowloon, Hong Kong	16	27	7	742	87*	37.10
T. L. Penney	Salisbury, Rhodesia	15	27	5	761	135*	34.59
‡D. P. Ostler	Solihull	17	32	2	1,024	174	34.13
‡Asif Din	Kampala, Uganda	6	9	0	291	66	32.33
J. D. Ratcliffe	Solihull	17	32	0	960	101	30.00
P. C. L. Holloway	Helston	2	4	1	68	44	22.66
‡N. M. K. Smith	Birmingham	16	25	2	420	51*	18.26
P. A. Booth	Huddersfield	6	11	3	144	49*	18.00
A. F. Giles	Chertsey	2	4	1	53	23	17.66
‡P. A. Smith	Jesmond	9	15	0	253	55	16.86
‡K. J. Piper	Leicester	10	14	1	183	52	14.07
‡R. G. Twose	Torquay	9	16	0	184	37	11.50
M. Burns	Barrow-in-Furness	5	9	0	89	22	9.88
‡G. C. Small	St George, Barbados	12	18	3	140	39	9.33
M. A. V. Bell	Birmingham	8	12	5	60	22*	8.57
‡A. A. Donald§	Bloemfontein, SA	9	11	3	63	19	7.87
‡T. A. Munton	Melton Mowbray	11	13	5	51	18	6.37

* *Signifies not out.* ‡ *Denotes county cap.* § *Overseas player.*

The following played a total of five three-figure innings for Warwickshire in County
Championship matches – A. J. Moles 2, D. P. Ostler 1, T. L. Penney 1, J. D. Ratcliffe 1.

BOWLING

	O	M	R	W	BB	5W/i	Avge
D. A. Reeve	261.1	103	473	20	3-38	0	23.65
A. A. Donald	258.1	59	744	30	7-98	2	24.80
M. A. V. Bell	207.1	52	627	25	7-48	3	25.08
T. A. Munton	309.3	105	677	25	7-41	1	27.08
G. C. Small	238.4	68	589	20	4-39	0	29.45
P. A. Booth	163.5	44	380	11	2-16	0	34.54
P. A. Smith	124.5	18	484	14	4-35	0	34.57
N. M. K. Smith	562.2	143	1,522	44	6-122	3	34.59

Also bowled: Asif Din 4–1–12–0; M. Burns 7–4–8–0; A. F. Giles 41.3–6–128–3; A. J.
Moles 14–2–97–4; D. P. Ostler 6–1–16–0; T. L. Penney 2.1–0–13–0; J. D. Ratcliffe
18.3–3–106–2; R. G. Twose 88.2–13–241–8.

Wicket-keepers: K. J. Piper 14 ct; M. Burns 9 ct, 1 st; P. C. L. Holloway 6 ct.

Leading Fielders: D. A. Reeve 22, D. P. Ostler 17.

WARWICKSHIRE v NORTHAMPTONSHIRE

At Birmingham, April 29, 30, May 1, 2. Warwickshire won by 197 runs. Warwickshire 22 pts, Northamptonshire 4 pts. Toss: Northamptonshire.

Off-spinner Neil Smith adroitly exploited a pitch which turned appreciably for bowlers from the City End. His five for 81 completed the victory and was only his second "five-for" in an innings, in his 41st match; his first had come against Middlesex in the penultimate game of the 1992 season. Warwickshire batted solidly in both innings, especially Penney, whose stand of 132 with Reeve set up the declaration. Northamptonshire were asked to score 369 from 90 overs to win, and lost their first three wickets for 11 to Donald and Small. Loye underlined his glittering potential, making his maiden fifty as he added 122 with Fordham, but once he was caught behind Smith did the rest.

Close of play: First day, Warwickshire 256-5 (D. A. Reeve 19*, N. M. K. Smith 12*); Second day, Northamptonshire 191-5 (N. A. Felton 90*, D. Ripley 3*); Third day, Warwickshire 199-5 (D. A. Reeve 67*, N. M. K. Smith 13*).

Warwickshire

A. J. Moles c Ripley b Curran	47	– lbw b Taylor	1
R. G. Twose c Ripley b Taylor	5	– c Felton b Cook	6
J. D. Ratcliffe lbw b Capel	34	– c Felton b Cook	17
D. P. Ostler c and b Curran	46	– c Ripley b Cook	15
T. L. Penney c Lamb b Capel	68	– c Bailey b Taylor	65
*D. A. Reeve c Felton b Curran	23	– not out	87
N. M. K. Smith c Bailey b Taylor	25	– not out	51
†K. J. Piper c Fordham b Curran	6		
G. C. Small c Curran b Cook	39		
A. A. Donald c Ripley b Penberthy	19		
T. A. Munton not out	3		
B 1, l-b 19, w 2, n-b 8	30	L-b 13, w 2, n-b 6	21

1/13 2/78 3/112 4/207 5/234   345   1/6 2/15 3/41   (5 wkts dec.) 263
6/274 7/274 8/288 9/321   4/46 5/178

Bonus points – Warwickshire 2, Northamptonshire 3 (Score at 120 overs: 275-7).

Bowling: *First Innings*—Taylor 32–10–82–2; Curran 35–10–64–4; Capel 25–6–66–2; Penberthy 22–7–50–1; Cook 21.5–7–50–1; Bailey 4–2–13–0. *Second Innings*—Taylor 22–6–76–2; Curran 16–6–51–0; Cook 19–5–51–3; Capel 14–5–30–0; Bailey 13–1–42–0.

Northamptonshire

A. Fordham c Donald b Munton	20	– lbw b Donald	55
N. A. Felton c Penney b Donald	93	– b Small	4
R. J. Bailey c Donald b Reeve	3	– c Munton b Donald	1
*A. J. Lamb c Penney b Munton	13	– c Munton b Donald	3
M. B. Loye c Moles b Small	44	– c Piper b Munton	63
D. J. Capel b Smith	1	– c Ostler b Smith	0
†D. Ripley c Piper b Munton	7	– (9) not out	11
K. M. Curran b Donald	0	– (7) b Smith	4
A. L. Penberthy c Reeve b Smith	7	– (8) c Donald b Smith	0
J. P. Taylor not out	12	– b Smith	0
N. G. B. Cook c and b Reeve	8	– c Munton b Smith	18
B 6, l-b 17, w 1, n-b 8	32	B 3, l-b 7, n-b 2	12

1/46 2/65 3/105 4/173 5/180   240   1/6 2/7 3/11 4/133 5/134   171
6/195 7/199 8/213 9/215   6/140 7/140 8/142 9/143

Bonus points – Northamptonshire 1, Warwickshire 4.

Bowling: *First Innings*—Donald 21–5–65–2; Small 14–4–38–1; Munton 30–13–50–3; Reeve 11.3–4–10–2; Smith 32–12–54–2. *Second Innings*—Donald 14–3–35–3; Small 12–3–33–1; Munton 7–5–12–1; Smith 20.2–4–81–5.

Umpires: M. J. Kitchen and D. R. Shepherd.

WARWICKSHIRE v DERBYSHIRE

At Birmingham, May 6, 7, 8. Derbyshire won by an innings and 72 runs. Derbyshire 24 pts, Warwickshire 3 pts. Toss: Warwickshire.

Warwickshire's inherent batting frailties were all too apparent on a slow pitch against a keen pace attack. All-rounder Cork shone with five wickets for 56 in the match, as well as 34 valuable runs. The inadequacy of a first-innings score of 192 was underlined when Morris and Adams added 161 for Derbyshire's third wicket, backed up by a confident 86 from O'Gorman. A lead of 187 was always likely to be conclusive, but Warwickshire's response was particularly feeble, even given the absence of Piper, who had dislocated his thumb trying to catch O'Gorman. They were bowled out for 115 in 45.2 overs before lunch on the third day. Ratcliffe offered the only resistance with a stylish 64.

Close of play: First day, Derbyshire 143-2 (J. E. Morris 64*, C. J. Adams 52*); Second day, Warwickshire 29-2 (J. D. Ratcliffe 23*, D. P. Ostler 5*).

Warwickshire

A. J. Moles c Adams b Griffith	16	– lbw b Malcolm	1
R. G. Twose c Cork b Griffith	26	– c O'Gorman b Malcolm	0
J. D. Ratcliffe lbw b Griffith	8	– lbw b Cork	64
D. P. Ostler lbw b Warner	57	– c Krikken b Warner	13
T. L. Penney lbw b Cork	15	– b Sladdin	8
D. A. Reeve b Malcolm	16	– lbw b Cork	0
N. M. K. Smith c Bowler b Warner	18	– lbw b Cork	2
*K. J. Piper not out	14	– absent injured	
G. C. Small b Warner	4	– (8) st Krikken b Sladdin	18
A. A. Donald c Barnett b Warner	1	– (9) c and b Sladdin	1
T. A. Munton lbw b Cork	2	– (10) not out	2
B 1, l-b 3, w 1, n-b 10	15	L-b 4, n-b 2	6

1/30 2/44 3/66 4/96 5/134   192   1/1 2/2 3/37 4/69 5/76   115
6/164 7/169 8/175 9/185   6/82 7/101 8/102 9/115

Bonus points – Derbyshire 4.

Bowling: *First Innings*—Malcolm 14-4-28-1; Cork 12.1-2-32-2; Warner 21-3-54-4; Griffith 9-1-32-3; Sladdin 21-5-42-0. *Second Innings*—Malcolm 12-4-28-2; Cork 14-3-24-3; Warner 6-1-23-1; Sladdin 13.2-3-36-3.

Derbyshire

*K. J. Barnett c Reeve b Donald	8		A. E. Warner b Smith	8
P. D. Bowler c Piper b Small	8		R. W. Sladdin not out	5
J. E. Morris c Ratcliffe b Small	95		D. E. Malcolm c Reeve b Donald	1
C. J. Adams lbw b Munton	65			
T. J. G. O'Gorman lbw b Munton	86		B 11, l-b 10, n-b 6	27
†A. Griffith b Smith	20			
†K. M. Krikken c and b Reeve	22			379
D. G. Cork b Smith	34			

1/16 2/20 3/181 4/191 5/244
6/306 7/342 8/361 9/374

Bonus points – Derbyshire 4, Warwickshire 3 (Score at 120 overs: 361-8).

Bowling: Donald 20.2-1-93-2; Small 16-2-60-2; Munton 34-12-72-2; Reeve 20-8-33-1; Smith 35-4-90-3; Twose 5-2-10-0.

Umpires: J. C. Balderstone and G. I. Burgess.

At Canterbury, May 13, 14, 15, 17. WARWICKSHIRE beat KENT by 110 runs.

At Liverpool, May 27, 28, 29, 31. WARWICKSHIRE drew with LANCASHIRE.

WARWICKSHIRE v SUSSEX

At Birmingham, June 3, 4, 5, 7. Drawn. Warwickshire 5 pts, Sussex 6 pts. Toss: Warwickshire.

A slow pitch of low bounce defied the efforts of both attacks and both captains, and a high-scoring draw was the inevitable result. Heavy overnight rain prevented play before lunch on the first day, but then Wells, who had scored 115 when the teams met 12 months before at Hove, helped himself to 130 – 82 of which came in boundaries. With Smith contributing an attractive 80, Sussex topped 400. A maiden Championship hundred from Ratcliffe, whose opening partnership with Moles was worth 153, confirmed his steady progress, though he had a nervous wait through lunch on 99 not out. Two declarations left Warwickshire to score 321 from a minimum of 61 overs, but Hemmings, who had played for them from 1966 to 1978, held them in check, bowling throughout the innings and taking four of the five wickets to fall before both sides settled for a draw.

Close of play: First day, Sussex 159-2 (D. M. Smith 66*, A. P. Wells 33*); Second day, Warwickshire 119-0 (A. J. Moles 60*, J. D. Ratcliffe 56*); Third day, Sussex 57-1 (C. W. J. Athey 35*, D. M. Smith 15*).

Sussex

C. W. J. Athey b Small	6	– c and b Twose	69
J. W. Hall lbw b Smith	42	– run out	4
D. M. Smith b Munton	80	– c Ratcliffe b Smith	71
*A. P. Wells b Munton	130	– not out	31
K. Greenfield c Reeve b Small	12	– not out	18
C. C. Remy lbw b Reeve	39		
F. D. Stephenson c Burns b Donald	37		
†P. Moores lbw b Twose	14		
A. C. S. Pigott c and b Reeve	13		
E. E. Hemmings not out	10		
E. S. H. Giddins b Reeve	1		
B 1, l-b 11, w 2, n-b 16	30	B 3, l-b 9, n-b 2	14

1/19 2/93 3/236 4/293 5/293   414   1/26 2/150 3/161   (3 wkts dec.) 207
6/353 7/383 8/397 9/409

Bonus points – Sussex 3, Warwickshire 2 (Score at 120 overs: 321-5).

Bowling: *First Innings*—Donald 23-3-100-1; Small 24-10-56-2; Munton 38-10-93-2; Reeve 20.4-6-47-3; Smith 26-7-68-1; Twose 14-2-38-1. *Second Innings*—Donald 7-1-18-0; Small 4-1-10-0; Munton 15-5-32-0; Smith 22-5-83-1; Reeve 12-4-32-0; Twose 5-0-20-1.

Warwickshire

A. J. Moles b Stephenson	77	– b Hemmings	29
J. D. Ratcliffe c Wells b Greenfield	101	– b Hemmings	27
R. G. Twose lbw b Stephenson	0	– (4) lbw b Greenfield	6
D. P. Ostler c Smith b Greenfield	23	– (5) c Smith b Hemmings	45
T. L. Penney run out	23	– (6) not out	33
*D. A. Reeve c sub b Pigott	27	– (7) not out	23
†M. Burns lbw b Hemmings	22	– (3) c and b Hemmings	18
N. M. K. Smith not out	15		
G. C. Small not out	4		
B 3, l-b 6	9	B 2, l-b 16	18

1/153 2/153 3/207 4/208 5/253   (7 wkts dec.) 301   1/62 2/87 3/88   (5 wkts) 199
6/282 7/286   4/118 5/154

A. A. Donald and T. A. Munton did not bat.

Bonus points – Warwickshire 3, Sussex 3.

Bowling: *First Innings*—Stephenson 30–7–81–2; Giddins 17–3–49–0; Pigott 15–7–27–1; Hemmings 33.3–8–75–1; Athey 3–1–9–0; Greenfield 20–6–51–2. *Second Innings*—Stephenson 12–3–30–0; Hemmings 33–10–70–4; Giddins 5–0–7–0; Pigott 9–2–33–0; Greenfield 7–1–41–1.

Umpires: J. H. Hampshire and R. A. White.

At Birmingham, June 9, 10, 11. WARWICKSHIRE drew with AUSTRALIANS (See Australian tour section).

At Oxford, June 12, 14, 15. WARWICKSHIRE drew with OXFORD UNIVERSITY.

WARWICKSHIRE v SURREY

At Birmingham, June 17, 18. Surrey won by eight wickets. Surrey 20 pts, Warwickshire 4 pts. Toss: Warwickshire.

Surrey won in only two days on a damp seaming pitch after 19 wickets fell on the first day. But the inadequacies of the batting hastened the game as much as the conditions. After Waqar Younis claimed six for 43 to dismiss Warwickshire for 88, Surrey were in turn reduced to 44 for six, four of the wickets falling to Small. However, the tailenders Bicknell, Kendrick and, next morning, Benjamin took the visitors to a lead of 87. Although Moles played grittily, and was again the top scorer, the rest of Warwickshire's batting was only marginally less tentative than in the first innings. Bicknell completed a fine all-round performance with six for 50 as the last nine wickets went down for 67; overall, Surrey had taken 20 wickets in 107.2 overs. They needed 71 to complete their third first-class win of the season, and Brown got them home in the final over of the second day with an unbeaten 42.

Close of play: First day, Surrey 128-9 (N. M. Kendrick 14*, J. E. Benjamin 0*).

Warwickshire

A. J. Moles c Kersey b Benjamin	29	– c Smith b M. P. Bicknell	42
J. D. Ratcliffe c Lynch b Waqar Younis	4	– c Thorpe b Benjamin	27
R. G. Twose c Kersey b Waqar Younis	0	– lbw b M. P. Bicknell	11
D. P. Ostler lbw b Benjamin	9	– lbw b M. P. Bicknell	34
T. L. Penney lbw b M. P. Bicknell	2	– lbw b Waqar Younis	2
*D. A. Reeve c Thorpe b Waqar Younis	14	– b Waqar Younis	3
†M. Burns c Ward b Waqar Younis	0	– c Kersey b M. P. Bicknell	17
N. M. K. Smith b Waqar Younis	3	– lbw b Benjamin	0
G. C. Small c Kersey b Waqar Younis	3	– c Ward b M. P. Bicknell	2
A. A. Donald c Lynch b Benjamin	9	– not out	4
T. A. Munton not out	7	– c Kersey b M. P. Bicknell	0
L-b 2, n-b 6	8	B 1, l-b 7, w 1, n-b 6	15
	88		**157**

1/5 2/15 3/39 4/42 5/57 6/60 7/67 8/70 9/71

1/62 2/90 3/91 4/102 5/112 6/143 7/144 8/149 9/153

Bonus points – Surrey 4.

Bowling: *First Innings*—Waqar Younis 15–3–43–6; M. P. Bicknell 14–7–27–1; Benjamin 9.4–5–16–3. *Second Innings*—Waqar Younis 15–3–32–2; M. P. Bicknell 22.4–5–50–6; Benjamin 20–8–36–2; Kendrick 11–2–31–0.

Surrey

D. J. Bicknell lbw b Donald	5	– not out	17
*M. A. Lynch c Ostler b Small	1	– c Small b Donald	0
G. P. Thorpe c Burns b Reeve	18	– b Donald	0
A. D. Brown b Small	10	– not out	42
D. M. Ward c Ratcliffe b Small	0		
A. W. Smith lbw b Small	13		
†G. J. Kersey lbw b Reeve	0		
M. P. Bicknell b Smith	37		
N. M. Kendrick not out	31		
Waqar Younis c Penney b Smith	9		
J. E. Benjamin c Burns b Munton	23		
B 10, l-b 4, n-b 14	28	B 9, n-b 3	12

1/6 2/6 3/23 4/31 5/44   175   1/1 2/1   (2 wkts) 71
6/44 7/82 8/114 9/128

Bonus points – Warwickshire 4.

Bowling: *First Innings*—Donald 20.3–6–56–1; Small 15–5–39–4; Munton 21.3–7–54–1; Reeve 4–4–0–2; Twose 1–1–0–0; Smith 4–1–12–2. *Second Innings*—Donald 6–1–11–2; Small 6–3–7–0; Smith 5.2–1–30–0; Munton 5–2–14–0.

Umpires: J. H. Harris and P. Willey.

At Ilford, June 24, 25, 26, 28. WARWICKSHIRE lost to ESSEX by three wickets.

WARWICKSHIRE v YORKSHIRE

At Birmingham, July 1, 2, 3, 5. Warwickshire won by six wickets. Warwickshire 23 pts, Yorkshire 3 pts. Toss: Warwickshire.

Donald's return to top form, bowling fast and full on a slow pitch, brought him match figures of ten for 129, and Warwickshire their third Championship win of the season. Their most dependable batsman, Moles, scored his first hundred for 13 months and the 23rd of his career. He and Ratcliffe put on 140 for the first wicket, and runs from Reeve and Smith helped towards an imposing total of 346. Donald, Munton and Reeve shared nine wickets to make Yorkshire follow on, and not even Richardson's maiden century for his county, which he brought up with a six off Donald, could prevent a comfortable Warwickshire win. The West Indies captain shared a fourth-wicket partnership of 174 with Moxon, but Donald was unstoppable.

Close of play: First day, Warwickshire 289-8 (P. C. L. Holloway 2*, N. M. K. Smith 0*); Second day, Yorkshire 10-1 (D. Byas 4*, D. Gough 5*); Third day, Warwickshire 11-1 (A. J. Moles 2*, P. C. L. Holloway 0*).

Warwickshire

A. J. Moles c Batty b Hartley	113	– c Byas b Hartley	6
J. D. Ratcliffe lbw b Gough	47	– c Stemp b Hartley	9
D. P. Ostler c Byas b Hartley	28	– (4) lbw b Hartley	17
T. L. Penney c and b Stemp	15	– (5) not out	32
*D. A. Reeve lbw b Jarvis	53	– (6) not out	2
P. A. Smith c Byas b Stemp	3		
R. G. Twose lbw b Gough	0		
T. A. Munton b Jarvis	0		
†P. C. L. Holloway not out	12	– (3) c Blakey b White	44
N. M. K. Smith c and b Stemp	30		
A. A. Donald b Jarvis	17		
B 4, l-b 11, w 3, n-b 10	28	B 3, l-b 2	5

1/140 2/195 3/204 4/250 5/266   346   1/10 2/15 3/37 4/112   (4 wkts) 115
6/287 7/287 8/289 9/322

Bonus points – Warwickshire 3, Yorkshire 3 (Score at 120 overs: 314-8).

Bowling: *First Innings*—Jarvis 30.1–7–95–3; Gough 26–5–75–2; Hartley 19–5–63–2; White 8–2–23–0; Stemp 38–19–43–3; Batty 17–5–32–0. *Second Innings*—Jarvis 7–3–8–0; Gough 9–1–32–0; Hartley 10–3–21–3; Stemp 6–2–18–0; Batty 7.2–1–25–0; White 3–1–6–1.

Yorkshire

*M. D. Moxon b Munton	15	– (4) lbw b Donald	72
A. A. Metcalfe c Munton b Donald	8	– c Reeve b Donald	0
R. B. Richardson c P. A. Smith b Donald	4	– (5) c Ostler b Munton	112
D. Byas c Holloway b Munton	18	– (1) c Holloway b Donald	9
†R. J. Blakey lbw b Reeve	19	– (6) b Donald	5
C. White b Reeve	10	– (7) b Donald	0
P. W. Jarvis b Donald	22	– (8) c Holloway b Donald	13
P. J. Hartley c Reeve b Munton	9	– (9) c Ratcliffe b N. M. K. Smith	4
D. Gough lbw b Reeve	1	– (3) lbw b Munton	20
R. D. Stemp not out	30	– not out	4
J. D. Batty b N. M. K. Smith	21	– c Holloway b Donald	10
B 5, l-b 6, n-b 10	21	B 10, l-b 3, n-b 20	33
	178		**282**

1/34 2/38 3/38 4/59 5/78   178   1/3 2/24 3/40 4/214 5/228   282
6/109 7/125 8/125 9/126   6/244 7/257 8/262 9/270

Bonus points – Warwickshire 4.

Bowling: *First Innings*—Donald 17–6–31–3; Munton 20–9–36–3; N. M. K. Smith 4–1–12–1; P. A. Smith 8–0–47–0; Reeve 17–8–38–3; Twose 3–1–3–0. *Second Innings*—Donald 29–7–98–7; Munton 25–9–55–2; P. A. Smith 13–0–52–0; Reeve 9–2–17–0; N. M. K. Smith 31–16–47–1.

Umpires: J. D. Bond and M. J. Kitchen.

WARWICKSHIRE v MIDDLESEX

At Birmingham, July 15, 16, 17, 19. Middlesex won by nine wickets. Middlesex 23 pts, Warwickshire 4 pts. Toss: Warwickshire.

The unexpected choice of a slow turning pitch, ideally suited to the Championship leaders, cost Warwickshire dearly. They were spun to defeat shortly after lunch on the fourth day, with Emburey and Tufnell sharing 15 wickets and predictably out-bowling the home spinners, Neil Smith and Booth. Mid-way through the second day, however, fiery bowling from Donald reduced Middlesex to 90 for six in reply to Warwickshire's 237. Carr engineered the recovery with a career-best unbeaten 192, including 23 fours, along with Emburey, whose obdurate 55 came out of 150 for the seventh wicket. Thanks to Carr, Middlesex added a further 147 after that. A lead of 150 proved too much against the quality off-spin of Emburey, despite a brave last-wicket stand of 50 between Booth and the injured Munton. Tufnell's match was not entirely happy. He was incensed when Moles scored four from a free hit at a ball which had slipped from his hand and run to square leg; it became six through the two-run penalty for a no-ball. Later that over, when Ratcliffe declined to walk before he was formally given out for a catch at the wicket, Tufnell lost his temper, shouted abuse at Ratcliffe and had to be restrained by team-mates.

Close of play: First day, Warwickshire 168-5 (P. A. Smith 5*, N. M. K. Smith 14*); Second day, Middlesex 205-6 (J. D. Carr 89*, J. E. Emburey 43*); Third day, Warwickshire 142-8 (P. A. Booth 10*, A. A. Donald 1*).

Warwickshire

A. J. Moles b Emburey	12	– c Carr b Emburey	23
J. D. Ratcliffe lbw b Tufnell	82	– c Brown b Tufnell	18
D. P. Ostler b Emburey	2	– c Carr b Emburey	6
T. L. Penney lbw b Tufnell	23	– c Roseberry b Emburey	19
*D. A. Reeve c Fraser b Emburey	11	– run out	19
P. A. Smith c Emburey b Tufnell	11	– b Emburey	0
N. M. K. Smith lbw b Fraser	34	– b Emburey	8
†K. J. Piper b Tufnell	0	– b Emburey	11
P. A. Booth c Ramprakash b Fraser	30	– not out	49
A. A. Donald c Ramprakash b Fraser	2	– c Roseberry b Tufnell	3
T. A. Munton not out	0	– b Fraser	18
B 4, l-b 7, w 1, n-b 18	30	B 6, l-b 12, n-b 14	32

1/27 2/33 3/105 4/149 5/149　　　　　237　　1/55 2/59 3/64 4/64 5/101　　　206
6/180 7/182 8/228 9/234　　　　　　　　　　　6/111 7/114 8/135 9/156

Bonus points – Warwickshire 1, Middlesex 4.

Bowling: *First Innings*—Fraser 16.4–5–42–3; Williams 15–6–25–0; Emburey 39–12–68–3; Tufnell 34–5–71–4; Feltham 10–3–20–0. *Second Innings*—Fraser 5.1–2–13–1; Williams 5–1–16–0; Tufnell 45–10–92–2; Emburey 48–15–61–6; Ramprakash 3–1–6–0.

Middlesex

D. L. Haynes b Donald	1	– c Reeve b Booth	2
M. A. Roseberry lbw b Donald	12	– not out	22
*M. W. Gatting lbw b N. M. K. Smith	4	– not out	33
M. R. Ramprakash c Reeve b Booth	16		
J. D. Carr not out	192		
†K. R. Brown c Reeve b N. M. K. Smith	5		
M. A. Feltham b Donald	11		
J. E. Emburey lbw b Reeve	55		
N. F. Williams c Donald b Booth	31		
A. R. C. Fraser c Ostler b N. M. K. Smith	12		
P. C. R. Tufnell b N. M. K. Smith	15		
B 17, l-b 7, w 3, n-b 6	33	L-b 3	3

1/9 2/18 3/28 4/40 5/51　　　　　　387　　1/5　　　　　　　(1 wkt) 60
6/90 7/240 8/319 9/341

Bonus points – Middlesex 3, Warwickshire 3 (Score at 120 overs: 308-7).

Bowling: *First Innings*—Donald 31–8–56–3; Munton 7–0–15–0; N. M. K. Smith 43.4–6–133–4; Booth 37–8–95–2; Reeve 17–5–35–1; P. A. Smith 6–2–29–0. *Second Innings*— N. M. K. Smith 7–1–18–0; Booth 8.5–1–33–1; Ratcliffe 2–1–6–0.

Umpires: K. E. Palmer and P. B. Wight.

At Leicester, July 22, 23, 24, 26. WARWICKSHIRE drew with LEICESTERSHIRE.

At Southampton, July 29, 30, 31, August 2. WARWICKSHIRE beat HAMPSHIRE by 80 runs.

At Cardiff, August 5, 6, 7. WARWICKSHIRE lost to GLAMORGAN by two wickets.

WARWICKSHIRE v GLOUCESTERSHIRE

At Birmingham, August 12, 13, 14, 16. Gloucestershire won by five wickets. Gloucestershire 20 pts, Warwickshire 6 pts. Toss: Warwickshire.

Gloucestershire struggled to avoid the follow-on but, in a match dominated by pace bowling, Walsh's extra hostility ultimately proved decisive; he led his team to their second successive win and off the bottom of the table. Moles put Warwickshire in a strong position with a patient century but on the second morning they lost seven wickets for 48. This statistic was echoed when the left-armer Bell took seven for 48, his career best, and bowled out Gloucestershire for 145. Broad and Russell scored more than half the runs off the bat; both were dropped by Asif Din, who acted as wicket-keeper when Burns was called on to bowl seamers while Reeve and Paul Smith were injured. Walsh led the way as Warwickshire were bowled out cheaply, and his batsmen responded when their turn came again. Though Reeve and Smith were now fit to bowl again, Hodgson and Broad set out with a stand of 92 and Hodgson, formerly with Warwickshire, stayed on for an unbeaten 85 in 97.4 overs.

Close of play: First day, Warwickshire 215-3 (A. J. Moles 109*, Asif Din 30*); Second day, Warwickshire 31-4 (T. L. Penney 10*, M. Burns 8*); Third day, Gloucestershire 155-3 (G. D. Hodgson 51*, M. W. Alleyne 13*).

Warwickshire

A. J. Moles b Walsh	117	– c Hancock b Babington		3
J. D. Ratcliffe c Russell b Alleyne	13	– lbw b Walsh		7
D. P. Ostler b Alleyne	29	– b Babington		1
T. L. Penney lbw b Walsh	24	– b Alleyne		26
Asif Din c Russell b Davies	53	– c Russell b Walsh		0
*D. A. Reeve retired hurt	1	– (9) b Walsh		36
P. A. Smith c Dawson b Walsh	5	– c Hodgson b Walsh		0
N. M. K. Smith b Walsh	0	– c Russell b Alleyne		5
†M. Burns c Russell b Alleyne	14	– (6) c Dawson b Walsh		14
P. A. Booth c Babington b Davies	7	– c Davies b Alleyne		3
M. A. V. Bell not out	0	– not out		22
B 1, l-b 1, n-b 15	17	L-b 1, n-b 6		7
	280			**124**

1/41 2/91 3/150 4/232 5/250 6/250 7/262 8/280 9/280

1/3 2/11 3/13 4/14 5/40 6/44 7/54 8/67 9/75

Bonus points – Warwickshire 2, Gloucestershire 4.

In the first innings D. A. Reeve retired hurt at 234.

Bowling: *First Innings*—Walsh 30-4-102-4; Babington 17-4-44-0; Alleyne 20-6-38-3; Davies 38.1-15-62-2; Wight 10-2-32-0. *Second Innings*—Walsh 24.2-5-59-5; Babington 23-7-30-2; Davies 5-1-9-0; Alleyne 12-5-25-3.

Gloucestershire

G. D. Hodgson c Ratcliffe b Bell	14	– (2) not out		85
S. G. Hinks c Reeve b Bell	4	– (4) c Burns b P. A. Smith		19
R. I. Dawson b Bell	5	– lbw b Reeve		8
B. C. Broad lbw b Bell	39	– (1) c Ostler b Bell		48
M. W. Alleyne c Moles b N. M. K. Smith	9	– c Penney b Reeve		43
T. H. C. Hancock lbw b N. M. K. Smith	0	– c Burns b Ratcliffe		43
†R. C. Russell lbw b Bell	25	– not out		10
R. M. Wight lbw b N. M. K. Smith	17			
*C. A. Walsh c Ostler b Bell	0			
M. Davies c N. M. K. Smith b Bell	2			
A. M. Babington not out	6			
B 5, l-b 10, w 3, n-b 6	24	B 8, l-b 8, w 2, n-b 16		34
	145	(5 wkts)		**263**

1/7 2/26 3/32 4/55 5/61 6/97 7/134 8/134 9/134

1/92 2/105 3/132 4/169 5/251

Bonus points – Warwickshire 4.

Bowling: *First Innings*—Bell 20.1–5–48–7; P. A. Smith 1–1–0–0; N. M. K. Smith 21–6–42–3; Burns 7–4–8–0; Booth 10–1–22–0; Asif Din 3–1–10–0. *Second Innings*—Bell 27.4–6–95–2; P. A. Smith 17–0–56–1; N. M. K. Smith 21–8–45–0; Reeve 17–4–28–1; Booth 12–6–17–0; Ratcliffe 3–1–6–1.

Umpires: B. Leadbeater and R. Palmer.

At Darlington, August 19, 20, 21, 23. WARWICKSHIRE lost to DURHAM by nine wickets.

WARWICKSHIRE v WORCESTERSHIRE

At Birmingham, August 26, 27, 28, 30. Worcestershire won by ten wickets. Worcestershire 21 pts, Warwickshire 3 pts. Toss: Warwickshire.

A weak Warwickshire attack – missing Munton and Paul Smith as well as Donald – was no match for Worcestershire, whose third consecutive victory lifted them to third place in the table. Another unusually dry Edgbaston pitch inhibited strokeplay, and batting became a perpetual grind which offered the holiday weekend crowd barely two runs an over. Warwickshire's perennial batting weakness surfaced yet again on the first day: the Worcestershire seamers were keen and lively, but not so threatening as to bowl a side out for 206. Though Worcestershire were struggling at 118 for five, thanks to three wickets from off-spinner Neil Smith, their later order turned the match with a seventh-wicket partnership of 152 between Rhodes, whose five-hour century was his second in consecutive innings, and Newport. Warwickshire's attempt to save the game was patchy, with only fifties from Ostler and Asif Din extending the game until the final afternoon.

Close of play: First day, Worcestershire 31-0 (T. S. Curtis 13*, M. J. Weston 17*); Second day, Worcestershire 243-6 (S. J. Rhodes 63*, P. J. Newport 40*); Third day, Warwickshire 104-3 (Asif Din 6*, K. J. Piper 4*).

Warwickshire

A. J. Moles lbw b Radford	12	–	c Rhodes b Illingworth	38
J. D. Ratcliffe c Rhodes b Tolley	5	–	c Leatherdale b Tolley	1
D. P. Ostler c and b Tolley	56	–	c Rhodes b Illingworth	50
Asif Din c Leatherdale b Radford	30	–	c Hick b Newport	63
*D. A. Reeve b Illingworth	12	–	(7) c Rhodes b Newport	6
R. G. Twose lbw b Newport	37	–	c Leatherdale b Illingworth	8
N. M. K. Smith c Weston b Tolley	2	–	(8) c Rhodes b Newport	3
†K. J. Piper c D'Oliveira b Newport	31	–	(5) b Illingworth	9
P. A. Booth b Newport	2	–	b Newport	3
G. C. Small c Leatherdale b Hick	0	–	st Rhodes b Hick	2
M. A. V. Bell not out	8	–	not out	11
B 1, l-b 8, n-b 2	11		B 2, l-b 6	8

1/18 2/18 3/96 4/115 5/137   206   1/2 2/85 3/99 4/117 5/135   201
6/149 7/179 8/185 9/190   6/146 7/150 8/156 9/173

Bonus points – Warwickshire 1, Worcestershire 4.

Bowling: *First Innings*—Radford 20–3–62–2; Tolley 16–4–29–3; Newport 18.4–3–49–3; Weston 3–2–9–0; Illingworth 20–8–29–1; Hick 10–3–19–1. *Second Innings*—Radford 7–0–28–0; Tolley 11–5–18–1; Hick 29–17–41–1; Newport 16.1–7–38–4; Illingworth 35–19–55–4; D'Oliveira 6–1–13–0.

Worcestershire

*T. S. Curtis lbw b Smith	13	– not out	6
M. J. Weston c Ratcliffe b Bell	31	– not out	5
G. A. Hick b Smith	46		
G. R. Haynes c Ostler b Smith	13		
D. B. D'Oliveira c Reeve b Booth	25		
D. A. Leatherdale c Reeve b Small	2		
†S. J. Rhodes b Smith	101		
P. J. Newport c Small b Smith	76		
C. M. Tolley c Asif Din b Booth	22		
R. K. Illingworth not out	39		
N. V. Radford b Twose	11		
B 6, l-b 12	18		

1/31 2/69 3/100 4/111 5/118   397   (no wkt) 11
6/166 7/318 8/319 9/374

Bonus points – Worcestershire 1, Warwickshire 2 (Score at 120 overs: 232-6).

Bowling: *First Innings*—Small 37–15–73–1; Bell 42–11–111–1; Smith 48–18–103–5; Reeve 18–9–27–0; Twose 12.2–1–29–1; Booth 29–12–36–2. *Second Innings*—Bell 2–0–6–0; Ostler 3–1–3–0; Ratcliffe 1.3–0–2–0.

Umpires: J. W. Holder and G. Sharp.

At Birmingham, September 7. WARWICKSHIRE v ZIMBABWEANS. No result (See Zimbabwean tour section).

WARWICKSHIRE v SOMERSET

At Birmingham, September 9, 10, 11, 13. Drawn. Warwickshire 2 pts, Somerset 4 pts. Toss: Warwickshire.

Rain and bad light had restricted play to 154.1 overs on the first three days and exchanged declarations set Somerset to score 340 on the final day. Overnight rain prevented any play before lunch; the umpires and Warwickshire wanted to start at 2 p.m., but Somerset disagreed. Believing his team could no longer win, acting-captain Harden objected to playing in conditions no different from those earlier deemed unfit. A telephone call to Lord's produced a ruling that upheld his view and Warwickshire's final home game was thus abandoned, leaving spectators baffled. During the match, Moles and Ratcliffe put on 162 in the first innings and 109 in the second – their fourth and fifth century partnerships of 1993 out of only eight for Warwickshire all season. Leg-spinner Mushtaq Ahmed bowled brilliantly for his six wickets on a slow pitch.

Close of play: First day, Warwickshire 111-0 (A. J. Moles 53*, J. D. Ratcliffe 44*); Second day, Warwickshire 128-0 (A. J. Moles 54*, J. D. Ratcliffe 55*); Third day, Warwickshire 118-1 dec.

Warwickshire

A. J. Moles c Lathwell b Mallender	75	– not out	52
J. D. Ratcliffe lbw b Mushtaq Ahmed	67	– c Harden b Lathwell	58
D. P. Ostler b Mushtaq Ahmed	14	– not out	1
Asif Din c sub b van Troost	9		
*D. A. Reeve not out	55		
P. A. Smith b Rose	14		
N. M. K. Smith c Fletcher b Mushtaq Ahmed	0		
†K. J. Piper lbw b Mushtaq Ahmed	4		
G. C. Small st Turner b Mushtaq Ahmed	0		
M. A. V. Bell c and b Mushtaq Ahmed	0		
T. A. Munton b Caddick	0		
B 6, l-b 15, w 1, n-b 22	44	B 4, w 1, n-b 2	7

1/162 2/180 3/190 4/210 5/250   282   1/109   (1 wkt dec.) 118
6/251 7/255 8/261 9/271

Bonus points – Warwickshire 2, Somerset 4.

Bowling: *First Innings*—Caddick 19.4–6–64–1; Mallender 23–7–30–1; Rose 12–3–47–1; van Troost 16–0–65–1; Mushtaq Ahmed 40–23–55–6. *Second Innings*—Caddick 7–0–38–0; Rose 4–0–20–0; Lathwell 11–3–40–1; Mushtaq Ahmed 5–2–16–0; Harden 0.3–0–0–0.

Somerset

M. N. Lathwell not out 29
N. A. Folland not out 32
$\overline{}$
(no wkt dec.) 61

A. N. Hayhurst, *R. J. Harden, I. Fletcher, †R. J. Turner, G. D. Rose, Mushtaq Ahmed, A. R. Caddick, N. A. Mallender and A. P. van Troost did not bat.

Bowling: Small 5–1–20–0; Munton 4–0–17–0; N. M. K. Smith 4–1–12–0; Ratcliffe 2–0–10–0; Asif Din 1–0–2–0.

Umpires: B. J. Meyer and G. A. Stickley.

At Nottingham, September 16, 17, 18, 20. WARWICKSHIRE drew with NOTTING-HAMSHIRE.

BIGGEST LEAPS IN THE COUNTY CHAMPIONSHIP

15 places	Worcestershire	17th to second	1993
14 places	Gloucestershire	16th to second	1969
13 places	Warwickshire	14th to first	1911
	Worcestershire	14th to first	1964
	Gloucestershire	16th to third	1976
	Kent	14th to first equal	1977
	Surrey	16th to third	1979
	Worcestershire	15th to second	1979
	Middlesex	14th to first	1980
	Hampshire	15th to second	1985
	Lancashire	15th to second	1987

WORCESTERSHIRE

Patron: The Duke of Westminster
President: G. H. Chesterton
Chairman: C. D. Fearnley
Chairman, Cricket Committee: M. G. Jones
Secretary: The Rev. Michael Vockins
Captain: T. S. Curtis
Coach: 1993 – K. J. Lyons
Head Groundsman: R. McLaren
Scorer: J. W. Sewter

Worcestershire's response to the advent of four-day Championship cricket, the year after finishing next to bottom, could hardly have been better. They ended the 1993 season with five successive victories and rose to be runners-up. Even the previously unbeaten champions, Middlesex, were no match for Worcestershire in the final game, being swept aside inside two days by an innings and 36 runs after being routed on the opening morning for just 68. It was the first time since their title season of 1965 that Worcestershire had strung together five straight Championship wins in a season, taking their total for the summer to nine, and all the more creditable for being attained with only minimal contributions from their overseas player, West Indian pace bowler Ken Benjamin. His recurring hamstring problems led to his release at the end of his first season at New Road, after taking 36 of his 37 wickets in his first eight games.

One can only surmise what Worcestershire might have achieved had they not lost so much time to rain and bad light. Yet for all their improvement in the first-class game, they were again found wanting in the three one-day competitions, where their brittle middle-order batting was time and again exposed. They succumbed by 55 runs to Leicestershire in the quarter-finals of the Benson and Hedges Cup, and by 104 runs to Glamorgan at the same stage in the NatWest Trophy. But their 16th place in the Sunday League was the major disappointment.

The tour game with the Australians typified Worcestershire's fluctuations. In the first innings they were all out for 90; following on, they were able to declare at 458 for four and lost with just one ball to spare.

Middle-order collapses were never far away in the Championship. But situations were regularly retrieved by spirited and determined rearguard actions from the lower order, with wicket-keeper Steve Rhodes and Phil Newport, in particular, both staking claims for higher batting berths in 1994. Rhodes's 848 runs included centuries in successive innings against Kent and Warwickshire, and helped clinch his selection for the England A tour to South Africa. Newport also averaged over 30, with six half-centuries. Inevitably, though, when the committee sat down to decide on an overseas player for 1994, the overwhelming evidence demanded the recruitment of a free-scoring batsman and prompted a renewed offer to the Australian Tom Moody – who actually could have been re-engaged in 1993 since he was not selected for the tour.

Newport's consistency with bat and ball – he was also the leading wicket-taker with 60 first-class victims – made him a worthy winner of the

Supporters' Association Player of the Year award. Richard Illingworth won the Dick Lygon award for the player judged to have done most for the county both on and off the field. Illingworth took a Championship-best six for 28 against Gloucestershire and became the first Worcestershire bowler to take a hat-trick in any of the one-day competitions, in the Sunday League match against Sussex at Hove. Gavin Haynes, who scored his maiden first-class century in making 158 against Kent, won the uncapped player of the year award, and should figure regularly in future.

Tim Curtis was again a model of consistency in his second season in charge, becoming the second batsman (after Graham Gooch) to complete centuries against the other 17 counties, when he made a hundred against Durham. He was the county's top first-class scorer with 1,553 runs at an average of 53.55, and also completed 5,000 runs in the Sunday League.

But the season's major records went to Graeme Hick who, despite his struggles for England, scored 2,353 runs in all cricket. His four centuries, taking his career total to 72, included a magnificent 187 against the Australians, and an unbeaten 104 against Leicestershire during which he became the game's youngest player to reach 20,000 first-class runs, aged 27 years and 20 days. Philip Weston followed his maiden century against Oxford University with a first Championship hundred against Derbyshire before his season was interrupted by illness. But a combined aggregate of 767 runs in 23 matches between Damian D'Oliveira and David Leatherdale, while Adam Seymour's top score was his unbeaten 54 against the tourists. Their failings left the way open for Second XI captain Martin Weston to revive his first-class career over the second half of his joint benefit season with D'Oliveira, before he was released at the end of his 15th season at New Road.

While Newport and Illingworth took the most wickets, Chris Tolley, who was capped during the season, and Neal Radford worked hard. Tolley never looked back after taking a wicket with his first ball of the season against the Australians, and produced two career-best performances within a week, returning five for 55 against Kent after scoring 78 against Surrey in the previous match. Radford reserved his best until last with six for 49 to complete Middlesex's rout. Stuart Lampitt also made several useful contributions. The highly-rated but injury-plagued Alex Wylie made his first-class debut in the opening Championship game against Nottinghamshire, but was then injured again.

At the end of the season Worcestershire announced the appointment of David Houghton, the former Zimbabwe captain, to run their Second XI cricket in 1994. It could prove an inspired move, not least if it has the desired effect on the future contentment of his fellow-countryman Hick. It may not have been a complete coincidence that initial talks with Houghton came in the wake of rumours on the county grapevine linking Hick with a move from New Road. However, following the resignation of Kevin Lyons, it was decided to go into the new season without a first-team coach. – Chris Moore.

WORCESTERSHIRE 1993

[*Bill Smith*]

Back row: T. Edwards, V. S. Solanki, K. R. Spiring, G. R. Haynes. *Middle row*: K. J. Lyons (*coach*), D. A. Leatherdale, C. J. Eyers, J. E. Brinkley, W. P. C. Weston, A. C. H. Seymour, A. Wylie, C. M. Tolley. *Front row*: M. J. Weston, R. K. Illingworth, N. V. Radford, S. J. Rhodes, T. S. Curtis (*captain*), D. B. D'Oliveira, G. A. Hick, P. J. Newport, S. R. Lampitt.

WORCESTERSHIRE RESULTS

All first-class matches – Played 19: Won 9, Lost 5, Tied 1, Drawn 4.

County Championship matches – Played 17: Won 9, Lost 4, Tied 1, Drawn 3.

Bonus points – Batting 32, Bowling 52.

Competition placings – Britannic Assurance County Championship, 2nd;
NatWest Bank Trophy, q-f; Benson and Hedges Cup, q-f;
AXA Equity & Law League, 16th.

BRITANNIC ASSURANCE CHAMPIONSHIP AVERAGES

BATTING

	Birthplace	*M*	*I*	*NO*	*R*	*HS*	*Avge*
‡G. A. Hick	Salisbury, Rhodesia	14	22	2	1,074	182	53.70
‡T. S. Curtis	Chislehurst	17	28	2	1,354	127	52.07
‡S. J. Rhodes	Bradford	17	26	3	848	101	36.86
‡P. J. Newport	High Wycombe	16	25	6	623	79*	32.78
G. R. Haynes	Stourbridge	8	12	0	334	158	27.83
‡R. K. Illingworth . . .	Bradford	16	22	8	376	58	26.85
W. P. C. Weston . . .	Durham	11	17	1	383	109	23.93
‡M. J. Weston	Worcester	7	13	1	277	59	23.08
‡C. M. Tolley	Kidderminster	16	22	5	381	78	22.41
‡D. B. D'Oliveira	Cape Town, SA	13	21	0	464	94	22.09
D. A. Leatherdale . . .	Bradford	10	15	1	303	119*	21.64
A. C. H. Seymour . . .	Royston	5	8	0	157	49	19.62
‡S. R. Lampitt	Wolverhampton	14	22	1	344	58	16.38
‡N. V. Radford	Luanshya, N. Rhodesia	11	13	5	102	29	12.75
K. C. G. Benjamin§	St John's, Antigua	11	11	3	85	26	10.62

Also batted: A. Wylie (*Tamworth*) (1 match) 0.

* *Signifies not out.*   ‡ *Denotes county cap.*   § *Overseas player.*

The following played a total of 12 three-figure innings for Worcestershire in County Championship matches – T. S. Curtis 4, G. A. Hick 3, S. J. Rhodes 2, G. R. Haynes 1, D. A. Leatherdale 1, W. P. C. Weston 1.

BOWLING

	O	*M*	*R*	*W*	*BB*	*5W/i*	*Avge*
P. J. Newport	509	128	1,337	56	6-63	1	23.87
K. C. G. Benjamin	283.5	42	911	37	6-70	2	24.62
R. K. Illingworth	574.1	200	1,192	48	6-28	1	24.83
N. V. Radford	222.5	36	797	29	6-49	1	27.48
C. M. Tolley	395.5	102	1,060	38	5-55	1	27.89
S. R. Lampitt	282	52	910	26	3-9	0	35.00
G. A. Hick	172.4	52	518	10	2-15	0	51.80

Also bowled: T. S. Curtis 1-0-7-0; D. B. D'Oliveira 38-8-107-5; G. R. Haynes 76-17-200-5; M. J. Weston 29-9-96-2; W. P. C. Weston 2-0-2-0; A. Wylie 22-3-73-1.

Wicket-keeper: S. J. Rhodes 39 ct, 6 st.

Leading Fielders: G. A. Hick 22, S. R. Lampitt 18, D. A. Leatherdale 17.

At Nottingham, April 29, 30, May 1, 2. WORCESTERSHIRE tied with NOTTINGHAM-
SHIRE.

At Worcester, May 5, 6, 7. WORCESTERSHIRE lost to AUSTRALIANS by five wickets
(See Australian tour section).

At Bradford, May 13, 14, 15, 17. WORCESTERSHIRE drew with YORKSHIRE.

WORCESTERSHIRE v SOMERSET

At Worcester, May 20, 21, 22, 24. Worcestershire won by two wickets. Worcestershire
20 pts, Somerset 5 pts. Toss: Worcestershire. Championship debut: J. I. D. Kerr.

Somerset were in sight of a third successive Championship win, which would have lifted
them to the top of the table, until Rhodes and Newport shared a match-winning partnership
of 77 in 17 overs. Tavaré's lunch-time declaration set Worcestershire 246 from 73 overs.
Their chances of making the highest score of the match appeared hopeless at 160 for six,
four wickets falling to Mushtaq Ahmed, who finished with a match return of ten for 145.
But the seventh-wicket pair set up a thrilling victory with four balls to spare. Rhodes made
an undefeated 54 off 72 balls, with Newport keeping pace until he fell to a juggling catch by
Harden at cover. By then Worcestershire required nine runs from the last two overs, though
they lost one more wicket getting there. The first day and a half had been lost to rain.
When the fire brigade had removed 5,000 gallons of water from blocked drains in the
outfield, Benjamin celebrated with six for 70. But he was promptly upstaged by Mushtaq,
whose five for 51 gave Somerset a first-innings lead of 94.

Close of play: First day, No play; Second day, Somerset 170-7 (N. D. Burns 41*,
A. Payne 1*); Third day, Somerset 82-3 (R. J. Harden 28*, N. A. Folland 21*).

Somerset

A. N. Hayhurst lbw b Lampitt	20	– lbw b Tolley	8
R. J. Turner c Curtis b Tolley	0	– lbw b Newport	17
R. J. Harden c Rhodes b Benjamin	10	– not out	72
*C. J. Tavaré c Tolley b Benjamin	46	– c Lampitt b Newport	0
N. A. Folland b Radford	24	– lbw b Newport	22
†N. D. Burns b Benjamin	44	– b Tolley	1
G. D. Rose lbw b Benjamin	7	– c Rhodes b Newport	4
J. I. D. Kerr c Rhodes b Benjamin	2	– lbw b Radford	6
A. Payne c Lampitt b Benjamin	17		
Mushtaq Ahmed lbw b Radford	36	– (9) b Tolley	8
A. P. van Troost not out	10		
B 1, l-b 11, w 2, n-b 6	20	L-b 8, w 1, n-b 4	13

1/3 2/20 3/48 4/86 5/148   236   1/25 2/31 3/31   (8 wkts dec.) 151
6/158 7/164 8/177 9/220   4/88 5/95 6/102
                              7/136 8/151

Bonus points – Somerset 1, Worcestershire 4.

Bowling: *First Innings*—Benjamin 26.5–5–70–6; Tolley 13–2–37–1; Newport 13–3–26–0;
Lampitt 12–4–24–1; Haynes 6–1–25–0; Radford 11–2–42–2. *Second Innings*—Benjamin
5–0–9–0; Tolley 25–6–55–3; Newport 22–7–31–4; Lampitt 6–1–22–0; Radford 6–0–24–1;
D'Oliveira 2–1–2–0.

Worcestershire

*T. S. Curtis lbw b Rose	35	– c Turner b Rose	45
W. P. C. Weston c Turner b van Troost	3	– c Burns b Rose	18
A. C. H. Seymour lbw b Kerr	1	– c Harden b Mushtaq Ahmed	13
D. B. D'Oliveira c Burns b Mushtaq Ahmed	13	– c Rose b Mushtaq Ahmed	31
G. R. Haynes c Turner b Mushtaq Ahmed	0	– c Harden b Mushtaq Ahmed	17
S. R. Lampitt lbw b Mushtaq Ahmed	11	– lbw b Mushtaq Ahmed	21
†S. J. Rhodes b Mushtaq Ahmed	24	– not out	54
P. J. Newport c Tavaré b Payne	10	– c Harden b Payne	36
C. M. Tolley not out	16	– c Payne b Mushtaq Ahmed	1
N. V. Radford c Burns b Payne	2	– not out	2
K. C. G. Benjamin c Kerr b Mushtaq Ahmed	13		
L-b 2, n-b 12	14	B 1, l-b 3, n-b 4	8

1/5 2/12 3/44 4/48 5/60	142	1/37 2/64 3/90 4/125	(8 wkts) 246
6/74 7/99 8/115 9/123		5/146 6/160 7/237 8/242	

Bonus points – Somerset 4.

Bowling: *First Innings*—van Troost 11–2–38–1; Kerr 5–0–15–1; Rose 10–4–21–1; Mushtaq Ahmed 21.2–9–51–5; Payne 6–1–15–2. *Second Innings*—van Troost 11–1–44–0; Kerr 9–2–34–0; Mushtaq Ahmed 33–7–94–5; Rose 13–1–57–2; Payne 6.2–2–13–1.

Umpires: J. H. Harris and G. Sharp.

At Gloucester, May 27, 28, 29, 31. WORCESTERSHIRE beat GLOUCESTERSHIRE by an innings and five runs.

At Northampton, June 3, 4, 5, 7. WORCESTERSHIRE lost to NORTHAMPTONSHIRE by six wickets.

WORCESTERSHIRE v LEICESTERSHIRE

At Worcester, June 10, 11, 12, 14. Drawn. Worcestershire 1 pt, Leicestershire 2 pts. Toss: Worcestershire.

Rain and flooding restricted play to just 75 overs. The first day ended in a storm which knocked out the scorers' computers, and the second and final days were washed out altogether; Worcestershire had lost five complete days and more than 900 overs to the weather in six Championship games. Hick, compiling an unbeaten 104, his 70th century, still had time to become the youngest player to complete 20,000 first-class runs, aged 27 years and 20 days. W. R. Hammond was 28 years and 13 days when he set the previous record in July 1931. Winston Benjamin took five of the six wickets to fall but was warned by umpire Julian for dissent over varying interpretations of the bouncer rule as the ball flew around helmet height.

Close of play: First day, Worcestershire 158-5 (G. A. Hick 82*, S. J. Rhodes 13*); Second day, No play; Third day, Worcestershire 207-6 (G. A. Hick 104*, R. K. Illingworth 5*).

Worcestershire

*T. S. Curtis c Parsons b Benjamin	6	†S. J. Rhodes c Benson b Benjamin	22
W. P. C. Weston c Boon b Benjamin	18	R. K. Illingworth not out	5
G. A. Hick not out	104	B 5, l-b 10, w 10, n-b 2	27
D. A. Leatherdale c and b Benjamin	0		
G. R. Haynes c Potter b Parsons	10	1/8 2/29 3/33 4/62	(6 wkts) 207
S. R. Lampitt c Whitaker b Benjamin	15	5/100 6/190	

C. M. Tolley, N. V. Radford and K. C. G. Benjamin did not bat.

Bonus points – Worcestershire 1, Leicestershire 2.

Bowling: Benjamin 28–11–67–5; Mullally 24–6–73–0; Parsons 14–5–27–1; Wells 9–4–25–0.

Leicestershire

T. J. Boon, *N. E. Briers, J. J. Whitaker, J. D. R. Benson, L. Potter, V. J. Wells, †P. A. Nixon, W. K. M. Benjamin, G. J. Parsons, A. D. Mullally and A. R. K. Pierson.

Umpires: R. Julian and R. A. White.

WORCESTERSHIRE v OXFORD UNIVERSITY

At Worcester, June 18, 19, 20. Drawn. Toss: Worcestershire. First-class debut: T. Edwards.
Starved of Championship cricket by the weather, Worcestershire took on the University with all their front-line batsmen except Hick, absent at the Lord's Test. But only Philip Weston, with his maiden first-class century, and Haynes seized the opportunity on the first day. Gallian again looked the part in holding together the students' reply before declaring 122 runs behind. But instead of giving his other batsmen time in the middle, Curtis compiled a century himself, off 103 balls, sharing an unbroken opening stand of 185 with Weston before setting Oxford a target of 308 in just over three hours plus 20 overs. A stand of 151 in 37 overs between Montgomerie, who made his second first-class century, and Lovell took them to 223 for two, but they gave up the chase after Lampitt took three wickets in two overs.

Close of play: First day, Worcestershire 303-6 (D. A. Leatherdale 17*, R. K. Illingworth 0*); Second day, Worcestershire 7-0 (T. S. Curtis 1*, W. P. C. Weston 5*).

Worcestershire

*T. S. Curtis run out	31	– not out	100
W. P. C. Weston c Yeabsley b Malik	113	– not out	81
A. C. H. Seymour c Lyons b Macdonald	20		
G. R. Haynes c Lyons b Jeh	49		
D. B. D'Oliveira c Lovell b Jeh	9		
D. A. Leatherdale not out	51		
S. R. Lampitt st Lyons b Trimby	22		
R. K. Illingworth c Lyons b Macdonald	13		
C. M. Tolley not out	0		
B 2, l-b 10, w 3, n-b 28	43	L-b 2, w 2	4

1/68 2/115 3/220 4/243   (7 wkts dec.) 351   (no wkt dec.) 185
5/264 6/301 7/346

N. V. Radford and †T. Edwards did not bat.

Bowling: *First Innings*—Jeh 23-0-93-2; Gallian 13-5-29-0; Yeabsley 20.3-3-87-0; Macdonald 16-6-29-2; Trimby 16-5-48-1; Malik 12-3-52-1; Montgomerie 1-0-1-0. *Second Innings*—Jeh 11-1-55-0; Gallian 9-1-30-0; Yeabsley 4-0-31-0; Trimby 5-0-29-0; Macdonald 4-0-22-0; Malik 2-0-16-0.

Oxford University

R. R. Montgomerie c Edwards b Tolley	2	– lbw b Lampitt	109
*J. E. R. Gallian c Curtis b Tolley	81	– c D'Oliveira b Illingworth	29
G. B. T. Lovell b Lampitt	16	– (4) c Leatherdale b Illingworth	71
C. L. Keey lbw b Radford	11	– (5) c Haynes b Lampitt	2
H. S. Malik c Weston b Radford	3	– (6) c Tolley b Lampitt	4
†C. W. J. Lyons c D'Oliveira b Illingworth	24	– (8) not out	4
C. M. Gupte not out	38	– (3) lbw b Weston	12
R. S. Yeabsley lbw b Lampitt	36	– (7) not out	4
M. P. W. Jeh lbw b Lampitt	0		
R. H. Macdonald not out	1		
B 5, l-b 4, n-b 8	17	B 4, l-b 6, n-b 4	14

1/5 2/46 3/79 4/93   (8 wkts dec.) 229   1/40 2/72 3/223   (6 wkts) 249
5/122 6/152 7/223 8/223   4/232 5/241 6/241

P. W. Trimby did not bat.

Bowling: *First Innings*—Radford 17–3–64–2; Tolley 18–4–46–2; Lampitt 18–5–44–3; Illingworth 19–7–32–1; Haynes 6–0–23–0; D'Oliveira 8–4–11–0; Leatherdale 1–1–0–0. *Second Innings*—Radford 8–1–42–0; Tolley 4–2–12–0; Illingworth 24–9–58–2; D'Oliveira 9–1–37–0; Weston 3–0–13–1; Lampitt 12–2–35–3; Curtis 6–2–15–0; Haynes 5–1–27–0.

Umpires: A. Clarkson and J. H. Hampshire.

At Stockton-on-Tees, June 24, 25, 26, 28. WORCESTERSHIRE beat DURHAM by three wickets.

WORCESTERSHIRE v DERBYSHIRE

At Kidderminster, July 1, 2, 3, 5. Worcestershire won by nine wickets. Worcestershire 24 pts, Derbyshire 2 pts. Toss: Derbyshire. First-class debut: A. S. Rollins.

Worcestershire prepared for their fourth Championship win of the season by plundering their highest-ever total at Kidderminster in 72 years and their best against Derbyshire. Hick, axed for the Third Test, responded with his 50th first-class century for Worcestershire at the club where he served his apprenticeship. His 173 off 176 balls, with 27 fours and four sixes, included 138 between lunch and tea on the second day. This left Durham as the only county against whom he had not scored a century and stole the limelight from Weston, who shared 175 with Curtis and 135 with Hick in completing his maiden Championship hundred. Derbyshire, having collapsed from 71 without loss to 251 all out despite debutant Adrian Rollins's unbeaten 46, required 309 to avoid an innings defeat. Barnett batted almost seven hours for his fourth century of the summer. But Benjamin took four wickets in 15 balls on the final morning, and Worcestershire reached the 50 runs needed in just 7.4 overs.

Close of play: First day, Worcestershire 118-0 (T. S. Curtis 49*, W. P. C. Weston 59*); Second day, Worcestershire 539-7 (C. M. Tolley 16*, R. K. Illingworth 9*); Third day, Derbyshire 289-5 (K. J. Barnett 137*, M. J. Vandrau 13*).

Derbyshire

*K. J. Barnett c Lampitt b Radford	36	– c Hick b Benjamin 168
P. D. Bowler c Rhodes b Benjamin	65	– c Rhodes b Radford 56
J. E. Morris c Lampitt b Newport	4	– c Lampitt b Illingworth 12
C. J. Adams b Lampitt	36	– c Hick b Illingworth 0
T. J. G. O'Gorman c Radford b Newport	7	– lbw b Radford 1
D. G. Cork c D'Oliveira b Newport	3	– c Rhodes b Tolley 57
M. J. Vandrau b Benjamin	4	– c Tolley b Radford 42
†A. S. Rollins not out	46	– not out 3
S. J. Base c Illingworth b Benjamin	15	– lbw b Benjamin 0
R. W. Sladdin c Hick b Lampitt	12	– lbw b Benjamin 0
O. H. Mortensen lbw b Lampitt	1	– c Hick b Benjamin 6
B 6, l-b 5, n-b 10	22	L-b 5, n-b 8 13

1/71 2/78 3/130 4/147 5/153   251   1/135 2/154 3/156 4/171 5/256   358
6/160 7/187 8/210 9/235   6/343 7/352 8/352 9/352

Bonus points – Derbyshire 2, Worcestershire 4.

Bowling: *First Innings*—Benjamin 20–1–84–3; Tolley 5–1–28–0; Radford 9–0–33–1; Newport 12–2–47–3; Lampitt 11.3–0–48–3. *Second Innings*—Benjamin 18–0–81–4; Tolley 11–4–35–1; Illingworth 42–24–53–2; Newport 14–2–60–0; Hick 8–4–13–0; Radford 19–2–85–3; Lampitt 5–0–24–0; Weston 2–0–2–0.

Worcestershire

*T. S. Curtis st Rollins b Sladdin	81	– c Rollins b Cork 5
W. P. C. Weston c Barnett b Adams	109	– not out 18
G. A. Hick c and b Vandrau	173	– not out 21
D. B. D'Oliveira lbw b Mortensen	26	
S. R. Lampitt lbw b Base	39	
†S. J. Rhodes b Base	38	
P. J. Newport c Rollins b Base	13	
C. M. Tolley b Base	27	
R. K. Illingworth lbw b Base	9	
N. V. Radford c Rollins b Base	3	
K. C. G. Benjamin not out	4	
B 6, l-b 18, n-b 14	38	N-b 6 6

1/175 2/310 3/389 4/431 5/490   **560**   1/8   **(1 wkt) 50**
6/509 7/516 8/544 9/552

Bonus points – Worcestershire 4 (Score at 120 overs: 389-2).

Bowling: *First Innings*—Cork 28–5–102–1; Base 31.2–7–82–5; Vandrau 28–6–72–1; Mortensen 31–10–59–1; Sladdin 39–5–185–1; Adams 7–0–36–1. *Second Innings*—Cork 4–1–11–1; Adams 2–0–21–0; Sladdin 1.4–0–18–0.

Umpires: G. A. Stickley and A. G. T. Whitehead.

At Portsmouth, July 15, 16, 17, 19. WORCESTERSHIRE drew with HAMPSHIRE.

WORCESTERSHIRE v GLAMORGAN

At Worcester, July 22, 23, 24, 26. Glamorgan won by one wicket. Worcestershire 6 pts, Glamorgan 20 pts. Toss: Worcestershire.

With one wicket and three balls to spare, Glamorgan reached the highest score of the game for a victory that lifted them into second place in the Championship. Set to make 331 on the final day, their cause looked lost at 92 for four before lunch. But Dale, opening in place of the injured James, hit 16 boundaries in his third century of the season – which made him the country's leading scorer. Even so the visitors still required ten from five overs, with their last pair at the wicket, before 18-year-old Thomas, whose first Championship appearance of the season brought him nine wickets including a career-best five for 76, swung the winning boundary over square leg. Tolley's four for 67 on the second day had secured Worcestershire a first-innings lead of 83. But it required a battling three-hour fifty by Newport and a last-wicket stand of 53 between Illingworth and Radford to rescue them from 78 for five in the second innings. Metson's nine catches in the match broke the Glamorgan record of eight dismissals which he had shared with H. G. Davies and E. W. Jones.

Close of play: First day, Worcestershire 267; Second day, Glamorgan 184; Third day, Worcestershire 247.

Worcestershire

*T. S. Curtis c Metson b Thomas	45	– lbw b Watkin 45
W. P. C. Weston c Metson b Dale	39	– (8) c Metson b Croft 1
G. A. Hick c Dale b Watkin	9	– c Metson b Watkin 9
D. B. D'Oliveira c Hemp b Thomas	73	– c Cottey b Thomas 13
M. J. Weston c Richards b Dale	4	– (2) c Richards b Thomas 0
S. R. Lampitt c Metson b Thomas	18	– (5) c Metson b Thomas 4
†S. J. Rhodes c Metson b Thomas	37	– (6) c and b Dale 25
P. J. Newport not out	20	– (7) c Richards b Thomas 54
C. M. Tolley c Metson b Watkin	0	– c Croft b Watkin 7
R. K. Illingworth c Metson b Watkin	4	– not out 42
N. V. Radford c Morris b Lefebvre	1	– b Thomas 29
L-b 4, w 5, n-b 8	17	B 1, l-b 11, w 4, n-b 2 ... 18

1/84 2/103 3/105 4/117 5/152   **267**   1/12 2/25 3/49 4/55 5/78   **247**
6/233 7/250 8/250 9/260   6/124 7/141 8/155 9/194

Bonus points – Worcestershire 2, Glamorgan 4.

Bowling: *First Innings*—Watkin 26–10–35–3; Thomas 25.5–8–84–4; Lefebvre 23.1–8–48–1; Croft 18–6–47–0; Dale 19–7–49–2. *Second Innings*—Watkin 26–7–63–3; Thomas 23.3–2–76–5; Lefebvre 22–9–30–0; Dale 9–1–27–1; Croft 21–8–39–1.

Glamorgan

A. Dale c Curtis b Tolley	44	– c Radford b Lampitt 124
*H. Morris c Rhodes b Newport	13	– c M. J. Weston b Tolley ... 15
M. P. Maynard st Rhodes b Illingworth	34	– c Rhodes b Newport 24
I. V. A. Richards c Lampitt b Newport	7	– lbw b Newport 0
P. A. Cottey lbw b Newport	4	– c Curtis b Lampitt 7
D. L. Hemp c Hick b Tolley	0	– b Radford 52
R. D. B. Croft c Hick b Tolley	1	– c Hick b Illingworth 43
†C. P. Metson c and b Tolley	9	– run out 22
R. P. Lefebvre c Newport b Illingworth	50	– not out 18
S. L. Watkin c D'Oliveira b Illingworth	14	– lbw b Lampitt 0
S. D. Thomas not out	5	– not out 9
L-b 1, n-b 2	3	L-b 8, n-b 12 20

1/23 2/93 3/100 4/104 5/104   **184**   1/28 2/73 3/79   **(9 wkts) 334**
6/104 7/106 8/141 9/175   4/92 5/180 6/269
                                    7/293 8/320 9/321

Bonus points – Worcestershire 4.

Bowling: *First Innings*—Newport 19–5–55–3; Tolley 21–3–67–4; Radford 7–0–35–0; Lampitt 5–0–15–0; Hick 3–1–9–0; Illingworth 6.4–4–2–3. *Second Innings*—Newport 21–4–60–2; Tolley 10–3–42–1; Illingworth 26.3–3–81–1; Lampitt 26–5–84–3; Hick 6–1–19–0; Radford 8–2–26–1; M. J. Weston 5–0–14–0.

Umpires: A. A. Jones and K. E. Palmer.

At Chelmsford, July 29, 30, 31, August 2. WORCESTERSHIRE lost to ESSEX by four wickets.

At Hove, August 5, 6, 7, 9. WORCESTERSHIRE lost to SUSSEX by nine wickets.

WORCESTERSHIRE v SURREY

At Worcester, August 12, 13, 14, 16. Worcestershire won by 65 runs. Worcestershire 21 pts, Surrey 8 pts. Toss: Worcestershire.

A fourth successive Championship defeat loomed over the home county as Thorpe and Darren Bicknell overhauled Surrey's 93-year-old record for the second wicket against Worcestershire, 272 by R. Abel and E. G. Hayes, adding 299 in 82 overs on the second day. But Newport swung the game next morning with a spell of four for ten in nine overs; Surrey lost their last seven wickets for 62 and their lead was just 21. A career-best 78 from stand-in opener Tolley enabled Curtis to set an enticing target of 293 in 64 overs. Surrey were still in the hunt as Ward and Martin Bicknell—who had claimed 11 wickets in the match—added 70 in 17 overs. But the last five wickets fell for 16 and Worcestershire triumphed with 23 balls remaining. Hick's 182 on the first day, as he passed 1,000 runs for the ninth successive season, included 26 fours and three sixes. It was his second century since he was dropped by England and was rewarded with a recall for the final Test.

Close of play: First day, Worcestershire 403-9 (R. K. Illingworth 5*); Second day, Surrey 365-3 (A. D. Brown 29*, J. Boiling 2*); Third day, Worcestershire 199-4 (D. A. Leatherdale 17*, S. R. Lampitt 12*).

Worcestershire

*T. S. Curtis b Waqar Younis	45 – lbw b Waqar Younis	0
M. J. Weston lbw b M. P. Bicknell	38 – (7) run out	0
G. A. Hick c Thorpe b M. P. Bicknell	182 – c Atkins b M. P. Bicknell	9
D. B. D'Oliveira b M. P. Bicknell	0 – lbw b Benjamin	50
D. A. Leatherdale c Thorpe b M. P. Bicknell	8 – c Brown b M. P. Bicknell	53
S. R. Lampitt c Atkins b Benjamin	5 – lbw b Waqar Younis	18
†S. J. Rhodes b M. P. Bicknell	20 – (8) b M. P. Bicknell	10
P. J. Newport c Boiling b M. P. Bicknell	52 – (9) not out	15
C. M. Tolley b Benjamin	0 – (2) c Kendrick b M. P. Bicknell	78
R. K. Illingworth not out	5 – c Thorpe b M. P. Bicknell	17
N. V. Radford lbw b Waqar Younis	1 – not out	10
B 9, l-b 12, w 1, n-b 28	50	B 5, l-b 14, n-b 34	53

1/94 2/100 3/102 4/118 5/136   406   1/0 2/11 3/154   (9 wkts dec.) 313
6/204 7/370 8/391 9/403   4/171 5/218 6/223
7/256 8/275 9/296

Bonus points – Worcestershire 4, Surrey 4.

Bowling: *First Innings*—Waqar Younis 20.5–4–75–2; M. P. Bicknell 31–9–86–6; Kendrick 18–6–71–0; Benjamin 24–3–107–2; Boiling 14–4–46–0. *Second Innings*—Waqar Younis 26–3–69–2; M. P. Bicknell 31–7–106–5; Thorpe 3–1–11–0; Benjamin 23–6–51–1; Kendrick 7–2–12–0; Boiling 17–4–45–0.

Surrey

D. J. Bicknell c Newport b Lampitt	130 – c Lampitt b Tolley	15
P. D. Atkins lbw b Radford	2 – c Rhodes b Newport	18
G. P. Thorpe run out	171 – lbw b Tolley	9
A. D. Brown c Newport b Radford	44 – (5) lbw b Radford	37
J. Boiling lbw b Lampitt	28 – (10) not out	8
*†A. J. Stewart c Rhodes b Newport	8 – (4) c Rhodes b Radford	54
D. M. Ward lbw b Lampitt	7 – (6) st Rhodes b Illingworth	29
M. P. Bicknell c Curtis b Newport	13 – (7) b Illingworth	39
N. M. Kendrick not out	1 – lbw b Lampitt	1
Waqar Younis c Lampitt b Newport	4 – (8) b Illingworth	0
J. E. Benjamin lbw b Newport	0 – b Newport	6
B 18, l-b 7, w 2, n-b 6	33	B 3, l-b 7, w 1	11

1/16 2/315 3/349 4/370 5/404   427   1/22 2/36 3/56 4/136 5/141   227
6/406 7/423 8/427 9/427   6/211 7/211 8/212 9/220

Bonus points – Surrey 4, Worcestershire 1 (Score at 120 overs: 393-4).

Bowling: *First Innings*—Tolley 19–8–42–0; Radford 31–8–85–2; Newport 33–11–86–4; Lampitt 21–4–71–3; Illingworth 25–4–77–0; Hick 10–2–41–0. *Second Innings*—Radford 14–0–64–2; Tolley 6–0–18–2; Newport 12.1–1–48–2; Illingworth 18–7–34–3; Lampitt 10–1–53–1.

Umpires: G. I. Burgess and K. E. Palmer.

WORCESTERSHIRE v KENT

At Worcester, August 19, 20, 21, 23. Worcestershire won by an innings and 130 runs. Worcestershire 24 pts, Kent 1 pt. Toss: Kent.

Kent paid the price for a madcap 50 minutes early in the second session when, despite the withdrawal of Benjamin with a hamstring injury, they squandered six wickets for 25 runs in 14 overs. Tolley was the chief beneficiary, returning five wickets for the first time. In contrast, Worcestershire took full advantage of the easy-paced pitch to compile a first-innings lead of 379, largely due to a stand of 262 in 78 overs between Haynes and Curtis. Haynes reached his maiden first-class century and Curtis his fifth of 1993. There was no respite for Kent's bowlers on the third day when Rhodes added an unbeaten hundred, the fourth of his career, as Worcestershire posted their biggest total of the season. Although reduced to ten men by Benson's knee injury, Kent delayed the inevitable until shortly after lunch on the final day when Illingworth, on his 30th birthday, bowled Fleming to secure Worcestershire's sixth Championship win, which carried them to fifth place.

Close of play: First day, Worcestershire 25-1 (T. S. Curtis 13*, G. R. Haynes 3*); Second day, Worcestershire 386-4 (D. B. D'Oliveira 20*, S. J. Rhodes 12*); Third day, Kent 143-4 (N. R. Taylor 1*, D. W. Headley 1*).

Kent

D. P. Fulton c Rhodes b Tolley	3	– c Rhodes b Illingworth	25
*M. R. Benson c D'Oliveira b Radford	24	– absent injured	
T. R. Ward c Newport b Tolley	38	– (2) c Illingworth b Tolley	30
C. L. Hooper c sub b Haynes	29	– c Haynes b Illingworth	38
N. R. Taylor c Leatherdale b Tolley	2	– lbw b Radford	26
N. J. Llong c Newport b Haynes	3	– (3) c Curtis b Illingworth	45
M. V. Fleming c Rhodes b Tolley	2	– b Illingworth	38
†S. A. Marsh c Rhodes b Tolley	8	– c sub b D'Oliveira	5
M. A. Ealham not out	54	– b Radford	15
D. W. Headley c Curtis b Newport	20	– (6) c Leatherdale b D'Oliveira	22
A. P. Igglesden c Rhodes b Radford	1	– (10) not out	2
L-b 3, w 2	5	L-b 2, w 1	3
	189		**249**

1/9 2/57 3/96 4/98 5/103   189   1/50 2/74 3/140 4/141 5/189   249
6/105 7/105 8/121 9/156   6/189 7/206 8/233 9/249

Bonus points – Worcestershire 4.

Bowling: *First Innings*—Benjamin 8–4–12–0; Tolley 21–5–55–5; Newport 15–4–33–1; Radford 19.1–8–53–2; Haynes 16–5–29–2; Weston 1–0–4–0. *Second Innings*—Radford 16–2–67–2; Tolley 14–4–32–1; Illingworth 34–16–68–4; Newport 16–3–48–0; Haynes 3–1–8–0; D'Oliveira 9–3–24–2.

Worcestershire

*T. S. Curtis c Fleming b Ealham	127	C. M. Tolley b Hooper	28
M. J. Weston c Marsh b Igglesden	9	R. K. Illingworth not out	24
G. R. Haynes c Hooper b Headley	158		
D. A. Leatherdale c Marsh b Headley	33	B 4, l-b 22, n-b 14	40
D. B. D'Oliveira c Headley b Fleming	45		
†S. J. Rhodes not out	100	1/21 2/283 3/341 4/360	(7 wkts dec.) 568
P. J. Newport c Taylor b Fleming	4	5/436 6/452 7/515	

N. V. Radford and K. C. G. Benjamin did not bat.

Bonus points – Worcestershire 4, Kent 1 (Score at 120 overs: 372-4).

Bowling: Igglesden 32–10–67–1; Headley 35–6–108–2; Fleming 41.5–10–128–2; Ealham 27–4–103–1; Hooper 37–6–117–1; Llong 6–1–19–0.

Umpires: J. C. Balderstone and B. Leadbeater.

At Birmingham, August 26, 27, 28, 30. WORCESTERSHIRE beat WARWICKSHIRE by ten wickets.

WORCESTERSHIRE v LANCASHIRE

At Worcester, August 31, September 1, 2, 3. Worcestershire won by one wicket. Worcestershire 23 pts, Lancashire 7 pts. Toss: Lancashire.

A scrambled bye off the fourth ball of the final over clinched a fourth successive Championship win for Worcestershire and lifted them into second place. On a fluctuating fourth day the odds were stacked against the home team when last man Benjamin, nursing a torn hamstring, limped out with a runner. They still needed 34 runs from 7.2 overs. But a succession of boundaries from Illingworth reduced the target to three from Wasim Akram's last over. Speak's first Championship century since June 1992 had put Lancashire in the driving seat and enabled Fairbrother, anxious to end a run of six defeats in seven Championship games, to set 329 in 76 overs. But Worcestershire wrested back the initiative as Curtis and Hick put on 124 in 21 overs. The balance shifted again after a brief shower when they lost five wickets to set up the thrilling finish. Before the match both teams stood in silence in memory of the former Lancashire player Ian Folley, who had died in hospital after an accident in a League game the previous day.

Close of play: First day, Lancashire 301-9 (G. Yates 3*, P. J. Martin 10*); Second day, Worcestershire 287-6 (S. J. Rhodes 29*, P. J. Newport 12*); Third day, Lancashire 255-4 (N. J. Speak 110*, M. Watkinson 39*).

Lancashire

G. D. Mendis c Rhodes b Illingworth	44	– c Rhodes b Newport	10
J. P. Crawley c D'Oliveira b Benjamin	36	– c Leatherdale b Haynes	27
M. A. Atherton lbw b Illingworth	1	– st Rhodes b Illingworth	0
*N. H. Fairbrother c Weston b Illingworth	0	– c Tolley b Hick	62
N. J. Speak c D'Oliveira b Hick	49	– c Rhodes b Newport	122
M. Watkinson c Leatherdale b Tolley	38	– c Hick b Illingworth	52
Wasim Akram c Leatherdale b Illingworth	22	– c Rhodes b Newport	0
P. A. J. DeFreitas c Hick b Newport	38	– c Leatherdale b Illingworth	2
†W. K. Hegg c Rhodes b Newport	42	– not out	23
G. Yates not out	6	– not out	18
P. J. Martin c Leatherdale b Newport	25		
L-b 12, w 1, n-b 6	19	L-b 11, w 3	14

1/74 2/76 3/76 4/104 5/175   320   1/20 2/21 3/51   (8 wkts dec.) 330
6/189 7/225 8/263 9/290   4/170 5/273 6/273
                                       7/280 8/289

Bonus points – Lancashire 3, Worcestershire 4.

Bowling: *First Innings*—Benjamin 15-0-68-1; Tolley 14-6-21-1; Newport 25.4-9-55-3; Illingworth 38-14-91-4; Haynes 11-3-37-0; Hick 6-3-13-1; D'Oliveira 1-0-5-0; Weston 6-2-18-0. *Second Innings*—Newport 31-7-73-3; Tolley 16-1-72-0; Illingworth 47-20-84-3; Haynes 16-2-36-1; Hick 10-0-54-1.

Worcestershire

*T. S. Curtis lbw b Martin	52	– b Yates	65
M. J. Weston hit wkt b DeFreitas	8	– c Fairbrother b Wasim Akram	15
G. A. Hick b Watkinson	91	– lbw b Yates	90
G. R. Haynes c Fairbrother b Watkinson	50	– c Hegg b Martin	0
D. B. D'Oliveira b Watkinson	13	– c DeFreitas b Martin	1
D. A. Leatherdale b Wasim Akram	13	– b Yates	10
†S. J. Rhodes c Hegg b DeFreitas	40	– c DeFreitas b Wasim Akram	13
P. J. Newport b DeFreitas	23	– c DeFreitas b Wasim Akram	39
C. M. Tolley not out	7	– c Crawley b DeFreitas	25
R. K. Illingworth b Wasim Akram	1	– not out	32
K. C. G. Benjamin c Fairbrother b DeFreitas	1	– not out	9
B 8, l-b 6, w 3, n-b 4	23	B 6, l-b 11, w 1, n-b 12	30

1/18 2/135 3/197 4/227 5/228   322   1/43 2/167 3/168   (9 wkts) 329
6/260 7/309 8/312 9/313   4/176 5/196 6/203
                                       7/241 8/264 9/295

Bonus points – Worcestershire 3, Lancashire 4.

Bowling: *First Innings*—Wasim Akram 28-4-80-2; DeFreitas 18.3-4-48-4; Martin 19-6-58-1; Watkinson 30-9-82-3; Yates 14-5-40-0. *Second Innings*—Wasim Akram 19.4-4-83-3; DeFreitas 15-1-73-1; Watkinson 13-1-51-0; Martin 16-2-63-2; Yates 12-2-42-3.

Umpires: R. Palmer and D. R. Shepherd.

WORCESTERSHIRE v MIDDLESEX

At Worcester, September 16, 17. Worcestershire won by an innings and 36 runs. Worcestershire 22 pts, Middlesex 4 pts. Toss: Worcestershire.

Their fifth successive victory, emphatically completed inside two days, proved enough to give Worcestershire second place in the Championship. Middlesex, who had clinched the title more than a fortnight earlier, set out to become the first champions since Hampshire 20 years before to finish the season unbeaten. But by 12.20 p.m. on the opening morning, after just 27.3 overs, they had been routed for 68, equalling the lowest score of the season, by Nottinghamshire at The Oval in July. The pitch was blameless but overcast conditions were ideal for swing bowling; Newport and Lampitt fully exploited them as Middlesex's last seven wickets fell for 26 runs. When bad light ended play Worcestershire were 125 runs ahead with three wickets remaining, a lead they stretched to 184 next day. A season's-best six for 49 from Radford then undid Middlesex a second time. Overall they lost 20 wickets in 87.4 overs; just three of their batsmen reached double figures and only Carr, whose 67 was the solitary half-century for either team, passed 20.

Close of play: First day, Worcestershire 193-7 (S. R. Lampitt 3*, C. M. Tolley 1*).

Middlesex

D. L. Haynes c Lampitt b Newport	17	– c Rhodes b Radford	9
M. A. Roseberry c Weston b Tolley	8	– (7) b Lampitt	20
*M. W. Gatting b Radford	6	– (4) c and b Radford	8
M. R. Ramprakash c Hick b Radford	4	– (3) lbw b Radford	6
J. D. Carr c Rhodes b Newport	10	– c Curtis b Illingworth	67
†K. R. Brown lbw b Lampitt	0	– c Rhodes b Newport	1
J. E. Emburey c Hick b Lampitt	0	– (8) c Illingworth b Radford	9
M. A. Feltham not out	3	– (2) c Leatherdale b Radford	2
R. L. Johnson b Newport	4	– c Weston b Lampitt	4
A. R. C. Fraser b Newport	4	– c Lampitt b Radford	7
P. C. R. Tufnell c Hick b Lampitt	4	– not out	6
L-b 1, w 2, n-b 5	8	L-b 2, w 1, n-b 6	9
	68		**148**

1/15 2/23 3/27 4/42 5/43   68
6/47 7/53 8/57 9/61

1/5 2/18 3/25 4/26 5/61   148
6/113 7/129 8/133 9/142

Bonus points – Worcestershire 4.

Bowling: *First Innings*—Radford 7–1–21–2; Tolley 7–3–17–1; Newport 7–0–20–4; Lampitt 6.3–1–9–3. *Second Innings*—Radford 16.1–3–49–6; Tolley 12–2–35–0; Newport 12–7–17–1; Lampitt 14–4–27–2; Illingworth 6–2–18–1.

Worcestershire

*T. S. Curtis c Brown b Tufnell	41	C. M. Tolley c Carr b Emburey	18
W. P. C. Weston c Brown b Johnson	17	R. K. Illingworth b Tufnell	35
G. A. Hick c Brown b Tufnell	41	N. V. Radford not out	3
G. R. Haynes b Emburey	5		
D. A. Leatherdale lbw b Tufnell	9	L-b 9, w 2, n-b 24	35
†S. J. Rhodes b Brown b Fraser	35		
P. J. Newport c Brown b Emburey	10	1/56 2/104 3/125 4/133	252
S. R. Lampitt b Fraser	3	5/154 6/186 7/190 8/193 9/239	

Bonus points – Worcestershire 2, Middlesex 4.

Bowling: Fraser 27–8–57–2; Feltham 21–7–58–0; Johnson 16–5–58–1; Emburey 11–3–30–3; Tufnell 20.1–6–40–4.

Umpires: J. D. Bond and M. J. Kitchen.

YORKSHIRE

Patron: HRH The Duchess of Kent
President and Chairman: Sir Lawrence Byford
Chairman, Cricket Committee: D. B. Close
Chief Executive: C. D. Hassell
Captain: M. D. Moxon
Director of Cricket: S. Oldham
Head Groundsman: K. Boyce
Scorer: J. T. Potter

Nothing is ever clear-cut so far as Yorkshire cricket is concerned. In the dark, grey corners of another disappointing season, arguments about the team's performances were overshadowed by controversy surrounding the departure of Paul Jarvis to Sussex.

The 28-year-old pace bowler began the summer by leading the side to victory over champions Essex and then playing for England in the one-day international series. But, taking into account another muscle strain, his poor fitness record throughout his career and the success of the other seamers, the committee released him with two years of his contract to run. Not everyone agreed with the decision, with questions being asked about management techniques. However, Ashley Metcalfe attracted greater public support: Yorkshire gave the experienced batsman the chance to move, too, but he opted to stay and serve the last year of his engagement, in the hope of winning back a regular place in a fragile batting line-up.

Undoubtedly the spectacular emergence of Darren Gough influenced the committee in their policy towards Jarvis. After taking only 16 Championship wickets at 35.50 runs each in his first eight matches and briefly disappearing, he returned when Jarvis was injured to take 39 more at 21.74 and earned a place on the England A tour to South Africa. Gough found an extra yard or so of pace, which, allied to improved accuracy, made him a dangerous competitor. In fact the seamers did well enough, with Mark Robinson – who took nine for 37 against his old county Northamptonshire – and Peter Hartley, once he had recovered from a persistent back strain, also enjoying great success.

Craig White, well established as a batsman, displayed some ability as an all-rounder, pushing the ball through quickly enough to have wicket-keeper Richard Blakey standing back, but off-spinner Jeremy Batty suffered from a lack of opportunity and, therefore, confidence. Left-arm spinner Richard Stemp, recruited from Worcestershire, began brightly before fading a bit, mainly due to bowling too short at times. Poor catching, especially close to the wicket, has been a long-standing weakness; nothing changed here, with Yorkshire missing a host of chances, some both straightforward and crucial. Blakey took 41 catches and made five stumpings but his wicket-keeping generally became patchy, as did his batting. Fluent and enterprising in the one-day matches, he became nervous and ill at ease in the four-day games.

In fact, the batsmen were to blame for most of the problems. Yorkshire were simply bowled out too cheaply too often and when they did score heavily they took far too long about it. A total of 21 batting points was the poorest by any county and they scored throughout at less than three an over in the Championship. This caution brought no reward, for the average runs per wicket amounted to a mere 28.14, despite the apparently formidable presence of Richie Richardson, the West Indies captain.

Richardson fell a long way short of expectations and enjoyed more than his share of good fortune in achieving a Championship average of 34.50. He never really came to terms with English conditions, hitting the ball in the air far too readily, yet Yorkshire re-engaged him for a second year, partly because there were few reasonable alternatives and partly because he did much better in the Sunday League.

Martyn Moxon had a moderate year as an opener and a poor one as captain, adopting a very defensive outlook. He was the only player to top 1,000 runs in the Championship – David Byas did so in all first-class matches – but his rate of progress would have got Geoff Boycott into trouble in the bitter past. Moxon set the tone of most innings and the scoring-rate was not helped by an experiment in which Paul Grayson served briefly as his first-wicket partner. Grayson as yet has no great weight of stroke and Yorkshire too often meekly surrendered the initiative to the opposition's attack. Moxon also let things drift in the field with a predictable approach. Thus Yorkshire, as for so many years, found themselves waiting on events instead of actively influencing them.

Things were so serious by early July that cricket chairman Brian Close and chief executive Chris Hassell held an emergency meeting with the players. Any suggestion of a crisis was dismissed, yet Hassell admitted at the time: "Everyone at Headingley is extremely concerned about the way things have gone on the field." The membership's worries were heightened because they went for more than a year without a home win on a Sunday and endured a barren home period almost as long in the Championship; both sequences ended with victories over Northamptonshire in mid-July.

Matters took a slight turn for the better in that Gloucestershire were defeated in the NatWest Trophy, but Yorkshire handed a quarter-final victory to Warwickshire and the season drifted on into sad anticlimax. Inevitably, there was a good deal of papering over the cracks: officially some encouragement was drawn from improvement in the final Championship and Sunday League placings. Yorkshire climbed from 16th to 12th in the one and 15th to ninth in the other but, measured against the yardstick of the county's history, such modest achievement hardly merited applause.

Moxon had insisted at the start of the campaign that his side could well win a one-day competition and should reach the top six in the Championship. In the event, they never threatened to do anything of the sort. Individually, all the front-line players did something worthwhile, but collectively Yorkshire were erratic, lacking application and spirit. If they are to make a challenge for honours in 1994, they will have to be much more positive and imaginative. – John Callaghan.

YORKSHIRE 1993

[*D. J. Williams*]

Back row: W. P. Morton (*physiotherapist*), B. Parker, M. Broadhurst, M. J. Foster, M. P. Vaughan, S. M. Milburn, R. A. Kettleborough, C. A. Chapman. *Middle row:* D. E. V. Padgett (*coach*), C. White, S. Bartle, M. A. Robinson, D. Byas, S. A. Kellett, J. D. Batty, D. Gough, M. K. Bore (*academy coach*). *Front row:* P. J. Hartley, R. J. Blakey, P. Carrick, M. D. Moxon (*captain*), S. Oldham (*director of cricket*), R. B. Richardson, A. A. Metcalfe, P. W. Jarvis.

YORKSHIRE RESULTS

All first-class matches – Played 19: Won 6, Lost 4, Drawn 9.

County Championship matches – Played 17: Won 5, Lost 4, Drawn 8.

Bonus points – Batting 21, Bowling 56.

Competition placings – Britannic Assurance County Championship, 12th;
NatWest Bank Trophy, q-f; Benson and Hedges Cup, 1st round;
AXA Equity & Law League, 9th.

BRITANNIC ASSURANCE CHAMPIONSHIP AVERAGES

BATTING

	Birthplace	M	I	NO	R	HS	Avge
‡M. D. Moxon	Barnsley	16	27	2	1,081	171*	43.24
‡C. White	Morley	17	28	6	816	146	37.09
‡R. B. Richardson§ . .	Five Islands, Antigua	14	23	1	759	112	34.50
‡D. Byas	Kilham	17	30	3	891	156	33.00
M. P. Vaughan	Manchester	2	4	0	118	64	29.50
‡S. A. Kellett	Mirfield	3	6	0	167	85	27.83
‡P. J. Hartley	Keighley	13	21	6	400	102	26.66
‡R. J. Blakey	Huddersfield	17	28	0	712	74	25.42
‡A. A. Metcalfe	Horsforth	8	13	0	320	76	24.61
A. P. Grayson	Ripon	10	17	0	386	64	22.70
‡P. W. Jarvis	Redcar	8	12	1	189	76	17.18
R. D. Stemp	Birmingham	15	21	6	254	37	16.93
J. D. Batty	Bradford	13	17	2	208	50	13.86
‡D. Gough	Barnsley	14	21	3	227	39	12.61
‡M. A. Robinson	Hull	16	20	8	43	16*	3.58

Also batted: ‡P. Carrick (*Armley*) (2 matches) 15, 0, 14*; M. J. Foster (*Leeds*) (1 match) 6; C. E. W. Silverwood (*Pontefract*) (1 match) 0.

* *Signifies not out.*   ‡ *Denotes county cap.*   § *Overseas player.*

The following played a total of five three-figure innings for Yorkshire in County Championship matches – D. Byas 1, P. J. Hartley 1, M. D. Moxon 1, R. B. Richardson 1, C. White 1.

BOWLING

	O	M	R	W	BB	5W/i	Avge
C. White	120	35	292	12	3-9	0	24.33
D. Gough	458.5	96	1,416	55	7-42	3	25.74
M. A. Robinson	500	127	1,324	48	9-37	3	27.58
P. J. Hartley	351.4	91	1,027	37	5-51	1	27.75
P. W. Jarvis	238.1	56	644	23	4-51	0	28.00
R. D. Stemp	472.3	165	1,060	31	5-89	1	34.19
J. D. Batty	302.2	78	861	20	4-27	0	43.05

Also bowled: P. Carrick 60–24–108–2; M. J. Foster 17–3–50–3; A. P. Grayson 5–3–7–0; R. B. Richardson 7–0–23–1; C. E. W. Silverwood 20–3–75–1; M. P. Vaughan 13–4–42–1.

Wicket-keepers: R. J. Blakey 38 ct, 3 st; C. White 1 ct.

Leading Fielder: D. Byas 15.

At Cambridge, April 17, 18, 19. YORKSHIRE drew with CAMBRIDGE UNIVERSITY.

YORKSHIRE v LANCASHIRE

Non-Championship Match

At Leeds, April 29, 30, May 1, 3. Yorkshire won by 116 runs. Toss: Lancashire.

Even though the counties were due to meet only once in the new-style Championship, Yorkshire and Lancashire were anxious to preserve Roses rivalry on both sides of the Pennines and instituted this challenge match, granted first-class status by the TCCB. They were competing for a vase newly commissioned from Aynsley China and sponsored, on this occasion, by Trans-Pennine Express. Yorkshire became the first holders because they had the better spin bowling on a slow pitch allowing some turn. Blakey, improvising more readily than his colleagues, gave Yorkshire's first innings some momentum against Watkinson (bowling off-breaks) and Barnett, although the last six wickets went for 42 runs. In reply, Lloyd batted superbly to score 116 from 159 balls, hitting 15 fours, and rescue his side almost single-handedly from 85 for six. Even so, Yorkshire gained a decisive lead through the spinners Batty and Stemp. Martin took five wickets in an innings for the first time when Yorkshire batted again, but Moxon, though having to retire after being hit on the foot when 64, made sure that his team maintained their advantage. Set 378, Lancashire never came to terms with the persistent Stemp, despite another attacking flourish from Lloyd. Stemp, Yorkshire's Birmingham-born recruit, finished the match with nine wickets.

Close of play: First day, Yorkshire 279-7 (P. W. Jarvis 2*, R. D. Stemp 0*); Second day, Yorkshire 16-0 (M. D. Moxon 11*, A. A. Metcalfe 3*); Third day, Lancashire 21-0 (G. D. Mendis 13*, M. A. Atherton 8*).

Yorkshire

*M. D. Moxon c Atherton b Barnett	48	– c Hegg b Martin	91
A. A. Metcalfe b DeFreitas	9	– lbw b DeFreitas	5
S. A. Kellett st Hegg b Barnett	62	– c Hegg b Martin	19
C. White lbw b Barnett	6	– b DeFreitas	25
†R. J. Blakey b Watkinson	95	– b Chapple	11
D. Byas c and b Watkinson	44	– c Lloyd b Watkinson	48
P. W. Jarvis c Atherton b Barnett	11	– b Martin	7
D. Gough c Mendis b Barnett	0	– c Watkinson b DeFreitas	11
R. D. Stemp b Watkinson	5	– b Martin	6
J. D. Batty lbw b DeFreitas	13	– b Martin	0
M. A. Robinson not out	8	– not out	2
B 3, l-b 13, n-b 2	18	B 2, l-b 19, n-b 12	33
	319		**258**

1/23 2/89 3/115 4/174 5/277   319   1/20 2/85 3/131 4/156 5/223   258
6/278 7/279 8/294 9/298   6/229 7/249 8/251 9/251

In the second innings M. D. Moxon, when 64, retired hurt at 114 and resumed at 156.

Bowling: *First Innings*—DeFreitas 18-6-49-2; Martin 18-8-35-0; Chapple 16-4-47-0; Watkinson 33-8-89-3; Barnett 40-12-83-5. *Second Innings*—DeFreitas 19-3-52-3; Martin 20-8-35-5; Watkinson 24-3-72-1; Barnett 30-12-63-0; Chapple 12-5-15-1.

Lancashire

G. D. Mendis c Blakey b Batty	16	– c Moxon b Stemp	22
M. A. Atherton c Kellett b Batty	19	– b Robinson	37
N. J. Speak b Stemp	6	– c Byas b Batty	39
*N. H. Fairbrother c Byas b Batty	0	– c Byas b Batty	2
G. D. Lloyd c Gough b Stemp	116	– c Batty b Stemp	88
†W. K. Hegg lbw b Jarvis	0	– b Stemp	1
M. Watkinson b Jarvis	0	– b Batty	2
P. A. J. DeFreitas c and b White	12	– st Blakey b Stemp	9
P. J. Martin lbw b Jarvis	21	– not out	38
G. Chapple not out	1	– c Byas b Stemp	16
A. A. Barnett lbw b Jarvis	0	– lbw b Stemp	0
L-b 7, n-b 2	9	B 2, l-b 4, w 1	7
	200		**261**

1/28 2/41 3/41 4/49 5/84   200   1/55 2/59 3/73 4/139 5/146   261
6/85 7/131 8/198 9/200   6/161 7/202 8/205 9/261

Bowling: *First Innings*—Jarvis 13.3–4–20–3; Gough 12–3–24–0; Robinson 8–1–14–0; Stemp 25–10–55–3; Batty 18–3–75–3; White 2–1–5–1. *Second Innings*—Jarvis 16–2–41–0; Gough 12–6–31–0; Stemp 42.3–13–92–6; Batty 32–8–83–3; Robinson 6–3–8–1.

Umpires: D. O. Oslear and P. Willey.

At Chelmsford, May 6, 7, 8, 10. YORKSHIRE beat ESSEX by 239 runs.

YORKSHIRE v WORCESTERSHIRE

At Bradford, May 13, 14, 15, 17. Drawn. Yorkshire 4 pts, Worcestershire 1 pt. Toss: Yorkshire. Championship debuts: R. B. Richardson; K. C. G. Benjamin.

Rain affected every day and completely washed out the second. Robinson's new-ball burst of three for 16 in ten overs undermined Worcestershire on a good pitch which allowed a little movement off the seam, and he went on to take a career-best seven for 47. Curtis resisted for 40 overs, but it was Rhodes and Lampitt who gave the innings some respectability by adding 52 in 19 overs. Moxon and Metcalfe made untroubled progress to 130, their 21st century opening stand, as Benjamin, on his Championship debut, experienced some problems with his line. His Test captain, Richardson, also disappointed, scoring one on his first first-class appearance for Yorkshire. There was never any chance of a positive finish, however; Yorkshire did not even make a serious attempt to gain a batting point on the restricted last day. The Friends of Park Avenue, who organise this fixture, employed their own security guards to prevent a repetition of the previous year's events, when thieves broke in to about 20 cars.

Close of play: First day, Worcestershire 185-7 (S. J. Rhodes 49*, P. J. Newport 13*); Second day, No play; Third day, Yorkshire 114-0 (M. D. Moxon 41*, A. A. Metcalfe 67*).

Worcestershire

*T. S. Curtis c Blakey b Robinson	25	R. K. Illingworth lbw b Robinson	4
W. P. C. Weston b Robinson	4	P. J. Newport not out	19
G. A. Hick lbw b Robinson	3	C. M. Tolley b Robinson	0
D. B. D'Oliveira lbw b Jarvis	10	K. C. G. Benjamin lbw b Jarvis	1
A. C. H. Seymour c Richardson		B 3, l-b 16, n-b 8	27
b Robinson	13		
S. R. Lampitt b Stemp	37	1/6 2/10 3/25 4/48 5/89	192
†S. J. Rhodes c Batty b Robinson	49	6/141 7/160 8/187 9/191	

Bonus points – Yorkshire 4.

Bowling: Jarvis 21.2–3–56–2; Robinson 26–7–47–7; Gough 21–5–45–0; White 10–3–13–0; Stemp 6–3–12–1.

Yorkshire

*M. D. Moxon b Tolley	51	C. White not out	21
A. A. Metcalfe c Hick b Benjamin	76	L-b 4, w 1, n-b 4	9
R. B. Richardson c D'Oliveira b Tolley	1		
D. Byas not out	34	1/130 2/134 (4 wkts)	196
†R. J. Blakey c Lampitt b Benjamin	4	3/137 4/146	

P. W. Jarvis, D. Gough, R. D. Stemp, J. D. Batty and M. A. Robinson did not bat.

Bonus point – Worcestershire 1.

Bowling: Benjamin 16–3–54–2; Newport 10–1–31–0; Lampitt 6–3–18–0; Tolley 18–4–39–2; Illingworth 14.4–5–33–0; Hick 4–0–17–0; D'Oliveira 1–1–0–0.

Umpires: D. R. Shepherd and G. A. Stickley.

At Southampton, May 20, 21, 22, 24. YORKSHIRE beat HAMPSHIRE by six wickets.

YORKSHIRE v GLAMORGAN

At Middlesbrough, June 3, 4, 5, 7. Glamorgan won by 121 runs. Glamorgan 21 pts, Yorkshire 5 pts. Toss: Glamorgan.

Glamorgan scored their first away win over Yorkshire in 23 years and joined Middlesex at the top of the table after bowling out Yorkshire on the final day. After Morris had scored a well-organised century and declared, Yorkshire were set 314 in a minimum of 83 overs. But they collapsed against Watkin, a class above any other bowler in the match, and Lefebvre. Richards completed the triumph with his off-breaks. The Glamorgan first innings had been built on a 139-run stand between James and Dale and they gained an unexpected lead when Yorkshire collapsed, losing their last six wickets for 30. Before that, Moxon completed his fourth successive Championship half-century and Richardson mixed caution with bursts of aggression. However, there was no pattern to the Yorkshire first innings and Blakey managed only one scoring stroke in an hour during a stand of 119 with White.

Close of play: First day, Glamorgan 302-7 (R. P. Lefebvre 0*, C. P. Metson 7*); Second day, Yorkshire 265-4 (R. J. Blakey 42*, C. White 58*); Third day, Glamorgan 230-3 (H. Morris 104*, I. V. A. Richard 3*).

Glamorgan

S. P. James c Byas b Jarvis	76	– c Blakey b Jarvis	3
*H. Morris c sub b Robinson	29	– not out	134
A. Dale c Byas b Stemp	100	– c White b Batty	49
M. P. Maynard c Stemp b Jarvis	3	– b Batty	58
I. V. A. Richards b Gough	27	– not out	43
P. A. Cottey c White b Robinson	22		
R. D. B. Croft c Moxon b Stemp	3		
R. P. Lefebvre c Batty b Jarvis	1		
†C. P. Metson c Blakey b Stemp	15		
S. L. Watkin not out	9		
S. R. Barwick c White b Stemp	2		
B 4, l-b 8, w 2, n-b 22	36	B 1, l-b 8, n-b 8	17

1/52 2/191 3/201 4/247 5/277   323   1/8 2/119 3/219   (3 wkts dec.) 304
6/290 7/295 8/307 9/319

Bonus points – Glamorgan 3, Yorkshire 3 (Score at 120 overs: 315-8).

Bowling: *First Innings*—Jarvis 25-4-61-3; Gough 20-3-65-1; Robinson 22-5-52-3; White 4-2-6-0; Stemp 30-10-51-3; Batty 25-4-76-0. *Second Innings*—Jarvis 14-3-52-1; Gough 8-3-19-0; Batty 22-5-72-2; Stemp 28-4-36-0; Robinson 23-4-68-0.

Yorkshire

*M. D. Moxon c Cottey b Barwick	51	– c Maynard b Lefebvre	30
A. A. Metcalfe c Maynard b Watkin	6	– c Metson b Lefebvre	56
R. B. Richardson c Metson b Watkin	81	– lbw b Lefebvre	42
D. Byas lbw b Dale	16	– c and b Richards	5
†R. J. Blakey c Richards b Lefebvre	50	– c Maynard b Watkin	16
C. White c Morris b Barwick	67	– b Watkin	18
P. W. Jarvis c Morris b Lefebvre	13	– b Watkin	0
D. Gough b Barwick	5	– c Dale b Richards	0
R. D. Stemp c Maynard b Watkin	1	– not out	11
J. D. Batty c Maynard b Watkin	8	– c Lefebvre b Watkin	8
M. A. Robinson not out	1	– c Maynard b Richards	1
B 7, l-b 4, n-b 4	15	B 1, l-b 4	5

1/11 2/102 3/153 4/165 5/284   314   1/44 2/126 3/137 4/137 5/161   192
6/290 7/302 8/305 9/305   6/161 7/172 8/172 9/185

Bonus points – Yorkshire 2, Glamorgan 2 (Score at 120 overs: 294-6).

Bowling: *First Innings*—Watkin 29.3-8-59-4; Lefebvre 28-12-53-2; Barwick 37-19-55-3; Croft 27-5-106-0; Dale 9-3-30-1. *Second Innings*—Watkin 22-8-59-4; Lefebvre 11-6-11-3; Barwick 12-4-45-0; Croft 17-6-50-0; Richards 16-5-22-3.

Umpires: G. I. Burgess and G. Sharp.

At Chesterfield, June 10, 11, 12, 14. YORKSHIRE drew with DERBYSHIRE.

YORKSHIRE v GLOUCESTERSHIRE

At Sheffield, June 17, 18, 19, 21. Drawn. Yorkshire 6 pts, Gloucestershire 3 pts. Toss Gloucestershire.

A very slow, low pitch dictated the course of the contest, with Yorkshire building steadily after being put in. Off-spinner Wight achieved impressive accuracy and posed some problems in flight before Hartley, recently recovered from a back strain, enlivened the proceedings. He made his 102 from only 159 balls, adding 111 in 30 overs with Jarvis Hodgson and Alleyne, who was missed on both 36 and 37, gave Gloucestershire's reply some backbone with a stand of 123, but the innings fell into confusion against Batty's off breaks as wickets fell to careless strokes and the visitors were dismissed for only 241, 204 behind. Broad and Alleyne prevented further embarrassment when Gloucestershire followed on and the game had already developed into a tedious stalemate when Alleyne gave Richardson his first first-class wicket in this country.

Close of play: First day, Yorkshire 282-6 (P. W. Jarvis 30*, P. J. Hartley 13*); Second day, Gloucestershire 105-1 (G. D. Hodgson 45*, M. W. Alleyne 46*); Third day, Gloucestershire 241-9 (M. Davies 18*, J. M. de la Pena 7*).

Yorkshire

*M. D. Moxon lbw b Wight	23	R. D. Stemp c Russell b Cooper ... 20
A. A. Metcalfe c Hancock b Cooper ...	63	J. D. Batty b Cooper	3
R. B. Richardson st Russell b Wight ...	54	M. A. Robinson not out	2
D. Byas lbw b Cooper	1		
†R. J. Blakey b Walsh	28	B 2, l-b 5, w 3, n-b 10 20
C. White b Cooper	53	
P. W. Jarvis lbw b Davies	76	1/42 2/148 3/150 4/164 5/197 449
P. J. Hartley lbw b Wight	102	6/263 7/374 8/425 9/441

Bonus points — Yorkshire 3, Gloucestershire 2 (Score at 120 overs: 304-6).

Bowling: Walsh 34–7–87–1; Cooper 40–11–83–5; Wight 27.4–6–71–3; de la Pena 14–1–79–0; Davies 38–13–95–1; Alleyne 5–2–23–0.

Gloucestershire

B. C. Broad c Richardson b Jarvis	5	– c Blakey b Robinson	87
G. D. Hodgson b Jarvis	57	– lbw b Stemp	21
M. W. Alleyne c Stemp b Jarvis	62	– c and b Richardson	78
T. H. C. Hancock b White	22	– not out	29
*A. J. Wright c Blakey b White	4	– not out	0
†R. C. Russell lbw b Batty	17		
R. M. Wight lbw b Batty	29		
C. A. Walsh c White b Batty	0		
M. Davies b Hartley	18		
K. E. Cooper lbw b Batty	0		
J. M. de la Pena not out	7		
L-b 4, n-b 16	20	L-b 10, n-b 10	20

1/6 2/129 3/136 4/153 5/166   241   1/68 2/161 3/235   (3 wkts) 235
6/185 7/191 8/226 9/226

Bonus points — Gloucestershire 1, Yorkshire 3 (Score at 120 overs: 218-7).

Bowling: *First Innings*—Jarvis 34–12–78–3; Robinson 32–14–48–0; Hartley 19.1–1–10–39–1; Batty 31–15–27–4; Stemp 13.4–13–0; White 16–6–32–2. *Second Innings*—Jarvis 17–3–33–0; Hartley 7–1–22–0; White 6–0–15–0; Robinson 12–4–52–1; Stemp 21–7–47–1; Batty 18–3–51–0; Richardson 2–0–5–1.

Umpires: D. J. Constant and R. A. White.

YORKSHIRE v KENT

At Leeds, June 24, 25, 26, 28. Drawn. Yorkshire 5 pts, Kent 6 pts. Toss: Yorkshire.

Igglesden recovered after bowling an untidy spell with the new ball to gain impressive movement away from the bat on a good, firm pitch. He proved too much for Yorkshire's upper order, though Hartley organised some late resistance. Yorkshire dropped Benson before he had scored and appeared to be in serious trouble as Hooper steered Kent into the lead. But the visitors lost their last seven wickets for 40 runs, with Jarvis bowling both quick and straight, and had to settle for a lead of 89. When Yorkshire batted again Kent lost both Igglesden and McCague to injury and Moxon batted more than eight hours to set up the declaration. Required to score 322 in 75 overs, Kent were immediately forced on to the defensive. Hooper resisted for 27 overs before losing patience and Yorkshire missed a crucial chance when Marsh, on three, was dropped by Stemp at slip. Marsh then stood firm with Fleming to ensure a draw.

Close of play: First day, Kent 39-0 (T. R. Ward 29*, M. R. Benson 5*); Second day, Yorkshire 18-0 (M. D. Moxon 7*, A. A. Metcalfe 8*); Third day, Yorkshire 318-4 (M. D. Moxon 128*, C. White 1*).

Yorkshire

*M. D. Moxon c Davis b Headley	8	– not out	171
A. A. Metcalfe c McCague b Igglesden	9	– lbw b Igglesden	9
R. B. Richardson lbw b Igglesden	23	– lbw b Davis	51
D. Byas c Hooper b McCague	11	– c Hooper b Igglesden	22
†R. J. Blakey c Marsh b Igglesden	19	– b Hooper	71
C. White c McCague b Igglesden	16	– c Benson b Fleming	38
P. W. Jarvis c Marsh b Igglesden	8	– run out	1
P. J. Hartley lbw b Hooper	54	– not out	9
D. Gough run out	19		
R. D. Stemp c Benson b Davis	29		
M. A. Robinson not out	1		
L-b 7, w 1, n-b 4	12	B 7, l-b 4, w 5, n-b 22	38

1/10 2/37 3/49 4/62 5/85   209   1/20 2/87 3/124   (6 wkts dec.) 410
6/93 7/110 8/151 9/207   4/303 5/369 6/377

Bonus points – Yorkshire 1, Kent 4.

Bowling: *First Innings*—McCague 25-6-46-1; Igglesden 25-5-66-5; Headley 23-8-43-1; Fleming 7-1-19-0; Hooper 4-2-7-1; Davis 3.4-0-21-1. *Second Innings*—McCague 16.5-1-74-0; Igglesden 14-1-31-2; Headley 28-5-95-0; Fleming 18-1-68-1; Davis 53-18-94-1; Hooper 13.1-0-29-1; Llong 1-0-8-0.

Kent

T. R. Ward c White b Jarvis	68	– c Metcalfe b Robinson	5
*M. R. Benson b Stemp	34	– c Byas b Jarvis	18
N. R. Taylor c Blakey b Robinson	21	– b Gough	11
C. L. Hooper b White	99	– lbw b Robinson	35
N. J. Llong c Metcalfe b Gough	39	– c Byas b Gough	28
M. V. Fleming c Blakey b White	7	– b Gough	20
†S. A. Marsh b Stemp	1	– not out	29
D. W. Headley b Jarvis	7	– not out	0
R. P. Davis b Jarvis	0		
M. J. McCague b Jarvis	1		
A. P. Igglesden not out	0		
B 3, l-b 4, n-b 14	21	L-b 6, w 1, n-b 14	21

1/106 2/120 3/185 4/258 5/268   298   1/24 2/30 3/43   (6 wkts) 167
6/273 7/288 8/288 9/296   4/101 5/111 6/153

Bonus points – Kent 2, Yorkshire 4.

Bowling: *First Innings*—Jarvis 22–7–51–4; Gough 16.5–3–40–1; Robinson 16–3–36–1; Hartley 14–2–41–0; Stemp 36–8–97–2; White 11–4–26–2. *Second Innings*—Jarvis 18–7–33–1; Hartley 9–1–21–0; Stemp 12–8–27–0; Robinson 12–3–24–2; Gough 18.3–5–47–3; White 5–2–9–0.

Umpires: G. I. Burgess and B. Leadbeater.

At Birmingham, July 1, 2, 3, 5. YORKSHIRE lost to WARWICKSHIRE by six wickets.

YORKSHIRE v NORTHAMPTONSHIRE

At Harrogate, July 15, 16, 17, 19. Yorkshire won by four wickets. Yorkshire 20 pts, Northamptonshire 4 pts. Toss: Yorkshire.

Rain washed out the first day and seeped through the covers, making the toss crucial. Jarvis retired after three overs with a leg strain, but the conditions were ideal for Robinson, a natural full-length bowler. Despite a foot injury he achieved figures of nine for 37, the best figures for Yorkshire since Wardle took nine for 25 against Lancashire in 1954. He twice claimed wickets with successive deliveries and his old county were bowled out inside 35 overs. But with the ball continuing to lift and seam in the afternoon Yorkshire found Curran almost equally unplayable as he matched his previous best analysis of seven for 47. Byas and Richardson, adding 84, built an important lead, before Northamptonshire made the most of improved conditions next day. Loye batted particularly well until brilliantly caught in the covers off Hartley, who maintained a demanding accuracy. Further heavy rain delayed Yorkshire's run-chase on the last day and finally left them only 41 overs to score 235. Byas and Blakey took them most of the way, sharing 145 in 22 overs. Despite Northamptonshire's attempts to close down the game and a series of head-high bouncers from Curran, the scores were level when he bowled the last possible ball: White struck it to the mid-wicket boundary.

Close of play: First day, No play; Second day, Yorkshire 168; Third day, Northamptonshire 305.

Northamptonshire

A. Fordham c Richardson b Robinson	23	– c Blakey b Hartley	9
N. A. Felton c Blakey b Robinson	10	– c Blakey b Hartley	66
R. J. Bailey c Blakey b Robinson	0	– b Hartley	68
*A. J. Lamb b Hartley	16	– c Blakey b Robinson	25
M. B. Loye c Byas b Robinson	1	– c White b Hartley	48
K. M. Curran c Richardson b Robinson	0	– c Richardson b Robinson	0
A. L. Penberthy c Moxon b Robinson	10	– b Batty	7
†D. Ripley c Blakey b Robinson	1	– c Hartley b Robinson	38
A. R. Roberts c Richardson b Robinson	8	– (10) c Grayson b Batty	11
M. N. Bowen c Blakey b Robinson	19	– (9) c Blakey b Hartley	1
J. P. Taylor not out	0	– not out	7
B 4, l-b 3, n-b 2	9	B 6, l-b 1, w 2, n-b 16	25
	97		**305**

1/38 2/38 3/43 4/45 5/45   1/26 2/133 3/162 4/221 5/227
6/59 7/64 8/71 9/94   6/238 7/244 8/246 9/275

Bonus points – Yorkshire 4.

Bowling: *First Innings*—Jarvis 3–0–16–0; Hartley 17–6–37–1; Robinson 14.2–3–37–9. *Second Innings*—Hartley 23–6–51–5; Robinson 28.5–6–87–3; Jarvis 7–2–21–0; Batty 27–8–89–2; White 6–2–21–0; Stemp 9–2–29–0.

Yorkshire

M. D. Moxon b Curran	1	– b Bowen	29
A. P. Grayson c Fordham b Curran	11	– c Loye b Bowen	12
R. B. Richardson lbw b Bowen	58	– c Felton b Bowen	12
D. Byas c and b Penberthy	54	– run out	71
R. J. Blakey c Fordham b Bowen	0	– c Roberts b Curran	74
C. White c Loye b Curran	15	– not out	14
*W. Jarvis c Ripley b Curran	17	– c Loye b Taylor	2
P. J. Hartley not out	2	– not out	3
R. D. Stemp c Ripley b Curran	0		
D. Batty b Curran	0		
M. A. Robinson lbw b Curran	0		
L-b 4, n-b 6	10	B 1, l-b 8, n-b 12	21

1/3 2/31 3/115 4/115 5/143   168   1/48 2/53 3/62   (6 wkts) 238
6/165 7/168 8/168 9/168   4/207 5/224 6/230

Bonus points – Northamptonshire 4.

Bowling: *First Innings*—Taylor 12–3–35–0; Curran 19–4–47–7; Bowen 14–3–37–2; Bailey 3–0–11–0; Penberthy 13–3–34–1. *Second Innings*—Taylor 12–2–52–1; Curran 14–1–80–1; Bowen 13–1–82–3; Penberthy 2–0–15–0.

Umpires: V. A. Holder and N. T. Plews.

At Taunton, July 29, 30, 31, August 2. YORKSHIRE beat SOMERSET by 48 runs.

At Nottingham, August 5, 6, 7, 9. YORKSHIRE lost to NOTTINGHAMSHIRE by 115 runs.

YORKSHIRE v MIDDLESEX

At Scarborough, August 12, 13, 14, 16. Drawn. Yorkshire 4 pts, Middlesex 8 pts. Toss: Yorkshire.

Yorkshire were totally outplayed on a pitch offering little assistance to the bowlers and only rain, which restricted the first day to 33.3 overs and the last to 42, thwarted Middlesex's hopes of a seventh consecutive Championship win. Although there was no turn, Tufnell unnerved Yorkshire with three for two in 11 balls before sturdy resistance from the tail achieved a second batting point. Gatting and Ramprakash, who were warned for running on the line of the stumps, then put on 321 from 87 overs, plundering the bowling for two sixes and 43 fours between them. After Gatting declared 183 ahead Yorkshire lost four wickets for 63, three of them in ten balls from Fraser, who was put on standby for the Oval Test two days later. When play eventually began on the last evening, Yorkshire surrendered feebly. Moxon, although reaching 93, refused some easy singles that might have made his side safe and Middlesex steadily worked their way through half-hearted resistance. But in a desperate finish Carr, at slip, dropped Batty, who then struck Williams for four and three to avert an innings defeat when there were only eight balls remaining and no time for Middlesex to bat again.

Close of play: First day, Yorkshire 89-5 (D. Byas 28*, P. J. Hartley 5*); Second day, Middlesex 138-2 (M. W. Gatting 50*, M. R. Ramprakash 34*); Third day, Yorkshire 110-4 (M. D. Moxon 68*, C. White 13*).

Yorkshire

*M. D. Moxon c Emburey b Tufnell	17	– c Brown b Emburey	93
A. P. Grayson c Brown b Fraser	10	– c Emburey b Fraser	0
R. B. Richardson lbw b Tufnell	5	– c and b Fraser	7
D. Byas b Feltham	76	– b Fraser	0
†R. J. Blakey c and b Tufnell	0	– b Williams	9
C. White c Ramprakash b Emburey	6	– c Ramprakash b Fraser	21
P. J. Hartley c Carr b Fraser	30	– c and b Williams	0
D. Gough lbw b Williams	28	– c Carr b Emburey	0
R. D. Stemp not out	26	– c Carr b Emburey	4
J. D. Batty c Brown b Fraser	18	– not out	11
M. A. Robinson c Carr b Fraser	4	– not out	0
B 4, l-b 5, w 1, n-b 26	36	B 6, l-b 5, n-b 28	39

1/27 2/42 3/51 4/51 5/77   256   1/9 2/17 3/25   (9 wkts) 184
6/144 7/201 8/201 9/250   4/63 5/123 6/143
                                                    7/148 8/170 9/177

Bonus points – Yorkshire 2, Middlesex 4.

Bowling: *First Innings*—Fraser 17–8–25–4; Williams 33–6–94–1; Tufnell 16–5–27–3; Emburey 9–2–23–1; Feltham 20–4–78–1. *Second Innings*—Fraser 16–5–49–4; Feltham 6–3–14–0; Tufnell 24–14–30–0; Williams 14.4–3–35–2; Emburey 18–6–34–3; Ramprakash 2–0–11–0.

Middlesex

D. L. Haynes c Blakey b Hartley	4	†K. R. Brown not out	18
M. A. Roseberry b Gough	28	J. E. Emburey not out	5
*M. W. Gatting c Stemp b Gough	182	B 7, l-b 4, n-b 26	37
M. R. Ramprakash c Richardson b Gough	140	
J. D. Carr c Moxon b Robinson	25	1/16 2/59 3/380 (5 wkts dec.) 439
		4/389 5/431

M. A. Feltham, N. F. Williams, A. R. C. Fraser and P. C. R. Tufnell did not bat.

Bonus points – Middlesex 4, Yorkshire 2.

Bowling: Hartley 23–4–85–1; Gough 22–4–78–3; Robinson 26–6–95–1; Stemp 30–10–107–0; Batty 9–1–47–0; White 6–1–16–0.

Umpires: D. O. Oslear and R. A. White.

At Manchester, August 19, 20, 21, 23. YORKSHIRE beat LANCASHIRE by 19 runs.

YORKSHIRE v DURHAM

At Leeds, August 26, 27, 28, 30. Drawn. Yorkshire 7 pts, Durham 5 pts. Toss: Yorkshire.

Bainbridge was the dominant figure, returning figures of nine for 118 with his apparently innocuous medium-pace and scoring an unbeaten hundred on the last day to secure a draw for Durham. Yorkshire had laboured through their first innings on an easy-paced pitch: White, capped two weeks earlier, hit a maiden century, batting five hours, but Yorkshire never gained control and Bainbridge reduced them from 390 for five to 400 all out, claiming five for one in 21 balls. Fowler, missed on 54 and 113, held Durham's reply together with his first century for the county, while Hutton, dropped at slip when one, helped him add 205. Durham's catching was no better: Kellett had four escapes in his 85. But Bainbridge was again rewarded for doing little more than maintain length and line. Durham abandoned the chase for 297 in 77 overs after losing three early wickets. With Yorkshire setting surprisingly defensive fields, however, Bainbridge battled resolutely and Hutton – dropped again on 29 – lent splendid support.

Close of play: First day, Yorkshire 326-4 (C. White 108*, P. J. Hartley 49*); Second day, Durham 232-3 (G. Fowler 128*, P. Bainbridge 2*); Third day, Yorkshire 168-6 (S. A. Kellett 82*, P. J. Hartley 3*).

Yorkshire

M. D. Moxon lbw b Brown	77	– c Graveney b Hughes	0
A. Kellett c Larkins b Graveney	15	– c Hutton b Bainbridge	85
D. Byas b Wood	36	– lbw b Brown	17
C. White c Larkins b Bainbridge	41	– c Hutton b Bainbridge	41
R. J. Blakey b Wood	37	– c Larkins b Bainbridge	0
P. J. Hartley b Wood	49	– (8) c Smith b Wood	29
A. P. Grayson c Larkins b Bainbridge	29	– (6) b Smith	11
D. Gough c Scott b Bainbridge	0	– (9) not out	13
R. D. Stemp c Hughes b Bainbridge	4	– (7) b Bainbridge	1
J. D. Batty c Hutton b Bainbridge	0	– not out	16
M. A. Robinson not out	0		
B 1, l-b 4, n-b 2	7	B 1, l-b 12, w 2	15

1/54 2/123 3/138 4/210 5/330	400	1/1 2/39 3/144 (8 wkts dec.)	228
6/390 7/390 8/397 9/399		4/146 5/163 6/164	
		7/197 8/203	

Bonus points – Yorkshire 3, Durham 2 (Score at 120 overs: 348-5).

Bowling: *First Innings*—Wood 27-4-87-3; Hughes 24-6-61-0; Brown 29-2-114-1; Graveney 24-5-64-1; Bainbridge 27.4-9-53-5; Smith 6-1-16-0. *Second Innings*—Wood 8-3-41-1; Hughes 16-2-48-1; Brown 12-2-31-1; Bainbridge 26-9-65-4; Graveney 3-2-20-0; Smith 8-4-10-1.

Durham

G. Fowler c White b Robinson	138	– c Byas b Hartley	4
W. Larkins c Kellett b Gough	2	– c Stemp b Gough	4
P. W. G. Parker b Gough	6	– lbw b Hartley	15
S. Hutton lbw b Hartley	73	– b Hartley	48
P. Bainbridge c Hartley b Stemp	36	– not out	103
I. Smith c Blakey b White	4	– b Robinson	23
C. W. Scott lbw b Gough	9	– lbw b Robinson	0
J. Wood b Robinson	2	– b White	4
D. A. Graveney b Gough	10	– not out	4
S. J. E. Brown lbw b Gough	0		
S. P. Hughes not out	0		
B 9, l-b 15, n-b 4	28	B 9, l-b 10, w 1, n-b 4	24

1/4 2/20 3/225 4/246 5/259	332	1/8 2/8 3/31 4/126 (7 wkts)	229
6/287 7/312 8/332 9/332		5/184 6/193 7/203	

Bonus points – Durham 3, Yorkshire 4.

Bowling: *First Innings*—Hartley 32-15-50-1; Gough 28-6-79-5; White 10-1-27-1; Robinson 24.5-1-89-2; Stemp 15-3-48-1; Batty 9-3-15-0. *Second Innings*—Hartley 9-7-35-3; Gough 22.4-4-68-1; White 6-2-17-1; Robinson 15-1-36-2; Stemp 12-3-46-0; Batty 2-0-8-0.

Umpires: J. C. Balderstone and H. D. Bird.

At Leicester, August 31, September 1, 2, 3. YORKSHIRE lost to LEICESTERSHIRE by 74 runs.

YORKSHIRE v SUSSEX

At Scarborough, September 9, 10, 11, 13. Drawn. Yorkshire 4 pts, Sussex 8 pts. Toss: Sussex.

Athey scored his fifth century of the season, and his fourth against his native county since leaving them in 1983. After a rain-interrupted first day he and Alan Wells – with his sixth hundred of 1993 – completely dominated some poor bowling on a pitch of little pace and low bounce. They shared 230 in 77 overs. Wells was missed three times, Athey twice and

Yorkshire looked distinctly ragged. When they came to bat they were soon struggling against the spin of Hemmings and Salisbury, given little assistance from the pitch but tremendous back-up from their fielders, who snapped up ten catches – Athey, who had taken over the captaincy when Wells damaged his knee, claimed three. When Yorkshire followed on Byas thrashed 55 from only 48 deliveries to put the conditions into perspective, but Yorkshire were still in danger until rain washed out the last day.

Close of play: First day, Sussex 97-2 (C. W. J. Athey 30*, A. P. Wells 3*); Second day, Yorkshire 43-1 (M. D. Moxon 21*, R. B. Richardson 21*); Third day, Yorkshire 97-1 (M. D. Moxon 28*, R. B. Richardson 8*).

Sussex

N. J. Lenham c Stemp b Hartley	27	I. D. K. Salisbury c Hartley b Stemp	1
C. W. J. Athey c Grayson b Gough	112	F. D. Stephenson not out	
K. Greenfield b Hartley	26	B 7, l-b 6, n-b 22	35
*A. P. Wells c Grayson b Gough	123		
M. P. Speight c White b Gough	18	1/30 2/82 3/312	(8 wkts dec.) 397
C. C. Remy c Grayson b Stemp	17	4/341 5/341 6/382	
†P. Moores run out	25	7/387 8/397	

E. E. Hemmings and E. S. H. Giddins did not bat.

Bonus points – Sussex 4, Yorkshire 3.

Bowling: Hartley 29–5–97–2; Gough 28–10–82–3; Robinson 20–5–78–0; Stemp 26.2–6–63–2; White 1–0–8–0; Batty 9–2–35–0; Richardson 5–0–18–0; Grayson 1–0–3–0.

Yorkshire

*M. D. Moxon c Moores b Hemmings	63	– not out	28
D. Byas c Speight b Stephenson	0	– lbw b Stephenson	55
R. B. Richardson c Speight b Giddins	36	– not out	8
C. White c Greenfield b Salisbury	10		
†R. J. Blakey c Athey b Hemmings	11		
A. P. Grayson c Hemmings b Salisbury	32		
P. J. Hartley c Speight b Hemmings	31		
D. Gough c Greenfield b Salisbury	0		
R. D. Stemp not out	14		
J. D. Batty c Athey b Hemmings	20		
M. A. Robinson c Athey b Salisbury	0		
B 2, l-b 5	7	N-b 6	6
1/2 2/72 3/96 4/121 5/142	224	1/81	(1 wkt) 97
6/190 7/190 8/192 9/223			

Bonus points – Yorkshire 1, Sussex 4.

Bowling: *First Innings*—Stephenson 14–2–41–1; Giddins 7–2–14–1; Remy 4–1–16–0; Hemmings 38–15–89–4; Greenfield 1–0–4–0; Salisbury 30–13–53–4. *Second Innings*—Stephenson 9–1–27–1; Giddins 2–0–19–0; Remy 2–0–28–0; Hemmings 6.3–0–17–0; Salisbury 2–0–6–0.

Umpires: J. D. Bond and V. A. Holder.

At The Oval, September 16, 17, 18, 20. YORKSHIRE drew with SURREY.

NATWEST BANK TROPHY, 1993

The final that no non-partisan spectator wanted turned into the one that no one will ever forget when Warwickshire, chasing the highest total ever made in a Lord's final, 321, hit the winning runs off the final ball. For hours, Sussex had looked near-certainties to stage a triumphant celebration of the 30th anniversary of their victory in the first Cup final. Instead, they were foiled by a century from Asif Din, a cricketer who was not even sure of his future on the Warwickshire staff, never mind in the team.

The draw for the semi-finals had created anticipation of something entirely different: a final between Somerset and Glamorgan, which would have meant Viv Richards bowing out at Lord's against the county that, famously, had sacked him seven years earlier. Instead, Warwickshire had a comfortable win over Somerset and Sussex dramatically beat Glamorgan when their captain Alan Wells scored a magnificent century to save them from a position as apparently hopeless as Warwickshire's was to be in the final.

Warwickshire's fourth success in a September final had echoes of Derbyshire's win in the Benson and Hedges final two months earlier: both teams were little fancied at the start of the competition, underdogs in the final and competing without their overseas players – Bishop of Derbyshire had been injured; Donald of Warwickshire was on tour with South Africa.

The marvellous end to the tournament was in total contrast to the early stages: the 14 minor teams failed not only to beat any of the first-class counties but even to trouble them. In the second round, all eight captains who won the toss opted to bat first and all eight led their teams to defeat.

Prize money

£30,000 for winners: WARWICKSHIRE.
£15,000 for runners-up: SUSSEX.
£7,500 for losing semi-finalists: GLAMORGAN and SOMERSET.
£3,750 for losing quarter-finalists: NORTHAMPTONSHIRE, SURREY, WORCESTER-
SHIRE and YORKSHIRE.

Man of the Match award winners received £600 in the final, £325 in the semi-finals, £275 in the quarter-finals, £165 in the second round and £135 in the first round. The prize money was increased from £73,350 in the 1992 tournament to £80,830.

FIRST ROUND

BUCKINGHAMSHIRE v LEICESTERSHIRE

At Marlow, June 22. Leicestershire won by 75 runs. Toss: Leicestershire.
Boon might have been out first ball, but Booden dropped him at second slip off Roshier and he went on to his maiden hundred in the competition. Leicestershire threw the bat in the final ten overs, scoring 84 runs while losing six wickets: Robinson hit 42 from 28 balls. Buckinghamshire could not build on a solid opening stand of 85, though Burrow reached an unbeaten 57 from 61 balls.
Man of the Match: T. J. Boon.

Leicestershire

T. J. Boon c Shearman b Scriven	117	V. J. Wells c Shearman b Roshier		9
*N. E. Briers b Barry	22	G. J. Parsons not out		5
J. J. Whitaker b Burrow	35	A. D. Mullally not out		19
J. D. R. Benson c and b Burrow	13	B 1, l-b 6, w 3, n-b 4		14
P. E. Robinson c Black b Barry	42			
L. Potter c Black b Scriven	4	1/56 2/143 3/167	(9 wkts, 60 overs)	289
W. K. M. Benjamin run out	2	4/239 5/244 6/248		
†P. A. Nixon run out	7	7/255 8/256 9/267		

Bowling: Roshier 10–2–53–1; Booden 8–2–30–0; Barry 9–0–43–2; Black 5–1–17–0; Burrow 12–1–69–2; Percy 5–0–16–0; Scriven 11–0–54–2.

Buckinghamshire

M. J. Roberts c Nixon b Wells	54	T. J. Barry c Boon b Benson		9
P. F. J. Strong c Benson b Parsons	42	P. G. Roshier not out		2
T. J. A. Scriven b Potter	10			
S. Burrow not out	57	L-b 6, w 5, n-b 8		19
S. M. Shearman b Wells	15			
B. S. Percy c and b Benjamin	1	1/85 2/112 3/122	(8 wkts, 60 overs)	214
†T. P. Russell c Boon b Benson	5	4/177 5/180 6/190		
*G. R. Black c Benjamin b Benson	0	7/191 8/206		

C. D. Booden did not bat.

Bowling: Benjamin 10–3–25–1; Mullally 12–4–32–0; Parsons 12–0–60–1; Potter 12–2–32–1; Wells 12–1–46–2; Benson 2–0–13–3.

Umpires: M. A. Johnson and R. Palmer.

CHESHIRE v NOTTINGHAMSHIRE

At Warrington, June 22. Nottinghamshire won by 62 runs. Toss: Cheshire.

Nottinghamshire's two international all-rounders met with contrasting fortunes: the New Zealander Cairns scored 64 after surviving a narrow decision on a run-out and later took four for 18, but Lewis strained his neck and shoulder in pre-match practice, scored nought in four balls and could not bowl. For Cheshire, both the former England player Miller and the less celebrated Potts bowled tightly and the captain, Cockbain, scored a fifty.

Man of the Match: C. L. Cairns.

Nottinghamshire

P. R. Pollard c Standing b Peel	17	†B. N. French lbw b Miller		0
M. Saxelby c Hignett b Crawley	17	R. A. Pick not out		14
*R. T. Robinson b Potts	19	J. A. Afford not out		0
P. Johnson c Gray b Crawley	13	B 1, l-b 5, w 14		20
G. F. Archer c and b O'Brien	39			
C. L. Cairns c Bean b Peel	64	1/27 2/56 3/67	(9 wkts, 60 overs)	208
C. C. Lewis c and b O'Brien	0	4/87 5/168 6/168		
K. P. Evans c and b O'Brien	5	7/178 8/179 9/204		

Bowling: Peel 12–1–45–2; Potts 12–3–34–1; Crawley 9–1–28–2; Miller 12–3–33–1; O'Brien 11–1–45–3; Bostock 4–0–17–0.

Cheshire

T. J. Bostock c French b Pick	8	J. F. M. O'Brien not out		13
S. T. Crawley lbw b Cairns	9	†T. P. A. Standing c Pollard b Cairns		2
*I. Cockbain c Johnson b Evans	57	N. D. Peel b Cairns		0
G. Miller b Pick	4	L-b 3, w 14		17
J. D. Gray lbw b Pick	2			
J. D. Bean c Evans b Saxelby	19	1/12 2/31 3/38	(55.3 overs)	146
R. G. Hignett b Cairns	14	4/41 5/78 6/98		
J. Potts lbw b Afford	1	7/115 8/142 9/146		

Bowling: Evans 12–4–30–1; Cairns 9.3–5–18–4; Pick 10–1–29–3; Afford 12–3–15–1; Saxelby 9–0–42–1; Pollard 3–0–9–0.

Umpires: G. I. Burgess and V. A. Holder.

DEVON v DERBYSHIRE

At Exmouth, June 22. Derbyshire won by 133 runs. Toss: Derbyshire.

Barnett and Bowler launched Derbyshire with their 15th century opening stand in limited-overs matches, and O'Gorman took an unbeaten 68 off 46 balls. Roebuck, the former Somerset captain, removed Barnett and later Cork and Griffith with consecutive deliveries. But Cork had his revenge when he bowled Roebuck, in a spell of four wickets in 25 balls which reduced Devon from 30 without loss to 45 for five. Malcolm finished them off with three wickets in nine balls.

Man of the Match: D. G. Cork.

Derbyshire

*K. J. Barnett c White b Roebuck	60	M. J. Vandrau run out		21
P. D. Bowler c Ward b Cottam	58	†B. J. M. Maher not out		0
J. E. Morris c Pritchard b Allin	21	B 2, l-b 5, w 4		11
C. J. Adams c Cottam b Ward	13			
T. J. G. O'Gorman not out	68	1/108 2/143 3/152	(7 wkts, 60 overs)	266
D. G. Cork c Ward b Roebuck	14	4/176 5/203		
F. A. Griffith c Wyatt b Roebuck	0	6/203 7/263		

D. E. Malcolm and O. H. Mortensen did not bat.

Bowling: Donohue 10–0–57–0; Ward 12–0–70–1; Allin 12–3–33–1; Cottam 12–0–45–1; Roebuck 12–1–37–3; Wyatt 2–0–17–0.

Devon

J. G. Wyatt lbw b Griffith	9	A. C. Cottam b Malcolm		2
S. M. Willis b Cork	20	A. W. Allin b Malcolm		0
G. W. White lbw b Cork	0	†C. S. Pritchard not out		1
A. J. Pugh lbw b Cork	0	B 1, l-b 3, w 6, n-b 2		12
D. E. L. Townsend b Vandrau	29			
*P. M. Roebuck b Cork	12	1/30 2/30 3/32	(43.4 overs)	133
K. Donohue b Mortensen	31	4/32 5/45 6/87		
T. W. Ward c O'Gorman b Malcolm	17	7/126 8/130 9/130		

Bowling: Mortensen 7–0–30–1; Malcolm 7.4–1–29–3; Cork 8–1–18–4; Griffith 6–3–13–1; Barnett 8–0–30–0; Vandrau 7–4–9–1.

Umpires: D. J. Halfyard and P. B. Wight.

GLAMORGAN v OXFORDSHIRE

At Swansea, June 22. Glamorgan won by 131 runs. Toss: Oxfordshire.

Richards arrived when Glamorgan were 40 for three and transformed the innings with an unbeaten 162, a score surpassed only four times in the competition's 31 seasons. It was also the highest for Glamorgan in any limited-overs competition. Richards reached 100 in 144 balls, and took only 21 more to get to 162, smashing 24 off the final over, when he hit two balls out of the ground. In all he hit two sixes and 15 fours and shared century partnerships with both Maynard and Cottey. Chasing 322, Oxfordshire's openers knocked off 121 before they were dismissed in successive overs.

Man of the Match: I. V. A. Richards.

Glamorgan

S. P. James c Waterton b Arnold	5	R. D. B. Croft not out		12
*H. Morris c Curtis b Hartley	6			
A. Dale run out	9	L-b 7, w 13		20
M. P. Maynard c Laudat b Savin	67			
I. V. A. Richards not out	162	1/8 2/24 3/40	(5 wkts, 60 overs)	322
P. A. Cottey run out	41	4/145 5/252		

R. P. Lefebvre, †C. P. Metson, S. L. Watkin and S. R. Barwick did not bat.

Bowling: Arnold 12–2–46–1; Joyner 7–1–49–0; Savin 9–0–42–1; Hartley 11–2–66–1; Laudat 2–0–16–0; Evans 11–0–56–0; Curtis 8–1–40–0.

Oxfordshire

D. A. J. Wise c Metson b Lefebvre	68	*P. J. Garner not out		6
†S. N. V. Waterton st Metson b Croft	41			
S. V. Laudat not out	24	B 1, l-b 13, w 3		17
T. A. Lester c Lefebvre b Dale	25			
G. P. Savin b Dale	8	1/121 2/121 3/156	(5 wkts, 60 overs)	191
J. S. Hartley lbw b Richards	2	4/166 5/177		

S. G. Joyner, R. A. Evans, K. A. Arnold and I. J. Curtis did not bat.

Bowling: Watkin 6–3–9–0; Lefebvre 10–5–14–1; Dale 12–2–49–2; Barwick 8–0–43–0; Richards 12–2–30–1; Croft 12–1–32–1.

Umpires: D. J. Dennis and B. J. Meyer.

GLOUCESTERSHIRE v HERTFORDSHIRE

At Bristol, June 22. Gloucestershire won by 110 runs. Toss: Hertfordshire.

Harris removed both Gloucestershire openers but Alleyne and Hancock steadied the innings with a stand of 103 and in the closing stages Walsh hit out for 37. Hertfordshire were pinned down by some tight bowling, especially from Smith, and only Gouldstone, once of Northamptonshire, made a significant score.

Man of the Match: M. W. Alleyne.

Gloucestershire

B. C. Broad lbw b Harris	14	C. A. Walsh b Jahangir		37
G. D. Hodgson c Harvey b Harris	9	A. M. Smith not out		8
M. W. Alleyne c and b Jahangir	73	A. M. Babington not out		1
T. H. C. Hancock c Harvey b Cavener	45	L-b 9, w 17, n-b 6		32
*A. J. Wright hit wkt b Walshe	14			
†R. C. Russell lbw b Walshe	2	1/21 2/26 3/129	(9 wkts, 60 overs)	274
R. J. Scott c Gouldstone b Jahangir	21	4/159 5/161 6/186		
R. M. Wight b Jahangir	18	7/207 8/259 9/264		

Bowling: Walshe 12–1–67–2; Harris 12–2–32–2; Jahangir 12–1–57–4; Surridge 12–1–53–0; Cavener 12–0–56–1.

Hertfordshire

M. James c Hancock b Walsh	16	M. J. Walshe c Russell b Alleyne		1
R. G. P. Ellis lbw b Babington	6	G. A. R. Harris c Smith b Hancock		10
M. R. Gouldstone not out	68	*D. Surridge c Russell b Hancock		2
N. J. Ilott c Smith b Wight	14	L-b 4, w 3, n-b 16		23
N. Gilbert b Smith	3			
K. Jahangir lbw b Smith	0	1/12 2/26 3/79	(57.5 overs)	164
C. N. Cavener c Wright b Scott	1	4/87 5/87 6/97		
†J. D. Harvey c Wight b Walsh	20	7/135 8/144 9/162		

Bowling: Walsh 9–1–27–2; Babington 10–2–29–1; Scott 10–0–37–1; Smith 12–6–17–2; Wight 12–0–34–1; Alleyne 3–0–9–1; Hancock 1.5–0–7–2.

Umpires: J. H. Harris and A. G. T. Whitehead.

KENT v MIDDLESEX

At Canterbury, June 22. Kent won by 166 runs. Toss: Kent.

Being dismissed for 116 with 24 overs to spare was a fate more fitting for a minor county than the powerful Middlesex batting line-up. McCague, in his best one-day bowling for Kent, removed Keech and Ramprakash early on, and then returned to dismiss Carr when he made the first ball of his second spell lift awkwardly. In the previous two overs Haynes had been bowled by Hooper and Gatting – batting at No. 5 after he injured his knee running into a boundary board – caught behind off Headley, who took three wickets against his old county. There was no recovery from 83 for five. Kent had batted solidly, on an easy-looking pitch, with all their top order firing except Fleming.

Man of the Match: M. J. McCague.

Kent

T. R. Ward c Weekes b Emburey	34	M. A. Ealham c Ramprakash b Cowans	0
*M. R. Benson c Fraser b Weekes	60	D. W. Headley not out	1
C. L. Hooper b Emburey	62	B 1, l-b 4, w 11, n-b 2	18
M. V. Fleming c Gatting b Weekes	5		
N. R. Taylor c Weekes b Emburey	57	1/65 2/124 3/136 (7 wkts, 60 overs)	282
N. J. Llong not out	27	4/222 5/242	
†S. A. Marsh c Ramprakash b Fraser	18	6/276 7/279	

M. J. McCague and A. P. Igglesden did not bat.

Bowling: Fraser 11–1–53–1; Cowans 11–0–47–1; Johnson 10–0–44–0; Emburey 12–0–59–3; Weekes 7–0–36–2; Keech 9–0–38–0.

Middlesex

D. L. Haynes b Hooper	41	R. L. Johnson c Fleming b McCague	5
M. Keech lbw b McCague	3	A. R. C. Fraser not out	2
M. R. Ramprakash c Benson b McCague	5	N. G. Cowans c Fleming b Hooper	2
J. D. Carr c Hooper b McCague	25	L-b 3, w 10, n-b 4	17
*M. W. Gatting c Marsh b Headley	2		
†K. R. Brown c Fleming b Headley	10	1/6 2/12 3/80 (36 overs)	116
P. N. Weekes c Llong b Headley	2	4/83 5/83 6/101	
J. E. Emburey b McCague	2	7/103 8/110 9/111	

Bowling: Igglesden 7–1–20–0; McCague 12–3–26–5; Headley 11–1–45–3; Ealham 3–0–10–0; Hooper 3–0–12–2.

Umpires: K. E. Palmer and G. A. Stickley.

NORFOLK v WARWICKSHIRE

At Lakenham, June 22. Warwickshire won by 143 runs. Toss: Warwickshire.

A century by Ostler in 99 balls underpinned Warwickshire's total of 285, though they only just lasted out their full 60 overs. The Norfolk captain Thomas and Bunting, formerly with Sussex, collected three wickets each. But the minor county's batting was less impressive, and was unable to cope with Neil Smith.

Man of the Match: D. P. Ostler.

Warwickshire

A. J. Moles b Fox	44	G. C. Small b Bunting	0
J. D. Ratcliffe run out	40	A. A. Donald not out	2
D. P. Ostler c Rogers b Thomas	104	T. A. Munton not out	1
P. A. Smith c Crowley b Bunting	25	L-b 6, w 13, n-b 2	21
*D. A. Reeve c Crowley b Cole	17		
T. L. Penney b Thomas	14	1/87 2/114 3/182 (9 wkts, 60 overs)	285
†P. C. L. Holloway b Thomas	16	4/226 5/256 6/271	
N. M. K. Smith c Goldsmith b Bunting	1	7/275 8/282 9/284	

Bowling: Cole 12–1–71–1; Bunting 12–1–40–3; Thomas 8–0–34–3; Goldsmith 12–1–59–0; Plumb 12–1–52–0; Fox 4–1–23–1.

Norfolk

C. J. Rogers lbw b Reeve	19	R. A. Bunting not out	18
S. G. Plumb b Small	5	A. P. Cole c Holloway b Ostler	4
S. C. Goldsmith c and b N. M. K. Smith	32	†S. C. Crowley run out	0
R. J. Finney lbw b Munton	2	L-b 13, w 5, n-b 6	24
R. D. E. Farrow b N. M. K. Smith	16		
S. B. Dixon c Ostler b N. M. K. Smith	6	1/6 2/46 3/49	(53.3 overs) 142
*D. R. Thomas c and b N. M. K. Smith	15	4/81 5/92 6/100	
N. Fox b N. M. K. Smith	1	7/106 8/111 9/134	

Bowling: Donald 7–2–13–0; Small 6–0–18–1; Reeve 5–1–16–1; Munton 12–1–33–1; P. A. Smith 6–1–12–0; N. M. K. Smith 12–5–17–5; Ratcliffe 4–0–16–0; Ostler 1.3–0–4–1.

Umpires: J. W. Holder and H. J. Rhodes.

NORTHAMPTONSHIRE v LANCASHIRE

At Northampton, June 22. Northamptonshire won by six wickets. Toss: Northamptonshire.

Bailey's unbeaten 96 ensured that holders Northamptonshire would win through, despite having to endure one of the two all-first-class encounters in the round. He hit a six and ten fours, despite being hit on the instep by two yorkers from DeFreitas, and added 117 with Fordham for the second wicket. The home county's only anxious moments came when the slow left-armer Barnett dismissed Fordham and Lamb in successive overs, with the help of wicket-keeper Hegg, and Atherton ran out Loye. But Lancashire had set too low a target. Only Atherton had the patience to survive in early damp conditions, and Watkinson's 71-run partnership with Austin came too late.

Man of the Match: R. J. Bailey.

Lancashire

M. A. Atherton c Bailey b Penberthy	37	M. Watkinson not out	60
S. P. Titchard c and b Taylor	4	I. D. Austin not out	38
N. J. Speak b Penberthy	0	B 1, l-b 2, w 5	8
*N. H. Fairbrother c Ripley b Curran	22		
G. D. Lloyd b Curran	1	1/16 2/16 3/45	(7 wkts, 60 overs) 178
Wasim Akram run out	4	4/56 5/56	
P. A. J. DeFreitas lbw b Ambrose	8	6/70 7/107	

†W. K. Hegg and A. A. Barnett did not bat.

Bowling: Taylor 12–4–35–1; Ambrose 12–3–34–1; Curran 12–3–39–2; Penberthy 12–3–33–2; Cook 12–1–34–0.

Northamptonshire

A. Fordham st Hegg b Barnett	39	K. M. Curran not out	23
N. A. Felton lbw b DeFreitas	3	B 4, l-b 5, w 1, n-b 2	12
R. J. Bailey not out	96		
*A. J. Lamb c Hegg b Barnett	4	1/4 2/121	(4 wkts, 56.5 overs) 181
M. B. Loye run out	4	3/125 4/137	

A. L. Penberthy, †D. Ripley, C. E. L. Ambrose, J. P. Taylor and N. G. B. Cook did not bat.

Bowling: Austin 11.5–3–36–0; DeFreitas 11–3–31–1; Watkinson 11–0–41–0; Wasim Akram 11–2–35–0; Barnett 12–2–29–2.

Umpires: H. D. Bird and A. A. Jones.

SCOTLAND v WORCESTERSHIRE

At Myreside, Edinburgh, June 22. Worcestershire won by 76 runs. Toss: Worcestershire.

Neither team found batting easy, with Hick scoring the only fifty, though Curtis was run out by Stanger when two short. Curtis and Weston had put on 92, and Hick added 83 with D'Oliveira, but there were no other major partnerships; Storie and Patterson shared 57 for Scotland's second wicket, but took 30 overs, leaving their colleagues far too much to do.

Man of the Match: G. A. Hick.

Worcestershire

*T. S. Curtis run out	48	R. K. Illingworth not out		2
W. P. C. Weston c Duthie b Govan	31	C. M. Tolley not out		9
G. A. Hick c Hamilton b Bevan	51			
D. B. D'Oliveira c Russell b Stanger	32	B 5, l-b 3, w 11		19
D. A. Leatherdale b Duthie	22			
†S. J. Rhodes c Salmond b Hamilton	18	1/92 2/95 3/178	(8 wkts, 60 overs)	238
S. R. Lampitt c Russell b Hamilton	4	4/195 5/220 6/224		
N. V. Radford c Storie b Duthie	2	7/226 8/227		

K. C. G. Benjamin did not bat.

Bowling: Stanger 11–3–35–1; Hamilton 9–2–44–2; Duthie 11–1–53–2; Bevan 12–1–47–1; Govan 12–2–31–1; Russell 5–0–20–0.

Scotland

†I. L. Philip c Leatherdale b Tolley	6	I. R. Beven not out		16
*A. C. Storie b Radford	32	P. G. Duthie not out		21
B. M. W. Patterson lbw b Illingworth	23	B 4, l-b 7, w 12		23
J. D. Love b Lampitt	16			
G. Salmond c Illingworth b Lampitt	18	1/18 2/75 3/83	(7 wkts, 60 overs)	162
A. B. Russell b Lampitt	2	4/115 5/117		
J. W. Govan c Benjamin b Hick	5	6/121 7/127		

I. M. Stanger and G. M. Hamilton did not bat.

Bowling: Benjamin 4–1–11–0; Tolley 10–3–15–1; Hick 12–3–32–1; Lampitt 12–2–23–3; Illingworth 12–3–32–1; Radford 7–0–26–1; Leatherdale 2–0–8–0; D'Oliveira 1–0–4–0.

Umpires: J. D. Bond and T. G. Wilson.

SHROPSHIRE v SOMERSET

At Telford, June 22. Somerset won by 116 runs. Toss: Shropshire.

Lathwell reached his maiden hundred in limited-overs competitions before lunch, helped by Shropshire's over-rate: they bowled 47 overs in two and a quarter hours. Lathwell hit 12 fours and a six and, though he was out just after the interval, Clive Lloyd urged his immediate selection for England when he named him as Man of the Match. Rose, with 52 in 38 balls, and Tavaré, with 56 in 48, took Somerset to 300. Shropshire opener Jones batted gamely for 47 overs to score 66.

Man of the Match: M. N. Lathwell.

Somerset

M. N. Lathwell c Sharp b Byram	103	K. A. Parsons not out		0
N. A. Folland lbw b Shantry	19	B 1, l-b 3, w 2		6
R. J. Harden c Parton b Byram	65			
G. D. Rose c Byram b Shantry	52	1/39 2/171	(4 wkts, 60 overs)	301
*C. J. Tavaré not out	56	3/198 4/300		

†N. D. Burns, Mushtaq Ahmed, A. R. Caddick, N. A. Mallender and A. P. van Troost did not bat.

Bowling: Shantry 7–1–36–2; Marsh 11–0–51–0; Byram 12–1–41–2; Edmunds 12–1–50–0; Sharp 10–0–50–0; Blakeley 8–0–69–0.

Shropshire

J. B. R. Jones c Mushtaq Ahmed b Parsons	66	†M. J. Davidson b Parsons		0
T. Parton c Burns b Caddick	5	B. K. Shantry c Tavaré b Lathwell		4
K. Sharp lbw b Rose	14	A. B. Byram b Mushtaq Ahmed		22
D. Marsh lbw b Rose	0	G. Edmunds not out		24
*M. R. Davies lbw b van Troost	1	B 4, l-b 6, w 6, n-b 8		26
A. N. Johnson b Rose	0			
P. M. Blakeley st Burns b Mushtaq Ahmed	23	1/28 2/51 3/52	(59.4 overs)	185
		4/53 5/60 6/111		
		7/122 8/135 9/148		

Bowling: Caddick 6–2–21–1; Mallender 6–1–10–0; van Troost 6–2–16–1; Rose 6–3–11–3; Parsons 12–0–47–2; Lathwell 11–4–23–1; Mushtaq Ahmed 8.4–3–16–2; Harden 3–0–23–0; Tavaré 1–0–6–0.

Umpires: R. A. White and P. Willey.

STAFFORDSHIRE v HAMPSHIRE

At Stone, June 22. Hampshire won by seven wickets. Toss: Hampshire.

Hampshire beat the Minor Counties champions with more than 15 overs to spare, thanks to an unbeaten century from Smith. He outscored Middleton by more than three to one in their second-wicket partnership of 117. Staffordshire were given a good start by openers Dean and Shaw, but after a mid-innings rally slipped from 138 for four to lose their last six wickets for 27 runs.

Man of the Match: R. A. Smith.

Staffordshire

S. J. Dean lbw b Udal	40	R. A. Spiers c Smith b Connor	0
P. F. Shaw lbw b Ayling	29	P. J. W. Allott run out	3
J. A. Waterhouse c Smith b James	4	N. P. Hackett not out	0
S. D. Myles lbw b James	7	L-b 12, w 8	20
A. J. Dutton c Terry b Ayling	24		
*N. J. Archer st Aymes b Udal	25	1/51 2/87 3/95	(59.1 overs) 165
P. G. Newman c Udal b Connor	9	4/96 5/138 6/149	
†M. I. Humphries c Nicholas b Connor	4	7/162 8/162 9/165	

Bowling: Marshall 11.1–0–28–0; James 12–2–29–2; Udal 12–1–24–2; Connor 12–3–21–3; Ayling 12–1–51–2.

Hampshire

V. P. Terry b Newman	12	*M. C. J. Nicholas not out	3
T. C. Middleton c Dean b Dutton	34	L-b 1	1
R. A. Smith not out	105		
D. I. Gower c Hackett b Allott	11	1/18 2/135 3/153	(3 wkts, 44.5 overs) 166

M. D. Marshall, K. D. James, †A. N. Aymes, J. R. Ayling, S. D. Udal and C. A. Connor did not bat.

Bowling: Newman 8–1–36–1; Hackett 6–1–20–0; Allott 12–2–45–1; Spiers 7–1–22–0; Dutton 11.5–0–42–1.

Umpires: A. Clarkson and B. Leadbeater.

SUFFOLK v ESSEX

At Bury St Edmunds, June 22. Essex won by 121 runs. Toss: Suffolk.

Essex won comfortably against their neighbours, a familiar crew including five of their own former players: Butler, Miller, Golding, East and Brown. Of these the less distinguished of the two slow left-armers, Golding, outshone East, conceding only 15 runs in 12 overs and dismissing Prichard and Hussain. For Essex, opener Stephenson made 84, the highest score of the game. But Salim Malik claimed the honours, with 74 in 70 balls, followed by four wickets, his best one-day analysis for the county. Only Caley prevented a total rout.

Man of the Match: Salim Malik.

Essex

P. J. Prichard b Golding	24	M. C. Ilott run out	5
J. P. Stephenson c Clements b Graham	84	P. M. Such not out	0
N. Hussain c East b Golding	17	S. J. W. Andrew not out	1
Salim Malik c East b Graham	74	L-b 7, w 3, n-b 6	16
*G. A. Gooch c Butler b Miller	14		
D. R. Pringle c Squire b Graham	2	1/64 2/105 3/175 (9 wkts, 60 overs) 251	
†M. A. Garnham c Halliday b Miller	6	4/210 5/224 6/230	
T. D. Topley c East b Graham	8	7/245 8/245 9/250	

Bowling: Graham 12–0–66–4; Douglas 12–0–54–0; Miller 12–0–61–2; Golding 12–4–15–2; East 12–1–48–0.

Suffolk

S. J. Halliday lbw b Ilott	2	*R. E. East c and b Salim Malik	13
S. M. Clements b Andrew	7	†A. D. Brown lbw b Salim Malik	0
K. A. Butler c Garnham b Topley	17	P. J. Douglas st Garnham b Salim Malik	2
P. J. Caley not out	54	L-b 3, w 4, n-b 12	19
A. J. Squire lbw b Topley	1		
I. D. Graham c Garnham b Topley	1	1/2 2/20 3/38 (48.2 overs) 130	
C. A. Miller st Garnham b Such	7	4/45 5/49 6/60	
A. K. Golding c Hussain b Salim Malik	7	7/89 8/111 9/117	

Bowling: Ilott 6–2–7–1; Pringle 6–2–8–0; Andrew 5–2–12–1; Topley 11–2–34–3; Such 7–3–15–1; Stephenson 7–1–26–0; Salim Malik 6.2–0–25–4.

Umpires: P. Adams and J. C. Balderstone.

SURREY v DORSET

At The Oval, June 22. Surrey won by ten wickets. Toss: Surrey.

A brutal century by Stewart, which formed almost two-thirds of a first-wicket stand of 164, hustled Surrey to victory with almost indecent haste inside 29 overs. It was the 12th ten-wicket win in the competition's history. Stewart reached 100 in 79 balls and hit 16 fours. His innings totally eclipsed a fine fifty from the much-travelled Hardy, who used his experience with Hampshire, Somerset and Gloucestershire to give Dorset some backbone. Waqar Younis, whose first 11 overs had been despatched for 59 runs, mopped up the tail with three wickets in four balls.

Man of the Match: A. J. Stewart.

Dorset

G. S. Calway lbw b Murphy	26	S. R. Walbridge b Waqar Younis	3
T. W. Richings b M. P. Bicknell	8	O. T. Parkin b Waqar Younis	0
A. Willows run out	12	P. L. Garlick b Waqar Younis	0
J. J. E. Hardy c Ward b M. P. Bicknell	73		
*†G. D. Reynolds lbw b Murphy	0	W 4	4
S. W. D. Rintoul c Stewart b M. P. Bicknell	36	1/18 2/33 3/73 (58.5 overs) 163	
R. A. Pyman b Benjamin	0	4/75 5/158 6/159	
J. H. Shackleton not out	1	7/159 8/163 9/163	

Bowling: M. P. Bicknell 12–4–26–3; Benjamin 12–2–24–1; Waqar Younis 11.5–0–59–3; Murphy 11–2–27–2; Boiling 12–1–27–0.

Surrey

D. J. Bicknell not out	54
*†A. J. Stewart not out	104
L-b 4, w 2	6

(no wkt, 28.4 overs) 164

G. P. Thorpe, M. A. Lynch, A. D. Brown, D. M. Ward, M. P. Bicknell, Waqar Younis, J. Boiling, A. J. Murphy and J. E. Benjamin did not bat.

Bowling: Garlick 3–0–17–0; Shackleton 6–1–28–0; Parkin 2–0–23–0; Walbridge 9.4–1–44–0; Willows 6–0–41–0; Pyman 2–0–7–0.

Umpires: J. H. Hampshire and M. K. Reed.

SUSSEX v WALES MINOR COUNTIES

At Hove, June 22. Sussex won by 114 runs. Toss: Sussex.

Wales, making their debut in the tournament, managed to bat throughout their 60 overs, though their recovery from 89 for six, after 42 overs, was helped by Wells's decision to experiment with his bowlers. Earlier, Athey hit nine fours and a six as he added 135 with Greenfield, who showed less urgency and remained four short of a hundred when the innings ended.

Man of the Match: K. Greenfield.

Sussex

C. W. J. Athey c Puddle b Smith	92	I. D. K. Salisbury c Edwards b Griffiths .. 0
J. W. Hall c Griffiths b Edwards	3	A. N. Jones not out 0
K. Greenfield not out	96	B 5, l-b 11, w 2, n-b 8 26
*A. P. Wells run out	8	
J. A. North c and b Derrick	20	1/24 2/159 3/171 (7 wkts, 60 overs) 257
F. D. Stephenson c Puddle b Griffiths ..	3	4/222 5/230
†P. Moores c Smith b Griffiths	9	6/255 7/256

E. S. H. Giddins and E. E. Hemmings did not bat.

Bowling: Derrick 12–1–35–1; Edwards 12–4–36–1; Ikram 6–1–33–0; Griffiths 12–3–57–3; Smith 12–1–41–1; Lloyd 6–0–39–0.

Wales Minor Counties

A. J. Jones run out	23	W. G. Edwards not out 28
†A. W. Harris c Moores b Jones	1	B. J. Lloyd not out................ 31
B. Metcalf c Moores b Salisbury	30	L-b 8, w 4 12
J. Derrick b Salisbury	4	
K. M. Bell lbw b Hemmings	13	1/4 2/51 3/58 (6 wkts, 60 overs) 143
*A. C. Puddle lbw b Giddins	1	4/72 5/73 6/89

A. D. Griffiths, A. Smith and A. Ikram did not bat.

Bowling: Jones 7–2–10–1; Giddins 12–2–24–1; North 2–0–17–0; Stephenson 5–2–4–0; Salisbury 8–1–17–2; Hemmings 12–4–15–1; Greenfield 7–0–23–0; Athey 7–0–25–0.

Umpires: T. E. Jesty and N. T. Plews.

WILTSHIRE v DURHAM

At Trowbridge, June 22. Durham won by 103 runs. Toss: Wiltshire.

Hutton, yet to appear in the Championship in 1993, scored a storming 95 with five sixes, including three in one over from Barnes. He added 166 in 29 overs with Bainbridge as Durham's gathering momentum carried them past 300 for the third year running in the first round. They took 121 runs from the final ten overs. Smith batted well for Wiltshire before he and Perrin were dismissed by Hughes with consecutive balls.

Man of the Match: S. Hutton.

Durham

I. T. Botham c Foyle b Prigent	55	A. C. Cummins not out 20
W. Larkins c Perrin b North	35	
P. W. G. Parker c Savage b Prigent	4	L-b 11, w 7, n-b 6............ 24
S. Hutton c Foyle b Tomlins	95	
P. Bainbridge b Tomlins	82	1/90 2/107 3/107 (5 wkts, 60 overs) 320
J. D. Glendenen not out	5	4/273 5/296

†C. W. Scott, J. Wood, S. P. Hughes and *D. A. Graveney did not bat.

Bowling: Barnes 12–0–93–0; Sheppard 4–0–41–0; Tomlins 12–2–51–2; Prigent 12–2–38–2; North 12–2–44–1; Simpkins 3–0–14–0; Marsh 5–0–28–0.

Wiltshire

L. K. Smith b Hughes	73	N. Prigent not out	14
P. M. Marsh b Hughes	2	G. Sheppard not out	2
*K. N. Foyle c Scott b Wood	0		
K. P. Tomlins c and b Graveney	28	L-b 4, w 6, n-b 14	24
R. R. Savage c Hutton b Bainbridge	26		
†S. M. Perrin b Hughes	0	1/6 2/7 3/82	(8 wkts, 60 overs) 217
D. P. Simpkins b Cummins	48	4/125 5/125 6/171	
P. D. North b Bainbridge	0	7/175 8/211	

S. N. Barnes did not bat.

Bowling: Wood 12–3–35–1; Hughes 11–3–29–3; Bainbridge 12–1–65–2; Cummins 12–3–38–1; Graveney 12–0–40–1; Glendenen 1–0–6–0.

Umpires: D. O. Oslear and G. Sharp.

YORKSHIRE v IRELAND

At Leeds, June 22. Yorkshire won by 85 runs. Toss: Ireland.

Moxon and Metcalfe opened strongly with 132 in 36 overs but, despite fifties from Richardson and Byas, Yorkshire did not accelerate conspicuously in the second half of their innings. Ireland's captain, Warke, batted into the 55th over for his 64, and had the minor satisfaction of seeing his team overtake their previous highest score in the competition, 186 against Gloucestershire in 1988, off the final ball.

Man of the Match: A. A. Metcalfe.

Yorkshire

*M. D. Moxon c Nelson b Curry	63
A. A. Metcalfe c P. McCrum b Harrison	77
R. B. Richardson c Curry b P. McCrum	54
D. Byas b P. McCrum	54
†R. J. Blakey not out	0
L-b 5, w 9, n-b 10	24

1/132 2/166   (4 wkts, 60 overs) 272
3/266 4/272

C. White, P. W. Jarvis, P. J. Hartley, D. Gough, J. D. Batty and M. A. Robinson did not bat.

Bowling: P. McCrum 10–0–51–2; Moore 10–2–47–0; Harrison 12–0–48–1; Nelson 10–0–45–0; Curry 6–0–28–1; C. McCrum 12–1–48–0.

Ireland

M. F. Cohen run out	15	G. D. Harrison not out	7
M. P. Rea c Byas b Hartley	9		
*S. J. S. Warke b Jarvis	64	B 1, l-b 18, w 5, n-b 6	30
D. A. Lewis lbw b White	1		
D. J. Curry lbw b Hartley	22	1/18 2/38 3/52	(5 wkts, 60 overs) 187
C. McCrum not out	39	4/96 5/170	

†P. B. Jackson, P. McCrum, A. N. Nelson and E. R. P. Moore did not bat.

Bowling: Jarvis 11–1–25–1; Hartley 9–1–25–2; Robinson 12–1–26–0; Gough 12–2–34–0; White 11–0–41–1; Batty 5–2–17–0.

Umpires: B. Dudleston and C. T. Spencer.

SECOND ROUND

ESSEX v NORTHAMPTONSHIRE

At Chelmsford, July 7. Northamptonshire won by five wickets. Toss: Essex.

Lamb sealed a magnificent Northamptonshire victory with an innings of the highest quality, his biggest in the competition. He came in when his team were 46 for three, and scored 124 off 127 deliveries. The ease with which he found the gaps was illustrated by the fact that he hit only a dozen boundaries. The 20-year-old Loye provided his main support, during a stand of 137 in 30 overs, and Penberthy took 41 from 45 balls to help Lamb finish things off with nearly two overs to spare. Such a result was hardly what Essex expected when Prichard and Stephenson had launched their innings with an opening partnership of 187 in 46 overs. Both lost momentum and were out in the nineties before Hussain's fifty from 43 balls injected impetus.

Man of the Match: A. J. Lamb.

Essex

P. J. Prichard lbw b Ambrose	92	D. R. Pringle c Curran b Ambrose		13
J. P. Stephenson b Bailey	90	L-b 2, w 6, n-b 2		10
N. Hussain b Taylor	50			
Salim Malik c Penberthy b Bailey	19	1/187 2/189 3/246	(5 wkts, 60 overs)	286
*G. A. Gooch not out	12	4/270 5/286		

†M. A. Garnham, S. J. W. Andrew, M. C. Ilott, T. D. Topley and P. M. Such did not bat.

Bowling: Ambrose 12–0–47–2; Taylor 11–2–45–1; Penberthy 9–1–47–0; Curran 11–2–54–0; Cook 7–0–42–0; Bailey 10–0–49–2.

Northamptonshire

A. Fordham lbw b Pringle	0	A. L. Penberthy not out		41
N. A. Felton c Gooch b Topley	10			
R. J. Bailey run out	31	L-b 6, w 4, n-b 6		16
M. B. Loye c Garnham b Andrew	65			
*A. J. Lamb not out	124	1/0 2/39 3/46	(5 wkts, 57.5 overs)	290
K. M. Curran lbw b Such	3	4/183 5/196		

†D. Ripley, C. E. L. Ambrose, J. P. Taylor and N. G. B. Cook did not bat.

Bowling: Pringle 12–1–53–1; Ilott 10.5–0–59–0; Topley 11–0–54–1; Stephenson 8–0–39–0; Such 12–0–54–1; Andrew 4–0–25–1.

Umpires: G. I. Burgess and D. O. Oslear.

GLAMORGAN v DURHAM

At Cardiff, July 7. Glamorgan won by seven wickets. Toss: Durham.

Maynard guided Glamorgan to their fourth successive NatWest quarter-final with a chanceless century from 103 deliveries, sharing partnerships of 100 with James and 85 in 15 overs with Richards. When he was out Glamorgan needed only seven from five overs. It completed a day of added responsibility for him; he had taken over the captaincy in the field when Morris twisted an ankle, an injury which prevented him from batting. Durham's efforts depended largely on Larkins and Parker, who put on 107 in 24 overs for the second wicket, and Botham, who scored 33 from 27 balls, including a six off Richards, before he was caught – also by Richards. Both men had announced their retirement, the former Somerset team-mates were not due to oppose each other in county cricket again, and they embraced as they left the field after Richards hit the winning runs.

Man of the Match: M. P. Maynard.

Durham

G. Fowler c and b Croft	24	S. Hutton not out	18
W. Larkins b Lefebvre	75		
P. W. G. Parker not out	73	B 4, l-b 4, w 2	10
I. T. Botham c Richards b Watkin	33		
P. Bainbridge c Cottey b Lefebvre	10	1/41 2/148 3/196 (5 wkts, 60 overs)	245
A. C. Cummins c Metson b Barwick	2	4/220 5/226	

†C. W. Scott, P. J. Berry, *D. A. Graveney and S. P. Hughes did not bat.

Bowling: Watkin 11–1–33–1; Lefebvre 12–4–31–2; Barwick 12–2–44–1; Croft 12–1–42–1; Dale 4–0–24–0; Richards 9–0–63–0.

Glamorgan

S. P. James lbw b Berry	48	P. A. Cottey not out	0
A. Dale run out	29	B 2, l-b 18, w 1, n-b 4	25
M. P. Maynard c Larkins b Berry	101		
I. V. A. Richards not out	45	1/54 2/154 3/239 (3 wkts, 57.1 overs)	248

*H. Morris, R. D. B. Croft, R. P. Lefebvre, †C. P. Metson, S. L. Watkin and S. R. Barwick did not bat.

Bowling: Cummins 12–1–43–0; Hughes 9–0–27–0; Botham 12–1–49–0; Graveney 10.1–0–47–0; Berry 7–0–35–2.

Umpires: D. J. Constant and J. H. Harris.

GLOUCESTERSHIRE v YORKSHIRE

At Bristol, July 7. Yorkshire won by two wickets. Toss: Gloucestershire.

Hartley struck the winning boundary with two balls left, the fifth time in 1993 that Gloucestershire had lost in the final over. Wright, the home captain, was bowled for nought and his misery was compounded when he collided with an umpire and left the field with concussion. Two days later he resigned the captaincy, saying he wanted to concentrate more on his own play. But the day began with promise for Gloucestershire; Broad, who batted the full 60 overs, and Hodgson opened with a stand of 165. However, an attractive 90 from Richardson, supported by Blakey and White, put Yorkshire well on course until Alleyne ended his innings with a fine return catch and two balls later had White taken at midwicket. Yorkshire needed 23 off the last two overs but found the composure they needed to score them.

Man of the Match: B. C. Broad.

Gloucestershire

B. C. Broad not out	114	S. G. Hinks not out	19
G. D. Hodgson c White b Robinson	62	B 1, l-b 7, w 2, n-b 4	14
M. W. Alleyne c Moxon b Gough	32		
*A. J. Wright b Gough	0	1/165 2/210 3/210 (3 wkts, 60 overs)	241

†R. C. Russell, R. J. Scott, R. M. Wight, C. A. Walsh, A. M. Smith and K. E. Cooper did not bat.

Bowling: Jarvis 12–1–57–0; Gough 10–3–31–2; Hartley 12–0–60–0; Robinson 12–2–31–1; Stemp 10–0–42–0; White 4–1–12–0.

Yorkshire

*M. D. Moxon c and b Wight	29	D. Gough run out	2
A. P. Grayson b Cooper	12	R. D. Stemp not out	1
R. B. Richardson c and b Alleyne	90		
S. A. Kellett b Walsh	3	L-b 8, w 5, n-b 2	15
†R. J. Blakey c sub b Alleyne	28		
C. White c Walsh b Alleyne	28	1/33 2/60 3/92 (8 wkts, 59.4 overs)	243
P. W. Jarvis c Alleyne b Walsh	13	4/139 5/200 6/201	
P. J. Hartley not out	22	7/217 8/222	

M. A. Robinson did not bat.

Bowling: Cooper 12–3–35–1; Walsh 11.4–1–40–2; Smith 12–1–58–0; Scott 6–0–30–0; Wight 8–1–24–1; Alleyne 10–0–48–3.

Umpires: R. Julian and P. Willey.

LEICESTERSHIRE v SURREY

At Leicester, July 7. Surrey won by seven wickets. Toss: Leicestershire.

The 1992 finalists batted miserably, although another disappointing Grace Road pitch did not help. Cracks in the one prepared for the game prompted a switch to the wicket on which Leicestershire had just beaten Lancashire in three days. This offered prodigious turn but negligible pace: nine out of 13 wickets fell to spin. Even so, Waqar Younis remained a potent threat. Once he had bowled Briers behind his legs, only Boon held firm. Surrey's three off-spinners, Boiling, Smith and Lynch, exploited the conditions and Smith earned the match award on his NatWest debut. With only 129 to defend Leicestershire had to bowl accurately; instead they conceded 48 in the first eight overs – Benjamin gave away 33 in four – leaving their own spinners, Potter and Pierson, a near-impossible task. Stewart scored 56 off 38 balls, with 12 fours, and his team won before tea.

Man of the Match: A. W. Smith.

Leicestershire

T. J. Boon c D. J. Bicknell b Smith....	45	G. J. Parsons b Waqar Younis........	2
*N. E. Briers b Waqar Younis........	17	A. R. K. Pierson c Thorpe	
J. J. Whitaker c Thorpe b Boiling.....	22	b M. P. Bicknell.	1
J. D. R. Benson c Lynch b Smith.....	2	A. D. Mullally b Waqar Younis.......	4
L. Potter c Thorpe b Boiling..........	1	B 1, l-b 2, w 1..............	4
V. J. Wells not out...................	17		
W. K. M. Benjamin b Smith	10	1/29 2/61 3/75 4/84 5/94 (46.5 overs) 129	
†P. A. Nixon lbw b Lynch	4	6/104 7/119 8/123 9/124	

Bowling: Waqar Younis 7.5–1–18–3; M. P. Bicknell 8–2–26–1; Benjamin 3–0–18–0; Boiling 12–1–29–2; Smith 12–4–25–3; Lynch 4–0–10–1.

Surrey

D. J. Bicknell b Potter	19	A. D. Brown not out	14
*†A. J. Stewart b Potter	56	L-b 1, w 2, n-b 4............	7
G. P. Thorpe c Nixon b Pierson	10		
M. A. Lynch not out	25	1/75 2/88 3/96 (3 wkts, 32.1 overs) 131	

D. M. Ward, A. W. Smith, M. P. Bicknell, Waqar Younis, J. Boiling and J. E. Benjamin did not bat.

Bowling: Benjamin 4–0–33–0; Mullally 4–2–15–0; Pierson 12–1–38–1; Potter 12–0–40–2; Parsons 0.1–0–4–0.

Umpires: V. A. Holder and P. B. Wight.

NOTTINGHAMSHIRE v SOMERSET

At Nottingham, July 7. Somerset won by three wickets. Toss: Nottinghamshire.

Somerset, who had pushed Nottinghamshire out of the Benson and Hedges Cup in May, completed a knockout double, with Folland playing a major role again. The match was played on the Trent Bridge Test pitch and was in its sixth day of use, but Nottinghamshire seemed well on course for a big total as Cairns and Robinson took them to 162 for three. Cairns hit six fours and a six in his 71, and was rewarded with his county cap at lunch and the match award – for the second time running – later. But his team lost that impetus against the tight seam bowling of Mallender and Rose. Although 204 was still a testing target, Folland, who struck nine fours, set Somerset on the path to a victory they achieved with 13 balls to spare.

Man of the Match: C. L. Cairns.

Nottinghamshire

D. W. Randall c Folland b Mallender	..	5	R. A. Pick c Folland b Rose	 0
P. R. Pollard c Burns b Caddick	...	22	M. G. Field-Buss not out	 5
*R. T. Robinson c Lathwell b Mallender		41	J. A. Afford b Mallender	 1
P. Johnson c Burns b van Troost	.....	19	L-b 6, w 8, n-b 8	 22
C. L. Cairns b Caddick	....	71		
M. A. Crawley b van Troost	....	8	1/27 2/27 3/65	(55.4 overs) 203
C. C. Lewis lbw b Rose	....	7	4/162 5/175 6/189	
†B. N. French lbw b Rose	....	2	7/189 8/190 9/192	

Bowling: Caddick 10–2–34–2; Mallender 10.4–2–33–3; van Troost 11–1–45–2; Mushtaq Ahmed 12–1–44–0; Rose 12–0–41–3.

Somerset

M. N. Lathwell c French b Pick	......	8	Mushtaq Ahmed not out	 5
N. A. Folland lbw b Lewis	....	63	A. R. Caddick not out	 0
R. J. Harden lbw b Lewis	....	31	L-b 16, w 4, n-b 4	 24
*C. J. Tavaré b Pick	....	30		
K. A. Parsons b Cairns	....	33	1/36 2/110 3/115	(7 wkts, 57.5 overs) 204
†N. D. Burns b Cairns	....	2	4/184 5/185	
G. D. Rose c Pollard b Lewis	....	8	6/195 7/199	

N. A. Mallender and A. P. van Troost did not bat.

Bowling: Lewis 11–1–24–3; Cairns 10.5–1–39–2; Pick 12–1–38–2; Afford 11–1–39–0; Field-Buss 12–1–44–0; Crawley 1–0–4–0.

Umpires: N. T. Plews and G. A. Stickley.

SUSSEX v HAMPSHIRE

At Hove, July 7. Sussex won by nine wickets. Toss: Hampshire.

Sussex strolled to a crushing victory after David Smith and Athey broke the tournament record for the first wicket. Smith led from the front while Athey, dropped twice on 55, hit the shot of the day, a thundering cover drive off Shine. Their partnership was the first double-century for any Sussex wicket in limited-overs competitions, and among the first to congratulate them afterwards was 83-year-old John Langridge, whose first-wicket partnership of 490 with E. H. Bowley in 1933 remains a county record. They had put on 248 when, with the scores level, Smith was yorked by Connor for 123. Speight hit the winning boundary. Another Smith, Robin of Hampshire, hit an undefeated 104. But Gower and Nicholas were out cheaply after lunch and although Smith and Marshall added 59 in the final ten overs, a total of 248 never looked sufficient on a Hove belter. This was only Sussex's second win over a first-class county in the NatWest since they last won it in 1986.

Man of the Match: D. M. Smith.

Hampshire

T. C. Middleton c Moores b Stephenson		9	M. D. Marshall not out	 31
V. P. Terry c Moores b Stephenson	....	71	L-b 7, w 6, n-b 6	 19
R. A. Smith not out	....	104		
D. I. Gower c Smith b Jones	....	2	1/20 2/146	(4 wkts, 60 overs) 248
*M. C. J. Nicholas c Jones b Salisbury	.	12	3/157 4/179	

K. D. James, †A. N. Aymes, S. D. Udal, C. A. Connor and K. J. Shine did not bat.

Bowling: Stephenson 12–3–52–2; Giddins 12–3–41–0; Jones 12–1–60–1; Salisbury 12–3–41–1; Greenfield 6–0–24–0; C. M. Wells 6–0–23–0.

Sussex

D. M. Smith b Connor	....	123
C. W. J. Athey not out	....	107
M. P. Speight not out	....	4
L-b 2, w 2, n-b 14	....	18

1/248   (1 wkt, 58.5 overs) 252

*A. P. Wells, K. Greenfield, C. M. Wells, F. D. Stephenson, †P. Moores, I. D. K. Salisbury, A. N. Jones and E. S. H. Giddins did not bat.

Bowling: Marshall 12–0–36–0; Connor 11.5–0–59–1; Shine 9.3–0–61–0; James 12–1–47–0; Udal 12–0–42–0; Nicholas 1.3–0–5–0.

Umpires: A. A. Jones and G. Sharp.

WARWICKSHIRE v KENT

At Birmingham, July 7. Warwickshire won by five wickets. Toss: Kent.

Warwickshire won a fluctuating tie to knock Kent out of the NatWest Trophy for the second year running thanks to Paul Smith and Reeve, who shared a stand of 79 in 16 overs. Reeve remained to add another 78 with the unorthodox Twose, steer his side home with three balls to spare and win the match award. In the morning Ward and Hooper set off at a frantic pace but Kent did well to reach 262 for nine after tottering at 172 for seven in the 48th over. Fleming started the recovery with 34, and Ealham completed it with his first one-day fifty, hitting three sixes and three fours, in 48 balls. The early loss of Warwickshire's top three revived Kent's hopes until Smith's 61 reshaped the innings.

Man of the Match: D. A. Reeve.

Kent

T. R. Ward c Penney b Donald	....	50	M. A. Ealham not out	....	58
*M. R. Benson c Piper b Munton	......	16	D. W. Headley c Piper b Donald	......	0
C. L. Hooper c Reeve b Donald	....	38	M. J. McCague not out	....	6
N. R. Taylor c Piper b Munton	....	25	B 4, l-b 6, w 7, n-b 6	....	23
N. J. Llong c Penney b Twose	....	1			
G. R. Cowdrey c Penney b Twose	.....	5	1/41 2/99 3/118	(9 wkts, 60 overs) 262
M. V. Fleming c Munton b Donald	....	34	4/123 5/137 6/150	
†S. A. Marsh b P. A. Smith	....	6	7/172 8/226 9/227	

Bowling: Donald 11–1–69–4; Munton 12–3–25–2; Reeve 10–2–28–0; N. M. K. Smith 7–0–40–0; Twose 12–3–30–2; P. A. Smith 8–0–60–1.

Warwickshire

A. J. Moles c and b Fleming	....	37	T. L. Penney not out	....	7
J. D. Ratcliffe c Marsh b McCague	....	18			
D. P. Ostler lbw b Headley	....	10	B 1, l-b 20, w 2, n-b 2	....	25
P. A. Smith c Marsh b Ealham	....	61			
*D. A. Reeve not out	....	72	1/32 2/58 3/95	(5 wkts, 59.3 overs) 265
R. G. Twose run out	....	35	4/174 5/252	

N. M. K. Smith, †K. J. Piper, A. A. Donald and T. A. Munton did not bat.

Bowling: McCague 12–1–54–1; Headley 12–2–48–1; Hooper 11.3–1–49–0; Ealham 12–1–38–1; Fleming 12–1–55–1.

Umpires: D. R. Shepherd and A. G. T. Whitehead.

WORCESTERSHIRE v DERBYSHIRE

At Worcester, July 7. Worcestershire won by four wickets. Toss: Derbyshire.

Curtis had not yet translated his prolific form in the Championship into the limited-overs game, but he chose the ideal occasion for his first one-day fifty of the season, steering Worcestershire with this sixth. Hick, with 48 in 53 balls, had helped him put on 82 for the second wicket, but Curtis's 82 was the decisive innings – though after he was dismissed 19 runs short of victory two more wickets fell before Worcestershire got home. Adams and Morris atoned for the early loss of both openers by adding 162 in 40 overs. But from 175 for two with 13 overs remaining Derbyshire managed only 69 more runs – not the best preparation for the Benson and Hedges final three days later.

Man of the Match: T. S. Curtis.

Derbyshire

*K. J. Barnett c Rhodes b Benjamin ...	1	A. E. Warner lbw b Tolley	2
P. D. Bowler c Rhodes b Tolley	6	D. E. Malcolm b Tolley	0
J. E. Morris b Newport.............	71	O. H. Mortensen not out............	4
C. J. Adams b Radford	93		
T. J. G. O'Gorman c Illingworth		L-b 13, w 9, n-b 4..........	26
b Newport .	1		
D. G. Cork b Benjamin	23	1/10 2/13 3/175 (9 wkts, 60 overs) 244	
F. A. Griffith c Leatherdale b Newport .	8	4/177 5/198 6/223	
†K. M. Krikken not out	9	7/233 8/235 9/236	

Bowling: Benjamin 12–3–38–2; Tolley 9–1–25–3; Newport 11–0–72–3; Radford 12–1–52–1; Illingworth 12–1–22–0; Hick 4–0–22–0.

Worcestershire

*T. S. Curtis b Warner	82	P. J. Newport not out	13
W. P. C. Weston c Warner b Griffith ..	27	N. V. Radford not out.............	4
G. A. Hick c Barnett b Malcolm	48	L-b 3, w 4, n-b 12..........	19
D. B. D'Oliveira lbw b Mortensen.....	15		
D. A. Leatherdale run out	36	1/67 2/149 3/174 (6 wkts, 57.2 overs) 245	
†S. J. Rhodes c Mortensen b Cork.....	1	4/226 5/228 6/228	

R. K. Illingworth, C. M. Tolley and K. C. G. Benjamin did not bat.

Bowling: Warner 12–1–33–1; Malcolm 11–1–77–1; Cork 12–2–55–1; Griffith 10.2–0–46–1; Mortensen 12–2–31–1.

Umpires: M. J. Kitchen and B. Leadbeater.

QUARTER-FINALS

GLAMORGAN v WORCESTERSHIRE

At Swansea, July 27, 28. Glamorgan won by 104 runs. Toss: Worcestershire.

Glamorgan qualified for the semi-finals for only the second time in the competition's 31 seasons – the other being in 1977 – with an easy win against a team they had just defeated in both the County Championship and Sunday League. When play began at 2.15 p.m. Glamorgan capitalised on a good start with James, overcoming a broken thumb, and Dale putting on 84 for the second wicket. Then Maynard struck nine fours in an entertaining 65-ball 84. Worcestershire struggled to 40 for two from 23 overs by the close, their progress restricted by Lefebvre, whose opening eight overs conceded only four runs and claimed Curtis, bowled. Their hopes ended when Hick was caught in the third over next morning; only a last-wicket partnership of 31 saved them from a worse defeat.

Man of the Match: M. P. Maynard.

Close of play: Worcestershire 40-2 (23 overs) (G. A. Hick 3*, D. B. D'Oliveira 0*).

Glamorgan

S. P. James c Leatherdale b Newport	68	R. P. Lefebvre not out	8
*H. Morris c Rhodes b Lampitt	39	S. L. Watkin c Rhodes b Lampitt	0
A. Dale c and b Newport	41		
M. P. Maynard run out	84	B 1, l-b 7, w 6, n-b 2	16
I. V. A. Richards b Radford	12		
P. A. Cottey c Rhodes b Radford	11	1/66 2/150 3/175	(9 wkts, 60 overs) 279
R. D. B. Croft lbw b Radford	0	4/204 5/228 6/228	
†C. P. Metson lbw b Illingworth	0	7/233 8/279 9/279	

S. R. Barwick did not bat.

Bowling: Newport 12–1–41–2; Tolley 10–0–40–0; Radford 12–1–55–3; Lampitt 12–2–56–2; Illingworth 11–1–64–1; Hick 3–0–15–0.

Worcestershire

*T. S. Curtis b Lefebvre	10	P. J. Newport b Croft	2
W. P. C. Weston c and b Dale	25	R. K. Illingworth run out	18
G. A. Hick c Lefebvre b Dale	11	C. M. Tolley not out	12
D. B. D'Oliveira c Lefebvre b Barwick	24		
D. A. Leatherdale b Dale	20	B 1, l-b 8	9
†S. J. Rhodes c and b Barwick	19	1/21 2/40 3/59	(50.5 overs) 175
S. R. Lampitt c Metson b Lefebvre	17	4/86 5/101 6/127	
N. V. Radford run out	0	7/141 8/144 9/144	

Bowling: Watkin 9–2–31–0; Lefebvre 11–5–13–2; Barwick 10–0–39–2; Dale 12–0–54–3; Richards 3.5–1–13–0; Croft 5–1–16–1.

Umpires: R. Julian and B. J. Meyer.

NORTHAMPTONSHIRE v SUSSEX

At Northampton, July 27, 28. Sussex won by 40 runs. Toss: Northamptonshire.

Sussex fought back magnificently in the field to defeat the Trophy holders after bad light sent the match into a second day. Northamptonshire were well placed when they opted to come off, requiring a further 85 off 20 overs with seven wickets in hand. But the loss of Lamb, run out by Alan Wells's throw just before play was suspended, proved crucial. Dropped at slip on nought, Lamb hit 71 in 88 balls and dominated a 112-run stand with Felton. Next morning, inspired by Stephenson, Sussex applied steady pressure and Northamptonshire cracked. Felton finally lost patience after 53 runs in 52 overs, holing out at long-on, and the last seven wickets fell for 43 runs in 14 overs. Sussex had compiled a defensible though not impregnable total on a slow pitch; Smith and Athey provided a solid start and Speight hit 34 off 26 deliveries.

Man of the Match: F. D. Stephenson.

Close of play: Northamptonshire 146-3 (40 overs) (N. A. Felton 40*, M. B. Loye 7*).

Sussex

D. M. Smith b Cook	47	I. D. K. Salisbury run out	3
C. W. J. Athey st Ripley b Cook	42	A. C. S. Pigott b Taylor	3
M. P. Speight c Ripley b Ambrose	34	E. S. H. Giddins not out	0
*A. P. Wells run out	23	B 1, l-b 7, w 5, n-b 4	17
C. M. Wells c Lamb b Cook	7		
J. A. North c Lamb b Curran	11	1/88 2/121 3/135	(9 wkts, 60 overs) 230
F. D. Stephenson run out	18	4/152 5/171 6/181	
†P. Moores not out	25	7/212 8/216 9/225	

Bowling: Ambrose 12–4–25–1; Taylor 12–2–44–1; Curran 12–1–38–1; Penberthy 6–0–35–0; Cook 12–1–53–1; Bailey 6–1–27–0.

Northamptonshire

A. Fordham b Giddins	16	C. E. L. Ambrose b Stephenson	0
N. A. Felton c sub b Salisbury	53	J. P. Taylor b Salisbury	1
R. J. Bailey c Moores b Stephenson	4	N. G. B. Cook c Moores b Pigott	1
*A. J. Lamb run out	71	L-b 12, w 8, n-b 2	22
M. B. Loye c Moores b Pigott	8		
K. M. Curran c Moores b Giddins	1	1/17 2/26 3/138	(55.2 overs) 190
A. L. Penberthy run out	3	4/147 5/156 6/167	
†D. Ripley not out	10	7/177 8/177 9/180	

Bowling: Stephenson 11–5–25–2; Giddins 10–3–21–2; Salisbury 12–0–49–2; C. M. Wells 12–0–43–0; Pigott 10.2–1–40–2.

Umpires: R. Palmer and D. R. Shepherd.

SOMERSET v SURREY

At Taunton, July 27, 28. Somerset won by 43 runs. Toss: Surrey.

In dull, threatening weather Somerset had problems against a lively attack on a slightly fresh pitch after rain delayed the start until 2.30 p.m. But after Lathwell fell to a brilliant catch by Boiling, who also bowled demandingly, Harden and Tavaré put on 65 in 18 overs and important impetus came from Mushtaq Ahmed, with a jaunty 35 in 31 balls, and van Troost, who hit four fours from five deliveries. Stewart was dismissed on the first evening but, resuming in much better conditions, Thorpe shared productive stands with Darren Bicknell and Brown. At 144 for three in the 45th over Surrey were firm favourites. But three overs spanning lunch turned the match. In the final over of a beautiful spell, Mushtaq had Brown stumped; then Mallender trapped Ward lbw and – the critical dismissal – Caddick had Thorpe superbly caught in the gully by the substitute Trump. Surrey found no way back from 153 for six, and Caddick finished them off, taking five for 30.

Man of the Match: Mushtaq Ahmed.

Close of play: Surrey 26-1 (9.5 overs) (D. J. Bicknell 5*, G. P. Thorpe 3*).

Somerset

A. N. Hayhurst b Waqar Younis	3	A. R. Caddick c Butcher	
M. N. Lathwell c Boiling b Butcher	34	b M. P. Bicknell	8
N. A. Folland c Waqar Younis b Boiling	17	N. A. Mallender not out	8
R. J. Harden c Lynch b M. P. Bicknell	33	A. P. van Troost not out	17
*C. J. Tavaré lbw b Lynch	29	L-b 12, w 10, n-b 4	26
†N. D. Burns c Lynch b M. P. Bicknell	2		
G. D. Rose c M. P. Bicknell b Butcher	18	1/19 2/60 3/63	(9 wkts, 60 overs) 230
Mushtaq Ahmed c Butcher		4/128 5/134 6/134	
b M. P. Bicknell	35	7/174 8/199 9/206	

Bowling: Waqar Younis 12–1–44–1; M. P. Bicknell 12–2–35–4; Benjamin 7–0–38–0; Butcher 12–2–57–2; Boiling 12–1–22–1; Lynch 5–1–22–1.

Surrey

D. J. Bicknell c Burns b Caddick	32	Waqar Younis b Rose	3
*†A. J. Stewart c Burns b Caddick	15	J. Boiling b Caddick	2
G. P. Thorpe c sub b Caddick	58	J. E. Benjamin not out	1
M. A. Lynch c and b Mushtaq Ahmed	5		
A. D. Brown st Burns		L-b 6, w 7, n-b 2	15
b Mushtaq Ahmed	26		
D. M. Ward lbw b Mallender	3	1/23 2/89 3/102	(56.5 overs) 187
M. A. Butcher c Burns b Mallender	15	4/144 5/149 6/153	
M. P. Bicknell b Caddick	12	7/176 8/181 9/186	

Bowling: Caddick 10.5–1–30–5; Mallender 12–3–28–2; Rose 12–1–42–1; van Troost 10–0–45–0; Mushtaq Ahmed 12–2–36–2.

Umpires: J. D. Bond and J. H. Hampshire.

YORKSHIRE v WARWICKSHIRE

At Leeds, July 27, 28. Warwickshire won by 21 runs. Toss: Warwickshire.

Warwickshire reached the semi-finals for the third successive year after a game that Yorkshire may have lost mentally before the start. Expressing concern about Headingley pitches, the players had wanted the tie moved to Scarborough. But after a bad start by Warwickshire the pitch played well enough, Ratcliffe and Reeve sharing a decisive stand of 136 and Ratcliffe going on to a maiden limited-overs century, with a six and eight fours. Thanks to the rain which delayed the start, Yorkshire had to resume on the second day. The match was all but lost already, however, after they slumped to 69 for five in 29 overs of strokeless indecision, especially against Donald, in his last match before joining South Africa in Sri Lanka. The final act of folly came when Byas ran himself out off the last ball of the day, attempting a suicidal second to Paul Smith. Smith also bowled accurately next morning, when Blakey and White revived Yorkshire by adding 105, a brave effort which equalled the sixth-wicket record for the competition but came too late.

Man of the Match: J. D. Ratcliffe.

Close of play: Yorkshire 69-5 (29 overs) (R. J. Blakey 2*).

Warwickshire

A. J. Moles c Blakey b Gough	2	†K. J. Piper b Hartley	1
J. D. Ratcliffe b White	105	G. C. Small b Gough	2
D. P. Ostler c White b Hartley	2	A. A. Donald lbw b Gough	0
P. A. Smith run out	6	L-b 5, w 2, n-b 12	19
*D. A. Reeve c Metcalfe b Robinson . .	50		
R. G. Twose lbw b Hartley	36	1/5 2/14 3/31	(59.4 overs) 245
T. L. Penney c Batty b White	10	4/167 5/182 6/204	
N. M. K. Smith not out	14	7/238 8/240 9/245	

Bowling: Hartley 12-0-64-3; Gough 11.4-2-31-3; Robinson 12-3-35-1; Batty 10-0-63-0; White 12-1-41-2; Grayson 2-0-6-0.

Yorkshire

*M. D. Moxon c Ratcliffe b Small	7	D. Gough c N. M. K. Smith	
A. P. Grayson b Donald	5	b P. A. Smith .	16
R. B. Richardson c Penney b Reeve . .	8	J. D. Batty c Penney b P. A. Smith . .	3
D. Byas run out	20	M. A. Robinson not out	0
A. A. Metcalfe lbw b P. A. Smith	12	B 1, l-b 12, w 15, n-b 2	30
†R. J. Blakey c Ostler b P. A. Smith . .	75		
C. White c Ostler b N. M. K. Smith . . .	46	1/9 2/23 3/31 4/59 5/69	(59.2 overs) 224
P. J. Hartley b Donald	2	6/174 7/187 8/203 9/224	

Bowling: Donald 12-3-38-2; Small 12-2-38-1; Reeve 12-3-42-1; P. A. Smith 11.2-1-37-4; Twose 8-0-39-0; N. M. K. Smith 4-0-17-1.

Umpires: J. W. Holder and R. A. White.

SEMI-FINALS

SOMERSET v WARWICKSHIRE

At Taunton, August 10. Warwickshire won by 52 runs. Toss: Warwickshire.

Warwickshire, losing semi-finalists in 1991 and 1992, reached Lord's at last – and a key player was their captain, Reeve, who had retired with concussion. He collided with the wicket-keeper, Burns, while batting, but returned in the 56th over, quickly dispensed with his runner and flourished to reach 28. Later he added three wickets. Warwickshire recovered splendidly after losing their openers for 27 runs in 15 overs. Ostler's excellent 90-ball fifty held the innings together. Somerset put up a fine performance in the field, with two excellent catches by Harden, a superb stumping by Burns and Caddick's direct hit from the boundary to run out Penney. Small limped off after bowling five overs of the Somerset innings, but had already dismissed both openers, aided by a brilliant slip catch by Ostler. Against determined and well-organised out-cricket, Somerset gradually fell behind the clock, despite the fighting performance of Folland. He found only two partners to stay with him: Harden and Burns. Folland was ninth out for 61, the highest score of the match.

Man of the Match: D. P. Ostler.

Warwickshire

Asif Din c Burns b van Troost	15	G. C. Small b Rose	11
J. D. Ratcliffe c Harden b van Troost	4	†K. J. Piper not out	4
D. P. Ostler c Harden b Mallender	58		
P. A. Smith st Burns b Mushtaq Ahmed	33	B 4, l-b 15, w 12, n-b 4	35
*D. A. Reeve not out	28		
R. G. Twose b van Troost	41	1/20 2/27 3/89 (8 wkts, 60 overs)	252
T. L. Penney run out	6	4/154 5/183 6/216	
N. M. K. Smith c and b Rose	17	7/216 8/236	

T. A. Munton did not bat.

D. A. Reeve, when 11, retired hurt at 125 and resumed at 216-6.

Bowling: Caddick 12–2–41–0; Mallender 12–4–32–1; van Troost 12–1–57–3; Rose 12–0–63–2; Mushtaq Ahmed 12–0–40–1.

Somerset

A. N. Hayhurst c Ostler b Small	2	A. R. Caddick lbw b Reeve	0
M. N. Lathwell lbw b Small	12	N. A. Mallender not out	11
N. A. Folland c Munton b P. A. Smith	61	A. P. van Troost b Twose	3
R. J. Harden c Twose b P. A. Smith	29	B 1, l-b 9, w 8, n-b 12	30
*C. J. Tavaré run out	1		
G. D. Rose c and b N. M. K. Smith	6	1/17 2/20 3/73 (56.3 overs)	200
Mushtaq Ahmed lbw b Reeve	14	4/86 5/99 6/122	
†N. D. Burns c P. A. Smith b Reeve	31	7/182 8/182 9/195	

Bowling: Small 5–2–9–2; Munton 10–3–23–0; Reeve 12–0–37–3; P. A. Smith 12–1–40–2; Ratcliffe 1–0–4–0; N. M. K. Smith 11–1–51–1; Twose 5.3–0–26–1.

Umpires: D. J. Constant and B. Dudleston.

SUSSEX v GLAMORGAN

At Hove, August 10. Sussex won by three wickets. Toss: Glamorgan.

Sussex reached their eighth NatWest final with four balls to spare after a thrilling game that was swinging Glamorgan's way until Lenham and Wells came together with Sussex 110 for six. They had just 15 overs to double it, but Lenham immediately got on to the front foot. Richards, looking for a farewell appearance at Lord's, was hit for 25 in his three overs, and once Sussex got up a head of steam there was no stopping them. Welsh voices in the crowd of 5,500 fell silent as their bowlers wilted. Earlier, Maynard had propped up Glamorgan with 84 after they batted first on a good wicket. James and Morris had opened solidly but, when Richards was caught and bowled, the initiative was with Sussex. Stephenson's bowling was outstanding and keen fielding made Glamorgan work for every run. In reply Sussex were reeling at 42 for three after 26 overs against the excellent line and length of Watkin, Lefebvre and Barwick. Although Wells increased the tempo, wickets were falling until Lenham joined him. Wells's 106 runs came from 131 balls with eight fours and a six. It was a brilliant one-day innings in which he manipulated the ball masterfully and Lenham, who finished with 47 off 43 balls, gave him excellent support.

Man of the Match: A. P. Wells.

Glamorgan

S. P. James lbw b Lenham	31	R. P. Lefebvre not out		8
*H. Morris b Pigott	21	S. L. Watkin b Stephenson		2
A. Dale c Smith b Pigott	1	S. R. Barwick b Pigott		1
M. P. Maynard c Wells b Stephenson	84	L-b 15, w 6		21
I. V. A. Richards c and b Greenfield	22			
P. A. Cottey b Greenfield	1	1/54 2/56 3/71	(60 overs)	220
R. D. B. Croft b Salisbury	20	4/124 5/138 6/195		
†C. P. Metson c Wells b Stephenson	8	7/204 8/208 9/216		

Bowling: Stephenson 12-1-25-3; Giddins 12-2-46-0; Lenham 7-0-31-1; Pigott 9-1-23-3; Salisbury 11-1-45-1; Greenfield 9-1-35-2.

Sussex

D. M. Smith b Watkin	8	N. J. Lenham b Lefebvre		47
C. W. J. Athey c Maynard b Dale	17	I. D. K. Salisbury not out		2
M. P. Speight c Lefebvre b Watkin	0	L-b 4, w 4, n-b 2		10
*A. P. Wells not out	106			
K. Greenfield run out	1	1/12 2/12 3/42	(7 wkts, 59.2 overs)	224
F. D. Stephenson c Cottey b Watkin	25	4/47 5/86		
†P. Moores c Richards b Dale	8	6/110 7/217		

A. C. S. Pigott and E. S. H. Giddins did not bat.

Bowling: Watkin 12-2-43-3; Lefebvre 12-4-24-1; Barwick 11.2-1-33-0; Dale 12-3-43-2; Croft 9-0-52-0; Richards 3-0-25-0.

Umpires: J. C. Balderstone and K. E. Palmer.

FINAL

SUSSEX v WARWICKSHIRE

At Lord's, September 4. Warwickshire won by five wickets. Toss: Warwickshire.

The 53rd one-day final at Lord's was widely regarded as the greatest ever played. Off the last ball, Warwickshire overhauled the Sussex total of 321 for six, the highest score in a Cup final. The result has to be judged in the context of poor Sussex fielding and some unimaginative captaincy by Wells, but the magnificence of the victory and the thrilling nature of the cricket was beyond dispute.

The eighth consecutive win in this final for the team batting second came after Warwickshire had chosen to bowl first in the hope that, even without their customary match-winner Donald, their seamers would be able to make use of the morning dampness. This did not happen. Munton dismissed Athey with just four on the board but this almost looked like an own goal when Speight came in to play the innings that set the tone of the match. Pulling off the front foot and jumping down the wicket to the bemused Munton as if he were a spinner, Speight scored 50 off 51 deliveries and allowed David Smith, less pugilistic than normal, to provide the backbone of the innings.

Smith, who averages over 50 in the competition after a career spanning 20 years and three counties, returned from injury to score 124, full of powerful drives. He shared stands of 103 with Speight, at a run a ball, and 119 in 16 overs with Lenham, who played a depth charge of an innings: 58 from 51 balls. The fielders were demoralised and Sussex scored 83 from the final ten overs. Smith was run out off the final ball – which hours later attained far more significance than anyone imagined at the time.

Warwickshire's task looked hopeless, the more so when they lost both openers with the score on 18. Paul Smith, all long hair and long handle, then added 75 in 16 overs with Ostler and, when Ostler clipped Salisbury to mid-wicket, Asif Din entered to play the innings of his life. It was only after tea that Sussex first realised the awful possibility of defeat. Smith, with flowing off-drives, and Asif Din, with wristy improvisation, added 71 in 15 overs. Sussex, bowlers and fielders, were haemorrhaging runs although Wells might have staunched the flow if he had switched his bowlers more: Greenfield, in particular, could have been introduced earlier.

[*Patrick Eagar*]

Roger Twose hits the winning runs at the end of the thrilling NatWest final.

Smith was fourth out at 164 in the 36th over and Asif Din and Reeve were required to score at more than a run a ball. They kept going, but, with 20 needed from two twilit overs Sussex still held a slender advantage. They strengthened their position in the 59th when Giddins conceded just five runs and had Asif Din caught at deep cover. He had scored 104 from 106 balls and added 142 in 23 overs with his captain Reeve. Fifteen were needed from the last over: Reeve, without Ian Botham's outrageous talent but with much of his competitive sense, scored 13 from the first five deliveries. Twose, facing his first and last ball, sliced it through the close off-side field for two to give Warwickshire their victory; stumps were pulled at both ends before the completion of the second run, and Warwickshire should have been awarded the match through losing fewer wickets. However, it was a day for romance rather than technicalities. – Paul Weaver

Man of the Match: Asif Din.　　*Attendance:* 25,908; *receipts* £670,950.

Sussex

D. M. Smith run out	124	K. Greenfield not out		8
C. W. J. Athey c Piper b Munton	0			
M. P. Speight c Piper b Reeve	50	L-b 11, w 18, n-b 16		45
*A. P. Wells b N. M. K. Smith	33			
F. D. Stephenson c N. M. K. Smith		1/4 (2) 2/107 (3)	(6 wkts, 60 overs)	321
b Twose	4	3/183 (4) 4/190 (5)		
N. J. Lenham lbw b Reeve	58	5/309 (6) 6/321 (1)		

†P. Moores, I. D. K. Salisbury, A. C. S. Pigott and E. S. H. Giddins did not bat.

Bowling: Small 12–0–71–0; Munton 9–0–67–1; P. A. Smith 7–0–45–0; Reeve 12–1–60–2; N. M. K. Smith 12–1–37–1; Twose 8–1–30–1.

Warwickshire

A. J. Moles c Moores b Pigott	2	R. G. Twose not out		2
J. D. Ratcliffe b Stephenson	13	B 3, l-b 13, w 13, n-b 6		35
D. P. Ostler c Smith b Salisbury	25			
P. A. Smith c Moores b Stephenson	60	1/18 (2) 2/18 (1)	(5 wkts, 60 overs)	322
Asif Din c Speight b Giddins	104	3/93 (3) 4/164 (4)		
*D. A. Reeve not out	81	5/306 (5)		

N. M. K. Smith, †K. J. Piper, G. C. Small and T. A. Munton did not bat.

Bowling: Giddins 12–0–57–1; Stephenson 12–2–51–2; Pigott 11–0–74–1; Salisbury 11–0–59–1; Greenfield 7–0–31–0; Lenham 7–0–34–0.

Umpires: H. D. Bird and M. J. Kitchen.

NATWEST BANK TROPHY RECORDS

(Including Gillette Cup, 1963-80)

Batting

Highest individual scores: 206, A. I. Kallicharran, Warwickshire v Oxfordshire, Birmingham, 1984; 177, C. G. Greenidge, Hampshire v Glamorgan, Southampton, 1975; 172*, G. A. Hick, Worcestershire v Devon, Worcester, 1987; 165*, V. P. Terry, Hampshire v Berkshire, Southampton, 1985; 162*, I. V. A. Richards, Glamorgan v Oxfordshire, Swansea, 1993; 162*, C. J. Tavaré, Somerset v Devon, Torquay, 1990; 159, C. L. Smith, Hampshire v Cheshire, Chester, 1989; 158, G. D. Barlow, Middlesex v Lancashire, Lord's, 1984; 158, Zaheer Abbas, Gloucestershire v Leicestershire, Leicester, 1983; 156, D. I. Gower, Leicestershire v Derbyshire, Leicester, 1984; 155, J. J. Whitaker, Leicestershire v Wiltshire, Swindon, 1984; 154*, H. Morris, Glamorgan v Staffordshire, Cardiff, 1989; 154, P. Willey, Leicestershire v Hampshire, Leicester, 1987; 153, A. Hill, Derbyshire v Cornwall, Derby, 1986; 151*, M. P. Maynard, Glamorgan v Durham, Darlington, 1991. (93 hundreds were scored in the Gillette Cup; 139 hundreds have been scored in the NatWest Bank Trophy.)

Most runs: 2,287, G. A. Gooch; 1,953, M. W. Gatting; 1,950, D. L. Amiss.

Fastest hundred: G. D. Rose off 36 balls, Somerset v Devon, Torquay, 1990.

Most hundreds: 7, C. L. Smith; 6, G. A. Gooch; 5, D. I. Gower, I. V. A. Richards and G. M. Turner.

Highest totals (off 60 overs): 413 for four, Somerset v Devon, Torquay, 1990; 404 for three, Worcestershire v Devon, Worcester, 1987; 392 for five, Warwickshire v Oxfordshire, Birmingham, 1984; 386 for five, Essex v Wiltshire, Chelmsford, 1988; 372 for five, Lancashire v Gloucestershire, Manchester, 1990; 371 for four, Hampshire v Glamorgan, Southampton, 1975; 365 for three, Derbyshire v Cornwall, Derby, 1986; 361 for eight, Essex v Cumberland, Chelmsford, 1992; 360 for two, Northamptonshire v Staffordshire, Northampton, 1990; 359 for four, Kent v Dorset, Canterbury, 1989; 354 for seven, Leicestershire v Wiltshire, Swindon, 1984; 349 for six, Lancashire v Gloucestershire, Bristol, 1984; 345 for two, Glamorgan v Durham, Darlington, 1991; 341 for six, Leicestershire v Hampshire, Leicester, 1987; 339 for four, Hampshire v Berkshire, Southampton, 1985; 336 for five, Worcestershire v Cumberland, Worcester, 1988; 336 for seven, Warwickshire v Hertfordshire, St Albans, 1990; 330 for four, Somerset v Glamorgan, Cardiff, 1978. *In the final:* 322 for five, Warwickshire v Sussex, Lord's, 1993.

Highest total by a minor county: 305 for nine, Durham v Glamorgan, Darlington, 1991.

Highest total by a side batting first and losing: 321 for six (60 overs), Sussex v Warwickshire, Lord's, 1993 (*in the final*)

Highest totals by a side batting second: 326 for nine (60 overs), Hampshire lost to Leicestershire, Leicester, 1987; 322 for five (60 overs), Warwickshire beat Sussex, Lord's, 1993 (*in the final*); 319 for nine (59.5 overs), Essex beat Lancashire, Chelmsford, 1992; 307 for five (60 overs), Hampshire beat Essex, Chelmsford, 1990; 306 for six (59.3 overs), Gloucestershire beat Leicestershire, Leicester, 1983; 305 for nine (60 overs), Durham lost to Glamorgan, Darlington, 1991; 298 (59 overs), Lancashire lost to Worcestershire, Manchester, 1985; 297 for four (57.1 overs), Somerset beat Warwickshire, Taunton, 1978; 296 for four (58 overs), Kent beat Surrey, Canterbury, 1985; 290 for seven (59.3 overs), Yorkshire beat Worcestershire, Leeds, 1982.

Lowest total in the final: 118 (60 overs), Lancashire v Kent, 1974.

Lowest completed totals: 39 (26.4 overs), Ireland v Sussex, Hove, 1985; 41 (20 overs), Cambridgeshire v Buckinghamshire, Cambridge, 1972; 41 (19.4 overs), Middlesex v Essex, Westcliff, 1972; 41 (36.1 overs), Shropshire v Essex, Wellington, 1974.

Lowest total by a side batting first and winning: 98 (56.2 overs), Worcestershire v Durham, Chester-le-Street, 1968.

Shortest innings: 10.1 overs (60 for one), Worcestershire v Lancashire, Worcester, 1963.

Matches re-arranged on a reduced number of overs are excluded from the above.

Record partnerships for each wicket

248 for 1st	D. M. Smith and C. W. J. Athey, Sussex v Hampshire at Hove	1993
286 for 2nd	I. S. Anderson and A. Hill, Derbyshire v Cornwall at Derby	1986
259* for 3rd	H. Morris and M. P. Maynard, Glamorgan v Durham at Darlington	1991
234* for 4th	D. Lloyd and C. H. Lloyd, Lancashire v Gloucestershire at Manchester	1978
166 for 5th	M. A. Lynch and G. R. J. Roope, Surrey v Durham at The Oval	1982
105 for 6th {	G. S. Sobers and R. A. White, Nottinghamshire v Worcestershire at Worcester	1974
	R. J. Blakey and C. White, Yorkshire v Warwickshire at Leeds	1993
160* for 7th	C. J. Richards and I. R. Payne, Surrey v Lincolnshire at Sleaford ..	1983
83 for 8th	S. N. V. Waterton and D. A. Hale, Oxfordshire v Gloucestershire at Oxford	1989
87 for 9th	M. A. Nash and A. E. Cordle, Glamorgan v Lincolnshire at Swansea	1974
81 for 10th	S. Turner and R. E. East, Essex v Yorkshire at Leeds	1982

Bowling

Most wickets: 81, G. G. Arnold; 79, J. Simmons.

Best bowling (12 overs unless stated): eight for 21 (10.1 overs), M. A. Holding, Derbyshire v Sussex, Hove, 1988; eight for 31 (11.1 overs), D. L. Underwood, Kent v Scotland, Edinburgh, 1987; seven for 15, A. L. Dixon, Kent v Surrey, The Oval, 1967; seven for 15 (9.3 overs), R. P. Lefebvre, Somerset v Devon, Torquay, 1990; seven for 19, N. V. Radford, Worcestershire v Bedfordshire, Bedford, 1991; seven for 30, P. J. Sainsbury, Hampshire v Norfolk, Southampton, 1965; seven for 32, S. P. Davis, Durham v Lancashire, Chester-le-Street, 1983; seven for 33, R. D. Jackman, Surrey v Yorkshire, Harrogate, 1970; seven for 37, N. A. Mallender, Northamptonshire v Worcestershire, Northampton, 1984.

Most economical analysis: 12–9–3–1, J. Simmons, Lancashire v Suffolk, Bury St Edmunds, 1985.

Most expensive analysis: 12–0–106–2, D. A. Gallop, Oxfordshire v Warwickshire, Birmingham, 1984.

Hat-tricks (7): J. D. F. Larter, Northamptonshire v Sussex, Northampton, 1963; D. A. D. Sydenham, Surrey v Cheshire, Hoylake, 1964; R. N. S. Hobbs, Essex v Middlesex, Lord's, 1968; N. M. McVicker, Warwickshire v Lincolnshire, Birmingham, 1971; G. S. le Roux, Sussex v Ireland, Hove, 1985; M. Jean-Jacques, Derbyshire v Nottinghamshire, Derby, 1987; J. F. M. O'Brien, Cheshire v Derbyshire, Chester, 1988.

Four wickets in five balls: D. A. D. Sydenham, Surrey v Cheshire, Hoylake, 1964.

Wicket-keeping and Fielding

Most dismissals: 66 (58 ct, 8 st), R. W. Taylor; 65 (59 ct, 6 st), A. P. E. Knott.

Most dismissals in an innings: 6 (5 ct, 1 st), R. W. Taylor, Derbyshire v Essex, Derby, 1981; 6 (4 ct, 2 st), T. Davies, Glamorgan v Staffordshire, Stone, 1986.

Most catches by a fielder: 26, J. Simmons; 25, G. Cook; 24, P. J. Sharpe.

Most catches by a fielder in an innings: 4 – A. S. Brown, Gloucestershire v Middlesex, Bristol, 1963; G. Cook, Northamptonshire v Glamorgan, Northampton, 1972; C. G. Greenidge, Hampshire v Cheshire, Southampton, 1984; D. C. Jackson, Durham v Northamptonshire, Darlington, 1984; T. S. Smith, Hertfordshire v Somerset, St Albans, 1984; H. Morris, Glamorgan v Scotland, Edinburgh, 1988; C. C. Lewis, Nottinghamshire v Worcestershire, Nottingham, 1992.

Results

Largest victories in runs: Somerset by 346 runs v Devon, Torquay, 1990; Worcestershire by 299 runs v Devon, Worcester, 1987; Essex by 291 runs v Wiltshire, Chelmsford, 1988; Sussex by 244 runs v Ireland, Hove, 1985; Lancashire by 241 runs v Gloucestershire, Manchester, 1990; Warwickshire by 227 runs v Oxfordshire, Birmingham, 1984; Essex by 226 runs v Oxfordshire, Chelmsford, 1985; Northamptonshire by 216 runs v Staffordshire, Northampton, 1990; Leicestershire by 214 runs v Staffordshire, Longton, 1975; Hampshire by 209 runs v Dorset, Southampton, 1987; Derbyshire by 204 runs v Cornwall, Derby, 1986; Gloucestershire by 204 runs v Cheshire, Bristol, 1992; Warwickshire by 201 runs v Buckinghamshire, Birmingham, 1987; Sussex by 201 runs v Buckinghamshire, Beaconsfield, 1992; Sussex by 200 runs v Durham, Hove, 1964. *In the final:* 175 runs, Yorkshire v Surrey, Lord's, 1965.

Victories by ten wickets (12): Northamptonshire v Leicestershire, Leicester, 1964; Warwickshire v Cambridgeshire, Birmingham, 1965; Sussex v Derbyshire, Hove, 1968; Hampshire v Nottinghamshire, Southampton, 1977; Middlesex v Worcestershire, Worcester, 1980; Yorkshire v Cheshire, Birkenhead, 1985; Yorkshire v Berkshire, Finchampstead, 1988; Yorkshire v Norfolk, Leeds, 1990; Yorkshire v Warwickshire, Leeds, 1990; Hampshire v Berkshire, Reading, 1991; Warwickshire v Hertfordshire, Birmingham, 1991; Surrey v Dorset, The Oval, 1993.

Earliest finishes: both at 2.20 p.m. Worcestershire beat Lancashire by nine wickets at Worcester, 1963; Essex beat Middlesex by eight wickets at Westcliff, 1972.

Scores level (9): Nottinghamshire 215, Somerset 215 for nine at Taunton, 1964; Surrey 196, Sussex 196 for eight at The Oval, 1970; Somerset 287 for six, Essex 287 at Taunton, 1978; Surrey 195 for seven, Essex 195 at Chelmsford, 1980; Essex 149, Derbyshire 149 for eight at Derby, 1981; Northamptonshire 235 for nine, Derbyshire 235 for six in the final at Lord's, 1981; Middlesex 222 for nine, Somerset 222 for eight at Lord's, 1983; Hampshire 224 for eight, Essex 224 for seven at Southampton, 1985; Essex 307 for six, Hampshire 307 for five at Chelmsford, 1990. Under the rules the side which lost fewer wickets won.

Wins by a minor county over a first-class county (8): Durham v Yorkshire (by five wickets), Harrogate, 1973; Lincolnshire v Glamorgan (by six wickets), Swansea, 1974; Hertfordshire v Essex (by 33 runs), 2nd round, Hitchin, 1976; Shropshire v Yorkshire (by 37 runs), Telford, 1984; Durham v Derbyshire (by seven wickets), Derby, 1985; Buckinghamshire v Somerset (by seven runs), High Wycombe, 1987; Cheshire v Northamptonshire (by one wicket), Chester, 1988; Hertfordshire v Derbyshire (2-1 in a bowling contest after the match was abandoned), Bishop's Stortford, 1991.

WINNERS

Gillette Cup

1963   SUSSEX beat Worcestershire by 14 runs.
1964   SUSSEX beat Warwickshire by eight wickets.
1965   YORKSHIRE beat Surrey by 175 runs.
1966   WARWICKSHIRE beat Worcestershire by five wickets.
1967   KENT beat Somerset by 32 runs.
1968   WARWICKSHIRE beat Sussex by four wickets.
1969   YORKSHIRE beat Derbyshire by 69 runs.
1970   LANCASHIRE beat Sussex by six wickets.
1971   LANCASHIRE beat Kent by 24 runs.
1972   LANCASHIRE beat Warwickshire by four wickets.
1973   GLOUCESTERSHIRE beat Sussex by 40 runs.
1974   KENT beat Lancashire by four wickets.
1975   LANCASHIRE beat Middlesex by seven wickets.
1976   NORTHAMPTONSHIRE beat Lancashire by four wickets.
1977   MIDDLESEX beat Glamorgan by five wickets.
1978   SUSSEX beat Somerset by five wickets.
1979   SOMERSET beat Northamptonshire by 45 runs.
1980   MIDDLESEX beat Surrey by seven wickets.

NatWest Bank Trophy

1981   DERBYSHIRE beat Northamptonshire by losing fewer wickets with the scores level.
1982   SURREY beat Warwickshire by nine wickets.
1983   SOMERSET beat Kent by 24 runs.
1984   MIDDLESEX beat Kent by four wickets.
1985   ESSEX beat Nottinghamshire by one run.
1986   SUSSEX beat Lancashire by seven wickets.
1987   NOTTINGHAMSHIRE beat Northamptonshire by three wickets.
1988   MIDDLESEX beat Worcestershire by three wickets.
1989   WARWICKSHIRE beat Middlesex by four wickets.
1990   LANCASHIRE beat Northamptonshire by seven wickets.
1991   HAMPSHIRE beat Surrey by four wickets.
1992   NORTHAMPTONSHIRE beat Leicestershire by eight wickets.
1993   WARWICKSHIRE beat Sussex by five wickets.

TEAM RECORDS 1963-93

	Rounds reached				Matches		
	W	F	SF	QF	P	W	L
Derbyshire	1	2	3	8	58*	28	30
Durham	0	0	0	1	32	9	23
Essex	1	1	4	13	65	35	30
Glamorgan	0	1	2	11	62	31	31
Gloucestershire	1	1	5	13	64	34	30
Hampshire	1	1	8	19	80	50	30
Kent	2	5	6	13	71	42	29
Lancashire	5	8	13	17	86	60	26
Leicestershire	0	1	3	14	63	32	31
Middlesex	4	6	13	17	85	58	27
Northamptonshire	2	6	9	17	78	49	29
Nottinghamshire	1	2	3	11	65	35	30
Somerset	2	4	9	15	75	46	29
Surrey	1	4	8	18	76*	46	30
Sussex	4	8	12	17	82	55	27
Warwickshire	4	7	13	17	84	57	27
Worcestershire	0	3	9	13	69	38	31
Yorkshire	2	2	4	13	62	33	29

* Derbyshire and Surrey totals each include a bowling contest after their first-round matches were abandoned in 1991; Derbyshire lost to Hertfordshire and Surrey beat Oxfordshire.

MINOR COUNTY RECORDS

From 1964 to 1979 the previous season's top five Minor Counties were invited to take part in the competition. In 1980 these were joined by Ireland, and in 1983 the competition was expanded to embrace 13 Minor Counties, Ireland and Scotland. The number of Minor Counties dropped to 12 in 1992 when Durham attained first-class status.

Between 1964 and 1991 Durham qualified 21 times, including 15 years in succession from 1977-1991. They reached the second round a record six times.

Of the other Minor Counties, Hertfordshire have qualified 18 times, Oxfordshire 17, Staffordshire 16, Buckinghamshire and Devon 15, Berkshire, Cambridgeshire, Cheshire and Suffolk 14, Norfolk 13, Shropshire and Wiltshire 12, Bedfordshire, Dorset and Lincolnshire 10, Cumberland and Northumberland 8, Cornwall 5 and Wales Minor Counties twice. These figures include the 1994 NatWest Trophy.

Only Hertfordshire have reached the quarter-finals, beating Berkshire and then Essex in 1976.

BENSON AND HEDGES CUP, 1993

Derbyshire won the Benson and Hedges Cup for the first time in the 2 years of the competition, upsetting the hot favourites Lancashire in a fin that contained far more than routine Cup-tie rivalry. After a Championsh match less than two weeks earlier, Derbyshire had reacted to one of Wasi Akram's spectacular bowling performances by sending the ball to Lord' The hint of alleged malpractice incensed Lancashire but it failed galvanise the team at Lord's. They allowed a strong position to slide awa fielded with uncharacteristic ineptitude and, after their defeat, failed regain form all season.

Derbyshire's win was more than normally welcome. Six weeks before th final the club announced that they had a financial crisis that could threate their survival and made three senior officials redundant. They were als without an overseas star: their West Indian fast bowler Ian Bishop wa injured and played only one match all season. None the less, the first-cla county with the lowest membership were able to beat the county with th highest. Derbyshire's success leaves Glamorgan, Sussex, Warwickshire an Durham as the only counties never to win the Benson and Hedges Cup.

The 1993 competition was the first played after the implementation o the Murray Report, which abolished the group matches and turned the Cu into a straight knockout. This avoided a lot of messing around with decim points to work out comparative run-rates. But the move was unpopular i many quarters: Kent and Gloucestershire found themselves knocked out a major tournament while it was still April; the makeweight teams Combined Universities, Minor Counties and Scotland – had less chance success than ever when forced to face full-time professionals in a singl match so early in the season; and several county officials regretted the lo of revenue. There were only 20 matches compared to 52 under the ol system. However, the format is to remain unchanged in 1994, except for th entry of Ireland who will become the 22nd competing team.

The tournament also became the first to veer away from the tradition o inviting well-known retired cricketers to judge Man of the Match prize The 1993 Gold Awards were decided by members of the Cricket Writer Club.

Prize money

£30,000 for winners: DERBYSHIRE.
£15,000 for runners-up: LANCASHIRE.
£7,500 for losing semi-finalists: LEICESTERSHIRE and NORTHAMPTONSHIRE.
£3,750 for losing quarter-finalists: HAMPSHIRE, SOMERSET, SUSSEX an WORCESTERSHIRE.

There was also £1,200 each for the winners of first-round matches and £900 for the winne of each preliminary match. Gold Award winners received £600 in the final, £325 in th semi-finals, £275 in the quarter-finals, £165 in the first round and £135 in the preliminar round. The £93,445 prize money was reduced from £115,150 in the 1992 tournament becaus of the reduction in matches. The total sponsorship, however, rose from £596,148 t £614,032.

PRELIMINARY ROUND

DURHAM v MINOR COUNTIES

At Hartlepool, April 27, 28. Durham won by six wickets. Toss: Minor Counties.

In a match delayed 24 hours by mist and a saturated ground, Durham needed all but seven deliveries of their 55 overs to reach their target of 157. Batting was never easy on the rain-affected pitch and there was a brief flutter in the home camp when Bainbridge was out for 34 off the first ball of the 53rd over with 15 still needed. But Botham finished the job in the next over, clipping his second six over mid-wicket to finish on 35 not out. Wicket-keeper Fothergill won the Gold Award for four excellent catches and a stumping.

Gold Award: A. R. Fothergill.

Minor Counties

S. J. Dean c Fothergill b Brown	5		G. Miller not out	22
N. R. Gaywood c Botham b Brown	4		†M. I. Humphries b Wood	27
M. J. Roberts c Fothergill b Hughes	18		K. A. Arnold not out	4
*I. Cockbain c Fothergill b Bainbridge	33		B 1, l-b 7, w 5	13
N. J. Adams c Fothergill b Hughes	11			
J. Derrick c Fowler b Bainbridge	13		1/5 2/17 3/35 (8 wkts, 55 overs)	156
P. G. Newman st Fothergill			4/55 5/79 6/95	
b Bainbridge	6		7/100 8/145	

A. Smith did not bat.

Bowling: Wood 8–2–19–1; Brown 9–2–32–2; Botham 6–0–21–0; Hughes 10–2–35–2; Graveney 11–2–17–0; Bainbridge 11–1–24–3.

Durham

W. Larkins lbw b Newman	42		P. W. G. Parker not out	3
G. Fowler lbw b Newman	0		L-b 7, w 2	9
I. Smith c Humphries b Smith	34			
P. Bainbridge c Cockbain b Miller	34		1/0 2/66 (4 wkts, 53.5 overs)	157
I. T. Botham not out	35		3/89 4/142	

†A. R. Fothergill, J. Wood, *D. A. Graveney, S. P. Hughes and S. J. E. Brown did not bat.

Bowling: Newman 10–3–23–2; Arnold 10.5–2–45–0; Miller 11–1–29–1; Derrick 11–2–30–0; Smith 11–2–23–1.

Umpires: B. J. Meyer and P. Willey.

GLOUCESTERSHIRE v DERBYSHIRE

At Bristol, April 27. Derbyshire won by virtue of losing fewer wickets. Toss: Derbyshire.

For Gloucestershire, it was a cruel way to start the season – knocked out of the Cup before May, even though the totals were level at the finish: Derbyshire went through because they had lost five wickets to Gloucestershire's seven. They made hard work of it after a century opening stand, needing 14 runs off the last two overs and still being one run behind when the last ball was bowled. Bowler, run out eight short of his hundred, held the innings together at his own unhurried pace. Gloucestershire's two recruits from Nottingham-shire made an encouraging, if unavailing, mark on the game. Broad, on his return to the West, scored a composed half-century; Cooper was by far the tightest and most threatening of their bowlers. For Derbyshire, Malcolm bowled more sharply than his figures suggested.

Gold Award: P. D. Bowler.

Gloucestershire

B. C. Broad c Cork b Griffith	58	M. C. J. Ball b Malcolm	1
S. G. Hinks c Krikken b Cork	6	A. M. Smith not out	(
R. J. Scott c Barnett b Griffith	44	L-b 6, w 6	1
M. W. Alleyne not out	30		
*A. J. Wright c Griffith b Mortensen	6	1/19 2/113 3/114 (7 wkts, 55 overs) 19	
T. H. C. Hancock lbw b Cork	23	4/121 5/155	
†R. C. Russell run out	2	6/160 7/180	

K. E. Cooper and M. J. Gerrard did not bat.

Bowling: Malcolm 11-1-42-1; Cork 11-2-39-2; Mortensen 11-2-30-1; Warne 11-2-33-0; Griffith 11-2-48-2.

Derbyshire

*K. J. Barnett c Ball b Smith	40	†K. M. Krikken not out	
P. D. Bowler run out	92		
J. E. Morris c Wright b Cooper	1	B 1, l-b 6, w 6	1
C. J. Adams lbw b Ball	1		
T. J. G. O'Gorman run out	34	1/101 2/110 3/117 (5 wkts, 55 overs) 19	
F. A. Griffith not out	13	4/170 5/186	

D. G. Cork, A. E. Warner, D. E. Malcolm and O. H. Mortensen did not bat.

Bowling: Cooper 11-3-20-1; Gerrard 11-1-44-0; Smith 11-0-43-1; Ball 11-1-32-1; Scott 11-0-52-0.

Umpires: J. C. Balderstone and J. D. Bond.

HAMPSHIRE v COMBINED UNIVERSITIES

At Southampton, April 27. Hampshire won by nine wickets. Toss: Combined Universities.
Hampshire comfortably cleared the first hurdle in their defence of the Cup. The student were contained by some steady bowling; their highest innings was a fifty from Snape, which ended when Smith caught him on the boundary. Taking the catch, Smith gashed his head on an advertising hoarding and went off for stitches. Middleton then batted with the fluency which had earned him selection for England A rather than the disappointing form he showed on tour, reaching his highest score in the competition, and Hampshire cruised home with five overs to spare. It completed a frustrating four days for the Combined Universities; friendly games against Middlesex and Northamptonshire, arranged before this fixture to compensate them for the abolition of their group matches, had been washed out.

Gold Award: T. C. Middleton.

Combined Universities

R. R. Montgomerie c Terry b Connor	0	J. C. Hallett c Aymes b Marshall	2
*J. P. Crawley c Marshall b Ayling	41	M. P. W. Jeh not out	1
G. B. T. Lovell c Aymes b Turner	18	B 1, l-b 7, w 3	1
J. N. Snape c Smith b Udal	52		
C. L. Keey b Udal	1	1/5 2/41 3/116 (7 wkts, 55 overs) 17	
G. M. Charlesworth b Marshall	14	4/117 5/128	
†S. F. Shephard not out	30	6/147 7/151	

R. M. Pearson and R. H. Macdonald did not bat.

Bowling: Marshall 11-4-24-2; Connor 11-2-36-1; Turner 11-0-41-1; Ayling 11-0-29-1; Udal 11-1-39-2.

Hampshire

V. P. Terry c Snape b Macdonald	.....	30
T. C. Middleton not out	....	91
D. I. Gower not out	....	41
B 1, w 7, n-b 8	....	16

1/67   (1 wkt, 50 overs) 178

R. A. Smith, *M. C. J. Nicholas, M. D. Marshall, J. R. Ayling, †A. N. Aymes, S. D. Udal, I. J. Turner and C. A. Connor did not bat.

Bowling: Pearson 11–2–34–0; Jeh 5–0–34–0; Hallett 7–0–16–0; Macdonald 8–2–20–1; Snape 11–1–47–0; Charlesworth 7–0–26–0; Montgomerie 1–1–0–0.

Umpires: M. J. Kitchen and G. Sharp.

KENT v GLAMORGAN

At Canterbury, April 27. Glamorgan won by 104 runs. Toss: Kent.

Kent's interest in the competition, in which they had previously reached the semi-finals more often than not was short-lived in 1993. They lost their last six wickets for only 25 runs, against tight and accurate Glamorgan out-cricket and a match-winning return of four for 15 from Barwick. Maynard scored 89 off 100 balls to give Glamorgan the ideal start after the early loss of James. Despite solid contributions from Taylor and Cowdrey, Kent were never up with the rate, and Metson stumped Fleming down the leg side off a wide to remove a dangerous hitter.

Gold Award: M. P. Maynard.

Glamorgan

S. P. James c and b McCague	....	3	R. P. Lefebvre c Penn b Fleming	8
*H. Morris c Llong b Fleming	....	44	†C. P. Metson not out	1
A. Dale lbw b Fleming	....	19	L-b 12, w 5, n-b 10..........	27
M. P. Maynard c Igglesden b McCague		89		
I. V. A. Richards c Benson b Igglesden		21	1/11 2/44 3/135 (7 wkts, 55 overs) 236	
P. A. Cottey b McCague	....	14	4/170 5/217	
R. D. B. Croft not out	....	10	6/218 7/232	

S. L. Watkin and S. R. Barwick did not bat.

Bowling: Igglesden 11–2–31–1; McCague 11–0–39–3; Penn 11–1–54–0; Fleming 11–1–52–3; Davis 11–0–48–0.

Kent

T. R. Ward c Maynard b Lefebvre	....	0	C. Penn b Watkin	0
*M. R. Benson c Lefebvre b Croft	....	13	M. J. McCague c Cottey b Richards ...	0
N. R. Taylor b Barwick	....	42	A. P. Igglesden c Dale b Barwick	1
N. J. Llong c Watkin b Barwick	.....	5	L-b 3, w 4	7
G. R. Cowdrey c Cottey b Richards	...	33		
M. V. Fleming st Metson b Barwick	...	7	1/1 2/26 3/35 (49.4 overs) 132	
†S. A. Marsh c Richards b Watkin	....	6	4/96 5/107 6/109	
R. P. Davis not out	....	18	7/114 8/121 9/121	

Bowling: Lefebvre 9–2–15–1; Watkin 11–2–35–2; Barwick 9.4–3–15–4; Croft 11–3–27–1; Dale 4–0–19–0; Richards 5–1–18–2.

Umpires: B. Dudleston and G. A. Stickley.

SCOTLAND v ESSEX

At Forfar, April 27. Essex won by nine wickets. Toss: Scotland.

Ilott had reduced Scotland to 14 for three when Jim Love, the former Yorkshire batsman and the Scottish Cricket Union's director of cricket, came to the wicket. His 44, supported by Govan, averted complete embarrassment, but he too fell to Ilott, who finished his second spell with five wickets in an innings for the first time in limited-overs competitions. A target of 107 detained Essex for little more than half their allotted overs.

Gold Award: M. C. Ilott.

Scotland

B. M. W. Patterson c Hussain b Ilott	3	A. Bee b Ilott		0
I. L. Philip c Gooch b Topley	17	I. M. Stanger not out		2
G. N. Reifer lbw b Ilott	0			
G. Salmond lbw b Ilott	0	L-b 3, w 6		9
J. D. Love b Ilott	44			
*A. B. Russell b Gooch	10	1/12 2/12 3/14	(8 wkts, 55 overs)	106
†D. A. Orr c Garnham b Gooch	0	4/30 5/53 6/59		
J. W. Govan not out	21	7/99 8/99		

G. M. Hamilton did not bat.

Bowling: Ilott 11–2–21–5; Pringle 11–4–20–0; Topley 11–1–29–1; Stephenson 11–5–13–0; Such 5–0–9–0; Gooch 6–2–11–2.

Essex

*G. A. Gooch c Stanger b Russell	41
J. P. Stephenson not out	50
P. J. Prichard not out	8
L-b 5, w 3	8

1/82   (1 wkt, 29.3 overs) 107

Salim Malik, N. Hussain, N. V. Knight, †M. A. Garnham, D. R. Pringle, T. D. Topley, M. C. Ilott and P. M. Such did not bat.

Bowling: Bee 5–0–20–0; Stanger 5–2–12–0; Hamilton 4–0–15–0; Reifer 5–0–15–0; Govan 6–2–13–0; Russell 4.3–0–27–1.

Umpires: J. H. Hampshire and J. W. Holder.

FIRST ROUND

DERBYSHIRE v MIDDLESEX

At Derby, May 11. Derbyshire won by 14 runs. Toss: Middlesex.

Chasing a target of 4.6 an over, Middlesex began by hitting 26 off the first two. Roseberry hit his first three balls from Malcolm for four and Haynes hit three fours off Cork. Middlesex were still strongly placed when the openers reached 100 in the 23rd over. However, Warner had already begun a controlled spell of 11 overs for 29 and Griffith changed the picture by dismissing Haynes and Ramprakash with successive balls. Bishop, in his only game of the season, had Carr caught at mid-off and, with Gatting still injured, Middlesex's batting finally proved too brittle. The Derbyshire innings had been dominated by Morris and Adams, who put on 97 in 18 overs. But Cork's late runs were also vital.

Gold Award: C. J. Adams.

Derbyshire

*K. J. Barnett c Carr b Williams	29	I. R. Bishop not out	12
P. D. Bowler b Keech	30	A. E. Warner not out	2
J. E. Morris c Emburey b Feltham	57		
C. J. Adams c Roseberry b Fraser	58	B 8, l-b 6, w 7, n-b 4	25
T. J. G. O'Gorman c Brown b Fraser	8		
F. A. Griffith c Carr b Feltham	8	1/55 2/84 3/181	(8 wkts, 55 overs) 253
†K. M. Krikken run out	1	4/198 5/209 6/215	
D. G. Cork b Fraser	23	7/216 8/244	

D. E. Malcolm did not bat.

Bowling: Feltham 11–1–39–2; Fraser 11–0–50–3; Williams 10–2–50–1; Emburey 11–0–45–0; Keech 8–0–37–1; Weekes 4–0–18–0.

Middlesex

D. L. Haynes lbw b Griffith	60	J. E. Emburey c Griffith b Bishop	17
M. A. Roseberry b Malcolm	58	N. F. Williams not out	0
M. R. Ramprakash c Barnett b Griffith	0	A. R. C. Fraser not out	1
*J. D. Carr c Cork b Bishop	41	L-b 6, w 14, n-b 6	26
P. N. Weekes b Malcolm	0		
M. Keech run out	7	1/100 2/100 3/161	(9 wkts, 55 overs) 239
†K. R. Brown c Krikken b Malcolm	24	4/161 5/179 6/185	
M. A. Feltham run out	5	7/191 8/232 9/238	

Bowling: Malcolm 11–1–62–3; Cork 11–0–56–0; Bishop 11–1–37–2; Warner 11–2–29–0; Griffith 11–0–49–2.

Umpires: G. I. Burgess and D. J. Constant.

DURHAM v HAMPSHIRE

At Stockton-on-Tees, May 11. Hampshire won by three wickets. Toss: Hampshire.

Hampshire won with five balls to spare after taking nine off the penultimate over, bowled by Hughes, who had given Durham hope in his previous over by removing Terry for 79. Terry shared crucial stands with James and Aymes after Hampshire had been reduced to 113 for five, Cummins taking two wickets in his second spell on his home debut. His triumphant dance on bowling fellow-Barbadian Marshall was one of the features of the match. Had he been allowed to complete his remaining three overs at that point the outcome might have been different; he was all too clearly struggling against the evening chill when he returned. Durham were left to regret losing the toss: in the morning extravagant movement off the seam had reduced them to 39 for three, and Larkins showed admirable application in reaching an unbeaten century, Durham's first in the competition.

Gold Award: W. Larkins.

Durham

W. Larkins not out	110	A. C. Cummins not out	3
G. Fowler c Smith b Marshall	7		
P. W. G. Parker c Aymes b Marshall	0	L-b 8, w 6, n-b 6	20
P. Bainbridge c Gower b Jean-Jacques	5		
I. Smith b Ayling	15	1/20 2/20 3/39	(5 wkts, 55 overs) 196
I. T. Botham b Connor	36	4/83 5/170	

†A. R. Fothergill, J. Wood, *D. A. Graveney and S. P. Hughes did not bat.

Bowling: Connor 11–2–34–1; Marshall 11–1–29–2; Ayling 11–4–39–1; Jean-Jacques 11–0–59–1; Udal 11–1–27–0.

Hampshire

V. P. Terry c Graveney b Hughes	79	†A. N. Aymes not out		23
T. C. Middleton c Fothergill b Cummins	8	S. D. Udal not out		9
R. A. Smith c Smith b Bainbridge	29	L-b 4, w 6, n-b 2		12
D. I. Gower c Graveney b Botham	4			
J. R. Ayling c Parker b Cummins	16	1/26 2/61 3/68	(7 wkts, 54.1 overs)	197
*M. D. Marshall b Cummins	4	4/105 5/113		
K. D. James run out	13	6/144 7/179		

M. Jean-Jacques and C. A. Connor did not bat.

Bowling: Cummins 11–1–36–3; Wood 6–0–23–0; Hughes 11–2–33–1; Botham 11–1–36–1; Bainbridge 10.1–1–41–1; Graveney 5–0–24–0.

Umpires: J. D. Bond and V. A. Holder.

GLAMORGAN v SUSSEX

At Cardiff, May 11. Sussex won by 33 runs. Toss: Sussex.

Sussex avenged their Championship defeat the previous weekend, though Glamorgan contributed to their own downfall with two self-inflicted run-outs. The game started with an opening partnership of 96 from Smith and Stephenson, a solid innings from Alan Wells and an accurate first spell of seven overs for 13 runs from Salisbury. Stephenson also bowled Maynard, who looked capable of winning the game for Glamorgan after Speight's two smart catches had accounted for Morris and James. Dale and Cottey were run out from the deep by Lenham as Glamorgan's chance faded away.

Gold Award: I. D. K. Salisbury.

Sussex

D. M. Smith b Dale	55	I. D. K. Salisbury not out		16
F. D. Stephenson b Dale	43	N. J. Lenham not out		15
M. P. Speight b Dale	17	B 1, l-b 9, w 13		23
*A. P. Wells c Lefebvre b Watkin	53			
C. M. Wells c Richards b Barwick	23	1/96 2/107 3/130	(7 wkts, 55 overs)	263
K. Greenfield b Lefebvre	10	4/197 5/217		
†P. Moores run out	8	6/229 7/231		

A. N. Jones and E. S. H. Giddins did not bat.

Bowling: Watkin 10–0–47–1; Lefebvre 8–1–33–1; Barwick 11–0–62–1; Croft 8–0–44–0; Dale 11–1–37–3; Richards 7–0–30–0.

Glamorgan

S. P. James c Speight b Jones	21	†C. P. Metson b Stephenson		1
*H. Morris c Speight b Lenham	28	S. L. Watkin b Stephenson		0
A. Dale run out	23	S. R. Barwick b Giddins		0
M. P. Maynard b Stephenson	57	L-b 6, w 4, n-b 8		18
I. V. A. Richards b Giddins	17			
P. A. Cottey run out	23	1/40 2/75 3/88	(52.2 overs)	230
R. D. B. Croft c Speight b Salisbury	23	4/130 5/174 6/183		
R. P. Lefebvre not out	19	7/225 8/229 9/229		

Bowling: Stephenson 10–0–48–3; C. M. Wells 4–0–20–0; Giddins 9.2–0–42–2; Jones 7–0–36–1; Lenham 11–0–50–1; Salisbury 11–1–28–1.

Umpires: R. A. White and P. Willey.

LEICESTERSHIRE v WARWICKSHIRE

At Leicester, May 11. Leicestershire won by virtue of losing fewer wickets. Toss: Leicestershire.

After bowling the last delivery of the match, Benjamin retrieved the ball and beat Donald's attempt to run the winning single with a direct hit on the stumps at the bowler's end. The scores remained tied and Leicestershire went through with a two-wicket advantage. Having chosen to bat on a slow pitch, Leicestershire had found scoring difficult, particularly against Small, who removed Boon and Whitaker in a mean opening spell. Robinson overcame early uncertainties to lead a recovery from 34 for three, adding 95 with Smith for the fourth wicket. Even so, a modest 207 should have been well within Warwickshire's compass, especially with Moles providing a typically sturdy foundation. However, after Ostler and Penney had brought the target within what seemed comfortable reach, a series of misjudgments in running, compounded by Burns throwing away his wicket with only nine wanted from two overs, undid the visitors.

Gold Award: P. E. Robinson.

Leicestershire

T. J. Boon b Small	19		W. K. M. Benjamin not out			3
*N. E. Briers c Donald b Munton	5		A. R. K. Pierson not out			1
J. J. Whitaker c Twose b Small	7					
P. E. Robinson lbw b P. A. Smith	70			B 3, l-b 6, w 5, n-b 2		16
B. F. Smith c Twose b P. A. Smith	43					
L. Potter c Burns b P. A. Smith	6		1/10 2/27 3/34	(8 wkts, 55 overs)		206
V. J. Wells c Penney b Donald	15		4/129 5/142 6/168			
†P. A. Nixon b Donald	21		7/188 8/204			

A. D. Mullally did not bat.

Bowling: Donald 11–0–47–2; Munton 11–1–40–1; Small 11–2–27–2; Reeve 9–2–20–0; Twose 3–0–10–0; N. M. K. Smith 4–1–20–0; P. A. Smith 7–0–33–3.

Warwickshire

A. J. Moles b Benjamin	63		G. C. Small run out			8
R. G. Twose c Potter b Pierson	12		A. A. Donald run out			9
N. M. K. Smith st Nixon b Pierson	8		T. A. Munton not out			5
*D. A. Reeve c Boon b Potter	8		L-b 4, w 2, n-b 4			10
D. P. Ostler b Pierson	36					
T. L. Penney b Pierson	22		1/45 2/70 3/96	(55 overs)		206
P. A. Smith run out	3		4/98 5/147 6/160			
†M. Burns b Wells	22		7/162 8/179 9/198			

Bowling: Benjamin 11–0–43–1; Mullally 11–1–43–0; Wells 11–1–37–1; Pierson 11–1–42–3; Potter 11–1–37–2.

Umpires: R. Julian and N. T. Plews.

NOTTINGHAMSHIRE v SOMERSET

At Nottingham, May 11. Somerset won by one wicket. Toss: Nottinghamshire. County debut: Mushtaq Ahmed.

A brilliant innings by Lathwell, who hit 77 from 59 balls and put on 137 with Folland, gave Somerset a flying start. When Harden and Tavaré extended that to 237 for two, a target of 280 looked easy. But then Mike, with a one-day best performance of four for 44, reduced them to 254 for six and suddenly there was a fight on. Somerset entered the final over still needing seven runs, with two wickets in hand; Pick bowled Caddick but, with the scores level, van Troost struck four from his last ball. Nottinghamshire's innings was dominated by 80 from Pollard; they were helped when Hayhurst broke down with a groin injury in his second over (he later batted with a runner). Tavaré fell back on Lathwell as an emergency bowler, and he conceded 49 in four overs.

Gold Award: M. N. Lathwell.

Nottinghamshire

D. W. Randall c Tavaré b Caddick	5	M. A. Crawley not out	26
P. R. Pollard lbw b Caddick	80	G. W. Mike not out	25
*R. T. Robinson b van Troost	29	B 4, l-b 11, w 10, n-b 4	29
P. Johnson c Burns b Rose	59		
C. C. Lewis c Folland b van Troost	25	1/22 2/102 3/164 (6 wkts, 55 overs) 279
C. L. Cairns c Trump b Rose	1	4/214 5/217 6/227

†B. N. French, R. A. Pick and J. A. Afford did not bat.

Bowling: Caddick 11–2–36–2; van Troost 10.4–0–38–2; Mushtaq Ahmed 11–0–50–0; Rose 11–1–45–2; Hayhurst 1.2–0–17–0; Trump 6–0–29–0; Lathwell 4–0–49–0.

Somerset

M. N. Lathwell lbw b Lewis	77	Mushtaq Ahmed c Pollard b Cairns	7
N. A. Folland c and b Afford	83	A. P. van Troost not out	9
R. J. Harden lbw b Mike	49	H. R. J. Trump not out	0
*C. J. Tavaré b Mike	19	B 1, l-b 6, w 4, n-b 4	15
†N. D. Burns c Pollard b Mike	2		
G. D. Rose c Mike b Cairns	13	1/137 2/179 3/237 (9 wkts, 55 overs) 283
A. N. Hayhurst c Pollard b Mike	5	4/238 5/239 6/254
A. R. Caddick b Pick	4	7/262 8/271 9/278

Bowling: Lewis 11–0–34–1; Cairns 11–0–63–2; Mike 11–1–44–4; Afford 9–1–56–1; Crawley 3–0–19–0; Pick 10–0–60–1.

Umpires: J. W. Holder and A. G. T. Whitehead.

SURREY v LANCASHIRE

At The Oval, May 11. Lancashire won by six runs. Toss: Surrey.

Lancashire achieved one of the most dramatic one-day victories of all time after the Surrey innings went from the sublime to the farcical. They were only 25 runs short of victory thanks to a 212-run partnership between Stewart and Thorpe; they then contrived to lose nine wickets for just 18 runs – and the match. Only Lynch, who walked for a leg-side catch by Hegg, could claim not to have thrown his wicket away. The remainder had no excuses. Thorpe's magnificent three-hour century was wasted, and he lost the Gold Award to Fairbrother, for a fine 87 which held Lancashire together. Stewart's 95 should have been turned into a century; instead the loss of his off stump began the tumble of wickets. Lynch and Thorpe fell in Wasim Akram's tenth over; Austin's medium pace accounted for Ward, Brown and Butcher; Watkinson whipped out Waqar Younis while Bicknell and Boiling were run out. The TCCB used the game for the first experiment in Britain with a third umpire replaying difficult line decisions on television and communicating with his colleagues on the field by two-way radio. But Allan Jones's only involvement proved that the camera could be as uncertain as the human eye. He was unable to judge whether Wasim should be given run out, and ruled that he should stay. A photograph taken from another angle suggested that Wasim had been lucky.

Gold Award: N. H. Fairbrother.

Lancashire

G. D. Mendis c Boiling b Butcher	19	Wasim Akram run out	38
M. A. Atherton c Stewart b M. P. Bicknell	11	†W. K. Hegg run out	0
N. J. Speak b M. P. Bicknell	0	I. D. Austin b M. P. Bicknell	0
*N. H. Fairbrother c Lynch b Waqar Younis	87	P. J. Martin not out	10
G. D. Lloyd c Stewart b Waqar Younis	25	B 4, l-b 15, w 5, n-b 6	30
M. Watkinson c Stewart b Butcher	1	1/34 2/34 3/50 (54.1 overs) 236
P. A. J. DeFreitas b Boiling	15	4/146 5/153 6/164
		7/200 8/203 9/203

Bowling: Waqar Younis 10.1–3–27–2; M. P. Bicknell 11–5–27–3; Benjamin 11–3–30–0; Butcher 11–2–41–2; Thorpe 2–0–16–0; Boiling 9–0–76–1.

Surrey

D. J. Bicknell b DeFreitas	0	Waqar Younis b Watkinson	3
*†A. J. Stewart b Martin	95	J. E. Benjamin not out	4
G. P. Thorpe c Martin		J. Boiling run out	1
b Wasim Akram	.103		
M. A. Lynch c Hegg b Wasim Akram	2	B 5, l-b 6, w 4, n-b 2	17
D. M. Ward c Martin b Austin	0		
A. D. Brown lbw b Austin	1	1/0 2/212 3/215	(55 overs) 230
M. A. Butcher b Austin	1	4/216 5/216 6/219	
M. P. Bicknell run out	3	7/220 8/225 9/229	

Bowling: DeFreitas 11–2–37–1; Martin 11–2–29–1; Austin 11–0–40–3; Wasim Akram 11–1–47–2; Watkinson 11–0–66–1.

Umpires: B. Dudleston and G. Sharp.

WORCESTERSHIRE v ESSEX

At Worcester, May 11. Worcestershire won by nine wickets. Toss: Worcestershire. County debut: K. C. G. Benjamin.

Rarely can the favourites of any competition have been so comprehensively outplayed. Worcestershire imposed such an early stranglehold that the reigning county champions managed only one run off 57 balls from Illingworth and Lampitt. With Salim Malik then brilliantly run out by Hick, and West Indian pace bowler Kenny Benjamin celebrating his belated debut for Worcestershire by bowling Hussain, there was never going to be an escape route after Essex had lurched to 73 for seven just after lunch. Curtis and Weston reduced Worcestershire's target of 116 by 31 before Hick plundered a demoralised attack to complete the rout. His unbeaten 62 came off just 54 balls and included 12 boundaries. The one-sided contest was won with 22.5 overs to spare.

Gold Award: G. A. Hick.

Essex

*G. A. Gooch c Rhodes b Newport	13	N. A. Foster c Weston b Newport	9
J. P. Stephenson lbw b Illingworth	16	M. C. Ilott b Illingworth	14
P. J. Prichard b Lampitt	6	P. M. Such c Hick b Illingworth	3
Salim Malik run out	1	B 1, l-b 4, w 6	11
N. Hussain b Benjamin	10		
D. R. Pringle c Rhodes b Tolley	11	1/26 2/37 3/38	(53.3 overs) 115
N. V. Knight c Hick b Benjamin	5	4/45 5/52 6/69	
†M. A. Garnham not out	16	7/73 8/82 9/107	

Bowling: Benjamin 11–2–28–2; Tolley 11–3–13–1; Newport 11–4–20–2; Lampitt 10–3–28–1; Illingworth 10.3–2–21–3.

Worcestershire

*T. S. Curtis lbw b Pringle	20
W. P. C. Weston not out	32
G. A. Hick not out	62
L-b 2, w 1	3
1/31	(1 wkt, 32.1 overs) 117

D. B. D'Oliveira, A. C. H. Seymour, S. R. Lampitt, †S. J. Rhodes, R. K. Illingworth, P. J. Newport, K. C. G. Benjamin and C. M. Tolley did not bat.

Bowling: Foster 8–0–17–0; Ilott 6–1–21–0; Pringle 7–3–21–1; Such 6–1–20–0; Stephenson 5.1–0–36–0.

Umpires: J. C. Balderstone and D. R. Shepherd.

YORKSHIRE v NORTHAMPTONSHIRE

At Leeds, May 11. Northamptonshire won by 34 runs. Toss: Yorkshire. County debut: R. B. Richardson.

Felton and Lamb put Northamptonshire in a strong position on a slow pitch, adding 118 from 30 overs for the third wicket. Yorkshire, however, recovered lost ground as White bowled very accurately and seven wickets fell for 42 runs in the next ten. Moxon and Richardson appeared to be winning the game as they shared a partnership of 104. But Lamb handled his bowlers skilfully, and both batsmen were out to errors of judgment within the space of three overs. As panic set in Yorkshire in turn collapsed, their last eight wickets producing just 63 runs. Richardson was awarded his Yorkshire cap before playing for the county at all, a break with ancient tradition but perhaps only fair under the circumstances: the club had forbidden him to wear his familiar maroon sunhat.

Gold Award: N. A. Felton.

Northamptonshire

A. Fordham lbw b Robinson	23	C. E. L. Ambrose not out		16
N. A. Felton b Robinson	62	J. P. Taylor run out		0
R. J. Bailey lbw b Silverwood	6	N. G. B. Cook not out		1
*A. J. Lamb c Byas b White	54	B 4, l-b 8, w 5, n-b 2		19
M. B. Loye b Gough	9			
D. J. Capel c Blakey b White	3	1/29 2/40 3/158	(9 wkts, 55 overs)	211
K. M. Curran lbw b Robinson	3	4/159 5/162 6/165		
†D. Ripley run out	15	7/190 8/199 9/200		

Bowling: Jarvis 9-0-40-0; Gough 9-2-27-1; Robinson 11-1-51-3; Silverwood 7-1-19-1; Grayson 8-1-32-0; White 11-0-30-2.

Yorkshire

*M. D. Moxon run out	52	D. Gough c Ripley b Taylor		1
S. A. Kellett c Ripley b Ambrose	7	M. A. Robinson not out		3
R. B. Richardson c Cook b Curran	52	C. E. W. Silverwood run out		2
D. Byas lbw b Capel	12	L-b 5, w 3		8
†R. J. Blakey lbw b Capel	0			
C. White c Ambrose b Capel	16	1/10 2/114 3/122	(52.1 overs)	177
A. P. Grayson run out	20	4/125 5/142 6/151		
P. W. Jarvis c Ripley b Taylor	4	7/171 8/171 9/174		

Bowling: Ambrose 9.1-2-21-1; Curran 11-0-25-1; Taylor 10-2-26-2; Capel 10-0-54-3; Cook 8-0-27-0; Bailey 4-0-19-0.

Umpires: B. J. Meyer and G. A. Stickley.

QUARTER-FINALS

HAMPSHIRE v NORTHAMPTONSHIRE

At Southampton, May 25, 26. Northamptonshire won by seven wickets. Toss: Northamptonshire.

For the third year running Lamb chose to take Northamptonshire off for bad light and resume next day in a crucial limited-overs game; for the first time he got it right. When play finally resumed after lunch on the second day, Lamb and Loye scampered home with eight balls to spare. Hampshire had always been in difficulties. Of their batsmen, only Terry mastered the murky conditions and an attack spearheaded by Ambrose. Northamptonshire reached 157 for one with no great difficulty and Felton and Bailey turned down an earlier offer of the light because they were behind on scoring-rate. But their dismissal in successive overs persuaded Lamb to sleep on it and hope that conditions would improve – they did.

Gold Award: N. A. Felton.

Close of play: Northamptonshire 160-3 (44.3 overs) (A. J. Lamb 2*, M. B. Loye 0*).

Hampshire

T. C. Middleton c Bailey b Taylor	3	S. D. Udal not out	4
V. P. Terry c Cook b Ambrose	76	†A. N. Aymes not out	1
R. A. Smith b Cook	30	B 5, l-b 2, w 10	17
D. I. Gower b Loye b Curran	31		
*M. C. J. Nicholas run out	27	1/7 2/93 3/137 (7 wkts, 55 overs) 223	
J. R. Ayling c Loye b Ambrose	25	4/170 5/194	
M. D. Marshall lbw b Taylor	9	6/216 7/216	

C. A. Connor and I. J. Turner did not bat.

Bowling: Ambrose 11–3–30–2; Taylor 11–2–34–2; Curran 11–3–38–1; Penberthy 11–0–53–0; Bailey 6–0–28–0; Cook 5–0–33–1.

Northamptonshire

A. Fordham c Aymes b Connor	30	M. B. Loye not out	31
N. A. Felton st Aymes b Turner	73	L-b 3, w 5, n-b 9	17
R. J. Bailey run out	45		
*A. J. Lamb not out	31	1/74 2/157 3/160 (3 wkts, 53.4 overs) 227	

K. M. Curran, A. L. Penberthy, †D. Ripley, C. E. L. Ambrose, J. P. Taylor and N. G. B. Cook did not bat.

Bowling: Marshall 11–1–48–0; Connor 10.4–1–43–1; Udal 11–1–44–0; Ayling 10–0–37–0; Turner 11–0–52–1.

Umpires: M. J. Kitchen and K. E. Palmer.

LEICESTERSHIRE v WORCESTERSHIRE

At Leicester, May 25. Leicestershire won by 55 runs. Toss: Leicestershire.

On a lifeless pitch that did nothing to improve Grace Road's reputation, Leicestershire's batting remained laboured until the last five overs yielded 58 runs, the same number Briers had ground out during the first 44. Kenny Benjamin gave away only seven in his first seven overs. But when the shackles came off at last, Nixon and Winston Benjamin put on 36 in 13 balls, Benjamin taking 20 off six; his second six lodged in the guttering of the new cricket school. The Leicestershire Benjamin then had both openers caught behind off his first and seventh deliveries. Worcestershire never posed a genuine threat, despite the admirable efforts of Hick, who brought them to the last 14 overs needing 77 with five wickets in hand. But all hope disappeared when Hick spooned a catch to mid-on.

Gold Award: W. K. M. Benjamin.

Leicestershire

T. J. Boon c D'Oliveira b Benjamin	1	W. K. M. Benjamin run out	20
*N. E. Briers lbw b Illingworth	58	G. J. Parsons not out	10
J. J. Whitaker c Rhodes b Benjamin	5	A. D. Mullally not out	1
P. E. Robinson b Newport	17	L-b 8, w 5, n-b 6	19
B. F. Smith lbw b Lampitt	34		
L. Potter c Illingworth b Lampitt	3	1/7 2/17 3/51 (9 wkts, 55 overs) 205	
†P. A. Nixon run out	27	4/127 5/130 6/139	
V. J. Wells b Tolley	10	7/156 8/192 9/197	

Bowling: Benjamin 11–4–37–2; Tolley 11–2–48–1; Newport 11–0–24–1; Lampitt 9–0–50–2; Illingworth 11–0–30–1; Hick 2–0–8–0.

Worcestershire

*T. S. Curtis c Nixon b Benjamin	0	C. M. Tolley b Wells	2
W. P. C. Weston c Nixon b Benjamin	1	K. C. G. Benjamin c Benjamin	
G. A. Hick c Boon b Wells	82	b Parsons	2
D. B. D'Oliveira lbw b Wells	9		
A. C. H. Seymour c Benjamin b Potter	3	L-b 13, w 2	15
S. R. Lampitt b Mullally	14		
†S. J. Rhodes run out	11	1/0 2/3 3/44 (48.2 overs) 150	
P. J. Newport not out	8	4/47 5/96 6/129	
R. K. Illingworth b Wells	3	7/129 8/143 9/147	

Bowling: Benjamin 9–3–13–2; Mullally 8–2–21–1; Parsons 10.2–2–25–1; Wells 10–0–37–4; Potter 11–1–41–1.

Umpires: B. Leadbeater and P. B. Wight.

SOMERSET v DERBYSHIRE

At Taunton, May 25, 26. Derbyshire won 6–3 in a bowling contest, after the match was abandoned.

On the first day rain permitted Derbyshire only 20.3 overs, in which they reached 69 without loss (K. J. Barnett 35*, P. D. Bowler 25*). After further rain, that match was declared void, and with the captains unable to agree whether to start a 20-over or ten-over match, and the TCCB refusing permission to postpone the game for a week, the umpires resorted to a bowl-out. Five players from each county had to deliver two balls each at an unguarded wicket. Derbyshire had been removed from the NatWest Trophy in 1991 by this method, when their bowlers achieved only one hit in ten attempts; this time they relied more on their batsmen, who proved far more accurate. All of their choices managed one hit, and Adams had two, whereas Somerset's nominees scored one hit each apart from Hayhurst, who missed twice.

The bowlers in the deciding contest were: Derbyshire – M. J. Vandrau, C. J. Adams, K. J. Barnett, D. G. Cork and P. D. Bowler; Somerset – H. R. J. Trump, M. N. Lathwell, A. N. Hayhurst and A. R. Caddick (Mushtaq Ahmed was not required to bowl).

SUSSEX v LANCASHIRE

At Hove, May 25. Lancashire won by five wickets. Toss: Lancashire.

Wasim Akram, newly returned from a week's break in Lahore, inspired Lancashire to a comfortable victory. Sussex never really recovered from losing their two most influential strokeplayers, Wells and Speight, to run-outs. Despite a good pitch it was only the steely determination of Athey, who hit an unbeaten 61, that allowed them to make as much as 178. Wasim, bowling with great fire, took two for 27 from his 11 overs and ran out Wells with a direct hit; keen Lancashire fielding made the batsmen struggle for every run. Sussex were briefly back in the hunt when Fairbrother and Speak were bowled in quick succession by Salisbury. But Wasim immediately hit an enormous six off Salisbury into an adjoining garden. He offered Wells a difficult chance on 30 but, when he was eventually bowled by Stephenson, for 46 off 47 balls, Lloyd steered Lancashire to the semi-finals with three overs to spare.

Gold Award: Wasim Akram.

Sussex

D. M. Smith b Wasim Akram	10	N. J. Lenham lbw b Martin		20
F. D. Stephenson lbw b Martin	13	I. D. K. Salisbury not out		2
M. P. Speight run out	4	L-b 10, w 3, n-b 8		21
*A. P. Wells run out	23			
C. W. J. Athey not out	61	1/21 2/38 3/39	(7 wkts, 55 overs)	178
C. M. Wells lbw b Watkinson	2	4/75 5/77		
†P. Moores lbw b Wasim Akram	22	6/126 7/171		

E. S. H. Giddins and E. E. Hemmings did not bat.

Bowling: DeFreitas 11–1–31–0; Martin 11–0–50–2; Wasim Akram 11–2–27–2; Watkinson 11–1–19–1; Barnett 11–0–41–0.

Lancashire

M. A. Atherton b C. M. Wells	38	M. Watkinson not out		8
S. P. Titchard c Speight b Hemmings	19			
N. J. Speak b Salisbury	20	L-b 6, w 2, n-b 2		10
*N. H. Fairbrother b Salisbury	9			
G. D. Lloyd not out	32	1/34 2/79 3/92	(5 wkts, 52 overs)	182
Wasim Akram b Stephenson	46	4/95 5/174		

†W. K. Hegg, P. A. J. DeFreitas, P. J. Martin and A. A. Barnett did not bat.

Bowling: Giddins 10–1–33–0; Stephenson 11–2–44–1; Hemmings 11–3–31–1; Salisbury 11–3–41–2; C. M. Wells 9–1–27–1.

Umpires: H. D. Bird and A. G. T. Whitehead.

SEMI-FINALS

DERBYSHIRE v NORTHAMPTONSHIRE

At Derby, June 8. Derbyshire won by eight wickets. Toss: Derbyshire.

Morris and Adams sent Derbyshire surging to their third final with an exhilarating partnership of 95 in 12 overs. Adams reached his half-century from 36 balls, with two sixes and five fours, and hit the winning runs with 21 balls to spare. Before them, only Lamb was able to score freely on a slow pitch. Malcolm dismissed the Northamptonshire openers in his first spell as Lamb made 60 from 69 balls and Derbyshire were pleased to see him fall to a fine catch by Krikken. That wicket, with Loye following before lunch, gave Derbyshire control and the only other significant contribution came from a restrained Bailey. Barnett and Bowler, both badly dropped, shared their 14th century partnership in one-day competitions, but Derbyshire needed 92 from the last 15 overs. Morris began the charge and Adams picked up the tempo eagerly.

Gold Award: J. E. Morris.

Northamptonshire

A. Fordham lbw b Malcolm	10	†D. Ripley c Barnett b Malcolm	9
N. A. Felton c Krikken b Malcolm	8	J. P. Taylor not out	6
R. J. Bailey c Barnett b Cork	51	C. E. L. Ambrose c Adams b Warner	3
*A. J. Lamb c Krikken b Cork	60	L-b 9, w 9, n-b 8	26
M. B. Loye lbw b Vandrau	8		—
D. J. Capel c Adams b Griffith	12	1/19 2/22 3/121 (53.2 overs) 210
K. M. Curran b Cork	15	4/137 5/160 6/180
A. L. Penberthy run out	2	7/191 8/197 9/203

Bowling: Warner 9.2–3–19–1; Malcolm 10–3–23–3; Cork 11–0–46–3; Vandrau 11–1–46–1; Griffith 9–0–49–1; Adams 3–0–18–0.

Derbyshire

*K. J. Barnett b Taylor	61
P. D. Bowler run out	45
J. E. Morris not out	48
C. J. Adams not out	53
B 3, l-b 3, w 1	7

1/102 2/119   (2 wkts, 51.3 overs) 214

T. J. G. O'Gorman, F. A. Griffith, D. G. Cork, †K. M. Krikken, M. J. Vandrau, A. E. Warner and D. E. Malcolm did not bat.

Bowling: Ambrose 10–2–27–0; Taylor 9.3–3–34–1; Capel 5–0–20–0; Penberthy 10–0–49–0; Curran 9–0–49–0; Bailey 8–0–29–0.

Umpires: A. A. Jones and R. Palmer.

LEICESTERSHIRE v LANCASHIRE

At Leicester, June 8. Lancashire won by 110 runs. Toss: Lancashire.

Another dead Grace Road pitch discouraged good cricket, but two outstanding performances enabled Lancashire to sweep through to their third Benson and Hedges final in four years with 15 overs to spare. Fairbrother was the only batsman to get to grips with the surface, confirming his reputation as a limited-overs batsman of supreme merit with an unbeaten 64 off 80 balls. His innings was chanceless save for a run-out appeal on 43, which was referred to Chris Balderstone in the pavilion, as TCCB trials with the television umpire continued. None of Fairbrother's partners found fluent strokeplay possible, but their modest achievements looked more than respectable against the limited efforts of their counterparts. Only Whitaker kept his side in remote contention, but by the time he was yorked by Wasim Akram, Leicestershire were already in trouble against Barnett's left-arm spin. This launched a devastating spell of five for two in nine balls – three bowled, two leg-before – which earned Wasim figures of five for ten as the second half of Leicestershire's batting surrendered for 15 runs.

Gold Award: N. H. Fairbrother.

Lancashire

G. D. Mendis c Robinson b Mullally ..	11	M. Watkinson b Wells	16
M. A. Atherton c Smith b Parsons	33	P. A. J. DeFreitas not out...........	7
N. J. Speak c Boon b Wells	27	L-b 13, w 4, n-b 4.............	21
*N. H. Fairbrother not out...........	64		—
G. D. Lloyd c Smith b Parsons	34	1/26 2/66 3/102 (6 wkts, 55 overs)	218
Wasim Akram c Robinson b Parsons ..	5	4/163 5/176 6/201	

†W. K. Hegg, I. D. Austin and A. A. Barnett did not bat.

Bowling: Benjamin 11–0–46–0; Mullally 11–1–44–1; Potter 11–2–35–0; Parsons 11–4–21–3; Wells 11–1–59–2.

Leicestershire

T. J. Boon st Hegg b Barnett	21	V. J. Wells not out.................	15
*N. E. Briers c Hegg b DeFreitas	5	G. J. Parsons b Wasim Akram	0
J. J. Whitaker b Wasim Akram	32	A. D. Mullally b Wasim Akram.......	0
P. E. Robinson b Barnett	9		
B. F. Smith b Austin	7	L-b 6, w 2, n-b 4.............	12
L. Potter c Austin b Barnett	6		—
W. K. M. Benjamin		1/19 2/47 3/59 (40 overs)	108
lbw b Wasim Akram .	1	4/72 5/86 6/93	
†P. A. Nixon lbw b Wasim Akram	0	7/93 8/108 9/108	

Bowling: DeFreitas 6–2–13–1; Austin 9–2–10–1; Watkinson 7–0–26–0; Wasim Akram 7–2–10–5; Barnett 11–0–43–3.

Umpires: J. H. Hampshire and N. T. Plews.

FINAL

DERBYSHIRE v LANCASHIRE

At Lord's, July 10. Derbyshire won by six runs. Toss: Lancashire.

Derbyshire, clear outsiders at 11 a.m., took possession of the Benson and Hedges Cup for the first time in their history nearly nine and a half hours later after a contest which, though lacking technical excellence, was high on drama, excitement and controversy. For the victors it was third time lucky after their defeats of 1978 and 1988.

Much of the pre-match publicity surrounded events on the last afternoon of a Championship match between the two counties less than a fortnight before the final. Derbyshire had sent a ball used with startling effect by Wasim Akram during their second-innings destruction to the TCCB for examination. Inevitable rumours of malpractice were quickly knocked down by the Board, but the mysterious saga and the ill-feeling it generated spilled into the final. Derbyshire supporters, however, thought they were back to more distant history when their top four had gone for 66 inside 16 overs. The 1988 team had all but lost by lunch against Hampshire and, five years later, a repeat seemed likely. One of those dismissed was Adams, though not before he had been struck on the back of his left shoulder while trying to avoid a full toss from Wasim. Had umpire Meyer considered the ball an intentional beamer, Wasim would not have been allowed to bowl again. As it was, the Pakistani suffered punishment of a different kind. Far from proving a match-winner, he was the day's most expensive bowler, coming under the cosh as Derbyshire's middle order launched a superb recovery. Cork led the way, choosing a perfect time to record his highest score to date in any competition. The young all-rounder, who faced 124 balls and struck seven fours, received excellent support from first O'Gorman and then Krikken, as stands of 109 and 77 took Derbyshire past 250. Lancashire's fielding fell well below its normal standard but, even so, Cork's innings was a gem; his leg glance from outside off stump against Wasim went down as the shot of the day.

Lancashire quickly lost Titchard and were always behind the required asking-rate. But when rain interrupted play for just over an hour they still looked favourites, with 112 runs needed off 17 overs and eight wickets in hand. Sterling work by the groundstaff prevented the final from going into a second day – and, soon after play resumed, Griffith removed Atherton to end a threatening stand of 70 with Fairbrother. It was a vital breakthrough and when Warner, who bowled splendidly, removed Lloyd and Wasim (who had been dropped by Cork off a skier the previous ball), Fairbrother posed the only threat. Cork deprived him of Watkinson's company during a tight 52nd over but Fairbrother was still there as Griffith stepped up to bowl the last six deliveries, in semi-darkness, with 11 runs required. He managed a single off the second ball; DeFreitas fell to the third, and though John Holder's TV replay verdict went Fairbrother's way as he flung himself towards the crease on the fourth, the glory by now was definitely Derbyshire's. – David Lloyd.

Gold Award: D. G. Cork. *Attendance:* 24,321; *receipts* £662,917.

Derbyshire

*K. J. Barnett b Wasim Akram	19		†K. M. Krikken not out		37
P. D. Bowler lbw b DeFreitas	4				
J. E. Morris c Hegg b Watkinson	22		B 1, l-b 11, w 1, n-b 5		18
C. J. Adams b Watkinson	11				—
T. J. G. O'Gorman c Hegg b DeFreitas	49		1/7 (2) 2/32 (1)	(6 wkts, 55 overs)	252
D. G. Cork not out	92		3/61 (3) 4/66 (4)		
F. A. Griffith c Hegg b DeFreitas	0		5/175 (5) 6/175 (7)		

A. E. Warner, D. E. Malcolm and O. H. Mortensen did not bat.

Bowling: Austin 11-2-47-0; DeFreitas 11-2-39-3; Wasim Akram 11-0-65-1; Watkinson 11-2-44-2; Barnett 11-0-45-0.

Lancashire

M. A. Atherton c and b Griffith	54		I. D. Austin not out		0
S. P. Titchard c Adams b Warner	0				
N. J. Speak b Mortensen	42		L-b 11, w 3, n-b 6		20
*N. H. Fairbrother not out	87				—
G. D. Lloyd lbw b Warner	5		1/9 (2) 2/80 (3)	(7 wkts, 55 overs)	246
Wasim Akram c and b Warner	10		3/150 (1) 4/159 (5)		
M. Watkinson b Cork	12		5/184 (6) 6/218 (7)		
P. A. J. DeFreitas c Krikken b Griffith	16		7/243 (8)		

†W. K. Hegg and A. A. Barnett did not bat.

Bowling: Malcolm 11-0-53-0; Warner 11-1-31-3; Cork 11-1-50-1; Mortensen 11-0-41-1; Griffith 11-0-60-2.

Umpires: B. J. Meyer and D. R. Shepherd.

BENSON AND HEDGES CUP RECORDS

Batting

Highest individual scores: 198*, G. A. Gooch, Essex v Sussex, Hove, 1982; 177, S. J. Cook, Somerset v Sussex, Hove, 1990; 173*, C. G. Greenidge, Hampshire v Minor Counties (South), Amersham, 1973; 158*, B. F. Davison, Leicestershire v Warwickshire, Coventry, 1972; 155*, M. D. Crowe, Somerset v Hampshire, Southampton, 1987; 155*, R. A. Smith, Hampshire v Glamorgan, Southampton, 1989; 154*, M. J. Procter, Gloucestershire v Somerset, Taunton, 1972; 154*, C. L. Smith, Hampshire v Combined Universities, Southampton, 1990. *In the final:* 132*, I. V. A. Richards, Somerset v Surrey, 1981. (228 hundreds have been scored in the competition. The most hundreds in one season is 24 in 1991.)

Most runs: 4,456, G. A. Gooch; 2,761, C. J. Tavaré; 2,663, D. W. Randall; 2,550, M. W. Gatting; 2,532, A. J. Lamb.

Fastest hundred: M. A. Nash in 62 minutes, Glamorgan v Hampshire at Swansea, 1976.

Most hundreds: 11, G. A. Gooch; 6, W. Larkins; 5, C. G. Greenidge, A. J. Lamb and N. R. Taylor.

Highest totals: 388 for seven, Essex v Scotland, Chelmsford, 1992; 366 for four, Derbyshire v Combined Universities, Oxford, 1991; 350 for three, Essex v Oxford & Cambridge Univs, Chelmsford, 1979; 333 for four, Essex v Oxford & Cambridge Univs, Chelmsford, 1985; 331 for five, Surrey v Hampshire, The Oval, 1990; 330 for four, Lancashire v Sussex, Manchester, 1991; 327 for four, Leicestershire v Warwickshire, Coventry, 1972; 327 for two, Essex v Sussex, Hove, 1982; 325 for five, Middlesex v Leicestershire, Leicester, 1992; 321 for one, Hampshire v Minor Counties (South), Amersham, 1973; 321 for five, Somerset v Sussex, Hove, 1990. *In the final:* 290 for six, Essex v Surrey, 1979.

Highest total by a side batting second and winning: 291 for five (53.5 overs), Warwickshire v Lancashire (288 for nine), Manchester, 1981. *In the final:* 244 for six (55 overs), Yorkshire v Northamptonshire (244 for seven), 1987; 244 for seven (55 overs), Nottinghamshire v Essex (243 for seven), 1989.

Highest total by a side batting second and losing: 303 for seven (55 overs), Derbyshire v Somerset (310 for three), Taunton, 1990. *In the final:* 255 (51.4 overs), Surrey v Essex (290 for six), 1979.

Highest match aggregates: 613 for ten wickets, Somerset (310-3) v Derbyshire (303-7), Taunton, 1990; 602 runs for 14 wickets, Essex (307-4) v Warwickshire (295), Birmingham, 1991; 601 runs for 13 wickets, Somerset (307-6) v Gloucestershire (294-7), Taunton, 1982; 600 runs for 16 wickets, Derbyshire (300-6) v Northamptonshire (300), Derby, 1987.

Lowest totals: 50 in 27.2 overs, Hampshire v Yorkshire, Leeds, 1991; 56 in 26.2 overs, Leicestershire v Minor Counties, Wellington, 1982; 59 in 34 overs, Oxford & Cambridge Univs v Glamorgan, Cambridge, 1983; 61 in 26 overs, Sussex v Middlesex, Hove, 1978; 61 in 25.3 overs, Essex v Lancashire, Chelmsford, 1992; 62 in 26.5 overs, Gloucestershire v Hampshire, Bristol, 1975. *In the final:* 117 in 46.3 overs, Derbyshire v Hampshire, 1988.

Shortest completed innings: 21.4 overs (156), Surrey v Sussex, Hove, 1988.

Record partnership for each wicket

252	for 1st	V. P. Terry and C. L. Smith, Hampshire v Combined Universities at Southampton	1990
285*	for 2nd	C. G. Greenidge and D. R. Turner, Hampshire v Minor Counties (South) at Amersham	1973
269*	for 3rd	P. M. Roebuck and M. D. Crowe, Somerset v Hampshire at Southampton	1987
184*	for 4th	D. Lloyd and B. W. Reidy, Lancashire v Derbyshire at Chesterfield .	1980
160	for 5th	A. J. Lamb and D. J. Capel, Northamptonshire v Leicestershire at Northampton	1986
121	for 6th	P. A. Neale and S. J. Rhodes, Worcestershire v Yorkshire at Worcester	1988
149*	for 7th	J. D. Love and C. M. Old, Yorkshire v Scotland at Bradford	1981
109	for 8th	R. E. East and N. Smith, Essex v Northamptonshire at Chelmsford .	1977
83	for 9th	P. G. Newman and M. A. Holding, Derbyshire v Nottinghamshire at Nottingham	1985
80*	for 10th	D. L. Bairstow and M. Johnson, Yorkshire v Derbyshire at Derby . .	1981

Bowling

Most wickets: 147, J. K. Lever; 132, I. T. Botham.

Best bowling: Seven for 12, W. W. Daniel, Middlesex v Minor Counties (East), Ipswich, 1978; seven for 22, J. R. Thomson, Middlesex v Hampshire, Lord's, 1981; seven for 32, R. G. D. Willis, Warwickshire v Yorkshire, Birmingham, 1981. *In the final:* Five for 13, S. T. Jefferies, Hampshire v Derbyshire, 1988.

Hat-tricks (10): G. D. McKenzie, Leicestershire v Worcestershire, Worcester, 1972; K. Higgs, Leicestershire v Surrey in the final, Lord's, 1974; A. A. Jones, Middlesex v Essex, Lord's, 1977; M. J. Procter, Gloucestershire v Hampshire, Southampton, 1977; W. Larkins, Northamptonshire v Oxford & Cambridge Univs, Northampton, 1980; E. A. Moseley, Glamorgan v Kent, Cardiff, 1981; G. C. Small, Warwickshire v Leicestershire, Leicester, 1984; N. A. Mallender, Somerset v Combined Universities, Taunton, 1987; W. K. M. Benjamin, Leicestershire v Nottinghamshire, Leicester, 1987; A. R. C. Fraser, Middlesex v Sussex, Lord's, 1988.

Wicket-keeping and Fielding

Most dismissals: 122 (117 ct, 5 st), D. L. Bairstow.

Most dismissals in an innings: 8 (all ct), D. J. S. Taylor, Somerset v Oxford & Cambridge Univs, Taunton, 1982.

Most catches by a fielder: 62, G. A. Gooch; 54, C. J. Tavaré; 53, I. T. Botham.

Most catches by a fielder in an innings: 5, V. J. Marks, Oxford & Cambridge Univs v Kent, Oxford, 1976.

Results

Largest victories in runs: Essex by 272 runs v Scotland, Chelmsford, 1992, and by 214 runs v Oxford & Cambridge Univs, Chelmsford, 1979; Derbyshire by 206 runs v Combined Universities, Oxford, 1991; Yorkshire by 189 runs v Hampshire, Leeds, 1991; Sussex by 186 runs v Cambridge University, Hove, 1974.

Victories by ten wickets (16): By Derbyshire, Essex (twice), Glamorgan, Hampshire, Kent, Lancashire, Leicestershire (twice), Middlesex, Northamptonshire, Somerset, Warwickshire, Worcestershire, Yorkshire (twice).

WINNERS 1972-93

1972 LEICESTERSHIRE beat Yorkshire by five wickets.
1973 KENT beat Worcestershire by 39 runs.
1974 SURREY beat Leicestershire by 27 runs.
1975 LEICESTERSHIRE beat Middlesex by five wickets.
1976 KENT beat Worcestershire by 43 runs.
1977 GLOUCESTERSHIRE beat Kent by 64 runs.
1978 KENT beat Derbyshire by six wickets.
1979 ESSEX beat Surrey by 35 runs.
1980 NORTHAMPTONSHIRE beat Essex by six runs.
1981 SOMERSET beat Surrey by seven wickets.
1982 SOMERSET beat Nottinghamshire by nine wickets.
1983 MIDDLESEX beat Essex by four runs.
1984 LANCASHIRE beat Warwickshire by six wickets.
1985 LEICESTERSHIRE beat Essex by five wickets.
1986 MIDDLESEX beat Kent by two runs.
1987 YORKSHIRE beat Northamptonshire, having taken more wickets with the scores tied.

1988 HAMPSHIRE beat Derbyshire by seven wickets.
1989 NOTTINGHAMSHIRE beat Essex by three wickets.
1990 LANCASHIRE beat Worcestershire by 69 runs.
1991 WORCESTERSHIRE beat Lancashire by 65 runs.
1992 HAMPSHIRE beat Kent by 41 runs.
1993 DERBYSHIRE beat Lancashire by six runs.

WINS BY UNIVERSITIES

1973 { OXFORD beat Northamptonshire at Northampton by two wickets.
1975 { OXFORD & CAMBRIDGE beat Worcestershire at Cambridge by 66 runs.
      { OXFORD & CAMBRIDGE beat Northamptonshire at Oxford by three wickets.
1976 OXFORD & CAMBRIDGE beat Yorkshire at Barnsley by seven wickets.
1984 OXFORD & CAMBRIDGE beat Gloucestershire at Bristol by 27 runs.
1989 { COMBINED UNIVERSITIES beat Surrey at Cambridge by nine runs.
      { COMBINED UNIVERSITIES beat Worcestershire at Worcester by five wickets.
1990 COMBINED UNIVERSITIES beat Yorkshire at Leeds by two wickets.

WINS BY MINOR COUNTIES AND SCOTLAND

1980 MINOR COUNTIES beat Gloucestershire at Chippenham by three runs.
1981 MINOR COUNTIES beat Hampshire at Southampton by three runs.
1982 MINOR COUNTIES beat Leicestershire at Wellington by 131 runs.
1986 SCOTLAND beat Lancashire at Perth by three runs.
1987 MINOR COUNTIES beat Glamorgan at Oxford (Christ Church) by seven wickets.
1990 SCOTLAND beat Northamptonshire at Northampton by two runs.
1992 MINOR COUNTIES beat Sussex at Marlow by 19 runs.

TEAM RECORDS 1972-93

	Rounds reached					Matches		
	W	F	SF	QF	P	W	L	NR
Derbyshire	1	3	4	8	101	54	40	7
Durham	0	0	0	0	6	3	3	0
Essex	1	5	8	13	112	71	40	1
Glamorgan	0	0	1	7	94	40	50	4
Gloucestershire	1	1	2	5	94	44	47	3
Hampshire	2	2	4	11	103	55	44	4
Kent	3	6	11	14	116	73	41	2
Lancashire	2	4	8	14	111	67	38	6
Leicestershire	3	4	6	9	105	59	40	6
Middlesex	2	3	5	13	107	57	42	8
Northamptonshire	1	2	4	9	100	46	46	8
Nottinghamshire	1	2	5	11	103	61	37	5
Somerset	2	2	7	11	105	58	45	2
Surrey	1	3	6	9	104	55	45	4
Sussex	0	0	1	9	96	48	47	1
Warwickshire	0	1	5	11	102	55	42	5
Worcestershire	1	4	6	13	108	56	48	4
Yorkshire	1	2	5	8	100	52	42	6
Cambridge University	0	0	0	0	8	0	8	0
Oxford University	0	0	0	0	4	1	3	0
Oxford & Cambridge Universities	0	0	0	0	48	4	42	2
Combined Universities	0	0	0	1	26	3	22	1
Minor Counties	0	0	0	0	54	5	46	3
Minor Counties (North)	0	0	0	0	20	0	20	0
Minor Counties (South)	0	0	0	0	20	0	19	1
Minor Counties (East)	0	0	0	0	12	0	12	0
Minor Counties (West)	0	0	0	0	12	0	12	0
Scotland	0	0	0	0	53	2	48	3

Middlesex beat Gloucestershire on the toss of a coin in their quarter-final in 1983.
Derbyshire and Somerset totals each include a bowling contest after their 1993 quarter-final
was abandoned; Derbyshire beat Somerset.

AXA EQUITY & LAW LEAGUE, 1993

The Sunday League, under its sixth official name and its third sponsor, was even more derided than usual in its 25th season. The revamped format was disliked by almost everyone for different reasons: traditionalists loathed the coloured clothes and white ball; the players hated the switch from 40 overs to 50 and complained of being worn out before the final days of Championship cricket on Mondays; and spectators, used to turning up to Sunday matches after lunch, never got the hang of the twelve o'clock starts.

None the less, the problems were entirely forgotten during a magnificent finale. By glorious chance, the two top teams – Kent and Glamorgan – were playing each other, winner take all, on the final Sunday of the season. With 12,000 people packed into the St Lawrence Ground, Glamorgan won their first-ever one-day trophy and Viv Richards, on his penultimate day of county cricket, played the vital innings and was there when the winning runs were hit.

Glamorgan's triumph stunned everyone except those Welshmen who had the confidence to believe that the club's quiet team-building was finally about to produce dividends. Before the League season began, they were between 100 and 200 to 1 in the betting. At the beginning of June, following two defeats and a washout, it was possible to back them at 500 to 1, the odds made famous by England's Test win at Headingley in 1981.

Continued overleaf

AXA EQUITY & LAW LEAGUE

	M	W	L	T	NR	Pts	Run-Rate
1 – Glamorgan (16)	17	13	2	0	2	56	75.41
2 – Kent (5)	17	12	3	0	2	52	81.65
3 – Surrey (4)	17	11	4	0	2	48	73.05
4 – Sussex (11)	17	10	5	1	1	44	78.32
5 – Northamptonshire (13).....	17	9	5	1	2	42	71.15
6 – Lancashire (11)...........	17	8	5	1	3	40	68.41
7 – Durham (8)	17	8	7	0	2	36	70.64
8 – Middlesex (1)	17	7	6	2	2	36	70.93
9 – Yorkshire (15)............	17	8	8	0	1	34	71.81
10 – Warwickshire (8)	17	7	8	0	2	32	70.51
11 – Derbyshire (13)..........	17	7	8	0	2	32	68.70
12 – Essex (2)	17	7	8	1	1	32	66.66
13 – Gloucestershire (8)	17	5	9	1	2	26	64.19
14 – Leicestershire (18)......	17	5	10	0	2	24	69.93
15 – Hampshire (3)............	17	4	9	0	4	24	68.85
16 – Worcestershire (7)	17	4	10	1	2	22	65.07
17 – Nottinghamshire (17).....	17	4	12	0	1	18	74.64
18 – Somerset (5)	17	2	12	0	3	14	62.02

1992 positions are shown in brackets.

When two or more counties finish with an equal number of points, the positions are decided by a) *most wins,* b) *runs per 100 balls.*

No play was possible in the following three matches: May 30 – Derbyshire v Hampshire at Checkley, Somerset v Glamorgan at Taunton; September 12 – Hampshire v Leicestershire at Southampton.

Glamorgan won their next 12 matches. The batting, led by the captain Hugh Morris, was exceptionally consistent and they had no need of the gimmicks used by other counties who promoted tail-end sloggers to take advantage of the new rule allowing only two men outside the circle in the first 15 overs. The bowling grew in assurance, with Lefebvre and Barwick particularly effective, and the fielding occasionally touched heights of brilliance. Above all, perhaps, Richards, the only man in the team accustomed to success, passed on to his team-mates the belief that failure was not inevitable. This was backed up by growing enthusiasm from the crowds on the seven different home grounds the county used in the League.

Their sequence of victories equalled the record run with which Middlesex, the deposed champions, began the 1992 season. Though Glamorgan's penultimate game was washed out, the victory at Canterbury took their unbeaten sequence to 14, beating the record established by Leicestershire in 1974. Their success left Gloucestershire, Northamptonshire and Surrey, along with Durham, as the only counties never to have won the League. Glamorgan will remain 50-over champions indefinitely; the TCCB decided in December to switch back to 40 overs in 1994.

Glamorgan had never before finished above joint fifth and in the previous four seasons had not been out of the bottom three, winning just 14 games and losing 43. They still have the worst League record of all the counties. Kent, the only team to keep pace with them, were unbeaten from June 20 until the final match. Their overseas player, Carl Hooper, with 854 runs and 19 economical wickets, was easily the League's most successful performer. Sussex, the only other team who ever looked like potential champions, started strongly, as they had in 1992, and shared the lead from May 23 until June 27. In the end, they finished fourth, just behind Surrey who, like Glamorgan, had never previously finished in the top three.

Durham, bottom of the Championship, finished with six consecutive wins to move into the top half. In contrast, Leicestershire had a sequence of losing eight in a row; Worcestershire lost their last four, just as they were putting together a marvellous winning sequence in the Championship; Nottinghamshire produced several blazing batting displays but still won only four times, continuing their dramatic decline since winning the League in 1991; and Somerset – in their time champions of the 40, 55 and 60-over games – completely failed to master the 50-over variant and finished bottom of the League for the first time.

The theory that counties out of the running would try and expend less energy on the 50-over competition was backed up by the fact that a record 53 players made their League debuts in the season, nine of them for Somerset.

Under TCCB regulations, two extras were scored for every no-ball bowled whether scored off or not. Any runs scored off the bat were credited to the batsman, while byes and leg-byes were counted as no-balls, in accordance with Law 24.9, in addition to the initial penalty. These regulations applied to all the one-day competitions in 1993, as well as the Championship.

Leading run-scorers: C. L. Hooper 854; P. D. Bowler 768; A. P. Wells 738; H. Morris 737; T. R. Ward 720; J. P. Stephenson 663; C. J. Adams 652; R. J. Blakey 606; P. Johnson 600.

Leading wicket-takers: F. D. Stephenson 31; A. C. Cummins 29; N. M. K. Smith 27; Waqar Younis and Wasim Akram 26; P. Bainbridge, S. R. Barwick, J. Boiling, E. S. H. Giddins and P. N. Weekes 25.

Most economical bowlers (runs per over, minimum 100 overs): R. P. Lefebvre 2.83; O. H. Mortensen 3.28; C. L. Hooper 3.30; Mushtaq Ahmed 3.37; T. A. Munton 3.38; F. D. Stephenson 3.42.

Leading wicket-keepers: C. P. Metson 28 (21 ct, 7 st); K. R. Brown 23 (18 ct, 5 st); S. J. Rhodes 23 (18 ct, 5 st).

Leading fielders: R. P. Lefebvre 14; C. L. Hooper 12; J. D. Carr and M. A. Lynch 11.

Prize money

£30,000 for winners: GLAMORGAN.
£15,000 for runners-up: KENT.
£7,500 for third place: SURREY.
£3,750 for fourth place: SUSSEX.
£375 for the winners of each match, shared if tied or no result.

SUMMARY OF RESULTS, 1993

	Derbyshire	Durham	Essex	Glamorgan	Gloucestershire	Hampshire	Kent	Lancashire	Leicestershire	Middlesex	Northamptonshire	Nottinghamshire	Somerset	Surrey	Sussex	Warwickshire	Worcestershire	Yorkshire
Derbyshire	—	L	W	W	W	N	W	L	L	L	N	L	W	L	W	L	W	L
Durham	W	—	L	L	L	N	N	L	L	W	W	W	W	L	L	W	W	W
Essex	L	W	—	N	W	W	L	W	W	T	L	W	L	L	L	L	L	W
Glamorgan	L	W	N	—	W	W	W	W	W	L	W	L	N	W	W	W	W	W
Gloucestershire	L	W	L	L	—	W	L	T	L	N	L	N	W	L	L	W	L	W
Hampshire	N	N	L	L	L	—	W	L	L	W	L	W	W	L	W	W	N	L
Kent	L	N	L	W	L	W	—	W	W	W	W	L	W	N	W	W	W	W
Lancashire	W	W	L	L	T	W	L	—	W	N	L	W	N	L	N	L	W	W
Leicestershire	W	W	L	L	W	N	L	L	—	L	L	W	L	N	L	L	W	L
Middlesex	W	L	T	L	N	W	L	N	W	—	L	W	W	L	T	W	W	L
Northamptonshire	N	L	W	W	W	L	W	W	W	—	W	W	N	L	L	L	T	L
Nottinghamshire	W	L	L	L	N	L	W	L	L	L	L	—	W	L	L	N	L	L
Somerset	L	L	W	N	L	L	L	L	N	W	N	W	—	L	W	L	L	W
Surrey	W	W	W	L	W	W	L	W	W	L	L	L	L	—	W	L	L	W
Sussex	L	W	W	W	L	W	L	N	L	W	T	W	W	W	—	W	W	L
Warwickshire	W	L	W	L	L	L	L	N	W	L	N	W	L	L	L	—	W	W
Worcestershire	L	L	W	L	W	N	L	L	L	L	T	L	W	L	W	L	—	N
Yorkshire	W	L	L	L	L	W	L	L	W	W	W	W	W	L	W	L	N	—

Home games in bold, away games in italics. W = Won, L = Lost, T = Tied, N = No result.

DERBYSHIRE

At Birmingham, May 9. DERBYSHIRE lost to WARWICKSHIRE by three wickets.

DERBYSHIRE v GLAMORGAN

At Derby, May 16. Derbyshire won by three runs. Toss: Glamorgan.

Derbyshire survived an extraordinary collapse in the closing stages of their innings to peg Glamorgan back just enough; Metson was caught off the final ball looking for the winning boundary. Derbyshire had plunged from 209 for two to 215 all out in 18 balls; five of those eight wickets went to Barwick, whose six for 28 was his best one-day analysis. Bowler was out for 96 for the second time in three days.

Derbyshire

*K. J. Barnett c Dale b Barwick	32	†B. J. M. Maher b Barwick		2
P. D. Bowler run out	96	S. J. Base not out		3
J. E. Morris b Croft	27	D. E. Malcolm c Hemp b Barwick		0
C. J. Adams c Dale b Watkin	52	L-b 2		2
A. E. Warner c Morris b Barwick	0			—
T. J. G. O'Gorman lbw b Barwick	0	1/69 2/111 3/209	(49.3 overs)	215
F. A. Griffith b Barwick	1	4/209 5/209 6/210		
D. G. Cork run out	0	7/210 8/210 9/215		

Bowling: Watkin 10–0–38–1; Lefebvre 10–1–43–0; Croft 10–0–28–1; Barwick 9.3–2–28–6; Dale 6–0–48–0; Richards 4–0–28–0.

Glamorgan

S. P. James c Maher b Malcolm	0	R. P. Lefebvre not out		1
*H. Morris c Barnett b Malcolm	70	†C. P. Metson c Cork b Griffith		1
A. Dale b Griffith	12	L-b 5, w 1, n-b 8		14
M. P. Maynard b Cork	69			
I. V. A. Richards c Maher b Griffith	30	1/0 2/37 3/133	(8 wkts, 50 overs)	212
R. D. B. Croft c Barnett b Griffith	13	4/188 5/197 6/205		
D. L. Hemp b Cork	2	7/210 8/212		

S. L. Watkin and S. R. Barwick did not bat.

Bowling: Malcolm 10–1–35–2; Warner 10–1–41–0; Cork 10–1–30–2; Griffith 10–0–48–4; Base 10–0–53–0.

Umpires: D. J. Constant and N. T. Plews.

At Chelmsford, May 23. DERBYSHIRE beat ESSEX by two wickets.

DERBYSHIRE v HAMPSHIRE

At Checkley, May 30. No result (abandoned). Toss: Derbyshire.

The game was originally reduced to 41 overs a side but then abandoned without a ball bowled.

At Lord's, June 6. DERBYSHIRE lost to MIDDLESEX by two wickets.

DERBYSHIRE v YORKSHIRE

At Chesterfield, June 13. Yorkshire won by nine wickets. Toss: Yorkshire.

A stand of 165 in 35 overs from Yorkshire's openers ensured an easy victory. Byas hit a six and 12 fours in his maiden limited-overs century, and his captain Moxon struck 12 fours. Derbyshire were unable to build on a good start after Adams went for 56 from 61 balls, though O'Gorman hit three sixes.

Derbyshire

P. D. Bowler c Hartley b Grayson	55	†B. J. M. Maher not out 14
C. J. Adams c Blakey b Jarvis	56	S. J. Base not out 2
J. E. Morris b Jarvis	1	L-b 3, n-b 6 9
T. J. G. O'Gorman b Jarvis	45	
*K. J. Barnett c Richardson b Batty	5	1/85 2/93 3/152 (7 wkts, 50 overs) 207
M. J. Vandrau c White b Hartley	13	4/159 5/182
A. E. Warner run out	7	6/186 7/197

O. H. Mortensen and R. W. Sladdin did not bat.

Bowling: Robinson 5-0-30-0; Jarvis 10-0-44-3; Hartley 10-0-40-1; White 5-1-25-0; Batty 10-0-34-1; Grayson 10-0-31-1.

Yorkshire

*M. D. Moxon c Maher b Warner	80
D. Byas not out	106
R. B. Richardson not out	8
L-b 5, w 3, n-b 6	14
1/165	(1 wkt, 43.3 overs) 208

A. A. Metcalfe, †R. J. Blakey, C. White, A. P. Grayson, P. W. Jarvis, P. J. Hartley, J. D. Batty and M. A. Robinson did not bat.

Bowling: Warner 8-0-34-1; Mortensen 10-2-33-0; Base 10-1-39-0; Vandrau 6.3-0-47-0; Sladdin 9-0-50-0.

Umpires: A. A. Jones and P. B. Wight.

At Canterbury, June 20. DERBYSHIRE beat KENT by three runs.

DERBYSHIRE v LANCASHIRE

At Derby, June 27. Lancashire won by 161 runs. Toss: Derbyshire.

It took Derbyshire barely half their allotted 50 overs to capitulate for 73 against Lancashire, the team they were to face in the Benson and Hedges Cup final a fortnight later. DeFreitas returned his best figures in the League, taking Derbyshire's first four wickets. Earlier, Atherton had scored 105, his second century in four days off Derbyshire's bowling.

Lancashire

M. A. Atherton b Griffith	105	P. A. J. DeFreitas not out 15
S. P. Titchard c Adams b Base	10	M. Watkinson not out 4
G. D. Lloyd lbw b Cork	6	B 7, l-b 7 14
*N. H. Fairbrother c Barnett b Malcolm	26	
N. J. Speak b Cork	21	1/42 2/53 3/104 (6 wkts, 50 overs) 234
Wasim Akram c Cork b Griffith	33	4/148 5/203 6/225

†W. K. Hegg, I. D. Austin and A. A. Barnett did not bat.

Bowling: Mortensen 10-0-52-0; Malcolm 10-2-44-1; Base 10-2-38-1; Cork 10-0-38-2; Griffith 10-1-48-2.

Derbyshire

P. D. Bowler c Austin b DeFreitas	0	†B. J. M. Maher c DeFreitas b Barnett		1
C. J. Adams c Titchard b DeFreitas	4	D. E. Malcolm b Wasim Akram		0
J. E. Morris c Speak b DeFreitas	4	O. H. Mortensen c and b Barnett		3
T. J. G. O'Gorman not out	34			
*K. J. Barnett c Hegg b DeFreitas	2	L-b 3, w 1		4
F. A. Griffith c Fairbrother				
b Watkinson	10	1/4 2/6 3/9	(26.5 overs)	73
D. G. Cork b Barnett	11	4/15 5/35 6/57		
S. J. Base b Wasim Akram	0	7/60 8/65 9/66		

Bowling: Austin 5–2–6–0; DeFreitas 7–1–16–4; Watkinson 4–0–12–1; Wasim Akram 6–0–21–2; Barnett 4.5–0–15–3.

Umpires: V. A. Holder and G. Sharp.

At Worcester, July 4. DERBYSHIRE beat WORCESTERSHIRE by five wickets.

DERBYSHIRE v SUSSEX

At Derby, July 25. Derbyshire won by 81 runs. Toss: Sussex.

Rain interrupted Derbyshire's innings four times in the first 15 overs, reducing the match to 38 overs a side. Malcolm settled the match with a spell of three wickets for no runs in seven balls.

Derbyshire

P. D. Bowler run out	57	*K. J. Barnett not out		11
C. J. Adams c Wells b Stephenson	43	†K. M. Krikken not out		1
J. E. Morris c Wells b North	6	L-b 6, w 2, n-b 4		12
T. J. G. O'Gorman c Athey b Giddins	60			
D. G. Cork b Stephenson	8	1/59 2/68 3/168	(6 wkts, 38 overs)	199
A. E. Warner b Stephenson	1	4/176 5/184 6/195		

S. J. Base, D. E. Malcolm and O. H. Mortensen did not bat.

Bowling: Giddins 10–0–65–1; Stephenson 10–0–44–3; Pigott 10–0–36–0; North 1–0–8–1; Salisbury 7–0–40–0.

Sussex

D. M. Smith lbw b Malcolm	10	I. D. K. Salisbury b Mortensen		18
M. P. Speight c Warner b Malcolm	14	A. C. S. Pigott c Base b Mortensen		2
C. W. J. Athey lbw b Malcolm	0	E. S. H. Giddins not out		0
*A. P. Wells lbw b Warner	0	L-b 3, w 3, n-b 4		10
J. A. North c Krikken b Cork	48			
N. J. Lenham c Krikken b Warner	1	1/23 2/23 3/24	(29.2 overs)	118
F. D. Stephenson c and b Malcolm	4	4/36 5/46 6/51		
†P. Moores c Morris b Cork	11	7/90 8/102 9/109		

Bowling: Warner 8–1–29–2; Malcolm 8–1–42–4; Cork 7–0–24–2; Mortensen 6.2–0–20–2.

Umpires: M. J. Kitchen and B. J. Meyer.

At Cheltenham, August 1. DERBYSHIRE beat GLOUCESTERSHIRE by eight wickets.

At Durham University, August 8. DERBYSHIRE lost to DURHAM by 112 runs.

DERBYSHIRE v SOMERSET

At Derby, August 15. Derbyshire won by 113 runs. Toss: Somerset.

Somerset went down to their eighth consecutive Sunday defeat after an opening stand of 201 between Bowler and Adams. Bowler's career-best one-day score came off 154 balls with two sixes and 15 fours. Caddick was treated most harshly, conceding 74 from nine overs. Somerset then crumpled to 64 for six.

Derbyshire

P. D. Bowler not out	138	A. S. Rollins not out	13
C. J. Adams c Mallender b Rose	93		
*J. E. Morris c Lathwell b Mallender	14	L-b 8, w 8, n-b 6	22
T. J. G. O'Gorman c Turner			
b Mallender	1	1/201 2/235 3/256 (3 wkts, 50 overs)	281

M. J. Vandrau, †K. M. Krikken, D. G. Cork, O. H. Mortensen, S. J. Base and D. E. Malcolm did not bat.

Bowling: Caddick 9-0-74-0; Mallender 10-1-28-2; Rose 7-1-44-1; Kerr 6-0-36-0; Payne 8-0-51-0; Mushtaq Ahmed 10-0-40-0.

Somerset

M. N. Lathwell c Krikken b Mortensen	4	A. R. Caddick b Vandrau	17
I. Fletcher c Krikken b Cork	26	J. I. D. Kerr b Malcolm	1
N. A. Folland c Krikken b Base	0	N. A. Mallender not out	0
*R. J. Harden c Krikken b Mortensen	16	B 1, w 7, n-b 2	10
G. D. Rose b Vandrau	52		
Mushtaq Ahmed b Mortensen	9	1/6 2/7 3/49 (38.1 overs)	168
A. Payne lbw b Cork	0	4/49 5/63 6/64	
†R. J. Turner c Krikken b Base	33	7/141 8/166 9/168	

Bowling: Mortensen 10-1-39-3; Base 7-2-17-2; Cork 7-0-20-2; Malcolm 7.1-0-41-1; Vandrau 7-0-50-2.

Umpires: P. B. Wight and P. Willey.

DERBYSHIRE v SURREY

At Ilkeston, August 22. Surrey won by five wickets. Toss: Surrey.

For the second Sunday running, Bowler and Adams shared a century opening stand; Adams scored his eighth fifty of the season in the competition and Bowler carried his bat. However, Morris was the only other Derbyshire player to reach double figures. Surrey started badly but Ward and Smith put on 113 in 27 overs.

Derbyshire

*P. D. Bowler not out	76	A. E. Warner lbw b Waqar Younis	6
C. J. Adams lbw b Boiling	66	S. J. Base run out	0
J. E. Morris lbw b Hollioake	14	O. H. Mortensen run out	1
T. J. G. O'Gorman b Hollioake	8		
A. S. Rollins run out	0	L-b 9, w 5, n-b 2	16
D. G. Cork b Benjamin	8		
F. A. Griffith b Waqar Younis	3	1/104 2/125 3/137 (45.4 overs)	201
†K. M. Krikken c Kersey		4/147 5/162 6/168	
b Waqar Younis	3	7/183 8/191 9/191	

Bowling: Butcher 9-0-50-0; Benjamin 7.4-1-26-1; Hollioake 9-0-43-2; Waqar Younis 10-1-33-3; Boiling 10-0-40-1.

Surrey

D. J. Bicknell lbw b Mortensen	0	M. A. Butcher not out		27
A. D. Brown c Cork b Base	5			
D. M. Ward not out	81	B 1, l-b 6, w 13, n-b 8		28
*M. A. Lynch b Base	3			
A. W. Smith c and b Cork	58	1/1 2/10 3/16	(5 wkts, 45.1 overs)	203
A. J. Hollioake lbw b Base	1	4/129 5/132		

†G. J. Kersey, Waqar Younis, J. Boiling and J. E. Benjamin did not bat.

Bowling: Mortensen 10–2–21–1; Base 10–0–34–3; Warner 9–1–40–0; Griffith 6.1–0–53–0; Cork 10–1–48–1.

Umpires: R. Julian and D. O. Oslear.

At Nottingham, August 29. DERBYSHIRE lost to NOTTINGHAMSHIRE by 142 runs.

DERBYSHIRE v NORTHAMPTONSHIRE

At Derby, September 12. No result. Toss: Northamptonshire.
Before heavy rain ended play there was time for Bowler, when 19, to pass his captain Barnett's Derbyshire record of 700 Sunday League runs in a season, set in 1986.

Derbyshire

P. D. Bowler c Ripley b Cook	40	M. J. Vandrau not out		14
C. J. Adams b Ambrose	9	†K. M. Krikken not out		14
*K. J. Barnett c Lamb b Bowen	79			
T. J. G. O'Gorman c Lamb b Bowen	17	L-b 5, w 18, n-b 2		25
A. S. Rollins b Cook	6			
D. G. Cork run out	2	1/34 2/87 3/144	(8 wkts, 50 overs)	214
A. E. Warner c Ripley b Bowen	4	4/171 5/173 6/176		
I. G. S. Steer b Ambrose	4	7/180 8/184		

S. J. Base did not bat.

Bowling: Ambrose 10–1–35–2; Bowen 10–2–35–3; Curran 10–2–23–0; Taylor 10–0–60–0; Cook 10–0–56–2.

Northamptonshire

A. Fordham, M. B. Loye, R. J. Bailey, R. J. Warren, *A. J. Lamb, K. M. Curran, †D. Ripley, M. N. Bowen, C. E. L. Ambrose, J. P. Taylor and N. G. B. Cook.

Umpires: B. Leadbeater and D. R. Shepherd.

At Leicester, September 19. DERBYSHIRE lost to LEICESTERSHIRE by 14 runs.

DURHAM

At Manchester, May 9. DURHAM lost to LANCASHIRE by 12 runs.

DURHAM v HAMPSHIRE

At Stockton-on-Tees, May 16. No result. Toss: Durham.
Durham were frustrated by rain when they were scenting their first victory over another first-class county since August 9. The match had already been reduced to 34 overs a side, but Cummins bowled well to take four wickets and Hampshire were kept well short of four an over. The Durham openers were coasting ahead of the rate when the conditions, already poor, became impossible.

Hampshire

V. P. Terry c Smith b Cummins	12	M. D. Marshall b Cummins	3
C. C. Middleton c Parker b Cummins	12	S. D. Udal not out	1
R. A. Smith not out	53		
D. I. Gower b Hughes	8	B 2, l-b 3, w 4, n-b 6	15
*M. C. J. Nicholas c Cummins			
b Bainbridge	13	1/20 2/32 3/53	(6 wkts, 34 overs) 127
R. Ayling c Bainbridge b Cummins	10	4/82 5/105 6/118	

†A. N. Aymes, M. Jean-Jacques and C. A. Connor did not bat.

Bowling: Hughes 8-0-38-1; Cummins 10-3-24-4; Berry 9-0-31-0; Bainbridge 7-0-29-1.

Durham

G. Fowler not out	23
W. Larkins not out	21
B 1, l-b 3	4

(no wkt, 11 overs) 48

P. W. G. Parker, P. Bainbridge, I. Smith, J. D. Glendenen, †A. R. Fothergill, A. C. Cummins, P. J. Berry, *D. A. Graveney and S. P. Hughes did not bat.

Bowling: Marshall 5-1-12-0; Connor 2-0-11-0; Udal 3-0-15-0; Ayling 1-0-6-0.

Umpires: V. A. Holder and B. J. Meyer.

At Bristol, May 23. DURHAM lost to GLOUCESTERSHIRE by five wickets.

DURHAM v KENT

At Darlington, May 30. No result. Toss: Durham.

A fierce assault from Ward and Fleming, who hit 46 from 24 balls, had the 100 up in 13 overs and laid the groundwork for Kent's first total of 300 in the Sunday League. Undaunted, Botham, with 45 from 34 balls, and Larkins gave Durham a blazing start as well before a 30-minute downpour left the field unfit.

Kent

T. R. Ward c Glendenen b Bainbridge	49	M. A. Ealham not out	12
M. V. Fleming c Bainbridge b Botham	46	D. W. Headley not out	9
C. L. Hooper c Smith b Hughes	85	B 4, l-b 10, w 6	20
N. R. Taylor c and b Smith	22		
N. J. Llong lbw b Graveney	20	1/76 2/110 3/156	(7 wkts, 50 overs) 300
*M. R. Benson c Parker b Bainbridge	18	4/195 5/235	
†S. A. Marsh c Fothergill b Cummins	19	6/278 7/278	

M. J. McCague and A. P. Igglesden did not bat.

Bowling: Cummins 10-1-78-1; Hughes 9-0-61-1; Botham 10-0-45-1; Bainbridge 9-1-38-2; Smith 4-0-27-1; Graveney 8-0-37-1.

Durham

I. T. Botham not out	45
W. Larkins not out	38
L-b 5, w 3	8

(no wkt, 12.3 overs) 91

G. Fowler, P. W. G. Parker, P. Bainbridge, I. Smith, J. D. Glendenen, A. C. Cummins, †A. R. Fothergill, *D. A. Graveney and S. P. Hughes did not bat.

Bowling: McCague 6-0-39-0; Igglesden 6-0-45-0; Hooper 0.3-0-2-0.

Umpires: J. C. Balderstone and R. A. White.

At Leicester, June 6. DURHAM lost to LEICESTERSHIRE by three runs.

DURHAM v MIDDLESEX

At Gateshead Fell, June 13. Durham won by six wickets. Toss: Durham.

In beating the reigning champions, Durham won their first victory over a first-class county for ten months and 21 matches – their last success was over Warwickshire in the Sunday League on August 9, 1992. Botham got them off to a good start by removing Gatting and Haynes quickly. Durham's reply to a mediocre 158 centred on a 93-run stand from Hutton and Bainbridge; Hutton remained until only 12 runs were required and Bainbridge hit the winning boundary in the next over.

Middlesex

*M. W. Gatting lbw b Botham	4	J. E. Emburey not out		17
D. L. Haynes c Briers b Botham	9	N. F. Williams not out		8
M. R. Ramprakash c Fothergill b Wood	14	B 1, l-b 5, w 3, n-b 2		11
J. D. Carr c and b Bainbridge	26			
P. N. Weekes b Hughes	36	1/10 2/23 3/54	(7 wkts, 50 overs)	158
†K. R. Brown run out	10	4/79 5/103		
M. Keech c Graveney b Cummins	23	6/123 7/143		

N. G. Cowans and A. R. C. Fraser did not bat.

Bowling: Botham 10–2–25–2; Cummins 8–1–26–1; Wood 5–0–14–1; Hughes 9–0–29–1; Bainbridge 9–3–24–1; Graveney 9–0–34–0.

Durham

I. T. Botham b Williams	11	M. P. Briers not out		1
W. Larkins lbw b Cowans	1	B 1, l-b 13, w 2, n-b 2		18
P. W. G. Parker c Cowans b Fraser	31			
S. Hutton c and b Weekes	44	1/2 2/26	(4 wkts, 46.5 overs)	159
P. Bainbridge not out	53	3/54 4/147		

A. C. Cummins, †A. R. Fothergill, J. Wood, *D. A. Graveney and S. P. Hughes did not bat.

Bowling: Williams 8–3–15–1; Cowans 10–3–15–1; Keech 10–1–31–0; Emburey 7.5–0–35–0; Fraser 8–0–30–1; Weekes 3–0–19–1.

Umpires: B. Leadbeater and P. Willey.

At Colwyn Bay, June 20. DURHAM lost to GLAMORGAN by 166 runs.

DURHAM v WORCESTERSHIRE

At Stockton-on-Tees, June 27. Durham won by five runs. Toss: Worcestershire.

Benjamin removed Botham with the first ball of the match, but was unable to hit the last one for six, leaving Durham as winners. Fowler, who passed 5,000 Sunday League runs, and Parker had dominated their innings with 105 for the second wicket. Replying, Worcestershire's experimental opener, Radford, hit his highest score in the Sunday League but his county faltered, with three run-outs in the final stages.

Durham

I. T. Botham c Hick b Benjamin	0	J. Wood not out		11
G. Fowler c Lampitt b Illingworth	52	†A. R. Fothergill not out		13
P. W. G. Parker c Lampitt b Newport	72	L-b 10, w 3, n-b 6		19
S. Hutton b Newport	0			
P. Bainbridge c Leatherdale b Newport	5	1/0 2/105 3/160	(7 wkts, 50 overs)	232
A. C. Cummins c Rhodes b Newport	22	4/167 5/176		
J. D. Glendenen lbw b Benjamin	8	6/203 7/213		

*D. A. Graveney and S. P. Hughes did not bat.

Bowling: Benjamin 10–3–35–2; Radford 9–0–50–0; Newport 10–0–46–4; Lampitt 0–25–0; Illingworth 9–0–48–1; Haynes 3–0–18–0.

Worcestershire

T. S. Curtis lbw b Cummins	1	P. J. Newport run out	5
N. V. Radford c Graveney b Bainbridge	70	K. C. G. Benjamin not out	0
G. A. Hick c Fothergill b Hughes	32	R. K. Illingworth not out	0
D. B. D'Oliveira c and b Bainbridge	25	B 1, l-b 9, w 4, n-b 6	20
D. A. Leatherdale c Wood b Graveney	0		
S. J. Rhodes run out	40	1/2 2/99 3/142 (9 wkts, 50 overs) 227	
S. R. Lampitt c Wood b Cummins	29	4/143 5/151 6/215	
G. R. Haynes lbw b Cummins	5	7/220 8/225 9/227	

Bowling: Botham 8–1–37–0; Cummins 10–1–46–2; Hughes 10–0–39–1; Wood 7–0–33–0; Bainbridge 8–0–32–2; Graveney 7–0–30–1.

Umpires: J. D. Bond and B. Dudleston.

At The Oval, July 4. DURHAM lost to SURREY by 36 runs.

At Chelmsford, July 25. DURHAM lost to ESSEX by six wickets.

DURHAM v SUSSEX

At Durham University, August 1. Sussex won by two wickets. Toss: Durham.
   Lenham took five wickets as his lively medium pace scattered Durham's middle order. Graveney helped make the game a contest by hitting four fours off the last over from Giddins but then Lenham helped Wells effect a recovery from 45 for three and Sussex scraped to victory in the last over.

Durham

G. Fowler c Moores b Giddins	6	†C. W. Scott c Wells b Pigott	17
W. Larkins c Speight b Lenham	44	*D. A. Graveney not out	33
A. C. Cummins c Pigott b North	11	S. P. Hughes not out	14
S. Hutton c Salisbury b Lenham	33	L-b 6, w 12, n-b 4	22
P. Bainbridge lbw b Lenham	6		
P. W. G. Parker c Wells b Salisbury	5	1/13 2/50 3/78 (9 wkts, 50 overs) 194	
I. Smith b Lenham	1	4/86 5/100 6/103	
J. Wood c Speight b Lenham	2	7/116 8/120 9/156	

Bowling: Stephenson 10–2–30–0; Giddins 10–2–40–1; Pigott 8–0–40–1; North 2–0–16–1; Lenham 10–0–28–5; Salisbury 10–0–34–1.

Sussex

D. M. Smith lbw b Cummins	15	I. D. K. Salisbury b Bainbridge	6
M. P. Speight c Bainbridge b Hughes	10	A. C. S. Pigott not out	2
C. W. J. Athey lbw b Cummins	13		
*A. P. Wells not out	69	L-b 1, w 6, n-b 16	23
N. J. Lenham c Scott b Hughes	34		
J. A. North lbw b Cummins	11	1/22 2/41 3/45 (8 wkts, 49.3 overs) 195	
F. D. Stephenson b Bainbridge	9	4/118 5/138 6/167	
†P. Moores c Graveney b Bainbridge	3	7/174 8/186	

E. S. H. Giddins did not bat.

Bowling: Hughes 10–2–44–2; Cummins 10–0–37–3; Bainbridge 10–3–21–3; Wood 9.3–1–59–0; Graveney 10–1–33–0.

Umpires: J. W. Holder and V. A. Holder.

DURHAM v DERBYSHIRE

At Durham University, August 8. Durham won by 112 runs. Toss: Durham.

Durham's highest Sunday total was founded on a first-wicket stand of 204, of which Fowler and Parker shared 184 after Larkins retired, hit on the hand by Malcolm. At one stage they hit 90 in ten overs. Fowler made his highest Sunday League score and the highest yet by a Durham batsman, with two sixes and six fours from 152 balls.

Durham

G. Fowler run out 124	S. Hutton not out	8
W. Larkins retired hurt 1	B 2, l-b 9, w 7, n-b 4	22
P. W. G. Parker run out 92		
P. Bainbridge not out 34	1/204 2/267 (2 wkts, 50 overs) 281

I. Smith, A. C. Cummins, †C. W. Scott, *D. A. Graveney, S. P. Hughes and S. J. E. Brown did not bat.

W. Larkins retired hurt at 20.

Bowling: Malcolm 10–0–52–0; Base 10–1–54–0; Mortensen 8–1–25–0; Adams 9–0–51–0; Sladdin 7–0–42–0; Vandrau 6–0–46–0.

Derbyshire

P. D. Bowler c Hughes b Bainbridge . . 32	R. W. Sladdin b Cummins	16
C. J. Adams c Scott b Cummins 16	O. H. Mortensen c Scott b Brown	0
*J. E. Morris c Scott b Bainbridge. 17	D. E. Malcolm not out	5
T. J. G. O'Gorman c Hughes		
b Bainbridge. 31	B 1, l-b 6, n-b 2	9
A. S. Rollins b Graveney 31		
M. J. Vandrau st Scott b Graveney 7	1/36 2/59 3/76 (44 overs) 165
†K. M. Krikken c Hughes b Graveney . 1	4/112 5/140 6/144
S. J. Base c Parker b Brown 4	7/144 8/148 9/148

Bowling: Hughes 7–0–30–0; Cummins 7–0–26–2; Bainbridge 10–0–36–3; Brown 10–1–35–2; Graveney 10–1–35–3.

Umpires: H. D. Bird and R. A. White.

At Northampton, August 15. DURHAM beat NORTHAMPTONSHIRE by 48 runs.

DURHAM v WARWICKSHIRE

At Darlington, August 22. Durham won by two wickets. Toss: Durham.

Cummins took four wickets for the second week running as Warwickshire were restricted to 195. Durham overtook their visitors with only four balls to spare.

Warwickshire

A. J. Moles b Hughes 4	D. R. Brown run out	6
J. D. Ratcliffe c Fowler b Bainbridge . . 6	M. A. V. Bell c Cummins.	3
D. P. Ostler c Scott b Brown 20	*T. A. Munton b Cummins	0
P. A. Smith c sub b Bainbridge 39	L-b 2, w 2	4
Asif Din b Cummins. 66		
R. G. Twose b Smith 25	1/11 2/20 3/46 (50 overs) 195
N. M. K. Smith b Cummins. 17	4/101 5/155 6/179
†M. Burns not out 5	7/182 8/189 9/195

Bowling: Hughes 10–3–29–1; Cummins 10–2–29–4; Brown 10–1–37–1; Bainbridge 10–2–49–2; Graveney 8–1–32–0; Smith 2–0–17–1.

Durham

G. Fowler c Munton b N. M. K. Smith	38
W. Larkins c N. M. K. Smith b Bell	43
P. W. G. Parker b N. M. K. Smith	3
P. Bainbridge run out	32
S. Hutton c Twose b N. M. K. Smith	9
I. Smith b Twose	17
A. C. Cummins c Burns b Twose	19
†C. W. Scott c Munton b Twose	15

*D. A. Graveney not out	4
S. J. E. Brown not out	0
B 2, l-b 9, w 4, n-b 2	17

1/69 2/75 3/124   (8 wkts, 49.2 overs) 197
4/130 5/144 6/166
7/189 8/193

S. P. Hughes did not bat.

Bowling: Munton 9.2-1-28-0; Brown 7-3-23-0; P. A. Smith 6-0-36-0; Bell 10-1-40-1; N. M. K. Smith 10-1-28-3; Twose 7-0-31-3.

Umpires: G. I. Burgess and J. H. Hampshire.

At Leeds, August 29. DURHAM beat YORKSHIRE by 13 runs.

DURHAM v NOTTINGHAMSHIRE

At Chester-le-Street, September 5. Durham won by three wickets. Toss: Nottinghamshire.
Saxelby's hundred was upstaged by Larkins's second successive Sunday century, off 108 balls. It was his 12th in the competition, taking him past the record of 11 held by Gordon Greenidge and Graham Gooch.

Nottinghamshire

P. R. Pollard b Cummins	40
P. Johnson c Brown b Hughes	17
*R. T. Robinson c Fothergill b Brown	14
M. Saxelby not out	100
M. A. Crawley run out	17
G. W. Mike st Fothergill b Graveney	13

M. P. Dowman c Fothergill b Hughes	31
†B. N. French not out	17
B 1, l-b 7, w 1, n-b 2	11

1/31 2/73 3/75   (6 wkts, 50 overs) 260
4/115 5/142 6/216

D. B. Pennett, R. T. Bates and R. A. Pick did not bat.

Bowling: Hughes 10-0-58-2; Cummins 10-1-62-1; Brown 10-1-31-1; Bainbridge 10-0-47-0; Graveney 6-1-29-1; Smith 4-0-25-0.

Durham

G. Fowler c and b Pick	22
W. Larkins b Pick	128
P. W. G. Parker lbw b Pick	18
P. Bainbridge c Bates b Dowman	9
S. Hutton lbw b Crawley	48
I. Smith not out	5
A. C. Cummins c French b Crawley	4

†A. R. Fothergill b Pick	1
*D. A. Graveney not out	4
L-b 10, w 7, n-b 6	23

1/65 2/92 3/115   (7 wkts, 48.1 overs) 262
4/232 5/242
6/251 7/257

S. P. Hughes and S. J. E. Brown did not bat.

G. Fowler, when 4, retired hurt at 9 and resumed at 65.

Bowling: Mike 9-0-43-0; Pennett 10-0-42-0; Pick 10-0-68-4; Crawley 9.1-0-36-2; Dowman 7-0-33-1; Bates 3-0-30-0.

Umpires: J. D. Bond and B. J. Meyer.

DURHAM v SOMERSET

At Hartlepool, September 19. Durham won by seven wickets. Toss: Durham.

Larkins again dominated with an innings of 52 in 41 balls as Durham swept to their sixth successive win in the League with 15 overs to spare. Somerset were saved from total embarrassment by an unbroken eighth-wicket partnership of 64 from Mallender and Caddick, but it was never enough.

Somerset

M. N. Lathwell c and b Hughes	5	N. A. Mallender not out	31
G. W. White c Brown b Graveney	40	A. R. Caddick not out	36
N. A. Folland c Hutton b Brown	6	L-b 3, w 4	7
*R. J. Harden b Brown	0		
G. D. Rose b Smith	30	1/14 2/32 3/32	(7 wkts, 50 overs) 164
†R. J. Turner b Parker b Smith	7	4/72 5/87	
Mushtaq Ahmed lbw b Smith	2	6/89 7/100	

H. R. J. Trump and A. P. van Troost did not bat.

Bowling: Hughes 10–1–31–1; Cummins 10–1–41–0; Brown 10–2–25–2; Graveney 10–2–25–1; Smith 10–0–39–3.

Durham

G. Fowler c Folland b Mallender	15	P. W. G. Parker not out	28
W. Larkins c Folland b Rose	52	L-b 3, w 1, n-b 6	10
I. Smith c Harden b Trump	25		
S. Hutton not out	38	1/24 2/72 3/112	(3 wkts, 35 overs) 168

D. A. Blenkiron, A. C. Cummins, *D. A. Graveney, †A. R. Fothergill, S. P. Hughes and S. J. E. Brown did not bat.

Bowling: Mallender 6–0–32–1; Caddick 5–0–32–0; van Troost 4–0–20–0; Rose 4–1–13–1; Trump 8–3–15–1; Mushtaq Ahmed 6–0–38–0; Lathwell 2–0–15–0.

Umpires: B. Leadbeater and N. T. Plews.

ESSEX

ESSEX v YORKSHIRE

At Chelmsford, May 9. Essex won by 22 runs. Toss: Yorkshire. First-team debut: C. E. W. Silverwood.

Though Essex began with 40 from eight overs in a rain-affected match, they then faltered until Pringle struck 72 off 68 balls. But Yorkshire never recovered from the loss of Moxon, and Such claimed his first five-wicket return in limited-overs competitions.

Essex

*G. A. Gooch c Blakey b Robinson	29	T. D. Topley c Blakey b Jarvis	1
J. P. Stephenson st Blakey b Batty	37	M. C. Ilott c White b Gough	1
Salim Malik lbw b Gough	18	P. M. Such not out	0
N. Hussain c Grayson b Batty	8	B 3, w 1, n-b 2	6
D. R. Pringle c Silverwood b Gough	72		
N. V. Knight c Grayson b Silverwood	9	1/40 2/66 3/87	(46.5 overs) 192
N. A. Foster c Jarvis b Batty	0	4/104 5/141 6/148	
†M. A. Garnham lbw b Jarvis	11	7/179 8/181 9/185	

Bowling: Robinson 10–0–45–1; Jarvis 9–1–26–2; Silverwood 9–1–40–1; Gough 8.5–1–23–3; Batty 10–0–55–3.

Yorkshire

*M. D. Moxon c Salim Malik b Topley.	47		J. D. Batty c Foster b Such		3
S. A. Kellett lbw b Foster	11		M. A. Robinson not out		6
D. Byas lbw b Such	25		C. E. W. Silverwood b Ilott		0
†R. J. Blakey c Garnham b Such	7		B 2, l-b 3, w 5		10
C. White run out	30				
A. P. Grayson c Hussain b Such	11		1/42 2/78 3/93	(46.5 overs)	170
P. W. Jarvis b Pringle	5		4/98 5/135 6/145		
D. Gough st Garnham b Such	15		7/150 8/163 9/165		

Bowling: Foster 8–1–28–1; Ilott 9.5–0–38–1; Pringle 9–1–27–1; Stephenson 5–0–22–0; Topley 5–0–18–1; Such 10–1–32–5.

Umpires: A. A. Jones and B. Leadbeater.

At The Oval, May 16. ESSEX lost to SURREY by two wickets.

ESSEX v DERBYSHIRE

At Chelmsford, May 23. Derbyshire won by two wickets. Toss: Derbyshire.

A ninth-wicket stand of 31 in 25 balls between Derbyshire's two English-born, South African-bred players, Vandrau and Base, salvaged their injury-hit team's efforts to overtake a meagre total of 142. Essex were disheartened by the loss of Hussain, struck on the finger by Adams; Knight reached his maiden Sunday fifty without any boundaries.

Essex

*P. J. Prichard c Maher b Warner	3		M. C. Ilott c O'Gorman b Adams		4
J. P. Stephenson lbw b Warner	5		P. M. Such b Adams		2
Salim Malik c Maher b Warner	13		S. J. W. Andrew not out		0
N. Hussain retired hurt	29		L-b 5, w 5		10
N. V. Knight c Bowler b Malcolm	54				
†M. A. Garnham c Adams b Base	14		1/4 2/21 3/22	(49.4 overs)	142
N. A. Foster lbw b Base	1		4/118 5/123 6/134		
T. D. Topley run out	7		7/134 8/141 9/142		

N. Hussain retired hurt at 78.

Bowling: Malcolm 10–0–31–1; Warner 10–5–11–3; Griffith 10–1–31–0; Base 10–0–29–2; Vandrau 5–0–20–0; Adams 4.4–0–15–2.

Derbyshire

*K. J. Barnett b Andrew	42		†B. J. M. Maher b Topley		4
P. D. Bowler b Andrew	7		S. J. Base not out		14
J. E. Morris c Salim Malik b Stephenson	20				
C. J. Adams c Salim Malik b Such	9		L-b 7, n-b 2		9
T. J. G. O'Gorman lbw b Andrew	1				
F. A. Griffith b Stephenson	16		1/10 2/56 3/68	(8 wkts, 49.2 overs)	145
A. E. Warner b Stephenson	0		4/72 5/98 6/98		
M. J. Vandrau not out	23		7/107 8/114		

D. E. Malcolm did not bat.

Bowling: Ilott 10–1–24–0; Andrew 10–1–25–3; Topley 10–1–42–1; Stephenson 9.2–2–25–3; Such 10–2–22–1.

Umpires: J. H. Hampshire and P. Willey.

ESSEX v SOMERSET

At Chelmsford, June 6. Somerset won by 22 runs. Toss: Somerset.

After losing to the same opponents inside three days in the Championship, Somerset secured their first Sunday win of the season. Harden set up their total of 201 while Mushtaq Ahmed conceded only 16 from ten overs of leg-spin.

Somerset

M. N. Lathwell run out	27	J. I. D. Kerr b Pringle	4
N. A. Folland c Shahid b Pringle	0	N. A. Mallender not out	6
R. J. Harden c Prichard b Stephenson	89	H. R. J. Trump not out	10
*C. J. Tavaré lbw b Topley	1		
†N. D. Burns run out	22	L-b 15, n-b 2	17
G. D. Rose b Stephenson	24		
Mushtaq Ahmed st Garnham b Stephenson	0	1/1 2/40 3/44 (9 wkts, 50 overs) 201 4/103 5/172 6/172
A. Payne lbw b Topley	1	7/175 8/181 9/186

Bowling: Pringle 10–3–36–2; Ilott 10–1–37–0; Topley 10–0–22–2; Stephenson 10–2–31–3; Childs 10–0–60–0.

Essex

*P. J. Prichard lbw b Kerr	16	T. D. Topley b Mallender	1
J. P. Stephenson c Tavaré b Rose	23	M. C. Ilott b Mallender	12
Salim Malik lbw b Rose	22	J. H. Childs b Payne	7
N. Hussain c Burns b Kerr	17		
D. R. Pringle b Mushtaq Ahmed	1	L-b 11, w 4, n-b 4	19
†M. A. Garnham lbw b Mushtaq Ahmed	18	1/20 2/60 3/76 (48.5 overs) 179
N. V. Knight not out	42	4/78 5/108 6/113
N. Shahid c and b Kerr	1	7/116 8/119 9/149

Bowling: Mallender 10–2–35–2; Kerr 10–1–34–3; Rose 9–1–31–2; Payne 9.5–1–52–1; Mushtaq Ahmed 10–1–16–2.

Umpires: V. A. Holder and A. G. T. Whitehead.

At Manchester, June 13. ESSEX beat LANCASHIRE by 60 runs.

At Nottingham, June 20. ESSEX beat NOTTINGHAMSHIRE by 75 runs.

ESSEX v WARWICKSHIRE

At Ilford, June 27. Warwickshire won by 46 runs. Toss: Warwickshire.

Warwickshire's second Sunday win of the season was founded on a second-wicket partnership of 107 in 17 overs from Moles and Ostler. They advanced to 253 for nine before dismissing six Essex batsmen for 99 runs. Stephenson batted through the innings and was last out for 90, but he had little useful support.

Warwickshire

A. J. Moles st Garnham b Such	66	G. C. Small c Pringle b Ilott	6
Asif Din b Ilott	20	P. A. Booth not out	5
D. P. Ostler run out	69		
P. A. Smith lbw b Stephenson	7	L-b 8, w 5, n-b 6	19
*D. A. Reeve b Topley	18		
R. G. Twose c Pringle b Ilott	42	1/42 2/149 3/161 (9 wkts, 50 overs) 253
†P. C. L. Holloway run out	1	4/181 5/209 6/215
N. M. K. Smith b Pringle	0	7/215 8/231 9/253

T. A. Munton did not bat.

Bowling: Pringle 10–2–44–2; Ilott 8–3–45–3; Topley 5–0–31–0; Such 10–0–47–1; Childs 7–0–41–0; Stephenson 10–0–37–1.

Essex

P. J. Prichard b Small	16	T. D. Topley b Reeve		20
J. P. Stephenson c P. A. Smith		M. C. Ilott run out		12
b Munton	90	J. H. Childs c Reeve b Twose		0
N. Hussain c Booth b Small	5	P. M. Such not out		14
Salim Malik c Asif Din		L-b 4, w 9, n-b 2		15
b N. M. K. Smith	9			—
*G. A. Gooch c and b N. M. K. Smith	21	1/22 2/35 3/57	(46.2 overs)	207
D. R. Pringle c Reeve b P. A. Smith	1	4/87 5/95 6/99		
†M. A. Garnham b P. A. Smith	4	7/133 8/158 9/164		

Bowling: Reeve 9–1–50–1; Munton 8.2–1–17–1; Small 6–0–11–2; P. A. Smith 8–0–32–2; N. M. K. Smith 8–0–48–2; Booth 3–0–19–0; Twose 4–0–26–1.

Umpires: A. A. Jones and G. A. Stickley.

At Maidstone, July 4. ESSEX lost to KENT by 157 runs.

ESSEX v LEICESTERSHIRE

At Southend, July 18. Essex won by 26 runs. Toss: Essex.

On a slow, low pitch all the batsmen struggled and Benjamin was particularly economical. Only Prichard and Boon passed 30.

Essex

P. J. Prichard run out	32	T. D. Topley b Benjamin		3
J. P. Stephenson c and b Benson	26	M. C. Ilott b Mullally		7
N. Hussain lbw b Pierson	21	P. M. Such not out		1
Salim Malik lbw b Pierson	22	B 4, l-b 2, w 7, n-b 2		15
*G. A. Gooch run out	20			—
D. R. Pringle c Benson b Benjamin	20	1/41 2/86 3/89	(48.5 overs)	192
N. V. Knight lbw b Benjamin	19	4/127 5/141 6/170		
†M. A. Garnham b Mullally	6	7/175 8/179 9/190		

Bowling: Benjamin 10–2–13–3; Mullally 6.5–0–35–2; Parsons 9–0–30–0; Benson 3–1–18–1; Potter 10–0–46–0; Pierson 10–0–44–2.

Leicestershire

J. D. R. Benson c Gooch b Pringle	7	G. J. Parsons b Topley		10
*N. E. Briers lbw b Stephenson	28	A. R. K. Pierson c Garnham b Pringle		4
T. J. Boon run out	32	A. D. Mullally not out		4
B. F. Smith b Stephenson	13	B 1, l-b 11, w 6		18
P. E. Robinson lbw b Stephenson	0			—
L. Potter run out	25	1/11 2/59 3/86	(48.1 overs)	166
W. K. M. Benjamin c Knight b Such	7	4/86 5/94 6/105		
†P. A. Nixon c Stephenson b Pringle	18	7/134 8/148 9/158		

Bowling: Pringle 9.1–1–16–3; Ilott 9–0–35–0; Topley 10–2–33–1; Stephenson 10–1–40–3; Such 10–1–30–1.

Umpires: J. W. Holder and G. A. Stickley.

ESSEX v DURHAM

At Chelmsford, July 25. Essex won by six wickets, their target having been revised to 134 from 41 overs. Toss: Essex.

Salim Malik's 71 from 70 balls was the only innings of authority on a sluggish pitch. The match was interrupted by rain when Essex had reached 114 from 36.4 overs. Twenty rowdy Durham supporters – most wearing Newcastle United football shirts – were ejected from the ground during the game.

Durham

G. Fowler c Lewis b Topley	20	*D. A. Graveney not out	19
W. Larkins c Such b Topley	9	S. J. E. Brown c Garnham b Topley	7
P. W. G. Parker c Stephenson b Boden	12	S. P. Hughes lbw b Pringle	5
P. Bainbridge c Boden b Stephenson	20	L-b 4, w 5, n-b 4	13
S. Hutton c Garnham b Boden	1		
I. Smith c Knight b Such	37	1/20 2/36 3/48	(48.1 overs) 163
A. C. Cummins c Knight b Such	11	4/52 5/91 6/112	
†C. W. Scott c Shahid b Such	9	7/122 8/141 9/149	

Bowling: Pringle 9.1–3–18–1; Topley 10–0–43–3; Boden 10–0–48–2; Stephenson 9–1–25–1; Such 10.2–25–3.

Essex

*P. J. Prichard c Hutton b Bainbridge	13	N. Shahid not out	20
J. P. Stephenson c Smith b Hughes	4	L-b 6, w 4, n-b 2	12
N. V. Knight c Larkins b Graveney	16		
Salim Malik not out	71	1/16 2/27	(4 wkts, 39.5 overs) 137
D. R. Pringle c Larkins b Brown	1	3/64 4/65	

J. J. B. Lewis, †M. A. Garnham, T. D. Topley, D. J. P. Boden and P. M. Such did not bat.

Bowling: Hughes 10–4–26–1; Cummins 9.5–2–34–0; Brown 10–2–35–1; Bainbridge 5–1–14–1; Graveney 5–0–22–1.

Umpires: D. R. Shepherd and P. B. Wight.

ESSEX v WORCESTERSHIRE

At Chelmsford, August 1. Worcestershire won by four wickets. Toss: Essex.

After Stephenson had dominated the Essex innings with 103 not out, including nine fours, Hick scored a Sunday-best unbeaten 120 off 116 balls, and became the youngest man to reach 4,000 League runs. He won the match with his fifth six – off the bowling of Stephenson.

Essex

P. J. Prichard run out	40	D. R. Pringle not out	7
J. P. Stephenson not out	103	B 4, l-b 1, w 5, n-b 2	12
N. Hussain c Rhodes b Newport	40		
Salim Malik c D'Oliveira b Tolley	27	1/82 2/166	(4 wkts, 50 overs) 248
*G. A. Gooch run out	19	3/214 4/241	

N. V. Knight, †M. A. Garnham, T. D. Topley, M. C. Ilott and P. M. Such did not bat.

Bowling: Tolley 5–0–34–1; Newport 10–0–56–1; Hick 10–0–41–0; Lampitt 10–0–49–0; D'Oliveira 5–0–19–0; Illingworth 10–0–44–0.

Worcestershire

*T. S. Curtis run out	23	S. R. Lampitt c Garnham b Topley	0
D. B. D'Oliveira c Such b Pringle	22	G. R. Haynes not out	28
G. A. Hick not out	120	L-b 8, w 3	11
D. A. Leatherdale c Garnham b Topley	5		
†S. J. Rhodes c Gooch b Such	31	1/45 2/48 3/61 (6 wkts, 48.3 overs) 250	
M. J. Weston c Salim Malik b Topley	10	4/132 5/180 6/180	

P. J. Newport, R. K. Illingworth and C. M. Tolley did not bat.

Bowling: Pringle 9-0-48-1; Ilott 3-0-22-0; Topley 10-2-24-3; Stephenson 8.3-0-47-0; Such 8-0-45-1; Salim Malik 10-0-56-0.

Umpires: R. Palmer and R. A. White.

At Northampton, August 8. ESSEX lost to NORTHAMPTONSHIRE by 134 runs.

At Bristol, August 22. ESSEX beat GLOUCESTERSHIRE by three wickets.

ESSEX v MIDDLESEX

At Colchester, August 29. Tied. Toss: Middlesex.

Middlesex's second Sunday tie in 1993 was a record fourth in the season. Essex needed ten off the last two overs with five wickets in hand, but lost them all for nine: Boden was run out going for a third run off the last ball. Weekes took four wickets after putting on 121 for the first wicket with Haynes, whose 101 took 109 balls.

Middlesex

P. N. Weekes b Stephenson	46	J. E. Emburey st Garnham b Ilott	0
D. L. Haynes c Boden b Salim Malik	101	R. L. Johnson not out	0
M. R. Ramprakash c Such b Ilott	53	B 1, l-b 1, w 8, n-b 2	12
*M. W. Gatting c Gooch b Salim Malik	15		
J. D. Carr c Gooch b Salim Malik	6	1/121 2/186 3/216 (6 wkts, 50 overs) 236	
†K. R. Brown not out	3	4/232 5/234 6/236	

A. R. C. Fraser, P. C. R. Tufnell and C. W. Taylor did not bat.

Bowling: Ilott 10-1-37-2; Topley 5-0-31-0; Boden 4-1-29-0; Stephenson 7-0-30-1; Such 10-0-41-0; Knight 5-0-30-0; Salim Malik 9-0-36-3.

Essex

P. J. Prichard c Brown b Johnson	23	M. C. Ilott b Johnson	3
J. P. Stephenson c sub b Taylor	41	P. M. Such b Johnson	0
Salim Malik c and b Weekes	67	D. J. P. Boden run out	2
*G. A. Gooch c Gatting b Tufnell	10	L-b 8, w 5, n-b 8	21
N. Shahid c Fraser b Weekes	40		
N. V. Knight c Brown b Weekes	15	1/33 2/86 3/111 (50 overs) 236	
†M. A. Garnham not out	12	4/193 5/207 6/227	
T. D. Topley lbw b Weekes	2	7/229 8/234 9/234	

Bowling: Fraser 8-0-40-0; Johnson 7-0-35-3; Taylor 5-0-20-1; Emburey 10-0-40-0; Weekes 10-0-46-4; Tufnell 10-0-47-1.

Umpires: B. Dudleston and N. T. Plews.

At Hove, September 7. ESSEX lost to SUSSEX on scoring-rate.

At Cardiff, September 12. GLAMORGAN v ESSEX. No result.

ESSEX v HAMPSHIRE

At Chelmsford, September 19. Essex won by 99 runs. Toss: Hampshire.

Essex compiled a formidable total thanks to Stephenson's second Sunday century of the season. Hampshire had no answer as Ilott made early inroads before Such recorded his second five-wicket haul in the Sunday League.

Essex

*P. J. Prichard c and b Thursfield	71	N. V. Knight not out	1
J. P. Stephenson not out	102	L-b 5, w 9	14
G. A. Gooch c Aymes b James	37		
N. Hussain c Terry b Thursfield	50	1/128 2/195	(4 wkts, 50 overs) 287
N. Shahid run out	12	3/268 4/284	

†R. J. Rollins, T. D. Topley, M. C. Ilott, P. M. Such and S. J. W. Andrew did not bat.

Bowling: Connor 10-2-37-0; Thursfield 10-0-50-2; James 10-1-50-1; Bovill 7-0-55-0; Udal 9-0-66-0; Nicholas 4-0-24-0.

Hampshire

T. C. Middleton b Such	33	C. A. Connor c Prichard b Such	2
V. P. Terry c Rollins b Ilott	2	M. J. Thursfield c and b Gooch	4
R. M. F. Cox c Rollins b Ilott	10	J. N. B. Bovill not out	7
*M. C. J. Nicholas c Stephenson b Topley	18	L-b 10, w 7, n-b 12	29
J. S. Laney c Knight b Such	12		
K. D. James st Rollins b Such	11	1/5 2/45 3/82	(49 overs) 188
†A. N. Aymes c Topley b Knight	44	4/90 5/106 6/110	
S. D. Udal b Such	16	7/145 8/153 9/168	

Bowling: Andrew 7-0-36-0; Ilott 6-1-15-2; Topley 10-1-32-1; Stephenson 10-1-33-0; Such 10-0-33-5; Gooch 3-0-15-1; Knight 3-0-14-1.

Umpires: J. H. Hampshire and G. Sharp.

GLAMORGAN

At Derby, May 16. GLAMORGAN lost to DERBYSHIRE by three runs.

GLAMORGAN v NORTHAMPTONSHIRE

At Pentyrch, May 23. Northamptonshire won by three wickets. Toss: Glamorgan.

Three wickets in the closing overs left the Northamptonshire tail to avert what would have been an unexpected victory for Glamorgan in their first game at Pentyrch. The home team had been pegged back by tight bowling on an uncertain pitch, especially from Cook, whose figures of four for 22 were the best of his limited-overs career.

Glamorgan

S. P. James lbw b Curran	26	†C. P. Metson c and b Taylor	2
*H. Morris c Felton b Taylor	2	S. L. Watkin run out	0
A. Dale c and b Cook	43	S. R. Barwick not out	1
M. P. Maynard c and b Cook	7	B 1, l-b 12, w 10, n-b 4	27
I. V. A. Richards c Felton b Cook	2		
P. A. Cottey c Ripley b Cook	14	1/8 2/62 3/73	(9 wkts, 50 overs) 169
R. D. B. Croft c Penberthy b Taylor	9	4/75 5/98 6/103	
R. P. Lefebvre not out	36	7/124 8/164 9/168	

Bowling: Taylor 9-1-32-3; Ambrose 10-1-20-0; Capel 9-0-28-0; Curran 7-0-43-1; Cook 10-3-22-4; Penberthy 5-0-11-0.

Northamptonshire

A. Fordham c Dale b Croft	19	†D. Ripley not out	5
N. A. Felton c Metson b Watkin	4	C. E. L. Ambrose not out	2
R. J. Bailey c and b Richards	49	L-b 6, w 4	10
D. J. Capel c Maynard b Watkin	47		
K. M. Curran run out	19	1/11 2/45 3/113 (7 wkts, 49.4 overs) 170	
*A. J. Lamb st Metson b Richards	8	4/128 5/153	
A. L. Penberthy run out	7	6/156 7/167	

N. G. B. Cook and J. P. Taylor did not bat.

Bowling: Watkin 10–3–28–2; Lefebvre 10–3–20–0; Croft 8–0–29–1; Barwick 10–0–33–0; Richards 8.4–0–36–2; Dale 3–0–18–0.

Umpires: J. D. Bond and R. A. White.

At Taunton, May 30. SOMERSET v GLAMORGAN. No result (abandoned).

At Middlesbrough, June 6. GLAMORGAN beat YORKSHIRE by 25 runs.

At The Oval, June 13. GLAMORGAN beat SURREY by ten wickets.

GLAMORGAN v DURHAM

At Colwyn Bay, June 20. Glamorgan won by 166 runs. Toss: Durham.

Dale took six wickets for ten runs in 29 balls, including a hat-trick, with his unregarded medium-pace to reduce Durham from 36 for two to 57 for eight. It was easily his best bowling in any competition, as well as Glamorgan's best in one-day cricket, and secured their biggest win in the Sunday League. The sequence began when Metson stumped Botham, who had just passed 5,000 runs in the competition, and Dale then ran quickly through the middle order, removing Hutton, Glendenen and Cummins with successive deliveries. Glamorgan won with nearly ten overs to spare. Earlier, Maynard had set up their total of 271 with 79 off 66 balls, including four sixes.

Glamorgan

S. P. James c Fothergill b Wood	58	R. P. Lefebvre lbw b Wood	3
*H. Morris c Larkins b Hughes	59	R. D. B. Croft not out	1
M. P. Maynard c Graveney b Cummins	79	B 1, l-b 9, w 1, n-b 2	13
A. Dale c Hutton b Bainbridge	7		
I. V. A. Richards not out	49	1/94 2/154 3/187 (6 wkts, 50 overs) 271	
P. A. Cottey b Hughes	2	4/224 5/235 6/268	

†C. P. Metson, S. L. Watkin and D. L. Hemp did not bat.

Bowling: Botham 10–0–39–0; Cummins 10–1–47–1; Graveney 7–0–49–0; Hughes 10–0–53–2; Wood 8–0–39–2; Bainbridge 5–0–34–1.

Durham

I. T. Botham st Metson b Dale	18	†A. R. Fothergill lbw b Dale	2
W. Larkins c Hemp b Watkin	7	*D. A. Graveney c Richards b Lefebvre	21
P. W. G. Parker c James b Lefebvre	0	S. P. Hughes not out	9
S. Hutton c Metson b Dale	11	B 1, l-b 3	4
P. Bainbridge c Metson b Richards	31		
J. D. Glendenen b Dale	1	1/13 2/14 3/36 (40.1 overs) 105	
A. C. Cummins b Dale	0	4/43 5/47 6/47	
J. Wood c Metson b Dale	1	7/49 8/57 9/83	

Bowling: Watkin 7–2–16–1; Lefebvre 9.1–3–22–2; Dale 10–1–22–6; Croft 9–1–19–0; Richards 5–0–22–1.

Umpires: R. Julian and A. G. T. Whitehead.

GLAMORGAN v NOTTINGHAMSHIRE

At Swansea, June 27. Glamorgan won by three wickets. Toss: Nottinghamshire.

Glamorgan, more used to settling at the bottom of the Sunday League table, rose to joint second place with this win. Metson made four catches and two stumpings, and Nottinghamshire fell from 170 for four to 175 for eight. Maynard again dominated Glamorgan's batting.

Nottinghamshire

P. R. Pollard c Richards b Croft	37	K. P. Evans c Lefebvre b Barwick	10
P. Johnson b Lefebvre	32	R. A. Pick not out	21
*R. T. Robinson c Metson b Lefebvre	6	M. G. Field-Buss st Metson b Lefebvre	5
G. F. Archer c Metson b Croft	10	L-b 5, w 2, n-b 2	9
C. L. Cairns c Metson b Richards	53		
C. C. Lewis c Morris b Dale	26	1/57 2/65 3/80	(50 overs) 210
G. W. Mike st Metson b Richards	1	4/89 5/170 6/170	
†B. N. French c Metson b Watkin	0	7/171 8/175 9/192	

Bowling: Watkin 10–0–57–1; Lefebvre 10–2–31–3; Barwick 10–0–36–1; Croft 10–0–29–2; Dale 5–0–40–1; Richards 5–1–12–2.

Glamorgan

S. P. James b Cairns	18	R. P. Lefebvre b Pick	10
*H. Morris c Mike b Field-Buss	30	†C. P. Metson not out	24
A. Dale b Cairns	3	B 1, l-b 5, w 7, n-b 6	19
M. P. Maynard not out	72		
I. V. A. Richards b Evans	2	1/45 2/49 3/78	(7 wkts, 48.5 overs) 211
P. A. Cottey c French b Evans	9	4/82 5/98	
R. D. B. Croft lbw b Lewis	24	6/140 7/158	

S. L. Watkin and S. R. Barwick did not bat.

Bowling: Lewis 10–0–60–1; Cairns 10–0–31–2; Pick 8–1–30–1; Field-Buss 10–0–45–1; Evans 6.5–1–22–2; Mike 4–0–17–0.

Umpires: J. H. Harris and D. O. Oslear.

GLAMORGAN v MIDDLESEX

At Cardiff, July 4. Glamorgan won by 121 runs. Toss: Middlesex.

Glamorgan's batsmen continued where they had left off in the first innings of their Championship match, taking 287, their highest Sunday score, off the Middlesex bowling. It was their fifth successive League win. James and Dale shared 172, a second-wicket record for Glamorgan in one-day cricket, in 34 overs, and Maynard hit 43 from 33 balls. Haynes, Roseberry and Gatting were all out in the first eight overs and Middlesex's position was hopeless.

Glamorgan

S. P. James run out	94	†C. P. Metson lbw b Emburey	2
*H. Morris c Brown b Cowans	3	S. L. Watkin not out	2
A. Dale b Weekes	61		
M. P. Maynard c and b Weekes	43	B 4, l-b 24, w 9, n-b 2	39
I. V. A. Richards c Keech b Weekes	18		
P. A. Cottey c Fraser b Emburey	13	1/10 2/182 3/199	(8 wkts, 50 overs) 287
R. D. B. Croft c Emburey b Weekes	8	4/248 5/268 6/271	
R. P. Lefebvre not out	4	7/280 8/282	

S. R. Barwick did not bat.

Bowling: Cowans 10–0–38–1; Feltham 10–1–54–0; Fraser 10–1–42–0; Emburey 10–0–42–2; Keech 3–0–22–0; Weekes 7–0–61–4.

Middlesex

D. L. Haynes c Maynard b Lefebvre	6	J. E. Emburey st Metson b Richards	28
M. A. Roseberry c Metson b Watkin	2	A. R. C. Fraser c Watkin b Richards	14
*M. W. Gatting b Lefebvre	2	N. G. Cowans not out	2
M. R. Ramprakash run out	8	B 1, l-b 2, w 2	5
P. N. Weekes c Lefebvre b Croft	24		
†K. R. Brown c Croft b Dale	16	1/7 2/8 3/14	(48.3 overs) 166
M. Keech c Lefebvre b Croft	34	4/31 5/57 6/60	
M. A. Feltham c Barwick b Richards	25	7/108 8/124 9/160	

Bowling: Watkin 9-3-19-1; Lefebvre 8-3-10-2; Barwick 9-1-32-0; Croft 10-0-44-2; Dale 7-0-35-1; Richards 5.3-0-23-3.

Umpires: J. C. Balderstone and V. A. Holder.

GLAMORGAN v SUSSEX

At Llanelli, July 11. Glamorgan won by 50 runs. Toss: Glamorgan.

A county record sixth win in succession set Glamorgan alongside Kent at the top of the table for the first time. Their total was founded on an opening partnership of 120 in 26 overs between James and Morris, followed by 82 in 13 overs between James and Maynard. James progressed from his fifth fifty in six League matches to 107 in 126 balls with eight fours. Sussex were never really in the chase.

Glamorgan

S. P. James c Moores b Jones	107	R. P. Lefebvre run out	12
*H. Morris c Athey b Giddins	67	†C. P. Metson not out	13
M. P. Maynard c A. P. Wells		S. L. Watkin not out	1
b Stephenson	31	B 1, l-b 3, w 2	6
I. V. A. Richards b Salisbury	22		
A. Dale run out	2	1/120 2/202 3/210	(8 wkts, 50 overs) 269
P. A. Cottey b Stephenson	4	4/230 5/234 6/241	
R. D. B. Croft b Giddins	4	7/241 8/266	

S. R. Barwick did not bat.

Bowling: Stephenson 10-3-32-2; Giddins 10-0-59-2; Jones 10-0-68-1; C. M. Wells 10-0-58-0; Salisbury 10-0-48-1.

Sussex

D. M. Smith run out	42	I. D. K. Salisbury c Lefebvre b Dale	17
F. D. Stephenson c Metson b Watkin	18	A. N. Jones b Dale	3
M. P. Speight c Cottey b Lefebvre	14	E. S. H. Giddins not out	0
*A. P. Wells st Metson b Barwick	51	L-b 8, w 2, n-b 2	12
C. M. Wells c Barwick b Croft	0		
C. W. J. Athey b Dale	0	1/31 2/54 3/112	(45.2 overs) 219
K. Greenfield c Metson b Barwick	0	4/117 5/139 6/139	
†P. Moores run out	56	7/153 8/210 9/219	

Bowling: Watkin 10-0-53-1; Lefebvre 8-1-25-1; Barwick 8-1-27-2; Croft 7-0-33-1; Dale 9.2-1-38-3; Richards 3-0-35-0.

Umpires: G. I. Burgess and R. Julian.

At Manchester, July 18. GLAMORGAN beat LANCASHIRE by eight wickets.

At Worcester, July 25. GLAMORGAN beat WORCESTERSHIRE by 27 runs.

GLAMORGAN v WARWICKSHIRE

At Neath, August 8. Glamorgan won by four wickets. Toss: Glamorgan. First-team debut: A. J. Jones.

The home fielding was outstanding, especially that of Dale and Lefebvre, who took stunning tumbling catches in the outfield, and Richards, who took a left-handed reflex return drive from Neil Smith. Warwickshire's below-strength attack was unable to prevent Glamorgan overtaking their meagre total.

Warwickshire

J. D. Ratcliffe b Lefebvre	1	†M. Burns not out	23
Asif Din c Cottey b Lefebvre	2	M. A. V. Bell not out	6
D. P. Ostler c Dale b Croft	27		
*D. A. Reeve c Barwick b Croft	22	L-b 2	2
A. J. Moles c Dale b Croft	12		
R. G. Twose c Lefebvre b Dale	34	1/1 2/18 3/44 (8 wkts, 50 overs) 163	
T. L. Penney b Barwick	28	4/52 5/89 6/114	
N. M. K. Smith c and b Richards	6	7/127 8/138	

T. A. Munton did not bat.

Bowling: Watkin 8–1–28–0; Lefebvre 10–3–22–2; Barwick 10–2–30–1; Croft 10–1–38–3; Dale 9–1–30–1; Richards 3–0–13–1.

Glamorgan

S. P. James run out	14	A. J. Jones lbw b Twose	3
*H. Morris c Ostler b Bell	46	†C. P. Metson not out	6
A. Dale c and b Ratcliffe	54	B 3, l-b 7, w 9	19
I. V. A. Richards c Ratcliffe b Smith	2		
P. A. Cottey c Twose b Ratcliffe	14	1/38 2/86 3/101 (6 wkts, 48 overs) 164	
R. D. B. Croft not out	6	4/143 5/150 6/155	

R. P. Lefebvre, S. L. Watkin and S. R. Barwick did not bat.

Bowling: Reeve 7–0–20–0; Munton 8–0–28–0; Bell 10–0–40–1; Smith 10–0–27–1; Twose 7–1–25–1; Asif Din 1–0–3–0; Ratcliffe 5–0–11–2.

Umpires: G. I. Burgess and R. Julian.

At Leicester, August 15. GLAMORGAN beat LEICESTERSHIRE by eight runs.

GLAMORGAN v HAMPSHIRE

At Swansea, August 22. Glamorgan won by six wickets. Toss: Glamorgan.

Glamorgan's 11th successive Sunday win was their 15th in the season in one-day competitions – a county record. Marshall's promotion to open for Hampshire was not a success but Smith, out of the Test team, came in and hit five sixes. However, Morris shepherded Glamorgan home. When 67, he passed Maynard's 1992 county record of 650 runs in a Sunday League season.

Hampshire

M. D. Marshall c Metson b Lefebvre	8	S. D. Udal c Metson b Lefebvre	0
V. P. Terry c Barwick b Dale	48	M. Jean-Jacques c Cottey b Barwick	4
R. A. Smith c Cottey b Dale	75	C. A. Connor not out	6
J. R. Wood b Dale	8	B 2, l-b 15, w 11	28
*M. C. J. Nicholas c Lefebvre b Barwick	21	1/14 2/131 3/152 (8 wkts, 48 overs) 207	
R. M. F. Cox b Richards	2	4/167 5/176 6/186	
†A. N. Aymes not out	7	7/188 8/201	

I. J. Turner did not bat.

Bowling: Bastien 10–1–33–0; Lefebvre 10–2–22–2; Croft 8–0–46–0; Barwick 9–1–49–2; Dale 6–0–25–3; Richards 7–0–15–1.

Glamorgan

S. P. James run out	4	R. D. B. Croft not out	6
*H. Morris run out	81	L-b 3, w 1, n-b 14	18
A. Dale lbw b Jean-Jacques	20		
I. V. A. Richards c Nicholas b Turner	5	1/8 2/57 (4 wkts, 47.3 overs)	209
P. A. Cottey not out	75	3/76 4/187	

D. L. Hemp, R. P. Lefebvre, †C. P. Metson, S. Bastien and S. R. Barwick did not bat.

Bowling: Connor 10-0-53-0; Marshall 9.3-2-32-0; Jean-Jacques 10-0-47-1; Turner 10-0-41-1; Udal 8-0-33-0.

Umpires: J. W. Holder and P. B. Wight.

GLAMORGAN v GLOUCESTERSHIRE

At Ebbw Vale, August 29. Glamorgan won by 31 runs. Toss: Glamorgan.

Glamorgan's 12th successive Sunday victory equalled Middlesex's record run in 1992, and was greatly enjoyed by a packed, beery crowd of about 4,000. Another county record fell when Metson caught Dawson for his 25th dismissal of the season. After James and Dale had put on 72 in 15 overs, Maynard took control, hitting 69 in 73 balls. Hinks was even more aggressive for Gloucestershire – his 62 took only 51 balls – but when he was out the innings fell away.

Glamorgan

S. P. James b Smith	38	†C. P. Metson c Williams b Smith	1
*H. Morris c Russell b Walsh	5	S. L. Watkin not out	2
A. Dale c Russell b Williams	29	S. R. Barwick not out	4
M. P. Maynard c Hancock b Babington	69	L-b 6, w 2, n-b 14	22
I. V. A. Richards c Walsh b Williams	14		
P. A. Cottey c Russell b Walsh	19	1/12 2/84 3/88 (9 wkts, 50 overs)	242
R. D. B. Croft c Hinks b Smith	20	4/107 5/145 6/187	
R. P. Lefebvre b Smith	19	7/217 8/234 9/234	

Bowling: Babington 10-0-53-1; Walsh 10-1-45-2; Smith 10-1-56-4; Williams 10-0-37-2; Scott 6-1-21-0; Alleyne 4-0-24-0.

Gloucestershire

S. G. Hinks c Richards b Dale	62	*C. A. Walsh c and b Dale	8
A. J. Wright c Richards b Watkin	11	A. M. Smith not out	14
R. I. Dawson c Metson b Lefebvre	6	A. M. Babington c Watkin b Lefebvre	2
M. W. Alleyne b Croft	28	L-b 4, w 5	9
R. J. Scott b Watkin	26		
T. H. C. Hancock lbw b Watkin	23	1/41 2/79 3/82 (47.5 overs)	211
†R. C. Russell c Cottey b Barwick	0	4/128 5/157 6/164	
R. C. Williams lbw b Dale	0	7/167 8/183 9/202	

Bowling: Watkin 10-0-55-3; Lefebvre 8.5-3-23-2; Barwick 9-1-49-1; Croft 10-1-33-1; Dale 9-0-41-3; Richards 1-0-6-0.

Umpires: K. E. Palmer and G. A. Stickley.

GLAMORGAN v ESSEX

At Cardiff, September 12. No result. Toss: Glamorgan.

Officials put in 4,000 extra seats but it began raining at 11.20 a.m. – September matches were starting at 11.00 – and the match was abandoned in mid-afternoon, ending Glamorgan's sequence of wins and leaving them behind Kent on run-rate pending their showdown for the title at Canterbury the following week.

Essex

P. J. Prichard c Metson b Watkin	3
J. P. Stephenson not out	1
†N. Shahid c James b Watkin	0
N. Hussain not out	0
W 3	3

1/5 2/7   (2 wkts, 5 overs) 7

*G. A. Gooch, N. V. Knight, J. J. B. Lewis, T. D. Topley, M. C. Ilott, P. M. Such and S. J. W. Andrew did not bat.

Bowling: Watkin 3–0–7–2; Lefebvre 2–2–0–0.

Glamorgan

S. P. James, *H. Morris, A. Dale, M. P. Maynard, I. V. A. Richards, P. A. Cottey, R. D. B. Croft, †C. P. Metson, R. P. Lefebvre, S. L. Watkin and S. R. Barwick.

Umpires: M. J. Kitchen and R. Palmer.

At Canterbury, September 19. GLAMORGAN beat KENT by six wickets.

GLOUCESTERSHIRE

At Northampton, May 9. GLOUCESTERSHIRE lost to NORTHAMPTONSHIRE by 62 runs.

GLOUCESTERSHIRE v DURHAM

At Bristol, May 23. Gloucestershire won by five wickets. Toss: Gloucestershire.
    Hodgson's maiden Sunday hundred saved Gloucestershire after they had been 38 for three. He added 135 with Wright, and then had some rapid assistance from Russell, who struck 27 from 16 balls, including two sixes in an over from Graveney. Durham's innings had followed the opposite path, subsiding from 142 for one, after a 130-run stand between Fowler and Parker, to 215 all out.

Durham

G. Fowler c Russell b Alleyne	91	J. Wood c Wright b Scott	11
W. Larkins c Russell b Smith	1	*D. A. Graveney c Russell b Scott	2
P. W. G. Parker c Scott b Alleyne	53	S. P. Hughes not out	1
P. Bainbridge run out	4	L-b 7, w 2, n-b 10	19
I. T. Botham b Williams	7		
A. C. Cummins c Alleyne b Williams	9	1/12 2/142 3/153 (50 overs) 215
I. Smith lbw b Williams	8	4/172 5/172 6/187
†A. R. Fothergill b Smith	9	7/189 8/209 9/212

Bowling: Gerrard 8–2–36–0; Smith 9–0–33–2; Scott 10–1–35–2; Williams 10–0–46–3; Alleyne 10–0–30–2; Ball 3–0–28–0.

Gloucestershire

B. C. Broad c Bainbridge b Cummins	2	T. H. C. Hancock not out	4
G. D. Hodgson not out	104		
R. J. Scott run out	0	L-b 5, w 5, n-b 2	12
M. W. Alleyne c Hughes b Wood	6		
*A. J. Wright c Smith b Graveney	61	1/4 2/11 3/38 (5 wkts, 48.5 overs) 216
†R. C. Russell c Larkins b Cummins	27	4/173 5/211

A. M. Smith, R. C. J. Williams, M. C. J. Ball and M. J. Gerrard did not bat.

Bowling: Cummins 9–1–40–2; Hughes 9–1–31–0; Botham 10–0–31–0; Wood 5–1–17–1; Bainbridge 6–0–29–0; Graveney 9.5–0–63–1.

Umpires: G. I. Burgess and D. O. Oslear.

GLOUCESTERSHIRE v WORCESTERSHIRE

At Gloucester, May 30. Worcestershire won by 15 runs. Toss: Gloucestershire.

Hick, who reached his fifty in 31 balls, effectively settled a match reduced to ten overs a side. When the rain finally allowed the match to start, the first over, bowled by Ricardo Williams of Gloucestershire, yielded 17 runs. Lampitt of Worcestershire also conceded 17 in his only over but an asking rate of 10.9 an over – the highest ever set from ten overs – still proved too much for the home team.

Worcestershire

G. A. Hick c Hodgson b Scott 59	D. A. Leatherdale not out	0
K. C. G. Benjamin st Russell b Cooper . 20	L-b 1, w 1, n-b 7	9
N. V. Radford c Hodgson b Smith 13		
*T. S. Curtis not out 7	1/36 2/60 3/107 (3 wkts, 10 overs) 108	

W. P. C. Weston, C. M. Tolley, S. R. Lampitt, †S. J. Rhodes, R. K. Illingworth and P. J. Newport did not bat.

Bowling: Williams 1–0–17–0; Walsh 2–0–14–0; Alleyne 2–0–20–0; Cooper 2–0–14–1; Smith 2–0–30–1; Scott 1–0–12–1.

Gloucestershire

M. W. Alleyne c W. P. C. Weston	C. A. Walsh not out	0
b Benjamin . 5		
†R. C. Russell c Illingworth b Newport . 26	L-b 2	2
*A. J. Wright not out 33		
T. H. C. Hancock c Lampitt b Radford . 27	1/6 2/48 3/93 (3 wkts, 10 overs) 93	

B. C. Broad, G. D. Hodgson, R. J. Scott, R. C. Williams, A. M. Smith and K. E. Cooper did not bat.

Bowling: Benjamin 2–0–15–1; Tolley 1–0–8–0; Newport 2–0–12–1; Illingworth 2–0–23–0; Lampitt 1–0–17–0; Radford 2–0–16–1.

Umpires: M. J. Kitchen and P. B. Wight.

At Tunbridge Wells, June 6. GLOUCESTERSHIRE lost to KENT by seven wickets.

At Sheffield, June 20. GLOUCESTERSHIRE beat YORKSHIRE by seven wickets.

At Leicester, June 27. GLOUCESTERSHIRE lost to LEICESTERSHIRE by 31 runs.

GLOUCESTERSHIRE v HAMPSHIRE

At Bristol, July 4. Gloucestershire won by 24 runs. Toss: Hampshire.

Both sides made a good start to their innings: Gloucestershire's openers Hodgson and Hinks shared a stand of 113, while Middleton and Gower put on 108 for the first wicket in 23 overs. But after Gower was run out Hampshire's batsmen were unable to keep up with the rate required.

Gloucestershire

G. D. Hodgson c Terry b Jean-Jacques	47	C. A. Walsh b Connor	0
S. G. Hinks c Nicholas b Udal	74		
M. W. Alleyne c Udal b James	36	L-b 7, w 7, n-b 2	16
*A. J. Wright c Terry b Jean-Jacques	21		
R. I. Dawson not out	21	1/113 2/135 3/176 (7 wkts, 50 overs) 240	
†R. C. Russell c Terry b James	7	4/189 5/204	
R. J. Scott c Udal b Connor	18	6/239 7/240	

M. Davies, A. M. Smith and A. M. Babington did not bat.

Bowling: Marshall 10–1–44–0; Connor 10–1–38–2; Jean-Jacques 10–1–59–2; James 10–0–52–2; Udal 10–0–40–1.

Hampshire

T. C. Middleton b Davies	54	S. D. Udal lbw b Walsh	0
D. I. Gower run out	60	M. Jean-Jacques c Wright b Smith	0
J. R. Wood b Alleyne	25	C. A. Connor b Walsh	1
V. P. Terry c Alleyne b Babington	27		
*M. C. J. Nicholas c Dawson		L-b 4, w 9, n-b 8	21
b Babington	9		
M. D. Marshall run out	0	1/108 2/138 3/148 (47.3 overs) 216	
K. D. James run out	9	4/170 5/170 6/183	
†A. N. Aymes not out	10	7/205 8/209 9/214	

Bowling: Babington 10–0–41–2; Walsh 9.3–2–38–2; Scott 7–0–29–0; Smith 9–0–39–1; Davies 6–0–35–1; Alleyne 6–0–30–1.

Umpires: H. D. Bird and P. B. Wight.

GLOUCESTERSHIRE v MIDDLESEX

At Moreton-in-Marsh, July 11. No result. Toss: Gloucestershire.

Heavy rain ended play before Middlesex could begin their reply. Walsh, captaining Gloucestershire after Wright's resignation two days earlier, thrashed 24 off 12 balls, with a six and four fours.

Gloucestershire

B. C. Broad c Roseberry b Tufnell	47	R. C. Williams run out	1
S. G. Hinks c Brown b Cowans	26	A. M. Smith st Brown b Weekes	1
M. W. Alleyne c Emburey b Tufnell	14	A. M. Babington b Fraser	1
A. J. Wright c Roseberry b Tufnell	36	B 1, l-b 4, n-b 4	9
R. J. Scott c Emburey b Tufnell	42		
†R. C. Russell b Cowans	31	1/54 2/85 3/93 (50 overs) 243	
*C. A. Walsh c Carr b Cowans	24	4/155 5/185 6/218	
R. M. Wight not out	11	7/232 8/236 9/238	

Bowling: Fraser 7–0–43–1; Cowans 10–1–49–3; Keech 3–1–21–0; Tufnell 10–0–44–4; Emburey 10–1–34–0; Weekes 10–0–47–1.

Middlesex

M. A. Roseberry, J. D. Carr, *M. W. Gatting, M. R. Ramprakash, P. N. Weekes, †K. R. Brown, M. Keech, J. E. Emburey, A. R. C. Fraser, N. G. Cowans and P. C. R. Tufnell.

Umpires: H. D. Bird and R. Palmer.

At Guildford, July 18. GLOUCESTERSHIRE lost to SURREY by nine wickets.

GLOUCESTERSHIRE v DERBYSHIRE

At Cheltenham, August 1. Derbyshire won by eight wickets. Toss: Derbyshire.

None of Gloucestershire's top five batsmen passed seven as they were tumbled out for 99 – and even that was better than looked likely when they were 26 for five. Base was the chief destroyer, matching his best limited-overs figures with four for 14 from ten overs. Despite fielding a much weakened team, Derbyshire romped home. Adams's 58 took only 42 balls and the match was over at 3.48 p.m.

Gloucestershire

B. C. Broad c Bowler b Base	2	M. Davies not out	13
G. D. Hodgson run out	7	A. M. Smith b Base	0
M. W. Alleyne c Krikken b Base	5	A. M. Babington c Adams b Griffith	10
R. I. Dawson c Krikken b Mortensen	5	L-b 6, w 4	10
A. J. Wright c Adams b Mortensen	3		
T. H. C. Hancock lbw b Base	36	1/7 2/12 3/18	(36 overs) 99
†R. C. Russell c Krikken b Sladdin	4	4/25 5/26 6/44	
*C. A. Walsh c Rollins b Sladdin	4	7/52 8/81 9/81	

Bowling: Mortensen 10-2-20-2; Base 10-3-14-4; Griffith 8-1-33-1; Sladdin 8-1-26-2.

Derbyshire

P. D. Bowler c Russell b Smith	3
C. J. Adams c Babington b Smith	58
*J. E. Morris not out	35
T. J. G. O'Gorman not out	0
N-b 4	4

1/47 2/81   (2 wkts, 14.5 overs) 100

I. G. S. Steer, A. S. Rollins, F. A. Griffith, †K. M. Krikken, S. J. Base, O. H. Mortensen and R. W. Sladdin did not bat.

Bowling: Babington 5-1-27-0; Walsh 3-0-28-0; Smith 3.5-0-26-2; Davies 3-0-19-0.

Umpires: J. C. Balderstone and J. H. Harris.

GLOUCESTERSHIRE v LANCASHIRE

At Cheltenham, August 8. Tied. Toss: Lancashire.

Fairbrother took Lancashire to within 26 runs of victory with five overs and five wickets remaining, and when the last over began at 200 for seven, victory seemed almost assured. However, Alleyne conceded only two runs and removed Watkinson and Hegg, and Austin was run out off the last ball to bring about the third tied Sunday League match of the season. Earlier, Gloucestershire had lost their last eight wickets for 33.

Gloucestershire

B. C. Broad c Hegg b Austin	44	†R. C. Russell c Hegg b DeFreitas	0
S. G. Hinks c Wasim Akram		*C. A. Walsh b Yates	1
b DeFreitas	92	M. Davies c Hegg b Austin	4
M. G. N. Windows c Crawley		A. M. Smith not out	0
b Watkinson	6	A. M. Babington b Wasim Akram	3
M. W. Alleyne c Fairbrother		L-b 10, w 10, n-b 4	24
b Watkinson	16		
T. H. C. Hancock c Crawley		1/102 2/123 3/169	(47.2 overs) 202
b DeFreitas	3	4/178 5/180 6/182	
R. J. Scott b Wasim Akram	9	7/183 8/199 9/199	

Bowling: DeFreitas 10-0-31-3; Austin 9-1-33-2; Wasim Akram 8.2-0-40-2; Watkinson 10-0-56-2; Yates 10-1-32-1.

Lancashire

J. P. Crawley c Russell b Babington ...	6	†W. K. Hegg c Russell b Alleyne...... 8
S. P. Titchard b Walsh	5	I. D. Austin run out................. 1
G. D. Lloyd c Hancock b Scott	12	G. Yates not out 1
*N. H. Fairbrother c Hinks b Davies ..	81	L-b 3, w 5, n-b 4 12
N. J. Speak b Alleyne	30	
Wasim Akram run out	34	1/11 2/12 3/45 (50 overs) 202
M. Watkinson c Babington b Alleyne ..	11	4/123 5/177 6/181
P. A. J. DeFreitas c Russell b Walsh ..	1	7/185 8/200 9/200

Bowling: Babington 10–1–28–1; Walsh 10–1–38–2; Scott 10–0–46–1; Smith 10–1–34–0; Alleyne 9–0–42–3; Davies 1–0–11–1.

Umpires: B. Dudleston and M. J. Kitchen.

At Birmingham, August 15. GLOUCESTERSHIRE beat WARWICKSHIRE by 11 runs.

GLOUCESTERSHIRE v ESSEX

At Bristol, August 22. Essex won by three wickets. Toss: Essex.

Gloucestershire lost their first four batsmen for single figures and, although Essex made a better start, a middle-order collapse left them struggling before Ilott hit out to see them through.

Gloucestershire

B. C. Broad b Topley	3	*C. A. Walsh run out 18
G. D. Hodgson b Ilott.............	2	M. Davies st Garnham b Stephenson .. 9
S. G. Hinks c Childs b Topley.......	4	A. M. Smith not out 0
M. W. Alleyne c Garnham b Boden ...	4	L-b 5, w 2, n-b 6............ 13
R. J. Scott b Stephenson	45	
T. H. C. Hancock lbw b Childs	10	1/5 2/11 3/15 (49.1 overs) 135
†R. C. Russell run out	27	4/30 5/49 6/97
R. C. Williams lbw b Stephenson	0	7/97 8/114 9/134

Bowling: Ilott 10–2–16–1; Topley 10–3–40–2; Boden 10–1–31–1; Stephenson 9.1–1–24–3; Childs 11–1–19–1.

Essex

N. V. Knight c Russell b Williams	22	T. D. Topley c Alleyne b Smith 2
J. P. Stephenson c Smith b Williams ...	35	M. C. Ilott not out.................. 17
N. Shahid st Russell b Alleyne........	18	L-b 3, w 3, n-b 2 8
Salim Malik lbw b Davies	12	
*P. J. Prichard lbw b Alleyne.........	8	1/59 2/59 3/82 (7 wkts, 49.1 overs) 139
†M. A. Garnham lbw b Smith	4	4/98 5/100
J. J. B. Lewis not out	13	6/109 7/113

D. J. P. Boden and J. H. Childs did not bat.

Bowling: Smith 9.1–3–33–2; Walsh 10–1–25–0; Scott 10–3–17–0; Williams 10–3–29–2; Davies 4–0–17–1; Alleyne 6–0–15–2.

Umpires: J. D. Bond and R. A. White.

At Ebbw Vale, August 29. GLOUCESTERSHIRE lost to GLAMORGAN by 31 runs.

At Taunton, September 5. GLOUCESTERSHIRE beat SOMERSET by three wickets.

GLOUCESTERSHIRE v NOTTINGHAMSHIRE

At Bristol, September 12. No result. Toss: Nottinghamshire.
Lewis removed Hinks with the first ball of a match that was washed out in the 12th over.

Gloucestershire

S. G. Hinks c Pollard b Lewis	0
A. J. Wright not out	14
M. G. N. Windows not out	24
L-b 4, w 1	5

1/0 (1 wkt, 11.5 overs) 43

M. W. Alleyne, T. H. C. Hancock, †R. C. Russell, R. C. Williams, *C. A. Walsh, M. C. J. Ball, A. M. Smith and A. M. Babington did not bat.

Bowling: Lewis 6-2-12-1; Mike 4-0-19-0; Pick 1.5-0-8-0.

Nottinghamshire

P. R. Pollard, P. Johnson, *R. T. Robinson, M. Saxelby, C. C. Lewis, G. W. Mike, C. L. Cairns, M. A. Crawley, †B. N. French, R. T. Bates and R. A. Pick.

Umpires: R. Julian and N. T. Plews.

At Hove, September 19. GLOUCESTERSHIRE lost to SUSSEX by 32 runs.

HAMPSHIRE

At Stockton-on-Tees, May 16. HAMPSHIRE v DURHAM. No result.

HAMPSHIRE v YORKSHIRE

At Southampton, May 23. Yorkshire won by 30 runs. Toss: Hampshire.
Yorkshire's total of 200 depended heavily on Richardson, whose 81 was his highest score yet for the county. He was dropped on 25 by Marshall, who was deputising as captain for the injured Nicholas. Marshall had a mixed day: he bowled tightly, and made his maiden fifty in the competition, 14 years after his debut, but Hampshire subsided rapidly after he was run out, with Gough taking four for 25.

Yorkshire

*M. D. Moxon c Terry b James	38	M. J. Foster b Marshall	2
A. A. Metcalfe c Terry b Marshall	3	J. D. Batty not out	3
R. B. Richardson c Udal b Connor	81		
D. Byas run out	2		
†R. J. Blakey c Middleton b Ayling	38	L-b 5, w 3	8
C. White not out	19	1/3 2/73 3/78 (8 wkts, 50 overs) 200
A. P. Grayson st Aymes b Udal	0	4/159 5/167 6/170
D. Gough c Ayling b Udal	6	7/187 8/190

M. A. Robinson did not bat.

Bowling: Marshall 10-3-26-2; Connor 8-0-26-1; Ayling 10-1-42-1; James 7-0-36-1; Turner 5-0-14-0; Udal 10-0-51-2.

Hampshire

T. C. Middleton b Gough	10	S. D. Udal lbw b Gough		3
V. P. Terry c and b White	13	C. A. Connor b Gough		12
D. I. Gower c White b Batty	27	I. J. Turner not out		1
J. R. Ayling c and b Batty	0	B 4, l-b 9, w 1		14
J. R. Wood c Batty b Gough	20			
*M. D. Marshall run out	59	1/13 2/51 3/56	(47.4 overs)	170
K. D. James run out	6	4/59 5/116 6/138		
†A. N. Aymes c Gough b Grayson	5	7/150 8/155 9/169		

Bowling: Robinson 6–1–10–0; Gough 7.4–0–25–4; Foster 7–0–34–0; White 10–0–24–1; Batty 10–0–34–2; Grayson 7–0–30–1.

Umpires: R. Julian and A. G. T. Whitehead.

At Checkley, May 30. DERBYSHIRE v HAMPSHIRE. No result (abandoned).

At Nottingham, June 6. HAMPSHIRE beat NOTTINGHAMSHIRE by eight wickets.

HAMPSHIRE v KENT

At Basingstoke, June 13. Kent won by seven wickets. Toss: Kent.

Hampshire's day went wrong from the moment they lost the toss. Ealham removed both their openers cheaply, and went on to return his best figures in any competition when he bowled Udal, Connor and Aymes in the last five balls of the innings. Then Ward and Fleming – who was dropped before scoring – put on 107 from just 13 overs while the field placings were still restricted. Ward's 112, his second Sunday hundred of the season, came from 91 balls with six sixes and 12 fours; Fleming hit 58 off 37 balls.

Hampshire

R. A. Smith c Ward b Ealham	15	S. D. Udal b Ealham		7
T. C. Middleton c Benson b Ealham	16	C. A. Connor b Ealham		0
J. R. Wood b Penn	33	†A. N. Aymes b Ealham		0
V. P. Terry c McCague b Hooper	23	L-b 6, w 4, n-b 4		14
*M. C. J. Nicholas c and b Hooper	31			
J. R. Ayling c Penn b McCague	15	1/33 2/44 3/86	(50 overs)	198
M. D. Marshall c Hooper b Ealham	27	4/108 5/130 6/150		
K. D. James not out	17	7/189 8/198 9/198		

Bowling: McCague 10–0–35–1; Ealham 10–1–53–6; Penn 10–2–27–1; Fleming 10–2–45–0; Hooper 10–1–32–2.

Kent

T. R. Ward b Ayling	112	N. J. Llong not out		16
M. V. Fleming c Aymes b James	58	L-b 3, n-b 2		5
C. L. Hooper run out	0			
N. R. Taylor not out	11	1/107 2/107 3/181	(3 wkts, 34 overs)	202

*M. R. Benson, G. R. Cowdrey, †S. A. Marsh, M. A. Ealham, M. J. McCague and C. Penn did not bat.

Bowling: Marshall 5–0–35–0; Connor 6–1–53–0; James 7–0–33–1; Ayling 6–0–45–1; Udal 10–0–33–0.

Umpires: J. H. Harris and D. O. Oslear.

At Northampton, June 20. HAMPSHIRE lost to NORTHAMPTONSHIRE by four wickets.

At Bristol, July 4. HAMPSHIRE lost to GLOUCESTERSHIRE by 24 runs.

HAMPSHIRE v SOMERSET

At Southampton, July 11. Hampshire won by seven wickets. Toss: Somerset.

Somerset's later batsmen were unable to capitalise on a century opening stand in 25 overs between Lathwell and the enterprising Folland. Hampshire, in contrast, lost three quick wickets before Terry and Nicholas took them to victory with a stand of 169 in 30 overs.

Somerset

M. N. Lathwell c Marshall b James ... 46	A. R. Caddick c Aymes b Marshall.... 11
N. A. Folland c Udal b James 60	N. A. Mallender c Marshall b Turner .. 13
G. D. Rose c Nicholas b Turner 9	H. R. J. Trump lbw b Turner........ 0
R. J. Harden b Udal 27	B 5, l-b 5, n-b 2 12
K. A. Parsons b Connor b Udal 14	
A. Payne c and b James 3	1/107 2/126 3/129 (49.4 overs) 214
*C. J. Tavaré c Aymes b Connor..... 7	4/162 5/170 6/172
†N. D. Burns not out.............. 12	7/182 8/195 9/214

Bowling: Marshall 10-2-26-1; Connor 10-2-40-1; Turner 9.4-1-58-3; James 10-0-46-3; Udal 10-0-34-2.

Hampshire

T. C. Middleton c Trump b Rose...... 9	*M. C. J. Nicholas not out........... 84
D. I. Gower b Rose................ 33	L-b 2, w 4 6
R. A. Smith c Burns b Payne 0	
V. P. Terry not out 83	1/36 2/37 3/46 (3 wkts, 48.5 overs) 215

K. D. James, M. D. Marshall, †A. N. Aymes, S. D. Udal, C. A. Connor and I. J. Turner did not bat.

Bowling: Caddick 9.5-0-38-0; Mallender 9-2-32-0; Rose 9-1-43-2; Payne 10-0-34-1; Trump 6-0-36-0; Parsons 5-0-30-0.

Umpires: J. C. Balderstone and G. A. Stickley.

HAMPSHIRE v WORCESTERSHIRE

At Portsmouth, July 18. No result. Toss: Worcestershire.

Before the rain set in Smith and Wood put on 105 for the third wicket.

Hampshire

V. P. Terry c D'Oliveira b Tolley...... 29	K. D. James not out 5
D. I. Gower c Radford b Tolley....... 27	
R. A. Smith c sub b Tolley.......... 79	L-b 9, w 3, n-b 2 14
J. R. Wood c and b Newport 44	
*M. C. J. Nicholas c Newport b Tolley. 2	1/53 2/81 3/186 (5 wkts, 42 overs) 203
S. D. Udal not out................ 3	4/195 5/196

†A. N. Aymes, C. A. Connor, M. Jean-Jacques and M. J. Thursfield did not bat.

Bowling: Benjamin 8-0-35-0; Radford 9-0-47-0; Tolley 10-1-50-4; Newport 8-1-25-1; Illingworth 7-0-37-0.

Worcestershire

*T. S. Curtis, N. V. Radford, G. A. Hick, D. B. D'Oliveira, S. R. Lampitt, M. J. Weston, †S. J. Rhodes, P. J. Newport, K. C. G. Benjamin, C. M. Tolley and R. K. Illingworth.

Umpires: D. J. Constant and P. Willey.

At Lord's, July 25. HAMPSHIRE lost to MIDDLESEX by 81 runs.

HAMPSHIRE v WARWICKSHIRE

At Southampton, August 1. Hampshire won by nine wickets. Toss: Warwickshire.

Warwickshire's innings was dominated by Asif Din, whose undefeated 132 off 141 balls was the highest in the competition by a Warwickshire batsman, passing John Jameson's 123 not out against Nottinghamshire in 1973. No one else reached 25. Yet his effort was upstaged by Robin Smith's unbeaten 118 off 118 balls, with a six and 14 fours. Smith shared in an unbroken partnership of 194 with Terry.

Warwickshire

J. D. Ratcliffe c Nicholas b Thursfield	14	T. L. Penney lbw b Connor	18
Asif Din not out	132	N. M. K. Smith not out	23
D. P. Ostler c Aymes b Thursfield	4	L-b 5, w 3	8
P. A. Smith lbw b Udal	21		
R. G. Twose b Turner	9	1/42 2/57 3/103 (6 wkts, 50 overs)	232
*D. A. Reeve c Connor b Turner	3	4/124 5/134 6/180	

†K. J. Piper, G. C. Small and T. A. Munton did not bat.

Bowling: Marshall 10–0–50–0; Connor 10–2–46–1; Thursfield 10–0–42–2; Turner 10–0–51–2; Udal 10–0–38–1.

Hampshire

D. I. Gower c Ostler b Small	26
V. P. Terry not out	74
R. A. Smith not out	118
B 2, l-b 8, w 1, n-b 4	15
1/39 (1 wkt, 44.5 overs)	233

J. R. Wood, *M. C. J. Nicholas, M. D. Marshall, †A. N. Aymes, S. D. Udal, C. A. Connor, I. J. Turner and M. J. Thursfield did not bat.

Bowling: Reeve 7–1–31–0; Munton 8–0–37–0; Small 7–1–21–1; P. A. Smith 6–0–30–0; N. M. K. Smith 9–0–53–0; Twose 4–0–20–0; Asif Din 3.5–0–31–0.

Umpires: J. D. Bond and R. Julian.

HAMPSHIRE v LANCASHIRE

At Southampton, August 15. Lancashire won by six wickets. Toss: Lancashire.

Hampshire were in a parlous position at 39 for six when Nicholas and Udal came together in a spirited 83-run partnership for the seventh wicket. The other nine batsmen managed only 23 between them as DeFreitas, bowling with genuine zip, took five wickets and Lancashire won comfortably.

Hampshire

D. I. Gower c and b Austin	1	M. J. Thursfield b Watkinson	9
V. P. Terry lbw b DeFreitas	4	C. A. Connor b DeFreitas	1
R. A. Smith c Atherton b DeFreitas	1	I. J. Turner lbw b DeFreitas	0
J. R. Wood c Hegg b Austin	0	B 4, l-b 6, w 5, n-b 12	27
*M. C. J. Nicholas not out	64		
M. D. Marshall lbw b DeFreitas	6	1/8 2/11 3/12 (47 overs)	158
†A. N. Aymes lbw b Watkinson	1	4/12 5/30 6/39	
S. D. Udal b Wasim Akram	44	7/122 8/151 9/158	

Bowling: Austin 8–0–22–2; DeFreitas 10–4–26–5; Watkinson 10–1–29–2; Wasim Akram 9–0–37–1; Yates 10–0–34–0.

Lancashire

M. A. Atherton c Connor b Udal	51	Wasim Akram not out 17
S. P. Titchard run out	31	L-b 3, w 3 6
J. P. Crawley c Terry b Thursfield	19	
*N. H. Fairbrother not out	25	1/77 2/85 (4 wkts, 47.4 overs) 159
N. J. Speak b Marshall	10	3/111 4/128

M. Watkinson, P. A. J. DeFreitas, †W. K. Hegg, I. D. Austin and G. Yates did not bat.

Bowling: Marshall 9–1–25–1; Connor 8.4–1–37–0; Thursfield 10–1–46–1; Turner 10–0–24–0; Udal 10–1–24–1.

Umpires: D. J. Constant and V. A. Holder.

At Swansea, August 22. HAMPSHIRE lost to GLAMORGAN by six wickets.

HAMPSHIRE v SUSSEX

At Portsmouth, August 29. Hampshire won by eight wickets. Toss: Hampshire.

A high-scoring match, the second of the season in which both sides passed 300, included three centuries, the first a Sunday League best for Wells, who put on 161 with Lenham in what looked like a winning total for Sussex. But they were overshadowed by a decisive 235 in 38 overs for the second wicket between Terry and Smith, as Hampshire took advantage of an injury to Hemmings and raced to victory with one ball to spare. Smith's 129 required only 108 balls. Six days later, in the NatWest final, Sussex reached 321 and lost again.

Sussex

F. D. Stephenson c Terry b Turner	59	I. D. K. Salisbury c Terry b Udal 2
M. P. Speight c Nicholas b Connor	8	E. E. Hemmings not out 1
C. W. J. Athey c Turner b Connor	0	
*A. P. Wells b Turner	127	B 1, l-b 6, w 2, n-b 2 11
N. J. Lenham c Cox b Connor	69	
K. Greenfield st Aymes b Udal	9	1/29 2/29 3/112 (8 wkts, 50 overs) 312
†P. Moores b Connor	12	4/273 5/275 6/288
J. A. North not out	14	7/296 8/299

E. S. H. Giddins did not bat.

Bowling: Connor 10–0–69–4; Shine 10–0–87–0; James 10–1–37–0; Turner 10–0–51–2; Udal 10–0–61–2.

Hampshire

V. P. Terry not out	124
J. R. Wood c Salisbury b Giddins	7
R. A. Smith c Athey b North	129
*M. C. J. Nicholas not out	28
B 11, l-b 5, w 9	25

1/20 2/255 (2 wkts, 49.5 overs) 313

K. D. James, R. M. F. Cox, †A. N. Aymes, S. D. Udal, C. A. Connor, K. J. Shine and I. J. Turner did not bat.

Bowling: Giddins 10–0–56–1; Stephenson 9.5–1–39–0; North 6–0–48–1; Hemmings 7.3–0–26–0; Salisbury 10–0–73–0; Lenham 3–0–19–0; Greenfield 3.3–0–36–0.

Umpires: A. A. Jones and D. R. Shepherd.

At The Oval, September 5. HAMPSHIRE lost to SURREY by 77 runs.

HAMPSHIRE v LEICESTERSHIRE

At Southampton, September 12. No result (abandoned).

At Chelmsford, September 19. HAMPSHIRE lost to ESSEX by 99 runs.

KENT

At Lord's, May 9. KENT beat MIDDLESEX by nine wickets.

KENT v WARWICKSHIRE

At Canterbury, May 16. Kent won by 66 runs. Toss: Kent.

Kent's second victory in two games made them the early League leaders. Ward fell one short of a maiden Sunday century. He and Benson had put on 67 in the first 15 overs, when the additional new fielding restrictions applied. The same rules later gave Warwickshire two no-balls when Spencer stepped outside one of the semi-circles. Donald dislocated a finger while bowling, and Warwickshire's batting had a makeshift look, with Burns, the deputy wicket-keeper playing for the injured Piper, promoted to open.

Kent

T. R. Ward c Twose b Donald	99	†S. A. Marsh c N. M. K. Smith	
*M. R. Benson lbw b P. A. Smith	40	b Munton	4
C. L. Hooper st Burns b N. M. K. Smith	29	D. J. Spencer run out	4
M. V. Fleming b N. M. K. Smith	14	B 3, l-b 6, w 15, n-b 4	28
N. R. Taylor not out	50		
G. R. Cowdrey c Penney		1/86 2/164 3/192 (8 wkts, 49 overs) 289	
b N. M. K. Smith	4	4/200 5/213 6/256	
N. J. Llong b Reeve	17	7/271 8/289	

D. W. Headley and A. P. Igglesden did not bat.

Bowling: Munton 9-0-55-1; Reeve 7-0-41-1; Donald 8.4-2-39-1; Bell 7-0-49-0; P. A. Smith 7-0-54-1; N. M. K. Smith 10-0-40-3; Twose 0.2-0-2-0.

Warwickshire

A. J. Moles c Marsh b Igglesden	14	M. A. V. Bell b Fleming	4
†M. Burns c Llong b Igglesden	4	T. A. Munton b Fleming	13
R. G. Twose run out	7	A. A. Donald absent injured	
D. P. Ostler c Ward b Fleming	44	L-b 16, w 8, n-b 2	26
T. L. Penney not out	83		
*D. A. Reeve st Marsh b Llong	4	1/12 2/25 3/33 (46.1 overs) 223	
P. A. Smith run out	1	4/104 5/117 6/120	
N. M. K. Smith b Headley	23	7/168 8/195 9/223	

Bowling: Igglesden 8-0-31-2; Headley 9-0-38-1; Hooper 10-0-42-0; Spencer 4-0-17-0; Fleming 9.1-0-39-3; Llong 6-0-40-1.

Umpires: B. Dudleston and G. Sharp.

At Nottingham, May 23. KENT lost to NOTTINGHAMSHIRE by nine wickets.

At Darlington, May 30. DURHAM v KENT. No result.

KENT v GLOUCESTERSHIRE

At Tunbridge Wells, June 6. Kent won by seven wickets. Toss: Kent.

Kent maintained their position as joint League leaders with a comfortable win. Hooper and Taylor put on 147 in 37 overs for the third wicket, after Gloucestershire had lost their last five wickets in 15 balls. The home team's only disappointment was the loss of Headley to a sprained ankle.

Gloucestershire

B. C. Broad c and b Hooper	52	C. A. Walsh run out		0
G. D. Hodgson b Ealham	15	K. E. Cooper b Fleming		1
*A. J. Wright c Marsh b Penn	16	A. M. Babington b Ealham		3
M. W. Alleyne c Hooper b Ealham	78	L-b 4, w 3		7
R. J. Scott c Taylor b Hooper	5			
T. H. C. Hancock lbw b Penn	13	1/28 2/75 3/99	(48.4 overs)	204
†R. C. Russell not out	13	4/113 5/163 6/194		
R. M. Wight run out	1	7/196 8/196 9/198		

Bowling: Headley 8–1–15–0; Ealham 9.4–0–41–3; Penn 9–0–58–2; Hooper 10–2–23–2; Fleming 9–0–50–1; Llong 3–0–13–0.

Kent

T. R. Ward c Broad b Walsh	23	N. J. Llong not out		11
M. V. Fleming c Babington b Walsh	9	L-b 7, w 1, n-b 6		14
C. L. Hooper not out	70			
N. R. Taylor c Wright b Wight	80	1/30 2/40 3/187	(3 wkts, 47.2 overs)	207

*M. R. Benson, G. R. Cowdrey, †S. A. Marsh, D. W. Headley, M. A. Ealham and C. Penn did not bat.

Bowling: Cooper 7–0–47–0; Walsh 8–1–31–2; Babington 10–2–23–0; Wight 10–1–41–1; Scott 6.2–1–25–0; Alleyne 6–0–33–0.

Umpires: B. J. Meyer and P. Willey.

At Basingstoke, June 13. KENT beat HAMPSHIRE by seven wickets.

KENT v DERBYSHIRE

At Canterbury, June 20. Derbyshire won by three runs. Toss: Kent.

Adams dominated the game with 92 runs from 85 balls and then three spectacular catches at short cover to reduce Kent to 46 for three. But Hooper, Cowdrey and Ealham later brought the target of 249 within sight; Ealham needed six from the final ball, but managed only two. Derbyshire could also be grateful for their narrow win to Base and Vandrau, who had prefaced their five wickets with a stand of 55 in ten overs.

Derbyshire

P. D. Bowler c Marsh b Ealham	18	S. J. Base b Fleming		31
C. J. Adams lbw b Fleming	92	R. W. Sladdin not out		5
J. E. Morris c McCague b Ealham	12			
T. J. G. O'Gorman run out	17	L-b 2, w 7, n-b 4		13
*K. J. Barnett c Llong b Igglesden	6			
F. A. Griffith b McCague	20	1/67 2/90 3/137	(8 wkts, 50 overs)	248
M. J. Vandrau not out	32	4/144 5/171 6/171		
†B. J. M. Maher c Marsh b McCague	2	7/186 8/241		

O. H. Mortensen did not bat.

Bowling: McCague 10–1–45–2; Igglesden 10–0–50–1; Hooper 10–0–44–0; Ealham 10–1–55–2; Fleming 10–0–52–2.

Kent

T. R. Ward c Adams b Base	....	15
M. V. Fleming c Adams b Mortensen	..	4
C. L. Hooper c Sladdin b Vandrau	....	72
N. R. Taylor c Adams b Base	....	6
N. J. Llong b Sladdin		3
*M. R. Benson b Vandrau	....	8
G. R. Cowdrey b Base		57
†S. A. Marsh c Mortensen b Griffith	...	28

M. A. Ealham not out 31
M. J. McCague not out 11

L-b 1, w 5, n-b 4 10

1/5 2/22 3/46   (8 wkts, 50 overs) 245
4/59 5/84 6/135
7/201 8/205

A. P. Igglesden did not bat.

Bowling: Mortensen 10–1–36–1; Base 10–0–60–3; Sladdin 10–1–37–1; Vandrau 10–1–39–2; Griffith 10–0–72–1.

Umpires: K. E. Palmer and N. T. Plews.

At Leeds, June 27. KENT beat YORKSHIRE by eight runs.

KENT v ESSEX

At Maidstone, July 4. Kent won by 157 runs. Toss: Kent.

Hooper's all-round form confirmed Kent's position at the head of the table as they scored 309, their highest Sunday total, and dismissed Essex for less than half that. Hooper made 103, his second hundred in two days off Essex, in 111 balls, and put on 126 with Ward, who hit four sixes in his 79-ball 86. Andrew was particularly hard hit. Later Hooper's off-spin claimed five for 41 and made him the first man to score a century and take five wickets in a Sunday League match.

Kent

T. R. Ward c Shahid b Cousins	....	86
M. V. Fleming c Childs b Pringle	......	0
C. L. Hooper c Prichard b Stephenson	.	103
N. J. Llong c Prichard b Childs	....	16
*M. R. Benson c Prichard b Childs	....	19
N. R. Taylor c Childs b Topley	....	15
G. R. Cowdrey not out	....	45

M. A. Ealham b Topley 3
D. W. Headley not out 8
B 3, l-b 9, n-b 2 14

1/17 2/143 3/171   (7 wkts, 50 overs) 309
4/215 5/245
6/268 7/279

†R. J. Parks and R. P. Davis did not bat.

Bowling: Pringle 10–2–42–1; Andrew 5–0–59–0; Stephenson 8–0–46–1; Cousins 7–0–31–1; Topley 10–1–61–2; Childs 10–0–58–2.

Essex

*P. J. Prichard c Taylor b Hooper	.....	67
J. P. Stephenson c Cowdrey b Headley	.	16
J. J. B. Lewis lbw b Ealham	....	0
N. Shahid b Hooper	....	16
D. D. J. Robinson b Hooper	....	2
D. R. Pringle run out	....	11
†M. A. Garnham b Hooper	....	8
T. D. Topley st Parks b Hooper	....	8

S. J. W. Andrew c Fleming b Davis . . . 14
D. M. Cousins c Hooper b Llong 1
J. H. Childs not out 6
L-b 1, n-b 2 3

1/43 2/44 3/73   (38.2 overs) 152
4/81 5/98 6/123
7/123 8/142 9/145

Bowling: Headley 8–0–35–1; Ealham 7–0–22–1; Fleming 5–0–27–0; Hooper 10–0–41–5; Davis 7–0–25–1; Llong 1.2–0–1–1.

Umpires: D. J. Constant and R. Julian.

At Hove, July 18. SUSSEX v KENT. No result.

At Taunton, July 25. KENT beat SOMERSET by three wickets.

KENT v LEICESTERSHIRE

At Canterbury, August 1. Kent won by 63 runs. Toss: Kent.

Hooper saw Kent well on their way to their highest Sunday score with 64 off 59 balls before Fleming and Cowdrey, with a six and six fours off 19 balls, put on a whirlwind 75 in five overs. Boon batted throughout Leicestershire's reply for 135 off 138 balls, but they were never up with the asking-rate. This victory saw Kent return to the top of the table ahead of Glamorgan, who had a game in hand.

Kent

T. R. Ward c Benson b Mullally	18		G. R. Cowdrey c Boon b Parsons		43
*M. R. Benson c Nixon b Wells	30		†S. A. Marsh not out		4
C. L. Hooper c Whitaker b Benson	64		B 3, l-b 10, w 6, n-b 12		31
N. R. Taylor b Wells	57				
N. J. Llong run out	13		1/33 2/102 3/155	(6 wkts, 50 overs)	327
M. V. Fleming not out	67		4/191 5/225 6/300		

M. A. Ealham, A. P. Igglesden and C. Penn did not bat.

Bowling: Mullally 10–0–53–1; Parsons 10–2–56–1; Wells 10–0–54–2; Dakin 7–0–64–0; Potter 9–0–57–0; Benson 4–0–30–1.

Leicestershire

T. J. Boon not out	135		V. J. Wells not out		24
*N. E. Briers c Fleming b Hooper	63				
J. J. Whitaker b Penn	14		L-b 8, w 1		9
P. E. Robinson b Ealham	15				
J. D. R. Benson c Cowdrey b Fleming	3		1/138 2/177 3/201	(5 wkts, 50 overs)	264
†P. A. Nixon b Ealham	1		4/210 5/213		

L. Potter, J. M. Dakin, G. J. Parsons and A. D. Mullally did not bat.

Bowling: Igglesden 10–1–36–0; Ealham 10–0–45–2; Penn 10–0–49–1; Hooper 10–0–60–1; Fleming 10–0–66–1.

Umpires: M. J. Kitchen and N. T. Plews.

KENT v SURREY

At Canterbury, August 8. Kent won by 54 runs. Toss: Surrey.

An extraordinary first over from Spencer turned the match: it consisted of nine balls and cost 14 runs and yielded two valuable wickets, two no-balls, a wide and five consecutive short-pitched balls. Hollioake and Kersey effected a recovery from 70 for five but Headley and Fleming then demolished the tail. Kent's total had been helped by a late flurry from Ealham, who hit three sixes off Murphy; 56 runs came in the last five overs.

Kent

T. R. Ward lbw b Holliake	43		D. J. Spencer not out		16
*M. R. Benson b Murphy	3		D. W. Headley not out		4
C. L. Hooper st Kersey b Boiling	51				
N. R. Taylor c Brown b Boiling	36		B 3, l-b 8, w 11		22
N. J. Llong c Kersey b Holliake	2				
M. V. Fleming b Benjamin	24		1/8 2/98 3/111	(8 wkts, 50 overs)	248
†S. A. Marsh c Lynch b Murphy	15		4/116 5/162 6/187		
M. A. Ealham b Waqar Younis	32		7/189 8/244		

A. P. Igglesden did not bat.

Bowling: Murphy 10–3–54–2; Benjamin 10–2–37–1; Waqar Younis 10–1–43–1; Holliake 10–0–44–2; Boiling 10–0–59–2.

Surrey

D. J. Bicknell b Ealham	21	J. E. Benjamin c Llong b Fleming	1
A. D. Brown b Igglesden	0	J. Boiling not out	2
D. M. Ward b Spencer	26	A. J. Murphy lbw b Headley	0
*M. A. Lynch c Fleming b Spencer	9	B 2, l-b 2, w 8, n-b 8	20
A. W. Smith run out	2		
A. J. Hollioake lbw b Headley	58	1/1 2/39 3/59	(45.1 overs) 194
†G. J. Kersey c Benson b Headley	49	4/62 5/70 6/180	
Waqar Younis c Spencer b Fleming	6	7/191 8/192 9/192	

Bowling: Igglesden 10-2-47-1; Ealham 8-2-27-1; Headley 9.1-0-32-3; Spencer 4-1-29-2; Hooper 6-0-23-0; Fleming 8-0-32-2.

Umpires: V. A. Holder and A. A. Jones.

At Worcester, August 22. KENT beat WORCESTERSHIRE on scoring-rate.

At Manchester, August 29. KENT beat LANCASHIRE by six wickets.

KENT v NORTHAMPTONSHIRE

At Canterbury, September 5. Kent won by three wickets. Toss: Northamptonshire.

Kent's victory put them back ahead of Glamorgan and made it inevitable that the title should be decided at Canterbury two weeks later. Llong was the only player on either side to pass 22, scoring 64; the inexperienced Bowen was particularly economical, taking two for 12 in his ten overs.

Northamptonshire

A. Fordham c Headley b Ealham	19	A. Walker not out	9
M. B. Loye c Ealham b Fleming	22	N. G. B. Cook not out	1
R. J. Bailey c Marsh b Ealham	1		
R. J. Warren b Hooper	21	L-b 4, w 5, n-b 4	13
*A. J. Lamb run out	19		
†D. Ripley b Headley	19	1/35 2/36 3/62	(8 wkts, 50 overs) 165
J. G. Hughes c Spencer b Headley	21	4/80 5/94 6/122	
M. N. Bowen c Hooper b Fleming	20	7/147 8/163	

J. P. Taylor did not bat.

Bowling: Igglesden 10-0-30-0; Ealham 7-3-21-2; Spencer 7-0-21-0; Fleming 6-0-26-2; Hooper 10-0-26-1; Headley 10-0-37-2.

Kent

T. R. Ward c Lamb b Bowen	22	*†S. A. Marsh lbw b Bailey	13
M. V. Fleming c Fordham b Walker	8	D. J. Spencer not out	17
C. L. Hooper c Fordham b Bowen	17	L-b 4, w 8	12
D. P. Fulton c Ripley b Cook	5		
N. J. Llong not out	64	1/9 2/48 3/49	(7 wkts, 47 overs) 166
G. R. Cowdrey run out	1	4/64 5/69	
M. A. Ealham c Ripley b Taylor	7	6/114 7/141	

D. W. Headley and A. P. Igglesden did not bat.

Bowling: Walker 9-1-38-1; Taylor 8-0-38-1; Bowen 10-4-12-2; Cook 10-1-30-1; Bailey 10-0-44-1.

Umpires: J. H. Harris and V. A. Holder.

KENT v GLAMORGAN

At Canterbury, September 19. Glamorgan won by six wickets. Toss: Kent.

A crowd of 12,000 which began queuing at four in the morning watched the first season of the revamped Sunday League end in the most dramatic and romantic way imaginable. Fate had brought the top two teams together on the final day of the season; destiny ensured that Vivian Richards would round off his magnificent career by taking Glamorgan to their first trophy since 1969, after 23 seasons of often abject failure. Kent, themselves without a trophy since 1978, began the day as favourites: a washout would have made them champions on run-rate. But the day was fine enough for Kent to feel emboldened to bat first. With Hooper, the League's leading run-scorer, well-set after reaching his ninth fifty, Kent had a chance of a good total despite a slow pitch. However, from 168 for four after 41 overs, Kent lost five wickets for 14 and only the last pair's efforts enabled them to scrape to 200. Glamorgan quickly lost James and struggled to get any runs at all against Igglesden and Ealham, before Dale and Morris eventually began to push ahead. The game was far from won when Richards sauntered to the crease in his familiar gunslinger's manner at 98 for three. He was nowhere near his best and was given an especially hard time by the pacy Anglo-Australian Spencer: he was both hit in the chest and caught off a no-ball. Richards prevailed, however, and an unbroken stand of 60 in ten overs with Cottey gave Glamorgan victory. The winning runs came from a top edge over the wicket-keeper but by that stage the result was no longer in doubt. Richards marched off punching the air and a heavy night of Welsh celebration began.

Kent

T. R. Ward c Metson b Watkin	11	D. P. Fulton c and b Lefebvre	1
M. V. Fleming c Morris b Croft	44	D. W. Headley not out	10
C. L. Hooper c Dale b Barwick	60	A. P. Igglesden not out	6
N. J. Llong b Dale	25	L-b 8, w 1	9
M. A. Ealham lbw b Croft	13		
G. R. Cowdrey c Metson b Dale	10	1/29 2/72 3/103 (9 wkts, 50 overs) 200
†S. A. Marsh c Lefebvre b Watkin	6	4/123 5/168 6/170
D. J. Spencer c Richards b Watkin	5	7/180 8/180 9/182

Bowling: Lefebvre 10-0-43-1; Watkin 10-1-33-3; Barwick 10-1-33-1; Croft 10-1-42-2; Dale 10-1-41-2.

Glamorgan

S. P. James c Cowdrey b Igglesden	3	P. A. Cottey not out	33
H. Morris c Fleming b Ealham	67	B 7, l-b 1, w 7, n-b 4	19
A. Dale c Marsh b Headley	31		
M. P. Maynard lbw b Spencer	2	1/6 2/84 (4 wkts, 47.4 overs) 201
R. B. Richards not out	46	3/98 4/141

R. D. B. Croft, †C. P. Metson, R. P. Lefebvre, S. L. Watkin and S. R. Barwick did not bat.

Bowling: Igglesden 10-1-43-1; Ealham 10-3-20-1; Headley 10-0-43-1; Hooper 10-0-44-0; Spencer 8.4-1-43-1.

Umpires: D. J. Constant and G. A. Stickley.

LANCASHIRE

LANCASHIRE v DURHAM

At Manchester, May 9. Lancashire won by 12 runs. Toss: Durham. County debut: A. C. Cummins.

The Reds gained victory at a crowded Old Trafford, a common occurrence in soccer but, with coloured clothing, a new development in cricket. Lancashire's total was dominated by a fine 96 from Atherton. Durham newcomer Anderson Cummins took no wickets, but gave a peak a bruised finger. Bainbridge's patient innings seemed enough to see Durham home, but after Smith was out no one gave him sufficient support.

Lancashire

M. A. Atherton c Brown b Hughes	....	96	†W. K. Hegg c Parker b Brown	......	14
N. J. Speak retired hurt	....	0	I. D. Austin not out	....	22
*N. H. Fairbrother c Larkins			P. J. Martin not out	....	0
	b Bainbridge	29	B 1, l-b 7, w 4, n-b 15	......	27
G. D. Lloyd b Botham	....	24			
M. Watkinson c Parker b Bainbridge	..	9	1/78 2/119 3/134	(7 wkts, 50 overs)	229
P. A. J. DeFreitas c Fothergill b Botham		6	4/167 5/176		
Wasim Akram c Parker b Botham	....	2	6/194 7/228		

A. A. Barnett did not bat.

N. J. Speak retired hurt at 9.

Bowling: Cummins 10–1–35–0; Hughes 10–1–41–1; Brown 10–0–64–1; Bainbridge 10–1–40–2; Botham 10–0–41–3.

Durham

W. Larkins c Hegg b Austin	....	28	M. P. Briers b Wasim Akram	....	15
G. Fowler c Fairbrother b Martin	......	19	A. C. Cummins not out	....	5
I. Smith c Watkinson b Martin	......	36	B 1, l-b 12, w 10, n-b 8	......	31
P. Bainbridge not out	....	69			
I. T. Botham b Watkinson	....	1	1/50 2/58 3/151	(6 wkts, 50 overs)	217
*P. W. G. Parker run out	....	13	4/157 5/185 6/212		

†A. R. Fothergill, S. P. Hughes and S. J. E. Brown did not bat.

Bowling: Wasim Akram 10–0–47–1; DeFreitas 10–2–26–0; Austin 9–0–38–1; Martin 8–0–32–2; Watkinson 10–1–38–1; Barnett 3–0–23–0.

Umpires: N. T. Plews and A. G. T. Whitehead.

At Taunton, May 16. SOMERSET v LANCASHIRE. No result.

LANCASHIRE v WARWICKSHIRE

At Manchester, May 30. No result. Toss: Warwickshire.

Rain intervened after off-spinner Neil Smith took five wickets in one-day cricket for the first time, reducing Lancashire to 130 for six. Atherton and Titchard had opened with 58 in 16 overs, including 22 off Donald's first two.

Lancashire

M. A. Atherton c and b Reeve	....	31	P. A. J. DeFreitas not out	....	21
S. P. Titchard b N. M. K. Smith	....	34	†W. K. Hegg not out	....	2
N. J. Speak lbw b N. M. K. Smith	....	17	B 2, l-b 10, w 10, n-b 6	....	24
*N. H. Fairbrother b N. M. K. Smith	.	16			
G. D. Lloyd st Burns b N. M. K. Smith		3	1/58 2/85 3/107	(7 wkts, 44.4 overs)	174
Wasim Akram c Burns b Munton	.....	24	4/108 5/113		
M. Watkinson c Moles			6/130 7/157		
	b N. M. K. Smith	2			

P. J. Martin and G. Chapple did not bat.

Bowling: Reeve 8–1–17–1; Munton 9–1–33–1; Donald 10–0–59–0; Small 9.4–0–31–0; N. M. K. Smith 8–0–26–5.

Warwickshire

A. J. Moles, †M. Burns, R. G. Twose, D. P. Ostler, T. L. Penney, *D. A. Reeve, P. A Smith, N. M. K. Smith, G. C. Small, A. A. Donald and T. A. Munton.

Umpires: J. H. Harris and D. J. Constant.

At The Oval, June 6. LANCASHIRE lost to SURREY by 165 runs.

LANCASHIRE v ESSEX

At Manchester, June 13. Essex won by 60 runs. Toss: Lancashire.

Two Essex bowlers just named in the party for the Lord's Test won the match. Ilott returned the remarkably economical figures of 6.5–2–8–2, while Such collected four wickets on the ground where he had taken eight for England a week earlier. Lancashire were dismissed with six overs to spare. Earlier Essex's batting leant heavily on Stephenson and Gooch, who came in at No. 5. They shared 116 for the fourth wicket, and alone of the top seven batsmen escaped the gloves of wicket-keeper Hegg. DeFreitas, dropped by England, bowled with his hand bandaged after slipping on the stairs and putting it through a window overlooking the Essex dressing-room.

Essex

J. P. Stephenson b Austin	93	M. C. Ilott b Wasim Akram	1
N. V. Knight c Hegg b DeFreitas	3	P. M. Such b Wasim Akram	8
N. Hussain c Hegg b Austin	5	S. J. W. Andrew not out	9
Salim Malik c Hegg b Wasim Akram	5	L-b 6, w 4, n-b 2	12
*G. A. Gooch c DeFreitas b Martin	67		
D. R. Pringle c Hegg b DeFreitas	17	1/28 2/52 3/57	(49.5 overs) 222
†M. A. Garnham c Hegg b Martin	2	4/173 5/197 6/202	
T. D. Topley lbw b Martin	0	7/202 8/205 9/205	

Bowling: DeFreitas 10–1–38–2; Martin 10–1–52–3; Austin 10–0–37–2; Wasim Akram 9.5–0–36–3; Barnett 10–0–53–0.

Lancashire

M. A. Atherton lbw b Such	38	†W. K. Hegg c Garnham b Stephenson	23
G. D. Mendis c Knight b Ilott	8	P. J. Martin not out	9
N. J. Speak c Garnham b Andrew	12	A. A. Barnett c Gooch b Ilott	0
*N. H. Fairbrother run out	15	L-b 2, w 2, n-b 3	7
G. D. Lloyd c Stephenson b Such	24		
Wasim Akram c Topley b Such	18	1/12 2/64 3/64	(43.5 overs) 162
P. A. J. DeFreitas lbw b Such	1	4/95 5/110 6/122	
I. D. Austin b Stephenson	7	7/122 8/138 9/161	

Bowling: Ilott 6.5–2–8–2; Pringle 6–1–16–0; Andrew 10–0–46–1; Topley 5–0–29–0; Such 10–2–38–4; Stephenson 6–0–23–2.

Umpires: J. D. Bond and B. J. Meyer.

LANCASHIRE v SUSSEX

At Manchester, June 20. Lancashire won by six wickets. Toss: Sussex.

Sussex lost their unbeaten record in the League with 19 overs to spare. As in their Benson and Hedges quarter-final a few weeks earlier they fell victim to the all-round power of Wasim Akram, who took four for 20 and won the match with an unbeaten 39. Tight bowling by Lancashire's seamers prevented the Sussex openers from making their usual rapid start and Wasim's first spell left them at 26 for five from 21 overs.

Sussex

C. W. J. Athey b Wasim Akram	5	A. C. S. Pigott run out	26
F. D. Stephenson b Austin	10	A. N. Jones b Wasim Akram	5
K. Greenfield b Watkinson	1	E. S. H. Giddins not out	1
*A. P. Wells c Hegg b Wasim Akram	1	L-b 6, w 6, n-b 4	16
J. A. North b Wasim Akram	1		
N. J. Lenham st Hegg b Barnett	24	1/17 2/20 3/20	(49.1 overs) 118
†P. Moores b Irani	9	4/23 5/26 6/57	
T. P. Donelan b DeFreitas	19	7/67 8/103 9/113	

Bowling: Austin 10–3–19–1; DeFreitas 8–3–10–1; Wasim Akram 10–4–20–4; Watkinson 9.1–3–17–1; Barnett 10–1–33–1; Irani 2–0–13–1.

Lancashire

S. P. Titchard not out	38	Wasim Akram not out	39
R. C. Irani c Lenham b Pigott	27		
G. D. Lloyd b Pigott	1	B 1, l-b 1, w 2, n-b 4	8
*N. H. Fairbrother c Greenfield b Donelan	9	1/49 2/57	(4 wkts, 31 overs) 122
N. J. Speak b Jones	0	3/68 4/70	

M. Watkinson, P. A. J. DeFreitas, †W. K. Hegg, I. D. Austin and A. A. Barnett did not bat.

Bowling: Stephenson 5–1–16–0; Giddins 5–0–22–0; Donelan 10–0–27–1; Pigott 5–1–16–2; Jones 5–0–26–1; North 1–0–13–0.

Umpires: G. I. Burgess and B. Leadbeater.

At Derby, June 27. LANCASHIRE beat DERBYSHIRE by 161 runs.

At Leicester, July 4. LANCASHIRE beat LEICESTERSHIRE by 83 runs.

LANCASHIRE v GLAMORGAN

At Manchester, July 18. Glamorgan won by eight wickets. Toss: Glamorgan.
Lancashire, without Wasim Akram and Fairbrother, were completely outplayed; only acting-captain Atherton batted with any authority. After the loss of Dale in the first over, Morris and Maynard found no problems with the pitch and added 145 in 26 overs.

Lancashire

S. P. Titchard b Croft	24	†W. K. Hegg c Morris b Lefebvre	18
R. C. Irani run out	6	G. Chapple not out	9
G. D. Lloyd c Metson b Watkin	0	A. A. Barnett not out	10
*M. A. Atherton b Watkin	64	L-b 6, w 2	8
N. J. Speak c Cottey b Barwick	9		
M. Watkinson lbw b Richards	7	1/20 2/21 3/48	(9 wkts, 50 overs) 167
P. A. J. DeFreitas b Richards	8	4/78 5/104 6/118	
I. D. Austin c Metson b Watkin	4	7/126 8/135 9/149	

Bowling: Watkin 10–1–26–3; Lefebvre 10–1–40–1; Croft 10–1–28–1; Barwick 10–0–25–1; Dale 6–0–23–0; Richards 4–0–19–2.

Glamorgan

A. Dale lbw b Chapple	0		
*H. Morris not out	87		
M. P. Maynard c Austin b Irani	72		
I. V. A. Richards not out	5		
L-b 1, w 3	4		
1/1 2/146		(2 wkts, 33.4 overs) 168	

D. L. Hemp, P. A. Cottey, R. D. B. Croft, R. P. Lefebvre, †C. P. Metson, S. L. Watkin and S. R. Barwick did not bat.

Bowling: Chapple 8.4–0–42–1; DeFreitas 6–0–40–0; Austin 6–1–29–0; Watkinson 5–0–22–0; Barnett 4–0–27–0; Irani 4–1–7–1.

Umpires: B. Leadbeater and B. J. Meyer.

LANCASHIRE v NOTTINGHAMSHIRE

At Manchester, July 25. Lancashire won by 26 runs. Toss: Nottinghamshire. County debut: S. A. Sylvester.

Rain reduced this match to a 15-over slog, which was effectively won for Lancashire by John Crawley in his first Sunday game of the season. Missed off his brother Mark when five, he smote 44 off 23 balls after DeFreitas and Austin had pulled Lancashire back from 12 for four. Nottinghamshire made a flying start with 36 for one off the first four overs, when the fielding restrictions were in force, but could not maintain that rate against Wasim Akram.

Lancashire

G. D. Lloyd c Crawley b Lewis	8	S. P. Titchard c French b Evans	1
N. J. Speak c French b Lewis	0	†W. K. Hegg not out	16
*M. Watkinson c Sylvester b Mike	0	L-b 6, w 1	7
Wasim Akram b Mike	3		
P. A. J. DeFreitas c French b Field-Buss	28	1/1 2/4 3/10 (7 wkts, 15 overs) 122
I. D. Austin c French b Evans	15	4/12 5/55
J. P. Crawley not out	44	6/61 7/63

P. J. Martin and G. Chapple did not bat.

Bowling: Lewis 3-0-12-2; Mike 3-0-27-2; Sylvester 2-0-19-0; Field-Buss 2-0-16-1; Evans 2-0-21-2; Crawley 2-0-21-0.

Nottinghamshire

P. R. Pollard c Watkinson b Austin	12	K. P. Evans b Wasim Akram	4
P. Johnson b DeFreitas	12	M. G. Field-Buss b Wasim Akram	0
D. W. Randall c Wasim Akram b Watkinson	11	S. A. Sylvester not out	1
C. C. Lewis run out	8	L-b 1, n-b 2	3
*R. T. Robinson b Chapple	11	
G. W. Mike c Titchard b Martin	14	1/15 2/36 3/44 (9 wkts, 15 overs) 96
M. A. Crawley not out	16	4/47 5/69 6/75
†B. N. French b Austin	4	7/88 8/95 9/95

Bowling: DeFreitas 3-0-17-1; Austin 3-0-31-2; Watkinson 3-0-20-1; Wasim Akram 3-0-8-2; Martin 2-0-15-1; Chapple 1-0-4-1.

Umpires: G. Sharp and R. A. White.

At Cheltenham, August 8. LANCASHIRE tied with GLOUCESTERSHIRE.

At Southampton, August 15. LANCASHIRE beat HAMPSHIRE by six wickets.

LANCASHIRE v YORKSHIRE

At Manchester, August 22. Lancashire won by three wickets. Toss: Lancashire.

In a match reduced to 45 overs, after rain delayed the start, Lancashire were hurried to victory by a hard-hit fifty from Wasim Akram.

Yorkshire

D. Byas c Barnett b DeFreitas	12	R. D. Stemp not out	12
M. P. Vaughan lbw b DeFreitas	6	J. D. Batty c Fairbrother b DeFreitas	3
M. J. Foster hit wkt b Wasim Akram	7	M. A. Robinson not out	0
*M. D. Moxon lbw b Yates	35	B 2, l-b 7, w 7, n-b 2	18
†R. J. Blakey c Yates b Barnett	38	
A. P. Grayson st Hegg b Barnett	3	1/18 2/18 3/32 (9 wkts, 45 overs) 173
C. White st Hegg b Yates	24	4/88 5/104 6/119
D. Gough run out	15	7/144 8/166 9/171

Bowling: DeFreitas 8-0-31-3; Austin 5-3-7-0; Watkinson 9-2-26-0; Wasim Akram 9-0-30-1; Barnett 5-0-35-2; Yates 9-0-35-2.

Lancashire

S. P. Titchard b White	18	P. A. J. DeFreitas b Robinson	3	
I. D. Austin b Foster	25	†W. K. Hegg not out	3	
J. P. Crawley c and b White	11	B 4, l-b 3, w 3, n-b 6	16	
*N. H. Fairbrother c Byas b Batty	32			
N. J. Speak run out	14	1/46 2/56 3/69	(7 wkts, 43.4 overs) 174	
Wasim Akram not out	51	4/98 5/147		
M. Watkinson run out	1	6/149 7/166		

A. A. Barnett and G. Yates did not bat.

Bowling: Gough 8.4–1–27–0; Robinson 9–1–44–1; Foster 5–0–20–1; White 9–1–35–2; Stemp 4–0–14–0; Batty 8–0–27–1.

Umpires: H. D. Bird and K. E. Palmer.

LANCASHIRE v KENT

At Manchester, August 29. Kent won by six wickets. Toss: Kent.
For Lancashire only Lloyd batted with any freedom against a tight Kent attack. Kent suffered three run-outs before Hooper and Llong settled matters with 82 in 13 overs.

Lancashire

M. A. Atherton c Marsh b Igglesden	1	I. D. Austin c Headley b Fleming	7	
G. D. Lloyd run out	53	†W. K. Hegg not out	5	
J. P. Crawley c Marsh b Headley	12	G. Yates run out	8	
*N. H. Fairbrother c Longley b Headley	3	L-b 7, w 2	9	
N. J. Speak c Igglesden b Fleming	24			
Wasim Akram b Igglesden	29	1/5 2/38 3/44	(49.5 overs) 192	
M. Watkinson c Fulton b Fleming	20	4/93 5/100 6/140		
P. A. J. DeFreitas c Fulton b Fleming	21	7/165 8/179 9/180		

Bowling: Igglesden 10–3–39–2; Ealham 10–2–29–0; Headley 9.5–1–50–2; Fleming 10–0–46–4; Hooper 10–1–21–0.

Kent

T. R. Ward c Hegg b DeFreitas	12	N. J. Llong not out	44	
D. P. Fulton run out	29	B 1, l-b 4, w 3	8	
C. L. Hooper not out	87			
J. I. Longley run out	7	1/13 2/68	(4 wkts, 42.3 overs) 193	
M. A. Ealham run out	6	3/97 4/111		

G. R. Cowdrey, M. V. Fleming, *†S. A. Marsh, D. W. Headley and A. P. Igglesden did not bat.

Bowling: Austin 8–0–37–0; DeFreitas 10–0–42–1; Wasim Akram 7–0–28–0; Yates 9–2–34–0; Watkinson 8.3–0–47–0.

Umpires: J. D. Bond and P. Willey.

At Worcester, September 5. LANCASHIRE beat WORCESTERSHIRE by six wickets.

At Lord's, September 12. MIDDLESEX v LANCASHIRE. No result.

LANCASHIRE v NORTHAMPTONSHIRE

At Manchester, September 19. Northamptonshire won by five wickets. Toss: Northamptonshire.

Northamptonshire's first win at Old Trafford in any limited-overs competition was achieved with one ball to spare, and was founded on a fourth-wicket partnership of 117 in 16 overs between Bailey and Warren, after Loye and Bailey had shared a second-wicket stand of 81.

Lancashire

G. D. Lloyd b Curran	69	P. A. J. DeFreitas c Ambrose b Bowen	5
M. A. Atherton c Ripley b Bowen	12	I. D. Austin not out	20
J. P. Crawley c Lamb b Cook	29	B 2, l-b 4, w 2, n-b 6	14
N. H. Fairbrother c Lamb b Cook	9		
N. J. Speak not out	63	1/48 2/95 3/120 (7 wkts, 50 overs) 246	
Wasim Akram c Warren b Cook	10	4/134 5/163	
M. Watkinson c Warren b Taylor	15	6/202 7/212	

W. K. Hegg and G. Yates did not bat.

Bowling: Ambrose 10-0-48-0; Bowen 10-1-57-2; Taylor 10-0-54-1; Curran 10-1-38-1; Cook 10-0-43-3.

Northamptonshire

A. Fordham c Lloyd b Austin	12	†D. Ripley not out	3
I. B. Loye c Lloyd b Yates	56		
R. J. Bailey b Wasim Akram	93	B 2, l-b 3, w 3, n-b 10	18
*A. J. Lamb c Hegg b Wasim Akram	0		
R. J. Warren c Atherton b Austin	56	1/29 2/110 3/110 (5 wkts, 49.5 overs) 247	
C. M. Curran not out	9	4/227 5/237	

J. N. Bowen, C. E. L. Ambrose, N. G. B. Cook and J. P. Taylor did not bat.

Bowling: DeFreitas 10-0-49-0; Austin 10-3-23-2; Watkinson 10-0-54-0; Wasim Akram 9.5-1-41-2; Yates 10-0-75-1.

Umpires: J. C. Balderstone and P. B. Wight.

LEICESTERSHIRE

LEICESTERSHIRE v NOTTINGHAMSHIRE

At Leicester, May 9. Leicestershire won by 90 runs. Toss: Nottinghamshire.

Leicestershire won for the first time at home in the Sunday League since May 19, 1991, despite losing both openers with two runs on the board. Nottinghamshire gave up their last nine wickets for only 64, with the slow left-armer Potter bowling four key batsmen for figures of five for 28. Umpire Don Oslear marked his first appearance in a blue polyester jacket by walking out with a crate of bottles calling "Milko!".

Leicestershire

T. J. Boon c French b Cairns	0	†P. A. Nixon not out	37
*N. E. Briers c and b Pennett	1	G. J. Parsons not out	6
J. J. Whitaker c Crawley b Pick	50	B 5, l-b 4, w 3, n-b 4	16
P. E. Robinson b Mike	22		
B. F. Smith c and b Field-Buss	30	1/0 2/2 3/49 (7 wkts, 50 overs) 216	
L. Potter b Cairns	37	4/107 5/111	
V. J. Wells c Johnson b Pennett	17	6/147 7/203	

A. R. K. Pierson and A. D. Mullally did not bat.

Bowling: Cairns 10-1-30-2; Pennett 10-1-42-2; Pick 10-0-41-1; Mike 10-1-50-1; Field-Buss 10-0-44-1.

Nottinghamshire

P. R. Pollard lbw b Parsons	1	R. A. Pick c Robinson b Pierson	5
D. W. Randall c Nixon b Mullally	33	M. G. Field-Buss c Briers b Parsons	4
*R. T. Robinson b Potter	41	D. B. Pennett not out	3
P. Johnson b Potter	15	B 3, l-b 7, w 2	12
M. A. Crawley b Potter	5		
C. L. Cairns b Potter	4	1/1 2/62 3/88	(41.5 overs) 126
G. W. Mike c Potter b Pierson	2	4/99 5/105 6/111	
†B. N. French st Nixon b Potter	1	7/113 8/113 9/121	

Bowling: Mullally 8–2–14–1; Parsons 6.5–0–25–2; Pierson 9–0–33–2; Wells 8–0–16–0; Potter 10–2–28–5.

Umpires: D. O. Oslear and G. A. Stickley.

At Horsham, May 23. LEICESTERSHIRE lost to SUSSEX by 63 runs.

LEICESTERSHIRE v DURHAM

At Leicester, June 6. Leicestershire won by three runs. Toss: Leicestershire.

Parsons claimed most of the credit for stopping Durham's steady progress towards a target of 218. He dismissed Glendenen and Bainbridge, who had added 76 in 16 overs, with successive balls in the 38th over (the batsmen had crossed), and then in his final over restricted Ian Smith and Hughes to seven when they needed 11.

Leicestershire

J. D. R. Benson c Graveney b Hughes	42	V. J. Wells b Cummins	4
*N. E. Briers c Bainbridge b Graveney	31	G. J. Parsons not out	23
J. J. Whitaker c Daley b Bainbridge	23	B 1, l-b 10, w 1, n-b 4	16
P. E. Robinson c Graveney	2		
†P. A. Nixon c Glendenen b Bainbridge	17	1/76 2/76 3/89	(7 wkts, 50 overs) 217
B. F. Smith not out	51	4/111 5/123	
L. Potter st Fothergill b Bainbridge	8	6/158 7/166	

J. M. Dakin and A. D. Mullally did not bat.

Bowling: Botham 10–0–47–0; Cummins 10–1–46–1; Hughes 10–2–33–1; Graveney 10–0–35–2; Bainbridge 10–0–45–3.

Durham

I. T. Botham c Briers b Dakin	28	†A. R. Fothergill run out	0
P. W. G. Parker lbw b Mullally	2	*D. A. Graveney b Wells	10
J. A. Daley c Nixon b Dakin	10	S. P. Hughes not out	4
P. Bainbridge lbw b Parsons	61	B 6, l-b 10, w 1, n-b 2	19
S. Hutton lbw b Wells	5		
J. D. Glendenen c Dakin b Parsons	28	1/11 2/39 3/56	(9 wkts, 50 overs) 214
I. Smith not out	34	4/67 5/143 6/143	
A. C. Cummins run out	13	7/170 8/171 9/201	

Bowling: Mullally 10–0–50–1; Parsons 10–0–32–2; Dakin 10–1–50–2; Wells 10–1–29–2; Potter 10–0–37–0.

Umpires: A. A. Jones and R. Palmer.

At Worcester, June 13. LEICESTERSHIRE beat WORCESTERSHIRE by four runs.

LEICESTERSHIRE v GLOUCESTERSHIRE

At Leicester, June 27. Leicestershire won by 31 runs. Toss: Leicestershire.

Benjamin hit a 35-ball 55 to re-establish Leicestershire's innings from 66 for five and then took three Gloucestershire wickets in his first five overs. Though Alleyne and Wright staged a similar rescue operation for Gloucestershire, the seamer Benson demolished the tail.

Leicestershire

J. D. R. Benson c Russell b Walsh	3	V. J. Wells not out	17
*N. E. Briers c Russell b Walsh	7	G. J. Parsons not out	19
T. J. Boon c Wright b Smith	17		
J. J. Whitaker c Russell b Scott	26	B 1, l-b 7, w 4	12
B. F. Smith b Scott	9		
L. Potter b Babington	45	1/5 2/12 3/51 (8 wkts, 50 overs)	214
W. K. M. Benjamin b Alleyne	55	4/59 5/66 6/151	
†P. A. Nixon c Hancock b Alleyne	4	7/161 8/184	

A. D. Mullally did not bat.

Bowling: Babington 10–1–37–1; Walsh 10–3–31–2; Smith 10–0–52–1; Scott 6–0–24–2; Wright 4–1–18–0; Alleyne 10–0–44–2.

Gloucestershire

B. C. Broad c Nixon b Benjamin	3	R. M. Wight c Briers b Benson	1
G. D. Hodgson c Benson b Benjamin	6	A. M. Smith not out	12
M. W. Alleyne c Nixon b Mullally	41	A. M. Babington b Benjamin	0
T. H. C. Hancock c Benson b Benjamin	2	B 1, l-b 6, w 12	19
*A. J. Wright c Potter b Benson	51		
†R. C. Russell c Whitaker b Wells	41	1/8 2/9 3/17 (48.2 overs)	183
R. J. Scott c Briers b Benson	6	4/105 5/107 6/136	
C. A. Walsh c Briers b Benson	1	7/138 8/140 9/183	

Bowling: Benjamin 9.2–3–35–4; Mullally 8–2–19–1; Wells 9–1–31–1; Parsons 9–1–31–0; Potter 6–0–33–0; Benson 7–0–27–4.

Umpires: J. C. Balderstone and A. G. T. Whitehead.

LEICESTERSHIRE v LANCASHIRE

At Leicester, July 4. Lancashire won by 83 runs. Toss: Lancashire.

Openers Titchard and Irani got Lancashire going with 79 in their first 15 overs; Titchard scored 84, his maiden League fifty, despite needing a runner after a blow to his foot from Benjamin. Wasim Akram and the later order took 90 runs off the last ten to reach Lancashire's highest Sunday score and the seamers claimed enough early Leicestershire wickets to make the later stages academic.

Lancashire

S. P. Titchard b Mullally	84	P. A. J. DeFreitas c Robinson	
R. C. Irani b Wells	34	b Benjamin	16
G. D. Lloyd run out	15	I. D. Austin not out	0
*N. H. Fairbrother c Robinson		B 4, l-b 11, w 4, n-b 7	26
b Benson	25		
N. J. Speak c Nixon b Parsons	36	1/83 2/124 3/164 (7 wkts, 50 overs)	300
Wasim Akram not out	42	4/208 5/222	
M. Watkinson c Parsons b Mullally	22	6/260 7/292	

†W. K. Hegg and A. A. Barnett did not bat.

Bowling: Benjamin 10–0–61–1; Mullally 9–0–61–2; Wells 9–1–46–1; Parsons 10–0–39–1; Potter 7–0–41–0; Benson 5–0–37–1.

Leicestershire

T. J. Boon b DeFreitas	8	
J. D. R. Benson c Fairbrother b Austin	22	
*J. J. Whitaker c Fairbrother		
b DeFreitas	8	
P. E. Robinson b Wasim Akram	13	
B. F. Smith c Speak b Barnett	38	
W. K. M. Benjamin b Wasim Akram	0	
L. Potter b Barnett	19	
†P. A. Nixon c and b Watkinson	13	

V. J. Wells c Wasim Akram		
b Watkinson	31	
G. J. Parsons not out	38	
A. D. Mullally c Hegg b Irani	2	
B 4, l-b 8, w 5, n-b 8	25	

(47.2 overs) 217

1/20 2/42 3/42
4/68 5/68 6/104
7/131 8/137 9/215

Bowling: DeFreitas 6–1–21–2; Austin 10–1–44–1; Watkinson 8–0–39–2; Wasim Akram 10–1–26–2; Barnett 10–0–58–2; Irani 3.2–0–17–1.

Umpires: J. H. Hampshire and N. T. Plews.

LEICESTERSHIRE v SURREY

At Leicester, July 11. No result. Toss: Surrey.
  The match was abandoned after 40 minutes when, as Waqar Younis prepared to bowl first change, both captains approached the umpires, who agreed that the Grace Road pitch was too dangerous for them to continue. Both this pitch and an alternative prepared for the match had become flooded when heavy rain seeped under the covers on the Thursday night, leaving them cracked with bare and grassy patches. The TCCB rejected a request by both counties to replay the match two days later.

Leicestershire

T. J. Boon c Thorpe b Benjamin	2	
*N. E. Briers not out	11	
J. J. Whitaker not out	9	
B 4	4	

1/3   (1 wkt, 11 overs) 26

B. F. Smith, J. D. R. Benson, L. Potter, V. J. Wells, †P. A. Nixon, W. K. M. Benjamin, G. J. Parsons and A. D. Mullally did not bat.

Bowling: M. P. Bicknell 6–1–9–0; Benjamin 5–2–13–1.

Surrey

D. J. Bicknell, A. D. Brown, *†A. J. Stewart, G. P. Thorpe, M. A. Lynch, D. M. Ward, A. W. Smith, M. P. Bicknell, Waqar Younis, J. Boiling and J. E. Benjamin.

Umpires: J. D. Bond and D. J. Constant.

At Southend, July 18. LEICESTERSHIRE lost to ESSEX by 26 runs.

LEICESTERSHIRE v WARWICKSHIRE

At Leicester, July 25. Warwickshire won by four wickets, their target having been revised to 121 from 24 overs. Toss: Warwickshire.
  Leicestershire were 31 for two off 15 overs when the first interruption for rain reduced the match to 34 overs. They accelerated through Whitaker, who hit 83 off 88 balls, with three sixes and seven fours, while Paul Smith took regular wickets at the other end. Further rain reduced Warwickshire's target, the final calculation leaving them to score nine in 2.1 overs. Neil Smith responded by hitting Benjamin for three fours in five balls.

eicestershire

J. Boon b Small	4	W. K. M. Benjamin not out	6
N. E. Briers b P. A. Smith	10	V. J. Wells not out	1
J. Whitaker c Moles b Donald	83	B 1, l-b 5, w 3	9
D. R. Benson c Small b P. A. Smith	10		
E. Robinson c Small b P. A. Smith	22	1/8 2/30 3/42 (7 wkts, 34 overs) 170	
Potter c Donald b P. A. Smith	2	4/83 5/90	
P. A. Nixon c Penney b P. A. Smith	23	6/161 7/162	

. J. Parsons and A. D. Mullally did not bat.

Bowling: Reeve 10–2–40–0; Small 7–2–11–1; P. A. Smith 10–1–54–5; N. M. K. Smith -0–21–0; Donald 5–0–38–1.

Varwickshire

J. Moles b Mullally	8	T. L. Penney b Parsons	5
sif Din c Parsons b Wells	23	N. M. K. Smith not out	18
P. Ostler lbw b Parsons	24	L-b 2, w 2, n-b 2	6
A. Smith run out	25		
O. A. Reeve not out	15	1/17 2/55 3/67 (6 wkts, 22.5 overs) 124	
G. Twose b Wells	0	4/87 5/87 6/94	

K. J. Piper, G. C. Small and A. A. Donald did not bat.

Bowling: Benjamin 6.5–1–41–0; Mullally 3–0–19–1; Parsons 8–1–38–2; Wells 5–0–24–2.

Umpires: V. A. Holder and A. G. T. Whitehead.

t Canterbury, August 1. LEICESTERSHIRE lost to KENT by 63 runs.

t Lord's, August 8. LEICESTERSHIRE lost to MIDDLESEX by eight wickets.

LEICESTERSHIRE v GLAMORGAN

t Leicester, August 15. Glamorgan won by eight runs. Toss: Leicestershire.
Glamorgan's total on a slow pitch featured contrasting half-centuries from Dale and the ore dashing Maynard – who faced just 46 balls – plus a whirlwind 27 in 15 balls from efebvre. Whitaker revived Leicestershire's challenge, but they eventually needed 18 off the st over, which proved too much when Whitaker, having taken six off the first two balls, as well caught at extra cover.

Glamorgan

P. James c Nixon b Millns	7	R. P. Lefebvre not out	27
H. Morris c Nixon b Dakin	14	†C. P. Metson not out	3
Dale run out	56	B 4, l-b 5, w 8	17
P. Maynard c Boon b Benson	54		
A. Cottey c Nixon b Dakin	27	1/11 2/42 3/128 (7 wkts, 50 overs) 228	
L. Hemp b Parsons	16	4/167 5/179	
D. B. Croft c and b Dakin	7	6/191 7/205	

L. Watkin and S. R. Barwick did not bat.

Bowling: Parsons 10–0–39–1; Millns 4–0–14–1; Dakin 10–2–45–3; Wells 10–1–47–0; erson 10–0–39–0; Benson 6–0–35–1.

Leicestershire

T. J. Boon c Lefebvre b Barwick	19	†P. A. Nixon c Lefebvre b Barwick		0
J. D. R. Benson b Lefebvre	1	G. J. Parsons not out		0
*J. J. Whitaker c Morris b Barwick	117	L-b 3, w 5		8
P. E. Robinson b Dale	24			
B. F. Smith c Lefebvre b Barwick	35	1/3 2/32 3/109	(7 wkts, 50 overs)	220
J. M. Dakin c Croft b Dale	4	4/179 5/189		
V. J. Wells not out	12	6/217 7/218		

A. R. K. Pierson and D. J. Millns did not bat.

Bowling: Lefebvre 10–4–20–1; Watkin 10–0–41–0; Barwick 10–0–46–4; Croft 10–0–42–0; Dale 10–0–68–2.

Umpires: H. D. Bird and B. Dudleston.

At Weston-super-Mare, August 22. LEICESTERSHIRE lost to SOMERSET by 96 runs.

At Northampton, August 29. LEICESTERSHIRE lost to NORTHAMPTONSHIRE by seven wickets.

LEICESTERSHIRE v YORKSHIRE

At Leicester, September 5. Yorkshire won by 65 runs. Toss: Leicestershire.

A Sunday League record fifth-wicket partnership of 190 in 21 overs between Blakey and Foster was the basis of Yorkshire's first 300 total in the competition. Blakey went 34 balls without scoring, before breaking loose to hit two sixes and ten fours, while Foster's first one-day hundred came off 70 balls, with eight straight sixes and seven fours; 186 runs were added in the last 20 overs. This was Leicestershire's eighth consecutive defeat in the competition.

Yorkshire

*M. D. Moxon b Mullally	15	B. Parker c Whitaker b Millns		5
D. Byas c Pierson b Parsons	8	D. Gough not out		3
M. P. Vaughan c Nixon b Parsons	11	L-b 16, w 11, n-b 10		37
†R. J. Blakey c Hepworth b Pierson	96			
C. White c Mullally b Pierson	15	1/11 2/43 3/43	(7 wkts, 50 overs)	318
M. J. Foster c Millns b Pierson	118	4/106 5/296		
P. J. Hartley not out	10	6/297 7/314		

A. P. Grayson and M. A. Robinson did not bat.

Bowling: Parsons 10–4–38–2; Mullally 10–0–70–1; Millns 10–0–48–1; Dakin 10–0–64–0; Pierson 10–0–82–3.

Leicestershire

T. J. Boon b White	26	A. R. K. Pierson c Byas b Hartley		7
*J. J. Whitaker b Grayson	49	D. J. Millns run out		10
†P. A. Nixon c Blakey b White	0	A. D. Mullally b Gough		2
P. E. Robinson c Blakey b Gough	71	B 2, l-b 9, w 19		30
B. F. Smith c Blakey b White	4			
P. N. Hepworth c White b Robinson	17	1/56 2/60 3/115	(47.5 overs)	253
J. M. Dakin c Blakey b Robinson	9	4/130 5/175 6/196		
G. J. Parsons not out	28	7/207 8/224 9/249		

Bowling: Hartley 10–0–41–1; Gough 9.5–0–67–2; Robinson 10–2–38–2; White 8–0–52–3; Grayson 10–0–44–1.

Umpires: D. O. Oslear and R. Palmer.

At Southampton, September 12. HAMPSHIRE v LEICESTERSHIRE. No result (abandoned).

LEICESTERSHIRE v DERBYSHIRE

At Leicester, September 19. Leicestershire won by 14 runs. Toss: Derbyshire. First-team debut: A. Sheriyar.

Leicestershire's narrow win was their first since June 27. They owed much to Smith, who added an unbroken 112 in 18 overs with Parsons. Derbyshire conceded 18 wides, including seven in one over by Steer.

Leicestershire

*J. J. Whitaker c and b Warner	10	†P. A. Nixon lbw b Barnett	3
P. N. Hepworth lbw b Mortensen	14	G. J. Parsons not out	37
V. J. Wells c and b Vandrau	50	B 1, l-b 5, w 18	24
P. E. Robinson c Bowler b Mortensen	8		
B. F. Smith not out	97	1/25 2/27 3/57 (6 wkts, 50 overs) 246	
D. L. Maddy c Krikken b Vandrau	3	4/109 5/114 6/134	

A. R. K. Pierson, M. T. Brimson and A. Sheriyar did not bat.

Bowling: Warner 10–0–59–1; Mortensen 10–1–20–2; Griffith 10–0–67–0; Vandrau 10–1–46–2; Barnett 6–0–27–1; Steer 4–1–21–0.

Derbyshire

P. D. Bowler b Brimson	46	F. A. Griffith not out	11
D. G. Cork c Maddy b Wells	21	†K. M. Krikken run out	2
T. J. G. O'Gorman b Wells	39	O. H. Mortensen c Hepworth b Wells	2
*K. J. Barnett c Whitaker b Pierson	31	B 1, l-b 8, w 7, n-b 2	18
A. S. Rollins run out	3		
I. G. S. Steer c Smith b Parsons	19	1/47 2/91 3/137 (49.5 overs) 232	
M. J. Vandrau lbw b Parsons	30	4/149 5/159 6/200	
A. E. Warner run out	10	7/216 8/218 9/230	

Bowling: Parsons 10–0–41–2; Sheriyar 5–0–29–0; Wells 9.5–0–57–3; Brimson 10–2–28–1; Pierson 10–1–42–1; Hepworth 5–0–26–0.

Umpires: J. W. Holder and B. J. Meyer.

MIDDLESEX

MIDDLESEX v KENT

At Lord's, May 9. Kent won by nine wickets. Toss: Kent. First-team debut: D. J. Spencer.

Lord's responded to its first League match in coloured clothing with a smaller-than-average Sunday crowd. The teams were dressed in the same shade of powder blue, and each included a newly-returned West Indian Test player, but Hooper was to prove more effective than Haynes and Kent won a one-sided contest. Drizzle reduced the match to 44 overs a side and enabled Igglesden to dismiss Keech and Ramprakash with consecutive balls of his first over, separated by 50 minutes. After that, Middlesex – who began 1992 with 12 successive Sunday wins – were never in the game.

Middlesex

M. A. Roseberry lbw b McCague	20	N. F. Williams c Marsh b Spencer	8
M. Keech c Cowdrey b Igglesden	0	R. L. Johnson not out	11
M. R. Ramprakash c Marsh b Igglesden	0	A. R. C. Fraser c and b Fleming	2
D. L. Haynes lbw b McCague	3	L-b 6, w 4, n-b 4	14
*J. D. Carr b McCague	25		
†K. R. Brown c Marsh b Fleming	5	1/4 2/4 3/22 (41.1 overs) 104	
M. A. Feltham c Taylor b Hooper	16	4/31 5/47 6/72	
J. E. Emburey c and b Hooper	0	7/75 8/84 9/93	

Bowling: Igglesden 8–3–19–2; McCague 10–2–18–3; Fleming 6.1–0–15–2; Spencer 8–0–28–1; Hooper 9–2–18–2.

Kent

T. R. Ward c Carr b Williams	16
*M. R. Benson not out	42
C. L. Hooper not out	37
B 3, l-b 1, w 2, n-b 4	10

1/23   (1 wkt, 26.4 overs) 105

N. R. Taylor, G. R. Cowdrey, N. J. Llong, M. V. Fleming, †S. A. Marsh, D. J. Spencer, A. P. Igglesden and M. J. McCague did not bat.

Bowling: Williams 6–0–22–1; Fraser 6–0–24–0; Feltham 6–1–23–0; Johnson 6–0–22–0; Emburey 1.4–0–7–0; Keech 1–0–3–0.

Umpires: J. H. Harris and M. J. Kitchen.

MIDDLESEX v NOTTINGHAMSHIRE

At Lord's, May 16. Middlesex won by five runs. Toss: Nottinghamshire.

Ramprakash and Carr added 165 in 29 overs, a third-wicket record for Middlesex in limited-overs cricket. Mike contributed his maiden one-day fifty to Nottinghamshire's reply, but, needing six from the last ball, he could only block it.

Middlesex

D. L. Haynes c Johnson b Cairns	17	J. E. Emburey not out	7
M. Keech lbw b Cairns	0		
M. R. Ramprakash c French b Lewis	88	B 2, l-b 3, w 2	7
*J. D. Carr c French b Lewis	92		
R. J. Sims b Lewis	15	1/10 2/27 (6 wkts, 50 overs) 257	
†K. R. Brown c Pollard b Lewis	26	3/192 4/205	
P. N. Weekes not out	5	5/244 6/250	

R. L. Johnson, N. F. Williams and A. R. C. Fraser did not bat.

Bowling: Lewis 10–3–45–4; Cairns 10–1–34–2; Evans 7–0–57–0; Field-Buss 10–0–39–0; Mike 10–0–60–0; Crawley 3–0–17–0.

Nottinghamshire

C. C. Lewis c Weekes b Williams	19	†B. N. French b Johnson	7
M. Saxelby c Brown b Weekes	37	K. P. Evans not out	17
*R. T. Robinson b Fraser	1		
P. Johnson c Haynes b Keech	42	B 5, l-b 25, w 14, n-b 2	46
C. L. Cairns c Brown b Keech	2		
P. R. Pollard lbw b Weekes	8	1/24 2/29 3/120 (8 wkts, 50 overs) 252	
M. A. Crawley c Brown b Williams	22	4/120 5/131 6/131	
G. W. Mike not out	51	7/189 8/215	

M. G. Field-Buss did not bat.

Bowling: Williams 10–1–36–2; Fraser 10–1–50–1; Johnson 5–0–31–1; Emburey 10–1–38–0; Keech 9–2–34–2; Weekes 6–0–33–2.

Umpires: R. Julian and P. Willey.

MIDDLESEX v SUSSEX

At Lord's, May 30. Tied. Toss: Sussex.

Sussex needed ten runs from Emburey's last over, and lost Lenham to his second ball, but they reduced the target to four from the final delivery, off which Pigott managed three to earn the Sunday League's highest-scoring tie. Gatting had hit 91 from 104 balls, adding 81 with Carr and then 93 in 13 overs with Brown. He walked when Lenham and the umpires were hesitating over a boundary catch. Sussex's bid for victory rested largely with Athey.

Middlesex

D. L. Haynes b Stephenson	10	M. Keech not out	14
M. R. Ramprakash c Moores b Giddins	28	R. L. Johnson not out	8
*M. W. Gatting c Lenham b Giddins	91	B 1, l-b 12, w 4, n-b 2	19
J. D. Carr b Athey	43		
P. N. Weekes lbw b C. M. Wells	0	1/34 2/42 3/123 (7 wkts, 49 overs)	247
†K. R. Brown c C. M. Wells b Pigott	33	4/130 5/223	
J. E. Emburey b Pigott	1	6/224 7/231	

N. F. Williams and A. R. C. Fraser did not bat.

Bowling: Stephenson 10-1-48-1; Giddins 10-0-38-2; Pigott 10-0-42-2; C. M. Wells 7-1-41-1; Lenham 6-0-26-0; Athey 6-0-39-1.

Sussex

D. M. Smith c sub b Weekes	27	N. J. Lenham c Weekes b Emburey	0
F. D. Stephenson c Gatting b Williams	13	A. C. S. Pigott not out	5
C. W. J. Athey b Fraser	85		
M. P. Speight c Fraser b Weekes	13	L-b 15, w 7, n-b 2	24
*A. P. Wells c Weekes b Emburey	40		
K. Greenfield b Emburey	6	1/19 2/55 3/85 (8 wkts, 49 overs)	247
†P. Moores c Williams b Weekes	19	4/160 5/175 6/223	
C. M. Wells not out	15	7/238 8/239	

E. S. H. Giddins did not bat.

Bowling: Williams 10-3-43-1; Fraser 10-0-52-1; Emburey 10-0-55-3; Weekes 9-0-39-3; Johnson 10-1-43-0.

Umpires: D. O. Oslear and G. A. Stickley.

MIDDLESEX v DERBYSHIRE

At Lord's, June 6. Middlesex won by two wickets. Toss: Derbyshire.

It took a late stand of 38 between Keech and Johnson to rescue Middlesex after Malcolm took three wickets in seven balls during his second spell. The middle order had almost squandered the advantage given them by Ramprakash's 84. Until Malcolm's burst it had been a day for batsmen. Bowler scored his maiden Sunday hundred, sharing 141 with his fellow-opener Adams, who had a lucky escape when 41; he was bowled by Fraser, but umpire Bond called him back, ruling that the delivery was a beamer and therefore a no-ball.

Derbyshire

P. D. Bowler not out	104
C. J. Adams c Haynes b Weekes	80
J. E. Morris b Weekes	4
T. J. G. O'Gorman not out	38
L-b 5, w 1, n-b 8	14

1/141 2/148 (2 wkts, 50 overs) 240

*K. J. Barnett, †K. M. Krikken, M. J. Vandrau, S. J. Base, A. E. Warner, R. W. Sladdin and D. E. Malcolm did not bat.

Bowling: Williams 7-1-18-0; Johnson 7-3-20-0; Fraser 9-1-54-0; Emburey 10-1-52-0; Keech 9-0-47-0; Weekes 8-0-44-2.

Middlesex

D. L. Haynes lbw b Warner 15	R. L. Johnson c Morris b Barnett 18
J. C. Pooley c Krikken b Malcolm 2	N. F. Williams not out 0
M. R. Ramprakash b Warner 84	
*J. D. Carr st Krikken b Sladdin 41	L-b 10, w 3 13
P. N. Weekes b Malcolm 40	
†K. R. Brown b Malcolm 6	1/12 2/20 3/102 (8 wkts, 48.5 overs) 241
M. Keech not out 21	4/187 5/193 6/196
J. E. Emburey c Adams b Malcolm 1	7/198 8/236

A. R. C. Fraser did not bat.

Bowling: Warner 9.5–0–49–2; Malcolm 10–0–36–4; Base 8–0–44–0; Vandrau 10–0–38–0; Sladdin 10–0–62–1; Barnett 1–0–2–1.

Umpires: J. D. Bond and D. R. Shepherd.

At Gateshead Fell, June 13. MIDDLESEX lost to DURHAM by six wickets.

At Bath, June 20. MIDDLESEX beat SOMERSET by eight wickets.

MIDDLESEX v SURREY

At Lord's, June 27. Surrey won by seven wickets. Toss: Surrey.

The Bicknell brothers dominated the match, with Martin dismissing Haynes and Gatting in six balls and Darren batting 45 overs for his unbeaten 65. Weekes and Brown added 97 for Middlesex's fifth wicket, but Martin Bicknell returned to remove Brown and a target of 173 left his elder brother few problems.

Middlesex

D. L. Haynes c Stewart b M. P. Bicknell 0	M. Keech c Stewart b Benjamin 2
M. A. Roseberry c D. J. Bicknell	J. E. Emburey not out 9
b Butcher . 19	
*M. W. Gatting b M. P. Bicknell 4	B 2, l-b 2, w 13 17
J. D. Carr c M. P. Bicknell b Butcher . . 18	
P. N. Weekes not out 66	1/4 2/10 3/36 (6 wkts, 49 overs) 172
†K. R. Brown b M. P. Bicknell 37	4/47 5/144 6/154

N. G. Cowans, A. R. C. Fraser and R. L. Johnson did not bat.

Bowling: M. P. Bicknell 10–2–18–3; Benjamin 10–1–31–1; Waqar Younis 9–1–46–0; Butcher 10–2–29–2; Boiling 10–0–44–0.

Surrey

D. J. Bicknell not out 65	M. A. Lynch not out 6
A. D. Brown b Johnson 54	L-b 10, w 4, n-b 4 18
*†A. J. Stewart c Roseberry b Emburey . 9	
G. P. Thorpe c Roseberry b Keech 21	1/90 2/105 3/157 (3 wkts, 45 overs) 173

D. M. Ward, M. A. Butcher, M. P. Bicknell, Waqar Younis, J. Boiling and J. E. Benjamin did not bat.

Bowling: Cowans 5–0–25–0; Fraser 7–0–33–0; Johnson 10–1–42–1; Emburey 8–0–31–1; Weekes 8–1–20–0; Keech 7–2–12–1.

Umpires: H. D. Bird and N. T. Plews.

At Cardiff, July 4. MIDDLESEX lost to GLAMORGAN by 121 runs.

At Moreton-in-Marsh, July 11. GLOUCESTERSHIRE v MIDDLESEX. No result.

At Birmingham, July 18. MIDDLESEX beat WARWICKSHIRE on scoring-rate.

MIDDLESEX v HAMPSHIRE

At Lord's, July 25. Middlesex won by 81 runs. Toss: Middlesex.

Gatting and Ramprakash, coming together at 61 for three, added an unbroken 185. Gatting was at his pugnacious best, hitting 11 fours and a six in his 95-ball hundred; while Ramprakash's half-century included only one boundary. Udal had an especially bad day: he injured a hand attempting a return catch and conceded 26 in the three overs after returning, bandaged. Brown dismissed five batsmen as Hampshire, bowled out for 88 the day before, subsided.

Middlesex

D. L. Haynes b Thursfield	21	*M. W. Gatting not out	104
M. A. Roseberry lbw b Turner	31	B 4, l-b 11, w 6	21
M. R. Ramprakash not out	69		
J. D. Carr c Aymes b James	0	1/39 2/60 3/61 (3 wkts, 50 overs)	246

†K. R. Brown, P. N. Weekes, J. E. Emburey, A. R. C. Fraser, N. G. Cowans and P. C. R. Tufnell did not bat.

Bowling: Connor 10-1-24-0; Thursfield 10-0-44-1; James 10-0-48-1; Turner 10-1-47-1; Udal 9.1-1-60-0; Nicholas 0.5-0-8-0.

Hampshire

T. C. Middleton c Brown b Fraser	0	M. J. Thursfield st Brown b Tufnell	4
D. I. Gower c Brown b Fraser	17	C. A. Connor b Tufnell	25
J. R. Wood c Brown b Fraser	9	I. J. Turner lbw b Fraser	2
V. P. Terry c Brown b Emburey	9	B 1, l-b 14, w 3	18
*M. C. J. Nicholas c Emburey b Weekes	14		
K. D. James c Carr b Tufnell	32	1/0 2/12 3/35 (44.5 overs)	165
†A. N. Aymes b Tufnell	17	4/50 5/60 6/106	
S. D. Udal not out	18	7/119 8/125 9/162	

Bowling: Fraser 8.5-2-17-4; Cowans 7-1-20-0; Emburey 10-2-25-1; Weekes 9-1-38-1; Tufnell 10-0-50-4.

Umpires: G. I. Burgess and J. H. Hampshire.

MIDDLESEX v LEICESTERSHIRE

At Lord's, August 8. Middlesex won by eight wickets. Toss: Leicestershire.

The match was dominated by Ramprakash. First he took five for 38 with his off-breaks, sharing the wickets with Tufnell, whose five for 28 were, like Ramprakash's, his best in limited-overs cricket. He then scored 89 not out, putting on 125 in 33 overs with Roseberry. The only precedent for two bowlers taking five each in a Sunday League game was when Sarfraz Nawaz and Neil Mallender shared the wickets for Northamptonshire against Middlesex at Tring in 1981.

Leicestershire

T. J. Boon c Carr b Tufnell	13	A. R. K. Pierson c Brown	
*J. J. Whitaker st Brown b Tufnell	78	b Ramprakash	1
V. J. Wells lbw b Tufnell	0	D. J. Millns b Ramprakash	7
J. M. Dakin st Brown b Ramprakash	27		
P. E. Robinson c Carr b Ramprakash	2	L-b 5, w 5	10
B. F. Smith b Ramprakash	27		
J. D. R. Benson b Tufnell	2	1/45 2/52 3/98 (49 overs)	179
†P. A. Nixon c Brown b Tufnell	6	4/106 5/138 6/144	
G. J. Parsons not out	6	7/162 8/162 9/166	

Bowling: Fraser 7–2–17–0; Feltham 7–1–24–0; Cowans 10–0–45–0; Tufnell 10–3–28–5; Keech 7–0–22–0; Ramprakash 8–1–38–5.

Middlesex

D. L. Haynes c Nixon b Millns	1
M. A. Roseberry c and b Pierson	47
M. R. Ramprakash not out	89
J. D. Carr not out	23
B 6, l-b 3, w 12, n-b 2	23

1/2 2/127   (2 wkts, 46 overs) 183

*M. W. Gatting, †K. R. Brown, M. A. Feltham, M. Keech, A. R. C. Fraser, N. G. Cowans and P. C. R. Tufnell did not bat.

Bowling: Parsons 10–3–24–0; Millns 8–0–45–1; Dakin 7–0–22–0; Wells 9–1–40–0; Pierson 10–1–28–1; Benson 2–0–15–0.

Umpires: J. D. Bond and B. Leadbeater.

At Scarborough, August 15. MIDDLESEX lost to YORKSHIRE by 77 runs.

MIDDLESEX v NORTHAMPTONSHIRE

At Lord's, August 22. Northamptonshire won by four wickets, their target having been revised to 171 from 35 overs. Toss: Northamptonshire.

Rain, which had delayed the start, again intervened during Northamptonshire's innings. They were lagging behind the required rate until Lamb arrived to settle the issue with 65 off 43 balls, winning the match with a six and a four.

Middlesex

J. C. Pooley c Taylor b Ambrose	3	†K. R. Brown not out	10
D. L. Haynes c Ambrose b Taylor	67	M. Keech not out	2
P. N. Weekes b Curran	36	B 2, l-b 6, w 6, n-b 4	18
J. D. Carr c Fordham b Bailey	32		
A. Habib c Loye b Taylor	15	1/16 2/119 3/124 (6 wkts, 38 overs) 185
*M. W. Gatting b Ambrose	2	4/160 5/163 6/182

R. L. Johnson, N. G. Cowans and C. W. Taylor did not bat.

Bowling: Walker 7–1–38–0; Ambrose 8–1–18–2; Curran 8–0–46–1; Taylor 8–0–37–2; Cook 4–0–26–0; Bailey 3–0–12–1.

Northamptonshire

A. Fordham c Gatting b Keech	36	†D. Ripley run out	0
M. B. Loye c Weekes b Taylor	11	C. E. L. Ambrose not out	1
R. J. Bailey b Weekes	7	B 7, l-b 7, w 10	24
R. J. Warren c Carr b Taylor	12		
*A. J. Lamb not out	65	1/33 2/46 3/80 (6 wkts, 34.2 overs) 173
K. M. Curran st Brown b Keech	17	4/140 5/140 6/157

A. Walker, J. P. Taylor and N. G. B. Cook did not bat.

A. Fordham, when 36, retired hurt at 91 and resumed at 140-4.

Bowling: Johnson 7.2–1–46–0; Cowans 7–3–30–0; Taylor 8–0–33–2; Weekes 8–1–28–1; Keech 4–0–22–2.

Umpires: D. J. Constant and A. G. T. Whitehead.

At Colchester, August 29. MIDDLESEX tied with ESSEX.

MIDDLESEX v LANCASHIRE

At Lord's, September 12. No result. Toss: Lancashire.

Roseberry's partners contributed just 17 runs between them as he raced to a half-century before rain ended play.

Middlesex

M. A. Roseberry c Hegg b Martin	51	*M. W. Gatting not out		0
P. N. Weekes c Lloyd b Austin	0			
M. R. Ramprakash c Watkinson		L-b 1, w 2, n-b 4		7
b DeFreitas	8			
D. L. Haynes c Hegg b Austin	4	1/3 2/32	(4 wkts, 20 overs)	75
J. D. Carr not out	5	3/37 4/75		

†K. R. Brown, R. L. Johnson, A. R. C. Fraser, C. W. Taylor and P. C. R. Tufnell did not bat.

Bowling: Austin 7–2–25–2; DeFreitas 5–1–22–1; Wasim Akram 3–0–20–0; Watkinson 3–1–5–0; Martin 2–0–2–1.

Lancashire

J. P. Crawley, M. A. Atherton, N. J. Speak, *N. H. Fairbrother, G. D. Lloyd, Wasim Akram, M. Watkinson, P. A. J. DeFreitas, I. D. Austin, †W. K. Hegg and P. J. Martin.

Umpires: J. W. Holder and A. A. Jones.

At Worcester, September 19. MIDDLESEX beat WORCESTERSHIRE by six wickets.

NORTHAMPTONSHIRE

NORTHAMPTONSHIRE v GLOUCESTERSHIRE

At Northampton, May 9. Northamptonshire won by 62 runs. Toss: Gloucestershire.

Penberthy, who might not have played but for Ambrose's flu, took five wickets for the first time in any competition, and ensured that Gloucestershire fell well short of a target of 186 from 37 overs, in a game curtailed by rain.

Northamptonshire

A. Fordham c Smith b Scott	66	K. M. Curran not out		6
N. A. Felton c Hancock b Babington	4			
M. B. Loye b Scott	36	L-b 2, w 2, n-b 2		6
*A. J. Lamb b Gerrard	27			
R. J. Bailey c Alleyne b Smith	18	1/27 2/110 3/117	(5 wkts, 37 overs)	185
D. J. Capel not out	22	4/154 5/158		

A. L. Penberthy, †D. Ripley, J. P. Taylor and N. G. B. Cook did not bat.

Bowling: Babington 10–2–34–1; Gerrard 10–1–42–1; Smith 7–0–51–1; Ball 2–0–15–0; Scott 8–1–41–2.

Gloucestershire

B. C. Broad lbw b Penberthy	22	M. C. J. Ball not out		10
S. G. Hinks run out	4	A. M. Babington c Ripley b Penberthy		10
R. J. Scott c Fordham b Capel	25	M. J. Gerrard lbw b Cook		4
M. W. Alleyne lbw b Penberthy	12	B 1, l-b 3, w 3		7
*A. J. Wright lbw b Penberthy	10			
T. H. C. Hancock lbw b Taylor	5	1/20 2/39 3/61	(34.2 overs)	123
†R. C. Russell b Cook	3	4/67 5/80 6/84		
A. M. Smith b Penberthy	11	7/95 8/100 9/112		

Bowling: Taylor 8–3–11–1; Curran 6–0–24–0; Capel 6–0–29–1; Penberthy 10–0–36–5; Cook 3.2–0–13–2; Bailey 1–0–6–0.

Umpires: J. H. Hampshire and J. W. Holder.

At Pentyrch, May 23. NORTHAMPTONSHIRE beat GLAMORGAN by three wickets.

NORTHAMPTONSHIRE v WORCESTERSHIRE

At Northampton, June 6. Tied. Toss: Northamptonshire.

A low-scoring match produced the second tie of the Sunday League season and Worcestershire's fourth in all competitions in just over two years. But it was not the expected result when they needed only four from the last over, with D'Oliveira 81 not out. He took a single from Taylor's first ball, then crossed with Newport's runner as Ripley held a skied catch. He ran another from the third, but had to watch as Tolley was bowled and Benjamin run out. Illingworth could manage only a single from the last ball. Taylor and Ripley had also played a significant role with the bat, after Northamptonshire had been 109 for seven.

Northamptonshire

A. Fordham c Rhodes b Benjamin	4		J. P. Taylor b Lampitt	24	
N. A. Felton b Tolley	3		A. Walker not out	8	
R. J. Bailey b Illingworth	43				
*A. J. Lamb b Radford	19		L-b 9, w 5, n-b 4	18	
D. J. Capel c Leatherdale b Illingworth	17				
K. M. Curran lbw b Illingworth	2		1/4 2/12 3/45	(9 wkts, 50 overs) 168	
A. L. Penberthy run out	6		4/86 5/90 6/106		
†D. Ripley c Leatherdale b Lampitt	24		7/109 8/148 9/168		

N. G. B. Cook did not bat.

Bowling: Benjamin 10–2–35–1; Tolley 5–3–13–1; Radford 9–3–27–1; Newport 8–0–24–0; Illingworth 10–1–23–3; Lampitt 8–0–37–2.

Worcestershire

W. P. C. Weston lbw b Curran	5		C. M. Tolley b Taylor	0	
A. C. H. Seymour run out	1		K. C. G. Benjamin run out	0	
D. A. Leatherdale b Curran	4		R. K. Illingworth not out	1	
D. B. D'Oliveira not out	83		B 1, l-b 6, w 6	13	
*†S. J. Rhodes c and b Cook	23				
S. R. Lampitt b Penberthy	28		1/5 2/12 3/24	(9 wkts, 50 overs) 168	
N. V. Radford b Capel	5		4/62 5/142 6/150		
P. J. Newport c Ripley b Taylor	5		7/166 8/167 9/167		

Bowling: Walker 3–0–4–0; Taylor 10–1–24–2; Curran 9–0–42–2; Penberthy 10–0–30–1; Cook 10–1–31–1; Capel 5–0–18–1; Bailey 3–0–12–0.

Umpires: D. O. Oslear and N. T. Plews.

At Hove, June 13. NORTHAMPTONSHIRE lost to SUSSEX by five wickets.

NORTHAMPTONSHIRE v HAMPSHIRE

At Northampton, June 20. Northamptonshire won by four wickets. Toss: Northamptonshire.

On his 39th birthday, Lamb hit an unbeaten 96 from 103 balls, taking his county to a victory that seemed improbable after they lost three early wickets. They still needed 11 off the final over but Ripley took five from the first two balls before his captain hit successive fours. Wood batted through nearly all Hampshire's innings for 92 not out.

Hampshire

T. C. Middleton c Bailey b Curran	....	69
K. D. James c Felton b Taylor	....	7
J. R. Wood not out	....	92
V. P. Terry not out	....	49
L-b 5, w 2, n-b 2	....	9

1/18 2/129   (2 wkts, 50 overs) 226

*M. C. J. Nicholas, J. R. Ayling, M. D. Marshall, †A. N. Aymes, S. D. Udal, C. A. Connor and K. J. Shine did not bat.

Bowling: Ambrose 10-0-36-0; Taylor 10-2-40-1; Curran 9-0-49-1; Penberthy 8-0-44-0; Cook 10-1-35-0; Bailey 3-0-17-0.

Northamptonshire

A. Fordham b Shine	....	18	A. L. Penberthy lbw b Connor	....	35
N. A. Felton lbw b Marshall	....	7	†D. Ripley not out	....	11
R. J. Bailey c Aymes b Shine	....	14	B 2, l-b 7, w 9, n-b 2	....	20
*A. J. Lamb not out	....	96			
M. B. Loye lbw b Udal	....	24	1/10 2/39 3/41 (6 wkts, 49.4 overs) 229		
K. M. Curran c Udal b Ayling	....	4	4/103 5/116 6/202		

C. E. L. Ambrose, J. P. Taylor and N. G. B. Cook did not bat.

Bowling: Connor 10-4-25-1; Marshall 9.4-0-46-1; Shine 5-0-15-2; James 7-0-45-0; Udal 10-0-47-1; Ayling 8-0-42-1.

Umpires: J. W. Holder and R. Palmer.

NORTHAMPTONSHIRE v SOMERSET

At Luton, June 27. Northamptonshire won by 17 runs. Toss: Somerset.

Promoted to open, Loye responded with his maiden limited-overs century, striking 15 fours and a six from 128 balls. He added 182 in 34 overs with Bailey, acting-captain because of a shoulder injury to Lamb. Though Somerset's innings started well, Ambrose and Taylor shared six wickets to end their hopes.

Northamptonshire

A. Fordham c Harden b Rose	....	10	†D. Ripley not out	....	7
M. B. Loye c Rose b Kerr	....	122	C. E. L. Ambrose not out	....	6
*R. J. Bailey b Caddick	....	72	L-b 8, w 5, n-b 2	....	15
K. M. Curran b Folland b Caddick	....	9			
N. A. Stanley lbw b Caddick	....	2	1/27 2/209 3/212 (7 wkts, 50 overs) 263		
A. L. Penberthy c Burns b Rose	.....	4	4/222 5/227		
N. A. Felton c Burns b Kerr	....	16	6/231 7/252		

J. P. Taylor and N. G. B. Cook did not bat.

Bowling: Caddick 10-1-41-3; Rose 10-0-61-2; Mallender 10-0-44-0; Kerr 10-0-63-2; Trump 10-0-46-0.

Somerset

M. N. Lathwell c Loye b Penberthy	40	A. R. Caddick b Taylor	9
N. A. Folland lbw b Taylor	69	N. A. Mallender b Ambrose	1
R. J. Harden run out	2	H. R. J. Trump not out	2
*C. J. Tavaré b Taylor	39	L-b 6, w 2, n-b 8	16
K. A. Parsons c Ripley b Ambrose	3		
G. D. Rose lbw b Ambrose	37	1/61 2/73 3/150	(49.4 overs) 246
†N. D. Burns c Cook b Curran	11	4/158 5/162 6/181	
J. I. D. Kerr run out	17	7/224 8/235 9/240	

Bowling: Ambrose 10-2-30-3; Taylor 9.4-1-40-3; Curran 10-2-43-1; Penberthy 8-0-65-1; Bailey 9-0-39-0; Cook 3-0-23-0.

Umpires: J. H. Hampshire and K. E. Palmer.

NORTHAMPTONSHIRE v NOTTINGHAMSHIRE

At Northampton, July 4. Northamptonshire won by 63 runs. Toss: Northamptonshire.
Nottinghamshire's desperate Sunday sequence since winning the title in 1991 continued with their 17th defeat in 21 completed matches. Loye and Curran underpinned the winning total of 227, quite enough to overwhelm Nottinghamshire.

Northamptonshire

A. Fordham lbw b Afford	17	†W. M. Noon c Afford b Lewis	7
M. B. Loye lbw b Evans	85	C. E. L. Ambrose not out	0
R. J. Bailey b Afford	15	B 2, l-b 10, w 9, n-b 2	23
N. A. Felton c Archer b Field-Buss	0		
*A. J. Lamb c and b Afford	14	1/42 2/82 3/83	(7 wkts, 50 overs) 227
K. M. Curran not out	65	4/106 5/175	
A. L. Penberthy lbw b Evans	1	6/177 7/216	

J. P. Taylor and N. G. B. Cook did not bat.

Bowling: Lewis 10-2-32-1; Cairns 10-0-48-0; Evans 10-1-60-2; Afford 10-2-33-3; Field-Buss 10-0-42-1.

Nottinghamshire

P. R. Pollard c Bailey b Taylor	4	†B. N. French b Curran	12
M. Saxelby run out	39	M. G. Field-Buss lbw b Curran	1
*R. T. Robinson c and b Curran	27	J. A. Afford not out	0
P. Johnson b Cook	8	B 1, l-b 7, w 2	10
C. L. Cairns c Loye b Penberthy	47		
C. C. Lewis lbw b Penberthy	6	1/8 2/47 3/70	(44 overs) 164
G. F. Archer c Lamb b Cook	1	4/88 5/103 6/104	
K. P. Evans b Ambrose	9	7/131 8/159 9/162	

Bowling: Taylor 8-2-29-1; Ambrose 8-1-26-1; Curran 8-1-25-3; Penberthy 9-0-38-2; Cook 10-0-27-2; Bailey 1-0-11-0.

Umpires: A. A. Jones and D. R. Shepherd.

At Birmingham, July 11. NORTHAMPTONSHIRE lost to WARWICKSHIRE by eight wickets.

At Leeds, July 18. NORTHAMPTONSHIRE lost to YORKSHIRE by nine wickets.

NORTHAMPTONSHIRE v SURREY

At Northampton, July 25. No result. Toss: Surrey.

After Waqar Younis had reduced Northamptonshire to 85 for six, they were helped to respectability by Loye and Ripley, before rain ended play. Lamb, having lost the toss five times running, had sent Bailey out to call, but with no better luck.

Northamptonshire

A. Fordham c Butcher b Hollioake	21	C. E. L. Ambrose c Hollioake	
M. B. Loye st Kersey b Boiling	64	b Waqar Younis	16
R. J. Bailey c Lynch b Murphy	6	J. P. Taylor b Murphy	6
*A. J. Lamb c Boiling		N. G. B. Cook not out	1
b Waqar Younis	0	L-b 7, w 8, n-b 2	17
K. M. Curran c Lynch b Waqar Younis	10		
N. A. Felton c Kersey b Waqar Younis	0	1/33 2/45 3/58 (9 wkts, 48 overs)	193
A. L. Penberthy b Boiling	0	4/84 5/84 6/85	
†D. Ripley not out	52	7/131 8/171 9/192	

Bowling: Hollioake 8–0–37–1; Murphy 10–1–44–2; Butcher 10–0–46–0; Waqar Younis 10–1–38–4; Boiling 10–0–21–2.

Surrey

D. J. Bicknell, A. D. Brown, D. M. Ward, *M. A. Lynch, A. W. Smith, †G. J. Kersey, M. A. Butcher, Waqar Younis, J. Boiling, A. J. Hollioake and A. J. Murphy.

Umpires: J. C. Balderstone and R. Julian.

NORTHAMPTONSHIRE v ESSEX

At Northampton, August 8. Northamptonshire won by 134 runs. Toss: Northamptonshire.

Looking a makeshift side without five of their senior players, Essex were never within sight of Northamptonshire's total and were all out with 15.4 overs remaining. The first over of the innings, bowled by Taylor, comprised 11 balls, including five wides and the wicket of Prichard. Cook and Snape then took command. Earlier, Lamb had passed 5,000 runs in the Sunday League.

Northamptonshire

A. Fordham b Topley	50	R. J. Warren not out	44
M. B. Loye c Pringle b Childs	44	L-b 5, w 6, n-b 10	21
R. J. Bailey not out	58		
*A. J. Lamb c Garnham b Boden	24	1/105 2/125 (4 wkts, 50 overs)	241
K. M. Curran run out	0	3/166 4/166	

†D. Ripley, J. N. Snape, C. E. L. Ambrose, J. P. Taylor and N. G. B. Cook did not bat.

Bowling: Andrew 10–1–39–0; Pringle 10–2–40–0; Boden 10–0–54–1; Topley 10–1–68–1; Childs 10–1–35–1.

Essex

*P. J. Prichard c Lamb b Taylor	4	D. J. P. Boden b Bailey	2
N. V. Knight c Ripley b Ambrose	1	S. J. W. Andrew c Curran b Snape	9
N. Shahid lbw b Cook	11	J. H. Childs not out	0
Salim Malik st Ripley b Cook	9	B 3, l-b 4, w 13	20
D. R. Pringle c Ripley b Curran	20		
J. J. B. Lewis c Fordham b Cook	15	1/5 2/19 3/39 (34.2 overs)	107
†M. A. Garnham c Bailey b Snape	9	4/40 5/68 6/89	
T. D. Topley c Fordham b Snape	7	7/89 8/96 9/106	

Bowling: Taylor 4–1–25–1; Ambrose 6–3–8–1; Curran 6–1–23–1; Cook 10–0–17–3; Snape 7–2–25–3; Bailey 1.2–0–2–1.

Umpires: B. J. Meyer and D. O. Oslear.

NORTHAMPTONSHIRE v DURHAM

At Northampton, August 15. Durham won by 48 runs. Toss: Northamptonshire.

Fowler and Larkins gave Durham a sound start with 80 in 18 overs before Smith struck 45 off 28 balls. Northamptonshire vainly struggled to overtake them, despite a stand of 90 in 23 overs between Curran and Bailey, who was top-scorer in his benefit match.

Durham

G. Fowler run out	42	†C. W. Scott not out	12
W. Larkins c Loye b Curran	45	*D. A. Graveney not out	1
P. W. G. Parker c and b Cook	43	B 1, l-b 7, w 9	17
P. Bainbridge c Curran b Ambrose	16		
S. Hutton c Walker b Taylor	23	1/80 2/118 3/144 (7 wkts, 50 overs) 246	
I. Smith b Ambrose	45	4/169 5/230	
A. C. Cummins c Walker b Taylor	2	6/230 7/242	

S. P. Hughes and S. J. E. Brown did not bat.

Bowling: Ambrose 10-0-50-2; Taylor 10-0-45-2; Walker 10-0-67-0; Curran 10-1-39-1; Cook 10-0-37-1.

Northamptonshire

R. R. Montgomerie c Smith b Hughes	0	A. Walker b Hughes	30
M. B. Loye c Scott b Cummins	3	N. G. B. Cook b Cummins	5
R. J. Bailey c and b Graveney	48	J. P. Taylor not out	3
*A. J. Lamb c Larkins b Cummins	5	L-b 12, w 11, n-b 2	25
K. M. Curran c Smith b Bainbridge	39		
R. J. Warren c Hutton b Bainbridge	5	1/0 2/8 3/14 (46.5 overs) 198	
†D. Ripley c Fowler b Graveney	9	4/104 5/115 6/122	
C. E. L. Ambrose c Parker b Cummins	26	7/148 8/166 9/187	

Bowling: Hughes 8.5-2-28-2; Cummins 9-3-27-4; Brown 10-1-46-0; Bainbridge 10-2-32-2; Graveney 9-0-53-2.

Umpires: J. H. Harris and G. A. Stickley.

At Lord's, August 22. NORTHAMPTONSHIRE beat MIDDLESEX by four wickets.

NORTHAMPTONSHIRE v LEICESTERSHIRE

At Northampton, August 29. Northamptonshire won by seven wickets. Toss: Leicestershire.

Northamptonshire secured a comfortable victory, thanks to an unbroken 93-run partnership in 15 overs between Lamb and Warren. Leicestershire conceded 25 in wides and no-balls.

Leicestershire

T. J. Boon lbw b Walker	8	J. M. Dakin run out	16
†P. A. Nixon lbw b Curran	24	G. J. Parsons not out	24
*J. J. Whitaker c Felton b Walker	0	B 1, l-b 8, w 9	18
P. E. Robinson b Taylor	18		
V. J. Wells b Bailey	35	1/20 2/24 3/47 (6 wkts, 50 overs) 196	
B. F. Smith not out	53	4/69 5/121 6/145	

D. J. Millns, A. D. Mullally and A. R. K. Pierson did not bat.

Bowling: Walker 7-0-30-2; Curran 7-1-29-1; Taylor 10-0-45-1; Bowen 6-0-24-0; Cook 10-1-34-0; Bailey 10-3-25-1.

Northamptonshire

A. Fordham run out	10		*A. J. Lamb not out	42
N. A. Felton st Nixon b Pierson	37		B 2, l-b 2, w 13, n-b 12	29
R. J. Bailey c Nixon b Mullally	11			
R. J. Warren not out	71		1/24 2/49 3/107 (3 wkts, 43.4 overs)	200

K. M. Curran, †W. M. Noon, M. N. Bowen, A. Walker, J. P. Taylor and N. G. B. Cook did not bat.

Bowling: Millns 6–0–35–0; Parsons 10–0–32–0; Mullally 8–0–37–1; Wells 4–0–14–0; Pierson 10–0–48–1; Dakin 5.4–0–30–0.

Umpires: G. I. Burgess and P. B. Wight.

At Canterbury, September 5. NORTHAMPTONSHIRE lost to KENT by three wickets.

At Derby, September 12. DERBYSHIRE v NORTHAMPTONSHIRE. No result.

At Manchester, September 19. NORTHAMPTONSHIRE beat LANCASHIRE by five wickets.

NOTTINGHAMSHIRE

At Leicester, May 9. NOTTINGHAMSHIRE lost to LEICESTERSHIRE by 90 runs.

At Lord's, May 16. NOTTINGHAMSHIRE lost to MIDDLESEX by five runs.

NOTTINGHAMSHIRE v KENT

At Nottingham, May 23. Nottinghamshire won by nine wickets. Toss: Nottinghamshire. Johnson scored 167 not out from 106 balls, with 20 fours and seven sixes, to give Nottinghamshire a brilliant victory. His century came from just 64 balls, and he put on 213 for the second wicket with Robinson in 28 overs. It was the highest score for the county in any one-day competition. Kent had also enjoyed a double-century stand for the second wicket, from Ward and Hooper; Ward reached the maiden League hundred that had eluded him a week earlier, hitting 15 fours and a six. But Kent lost their next eight wickets in six overs, Cairns taking five of them in 14 balls.

Kent

T. R. Ward b Cairns	131		D. W. Headley run out	2
*M. R. Benson c Pollard b Cairns	3		M. J. McCague not out	4
C. L. Hooper c Johnson b Pick	94			
M. V. Fleming c and b Cairns	0		B 2, l-b 13, w 6	21
N. R. Taylor run out	6			
G. R. Cowdrey lbw b Cairns	0		1/15 2/233 3/237 (9 wkts, 50 overs)	264
N. J. Llong b Cairns	2		4/250 5/250 6/251	
†S. A. Marsh c Robinson b Cairns	1		7/253 8/258 9/264	

A. P. Igglesden did not bat.

Bowling: Cairns 10–0–52–6; Mike 8–0–38–0; Pick 10–0–48–1; Field-Buss 9–0–50–0; Evans 9–1–41–0; Crawley 4–0–20–0.

Nottinghamshire

P. Johnson not out................	.167
M. Saxelby c Hooper b Igglesden......	8
*R. T. Robinson not out............	63
L-b 6, w 9, n-b 12..........	27

1/52   (1 wkt, 35.2 overs) 265

P. R. Pollard, C. L. Cairns, M. A. Crawley, G. W. Mike, R. A. Pick, †B. N. French, K. P. Evans and M. G. Field-Buss did not bat.

Bowling: Igglesden 8–1–37–1; Headley 4–0–30–0; McCague 7–0–67–0; Fleming 7.2–0–72–0; Hooper 9–0–53–0.

Umpires: V. A. Holder and P. B. Wight.

NOTTINGHAMSHIRE v HAMPSHIRE

At Nottingham, June 6. Hampshire won by eight wickets. Toss: Hampshire.

The visitors registered their first Sunday win of the season after Connor removed Nottinghamshire's top three. Then Gower struck 59, including nine fours, as he and his opening partner Middleton took Hampshire almost halfway to victory on their own.

Nottinghamshire

P. Johnson c Aymes b Connor........	31	R. A. Pick c Nicholas b Ayling......	9
P. R. Pollard b Connor............	17	D. B. Pennett not out..............	1
*R. T. Robinson b Connor..........	66	M. G. Field-Buss b Udal..........	0
C. L. Cairns lbw b James..........	10	L-b 8, w 6.................	14
G. F. Archer b Turner.............	17		
M. A. Crawley retired hurt.........	7	1/47 2/52 3/76 (50 overs) 204
G. W. Mike b Udal...............	0	4/118 5/134 6/168
†B. N. French lbw b Udal..........	32	7/189 8/204 9/204

M. A. Crawley retired hurt at 128.

Bowling: Connor 10–3–23–3; Thursfield 6–0–38–0; Ayling 10–0–38–1; James 7–0–23–1; Udal 10–0–45–3; Turner 7–0–29–1.

Hampshire

T. C. Middleton b Mike............	48
D. I. Gower c French b Field-Buss....	59
*M. C. J. Nicholas not out..........	46
V. P. Terry not out................	46
L-b 5, w 4.................	9

1/99 2/126   (2 wkts, 47.4 overs) 208

K. D. James, J. R. Ayling, †A. N. Aymes, S. D. Udal, C. A. Connor, I. J. Turner and M. J. Thursfield did not bat.

Bowling: Pennett 10–1–51–0; Cairns 9.4–0–43–0; Pick 9–1–26–0; Mike 9–0–36–1; Field-Buss 10–1–47–1.

Umpires: J. C. Balderstone and B. Leadbeater.

NOTTINGHAMSHIRE v ESSEX

At Nottingham, June 20. Essex won by 75 runs. Toss: Nottinghamshire.

Acting-captain Prichard batted all but three overs of Essex's 50 for his second century in the League. Then his bowlers quickly had Nottinghamshire in trouble, sending them to their fourth defeat in five Sunday games.

Essex

*P. J. Prichard c Mike b Pick	107	T. D. Topley not out		7
J. P. Stephenson c Johnson b Pick	30	M. C. Ilott run out		5
N. Hussain c Archer b Mike	20	L-b 4, w 5, n-b 2		11
Salim Malik run out	23			
D. R. Pringle c Mike b Field-Buss	37	1/42 2/78 3/129	(8 wkts, 50 overs)	261
N. Shahid b Field-Buss	1	4/204 5/207 6/244		
†M. A. Garnham b Cairns	20	7/251 8/261		

S. J. W. Andrew and J. H. Childs did not bat.

Bowling: Cairns 10–0–50–1; Evans 10–0–54–0; Pick 10–0–55–2; Mike 10–1–53–1; Field-Buss 10–0–45–2.

Nottinghamshire

P. Johnson b Ilott	6	K. P. Evans c Prichard b Andrew		17
M. Saxelby b Pringle	11	R. A. Pick b Stephenson		2
*R. T. Robinson b Childs	52	M. G. Field-Buss not out		7
C. L. Cairns c Garnham b Topley	11	L-b 4, n-b 4		8
G. F. Archer c Stephenson b Topley	18			
P. R. Pollard lbw b Childs	24	1/10 2/30 3/69	(45.3 overs)	186
G. W. Mike b Childs	18	4/101 5/111 6/145		
†B. N. French b Childs	12	7/150 8/167 9/170		

Bowling: Ilott 6–2–30–1; Pringle 6–1–17–1; Topley 10–0–38–2; Andrew 6.3–0–28–1; Childs 10–0–38–4; Stephenson 7–0–31–1.

Umpires: H. D. Bird and B. Dudleston.

At Swansea, June 27. NOTTINGHAMSHIRE lost to GLAMORGAN by three wickets.

At Northampton, July 4. NOTTINGHAMSHIRE lost to NORTHAMPTONSHIRE by 63 runs.

NOTTINGHAMSHIRE v WORCESTERSHIRE

At Nottingham, July 11. Nottinghamshire won by four wickets. Toss: Nottinghamshire.

For their second Sunday win of the season Nottinghamshire were indebted to Cairns, who alone coped confidently with the variable bounce and pace to score 47 after taking three wickets. Randall, making a rare appearance, became the third player after Graham Gooch and Dennis Amiss to reach 7,000 runs in the Sunday League.

Worcestershire

*T. S. Curtis c and b Cairns	14	K. C. G. Benjamin b Cairns		14
N. V. Radford b Pick	28	C. M. Tolley c and b Lewis		2
G. A. Hick c Mike b Crawley	27	R. K. Illingworth not out		2
D. B. D'Oliveira c Field-Buss b Crawley	15	B 1, l-b 2, w 4, n-b 10		17
D. A. Leatherdale c French b Field-Buss	9			
†S. J. Rhodes c and b Field-Buss	2	1/29 2/73 3/91	(47.2 overs)	155
M. J. Weston b Cairns	19	4/106 5/108 6/110		
P. J. Newport c Lewis b Field-Buss	6	7/124 8/146 9/151		

Bowling: Lewis 8.2–1–28–1; Cairns 8–0–32–3; Pick 8–0–26–1; Mike 5–0–20–0; Crawley 10–2–21–2; Field-Buss 8–2–25–3.

Nottinghamshire

P. Johnson b Benjamin	3	C. C. Lewis c Weston b Benjamin	12
M. Saxelby c Rhodes b Benjamin	12	G. W. Mike not out	11
*R. T. Robinson st Rhodes b Illingworth	22	L-b 4, w 6, n-b 4	14
C. L. Cairns c Leatherdale b Hick	47		
M. A. Crawley b Newport	7	1/4 2/15 3/80 (6 wkts, 48.3 overs) 158	
D. W. Randall not out	30	4/96 5/109 6/130	

†B. N. French, R. A. Pick and M. G. Field-Buss did not bat.

Bowling: Benjamin 10-2-25-3; Tolley 9-0-43-0; Illingworth 10-3-23-1; Newport 10-2-31-1; Hick 9.3-0-32-1.

Umpires: J. H. Hampshire and A. G. T. Whitehead.

NOTTINGHAMSHIRE v SOMERSET

At Nottingham, July 18. Nottinghamshire won by four wickets. Toss: Nottinghamshire.
An aggressive 73 off 88 balls by Cairns saw Nottinghamshire to victory with 7.2 overs to spare.

Somerset

M. N. Lathwell c Pollard b Lewis	12	A. Payne b Lewis	17
N. A. Folland b Evans	29	A. R. Caddick b Pick	1
*C. J. Tavaré b Cairns	37	L-b 8, w 9	17
R. J. Harden b Field-Buss	20		
K. A. Parsons c Randall b Field-Buss	16	1/18 2/50 3/106 (9 wkts, 50 overs) 200	
†N. D. Burns run out	0	4/110 5/111 6/133	
G. D. Rose not out	50	7/146 8/195 9/200	
Mushtaq Ahmed c Pollard b Field-Buss	1		

N. A. Mallender did not bat.

Bowling: Lewis 10-1-35-2; Cairns 10-0-35-1; Pick 7-0-37-1; Evans 10-0-32-1; Crawley 3-0-21-0; Field-Buss 10-0-32-3.

Nottinghamshire

P. R. Pollard c Burns b Mallender	19	C. C. Lewis not out	20
P. Johnson c and b Rose	34	K. P. Evans not out	12
*R. T. Robinson lbw b Rose	5	B 1, l-b 2, w 1, n-b 2	6
C. L. Cairns lbw b Mallender	73		
D. W. Randall b Mushtaq Ahmed	22	1/55 2/55 3/60 (6 wkts, 42.4 overs) 203	
M. A. Crawley lbw b Rose	12	4/117 5/163 6/187	

†B. N. French, R. A. Pick and M. G. Field-Buss did not bat.

Bowling: Caddick 8.4-0-50-0; Mallender 10-0-49-2; Rose 10-2-36-3; Mushtaq Ahmed 10-1-48-1; Payne 4-1-17-0.

Umpires: R. Julian and M. J. Kitchen.

At Manchester, July 25. NOTTINGHAMSHIRE lost to LANCASHIRE by 26 runs.

At The Oval, August 1. NOTTINGHAMSHIRE lost to SURREY by four wickets.

NOTTINGHAMSHIRE v YORKSHIRE

At Nottingham, August 8. Yorkshire won by six wickets. Toss: Yorkshire. First-team debut: M. P. Dowman.

A solid 83 from Robinson and Johnson's fifty in 24 balls were upstaged by Richardson's first one-day hundred for Yorkshire, which came in 86 balls with three sixes and six fours. Even so, Yorkshire won with only two balls to spare.

Nottinghamshire

P. R. Pollard c and b Hartley	12	†B. N. French b Gough	6
P. Johnson b Hartley	55	R. A. Pick not out	0
*R. T. Robinson b Robinson	83		
C. L. Cairns run out	28	B 4, n-b 2	6
C. C. Lewis b Gough	65		
G. W. Mike c Byas b Hartley	0	1/42 2/75 3/142 (8 wkts, 50 overs) 261
M. P. Dowman b Hartley	6	4/233 5/236 6/249
R. T. Bates not out	0	7/251 8/257

D. B. Pennett did not bat.

Bowling: Hartley 10-0-54-4; Gough 8-1-59-2; Robinson 10-1-47-1; Foster 4-0-21-0; Stemp 10-0-40-0; Grayson 8-0-36-0.

Yorkshire

*M. D. Moxon c Johnson b Mike	14	C. White not out	27
D. Byas c Cairns b Pennett	21	L-b 5, w 5	10
R. B. Richardson c and b Mike	103		
A. P. Grayson b Dowman	32	1/30 2/42 (4 wkts, 49.4 overs) 264
†R. J. Blakey not out	57	3/128 4/192

M. J. Foster, P. J. Hartley, D. Gough, R. D. Stemp and M. A. Robinson did not bat.

Bowling: Lewis 10-2-29-0; Pick 10-0-49-0; Mike 9.4-0-65-2; Pennett 4-0-26-1; Bates 10-0-48-0; Dowman 6-0-42-1.

Umpires: D. J. Constant and J. W. Holder.

At Eastbourne, August 15. NOTTINGHAMSHIRE lost to SUSSEX by 94 runs.

NOTTINGHAMSHIRE v DERBYSHIRE

At Nottingham, August 29. Nottinghamshire won by 142 runs. Toss: Nottinghamshire.

Nottinghamshire's spectacular victory was founded on their highest one-day total, their second of the season over 300 and the season's highest by any side. They were given a flying start by Johnson and Pollard, who opened with 169 in 17 overs, and were especially hard on Cork, whose figures of 8-0-96-1 were the most expensive ever in the Sunday League, passing Geoff Miller's 7.5-0-89-3, also for Derbyshire, in 1984. Derbyshire were never in the hunt, despite a maiden fifty from Rollins.

Nottinghamshire

P. Johnson c Barnett b Mortensen	75	K. P. Evans c Bowler b Warner	7
P. R. Pollard lbw b Steer	91	†B. N. French not out	6
*R. T. Robinson not out	78	L-b 5, w 3, n-b 18	26
M. Saxelby c Cork b Base	30		
G. W. Mike c Krikken b Base	0	1/169 2/201 3/264 (6 wkts, 50 overs) 329
M. A. Crawley c Adams b Cork	16	4/264 5/294 6/303

R. T. Bates, R. A. Pick and D. B. Pennett did not bat.

Bowling: Mortensen 10-0-53-1; Base 10-0-62-2; Cork 8-0-96-1; Warner 8-0-52-1; Adams 7-0-28-0; Steer 7-0-33-1.

Derbyshire

P. D. Bowler b Pennett	5	A. E. Warner c French b Bates	15
C. J. Adams c Pick b Mike	11	S. J. Base c Pollard b Bates	23
*K. J. Barnett lbw b Pick	28	O. H. Mortensen not out	2
T. J. G. O'Gorman c French b Pick	5	L-b 10, w 8	18
A. S. Rollins b Mike	57		
I. G. S. Steer c Bates b Crawley	3	1/5 2/24 3/36	(45.5 overs) 187
D. G. Cork b Evans	4	4/75 5/93 6/111	
†K. M. Krikken lbw b Bates	16	7/138 8/160 9/171	

Bowling: Mike 9.2–0–46–2; Pennett 8–2–18–1; Pick 8–2–20–2; Bates 6.5–0–43–3; Crawley 8–0–33–1; Evans 5.4–0–17–1.

Umpires: V. A. Holder and R. Palmer.

At Chester-le-Street, September 5. NOTTINGHAMSHIRE lost to DURHAM by three wickets.

At Bristol, September 12. GLOUCESTERSHIRE v NOTTINGHAMSHIRE. No result.

NOTTINGHAMSHIRE v WARWICKSHIRE

At Nottingham, September 19. Warwickshire won by 160 runs. Toss: Warwickshire. County debut: S. J. Dean.

Bell's first five-wicket return on a Sunday brought the downfall of Nottinghamshire, as he and Neil Smith removed their last eight batsmen for 21. Randall, in his last match before retiring, captained the side and was lbw to Munton for three. He batted in a shirt borrowed from a team-mate with "Bates" across his back, though it is unlikely that anyone was fooled. Earlier, Warwickshire had been taken towards their highest total of the season by an explosive 60 off 54 balls from Asif Din.

Warwickshire

S. J. Dean b Pennett	17	N. M. K. Smith not out	12
†M. Burns c Cairns b Pick	26	M. A. V. Bell c Pick b Cairns	6
D. P. Ostler b Bates	53		
P. A. Smith c French b Pennett	46	B 5, l-b 6, w 2, n-b 4	17
Asif Din b Bates	60		
R. G. Twose c Johnson b Pennett	0	1/33 2/82 3/118	(9 wkts, 50 overs) 276
*D. A. Reeve lbw b Cairns	22	4/213 5/215 6/215	
T. L. Penney c Johnson b Lewis	17	7/251 8/262 9/276	

T. A. Munton did not bat.

Bowling: Pick 10–1–61–1; Lewis 10–1–39–1; Cairns 10–0–55–2; Pennett 10–0–32–3; Bates 10–1–78–2.

Nottinghamshire

P. R. Pollard c Asif Din b Reeve	12	R. A. Pick st Burns b N. M. K. Smith	2
P. Johnson c Burns b Bell	47	D. B. Pennett c Penney	
*D. W. Randall lbw b Munton	3	b N. M. K. Smith	0
M. Saxelby st Burns b N. M. K. Smith	23		
C. L. Cairns c Twose b Bell	7	L-b 7, w 2, n-b 4	13
M. P. Dowman b Bell	2		
C. C. Lewis not out	6	1/20 2/42 3/95	(28 overs) 116
R. T. Bates c Ostler b Bell	1	4/99 5/106 6/107	
†B. N. French c Burns b Bell	0	7/109 8/113 9/116	

Bowling: Reeve 7–1–30–1; Munton 8–0–48–1; Bell 7–1–21–5; N. M. K. Smith 6–0–10–3.

Umpires: B. Dudleston and A. A. Jones.

SOMERSET

SOMERSET v LANCASHIRE

At Taunton, May 16. No result. Toss: Somerset. First-team debut: J. I. D. Kerr.

Rain delayed the start, and returned just before the end of Lancashire's shortened innings. The highlight of the day was van Troost's one-handed catch on the boundary to remove Wasim Akram.

Lancashire

P. Titchard c Burns b Rose	16	†W. K. Hegg lbw b Payne	1
M. A. Atherton c Burns b Kerr	28	I. D. Austin not out	16
N. J. Speak c Burns b Mushtaq Ahmed	40	P. J. Martin not out	13
G. D. Lloyd b Payne	28	L-b 10, w 6, n-b 2	18
M. Watkinson b Caddick	27		
Wasim Akram c van Troost		1/44 2/62 3/117 (8 wkts, 44.1 overs) 210	
b Mushtaq Ahmed	9	4/121 5/137 6/168	
P. A. J. DeFreitas c Folland b Caddick	14	7/171 8/182	

G. Chapple did not bat.

Bowling: Caddick 9–0–44–2; van Troost 5.1–0–33–0; Kerr 5–0–21–1; Rose 8–2–22–1; Mushtaq Ahmed 9–1–37–2; Payne 8–0–43–2.

Somerset

M. N. Lathwell, R. J. Harden, N. A. Folland, *C. J. Tavaré, †N. D. Burns, G. D. Rose, J. I. D. Kerr, Mushtaq Ahmed, A. Payne, A. R. Caddick and A. P. van Troost.

Umpires: J. C. Balderstone and R. Palmer.

At Worcester, May 23. SOMERSET lost to WORCESTERSHIRE by four wickets.

SOMERSET v GLAMORGAN

At Taunton, May 30. No result (abandoned).

Though rain prevented any play, Viv Richards accepted honorary life membership of Somerset and a commemorative plaque on his return to his former county, marking the formal end to the feud that began when he and Joel Garner were sacked in 1986.

At Chelmsford, June 6. SOMERSET beat ESSEX by 22 runs.

SOMERSET v MIDDLESEX

At Bath, June 20. Middlesex won by eight wickets. Toss: Somerset.

Ramprakash and Carr secured victory with 16.3 overs to spare after Mallender had removed both Middlesex openers with five on the board. Somerset had collapsed to 47 for five, with two run-outs, as they struggled against some supremely economical bowling from Cowans and Emburey. Tavaré reached 6,000 runs in the competition when he was six.

Somerset

M. N. Lathwell lbw b Cowans	8	N. A. Mallender c Ramprakash	
N. A. Folland run out	7	b Williams	20
R. J. Harden c Brown b Williams	1	H. R. J. Trump not out	6
*C. J. Tavaré run out	12		
†N. D. Burns c Carr b Fraser	4	L-b 4, w 7, n-b 6	17
G. D. Rose c Carr b Fraser	28		
Mushtaq Ahmed c Sims b Emburey	32		
A. Payne c Williams b Weekes	9		
J. I. D. Kerr b Keech	0		

1/14 2/24 3/36 4/44 5/47 6/84 7/99 8/99 9/127 　　(50 overs) 144

Bowling: Cowans 10–4–12–1; Williams 10–1–42–2; Fraser 10–1–36–2; Emburey 10–5–10–1; Weekes 6–0–27–1; Keech 4–0–13–1.

Middlesex

D. L. Haynes c Burns b Mallender	0
R. J. Sims c Rose b Mallender	3
M. R. Ramprakash not out	73
*J. D. Carr not out	57
B 8, l-b 1, w 1, n-b 2	12

1/0 2/5 　　　　　(2 wkts, 33.3 overs) 145

P. N. Weekes, †K. R. Brown, M. Keech, J. E. Emburey, N. F. Williams, A. R. C. Fraser and N. G. Cowans did not bat.

Bowling: Mallender 6–3–11–2; Kerr 5–0–31–0; Mushtaq Ahmed 6–0–32–0; Rose 4.3–0–15–0; Trump 8–1–30–0; Payne 4–0–17–0.

Umpires: B. J. Meyer and G. Sharp.

At Luton, June 27. SOMERSET lost to NORTHAMPTONSHIRE by 17 runs.

SOMERSET v SUSSEX

At Taunton, July 4. Sussex won by 105 runs. Toss: Sussex.

Speight reached 100 from only 47 balls, the second fastest in League history, behind Graham Rose of Somerset's 46-ball century against Glamorgan in 1990; Rose this time was one of the suffering bowlers. Speight had to retire hurt on 93 and returned with his back in plaster and accompanied by a runner; but he hit just as hard afterwards, finishing with four sixes and 20 fours. His efforts took Sussex to 302. Later Jones took four for 26 against his old county.

Sussex

D. M. Smith c Mallender b Kerr	9	A. C. S. Pigott not out	9
F. D. Stephenson c Burns b Mallender	16	A. N. Jones not out	13
M. P. Speight c Parsons b Kerr	126		
C. W. J. Athey c Trump b Parsons	23	L-b 10, w 5, n-b 2	17
*A. P. Wells c Tavaré b Trump	19		
K. Greenfield b Mallender	15	1/22 2/65 3/147 　　(8 wkts, 50 overs) 302	
C. M. Wells c Trescothick b Kerr	35	4/182 5/188 6/232	
†P. Moores b Hallett	20	7/277 8/278	

E. S. H. Giddins did not bat.

M. P. Speight, when 93, retired hurt at 143 and resumed at 232.

Bowling: Mallender 10–1–52–2; Rose 10–0–50–0; Kerr 10–0–67–3; Hallett 6–0–61–1; Trump 10–0–43–1; Parsons 4–0–19–1.

Somerset

N. A. Folland c Moores b Giddins	5	J. C. Hallett c Greenfield b Athey	26
M. E. Trescothick c C. M. Wells b Jones	28	N. A. Mallender c C. M. Wells b Athey	20
R. J. Harden c Giddins b Jones	21	H. R. J. Trump not out	13
G. D. Rose b Jones	5		
C. J. Tavaré c Moores b Jones	13	L-b 6, w 4, n-b 2	12
A. Parsons lbw b C. M. Wells	34		
N. D. Burns c Greenfield b C. M. Wells	5	(48.2 overs) 197	
I. D. Kerr b Greenfield	15		

1/16 2/59 3/61
4/78 5/81 6/92
7/120 8/146 9/169

Bowling: Stephenson 6-1-21-0; Giddins 5-0-19-1; Jones 8-2-26-4; C. M. Wells 10-0-48-2; Pigott 5-0-16-0; Greenfield 10-0-37-1; Athey 4.2-0-24-2.

Umpires: J. H. Harris and J. W. Holder.

At Southampton, July 11. SOMERSET lost to HAMPSHIRE by seven wickets.

At Nottingham, July 18. SOMERSET lost to NOTTINGHAMSHIRE by four wickets.

SOMERSET v KENT

At Taunton, July 25. Kent won by three wickets. Toss: Kent.

Somerset slumped to 71 for six before Rose and Payne rallied the innings. Hooper conceded only eight runs in his ten overs but the medium-pacers were less effective: Payne hit three sixes while Rose, who took 12 overs to reach seven, cut loose to take 17 off an over from Fleming and 19 from one of Ealham's. Later, Rose took four wickets and ran out Llong. Kent were also in early trouble, but Taylor and Llong put on 96 before Marsh and Ealham knocked off the 50 needed from the last eight overs with nine balls to spare.

Somerset

G. W. White lbw b Headley	1	Mushtaq Ahmed c Marsh b Fleming	0
C. J. Tavaré c Fleming b Hooper	15	A. Payne not out	55
N. D. Burns c Marsh b Ealham	2	L-b 8, w 2, n-b 2	12
K. J. Parsons lbw b Penn	22		
A. N. Hayhurst c and b Fleming	8	1/2 2/7 3/47 (6 wkts, 50 overs) 193	
G. D. Rose not out	78	4/48 5/65 6/71	

N. A. Mallender, A. P. van Troost and A. C. Cottam did not bat.

Bowling: Headley 10-3-30-1; Ealham 10-2-44-1; Penn 8-1-19-1; Hooper 10-5-8-1; Fleming 8-0-57-2; Llong 4-0-27-0.

Kent

T. R. Ward c Payne b van Troost	4	†S. A. Marsh not out	20
M. V. Fleming c Burns b Rose	18	M. A. Ealham not out	32
C. L. Hooper c and b Mallender	6	L-b 8, w 5, n-b 12	25
*M. R. Benson c Burns b Rose	4		
N. R. Taylor lbw b Rose	44	1/5 2/33 3/38 (7 wkts, 48.3 overs) 196	
N. J. Llong run out	42	4/44 5/140	
G. R. Cowdrey c White b Rose	1	6/141 7/144	

D. W. Headley and C. Penn did not bat.

Bowling: Mallender 10-1-24-1; van Troost 9-0-45-1; Rose 10-2-26-4; Payne 7-1-31-0; Cottam 6-0-24-0; Mushtaq Ahmed 6.3-0-38-0.

Umpires: J. D. Bond and B. Dudleston.

SOMERSET v YORKSHIRE

At Taunton, August 1. Yorkshire won by four wickets. Toss: Somerset.

From 123 for six, Yorkshire were swept to victory by Richardson and Hartley whose unbroken 80 for the seventh wicket came in 12 overs. With 17 needed as Payne began the penultimate over, Richardson took one and Hartley hit the other 16 off five balls, to finish the match with an over to spare. Mushtaq Ahmed conceded only 15 in his ten overs.

Somerset

A. N. Hayhurst c Byas b Robinson	80	*C. J. Tavaré c Foster b Hartley	4
M. N. Lathwell b Gough	13	†N. D. Burns not out	
N. A. Folland b Batty	38	B 2, l-b 6, w 3, n-b 4	15
R. J. Harden not out	47		
Mushtaq Ahmed c Batty b Hartley	2	1/16 2/121 3/176 (6 wkts, 50 overs) 207	
A. Payne b Hartley	0	4/180 5/181 6/197	

A. R. Caddick, N. A. Mallender and H. R. J. Trump did not bat.

Bowling: Hartley 10-0-40-3; Gough 10-2-39-1; Robinson 8-3-26-1; Foster 9-1-39-0; Batty 10-1-41-1; Grayson 3-0-9-0.

Yorkshire

*M. D. Moxon c Tavaré b Payne	21	M. J. Foster lbw b Caddick	0
D. Byas b Mushtaq Ahmed	31	P. J. Hartley not out	46
R. B. Richardson not out	58	B 5, l-b 7, w 13, n-b 4	29
C. White lbw b Mushtaq Ahmed	1		
†R. J. Blakey c and b Trump	5	1/50 2/66 3/75 (6 wkts, 49 overs) 203	
A. P. Grayson b Caddick	12	4/86 5/123 6/123	

D. Gough, J. D. Batty and M. A. Robinson did not bat.

Bowling: Caddick 10-0-51-2; Mallender 5-0-20-0; Payne 5-1-30-1; Mushtaq Ahmed 10-5-15-2; Trump 10-0-38-1; Lathwell 9-0-37-0.

Umpires: J. H. Hampshire and K. E. Palmer.

At Derby, August 15. SOMERSET lost to DERBYSHIRE by 113 runs.

SOMERSET v LEICESTERSHIRE

At Weston-super-Mare, August 22. Somerset won by 96 runs. Toss: Leicestershire.

Somerset's second Sunday League win of the season, and their first at home since August 16, 1992, ended their run of eight consecutive defeats in the competition. Instead, Leicestershire recorded their sixth in succession. Somerset were indebted to a second-wicket stand of 102 between Lathwell and Folland, whose maiden Sunday hundred came in 119 balls. Kerr at No. 10, was their only other batsman to reach double figures.

Somerset

I. Fletcher c Nixon b Parsons	5	†R. J. Turner run out	0
M. N. Lathwell b Pierson	75	J. I. D. Kerr not out	15
N. A. Folland not out	107		
*R. J. Harden c Nixon b Mullally	3	B 7, l-b 3, w 5, n-b 6	21
G. D. Rose c Benson b Parsons	6		
M. E. Trescothick lbw b Pierson	4	1/18 2/120 3/137 (8 wkts, 50 overs) 246	
Mushtaq Ahmed c Wells b Parsons	3	4/174 5/192 6/208	
A. Payne b Parsons	0	7/211 8/213	

A. P. van Troost did not bat.

Bowling: Parsons 10-1-31-4; Mullally 10-2-42-1; Dakin 6-0-38-0; Wells 10-0-51-0; Pierson 10-0-55-2; Benson 4-0-13-0.

eicestershire

J. Boon c Harden b Kerr	14	G. J. Parsons c Lathwell b Kerr	7
D. R. Benson c Turner b van Troost	13	A. R. K. Pierson c Turner b van Troost	0
*. J. Whitaker c Harden b van Troost	0	A. D. Mullally not out	0
E. Robinson lbw b Rose	18	B 1, l-b 8, w 4, n-b 2	15
F. Smith lbw b Mushtaq Ahmed	25		
J. Wells run out	39	1/23 2/23 3/37	(41.3 overs) 144
P. A. Nixon b Mushtaq Ahmed	11	4/78 5/83 6/126	
M. Dakin run out	2	7/129 8/143 9/144	

Bowling: Rose 8–1–28–1; van Troost 7.3–1–17–3; Kerr 8–0–33–2; Payne 6–0–15–0; Mushtaq Ahmed 10–1–28–2; Lathwell 2–0–14–0.

Umpires: N. T. Plews and D. R. Shepherd.

t The Oval, August 29. SOMERSET lost to SURREY by five wickets.

SOMERSET v GLOUCESTERSHIRE

t Taunton, September 5. Gloucestershire won by three wickets. Toss: Somerset.
Everyone struggled for runs on an unpredictable pitch, considered poor but not unsuitable
y the umpires. Gloucestershire looked unlikely to pass even Somerset's paltry 111 when
ey were 68 for six. However, Scott and Russell resisted for 12 overs and a late flurry from
all saw them home at 4.15 p.m.

Somerset

Fletcher c Windows b Babington	11	A. R. Caddick c Alleyne b Ball	2
I. N. Lathwell run out	36	H. R. J. Trump b Alleyne	0
I. E. Trescothick c Hinks b Babington	0	A. P. van Troost lbw b Ball	0
A. N. Hayhurst c Hancock b Williams	2	L-b 3, w 5, n-b 4	12
A. Parsons c Russell b Ball	15		
I. D. Rose b Alleyne	20	1/26 2/26 3/51	(41.5 overs) 111
Mushtaq Ahmed c Hancock b Alleyne	2	4/55 5/89 6/94	
R. J. Turner not out	11	7/101 8/107 9/108	

Bowling: Babington 6–2–13–2; Smith 6–2–19–0; Williams 8–0–30–1; Scott 5–0–14–0; Ball 5–0–24–3; Alleyne 7–2–8–3.

Gloucestershire

G. Hinks b Caddick	7	R. C. Williams lbw b Mushtaq Ahmed	4
.. J. Wright lbw b Caddick	7	*†R. C. Russell lbw b van Troost	12
I. G. N. Windows c Turner b van Troost	9	M. C. J. Ball not out	15
I. W. Alleyne b Mushtaq Ahmed	14	L-b 4, w 5, n-b 10	19
. H. C. Hancock c Turner b Mushtaq Ahmed	7		
. J. Scott not out	21	1/10 2/27 3/37	(7 wkts, 35 overs) 115
		4/58 5/64	
		6/68 7/96	

A. M. Smith and A. M. Babington did not bat.

Bowling: van Troost 8–1–43–2; Caddick 8–0–31–2; Mushtaq Ahmed 10–4–17–3; Trump 7–4–20–0.

Umpires: R. Julian and P. B. Wight.

t Birmingham, September 12. WARWICKSHIRE v SOMERSET. No result.

t Hartlepool, September 19. SOMERSET lost to DURHAM by seven wickets.

SURREY

At Hove, May 9. SURREY lost to SUSSEX by 65 runs.

SURREY v ESSEX

At The Oval, May 16. Surrey won by two wickets. Toss: Essex.

Essex had omitted Hussain for disciplinary reasons. The revised batting line-up manage only 207. Brown revealed his hitting power in a 38-ball fifty to put Surrey on course, an they won with three overs to spare.

Essex

P. J. Prichard c Boiling b Benjamin	16	T. D. Topley b Waqar Younis	
J. P. Stephenson b Boiling	37	M. C. Ilott not out	
Salim Malik b Benjamin	7	P. M. Such not out	
D. R. Pringle b Waqar Younis	16	B 1, l-b 8, w 8	
*G. A. Gooch c Butcher b Murphy	65		
N. V. Knight c Lynch b Boiling	6	1/22 2/32 3/63	(9 wkts, 50 overs) 20
†M. A. Garnham lbw b Thorpe	0	4/102 5/123 6/124	
J. J. B. Lewis b Thorpe	7	7/148 8/182 9/199	

Bowling: Benjamin 7–1–23–2; Murphy 8–3–25–1; Butcher 10–0–39–0; Waqar Youn 9–1–46–2; Boiling 9–0–38–2; Thorpe 7–0–27–2.

Surrey

D. J. Bicknell c Stephenson b Pringle	8	J. Boiling b Ilott	
A. D. Brown b Topley	52	J. E. Benjamin not out	
*†A. J. Stewart b Topley	53		
G. P. Thorpe st Garnham b Such	27	L-b 8, w 6, n-b 2	
M. A. Lynch c Lewis b Stephenson	14		
D. M. Ward st Garnham b Stephenson	1	1/10 2/83 3/137	(8 wkts, 46.5 overs) 20
M. A. Butcher not out	27	4/165 5/165 6/173	
Waqar Younis b Ilott	9	7/200 8/200	

A. J. Murphy did not bat.

Bowling: Ilott 9.5–0–53–2; Pringle 9–1–37–1; Stephenson 8–0–42–2; Topley 10–1–41–; Such 10–2–27–1.

Umpires: G. I. Burgess and J. W. Holder.

SURREY v LANCASHIRE

At The Oval, June 6. Surrey won by 165 runs. Toss: Surrey.

Lancashire were bowled out in barely half their allotted 50 overs on a day when tw young Surrey players shone. Brown reached his century from only 60 balls and took thre catches, while 21-year-old seamer Adam Hollioake claimed four for 33, after Benjamin an Martin Bicknell had initiated the Lancashire collapse. Brown's characteristically rap innings included 15 fours and a six, and he raised the 100 in 13 overs with Darren Bickne

Surrey

D. J. Bicknell lbw b Austin	30	Waqar Younis lbw b Austin	
A. D. Brown b Wasim Akram	103	J. Boiling not out	
G. P. Thorpe c Hegg b Wasim Akram	15	J. E. Benjamin not out	
*M. A. Lynch c Barnett b Watkinson	5		
D. M. Ward b Wasim Akram	55	L-b 6, w 7	
A. J. Hollioake c Wasim Akram b Barnett	6	1/100 2/149 3/161	(9 wkts, 50 overs) 25
†G. J. Kersey lbw b Martin	15	4/162 5/182 6/233	
M. P. Bicknell b Wasim Akram	8	7/249 8/254 9/256	

Bowling: Wasim Akram 10–0–32–4; Martin 5–0–48–1; Austin 10–1–43–2; Watkinson –1–49–1; Barnett 10–1–43–1; Chapple 5–0–38–0.

ancashire

N. H. Fairbrother b Benjamin	11	P. J. Martin c Brown b Hollioake	6
D. Lloyd c Benjamin		G. Chapple b Hollioake	3
b M. P. Bicknell	11	A. A. Barnett not out	11
J. Speak c Brown b M. P. Bicknell	1		
P. Titchard c Thorpe b Benjamin	2	L-b 4, w 3	7
asim Akram c Kersey b Hollioake	11		
Watkinson c Brown b Waqar Younis	8	1/23 2/23 3/29	(25.4 overs) 94
W. K. Hegg c Kersey b Hollioake	0	4/29 5/49 6/49	
D. Austin c and b Boiling	23	7/54 8/66 9/79	

Bowling: M. P. Bicknell 6–1–25–2; Benjamin 5–1–19–2; Waqar Younis 7–2–13–1; ollioake 7–1–33–4; Boiling 0.4–0–0–1.

Umpires: R. Julian and G. A. Stickley.

SURREY v GLAMORGAN

t The Oval, June 13. Glamorgan won by ten wickets. Toss: Surrey.
James and Morris had no difficulty knocking off 169 after some ineffectual Surrey atting, except from Stewart and Thorpe.

urrey

J. Bicknell c Richards b Watkin	6	Waqar Younis c Cottey b Watkin	1
D. Brown c Cottey b Watkin	12	J. Boiling not out	3
A. J. Stewart run out	39	J. E. Benjamin c Metson b Barwick	4
P. Thorpe b Lefebvre	75	L-b 1, w 3	4
A. Lynch c Watkin b Dale	15		
M. Ward run out	4	1/17 2/20 3/88	(49 overs) 168
J. Hollioake run out	1	4/131 5/146 6/151	
P. Bicknell b Barwick	4	7/160 8/160 9/162	

Bowling: Watkin 10–2–38–3; Lefebvre 9–0–21–1; Barwick 10–1–22–2; Croft 4–0–21–0; ichards 8–1–34–0; Dale 8–0–31–1.

lamorgan

P. James not out	65	
H. Morris not out	98	
L-b 2, w 4	6	
(no wkt, 46.2 overs)	169	

Dale, D. L. Hemp, I. V. A. Richards, P. A. Cottey, R. D. B. Croft, R. P. Lefebvre, †C. P. Metson, S. L. Watkin and S. R. Barwick did not bat.

Bowling: M. P. Bicknell 10–3–28–0; Benjamin 10–2–40–0; Boiling 10–0–29–0; Waqar ounis 7–0–32–0; Hollioake 6–0–24–0; Lynch 3.2–0–14–0.

Umpires: J. H. Hampshire and R. Palmer.

t Birmingham, June 20. SURREY beat WARWICKSHIRE by 18 runs.

t Lord's, June 27. SURREY beat MIDDLESEX by seven wickets.

SURREY v DURHAM

At The Oval, July 4. Surrey won by 36 runs. Toss: Surrey.

Durham hoped for their third Sunday win of the season when they had Surrey at 63 fo
five, three of the wickets going to Botham. But Lynch's 78 and Kersey's maiden fifty pu
the home team back on course, and there were to be no batting heroics from Botham, wh
struck out at his stumps in annoyance when he was bowled but received a standing ovatio
after what was assumed to be his last innings at The Oval.

Surrey

D. J. Bicknell c Scott b Botham	16	Waqar Younis b Hughes		
A. D. Brown b Botham	5	J. Boiling b Hughes		
D. M. Ward c Fowler b Hughes	25	J. E. Benjamin not out		
*M. A. Lynch c Fowler b Brown	78	L-b 7, w 1, n-b 2		
A. W. Smith lbw b Botham	4			
M. A. Butcher b Cummins	1	1/13 2/46 3/52	(9 wkts, 50 overs) 20	
†G. J. Kersey c Berry b Brown	50	4/56 5/63 6/182		
M. P. Bicknell not out	7	7/194 8/204 9/204		

Bowling: Botham 10–4–22–3; Cummins 8–2–33–1; Hughes 10–1–41–3; Bainbridg
9–1–29–0; Berry 8–0–43–0; Brown 5–0–30–2.

Durham

I. T. Botham b Butcher	19	P. J. Berry b Waqar Younis		
G. Fowler b M. P. Bicknell	5	S. P. Hughes not out		
*P. W. G. Parker c Ward b Benjamin	8	S. J. E. Brown c Butcher b Benjamin		
S. Hutton b Butcher	25	L-b 5, w 6, n-b 4		1
P. Bainbridge st Kersey b Boiling	46			
A. C. Cummins c Kersey b Butcher	3	1/8 2/27 3/36	(48.3 overs) 16	
I. Smith lbw b M. P. Bicknell	21	4/96 5/100 6/125		
†C. W. Scott lbw b M. P. Bicknell	5	7/144 8/145 9/154		

Bowling: Waqar Younis 10–2–20–1; M. P. Bicknell 9–2–22–3; Benjamin 9.3–1–33–2
Butcher 10–1–35–3; Boiling 10–0–54–1.

Umpires: K. E. Palmer and R. A. White.

At Leicester, July 11. LEICESTERSHIRE v SURREY. No result.

SURREY v GLOUCESTERSHIRE

At Guildford, July 18. Surrey won by nine wickets, their target having been revised to 10
from 34 overs. Toss: Surrey.

Two attempts at a restart after rain interrupted Surrey's innings eventually left them 11.
overs in which to score eight runs; they hit ten off six balls. Gloucestershire lost their las
eight wickets for 53 runs.

Gloucestershire

B. C. Broad c Butcher b Boiling	39	*C. A. Walsh lbw b M. P. Bicknell		
S. G. Hinks b Butcher	14	A. M. Smith c Lynch b Benjamin		
M. W. Alleyne c Lynch b Boiling	36	A. M. Babington b Benjamin		
A. J. Wright st Stewart b Boiling	7	L-b 4, w 7, n-b 4		1
R. J. Scott c Stewart b Waqar Younis	3			
R. I. Dawson c Lynch b Benjamin	4	1/37 2/79 3/102	(49 overs) 15	
†R. C. Russell not out	22	4/111 5/115 6/124		
R. M. Wight c Stewart b M. P. Bicknell	4	7/135 8/135 9/151		

Bowling: M. P. Bicknell 9–2–23–2; Benjamin 10–1–34–3; Butcher 10–0–29–1; Waqa
Younis 10–0–37–1; Boiling 10–1–28–3.

Surrey

D. J. Bicknell not out	44
A. D. Brown c Hinks b Walsh	32
D. M. Ward not out	24
L-b 3, w 1, n-b 6	10

1/47   (1 wkt, 23.3 overs) 110

*†A. J. Stewart, G. P. Thorpe, M. A. Lynch, M. A. Butcher, M. P. Bicknell, J. Boiling, Waqar Younis and J. E. Benjamin did not bat.

Bowling: Babington 8-0-40-0; Walsh 7.3-1-34-1; Smith 4-0-17-0; Alleyne 4-0-16-0.

Umpires: G. Sharp and D. R. Shepherd.

At Northampton, July 25. NORTHAMPTONSHIRE v SURREY. No result.

SURREY v NOTTINGHAMSHIRE

At The Oval, August 1. Surrey won by four wickets. Toss: Surrey.

Nottinghamshire, beaten by Surrey in the Championship on Saturday, lost again despite amassing their highest total in the League. Pollard and Johnson set the pace with 99 off 11.3 overs, Cairns increased it with his maiden one-day century – 126 off 111 balls including seven sixes. French joined him in a Sunday League record eighth-wicket stand of 110 unbroken, with 75 coming off the last four overs. Surrey then staged their own pyrotechnics to compile the highest total by a side batting second in the Sunday League. Thorpe (83 balls, two sixes, eight fours) and Ward (three sixes and eight fours in 91 balls) were the leaders, putting on 159 for the fifth wicket in 20 overs. The aggregate of 631 runs for the match was a record for the competition, passing by 27 that set by Surrey and Warwickshire, also at The Oval, in 1985.

Nottinghamshire

P. R. Pollard c Stewart b Benjamin	74	K. P. Evans b Hollioake	11
P. Johnson c Thorpe b Boiling	55	†B. N. French not out	19
*R. T. Robinson b Waqar Younis	1	B 5, l-b 6, w 1, n-b 9	21
C. L. Cairns not out	126		
D. W. Randall lbw b Boiling	1	1/99 2/100 3/169 (7 wkts, 48 overs) 314	
M. A. Crawley c Stewart b Benjamin	1	4/172 5/173	
C. C. Lewis c Stewart b M. P. Bicknell	5	6/184 7/204	

M. G. Field-Buss and R. A. Pick did not bat.

Bowling: M. P. Bicknell 10-0-73-1; Benjamin 9-1-62-2; Waqar Younis 9-0-64-1; Boiling 10-0-39-2; Hollioake 10-0-65-1.

Surrey

D. J. Bicknell b Lewis	7	*†A. J. Stewart not out	42
A. D. Brown run out	1	M. P. Bicknell not out	7
A. J. Hollioake c Pollard b Lewis	14	B 1, l-b 7, w 8	16
G. P. Thorpe c French b Cairns	94		
M. A. Lynch lbw b Cairns	35	1/2 2/17 3/26 (6 wkts, 46 overs) 317	
D. M. Ward b Lewis	101	4/88 5/247 6/282	

J. Boiling, Waqar Younis and J. E. Benjamin did not bat.

Bowling: Pick 9-1-59-0; Lewis 10-0-42-3; Cairns 10-0-61-2; Evans 9-0-70-0; Field-Buss 4-0-40-0; Crawley 4-0-37-0.

Umpires: B. Leadbeater and B. J. Meyer.

At Canterbury, August 8. SURREY lost to KENT by 54 runs.

At Worcester, August 15. SURREY lost to WORCESTERSHIRE by 37 runs.

At Ilkeston, August 22. SURREY beat DERBYSHIRE by five wickets.

SURREY v SOMERSET

At The Oval, August 29. Surrey won by five wickets. Toss: Somerset.
Lathwell's 85, with 12 fours, formed the backbone of Somerset's innings, in which Waqar Younis took four for 25. Bicknell and Atkins then gave Surrey a sound start but the innings lost momentum and, with 72 still needed from seven overs, they were indebted for their narrow win to Hollioake's mature batting.

Somerset

M. N. Lathwell c and b Butcher 85	†R. J. Turner not out 5
I. Fletcher c Kersey b Hollioake 15	J. I. D. Kerr not out 1
G. W. White b Waqar Younis 0	
*R. J. Harden b Waqar Younis 39	B 4, l-b 5, w 3, n-b 6 18
G. D. Rose c Smith b Murphy 31	
K. A. Parsons c Kersey b Waqar Younis 1	1/55 2/56 3/142 (8 wkts, 49 overs) 238
Mushtaq Ahmed c Smith b Butcher. . . . 29	4/160 5/173 6/209
A. Payne b Waqar Younis 14	7/229 8/235

H. R. J. Trump did not bat.

Bowling: Murphy 10–2–48–1; Butcher 10–0–71–2; Hollioake 10–2–44–1; Waqar Younis 9–2–25–4; Boiling 10–0–41–0.

Surrey

D. J. Bicknell c Trump b Payne 76	A. J. Hollioake not out 47
P. D. Atkins st Turner b Trump 55	M. A. Butcher not out 22
A. D. Brown st Turner	
b Mushtaq Ahmed . 26	L-b 3, w 1, n-b 2. 6
*M. A. Lynch c Trump	
b Mushtaq Ahmed . 0	1/109 2/150 3/150 (5 wkts, 48.3 overs) 241
A. W. Smith b Mushtaq Ahmed 9	4/162 5/178

†G. J. Kersey, Waqar Younis, J. Boiling and A. J. Murphy did not bat.

Bowling: Rose 9.3–2–33–0; Kerr 10–1–57–0; Payne 9–0–55–1; Trump 10–0–56–1; Mushtaq Ahmed 10–2–37–3.

Umpires: D. J. Constant and D. O. Oslear.

SURREY v HAMPSHIRE

At The Oval, September 5. Surrey won by 77 runs. Toss: Hampshire. First-team debut: J. N. B. Bovill.
Stewart's 83 was eclipsed by a fine all-round contribution by Waqar Younis. Like Stewart he hit three sixes and followed with three wickets, including those of Connor and Bovill from successive unplayable deliveries. Hampshire were well beaten with nine overs remaining.

Surrey

D. J. Bicknell c Terry b Connor	1	J. Boiling run out	8
A. D. Brown b Shine	6	J. E. Benjamin c Aymes b Bovill	8
*†A. J. Stewart c Cox b Udal	83	A. J. Murphy not out	1
G. P. Thorpe c Nicholas b Connor	2	B 1, l-b 4, w 5, n-b 4	14
D. M. Ward b Connor	7		
A. W. Smith c Aymes b Bovill	28	1/7 2/7 3/14	(50 overs) 213
M. A. Butcher lbw b Udal	16	4/31 5/105 6/149	
Waqar Younis c Udal b Bovill	39	7/156 8/170 9/203	

Bowling: Shine 10–0–54–1; Connor 10–2–33–3; James 10–0–47–0; Bovill 10–0–40–3; Udal 10–0–34–2.

Hampshire

V. P. Terry lbw b Murphy	5	C. A. Connor b Waqar Younis	0
J. R. Wood c Stewart b Murphy	10	J. N. B. Bovill b Waqar Younis	0
R. A. Smith b Boiling	30	K. J. Shine not out	1
K. D. James c Smith b Waqar Younis	12	L-b 2, w 7, n-b 2	11
*M. C. J. Nicholas c Brown b Boiling	28		
R. M. F. Cox b Boiling	3	1/10 2/17 3/61	(41 overs) 136
†A. N. Aymes c Benjamin b Boiling	21	4/65 5/73 6/111	
S. D. Udal run out	15	7/130 8/134 9/134	

Bowling: Benjamin 8–0–44–0; Murphy 8–3–12–2; Waqar Younis 8–0–29–3; Butcher 7–0–23–0; Boiling 10–1–26–4.

Umpires: G. I. Burgess and N. T. Plews.

SURREY v YORKSHIRE

At The Oval, September 19. Surrey won by five wickets. Toss: Surrey.

One of Brown's customarily forthright half-centuries, off 58 balls, helped Surrey shrug off the loss of Bicknell in the first over and they cruised to the victory which gave them third place in the League, their highest ever.

Yorkshire

*M. D. Moxon c Smith b Butcher	3	†C. A. Chapman not out	22
D. Byas c Brown b Murphy	0	D. Gough b Hollioake	8
R. J. Blakey c Smith b Hollioake	41	M. A. Robinson c Smith b Hollioake	0
R. B. Richardson c Ward b Murphy	1	L-b 6, w 5	11
M. J. Foster c Brown b Murphy	7		
C. White c Waqar Younis b Boiling	41	1/3 2/3 3/14	(49.5 overs) 185
A. P. Grayson c Smith b Hollioake	36	4/36 5/67 6/117	
P. J. Hartley c Stewart b Waqar Younis	15	7/144 8/162 9/185	

Bowling: Murphy 10–1–36–3; Butcher 10–4–34–1; Waqar Younis 10–0–34–1; Hollioake 9.5–1–42–4; Boiling 10–0–33–1.

Surrey

D. J. Bicknell c Byas b Hartley	4	A. J. Hollioake not out	21
A. D. Brown run out	52	B 1, l-b 4, w 1	6
*†A. J. Stewart c Moxon b Grayson	35		
G. P. Thorpe c Chapman b Gough	16	1/4 2/91 3/96	(5 wkts, 47.3 overs) 188
D. M. Ward b Foster	24	4/122 5/146	
A. W. Smith not out	30		

M. A. Butcher, Waqar Younis, J. Boiling and A. J. Murphy did not bat.

Bowling: Hartley 9–2–41–1; Gough 10–2–27–1; Robinson 10–1–35–0; White 7.3–1–37–0; Grayson 6–0–23–1; Foster 5–0–20–1.

Umpires: J. H. Harris and R. Palmer.

SUSSEX

SUSSEX v SURREY

At Hove, May 9. Sussex won by 65 runs. Toss: Surrey.

Promoting Stephenson to open paid off brilliantly for Sussex; his maiden League hundred, from 79 balls, with 15 fours, enabled them to set Surrey a target of 6.34 an over. Stephenson and Smith had the century stand up in the 13th over. After they had gone, Speight and Colin Wells kept up the momentum with 67 in eight, taking Sussex to their highest Sunday score. For Surrey, only Ward and Lynch could approach the required rate. Hemmings, the only player to have appeared in every season of the Sunday League since its inception in 1969, when he was a 20-year-old with Warwickshire, made his debut in the competition for his third county, Sussex, aged 44 years and 78 days.

Sussex

D. M. Smith c Boiling b Butcher	52	A. N. Jones b Murphy	2
F. D. Stephenson c Thorpe b Boiling	103	E. E. Hemmings not out	2
M. P. Speight b Butcher	55	E. S. H. Giddins not out	0
*A. P. Wells c Lynch b Butcher	10		
C. M. Wells b Boiling	31	L-b 7, w 3, n-b 8	18
K. Greenfield lbw b M. P. Bicknell	18		
†P. Moores c and b Boiling	3	1/162 2/174 3/191 (9 wkts, 49 overs) 310
I. D. K. Salisbury c Butcher		4/258 5/275 6/283	
b M. P. Bicknell	16	7/292 8/305 9/310	

Bowling: M. P. Bicknell 10-1-63-2; Benjamin 10-0-66-0; Murphy 9-0-70-1; Butcher 10-0-52-3; Boiling 10-0-52-3.

Surrey

D. J. Bicknell lbw b Giddins	15	J. Boiling b Giddins	0
A. D. Brown c and b Giddins	15	J. E. Benjamin not out	2
D. M. Ward lbw b Stephenson	73	A. J. Murphy c Jones b Salisbury	0
*†A. J. Stewart c Moores b Jones	17	L-b 17, w 10, n-b 6	33
G. P. Thorpe c Moores b Hemmings	18		
M. A. Lynch c sub b Salisbury	54	1/25 2/44 3/78 (43.5 overs) 245
M. A. Butcher b Salisbury	8	4/127 5/201 6/231	
M. P. Bicknell c and b Salisbury	10	7/231 8/232 9/245	

Bowling: Stephenson 9-0-48-1; Giddins 9-0-42-3; Jones 7-0-24-1; C. M. Wells 4-0-22-0; Hemmings 6-0-43-1; Salisbury 8.5-1-49-4.

Umpires: G. Sharp and P. B. Wight.

SUSSEX v LEICESTERSHIRE

At Horsham, May 23. Sussex won by 63 runs. Toss: Sussex.

Sussex were on top from the start when Smith and Stephenson put on 61 in ten overs, laying the foundations for a total of 283. Leicestershire soon stumbled to 91 for five, and could aim only for respectability.

Sussex

D. M. Smith b Mullally	75	†P. Moores c Boon b Parsons	1
F. D. Stephenson c Whitaker b Wells	30	I. D. K. Salisbury lbw b Mullally	
M. P. Speight c Boon b Potter	52	B 4, l-b 8, w 2	1
*A. P. Wells c Wells b Dakin	21		
C. M. Wells b Parsons	30	1/61 2/145 3/185 (8 wkts, 50 overs) 28
C. W. J. Athey c sub b Wells	19	4/194 5/240 6/243	
N. J. Lenham not out	24	7/265 8/283	

A. C. S. Pigott and E. S. H. Giddins did not bat.

Bowling: Mullally 10-0-52-2; Parsons 10-0-72-2; Dakin 10-1-62-1; Potter 10-0-31-; Wells 10-0-54-2.

Leicestershire

T. J. Boon c Moores b C. M. Wells	29	V. J. Wells not out	39
*N. E. Briers c Lenham b Stephenson	4	J. M. Dakin not out	20
B. F. Smith run out	2	B 1, l-b 21, w 8	30
P. E. Robinson lbw b C. M. Wells	22		
J. J. Whitaker c Athey b C. M. Wells	12	1/4 2/8 3/66 (7 wkts, 50 overs) 220	
L. Potter c Moores b Stephenson	25	4/75 5/91	
†P. A. Nixon b Stephenson	37	6/150 7/159	

G. J. Parsons and A. D. Mullally did not bat.

Bowling: Giddins 10–4–32–0; Stephenson 10–1–29–3; C. M. Wells 10–0–34–3; Salisbury 10–0–34–0; Pigott 10–0–69–0.

Umpires: J. C. Balderstone and D. J. Constant.

At Lord's, May 30. SUSSEX tied with MIDDLESEX.

At Birmingham, June 6. SUSSEX beat WARWICKSHIRE by two wickets.

SUSSEX v NORTHAMPTONSHIRE

At Hove, June 13. Sussex won by five wickets. Toss: Sussex.

Both counties entered the match unbeaten in the League, but the visitors were soon two for two, before Bailey and Lamb put on 102. Sussex also lost two early wickets, but their captain Wells's unbeaten 92 proved decisive.

Northamptonshire

A. Fordham c Smith b Stephenson	1	M. N. Bowen b Stephenson	1
N. A. Felton c Moores b Stephenson	0	J. P. Taylor not out	1
R. J. Bailey c Moores b North	47	N. G. B. Cook b Giddins	0
*A. J. Lamb c Greenfield b North	60		
D. J. Capel c Athey b Giddins	20	L-b 8, w 1, n-b 2	11
K. M. Curran b Pigott	43		
A. L. Penberthy c Greenfield		1/1 2/2 3/104 (49.5 overs) 214	
b Stephenson	22	4/120 5/145 6/196	
†D. Ripley b Giddins	8	7/201 8/206 9/214	

Bowling: Stephenson 10–1–27–4; Giddins 9.5–2–44–3; Pigott 10–0–56–1; Jones 10–0–30–0; North 10–0–49–2.

Sussex

D. M. Smith lbw b Cook	52	J. A. North not out	9
F. D. Stephenson c Ripley b Curran	2		
C. W. J. Athey c Lamb b Taylor	1	L-b 2, w 4, n-b 2	8
*A. P. Wells not out	92		
K. Greenfield run out	48	1/10 2/17 3/87 (5 wkts, 48 overs) 217	
†P. Moores c Lamb b Capel	5	4/182 5/192	

A. C. S. Pigott, B. T. P. Donelan, A. N. Jones and E. S. H. Giddins did not bat.

Bowling: Taylor 9–3–27–1; Curran 9–1–37–1; Penberthy 8–0–51–0; Capel 10–1–48–1; Cook 7–0–34–1; Bowen 5–0–18–0.

Umpires: D. J. Constant and B. Dudleston.

At Manchester, June 20. SUSSEX lost to LANCASHIRE by six wickets.

At Taunton, July 4. SUSSEX beat SOMERSET by 105 runs.

At Llanelli, July 11. SUSSEX lost to GLAMORGAN by 50 runs.

SUSSEX v KENT

At Hove, July 18. No result. Toss: Kent.

Rain, having earlier delayed the start and reduced the match to 48 overs, returned to en
play. Llong's best Sunday return had led to a Sussex collapse from 116 for two to 177 all ou

Sussex

D. M. Smith run out	8	I. D. K. Salisbury c Ward b Llong	....
M. P. Speight c Marsh b Ealham	32	A. C. S. Pigott c Hooper b McCague	....
C. W. J. Athey c Llong b Hooper	42	E. S. H. Giddins c McCague b Fleming	
*A. P. Wells c Marsh b Hooper	33	L-b 4, w 3, n-b 2	
J. A. North c Headley b Llong	20		
F. D. Stephenson c Hooper b Llong	2	1/34 2/48 3/116	(46.3 overs) 1?
†P. Moores b Llong	0	4/131 5/134 6/134	
B. T. P. Donelan not out	17	7/151 8/160 9/173	

Bowling: McCague 10-0-54-1; Ealham 6-1-31-1; Headley 8-1-30-0; Flemin
3.3-0-12-1; Hooper 10-2-22-2; Llong 9-1-24-4.

Kent

T. R. Ward not out	3
M. V. Fleming not out	0

(no wkt, 1.1 overs) 3

C. L. Hooper, N. J. Llong, *M. R. Benson, N. R. Taylor, G. R. Cowdrey, M. A. Ealhar
D. W. Headley, †S. A. Marsh and M. J. McCague did not bat.

Bowling: Stephenson 1-0-1-0; Giddins 0.1-0-2-0.

Umpires: R. Palmer and A. G. T. Whitehead.

At Derby, July 25. SUSSEX lost to DERBYSHIRE by 81 runs.

At Durham University, August 1. SUSSEX beat DURHAM by two wickets.

SUSSEX v WORCESTERSHIRE

At Hove, August 8. Sussex won by 29 runs. Toss: Sussex.

The Sussex innings came to a sudden end when Illingworth took the last three wicke
with a hat-trick – the first for Worcestershire in one-day cricket. Hick raced along in rep
before falling to a superb catch on the boundary by Lenham.

Sussex

D. M. Smith lbw b Newport	3	I. D. K. Salisbury not out	....
M. P. Speight lbw b Haynes	32	A. C. S. Pigott b Illingworth	....
C. W. J. Athey c and b Weston	64	E. S. H. Giddins lbw b Illingworth	....
*A. P. Wells c Lampitt b Tolley	86	L-b 4, w 3	
F. D. Stephenson run out	6		
K. Greenfield c Curtis b Tolley	14	1/20 2/40 3/165	(48.4 overs) 2
†P. Moores b Illingworth	34	4/181 5/198 6/240	
N. J. Lenham st Rhodes b Illingworth	9	7/250 8/261 9/261	

Bowling: Newport 9–0–39–1; Haynes 10–1–42–1; Weston 10–0–49–1; Lampitt 6–0–35–0; Illingworth 5.4–0–37–4; Tolley 8–0–55–2.

Worcestershire

*T. S. Curtis c Smith b Pigott	30	S. R. Lampitt b Stephenson	2
D. B. D'Oliveira c Salisbury		R. K. Illingworth b Greenfield	22
b Stephenson	11	C. M. Tolley not out	5
G. A. Hick c Lenham b Giddins	66	P. J. Newport b Giddins	3
D. A. Leatherdale c Greenfield		B 4, l-b 2, w 8	14
b Salisbury	13		
†S. J. Rhodes lbw b Greenfield	24	1/27 2/72 3/89	(48.3 overs) 232
M. J. Weston c Wells b Stephenson	35	4/144 5/158 6/170	
G. R. Haynes b Greenfield	7	7/173 8/216 9/226	

Bowling: Stephenson 10–1–36–3; Giddins 9.3–0–46–2; Lenham 5–0–37–0; Pigott 10–0–39–1; Salisbury 4–0–24–1; Greenfield 10–1–44–3.

Umpires: G. A. Stickley and P. B. Wight.

SUSSEX v NOTTINGHAMSHIRE

At Eastbourne, August 15. Sussex won by 94 runs. Toss: Nottinghamshire.

Speight helped put the game out of Nottinghamshire's reach by hitting 12 fours in an explosive 57 off 42 balls, as Sussex swept to 118 in the first 15 overs. Nottinghamshire were pegged down by tight bowling from Giddins and Stephenson.

Sussex

D. M. Smith b Afford	25	†P. Moores not out	19
M. P. Speight c French b Mike	57	I. D. K. Salisbury run out	10
F. D. Stephenson c Pick b Mike	35	E. S. H. Giddins run out	1
C. W. J. Athey c Pick b Bates	6	L-b 6, w 12, n-b 4	22
*A. P. Wells c Crawley b Bates	24		
K. Greenfield c Pollard b Crawley	35	1/77 2/123 3/134	(48.3 overs) 262
N. J. Lenham c French b Crawley	28	4/138 5/180 6/216	
J. A. North c French b Mike	0	7/218 8/232 9/253	

Bowling: Lewis 5.3–0–46–0; Pick 10–1–57–0; Mike 9–0–55–3; Bates 10–0–38–2; Afford 4–0–10–1; Crawley 10–0–50–2.

Nottinghamshire

P. R. Pollard c Moores b Stephenson	2	R. T. Bates c Moores b Salisbury	1
P. Johnson lbw b Giddins	1	R. A. Pick not out	11
*R. T. Robinson c Wells b Salisbury	51	J. A. Afford c Athey b North	1
C. L. Cairns b Giddins	4	L-b 12, w 7	19
C. C. Lewis c Lenham b Stephenson	14		
M. A. Crawley c Moores b Salisbury	22	1/3 2/3 3/7	(45.1 overs) 168
G. W. Mike c Moores b Lenham	9	4/34 5/69 6/90	
†B. N. French c and b Greenfield	33	7/137 8/140 9/164	

Bowling: Giddins 8–3–16–2; Stephenson 7–2–17–2; Lenham 10–0–54–1; Salisbury 10–0–30–3; Greenfield 10–0–39–1; North 0.1–0–0–1.

Umpires: D. R. Shepherd and A. G. T. Whitehead.

At Portsmouth, August 29. SUSSEX lost to HAMPSHIRE by eight wickets.

SUSSEX v ESSEX

At Hove, September 7. Sussex won on scoring-rate, Essex's target having been revised to 256 from 44 overs. First-team debut: K. Newell.

The match was played on Tuesday because Sussex had been in the NatWest final at the weekend. Essex were set a rain-revised target. They seemed well set at 200 for four but then lost four wickets for no runs. They were undone by Franklyn Stephenson, whose best one-day figures included a spell of three wickets in an over.

Sussex

D. M. Smith b Andrew	51	C. C. Remy c Knight b Ilott		19
F. D. Stephenson c Topley b Andrew	16			
M. P. Speight b Andrew	24	L-b 15, w 6, n-b 16		37
*A. P. Wells lbw b Such	39			
C. W. J. Athey c Rollins b Stephenson	15	1/57 2/92 3/145	(7 wkts, 50 overs)	290
K. Greenfield not out	65	4/163 5/219		
†P. Moores run out	24	6/236 7/290		

K. Newell, I. D. K. Salisbury and E. S. H. Giddins did not bat.

Bowling: Andrew 10–0–56–3; Ilott 10–0–72–1; Topley 10–1–54–0; Stephenson 10–0–58–1; Such 10–1–35–1.

Essex

P. J. Prichard c Remy b Giddins	18	M. C. Ilott b Stephenson		0
J. P. Stephenson c Moores b Stephenson	20	P. M. Such run out		19
N. Shahid c Giddins b Remy	64	S. J. W. Andrew b Stephenson		0
*G. A. Gooch b Salisbury	58	L-b 1, w 1, n-b 8		10
N. V. Knight not out	25			
J. J. B. Lewis b Stephenson	15	1/33 2/51 3/154	(40.3 overs)	229
†R. J. Rollins b Stephenson	0	4/177 5/200 6/200		
T. D. Topley run out	0	7/200 8/200 9/227		

Bowling: Stephenson 9.3–1–23–5; Giddins 8–0–53–1; Remy 10–1–44–1; Newell 6–0–44–0; Greenfield 1–0–20–0; Salisbury 6–0–44–1.

Umpires: D. J. Constant and B. Dudleston.

At Scarborough, September 12. SUSSEX lost to YORKSHIRE by 21 runs.

SUSSEX v GLOUCESTERSHIRE

At Hove, September 19. Sussex won by 32 runs. Toss: Gloucestershire.

Stephenson made a significant all-round contribution to a victory which saw Sussex hold fourth place in the League. He opened both batting and bowling for 81 and three wickets. Stephenson finished the season with 31 Sunday League wickets, two more than the previous county record of 29, set by Garth le Roux in 1982. Alan Wells took his season's tally of runs to 738, also a county record; the previous best was 699 by Roger Knight in 1976.

Sussex

N. J. Lenham run out	12	I. D. K. Salisbury lbw b Walsh		13
F. D. Stephenson c and b Ball	81	E. E. Hemmings not out		4
M. P. Speight c Ball b Smith	12	E. S. H. Giddins b Walsh		0
*A. P. Wells run out	15	B 1, l-b 4, w 2, n-b 14		21
K. Greenfield run out	18			
C. W. J. Athey st Russell b Ball	0	1/24 2/48 3/91	(49.3 overs)	224
†P. Moores b Walsh	48	4/145 5/146 6/169		
C. C. Remy run out	0	7/172 8/213 9/224		

Bowling: Smith 10–1–52–1; Walsh 9.3–1–33–3; Williams 10–0–51–0; Alleyne 8–0–46–0; Ball 10–0–30–2; Hancock 2–0–7–0.

Gloucestershire

S. G. Hinks b Giddins	60	R. C. Williams b Giddins	4
A. J. Wright c Moores b Giddins	2	M. C. J. Ball not out	10
M. G. N. Windows b Stephenson	6	A. M. Smith b Giddins	3
M. W. Alleyne c Athey b Hemmings	8	L-b 9, w 1, n-b 2	12
T. H. C. Hancock c Speight b Salisbury	46		
R. J. Cunliffe c Hemmings b Stephenson	22	1/10 2/31 3/58	(47.1 overs) 192
†R. C. Russell c Giddins b Salisbury	3	4/124 5/141 6/149	
*C. A. Walsh b Stephenson	16	7/171 8/174 9/186	

Bowling: Stephenson 9–3–30–3; Giddins 8.1–1–36–4; Hemmings 10–0–44–1; Remy 6–1–28–0; Salisbury 10–1–28–2; Greenfield 4–0–17–0.

Umpires: K. E. Palmer and P. Willey.

WARWICKSHIRE

WARWICKSHIRE v DERBYSHIRE

At Birmingham, May 9. Warwickshire won by three wickets. Toss: Warwickshire. First-team debut: A. S. Rollins.

Warwickshire laboured longer over a target of 174 than they might have done, and came to the final two overs still needing 24. The afternoon began with Munton removing Barnett and Adams for no score, and Derbyshire did not manage a run until the eighth over. Bowler's 77 helped them to recover, but the later order fell foul of a curious "hat-trick": Rollins was dismissed by Small, Krikken by Reeve and Warner was run out off consecutive balls of one over, which Reeve completed after Small injured his wrist.

Derbyshire

*K. J. Barnett c Burns b Munton	0	A. E. Warner run out	0
P. D. Bowler b Reeve	77	S. J. Base not out	6
C. J. Adams c Penney b Munton	0	D. E. Malcolm not out	7
T. J. G. O'Gorman c Reeve b Small	15		
F. A. Griffith c Burns b Small	1	B 5, l-b 3, w 4, n-b 4	16
D. G. Cork c Small b P. A. Smith	26		
A. S. Rollins c Twose b Small	18	1/0 2/0 3/38	(9 wkts, 49 overs) 173
†K. M. Krikken c N. M. K. Smith b Reeve	7	4/44 5/92 6/139	
		7/160 8/160 9/160	

Bowling: Munton 10–5–32–2; Reeve 6.3–3–23–2; Donald 10–1–30–0; Small 8.3–1–27–3; N. M. K. Smith 7–0–22–0; P. A. Smith 7–0–31–1.

Warwickshire

A. J. Moles c Griffith b Cork	28	N. M. K. Smith not out	7
R. G. Twose c Adams b Cork	65	G. C. Small not out	4
P. A. Smith c Krikken b Base	7	B 1, l-b 4, w 5, n-b 2	12
D. P. Ostler c Krikken b Griffith	3		
T. L. Penney c Barnett b Griffith	23	1/62 2/71 3/77	(7 wkts, 48.5 overs) 174
*D. A. Reeve c Base b Griffith	3	4/127 5/135	
†M. Burns c Bowler b Warner	22	6/150 7/163	

A. A. Donald and T. A. Munton did not bat.

Bowling: Malcolm 10–3–15–0; Warner 9–1–48–1; Cork 9.5–0–34–2; Base 10–0–35–1; Griffith 10–0–37–3.

Umpires: J. C. Balderstone and G. I. Burgess.

At Canterbury, May 16. WARWICKSHIRE lost to KENT by 66 runs.

At Manchester, May 30. LANCASHIRE v WARWICKSHIRE. No result.

WARWICKSHIRE v SUSSEX

At Birmingham, June 6. Sussex won by two wickets. Toss: Warwickshire.

Sussex remained unbeaten despite needing all but one of their overs to reach an insignificant target.

Warwickshire

A. J. Moles b Stephenson	7	G. C. Small c Moores b Pigott	6
J. D. Ratcliffe c Moores b Jones	25	A. A. Donald b Donelan	1
R. G. Twose run out	5	T. A. Munton not out	2
D. P. Ostler b Jones	13	B 2, l-b 10, w 3, n-b 4	19
T. L. Penney lbw b Jones	2		
*D. A. Reeve b Giddins	38	1/20 2/39 3/45	(47.1 overs) 133
†M. Burns c Moores b Jones	0	4/63 5/67 6/67	
N. M. K. Smith b Pigott	15	7/103 8/115 9/116	

Bowling: Stephenson 9–2–18–1; Giddins 7.1–1–19–1; Jones 10–2–24–4; Pigott 10–2–21–2; Donelan 8–1–25–1; Athey 3–0–14–0.

Sussex

D. M. Smith lbw b Small	23	A. C. S. Pigott c Moles b Reeve	6
F. D. Stephenson c Burns b Small	17	A. N. Jones not out	5
C. W. J. Athey b Munton	2		
*A. P. Wells run out	31	B 4, l-b 10, w 8, n-b 4	26
K. Greenfield lbw b Munton	0		
†P. Moores c Reeve b Munton	3	1/50 2/53 3/53	(8 wkts, 49 overs) 134
J. W. Hall lbw b Smith	10	4/54 5/68 6/84	
B. T. P. Donelan not out	11	7/109 8/122	

E. S. H. Giddins did not bat.

Bowling: Donald 10–2–33–0; Small 10–1–28–2; Munton 10–6–11–3; Reeve 10–3–26–1; Smith 9–2–22–1.

Umpires: J. H. Hampshire and R. A. White.

WARWICKSHIRE v SURREY

At Birmingham, June 20. Surrey won by 18 runs. Toss: Surrey.

Warwickshire were 150 for three, needing 45 from seven overs. But once Waqar Younis removed Paul Smith, who had added 92 with Penney, the remaining six wickets swiftly followed, three of them falling in four balls to Martin Bicknell. Surrey's highest score was 33 from Andrew Smith in his first Sunday League appearance.

Surrey

D. J. Bicknell b Donald	20	Waqar Younis not out	4
A. D. Brown lbw b Small	26	J. Boiling run out	3
G. P. Thorpe c and b N. M. K. Smith	30	J. E. Benjamin c Ratcliffe	
*M. A. Lynch c Holloway b Small	2	b N. M. K. Smith	0
D. M. Ward c Ratcliffe			
b N. M. K. Smith	26	B 9, l-b 9, w 14	32
A. W. Smith c Holloway b Donald	33		
†G. J. Kersey lbw b P. A. Smith	14	1/49 2/49 3/51	(48.5 overs) 194
M. P. Bicknell c Munton		4/111 5/123 6/167	
b N. M. K. Smith	4	7/181 8/184 9/193	

Bowling: Donald 10–0–27–2; Munton 9–1–46–0; Small 10–1–27–2; P. A. Smith 10–0–55–1; N. M. K. Smith 9.5–1–21–4.

Warwickshire

A. J. Moles run out	10	G. C. Small c Kersey b M. P. Bicknell	0
J. D. Ratcliffe b Boiling	24	A. A. Donald c and b Waqar Younis	0
D. P. Ostler b Boiling	17	*T. A. Munton not out	3
P. A. Smith c Thorpe b Waqar Younis	49		
T. L. Penney c Ward b Thorpe	41	L-b 5, w 6, n-b 2	13
R. G. Twose c Kersey b M. P. Bicknell	14		
†P. C. L. Holloway lbw b M. P. Bicknell	1	1/23 2/51 3/58	(48.5 overs) 176
N. M. K. Smith c Kersey		4/150 5/151 6/160	
b M. P. Bicknell	4	7/164 8/165 9/170	

Bowling: M. P. Bicknell 9.5–2–19–4; Benjamin 10–0–39–0; Waqar Younis 10–1–34–2; Boiling 10–0–40–2; Thorpe 9–0–39–1.

Umpires: J. H. Harris and P. Willey.

At Ilford, June 27. WARWICKSHIRE beat ESSEX by 46 runs.

WARWICKSHIRE v YORKSHIRE

At Birmingham, July 4. Warwickshire won by eight wickets. Toss: Yorkshire.
Yorkshire's scoring-rate of 2.62 was the lowest yet in the League over a full 50 overs. Ostler easily steered Warwickshire to victory.

Yorkshire

D. Byas c Twose b P. A. Smith	18	D. Gough lbw b Donald	2
A. P. Grayson run out	3	R. D. Stemp not out	23
R. B. Richardson c Piper b P. A. Smith	23	M. A. Robinson not out	2
A. A. Metcalfe c Piper b Twose	12	L-b 5, w 6, n-b 2	13
†R. J. Blakey c and b P. A. Smith	7		
C. White b P. A. Smith	27	1/9 2/43 3/44	(9 wkts, 50 overs) 131
*P. W. Jarvis c Moles b N. M. K. Smith	1	4/63 5/78 6/82	
P. J. Hartley b Donald	0	7/84 8/92 9/126	

Bowling: Reeve 5–2–9–0; Munton 10–2–24–0; Donald 10–2–27–2; P. A. Smith 10–2–33–4; Twose 7–2–11–1; N. M. K. Smith 8–0–22–1.

Warwickshire

A. J. Moles b Robinson	7
Asif Din b Jarvis	0
D. P. Ostler not out	81
P. A. Smith not out	38
B 4, w 1, n-b 4	9

1/1 2/34   (2 wkts, 32.3 overs) 135

*D. A. Reeve, T. L. Penney, R. G. Twose, N. M. K. Smith, †K. J. Piper, A. A. Donald and T. A. Munton did not bat.

Bowling: Jarvis 7–1–23–1; Hartley 7.3–1–44–0; Gough 5–0–22–0; Robinson 6–2–11–1; White 4–0–9–0; Stemp 3–0–22–0.

Umpires: J. D. Bond and M. J. Kitchen.

WARWICKSHIRE v NORTHAMPTONSHIRE

At Birmingham, July 11. Warwickshire won by eight wickets, their target having been revised to 180 from 43 overs. Toss: Warwickshire.
Rain intervened twice, lopping three overs off Northamptonshire's innings and then interrupting Warwickshire's reply. They sped to their reduced target thanks to an unbroken partnership of 132 between Ostler and Paul Smith.

Northamptonshire

A. Fordham lbw b Donald	33	†D. Ripley not out	16
M. B. Loye c Piper b Munton	1	C. E. L. Ambrose not out	2
R. J. Bailey b Reeve	69	B 2, l-b 5, w 4, n-b 4	15
*A. J. Lamb b Donald	0		
K. M. Curran c Piper b Donald	5	1/10　2/64　3/64　　(7 wkts, 47 overs) 196
N. A. Felton c Asif Din b Munton	32	4/73　5/145
A. L. Penberthy b Reeve	23	6/170　7/191

J. P. Taylor and A. Walker did not bat.

Bowling: Reeve 10–3–41–2; Munton 10–3–46–2; Donald 10–0–41–3; P. A. Smith 7–1–26–0; Twose 4–0–16–0; N. M. K. Smith 6–1–19–0.

Warwickshire

A. J. Moles c Loye b Walker	21
Asif Din c Ripley b Curran	19
D. P. Ostler not out	68
P. A. Smith not out	63
L-b 7, w 3, n-b 2	12

1/35　2/51　　　　(2 wkts, 40.1 overs) 183

*D. A. Reeve, T. L. Penney, R. G. Twose, N. M. K. Smith, †K. J. Piper, A. A. Donald and T. A. Munton did not bat.

Bowling: Ambrose 8–1–30–0; Taylor 9–2–28–0; Walker 9–1–39–1; Curran 9.1–0–50–1; Bailey 3–0–18–0; Penberthy 2–0–11–0.

Umpires: B. Leadbeater and K. E. Palmer.

WARWICKSHIRE v MIDDLESEX

At Birmingham, July 18. Middlesex won on scoring-rate when rain ended play. Toss: Middlesex.

Persistent heavy rain denied Warwickshire the chance to attempt nine runs off the last over with two wickets in hand. Earlier, batsmen had prospered. Haynes made his highest Sunday League score of 142 not out off 167 balls and put on 175 for the first wicket with Roseberry. After Moles had gone for no score, Ostler hit his fourth consecutive Sunday fifty.

Middlesex

D. L. Haynes not out	142
M. A. Roseberry c Ostler b Donald	66
M. R. Ramprakash b N. M. K. Smith	8
J. D. Carr not out	16
B 8, l-b 7, w 6, n-b 8	29

1/175　2/211　　　　(2 wkts, 50 overs) 261

*M. W. Gatting, †K. R. Brown, P. N. Weekes, J. E. Emburey, A. R. C. Fraser, N. G Cowans and R. L. Johnson did not bat.

Bowling: Reeve 7–0–43–0; Twose 4–0–20–0; Donald 10–1–46–1; P. A. Smith 9–1–40–0; N. M. K. Smith 10–0–49–1; Booth 10–0–48–0.

Warwickshire

A. J. Moles c Brown b Fraser	0	†K. J. Piper b Cowans	0
Asif Din c Carr b Weekes	94	P. A. Booth not out	0
D. P. Ostler c Emburey b Weekes	83		
P. A. Smith c Carr b Weekes	7		
*D. A. Reeve c Carr b Johnson	20	L-b 5, w 4, n-b 6	15
R. G. Twose lbw b Weekes	0		
T. L. Penney not out	27	1/0 2/161 3/171 (8 wkts, 49 overs) 253	
N. M. K. Smith c Ramprakash		4/216 5/216 6/220	
b Cowans	7	7/233 8/236	

A. A. Donald did not bat.

Bowling: Fraser 10–2–36–1; Cowans 10–2–58–2; Emburey 9–0–43–0; Johnson 10–0–62–1; Weekes 10–0–49–4.

Umpires: K. E. Palmer and P. B. Wight.

At Leicester, July 25. WARWICKSHIRE beat LEICESTERSHIRE by four wickets.

At Southampton, August 1. WARWICKSHIRE lost to HAMPSHIRE by nine wickets.

At Neath, August 8. WARWICKSHIRE lost to GLAMORGAN by four wickets.

WARWICKSHIRE v GLOUCESTERSHIRE

At Birmingham, August 15. Gloucestershire won by 11 runs. Toss: Warwickshire.
Gloucestershire squeezed home with two balls to spare, despite Neil Smith's fifty from 36 balls, including three sixes. The unbroken half-century partnership in seven overs between Alleyne and Russell proved decisive.

Gloucestershire

B. C. Broad c Penney b Twose	36	†R. C. Russell not out	34
G. D. Hodgson b Munton	20		
S. G. Hinks b N. M. K. Smith	42		
M. W. Alleyne not out	52	L-b 8, w 6, n-b 4	18
R. J. Scott c Burns b Twose	2		
T. H. C. Hancock c N. M. K. Smith		1/39 2/106 3/113 (5 wkts, 50 overs) 232	
b Brown	28	4/122 5/181	

*C. A. Walsh, M. Davies, A. M. Smith and A. M. Babington did not bat.

Bowling: Munton 10–4–29–1; Brown 10–1–37–1; P. A. Smith 10–0–47–0; Twose 10–0–50–2; N. M. K. Smith 10–1–61–1.

Warwickshire

*J. D. Ratcliffe run out	22	†M. Burns b Smith	1
Asif Din c sub b Walsh	6	D. R. Brown not out	8
D. P. Ostler c Russell b Babington	0	T. A. Munton run out	10
P. A. Smith c Hinks b Davies	50	B 1, l-b 2, w 2, n-b 2	7
A. J. Moles b Alleyne	26		
R. G. Twose b Babington	10	1/10 2/15 3/34 (49.4 overs) 221	
T. L. Penney b Walsh	27	4/104 5/104 6/119	
N. M. K. Smith c Scott b Smith	54	7/197 8/202 9/206	

Bowling: Babington 10–0–33–2; Walsh 9.4–4–21–2; Smith 10–0–54–2; Scott 5–0–17–0; Alleyne 10–0–55–1; Davies 5–0–38–1.

Umpires: B. Leadbeater and R. Palmer.

At Darlington, August 22. WARWICKSHIRE lost to DURHAM by two wickets.

WARWICKSHIRE v WORCESTERSHIRE

At Birmingham, August 29. Warwickshire won by 44 runs. Toss: Warwickshire.

Paul Smith bowled Warwickshire to victory on a slow pitch with his best return in the Sunday League.

Warwickshire

A. J. Moles run out	6	N. M. K. Smith c Haynes b Radford	0
J. D. Ratcliffe lbw b Haynes	5	†K. J. Piper not out	10
D. P. Ostler c Haynes b Radford	43	L-b 8, w 8, n-b 2	18
P. A. Smith lbw b Haynes	11		
Asif Din c Rhodes b Radford	42	1/14 2/16 3/78	(7 wkts, 50 overs) 188
*D. A. Reeve b Illingworth	21	4/106 5/144	
R. G. Twose not out	32	6/144 7/148	

D. R. Brown and T. A. Munton did not bat.

Bowling: Newport 10–5–24–0; Haynes 10–1–21–2; Illingworth 10–0–45–1; Lampitt 10–1–48–0; Radford 10–1–42–3.

Worcestershire

*T. S. Curtis lbw b P. A. Smith	16	P. J. Newport b Twose	9
D. B. D'Oliveira c Piper b Munton	5	R. K. Illingworth not out	4
G. A. Hick c Ostler b P. A. Smith	17	N. V. Radford c and b Reeve	0
G. R. Haynes c N. M. K. Smith b Twose	28	B 2, l-b 4, w 3, n-b 10	19
D. A. Leatherdale lbw b P. A. Smith	5		
†S. J. Rhodes b P. A. Smith	4	1/12 2/38 3/47	(46.3 overs) 144
M. J. Weston c and b Twose	18	4/55 5/66 6/92	
S. R. Lampitt c Ostler b P. A. Smith	19	7/122 8/134 9/144	

Bowling: Reeve 5.3–1–12–1; Munton 8–3–11–1; Brown 8–1–23–0; P. A. Smith 10–0–36–5; Twose 10–1–35–3; N. M. K. Smith 5–1–21–0.

Umpires: J. W. Holder and G. Sharp.

WARWICKSHIRE v SOMERSET

At Birmingham, September 12. No result. Toss: Somerset.

Rain thwarted Somerset's chances of escaping from the bottom of the table.

Somerset

M. N. Lathwell c Reeve b Munton	32	†R. J. Turner c Twose b Brown	14
I. Fletcher run out	0	N. A. Mallender not out	5
N. A. Folland c and b N. M. K. Smith	27	L-b 4, w 1, n-b 2	7
*R. J. Harden not out	41		
G. D. Rose run out	4	1/2 2/49 3/75	(6 wkts, 40 overs) 133
Mushtaq Ahmed c Ostler b N. M. K. Smith	3	4/83 5/86 6/122	

A. R. Caddick, H. R. J. Trump and A. P. van Troost did not bat.

Bowling: Munton 10–3–17–1; Brown 5–0–25–1; Bell 6–0–36–0; N. M. K. Smith 10–0–26–2; P. A. Smith 8–1–23–0; Twose 1–0–2–0.

Warwickshire

Asif Din, †M. Burns, D. P. Ostler, P. A. Smith, *D. A. Reeve, R. G. Twose, T. L. Penney, N. M. K. Smith, D. R. Brown, M. A. V. Bell and T. A. Munton.

Umpires: B. J. Meyer and G. A. Stickley.

At Nottingham, September 19. WARWICKSHIRE beat NOTTINGHAMSHIRE by 160 runs.

WORCESTERSHIRE

At Leeds, May 16. YORKSHIRE v WORCESTERSHIRE. No result.

WORCESTERSHIRE v SOMERSET

At Worcester, May 23. Worcestershire won by four wickets. Toss: Worcestershire.

Both teams found batting a trial on a grudging pitch. Somerset did not even reach three figures, and were dismissed with nearly 15 overs left. But Worcestershire lost their first five wickets for 54, before Rhodes came in to make the highest innings of the game, an unbeaten 24.

Somerset

A. N. Hayhurst c Seymour b Lampitt ..	10	A. Payne not out	10
N. A. Folland c D'Oliveira b Radford..	11	J. I. D. Kerr c and b Newport........	7
R. J. Harden c Leatherdale b Lampitt..	6	A. P. van Troost c Rhodes b Tolley....	8
*C. J. Tavaré c D'Oliveira b Lampitt ..	1		
†N. D. Burns c Rhodes b Radford.....	5	L-b 5, w 8, n-b 8............	21
G. D. Rose c D'Oliveira b Newport ...	14		
K. A. Parsons lbw b Radford.........	0	1/25 2/36 3/36	(35.1 overs) 99
Mushtaq Ahmed c M. J. Weston		4/39 5/51 6/51	
b D'Oliveira .	6	7/62 8/74 9/87	

Bowling: Radford 10–2–25–3; Tolley 3.1–0–11–1; Lampitt 6–2–12–3; D'Oliveira 8–0–27–1; Newport 8–2–19–2.

Worcestershire

*T. S. Curtis c Tavaré b Kerr	12	†S. J. Rhodes not out	24
W. P. C. Weston lbw b Kerr	22	N. V. Radford not out..............	1
A. C. H. Seymour lbw b Rose	2		
D. B. D'Oliveira c Tavaré		L-b 6, w 3, n-b 10..........	19
b Mushtaq Ahmed .	5		
M. J. Weston b Mushtaq Ahmed......	3	1/21 2/24 3/49	(6 wkts, 41.4 overs) 100
S. R. Lampitt c Burns b van Troost...	12	4/54 5/54 6/92	

D. A. Leatherdale, P. J. Newport and C. M. Tolley did not bat.

Bowling: van Troost 9.4–0–36–1; Kerr 6–2–13–2; Rose 10–3–18–1; Mushtaq Ahmed 10–3–17–2; Payne 6–2–10–0.

Umpires: J. H. Harris and G. Sharp.

At Gloucester, May 30. WORCESTERSHIRE beat GLOUCESTERSHIRE by 15 runs.

At Northampton, June 6. WORCESTERSHIRE tied with NORTHAMPTONSHIRE.

WORCESTERSHIRE v LEICESTERSHIRE

At Worcester, June 13. Leicestershire won by four runs. Toss: Worcestershire.

Another dead slow New Road pitch kept the batsmen struggling. Worcestershire made little headway chasing a mere 179 until their ninth-wicket pair, Lampitt and Illingworth, smashed 51 in their 8.4 overs together. They needed 18 off the last over and only narrowly failed.

Leicestershire

J. D. R. Benson c Leatherdale		
b Benjamin .	31	
*N. E. Briers c Curtis b Radford	5	
T. J. Boon run out	66	
J. J. Whitaker c Illingworth b Radford .	1	
B. F. Smith c D'Oliveira b Radford . . .	5	
L. Potter c Leatherdale b Illingworth . .	26	
W. K. M. Benjamin run out	16	
†P. A. Nixon lbw b Tolley	19	

V. J. Wells lbw b Benjamin	0
G. J. Parsons b Radford	0
A. D. Mullally not out	2
L-b 1, w 2, n-b 4	7
	(46.1 overs) 178
1/32 2/43 3/48	
4/57 5/123 6/146	
7/173 8/176 9/176	

Bowling: Benjamin 8.1–2–15–2; Tolley 10–0–61–1; Radford 9–0–26–4; Lampitt 9–0–36–0; Illingworth 10–1–39–1.

Worcestershire

*T. S. Curtis b Parsons	12	
W. P. C. Weston c Potter b Mullally . . .	5	
G. A. Hick b Mullally	11	
D. B. D'Oliveira b Potter	30	
D. A. Leatherdale c Wells b Potter . . .	1	
†S. J. Rhodes lbw b Potter	20	
S. R. Lampitt not out	41	
N. V. Radford b Parsons	7	

K. C. G. Benjamin b Parsons	1
R. K. Illingworth b Wells	30
C. M. Tolley not out	2
B 3, l-b 8, w 1, n-b 2	14
	(9 wkts, 50 overs) 174
1/10 2/26 3/44	
4/54 5/75 6/94	
7/107 8/109 9/160	

Bowling: Benjamin 10–1–41–0; Mullally 10–3–30–2; Parsons 10–1–32–3; Wells 10–0–30–1; Potter 10–1–30–3.

Umpires: R. Julian and R. A. White.

At Stockton-on-Tees, June 27. WORCESTERSHIRE lost to DURHAM by five runs.

WORCESTERSHIRE v DERBYSHIRE

At Worcester, July 4. Derbyshire won by five wickets. Toss: Worcestershire.

Derbyshire bowled tightly to keep Worcestershire down to 190. Adams scored his fifth Sunday fifty of the season to set up Derbyshire's reply, and Barnett steered them home in the final over.

Worcestershire

*T. S. Curtis c Krikken b Mortensen . .	8	
N. V. Radford c Mortensen b Base	17	
G. A. Hick lbw b Base	30	
W. P. C. Weston c Base b Griffith . . .	9	
D. B. D'Oliveira c Base b Warner	27	
D. A. Leatherdale run out	28	
†S. J. Rhodes b Mortensen	8	
S. R. Lampitt not out	17	

C. M. Tolley b Warner	0
P. J. Newport run out	7
R. K. Illingworth not out	14
B 9, l-b 12, w 4	25
	(9 wkts, 50 overs) 190
1/15 2/48 3/70	
4/81 5/139 6/145	
7/150 8/151 9/165	

Bowling: Mortensen 10–2–24–2; Cork 10–0–53–0; Warner 10–2–23–2; Base 10–0–30–2; Griffith 10–0–39–1.

Derbyshire

P. D. Bowler lbw b Illingworth	14	
C. J. Adams st Rhodes b Illingworth . .	63	
J. E. Morris b Illingworth	4	
T. J. G. O'Gorman c Lampitt		
b Newport .	27	
F. A. Griffith st Rhodes b Hick	20	

*K. J. Barnett not out	34
†K. M. Krikken not out	20
B 2, l-b 3, w 3, n-b 4	12
	(5 wkts, 49.3 overs) 194
1/74 2/80 3/93	
4/138 5/138	

D. G. Cork, O. H. Mortensen, A. E. Warner and S. J. Base did not bat.

Bowling: Radford 8–1–37–0; Tolley 9.3–0–45–0; Newport 7–1–29–1; Lampitt 5–0–16–0; Illingworth 10–0–29–3; Hick 10–1–33–1.

Umpires: G. A. Stickley and A. G. T. Whitehead.

At Nottingham, July 11. WORCESTERSHIRE lost to NOTTINGHAMSHIRE by four wickets.

At Portsmouth, July 18. HAMPSHIRE v WORCESTERSHIRE. No result.

WORCESTERSHIRE v GLAMORGAN

At Worcester, July 25. Glamorgan won by 27 runs. Toss: Glamorgan.

Richards dominated this match between the counties who were to meet two days later in the NatWest quarter-finals. First he hit a rapid 63, including four consecutive fours as he took 19 off the penultimate over, bowled by Radford. He ran out Hick as both openers went in the third over, and rounded off his day with two wickets and a brilliant running catch to dismiss Newport. Dale and Morris had put on 150 for Glamorgan's first wicket and Worcestershire were never up with the required rate.

Glamorgan

A. Dale run out	57	R. P. Lefebvre not out		4
*H. Morris c Rhodes b Weston	87	†C. P. Metson not out		0
M. P. Maynard c Rhodes b Hick	0	L-b 4, w 9, n-b 2		15
I. V. A. Richards c Curtis b Lampitt	63			
P. A. Cottey c Rhodes b Hick	5	1/150 2/152 3/171	(7 wkts, 50 overs)	259
D. L. Hemp c Tolley b Newport	12	4/186 5/210		
R. D. B. Croft c Leatherdale b Lampitt	16	6/255 7/255		

S. L. Watkin and S. R. Barwick did not bat.

Bowling: Newport 10–1–37–1; Tolley 8–0–41–0; Lampitt 4–0–25–2; Radford 5–0–38–0; Illingworth 10–0–51–0; Hick 10–0–49–2; Weston 3–0–14–1.

Worcestershire

G. A. Hick run out	5	P. J. Newport c Richards b Watkin		3
N. V. Radford c Metson b Lefebvre	6	R. K. Illingworth not out		13
*T. S. Curtis c Dale b Richards	62	C. M. Tolley b Lefebvre		3
D. B. D'Oliveira st Metson b Croft	26	B 2, l-b 8, w 7		17
D. A. Leatherdale c Morris b Richards	38			
†S. J. Rhodes c Hemp b Lefebvre	37	1/12 2/12 3/75	(49.1 overs)	232
M. J. Weston run out	1	4/141 5/157 6/172		
S. R. Lampitt c Lefebvre b Watkin	21	7/200 8/205 9/221		

Bowling: Lefebvre 9.1–0–38–3; Watkin 10–1–33–2; Barwick 10–1–43–0; Croft 5–0–27–1; Dale 9–0–54–0; Richards 6–0–27–2.

Umpires: A. A. Jones and K. E. Palmer.

At Chelmsford, August 1. WORCESTERSHIRE beat ESSEX by four wickets.

At Hove, August 8. WORCESTERSHIRE lost to SUSSEX by 29 runs.

WORCESTERSHIRE v SURREY

At Worcester, August 15. Worcestershire won by 37 runs. Toss: Surrey.

Only Hick came to terms with the uneven bounce of the New Road pitch and, once he had gone, Worcestershire collapsed to 144 for nine. But they were helped by Lampitt and Newport, whose tenth-wicket partnership of 50 in 10.4 overs was a League record for Worcestershire. Surrey in turn subsided to 76 for six and could never catch up. Curtis, when four, reached 5,000 runs in the League in 140 innings – only three more than the record of 137 innings set by Glenn Turner, also of Worcestershire, in 1980.

Worcestershire

*T. S. Curtis c Stewart b Benjamin	8	R. K. Illingworth c Lynch	
D. B. D'Oliveira c Ward b Benjamin	9	b Waqar Younis	8
G. A. Hick c Lynch b Boiling	64	C. M. Tolley b Waqar Younis	0
G. R. Haynes b Murphy	32	P. J. Newport not out	26
D. A. Leatherdale c Lynch		L-b 6, w 7, n-b 2	15
b Hollioake	1		
†S. J. Rhodes c Stewart b Hollioake	0	1/11 2/32 3/115	(48.4 overs) 194
N. V. Radford lbw b Hollioake	3	4/117 5/121 6/125	
S. R. Lampitt lbw b Benjamin	28	7/129 8/144 9/144	

Bowling: Benjamin 9.4–0–40–3; Murphy 9–0–27–1; Waqar Younis 10–1–37–2; Hollioake 10–2–37–3; Boiling 10–1–47–1.

Surrey

D. J. Bicknell run out	18	J. Boiling not out	23
A. D. Brown c D'Oliveira b Newport	19	J. E. Benjamin c Curtis b Radford	12
G. P. Thorpe lbw b Haynes	8	A. J. Murphy b Illingworth	9
*†A. J. Stewart run out	7	L-b 9, w 8	17
D. M. Ward lbw b Radford	3		
M. A. Lynch c Rhodes b Lampitt	4	1/34 2/46 3/56	(44.1 overs) 157
A. J. Hollioake b Illingworth	16	4/59 5/63 6/76	
Waqar Younis c Rhodes b Radford	21	7/112 8/113 9/128	

Bowling: Newport 9–3–26–1; Haynes 10–1–39–1; Lampitt 7–2–8–1; Radford 10–1–39–3; Tolley 2–0–15–0; Illingworth 6.1–0–21–2.

Umpires: G. I. Burgess and K. E. Palmer.

WORCESTERSHIRE v KENT

At Worcester, August 22. Kent won on scoring-rate when rain ended play. Toss: Worcestershire.

Had Fleming not hit two off the last possible ball before the rain set in, Worcestershire would have won on scoring-rate. As it was, they were 0.04 behind with 3.72 as opposed to Kent's 3.76. Worcestershire lost four of their top five to Igglesden and batted at a funereal pace; they hit only six fours in all, a number passed by Kent within eight overs.

Worcestershire

*T. S. Curtis c Llong b Igglesden	6	P. J. Newport b Headley	14
D. B. D'Oliveira c Cowdrey b Igglesden	25	N. V. Radford b Headley	6
A. C. H. Seymour b Headley	20	R. K. Illingworth not out	3
G. R. Haynes c and b Igglesden	4	B 4, l-b 12, w 4, n-b 4	24
D. A. Leatherdale lbw b Igglesden	0		
†S. J. Rhodes c Cowdrey b Hooper	35	1/28 2/35 3/51	(9 wkts, 50 overs) 186
M. J. Weston b Igglesden	24	4/51 5/77 6/123	
S. R. Lampitt not out	23	7/129 8/161 9/175	

Bowling: Igglesden 10–1–29–5; Ealham 10–2–43–0; Fleming 10–0–25–0; Headley 10–0–47–3; Hooper 10–1–26–1.

Kent

T. R. Ward c D'Oliveira b Newport	... 27	M. V. Fleming not out	11
N. J. Llong c Rhodes b Haynes	6		
C. L. Hooper run out	47	L-b 11, w 2	13
N. R. Taylor lbw b Haynes	9		
J. I. Longley c Rhodes b Lampitt	20	1/8 2/46 3/65	(5 wkts, 38 overs) 143
G. R. Cowdrey not out	10	4/110 5/124	

*†S. A. Marsh, M. A. Ealham, D. W. Headley and A. P. Igglesden did not bat.

Bowling: Newport 8–1–34–1; Haynes 10–2–30–2; Radford 9–0–35–0; Lampitt 9–0–21–1; Illingworth 2–0–12–0.

Umpires: J. C. Balderstone and B. Leadbeater.

At Birmingham, August 29. WORCESTERSHIRE lost to WARWICKSHIRE by 44 runs.

WORCESTERSHIRE v LANCASHIRE

At Worcester, September 5. Lancashire won by six wickets. Toss: Worcestershire.
In another low-scoring match at New Road, only Fairbrother and Speak made fifties; they shared in a match-winning partnership of 118.

Worcestershire

*T. S. Curtis c Lloyd b Austin	4	P. J. Newport c Atherton b DeFreitas	0
W. P. C. Weston b Wasim Akram	26	R. K. Illingworth b Austin	25
G. A. Hick b Wasim Akram	35	C. M. Tolley not out	1
G. R. Haynes not out	41	B 4, l-b 16, w 5, n-b 10	35
A. C. H. Seymour run out	0		
D. A. Leatherdale c DeFreitas b Yates	18	1/5 2/71 3/95	(9 wkts, 50 overs) 188
†S. J. Rhodes c and b Yates	3	4/97 5/130 6/139	
S. R. Lampitt lbw b Yates	0	7/139 8/141 9/187	

Bowling: DeFreitas 10–2–26–1; Austin 10–0–42–2; Watkinson 10–1–25–0; Wasim Akram 10–0–48–2; Yates 10–0–27–3.

Lancashire

M. A. Atherton c Rhodes b Lampitt	... 25	Wasim Akram not out	0
G. D. Lloyd c Rhodes b Hick	35	B 1, l-b 4, w 7, n-b 4	16
J. P. Crawley b Hick	4		
*N. H. Fairbrother not out	56	1/52 2/68	(4 wkts, 49.2 overs) 191
N. J. Speak c Rhodes b Weston	55	3/69 4/187	

M. Watkinson, P. A. J. DeFreitas, I. D. Austin, †W. K. Hegg and G. Yates did not bat.

Bowling: Newport 10–2–35–0; Haynes 7–0–47–0; Lampitt 9.2–3–18–1; Tolley 4–1–17–0; Hick 8–0–26–2; Illingworth 10–1–41–0; Weston 1–0–2–1.

Umpires: A. A. Jones and P. Willey.

WORCESTERSHIRE v MIDDLESEX

At Worcester, September 19. Middlesex won by six wickets. Toss: Worcestershire. First-team debuts: V. S. Solanki, K. R. Spring; T. A. Radford.
Only two balls remained when Middlesex overtook Worcestershire, who thus equalled their worst record in the Sunday League with only four wins. Johnson recorded his first four-wicket return and Ramprakash scored his seventh Sunday League fifty of the season. Vikram Solanki, who made 22, was the youngest player ever to appear in the League for Worcestershire, aged 17 years and 171 days.

Worcestershire

W. P. C. Weston c Brown b Fraser	2	N. V. Radford c Brown b Johnson	22
K. R. Spiring c Gatting b Taylor	7	R. K. Illingworth run out	6
G. A. Hick c Tufnell b Johnson	17	P. J. Newport not out	0
G. R. Haynes b Weekes	48	L-b 2, w 7, n-b 2	11
V. S. Solanki c Taylor b Tufnell	22		
M. J. Weston c Brown b Johnson	42	1/5 2/15 3/35	(49.3 overs) 197
*†S. J. Rhodes c Fraser b Johnson	15	4/92 5/109 6/146	
S. R. Lampitt c Roseberry b Fraser	5	7/162 8/184 9/195	

Bowling: Fraser 10–2–31–2; Taylor 9.3–2–24–1; Johnson 10–0–66–4; Tufnell 10–0–34–1; Weekes 10–0–40–1.

Middlesex

M. A. Roseberry b Haynes	20	†K. R. Brown not out	23
T. A. Radford c and b Illingworth	38	B 2, l-b 5, w 7	14
M. R. Ramprakash c and b Illingworth	63		
P. N. Weekes st Rhodes b Hick	3	1/22 2/101	(4 wkts, 49.4 overs) 199
*J. D. Carr not out	38	3/128 4/147	

M. W. Gatting, C. W. Taylor, R. L. Johnson, A. R. C. Fraser and P. C. R. Tufnell did not bat.

Bowling: Haynes 10–2–32–1; Newport 10–1–35–0; Lampitt 5–0–29–0; Radford 7.4–0–36–0; Illingworth 10–0–26–2; Hick 4–0–17–1; M. J. Weston 3–0–17–0.

Umpires: J. D. Bond and M. J. Kitchen.

YORKSHIRE

At Chelmsford, May 9. YORKSHIRE lost to ESSEX by 22 runs.

YORKSHIRE v WORCESTERSHIRE

At Leeds, May 16. No result. Toss: Worcestershire.

Much of the match was played in drizzle. Worcestershire's innings was finally ended when they were well placed but three overs short of the minimum needed for a result.

Yorkshire

*M. D. Moxon c Lampitt b Newport	20	P. W. Jarvis not out	7
A. A. Metcalfe lbw b Newport	22	D. Gough not out	2
R. B. Richardson lbw b Illingworth	17	L-b 8, w 2, n-b 4	14
D. Byas c Seymour b Tolley	38		
†R. J. Blakey b Benjamin	43	1/46 2/63 3/71	(7 wkts, 50 overs) 187
C. White c Lampitt b Benjamin	20	4/122 5/168	
A. P. Grayson c Rhodes b Tolley	4	6/176 7/178	

M. A. Robinson and C. E. W. Silverwood did not bat.

Bowling: Benjamin 10–3–29–2; Tolley 10–0–50–2; Newport 10–0–38–2; Lampitt 10–1–48–0; Illingworth 10–3–14–1.

Worcestershire

*T. S. Curtis b Robinson	31
W. P. C. Weston not out	15
G. A. Hick not out	0
B 1, l-b 4, n-b 4	9

1/54   (1 wkt, 17 overs) 55

D. B. D'Oliveira, A. C. H. Seymour, S. R. Lampitt, †S. J. Rhodes, R. K. Illingworth, P. J. Newport, K. C. G. Benjamin and C. M. Tolley did not bat.

Bowling: Jarvis 5–1–9–0; Gough 5–1–14–0; Robinson 4–1–16–1; Silverwood 3–1–11–0.

Umpires: D. R. Shepherd and G. A. Stickley.

t Southampton, May 23. YORKSHIRE beat HAMPSHIRE by 30 runs.

YORKSHIRE v GLAMORGAN

t Middlesbrough, June 6. Glamorgan won by 25 runs. Toss: Glamorgan.

Glamorgan lifted themselves off the bottom of the table with their first Sunday win of 993 as Yorkshire collapsed. The margin might have been greater if Grayson had not been ropped off his first ball when Yorkshire were 67 for five; he remained to add 58 with lakey. Glamorgan's difficulties had come at the end of their innings, as they subsided from 4 for four.

Glamorgan

P. James c Metcalfe b Batty	51	†C. P. Metson not out	14
H. Morris c White b Robinson	21	S. R. Barwick b Gough	0
. Dale st Blakey b Batty	39	M. Frost not out	1
. P. Maynard c Jarvis b Batty	27	B 1, l-b 3, w 3, n-b 2	9
V. A. Richards b Jarvis	20		
. A. Cottey b Gough	24	1/34 2/106 3/126 (9 wkts, 50 overs) 208	
. D. B. Croft c Blakey b Jarvis	0	4/159 5/184 6/184	
. P. Lefebvre lbw b Robinson	2	7/187 8/207 9/207	

Bowling: Jarvis 10–1–28–2; Gough 9–1–53–2; Robinson 10–1–36–2; White 7–0–29–0; Grayson 4–0–17–0; Batty 10–0–41–3.

Yorkshire

M. D. Moxon c Lefebvre b Frost	6	D. Gough lbw b Richards	6
. A. Metcalfe c James b Barwick	16	J. D. Batty b Lefebvre	3
. B. Richardson c Lefebvre b Barwick	20	M. A. Robinson b Lefebvre	1
). Byas c Morris b Barwick	6	L-b 6, w 7	13
R. J. Blakey b Richards	44		
. White c Morris b Barwick	8	1/9 2/45 3/54 (48.5 overs) 183	
. P. Grayson c Morris b Richards	22	4/55 5/67 6/125	
. W. Jarvis not out	38	7/136 8/168 9/173	

Bowling: Frost 8–1–40–1; Lefebvre 9.5–3–28–2; Barwick 10–1–27–4; Croft 10–1–28–0; Dale 5–0–33–0; Richards 6–1–21–3.

Umpires: G. I. Burgess and G. Sharp.

At Chesterfield, June 13. YORKSHIRE beat DERBYSHIRE by nine wickets.

YORKSHIRE v GLOUCESTERSHIRE

At Sheffield, June 20. Gloucestershire won by seven wickets. Toss: Gloucestershire.

Yorkshire set Gloucestershire a target of only 3.34 an over and, though they lost three heap wickets, opener Broad and captain Wright saw them home with an unbroken fourth-wicket stand of 123.

Yorkshire

*M. D. Moxon lbw b Babington	0	A. P. Grayson c Hancock b Walsh . . . .
D. Byas run out	50	D. Gough not out . . . .
R. B. Richardson c Russell b Smith . . .	24	L-b 2, w 8, n-b 4 . . . .
A. A. Metcalfe b Scott	3	
†R. J. Blakey b Wight	31	1/4 2/39 3/53 (8 wkts, 50 overs) 1
C. White b Walsh	23	4/105 5/125 6/153
P. J. Hartley c Scott b Smith	11	7/161 8/166

J. D. Batty and C. E. W. Silverwood did not bat.

Bowling: Walsh 10–1–20–2; Babington 10–2–38–1; Smith 9–1–29–2; Scott 10–2–24– Alleyne 4–0–20–0; Wight 7–0–33–1.

Gloucestershire

B. C. Broad not out	75	*A. J. Wright not out . . . .
G. D. Hodgson b Gough	0	L-b 5, w 3, n-b 4 . . . .
M. W. Alleyne lbw b White	6	
T. H. C. Hancock lbw b White	1	1/9 2/30 3/44 (3 wkts, 48 overs) 1

R. J. Scott, †R. C. Russell, R. M. Wight, C. A. Walsh, A. M. Smith and A. M. Babingt did not bat.

Bowling: Gough 10–1–39–1; Hartley 10–2–30–0; White 10–1–21–2; Silverwood 4–1–19– Batty 10–1–40–0; Grayson 4–0–13–0.

Umpires: D. J. Constant and R. A. White.

YORKSHIRE v KENT

At Leeds, June 27. Kent won by eight runs. Toss: Kent.

Kent claimed undisputed leadership of the League table through their narrow win. Wa made 49 from 52 balls, including ten fours, most of them superbly driven. Most of the oth batsmen, on both sides, struggled to time the ball.

Kent

T. R. Ward c Richardson b Batty	49	M. A. Ealham not out . . . .
M. V. Fleming lbw b Gough	1	D. W. Headley c Foster b Hartley . . . . .
C. L. Hooper c Gough b Batty	32	M. J. McCague not out . . . .
N. R. Taylor c White b Stemp	35	L-b 3, w 5 . . . .
N. J. Llong c Moxon b Batty	4	
*M. R. Benson c Byas b White	20	1/6 2/67 3/92 (9 wkts, 50 overs) 2
G. R. Cowdrey run out	9	4/111 5/138 6/151
†S. A. Marsh run out	17	7/169 8/186 9/198

Bowling: Hartley 10–1–44–1; Gough 10–2–38–1; White 9–0–30–1; Foster 1–0–13–0; Ba 10–1–29–3; Stemp 10–0–43–1.

Yorkshire

*M. D. Moxon c Fleming b Hooper . . .	40	P. J. Hartley c Hooper b Fleming . . . . .
D. Byas b Headley	3	D. Gough not out . . . .
R. B. Richardson c Fleming b Hooper .	20	L-b 12, w 3 . . . .
A. A. Metcalfe c Hooper b McCague . .	45	
†R. J. Blakey not out	41	1/16 2/64 3/67 (7 wkts, 50 overs) 1
C. White c Llong b McCague	2	4/135 5/139
M. J. Foster run out	1	6/144 7/192

R. D. Stemp and J. D. Batty did not bat.

Bowling: McCague 10–1–29–2; Headley 10–2–29–1; Ealham 10–1–52–0; Hoop 10–1–23–2; Fleming 10–1–47–1.

Umpires: G. I. Burgess and B. Leadbeater.

At Birmingham, July 4. YORKSHIRE lost to WARWICKSHIRE by eight wickets.

YORKSHIRE v NORTHAMPTONSHIRE

At Leeds, July 18. Yorkshire won by nine wickets. Toss: Yorkshire.

Northamptonshire were put in trouble by their former bowler Robinson but recovered a little when Ripley and Cook came together in a ninth-wicket stand of 62. Inspired by the threat of rain, Moxon and Byas then launched a furious assault, with a stand of 165 from 31 overs. Moxon fell with just eight runs needed, but Yorkshire won two-thirds of the way through their allocation.

Northamptonshire

A. Fordham run out	17	J. P. Taylor b Gough	1
M. B. Loye lbw b Robinson	32	N. G. B. Cook run out	20
R. J. Bailey b Robinson	16	A. Walker not out	3
*A. J. Lamb lbw b Robinson	5	B 2, l-b 10, w 1, n-b 6	19
K. M. Curran c Blakey b Foster	0		
N. A. Felton c White b Batty	12	1/55 2/60 3/72	(9 wkts, 50 overs) 172
A. L. Penberthy lbw b Robinson	0	4/73 5/81 6/81	
†D. Ripley not out	47	7/104 8/106 9/168	

Bowling: Hartley 10-3-37-0; Gough 10-1-21-1; Robinson 10-2-23-4; White 7-1-31-0; Foster 9-1-33-1; Batty 4-0-15-1.

Yorkshire

*M. D. Moxon b Taylor	70
D. Byas not out	88
R. B. Richardson not out	5
L-b 5, w 5, n-b 2	12
1/165	(1 wkt, 33.4 overs) 175

A. P. Grayson, †R. J. Blakey, C. White, M. J. Foster, P. J. Hartley, D. Gough, J. D. Batty and M. A. Robinson did not bat.

Bowling: Taylor 9-2-33-1; Walker 8.4-2-36-0; Curran 5-0-28-0; Cook 5-1-21-0; Penberthy 3-0-31-0; Bailey 3-0-21-0.

Umpires: V. A. Holder and N. T. Plews.

At Taunton, August 1. YORKSHIRE beat SOMERSET by four wickets.

At Nottingham, August 8. YORKSHIRE beat NOTTINGHAMSHIRE by six wickets.

YORKSHIRE v MIDDLESEX

At Scarborough, August 15. Yorkshire won by 77 runs. Toss: Middlesex.

An unbroken partnership of 132 from 12 overs – including 92 off the last seven – between Richardson and Blakey proved decisive in a match reduced by rain to 37 overs a side. Richardson struck four sixes and Blakey, who faced only 38 balls, six. This was Yorkshire's fourth successive Sunday win.

Yorkshire

*M. D. Moxon c Roseberry		†R. J. Blakey not out.................	6
b Ramprakash .	50	L-b 1, w 9, n-b 6...........	1
D. Byas c Keech b Emburey	22		
R. B. Richardson not out	88	1/45 2/113 (2 wkts, 37 overs) 24

A. P. Grayson, C. White, M. J. Foster, P. J. Hartley, R. D. Stemp, D. Gough and M. A Robinson did not bat.

Bowling: Fraser 8–1–39–0; Feltham 7–0–57–0; Cowans 8–0–52–0; Emburey 7–1–50–1 Keech 3–0–16–0; Ramprakash 4–0–30–1.

Middlesex

D. L. Haynes b Stemp.............	60	M. Keech st Blakey b Stemp	
M. A. Roseberry lbw b Gough........	2	A. R. C. Fraser b White.............	1
M. R. Ramprakash c Moxon b Hartley .	0	N. G. Cowans b White	
J. D. Carr c Blakey b Robinson.......	13	B 5, l-b 5, w 2, n-b 4	1
*M. W. Gatting c Richardson b Stemp .	14		
†K. R. Brown c Blakey b Robinson ..	13	1/20 2/21 3/51 (32.3 overs)
J. E. Emburey not out	36	4/81 5/103 6/120	
M. A. Feltham c White b Robinson ..	2	7/123 8/127 9/168	

Bowling: Hartley 6–1–22–1; Gough 6–0–31–1; Robinson 8–0–28–3; Stemp 8–0–41–3 White 2.3–0–12–2; Grayson 2–0–24–0.

Umpires: D. O. Oslear and R. A. White.

At Manchester, August 22. YORKSHIRE lost to LANCASHIRE by three wickets.

YORKSHIRE v DURHAM

At Leeds, August 29. Durham won by 13 runs. Toss: Durham.

Larkins made 114 from 115 balls but hit only one six and four fours. He and Parke added 139 in 26 overs before seven wickets fell for 18 runs. Yorkshire lagged behind the scoring-rate and found the task of 82 from the last ten overs too demanding.

Durham

G. Fowler c Blakey b Robinson	15	*D. A. Graveney not out	
W. Larkins c Kellett b Robinson 114		S. J. E. Brown b Gough	
P. W. G. Parker b Foster	54	S. P. Hughes not out	
P. Bainbridge c Blakey b Grayson.....	17	B 1, l-b 13, w 1.............	1
S. Hutton st Blakey b Grayson.......	3		
I. Smith c Robinson b Hartley	4	1/47 2/186 3/212 (9 wkts, 50 overs) 23
A. C. Cummins c Grayson b Hartley ...	2	4/215 5/219 6/221	
†A. R. Fothergill run out	1	7/223 8/226 9/229	

Bowling: Hartley 10–3–23–2; Gough 10–1–40–1; Robinson 10–1–36–2; White 10–0–43–0 Batty 3–0–27–0; Foster 4–0–29–1; Grayson 3–0–18–2.

Yorkshire

*M. D. Moxon st Fothergill b Graveney	64	D. Gough run out	
D. Byas c and b Bainbridge	28	J. D. Batty run out	
†R. J. Blakey c Hutton b Bainbridge ...	28	M. A. Robinson not out	
S. A. Kellett c Fothergill b Smith	6	L-b 4, w 1, n-b 4...........	
C. White c Brown b Graveney	21		
P. J. Hartley b Cummins	21	1/91 2/103 3/114 (9 wkts, 50 overs) 21
A. P. Grayson not out.............	18	4/149 5/166 6/176	
M. J. Foster c Smith b Cummins	17	7/200 8/209 9/210	

Bowling: Hughes 10–0–39–0; Cummins 10–0–51–2; Brown 6–0–33–0; Bainbridge ▮–2–41–2; Graveney 10–0–32–2; Smith 4–0–17–1.

Umpires: J. C. Balderstone and H. D. Bird.

▮ Leicester, September 5. YORKSHIRE beat LEICESTERSHIRE by 65 runs.

YORKSHIRE v SUSSEX

▮ Scarborough, September 12. Yorkshire won by 21 runs. Toss: Sussex.
This fixture, played in sunshine, was the only one of the day to produce a result. ▮ichardson and Blakey rescued Yorkshire from a poor start with a fourth-wicket ▮rtnership of 146 in 29 overs. Hartley then removed Stephenson first ball and went on to ▮e five for 36.

orkshire

▮. D. Moxon b Stephenson	4	A. P. Grayson run out	2
Byas c Moores b Stephenson	24	†C. A. Chapman not out	15
B. Richardson b Remy	89	L-b 5, w 2	7
▮. J. Foster c Greenfield b Stephenson	21		
J. Blakey c Moores b Giddins	61	1/14 2/29 3/57 (7 wkts, 50 overs) 255	
J. Hartley b Remy	0	4/203 5/203	
White not out	32	6/205 7/214	

. Gough and M. A. Robinson did not bat.

Bowling: Stephenson 10–2–39–3; Giddins 10–0–44–1; Remy 10–0–48–2; Salisbury ▮0–27–0; C. M. Wells 10–0–51–0; Lenham 6–0–41–0.

ussex

D. Stephenson c Foster b Hartley	0	C. C. Remy b Hartley	1
W. J. Athey c Moxon b Hartley	51	I. D. K. Salisbury lbw b Hartley	0
▮. P. Speight c Byas b Hartley	10	E. S. H. Giddins not out	9
▮. P. Wells c Richardson b Grayson	80	L-b 6, w 3, n-b 4	13
M. Wells b Gough	0		
J. Lenham run out	30	1/0 2/19 3/128 (48.4 overs) 234	
. Greenfield run out	40	4/128 5/168 6/203	
▮. Moores b White	0	7/213 8/220 9/220	

Bowling: Hartley 9.4–1–36–5; Gough 9–2–20–1; White 10–0–56–1; Robinson 10–0–41–0; ▮rayson 10–0–75–1.

Umpires: J. D. Bond and V. A. Holder.

▮ The Oval, September 19. YORKSHIRE lost to SURREY by five wickets.

SUNDAY LEAGUE RECORDS

Batting

Highest score: 176 – G. A. Gooch, Essex v Glamorgan (Southend), 1983.

Most hundreds: 12 – W. Larkins; 11 – C. G. Greenidge and G. A. Gooch; 9 – K. S. McEwan and B. A. Richards. 427 hundreds have been scored in the League. The most in one season is 40 in 1990.

Most runs: G. A. Gooch 7,491; D. W. Randall 7,062; D. L. Amiss 7,040; W. Larkins 6,957; C. W. J. Athey 6,752; C. T. Radley 6,650; D. R. Turner 6,639; P. Willey 6,506; C. G. Greenidge 6,344; C. E. B. Rice 6,265; G. M. Turner 6,144.

Most runs in a season: 917 – T. M. Moody (Worcestershire), 1991.

Most sixes in an innings: 13 – I. T. Botham, Somerset v Northamptonshire (Wellingborough School), 1986.

Most sixes by a team in an innings: 18 – Derbyshire v Worcestershire (Knypersley), 1985.

Most sixes in a season: 26 – I. V. A. Richards (Somerset), 1977.

Highest total: 360 for three – Somerset v Glamorgan (Neath), 1990.

Highest total – batting second: 317 for six – Surrey v Nottinghamshire (The Oval), 1993 (50-overs match).

Highest match aggregate: 631 – Nottinghamshire (314 for seven) v Surrey (317 for six) (The Oval), 1993 (50-overs match).

Lowest total: 23 (19.4 overs) – Middlesex v Yorkshire (Leeds), 1974.

Shortest completed innings: 16 overs – Northamptonshire 59 v Middlesex (Tring), 1974.

Shortest match: 2 hr 13 min (40.3 overs) – Essex v Northamptonshire (Ilford), 1971.

Biggest victories: 220 runs, Somerset beat Glamorgan (Neath), 1990.
  There have been 24 instances of victory by ten wickets – by Derbyshire, Essex (three times), Glamorgan (twice), Hampshire, Leicestershire (twice), Middlesex (twice), Northamptonshire, Nottinghamshire, Somerset (twice), Surrey (twice), Warwickshire, Worcestershire (three times) and Yorkshire (three times). This does not include those matches in which the side batting second was set a reduced target but does include matches where both sides faced a reduced number of overs.

Ties: There have been 37 tied matches. Lancashire and Worcestershire have each tied eight times; only Durham have yet to tie.

Record partnerships for each wicket

239	for 1st	G. A. Gooch and B. R. Hardie, Essex v Nottinghamshire at Nottingham	1989
273	for 2nd	G. A. Gooch and K. S. McEwan, Essex v Nottinghamshire at Nottingham	1983
223	for 3rd	S. J. Cook and G. D. Rose, Somerset v Glamorgan at Neath	1990
219	for 4th	C. G. Greenidge and C. L. Smith, Hampshire v Surrey at Southampton	1987
190	for 5th	R. J. Blakey and M. J. Foster, Yorkshire v Leicestershire at Leicester	1993
124*	for 6th	J. J. Whitaker and P. A. Nixon, Leicestershire v Surrey at The Oval	1991
132	for 7th	K. R. Brown and N. F. Williams, Middlesex v Somerset at Lord's	1988
110*	for 8th	C. L. Cairns and B. N. French, Nottinghamshire v Surrey at The Oval	1993
105	for 9th	D. G. Moir and R. W. Taylor, Derbyshire v Kent at Derby	1984
57	for 10th	D. A. Graveney and J. B. Mortimore, Gloucestershire v Lancashire at Tewkesbury	1973

owling

st analyses: eight for 26, K. D. Boyce, Essex v Lancashire (Manchester), 1971; seven for 15, R. A. Hutton, Yorkshire v Worcestershire (Leeds), 1969; seven for 39, A. Hodgson, Northamptonshire v Somerset (Northampton), 1976; seven for 41, A. N. Jones, Sussex v Nottinghamshire (Nottingham), 1986; six for six, R. W. Hooker, Middlesex v Surrey (Lord's), 1969; six for seven, M. Hendrick, Derbyshire v Nottinghamshire (Nottingham), 1972; six for nine, N. G. Cowans, Middlesex v Lancashire (Lord's), 1991.

ur wickets in four balls: A. Ward, Derbyshire v Sussex (Derby), 1970.

at-tricks (23): A. Ward, Derbyshire v Sussex (Derby), 1970; R. Palmer, Somerset v Gloucestershire (Bristol), 1970; K. D. Boyce, Essex v Somerset (Westcliff), 1971; G. D. McKenzie, Leicestershire v Essex (Leicester), 1972; R. G. D. Willis, Warwickshire v Yorkshire (Birmingham), 1973; W. Blenkiron, Warwickshire v Derbyshire (Buxton), 1974; A. Buss, Sussex v Worcestershire (Hastings), 1974; J. M. Rice, Hampshire v Northamptonshire (Southampton), 1975; M. A. Nash, Glamorgan v Worcestershire (Worcester), 1975; A. Hodgson, Northamptonshire v Somerset (Northampton), 1976; A. E. Cordle, Glamorgan v Hampshire (Portsmouth), 1979; C. J. Tunnicliffe, Derbyshire v Worcestershire (Derby), 1979; M. D. Marshall, Hampshire v Surrey (Southampton), 1981; I. V. A. Richards, Somerset v Essex (Chelmsford), 1982; P. W. Jarvis, Yorkshire v Derbyshire (Derby), 1982; R. M. Ellison, Kent v Hampshire (Canterbury), 1983; G. C. Holmes, Glamorgan v Nottinghamshire (Ebbw Vale), 1987; K. Saxelby, Nottinghamshire v Worcestershire (Nottingham), 1987; K. M. Curran, Gloucestershire v Warwickshire (Birmingham), 1989; M. P. Bicknell, Surrey v Derbyshire (The Oval), 1992; M. J. McCague, Kent v Glamorgan (Swansea), 1992; A. Dale, Glamorgan v Durham (Colwyn Bay), 1993; R. K. Illingworth, Worcestershire v Sussex (Hove), 1993.

ost economical analysis: 8–8–0–0, B. A. Langford, Somerset v Essex (Yeovil), 1969.

ost expensive analyses: 8–0–96–1, D. G. Cork, Derbyshire v Nottinghamshire (Nottingham), 1993; 7.5–0–89–3, G. Miller, Derbyshire v Gloucestershire (Gloucester), 1984; 8–0–88–1, E. E. Hemmings, Nottinghamshire v Somerset (Nottingham), 1983.

ost wickets in a season: 34 – R. J. Clapp (Somerset), 1974, and C. E. B. Rice (Nottinghamshire), 1986.

ost wickets: J. K. Lever 386; D. L. Underwood 346; J. E. Emburey 329; J. Simmons 307; S. Turner 303; N. Gifford 284; E. E. Hemmings 276; J. N. Shepherd 267; I. T. Botham 256; T. E. Jesty 249; R. D. Jackman 234; P. Willey 234.

icket-keeping and Fielding

ost dismissals: D. L. Bairstow 257 (234 ct, 23 st); R. W. Taylor 236 (187 ct, 49 st); E. W. Jones 223 (184 ct, 39 st).

ost dismissals in a season: 29 (26 ct, 3 st) – S. J. Rhodes (Worcestershire), 1988.

ost dismissals in an innings: 7 (6 ct, 1 st) – R. W. Taylor, Derbyshire v Lancashire (Manchester), 1975.

ost catches in an innings: 6 – K. Goodwin, Lancashire v Worcestershire (Worcester), 1969; R. W. Taylor, Derbyshire v Lancashire (Manchester), 1975.

ost stumpings in an innings: 4 – S. J. Rhodes, Worcestershire v Warwickshire (Birmingham), 1986; N. D. Burns, Somerset v Kent (Taunton), 1991.

ost catches by a fielder (not a wicket-keeper): J. F. Steele 101; D. P. Hughes 97; G. Cook 94; C. T. Radley 91.

ost catches in a season: 16 – J. M. Rice (Hampshire), 1978.

ost catches in an innings: 5 – J. M. Rice, Hampshire v Warwickshire (Southampton), 1978.

CHAMPIONS 1969-93

John Player's County League
1969 Lancashire
John Player League
1970 Lancashire
1971 Worcestershire
1972 Kent
1973 Kent
1974 Leicestershire
1975 Hampshire
1976 Kent
1977 Leicestershire
1978 Hampshire
1979 Somerset
1980 Warwickshire
1981 Essex
1982 Sussex

1983 Yorkshire
John Player Special League
1984 Essex
1985 Essex
1986 Hampshire
Refuge Assurance League
1987 Worcestershire
1988 Worcestershire
1989 Lancashire
1990 Derbyshire
1991 Nottinghamshire
Sunday League
1992 Middlesex
AXA Equity & Law League
1993 Glamorgan

MATCH RESULTS 1969-93

		Matches				*League positions*		
	P	W	L	T	NR	*1st*	*2nd*	*3i*
Derbyshire	402	172	190	2	38	1	0	
Durham	34	15	14	0	5	0	0	
Essex	402	216	145	5	36	3	5*	
Glamorgan	402	137	219	3	43	1	0	
Gloucestershire	402	141	210	4	47	0	1	
Hampshire	402	204	157	6	35	3	1	
Kent	402	212	144	5	41	3	3	
Lancashire	402	198	149	8	47	3	2	
Leicestershire	402	171	178	2	51	2	2*	
Middlesex	402	188	165	6	43	1	1	
Northamptonshire	402	154	203	3	42	0	0	
Nottinghamshire	402	167	197	3	35	1	2	
Somerset	402	193	166	2	41	1	6*	
Surrey	402	175	181	4	42	0	0	
Sussex	402	178	176	5	43	1	2*	
Warwickshire	402	154	196	6	46	1	0	
Worcestershire	402	191	169	8	34	3	2	
Yorkshire	402	174	181	2	45	1	1	

* Includes one shared 2nd place in 1976.

THE UNIVERSITIES IN 1993

OXFORD

President: M. J. K. Smith (St Edmund Hall)
Hon. Treasurer: Dr S. R. Porter (Nuffield College)

Captain: J. E. R. Gallian (Pittwater House, Sydney and Keble)
Secretary: C. J. Townsend (Dean Close, Cheltenham and Brasenose)

Captain for 1994: R. R. Montgomerie (Rugby and Worcester)
Secretary: R. S. Yeabsley (Haberdashers' Aske's, Elstree and Keble)

Oxford University enjoyed one of their most successful seasons for many years, culminating in an emphatic nine-wicket win over Cambridge in the Varsity Match, their first since 1984. This followed an exciting victory over Nottinghamshire by seven wickets, and against Hampshire they were within ten runs of a third win.

Traditionally pace bowling has been the chief weakness at The Parks, but for the first time since 1977 it was Oxford's strength. The Australian-born captain Jason Gallian was fortunate in having four good seamers, who enabled the University to bowl out three county sides – Durham, Hampshire and Middlesex – on the first day. Michael Jeh, quicker and more accurate than the previous year, was the leading wicket-taker with 24, while Richard Yeabsley, a Freshman, collected 20. Rob Macdonald was far more effective than in 1992, when he was troubled for much of the season with a foot injury. Gallian completed the quartet and he also picked up some useful wickets.

Midway through the season, Patrick Trimby, a leg-spinner, was promoted to the first team after some good performances for the Authentics. He impressed many county batsmen with his control and ability to conceal the googly, and was amply rewarded with six wickets in the Varsity Match. The bowling was supported throughout by fielding of a high standard, and in Craig Lyons, a South African, Oxford had one of the best wicket-keepers seen at The Parks in many years. His 24 dismissals helped Oxford to take over a hundred wickets, the most since 1977, and at times he scored valuable runs.

For much of the season Oxford were without their most experienced batsmen, Richard Montgomerie and Geoff Lovell, the 1992 captain, who were preparing for their final examinations. The batting was further weakened when Gallian himself broke a thumb during the match against Lancashire, the county he joined full-time at the end of term. But when they returned the batting was as strong as the bowling. Five hundreds were scored during the season. The highlight at Oxford was Gallian's magnificent unbeaten 141 against Nottinghamshire. Chris Keey hit 111 off Northamptonshire and Montgomerie 109 at Worcester. At Lord's, where Oxford's easy win was arguably an accurate representation of the difference between the sides, Gallian scored 115 and Lovell 114 as Oxford amassed 400 for six declared before lunch on the second day. Chinmay Gupte and Hasnain Malik were solid in the middle of the innings and, although there was some surprise when Gregor Macmillan was preferred to Malik at Lord's, it proved an inspired selection; he hit 63 and took three wickets.

OXFORD UNIVERSITY 1993

[*Bill Smith*]

Back row: L. J. Lenham (*coach*), C. M. Gupte, C. W. J. Lyons, C. L. Keey, R. S. Yeabsley, G. I. Macmillan, P. W. Trimby, H. S. Malik, G. S. Gordon (*scorer*). *Front row*: R. H. Macdonald, R. R. Montgomerie, J. E. R. Gallian (*captain*), G. B. T. Lovell, M. P. W. Jeh.

Oxford's fine season was in no small measure due to Gallian's leadership. Montgomerie took over the difficult task of trying to lessen the gulf between the universities and the first-class counties. Half the side has disappeared but the new captain will have at his disposal another strong intake of Freshmen, and the second Bradman Scholar, Andrew Ridley, who arrived from Sydney as Lovell's successor. – Paton Fenton.

OXFORD UNIVERSITY RESULTS

First-class matches – Played 10: Won 2, Drawn 8.

FIRST-CLASS AVERAGES

BATTING AND FIELDING

	Birthplace	M	I	NO	R	HS	Avge	Ct/St
E. R. Gallian	Sydney, Australia	9	15	2	643	141*	49.46	4
R. R. Montgomerie	Rugby	6	11	1	371	109	37.10	2
G. B. T. Lovell	Sydney, Australia	7	11	1	365	114	36.50	8
M. Gupte	Poona, India	9	16	3	397	61	30.53	3
G. I. Macmillan	Guildford	9	14	1	336	63	25.84	5
S. Malik	Sargodha, Pakistan	9	13	3	234	64*	23.40	6
C. L. Keey	Johannesburg, SA	10	16	1	341	111	22.73	4
R. S. Yeabsley	St Albans	10	13	4	138	36	15.33	5
W. J. Lyons	Johannesburg, SA	9	12	4	108	28	13.50	22/2
P. W. Jeh	Colombo, Sri Lanka	10	10	4	26	9	4.33	2
R. H. Macdonald	Cape Town, SA	9	7	2	18	11	3.60	0

Also batted: E. R. Fowler (*Northampton*) (2 matches) 9, 5, 5; A. W. MacLay (*Salisbury*) (1 match) 0*; R. D. Oliphant-Callum (*Twickenham*) (2 matches) 13, 5, 2; C. J. Townsend (*Wokingham*) (1 match) 0* (2 ct); P. W. Trimby (*Shrewsbury*) (6 matches) 2*, 1* (2 ct). C. A. Ellison (*King's Lynn*) (1 match) did not bat.

* *Signifies not out.*

The following played a total of five three-figure innings for Oxford University – J. E. R. Gallian 2, C. L. Keey 1, G. B. T. Lovell 1, R. R. Montgomerie 1.

BOWLING

	O	M	R	W	BB	5W/i	Avge
G. I. Macmillan	67.2	14	211	7	3-13	0	30.14
R. H. Macdonald	216	64	562	16	5-20	1	35.12
R. S. Yeabsley	237.1	53	762	20	3-30	0	38.10
P. W. Trimby	143.2	31	469	12	3-72	0	39.08
E. R. Gallian	166	43	464	10	3-52	0	46.40
P. W. Jeh	297	48	1,140	24	5-63	1	47.50
S. Malik	117.5	28	414	7	2-18	0	59.14

Also bowled: B. C. A. Ellison 11-1-40-2; C. M. Gupte 1-0-7-0; A. W. MacLay 2-0-51-1; R. R. Montgomerie 2-0-6-0.

Note: Matches in this section which were not first-class are signified by a dagger.

†At Oxford, April 10. Oxford University v Middlesex. Abandoned without a ball bowled owing to rain.

†At Oxford, April 12. Oxford University won by three wickets. Toss: Durham University. Durham University 108 (A. Newman 31; H. S. Malik four for 27); Oxford University 110 for seven (R. S. Yeabsley 32; R. C. Stanley four for 14).

OXFORD UNIVERSITY v DURHAM

At Oxford, April 14, 15, 16. Drawn. Toss: Oxford University. First-class debuts: G. I. Macmillan, R. S. Yeabsley. County debut: G. Fowler.

The TCCB's computerised scoring system was among the first-class debutants, though the telephone line connecting the scorers to the central computer was installed only half an hour before play began. Oxford's delight in dismissing Durham for 191 evaporated as they lost five for 34 by the close. Their eventual 86 was the University's lowest total of the season, with six ducks. Batsmen fared better in the second innings. Fowler took three hours over his first fifty for Durham, and a flurry of four wickets for nine runs helped Jeh record career-best figures, but Oxford were set to chase 357 in 290 minutes. After a poor start, Keey and Macmillan rescued them with 123 in 33 overs; Macmillan atoned for his duck on debut with a maiden half-century. Graveney, who returned his best figures for Durham, settled for a draw with three overs remaining.

Close of play: First day, Oxford University 34-5 (C. M. Gupte 5*); Second day, Durham 204-6 (I. Smith 13*, P. J. Berry 28*).

Durham

G. Fowler run out	2	– c Malik b Jeh	50
W. Larkins c Gupte b Jeh	21	– c Montgomerie b Gallian	36
P. W. G. Parker c Macmillan b Macdonald	17	– c Lovell b Jeh	39
P. Bainbridge c Lovell b Macdonald	4	– b Jeh	27
J. A. Daley c Townsend b Macmillan	41	– c Jeh b Malik	1
I. Smith b Macdonald	15	– b Jeh	34
†C. W. Scott c Lovell b Macmillan	17	– c Lovell b Malik	1
P. J. Berry c Townsend b Macmillan	33	– not out	39
J. Wood lbw b Jeh	3	– not out	12
*D. A. Graveney c Lovell b Yeabsley	13		
S. J. E. Brown not out	2		
B 10, l-b 6, w 5, n-b 2	23	B 2, l-b 6, n-b 4	12

1/2 2/42 3/42 4/52 5/69   191   1/52 2/119 3/160   (7 wkts dec.) 251
6/116 7/133 8/136 9/163   4/161 5/165
                                     6/169 7/233

Bowling: *First Innings*—Jeh 19-3-46-2; Gallian 15-5-27-0; Macdonald 17-7-28-3; Yeabsley 20-6-46-1; Malik 3-1-7-0; Macmillan 9.2-1-21-3. *Second Innings*—Jeh 28-8-46-4; Gallian 13-3-50-1; Macmillan 10-1-44-0; Macdonald 19-6-48-0; Yeabsley 11-3-37-0; Malik 11-6-18-2.

Oxford University

R. R. Montgomerie lbw b Wood	12	– c Parker b Berry	29
*J. E. R. Gallian lbw b Wood	0	– st Scott b Graveney	23
G. I. Macmillan lbw b Brown	0	– c Parker b Graveney	51
G. B. T. Lovell b Brown	0	– b Graveney	17
C. L. Keey c Bainbridge b Wood	16	– c Graveney b Smith	70
C. M. Gupte run out	0	– c Smith b Graveney	7
M. P. W. Jeh lbw b Brown	0	– (8) not out	2
H. S. Malik c Larkins b Bainbridge	25	– (7) not out	13
R. S. Yeabsley b Berry	0		
†C. J. Townsend not out	0		
R. H. Macdonald st Scott b Bainbridge	0		
L-b 7, w 2, n-b 2	11	L-b 3, w 5, n-b 6	14

1/1 2/4 3/12 4/12 5/34	86	1/52 2/60 3/79 (6 wkts) 226
6/35 7/81 8/82 9/86		4/202 5/202 6/221

Bowling: *First Innings*—Wood 13–1–41–3; Brown 13–2–19–3; Berry 6–1–9–1; Bainbridge 5.5–0–10–2. *Second Innings*—Wood 3–0–7–0; Brown 12–1–46–0; Smith 11–1–35–1; Graveney 35–16–49–4; Bainbridge 5–1–24–0.

Umpires: M. J. Kitchen and P. Willey.

OXFORD UNIVERSITY v LANCASHIRE

At Oxford, April 17, 19, 20. Drawn. Toss: Lancashire. First-class debut: C. W. J. Lyons.

Oxford paid heavily for dropping Atherton three times, on 17, 27 and 89. He went on to 107 out of Lancashire's 309 for four. Worse, one of those missed chances resulted in Gallian breaking his thumb; he did not bat, though he still opened the bowling in the second innings and took Lancashire's first two wickets. He and his colleagues made the county work hard to build on a lead of 115. The one batsman they could not dislodge, however, was Lloyd, who completed an unbeaten century with 13 fours before Fairbrother set the University a target of 310 in 220 minutes. Montgomerie scored his second half-century of the match, sharing a first-wicket stand of 85 with Gupte, who opened instead of Gallian. The game petered out into a draw with ten overs left.

Close of play: First day, Lancashire 309-4 (N. H. Fairbrother 44*, W. K. Hegg 17*); Second day, Lancashire 45-2 (G. D. Lloyd 19*, M. Watkinson 17*).

Lancashire

G. D. Mendis b Yeabsley	26	– b Gallian	1
M. A. Atherton b Macdonald	107		
N. J. Speak c Lyons b Malik	87		
*N. H. Fairbrother not out	44		
G. D. Lloyd c sub b Macmillan	20	– (2) not out	100
†W. K. Hegg not out	17	– (3) c Lyons b Gallian	8
M. Watkinson (did not bat)		– (4) c Malik b Yeabsley	18
P. A. J. DeFreitas (did not bat)		– (5) c Lyons b Yeabsley	5
I. D. Austin (did not bat)		– (6) lbw b Yeabsley	20
P. J. Martin (did not bat)		– (7) b Malik	30
A. A. Barnett (did not bat)		– (8) not out	11
B 1, l-b 1, w 2, n-b 4	8	B 1	1

1/56 2/216 3/230 4/261	(4 wkts dec.) 309	1/3 2/11 3/48 (6 wkts dec.) 194
		4/68 5/116 6/168

Bowling: *First Innings*—Jeh 22–4–74–0; Gallian 9–2–20–0; Macdonald 21–6–58–1; Yeabsley 19–5–48–1; Malik 19–3–50–1; Macmillan 18–1–57–1. *Second Innings*—Jeh 10–3–51–0; Gallian 16–5–42–2; Macdonald 10–3–27–0; Malik 7.5–2–30–1; Yeabsley 12–2–30–3; Macmillan 3–0–13–0.

Oxford University

R. R. Montgomerie c Lloyd b Martin	65 – not out	75
C. M. Gupte b Martin	2 – c Atherton b Barnett	39
G. I. Macmillan c Atherton b Martin	21 – lbw b Barnett	5
G. B. T. Lovell b Martin	0 – c Hegg b Atherton	28
C. L. Keey c Mendis b Watkinson	27 – not out	3
†C. W. J. Lyons b Watkinson	28	
H. S. Malik not out	18	
M. P. W. Jeh lbw b DeFreitas	2	
R. S. Yeabsley lbw b DeFreitas	2	
R. H. Macdonald run out	1	
*J. E. R. Gallian absent injured		
B 11, l-b 6, w 5, n-b 6	28	B 4, l-b 1, w 1, n-b 8 14
	194	(3 wkts) 164

1/18 2/97 3/97 4/104 5/148   1/85 2/101 3/148
6/165 7/180 8/186 9/194

Bowling: *First Innings*—DeFreitas 19-5-57-2; Martin 17-7-42-4; Watkinson 17.4-5-29-2; Austin 4-1-18-0; Barnett 12-2-31-0. *Second Innings*—DeFreitas 6-1-21-0; Martin 5-1-11-0; Austin 8-1-36-0; Barnett 19-4-40-2; Watkinson 16-2-43-0; Atherton 5-0-8-1.

Umpires: M. J. Kitchen and P. Willey.

OXFORD UNIVERSITY v GLAMORGAN

At Oxford, April 21, 22, 23. Drawn. Toss: Glamorgan. First-class debut: A. W. MacLay. County debut: R. P. Lefebvre.

Rain saved Oxford from a heavy defeat. Glamorgan spent the first day compiling 463 – seven runs more than their previous best in The Parks, in 1985 – with centuries from Morris, Maynard and Richards. The bowling was softened up by Morris and Dale, who added 142, and after Morris retired at tea with a knee injury, Richards and Maynard plundered an unbroken 233 off 33 overs. Maynard reached three figures in 96 balls and Richards in 94. When 23, Richards joined C. G. Greenidge and R. E. Marshall as the only West Indians to have scored 35,000 first-class runs. Oxford, lacking regular openers Gallian and Montgomerie, were skittled for 99, with 49 from acting-captain Lovell. Glamorgan waived the follow-on, but declared on the final morning with a lead of 479 before further play was washed out.

Close of play: First day, Glamorgan 463-2 (M. P. Maynard 110*, I. V. A. Richards 109*); Second day, Glamorgan 115-3 (R. P. Lefebvre 9*, C. P. Metson 1*).

Glamorgan

S. P. James c Malik b Yeabsley	41 – c Lyons b Jeh	15
*H. Morris retired hurt	109	
A. Dale b Malik	67	
M. P. Maynard not out	110	
I. V. A. Richards not out	109	
P. A. Cottey (did not bat)	– (2) c Lyons b MacLay	60
R. D. B. Croft (did not bat)	– (3) lbw b Jeh	27
R. P. Lefebvre (did not bat)	– (4) not out	9
†C. P. Metson (did not bat)	– (5) not out	1
B 3, l-b 6, w 4, n-b 14	27	L-b 2, w 1	3
	(2 wkts dec.) 463	(3 wkts dec.) 115

1/78 2/220   1/25 2/67 3/106

S. L. Watkin and S. R. Barwick did not bat.

In the first innings H. Morris retired hurt at 230.

Bowling: *First Innings*—Jeh 31-5-156-0; Macdonald 22-6-66-0; MacLay 9-0-40-0; Yeabsley 18-3-101-1; Macmillan 9-4-20-0; Malik 15-1-71-1. *Second Innings*—Jeh 12-1-47-2; Yeabsley 8-3-23-0; Malik 7-3-32-0; MacLay 3-0-11-1.

Oxford University

†C. W. J. Lyons run out	0		R. S. Yeabsley c Maynard b Barwick	10
C. M. Gupte c Maynard b Lefebvre	4		R. H. Macdonald lbw b Croft	0
H. S. Malik b Dale	9		A. W. MacLay not out	0
*G. B. T. Lovell c Metson b Barwick	49			
C. L. Keey c Cottey b Watkin	3		L-b 3	3
R. D. Oliphant-Callum run out	13			
G. I. Macmillan c Richards b Croft	8		1/0 2/11 3/19 4/26 5/77	99
M. P. W. Jeh c James b Barwick	0		6/88 7/88 8/88 9/89	

Bowling: Watkin 13–6–11–1; Lefebvre 17–8–22–1; Barwick 19.4–9–26–3; Croft 22–13–23–2; Dale 6–2–14–1.

Umpires: J. W. Holder and V. A. Holder.

†At Oxford, April 29. Oxford University won by six wickets. Toss: Berkshire. Berkshire 143 (M. P. W. Jeh three for 17, B. C. A. Ellison three for 37); Oxford University 144 for four (E. R. Fowler 52, H. S. Malik 56 not out).

OXFORD UNIVERSITY v HAMPSHIRE

At Oxford, May 5, 6, 7. Drawn. Toss: Hampshire. First-class debut: E. R. Fowler. County debut: M. Jean-Jacques.

Oxford finished ten short of their fourth victory in 41 encounters with Hampshire, after a sporting declaration by Nicholas set them 176 off 43 overs. Impressive seam bowling reduced the county to 27 for four and eventually dismissed them for 169, thanks to Jeh's first-ever five-wicket haul. With Gupte and Macmillan backing Gallian up in partnerships of 68 and 53, the University could afford the luxury of declaring 61 ahead. Middleton and Terry, who reached 117 before retiring, hit off the arrears in an opening stand of 166. Oxford's run-chase started poorly when they lost Gallian in the first over, but Gupte and Macmillan kept them in contention with 61 in 15 overs. Then Malik launched a late assault with his maiden half-century. He was unbeaten at the end, but it did not help that four of his partners were run out.

Close of play: First day, Oxford University 33-0 (C. M. Gupte 13*, J. E. R. Gallian 15*); Second day, Hampshire 27-0 (T. C. Middleton 13*, V. P. Terry 11*).

Hampshire

T. C. Middleton b Jeh	0	– b Yeabsley	63
V. P. Terry b Jeh	11	– retired out	117
R. A. Smith c Lyons b Gallian	3	– not out	15
*M. C. J. Nicholas c Lyons b Macdonald	62		
J. R. Ayling b Jeh	0	– (4) not out	27
K. D. James c Keey b Malik	32		
†A. N. Aymes b Jeh	2		
S. D. Udal c Yeabsley b Macdonald	6		
M. Jean-Jacques not out	21		
I. J. Turner c Macmillan b Jeh	5		
K. J. Shine lbw b Macdonald	7		
L-b 3, w 3, n-b 14	20	B 2, l-b 7, w 1, n-b 4	14

1/3 2/13 3/27 4/27 5/126   169   1/166 2/207   (2 wkts dec.) 236
6/126 7/129 8/143 9/152

Bowling: *First Innings*—Jeh 23–8–63–5; Gallian 11–4–16–1; Yeabsley 14–4–21–0; Macdonald 15.1–3–36–3; Malik 14–6–30–1. *Second Innings*—Jeh 21–5–60–0; Gallian 7–1–20–0; Macmillan 6–0–33–0; Yeabsley 22–5–49–1; Macdonald 11.4–3–26–0; Malik 7–1–32–0; Gupte 1–0–7–0.

Oxford University

C. M. Gupte lbw b Udal	29	– c Turner b Udal	36
*J. E. R. Gallian st Aymes b Turner	83	– lbw b Jean-Jacques	0
G. I. Macmillan c sub b Turner	30	– c Jean-Jacques b Turner	26
C. L. Keey run out	0	– c sub b Udal	23
H. S. Malik lbw b Udal	23	– not out	64
E. R. Fowler b Udal	9	– (7) run out	5
R. D. Oliphant-Callum c Aymes b Jean-Jacques	5	– (9) run out	2
†C. W. J. Lyons b Shine	8	– run out	2
R. S. Yeabsley c Aymes b James	26	– (6) run out	1
M. P. W. Jeh not out	5	– not out	3
R. H. Macdonald not out	4		
B 1, l-b 5, n-b 2	8	L-b 4	4

1/68 2/121 3/126 4/156 5/177   (9 wkts dec.) 230   1/1 2/62 3/62 4/107   (8 wkts) 166
6/182 7/192 8/204 9/225   5/126 6/142 7/152 8/158

Bowling: *First Innings*—Shine 16–6–41–1; Jean-Jacques 21–6–45–1; Ayling 15–7–13–0; James 13–5–20–1; Turner 25–11–43–2; Udal 28–7–62–3. *Second Innings*—Jean-Jacques 6–0–16–1; Shine 5–0–26–0; Turner 10–3–29–1; Udal 15.5–2–64–2; James 6–0–27–0.

Umpires: D. J. Constant and M. K. Reed.

†At Oxford, May 10. Oxford University v Club Cricket Conference Under-25. Abandoned without a ball bowled, owing to rain.

†At Oxford, May 13. Oxford University v Loughborough University. Cancelled.

†At Oxford, May 14. Oxford University won by 55 runs. Toss: Oxfordshire. Oxford University 170 (C. M. Gupte 36, J. E. R. Gallian 38; I. J. Curtis five for 26); Oxfordshire 115 (S. G. Joyner 38).

OXFORD UNIVERSITY v NORTHAMPTONSHIRE

At Oxford, May 15, 17, 18. Drawn. Toss: Northamptonshire. First-class debut: P. W. Trimby.

Oxford's first century of the season, and the first of Keey's first-class career, was not quite enough to avert the follow-on; they fell five short. But Bailey preferred to give his middle order batting practice before challenging the students to score 244 from 66 overs. They made 123 for two before the last 20, but abandoned the chase when two more wickets fell. Though they subsided a little further, to 147 for six, Northamptonshire had no interest in pursuing the match to a conclusion. On the first day Lamb and Bailey steadied the county with a 124-run stand, after Yeabsley removed Felton and Fordham in his first four overs. Later, Loye and Ripley added an unbeaten 116, with Ripley reaching the first of two unbeaten half-centuries in the game.

Close of play: First day, Oxford University 17-2 (J. E. R. Gallian 6*, C. L. Keey 0*). Second day, Oxford University 169-6 (C. L. Keey 107*, R. S. Yeabsley 0*).

Northamptonshire

A. Fordham c Trimby b Yeabsley	28			
N. A. Felton lbw b Yeabsley	16			
R. J. Bailey b Gallian	91			
A. J. Lamb c Gupte b Trimby	46			
M. B. Loye not out	57	– not out	20	
A. L. Penberthy run out	3	– (2) c Montgomerie b Jeh	0	
D. Ripley not out	62	– (3) not out	50	
A. R. Roberts (did not bat)		– (1) c Lyons b Yeabsley	3	
N. G. B. Cook (did not bat)		– (4) c Lyons b Yeabsley	2	
B 1, l-b 4, w 2, n-b 24	31	W 2, n-b 12	14	

1/46 2/69 3/193 4/213 5/218 (5 wkts dec.) 334 1/3 2/3 3/21 (3 wkts dec.) 89

A. Walker and J. P. Taylor did not bat.

Bowling: *First Innings*—Jeh 9-1-56-0; Gallian 14-4-42-1; Yeabsley 18-4-52-2; Macdonald 15-5-56-0; Trimby 18-1-73-1; Malik 12-1-50-0. *Second Innings*—Jeh 6-0-33-1; Yeabsley 6-3-12-2; Trimby 6-1-17-0; Montgomerie 1-0-5-0; Macdonald 4-0-22-0.

Oxford University

R. R. Montgomerie c Loye b Taylor	9	– c Lamb b Cook	40	
J. E. R. Gallian lbw b Roberts	11	– c Walker b Cook	27	
C. M. Gupte c Ripley b Taylor	1	– c Ripley b Taylor	37	
C. L. Keey b Taylor	111	– b Cook	20	
G. I. Macmillan c Cook b Roberts	13	– (6) st Ripley b Roberts	9	
H. S. Malik b Penberthy	13	– (5) b Penberthy	4	
*C. W. J. Lyons b Walker	4			
R. S. Yeabsley run out	2	– (7) not out	2	
M. P. W. Jeh lbw b Walker	1			
R. H. Macdonald b Walker	1			
W. Trimby not out	2			
B 2, l-b 4, w 1, n-b 2	9	B 1, l-b 5, n-b 2	8	

1/12 2/14 3/22 4/64 5/118 180 1/48 2/89 3/123 (6 wkts) 147
6/156 7/171 8/177 9/177   4/128 5/145 6/147

Bowling: *First Innings*—Taylor 19-10-27-3; Walker 20.5-6-62-3; Roberts 20-7-33-2; Penberthy 10-4-23-1; Cook 6-3-7-0; Bailey 6-1-22-0. *Second Innings*—Taylor 11-2-32-1; Walker 4-0-16-0; Cook 18-5-34-3; Penberthy 10-1-37-1; Roberts 11.1-4-22-1.

Umpires: R. A. White and A. G. T. Whitehead.

At Wormsley, May 16. Drawn. J. Paul Getty's XI 211 for seven dec. (T. J. Boon 59, N. E. Briers 34); Oxford University 196 for nine (J. E. R. Gallian 71, M. P. W. Jeh 30; S. Watkinson four for 40).

OXFORD UNIVERSITY v MIDDLESEX

At Oxford, May 19, 20, 21. Drawn. Toss: Middlesex.

Reciprocal declarations kept the match alive after rain prevented any play on the second day or before lunch on the third. But Oxford's hopes of repeating the previous year's win came to nothing. They took the honours, dismissing a first-class county inside the first day for the third time in 1993. Macdonald, with his best career analysis yet, and Yeabsley shared eight wickets. Gatting scored 60 on his first appearance since injuring his arm while playing the Australians. On the final day Oxford declared at their overnight score and Gatting closed the second innings after six overs, leaving a target of 231 in 205 minutes. A determined effort by Gallian and Gupte, who reached his highest score, ended when Gallian was caught and Fraser claimed Gupte and Macmillan.

Close of play: First day, Oxford University 37-1 (C. M. Gupte 28*, C. W. J. Lyons 0*); second day, No play.

Middlesex

M. Keech c Malik b Yeabsley	12	– (2) not out	15
J. C. Pooley lbw b Macdonald	49		
R. J. Sims c Keey b Macdonald	28		
†K. R. Brown c Macmillan b Macdonald	1	– (1) not out	10
P. N. Weekes c Lyons b Macdonald	4		
*M. W. Gatting c Yeabsley b Jeh	60		
N. F. Williams c Lyons b Yeabsley	6		
A. R. C. Fraser c Keey b Yeabsley	15		
C. W. Taylor not out	28		
P. C. R. Tufnell c Yeabsley b Trimby	12		
N. G. Cowans c Lyons b Macdonald	14		
B 4, l-b 2, w 1	7	L-b 1, w 1, n-b 4	6

1/30 2/85 3/89 4/94 5/101   236   (no wkt dec.) 31
6/118 7/164 8/195 9/218

Bowling: *First Innings*—Jeh 11–0–55–1; Yeabsley 20–1–74–3; Gallian 13–4–41–0; Macdonald 16.1–7–20–5; Trimby 14–3–37–1; Malik 2–1–3–0. *Second Innings*—Jeh 3–0–14–0; Yeabsley 3–0–16–0.

Oxford University

C. M. Gupte not out	28	– c and b Fraser	61
*J. E. R. Gallian lbw b Cowans	6	– c Gatting b Taylor	47
†C. W. J. Lyons not out	0	– (8) not out	4
G. I. Macmillan (did not bat)		– (3) b Fraser	27
C. L. Keey (did not bat)		– (4) c Pooley b Weekes	9
H. S. Malik (did not bat)		– (5) c Brown b Fraser	1
R. S. Yeabsley (did not bat)		– (6) not out	11
E. R. Fowler (did not bat)		– (7) c Keech b Weekes	5
L-b 3	3	B 4, l-b 2, n-b 6	12

1/34   (1 wkt dec.) 37   1/93 2/144 3/151   (6 wkts) 177
                             4/156 5/160 6/169

M. P. W. Jeh, R. H. Macdonald and P. W. Trimby did not bat.

Bowling: *First Innings*—Taylor 7–2–16–0; Williams 5–3–5–0; Cowans 4–1–12–1; Tufnell 1–1–0–0; Weekes 1–0–1–0. *Second Innings*—Taylor 11–3–25–1; Fraser 14–1–38–3; Weekes 20–1–55–2; Williams 6–1–29–0; Cowans 8–0–20–0; Keech 2–1–4–0.

Umpires: T. E. Jesty and R. Palmer.

†At Oxford, May 22. Oxford University won by 129 runs. Toss: Oxford University. Oxford University 253 for three dec. (G. I. Macmillan 77, H. S. Malik 95, J. T. A. Martin-Jenkins 34 not out); Free Foresters 124 (C. Rowe 30; P. W. Trimby five for 50).

†At Oxford, May 25. Drawn. Toss: Oxford University. Oxford University 277 for four dec. (C. L. Keey 42, J. E. R. Gallian 112, E. R. Fowler 30, H. S. Malik 53; P. Harrisor three for 60); Midlands Club Cricket Conference 221 for eight (D. A. Thorne 31, G. J. Toogood 58, J. S. Hartley 38; H. S. Malik four for 60).

†At Oxford, May 27. Oxford University v Royal Navy. Abandoned without a bal bowled, owing to rain.

OXFORD UNIVERSITY v NOTTINGHAMSHIRE

At Oxford, May 29, 31, June 1. Oxford University won by seven wickets. Toss: Oxford University. First-class debut: R. T. Bates.

A magnificent unbeaten century from Gallian steered Oxford to their first first-class win of the season, and their second over a first-class county since 1974. Gallian's career-best 141, from 214 balls with 15 fours, was well supported by Gupte (dropped in the first over) and Macmillan, in stands of 87 and 104. Their target of 257 in the final two sessions was achieved with three overs to spare. Asked to bat, Nottinghamshire reached 249 on the first day, with half-centuries from Saxelby and Robinson. On Monday, the University struggled to 39 for five by lunch. Both openers fell to Lewis, returning after his injury in the one-day internationals. Malik revived the innings, which eventually totalled 151, and Robinson was confident enough to declare after extending their lead to 256 on the final morning.

Close of play: First day, Nottinghamshire 249-7 (R. T. Bates 33*, K. P. Evans 1*); Second day, Nottinghamshire 53-2 (P. R. Pollard 29*, C. C. Lewis 6*).

Nottinghamshire

P. R. Pollard c Lyons b Gallian	22	– not out	64
M. Saxelby c Gallian b Yeabsley	56	– st Lyons b Trimby	7
*R. T. Robinson c Jeh b Yeabsley	60		
P. Johnson c Lyons b Trimby	6	– (5) c Lyons b Yeabsley	4
M. A. Crawley c Gallian b Yeabsley	0	– (3) b Jeh	0
G. F. Archer lbw b Gallian	31	– not out	13
R. T. Bates not out	33		
C. C. Lewis c Lyons b Macdonald	25	– (4) c Malik b Yeabsley	51
K. P. Evans not out	1		
L-b 4, w 3, n-b 8	15	B 6, l-b 2, w 3, n-b 8	19

1/42 2/139 3/156 4/156 5/156   (7 wkts dec.) 249   1/40 2/45   (4 wkts dec.) 158
6/206 7/246   3/135 4/139

†S. Bramhall and R. A. Pick did not bat.

Bowling: *First Innings*—Jeh 12-4-37-0; Macdonald 17-4-59-1; Gallian 13-3-40-2; Yeabsley 16-6-33-3; Trimby 17-2-53-1; Malik 6-0-23-0; Macmillan 1-1-0-0. *Second Innings*—Jeh 11-0-54-1; Gallian 4-2-12-0; Trimby 10-4-28-1; Macdonald 9-3-20-0; Yeabsley 13-3-36-2.

Oxford University

C. M. Gupte b Lewis	0	– c Robinson b Crawley	38
*J. E. R. Gallian lbw b Lewis	7	– not out	141
G. I. Macmillan lbw b Evans	14	– c Evans b Crawley	51
C. L. Keey b Crawley	1	– c Lewis b Crawley	3
G. B. T. Lovell c Lewis b Evans	13	– not out	18
H. S. Malik b Evans	48		
R. S. Yeabsley c Pollard b Bates	24		
†C. W. J. Lyons c Archer b Crawley	5		
M. P. W. Jeh c Bramhall b Lewis	9		
R. H. Macdonald b Lewis	11		
P. W. Trimby not out	1		
B 3, l-b 11, n-b 4	18	B 2, l-b 2, w 2	6

1/0 2/15 3/18 4/28 5/37   151   1/87 2/191 3/208   (3 wkts) 257
6/82 7/114 8/120 9/148

Bowling: *First Innings*—Lewis 19.5-4-51-4; Evans 23-11-31-3; Pick 13-3-27-0; Crawley 10-3-13-2; Bates 16-11-15-1. *Second Innings*—Lewis 16-1-50-0; Pick 15-2-69-0; Crawley 24.3-5-86-3; Bates 14-2-48-0.

Umpires: P. Adams and A. G. T. Whitehead.

†At Oxford, June 3. Wiltshire won by five wickets. Toss: Oxford University. Oxford University 102 (35.5 overs) (G. Sheppard four for 29); Wiltshire 103 for five (41.5 overs).

†At Oxford, June 8, 9, 10. Drawn. Toss: MCC. MCC 355 for four dec. (A. W. Brown 31, A. Flower 156, A. J. Goldsmith 121) and 243 for eight dec. (P. W. Romaines 44, G. J. Toogood 36, S. D. Welch 34 not out); Oxford University 320 for nine dec. (J. E. R. Gallian 60, H. S. Malik 30, C. W. J. Lyons 78, B. Lawrence 52; S. D. Jack three for 52, K. G. Sedgbeer three for 59) and 20 for two.

OXFORD UNIVERSITY v WARWICKSHIRE

At Oxford, June 12, 14, 15. Drawn. Toss: Oxford University. First-class debut: B. C. A. Ellison.

Oxford's last first-class match of the season at The Parks was ruined by rain, which wiped out the first two days. In an uneventful one-innings game played on the Tuesday, Moles top-scored with 79 out of Warwickshire's 177 for three; Oxford had reached 118 for six when Munton and Gallian settled for the draw with three overs to play.

Close of play: First day, No play; Second day, No play.

Warwickshire

A. J. Moles b Ellison	79	T. L. Penney not out	16
J. D. Ratcliffe c Lyons b Trimby	37	W 1, n-b 10	11
R. G. Twose c Malik b Ellison	11		
D. P. Ostler not out	23	1/108 2/135 3/136 (3 wkts. dec.)	177

P. A. Smith, †P. C. L. Holloway, N. M. K. Smith, P. A. Booth, M. A. V. Bell and *T. A. Munton did not bat.

Bowling: Jeh 13–1–49–0; Gallian 8–2–29–0; Yeabsley 6–1–26–0; Trimby 18–6–33–1; Ellison 11–1–40–2.

Oxford University

R. R. Montgomerie c Ostler b Munton	6	R. S. Yeabsley lbw b Twose	0
*J. E. R. Gallian c Ostler b Booth	20	M. P. W. Jeh not out	4
G. B. T. Lovell lbw b Twose	39	B 2, l-b 1, w 1	4
C. L. Keey c Twose b N. M. K. Smith	9		
H. S. Malik c P. A. Smith b Twose	9	1/19 2/40 3/63 (6 wkts)	118
†C. W. J. Lyons not out	27	4/78 5/91 6/91	

G. I. Macmillan, B. C. A. Ellison and P. W. Trimby did not bat.

Bowling: Bell 5–0–22–0; Munton 5–3–6–1; Booth 11–5–16–1; P. A. Smith 6–0–21–0; N. M. K. Smith 10–4–16–1; Twose 6–0–34–3.

Umpires: P. Adams and H. D. Bird.

†At Oxford, June 16, 17. Drawn. Toss: Oxford University. Oxford University 282 for four dec. (R. R. Montgomerie 113, G. B. T. Lovell 71, H. S. Malik 31; J. P. Pearce three for 117); Harlequins 217 for five (J. Ricketts 31, N. Martin 131, R. Turnill 33).

At Worcester, June 18, 19, 20. OXFORD UNIVERSITY drew with WORCESTERSHIRE.

†At Aldershot, June 26, 27, 28. Oxford University won by 182 runs. Toss: Oxford University. Oxford University 350 for eight dec. (R. R. Montgomerie 180, J. E. R. Gallian 84, C. L. Keey 31) and 218 for seven dec. (C. M. Gupte 40, G. I. Macmillan 40, C. W. J. Lyons 71 not out; AEM J. Mann four for 60); Combined Services 254 (Capt. R. J. Greatorex 58, FS B. Phillips 32; M. P. W. Jeh five for 80) and 132 (H. S. Malik three for 25).

At Lord's, June 30, July 1, 2. OXFORD UNIVERSITY beat CAMBRIDGE UNIVERSITY by nine wickets.

CAMBRIDGE

President: Professor A. D. Buckingham (Pembroke)

Captain: J. P. Crawley (Manchester GS and Trinity)
Secretary: C. M. Pitcher (St Edward's, Oxford and Selwyn)

Captain for 1994: A. R. Whittall (Falcon College, Zimbabwe and Trinity)
Secretary: R. Q. Cake (KCS, Wimbledon and St John's)

Although Cambridge lost only two of their ten first-class fixtures, 1993 was a season of under-achievement for a team that had promised to be one of the strongest of recent years. Significantly, the two losses, at the hands of Kent and Oxford, who were both keen to avenge defeats the previous year, came on the two occasions Cambridge were asked to follow on.

It was the batting, leaning so heavily on John Crawley, that proved to be the big disappointment. The captain led from the front, having moved up from No. 3 to open. From there he dominated the run-making, scoring 828 runs at an average of 69. He amply illustrated his ability and the potential to emulate Mike Atherton, his predecessor at Manchester Grammar School as well as Cambridge, and his team-mate at Lancashire. Inevitably it was Crawley who scored the University's only first-class century of the summer, a career-best 187 not out against Sussex at Hove, in the last county match of the term. Unfortunately, he could not quite repeat the feat in the next game at Lord's, where his team was comprehensively outplayed by a much stronger Oxford side.

Russell Cake, a hockey-playing Freshman from King's College School, Wimbledon, emerged as the best of the rest. The highlight of his debut season was a century for the Combined Universities against the Australian tourists at Oxford. Disappointingly, he too failed to rise to the occasion at Lord's, where he bagged a pair. Mike Jarrett repaid his captain's loyalty, playing several match-saving innings; however, Graham Charlesworth, a one-year graduate student who had previously appeared for several county second elevens and for Griqualand West in South Africa, was generally disappointing. Charlesworth and the obdurate opener, Garri Jones, were the only others to top 200 runs.

While batting was a problem, Cambridge possessed greater bowling strength than for some years. Five players shared the 75 wickets which fell to bowlers, with off-spinners Richard Pearson and Andy Whittall claiming 39 of them in 620 overs – almost half the 1,325 bowled, reflecting Cambridge's recent reliance on spin. But no one took more than three wickets in an innings and Charlesworth's three for 33 against Leicestershire was the best return of the season.

Cambridge were not always helped by the weather, nor by the slow pitches at Fenner's. But there were signs of changing times. In an effort to improve the quality of the square, the club had decided to re-lay a small area and the opening match of the season, against Derbyshire, was played on a new pitch. Its pace and bounce so impressed the umpires that they sent a complimentary report to the TCCB. Encouraged, the university hoped to lay more new pitches during the next few winters. – David Hallett.

CAMBRIDGE UNIVERSITY 1993

[Bill Smith]

Back row: G. J. Saville (*coach*), G. W. Jones, J. P. Arscott, R. H. J. Jenkins, G. M. Charlesworth, A. R. Whittall, N. J. Haste, R. Q. Cake, A. R. May (*scorer*). *Front row*: J. P. Carroll, R. M. Pearson, J. P. Crawley (*captain*), C. M. Pitcher, M. E. D. Jarrett.

CAMBRIDGE UNIVERSITY RESULTS

First-class matches – Played 10: Lost 2, Drawn 8.

FIRST-CLASS AVERAGES

BATTING AND FIELDING

	Birthplace	M	I	NO	R	HS	Avge	Ct/St
J. P. Crawley	Maldon	9	15	3	828	187*	69.00	6
R. Q. Cake	Chertsey	10	17	3	348	83	31.63	5
M. E. D. Jarrett	London	8	13	1	277	51	23.08	3
G. M. Charlesworth....	Ashow, Warwicks.	10	15	3	250	49	20.83	3
G. W. Jones	Birmingham	10	16	1	241	45*	16.06	1
J. P. Arscott	Tooting	10	12	3	105	22*	11.66	12/1
R. M. Pearson	Batley	9	9	1	93	31	11.62	3
A. R. Whittall	Umtali, Rhodesia	10	9	2	80	40	11.42	2
C. M. Pitcher	Croydon	9	8	2	61	27*	10.16	5
N. J. Haste	Northampton	10	9	1	76	36	9.50	5
J. Leppard	South Benfleet	5	6	0	55	20	9.16	0
J. P. Carroll	Bebington	8	12	1	69	21	6.27	1

Also batted: P. M. C. Millar (*Westminster*) (1 match) 2. R. H. J. Jenkins (*Leicester*) (1 match) did not bat.

* *Signifies not out.*

J. P. Crawley played the only three-figure innings for Cambridge University.

BOWLING

	O	M	R	W	BB	5W/i	Avge
R. M. Pearson	310.3	67	876	20	3-61	0	43.80
C. M. Pitcher	203.1	35	698	14	3-50	0	49.85
A. R. Whittall	309.3	63	969	19	3-79	0	51.00
G. M. Charlesworth....	229.5	52	645	12	3-33	0	53.75
N. J. Haste	225	43	715	10	2-44	0	71.50

Also bowled: R. H. J. Jenkins 16–1–77–0; J. Leppard 11–0–40–0; P. M. C. Millar 20–4–61–0.

Note: Matches in this section which were not first-class are signified by a dagger.

†At Cambridge, April 8. Cambridge University won by 48 runs. Toss: Cambridge University. Cambridge University 185 for three (50 overs) (J. P. Crawley 36, J. P. Carroll 50 not out, R. Q. Cake 42; J. Barr three for 24); Loughborough University 137 (49.1 overs) (C. M. Pitcher four for 29, G. M. Charlesworth three for 26).

†At Cambridge, April 9. No result, rain having stopped play. Toss: Cambridge University. Cambridge University 44 for two (18 overs) v Loughborough University.

†At Cambridge, April 10. Cambridge University v Durham University. Abandoned without a ball bowled, owing to rain.

†At Cambridge, April 11. Durham University won by six wickets. Toss: Cambridge University. Cambridge University 116 for nine (35 overs) (J. P. Crawley 56); Durham University 117 for four (33.3 overs) (A. C. Richards 61).

CAMBRIDGE UNIVERSITY v DERBYSHIRE

At Cambridge, April 14, 15, 16. Drawn. Toss: Cambridge University. First-class debuts: R. Q. Cake, N. J. Haste, J. Leppard, P. M. C. Millar, A. R. Whittall.

The match provided early-season practice for Derbyshire's batsmen and the new computerised scoring system, which suffered occasional glitches, aggravated by having to share the electricity supply with a hamburger van. Morris and O'Gorman promptly embarked with centuries on April 14, the earliest date for a Derbyshire hundred. Morris, the more aggressive, hit two sixes and 18 fours in his 30th first-class century, as they added 174 for the third wicket. Crawley dominated Cambridge's reply, batting for 83 of their 88.4 overs and scoring more than half the total of 140. Barnett chose not to enforce the follow-on: instead he and Bowler ran up their 17th first-class century opening stand before a lunchtime declaration set Cambridge 378 in four hours. They were happy to survive, with Jones scoring 17 runs in nearly three hours.

Close of play: First day, Derbyshire 380-5 (T. J. G. O'Gorman 130*); Second day, Derbyshire 41-0 (K. J. Barnett 10*, P. D. Bowler 29*).

Derbyshire

P. D. Bowler b Pearson	15	– (2) not out	73
C. J. Adams c Arscott b Charlesworth	5	– (3) c Crawley b Whittall	16
J. E. Morris b Charlesworth	136		
T. J. G. O'Gorman not out	130		
F. A. Griffith c Charlesworth b Whittall	25		
D. G. Cork c Arscott b Haste	56	– (1) c Crawley b Whittall	42
*K. J. Barnett (did not bat)		–	
B 4, l-b 7, n-b 2	13	L-b 6	6

1/5 2/55 3/229   (5 wkts. dec.) 380   1/115 2/137   (2 wkts. dec.) 137
4/297 5/380

†K. M. Krikken, A. E. Warner, R. W. Sladdin and S. J. Base did not bat.

Bowling: *First Innings*—Charlesworth 20-2-74-2; Haste 19-2-67-1; Pearson 21-3-80-1; Millar 14-4-41-0; Whittall 26-4-78-1; Leppard 8-0-29-0. *Second Innings*—Charlesworth 13-3-29-0; Haste 10-2-28-0; Whittall 10.1-4-26-2; Millar 6-0-20-0; Pearson 14-1-28-0.

Cambridge University

*J. P. Crawley c Griffith b Base	73	– c O'Gorman b Sladdin	32
G. W. Jones lbw b Cork	0	– lbw b Morris	17
J. P. Carroll c and b Cork	4	– b Sladdin	13
G. M. Charlesworth c Bowler b Griffith	17	– not out	20
R. Q. Cake lbw b Sladdin	1	– not out	10
J. Leppard c Krikken b Cork	5		
†J. P. Arscott c Krikken b Sladdin	21		
N. J. Haste b Base	3		
R. M. Pearson st Krikken b Sladdin	6		
A. R. Whittall not out	2		
P. M. C. Millar lbw b Griffith	2		
L-b 3, w 3	6	B 2, w 4	6

1/1 2/11 3/66 4/72 5/83   140   1/37 2/59 3/84   (3 wkts.) 98
6/120 7/124 8/135 9/137

Bowling: *First Innings*—Cork 15.4-4-21-3; Warner 16-11-9-0; Griffith 15.4-6-31-2; Base 12-3-20-2; Sladdin 30-11-56-3. *Second Innings*—Cork 10.4-4-17-0; Warner 8-4-16-0; Sladdin 24-15-20-2; Griffith 8-1-16-0; Adams 8-2-10-0; Bowler 2-0-8-0; Morris 6-1-6-1; Base 2-1-3-0.

Umpires: P. Adams and B. J. Meyer.

CAMBRIDGE UNIVERSITY v YORKSHIRE

At Cambridge, April 17, 18, 19. Drawn. Toss: Cambridge University.

The final afternoon became a frustrating one for Yorkshire's batsmen: Byas came off with a "migraine" to give Carrick a chance of reaching the 51 runs he needed to complete 10,000 for the county. But Carrick made only 16, and though Byas recovered he perished in the attempt to reach 100 before Moxon declared at tea. On the first day Metcalfe made his bid to reclaim the opener's job by batting more than four hours for an unbeaten 133. The Yorkshire-born off-spinner Pearson bowled 26 overs for 39 runs without claiming a wicket, but his counterpart Batty took five when Cambridge replied and slid from 61 without loss to 94 for seven. Despite the loss of Broadhurst, with bruised ribs, after he had bowled only seven balls, Yorkshire dismissed Cambridge for 137.

Close of play: First day, Yorkshire 172-3 (A. A. Metcalfe 77*, R. J. Blakey 7*); Second day, Cambridge University 126-8 (R. Q. Cake 21*, A. R. Whittall 0*).

Yorkshire

*M. D. Moxon c Carroll b Pitcher	4	– c Haste b Whittall		27
A. A. Metcalfe not out	133			
S. A. Kellett c Crawley b Whittall	53			
C. White c Arscott b Haste	15	– (3) b Pearson		34
†R. J. Blakey not out	41	– (6) not out		0
D. Byas (did not bat)		– (2) c Jones b Pearson		90
P. Carrick (did not bat)		– (4) not out		16
D. Gough (did not bat)		– (5) c Arscott b Pitcher		10
B 5, l-b 10, w 1, n-b 8	24	L-b 1, w 1, n-b 2		4

1/5 2/108 3/147   (3 wkts dec.) 270   1/53 2/148   (4 wkts dec.) 181
                                                 3/163 4/180

J. D. Batty, M. Broadhurst and S. M. Milburn did not bat.

In the second innings D. Byas, when 77, retired ill at 141 and resumed at 163.

Bowling: *First Innings*—Charlesworth 12–3–40–0; Pitcher 17–4–63–1; Haste 24–7–43–1; Whittall 28–8–70–1; Pearson 26–8–39–0. *Second Innings*—Haste 7–3–27–0; Charlesworth 17–6–32–0; Pitcher 10–0–36–1; Whittall 12–3–40–1; Pearson 18–2–45–2.

Cambridge University

*J. P. Crawley st Blakey b Batty	30	– not out		33
G. W. Jones lbw b White	17			
J. P. Carroll c Byas b Batty	2			
G. M. Charlesworth lbw b Batty	5			
R. Q. Cake not out	29	– (2) not out		25
J. Leppard c Blakey b Batty	0			
†J. P. Arscott c White b Batty	8			
N. J. Haste lbw b Carrick	5			
R. M. Pearson b Gough	22			
A. R. Whittall b White	0			
C. M. Pitcher c Blakey b Gough	2			
B 4, l-b 8, w 1, n-b 4	17	L-b 1, n-b 3		4

1/61 2/61 3/68 4/73 5/73   137   (no wkt) 62
6/81 7/94 8/121 9/128

Bowling: *First Innings*—Gough 18.4–7–37–2; Broadhurst 1.1–0–7–0; Milburn 11.5–7–18–0; Batty 25–7–36–5; White 8–0–13–2; Carrick 12–6–14–1. *Second Innings*—Gough 6–3–9–0; Milburn 6–1–17–0; Moxon 4–2–7–0; Byas 2–0–18–0; Batty 6–1–10–0; Carrick 5–5–0–0.

Umpires: B. J. Meyer and M. K. Reed.

CAMBRIDGE UNIVERSITY v KENT

At Cambridge, April 21, 22, 23. Kent won by an innings and 34 runs. Toss: Cambridge University.

Cambridge had brief hopes of repeating their 1992 victory over Kent when they reduced them to 107 for five, but a stand of 125 between Llong and Marsh permitted a more respectable 273 by the close. Early next morning, the left-hander Llong completed his maiden first-class century before Marsh declared at 300. The University's batting, already weakened by the absence of Crawley, who was playing for England A at Chelmsford, and deprived of Jones until he had finished his morning exam, succumbed for 142. That represented a recovery from 97 for nine, but left them nine short of avoiding the follow-on, which Marsh did not hesitate to enforce. Cambridge were all out for 124, with Davis claiming five for 26 in 24 overs and fellow-spinner Llong rounding off his game with a career-best three for 29.

Close of play: First day, Kent 273-6 (N. J. Llong 99*, D. W. Headley 18*); Second day, Cambridge University 37-1 (R. Q. Cake 11*, M. E. D. Jarrett 22*).

Kent

T. R. Ward c Arscott b Charlesworth	17	*†S. A. Marsh c Arscott b Whittall	57
J. I. Longley b Pitcher	2	D. W. Headley not out	26
N. R. Taylor lbw b Pearson	34	B 3, l-b 6, w 1, n-b 8	18
G. R. Cowdrey c Haste b Charlesworth	13		
N. J. Llong not out	116	1/6 2/22 3/63	(6 wkts dec.) 300
M. V. Fleming c Whittall b Pearson	17	4/83 5/107 6/232	

R. P. Davis, C. Penn and A. P. Igglesden did not bat.

Bowling: Charlesworth 22–7–52–2; Pitcher 12–5–30–1; Whittall 35–10–84–1; Haste 20–4–55–0; Pearson 28–7–70–2.

Cambridge University

R. Q. Cake b Igglesden	2	– (2) c Ward b Llong	27
M. E. D. Jarrett c Longley b Penn	1	– (3) c and b Davis	38
G. M. Charlesworth c Marsh b Penn	5	– (4) not out	18
J. P. Carroll c Marsh b Fleming	6	– (5) c and b Davis	1
J. Leppard c Longley b Penn	16	– (6) st Marsh b Davis	8
G. W. Jones c Marsh b Headley	38	– (1) c Marsh b Igglesden	2
†J. P. Arscott b Penn	8	– c Llong b Davis	5
N. J. Haste not out	26	– c Marsh b Davis	0
*R. M. Pearson c and b Davis	5	– c Penn b Llong	10
C. M. Pitcher run out	0	– c Davis b Llong	4
A. R. Whittall run out	27	– lbw b Igglesden	1
B 5, l-b 3	8	L-b 10	10

1/2 2/4 3/8 4/20 5/38	142	1/4 2/67 3/71 4/78 5/90	124
6/50 7/88 8/97 9/97		6/98 7/98 8/115 9/123	

Bowling: *First Innings*—Igglesden 10–1–27–1; Penn 12–7–12–4; Fleming 11–6–12–1; Headley 14–5–28–1; Davis 11–4–28–1; Llong 6–1–27–0. *Second Innings*—Igglesden 13.5–5–14–2; Penn 13–3–21–0; Headley 4–0–17–0; Fleming 5–2–7–0; Davis 24–11–26–5; Llong 23–10–29–3.

Umpires: J. H. Hampshire and D. O. Oslear.

CAMBRIDGE UNIVERSITY v ESSEX

At Cambridge, May 1, 2, 3. Drawn. Toss: Essex.

When told that his 100th first-class century, scored at Cuttack in January, was only reckoned to be his 99th by ICC, who did not recognise his matches for the South African Breweries XI as first-class, Gooch replied that he would have to get another against Cambridge. He duly passed the landmark with his second six and immediately walked off, disdaining the pretence of an injury; under Law 2.9, he was thus regarded as out. Hussain, who had partnered him in a stand of 159, also reached a century, though Cambridge removed Essex's last five wickets for 35 runs. But the University could only muster 105, the bulk of it once again from Crawley. Essex took some extra batting practice before setting Cambridge a notional 447 in four hours. This time Crawley had some support, from Jarrett, and saved the game.

Close of play: First day, Cambridge University 37-1 (J. P. Crawley 32*, M. E. D. Jarrett 4*); Second day, Essex 96-0 (P. J. Prichard 44*, N. V. Knight 51*).

Essex

*G. A. Gooch retired out	105		
P. J. Prichard c Crawley b Haste	6	– (1) c Whittall b Haste	54
N. V. Knight lbw b Charlesworth	11	– (2) c Haste b Pearson	94
N. Hussain c Haste b Whittall	111		
N. Shahid c Cake b Pearson	4	– (4) lbw b Pearson	8
†M. A. Garnham lbw b Pitcher	10	– (3) c Pitcher b Pearson	18
N. A. Foster c Arscott b Whittall	37	– (5) not out	26
T. D. Topley b Pearson	25	– (6) not out	19
P. M. Such c Arscott b Charlesworth	0		
S. J. W. Andrew c Jarrett b Whittall	1		
J. H. Childs not out	1		
B 4, l-b 5, w 1, n-b 2	12	B 2, l-b 5, n-b 2	9

1/17 2/40 3/199 4/217 5/246	323	1/132 2/163	(4 wkts dec.) 228
6/288 7/297 8/304 9/307		3/181 4/190	

Bowling: *First Innings*—Haste 15-1-48-1; Charlesworth 19-5-55-2; Pitcher 13-1-49-1; Whittall 23-6-85-3; Pearson 19.3-0-77-2. *Second Innings*—Haste 16-6-38-1; Charlesworth 7-1-14-0; Pitcher 10-0-48-0; Pearson 17-2-70-3; Whittall 16-4-51-0.

Cambridge University

*J. P. Crawley b Childs	63	– c Shahid b Childs	60
G. W. Jones c Garnham b Andrew	1	– c Knight b Childs	9
M. E. D. Jarrett c Garnham b Foster	10	– lbw b Such	47
R. Q. Cake c Knight b Andrew	0	– not out	14
G. M. Charlesworth b Andrew	0	– not out	1
J. P. Carroll c Gooch b Topley	5		
†J. P. Arscott lbw b Childs	0		
N. J. Haste c and b Childs	1		
R. M. Pearson b Hussain b Topley	5		
C. M. Pitcher not out	10		
A. R. Whittall c Garnham b Topley	9		
L-b 1	1	B 3, l-b 11	14

1/8 2/63 3/66 4/70 5/77	105	1/54 2/95 3/139	(3 wkts) 145
6/78 7/79 8/84 9/88			

Bowling: *First Innings*—Foster 12-4-30-1; Andrew 20-4-47-3; Such 1-0-1-0; Topley 12.4-8-15-3; Childs 13-7-11-3. *Second Innings*—Foster 12-2-40-0; Andrew 6-5-1-0; Topley 5-1-12-0; Such 17-4-44-1; Childs 18-8-28-2; Shahid 6-4-6-0.

Umpires: P. Adams and R. Julian.

CAMBRIDGE UNIVERSITY v GLAMORGAN

At Cambridge, May 5, 6, 7. Drawn. Toss: Glamorgan.

Another competent, if not inspired, performance in the field from Cambridge kept Glamorgan to 298 for eight on the first day. The county owed much of that to the efforts of Croft, who batted three hours for his maiden century, striking 14 fours from 164 balls. But the University's usual middle-order vulnerability emphasised their reliance on Crawley, who just missed his fifty, and Cake, who reached one for the first time. Glamorgan eventually set Cambridge 314 in a little over three and a half hours, and Crawley responded by setting off at a run a minute. But when he fell for 49 a second time, Jarrett settled down to keep out the Glamorgan attack.

Close of play: First day, Glamorgan 298-8 (C. P. Metson 14*, S. L. Watkin 2*); Second day, Glamorgan 46-1 (D. L. Hemp 14*, P. A. Cottey 3*).

Glamorgan

S. P. James b Pitcher	31	– (6) lbw b Pitcher	6
*H. Morris c and b Pearson	51		
M. P. Maynard b Pitcher	20		
P. A. Cottey st Arscott b Pearson	5	– (3) retired hurt	13
D. L. Hemp c Charlesworth b Whittall	19	– (2) c and b Pearson	33
R. D. B. Croft c Cake b Whittall	107	– (8) not out	24
A. Dale c sub b Charlesworth	29	– (5) c Arscott b Pitcher	17
R. P. Lefebvre lbw b Charlesworth	14	– (4) c Crawley b Pitcher	35
†C. P. Metson not out	14	– (1) b Charlesworth	25
S. L. Watkin not out	2	– (7) not out	24
L-b 3, w 1, n-b 2	6	B 7, l-b 1, n-b 2	10

1/83 2/103 3/109 4/111 5/170   (8 wkts dec.) 298   1/31 2/77 3/129   (5 wkts dec.) 187
6/239 7/267 8/282   4/134 5/137

S. R. Barwick did not bat.

In the second innings P. A. Cottey retired hurt at 66.

Bowling: *First Innings*—Haste 15-1-41-0; Charlesworth 21-5-51-2; Pearson 29-9-68-2; Pitcher 17-3-58-2; Whittall 23-3-77-2. *Second Innings*—Haste 13-4-45-0; Charlesworth 7-1-17-1; Pearson 21-6-53-1; Whittall 6-3-14-0; Pitcher 13-2-50-3.

Cambridge University

*J. P. Crawley lbw b Lefebvre	49	– c Maynard b Croft	49
G. W. Jones c Lefebvre b Croft	24	– c Maynard b Barwick	7
M. E. D. Jarrett b Barwick	5	– not out	43
R. Q. Cake not out	57	– c and b Croft	9
G. M. Charlesworth lbw b Lefebvre	0	– b Dale	25
J. P. Carroll c Metson b Croft	1	– c Maynard b Dale	0
†J. P. Arscott c Lefebvre b Watkin	6	– not out	15
N. J. Haste b Watkin	0		
C. M. Pitcher c Maynard b Watkin	18		
A. R. Whittall c Morris b Barwick	1		
R. M. Pearson lbw b Watkin	0		
B 4, l-b 7	11	B 2, l-b 3	5

1/46 2/54 3/93 4/93 5/102   172   1/53 2/61 3/79   (5 wkts) 153
6/111 7/112 8/162 9/171   4/122 5/122

Bowling: *First Innings*—Watkin 21-8-36-4; Lefebvre 16-4-31-2; Barwick 22-5-39-2; Croft 25-13-39-2; Dale 5-1-16-0. *Second Innings*—Watkin 10-2-33-0; Lefebvre 8-5-22-0; Barwick 10-2-31-1; Croft 20-11-32-2; Dale 12-5-30-2.

Umpires: B. Dudleston and T. E. Jesty.

†At Cambridge, May 9. Cryptics won by six wickets. Toss: Cambridge University. Cambridge University 199 for seven dec. (J. P. Arscott 42, D. E. Stanley 68; J. P. Pearce three for 53); Cryptics 200 for four (J. A. Claughton 100, D. C. Elstone 31, J. Drake-Brockman 34).

†At Cambridge, May 10, 11, 12. Cambridge University won by four wickets. Toss: MCC. MCC 265 for four dec. (R. A. McGregor 114, C. F. B. P. Rudd 116) and 220 for four dec. (K. T. Medlycott 58, P. J. Hacker 82 not out, S. D. Jack 39 not out); Cambridge University 247 for two dec. (G. W. Jones 46, R. Q. Cake 125 not out, G. M. Charlesworth 37 not out, Extras 31) and 242 for six (J. P. Arscott 46, G. M. Charlesworth 34, R. Q. Cake 67 not out, C. M. Pitcher 34 not out).

†At Cambridge, May 13. Cambridge University won by 11 runs. Toss: Cambridge University. Cambridge University 222 for six (55 overs) (R. D. Mann 53, J. P. Carroll 33, G. M. Charlesworth 48, J. P. Arscott 41 not out; S. V. Aldis three for 38); Cambridgeshire 211 (55 overs) (N. T. Gadsby 34, T. C. Williams 61, Extras 33).

CAMBRIDGE UNIVERSITY v LEICESTERSHIRE

At Cambridge, May 15, 16, 17. Drawn. Toss: Cambridge University. First-class debut: J. M. Dakin.

For the first time in two years Cambridge elected to bat against a county and, despite the early loss of both openers, Jarrett and Charlesworth led them towards 179. That total looked healthier when they reduced Leicestershire to 111 for six. But Potter and acting-captain Parsons restored sanity, though both were dropped behind the wicket in a strong wind. Potter had just reached his century when Leicestershire were bowled out for 282. But with play curtailed by the weather Cambridge spent the final day compiling 256, their first total over 200 of the season, thanks to eighties from Crawley and Cake.

Close of play: First day, Leicestershire 40-2 (B. F. Smith 7*, P. E. Robinson 4*); Second day, Cambridge University 2-0 (J. P. Crawley 0*, G. W. Jones 2*).

Cambridge University

*J. P. Crawley c Nixon b Mullally	6	– b Parsons	86
G. W. Jones lbw b Dakin	0	– lbw b Mullally	7
M. E. D. Jarrett c Benson b Pierson	51	– c Benson b Parsons	9
R. Q. Cake c Potter b Parsons	22	– b Robinson	83
G. M. Charlesworth lbw b Dakin	49	– lbw b Hepworth	27
†J. P. Arscott c Nixon b Dakin	0	– (7) not out	22
J. Leppard c Benson b Potter	20	– (6) lbw b Wells	6
N. J. Haste c Parsons b Dakin	5		
R. M. Pearson not out	13		
C. M. Pitcher c Benson b Parsons	0		
A. R. Whittall st Nixon b Potter	0		
B 1, l-b 5, w 1, n-b 6	13	L-b 8, w 4, n-b 4	16

1/2 2/16 3/50 4/111 5/114   179   1/55 2/91 3/116   (6 wkts dec.) 256
6/143 7/157 8/169 9/174   4/176 5/186 6/256

Bowling: *First Innings*—Mullally 13–6–28–1; Dakin 22–9–45–4; Parsons 11–6–23–2; Smith 7–2–22–0; Potter 11.4–4–17–2; Pierson 17–5–38–1. *Second Innings*—Mullally 16–7–42–1; Dakin 12–1–39–0; Potter 18–8–34–0; Pierson 15–5–46–0; Hepworth 9–1–26–1; Wells 7–2–12–1; Robinson 1–0–13–1.

Leicestershire

J. D. R. Benson lbw b Haste	11	J. M. Dakin lbw b Charlesworth	5
P. N. Hepworth b Haste	18	A. R. K. Pierson b Pearson	15
B. F. Smith b Pearson	17	A. D. Mullally c Arscott b Pitcher	7
P. E. Robinson lbw b Charlesworth	33		
V. J. Wells lbw b Pitcher	1	B 8, l-b 3, n-b 2	13
L. Potter not out	103		
†P. A. Nixon c Crawley b Charlesworth		1/25 2/34 3/61 4/64 5/111	282
*G. J. Parsons run out	59	6/111 7/218 8/232 9/257	

Bowling: Pitcher 22.1–5–72–2; Haste 14–5–44–2; Pearson 26–5–77–2; Charlesworth 21–6–33–3; Whittall 18–6–34–0; Leppard 3–0–11–0.

Umpires: A. Clarkson and D. O. Oslear.

CAMBRIDGE UNIVERSITY v LANCASHIRE

At Cambridge, May 19, 20, 21. Drawn. Toss: Cambridge University.

Rain prevented any play after the first day, when Lancashire reached 342 for three. Mendis scored what was to be the only century of his benefit season after sharing an opening stand of 173 with Atherton, leading the county against his old university. Atherton had been only nine short of his own hundred when he judged it prudent to retire with a back muscle spasm.

Close of play: First day, Lancashire 342-3 (W. K. Hegg 26*, M. Watkinson 31*); Second day, No play.

Lancashire

G. D. Mendis c Jarrett b Haste	106	M. Watkinson not out 31
*M. A. Atherton retired hurt	91	
N. J. Speak c Arscott b Haste	35	L-b 3, w 2, n-b 2 7
G. D. Lloyd c Pearson b Whittall	46	
†W. K. Hegg not out	26	1/228 2/281 3/289 (3 wkts) 342

P. A. J. DeFreitas, P. J. Martin, S. D. Fletcher, G. Chapple and A. A. Barnett did not bat.

M. A. Atherton retired hurt at 173.

Bowling: Pitcher 17–3–55–0; Charlesworth 19–2–65–0; Pearson 28–8–80–0; Haste 20–3–56–2; Whittall 20–2–83–1.

Cambridge University

*J. P. Crawley, G. W. Jones, M. E. D. Jarrett, R. Q. Cake, G. M. Charlesworth, J. Leppard, †J. P. Arscott, N. J. Haste, C. M. Pitcher, R. M. Pearson and A. R. Whittall.

Umpires: A. Clarkson and J. W. Holder.

†At Cambridge, June 6. Drawn. Toss: Cambridge University. Cambridge University 242 for two dec. (G. W. Jones 100, G. M. Charlesworth 101 not out); Free Foresters 228 for six (R. McLeay 65, D. C. Sandiford 70).

†At Arundel, June 10. Cambridge University won by nine wickets. Toss: Lavinia, Duchess of Norfolk's XI. Lavinia, Duchess of Norfolk's XI 165 for seven dec. (D. Briance 39, C. Light 42, S. Savant 34; C. M. Pitcher four for 40, R. H. J. Jenkins three for 56); Cambridge University 169 for one (J. P. Crawley 108 not out, G. W. Jones 44).

CAMBRIDGE UNIVERSITY v NOTTINGHAMSHIRE

At Cambridge, June 12, 13, 14. Drawn. Toss: Cambridge University.

Play was only possible on the second day, when Pollard completed an unbeaten four-hour century for Nottinghamshire. Pick's early declaration gave Cambridge 25 overs' batting, in which Crawley reached 28 not out; the next day's weather deprived him of his final chance to score a first-class hundred at Fenner's while a student.

Close of play: First day, No play; Second day, Cambridge University 51-2 (J. P. Crawley 28*, R. Q. Cake 6*).

Nottinghamshire

P. R. Pollard not out	104	M. G. Field-Buss not out		20
M. Saxelby lbw b Pearson	31			
G. F. Archer b Pearson	1	B 8, l-b 6, w 1, n-b 2		17
W. A. Dessaur b Whittall	0			—
K. P. Evans c Jarrett b Whittall	24	1/79 2/83 3/84	(5 wkts dec.)	200
G. W. Mike c Pitcher b Pearson	3	4/130 5/141		

*R. A. Pick, †S. Bramhall, D. B. Pennett and J. A. Afford did not bat.

Bowling: Charlesworth 9–5–9–0; Pitcher 17–1–48–0; Whittall 21–3–57–2; Haste 4–0–11–0; Pearson 24–5–61–3.

Cambridge University

*J. P. Crawley not out	28
G. W. Jones b Pennett	5
M. E. D. Jarrett b Evans	8
R. Q. Cake not out	6
B 1, l-b 1, n-b 2	4
1/9 2/38 (2 wkts)	51

G. M. Charlesworth, J. P. Carroll, †J. P. Arscott, N. J. Haste, C. M. Pitcher, R. M. Pearson and A. R. Whittall did not bat.

Bowling: Pennett 6–1–14–1; Pick 6–0–18–0; Mike 5–2–10–0; Evans 4–1–6–1; Afford 2–2–0–0; Field-Buss 2–1–1–0.

Umpires: A. Clarkson and K. E. Palmer.

†At Cambridge, June 15, 16, 17. Cambridge University won by 20 runs. Toss: Combined Services. Cambridge University 131 (J. P. Arscott 51; Cpl M. King four for 29) and 133 for two dec. (R. Q. Cake 66, J. P. Carroll 49 not out); Combined Services 70 for three dec. (Cpl A. Elks 35 not out) and 174 (A. R. Whittall seven for 80).

†At Cambridge, June 19. Cambridge University won by five wickets. Toss: Sydney University. Sydney University 138 for eight (50 overs) (T. Watkins 42; A. R. Whittall three for 18); Cambridge University 142 for five (39.1 overs) (J. P. Crawley 74).

†At Cambridge, June 20. Cambridge University won by five wickets. Toss: Quidnuncs. Quidnuncs 223 (R. Heap 30, M. J. Morris 55, J. C. M. Atkinson 42; A. R. Whittall six for 87); Cambridge University 227 for five (G. M. Charlesworth 117, J. Leppard 33).

†At Cambridge, June 21. Club Cricket Conference won by ten wickets. Toss: Cambridge University. Cambridge University 212 for three (50 overs) (J. P. Carroll 58, M. E. D. Jarrett 38, J. Leppard 40, R. Q. Cake 55 not out); Club Cricket Conference 213 for no wkt (45.4 overs) (S. Brewster 104 not out, A. Small 100 not out).

At Hove, June 26, 27, 28. CAMBRIDGE UNIVERSITY drew with SUSSEX.

THE UNIVERSITY MATCH, 1993

OXFORD UNIVERSITY v CAMBRIDGE UNIVERSITY

At Lord's, July 30, July 1, 2. Oxford University won by nine wickets. Toss: Cambridge University.

Oxford secured a comprehensive victory after taking control on the first day. The match was dominated by the captains, both of them on Lancashire's books even though Gallian was born and bred in Australia. Crawley, who had led Cambridge to an unexpected win the previous year chasing a target, gave Oxford first use of a good pitch. At first it looked as if his gamble might come off; in the third over of the match, Montgomerie was run out answering Gallian's call for a quick single, and Oxford resisted the temptation to hammer some rather ordinary bowling. But Cambridge had to wait 167 runs for the next wicket, when Macmillan fell for a steady 63. He was soon followed by Gallian, after his third first-class century, which included 14 fours and a six. Lovell, another Australian and the previous season's captain, also reached three figures on the second morning, before Gallian declared at 400. Cambridge were dismissed inside 68 overs, struggling against Jeh's pace, Trimby's leg-spin and the off-breaks of Macmillan. The only significant batting came from Crawley, fresh from his career-best 187 against Sussex. In the first innings, he scored 63 from 76 balls, out of 95 while he was at the crease. After his team lost their last four wickets for 12 runs and followed on, he made 49 out of 67. But Gallian trapped him lbw, the second wicket in his spell of three in 22 balls. Only a last-wicket stand of 70 in 15 overs from Pitcher and Whittall set Oxford any sort of target; they knocked off the 97 runs needed inside an hour.

Close of play: First day, Oxford University 308-4 (G. B. T. Lovell 80*, C. M. Gupte 7*); Second day, Cambridge University 35-0 (J. P. Crawley 30*, G. W. Jones 2*).

Oxford University

R. R. Montgomerie (*Rugby and Worcester*) run out 1	– c Cake b Pearson	23
*J. E. R. Gallian (*Pittwater House, Sydney and Keble*) c Cake b Whittall 115	– not out	53
G. I. Macmillan (*Guildford CS, Charterhouse, Southampton U. and Keble*) c Cake b Whittall . 63	– not out	15
G. B. T. Lovell (*Sydney C. of E. GS, Sydney U. and Exeter*) c Haste b Pitcher 114		
C. L. Keey (*Harrow, Durham U. and Keble*) b Pearson 33		
C. M. Gupte (*John Lyon S. and Pembroke*) not out................................... 43		
†C. W. J. Lyons (*King Edward VII S., Johannesburg, Witwatersrand and Keble*) run out 2		
R. S. Yeabsley (*Haberdashers' Aske's, Elstree and Keble*) not out 20		
B 2, l-b 5, n-b 2 9	B 4, l-b 1, w 4	9

1/3 2/170 3/186 4/276   (6 wkts dec.) 400   1/59   (1 wkt) 100
5/356 6/371

M. P. W. Jeh (*Brisbane State High, Griffith U. and Keble*), R. H. Macdonald (*Rondebosch Boys' HS, Cape Town U., Durham U. and Keble*) and P. W. Trimby (*Shrewsbury and Worcester*) did not bat.

Bowling: *First Innings*—Pitcher 27-3-90-1; Charlesworth 25.5-4-104-0; Pearson 30-10-77-1; Haste 13-1-61-0; Whittall 20-0-61-2. *Second Innings*—Pitcher 1-0-13-0; Pearson 9-1-51-1; Whittall 8.2-2-31-0.

Cambridge University

J. P. Crawley (Manchester GS and Trinity) lbw b Jeh	63	lbw b Gallian	49
G. W. Jones (King's, Chester and Gonville & Caius) c Trimby b Macmillan	39	lbw b Gallian	2
M. E. D. Jarrett (Harrow and Girton) b Trimby	22	c Lyons b Trimby	25
R. Q. Cake (KCS, Wimbledon and St John's) c Macmillan b Trimby	0	c Lyons b Gallian	0
G. M. Charlesworth (Bablake, Durham U. and Hughes Hall) lbw b Jeh	49	b Macdonald	17
M. P. Carroll (Rendcomb and Homerton) c Lovell b Macmillan	0	c Gallian b Jeh	21
*J. P. Arscott (Tonbridge and Magdalene) c Keey b Macmillan	0	c Gupte b Trimby	14
N. J. Haste (Wellingborough and Pembroke) b Jeh	36	c Gallian b Trimby	0
R. M. Pearson (Batley GS and St John's) c Yeabsley b Jeh	1	c Lovell b Jeh	31
C. M. Pitcher (St Edward's, Oxford and Selwyn) lbw b Trimby	0	not out	27
A. R. Whittall (Falcon, Zimbabwe and Trinity) not out	0	c Macmillan b Yeabsley	40
B 4, l-b 8, w 1, n-b 18	31	L-b 8, w 5, n-b 16	29
	241		**255**

1/95 2/136 3/144 4/160 5/168
6/168 7/229 8/238 9/241

1/44 2/67 3/67 4/103 5/138
6/138 7/138 8/181 9/185

Bowling: *First Innings*—Jeh 14·2–2–61–4; Gallian 5–0–14–0; Yeabsley 5–0–40–0; Trimby 24.2–8–79–3; Macdonald 10–2–22–0; Macmillan 9–5–13–3. *Second Innings*—Jeh 18–2–90–2; Gallian 16–2–52–3; Macdonald 8–3–23–1; Trimby 15–1–72–3; Macmillan 2–1–10–0; Yeabsley 1.4–1–0–1.

Umpires. G. I. Burgess and G. Sharp.

OXFORD v CAMBRIDGE, NOTES

Since the war Cambridge have won nine times (1949, 1953, 1957, 1958, 1972, 1979, 1982, 1986 and 1992) and Oxford eight (1946, 1948, 1951, 1959, 1966, 1976, 1984, and 1993). All other matches have been drawn; the 1988 fixture was abandoned without a ball being bowled.

Ninety-six three-figure innings have been played in the University matches. For the fullest lists see the 1940 and 1993 *Wisdens*. There have been three double-centuries for Cambridge (211 by G. Goonesena in 1957, 201 by A. Ratcliffe in 1931 and 200 by Majid Khan in 1970) and two for Oxford (238* by Nawab of Pataudi, sen. in 1931 and 201* by M. J. K. Smith in 1954). Ratcliffe's score was a record for the match for only one day, before being beaten by Pataudi's. M. J. K. Smith and R. J. Boyd-Moss (Cambridge) are the only players to score three hundreds.

The highest totals in the fixture are 503 in 1900, 457 in 1947 and 453 for eight in 1931, all by Oxford. Cambridge's highest is 432 for nine in 1936. The lowest totals are 32 by Oxford in 1878 and 39 by Cambridge in 1858.

F. C. Cobden, in the Oxford v Cambridge match in 1870, performed the hat-trick by taking the last three wickets and won an extraordinary game for Cambridge by two runs. The feat is without parallel in first-class cricket. Other hat-tricks, all for Cambridge, have been credited to A. G. Steel (1879), P. H. Morton (1880), J. F. Ireland (1911), and R. G. H. Lowe (1926). S. E. Butler, in the 1871 match, took all the wickets in the Cambridge first innings. D. W. Jarrett (Oxford 1975, Cambridge 1976), S. M. Wookey (Cambridge 1975-76, Oxford 1978) and G. Pathmanathan (Oxford 1975-78, Cambridge 1983) are alone in gaining cricket Blues for both Universities.

A full list of Blues from 1837 may be found in Wisdens *published between 1923 and 1939. The lists thereafter were curtailed:* Wisdens *from 1948 to 1972 list Blues since 1880; from 1972 to 1982 since 1919; from 1982 to 1992 since 1946.*

THE COMMERCIAL UNION
UAU CHAMPIONSHIP, 1993

By GRENVILLE HOLLAND

The 1993 season was a difficult and unsatisfactory one for Universitie
Athletic Union cricket. A much enlarged competition, coupled with som
poor and belated decisions, harmed the reputation of UAU.

Even before 1993, with over 40 universities competing for th
championship in the short examination-ridden summer term, it had ofte
been hard enough to get the season finished before the students went dow
In 1993, however, with the new universities and the Scottish universities a
joining in, the administrative difficulties were compounded. Unfortunatel
UAU's reaction was to shorten the season by a week, so that the fin
clashed with exam time. This was supposed to avoid a clash with th
Combined Universities v Australians fixture; in fact a switch of one da
would have averted this. Recognising the pressures, UAU also introduced
"no replay" rule for the league programme but they took this decision withou
giving adequate notice and this just added to the confusion.

The net effect was to render the 1993 competition almost meaningles
Durham won, for the fourth successive year, but their opponents in th
final, Manchester, had to field a much weakened side. And had it not bee
for the sportsmanship of the Newcastle captain, Graham Wilson, Durha
would not even have reached the last 16. Their first three games were calle
off and though Durham did secure wins against York and Hull – with 11
from Alex Richards – they needed a victory against Newcastle to qualif
The match took place on a dismal day and after Jeremy Hallett had tak
five for 31 to restrict Newcastle to 113 for six, heavy rain was sweepin
across the Racecourse ground. However, Newcastle volunteered to take th
field. Mercifully, their soaking lasted only 33 minutes as Toby Peirce an
Richards made the runs in 11 overs and hustled Durham into the nex
round.

They beat St Andrews and Loughborough, where the spinners Crai
Stanley and Matthew Brimson made the most of a wet, uncovered wicket t
reach the semi-finals. Their opponents there, Swansea, had been carrie
through by some excellent bowling from Scott Moffat, who took seven fo
51 against Cardiff Institute and five for 21 against Reading, the 1992 sem
finalists. This had been a tricky game for Swansea. They had restricte
Reading to 122 for eight in a match reduced to 50 overs but Swanse
themselves slid to 68 for six, before Treharne Parker and the captai
Duncan Verry carefully restored the position.

Manchester had a series of easy wins in the north-west, with Tor
Harrison in top form. Harrison made 117 out of a total of 310 for si
against Liverpool. Manchester's other group games (except for two wash
outs) consisted of them bowling out the opposition cheaply and winnin
by eight or nine wickets. Harrison then turned in an all-round performanc
in the challenge round against Edinburgh, scoring 97 and taking fou
wickets in a 159-run victory. In the quarter-final against Salford, Harriso
made 120.

Their next opponents were Kent, a growing force in UAU cricket for several years, who reached their third successive semi-final. However, Kent had made a bad start to the summer when they lost to Sussex by five wickets in the opening game. Gradually, their batsmen, led by the Kent county player David Fulton, began to establish some control. Fulton made 51 not out against West London Institute, when his team-mate Joe Owen made 87 not out. Fulton then scored an unbeaten century against City, 79 not out against LSE and 73 not out against Nottingham in the challenge round. In the quarter-final Kent met Sussex again and they had their revenge in spectacular fashion. Andy Whyte scored 147 not out and Fulton 105 out of a total of 305 for four. The target was well beyond Sussex, who were bowled out for 195 with spinner John Collins taking four for 30.

The semi-finals were scheduled for June 16 but heavy rain prevented play in either fixture that day. To get a start the following day, the Kent–Manchester match had to be switched from St Albans to Southgate, where they were lucky to find a well-covered wicket that enabled them to start almost on time. Fraser Stewart scored 65 not out for Manchester, which turned out to be the match-winning innings as the accuracy of their spinners tied Kent down. Durham, meanwhile, had an easy win over Swansea on a green pitch at Letchworth; after a slow start, the openers, Peirce and Richards, assumed command and it was the 46th over before they were parted.

This set up the final and Durham were able to celebrate the 150th anniversary of cricket at the university in some style. They had already claimed the indoor UAU and NCA titles. But it was an unsatisfactory result and unfair on Manchester. With some universities now contemplating "semesterisation", dividing the year into two terms instead of three, all summer sport – not just cricket – is facing even graver dangers in the future.

SEMI-FINALS

At Letchworth, June 17. Durham won by 117 runs. Toss: Durham. Durham 257 for three (58 overs) (M. T. E. Peirce 88, A. C. Richards 102); Swansea 140 for six (58 overs) (S. Moffat 46; J. N. Snape five for 33).

At Southgate, June 17. Manchester won by 39 runs. Toss: Manchester. Manchester 161 for nine (51 overs) (F. L. Stewart 65 not out; J. Owen three for 28); Kent 122 (46 overs) (R. Archer 38; J. M. S. Whittington five for 49, F. Irfan three for 40).

FINAL

DURHAM v MANCHESTER

At Southgate, June 18. Durham won by 210 runs. Toss: Durham.
Manchester were fatally weakened by the loss of three key players: Irfan and Whittington, who had taken eight wickets between them in the semi-final, and the opener Moore, all of whom had to return north to finish their exams. They were thus in no position to compete with Durham. Though the game was one-sided it was played in an excellent spirit. Knowing the Manchester bowling was frail, Durham chose to bat on a good wicket and, although Harrison bowled splendidly, they were rarely in trouble. Peirce and Richards put on 116 for the first wicket until Richards was out to Manchester's captain Hagen in the

24th over. On 154, Peirce, who had been steadiness personified, was surprised by a ball from Harrison and bowled for 83. However, Ecclestone, Windows and the talented Snape just added to Manchester's woes as Durham cruised to 316 for five in the available 60 overs. It was far too much for Manchester, who lost Cooper to a vicious, rising ball in the opening over from Stanley and could never meet the challenge. The spin of Snape and Brimson accounted for six wickets as Manchester were dismissed for 106.

Durham

M. T. E. Peirce b Harrison	83	C. J. Hawkes b Moore	
A. C. Richards c Hall b Hagen	50	R. J. Ballinger not out	
*S. C. Ecclestone b Harrison	20	B 7, l-b 12, w 4, n-b 1	2
J. N. Snape not out	88		
M. G. N. Windows c Jouning		1/116 2/154 3/187 (5 wkts, 60 overs) 316
b Harrison	49	4/278 5/299	

J. C. Hallett, †J. N. Batty, M. T. Brimson and R. C. Stanley did not bat.

Bowling: Harrison 23–2–76–3; Moore 21–0–121–1; Jouning 7–0–44–0; Hagen 9–0–56–1.

Manchester

J. B. Jouning c Batty b Ballinger	14	P. F. Moore c Snape b Brimson	
W. C. Cooper c Hawkes b Stanley	0	D. Witherspoon st Batty b Snape	
F. L. Stewart c Peirce b Hallett	17	A. A. G. Logan not out	
T. W. Harrison c Hallett b Brimson	27	B 3, l-b 7, w 5, n-b 5	
*N. R. Hagen c Batty b Ballinger	0		
†B. G. Blyth lbw b Snape	12	1/2 2/42 3/42 (42.4 overs) 106
M. J. Hall c Brimson b Snape	3	4/44 5/83 6/87	
T. E. Kerry c Brimson b Snape	6	7/99 8/104 9/106	

Bowling: Stanley 6–2–19–1; Hallett 5–1–17–1; Ballinger 8–2–22–2; Snape 13.4–4–17–; Brimson 10–3–21–2.

Umpires: K. Hopley and S. Poole.

WINNERS 1927–93

1927	Manchester	1955	Birmingham	1974	Durham
1928	Manchester	1956	Null and void	1975	Loughborough Colls.
1929	Nottingham	1957	Loughborough Colls.	1976	Loughborough
1930	Sheffield	1958	Null and void	1977	Durham
1931	Liverpool	1959	Liverpool	1978	Manchester
1932	Manchester	1960	Loughborough Colls.	1979	Manchester
1933	Manchester	1961	Loughborough Colls.	1980	Exeter
1934	Leeds	1962	Manchester	1981	Durham
1935	Sheffield	1963	Loughborough Colls.	1982	Exeter
1936	Sheffield	1964	Loughborough Colls.	1983	Exeter
1937	Nottingham	1965	Hull	1984	Bristol
1938	Durham	1966 {	Newcastle	1985	Birmingham
1939	Durham		Southampton	1986	Durham
1946	Not completed	1967	Manchester	1987	Durham
1947	Sheffield	1968	Southampton	1988	Swansea
1948	Leeds	1969	Southampton	1989	Loughborough
1949	Leeds	1970	Southampton	1990	Durham
1950	Manchester	1971	Loughborough Colls.	1991	Durham
1951	Manchester	1972	Durham	1992	Durham
1952	Loughborough Colls.	1973 {	Leicester	1993	Durham
1953	Durham		Loughborough Colls.		
1954	Manchester				

OTHER FIRST-CLASS MATCH, 1993

IRELAND v SCOTLAND

Eglinton, June 12, 13, 14. Drawn. Toss: Ireland. First-class debuts: D. J. Curry, N. G. ak, E. R. Moore; I. R. Beven, G. M. Hamilton.

While nine out of ten first-class matches in England were washed out on the Monday, ay continued across the Irish Sea. However, Ireland failed to make the most of the vantage they had built up in the previous two days of their annual first-class fixture with otland. They extended a lead of 111 to 279 before declaring, but left themselves only 55 ers to dismiss Scotland again. Though the run-chase was abandoned by tea, Alastair orie comfortably saved the game. On the first day Michael Rea scored his maiden first-ass century, adding 127 with Stephen Warke for the second wicket. Scotland were seven wn before they averted the follow-on, with Jim Govan their top scorer on 50. Govan's -spin then claimed four Irish wickets, including Alan Lewis, who had completed his cond fifty of the match.

Close of play: First day, Ireland 266-4 (D. A. Lewis 29*, G. D. Harrison 16*); Second y, Scotland 211-9 (D. A. Orr 13*, A. Bee 8*).

eland

. F. Cohen b Govan	37	– (6) not out	1
P. Rea c Bee b Beven	115	– (1) run out	2
J. S. Warke b Bee	47	– (5) b Govan	14
A. Lewis not out	56	– (3) st Orr b Govan	73
J. Curry b Beven	4	– (2) c Orr b Govan	41
D. Harrison c Storie b Hamilton	32		
G. Doak c Storie b Hamilton	25	– (4) st Orr b Govan	25
. B. Jackson lbw b Hamilton	0		
McCrum b Hamilton	5		
J. Hoey b Hamilton	5		
B 7, l-b 11, n-b 6	24	L-b 11, w 1	12

83 2/210 3/218 4/229 5/303   (9 wkts dec.) 327   1/7 2/57 3/129   (5 wkts dec.) 168
311 7/311 8/321 9/327   4/161 5/168

R. Moore did not bat.

Bowling: First Innings—Bee 27-4-86-1; Hamilton 24.3-6-65-5; Beven 42-14-93-2; ovan 19-3-62-1; Russell 1-0-3-0. *Second Innings*—Bee 11-0-55-0; Hamilton 11-3-35-0; ven 3-0-14-0; Russell 5-0-19-0; Govan 15.5-4-34-4.

cotland

M. W. Patterson c Jackson b McCrum	0	– c Warke b Hoey	43
L. Philip lbw b McCrum	16	– b Harrison	14
. C. Storie c Doak b McCrum	19	– not out	40
Salmond c Doak b Hoey	39	– c Hoey b Harrison	6
D. Love b Hoey	14	– not out	14
B. Russell b Curry	9		
W. Govan c Lewis b Harrison	50		
R. Beven c Jackson b Moore	14		
. A. Orr c Rea b Hoey	14		
M. Hamilton c Jackson b Harrison	0		
Bee not out	12		
L-b 9, w 4, n-b 14	27	B 1, l-b 6, w 2, n-b 4	13

0 2/31 3/65 4/95 5/110   216   1/59 2/63 3/80   (3 wkts) 130
24 7/165 8/200 9/200

Bowling: First Innings—McCrum 17-4-56-3; Moore 20-11-34-1; Hoey 32.1-12-68-3; wis 2-0-17-0; Harrison 19-7-20-2; Curry 6-4-12-1. *Second Innings*—McCrum –3-26-0; Moore 9-4-19-0; Harrison 10-2-31-2; Hoey 14-0-43-1; Curry 4-3-4-0; Doak 1-0-0; Cohen 1-1-0-0.

Umpires: W. B. Arlow and H. J. Henderson.

MCC MATCHES IN 1993

The highlight of the season was undoubtedly the victory over Melbour Cricket Club. It was a remarkable fact that, in the long history of the tw MCCs – a combined 361 years – the clubs had never played against ea other. After the success of this year's fixture, it was agreed that in future match should take place during every Ashes series.

The inaugural game was played at Lord's two days after the Second Te Marylebone were given a solid foundation by an opening stand of 1 between Chris Broad, who made 116, and Anthony Ellison. A late flouri from Giles Toogood and Neil Trestrail, who put on 52 for the fifth wicke enabled the innings to reach 251. Melbourne made a spirited attempt beat that, led by Steve McCooke, who scored a magnificent 104. But t lower order collapsed, with five wickets falling for 41 runs, and th finished seven short of their target at the end of their allotted 55 overs.

In May, MCC played Hertfordshire at the minor county's ne headquarters at Shenley Park, where a splendid pavilion was opened by S Colin Cowdrey. Honours were even at the close; a sound partnersh between Malcolm Roberts and Bill Athey had enabled MCC to declare 231 for three, and Hertfordshire were ultimately unable to master t bowling, despite a well-struck hundred from Nigel Ilott, brother of t Essex player.

Once again MCC played no first-class cricket, but had a full programm with 319 matches in all. They won 117, drew 114 and lost 54, with abandoned. Four of these games were played at Lord's: apart from the w against Melbourne, MCC lost to MCC Young Cricketers and drew wi MCC Schools and Ireland. – John Jameson.

Note: Matches in this section were not first-class.

At Lord's, May 5. MCC Young Cricketers won by one wicket. Toss: MCC. MCC 251 five dec. (J. E. M. Nicholson 72, P. W. G. Parker 73, G. V. Palmer 39 not out); MC Young Cricketers 252 for nine (R. W. Lawson 95, S. D. Welch 37; C. E. Sketchley four f 96, S. C. Wundke three for 38).

At Cambridge, May 10, 11, 12. MCC lost to CAMBRIDGE UNIVERSITY by fo wickets (See The Universities in 1993).

At Tunbridge Wells, May 14. Drawn. Toss: Club Cricket Conference. MCC 206 for s dec. (D. C. Briance 74, N. R. C. MacLaurin 62; M. J. Roberts three for 21); Club Crick Conference 92 for one (J. Chambers 40).

At Shenley Park, May 18. Drawn. Toss: Hertfordshire. MCC 231 for three dec. (M. Roberts 60, C. W. J. Athey 70, A. J. Wright 36, L. Potter 31 not out, K. G. Sedgbeer 30 r out); Hertfordshire 212 for seven (N. J. Ilott 105; K. T. Medlycott four for 78).

At Oxford, June 8, 9, 10. MCC drew with OXFORD UNIVERSITY (See T Universities in 1993).

At Durham, June 14, 15. Drawn, after both teams forfeited their first innings because rain. Toss: Durham University. MCC 220 for five dec. (J. Foster 95, A. Flower 3 Durham University 179 for eight (M. G. N. Windows 35, S. C. Ecclestone 47; K. Williams three for 29).

At Lord's, June 23. MCC won by six runs. Toss: Melbourne CC. MCC 251 for five (55 overs) (B. C. Broad 116, A. F. D. Ellison 41, N. J. L. Trestrail 30; M. Anderson three for); Melbourne CC 245 for nine (55 overs) (M. Sholly 41, S. McCooke 104, R. Templeton .

At Arundel, July 4. Lavinia, Duchess of Norfolk's XI won by three wickets. Toss: MCC. CC 254 for five dec. (A. G. Warrington 36, J. A. Waterhouse 84 not out, S. P. Henderson Mushtaq Mohammad 43); Lavinia, Duchess of Norfolk's XI 257 for seven (K. Newell M. Newell 69, C. Light 61; J. Simmons five for 53).

At Finchampstead, July 7. Drawn. Toss: National Association of Young Cricketers. CC 276 for four dec. (H. Cartwright 83, J. L. P. Meadows 129); National Association of ung Cricketers 256 for eight (H. K. Adamjee 33, M. H. Colclough 57, A. N. Muggleton , P. J. Nicholson 52; P. A. Veness four for 55).

At Lord's, July 13. MCC drew with MCC SCHOOLS (See Schools Cricket in 1993).

At Wormsley, July 18. Drawn. Toss: J. Paul Getty's XI. MCC 181 for five dec. (J. D. binson 81); J. Paul Getty's XI 50 for three.

At High Wycombe, July 28, 29. Wales won by one wicket. Toss: MCC. MCC 197 for e dec. (T. Brown 49, D. A. Banks 44, P. J. Mir 50 not out; M. J. Ennion three for 64) d 223 for five dec. (J. D. Robinson 98); Wales 198 (T. Parker 82, M. J. Ennion 65; R. A. y four for 47, C. K. Bullen four for 54) and 224 for nine (B. J. Lloyd 64; C. K. Bullen six 99).

At Halesowen, August 5. Drawn. Toss: MCC. MCC 216 for six dec. (D. L. Houghton 56, J. Roberts 59); Midlands Club Cricket Conference 172 for nine (J. Hartley 39, N. artin 57 not out; K. Bird three for 24).

At Feethams, Darlington, August 11. North Yorkshire and South Durham Cricket ague v MCC. Abandoned.

At RAF Vine Lane, Uxbridge, August 12. MCC won by eight runs. Toss: Combined rvices. MCC 211 for six (45 overs) (D. C. Briance 75, J. D. Robinson 39); Combined rvices 203 for nine (45 overs) (Capt. R. J. Greatorex 57, 2nd Lt C. H. G. St George 34, pt. I. S. Fielding 32; C. K. Bullen three for 28, R. M. O. Cooke four for 37).

At Lord's, August 15, 16. Drawn. Toss: Ireland. MCC 260 for five dec. (M. S. A. cEvoy 33, M. J. Roberts 114, J. D. Robinson 51; A. R. Dunlop three for 60) and 214 for ar dec. (M. S. A. McEvoy 54, D. L. Houghton 30, C. K. Bullen 53); Ireland 190 for six c. (M. P. Rea 86, C. McCrum 35; K. P. Dutch five for 76) and 264 for nine (M. F. hen 63, S. J. S. Warke 85; K. P. Dutch eight for 114).

At Southport and Birkdale CC, August 18. Drawn. Toss: MCC. MCC 239 for two dec. . P. Tubbs 100 not out, J. A. Waterhouse 91 not out); National Association of Young icketers 143 for six (J. D. Cokayne 70, P. J. Nicholson 32 not out; M. G. Boocock four 50).

At Forfar, August 18, 19, 20. Drawn. Toss: Scotland. MCC 238 for five dec. (A. Flower D. A. Banks 63, G. J. Toogood 63 not out, R. P. Gofton 32 not out; I. R. Beven three 61) and 215 for six dec. (A. Flower 50, D. L. Houghton 62, P. J. Mir 50); Scotland 177 five dec. (A. C. Storie 89 not out; P. J. Heaton three for 40) and 236 for four (A. C. orie 103, G. N. Reifer 70).

OTHER MATCHES, 1993

Note: Matches in this section were not first-class.

At The Oval, April 20, 21, 22, 23. Surrey Second XI won by six wickets. Toss: England Under-19. England Under-19 586 for nine dec. (M. P. Dowman 79, M. P. Vaughan 16? M. J. Walker 50, J. A. Daley 94, C. J. Rika 36, G. Chapple 72, Extras 42; M. ? Bainbridge three for 105) and 135 for four dec. (M. P. Vaughan 45, C. J. Rika 35 not out? Surrey Second XI 422 (P. D. Atkins 80, A. W. Smith 55, M. A. Butcher 85 retired, G. ? Kersey 50, D. J. M. Kelleher 80, Extras 39; J. E. Hindson three for 102, G. Keedy three f? 128) and 300 for four (R. I. Alikhan 102, P. D. Atkins 32, G. J. Kersey 71, I. J. Ward ? not out, K. T. Medlycott 30 not out).

TETLEY BITTER TROPHY

A 55-over competition contested by four invited counties.

At Harrogate, July 12. Nottinghamshire won by 13 runs. Toss: Nottinghamshir? Nottinghamshire 299 for eight (55 overs) (M. A. Crawley 113, P. Johnson 42, C. C. Lew? 55, C. L. Cairns 34; V. J. Wells five for 57); Leicestershire 286 for nine (55 overs) (T. ? Boon 84, J. J. Whitaker 69, B. F. Smith 39; C. L. Cairns four for 48).

At Harrogate, July 13. Yorkshire won by six wickets. Toss: Durham. Durham 235 f? seven (55 overs) (G. Fowler 51, S. Hutton 46, D. A. Blenkiron 36, C. W. Scott 36 not ou? P. J. Hartley three for 33); Yorkshire 238 for four (47.2 overs) (A. P. Grayson 49, R. ? Richardson 77, D. Byas 80).

At Harrogate, July 14. **Final:** Nottinghamshire won on scoring-rate. Toss: Yorkshir? Nottinghamshire 159 for nine (50 overs) (J. D. Batty four for 20); Yorkshire 43 for fi? (21 overs).

JESMOND FESTIVAL

At Jesmond, July 13. Rest of the World XI won by 37 runs. Toss: Rest of the World X? Rest of the World XI 309 for five (55 overs) (P. V. Simmons 104, A. D. Jadeja 87, C. ? Greenidge 59; M. C. Ilott three for 56); England XI 272 for nine (55 overs) (M. ? Atherton 33, M. W. Gatting 90, S. J. Rhodes 35; A. A. Donald three for 48, R. A. Harp? four for 67).

At Jesmond, July 14. No result. Toss: Rest of the World XI. Rest of the World XI 14? for four (25 overs) (P. V. Simmons 58) v England XI.

SEEBOARD TROPHY

A 50-over competition contested by Sussex and two other invited counties.

At Canterbury, July 14. Surrey won by five wickets. Toss: Surrey. Kent 209 for eig? (50 overs) (N. R. Taylor 40, G. R. Cowdrey 30, N. J. Llong 47, S. A. Marsh 50; M. ? Bicknell three for 32); Surrey 213 for five (43.1 overs) (P. D. Atkins 31, D. J. Bicknell 3? M. A. Lynch 47, A. J. Stewart 53).

At Hove, August 4. **Final:** Surrey won by seven wickets after their target was revised ? 150 from 32 overs. Toss: Surrey. Sussex 233 for nine (50 overs) (M. P. Speight 46, C. W. ? Athey 39, A. P. Wells 52, N. J. Lenham 35; A. J. Hollioake four for 46); Surrey 153 f? three (26.2 overs) (P. D. Atkins 56 not out, M. A. Lynch 30, A. D. Brown 53 not out).

JOSHUA TETLEY FESTIVAL TROPHY

A 50-over competition contested by Yorkshire and three other invited counties.

At Scarborough, September 6. Yorkshire won by nine wickets. Toss: Yorkshire. Derbyshire 198 for seven (50 overs) (A. S. Rollins 91 not out, K. J. Barnett 59; P. J. Hartley four for 35); Yorkshire 199 for one (33.4 overs) (M. D. Moxon 86 not out, D. Byas 78 not out).

At Scarborough, September 7. Gloucestershire won by two runs. Toss: Durham. Gloucestershire 219 for nine (50 overs) (A. J. Wright 59, M. W. Alleyne 35; S. J. E. Brown three for 26); Durham 217 (49.5 overs) (A. C. Cummins 107, S. J. E. Brown 43 not out; A. M. Babington six for 44).

At Scarborough, September 8. **Final:** Yorkshire won by 60 runs. Toss: Gloucestershire. Yorkshire 228 for eight (45 overs) (M. D. Moxon 41, A. P. Grayson 67 not out, M. J. Foster 41; C. A. Walsh five for 24); Gloucestershire 168 (35.4 overs) (M. G. N. Windows 38, M. W. Alleyne 49; D. Gough four for 32).

I ZINGARI RESULTS, 1993

Matches 23: Won 8, Lost 7, Drawn 8. Abandoned 2.

May 4	Eton College	Lost by three wickets
May 15	Royal Artillery	Lost by two wickets
May 16	Staff College	Won by two wickets
May 22	Eton Ramblers	Drawn
June 3	Harrow School	Won by five wickets
June 5	Hurlingham CC	Lost by 69 runs
June 6	Earl of Carnarvon's XI	Lost by one run
June 13	Sandhurst Wanderers	Won by 116 runs
June 19	Guards CC	Lost by 32 runs
June 19	Charterhouse	Won by one wicket
June 27	J. Paul Getty's XI	Drawn
June 30	Winchester College	Drawn
July 4	Hagley CC	Won by five wickets
July 10	Green Jackets Club	Won by five wickets
July 11	Rickling Green CC	Drawn
July 17	Leicester Gentlemen	Won by 31 runs
July 18	Sir John Starkey's XI	Lost by seven wickets
July 25	Lavinia, Duchess of Norfolk's XI	Drawn
July 31	Lord Kingsdown's XI	Abandoned
August 1	Band of Brothers	Drawn
August 5	The Frogs	Drawn
August 7, 8	South Wales Hunts XI	Drawn
August 15	Captain R. H. Hawkins's XI	Lost by five wickets
August 22	Royal Navy CC	Abandoned
September 5	J. H. Pawle's XI	Won by three wickets

LORDS AND COMMONS RESULTS, 1993

Matches 17: Won 6, Lost 7, Tied 1, Drawn 3, Abandoned 1, Cancelled 5.

At Roedean School, Brighton, April 24. Lords and Commons won by 17 runs. Lords and Commons 129 for six (G. W. Allen 53 retired, not out); Roedean School 112 for eight.

At St Paul's School, Barnes, April 28. St Paul's School won by eight wickets. Lords and Commons 158 for seven (C. F. Horne 68, R. R. Kershaw 39); St Paul's School 162 for two.

At Vincent Square, May 4. Tied. Westminster School 154 (G. W. Allen three for 31, Hon. E. Brassey three for 28); Lords and Commons 154 for seven (R. R. Kershaw 44).

At Civil Service Ground, Chiswick, May 12. ACAS won by six wickets. Lords and Commons 104 for six (D. J. Fatchett 49); ACAS 107 for four.

At The Oval, May 19. Drawn. Lords XIII 225 for seven dec. (Lord Stafford 100, Lord Williams of Elvel 32 not out); Commons XIV 186 for nine (D. J. C. Faber 93; Duke of Roxburghe four for 49).

At Motspur Park, May 25. Lords and Commons won by four wickets. BBC Westminster 166 for five; Lords and Commons 167 for six (G. W. Allen 68, C. F. Horne 37, J. Rivington 34).

At Wormsley, May 30. Drawn. J. Paul Getty's XI 158 for five dec.; Lords and Commons 151 for nine (Hon. M. Rawlinson 46 not out).

At Bank of England Ground, Roehampton, June 8. Lords and Commons won by eight wickets. Mandarins 117 for nine (E. A. Kent-Jones three for 14); Lords and Commons 119 for two (D. J. C. Faber 39).

At Gymkhana Ground, Osterley, June 10. Indian High Commission v Lords and Commons. Cancelled.

At Bank of England Ground, Roehampton, June 16. Conservative Agents v Lords and Commons. Cancelled due to three-line whip.

At Civil Service Ground, Eltham, June 23. Parliamentary Staff won by two runs. Parliamentary Staff 167 for six; Lords and Commons 165 for six (P. Sterner 92).

At The Hague CC, June 25. Drawn. Dutch Parliament 200 for seven dec. (G. W. Allen three for 35); Lords and Commons 165 for nine (M. H. Meacher 35, Hon. M. Trafford 33).

At Bloemendaal, June 26. Dutch Parliament won by 59 runs. Dutch Parliament 233 for seven dec. (B. Mustill three for 66); Lords and Commons 174 (G. W. Allen 63, Hon. M. Trafford 53, M. Evans 32 not out).

At Burton Court, June 30. Lords and Commons won by 16 runs. Lords and Commons 249 (S. J. D. Yorke 36, R. R. Kershaw 30, D. J. C. Faber 35, Hon. M. Rawlinson 38); Guards CC 233 (Hon. E. Brassey five for 52).

At Vincent Square, July 8. MCC won by 47 runs. MCC 261 for five dec. (P. H. Edmonds three for 55); Lords and Commons 214 (D. J. C. Faber 38, M. Bowers 34).

At Vincent Square, July 15. Old Westminsters v Lords and Commons. Abandoned.

At Burton Court, July 21. Lords and Commons won by 173 runs. Lords and Commons 225 for three dec. (P. A. G. Jackson 91 not out, Earl Fortescue 58 not out, Hon. M. Rawlinson 31); Eton Ramblers 52 (P. H. Edmonds eight for 13).

At Lower Ground, Tunbridge Wells, July 23. Fleet Street v Lords and Commons. Cancelled due to vote of confidence.

At Old Emmanuel, New Malden, August 18. Law Society won by 105 runs. Law Society 193 for eight dec. (T. Azam three for 34, B. Mustill three for 40); Lords and Commons 88.

At Harrow School, September 3. Lords and Commons won by two wickets. Harrow Wanderers 150 (D. R. Dover three for 30, Hon. E. Brassey three for 32, R. J. Atkins three for 12); Lords and Commons 152 for eight (R. R. Kershaw 76).

At Highclere, Hampshire, September 5. Earl of Carnarvon's XII won by 86 runs. Earl of Carnarvon's XII 225 for ten dec. (Hon. T. M. Lamb three for six, Hon. E. Brassey three for 49); Lords and Commons 139.

At Armoury House, September 8. Winged Fellowship v Lords and Commons. Cancelled.

At Lord's, Nursery Ground, October 2. Cross Arrows v Lords and Commons. Cancelled.

THE MINOR COUNTIES IN 1993

By MICHAEL BERRY and ROBERT BROOKE

Staffordshire's domination of Minor Counties cricket brought their third consecutive title in 1993, and their second Championship and knockout cup double in those three years. Worcestershire, in the years immediately before they joined the County Championship in 1899, were the last team to win in three successive years. Staffordshire are also listed as winning three successive Championships, in 1914, 1920 and 1921, though some sources now cast doubt on whether the 1914 season was properly completed.

Staffordshire added Paul Allott to their formidable squad, but the former Lancashire and England bowler appeared in only one Championship match. Instead it was another bowler with first-class experience, the former Derbyshire paceman, Paul Newman, who was their match-winning spearhead. Newman, who bowled with venom and hostility, became the first Staffordshire player for 23 years to take 50 Championship wickets in a season when he claimed a match return of nine for 57 in the final Eastern Division fixture against Cumberland. They came at a cost of just 13.44 each and won Newman the Frank Edwards bowling trophy. Steve Dean, who was in record-breaking form in the Birmingham League, scored 579 runs to earn himself a Sunday League appearance for Warwickshire at the end of the summer, and David Banks amassed 425 in only four Championship appearances. Simon Myles, Staffordshire's hero in the Championship play-off win over Cheshire, made vital contributions with bat and ball as Staffordshire won four of their last six matches.

Continued over

MINOR COUNTIES CHAMPIONSHIP, 1993

Eastern Division	M	W	L	D	NR	Bonus Points Batting	Bowling	Total Points
Staffordshire[NW]	9	5	1	3	0	22	18	120
Norfolk[NW]	9	3	1	5	0	26	25	99
Cambridgeshire[NW]	9	2	0	6	1	20	23	80
Northumberland[NW]	9	2	3	4	0	17	20	69
Cumberland[NW]	9	2	3	3	1	17	15	69
Lincolnshire[NW]	9	2	3	4	0	17	15	67
Bedfordshire[NW]	9	2	3	4	0	9	15	56
Hertfordshire	9	1	2	6	0	16	22	54
Buckinghamshire	9	1	2	6	0	20	16	52
Suffolk	9	1	3	5	0	10	17	43

Western Division	M	W	L	D	NR	Bonus Points Batting	Bowling	Total Points
Cheshire[NW]	9	4	2	2	1	21	23	113
Oxfordshire[NW]	9	4	0	4	1	19	22	110
Wales[NW]	9	3	0	3	3	8	16	87
Berkshire[NW]	9	2	3	4	0	17	24	73
Devon[NW]	9	2	1	5	1	11	22	70
Wiltshire	9	1	0	6	2	20	19	49*
Shropshire	9	1	2	6	0	11	17	44
Herefordshire	9	0	3	5	1	17	21	43
Dorset	9	0	3	6	0	12	27	39
Cornwall	9	0	3	5	1	10	13	28

* 16 points deducted for breach of regulations.

Win = 16 pts. No result (including abandoned games) = 5 pts.
[NW] *Denotes qualified for NatWest Bank Trophy in 1994.*

A Derbyshire connection was also the key to **Norfolk** finishing as runners-up to Staffordshire in the Eastern Division table. Steve Goldsmith crowned his first season in Minor Counties cricket with 917 runs, the best aggregate of the summer. The highlight was his innings of 200 not out against Cumberland at Lakenham, which was part of a county record unbroken third-wicket partnership of 290 with Roger Finney (107 not out). Finney (522 runs), Steve Plumb (586) and Carl Rogers (607) reflected Norfolk's batting strength, while Rodney Bunting (36 wickets) and David Thomas, their captain, both produced some penetrative bowling. Thomas took his 24 wickets at 14.87 each.

Stuart Turner showed no signs of losing his hunger for Minor Counties wickets, despite the fact that he celebrated his 50th birthday during the season. Turner captured 28 wickets in six matches for **Cambridgeshire**, and his seven for 31 return against Northumberland at Jesmond included a hat-trick. Cambridgeshire, who recruited Brian Hardie, one of Turner's former colleagues at Essex, but lost off-spinner Adrian Pierson to Leicestershire, were well served with the bat by Giles Ecclestone (481 runs) and Bruce Roberts (444).

Northumberland, one of five current Minor Counties sides never to have won the title, raised their hopes of breaking that duck when a remarkable victory over Lincolnshire took them to the top of the Eastern Division at the end of June. Chasing 307 in 58 overs at Jesmond, they won by eight wickets with 29 balls to spare. But they soon slipped out of contention, and only a last-match win over Suffolk secured a place in the 1994 NatWest Trophy. Paul Dutton scored 408 runs and Mike Younger, who had stood down as captain to allow Graeme Morris to take over, made 402 at an average of 57.42. Five different players compiled centuries, including Andrew Roseberry, who became only the second Northumberland player to reach three figures on his debut. In the same fixture, against Bedfordshire, Younger made his first county hundred in his 141st Championship appearance. Ian Conn (28) and Graeme Angus (22) shared 50 wickets.

Cumberland, one of four Eastern Division counties who won two matches but lost three, made little impact with the ball. However, David Pearson, with 590 runs, and captain Simon Dutton, who made 455, were the front-line batsmen, and Mike Ingham, a newcomer, collected 254 runs in just three appearances. Bernard Reidy, having taken a decision to retire from Minor Counties cricket at the end of the 1992 season, had a change of mind and played in two Championship matches.

Lincolnshire's results mirrored those of Cumberland, but in Russell Evans they possessed one of the success stories of the summer. Evans, the former Nottinghamshire right-hander, finished with 819 runs at 91.00 to establish a new county record and take the Wilfred Rhodes Trophy for topping the Minor Counties batting averages. Evans accumulated four centuries, one of which came on his Championship debut against Cumberland, and surpassed Geoff Robinson's record of 815 runs in a season for Lincolnshire, achieved both in 1970 and 1980. Evans (153 not out) and Steve Bradford (151) were partners in a third-wicket stand of 308 against Buckinghamshire at Burghley Park in Stamford. Lincolnshire used 20 different bowlers, of whom only Bradford, a slow left-armer, managed to reach 20 wickets, while Keith Medlycott, the former Surrey left-arm spinner, made just one unsuccessful appearance. Phil Heseltine stood in for the new captain, Nigel Illingworth, who played only one Championship game owing to a back injury.

Chris Bullen, another who played for Surrey, excelled with the bat in helping **Bedfordshire** enjoy the unaccustomed role of Eastern Division leaders at one stage during the season. Bullen's tally of 613 runs contained a brilliant unbeaten 100 against Lincolnshire that took Bedfordshire to the top of the table. But thereafter they faded after being comprehensively beaten by Staffordshire. Bedfordshire had a new captain in Philip Hoare, while Peter Thomas, an off-spinner returning to the side after failing to appear in 1992, was leading wicket-taker with 22 victims.

Hertfordshire fielded 27 players during a moderate season, with Mark Gouldstone and Ray Kingshott the two major newcomers. Gouldstone, who had rarely produced his best form with Bedfordshire, relished the switch to make 602 runs, but Kingshott, a slow left-arm bowler who had been a prolific wicket-taker at Norfolk, struggled with his bowling delivery and finished with only 12 wickets. The estimable Andy Needham scored 557 runs and took 32 wickets.

Tim Scriven (656) and Malcolm Roberts (547) supplied the bulk of the **Buckinghamshire** runs, with Jason Harrison also displaying his immense potential in contributing 445 in four matches at an average of 74.16. But Buckinghamshire lacked on the bowling front and possibly the most notable highlight of their season was when Neil Hames, their 43-year-old former captain, appeared in the same side as his 18-year-old son Brett in their solitary victory over Cumberland.

Suffolk's season ended with their being bowled out for 88 on the way to a six-wicket defeat in their final fixture at Northumberland. It was in stark contrast to their successful pursuit of a 322 target to beat Cumberland, and meant that they suffered the ignominy of collecting the Eastern Division wooden spoon for the first time. Simon Clements hit 544 runs, and in the process overhauled Tony Warrington's career record of 7,623 to become the highest run-scorer in Suffolk's history with 7,738. Andy Squire made 468, while Andrew Golding took 28 wickets and Rob Gregg backed him up with 22. Keith Butler, previously of Essex, was one of Suffolk's new faces in their last season under the captaincy of Ray East. Phil Caley takes over as captain for 1994.

Cheshire took an early grip on the Western Division table with 60 points gleaned from their first three matches as Cornwall, Shropshire and Herefordshire were all beaten. Their only other win was a nail-biting last-ball triumph over Berkshire, although their maximum haul of eight bonus points in their final fixture with Wiltshire proved sufficient to see off the late challenge of Oxfordshire, who had inched in front of Ian Cockbain's side after winning three of their last four matches, including an eight-wicket victory over Cheshire. Andrew Hall, who had captained the English Schools Under-19 side in 1991, scored 96 and then 109 in his first two games, going on to finish with 525 runs. Inevitably, Cheshire's greatest trump card was their slow bowling. John O'Brien claimed 36 wickets, and Geoff Miller took 35.

Bowlers were also the springboard for **Oxfordshire's** late rally. Ian Curtis (33 wickets), Keith Arnold (28) and Rupert Evans (24) showed no signs that their appetite for Western Division batsmen was on the wane, with Arnold returning match figures of nine for 56 in the win over Herefordshire. The reliable Stuart Waterton laid the foundations of the Oxfordshire run-making with 693, although victory in their final match against Devon was down to off-spinner Evans, whose career-best 66 not out revived them from 59 for five to a match-winning 234 for nine. Evans won the game by lifting the second and third balls of the final over from Tony Allin for two sixes.

Wales were realistic contenders for the Western Division title after three wins in their first five matches. Individually, Andrew Harris (405 runs), Tony Smith (28 wickets) and Jude Chaminde, a Sri-Lankan born teenager, who made 284 runs in four appearances, all stood out and, in finishing third behind Cheshire and Oxfordshire, Wales showed that they have completed their apprenticeship at the two-day game. Although they struggled for bonus points – particularly of the batting variety – their tally of three wins reflected their best season since joining the Championship in 1988.

Berkshire, languishing in the lower reaches for the large part of the season, leapfrogged up into fourth place after winning their final two fixtures against Dorset and Herefordshire. David Mercer (543) and Gary Loveday (519) found their form with the bat, and James Hodgson, a 21-year-old graduate of Berkshire's youth set-up, scored his 433 runs at an impressive average of 72.16. Peter Lewington, their 43-year-old off-spinner, collected 35 wickets to extend his career tally to 574. He is now only nine away from equalling the Berkshire record of Robert Relf, who claimed 583 victims between 1923 and 1946.

Nick Folland's departure to Somerset coincided with **Devon** disappearing from the limelight. Peter Roebuck, formerly Somerset's captain, took over the role at Devon from Folland and led by example by scoring 377 runs and taking 21 wickets. Nick Gaywood, who had been close to scoring 1,000 Championship runs in 1992, was far less productive, and Julian Wyatt, another former Somerset man, took time to settle in, despite making a match-winning century in the MCC Trophy tie against Dorset. As well as Roebuck, five other Devon bowlers claimed more than ten wickets apiece.

Wiltshire will remember 1993 for all the wrong reasons, despite the fact that they reached the one-day final for the first time. Their big day at Lord's was ruined by both a crushing defeat by Staffordshire, and an ill-timed teatime announcement that 16 points had been deducted from their Championship total for "a breach of regulations". The charge was that Wiltshire had not merely fed Berkshire "joke" runs in a bid to make up for lost time in a rain-hit fixture at Finchampstead, but had done so in an unsubtle and mocking manner. They presented Berkshire with 203 runs in 19.4 overs of non-bowling, and the lost point cost Wiltshire a place in the 1994 NatWest Trophy. Lawrence Smith amassed 702 runs the highest total by a Western Division batsman – Rob Savage made 519, and Grant Sheppard, a new-ball bowler, continued his promising progress with 22 wickets. The versatile talents of Paul Marsh (580 runs and 16 wickets) also shone brightly for a Wiltshire side who had recruited Keith Tomlins (ex-Middlesex), Stuart Barnes (ex-Gloucestershire) and Philip North, formerly of Glamorgan and Wales, prior to the season.

Shropshire, with a new captain in Mark Davies, enlisted Kevin Sharp to replace Alvin Kallicharran as their professional, and the former Yorkshire player was one of three newcomers to perform with distinction. Sharp's tally of 564 runs contained a decisive 131 not out that led Shropshire to their lone victory over Dorset, local lad Andrew Breakwell scored 425 in only four games at an average of 85.00 and Paul Blakeley, a swing bowler recommended by Sharp, was the leading wicket-taker with 23 victims. While the win over Dorset was the high spot, the low point came when Shropshire's brittle batting collapsed to 64 all out in the defeat by Devon at Shifnal.

Kallicharran's change of surroundings brought him 486 runs for **Herefordshire**, but their lack of genuine match-winners meant that they failed to register a single Championship victory in their second season in the Minor Counties game. Apart from Kallicharran, no other batsman reached 300 runs, and the wickets were evenly distributed, with no bowler taking 15. Philip Thorn, the former Wiltshire captain, returned to Minor Counties cricket after a nine-year gap when he made two appearances for Herefordshire in the second half of the season.

Dorset and Cornwall also completed the season without tasting victory in the Championship. Giles Reynolds succeeded Barry Lewis as the captain of **Dorset**, for whom Tim Richings (615) and Jon Hardy (557) both scored freely. Sean Walbridge, a slow left-armer, again performed consistently to finish with 28 wickets, and Viv Pike, a leg-spinner, was an interesting new recruit as Dorset bagged a healthy 27 bowling bonus points.

Ricky Bartlett was the only bright spot of another unfulfilled summer for **Cornwall**. The former Somerset batsman compiled two centuries amongst his 598 runs, but was given little support. David Toseland, their evergreen off-spinner, claimed 18 wickets and strike bowler Chris Lovell's three appearances realised 16, but Cornwall finished holding up the rest of the Western Division table for the ninth time in 11 years. Cornwall, who were in a strong position against Shropshire when rain intervened at the start of the final hour, also provided one of the oddest memories of the campaign, with an inexplicable first-innings declaration at 68 for six against Wales at Falmouth.

CHAMPIONSHIP FINAL

CHESHIRE v STAFFORDSHIRE

At Worcester, September 12, 13. Staffordshire won by five wickets. Toss: Cheshire.

Simon Myles, a Mansfield-born all-rounder who represented Hong Kong in the 1986 ICC Trophy, conjured up an act of cricketing escapology to steer Staffordshire to a hat-trick of title wins. For the second year in succession, play spilled into the reserve day, with Cheshire recovering from an overnight 66 for four off 33 overs to reach 174 for six. Rain intervened again, washing out Monday's afternoon session, and with the weather still far from certain, Staffordshire lurched to 40 for five on an unpredictable wicket. But then Myles and Newman revived them with an unbroken sixth-wicket partnership of 138 in 21 overs and victory arrived in the gloom of a 7.20 p.m. finish.

Cheshire

S. T. Crawley lbw b Newman	2	A. J. Murphy not out	6
A. J. Hall c Humphries b Heap	9	J. F. M. O'Brien not out	1
T. J. Bostock b Myles	19	L-b 12, w 9, n-b 2	23
*I. Cockbain c Myles b Heap	8		
J. D. Gray c Newman b Heap	54	1/4 2/15 3/29 (6 wkts, 55 overs) 174		
R. G. Hignett b Newman	52	4/54 5/167 6/169		

G. Miller, †T. P. A. Standing and N. D. Peel did not bat.

Bowling: Newman 11–4–34–2; Hackett 11–2–20–0; Heap 11–3–37–3; Myles 11–0–38–1; Dutton 11–2–33–0.

Staffordshire

S. J. Dean b Murphy	0	*P. G. Newman not out	33
D. Cartledge c Crawley b Murphy	5		
D. A. Banks b Miller	7	B 2, l-b 12, w 15, n-b 4	33
S. D. Myles not out	94		
P. F. Shaw c Standing b Hignett	0	1/0 2/17 3/17 (5 wkts, 46.1 overs) 178		
A. J. Dutton c Cockbain b Hignett	6	4/25 5/40		

†M. I. Humphries, T. M. Heap, R. A. Spiers and N. P. Hackett did not bat.

Bowling: Murphy 10–3–25–2; Miller 9.1–2–23–1; Peel 7–1–24–0; Hignett 9–0–46–2; O'Brien 9–1–36–0; Crawley 2–0–10–0.

Umpires: P. Adams and T. G. Wilson.

MCC TROPHY FINAL

STAFFORDSHIRE v WILTSHIRE

At Lord's, August 25. Staffordshire won by 69 runs. Toss: Staffordshire.

Steve Dean missed what would have been one of the greatest Minor Counties centuries through a bizarre dismissal. Dean had made 99 out of Staffordshire's 149 for nought when he straight drove slow left-armer North in the 25th over. The ball looped off the ankle of his opening partner, Cartledge, who was trying to take evasive action at the non-striker's end, and North took an unexpected caught and bowled. Staffordshire's total of 326 for seven was the second-highest in the 11-year history of the competition, and put the game out of Wiltshire's reach, despite the commendable efforts of Smith and Tomlins.

Staffordshire

S. J. Dean c and b North	99	*N. J. Archer not out	4
D. Cartledge lbw b Tomlins	55	T. M. Heap not out	10
D. A. Banks c Foyle b Tomlins	26	L-b 6, w 4, n-b 10	20
S. D. Myles lbw b Tomlins	38		
A. J. Dutton b Barnes	30	1/149 2/173 3/233 (7 wkts, 55 overs) 326		
P. G. Newman c Savage b Barnes	33	4/242 5/295		
†M. I. Humphries b Barnes	11	6/301 7/316		

R. A. Spiers and N. P. Hackett did not bat.

Bowling: Barnes 10–0–76–3; Sheppard 10–2–48–0; Marsh 6–0–37–0; Prigent 7–0–48–0; North 11–1–58–1; Tomlins 11–0–53–3.

Wiltshire

L. K. Smith c Dean b Myles	74	P. D. North b Newman	14
P. M. Marsh c Archer b Heap	38	N. Prigent not out	1
K. P. Tomlins c Banks b Myles	60	L-b 11, w 5	16
†S. M. Perrin b Newman	9		
R. R. Savage lbw b Newman	0	1/75 2/141 3/164 (7 wkts, 55 overs) 257		
P. D. Simpkins b Myles	16	4/164 5/193		
*K. N. Foyle not out	29	6/221 7/245		

G. Sheppard and S. N. Barnes did not bat.

Bowling: Newman 11–0–30–3; Hackett 11–4–27–0; Heap 9–0–44–1; Spiers 7–0–43–0; Myles 11–0–68–3; Dutton 6–0–34–0.

Umpires: P. Adams and D. J. Halfyard.

BEDFORDSHIRE

Matches 9: Won – Buckinghamshire, Lincolnshire. Lost – Cambridgeshire, Cumberland, Staffordshire. Drawn – Hertfordshire, Norfolk, Northumberland, Suffolk.

Batting Averages

	M	I	NO	R	HS	100s	50s	Avge
C. K. Bullen	9	15	3	613	126*	2	3	51.08
R. N. Dalton	5	8	1	280	73	0	2	40.00
N. G. Folland	6	10	2	212	66*	0	1	26.50
D. R. Clarke	6	10	0	261	66	0	2	26.10
R. J. Plowman	7	9	6	78	23*	0	0	26.00
R. Swann	5	9	0	216	63	0	1	24.00
P. A. Thomas	4	8	0	178	50	0	1	22.25
*P. D. B. Hoare	9	16	2	270	50	0	1	19.28
S. D. L. Davis	5	9	0	172	56	0	1	19.11
C. J. Birt	8	14	1	176	63*	0	1	13.53
P. D. Thomas	5	8	1	80	27	0	0	11.42

Played in seven matches: †G. D. Sandford 0, 0*, 0*, 4*, 4; M. R. White 0, 3*, 3, 0*. Played in four matches: P. A. Owen 0, 4, 2. Played in three matches: B. L. Marvin 9, 1, 9, 15. Played in two matches: B. C. Banks 1; †E. R. Osborn 10*, 0, 24*; M. C. Vincent 20, 24*, 2, 11. Played in one match: D. Bhagvantass 11*, 16; K. Gentle 9, 15; L. A. Selfe 0.

Bowling Averages

	O	M	R	W	BB	5W/i	Avge
P. D. Thomas	120.1	18	501	22	6-121	3	22.77
M. R. White	128.5	15	418	12	6-64	1	34.83
C. K. Bullen	217.5	54	629	18	4-47	0	34.94

Also bowled: B. C. Banks 16–3–59–1; R. N. Dalton 45–6–160–3; B. L. Marvin 32.5–6–178–5; P. A. Owen 70–8–324–8; R. J. Plowman 139.1–28–416–5; L. A. Selfe 6.5–0–38–0; R. Swann 81–16–257–9.

BERKSHIRE

Matches 9: Won – Dorset, Herefordshire. Lost – Cheshire, Devon, Wales. Drawn – Cornwall, Oxfordshire, Shropshire, Wiltshire.

Batting Averages

	M	I	NO	R	HS	100s	50s	Avge
J. S. Hodgson	6	9	3	433	101*	1	4	72.16
B. S. Jackson	5	6	2	214	65*	0	2	53.50
D. A. Shaw	4	7	1	301	132*	1	1	50.16
D. J. M. Mercer	8	14	3	543	118*	2	1	49.36
P. J. Oxley	5	7	4	122	35*	0	0	40.66
G. E. Loveday	9	16	2	519	157*	1	1	37.07
G. T. Headley	7	12	0	374	75	0	3	31.16
†N. D. J. Cartmell	4	6	3	88	53*	0	1	29.33
*M. L. Simmons	8	11	0	224	41	0	0	20.36
M. Sagheer	8	12	3	138	44	0	0	15.33

Played in eight matches: P. J. Lewington 1*, 3. Played in five matches: R. O'Toole 1*, 8, 13*, 5, 0*. Played in four matches: J. K. Barrow 27, 0, 0, 12*; N. A. Fusedale 11, 17, 4, 3; D. J. B. Hartley 0, 2; †N. P. Harvey 3, 2. Played in three matches: M. G. Lickley 10, 30, 11. Played in two matches: N. Pitcher did not bat. Played in one match: †M. E. Stevens 0.

Bowling Averages

	O	M	R	W	BB	5W/i	Avge
P. J. Lewington	232.1	54	693	35	6-42	4	19.80
K. Barrow	87.5	13	304	12	4-36	0	25.33
N. A. Fusedale	80.3	18	309	11	7-98	1	28.09
M. Sagheer	124.4	20	489	15	4-19	0	32.60
D. J. B. Hartley	101.2	12	479	13	3-34	0	36.84

Also bowled: G. T. Headley 13–1–72–1; J. S. Hodgson 20–2–75–1; B. S. Jackson 37–10–271–8; M. G. Lickley 17–5–41–2; R. O'Toole 47.1–9–165–0; P. J. Oxley 27–9–103–0; N. Pitcher 42–11–125–6; D. A. Shaw 4–0–25–0.

BUCKINGHAMSHIRE

Matches 9: Won – Cumberland. Lost – Bedfordshire, Hertfordshire. Drawn – Cambridgeshire, Lincolnshire, Norfolk, Northumberland, Staffordshire, Suffolk.

Batting Averages

	M	I	NO	R	HS	100s	50s	Avge
N. C. Harrison	4	8	2	445	111*	1	3	74.16
M. J. Roberts	6	12	1	547	112*	1	5	49.72
T. J. A. Scriven	9	17	2	656	94	0	5	43.73
D. Burrow	8	13	4	307	72*	0	1	34.11
R. R. Baigent	5	9	1	246	66	0	1	30.75
N. W. Farrow	6	8	1	175	43*	0	0	25.00
T. P. Russell	9	9	4	116	50	0	1	23.20
B. S. Percy	5	8	3	114	44	0	0	22.80
C. J. Barry	6	10	4	117	38*	0	0	19.50
S. M. Shearman	8	12	1	210	47	0	0	19.09
*G. R. Black	8	7	2	61	15	0	0	12.20

Played in five matches: C. D. Booden 0*, 0*, 0; D. M. Owen 6, 2, 2, 4*. Played in four matches: P. G. Roshier 21*, 2, 12*, 0, 14. Played in three matches: G. D. T. Paskins 6, 14, 3, 111, 0. Played in two matches: B. A. Hames 12, 7, 41. Played in one match: M. A. Farnon 11*; N. G. Hames 23; J. W. D. Lishman 0; S. G. Lynch 21; P. F. J. Strong 28, 54; J. N. B. Bovill did not bat.

Bowling Averages

	O	M	R	W	BB	5W/i	Avge
T. J. A. Scriven	197.2	58	579	19	4-43	0	30.47
C. D. Booden	116.4	18	370	12	3-67	0	30.83
S. Burrow	128.3	23	465	14	3-32	0	33.21
D. M. Owen	108.1	19	347	10	5-28	1	34.70

Also bowled: T. J. Barry 85.3–10–323–7; G. R. Black 96.5–19–326–9; J. N. B. Bovill 15–2–59–1; M. A. Farnon 2–1–6–1; B. A. Hames 4–1–20–0; J. C. Harrison 21–2–103–3; J. W. D. Lishman 12–2–44–3; S. G. Lynch 2–0–16–0; B. S. Percy 18–2–72–1; P. G. Roshier 99.1–14–357–9; S. M. Shearman 1–0–4–0.

CAMBRIDGESHIRE

Matches 9: Won – Bedfordshire, Lincolnshire. Drawn – Buckinghamshire, Hertfordshire, Norfolk, Northumberland, Staffordshire, Suffolk. No result – Cumberland.

Batting Averages

	M	I	NO	R	HS	100s	50s	Avg
B. Roberts	7	12	3	444	87	0	5	49.3
G. W. Ecclestone....	8	16	4	481	104*	2	1	40.0
D. P. Norman	8	13	2	382	94	0	3	34.7
B. R. Hardie	5	9	0	289	93	0	2	32.1
S. C. Ecclestone	5	7	2	134	44	0	0	26.8
*N. T. Gadsby.......	8	15	3	310	86*	0	1	25.8
N. J. Adams	4	6	0	102	32	0	0	17.0
T. S. Smith.........	4	6	1	50	31	0	0	10.0

Played in six matches: †M. W. C. Olley 24, 0*, 17, 4*; D. F. Ralfs 3, 4*, 5*, 4*; S. Turner 24, 13*, 2, 0. Played in five matches: A. Akhtar 8*, 3, 1, 1, 0. Played in four matches: C. R. F. Green 0, 7*, 1. Played in three matches: R. A. Milne 10, 0, 3*, 3, 0. Played in two matches: †C. J. Malton 13*, 1; R. P. Merriman 5, 16, 7; Nadeem Mohammed 29, 20, 4*, 0. Played in one match: D. W. S. Pimblett 0*, 8; T. C. Williams 2, 18; A. Cowan did not bat.

Bowling Averages

	O	M	R	W	BB	5W/i	Avg
S. Turner	245.1	76	523	28	7-31	2	18.6
B. Roberts	100.5	19	334	15	5-77	1	22.2
T. S. Smith.........	117	28	284	12	3-58	0	23.6
D. F. Ralfs	125	19	405	15	4-34	0	27.0
A. Akhtar	104	28	307	11	3-27	0	27.9

Also bowled: N. J. Adams 12-1-64-1; A. Cowan 36-10-98-4; S. C. Ecclestone 65-11-263-6; N. T. Gadsby 9-1-42-0; C. R. F. Green 97-23-267-9; R. P. Merriman 7-1-43-0; D. P. Norman 10-0-44-0; T. C. Williams 15-1-65-4.

CHESHIRE

Matches 9: Won – Berkshire, Cornwall, Herefordshire, Shropshire. Lost – Oxfordshire, Wiltshire. Drawn – Devon, Dorset. No result – Wales.

Batting Averages

	M	I	NO	R	HS	100s	50s	Avg
T. J. Bostock	7	9	2	329	97	0	3	47.0
R. G. Hignett	9	14	5	359	71*	0	1	39.8
J. D. Gray	9	13	3	390	72	0	1	39.0
A. J. Hall	8	14	0	525	109	1	3	37.5
J. D. Bean	7	11	4	244	60*	0	2	34.8
*I. Cockbain	9	15	1	443	130*	1	1	31.6
S. T. Crawley	7	11	0	326	75	0	1	29.6
G. Miller	9	6	3	81	22*	0	0	27.0
I. B. Middlehurst	5	8	3	131	29*	0	0	26.2
J. F. M. O'Brien	9	6	2	50	16*	0	0	12.5

Played in nine matches: †T. P. A. Standing 4, 1*, 0, 6. Played in six matches: N. D. Peel 0, 14*. Played in two matches: C. Lamb 0. Played in one match: E. S. Garnett 2*; B. N. Kingham 18; J. Potts did not bat.

Bowling Averages

	O	M	R	W	BB	5W/i	Avg
G. Miller	319.1	104	648	35	5-26	4	18.5
J. F. M. O'Brien	297.3	81	801	36	5-58	1	22.2
R. G. Hignett	106.5	19	440	11	3-27	0	40.0

Also bowled: T. J. Bostock 28.4-5-141-1; I. Cockbain 2-1-4-0; S. T. Crawley 26-5-84-4; E. S. Garnett 17-5-57-1; J. D. Gray 3-0-29-1; A. J. Hall 30.4-2-188-3; B. N. Kingham 2-0-20-1; C. Lamb 32-7-84-3; I. B. Middlehurst 2-0-17-1; N. D. Peel 139-25-400-10; J. Potts 11.2-3-35-3.

CORNWALL

Matches 9: Lost – Cheshire, Oxfordshire, Wales. Drawn – Berkshire, Devon, Dorset, Hereford-shire, Shropshire. No result – Wiltshire.

Batting Averages

	M	I	NO	R	HS	100s	50s	Avge
R. J. Bartlett	8	13	2	598	146*	2	4	54.36
R. G. Furse	9	12	6	237	76*	0	1	39.50
K. R. Blackburn	5	8	1	229	63*	0	2	32.71
S. M. Williams	9	16	1	393	89	0	2	26.20
R. T. Walton	6	9	2	179	57	0	1	25.57
J. E. M. Nicolson	7	11	2	210	51*	0	1	21.33
†D. J. Rowe	7	10	3	142	43*	0	0	20.28
S. Wherry	5	8	0	152	59	0	1	19.00
J. F. Grigg	5	9	1	91	36*	0	0	11.37
*G. G. Watts	8	9	2	66	18*	0	0	9.42
C. C. Lovell	3	6	0	50	30	0	0	8.33

Played in six matches: D. A. Toseland 2, 0*, 2, 1*. Played in three matches: J. P. Kent 4*, 32, 8, 6*, 5; G. C. Trenwith 0, 0*, 23, 8*. Played in two matches: R. M. H. Bell 0; †D. J. Hollyoak 0; S. A. Hunt 1; A. J. Martin 4; G. M. Thomas 24, 66, 21, 10; T. F. Boston did not bat. Played in one match: S. Hooper 7; D. H. Pascoe 17; K. J. Willcock 8, 0*.

Bowling Averages

	O	M	R	W	BB	5W/i	Avge
C. C. Lovell	91.5	14	328	16	6-85	2	20.50
R. G. Furse	135.3	30	465	15	2-8	0	31.00
D. A. Toseland	160	18	592	18	4-78	0	32.88
G. G. Watts	158.2	24	602	15	6-62	1	40.13

Also bowled: R. J. Bartlett 11.4–3–35–2; R. M. H. Bell 28–6–95–2; T. F. Boston 29–2–131–1; S. A. Hunt 4–0–24–0; J. P. Kent 28.3–2–129–1; A. J. Martin 25–2–89–2; D. H. Pascoe 3–0–27–0; G. C. Trenwith 70–19–213–5; K. J. Willcock 39–11–121–3.

CUMBERLAND

Matches 9: Won – Bedfordshire, Northumberland. Lost – Buckinghamshire, Staffordshire, Suffolk. Drawn – Hertfordshire, Lincolnshire, Norfolk. No result – Cambridgeshire.

Batting Averages

	M	I	NO	R	HS	100s	50s	Avge
M. J. Ingham	3	6	1	254	127*	1	1	50.80
*†S. M. Dutton	7	13	4	455	62	0	5	50.55
D. J. Makinson	8	12	5	323	78*	0	2	46.14
†D. J. Pearson	8	15	2	590	114*	2	1	45.38
D. Patel	4	7	1	217	73	0	1	36.16
G. Fisher	7	13	0	324	87	0	2	24.92
D. T. Smith	4	7	1	136	56*	0	1	22.66
S. James	8	9	2	145	61	0	1	20.71
P. Beech	4	6	1	96	59	0	1	19.20
S. Wall	4	8	3	63	20	0	0	12.60
J. M. Lewis	4	7	1	72	36	0	0	12.00

Played in five matches: M. D. Woods 10*, 8, 0, 0. Played in three matches: S. Sharp 60, 28, 29, 21, 2. Played in two matches: I. Jackson 6, 0*; J. R. Moyes 1*, 10, 20; B. W. Reidy 1, 33, 34*; M. G. Scothern 14; D. M. Wheatman 0*; R. Ellwood and W. G. Lovell did not bat. Played in one match: M. Burns 28, 37; A. Hall 8, 0; I. J. Houseman 0.

Bowling Averages

	O	M	R	W	BB	5W/i	Avge
P. Beech	70.3	9	288	11	6-46	1	26.18
M. D. Woods	149.3	32	476	17	5-36	1	28.00
D. J. Makinson	163	32	551	14	4-66	0	39.35

Also bowled: M. Burns 31–9–105–5; S. M. Dutton 4–0–40–0; R. Ellwood 21–4–83–1; G. Fisher 4.5–0–62–0; I. J. Houseman 27–5–104–3; I. Jackson 29–3–118–4; S. James 54.2–14–257–7; J. M. Lewis 54.1–12–181–8; W. G. Lovell 51.1–3–228–4; D. Patel 16–2–84–3; B. W. Reidy 20–11–45–3; M. G. Scothern 44–11–139–3; D. T. Smith 6–1–37–0; S. Wall 82–16–325–5; D. M. Wheatman 34.4–14–158–0.

DEVON

Matches 9: Won – Berkshire, Shropshire. Lost – Oxfordshire. Drawn – Cheshire, Cornwall, Dorset, Herefordshire, Wales. No result – Wiltshire.

Batting Averages

	M	I	NO	R	HS	100s	50s	Avge
*P. M. Roebuck......	9	13	6	377	92*	0	2	53.85
S. M. Willis	8	16	2	551	127*	1	3	39.35
A. J. Pugh	8	15	2	431	83	0	3	33.15
N. R. Gaywood	9	17	0	477	80	0	3	28.05
K. Donohue	7	10	3	192	65	0	2	27.42
J. G. Wyatt	9	17	2	402	76*	0	3	26.80
M. C. Woodman	9	8	4	102	41	0	0	25.50
G. W. White	3	6	0	128	43	0	0	21.33
D. E. L. Townsend ...	4	6	0	87	27	0	0	14.50

Played in nine matches: †C. S. Pritchard 5*, 4, 22*, 4, 7*. Played in five matches: T. W. Ward 0, 14, 2, 39, 0. Played in four matches: D. N. Butcher 3*, 10, 0*. Played in three matches: A. C. Cottam 37*, 26, 33*, 1*; J. Rhodes 13, 18, 6, 21*, 4*. Played in two matches: A. W. Allin 2, 6*; R. I. Dawson 21, 52; D. A. Tall 5, 1, 9. Played in one match: I. Gompertz 0, 3*; A. O. F. Le Fleming 12, 1; M. J. Record 0.

Bowling Averages

	O	M	R	W	BB	5W/i	Avge
D. N. Butcher	75	18	228	13	6-43	1	17.53
A. W. Allin	69.2	25	201	11	4-33	0	18.27
P. M. Roebuck	195.4	68	441	21	3-42	0	21.00
A. C. Cottam	93	24	305	14	4-41	0	21.78
M. C. Woodman	169	48	392	16	4-36	0	24.50
K. Donohue	137.2	30	373	14	3-12	0	26.64

Also bowled: R. I. Dawson 13–2–51–2; N. R. Gaywood 11–2–71–3; I. Gompertz 0.1–0–0–0; A. O. F. Le Fleming 12–1–51–1; A. J. Pugh 2–0–15–0; M. J. Record 14–1–69–2; J. Rhodes 39.4–3–176–7; D. A. Tall 19–2–74–3; T. W. Ward 34–3–123–3; G. W. White 22.2–2–100–4; S. M. Willis 1–0–18–0; J. G. Wyatt 6–0–43–1.

DORSET

Matches 9: Lost – Berkshire, Shropshire, Wales. Drawn – Cheshire, Cornwall, Devon, Herefordshire, Oxfordshire, Wiltshire.

Batting Averages

	M	I	NO	R	HS	100s	50s	Avge
J. J. E. Hardy	9	18	5	557	75	0	3	42.84
T. W. Richings	9	18	2	615	102	2	4	38.43
*†G. D. Reynolds	9	16	5	422	85	0	3	38.36
J. Cassell	8	13	1	335	105*	1	1	27.91
G. S. Calway	4	8	1	176	57*	0	1	25.14
J. A. Claughton	5	10	0	251	77	0	2	25.10
V. J. Pike	5	6	2	86	51*	0	1	21.50
A. Willows	9	13	1	203	58*	0	1	16.91
S. R. Walbridge	9	8	1	62	18	0	0	8.85
P. L. S. Norris	5	6	2	34	22	0	0	8.50

Played in seven matches: P. L. Garlick 1*, 0, 15*, 0*, 0*. Played in six matches: J. W. Dike 8*, 18, 2, 0, 0. Played in four matches: J. H. Shackleton 13, 13*, 21*. Played in two matches: G. A. Bucknall 16, 11, 46*, 7; O. T. Parkin 0, 1*, 2; R. A. Pyman 0, 8; S. W. D. Rintoul 1, 7. Played in one match: S. J. Ball 3; R. V. Morgan 2.

Bowling Averages

	O	M	R	W	BB	5W/i	Avge
J. W. Dike	105.1	22	308	15	7-58	1	20.53
S. R. Walbridge	239.3	62	719	28	4-34	0	25.67
V. J. Pike	154	39	566	16	5-51	1	35.37

Also bowled: S. J. Ball 35.2–5–95–3; G. S. Calway 12–4–22–1; P. L. Garlick 101–24–317–8; P. L. S. Norris 37–9–143–3; O. T. Parkin 53–13–130–6; R. A. Pyman 42–9–113–5; J. H. Shackleton 77.1–17–225–7; A. Willows 69.1–5–276–5.

HEREFORDSHIRE

Matches 9: Lost – Berkshire, Cheshire, Oxfordshire. Drawn – Cornwall, Devon, Dorset, Shropshire, Wiltshire. No result – Wales.

Batting Averages

	M	I	NO	R	HS	100s	50s	Avge
†R. Hall	4	8	0	295	94	0	2	36.87
A. I. Kallicharran	8	15	0	486	102	1	2	32.40
S. M. Brogan	5	10	1	266	69	0	2	29.55
M. C. Abberley	4	8	0	223	60	0	2	27.87
M. J. Bailey	5	8	3	132	33	0	0	26.40
M. G. Fowles	4	7	2	121	32	0	0	24.20
D. J. Martindale	4	8	0	178	50	0	1	22.25
M. F. Robinson	3	6	2	82	29	0	0	20.50
M. Dalloway	5	9	1	145	85*	0	1	18.12
*R. P. Skyrme	8	15	3	201	40*	0	0	16.75
R. G. R. Barlow	5	9	0	148	56	0	1	16.44
†J. R. Tegg	5	8	0	62	19	0	0	7.75

Played in three matches: R. M. Cox 10, 41, 7, 24, 18; A. Herbert 0*; P. J. Humphries 4, 10*, 12*, 1*; P. J. B. Hunt 27, 11, 7*, 12, 3; N. M. Husbands 2*, 0*, 0. Played in two matches: L. R. James 2, 5; E. N. R. Symonds 16, 13, 26; P. L. Thorn 19*, 50, 35, 38; S. G. Watkins 1, 11, 76, 65. Played in one match: J. M. Connor 7, 27*; R. Holdsworth 2*, 3; E. P. M. Holland 2; I. O. Maklin 4, 0*; D. C. M. Robinson 2.

Bowling Averages

	O	M	R	W	BB	5W/i	Avge
P. J. Humphries......	76.3	13	256	13	5-71	1	19.69
A. Herbert	62.4	6	257	10	4-43	0	25.70
M. F. Robinson	77	13	340	11	4-66	0	30.90
M. J. Bailey	110	18	426	12	4-64	0	35.50

Also bowled: R. G. R. Barlow 24–3–127–2; R. M. Cox 27.2–3–117–2; M. G. Fowles 83.3–11–313–8; R. Holdsworth 17–2–77–1; E. P. M. Holland 18–2–71–1; P. J. B. Hunt 20–1–105–2; N. M. Husbands 87–19–337–9; L. R. James 19–3–65–0; A. I. Kallicharran 103–18–366–8; D. C. M. Robinson 27.5–8–54–3; R. P. Skyrme 10.5–1–68–2; P. L. Thorn 57.1–17–216–7; S. G. Watkins 33–2–140–0.

HERTFORDSHIRE

Matches 9: Won – Buckinghamshire. Lost – Norfolk, Staffordshire. Drawn – Bedfordshire, Cambridgeshire, Cumberland, Lincolnshire, Northumberland, Suffolk.

Batting Averages

	M	I	NO	R	HS	100s	50s	Avge
A. Needham	9	16	8	557	110	1	5	69.62
M. R. Gouldstone . . .	9	17	5	602	116*	1	4	50.16
M. A. Everett	5	9	2	224	86*	0	2	32.00
N. J. Ilott	7	11	0	306	78	0	3	27.81
M. James	8	15	0	360	100	1	2	24.00
R. G. P. Ellis	7	12	2	230	93*	0	1	23.00
C. N. Cavener	5	6	3	62	45*	0	0	20.66

Played in eight matches: *D. Surridge 2*, 6, 2*, 0*. Played in five matches: K. Jahangir 2, 71*, 6, 0, 61*; R. Kingshott 1, 0, 1. Played in four matches: †A. D. Griffin 30, 2, 17, 0. Played in three matches: †J. D. Harvey 1*, 10, 0, 3; G. A. R. Harris did not bat. Played in two matches: †P. A. Bashford 1; G. A. Buchanan 12, 29*; N. Gilbert 23, 24, 21; E. P. Neal 2, 7*; M. J. Walshe 0, 16; P. A. Waterman 15; M. C. G. Wright 4, 5, 43. Played in one match: M. M. Blackburn 14, 1; S. P. Ducat 103*, 0; M. R. Evans 0, 9; I. J. Fantham 0; S. P. Moffat 0, 5; S. P. Page 4, 40; R. Premadasa 11.

Bowling Averages

	O	M	R	W	BB	5W/i	Avge
C. N. Cavener	85	10	329	15	4–40	0	21.93
A. Needham	245.2	62	734	32	6–63	2	22.93
D. Surridge	140.3	29	402	15	5–32	2	26.80
R. Kingshott	114	20	393	12	5–74	1	32.75

Also bowled: M. M. Blackburn 8.4–0–57–0; M. R. Evans 17–3–59–1; M. A. Everett 17–1–115–3; I. J. Fantham 14–2–55–1; M. R. Gouldstone 3–0–14–1; G. A. R. Harris 83.4–20–237–3; J. D. Harvey 7–2–15–0; K. Jahangir 65.3–13–235–9; M. James 3–0–33–0; E. P. Neal 50.5–9–177–5; R. Premadasa 22.1–3–91–5; M. J. Walshe 39–7–126–3; P. A. Waterman 23–5–79–2.

LINCOLNSHIRE

Matches 9: Won – Staffordshire, Suffolk. Lost – Bedfordshire, Cambridgeshire, Northumberland. Drawn – Buckinghamshire, Cumberland, Hertfordshire, Norfolk.

Batting Averages

	M	I	NO	R	HS	100s	50s	Avge
R. J. Evans	7	13	4	819	153*	4	3	91.00
S. A. Bradford	8	8	4	261	151	1	1	65.25
M. A. Fell	7	12	5	327	72*	0	2	46.71
*P. J. Heseltine	8	12	4	297	116	1	0	37.12

	M	I	NO	R	HS	100s	50s	Avge
D. B. Storer	4	7	1	201	62*	0	2	33.50
N. J. C. Gandon	6	9	0	198	53	0	2	28.28
D. A. Christmas	6	6	2	107	50*	0	1	26.75
S. N. Warman	8	9	2	179	54	0	1	25.57
J. R. Robinson.......	4	8	0	181	60	0	1	22.62
P. A. Rawden	7	11	1	201	37	0	0	20.10
†N. P. Dobbs........	8	6	4	25	9*	0	0	12.50

Played in seven matches: P. J. Hacker 1, 16, 19, 16, 0. Played in three matches: J. R. Wileman 9, 22, 53*, 121. Played in two matches: D. R. Brewis 6; D. Gillett 14, 25, 6*; M. Irving 5*; P. D. McKeown 4. Played in one match: A. C. Ellis 0*; G. M. Evison 6, 0; *N. J. B. Illingworth 6, 2; K. T. Medlycott 17, 15; C. Wicks 0; †M. Allison, M. Blackbourn and K. V. Tillison did not bat.

Bowling Averages

	O	M	R	W	BB	5W/i	Avge
M. A. Fell	136.4	29	410	16	4-38	0	25.62
S. A. Bradford	206.1	43	709	20	4-58	0	35.45
P. J. Hacker	145.4	28	451	12	3-53	0	37.58
D. A. Christmas	135	24	428	10	3-24	0	42.80

Also bowled: M. Blackbourn 8-1-39-0; D. R. Brewis 13-4-49-1; A. C. Ellis 13-1-66-1; R. J. Evans 4-0-25-1; N. J. C. Gandon 23.1-2-156-3; D. Gillett 0.1-0-4-0; P. J. Heseltine 2-0-5-0; N. J. B. Illingworth 24.1-3-109-2; M. Irving 23.3-3-83-1; P. D. McKeown 34-6-152-2; K. T. Medlycott 37-5-113-1; P. A. Rawden 14-3-48-0; J. R. Robinson 24.4-3-103-8; K. V. Tillison 5-0-26-0; S. N. Warman 19-1-142-1; J. R. Wileman 43.1-8-116-7.

NORFOLK

Matches 9: Won – Hertfordshire, Northumberland, Suffolk. Lost – Staffordshire. Drawn – Bedfordshire, Buckinghamshire, Cambridgeshire, Cumberland, Lincolnshire.

Batting Averages

	M	I	NO	R	HS	100s	50s	Avge
S. C. Goldsmith	9	17	4	917	200*	1	8	70.53
R. J. Finney........	9	15	4	522	107*	1	2	47.45
S. G. Plumb	9	18	4	586	107*	1	3	41.85
C. J. Rogers	9	18	2	607	89*	0	6	37.93
R. D. E. Farrow	8	10	2	164	35	0	0	20.50
*D. R. Thomas	8	7	3	64	26*	0	0	16.00
S. B. Dixon	5	7	3	58	42*	0	0	14.50
N. Fox	9	6	1	48	25	0	0	9.60
R. A. Bunting	9	6	2	16	11	0	0	4.00

Played in six matches: †J. P. Garner 0. Played in four matches: C. Amos 1*, 3, 2, 27, 0*. Played in three matches: †S. C. Crowley 6; D. J. C. Logan 1*, 0*, 16*. Played in two matches: A. P. Cole 13*; M. C. Earthy did not bat. Played in one match: D. J. Adams 3*; S. R. Harvey 8, 3; M. R. Tipping 1*; C. S. Carey did not bat.

Bowling Averages

	O	M	R	W	BB	5W/i	Avge
D. R. Thomas	137.3	40	357	24	6-36	2	14.87
R. A. Bunting	254.4	45	895	36	5-38	2	24.86
S. G. Plumb	196.3	52	602	21	3-18	0	28.66
N. Fox	71.2	12	296	10	5-43	1	29.60

Also bowled: D. J. Adams 24.3-7-73-4; C. S. Carey 7-2-27-0; A. P. Cole 41-10-150-4; M. C. Earthy 26.4-3-87-3; R. D. E. Farrow 1.1-0-9-0; R. J. Finney 4-0-44-1; S. C. Goldsmith 151.3-30-497-8; D. J. C. Logan 29-3-175-4; C. J. Rogers 1-0-5-0.

NORTHUMBERLAND

Matches 9: Won – Lincolnshire, Suffolk. Lost – Cumberland, Norfolk, Staffordshire. Drawn – Bedfordshire, Buckinghamshire, Cambridgeshire, Hertfordshire.

Batting Averages

	M	I	NO	R	HS	100s	50s	Avge
J. P. Barrett	3	6	2	262	151	1	1	65.50
M. E. Younger.......	7	11	4	402	101*	1	3	57.42
T. A. S. Brown	8	13	3	386	135*	1	2	38.60
P. N. S. Dutton	8	14	1	408	102	1	1	31.38
A. Roseberry	7	13	1	357	102	1	3	29.75
M. J. Green	9	13	1	330	49	0	0	27.50
*G. R. Morris	6	10	0	239	48	0	0	23.90
I. E. Conn	9	10	2	168	33	0	0	21.00
G. Angus	8	6	2	56	20*	0	0	14.00
†P. J. Nicholson	7	8	3	40	16*	0	0	8.00

Played in seven matches: P. C. Graham 0*, 1. Played in three matches: N. B. Campbell 0, 1, 8*, 5; R. A. Darling 4*, 6, 2*, 2*; C. Stanley 0, 0; M. S. Tiffin 19, 29, 31, 2; O. S. Youll 4, 17, 11. Played in two matches: W. Falla 0, 14. Played in one match: †T. W. Adcock 71*, 11*; P. G. Cormack 16, 0; †B. Storey 12.

Bowling Averages

	O	M	R	W	BB	5W/i	Avge
I. E. Conn	198.5	37	693	28	4-48	0	24.75
P. C. Graham	170.5	37	451	17	4-15	0	26.52
G. Angus	160.5	30	619	22	3-33	0	28.13

Also bowled: N. B. Campbell 49–11–191–3; R. A. Darling 61–16–156–6; P. N. S. Dutton 23.3–4–78–3; W. Falla 25–3–128–1; C. Stanley 65.1–9–281–8; O. S. Youll 6–0–32–1; M. E. Younger 82–22–283–5.

OXFORDSHIRE

Matches 9: Won – Cheshire, Cornwall, Devon, Herefordshire. Drawn – Berkshire, Dorset, Shropshire, Wiltshire. No result – Wales.

Batting Averages

	M	I	NO	R	HS	100s	50s	Avge
R. J. Cunliffe	4	7	3	275	117*	1	1	68.75
†S. N. V. Waterton ...	9	16	2	693	100*	1	8	49.50
R. A. Evans	9	9	6	117	66*	0	1	39.00
*P. J. Garner	9	12	3	298	66*	0	3	33.11
D. A. J. Wise........	9	16	1	439	90	0	4	29.26
G. P. Savin	9	12	0	230	43	0	0	25.55
J. S. Hartley	9	11	4	162	64*	0	1	23.14
T. A. Lester	8	11	1	230	51	0	2	23.00

Played in nine matches: I. J. Curtis 8, 2*, 1*. Played in eight matches: K. A. Arnold 5, 14, 13, 12. Played in four matches: S. V. Laudat 19, 2, 1. Played in three matches: J. M. Campbell 20*, 11, 16; I. M. Henderson 2*. Played in two matches: J. N. Batty 28, 4; P. M. Jobson 1, 1, 4. Played in one match: T. H. C. Hancock 22; S. G. Joyner did not bat.

Bowling Averages

	O	M	R	W	BB	5W/i	Avge
K. A. Arnold	212.4	56	507	28	5-30	1	18.10
I. J. Curtis	209.2	49	630	33	5-62	1	19.09
R. A. Evans	213.3	57	555	24	5-29	2	23.12

Also bowled: J. M. Campbell 21-5-55-1; P. J. Garner 11.3-4-46-0; T. H. C. Hancock 21-5-55-4; J. S. Hartley 62.3-13-189-3; I. M. Henderson 42-7-207-4; S. G. Joyner 15-2-41-1; S. V. Laudat 26-2-107-6; T. A. Lester 2-0-21-0; G. P. Savin 40-4-173-2; D. A. J. Wise 1-0-10-0.

SHROPSHIRE

Matches 9: Won – Dorset. Lost – Cheshire, Devon. Drawn – Berkshire, Cornwall, Hereford-shire, Oxfordshire, Wales, Wiltshire.

Batting Averages

	M	I	NO	R	HS	100s	50s	Avge
A. D. Breakwell	4	8	3	425	108*	1	4	85.00
K. Sharp	8	15	5	564	136*	2	2	56.40
*M. R. Davies	9	17	3	398	90	0	2	28.42
J. B. R. Jones	6	12	1	302	112	1	0	27.45
J. Foster	5	10	0	223	49	0	0	22.30
T. Parton	7	13	0	235	69	0	2	18.07
P. M. Blakeley	7	10	0	147	47	0	0	14.70
A. B. Byram	9	13	5	109	49	0	0	13.62
†M. J. Davidson	7	9	2	82	21	0	0	11.71
G. Edmunds	9	6	2	39	12*	0	0	9.75

Played in six matches: P. A. Thomas 2, 0*. Played in four matches: A. S. Barnard 6*, 7*, 6; B. K. Shantry 0*, 8, 0. Played in three matches: A. N. Johnson 75*, 23, 13, 1; A. R. Williams 12, 36, 12, 2, 4. Played in two matches: †N. K. Armstrong 12; D. Marsh 66*, 2, 18; M. J. Turner 9, 0, 0. Played in one match: G. L. Home 6, 18; P. T. Massey 6, 1.

Bowling Averages

	O	M	R	W	BB	5W/i	Avge
P. M. Blakeley	162.1	48	492	23	4-42	0	21.39
P. A. Thomas	149	25	572	14	3-76	0	40.85
A. B. Byram	198.5	32	778	19	6-76	1	40.94
G. Edmunds	186	42	689	14	3-33	0	49.21

Also bowled: A. S. Barnard 66.1-14-218-6; M. R. Davies 3-1-31-0; A. N. Johnson 0.1-0-4-0; J. B. R. Jones 1.2-0-11-0; D. Marsh 48-14-156-4; P. T. Massey 13-3-48-0; T. Parton 1-0-6-0; B. K. Shantry 89-25-212-9; K. Sharp 37.4-4-182-5.

STAFFORDSHIRE

Matches 9: Won – Bedfordshire, Cumberland, Hertfordshire, Norfolk, Northumberland. Lost – Lincolnshire. Drawn – Buckinghamshire, Cambridgeshire, Suffolk.

Batting Averages

	M	I	NO	R	HS	100s	50s	Avge
D. A. Banks	4	7	4	425	97*	0	4	141.66
S. D. Myles	8	14	4	494	91	0	3	49.40
S. J. Dean	7	13	0	579	86	0	6	44.53
P. G. Newman	9	8	5	127	35	0	0	42.33
D. Cartledge.........	8	15	1	469	67	0	4	33.50
P. F. Shaw	8	12	3	290	98	0	2	32.22
R. D. Salmon	3	6	1	125	50	0	1	25.00
A. J. Dutton........	5	6	1	115	81	0	1	23.00
†M. I. Humphries	9	6	1	35	16	0	0	7.00

Played in eight matches: N. P. Hackett 0*. Played in seven matches: *N. J. Archer 6, 4, 35*, 22*, 2. Played in six matches: T. M. Heap 8, 0*. Played in five matches: R. A. Spiers 20, 8. Played in three matches: D. J. Brock 0*; M. P. Clewley did not bat. Played in two matches: J. P. Addison 36, 121*, 8, 1*; J. A. Waterhouse 15, 6, 50*. Played in one match: P. J. W. Allott 0; P. R. Oliver 12.

Bowling Averages

	O	M	R	W	BB	5W/i	Avge
S. D. Myles	61.2	19	171	15	3-22	0	11.40
P. G. Newman	308.2	83	672	50	6-14	3	13.44
D. J. Brock	66	12	202	10	3-17	0	20.20
T. M. Heap	96.5	16	348	11	2-33	0	31.63
N. P. Hackett	183	41	584	14	4-52	0	41.71

Also bowled: J. P. Addison 21.5–2–96–1; P. J. W. Allott 38–16–65–4; D. Cartledge 36–8–138–3; M. P. Clewley 49.3–16–147–6; A. J. Dutton 27.2–8–74–6; R. A. Spiers 123.2–27–365–9.

SUFFOLK

Matches 9: Won – Cumberland. Lost – Lincolnshire, Norfolk, Northumberland. Drawn – Bedfordshire, Buckinghamshire, Cambridgeshire, Hertfordshire, Staffordshire.

Batting Averages

	M	I	NO	R	HS	100s	50s	Avge
A. J. Squire	8	15	2	468	88*	0	1	36.00
S. M. Clements	9	17	0	544	154	1	3	32.00
†S. J. Halliday	5	9	2	191	67	0	2	27.28
P. J. Caley	8	15	2	350	100*	1	2	26.92
M. J. Peck	8	16	5	292	74	0	2	26.54
C. A. Miller	9	13	1	298	84	0	2	24.83
K. A. Butler	8	15	1	346	70	0	3	24.71
I. D. Graham........	5	8	1	157	91*	0	1	22.42
A. K. Golding	6	8	3	59	19*	0	0	11.80
R. R. Gregg	9	15	1	127	61	0	1	9.07
*R. E. East	7	7	1	51	32	0	0	8.50

Played in six matches: †A. D. Brown 3*, 0*, 1*, 18. Played in four matches: P. J. Douglas 0, 9*, 1*. Played in three matches: S. Leggett 0, 1*, 0. Played in two matches: †M. J. Holland 0*, 12. Played in one match: W. J. Earl 1*, 9; R. Robinson 0.

Bowling Averages

	O	M	R	W	BB	5W/i	Avge
A. K. Golding	218.3	57	577	28	7-44	2	20.60
I. D. Graham........	76.1	13	288	11	4-34	0	26.18
R. R. Gregg	175.5	15	664	22	6-60	1	30.18

Also bowled: K. A. Butler 3–0–48–0; P. J. Caley 50–9–226–3; S. M. Clements 4–0–27–0; P. J. Douglas 60–4–261–4; R. E. East 75.5–12–223–0; S. J. Halliday 1–0–3–0; S. Leggett 46–5–214–3; C. A. Miller 111.4–8–477–7; M. J. Peck 5.3–1–45–3; R. Robinson 28–1–121–3.

WALES MINOR COUNTIES

Matches 9: Won – Berkshire, Cornwall, Dorset. Drawn – Devon, Shropshire, Wiltshire. No result – Cheshire, Herefordshire, Oxfordshire.

Batting Averages

	M	I	NO	R	HS	100s	50s	Avge
J. Chaminde	4	6	1	284	90	0	3	56.80
J. Derrick	6	10	3	294	110*	1	1	42.00
†A. W. Harris	6	11	1	405	88	0	3	40.50
*A. C. Puddle	8	12	1	399	97	0	3	36.27
A. Smith	7	6	4	46	22*	0	0	23.00
K. M. Bell	8	14	3	228	62	0	1	20.72
M. Newbold	4	6	1	69	22*	0	0	13.80
J. P. J. Sylvester	5	9	0	99	40	0	0	11.00

Played in seven matches: A. D. Griffiths 6, 12, 2, 31. Played in five matches: W. G. Edwards 2, 11, 14*, 0, 19*; A. Ikram 14, 12, 3; †A. J. P. Richards 16*, 27*, 10*, 22*, 10*. Played in four matches: B. J. Lloyd 3, 15*, 0. Played in three matches: M. J. Ennion 13, 29, 0, 13; S. Evans 73, 16, 7, 23, 1. Played in two matches: B. Metcalf 0, 2, 6, 20; B. S. Phelps 5*, 10*; P. S. Jones did not bat. Played in one match: A. Dalton 9, 23; D. L. Hemp 65, 21.

Bowling Averages

	O	M	R	W	BB	5W/i	Avge
A. Smith	184.5	48	555	28	6-37	2	19.82
A. D. Griffiths	137	10	452	15	3-57	0	30.13
J. Derrick	154	33	435	12	4-78	0	36.25

Also bowled: K. M. Bell 2–0–18–0; A. Dalton 0.4–0–6–0; W. G. Edwards 79–29–161–8; A. Ikram 95–27–249–9; P. S. Jones 46–7–153–8; B. J. Lloyd 50.2–13–139–4; M. Newbold 3–0–16–0; B. S. Phelps 23.3–4–94–1; A. C. Puddle 1–0–10–1; J. P. J. Sylvester 47.3–5–218–8.

WILTSHIRE

Matches 9: Won – Cheshire. Drawn – Berkshire, Dorset, Herefordshire, Oxfordshire, Shropshire, Wales. No result – Cornwall, Devon.

Batting Averages

	M	I	NO	R	HS	100s	50s	Avge
R. R. Savage	8	15	4	519	114*	2	0	47.18
L. K. Smith	9	16	0	702	119	2	3	43.87
P. M. Marsh	9	16	0	580	126	1	2	36.25
†S. M. Perrin	9	16	2	440	67	0	4	31.42
K. P. Tomlins	5	9	1	214	81*	0	1	26.75
P. D. North	9	13	3	265	77	0	1	26.50
G. Sheppard	9	9	4	131	35	0	0	26.20
D. Perryman	7	6	4	36	29	0	0	18.00
D. P. Simpkins	9	15	3	193	47	0	0	16.08
*K. N. Foyle	8	12	0	172	64	0	1	14.33
J. Lewis	6	6	1	22	12	0	0	4.40

Played in six matches: S. N. Barnes 6, 7, 0, 6*. Played in three matches: N. Prigent 3*, 4, 6*. Played in one match: R. Greatorex 40, 60; J. J. Newman 22.

Bowling Averages

	O	M	R	W	BB	5W/i	Avge
D. Perryman	97.5	20	412	17	5-32	1	24.23
P. D. North	125	37	342	13	5-58	1	26.30
P. M. Marsh	109.4	24	425	16	4-44	0	26.56
G. Sheppard	191	26	804	22	5-70	1	36.54
S. N. Barnes	133	30	524	12	4-66	0	43.66

Also bowled: K. N. Foyle 6–0–37–0; J. Lewis 86–20–275–9; S. M. Perrin 9.4–0–118–0; N. Prigent 41.5–8–128–3; R. R. Savage 4–0–48–0; D. P. Simpkins 9–0–40–1; L. K. Smith 30–6–91–4; K. P. Tomlins 26.5–3–115–1.

LEADING MINOR COUNTIES CHAMPIONSHIP AVERAGES, 1993

BATTING

(Qualification: 8 innings)

	M	I	NO	R	HS	100s	Avge
R. J. Evans (*Lincolnshire*)	7	13	4	819	153*	4	91.00
A. D. Breakwell (*Shropshire*)	4	8	3	425	108*	1	85.00
J. C. Harrison (*Buckinghamshire*)....	4	8	2	445	111*	1	74.16
J. S. Hodgson (*Berkshire*)	6	9	3	433	101*	1	72.16
S. C. Goldsmith (*Norfolk*)	9	17	4	917	200*	1	70.53
A. Needham (*Hertfordshire*)	9	16	8	557	110	1	69.62
S. A. Bradford (*Lincolnshire*)	8	8	4	261	151	1	65.25
M. E. Younger (*Northumberland*)	7	11	4	402	101*	1	57.42
K. Sharp (*Shropshire*)	8	15	5	564	136*	2	56.40
R. J. Bartlett (*Cornwall*)	8	13	2	598	146*	2	54.36

BOWLING

(Qualification: 20 wickets)

	O	M	R	W	BB	Avge
P. G. Newman (*Staffordshire*)..	308.2	83	672	50	6-14	13.44
D. R. Thomas (*Norfolk*)	137.3	40	357	24	6-36	14.87
K. A. Arnold (*Oxfordshire*)....	212.4	56	507	28	5-30	18.10
G. Miller (*Cheshire*)	319.1	104	648	35	5-26	18.51
S. Turner (*Cambridgeshire*)	245.1	76	523	28	7-31	18.67
I. J. Curtis (*Oxfordshire*)	209.2	49	630	33	5-62	19.09
P. J. Lewington (*Berkshire*)....	232.1	54	693	35	6-42	19.80
A. Smith (*Wales*)	184.5	48	555	28	6-37	19.82
A. K. Golding (*Suffolk*)	218.3	57	577	28	7-44	20.60

THE MINOR COUNTIES CHAMPIONS

1895	Norfolk	1926	Durham	1963	Cambridgeshire
	Durham	1927	Staffordshire	1964	Lancashire II
	Worcestershire	1928	Berkshire	1965	Somerset II
1896	Worcestershire	1929	Oxfordshire	1966	Lincolnshire
1897	Worcestershire	1930	Durham	1967	Cheshire
1898	Worcestershire	1931	Leicestershire II	1968	Yorkshire II
1899	Northamptonshire	1932	Buckinghamshire	1969	Buckinghamshire
	Buckinghamshire	1933	Undecided	1970	Bedfordshire
1900	Glamorgan	1934	Lancashire II	1971	Yorkshire II
	Durham	1935	Middlesex II	1972	Bedfordshire
	Northamptonshire	1936	Hertfordshire	1973	Shropshire
1901	Durham	1937	Lancashire II	1974	Oxfordshire
1902	Wiltshire	1938	Buckinghamshire	1975	Hertfordshire
1903	Northamptonshire	1939	Surrey II	1976	Durham
1904	Northamptonshire	1946	Suffolk	1977	Suffolk
1905	Norfolk	1947	Yorkshire II	1978	Devon
1906	Staffordshire	1948	Lancashire II	1979	Suffolk
1907	Lancashire II	1949	Lancashire II	1980	Durham
1908	Staffordshire	1950	Surrey II	1981	Durham
1909	Wiltshire	1951	Kent II	1982	Oxfordshire
1910	Norfolk	1952	Buckinghamshire	1983	Hertfordshire
1911	Staffordshire	1953	Berkshire	1984	Durham
1912	In abeyance	1954	Surrey II	1985	Cheshire
1913	Norfolk	1955	Surrey II	1986	Cumberland
1914	Staffordshire	1956	Kent II	1987	Buckinghamshire
1920	Staffordshire	1957	Yorkshire II	1988	Cheshire
1921	Staffordshire	1958	Yorkshire II	1989	Oxfordshire
1922	Buckinghamshire	1959	Warwickshire II	1990	Hertfordshire
1923	Buckinghamshire	1960	Lancashire II	1991	Staffordshire
1924	Berkshire	1961	Somerset II	1992	Staffordshire
1925	Buckinghamshire	1962	Warwickshire II	1993	Staffordshire

UMPIRES FOR 1994

FIRST-CLASS UMPIRES

J. C. Balderstone, H. D. Bird, J. D. Bond, G. I. Burgess, D. J. Constant, B. Dudleston, J. H. Hampshire, J. H. Harris, J. W. Holder, V. A. Holder, T. E. Jesty, A. A. Jones, R. Julian, M. J. Kitchen, B. Leadbeater, K. J. Lyons, B. J. Meyer, K. E. Palmer, R. Palmer, N. T. Plews, G. Sharp, D. R. Shepherd, R. A. White, A. G. T. Whitehead, P. B. Wight and P. Willey. *Reserves:* P. Adams, A. Clarkson, M. J. Harris, M. K. Reed and J. F. Steele.

Note: The panel of umpires for Test matches and one-day internationals was not available at the time *Wisden* went to press.

MINOR COUNTIES UMPIRES

P. Adams, K. Bray, P. Brown, D. L. Burden, R. K. Curtis, J. B. Foulkes, D. J. Halfyard, M. A. Johnson, B. Knight, S. W. Kuhlmann, G. I. McLean, M. P. Moran, D. Norton, C. T. Puckett, G. P. Randall-Johnson, M. K. Reed, K. S. Shenton, C. Smith, C. T. Spencer, C. Stone, D. S. Thompsett, J. M. Tythcott, G. Williams, T. G. Wilson and R. Wood. *Reserves:* A. R. Bundy, A. Carter, S. P. Chitty, A. R. Clark, K. Coburn, A. G. Forster, J. A. Gurney, K. R. Jenkins, C. S. Kelly, R. E. Lawson, D. Lea, G. Lowden, P. R. Mitchell, J. G. Reed, G. B. Smith, M. D. Smith, K. G. Sutherland, T. J. White, B. H. Willey and N. J. Williams.

RAPID CRICKETLINE SECOND ELEVEN CHAMPIONSHIP, 1993

Middlesex Second Eleven emulated their first team's performance and won the Championship, finishing 21 points clear of their nearest rivals, Lancashire. Only Kent had done that particular double before – in 1970. It was a third success for Middlesex, who had won the title in 1974 and 1989, when their first team had come sixth and third respectively. The Bain Clarkson Trophy went to Leicestershire, who had qualified for the semi-finals only as the best of the group runners-up. They overwhelmed Sussex in a one-sided final, having squeezed past Hampshire in their semi-final. Sussex had beaten Nottinghamshire, also by a narrow margin. Neither finalist had reached that stage before, and Leicestershire were the eighth new holders in as many years of the competition. None of the front-runners in the one-day competition did particularly well in the Championship, in which Leicestershire were 13th and Sussex eighth.

The season was seriously affected by rain, with as many as eight matches abandoned without a ball bowled; Warwickshire were particularly hard hit, being involved in three of those. Of the four counties who had two matches completely washed out – Middlesex, Lancashire, Surrey and Worcestershire – the first two were still able to take their places at the top of the table. With such interference from the weather, it was probably not surprising that only two batsmen scored 1,000 runs. Jonathan Longley of Kent was the most prolific with 1,061 in 24 innings, closely followed by Nottinghamshire's Graeme Archer, who had three fewer innings for his 1,054. Ashley Metcalfe fell just one short of four figures with 999 for Yorkshire in only 17 innings. Metcalfe's total was boosted by five hundreds, the same number that Wayne Dessaur struck for Nottinghamshire. His team-mate, Mark Saxelby, made the highest score of the season, his 238 not out being one of eight double-hundreds in the Championship. The highest average was recorded by Tim

SECOND ELEVEN CHAMPIONSHIP, 1993

					Bonus points		
Win = 16 points	M	W	L	D	Batting	Bowling	Points
1 – Middlesex (6)	17	7	1	9†	50	44	206
2 – Lancashire (10)	17	6	2	9†	42	47	185
3 – Yorkshire (5)	17	6	1	10	45	45	182
4 – Gloucestershire (3) ...	17	4	1	12	50	63	177
5 – Nottinghamshire (14) .	17	5	4	8	42	54	176
6 – Surrey (1)...........	17	5	4	8†	39	52	171
7 – Essex (18)	17	5	7	5	34	54	168
8 – Sussex (9)..........	17	4	7	6	42	45	151
9 – Somerset (12)........	17	4	4	9*	44	42	150
10 – Hampshire (4).......	17	3	1	13	40	48	136
11 – Kent (8)	17	3	4	10*	40	37	125
12 – Northamptonshire (2) .	17	3	2	12	33	36	123
13 – Leicestershire (15)....	17	3	5	9*	26	47	117
14 – Durham (6)	17	2	6	9	38	46	116
15 – Warwickshire (12)....	17	2	4	11‡	38	43	113
16 – Worcestershire (16)...	17	3	3	11†	28	34	110
17 – Derbyshire (11)	17	1	2	14*	35	39	86
18 – Glamorgan (17)......	17	1	9	7*	28	39	83

1992 positions are shown in brackets.

The totals for Derbyshire, Leicestershire and Yorkshire include 12 points for a win in a one-innings match. The total for Northamptonshire includes 6 points for batting second in a one-innings match drawn with the scores level.

* Indicates one match abandoned without a ball bowled.

† Indicates two matches abandoned without a ball bowled.

‡ Indicates three matches abandoned without a ball bowled.

O'Gorman, whose 494 runs in seven innings for Derbyshire came at an average of 123.50, but only Toby Radford of Middlesex managed more than 500 runs at a three-figure average, with 734 at 104.85 in 11 innings.

Again, it was not a vintage year for the bowlers; only two took 50 wickets, as in 1992, but this year none reached 55. Nottinghamshire's James Hindson was the most successful, taking 52 at 29.25, which was one more than fell to the Middlesex all-rounder, Keith Dutch (51 at 25.66), who also scored 420 runs and was named the Rapid Cricketline Second Eleven Championship Player of the Year. Hindson sent down the most overs, with 500, Rajesh Maru of Hampshire delivered 479.1 for his 38 wickets and Dutch bowled 469.1. Of the bowlers who took at least 25 wickets, Yorkshire's captain, Phil Carrick, was the most economical with 25 at 9.24, followed by Gary Yates of Lancashire who took 31 at 13.90 as well as scoring 326 runs in nine innings. Championship hat-tricks were recorded by Kent's Duncan Spencer, Northamptonshire's Tim Walton and Warwickshire's Graeme Welch, while James Brinkley performed the feat for Worcestershire in the Bain Clarkson Trophy.

The leading all-rounder was Ricardo Williams of Gloucestershire, who collected 639 runs and 47 wickets in 14 matches, while Paul Weekes of Middlesex needed only ten matches for his 612 runs and 38 wickets. Surrey's Neil Sargeant was the leading wicket-keeper with 49 dismissals (all caught), as well as 709 runs, while Paul Farbrace of Middlesex, fifth in the wicket-keeping table, hit 707 to set alongside his 35 dismissals. Richard Williams followed Sargeant with 47 for Gloucestershire, while Shaun Humphries effected 43 for Sussex. Sargeant, Farbrace and Humphries, along with eight other players, appeared in all their team's matches. In the field, Maru was outstanding with 26 catches, the fourth-most by a fielder in one season and the most since 1984. Jason Harrison of Middlesex was next with 21.

Twelve players batted in Nottinghamshire's first innings in the match against Gloucestershire at Bristol on August 25, 26, 27. David Pennett, nought not out overnight, was called up for a first-team game, being replaced on the second morning by Steven Musgrove, who, however, was lbw for nought. There was an absurd episode in the match between Yorkshire and Lancashire at Todmorden on July 7, 8, 9 after Lancashire had passed 450 on the first day and rain had washed out the second. On the third day, in a ridiculous attempt to feed runs and perhaps produce a result, Mark Harvey bowled 18 consecutive no-balls, all of which went to the boundary. The over was never completed and his bowling figures for the season read an unlikely 5.4-0-140-0.

Derbyshire had a difficult season, being hampered by injuries, and had to call on 48 players. They did not win until their last game, against Sussex at Chesterfield, which enabled them to finish ahead of Glamorgan. The pick of the batsmen were Tim O'Gorman and Gary Steer. Alastair Richardson, at medium pace, and the off-spinner Paul Whitaker bore the brunt of the attack.

Durham failed to maintain the form of their first season and slipped down eight places, though some of their individual performances were personally satisfying: Ian Smith scored 160 against his former county, Glamorgan, at Boldon while the newcomer Peter Wilcock, who also played for English Schools, made his mark with 116 not out against Hampshire. Phil Berry played in only two matches but took six for ten against Leicestershire at Chester-le-Street.

In contrast to their first team, **Essex** improved, despite often fielding a depleted side because uncapped players had to be drafted into the first team. The Canadian-born Muneeb Diwan scored consistently, with eight fifties but no hundred – though he was stranded on 99 not out against Middlesex. Andrew Hibbert and the outstanding wicket-keeper Robert Rollins also made maiden centuries. The slow left-armer Mark Powell became the leading wicket-taker after coming down from college in Southampton, taking 37 wickets including six for 67 against Warwickshire and seven for 71 against Middlesex. In September, he scored his maiden century against Durham. At Colchester, against Somerset, the team was strengthened by the improbable figure of Graham Gooch, for the first time in 15 years – he was worried about his form after the one-day internationals. However, he made only 25 and 23.

Glamorgan's form was also in contrast to the first team's performance. They came bottom and, like Derbyshire, did not win until their final match. James Williams was voted their Second Eleven Player of the Year, with 703 runs including a century against Durham. But only Leicestershire registered fewer batting points and the bowling was also disappointing,

Second Eleven Championship, 1993

though Steve Bastien took 30 wickets. Adrian Shaw, ever-present, kept wicket competently and passed 500 runs for the first time.

Gloucestershire maintained their improvement, winning four games; but for the weather they might easily have won three more. They had more bonus points than anyone else. They often did less well in the second innings. Ricardo Williams was again the outstanding all-rounder and Kamran Sheeraz and the English Schools captain Michael Cawdron showed promise towards the end of the season.

It was a frustrating season for **Hampshire**, who drew 13 matches and showed a disturbing inability to winkle out tailenders. The leading run-scorer was the left-hander Julian Wood, who sometimes batted brilliantly but lacked consistency; Rupert Cox also scored heavily. Encouraging first full seasons were recorded by the wicket-keeper Mark Garaway and William Kendall, who hit a fighting 103 against Nottinghamshire. The mainstay of the bowling was the experienced Rajesh Maru. At Boldon, Durham were dismissed for 53 with fast-medium bowler Jim Bovill recording match figures of ten for 69. Liam Botham showed promise in his first season. Hampshire used 27 players, the fewest of any county.

Although many players with first-team experience were available during the season, **Kent** slipped down the table. Jonathan Longley was the backbone of the batting with a thousand runs for the second successive year, including four centuries. Richard Ellison and Graham Cowdrey also scored well. But the highest innings, 191, came from the Western Australian, Robert Kelly, against Middlesex at Eltham. Among the youngsters, David Fulton passed 500 runs while the wicket-keeper Simon Willis made a century against Derbyshire at Folkestone. The Australian-bred pace bowler Duncan Spencer had a memorable match against Leicestershire at Oakham, scoring 93 and taking six for 26, including a hat-trick.

Lancashire rose from tenth place to be runners-up. They dominated all but two of their matches but were affected by their traditional weather. Their most successful batsman, Ronnie Irani, scored 203 not out against Kent at Manchester but left after the season to join Essex. He passed 800 runs, as did Stephen Titchard. The off-spinner Gary Yates headed the bowling averages and Nick Derbyshire produced some performances of genuine pace and accuracy in the latter part of the season. Mark Harvey, the England Under-19 player, fielded excellently and made a maiden century in the two-day win over Durham.

Although **Leicestershire** came only 13th in the Championship, their team spirit and determination won them the Bain Clarkson Trophy. Two all-rounders stood out, Jonathan Dakin and Warwick Adlam, who took five wickets in an innings four times. A young fast bowler, Adlam was on a reciprocal scholarship from Australia, under which Ben Smith was to go to New South Wales in the winter. Smith himself scored 200 not out against Durham. The best bowling return was five for 14 against Durham from Niroshan de Silva, a leg-spinner and son of the former Sri Lankan captain D. S. de Silva.

Middlesex's third Championship was based, like their first team's success, on a well-balanced side. The batting was strong: seven players made hundreds, with three double-centuries. Robin Sims, a dashing left-hander, made 213 against Sussex at Harrow, while Jason Pooley and Jason Harrison both scored 203 not out at Uxbridge, against Glamorgan and Hampshire respectively. Harrison and Pooley put on an unbroken 329 for the first wicket in the Glamorgan match, with Harrison scoring 102 not out. Toby Radford joined the side after the university term and averaged a phenomenal 104.85, adding freedom to an already solid technique. Paul Farbrace had an excellent season behind the stumps while Matthew Keech was a revelation for someone who took up bowling only two years ago and headed the averages with his medium pace. Keith Dutch's 51 wickets included six for 75 against Somerset.

Northamptonshire, runners-up in 1992, slipped to 12th. Wayne Noon, however, was outstanding. He captained the side for most of the season, kept wicket and headed the batting averages with 785 runs. His form was not good enough, though, to displace the first-team keeper David Ripley and he retreated to Nottinghamshire. Richard Montgomerie also

roduced some splendid innings when he came down from Oxford, notably 138 not out
gainst Yorkshire at Wellingborough School. The outstanding bowler was Mark Bowen,
who performed with more consistency and pace than in the past. Another bowling highlight
was a hat-trick by Tim Walton, spread over two innings against Leicestershire.

Under the captaincy of Mike Newell, **Nottinghamshire** returned to their accustomed place
on the top part of the table, finishing fifth. The outstanding innings was Mark Saxelby's 238
not out, which was a record for the county and equalled the seventh-highest score in the
Championship. Coming in the fourth innings against Gloucestershire at Bristol, it
contributed to a winning total of 400 for six, after Nottinghamshire had been bowled out for
1 in the first innings. Saxelby totalled 875 in nine matches but both Graeme Archer, with
,054, and Wayne Dessaur, with 897 including five hundreds, scored more overall. Richard
Bates, who missed 1992 through injury, scored a maiden century against Worcestershire and
took 39 wickets with his off-spin, including four for four when Derbyshire were bowled out
for 46 at Newark. However, the outstanding bowler was the slow left-armer James Hindson,
who had 52 wickets.

Somerset's leading batsmen were the identical twins, Keith and Kevin Parsons, but there
were also centuries from Marcus Trescothick, Giles White and Kevin Sedgbeer, and from
Neil Burns, who came down from the first team to score an unbeaten 225 against
Middlesex. The left-arm spinner Andy Cottam was the leading bowler, with 35 wickets, but
subsequently moved on to Northamptonshire.

The 1992 champions **Surrey** dropped to sixth. The most prolific batsman was Rehan
Alikhan while another senior player, David Ward, became the only player to hit a hundred
in each innings in the Championship. David Thompson was the most successful bowler
with 41 wickets, while Mark Bainbridge collected 35, somewhat expensively.

Like their first team, **Sussex** reached the one-day final but lost, and performed moderately
in the Championship. Keith Greenfield was the leading run-scorer but a feature of the
season was the form of the left-hander Toby Peirce, who made 726 runs after his return
from Durham University. Shaun Humphries, a young wicket-keeper who played in every
match, effected 43 dismissals and another ever-present, left-arm spinner Jacob Dean, took
the most wickets.

With their three washouts, **Warwickshire** were always struggling. When they did play,
many batsmen were inconsistent and the bowling lacked penetration. There were two
notable performances from the pace bowlers: Paul Aldred took six for 47 against
Glamorgan at Moseley and Graeme Welch had a hat-trick against Durham. Two left-
armers took the most wickets, Michael Bell and the spinner Ashley Giles.

Worcestershire remained in 16th place but there was some encouragement. With a small
professional staff, the club offered plenty of opportunities to non-staff players, of whom
seam bowlers Parvez Mirza and Matt Brooke did well enough to be offered engagements for
1994, while Ben McCorkill, a left-arm spinner, earned a summer contract. Tim Edwards, in
his first season on the staff, kept wicket well and was a gutsy batsman.

Yorkshire's young team did well to move up to third place, three points behind
Lancashire. Ashley Metcalfe finished one short of 1,000 runs in just ten matches. He was
one of two players in the Championship to score five centuries. Colin Chapman, the wicket-
keeper, made 40 dismissals and hit a century against Durham at Marske-by-Sea. He played
in all the matches, along with Bradley Parker and the left-hander Richard Kettleborough,
who both scored more than 800 runs.

DERBYSHIRE SECOND ELEVEN

*Matches 17: Won – Sussex. Lost – Kent, Nottinghamshire. Drawn – Durham, Essex,
Glamorgan, Gloucestershire, Hampshire, Lancashire, Leicestershire, Middlesex, Northamptonshire, Somerset, Surrey, Warwickshire, Yorkshire. Abandoned – Worcestershire.*

Batting Averages

	M	I	NO	R	HS	100s	Avge
T. J. G. O'Gorman ...	4	7	3	494	156*	2	123.50
G. R. Hill	3	5	2	198	91	0	66.00
I. G. S. Steer	6	11	1	566	139	2	56.60
A. Roseberry	7	11	1	434	136	1	43.40
G. M. Pooley	7	12	3	390	100*	1	43.33
*†B. J. M. Maher	12	10	8	80	30*	0	40.00
T. A. Tweats	10	18	2	613	113	1	38.31
A. S. Rollins	11	18	1	610	78	0	35.88
P. R. Whitaker	15	20	0	493	86	0	24.65
S. C. Goldsmith	3	4	0	97	82	0	24.25
M. J. Vandrau	2	3	0	72	38	0	24.00
D. J. Shadford	3	6	1	111	28	0	22.20
†M. Gilliver	2	3	0	65	32	0	21.66
N. Johnson	3	4	1	56	22	0	18.66
A. J. Harris	8	9	1	138	30	0	17.25
M. Taylor	6	8	2	98	49	0	16.33
P. J. Bennett	6	8	0	130	65	0	16.25
†P. G. T. Davies	2	3	0	47	30	0	15.66
J. D. Cokayne	2	3	0	45	42	0	15.00
D. J. Lovell	8	10	0	125	39	0	12.50
S. A. Stoneman	11	12	2	117	24	0	11.70
L. J. Henshaw	5	6	0	69	28	0	11.50
R. W. Sladdin	4	5	1	36	20*	0	9.00
A. W. Richardson	10	11	2	45	14	0	5.00

Played in two matches: C. R. Miller 0; G. V. Palmer 27*. Played in one match R. Bhanabhai 6, 1*; S. M. Brogan 4, 34; A. M. Brown 18, 4; B. St A. Browne 13, 3; B. A. Cruse 23, 18; K. Dean 0, 0; V. C. Drakes 28, 71; S. Jack 1, 20*; †S. Kulkarni 11; S. Lacey 4, 3; †J. Moyes 0, 1*; N. Podmore 1, 0; G. M. Roberts 4*; K. Semple 35*, 7; G. F. Shephard 7, 3*; J. I. M. Smith 1*; D. Thakur 4*; J. A. Waterhouse 0, 7; M. A. Wintle 39 5; N. Hanson, †C. Marples and A. Richardson did not bat.

Bowling Averages

	O	M	R	W	BB	Avge
B. St A. Browne	29	5	83	5	5-41	16.60
N. Podmore	58.5	13	133	8	5-98	16.62
D. Thakur	23.3	5	96	4	4-96	24.00
R. W. Sladdin	133.2	32	404	15	4-109	26.93
M. Taylor	120	28	352	13	5-33	27.07
M. J. Vandrau	66	26	149	5	2-21	29.80
A. W. Richardson	250.3	32	1,017	32	5-60	31.78
V. C. Drakes	27	1	133	4	3-43	33.25
S. A. Stoneman	160.4	25	529	14	3-57	37.78
P. R. Whitaker	296.3	103	1,159	30	5-120	38.63
D. J. Lovell	63.4	19	194	4	2-22	48.50
L. J. Henshaw	65.4	11	259	5	3-51	51.80
A. S. Rollins	85	10	385	7	2-24	55.00
A. J. Harris	145.5	25	620	10	2-27	62.00

Also bowled: R. Bhanabhai 21-1-86-0; B. A. Cruse 1-0-8-0; K. Dean 24-10-69-2 S. C. Goldsmith 35-6-108-3; N. Hanson 19-3-100-2; S. Jack 24-3-97-1; N. Johnson 39-6-124-3; B. J. M. Maher 12-0-55-2; C. R. Miller 20.1-2-85-2; G. V. Palmer 36-4-127-3; A. Richardson 7-0-31-1; G. M. Roberts 21-1-93-2; K. Semple 11.3-4-30-0 D. J. Shadford 31.4-7-95-2; G. F. Shephard 14-0-61-2; J. I. M. Smith 21-4-66-0 I. G. S. Steer 32.3-5-127-2; J. A. Waterhouse 3-0-19-0.

DURHAM SECOND ELEVEN

Matches 17: Won – Glamorgan, Nottinghamshire. Lost – Essex, Gloucestershire, Lancashire, Middlesex, Somerset, Surrey. Drawn – Derbyshire, Hampshire, Kent, Leicestershire, Northamptonshire, Sussex, Warwickshire, Worcestershire, Yorkshire.

Batting Averages

	M	I	NO	R	HS	100s	Avge
S. M. McEwan........	3	5	3	122	68*	0	61.00
J. A. Daley..........	3	6	0	268	110	2	44.66
P. J. Wilcock	3	6	1	218	116*	1	43.60
J. D. Glendenen	7	13	0	517	106	1	39.76
S. Hutton	6	11	0	423	134	1	38.45
M. P. Briers	12	23	3	667	158*	1	33.35
I. Smith	8	15	0	471	160	1	31.40
G. Wigham	7	11	5	163	43*	0	27.16
R. M. S. Weston	7	13	1	318	88	0	26.50
S. D. Birbeck	5	10	1	221	83	0	24.55
D. A. Blenkiron	17	33	1	747	69	0	23.34
P. W. Henderson	14	26	1	580	93	0	23.20
G. J. Weeks	3	6	0	129	38	0	21.50
†A. R. Fothergill	10	18	3	286	62	0	19.06
S. Lugsden	7	8	5	55	39*	0	18.33
K. A. Butler	3	6	0	103	69	0	17.16
†M. W. Garside	3	6	1	84	28	0	16.80
D. Bates	2	4	0	65	34	0	16.25
D. M. Cox	15	24	3	339	49	0	16.14
J. Wood	8	13	4	98	32*	0	10.88
M. M. Betts	10	14	3	115	32	0	10.45
J. P. Searle	10	11	4	40	18	0	5.71

Played in three matches: R. D. Wild 0*, 5, 2. Played in two matches: P. J. Berry 1, 1; G. Cook 34, 0; H. T. R. Davis 13*, 3, 2; †C. W. Scott 0, 16*, 5*; N. J. Trainor 6, 5, 51*. Played in one match: S. Chapman 2, 90; G. Fowler 1, 43; D. M. Jones 73; N. Killeen 1; G. R. Mason 12; N. Pratt 54, 21; †R. J. Storr 0, 1; †G. Thomas 38*, 9*; D. T. Wyrill 4, 0; G. D. Yates 7, 5; S. A. J. Boswell and R. H. Carlson did not bat.

Note: In the match v Surrey at Felling I. Smith, called up for a first-team match, was replaced in the second innings by N. J. Trainor.

Bowling Averages

	O	M	R	W	BB	Avge
P. J. Berry	71.2	30	125	9	6-10	13.88
D. A. Blenkiron	24.4	4	101	4	2-17	25.25
M. M. Betts	208	38	720	26	4-15	27.69
M. P. Briers	153.5	35	529	19	4-56	27.84
S. D. Birbeck	83	18	302	10	3-86	30.20
S. Lugsden	155.1	43	468	14	3-21	33.42
D. M. Cox	428.3	130	1,268	35	5-59	36.22
I. Smith	73	17	225	6	3-25	37.50
G. Wigham	146.4	25	461	11	3-60	41.90
J. P. Searle	270	58	833	19	4-91	43.84
J. Wood	183.3	24	728	16	2-25	45.50
P. W. Henderson	162	23	711	10	4-81	71.10

Also bowled: S. A. J. Boswell 23–7–66–1; R. H. Carlson 15–2–58–3; H. T. R. Davis 27–5–68–3; D. M. Jones 6–0–28–0; N. Killeen 11–0–45–0; S. M. McEwan 43–14–94–3; G. R. Mason 8–3–28–0; R. M. S. Weston 15–2–47–2; R. D. Wild 48–16–154–1; G. D. Yates 6–1–21–1.

ESSEX SECOND ELEVEN

Matches 17: Won – Durham, Leicestershire, Middlesex, Nottinghamshire, Sussex. Lost – Glamorgan, Hampshire, Lancashire, Northamptonshire, Surrey, Worcestershire, Yorkshire. Drawn – Derbyshire, Gloucestershire, Kent, Somerset, Warwickshire.

Batting Averages

	M	I	NO	R	HS	100s	Avge
J. J. B. Lewis	4	7	1	372	161	1	62.00
N. V. Knight	9	18	3	858	145	2	57.20
M. Diwan	15	29	5	934	99*	0	38.91
N. Shahid	12	23	1	713	147	2	32.40
*A. R. Butcher	10	15	2	415	63	0	31.92
P. J. Ayres	3	6	1	156	65*	0	31.20
D. D. J. Robinson	13	26	1	776	68	0	31.04
A. J. E. Hibbert	3	6	0	176	125	1	29.33
K. T. Medlycott	3	5	2	80	54*	0	26.66
†R. J. Rollins	12	22	3	444	104	1	23.36
T. D. Topley	4	7	1	134	52*	0	22.33
A. G. J. Fraser	4	7	0	151	84	0	21.57
G. A. Khan	9	16	0	317	74	0	19.81
M. Powell	13	20	3	275	106	1	16.17
D. J. P. Boden	10	15	2	158	34	0	12.15
C. G. Feltham	6	11	1	114	37	0	11.40
L. Tennant	12	19	6	139	24	0	10.69
S. J. W. Andrew	7	10	2	85	38	0	10.62
C. Patel	3	5	0	26	16	0	5.20
D. M. Cousins	10	12	4	30	10	0	3.75

Played in three matches: R. M. Atkinson 0, 14*, 20*, 12, 11*. Played in two matches: D. W. Ayres 17*, 2; A. Cowan 8*, 3; A. K. Golding 0, 2. Played in one match: B. St A. Browne 3*; A. K. Durgacharran 1; S. C. Ecclestone 20, 0; R. Ellwood 10; M. A. Garnham 9, 80*; G. A. Gooch 25, 23; C. P. Harvey 9, 21; I. J. Harvey 10*, 0*; B. J. Hyam 3*, 32; S. K. Mohammed 2*; G. Norris 8, 4; A. Pratt 17, 0; P. R. Shaw 1; M. J. Walshe 1*; J. H. Childs, D. J. Foster and N. P. Harvey did not bat.

Note: In the match v Sussex at Chelmsford J. J. B. Lewis, called up for a first-team match, was replaced by J. H. Childs.

Bowling Averages

	O	M	R	W	BB	Avge
J. H. Childs	39	25	52	8	6-28	6.50
A. K. Golding	47.3	9	111	8	3-13	13.87
T. D. Topley	106	31	273	15	6-51	18.20
A. Cowan	37	6	146	7	3-39	20.85
N. V. Knight	28.2	6	88	4	2-18	22.00
S. J. W. Andrew	163.5	38	462	18	4-65	25.66
M. Powell	420.1	112	1,124	37	7-71	30.37
L. Tennant	254	28	932	30	4-44	31.06
K. T. Medlycott	43	8	157	5	3-73	31.40
D. M. Cousins	239	51	726	22	4-79	33.00
N. Shahid	125.4	30	330	10	3-22	33.00
D. J. P. Boden	249	46	817	24	4-37	34.04
C. G. Feltham	154.4	43	424	10	3-57	42.40

Also bowled: R. M. Atkinson 62.3–8–234–1; D. W. Ayres 18–3–72–2; B. St A. Browne 30.3–2–149–3; R. Ellwood 26–7–84–3; D. J. Foster 16–2–66–2; A. G. J. Fraser 9–2–45–0; G. A. Gooch 13–4–15–2; I. J. Harvey 4–0–23–0; J. J. B. Lewis 3–0–30–1; S. K. Mohammed 12–2–29–2; C. Patel 72–6–335–3; D. D. J. Robinson 26–5–121–2; M. J. Walshe 16.2–3–51–0.

GLAMORGAN SECOND ELEVEN

Matches 17: Won – Essex. Lost – Durham, Hampshire, Lancashire, Northamptonshire, Somerset, Surrey, Sussex, Warwickshire, Worcestershire. Drawn – Derbyshire, Gloucestershire, Kent, Middlesex, Nottinghamshire, Yorkshire. Abandoned – Leicestershire.

Batting Averages

	M	I	NO	R	HS	100s	Avge
D. L. Hemp	8	14	1	639	106*	2	49.15
R. O. Jones	8	13	3	371	87	0	37.10
G. P. Butcher	11	21	2	647	154	2	34.05
J. R. A. Williams	11	22	1	703	108*	1	33.47
A. J. Jones	6	12	1	323	67	0	29.36
I. Bishop	10	19	2	452	80	0	26.58
G. H. J. Rees	5	9	1	184	73	0	23.00
J. P. J. Sylvester	9	15	2	282	66	0	21.69
A. J. Dalton	15	27	2	542	53*	0	21.68
†A. D. Shaw	16	27	2	508	64	0	20.32
J. Davies	2	4	0	81	47	0	20.25
A. M. Brown	5	9	0	182	42	0	20.22
B. S. Phelps	6	9	2	117	46	0	16.71
S. D. Thomas	4	6	1	80	24	0	16.00
A. D. Rowlands	3	5	1	56	35	0	14.00
M. Frost	8	9	3	68	21	0	11.33
S. Bastien	13	22	4	198	33	0	11.00
G. M. Roberts	3	5	0	49	32	0	9.80
S. Purdie	6	11	1	71	24	0	7.10
O. T. Parkin	5	6	2	24	11*	0	6.00
E. P. M. Holland	6	9	2	35	12	0	5.00

Played in five matches: J. F. Steele 9*, 3*, 31*, 15*, 0*, 11*, 10*. Played in two matches: A. Roseberry 149, 20, 25. Played in one match: G. Angus 2, 12*; A. B. Byram 6, 0; S. Dhaniram 2, 0; D. H. Evans 2, 4; P. S. Jones 4; T. A. Roach 25; J. M. S. Whittington 1; N. J. Wood 22; B. Zuiderent 9, 0.

Bowling Averages

	O	M	R	W	BB	Avge
G. M. Roberts	79	28	190	9	4-95	21.11
O. T. Parkin	120	21	417	16	5-49	26.06
M. Frost	222	38	786	24	4-52	32.75
S. Bastien	355.2	86	1,062	30	6-56	35.40
E. P. M. Holland	132.5	21	475	12	4-119	39.58
R. O. Jones	244.5	50	799	20	4-71	39.95
S. D. Thomas	106.4	17	418	9	4-83	46.44
B. S. Phelps	192.5	45	647	13	5-89	49.76
J. P. J. Sylvester	113	39	309	6	2-50	51.50

Also bowled: G. Angus 20–5–50–2; G. P. Butcher 51.4–7–172–3; A. B. Byram 32–11–98–1; A. J. Dalton 61–10–248–3; D. L. Hemp 7–0–34–0; P. S. Jones 16–1–69–1; S. Purdie 87–8–385–4; T. A. Roach 6–0–24–0; A. D. Rowlands 37–6–143–1; J. M. S. Whittington 9–0–39–0; N. J. Wood 37.5–13–63–5.

GLOUCESTERSHIRE SECOND ELEVEN

Matches 17: Won – Durham, Leicestershire, Sussex, Warwickshire. Lost – Nottinghamshire. Drawn – Derbyshire, Essex, Glamorgan, Hampshire, Kent, Lancashire, Middlesex, Northampton-shire, Somerset, Surrey, Worcestershire, Yorkshire.

Batting Averages

	M	I	NO	R	HS	100s	Avge
M. J. Gerrard	7	4	3	70	42	0	70.00
G. D. Hodgson	4	6	0	411	120	2	68.50
A. J. Wright	6	10	2	518	101*	1	64.75
R. J. Scott	10	16	2	851	132	3	60.78
M. G. N. Windows ...	6	9	1	458	143	2	57.25
R. J. Cunliffe	11	14	2	509	114	1	42.41
D. R. Hewson	7	10	2	324	86	0	40.50
R. C. Williams	14	20	4	639	109	2	39.93
R. I. Dawson	7	10	0	377	111	1	37.70
†R. C. J. Williams	16	21	8	394	56*	0	30.30
R. M. Wight	11	12	3	267	79*	0	29.66
J. Shepherd	2	4	0	117	48	0	29.25
M. C. J. Ball	11	10	3	185	40*	0	26.42
T. H. C. Hancock	4	5	0	129	70	0	25.80
U. Sisodia	8	12	0	251	62	0	20.91
Z. A. Sher	6	7	0	128	59	0	18.28
A. M. Babington	7	4	1	30	21*	0	10.00
J. M. de la Pena	11	7	1	51	10	0	8.50
R. Horrell	10	7	0	54	33	0	7.71
A. M. Smith	8	7	2	37	8*	0	7.40

Played in five matches: M. Davies 7, 49, 8*. Played in four matches: M. J. Cawdron 5, 8*. Played in three matches: S. G. Hinks 55, 17, 12; K. P. Sheeraz 13*, 53, 6*. Played in two matches: J. A. Beard 29, 46; H. J. Morgan 10, 0*, 34. Played in one match: A. J. Collins 4, 2; †A. C. Walker did not bat.

Bowling Averages

	O	M	R	W	BB	Avge
M. Davies	137.5	50	271	17	6-26	15.94
K. P. Sheeraz	89	32	220	12	4-37	18.33
A. M. Smith	228.1	49	647	34	5-73	19.02
R. C. Williams	358.3	88	991	47	6-84	21.08
M. J. Gerrard	188.2	43	425	18	3-22	23.61
M. C. J. Ball	243.4	54	599	25	5-45	23.96
M. J. Cawdron	91	20	303	12	5-25	25.25
A. M. Babington	216.5	58	546	19	5-56	28.73
R. J. Scott	96	22	269	9	2-17	29.88
R. M. Wight	357	100	882	25	7-106	35.28
J. M. de la Pena	205.2	36	764	21	6-51	36.38

Also bowled: A. J. Collins 12-1-59-1; R. I. Dawson 5-1-20-0; T. H. C. Hancock 15-4-45-2; D. R. Hewson 3-1-5-0; R. Horrell 82-17-215-4; Z. A. Sher 26.2-7-86-4; U. Sisodia 52-7-216-3; M. G. N. Windows 3-0-23-0; A. J. Wright 0.3-0-2-0.

HAMPSHIRE SECOND ELEVEN

Matches 17: Won – Essex, Glamorgan, Surrey. Lost – Middlesex. Drawn – Derbyshire, Durham, Gloucestershire, Kent, Lancashire, Leicestershire, Northamptonshire, Nottinghamshire, Somerset, Sussex, Warwickshire, Worcestershire, Yorkshire.

Batting Averages

	M	I	NO	R	HS	100s	Avge
T. C. Middleton	7	11	1	514	93	0	51.40
R. T. P. Miller	2	3	1	93	50	0	46.50
R. S. M. Morris	10	14	2	498	126	1	41.50
J. S. Laney	11	15	2	515	126*	1	39.61
*R. M. F. Cox	13	21	2	710	118*	3	37.36

	M	I	NO	R	HS	100s	Avge
R. Wood	14	23	3	739	152	1	36.95
J. S. Kendall	15	21	4	584	103	1	34.35
M. Garaway	16	24	2	658	121	1	29.90
I. J. Thursfield	11	13	4	169	57	0	18.77
R. J. Maru	16	21	6	265	55	0	17.66
P. Kent	5	6	0	89	33	0	14.83
J. Turner	10	8	3	68	33*	0	13.60
N. B. Bovill	10	8	2	81	26	0	13.50
J. N. Batty	4	6	1	65	21	0	13.00
M. Jean-Jacques	11	9	3	77	32	0	12.83
P. J. Flint	6	7	4	37	28*	0	12.33
R. Byrne	10	10	4	63	18	0	10.50
K. J. Shine	3	1	1	20	17*	0	6.66

Played in four matches: L. J. Botham 2, 0, 0. Played in three matches: C. A. Connor 73. Played in two matches: J. R. Ayling 114, 7; L. B. Linton 15, 0. Played in one match: V. C. Drakes 42; K. D. James 45, 22; C. G. Knight 0; H. S. Malik 16, 1; G. M. Pooley 29.

Note: Owing to first-team calls, R. S. M. Morris was replaced by L. B. Linton in the match v Derbyshire at Derby, M. Jean-Jacques was replaced by J. R. Byrne in the match v Yorkshire at Portsmouth and R. S. M. Morris was replaced by L. B. Linton in the match v Leicestershire at Hinckley.

Bowling Averages

	O	M	R	W	BB	Avge
K. D. James	25	11	45	5	3-39	9.00
P. J. Flint	140.2	41	357	18	6-32	19.83
N. B. Bovill	235.1	68	648	31	6-30	20.90
I. J. Thursfield	292.4	85	769	31	6-101	24.80
J. Shine	62	15	166	6	3-41	27.66
R. J. Maru	479.1	150	1,068	38	6-24	28.10
J. Turner	297.4	105	622	20	4-11	31.10
M. Jean-Jacques	289.4	80	818	24	5-29	34.08
C. A. Connor	77	18	253	7	5-25	36.14
L. J. Botham	65	8	240	6	4-63	40.00

Also bowled: J. R. Ayling 20-5-46-1; R. M. F. Cox 2-0-13-0; V. C. Drakes 14-4-34-1; W. S. Kendall 1-0-7-1; J. P. Kent 1-0-9-0; C. G. Knight 12-1-25-1; J. S. Laney 7-7-148-3; H. S. Malik 3-0-17-0; R. T. P. Miller 5-1-22-0; R. S. M. Morris 2-0-29-1; R. Wood 9.3-0-50-1.

KENT SECOND ELEVEN

Matches 17: Won – Derbyshire, Leicestershire, Warwickshire. Lost – Lancashire, Nottinghamshire, Somerset, Sussex. Drawn – Durham, Essex, Glamorgan, Gloucestershire, Hampshire, Middlesex, Northamptonshire, Worcestershire, Yorkshire. Abandoned – Surrey.

Batting Averages

	M	I	NO	R	HS	100s	Avge
G. R. Cowdrey	6	10	1	705	169	3	78.33
C. C. Kelly	3	4	0	259	191	1	64.75
A. J. Planck	5	6	2	229	86*	0	57.25
I. I. Longley	14	24	5	1,061	173*	4	55.84
D. P. Fulton	7	12	1	521	126	1	47.36
D. J. Spencer	10	15	4	451	95	0	41.00
R. M. Ellison	11	17	2	514	101	1	34.26
M. A. Ealham	4	6	1	145	52	0	29.00

	M	I	NO	R	HS	100s	Avg
C. Penn	7	6	0	169	93	0	28.1
†S. C. Willis	15	20	2	475	102	1	26.3
M. J. Walker	12	20	0	483	93	0	24.1
P. J. Wilcock	5	8	1	136	51	0	19.4
N. W. Preston	6	8	5	43	16*	0	14.3
R. P. Davis	5	8	0	114	50	0	14.2
G. J. J. Sheen	2	4	0	55	23	0	13.7
E. J. Stanford	10	11	4	88	21*	0	12.5
A. G. E. Ealham	6	5	2	23	18	0	7.6
T. N. Wren	15	17	4	93	26	0	7.1
C. H. Badenhorst	1	2	0	13	11	0	6.5
M. M. Patel	11	9	0	48	23	0	5.3
L. E. Robson	2	3	0	14	9	0	4.6

Played in three matches: I. Baldock 45, 17. Played in two matches: L. A. K. Clarke 2, 0; J. B. Thompson 13, 1*. Played in one match: J. D. Boreham 41; D. W. Headley 33, 1; A. P. Igglesden 7; A. J. Jordan 4; J. A. Knott 11, 4; N. J. Llong 16; S. G. Milroy 43, 2; D. Pask 4, 1; B. J. Phillips 15, 5*; †M. A. Roberts 4; N. R. Taylor 14; A. Tutt 1; T. R. Ward 62.

Note: In the match v Hampshire at Basingstoke M. M. Patel, called up for a first-team match, was replaced by A. Jordan.

Bowling Averages

	O	M	R	W	Avg
M. A. Ealham	78	29	236	9	26.2
M. M. Patel	461	163	1,003	36	27.8
R. M. Ellison	154.4	35	462	16	28.8
R. P. Davis	217.5	53	635	21	30.2
D. J. Spencer	225.2	40	780	25	31.2
C. Penn	113	30	290	7	41.4
T. N. Wren	311	64	1,096	25	43.8
N. W. Preston	117.5	19	376	8	47.0
E. J. Stanford	229.4	49	754	14	53.8

Also bowled: C. H. Badenhorst 28–5–107–1; J. D. Boreham 13–2–44–0; L. A. K. Clark 24–5–109–0; G. R. Cowdrey 6.2–3–13–1; D. P. Fulton 3.3–0–14–1; D. W. Headley 29–6–76–3; A. P. Igglesden 27–6–60–2; A. J. Jordan 5.5–0–27–1; R. C. Kelly 11–0–55–4; N. J. Llong 24.9–60–2; J. I. Longley 0.1–0–6–0; S. G. Milroy 6–1–20–0; B. J. Phillips 21–1–78–1; A. J. Planck 28.2–123–1; L. E. Robson 19–2–93–1; G. J. J. Sheen 4–0–33–0; J. B. Thompson 25–6–73–1; A. Tutt 4–2–10–0; T. R. Ward 12–2–30–1.

LANCASHIRE SECOND ELEVEN

Matches 17: Won – Durham, Essex, Glamorgan, Kent, Northamptonshire, Surrey. Lost Somerset, Sussex. Drawn – Derbyshire, Gloucestershire, Hampshire, Leicestershire, Nottinghamshire, Worcestershire, Yorkshire. Abandoned – Middlesex, Warwickshire.

Batting Averages

	M	I	NO	R	HS	100s	Avg
J. E. R. Gallian	7	12	1	708	120	2	64.3
S. P. Titchard	11	19	5	839	168*	3	59.9
R. C. Irani	13	21	5	876	203*	3	54.7
G. D. Lloyd	4	6	0	275	146	1	45.8
J. D. Fitton	13	18	3	622	90	0	41.4
G. Yates	10	9	1	326	132*	1	40.7
N. T. Wood	5	8	1	225	69	0	32.1
G. J. Cordingley	2	3	1	61	35*	0	30.5
I. D. Austin	13	18	3	434	63*	0	28.9

	M	I	NO	R	HS	100s	Avge
J. Martin	2	3	0	85	47	0	28.33
J. Green	6	7	2	139	49*	0	27.80
E. Harvey	10	15	0	413	101	1	27.53
M. McDowell	2	3	0	78	41	0	26.00
Chapple	5	4	1	52	22	0	17.33
†J. Stanworth	11	11	2	151	59*	0	16.77
D. Fletcher	12	12	3	116	61*	0	12.88
A. Derbyshire	14	11	3	81	23	0	10.12
M. Fielding	13	14	5	87	24*	0	9.66

Played in six matches: M. A. Sharp 1*, 0*. Played in two matches: †N. P. Harvey 58*, 6; M. James 6*, 4*. Played in one match: A. A. Barnett 3; J. P. Crawley 23; A. Flintoff 6, 13; J. A. L. Henderson 21; C. J. McDonald 4; L. J. Marland 7, 13; J. Ratledge 33; J. Shadford 26*, 3; C. Brown did not bat.

Note: Owing to first-team calls, G. Chapple was replaced by N. A. Derbyshire in the match v Somerset at Taunton, S. P. Titchard and P. J. Martin were replaced by G. Yates and G. J. Cordingley in the match v Derbyshire at Chesterfield, I. D. Austin was replaced by G. J. Cordingley in the match v Nottinghamshire at Manchester, I. D. Austin and G. Yates were replaced by N. T. Wood and S. D. Fletcher in the match v Hampshire at Blackpool and R. C. Irani was replaced by N. T. Wood in the match against Sussex at Eastbourne.

Bowling Averages

	O	M	R	W	BB	Avge
G. Yates	187.2	62	431	31	7-44	13.90
I. D. Austin	186	58	470	27	5-16	17.40
M. Fielding	198.2	48	557	25	4-33	22.28
M. A. Sharp	82	33	181	8	3-44	22.62
A. M. James	52.2	16	129	5	2-24	25.80
N. A. Derbyshire	225.1	38	812	29	5-26	28.00
D. Fitton	204.5	51	649	21	4-49	30.90
P. J. Martin	43	6	138	4	2-52	34.50
S. D. Fletcher	249	51	784	21	4-22	37.33
G. Chapple..........	71	18	231	5	2-42	46.20

Also bowled: A. A. Barnett 25–7–77–1; C. Brown 17–5–48–2; G. J. Cordingley 2–0–79–0; J. E. R. Gallian 45–8–127–2; R. J. Green 2–0–26–0; M. E. Harvey 54.4–0–140–0; J. A. L. Henderson 10–1–29–0; R. C. Irani 52.3–11–155–3; G. D. Lloyd 5–0–32–1; D. J. Shadford 17–1–79–0; S. P. Titchard 5.3–0–21–0; N. T. Wood 17.1–1–152–3.

LEICESTERSHIRE SECOND ELEVEN

Matches 17: Won – Sussex, Warwickshire, Yorkshire. Lost – Essex, Gloucestershire, Kent, Middlesex, Northamptonshire. Drawn – Derbyshire, Durham, Hampshire, Lancashire, Nottinghamshire, Somerset, Surrey, Worcestershire. Abandoned – Glamorgan.

Batting Averages

	M	I	NO	R	HS	100s	Avge
J. D. R. Benson	9	16	0	672	101	2	42.00
B. F. Smith	4	8	1	276	200*	1	39.42
Imtiaz Ahmed	2	4	1	117	49	0	39.00
J. M. Dakin	15	22	3	685	120	2	36.05
D. L. Maddy	14	23	2	705	100	1	33.57
W. J. Adlam	12	17	1	519	100	1	32.43
I. J. Sutcliffe	5	9	1	256	80*	0	32.00
P. N. Hepworth	11	19	4	475	83	0	31.66
P. E. Robinson	3	4	1	94	58	0	31.33
A. F. Haye	13	17	2	394	95	0	26.26
†P. Whitticase	13	16	1	332	60	0	22.13
S. Schofield..........	7	7	0	137	44	0	19.57

	M	I	NO	R	HS	100s	Avge
M. T. Brimson	4	5	0	76	27	0	15.20
C. D. Crowe	5	8	1	99	30	0	14.14
S. Atkinson	10	12	4	112	35	0	14.00
A. Sheriyar	7	8	5	42	20*	0	14.00
N. S. de Silva	10	9	4	50	15*	0	10.00
T. J. Mason	2	4	0	37	29	0	9.25
M. D. R. Sutliff	3	6	0	55	31	0	9.16
I. M. Stanger	3	4	1	27	14	0	9.00

Played in two matches: B. Leech 0*; D. J. Millns 13, 0; K. S. Newbold 14; G. J. Parsons 23. Played in one match: R. A. Cobb 33, 11*; A. Cowans 7, 0*; G. N. P. Harvey 21*; N. Jackson 15, 3; B. B. Moore 21, 7*; †P. A. Nixon 8; L. Potter 72; N. Pratt 25, 0; P. G. Roshier 23*; G. F. Sheppard 0; V. Walsh 2; V. J. Wells 48, 43*; P. S. Widdowson 7, 0; I. Critchley, M. K. Davies and M. M. Meetham did not bat.

Bowling Averages

	O	M	R	W	BB	Avge
V. Walsh	21	8	43	4	3-38	10.75
V. J. Wells	25.2	7	71	6	5-26	11.83
G. J. Parsons	26	8	63	5	5-47	12.60
N. S. de Silva	119.3	42	261	19	5-14	13.73
D. J. Millns	56.1	15	176	11	5-55	16.00
W. J. Adlam	229.3	61	633	33	5-30	19.18
M. T. Brimson	131	53	245	12	3-44	20.41
S. Atkinson	169.2	49	468	17	4-29	27.52
J. M. Dakin	321.2	76	1,032	35	5-69	29.48
I. M. Stanger	74	22	220	6	2-43	36.66
P. N. Hepworth	107.3	32	307	7	2-22	43.85
A. Sheriyar	124	23	405	8	2-75	50.62
A. F. Haye	85.1	10	357	5	2-57	71.40

Also bowled: J. D. R. Benson 40–13–116–2; A. Cowans 21–2–99–1; I. Critchley 3–1–13–0; C. D. Crowe 16–3–64–2; M. K. Davies 3–0–25–1; B. Leech 25–9–68–1; D. L. Maddy 4–0–22–0; T. J. Mason 43–19–77–1; K. S. Newbold 33–13–106–2; L. Potter 19–8–40–2; N. Pratt 7–0–46–0; P. G. Roshier 15–3–52–1; S. Schofield 5–0–18–0; G. F. Sheppard 13–3–47–3; B. F. Smith 1–1–0–0; P. S. Widdowson 20–4–93–2.

MIDDLESEX SECOND ELEVEN

Matches 17: Won – Durham, Hampshire, Leicestershire, Somerset, Surrey, Sussex, Worcestershire. Lost – Essex. Drawn – Derbyshire, Glamorgan, Gloucestershire, Kent, Northamptonshire, Nottinghamshire, Yorkshire. Abandoned – Lancashire, Warwickshire.

Batting Averages

	M	I	NO	R	HS	Avge
T. A. Radford	7	11	4	734	155*	104.85
*J. C. Pooley	13	22	2	845	203*	42.25
R. J. Sims	10	16	2	590	213	42.14
A. Habib	14	21	4	705	123	41.47
P. N. Weekes	10	16	1	612	118	40.80
†P. Farbrace	15	20	1	707	132	37.21
K. P. Dutch	13	17	5	420	61	35.00
J. C. Harrison	14	22	2	686	203*	34.30
R. S. Yeabsley	6	7	3	129	39*	32.25
M. Keech	10	15	3	327	84*	27.25
I. J. Gould	7	6	2	68	26	17.00

	M	I	NO	R	HS		Avge
. W. Taylor	11	11	3	126	26		15.75
. A. Khan	2	4	1	44	20		14.66
. L. Johnson	4	3	0	35	20		11.66
. C. Usher	7	8	4	12	5*		3.00

Played in four matches: D. A. Walker 15, 14. Played in three matches: S. K. Mohammed 5, 1. Played in two matches: J. Angel 20; R. J. Ballinger 17, 0; N. G. Cowans 7, 0; Patel 2*, 0. Played in one match: C. Banton 34; R. A. Davidson 2*; M. A. Feltham 59; A. Kidd 10; G. M. Pooley 28; U. Rhashid 21; A. Roseberry 46*.

Bowling Averages

	O	M	R	W	BB	Avge
. Keech	165.5	39	431	22	5-28	19.59
. L. Johnson	106.3	25	330	15	4-24	22.00
N. Weekes	386.3	116	837	38	5-43	22.02
S. Yeabsley	103.3	26	314	13	5-32	24.15
. P. Dutch	469.1	137	1,309	51	6-75	25.66
. C. Usher	121.2	25	364	12	5-40	30.33
. W. Taylor	256.2	59	809	26	3-37	31.11

Also bowled: J. Angel 52-7-166-3; R. J. Ballinger 41-6-153-7; N. G. Cowans 4-19-131-6; R. A. Davidson 25-1-117-1; M. A. Feltham 28-8-67-6; I. J. Gould 4-6-54-2; A. Habib 11-3-36-1; J. C. Harrison 36.3-6-129-2; A. A. Khan 48-9-137-5; K. Mohammed 58-10-184-5; S. Patel 22-8-78-3; J. C. Pooley 1-0-9-0; U. Rhashid 5-2-50-0; R. J. Sims 0.1-0-0-0; D. A. Walker 45.5-12-139-1.

NORTHAMPTONSHIRE SECOND ELEVEN

Matches 17: Won – Essex, Glamorgan, Leicestershire. Lost – Lancashire, Yorkshire. Drawn – Derbyshire, Durham, Gloucestershire, Hampshire, Kent, Middlesex, Nottinghamshire, Somerset, Surrey, Sussex, Warwickshire, Worcestershire.

Batting Averages

	M	I	NO	R	HS	100s	Avge
†W. M. Noon.......	13	15	5	785	133	4	78.50
J. G. B. Cook	6	5	3	96	34*	0	48.00
. R. Roberts........	4	5	2	139	69*	0	46.33
R. Montgomerie ...	9	18	3	604	138*	1	40.26
. P. Fleming	9	13	2	439	85	0	39.90
. J. Warren	10	17	6	414	88	0	37.63
. L. Penberthy	6	11	2	334	99	0	37.11
. J. Innes	12	17	4	475	69*	0	36.53
. A. Stanley	10	16	4	423	104	1	35.25
. C. Walton	15	18	1	520	71	0	30.58
. G. Hughes	11	13	3	305	55*	0	30.50
N. Snape	7	12	1	295	74	0	26.81
. N. Bowen	11	10	2	211	67	0	26.37
. W. Harrison	5	8	1	173	56	0	24.71
. J. Rika..........	11	11	2	173	34	0	19.22
. Walker..........	15	16	4	146	50	0	12.16
M. Attfield	3	4	0	47	29	0	11.75
. M. Pearson	8	6	3	17	9*	0	5.66

Played in eight matches: J. Tomlinson 0*, 24*, 1. Played in three matches: R. M. Carter 22*. Played in two matches: V. C. Drakes 32, 10; †W. J. Hearsey 0*, 1, 3; R. J. Pack 3, 0*, 2. Played in one match: R. N. Dalton 6; †S. Platt 15; D. Roberts 30*, 0; R. J. Williams 0; D. M. Benkenstein and R. D. Wild did not bat.

Note: In the match v Hampshire at Southampton R. J. Warren, called up for a first-team match, was replaced by J. G. Hughes.

Bowling Averages

	O	M	R	W	BB	Avg
A. L. Penberthy	127.4	31	360	16	4-25	22.5
M. N. Bowen	274.1	61	789	33	6-38	23.9
R. M. Pearson	143.3	32	436	14	5-82	31.1
A. Walker	366.2	97	1,049	33	4-26	31.7
T. C. Walton	133.1	24	504	15	4-20	33.6
J. G. Hughes	101	18	394	11	2-16	35.8
A. R. Roberts	104.1	25	305	7	4-69	43.5
J. Tomlinson	94	18	365	8	3-67	45.6
J. N. Snape	180.1	51	558	12	4-46	46.5
N. G. B. Cook	147.5	54	328	7	2-53	46.8
C. J. Rika	55.1	6	225	4	2-18	56.2
K. J. Innes	106	17	399	7	2-23	57.0

Also bowled: J. M. Attfield 1–0–3–0; D. M. Benkenstein 8–0–33–1; R. N. Dalton 12–1–49–1; V. C. Drakes 23–4–104–1; T. W. Harrison 22–4–91–0; R. J. Pack 22–0–68–1; N. A. Stanley 29.2–11–82–2; R. D. Wild 10–2–23–1.

NOTTINGHAMSHIRE SECOND ELEVEN

Matches 17: Won – Derbyshire, Gloucestershire, Kent, Sussex, Worcestershire. Lost – Durham, Essex, Surrey, Yorkshire. Drawn – Glamorgan, Hampshire, Lancashire, Leicestershire, Middlesex, Northamptonshire, Somerset, Warwickshire.

Batting Averages

	M	I	NO	R	HS	100s	Avg
K. P. Evans	3	4	2	172	88*	0	86.00
M. A. Crawley	5	8	1	449	114*	2	64.1
M. Saxelby	9	16	1	875	238*	2	58.3
G. F. Archer	12	21	2	1,054	139*	3	55.4
W. A. Dessaur	13	22	4	897	120*	5	49.8
M. P. Dowman	12	19	2	627	154	2	36.8
G. W. Mike	7	11	2	276	60*	0	30.6
*M. Newell	15	19	9	290	62*	0	29.0
K. P. T. Thomas	2	4	0	83	76	0	20.7
R. J. Chapman	14	15	5	187	28	0	18.7
R. T. Bates	15	22	3	340	100*	1	17.8
J. E. Hindson	14	18	4	248	50	0	17.7
†S. Bramhall	16	23	2	346	95	0	16.4
L. N. Walker	6	12	1	179	42	0	16.2
R. A. Pick	5	3	0	45	28	0	15.0
D. B. Pennett	13	16	4	140	33	0	11.6
S. J. Musgrove	3	6	1	34	13*	0	6.8
S. A. Sylvester	14	12	4	40	12	0	5.00
R. W. J. Howitt	2	4	0	11	7	0	2.7

Played in two matches: U. Afzaal 10*, 0. Played in one match: S. M. Brogan 51, 1; P. Johnson 66, 2; P. R. Pollard 33; D. W. Randall 98, 19; G. E. Welton 7, 0; J. R. Wileman 73, 21; G. D. Yates 12, 4.

Note: In the match v Gloucestershire at Bristol R. T. Bates and D. B. Pennett, called up for a first-team match, were replaced by S. J. Musgrove and M. Newell.

Bowling Averages

	O	M	R	W	BB	Avge
K. P. Evans	88.1	31	192	11	5-45	17.45
R. A. Pick	135	26	352	17	5-41	20.70
U. Afzaal	66	23	140	6	4-97	23.33
D. B. Pennett	282	77	833	30	5-39	27.76
J. E. Hindson	500	108	1,521	52	8-131	29.25
R. T. Bates	412.3	101	1,159	39	6-65	29.71
G. W. Mike	141.1	40	378	12	3-32	31.50
S. A. Sylvester	313	62	989	27	3-25	36.62
R. J. Chapman	251	51	832	13	3-26	64.00

Also bowled: M. A. Crawley 46-8-123-3; W. A. Dessaur 2-1-6-0; M. P. Dowman 23.2-10-68-3; M. Newell 29.2-4-141-1; G. D. Yates 21-5-46-3.

SOMERSET SECOND ELEVEN

Matches 17: Won – Durham, Glamorgan, Kent, Lancashire. Lost – Middlesex, Surrey, Worcestershire, Yorkshire. Drawn – Derbyshire, Essex, Gloucestershire, Hampshire, Leicestershire, Northamptonshire, Nottinghamshire, Sussex. Abandoned – Warwickshire.

Batting Averages

	M	I	NO	R	HS	100s	Avge
†N. D. Burns	4	8	3	461	225*	1	92.20
K. A. Parsons	10	20	4	800	164	2	50.00
M. E. Trescothick	10	16	1	663	109	1	44.20
J. I. D. Kerr	5	8	2	252	80	0	42.00
G. W. White	10	18	1	675	123	1	39.70
K. G. Sedgbeer	5	8	0	276	103	1	34.50
I. Fletcher	2	3	0	94	92	0	31.33
K. J. Parsons	16	27	4	720	87	0	31.30
J. C. Hallett	8	9	6	86	34	0	28.66
V. P. Clarke	10	14	1	357	70*	0	27.46
*†R. J. Turner	11	19	3	423	62	0	26.43
A. C. Cottam	11	14	4	248	74	0	24.80
G. M. Bennett	11	15	3	295	51	0	24.58
A. Payne	10	15	1	293	77	0	20.92
R. J. Harding	7	4	0	81	36	0	20.25
I. R. Dalwood	3	3	1	31	15	0	15.50
P. Clifford	8	7	4	45	42*	0	15.00
A. C. Winstone	3	5	1	28	20*	0	7.00
M. Dimond	6	7	1	37	21	0	6.16
M. J. Walshe	4	4	0	6	4	0	1.50

Played in six matches: H. R. J. Trump 8*, 0, 0. Played in two matches: A. N. Hayhurst 181, 45; P. J. Robinson, 2*, 1*. Played in one match: I. A. Bond 8; G. Brown 2, 0; S. P. Griffiths 7, 3; N. A. Mallender 59; N. Sen 0; L. D. Sutton 33; G. Swinney 35, 2; M. G. Warburton 5, 0; B. M. Wellington 0; J. G. Wyatt 76; P. Turner and R. P. van Niekerk did not bat.

Bowling Averages

	O	M	R	W	BB	Avge
M. G. Warburton	33	6	114	7	7-114	16.28
A. N. Hayhurst	38	10	97	5	3-28	19.40
A. C. Cottam	311.3	89	905	35	6-115	25.85
R. J. Harding	214	56	581	22	5-76	26.40
A. Payne	210.1	41	696	25	5-64	27.84
M. Dimond	96	17	346	11	5-47	31.45

	O	M	R	W	BB	Avge
H. R. J. Trump	229.1	50	683	20	4-108	34.15
P. Clifford.	90	18	278	8	2-15	34.75
G. M. Bennett	163.3	45	454	13	3-28	34.92
J. C. Hallett	230.4	46	781	22	5-71	35.50
K. A. Parsons	73.3	22	199	5	1-16	39.80
M. J. Walshe	68	7	272	4	2-21	68.00
J. I. D. Kerr	109.5	15	396	4	2-26	99.00

Also bowled: I. A. Bond 27.2–5–103–3; V. P. Clarke 79–16–288–3; J. R. Dalwood 12–1–72–40–0; N. A. Mallender 19–3–41–1; P. J. Robinson 15.4–4–45–1; K. G. Sedgbeer 16–2–50–2; N. Sen 5–2–11–0; G. Swinney 9–6–13–1; P. Turner 16–1–61–1; B. M. Wellington 4–0–17–2; G. W. White 2–0–20–0; A. C. Winstone 79.2–21–205–3.

SURREY SECOND ELEVEN

Matches 17: Won – Durham, Essex, Glamorgan, Nottinghamshire, Somerset. Lost – Hampshire, Lancashire, Middlesex, Warwickshire. Drawn – Derbyshire, Gloucestershire, Leicestershire, Northamptonshire, Sussex, Yorkshire. Abandoned – Kent, Worcestershire.

Batting Averages

	M	I	NO	R	HS	100s	Avge
D. M. Ward	4	6	2	396	120*	2	99.00
R. I. Alikhan	9	13	2	770	156	3	70.00
P. D. Atkins.	5	8	1	298	153	1	42.57
†G. J. Kersey	6	7	1	238	122	1	39.66
†N. F. Sargeant	15	24	3	709	85	0	33.76
A. J. Hollioake.	11	14	1	426	105	1	32.76
G. J. Kennis	4	7	1	195	68	0	32.50
M. A. Butcher	7	9	1	257	70*	0	32.12
M. R. Bainbridge.	15	19	7	305	58*	0	25.41
I. J. Ward	14	20	4	343	59	0	21.43
D. J. M. Kelleher	11	13	1	221	70	0	18.41
Z. Sadiq	2	4	1	54	31	0	18.00
P. G. Roshier	4	4	1	46	43	0	15.33
R. Skidmore	5	6	1	67	33*	0	13.40
M. J. Church	3	4	0	27	17	0	6.75
D. J. Thompson	13	11	5	35	11*	0	5.83

Played in four matches: J. Boiling 10, 4, 3; N. M. Kendrick 20, 2; A. J. Murphy 17, 9* 0. Played in three matches: S. Babar 11; G. S. Clinton 25, 4; M. Kenlock 9*, 4*; S. J Pawson 25, 7, 0. Played in two matches: A. N. Muggleton 6*, 6, 0; R. W. Nowell 28, 9, 1* A. W. Smith 62, 1, 12. Played in one match: P. J. Atherley 1, 13; T. B. M. de Leede 25 30*; A. J. Hall 9, 22; G. Luxon 19; M. A. Lynch 69; K. T. Medlycott 43; N. Mughal 9, 6* S. Pratt 12, 14; D. J. Tomlinson 0.

Note: Owing to first-team calls, J. Boiling was replaced by G. J. Kennis in the match Gloucestershire at Bristol and N. M. Kendrick was replaced by S. Pratt in the match Leicestershire at Leicester.

Bowling Averages

	O	M	R	W	BB	Avge
J. Boiling	95.3	45	101	10	4-13	10.1
N. M. Kendrick	71.3	21	186	11	6-69	16.9
A. J. Murphy	152.5	40	370	20	4-40	18.5
P. G. Roshier	114.5	18	333	16	5-46	20.8
M. A. Butcher	125.2	26	354	17	4-18	20.8
D. J. Thompson	314.3	53	1,127	41	5-39	27.4

	O	M	R	W	BB	Avge
A. J. Hollioake.......	290.1	61	936	33	5-68	28.36
A. Kenlock	90	27	220	7	2-34	31.42
A. R. Bainbridge.....	425.5	111	1,118	35	5-72	31.94
J. M. Kelleher	285.2	73	821	20	3-49	41.05

Also bowled: R. I. Alikhan 29–6–84–4; S. Babar 26–5–85–1; G. S. Clinton 0.5–0–6–0; T. B. M. de Leede 12–3–51–1; G. J. Kennis 39–9–123–1; A. N. Muggleton 23–6–65–2; N. Mughal 4–1–29–0; R. W. Nowell 24–9–32–1; S. J. Pawson 18–3–73–1; N. F. Sargeant 7–0–36–0; R. Skidmore 2–0–13–0; A. W. Smith 42–17–82–0; D. J. Tomlinson 2–0–16–0; D. M. Ward 4.4–2–26–0; I. J. Ward 44.4–6–168–1.

SUSSEX SECOND ELEVEN

Matches 17: Won – Glamorgan, Kent, Lancashire, Worcestershire. Lost – Derbyshire, Essex, Gloucestershire, Leicestershire, Middlesex, Nottinghamshire, Yorkshire. Drawn – Durham, Hampshire, Northamptonshire, Somerset, Surrey, Warwickshire.

Batting Averages

	M	I	NO	R	HS	100s	Avge
N. J. Lenham	4	6	3	300	138	2	100.00
*K. Greenfield	10	16	3	810	144*	3	62.30
A. C. S. Pigott	4	5	2	154	80*	0	51.33
G. Norris	2	4	0	186	80	0	46.50
M. T. E. Peirce	12	19	0	726	141	2	38.21
J. W. Hall	8	12	0	447	184	1	37.25
B. T. P. Donelan	11	17	3	515	78	0	36.78
J. A. North	9	16	2	503	120	1	35.92
C. M. Wells	10	15	2	467	117	1	35.92
K. Newell	14	22	0	582	114	1	26.45
C. C. Remy	12	21	0	552	67	0	26.28
M. Newell..........	7	12	3	194	55*	0	21.55
D. R. Law	11	13	2	221	81	0	20.09
N. R. Marchant	3	6	0	110	33	0	18.33
J. W. Dean	17	18	5	194	61	0	14.92
P. G. Hudson	2	3	1	27	17*	0	13.50
†S. Humphries	17	20	6	161	29*	0	11.50
R. S. C. Martin-Jenkins ..	3	4	1	25	21*	0	8.33
N. C. Phillips	10	10	2	61	29	0	7.62
R. J. Kirtley	4	5	2	11	9*	0	3.66
V. C. Drakes	3	3	3	68	27*	0	–

Played in three matches: S. Warmington 5; C. E. Waller did not bat. Played in two matches: J. D. Lewry 1. Played in one match: C. W. J. Athey 87, 13; R. Harding 3; A. N. Jones 86*, 34*; N. Pratt 14, 8; M. P. Speight 168*, 31; P. Wicker 1, 0; E. S. H. Giddins did not bat.

Note: In the match v Essex at Colchester K. Greenfield, called up for a first-team match, was replaced by J. W. Dean.

Bowling Averages

	O	M	R	W	BB	Avge
J. A. North	95.5	23	336	20	4-5	16.80
M. T. E. Peirce	30	8	93	5	2-20	18.60
E. S. H. Giddins	35.5	7	123	5	4-43	24.60
D. R. Law	247.2	43	810	30	5-51	27.00
C. M. Wells	133.2	42	304	10	4-18	30.40
J. W. Dean..........	402.5	115	1,154	37	3-18	31.18
R. J. Kirtley	51.5	8	197	6	2-31	32.83

	O	M	R	W	BB	Avge
K. Greenfield	61	7	241	7	3-62	34.4
B. T. P. Donelan	339.4	72	1,096	31	4-80	35.3
V. C. Drakes	42	6	150	4	3-50	37.5
K. Newell	115.4	28	365	9	5-77	40.5
N. C. Phillips	218.4	59	694	15	4-46	46.2
C. C. Remy	159.4	24	546	10	2-31	54.6

Also bowled: P. G. Hudson 7–2–17–0; A. N. Jones 20–10–33–2; N. J. Lenham 10–1–26–0; J. D. Lewry 30–8–78–3; A. C. S. Pigott 44–10–146–1; N. Pratt 4–1–19–0; C. E. Waller 7–0–30–1; S. Warmington 15–5–34–0.

WARWICKSHIRE SECOND ELEVEN

Matches 17: Won – Glamorgan, Surrey. Lost – Gloucestershire, Kent, Leicestershire, Yorkshire. Drawn – Derbyshire, Durham, Essex, Hampshire, Northamptonshire, Nottinghamshire, Sussex, Worcestershire. Abandoned – Lancashire, Middlesex, Somerset.

Batting Averages

	M	I	NO	R	HS	100s	Avge
*P. A. Smith	5	8	1	454	107	1	64.8
†P. C. L. Holloway . . .	9	16	0	633	118	1	39.5
†M. Burns	10	17	0	637	172	1	37.4
J. M. A. Inglis	4	7	1	220	71	0	36.6
A. F. Giles	12	20	4	552	81*	0	34.5
*Asif Din	8	15	0	506	120	1	33.7
R. G. Twose	5	8	0	245	74	0	30.6
P. A. Booth	5	7	2	147	50*	0	29.4
D. R. Brown	8	14	2	350	81	0	29.1
N. R. Newman	3	6	2	111	71	0	27.7
C. E. Mulraine	13	22	2	545	86	0	27.2
A. Singh	2	3	0	77	39	0	25.6
G. Welch	13	22	5	422	88	0	24.8
W. G. Khan	13	25	1	572	63	0	23.8
M. A. V. Bell	7	8	2	139	58	0	23.1
M. F. Robinson	9	11	4	89	41*	0	12.7
D. R. Maynard	2	4	2	25	8	0	12.5
P. Aldred	6	4	2	19	19	0	9.5
M. J. Powell	4	6	0	29	12	0	4.8

Played in four matches: D. A. Alltree 2*, 0*, 0*. Played in three matches: S. McDonald 12*, 0. Played in two matches: †A. Frost 14*, 14; C. W. Henderson did not bat. Played in one match: D. Barr 23, 3; F. Napier 10, 7; †K. J. Piper 40*, 36; P. J. L. Radley 12, 1*; I. M. Stanger 6*, 0; P. A. Thomas 1; M. A. Wagh 27*, 26; R. N. Abberley and C. W. Wilkinson did not bat.

Note: Owing to first-team calls, R. N. Abberley replaced A. F. Giles in the match v Kent at Maidstone, J. M. A. Inglis replaced R. G. Twose in the match v Yorkshire at Sheffield, P. J. L. Radley replaced M. Burns in the match v Gloucestershire at Studley and S. McDonald replaced R. G. Twose in the match v Worcestershire at Worcester.

Bowling Averages

	O	M	R	W	BB	Avge
D. A. Alltree	88.1	25	237	16	5-39	14.8
I. M. Stanger	28	3	116	6	3-50	19.3
C. W. Wilkinson	38	12	100	5	3-49	20.0
P. Aldred	160.2	35	412	20	6-47	20.6
M. A. V. Bell	215.1	55	609	29	5-34	21.0

	O	M	R	W	BB	Avge
D. R. Brown	140.3	37	417	19	3-17	21.94
P. A. Smith	100.1	18	331	14	5-33	23.64
P. C. L. Holloway	37	13	96	4	3-20	24.00
P. A. Booth	174.3	71	304	11	4-34	27.63
N. R. Newman	94.3	26	224	8	3-30	28.00
A. F. Giles	307.5	84	824	25	4-54	32.96
R. G. Twose........	65	9	231	5	2-35	46.20
G. Welch	284.5	55	920	17	4-33	54.11
M. F. Robinson	149.4	24	575	10	3-15	57.50

Also bowled: Asif Din 32.3–6–130–2; M. Burns 7–2–18–0; C. W. Henderson 29.5–10–66–3; S. McDonald 34–5–142–1; D. R. Maynard 41–7–129–1; P. A. Thomas 7–3–34–0.

WORCESTERSHIRE SECOND ELEVEN

Matches 17: Won – Essex, Glamorgan, Somerset. Lost – Middlesex, Nottinghamshire, Sussex. Drawn – Durham, Gloucestershire, Hampshire, Kent, Lancashire, Leicestershire, Northamptonshire, Warwickshire, Yorkshire. Abandoned – Derbyshire, Surrey.

Batting Averages

	M	I	NO	R	HS	Avge
W. P. C. Weston	2	4	0	357	140	89.25
G. R. Haynes........	8	14	4	619	127	61.90
J. M. Connor	2	3	1	92	36	46.00
N. J. Bratt	4	3	2	43	35*	43.00
D. A. Leatherdale	4	6	0	247	109	41.16
*M. J. Weston	8	11	1	404	96	40.40
G. A. Pollock	11	17	2	576	117	38.40
T. W. Harrison	2	4	1	112	50*	37.33
V. S. Solanki	6	11	2	327	82	36.33
A. C. H. Seymour	9	18	0	581	114	32.27
D. B. D'Oliveira	2	3	1	63	42	31.50
K. R. Spiring	8	16	1	456	121*	30.40
S. Ahmed	3	5	2	87	30	29.00
R. L. Robinson	4	7	1	163	82	27.16
†T. Edwards........	13	16	3	352	100*	27.07
C. W. Boroughs......	2	3	0	74	42	24.66
G. Salmond	3	5	1	82	46	20.50
T. M. Heap	8	8	0	163	80	20.37
J. E. Brinkley........	13	15	4	206	37	18.72
S. Janes.............	3	5	0	90	41	18.00
A. G. Pollock	2	3	0	44	30	14.66
C. J. Eyers	7	8	1	79	34	11.28
A. D. Bairstow.......	4	4	0	39	24	9.75
G. R. Hill..........	4	7	1	56	37	9.33
M. P. Brooke	6	8	4	21	13*	5.25
B. M. McCorkill	6	5	1	17	7*	4.25

Played in three matches: S. W. K. Ellis 2, 1*; A. Wylie 0*, 0, 0. Played in two matches: I. J. Houseman 4*; T. K. Marriott 3*; D. J. Shadford 12, 6; E. N. R. Symonds 2*, 2. Played in one match: A. J. L. Barr 18, 2; N. M. Davies 12*, 1; C. G. R. Lightfoot 5, 3*; P. Mirza 1; N. V. Radford 46*, 7; C. M. B. Tetley 5*; M. R. Gill did not bat.

Bowling Averages

	O	M	R	W	Avge
P. Mirza	41.2	7	147	8	18.37
T. W. Harrison	43.1	7	149	7	21.28
N. J. Bratt	89	26	275	10	27.50
G. R. Haynes	185.1	39	482	16	30.12
A. Wylie	61	9	237	7	33.85
C. J. Eyers	106.5	15	446	12	37.16
B. M. McCorkill	193.4	38	638	17	37.52
G. A. Pollock	109.1	21	348	9	38.66
M. P. Brooke	165	26	592	14	42.28
A. G. Pollock	66	9	207	4	51.75
T. M. Heap	192.1	37	609	11	55.36
J. E. Brinkley	300.1	64	1,049	17	61.70
V. S. Solanki	69.2	13	216	3	72.00

Also bowled: A. J. L. Barr 4–1–17–1; N. M. Davies 5.4–2–5–3; D. B. D'Oliveira 19–4–56–1; S. W. K. Ellis 55–3–241–3; I. A. Houseman 28.1–3–107–3; D. A. Leatherdale 9–3–19–2; C. G. R. Lightfoot 9–0–34–0; T. K. Marriott 30–5–90–2; N. V. Radford 27–7–64–0; C. M. B. Tetley 20–7–62–1; M. J. Weston 27–7–64–0.

YORKSHIRE SECOND ELEVEN

Matches 17: Won – Essex, Northamptonshire, Nottinghamshire, Somerset, Sussex, Warwickshire. Lost – Leicestershire. Drawn – Derbyshire, Durham, Glamorgan, Gloucestershire, Hampshire, Kent, Lancashire, Middlesex, Surrey, Worcestershire.

Batting Averages

	M	I	NO	R	HS	100s	Avge
A. P. Grayson	7	11	2	577	90	0	64.11
*A. A. Metcalfe	10	17	0	999	160	5	58.76
S. Bartle	5	6	3	146	56	0	48.66
M. P. Vaughan	9	17	2	683	123	1	45.53
S. A. Kellett	9	15	0	647	89	0	43.13
R. A. Kettleborough . .	17	27	5	855	115	1	38.86
B. Parker	17	28	5	866	204	1	37.65
A. I. Ditta	5	5	2	99	41	0	33.00
A. McGrath	5	7	0	229	87	0	32.71
†C. A. Chapman	17	25	8	553	100	1	32.52
*P. Carrick	5	6	3	96	46*	0	32.00
M. J. Foster	12	17	4	414	74*	0	31.84
S. J. Foster	2	3	0	91	50	0	30.33
P. W. Jarvis	3	3	1	53	28	0	26.50
G. M. Hamilton	5	5	2	50	24*	0	16.66
M. Broadhurst	8	7	3	52	31	0	13.00
C. J. Schofield	4	7	1	77	24	0	12.83
M. I. Bradford	9	6	0	72	23	0	12.00
C. E. W. Silverwood . .	13	7	3	35	10	0	8.75
G. Keedy	6	2	0	14	10	0	7.00
P. J. Hartley	2	3	0	20	11	0	6.66

Played in four matches: A. Wharf 8. Played in three matches: J. D. Batty 34*. Played in two matches: I. D. Fisher 15, 0*; S. Oldham 1*; M. R. Steel 4. Played in one match: D. Bates 2, 0; D. Byas 24*, 4; D. Gough 27*; A. C. Morris 0; R. M. Atkinson and S. M. Milburn did not bat.

Note: Owing to first-team calls, A. P. Grayson was replaced by A. I. Ditta in the match v Essex at Leeds and M. J. Foster was replaced by M. I. Bradford in the match v Gloucestershire at Bristol.

Bowling Averages

	O	M	R	W	BB	Avge
P. Carrick	196.3	99	231	25	5-16	9.24
G. M. Hamilton	65.1	18	210	9	3-50	23.33
P. J. Hartley	41	13	104	4	2-22	26.00
J. D. Batty	158.3	41	454	17	6-69	26.70
C. E. W. Silverwood	234	43	851	28	4-31	30.39
I. D. Fisher	69	11	216	7	5-84	30.85
M. P. Vaughan	271.3	77	743	23	4-72	32.30
G. Keedy	311.4	99	676	18	4-64	37.55
A. Wharf	69	13	270	7	2-20	38.57
M. I. Bradford	139	39	480	11	3-48	43.63
M. J. Foster	218.3	47	689	15	3-36	45.93
P. W. Jarvis	96.4	29	279	6	4-106	46.50
A. P. Grayson	143.2	51	337	7	3-44	48.14
M. Broadhurst	159	28	553	10	4-75	55.30

Also bowled: R. M. Atkinson 17–3–80–2; S. Bartle 30–5–138–2; D. Bates 3–0–18–0; A. I. Ditta 45–11–152–3; D. Gough 32–9–65–3; R. A. Kettleborough 22–3–82–3; S. M. Milburn 17.2–3–63–3; A. C. Morris 5–2–8–1; M. R. Steel 26–3–112–0.

SECOND ELEVEN CHAMPIONS

1959	Gloucestershire	1971	Hampshire	1983	Leicestershire
1960	Northamptonshire	1972	Nottinghamshire	1984	Yorkshire
1961	Kent	1973	Essex	1985	Nottinghamshire
1962	Worcestershire	1974	Middlesex	1986	Lancashire
1963	Worcestershire	1975	Surrey	1987	{ Kent / Yorkshire }
1964	Lancashire	1976	Kent		
1965	Glamorgan	1977	Yorkshire	1988	Surrey
1966	Surrey	1978	Sussex	1989	Middlesex
1967	Hampshire	1979	Warwickshire	1990	Sussex
1968	Surrey	1980	Glamorgan	1991	Yorkshire
1969	Kent	1981	Hampshire	1992	Surrey
1970	Kent	1982	Worcestershire	1993	Middlesex

BAIN CLARKSON TROPHY, 1993

North Zone	P	W	L	NR	Points	Runs/100b
Nottinghamshire	10	7	2	1	15	63.57
Leicestershire	10	6	2	2	14	61.56
Yorkshire	10	5	2	3	13	74.93
Lancashire	10	4	4	2	10	74.61
Derbyshire	10	3	6	1	7	57.02
Durham	10	0	9	1	1	59.63

South-West Zone	P	W	L	NR	Points	Runs/100b
Hampshire	12	7	3	2	16	69.44
Gloucestershire	12	7	3	2	16	67.85
Warwickshire	12	7	5	0	14	64.94
Somerset	12	6	6	0	12	68.77
Northamptonshire	12	6	6	0	12	59.83
Glamorgan	12	3	7	2	8	57.25
Worcestershire	12	3	9	0	6	66.19

Bain Clarkson Trophy, 1993

South-East Zone	P	W	L	NR	Points	Runs/100b
Sussex	10	6	3	1	13	57.11
Middlesex	10	6	4	0	12	67.25
Kent	10	5	4	1	11	77.12
Surrey	10	5	4	1	11	76.18
Essex	10	4	5	1	9	63.48
MCC Young Cricketers	10	1	7	2	4	68.28

Notes: Leicestershire qualified for the semi-finals as the best runners-up after the zone matches.

Counties are restricted to players qualified for England and for competitive county cricket, only two of whom may be capped players. The matches are of 55 overs per side.

SEMI-FINALS

At Southampton, August 17. Leicestershire won by five runs. Toss: Leicestershire. Leicestershire 211 (51.2 overs) (P. E. Robinson 57, P. A. Nixon 38; M. Jean-Jacques three for 46, J. N. B. Bovill four for 35); Hampshire 206 (54.5 overs) (R. M. F. Cox 107; V. J. Wells three for 30, P. N. Hepworth three for 47).

At Nottingham, August 17. Sussex won by ten runs. Toss: Nottinghamshire. Sussex 197 for nine (55 overs) (K. Greenfield 45, K. Newell 41, N. C. Phillips 34 not out; D. B. Pennett three for 46); Nottinghamshire 187 for nine (55 overs) (M. Saxelby 69, G. F. Archer 34; K. Newell four for 19, E. S. H. Giddins three for 28).

FINAL

LEICESTERSHIRE v SUSSEX

At Leicester, September 6. Leicestershire won by 142 runs. Toss: Sussex.
Man of the Match: V. J. Wells.

Leicestershire

P. N. Hepworth c Humphries b Remy	28	*G. J. Parsons not out	3
D. L. Maddy c Humphries b Newell	51	A. R. K. Pierson not out	1
V. J. Wells b Greenfield	114		
P. E. Robinson c Donelan b North	46	L-b 13, w 10, n-b 10	33
B. F. Smith b Greenfield	9		
†P. A. Nixon c Hall b Greenfield	11	1/99 2/109 3/235 (8 wkts, 55 overs) 308
J. M. Dakin b Giddins	4	4/281 5/282 6/287
A. F. Haye c Humphries b Giddins	8	7/297 8/306

M. T. Brimson did not bat.

Bowling: Giddins 8-0-54-2; Law 5-1-20-0; Wells 6-0-26-0; Remy 8-0-30-1; Donelan 4-0-28-0; Newell 8-1-32-1; Greenfield 11-0-60-3; North 5-0-45-1.

Sussex

J. W. Hall c Maddy b Dakin	19	D. R. Law c Maddy b Brimson	0
C. C. Remy b Haye	0	†S. Humphries not out	1
*K. Greenfield b Wells	41	E. S. H. Giddins c Haye b Brimson	0
C. M. Wells c Dakin b Pierson	44	L-b 5, w 12, n-b 2	19
J. A. North c Smith b Parsons	18		
M. T. E. Peirce c Hepworth b Parsons	11	1/0 2/45 3/117 (43.1 overs) 166
K. Newell c Hepworth b Parsons	0	4/132 5/146 6/147
B. T. P. Donelan c Dakin b Parsons	13	7/161 8/163 9/166

Bowling: Parsons 10-4-21-4; Haye 8-0-33-1; Dakin 6-0-23-1; Brimson 8.1-1-26-2; Pierson 6-0-31-1; Wells 5-0-27-1.

Umpires: J. C. Balderstone and K. E. Palmer.

WINNERS 1986-93

1986 NORTHAMPTONSHIRE beat Essex by 14 runs at Chelmsford.
1987 DERBYSHIRE beat Hampshire by seven wickets at Southampton.
1988 YORKSHIRE beat Kent by seven wickets at Leeds.
1989 MIDDLESEX beat Kent by six wickets at Canterbury.
1990 LANCASHIRE beat Somerset by eight wickets at Manchester.
1991 NOTTINGHAMSHIRE beat Surrey by eight wickets at The Oval.
1992 SURREY beat Northamptonshire by eight wickets at The Oval.
1993 LEICESTERSHIRE beat Sussex by 142 runs at Leicester.

CAREER FIGURES

Players retiring from county cricket or not retained

BATTING

	M	I	NO	R	HS	100s	Avge	1,000r/ season
R. I. Alikhan	105	181	14	4,696	138	2	28.11	1
P. D. Atkins	24	44	3	1,081	114*	1	26.36	0
J. R. Ayling	60	90	12	2,082	121	1	26.69	0
J. D. R. Benson . . .	56	83	8	2,097	153	4	27.96	0
P. A. Booth	59	80	18	830	62	0	13.38	0
I. T. Botham	402	617	46	19,399	228	38	33.97	4
M. P. Briers	17	30	4	462	62*	0	17.76	0
P. Carrick	444	572	104	10,300	131*	3	22.00	0
B. T. P. Donelan . .	52	65	21	1,105	68*	0	25.11	0
J. D. Fitton	52	61	15	872	60	0	18.95	0
S. D. Fletcher	114	96	32	476	28*	0	7.43	0
N. A. Foster	230	269	59	4,343	107*	2	20.68	0
A. G. J. Fraser	10	10	5	137	52*	0	27.40	0
M. Frost	64	52	19	106	12	0	3.21	0
M. J. Gerrard	20	26	10	107	42	0	6.68	0
J. D. Glendenen . . .	21	34	2	648	117	1	20.25	0
D. I. Gower	448	727	70	26,339	228	53	40.08	13
S. P. Hughes	205	226	70	1,775	53	0	11.37	0
A. N. Jones	175	153	62	1,037	43*	0	11.39	0
S. M. McEwan	65	48	17	407	54	0	13.12	0
G. D. Mendis	366	643	61	21,436	209*	41	36.83	13
L. Potter	223	354	42	9,027	165*	8	28.93	3
D. R. Pringle	295	405	78	9,243	128	10	28.26	0
D. W. Randall	488	827	81	28,456	237	52	38.14	13
I. V. A. Richards . .	507	796	62	36,212	322	114	49.33	14+3
A. G. Robson	7	7	3	3	3	0	0.75	0
R. J. Scott	72	123	9	2,719	127	3	23.85	0
N. A. Stanley	21	35	4	1,019	132	1	32.87	0
C. J. Tavaré	431	717	75	24,906	219	48	38.79	16
L. Tennant	10	13	5	110	23*	0	13.75	0
I. J. Turner	24	27	8	159	39*	0	8.36	0
M. J. Weston	161	258	24	5,597	145*	3	23.91	1
J. R. Wood	27	36	3	960	96	0	29.09	0

* *Signifies not out.*

BOWLING AND FIELDING

	R	W	BB	Avge	5W/i	10W/m	Ct/St
R. I. Alikhan	289	8	2-19	36.12	—	—	57
P. D. Atkins	—	—	—	—	—	—	9
J. R. Ayling	3,405	134	5-12	25.41	1	0	17
J. D. R. Benson . . .	488	8	2-24	61.00	—	—	65
P. A. Booth	4,200	103	5-98	40.77	1	0	19
I. T. Botham	31,902	1,172	8-34	27.22	59	8	354
M. P. Briers	690	12	3-109	57.50	—	—	8
P. Carrick	32,237	1,081	8-33	29.82	47	5	197
B. T. P. Donelan . .	4,568	105	6-62	43.50	4	1	14
J. D. Fitton	4,359	82	6-59	53.15	3	0	11
S. D. Fletcher	8,375	240	8-58	34.89	5	0	27
N. A. Foster	22,196	908	8-99	24.44	50	8	116
A. G. J. Fraser	386	12	3-46	32.16	—	—	1
M. Frost	6,005	169	7-99	35.53	4	2	7
M. J. Gerrard	1,381	36	6-40	38.36	1	1	7
J. D. Glendenen . . .							6
D. I. Gower	227	4	3-47	56.75	—	—	280/1
S. P. Hughes	15,139	466	7-35	32.48	10	0	50
A. N. Jones	13,516	410	7-30	32.96	12	1	42
S. M. McEwan	4,869	156	6-34	31.21	3	0	24
G. D. Mendis	158	1	1-65	158.00	—	—	145/1
L. Potter	6,879	177	5-45	38.86	1	0	190
D. R. Pringle	20,230	761	7-18	26.58	25	3	153
D. W. Randall	413	13	3-15	31.76	—	—	361
I. V. A. Richards . .	10,070	223	5-88	45.15	1	0	464/1
A. G. Robson	508	9	4-37	56.44	—	—	1
R. J. Scott	2,031	43	3-43	47.23	—	—	34
N. A. Stanley	19	0	—	—	—	—	9
C. J. Tavaré	722	5	1-3	144.40	—	—	418
L. Tennant	503	15	4-54	33.53	—	—	1
I. J. Turner	1,965	54	5-81	36.38	1	0	12
M. J. Weston	3,204	82	4-24	39.07	—	—	76
J. R. Wood	38	1	1-5	38.00	—	—	13

Note: I. T. Botham, once, and N. A. Foster, twice, were the only bowlers from this list to take 100 wickets in a season.

HONOURS' LIST, 1993-94

In 1993-94, the following were decorated for their services to cricket:

New Year's Honours, 1993: G. H. G. Doggart (former treasurer of MCC and president of English Schools' Cricket Association) OBE, M. J. Stewart (England – former England manager) OBE.

Queen's Birthday Honours: H. Larwood (England) MBE, B. J. Paterson (former chair of New Zealand Cricket Council) OBE.

New Year's Honours, 1994: H. T. Brind (Surrey groundsman and TCCB inspector of pitches) MBE, J. R. Murray (West Indies) MBE (Grenada list), B. A. Hosking (services to New Zealand cricket and electric power industry) OBE, I. D. S. Smith (New Zealand) MBE, K. Smithies (England women's captain) MBE, Lt-Col. J. R. Stephenson (retiring secretary of MCC) CBE, E. W. Swanton (cricket writer) CBE, M. A. Youdell (Nottinghamshire chairman – services to youth clubs) MBE.

Clyde Walcott (West Indies) became a Knight of St Andrew on November 30, Barbados's Independence Day.

THE LANCASHIRE LEAGUES, 1994

By CHRIS ASPIN

The coldest summer most league followers could remember was a memorable one thanks to several overseas professionals. In the Lancashire League, Michael Bevan, the New South Wales batsman, making his league debut at Rawtenstall, left crowds wondering why he was not touring with Australia. Meanwhile, in the Central Lancashire League, Middleton professional Peter Sleep, who had given up first-class cricket in Australia at the age of 36, showed his juniors that he remained a master of the limited-overs game. West Indian Test players Phil Simmons of Haslingden, Keith Arthurton of Ramsbottom and Roger Harper of Bacup braved the sunless afternoons to bring the three major trophies to the Rossendale Valley.

Haslingden, despite lacking their two leading amateur bowlers for most of the campaign, regained the championship for the seventh time in the last 11 years; they have been runners-up three times in the same period. Ramsbottom and Rawtenstall tied three points behind Haslingden, but Ramsbottom took the Holland Cup, having won one more match. The Jennings Worsley Cup went to Bacup for the first time after a one-sided final at Rawtenstall. Before a crowd that paid a record £3,295 at the gate, Harper bowled unchanged and then completed an unbeaten century in heavy drizzle, as Bacup overhauled Rawtenstall's 192 with only one wicket down.

Rawtenstall also took part in a record-breaking league match against Lowerhouse. Batting first, Bevan and Peter Wood scored centuries in a second-wicket stand of 227 to set up a total of 319 for six. While Lowerhouse professional Cameron Williamson was making the third century of the game it looked as if even that could be beaten. But after his dismissal they fell 56 short. Rawtenstall's total and the match aggregate of 583 were both league records, and 227 was the club's highest ever stand.

Bevan set another club record with his 1,346 runs at 70.84 and earned more than £700 in collections, but departed under a cloud. He drove off from the Bacup ground during a vital match when out for five. "I got myself out cheaply," Bevan explained. "It was anguish, and I had to cool off." After a special meeting the club committee fined him and broke off negotiations in respect of a contract for 1994. However, following much internal debate, they changed their minds and re-signed him in December.

Batsmen had the upper hand throughout the season, with five professionals – the four from Rossendale already mentioned plus South Australian Greg Blewett at Rishton – topping 1,000 runs. Damien Fleming, the Victorian seamer, bowled impressively to head the averages, with 79 wickets for Enfield at 11.68. Only three amateurs scored more than 700 runs: Ian Bell of Ramsbottom, Wood of Rawtenstall and Michael Ingham of Haslingden. By the end of his 21st season, the 41-year-old Wood had become the league's most prolific run-maker, edging past the 13,091 made by Bryan Knowles of Haslingden to set a new record of 13,250.

In the Central Lancashire League, Sleep, in his second season with Middleton, headed both batting and bowling averages – and also the aggregate lists. He was the only player to do the double – 1,748 runs at 92.00 and 100 wickets at 13.99. But Middleton finished fourth and the cup medal which seemed to be within Sleep's grasp until the closing moments of the Lees Wood final against Heywood eluded him. This match, the most exciting of the season, swung back and forth until the last over. Underdogs Heywood looked daunted by Middleton's 176 until Sleep was hit out of the ground several times; they won off the penultimate ball with two wickets standing.

Rochdale, helped by 1,261 runs and 56 wickets from New Zealander Chris Harris, won their third championship in four years. Their 101 points put them seven ahead of Littleborough. But after congratulating Rochdale, the league committee fined them £500 for playing their final match without a professional – a long-standing league requirement. Harris was not involved in the dispute; he had signed his contract on the understanding that he could leave early.

MARSDEN BS LANCASHIRE LEAGUE

	P	W	L	NR	Bonus Pts	Pts	Professional	Runs	Avge	Wkts	Avge
Haslingden ...	26	19	5	2	8	86	P. V. Simmons ...	1,046	61.52	54	18.87
Ramsbottom..	26	19	5	2	5	83	K. L. T. Arthurton	1,132	75.46	40	18.70
Rawtenstall ..	26	18	6	2	9	83	M. G. Bevan ...	1,346	70.84	63	22.44
Nelson	26	17	7	2	9	79	J. C. Scuderi ...	850	42.50	61	17.22
Bacup	26	16	9	1	7	72	R. A. Harper	1,120	70.00	72	13.69
Burnley	26	15	8	3	4	67	J. Angel........	394	43.77	62	16.69
East Lancs ...	26	11	13	2	6	52	D. Clarke........	393	20.68	53	18.54
Enfield	26	10	14	2	6	48	D. W. Fleming ...	805	44.72	79	11.68
Accrington ...	26	10	15	1	6	47	N. Johnson	803	36.50	70	16.34
Lowerhouse ..	26	8	16	2	7	41	C. Williamson	788	34.26	75	14.33
Todmorden...	26	8	17	1	4	37	P. J. W. Allott ...	336	17.68	52	17.71
Church	26	7	18	1	5	34	C. D. Matthews ...	587	24.45	77	17.45
Rishton	26	7	18	1	4	33	G. S. Blewett	1,104	48.00	52	24.84
Colne	26	5	19	2	2	24	M. J. Pawson	562	28.10	46	22.60

Note: Four points awarded for a win; one point for a no-result; one point for dismissing the opposition.

CENTRAL LANCASHIRE LEAGUE

	P	OW	LW	L	D	Pts	Professional	Runs	Avge	Wkts	Avge
Rochdale ...	30	5	16	3	6	101	C. Z. Harris	1,261	60.04	56	18.10
Littleborough	30	10	9	7	4	94	S. G. Law........	1,122	46.75	68	17.94
Milnrow	30	10	7	6	7	93*	A. G. Daley	628	29.90	73	20.83
Middleton ..	30	8	10	7	5	90	P. R. Sleep	1,748	92.00	100	13.99
Norden	30	6	12	7	5	88	D. K. Morrison ...	420	30.00	60	20.58
Unsworth ...	30	9	7	8	6	85	C. Williams	621	31.05	72	15.66
Radcliffe....	30	7	8	7	8	83	G. I. Foley	1,516	79.78	31	27.77
Stockport ...	30	7	5	12	6	68*	Ijaz Akhtar	427	17.08	92	15.66
Heywood ...	30	6	2	15	7	52	A. Flower	1,180	42.14	64	15.40
Ashton	30	4	6	16	4	52	B. Roberts	927	34.33	47	22.44
Oldham	30	5	3	15	7	51	Sajjad Ahmed	1,050	38.88	35	27.65
Royton	30	5	3	15	7	51	J. Grant........	243	12.15	53	22.18
Stand	30	7	1	17	5	49	M. Warden	331	18.38	99	15.50
Walsden	30	5	2	17	6	45	B. White	714	29.75	69	18.15
Werneth	30	4	1	19	6	36	C. J. P. G. van Zijl.	868	36.16	53	22.75
Crompton...	30	1	1	21	7	23	S. J. O'Shaughnessy	719	35.95	42	24.11

* Includes three points for a tie.

Notes: Five points awarded for an outright win; four points for a limited win; two points for a draw. An outright win is gained when a team bowls the opposition out. Averages include cup games.

LEAGUE CRICKET IN ENGLAND AND WALES, 1993

By GEOFFREY DEAN

It was not just in the Ashes series that Australians played a dominant role in 1993. Scores of Australian club cricketers invaded the English and Welsh leagues and made big impressions, breaking numerous records. One of the reasons for their success must be the fact that Australian league, or grade, cricket is almost entirely non-limited overs, with most games spread over two days on separate weekends. In England, still, few leagues even begin matches in the mornings, discouraging the emergence of wicket-taking bowlers and inducing batsmen to sell their wickets much less dearly.

There were demands in several places for restrictions to be placed on the number of overseas players, as in county cricket. Some officials were terrified about the consequences of introducing complicated and hard-to-enforce rules about registration. However, the Somerset League, one of those most affected, voted in November to limit overseas players to one per team. The League secretary Terry Mockridge was writing to the TCCB for help in framing a definition of who should and should not count as a home player. "For little leagues like ours it promises a lot of grey areas," said Mockridge. "I was dead against the proposal." But the problem in his League was obvious.

Of the top eight in the batting averages five were Australian, with Murray Christie of Uphill Castle (796) and Minehead's Shaun Deitz (786) the leading run-scorers. The man who helped Glastonbury win the title for the first time was not an Australian but not an Englishman either: the former West Indian Test player Joel Garner scored 488 runs at 44 and took 67 wickets at 12. However, Milverton's Vince Pike not only took more wickets (74) than Garner but also boasted a better strike rate.

Elsewhere in the south-west, Clifton Flax Bourton took the Western League title, winning every game except their last against Westbury-on-Trym, when they paid the penalty for reversing the batting order, and lost. Pushed hard by Lansdown, they did not become champions until their penultimate game of the season against Stroud when Mark Newton produced one of the all-round performances of the season, following 65 with eight for 57. In the Cornwall League, Falmouth's attempt to win a third successive championship was thwarted by St Austell. Exmouth, however, made it four Devon League titles in a row and were unbeaten until the final Saturday, when runners-up Exeter defeated them by nine wickets. Chepstow had to win their last match against the 1992 champions, Panteg, to be Three Counties League champions for the first time. Adrian Dale, Glamorgan player and Chepstow boy, came back to help the club: he made nought but captain Rob Moore scored 121, finishing with 976 for the season, and Chepstow won.

Two outstanding English amateurs became only the seventh and eighth batsmen since the Second World War to pass 1,000 runs in the Birmingham League. Steve Dean, the Staffordshire and England Amateur opener, amassed 1,166 runs for Walsall, beating by 14 the club record, held by former Australian Test captain Graham Yallop. Jon Wright finished with 1,006 runs. But his club Old Hill, the National Club Championship winners, had to be content with second place in the League behind West Bromwich Dartmouth, the side they beat in the final at Lord's. Old Hill finished just four points behind; "I only won six tosses out of 22," said their captain, David Banks, ruefully. It was Dartmouth's first title for 19 years. Top of the batting averages was Anthony Pollock, son of former South African Test batsman, Graeme, who made 872 runs at 67 for Worcester City.

Mark Gouldstone was just 17 short of becoming the fifth batsman in the Northants County League's history to score 1,000 runs in a season. He ran out of overs in Overstone's final match against Isham, when he made an unbeaten 117 out of 165 for seven. Andrew Churchill, of Romford & Gidea Park, narrowly failed to become the first Englishman in the Essex League to pass 1,000, needing only nine from his final innings but falling for a duck. Two weeks earlier, Neil Barry of Hadleigh & Thundersley (and Guyana) was the first of any nationality to reach the same milestone.

The Essex League featured one of the most exciting finishes of the season when the top two teams met on the final Saturday. Chelmsford had to beat leaders Fives & Heronians to retain their title and, after winning a vital toss, did so by seven wickets after dismissing Fives for 117. By a strange quirk, the Fives and Chelmsford Second XIs met on the same day in an identical title decider. Chelmsford, needing 19 off the final 15 balls with five wickets in hand, did not complete their innings because Fives' Jeff Rodrigues broke a leg while fielding. He could not be moved and, by the time the ambulance arrived, it was dark and Fives secured the draw they needed to be Second XI champions.

In the north-east, the Tyneside Senior League was tied for the first time since 1967. For Sacriston, joint winners with Shotley Bridge, Western Australian Steve Russell almost did the double with 1,084 runs and 98 wickets. Dennison Thomas, of third-placed South Moor, did manage the feat with 1,009 runs and a league record of 108 wickets. The former West Indian Test player Derick Parry claimed 84 victims and saw Horden to the Durham Senior League title ahead of Eppleton, for whom Jimmy Adams scored 1,130 runs and took 43 wickets. Ashington, winners of the Northumberland County League, owed much to Australian professional Scott Kay's 1,009 runs and wicket-keeper Bruce Storey's record 44 victims.

Another keeper to excel was Neil Priestley of Yorkshire League champions Sheffield Collegiate, who scored 782 runs and accounted for 32 batsmen. Cleethorpes hope they have unearthed a rare talent in Guy Welton who, at the age of 15, began his Yorkshire League career with 56 against York and 110 against Hull in the same August Bank Holiday weekend. Bradford League winners, East Bierley, were indebted to spinner David Jay, who took 75 wickets at 15. Peter Graham of Yeadon topped the bowling averages with 63 victims at 11. Russell Evans of Farsley finished with a league record aggregate of 1,376 runs. Another record went in the Leeds League where an Australian fast bowler, Darin Turner of champions Woodhouse, claimed 114 wickets. Gomersal won the Central Yorkshire League championship with James Pamment totalling 1,314 runs and Steve Foster 1,104.

The tragic death of the former Lancashire all-rounder, Ian Folley, in a North Lancashire League match overshadowed everything else there. However, Surendra Bhave set a league record of 1,853 runs for Vickers Sports. Millom won the title for the fifth successive year. Mel Whittle, 48, became the first amateur in the 64-year history of the Bolton League to take 100 wickets, finishing with 102 for the champions, Kearsley. Kendal won their first Northern League title since 1959. Macclesfield's prolific Australian, Darren Berry, helped his club to a second successive Cheshire County League championship. Berry made 196 not out against Poynton out of a league record total of 309 for three, but Poynton actually beat the record themselves 48 hours later with 312 for seven against Hyde. At the other end of the scale, a new South Lancashire League low was set by Massey Ferguson who succumbed for just 12 against Metrovicks.

In the East Midlands, Notts. Unity Casuals won the Notts. Alliance League for the first time after a dramatic last Saturday finish. Victory over Collingham by ten wickets coincided with a surprise two-wicket defeat at Notts. Forest for

Kimberley Institute, who had led the table for the previous eight weeks. In the Derbyshire County League, the Glenn brothers of Denby had a major impact with Philip amassing 1,145 runs and Michael topping the league bowling averages with 51 wickets. Langley Mill's Andrew Brown hit 960 runs and Ockbrook's David Hallack 941.

Esher's charge to the Surrey Championship title was brought about by victories in ten of their last 13 games. Andrew Bernard's 960 runs were important, as were Dexter Toppin's 56 wickets. Bromley became the first side to win the Kent League for three successive seasons, and Finchley retained their Middlesex League title. Luton Town were joint champions of the Hertfordshire League with St Albans, who would have won the title outright in their final game if they had taken just two more Stevenage wickets in a draw. Stevenage slipped to 78 for six, but the seventh-wicket pair survived the final hour.

Former Hampshire all-rounder Jon Ayling helped Portsmouth to the Southern League title with three hundreds in his eight innings; Barry Boorah took six wickets in a game four times for the champions. The league's batting award went to Chris Elward of Bournemouth, who played in two leagues and won the Dorset League in which they compete on Sundays. Former Hampshire seamer Steve Malone of Lymington was banned by the Southern League following verbal abuse of a Hambledon batsman. Swansea won the South Wales Cricket Association for a seventh time, preventing runners-up Neath from equalling Maesteg Celtic's record of four successive titles.

LEAGUE WINNERS, 1993

League	Winners	League	Winners
Airedale & Wharfedale	Otley	Midland Combined Counties	Highway
Bassetlaw	Welbeck Colliery	Norfolk Alliance	Vauxhall Mallards
Birmingham	W. Bromwich Dartmouth	Northants County	County Colts
Bolton	Kearsley	Northern	Kendal
Bradford	East Bierley	North Lancashire	Millom
Central	Bedworth	North Staffs. & South Cheshire	Cheadle
Central Yorkshire	Gomersal	Northumberland County	Ashington
Cherwell	North Oxford	North Wales	Marchwiel
Cheshire County	Macclesfield	North Yorks. & South Durham	Middlesbrough
Cornwall	St Austell	Notts. Alliance	Notts. Unity Casuals
Derbyshire County	Quarndon	Ribblesdale	Baxenden
Devon	Exmouth	Saddleworth	Heyside
Dorset Premier	Bournemouth	Somerset	Glastonbury
Durham County	Sedgefield	Southern	Portsmouth
Durham Senior	Horden	South Thames	RACS Eltham
Essex	Chelmsford	South Wales Association	Swansea
Hertfordshire	{ Luton Town / St Albans	Surrey Championship	Esher
		Sussex	Chichester
Huddersfield	Lascelles Hall	Thames Valley	Beaconsfield
Kent	Bromley	Three Counties	Chepstow
Lancashire & Cheshire	Longsight	Two Counties (Suffolk/Essex)	Halstead
Leeds	Woodhouse	Tyneside Senior	{ Sacriston / Shotley Bridge
Liverpool Competition	New Brighton		
Manchester Association	Bolton	Western	Clifton Flax Bourton
Middlesex	Finchley	Yorkshire	Sheffield Collegiate
Midland Club Championship	Sutton Coldfield		

Note: To avoid confusion traditional League names have been given in this list and sponsors' names omitted.

NATIONAL CLUB CHAMPIONSHIP, 1993

The West Midlands club Old Hill won the Championship for the fourth time in ten years and thus the Abbot Ale Cup, which was being awarded for the first time, when they beat West Bromwich Dartmouth, their local rivals, whose ground is barely five miles away from Old Hill. Dartmouth had to contest the final without their star player, the former Zimbabwean captain David Houghton, barred under the competition rules as an overseas player. The victory reversed the Birmingham League placings; Dartmouth were champions, with Old Hill just four points behind.

The clubs became joint favourites even before the quarter-finals, when Old Hill beat Brentham from Middlesex in a match marred by acrimony over a disputed catch. Then they held off a gallant challenge from Chichester Priory Park, who fell short of reaching a total of 221 for seven by just 18 runs. West Bromwich Dartmouth had easy wins over the Yorkshire club Slaithwaite and Alnwick of Northumberland before the final. The 1992 finalists never came close. The champions Optimists went out to their Western League rivals Clifton Flax Bourton in the first round; Kendal, the runners-up, reached their group semi-finals but then went out to Fleetwood.

St Fagans from Glamorgan, three-time winners of the Village Championship, graduated to the senior competition in style with a victory over Cheltenham before losing to Chichester Priory Park. Another team who put together a good run were Fives and Heronians from Essex who beat two of the most powerful Middlesex clubs, Finchley and Enfield. Needing 56 off five overs against Enfield and 20 off the last, they won the match with a last-ball four. The quarter-final draw, for the first time, was carried live on BBC Radio Five. – Russell Grant.

FINAL

OLD HILL v WEST BROMWICH DARTMOUTH

At Lord's, August 27. Old Hill won by seven wickets. Toss: West Bromwich Dartmouth.

In a match far removed from these two teams' usual tight battles, Old Hill took the advantage early on and never let it slip. Dartmouth struggled on a typically slow Lord's pitch against the accurate medium pace of 41-year-old Peter Bagley, who finished with four for 19. Old Hill's experienced batsmen made the runs in comfort. After the openers had been parted, Graeme Calway, who plays for Dorset, and the former Worcestershire batsman Mark Scott, put on 69 until Calway was out with the scores level. To add to the feeling of anticlimax, a wide decided the match. Following the tradition of the competition, the Man of the Match award – presented by Geoff Boycott – went to a player on the losing side, the Dartmouth top scorer Justin Inglis.

West Bromwich Dartmouth

R. M. Cox b Bagley	14	P. Mirza not out		5
*K. N. Patel run out	8	†P. A. Swainson lbw b Bagley		2
J. M. A. Inglis b Bagley	34	D. Parsons run out		1
A. Farooque run out	21	L-b 11, w 6		17
M. Sheikh b Calway	14			
N. Sajjad c Banks b Humphries	13	1/10 2/49 3/78	(45 overs)	133
R. M. Cooper lbw b Bagley	4	4/99 5/107 6/123		
A. J. Mackay b Humphries	0	7/123 8/125 9/129		

Bowling: Humphries 8–3–16–2; Proud 9–2–16–0; Derham 9–0–35–0; Bagley 9–2–19–4; Calway 6–0–25–1; Wright 4–0–11–0.

Old Hill

W. G. Khan c Farooque b Sajjad	27	*D. A. Banks not out	0
J. Wright b Sajjad	28	L-b 10, w 7, n-b 2	19
G. S. Calway c Parsons b Cooper	32		
M. S. Scott not out	28	1/42 2/64 3/133 (3 wkts, 34.5 overs) 134

A. E. Brookes, †J. Robinson, S. Derham, P. Humphries, P. R. Bagley and S. Proud did not bat.

Bowling: Mirza 9–1–35–0; Mackay 7–2–20–0; Sheikh 3–0–8–0; Sajjad 7–1–29–2; Parsons 2–0–14–0; Farooque 4–1–11–0; Cooper 2.5–0–7–1.

Umpires: K. Bray and E. Wilson.

WINNERS 1969–93

1969	Hampstead	1978	Cheltenham	1987	Old Hill
1970	Cheltenham	1979	Scarborough	1988	Enfield
1971	Blackheath	1980	Moseley	1989	Teddington
1972	Scarborough	1981	Scarborough	1990	Blackpool
1973	Wolverhampton	1982	Scarborough	1991	Teddington
1974	Sunbury	1983	Shrewsbury	1992	Optimists
1975	York	1984	Old Hill	1993	Old Hill
1976	Scarborough	1985	Old Hill		
1977	Southgate	1986	Stourbridge		

NATIONAL VILLAGE CRICKET CHAMPIONSHIP, 1993

Old-fashioned local rivalry added spice to the 22nd Village Cricket Championship; for the first time in its history, the final was contested by teams from the same league, Three Counties. Kington of Herefordshire and Frocester of Gloucestershire were both making their debut at Lord's, after Kington defeated 1985 winners Freuchie in their semi-final and Frocester beat Rowledge, who were runners-up the same year. A pulsating match saw Kington victors by two runs.

Too many results in the earlier rounds had been governed by the weather: in Lancashire, Bromborough Pool beat Brinscall on the toss of a coin, while Croston lost a bowl-out when their innings was abandoned at 20 without loss after they had dismissed their opponents for 59. Meanwhile, Goatacre, winners in 1988 and 1990, lost heavily early on to Winsley. Hawridge & Cholesbury and Hatfield Peverel, both disqualified for inadvertently infringing competition rules, took consolation in a friendly match on the day of the final. Sussex side Fletching, in true village spirit, kept things in the family; five Horscroft brothers played in the team, while their father Brian, formerly club captain, is now the groundsman and vice-chairman. In Durham, a rush of applicants to field at deep fine leg during the regional final between Mainsforth and Liverton Mines was attributed to a topless blonde sunbathing by the boundary rope.

A total of 639 teams took part in the competition, which was organised by *The Cricketer* and sponsored, for the last time, by Rothmans. – Amanda Ripley.

FINAL

FROCESTER v KINGTON

At Lord's, August 29. Kington won by two runs. Toss: Frocester.

Put in, Kington made 191 for six, after a solid start from opener Mark Porteous and a frenetic finish by Nigel Scott and Jim Lewis, who put on 25 runs for the seventh wicket in the last few overs. In reply, Frocester lost three wickets for 73, but John Evans and Ian Smith added 75 for the fourth to keep pace with the asking-rate. With 44 required from the last six overs Kington captain Edward Price called on leg-spinner Clive Scott. With his first ball he stemmed the flow, having Evans caught bowled for 73, made from only 80 balls. Scott took two more wickets and conceded only two runs from the penultimate over. That left Frocester needing 11. Even then they were in sight of victory as Smith heaved Rob Johnston's first ball for six. But with nine wickets down and three runs required from the final ball, tailender Basil Norbury was bowled.

Kington

†M. S. Porteous c Smith b Hudd	45	R. E. Johnston b Hutchings	7	
C. J. Scott c Reed b Hudd	24	J. W. Lewis not out	17	
M. J. Powell b Hudd	24	L-b 13, w 5, n-b 1	19	
*E. D. Price st Reed b Woodmason	29			
D. J. Morgan c Reed b Camm	1	1/55 2/104 3/106	(6 wkts, 40 overs) 191	
N. I. Scott not out	25	4/115 5/144 6/166		

A. G. Stansbury-Stokes, K. J. Gwynne and M. R. Cronin did not bat.

Bowling: Norbury 9-3-24-0; Woodmason 9-0-38-1; Hudd 9-0-36-3; Camm 8-0-35-1; Hutchings 5-0-45-1.

Frocester

C. St J. Lamden run out	17	B. J. Norbury b Johnston	0	
D. M. Whincup c Porteous b Price	13	E. P. Woodmason run out	1	
*J. A. Evans c Porteous b C. J. Scott	73	N. J. Hutchings not out	1	
†S. J. Reed b Cronin	4	B 2, l-b 5, w 10	17	
I. D. Smith b Johnston	53			
P. D. Spyvee lbw b Johnston	1	1/25 2/56 3/73	(40 overs) 189	
M. C. Camm st Porteous b C. J. Scott	8	4/148 5/150 6/179		
G. Hudd c Price b C. J. Scott	0	7/181 8/187 9/188		

Bowling: Gwynne 7-0-27-0; Price 9-1-26-1; Cronin 9-4-19-1; Stansbury-Stokes 4-0-34-0; Johnston 8-0-66-3; C. J. Scott 3-0-10-3.

Umpires: P. Adams and K. Coburn.

WINNERS 1972-93

1972 Troon (Cornwall)
1973 Troon (Cornwall)
1974 Bomarsund (Northumberland)
1975 Gowerton (Glamorgan)
1976 Troon (Cornwall)
1977 Cookley (Worcestershire)
1978 Linton Park (Kent)
1979 East Bierley (Yorkshire)
1980 Marchwiel (Clwyd)
1981 St Fagans (Glamorgan)
1982 St Fagans (Glamorgan)

1983 Quarndon (Derbyshire)
1984 Marchwiel (Clwyd)
1985 Freuchie (Fife)
1986 Forge Valley (Yorkshire)
1987 Longparish (Hampshire)
1988 Goatacre (Wiltshire)
1989 Toft (Cheshire)
1990 Goatacre (Wiltshire)
1991 St Fagans (Glamorgan)
1992 Hursley Park (Hampshire)
1993 Kington (Herefordshire)

IRISH CRICKET IN 1993

By DEREK SCOTT

Ireland was elected an Associate Member of the International Cricket Conference at the July meeting, a much-needed boost offering its cricketers the chance to compete in the ICC Trophy, and possibly qualify for the World Cup. In preparation for the 1994 Trophy in Kenya, the team played a record 12 matches.

In mid-June Ireland hosted their annual first-class fixture with Scotland but, despite outplaying them for much of the match, they left their declaration too late to force a victory. Michael Rea made a fine century and Alan Lewis two fifties. Next came four defeats in a row – by Yorkshire in the NatWest Trophy, Barbados (twice) and the Australian tourists, though a huge Dublin crowd, which included President Mary Robinson, at least had a 45-minute hundred from Allan Border to enjoy.

In July Ireland travelled to the English Midlands for the inaugural and highly successful Triple Crown Tournament with Scotland, Wales and an England Amateur XI. As so often in rugby, Wales blocked their way to the crown. After a comfortable win over Scotland and a thrilling one against England, Ireland lost their final rain-affected match with the Welsh, who had not won before, and yielded the handsome trophy to England on strike-rate by the tiniest fraction. After a draw with Lavinia, Duchess of Norfolk's XI, at Arundel in August, Ireland arrived at Lord's and made a determined attempt to meet MCC's challenge of 285 on a good pitch near the Tavern boundary, until a late flurry of wickets left the last pair to survive eight balls.

A visit to The Hague concluded the season. Ireland had defeated the Dutch four times in the 1970s but found their native players much improved and augmented by some formidable residentially qualified foreigners. With no time to master the technique of batting and bowling on a mat laid on shale, the Irish lost two limited-overs matches heavily.

The selectors tried out 20 players during the season before reaching a shortlist of 16 for Kenya. For the second successive year, Michael Rea passed 400 runs, with 491 at 37.76. Stephen Warke, who captained Ireland for a record 39th time, scored 416 at 34.66. The bowling was weaker, with each wicket costing nearly 40 runs. Leg-spinner Conor Hoey took 14 at just over 30 while Desmond Curry – perhaps underused – had nine at 24 each.

The Senior Interprovincial competition was plagued by rain, with only four positive results in 15 matches. North-West retained the title on bonus points, with the help of their Indian Test player, M. V. Narasimha Rao – known in Ireland as Bobby. The Leinster Union swept the board at Under-18, Under-15 and Under-13 levels. North Down won a disappointing final against Brigade in the All-Ireland Cup, sponsored by Schweppes for the last time. In club cricket YMCA won two separate league titles in Leinster, with Angus Dunlop reaching 1,000 runs for the second year running. Pembroke beat Old Belvedere to regain the Leinster Cup after ten years. In the Northern Union, Waringstown won their 19th cup, but lost the league title by a single point to Lisburn. In the North-West, Strabane won their tenth cup; Donemana created an All-Ireland record by winning the league for the ninth successive year. Church of Ireland won the Munster League for the first time since 1981 and Cork County took the cup.

SCOTTISH CRICKET IN 1993

By J. WATSON BLAIR

This was a disappointing year for Scotland. The International Cricket Council refused to grant them Associate Membership, saying there were doubts about the constitutional position, which was a demoralising blow. The Scottish Cricket Union, which had carried out changes recommended by ICC in 1992, was baffled but renewed its efforts.

The abolition of the Benson and Hedges Cup's zonal round reduced Scotland to two matches against English first-class counties. In late April they were knocked out of the cup by Essex, in a nine-wicket defeat at Forfar, while on a bitterly cold June day Worcestershire achieved a 76-run victory at Edinburgh in the NatWest Trophy. The only first-class fixture, against Ireland at Eglinton in mid-June, saw Scotland salvage a draw after Ireland set them a formidable 280 in 55 overs. Bruce Russell was unexpectedly removed from the captaincy, which he had held since 1991, before the match, though he retained his place; Alastair Storie, an experienced player in England and South Africa, took over.

Barbados visited Glasgow in the same month, when a glorious century from former Scotland professional Gordon Greenidge set up a narrow win for the West Indians. MCC's biennial trip to Scotland, in August, was transferred from Aberdeen to Forfar because of rain. After three declarations, Scotland were stranded 41 short of victory with six wickets in hand; Storie struck 103. In July, Scotland took part in the inaugural Triple Crown Tournament, where they lost to Ireland and an England Amateur XI, who claimed the trophy, and defeated Wales. The international team had made a second pre-season tour of South Africa, based in Cape Town. They won two and lost four of eight scheduled matches. More importantly, Jim Love, the SCU's new director of cricket, familiarised himself with the squad. A trip to Zimbabwe was planned for March 1994.

On the domestic scene Grange won the Whyte and Mackay Scottish Cup for the fourth successive year (including a shared title in 1992) after a thrilling final with Arbroath. Colts took the Kelly's Copiers Small Clubs Cup. The Royal Bank of Scotland Quaich for the Scottish Area Championship – played under a successful new format – went to Strathclyde East. Arbroath won the Scottish Counties Championship, Greenock the Western Union, Grange the East League, Dumfries the Border League, Dundee HSFP the Strathmore Union, Buckie the North of Scotland League and Glasgow High and Kelvinside the Glasgow and District League.

Grange were Famous Grouse's Team of the Year for the fourth time running, and Storie Batsman of the Year. The bowling, all-round and wicket-keeping awards went to Clarence Parfitt, Jim Govan and Donald Orr respectively. Ian Stanger was Young Player of the Year again and also leading amateur bowler in the D. M. Hall Western Union awards, which named Ian Kennedy best amateur batsman and Greenock top club. The Scottish Cricket Writers Association, founded in August 1992, gave awards to George Salmond, Mark Kelaher, Parfitt and Colin Mair.

A bright note came from West District's victory over Hampshire in the NCA County Championship final in early September – which earned them a civic reception from the Lord Provost and Glasgow City Council. Freuchie reached the semi-final of the National Village Championship, which they won in 1985.

THE TRIPLE CROWN TOURNAMENT, 1993

By GARETH A. DAVIES

The inaugural Triple Crown Tournament, for the senior teams of Ireland, Scotland and Wales and the England Amateur XI, was hosted by the National Cricket Association in the Midlands in July. England won because of their bowlers' marginally higher strike-rate after tying on points with Ireland. Going into the final day Ireland had a clear advantage, having already beaten Scotland and England, and their opponents Wales had lost twice. But Ireland's luck ran out on a damp Friday. Welsh all-rounder Jamie Sylvester rattled up 68 and then finished off the batting with two wickets.

An unbeaten century against Scotland from Malcolm Roberts set up victory for the English, whose bowlers then claimed eight wickets – their minimum arithmetical requirement. The trophy had to be redirected from Wolverhampton, where Ireland were playing, to England's game at Moseley. The 1994 tournament is to be staged by the Scottish Cricket Union.

Results

At Old Hill CC, July 21. England Amateur XI won by nine wickets. Toss: England Amateur XI. Wales 143 (54 overs) (J. Derrick 34; N. P. Hackett three for 32); England Amateur XI 144 for one (34 overs) (S. J. Dean 85 not out, M. J. Roberts 52 not out).

At Stratford-upon-Avon, July 21. Ireland won by five wickets. Toss: Ireland. Scotland 156 for eight (55 overs) (G. N. Reifer 52 not out; D. A. Lewis four for 21); Ireland 157 for five (48.2 overs) (M. P. Rea 72 not out, S. G. Smyth 31 not out).

At Edgbaston, July 22. Ireland won by 13 runs. Toss: Ireland. Ireland 194 for six (55 overs) (M. F. Cohen 42, S. J. S. Warke 39 not out); England Amateur XI 181 (52.4 overs) (S. N. V. Waterton 66; C. McCrum four for 27).

At Walsall CC, July 22. Scotland won by six runs. Toss: Wales. Scotland 179 (55 overs) (A. C. Storie 62, A. B. Russell 59); Wales 173 (54.2 overs) (A. W. Harris 43, M. J. Newbold 54; G. N. Reifer three for 24, K. L. P. Sheridan three for 52).

At Moseley CC, July 23. England Amateur XI won by 23 runs. Toss: England Amateur XI. England Amateur XI 207 for five (30 overs) (M. J. Roberts 111 not out; P. G. Duthie three for 30); Scotland 184 for eight (30 overs) (J. D. Love 87).

At Wolverhampton, July 23. Wales won by 19 runs. Toss: Ireland. Wales 180 for eight (45 overs) (S. Evans 41, J. P. J. Sylvester 68); Ireland 161 (42.3 overs) (S. J. S. Warke 39, S. G. Smyth 46).

FINAL TABLE

	Played	Won	Lost	Points	Strike-rate
England Amateur XI......	3	2	1	4	35.3
Ireland	3	2	1	4	36.5
Wales	3	1	2	2	37.9
Scotland	3	1	2	2	41.1

Strike-rate was calculated by dividing the balls bowled, including wides and no-balls, by wickets taken.

WEST INDIES UNDER-19 IN ENGLAND, 1993

By GERALD HOWAT

he West Indian Under-19 side which toured England in 1993 did not chieve the standards normally synonymous with Caribbean cricket or even lfil the expectations raised when they won their first three matches. Their redecessors of 1982 – who included Courtney Walsh, Phil Simmons and oger Harper – had won the "Test" series 2-0 and England had not beaten West Indian Under-19 side in a full-length game since 1978. But England on the two one-day internationals easily and gained the only victory in the ests, although West Indies led on first innings in both drawn games. All neir opponents on the tour presented a serious challenge, especially the aree different Development of Excellence teams and England Under-18.

The tour party had been picked after a youth tournament in St Kitts in uly. Although six players had already appeared at first-class level, the side acked experienced opening batsmen and a strong attack. Much depended n Shivnarine Chanderpaul, an elegant, slightly built player from Guyana nd one of six left-handers in the party. He scored 753 runs at 57.92, nough he reserved his best for the Tests in which he averaged 124.00. nother Guyanese left-hander, Andre Percival, who averaged 78.50, was oth an attacking batsman and difficult to shift. Though uneasy at his romotion to open, Mario Ventura scored 487. Juni Mitchum demonstrated ome attractive strokeplay while Anil Balliram and Raymond Griffith had neir moments of success.

Of the bowlers, the Guyanese Colin Stuart was much the most successful his 28 wickets at 26.85 were more than the other seamers, who averaged ver 40, took between them. He had pace and the ability to bowl long pells, though he could not force the England batsmen on to the back foot ntil the final match. The tall Mervyn Dillon was hampered by injury. As ith the Sri Lankans in 1992 – though more surprisingly – the strength of ne bowling lay in the spinners. Leg-spinner Dinanath Ramnarine, who ook 19 wickets at 28.78, bowled impressively at Hove, claiming five for 41 as England scored 561 on a placid pitch. He often bowled in harness ith one of two other leg-spinners, Rawl Lewis, who finished with 15 vickets at 32.20, and Chanderpaul.

The captain, Ian Bradshaw, from Harrison College, Barbados, was the nly productive all-rounder. He scored 459 useful runs in the middle order nd, as a fast left-armer, took his share in the attack, if rather expensively. Iis captaincy, at first rather rigid, became flexible and imaginative. In the ield the team – who obviously felt the cold – suffered by comparison with ngland. Wicket-keeper Andre Coley lacked the polished glove-work of Robert Rollins, of Essex, and little was seen of his deputy, Kester Sylvester, espite his first-class experience for Windward Islands.

Relations between the tourists and their various opponents were good nd they set a high standard in personal appearance and conduct on the ield. Cricket, they reported, was losing out among their contemporaries at ome to basketball and American football, which are popularised by elevision. These young players, however, showed much dedication and the hree Guyanese representatives at least, Chanderpaul, Percival and Stuart, hould be seen again. The tour was sponsored by Northern Telecom.

TOUR PARTY

I. Bradshaw (Barbados) (*captain*), A. Givance (Jamaica) (*vice-captain*), A. Balliram (Trinidad & Tobago), S. Chanderpaul (Guyana), R. Christopher (Leeward Island A. Coley (Jamaica), M. Dillon (Trinidad & Tobago), R. Griffith (Barbados), R. N Lewis (Windward Islands), J. Mitchum (Leeward Islands), A. R. Percival (Guyan D. Ramnarine (Trinidad & Tobago), C. Stuart (Guyana), K. K. Sylvester (Windwa Islands) and M. D. Ventura (Jamaica).

Manager: G. Sterling. *Coach:* W. A. Bourne.

RESULTS

Matches – Played 13: Won 3, Lost 5, Drawn 5.

Note: None of the matches played was first-class.

v MCC Young Cricketers: at Wellington College, July 31. West Indies Under-19 won seven wickets. MCC Young Cricketers 154 for eight (55 overs) (M. J. Church 32; R. Lewis three for 23); West Indies Under-19 156 for three (55 overs) (A. Balliram 77 not ou R. Griffith 33).

v English Schools CA Under-19: at Wellington College, August 2. West Indies Under-19 wo by 13 runs. West Indies Under-19 246 for four (55 overs) (M. D. Ventura 90, R. Griffith not out); English Schools CA Under-19 233 for eight (55 overs) (D. J. Shadford 3 A. Singh 48).

v Wales Minor Counties: at Wellington College, August 3. West Indies Under-19 won by runs. West Indies Under-19 238 for nine (55 overs) (M. D. Ventura 100, A. Balliram 68 Wales Minor Counties 159 (55 overs).

v England Under-19: (First one-day "international"): at Leicester, August 5. England Unde 19 won by 90 runs. England Under-19 292 for five (55 overs) (M. P. Vaughan 122, M. Dowman 63, M. J. Walker 35; C. Stuart three for 53); West Indies Under-19 202 for eig (55 overs) (S. Chanderpaul 37, A. R. Percival 35, I. Bradshaw 56 not out).

v England Under-19: (Second one-day "international"): at Chelmsford, August 7. Englan Under-19 won by 140 runs. England Under-19 241 for six (55 overs) (M. P. Vaughan 5 M. J. Walker 84, J. A. Daley 32); West Indies Under-19 101 (37.5 overs) (A. Balliram 3 G. Keedy three for 23).

v League Cricket Conference Under-25: at Shenley, August 8, 9, 10. League Crick Conference Under-25 won by one wicket. West Indies Under-19 300 (S. Chanderpaul 8 I. Bradshaw 88; S. Shah five for 72, A. Bird three for 74) and 134 for five dec.; Leag Cricket Conference Under-25 219 for four dec. (N. J. Heaton 86 not out, N. T. Wood 4 and 216 for nine (N. T. Wood 58, P. J. Wilcock 41; D. Ramnarine six for 58).

ENGLAND UNDER-19 v WEST INDIES UNDER-19

First "Test" Match

t Nottingham, August 12, 13, 14, 15. Drawn. Toss: England Under-19.

An overnight thunderstorm prevented any play on the fourth day though a positive result as already unlikely. England put themselves in a strong position by scoring 243 for four on he first day; Vaughan of Yorkshire added another century to his 122 a week earlier in the ne-day international at Leicester. His partnership of 134 with Walker for the second icket set a new Under-19 record. The West Indian fielders clearly struggled in the cold eather, but Bradshaw, Christopher and especially Stuart managed to bowl some well-ontrolled pace. England added another 103 next day before their innings ended with nine ickets down – Thomas had an injured hand and was unable to bat. Walker set an ttacking field for his pace bowlers, Broadhurst and Chapple, an experienced opening pair t this level, but it was the spinners, notably Phillips, who broke through. With Ventura run ut at 87 for three, West Indies ended the second day in danger of following on. On what roved to be the final day, Bradshaw and Chanderpaul removed that possibility before unch, with Chanderpaul completing an undefeated double-century, containing 28 fours, just efore the close. While West Indies needed a large total to enable their spinners to attack ngland, their slow scoring in the evening belied their ambition.

ngland Under-19

1. P. Vaughan c Coley b Bradshaw	...119	M. Broadhurst b Stuart	13
1. P. Dowman lbw b Bradshaw	4	G. Keedy not out	1
M. J. Walker b Ramnarine	43	S. D. Thomas absent injured	
. A. Daley b Bradshaw	88		
. J. Cunliffe b Stuart	18	B 4, l-b 7, w 6, n-b 8	25
. C. Phillips b Stuart	3		
. Chapple c Chanderpaul b Ramnarine	17	1/7 2/141 3/206 4/240 5/253	346
R. J. Rollins lbw b Ramnarine	15	6/286 7/316 8/328 9/346	

Bowling: Stuart 23.4–5–71–3; Bradshaw 28–8–50–3; Christopher 15–3–48–0; Chanderpaul 5–3–44–0; Givance 8–0–24–0; Ramnarine 39–5–98–3.

Vest Indies Under-19

. Balliram b Phillips	17	†A. Coley c Vaughan b Phillips	3
1. D. Ventura run out	36	D. Ramnarine not out	16
. Mitchum b Phillips	20		
. Chanderpaul not out	...203	B 4, l-b 12, w 6	22
. Griffith c Walker b Chapple	13		
I. Bradshaw c Phillips b Chapple	34	1/48 2/80 3/87 4/158	(7 wkts) 379
. Givance c Dowman b Phillips	15	5/250 6/300 7/311	

. Stuart and R. Christopher did not bat.

Bowling: Chapple 28–9–69–2; Broadhurst 16–1–56–0; Thomas 16–3–48–0; Phillips 4–14–102–4; Keedy 41–15–73–0; Vaughan 6–1–12–0; Dowman 2–0–3–0.

Umpires: J. C. Balderstone and A. A. Jones.

Development of Excellence XI: at Oundle School, August 17, 18, 19. Drawn. West Indies nder-19 295 for six dec. (A. Balliram 89, I. Bradshaw 66, K. K. Sylvester 47; D. J. hadford three for 63) and 240 for six dec. (J. Mitchum 40, A. R. Percival 113 not out; . J. Innes four for 56); Development of Excellence XI 254 for four dec. (G. P. Butcher 109 ot out, D. J. Shadford 61 not out) and 193 for eight (T. A. Tweats 52; C. Stuart four or 68).

Development of Excellence XI: at Oundle School, August 21, 22, 23. Drawn. West Indies nder-19 320 for five dec. (M. D. Ventura 52, S. Chanderpaul 153 not out) and 152 for ree dec. (A. R. Percival 70 not out); Development of Excellence XI 157 for three dec. D. A. Blenkiron 64, C. J. Rika 60) and 154 for seven (R. S. Yeabsley 71 not out; . Chanderpaul three for 29).

ENGLAND UNDER-19 v WEST INDIES UNDER-19

Second "Test" Match

At Hove, August 26, 27, 28, 29. England Under-19 won by nine wickets. Toss: England Under-19.

In sun warm enough for even the West Indians to remove their sweaters, England won comfortably on the last afternoon, after some resistance by Chanderpaul had given the tourists an outside chance of the draw. England reached an impregnable 425 for three on the first day, with Mathew Dowman of Nottinghamshire batting throughout for 230. His eventual 267, with 34 fours, was the highest score for any international side at this level. He cut and hooked to great effect while Cunliffe, a powerful batsman who plays the ball late, shared with him in a stand of 266, an Under-19 record for any wicket. For West Indies, Mitchum, finding form at last, curbed his natural instinct to play strokes to make a patient century. On the third day the pace of Thomas and Law, on his home ground, and the left-arm spin of Keedy removed the last six West Indian wickets for 45 and then demolished their top five for 87 when they followed on, 196 behind. Chanderpaul, who played a fighting 91 with some thundering square cuts, kept up their hopes on the last day. Once he had gone, England coasted to their first victory over West Indies since 1978, a fair reflection of their undoubted batting and bowling superiority.

England Under-19

M. P. Dowman c Balliram b Ramnarine	267	– c Ventura b Christopher	3
M. P. Vaughan lbw b Ramnarine	21	– not out	21
*M. J. Walker b Coley b Ramnarine	26	– not out	30
J. A. Daley c Balliram b Stuart	35		
R. J. Cunliffe c Ramnarine b Givance	98		
M. E. Trescothick c Mitchum b Givance	17		
G. Chapple c Percival b Ramnarine	7		
†R. J. Rollins c Percival b Givance	27		
D. R. Law not out	0		
S. D. Thomas run out	0		
G. Keedy lbw b Ramnarine	0		
B 11, l-b 14, n-b 38	63	L-b 1, n-b 6	7

1/61 2/119 3/220 4/486 5/522   561   1/9   (1 wkt) 61
6/523 7/549 8/561 9/561

Bowling: First Innings—Stuart 22-2-120-1; Bradshaw 10-0-52-0; Christopher 9-0-49-0; Ramnarine 45.1-6-141-5; Givance 47-7-153-3; Chanderpaul 3-0-20-0; Balliram 1-0-1-0. *Second Innings*—Stuart 5-0-28-0; Christopher 4-0-25-1; Ramnarine 3.2-1-7-0.

West Indies Under-19

A. Balliram run out	41	– lbw b Keedy	11
M. D. Ventura st Rollins b Keedy	25	– c Vaughan b Thomas	38
J. Mitchum lbw b Chapple	105	– lbw b Law	5
S. Chanderpaul c Cunliffe b Law	22	– (6) c Rollins b Keedy	91
A. R. Percival c Thomas b Law	79	– (7) c Law b Thomas	12
*I. Bradshaw c Rollins b Thomas	27	– (4) c Daley b Keedy	4
A. Givance c Vaughan b Law	0	– (8) c Trescothick b Vaughan	25
D. Ramnarine lbw b Keedy	12	– (5) c Dowman b Law	16
†A. Coley not out	7	– lbw b Keedy	25
C. Stuart b Thomas	0	– not out	1
R. Christopher b Keedy	11	– c Law b Chapple	0
B 8, l-b 5, w 5, n-b 18	36	B 1, l-b 1, w 4, n-b 12	18

1/57 2/116 3/165 4/299 5/320   365   1/23 2/62 3/67 4/85 5/87   256
6/320 7/346 8/346 9/346   6/123 7/163 8/246 9/253

Bowling: First Innings—Chapple 20-4-70-1; Law 25-7-63-3; Thomas 26-7-96-2; Keedy 42-16-79-3; Vaughan 9-3-21-0; Dowman 6-0-23-0. *Second Innings*—Law 16-1-82-2; Chapple 16.2-6-37-1; Vaughan 16-7-30-1; Keedy 43-16-71-4; Thomas 11-3-34-2.

Umpires: R. Julian and R. A. White.

Development of Excellence XI: at Sleaford CC, September 1, 2, 3. Development of xcellence XI won by four wickets. West Indies Under-19 363 for nine dec. (A. Balliram 2, A. R. Percival 115 not out, R. N. Lewis 56) and 166 for eight dec. (R. Griffith 64; J. Killeen three for 78); Development of Excellence XI 290 (I. J. Sutcliffe 78, K. R. piring 71; C. Stuart six for 105) and 240 for six (C. J. Schofield 73, A. J. E. Hibbert 59).

England Under-18: at Southport CC, September 6, 7, 8. Drawn. West Indies Under-19 148 A. Balliram 37; T. J. Mason five for 44, B. S. Phelps five for 46) and 108 for five R. Griffith 65; T. J. Mason three for 35); England Under-18 367 for seven dec. (A. D. airstow 100 not out, A. Morris 80, Extras 81).

ENGLAND UNDER-19 v WEST INDIES UNDER-19

Third "Test" Match

At Manchester, September 10, 11, 12, 13. Drawn. Toss: England Under-19.

Frequent stoppages for rain and bad light denied West Indies the chance to capitalise on heir best start of the tour. They had removed nine England wickets for 78, with Stuart bowling extremely fast, before Chapple and Keedy, the last-wicket pair from Lancashire nd Yorkshire, scored a run a minute, almost doubling the total. When West Indies replied, hree left-handers, Ventura, Chanderpaul and Bradshaw, all made half-centuries to take hem into a comfortable lead. With a left-hander at the wicket throughout the innings, Law vas the most effective of the England bowlers, getting some lift and using the wind. He vent into lunch on the third day on a hat-trick, after two fine leg-side catches by Rollins nd helped him to four wickets for seven in 32 balls. Declaring on the last morning, in the ope of bowling England out in a day, West Indies were thwarted by rain after Vaughan nd Dowman had reduced the deficit to 81. The pair completed 771 runs between them in heir five internationals against the tourists, Dowman passing 400 just before the match was bandoned in mid-afternoon.

England Under-19

M. P. Vaughan b Stuart	0	– not out	27
M. P. Dowman c Ramnarine b Dillon	25	– not out	35
M. J. Walker c Coley b Bradshaw	1		
C. J. Cunliffe b Stuart	17		
M. E. Trescothick c Coley b Stuart	9		
N. T. Wood c Mitchum b Lewis	2		
G. Chapple not out	39		
R. J. Rollins c Coley b Bradshaw	0		
O. R. Law c Coley b Bradshaw	0		
N. C. Phillips c Ventura b Lewis	1		
G. Keedy c Stuart b Ramnarine	25		
B 9, l-b 2, w 4, n-b 10	25	N-b 4	4
1/4 2/9 3/38 4/60 5/62	144	(no wkt)	66
1/72 7/77 8/77 9/78			

Bowling: *First Innings*—Bradshaw 17-3-36-3; Stuart 18-6-43-3; Dillon 11-4-19-1; Lewis 15-6-28-2; Ramnarine 2.1-0-7-1. *Second Innings*—Bradshaw 5-2-11-0; Stuart 4-0-23-0; Dillon 2-0-16-0; Ramnarine 2.1-0-9-0; Lewis 2-0-7-0.

West Indies Under-19

M. D. Ventura lbw b Law	55	†A. Coley not out	16
J. Mitchum c Rollins b Keedy	21	C. Stuart not out	3
R. Griffith lbw b Keedy	7		
S. Chanderpaul c Rollins b Law	56	B 11, l-b 9, w 2, n-b 9	31
A. R. Percival c Phillips b Law	0		
I. Bradshaw c Dowman b Keedy	76	1/38 2/57 3/128	(8 wkts dec.) 291
R. N. Lewis c Rollins b Law	0	4/128 5/185 6/185	
D. Ramnarine c Rollins b Chapple	26	7/245 8/283	

M. Dillon did not bat.

Bowling: Chapple 24-9-64-1; Law 26-7-74-4; Keedy 35-11-55-3; Phillips 25-11-42-0; Dowman 5-0-23-0; Vaughan 5-2-13-0.

Umpires: J. H. Hampshire and D. O. Oslear.

NAYC UNDER-19 COUNTY FESTIVALS, 1993

By PHILIP HOARE

Lancashire regained the NAYC Under-19 County title which they won in 1986, its inaugural year, through their strong spin attack and the batting talents of Darren Shadford and their captain, Lee Marland. The final was a close call after a relative failure in their own innings: Durham, who had passed 200 in four of their previous five matches, needed only 160 from 60 overs. But the spinners, Matthew Taylor and Chris Brown, put the brake on and then dismissed them for a mere 83.

In the Cambridge festival, Shadford passed fifty in every match except one, and he made 107 against Cambridgeshire, when Lancashire ran up 308 and Marland contributed 121. Off-spinner Brown warmed up with six for 81 to dismiss Nottinghamshire in the opening match, and slow left-arme Taylor claimed five as Lancashire defeated Essex in the area final. At Oxford, Durham's star was Paul Dumighan, who averaged over 100, with scores of 76 against Cornwall, 122 not out against Oxfordshire and, in the final, 87 not out, as Durham swept past a Warwickshire total of 211 with eight wickets to spare. He had valuable support from Nick Trainor, with scores of 61 not out, 102 and 82, and Martin Hood, who scored 114 against Derbyshire.

Among the 32 other counties taking part in the two festivals, which run concurrently at various grounds round the two university cities, Warwickshire had another strong batting line-up. Mark Wagh and Michael Powell scored 141 not out and 128, the highest scores of the week, in their victory over Shropshire. There were two centuries each for Luke Sutton of Somerset, who scored 104 against Devon and 101 against Hertfordshire and James Cokayne of Derbyshire, with 122 not out against Cornwall and 115 against Durham. Several bowlers took six wickets in an innings, but the best figures of the week were Navid Bashir's seven for 68 for Buckinghamshire against Berkshire.

Once more the festivals were affected by rain, though not as severely as in 1992. At Cambridge all eight of Thursday's play-offs were washed out after torrential overnight rain and further showers during the day. The last casualty was Lancashire's match with defending champions Yorkshire reluctantly abandoned after tea. Lancashire and Essex went through to the area final as the only teams unbeaten in the group matches.

The Hilda Overy Championship, which ran throughout the summer but included matches at the festivals, was won by Glamorgan, unbeaten over seven matches with six wins and a tie. Their points average kept them ahead of Yorkshire and Durham, who both won six matches out of seven and Sussex, who had the highest points total with nine out of 11.

AREA FINALS

At Clare College, Cambridge, August 13. Lancashire won by 23 runs. Toss: Lancashire. Lancashire 209 for eight (60 overs) (L. J. Marland 44, M. Ramsbottom 89; G. Goodwin three for 60); Essex 186 for nine (60 overs) (I. Harvey 59 not out; C. Brown four for 91, M. Taylor five for 68).

At Jesus College, Oxford, August 13. Durham won by eight wickets. Toss: Warwickshire. Warwickshire 211 for seven (60 overs) (M. J. Powell 72, M. A. Wagh 45); Durham 215 for two (58.3 overs) (P. R. Dumighan 87 not out, N. J. Trainor 82).

FINAL

DURHAM v LANCASHIRE

At Christ Church, Oxford, August 14. Lancashire won by 76 runs. Toss: Lancashire.

Durham had high hopes after dismissing Lancashire for only 159, but quite failed to master the Lancashire spinners on a pitch which helped all the bowlers. Lancashire chose to bat and made solid progress until lunch, chiefly thanks to Shadford's 60, but they were unable to accelerate. Seamer Paul Collingwood returned four for 42, assisted by wicket-keeper Phil Nicholson with five dismissals. Durham started confidently, with opener Paul Dumighan looking to follow up his form earlier in the week. But once he went for 23 and slow left-armer Matthew Taylor joined the taller off-spinner Chris Brown, who bowled throughout the innings, Durham fell quickly behind a modest asking-rate of 2.66. Taylor claimed the match award with five wickets for 19 runs in 15 overs. The last wicket fell to Brown, with more than eight overs to spare when Richard Ankers stumped Nick Taylor; Ankers was standing in for James Moyes, who had to miss his team's triumph after being hit in the mouth and needing stitches.

Lancashire

L. J. Marland lbw b Taylor	7	C. Brown st Nicholson b Collingwood	1
M. Ramsbottom lbw b Killeen	6	M. Taylor run out	15
D. J. Shadford c Nicholson b Collingwood	60	†J. R. Moyes not out	7
I. Ratledge c Hood b Collingwood	21	L-b 3, w 9	12
A. J. Green c Nicholson b Collingwood	21		
A. D. Mawson run out	3	1/11 2/24 3/94 (59.4 overs) 159	
R. W. J. Ankers st Nicholson b Trainor	6	4/106 5/116 6/129	
P. J. Seal st Nicholson b Trainor	0	7/129 8/133 9/134	

Bowling: Killeen 9.4-3-17-1; Taylor 7-0-21-1; Hughes 10-1-38-0; Trainor 11-0-38-2; Collingwood 22-6-42-4.

Durham

P. R. Dumighan st Moyes b Taylor	23	P. D. Collingwood run out	8
M. Hood lbw b Seal	3	H. Hubber not out	5
N. J. Trainor b Seal	1	N. C. F. Taylor st Ankers b Brown	1
W. Ritzema c Shadford b Taylor	14	B 3, l-b 2, w 1, n-b 2	8
A. A. Hawthorne c and b Taylor	2		
N. Killeen b Taylor	4	1/3 2/21 3/38 (51.4 overs) 83	
Q. J. Hughes b Shadford b Taylor	1	4/43 5/47 6/47	
P. J. Nicholson run out	13	7/64 8/77 9/77	

Bowling: Seal 11-5-16-2; Brown 25.4-9-43-1; Taylor 15-8-19-5.

Umpires: J. W. Holder and R. Julian.

PAST WINNERS

1986	Lancashire	1990	Essex
1987	Yorkshire	1991	Middlesex
1988	Warwickshire	1992	Yorkshire
1989	Warwickshire	1993	Lancashire

SCHOOLS CRICKET IN 1993

To get to "Oxford" as a cricketer – never mind as a scholar – represents excellence in itself for the 44 boys invited annually to the MCC Oxford Festival, which leads up to three matches at Lord's. The 1993 Festival was badly hit by the weather, as it had been in 1992. Boys who had hoped to play on two or even three occasions at Lord's had their aspirations curtailed at tea on the first day, with no further play possible on the following days.

Nor did the weather at Oxford, in the preceding trials, give the selectors as much time as they would have liked for players to display their talents, batsmen not getting to the wicket and bowlers not invited to perform have scant opportunity to press their claims. There may be a case – whatever the weather – for selectors asking a batsman to retire or a bowler to be withdrawn from the attack. Equity would demand that such players would be in the squad for Lord's in that their performances had told the selectors all they wished to know.

Those who came to Oxford broadly represented the best schoolboy talent of the year. One says "broadly" for several reasons: Jonathan Henderson (Hulme GS, Oldham), Robin Weston (Durham) and Nathan Wood (William Hulme's GS, Manchester) were unavailable because of their commitment to the England Under-18 International Youth Tournament. Wood, indeed, later made his debut as an England Under-19 player against West Indies at Old Trafford. The basic selection requires that 22 come from the English Schools Cricket Association (ESCA) sector and 22 from the Headmasters' Conference Schools (HMC). The latter selection depends much upon reports from schools; objective judgments must be made from what can be subjective submissions. After four days of intermittent cricket at Oxford, the following were selected to play in at least one match at Lord's: Andrew Bairstow, Scott Boswell, Michael Cawdron, Dominic Hewson, Quentin Hughes, Barry Hyam, Neil Killeen, Anthony McGrath, Tim Mason, Alex Morris, Richard Nowell, Ben Phillips, Spencer Platt, Darren Shadford, Anurag Singh, Matthew Taylor and Peter Wilcock. Their schools may be found in the scorecards that follow. – Gerald Howat.

HMC SOUTHERN SCHOOLS v HMC NORTHERN SCHOOLS

At Wadham College, Oxford, July 9, 10. Drawn.

Rain delayed the start until after lunch and the first innings was limited to 35 overs each. No batsman was able to establish himself although all the openers played with some purpose. The slow bowlers on each side, especially James and Nowell, proved the most successful. Hames and Hewson, in the Southern second innings, shared in a partnership of 89 while the seamer Boswell bowled a good line. More rain, on the second afternoon, made any result academic, but Bairstow compiled an excellent half-century for the Northern side in difficult conditions.

HMC Southern Schools

B. A. Hames (*Lord Wandsworth*) c Bairstow b Dennison .	17 – b Boswell	55
A. D. Pierce (*Lancing*) b Dennison	22 – (6) b James	0
D. R. Hewson (*Cheltenham*) c Boswell b James .	6 – b Carpenter	98
G. A. Bucknell (*Bryanston*) c Carpenter b Dennison .	0 – (2) c Carpenter b Boswell	0
*M. J. Cawdron (*Cheltenham*) b James	21 – (7) not out	21
G. R. Treagus (*King Edward VI, Southampton*) c Simpson b James	0 – (4) b James	26
R. W. Nowell (*Trinity*) lbw b James	8 – (5) lbw b James	11
T. J. Mason (*Denstone*) b Taylor	19 – (9) c Hector b Boswell	0
G. W. Francis (*Alleyn's*) c Dennison b James .	5	
J. Harvey (*Chigwell*) not out	0 – (8) c Wagh b Boswell	0
F. M. J. Costeloe (*Sherborne*) c Hodgson b James	2	
Extras	6	Extras 13

	106	(8 wkts dec.) 224

1/43 2/43 3/43 4/69 5/69
6/70 7/95 8/101 9/104

1/9 2/98 3/146
4/164 5/178 6/204
7/209 8/222

Bowling: *First Innings*—Taylor 6-0-19-1; Boswell 5-3-8-0; Dennison 6-3-19-3; Carpenter 6-2-15-0; Wagh 5-0-21-0; James 6-2-22-6. *Second Innings*—Taylor 16-5-55-0; Boswell 15-1-40-4; James 19-2-60-3; Dennison 2-0-13-0; Carpenter 11-1-36-1; Wagh 4-0-14-0.

HMC Northern Schools

L. J. Marland (*Manchester GS*) b Mason	27 – (3) c Francis b Costeloe	0
A. D. Bairstow (*Woodhouse Grove*) c Mason b Nowell .	27 – (4) not out	57
T. A. Simpson (*Eton*) c Hewson b Nowell	11 – (1) c Bucknell b Costeloe	1
*P. Hodgson (*Wellington C.*) st Francis b Mason .	7 – (2) c Francis b Nowell	11
M. A. Wagh (*King Edward's, Birmingham*) not out	4 – not out	10
*Dennison (*Royal GS, Lancaster*) c Pierce b Nowell .	1	
R. Carpenter (*Birkenhead*) not out	0	
Extras	7	Extras 7

	(5 wkts dec.) 84	(3 wkts) 86

1/56 2/66 3/79 4/79 5/83

1/1 2/1 3/32

*G. D. Hector (*Taunton*), S. A. J. Boswell (*Pocklington*), N. C. F. Taylor (*Durham*) and A. M. James (*King's, Macclesfield*) did not bat.

Bowling: *First Innings*—Costeloe 5-0-15-0; Harvey 5-1-12-0; Cawdron 5-1-18-0; Mason 12-2-24-2; Nowell 8-3-9-3. *Second Innings*—Harvey 4-1-12-0; Costeloe 4-1-14-2; Cawdron 8-1-16-0; Nowell 6-0-22-1; Mason 8-4-21-0.

ESCA NORTH v ESCA SOUTH

At St Edward's School, Oxford, July 9, 10. ESCA North won by 174 runs.

This became a one-innings match because of rain. The North proved the stronger side by far, as nearly all their batsmen played an innings of substance, especially Morris, and almost every wicket-partnership achieved something. Only Swann, in a determined innings, contributed much to the South's reply against a varied attack which included the pace of Richardson, the leg-spin of Lapsia and the slow left-armers of Taylor. Shadford, though not getting wickets on this occasion, showed his all-round potential.

ESCA North

*P. J. Wilcock (*Hopwood Hall; Lancs.*) c Hyam b Phillips . 24	S. K. Lapsia (*Stockport GS; Cheshire*) b Thorpe . 4
D. J. Shadford (*Oldham C. of T.; Lancs.*) c Platt b Phillips . 44	Q. J. Hughes (*Durham Johnston; Durham*) not out . 3
A. Singh (*King Edward's, Birmingham; Warwicks.*) lbw b Phillips . 4	N. Killeen (*Derwentside; Durham*) b Thorpe . 2
A. McGrath (*Yorkshire Martyrs; Yorks.*) c Platt b Hudson . 53	M. Taylor (*Bolton SFC; Lancs.*) run out
A. Morris (*Holgate; Yorks.*) c Platt b Phillips . 57	Extras 1
†T. Gane (*Stockport C.; Cheshire*) c Fossey b Hudson . 3	1/29 2/34 3/126 (9 wkts dec.) 30
A. Richardson (*Stafford CFE; Staffs.*) did not bat.	4/161 5/184 6/213
	7/263 8/293 9/302

Bowling: Fossey 17–2–74–0; Phillips 29–10–53–4; Batteley 6–1–15–0; Thorpe 17–3–71–2; Byrne 11–2–32–0; Dibden 9–1–30–0; Hudson 9–4–20–2.

ESCA South

*S. T. Platt (*Coundon Court; Warwicks.*) c Singh b Lapsia . 13	†B. J. Hyam (*Havering SFC; Essex*) b Richardson .
A. Swann (*Sponne; Northants*) b Richardson . 36	R. Dibden (*Barton Peveril; Hants*) lbw b Hughes . 2
D. Roberts (*Mullion; Cornwall*) c Shadford b Taylor . 1	C. Batteley (*Bromsgrove; Worcs.*) c McGrath b Lapsia .
S. Byrne (*London Oratory; London*) c Shadford b Taylor . 0	B. Phillips (*Langley Park; Kent*) not out .
D. Fossey (*Daventry SFC; Northants*) c Killeen b Hughes . 29	
P. Hudson (*Collyers SFC; Sussex*) c Killeen b Richardson . 0	Extras . . . .
G. Thorpe (*N. Warwicks CAT; Warwicks.*) c McGrath b Lapsia . 20	1/31 2/34 3/38 4/80 5/80 12 6/82 7/93 8/119 9/123

Bowling: Killeen 7–2–13–0; Shadford 8–1–32–0; Lapsia 14–6–26–3; Taylor 17–7–29–2; Richardson 9–3–18–3; Hughes 4–0–8–2.

At St John's College, Oxford, July 11. P. J. Wilcock's XI won by nine wickets. M. J. Cawdron's XI 207 for nine dec. (S. T. Platt 57, B. J. Hyam 62; R. W. Nowell four for 29); P. J. Wilcock's XI 208 for one (D. Roberts 51, A. D. Pierce 96 not out, P. J. Wilcock 3 retired hurt).

At St Edward's School, Oxford, July 11. Drawn. L. J. Marland's XI 255 for five dec. (L. J. Marland 45, A. Singh 81, S. Byrne 32, A. Morris 48; N. C. F. Taylor four for 85); T. J. Mason's XI 136 for four (G. A. Bucknell 60 not out).

At Christ Church, Oxford, July 12. MCC Schools West won by three wickets in a 12-a-side match. MCC Schools East 236 for five dec. (A. D. Bairstow 62 retired hurt, A. Singh 73, D. J. Shadford 59); MCC Schools West 237 for eight (S. T. Platt 68, A. Morris 89, M. Taylor three for 54).

MCC v MCC SCHOOLS

At Lord's, July 13. Drawn. Toss: MCC.

MCC fielded a cosmopolitan XI, led by John Barclay, with two former Test players, a Bangladesh Under-19 representative and four more with English county experience. Terry and Dracup dominated play until mid-afternoon. Terry, reaching his century just before lunch, drove more strongly than schoolboys were used to and runs might have been saved had the field been set deeper. The off-spinner Mason, bowling rather faster than one might expect, had Terry caught as he induced a collapse from 173 for two to 188 for six. Williamson and Black, however, hit strongly before the declaration after 63 overs – mindful, perhaps, that the Schools had successfully chased 216 two years earlier. Wilcock and Bairstow were in no trouble and what might have been an interesting finish was spoilt when the rain came – as predicted exactly by the weathermen – at four o'clock.

MCC

A. S. A. McEvoy c Wilcock b Killeen .	9	*J. R. T. Barclay c and b Mason	8
J. P. Terry c Nowell b Mason	113	G. R. Black not out	31
B. H. Dracup c McGrath b Shadford	32	B 2, l-b 5, n-b 1	8
D. Robinson b Mason	14		
S. Hassan b Mason	0	1/19 2/137 3/173 (6 wkts dec.) 244	
D. Williamson not out	29	4/174 5/174 6/188	

D. R. Doshi, †D. J. Goldsmith and M. E. Allbrook did not bat.

Bowling: Killeen 11–2–34–1; Phillips 10–3–39–0; Nowell 11–1–57–0; Cawdron 6–1–18–0; Mason 18–5–61–4; Shadford 7–0–28–1.

MCC Schools

P. J. Wilcock (*Hopwood Hall*) not out . .	22
A. D. Bairstow (*Woodhouse Grove*) not out . .	32
L-b 1	1

(no wkt) 55

A. McGrath (*Yorkshire Martyrs*), A. Morris (*Holgate*), *M. J. Cawdron (*Cheltenham*), D. J. Shadford (*Oldham C. of T.*), †S. T. Platt (*Coundon Court*), R. W. Nowell (*Trinity*), T. J. Mason (*Denstone*), N. Killeen (*Derwentside*) and B. Phillips (*Langley Park*) did not bat.

Bowling: Black 7–2–14–0; Robinson 4–0–30–0; Allbrook 2–0–10–0.

Umpires: R. H. Duckett and B. Wilson.

MCC SCHOOLS v NATIONAL ASSOCIATION OF YOUNG CRICKETERS

At Lord's, July 14. Abandoned. No play was possible, owing to rain.

MCC Schools

A. D. Bairstow (*Woodhouse Grove*), S. T. Platt (*Coundon Court*), A. Singh (*King Edward's, Birmingham*), D. R. Hewson (*Cheltenham*), *M. J. Cawdron (*Cheltenham*), D. J. Shadford (*Oldham C. of T.*), †B. J. Hyam (*Havering*), T. J. Mason (*Denstone*), Q. J. Hughes (*Durham Johnston*), M. Taylor (*Bolton SFC*) and S. A. J. Boswell (*Pocklington*).

National Association of Young Cricketers

J. K. Adamjee (*Notts.*), W. J. Earl (*Suffolk*), *M. H. Colclough (*Staffs.*), G. R. Treagus (*Hants*), J. D. Cokayne (*Derbys.*), S. J. Lacey (*Derbys.*), †P. J. Nicholson (*Durham*), A. N. Muggleton (*Surrey*), I. Gompertz (*Devon*), C. Brown (*Lancs.*) and N. J. Bratt (*Staffs.*).

The match between NCA Young Cricketers and Combined Services, scheduled for July 15, was abandoned.

At Dublin, July 5, 6, 7. Welsh Schools won by six wickets. Irish Schools Under-19 267 for nine dec. (R. O'Reilly 70, G. O'Mara 32, R. Eagleson 51; B. S. Phelps four for 59) and 117 for eight dec. (G. Cooke 50; Adrian J. Harries three for 24); Welsh Schools Under-19 118 (S. Jenkins 35, H. Evans 30; J. Cunningham three for 16, R. Eagleson three for 13) and 268 for four (G. Lewis 136, H. Evans 94).

At Lensbury Club, Teddington, July 19, 20. Drawn. English Schools Under-19 189 for seven (A. D. Bairstow 52, S. Platt 46, D. R. Hewson 35; Andrew Harries four for 75) and 156 for seven dec. (S. T. Platt 34, D. J. Shadford 40; Andrew Harries three for 50); Welsh Schools Under-19 136 for nine (D. J. Shadford three for 41, M. Taylor three for 28) and 139 for seven (M. J. Ennion 37, J. Chaminde 51; B. Phillips three for 15, M. Taylor four for 34).

At Abergavenny, July 27, 28, 29. Welsh Schools Under-19 won by three wickets. Scotland Young Cricketers 276 (D. W. Hodge 54, M. J. Leonard 40, D. R. Lockhart 52, C. J. Mearns 42; B. S. Phelps six for 77) and 162 (J. M. Gayfer 51, M. J. Leonard 35; Adrian J. Harries three for 50, Andrew Harries four for 22); Welsh Schools Under-19 265 (G. Lewis 88, A. Evans 86; N. Smith three for 38) and 174 for seven (S. Jenkins 60, A. Evans 34).

At Clydesdale, Glasgow, August 5, 6. Drawn, rain having ended play after the first day. English Schools Under-19 303 for six (D. R. Hewson 110, P. J. Wilcock 104, A. Singh 40; C. J. Mearns three for 91) and two for no wkt; Scotland Young Cricketers 205 for eight (J. N. Gayfer 55, C. J. Mearns 30; T. M. A. Mason three for 48, M. Taylor three for 73).

ETON v HARROW

At Lord's, June 29. Drawn. Toss: Harrow.

Eton held the advantage from the start, thanks to Machin, who scored their first century at Lord's since 1968. At lunch they were 127 without loss; Harrow's best chance had come in the seventh over when only their inept fielding prevented a run-out. Machin lost Simpson when they had put on 149 but proceeded, with gathering speed, to score 150, including 13 fours, from 193 balls over nearly four hours. It was the highest score since the fixture was reduced to one innings in 1982. Simpson immediately declared, setting a target of 255 in three hours. Harrap was run out in the third over and Chittenden caught behind off the sixth ball from Lightfoot, the spinner, who worried the batsmen so much that he did not concede a run until his fifth over. By then McIntosh had retired, felled by Douglas's pace, and the loss of Foster, their century-maker in 1992, left Harrow effectively 21 for four with Renshaw leading a fight for survival. But he batted for 130 minutes, reaching fifty just before the close, and had support from Barker and then Henson, who defended for an hour and three runs to keep Eton out.

Eton

*T. A. Simpson c Chittenden b Barker	52
H. V. Machin not out	150
C. E. Steel c Henson b Hollway	19
†O. W. R. Clayton not out	10
B 7, l-b 5, w 5, n-b 6	23

1/149 2/239   (2 wkts dec.) 254

C. G. R. Lightfoot, H. G. Duberly, J. N. P. Moffatt, T. M. A. Wemyss, N. S. Burgess, B. J. Cowen and A. F. Douglas did not bat.

Bowling: Hollway 19-1-64-1; Barker 18.1-2-84-1; Tregoning 16-5-51-0; Blake 6-0-24-0; Roundell 5-0-19-0.

Harrow

A. I. H. McIntosh retired hurt	7	S. D. Henson not out	3
N. G. Harrap run out	3		
†O. H. Chittenden c Clayton b Lightfoot	1	B 7, w 3, n-b 2	12
H. St J. R. Foster c Clayton b Douglas	6		
*J. A. J. Renshaw not out	57	1/10 2/14	(4 wkts) 114
M. P. Barker b Duberly	25	3/21 4/67	

N. W. Blake, S. F. Roundell, B. A. Hollway and G. R. Tregoning did not bat.

A. I. H. McIntosh retired hurt at 16.

Bowling: Douglas 16–6–24–1; Burgess 8–2–14–0; Lightfoot 15–9–16–1; Cowen 3–1–6–0; Duberly 6–3–11–1; Steel 4–0–26–0; Wemyss 2–1–3–0; Simpson 1–0–7–0.

Umpires: D. J. Dennis and R. Wood.

Of the 158 matches played between the two schools since 1805, Eton have won 52, Harrow 44 and 62 have been drawn. Matches during the two world wars are excluded from the reckoning. The fixture was reduced from a two-day, two-innings-a-side match to a one-day fixture in 1982. Forty-seven centuries have been scored, the highest being 183 by D. C. Boles of Eton in 1904; M. C. Bird of Harrow is the only batsman to have made two hundreds in a match, in 1907. The highest score since the First World War is 161 not out by M. K. Fosh of Harrow in 1975, Harrow's last victory. Since then Eton have won in 1977, 1985, 1990 and 1991; all other games have been drawn. A full list of centuries since 1918 and results from 1950 can be found in Wisdens prior to 1994.

HIGHLIGHTS FROM THE SCHOOLS

Despite wet weather, it was a summer for the batsmen, with 11 schoolboys passing 1,000 runs – the same number as in the record-breaking summer of 1990. I. C. Sutcliffe of Leeds GS was the most prolific with 1,623 at 101.43, followed by G. R. Treagus of King Edward's, Southampton (1,613 at 84.89), C. Clark of Durham (1,246 at 77.87), M. V. Steele of Wellingborough (1,174 at 83.85), A. D. Pierce of Lancing (1,125 at 66.17), W. Ritzema of Durham (1,124 at 62.44), J. E. Phillips of Royal GS, Worcester (1,024 at 53.89), L. J. Marland of Manchester GS (1,016 at 127.00), C. E. Mear of Kimbolton (1,007 at 50.35), R. J. Howell of Newcastle-under-Lyme (1,004 at 66.93) and J. J. Bull of Oakham (1,001 at 58.88). Treagus played the most innings with 25 and all had 20 or more except for Marland, who played just 13, and Steele with 19. Marland and Sutcliffe were two of five batsmen to record three-figure averages, the others being R. M. S. Weston of Durham, with 581 runs at 145.25 in only seven innings, N. T. Wood of William Hulme's GS, with 939 at 117.37, and G. A. Bucknell of Bryanston with 803 at 100.37.

There were two double-centuries; the highest, 208 not out from Marland, was closely followed by Ritzema's 207. In addition, 23 batsmen scored three or more hundreds, the most being eight by Sutcliffe (a rate of a hundred every three innings), six by Treagus and five by J. M. Connor for Royal GS, Worcester. Four others made four centuries, including Wood, who also averaged one every three innings.

It is perhaps not surprising, given these statistics, that the bowlers fared less well in 1993. Only 11 took 50 wickets and just two passed 60: T. J. Mason of Denstone with 63 at 11.79, and J. R. Carpenter of Birkenhead, also with 63 at 13.65. These two sent down 292 and 301 overs respectively and only M. J. Cawdron of Cheltenham needed as few as 200 overs for his 50 wickets at 10.56.

Five of the bowlers who took 30 or more wickets recorded single-figure averages. C. M. Gammell of Charterhouse Girls was the most economical with 42 at 5.02. Among the boys, I. D. Shambrook of Dartford GS led with 34 at 8.58, followed by A. J. Terrington of Exeter with 30 at 8.90, A. Sahai of Westminster with 30 at 8.96 and N. N. Bielby of Simon Langton GS with 36 at 9.38. Six bowlers took hat-tricks, of whom B. W. Gannon performed the feat twice for Abingdon. The others were M. Cassidy of Glasgow Academy, J. A. Floyd of Bishop's Stortford, S. R. Hall of Manchester GS, P. Jack of Bromsgrove and N. Stanger of Reed's. No nine-wicket returns were reported, although 12 bowlers took eight in an innings, the best figures being eight for ten by G. P. Brooks of Plymouth College.

When some schools play more than 20 matches and others fewer than 12, it is not always easy to compare all-rounders. However, two who especially caught the eye, maintaining the best averages as well as the highest totals, were Cawdron (887 runs at 73.91, 50 wickets at 10.56) and Mason (800 runs at 61.53, 63 wickets at 11.79). Of those who played in fewer than 15 matches, D. Spencer of Kingston GS collected 612 runs at 51 and 45 wickets at 13.40, while R. J. Nowell of Trinity had 597 runs at 45.92 and 51 wickets at 16.90. The winner of the Cricket Society's Wetherell Award was W. J. House of Sevenoaks, who scored 612 runs at 76.50 and took 28 wickets at 10.07.

Again it was encouraging to note the increasing fixture lists in which 27 schools played more than 20 matches, and King Edward VI, Southampton, played 27. Nineteen schools won more than half their games; Simon Langton GS won 71 per cent, with Barnard Castle and Woodhouse Grove winning 70 per cent. Woodhouse Grove were unbeaten, as were ten other sides, although in some instances the number of drawn games suggests that the unbeaten record was more the result of negative play than of a side's strength. Several schools expressed frustration at the negative attitudes of opposing sides, some of whom would bat defensively until well after tea, leaving them only a third or even a quarter of the overs in which to chase an unreasonable target. Other unbeaten sides who won more than half their matches were Abingdon, Colfe's, Eton and Oundle, while at the other end of the scale, with no victories, were Bristol GS, Christ College Brecon, Kingswood, Shiplake, Trent, Woodbridge and Wycliffe.

Many batting records and some bowling records were broken during the season; these and a number of other outstanding performances may be found in the returns from the schools which follow.

THE SCHOOLS

(Qualification: Batting 150 runs; Bowling 15 wickets)

* On name indicates captain.   * On figures indicates not out.

Note: The line for batting reads Innings–Not Outs–Runs–Highest Score–100s–Average; that for bowling reads Overs–Maidens–Runs–Wickets–Best Bowling–Average.

ABINGDON SCHOOL

Played 21: Won 14, Lost 0, Drawn 7. Abandoned 2

Master i/c: A. M. Broadbent

An excellent all-round contribution resulted in what was thought to be Abingdon's most successful season: unbeaten and victorious in 14 of 21 matches. Ben Gannon, a genuinely fast strike bowler, took hat-tricks against Berkshire Gentlemen and Old Abingdonians. He was well supported by Luke List, who also headed the batting averages, while Adam Janisch's 626 runs included five fifties in his last ten innings.

Wins v: Magdalen College S.; Oratory (twice); Reading; Henry Box, Witney; Berkshire Gentlemen; Lord Williams's, Thame; Burford; UCS, Hampstead; RGS, High Wycombe; Cherwell; Merchiston Castle; Sedbergh; South Oxfordshire Amateurs.

Batting—L. R. J. List 18–7–608–102*–1–55.27; *A. N. Janisch 19–5–626–96–0–44.71; T. C. B. Pollard 18–4–437–110*–1–31.21; A. P. Harding 15–4–299–71*–0–27.18; G. J. Horton 10–2–165–76*–0–20.62; N. J. Watts 18–1–324–44–0–19.05.

Bowling—B. W. Gannon 261.5–100–477–46–5/12–10.36; L. R. J. List 154.5–43–362–31–6/22–11.67; G. J. Horton 113–34–331–23–4/16–14.39; B. M. Fuggles 145.2–28–392–19–4/14–20.63.

ALDENHAM SCHOOL

Played 14: Won 4, Lost 6, Drawn 4

Master i/c: P. K. Smith

Wins v: UCS, Hampstead; Common Room; King William's, IoM; Liverpool.

Batting—C. A. Hill 10–6–169–52*–0–42.25; *T. J. McAllister 13–1–284–76–0–23.66; J. I. Springer 14–0–256–50–0–18.28; I. M. Hubbard 14–1–234–60*–0–18.00; A. P. Tennant 11–1–160–42–0–16.00; S. Wenzel 13–1–176–59–0–14.66.

Bowling—T. C. M. Britton 89.1–20–175–15–4/27–11.66; T. J. McAllister 90.2–15–340–15–5/24–22.66; M. R. N. Lycett 160.3–35–447–15–4/22–29.80.

ALLEYN'S SCHOOL

Played 13: Won 4, Lost 4, Drawn 5. Abandoned 1

Master i/c: S. E. Smith   Cricket professional: P. Edwards

Wins v: St John's, Leatherhead; Wilsons; Wallington; Highgate.

Batting—R. McGill 12–3–410–80*–0–45.55; *G. W. Francis 12–2–419–123*–1–41.90; B. McGill 10–1–205–69*–0–22.77; S. Z. Tabassum 10–0–223–60–0–22.30; M. H. Berglund 11–2–179–38*–0–19.88.

Bowling—J. T. Bodinetz 96.3–25–303–17–5/28–17.82; B. McGill 102–21–351–15–6/36–23.40.

ARDINGLY COLLEGE

Played 22: Won 7, Lost 6, Drawn 9

Master i/c: R. A. King   Cricket professional: G. A. Tedstone

Prominent at Ardingly were identical twins Jason and Bruce Hubbard, who have represented Sussex at tennis.

Wins v: Eastbourne; St George's, Weybridge; Seaford; Christ's Hospital; Reigate GS; Headmaster's XI; St Peter's, York.

Batting—J. Hubbard 20–1–814–112–2–42.84; J. Zang 20–4–632–93–0–39.50; B. Hubbard 18–5–407–82*–0–31.30; P. Carvalho 12–1–263–51*–0–23.90; *T. Elliott 14–5–191–57*–0–21.22; N. Kithakye 11–0–224–51–0–20.36; M. Oshitola 17–0–339–71–0–19.94; G. Best 18–3–287–45–0–19.13.

Bowling—A. Warren 179.3–42–614–25–6/32–24.56; M. Oshitola 175–32–606–24–3/35–25.25; T. Elliott 185.2–40–563–19–4/27–29.63.

ARNOLD SCHOOL

Played 19: Won 4, Lost 7, Drawn 8. Abandoned 3

Master i/c: S. Burnage   Cricket professional: J. Simmons

A highlight for a young side was a second tour of Northern Ireland.

Wins v: King Edward VII, Lytham; Belfast RA; QEGS, Blackburn; Old Arnoldians.

Batting—R. E. Parkin 17–1–383–76*–0–23.93; D. Fielding 19–2–396–69–0–23.29; M. D. Grimshaw 19–3–287–87*–0–17.93; A. L. Taylor 18–3–244–42–0–16.26; J. Gregson 18–1–269–61–0–15.82; N. Gourlay 17–0–215–51–0–12.64.

Bowling—N. Gourlay 214–50–620–27–6/32–22.96; N. Scaife 195.3–32–713–28–5/31–25.46; D. Fielding 201.4–38–722–27–5/31–26.74.

ASHVILLE COLLEGE

Played 19: Won 2, Lost 7, Drawn 10

Master i/c: J. S. Herrington

Wins v: XL Club; South Craven.

Batting—J. Cousen 19-2-433-92*-0-25.47; R. Smart 18-2-375-88*-0-23.43; S. Crebe 18-4-269-44*-0-19.21; S. Kay 18-2-309-59-0-17.31; R. Barratt 18-2-267-51-0-16.68.

Bowling—S. Creber 147-22-503-17-4/29-29.58.

BABLAKE SCHOOL

Played 17: Won 11, Lost 2, Drawn 4. Abandoned 2

Master i/c: B. J. Sutton   Cricket professional: D. J. Bar

Bablake School retained the Warwickshire Cup and inflicted a rare home defeat on RGS Worcester. They attributed their success to a penetrative attack and batting right down th order.

Wins v: RGS, Worcester; Woodlands; Loughborough GS; Wolverhampton GS; Kin, Edward's, Five Ways; Bishop Vesey's GS; King Edward's, Birmingham; Solihull Handsworth GS; King Edward's, Nuneaton; North Warwickshire C.

Batting—S. N. Smyth 12-4-223-46-0-27.87; P. W. Twiney 16-2-376-95-0-26.85 R. M. Tewkesbury 18-3-384-56-0-25.60; D. J. Keenan 15-1-358-98-0-25.57; *J. Har 14-5-195-44*-0-21.66; C. J. Gardiner 14-0-276-49-0-19.71; S. P. Arkel 13-2-155-40*-0-14.09.

Bowling—R. D. East 130.3-34-366-35-5/26-10.45; P. W. Twiney 91-15-248-22-4/27-11.27 J. Hart 120-35-229-20-4/6-11.45; W. E. Wood 112.5-20-393-33-4/23-11.90; Omar Ahma 142-26-363-23-4/13-15.78.

BANCROFT'S SCHOOL

Played 18: Won 5, Lost 3, Drawn 10

Master i/c: J. G. Bromfield   Cricket professional: J. K. Leve

Three school records were broken by C. S. Greenhill in his fourth full season. His 805 runs which improved on his own record of 705 set in 1992, took his total for the XI to 2,800 from 74 innings; the previous best was 2,554 by P. J. Carvell from 76 innings between 1945 an 1950. Greenhill's three hundreds took his tally for the XI to five, another record, althoug it was A. A. Khan who broke the individual innings record with his 130 against Ol Bancroftians. After an erratic start, Khan bowled his left-arm spin to good effect an became the leading wicket-taker. A tour to South Africa was planned for December.

Wins v: Essex Under-16; Brentwood; St Dunstan's; XL Club; Incogniti.

Batting—*C. S. Greenhill 18-9-805-121*-3-89.44; P. D. Baker 18-1-433-104*-1-25.47 A. A. Khan 17-1-394-130-1-24.62; P. Eacott 14-2-204-57*-0-17.00; P. T. Vohman 16-2-237-60*-0-16.92.

Bowling—S. M. Greenhill 95-22-237-15-5/26-15.80; E. D. Man 176-34-525-26-6/53-20.19; C. S. Greenhill 117.5-30-336-16-4/62-21.00; M. J. Ti 114-24-425-20-3/17-21.25; A. A. Khan 211.3-49-761-35-7/48-21.74.

BANGOR GRAMMAR SCHOOL

Played 18: Won 12, Lost 3, Drawn 3. Abandoned 7

Master i/c: C. C. J. Harte

The captain, Jan Cunningham, played for Ireland Under-21 and Under-19. His younger brother, Ross, is expected to take over the captaincy in 1994, while the youngest brother, Bryn, made his First XI debut and represented Ireland Under-15.

Wins v: Arnold; Ballymena Acad.; Campbell; Down HS; Friends, Lisburn; Limavady GS (twice); MCB; Munster Under-19; Royal Belfast AI; The Staff; Sullivan Upper.

Batting—M. L. Edwards 12-3-349-58-0-38.77; *J. L. Cunningham 15-4-305-83-0-27.72; W. P. McMillan 18-0-415-74-0-23.05; A. M. Hopper 16-4-240-42-0-20.00; R. C. Cunningham 12-2-158-59*-0-15.80; K. M. Miskelly 14-1-193-33-0-14.84; M. N. Scott 15-0-191-47-0-12.73.

Bowling—M. J. Williamson 94-23-210-24-6/24-8.75; C. M. Kennedy 119-19-360-30-5/19-12.00; J. W. Martin 85.4-18-274-22-5/31-12.45; S. J. Armour 105.3-35-249-17-6/26-14.64; J. L. Cunningham 125.1-27-352-18-4/4-19.55.

BARNARD CASTLE SCHOOL

Played 17: Won 12, Lost 3, Drawn 2. Abandoned 2

Master i/c: C. P. Johnson

All-round contributions and excellent team spirit resulted in a far better season than had been expected, the 12 wins including a rare victory over Durham.

Wins v: Ashville; Durham; Pocklington; Edinburgh Acad.; St Bees; Lomond; Barnard Castle CC; Durham Pilgrims; UCS, Hampstead (twice); King Edward's, Lytham; Woodbridge.

Batting—*N. R. Walker 16-6-516-100*-1-51.60; J. Benson 18-2-402-64-0-25.12; J. W. Hatch 16-1-357-53-0-23.80; S. E. W. Taylor 10-2-158-36-0-19.75; A. D. Ballantyne 15-0-199-38-0-13.26.

Bowling—A. D. Ballantyne 169.5-54-400-36-5/17-11.11; J. W. Hatch 150.2-33-377-33-4/21-11.42; J. Benson 136-34-394-26-6/58-15.15; N. R. Walker 152-34-452-28-5/48-16.14.

BEDFORD SCHOOL

Played 15: Won 4, Lost 4, Drawn 7. Abandoned 2

Master i/c: D. W. Jarrett   Cricket professional: R. G. Caple

In the last week of the season hundreds were scored by the captain M. R. Evans, the England Under-15 captain M. E. Snell and the England Under-19 rugby captain A. C. T. Gomarsall. J. A. C. Piachaud, son of the Hampshire bowler J. D. Piachaud, looked a promising off-spinner, while the wicket-keeper T. M. B. Bailey effected 30 dismissals, a third of which were stumpings.

Wins v: Rugby; Felsted; XL Club; Stowe.

Batting—*M. R. Evans 17-2-630-113-1-42.00; M. E. Snell 16-4-486-122*-1-40.50; R. M. Pape 11-6-169-34*-0-33.80; T. M. B. Bailey 15-2-435-56*-0-33.46; A. C. T. Gomarsall 16-1-496-116-1-33.06; B. Cheema 14-6-211-47-0-26.37.

Bowling—S. C. Laite 212-41-701-32-4/25-21.90; M. R. Evans 184-44-530-22-5/46-24.09; J. A. C. Piachaud 127-17-473-15-4/53-31.53.

BEDFORD MODERN SCHOOL

Played 18: Won 5, Lost 0, Drawn 13. Abandoned 3

Master i/c: N. J. Chinneck

J. R. Whitbread played some destructive innings, while B. J. Young (89) and G. S. Pilgrim (64) shared in a rapid opening partnership of 157 in a comfortable victory over Wellingborough.

Wins v: Christ's C., Cambridge; Selwyn C.; Wellingborough; Stamford; MCC.

Batting—J. R. Whitbread 18–2–634–101–1–39.62; B. J. Young 16–1–520–89–0–34.66; *G. S. Pilgrim 17–2–519–72*–0–34.60; M. J. Brownridge 17–5–316–41*–0–26.33; I. R. Chadwick 12–5–179–40–0–25.57; S. J. Robinson 10–4–152–53–0–25.33; A. G. Brown 14–1–295–71–0–22.69.

Bowling—M. J. Brownridge 214–51–533–26–6/34–20.50; N. T. Wildman 222–38–739–34–6/104–21.73; B. J. Young 120–26–445–16–3/7–27.81.

BEECHEN CLIFF SCHOOL

Played 10: Won 5, Lost 0, Drawn 5. Abandoned 3

Master i/c: K. J. L. Mabe   Cricket professional: P. J. Colbourne

One highlight in an unbeaten season was the successful pursuit of 265 to beat MCC by one wicket off the last ball. Another was the school record unbeaten 178 off 83 balls, with ten sixes, hit by Darren Barnes against St Wilfred's, Blackburn, in his last innings for the XI.

Wins v: Kingswood; Dauntsey's; Wells Cathedral S.; St Wilfred's, Blackburn; MCC.

Batting—D. M. Barnes 8–1–351–178*–1–50.14; N. J. Bursell 5–0–237–75–0–47.40; B. R. Staunton 10–3–254–73*–0–36.28.

Bowling—N. G. Priscott 81–22–337–22–6/14–15.31; M. J. Prentice 98.4–22–278–18–4/10–15.44.

BERKHAMSTED SCHOOL

Played 15: Won 6, Lost 6, Drawn 3

Master i/c: J. G. Tolchard   Cricket professional: M. Herring

The XI won the Cowell Trophy at their festival, in which the guests were Framlingham, Kimbolton, Monmouth and Winchester.

Wins v: Mill Hill; Framlingham; Aldenham; Monmouth; Magdalen College S.; Kimbolton.

Batting—N. A. Wolstenholme 15–2–682–114–2–52.46; J. A. Crowther 15–2–355–55–0–27.30; *D. T. L. Pountney 13–3–267–44–0–26.70; B. A. King 15–1–357–120*–1–25.50; R. D. Mackintosh 11–0–181–51–0–16.45.

Bowling—E. N. Tolchard 95.1–13–404–18–5/19–22.44; N. A. Reed 150.2–23–492–19–5/25–25.89.

BETHANY SCHOOL

Played 13: Won 4, Lost 4, Drawn 5. Abandoned 2

Master i/c: P. Norgrove   Cricket professional: G. Campbell

Wins v: Harvey GS; City of London Freeman's; Ewell Castle; Rochester Clergy.

Batting—*G. R. Newell 10–3–467–89–0–66.71; A. Owen 13–2–369–82–0–33.54; F. Sadiqeen 12–2–214–50–0–21.40; B. Chater 13–1–254–59*–0–21.16.

Bowling—G. R. Newell 116.4–26–319–27–7/23–11.81; F. Sadiqeen 121.5–28–398–26–3/16–15.30; M. Roche 132–22–441–16–5/23–27.56.

BIRKENHEAD SCHOOL

Played 19: Won 8, Lost 5, Drawn 6

Master i/c: P. A. Whittel   Cricket professional: G. Rennie

Wins v: Ellesmere; Ormskirk GS; Wirral GS; Manchester GS; William Hulme's GS; Liverpool C; King's, Chester; Foyle and Londonderry.

Batting—*J. R. Carpenter 19–2–688–104*–1–40.47; Z. R. Feather 14–2–469–79–0–39.08; J. G. Boumphrey 13–3–377–100*–2–37.70; E. J. N. Roberts 16–0–432–84–0–27.00; E. J. Clarke 17–4–308–38–0–23.69; P. L. Higgins 16–0–240–43–0–15.00.

Bowling—J. R. Carpenter 301–75–860–63–7/30–13.65; A. B. Birley 147–39–336–21–5/28–16.00; Z. R. Feather 138–25–422–23–5/38–18.34.

BISHOP'S STORTFORD COLLEGE

Played 21: Won 9, Lost 1, Drawn 11. Abandoned 1

Master i/c: D. A. Hopper   Cricket professional: C. S. Bannister

Nine victories equalled the school record, but rain frustrated efforts to add the elusive tenth. The side's strength was their batting: seven times they successfully chased a target. Ian Bateman was a positive captain, always prepared to risk defeat, and made a significant all-round contribution, his century against The Perse being especially dominant. In the match against The Leys, James Lamb scored 158 not out and leg-spinner Julian Floyd took four wickets in five balls, including the side's first hat-trick since the war. Tim Laverack took three in four balls to frustrate Framlingham's victory bid.

Wins v: Brentwood; Aldenham; St Edmund's, Ware; Berkhamsted; XL Club; Chigwell; The Perse; Wrekin; Bromsgrove.

Batting—J. D. Lamb 22–2–946–158*–2–47.30; *I. M. Bateman 18–1–698–113–1–41.05; R. M. Webb 20–6–559–67–0–39.92; J. A. Floyd 18–6–440–68–0–36.66; J. S. W. Toombs 21–1–352–54–0–17.60; W. E. Ayres 17–5–162–33*–0–13.50.

Bowling—M. Bashford 190–56–422–32–6/39–13.18; I. M. Bateman 112–25–343–22–4/23–15.59; T. E. Laverack 267.2–51–823–39–7/46–21.10; P. R. Stoddart 104.2–20–321–15–5/25–21.40; S. J. C. Fishpool 111.4–19–450–15–4/87–30.00; J. A. Floyd 228–48–697–20–6/65–34.85.

BLOXHAM SCHOOL

Played 17: Won 5, Lost 3, Drawn 9. Abandoned 1

Master i/c: J. P. Horton

Wins v: St Bartholomew's, Newbury; Dean Close; Magdalen College S.; Rendcomb; South Oxfordshire Amateurs.

Batting—O. R. Cripps 14–8–221–51*–0–36.83; A. R. Hurst 17–2–508–153*–1–33.86; M. D. Belcher 16–1–368–64*–0–24.53; *A. J. R. Hicks 17–3–324–57–0–23.14; R. S. Tarrant 16–3–287–52–0–22.07; A. A. Adejumo 16–1–259–47–0–17.26; C. W. Huntingford 14–0–237–64–0–16.92.

Bowling—M. D. Belcher 130.3–35–372–23–4/33–16.17; I. A. R. Adams 151.1–38–448–21–5/27–21.33; A. J. R. Hicks 114–19–438–20–5/71–21.90; P. R. Arber 184–22–733–23–3/24–31.86; G. J. Jones 160.2–30–592–15–2/23–39.46.

BLUNDELL'S SCHOOL

Played 17: Won 6, Lost 3, Drawn 8. Abandoned 1

Master i/c: R. F. Harriott   Cricket professional: N. A. Folland

Although unable to repeat their record of 1992, when they were undefeated by schools, the side were satisfied with their season. Ian Gompertz took the honours in a strong batting line-up, his score of 156 against Plymouth College being a highlight. Rafe Clifford-Jones and James Stormonth put on 210 unbroken for the fourth wicket in the festival game against Canford, whose final pair held on for a draw. Stormonth again headed the bowling averages, with 39 wickets to add to his 41 in 1992. He was ably supported by the pace of Tam Blair and spin of Peter Beale. Gompertz was selected to play for NAYC at Lord's and represented Devon.

Wins v: Exeter; Royal Marines; Wellington S.; Taunton; Sherborne; Ampleforth.

Batting—I. Gompertz 15–1–753–156–2–53.78; R. Clifford-Jones 15–4–583–115–2–53.00; I. Bransdon 14–2–464–111–1–38.66; J. Stormonth 14–3–297–93*–0–27.00; E. Dorey 16–1–345–56*–0–23.00; G. Vaughan 10–2–157–32*–0–19.62.

Bowling—J. Stormonth 169.1–28–634–39–6/34–16.25; T. Blair 136.2–29–431–26–5/38–16.57; P. Beale 95–13–347–18–4/61–19.27; I. Gompertz 110–24–324–16–4/23–20.25.

BRADFIELD COLLEGE

Played 15: Won 4, Lost 3, Drawn 8. Abandoned 1

Master i/c: F. R. Dethridge   Cricket professional: J. F. Harvey

The batting averages were headed by A. W. Mence, son of M. D. Mence of Warwickshire and Gloucestershire.

Wins v: Charterhouse; Stowe; Oratory; St Edward's, Oxford.

Batting—A. W. Mence 10–1–225–70*–0–25.00; D. S. R. Robinson 11–3–195–31–0–24.37; C. S. Williams 14–1–278–72–0–21.38; E. A. Petter 14–0–277–73–0–19.78; A. M. Parkinson 14–2–222–57–0–18.50; T. P. Dellor 15–1–214–80–0–15.28.

Bowling—T. P. Dellor 68.5–10–244–15–5/44–16.26; A. C. Murray 100–22–306–15–6/22–20.40; E. J. Kendall 177.4–50–473–22–4/29–21.50; A. M. Parkinson 142.2–25–447–17–4/40–26.29.

BRADFORD GRAMMAR SCHOOL

Played 24: Won 3, Lost 5, Drawn 16

Master i/c: A. G. Smith

A young XI saw two records broken: M. J. Anderson's aggregate of 897, including nine fifties, was a best for the school, as was his opening partnership of 190 unbroken with S. E. P. Davies in the ten-wicket victory over RGS, Lancaster.

Wins v: Silcoates; RGS, Lancaster; Parents XI.

Batting—M. J. Anderson 23–2–897–93–0–42.71; *A. J. Brosnan 23–3–783–110*–1–39.15; S. E. P. Davies 24–3–674–86*–0–32.09; D. J. Groom 20–3–354–48–0–20.82; S. A. Marshall 23–2–394–46–0–18.76; A. J. Myers 15–4–195–57–0–17.72; J. R. I. McIntosh 19–2–211–64–0–12.41.

Bowling—A. J. Myers 222.5–57–731–31–7/61–23.58; D. C. Illingworth 207.3–40–772–31–5/61–24.90; G. S. Kinvig 173.2–30–631–24–4/83–26.29; J. R. Cockcroft 194.3–29–817–22–4/38–37.13.

BRENTWOOD SCHOOL

Played 18: Won 4, Lost 4, Drawn 10

Master i/c: B. R. Hardie

Wins v: Royal Anglian Regiment; Old Brentwoods (twice); Brentwood '79.

Batting—*J. E. B. Vereker 17–2–437–65*–0–29.13; B. Weller 17–1–358–85*–0–22.37; T. M. Witney 17–0–323–87–0–19.00; A. K. Amin 13–3–189–66–0–18.90; B. J. Tappin 15–3–183–59–0–15.25.

*Bowling—*L. D. Waite 237.1–65–630–28–4/16–22.50; N. C. Ellis-Calcott 91–14–358–15–3/36–23.86; J. E. B. Vereker 198.3–37–713–22–5/74–32.40; B. J. Tappin 207.1–49–692–19–2/42–36.42.

BRIGHTON COLLEGE

Played 22: Won 8, Lost 5, Drawn 9

Master i/c: J. Spencer   Cricket professional: J. D. Morley

A season of fluctuating fortunes included a run of five consecutive wins against schools mid-term. Clare Connor became the first girl to command a regular place in the First XI.

Wins v: Common Room; Worth; Whitgift; Ardingly; Portsmouth GS; Eastbourne; Ipswich; Edinburgh Acad.

*Batting—*M. N. Dovey 21–0–752–108–1–35.80; A. D. King 21–1–604–98–0–30.20; E. S. Hart 21–4–436–95*–0–25.64; A. R. Bidwell 20–2–395–74–0–21.94; G. F. Hudson 17–4–277–59*–0–21.30; S. E. Green 15–4–159–70–0–14.45; P. E. Fokes 17–2–181–28–0–12.06.

*Bowling—*E. S. Hart 199–41–559–41–6/43–13.63; Miss C. J. Connor 89–11–304–17–4/33–17.88; R. A. Stoner 148.1–23–474–25–4/12–18.96; P. E. Fokes 173.5–34–541–21–3/28–25.76; T. A. G. Middleton 187.2–18–703–27–6/42–26.03.

BRISTOL GRAMMAR SCHOOL

Played 14: Won 0, Lost 6, Drawn 8. Abandoned 3

Master i/c: K. Blackburn

Batting—*S. Meredith 14–1–505–87–0–38.84; M. Sutherland 13–0–291–83–0–22.38; R. Coe 12–0–236–48–0–19.66; S. Eastman 11–1–170–40–0–17.00; G. Axson 13–0–220–55–0–16.92.

*Bowling—*A. Mitchell 157.4–26–564–24–4/53–23.50.

BROMSGROVE SCHOOL

Played 17: Won 5, Lost 4, Drawn 8

Master i/c: P. Newman

A hat-trick by P. Jack was instrumental in the long-awaited victory over MCC.

Wins v: Dean Close; Wrekin; Bromsgrove Martlets; MCC; Stamford.

*Batting—*W. Glover 15–3–627–86–0–52.25; S. Davis 14–2–401–111–3–33.41; P. Hoy 12–1–346–93–0–31.45; A. Haji 13–2–245–81*–0–22.27; E. Sawtell 8–0–177–57–0–22.12; G. Davies 14–2–262–50–0–21.83; M. Eckersley 13–2–210–62*–0–19.09.

*Bowling—*P. Jack 158.1–23–584–29–4/37–20.13; C. Battelley 209.4–47–621–28–4/33–22.17; T. Davis 130.1–18–452–19–4/17–23.78.

BRYANSTON SCHOOL

Played 12: Won 4, Lost 0, Drawn 8. Abandoned 3

Master i/c: T. J. Hill

Guy Bucknell's three centuries took him past 3,000 runs in First XI and Under-19 schools representative cricket. Against Canford, Bryanston were reduced to 11 for five before Richard White (140 not out) held the innings together, being joined by Joe Cooke (33) in a record unbroken ninth-wicket stand of 131. Declaring at 201 for eight, Bryanston then dismissed Canford for 175 with ten overs to spare. The side came eighth in the Sir Garfield Sobers Tournament in Barbados, where Charlie Austin captained the English Schools' Festival side to victory over the West Indies Festival side.

Wins v: XL Club; Canford; Free Foresters; Milton Abbey.

Batting—G. A. Bucknell 11–3–803–135–3–100.37; R. J. White 5–1–176–140*–1–44.00; R. J. Hannon 11–4–199–68*–0–28.42; R. J. Wagstaffe 12–0–334–83–0–27.83; E. O. G. Hunt 10–1–226–81*–0–25.11; T. C. Z. Lamb 12–1–253–54–0–23.00.

Bowling—T. P. W. Brunner 120.4–32–310–19–4/55–16.31; *C. F. Austin 149.5–37–421–21–4/43–20.04; M. W. Davis 162–25–596–26–3/46–22.92.

CAMPBELL COLLEGE

Played 15: Won 9, Lost 2, Drawn 4

Master i/c: E. T. Cooke

Wins v: Ballymena Acad.; Coleraine AI; Regent House; Down High; King William's, IOM; Solihull; Dungannon Royal; Royal Belfast AI; Methodist C.

Batting—R. H. Lucas 14–5–515–82*–0–57.22; A. E. Logan 14–1–443–72*–0–34.07; S. D. Hughes 14–0–211–53–0–15.07.

Bowling—S. R. J. Flanagan 117–27–271–26–6/8–10.42; N. J. Brown 105–11–300–28–5/17–10.71; R. H. Lucas 74–11–239–17–6/18–14.05.

CANFORD SCHOOL

Played 17: Won 3, Lost 5, Drawn 9. Abandoned 2

Master i/c: S. J. Turrill   Cricket professional: J. J. E. Hardy

A highlight in a disappointing season was an innings of 122 not out by Richard Blacker against a strong Uppingham side at the Blundell's Festival.

Wins v: Milton Abbey; XL Club; King's, Bruton.

Batting—G. P. A. Herring 14–3–350–63–0–31.81; T. W. Cutler 16–1–470–57–0–31.33; R. C. H. Blacker 14–2–364–122*–1–30.33; S. J. Neal 17–1–410–53–0–25.62; M. B. G. Oliver 15–2–218–81*–0–16.76.

Bowling—G. P. A. Herring 93.2–15–303–17–4/0–17.82; *W. R. S. White-Cooper 176.4–31–521–28–5/23–18.60; T. W. Cutler 199.3–46–563–28–4/13–20.10; A. C. Major 201–40–710–16–4/60–44.37.

CATERHAM SCHOOL

Played 16: Won 7, Lost 5, Drawn 4. Abandoned 1

Master i/c: A. G. Tapp   Cricket professional: Wasim Raja

Wins v: Reed's; Alleyn's; King's, Rochester; Christ's Hospital; Whitgift; Kingston GS; Radford C., Canberra.

Batting—D. Sales 13–5–647–125*–2–80.87; *G. Owen 14–2–587–115*–1–48.91; J. Winter 15–3–358–83*–0–29.83; J. Coppin 13–0–232–48–0–17.84.

Bowling—D. Sales 127–32–409–27–4/14–15.14; K. Barton 234.3–58–766–30–4/49–25.53.

CHARTERHOUSE (BOYS)
Played 22: Won 2, Lost 8, Drawn 12

Master i/c: J. M. Knight

Cricket professional: R. V. Lewis

Wins v: Grasshoppers; Winchester.

Batting—G. H. Tassell 23–3–716–87*–0–35.80; *L. J. Webb 23–0–769–125–1–33.43; A. R. Younie 23–0–588–126–1–25.56; J. O. A. Willson 14–1–320–45–0–24.61; M. C. Goodwin 12–0–215–39–0–17.91; B. I. Wakeham 22–2–356–46–0–17.80; M. A. Souter 17–6–185–50–0–16.81.

Bowling—M. A. Souter 181.3–32–590–37–5/16–15.94; G. A. Ladenburg 202–33–691–26–6/42–26.57; W. M. J. Rowlandson 124–22–479–15–4/51–31.93; J. O. A. Willson 147–23–514–15–2/18–34.26.

CHARTERHOUSE (GIRLS)
Played 10: Won 6, Lost 3, Drawn 1. Abandoned 1

Mistress i/c: Mrs F. C. Noble

Cricket professional: R. V. Lewis

The side won the Emma Durden-Smith/Camilla Heazell Challenge Trophy for the third successive season. AnnaLisa Williams and Caroline Gammell broke school records for batting and bowling respectively.

Wins v: Bromsgrove; St Bede's; Dunottar; Cranleigh; Wellington; Verites.

Batting—A. B. Williams 9–1–165–54–0–20.62.

Bowling—C. M. Gammell 94–18–211–42–7/15–5.02; S. J. Lawrence 53.3–8–135–16–4/10–8.43.

CHELTENHAM COLLEGE
Played 19: Won 13, Lost 3, Drawn 3

Master i/c: M. W. Stovold

Cricket professional: G. Brown

In what was probably their best season ever, the XI won 13 of their 19 matches, many by significant margins. The captain, M. J. Cawdron, was outstanding with 887 runs and 50 wickets. He hit 135 not out against Dean Close, 120 against Rendcomb and 175 against Radley. This last included 27 boundaries and was the highest for the college since the war. D. E. A. Lawrence was almost as prolific and the pair featured in two notable opening partnerships: 282 against Rendcomb, including 200 before lunch, and what is believed to be a record of 294 against Radley, 259 coming before lunch. Both Cawdron and D. R. Hewson played for Gloucestershire Second XI, English Schools and MCC Schools, with Cawdron captaining the schools sides.

Wins v: Dean Close; Rendcomb; Malvern; Radley; Pate's GS; Rugby; Repton; Bishop's, Cape Town; Shrewsbury; St Edward's, Oxford; Sherborne; Marlborough; Haileybury.

Batting—*M. J. Cawdron 17–5–887–175–3–73.91; D. E. A. Lawrence 19–3–812–145*–2–50.75; D. R. Hewson 17–7–463–67*–0–46.30; A. J. Hingston 10–3–160–48–0–22.85; T. E. Phillips 14–3–213–77*–0–19.36.

Bowling—M. J. Cawdron 200–52–528–50–7/58–10.56; M. E. Snape 105.3–33–230–21–5/9–10.95; A. J. Hingston 166–42–409–34–6/17–12.02; E. T. Miles 94.1–17–382–16–5/29–23.87.

CHIGWELL SCHOOL

Played 16: Won 4, Lost 4, Drawn 8. Abandoned 5

Master i/c: D. N. Morrison

Cricket professional: F. A. Griffith

Wins v: Brentwood; Forest; St Edmund's, Ware; William Hulme's GS.

Batting—I. J. Harvey 7–1–369–135*–1–61.50; *G. Offen 15–1–755–115–1–53.92; I. R. Mufti 11–4–188–57*–0–26.85; S. Malhan 13–1–184–42*–0–15.33; A. D. Mandrekar 14–3–158–35*–0–14.36; J. S. Healy 13–2–150–57*–0–13.63.

Bowling—I. J. Harvey 98.4–22–262–25–8/27–10.48; S. Malhan 172.3–28–560–22–4/18–25.45.

CHRIST COLLEGE, BRECON

Played 15: Won 0, Lost 9, Drawn 6. Abandoned 2

Master i/c: C. W. Kleiser

Cricket professional: S. R. Barwick

The side suffered a second successive season with no wins, creating an unenviable record for the captain, Robert Strawbridge. In fact, 1993 was considered even more disappointing than 1992, for they never once reached a winning position. With talent in evidence lower down the school, the future looks brighter.

Batting—G. A. R. Davies 14–1–354–58*–0–27.23; *R. Strawbridge 14–0–304–85–0–21.71; D. Lally 14–1–278–54–0–21.38; D. Bartlett 15–2–194–39*–0–14.92.

Bowling—D. Bartlett 181.3–43–550–28–4/28–19.64.

CHRIST'S HOSPITAL

Played 13: Won 3, Lost 6, Drawn 4. Abandoned 2

Master i/c: H. Holdsworth

Cricket professionals: K. G. Suttle and P. J. Graves

Wins v: Worth; Worthing SFC; Alberton HS, Transvaal.

Batting—*R. Howard 12–1–277–56–0–25.18; T. Smith 13–1–278–49–0–23.16; J. A. Cordner 13–0–267–56–0–20.53; J. Edwards 12–1–160–42–0–14.54.

Bowling—R. Howard 104–32–286–17–5/13–16.82; A. Walker 139.4–30–489–22–5/42–22.22.

CLIFTON COLLEGE

Played 18: Won 9, Lost 2, Drawn 7

Master i/c: C. M. E. Colquhoun

Cricket professional: F. J. Andrew

With the emphasis on entertaining and positive cricket, the college won a record nine matches. They owed much to James Kirtley, an outstanding fast bowler who played for Sussex Second XI and whose tally of 59 wickets for the college was a post-war record. Few opponents could cope with his pace and many sides failed to total 120, which somewhat restricted opportunities for the Clifton batsmen. Gareth Rees, the Welsh Schools and Glamorgan Second XI representative, was the most prolific, while Philip Hosegood also impressed and sound support came from Rupert Swetman, son of the former England wicket-keeper, Roy Swetman.

Wins v: Colston's; Malvern; Blundell's; King's, Bruton; Taunton; Monmouth; Rugby; Clifton CC; Free Foresters.

Batting—G. H. J. Rees 18–2–788–112–1–49.25; P. J. Hosegood 17–4–544–127*–2–41.84; R. W. Swetman 13–3–373–103*–1–37.30; D. J. R. England 18–6–311–55–0–25.91; A. J. C. Turner 10–2–195–45*–0–24.37; A. N. Baker 13–3–179–38–0–17.90.

Bowling—*R. J. Kirtley 228.5–55–618–59–8/35–10.47; A. N. Baker 126.4–32–354–25–6/71–14.16; B. R. Harris 73–12–248–15–5/40–16.53.

COLFE'S SCHOOL

Played 14: Won 8, Lost 0, Drawn 6. Abandoned 2

Master i/c: D. P. H. Meadows

A highlight for the unbeaten Colfe's XI was the match against Trinity in which Paul Thompson followed an innings of 117 not out with a return of six for 25.

Wins v: Wilson's; Kingston GS; Trinity; Alleyn's; Eltham; Hampton; XL Club; Watson's XI.

Batting—S. Groves 14-3-456-90-0-41.45; P. Thompson 13-1-429-117*-1-35.75; *P. Scott 14-5-267-53*-0-29.66; J. Butterfill 12-0-223-76-0-18.58; M. Quilter 11-0-179-63-0-16.27.

Bowling—P. Scott 187.2-51-500-40-6/61-12.50; P. Gaston 148.2-48-402-27-7/49-14.88; C. Battarbee 147-34-398-16-5/19-24.87.

COLSTON'S COLLEGIATE SCHOOL

Played 20: Won 9, Lost 3, Drawn 8. Abandoned 2

Masters i/c: M. P. B. Tayler and A. J. Palmer

Christopher Taylor's 900 runs, the most by a Colston's fifth-former, were instrumental in the side's record nine wins. Against the XL Club, Taylor and Alexander Nicholls opened with 261, which was the best by the school for any wicket.

Wins v: Dauntsey's; King Edward's, Bath; Christ's C., Brecon; Monmouth; Wycliffe; Merchant Venturers' XI; Balliol C.; Hutton GS; William Hulme's GS.

Batting—C. G. Taylor 20-4-900-141-3-56.25; A. J. C. Bell 15-2-389-89-0-29.92; *J. Barnes 17-3-359-69-0-25.64; D. S. C. Bell 18-2-390-101*-1-24.37; M. J. Baldwin 13-3-240-67-0-24.00; A. R. Nicholls 18-1-407-114-2-23.94; C. P. Wyatt 12-3-206-65-0-22.88.

Bowling—M. J. Wherlock 111.1-21-334-21-4/30-15.90; A. J. C. Bell 84-20-274-15-4/20-18.26; C. G. Taylor 157-36-482-20-4/48-24.10; D. S. C. Bell 131.1-21-460-19-3/48-24.21; R. M. Bryan 126.3-25-451-16-3/59-28.18.

CRANBROOK SCHOOL

Played 20: Won 9, Lost 4, Drawn 7. Abandoned 1

Master i/c: A. J. Presnell

Wins v: Shebbear (twice); Grenville; Cowley; Harvey GS; Maidstone GS; Gravesend GS; Incogniti; Kent C.

Batting—*J. Steed 16-2-465-83-0-33.21; P. Brenchley 16-2-419-88*-0-29.92; N. Byrom 16-2-384-55-0-27.42; T. Piper 17-1-331-54-0-20.68.

Bowling—B. Trajett 106-40-236-21-5/3-11.23; S. Draker 194-56-451-38-6/16-11.86; W. Souter 195-48-499-41-5/37-12.17; J. Steed 124-21-401-28-5/22-14.32.

CRANLEIGH SCHOOL

Played 18: Won 5, Lost 1, Drawn 12. Abandoned 2

Master i/c: D. C. Williams

Wins v: Charterhouse; Eastbourne; St John's; Kings, Canterbury; XL Club.

Batting—N. J. G. Read 18–4–795–136*–1–56.78; A. Riva 18–4–476–82–0–34.00; A. N. Price 16–4–368–75*–0–30.66; P. C. Butcher 12–2–220–61–0–22.00; C. E. J. Oliver 18–0–341–56–0–18.94; S. J. S. Hilton 13–3–182–55–0–18.20; G. A. N. Brown 17–2–255–69–0–17.00.

Bowling—N. J. G. Read 171.2–35–515–28–7/50–18.39; A. N. Price 260.4–75–786–33–6/44–23.81; K. Akram 143.2–28–508–18–4/19–28.22; T. W. P. Evans 199.3–41–567–20–5/95–28.35.

CULFORD SCHOOL

Played 12: Won 2, Lost 4, Drawn 6. Abandoned 1

Master i/c: R. P. Shepperson

Wins v: Gentlemen of Suffolk; Old Culfordians.

R. W. Pineo 12–3–322–77–0–35.77; J. J. W. Sallis 12–1–357–113*–1–32.45; I. C. Eneli 7–1–165–78–0–27.50; B. R. Lindley 10–0–193–61–0–19.30.

Bowling—R. W. Pineo 103.2–20–266–19–3/15–14.00; G. A. Ornbo 115.5–29–350–18–5/52–19.44; M. J. White 98.3–11–430–15–4/72–28.66.

DARTFORD GRAMMAR SCHOOL

Played 22: Won 11, Lost 2, Drawn 9

Masters i/c: C. J. Plummer and G. T. Prout

Wins v: Rochester MS; Oakwood Park GS; Langley Park (twice); Campion; Judd; XL Club; St George's; BETH; St Olave's GS; Staff XI.

Batting—J. J. Snowden 14–1–470–100–1–36.15; K. M. Ring 20–2–487–84–0–27.05; *D. M. Rye 21–2–504–67–0–26.52; I. D. Shambrook 16–6–211–41*–0–21.10; M. J. Dixon 16–2–281–100*–1–20.07; A. D. Bowers 15–2–177–31–0–13.61; S. J. Pollard 18–1–211–34*–0–12.41.

Bowling—I. D. Shambrook 116.4–28–292–34–5/21–8.58; J. J. Snowden 77–20–226–16–4/24–14.12; J. H. Moore 64.5–6–346–20–4/38–17.30; L. P. Jeffs 127.2–18–413–19–5/40–21.73.

DAUNTSEY'S SCHOOL

Played 12: Won 5, Lost 4, Drawn 3

Master i/c: D. C. R. Baker   Cricket professional: P. Knowles.

Wins v: King Edward's, Bath; XL Club; DCRB XI; Trinity; Old Dauntseians XI.

Batting—A. Darbyshire 11–3–367–108*–1–45.87; J. Thornton 12–1–486–92*–0–44.18; J. Gaiger 12–0–251–58–0–20.91; M. Gauguier 11–0–152–32–0–13.81.

Bowling—A. Darbyshire 120.3–36–330–29–5/22–11.37.

DEAN CLOSE SCHOOL

Played 14: Won 3, Lost 7, Drawn 4. Abandoned 2

Master i/c: C. M. Kenyon   Cricket professional: S. Hansford.

Highlights for a young side were the dismissal of Monmouth for 95 and the match against Pate's GS, in which Ben Hyde brought up his century with the winning hit off the last ball.

Wins v: Pate's GS; Staff Common Room; Wycliffe.

Batting—*B. M. Hyde 11–2–300–100*–1–33.33; L. M. Simmonds 14–0–422–97–0–30.14; C. S. Olliver 9–0–216–87–0–24.00; S. H. Kenworthy 10–0–191–76–0–19.10.

*Bowling—*T. N. Johnson 94–15–278–18–5/20–15.44.

DENSTONE COLLEGE (BOYS)

Played 20: Won 7, Lost 0, Drawn 13. Abandoned 4

Master i/c: A. N. James

Century partnerships abounded at Denstone for whom T. O. Kemp's aggregate of 914 runs was a college record and T. J. Mason was their best all-rounder of all time with 800 runs and 63 wickets (off-spin). These two put on 166 against Tettenhall and 156 against Worksop, while Mason shared in 149 unbroken with R. J. Davies against an Old Denstonian side containing J. N. Snape of Northamptonshire. The highest stand, though, was 176 for the first wicket against Wrekin between Kemp and the Nottinghamshire Under-16 representative, R. W. J. Howitt—just one of their eight half-century opening partnerships, three of which were extended to three figures. Mason went on to play for Leicestershire Second XI, English Schools and MCC Schools.

Wins v: Newcastle-under-Lyme; Worksop; Old Swinford Hospital S.; King Edward VI, Aston; Magdalen College S.; MCC; Tettenhall.

Batting—*T. J. Mason 19–6–800–103–2–61.53; T. O. Kemp 19–3–914–108–1–57.12; R. J. Davies 11–6–160–49*–0–32.00; R. W. J. Howitt 19–0–553–62–0–29.10; P. A. Handford 16–5–308–89*–0–28.00; D. J. O'Keefe 11–3–153–38–0–19.12.

Bowling— T. J. Mason 292–88–743–63–7/61–11.79; A. T. Griffin 141–34–484–21–4/29–23.04; J. A. J. Cure 153.5–30–537–19–3/21–28.26.

DENSTONE COLLEGE (GIRLS)

Played 8: Won 6, Lost 2, Drawn 0. Abandoned 2

Mistress i/c: Miss J. R. Morris

Wins v: Charterhouse; Sevenoaks; Tunbridge Wells; Moreton Hall; Malvern; Repton.

*Batting—*K. M. Grandfield 7–4–157–64*–0–52.33.

Bowling—*A. L. Bennett 50.3–10–130–24–7/11–5.41; K. M. Grandfield 61.2–12–149–22–5/7–6.77.

DOUAI SCHOOL

Played 12: Won 2, Lost 3, Drawn 7. Abandoned 1

Master i/c: J. Shaw

Wins v: Berkshire Gentlemen; Cokethorpe.

*Batting—*O. Scott 11–5–236–68–0–39.33; *R. Leach 11–0–289–68–0–26.27; D. McClement 11–2–184–74–0–20.44; J. Wicks 11–2–175–39–0–19.44; C. Nicoll 11–1–193–38–0–19.30.

*Bowling—*R. Leach 82.5–5–322–18–5/48–17.88.

DOVER COLLEGE

Played 15: Won 5, Lost 5, Drawn 5. Abandoned 1

Master i/c: D. C. Butler

A young well-balanced side recorded the most victories since 1984, including one over King's, Rochester, who subsided from 118 for two to 131 all out in pursuit of 146. They were undone by Matthew Craig (fast-medium), who took four for seven, including three wickets in four balls and a spell of four for one, and Dion Sessford (slow left-arm), who returned three for five. Adam Sims completed two seasons in the XI with a tally of 1,045 runs.

Wins v: Kent C; King's, Rochester; Chatham House GS; Dover CC; XL Club.

Batting—A. N. Sims 13–0–496–83–0–38.15; M. T. Telford 14–2–342–75*–0–28.50; *A. M. F. Sambucci 15–0–360–52–0–24.00; A. J. T. Stanley 15–2–207–39*–0–15.92; R. T. P. Chappell 14–1–174–48–0–13.38.

Bowling—R. T. P. Chappell 115.3–19–420–24–5/60–17.50; M. G. Craig 129–22–352–15–4/20–23.46; D. J. L. Sessford 297–64–827–31–7/36–26.67.

DOWNSIDE SCHOOL

Played 17: Won 1, Lost 7, Drawn 9

Master i/c: K. J. M. Burke   Cricket professional: B. Bing

Win v: Downside Wanderers.

Batting—M. G. F. Walker 17–3–547–81*–0–39.07; C. P. Reid 12–2–242–51–0–24.20; *J. P. Burke 17–1–324–75–0–20.25; J. W. J. Hynes 13–1–203–44–0–16.91; W. B. J. Mostyn 11–1–163–58–0–16.30; C. H. McEwen 14–1–175–28–0–13.46.

Bowling—T. F. Molony 141.1–24–450–26–6/31–17.30; M. G. F. Walker 144.2–28–449–17–3/8–26.41; C. P. Reid 199–42–564–21–3/14–26.85; M. A. Melough 127–12–547–15–3/51–36.46.

DUKE OF YORK'S ROYAL MILITARY SCHOOL

Played 14: Won 1, Lost 3, Drawn 10. Abandoned 2

Master i/c: S. Salisbury   Cricket professional: M. Garnaut

Win v: St Augustine's.

Batting—E. J. Budd 11–1–354–72–0–35.40; J. J. Stones 12–0–254–59–0–21.16; *C. M. G. Pollock 12–1–209–61–0–19.00; R. J. J. Martindale 13–2–175–48–0–15.90.

Bowling—E. J. Budd 56.4–8–182–18–4/22–10.11; R. J. J. Martindale 144–29–432–27–6/11–16.00; J. J. Stones 127–36–372–19–3/36–19.57.

DURHAM SCHOOL

Played 20: Won 13, Lost 1, Drawn 6. Abandoned 1

Master i/c: N. J. Willings   Cricket professional: M. Hirsch

The school's finest XI yet won a record 13 matches, including the first seven of the season. They scored 200 on 16 occasions, 300 three times and lost only on a very poor wicket at Barnard Castle, where they were bowled out for an uncharacteristic 78. At the request of the county club, Robin Weston played only in mid-week matches, which gave Chris Clark and Wayne Ritzema the opportunity to shine—and they did, with 1,246 and 1,124 runs respectively and seven century opening partnerships. The highest of these was 340 against the Old Dunelmians (Ritzema 207, Clark 120 not out). Clark hit five hundreds and Ritzema three, including one of only two double-centuries reported in *Wisden*; Weston, in his seven appearances, played two three-figure innings, and averaged 145.25. As well as representing the county side, Weston played for England Under-18. With Clark and Ritzema returning and plenty of younger talent coming through, prospects are excellent.

Wins v: Giggleswick; Hild/Bede; Ampleforth; MCC; Sedbergh; Dame Allan's; Pocklington; New C.; Old Dunelmians XI; Rossall; St Bees; Young Waratahs; President's XI.

Batting—R. M. S. Weston 7–3–581–146–2–145.25; C. Clark 20–4–1,246–141*–5–77.87; W. Ritzema 20–2–1,124–207–3–62.44; J. B. Windows 13–5–310–55–0–38.75; J. W. M. Taylor 17–6–409–92–0–37.18.

Bowling—J. W. M. Taylor 165.1–45–415–33–6/25–12.57; J. B. Windows 101.3–28–289–20–4/17–14.45; J. H. C. Bailey 85–22–316–19–4/14–16.63; N. C. F. Taylor 213–72–490–27–5/34–18.14; M. Coates 117–28–456–16–4/41–28.50.

EASTBOURNE COLLEGE

Played 20: Won 6, Lost 8, Drawn 6

Master i/c: N. L. Wheeler   Cricket professional: J. N. Shepherd

A. J. H. Bogdanovski, nephew of P. H. Edmonds, was the outstanding all-rounder on whom the young, inexperienced side relied heavily. He was well supported with the bat by T. J. White and C. J. Bott, who shared in an unbeaten stand of 162 in the seven-wicket win over Tonbridge.

Wins v: Tonbridge; Worth; Cranbrook; Sussex Martlets; Stragglers of Asia; Victoria C., Jersey.

Batting—T. J. White 20–3–603–96–0–35.47; A. J. H. Bogdanovski 20–1–661–102–1–34.78; C. J. Bott 19–2–565–87*–0–33.23; C. J. Dyer 15–4–208–35–0–18.90; A. S. Wood 15–5–166–26*–0–16.60; C. J. H. Baker 16–0–215–35–0–13.43; I. P. Sands 18–1–227–51*–0–13.35.

Bowling—*O. J. Kayes 204.5–54–609–26–5/45–23.42; A. J. H. Bogdanovski 181.2–21–734–25–3/77–29.36; C. J. A. Dawson 197.5–32–760–19–4/45–40.00.

THE EDINBURGH ACADEMY

Played 15: Won 4, Lost 5, Drawn 6. Abandoned 6

Master i/c: G. R. Bowe

Wins v: George Watson's; Kelvinside Acad.; Fettes; Rector's XI.

Batting—J. S. D. Moffat 14–1–316–66–0–24.30; A. S. Eaton 13–1–286–58*–0–23.83; *R. E. Boyd 15–1–328–85–0–23.42; J. A. K. Macleod 14–0–316–77–0–22.57; P. A. T. G. Rutherford 13–3–221–69–0–22.10.

Bowling—J. A. K. Macleod 164–38–485–27–7/24–17.96; J. S. D. Moffat 99.4–26–326–17–5/39–19.17.

ELIZABETH COLLEGE, GUERNSEY

Played 22: Won 9, Lost 2, Drawn 11. Abandoned 2

Master i/c: M. E. Kinder

The side's strength lay in their batting and ability to chase totals in excess of 200. Simon Beck's total of 808 runs was the highest in recent years, while Stephen Pitt made an outstanding all-round contribution with 678 runs and 43 wickets.

Wins v: Old Elizabethans; King Edward VI, Southampton; Lord Wandsworth; GICC; GCA; Bodicote; Police CC; Occasionals (London); Second XI.

Batting—S. A. Beck 18–1–808–124–2–47.52; S. R. Pitt 17–1–678–115–2–42.37; R. J. Newbould 18–5–428–63–0–32.92; W. D. Martel 16–7–236–35*–0–26.22; T. M. Carey 17–4–321–105*–1–24.69; J. M. Arnold 10–0–203–53–0–20.30; S. J. Fooks 12–2–176–69*–0–17.60.

Bowling—S. R. Pitt 237–44–737–43–6/49–17.13; R. J. Newbould 174–35–562–32–5/47–17.56; T. J. Martel 97.4–11–456–21–4/59–21.71.

ELLESMERE COLLEGE

Played 17: Won 3, Lost 8, Drawn 6. Abandoned 1

Master i/c: E. Marsh   Cricket professional: R. G. Mapp

Matthew Gillison broke three college records: his aggregate of 987 surpassed his own 770 in 1992, his four centuries were the most in a season for the College, and his 154 against Bloxham was the highest by an Ellesmere batsman.

Wins v: King's, Macclesfield; Bloxham; MCC.

Batting—*M. E. Gillison 15–1–987–154–4–70.50; T. J. Downes 16–1–285–81–0–19.00; T. A. M. E. Benzie 11–2–160–47–0–17.77; J. P. Terry 16–0–275–45–0–17.18; T. F. Stewart 14–3–156–53–0–14.18.

Bowling—P. R. Harper 147–32–474–23–5/31–20.60; J. R. C. Maddocks 126–29–410–15–5/25–27.33; T. F. Stewart 152–11–590–19–4/50–31.05.

ELTHAM COLLEGE

Played 19: Won 5, Lost 4, Drawn 10. Abandoned 1

Masters i/c: P. McCartney and   Cricket professionals: R. W. Hills and
B. Withecombe   R. Winup

Wins v: Bancroft's; St Olave's; Thomas Tallis; Old Elthamians; Newington C., Australia.

Batting—T. W. Barwick 19–4–546–68–0–36.40; T. B. Beames 16–5–277–52*–0–25.18; *G. P. Martin 17–0–366–89–0–21.52; J. D. Nicholls 15–1–247–73–0–17.64; J. M. Bensted 19–1–304–37–0–16.88.

Bowling—J. M. Bensted 137.1–38–368–21–4/23–17.52; B. P. Cartwright 202.3–45–670–35–7/17–19.14; D. J. Hadley 97.3–9–394–15–4/30–26.26; T. B. Beames 158.4–18–570–15–4/59–38.00.

EMANUEL SCHOOL

Played 18: Won 7, Lost 4, Drawn 7. Abandoned 1

Master i/c: J. R. Cremer

In the match against John Fisher, Tim Seaton scored 127 not out and, bowling medium pace, took five wickets for six runs.

Wins v: Tiffin; Latymer Upper; John Fisher; Esher; Rutlish; Richmond; Masters XI.

Batting—T. Seaton 18–3–580–127*–1–38.66; N. Deshpande 18–1–568–107–1–33.41; D. Darriba 20–1–430–47*–0–23.84; *R. Young 18–1–394–93–0–23.17; R. Pharoah 15–1–297–68–0–21.21.

Bowling—S. Dillsworth 140.2–40–367–32–5/13–11.46; T. Seaton 155.3–39–393–31–5/6–12.67; R. Pharoah 96–23–229–15–3/15–15.26; D. Darriba 179.3–43–496–22–4/10–22.54; C. Astwood 131.4–15–532–17–5/39–31.29.

ENFIELD GRAMMAR SCHOOL

Played 23: Won 3, Lost 2, Drawn 18. Abandoned 1

Master i/c: J. J. Conroy

Wins v: John Lyon; Enfield CC; Verulam.

Batting—L. Beskeen 21–6–586–108–1–39.06; A. Laraman 19–2–472–83–0–27.76; J. Barbe 20–1–379–71–0–19.94; P. Honnor 12–3–159–36–0–17.66; D. Evans 21–2–287–50–0–15.10.

Bowling—R. Baker 135.1–28–399–31–5/36–12.87; M. Nicholls 116–18–349–22–5/29–15.86; J. Mitchell 134.5–26–450–27–5/23–16.66; L. Beskeen 149.3–29–473–26–5/17–18.19; S. Berryman 163.5–29–508–23–5/28–22.08.

EPSOM COLLEGE

Played 11: Won 3, Lost 2, Drawn 6

Master i/c: M. D. Hobbs

Wins v: MCC; Old Epsomians; Eastbourne.

Batting—N. F. Harris 10–1–354–104*–1–39.33; N. S. F. Wherry 10–4–224–58–0–37.33; A. R. Harris 10–3–203–107*–1–29.00; J. D. Relleen 11–1–185–27–0–18.50; Z. Zainudin 10–0–179–35–0–17.90; M. J. Stacey 10–0–157–37–0–15.70.

Bowling—N. S. F. Wherry 145.3–29–468–29–5/33–16.13; J. D. Bushell 104–12–454–16–5/63–28.37.

ETON COLLEGE

Played 17: Won 9, Lost 0, Drawn 8

Master i/c: J. A. Claughton   Cricket professional: J. M. Rice

The record of nine won, none lost went one better than the previous best of nine won, one lost set in 1991. Tom Simpson played a significant role as captain and a consistent batsman; he and his opening partner, Hugo Machin, put on 149 against Harrow and 240 against Radford College, Canberra. Machin's last four innings were 150 not out and 132 in those two matches respectively, plus another two half-centuries as Eton retained the Silk Trophy at Radley.

Wins v: St Edward's, Oxford; I Zingari; Marlborough; Northamptonshire Under-19; Winchester; Tonbridge; Radford C., Canberra; Radley; Shrewsbury.

Batting—*T. A. Simpson 17–1–835–105–1–52.18; H. V. Machin 17–3–660–150*–2–47.14; O. W. R. Clayton 14–6–209–31–0–26.12; C. G. R. Lightfoot 12–4–180–55–0–22.50; C. E. Steel 16–5–235–59*–0–21.36.

Bowling—H. G. Duberly 54–11–169–15–3/6–11.26; N. S. Burgess 167–31–421–27–3/15–15.59; C. G. R. Lightfoot 289.5–92–629–40–6/23–15.72; A. F. Douglas 235–68–479–30–4/22–15.96; B. J. Cowen 128–28–357–15–3/16–23.80.

EXETER SCHOOL

Played 16: Won 7, Lost 3, Drawn 6. Abandoned 4

Master i/c: M. C. Wilcock

Wins v: Kelly C.; Taunton; Exeter St James CC; Queen's, Taunton; Sidmouth CC; Wells Cathedral S.; Herefordshire CA XI.

Batting—A. O. F. Le Fleming 11–2–594–134*–1–66.00; J. D. Evennett 12–4–313–102–1–39.12; J. P. Janion 10–5–181–51*–0–36.20; M. H. Price 10–3–218–58*–0–31.14; S. R. Irvin 8–2–180–65–0–30.00; D. R. Rosslee 11–2–266–86–0–29.55; B. S. Richards 13–3–278–57*–0–27.80; *R. J. Moody 12–2–169–57–0–16.90.

Bowling—A. J. Terrington 117–38–267–30–7/34–8.90; J. D. Evennett 153.2–40–405–36–5/39–11.25; A. O. F. Le Fleming 99.1–28–266–20–8/51–13.30.

FELSTED SCHOOL

Played 16: Won 5, Lost 4, Drawn 7. Abandoned 1

Master i/c: F. C. Hayes   Cricket professional: G. O. Barker

A young side boasted all-round strength. G. J. A. Goodwin (left-arm spin) played for Essex Second XI, Essex Under-19 and Under-16, where he was joined by E. J. Wilson and 14-year-old R. F. C. Hayes, son of the England player F. C. Hayes.

Wins v: RGS, Colchester; Bishop's Stortford; Merchant Taylors', Northwood; Ipswich; Gentlemen of Essex.

Batting—S. D. Wild 16-1-523-80*-0-34.86; E. J. Wilson 17-2-514-59*-0-34.26; J. D. G. Goodwin 17-1-518-80*-0-32.37; J. P. Ward 16-0-404-69-0-25.25; *S. Edwards 14-4-215-51*-0-21.50; R. F. C. Hayes 10-1-167-26-0-18.55; J. C. Forrester 13-2-162-24-0-14.72; J. J. H. Ward 15-2-176-58-0-13.53.

Bowling—G. J. A. Goodwin 288.3-89-764-37-6/40-20.64; B. J. Coward-Talbott 173-36-505-23-4/39-21.95; J. A. Crafford 157.2-33-479-20-5/70-23.95; S. Edwards 146.1-34-498-19-4/48-26.21.

FETTES COLLEGE

Played 13: Won 1, Lost 10, Drawn 2. Abandoned 2

Master i/c: C. H. Carruthers — Cricket professional: J. van Geloven

Win v: Stewart's Melville.

Batting—A. I. F. Nelson 12-1-186-55-0-16.90; *T. F. White 14-0-171-26-0-12.21.

Bowling—T. F. White 185.4-41-479-30-5/28-15.96; A. I. F. Nelson 146-35-387-23-4/25-16.82; I. E. G. Forbes 138-29-397-19-3/47-20.89.

FOREST SCHOOL

Played 17: Won 6, Lost 2, Drawn 9. Abandoned 3

Master i/c: S. Turner

Steady rather than outstanding performances resulted in a better season than had been expected, in which the side won six matches and had the advantage in five of the draws.

Wins v: Gentlemen of Essex; Ilford CHS; Essex Under-16; Wellingborough; Ipswich; Culford.

Batting—*S. Moss 17-1-475-98*-0-29.68; N. Sims 17-0-474-59-0-27.88; G. Kilby 14-6-190-65*-0-23.75; J. McKay 13-2-261-62-0-23.72; W. Rogers 13-4-202-42-0-22.44; D. Pratt 16-1-296-66-0-19.73; M. Butler 16-0-305-51-0-19.06.

Bowling—D. Pratt 207-49-521-27-5/31-19.29; W. Rogers 135.4-24-441-20-4/31-22.05; D. Ducat 146.5-28-578-19-4/58-30.42.

FOYLE AND LONDONDERRY COLLEGE

Played 15: Won 8, Lost 5, Drawn 2

Masters i/c: G. McCarter and I. McCracken

Wins v: Ballymena Acad.; St Johnston; Strabane; Belfast HS; Friends; Limavady GS; Ruthin; Wirral.

Batting—J. Torrens 16-4-501-70-0-41.75; A. M. G. Henderson 15-1-204-79-0-14.57; L. A. C. Lindsay 15-0-174-31-0-11.60.

Bowling—A. M. G. Henderson 92-11-260-27-5/16-9.62; B. Galbraith 128-35-287-29-7/33-9.89; *A. Tosh 86-21-230-18-4/22-12.77; J. Torrens 134-33-298-22-5/15-13.54.

FRAMLINGHAM COLLEGE

Played 16: Won 8, Lost 4, Drawn 4. Abandoned 1

Master i/c: P. J. Hayes   Cricket professional: C. Rutterford

Ashley Cowan (140 not out) and Jonathan Phillips (73 not out) put on 232 unbroken in 28 overs to beat St Joseph's, Ipswich. Against Woodbridge, Cowan, who headed both averages, took five for seven as the opposition were tumbled out for just 35.

Wins v: St Joseph's, Ipswich; Colchester; Old Framlinghamians; Royal Anglian Regiment; Woodbridge; Gentlemen of Suffolk; Winchester; Kimbolton.

Batting—*A. P. Cowan 10–2–595–140*–1–74.37; J. H. Phillips 15–3–511–85–0–42.58; J. H. Pearl 12–3–302–85–0–33.55; W. D. Buck 11–4–156–59*–0–22.28; J. R. Roberts 13–1–235–65–0–19.58; D. M. Vipond 12–2–162–49–0–16.20.

Bowling—A. P. Cowan 120.1–38–325–27–8/42–12.03; B. A. Emblin 147.3–27–422–20–4/68–21.10; W. D. Buck 183–47–583–18–3/62–32.38.

GIGGLESWICK SCHOOL

Played 12: Won 6, Lost 2, Drawn 4. Abandoned 2

Master i/c: C. Green   Cricket professional: S. Pearce

Wins v: St Bees; Ashville; Old Giggleswickians; Gestingthorpe CC; XL Club; R. C. Green's XI.

Batting—S. J. Nesbitt 11–0–260–74–0–23.63; S. J. Taylor 10–2–186–47–0–23.25; J. A. E. Caton 12–1–251–84–0–22.81; *O. J. B. Jackson 12–1–173–43–0–15.72.

Bowling—S. J. Nesbitt 107–15–278–22–5/46–12.63; J. B. Savage 111–25–295–18–3/23–16.38; O. J. B. Jackson 107–14–432–24–6/49–18.00; S. J. Taylor 96–11–329–18–5/50–18.27.

THE GLASGOW ACADEMY

Played 10: Won 5, Lost 2, Drawn 3. Abandoned 4

Master i/c: J. Pawson   Cricket professional: V. Hariharan

M. Cassidy's four five-wicket returns in eight matches included a hat-trick in figures of six for 13 against George Watson's. He also broke the 43-year-old school record for throwing the cricket ball with a throw of 94.80 metres. D. R. Lockhart, who scored an unbeaten century against Morrison's Academy, was selected for Scotland Under-19.

Wins v: Glasgow HS; Morrison's Acad.; Hutcheson's GS; George Watson's; Glasgow Acad. FP XI.

Batting—*D. R. Lockhart 8–4–396–100*–1–99.00.

Bowling—M. Cassidy 86–23–212–26–6/13–8.15; J. Graham 103.3–15–233–24–5/11–9.70.

GLENALMOND

Played 10: Won 2, Lost 5, Drawn 3

Master i/c: J. D. Bassett   Cricket professional: Piyush Kharkha

A highlight was the match against Dollar Academy who were dismissed for 27 in reply to 77 for five declared, J. I. M. Gully returning six for 15 and A. K. P. Young taking four for eight.

Wins v: Strathallan; Dollar Acad.

Batting—J. Gibbs 9–2–172–66*–0–24.57; *J. I. M. Gully 11–0–184–41–0–16.72.

Bowling—J. I. M. Gully 147.5–36–386–30–6/15–12.86; A. K. P. Young 39–25–371–25–4/8–14.84.

GORDONSTOUN SCHOOL

Played 10: Won 3, Lost 3, Drawn 4, Abandoned 2

Master i/c: C. J. Barton

Some excellent cricket was played by the young side, who did not allow themselves to be discouraged by Morayshire's wettest season for 50 years.

Wins v: Robert Gordon's; XL Club; Headmaster's XI.

Batting—S. A. Walton 10–1–257–76*–0–28.55; R. Dhar 10–2–202–58*–0–25.25.

Bowling—B. G. Clarke 91–22–219–25–5/45–8.76; J. L. Shrago 96–18–353–25–6/36–14.12.

GRENVILLE COLLEGE

Played 8: Won 3, Lost 3, Drawn 2, Abandoned 2

Master i/c: C. R. Beechey

Wins v: Gremlins; North Devon CC; Braunton.

Batting—J. P. Eyer 8–1–281–80–0–40.14.

Bowling—D. Hooper 56.4–12–182–16–5/61–11.37; J. P. Eyer 70–7–212–18–5/28–11.77.

GRESHAM'S SCHOOL

Played 16: Won 3, Lost 7, Drawn 6, Abandoned 1

Master i/c: A. M. Ponder

Wins v: Wymondham; Culford; King Edward VII.

Batting—B. J. Threlfall 16–2–589–111–1–42.07; *S. E. Child 16–2–531–109–1–37.92; J. Arnold 15–1–238–69–0–17.00; G. Marsom 13–2–187–50–0–17.00; D. Jackson 13–1–202–43*–0–16.83.

Bowling—T. Puce 104–22–288–19–4/16–15.15; D. Jackson 181.2–33–600–38–7/37–15.78.

HABERDASHERS' ASKE'S SCHOOL

Played 16: Won 6, Lost 1, Drawn 9, Abandoned 3

Masters i/c: S. D. Charlwood and D. I. Yeabsley

The captain, Chris Harris, completed four years in the XI with a total of 1,862 runs (a record in recent years) and 77 wickets.

Wins v: Queen Elizabeth, Barnet; Berkhamsted; Gents of Herts; UCS, Hampstead; Merchant Taylors', Northwood; Beacon House GS, Pakistan.

Batting—*C. V. Harris 14–4–748–105–1–74.80; N. J. Fielden 16–2–489–118*–1–34.92; S. J. Liddle 12–0–328–101–1–27.33; S. F. Byrne 12–3–215–73–0–23.88; N. J. Wes 13–3–212–67*–0–21.20; G. I. Smart 11–1–156–42–0–15.60.

Bowling—D. R. Bernard 130.4–27–387–26–5/42–14.88; C. V. Harri 96.5–22–293–19–4/42–15.42; S. J. Liddle 184.4–45–511–29–4/6–17.62; N. J. Wes 166–45–460–17–2/17–27.05.

HAILEYBURY

Played 18: Won 1, Lost 7, Drawn 10

Master i/c: M. S. Seymour

Cricket professional: P. M. Ellis

Win v: Westminster.

Batting—P. A. Bhatia 11–3–532–79*–0–66.50; A. S. Lewis 18–1–549–104*–1–32.29; G. B. J. Mitchell 19–1–441–100*–1–24.50; R. E. Walker 15–1–297–77*–0–21.21; P. D. Stafford 17–1–324–59–0–20.25.

Bowling—*M. D. Fettes 174–45–485–17–4/39–28.52; R. E. Walker 223–59–683–23–5/41–29.69.

HAMPTON SCHOOL

Played 20: Won 6, Lost 3, Drawn 11

Master i/c: A. J. Cook

Cricket professional: P. Farbrace

A match-winning 129 not out from M. P. Hall against MCC early in the season inspired a young and inexperienced XI. They went on to win five more, the most memorable being the successful pursuit of 253 off the last ball against Latymer. T. J. Green took 41 wickets in his first season and A. C. King, who had not passed six in his two previous seasons, found the consistency to score 618 runs as well as taking 29 wickets.

Wins v: MCC; Latymer; RGS, Guildford; Headmaster's XI; King Edward VI, Southampton; Adullamites.

Batting—*A. C. King 19–3–618–105–1–38.62; M. P. Hall 18–1–647–129*–1–38.05; A. S. Barnes 15–3–419–96–0–34.91; J. Dave 18–1–481–63–0–28.29; A. T. Pagnamenta 10–3–172–46*–0–24.57; T. J. Green 15–5–226–59*–0–22.60; M. J. Templeman 17–0–203–62–0–11.94.

Bowling—T. J. Green 212–42–730–41–5/34–17.80; S. M. O. Evans 206–35–675–26–5/29–25.96; A. C. King 238.3–56–896–29–5/63–30.89.

HARROW SCHOOL

Played 15: Won 3, Lost 3, Drawn 9. Abandoned 1

Master i/c: W. Snowden

Cricket professional: R. K. Sethi

Wins v: Haileybury; Diocesan C., Cape Town; MCC.

Batting—N. W. Blake 11–5–331–70*–0–55.16; H. St J. R. Foster 14–2–472–73–0–39.33; M. P. Barker 11–2–253–53–0–28.11; O. H. Chittenden 7–0–169–71–0–24.14; N. G. Harrap 15–0–250–59–0–16.66.

Bowling—G. R. Tregoning 190.2–55–478–24–7/19–19.91; B. A. Hollway 75–40–506–24–5/29–21.08; N. W. Blake 104–15–354–16–6/28–22.12; M. P. Barker 182.3–33–592–19–3/30–31.15.

THE HARVEY GRAMMAR SCHOOL

Played 21: Won 5, Lost 3, Drawn 13

Master i/c: P. J. Harding

The captain, L. Stone, was dominant, with 577 runs and 51 wickets.

Wins v: Homewood; Dover GS; Duke of York's Military S.; XL Club; Morebath CC.

Batting—*L. Stone 17–4–577–95–0–44.38; J. Hughes 20–1–400–67–0–21.05; J. Smith 19–2–348–45–0–20.47; D. R. Himsworth 18–5–249–51–0–19.15; E. Johnson 19–3–302–72*–0–18.87.

Bowling—L. Stone 251.3–68–683–51–5/21–13.39; J. Mabberley 50–5–203–15–6/20–13.53; J. Wood 173.4–48–522–22–4/14–23.72.

HEREFORD CATHEDRAL SCHOOL

Played 16: Won 7, Lost 6, Drawn 3

Master i/c: A. Connop

Wins v: King's, Gloucester; Llandovery; King's, Worcester; Christ C., Brecon; XL Club; Bristol Cathedral S.; Herefordshire Gents.

Batting—B. J. P. Albright 13–2–495–102*–1–45.00; D. F. Kings 15–1–389–103–1–27.78; T. I. Hall 14–3–239–54–0–21.72; J. C. Andrews 16–2–301–60–0–21.50; *S. E. Albright 14–0–251–65–0–17.92; N. C. Creaser 14–2–159–24*–0–13.25.

Bowling—J. Butlin 118.2–28–316–19–6/36–16.63; D. F. Kings 165.5–42–503–22–4/15–22.86; J. L. Rees 150.5–32–487–19–6/25–25.63; S. E. Albright 150.5–29–568–17–4/46–33.41.

HIGHGATE SCHOOL

Played 16: Won 4, Lost 6, Drawn 6

Masters i/c: R. J. Davis and R. G. W. Marsh   Cricket professional: R. E. Jones

The unbroken partnership of 204 between M. J. Robinson (145*) and T. O. Jenkins (82*) against the XL Club was a school record.

Wins v: Latymer; Christ C., Finchley; Trinity GS, Sydney; Incogniti.

Batting—*M. J. Robinson 14–1–529–145*–2–40.69; T. O. Jenkins 15–3–302–82*–0–25.16; G. J. A. Chapman 14–1–229–63–0–17.61.

Bowling—T. O. Jenkins 86–12–346–15–4/68–23.06; M. J. Robinson 111–12–420–15–3/9–28.00.

HURSTPIERPOINT COLLEGE

Played 21: Won 14, Lost 2, Drawn 5. Abandoned 1

Master i/c: M. E. Allbrook   Cricket professional: D. J. Semmence

The most successful season in their 144-year history saw the XI win a record 14 matches, three more than the previous best. Justin Bates stood out with 911 runs and 31 wickets, bowling off-breaks, while Simon Cross captained the side with panache as well as scoring prolifically.

Wins v: Ardingly; Seaford (twice); Old Boys; Worth; Brighton; Whitgift; St John's, Leatherhead; Reigate GS; MCC; Bishop's, Cape Town; Ellesmere; Bloxham; Worksop.

Batting—J. J. Bates 20–2–911–100–1–50.61; *S. J. Cross 20–2–737–129–1–40.94; A. D. Earl 17–3–558–77–0–39.85; N. J. Jenkin 14–9–168–51*–0–33.60; R. E. L. Willsdon 20–1–430–83–0–22.63; J. E. R. Paterson 18–3–303–49–0–20.20; S. P. May 17–6–193–49–0–17.54.

Bowling—J. E. R. Paterson 243–50–692–33–5/22–20.96; J. J. Bates 226.4–48–736–31–5/21–23.74; L. J. Atkins 236.1–44–744–31–6/34–24.00; A. C. Scoones 100–16–416–17–2/17–24.47; E. R. Power 134–14–521–18–3/43–28.94.

IPSWICH SCHOOL

Played 16: Won 3, Lost 6, Drawn 7. Abandoned 1

Master i/c: A. K. Golding   Cricket professional: R. E. East

Wins v: Gresham's; Old Ipswichians; Edinburgh Acad.

Batting—A. Prabhakar 13–2–497–111–1–45.18; B. Maddison 14–0–456–104–1–32.57; R. Robinson 16–1–450–73–0–30.00; *D. Douglas 17–1–373–49–0–23.31; G. McCartney 17–0–330–42–0–19.41; J. Lear 13–2–204–38–0–18.54.

Bowling—R. Robinson 228–46–610–38–7/46–16.05; J. East 100–26–297–16–3/30–18.56; N. Maper 172–42–511–21–5/48–24.33.

ISLEWORTH AND SYON SCHOOL

Played 16: Won 9, Lost 4, Drawn 3

Master i/c: B. A. Goldsby

Thirteen-year-old O. A. Shah showed exceptional talent, scoring five fifties in ten innings and heading the batting averages.

Wins v: Longford; Hampton XI; Ealing C.; Glyn; Preston Manor; Latymer Upper; Heathland; Christ's C.; Lampton.

Batting—O. A. Shah 10–1–367–87–0–40.77; B. M. Goldsby 13–2–223–65*–0–20.27; H. Ally 13–2–219–50*–0–19.90; *S. I. Tailor 12–0–218–40–0–18.16; O. Ghaffar 12–1–159–40–0–14.45.

Bowling—B. M. Goldsby 93.5–16–371–21–4/13–17.66; M. I. Tailor 93.4–12–307–15–4/31–20.46.

KELLY COLLEGE

Played 11: Won 3, Lost 2, Drawn 6

Master i/c: G. C. L. Cooper

Wins v: Shebbear; Allhallows; Truro.

Batting—*D. S. Edwards 9–3–247–66*–0–41.16; J. G. Evans 10–1–299–134*–1–33.22; J. L. Rove 9–2–207–77–0–29.57; D. A. Parnwell 10–2–197–59–0–24.62.

Bowling—J. M. Rowan 162–30–469–33–6/31–14.21; J. L. Rove 109–17–332–17–5/45–19.52.

KIMBOLTON SCHOOL

Played 22: Won 7, Lost 9, Drawn 6. Abandoned 2

Master i/c: R. P. Merriman   Cricket professional: M. E. Latham

Prepared to risk defeat in pursuit of victory, the XI achieved a positive result in 16 of their 22 matches, many of which were extremely close. The captain, Charles Mear, led by example, creating a school record with 1,007 runs at an average of 50.35.

Wins v: R. P. Merriman's XI; XL Club; Old Kimboltonians; Gentlemen of Bedfordshire; Wisbech GS; Leicestershire CCC Club & Ground XI; Monmouth.

Batting—*C. E. Mear 22–2–1,007–110–1–50.35; A. J. Scott 16–0–530–101–1–33.12; R. J. Caswell 20–7–356–71–0–27.38; D. R. Ford 18–1–368–59*–0–21.64; P. S. Pippard 18–5–266–47*–0–20.46; J. P. Latham 21–2–361–54–0–19.00; R. K. Kanani 18–1–241–34–0–14.17.

Bowling—J. P. Latham 280.3–42–989–41–5/37–24.12; R. K. Kanani 171–32–594–22–4/24–27.00; J. C. R. Follett 219.4–31–818–22–4/58–37.18.

KING EDWARD VI COLLEGE, STOURBRIDGE

Played 14: Won 4, Lost 2, Drawn 8. Abandoned 4

Master i/c: R. A. Williams

The victory over Wyggeston & Queen Elizabeth I SFC was memorable for the contribution of the wicket-keeper, M. J. Porter: he followed a maiden century with two catches and four stumpings.

Wins v: Worcester SFC; King Henry VIII, Coventry; Wyggeston & Queen Elizabeth I SFC; Worcestershire Under-15.

Batting—M. J. Porter 12–2–284–100*–1–28.40; R. J. Parker 11–0–226–57–0–20.54; D. R. Vaux 10–0–204–39–0–20.40; H. A. Williams 13–3–204–50*–0–20.40; J. D. Cutler 12–0–188–61–0–15.66.

Bowling—R. J. Young 86.4–21–189–17–5/12–11.11; H. A. Williams 94.4–20–282–19–4/9–14.84; C. P. W. Jonkers 106.3–25–272–15–3/24–18.13.

KING EDWARD VI SCHOOL, SOUTHAMPTON

Played 27: Won 9, Lost 6, Drawn 12. Abandoned 5

Master i/c: R. J. Putt

Glyn Treagus was again outstanding and finished with five school records to his name. His season's total of 1,613 passed the previous record of 1,188 by Mark O'Connor in 1984, while his tally of 3,329 for the XI similarly improved upon O'Connor's 2,534. He hit six hundreds – 100, 130, 134 not out, 112 not out, 128 not out and 115 – the three biggest of which were all higher than the previous best and the second, third and fourth were in consecutive innings. He also featured in the XI's highest partnership of 238 unbroken against Lord Wandsworth, with David Wickes, who made 83 not out. Continuing his excellence in the field, Treagus held 24 catches for the First XI – the most by a non-wicket-keeper. He played for NAYC, Hampshire Under-19 and captained Hampshire and West of England Schools.

Wins v: Cricklade; Peter Symonds; Taunton's C.; Brockenhurst; Barton Peveril; Winchester; Portsmouth GS; Old Edwardians; Staff XI.

Batting—*G. R. Treagus 25–6–1,613–134*–6–84.89; M. Holden 23–2–495–56*–0–23.57; D. J. Wickes 14–1–297–83*–0–22.84; R. E. Harris 13–1–272–75–0–22.66; J. P. Atkins 19–3–315–59*–0–19.68; D. J. Mansbridge 13–1–215–34–0–17.91; T. R. Osman 21–1–293–44–0–14.65.

Bowling—A. J. Hill 119.1–23–433–25–5/44–17.32; A. K. Parkinson 159.2–24–578–32–6/35–18.06; G. R. Treagus 189.4–41–598–32–5/25–18.68; E. T. A. Freeman 228–58–674–26–4/38–25.92; S. J. Andrews 115.4–20–423–16–4/27–26.43; A. R. Grapes 204.5–52–599–21–5/38–28.52.

KING EDWARD VII SCHOOL, LYTHAM

Played 15: Won 5, Lost 4, Drawn 6

Master i/c: A. Crowther

Wins v: Habergham; Silcoates; Kirkham GS; UCS, Hampstead; Woodbridge.

Batting—*G. D. Maitland 15–3–787–118*–2–65.58; D. J. Tomlinson 15–4–326–67*–0–29.63; R. J. Macauley 14–3–276–85–0–25.09; P. Kay 13–0–240–74–0–18.46.

Bowling—D. J. Tomlinson 240.5–64–620–35–7/45–17.71; M. J. Eastham 106–12–398–18–5/41–22.11; R. J. Thomas 108.3–12–437–16–3/15–27.31.

KING EDWARD'S SCHOOL, BIRMINGHAM

Played 24: Won 8, Lost 5, Drawn 11. Abandoned 1

Master i/c: M. D. Stead   Cricket professional: D. A. Houghton

A. Singh made the highest post-war score of 153 against Denstone, totalling 787 runs and taking 47 wickets. He scored three hundreds altogether, as did M. A. Wagh, who, with N. M. Lineham, gave notable all-round support. Singh was selected for MCC Schools and with Wagh, played for Warwickshire Second XI.

Wins v: Warwickshire CA XI; Shrewsbury; Warwick; Repton; Pocklington; Old Edwardians Association; King Edward VI, Aston; Hereford Cathedral S.

Batting—M. A. Wagh 19–5–794–114*–3–56.71; A. Singh 17–3–787–153–3–56.21; *N. M. Linehan 20–6–692–96–0–49.42; C. D. J. Taylor 19–1–260–44–0–14.44; M. S. Kazi 20–2–183–25–0–10.16; T. Robinson 18–2–152–27–0–9.50.

Bowling—A. Singh 226.5–50–709–47–7/42–15.08; N. M. Linehan 265.5–60–694– 34–6/47–20.41; M. A. Wagh 258.3–70–739–33–5/21–22.39; N. A. Bovaird 148–21–558–20–5/46–27.90.

KING HENRY VIII SCHOOL, COVENTRY

Played 15: Won 3, Lost 3, Drawn 9. Abandoned 1

Master i/c: G. P. C. Courtois

Wins v: King Edward VI, Stratford; King Edward VI, Five Ways; Coventry and North Warwickshire CC.

Batting—J. D. Ham 14–4–751–112*–2–75.10; J. A. Taplin 15–4–633–117–1–57.54.

Bowling—N. S. Lightowler 89.2–23–359–21–7/5–17.09; J. A. Taplin 137–37–395–23–5/36–17.17; S. Park 106.4–21–326–16–3/30–20.37.

KING WILLIAM'S COLLEGE

Played 12: Won 5, Lost 3, Drawn 4. Abandoned 2

Master i/c: A. Maree   Cricket professional: D. Mark

Wins v: Peel CC; Belvedere, Dublin; Silcoates; Liverpool; King's, Chester.

Batting—B. J. Mitchell 11–2–514–129–2–57.11; K. S. Moore 6–0–164–87–0–27.33; S. Caveney 7–0–184–62–0–26.28; B. J. Manuja 9–1–152–31–0–19.00.

Bowling—J. F. K. Bregazzi 101–32–265–21–4/24–12.61; A. P. Jackson 131.4–27–340–21–4/17–16.19; B. A. Moffett 79.2–6–359–15–4/38–23.93.

KING'S COLLEGE, TAUNTON

Played 18: Won 4, Lost 2, Drawn 12

Master i/c: R. J. R. Yeates   Cricket professional: D. Breakwell

Both batting and bowling records were broken, respectively by J. G. M. Ross, with 702 runs, and fourth-former S. H. Diment, whose tally of 55 wickets was more than three times greater than the next highest.

Wins v: Queen's, Taunton; Taunton; Habergham; Royal Marines.

Batting—*J. G. M. Ross 16–1–702–105–1–46.80; B. W. Hiles 11–5–222–52–0–37.00; T. A. Scourfield 15–2–444–78*–0–34.15; A. T. Dart 15–1–376–96–0–26.85; M. J. Hockin 14–0–340–104–2–24.28; C. J. D. Ross 10–1–214–44–0–23.77; D. J. Bostock 16–3–260–62–0–20.00; T. W. J. Farley 15–5–172–36*–0–17.20; M. J. Wrout 12–2–154–42–0–15.40.

Bowling—S. H. Diment 299.2–70–896–55–8/29–16.29; J. G. M. Ross 149.5–29–388–16–5/55–24.25; M. J. Wrout 143.5–26–465–16–3/18–29.06.

KING'S COLLEGE SCHOOL, WIMBLEDON

Played 23: Won 11, Lost 3, Drawn 9

Master i/c: G. C. McGinn   Cricket professional: L. J. Moody

Continuing their successful ways, the side owed much to Ben Howland, who took over the captaincy from his brother and headed the batting. David Gorrod, the leading bowler with 44 wickets, was also a prolific batsman as was Paul Redwood, who scored the side's only hundred. The season finished with a third consecutive success in the Surrey Under-18 Cup and a marvellous victory off the last ball over MCC, who were captained by Howland's father, Peter.

Wins v: Kingston GS; UCS, Hampstead; Emanuel; Reed's; Whitgift; Wimbledon C.; Caterham; MCC; St Paul's; Wimbledon XI; GICC.

Batting—*B. J. Howland 21–4–797–94–0–46.88; D. E. Gorrod 23–3–675–81–0–33.75; P. J. D. Redwood 21–2–607–110–1–31.94; L. A. Whitaker 8–2–158–68–0–26.33; C. Strickland 11–1–256–67–0–25.60; R. Sleigh 20–0–448–71–0–22.40; S. H. Cosh 16–7–168–24–0–18.66; O. B. Gobat 20–6–161–45–0–11.50.

Bowling—D. E. Gorrod 267–52–862–44–6/27–19.59; O. B. Gobat 116–19–487–24–4/19–20.29; T. W. Flower 107–12–391–18–3/23–21.72; S. H. Cosh 81–3–371–17–6/38–21.82; S. J. Foster 144–32–425–18–3/27–23.61; B. J. Howland 182–35–614–22–5/55–27.90.

KING'S SCHOOL, BRUTON

Played 16: Won 6, Lost 3, Drawn 7. Abandoned 1

Master i/c: P. Platts-Martin   Cricket professional: N. J. Lockhart

Wins v: Taunton; Downside; Monkton Combe; Queen's, Taunton; XL Club; Headmaster's XI.

Batting—O. R. Fowlston 16–4–475–101*–1–39.58; C. J. S. Upton 13–0–370–115–1–28.46; A. E. Hughes 14–1–341–64–0–26.23; T. W. Vine 14–4–201–52–0–20.10; *J. K. Fleming 15–2–253–39*–0–19.46.

Bowling—L. C. Crofts 75–18–239–17–5/32–14.05; J. P. Thomas 135.1–31–348–23–6/19–15.13; O. R. Fowlston 180.2–47–466–28–6/44–16.64; A. E. Hughes 154–39–439–18–3/46–24.38.

THE KING'S SCHOOL, CANTERBURY

Played 12: Won 6, Lost 2, Drawn 4. Abandoned 2

Master i/c: A. W. Dyer   Cricket professional: A. G. E. Ealham

Much depended on the batting of the wicket-keeper Ben Craddock, whose 117 not out was instrumental in the successful pursuit of 182 in two hours against Highgate.

Wins v: Dover; Eastbourne; Highgate; Sutton Valence; Old King's Scholars; Stragglers of Asia.

Batting—B. W. M. Craddock 13–3–520–117*–1–52.00; J. W. Lewis-Jones 11–0–314–66–0–28.54; J. B. Rayner 13–1–312–56*–0–26.00; E. P. G. Sayer 10–4–150–51*–0–25.00; R. J. Weston 13–0–223–50–0–17.15.

Bowling—A. R. Wilson 133–32–385–21–4/21–18.33; E. P. G. Sayer 176.4–46–459–23–5/24–19.95; R. J. Weston 131.2–25–440–18–5/52–24.44.

THE KING'S SCHOOL, CHESTER

Played 18: Won 4, Lost 11, Drawn 3. Abandoned 1

Master i/c: K. H. Mellor

Wins v: Ellesmere; Tattenhall; Aldenham; Liverpool.

Batting—A. C. Richardson 17–1–620–113*–1–38.75; S. J. McCormick 15–1–402–78–0–28.71; *E. J. Spencer 15–0–378–69–0–25.20; P. R. T. Brotherhood 17–2–235–51*–0–15.66; C. J. Evans 17–3–206–66*–0–14.71; D. J. Atkin 15–3–159–34*–0–13.25.

Bowling—J. Connerty 101.2–15–376–22–5/21–17.09; D. J. Atkin 193.2–51–496–25–3/10–19.84; J. Cornelius 164–38–559–24–5/28–23.29; A. J. Douglas 119.3–16–421–17–6/40–24.76.

THE KING'S SCHOOL, ELY

Played 17: Won 3, Lost 3, Drawn 11. Abandoned 2

Masters i/c: C. J. Limb and W. J. Marshall   Cricket professional: T. G. A. Morley

A young side won the Solway Cup for Cambridgeshire Schools Under-19 sides.

Wins v: Wisbech GS; Hills Road SFC; Long Road SFC.

Batting—C. J. Kisby 13–2–414–74–0–37.63; C. D. Marshall 17–1–452–69–0–28.25; C. W. Kisby 14–6–183–35–0–22.87; M. C. Parker 16–2–312–52*–0–22.28; C. D. Sutton 16–1–194–52–0–12.93.

Bowling—D. J. Parker 79–25–216–16–5/17–13.50; A. R. Cable 91–12–329–16–4/28–20.56; M. C. Parker 145.4–29–470–22–3/16–21.36; C. J. Kisby 114.5–10–407–18–3/35–22.61.

THE KING'S SCHOOL, MACCLESFIELD

Played 21: Won 7, Lost 1, Drawn 13. Abandoned 1

Master i/c: D. M. Harbord   Cricket professional: S. Moores

The side was ably led by Andrew James, whose left-arm spin brought him 54 wickets and who went on to play for Lancashire Second XI.

Wins v: William Hulme's GS; Arnold; Bolton; King's, Chester; Brighton; Edinburgh Acad.; Old Boys.

Batting—M. C. Mason 18–4–559–100*–1–39.92; C. M. Watson 18–5–494–79–0–38.00; A. S. Bones 21–2–511–67–0–26.89; N. E. Sentance 21–4–445–61*–0–26.17; R. J. Bones 16–4–268–67*–0–22.33; *A. M. James 12–4–157–36–0–19.62.

Bowling—A. M. James 265.5–88–556–54–7/21–10.29; C. M. Watson 227.3–42–671–27–4/30–24.85; P. M. Daniels 131.3–23–450–18–3/12–25.00; K. B. S. Spreckley 146–13–634–21–4/85–30.19.

KING'S SCHOOL, WORCESTER

Played 21: Won 6, Lost 5, Drawn 10. Abandoned 2

Master i/c: D. P. Iddon

Wins v: Wrekin; Christ C., Brecon; Hereford Cathedral S.; Camels CC; Gentlemen of Worcester CC; Victoriana CC.

Batting—L. R. Chivers 19–7–330–63*–0–27.50; A. Fiaz 20–0–485–73–0–24.25; M. T. Richardson 20–1–421–67*–0–22.15; *P. A. Judge 21–2–404–64*–0–21.26; C. W. Gough 16–3–241–54–0–18.53; T. P. Bawden 15–4–188–32–0–17.09; R. B. Cook 19–0–316–54–0–16.63; S. J. P. Buckland 13–2–178–48*–0–16.18.

Bowling—S. J. P. Buckland 192.4–41–624–41–7/40–15.21; T. P. Bawden 206.5–33–723–33–4/30–21.90; R. J. Firth 104.1–18–475–20–5/57–23.75; A. Fiaz 100–15–400–15–3/31–26.66.

KINGSTON GRAMMAR SCHOOL

Played 14: Won 6, Lost 5, Drawn 3. Abandoned 2

Master i/c: J. A. Royce   Cricket professional: C. Mutucumarana

Leading by example, Dean Spencer collected 612 runs and 45 wickets, going on to play for Surrey Under-19 and Surrey YC.

Wins v: Tiffin; St Benedict's; Sutton GS; Glyn; Isleworth & Syon; Old Boys.

Batting—*D. Spencer 14–2–612–130–1–51.00; P. D. Flanagan 11–4–181–56*–0–25.85; G. T. Fordham 12–0–211–59–0–17.58; D. J. S. Roberts 11–1–170–65–0–17.00; D. J. Hall 12–0–173–76–0–14.41.

Bowling—B. J. Honour 186.2–38–492–39–6/43–12.61; D. Spencer 228.2–57–603–45–8/46–13.40.

KINGSWOOD SCHOOL

Played 8: Won 0, Lost 3, Drawn 5

Master i/c: R. J. Lewis

Batting—R. K. Carter 8–3–175–82–0–35.00; *T. Ross 7–0–158–58–0–22.57.

Bowling—No bowler took 15 wickets.

LANCING COLLEGE

Played 22: Won 11, Lost 5, Drawn 6

Master i/c: M. Bentley   Cricket professional: R. Davis

Adam Pierce became the first to score 1,000 runs in a season for the college, passing the previous record of 981 set by G. H. Heslop in 1914. His innings of 170 out of 261 for six against Eastbourne was the highest by an individual in the Langdale Cup, which Lancing won. Other big innings were his unbeaten 141 out of 213 for four against Sussex Martlets and 114 out of 259 for eight against Malvern. On another occasion he was out handled the ball against Charterhouse, when he knocked the ball away from his stumps. He was followed in the batting by the side's other centurion, Ed Davies, while the most successful bowler was Mark Gurney, whose identical twin David was also in the XI. Nick Hayday played for England Under-16 and Sussex Under-19.

Wins v: Ardingly; Eastbourne (twice); Hurstpierpoint; Reigate GS; Christ's Hospital; Worth; Free Foresters; Sussex Martlets; Malvern; Charterhouse.

Batting—A. D. Pierce 21–4–1,125–170–3–66.17; E. Davies 15–3–522–125*–1–43.50; D. Gurney 14–3–376–77–0–34.18; *J. Southon 20–2–475–88–0–26.38; M. Gurney 13–6–152–36–0–21.71; N. Hayday 17–1–316–52–0–19.75.

Bowling—E. Fleming 104–18–464–24–4/37–19.33; H. Tatham 178–33–586–27–3/6–21.70; J. Souter 313–101–924–42–7/50–22.00; M. Gurney 341–90–1,108–48–6/55–23.08; G. Robinson 180–48–485–18–5/34–26.94.

LANGLEY PARK SCHOOL

Played 12: Won 5, Lost 4, Drawn 3

Master i/c: C. H. Williams

Ben Phillips, who scored the side's only hundred and headed the bowling averages, played for Kent Second XI, MCC Schools and English Schools.

Wins v: St Columba; Eltham; Chislehurst & Sidcup GS; St Olave's GS; Old Boys.

Batting—J. Martin 8–4–156–52–0–39.00; J. Evans 12–3–332–60*–0–36.88; B. Phillips 8–1–213–100–1–30.42; P. Kendrick 8–2–173–79–0–28.83; G. Butler 11–0–259–64–0–23.54.

Bowling—B. Phillips 69.3–20–134–20–7/36–6.70.

LATYMER UPPER SCHOOL

Played 17: Won 3, Lost 7, Drawn 7

Master i/c: A. M. Weston   Cricket professional: K. Mayers

Aftab Choudry could not match his bowling success of 1992, but still shared 78 wickets with the promising all-rounder, Matthew Pryor. However, the highlight of Choudhry's season was a century in his last match, against RGS, High Wycombe, his previous highest score having been 17.

Wins v: St Benedict's; Old Latymerians; Enfield GS.

Batting—L. Buchanan 17–0–503–82–0–29.58; M. Pryor 11–3–207–56*–0–25.87; *A. Choudry 10–2–158–105*–1–19.75; I. Bolton 17–2–254–48–0–16.93; J. Hall 16–0–248–46–0–15.50; M. Thein 10–0–153–58–0–15.30; J. Woolard 13–1–155–36–0–12.91.

Bowling—M. Pryor 176.3–48–420–41–6/48–10.24; A. Choudry 207.4–62–584–37–6/14–15.78.

LEEDS GRAMMAR SCHOOL

Played 25: Won 9, Lost 7, Drawn 9

Master i/c: R. Hill

Iain Sutcliffe was an outstanding batsman. He left to take up a place at Oxford with a record total of 3,328 runs at 64, having added 1,623, also a record, in his last season. He scored eight hundreds – against Hymers, Nottingham HS, Ashville, and the Past XI in England plus four during a successful nine-match tour of Kenya. His opening partner, David Gait, was the next most prolific with 703 runs and the two shared eight three-figure stands, the highest being 201 against Ashville College.

Wins v: Silcoates; Ermysteds GS; Pocklington; Nottingham HS; Barnard Castle; Rift Valley CC; Mombasa CC; Trafalgar House, Cape Town (twice).

Batting—I. C. Sutcliffe 24–8–1,623–161–8–101.43; D. L. Peters 6–0–226–114–1–37.66; D. P. Gait 20–1–703–107–1–37.00; O. T. Robertson 18–2–463–63–0–28.93; T. E. Limbert 13–5–156–40*–0–19.50; B. Patel 17–3–267–44–0–19.07; D. P. Kershaw 19–3–249–50*–0–15.56; J. S. Wood 17–4–165–28–0–12.69.

Bowling—P. J. Miller 135–23–515–26–4/28–19.80; T. E. Limbert 285–45–926–44–7/33–21.04; B. G. Williams 158–32–487–20–3/26–24.35; E. J. A. Smith 130.4–13–419–16–5/25–26.18; D. P. Kershaw 176–33–721–23–4/69–31.34.

LEIGHTON PARK SCHOOL

Played 12: Won 3, Lost 5, Drawn 4

Master i/c: M. J. Morris

A young and enthusiastic side enjoyed their cricket.

Wins v: Old Leightonians; Staff XI; M. Beer's XI.

Batting—A. Butt 10–2–361–73*–0–45.12; G. Dias 11–2–230–72*–0–25.55; *P. Samuels 9–1–152–56–0–19.00; D. Paton 9–0–161–43–0–17.88.

Bowling—D. Paton 84–20–214–15–5/13–14.26; A. Butt 93–17–348–17–5/9–20.47.

THE LEYS SCHOOL

Played 15: Won 4, Lost 1, Drawn 10. Abandoned 2

Master i/c: T. Firth   Cricket professional: D. Gibson

The leading batsman was T. C. W. Keates, whose 739 runs included three hundreds and an unbeaten 99.

Wins v: Oakham; MCC; Gresham's; Fettes.

Batting—T. C. W. Keates 15–2–739–118–3–56.84; T. H. Fairey 13–3–407–67–0–40.70; *D. M. Wingfield 14–2–369–82*–0–30.75; R. W. Erlebach 14–1–303–56–0–23.30; A. O. Newman 11–2–199–50*–0–22.11.

Bowling—A. O. Newman 144.1–41–372–24–5/6–15.50; S. E. Graham 15–21–287–17–3/30–16.88; T. H. Fairey 83–15–292–17–4/33–17.17; D. M. Wingfield 142.2–35–505–25–5/37–20.20.

LIVERPOOL COLLEGE

Played 12: Won 1, Lost 7, Drawn 4. Abandoned 3

Master i/c: Rev. J. R. Macaulay

Win v: St Anselm's.

Batting—J. L. Perry 12–0–254–70–0–21.16; M. Chang 9–0–177–51–0–19.66; R. Cairns 12–0–198–50–0–16.50; A. Beacham 12–1–156–26–0–14.18; *A. Godson 12–0–166–41–0–13.83.

Bowling—J. L. Perry 109–16–394–23–6/50–17.13; M. Goel 102–18–384–15–3/28–25.60.

LLANDOVERY COLLEGE

Played 12: Won 3, Lost 2, Drawn 7

Master i/c: T. G. Marks

Never bowled out but lacking penetration, the side were too often unable to force a result. Three consistent batsmen, Shaun Howells, Russell Mably and Gethin Watts, were selected to play for the Welsh Independent Schools XI. Howells also took 23 wickets and shared with Watts in a partnership of 147 against Christ College, Brecon. Richard Teifi Davies impressed with both bat and ball, highlights being his unbeaten century against Llandovery CC and a return of six for 26 against MCC, who were beaten for the first time.

Wins v: MCC; XL Club; B. T. Edwards's XI.

Batting—S. C. Howells 12–4–541–93–0–67.62; R. D. Mably 9–2–256–79–0–36.57; G. A. Watts 12–0–288–58–0–24.00; R. T. Davies 12–1–176–101*–1–16.00.

Bowling—R. T. Davies 82–11–334–30–6/26–11.13; S. C. Howells 114–30–304–23–4/49–13.21.

LORD WANDSWORTH COLLEGE

Played 11: Won 3, Lost 3, Drawn 5. Abandoned 1

Master i/c: G. R. Smith

The England Under-16 representative, David Thomas, headed the bowling and scored the most runs.

Wins v: Churcher's; Portsmouth GS; St John's, Southsea.

Batting—S. Butler 11–5–268–55–0–44.66; D. A. Thomas 11–3–338–96*–0–42.25; B. A. Hames 7–0–222–102–0–31.71; M. Palmer 11–2–214–89–0–23.77; S. English 11–1–221–64–0–22.10.

Bowling—D. A. Thomas 141.2–23–482–29–7/54–16.62.

LORD WILLIAMS'S SCHOOL

Played 11: Won 2, Lost 4, Drawn 5

Master i/c: J. E. Fulkes

The most entertaining match was that against the touring Northwood HS from Durban, Robin Smith's old school.

Wins v: Desborough; Thame Town CC.

Batting—C. M. Pigden 11–0–253–58–0–23.00; J. H. C. Borgnis 11–0–215–55–0–19.54; M. F. White 11–0–199–39–0–18.09.

Bowling—No bowler took 15 wickets.

LORETTO SCHOOL

Played 17: Won 5, Lost 3, Drawn 9. Abandoned 2

Master i/c: R. P. Whait

Wins v: Glenalmond; Fettes; Kelvinside Acad.; George Watson's; XL Club.

Batting:—*N. A. S. Smith 13–5–558–106*–2–69.75; R. A. G. Grant 15–2–354–68–0–27.23; M. R. Stewart 10–0–235–59–0–23.50; R. S. F. Steenberg 14–3–157–41–0–14.27.

Bowling:—A. G. Shaw 185.4–45–424–37–6/24–11.45; N. A. S. Smith 128–29–290–20–5/13–14.50; J. D. Hare 151–44–409–28–4/2–14.60.

LOUGHBOROUGH GRAMMAR SCHOOL

Played 18: Won 6, Lost 6, Drawn 6. Abandoned 3

Master i/c: J. S. Weitzel

Wins v: Stamford; Bishop Vesey's; XL Club; King Edward's, Birmingham; Old Loughburians; Trinity GS, Sydney.

Batting:—J. P. C. Young 17–4–475–89*–0–36.53; *P. J. Noon 16–3–377–60–0–29.00; R. A. J. Parkin 17–0–355–60–0–20.88; M. K. Davies 16–2–279–44–0–19.92; S. A. Bajwa 15–1–229–62–0–16.35; R. A. Jolob 16–2–172–42–0–12.28.

Bowling:—S. A. Bajwa 198–57–491–37–5/27–13.27; M. S. Cooper 162–54–485–26–7/67–18.65; J. L. Taylor 119.2–20–409–18–4/24–22.72; M. K. Davies 196.3–56–589–25–5/62–23.56.

MAGDALEN COLLEGE SCHOOL

Played 18: Won 3, Lost 5, Drawn 10. Abandoned 2

Master i/c: P. Askew

Highlights were the first win for more than 20 years over MCC and the school's first two-day game – against Sedbergh. More than 800 runs were scored and, although the match was drawn, the XI were within sight of their target as the last over was bowled.

Wins v: Dean Close; MCC; Old Waynfletes.

Batting:—S. R. D. Hayes 20–1–630–119–2–33.15; *D. R. Bixby 20–4–481–64*–0–30.06; W. W. Hopkin 8–1–173–50–0–24.71; J. D. R. Adcock 8–1–159–48–0–22.71; A. Booth 15–2–285–73–0–21.92; S. R. Sharpe 17–2–284–92*–0–18.93; S. M. Ison 17–1–287–72–0–17.93; D. D. Harris 16–3–191–34–0–14.69.

Bowling:—J. J. Waterman 194–38–606–27–4/13–22.44; J. L. D. Sherwood 194.5–40–633–27–7/52–23.44; A. Booth 154.1–19–712–30–5/75–23.73; N. J. Carlsen 134–26–458–18–5/52–25.44.

MALVERN COLLEGE

Played 15: Won 1, Lost 5, Drawn 9

Master i/c: A. J. Murtagh   Cricket professional: R. W. Tolchard

Win v: Shrewsbury.

Batting:—J. Robbins 15–2–450–75–0–34.61; M. Smart 15–1–331–70*–0–23.64; P. Hardinges 14–3–231–64*–0–21.00; J. Morgan 11–0–155–43–0–14.09; *T. Sheehan 15–0–161–42–0–10.73.

Bowling:—T. Sheehan 128–26–365–20–4/21–18.25; C. Hurst 99–21–325–16–3/46–20.31; M. Smart 255–81–672–30–6/68–22.40; J. Mackie 143–28–454–15–3/36–30.26.

MANCHESTER GRAMMAR SCHOOL

Played 15: Won 9, Lost 1, Drawn 5. Abandoned 3

Master i/c: D. Moss

This was an excellent season, despite there being fewer matches owing to a wet May and lack of an end-of-season tour. The batting was strong, as had been expected, although the dominance of Lee Marland sometimes limited opportunities for others. Marland, who went on to play for Lancashire Second XI, was outstanding both as captain and batsman. Despite having only 13 innings he became the third after Mike Atherton and Mark Crawley to score 1,000 runs for the school and his 208 not out against William Hulme's GS was a record, although he played other equally impressive innings to achieve stiff targets. The bowling was also strong, with Stephen Hall proving remarkably fast and accurate. His six for 10 against Bury GS included the first hat-trick for many years, while leg-spinner Charles Sinton, who completed a record number of matches for the First XI, took seven for 15 against Stockport GS. They were supported by high-quality fielding, led by the improving Philip Knott behind the stumps.

Wins v: Bolton; Ellesmere; MCC; Stockport GS; Bury GS; King Edward's, Lytham; RGS, Lancaster; Pocklington; Leeds GS.

Batting—*L. J. Marland   13–5–1,016–208*–3–127.00;   S. A. Richardson 9–5–166–50*–0–41.50;   M. J. Chilton   14–3–395–58–0–35.90;   R. C. Wilcock 14–1–396–103*–1–30.46; P. D. Knott 11–3–208–40–0–26.00.

*Bowling—*S. R. Hall   167.4–36–477–33–6/10–14.45;   M. J. Chilton   81.1–21–248– 16–4/35–15.50;   C. F. Sinton   205.1–52–642–32–7/15–20.06;   R. M. Bipul 105.2–22–368–15–4/76–24.53.

MARLBOROUGH COLLEGE

Played 15: Won 5, Lost 4, Drawn 6. Abandoned 2

Masters i/c: R. B. Pick and J. A. Genton   Cricket professional: R. M. Ratcliffe

A young and talented side played entertaining cricket. Gaurav Murgai, an Indian international squash player, scored 930 runs in 15 innings, of which his 172 against Clifton was the highest for Marlborough since G. E. Hewan's 205 in 1934. Lee Ratcliffe, son of R. M. Ratcliffe of Lancashire, was hampered by a back injury which restricted his bowling, but he excelled with the bat once he was promoted to open after half term.

Wins v: Marlborough CC; Romany; R. B. Pick's XI; Mid Glamorgan; Haileybury.

*Batting—*G. Murgai 15–4–930–172–2–84.54; L. J. Ratcliffe 14–2–584–106–2–48.66; A. M. Wade 13–0–267–61–0–20.53; C. A. Gough 14–2–230–69*–0–19.16; R. L. A. Spender 13–0–162–58–0–12.46.

Bowling—*T. A. Leslie   109.3–23–374–17–3/34–22.00;   A. T. Murphy 97.1–8–378–16–3/22–23.62.

MERCHANT TAYLORS' SCHOOL, CROSBY

Played 17: Won 4, Lost 1, Drawn 12. Abandoned 1

Master i/c: Rev. D. A. Smith   Cricket professional: G. W. Flowe

N. A. Doggett, the leading wicket-taker for the third time, took his tally for the school pas 100. A less enviable landmark was made by the Delaney brothers, who each out for a duck in the same innings twice.

Wins v: Liverpool; King's, Chester; Northern Nomads; XL Club.

Batting—G. A. Edwards 16–2–583–95–0–41.64; N. C. Delaney 16–5–239–45–0–21.72; P. K. Delaney 16–4–258–63*–0–21.50; A. Sharma 15–0–296–68–0–19.73; T. M. Wilson 13–5–150–24*–0–18.75; S. B. Howard 9–0–168–55–0–18.66; *N. A. Doggett 12–3–163–56–0–18.11.

Bowling—N. A. Doggett 194–61–537–28–5/86–19.17; G. R. Ball 118–30–403–19–5/5–21.21; N. C. Delaney 180–41–643–20–3/29–32.15.

MERCHANT TAYLORS' SCHOOL, NORTHWOOD

Played 24: Won 8, Lost 4, Drawn 12

Master i/c: W. M. B. Ritchie   Cricket professional: H. C. Latchman

Anthony Smee captained the side intelligently and with panache. He was also their leading batsman, while the attack was headed by Thushara Hewage, who bowled his seamers accurately and to good effect.

Wins v: Latymer Upper; St Albans; Watford GS; Enfield GS; UCS, Hampstead; Berkhamsted; Mill Hill; Westminster.

Batting—*A. J. M. Smee 21–3–728–106–2–40.44; P. C. Smith 19–3–457–88*–0–28.56; D. C. Ellis 18–2–408–72–0–25.50; D. J. Grundy 10–0–218–49–0–21.80; P. V. Harris 20–3–366–53–0–21.52; P. Parekh 15–6–150–26*–0–16.66; T. N. S. Hewage 15–4–172–47–0–15.63; Navin P. Sapra 22–5–255–57–0–15.00.

Bowling—T. N. S. Hewage 284–81–646–46–6/43–14.04; Neeraj P. Sapra 168.4–47–472–27–6/28–17.48; A. W. Crockford 186–42–530–27–5/47–19.62; N. J. Perin 150–27–438–19–5/38–23.05; P. Parekh 120.4–19–441–16–4/45–27.56.

MERCHISTON CASTLE SCHOOL

Played 15: Won 6, Lost 5, Drawn 4. Abandoned 3

Master i/c: C. W. Swan

Wins v: George Watson's; George Heriot's; Glenalmond; Dundee HS; Fettes; Sedbergh.

Batting—A. A. W. Boyle 13–5–214–38–0–26.75; *K. C. M. Roger 15–1–346–66–0–24.71; A. J. Turner 15–2–268–100*–1–20.61; E. J. W. Weston 16–1–294–52–0–19.60; J. A. M. Kerr 15–1–234–59–0–16.71; D. B. Finlay 13–1–189–67–0–15.75.

Bowling—R. F. A. Dobson 170–47–421–37–8/48–11.37; G. F. A. Milligan 187–59–412–34–6/34–12.11; A. P. Paterson 162–37–455–29–6/34–15.68.

MILL HILL SCHOOL

Played 24: Won 10, Lost 4, Drawn 10

Master i/c: S. T. Plummer   Cricket professional: I. J. F. Hutchinson

Wins v: Latymer Upper; Millers' CC; Kingsbury; UCS, Hampstead; St Ignatius; Highgate; Queen Elizabeth's, Barnet; Old Millhillians; Richmond; Downside.

Batting—D. L. Goodwin 22–1–808–139*–2–38.47; K. B. Patel 21–3–483–73–0–26.83; S. V. Harvey 20–4–334–94–0–20.87; S. Sandhu 13–3–171–48–0–17.10; J. Romeu 15–5–167–46*–0–16.70; N. Kamath 24–1–320–55–0–13.91; L. J. Baldwin 15–2–166–29–0–12.76; J. H. Morgan 15–2–150–25–0–11.53.

Bowling—R. J. Peach 140–39–348–28–5/9–12.42; M. A. Parkinson 219–55–539–38–5/38–14.18; L. J. Baldwin 150–25–453–22–7/65–20.59; K. B. Patel 126–24–379–16–3/18–23.68; N. Kamath 197–32–586–22–4/69–26.63.

MILLFIELD SCHOOL

Played 19: Won 8, Lost 1, Drawn 10

Master i/c: A. D. Curtis

Cricket professional: G. C. Wilson

The youngest XI ever to represent the school enjoyed a memorable season. The captain, Paul Mitchell, was by far the most prolific batsman and was selected to play for Young Zimbabwe against Young England. With the ball, it was the 16-year-old left-arm spinner, Ben McCorkill, who excelled: he took 43 wickets and went on to play for Worcestershire Second XI, while the all-rounder, Duncan Ayres, played for Essex Second XI.

Wins v: King's, Taunton; Taunton; MCC; Incogniti; Monmouth; Selborne C., South Africa; Trinity GS, Sydney; Old Boys.

Batting—*P. M. Mitchell 20–0–921–124–2–46.05; J. P. Hart 17–4–353–45–0–27.15; T. D. Martin 16–4–325–74–0–27.08; K. A. O. Barrett 15–1–350–103–1–25.00; L. Sutton 19–2–401–74–0–23.58; D. W. Ayres 17–6–246–40–0–22.36.

Bowling—B. M. McCorkill 279–70–772–43–6/17–17.95; F. J. Black 91–17–299–15–4/26–19.93; C. J. Chandler 205–50–544–26–4/9–20.92; J. P. Hart 161–40–490–20–3/12–24.50; D. W. Ayres 125–20–429–17–5/49–25.23.

MILTON ABBEY SCHOOL

Played 14: Won 2, Lost 8, Drawn 4. Abandoned 1

Master i/c: P. W. Wood

Wins v: Allhallows; Old Boys.

Batting—M. N. Amin 11–0–260–80–0–23.63; J. Dooley 13–0–264–53–0–20.30; O. H. W. Williams 14–2–224–59–0–18.66; D. K. Maxwell 12–1–187–58–0–17.00; *N. K. G. Tomlin 14–1–175–41–0–15.90.

Bowling—J. N. Butler 119.2–19–357–21–4/45–17.00; O. H. W. Williams 115–18–409–24–5/50–17.04.

MONKTON COMBE SCHOOL

Played 15: Won 2, Lost 4, Drawn 9. Abandoned 2

Master i/c: N. D. Botton

A highlight was the partnership of 197 against Colston's between Jonathan St John (100) and 14-year-old Chris Taarnby (103); it was 50 runs more than the previous best for the school and was the first time two batsmen had scored centuries in the same match.

Wins v: Fettes; Old Monktonians.

Batting—J. F. A. St John 15–1–610–100–1–43.57; G. R. Arscott 8–2–213–66*–0–35.50; C. R. Taarnby 12–0–316–103–1–26.33; K. Mok 10–3–174–56*–0–24.85; J. E. Cary 14–0–220–61–0–15.71.

Bowling—C. E. Page 147.5–22–552–26–6/33–21.23; J. F. A. St John 126–32–430–19–5/7–22.63; J. R. C. Meredith 159.2–44–497–19–3/14–26.15.

MONMOUTH SCHOOL

Played 23: Won 12, Lost 7, Drawn 4

Master i/c: D. H. Messenger

Cricket professional: G. I. Burgess

The sequence of eight wins at the beginning of the school's most successful season to date was one of several records to fall. Anu Mohindru's 755 runs included a school record three centuries, while Reuben Spiring took his tally for the XI to a record 1,605 before going on to take up a professional contract with Worcestershire. Paul Davies was the outstanding bowler, his 58 wickets falling just one short of the school record. The XI reached the final of the Chesterton Trophy for the second time in three years, losing to RGS, Worcester.

Wins v: G. I. Burgess XI; Christ C., Brecon; Cheltenham; Wycliffe; Rendcomb; Gloucester Gypsies; Dean Close; Queen's, Taunton; Malvern; Bristol GS; Framlingham; Winchester.

Batting—*A. Mohindru 16–2–755–116–3–53.92; K. R. Spiring 15–2–471–105*–1–36.23; D. J. R. Price 21–3–449–66*–0–24.94; I. E. Mackinlay 22–3–360–57–0–18.94; J. A. Hughes 16–4–166–65–0–13.83.

Bowling—P. W. Davies 267.3–62–691–58–7/27–11.91; A. Mohindru 84–25–258–15–5/6–17.20; I. J. Plumley 121.4–23–411–22–4/29–18.68; D. J. R. Price 168.5–37–481–22–5/2–21.86; I. E. Mackinlay 205.2–31–695–22–4/53–31.59.

NEWCASTLE-UNDER-LYME SCHOOL (BOYS' XI)

Played 20: Won 4, Lost 1, Drawn 15

Master i/c: S. A. Robson

Cricket professional: C. Coutts

R. J. Howell became the first batsman to top four figures in a season for the XI and equalled his own school record of two centuries. He shared in six half-century opening partnerships with R. G. Feltbower, who also headed the bowling averages. The unbroken eighth-wicket partnership of 69 against Tettenhall College between S. S. Shah and D. G. Bailey was another school record. The side were often frustrated by the negative tactics of opposing sides. It may be that Howell's reputation made them cautious, but on one notorious occasion, their opponents batted for 74 overs in making 202 for eight, leaving them just 35 overs – in which they made 192 for five.

Wins v: Bishop Vesey's GS; MCC; Solihull; Kelvinside Acad.

Batting—*R. J. Howell 20–5–1,004–111*–2–66.93; S. S. Shah 13–7–258–50–0–43.00; A. J. G. Cheetham 16–4–331–62*–0–27.58; N. S. J. Clarke 15–2–329–101*–1–25.30; R. G. Feltbower 20–1–374–55–0–19.68; R. Singh 14–3–196–48–0–17.81.

Bowling—R. G. Feltbower 226–80–496–30–4/17–16.53; R. Singh 107–28–304–18–4/44–16.88; D. A. Spence 153–39–448–16–2/23–28.00; R. J. Howell 186–37–572–17–4/44–33.64.

NEWCASTLE-UNDER-LYME SCHOOL (GIRLS' XI)

Played 6: Won 5, Lost 1, Drawn 0. Abandoned 1

Staff i/c: E. A. Cook and R. G. Jones

Tracy Phillips became the first girl to score a century for the school when she made 102 not out against Bromsgrove.

Wins v: Wrekin; Tettenhall; Bromsgrove; Staff XI; Denstone.

Batting—T. Phillips 4–3–224–102*–1–224.00; K. Scarpello 6–1–193–55*–0–38.60.

Bowling—T. Phillips 37.4–8–78–15–7/7–5.20; *S. Braithwaite 42.1–7–141–15–5/30–9.40.

NOTTINGHAM HIGH SCHOOL

Played 15: Won 5, Lost 1, Drawn 9. Abandoned 4

Master i/c: J. Lamb

Cricket professional: K. Poole

The batting was headed by David Smit, brother of the England women's wicket-keeper Jane Smit.

Wins v: Stamford; Loughborough GS; Bishop Vesey's; Trent; Forest Amateurs.

Batting—D. Smit 12–1–543–97–0–49.36; D. T. Wootton 13–4–362–72–0–40.22; A. H. Rose 12–1–401–65–0–36.45; P. M. Dunn 10–1–247–81–0–27.44; M. J. Allen 9–2–179–71–0–25.57; S. H. Ferguson 11–2–152–35–0–16.88.

Bowling—A. H. Rose 121–22–387–19–4/40–20.36; P. W. McNaughton 96–20–308–15–3/29–20.53.

OAKHAM SCHOOL

Played 22: Won 5, Lost 6, Drawn 11

Master i/c: J. Wills

Cricket professional: D. S. Steele

Records tumbled in an enjoyable season in which 22 matches were played – the most yet. James Bull set a new batting record with 1,001 runs, including three centuries, and also took 31 wickets. Cristian Durant, who followed him in the batting averages and also made a hundred, effected 31 dismissals behind the stumps. This figure was the highest since records began in 1884, as were his 20 stumpings.

Wins v: Trent; Mount St Mary's; XL Club; Old Oakhamians; Derby Friars.

Batting—*J. J. Bull 21–4–1,001–116*–3–58.88; C. D. Durant 17–1–433–100–1–27.06; H. D. Patel 14–3–249–70*–0–22.63; S. Greenwood 8–0–154–56–0–19.25; A. Bhatia 21–2–348–55*–0–18.31.

*Bowling—*A. James 178.2–42–599–32–4/17–18.71; H. D. Patel 212.5–41–691–32–6/17–21.59; J. J. Bull 253.2–64–720–31–5/38–23.22; S. Evans 156–35–532–18–3/35–29.55.

THE ORATORY SCHOOL

Played 19: Won 10, Lost 2, Drawn 7. Abandoned 3

Master i/c: P. L. Tomlinson

Cricket professional: J. B. K. Howell

The Tomlinson brothers were pre-eminent. The captain, J. P. S. Tomlinson, scored three centuries in his 814 runs and passed 2,000 runs for the XI. He will be looking for another 642 in 1994 to reach 3,000. His younger brother, S. C. B. Tomlinson, a fast bowler who went on to play for England Under-14, marked his debut in the XI with a return of six for seven v St Edmund's and went on to take the most wickets, as well as scoring 322 runs. The brothers shared in a record partnership of 203 for the fourth wicket against Emeriti.

Wins v: Berkhamsted; MCC; Douai; Magdalen College S.; RGS, High Wycombe; South Oxfordshire Amateurs; XL Club; Merchiston Castle; Berkshire Gentlemen; Leighton Park.

Batting—*J. P. S. Tomlinson 19–5–814–135–3–58.14; S. C. B. Tomlinson 10–2–322–79–0–40.25; R. W. Atkins 14–3–380–75*–0–34.54; R. D. Louisson 17–1–431–102–1–26.93; D. H. Orchard 14–0–204–47–0–14.57; S. F. Hasslacher 11–0–156–47–0–14.18; J. A. D. Urquhart 12–0–162–32–0–13.50.

*Bowling—*S. C. B. Tomlinson 151–31–472–38–6/7–12.42; J. A. D. Urquhart 112–9–431–19–4/31–22.68; D. H. Orchard 93–7–380–16–5/27–23.75; N. J. Watson 76–3–387–16–4/38–24.18; S. F. Hasslacher 58–5–380–15–3/31–25.33.

OUNDLE SCHOOL

Played 20: Won 11, Lost 0, Drawn 9. Abandoned 1

Master i/c: J. R. Wake

Cricket professional: A. Howorth

Entertaining and attacking cricket was in evidence under the intelligent captaincy of the South African-born Colin McInnes, the reward being a record number of 11 wins. Eight batsmen passed 200 runs, five averaged more than 30, and four bowlers took 127 wickets between them. McInnes totalled 873 runs including hundreds against Repton (103), Gentlemen of Leicestershire (113 not out), Felsted (115 not out) and Bedford (104). Spin bowlers Harry Preston (left-arm) and George Gilroy (off-spin) shared 68 wickets and won the game against MCC with a record unfinished eighth-wicket partnership of 139.

Wins v: Stamford; Kimbolton; Repton; MCC; Oakham; Gentlemen of Leicestershire; Uppingham; XL Club; Oundle Rovers; Hamilton Schools, Victoria; Antipodeans, Sydney.

Batting—*C. G. McInnes 20–3–873–115*–4–51.35; B. B. Briggs 9–2–312–108*–1–44.57; G. P. M. Gilroy 9–4–213–96–0–42.60; J. E. Murray 12–4–277–65*–0–34.62; H. C. Preston 11–6–161–74*–0–32.20; O. P. Pugh 17–1–446–76–0–27.87; A. S. Steele 15–2–343–81–0–26.38; A. M. MacLeod-Smith 17–3–331–46–0–23.64; J. P. Samworth 10–1–208–70–0–23.11; T. J. Rayden 13–4–181–39–0–20.11.

Bowling—J. S. Hicks 222.3–31–334–29–5/58–11.51; G. P. M. Gilroy 161.5–31–588–29–6/60–20.27; H. C. Preston 286.3–39–832–39–6/26–21.33; A. M. MacLeod-Smith 225.5–30–740–30–6/53–24.66.

THE PERSE SCHOOL

Played 14: Won 3, Lost 3, Drawn 8. Abandoned 2

Master i/c: A. C. Porter

Cricket professional: D. C. Collard

Wins v: Old Perseans; Kimbolton; XL Club.

Batting—*R. T. Ragnauth 14–3–431–115*–1–39.18; P. Horsley 11–0–400–96–0–36.36; T. B. Sheppard 14–2–362–105*–1–30.16; J. Stobbs 9–2–194–52–0–27.71; J. R. Small 12–2–214–62–0–21.40.

Bowling—J. R. Mayer 126–22–395–20–5/26–19.75; J. R. N. Jack 122–16–430–17–5/98–25.29.

PLYMOUTH COLLEGE

Played 16: Won 7, Lost 0, Drawn 9

Master i/c: T. J. Stevens

Wins v: St Mark & St John; Plymouth Corporate Officers; Old Suttonians; Keyham; Philanthropists; Queen's, Taunton; Plymouth Hospitals.

Batting—J. G. Fabian 12–1–429–85–0–39.00; M. J. Ross 16–2–503–102*–1–35.92; P. E. Jefford 15–2–429–102*–1–33.00; *C. J. Pope 15–2–421–102*–1–32.38; E. A. James 11–3–168–45–0–21.00.

Bowling—P. E. Jefford 106–27–234–22–6/54–10.63; G. P. Brooks 58–13–228–15–8/10–15.20; C. S. Irish 176–44–528–32–4/45–16.50; K. G. Willcock 123–31–347–20–4/56–17.35.

POCKLINGTON SCHOOL

Played 19: Won 6, Lost 7, Drawn 6

Master i/c: D. Nuttall

In a promising young side, the English Schools representative Scott Boswell headed both averages, deserving more than the 43 wickets he took. Slightly more prolific with the bat was the captain, Matthew Atkinson, also an outstanding wicket-keeper, who scored centuries against Ampleforth, Sedbergh and RGS, Newcastle. Boswell went on to play for Durham Second XI and has been offered an extended trial with Northamptonshire for 1994.

Wins v: QEGS, Wakefield; Ashville; RGS, Newcastle; Old Wyvernians; Saints CC; Old Pocklingtonians.

Batting—S. A. J. Boswell 19–4–677–98*–0–45.13; *M. T. Atkinson 18–0–698–115–3–38.77; R. S. Milne 17–4–282–54–0–21.69; D. Clappison 16–4–228–46–0–19.00; M. B. Stacey 17–0–318–66–0–18.70; J. A. Etty 14–3–180–55*–0–16.36.

Bowling—S. A. J. Boswell 209–34–696–43–6/15–16.18.

PORTSMOUTH GRAMMAR SCHOOL

Played 18: Won 5, Lost 7, Drawn 6

Master i/c: G. D. Payne

Cricket professional: R. J. Parks

Wins v: Churcher's; Christ's Hospital; Southdowns; United Services Portsmouth; XL Club.

Batting—E. J. Anderson 6–0–198–65–0–33.00; R. D. Saulet 16–0–390–86–0–24.37; J. C. E. Moon 14–3–237–56–0–21.54; R. J. Taylor 15–1–286–44–0–20.42; J. S. Greer 16–3–255–53–0–19.61; N. D. Plummer 16–4–214–51*–0–17.83; A. D. N. Horstead 13–4–160–30–0–17.77.

Bowling—R. D. Saulet 167.2–24–636–40–6/42–15.90; S. J. I. Richardson 99–21–307–15–4/16–20.46; *S. J. Lippiett 98.5–14–374–15–3/22–24.93.

PRIOR PARK COLLEGE

Played 15: Won 4, Lost 1, Drawn 10

Master i/c: D. R. Holland

Wins v: Kingswood; Headmaster's XI; King Edward's, Bath; Prior Park Association.

Batting—I. Okoli 11–1–359–88–0–35.90; L. Dokic 10–4–212–51–0–35.33; *P. B. Bennett 11–0–239–56–0–21.72; T. A. O. Lamb 12–0–166–48–0–13.83.

Bowling—J. Chippendale 57.1–14–146–15–8/46–9.73; L. Dokic 163–38–380–30–5/10–12.66.

QUEEN ELIZABETH GRAMMAR SCHOOL, WAKEFIELD

Played 18: Won 3, Lost 4, Drawn 11

Master i/c: T. Barker

Wins v: William Hulme's GS; Ashville; South Craven.

Batting—A. M. R. Birkby 14–5–275–55*–0–30.55; *D. A. Woffinden 18–2–444–60*–0–27.75; S. K. Mandal 17–0–468–92–0–27.52; G. R. J. Dawson 15–6–236–48–0–26.22; K. Jayarajasingam 14–0–360–70–0–25.71; G. A. Daniels 17–3–261–55*–0–18.64.

Bowling—J. E. Mardling 90–18–274–23–6/19–11.91; S. K. Mandal 140–38–409–27–5/46–15.14; N. R. Stoner 85–21–233–15–3/12–15.53; K. Jayarajasingam 149.4–36–360–18–4/36–20.00; D. A. Woffinden 146–22–470–20–6/49–23.50.

QUEEN'S COLLEGE, TAUNTON

Played 15: Won 3, Lost 7, Drawn 5

Master i/c: J. W. Davies

Richard Jones, the most prolific batsman for more than 20 years, was well supported by Neil Barnes, who developed into a useful all-rounder. However, the bowling was rarely penetrative enough to capitalise on batting strength.

Wins v: Bristol GS; Kennicott; Trinity GS, Sydney.

Batting—*R. G. Jones 15–3–677–125*–2–56.41; N. A. Barnes 15–7–390–80*–0–48.75; H. P. Bowden 10–4–217–49–0–36.16; O. D. Watts 12–1–247–72–0–22.45; J. C. Kelly 15–0–273–69–0–18.20.

Bowling—G. Lewis 77–20–207–16–4/14–12.93; P. Spencer-Ward 127–18–423–17–4/32–24.88.

RADLEY COLLEGE

Played 12: Won 4, Lost 1, Drawn 7. Abandoned 1

Master i/c: W. J. Wesson   Cricket professionals: A. G. Robinson and A. R. Wagner

Despite his inability to bowl for much of the season, owing to a back injury, R. S. C. Martin-Jenkins still managed to send down 112 overs for 15 wickets and headed the batting averages. He went on to play for Sussex Second XI and England Under-17, while another member of the XI, M. P. Borwick, was an international polo player.

Wins v: Stowe; Bradfield; Radley Rangers; Free Foresters.

Batting—R. S. C. Martin-Jenkins 11–2–511–139–1–56.77; J. A. H. Boyle 12–2–329–83–0–32.90; A. J. Strauss 12–1–349–86–0–31.72; J. M. M. Coutts 10–4–158–55*–0–26.33; M. P. Borwick 9–1–184–49*–0–23.00; *C. L. Busk 10–0–195–44–0–19.50.

Bowling—M. P. E. O'Connor 65.3–16–167–15–7/23–11.13; M. R. Bellhouse 164–31–478–25–4/32–19.12; R. S. C. Martin-Jenkins 111.5–25–336–15–5/75–22.40.

RATCLIFFE COLLEGE

Played 16: Won 4, Lost 1, Drawn 11

Master i/c: R. M. Hughes

Much depended on E. J. Meredith, who topped the batting averages for a record fifth season and was also the leading bowler.

Wins v: Wyggeston & Queen Elizabeth I SFC; Rearsby CC; Glenthorpe CC; R. M. Hughes' XI.

Batting—*E. J. Meredith 15–1–774–109–2–55.28; S. Mudd 13–1–341–95–0–28.41; E. G. Davies 15–1–256–58*–0–18.28; M. Ferrari 13–2–195–41–0–17.72; A. Clough 12–0–181–59–0–15.08.

Bowling—E. J. Meredith 118–20–362–26–6/18–13.92; A. B. Hall 149.3–20–540–24–4/67–22.50.

READING SCHOOL

Played 13: Won 3, Lost 4, Drawn 6. Abandoned 3

Master i/c: S. B. Marfleet

Wins v: Shiplake; Reading Bluecoat; Eton III.

Batting—*B. Mayhew 12–2–345–74–0–34.50; B. Clacy 11–0–367–83–0–33.36; D. Airey 12–0–282–60–0–23.50; S. Patel 11–0–156–54–0–14.18.

Bowling—R. Pilkington 107.4–13–443–18–4/33–24.61; S. Patel 142.2–32–419–17–4/83–24.64.

REED'S SCHOOL

Played 14: Won 3, Lost 6, Drawn 5. Abandoned 2

Master i/c: S. G. Wilson

N. Stanger's return of seven for 15 in the victory over King Edward's, Witley, included a hat-trick. Two batting records were broken when R. Webster and T. Makhzangi added 162 unbroken for the third wicket against John Fisher and R. S. Page and C. Hugall opened with 113 against Stock Exchange CC.

Wins v: Glyn; King Edward's, Witley; Guernsey CA.

Batting—R. S. Page 12–2–319–53*–0–31.90; T. Makhzangi 14–3–311–81*–0–28.27; R. Webster 14–2–337–85–0–28.08; C. Hugall 13–0–287–61–0–22.07; B. Woolnough 14–0–296–60–0–21.14; *D. Keep 11–1–194–45*–0–19.40.

Bowling—N. Stanger 91.5–16–286–17–7/15–16.82.

REIGATE GRAMMAR SCHOOL

Played 20: Won 1, Lost 7, Drawn 12. Abandoned 1

Master i/c: D. C. R. Jones

Cricket professional: H. Newton

In the most disappointing season for 30 years, the XI won only once – against potentially the strongest opposition. M. H. Hetherington, the wicket-keeper, three times claimed five victims in an innings and established a school record with seven (4 ct, 3 st) against RGS, Guildford – in an innings extended by rain to six hours.

Win v: Surrey YC.

Batting—*J. B. Drewett 19-0-573-97-0-30.15; R. J. Callcut 16-3-321-53-0-24.69; M. H. Hetherington 19-0-450-69-0-23.68; D. M. P. Wilson 10-1-201-45-0-22.33; S. N. Teasdale 18-1-357-78-0-21.00; D. C. Jackson 13-1-217-50-0-18.08; R. J. C. Lowe 12-0-187-40-0-15.58; T. J. H. Martin 19-1-246-34-0-13.66.

Bowling—A. P. Chalkley 137.4-19-564-22-6/36-25.63; D. C. Sainsbury 196-37-634-23-5/63-27.56; T. J. H. Martin 175.5-23-681-18-4/41-37.83.

RENDCOMB COLLEGE

Played 15: Won 2, Lost 6, Drawn 7. Abandoned 1

Master i/c: C. Burden

Cricket professional: D. Essenhigh

Mark Valentine scored 104 out of 148, against Gloucestershire Gypsies, 136 being added while he was at the wicket; he passed 40 seven times in his last eight innings. The other player to score a century was the Under-15 wicket-keeper Francis Newcombe, who hit 117 against King's, Gloucester.

Wins v: Dean Close; Pate's GS.

Batting—*M. Valentine 14-2-575-104-1-47.91; C. Lawton 14-4-211-58*-0-21.10; P. Roberts 15-1-292-66*-0-20.85; M. Giggs 11-1-172-55*-0-17.20.

Bowling—D. Morris 86.5-19-282-20-5/7-14.10; C. Lawton 162-42-537-26-4/47-20.65; I. Kwelagobe 116.5-15-477-22-4/30-21.68.

REPTON SCHOOL

Played 14: Won 4, Lost 4, Drawn 6. Abandoned 1

Master i/c: M. Stones

Cricket professional: M. K. Kettle

Jonathan Sheard scored three centuries in successive matches in eight days in May.

Wins v: MCC; Malvern; Bromsgrove; Oakham.

Batting—J. F. Sheard 14-0-789-119-3-56.35; C. J. Gilbert 8-3-228-77*-0-45.60; S. A. Twigg 13-0-386-122-1-29.69; M. Redfern 11-1-266-46-0-26.60; E. C. Bloor 14-2-218-47-0-18.16.

Bowling—J. W. S. Piper 131.3-19-513-17-5/43-30.17.

ROEDEAN SCHOOL

Played 13: Won 3, Lost 8, Drawn 2. Abandoned 1

Staff i/c: A. S. England and A. F. Romanov

The captain, Nicky Bowes, played for Sussex Under-19 Girls.

Wins v: Ansty LCC; Sevenoaks; Fathers' XI.

Batting—*N. J. Bowes 10-3-156-31-0-22.28.

Bowling—G. M. Baker 53-1-185-18-4/16-10.27; N. J. Bowes 54.1-3-234-16-4/13-14.62.

ROSSALL SCHOOL

Played 18: Won 6, Lost 2, Drawn 10. Abandoned 4

Master i/c: A. T. Crouch

Patrick McKeown's 952 runs were a record for the school, surpassing the previous best of 911 by former MCC President M. E. L. Melluish. Liam Botham (son of Ian) had an outstanding all-round season with 604 runs and 35 wickets. Both he and McKeown played for Hampshire Second XI.

Wins v: Stonyhurst; Bolton; Old Rossallians; XL Club; Loretto; Merchant Taylors', Northwood.

Batting—P. McKeown 21–6–952–143*–3–63.46; L. Botham 17–3–604–82–0–43.14; J. Birch 9–3–161–63–0–26.83; M. Denley 13–4–223–64*–0–24.77; N. Roberts 12–5–165–50*–0–23.57; L. Powell 16–3–208–29*–0–16.00; N. Perry 15–1–192–53–0–13.71.

Bowling—M. Dewhurst 49.3–7–149–15–5/18–9.93; L. Botham 281.2–65–684–35–4/34–19.54.

THE ROYAL GRAMMAR SCHOOL, GUILDFORD

Played 16: Won 5, Lost 4, Drawn 7. Abandoned 2

Master i/c: S. B. R. Shore

Wins v: Portsmouth; Emanuel; John Fisher; Kingston GS; RGS, High Wycombe.

Batting—A. Moss 19–2–643–67–0–37.82; N. Griffiths 17–2–509–94–0–33.93; R. Kitzinger 14–3–272–58–0–24.72; B. Fraser 17–0–367–82–0–21.58; M. McGrory 18–2–288–44–0–18.00.

Bowling—I. Nordon 156–39–546–34–5/41–16.05; A. Moss 205–53–618–34–6/24–18.17; D. Honey 150–24–462–23–4/24–20.08.

THE ROYAL GRAMMAR SCHOOL, NEWCASTLE

Played 19: Won 10, Lost 2, Drawn 7. Abandoned 1

Master i/c: D. W. Smith   Cricket professional: R. Ford

A record aggregate of 685 was achieved by J. C. Hammill, closely followed by B. A. Jones-Lee, a fifth-former.

Wins v: Dame Allan's (twice); Edinburgh Acad.; Austin Friars; Yarm; Hexham; King's, Tynemouth; Lomond; RGS, Worcester; RGS, Lancaster.

Batting—B. A. Jones-Lee 17–5–656–82–0–54.66; *J. C. Hammill 16–1–685–88–0–45.66; N. R. Gandy 17–4–471–77*–0–36.23; M. J. Smalley 16–3–197–48–0–15.15.

Bowling—K. Walton 200.5–41–578–33–7/13–17.51; M. J. Smalley 230.3–69–542–29–4/15–18.68.

THE ROYAL GRAMMAR SCHOOL, WORCESTER

Played 25: Won 15, Lost 3, Drawn 7

Master i/c: B. M. Rees   Cricket professional: M. J. Horton

In another successful season, the XI again equalled their record of 15 wins, dominated the RGS Festival in Wycombe and retained the Chesterton Cup by beating Monmouth in an exciting final. J. E. Phillips became the first to pass 1,000 runs in successive seasons and was closely followed in the averages by J. M. Connor, whose five centuries were also a record. The captain, N. M. Davies, was the leading bowler with 53 wickets, as well as making a useful contribution with the bat.

Wins v: RGS, Colchester (twice); Malvern; Bromsgrove; King's, Worcester; Hereford Cathedral S.; King Henry VIII, Coventry; Christ C., Brecon; King Edward's, Birmingham; Monmouth; Solihull; Old Elizabethans; RGS, Guildford; RGS, Lancaster; RGS, High Wycombe.

Batting—J. E. Phillips 24–5–1,024–127*–1–53.89; J. M. Connor 24–6–933–118–5–51.83; D. J. Protherough 15–4–388–106–1–35.27; *N. M. Davies 21–0–618–98–0–29.42; L. P. Wilks 23–1–471–81–0–21.40; D. T. Fidoe 16–6–197–46*–0–19.70.

Bowling—N. M. Davies 286.5–53–969–53–8/51–18.28; M. J. Sellek 118–25–341–16–2/8–21.31; D. T. Fidoe 201.2–41–698–30–4/21–23.26; I. H. Duckhouse 177.5–33–562–22–5/42–25.54; L. P. Wilks 166.5–22–626–23–4/6–27.21.

RUGBY SCHOOL

Played 15: Won 1, Lost 5, Drawn 9

Master i/c: K. Siviter   Cricket professional: W. J. Stewart

Win v: King Edward VI, Birmingham.

Batting—*C. J. C. Robards 17–2–661–133–2–44.06; E. J. Lowe 16–2–493–102–1–35.21; J. N. Plews 13–3–297–80–0–29.70; H. D. Meech 15–0–377–80–0–25.13; H. L. Green 16–0–358–53–0–22.37; J. A. Roper 14–0–182–46–0–13.00.

Bowling—E. J. Lowe 239.3–56–779–33–5/44–23.60.

RYDAL SCHOOL

Played 10: Won 2, Lost 0, Drawn 8

Master i/c: M. T. Leach   Cricket professional: R. W. C. Pitman

M. G. Macdonald completed his fifth season in the XI.

Wins v: Liverpool; Oswestry.

Batting—M. G. Macdonald 9–2–204–61–0–29.14; *M. H. Bennett 10–0–282–63–0–28.20.

Bowling—M. H. Bennett 87–23–215–15–3/14–14.33; S. M. Ashley 100–18–332–17–5/30–19.52.

ST ALBANS SCHOOL

Played 18: Won 9, Lost 3, Drawn 6

Master i/c: I. Jordan

Batting records tumbled during the season. M. J. Seller (105 not out) and fourth-former J. Freedman (118 not out) put on 226 unbroken for the fourth wicket against the Gentlemen of Hertfordshire. The previous school record for any wicket, 190, was also exceeded in a record second-wicket partnership of 192 by Freedman (103) and R. Bee (87) against MCC. The eventual total of 257 for eight in that match was another St Albans record.

Wins v: Roundwood; St Columba's; Dr Challoner's; Queen Elizabeth, Barnet; St Benedict's; Gentlemen of Hertfordshire; John Lyon (twice); MCC.

Batting—J. Freedman 12–3–437–118*–2–48.55; *M. J. Seller 17–4–597–105*–1–45.92; S. Chapman 13–2–318–87–0–28.90; R. Bee 15–1–335–87–0–23.92; J. Mote 16–2–228–74*–0–16.28.

Bowling—No bowler took 15 wickets.

ST DUNSTAN'S COLLEGE

Played 15: Won 2, Lost 6, Drawn 7

Masters i/c: C. Matten and O. T. Price

Wins v: Eltham; Caterham.

Batting—J. Bennett 15–1–559–120*–2–39.92; P. Gaskell 10–0–331–87–0–33.10; *P. A. R. Hobson 12–1–345–86–0–31.36; I. Pressney 12–2–199–57–0–19.90; L. Speed 12–1–203–94–0–18.45; C. Beales 13–2–184–52–0–16.72; N. Kirby 12–1–169–50–0–15.36.

Bowling—J. Bennett 134.4–31–557–25–4/23–22.28; J. North 150.1–52–539–19–5/42–28.36.

ST EDWARD'S SCHOOL, OXFORD

Played 12: Won 3, Lost 5, Drawn 4. Abandoned 1

Master i/c: M. D. Peregrine   Cricket professional: G. V. Palmer

Wins v: Cryptics; Stowe; St Edward's Martyrs.

Batting—N. S. Platt 6–2–175–68–0–43.75; O. M. Slipper 12–0–470–100–1–39.16; A. R. Phillips 9–2–166–41–0–23.71; *J. G. Drake-Brockman 11–2–209–47–0–23.22; A. S. Peebles 10–1–190–52–0–21.11; P. E. H. Franks 10–2–161–59–0–20.12; G. H. Malec 10–0–184–51–0–18.40; C. D. H. Jolly 11–1–154–58–0–15.40.

Bowling—N. Obolensky 151.3–32–393–22–7/46–17.86; J. G. Drake-Brockman 131.5–36–368–18–6/42–20.44.

ST GEORGE'S COLLEGE, WEYBRIDGE

Played 18: Won 6, Lost 5, Drawn 7. Abandoned 2

Master i/c: D. G. Ottley

Wins v: Tercels; Sussex Martlets; Grasshoppers; Aldenham; Emeriti; Old Georgians.

Batting—G. Henderson 14–4–563–149*–2–56.30; *N. Hoyle 14–2–584–103–2–48.66; C. Fletcher 10–0–303–114–1–30.30; A. Watts 12–1–286–94–0–26.00; J. Stephens 13–2–196–47–0–17.81; M. Nicholson 9–0–160–39–0–17.77.

Bowling—N. Hoyle 225–63–780–39–8/29–20.00; G. Henderson 168–36–732–30–7/55–24.40.

ST JOHN'S SCHOOL, LEATHERHEAD

Played 14: Won 2, Lost 4, Drawn 8. Abandoned 2

Master i/c: A. B. Gale   Cricket professional: E. Shepperd

The 750 runs accumulated by William Letts included 123 against Old Johnians, 100 not out against the Headmaster's XI and 130 not out against the XL Club, in which match he and Mark Edsall opened with a school record stand of 202. The leading bowler, Geoff Thompson, played for Surrey Young Cricketers.

Wins v: Headmaster's XI; St Benedict's.

Batting—W. Letts 14–2–750–130*–3–62.50; *M. I. Ridgway 13–2–376–66*–0–34.18; S. J. Speller 12–3–248–51*–0–27.55; M. D. Edsall 14–0–305–74–0–21.78.

Bowling—G. J. Thompson 248–75–617–37–5/32–16.67; S. J. Speller 173–50–452–19–5/55–23.78.

ST JOSEPH'S COLLEGE, IPSWICH

Played 19: Won 11, Lost 4, Drawn 4. Abandoned 2

Master i/c: G. A. Corner

The 11 wins were a record for the college, as was A. M. P. Heyland's aggregate of 687 runs, surpassing the 682 scored by J. McLoughlin in 1990. When J. Payne took six for 22 against Wymondham College, all six were bowled.

Wins v: Attleborough CC; Woodbridge; Suffolk Under-16; Kessingland CC; Suffolk Club & Ground; East Bergholt CC; Royal Hospital S.; Pimpernels; J. Bidwell's XI; Old Oakhillians; Wymondham.

Batting—*A. M. P. Heyland 17–3–687–110–1–49.07; B. G. J. Leary 11–4–300–56–0–42.85; E. G. Manning 18–2–403–60–0–25.18; N. K. Marshall 16–4–278–74*–0–23.16; M. J. Fair 18–5–276–59*–0–21.23; J. A. A. S. Akin-George 12–1–180–70–0–16.36.

Bowling—B. G. J. Leary 157–38–337–29–6/34–11.62; J. Payne 79.2–10–265–19–6/22–13.94; M. S. Blake 76–10–260–15–3/20–17.33; C. M. Jack 122–13–397–18–5/24–22.05; E. G. Manning 142–16–580–18–3/30–32.22.

ST LAWRENCE COLLEGE, RAMSGATE

Played 15: Won 9, Lost 2, Drawn 4

Master i/c: N. O. S. Jones   Cricket professional: A. P. E. Knott

The side was dominated by Kevin Vandrau, brother of the Derbyshire all-rounder. As well as captaining the XI, he scored the most runs and took the most wickets with his seam bowling. Benedict Swindells, the Kent Under-15 captain, opened the batting and kept wicket competently.

Wins v: XL Club; St Augustine's; Duke of York's RMS; Dover; King's, Rochester; St Edmund's, Canterbury; Old Lawrentians; King's, Canterbury; Gravesend GS.

Batting—P. W. Spencer 15–8–457–83*–0–65.28; *K. M. Vandrau 15–3–711–113–1–59.25; B. C. Swindells 15–1–453–81*–0–32.35; A. J. Boaler 15–0–353–49–0–23.53.

Bowling—K. M. Vandrau 226.4–42–736–44–7/35–16.72; J. E. S. Foot 141–26–391–17–5/22–23.00; P. W. Spencer 165.3–43–449–18–3/21–24.94; J. A. S. Clifford 105.5–13–411–16–3/30–25.68.

ST PAUL'S SCHOOL

Played 16: Won 7, Lost 2, Drawn 7. Abandoned 1

Master i/c: G. Hughes   Cricket professional: M. Heath

Wins v: Highgate; Lords and Commons; Buccaneers; Old Paulines; The Masters; MCC; Monkton Combe.

Batting—J. F. A. Poulet 16–2–649–82*–0–46.35; R. S. Stanier 16–0–648–100–1–40.50; T. B. Peters 16–3–451–80–0–34.69; A. J. Baldock 12–3–221–52–0–24.55; F. A. Badat 12–1–265–66–0–24.09.

Bowling—J. F. A. Poulet 84–25–254–17–4/41–14.94; *D. C. Hitchins 192.5–51–524–31–7/48–16.90; S. A. Hurll 141.2–27–433–25–5/31–17.32; T. B. Peters 160–36–597–22–5/17–27.13.

ST PETER'S SCHOOL, YORK

Played 18: Won 4, Lost 1, Drawn 13. Abandoned 2

Master i/c: D. Kirby   Cricket professional: K. F. Mohan

Michael Davies, who scored four of the side's seven centuries, set two new records. His innings of 169 not out against Bradford GS was the highest by a Peterite and his aggregate of 983 overtook Norman Yardley's 973 in 1933.

Wins v: Ampleforth; Old Peterites; President's XI; Loretto.

Batting—*M. J. Davies 19–1–983–169*–4–54.61; R. F. T. Musgrave 18–4–632–124*–2–45.14; T. W. F. Cockcroft 12–3–298–120–1–33.11; J. Lovell 9–2–177–42–0–25.28; T. J. Archer 17–1–321–81–0–20.06; M. S. Bradley 13–3–200–52*–0–20.00; A. L. T. Kay 15–3–182–40*–0–15.16.

Bowling—R. F. T. Musgrave 178–33–577–30–3/25–19.23; J. Lovell 220.1–62–570–24–6/25–23.75; N. J. Ogden 140.3–28–521–20–4/14–26.05.

SEVENOAKS SCHOOL

Played 16: Won 6, Lost 1, Drawn 9. Abandoned 2

Master i/c: I. J. B. Walker

Captained by Hesham Iqbal, son of Asif Iqbal, the side lost only to a strong Sevenoaks Vine XI – off the fifth ball of the last over. William House won the Cricket Society's Wetherell Award for his outstanding all-round performance.

Wins v: XL Club; Cranbrook; Pioneers CC; Old Sennockians; St Dunstan's; Skinners'.

Batting—*Hesham Iqbal 15–7–647–90*–0–80.87; W. J. House 13–5–612–108–2–76.50; T. M. Briggs 12–4–251–65–0–31.37; G. J. Streatfeild 11–0–276–58–0–25.09; D. M. Thomas 10–0–152–43–0–15.20.

Bowling—W. J. House 124–34–282–28–5/31–10.07; T. M. Briggs 111–30–299–19–3/18–15.73; J. S. Smeeton 171–45–437–23–4/16–19.00.

SHERBORNE SCHOOL

Played 14: Won 6, Lost 3, Drawn 5. Abandoned 1

Master i/c: G. C. Allen   Cricket professional: A. Willows

Highlights were a victory over a strong MCC side and their first win for some 50 years over Sherborne Town. The bowling was dominated by the captain, F. M. J. Costeloe, while hundreds were scored by G. W. Garrett and N. I. Gavin-Brown, the latter doing so against MCC on his promotion to the XI.

Wins v: King's, Bruton; Sherborne Town; Free Foresters; Downside; MCC; Sherborne Pilgrims.

Batting—G. W. Garrett 14–1–439–100*–1–33.76; A. S. Cossins 14–2–377–90–0–31.41; N. I. Gavin-Brown 6–0–183–109–1–30.50; S. W. Giles 14–3–279–58–0–25.36; T. G. Rankine 13–0–318–70–0–24.46; T. J. Percival 9–1–171–48–0–21.37; C. J. S. Firebrace 9–0–176–54–0–19.55.

Bowling—*F. M. J. Costeloe 251.2–45–769–40–6/59–19.22; A. J. Robertson 172–19–659–27–6/46–24.40.

SHIPLAKE COLLEGE

Played 13: Won 0, Lost 6, Drawn 7

Master i/c: P. M. Davey

Cricket professional: M. J. Hobbs

Batting—D. Jacobs 6–1–371–114*–1–74.20; *T. P. Caston 13–0–465–106–1–35.76.

Bowling—No bowler took 15 wickets.

SHREWSBURY SCHOOL

Played 19: Won 8, Lost 5, Drawn 6. Abandoned 1

Master i/c: S. M. Holroyd

Cricket professional: A. P. Pridgeon

Wins v: Wrekin; Ellesmere; MCC; Trent; Radley; Radford C., Canberra; A. P. Pridgeon's XI; Shropshire Gentlemen.

Batting—B. E. Hughes 17–4–456–100*–1–35.07; M. R. H. Pike 20–0–562–93–0–28.10; S. W. K. Ellis 20–2–505–85–0–28.05; M. C. Whitehurst 15–2–335–101–1–25.76; N. J. B. Green 10–1–210–66*–0–23.33; C. J. Clarke 19–0–381–77–0–20.05; M. A. Randall 15–3–155–34*–0–12.91; *S. C. Belfield 16–3–164–54–0–12.61.

Bowling—S. W. K. Ellis 226–42–689–39–5/36–17.66; I. S. Dhariwal 207–41–609–30–7/50–20.30; M. A. Randall 127.4–13–470–19–3/20–24.73; C. E. Mann 158.4–29–506–15–2/17–33.73.

SIMON LANGTON GRAMMAR SCHOOL

Played 21: Won 15, Lost 1, Drawn 5. Abandoned 1

Master i/c: R. H. Green

Fifteen of 21 matches were won, the only loss coming in the last over against Old Langtonians. The XI won the Lemon Cup and Kent Schools Under-19 League. The captain, N. N. Bielby, registered most runs and most wickets.

Wins v: Cranbook GS; Kent C.; Chatham GS (twice); Harvey GS; Dartford GS; QES, Faversham; Sir Joseph Williamson's MS; Norton Knatchbull; Bexley-Erith THS; Judd; St Augustine's; Sir Roger Manwood's; Bishop's Stortford HS; Simon Langton Staff.

Batting—J. J. Cattell 18–6–487–60–0–40.58; S. C. Tophill 14–3–392–66–0–35.63; *N. N. Bielby 21–3–620–116*–2–34.44; R. E. White 15–2–346–43*–0–26.61; D. R. Mathews 17–1–369–79–0–23.06; B. T. Ralph 15–3–203–38–0–16.91; R. J. Marsh 14–3–183–54*–0–16.63.

Bowling—A. Claridge 88.2–32–191–24–5/12–7.95; J. J. Cattell 37–3–143–16–4/28–8.93; N. N. Bielby 124.5–25–338–36–7/37–9.38; R. J. Marsh 162–34–421–34–7/33–12.38; D. L. Churchward 94.3–15–381–28–6/40–13.60.

SOLIHULL SCHOOL

Played 14: Won 1, Lost 5, Drawn 8. Abandoned 5

Master i/c: D. J. Dunn

Cricket professional: S. Perryman

Win v: Recent Old Boys.

Batting—*S. J. Legg 13–2–480–107*–1–43.63; A. S. Prescott 13–1–435–99–0–36.25; P. S. Amiss 12–1–345–76–0–31.36; C. R. Briggs 13–1–365–105*–1–30.41; J. R. Vaughan 10–1–201–46–0–22.33.

Bowling—E. J. Dawes 129–24–478–15–4/34–31.86.

SOUTH CRAVEN SCHOOL

Played 8: Won 3, Lost 3, Drawn 2. Abandoned 1

Master i/c: D. M. Birks

The second-wicket partnership of 102 between Malcolm Birks (73 not out) and Neil Spragg (42) against Ermysted's GS was a school record.

Wins v: Rotherham SFC; Ermysted's GS; Scarborough SFC.

Batting—N. Spragg 5–2–202–66–0–67.33; I. Spragg 6–0–218–90–0–36.33; *M. J. Birks 7–1–200–73*–0–33.33.

Bowling—No bowler took 15 wickets.

STAMFORD SCHOOL

Played 15: Won 2, Lost 7, Drawn 6

Master i/c: P. D. McKeown

Wins v: The Leys; XL Club.

Batting—J. P. Moore 12–1–377–110*–1–34.27; T. E. Smith 5–0–154–68–0–30.80; L. H. Jackson 14–2–326–60–0–27.16; *B. T. Bonney-James 15–2–334–86–0–25.69; E. J. Detoney 14–4–173–52–0–17.30; J. M. Lusby 13–0–212–36–0–16.30; G. S. Paulson 15–5–151–42–0–15.10.

Bowling—P. Holland 211–45–699–30–5/59–23.30; L. H. Jackson 136–16–636–21–5/74–30.28; G. S. Paulson 213–50–762–15–4/135–50.80.

STOCKPORT GRAMMAR SCHOOL

Played 12: Won 1, Lost 3, Drawn 8. Abandoned 3

Master i/c: S. Teasdale   Cricket professional: D. J. Makinson

Win v: Stockport GS Old Boys.

Batting—*S. K. Lapsia 10–1–276–51–0–30.66; N. S. Thompson 12–2–227–59–0–22.70.

Bowling—S. K. Lapsia 89.5–28–262–23–6/21–11.39; A. J. Wallace 91–13–295–17–5/41–17.35; N. S. Thompson 148.2–30–493–25–5/49–19.72.

STOWE SCHOOL

Played 14: Won 3, Lost 6, Drawn 5. Abandoned 1

Master i/c: M. J. Harris

Wins v: Northamptonshire Under-19; MCC; Old Stoics.

Batting—P. Denning 13–2–291–70*–0–26.45; G. Smith-Walker 12–0–293–57–0–24.41; E. Rogers 13–1–272–51*–0–22.66; J. Nash 13–0–227–59–0–17.46; G. Passmore 14–1–207–76*–0–15.92; S. Gerrard 13–0–194–35–0–14.92.

Bowling—C. Howie 187–41–457–25–5/42–18.28; E. Rogers 170–35–504–15–3/23–33.60.

STRATHALLAN SCHOOL

Played 11: Won 3, Lost 3, Drawn 5. Abandoned 7

Master i/c: R. J. W. Proctor

A very young side suffered a disappointing season, seriously disrupted by rain, which completely washed out seven of their 18 fixtures.

Wins v: Fettes; Stewart's Melville; Coleraine.

Batting—S. G. Cooksley 11–1–236–54–0–23.60; *N. A. Gray 11–0–189–69–0–17.18.

Bowling—D. G. Forbes 65.4–8–282–18–5/33–15.66; A. S. Doodson 116–34–258–15–5/46–17.20; R. J. D. Barr 102.5–32–279–16–5/13–17.43; J. D. Henderson 120.3–31–343–18–5/24–19.05.

SUTTON VALENCE SCHOOL

Played 15: Won 3, Lost 8, Drawn 4

Master i/c: D. Pickard

Wins v: St Bede's; Old Suttonians; Dover.

Batting—W. G. Waters 15–1–568–93–0–40.57; *A. R. Barr 13–2–304–79–0–27.63; B. Painter 12–0–327–52–0–27.25; T. Thomson 11–1–151–43–0–15.10.

Bowling—A. R. Barr 95–25–257–15–3/22–17.13; B. Painter 146–28–464–27–7/12–17.18; W. G. Waters 171–26–614–27–4/33–22.74; M. Fox 136–25–419–15–3/30–27.93.

TAUNTON SCHOOL

Played 13: Won 3, Lost 6, Drawn 4. Abandoned 1

Master i/c: D. Baty   Cricket professional: A. Kennedy

Wins v: Canford; Old Tauntonians; Burnley Habergham.

Batting—G. D. Hector 13–0–359–65–0–27.61; T. Phillips 12–2–216–101–1–21.60; J. Ord 13–2–179–55–0–16.27; G. A. Manchip 12–0–156–34–0–13.00.

Bowling—J. Ord 221.3–56–580–32–6/33–18.12; M. R. Thomas 168–36–462–22–5/33–21.00.

TIFFIN SCHOOL

Played 19: Won 4, Lost 3, Drawn 12. Abandoned 1

Master i/c: M. J. Williams

Despite the preponderance of draws, Tiffin reported an entertaining season in which team spirit was excellent and the Hampton 6-a-side trophy was won in July.

Wins v: St Benedict's; Reed's; KCS, Wimbledon; Desborough.

Batting—N. Evans 17–4–672–100*–1–51.69; R. C. Ward 19–4–604–100*–1–40.26; *M. A. Rafique 19–1–577–91–0–32.05; S. E. Schollar 17–7–223–57–0–22.30; O. W. Burley 12–1–213–39–0–19.36; S. Amfo-Okoampah 19–1–340–50*–0–18.88.

Bowling—O. W. Burley 194–55–662–35–4/22–18.91; J. C. N. Gray 187.2–33–668–32–7/24–20.87; P. W. Haylock 183.4–38–623–25–4/13–24.92.

TONBRIDGE SCHOOL

Played 19: Won 13, Lost 3, Drawn 3. Abandoned 1

Master i/c: I. S. MacEwen   Cricket professional: C. Stone

Thirteen victories beat the previous best of 12 achieved by Chris Cowdrey's 1975 XI. The captain, J. D. Chaplin, made an outstanding all-round contribution, while J. A. Ford headed both averages and M. J. Barham took the most wickets.

Wins v: Lancing; Charterhouse; Bedford; Haileybury; Wellington C.; Caulfield GS, Melbourne; MCC; Old Tonbridgians; Clifton; Felsted; Antipodeans, Sydney; Bradford GS; Alberton Schools, Transvaal.

Batting—J. A. Ford 20–6–754–118*–1–53.85; *J. D. Chaplin 20–2–834–122–1–46.33; C. D. Walsh 20–3–670–93–0–39.41; C. S. Charlton 12–5–183–74*–0–26.14; R. A. Arscott 18–3–222–39–0–14.80.

Bowling—J. A. Ford 92.4–26–239–19–4/36–12.57; J. D. Chaplin 216.1–70–513–39–6/37–13.15; W. M. Fyfe 85–17–216–15–3/10–14.40; H. R. G. Moxon 211.5–57–481–33–5/29–14.57; M. J. Barham 349.3–133–709–41–7/71–17.29.

TRENT COLLEGE

Played 13: Won 0, Lost 7, Drawn 5, Tied 1. Abandoned 2

Master i/c: Dr T. P. Woods   Cricket professional: G. Miller

The batting averages were headed by N. A. Gie, the HMC Under-16 captain and son of C. A. Gie who played for Western Province and Natal.

Batting—N. A. Gie 12–0–588–153–1–49.00; K. G. Reesby 12–3–261–57–0–29.00; B. L. Spendlove 6–0–168–50–0–28.00; A. M. Lock 11–0–197–52–0–17.90; B. G. Martin 13–0–203–69–0–15.61.

Bowling—N. C. M. Owen 124.2–14–466–15–5/44–31.06.

TRINITY SCHOOL

Played 22: Won 10, Lost 3, Drawn 8, Tied 1. Abandoned 2

Masters i/c: I. W. Cheyne and B. Widger

Although not as spectacular as in 1992, the XI enjoyed another fine season. Despite missing some of the matches and the tour to Holland, R. W. Nowell still managed to score 597 runs and take 51 wickets with his left-arm spin. He extended his record for the XI to 3,513 runs and 203 wickets, a post war record and just 14 behind the overall record. He is expected to add to those figures in his final year in 1994. It was encouraging to note that the XI continued to perform well in his absence, ably led by D. O. Dyer, whose left-arm spin brought him 42 wickets and who played some fine innings, especially against Caterham and Whitgift. The six centuries were shared between four boys, of whom D. L. Fifield and P. J. McDonnell both made hundreds against Reigate. Nowell played for Surrey Second XI, England Under-17, English Schools and NAYC.

Wins v: St Dunstan's; Wallington HS; Whitgift; Caterham; John Fisher; Emanuel; Reigate; Past Captain's XI; Hague CC; VOC Rotterdam.

Batting—R. W. Nowell 14–1–597–102–1–45.92; *D. O. Dyer 18–4–610–129*–2–43.57; P. J. McDonnell 18–5–564–100*–1–43.38; D. L. Fifield 21–0–704–145–2–33.52; S. Higgins 17–4–343–73*–0–26.38.

Bowling—R. W. Nowell 296–61–862–51–6/41–16.90; D. O. Dyer 318.2–86–764–42–6/55–18.19; A. J. T. Clark 248–70–609–28–5/51–21.75.

TRURO SCHOOL

Played 10: Won 3, Lost 4, Drawn 3. Abandoned 2

Master i/c: D. M. Phillips

Wins v: Truro School Society; Old Boys; Common Room XI.

Batting—*R. A. Atkins 10–2–324–107*–1–40.50; T. G. Sharp 6–0–151–41–0–25.16; S. J. Perkins 8–1–157–60*–0–22.42.

Bowling—S. J. Perkins 120.2–23–278–19–7/35–14.63.

UNIVERSITY COLLEGE SCHOOL

Played 18: Won 1, Lost 12, Drawn 5

Master i/c: S. M. Bloomfield   Cricket professional: W. G. Jones

A young side bowled well but were let down by weak batting and poor catching. N. D. Modi and G. M. J. Taylor set a tenth-wicket record of 77 against Abingdon.

Win v: Woodbridge.

Batting—B. J. Marshall 15–4–261–53*–0–23.72; *A. R. Gishen 19–0–396–113–1–20.84; F. J. Renton 19–0–361–45–0–19.00; C. F. B. Miller 15–3–224–41*–0–18.66.

Bowling—A. M. Quint 144–40–341–20–5/41–17.05; G. M. J. Taylor 225.2–47–764–35–5/58–21.82; G. M. Joseph 196.4–37–620–24–7/20–25.83.

UPPINGHAM SCHOOL

Played 17: Won 7, Lost 1, Drawn 9. Abandoned 2

Master i/c: I. E. W. Sanders   Cricket professional: M. R. Hallam

In Uppingham's best season for many years, James Beaumont scored 860 runs, his 748 in term-time overtaking James Whitaker's record of 747 in 1980.

Wins v: Trent; Felsted; Gentlemen of Leicestershire; Stamford; Bedford; Blundell's; Ampleforth.

Batting—*J. N. Beaumont 18–3–860–108*–1–57.33; E. W. R. Hill 18–2–492–73–0–30.75; A. D. J. Dawe 16–5–317–62*–0–28.81; A. L. Perkins 14–4–273–104*–1–27.30; B. P. Aspell 17–1–387–77–0–24.18; T. A. Norris 8–0–164–36–0–20.50; M. Bird 14–2–198–35*–0–16.50.

Bowling—M. Bird 269.1–50–871–37–6/63–23.54; S. C. Debenham 279.5–69–847–33–5/34–25.66.

VICTORIA COLLEGE, JERSEY

Played 17: Won 3, Lost 5, Drawn 9

Master i/c: D. A. R. Ferguson

Wins v: P. Coyne's XI; Abbotsholme; Portsmouth GS.

Batting—*C. Jones 15–3–759–128*–3–63.25; S. A. Ramskill 11–4–283–80–0–40.42; C. J. D. O'Brien 16–3–413–94–0–31.76; C. N. A. Gothard 17–1–347–64–0–21.68; T. J. George 11–1–193–59*–0–19.30; A. Skilton 16–0–171–31–0–10.68.

Bowling—C. Jones 140–30–252–17–6/34–14.82; G. M. Carnegie 100–16–316–15–3/20–21.06; S. A. Ramskill 238–44–834–29–5/79–28.75.

WARWICK SCHOOL

Played 15: Won 3, Lost 2, Drawn 9, Tied 1. Abandoned 1

Master i/c: D. C. Elstone

A highlight in a season of close finishes was the tie against Trent College, who, needing ten runs off the last six overs with five wickets in hand, lost their last wicket off the last ball. Lewis Edwards was an excellent captain, Eddie Butcher proved to be a quality all-rounder and John Moffatt headed the batting as well as keeping wicket.

Wins v: Loughborough GS; Old Warwickians; Cryptics.

Batting—J. Moffatt 14–2–529–103*–2–44.08; E. Butcher 14–2–391–85–0–32.58; P. Mayo 14–4–299–67*–0–29.90; *L. A. J. Edwards 13–2–213–47*–0–19.36; H. Munton 10–1–152–50*–0–16.88; W. Hayes 13–0–215–50–0–16.53.

Bowling—E. Butcher 188–45–541–32–5/30–16.90; E. Rushton 99.1–19–345–16–5/40–21.56.

WELLINGBOROUGH SCHOOL

Played 19: Won 6, Lost 2, Drawn 11

Master i/c: M. H. Askham

Cricket professional: J. C. J. Dye

Mark Steele, son of the Test player David Steele, was outstanding. As well as opening the bowling, he broke the school batting record wth 1,174 runs, overtaking the 1990 record of 1,116 by Jeremy Attfield.

Wins v: Wisbech GS; Ratcliffe; Brentwood; XL Club; Lord Williams's, Thame; William Hulme's GS.

Batting—M. V. Steele 19–5–1,174–122*–2–83.85; K. G. Potter 18–1–480–81–0–28.23; M. A. R. Prabhu 11–5–152–38–0–25.33; S. L. Shah 12–1–260–83*–0–23.63; P. S. Smith 18–2–375–56–0–23.43.

Bowling—M. V. Steele 154.1–26–455–23–3/29–19.78; J. R. E. Wilson 153.5–28–627–27–4/36–23.22; D. W. Hallworth 239–45–839–23–4/23–36.47.

WELLINGTON COLLEGE

Played 18: Won 10, Lost 1, Drawn 7. Abandoned 1

Masters i/c: C. M. St G. Potter and R. I. H. B. Dyer

Cricket professional: P. J. Lewington

A strong XI had their best season ever, with two wins more than the previous best of eight.

Wins v: Free Foresters; Winchester; Harrow; Bradfield; Caulfield GS, Melbourne; Haileybury; Melbourne GS, Australia; Stowe; Bedford; Northwood HS, South Africa.

Batting—T. P. Hodgson 18–2–773–129*–1–48.31; D. R. H. Churton 18–3–669–103*–1–44.60; *T. P. Newman 18–3–576–89–0–38.40; D. R. L. B. Lamb 15–2–396–84*–0–30.46; S. R. Pearce 9–2–188–53*–0–26.85; S. D. M. Brownrigg 14–2–301–55–0–25.08; W. G. M. Sawrey-Cookson 15–5–201–35–0–20.10.

Bowling—H. J. Bishop 140.1–21–400–25–4/19–16.00; D. M. Simpson 214.3–53–579–34–6/30–17.02; T. P. Newman 190.5–43–568–24–6/48–23.66; S. D. M. Brownrigg 217.2–42–593–24–4/22–24.70; B. St J. Morris 150.4–29–471–19–4/37–24.78.

WELLINGTON SCHOOL

Played 17: Won 7, Lost 2, Drawn 8

Master i/c: P. M. Pearce

Jeremy Clarke established a school record of 58 wickets in the season.

Wins v: Mallards CC; Queen Elizabeth's Hospital; West Buckland; Queen's, Taunton; Allhallows; Colston's; Habergham.

Batting—A. Fulker 16–3–411–79*–0–31.61; *D. Davidson 17–2–415–75–0–27.66; L. Wardell 16–0–327–43–0–20.43; R. Cooper 16–0–313–63–0–19.56; G. Scott 15–1–181–48–0–12.92; B. Hartley 14–1–156–25–0–12.00.

Bowling—B. Rudall 189–10–189–22–6/31–8.59; J. Clarke 252–62–758–58–8/30–13.06; D. Hewitt 153–32–302–16–4/26–18.87; D. Davidson 167–38–536–21–4/54–25.52.

WELLS CATHEDRAL SCHOOL

Played 14: Won 4, Lost 4, Drawn 6. Abandoned 1

Master i/c: M. Stringer

Wins v: XL Club; Wells CC; Millfield; Somerset Stragglers.

Batting—A. Frankpitt 15–4–431–89–0–39.18; J. Stone 6–1–151–78–0–30.20; A. Murphy 15–0–341–64–0–22.73; J. Pym 14–0–305–78–0–21.78; B. Maddison 13–0–255–70–0–19.61; R. Bates 12–3–162–52–0–18.00.

Bowling—J. Keen 168.3–39–556–40–7/55–13.90.

WESTMINSTER SCHOOL

Played 11: Won 3, Lost 2, Drawn 6

Master i/c: D. Cook   Cricket professional: R. O. Butcher

Alex Worthington completed four seasons in the XI with a total of 1,571 runs, more than any other batsman in recent times.

Wins v: Kingston GS; UCS, Hampstead; Westminster City S.

Batting—*A. Worthington 11–3–308–90–0–38.50; K. Karmali 7–2–167–58*–0–33.40; S. Khan 9–2–157–48–0–22.42; D. Mahoney 11–0–173–56–0–15.72.

Bowling—A. Sahai 99.2–27–269–30–6/22–8.96; M. Cornes 71.1–13–248–15–5/25–16.53; D. Mahoney 91.1–14–296–15–4/23–19.73.

WHITGIFT SCHOOL

Played 16: Won 3, Lost 7, Drawn 6. Abandoned 1

Master i/c: P. C. Fladgate   Cricket professional: C. J. Franklin

Weak batting hampered progress and resulted in a rather disappointing season. A highlight was the opening partnership of 175 against Reigate GS between M. G. Courtenay (90) and T. R. K. Hird (77).

Wins v: Honesti; OWA; Kingston GS.

Batting—T. R. K. Hird 14–0–309–90–0–22.07; *C. E. Catling 17–2–312–49*–0–20.80; B. Goward 13–1–232–71–0–19.33; T. C. Dobson 17–0–306–41–0–18.00; J. P. Blasco 15–1–241–50–0–17.21; P. E. Bulteel 15–3–199–62*–0–16.58.

Bowling—G. K. Spring 208.3–56–564–31–6/51–18.19; T. R. K. Hird 153–32–465–23–5/35–20.21; J. P. Blasco 140.3–27–474–18–4/46–26.33; A. A. Chmielowski 150–43–395–15–4/27–26.33.

WILLIAM HULME'S GRAMMAR SCHOOL

Played 14: Won 3, Lost 6, Drawn 5. Abandoned 3

Master i/c: H. W. Timm   Cricket professional: R. Collins

New records were set by Nathan Wood, son of the Test player Barry Wood. His innings of 145 not out against Bury GS passed the previous highest of 144 not out, but he later improved on that again with 163 not out against the XL Club. His innings against Bury GS featured in a record-breaking opening stand of 241, while his other hundreds were 130 not out against Old Hulmeians and 112 out of the first 140 scored against St Bede's. He played for England Under-18, England Under-19 and Lancashire Second XI, having a full contract with the county for 1994.

Wins v: King's, Chester; Bradford GS; XL Club.

Batting—N. T. Wood 12–4–939–164*–4–117.37; P. D. Warren 14–2–535–99–0–44.58; I. Cooke 13–3–198–48–0–19.80.

Bowling—T. Allen 123.4–24–388–23–5/34–16.86; C. Bell 118.2–25–426–24–5/31–17.75.

WINCHESTER COLLEGE

Played 20: Won 3, Lost 7, Drawn 10. Abandoned 1

Master i/c: K. N. Foyle   Cricket professional: I. C. D. Stuart

There was plenty of effort but little class in the XI, whose lack of penetration and brittle batting brought disappointing results. Too much depended on the experienced N. D. Freebody, who headed the batting, and R. J. A. T. Chaffey, who managed the only five-wicket return of the season, but with some promising colts coming through, prospects look good.

Wins v: Old Wykehamists; Kimbolton; Berkhamsted.

Batting—N. D. Freebody 20-1-719-106*-1-37.84; A. B. P. Miller 13-2-383-57*-0-34.81; R. J. A. T. Chaffey 20-3-415-124*-1-24.41; C. F. P. Villiers 18-6-259-31-0-21.58.

Bowling—R. J. A. T. Chaffey 154-32-494-19-5/64-26.00; N. D. Freebody 197-59-543-17-3/26-31.94; G. W. Phillips 157.3-20-604-16-3/24-37.75.

WOODBRIDGE SCHOOL

Played 15: Won 0, Lost 8, Drawn 7

Master i/c: P. Kesterton

Batting—B. D. Harper 15-1-318-78-0-22.71; G. A. Holloway 8-0-164-47-0-20.50; G. A. Haggart 14-1-163-45-0-12.53.

Bowling—*P. A. Birchley 136.1-25-439-22-5/36-19.95; T. E. Percival 113-12-435-15-2/18-29.00.

WOODHOUSE GROVE SCHOOL

Played 17: Won 12, Lost 0, Drawn 5

Master i/c: E. R. Howard   Cricket professional: N. Pretorius

All-round excellence was the key to the most successful season in the school's history. Innings were regularly given a solid foundation by the left-handed openers David Webster and Andrew Bairstow, son of the former Yorkshire wicket-keeper. Ned Taylor had a fine all-round season and considerable promise was shown by the Under-15 player Daniel Brier. Webster was an imaginative captain, who regularly used at least seven bowlers and whose off-spin lent variety to the attack. Bairstow went on to play for MCC Schools and English Schools.

Wins v: Ashville; Hymers; QEGS, Wakefield; Barnard Castle; Batley GS; Giggleswick; Newingham; Hawks CC; Craven Gentlemen; XL Club; Old Boys; Headmaster's XI.

Batting—*D. J. Webster 13-3-554-112*-1-55.40; A. D. Bairstow 15-4-543-109-1-49.36; N. B. Taylor 13-7-285-60*-0-47.50; S. J. Nesbit 12-2-273-75-0-27.30; A. M. Cadman 15-2-306-59-0-23.53; D. T. Brier 10-2-156-59-0-19.50.

Bowling—N. B. Taylor 90.4-21-263-26-5/12-10.11; M. C. Tetley 132.2-31-375-22-4/21-17.04; D. J. Webster 129-26-339-17-3/7-19.94; R. D. Graves 128-25-368-15-3/15-24.53.

WORKSOP COLLEGE

Played 19: Won 5, Lost 3, Drawn 11

Master i/c: C. G. Paton   Cricket professional: A. Kettleborough

The First XI was coached by the headmaster, MCC secretary-designate and former captain of Surrey, R. D. V. Knight.

Wins v: Ampleforth; Mount St Mary's; XL Club; Repton; Ellesmere.

Batting—D. J. Smith 7–3–161–97*–0–40.25; J. S. Berry 17–2–504–124–1–33.60; *R. J. Fox-Andrews 15–0–450–67–0–30.00; I. P. Jenkinson 8–0–209–83–0–26.12; M. A. Czernek 9–1–207–64*–0–25.87; A. P. Scrini 15–2–279–57–0–21.46; A. S. Hunter 15–2–194–43*–0–14.92; A. J. Fairbrother 16–0–218–70–0–13.62; J. W. Ireland 14–2–152–41–0–12.66.

Bowling—L. F. H. Wilkinson 132.4–38–386–23–5/10–16.78; A. S. Hunter 191.1–42–624–32–4/14–19.50; L. Mackay 84–8–346–17–4/42–20.35; R. J. Fox-Andrews 93–13–354–15–4/33–23.60.

WREKIN COLLEGE

Played 18: Won 3, Lost 7, Drawn 8

Master i/c: M. de Weymarn   Cricket professional: D. A. Banks

Wins v: MCC; Chase HS; Hereford Cathedral S.

Batting—*C. M. Ingram 15–4–484–86*–0–44.00; R. P. L. Burton 18–1–398–57–0–23.41; R. M. I. Davies 14–0–316–44–0–22.57; J. W. Marshall 17–1–358–88–0–22.37; I. W. McArthur 12–3–153–28–0–17.00.

Bowling—I. H. McArthur 178–23–632–29–6/39–21.79; R. P. L. Burton 167–29–575–22–4/51–26.13; B. J. Morley 172–21–584–20–4/52–29.20.

WYCLIFFE COLLEGE

Played 12: Won 0, Lost 4, Drawn 7, Tied 1. Abandoned 2

Master i/c: M. C. Russell   Cricket professional: A. G. Lawson

The weakest XI for some years suffered from the lack of an experienced bowler. The captain, P. W. Lewis, son of the former Glamorgan leg-spin bowler D. W. Lewis, led the side confidently but had a wretched season with the bat. Much therefore depended on I. M. Collins, who passed 500 runs with three centuries, despite having missed nearly three weeks owing to an injury.

Batting—I. M. Collins 10–1–538–114–3–59.77; P. Smith 11–3–174–38–0–21.75; *P. W. Lewis 11–0–159–40–0–14.45.

Bowling—No bowler took 15 wickets.

WYGGESTON & QUEEN ELIZABETH I SIXTH FORM COLLEGE

Played 10: Won 3, Lost 4, Drawn 3. Abandoned 2

Master i/c: G. G. Wells

Wins v: Bosworth; Masters' XI; High Pavement.

Batting—M. D. R. Sutliff 6–0–246–102–1–41.00; J. D. Hanger 9–0–259–60–0–28.77; *J. D. Lawrence 8–1–164–50*–0–23.42.

Bowling—No bowler took 15 wickets.

WOMEN'S CRICKET, 1993

By CAROL SALMON

WORLD CUP, 1993

England finally broke Australia's stranglehold on women's cricket when they beat New Zealand in the final at Lord's by 67 runs. After England's win in the inaugural competition, at home in 1973, they had lost the next three finals to Australia. This time the Australians lost two crucial preliminary matches and went out; not only was it refreshing to see someone other than an Australian lift the World Cup, it was a fine achievement by New Zealand to deny their trans-Tasman rivals a final place for the first time.

Around 4,500 people attended the final, beyond all expectations, thanks to excellent media coverage. With England's men 3-0 down against Australia, English newspapers, television and radio eagerly portrayed the women's team as the country's cricketing salvation. But only an eleventh-hour contribution of £90,000 from the Foundation for Sports and the Arts had enabled the tournament to go ahead in the first place, though later it received substantial support from the Sports Council and MCC. They were all gratefully acknowledged by Audrey Collins, retiring president of the Women's Cricket Association, in her presentation speech in front of the Lord's Pavilion.

New Zealand had a magnificent qualifying run, winning all their seven games and conceding just 1.61 runs an over. Their 25-run victory over England at Beckenham featured the best fielding – there were five run-outs – and bowling of the tournament, when they prevented England performing the seemingly routine task of scoring 128 in 60 overs. England were no match for New Zealand that day; nor, surprisingly, were the Australians in their final qualifying match. Having lost to England, Australia needed to win to have a chance of reaching the final. Instead they lost by an amazing ten wickets, bowled out for 77. Going for their shots, New Zealand reached their target in only 18.2 overs.

The Australians' fall from grace was spectacular; coach Peter Bakker acknowledged that their late arrival in England, reducing the opportunity for warm-up matches, was a major factor. But too many players did not perform up to past standards and there was a feeling that they had enjoyed too much success and lost their appetite. Denise Annetts, who came with a formidable reputation, played only one significant innings and their highest scorer was Belinda Clark, with 199 runs at 33.16, while their chief wicket-taker was leg-spinner Sharyn Bow, with 11 at 12.36.

The leading run-scorer of the competition was England's 34-year-old opener Janette Brittin, with 410 runs at 51.25. During the final at Lord's she became the first player to pass 1,000 World Cup runs; she earlier overtook Rachael Heyhoe-Flint's record of 2,457 runs in all internationals for England, reaching 2,789. She hit only 16 boundaries in her eight innings but her approach throughout was mature and thoughtful. She scored two hundreds, one against Denmark, who conceded 286 and lost their first-ever World Cup match by 239 runs; the second came in a much closer game with India, which England won by three runs in the final over. Carole

Hodges, who also scored two centuries, was second in the run aggregates, with 334 runs at 47.71. Her match-winning 105 not out in 141 balls against Australia at Guildford was probably her finest for England. The other heroine of the victory over Australia – which was seized on by the press, as it came on the day England lost the Ashes and Gooch resigned – was Gill Smith, who destroyed their batting with five for 30. The all-rounder Jo Chamberlain played below her best in the early matches, but hit peak form by the final, where she won the match award for a spectacular 38, followed by a wicket, a run-out and a catch. Captain Karen Smithies was England's player of the tournament. Her 77 overs of seam cost just 1.54 runs each and she took 15 wickets at 7.93. Her contribution to women's cricket was recognised with an OBE in the New Year's honours. Clare Taylor, who conceded just 1.81 an over, and Smith had 14 wickets each, and off-spinner Hodges, who often opened the bowling, had a hat-trick against Denmark. Wicket-keeper Jane Smit justified her surprise selection ahead of Lisa Nye with quiet efficiency, making 12 dismissals, nine caught and three stumped.

The impressive New Zealand wicket-keeper and captain Sarah Illingworth set a World Cup record of six dismissals (four stumped and two caught) against Australia. However, this was equalled only 16 minutes later, at Ealing, when India's Kalpana claimed the last of her five catches and a stumping against Denmark. Like Smithies, Julie Harris finished with 15 wickets, including a hat-trick of lbws against West Indies. New Zealand's leading scorer was Debbie Hockley, with 229 at 45.80. But many of her middle-order colleagues had too little time in the middle; until the final they never had to chase more than 96.

India, led by the experienced Diana Edulji, who claimed 14 wickets, improved with every match. They lost only to the big three – Australia, England and New Zealand – and it looked as though they would be a force to be reckoned with when they host the next World Cup, in December 1997. West Indies could also have a bright future, given more regular competition. They boasted a promising spin attack, led by Desirée Luke and Cherry-Ann Singh. Of the Europeans, Ireland were disappointed to win only twice, against Denmark and Holland, after reaching the third-place play-off against New Zealand in 1988-89. Denmark entered their first World Cup with expectations that were not realised, while Holland, who had a good win over West Indies, must have sunk to a world's worst in taking 54.2 overs to score 40 after deciding to bat.

Results

At Warrington, July 20. Australia won by ten wickets. Toss: Australia. Holland 53 (49.3 overs) (B. Calver four for eight, S. Bow three for 11); Australia 56 for no wkt (16.5 overs) (B. Clark 37 not out).

At Banstead, July 20. England won by 239 runs. Toss: Denmark. England 286 for three (60 overs) (J. A. Brittin 104, H. C. Plimmer 77, B. A. Daniels 60 not out); Denmark 47 (33.5 overs) (C. E. Taylor four for 13, C. A. Hodges four for three, including a hat-trick).

At John Player Ground, Nottingham, July 20. India won by 63 runs. Toss: West Indies. India 155 for five (52.3 overs) (A. Jain 84 not out); West Indies 92 (48.4 overs) (D. Edulji three for 15).

At Shenley, July 20. New Zealand won by seven wickets. Toss: New Zealand. Ireland 82 for six (39 overs) (S. Reamsbottom 35); New Zealand 83 for three (19.3 overs) (M. A. M. Lewis 32, S. L. Illingworth 32 not out).

At Collingham, July 21. Australia won by seven wickets. Toss: India. India 108 (58.4 overs) (S. Gupta 32 not out; K. M. Brown three for 19, S. Bow three for 28); Australia 114 for three (38.3 overs) (B. Clark 35, D. A. Annetts 40 not out).

At Christ Church, Oxford, July 21. Ireland won by 70 runs. Toss: Denmark. Ireland 234 for six (60 overs) (S. Owens 61, M. Grealey 63 not out; J. Jonsson three for 34); Denmark 164 for nine (60 overs) (M. Frost 37, V. Nielsen 33; S. Bray three for 22).

At Lloyds Bank Ground, Beckenham, July 21. New Zealand won by 25 runs. Toss: England. New Zealand 127 (54.5 overs) (G. A. Smith three for 16, K. Smithies three for 23); England 102 (57.2 overs).

At Stoke-on-Trent, July 21. Holland won by 70 runs. Toss: Holland. Holland 158 (59.5 overs) (P. Te Beest 62; C.-A. James three for 17); West Indies 88 (45.4 overs) (A. Beecheno van Lier four for 24).

At Tunbridge Wells, July 24. Australia won by eight wickets. Toss: West Indies. West Indies 131 for nine (60 overs) (A. Browne 65 not out; B. Calver four for four); Australia 133 for two (29.5 overs) (B. Clark 53).

At Wellington College, July 24. New Zealand won by nine wickets. Toss: Denmark. Denmark 93 (58.1 overs) (J. E. Harris three for 13, C. A. Campbell three for 25); New Zealand 94 for one (17.5 overs) (P. D. Kinsella 43 not out, D. A. Hockley 44).

At Reading, July 24. England won on scoring-rate, Ireland's target having been revised to 243 from 56 overs. Toss: Ireland. England 259 for four (60 overs) (C. A. Hodges 113, H. C. Plimmer 118); Ireland 80 for nine (56 overs) (J. M. Chamberlain three for 14, K. Smithies three for six).

At Beaconsfield, July 24. India won by 17 runs. Toss: Holland. India 93 for four (35 overs) (S. Agarwal 42 not out); Holland 76 (34.1 overs).

At Roehampton, July 25. Australia won by 49 runs. Toss: Australia. Australia 194 for eight (60 overs) (L. A. Larsen 62, Z. J. Goss 69); Ireland 145 for four (60 overs) (C. O'Neill 44 not out).

At Lloyds Bank Ground, Beckenham, July 25. West Indies won by 44 runs. Toss: Denmark. West Indies 120 (45.3 overs) (L. Slebsager three for 25, S. Nielsen three for 23); Denmark 76 (52.1 overs) (E. Cunningham three for 16).

At Finchampstead, July 25. England won by three runs. Toss: India. England 179 (59.5 overs) (J. A. Brittin 100; D. Edulji four for 12); India 176 (59.5 overs) (S. Agarwal 57, P. Janardhan 31 not out).

At Lindfield, July 25. New Zealand won by ten wickets. Toss: Holland. Holland 40 (54.2 overs) (J. A. Turner five for five, J. E. Harris three for five); New Zealand 41 for no wkt (13.2 overs).

At Guildford, July 26. England won by 43 runs. Toss: England. England 208 for five (60 overs) (J. A. Brittin 61, C. A. Hodges 105 not out); Australia 165 (53.5 overs) (B. J. Haggett 41, S. Griffiths 34, B. Calver 34 not out; K. Smithies three for 13, G. A. Smith five for 30).

At Wellington College, July 26. Denmark won by 30 runs. Toss: Denmark. Denmark 152 for seven (60 overs) (K. Mikkelsen 36; N. Payne three for 20); Holland 122 (55.1 overs) (A. van Noortwijk 52; S. Nielsen three for 36).

At Wellington College, July 26. India won by four wickets. Toss: Ireland. Ireland 151 (58.4 overs) (S. Reamsbottom 46, M.-P. Moore 37 not out; P. Janardhan three for 26); India 152 for six (57.3 overs) (R. Venugopal 54).

At Chiswick, July 26. New Zealand won by seven wickets. Toss: West Indies. West Indies 96 (57.1 overs) (A. Browne 43; J. E. Harris three for 18, including a hat-trick, E. Musson three for 22); New Zealand 97 for three (26.4 overs) (D. A. Hockley 35, K. Bond 0 not out).

At Dulwich, July 28. Australia won by seven wickets. Toss: Denmark. Denmark 76 (54 overs) (V. Nielsen 26; S. Bow four for 21, L. Hunter three for 19); Australia 77 for three (8.5 overs) (B. Clark 44).

At Arundel, July 28. England won by four wickets. Toss: England. West Indies 120 (59.4 overs); England 123 for six (46.1 overs) (J. A. Brittin 46, J. M. Chamberlain 34 not out; D. Luke three for 27).

At Marlow, July 28. Ireland won by two wickets. Toss: Ireland. Holland 134 for eight (60 overs) (N. Payne 46; E. Owens three for 24); Ireland 136 for eight (56.3 overs) (A. van Noortwijk four for 21).

At Ealing, July 28. New Zealand won by 42 runs. Toss: New Zealand. New Zealand 154 for eight (60 overs) (D. A. Hockley 53 not out; P. Janardhan four for 26); India 112 (54.3 overs).

At Hong Kong & Shanghai Bank Ground, Beckenham, July 29. New Zealand won by ten wickets. Toss: Australia. Australia 77 (51.3 overs) (Z. J. Goss 31; J. E. Harris three for 15); New Zealand 78 for no wkt (18.2 overs) (P. D. Kinsella 35 not out, D. A. Hockley 38 not out).

At Slough, July 29. India won by nine wickets. Toss: India. Denmark 116 (57.5 overs) (S. Dabir four for 22); India 117 for one (40.5 overs) (S. Agarwal 58 not out).

At Ealing, July 29. England won by 133 runs. Toss: Holland. England 207 for five (60 overs) (J. A. Brittin 35, C. A. Hodges 38, B. A. Daniels 52, K. Smithies 36 not out; W. Gerritsen three for 38); Holland 74 (53.5 overs) (S. J. Kitson three for 14).

At Dorking, July 29. West Indies won by 19 runs. Toss: Ireland. West Indies 208 for six (60 overs) (E. Caesar 78, C.-A. James 54 not out); Ireland 189 for nine (60 overs) (S. Reamsbottom 60; C.-A. Singh five for 36).

QUALIFYING TABLE

	Played	Won	Lost	Points
New Zealand	7	7	0	28
England	7	6	1	24
Australia	7	5	2	20
India	7	4	3	16
West Indies	7	2	5	8
Ireland	7	2	5	8
Denmark	7	1	6	4
Holland	7	1	6	4

ENGLAND v NEW ZEALAND

Final

At Lord's, August 1. England won by 67 runs. Toss: New Zealand.

New Zealand entered the final as favourites, having been unbeaten in the qualifying matches, including a notable victory over England. But the occasion proved too much for an inexperienced team; their earlier sure fielding and line and length bowling were rarely in evidence. Watson was dropped in the first over and, though she was bowled soon afterwards, Brittin and Hodges added 85, slowly but surely swinging the match England's way. Still, their final total of 195 was made possible only by Chamberlain scoring 38 from just 33 balls, complemented by intelligent running between the wickets from newcomer Daniels; England took 71 off the final ten overs. New Zealand's target did not look too formidable when they reached 50 with only one down in the 20th over. But two magical moments all but ensured it would be England's day. First, Kitson flung herself wide to her ft in the gully to dismiss Bond with a spectacular catch off Chamberlain's bowling. Then hamberlain ran out New Zealand's top bat, Hockley, with a fine pick-up and direct hit om extra cover. There proved to be no way back for New Zealand, who were bowled out r 128 with nearly five overs to spare.

Player of the Match: J. M. Chamberlain.

ngland

A. Brittin c Gunn b McLauchlan	48	*K. Smithies not out	10
A. Watson b McLauchlan	5		
A. Hodges st Illingworth b Campbell	45	B 8, 1-b 7, w 2	17
C. Plimmer run out	11		—
M. Chamberlain b Harris	38	1/11 2/96 3/114 (5 wkts, 60 overs) 195	
A. Daniels not out	21	4/118 5/175	

. Smit, C. E. Taylor, G. A. Smith and S. J. Kitson did not bat.

Bowling: Turner 8-1-32-0; Harris 12-3-31-1; McLauchlan 10-2-25-2; Campbell 2-2-45-1; Gunn 12-5-33-0; Drumm 6-1-14-0.

lew Zealand

D. Kinsella c Smit b Taylor	15	J. A. Turner c Taylor b Smith	2
A. Hockley run out	24	J. E. Harris not out	5
Bond c Kitson b Chamberlain	12	C. A. Campbell c Brittin b Kitson	6
A. M. Lewis lbw b Taylor	28	L-b 8, w 5	13
S. L. Illingworth c and b Smithies	4		—
C. Drumm c Chamberlain b Smith	0	1/25 2/51 3/60 (55.1 overs) 128	
V. Gunn b Smith	19	4/70 5/71 6/110	
McLauchlan c Brittin b Kitson	0	7/112 8/114 9/120	

Bowling: Taylor 12-3-27-2; Hodges 5-2-11-0; Chamberlain 9-2-28-1; Smithies 2-4-14-1; Smith 12-1-29-3; Kitson 5.1-1-11-2.

Umpires: J. West and V. Williams.

ENGLISH WOMEN'S CRICKET, 1993

fter the excitement of England's victory over New Zealand in the World 'up final at Lord's, the country's foremost all-rounder for the past decade, 'arole Hodges, announced her retirement at the age of 34. She had played 8 Tests for England since 1984, scoring 1,164 runs at 40.13. Her highest core was an unbeaten 158 in her debut series, against New Zealand. Her ff-spin claimed 23 wickets at 29.47 and some outstanding fielding earned er 25 catches, an England record.

Though captain of Lancashire and Cheshire, Hodges played for Wakeeld in Yorkshire and was instrumental in establishing their domination of he domestic scene. She signed off at club level in September, helping Vakefield to their third League and Cup double in five seasons; they also von the League in 1992, when there was no Cup competition. In 1993 their ouble success came at the expense of two London clubs. In the National Knockout Cup final Hodges and the promising Katherine Leng put on 104 or the first wicket to set up victory with ten overs to spare over Gunnersbury; in the National League final against Riverside they opened vith 72 in 20 overs on a wet wicket, Hodges finishing unbeaten on 65 in esting conditions. Riverside took 14 runs off their first over but the loss of he big-hitting Sandra Bednarek and Ros Heggs proved crucial.

Hodges and Leng had also played crucial roles in the North's triumph at the territorial tournament in Oxford at the end of August. The North won all three of their games, against the South, the East and the Mid-West. Hodges made an unbeaten 97 against the South, while Leng, in addition to her batting, earned a total of six wickets with leg-spin. Another Northern youngster, Melissa Reynard, also took six wickets in the tournament, as did England and Mid-West captain Karen Smithies. England players Wendy Watson and Jane Smit both reached the 90s for the Mid-West against the South, but the only century came from Surrey's Ruth Lupton, who was run out for 109 in the South's game with the North.

Earlier in the season the area championship was won by Yorkshire. They met East Midlands in the final for the fourth consecutive year and beat them for the second year running, after removing their last eight wickets for 37 – including five ducks. Surrey beat Middlesex in the third-place play-off. Twelve teams took part, including a Yorkshire Second XI, as the England selectors made their final choice for the World Cup squad.

Note: Matches in this section were not first-class.

AREA CHAMPIONSHIP FINAL

At Wellingborough School, June 2. Yorkshire won by ten wickets. East Midlands 112 (49.4 overs) (W. A. Watson 36; J. Tedstone four for 17); Yorkshire 113 for no wkt (45.4 overs) (D. Maybury 77 not out).

TERRITORIAL TOURNAMENT

At Oxford, August 28. The Mid-West won by seven wickets. The East 200 for five (55 overs) (A. Bainbridge 48, J. Godman 57; K. Smithies three for 56); The Mid-West 202 for three (53.5 overs) (B. A. Daniels 89 not out).

At Oxford, August 28. The North won by 14 runs. The North 275 for five (55 overs) (K. Leng 68, C. A. Hodges 97 not out, D. Maybury 56); The South 261 for two (55 overs) (R. Lupton 109, J. A. Brittin 87 not out, S. Bednarek 36).

At Oxford, August 29. The North won by 59 runs. The North 223 for nine (55 overs) (D. Maybury 76, C. A. Hodges 39); The East 164 for nine (55 overs) (M. Reynard three for 47, K. Leng three for 38).

At Oxford, August 29. The Mid-West won by 117 runs. The Mid-West 248 for five (55 overs) (W. A. Watson 90, J. Smit 97; S. Bayton three for 48); The South 131 (43.5 overs) (R. Lupton 32; K. Smithies three for 13, C. Handley three for 10).

At Oxford, August 30. The East won by eight wickets. The South 154 for nine (55 overs) (J. A. Brittin 41, S. Bayton 39; A. Bainbridge three for 21); The East 158 for two (48.5 overs) (A. Bainbridge 66 not out, A. Godliman 45).

At Oxford, August 30. The North won by nine wickets. The Mid-West 131 (55 overs) (K. Leng three for 30); The North 132 for one (34.5 overs) (H. C. Plimmer 69 not out).

NATIONAL CLUB KNOCKOUT FINAL

At Polegate CC, Sussex, September 4. Wakefield won by six wickets. Toss: Wakefield. Gunnersbury 131 for nine (40 overs) (D. Stock 40; C. E. Taylor three for 18); Wakefield 132 for four (30 overs) (C. A. Hodges 59, K. Leng 42).

NATIONAL LEAGUE FINAL

At Newark and Sherwood CC, Nottingham, September 19. Wakefield won by 28 runs. Toss: Riverside. Wakefield 161 for four (40 overs) (C. A. Hodges 65 not out, K. Leng 38, M. P. Moore 34 not out); Riverside 133 (38.4 overs) (R. Heggs 35, S. Bednarek 30).

PART FOUR: OVERSEAS CRICKET IN 1992-93

FEATURES OF 1992-93

Double-Hundreds (23)

S. S. Bhave	220	Maharashtra v Saurashtra at Bhavnagar.
S. J. Cook	228	Transvaal v Northern Transvaal at Pretoria.
R. David	201*	Nondescripts v Rio SC at Colombo.
P. A. de Silva	231	President's XI v Under-23 XI at Colombo.
R. S. Dravid	200*	Karnataka v Andhra at Bangalore.
A. D. Jadeja	254*	Indians v Combined Bowl XI at Springs.
V. G. Kambli (3)†	202*	Bombay v Maharashtra at Pune.
	224	India v England at Bombay.
	227	India v Zimbabwe at Delhi.
A. R. Khurasia	238	Madhya Pradesh v Vidarbha at Korba.
H. A. Kinikar	205*	Maharashtra v Railways at Pune.
T. P. Kodikara	236*	Antonians v Rio SC at Colombo.
A. J. Lamb	206*	Western Province v Northern Transvaal at Cape Town.
C. B. Lambert	263*	Guyana v Windward Islands at Berbice.
B. C. Lara	277	West Indies v Australia at Sydney.
J. V. Paranjpe	218	Bombay v Gujarat at Bombay.
W. N. Phillips	205	Victoria v New South Wales at Sydney.
A. Ranatunga	238*	Sinhalese SC v Sebastianites at Colombo.
Sajid Ali	203*	Karachi v Lahore at Karachi.
Sher Ali	201*	Bahawalpur v Islamabad at Islamabad.
M. E. Waugh	200*	New South Wales v West Indians at Sydney.
M. Yachad	200	Transvaal v Orange Free State at Bloemfontein.
Yusuf Ali Khan	203	Railways v Madhya Pradesh at Delhi.

† *V. G. Kambli scored 224 and 227 in consecutive innings.*

Hundred on First-Class Debut

Z. Bharucha	100	Bombay v Baroda at Bombay.
H. A. Kinikar	110	Maharashtra v Saurashtra at Bhavnagar.
J. D. Nel	104	Western Transvaal v Eastern Transvaal at Springs.
Parashar Patel	123	Gujarat v Bombay at Bombay.

Three Hundreds in Successive Innings

A. Malhotra (Bengal) .... 100* v Bihar at Calcutta, 109 v Assam at Gauhati, 100* v Orissa at Calcutta.

Hundred in Each Innings of a Match

Asif Mujtaba	102*	125*	Pakistanis v Queensland at Brisbane.
F. J. C. Cronje	138	121*	Griqualand West v W. Transvaal at Potchefstroom.
M. D. Crowe	152	137*	Wellington v Canterbury at Christchurch.
D. R. Martyn	133*	112	Western Australia v Queensland at Brisbane.
R. T. Ponting	107	100*	Tasmania v Western Australia at Hobart.
M. J. R. Rindel	106	111	Northern Transvaal v Natal at Durban.
Shahid Tanvir	113	142	National Bank v PACO at Lahore.
Sohail Jaffer	160	102*	PNSC v National Bank at Sahiwal.

Carrying Bat Through Completed Innings

Ghulam Ali . . . . 135*   PACO (224) v PIA at Multan.
A. F. G. Griffith . . . 37*   Barbados (79) v Trinidad & Tobago at Bridgetown.
D. L. Haynes . . . . . . 143*   West Indies (382) v Pakistan at Port-of-Spain.
D. J. Murray . . . . . . 106*   Canterbury (233) v Northern Districts at Hamilton.

First-Wicket Partnership of 100 in Each Innings

116   102   M. J. Greatbatch/R. T. Latham, New Zealand v Zimbabwe at Bulawayo.

Other Notable Partnerships

Second Wicket
415   A. D. Jadeja/S. V. Manjrekar, Indians v Combined Bowl XI at Springs.
289   W. A. M. P. Perera/T. P. Kodikara, Antonians v Rio SC at Colombo.
261   A. V. Vijayvargiya/A. R. Khurasia, Madhya Pradesh v Vidarbha at Korba.

Third Wicket
293   H. P. Tillekeratne/P. A. de Silva, President's XI v Under-23 XI at Colombo.
293   R. B. Richardson/B. C. Lara, West Indies v Australia at Sydney.
291   A. P. Gurusinha/A. Ranatunga, Sinhalese SC v Sebastianites at Colombo.

Fourth Wicket
282   Vikram Rathore/Bhupinder Singh, jun. Punjab v Himachal Pradesh at Una.

Fifth Wicket
267   A. J. Lamb/A. P. Kuiper, Western Province v N. Transvaal at Cape Town.
259   A. S. Kaypee/V. S. Yadav, Haryana v Uttar Pradesh at Ghaziabad.

Seventh Wicket
217   Tahir Rashid/Akram Raza, Habib Bank v PIA at Karachi.

Eighth Wicket
171*   Shahid Nawaz/Umer Rashid, PACO v HBFC at Lahore.

Tenth Wicket
135   S. S. Karim/Hilalali Khan, Bihar v Orissa at Dhanbad.
113   S. Subramaniam/M. Sanjay, Tamil Nadu v Assam at Madras.
112   G. P. Wickremasinghe/P. K. Wijetunge, Sinhalese SC v Colts at Colombo.
107   K. K. Sharma/D. S. Mishra, Railways v Rajasthan at Jaipur.
106   C. L. Hooper/C. A. Walsh, West Indies v Pakistan at St John's.

   * *Unbroken partnership.*

Twelve or More Wickets in a Match

Amin Lakhani 12-176   PNSC v PACO at Sahiwal.
U. Chatterjee 13-87   Bengal v Tripura at Agartala.
R. P. de Groen 13-99   Northern Districts v Otago at Alexandra.
A. A. Donald 12-139   South Africa v India at Port Elizabeth.
F. Ghayas . . . . 13-110†   Delhi v Services at Delhi.
C. D. Hathurusinghe 13-77   Tamil Union v Rio SC at Colombo.
A. P. Igglesden 12-66   Boland v Griqualand West at Kimberley.
Avinash Kumar 13-316   Bihar v Tripura at Ranchi.
A. Kumble 13-138   Rest of India v Delhi at Delhi.
Manzoor Elahi 12-165   ADBP v PNSC at Lahore.
S. L. V. Raju 12-117   South Zone v East Zone at Vishakhapatnam.
S. Subramaniam 14-118   Tamil Nadu v Assam at Madras.
Waqar Younis 12-176   United Bank v PNSC at Sahiwal.
K. I. W. Wijegunawardene . 12-117   Colombo CC v Under-23 XI at Colombo.

   † *On debut.*

Eight or More Wickets in an Innings

Amin Lakhani	8-60	PNSC v PACO at Sahiwal.
C. D. Hathurusinghe	8-40	Tamil Union v Rio SC at Colombo.
G. R. J. Matthews	8-52	New South Wales v Western Australia at Sydney.
Zakir Khan	9-45	ADBP v Habib Bank at Peshawar.

Hat-Tricks

A. J. Gale	Otago v Canterbury at Dunedin.
S. Subramaniam	Tamil Nadu v Kerala at Tiruvalla.

Most Overs Bowled in a Match

103.1-38-230-8	Arshad Ayub	Hyderabad v Baroda at Baroda.
100-46-139-8	G. R. J. Matthews	New South Wales v Tasmania at Sydney.

Nine Wicket-Keeping Dismissals in a Match

P. W. Anderson	(8 ct, 1 st)	Queensland v South Australia at Adelaide.
L. K. Germon	(9 ct)	Canterbury v Northern Districts at Christchurch.
D. J. Richardson	(9 ct)	South Africa v India at Port Elizabeth.
Tahir Rashid	(8 ct, 1 st)	Habib Bank v PACO at Gujranwala.

Six or More Wicket-Keeping Dismissals in an Innings

M. Badat	(5 ct, 1 st)	South African Invitation XI v Indians at Bloemfontein.
L. K. Germon	(6 ct)	Canterbury v Northern Districts at Christchurch.
K. S. More	(5 ct, 1 st)	Indians v UCBSA President's XI at Verwoerdburg.
S. Rajapakse	(6 ct)	Nondescripts CC v Burgher RC at Colombo.
Tahir Rashid (2)	(8 ct, 1 st)†	Habib Bank v PACO at Gujranwala.
	(6 ct)	Habib Bank v United Bank at Karachi.

† *World record.*

Seven Catches in a Match in the Field

H. P. Tillekeratne	Sri Lanka v New Zealand at Colombo.

Five Catches in an Innings in the Field

V. G. Kambli	Rest of India v Delhi at Delhi.
S. Soysa	Moratuwa v Kurunegala SC at Moratuwa.

Match Double (100 Runs and 10 Wickets)

T. B. Arothe	20, 154; 6-75, 5-102	Baroda v Gujarat at Surat.
Maninder Singh	102*; 7-54, 3-22	Delhi v Haryana at Gurgaon.
K. Bharathan	107; 7-39, 4-58	Railways v Rajasthan at Jaipur.

No Byes Conceded in Total of 500 or More

B. D. Mohanty	Orissa v Bengal (636-7 dec.†) at Calcutta.
M. Parmar	Saurashtra v Maharashtra (591-5 dec.) at Bhavnagar.
R. J. Blakey	England v India (560-6 dec.) at Madras.
Moin Khan	Pakistanis v President's XI (508-5 dec.) at Georgetown.

† *Including 16 penalty runs for slow over-rate.*

Highest Innings Totals

683 . . . . Habib Bank v ADBP at Lahore.
636-7 dec.†. . . Bengal v Orissa at Calcutta.
635-9 dec.†. . . Bombay v Gujarat at Bombay.
606 . . . . West Indies v Australia at Sydney.

 † *Bengal's total included 16 and Bombay's total eight penalty runs for slow over-rate.*

Lowest Innings Totals

42 . . . . . . Canterbury v Otago at Dunedin.
50 . . . . . Karachi v Faisalabad at Karachi.
64 . . . . . Eastern Transvaal v Boland at Brackenfell.
71 . . . . . . Natal v Transvaal at Johannesburg.
75 . . . . . Queensland v New South Wales at Sydney.
85† . . . . . . Hyderabad v Punjab at Ludhiana.
86† . . . . . Orissa v Bengal at Calcutta.

 † *Excluding penalty runs for slow over-rate, Hyderabad's total was 75 and Orissa's 74.*

Victory Losing Only One Wicket

Nondescripts (418-1 dec.) beat Rio SC by an innings and 214 runs at Colombo.

50 Extras in an Innings

	b	l-b	w	n-b	
61	0	6	10	45†	Tasmania (298-6 dec.) v South Australia at Adelaide.
58	0	23	1	34	Australia (471) v Sri Lanka at Colombo.
56	4	10	2	40†	W. Australia (298) v Queensland at Perth (first inns).
55	10	16	1	28†	Tasmania (335) v Queensland at Brisbane.
54	1	7	8	38†	South Australia (271) v Tasmania at Hobart.
52	10	26	6	10	HBFC (405) v National Bank at Rawalpindi.
52	7	10	1	34†	W. Australia (318-3) v Queensland at Perth (second inns).
52	1	27	1	23	Auckland (423-7 dec.) v Wellington at Wellington.
50	22	11	0	17	Punjab (390) v Delhi at Delhi.

 † *Under Australian Cricket Board playing conditions, two extras were scored for every no-ball excluding runs scored off the delivery.*

Note: The following Features of 1991-92 were received too late for inclusion in the 1993 edition of *Wisden*.

Notable Partnerships

Fourth Wicket
267* A. Ranatunga/M. S. Atapattu, Sinhalese SC v Sebastianites at Colombo.

Tenth Wicket
118 A. W. Ekanayake/D. Amaraseena, Kurungala Youth v Antonians at Colombo.

Twelve Wickets in a Match

A. W. Ekanayake 12-151 . . . . North-Western Province v Central Province c Kurungala.

Nine Wicket-Keeping Dismissals in a Match

S. Peiris   (8 ct, 1 st) . . . . Antonians v Kurungala Youth at Colombo.

Five Catches in an Innings in the Field

J. Bandara . . . . Central Province v Western Province South at Moratuwa.

ENGLAND IN INDIA AND SRI LANKA, 1992-93

By PETER HAYTER

On March 10, 1993, while England were going down to a terrible defeat in a one-day international in Sri Lanka, the Test and County Cricket Board met at Lord's to discuss the England team's spectacular failure on the three-month tour of the sub-continent. There was widespread speculation that Ted Dexter, the chairman of selectors, would be forced to resign.

A. C. Smith, the chief executive, insisted that the debate on England matters had been "lengthy, wide-ranging and, above all, constructive". Unfortunately, this was not what came through in the newspapers. The main item of news to emerge from this meeting was nothing to do with the cricket. "There is a modern fashion for designer stubble," Dexter was quoted as saying, "and some people believe it to be very attractive. But it is aggravating to others and we will be looking at the whole question of people's facial hair."

Thousands of miles away, even the tour manager Bob Bennett had been criticised after he was pictured wearing a T-shirt and ill-fitting shorts at a press conference. He had already written to the Board to say "the players have been made aware of their responsibilities" concerning their appearance. One of the players expressed relief: "At least now we know we didn't lose because we played terribly," he said.

In fact, England did play terribly. They became the first team ever to lose all their matches in a Test series in India, going down 3-0, each time by a huge margin. They then lost a Test match to Sri Lanka for the first time. Many would say they effectively lost before they even set out. In most cases where the selection of a Test side or tour party comes in for heavy criticism, it is made with the benefit of hindsight. Any numbskull can say that Jones should never have played after Jones has been out first ball for nought in both innings. But rarely, if ever, have so much scorn, indignation and fury been heaped on the selection of a touring team before it even boarded the plane, let alone played a match, as happened when it was announced that David Gower, Jack Russell and Ian Salisbury had been left out.

The belief that Gower's left-handedness, skill against the turning ball and experience as England's leading scorer in Test history would be invaluable in the conditions peculiar to India had nothing to do with hindsight. Nor did the argument that, on turning pitches, the best wicket-keeper available had to be selected and the best wicket-keeper available was Russell. It was foresight the selectors lacked, and they combined this failure with high-handedness in declining to present a credible case. The assertion that 35-year-old Gower was not considered on the grounds of age appeared simply ridiculous when Graham Gooch (aged 39) and Mike Gatting (35) were included along with 40-year-old John Emburey. Gatting and Emburey were returning to the squad at the earliest possible moment after serving a ban for touring South Africa. It so incensed a group of "rebel" MCC members, led by Dennis Oliver, that they forced a Special General Meeting of that club at which a motion of no confidence in England's Test selectors was debated. It was carried in the hall, despite vigorous opposition from the committee. Postal votes ensured that it was narrowly rejected overall.

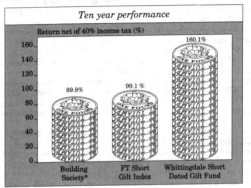

At least the muddle was consistent. The selectors at home made a mess of the original choice by trying to balance the requirements of Test and one-day cricket – hence the selection of Dermot Reeve and Richard Blakey ahead of Gower and Russell. The tour selectors – Keith Fletcher, as manager, Gooch, Alec Stewart, as vice-captain, and Gatting – maintained that standard of muddled thinking throughout the trip. For the First Test at Calcutta, they somehow came to the conclusion that the attack best suited to exploit the spin offered by a bare, dry pitch should contain four seamers. Then, to ensure balance, they chose Salisbury, who had only recently been elevated in status from net bowler to full member of the squad, at the expense of the two spinners, Tufnell and Emburey, they had originally selected ahead of him. In Madras, when Gooch was laid low by food poisoning, they left out the experienced Atherton; likewise in Bombay, the omission of Jarvis, hitherto their most dangerous bowler, in favour of DeFreitas, who had hardly bowled a ball in anger all tour, again defied all logic.

The confusion over Stewart's role caused disruption throughout. Originally understood to have been chosen as wicket-keeper first and middle-order batsman second, he was pushed up the order to open in place of the unwell Atherton in Calcutta. But when Gooch pulled out on the morning of the Second Test in Madras, Stewart still stayed as opener with Smith. Atherton was kept out. Thus Blakey, who would not have been rated among the top ten wicket-keepers in county cricket, was selected as England's first-choice wicket-keeper-batsman. He kept his place in Bombay too. He made seven runs in four innings and, not surprisingly, looked unconvincing as a wicket-keeper as well.

Certainly, it was a strenuous tour physically and a stressful one mentally. The mood of the party was not helped by the news they received on arrival in Delhi, that Gooch's long-standing and apparently solid marriage had foundered. At the start of a long haul, during which players would be separated from wives and young children in sometimes less-than-hospitable circumstances, this may have affected some of them more than was at first imagined. In the bar of the team's hotel on New Year's Eve, one of the less experienced members of the party was in such distress that he was already longing for home a mere four days into the tour. The communal violence in the wake of the destruction of the temple of Ayodhya that resulted in hundreds of deaths all over India also created an unsettled atmosphere among the squad. Their fears were heightened when the first international match, due to be played in Ahmedabad, was cancelled because the safety of the players could not be guaranteed. As a result of this and crowd disturbances at games that did take place, some of the party simply gave up trying to come to terms with a country that, at the best of times, can be quite overwhelming.

They were also subjected to a bizarre itinerary, drawn up by the Indian Board in the belief that the Test matches would be unpopular. India's successes proved this quite mistaken. The trip would have been exhausting even if Indian Airlines pilots had not been on strike. For instance, in less than a fortnight before the first Test in Calcutta, England travelled from Delhi to Jaipur, Jaipur to Delhi, Delhi to Chandigarh, Chandigarh to Delhi, Delhi to Bhubaneshwar, Bhubaneshwar to Cuttack and finally Cuttack to Calcutta, all of which would have been draining even without two one-day internationals and a three-day match in the process.

In any circumstances other than dire necessity Gooch would not have played in Calcutta, and he did not in Madras. Every member of the party went down with stomach problems at some stage and all suffered from the 'flu virus that, after he had witnessed at first hand the smog in the City of Joy, led Dexter to announce a study into the effects of air pollution on cricketers. The pollution was something for which, no matter how long the England party had trained beforehand in the Whittingdale scheme at Lilleshall, they could not have been prepared. Some suggested that, in future, any player fortunate enough to be selected for India should acclimatise by revving a car engine in a locked garage. Even the scorer, Clem Driver of Essex, collapsed during the First Test and returned home; Monica Reeve, mother of Dermot, took over the scorebook.

But it was in their specific technical preparation that England were badly let down and, as a result, left completely exposed against the Indian spinners. The batsmen had spent many hours of intensive practice at Lilleshall facing the England spinners on artificial surfaces known as "spinmats". These took spin, but they also had bounce and pace. Consequently, while the batsmen became used to waiting until the last minute before playing the ball off the wicket on the back foot, the bowlers also got into a rhythm in conditions which bore no resemblance to the ones they would actually encounter. When they faced real Indian spinners in real Indian conditions, the batsmen were bamboozled. Instead of using their feet to go forward or padding the ball away with a huge forward lunge, too many stayed rooted to the spot and paid the price. The pattern never changed.

India had formulated a plan to get the best out of their players on wickets designed for them and they carried it out to perfection. The excellent Azharuddin, under pressure at the start of the series following the disastrous tour to South Africa, led them well and played the decisive innings of the series to give his bowlers enough runs to put England's batsmen under pressure in the First Test. England's failure to make the 172 required to avoid the follow-on cost them the match and decided the course of future events. Thereafter, Tendulkar and Sidhu in Madras and Kambli in Bombay played similarly crucial innings against bowling that, in its failure to adhere to the fundamentals of length and line, was hugely disappointing throughout, thereby enabling the spinners to take full control. All three bowled brilliantly on occasions and they finished the series having taking 46 of the 58 England wickets which fell to bowlers. The tourists did no better in Colombo, where the spinners took 15 wickets in England's first-ever Test defeat by Sri Lanka, sandwiched between two further one-day international defeats. Gooch had already left for home, as he had always planned, which also did not help. Kumble was the best of the spinners England met in all four Tests, taking 21 at 19.80. His success set the seal on an unhappy first tour for new team manager Keith Fletcher. After having returned from a costly spying mission to watch India's Test in Johannesburg, Fletcher announced the following verdict on the bespectacled leg-spinner: "I didn't see him turn a single ball from leg to off. I don't believe we will have much problem with him." Fortunately for Fletcher, on a tour like this, such a statement seemed merely a routine misjudgment.

ENGLAND TOURING PARTY

G. A. Gooch (Essex) (*captain*), A. J. Stewart (Surrey) (*vice-captain*), M. A. Atherton (Lancashire), R. J. Blakey (Yorkshire), P. A. J. DeFreitas (Lancashire), J. E. Emburey (Middlesex), N. H. Fairbrother (Lancashire), M. W. Gatting (Middlesex), G. A. Hick (Worcestershire), P. W. Jarvis (Yorkshire), C. C. Lewis (Nottinghamshire), D. E. Malcolm (Derbyshire), D. A. Reeve (Warwickshire), R. A. Smith (Hampshire), J. P. Taylor (Northamptonshire), P. C. R. Tufnell (Middlesex).

I. D. K. Salisbury (Sussex), who travelled out with the party to India but was intended to join England A in Australia, was later asked to remain on the senior tour.

Tour manager: R. M. Bennett (Lancashire). *Team manager:* K. W. R. Fletcher. *Scorers:* C. F. Driver (Essex) and Mrs M. Reeve. *Physiotherapist:* D. Roberts (Worcestershire).

ENGLAND TOUR RESULTS

Test matches – Played 4: Lost 4.

First-class matches – Played 8: Lost 4, Drawn 4.

Losses – India (3), Sri Lanka.

Draws – Delhi, Indian Board President's XI, Indian Under-25 XI, Rest of India.

One-day internationals – Played 8: Won 3, Lost 5. *Wins* – India (3). *Losses* – India (3), Sri Lanka (2).

Other non first-class matches – Played 2: Won 1, Lost 1. *Win* – B. S. Bedi's Select XI. *Loss* – Indian Board President's XI.

TEST MATCH AVERAGES – INDIA v ENGLAND

INDIA – BATTING

	T	I	NO	R	HS	100s	Avge	Ct/St
V. G. Kambli	3	4	1	317	224	1	105.66	0
S. R. Tendulkar....	3	4	1	302	165	1	100.66	4
M. Azharuddin	3	3	0	214	182	1	71.33	3
N. S. Sidhu	3	4	0	235	106	1	58.75	0
Kapil Dev	3	3	1	101	66*	0	50.50	3
P. K. Amre	3	3	0	147	78	0	49.00	4
M. Prabhakar	3	4	0	130	46	0	32.50	3
K. S. More........	3	3	2	30	26*	0	30.00	9/4

Played in three Tests: R. K. Chauhan 2, 15; A. Kumble 0, 16 (1 ct); S. L. V. Raju 1, 0*.

* *Signifies not out.*

BOWLING

	O	M	R	W	BB	5W/i	Avge
Kapil Dev	51.2	15	133	7	3-35	0	19.00
A. Kumble	181	53	416	21	6-64	1	19.80
M. Prabhakar	48	17	127	5	3-28	0	25.40
S. L. V. Raju	210	62	468	16	4-103	0	29.25
R. K. Chauhan....	169.4	64	323	9	3-30	0	35.88

Also bowled: S. R. Tendulkar 4–2–9–0.

ENGLAND – BATTING

	T	I	NO	R	HS	100s	Avge	Ct/St
G. A. Hick	3	6	0	315	178	1	52.50	5
M. W. Gatting	3	6	0	219	81	0	36.50	1
C. C. Lewis.........	3	6	0	206	117	1	34.33	3
N. H. Fairbrother....	2	4	0	134	83	0	33.50	0
P. C. R. Tufnell	2	4	3	28	22*	0	28.00	0
A. J. Stewart........	3	6	0	146	74	0	24.33	0/1
R. A. Smith	3	6	0	146	62	0	24.33	2
I. D. K. Salisbury....	2	4	0	70	28	0	17.50	2
G. A. Gooch........	2	4	0	47	18	0	11.75	1
P. W. Jarvis	2	4	0	20	8	0	5.00	1
D. E. Malcolm	2	4	2	4	4*	0	2.00	0
R. J. Blakey	2	4	0	7	6	0	1.75	2

Played in one match: M. A. Atherton 37, 11 (2 ct); P. A. J. DeFreitas 11, 12 (2 ct); J. E. Emburey 12, 1; J. P. Taylor 17, 17*.

* Signifies not out.

BOWLING

	O	M	R	W	BB	5W/i	Avge
G. A. Hick	76.5	11	202	8	3-19	0	25.25
P. W. Jarvis	60.2	13	167	4	2-72	0	41.75
D. E. Malcolm	57	11	170	3	3-67	0	56.66
P. C. R. Tufnell	80.3	9	274	4	4-142	0	68.50
C. C. Lewis.........	79	16	223	3	2-114	0	74.33
I. D. K. Salisbury...	52	6	230	3	2-142	0	76.66

Also bowled: P. A. J. DeFreitas 20–4–75–0; J. E. Emburey 59–14–144–2; J. P. Taylor 22–3–74–1.

ENGLAND AVERAGES – FIRST-CLASS MATCHES

Note: The following averages include the Test match between England and Sri Lanka in Colombo.

BATTING

	M	I	NO	R	HS	100s	Avge	Ct/St
R. A. Smith	7	12	2	579	149*	2	57.90	3
M. W. Gatting	7	13	2	470	115	1	42.72	5
G. A. Hick	7	13	1	501	178	1	41.75	9
G. A. Gooch........	5	8	1	278	102*	1	39.71	4
C. C. Lewis.........	7	11	1	299	117	1	29.90	6
J. E. Emburey.......	4	6	1	146	59	0	29.20	2
M. A. Atherton	5	10	1	253	80*	0	28.11	5
N. H. Fairbrother....	6	10	1	237	83	0	26.33	2
A. J. Stewart........	8	15	1	296	74	0	21.14	9/4
I. D. K. Salisbury....	4	5	1	75	28	0	18.75	3
P. A. J. DeFreitas ...	3	4	0	70	45	0	17.50	2
R. J. Blakey	3	5	1	70	63*	0	17.50	3
P. C. R. Tufnell	7	8	5	38	22*	0	12.66	1
D. E. Malcolm	6	7	3	27	13	0	6.75	1
P. W. Jarvis	4	7	0	24	8	0	3.42	2

Played in three matches: J. P. Taylor 2*, 17, 17*. Played in two matches: D. A. Reeve 19, 3, 21*.

* Signifies not out.

BOWLING

	O	M	R	W	BB	5W/i	Avge
P. W. Jarvis	128.1	28	335	12	3-61	0	27.91
J. P. Taylor	65.4	11	217	7	5-46	1	31.00
C. C. Lewis	181	33	478	14	4-66	0	34.14
G. A. Hick	115.5	20	315	9	3-19	0	35.00
D. E. Malcolm	140	34	392	10	3-3	0	39.20
I. D. K. Salisbury....	87	11	362	9	3-54	0	40.22
P. C. R. Tufnell	227.5	36	746	14	4-95	0	53.28
J. E. Emburey	149	31	442	7	2-48	0	63.14

Also bowled: P. A. J. DeFreitas 63–13–194–0; M. W. Gatting 4–0–19–0; G. A. Gooch 5–3–2–2; D. A. Reeve 13–3–33–0.

Note: Matches in this section which were not first-class are signified by a dagger.

DELHI v ENGLAND XI

At Faridabad, January 3, 4, 5. Drawn. Toss: England XI.

England had the worst of their opening match against Delhi, the Ranji Trophy champions, in the concrete saucer of the Nahar Singh stadium. Intermittent black smoke from a nearby clay chimney was one worrying portent for England. There were others: the four-man seam attack failed to move the ball off the straight throughout the first day when Delhi crawled to 190 for three. When England replied, the spin of Maninder Singh and Kirti Azad (whose six for 30 was his best return since he took seven for 63 against Fletcher's side at Nagpur in 1981-82) caused such problems that, Atherton apart, none of the top order got past 25 in a total of 194. Delhi extended their lead to 232 with ease, mainly against some non-spinning spin from Tufnell, then took three wickets in England's brief second innings.

Close of play: First day, Delhi 190-3 (Hitesh Sharma 87*, K. Bhaskar Pillai 22*); Second day, England XI 154-5 (G. A. Hick 11*).

Delhi

M. Nayyar c Stewart b Jarvis..................	11	– c Hick b Jarvis................	12
Hitesh Sharma lbw b Lewis...................	88	– c Hick b Jarvis................	4
Bantoo Singh c Lewis b Hick...............	15	– not out........................	50
Ajay Sharma c Hick b Lewis	30	– not out........................	61
K. Bhaskar Pillai lbw b Jarvis	27		
*K. Azad c Stewart b Jarvis...............	4		
V. Razdan c Fairbrother b Lewis	8		
Maninder Singh c Hick b Malcolm	26		
A. S. Wassan lbw b Tufnell	30		
F. Ghayas st Stewart b Tufnell............	6		
†M. G. Chaturvedi not out.................	8		
B 2, l-b 14, w 2, n-b 15	33	B 4, l-b 4, n-b 5	13

1/28 2/95 3/151 4/195 5/201   286   1/16 2/23   (2 wkts dec.) 140
6/209 7/211 8/272 9/272

Bowling: *First Innings*—Malcolm 24-9-50-1; Jarvis 25-8-61-3; Lewis 26-3-70-3; Tufnell 23.4-4-66-2; Reeve 6-2-11-0; Hick 10-5-12-1. *Second Innings*—Malcolm 3-1-10-0; Jarvis 9-4-17-2; Tufnell 16-3-52-0; Hick 9-2-32-0; Lewis 5-2-21-0.

England XI

*G. A. Gooch c Maninder Singh b Razdan	24	– b Ghayas	28
M. A. Atherton c Hitesh Sharma b Azad	59	– c Chaturvedi b Maninder Singh	18
†A. J. Stewart lbw b Wassan	19	– c Chaturvedi b Ghayas	1
M. W. Gatting b Azad	25	– not out	11
G. A. Hick c Bhaskar Pillai b Maninder Singh	24	– not out	4
P. W. Jarvis b Azad	1		
N. H. Fairbrother c Bhaskar Pillai b Azad	0		
D. A. Reeve c Bhaskar Pillai b Maninder Singh	19		
C. C. Lewis c Hitesh Sharma b Azad	0		
P. C. R. Tufnell not out	1		
D. E. Malcolm c Bhaskar Pillai b Azad	2		
B 4, l-b 7, n-b 9	20	L-b 1	1
	194	(3 wkts)	63

1/42 2/86 3/139 4/150 5/154   194   1/40 2/46 3/50   (3 wkts) 63
6/154 7/186 8/191 9/191

Bowling: *First Innings*—Razdan 13–4–23–1; Wassan 14–2–37–1; Ghayas 6–0–28–0; Maninder Singh 29–5–65–2; Azad 17–6–30–6. *Second Innings*—Wassan 3–0–25–0; Razdan 2–0–7–0; Maninder Singh 9–2–13–1; Ghayas 8–1–17–2.

Umpires: V. K. Ramaswamy and R. S. Rathore.

INDIAN BOARD PRESIDENT'S XI v ENGLAND XI

At Lucknow, January 8, 9, 10. Drawn. Toss: Indian Board President's XI.

As communal violence mounted in Ahmedabad, eventually prompting the cancellation of the following week's one-day international there, some England players struggled to concentrate against a side containing five Test cricketers and two, the left-handed batsman Kambli and off-spinner Chauhan, who were to play a significant part in the series. Lucknow is only 80 miles from Ayodhya, the centre of the communal troubles: players were advised not to leave their hotel without a police escort and the crowd of 20,000 each day contained 5,000 armed guards. Kambli's exciting strokeplay as he scored 61 from 65 balls was a foretaste of some brilliant innings to come, but England's bowlers were deceived by his flashing outside off-stump into thinking he could be got out cheaply with the right ball. On the second morning, Taylor's spell of five for 19 from 9.4 overs ensured his Test debut in Calcutta, while Gatting's first century for an England team since 1987 distracted from the ineptitude of his team-mates against the spinners. This was in stark contrast to Sidhu's calculated assault – four sixes in each innings – on Emburey.

Close of play: First day, Indian Board President's XI 178-3 (Ajay Sharma 0*, N. R. Mongia 45*); Second day, England XI 168-3 (M. W. Gatting 85*, P. A. J. DeFreitas 0*).

Indian Board President's XI

S. S. Bhave c Stewart b Lewis	1	– c and b Tufnell	17
N. S. Sidhu c Gatting b Emburey	36	– not out	57
V. G. Kambli retired hurt	61		
Ajay Sharma c Gatting b Taylor	0		
R. S. Dravid st Stewart b Gooch	27	– (3) not out	28
†N. R. Mongia b Taylor	55		
R. K. Chauhan c Stewart b Taylor	0		
*Maninder Singh b Gooch	15		
S. A. Ankola c Gooch b Taylor	3		
P. S. Vaidya b Taylor	13		
N. D. Hirwani not out	1		
B 2, l-b 6, w 1, n-b 2	11	N-b 5	5
	223	(1 wkt)	107

1/1 2/105 3/177 4/178 5/178   223   1/29   (1 wkt) 107
6/197 7/201 8/219 9/223

In the first innings V. G. Kambli retired hurt at 85. Ajay Sharma also retired hurt at 85, but resumed at 177.

Bowling: First Innings—DeFreitas 20–5–59–0; Lewis 11–2–35–1; Emburey 14–4–44–1; Taylor 15.4–4–46–5; Tufnell 11–1–29–0; Gooch 5–3–2–2. *Second Innings*—DeFreitas 7–3–8–0; Lewis 5–1–5–0; Tufnell 12–4–24–1; Taylor 6–0–25–0; Emburey 8–1–36–0; Hick 4–1–9–0.

England XI

*G. A. Gooch st Mongia b Hirwani ... 77	J. E. Emburey lbw b Maninder Singh .. 20
M. W. Gatting b Maninder Singh 115	J. P. Taylor not out 2
†A. J. Stewart lbw b Hirwani......... 4	P. C. R. Tufnell not out 7
R. A. Smith lbw b Hirwani 1	
P. A. J. DeFreitas c Ajay Sharma	B 16, l-b 6 22
b Hirwani. 45	
G. A. Hick lbw b Maninder Singh 12	1/131 2/135 3/164 (9 wkts dec.) 307
N. H. Fairbrother b Chauhan 2	4/226 5/252 6/265
C. C. Lewis b Chauhan............... 0	7/265 8/296 9/298

Bowling: Vaidya 10–1–31–0; Ankola 17–5–39–0; Chauhan 16–4–57–2; Maninder Singh 32–10–80–3; Hirwani 27–4–78–4.

Umpires: P. D. Reporter and S. Venkataraghavan.

†At Feroz Shah Kotla, Delhi, January 13. Indian Board President's XI won by nine wickets. Toss: England XI. England XI 245 for eight (50 overs) (G. A. Gooch 85, A. J. Stewart 36); Indian Board President's XI 246 for one (47.4 overs) (N. S. Sidhu 130 not out, Ajay Sharma 75 not out).

†At Feroz Shah Kotla, Delhi, January 15. England XI won by two wickets. Toss: England XI. B. S. Bedi's Select XI 202 for six (50 overs) (Kapil Dev 33, Ajay Sharma 45, S. Chopra 50 not out); England XI 203 for eight (49.4 overs) (R. A. Smith 30, G. A. Hick 93).
The match was arranged to provide the England players with practice after the one-day international at Ahmedabad was cancelled. B. S. Bedi's XI drew on 15 players; Kapil Dev did not appear in the field.

†INDIA v ENGLAND

First One-day International

At Jaipur, January 18. England won by four wickets. Toss: England.

A scrambled single off bat and pad from the last ball of the match gave England victory in front of a capacity crowd at the Sawai Man Singh stadium. Thousands were locked out, many in possession of forged tickets and some with valid ones, and lathi-wielding police employed riot control tactics to dissuade them from climbing the walls. This furious activity, sending up huge dust clouds, was matched by the excited cacophony inside the stadium. Jarvis was much the best of England's bowlers. The yorker which splayed Sidhu's stumps in the second over caused widespread relief, particularly for Emburey, and his fast-medium in-swing might well have caused a collapse, had Hick accepted a simple catch at slip to dismiss Kambli. In the event Kambli celebrated his 21st birthday with an unbeaten hundred. His 164-run partnership with his schoolfriend Tendulkar took India to a sizeable total. Stewart's 91 was the backbone of England's reply, and he used his feet well to hit left-arm spinner Raju over the ropes twice. Later, Fairbrother supplied the necessary acceleration. England needed six from the last over, and Prabhakar was left to rue an overthrow off his own penultimate delivery, which enabled them to draw level.

Man of the Match: V. G. Kambli.

India

M. Prabhakar b Jarvis		25
N. S. Sidhu b Jarvis		0
V. G. Kambli not out		100
*M. Azharuddin lbw b Lewis		6
S. R. Tendulkar not out		82
B 2, l-b 7, w 1		10

1/0 (2) 2/31 (1)   (3 wkts, 48 overs) 223
3/59 (4)

P. K. Amre, Kapil Dev, †V. S. Yadav, J. Srinath, A. Kumble and S. L. V. Raju di
not bat.

Bowling: DeFreitas 9-3-40-0; Jarvis 10-0-49-2; Reeve 10-0-37-0; Lewis 9-0-26-1
Emburey 8-0-49-0; Gooch 2-0-13-0.

England

*G. A. Gooch lbw b Kapil Dev	4		C. C. Lewis not out	
†A. J. Stewart c Yadav b Kapil Dev	91			
R. A. Smith c and b Prabhakar	16		B 1, l-b 8, w 3, n-b 2	
M. W. Gatting b Kumble	30			
N. H. Fairbrother not out	46		1/29 (1) 2/85 (3) (6 wkts, 48 overs) 22	
G. A. Hick run out	13		3/145 (2) 4/161 (4)	
D. A. Reeve b Prabhakar	2		5/200 (6) 6/203 (7)	

P. A. J. DeFreitas, J. E. Emburey and P. W. Jarvis did not bat.

Bowling: Kapil Dev 10-1-36-2; Prabhakar 10-0-43-2; Srinath 10-0-47-0; Raj
8-1-35-0; Kumble 10-0-54-1.

Umpires: S. K. Bansal and S. Venkataraghavan.

†INDIA v ENGLAND

Second One-day International

At Chandigarh, January 21. India won by five wickets. Toss: India.

A match effectively decided by the toss was won by India with five wickets and almo
five overs to spare. The pitch was still conspicuously damp when play began at 9 a.m. an
Kapil Dev, Prabhakar and Srinath swung and seamed the ball alarmingly. England nev
recovered from the loss of four leading batsmen for 49 and only a stand of 83 betwee
Smith and Hick prevented a rout. As conditions for batting improved, India ma
unhurried progress to their target. Sidhu's 76 included two more sixes, off Salisbury, to ta
his tally against England's attack to 13. Otherwise, Salisbury, recently co-opted to t
squad as Emburey and Tufnell struggled to adapt to India, bowled tidily. Chaotic crow
control resulted in a fatal shooting. Nearly 10,000 people attempted to force their way int
the Sector 16 Stadium, already jam-packed to its 25,000 capacity, and as a path was bei
cleared for the Governor of Punjab, a pistol shot wounded two policemen, one of whom la
died in hospital.

Man of the Match: N. S. Sidhu.

England

*G. A. Gooch c Tendulkar b Srinath	7		D. A. Reeve not out	
†A. J. Stewart c Azharuddin			C. C. Lewis not out	
b Kapil Dev	7		L-b 13, w 13, n-b 4	
R. A. Smith lbw b Kumble	42			
M. W. Gatting c and b Srinath	0		1/19 (2) 2/20 (1) (6 wkts, 50 overs)	
N. H. Fairbrother lbw b Raju	7		3/22 (4) 4/49 (5)	
G. A. Hick b Kapil Dev	56		5/132 (3) 6/153 (6)	

P. A. J. DeFreitas, P. W. Jarvis and I. D. K. Salisbury did not bat.

Bowling: Kapil Dev 10-2-40-2; Prabhakar 8-0-30-0; Srinath 10-2-34-2; Tendul
3-0-16-0; Raju 9-0-28-1; Kumble 10-0-37-1.

India

N. S. Sidhu c Reeve b DeFreitas	76	Kapil Dev not out	5
M. Prabhakar c Reeve b Lewis	36	L-b 3, w 5, n-b 6	14
V. G. Kambli c and b Jarvis	9		
*M. Azharuddin lbw b Reeve	36	1/79 (2) 2/99 (3) (5 wkts, 45.1 overs) 201	
S. R. Tendulkar lbw b DeFreitas	1	3/148 (1) 4/161 (5)	
P. K. Amre not out	24	5/195 (4)	

†V. S. Yadav, A. Kumble, J. Srinath and S. L. V. Raju did not bat.

Bowling: DeFreitas 10–1–31–2; Jarvis 10–1–43–1; Reeve 6.1–0–33–1; Lewis 10–0–47–1; Salisbury 8–1–42–0; Gatting 1–0–2–0.

Umpires: R. V. Ramani and V. K. Ramaswamy.

INDIAN UNDER-25 XI v ENGLAND XI

At Cuttack, January 23, 24, 25. Drawn. Toss: England XI.

In contrast to the previous 22 men who had reached the target, Graham Gooch became the first batsman uncertain whether he had reached a hundred hundreds or not. He made 102 in England's first innings, just before his 100th Test. Celebrations were somewhat muted since ICC was due to pronounce the following week on his century on the rebel tour of South Africa 11 years earlier. (Subsequently, ICC said this was not first-class but the decision was rejected by most statistical authorities, including *Wisden*.) Gooch retired at tea, allowing other players to get in some practice. Smith also plundered some inexperienced bowling to make his first century of the tour. But Atherton, having been a stranger to his bat for 18 days through illness, went for nought in England's first innings of 408 for four declared. He made amends by scoring 80 not out at the second attempt. Malcolm, similarly short of time in the field, was selected despite being too ill to appear until the third morning, when he shot out the Indian Under-25 tail, taking three for three in the two overs he bowled. Meanwhile, another poor performance from Tufnell put his Test place under threat from Salisbury, who ended an excellent 103 from Khurasia.

Close of play: First day, England XI 312-3 (R. A. Smith 103*, G. A. Hick 4*); Second day, Indian Under-25 XI 224-4 (A. R. Khurasia 88*, G. K. Pandey 35*).

England XI

*G. A. Gooch retired hurt	102		
M. A. Atherton lbw b Zaidi	0	– (1) not out	80
†A. J. Stewart lbw b Gandhe	39	– c Dighe b Jadeja	21
R. A. Smith not out	149		
M. W. Gatting c Bahutule b Zaidi	41	– (4) not out	12
G. A. Hick c Puri b Kuruvilla	27	– (2) c Dighe b Zaidi	25
C. C. Lewis not out	26		
B 8, l-b 11, w 1, n-b 4	24	B 6, l-b 1, n-b 1	8

1/4 2/71 3/303 4/364   (4 wkts dec.) 408   1/46 2/82   (2 wkts dec.) 146

I. D. K. Salisbury, J. P. Taylor, P. C. R. Tufnell and D. E. Malcolm did not bat.

In the first innings G. A. Gooch retired hurt at 218.

Bowling: *First Innings*—Kuruvilla 28–2–91–1; Zaidi 29–5–91–2; Gandhe 20–2–87–1; Bahutule 35–9–86–0; Pandey 4–0–20–0; Jadeja 8–2–14–0. *Second Innings*—Zaidi 12–3–34–1; Kuruvilla 10–2–27–0; Gandhe 13–3–48–0; Jadeja 5–2–7–1; Bahutule 6–1–23–0.

Indian Under-25 XI

*A. D. Jadeja lbw b Lewis	48	– b Malcolm	0
A. R. Khurasia c Gooch b Salisbury	103		
J. V. Paranjpe lbw b Taylor	1	– not out	23
R. S. Dravid lbw b Lewis	15		
R. Puri retired hurt	13		
†S. S. Dighe c Lewis b Salisbury	8	– (2) not out	23
G. K. Pandey c Gooch b Malcolm	54		
S. V. Bahutule b Salisbury	4		
P. V. Gandhe not out	7		
A. W. Zaidi lbw b Malcolm	0		
A. Kuruvilla b Malcolm	0		
B 1, l-b 5, w 1, n-b 13	20	W 1, n-b 6	7

1/33 2/74 3/89 4/98 5/258   273   1/1   (1 wkt) 53
6/262 7/273 8/273 9/273

In the first innings A. R. Khurasia, when 6, retired hurt at 26 and resumed at 98. R. Puri retired hurt at 100.

Bowling: *First Innings*—Lewis 16–3–37–2; Taylor 22–4–72–1; Tufnell 15–4–56–0; Salisbury 15–2–77–3; Hick 6–1–22–0; Malcolm 2–1–3–3. *Second Innings*—Malcolm 7–0–25–1; Gatting 4–0–19–0; Tufnell 3–1–8–0; Salisbury 1–0–1–0.

Umpires: S. K. Bansal and A. L. Narasimhana.

INDIA v ENGLAND

First Test Match

At Calcutta, January 29, 30, 31, February 1, 2. India won by eight wickets. Toss: India. Test debuts: R. K. Chauhan, V. G. Kambli; J. P. Taylor.

England were beaten in the first Test, physically, mentally, technically and tactically as Azharuddin led his side to victory, only the second in their past 26 Tests. India were in control even before Gooch, who was clearly unwell throughout his 100th Test, lost the toss. The England selectors, deprived of Atherton by illness, added insanity to injury by choosing a four-man pace attack. All the signs, particularly the Indians' choice of three spinners, Kumble, Raju and Chauhan, indicated that long hours of toil lay that way.

England's bowling resources comprised Malcolm, Jarvis, Lewis and the debutant from Northamptonshire, Taylor, plus one spinner, Salisbury, who started the tour as a net bowler, and another, Hick, whose first-class haul in 1992 was eight wickets at 51.87 each. In the event Hick's return of five for 28 in the match merely underlined the folly of excluding both Emburey and Tufnell. The England management explained that their senior spinners had not bowled well enough, nor with sufficient confidence, to justify inclusion, ignoring the point that there is no surer way of regaining confidence than taking wickets in Tests.

In fact, England might have got away with their selection had it not been for Azharuddin, who came to the dry, brown but firm wicket with his side in some difficulty at 93 for three and his own captaincy in jeopardy after an unsuccessful tour to South Africa. He departed having thrilled the capacity crowd at Eden Gardens with an innings of 182 and batted England out of the game. This was a masterpiece of uninhibited strokeplay matched with watchful defence. He bided his time before taking his pick of the varied assortment of bad balls served up at regular intervals and, until he capitulated to Hick's off-spin with a tired shot, he never looked remotely troubled.

England needed a mere 172 to avoid the follow-on and in falling nine runs short effectively surrendered the match. Kapil Dev and Prabhakar completed the task of removing the shine from the new ball in 12 overs and inevitably made way for the Indian spinners to take control. England's batsmen, flummoxed by the turning ball delivered flat and at pace by Kumble and Raju and into the rough outside off stump (caused by the left-armer Taylor's follow-through) by Chauhan, too often fell betwixt and between playing forward or back. They collapsed to 88 for five at the end of the second day and recovered in to 163 all out. They were then dealt a body-blow when Gooch failed for the second time in wasteful fashion, having momentarily lifted his back foot from the batting crease to allow

More an unexpected but gleefully accepted opportunity to stump him. Thereafter Gatting, returning to Test cricket after his ban for touring South Africa, held out doggedly. He made good use of the sweep shot until, only 16 short of making India bat again, he attempted to play it at a wider delivery from Chauhan and dragged the ball on to his stumps. Hick, surmounting his first-innings disappointment and growing pressure on his place in the side, batted far more positively the second time, while Salisbury and Taylor, who hung around for a combined total of 225 minutes in a lost cause, demonstrated a refreshing simplicity of technique against spin. They thrust their front pads forward and played at nothing but those balls that demanded a response. They showed what might have been achieved by greater application from their supposed betters, who had batted as though certain that defeat was unavoidable.

Up to 25,000 spectators assembled on the final morning to watch India score the last 43 runs required for victory. Shortly after they had celebrated Calcutta-style – thunderflashes, firecrackers and all – Azharuddin's rehabilitation as a national hero was completed by his appointment for the remaining two Tests. Meanwhile, Ted Dexter, the chairman of the England committee, announced that, as a result of the continuing poor health of some England players, a study into air pollution levels in Indian cities had been commissioned. Some sceptical observers regarded this as nothing more than a smokescreen.

Man of the Match: M. Azharuddin.

Close of play: First day, India 263-4 (M. Azharuddin 114*, P. K. Amre 7*); Second day, England 88-5 (N. H. Fairbrother 17*, I. D. K. Salisbury 0*); Third day, England 128-2 (M. W. Gatting 48*, R. A. Smith 2*); Fourth day, India 36-0 (M. Prabhakar 12*, N. S. Sidhu 20*).

India

M. Prabhakar c Lewis b Salisbury	46	– b Hick	13
N. S. Sidhu c Hick b Taylor	13	– st Stewart b Hick	37
V. G. Kambli c Hick b Jarvis	16	– not out	18
S. R. Tendulkar c Hick b Malcolm	50	– not out	9
*M. Azharuddin c Gooch b Hick	182		
P. K. Amre c Hick b Jarvis	12		
†K. S. More not out	13		
A. Kumble b Malcolm	4		
R. K. Chauhan b Malcolm	0		
S. L. V. Raju c Salisbury b Hick	2		
B 6, l-b 6, w 10, n-b 10	32	L-b 4, n-b 1	5

1/49 (2) 2/78 (3) 3/93 (1) 4/216 (4)   371   1/51 (1) 2/62 (2)   (2 wkts) 82
5/278 (6) 6/346 (7) 7/362 (5)
8/368 (9) 9/370 (10) 10/371 (11)

Bowling: *First Innings*—Malcolm 24-3-67-3; Jarvis 27-5-72-2; Lewis 23-5-64-0; Taylor 19-2-65-1; Salisbury 17-2-72-1; Hick 12.5-5-19-3. *Second Innings*—Malcolm 6-1-16-0; Jarvis 5.2-1-23-0; Taylor 3-1-9-0; Salisbury 6-3-16-0; Lewis 3-1-5-0; Hick 6-1-9-2.

England

*G. A. Gooch c Azharuddin b Raju	17	– st More b Kumble	18
†A. J. Stewart b Prabhakar	0	– c Tendulkar b Kumble	49
M. W. Gatting b Chauhan	33	– b Chauhan	81
R. A. Smith c Amre b Kumble	1	– c More b Chauhan	8
G. A. Hick b Kumble	1	– lbw b Raju	25
N. H. Fairbrother c More b Kumble	17	– c sub (W. V. Raman) b Kumble	25
I. D. K. Salisbury c More b Chauhan	28	– (9) c More b Kapil Dev	26
C. C. Lewis b Raju	21	– (7) c Amre b Raju	16
P. W. Jarvis c Prabhakar b Raju	4	– (8) lbw b Raju	6
J. P. Taylor st More b Chauhan	17	– not out	17
D. E. Malcolm not out	4	– lbw b Kapil Dev	0
B 8, l-b 8, w 4	20	L-b 13, n-b 2	15

1/8 (2) 2/37 (1) 3/38 (4) 4/40 (5)   163   1/48 (1) 2/111 (2) 3/145 (4)   286
5/87 (3) 6/89 (6) 7/111 (8)   4/192 (3) 5/192 (5) 6/216 (7)
8/119 (9) 9/149 (10) 10/163 (7)   7/234 (8) 8/254 (6)
                                    9/286 (9) 10/286 (11)

Bowling: *First Innings*—Kapil Dev 6–1–18–0; Prabhakar 9–3–10–1; Kumble 29–8–50–3; Raju 27–14–39–3; Chauhan 29.1–15–30–3. *Second Innings*—Kapil Dev 8.2–5–12–2; Prabhakar 9–4–26–0; Chauhan 45–17–79–2; Raju 35–9–80–3; Kumble 40–16–76–3.

Umpires: P. D. Reporter and S. Venkataraghavan. Referee: C. W. Smith (West Indies).

REST OF INDIA v ENGLAND XI

At Vishakhapatnam, February 5, 6, 7. Drawn. Toss: England XI.

An opportunity for England to refresh themselves in the cleaner air of the coast turned into another series of disrupting distractions. On the second day, as the Rest of India were cruising past England's 253 for six declared, Tufnell, who was struggling to find form and rhythm, lost his temper. He was already seething after being no-balled 11 times; then Blakey missed a stumping chance against Tendulkar. Tufnell snatched his England cap from umpire Jayaprakash, kicked it along the ground and exchanged heated words with team-mates. He was subsequently fined £500 for the team management for "ungentlemanly conduct towards an umpire". After a meeting with the Rev. Andrew Wingfield Digby, the team's pastoral counsellor, and a night to reflect, Tufnell responded with his best bowling of the tour. He took four wickets in 5.3 overs as the Rest of India lost five for 11. Smith, Blakey and Emburey made runs for England in the first innings; Fairbrother made good use of the second innings as the game drifted away. However, the acting-captain Stewart had a game in which he faced nine balls, made a duck, burst a blood vessel in his finger and did not field. Emburey took over the captaincy.

Close of play: First day, England XI 230-5 (R. J. Blakey 55*, J. E. Emburey 43*); Second day, Rest of India 295-4 (J. V. Paranjpe 51*, A. R. Kapoor 33*).

England XI

M. A. Atherton c Paranjpe b Ankola	33	– (2) c Yadav b Prasad	.
*A. J. Stewart retired hurt	0	– (4) lbw b Padmanabhan	3
R. A. Smith lbw b Prasad	82	– (1) retired hurt	7!
N. H. Fairbrother b Kapoor	2	– (3) not out	2
D. A. Reeve lbw b Kapoor	3	– not out	.
†R. J. Blakey not out	63		
P. A. J. DeFreitas c Yadav b Prasad	5		
J. E. Emburey b Prasad	53		
I. D. K. Salisbury not out	5		
B 2, l-b 1, w 1, n-b 6	10	B 8, l-b 4, w 1	1
	(6 wkts dec.) 253	(2 wkts)	15

1/81 2/91 3/120 4/127 5/129 6/241   1/4 2/85

P. C. R. Tufnell and D. E. Malcolm did not bat.

In the first innings A. J. Stewart retired hurt at 5. In the second innings R. A. Smith retired hurt at 82.

Bowling: *First Innings*—Ankola 25–6–91–1; Prasad 22–10–39–3; Chatterjee 14–2–37–; Padmanabhan 19–6–31–0; Kapoor 21–5–45–2; Tendulkar 3–0–7–0. *Second Innings*—Ankola 8–3–13–0; Prasad 8.1–1–24–1; Kapoor 11–3–35–0; Chatterjee 9–3–31–0; Padmanabhan 14–2–35–1; Tendulkar 1–1–0–0.

Rest of India

W. V. Raman lbw b Malcolm	24	S. A. Ankola c Blakey b Tufnell	.
A. R. Khurasia b Atherton b Malcolm	10	K. N. A. Padmanabhan not out	.
S. V. Manjrekar c Emburey b Salisbury	96	V. Prasad not out	.
*S. R. Tendulkar c Atherton b Salisbury	61	L-b 6, w 1, n-b 15	
J. V. Paranjpe c Fairbrother b Tufnell	64		
A. R. Kapoor c Emburey b Tufnell	54	1/23 2/50 3/166	(9 wkts dec.)
†V. S. Yadav b Malcolm b Tufnell	1	4/216 5/328 6/332	
U. Chatterjee c and b Salisbury	6	7/336 8/339 9/339	

Bowling: Malcolm 19–4–63–2; DeFreitas 16–1–52–0; Reeve 7–1–22–0; Tufnell 26–4–95–4; Emburey 20–4–53–0; Salisbury 19–3–54–3.

Umpires: S. Chowdhary and A. V. Jayaprakash.

INDIA v ENGLAND

Second Test Match

At Madras, February 11, 12, 13, 14, 15. India won by an innings and 22 runs. Toss: India. Test debut: R. J. Blakey.

England were well beaten by 11 men and a plate of prawns as India won the match – and with it the series – by an innings and 22 runs. The night before the match Gooch and Gatting had eaten in the Chinese restaurant at the team's hotel; their meal included an extra plate of prawns. Shortly before the start of play Gooch, complaining of sickness and dizziness, was forced to withdraw from the game. Later, after acting-captain Stewart had lost the toss, Gatting and Smith, who had apparently eaten chicken in his room, both left the field feeling ill. There followed considerable debate as to whether the players had ignored the advice they were given about diet. But since the team had previously eaten plenty of both seafood and Chinese food (which is very common in India) with no ill effect, the management decided not to add disciplinary action to the players' troubles. England then started preparing their own lunchtime buffet for the players, consisting of corned beef, baked beans and nan bread served by manager Bob Bennett, physiotherapist David Roberts and chaplain Andrew Wingfield Digby in the dressing-room, known thereafter as Bob's Bistro.

This was the third time Gooch had been forced to drop out overseas since he became captain. The effect was predictable. In his absence from the final two Tests in the West Indies in 1989-90, England lost in Barbados and Antigua to surrender a 1-0 lead. They lost again in Brisbane in the First Test of the 1990-91 Ashes series, a defeat from which they never recovered. The sequence continued here after England exacerbated their problems with another piece of muddled selection. In the absence of their most experienced batsman and opener, and with Smith and Gatting both poorly, it seemed obvious to everyone outside the tour selection committee that the fit-again Atherton must play. However, Stewart's reluctance to open the batting, keep wicket and captain the side led them to include Blakey as wicket-keeper and Smith as Stewart's opening partner. Atherton was not even among the four substitutes used on the first day.

The pattern of play was much the same as it had been in Calcutta. Sidhu, on the first day, and Tendulkar, on the second, completed excellently-crafted centuries in India's first-innings total of 560 for six declared, their highest total against England at home. Tendulkar's six-hour 165 – including 24 fours and a six – was a gem but, had a third umpire, using TV replay, been on hand to review a run-out attempt by Lewis when he was on nine, India might not have made such a conclusive total. Kapil Dev, in his 122nd Test, made 66 not out; when he reached 35 he became the first man to score 5,000 Test runs and take 400 wickets. The lack of penetration in England's bowling was again disappointing. Tufnell, whose omission from the Calcutta Test had caused such controversy, finished wicketless after 41 overs, Salisbury bowled too many long hops and, on a pitch that was playing easily, Lewis, Jarvis and Malcolm posed no threat to the Indian batsmen.

England could take a little comfort in decent scores by Stewart, Hick, who was at last beginning to look the part, and Fairbrother, with his first Test fifty. But the loss of six wickets for 63, in the time-honoured fashion of England collapses, meant that they could not avoid the follow-on. After a fifty from Smith, the highlight of the second innings was an exciting maiden Test hundred by Lewis, who decided to attack on the basis that England had nothing to lose, and reached three figures with a six off Raju, shortly before the close of the fourth day, his 25th birthday. The Lewis interlude lasted only 170 minutes and it took India just 35 minutes of the final morning to finish the match. Again the spinners, Kumble, Raju and Chauhan, did the damage, exposing England's leaden-footed lack of technique; as in Calcutta, they took 17 of the 20 wickets. In the second innings the leg-spinner Kumble bowled quite beautifully to take six for 64 as England duly and meekly succumbed to their heaviest defeat by India and only their second by an innings. The previous instance was also at Madras, in 1951-52. Afterwards, Fletcher bemoaned the lack of turning pitches in domestic cricket which meant that England's batsmen were ill-equipped for these conditions.

Man of the Match: S. R. Tendulkar.

Close of play: First day, India 275-2 (N. S. Sidhu 104*, S. R. Tendulkar 70*); Second day, England 19-0 (R. A. Smith 6*, A. J. Stewart 10*); Third day, England 221-7 (N. H. Fairbrother 38*, P. W. Jarvis 0*); Fourth day, England 231-8 (C. C. Lewis 108*, P. C. R. Tufnell 10*).

India

M. Prabhakar c Blakey b Lewis	27	†K. S. More not out	26
N. S. Sidhu c Hick b Jarvis	106		
V. G. Kambli lbw b Hick	59	L-b 10, w 2, n-b 15	27
S. R. Tendulkar c and b Salisbury	165		
*M. Azharuddin c Smith b Jarvis	6	1/41 (1) 2/149 (3)	(6 wkts dec.) 560
P. K. Amre c Jarvis b Salisbury	78	3/296 (2) 4/324 (5)	
Kapil Dev not out	66	5/442 (4) 6/499 (6)	

A. Kumble, R. K. Chauhan and S. L. V. Raju did not bat.

Bowling: Malcolm 27-7-87-0; Jarvis 28-7-72-2; Lewis 11-1-40-1; Tufnell 41-3-132-0; Hick 29-2-77-1; Salisbury 29-1-142-2.

England

R. A. Smith lbw b Kumble		17 – c Amre b Kumble	56
*A. J. Stewart c sub (W. V. Raman) b Raju	74	74 – lbw b Kapil Dev	0
G. A. Hick lbw b Chauhan		64 – c Tendulkar b Kapil Dev	0
M. W. Gatting run out		2 – lbw b Raju	19
N. H. Fairbrother c Kapil Dev b Chauhan	83	83 – c Prabhakar b Kumble	9
†R. J. Blakey b Raju		0 – b Kumble	6
C. C. Lewis c Azharuddin b Raju		0 – c and b Kumble	117
I. D. K. Salisbury lbw b Kumble		4 – b Kumble	12
P. W. Jarvis c sub (W. V. Raman) b Raju	8	8 – c Tendulkar b Kumble	22
P. C. R. Tufnell c Azharuddin b Chauhan		2 – not out	2
D. E. Malcolm not out		0 – c sub (W. V. Raman) b Raju	0
B 14, l-b 16, n-b 2	32	B 4, l-b 5	9
	286		252

1/46 (1) 2/157 (3) 3/166 (4) 4/175 (2)   1/10 (2) 2/12 (3) 3/71 (4)
5/179 (6) 6/179 (7) 7/220 (8)   4/82 (1) 5/88 (6) 6/99 (5)
8/277 (9) 9/279 (5) 10/286 (10)   7/172 (8) 8/186 (9)
                                   9/241 (7) 10/252 (11)

Bowling: *First Innings*—Prabhakar 3-2-7-0; Kumble 25-9-61-2; Chauhan 39.3-16-69-3; Raju 54-21-103-4; Kapil Dev 4-0-11-0; Tendulkar 2-1-5-0. *Second Innings*—Prabhakar 3-2-4-0; Kapil Dev 11-5-36-2; Raju 23.1-3-76-2; Chauhan 21-4-59-0; Kumble 21-7-64-6; Tendulkar 2-1-4-0.

Umpires: V. K. Ramaswamy and R. S. Rathore. Referee: C. W. Smith (West Indies).

INDIA v ENGLAND

Third Test Match

At Bombay, February 19, 20, 21, 22, 23. India won by an innings and 15 runs. Toss: England.

England became the first side to lose every game of a Test series in India, despite the commanding century from Hick for which he and the England selectors had been waiting since he made his debut in the First Test of the 1991 series against West Indies. Hick knew that his performances on this tour might make or break his career after the disappointment of his baffling failure to bridge the gap between county and Test cricket. Pressure on him to live up to his undoubted but unproven potential was even greater because of the controversy over the omission of Gower. And when he arrived at the crease to play his 22nd Test innings, England, despite winning the toss and being able to select their first-choice batting order at last, were once again floundering in crisis at 58 for four. Gooch, Stewart, Smith and Gatting were out, Stewart through a run-out that appeared to sum up the division within the party after weeks of failure.

He and Atherton were considered rivals for the England captaincy after Gooch. Atherton had been Gooch's deputy in 1991, before missing the tour to New Zealand and the World Cup because of back surgery. He lost the job to Stewart, who was about to take over the side in Sri Lanka after Gooch's early departure from the tour. The uncertainty over the succession had created a dangerous undercurrent. There was a mix-up over a short single and both were stranded at the bowler's end; it reflected little credit on either that their wait for umpire Venkataraghavan's decision was conducted in stony silence with a telling lack of eye contact. Morally and technically, Atherton, the non-striker, should have gone, as initially responded to Stewart's call, and the batsmen had crossed before he thought better of it. But having been forced to sit out the previous two Tests, Atherton was in no mood to sacrifice his chance of an innings. The umpire decided that the conspicuously reluctant Stewart should depart.

It would not have been surprising, given the prevailing fatalistic mood of the party, had England simply folded then and there. Indeed, when Hick joined Atherton, the Indians must have felt that one more puff would bring the house down. But Hick survived the loss of his partner and Blakey two runs later when the board read 118 for six. Hick prospered in an excellent stand worth 93 with Lewis, followed by an unlikely one of 68 for the last wicket with Tufnell, who scored just two in 83 minutes. Ninety-nine overnight, Hick reached his maiden Test hundred, his 68th in first-class cricket, in the first over next day. After 501 minutes, 20 fours and a six, he was last man out for 178 of England's 347, a total that should have ensured a face-saving draw at least.

It did not because, once again, the Indian batsmen capitalised on some woeful bowling and fielding. Sidhu and Prabhakar put on 109 for the first wicket. On 174, Sidhu was picked up at silly point off Tufnell. In the next over, Kambli skied a simple catch to long-off and DeFreitas made a hash of it. The spill instantly drained the England players of their last dregs of optimism. Kambli went on to make 224 on his home ground, his first Test century in only his third Test. Only 11 men have scored more in their maiden Test century, and it was the highest score ever for India against England. The third-wicket partnership with his Bombay schoolfriend Tendulkar produced 194 runs, a partnership that produced special home-town delight for the crowd. Kambli's was an innings of rare quality, full of daring strokeplay executed with a joyfulness that rippled round the ground. He batted nearly ten hours, faced 411 balls and hit 23 fours. It enabled his team to reach 591 and leave their opponents completely demoralised.

Chasing the 244 required to make India bat again, England immediately slumped to 34 for three. Prabhakar slipped out Stewart, Gooch and Atherton in an opening spell of three for 27 in eight overs from which the innings never recovered. Smith, Gatting and Hick made a fist of survival, but the pitch, now taking considerable turn, enabled the spinners to complete the job shortly after lunch on the fifth day.

At least the margin of England's defeat was an improvement on Madras. There India's victory by an innings and 22 runs was their biggest over England. Here they had to be content with scraping home by an innings and 15. Gooch indicated afterwards that he took full responsibility for the 3-0 defeat. In a highly charged press conference at the team's hotel he suggested that he was uncertain whether to carry on as captain for the summer ahead. The issue was unresolved until well after the Australians arrived in England in April. Azharuddin, on the other hand, who was being abused by the Indian media and several former Indian Test players as the series began, might have allowed himself a quiet chuckle. His position, at one time considered untenable, had suddenly become unassailable.

Man of the Match: G. A. Hick. *Man of the Series:* A. Kumble.

Close of play: First day, England 239-7 (G. A. Hick 99*, J. E. Emburey 5*); Second day, India 144-1 (N. S. Sidhu 69*, V. G. Kambli 20*); Third day, India 397-3 (V. G. Kambli 164*, M. Azharuddin 14*); Fourth day, England 108-3 (R. A. Smith 39*, M. W. Gatting 31*).

England

*G. A. Gooch c More b Kapil Dev	4	– b Prabhakar	8
A. J. Stewart run out	13	– lbw b Prabhakar	10
M. A. Atherton c Prabhakar b Kumble	37	– c More b Prabhakar	11
R. A. Smith c More b Raju	2	– b Kumble	62
M. W. Gatting c Kapil Dev b Raju	23	– st More b Chauhan	61
G. A. Hick c Kapil Dev b Prabhakar	178	– c Amre b Kumble	47
†R. J. Blakey lbw b Kumble	1	– b Kumble	0
C. C. Lewis lbw b Kumble	49	– c More b Raju	3
J. E. Emburey c More b Kapil Dev	12	– c Tendulkar b Kumble	1
P. A. J. DeFreitas lbw b Kapil Dev	11	– st More b Raju	12
P. C. R. Tufnell not out	2	– not out	2
B 4, l-b 5, w 2, n-b 4	15	B 4, l-b 6, w 1, n-b 1	12
	347		**229**

1/11 (1) 2/25 (2) 3/30 (4) 4/58 (5)   1/17 (2) 2/26 (1) 3/34 (3)
5/116 (3) 6/118 (7) 7/211 (8)   4/155 (5) 5/181 (4) 6/181 (7)
8/262 (9) 9/279 (10) 10/347 (6)   7/206 (8) 8/214 (6)
                                              9/215 (9) 10/229 (10)

Bowling: *First Innings*—Kapil Dev 15–3–35–3; Prabhakar 13–2–52–1; Raju 44–8–102–2;
Kumble 40–4–95–3; Chauhan 23–7–54–0. *Second Innings*—Kapil Dev 7–1–21–0; Prabhakar
11–4–28–3; Raju 26.5–7–68–2; Kumble 26–9–70–4; Chauhan 12–5–32–1.

India

N. S. Sidhu c Smith b Tufnell	79	R. K. Chauhan c Atherton b Tufnell		15
M. Prabhakar c Blakey b Hick	44	S. L. V. Raju not out		0
V. G. Kambli c Gatting b Lewis	224			
S. R. Tendulkar lbw b Tufnell	78	B 5, l-b 14, w 5, n-b 6		30
*M. Azharuddin lbw b Lewis	26			
P. K. Amre c DeFreitas b Hick	57	1/109 (2) 2/174 (1) 3/368 (4)		591
Kapil Dev c DeFreitas b Emburey	22	4/418 (5) 5/519 (6) 6/560 (7)		
†K. S. More c Lewis b Emburey	0	7/560 (8) 8/563 (3)		
A. Kumble c Atherton b Tufnell	16	9/591 (9) 10/591 (10)		

Bowling: DeFreitas 20–4–75–0; Lewis 42–9–114–2; Emburey 59–14–144–2; Tufnell
39.3–6–142–4; Hick 29–3–97–2.

Umpires: P. D. Reporter and S. Venkataraghavan. Referee: C. W. Smith (West Indies).

†INDIA v ENGLAND

Third One-day International

At Bangalore, February 26. England won by 48 runs. Toss: India.

An unremarkable match provided England with their first success for five and a half
weeks in front of a passionate crowd of more than 50,000. In an experiment with the
batting order, England sent Gooch in at No. 6. From there, with the help of Hick, he
rebuilt the innings after the fast-medium Srinath had removed Smith, Stewart and Gatting
in a lively first spell. Srinath, a former pupil of Dennis Lillee who had missed the Test
series, finished with five for 41. Another neglected bowler, Jarvis, who had been omitted at
Bombay for DeFreitas, made his point by removing Kambli with his first ball – after
Lewis had dismissed Tendulkar in the next over – Azharuddin with his eighth. His five for
35 represented a match-winning performance. Kapil Dev and Kumble offered late but
ineffectual resistance. Both teams were fined by referee Cammie Smith for their slow over
rate: India 15 per cent of their match fees, England 30 per cent.

Men of the Match: P. W. Jarvis and J. Srinath.

England

R. A. Smith c More b Srinath	29	P. W. Jarvis c Azharuddin b Kapil Dev	
†A. J. Stewart lbw b Srinath	14	D. E. Malcolm not out	
G. A. Hick c Amre b Prabhakar	56		
M. W. Gatting b Srinath	7	L-b 15, w 4, n-b 8	2
N. H. Fairbrother run out	5		
*G. A. Gooch b Prabhakar	45	1/42 (2) 2/65 (1)	(9 wkts, 47 overs) 2
C. C. Lewis c Tendulkar b Srinath	19	3/79 (4) 4/102 (5)	
D. A. Reeve not out	13	5/157 (3) 6/185 (7)	
P. A. J. DeFreitas c Prabhakar b Srinath	2	7/210 (6) 8/213 (9) 9/218 9/218 (10)	

Bowling: Kapil Dev 8–1–27–1; Prabhakar 10–0–50–2; Srinath 9–1–41–5; Ra
10–0–46–0; Kumble 10–1–39–0.

India

M. Prabhakar run out	0	J. Srinath c Hick b Malcolm	2
N. S. Sidhu c Gooch b DeFreitas	40	S. L. V. Raju not out	1
V. G. Kambli c Stewart b Jarvis	33		
S. R. Tendulkar c Hick b Lewis	3	L-b 4, w 11, n-b 3	18
*M. Azharuddin lbw b Jarvis	1		
P. K. Amre c Hick b Jarvis	16	1/3 (1) 2/61 (3) 3/66 (4) (41.4 overs) 170
Kapil Dev c Gooch b Malcolm	32	4/67 (5) 5/100 (6) 6/114 (2)
†K. S. More lbw b Jarvis	0	7/115 (8) 8/160 (7)
A. Kumble b Jarvis	24	9/166 (10) 10/170 (9)

Bowling: Malcolm 9–1–47–2; DeFreitas 8–0–27–1; Lewis 10–0–32–1; Jarvis 8.4–1–35–5; Reeve 6–0–25–0.

Umpires: V. K. Ramaswamy and M. R. Singh.

†INDIA v ENGLAND

Fourth One-day International

At Jamshedpur, March 1. England won by six wickets. Toss: England.

England won a match shortened by rain and marred by crowd trouble to extend their lead in the series to 3-1 with two to play. During India's innings of 137 in 26 overs Malcolm, chasing a ball towards the boundary, narrowly escaped being hit by a six-inch metal bolt thrown from behind the fence. He was clearly shaken and Fletcher complained that "unless control is more effective, someone will be seriously hurt, or even killed". J. Y. Lele, joint secretary of the Indian Board, said the crowd had been incensed because stewards were hitting people. Yet more security was introduced for the final two matches at Gwalior. Fairbrother, hobbling after two painful blows on the knee which forced him to use a runner, was England's hero. He paced his unbeaten 53 from 52 balls perfectly, hitting only four fours, as he led the chase for 65 off the final ten overs.

Man of the Match: N. H. Fairbrother.

India

N. S. Sidhu c DeFreitas b Malcolm	18	†K. S. More not out	1
M. Prabhakar c Blakey b DeFreitas	2		
V. G. Kambli run out	23	L-b 6, w 3, n-b 1	10
S. R. Tendulkar b Jarvis	24		
*M. Azharuddin c Fairbrother b Lewis	23	1/11 (2) 2/46 (1) (7 wkts, 26 overs) 137
Kapil Dev not out	15	3/51 (3) 4/96 (5)
P. K. Amre c Gooch b Jarvis	19	5/99 (4) 6/122 (7)
S. A. Ankola run out	2	7/127 (8)

A. Kumble and J. Srinath did not bat.

Bowling: DeFreitas 4–0–17–1; Malcolm 6–0–17–1; Lewis 5–0–25–1; Reeve 6–0–32–0; Jarvis 5–0–40–2.

England

*G. A. Gooch c More b Kapil Kev	15	D. A. Reeve not out	17
R. A. Smith run out	17	L-b 8, w 5	13
G. A. Hick c Azharuddin b Ankola	1		
N. H. Fairbrother not out	53	1/27 (1) 2/33 (3) (4 wkts, 25.4 overs) 141
C. C. Lewis lbw b Prabhakar	25	3/43 (2) 4/93 (5)

M. W. Gatting, †R. J. Blakey, P. A. J. DeFreitas, P. W. Jarvis and D. E. Malcolm did not bat.

Bowling: Kapil Dev 4–1–10–1; Prabhakar 5.4–0–34–1; Srinath 6–0–38–0; Ankola 6–0–28–1; Kumble 4–0–23–0.

Umpires: L. Narasimhan and C. S. Sathe.

†INDIA v ENGLAND

Fifth One-day International

At Gwalior, March 4. India won by three wickets. Toss: India.

This match, which replaced the cancelled game at Ahmedabad, produced excellent cricket but was spoiled by more missile-throwing. This time Stewart was the victim, hit on the head, and slightly hurt, by a piece of concrete. The perpetrator somehow eluded the thousand extra police brought in after the incident at Jamshedpur. Smith's brilliant century, 129 from 145 balls including 12 fours and four sixes, was the substance of England's innings. But his dismissal at 246 for four started a collapse in which their last seven wickets went for ten runs in 20 balls. India looked doomed when Prabhakar and Kambli fell with only four runs on the board but Sidhu and Azharuddin put on 175 in 28.2 overs for the third wicket. Sidhu, magnificently imperturbable as wickets fell around him, finished unbeaten on 134 to lead India to victory with two overs to spare. It was his third hundred off England's attack on the tour.

Man of the Match: N. S. Sidhu.

England

R. A. Smith lbw b Srinath	129		P. A. J. DeFreitas not out	2
A. J. Stewart b Kumble	33		P. W. Jarvis b Prabhakar	0
G. A. Hick c More b Prabhakar	18		D. E. Malcolm b Prabhakar	0
N. H. Fairbrother c Maninder Singh			B 1, l-b 16, w 8, n-b 4	29
	b Srinath	37		
C. C. Lewis lbw b Prabhakar	4		1/101 (2) 2/154 (3)	(50 overs) 256
*G. A. Gooch run out	1		3/227 (4) 4/246 (1) 5/246 (5)	
D. A. Reeve run out	3		6/251 (6) 7/251 (8) 8/256 (7)	
†R. J. Blakey lbw b Srinath	0		9/256 (10) 10/256 (11)	

Bowling: Kapil Dev 9–0–39–0; Prabhakar 10–0–54–4; Srinath 10–0–41–3; Kumble 10–0–41–1; Maninder Singh 8–0–46–0; Ajay Sharma 3–0–18–0.

India

N. S. Sidhu not out	134		A. Kumble not out	19
M. Prabhakar lbw b DeFreitas	0			
V. G. Kambli c Gooch b Malcolm	2		B 2, l-b 9, w 8, n-b 1	20
*M. Azharuddin c Stewart b Malcolm	74			
S. R. Tendulkar b Jarvis	5		1/1 (2) 2/4 (3)	(7 wkts, 48 overs) 257
Ajay Sharma run out	0		3/179 (4) 4/189 (5)	
Kapil Dev c Hick b Jarvis	2		5/190 (6) 6/202 (7)	
†K. S. More c Hick b Malcolm	1		7/205 (8)	

Maninder Singh and J. Srinath did not bat.

Bowling: DeFreitas 10–0–52–1; Malcolm 10–0–40–3; Lewis 10–0–56–0; Jarvis 10–0–43–2; Reeve 6–0–37–0; Hick 2–0–18–0.

Umpires: A. V. Jayaprakash and P. D. Reporter.

†INDIA v ENGLAND

Sixth One-day International

At Gwalior, March 5. India won by four wickets. Toss: India.

India squared the series 3–3 thanks to an inspired innings from Azharuddin, who took his side to victory with eight balls to spare. Just as happened 24 hours earlier, after England had been inserted on a dry, bare pitch, Smith set about the bowling with gusto. This time he was overshadowed by a thrilling unbeaten century by Hick, whose 105 came in 109 balls. But even these innings rapidly slipped from memory once Azharuddin started to impose his genius on the proceedings. The Indian captain came to the wicket at 99 for two, with 167 required in 24 overs. He ripped the England attack to pieces – his 95 not out came from just 63 balls. Thus England's tour of India ended in their sixth defeat in nine international matches, and all their plans in tatters.

Man of the Match: M. Azharuddin.

Man of the Series: N. S. Sidhu.

England

R. A. Smith c Ajay Sharma		M. W. Gatting c Sidhu b Srinath	6
b Maninder Singh	72	C. C. Lewis not out	3
†A. J. Stewart c More b Srinath	11	L-b 8, w 17, n-b 2	27
G. A. Hick not out	105		
N. H. Fairbrother c Kapil Dev		1/42 (2) 2/158 (1) (4 wkts, 48 overs) 265	
b Srinath	41	3/246 (4) 4/258 (5)	

*G. A. Gooch, D. A. Reeve, P. A. J. DeFreitas, P. W. Jarvis and D. E. Malcolm did not bat.

Bowling: Kapil Dev 10-2-48-0; Prabhakar 9-0-52-0; Srinath 9-0-37-3; Maninder Singh 10-0-62-1; Kumble 10-0-58-0.

India

M. Prabhakar b Jarvis	73	Ajay Sharma c Gooch b Jarvis	2
N. S. Sidhu c Hick b Lewis	19	†K. S. More not out	10
V. G. Kambli c Reeve b DeFreitas	22	L-b 1, w 7, n-b 2	10
*M. Azharuddin not out	95		
S. R. Tendulkar c sub (J. P. Taylor)		1/41 (2) 2/99 (3) (6 wkts, 46.4 overs) 267	
b Lewis	34	3/166 (1) 4/245 (5)	
Kapil Dev c Reeve b Jarvis	2	5/251 (6) 6/253 (7)	

A. Kumble, J. Srinath and Maninder Singh did not bat.

Bowling: Malcolm 8-0-56-0; Lewis 10-1-51-2; Jarvis 10-0-39-3; Reeve 8.4-0-64-0; DeFreitas 10-0-56-1.

Umpires: S. K. Bansal and S. Venkataraghavan.

†SRI LANKA v ENGLAND

First One-day International

At Khettarama Stadium, Colombo, March 10 (day/night). Sri Lanka won on scoring-rate. Toss: Sri Lanka.

The Sri Lankan leg, with Gooch safely back in England and Stewart taking over the captaincy, began with England's worst one-day performance of the tour so far. It ensured a losing double for team manager Fletcher, who was captain when Sri Lanka gained their only other one-day international victory over England in 1981-82, and Gatting, who played in both matches. The bowling in the closing stages of Sri Lanka's innings was particularly inept. England bowled ten wides and 11 no-balls in all; DeFreitas was entrusted with only three overs and Jarvis and Reeve were hit especially hard. The only other survivor of Sri Lanka's previous win, their captain Ranatunga, feasted on the bowling before Tillekeratne and Jayasuriya gorged themselves in an unbeaten sixth-wicket stand of 70 in just six overs. Heavy rain interrupted England's reply at 67 for three in the 20th over, reducing their target from 251 in 47 to an eminently achievable 203 in 38. But once Hick and Fairbrother were out the rest was a formality.

Man of the Match: H. P. Tillekeratne.

Sri Lanka

R. S. Mahanama c Hick b Malcolm	...	7	
U. C. Hathurusinghe lbw b Emburey	..	43	
A. P. Gurusinha c DeFreitas b Jarvis	..	5	
P. A. de Silva c and b Reeve	....	34	
*A. Ranatunga c Stewart b Lewis	.....	36	
H. P. Tillekeratne not out	....	66	

S. T. Jayasuriya not out	 34
B 3, l-b 4, w 10, n-b 8	 25

1/16 (1) 2/33 (3)	(5 wkts, 47 overs)	250
3/101 (4) 4/109 (2)		
5/180 (5)		

†A. M. de Silva, R. S. Kalpage, C. P. H. Ramanayake and G. P. Wickremasinghe did not bat.

Bowling: Malcolm 7–1–32–1; Lewis 9–0–40–1; Jarvis 9–0–57–1; DeFreitas 3–0–25–0; Emburey 10–1–42–1; Reeve 9–1–47–1.

England

R. A. Smith c and b Wickremasinghe	..	3	
*A. J. Stewart lbw b Ramanayake	....	5	
G. A. Hick c Mahanama			
	b Hathurusinghe	31	
N. H. Fairbrother lbw b Jayasuriya	....	34	
M. W. Gatting b Kalpage	....	1	
C. C. Lewis b Kalpage	....	16	
D. A. Reeve c Ranatunga b Kalpage	..	16	
P. A. J. DeFreitas c Ranatunga			
	b Wickremasinghe	21	

J. E. Emburey st A. M. de Silva	
	b Jayasuriya . 10
P. W. Jarvis not out	 16
D. E. Malcolm run out	 2
L-b 10, w 4, n-b 1	 15

1/7 (2) 2/9 (1) 3/67 (3)	(36.1 overs)	170
4/71 (5) 5/99 (4) 6/103 (6)		
7/120 (7) 8/137 (9)		
9/152 (8) 10/170 (11)		

Bowling: Ramanayake 7–0–25–1; Wickremasinghe 6.1–1–21–2; Hathurusinghe 6–0–28–1; Gurusinha 2–0–7–0; Kalpage 8–0–34–3; Jayasuriya 7–0–45–2.

Umpires: K. T. Francis and S. Ponnadurai.

SRI LANKA v ENGLAND

Test Match

At Sinhalese Sports Club, Colombo, March 13, 14, 15, 17, 18. Sri Lanka won by five wickets. Toss: England. Test debut: A. M. de Silva.

Sri Lanka comprehensively outplayed England and thoroughly deserved their first win against them in five Tests and their fourth in the 43 they had contested since attaining Test status 11 years previously. England joined India, Pakistan and New Zealand on the list of Sri Lankan conquests.

Although there were individual performances of some merit from England, collectively this was another bad display. The tourists once again failed to produce the standard of performance required to compete with technically skilled and highly motivated opposition in a hostile environment. In Calcutta the climatic peculiarity that had caused so much consternation was smog; here it was the steamy heat. The shirts of the England players were soaked in perspiration throughout the match as temperatures soared into the high 90s and the humidity became quite exhausting. It was hard to disagree with team manager Fletcher's assertion, supported by the fact that England's highest scorers were born in Southern Africa, that: "It's very nearly too hot here for Europeans to play cricket."

There were also further murmurings regarding the impartiality of Sri Lankan umpiring and the bowling action of Sri Lankan off-spinners Warnaweera and Muralitharan. But overall, England had nothing and no one to blame but themselves. They had been given a substantial platform by Smith, who scored his first century as a Test opener. In partnerships of 112 with Hick and 122 with Stewart he played the anchor role to perfection. His first Test hundred overseas, and his eighth in all, lasted seven and a half hours, a tribute to his stamina as well as his skill. But after he was dismissed at 316 for four the innings soon folded: the last seven wickets fell for 64 runs.

The Sri Lankan batting lived up to its high reputation against some of England's best bowling on the entire tour, particularly from Lewis and Tufnell. De Silva and Ranatunga, their two senior batsmen, displayed the determination to build long innings as well as the exquisite wristy strokeplay so widely admired in world cricket. But the decline of the innings from 330 for three to 376 for eight indicated a brittleness in the lower order to match England's until the fourth morning of the match. England needed almost two hours to take the wickets of two tailenders who enabled Tillekeratne to finish unbeaten on 93 and build a first-innings lead of 89.

England's batting self-destructed again. Against some penetrative off-spin from Warnaweera, they slumped initially to 96 for five. Atherton completed a miserable tour by adding two to his first-innings 13 to finish with a Test average for the tour of 15.75, while Gatting, Smith and Hick all got out when well set through careless shots. Lewis and Emburey made sure the innings achieved a modicum of respectability at 228 all out on the final morning.

Their efforts might have led to greater things had Sri Lanka, struggling at 61 for four with 79 still required to win, performed as they had done against Australia on the same ground in August 1992. Then they needed 181 to win, reached 127 for two and lost. This time, however, in front of substantially the biggest crowd of the match – some 10,000 who arrived to witness the historic moment of victory – there was to be no repetition. The England bowlers once more found Tillekeratne impossible to get out. Tufnell and Emburey bowled well in tandem, but Tillekeratne had their measure, cutting hard at anything fractionally short and dancing down the wicket if the opportunity to drive presented itself. At the other end, Ranatunga was batting as though his life depended on it. For him, victory meant too much to be allowed to slip through his grasp. His obvious sadness when he was caught with only four runs needed soon disappeared as Jayasuriya pulled Tufnell's next ball for six.

Man of the Match: H. P. Tillekeratne.

Close of play: First day, England 245-3 (R. A. Smith 91*, A. J. Stewart 26*); Second day, Sri Lanka 140-1 (U. C. Hathurusinghe 53*, A. P. Gurusinha 12*); Third day, Sri Lanka 408-8 (H. P. Tillekeratne 51*, M. Muralitharan 7*); Fourth day, England 226-9 (J. E. Emburey 57*, D. E. Malcolm 8*).

England

R. A. Smith b Muralitharan	128	– b Jayasuriya	35
M. A. Atherton lbw b Ramanayake	13	– c Tillekeratne b Gurusinha	2
M. W. Gatting c Jayasuriya b Muralitharan	29	– c Tillekeratne b Warnaweera	18
G. A. Hick c Tillekeratne b Muralitharan	68	– c Ramanayake b Warnaweera	26
*†A. J. Stewart c Tillekeratne b Warnaweera	63	– c Mahanama b Warnaweera	3
N. H. Fairbrother b Warnaweera	18	– run out	3
C. C. Lewis run out	22	– c Jayasuriya b Muralitharan	45
J. E. Emburey not out	1	– b Gurusinha	59
P. W. Jarvis lbw b Warnaweera	0	– st A. M. de Silva b Jayasuriya	3
P. C. R. Tufnell lbw b Muralitharan	1	– c A. M. de Silva b Warnaweera	1
D. E. Malcolm c Gurusinha b Warnaweera	13	– not out	8
B 5, l-b 3, w 1, n-b 15	24	B 4, l-b 2, w 1, n-b 18	25

1/40 (2) 2/82 (3) 3/194 (4) 4/316 (1)   380   1/16 (2) 2/38 (3) 3/83 (1)   228
5/323 (5) 6/358 (6) 7/366 (7) 8/366 (9)   4/91 (4) 5/96 (5) 6/130 (6)
9/367 (10) 10/380 (11)   7/153 (7) 8/173 (9)
     9/188 (10) 10/228 (8)

Bowling: First Innings—Ramanayake 17-2-66-1; Gurusinha 5-1-12-0; Warnaweera 40.1-11-90-4; Hathurusinghe 8-2-22-0; Muralitharan 45-12-118-4; Jayasuriya 12-1-53-0; Ranatunga 3-0-11-0. *Second Innings*—Ramanayake 3-0-16-0; Gurusinha 6-3-7-2; Warnaweera 25-4-98-4; Muralitharan 16-3-55-1; Jayasuriya 16-3-46-2.

Sri Lanka

R. S. Mahanama c Smith b Emburey	64	– c Stewart b Lewis	6
U. C. Hathurusinghe c Stewart b Lewis	59	– c Stewart b Tufnell	14
A. P. Gurusinha st Stewart b Tufnell	43	– b Emburey	29
P. A. de Silva c Stewart b Jarvis	80	– c Jarvis b Emburey	7
*A. Ranatunga c Stewart b Lewis	64	– c Gatting b Tufnell	35
H. P. Tillekeratne not out	93	– not out	36
S. T. Jayasuriya c Atherton b Lewis	4	– not out	6
†A. M. de Silva c Gatting b Emburey	9		
C. P. H. Ramanayake c Lewis b Jarvis	1		
M. Muralitharan b Lewis	19		
K. P. J. Warnaweera b Jarvis	1		
B 2, l-b 13, w 2, n-b 15	32	B 1, l-b 2, n-b 6	9

1/99 (1) 2/153 (2) 3/203 (3) 4/330 (4)   469 1/8 (1) 2/48 (3)   (5 wkts) 142
5/339 (5) 6/349 (7) 7/371 (8) 8/376 (9)   3/61 (4) 4/61 (2)
9/459 (10) 10/469 (11)   5/136 (5)

Bowling: *First Innings*—Malcolm 25-7-60-0; Jarvis 25.5-1-76-3; Lewis 31-5-66-4; Tufnell 33-5-108-1; Emburey 34-6-117-2; Hick 8-0-27-0. *Second Innings*—Lewis 8-1-21-1; Jarvis 8-2-14-0; Malcolm 3-1-11-0; Emburey 14-2-48-2; Tufnell 7.4-1-34-2; Hick 2-0-11-0.

Umpires: K. T. Francis and T. M. Samarasinghe. Referee: C. W. Smith (West Indies).

†SRI LANKA v ENGLAND

Second One-day International

At Moratuwa, March 20. Sri Lanka won by eight wickets. Toss: Sri Lanka.

England were thrashed by eight wickets with almost 15 overs to spare, after scoring a paltry 180 against a very weak attack comprising eight bowlers, but little quality. Six wickets went to Jayasuriya, hardly a front-line slow left-armer. In his first over since the Second Test in Madras 36 days earlier, Salisbury removed both openers, but when he had de Silva dropped by Smith in his next, England lost all heart. De Silva, treating the attack with barely disguised contempt, hit them for four sixes and seven fours and finished unbeaten on 75 from 68 balls. "We got hammered, didn't we?" said Stewart. For England's dazed and humiliated players, the flight to Heathrow the next morning could not come soon enough.

Man of the Match: S. T. Jayasuriya.

England

C. C. Lewis c Ramanayake b Wickremasinghe	8	I. D. K. Salisbury not out	2
R. A. Smith st A. M. de Silva b Jayasuriya	31	P. W. Jarvis c A. M. de Silva b Jayasuriya	4
G. A. Hick lbw b Kalpage	36	J. P. Taylor b Jayasuriya	1
N. H. Fairbrother c A. M. de Silva b Jayasuriya	21		
*†A. J. Stewart lbw b Tillekeratne	14	B 2, l-b 9, w 3, n-b 6	20
M. W. Gatting lbw b P. A. de Silva	2		
D. A. Reeve b Jayasuriya	20	1/23 (1) 2/77 (2) 3/85 (3) (48.5 overs) 180
J. E. Emburey c Ramanayake b Jayasuriya	21	4/111 (4) 5/114 (6) 6/125 (5)

7/168 (8) 8/172 (7)
9/177 (10) 10/180 (11)

Bowling: Ramanayake 4-0-20-0; Wickremasinghe 8-0-23-1; Gurusinha 4-0-21-0; Hathurusinghe 2-0-13-0; Kalpage 10-0-27-1; Jayasuriya 9.5-0-29-6; P. A. de Silva 7-1-22-1; Tillekeratne 4-0-14-1.

Sri Lanka

R. S. Mahanama c Stewart b Salisbury . 29
U. C. Hathurusinghe c and b Salisbury . 33
A. P. Gurusinha not out 35
P. A. de Silva not out 75
    B 1, l-b 2, w 2, n-b 6 11

1/66 (2) 2/68 (1)   (2 wkts, 35.2 overs) 183

*A. Ranatunga, H. P. Tillekeratne, S. T. Jayasuriya, †A. M. de Silva, R. S. Kalpage, C. P. H. Ramanayake and G. P. Wickremasinghe did not bat.

  Bowling: Lewis 7–1–13–0; Jarvis 4–0–22–0; Taylor 3–0–20–0; Emburey 6–0–29–0; Salisbury 4–0–36–2; Hick 6.2–1–36–0; Reeve 5–0–24–0.

          Umpires: B. C. Cooray and T. M. Samarasinghe.

ENGLAND UNDER-19 IN INDIA, 1992-93

England Under-19 toured India from January to March 1993, playing 11 games, with little more success than their senior counterparts. They won one, lost six and drew four. The three-match "Test" series included their solitary victory, an innings win in the opening match at Ghaziabad, and the series was drawn 1-1 after a draw at Delhi and India Under-19's innings win in the final game at Calcutta. India Under-19 won the one-day series 3-0. Two other one-day games were lost, and three three-day matches drawn.

The party of 15 for the tour was: M. J. Walker (Kent) (*captain*), M. Broadhurst (Yorkshire), R. J. Ballinger (Middlesex), G. Chapple (Lancashire), R. J. Cunliffe (Oxfordshire/ Gloucestershire), J. A. Daley (Durham), M. P. Dowman (Lincolnshire/Nottinghamshire), J. E. Hindson (Nottinghamshire), R. O. Jones (Cheshire/Lancashire), J. I. D. Kerr (Somerset), C. E. Mulraine (Warwickshire), A. Payne (Somerset), R. J. Rollins (Essex), M. P. Vaughan (Yorkshire) and P. J. Wilcock (Lancashire). *Manager:* S. P. Coverdale (Northamptonshire). *Coach:* G. J. Saville (Essex).

First Under-19 "Test": At Ghaziabad, January 28, 29, 30, 31. England Under-19 won by an innings and four runs. Toss: England Under-19. England Under-19 451 for eight dec. M. P. Dowman 142, M. P. Vaughan 43, M. J. Walker 37, J. A. Daley 35, R. J. Cunliffe 50, R. J. Rollins 43 not out, Extras 33; M. Rana three for 73); India Under-19 251 (P. Dave 40, T. Jabbar 32, P. Dharmani 73 not out; M. Broadhurst four for 77, J. E. Hindson four for 71) and 196 (P. Dave 67; G. Chapple three for 38, M. Broadhurst four for 71).

Second Under-19 "Test": At Delhi, February 4, 5, 6, 7. Drawn. Toss: England Under-19. England Under-19 347 (M. P. Dowman 39, M. J. Walker 45, J. A. Daley 55, J. I. D. Kerr 39, G. Chapple 50 not out, Extras 38; P. Thakur four for 91, S. Sriram five for 68) and 162 for five (R. J. Cunliffe 78 not out); India Under-19 421 for nine dec. P. Dave 132, A. Dani 111, T. Jabbar 42, A. Majumdar 52; M. Broadhurst three for 72).

Third Under-19 "Test": At Calcutta, February 16, 17, 18, 19. India Under-19 won by an innings and 155 runs. Toss: India Under-19. India Under-19 474 for eight dec. (P. Dave 75, A. Dani 70, T. Jabbar 89, A. Majumdar 65, P. Dharmani 85; M. P. Vaughan three for 83); England Under-19 164 (M. J. Walker 48, J. E. Hindson 51 not out; P. Thakur six for 51, R. Sanghvi three for 50) and 155 (M. J. Walker 49, R. J. Cunliffe 57 not out; R. Sanghvi three for 41, S. Sriram four for 27).

ENGLAND A IN AUSTRALIA, 1992-93

By BILL DAY

The England A tour to Australia was a major disappointment for several reasons. The itinerary was seriously flawed in the planning stage, most of the matches were played virtually in secret and some of the 15 players chosen for the voyage of discovery did nothing to enhance their reputations as potential Test cricketers.

The belief that the two-month tour could be sustained with no unofficial Test matches or representative fixtures was found to be misguided from the beginning. Add to that the decision not to make three of the seven longer matches first-class and the tour was stripped of the competitive edge that had prevailed on the more imaginatively organised England A tours to Kenya and Zimbabwe in 1989-90, Pakistan and Sri Lanka in 1990-91 and Bermuda and the West Indies in 1991-92.

Keith Fletcher, team manager of the three tours before his promotion to run the full England side, stressed on the earlier trips that, if England A team cricket was to have any credibility in the development of future Test players, there had to be an opportunity to play the five-day game. Four games on this tour were of four days but two of them, against the Australian Cricket Academy in Melbourne and a Western Australian XI in Perth, were declared non-first-class by the Australian Cricket Board, which showed less enthusiasm for the trip than their counterparts at Lord's. The England manager Mike Vockins's protest over the secondary status given the match in Melbourne, against Australia's most talented young players, was dismissed by the board in line with their policy that Academy cricket should not be first-class.

The tour's struggle for credibility reached almost farcical proportions in what should have been the climax of the programme in Perth, when Test bowler Bruce Reid, returning to fitness and hoping to make a late bid for a place on the Ashes tour, withdrew from the Western Australian XI midway through the match to take up more important Sheffield Shield duties in Adelaide. Lengthy explanations for his departure could not disguise the feeling among most English observers that here was a lost legion of cricketers ending a two-month tour that nobody down under seemed to care about. There was little or no advance publicity for matches in the state newspapers and, with the Australian authorities apparently reluctant to distribute information, most games were played in front of empty stands. The welcome offered at the games in Caloundra and Alice Springs proved that the Australians retained all their traditional hospitality for the Poms. But it was in sharp contrast to the big city take-it-or-leave-it attitude, which prompted one player to lament: "Does anybody know we're here? Does anybody care?"

Thankfully, the tour, admirably led by the benevolent Vockins and team manager Norman Gifford, proved a lot more fruitful than had at one time seemed possible. In the one-day matches, England A beat Northern Territory and Western Australian XIs and were defeated by New South Wales and Tasmania. They won two, lost two and drew two of the longer fixtures. Sadly, the victories came against the Australian Cricket Academy and a Western Australian XI in matches not ratified as first-class.

The rota system of team selection gave everyone a chance, but that policy, and the lack of any representative opposition – the Cricket Academy was the closest to that – denied the players the important individual competitive element. When have all men been equals on a cricket pitch? The three previous A tours had given players a chance to fight for places in the unofficial Tests played as the highlights of those trips. The guarantee of regular cricket for all 15 players did have its advantages and, at times, injuries to players determined that selection meetings were merely a rubber stamp – "if you're fit enough you're good enough" – exercise. The bowling attack was seriously depleted at times, as David Millns, who damaged his Achilles tendon, and James Boiling, with a broken toe, missed vital matches for three weeks. Dominic Cork and Mark Ilott were sidelined by injuries to the knee and lumbar region respectively. Batsmen fared better, with the only serious casualties Graham Lloyd, who split his hand webbing, and the captain Martyn Moxon, who broke his finger a year to the week after breaking his thumb on the trip to Bermuda.

If the purpose of these tours is to uncover players with the potential to play Test cricket, then that was accomplished. Mark Lathwell, the 21-year-old Somerset batsman, emerged as a major discovery. An exquisite timer, he scored a career-best 175 in Tasmania and a second tour century against New South Wales to enhance suggestions that he should be England material sooner rather than later. Not since David Gower emerged had a youngster quickened the pulse quite like Lathwell. Graham Thorpe of Surrey, an ever-present on four A tours, had something to prove to the selectors after failing to make the progress expected of him. He took up the challenge admirably, scoring 444 runs in the longer matches with more consistency than he had generally shown in his five seasons at The Oval. Graham Lloyd of Lancashire proved another exciting prospect, scoring dashing centuries against the Australian Cricket Academy and Western Australian XI with a *joie de vivre* not always evident in his father David's batting. Lloyd was subjected to a barrage of sledging during his innings of 105 in Perth. "The fielders taunted him as gutless as he ducked a stream of bouncers from Duncan Spencer: "I must have some guts," he said, "I've nicked a hundred off you."

Jack Russell, named vice-captain after the disappointment of his omission from the senior England tour, was given the added responsibility of leading the team in four matches after Moxon's finger injury – his first experience of captaincy – and had the satisfaction of supervising three of England A's four wins. He kept immaculately throughout the two months, and proved that specialist spinners deserve the support of a specialist wicket-keeper. Peter Such was the pick of the England bowlers, tying up most batsmen with immaculate line and length and no shortage of turn when conditions suited. Andy Caddick's outstanding pace bowling accounted for 21 victims in the longer matches. The left-armer Mark Ilott, returning after missing most of the 1991 season with a stress fracture of the back, produced unflattering bowling figures, rarely receiving the luck his efforts in beating the bat regularly demanded. But he showed considerable progress. As for several others, it was the prelude to full caps in very quick time.

ENGLAND A TOURING PARTY

M. D. Moxon (Yorkshire) (*captain*), R. C. Russell (Gloucestershire) (*vice-captain*), J. Boiling (Surrey), A. R. Caddick (Somerset), D. J. Capel (Northamptonshire), D. G. Cork (Derbyshire), M. C. Ilott (Essex), M. N. Lathwell (Somerset), G. D. Lloyd (Lancashire), T. C. Middleton (Hampshire), D. J. Millns (Leicestershire), P. J. Prichard (Essex), M. A. Roseberry (Middlesex), P. M. Such (Essex), G. P. Thorpe (Surrey).

Boiling was called up to replace I. D. K. Salisbury (Sussex), who had joined the senior England party in India.

Tour manager: The Rev. M. D. Vockins (Worcestershire). *Team manager:* N. Gifford (Sussex).

ENGLAND A TOUR RESULTS

First-class matches – Played 4: Lost 2, Drawn 2.
Losses – South Australia, New South Wales.
Draws – Tasmania, Queensland.
Other non first-class matches – Played 7: Won 4, Lost 2, Drawn 1. *Wins* – Australian Cricket Academy (four days), Northern Territory XI, Western Australian XI, Western Australian XI (four days). *Losses* – New South Wales XI, Tasmania. *Draws* – Australian Capital Territory (three days).

ENGLAND A AVERAGES – FIRST-CLASS MATCHES

BATTING

	M	I	NO	R	HS	100s	Avge	Ct/St
G. P. Thorpe	3	5	1	215	96	0	53.75	2
M. D. Moxon	3	6	2	194	62	0	48.50	1
M. N. Lathwell.....	4	7	0	332	175	2	47.42	1
G. D. Lloyd	2	4	1	140	60	0	46.66	0
M. A. Roseberry....	3	6	1	129	39	0	25.80	2
D. J. Millns........	3	5	1	90	30	0	22.50	0
D. J. Capel........	4	6	1	109	80*	0	21.80	1
R. C. Russell.......	4	6	1	103	51*	0	20.60	3/1
P. J. Prichard......	2	4	0	48	34	0	12.00	0
T. C. Middleton	4	8	0	88	21	0	11.00	1
D. G. Cork	3	4	0	28	22	0	7.00	0
P. M. Such	3	5	2	18	11*	0	6.00	1

Played in two matches: J. Boiling 5*, 3, 2 (1 ct); A. R. Caddick 16, 0, 0; M. C. Ilott 9*, 6, 23* (1 ct).

* *Signifies not out.*

BOWLING

	O	M	R	W	BB	5W/i	Avge
A. R. Caddick	61	18	143	5	3-68	0	28.6
D. J. Capel	87.2	8	249	6	4-72	0	41.5
P. M. Such	106.2	21	271	6	3-36	0	45.1
D. G. Cork	54.3	11	164	3	2-65	0	54.6
J. Boiling	87	19	232	4	3-93	0	58.0

Also bowled: M. C. Ilott 76–21–187–2; D. J. Millns 74.5–10–265–1; G. P. Thorpe 2–0–6–0.

Note: Matches in this section which were not first-class are signified by a dagger.

†At Bowral, January 31. New South Wales XI won by 28 runs. Toss: England A. New South Wales XI 193 for nine (50 overs) (R. Chee Quee 50, W. J. Adlam 30); England A 165 (48.4 overs) (M. A. Roseberry 37, P. J. Prichard 50).

†AUSTRALIAN CAPITAL TERRITORY v ENGLAND A

At Canberra, February 2, 3, 4. Drawn. Toss: Australian Capital Territory.

An impressive performance by England A failed to earn victory in their first full-length match. In blazing heat Moxon hooked McLeod for six to bring up what would have been his 34th century had the game been given first-class status, and put on 128 in 125 minutes with Russell. Then his pace bowlers gave Australian Capital Territory a gruelling time: Ilott and Caddick claimed four each as they swept aside the home team for 65. But they were denied victory by Nick Speak of Lancashire, playing Australian grade cricket after his omission from the touring party. Caught first ball in the collapse, he batted for five and a half hours during the second innings, running up 120 and sharing a 213-run stand with Solway. The frustrated tourists conceded the draw seven overs early, when ACT were 47 ahead with three wickets standing.

Close of play: First day, England A 326-5 (R. C. Russell 60*, D. G. Cork 3*); Second day, Australian Capital Territory 128-2 (P. Solway 50*, N. J. Speak 44*).

England A

T. C. Middleton c Irvine b McLeod ... 27	A. R. Caddick not out 25		
M. N. Lathwell c and b Irvine 35	J. Boiling not out 10		
*M. D. Moxon c King b Bull 123	B 9, l-b 9, w 2, n-b 12 32		
P. J. Prichard lbw b Bull 37			
G. D. Lloyd c McLeod b Bull 10	1/69 2/83 3/164	(7 wkts dec.) 379	
†R. C. Russell b McNamee b McLeod .. 67	4/194 5/322		
D. G. Cork b Bush 13	6/343 7/343		

M. C. Ilott and P. M. Such did not bat.

Bowling: Killen 30–13–55–0; McLeod 25–6–72–2; Irvine 18–5–51–1; Bull 22–4–81–3; Bush 28–6–75–1; Maxwell 9–1–27–0.

Australian Capital Territory

M. J. Frost b Ilott 4	– lbw b Caddick 2	
S. McNamee b Caddick 0	– lbw b Cork 9	
*P. Solway c Middleton b Ilott 0	– run out 104	
N. J. Speak c Middleton b Ilott 0	– c Russell b Caddick 120	
S. Maxwell not out 22	– not out 53	
. Bull c Russell b Caddick 0	– c Russell b Cork 8	
G. R. Irvine c Russell b Ilott 7	– b Such 16	
C. M. Killen c Caddick b Cork 4	– run out 0	
S. King c Lloyd b Caddick 7	– not out 10	
C. W. McLeod c Moxon b Caddick 0		
G. A. Bush c Russell b Cork 7		
L-b 5, w 5, n-b 4 14	B 4, l-b 14, w 1, n-b 20 .. 39	

1/4 2/6 3/6 4/7 5/12	65	1/2 2/22 3/235 4/268	(7 wkts) 361
6/26 7/39 8/56 9/56		5/281 6/322 7/322	

Bowling: First Innings—Ilott 12–4–12–4; Caddick 11–8–14–4; Such 1–0–3–0; Cork 2–1–31–2. Second Innings—Caddick 32–11–80–1; Cork 26–2–93–2; Ilott 24–2–77–1; Such 8–23–69–1; Boiling 23–10–24–0.

Umpires: G. Davidson and K. Duffy.

†At Launceston, February 7. Tasmania won by 24 runs. Toss: Tasmania. Tasmania 224 fo
three (50 overs) (D. F. Hills 45, J. Cox 57, R. T. Ponting 59 not out, M. J. Di Venuto 4
not out); England A 200 (49.2 overs) (G. P. Thorpe 78, D. G. Cork 54; S. B. Oliver thre
for 29).

*Umpires R. Donaldson and S. G. Randell mistakenly allowed I. M. Connell to bowl an 11t
over, during which Thorpe was run out.*

TASMANIA v ENGLAND A

At Launceston, February 8, 9, 10. Drawn. Toss: England A.

Mark Lathwell's highest score, and only the second century of his career, made such
deep impression on Ted Dexter, chairman of the England Committee and newly arrive
from India, that he went straight to the dressing-room to congratulate him. Lathwell score
175 and hit 25 fours in five hours, demonstrating the effortless timing that so excite
Somerset supporters in 1992. Moxon declared on the first evening at 420 for nine, and rai
forced two more declarations before Tasmania set out in pursuit of 354 in 78 overs. Gallar
centuries and a stand of 202 for the second wicket from Hills and Cox threatened an upse
But when Cox was run out Boiling halted their charge, dismissing Hills, Ponting an
Tucker in his next ten balls to force a draw.

Close of play: First day, England A 420-9 dec.; Second day, Tasmania 159-0 (D. F. Hil
77*, N. C. P. Courtney 73*).

England A

T. C. Middleton c Castle b Matthews	18	– c Courtney b Cooley	
M. A. Roseberry lbw b Matthews	39	– not out	3
*M. D. Moxon c Tucker b Matthews	10	– not out	3
G. P. Thorpe c sub (M. G. Farrell) b Matthews	96		
M. N. Lathwell c Hills b Castle	175		
D. J. Capel b Castle	1		
†R. C. Russell c Buckingham b Castle	10		
D. G. Cork c Cox b Courtney	1		
D. J. Millns c Atkinson b Courtney	25		
J. Boiling not out	5		
M. C. Ilott not out	9		
L-b 7, w 2, n-b 22	31	B 4, l-b 3, n-b 8	1

1/59 2/70 3/81 4/265 5/270   (9 wkts dec.) 420   1/20   (1 wkt dec.) 9
6/312 7/325 8/406 9/408

Bowling: *First Innings*—Cooley 18-3-73-0; Matthews 27-3-110-4; McPhee 19-5-55-
Cox 1-0-4-0; Castle 35-3-105-3; Tucker 2-0-16-0; Buckingham 4-0-28-0; Courtne
4-1-22-2. *Second Innings*—Cooley 8-3-15-1; Matthews 4-1-9-0; McPhee 4-0-15-
Courtney 2-0-8-0; Castle 2-0-6-0; Hills 3-1-6-0; Cox 3-0-18-0; Ponting 0.4-0-8-0.

Tasmania

D. F. Hills not out	77	– c Lathwell b Boiling	10
N. C. P. Courtney not out	73	– c Roseberry b Capel	2
J. Cox (did not bat)		– run out	11
R. T. Ponting (did not bat)		– lbw b Boiling	
D. J. Buckingham (did not bat)		– not out	
*R. J. Tucker (did not bat)		– c Ilott b Boiling	
†M. N. Atkinson (did not bat)		– not out	1
B 1, l-b 4, n-b 4	9	B 1, l-b 8, w 1, n-b 6	1

(no wkt dec.) 159   1/63 2/265 3/265   (5 wkts) 28
4/267 5/271

C. D. Matthews, P. T. McPhee, T. J. Cooley and D. J. Castle did not bat.

Bowling: *First Innings*—Millns 9-2-36-0; Ilott 16-5-37-0; Cork 15-5-38-0; Cap
7.3-0-30-0; Boiling 7-3-13-0. *Second Innings*—Ilott 20-3-64-0; Millns 5.5-1-22-0; Boilin
30-5-93-3; Cork 9.1-1-43-0; Capel 13-0-57-1.

Umpires: R. Donaldson and B. T. Knight.

†AUSTRALIAN CRICKET ACADEMY v ENGLAND A

At Melbourne, February 14, 15, 16, 17. England A won by 81 runs. Toss: England A.

Peter Such's career-best performance of seven for 82 was left unrecognised when the Australian Cricket Board insisted that the match was not first-class, even though all but one of the players had previous first-class experience. Such took six for 39 on the second evening as the Academy collapsed from 159 for one to 231 all out; the slump might have been worse had his spin partner, Boiling, not broken a toe while batting. England A were able to set a target of 276 in 85 overs after Prichard and Thorpe batted solidly and Lloyd hit a four-hour 124, including 15 fours and two sixes. This time the Academy reached 164 for three before losing seven wickets for 30, four of them to Such's wizardry, giving him match figures of 11 for 144. Three of his victims were stumped by Russell; the Academy wicket-keeper, Gilchrist, also had a good game, with one stumping and nine catches.

Close of play: First day, Australian Cricket Academy 7-0 (D. F. Hills 1*, M. J. Slater 4*); Second day, Australian Cricket Academy 231; Third day, England A 271-6 (G. D. Lloyd 124*, A. R. Caddick 27*).

England A

M. A. Roseberry c Gilchrist b McIntyre	14	– (2) c Corbett b Cook	1
*M. D. Moxon c Ponting b Bevan	30	– (1) lbw b Cook	2
P. J. Prichard c Gilchrist b Cook	77	– lbw b Stewart	43
G. P. Thorpe st Gilchrist b McIntyre	2	– c Gilchrist b Cook	63
G. D. Lloyd c Bevan b Stewart	17	– c Gilchrist b Corbett	124
D. J. Capel c Gilchrist b Stewart	10	– c Gilchrist b Cook	1
†R. C. Russell c Gilchrist b McIntyre	32	– c Ponting b Stewart	9
A. R. Caddick c Bevan b Corbett	13	– c Cook b McIntyre	39
J. Boiling not out	3	– absent injured	
M. C. Ilott c McIntyre b Corbett	3	– (9) c Gilchrist b Corbett	0
P. M. Such c Gilchrist b Cook	3	– (10) not out	2
L-b 9, w 3, n-b 4	16	L-b 2	2
	220		**286**

1/51 2/55 3/58 4/79 5/95   220   1/3 2/3 3/82 4/138 5/152   286
6/160 7/210 8/210 9/215   6/193 7/272 8/272 9/286

Bowling: *First Innings*—Cook 16.2–7–21–2; Corbett 20–8–27–2; Law 6–2–14–0; McIntyre 29–6–85–3; Bevan 6–1–13–1; Stewart 21–5–51–2. *Second Innings*—Cook 21–7–54–4; Corbett 21–7–42–2; McIntyre 28.3–6–79–1; Law 12–2–33–0; Stewart 20–4–55–2; Bevan 5–0–21–0.

Australian Cricket Academy

D. F. Hills c Thorpe b Capel	66	– c Prichard b Caddick	14
*M. J. Slater c Prichard b Such	43	– run out	41
G. S. Blewett c Russell b Capel	43	– lbw b Capel	25
M. G. Bevan st Russell b Such	2	– c Moxon b Such	53
R. T. Ponting c sub (T. C. Middleton) b Such	0	– lbw b Such	25
S. G. Law run out	15	– c Capel b Caddick	11
†A. C. Gilchrist st Russell b Such	12	– st Russell b Such	2
J. Stewart c Moxon b Such	10	– c Roseberry b Caddick	5
S. H. Cook c sub (T. C. Middleton) b Such	1	– lbw b Such	4
P. E. McIntyre b Such	5	– (11) b Caddick	1
T. F. Corbett not out	18	– (10) not out	0
B 1, l-b 12, w 1, n-b 2	16	L-b 5, n-b 8	13
	231		**194**

1/69 2/159 3/162 4/163 5/168   231   1/19 2/67 3/97 4/164 5/181   194
6/190 7/195 8/207 9/208   6/183 7/183 8/191 9/193

Bowling: *First Innings*—Caddick 23–4–56–0; Ilott 18–5–42–0; Such 35.4–9–82–7; Capel 15–4–38–2. *Second Innings*—Ilott 10–0–52–0; Caddick 16.1–5–46–4; Capel 12–3–29–1; Such 24–8–62–4.

Umpires: D. W. Holt and P. H. Jensen.

QUEENSLAND v ENGLAND A

At Caloundra, February 19, 20, 21, 22. Drawn. Toss: England A.

Heavy rain tested the Sunshine Coast's drainage severely and washed out the first five sessions. England A resisted pressure to turn a first-class fixture into two one-day games and play finally began after tea on the second day. Despite every attempt by the local club to create a carnival atmosphere, the match never really took off. The tourists recovered from ten for three through the solid efforts of Moxon, Thorpe and Capel, who was unbeaten on 80 with 11 fours and two sixes; the Queensland captain, Wellham, had bowled one over with the second new ball as he despaired of the declaration coming. His men responded with 296 for seven, including 66 from Hayden, who was bowled, for the first time in his 21 match first-class career. England A batted again on the final evening, when Moxon was struck painfully on the ankle.

Close of play: First day, No play; Second day, England A 64-3 (M. D. Moxon 11*, G. P. Thorpe 26*); Third day, Queensland 148-1 (M. L. Hayden 65*, W. A. Seccombe 2*).

England A

T. C. Middleton lbw b Kasprowicz	2	– run out	2
M. N. Lathwell c Seccombe b Law	0	– b Jackson	40
*M. D. Moxon c Wellham b Law	57	– retired hurt	0
P. J. Prichard b Bichel	3	– c Kingdon b Bichel	9
G. P. Thorpe c and b Jackson	45	– not out	33
G. D. Lloyd b Kasprowicz	30	– not out	9
D. J. Capel not out	80		
†R. C. Russell c Seccombe b Kasprowicz	5		
D. G. Cork st Seccombe b Law	4		
A. R. Caddick c Seccombe b Rackemann	16		
P. M. Such not out	0		
B 4, l-b 10, w 1, n-b 30	45	L-b 2, w 2, n-b 12	16

1/2 2/4 3/10   (9 wkts dec.) 287   1/3 2/23 3/71   (3 wkts dec.) 104
4/108 5/157 6/189
7/220 8/227 9/276

In the second innings M. D. Moxon retired hurt at 10.

Bowling: *First Innings*—Kasprowicz 26-5-64-3; Law 21-10-45-3; Bichel 16-2-64-1; Rackemann 11.1-1-25-1; Jackson 25-4-67-1; Wellham 1-0-8-0. *Second Innings*—Kasprowicz 5-0-28-0; Bichel 6-0-29-1; Jackson 7-1-19-1; Rackemann 5-0-26-0.

Queensland

M. L. Hayden b Cork	66	M. S. Kasprowicz b Capel	0
T. J. Barsby b Caddick	78	A. J. Bichel not out	1
†W. A. Seccombe c Thorpe b Cork	5	L-b 15, n-b 2	17
P. J. T. Goggin b Caddick	33		
S. G. Law c Moxon b Such	35	1/139 2/152 3/153 (7 wkts dec.) 255
*D. M. Wellham not out	42	4/209 5/227
D. R. Kingdon c and b Such	4	6/240 7/255

P. W. Jackson and C. G. Rackemann did not bat.

Bowling: Caddick 25-7-75-2; Cork 24-4-65-2; Such 38-7-96-2; Capel 20-3-45-1.

Umpires: A. J. McQuillan and P. D. Parker.

SOUTH AUSTRALIA v ENGLAND A

At Adelaide, February 26, 27, 28, March 1. South Australia won by seven wickets. Toss: England A.

The weakness of English batsmen against quality leg-spin was sharply exposed by Sleep and McIntyre. The tourists never recovered from their first-day collapse for 152, when Sleep conceded only 11 runs in 14 overs. Siddons steered his team to 308 for eight declared, top scoring with 74, and in the second innings England A were no match for McIntyre. He took full advantage of their leaden-footed and passive resistance to sharp turn to claim six for 43. Not even a visit from Sir Donald Bradman could inspire the tourists on a chilly Sunday when Moxon broke his finger and the talented Lathwell faced 79 balls and scored just six. They left South Australia a mere 70 to win.

Close of play: First day, South Australia 47-1 (A. J. Hammond 19*, J. A. Brayshaw 8*); Second day, England A 12-0 (T. C. Middleton 5*, M. A. Roseberry 5*); Third day, England A 136-6 (R. C. Russell 8*, D. G. Cork 0*).

England A

T. C. Middleton c Webber b Reeves	12	– lbw b Wigney	10
M. A. Roseberry lbw b Hickey	30	– lbw b Hickey	5
*M. D. Moxon c Hammond b Hickey	28	– c Wigney b Sleep	62
G. P. Thorpe run out	2	– b McIntyre	39
M. N. Lathwell c Wigney b Reeves	8	– b Brayshaw	6
D. J. Capel b Reeves	7	– c Siddons b McIntyre	0
†R. C. Russell c Nielsen b Hickey	22	– b McIntyre	10
D. G. Cork st Nielsen b Sleep	1	– lbw b McIntyre	22
D. J. Millns not out	21	– c Nielsen b McIntyre	30
M. C. Ilott lbw b Sleep	6	– not out	23
P. M. Such lbw b Reeves	2	– c Hammond b McIntyre	5
L-b 5, w 1, n-b 7	13	L-b 8, w 1, n-b 4	13

1/42 2/61 3/71 4/79 5/92   152   1/12 2/26 3/115 4/123 5/124   225
6/115 7/116 8/122 9/143   6/136 7/140 8/180 9/207

Bowling: First Innings—Reeves 13.4-2-57-4; Wigney 16-4-29-0; Hickey 13-4-34-3; McIntyre 8-4-16-0; Sleep 14-7-11-2. *Second Innings*—Reeves 8-2-54-0; Wigney 17-7-21-1; Hickey 16-2-38-1; Sleep 37-13-61-1; McIntyre 29-13-43-6; Brayshaw 1-1-0-1.

South Australia

G. S. Blewett b Cork	14	– st Russell b Such	23
A. J. Hammond lbw b Ilott	23	– c Middleton b Such	6
J. A. Brayshaw lbw b Ilott	49	– b Such	7
*J. D. Siddons c Thorpe b Capel	74		
D. S. Webber c Russell b Capel	55	– (4) not out	12
†T. J. Nielsen lbw b Capel	20	– (5) not out	15
P. R. Sleep c Roseberry b Capel	11		
D. A. Reeves not out	12		
B. N. Wigney run out	17		
B 2, l-b 5, n-b 26	33	L-b 1, n-b 6	7

1/29 2/67 3/136 4/214 5/265   (8 wkts dec.) 308   1/29 2/34 3/41   (3 wkts) 70
6/270 7/281 8/308

D. J. Hickey and P. E. McIntyre did not bat.

Bowling: First Innings—Ilott 30-10-64-2; Millns 24-3-93-0; Capel 27.5-2-72-4; Cork 6.2-1-18-1; Such 15.4-2-48-0; Thorpe 2-0-6-0. *Second Innings*—Millns 4-1-11-0; Ilott 10-3-22-0; Such 10.4-2-36-3.

Umpires: D. J. Harper and G. C. J. Robinson.

NEW SOUTH WALES v ENGLAND A

At Sydney, March 4, 5, 6, 7. New South Wales won by ten wickets. Toss: England A.

A second successive match offered proof that spin can undermine an Englishman abroad. Matthews, still an attacking off-spinner, and Freedman, the unorthodox left-armer, accounted for 15 wickets as England A crashed for 238 and 208. Freedman returned the best analysis of his two first-class seasons. Only Lathwell, who hit 17 fours in three hours for his second century of the tour, Lloyd, with two solid contributions, and Russell, who scored an unbeaten fifty in his first match as captain, emerged with credit. And Caddick was the sole bowler with respectable figures. New South Wales ran up 421 for six declared, including a career-best 170 from Bevan and 90 from Richard Chee Quee, an opener of Chinese origin making his first-class debut.

Close of play: First day, New South Wales 32-1 (R. Chee Quee 19*, A. C. Gilchrist 10*); Second day, New South Wales 295-3 (M. G. Bevan 105*, T. H. Bayliss 36*); Third day, England A 60-3 (P. J. Prichard 25*, J. Boiling 0*).

England A

T. C. Middleton c Chee Quee b Freedman	21	– c Emery b Freedman		20
M. A. Roseberry c and b Freedman	13	– lbw b Holdsworth		5
M. N. Lathwell b Matthews	103	– lbw b Holdsworth		0
P. J. Prichard b Matthews	7	– c Emery b Freedman		34
G. D. Lloyd c Gilchrist b Freedman	60	– (6) b Holdsworth		41
D. J. Capel c Emery b Matthews	0	– (7) lbw b Freedman		21
*†R. C. Russell lbw b Matthews	5	– (8) not out		51
A. R. Caddick c Emery b Freedman	0	– (9) lbw b Freedman		0
D. J. Millns b Matthews	0	– (10) c Bevan b Holdsworth		13
J. Boiling c Bayliss b Freedman	3	– (5) b Matthews		2
P. M. Such not out	11	– b Holdsworth		0
L-b 8, n-b 6	14	B 9, l-b 9, w 1, n-b 2		21
	238			**208**

1/39 2/50 3/68 4/174 5/182 238   1/15 2/17 3/54 4/71 5/73 208
6/220 7/221 8/221 9/226   6/102 7/171 8/176 9/208

Bowling: First Innings—Holdsworth 14-4-44-0; McGrath 16-4-47-0; Freedman 28.2-6-89-6; McNamara 6-3-10-0; Matthews 17-5-40-4; Bevan 1-1-0-0. *Second Innings*—Holdsworth 16-1-47-5; McGrath 5-0-12-0; Matthews 25-9-61-1; Freedman 32-11-59-4; Bayliss 3-1-11-0.

New South Wales

M. J. Slater c Russell b Caddick	2	– (2) not out		12
R. Chee Quee b Caddick	90	– (1) not out		10
A. C. Gilchrist c Capel b Boiling	47			
M. G. Bevan c Boiling b Millns	170			
T. H. Bayliss c Boiling b Caddick	52			
B. E. McNamara not out	22			
*†P. A. Emery c Russell b Such	15			
G. R. J. Matthews not out	6			
L-b 10, w 1, n-b 6	17	L-b 4		4
	(6 wkts dec.) 421			**(no wkt) 26**

1/5 2/110 3/194   (6 wkts dec.) 421   (no wkt) 26
4/356 5/387 6/412

D. A. Freedman, W. J. Holdsworth and G. D. McGrath did not bat.

Bowling: First Innings—Millns 32-3-103-1; Caddick 36-11-68-3; Capel 19-3-45-0; Such 39-10-84-1; Boiling 47-11-111-1. *Second Innings*—Such 3-0-7-0; Boiling 3-0-15-0.

Umpires: I. G. Jackson and I. S. Thomas.

†At Alice Springs, March 10. England A won by eight wickets. Toss: Northern Territory XI. Northern Territory XI 147 (49.3 overs) (M. L. Hayden 36; J. Boiling three for 19); England A 148 for two (M. A. Roseberry 67 not out).

†At Perth, March 12. England A won by five wickets. Toss: England A. Western Australian XI 213 for six (50 overs) (D. Virgo 55, W. S. Andrews 82); England A 214 for five (48.2 overs) (P. J. Prichard 42, G. P. Thorpe 44).

†WESTERN AUSTRALIAN XI v ENGLAND A

At Perth, March 14, 15, 16, 17. England A won by 260 runs. Toss: Western Australian XI.

The last match of the tour provided Russell with his third successive win as acting-captain, following the two one-day games. Asked to bat, his team scored 293 off a Western Australian attack containing Test bowler Bruce Reid, but otherwise effectively a second team. Thorpe, revelling in a fast, true and springy WACA pitch, fell just short of his first hundred of the tour. England A's pace attack also found conditions perfect and dismissed the home team for 192. After Reid departed to join Western Australia's Shield team, being replaced by Brinkley, the tourists amassed 300 in 264 minutes. Thorpe and Lloyd shared 172 at five an over and Russell smashed 58 from 26 balls before setting a near impossible target of 402 in just over a day. Dennis Lillee assisted the tourists' rousing finale. He coached their fast bowlers on the last morning and then watched Caddick take five for 38 as the Western Australians mustered only 141.

Close of play: First day, England A 262-8 (D. J. Millns 24*, M. C. Ilott 10*); Second day, Western Australian XI 190-7 (M. Goodwin 59*, W. Wishart 9*); Third day, Western Australian XI 19-1 (D. Fitzgerald 9*, R. Campbell 5*).

England A

T. C. Middleton hit wkt b Wishart	42	– run out		10
M. N. Lathwell c Fitzgerald b Reid	20	– c McDonald b Spencer		10
P. J. Prichard lbw b Reid	10	– c Herzberg b McDonald		12
G. P. Thorpe lbw b McDonald	97	– c Campbell b Spencer		67
G. D. Lloyd c Campbell b McDonald	9	– c Campbell b Spencer		105
*†R. C. Russell c Campbell b McDonald	18	– not out		58
D. G. Cork b McDonald	5	– not out		2
A. R. Caddick lbw b McDonald	0			
D. J. Millns c Fitzgerald b Reid	25			
M. C. Ilott b McDonald	30			
J. Boiling not out	9			
B 6, l-b 7, w 3, n-b 22	38	B 5, l-b 7, n-b 24		36

1/30 2/30 3/185 4/187 5/201   293   1/20 2/43 3/52   (5 wkts dec.) 300
6/215 7/217 8/225 9/263   4/224 5/277

Bowling: First Innings—Reid 24–5–58–3; Spencer 18–2–93–0; McDonald 30–15–36–6; Herzberg 13–3–41–0; Wishart 23–10–52–1. *Second Innings*—McDonald 18–4–36–1; Spencer 17–3–76–3; Andrews 7–1–19–0; Herzberg 3–0–28–0; Brinkley 8–1–34–0; Wishart 11–0–95–0.

Western Australian XI

D. Virgo c Boiling b Ilott	37	– lbw b Millns		4
D. Fitzgerald c Cork b Caddick	1	– c Russell b Ilott		23
†R. Campbell c Russell b Cork	24	– c Russell b Caddick		7
*W. S. Andrews c Russell b Caddick	19	– lbw b Cork		0
M. Goodwin c Russell b Ilott	59	– c Russell b Caddick		35
B. Rayner c Boiling b Ilott	15	– lbw b Ilott		34
D. J. Spencer run out	0	– b Caddick		0
S. Herzberg c Middleton b Millns	0	– b Caddick		0
W. Wishart c Thorpe b Millns	9	– c Russell b Ilott		0
J. E. Brinkley c Boiling b Millns	9	– b Caddick		13
C. L. McDonald not out	0	– c Russell b Caddick		2
L-b 7, w 3, n-b 8	18	L-b 5, w 1, n-b 4		10

1/4 2/42 3/72 4/105 5/135   192   1/8 2/22 3/52 4/64 5/114   141
6/141 7/172 8/190 9/192   6/126 7/126 8/126 9/126

B. A. Reid did not bat.

Bowling: First Innings—Millns 18.4–8–33–3; Caddick 18–7–39–2; Ilott 19–10–21–3; Cork 19–4–58–1; Boiling 10–2–34–0. *Second Innings*—Millns 10–3–22–1; Caddick 18.2–8–38–5; Cork 7–0–26–1; Ilott 11–4–46–3; Boiling 2–1–4–0.

Umpires: D. Johnston and B. Rennie.

THE AUSTRALIANS IN SRI LANKA, 1992-93

By MIKE COWARD

With good fortune on their side, Australia won their first Test series on the Indian sub-continent for 23 years, since Bill Lawry's team beat India 3-1 in 1969-70. It was a small step towards fulfilling their captain Allan Border's wish to redress the country's abysmal away record of the past 15 years – a mere ten wins against 27 defeats in 65 Tests, and only the Ashes series of 1989 settled in their favour. Australia won only one of the three Tests, the First, when the Sri Lankans lapsed into old, destructive ways at the very moment they were poised to come of age as a Test country. At one stage 76 without loss, in pursuit of 181 for their first victory against one of cricket's traditional powers, Sri Lanka lost by 16 runs. "It must be the greatest heist since the Great Train Robbery," said Border. For Sri Lankan cricket, defeat after four days in the ascendancy was terribly dispiriting.

Sri Lanka were playing their first home Test since the horrific bomb blast at a bus station in Colombo in 1987, and the defeat came just after the deaths of nine of the country's military chiefs in an explosion in the war-torn north. Security for the tour was comprehensive but unobtrusive; with gentle persuasion from Border, and manager Cam Battersby, the Australians rid themselves of some of the paranoia which characterised their visits to the region in the 1980s. As a diplomatic exercise at a sensitive time in the evolution of the game in Sri Lanka, the tour was an overwhelming success. While Border was alarmed at the disproportionately high number of lbw decisions against Australia compared to Sri Lanka – 16 to four in the Test series – he conceded that the umpires had been disadvantaged by the five-year hiatus and did not believe any malice was intended. Fêted wherever he travelled on his 11th, and presumably final, tour of the Indian sub-continent in 14 years, Border further endeared himself to the people when he declared Sri Lanka to be a more accomplished Test match than India.

Be that as it may, Sri Lanka's successes came in the limited-overs series which they won 2-1; their one defeat came under lights at Khettarama Stadium. With the notable exception of the final Test at the Tyronne Fernando Stadium at Moratuwa – the country's sixth and Greater Colombo's fifth Test match venue – crowds were much greater at the limited-overs games. In part this was due to the bold decision of the Sri Lankan board to show the Tests live on TV, to encourage sponsors and alert the community to the resumption of Test cricket. High prices and persistent rains were other factors in keeping the Test crowds low.

Without detracting from the wholehearted and, overall, encouraging efforts of Sri Lanka, Australia's performances were as uninspiring as they were unconvincing: they played "catch-up cricket" for the entire tour. With only 13 players, there was little room for manoeuvre. Among the bowlers, the omission of Merv Hughes raised a few eyebrows but was interpreted as a hint that he should attend to his fitness; his Victorian team-mate Tony Dodemaide was preferred.

The selectors had restructured the batting order, telling Border to bat at No. 6, elevating Tom Moody to open and compelling Dean Jones to accept greater responsibility at No. 4. Two months later, they were thinking again.

This was seen as Moody's big opportunity after five years on the fringe of the team, but he was exposed against the seaming ball. However, he was merely the most conspicuous of the failures. Only twice in six innings did Australia reach 110 without five wickets down and Greg Matthews and Ian Healy were effectively required to operate as specialist batsmen. Surprise at well-grassed and moist pitches that favoured seam bowlers could not entirely account for the failure of Moody, Mark Taylor and David Boon against the least glamorous attack in Test cricket.

Going into the series Champaka Ramanayake's best bowling return in ten Tests was two for 39, and his aggregate was 19, which he almost doubled to 36; Chandika Hathurusingha had taken only one wicket in six Tests but here he took eight; the slow left-armer Anurasiri had played in just eight Tests in six years, but now sent down more overs than anyone else; and Duleep Liyanage and Muttiah Muralitharan, the only Tamil in the team, were little known outside their provincial districts when the Tests began. The Sri Lankan selectors were amply vindicated in choosing Liyanage (who was coached by Dennis Lillee in Madras immediately after the tour) and Muralitharan, a prodigious spinner of the ball. They were less successful in resolving the wicket-keeping problem.

AUSTRALIAN TOUR PARTY

A. R. Border (Queensland) (*captain*), D. C. Boon (Tasmania), A. I. C. Dodemaide (Victoria), I. A. Healy (Queensland), D. M. Jones (Victoria), C. J. McDermott (Queensland), D. R. Martyn (Western Australia), G. R. J. Matthews (New South Wales), T. M. Moody (Western Australia), M. A. Taylor (New South Wales), S. K. Warne (Victoria), M. E. Waugh (New South Wales), M. R. Whitney (New South Wales).
Manager: Dr C. Battersby. *Coach:* R. B. Simpson.

AUSTRALIAN TOUR RESULTS

Test matches – Played 3: Won 1, Drawn 2.
First-class matches – Played 5: Won 1, Drawn 4.
Wins – Sri Lanka.
Draws – Sri Lanka (2), Board President's XI, Southern Districts XI.
One-day internationals – Played 3: Won 1, Lost 2.

TEST MATCH AVERAGES

SRI LANKA – BATTING

	T	I	NO	R	HS	100s	Avge	Ct
R. S. Kaluwitharana....	2	3	1	137	132*	1	68.50	4
A. P. Gurusinha.......	3	5	2	205	137	1	68.33	3
R. S. Mahanama.......	3	5	0	250	78	0	50.00	3
A. Ranatunga	3	4	0	193	127	1	48.25	3
P. A. de Silva	3	4	0	186	85	0	46.50	1
U. C. Hathurusinghe ...	3	5	0	172	67	0	34.40	0
S. T. Jayasuriya	2	3	1	22	19	0	11.00	5
C. P. H. Ramanayake ..	3	4	1	29	15*	0	9.66	1
S. D. Anurasiri	3	3	1	3	2*	0	1.50	1

Played in two Tests: D. K. Liyanage 4, 1; M. Muralitharan 0* (1 ct). Played in one Test: M. S. Atapattu 0, 1; A. W. R. Madurasinghe 5*, 0; H. P. Tillekeratne 82 (3 ct); G. P. Wickremasinghe 21, 2 (1 ct).

* Signifies not out.

BOWLING

	O	M	R	W	BB	5W/i	Avge
C. P. H. Ramanayake ..	145.4	28	434	17	5-82	1	25.52
D. K. Liyanage	76	14	223	8	4-56	0	27.87
U. C. Hathurusinghe . . .	95	27	236	8	4-66	0	29.50
S. D. Anurasiri	150	23	338	10	4-127	0	33.80
M. Muralitharan	73.1	12	225	4	2-109	0	56.25

Also bowled: A. P. Gurusinha 15-2-55-2; S. T. Jayasuriya 9-1-26-0; A. W. R. Madurasinghe 24-2-71-0; R. S. Mahanama 5-0-27-0; A. Ranatunga 1-0-9-0; G. P. Wickremasinghe 37-4-148-3.

AUSTRALIA – BATTING

	T	I	NO	R	HS	100s	Avge	Ct
D. M. Jones	3	6	1	276	100*	1	55.20	2
G. R. J. Matthews	3	6	0	329	96	0	54.83	2
I. A. Healy	3	6	2	202	71	0	50.50	7
A. R. Border	3	6	0	243	106	1	40.50	2
D. C. Boon	3	6	0	161	68	0	26.83	3
M. A. Taylor	3	6	0	148	43	0	24.66	1
S. K. Warne	2	3	0	66	35	0	22.00	0
C. J. McDermott	3	4	0	81	40	0	20.25	1
M. R. Whitney	2	3	1	24	13	0	12.00	0
T. M. Moody	3	6	0	71	54	0	11.83	3
M. E. Waugh	3	6	0	61	56	0	10.16	3

Played in two Tests: A. I. C. Dodemaide 16*, 13*, 2*.

* Signifies not out.

BOWLING

	O	M	R	W	BB	5W/i	Avge
C. J. McDermott	124	30	342	14	4-53	0	24.42
A. I. C. Dodemaide	53.5	15	150	6	4-65	0	25.00
G. R. J. Matthews	120	28	312	8	4-76	0	39.00

Also bowled: A. R. Border 19-4-51-1; T. M. Moody 31-4-79-1; S. K. Warne 38.1-8-158-3; M. E. Waugh 23-3-94-2; M. R. Whitney 58-15-159-2.

AUSTRALIAN AVERAGES – FIRST-CLASS MATCHES

BATTING

	M	I	NO	R	HS	100s	Avge	Ct/St
I. A. Healy	5	9	3	326	78*	0	54.33	9/1
G. R. J. Matthews	4	7	0	340	96	0	48.57	3
D. M. Jones	5	9	1	295	100*	1	36.87	2
A. R. Border	5	9	0	324	106	1	36.00	3
M. E. Waugh	5	9	0	291	118	1	32.33	5
D. C. Boon	5	9	0	235	68	0	26.11	3
C. J. McDermott	5	7	1	142	58*	0	23.66	0
M. A. Taylor	4	7	0	161	43	0	23.00	2
S. K. Warne	3	4	0	67	35	0	16.75	1
M. R. Whitney	4	6	4	30	13	0	15.00	1
A. I. C. Dodemaide	4	6	3	39	16*	0	13.00	1
T. M. Moody	5	9	0	106	54	0	11.77	4

Played in one match: D. R. Martyn 61, 13.

* Signifies not out.

BOWLING

	O	M	R	W	BB	5W/i	Avge
A. I. C. Dodemaide....	98.5	33	229	11	4-65	0	20.81
M. R. Whitney.......	102	31	246	9	4-34	0	27.33
C. J. McDermott.....	182	43	514	16	4-53	0	32.12
G. R. J. Matthews....	148	33	381	10	4-76	0	38.10

Also bowled: D. C. Boon 3–0–4–0; A. R. Border 23–6–60–1; D. M. Jones 0.5–0–1–1; T. M. Moody 39–7–99–1; S. K. Warne 38.1–8–158–3; M. E. Waugh 40–6–129–2.

Note: Matches in this section which were not first-class are signified by a dagger.

BOARD PRESIDENT'S XI v AUSTRALIANS

At Kandy, August 10, 11, 13. Drawn. Toss: Australians.

Rescheduled to incorporate a rest day for a religious festival, the match was disrupted first by the late arrival of the host team and then by poor weather. Steady rain during the previous month meant a damp pitch, uneven in bounce and pace, and a treacherously soft outfield. With the ball seaming and turning sharply from the start, an unheralded attack exposed flaws in the Australians' new-look batting order. Waugh, with 74 in two and a quarter hours, was the only specialist batsman to adjust to the conditions, although tailender McDermott's brash unbeaten 58 from 74 balls and a ninth-wicket stand of 79 with Healy ensured an acceptable score. Undeterred by frequent showers on the second day, when only 29 overs were bowled, Mahanama and Gurusinha took their partnership to 122, a solid foundation for Atapattu and Jayasuriya, who made half-centuries.

Close of play: First day, Australians 278-9 (C. J. McDermott 58*, M. R. Whitney 0*); Second day, Board President's XI 71-1 (R. S. Mahanama 38*, A. P. Gurusinha 20*).

Australians

M. A. Taylor c Mahanama b Hathurusinghe . 13	G. R. J. Matthews c and b Ekanayake . 11	
T. M. Moody c Jayasuriya b Weerakkody . 6	†I. A. Healy c Kaluwitharana b Liyanage . 31	
D. C. Boon c Hathurusinghe b Weerakkody . 17	A. I. C. Dodemaide b Muralitharan ... 0	
D. M. Jones c Kaluwitharana b Liyanage . 13	C. J. McDermott not out 58	
M. E. Waugh c Kaluwitharana b Ekanayake . 74	M. R. Whitney not out 0	
*A. R. Border b Liyanage 33	B 5, l-b 11, w 3, n-b 3 22	

1/14 2/36 3/54   (9 wkts dec.) 278
4/66 5/130 6/178
7/183 8/188 9/267

Bowling: Liyanage 18–5–55–3; Weerakkody 18–2–48–2; Hathurusinghe 10–3–27–1; Muralitharan 22–2–79–1; Gurusinha 2–1–7–0; Ekanayake 13–2–46–2.

Board President's XI

R. S. Mahanama lbw b Dodemaide.... 82	†R. S. Kaluwitharana c Taylor b Matthews . 19	
U. C. Hathurusinghe c Matthews b Whitney . 1	D. K. Liyanage not out	
*A. P. Gurusinha c Border b Whitney . 47	B 9, l-b 1, w 6, n-b 4 20	
H. P. Tillekeratne b Whitney 3		
M. S. Atapattu not out 64	1/7 2/129 3/133 (6 wkts) 293	
S. T. Jayasuriya st Healy b Matthews .. 51	4/165 5/251 6/287	

A. W. Ekanayake, A. K. Weerakkody and M. Muralitharan did not bat.

Bowling: McDermott 28–5–87–0; Whitney 24–6–53–3; Dodemaide 20–7–49–1; Matthews 28–5–69–2; Moody 5–3–11–0; Border 1–0–1–0; Waugh 7–2–13–0.

Umpires: S. Ponnadurai and K. T. P. Wijedasa.

†SRI LANKA v AUSTRALIA

First One-day International

At P. Saravanamuttu Stadium, Colombo, August 15. Sri Lanka won by four wickets. Toss: Sri Lanka.

Sri Lanka marked their first full international on home soil since April 1987 by claiming a thrilling victory with four balls in hand. Undeterred by the early loss of Mahanama and Tillekeratne, the flamboyant de Silva and Gurusinha turned the game with a third-wicket stand of 147. De Silva had reached 105 from 102 balls, with 12 fours and two sixes, when he was run out. But his captain, Ranatunga, tore 20 runs from McDermott's ninth over, including sixes over point and extra cover. After these exertions he complained of damaged stomach muscles and needed a runner. For Australia, Moody and Taylor had opened with 109 in the first 27 overs, when the going was hardest, and Taylor narrowly missed a maiden hundred in one-day internationals. But a total of 247 for five proved just too low to defend.

Man of the Match: P. A. de Silva.

Australia

T. M. Moody c and b Kalpage	54	*A. R. Border not out 19
M. A. Taylor c Tillekeratne b Kalpage	94	G. R. J. Matthews not out 1
D. M. Jones st Kaluwitharana		B 2, l-b 8, w 4, n-b 4 18
b Anurasiri	30	
D. C. Boon lbw b Ramanayake	0	1/109 2/175 3/176 (5 wkts, 50 overs) 247
M. E. Waugh b Wickremasinghe	31	4/216 5/244

†I. A. Healy, A. I. C. Dodemaide, C. J. McDermott and M. R. Whitney did not bat.

Bowling: Wickremasinghe 9-1-35-1; Ramanayake 10-0-54-1; Gurusinha 8-0-30-0; Ranatunga 3-0-22-0; Anurasiri 10-0-44-1; Kalpage 10-0-52-2.

Sri Lanka

R. S. Mahanama b Whitney	0	†R. S. Kaluwitharana b Dodemaide ... 1
H. P. Tillekeratne c Healy b McDermott	7	R. S. Kalpage not out 11
A. P. Gurusinha c Waugh b Matthews	53	B 4, l-b 10, w 8, n-b 3 25
P. A. de Silva run out	105	
*A. Ranatunga not out	45	1/3 2/12 3/159 (6 wkts, 49.2 overs) 251
M. S. Atapattu c Waugh b Whitney	4	4/202 5/212 6/214

C. P. H. Ramanayake, S. D. Anurasiri and G. P. Wickremasinghe did not bat.

Bowling: McDermott 9.2-1-64-1; Whitney 10-1-33-2; Dodemaide 10-0-50-1; Moody 7-1-36-0; Matthews 10-0-34-1; Border 3-0-20-0.

Umpires: B. C. Cooray and W. A. U. Wickremasinghe.

SRI LANKA v AUSTRALIA

First Test Match

At Sinhalese Sports Club, Colombo, August 17, 18, 19, 21, 22. Australia won by 16 runs. Toss: Sri Lanka. Test debut: R. S. Kaluwitharana.

The carelessness of Aravinda de Silva cost Sri Lanka what would have been their third and most famous victory since entering the Test arena in February 1982. With 54 runs needed from nearly 25 overs, de Silva, who had taken 37 from 32 balls with seven fours, attempted to strike McDermott for the second time over Border at mid-on. Border, at full stretch, ran 25 metres with the flight of the ball and held a magnificent catch over his shoulder.

From that moment Sri Lanka collapsed utterly, losing their last eight wickets for 37 runs. A crowd of 10,000, the biggest of the match, jeered them at the presentation ceremony. In just 17.4 overs they had squandered the impressive gains of the first three days, after Ranatunga had compelled the Australians to bat first on a damp pitch under overcast skies. The occasional seamer, Hathurusinghe, exploited the conditions with sharp and late movement to claim the wickets of Boon, Jones, Border and Waugh in just 24 balls as Australia were dismissed for 256 on the first day.

On a more docile pitch and beneath comparatively clear skies next day, the stylish Mahanama laid the foundations for Sri Lanka's first total of 500, in their 38th Test. Breaking further new ground, three of their number scored centuries in one innings. Gurusinha, wearing new contact lenses, played the anchor role, and batted eight hours 45 minutes for 137. With Ranatunga he added 230 for the fourth wicket – the second-highest partnership for Sri Lanka. Ranatunga and Kaluwitharana, on his debut, changed the tempo with audacious hundreds. Ranatunga took 127 from 192 balls, with 15 fours and three sixes; at the height of his assault, he thumped 29 off three overs from the leg-spinner, Warne. Meanwhile, Kaluwitharana, supposedly chosen as a specialist wicket-keeper, batted with breathtaking arrogance for an unbeaten 132 from 158 balls with 26 boundaries – nine against Warne and seven off McDermott.

Exhorted by Border to show greater "guts and determination", Australia scored 367 on the fourth day. Though they lost five batsmen in clearing a deficit of 291, they entered the final morning 102 ahead with three wickets in hand. Matthews's responsible 64, which took Australia from 269 for five to 431 for nine, was one of four fifties from the seven top-order batsmen, who could not muster 100 runs between them in the first innings, and gallant resistance from tailenders McDermott, Warne and Whitney proved the ideal complement. A final total of 471 set Sri Lanka 181 in 58 overs and gave the visitors just a little optimism. Then, after de Silva's fateful error, Matthews returned four for 76 and with Warne, who claimed three in 13 balls without conceding a run, he engineered an improbable victory. It was a fine comeback for Matthews, ignored by the Australian selectors for the past year; it was also one of Australia's greatest fightbacks. Only once before had they won a Test after trailing by more than 200 on the first innings: in Durban in 1949-50 they beat South Africa by five wickets despite being bowled out for 75 in response to 311.

Man of the Match: G. R. J. Matthews.

Close of play: First day, Sri Lanka 6-0 (R. S. Mahanama 6*, U. C. Hathurusinghe 3*); Second day, Sri Lanka 265-3 (A. P. Gurusinha 87*, A. Ranatunga 69*); Third day, Australia 26-0 (T. M. Moody 8*, M. A. Taylor 9*); Fourth day, Australia 393-7 (G. R. J. Matthews 51*, C. J. McDermott 28*).

Australia

M. A. Taylor lbw b Wickremasinghe	42	– (2) c Gurusinha b Anurasiri	43
T. M. Moody lbw b Ramanayake	1	– (1) b Ramanayake	13
D. C. Boon c Ramanayake b Hathurusinghe	32	– c Ranatunga b Anurasiri	68
D. M. Jones lbw b Hathurusinghe	10	– run out	57
M. E. Waugh c Kaluwitharana b Hathurusinghe	5	– c Kaluwitharana b Wickremasinghe	56
*A. R. Border b Hathurusinghe	3	– c Gurusinha b Anurasiri	15
G. R. J. Matthews lbw b Ramanayake	6	– c Kaluwitharana b Ramanayake	64
†I. A. Healy not out	66	– lbw b Hathurusinghe	12
C. J. McDermott c Ranatunga b Ramanayake	22	– lbw b Ramanayake	40
S. K. Warne c and b Anurasiri	24	– b Anurasiri	35
M. R. Whitney c and b Wickremasinghe	13	– not out	10
L-b 10, w 3, n-b 19	32	L-b 23, w 1, n-b 34	58
	256		471

1/8 (2) 2/84 (3) 3/94 (1) 4/96 (4)
5/109 (6) 6/118 (5) 7/124 (7)
8/162 (9) 9/207 (10) 10/256 (11)

1/41 (1) 2/107 (2) 3/195 (3)
4/233 (4) 5/269 (6) 6/319 (5)
7/361 (8) 8/417 (9)
9/431 (7) 10/471 (10)

Bowling: *First Innings*—Ramanayake 20-4-51-3; Wickremasinghe 18-4-69-2; Hathurusinghe 22-5-66-4; Madurasinghe 10-1-21-0; Gurusinha 2-0-17-0; Anurasiri 12-2-22-1. *Second Innings*—Ramanayake 37-10-113-3; Wickremasinghe 19-0-79-1; Hathurusinghe 27-7-79-1; Anurasiri 35-3-127-4; Madurasinghe 14-1-50-0.

Sri Lanka

R. S. Mahanama c Healy b Waugh	78	– c Boon b Matthews	39
U. C. Hathurusinghe c Taylor b Waugh	18	– run out	36
A. P. Gurusinha c Jones b Whitney	137	– not out	31
P. A. de Silva lbw b Matthews	6	– c Border b McDermott	37
*A. Ranatunga c Warne b Matthews	127	– c Border b McDermott	0
M. S. Atapattu b Matthews	0	– b Matthews	1
†R. S. Kaluwitharana not out	132	– b Matthews	4
C. P. H. Ramanayake c Healy b McDermott	0	– lbw b Matthews	6
G. P. Wickremasinghe c Matthews b McDermott	21	– c Waugh b Warne	2
A. W. R. Madurasinghe not out	5	– (11) c Matthews b Warne	0
S. D. Anurasiri (did not bat)		– (10) c Waugh b Warne	1
B 2, l-b 7, w 1, n-b 13	23	B 2, l-b 3, n-b 2	7
	(8 wkts dec.) 547		**164**

1/36 (2) 2/128 (1) 3/137 (4)
4/367 (5) 5/367 (6) 6/463 (3)
7/472 (8) 8/503 (9)

1/76 (1) 2/79 (2) 3/127 (4)
4/132 (5) 5/133 (6) 6/137 (7)
7/147 (8) 8/150 (9)
9/156 (10) 10/164 (11)

Bowling: *First Innings*—McDermott 40–9–125–2; Whitney 32–10–84–1; Moody 17–3–44–0; Waugh 17–3–77–2; Warne 22–2–107–0; Matthews 38–11–93–3; Border 4–1–8–0. *Second Innings*—McDermott 14-4-43-2; Whitney 5-2-13-0; Moody 5-0-10-0; Matthews 20-2-76-4; Waugh 2-0-6-0; Warne 5.1-3-11-3.

Umpires: K. T. Francis and T. M. Samarasinghe. Referee: F. J. Cameron (New Zealand).

SOUTHERN DISTRICTS XI v AUSTRALIANS

At Matara, August 24, 25, 26. Drawn. Toss: Australians.

Such was the public response to the Australians' visit to this southern fishing port that Sri Lankan officials proposed a limited-overs international should be played at the Uyanwatte Stadium in the future. Damien Martyn, in his only appearance of the tour, confirmed his potential with an impressive 61, Waugh made light of the oppressive humidity to score his 36th first-class century, and Healy batted three and a quarter hours for a gritty 78. They took the tourists to 312 after Wijegunawardene and Liyanage had reduced them to 70 for three. The Australians' own seamers, Whitney, who took four wickets in 24 balls, and Dodemaide, with three in his first eight overs, earned a useful first-innings lead of 148. This provided sufficient time for Boon and Border to regain their touch in the middle. Leg-spinner Warne could not bowl because of a foot injury.

Close of play: First day, Australians 312-9 (I. A. Healy 78*, M. R. Whitney 3*); Second day, Australians 40-2 (D. C. Boon 24*, D. M. Jones 0*).

Australians

T. M. Moody b Liyanage	28	– (2) c Jayasuriya b Liyanage	1
D. C. Boon b Wijegunawardene	0	– (1) c Kaluwitharana b de Silva	57
D. R. Martyn lbw b de Silva	61	– c Kaluwitharana b Ranatunga	13
D. M. Jones b Liyanage	0	– c Jayasuriya b Liyanage	6
M. E. Waugh c Wijegunawardene b Ranatunga	118	– (7) c Kaluwitharana b de Silva	38
*A. R. Border c Kumudu b Liyanage	3	– (5) c Kumudu b de Silva	45
†I. A. Healy not out	78	– (8) b Tilekeratne b Kalpage	15
C. J. McDermott lbw b Wijegunawardene	0	– (10) b Liyanage b Kalpage	3
A. I. C. Dodemaide c Atapattu b Wijegunawardene	0	– (6) lbw b de Silva	8
S. K. Warne lbw b Wijegunawardene	1	– absent injured	
M. R. Whitney not out	3	– (9) not out	3
B 1, l-b 11, w 2, n-b 6	20	B 2, l-b 6, w 1, n-b 6	15
	(9 wkts dec.) 312		**204**

1/4 2/70 3/70 4/124 5/132
6/257 7/278 8/280 9/289

1/14 2/38 3/53 4/130 5/137
6/150 7/195 8/199 9/204

Bowling: *First Innings*—Wijegunawardene 18-4-58-4; Liyanage 20-3-69-3; Ranatunga 20-3-51-1; de Silva 14-0-57-1; Kalpage 12-0-52-0; Jayasuriya 6-0-13-0. *Second Innings*—Wijegunawardene 10-0-45-0; Liyanage 14-2-42-2; Ranatunga 6-0-20-1; Kalpage 26.3-11-47-2; de Silva 19-5-42-4.

Southern Districts XI

C. Mendis b Dodemaide	17	– c Dodemaide b McDermott	4
W. M. J. Kumudu c Healy b Dodemaide	22	– c Waugh b Dodemaide	6
*†H. P. Tillekeratne c Waugh b Dodemaide	9	– not out	10
S. T. Jayasuriya lbw b Whitney	13	– not out	13
M. S. Atapattu c sub b McDermott	35		
R. S. Kaluwitharana c sub b Whitney	2		
R. S. Kalpage c Moody b Whitney	3		
N. Ranatunga c Healy b Whitney	0		
D. K. Liyanage run out	2		
E. A. R. de Silva not out	34		
K. I. W. Wijegunawardene c Whitney b Jones	17		
L-b 5, n-b 5	10	N-b 1	1

1/23 2/47 3/52 4/71 5/79   **164**   1/8 2/16   (2 wkts) **34**
6/84 7/86 8/90 9/130

Bowling: *First Innings*—McDermott 22-6-66-1; Whitney 20-10-34-4; Dodemaide 15-6-19-3; Moody 3-0-9-0; Waugh 10-1-22-0; Border 3-2-8-0; Jones 0.5-0-1-1. *Second Innings*—McDermott 8-2-19-1; Dodemaide 10-5-11-1; Boon 3-0-4-0.

Umpires: M. D. D. N. Guneratne and D. N. Pathirana.

SRI LANKA v AUSTRALIA

Second Test Match

At Khettarama Stadium, Colombo, August 28, 29, 30, September 1, 2. Drawn. Toss: Sri Lanka. Test debuts: M. Muralitharan, D. K. Liyanage.

The loss of more than six hours to rain and poor light stole any sense of occasion or excitement from the first Test match to be played at Khettarama, the stadium built on reclaimed marshland which became the 66th Test ground and the fourth in Colombo. Watched by the smallest crowds of the series, Australia once more struggled against an attack including the two newcomers: Duleep Liyanage, a pace bowler, and off-spinner Muttiah Muralitharan. From the moment Australia were required to bat first against the seaming ball on a pitch chosen at the eleventh hour by Anuruddha Polonowitta, who combined his role as supervisor of groundsmen with chairing the Sri Lankan selectors, there were striking similarities with the First Test. Indeed, it was the fourth time Ranatunga had won the toss and chosen to field in his four Tests as captain against Australia.

But for the diligent half-centuries by Jones and Matthews, Australia's early discomfort on the deceptively slow pitch would have been greater. As it was, their score of 247 in six hours and 50 minutes seemed hopelessly inadequate when Sri Lanka responded with 161 for two by tea on the third day. But Australia claimed seven wickets for 97 in the final session – the last five for 18 runs in 13 overs. Though Moody made the initial breakthrough by bowling the belligerent Hathurusinghe, it was McDermott who started the landslide. Using the old ball, and with Border sending down miserly slow left-arm spin from the other end, McDermott took four for 11, one bowled and three caught behind, in an outstanding seven-over spell. Apart from de Silva, who batted with both flair and responsibility for 85 in four hours, and Hathurusinghe, no one reached 30. Mahanama and Jayasuriya, in particular, fell to poor shots; Mahanama became Dodemaide's first Test wicket for nearly four years as he made an impressive return in place of Warne.

Errors in the field, notably by Kaluwitharana, who twice missed stumping Jones off Anurasiri, once before he had scored, cost Sri Lanka a priceless opportunity to press for victory. Australia floundered against the spinners Anurasiri and Muralitharan, who bowled 34 overs between them. Muralitharan removed Moody and Waugh with consecutive balls, and the tourists were a tremulous 149 for five during the final session of the fourth day, before Jones, who offered two more chances, and Matthews restored order with a sixth-wicket stand of 131 in 155 minutes. While Jones's undefeated 100 in four hours and 41 minutes was probably the least convincing of his 11 Test centuries (three in his five matches against Sri Lanka), it came at a vital time and finally put the match beyond the diffident Sri Lankans' reach. They made no attempt to meet Border's challenge of 286 in the time that remained.

Man of the Match: D. M. Jones.

Close of play: First day, Australia 177-5 (D. M. Jones 77*, G. R. J. Matthews 18*); Second day, Sri Lanka 0-0 (R. S. Mahanama 0*, U. C. Hathurusinghe 0*); Third day, Sri Lanka 258-9 (S. D. Anurasiri 2*, M. Muralitharan 0*); Fourth day, Australia 206-5 (D. M. Jones 48*, G. R. J. Matthews 23*).

Australia

T. M. Moody c Kaluwitharana b Liyanage	1	– (2) b Muralitharan	54
M. A. Taylor c Jayasuriya b Hathurusinghe	15	– (1) lbw b Hathurusinghe	26
D. C. Boon c Jayasuriya b Liyanage	28	– c Mahanama b Anurasiri	15
D. M. Jones lbw b Gurusinha	77	– not out	100
M. E. Waugh c Jayasuriya b Ramanayake	0	– lbw b Muralitharan	0
*A. R. Border b Liyanage	13	– lbw b Anurasiri	28
G. R. J. Matthews c Muralitharan b Ramanayake	55	– c Mahanama b Anurasiri	51
†I. A. Healy lbw b Gurusinha	0	– not out	4
C. J. McDermott lbw b Muralitharan	9		
A. I. C. Dodemaide not out	16		
M. R. Whitney lbw b Ramanayake	1		
B 10, l-b 14, w 2, n-b 6	32	B 4, l-b 9, n-b 5	18
	247	**(6 wkts dec.)**	**296**

1/1 (1) 2/34 (2) 3/69 (3) 4/72 (5)   1/61 (1) 2/102 (3)   (6 wkts dec.) 296
5/109 (6) 6/181 (4) 7/183 (8)   3/104 (2) 4/104 (5)
8/200 (9) 9/239 (7) 10/247 (11)   5/149 (6) 6/280 (7)

Bowling: First Innings—Ramanayake 23.3-7-64-3; Liyanage 30-10-66-3; Hathurusinghe 9-1-26-1; Gurusinha 9-2-18-2; Anurasiri 8-0-17-0; Muralitharan 17-2-32-1. *Second Innings*—Ramanayake 12-0-49-0; Liyanage 13-1-47-0; Hathurusinghe 12-4-12-1; Anurasiri 44-11-66-3; Muralitharan 34-7-109-2.

Sri Lanka

R. S. Mahanama c Moody b Dodemaide	14	– lbw b McDermott	69
U. C. Hathurusinghe b Moody	67	– c Moody b McDermott	49
A. P. Gurusinha c Healy b Whitney	29	– not out	8
P. A. de Silva c Healy b McDermott b Dodemaide	85		
*A. Ranatunga c sub (D. R. Martyn) b Dodemaide	18		
S. T. Jayasuriya c Healy b McDermott	19	– (4) not out	1
†R. S. Kaluwitharana c sub (D. R. Martyn) b Border	1		
C. P. H. Ramanayake b McDermott	8		
D. K. Liyanage c Healy b McDermott	4		
S. D. Anurasiri not out	2		
M. Muralitharan not out	0		
L-b 6, n-b 5	11	L-b 6, n-b 3	9
	(9 wkts dec.) 258	**(2 wkts)**	**136**

1/26 (1) 2/67 (3) 3/174 (2)   (9 wkts dec.) 258   1/110 (2) 2/129 (1)   (2 wkts) 136
4/211 (5) 5/240 (6) 6/243 (4)
7/243 (8) 8/255 (8) 9/258 (9)

Bowling: First Innings—McDermott 20-4-53-4; Whitney 16-1-49-1; Dodemaide 25-4-74-2; Matthews 10-2-20-0; Waugh 4-0-11-0; Moody 6-1-17-1; Border 11-3-28-1. *Second Innings*—McDermott 19-7-32-2; Whitney 5-2-13-0; Matthews 21-5-59-0; Dodemaide 5-2-11-0; Border 4-0-15-0.

Umpires: I. Anandappa and W. A. U. Wickremasinghe.
Referee: F. J. Cameron (New Zealand).

†SRI LANKA v AUSTRALIA

Second One-day International

At Khettarama Stadium, Colombo, September 4. Sri Lanka won on scoring-rate. Toss: Sri Lanka.

Australia were put in on a wet pitch hastily prepared after the intended strip was damaged by heavy traffic during the Test match which finished two days earlier. After a steady start they lost momentum against Hathurusinghe, who moved the ball sharply off the seam, and off-spinner Kalpage, who cleverly varied his length and pace and bowled with impressive economy. Jones played intelligently for 59, eliciting useful support from Boon and Border. Rain cut six overs and Sri Lanka's target was reduced to 191. They achieved it with seven balls to spare, thanks to the efficiency of de Silva, with 63 from 61 balls, and Hathurusinghe, who returned to bring up his fifty with the winning boundary after retiring with a severe bout of leg cramp.

Man of the Match: U. C. Hathurusinghe.

Australia

T. M. Moody c Tillekeratne b Gurusinha	17	†I. A. Healy run out	6
M. A. Taylor run out	30	C. J. McDermott not out	1
D. M. Jones not out	59		
D. C. Boon run out	35	B 1, l-b 15, w 3, n-b 8	27
M. E. Waugh lbw b Ramanayake	10		
*A. R. Border c Kalpage b Ramanayake	30	1/56 2/65 3/127 (7 wkts, 50 overs)	216
G. R. J. Matthews c Tillekeratne		4/149 5/194	
b Wickremasinghe	1	6/197 7/207	

A. I. C. Dodemaide and M. R. Whitney did not bat.

Bowling: Ramanayake 10–2–43–2; Wickremasinghe 10–0–40–1; Hathurusinghe 10–1–34–0; Gurusinha 4–1–21–1; Ranatunga 3–1–11–0; Anurasiri 5–0–20–0; Kalpage 8–0–31–0.

Sri Lanka

R. S. Mahanama run out	33	S. T. Jayasuriya b McDermott	2
U. C. Hathurusinghe not out	52	†H. P. Tillekeratne not out	2
A. P. Gurusinha lbw b Dodemaide	4	B 2, l-b 7, w 4, n-b 3	16
P. A. de Silva c Whitney b Matthews	63		
*A. Ranatunga c Dodemaide		1/71 2/77 3/172 (5 wkts, 42.5 overs)	194
b Matthews	22	4/176 5/190	

R. S. Kalpage, C. P. H. Ramanayake, G. P. Wickremasinghe and S. D. Anurasiri did not bat.

U. C. Hathurusinghe, when 48, retired hurt at 122 and resumed at 190.

Bowling: McDermott 9–0–44–1; Whitney 7–0–27–0; Dodemaide 10–1–39–1; Moody 9–0–35–0; Matthews 6.5–0–34–2; Waugh 1–0–6–0.

Umpires: B. C. Cooray and T. M. Samarasinghe.

†SRI LANKA v AUSTRALIA

Third One-day International

At Khettarama Stadium, Colombo, September 5 (day/night). Australia won by five wickets. Toss: Australia.

Having won the toss for the first time in the series, Border turned the tables on Ranatunga by asking him to bat. This set up a comfortable Australian victory in the first floodlit limited-overs international in Sri Lanka. The home team, in uniforms of faded turquoise with a white chest band, failed to build on a splendid foundation of 101 for the second wicket, laid by Hathurusinghe and Gurusinha after Mahanama had fallen first ball. The Australians – who wore a rich salmon strip with a broad grey band and called themselves the "Pink Panthers" – began uncertainly, and were 58 for three in the 18th over. But the next 18 overs brought an enterprising stand of 84 from Boon and Waugh. Boon remained unbeaten on 69 when Australia won with 13 balls to spare.

Man of the Match: D. C. Boon.

Sri Lanka

R. S. Mahanama c Taylor b McDermott	0	†H. P. Tillekeratne not out	35
U. C. Hathurusinghe c Boon		R. S. Kalpage not out	1
b Matthews	46		
A. P. Gurusinha lbw b Matthews	49	B 1, l-b 5, w 9	15
P. A. de Silva c Matthews b Dodemaide	39		
*A. Ranatunga b Whitney	15	1/0 2/101 3/112 (6 wkts, 50 overs) 207	
S. T. Jayasuriya b Whitney	7	4/137 5/145 6/197	

E. A. R. de Silva, C. P. H. Ramanayake and G. P. Wickremasinghe did not bat.

Bowling: McDermott 10-1-30-1; Dodemaide 10-1-44-1; Whitney 10-1-40-2; Matthews 10-1-33-2; Moody 7-0-38-0; Border 3-0-16-0.

Australia

M. A. Taylor c Gurusinha		*A. R. Border c Gurusinha	
b Hathurusinghe	14	b Ramanayake	14
T. M. Moody c Mahanama		G. R. J. Matthews not out	10
b Ramanayake	13		
D. M. Jones st Tillekeratne		B 4, l-b 7, w 4, n-b 4	19
b E. A. R. de Silva	17		
D. C. Boon not out	69	1/28 2/39 3/58 (5 wkts, 47.5 overs) 208	
M. E. Waugh run out	52	4/142 5/186	

†I. A. Healy, C. J. McDermott, A. I. C. Dodemaide and M. R. Whitney did not bat.

Bowling: Ramanayake 8.5-0-34-2; Wickremasinghe 9-0-32-0; Gurusinha 2-0-8-0; Hathurusinghe 10-0-38-1; E. A. R. de Silva 10-0-47-1; Kalpage 6-0-28-0; Jayasuriya 2-0-10-0.

Umpires: I. Anandappa and W. A. U. Wickremasinghe.

SRI LANKA v AUSTRALIA

Third Test Match

At Moratuwa, September 8, 9, 10, 12, 13. Drawn. Toss: Australia.

Rain carried by the south-west monsoon ruined a match pregnant with possibilities at the Tyronne Fernando Stadium, Test cricket's 67th ground. But the poor weather did not deter the largest crowds of the series. They generously applauded Border, who dragged the Australians back from the brink twice – coming in at 57 for four and nine for four. In the first innings, though Waugh departed almost at once, Border added 127 for the sixth wicket with Matthews and, with the pugnacious Healy, 67 for the seventh. Such was their defiance that Australia recovered from 58 for five to reach 337, after electing to have first use of the hardest and truest pitch they had encountered. Meanwhile, Border scored his 24th Test hundred in his 133rd match, becoming the first Australian to register centuries against six countries. It was his first Test hundred for four years, in which time he had played 36 Tests and made 21 fifties; his second-innings 78 made him the first player to amass 80 Test scores of fifty or more, beating S. M. Gavaskar's 79.

The opposing captain, Ranatunga, also reached a landmark; when 25 he became the first Sri Lankan to reach 2,000 runs in Test cricket. It was his 61st innings in his 36th match since making his Test debut, along with Sri Lanka, in February 1982. But his team's batting was indifferent, and they seemed to have lost their enthusiasm for the game; they eagerly accepted the offer of bad light against the spinners, and declined a suggestion that they might make up time on the rest day. Seemingly unalarmed by a first-innings deficit of 63, Sri Lanka raised the hopes of their supporters when Ramanayake and Liyanage again exposed the weaknesses in Australia's batting. Indeed, if Jayasuriya at silly point had not missed a sharp chance when Border was 19, off Anurasiri, Australia would have been in a far worse predicament at 51 for five. They were already in deep shock after Waugh was out for a pair for the second consecutive Test, a disaster that had previously befallen only five players (R. J. Crisp, W. M. Clark, R. G. Holland, R. Peel and P. I. Pocock), none of them of comparable batting distinction. But Matthews, with his fifth consecutive half-century of the series, and the dependable Healy eased any embarrassment after the loss of yet more time – three and a quarter hours – to rain on the final day. One joker added an extra touch to the statue of St Joseph positioned near the pavilion, supposedly to ward off foul weather: an umbrella.

Man of the Match: A. R. Border.

Close of play: First day, Australia 287-8 (I. A. Healy 43*, S. K. Warne 1*); Second day, Sri Lanka 143-4 (H. P. Tillekeratne 18*, A. Ranatunga 9*); Third day, Sri Lanka 215-4 (H. P. Tillekeratne 52*, A. Ranatunga 45*); Fourth day, Australia 147-6 (G. R. J. Matthews 20*, I. A. Healy 8*).

Australia

T. M. Moody b Ramanayake		0	– (2) c Tillekeratne b Ramanayake		2
M. A. Taylor c Ranatunga b Anurasiri		19	– (1) c Mahanama b Liyanage		3
D. C. Boon c de Silva b Ramanayake		18	– lbw b Liyanage		0
D. M. Jones lbw b Liyanage		11	– b Anurasiri		21
M. E. Waugh b Ramanayake		0	– c Tillekeratne b Liyanage		0
*A. R. Border b Ramanayake		106	– lbw b Ramanayake		78
G. R. J. Matthews run out		57	– b Ramanayake		96
†I. A. Healy c Jayasuriya b Muralitharan		71	– c Jayasuriya b Liyanage		49
C. J. McDermott c Tillekeratne b Hathurusinghe		10			
S. K. Warne c Gurusinha b Ramanayake		7			
A. I. C. Dodemaide not out		13	– (9) not out		2
B 3, l-b 9, w 3, n-b 10		25	L-b 4, w 1, n-b 15		20
		337		**(8 wkts)**	**271**

1/0 (1) 2/42 (2) 3/46 (3) 4/57 (4) 5/58 (5) 6/185 (7) 7/252 (6) 8/283 (9) 9/302 (10) 10/337 (8)

1/6 (1) 2/6 (2) 3/6 (3) (8 wkts) 271 4/9 (5) 5/60 (4) 6/132 (6) 7/261 (8) 8/271 (7)

Bowling: First Innings—Ramanayake 31-3-82-5; Liyanage 17-0-54-1; Hathurusinghe 21-8-50-1; Anurasiri 22-2-57-1; Muralitharan 15.1-2-58-1; Jayasuriya 2-0-9-0; Gurusinha 3-0-15-0. *Second Innings*—Ramanayake 22.1-4-75-3; Liyanage 16.3-3-56-4; Hathurusinghe 4-2-3-0; Gurusinha 1-0-5-0; Anurasiri 29-5-49-1; Muralitharan 7-1-26-0; Ranatunga 1-0-9-0; Jayasuriya 7-1-17-0; Mahanama 5-0-27-0.

Sri Lanka

R. S. Mahanama lbw b Matthews	50	C. P. H. Ramanayake not out		15
U. C. Hathurusinghe c Boon b McDermott	2	D. K. Liyanage c Moody b Dodemaide		1
A. P. Gurusinha c Healy b McDermott	0	S. D. Anurasiri b Dodemaide		0
P. A. de Silva b Dodemaide	58	L-b 8, w 3, n-b 5		16
†H. P. Tillekeratne c Waugh b Dodemaide	82		**(9 wkts dec.)**	**274**
*A. Ranatunga c Jones b McDermott	48			
S. T. Jayasuriya c Boon b McDermott	2			

1/4 (2) 2/4 (3) 3/111 (4) 4/116 (1) 5/232 (6) 6/234 (7) 7/262 (5) 8/274 (9) 9/274 (10)

M. Muralitharan did not bat.

Bowling: McDermott 31-6-89-4; Dodemaide 23.5-9-65-4; Moody 3-0-8-0; Matthews 31-8-64-1; Warne 11-3-40-0.

Umpires: B. C. Cooray and K. T. Francis. *Referee:* F. J. Cameron (New Zealand).

THE INDIANS IN ZIMBABWE AND SOUTH AFRICA, 1992-93

By RICHARD STREETON

A great deal of humdrum cricket failed to detract from the diplomatic and sporting history made when India embarked on a tour of Zimbabwe and South Africa late in 1992. Slow scoring and negative captaincy, coupled with moribund pitches, marred both Zimbabwe's inaugural Test and the first series staged in South Africa for 23 years. The continued failure of the Indians to do themselves justice away from home also militated against the representative games being worthy of these occasions. By the end of the tour India had gone 25 Test matches outside their own country without a win. In the wider context, though, this first tour to South Africa by a recognised non-white side was a success. The visit had the active support of the African National Congress and was almost entirely free from political rancour. More than £650,000 of the profits made by the United Cricket Board of South Africa (UCBSA) went into their development programme for black cricketers. The Indians undertook a heavy schedule of duties off the field, in townships and elsewhere, and proved fine ambassadors.

The tour will be remembered for the introduction of ICC's scheme for independent umpires and even more for the South African board's experiment using television replays to settle difficult line decisions. It was a successful innovation, welcomed by most players and officials after some initial reservations. Hitherto, for as long as the game has been played, batsmen have received the benefit of an umpire's doubt. When officials on the field felt unable to decide, a third umpire in the pavilion watched video replays to rule on run-outs, stumpings (and hit-wicket decisions, though none arose). A green light signalled that the batsman must go, and red that he was not out. Invariably the crowd buzzed with excitement as they waited and at some grounds they were able to watch the big-screen replays at the same time. The only major dispute arose when the West Indian umpire Steve Bucknor declined to call for a replay.

The dreary routine that characterised the Tests was started on a lifeless pitch in Harare. Zimbabwe set their sights on avoiding defeat through dour batting and defensive bowling. As it happened, they were in the box seat for long periods, primarily due to dominant performances from David Houghton and John Traicos, arguably their only players of true Test class. Indian shortcomings – unreliable batting and ineffectual bowling – were already discernible. Perhaps Zimbabwe could be excused a little for their caution, in view of their limited playing resources. Whether they justify their Test status will depend on the success of their schemes to find cricketers among the previously untapped African population.

India's problems were underlined more harshly when they reached South Africa, where they were beaten 1-0 in the four-match Test series and trounced 5-2 in the day/night internationals. The chief discrepancy between the teams was the accurate and spirited South African quick bowling, backed by spectacular catching and fielding. The tactical influence of Mike Procter, the team manager, was obvious as the Indian strokemakers found their favourite shots restricted. South Africa's batting was less reliable, but that innate combativeness their sportsmen have always possessed ensured that somebody played the innings required on the day. Often it was Kepler Wessels, whose experience proved vital, even if his captaincy was over-cautious. Hansie Cronje, Andrew Hudson, Jonty Rhodes, Brian McMillan and Daryll Cullinan all made telling contributions at different times.

McMillan, regularly, was a difficult man to dislodge. Also a consistently dangerous bowler and an outstanding second slip, he emerged as one of the best all-rounders in the world. He must have come close to being chosen as the man of the series. This award went to Allan Donald, the linchpin of the South African attack, who maintained his hostility and speed in a manner that was a tribute to his stamina as well as his skill. India's lack of confidence at the crease was most evident when he was bowling. His match figures of 12 for 139 in the Third Test at Port Elizabeth, together with a determined hundred by Cronje, clinched an emphatic victory and thus the series for South Africa. Rhodes led a zestful fielding side with numerous brilliant interceptions on the off side; but there were no weak links and the Indians were rendered jittery and unsure in their running between the wickets.

For all Mohammad Azharuddin's qualities as a diplomat, he failed to get his team to gel as a unit. The main batsmen often fell to a combination of poor technique and ill-chosen strokes. More than once, greater deter-mination was shown lower in the order. The averages demonstrate how Azharuddin and Ravi Shastri struggled for runs and Sanjay Manjrekar lost his touch after starting the tour well, scoring three hundreds. India suffered from their openers' inability to get a proper start and the No. 3 position also became a worry. Pravin Amre did little after an impressive century on debut in the First Test at Durban. Sachin Tendulkar scored a hundred in the Second Test at Johannesburg without looking at his best and he had a miserable time in the one-day games.

India's batting reached its lowest ebb in the Third Test at Port Elizabeth, apart from a memorable hundred by Kapil Dev in a losing cause. Kapil's bowling was always steady but he was unable to recapture the penetration he showed in Australia 12 months earlier. Manoj Prabhakar's swing brought him a rewarding spell on the first morning in Johannesburg, but he remained an inconsistent cricketer. Javagal Srinath was a whole-hearted trier; his deceptive pace and movement hinted at a promising future. The fast leg-spinner Anil Kumble had a busy tour and the batsmen's reactions suggested that India might have done well to include a slower, more orthodox leg-break bowler as well. There were also occasional debatable umpiring decisions. These were infrequent but they tended to go against the Indians.

The Durban Test was ruined by rain and in Johannesburg both captains spurned the chance of striking out for a result. Any hope that the final Test would provide some atonement was dashed when South Africa chose to sit on their lead. On another slow pitch India saw little point in trying to take the initiative. The outcome was one of the slowest-scoring and most boring Test matches in history. It did nothing to help promote the traditional game in South Africa after the long years in isolation. Fewer than 200,000 paid to see the four Test matches, while near-capacity crowds, 150,000 in all, packed the seven venues for the day/night series. But even these games were not especially exciting.

The second, at Port Elizabeth, saw the only discordant note on what the marketing men had called the "Friendship Tour": Kapil ran out Peter Kirsten at the bowler's end for backing up before the ball was bowled. Kirsten, who had been warned by Kapil in other games, was fined for dissent when he was given out. India lodged a complaint that Wessels had struck Kapil's shins with his bat later in the same over but Clive Lloyd, the match referee, found the charge unproven. Sir Colin Cowdrey, the ICC president, reversed previous policy and allowed the referees to clarify such incidents with the media. This realistic step had a hand in ensuring that the tour was so free of strife.

INDIAN TOURING PARTY

M. Azharuddin (Hyderabad) (*captain*), R. J. Shastri (Bombay) (*vice-captain*), P. K. Amre (Rajasthan), S. T. Banerjee (Bihar), A. D. Jadeja (Haryana), Kapil Dev (Haryana), A. Kumble (Karnataka), S. V. Manjrekar (Bombay), K. S. More (Baroda), M. Prabhakar (Delhi), S. L. V. Raju (Hyderabad), W. V. Raman (Tamil Nadu), Chetan Sharma (Haryana), J. Srinath (Karnataka), S. R. Tendulkar (Bombay), V. S. Yadav (Haryana).
   Manager: A. Mathur.   *Team manager:* A. L. Wadekar.

INDIAN TOUR RESULTS

Test matches – Played 5: Lost 1, Drawn 4.
First-class matches – Played 9: Won 1, Lost 1, Drawn 7.
Win – Combined Bowl XI.
Loss – South Africa.
Draws – Zimbabwe, South Africa (3), UCBSA President's XI, South African Invitation XI, South African Students XI.
One-day internationals – Played 8: Won 3, Lost 5. *Wins* – Zimbabwe, South Africa (2). *Losses* – South Africa (5).
Other non first-class matches – Played 3: Won 3. *Wins* – Zimbabwe Board President's XI, N. F. Oppenheimer's XI, UCBSA President's XI.

TEST MATCH AVERAGES – SOUTH AFRICA v INDIA

SOUTH AFRICA – BATTING

	T	I	NO	R	HS	100s	Avge	Ct
J. N. Rhodes	4	7	1	275	91	0	45.83	1
K. C. Wessels	4	8	1	295	118	1	42.14	5
W. J. Cronje	3	6	1	207	135	1	41.40	0
B. M. McMillan	4	6	1	194	98	0	38.80	8
C. R. Matthews	3	4	1	94	31	0	31.33	0
A. C. Hudson	4	8	0	245	55	0	30.62	5
D. J. Richardson	4	6	1	106	50	0	21.20	16
S. J. Cook	2	4	0	76	43	0	19.00	0
O. Henry	3	3	0	53	34	0	17.66	2
A. A. Donald	4	5	3	29	14*	0	14.50	0
P. N. Kirsten	4	7	1	76	26	0	12.66	2

   Played in two Tests: M. W. Pringle 33, 3*; B. N. Schultz 0*, 0*. Played in one Test: D. J. Cullinan 46, 28 (1 ct).

   * *Signifies not out.*

BOWLING

	O	M	R	W	BB	5W/i	Avge
A. A. Donald......	175	49	394	20	7-84	2	19.70
C. R. Matthews....	109	44	190	9	3-32	0	21.11
B. M. McMillan ..	155	55	307	13	4-74	0	23.61
B. N. Schultz......	51.4	16	101	4	2-37	0	25.25

Also bowled: W. J. Cronje 56.4–28–71–3; O. Henry 71.1–15–189–3; P. N. Kirsten 5–1–13–0; M. W. Pringle 34–10–67–1; J. N. Rhodes 1–0–5–0.

INDIA – BATTING

	T	I	NO	R	HS	100s	Avge	Ct
Kapil Dev	4	5	0	202	129	1	40.40	1
P. K. Amre	4	6	1	169	103	1	33.80	0
S. R. Tendulkar....	4	6	0	202	111	1	33.66	4
A. D. Jadeja.......	3	5	1	99	43	0	24.75	0
S. V. Manjrekar...	4	7	2	116	46	0	23.20	3
K. S. More	4	5	0	102	55	0	20.40	11
M. Azharuddin	4	6	0	120	60	0	20.00	6
S. L. V. Raju	2	3	2	20	18	0	20.00	0
M. Prabhakar	4	6	0	112	62	0	18.66	4
A. Kumble........	4	5	1	60	21*	0	15.00	1
R. J. Shastri	3	5	0	59	23	0	11.80	0
J. Srinath	3	3	2	6	5	0	6.00	3

Played in one Test: W. V. Raman 21, 0.

* *Signifies not out.*

BOWLING

	O	M	R	W	BB	5W/i	Avge
A. Kumble	254.3	87	467	18	6-53	1	25.94
J. Srinath	138.5	30	313	12	4-33	0	26.08
Kapil Dev.......	165	46	299	8	3-43	0	37.37
M. Prabhakar....	144	31	389	9	4-90	0	43.22
S. L. V. Raju ...	131	43	242	4	3-73	0	60.50

Also bowled: M. Azharuddin 0.1–0–4–0; S. V. Manjrekar 1–0–4–0; R. J. Shastri 31–4–74–2; S. R. Tendulkar 7–2–14–1.

INDIAN AVERAGES – FIRST-CLASS MATCHES

Note: The following averages include India v Zimbabwe in Harare.

BATTING

	M	I	NO	R	HS	100s	Avge	Ct/St
A. D. Jadeja.......	5	8	2	428	254*	1	71.33	2
S. V. Manjrekar....	8	12	3	604	186	3	67.11	4
Kapil Dev	6	6	0	262	129	1	43.66	1
S. R. Tendulkar ...	8	10	0	409	131	2	40.90	6
P. K. Amre	7	10	1	343	103	2	38.11	1
K. S. More........	7	8	0	168	55	0	21.00	21/1

	M	I	NO	R	HS	100s	Avge	Ct/St
R. J. Shastri	7	11	1	176	63	0	17.60	4
W. V. Raman	6	9	1	125	43	0	15.62	5
M. Azharuddin	8	10	1	132	60	0	14.66	13
M. Prabhakar	7	10	0	143	62	0	14.30	6
S. L. V. Raju	7	8	4	41	18	0	10.25	1
A. Kumble	7	8	1	65	21*	0	9.28	4
J. Srinath	7	7	3	28	8	0	7.00	3

Played in four matches: Chetan Sharma 25*, 14*, 17 (2 ct). Played in three matches: S. T. Banerjee 0 (1 ct). Played in two matches: V. S. Yadav 36, 0 (7 ct).

* *Signifies not out.*

BOWLING

	O	M	R	W	BB	5W/i	Avge
S. T. Banerjee	63	22	131	9	5-29	1	14.55
J. Srinath	261.3	60	623	26	4-33	0	23.96
R. J. Shastri	113	30	244	10	3-7	0	24.40
A. Kumble	355.5	118	675	26	6-53	1	25.96
M. Prabhakar	263.2	70	609	22	4-41	0	27.68
Kapil Dev	246	74	437	13	3-43	0	33.61
S. L. V. Raju	332.2	118	641	19	5-68	1	33.73
Chetan Sharma	98.4	17	319	8	4-56	0	39.87

Also bowled: P. K. Amre 1–0–10–0; M. Azharuddin 7.1–4–14–0; A. D. Jadeja 2–0–7–0; S. V. Manjrekar 1–0–4–0; S. R. Tendulkar 36.5–11–95–4.

Note: Matches in this section which were not first-class are signified by a dagger.

†At Harare, October 15. Indians won by 16 runs. Indians 203 for nine (50 overs) (R. J. Shastri 73); Zimbabwe Board President's XI 187 for nine (50 overs) (G. A. Briant 51 not out).

ZIMBABWE v INDIA

Inaugural Test Match

At Harare, October 18, 19, 20, 21, 22. Drawn. Toss: Zimbabwe. Test debuts: all Zimbabweans except A. J. Traicos.

Against expectation Zimbabwe held the upper hand for long periods in their inaugural Test match, played in very hot weather on a lifeless pitch. Both attacks were rendered innocuous and much of the batting was also excessively cautious, with a run-rate of barely two an over. Zimbabwe, however, had the satisfaction of gaining a first-innings lead of 149 and, as the ninth Test-playing country, went on to become the first to avoid defeat in their initial Test since Australia in 1876-77, when Test cricket began. Their captain, Houghton, became the first player to score a century on his country's debut since Charles Bannerman, on the same occasion. Houghton shared the individual honours with Manjrekar, who scored a hundred for India, and Traicos, the Zimbabwean off-spinner.

At the age of 45, Traicos became the 14th man to represent two countries at Test level, 22 years and 222 days since playing for South Africa in their last Test before exclusion from international cricket – a record gap between Test appearances. He took five for 86 in 50 overs marked by subtle changes of pace and flight. The game will also be remembered as the first Test to have three appointed umpires. A new sponsorship by the British company National Grid meant that Dickie Bird was flown out from England to stand in his 48th Test and equal the world record set by his compatriot, Frank Chester. Bird stood throughout and the two Zimbabwean umpires on alternate days. Attendances throughout the game were tiny.

India, still adjusting to the altitude and short on match preparation, could take only five wickets during the first two days. The Zimbabwean innings was launched by a stand of 100 from Arnott and Grant, the younger of the Flower brothers, who survived a chance to slip off Raju when 21 and had made 82 when he fell just before the close. An early wicket next morning brought in Houghton, for so long the mainstay of his country's batting, to make his Test debut at the age of 35. Curbing his natural attacking instincts, he reached a chanceless hundred in 305 minutes, with 12 fours. He had sound support from Andy Flower, who helped him to add 165 in 68 overs for the sixth wicket, but Zimbabwe quickly lost their last five wickets on the third morning. Houghton was seventh out when he edged a catch behind. He had batted watchfully for 414 minutes, permitting himself just the occasional lofted drive or pull; he hit 15 fours from 322 balls, and played the spinners especially well.

Zimbabwe's eventual total of 456 was easily the highest by a country on Test debut, beating Australia's 245. When they took the field they soon lost Brandes, their only fast bowler, who broke down after two overs and took no further part in the match. Yet they shrugged off this setback, as Traicos subdued the batsmen from the moment he came on; he held a good return catch to dismiss Tendulkar and then had Azharuddin taken at slip. India were thus reduced to 93 for four by the close, still needing 164 to avoid the follow-on. The left-arm seamer Crocker, included shortly before the toss when Shah pulled out because of a niggling groin strain, conceded only 11 in his first 13 overs, nine of which were maidens.

On the fourth day Traicos claimed the only three wickets to fall. Zimbabwe, though, lost the initiative for the first time when they took the new ball at 113 for five from 75 overs. The switch from Traicos's spin suited Kapil Dev, who made a forceful 60 in 95 balls. Prabhakar and More then stayed with Manjrekar as he dragged the game away from Zimbabwe, pushing and nudging towards his hundred just before the close after 500 minutes, the fourth-slowest Test century. He had faced 397 balls and hit only seven fours.

Though he was soon caught at backward point next morning, when India were all out in a further 45 minutes, Zimbabwe could only bat out the match.

Close of play: First day, Zimbabwe 188-3 (A. J. Pycroft 6*, M. G. Burmester 2*); Second day, Zimbabwe 406-5 (D. L. Houghton 110*, A. Flower 55*); Third day, India 93-4 (S. V. Manjrekar 27*, S. L. V. Raju 0*); Fourth day, India 278-7 (S. V. Manjrekar 100*, K. S. More 23*).

Zimbabwe

K. J. Arnott c Raman b Kumble	40	– b Prabhakar	32
G. W. Flower c More b Srinath	82	– c More b Kapil Dev	6
A. D. R. Campbell lbw b Kapil Dev	45	– b Kapil Dev	0
A. J. Pycroft c Azharuddin b Prabhakar	39	– lbw b Shastri	46
M. G. Burmester c Azharuddin b Prabhakar	7		
*D. L. Houghton c More b Srinath	121	– (5) not out	41
†A. Flower b Prabhakar	59	– (6) not out	1
G. J. Crocker not out	23		
E. A. Brandes lbw b Srinath	0		
A. J. Traicos b Kumble	5		
M. P. Jarvis c Raman b Kumble	0		
B 1, l-b 19, n-b 15	35	B 11, l-b 4, n-b 5	20

1/100 (1) 2/175 (3) 3/186 (2) 4/199 (5)   456   1/16 (2) 2/16 (3)   (4 wkts dec.) 146
5/252 (4) 6/417 (7) 7/445 (6)   3/93 (4) 4/119 (1)
8/445 (9) 9/454 (10) 10/456 (11)

Bowling: *First Innings*—Kapil Dev 39-13-71-1; Prabhakar 45-15-66-3; Srinath 39-12-89-3; Raju 39-15-79-0; Kumble 35.2-11-79-3; Shastri 17-3-52-0. *Second Innings*—Prabhakar 14.4-4-22-1; Kapil Dev 15-4-22-2; Tendulkar 4-3-8-0; Srinath 5-1-15-0; Kumble 9-1-15-0; Raju 7-2-17-0; Shastri 12-4-32-1.

India

R. J. Shastri c Pycroft b Burmester	11	†K. S. More c Traicos b Burmester 41
W. V. Raman b Crocker.............	43	A. Kumble c A. Flower b Burmester... 0
S. V. Manjrekar c sub (S. G. Davies)		J. Srinath not out................. 6
b Jarvis .	104	
S. R. Tendulkar c and b Traicos	0	B 2, l-b 9, n-b 1 12
*M. Azharuddin c G. W. Flower		
b Traicos .	9	1/29 (1) 2/77 (2) 3/78 (4) 4/93 (5) 307
S. L. V. Raju c Arnott b Traicos	7	5/101 (6) 6/197 (7)
Kapil Dev b Traicos	60	7/219 (8) 8/287 (3)
M. Prabhakar c Arnott b Traicos.....	14	9/294 (10) 10/307 (9)

Bowling: Brandes 2–0–3–0; Burmester 39.4–18–78–3; Jarvis 38–17–73–1; Crocker 35–18–41–1; Traicos 50–16–86–5; G. W. Flower 5–0–15–0.

Umpires: H. D. Bird (England), K. Kanjee and I. D. Robinson.
Referee: P. L. van der Merwe (South Africa).

†ZIMBABWE v INDIA

One-day International

At Harare, October 25. India won by 30 runs. Toss: Zimbabwe. International debuts: D. H. Brain, C. N. Evans.

A target of 240 always looked out of reach for Zimbabwe after their middle order failed. A crowd of 8,000 saw the Flower brothers give them a sound start, but only Crocker, with a forceful 50, hinted at the necessary acceleration later. Earlier, Crocker had taken four important wickets, Manjrekar had made 70 to anchor India's innings after both openers fell with one run on the board, and Tendulkar and Amre played some fine strokes.

India

R. J. Shastri c G. W. Flower		†K. S. More run out 22
b Burmester .	1	J. Srinath not out 1
A. D. Jadeja b Brain	0	A. Kumble run out 1
*M. Azharuddin c Brain b Crocker	29	
S. R. Tendulkar c Brain b Crocker ...	39	B 5, l-b 4, w 7 16
S. V. Manjrekar c A. Flower b Crocker	70	
P. K. Amre lbw b Traicos	36	1/1 2/1 3/75 (49.4 overs) 239
Kapil Dev c Evans b G. W. Flower ...	5	4/78 5/151 6/168
M. Prabhakar c sub (S. G. Peall)		7/211 8/223 9/238
b Crocker .	19	

Bowling: Brain 10–0–52–1; Burmester 6–0–38–1; Shah 10–1–23–0; Crocker 7.4–0–26–4; Traicos 10–0–48–1; G. W. Flower 6–0–43–1.

Zimbabwe

†A. Flower run out	62	A. D. R. Campbell b Srinath 0
G. W. Flower b Srinath	34	M. G. Burmester b Prabhakar 11
A. H. Shah run out	16	A. J. Traicos not out 0
*D. L. Houghton c Amre b Jadeja ...	4	B 1, l-b 6, w 4, n-b 3 14
A. C. Waller c Kumble b Prabhakar ...	9	
C. N. Evans c Azharuddin b Kumble ..	1	1/63 2/88 3/98 (49.1 overs) 209
G. J. Crocker b Kapil Dev	50	4/120 5/123 6/180
D. H. Brain b Srinath	8	7/196 8/196 9/209

Bowling: Kapil Dev 8.1–1–27–1; Prabhakar 10–0–43–2; Tendulkar 3–0–16–0; Srinath 10–1–35–3; Shastri 5–0–22–0; Jadeja 5–0–24–1; Kumble 8–1–35–1.

Umpires: I. D. Robinson and R. Tiffin.

†At Randjesfontein, October 29. Indians won by 80 runs. Indians batted first by mutual agreement. Indians 207 for six dec. (A. D. Jadeja 50, S. R. Tendulkar 100 not out; A. J. Kourie four for 50); N. F. Oppenheimer's XI 127 (H. H. Gibbs 36; Chetan Sharma three for 49, including a hat-trick, S. L. V. Raju four for 11).

COMBINED BOWL XI v INDIANS

At Springs, October 31, November 1, 2, 3. Indians won by an innings and 241 runs. Toss: Combined Bowl XI.

A second-wicket partnership of 415 in 114 overs between Jadeja and Manjrekar over-shadowed everything else in this match against a team drawn from the minor provinces. It was the highest stand for any wicket by an Indian side abroad and only the second above 400 in South Africa. Both Indians played attractive strokes all round the wicket against moderate bowling on a bland surface. Manjrekar hit 21 fours before he was caught at backward point after a seven-and-a-half-hour 186; Jadeja, making the most of a life at 24, was undefeated with 254, including 36 fours and a six, after 583 minutes and 437 balls. Cann, the Griqualand West and former Glamorgan player, resisted dourly in the Bowl XI's first innings, but the batting caved in when they went in again 326 behind.

Close of play: First day, Combined Bowl XI 224-9 (P. D. de Vaal 32*, H. Williams 16*); Second day, Indians 296-1 (A. D. Jadeja 132*, S. V. Manjrekar 134*); Third day, Combined Bowl XI 51-6 (T. A. Marsh 3*).

Combined Bowl XI

*M. J. Cann c and b Banerjee	94 – c Azharuddin b Banerjee	2
N. M. Snyman c Yadav b Kapil Dev	4 – c Azharuddin b Kapil Dev	2
H. M. de Vos c Yadav b Banerjee	1 – c Yadav b Kumble	21
W. S. Truter lbw b Sharma	18 – c Kumble b Banerjee	11
F. J. C. Cronje lbw b Raju	7 – lbw b Sharma	6
†B. Randall lbw b Kumble	20 – lbw b Raju	2
T. A. Marsh c Azharuddin b Sharma	10 – c Kumble b Banerjee	3
P. D. de Vaal not out	37 – not out	24
L. D. Botha c Kumble b Banerjee	4 – c Azharuddin b Banerjee	0
C. W. Henderson b Sharma	7 – c Yadav b Banerjee	0
H. Williams c Raman b Sharma	17 – b Kumble	6
B 6, l-b 5	11	B 4, l-b 1, w 3	8

1/5 2/16 3/60 4/67 5/102   230   1/5 2/5 3/23 4/35 5/44   85
6/132 7/186 8/190 9/204   6/51 7/58 8/70 9/70

Bowling: *First Innings*—Kapil Dev 15-5-29-1; Banerjee 15-6-41-3; Jadeja 2-0-7-0; Sharma 18.4-5-56-4; Raju 30-13-46-1; Kumble 20-7-34-1; Azharuddin 6-4-6-0. *Second Innings*—Kapil Dev 12-6-16-1; Banerjee 19-10-29-5; Sharma 7-2-22-1; Raju 4-4-0-1; Kumble 7-3-13-2.

Indians

W. V. Raman c Randall b Botha	11	*M. Azharuddin not out	1
A. D. Jadeja not out	254	B 8, l-b 12, w 4, n-b 15	39
S. V. Manjrekar c Snyman b Marsh ..	186		
S. R. Tendulkar c Randall b Williams..	65	1/15 2/430 3/553 (3 wkts dec.)	556

Kapil Dev, S. T. Banerjee, Chetan Sharma, †V. S. Yadav, A. Kumble and S. L. V. Raju did not bat.

Bowling: Botha 23-5-79-1; Williams 26-3-63-1; Marsh 31-4-112-1; Cronje 18-3-76-0; Henderson 21-1-94-0; de Vaal 10-1-48-0; Cann 13-0-64-0.

Umpires: W. Diedricks and K. E. Liebenberg.

UCBSA PRESIDENT'S XI v INDIANS

At Verwoerdburg, November 6, 7, 8, 9. Drawn. Toss: UCBSA President's XI.

The Indians needed 296 to win when rain washed out play on the final day to prevent an interesting finish. Earlier, they had conceded a lead of 104 as Brett Schultz, a 22-year-old hostile, left-arm fast bowler, earned selection for the First Test by taking five for 35. In the President's XI's first innings, Prabhakar swung the ball freely in the humidity, helping More to three of his six dismissals. One ball from Prabhakar, however, brought six byes: it struck a helmet on the ground behind More and the umpires unexpectedly ruled that the batsmen had completed a single before the five-run penalty came into force. Srinath and the highly economical Shastri bowled effectively on the third day, when more than two hours' play was lost to rain and Cronje completed a second restrained half-century.

Close of play: First day, UCBSA President's XI 268; Second day, UCBSA President's XI 77-2 (T. N. Lazard 43*, W. J. Cronje 20*); Third day, Indians 9-0 (R. J. Shastri 5*, W. V. Raman 2*).

UCBSA President's XI

P. J. R. Steyn c More b Banerjee	0	– c and b Prabhakar	0
T. N. Lazard c Tendulkar b Srinath	16	– lbw b Prabhakar	52
L. J. Koen c More b Prabhakar	49	– b Srinath	4
*W. J. Cronje c Sharma b Shastri	73	– c sub (A. D. Jadeja) b Srinath	53
M. J. R. Rindel c More b Prabhakar	0	– c More b Srinath	22
†E. L. R. Stewart c More b Prabhakar	41	– c Raju b Shastri	17
K. Mahuwa c Prabhakar b Raju	29	– c and b Shastri	32
D. B. Rundle b Shastri	12	– lbw b Srinath	1
T. Bosch st More b Raju	4	– (10) c sub (A. D. Jadeja) b Raju	2
R. A. Lyle c More b Srinath	22	– (9) lbw b Shastri	0
B. N. Schultz not out	4	– not out	0
B 7, l-b 5, n-b 6	18	L-b 13, n-b 4	17
	268		**200**

1/3 2/41 3/87 4/89 5/182   1/0 2/31 3/88 4/136 5/145
6/194 7/218 8/228 9/254   6/189 7/194 8/195 9/200

Bowling: *First Innings*—Prabhakar 17-5-38-3; Banerjee 13-3-26-1; Raju 18.5-5-57-2; Sharma 12-1-53-0; Srinath 14-4-58-2; Shastri 14-7-24-2. *Second Innings*—Prabhakar 16-3-42-2; Srinath 18-2-49-4; Sharma 12-0-45-0; Banerjee 4-0-12-0; Raju 13.3-3-32-1; Shastri 6-1-7-3.

Indians

R. J. Shastri c Stewart b Schultz	10	– not out	5
W. V. Raman c Rindel b Schultz	20	– not out	2
M. Prabhakar c Koen b Bosch	9		
S. R. Tendulkar c Stewart b Lyle	11		
*M. Azharuddin c Koen b Bosch	2		
P. K. Amre lbw b Schultz	23		
†K. S. More c Rindel b Lyle	20		
S. L. V. Raju b Schultz	0		
S. T. Banerjee c Bosch b Schultz	0		
Chetan Sharma not out	25		
J. Srinath c Lazard b Lyle	8		
B 4, l-b 2, w 1, n-b 29	36	W 2	2
	164	(no wkt)	**9**

1/39 2/42 3/68 4/71 5/74
6/115 7/115 8/117 9/138

Bowling: *First Innings*—Bosch 12-0-65-2; Schultz 17-7-35-5; Lyle 15.4-5-36-3; Rundle 10-2-22-0. *Second Innings*—Schultz 3-0-8-0; Lyle 2-1-1-0; Bosch 1-1-0-0.

Umpires: W. Diedricks and S. B. Lambson.

SOUTH AFRICA v INDIA

First Test Match

At Durban, November 13, 14, 15, 16, 17. Drawn. Toss: India. Test debuts: S. J. Cook, O. Henry, B. M. McMillan, J. N. Rhodes, B. N. Schultz; P. K. Amre, A. D. Jadeja.

A match of historic importance faded away into a draw after the fourth day was washed out. Even before that, the occasion made surprisingly little impact on Durban, with its huge Indian community: the total attendance was barely 30,000. It was a game of milestones, none the less: in South Africa's first home Test since March 1970 they included a non-white player for the first time, Omar Henry, who was their oldest debutant at 40 years and 295 days. It was also the first time television replays were used to settle awkward line decisions. On the second day Tendulkar changed his mind about a run and was trying to get back when Rhodes returned to Hudson. After a slight pause, Cyril Mitchley, the square-leg umpire, signalled to Karl Liebenberg, the umpire in the pavilion, by shaping a TV screen with his fingers. Thirty seconds later Liebenberg lit the green light to signify that Tendulkar was out.

The highlights of the actual game were centuries for Wessels, who became the first batsman to make a hundred for two countries, and Amre, on his debut, which ensured a rough equality in what cricket was possible. The game had a dramatic start and Jimmy Cook's long-awaited Test debut a disastrous one when he was caught at third slip from the game's first ball. No one had previously been out to the first ball of his first Test. But although more grass than expected had been left on the pitch it did not help the bowlers that much and Wessels stopped any possibility of a collapse.

Though Kirsten never settled, he stayed with his captain for more than two hours, before Rhodes helped add 82. Wessels's renowned composure was evident as he played every ball on its merits, with anything wayward nudged, deflected or, occasionally, driven. On 90, he broke out to hit three successive leg-side fours off Srinath, and was finally caught at slip 25 minutes before the close.

India made a wretched start, slumping to 38 for four, the wickets including that of Tendulkar, victim of the video replay. India were still in a parlous position when bad light ended play early at 128 for six on the third day. Their progress was slow but their self-control never wavered. Though South Africa were unfortunate to lose Schultz, who pulled a hamstring, the other bowlers delivered too many balls that could be left alone. As they tired, Amre began to drive and pull, and passed rapidly to his hundred. Several spectators ran on to congratulate him and a few cans were thrown on to the outfield as they were hustled off; Steve Bucknor, the West Indian umpire, helped get the intruders back behind the fence. Amre was caught soon afterwards at backward point. He had batted 378 minutes and hit 11 fours from 298 balls. More was last out, after five hours, but bad light and then the fourth-day washout prevented South Africa resuming until the final day, which effectively turned into a day of public practice.

Man of the Match: P. K. Amre.

Close of play: First day, South Africa 215-7 (D. J. Richardson 11*); Second day, India 128-6 (P. K. Amre 39*, M. Prabhakar 0*); Third day, India 277; Fourth day, No play.

South Africa

S. J. Cook c Tendulkar b Kapil Dev	0	– c and b Kumble	43
A. C. Hudson b Kapil Dev	14	– c More b Srinath	55
*K. C. Wessels c Azharuddin b Kumble	118	– c More b Srinath	32
P. N. Kirsten c More b Srinath	13	– not out	11
J. N. Rhodes c Azharuddin b Kumble	41	– not out	26
B. M. McMillan c Prabhakar b Shastri	3		
†D. J. Richardson lbw b Prabhakar	15		
O. Henry c Tendulkar b Shastri	3		
M. W. Pringle lbw b Kapil Dev	33		
A. A. Donald lbw b Prabhakar	1		
B. N. Schultz not out	0		
L-b 6, n-b 7	13	B 1, l-b 2, n-b 6	9
	254	(3 wkts)	**176**

1/0 (1) 2/41 (2) 3/101 (4) 4/183 (5)
5/194 (6) 6/206 (3) 7/215 (8) 8/251 (7)
9/253 (9) 10/254 (10)

1/68 (1) 2/129 (2) (3 wkts) 176
3/138 (3)

Bowling: *First Innings*—Kapil Dev 22-6-43-3; Prabhakar 24.4-7-47-2; Srinath 18-3-69-1; Kumble 28-8-51-2; Shastri 11-1-38-2. *Second Innings*—Kapil Dev 19-11-19-0; Prabhakar 14-3-47-0; Srinath 16-3-42-2; Kumble 16-4-36-1; Shastri 14-2-22-0; Tendulkar 2-1-3-0; Manjrekar 1-0-4-0.

India

R. J. Shastri lbw b Pringle	14	†K. S. More lbw b Henry	55	
A. D. Jadeja c McMillan b Schultz	3	A. Kumble b Henry	8	
S. V. Manjrekar lbw b McMillan	0	J. Srinath not out	1	
S. R. Tendulkar run out	11	B 1, l-b 7, w 4, n-b 19	31	
*M. Azharuddin run out	36			
P. K. Amre c Rhodes b McMillan	103	1/18 (2) 2/22 (3) 3/38 (4) 4/38 (1)	277	
Kapil Dev c Richardson b McMillan	2	5/125 (5) 6/127 (7) 7/146 (8)		
M. Prabhakar c McMillan b Donald	13	8/247 (6) 9/274 (10) 10/277 (9)		

Bowling: Donald 29-6-69-1; Schultz 14.5-7-25-1; McMillan 37-18-52-3; Pringle 34-10-67-1; Henry 19.1-3-56-2.

Umpires: S. A. Bucknor (West Indies), K. E. Liebenberg and C. J. Mitchley.
Referee: C. H. Lloyd (West Indies).

SOUTH AFRICAN INVITATION XI v INDIANS

At Bloemfontein, November 20, 21, 22, 23. Drawn. Toss: Indians.

Amre and Manjrekar scored attractive hundreds for the Indians on a pitch which became progressively easier and made the final day academic. On the first day, Amre's batting was invaluable after careless strokes reduced the touring team to 21 for three. In the second innings, though, Manjrekar was building on a stand of 130 from Shastri and Jadeja, the Indians' first substantial opening partnership of the tour. Rushmere batted well for the Invitation XI, scoring two fifties, and two non-whites, Dean MacHelm, a left-arm spinner, and Mehmood Badat, a wicket-keeper, made promising beginnings at this level. Badat took seven catches and stumped Manjrekar to give MacHelm his first wicket.

Close of play: First day, Indians 242-8 (Chetan Sharma 10*, S. L. V. Raju 2*); Second day, South African Invitation XI 204-9 (C. R. Matthews 12*, D. MacHelm 0*); Third day, Indians 226-4 (S. V. Manjrekar 47*, M. Prabhakar 4*).

Indians

*R. J. Shastri lbw b Snell	2	– c Wilkinson b MacHelm	63
A. D. Jadeja c Kuiper b van Zyl	7	– c Badat b Snell	68
W. V. Raman c Badat b Snell	7	– lbw b Snell	6
S. V. Manjrekar st Badat b MacHelm	53	– not out	102
P. K. Amre c Badat b Kuiper	101	– c Snell b Davids	20
M. Prabhakar c Matthews b MacHelm	0	– lbw b van Zyl	8
†V. S. Yadav c Rushmere b Davids	36	– b Snell	0
Chetan Sharma not out	14	– c Badat b Kuiper	17
A. Kumble c Badat b Snell	4	– c Kuiper b Davids	4
S. L. V. Raju c Badat b van Zyl	2	– not out	3
J. Srinath c Badat b van Zyl	3		
L-b 9, w 1, n-b 11	21	B 5, l-b 12, n-b 7	24

1/4 2/17 3/21 4/134 5/134	250	1/130 2/138 3/155 (8 wkts dec.) 312
6/217 7/223 8/229 9/242		4/209 5/236 6/238
		7/284 8/289

Bowling: *First Innings*—Snell 25-5-57-3; Matthews 17-1-60-0; van Zyl 18.1-5-32-3; MacHelm 18-2-46-2; Kuiper 15-3-41-1; Davids 3-2-5-1. *Second Innings*—Snell 26-4-63-3; van Zyl 27-8-56-1; Kuiper 18-7-44-1; Matthews 18-4-37-0; MacHelm 16-4-60-1; Davids 16.3-4-35-2.

South African Invitation XI

M. Yachad c Yadav b Prabhakar	12	– (2) not out	64
I. Munshi c Jadeja b Prabhakar	6	– (1) b Sharma	0
M. W. Rushmere c Yadav b Prabhakar	75	– not out	54
A. P. Kuiper b Srinath	6		
L. J. Wilkinson c Yadav b Sharma	9		
F. Davids lbw b Kumble	38		
C. J. P. G. van Zyl b Kumble	8		
R. P. Snell lbw b Srinath	0		
†M. Badat c Shastri b Raju	8		
*C. R. Matthews c Jadeja b Prabhakar	24		
D. MacHelm not out	1		
B 8, l-b 9, n-b 15	32	L-b 3, w 4, n-b 4	11

1/22 2/30 3/60 4/79 5/168   219   1/5   (1 wkt) 129
6/170 7/173 8/178 9/204

Bowling: First Innings—Prabhakar 22.2–9–41–4; Srinath 13–3–36–2; Sharma 20–5–41–1; Kumble 26–7–60–2; Raju 8–3–21–1; Shastri 1–0–3–0. *Second Innings*—Sharma 11–2–45–1; Prabhakar 5–3–11–0; Shastri 6–1–26–0; Raju 13–6–16–0; Srinath 8–3–21–0; Kumble 4–2–7–0.

Umpires: R. E. Koertzen and S. B. Lambson.

SOUTH AFRICA v INDIA

Second Test Match

At Johannesburg, November 26, 27, 28, 29, 30. Drawn. Toss: South Africa. Test debut: C. R. Matthews.

After four tense, hard-fought days, the match was deprived of the climax it deserved on the fifth by a negative approach from both captains. Two incidents shaped its course as South Africa redeemed an appalling start to their first innings. Rhodes was 28 when umpire Bucknor decided that he had not been run out by a direct hit by Srinath from mid-off. Television showed that Rhodes failed to make his ground by some six inches. Bucknor, who was poorly positioned, declined to call upon the third umpire's replay facilities, though the Indians pleaded with him to do so. Rhodes went on to make 91. The second significant event came when South Africa were reduced to three front-line bowlers: Pringle's eye socket bone was fractured when he top-edged a ball from Srinath into his face.

Superb swing bowling from Prabhakar was mainly responsible for South Africa crumbling to 26 for four on what was then a hard, pacy pitch. It later became slower, with only a suspicion of uneven bounce. The scoreline could have been worse: Rhodes gave a hard chance to More off Prabhakar before he scored. Unruffled by this or the run-out controversy, Rhodes shared useful stands with Cronje and McMillan, and was finally leg-before to Kumble after batting with a mixture of perkiness and resolution. McMillan chose his strokes with sound common sense and was even closer to a maiden Test hundred when he was last out, lifting a short ball to long leg.

The depleted South African attack, led by McMillan and Matthews, quickly had India in trouble, with Tendulkar providing the only resistance. He made a streaky start against Donald and at ten should have been caught in the slips, but always tried to wrest the initiative. When 33 he became, at 19 years 217 days, the youngest batsman to reach 1,000 Test runs, displacing Kapil Dev (21 years 27 days in 1979-80). Tendulkar was less positive on the third morning but completed his fourth Test hundred shortly after lunch.

South Africa had gained a lead of 65, but from the start of their second innings were too slow in consolidating it. A lengthy spell from Kumble never allowed them to break free on the fourth day. Kumble finished with six for 53. He seldom turned the ball much but his brisk top-spin and googlies came through at varying heights out of the rough. Richardson, the night-watchman, stayed two and a half hours for his fifty, but wickets fell when an attempt was finally made to accelerate. India required a further 303 on the fifth day to win. Their lack of ambition became clear when they added only 41 before lunch, with Shastri making three scoring strokes. Early in the afternoon they lost four wickets for five runs: Jadeja, Azharuddin and Shastri all played poor strokes and Tendulkar was beaten by Donald's pace. But Wessels retained defensive field placings as Manjrekar and Amre stood firm. A crowd of 12,000 was remarkably tolerant as the match fizzled out. A total attendance of 80,000 included 21,000 on the Saturday, when the president of the African National Congress, Nelson Mandela, was present, and 26,000 on Sunday.

Man of the Match: B. M. McMillan.

Close of play: First day, South Africa 226-7 (B. M. McMillan 69*, C. R. Matthews 15*); Second day, India 128-6 (S. R. Tendulkar 75*, Kapil Dev 1*); Third day, South Africa 75-1 (A. C. Hudson 35*, D. J. Richardson 2*); Fourth day, India 15-0 (R. J. Shastri 7*, A. D. Jadeja 8*).

South Africa

S. J. Cook c More b Prabhakar	2	– c More b Srinath	31
A. C. Hudson c Azharuddin b Prabhakar	8	– b Kumble	53
*K. C. Wessels c Azharuddin b Srinath	5	– (4) run out	11
P. N. Kirsten lbw b Prabhakar	0	– (5) b Kumble	26
J. N. Rhodes lbw b Kumble	91	– (6) b Kumble	13
W. J. Cronje c and b Kapil Dev	8	– (7) b Kumble	15
B. M. McMillan c Manjrekar b Srinath	98	– (8) c Prabhakar b Kumble	5
†D. J. Richardson lbw b Kumble	9	– (3) b Kumble	50
C. R. Matthews b Prabhakar	31	– c Tendulkar b Prabhakar	18
M. W. Pringle retired hurt	3	– absent injured	
A. A. Donald not out	14	– (10) not out	7
L-b 10, w 4, n-b 9	23	B 1, l-b 14, w 1, n-b 7	23
	292		**252**

1/10 (2) 2/11 (1) 3/11 (4) 4/26 (3) 5/73 (6)   1/73 (1) 2/108 (2) 3/138 (4)
6/158 (5) 7/186 (8) 8/251 (9) 9/292 (7)   4/170 (3) 5/194 (6) 6/199 (5)
   7/209 (8) 8/239 (7) 9/252 (9)

In the first innings M. W. Pringle retired hurt at 261.

Bowling: *First Innings*—Kapil Dev 25-4-62-1; Prabhakar 29-3-90-4; Srinath 26.5-6-60-2; Kumble 26-8-60-2; Shastri 4-0-10-0. *Second Innings*—Kapil Dev 24-6-50-0; Prabhakar 23.2-3-74-1; Srinath 26-2-58-1; Kumble 44-22-53-6; Tendulkar 1-0-2-0.

India

R. J. Shastri c Wessels b Matthews	7	– b Matthews	23
A. D. Jadeja lbw b McMillan	14	– c Wessels b Donald	43
S. V. Manjrekar b McMillan	7	– (5) not out	32
S. R. Tendulkar b Hudson b Cronje	111	– lbw b Donald	1
*M. Azharuddin c Wessels b Matthews	9	– (3) c Richardson b Matthews	1
P. K. Amre lbw b McMillan	7	– not out	35
M. Prabhakar c Richardson b Donald	2		
Kapil Dev c McMillan b Donald	25		
†K. S. More c Richardson b McMillan	10		
A. Kumble not out	21		
J. Srinath c Richardson b Donald	5		
L-b 4, w 4, n-b 1	9	B 2, l-b 2, n-b 2	6
	227	(4 wkts)	**141**

1/27 (1) 2/27 (2) 3/44 (3) 4/77 (5)   1/68 (2) 2/70 (3)
5/124 (6) 6/127 (7) 7/155 (8) 8/174 (9)   3/71 (1) 4/73 (4)
9/212 (4) 10/227 (11)

Bowling: *First Innings*—Donald 31-9-78-3; McMillan 29-11-74-4; Matthews 29-13-41-2; Cronje 17-10-22-1; Kirsten 2-0-8-0. *Second Innings*—Donald 20-6-43-2; McMillan 21-6-34-0; Matthews 20-10-23-2; Cronje 18-7-32-0; Kirsten 3-1-5-0.

Umpires: S. A. Bucknor (West Indies), S. B. Lambson and C. J. Mitchley.
Referee: C. H. Lloyd (West Indies).

†At Pietermaritzburg, December 4 (day/night). Indians won by six wickets. Toss: UCBSA President's XI. UCBSA President's XI 196 for eight (50 overs) (G. Kirsten 100); Indians 199 for four (47.3 overs) (W. V. Raman 47, M. Azharuddin 69 not out, S. R. Tendulkar 34).

After the crowd invaded the pitch, mistakenly believing the Indians had won at 195 for four, the President's XI captain, Peter Rawson, deliberately bowled a ball which went for four byes so that the players could escape.

†SOUTH AFRICA v INDIA

First One-day International

At Cape Town, December 7 (day/night). South Africa won by six wickets. Toss: India. International debuts: D. J. Callaghan, P. S. de Villiers.

A virtuoso performance by Cronje ensured that South Africa won their first home limited-overs international. His medium pace brought him five for 32 as India failed to build on a good start provided by Jadeja and Raman. Cronje later completed the victory, with three balls to spare, by hitting a six over mid-wicket. South Africa had been pegged back by steady bowling and reached the last two overs still needing 16. Earlier they owed much to Wessels and Kirsten, who both survived chances, though Wessels missed his fifty when he became the first batsman in a one-day international to be ruled out by the video replay.

Man of the Match: W. J. Cronje.

India

A. D. Jadeja c Kirsten b Cronje	48	†K. S. More c Kirsten b Donald		4
W. V. Raman b Cronje	47	A. Kumble not out		3
*M. Azharuddin c Richardson b Donald	9	J. Srinath run out		0
S. R. Tendulkar b McMillan	15	L-b 5, n-b 1		6
S. V. Manjrekar c Matthews b Cronje	13			
P. K. Amre c Hudson b Cronje	4	1/92 2/103 3/109	(50 overs)	184
Kapil Dev c Cronje b McMillan	27	4/133 5/140 6/140		
M. Prabhakar c Wessels b Cronje	8	7/153 8/158 9/184		

Bowling: Donald 10-2-32-2; de Villiers 7-2-24-0; Matthews 10-0-38-0; McMillan 10-0-42-2; Callaghan 3-0-11-0; Cronje 10-0-32-5.

South Africa

*K. C. Wessels run out	43	W. J. Cronje not out		12
A. C. Hudson c Prabhakar b Tendulkar	33	B 4, l-b 5, w 1, n-b 1		11
P. N. Kirsten c Raman b Prabhakar	56			
J. N. Rhodes c Tendulkar b Srinath	13	1/56 2/108	(4 wkts, 49.3 overs)	185
D. J. Callaghan not out	17	3/140 4/168		

B. M. McMillan, †D. J. Richardson, C. R. Matthews, A. A. Donald and P. S. de Villiers did not bat.

Bowling: Kapil Dev 10-1-43-0; Prabhakar 9.3-1-36-1; Tendulkar 10-1-25-1; Srinath 10-2-34-1; Kumble 10-0-38-0.

Umpires: S. B. Lambson and K. E. Liebenberg.

†SOUTH AFRICA v INDIA

Second One-day International

At Port Elizabeth, December 9 (day/night). South Africa won by six wickets. Toss: India.

A straightforward win by South Africa will be remembered less than the controversy which ensued when Kapil Dev ran out Kirsten for backing up before he bowled the ball. Kapil did not warn the batsman, having done so three times previously on the tour. Kirsten reacted angrily before walking off. Later in the same over Wessels appeared to collide with

Kapil as he turned for a second run. India lodged a complaint that Wessels had hit him on the shins with his bat. They also claimed that Kirsten had shown dissent and incited the crowd. Clive Lloyd, the match referee, announced the next day that Wessels had admitted his bat had come into contact with Kapil but had said it was unintentional. Lloyd had not seen the incident and, as the television cameras had been following the ball, he said the truth could not be established. Kirsten was fined 50 per cent of his match fee for unacceptable conduct. On a slow pitch India recovered from 84 for seven to reach 147, but they were always contained by tight South African out-cricket; McMillan took four wickets, held a good slip catch and was responsible for a run-out. South Africa, too, began slowly and were 70 for four before Callaghan and Cronje settled in.

Man of the Match: B. M. McMillan.

India

A. D. Jadeja c McMillan b Schultz	5	†K. S. More b McMillan		32
W. V. Raman b Matthews	33	A. Kumble b McMillan		7
*M. Azharuddin run out	5	J. Srinath not out		1
S. R. Tendulkar c Richardson				
b Callaghan	10	L-b 3, n-b 2		5
S. V. Manjrekar run out	17			
P. K. Amre run out	30	1/8 2/40 3/48	(49.4 overs)	147
Kapil Dev c Rhodes b McMillan	1	4/65 5/81 6/82		
M. Prabhakar c Richardson b McMillan	1	7/84 8/118 9/144		

Bowling: Donald 10-4-26-0; Schultz 9-1-35-1; Matthews 10-4-20-1; McMillan 9.4-0-32-4; Cronje 6-0-18-0; Callaghan 5-0-13-1.

South Africa

A. C. Hudson b Kapil Dev	5	W. J. Cronje not out		38
*K. C. Wessels c Jadeja b Prabhakar	30	B 2, l-b 4, w 3, n-b 3		12
P. N. Kirsten run out	5			
J. N. Rhodes lbw b Srinath	13	1/8 2/20	(4 wkts, 46.4 overs)	148
D. J. Callaghan not out	45	3/46 4/70		

B. M. McMillan, †D. J. Richardson, C. R. Matthews, A. A. Donald and B. N. Schultz did not bat.

Bowling: Kapil Dev 9-2-19-1; Prabhakar 8-0-30-1; Kumble 10-1-22-0; Srinath 10-1-31-1; Tendulkar 5-1-18-0; Jadeja 4.4-1-22-0.

Umpires: R. E. Koertzen and C. J. Mitchley.

†SOUTH AFRICA v INDIA

Third One-day International

At Verwoerdburg, December 11 (day/night). India won by four wickets. Toss: India.

A dominant and entertaining hundred by the left-hander Raman sealed India's victory on a hard, fast pitch, which suited both their strokemakers and spinners. India reached a target of 215 with five balls to spare; Shastri hit with good judgment after Raman was sixth out, and further justified his recall with the ball, bowling Kirsten for 19. Raman's first century for India included only one chance, at 106, and was full of orthodox driving and assured hitting on the leg side. He shared timely stands with Azharuddin and Tendulkar. South Africa had been given a good platform by Hudson and Wessels, but lost momentum against Kumble and Shastri.

Man of the Match: W. V. Raman.

South Africa

*K. C. Wessels b Kumble	34	B. M. McMillan not out		10
A. C. Hudson run out	87			
P. N. Kirsten b Shastri	19	L-b 7, w 1, n-b 6		14
J. N. Rhodes run out	18			—
D. J. Callaghan not out	32	1/92 2/124 3/163	(5 wkts, 50 overs)	214
W. J. Cronje b Kumble	0	4/180 5/181		

†D. J. Richardson, C. R. Matthews, A. A. Donald and P. S. de Villiers did not bat.

Bowling: Kapil Dev 5-1-19-0; Prabhakar 9-1-31-0; Srinath 9-0-38-0; Tendulkar 2-0-16-0; Jadeja 8-0-38-0; Kumble 10-0-29-2; Shastri 7-1-36-1.

India

A. D. Jadeja c Richardson b Matthews	20	R. J. Shastri not out		27
W. V. Raman c McMillan b Donald	113	†K. S. More not out		5
P. K. Amre c Donald b Cronje	1			
*M. Azharuddin b Matthews	18	L-b 1, w 4, n-b 3		8
S. R. Tendulkar c Richardson				—
b Matthews	22	1/56 2/72 3/123	(6 wkts, 49.1 overs)	215
Kapil Dev b de Villiers	1	4/168 5/171 6/194		

M. Prabhakar, A. Kumble and J. Srinath did not bat.

Bowling: Donald 10-1-45-1; de Villiers 10-1-33-1; Matthews 10-0-56-3; McMillan 9.1-0-36-0; Callaghan 3-0-13-0; Cronje 7-0-31-1.

Umpires: W. Diedricks and S. B. Lambson.

†SOUTH AFRICA v INDIA

Fourth One-day International

At Johannesburg, December 13 (day/night). South Africa won by six wickets. Toss: South Africa.

Tight bowling and fielding restricted India to 161, a total they could never defend, in the first day/night match staged in South Africa on a Sunday. It was hastily rescheduled when rain prevented play the previous day. There was no provision for this in the tour playing conditions, but the 32,000 tickets had long been sold and television coverage arranged. India's progress was always too slow on a soaked field and only Azharuddin made a sizable contribution. South Africa also took their time before Rhodes applied a spur and he finished the match with a six over long-off. Television's omnipotence was further demonstrated when the Indian fielders successfully appealed for Callaghan's run-out after watching the replay on the giant screen.

Man of the Match: J. N. Rhodes.

India

A. D. Jadeja lbw b Callaghan	18	†K. S. More run out		2
W. V. Raman b Donald	0	M. Prabhakar not out		5
P. K. Amre lbw b Donald	2	A. Kumble not out		7
*M. Azharuddin c Richardson				
b Matthews	49	B 1, l-b 5, w 11, n-b 2		19
S. R. Tendulkar c McMillan b Donald	21			—
R. J. Shastri c McMillan b de Villiers	17	1/9 2/12 3/61	(9 wkts, 50 overs)	161
Kapil Dev c Richardson b Matthews	18	4/107 5/108 6/136		
J. Srinath c Rhodes b McMillan	3	7/143 8/149 9/149		

Bowling: Donald 10-0-27-3; de Villiers 10-2-24-1; McMillan 10-0-39-1; Matthews 10-1-33-2; Callaghan 5-0-17-1; Cronje 5-0-15-0.

South Africa

A. C. Hudson c Azharuddin b Kumble .	22
*K. C. Wessels c Jadeja b Srinath	45
P. N. Kirsten lbw b Srinath	21
J. N. Rhodes not out	42
D. J. Callaghan run out	12

W. J. Cronje not out	11
L-b 9, w 2, n-b 1	12
1/47 2/88	(4 wkts, 48.3 overs) 165
3/95 4/133	

B. M. McMillan, †D. J. Richardson, C. R. Matthews, P. S. de Villiers and A. A. Donald did not bat.

Bowling: Kapil Dev 9-0-23-0; Prabhakar 8-1-24-0; Tendulkar 3-0-4-0; Kumble 9-1-33-1; Shastri 10-1-33-0; Srinath 9.3-1-39-2.

Umpires: K. E. Liebenberg and C. J. Mitchley.

†SOUTH AFRICA v INDIA

Fifth One-day International

At Bloemfontein, December 15 (day/night). South Africa won by eight wickets. Toss: South Africa. International debut: V. S. Yadav.

Hudson scored his country's first hundred in a limited-overs international as South Africa gained a decisive 4-1 lead in the series. Needing 208, they received a good start from Wessels and Hudson, who put on 125 in 33 overs – a stand which was interrupted for 15 minutes when the floodlights lost some power. Hudson always scored freely on the front and back foot before he was caught in the covers with only four runs required. He faced 147 balls and hit a six and eight fours. India had again been pinned down by accurate bowling before Azharuddin and Shastri accelerated in the last six overs. Unruly crowd behaviour marred the match with several pitch invasions as players reached milestones.

Man of the Match: A. C. Hudson.

India

A. D. Jadeja c McMillan b Donald	9
W. V. Raman c McMillan b Matthews .	16
M. Prabhakar run out	36
*M. Azharuddin not out	86
S. R. Tendulkar b de Villiers	32

R. J. Shastri not out	21
B 1, l-b 3, w 1, n-b 2	7
1/17 2/47	(4 wkts, 50 overs) 207
3/88 4/156	

Kapil Dev, P. K. Amre, †V. S. Yadav, A. Kumble and J. Srinath did not bat.

Bowling: Donald 10-2-36-1; de Villiers 10-0-29-1; Matthews 10-1-37-1; McMillan 10-0-59-0; Cronje 6-0-20-0; Callaghan 4-0-22-0.

South Africa

*K. C. Wessels c McMillan b Kumble	55
A. C. Hudson c Azharuddin b Srinath .	108
P. N. Kirsten not out	35
J. N. Rhodes not out	0
L-b 5, w 2, n-b 3	10

1/125 2/204   (2 wkts, 47.2 overs) 208

W. J. Cronje, D. J. Callaghan, B. M. McMillan, C. R. Matthews, †D. J. Richardson, A. A. Donald and P. S. de Villiers did not bat.

Bowling: Kapil Dev 9-1-35-0; Prabhakar 10-0-35-0; Srinath 9-0-43-1; Kumble 10-0-34-1; Shastri 5-0-25-0; Tendulkar 4-0-27-0; Amre 0.2-0-4-0.

Umpires: R. E. Koertzen and S. B. Lambson.

†SOUTH AFRICA v INDIA

Sixth One-day International

At Durban, December 17 (day/night). South Africa won by 39 runs. Toss: India.

For the first time in the series the team winning the toss and batting second failed to gain victory. Though Wessels and Kirsten added 93 in 23 overs for the second wicket, South Africa were unable to keep the initiative for long against a steady attack. Kapil Dev, in particular, bowled with exemplary control. Later, Donald and de Villiers were equally accurate and India were seldom allowed any leeway. The visitors required 217 but again failed to do themselves justice; only Azharuddin and Kapil Dev hinted India might mount a challenge, and Azharuddin fell victim to a spectacular catch by de Villiers.

Man of the Match: Kapil Dev.

South Africa

A. C. Hudson c Yadav b Kapil Dev	15	M. W. Pringle run out	9
*K. C. Wessels c Manjrekar		C. R. Matthews not out	1
b Prabhakar	78		
P. N. Kirsten c Manjrekar b Shastri	44	B 2, l-b 5, n-b 1	8
J. N. Rhodes c Shastri b Kapil Dev	16		
D. J. Callaghan st Yadav b Kumble	8	1/28 2/121 3/157 (8 wkts, 50 overs)	216
W. J. Cronje b Kapil Dev	25	4/162 5/173 6/198	
†D. J. Richardson run out	12	7/215 8/216	

P. S. de Villiers and A. A. Donald did not bat.

Bowling: Prabhakar 10-1-54-1; Kapil Dev 10-4-23-3; Raju 10-1-45-0; Sharma 4-0-18-0; Kumble 10-1-33-1; Shastri 6-0-36-1.

India

M. Prabhakar c Richardson b Matthews	21	Chetan Sharma c Rhodes b de Villiers	15
A. D. Jadeja c Richardson b Pringle	12	A. Kumble run out	0
S. V. Manjrekar run out	10	S. L. V. Raju not out	3
*M. Azharuddin c de Villiers b Cronje	41	B 1, l-b 4, w 2, n-b 7	14
S. R. Tendulkar c Cronje b Pringle	23		
Kapil Dev c Richardson b Donald	30	1/40 2/42 3/65 (47.5 overs)	177
R. J. Shastri c Kirsten b Pringle	5	4/110 5/127 6/144	
†V. S. Yadav b Matthews		7/153 8/172 9/173	

Bowling: Donald 9-3-18-1; de Villiers 8.5-3-22-1; Matthews 10-0-40-2; Pringle 10-0-51-3; Callaghan 4-0-21-0; Cronje 6-1-20-1.

Umpires: W. Diedricks and K. E. Liebenberg.

†SOUTH AFRICA v INDIA

Seventh One-day International

At East London, December 19 (day/night). India won by five wickets. Toss: India.

Positive strokeplay by Amre and Yadav gave India success, though it was too late to affect the series, which South Africa won 5-2. Chasing 204, India began shakily and were 80 for four before Kapil Dev helped Amre add 50 for the fifth wicket. Yadav then joined Amre and shared an unfinished stand of 74 in ten overs. In the final stages, South Africa missed McMillan: he had twisted an ankle soon after he started bowling, and decided to complete his quota unchanged before retiring. His team's innings was slowed by Kapil and the spinners, though Wessels became the only batsman on either side to pass 300 runs in the series, and Cronje later hit freely.

Man of the Match: P. K. Amre.   *Man of the Series:* K. C. Wessels.

South Africa

*K. C. Wessels c Tendulkar b Raju	57	†D. J. Richardson b Prabhakar		0
A. C. Hudson lbw b Prabhakar	8	C. R. Matthews run out		1
P. N. Kirsten c Banerjee b Raju	30	L-b 9, w 1, n-b 2		12
J. N. Rhodes c Kumble b Prabhakar	37			
D. J. Callaghan c Yadav b Raju	24	1/21 2/86 3/108	(8 wkts, 50 overs)	203
W. J. Cronje c Manjrekar b Kapil Dev	55	4/108 5/199 6/200		
B. M. McMillan not out	3	7/201 8/203		

A. A. Donald and P. S. de Villiers did not bat.

Bowling: Prabhakar 10-1-43-3; Kapil Dev 10-4-27-1; Sharma 8-0-34-0; Banerjee 3-0-20-0; Raju 10-0-37-3; Kumble 9-0-33-0.

India

M. Prabhakar b Donald	12	Kapil Dev lbw b Matthews		17
S. V. Manjrekar lbw b McMillan	6	†V. S. Yadav not out		34
S. R. Tendulkar c Richardson		L-b 4, w 1, n-b 1		6
b Matthews	21			
*M. Azharuddin run out	24	1/16 2/39 3/43	(5 wkts, 47.2 overs)	204
P. K. Amre not out	84	4/80 5/130		

Chetan Sharma, S. T. Banerjee, S. L. V. Raju and A. Kumble did not bat.

Bowling: Donald 10-0-49-1; de Villiers 8.2-3-26-0; McMillan 10-1-38-1; Matthews 10-2-44-2; Callaghan 5-0-21-0; Cronje 4-0-22-0.

Umpires: R. E. Koertzen and C. J. Mitchley.

SOUTH AFRICAN STUDENTS XI v INDIANS

At East London, December 21, 22, 23. Drawn. Toss: South African Students XI.

Tendulkar made a sound hundred in four and a half hours, but otherwise the Indian batsmen failed to take the chance of useful practice against a combined XI from South African Universities, Colleges and Techikons. The touring team were unable to force the victory which seemed probable as Raju's left-arm spin earned him nine wickets in the match. For the students, Johnson, a left-hander, batted solidly and the medium-fast Handman worked hard. Abrahams had a splendid first-class debut. He played two substantial undefeated innings and bowled his off-spin sturdily.

Close of play: First day, Indians 6-0 (R. J. Shastri 4*, W. V. Raman 0*); Second day, Indians 273-8 (S. L. V. Raju 9*).

South African Students XI

*M. C. Venter c More b Raju	6	– c Manjrekar b Srinath		9
P. H. Barnard lbw b Srinath	3	– b Raju		32
N. C. Johnson b Srinath	61	– c sub (V. S. Yadav) b Raju		16
S. Pope c Azharuddin b Raju	0	– c Amre b Raju		5
J. Payn lbw b Sharma	2	– b Raju		4
†E. L. R. Stewart b Raju	11	– c Raman b Raju		31
D. R. Laing c and b Shastri	21	– lbw b Tendulkar		19
R. E. Veenstra c and b Shastri	0	– c Raman b Tendulkar		1
S. Abrahams not out	35	– not out		48
M. W. Handman c Sharma b Raju	11	– run out		11
A. Huckle c and b Tendulkar	5			
L-b 5, w 2, n-b 12	19	L-b 10, n-b 3		13
1/6 2/20 3/20 4/25 5/55	174	1/38 2/46 3/52	(9 wkts)	207
6/107 7/109 8/133 9/164		4/85 5/98 6/135		
		7/142 8/155 9/207		

Bowling: *First Innings*—Banerjee 12-3-23-0; Srinath 13-2-28-2; Raju 33-13-63-4; Sharma 11-2-25-1; Shastri 16-2-21-2; Tendulkar 3.5-1-9-1. *Second Innings*—Srinath 12.4-3-14-1; Sharma 7-0-32-0; Shastri 10-8-5-0; Raju 35-11-68-5; Tendulkar 22-5-64-2; Azharuddin 1-0-4-0; Amre 1-0-10-0.

Indians

R. J. Shastri c Barnard b Huckle	26		S. L. V. Raju not out	9
W. V. Raman c Stewart b Handman	15		J. Srinath lbw b Handman	5
S. V. Manjrekar c Stewart b Handman	43			
S. R. Tendulkar c Abrahams b Handman	131		L-b 3, w 1, n-b 5	9
*M. Azharuddin run out	0			
P. K. Amre c Laing b Huckle	30		1/29 2/53 3/162 (8 wkts dec.)	273
†K. S. More lbw b Laing	5		4/163 5/216 6/239	
			7/267 8/273	

Chetan Sharma and S. T. Banerjee did not bat.

Bowling: Veenstra 7-2-17-0; Handman 21-7-59-4; Huckle 19-1-94-2; Laing 23-7-63-1; Abrahams 22-4-37-0.

Umpires: R. E. Koertzen and C. J. Mitchley.

SOUTH AFRICA v INDIA

Third Test Match

At Port Elizabeth, December 26, 27, 28, 29. South Africa won by nine wickets. Toss: South Africa.

Hostile fast bowling by Donald, who took 12 wickets, and a solid century by Cronje were the decisive performances as South Africa completed victory with a day to spare. It was their first Test win since they were readmitted to ICC; their last had been over Australia on the same ground in March 1970. Donald's figures were the fourth-best for South Africa, and Richardson was the first South African wicket-keeper to take nine catches in a Test. A flamboyant hundred by Kapil Dev, coming in when India were 27 for five in their second innings, prolonged the game, but otherwise India were badly let down by their batsmen. They were also handicapped by a knee injury to Shastri, who was able to bowl only two overs. Prabhakar was fined ten per cent of his match fee, about £20, for dissent on the fourth day when he was given out. Mike Smith, the match referee, had decided against taking unilateral action the previous day when two other apparent cases of dissent by Indians went unreported by the umpires.

South Africa never lost the initiative after taking eight wickets on the opening day, when Wessels surprised most people by asking India to bat in good conditions. Donald extracted plenty of life from a slow pitch, but several Indians got out playing loose strokes. An exception was Azharuddin who, though dropped behind when eight, went on to bat confidently until he fell to a leg-side catch, which he seemed to think had come off his shirt. It was his only first-class fifty of the tour. South Africa batted very slowly against marathon stints from the spinners Kumble and Raju. Wessels was out in the second over but Hudson and Cronje, promoted to No. 3, shared the first three-figure stand for South Africa in the series. Cronje's concentration and resolve never faltered. He faced 411 balls before he was last out after eight and threequarter hours.

Any satisfaction India felt at restricting their deficit to 63 quickly evaporated as the first six batsmen were out for single-figure scores in 21 overs before Kapil checked the collapse. Next morning, with commendable support from the tail, he punished the bowling in a thrilling exhibition of classical driving and forceful leg-side strokes. Despite an injured right hand Kapil claimed 96 of the 144 India added to their overnight 71 for six before he was caught at slip. In all he scored 129, his eighth Test hundred, out of 188 in 177 balls, less than half the number faced by Cronje. Assertive strokeplay by Wessels steered South Africa to a target of 153 with seven minutes left of the fourth day.

Man of the Match: A. A. Donald.

Close of play: First day, India 197-8 (K. S. More 15*, A. Kumble 5*); Second day, South Africa 163-3 (W. J. Cronje 75*, B. M. McMillan 19*); Third day, India 71-6 (Kapil Dev 33*, M. Prabhakar 10*).

India

R. J. Shastri c Henry b McMillan	10 – c Richardson b McMillan	5
W. V. Raman c Richardson b Donald	21 – b Donald	0
S. V. Manjrekar c Henry b McMillan	23 – lbw b Donald	6
S. R. Tendulkar c Richardson b Donald	6 – c Richardson b Schultz	0
*M. Azharuddin c Richardson b Donald	60 – c Wessels b Donald	7
P. K. Amre c McMillan b Donald	11 – c Richardson b Schultz	7
Kapil Dev c Kirsten b McMillan	12 – c McMillan b Donald	129
M. Prabhakar c McMillan b Matthews	11 – b Donald	17
†K. S. More b McMillan	20 – b Donald	17
A. Kumble c McMillan b Schultz	14 – c Richardson b Donald	17
S. L. V. Raju not out	0 – not out	2
L-b 13, w 4, n-b 7	24 L-b 4, w 1, n-b 3	8
	212	**215**

1/43 (1) 2/49 (2) 3/59 (4) 4/98 (3)   1/1 (2) 2/10 (3) 3/11 (4) 4/20 (5)
5/143 (6) 6/152 (5) 7/160 (7) 8/185 (8)   5/27 (6) 6/31 (1) 7/88 (8)
9/208 (9) 10/212 (10)   8/120 (9) 9/197 (10) 10/215 (7)

Bowling: *First Innings*—Donald 27-11-55-5; Schultz 20.5-4-39-1; McMillan 20-9-41-3; Matthews 17-7-34-1; Henry 11-2-30-0. *Second Innings*—Donald 28-4-84-7; Schultz 16-5-37-2; McMillan 12-2-30-1; Matthews 9-1-43-0; Henry 8-2-17-0.

South Africa

A. C. Hudson c Raju	52 – (2) c Azharuddin b Tendulkar	33
*K. C. Wessels b Prabhakar	0 – (1) not out	95
W. J. Cronje b Kumble	135 – not out	16
P. N. Kirsten c More b Raju	0	
B. M. McMillan lbw b Raju	25	
J. N. Rhodes c Prabhakar b Kumble	2	
†D. J. Richardson run out	1	
O. Henry lbw b Kapil Dev	16	
C. R. Matthews c Azharuddin b Kapil Dev	17	
A. A. Donald b Kumble	6	
B. N. Schultz not out	0	
B 2, l-b 13, n-b 6	21 B 8, l-b 3	11
	275 1/98 (2)	**(1 wkt) 155**

1/0 (2) 2/117 (1) 3/117 (4) 4/171 (5)
5/182 (6) 6/185 (7) 7/215 (8) 8/259 (9)
9/274 (10) 10/275 (3)

Bowling: *First Innings*—Kapil Dev 24-6-45-2; Prabhakar 15-3-57-1; Kumble 50.3-16-81-3; Raju 46-15-73-3; Tendulkar 1-1-0-0; Shastri 2-1-4-0. *Second Innings*—Kapil Dev 5-1-9-0; Prabhakar 5-2-7-0; Raju 18-5-50-0; Kumble 20-5-65-0; Tendulkar 3-0-9-1; Azharuddin 0.1-0-4-0.

Umpires: W. Diedricks, R. E. Koertzen and D. R. Shepherd (England).
Referee: M. J. K. Smith (England).

SOUTH AFRICA v INDIA

Fourth Test Match

At Cape Town, January 2, 3, 4, 5, 6. Drawn. Toss: South Africa. Test debut: D. J. Cullinan.

A slow-scoring series reached its nadir as the teams averaged 1.83 runs an over in a match which at times came close to being a travesty. South Africa clinched the series 1-0 by drawing and this was clearly their solitary ambition in spite of positive pre-match statements; the win money for drawn Tests was being added to the series-winners' pool, which gave South Africa an incentive to be negative. However, India batted even more slowly, their sights seemingly set only on a first-innings lead. They fell short by 84 runs after ten and a quarter hours of drudgery. A pitch lacking pace and bounce was another guilty party.

South Africa occupied the crease for most of the first two days as they compiled the first total of 300 in the series. A shaky start was partially redeemed by Rhodes and Cullinan, who added 99 in 40 overs for the fifth wicket. The innings meandered even more on the second day: McMillan, who was dropped twice, was in 69 overs for 52.

India's innings crawled along on the third day; hourly run-rates of 31, 21, 30, 18, 22 and 26 brought 148 runs in a six-hour day. Their most substantial stand, 85 in 58 overs, came from Manjrekar and Prabhakar. Manjrekar was two when he swept a ball from Henry into the grille of Hudson's helmet at short leg, where it was no longer in play under Law 23. Prabhakar batted nearly five and a quarter hours for 62.

There were two bursts of wickets, interrupted by a livelier stand between Tendulkar and Kapil Dev, but it was too late to help anyone. Srinath dismissed Hudson and Cronje before the close of the fourth day and contributed another fiery spell on the last day, but South Africa plodded on again, extracting only 71 runs from 59 overs before tea. Wessels made a token declaration 20 minutes after tea and the match was given up as early as possible. During the drinks break on the third morning, cricket and ANC officials had joined the players on the field to mark the death of Dr Danie Craven, the president of the South African Rugby Union.

Man of the Match: J. Srinath.   *Man of the Series:* A. A. Donald.

Close of play: First day, South Africa 189-5 (J. N. Rhodes 61*, B. M. McMillan 4*); Second day, India 13-0 (A. D. Jadeja 4*, M. Prabhakar 7*); Third day, India 161-5 (S. R. Tendulkar 9*, S. L. V. Raju 2*); Fourth day, South Africa 48-2 (K. C. Wessels 29*, P. N. Kirsten 7*).

South Africa

A. C. Hudson c and b Srinath	19	– (2) c More b Srinath	11
*K. C. Wessels b Prabhakar	0	– (1) c and b Srinath	34
W. J. Cronje c Manjrekar b Kumble	33	– c More b Srinath	0
P. N. Kirsten c More b Kapil Dev	13	– c Manjrekar b Kapil Dev	13
D. J. Cullinan c Prabhakar b Raju	46	– c More b Srinath	28
J. N. Rhodes c More b Srinath	86	– c Srinath b Kumble	16
B. M. McMillan c sub (V. S. Yadav) b Kumble	52	– not out	11
†D. J. Richardson c Tendulkar b Kumble	21	– not out	10
O. Henry run out	34		
C. R. Matthews not out	28		
A. A. Donald not out	1		
B 2, l-b 22, w 2, n-b 1	27	L-b 4, n-b 3	7

1/0 (2) 2/28 (1) 3/57 (4) 4/78 (3)   (9 wkts dec.) 360   1/20 (2) 2/28 (3)   (6 wkts dec.) 130
5/177 (5) 6/245 (6) 7/282 (8)   3/61 (4) 4/61 (1)
8/319 (7) 9/345 (9)   5/95 (6) 6/107 (5)

Bowling: *First Innings*—Kapil Dev 29-8-42-1; Prabhakar 23-6-48-1; Raju 47-15-94-1; Srinath 25-6-51-2; Kumble 47-13-101-3. *Second Innings*—Kapil Dev 17-4-29-1; Prabhakar 10-4-19-0; Srinath 27-10-33-4; Kumble 23-11-20-1; Raju 20-8-25-0.

India

A. D. Jadeja c Kirsten b McMillan	19	– not out	20
M. Prabhakar c Wessels b Henry	62	– c Richardson b Matthews	7
S. V. Manjrekar c Hudson b Donald	46	– not out	2
P. K. Amre c McMillan b Donald	6		
S. R. Tendulkar c Hudson b Cronje	73		
*M. Azharuddin c Richardson b McMillan	7		
S. L. V. Raju c Cullinan b Matthews	18		
Kapil Dev c Hudson b Cronje	34		
†K. S. More lbw b Matthews	0		
A. Kumble c Hudson b Matthews	0		
J. Srinath not out	0		
L-b 7, w 3, n-b 1	11		

1/44 (1) 2/129 (3) 3/138 (4) 4/144 (3)   276   1/21 (2)   (1 wkt) 29
5/153 (6) 6/200 (7) 7/275 (8) 8/276 (9)
9/276 (10) 10/276 (5)

Bowling: *First Innings*—Donald 36-13-58-2; McMillan 36-9-76-2; Matthews 28-12-32-3; Cronje 18.4-8-17-2; Henry 33-8-86-1. *Second Innings*—Donald 4-0-7-0; Matthews 6-1-17-1; Cronje 3-3-0-0; Rhodes 1-0-5-0.

Umpires: S. B. Lambson, K. E. Liebenberg and D. R. Shepherd (England).
Referee: M. J. K. Smith (England).

THE NEW ZEALANDERS IN ZIMBABWE AND SRI LANKA, 1992-93

By SRI KRISHNAMURTHI

What began as a confidence-boosting exercise to develop some of New Zealand's emerging players turned into a tour through a chamber of horrors. After their expected successes in Zimbabwe – whose promotion to Test status New Zealand had enthusiastically supported – Martin Crowe's youthful side arrived in Colombo prepared for stiffer competition in a three-Test series. But 36 hours later Sri Lanka lost all its idyllic enchantment.

On November 16 several players were taking breakfast on the balconies of their hotel in Colombo when, less than 50 metres away, Sri Lanka's naval commander, Vice-Admiral Clancy Fernando, and three other naval personnel were assassinated by a suicide bomber from the Tamil separatist movement. The tourists saw the horrific results at first hand. Dismembered bodies were strewn over the blood-stained street; even the balconies and walls of the hotel were stained with human debris. Many of the players went into shock.

New Zealand's previous tour of Sri Lanka, led by Crowe's brother Jeff in 1986-87, was abandoned after a bomb killed over 100 people at the crowded Pettah bus station, which the team had passed at a distance of 150 metres half an hour before. This time, though fewer people died, the incident was much closer. After seeking diplomatic advice, a majority of the tourists voted to leave.

But the chairman of New Zealand Cricket, Peter McDermott, having consulted government officials, flew out to insist that the tour should go on. McDermott was concerned about the cost to his board in tour guarantees and compensation to the Sri Lankan board; the government was concerned about trading relations with Sri Lanka, and particularly about a trade exhibition due to start in Colombo two days later. Despite public promises that there would be no pressure and no recriminations, McDermott was forceful in a three-and-a-half-hour meeting with the players, creating division and acrimony within their ranks. Mark Greatbatch was particularly angry at attempts to make him stay, and returned home with Rod Latham, Dipak Patel, Gavin Larsen and Willie Watson. Coach Warren Lees also left, and Crowe took over his duties. Ken Rutherford, one of those who changed their minds and stayed, warned other countries against touring Sri Lanka, though he later withdrew his remarks under pressure from ICC. The departed players were replaced by 38-year-old John Wright, who thought he had played his last Test cricket, Justin Vaughan, Michael Owens and Grant Bradburn. Vaughan, an English-born doctor who played for Gloucestershire in 1992, made himself useful on the flight over by attending a sick woman. A revised itinerary included two Tests instead of three, reducing the trip by a week. But the players' confidence and will never recovered. After winning all their matches in Zimbabwe apart from the drawn First Test, they lost all in Sri Lanka except the rain-curtailed First Test at Moratuwa and the first of the one-day internationals, washed out when Sri Lanka were in sight of victory. Most humiliating was their first-ever Test defeat by Sri Lanka, whose only previous two Test victories were over India and Pakistan, both in 1985-86.

Back in Zimbabwe, New Zealand had been encouraged by a maiden Test hundred from Latham in the First Test at Bulawayo (Kevin Arnott reciprocated with a century on the final day) and by the steady development of Patel. The Kenyan-born off-spinner, who had played such a major role in their World Cup campaign, took six wickets in an innings in both Tests and spun New Zealand to victory in the Second. Crowe scored his 14th Test century in Harare and his 15th, perhaps his best, in a vain attempt to stave off Sri Lanka's victory in Colombo. Rutherford battled more successfully than most through the Sri Lankan nightmare, scoring a long-overdue second Test hundred, and Wright's unexpected return enabled him to become the first New Zealander to score 5,000 Test runs. For the victorious Sri Lankans, opener Roshan Mahanama batted splendidly, scoring his first two Test centuries in successive innings and another hundred in the third limited-overs game. Former wicket-keeper Hashan Tillekeratne claimed his own place in the record books by equalling the Test record for a fielder of seven catches in a match.

NEW ZEALAND TOURING PARTY

M. D. Crowe (Wellington) (*captain*), A. H. Jones (Wellington) (*vice-captain*), S. B. Doull (Northern Districts), M. J. Greatbatch (Central Districts), C. Z. Harris (Canterbury), B. R. Hartland (Canterbury), M. J. Haslam (Auckland), G. R. Larsen (Wellington), R. T. Latham (Canterbury), D. J. Nash (Northern Districts), A. C. Parore (Auckland), D. N. Patel (Auckland), K. R. Rutherford (Otago), M. L. Su'a (Auckland), W. Watson (Auckland).

Doull and Haslam joined the party to tour Zimbabwe as replacements for C. L. Cairns (Canterbury) and D. K. Morrison (Auckland), who withdrew with injuries before the tour began. C. Pringle (Auckland) was summoned to Sri Lanka after Doull was injured in Zimbabwe. After the bombing outside the tourists' hotel in Colombo, Greatbatch, Larsen, Latham, Patel and Watson returned to New Zealand, to be replaced by G. E. Bradburn (Northern Districts), M. B. Owens (Canterbury), J. T. C. Vaughan (Auckland) and J. G. Wright (Auckland). Coach W. K. Lees also left Sri Lanka after the bomb.

Team manager: L. Dearsley. *Coach*: W. K. Lees.

NEW ZEALAND TOUR RESULTS

Test matches – Played 4: Won 1, Lost 1, Drawn 2.
First-class matches – Played 5: Won 2, Lost 1, Drawn 2.
Wins – Zimbabwe, Zimbabwe B.
Loss – Sri Lanka.
Draws – Zimbabwe, Sri Lanka.
One-day internationals – Played 5: Won 2, Lost 2, No result 1. *Wins* – Zimbabwe (2).
   Losses – Sri Lanka (2). *No result* – Sri Lanka.
Other non first-class matches – Played 3: Won 1, Lost 2. *Win* – Zimbabwe Country Districts.
   Losses – Sri Lankan Board XI (2).

NEW ZEALAND AVERAGES – FIRST-CLASS MATCHES

BATTING

	M	I	NO	R	HS	100s	Avge	Ct/St
M. J. Greatbatch....	3	6	1	392	126*	1	78.40	2
K. R. Rutherford....	5	10	2	415	105	1	51.87	2
R. T. Latham.......	3	6	1	257	119	1	51.40	3
A. H. Jones	5	9	3	297	81*	0	49.50	2

	M	I	NO	R	HS	100s	Avge	Ct/St
M. D. Crowe	4	8	0	386	140	2	48.25	2
J. G. Wright	2	4	0	133	50	0	33.25	0
C. Z. Harris	2	4	1	84	56	0	28.00	1
B. R. Hartland	3	6	0	130	52	0	21.66	3
A. C. Parore	5	6	0	91	60	0	15.16	12/3
M. L. Su'a	5	5	1	47	44	0	11.75	4

Played in three matches: M. J. Haslam 3 (2 ct); D. J. Nash 5, 11*, 4 (3 ct); D. N. Patel 11*, 6, 58* (4 ct). Played in two matches: S. B. Doull 2*, 2; M. B. Owens 0*, 0, 8*; W. Watson 3 (1 ct). Played in one match: G. E. Bradburn 1, 7 (1 ct); C. Pringle 0, 23; J. T. C. Vaughan 17, 0* (1 ct).

* Signifies not out.

BOWLING

	O	M	R	W	BB	5W/i	Avge
S. B. Doull	40	11	90	7	6-37	1	12.85
D. N. Patel	146.1	40	358	20	6-50	3	17.90
M. L. Su'a	135.1	32	327	12	5-85	1	27.25
M. B. Owens	53	11	200	7	4-101	0	28.57
D. J. Nash	84	20	247	5	2-72	0	49.40

Also bowled: G. E. Bradburn 40.4-5-142-3; M. D. Crowe 6-0-25-0; C. Z. Harris 18-5-81-0; M. J. Haslam 85-23-262-3; A. H. Jones 8.4-2-20-1; R. T. Latham 13-4-32-1; C. Pringle 34-8-90-1; J. T. C. Vaughan 14-0-56-0; W. Watson 42-13-85-2.

Note: Matches in this section which were not first-class are signified by a dagger.

†At South Harare Country Club, October 24. New Zealanders won by six wickets. Toss: Zimbabwe Country Districts. Zimbabwe Country Districts 207 for nine (50 overs) (M. H. Dekker 50, R. M. Bentley 53, C. M. Robertson 40; M. L. Su'a four for 20); New Zealanders 210 for four (47.5 overs) (M. J. Greatbatch 59, R. T. Latham 35, A. H. Jones 56 not out, A. C. Parore 34 not out).

ZIMBABWE B v NEW ZEALANDERS

At Old Georgian Sports Club, Harare, October 26, 27, 28. New Zealanders won by eight wickets. Toss: Zimbabwe B.

A whirlwind unbeaten hundred from Greatbatch saw the New Zealanders to an eight-wicket win in their opening first-class fixture. Greatbatch thumped 126, including 22 fours, to warm up for the First Test. Further good news for the tourists came from the off-spinner Patel, who took five wickets in the first innings, and the new seamer Simon Doull, with six for 37 in the second. Waller had chosen to bat, and James and Evans responded well with 115 for the home team's second wicket. Jones, acting-captain while Crowe recovered from a virus, declared 12 behind on the following afternoon, when he was unbeaten on 81, and then bowled Zimbabwe B's top scorer Evans just before the close. The New Zealanders' target was 207, and Greatbatch, supported by Rutherford and Latham, saw them home with 13 overs to spare.

Close of play: First day, New Zealanders 43-0 (B. R. Hartland 26*, M. J. Greatbatch 17*); Second day, Zimbabwe B 105-3 (E. A. Essop-Adam 28*, K. G. Duers 4*).

Zimbabwe B

M. H. Dekker run out	8	– lbw b Doull	0
†W. R. James st Parore b Patel	63	– c Hartland b Doull	4
C. N. Evans lbw b Patel	66	– b Jones	56
E. A. Essop-Adam lbw b Patel	4	– c sub (G. R. Larsen) b Latham	51
*A. C. Waller c and b Patel	4	– (6) c Jones b Doull	1
S. G. Davies lbw b Nash	11	– (7) c Hartland b Haslam	3
S. G. Peall c Nash b Patel	25	– (8) st Parore b Haslam	34
D. H. Brain c Patel b Nash	11	– (9) c Parore b Doull	16
J. A. Rennie not out	27	– (10) c Hartland b Doull	0
K. G. Duers not out	9	– (5) c Parore b Doull	11
H. Hira (did not bat)		– not out	2
B 1, l-b 8, w 2, n-b 7	18	B 8, l-b 4, n-b 4	16

1/20 2/135 3/141 4/147 5/158   (8 wkts dec.) 246   1/1 2/13 3/85 4/125 5/131   194
6/190 7/196 8/207   6/142 7/142 8/176 9/186

Bowling: *First Innings*—Su'a 14-3-50-0; Nash 19-4-72-2; Latham 2-1-1-0; Doull 4-1-16-0; Patel 27-9-54-5; Haslam 17-5-44-0. *Second Innings*—Doull 17-3-37-6; Su'a 4-0-9-0; Latham 8-1-25-1; Nash 11-1-35-0; Haslam 18-4-65-2; Jones 5-1-11-1.

New Zealanders

B. R. Hartland c Hira b Brain	33	– (2) c Essop-Adam b Peall	0
M. J. Greatbatch c Dekker b Brain	23	– (1) not out	126
*A. H. Jones not out	81		
K. R. Rutherford lbw b Brain	4	– (3) lbw b Rennie	34
R. T. Latham c Davies b Duers	28	– (4) not out	37
†A. C. Parore c Waller b Duers	9		
D. J. Nash c Evans b Peall	5		
M. L. Su'a c Duers b Peall	44		
S. B. Doull not out	2		
L-b 2, n-b 3	5	B 5, l-b 3, n-b 3	11

1/51 2/73 3/77 4/119 5/129   (7 wkts dec.) 234   1/6 2/79   (2 wkts) 208
6/151 7/222

M. J. Haslam and D. N. Patel did not bat.

Bowling: *First Innings*—Brain 15-4-68-3; Duers 20-9-43-2; Dekker 3-0-16-0; Peall 21-8-55-2; Hira 5-1-24-0; Rennie 7-2-26-0. *Second Innings*—Brain 3-0-20-0; Peall 25.5-3-86-1; Duers 7-2-16-0; Rennie 4-0-14-1; Hira 8-0-39-0; Davies 4-0-25-0.

Umpires: N. Fleming and R. Tiffin.

†ZIMBABWE v NEW ZEALAND

First One-day International

At Bulawayo, October 31. New Zealand won by 22 runs. Toss: Zimbabwe. International debuts: M. H. Dekker, S. G. Peall; S. B. Doull, D. J. Nash.

New Zealand eventually cantered home in a dreary encounter at the Bulawayo Athletic Club. Asked to bat on a slow, turning pitch, they made heavy going of it. Jones's 68 was his 25th fifty in 64 limited-overs internationals. He was supported by Latham and Crowe, who made 40 in his first match of the tour. A target of 245 from 50 overs was not over-demanding, though Zimbabwe slipped to 34 for three before spluttering into life. Dekker scored 79 on his international debut and it was only after his dismissal that the New Zealanders – who were struggling in the field because of the altitude – could be sure of victory.

New Zealand

M. J. Greatbatch c A. Flower b Brain .	21	D. J. Nash run out	3
R. T. Latham run out	45	S. B. Doull not out	2
A. H. Jones st A. Flower			
b G. W. Flower .	68	B 5, l-b 4, w 4, n-b 2	15
*M. D. Crowe c Dekker b G. W. Flower	40		
K. R. Rutherford not out	35	1/23 2/110 3/175 (7 wkts, 50 overs) 244	
D. N. Patel c Crocker b G. W. Flower .	4	4/192 5/200	
†A. C. Parore c Houghton b Shah	11	6/233 7/236	

G. R. Larsen and W. Watson did not bat.

Bowling: Brain 8–1–46–1; Peall 10–1–32–0; Crocker 3–0–17–0; Shah 9–0–57–1; Traicos 10–0–44–0; G. W. Flower 10–1–39–3.

Zimbabwe

†A. Flower b Patel.................	10	S. G. Peall b Watson...............	1
G. W. Flower c Greatbatch b Watson..	0	D. H. Brain not out...............	16
*D. L. Houghton c Watson b Patel	19	A. J. Traicos not out	7
M. H. Dekker lbw b Doull	79	L-b 8, w 3	11
A. C. Waller st Parore b Patel	23		
C. N. Evans st Parore b Latham	22	1/4 2/29 3/34 (9 wkts, 50 overs) 222	
A. H. Shah run out	25	4/75 5/126 6/163	
G. J. Crocker c Crowe b Doull	3	7/195 8/198 9/200	

Bowling: Doull 10–2–42–2; Watson 8–0–45–2; Patel 10–2–26–3; Larsen 6–0–33–0; Jones 10–0–36–0; Latham 5–0–27–1; Nash 1–0–5–0.

Umpires: K. Kanjee and I. D. Robinson.

ZIMBABWE v NEW ZEALAND

First Test Match

At Bulawayo, November 1, 2, 3, 4, 5. Drawn. Toss: New Zealand. Test debuts: A. H. Shah; S. B. Doull, M. J. Haslam.

Zimbabwe and New Zealand's first Test match ended in a listless draw, with ten hours' play lost as a result of solid rain and inadequate covering. Unusually, the rain was greeted with delight by the spectators; Zimbabwe's terrible drought was a matter of far more concern than the cricket.

The weather wiped out the first morning before play began, making the Bulawayo Athletic Club Test cricket's 69th venue and giving English umpire Dickie Bird his record 49th Test. New Zealand, who gave caps to Doull and left-arm spinner Mark Haslam, chose to bat on a sluggish pitch, and brought up 100 in their 19th over, with Greatbatch striking a blistering fifty from 39 balls. Zimbabwe, already missing their strike bowler, Brandes, lost their veteran off-spinner, Traicos, for the rest of the day when he injured his back after bowling eight overs for only nine runs. It seemed plain that they were already playing for the draw. This aim was assisted by further delay on the second day, after water seeped under the covers, but the stocky Latham nevertheless proceeded to his maiden Test hundred.

With Zimbabwe reluctant to field in damp conditions on the third day an exasperated Crowe was forced to declare when play started in the afternoon and watch his opponents move haltingly to 54 for one from 41 overs by stumps. Off-spinner Patel, who had shared the new ball with Su'a, breathed some life into the fourth day, returning career-best Test figures of six for 113. Zimbabwe were bowled out for 219, 106 behind, with Andy Flower's 81 the only significant contribution.

In a desperate bid to give themselves some chance of victory New Zealand raced to 163 for one by the close. Greatbatch and Latham became the first New Zealand openers to share a century opening stand in each innings of a Test. Next morning Crowe declared, setting Zimbabwe a target of 329 from 73 overs. Zimbabwe made no attempt to respond, preferring to maintain their unbeaten record while Arnott scored his maiden Test century.

Close of play: First day, New Zealand 205-1 (R. T. Latham 86*, A. H. Jones 30*); Second day, New Zealand 325-3 (A. H. Jones 67*, K. R. Rutherford 7*); Third day, Zimbabwe 54-1 (K. J. Arnott 25*, M. G. Burmester 0*); Fourth day, New Zealand 163-1 (M. J. Greatbatch 80*, A. H. Jones 31*).

New Zealand

M. J. Greatbatch c Campbell b Shah	87	– c Houghton b Jarvis	88
R. T. Latham run out	119	– c Houghton b G. W. Flower	48
A. H. Jones not out	67	– retired hurt	39
*M. D. Crowe c Jarvis b Traicos	42	– (5) c A. Flower b Jarvis	6
K. R. Rutherford not out	7	– (7) not out	11
†A. C. Parore (did not bat)		– (4) c Houghton b Jarvis	12
S. B. Doull (did not bat)		– (6) b Traicos	2
D. N. Patel (did not bat)		– not out	11
L-b 3	3	B 1, l-b 3, n-b 1	5

1/116 (1) 2/243 (2) 3/314 (4)   (3 wkts dec.) 325   1/102 (2) 2/181 (1) (5 wkts dec.) 222
3/193 (5) 4/196 (6)
5/204 (4)

M. J. Haslam, M. L. Su'a and W. Watson did not bat.

In the second innings A. H. Jones retired hurt at 175.

Bowling: *First Innings*—Jarvis 26.1-4-87-0; Burmester 14-1-71-0; Shah 14-6-46-1; Traicos 23.1-4-56-1; Crocker 14-1-57-0; Houghton 0.5-0-0-0; G. W. Flower 4-2-5-0. *Second Innings*—Jarvis 11-0-38-3; Shah 7-0-36-0; Crocker 5-0-30-0; Traicos 17-1-82-1; G. W. Flower 8-0-32-1.

Zimbabwe

K. J. Arnott c Crowe b Patel	30	– not out	101
G. W. Flower c Rutherford b Patel	29	– c Latham b Patel	45
M. G. Burmester c Haslam b Patel	0		
A. D. R. Campbell run out	0	– (3) not out	48
A. J. Pycroft b Doull	2		
*D. L. Houghton b Patel	36		
†A. Flower c Haslam b Su'a	81		
A. H. Shah c Parore b Su'a	28		
G. J. Crocker b Patel	1		
A. J. Traicos b Patel	4		
M. P. Jarvis not out	2		
L-b 4, n-b 2	6	L-b 2, w 1	3

1/54 (2) 2/56 (3) 3/59 (4) 4/62 (5)   219   1/92 (2)   (1 wkt) 197
5/64 (1) 6/134 (6) 7/194 (8)
8/213 (9) 9/213 (7) 10/219 (10)

Bowling: *First Innings*—Su'a 9-3-18-2; Patel 40.4-12-113-6; Doull 15-6-29-1; Watson 7-3-10-0; Haslam 21-8-44-0; Jones 1-0-1-0. *Second Innings*—Su'a 6.1-2-9-0; Doull 4-1-8-0; Patel 28-7-60-1; Haslam 19-4-76-0; Latham 3-2-6-0; Watson 7-2-21-0; Crowe 4-0-15-0.

Umpires: H. D. Bird (England), K. Kanjee and I. D. Robinson.
Referee: D. J. McGlew (South Africa).

ZIMBABWE v NEW ZEALAND

Second Test Match

At Harare Sports Club, November 7, 9, 10, 11, 12. New Zealand won by 177 runs. Toss: New Zealand. Test debuts: D. H. Brain; D. J. Nash.

Zimbabwe lost their record as Test cricket's only unbeaten nation in their third match. Panic and despondency – for no apparent reason – combined with a match-winning six for 50 from Patel saw them collapse for 137 on the final day. It was New Zealand's first Test victory in 11 Tests since they beat Australia at Wellington in 1989-90 and their first away from home since they beat India at Bombay in 1988-89.

New Zealand substituted Dion Nash for Doull, who had succumbed to a stress fracture of the back. After Crowe won the toss, he chose to bat and justified his confidence in the pitch's suitability to strokeplay with his 14th Test hundred, taking 96 runs between lunch and tea. In all he scored 140 from 163 balls, striking 17 fours and three sixes, and shared 168 in 36 overs with Rutherford for the fourth wicket. Next day, in the limited-overs international which – unprecedentedly – interrupted the Test, he made 94. Resuming the game on Monday, New Zealand lost their last four wickets for 21 runs; Rutherford complained that playing a one-day match in mid-Test innings was too taxing, both mentally and physically.

Zimbabwe recovered from the early loss of Grant Flower through a 107-run stand between Arnott and Campbell, who made his maiden Test fifty. But a burst of three wickets for no runs in seven balls from Su'a put his team back on course on the rain-shortened third day, on the way to his first five-wicket return in Tests. Houghton declared 52 behind and New Zealand set about building a target. Crowe, now limping with ankle and thigh strains, Rutherford and Patel took them to 262 in five and a quarter hours before asking Zimbabwe to score 315 in 71 overs. At lunch the home team were 25 for two, but disaster struck in the afternoon session as they slumped to 94 for eight. Patel had taken five for 32 and when he dismissed last man Traicos in the evening he improved his Test figures for the third match running. Dickie Bird could also celebrate as he became the first umpire to stand in 50 Tests.

Close of play: First day, New Zealand 314-6 (K. R. Rutherford 72*, D. J. Nash 0*); Second day, Zimbabwe 173-3 (A. J. Pycroft 38*, D. L. Houghton 7*); Third day, Zimbabwe 228-6 (A. Flower 8*, G. J. Crocker 8*); Fourth day, New Zealand 187-4 (K. R. Rutherford 57*, D. N. Patel 16*).

New Zealand

M. J. Greatbatch c A. Flower b Brain	55	– c Brandes b Brain	13
R. T. Latham c A. Flower b Crocker	15	– c Houghton b Brandes	10
A. H. Jones c Pycroft b Brandes	8	– st A. Flower b Traicos	28
*M. D. Crowe c Burmester b Crocker	140	– lbw b Traicos	61
K. R. Rutherford c A. Flower b Traicos	74	– c Arnott b Brandes	89
D. N. Patel c Campbell b Traicos	6	– not out	58
†A. C. Parore run out	2		
D. J. Nash not out	11		
M. L. Su'a c Arnott b Brandes	1		
W. Watson b Brain	3		
M. J. Haslam c A. Flower b Brain	3		
L-b 11, n-b 6	17	L-b 2, w 1	3

1/44 (2) 2/73 (3) 3/131 (4) 4/299 (4)   335   1/21 (2) 2/27 (1)   (5 wkts dec.) 262
5/306 (6) 6/313 (7) 7/321 (5)   3/77 (3) 4/132 (4)
8/327 (9) 9/330 (10) 10/335 (11)   5/262 (5)

Bowling: *First Innings*—Brandes 22–6–49–2; Brain 18–5–49–3; Crocker 15–1–65–2; Burmester 10–2–34–0; Traicos 23–1–82–2; G. W. Flower 6–0–45–0. *Second Innings*—Brandes 19.4–3–59–2; Brain 16–2–52–1; Crocker 7–0–24–0; Traicos 27–8–70–2; G. W. Flower 4–0–11–0; Burmester 9–1–44–0.

Zimbabwe

K. J. Arnott b Watson	68	– c Watson b Nash	10
G. W. Flower lbw b Su'a	5	– c Latham b Su'a	1
A. D. R. Campbell c Su'a b Patel	52	– c Greatbatch b Patel	35
A. J. Pycroft b Su'a	60	– c Latham b Watson	5
*D. L. Houghton c Su'a	21	– c Nash b Patel	2
†A. Flower c Patel b Nash	14	– c Parore b Patel	9
E. A. Brandes c Parore b Su'a	0	– c and b Patel	6
G. J. Crocker b Su'a	12	– c Greatbatch b Haslam	33
D. H. Brain c Su'a b Patel	11	– c Su'a b Patel	17
M. G. Burmester not out	30	– not out	17
A. J. Traicos not out	1	– lbw b Patel	0
L-b 7, n-b 2	9	L-b 2	2

1/7 (2) 2/114 (3) 3/136 (1)   (9 wkts dec.) 283   1/3 (2) 2/15 (1) 3/28 (4)   137
4/210 (4) 5/211 (5) 6/211 (7)   4/34 (5) 5/56 (6) 6/62 (7)
7/239 (8) 8/239 (6) 9/275 (9)   7/71 (3) 8/91 (9)
9/137 (8) 10/137 (11)

Bowling: *First Innings*—Su'a 37–8–85–5; Nash 28–10–59–1; Watson 25–6–51–1; Patel 33–7–81–2. *Second Innings*—Su'a 12–3–30–1; Nash 8–3–19–1; Watson 3–2–3–1; Patel 17.3–5–50–6; Haslam 10.2–2–33–1.

Umpires: H. D. Bird (England), K. Kanjee and I. D. Robinson.
Referee: D. J. McGlew (South Africa).

†ZIMBABWE v NEW ZEALAND

Second One-day International

At Harare Sports Club, November 8. New Zealand won by four wickets. Toss: Zimbabwe. International debuts: E. A. Essop-Adam, U. Ranchod.

For the first time in history a one-day international interrupted a Test match as the Zimbabwe authorities wanted to maximise revenue on the Sunday. New Zealand won it to take the series but it was an acrimonious game: Grant Flower was run out by Patel while backing up at the non-striker's end, after several warnings, and Crowe spoke to umpire Kantilal Kanjee after three run-out appeals were turned down. Zimbabwe's top four made fifties on a superb one-day pitch, with the Flower brothers' opening stand of 124 runs a record for the country in limited-overs internationals. New Zealand's openers countered with 98 before Crowe and Rutherford ensured victory with 130 for the fourth wicket. Crowe, though still affected by his illness, added an 88-ball 94 to his 140 in the Test the previous day.

Zimbabwe

†A. Flower c Parore b Patel	56	E. A. Essop-Adam not out	14
G. W. Flower run out	63	A. H. Shah not out	4
*D. L. Houghton c Greatbatch b Harris	50	L-b 7, w 3, n-b 5	15
M. H. Dekker c Parore b Su'a	55		
C. N. Evans c Latham b Watson	12		
E. A. Brandes b Harris	2	1/124 2/130 3/199 (6 wkts, 50 overs) 271

4/221 5/232 6/262

U. Ranchod, D. H. Brain and A. J. Traicos did not bat.

Bowling: Su'a 10–0–36–1; Patel 10–0–48–1; Watson 9–0–61–1; Larsen 10–0–45–0; Harris 10–0–60–2; Latham 1–0–14–0.

New Zealand

M. J. Greatbatch c A. Flower b Brandes	55	D. N. Patel not out 1
R. T. Latham c Essop-Adam b Ranchod	40	†A. C. Parore not out 3
B. R. Hartland c A. Flower b Brandes	5	
*M. D. Crowe b Brandes	94	L-b 8, w 10, n-b 3 21
K. R. Rutherford c Essop-Adam		
b G. W. Flower	37	1/98 2/113 3/114 (6 wkts, 46.5 overs) 272
C. Z. Harris b Brain	16	4/244 5/266 6/267

G. R. Larsen, M. L. Su'a and W. Watson did not bat.

Bowling: Brain 5–1–27–1; Ranchod 10–1–44–1; Shah 6–0–31–0; Brandes 8.5–0–74–3; Traicos 10–1–50–0; G. W. Flower 7–0–38–1.

Umpires: K. Kanjee and I. D. Robinson.

---

†At Matara, November 23. Sri Lankan Board President's XI won by 17 runs. Toss: New Zealanders. Sri Lankan Board President's XI 181 for seven (45 overs) (M. S. Atapattu 48); New Zealanders 164 for seven (45 overs) (C. Z. Harris 31, G. E. Bradburn 47 not out; R. S. Kalpage three for 24).

---

†At Matara, November 24. Sri Lankan Board President's XI won by one wicket. Toss: New Zealanders. New Zealanders 149 for eight (45 overs) (D. J. Nash 38 not out); Sri Lankan Board President's XI 152 for nine (44.1 overs) (C. Pringle four for 20, G. E. Bradburn three for 25).

SRI LANKA v NEW ZEALAND

First Test Match

At Moratuwa, November 27, 28, 29, December 1, 2. Drawn. Toss: Sri Lanka. Test debuts: C. Z. Harris, M. B. Owens, J. T. C. Vaughan.

A necessarily makeshift New Zealand line-up, playing their first first-class cricket since arriving in Sri Lanka, were relieved to escape with a draw. They had selected three new caps – Chris Harris, son of Test player P. G. Z. Harris, Michael Owens and Justin Vaughan. The last two had flown out to replace the players who had returned home after the shock of the bomb in Colombo. Rutherford had been reluctant to remain in Sri Lanka, but showed great maturity and adaptability in scoring only his second Test century and his first since 1987-88. With Harris, who made fifty on debut, he put on 151, to steer their team out of trouble after Ranatunga asked them to bat and they lost four wickets on a rain-shortened first day. Crowe caused consternation in the Sri Lankan camp when he suggested to umpire Francis that Warnaweera was throwing his off-cutters rather than bowling them. Francis was not swayed, pointing out that Warnaweera had toured India and New Zealand without being called. Soon afterwards Crowe fell to a diving catch as he tried to hit Warnaweera through mid-wicket. But he had more pressing problems when Sri Lanka batted. He admitted that it had been a mistake to omit his spinners, Haslam and Bradburn, and New Zealand's fielding was still short of its best. Crowe himself dropped Mahanama twice, and the Sri Lankan opener went on to his maiden Test century in his 15th match, converting it to 153 before he was run out. Meanwhile de Silva provided the pyrotechnics in a rapid 62.

Ranatunga declared early on the fourth day with a lead of 39. New Zealand battled meticulously to finish on 104 without loss; when 25, Wright, called up to extend his Test career in the crisis after the bomb, became the first New Zealander to score 5,000 Test runs. His opening partner, Hartland, regaining his confidence after being omitted in Zimbabwe, reached his maiden Test fifty. On the last day New Zealand eked out another 91 runs while losing five wickets, their cause assisted by rain which ended play early. Only Rutherford, who hit 53 from 62 balls, including nine fours and two sixes, showed much aggression in keeping Sri Lanka at bay.

Man of the Match: R. S. Mahanama.

Close of play: First day, New Zealand 139-4 (K. R. Rutherford 46*, C. Z. Harris 11*); Second day, Sri Lanka 10-0 (R. S. Mahanama 3*, U. C. Hathurusinghe 0*); Third day, Sri Lanka 299-4 (H. P. Tillekeratne 0*, A. Ranatunga 0*); Fourth day, New Zealand 104-0 (B. R. Hartland 50*, J. G. Wright 38*).

New Zealand

B. R. Hartland c de Silva b Liyanage	3	– lbw b Ramanayake	52
J. G. Wright c Gurusinha b Ramanayake	11	– st Wickremasinghe b Anurasiri	42
A. H. Jones c Mahanama b Liyanage	35	– c Wickremasinghe	
		b Ramanayake	14
*M. D. Crowe c Ranatunga b Warnaweera	19	– c Tillekeratne b Anurasiri	11
K. R. Rutherford c Wickremasinghe			
b Hathurusinghe	105	– lbw b Warnaweera	53
C. Z. Harris b Warnaweera	56	– (7) not out	0
J. T. C. Vaughan b Liyanage	17	– (6) not out	0
†A. C. Parore c Wickremasinghe b Anurasiri	3		
D. J. Nash c Wickremasinghe b Liyanage	4		
M. L. Su'a b Anurasiri	0		
M. B. Owens not out	0		
B 5, l-b 12, w 2, n-b 16	35	L-b 8, w 1, n-b 14	23

1/6 (1) 2/44 (2) 3/77 (3) 4/87 (4) 5/238 (5) 288   1/110 (1) 2/122 (2) (5 wkts) 195
6/265 (6) 7/273 (8) 8/283 (9)   3/136 (4) 4/160 (3)
9/286 (10) 10/288 (7)   5/194 (5)

Bowling: *First Innings*—Ramanayake 23-2-57-1; Liyanage 26.5-6-82-4; Hathurusinghe 8-4-12-1; Anurasiri 34-11-55-2; Warnaweera 34-15-46-2; de Silva 4-2-8-0; Gurusinha 1-0-6-0; Ranatunga 3-2-5-0. *Second Innings*—Ramanayake 17-6-27-2; Liyanage 17-4-48-0; Hathurusinghe 10-6-22-0; Ranatunga 7-2-26-0; Anurasiri 26-11-32-2; Warnaweera 25-15-31-1; Tillekeratne 1-0-1-0.

Sri Lanka

R. S. Mahanama run out	153	C. P. H. Ramanayake not out	10
U. C. Hathurusinghe c Jones b Nash	10		
A. P. Gurusinha c Vaughan b Su'a	43	L-b 7, w 9, n-b 16	32
P. A. de Silva c Nash b Su'a	62		
H. P. Tillekeratne b Owens	1	1/27 (2) 2/164 (3) (6 wkts dec.) 327
*A. Ranatunga c Parore b Owens	3	3/297 (4) 4/299 (1)
†A. G. D. Wickremasinghe not out	13	5/300 (5) 6/309 (6)

D. K. Liyanage, S. D. Anurasiri and K. P. J. Warnaweera did not bat.

Bowling: Su'a 25-6-62-2; Owens 17-3-63-2; Nash 18-2-62-1; Vaughan 14-0-56-0; Harris 15-5-64-0; Jones 1-0-3-0; Crowe 2-0-10-0.

Umpires: K. T. Francis and T. M. Samarasinghe. Referee: S. Venkataraghavan (India).

†SRI LANKA v NEW ZEALAND

First One-day International

At Khettarama Stadium, Colombo, December 4 (day/night). No result. Toss: Sri Lanka.

A downpour allowed New Zealand "to do a Houdini", according to Crowe, after a substandard performance. The match was abandoned when Sri Lanka were 41 for two wickets – both taken by Pringle, at his fiery best – from 10.2 overs and coasting: the original target was 167 from 50 overs, but to achieve a positive result they needed only 67 from 20. Ranatunga was enraged when umpires Francis – who was later replaced for the Second Test – and Manuel called off the game because of a soggy outfield, with Sri Lanka just 26 short. New Zealand were deprived of seam bowler Owens before the start; he lost two teeth in an accident while practising. Their revised line-up, in which Parore was promoted to open with Wright, batted dismally.

New Zealand

†A. C. Parore run out		20
J. G. Wright b G. P. Wickremasinghe		7
A. H. Jones st A. G. D.		
Wickremasinghe b Gurusinha		24
*M. D. Crowe		
c A. G. D. Wickremasinghe		
b G. P. Wickremasinghe		1
K. R. Rutherford c Liyanage b Kalpage		36
C. Z. Harris not out		32
J. T. C. Vaughan b Kalpage		6

G. E. Bradburn b Kalpage		6
D. J. Nash run out		9
M. L. Su'a lbw b Gurusinha		1
C. Pringle not out		3
L-b 8, w 13		21

1/23 2/37 3/39　　　(9 wkts, 50 overs) 166
4/99 5/108 6/124
7/136 8/148 9/155

Bowling: G. P. Wickremasinghe 10–0–39–2; Liyanage 6–0–24–0; Hathurusinghe 10–2–20–0; Anurasiri 5–0–21–0; Kalpage 10–0–29–3; Gurusinha 9–1–25–2.

Sri Lanka

R. S. Mahanama not out		11
U. C. Hathurusinghe c Parore b Pringle		5
A. P. Gurusinha c Harris b Pringle		0
P. A. de Silva not out		13
L-b 2, w 10		12

1/20 2/20　　　(2 wkts, 10.2 overs) 41

*A. Ranatunga, H. P. Tillekeratne, †A. G. D. Wickremasinghe, D. K. Liyanage, R. S. Kalpage, S. D. Anurasiri and G. P. Wickremasinghe did not bat.

Bowling: Pringle 5.2–0–15–2; Su'a 4–0–13–0; Nash 1–0–11–0.

Umpires: K. T. Francis and P. Manuel.

SRI LANKA v NEW ZEALAND

Second Test Match

At Sinhalese Sports Club, Colombo, December 6, 7, 8, 9. Sri Lanka won by nine wickets. Toss: Sri Lanka.

New Zealand's abysmal performance in their first innings enabled Sri Lanka to record a third victory in their 42nd Test, and their first over New Zealand, with four sessions to spare. The star of the Sri Lankan team was Tillekeratne, who had lost the wicket-keeper's job to Gamini Wickremasinghe, but equalled the record of seven field catches in a Test held by G. S. Chappell and Yajurvindra Singh – after making 93, his highest Test score. Mahanama followed up his maiden Test century at Moratuwa with a second in successive innings and the Sri Lankan spinners, Warnaweera, Muralitharan – called up to replace seamer Ramanayake – and Anurasiri, shared 15 wickets in the match.

Ranatunga had opted for first use of a pitch which was beginning to break up and turn by the close of the first day. By then Sri Lanka were already 303 for six, with Mahanama reaching a well-disciplined hundred in 128 balls to provide the platform for Sri Lanka's aspirations. Ranatunga himself contributed 76 and, after Tillekeratne had added 69 for the eighth wicket with Anurasiri, a Sri Lankan Test record, they reached a solid 394. New Zealand were 42 without loss at tea on the second day but lost seven wickets in the final session, four to Warnaweera and two to Muralitharan, with neither Crowe nor Rutherford scoring. Next morning their last three wickets went in 19 balls and New Zealand followed on 292 behind.

Fighting to save his team, Crowe played what he later acknowledged as probably his finest innings. But it did not escape controversy. When 39, Crowe appeared to be caught at silly point but, although umpire Anandappa gave him out, Crowe stood his ground, asking Gurusinha whether it was a fair catch. The fielder could not confirm it, and square-leg umpire Samarasinghe asked Anandappa to rescind his decision. Crowe proceeded to his 15th Test century, from 108 balls, including nine fours and four sixes, and added 159 with Wright for the third wicket. Had it not been for a hamstring injury he might have stayed long enough to save the game. But despite Wright's 50, an attractive 38 from Rutherford and Parore's maiden Test half-century, which helped to keep Sri Lanka out until lunch on the fourth day, New Zealand could set a target of no more than 70. Sri Lanka knocked them off in under 15 overs.

Man of the Match: H. P. Tillekeratne.

Close of play: First day, Sri Lanka 303-6 (H. P. Tillekeratne 43*, D. K. Liyanage 10*); Second day, New Zealand 100-7 (G. E. Bradburn 1*, M. L. Su'a 1*); Third day, New Zealand 277-6 (A. C. Parore 17*, G. E. Bradburn 5*).

Sri Lanka

R. S. Mahanama c Bradburn b Owens	109	– c Parore b Owens 29
U. C. Hathurusinghe c Harris b Owens	27	– not out 23
A. P. Gurusinha st Parore b Bradburn	22	– not out 14
P. A. de Silva c Parore b Pringle	3	
*A. Ranatunga c Parore b Su'a	76	
H. P. Tillekeratne c Parore b Bradburn	93	
†A. G. D. Wickremasinghe c Rutherford b Owens	2	
D. K. Liyanage c Parore b Su'a	16	
S. D. Anurasiri c Su'a b Owens	24	
M. Muralitharan not out	4	
K. P. J. Warnaweera c Crowe b Bradburn	5	
B 3, l-b 4, w 3, n-b 3	13	L-b 2, n-b 2 4

1/102 (2) 2/160 (3) 3/167 (4) 4/182 (1)　　394　　1/36 (1)　　　(1 wkt) 70
5/274 (5) 6/287 (7) 7/316 (8)
8/385 (6) 9/385 (5) 10/394 (11)

Bowling: *First Innings*—Su'a 26-7-50-2; Owens 30-7-101-4; Pringle 32-7-85-1; Bradburn 37.4-4-134-3; Harris 3-0-17-0. *Second Innings*—Owens 6-1-36-1; Pringle 2-1-5-0; Su'a 2-0-14-0; Bradburn 3-1-8-0; Jones 1.4-1-5-0.

New Zealand

B. R. Hartland c Gurusinha b Warnaweera	21	– c Muralitharan b Gurusinha 21
J. G. Wright c Wickremasinghe b Warnaweera	30	– c Mahanama b Muralitharan 50
A. H. Jones c Tillekeratne b Warnaweera	20	– c Tillekeratne b Warnaweera 5
*M. D. Crowe b Muralitharan	0	– c Tillekeratne b Muralitharan ...107
K. R. Rutherford c Tillekeratne b Warnaweera	0	– c sub (S. T. Jayasuriya) b Warnaweera . 38
C. Z. Harris run out	9	– lbw b Anurasiri 19
†A. C. Parore lbw b Muralitharan	5	– c Tillekeratne b Muralitharan .. 60
G. E. Bradburn c Tillekeratne b Liyanage	1	– c Wickremasinghe b Anurasiri .. 7
M. L. Su'a not out	2	– b Muralitharan 0
C. Pringle b Liyanage	0	– c Tillekeratne b Liyanage 23
M. B. Owens c Anurasiri b Muralitharan	0	– not out 8
L-b 4, w 1, n-b 9	14	B 2, l-b 8, n-b 13 23

1/57 (2) 2/60 (1) 3/63 (4) 4/64 (5)　　102　　1/23 (1) 2/30 (3) 3/189 (4)　　361
5/88 (6) 6/97 (3) 7/99 (7)　　　　　　　　4/196 (2) 5/240 (5) 6/261 (6)
8/100 (8) 9/100 (10) 10/102 (11)　　　　　7/285 (8) 8/286 (9)
　　　　　　　　　　　　　　　　　　　　9/317 (10) 10/361 (7)

Bowling: *First Innings*—Liyanage 9-3-9-2; Gurusinha 4-1-15-0; Anurasiri 6-1-13-0; Hathurusinghe 7-3-14-0; Warnaweera 14-3-25-4; Muralitharan 12.1-3-22-3. *Second Innings*—Liyanage 12-3-35-1; Gurusinha 8-1-19-1; Warnaweera 34-4-107-2; Muralitharan 40.5-13-134-4; Anurasiri 22-4-54-2; Hathurusinghe 3-2-2-0.

Umpires: I. Anandappa and T. M. Samarasinghe. Referee: S. Venkataraghavan (India).

†SRI LANKA v NEW ZEALAND

Second One-day International

At P. Saravanamuttu Stadium, Colombo, December 12. Sri Lanka won by eight wickets.
Toss: Sri Lanka.

Crowe pulled out of the last two matches of the tour, leaving Jones to lead a demoralised and injury-stricken side. The acting-captain admitted that the players were starting to think of home and a lifeless performance ended in defeat by eight wickets. Asked to bat, they scrambled an untidy 190 for seven, Hartland top-scoring with 54 and Nash unbeaten after a fighting 40 which included two sixes. Sri Lanka swept home with more than 12 overs to spare. Mahanama's rich form continued, as he struck seven fours and a six in his 84 not out, with de Silva also unbeaten on 43, hitting five fours and two sixes.

Man of the Match: R. S. Mahanama.

New Zealand

B. R. Hartland st A. G. D.			J. T. C. Vaughan c Hathurusinghe		
Wickremasinghe b Jayasuriya .	54		b Jayasuriya .	12
J. G. Wright run out	1		G. E. Bradburn not out	11
*A. H. Jones c Kalpage b Anurasiri . . .	37			
K. R. Rutherford c Mahanama			B 4, l-b 9, n-b 1	14
b Kalpage .	2			
C. Z. Harris c Mahanama b Kalpage . .	2		1/17 2/96 3/100	(7 wkts, 50 overs) 190
†A. C. Parore c Gurusinha b Jayasuriya	17		4/100 5/108	
D. J. Nash not out	40		6/134 7/150	

C. Pringle and M. L. Su'a did not bat.

Bowling: G. P. Wickremasinghe 7–1–29–0; Gurusinha 7–1–11–0; Hathurusinghe 3–0–16–0; Anurasiri 10–0–34–1; Ranatunga 5–0–20–0; Kalpage 10–2–34–2; Jayasuriya 8–0–33–3.

Sri Lanka

R. S. Mahanama not out	84		P. A. de Silva not out	43
U. C. Hathurusinghe c Rutherford			B 5, l-b 3, w 4, n-b 2	14
b Su'a .	14			
A. P. Gurusinha c Nash b Harris	37		1/46 2/120	(2 wkts, 37.4 overs) 192

*A. Ranatunga, H. P. Tillekeratne, S. T. Jayasuriya, †A. G. D. Wickremasinghe, R. S. Kalpage, G. P. Wickremasinghe and S. D. Anurasiri did not bat.

Bowling: Pringle 9.4–1–45–0; Nash 6–2–15–0; Su'a 5–0–28–1; Vaughan 4–0–26–0; Harris 5–0–34–1; Bradburn 8–0–36–0.

Umpires: I. Anandappa and S. Ponnadurai.

†SRI LANKA v NEW ZEALAND

Third One-day International

At Khettarama Stadium, Colombo, December 13 (day/night). Sri Lanka won by 31 runs. Toss: New Zealand.

A superb 127-ball hundred from Man of the Series Mahanama crushed New Zealand's hopes of leaving Sri Lanka with a win. Put in to bat, Mahanama and Gurusinha shared 166 for the second wicket. A total of 262 from 49 overs was much the best of the series. Despite a brave effort, especially from Harris, New Zealand were all out for 231 in the final over. They left for home early next day.

Man of the Match: R. S. Mahanama.

Sri Lanka

R. S. Mahanama c Jones b Harris	107	R. S. Kalpage not out	3
U. C. Hathurusinghe b Pringle	5		
A. P. Gurusinha b Haslam	76	L-b 2, w 5, n-b 2	9
P. A. de Silva c and b Pringle	20		
*A. Ranatunga c Jones b Pringle	16	1/9 2/175 3/203 (6 wkts, 49 overs) 262
S. T. Jayasuriya run out	26	4/218 5/246 6/262	

H. P. Tillekeratne, †A. G. D. Wickremasinghe, S. D. Anurasiri and G. P. Wickremasinghe did not bat.

Bowling: Owens 8-0-37-0; Pringle 8-0-59-3; Nash 6-0-44-0; Vaughan 10-1-27-0; Harris 10-0-48-1; Bradburn 2-0-17-0; Haslam 5-0-28-1.

New Zealand

B. R. Hartland c A. G. D. Wickremasinghe b Gurusinha	14	G. E. Bradburn run out	2
†A. C. Parore b Gurusinha	13	M. B. Owens st A. G. D. Wickremasinghe b Anurasiri	0
*A. H. Jones c Jayasuriya b Kalpage	32	M. J. Haslam c Ranatunga b Tillekeratne	9
K. R. Rutherford c and b Kalpage	30		
J. T. C. Vaughan st A. G. D. Wickremasinghe b Kalpage	33	L-b 14, w 4, n-b 1	19
C. Z. Harris not out	68	1/29 2/35 3/88 (48.5 overs) 231
D. J. Nash run out	8	4/108 5/165 6/187	
C. Pringle c Gurusinha b Anurasiri	3	7/194 8/199 9/203	

Bowling: G. P. Wickremasinghe 6-2-13-0; Gurusinha 7-1-29-2; Hathurusinghe 2-0-16-0; Anurasiri 10-0-45-2; Kalpage 10-0-46-3; Ranatunga 5-1-26-0; de Silva 6-0-31-0; Jayasuriya 2-1-8-0; Tillekeratne 0.5-0-3-1.

Umpires: K. T. Francis and P. Manuel.

AUSTRALIA UNDER-19 IN NEW ZEALAND, 1992-93

Note: These matches were not first-class.

First Under-19 "Test": At Napier. Abandoned.

Second Under-19 "Test": At Hamilton, February 25, 26, 27, 28. Drawn. Toss: Australia Under-19. Australia Under-19 303 (M. L. Love 30, N. W. Ashley 30, J. P. Maher 133; W. Wilson four for 92, R. A. Smith four for 71) and 321 for seven dec. (M. L. Love 132, S. Hodge 38, J. P. Maher 30, S. Lee 51); New Zealand Under-19 282 (R. A. Jones 49, S. P. Fleming 120, J. W. Wilson 31; S. Lee three for 56) and 243 for seven dec. (S. P. Fleming 84, J. M. Paul 100 not out; S. Lee five for 70).

Third Under-19 "Test": At Dunedin, March 7, 8, 9. New Zealand Under-19 won by an innings and 79 runs. Toss: New Zealand Under-19. New Zealand Under-19 298 (R. A. Lawson 72, S. P. Fleming 63, J. W. Wilson 31, R. A. Smith 44; M. Hatton three for 39); Australia Under-19 87 (C. Glasscock 33; J. W. Wilson four for 13, C. M. Brown three for 27) and 132 (B. Hodge 41; R. A. Smith three for 32).

New Zealand Under-19 won the "Test" series 1-0, while Australia Under-19 won the three-match limited-overs series 2-1.

THE WEST INDIANS IN AUSTRALIA, 1992-93

By TONY COZIER

A fledgling West Indian team, under a captain in his first full series, showed great resilience in winning the new Frank Worrell Trophy – the original had disappeared – and adding yet another World Series Cup to their collection. It was West Indies' first series against Australia since 1972-73 without the imposing batting talents of Vivian Richards and Gordon Greenidge, the first since 1979-80 without Jeffrey Dujon, their most successful wicket-keeper-batsman, and since 1983-84 without Malcolm Marshall, their leading taker of Test wickets. All had left the international scene since the teams last met in the Caribbean, less than two years earlier, and the failure of the reconstituted team, under new captain Richie Richardson, in the World Cup did not encourage hopes of a quick revival.

When Australia won the Second Test at Melbourne comfortably by 139 runs, having only just been denied victory in the First, and then amassed over 500 in their first innings of the Third at Sydney before removing the openers for 31, West Indies faced a stern test of character. An extraordinary double-century by the left-hander Brian Lara, assessed by many reputable judges as one of the finest innings of the modern era, revived them. Lara's 277, the fourth highest Test score by a West Indian, and his third-wicket partnership of 293 with Richardson led to a total of 606, undermined Australia's confidence and proved the turning point in the series. After securing a draw in Sydney, West Indies won every match: the final two Tests to take the series 2-1 and four consecutive World Series Cup games, including the two finals against Australia. A heart-stopping victory by one run, Test cricket's narrowest margin, in an unusually low-scoring match at Adelaide levelled the series. And as they had done in each of their three previous Tests in Perth, they overwhelmed their opponents on a characteristically fast and bouncy pitch.

While Lara's unforgettable performance changed the course of the series, Curtly Ambrose's flawless fast bowling was instrumental in winning it. Hindered by bad luck on unresponsive pitches in the first three Tests, he was irresistible in the more sympathetic conditions of Adelaide and Perth, claiming 19 wickets in the two matches at less than 11 runs each. Using his height to awkward effect, Ambrose was always capable of delivering the unplayable ball at the opportune time. When Australia required only 186 to win at Adelaide, he removed their two most reliable batsmen, David Boon and Allan Border, for a single between them. Then he settled the outcome of the Perth Test after lunch on the first day with a stunning spell of seven for one off 32 balls. He went on to equal the record of 33 wickets in an Australian–West Indian series held by Clarrie Grimmett and Alan Davidson. In the two one-day finals, he took eight wickets for 58.

West Indies could also take comfort from the positive and level-headed leadership of Richardson, and the advance of those batsmen still seeking to establish themselves. In their contrasting styles, the right-handed opener Phil Simmons, and the left-hander, Keith Arthurton, scored their maiden Test centuries. Jimmy Adams, yet another left-hander among the new brigade, batted solidly when given the chance. The batting failures of the experienced Desmond Haynes, in his eighth series against Australia, an

Carl Hooper, and the fact that the vice-captain, Gus Logie, was not chosen at all for the Tests emphasised the development of the new order. The bowling, heavily dependent on Ambrose, lacked the depth in quality pace of its predecessors, although Ian Bishop improved markedly each time he bowled on his return to international cricket following his lengthy lay-off through a back injury. In the circumstances, Hooper's off-spin was used more than ever and made a significant contribution.

Australia's eighth successive failure in a Worrell Trophy series was an understandable disappointment to them after coming so close – particularly to their captain, Border, who had been involved in the last seven series. Border's personal joy at Australia's triumph in Melbourne was enhanced by his first home Test century for five years, and he passed 10,000 Test runs a week later in Sydney. After that his fortunes slumped as markedly as his team's, culminating in his first "pair" in first-class cricket in the Perth Test when he was reported by the umpires for dissent for the second time in the series. Fined half his match fee by the referee, Raman Subba Row, after the First Test in Brisbane, he was merely reprimanded by Donald Carr, who had taken over before his second misdemeanour. The solid Boon, restored to his opening position, was the only Australian to bat consistently and the only one to emulate four of the West Indians and average over 40. He, Border and the Waugh twins each scored centuries but the Australian batting was always vulnerable to the extra bounce Ambrose and his associates extracted at Adelaide and Perth. Martyn and Langer, two Western Australians in their early twenties, were the new batsmen introduced and, though they achieved nothing spectacular, they were undaunted by the atmosphere of Test cricket.

The loss of Bruce Reid, the tall left-arm fast bowler who once more broke down after the First Test, appreciably weakened the Australian attack, especially since Craig McDermott threatened only in spells. The whole-hearted Merv Hughes seldom wavered, his 20 wickets at 21.60 runs each a deserving reward for his efforts, but the most incisive bowling came from the spinners. Shane Warne, still an apprentice in the difficult art of leg-spin, secured the Melbourne victory with his seven for 52 but managed only two wickets after that. Tim May, the off-spinner playing his first Test for four years, completed the rout of West Indies' second innings at Adelaide with five wickets for five runs, and appeared to have set up an Australian victory. A day later, he was at the non-striker's end when Courtney Walsh's dismissal of McDermott undid all his efforts.

In pleasant contrast to their previous series, which was marred by obvious antagonism between the teams, the spirit throughout was amicable, due largely to Richardson's attitude and the presence of the ICC referees. Border's reaction to the umpiring may have been unbecoming a captain but he was not alone in believing it to be sub-standard. There seemed to be a peculiar reluctance to invoke the lbw law: only 11 such decisions were given in the five Tests, opposed to 21 in the previous season's series against India. The perpetual popularity of the West Indians in Australia, Australia's initial success in the Test series and the presence in the World Series Cup of the World Cup champions, Pakistan, brought in large crowds. Average attendance for the 14 one-day internationals was about 20,000 and for the Tests just over 16,000 a day. They were encouraging statistics.

WEST INDIAN TOURING PARTY

R. B. Richardson (Leeward Islands) (*captain*), A. L. Logie (Trinidad & Tobago) (*vice-captain*), J. C. Adams (Jamaica), C. E. L. Ambrose (Leeward Islands), K. L. T. Arthurton (Leeward Islands), K. C. G. Benjamin (Leeward Islands), I. R. Bishop (Trinidad & Tobago), A. C. Cummins (Barbados), D. L. Haynes (Barbados), C. L. Hooper (Guyana), B. C. Lara (Trinidad & Tobago), J. R. Murray (Windward Islands), B. P. Patterson (Jamaica), P. V. Simmons (Trinidad & Tobago), C. A. Walsh (Jamaica), D. Williams (Trinidad & Tobago).

     Manager : D. A. J. Holford.   *Assistant manager :* R. B. Kanhai.

WEST INDIAN TOUR RESULTS

Test matches – Played 5: Won 2, Lost 1, Drawn 2.
First-class matches – Played 8: Won 3, Lost 1, Drawn 4. Abandoned 1.
Wins – Australia (2), Western Australia.
Loss – Australia.
Draws – Australia (2), Australian XI, New South Wales.
Abandoned – Victoria.
One-day internationals – Played 10: Won 7, Lost 3. *Wins* – Australia (4), Pakistan (3).
     Losses – Australia (2), Pakistan (1).
Other non first-class matches – Played 4: Won 3, Lost 1. *Wins* – ACB Chairman's XI, Western Australia, Australian Country XI. *Loss* – Prime Minister's XI.

TEST MATCH AVERAGES

AUSTRALIA – BATTING

	T	I	NO	R	HS	100s	Avge	Ct/St
D. C. Boon	5	10	2	490	111	1	61.25	5
M. E. Waugh	5	9	0	340	112	1	37.77	6
A. R. Border	5	9	0	298	110	1	33.11	0
D. R. Martyn	4	7	1	169	67*	0	28.16	1
S. R. Waugh	5	9	0	228	100	1	25.33	5
M. A. Taylor	4	8	1	170	46*	0	24.28	5
J. L. Langer	2	4	0	85	54	0	21.25	1
I. A. Healy	5	9	1	130	36*	0	16.25	19/4
M. G. Hughes	5	9	1	118	43	0	14.75	5
C. J. McDermott	5	8	2	82	18	0	13.66	1
S. K. Warne	4	7	0	42	14	0	6.00	3

     Played in two Tests: G. R. J. Matthews 30, 0, 79 (1 ct). Played in one Test: J. Angel 0 4*; T. B. A. May 6, 42*; B. A. Reid 1*, 1; M. R. Whitney 0, 13 (1 ct).

     * *Signifies not out.*

BOWLING

	O	M	R	W	BB	5W/i	Avge
T. B. A. May	20.5	4	50	7	5-9	1	7.1
B. A. Reid	53	9	151	7	5-112	1	21.5
M. G. Hughes	145.2	30	432	20	5-64	1	21.6
S. K. Warne	108.2	23	313	10	7-52	1	31.3
C. J. McDermott	167.1	29	615	18	4-35	0	34.1

     Also bowled: J. Angel 19-4-72-1; A. R. Border 15-1-48-0; G. R. J. Matthews 99-28-228-4; M. E. Waugh 22-2-84-4; S. R. Waugh 58-14-162-3; M. R. Whitney 23-6-59-2.

WEST INDIES – BATTING

	T	I	NO	R	HS	100s	Avge	Ct
B. C. Lara	5	8	1	466	277	1	58.25	6
K. L. T. Arthurton . .	5	8	1	365	157*	1	52.14	6
J. C. Adams	3	4	1	148	77*	0	49.33	2
R. B. Richardson	5	8	0	380	109	1	47.50	3
P. V. Simmons	5	8	0	283	110	1	35.37	7
J. R. Murray	3	4	1	97	49*	0	32.33	19
C. L. Hooper	4	7	0	130	47	0	18.57	7
D. L. Haynes	5	8	0	123	45	0	15.37	3
I. R. Bishop	5	8	1	57	16*	0	8.14	1
C. E. L. Ambrose . . .	5	8	2	47	16	0	7.83	1
C. A. Walsh	5	8	3	23	17	0	4.60	1
D. Williams	2	4	0	15	15	0	3.75	11

Played in one Test: K. C. G. Benjamin 15, 0; A. C. Cummins 3; B. P. Patterson 0.

* Signifies not out.

BOWLING

	O	M	R	W	BB	5W/i	Avge
C. E. L. Ambrose	260.3	77	542	33	7-25	3	16.42
I. R. Bishop	201	39	480	23	6-40	1	20.86
C. A. Walsh	175.1	42	467	12	4-91	0	38.91
C. L. Hooper	170.5	29	438	10	4-75	0	43.80

Also bowled: J. C. Adams 27–3–103–1; K. L. T. Arthurton 9–1–22–0; K. C. G. Benjamin 18–2–54–2; A. C. Cummins 15–3–55–1; B. C. Lara 2–0–4–0; B. P. Patterson 26–0–127–1; R. B. Richardson 1–0–4–0; P. V. Simmons 49–14–112–2.

WEST INDIAN AVERAGES – FIRST-CLASS MATCHES

BATTING

	M	I	NO	R	HS	100s	Avge	Ct/St
K. L. T. Arthurton	7	12	2	598	157*	2	59.80	6
B. C. Lara	7	12	0	586	277	1	48.83	9
R. B. Richardson	7	12	0	550	109	1	45.83	5
C. L. Hooper	7	13	2	460	124	1	41.81	7
P. V. Simmons	8	14	0	570	110	3	40.71	11
J. C. Adams	6	10	3	258	77*	0	36.85	4
A. L. Logie	3	5	0	168	99	0	33.60	3
J. R. Murray	4	5	1	122	49*	0	30.50	21
D. L. Haynes	7	12	0	356	79	0	29.66	4
I. R. Bishop	6	9	1	92	35	0	11.50	1
D. Williams	4	7	0	66	23	0	9.42	14/1
C. A. Walsh	6	10	3	42	17	0	6.00	1
C. E. L. Ambrose . . .	7	11	2	51	16	0	5.66	1

Played in three matches: K. C. G. Benjamin 13*, 4*, 15, 0 (2 ct); A. C. Cummins 4, 0, 4*, 3; B. P. Patterson 6, 0, 0.

* Signifies not out.

BOWLING

	O	M	R	W	BB	5W/i	Avge
C. E. L. Ambrose	315.3	87	689	38	7-25	3	18.13
I. R. Bishop	240.3	45	617	26	6-40	1	23.73
K. C. G. Benjamin	67	11	211	6	3-27	0	35.16
C. L. Hooper	313.2	57	803	22	5-72	1	36.50
C. A. Walsh	199.1	45	542	13	4-91	0	41.69
B. P. Patterson	73	4	304	6	2-23	0	50.66
A. C. Cummins	91	14	302	5	3-73	0	60.40

Also bowled: J. C. Adams 50–5–183–2; K. L. T. Arthurton 10–2–22–0; B. C. Lara 2–0–4–0; R. B. Richardson 3–1–8–0; P. V. Simmons 63–14–182–2.

Note: Matches in this section which were not first-class are signified by a dagger.

†At Lilac Hill, November 2. West Indians won by seven wickets. Toss: ACB Chairman's XI. ACB Chairman's XI 209 for nine (50 overs) (G. R. Marsh 72, T. M. Moody 31, D. R. Martyn 32; C. L. Hooper three for 42); West Indians 210 for three (44.2 overs) (B. C. Lara 106, R. B. Richardson 53).

†At Perth, November 4 (day/night). West Indians won by 28 runs. Toss: Western Australia. West Indians 199 (49 overs) (D. L. Haynes 44, R. B. Richardson 36, K. L. T. Arthurton 44; J. Angel four for 38); Western Australia 171 (45.5 overs) (D. R. Martyn 52, I. R. Bishop three for 21, C. L. Hooper three for 25).

WESTERN AUSTRALIA v WEST INDIANS

At Perth, November 6, 7, 8, 9. West Indians won by 236 runs. Toss: Western Australia.

The West Indians achieved only their third victory in eight matches against Western Australia after a century by Arthurton changed the game. The West Indians had faltered after a sound start built around fifties from Haynes and Lara, losing four wickets in six overs after lunch on the first day. They recovered slightly through Adams and Logie, who hit 49 including a six and eight fours off just 41 balls, but were still bowled out for 280 with Julian and Angel claiming five wickets each. However, the Western Australian batsmen were also struggling at 159 for six before Andrews and Julian added 65, allowing a sporting declaration early on the third day. Arthurton's tenth first-class century and his partnership of 123 with Hooper placed the tourists in an impregnable position and an opening burst of three wickets in 13 balls by Benjamin set up a West Indian win, with more than 24 overs to spare.

Close of play: First day, West Indians 280; Second day, Western Australia 188-6 (W. S. Andrews 32*, B. P. Julian 8*); Third day, West Indians 235-3 (C. L. Hooper 42*, K. L. T. Arthurton 50*).

West Indians

D. L. Haynes c Moody b Julian	52	– c Veletta b Julian	66
P. V. Simmons c Veletta b Julian	15	– b Alderman	19
B. C. Lara c Moody b Angel	55	– c Langer b Angel	46
C. L. Hooper c Moody b Angel	5	– c Martyn b Alderman	60
K. L. T. Arthurton c Zoehrer b Angel	7	– not out	104
*A. L. Logie b Angel	49		
J. C. Adams c Zoehrer b Julian	52	– (6) not out	19
†D. Williams lbw b Julian	19		
C. E. L. Ambrose c Zoehrer b Julian	0		
K. C. G. Benjamin not out	13		
B. P. Patterson b Angel	6		
L-b 1, n-b 6	7	B 4, l-b 4, n-b 4	12

1/40 2/117 3/131 4/132 5/139   280   1/54 2/124   (4 wkts dec.) 326
6/214 7/248 8/248 9/269   3/147 4/270

Bowling: *First Innings*—Reid 18–4–62–0; Alderman 18–3–52–0; Julian 20–3–72–5; Angel 20.4–6–59–5; Andrews 10–0–34–0. *Second Innings*—Reid 7–1–27–0; Julian 16–4–46–1; Alderman 21–4–68–2; Angel 14–4–37–1; Zoehrer 16–2–66–0; Andrews 14–1–74–0.

Western Australia

M. R. J. Veletta c Haynes b Hooper	51	– (2) c Lara b Benjamin	2
*G. R. Marsh c Lara b Ambrose	7	– (1) b Benjamin	7
J. L. Langer b Hooper	40	– b Ambrose	15
T. M. Moody b Hooper	15	– lbw b Benjamin	0
D. R. Martyn c Benjamin b Hooper	9	– c Simmons b Ambrose	40
W. S. Andrews c Benjamin b Adams	51	– not out	19
†T. J. Zoehrer c Williams b Ambrose	9	– st Williams b Hooper	31
B. P. Julian not out	32	– b Hooper	0
J. Angel not out	5	– c Williams b Patterson	0
T. M. Alderman (did not bat)		– b Patterson	0
B. A. Reid (did not bat)		– c sub (J. R. Murray) b Hooper	0
L-b 3, n-b 17	20	L-b 5, n-b 12	17

1/8 2/92 3/110 4/126 5/146 (7 wkts dec.) 239   1/8 2/11 3/11 4/73 5/76   131
6/159 7/224   6/124 7/124 8/128 9/128

Bowling: *First Innings*—Ambrose 25–3–58–2; Patterson 14–2–49–0; Hooper 30–9–61–4; Benjamin 16–3–66–0; Adams 2–1–2–1. *Second Innings*—Patterson 9–1–23–2; Benjamin 9–2–27–3; Hooper 16.5–2–45–3; Ambrose 8–2–31–2; Arthurton 1–1–0–0.

Umpires: R. A. Emerson and T. A. Prue.

†At Canberra, November 12. Prime Minister's XI won by three runs. Toss: Prime Minister's XI. Prime Minister's XI 233 for seven (50 overs) (D. M. Jones 76, M. G. Bevan 58); West Indians 230 for nine (50 overs) (D. L. Haynes 35, D. Williams 57, J. C. Adams 34; P. R. Reiffel four for 44).

AUSTRALIAN XI v WEST INDIANS

At Hobart, November 14, 15, 16, 17. Drawn. Toss: Australian XI.

Steve Waugh's 95 and five wickets from 39 overs by Hooper were the highlights of the combined team's first innings. But Simmons hit powerfully for a six and 17 fours in a century off 152 balls to put the West Indians ahead on first innings. Waugh then virtually guaranteed his Test selection on the last day by reaching the hundred that had eluded him in the first innings, in just two hours 50 minutes. His stand of 115 with Lehmann enabled Healy to declare, challenging the West Indians to get 253 off a minimum 52 overs to win. They seemed on course while Arthurton was running up 46 off 38 balls, with ten fours, but once he and Logie were dismissed by Hughes at the same score the tourists chose to take no further chances and abandoned the chase.

Close of play: First day, Australian XI 261-5 (S. R. Waugh 76*, I. A. Healy 13*); Second day, West Indians 254-6 (K. L. T. Arthurton 24*, A. L. Logie 15*); Third day, Australian XI 142-3 (S. R. Waugh 27*, D. R. Martyn 26*).

Australian XI

W. N. Phillips c Simmons b Hooper	40	– (2) c Simmons b Cummins	1
M. L. Hayden c Logie b Benjamin	46	– (1) lbw b Cummins	53
D. C. Boon c Simmons b Hooper	9	– c Logie b Cummins	30
S. R. Waugh c Murray b Bishop	95	– not out	100
D. R. Martyn run out	39	– c Murray b Bishop	44
D. S. Lehmann b Hooper	16	– not out	54
*†I. A. Healy c sub (B. C. Lara) b Hooper	21		
S. K. Warne c Logie b Hooper	6		
C. D. Matthews not out	26		
M. G. Hughes b Cummins	14		
D. A. Freedman b Adams b Bishop	3		
B 4, l-b 9, n-b 13	26	B 4, l-b 4, n-b 3	11

1/88 2/99 3/110 4/206 5/233   341   1/5 2/84   (4 wkts dec.) 293
6/286 7/292 8/303 9/319   3/93 4/178

Bowling: First Innings—Bishop 26.3–3–98–2; Benjamin 24–4–64–1; Cummins 26–6–73–1; Hooper 39–9–72–5; Adams 6–0–21–0. *Second Innings*—Bishop 13–3–39–1; Cummins 27–5–73–3; Simmons 14–0–70–0; Hooper 30.3–6–87–0; Adams 4–0–16–0.

West Indians

D. L. Haynes c Martyn b Waugh	36	– b Hughes	79
P. V. Simmons c Boon b Warne	106	– lbw b Matthews	8
*R. B. Richardson c Freedman b Hughes	43	– c Freedman b Warne	32
K. L. T. Arthurton lbw b Matthews	76	– b Hughes	46
C. L. Hooper c Matthews b Warne	22	– (6) not out	38
A. L. Logie c sub (D. F. Hills) b Warne	15	– (5) c Healy b Hughes	0
J. C. Adams lbw b Warne	4	– not out	6
†J. R. Murray c Waugh b Freedman	25		
I. R. Bishop b Hughes	35		
A. C. Cummins c Waugh b Hughes	4		
K. C. G. Benjamin not out	4		
B 1, l-b 9, n-b 2	12	L-b 3, w 1	4

1/89 2/188 3/191 4/226 5/261   382   1/13 2/92 3/160   (5 wkts) 213
6/269 7/316 8/358 9/371   4/160 5/197

Bowling: First Innings—Hughes 27–4–76–3; Matthews 24–3–86–1; Waugh 8–3–31–1; Freedman 19–3–75–1; Warne 33–8–104–4. *Second Innings*—Hughes 16–3–44–3; Matthews 7–0–26–1; Waugh 7–2–22–0; Warne 17–2–80–1; Freedman 6–1–38–0.

Umpires: D. B. Hair and S. G. Randell.

NEW SOUTH WALES v WEST INDIANS

At Sydney, November 20, 21, 22, 23. Drawn. Toss: New South Wales.

So thoroughly outplayed on the first two and a half days that they followed on 290 behind, the West Indians gave a thrilling exhibition of strokeplay in their second innings, at a scoring-rate of more than four an over. Their bowling had been flat and they dropped six catches in the New South Wales innings, three offered by Mark Waugh after he had reached three figures. He and Taylor added 132, and later Taylor declared as soon as Waugh had completed the state's first double-century against a West Indian team. He faced 304 balls, batting six hours and 55 minutes, hitting 12 fours. Only Hooper batted with anything like the same purpose in the West Indians' first innings, a misleading prelude to what followed. Simmons and Richardson set the pattern on the third afternoon with a partnership of 168 off 197 balls. Simmons was out just before the close, having struck a six and 17 fours. The onslaught was even more devastating next morning when 180 runs were added in the first two hours. Hooper and Logie, who gave four chances, carried their partnership to 193 in 127 minutes before Logie was run out attempting the single that would have given him a hundred from 98 balls. Hooper was more fortunate, reaching his maiden first-class century in Australia.

Close of play: First day, New South Wales 349-4 (M. E. Waugh 121*, G. R. J. Matthews 15*); Second day, West Indians 55-2 (P. V. Simmons 17*, C. L. Hooper 0*); Third day, West Indians 225-3 (C. L. Hooper 21*, A. L. Logie 7*).

New South Wales

S. M. Small c Lara b Patterson	23	– c Richardson b Patterson	8
*M. A. Taylor run out	101		
S. R. Waugh c Adams b Walsh	22		
M. E. Waugh not out	200		
M. G. Bevan c Richardson b Patterson	40	– (2) not out	17
G. R. J. Matthews c Williams b Ambrose	20		
†P. A. Emery not out	29	– (3) not out	4
B 1, l-b 20, w 1, n-b 16	38	L-b 2, n-b 3	5

1/45 2/89 3/221 4/313 5/374   (5 wkts dec.) 473   1/24   (1 wkt) 34

M. R. Whitney, W. J. Holdsworth, P. J. S. Alley and D. A. Freedman did not bat.

Bowling: First Innings—Ambrose 22-5-58-1; Patterson 20-1-92-2; Walsh 24-3-75-1; Cummins 20-0-87-0; Hooper 26.1-2-100-0; Adams 9-0-40-0. *Second Innings*—Patterson 4-0-13-1; Cummins 3-0-14-0; Adams 2-1-1-0; Richardson 2-1-4-0.

West Indians

P. V. Simmons c Bevan b Alley	30	– c Emery b Alley	109
B. C. Lara c Emery b Holdsworth	16	– c Emery b Holdsworth	3
*R. B. Richardson c Emery b Alley	20	– c S. R. Waugh b Matthews	75
C. L. Hooper not out	81	– c Emery b Freedman	124
A. L. Logie b Whitney	5	– run out	99
J. C. Adams b Holdsworth	7	– run out	22
†D. Williams c Matthews b Freedman	9	– c Bevan b Matthews	23
C. E. L. Ambrose b Freedman	4	– c S. R. Waugh b Matthews	0
A. C. Cummins c Emery b Freedman	5	– not out	14
C. A. Walsh b Matthews	5	– c Bevan b Matthews	14
B. P. Patterson b Matthews	0		
L-b 4, w 2	6	B 2, l-b 17, w 1, n-b 4	24

1/26 2/55 3/74 4/80 5/93   183   1/23 2/191 3/208   (9 wkts dec.) 507
6/131 7/139 8/139 9/146   4/401 5/444 6/452
                                       7/461 8/483 9/507

Bowling: First Innings—Holdsworth 11-1-53-2; Whitney 14-4-40-1; Alley 10-4-11-2; Matthews 11.1-2-49-2; Freedman 5-1-26-3. *Second Innings*—Holdsworth 11-0-80-1; Whitney 14-2-55-0; Alley 10-0-58-1; Matthews 49.3-12-148-4; S. R. Waugh 16-3-43-0; Freedman 19-4-64-1; Bevan 6-0-40-0.

Umpires: D. B. Hair and I. S. Thomas.

AUSTRALIA v WEST INDIES

First Test Match

At Brisbane, November 27, 28, 29, 30, December 1. Drawn. Toss: Australia. Test debut: D. R. Martyn.

An intensely fought contest ended with West Indies, who held a slight advantage for the first four days, desperately hanging on for a draw. Australian frustration at the refusal of several lbw appeals in the closing stages led the umpires to report Border and Hughes for dissent, for which the Australian captain, who did not attend the post-match hearing, was fined half his match fee, $A2,000, by match referee Raman Subba Row, and Hughes 10 per cent ($A400).

Australia, who unexpectedly omitted Dean Jones, failed to capitalise on ideal conditions when they batted first. Hooper, returning his best Test figures, dislodged Mark Waugh and Boon when both were at their most threatening. Border then shared successive half-century partnerships with the debutant Martyn, who eventually gave Ambrose his 150th Test wicket, and Matthews. But Border's run-out, attempting a sharp single, came as a crucial setback, and West Indies were batting just before lunch next day. They lost their top three for 58 before the left-handers Lara and Arthurton rebuilt the innings with a confident partnership of 112 that ended in controversy and confusion. Healy fumbled a leg-side stumping off Matthews but then knocked the wayward ball back towards the stumps; Lara was still short of his ground and umpire Prue ruled him out. Television replays showed the wicket-keeper's glove, not the ball, had dislodged the bails, and Healy later claimed he had told the umpire as much.

Arthurton dominated the rest of the innings, passing his maiden Test century in his seventh Test just before lunch on the third day and reaching his highest first-class score before running out of partners. Batting seven and a half hours, he hit a straight six off Border and 16 fours, mostly through the off side. His only chance was at 72, a return catch to Steve Waugh, although a few runs later he was lucky not to be given out by Prue, caught behind off the same bowler.

A spectacular hailstorm that turned the outfield white in minutes halted play on the third afternoon and the West Indian innings ended soon afterwards. They had a useful lead of 78 but a missed catch in the second over of the fourth morning was to cost them dearly. Boon, then six, edged Ambrose to second slip where Hooper dropped a two-handed chance to his left. Boon, solid as ever, proceeded to his 14th Test century, his third against West Indies. He and Mark Waugh put on 110 at a run a minute before a miscued pull by Boon off Bishop was well caught at cover point. Australia were building a strong position when Ambrose, armed with the new ball, removed three wickets for three runs in 11 deliveries before the close. The match was fascinatingly poised; half an hour before lunch on the final day West Indies were left 231 to win in a minimum of 63 overs.

By the interval Haynes, Simmons and Lara had been caught off the outside edge, with only three runs scored, and McDermott's third wicket, Arthurton bowled for nought off the inside edge, made it nine for four. Six of the nine runs had come from a vicious hook by Richardson off Reid. And the captain continued the counter-attack to such effect that, with Hooper his steady partner, West Indies had recovered to 93 for four at tea, 138 short of their goal. Only when Hooper and Williams were dismissed in successive overs on the resumption did Richardson abandon thoughts of winning, but he remained defiant for another hour and 20 minutes before he was seventh out, caught down the leg side, with six overs remaining. Reid accounted for Ambrose but Bishop could not be moved. Neither could Walsh, who nervously survived seven balls before his partner calmly played out the final over from Hughes.

Man of the Match: D. C. Boon.   *Attendance*: 31,749.

Close of play: First day, Australia 259-6 (G. R. J. Matthews 28*, I. A. Healy 2*); Second day, West Indies 195-4 (K. L. T. Arthurton 61*, C. L. Hooper 14*); Third day, Australia 21-0 (D. C. Boon 6*, M. A. Taylor 14*); Fourth day, Australia 266-6 (A. R. Border 6*, I. A. Healy 5*).

Australia

M. A. Taylor c Williams b Bishop	7	– (2) c Williams b Walsh	34
D. C. Boon c Simmons b Hooper	48	– (1) c Arthurton b Bishop	111
S. R. Waugh c Williams b Ambrose	10	– c Williams b Ambrose	20
M. E. Waugh c and b Hooper	39	– c Haynes b Ambrose	60
D. R. Martyn c Lara b Ambrose	36	– lbw b Ambrose	15
*A. R. Border run out	73	– c Williams b Walsh	17
G. R. J. Matthews c Arthurton b Bishop	30	– lbw b Ambrose	0
†I. A. Healy c Lara b Hooper	17	– c Williams b Bishop	18
M. G. Hughes c Bishop b Hooper	10	– c Williams b Ambrose	1
C. J. McDermott c Hooper b Patterson	3	– not out	16
B. A. Reid not out	1	– c Richardson b Hooper	1
B 3, l-b 4, n-b 12	19	B 4, l-b 2, n-b 9	15
	293		**308**

1/8 (1) 2/21 (3) 3/88 (4) 4/125 (2)   293   1/64 (2) 2/114 (3) 3/224 (1)   308
5/180 (5) 6/252 (6) 7/264 (7)   4/250 (4) 5/255 (5) 6/255 (7)
8/285 (8) 9/288 (10) 10/293 (9)   7/280 (8) 8/287 (9)
        9/295 (6) 10/308 (11)

Bowling: First Innings—Ambrose 29.1–12–53–2; Bishop 23–3–51–2; Patterson 19–0–83–1; Walsh 0.5–0–2–0; Hooper 30.1–4–75–4; Simmons 7–2–16–0; Arthurton 3–0–6–0. *Second Innings*—Ambrose 32–8–66–5; Bishop 27–6–58–2; Hooper 28.2–8–63–1; Walsh 24–3–64–2; Patterson 7–0–44–0; Arthurton 1–0–2–0; Simmons 1–0–5–0.

West Indies

D. L. Haynes c Taylor b Reid	8	– c Healy b McDermott	1
P. V. Simmons b Reid	27	– c Healy b Reid	1
*R. B. Richardson c Matthews b Hughes	17	– c Healy b Hughes	66
B. C. Lara st Healy b Matthews	58	– c Taylor b McDermott	0
K. L. T. Arthurton not out	157	– b McDermott	0
C. L. Hooper b S. R. Waugh	47	– c Boon b Matthews	32
†D. Williams c Hughes b Reid	15	– lbw b McDermott	0
I. R. Bishop b McDermott	5	– not out	16
C. E. L. Ambrose lbw b Reid	4	– c Hughes b Reid	4
B. P. Patterson c M. E. Waugh b Reid	0		
C. A. Walsh b Hughes	17	– (10) not out	0
L-b 6, n-b 10	16	L-b 7, n-b 6	13
	371	(8 wkts)	**133**

1/25 (1) 2/50 (3) 3/58 (2) 4/170 (4)
5/265 (6) 6/293 (7) 7/307 (8) 8/321 (9)
9/331 (10) 10/371 (11)

1/2 (1) 2/2 (2) 3/3 (4) (8 wkts) 133
4/9 (5) 5/95 (6) 6/96 (7)
7/123 (3) 8/128 (9)

Bowling: *First Innings*—McDermott 25-4-93-1; Reid 37-2-112-5; Hughes 18.3-3-58-2; Matthews 27-12-41-1; Border 1-0-7-0; S. R. Waugh 14-2-46-1; M. E. Waugh 2-0-8-0. *Second Innings*—McDermott 18-7-35-4; Reid 16-7-39-2; Hughes 13-4-28-1; Matthews 13-4-18-1; S. R. Waugh 5-2-6-0.

Umpires: T. A. Prue and S. G. Randell. Referee: R. Subba Row (England).

West Indies' matches v Australia and Pakistan in the Benson and Hedges World Series Cup (December 4–December 17) may be found in that section.

VICTORIA v WEST INDIANS

At Bendigo, December 19, 20, 21, 22. Abandoned. Rain prevented play on the first two days, and an electrical storm on the third caused the umpires to abandon the tourists' first first-class match for nearly three weeks.

AUSTRALIA v WEST INDIES

Second Test Match

At Melbourne, December 26, 27, 28, 29, 30. Australia won by 139 runs. Toss: Australia.

While Simmons and his captain, Richardson, were attacking in a second-wicket partnership of 134 on the final morning West Indies threatened a remarkable victory, but a target of 359 on a worn pitch was an enormous one. Once Warne, in his fifth Test, bowled Richardson with a top-spinner just before lunch, the effort disintegrated. The last nine wickets fell for 76 and by tea Australia were 1-0 up in the series. Warne was the destroyer with seven wickets, three from the North End and his last four, for three runs, from the South.

The platform for Australia's eventual win was built by Mark Waugh and Border, who came together at 115 for four on the first day to add 204. Waugh's century was his third in Tests, Border's his 25th. Both were let off by the wicket-keeper, Williams: Waugh on a stumping off Hooper when 23 and a catch off Bishop when 71, Border on a wide leg-side deflection off Ambrose when five. Waugh batted five hours 35 minutes and hit nine fours. Border's third hundred against West Indies, his first since 1983-84, lasted nearly six hours, included a six and five fours and came at an opportune time, just when his lengthy hold on the captaincy was being increasingly questioned by the media.

Hughes quickly accounted for Haynes, Simmons and Richardson on the second afternoon, which took him to 150 Test wickets. For the second successive Test Lara and Arthurton rescued the innings by adding over a hundred together; the slowness of the recently relaid outfield was reflected in the fact that they ran two fours and 11 threes. But West Indies lost their last five wickets for 41 once Arthurton was out to McDermott, who took four for 17 from his final seven overs.

Australia's suspicions of the pitch were confirmed by a shooter from Simmons which bowled a bemused Boon late on the third day, and they approached their task with utmost caution, in spite of a first-innings lead of 162. Taylor laboured four hours and ten minutes over 42 and when Border was sixth out the margin had advanced only to 264 and West Indies were back in contention. It was Martyn, in his second Test, who ignored the doubts of his seniors and stimulated a revival that brought 94 for the last four wickets at a run a minute.

The loss of Haynes in the 13 overs they faced on the fourth evening was a setback to West Indian hopes, but Simmons and Richardson lifted them again next morning. They were less than a quarter of an hour away from lunch, having added 111 on the day, when Richardson, playing from the crease, was deceived by Warne. Simmons went on to score his maiden Test hundred in his 20th innings but, by the time he became Warne's fourth victim, caught at mid-wicket, the decline was terminal. Less than an hour later, Australia had completed their ninth win in 12 Tests against West Indies on the ground.

Man of the Match: S. K. Warne.   *Attendance:* 137,134.

Close of play: First day, Australia 227-4 (M. E. Waugh 63*, A. R. Border 51*); Second day, West Indies 62-3 (B. C. Lara 14*, K. L. T. Arthurton 13*); Third day, Australia 26-1 (M. A. Taylor 9*, S. K. Warne 1*); Fourth day, West Indies 32-1 (P. V. Simmons 14*, R. B. Richardson 12*).

Australia

D. C. Boon c Williams b Walsh	46	(2) b Simmons	11
M. A. Taylor c Lara b Walsh	13	(1) b Bishop	42
S. R. Waugh c Lara b Ambrose	38	(4) c Simmons b Bishop	1
M. E. Waugh c Williams b Ambrose	112	(5) b Adams b Walsh	16
D. R. Martyn c Simmons b Ambrose	7	(6) not out	67
*A. R. Border c Williams b Bishop	110	(7) b Bishop	4
†I. A. Healy c Hooper b Walsh	24	(8) c and b Walsh	8
M. G. Hughes not out	9	(9) c Williams b Ambrose	15
S. K. Warne c Adams b Bishop	1	(3) c Arthurton b Ambrose	5
C. J. McDermott b Walsh	17	c Arthurton b Simmons	4
M. R. Whitney lbw b Bishop	0	run out	13
L-b 14, w 1, n-b 3	18	B 1, l-b 8, n-b 1	10
	395		**196**

1/38 (2) 2/100 (3) 3/104 (1) 4/115 (5)   1/22 (2) 2/40 (3) 3/41 (4)
5/319 (4) 6/362 (6) 7/366 (7)   4/73 (5) 5/90 (1) 6/102 (7)
8/369 (9) 9/394 (10) 10/395 (11)   7/121 (8) 8/154 (9)
                                                 9/167 (10) 10/196 (11)

Bowling: *First Innings*—Ambrose 35–10–70–3; Bishop 29–2–84–3; Simmons 10–2–23–0; Walsh 39–10–91–4; Hooper 36–3–95–0; Adams 4–0–18–0. *Second Innings*—Ambrose 30–9–57–2; Bishop 20–5–45–3; Walsh 21–7–42–2; Simmons 18–6–34–2; Hooper 2.4–1–9–0.

West Indies

D. L. Haynes c Hughes	7	c Healy b Hughes	5
P. V. Simmons c Boon b Hughes	6	c Boon b Warne	110
*R. B. Richardson c Healy b Hughes	15	b Warne	52
B. C. Lara lbw b Whitney	52	c Boon b Whitney	4
K. L. T. Arthurton c Healy b McDermott	71	st Healy b Warne	13
C. L. Hooper c and b S. R. Waugh	3	c Whitney b Warne	1
J. C. Adams c Boon b McDermott	47	c Taylor b McDermott	16
†D. Williams c Healy b McDermott	0	c M. E. Waugh b Warne	0
I. R. Bishop b McDermott	9	c Taylor b Warne	7
C. E. L. Ambrose c McDermott b Warne	7	not out	0
C. A. Walsh not out	0	c Hughes b Warne	0
L-b 10, n-b 6	16	B 3, l-b 2, n-b 1	6
	233		**219**

1/11 (1) 2/28 (2) 3/33 (3) 4/139 (4)   1/9 (1) 2/143 (4) 3/148 (4)
5/144 (6) 6/192 (5) 7/192 (8)   4/165 (5) 5/177 (6) 6/198 (2)
8/206 (9) 9/233 (10) 10/233 (7)   7/206 (7) 8/206 (8)
                                              9/219 (9) 10/219 (11)

Bowling: *First Innings*—McDermott 25.1–8–66–4; Hughes 19–5–51–3; Whitney 13–4–27–1; Warne 24–7–65–1; S. R. Waugh 4–1–14–1. *Second Innings*—McDermott 17–2–66–1; Hughes 18–7–41–1; Whitney 10–2–32–1; Warne 23.2–8–52–7; M. E. Waugh 3–0–23–0.

Umpires: S. G. Randell and C. D. Timmins. Referee: R. Subba Row (England).

AUSTRALIA v WEST INDIES

Third Test Match

At Sydney, January 2, 3, 4, 5, 6. Drawn. Toss: Australia. Test debut: J. R. Murray.

An innings of breathtaking quality by Brian Lara towered over everything else in a high-scoring match. It drastically altered the course of a series that was slipping away from his team when he joined Richardson in the second over of the third day. West Indies were 31 for two, replying to 503 for nine declared; only five days earlier they had been beaten in Melbourne, and they were deeply suspicious about the Sydney ground, where they had lost their two previous Tests in otherwise successful series.

In between breaks for rain Lara unleashed a dazzling array of strokes. He needed only 125 balls to reach his maiden Test century in his fifth match. By the end of the day, he was 121, Richardson 94 and their partnership of 217 already the highest for West Indies' third wicket in a Test in Australia. They had taken it to 293 when Richardson's hook off Hughes was caught at deep backward square leg. In five and a half hours at the wicket he hit 11 fours in his 15th Test century, and his eighth against Australia. "I can hardly remember my hundred," he said afterwards. "It was difficult playing and being a spectator at the same time." By this time Lara was scoring at will in all directions, dominating another partnership, of 124, with Arthurton. Australia were powerless to stop him until he committed himself to a single to cover off Matthews and could not beat Martyn's return to the wicket-keeper when Hooper sent him back. His 277 was the third-highest individual Test score against Australia (behind L. Hutton and R. E. Foster) and the highest for either side in Tests between Australia and West Indies. He struck 38 fours off 372 balls in seven hours 54 minutes. Lara's pre-eminence on the rain-shortened fourth day was such that he added 156 and struck 23 fours, outscoring his three partners by more than two to one. His solitary chance, low to Steve Waugh at gully off Hughes, was when he was 172.

Lara's approach contrasted markedly with the careful grafting of most of the Australians. Mark Waugh was the exception, scoring 57 out of a 94-run stand with his brother. But Steve Waugh worked diligently for four and a half hours over his fourth Test century, which included only five fours. After the loss of three wickets for 16, late on the first day, Border and Matthews regained the initiative, but they took nearly four hours over their partnership of 155. When Border drove Hooper to mid-on for his 21st run he reached 10,000 runs in his 136th Test, a landmark previously achieved only by India's S. M. Gavaskar. As the match drifted to a draw on the final afternoon, after West Indies were finally dismissed for 606, Boon became the eighth Australian to pass 5,000 Test runs.

Man of the Match: B. C. Lara.   *Attendance:* 83,115.

Close of play: First day, Australia 272-5 (A. R. Border 0*, G. R. J. Matthews 0*); Second day, West Indies 24-1 (D. L. Haynes 16*, R. B. Richardson 3*); Third day, West Indies 248-2 (R. B. Richardson 94*, B. C. Lara 121*); Fourth day, West Indies 488-5 (C. L. Hooper 7*, J. C. Adams 5*).

Australia

D. C. Boon c Murray b Adams	76	– (2) not out	63
M. A. Taylor c Murray b Bishop	20	– (1) not out	46
S. R. Waugh c Simmons b Ambrose	100		
M. E. Waugh run out	57		
D. R. Martyn b Ambrose	0		
*A. R. Border c Murray b Hooper	74		
G. R. J. Matthews c Murray b Hooper	79		
†I. A. Healy not out	36		
M. G. Hughes c Haynes b Bishop	17		
S. K. Warne c Simmons b Hooper	14		
B 2, l-b 23, n-b 5	30	B 1, l-b 2, n-b 5	8

1/42 (2) 2/160 (1) 3/254 (4)   (9 wkts dec.) 503   (no wkt) 117
4/261 (5) 5/270 (3) 6/425 (6)
7/440 (7) 8/469 (9) 9/503 (10)

C. J. McDermott did not bat.

Bowling: *First Innings*—Ambrose 35-8-87-2; Bishop 36-6-87-2; Walsh 30-8-86-0; Hooper 45.4-6-137-3; Adams 15-2-56-1; Simmons 10-2-25-0. *Second Innings*—Ambrose 6-2-10-0; Bishop 4-1-9-0; Simmons 3-2-9-0; Walsh 8-3-13-0; Hooper 10-2-22-0; Adams 8-1-29-0; Arthurton 5-1-14-0; Lara 2-0-4-0; Richardson 1-0-4-0.

[*Joe Mann, Allsport*

Brian Lara reaches his 200 on the way to 277 in the Sydney Test.

West Indies

D. L. Haynes b Matthews	22	
P. V. Simmons c Taylor b McDermott	3	
*R. B. Richardson c Warne b Hughes	109	
B. C. Lara run out	277	
K. L. T. Arthurton c Healy b Matthews	47	
C. L. Hooper b Warne	21	
J. C. Adams not out	77	
†J. R. Murray c Healy b Hughes	11	
I. R. Bishop run out	0	

C. E. L. Ambrose c Martyn		
b M. E. Waugh	16	
C. A. Walsh c Healy b Hughes	0	
B 4, l-b 9, w 1, n-b 8	22	
1/13 (2) 2/31 (1) 3/324 (3) 4/448 (5)		606
5/481 (4) 6/537 (6) 7/573 (8)		
8/577 (9) 9/603 (10) 10/606 (11)		

Bowling: McDermott 33–3–119–1; Hughes 16.4–1–76–3; Matthews 59–12–169–2; S. R. Waugh 11–1–43–0; Warne 41–6–116–1; Border 14–1–41–0; M. E. Waugh 10–1–29–1.

Umpires: D. B. Hair and T. A. Prue. Referee: D. B. Carr (England).

West Indies' matches v Australia and Pakistan in the Benson and Hedges World Series Cup (January 9–January 18) may be found in that section.

†At Newcastle, January 13. West Indians won by 51 runs. Toss: West Indians. West Indians 294 (50 overs) (D. L. Haynes 46, K. L. T. Arthurton 94, C. L. Hooper 33, A. C. Cummins 49; G. R. Irvine three for 50); Australian Country XI 243 (47.1 overs) (B. J. Spanner 68, G. R. Irvine 56; P. V. Simmons three for 58).

AUSTRALIA v WEST INDIES

Fourth Test Match

At Adelaide, January 23, 24, 25, 26. West Indies won by one run. Toss: West Indies. Test debut: J. L. Langer.

Adelaide 1992-93 took its place as one of the greatest of all Test matches when Craig McDermott failed to get out of the way of a lifter from Courtney Walsh and gloved a catch to give West Indies victory by one run, the narrowest victory anyone has achieved in 116 years of Test cricket.

But it had been a game of fluctuating fortunes throughout. When Australia, needing 186 to win, lost their eighth second-innings wicket for 102, it appeared to have made its decisive shift. But then the 22-year-old debutant Justin Langer, who came in only when Martyn was injured at pre-match practice, added 42 with the No. 10 Tim May, who was playing his first Test in four years. After that May and the last man McDermott put on another 40 to get Australia within two of their target.

The unfolding drama lifted the TV cricket ratings in Australia to a new record. And, with the Adelaide Oval within walking distance of the city centre, new spectators rushed to the ground. Finally, a short ball from Walsh, pitched on off stump, lifted to brush McDermott's hand on its way through to Murray. Umpire Hair upheld the appeal. The West Indians on the field celebrated emotionally. The crowd who had been singing "Waltzing Matilda" as Australia inched towards their goal were stunned into silence.

The Australian captain Border did not dispute Hair's decision, though he said that, like the result, it was a very close one. "What can you say – one run? I was very confident of getting 186 at the start of the day." His opposite number Richardson said: "I knew Walshy would get a wicket with that very ball. I never lost hope." Both leaders paid tribute to the man who made the result possible: Ambrose consolidated his reputation as the world's leading fast bowler with ten wickets in the match and a burst of three wickets in 19 balls after lunch to dismiss Steve Waugh, Border and Hughes. "I have never seen a bowler like him," said Richardson.

The pitch had been kept covered against unusually wet weather and was much fresher than is normal in Adelaide. But it was not only fast bowlers who prospered. The off-spinner May delighted his home crowd on his return to Test cricket by taking five wickets for five runs in 32 balls as the West Indians' second innings folded. West Indies' first-innings 252 was the highest total of the match, and that was disappointing after Haynes and Simmons had provided a comfortable start of 84. Hughes was rewarded for his persistence with five wickets but Australia had a foretaste of difficulties ahead as they lost Taylor in the second over and a stunning blow from Bishop split Langer's helmet shortly before the close.

Boon, hit on the forearm, was forced to retire hurt early on the rain-shortened second day. Returning when five wickets were down, he was left unbeaten as Australia conceded a lead of 39 on a remarkable third day which saw 17 wickets fall for 259 runs. An incisive opening spell by McDermott reduced West Indies to 65 for four and, after Richardson and Hooper added 59, the last six wickets collapsed for 22 in nine overs of spin, largely due to careless batting. May did most of the damage and took five of the wickets but the most crucial one belonged to Warne: Richardson for 72, having passed 5,000 Test runs.

On the fourth day, Australia started their quest for the victory that would have given them the Frank Worrell Trophy. They lost both openers cheaply and when four wickets fell for ten runs in the first half hour after lunch – three of them to Ambrose – it appeared certain that West Indies would square the series. Langer's determined resistance and his partnerships with Warne and May lifted Australian hopes, before May, batting with an injured hand, and McDermott brought them so close.

Man of the Match: C. E. L. Ambrose.   *Attendance:* 57,573.

Close of play: First day, Australia 2-1 (D. C. Boon 1*, J. L. Langer 0*); Second day, Australia 100-3 (S. R. Waugh 35*, A. R. Border 18*); Third day, West Indies 146.

West Indies

D. L. Haynes st Healy b May	45	– c Healy b McDermott	11
P. V. Simmons c Hughes b S. R. Waugh	46	– b McDermott	10
*R. B. Richardson lbw b Hughes	2	– c Healy b Warne	72
B. C. Lara c Healy b McDermott	52	– c S. R. Waugh b Hughes	7
K. L. T. Arthurton c S. R. Waugh b May	0	– c Healy b McDermott	0
C. L. Hooper c Healy b Hughes	2	– c Hughes b May	25
†J. R. Murray not out	49	– c M. E. Waugh b May	0
I. R. Bishop c M. E. Waugh b Hughes	13	– c M. E. Waugh b May	6
C. E. L. Ambrose c Healy b Hughes	0	– st Healy b May	1
K. C. G. Benjamin b M. E. Waugh	15	– c Warne b May	0
C. A. Walsh lbw b Hughes	5	– not out.	0
L-b 11, n-b 12	23	L-b 2, n-b 12	14
	252		**146**

1/84 (2) 2/99 (3) 3/129 (1) 4/130 (5)   1/14 (1) 2/49 (2) 3/63 (4)
5/134 (6) 6/189 (4) 7/206 (8)   4/65 (5) 5/124 (6) 6/137 (7)
8/206 (9) 9/247 (10) 10/252 (11)   7/145 (9) 8/146 (9)
    9/146 (10) 10/146 (8)

Bowling: *First Innings*—McDermott 16–1–85–1; Hughes 21.3–3–64–5; S. R. Waugh 13–4–37–1; May 14–1–41–2; Warne 2–0–11–0; M. E. Waugh 1–0–3–1. *Second Innings*—McDermott 11–0–66–3; Hughes 13–1–43–1; S. R. Waugh 5–1–8–0; May 6.5–3–9–5; Warne 6–2–18–1.

Australia

M. A. Taylor c Hooper b Bishop	1	– (2) c Murray b Benjamin	7
D. C. Boon not out	39	– (1) lbw b Ambrose	0
J. L. Langer c Murray b Benjamin	20	– c Murray b Bishop	54
M. E. Waugh c Simmons b Ambrose	0	– c Hooper b Walsh	26
S. R. Waugh c Murray b Ambrose	42	– c Arthurton b Ambrose	4
*A. R. Border c Hooper b Ambrose	19	– c Haynes b Ambrose	1
†I. A. Healy c Hooper b Ambrose	0	– b Walsh	0
M. G. Hughes c Murray b Hooper	43	– lbw b Ambrose	1
S. K. Warne lbw b Hooper	0	– lbw b Bishop	9
T. B. A. May c Murray b Ambrose	6	– not out	42
C. J. McDermott b Ambrose	14	– c Murray b Walsh	18
B 7, l-b 3, n-b 19	29	B 1, l-b 8, n-b 13	22
	213		**184**

1/1 (1) 2/16 (4) 3/46 (3) 4/108 (6)   1/5 (1) 2/16 (2) 3/54 (4)
5/108 (7) 6/112 (5) 7/181 (8)   4/64 (5) 5/72 (6) 6/73 (7)
8/181 (9) 9/197 (10) 10/213 (11)   7/74 (8) 8/102 (9)
    9/144 (3) 10/184 (11)

In the first innings D. C. Boon, when 2, retired hurt at 16-1 and resumed at 108-5.

Bowling: *First Innings*—Ambrose 28.2–6–74–6; Bishop 18–3–48–1; Benjamin 6–0–22–1; Walsh 10–3–34–0; Hooper 13.4–25–2. *Second Innings*—Ambrose 26–5–46–4; Bishop 17–3–41–2; Benjamin 12–2–32–1; Walsh 19.4–4–43–3; Hooper 5–1–12–0.

Umpires: D. B. Hair and L. J. King. Referee: D. B. Carr (England).

AUSTRALIA v WEST INDIES

Fifth Test Match

At Perth, January 30, 31, February 1. West Indies won by an innings and 25 runs. Toss: Australia. Test debuts: J. Angel; A. C. Cummins.

West Indies' fourth victory in their four Tests at the WACA ground was secured five minutes before lunch on the third day. It originated in one of Test cricket's most devastating spells, by Ambrose, which wrecked Australia on the first day and assured West Indies of retaining the Frank Worrell Trophy they had held since 1977-78. With the strong "Fremantle Doctor" breeze at his back, Ambrose took seven wickets, among them Border first ball, for one run off 32 balls. Six of the victims were caught either by the wicket-keeper or in the slips. Australia were reduced from 85 for two to 119 all out; by the close of play West Indies were already in the lead at 135 for one, and their batsmen had hit four sixes and 16 fours.

Richardson accounted for two sixes and seven fours in 47 off 40 balls and, though Haynes retired after hooking a bouncer into his face, Simmons had hit confidently for 80. Australia clawed back a little ground on the second morning when Simmons was among the four wickets that fell for 87. However, a dropped catch by Border at slip off Hughes allowed Murray to escape before he had scored, and the wicket-keeper and Arthurton consolidated West Indies' innings with a partnership of 75.

With a daunting deficit of 203, Australia lost four wickets by the end of the second day and their hopes of making a fight of it depended heavily on Boon and Border, their two most experienced batsmen. Bishop, generating extreme pace, despatched both in the same over and the rest was a formality as he completed his best figures in Test cricket. Bishop ended Boon's series ten runs short of 500, uprooting his off stump, and then bowled Border off the inside edge third ball. It was the first time in his 138 Tests the Australian captain had endured a pair, and he remained 50 short of passing S. M. Gavaskar's record of 10,122 Test runs. His disappointment was compounded when, along with Hughes, he was reported for the second time in the series for showing dissent, though they were only "severely reprimanded" rather than fined. Australia were also less than happy that such a fast, bouncy pitch should be presented to the West Indian bowlers for the decisive Test of the series. Meanwhile, the 16-man West Indian party all clambered aboard the station wagon that Ambrose won as Man of the Series and, with Ambrose at the wheel, did a lap of honour of the WACA. It was perhaps the only time since they arrived in Perth that they had been in any kind of danger.

Man of the Match: C. E. L. Ambrose.   *Man of the Series:* C. E. L. Ambrose.

Attendance: 44,197.

Close of play: First day, West Indies 135-1 (P. V. Simmons 45*, B. C. Lara 16*); Second day, Australia 75-4 (D. C. Boon 45*, D. R. Martyn 3*).

Australia

J. L. Langer c Murray b Bishop	10	– (2) c sub (A. L. Logie) b Ambrose	1
D. C. Boon c Richardson b Ambrose	44	– (1) b Bishop	52
S. R. Waugh c Murray b Bishop	13	– c sub (A. L. Logie) b Bishop	0
M. E. Waugh c Murray b Ambrose	9	– c Richardson b Bishop	21
D. R. Martyn c Simmons b Ambrose	13	– (6) c Ambrose b Cummins	31
*A. R. Border c Murray b Ambrose	0	– (7) b Bishop	0
†I. A. Healy c Lara b Ambrose	0	– (8) c Murray b Bishop	27
M. G. Hughes c Arthurton b Ambrose	0	– (9) c Murray b Walsh	22
S. K. Warne run out	13	– (5) c Murray b Ambrose	0
J. Angel c Murray b Ambrose	0	– not out	4
C. J. McDermott not out	2	– c Lara b Bishop	8
L-b 8, w 1, n-b 6	15	B 1, l-b 6, n-b 5	12

1/27 (1) 2/58 (3) 3/85 (4) 4/90 (2)   119   1/13 (2) 2/14 (3) 3/66 (4)   178
5/90 (6) 6/100 (7) 7/102 (8)   4/67 (5) 5/95 (1) 6/95 (7)
8/104 (5) 9/104 (10) 10/119 (9)   7/130 (6) 8/162 (9)
                                            9/170 (8) 10/178 (11)

Bowling: *First Innings*—Ambrose 18–9–25–7; Bishop 11–6–17–2; Walsh 11.2–2–45–0; Cummins 7–0–24–0. *Second Innings*—Ambrose 21–8–54–2; Bishop 16–4–40–6; Walsh 12–2–46–1; Cummins 8–3–31–1.

West Indies

D. L. Haynes c Healy b Hughes	24	A. C. Cummins c M. E. Waugh	
P. V. Simmons c S. R. Waugh b Angel	80	b Hughes	3
*R. B. Richardson c Langer		C. E. L. Ambrose not out	9
b McDermott	47	C. A. Walsh b Hughes	1
B. C. Lara c Warne b McDermott	16	B 4, l-b 10, n-b 6	20
K. L. T. Arthurton c S. R. Waugh			
b McDermott	77	1/111 (3) 2/136 (4) 3/184 (2)	322
J. C. Adams b Hughes	8	4/195 (6) 5/205 (1) 6/280 (7)	
†J. R. Murray c Healy b M. E. Waugh	37	7/286 (8) 8/301 (9)	
I. R. Bishop c Healy b M. E. Waugh	0	9/319 (5) 10/322 (11)	

D. L. Haynes, when 21, retired hurt at 34 and resumed at 195.

Bowling: McDermott 22–4–85–3; Hughes 25.4–6–71–4; Angel 19–4–72–1; Warne 12–0–51–0; S. R. Waugh 6–3–8–0; M. E. Waugh 6–1–21–2.

Umpires: S. G. Randell and C. D. Timmins. Referee: D. B. Carr (England).

THE COOPERS & LYBRAND RATINGS

Introduced in 1987, the Coopers & Lybrand Ratings (formerly the Deloitte Ratings) rank Test cricketers on a scale from 0 to 1,000 according to their performances in Test matches since 1981. The ratings are calculated by computer and take into account playing conditions, the quality of the opposition and the result of the matches. The value of a player's performance is assessed in relation to the Coopers & Lybrand Ratings of the opposing players and it also reflects his ability to score match-winning runs or take match-winning wickets. Updated after every Test match, with a player's most recent performances carrying more weight than his earlier ones, the Coopers & Lybrand Ratings endeavour to provide a current assessment of a Test cricketer's form and his place among his peers. A player cannot get a full rating until he has played 20 innings or taken 50 wickets in Tests.

The leading 20 batsmen and bowlers in the Ratings after the 1993-94 series between Sri Lanka and South Africa which ended on September 19 were:

	Batsmen	Rating		Bowlers	Rating
1.	D. L. Haynes (*WI*)	835	1.	Waqar Younis (*Pak.*)	903
2.	G. A. Gooch (*Eng.*)	819	2.	C. E. L. Ambrose (*WI*)	885
3.	R. B. Richardson (*WI*)	780	3.	A. Kumble (*Ind.*)	828
4.	D. C. Boon (*Aus.*)	722	4.	I. R. Bishop (*WI*)	810
5.	Salim Malik (*Pak.*)	706	5.	S. K. Warne (*Aus.*)	771
6.	S. R. Tendulkar (*Ind.*)	700	6.	A. A. Donald (*SA*)	755†
	B. C. Lara (*WI*)	700*	7.	M. G. Hughes (*Aus.*)	725
8.	M. D. Crowe (*NZ*)	655	8.	A. R. C. Fraser (*Eng.*)	674
9.	Javed Miandad (*Pak.*)	644	9.	Wasim Akram (*Pak.*)	669
10.	P. A. de Silva (*SL*)	641	10.	B. A. Reid (*Aus.*)	654
11.	A. R. Border (*Aus.*)	628	11.	T. B. A. May (*Aus.*)	650
12.	R. A. Smith (*Eng.*)	611	12.	B. N. Schultz (*SA*)	618†
13.	V. G. Kambli (*Ind.*)	597*	13.	C. A. Walsh (*WI*)	613
14.	M. E. Waugh (*Aus.*)	594	14.	Kapil Dev (*Ind.*)	611
15.	S. T. Jayasuriya (*SL*)	592*	15.	C. J. McDermott (*Aus.*)	602
16.	M. A. Atherton (*Eng.*)	583	16.	D. K. Morrison (*NZ*)	588
	H. P. Tillekeratne (*SL*)	583	17.	W. K. M. Benjamin (*WI*)	583†
18.	A. J. Stewart (*Eng.*)	567	18.	M. Prabhakar (*Ind.*)	562
19.	S. R. Waugh (*Aus.*)	563	19.	P. R. Reiffel (*Aus.*)	557†
20.	P. V. Simmons (*WI*)	560	20.	M. Muralitharan (*SL*)	555†

* Signifies the batsman has played fewer than 20 Test innings.
† Signifies the bowler has taken fewer than 50 wickets.

THE PAKISTANIS IN AUSTRALIA AND NEW ZEALAND, 1992-93

By TERRY POWER

Pakistan, the third team in the Australian one-day World Series Cup, employed the Christmas and New Year break in the tournament for the Australia–West Indies Tests to cross the Tasman for four internationals with New Zealand. After three one-day matches they took part in the earliest Test ever held in the country, at Hamilton starting on January 2, providing a new dimension to the season. Financially, the tour made what the chairman of New Zealand Cricket, Peter McDermott, called "a very minor loss" but officials were sufficiently encouraged to plan similar visits when the Test team had no other engagements.

Some of New Zealand's players had been home for less than a fortnight after their traumatic tour of Sri Lanka. Despite speculation that the five who had chosen to return early after the terrorist bombing near their hotel might have damaged their prospects of selection, all appeared against Pakistan. Cairns, who had missed the tour because of kidney surgery, was also selected but after two outings for Canterbury decided to withdraw.

The pace bowling on both sides was much stronger than the batting. Neither made more than 158 in any of the one-day games, and Mark Greatbatch's 133 on the second day of the Test was the only century for either team throughout the visit. Pakistan's captain and leading batsman, Javed Miandad, was conscientious and reasonably productive without ever being near top form; his opposite number, Martin Crowe, shone in the one-day series but missed the Test through injury. The dominance of the fast bowlers reached a climax on the fourth afternoon at Hamilton, when Wasim Akram and Waqar Younis gave a magnificently sustained exhibition to despatch New Zealand for 93 and earn a dramatic 33-run victory.

New Zealand won the limited-overs series 2-1 after Pakistan took the first match at Wellington. The one-day specialist Gavin Larsen – who had given up the chance of his long-awaited Test debut by coming back from Sri Lanka – made a big contribution, bowling 29 overs of slow-medium pace from his stiff-legged approach for only 65 runs. New Zealand's fielders had a clear edge in the one-day matches, but in the Test the vital chance for Pakistan was held and that for New Zealand dropped.

The tour may be most clearly remembered, however, for a regrettable landmark in cricket history. After Pakistan's limited-overs defeat at Napier, Aqib Javed became the first international cricketer to be suspended for his behaviour on field. Australian referee Peter Burge banned him from the deciding fixture of the series for obscene abuse of an umpire who had no-balled him. Aqib already had the unfortunate distinction of having been the first player to be fined under the same ICC rules, during the Old Trafford Test six months earlier. The Pakistanis had an unsuccessful tour of Australia. After one victory and a tie they lost their last six World Series matches, though they won their only first-class game, played over four days against Queensland. Before their next trip, to Sharjah and South Africa in February, Miandad was replaced as captain by Wasim. Waqar, who had helped him carry the team to victory in the Hamilton Test, was named as his deputy.

PAKISTANI TOURING PARTY

Javed Miandad (Karachi/Habib Bank) (*captain*), Ramiz Raja (Lahore/PNSC) (*vice-captain*), Aamir Sohail (Sargodha/Habib Bank), Aqib Javed (PACO), Asif Mujtaba (Karachi/PIA), Ata-ur-Rehman (Lahore/PACO), Inzamam-ul-Haq (Multan/United Bank), Mushtaq Ahmed (Multan/United Bank), Naved Anjum (Lahore/Habib Bank), Rashid Latif (Karachi/United Bank), Saeed Anwar (ADBP), Salim Malik (Lahore/Habib Bank), Shahid Saeed (Lahore/PACO), Waqar Younis (Multan/United Bank), Wasim Akram (Lahore/PIA).
Tour manager: Naushad Ali. *Assistant manager:* Iqbal Qasim.

PAKISTANI TOUR RESULTS

Test match – Played 1: Won 1.
First-class matches – Played 2: Won 2.
Wins – New Zealand, Queensland.
One-day internationals – Played 11: Won 2, Lost 8, Tied 1. *Wins* – West Indies, New Zealand. *Losses* – Australia (3), West Indies (3), New Zealand (2). *Tie* – Australia.
Other non first-class matches – Played 3: Won 3. *Wins* – Western Australian Country Combined XI, Western Australia, Northern Territory Invitation XI.

Note: Matches in this section which were not first-class are signified by a dagger.

†At Northam, November 29. Pakistanis won by one run. Pakistanis batted first by mutual agreement. Pakistanis 167 (44.1 overs) (Inzamam-ul-Haq 36, Saeed Anwar 30; B. Woods three for 10); Western Australian Country Combined XI 166 for six (45 overs) (J. L. Langer 36, M. P. Lavender 37, J. B. Szeliga 31, M. R. J. Veletta 31 not out; Salim Malik three for 37).

†At Perth, December 1 (day/night). Pakistanis won by 27 runs. Toss: Pakistanis. Pakistanis 270 for three (50 overs) (Aamir Sohail 49, Ramiz Raja 98, Salim Malik 38, Javed Miandad 69 not out); Western Australia 243 (47.5 overs) (W. S. Andrews 40, T. J. Zoehrer 83; Waqar Younis three for 33, Ata-ur-Rehman three for 58).

Pakistan's matches v Australia and West Indies in the Benson and Hedges World Series Cup (December 4–December 17) may be found in that section.

†At Alice Springs, December 6. Pakistanis won by 94 runs. Pakistanis batted first by mutual agreement. Pakistanis 273 for six (50 overs) (Saeed Anwar 135 retired out, Wasim Akram 50, Asif Mujtaba 32); Northern Territory Invitation XI 179 (45.5 overs) (T. J. Nielsen 34; Wasim Akram five for 33, including a hat-trick, all bowled, to finish the match).

QUEENSLAND v PAKISTANIS

At Brisbane, December 19, 20, 21, 22. Pakistanis won by five wickets. Toss: Queensland.
Set 291 in a minimum of 72 overs, the Pakistanis won with four balls to spare, raising their spirits after three successive World Series defeats. Wasim Akram led the team as Javed Miandad and Ramiz Raja were rested, but the victory was underpinned by two unbeaten centuries from left-hander Asif Mujtaba. Though overshadowed in the first innings by the flamboyance of Inzamam-ul-Haq, who scored 83 of their 129 for the third wicket, he steadied the tourists on the last day and then accelerated to add 133 in 109 minutes with Saeed Anwar. Queensland's first innings had fallen away in the face of

Mushtaq Ahmed's leg-spin, but they tackled him more confidently in the second. Barsby's 116, including 23 fours, came in 119 balls, and his second fifty just 21. Border's more sedate hundred confirmed his fitness after he had strained a hamstring in the First Test against West Indies.

Close of play: First day, Pakistanis 37-0 (Aamir Sohail 25*, Shahid Saeed 12*); Second day, Pakistanis 342-4 (Asif Mujtaba 84*, Rashid Latif 11*); Third day, Queensland 318-5 (A. R. Border 71*, S. C. Storey 15*).

Queensland

M. L. Hayden c Rashid Latif b Ata-ur-Rehman. 79	– (2) c Asif Mujtaba b Mushtaq Ahmed .	34
T. J. Barsby c Ata-ur-Rehman b Mushtaq Ahmed . 53	– (1) c Aamir Sohail b Mushtaq Ahmed .	116
P. J. T. Goggin c Rashid Latif b Wasim Akram 6	– c Asif Mujtaba b Mushtaq Ahmed .	2
S. G. Law c Rashid Latif b Ata-ur-Rehman 21	– c Rashid Latif b Wasim Akram .	15
A. R. Border c Aamir Sohail b Shahid Saeed . . 22	– not out.	116
*D. M. Wellham lbw b Shahid Saeed 16	– run out	49
S. C. Storey not out 29	– st Rashid Latif b Mushtaq Ahmed .	26
†I. A. Healy b Mushtaq Ahmed 15	– c Wasim Akram b Naved Anjum	14
C. J. McDermott c Aamir Sohail b Mushtaq Ahmed . 9	– not out	2
M. S. Kasprowicz c Saeed Anwar b Wasim Akram . 2		
G. J. Rowell b Mushtaq Ahmed 4		
L-b 3, n-b 1 4	B 8, l-b 5, w 1, n-b 10 . . .	24

1/89 2/127 3/153 4/176 5/196   260   1/101 2/157 3/160   (7 wkts dec.) 398
6/201 7/233 8/243 9/251   4/174 5/301
                                       6/350 7/381

Bowling: First Innings—Wasim Akram 19-4-45-2; Aqib Javed 10-4-38-0; Ata-ur-Rehman 15-4-60-2; Naved Anjum 5-1-15-0; Mushtaq Ahmed 18.5-2-70-4; Aamir Sohail 4-1-13-0; Shahid Saeed 4-0-16-2. *Second Innings*—Wasim Akram 21-7-43-1; Aqib Javed 12-2-34-0; Naved Anjum 18-0-107-1; Mushtaq Ahmed 30.3-3-136-4; Shahid Saeed 7-0-31-0; Aamir Sohail 2-0-19-0; Asif Mujtaba 5-1-15-0.

Pakistanis

Aamir Sohail run out 65	– c Healy b McDermott	5
Shahid Saeed lbw b Law 83	– c Goggin b Kasprowicz	14
Asif Mujtaba not out 102	– not out	125
Inzamam-ul-Haq c McDermott b Storey . . 83	– c Wellham b Storey	42
Saeed Anwar c Border b McDermott 13	– c Goggin b Kasprowicz	72
†Rashid Latif c and b Kasprowicz 19	– (7) not out	18
Naved Anjum c Healy b Kasprowicz 0		
Mushtaq Ahmed not out 0		
*Wasim Akram (did not bat)	– (6) b Kasprowicz	3
L-b 2, n-b 1 3	B 5, l-b 4, n-b 3	12

1/116 2/176 3/305   (6 wkts dec.) 368   1/7 2/33 3/109   (5 wkts) 291
4/325 5/360 6/360   4/242 5/248

Aqib Javed and Ata-ur-Rehman did not bat.

Bowling: First Innings—McDermott 26-4-95-1; Rowell 26-6-68-0; Kasprowicz 24-6-70-2; Storey 21-1-105-1; Law 8-4-12-1; Border 3-0-16-0. *Second Innings*—McDermott 17-5-50-1; Rowell 18-1-37-0; Storey 15-1-67-1; Border 11-2-45-0; Kasprowicz 17.2-4-60-3; Law 4-0-23-0.

Umpires: A. J. McQuillan and C. D. Timmins.

†NEW ZEALAND v PAKISTAN

First One-day International

At Wellington, December 26. Pakistan won by 50 runs. Toss: New Zealand.

Wasim Akram began with two wides in his first three deliveries but soon asserted the dominance that was to be vital in Pakistan's brief visit. His career-best one-day figures of five for 19 took his team to their sixth successive one-day victory over New Zealand. Pakistan scored at barely three an over on a new, two-paced pitch, with damp conditions helping the ball to swing; New Zealand lasted just 39.3 overs. For the first time in New Zealand a third umpire, Brian Aldridge, was appointed to observe proceedings on a television monitor but he had no decisions to make.

Man of the Match: Wasim Akram.

Pakistan

Aamir Sohail b Morrison	8	Waqar Younis not out	4
Ramiz Raja b Harris	50	Mushtaq Ahmed not out	1
Salim Malik run out	25		
*Javed Miandad c and b Morrison	46	B 4, l-b 3, w 3, n-b 1	11
Inzamam-ul-Haq c Jones b Watson	0		
Asif Mujtaba c Patel b Harris	0	1/14 2/57 3/116 (8 wkts, 49 overs) 158
Wasim Akram c Morrison b Harris	1	4/117 5/119 6/123
†Rashid Latif c Latham b Watson	12	7/152 8/153

Aqib Javed did not bat.

Bowling: Morrison 7-1-19-2; Watson 10-0-37-2; Patel 10-0-37-0; Larsen 10-0-30-0; Harris 10-1-24-3; Latham 2-0-4-0.

New Zealand

M. J. Greatbatch c Waqar Younis b Wasim Akram	7	†A. C. Parore c Salim Malik b Wasim Akram	14
R. T. Latham b Wasim Akram	1	G. R. Larsen c Rashid Latif b Wasim Akram	11
A. H. Jones c Rashid Latif b Wasim Akram	0	D. K. Morrison run out	3
*M. D. Crowe c Aamir Sohail b Aqib Javed	28	W. Watson not out	1
K. R. Rutherford b Aqib Javed	18	L-b 8, w 6, n-b 3	17
C. Z. Harris b Aqib Javed	7	1/10 2/11 3/19 (39.3 overs) 108
D. N. Patel c Inzamam-ul-Haq b Mushtaq Ahmed	1	4/60 5/73 6/74 7/77 8/97 9/106

Bowling: Wasim Akram 9-1-19-5; Waqar Younis 8-2-14-0; Aqib Javed 10-1-27-3; Mushtaq Ahmed 8-1-20-1; Aamir Sohail 4.3-0-20-0.

Umpires: R. S. Dunne and C. E. King.

†NEW ZEALAND v PAKISTAN

Second One-day International

At Napier, December 28. New Zealand won by six wickets. Toss: New Zealand.

The match was overshadowed by an incident which led to Aqib Javed becoming the first player to be suspended for breaches of the ICC Code of Conduct. New Zealand were chasing 137 and had lost both openers for 30 when Jones gave a lobbed, gloved slip catch off a short-pitched delivery from Aqib. Umpire Aldridge called a no-ball, judging that it was above shoulder-height, a verdict supported by television replays. After the match, Aldridge reported the bowler to the referee, Peter Burge. The non-striker, Crowe, and a nearby fieldsman, Ramiz Raja, attended a 75-minute hearing, where Crowe said Aqib had called the umpire an "effing cheat". To Aqib's defence that he was talking to himself, he commented: "It was a funny thing to call yourself." Burge suspended the bowler for the next international. Crowe's other major contribution to the day's entertainment was a match-winning 47 not out. New Zealand had kept Pakistan's score down on a pitch which was harder than in Wellington but grassy. Continuing wet weather reduced the contest to 42 overs each. Patel once again opened the attack with off-spin and, like the medium-pacer Larsen, conceded under two an over. More history was made when the first two decisions taken in New Zealand by a television umpire, Steve Dunne, came from successive deliveries. Shahid Saeed was narrowly out and Rashid Latif more comfortably home, both after run-out appeals.

Man of the Match: M. D. Crowe.

Pakistan

Aamir Sohail b Patel	9		Waqar Younis not out		0
Ramiz Raja c Parore b Patel	1		Mushtaq Ahmed not out		0
Salim Malik c Parore b Watson	39				
*Javed Miandad b Larsen	19		B 3, l-b 9, w 8		20
Inzamam-ul-Haq c Parore b Larsen	2				
Shahid Saeed run out	14		1/9 2/14 3/67	(8 wkts, 42 overs)	136
†Rashid Latif c Jones b Morrison	20		4/69 5/92 6/113		
Wasim Akram c Parore b Watson	12		7/128 8/135		

Aqib Javed did not bat.

Bowling: Morrison 8–1–30–1; Patel 9–2–16–2; Watson 8–0–39–2; Larsen 9–2–15–2; Harris 8–1–24–0.

New Zealand

M. J. Greatbatch c Rashid Latif			K. R. Rutherford c Ramiz Raja		
b Wasim Akram	0		b Shahid Saeed	34
R. T. Latham b Shahid Saeed	21		C. Z. Harris not out		3
A. H. Jones c Rashid Latif			B 1, l-b 1, w 5, n-b 8		15
b Waqar Younis	17				
*M. D. Crowe not out	47		1/0 2/30 3/71 4/133	(4 wkts, 37.4 overs)	137

D. N. Patel, †A. C. Parore, G. R. Larsen, D. K. Morrison and W. Watson did not bat.

Bowling: Wasim Akram 9–2–22–1; Waqar Younis 9–0–36–1; Aqib Javed 8–1–39–0; Shahid Saeed 7–0–20–2; Mushtaq Ahmed 4–0–16–0; Salim Malik 0.4–0–2–0.

Umpires: B. L. Aldridge and D. M. Quested.

†NEW ZEALAND v PAKISTAN

Third One-day International

At Auckland, December 30. New Zealand won by six wickets. Toss: New Zealand.

Javed Miandad's 30 was the highest score of Pakistan's innings as they subsided within 47.4 overs on a brown, slow pitch; none of the three strips supplied for the series complied with the usual limited-overs formula of quick runs. Watson bowled beautifully at medium-fast pace for four wickets. Although Greatbatch pulled Wasim Akram's first delivery of the New Zealand innings into the South Stand for six, three were out for 45. Then Crowe again rose above the difficulties facing the other players; his unbeaten 57 took him to 132 runs for once out in the series.

Man of the Match: M. D. Crowe.

Pakistan

Ramiz Raja b Watson	23		†Rashid Latif not out		9
Shahid Saeed run out	17		Waqar Younis c Crowe b Morrison		0
Salim Malik c Crowe b Larsen	23		Mushtaq Ahmed c Greatbatch b Watson	6
Saeed Anwar c Parore b Watson	0		L-b 5, n-b 3		8
*Javed Miandad c Parore b Watson	30				
Inzamam-ul-Haq run out	2		1/35 2/43 3/47	(47.4 overs)	139
Wasim Akram c Harris b Morrison	21		4/75 5/77 6/123		
Naved Anjum st Parore b Harris	0		7/123 8/127 9/128		

Bowling: Morrison 10–1–27–2; Patel 10–2–25–0; Watson 8.4–1–27–4; Larsen 10–2–20–1; Harris 6–1–22–1; Jones 2–0–6–0; Latham 1–0–7–0.

New Zealand

M. J. Greatbatch c Mushtaq Ahmed b Wasim Akram . 24	K. R. Rutherford b Mushtaq Ahmed . . 28	
R. T. Latham c Inzamam-ul-Haq b Waqar Younis . 0	C. Z. Harris not out 11	
	L-b 3, w 5, n-b 3 11	
A. H. Jones lbw b Naved Anjum 9	1/10 2/34 (4 wkts, 42.4 overs) 140	
*M. D. Crowe not out 57	3/45 4/105	

D. N. Patel, †A. C. Parore, G. R. Larsen, D. K. Morrison and W. Watson did not bat.

Bowling: Wasim Akram 9–2–28–1; Waqar Younis 10–2–27–1; Naved Anjum 10–1–30–1; Mushtaq Ahmed 9.4–1–34–1; Salim Malik 1–0–4–0; Shahid Saeed 3–0–14–0.

Umpires: B. L. Aldridge and D. B. Cowie.

NEW ZEALAND v PAKISTAN

Test Match

At Hamilton, January 2, 3, 4, 5. Pakistan won by 33 runs. Toss: New Zealand.

Wasim Akram and Waqar Younis swept Pakistan to victory on the fourth afternoon with a never-to-be-forgotten display of sustained, hostile fast bowling. Set only 127 to win, with more than two days remaining, New Zealand were 39 for three overnight. Rain delayed the resumption until the early afternoon, when the two pace bowlers attacked continuously for two hours to dismiss them for 93.

After 40 minutes without a wicket, Javed Miandad was about to turn to Mushtaq Ahmed's spin, then decided to give Waqar another chance. Jones turned the next delivery firmly to the on side, Asif Mujtaba at short leg thrust a hand to his left and the ball stuck. Wasim and Waqar took the last seven wickets for 28, overwhelming New Zealand with their pace and swing on a pitch on which the occasional delivery came through low. When Waqar bowled Harris it was his 100th wicket in his 20th Test.

Wright, omitted from the one-day squad, had broken a finger after being recalled, and Crowe also damaged a finger while fielding at Auckland – two experienced, in-form batsmen badly missed in a low-scoring match. Rutherford deputised as captain. After losing his fourth consecutive toss and watching Pakistan lose three for 12, Miandad batted responsibly for 221 minutes. He was skittled eight short of his century by left-armer Su'a, who returned his best international figures. Gaining considerable swing at fast-medium pace, he despatched Ramiz Raja with his third delivery and removed four of Pakistan's top six.

Greatbatch and Hartland began the reply at half past four on Saturday and were not separated before two o'clock the next day. Hartland's courage was more admirable than his technique against the bouncers that repeatedly struck his helmet – like being kicked in the head by a horse, he said. But Sunday was dominated by what seemed to be a match-winning hundred from Greatbatch. He batted for seven hours with characteristic pugnacity, unwilling to be tied down and skilful on his feet for one of his solid build. His best shot was a magnificent on-driven boundary off Wasim. Greatbatch's achievement was the greater against such fine bowling; once Mushtaq had Hartland stumped, the other four main batsmen struggled 99 minutes for 24 runs between them. Only Parore, eking out 16 in 113 minutes, offered any sense of security.

Pakistan kept New Zealand's lead to 48, but when Su'a removed Miandad again, just after noon on the second day, it was five down for 39 – still nine runs behind. The other four wickets went to Morrison, including Aamir Sohail first ball. Bowling genuinely fast, Morrison launched into a sequence of performances that carried him through the next series against Australia. Less than ten months earlier, Inzamam-ul-Haq's batting had ended New Zealand's World Cup run. So far he had offered no encore. But on the third afternoon he contributed 75 runs, which looked at the time like brave defiance. When he was 39 there came the moment which, combined with Mujtaba's catch next day, decided the Test. Rutherford, at short mid-wicket, dived and took Inzamam, but the ball was jogged out of his grasp as his elbow hit the ground. Needing 127, New Zealand lost both openers and night-watchman Morrison that evening, all to Wasim. Next day he and Waqar completed their improbable victory.

There had been volleys of none-too-cheery banter throughout the match; most of it seemed to come from Pakistanis, though Patel, at short leg, obviously baited Rashid Latif on the third afternoon. At the end of a tense day's play referee Peter Burge issued a statement warning both teams against sledging.

Man of the Match: Wasim Akram.

Close of play: First day, New Zealand 23-0 (M. J. Greatbatch 8*, B. R. Hartland 7*); Second day, New Zealand 256-8 (A. C. Parore 16*); Third day, New Zealand 39-3 (A. H. Jones 11*, A. C. Parore 0*).

Pakistan

Aamir Sohail c Owens b Morrison	0	– b Morrison	0
Ramiz Raja c Rutherford b Su'a	4	– c Parore b Morrison	8
Asif Mujtaba c Owens b Su'a	0	– lbw b Morrison	11
*Javed Miandad b Su'a	92	– lbw b Su'a	12
Salim Malik c Parore b Morrison	14	– c Su'a b Morrison	0
Inzamam-ul-Haq c Morrison b Su'a	23	– lbw b Owens	75
Wasim Akram c Greatbatch b Patel	27	– (8) b Patel	15
†Rashid Latif not out	32	– (7) c Rutherford b Su'a	33
Waqar Younis run out	13	– not out	4
Mushtaq Ahmed lbw b Su'a	2	– c Rutherford b Morrison	10
Aqib Javed c Greatbatch b Morrison	1	– c Hartland b Patel	2
W 4, n-b 4	8	L-b 2, n-b 2	4
	216		**174**

1/4 (2) 2/4 (1) 3/12 (3) 4/45 (5)   216   1/0 (1) 2/20 (2) 3/25 (3)   174
5/87 (6) 6/158 (7) 7/176 (4)   4/25 (5) 5/39 (4) 6/119 (7)
8/202 (9) 9/208 (10) 10/216 (11)   7/158 (6) 8/158 (8)
9/171 (10) 10/174 (11)

Bowling: *First Innings*—Morrison 19.3-4-42-3; Su'a 24-2-73-5; Owens 12-3-48-0; Patel 14-2-53-1. *Second Innings*—Morrison 15-2-41-5; Su'a 13-1-47-2; Owens 7-0-19-1; Patel 20.1-5-65-2.

New Zealand

M. J. Greatbatch lbw b Waqar Younis	133	– (2) c Aamir Sohail b Wasim Akram	8
B. R. Hartland st Rashid Latif b Mushtaq Ahmed	43	– (1) b Wasim Akram	9
A. H. Jones lbw b Wasim Akram	2	– c Asif Mujtaba b Waqar Younis	19
R. T. Latham lbw b Wasim Akram	2	– (6) b Waqar Younis	0
*K. R. Rutherford c Rashid Latif b Mushtaq Ahmed	14	– (7) c Aamir Sohail b Wasim Akram	9
C. Z. Harris lbw b Waqar Younis	6	– (8) b Wasim Akram	9
D. N. Patel lbw b Mushtaq Ahmed	12	– (9) b Waqar Younis	4
†A. C. Parore lbw b Wasim Akram	16	– (5) c Rashid Latif b Wasim Akram	13
M. L. Su'a c Rashid Latif b Waqar Younis	0	– (10) lbw b Waqar Younis	0
D. K. Morrison not out	3	– (4) lbw b Wasim Akram	0
M. B. Owens b Waqar Younis	0	– not out	0
B 1, l-b 15, w 1, n-b 16	33	B 1, l-b 11, n-b 10	22
	264		**93**

1/108 (2) 2/111 (3) 3/117 (4) 4/147 (5)   264   1/19 (2) 2/31 (3) 3/32 (4)   93
5/164 (6) 6/193 (7) 7/254 (1)   4/65 (5) 5/67 (6) 6/71 (6)
8/256 (9) 9/257 (8) 10/264 (11)   7/88 (7) 8/88 (8)
9/88 (10) 10/93 (9)

Bowling: *First Innings*—Wasim Akram 31-9-66-3; Waqar Younis 28-11-59-4; Mushtaq Ahmed 38-10-87-3; Aqib Javed 7-2-24-0; Aamir Sohail 5-2-12-0. *Second Innings*—Wasim Akram 22-4-45-5; Aqib Javed 8-2-14-0; Waqar Younis 13.3-4-22-5.

Umpires: B. L. Aldridge and R. S. Dunne. Referee: P. J. P. Burge (Australia).

Pakistan's matches v Australia and West Indies in the Benson and Hedges World Series Cup (January 9–January 14) may be found in that section.

THE AUSTRALIANS IN NEW ZEALAND, 1992-93

By PATRICK SMITHERS

Australia's third tour of New Zealand under Allan Border did not, at least, end in defeat like the previous two; but nor did the Australians exact revenge for previous frustrations, although New Zealand were a weaker side than they had been when the countries had last met in a Test series three years earlier. New Zealand were not even competitive in the First Test, which they lost by a gaping margin, but played with characteristic resolve thereafter to level the series 1-1 and maintain their 16-year unbeaten record at home against their nearest and keenest cricketing rivals. Border's consolation was strictly personal: he eclipsed Sunil Gavaskar's record to become Test cricket's leading run-scorer. Australia's consolation was a 3-2 scoreline in an exciting one-day tournament, which played to packed houses as it worked its way up the country.

New Zealand's fortunes revived after the defeat by an innings and 60 runs in Christchurch, despite several notable deficiencies in their team, which had just lost three Tests in succession – to Sri Lanka, Pakistan and Australia. The home side did not field a specialist sixth batsman throughout the series, instead relying, in turn, on a bowling all-rounder (Cairns), a wicket-keeper (Blain) and a spare-part player (Harris) to fill that post. Nor did they have an effective spin bowler until the final Australian innings of the series, when Martin Crowe invoked the spirit of New Zealand's World Cup campaign and gave Patel the new ball, unorthodox tactics that met with immediate success. This was, remarkably enough, New Zealand's first series against Australia that did not feature Richard Hadlee (although Hadlee did not play in the one-off Tests in Wellington in 1945-46 and 1989-90). And their situation looked particularly precarious when, during the anguished soul-searching that followed the loss in Christchurch, Crowe publicly invited the selectors to replace him as captain if they deemed it in the best interests of New Zealand cricket. The offer was declined. Then, after an honourable draw in Wellington, New Zealand's five-wicket win in Auckland struck a chord with the public. An estimated 8,000 turned up to Eden Park when the gates were thrown open on the last day of the series to watch New Zealand make the 33 runs needed to square the rubber and retain the Trans-Tasman trophy.

For the second time in the southern summer, Australia could blame their batting for allowing a series to slip. By the end of the Third Test, Australia had gone five matches without producing a century-maker. The sense of retarded progress was emphasised by the presence of Border, who batted at No. 6, at the top of the list of Australian averages and aggregates, Steve Waugh being the only other Australian to average more than 40. Merv Hughes came third in the averages. By the Third Test, Mark Waugh had been dropped, the culmination of two years of wasted opportunities, while Justin Langer completed a lean series in the No. 3 position with a pair at Auckland. The series' only century came from Ken Rutherford, appropriately enough, because the strokemaker from Otago was the outstanding batsman on either side, making 298 runs at 59.60 and continuing the courageous resurrection of a career almost sacrificed in the Caribbean in his teens. John Wright was the only other man to top 200 runs and, just as important for New Zealand, his average occupation of the crease was three and a quarter hours. He announced his retirement after the Third Test, when the technological age finally caught up with him – his 148th and last Test innings ended with the third umpire flashing a red light from the stand to signal that his 38-year-old legs had failed by a fraction to complete a single in time. Tony Blain, who returned to Test cricket at the age of 31 when Parore was injured, batted resolutely at important stages of the Second and Third Tests and kept wicket impressively, making him the find of the series for New Zealand.

The five-match one-day series was also keenly contested, and settled in Australia's favour only in the final game. Their batsmen, and Mark Waugh in particular, seemed to revel in the greater licence permitted to them; Waugh averaged over 60 when promoted to open, a move previously ruled out by team management.

The cricket throughout the tour was engaging, not for any sustained excellence, but for the intensity of the struggle. The man who did more than any other to entertain was Shane Warne, who somehow managed to combine that quality with a consistency not matched by any other player. After helping bowl Australia to victory in the Christchurch Test, he was unfortunate not to have more time in Wellington or more runs to defend in Auckland. His 17 wickets at 15.05 broke Dennis Lillee's record of 15 for the most by an Australian on a Test tour of New Zealand and equalled Craig McDermott's record for Australia against New Zealand in either country. Incredibly for a wrist-spinner, he conceded an average of only 1.61 runs per over. Danny Morrison, after a wayward start in Christchurch, fuelled New Zealand's comeback, taking career-best figures in Wellington and also finishing the series with 17 wickets; by the end of the Third Test he was a more menacing proposition than either of Australia's opening pair, McDermott, who was hampered by a hernia problem, and Hughes, each of whom took 13 wickets.

If Hughes appeared to breach the code of conduct during his altercation with Mark Greatbatch in the Third Test, ICC referee Javed Burki was unconcerned, saying that "you can enforce the code so strictly that you take all the fun out of the game". Overall, the series was played in an excellent spirit. Border walked at a crucial stage in the last Test, and Crowe reciprocated in the first one-day international, "out of respect for the Australians".

AUSTRALIAN TOURING PARTY

A. R. Border (Queensland) (*captain*), M. A. Taylor (New South Wales) (*vice-captain*), D. C. Boon (Tasmania), I. A. Healy (Queensland), M. G. Hughes (Victoria), J. L. Langer (Western Australia), D. R. Martyn (Western Australia), T. B. A. May (South Australia), C. J. McDermott (Queensland), P. R. Reiffel (Victoria), S. K. Warne (Victoria), M. E. Waugh (New South Wales), S. R. Waugh (New South Wales).

A. I. C. Dodemaide and D. M. Jones (both Victoria) replaced Langer and McDermott for the one-day international series.

Manager: I. H. McDonald.   *Coach:* R. B. Simpson.

AUSTRALIAN TOUR RESULTS

Test matches – Played 3: Won 1, Lost 1, Drawn 1.
First-class matches – Played 4: Won 2, Lost 1, Drawn 1.
Wins – New Zealand, New Zealand Board XI.
Loss – New Zealand.
Draw – New Zealand.
One-day internationals – Played 5: Won 3, Lost 2.
Other non first-class match – Lost v New Zealand President's XI.

TEST MATCH AVERAGES

NEW ZEALAND – BATTING

	T	I	NO	R	HS	100s	Avge	Ct/St
K. R. Rutherford....	3	6	1	298	102	1	59.60	1
J. G. Wright	3	6	1	237	72	0	47.40	2
M. D. Crowe	3	6	0	186	98	0	31.00	1
T. E. Blain	2	4	1	91	51	0	30.33	7/1
M. J. Greatbatch ..	3	6	0	126	61	0	21.00	3
D. N. Patel	3	5	1	83	35	0	20.75	0
A. H. Jones	3	6	0	110	42	0	18.33	4
D. K. Morrison	3	5	3	35	19	0	17.50	3
C. L. Cairns	2	3	0	48	21	0	12.00	1

Played in two Tests: M. B. Owens 0, 0*, 0 (1 ct); M. L. Su'a 0, 44, 3; W. Watson 3, 0.
Played in one Test: C. Z. Harris 13, 0 (1 ct); A. C. Parore 6, 5 (3 ct).

* *Signifies not out.*

BOWLING

	O	M	R	W	BB	5W/i	Avge
D. K. Morrison....	114.2	29	288	17	7-89	2	16.94
W. Watson	67	26	150	7	3-43	0	21.42
M. B. Owens	47	12	112	4	3-58	0	28.00
D. N. Patel	70	13	263	8	5-93	1	32.87

Also bowled: C. L. Cairns 55.3–12–164–1; C. Z. Harris 2–1–4–0; M. L. Su'a 65–12–189–2.

AUSTRALIA – BATTING

	T	I	NO	R	HS	100s	Avge	Ct/St
A. R. Border	3	4	0	189	88	0	47.25	3
S. R. Waugh	3	4	0	178	75	0	44.50	1
M. G. Hughes	3	4	1	117	45	0	39.00	0
M. A. Taylor	3	4	0	148	82	0	37.00	7
D. C. Boon	3	4	0	125	53	0	31.25	3
S. K. Warne	3	4	2	49	22*	0	24.50	1
J. L. Langer	3	4	0	87	63	0	21.75	1
I. A. Healy........	3	4	0	86	54	0	21.50	12/1
C. J. McDermott....	3	4	1	27	10	0	9.00	1
P. R. Reiffel	3	4	0	35	18	0	8.75	1

Played in two Tests: M. E. Waugh 13, 12. Played in one Test: D. R. Martyn 1, 74.

* *Signifies not out.*

BOWLING

	O	M	R	W	BB	5W/i	Avge
S. K. Warne	159	73	256	17	4-8	0	15.05
C. J. McDermott	125	36	326	13	3-54	0	25.07
M. G. Hughes	132.2	38	349	13	4-62	0	26.84
P. R. Reiffel	103	33	250	5	2-27	0	50.00

Also bowled: D. C. Boon 1-1-0-0; A. R. Border 18-8-26-0; D. R. Martyn 1-1-0-0; M. A. Taylor 4-2-15-0; M. E. Waugh 15-5-27-1; S. R. Waugh 41-18-71-2.

AUSTRALIAN AVERAGES – FIRST-CLASS MATCHES

BATTING

	M	I	NO	R	HS	100s	Avge	Ct/St
S. R. Waugh	4	6	1	250	75	0	50.00	2
I. A. Healy	4	5	1	173	87*	0	43.25	13/1
J. L. Langer	4	6	1	214	89	0	42.80	2
A. R. Border	4	5	0	189	88	0	37.80	4
M. A. Taylor	4	6	0	193	82	0	32.16	12
M. G. Hughes	4	5	1	127	45	0	31.75	1
D. C. Boon	3	4	0	125	53	0	31.25	3
S. K. Warne	4	5	2	51	22*	0	17.00	1
P. R. Reiffel	4	5	0	84	49	0	16.80	2
C. J. McDermott	3	4	1	27	10	0	9.00	1

Played in three matches: M. E. Waugh 0, 13, 12 (2 ct). Played in two matches: D. R. Martyn 9, 1, 74. Played in one match: T. B. A. May 1.

* *Signifies not out.*

BOWLING

	O	M	R	W	BB	5W/i	Avge
S. K. Warne	187.5	81	337	19	4-8	0	17.73
M. G. Hughes	171.2	55	405	19	4-21	0	21.31
S. R. Waugh	55	21	108	5	2-21	0	21.60
C. J. McDermott	125	36	326	13	3-54	0	25.07
P. R. Reiffel	142.4	47	367	12	5-78	1	30.58

Also bowled: D. C. Boon 1-1-0-0; A. R. Border 28-15-34-1; D. R. Martyn 1-1-0-0; T. B. A. May 33-6-83-0; M. A. Taylor 4-2-15-0; M. E. Waugh 18-6-45-1.

Note: Matches in this section which were not first-class are signified by a dagger.

NEW ZEALAND BOARD XI v AUSTRALIANS

At New Plymouth, February 16, 17, 18. Australians won by nine wickets. Toss: New Zealand Board XI.

The Board XI contrived to lose 19 wickets and the match inside the scheduled three days, despite fielding four of the top six batsmen who had recently played Pakistan, as well as Martin Crowe, who missed the Test through injury. The first day was blessed by a sparkling 163 from Crowe, who exploited the close proximity of the grassed terraces of Pukekura Park to hit 24 fours and three sixes, particularly punishing Warne. But his team-mates contributed only 93 between them. Their second attempt was even more dismal, thanks largely to Hughes, who bowled with pace and rhythm throughout. The Australians did not match Crowe's innings but demonstrated far greater consistency; even their No. 9, Reiffel, added 49 runs to his five first-innings wickets. The 20-year-old left-arm orthodox spinner, Haslam, enjoyed some heady success, taking three wickets, including Border's, in 14 deliveries, but could not keep this rate up. David Boon missed the match after flying back to Tasmania for the funeral of his father, Clarrie.

Close of play: First day, Australians 26-0 (M. A. Taylor 8*, J. L. Langer 16*); Second day, New Zealand Board XI 2-1 (M. J. Greatbatch 2*, A. H. Jones 0*).

New Zealand Board XI

B. R. Hartland b Hughes	6	– (2) c Taylor b Reiffel	0
M. J. Greatbatch b S. R. Waugh	21	– (1) c Taylor b S. R. Waugh	20
A. H. Jones c Hughes b S. R. Waugh	10	– lbw b Hughes	38
*M. D. Crowe b Border b Reiffel	163	– c Reiffel b Border	16
C. Z. Harris b Reiffel	29	– c Langer b Warne	8
†A. C. Parore c Taylor b Reiffel	0	– lbw b Reiffel	7
M. N. Hart b Hughes	15	– c S. R. Waugh b Hughes	24
D. J. Nash c Taylor b Reiffel	0	– not out	15
C. Pringle c Healy b Reiffel	8	– c M. E. Waugh b Hughes	9
M. J. Haslam not out	4	– c Taylor b Hughes	2
M. B. Owens (did not bat)		– c M. E. Waugh b Warne	0
B 1, l-b 3, n-b 4	8	B 5, l-b 5, w 1	11

1/12 2/30 3/55 4/192 5/192   (9 wkts dec.) 264   1/0 2/58 3/78 4/82 5/91   150
6/251 7/251 8/251 9/264   6/105 7/135 8/147 9/149

Bowling: *First Innings*—Hughes 20-7-35-2; Reiffel 23.4-8-78-5; S. R. Waugh 8-2-21-2; May 23-6-48-0; M. E. Waugh 3-1-18-0; Warne 16-1-60-0. *Second Innings*—Hughes 19-10-21-2; Reiffel 16-6-39-2; S. R. Waugh 6-1-16-1; May 10-0-35-0; Border 10-7-8-1; Warne 12.5-7-21-2.

Australians

M. A. Taylor c Hart b Owens	45	– (2) c Parore b Owens	0
J. L. Langer c Parore b Haslam	89	– (1) not out	38
S. R. Waugh c sub (T. Kennedy) b Nash	41	– not out	31
M. E. Waugh c sub (T. Kennedy) b Haslam	0		
D. R. Martyn b Haslam	9		
*A. R. Border c Jones b Haslam	0		
†I. A. Healy not out	87		
M. G. Hughes b Pringle	10		
P. R. Reiffel c Parore b Owens	49		
T. B. A. May b Owens	1		
S. K. Warne c Greatbatch b Pringle	2		
L-b 9, w 4, n-b 2	15		

1/119 2/182 3/183 4/195 5/197   348   1/7   (1 wkt) 69
6/206 7/217 8/315 9/317

Bowling: *First Innings*—Owens 21-4-85-3; Pringle 20.3-5-66-2; Nash 15-2-46-1; Haslam 26-3-101-4; Hart 14-2-36-0; Harris 1-0-5-0. *Second Innings*—Owens 5-0-25-1; Pringle 4-0-19-0; Haslam 3.5-0-19-0; Nash 2-0-6-0.

Umpires: C. E. King and D. M. Quested.

---

†At Nelson, February 22. New Zealand President's XI won by three wickets. Toss: Australians. Australians 222 for eight (50 overs) (D. C. Boon 75, M. E. Waugh 56; C. Pringle three for 23); New Zealand President's XI 223 for seven (48.4 overs) (K. R. Rutherford 97, B. A. Young 57; M. E. Waugh three for 18).

A one-day match was played after the first two days of the planned first-class fixture were washed out.

NEW ZEALAND v AUSTRALIA

First Test Match

At Christchurch, February 25, 26, 27, 28. Australia won by an innings and 60 runs. Toss: New Zealand.

For a contest so one-sided, this match had a surprising amount to recommend it. Border provided a sense of history, Rutherford batted gallantly in both innings against the tide and Warne reminded New Zealand of the exotic delights and dangers of quality leg-spin, such a rarity in this country that most of the batsmen responded like petrified rabbits. New Zealand, who lacked batting depth, went on the attack by naming five bowlers and sending Australia in on a wet pitch. After that, the strategy rang hollow, thanks to errant bowling and defensive field settings; a third man was preferred to short leg on the first morning. After several days sweating under the covers, the pitch was dark, damp and sprinkled with inviting green patches. But the fast bowlers were so profligate in their line that coach Warren Lees gave them a dressing down at lunch. Inevitably, the chatter in the stands centred on what Sir Richard Hadlee might have done on his old stamping ground.

The Australians kept their heads down until conditions eased. The left-handers Taylor and Langer played with pragmatism rather than panache and added 116 for the second wicket. If their scoring-rate was modest, Australia more than compensated on the second day, when their diligence enabled their colleagues to make an uninhibited assault. Australia added 149 in the middle session, in which Hughes clubbed 45 from 46 balls. Three of his four sixes were off Patel, including one on to the roof of a grandstand. Border, fortunate to survive a run-out chance on nine, top-scored with 88 out of 485, although it was his lofted sweep off Patel at 1.52 p.m. that drew the most attention. As the ball bounced into the fence at mid-wicket, Border reached 50 and overtook S. M. Gavaskar's 10,122 to become the leading run-scorer in Tests. Being Border, he painted the achievement as little more than a numerical inevitability for one who had played so many matches – this was his 139th Test. He saluted his team-mates in the stand, acknowledged the applause of the sparse crowd, shook hands with Healy and Parore, the nearest players, and continued his innings.

The Australian bowlers had no trouble finding their line. McDermott dismissed Greatbatch and Jones before stumps on the second day, and Hughes removed Crowe, sparring indecisively at a lifter, during a splendid spell early on the third. Picking up Crowe twice in the match was a considerable service. But no one made the New Zealanders more uncomfortable than Warne. Wright and Rutherford poked and prodded at his leg-spin with such suspicion that his first seven overs did not yield a run. Warne bowled unchanged in each innings, 22 overs in the first and 26 in the second, for match figures of seven wickets for 86. As New Zealand floundered for 182 and 243, only Rutherford prospered, save for some late-order hitting from Patel and Su'a. Rutherford's 57 on an improving pitch mocked his team-mates' efforts and included the shot of the series – an audacious back-foot cover drive off McDermott that cleared the fence. His 102 following on was even better. But his dismissals were instructive; Warne bowled him around his legs attempting to sweep in the first innings, and had him caught behind after spinning a leg-break sharply out of the footmarks coming round the wicket in the second.

Man of the Match: S. K. Warne.

Close of play: First day, Australia 217-3 (J. L. Langer 63*, S. R. Waugh 33*); Second day, New Zealand 30-2 (J. G. Wright 4*, M. D. Crowe 7*); Third day, New Zealand 37-3 (M. D. Crowe 5*, K. R. Rutherford 4*).

Australia

D. C. Boon c Parore b Owens	15	S. K. Warne not out	22
M. A. Taylor c Crowe b Morrison	82	C. J. McDermott c Jones b Cairns	4
J. L. Langer lbw b Morrison	63		
M. E. Waugh c Parore b Patel	13	B 2, l-b 6, w 5, n-b 6	19
S. R. Waugh lbw b Owens	62		
*A. R. Border c Parore b Morrison	88	1/33 (1) 2/149 (2) 3/170 (4)	485
†I. A. Healy c Morrison b Owens	54	4/217 (3) 5/264 (5) 6/363 (7)	
M. G. Hughes c Cairns b Patel	45	7/435 (6) 8/441 (8)	
P. R. Reiffel c Greatbatch b Su'a	18	9/480 (9) 10/485 (11)	

Bowling: Morrison 36–11–81–3; Su'a 33–5–106–1; Cairns 31.3–9–87–1; Owens 26–9–58–3; Patel 31–3–145–2.

New Zealand

M. J. Greatbatch	c Healy b McDermott	4	– c Reiffel b Hughes	0
J. G. Wright	lbw b Warne	39	– b McDermott	14
A. H. Jones	lbw b McDermott	8	– c Border b McDermott	10
*M. D. Crowe	c Taylor b Hughes	15	– lbw b Hughes	14
K. R. Rutherford	b Warne	57	– c Healy b Warne	102
C. L. Cairns	c Boon b McDermott	0	– c Taylor b Warne	21
D. N. Patel	c McDermott b Hughes	35	– (8) b Warne	8
†A. C. Parore	c Boon b Reiffel	6	– (7) c Boon b Warne	5
M. L. Su'a	c Healy b Reiffel	0	– b Hughes	44
D. K. Morrison	not out	4	– c Healy b Hughes	19
M. B. Owens	lbw b Warne	0	– not out	0
	B 2, l-b 4, w 4, n-b 4	14	L-b 2, n-b 4	6

1/4 (1) 2/18 (3) 3/53 (4) 4/124 (5)   182   1/0 (1) 2/19 (3) 3/24 (2)   243
5/128 (6) 6/138 (2) 7/150 (8) 8/152 (9)   4/51 (4) 5/92 (6) 6/110 (7)
9/181 (7) 10/182 (11)   7/144 (8) 8/190 (5)
                                                          9/242 (9) 10/243 (10)

Bowling: *First Innings*—McDermott 21–4–73–3; Hughes 21–10–44–2; Reiffel 18–8–27–2; S. R. Waugh 4–2–9–0; Warne 22–12–23–3. *Second Innings*—Hughes 24.5–6–62–4; McDermott 19–6–45–2; Reiffel 18–3–59–0; S. R. Waugh 2–2–0–0; Warne 26–7–63–4; M. E. Waugh 5–1–12–0.

Umpires: B. L. Aldridge and C. E. King. Referee: Javed Burki (Pakistan).

NEW ZEALAND v AUSTRALIA

Second Test Match

At Wellington, March 4, 5, 6, 7, 8. Drawn. Toss: Australia.

Going into the last day at the Basin Reserve, Australia were looking to Warne's leg-spin to bring them a second win to take the series. It was not an unreasonable expectation. New Zealand, fielding only five recognised batsmen, were three down with a lead of 71, Wright was in cotton wool with an ankle injury and the memory of Christchurch was fresh in everyone's minds. Yet, by the time the game was called off an hour before the scheduled close, New Zealand had drawn the match; indeed, had six hours not been lost, mostly to rain on the first day, they might even have won.

The rehabilitation of their fortunes started and ended with Wright, who walked out to open the batting on the first morning and hobbled off on the last afternoon. In between, he stood guard over embattled New Zealand's reputation for more than nine and a half hours. Sent in on a seaming pitch, he and Greatbatch opened with a disciplined 111 before Crowe moved to capitalise on their start. In an effort to make up for lost time, Crowe and Rutherford blazed 49 in the first 38 minutes on the third morning, but then Rutherford was caught behind and New Zealand lost seven wickets for 42. At one stage McDermott took three for five, including Crowe, bowled by an off-cutter for 98. Struck a nasty blow on the helmet by Hughes when nine, Crowe played a brave innings full of his trademark pulls. But he became bogged down in the 90s. While on 97 he was beaten by several superb deliveries from Warne.

An eventful fourth day, in which 11 wickets fell, was also notable for Crowe's temporary surrender of the captaincy – while he remained on the field – to Rutherford for half an hour after lunch. Morrison found his rhythm with the second new ball, taking the last six Australian wickets for a career-best seven for 89. The lifter that claimed Steve Waugh was decidedly unpleasant.

New Zealand led by 31 on the first innings, although they lost Greatbatch, Crowe and Rutherford before stumps; the batting order had been rearranged after Wright hurt his ankle in the field. Needing quick wickets to force a result, Border started with Warne into the wind on the last morning but, strangely, employed only one close fielder – a slip. It was strange, too, that Hughes was not introduced until after drinks in the middle session, when the game was all but dead. Jones and Blain survived a tense first hour without mishap, and only one wicket fell before lunch when Jones was lbw to Warne's flipper. Blain, flown in the day before the match to replace Parore, who was hit on the head in the nets, proved a doughty competitor, responding admirably to the challenge of batting at No. 5 when New Zealand could ill afford an outbreak of panic.

Man of the Match: D. K. Morrison.

Close of play: First day, New Zealand 28-0 (M. J. Greatbatch 13*, J. G. Wright 10*); Second day, New Zealand 237-3 (M. D. Crowe 62*, K. R. Rutherford 14*); Third day, Australia 107-2 (J. L. Langer 8*, M. E. Waugh 0*); Fourth day, New Zealand 40-3 (A. H. Jones 20*, T. E. Blain 2*).

New Zealand

M. J. Greatbatch c Taylor b Reiffel	61	– (2) b McDermott	0
J. G. Wright c Healy b Hughes	72	– (6) not out	46
A. H. Jones b Reiffel	4	– (1) lbw b Warne	42
*M. D. Crowe b McDermott	98	– (3) lbw b McDermott	3
K. R. Rutherford c Healy b Hughes	32	– (4) c Healy b Reiffel	11
†T. E. Blain b Hughes	1	– (5) c Healy b Warne	51
C. L. Cairns c Border b McDermott	13	– lbw b McDermott	14
D. N. Patel not out	13	– c Healy b M. E. Waugh	25
D. K. Morrison c Warne b McDermott	2	– not out	0
W. Watson c Taylor b Warne	3		
M. B. Owens b Warne	0		
B 7, l-b 11, w 2, n-b 10	30	B 8, l-b 8, w 1, n-b 1	18

1/111 (1) 2/120 (3) 3/191 (2) 4/287 (5)   329   1/4 (2) 2/9 (3) 3/30 (4)   (7 wkts) 210
5/289 (6) 6/307 (7) 7/308 (4)   4/101 (5) 5/131 (5)
8/314 (9) 9/329 (10) 10/329 (11)   6/154 (7) 7/202 (8)

Bowling: First Innings—McDermott 31-8-66-3; Hughes 35-9-100-3; Reiffel 23-8-55-2; S. R. Waugh 15-7-28-0; Warne 29-9-59-2; M. E. Waugh 2-1-3-0. *Second Innings*—McDermott 23-9-54-3; Hughes 11-5-22-0; Warne 40-25-49-2; Reiffel 16-7-27-1; Border 12-5-15-0; M. E. Waugh 8-3-12-1; Taylor 4-2-15-0; Boon 1-1-0-0.

Australia

M. A. Taylor run out	50	S. K. Warne c Greatbatch b Morrison	22
D. C. Boon c and b Morrison	37	C. J. McDermott not out	7
J. L. Langer c Blain b Watson	24		
M. E. Waugh c and b Owens	12	L-b 14, n-b 4	18
S. R. Waugh c Blain b Morrison	75		
*A. R. Border lbw b Morrison	30	1/92 (1) 2/105 (2) 3/128 (4)	298
†I. A. Healy c Rutherford b Morrison	8	4/154 (3) 5/229 (6) 6/237 (7)	
M. G. Hughes c Wright b Morrison	8	7/251 (8) 8/258 (9)	
P. R. Reiffel lbw b Morrison	7	9/271 (5) 10/298 (10)	

Bowling: Morrison 26.4-5-89-7; Cairns 24-3-77-0; Watson 29-12-60-1; Owens 21-3-54-1; Patel 1-0-4-0.

Umpires: B. L. Aldridge and R. S. Dunne. *Referee:* Javed Burki (Pakistan).

NEW ZEALAND v AUSTRALIA

Third Test Match

At Auckland, March 12, 13, 14, 15, 16. New Zealand won by five wickets. Toss: Australia.
Australia spent most of this engrossing Test trying to wriggle their way out of trouble after a calamitous opening day. Indeed, they almost wriggled into a winning position, setting New Zealand a thorny target of 201 on a bowlers' pitch. That the home side made the runs with five wickets to spare, and without succumbing to the tension of the occasion, was a measure of their improvement through the series.

Border's decision to bat looked reasonable after an uneventful first hour, but then the clouds enclosed Eden Park and the game underwent a personality change. New Zealand had learned the lessons of Christchurch and dismissed Australia for 139 in conditions conducive to swing and seam bowling. Morrison's lethal fast out-swingers brought him six for 37. This included his 100th Test wicket when he had Healy caught in the gully – though Border, his 99th, was given out caught behind to a delivery that clipped his off stump without removing the bails, the first of several decisions from umpire King that upset the Australians. Morrison became the eighth New Zealander to pass the milestone, in his 29th Test. New Zealand also benefited from the influence of the canny Watson; Martyn, who had replaced Mark Waugh, did well to get an edge to a Watson leg-cutter.

The impression that Eden Park was a swing bowler's paradise was reinforced next day by Steve Waugh, whose potent out-swinger had Crowe caught at first slip attempting to turn the ball to leg. Unfortunately, that resulted in Border holding back Warne – other than a maiden before lunch – until the last hour of the day, when New Zealand led by 39. Once again Warne changed a game's direction, taking four wickets for eight from 15 overs. Collectively the New Zealand batsmen had struck their best form of the series, but had little to show for it: the top five reached 20, but none passed Rutherford's 43, which ended when he danced recklessly down the pitch to Warne's second delivery.

In a bid to swing the delicately balanced series, Crowe tossed the new ball to his off-spinner, Patel. Crowe spoke later of the "eerie feeling" this created in the opposition, and certainly Australia appeared slightly spooked: Taylor was stumped in Patel's first over and Langer lbw in his second, neither offering a shot. Martyn responded with an aristocratic 74, dropping down on one knee to slap the bowling about. Boon made only 29 of their 107-run partnership before Martyn fell to Greatbatch's acrobatic catch at silly mid-off. But it still took determined contributions from Border and Hughes to scrape together the lead of 200 Australia thought they needed.

The series reached a climax with the heavyweight clash between Hughes and the New Zealand opener Greatbatch, who came out swinging like cowboys in a bar-room brawl. Hughes was affronted by Greatbatch's tactic of charging the bowling and the pair exchanged heated words, brushed chests and Hughes once spat on the ground in Greatbatch's direction. Greatbatch's most extraordinary shot came at the expense of McDermott, whom he charged and deposited into the terraces over wide mid-off. His 29 from 30 balls ended when Hughes uprooted his middle stump, but he had broken the ice. While never dominating Warne, the New Zealand batsmen made a better fist of his bowling than at any other stage in the series, and won in something close to comfort.

Men of the Match: D. K. Morrison and K. R. Rutherford.

Close of play: First day, Australia 139-9 (S. K. Warne 3*, C. J. McDermott 6*); Second day, New Zealand 206-8 (M. L. Su'a 0*, D. K. Morrison 0*); Third day, Australia 226-6 (A. R. Border 61*, M. G. Hughes 0*); Fourth day, New Zealand 168-5 (K. R. Rutherford 31*, T. E. Blain 19*).

Australia

D. C. Boon lbw b Watson	20	– lbw b Su'a	53
M. A. Taylor lbw b Morrison	13	– st Blain b Patel	3
J. L. Langer c Blain b Morrison	0	– lbw b Patel	0
D. R. Martyn c Blain b Watson	1	– c Greatbatch b Patel	74
S. R. Waugh c Jones b Watson	41	– lbw b Patel	0
*A. R. Border c Blain b Morrison	0	– c Harris b Watson	71
†I. A. Healy c Jones b Morrison	0	– c Blain b Patel	24
M. G. Hughes c Morrison b Patel	33	– not out	31
P. R. Reiffel c Blain b Morrison	9	– b Watson	1
S. K. Warne not out	3	– c Jones b Morrison	2
C. J. McDermott b Morrison	6	– c Wright b Watson	10
L-b 7, n-b 6	13	B 1, l-b 7, n-b 8	16
	139		**285**

1/38 (1) 2/38 (2) 3/39 (3) 4/39 (4)   1/5 (2) 2/8 (3) 3/115 (4)
5/43 (6) 6/48 (7) 7/101 (8) 8/121 (5)   4/119 (5) 5/160 (1) 6/225 (7)
9/ 133 (9) 10/139 (11)   7/261 (6) 8/271 (9)
          9/274 (10) 10/285 (11)

Bowling: *First Innings*—Morrison 18.4-5-37-6; Su'a 14-3-27-0; Watson 19-9-47-3; Patel 4-0-21-1. *Second Innings*—Morrison 33-8-81-1; Patel 34-10-93-5; Watson 19-5-43-3; Su'a 18-4-56-1; Harris 2-1-4-0.

New Zealand

J. G. Wright c Taylor b McDermott	33	– run out	33
M. J. Greatbatch c Border b Hughes	32	– b Hughes	29
A. H. Jones b Healy b Hughes	20	– b Warne	26
*M. D. Crowe c Taylor b Waugh	31	– c Langer b Warne	25
K. R. Rutherford st Healy b Warne	43	– not out	53
C. Z. Harris c Taylor b Warne	13	– lbw b Waugh	0
†T. E. Blain c Healy b McDermott	15	– not out	24
D. N. Patel c Healy b Warne	2		
M. L. Su'a c Waugh b Warne	3		
D. K. Morrison not out	10		
W. Watson lbw b Hughes	0		
B 7, l-b 10, n-b 5	22	L-b 10, n-b 1	11

1/60 (2) 2/91 (1) 3/97 (3) 4/144 (4)   224   1/44 (2) 2/65 (1)   (5 wkts) 201
5/178 (5) 6/200 (7) 7/205 (8) 8/206 (6)   3/109 (4) 4/129 (3)
9/224 (9) 10/224 (11)   5/134 (6)

Bowling: *First Innings*—McDermott 19-6-50-2; Hughes 24.5-6-67-3; Reiffel 22-6-63-0; Warne 15-12-8-4; Waugh 14-6-19-1; Martyn 1-1-0-0. *Second Innings*—McDermott 12-3-38-0; Hughes 15.4-2-54-1; Reiffel 6-1-19-0; Warne 27-8-54-2; Border 6-3-11-0; Waugh 6-1-15-1.

Umpires: C. E. King and S. J. Woodward. Referee: Javed Burki (Pakistan).

†NEW ZEALAND v AUSTRALIA

First One-day International

At Dunedin, March 19. Australia won by 129 runs. Toss: Australia. International debut: J. W. Wilson.

Australia shed the batting strait-jacket that had stifled their recent one-day performances with immediate success. A free-wheeling approach brought nine sixes and 12 fours, 102 out of their total of 258 for four. Mark Waugh enjoyed the opening berth; Taylor supported him in a partnership of 95, then added 104 with Jones, whose 52 came from 56 balls. Unhappily for the boisterous crowd of 14,414, New Zealand's chase was effectively buried in the fourth over, when Crowe was caught behind to leave them ten for three. To the annoyance of the Australians, umpire King gave Crowe not out, but he prevented a scene by walking. Dodemaide, like Jones newly flown in from Australia, dismissed four of the top six.

Man of the Match: A. I. C. Dodemaide.

Australia

M. E. Waugh c Crowe b Watson	60	*A. R. Border not out	14
M. A. Taylor run out	78	L-b 7, n-b 2	9
D. M. Jones c Greatbatch b Larsen	52		
S. R. Waugh not out	23	1/95 2/199 (4 wkts, 50 overs) 258	
D. R. Martyn b Wilson	22	3/200 4/236	

†I. A. Healy, M. G. Hughes, A. I. C. Dodemaide, P. R. Reiffel and T. B. A. May did not bat.

Bowling: Morrison 10-0-36-0; Wilson 10-0-58-1; Patel 8-0-40-0; Watson 10-0-58-1; Larsen 10-0-44-1; Latham 2-0-15-0.

New Zealand

M. J. Greatbatch c Jones b Hughes	0	G. R. Larsen st Healy b May	22
R. T. Latham c Healy b Dodemaide	1	D. K. Morrison not out	20
A. H. Jones b Reiffel	24	W. Watson c Martyn b May	21
*M. D. Crowe c Healy b Dodemaide	1	L-b 3, w 3, n-b 2	8
K. R. Rutherford b Dodemaide	21		
†T. E. Blain b Dodemaide	0	1/0 2/3 3/10 (42.2 overs) 129	
J. W. Wilson b Reiffel	0	4/46 5/46 6/49	
D. N. Patel c Martyn b May	11	7/52 8/72 9/97	

Bowling: Hughes 7–0–23–1; Dodemaide 10–4–20–4; Reiffel 9–2–17–2; S. R. Waugh 7–0–15–0; May 9.2–0–51–3.

Umpires: R. S. Dunne and C. E. King.

†NEW ZEALAND v AUSTRALIA

Second One-day International

At Christchurch, March 21, 22. Australia won by one wicket. Toss: New Zealand.

A day and a half into this "one-day" international, Australia scampered to victory with three balls to spare. Had Pringle's confident lbw appeal against Reiffel been upheld at the start of the over the match would have been tied. Near-Antarctic weather – one television cameraman was taken to hospital with hypothermia – first reduced the game to 45 overs and then forced it into a second day. Border had already chosen to sit it out. New Zealand were 75 for five after Reiffel took four wickets for three runs, including Jones and Harris with successive balls, but recovered thanks largely to Blain's 41. The bulk of Australia's runs came in a 103-run stand between Mark Waugh and Boon, who became the first Australian to be given out by a third umpire, watching TV. Healy and Dodemaide soon became the second and third. Hilariously, Healy was the subject of run-out appeals at each end off the same ball, both of which were referred. Fortunately, he was out to the first and no ruling was required on the second; no one was sure whether the ball was live or dead.

Man of the Match: P. R. Reiffel.

Close of play: Australia 51-2 (13.3 overs) (M. E. Waugh 32*, D. C. Boon 9*).

New Zealand

R. T. Latham c S. R. Waugh b Hughes	13	G. R. Larsen not out	23
M. J. Greatbatch c Jones b Reiffel	32	C. Pringle not out	2
A. H. Jones c Healy b Reiffel	22		
*M. D. Crowe b Reiffel	1	B 5, l-b 7, w 1, n-b 1	14
K. R. Rutherford b S. R. Waugh	35		
C. Z. Harris b Reiffel	0	1/22 2/65 3/74 (8 wkts, 45 overs) 196
†T. E. Blain c Jones b M. E. Waugh	41	4/75 5/75 6/139
D. N. Patel run out	13	7/163 8/191

D. K. Morrison did not bat.

Bowling: Hughes 9–3–27–1; Dodemaide 10-4–27–0; Reiffel 10-2–38–4; May 9–0–52–0; S. R. Waugh 6–0–35–1; M. E. Waugh 1–0–5–1.

Australia

*M. A. Taylor c Crowe b Patel	3	A. I. C. Dodemaide run out	8
M. E. Waugh st Blain b Harris	57	P. R. Reiffel not out	1
D. M. Jones b Morrison	6	T. B. A. May not out	0
D. C. Boon run out	55	B 1, l-b 13, w 4, n-b 3	21
S. R. Waugh b Morrison	30		
D. R. Martyn c Jones b Harris	1	1/7 2/19 3/122 (9 wkts, 44.3 overs) 197
†I. A. Healy run out	15	4/130 5/142 6/179
M. G. Hughes c and b Pringle	0	7/179 8/196 9/196

Bowling: Morrison 9–0–45–2; Patel 9–0–33–1; Larsen 9–2–28–0; Pringle 8.3–0–41–1; Harris 9–1–36–2.

Umpires: R. S. Dunne and D. M. Quested.

†NEW ZEALAND v AUSTRALIA

Third One-day International

At Wellington, March 25. New Zealand won by 88 runs. Toss: New Zealand.

New Zealand borrowed from their World Cup manual to construct a comfortable win around the batting prowess of Crowe and nagging slow-medium bowlers on a pitch so lifeless that Hughes and Morrison bowled only four overs each. Despite a knee injury, Crowe limped through from the 15th over to the end. He smashed 18 runs from the 48th over of the innings, bowled by Border, hitting a pair of sixes over long-off. The only other batsman to reach fifty in the match was Taylor, although he laboured 21 overs for 21 runs. Australia lacked the innovative hitting to counter the low pitch once Jones was caught behind off Larsen's second delivery and Steve Waugh was bowled by a grubber. Larsen was particularly hard to get away, taking three wickets for 17 in his ten overs.

Man of the Match: G. R. Larsen.

New Zealand

M. J. Greatbatch c S. R. Waugh b Dodemaide .	8
R. T. Latham lbw b Reiffel	21
A. H. Jones st Healy b Warne	29
*M. D. Crowe not out	91
C. Z. Harris run out	18
†T. E. Blain c and b Border	9
J. W. Wilson c S. R. Waugh b Warne	15
D. N. Patel c M. E. Waugh b Border	7
G. R. Larsen run out	4
C. Pringle run out	1
D. K. Morrison c Boon b Dodemaide	0
L-b 3, w 8	11

1/26 2/49 3/95 (50 overs) 214
4/127 5/140 6/168
7/178 8/205 9/213

Bowling: Hughes 4–0–21–0; Dodemaide 9–1–38–2; Reiffel 10–1–21–1; Warne 10–0–40–2; S. R. Waugh 7–0–37–0; Border 10–0–54–2.

Australia

M. E. Waugh b Morrison	0
M. A. Taylor c Latham b Patel	50
D. M. Jones c Blain b Larsen	25
D. C. Boon b Wilson	2
S. R. Waugh b Harris	9
*A. R. Border run out	0
†I. A. Healy c Wilson b Larsen	1
M. G. Hughes b Larsen	2
A. I. C. Dodemaide c Greatbatch b Patel	7
P. R. Reiffel not out	8
S. K. Warne b Wilson	3
B 4, l-b 5, w 7, n-b 3	19

1/0 2/42 3/55 (37.2 overs) 126
4/71 5/71 6/77
7/93 8/108 9/122

Bowling: Morrison 4–1–21–1; Pringle 5–1–11–0; Wilson 5.2–0–21–2; Larsen 10–3–17–3; Harris 8–1–33–1; Patel 5–0–14–2.

Umpires: C. E. King and D. M. Quested.

†NEW ZEALAND v AUSTRALIA

Fourth One-day International

At Hamilton, March 27. New Zealand won by three wickets. Toss: Australia.

In only his third international, Jeff Wilson, the athletic 19-year-old all-rounder from Otago, helped to pull off a remarkable win. Replying to Australia's 247 for seven on an ideal one-day pitch, not even another fine 91 from Crowe, still limping badly, was enough. When he was run out by a direct hit from Mark Waugh at backward point, New Zealand needed 76 from the last ten overs. Wilson hit 44 from 28 balls, including three fours and a crucial six off Steve Waugh in the 48th over. To the delight of a full house he squirted the same bowler to the fine-leg boundary for victory with two balls to spare. In Australia's innings, Mark Waugh and Jones had the New Zealand bowlers at their mercy, putting on 143 before Jones was run out by a deft flick out of the back of his hand by Harris. Mark Waugh's 108 was his maiden century in one-day internationals.

Man of the Match: M. D. Crowe.

Australia

*M. A. Taylor c Blain b Morrison	13
M. E. Waugh b Morrison	108
D. M. Jones run out	64
D. C. Boon c Morrison b Harris	2
S. R. Waugh b Pringle	19
D. R. Martyn c Blain b Morrison	17
†I. A. Healy lbw b Pringle	1
A. I. C. Dodemaide not out	1
M. G. Hughes not out	10
B 1, l-b 6, w 5	12

1/29 2/172 3/178 (7 wkts, 50 overs) 247
4/215 5/217
6/227 7/235

P. R. Reiffel and T. B. A. May did not bat.

Bowling: Morrison 9–0–35–3; Pringle 8–1–41–2; Larsen 10–0–42–0; Wilson 3–0–20–0; Patel 10–0–47–0; Harris 7–0–37–1; Jones 3–0–18–0.

New Zealand

M. J. Greatbatch c Healy b Hughes ...	13	D. N. Patel run out	4
A. H. Jones run out	18	G. R. Larsen not out	12
*M. D. Crowe run out	91	B 2, l-b 11, w 5	18
K. R. Rutherford c Healy b Reiffel ...	9		
C. Z. Harris c Healy b Reiffel	0	1/24 2/59 3/88 (7 wkts, 49.4 overs) 250	
†T. E. Blain b Dodemaide	41	4/94 5/172	
J. W. Wilson not out	44	6/196 7/210	

C. Pringle and D. K. Morrison did not bat.

Bowling: Hughes 10-3-28-1; Dodemaide 10-1-39-1; Reiffel 10-2-46-2; May 10-0-45-0; S. R. Waugh 7.4-0-59-0; M. E. Waugh 2-0-20-0.

Umpires: B. L. Aldridge and D. B. Cowie.

†NEW ZEALAND v AUSTRALIA

Fifth One-day International

At Auckland, March 28. Australia won by three runs. Toss: New Zealand.

Fittingly, the series remained live until the final ball, when Pringle needed a six to give New Zealand the trophy. Hughes, who had retained his sense of humour despite being pelted with fruit at fine leg, first pretended to repeat the infamous underarm of 1980-81. In the end, Pringle hit a more conventional ball for only two. Larsen and Pringle shared a ninth-wicket stand of 54, in under seven overs. Greatbatch hit May on to the roof of the northern stand, but the middle order was undermined by underarm throws to run out Rutherford and Blain. Mark Waugh continued his excellent form with 83 at a run a ball, although another mix-up with Jones ended their promising partnership. Latham's career-best figures of five for 32 included a double-wicket maiden.

Man of the Match: M. E. Waugh.

Australia

M. E. Waugh c Greatbatch b Latham ..	83	M. G. Hughes not out	12
M. A. Taylor c and b Morrison	1	P. R. Reiffel not out	2
D. M. Jones run out	25	B 1, l-b 5, w 5, n-b 1	12
D. C. Boon c Patel b Latham.........	40		
S. R. Waugh b Latham	39	1/7 2/71 3/145 (8 wkts, 50 overs) 232	
*A. R. Border c Patel b Latham	1	4/178 5/183 6/213	
†I. A. Healy c Crowe b Pringle	17	7/213 8/215	
A. I. C. Dodemaide c Crowe b Latham.	0		

T. B. A. May did not bat.

Bowling: Morrison 8-0-41-1; Wilson 7-0-36-0; Pringle 9-0-52-1; Larsen 10-1-32-0; Patel 6-0-33-0; Latham 10-1-32-5.

New Zealand

R. T. Latham c M. E. Waugh		D. N. Patel c M. E. Waugh	
b Hughes .	22	b S. R. Waugh .	8
M. J. Greatbatch c Border		G. R. Larsen not out	33
b S. R. Waugh .	68	C. Pringle not out	22
A. H. Jones st Healy b May	2	L-b 19, w 8, n-b 1	28
*M. D. Crowe lbw b May	11		
K. R. Rutherford run out	6	1/50 2/67 3/97 (8 wkts, 50 overs) 229	
†T. E. Blain run out	8	4/114 5/136 6/139	
J. W. Wilson c Border b Dodemaide ...	21	7/166 8/175	

D. K. Morrison did not bat.

Bowling: Hughes 10-0-46-1; Dodemaide 10-1-39-1; Reiffel 10-0-49-0; May 10-0-40-2; S. R. Waugh 8-1-27-2; M. E. Waugh 2-0-9-0.

Umpires: B. L. Aldridge and D. B. Cowie.

THE ZIMBABWEANS IN INDIA, 1992-93

By R. MOHAN

The Zimbabweans came to India to learn. Though they lost the Test match by an innings and the limited-overs series 3-0, the newcomers to Test cricket gained valuable experience from their first overseas tour at this level. It was a useful step forward after a debut Test season at home, in which they had announced their arrival by dominating the one-off Test against India in Harare. The conditions were very different. The well-rolled turf of the Harare Sports Club had denied help to all the bowlers, fast and slow, while the Feroz Shah Kotla in New Delhi held out something for the spinners. The Indians, fresh from their rousing 3-0 triumph over England, were hot favourites to win a fourth consecutive Test, and duly did so, by an innings and 13 runs.

However, the Flower brothers made a heroic attempt to deny the home side victory, after the Indian batsmen had run up another remorseless score to support their spinners. Vinod Kambli, the young left-hander and the lesser-known half of the famous unbroken schoolboy record partnership of 664 with Sachin Tendulkar, joined Walter Hammond and Sir Donald Bradman as the only batsmen to have scored double-centuries in successive Test innings. But most of the second day's play was wasted, due to light rain and an inadequate covering system, and a declaration by lunch on the third day left India a little more than half the scheduled playing time of 30 hours to force a win. A day later, Zimbabwe were 62 short of averting the follow-on. The Flowers had added 192, Andy reaching Zimbabwe's first overseas Test hundred and Grant poised to follow. But a solitary lapse of concentration on Andy Flower's part was sufficient to kill the momentum: he charged spinner Maninder Singh and was stumped. His younger brother was soon out too and Zimbabwe collapsed.

In the second innings, Andy Flower played a prominent role again, making an unbeaten 62, but India won with a little under two hours to spare.

The Zimbabweans were way behind in the one-day internationals. They lost the first and third conclusively, and could stretch India only in the rain-shortened second match at Gauhati, settled by a forceful and opportune innings from India's captain, Mohammad Azharuddin. With this success to cap four consecutive Test victories, India's finest-ever run, in the same season in which the side was outplayed in South Africa, he may have proved the adage that there is no place like home.

Public interest in the series was limited, despite the enthusiasm engendered during the Tests against England just beforehand. Crowds at the Test averaged around 5,000. And though the one-day internationals were all fairly full, they were played in secondary centres, where people are less blasé. The TV audience figures were poor and the tour was too short for the Zimbabweans to emerge as major personalities.

ZIMBABWEAN TOURING PARTY

D. L. Houghton (*captain*), A. Flower (*vice-captain*), K. J. Arnott, D. H. Brain, E. A. Brandes, G. A. Briant, A. D. R. Campbell, G. J. Crocker, M. H. Dekker, G. W. Flower, W. R. James, U. Ranchod, A. H. Shah, A. J. Traicos.
Tour manager: M. A. Meman.

ZIMBABWEAN TOUR RESULTS

Test match – Played 1: Lost 1.
One-day internationals – Played 3: Lost 3.

Note: Matches in this section which were not first-class are signified by a dagger.

INDIA v ZIMBABWE

Test Match

At Delhi, March 13, 14, 15, 16, 17. India won by an innings and 13 runs. Toss: India. Test debuts: V. S. Yadav; G. A. Briant, U. Ranchod.

The scoreboard read Zimbabwe 275 for three, A. Flower 115, G. W. Flower 96. About half an hour after lunch on the fourth day a draw was written all over the one-off Test and Feroz Shah Kotla seemed destined to mark the end of India's sequence of stirring triumphs. A sudden rush of blood came to Andy Flower's head, like some African gust of wind. He charged Maninder Singh, the slow left-armer, to be stumped by the wicket-keeper Vijay Yadav. The complexion of the contest changed decisively. The Flowers had been well set to join Ian and Greg Chappell and Mushtaq and Sadiq Mohammad as the third pair of brothers to make centuries in the same Test innings, but Grant was lbw in Maninder's next over. Zimbabwe's defiance of Indian spin was at an end. By tea the visitors were batting again.

For India it had been a battle against time. Almost a day was lost thanks to the primitive covers, which a minor shower penetrated to reach the pitch and render the run-ups soggy. The momentum on the opening day, which saw successive century partnerships for the second and third wickets, was arrested. But in the brief play possible on the second day Kambli took part in a third stand that went over 100, for the fourth wicket, before running out his captain, Azharuddin, while in the nervous 190s. He went on to emulate Hammond and Bradman in making a second successive Test double-century, before he fell victim to the veteran off-spinner Traicos. Kambli came three runs closer than he did against England in Bombay to breaking the record score by an Indian in Test cricket, S. M. Gavaskar's 236 not out against West Indies at Madras nine years earlier. But he remained third, behind V. Mankad's 231 against New Zealand at Madras in 1955-56. The accuracy of Traicos was the only check on the rampaging Indian batsmen until India called a halt at lunch on the third day, with Amre's quick fifty having taken them to an imposing 536.

Zimbabwe would have left satisfied at the close that evening. The Flowers had steadied the innings after Arnott was leg-before first ball, with Campbell and Houghton dismissed by the 34th over. The left-handed Andy and the right-handed Grant formed an effective combination to counter the spinners, and held them at bay for 192 runs and nearly 82 overs. Andy, who scored his 115 in 289 minutes from 236 balls, was the more aggressive foil to Grant, who made his 96 in 425 minutes and 359 balls.

Once the brothers had gone the spinners shared the spoils. But it was the last wicket, that of Shah attempting a second run against Sidhu's throwing arm at long leg, which sealed Zimbabwe's fate. They were left 15 short of saving the follow-on and they struggled throughout their second innings after Grant Flower was lbw in the second over. A bright 61 from Campbell and his stand of 64 with fellow left-hander Andy Flower, after Houghton went early on the final day, represented the height of resistance. Andy Flower's second, more subdued, innings lasted 214 minutes and 191 balls; it was defence of a high calibre on a wearing pitch. In all, he spent more than eight hours at the crease and ensured that Zimbabwe were far from disgraced. But Maninder took four for 66 and Kumble, mixing top-spinners with the occasional genuine leg-break, finished with five for 70 and eight in the match, giving him 53 in ten Tests, the quickest any Indian bowler has reached 50 wickets.

Man of the Match: V. G. Kambli.

Close of play: First day, India 340-3 (V. G. Kambli 176*, M. Azharuddin 29*); Second day, India 411-4 (V. G. Kambli 207*, P. K. Amre 12*); Third day, Zimbabwe 152-3 (G. W. Flower 47*, A. Flower 46*); Fourth day, Zimbabwe 62-2 (A. D. R. Campbell 31*, D. L. Houghton 1*).

India

M. Prabhakar c A. Flower b Brain	3	A. Kumble not out	18
N. S. Sidhu lbw b Traicos	61		
V. G. Kambli c and b Traicos	227	B 17, l-b 6, w 2	25
S. R. Tendulkar c Traicos b Ranchod	62		
*M. Azharuddin run out	42	1/19 (1) 2/126 (2)	(7 wkts dec.) 536
P. K. Amre not out	52	3/263 (4) 4/370 (5)	
Kapil Dev st A. Flower b Traicos	16	5/434 (3) 6/464 (7)	
†V. S. Yadav b Brain	30	7/507 (8)	

R. K. Chauhan and Maninder Singh did not bat.

Bowling: Brandes 26-4-93-0; Brain 34-1-146-2; Shah 10-3-43-0; Traicos 50-4-186-3; Ranchod 12-0-45-1.

Zimbabwe

K. J. Arnott lbw b Kapil Dev	0	b Maninder Singh	21
G. W. Flower lbw b Maninder Singh	96	lbw b Prabhakar	0
A. D. R. Campbell b Chauhan	32	c Amre b Kumble	61
*D. L. Houghton lbw b Kumble	18	c Amre b Kumble	1
†A. Flower st Yadav b Maninder Singh	115	not out	62
G. A. Briant st Yadav b Kumble	1	c Kambli b Maninder Singh	16
A. H. Shah run out	25	lbw b Kumble	6
E. A. Brandes c Sidhu b Kumble	8	c Chauhan b Maninder Singh	1
D. H. Brain c Kambli b Maninder Singh	0	lbw b Kumble	0
U. Ranchod b Chauhan	7	c Yadav b Maninder Singh	1
A. J. Traicos not out	0	lbw b Kumble	1
B 4, l-b 10, w 1, n-b 5	20	B 10, l-b 16, w 2, n-b 3	31
	322		201

1/0 (1) 2/53 (3) 3/83 (4) 4/275 (5)
5/276 (2) 6/276 (6) 7/286 (8)
8/287 (9) 9/318 (10) 10/322 (7)

1/2 (2) 2/53 (1) 3/62 (4)
4/126 (3) 5/159 (6) 6/167 (7)
7/176 (8) 8/177 (9)
9/188 (10) 10/201 (11)

Bowling: *First Innings*—Kapil Dev 13-4-37-1; Prabhakar 14-4-23-0; Chauhan 28.1-4-68-2; Kumble 43-12-90-3; Maninder Singh 32-4-79-3; Tendulkar 5-1-11-0. *Second Innings*—Kapil Dev 4-1-4-0; Prabhakar 4-3-5-1; Chauhan 14-5-30-0; Kumble 38.5-16-70-5; Maninder Singh 35-8-66-4.

Umpires: S. K. Bansal and S. Venkataraghavan. Referee: Asif Iqbal (Pakistan).

†INDIA v ZIMBABWE

First One-day International

At Faridabad, March 19. India won by 67 runs. Toss: Zimbabwe.

Houghton asked India to bat first and admitted later that he had made a mistake: he had followed the trend in India's one-day series with England, in which the chasing side won five games out of six. However, India made 249 in the 48 overs that Zimbabwe bowled, with the in-form Kambli plundering 80 off 74 balls to capitalise on a century opening stand between Sidhu and Prabhakar. Zimbabwe were never in the hunt after losing Andy Flower early. Houghton raised some hopes, but they died when he was run out backing up, with the bowler Prabhakar deflecting the ball onto the wicket.

Man of the Match: V. G. Kambli.

India

M. Prabhakar c Houghton b Traicos ...	56	A. Kumble c James b Brain	0
N. S. Sidhu c Brain b Crocker	56	S. A. Ankola not out	1
V. G. Kambli b Brain	80	B 7, l-b 8, w 8, n-b 1	24
*M. Azharuddin c and b G. W. Flower	8		
S. R. Tendulkar c and b G. W. Flower	3	1/114 2/149 3/183 (7 wkts, 48 overs) 249	
P. K. Amre c James b Brandes	2	4/204 5/207	
†V. S. Yadav not out	19	6/245 7/245	

J. Srinath and S. L. V. Raju did not bat.

Bowling: Brandes 10–0–32–1; Brain 9–0–36–2; Shah 4–0–26–0; Crocker 10–0–54–1; Traicos 10–0–61–1; G. W. Flower 5–0–25–2.

Zimbabwe

†A. Flower b Prabhakar	9	G. J. Crocker c Yadav b Srinath	2
G. W. Flower c Kumble b Raju	42	D. H. Brain st Yadav b Tendulkar	27
A. D. R. Campbell c Prabhakar b Raju	12	A. J. Traicos not out	7
*D. L. Houghton run out	23	B 8, l-b 14, w 6, n-b 1	29
M. H. Dekker c Azharuddin b Srinath	22		
W. R. James run out	0	1/20 2/71 3/84 (46.2 overs) 182	
A. H. Shah c Raju b Kumble	2	4/105 5/115 6/126	
E. A. Brandes lbw b Srinath	7	7/135 8/141 9/149	

Bowling: Srinath 10–1–38–3; Prabhakar 9–1–33–1; Ankola 7–1–20–0; Raju 10–0–26–2; Kumble 10–0–37–1; Tendulkar 0.2–0–6–1.

Umpires: N. Menon and S. C. Sharma.

†INDIA v ZIMBABWE

Second One-day International

At Gauhati, March 22. India won by seven wickets. Toss: India.

A truncated match was given an exciting finish when India squeezed home with three balls to spare. Nearly three hours were lost to overnight rain, which left wet patches on the pitch. When Zimbabwe were put in, the Flower brothers were among the runs again, and Grant reached the top score of the match, 57 off 67 balls. Though the target did not seem stiff for a side in form, India struggled after another good start. Azharuddin's coolness at the end tilted the scales. With 16 needed from the final two overs he pulled a ball of full length from Brain for six over mid-wicket.

Man of the Match: G. W. Flower.

Zimbabwe

†A. Flower c Kumble b Ankola	26	K. J. Arnott not out	1
G. W. Flower c Kambli b Kumble	57		
A. D. R. Campbell run out	29	B 1, l-b 12, w 3, n-b 2	18
*D. L. Houghton lbw b Kumble	8		
M. H. Dekker b Prabhakar	2	1/56 2/112 (6 wkts, 28 overs) 149	
G. A. Briant not out	6	3/137 4/137	
E. A. Brandes b Srinath	2	5/145 6/148	

D. H. Brain, G. J. Crocker and A. J. Traicos did not bat.

Bowling: Kapil Dev 6–0–21–0; Prabhakar 5–0–31–1; Srinath 5–0–19–1; Ankola 6–0–33–1; Kumble 6–0–32–2.

India

M. Prabhakar c Houghton b Brandes .. 51	S. R. Tendulkar not out 8
N. S. Sidhu b Crocker 25	B 1, l-b 6, w 10, n-b 2 19
V. G. Kambli b G. W. Flower 32	
*M. Azharuddin not out 15	1/67 2/122 3/128 (3 wkts, 27.3 overs) 150

P. K. Amre, Kapil Dev, †V. S. Yadav, A. Kumble, S. A. Ankola and J. Srinath did not bat.

Bowling: Brandes 6–0–14–1; Brain 6–0–39–0; Crocker 6–0–35–1; Traicos 6–0–32–0; G. W. Flower 3.3–0–23–1.

Umpires: S. Choudhury and P. N. Ramachandran.

†INDIA v ZIMBABWE

Third One-day International

At Pune, March 25. India won by eight wickets. Toss: India.

The home side met a target of 235 in 50 overs with a measure of comfort on a good pitch. The Zimbabweans had had their best batting day of the series. The Flower brothers gave them a rousing start against some wayward bowling and poor fielding. But after a brilliant throw by Azharuddin to run out Andy Flower the spinners put the brake on the scoring-rate. Raman, who had not played for India since their return from South Africa, led the way with an elegant half-century, an example followed by Ajay Sharma, whose utility left-arm spin had restricted Zimbabwe most effectively.

Man of the Match: Ajay Sharma.

Zimbabwe

†A. Flower run out 32	G. J. Crocker b Kapil Dev 1
G. W. Flower c Yadav b Kumble 50	D. H. Brain not out 12
A. D. R. Campbell st Yadav b Kumble 22	A. J. Traicos c Ankola b Srinath 4
*D. L. Houghton b Kapil Dev 46	B 2, l-b 14, w 17, n-b 4 37
M. H. Dekker run out 8	
G. A. Briant run out 16	1/58 2/122 3/129 (49.5 overs) 234
A. H. Shah c Yadav b Kapil Dev 1	4/154 5/196 6/199
E. A. Brandes c Kumble b Srinath ... 5	7/212 8/215 9/217

Bowling: Kapil Dev 10–1–54–3; Srinath 9.5–1–34–2; Ankola 6–0–32–0; Tendulkar 4–0–30–0; Ajay Sharma 10–0–34–0; Kumble 10–0–34–2.

India

W. V. Raman c G. W. Flower b Traicos	66
N. S. Sidhu run out	45
V. G. Kambli not out	47
Ajay Sharma not out	59
L-b 8, w 10, n-b 3	21

1/114 2/134   (2 wkts, 45.3 overs) 238

*M. Azharuddin, S. R. Tendulkar, Kapil Dev, †V. S. Yadav, A. Kumble, S. A. Ankola and J. Srinath did not bat.

Bowling: Brandes 10–0–31–0; Briant 9.3–0–47–0; G. W. Flower 5–0–39–0; Crocker 8–1–39–0; Shah 3–0–24–0; Traicos 10–0–50–1.

Umpires: K. Parthasarathi and S. Shastri.

THE PAKISTANIS IN ZIMBABWE, 1992-93

Note: This match was not first-class.

ZIMBABWE v PAKISTAN

One-day International

At Harare Sports Club, Harare, March 2. Pakistan won by seven wickets. Toss: Pakistan. International debut: G. A. Briant.

Pakistan beat Zimbabwe easily enough in a one-off game as they travelled back from South Africa after a triangular series involving West Indies. Their bowlers benefited from early dampness, extracting plenty of life from the pitch, while the home batsmen could reach the boundary only five times across a wet outfield. Three of those fours came from Houghton, who made 51 with support from Grant Flower. Flower's brother Andy was struck on the finger while batting; Gavin Briant, on his international debut, stood in as wicket-keeper. Zimbabwe's hopes rose when they took two early wickets, but a 115-run partnership between Shoaib Mohammad and Javed Miandad soon killed them off.

Man of the Match: Javed Miandad.

Zimbabwe

†A. Flower c and b Mushtaq Ahmed	10	S. G. Peall c Rashid Latif	
G. W. Flower c Aamir Sohail		b Waqar Younis	3
b Mushtaq Ahmed	35	E. A. Brandes b Waqar Younis	5
K. J. Arnott run out	17	D. H. Brain b Wasim Akram	1
*D. L. Houghton lbw b Waqar Younis	51	A. J. Traicos not out	0
G. A. Briant c Rashid Latif			
b Mushtaq Ahmed	0	B 2, l-b 7, w 13, n-b 4	26
M. H. Dekker c Rashid Latif			
b Aqib Javed	16	1/55 2/60 3/92 (49.1 overs)	164
A. H. Shah c Shoaib Mohammad		4/92 5/139 6/140	
b Wasim Akram	0	7/152 8/159 9/164	

A. Flower, when 6, retired hurt at 17 and resumed at 55.

Bowling: Wasim Akram 10–0–35–2; Aqib Javed 10–1–32–1; Waqar Younis 8.1–1–31–3; Mushtaq Ahmed 10–2–22–3; Aamir Sohail 10–0–30–0; Asif Mujtaba 1–0–5–0.

Pakistan

Aamir Sohail c Brandes b Shah	15	Zahid Fazal not out	8
Ramiz Raja c G. Flower b Brandes	0	B 2, l-b 3, w 8	13
Shoaib Mohammad c Traicos b Brain	43		
Javed Miandad not out	86	1/1 2/27 3/142 (3 wkts, 47.2 overs)	165

Asif Mujtaba, *Wasim Akram, †Rashid Latif, Waqar Younis, Mushtaq Ahmed and Aqib Javed did not bat.

Bowling: Brandes 8.2–1–33–1; Brain 10–3–29–1; Shah 10–0–26–1; Traicos 10–1–29–0; Peall 9–0–43–0.

Umpires: K. Kanjee and I. D. Robinson.

THE PAKISTANIS IN THE WEST INDIES, 1992-93

By DICKY RUTNAGUR

For the first time in four tours of the West Indies, Pakistan failed to distinguish themselves. They struck back spiritedly after going two down to tie the five-match one-day series, but they could not summon the same resilience in contesting the three-Test rubber, which was not quite the battle of giants it was expected to be.

On a pitch in Port-of-Spain that was decidedly poor, but which should have been less disadvantageous to Pakistan than West Indies, they lost the First Test in three days, by the overwhelming margin of 204 runs. In the Second, in Bridgetown, where they had always run West Indies close in the past, the gap was just as wide – ten wickets in four days. But for adverse weather, the Third, played on an amiable pitch in Antigua, might have ended in another rout. A dropped chance probably saved Pakistan from the follow-on. But the series produced a lot of entertaining cricket and its most heartening feature was the large attendance at every Test.

On the night the Pakistanis arrived in Grenada for their last match before the First Test, four members of the team – Wasim Akram, the captain, Waqar Younis, the vice-captain, Aqib Javed and Mushtaq Ahmed – were arrested on a beach, and charged with "constructive possession" of marijuana. They claimed they were frogmarched to the police station and taunted by officers and onlookers. The charges were dropped but the manager, Khalid Mahmood, maintained that the business had left the team without the "mental and physical strength" to play a series and further stated that the players wanted the rest of the tour called off. However, Wasim said the thought had not entered his mind. He was bitter about the incident, though: "We are accused of things wherever we go," he told a newspaper. "Last year in England it was ball-tampering and now this, which was 20 times worse. We are not bad human beings. We don't make trouble. All we are is good cricketers. Why are some people jealous of that?"

After negotiations, it was agreed that the start of the First Test be put back by a day to give the Pakistanis time to get over the trauma. Indeed, if the Pakistanis were depressed by the events in Grenada, their spirits should have been restored when on the first day they shot out West Indies for a mere 127. But that was to be their only taste of supremacy in the series.

There were other factors, more pertinent, that caused Pakistan's eclipse. Lack of experienced players in the tour party – the omission of Salim Malik and Shoaib Mohammad had raised some eyebrows – became a greater handicap because none of the remaining battle-hardened members of the team lived up to their reputations. Ramiz Raja's form dried up by the time the Tests began. Javed Miandad, troubled by injuries, lacked the footwork and reflexes which had made him such a formidable batsman. He batted as if from memory. Wasim was jaded and so lacked control that he did not have the confidence to run in to bowl at full throttle. Lack of self-assurance was most apparent when he was reluctant to bowl, as was Waqar, on the second day of the First Test, when West Indies blades were flailing. This was also when Mushtaq left the field, no longer able to bear the pain in his back.

Pakistan were hit very hard by injuries. Aqib, it would seem, had come on the tour without recovering from stress fractures in his back. Neither he nor Mushtaq completed the tour. In view of the known uncertainty of West Indian batsmen against wrist-spin, Mushtaq's absence significantly altered the balance between the two sides. Aamir Sohail, seen to advantage in the one-day series and in the First Test, was carrying an injury by the Second. Rashid Latif, the first-choice wicket-keeper, missed the first two Tests. Two catches that his deputy, Moin Khan, dropped in the fourth over of the Second Test put Pakistan in an irretrievable position.

The itinerary, too, was to the tourists' disadvantage. With the three Tests scheduled back to back, there was no scope to rest the injured or to bring their replacements into form. Shakeel Ahmed and Nadeem Khan played the final Test without having had any cricket for nearly three weeks. Indeed, most of the party had toured Australia, New Zealand, Sharjah and South Africa without playing more than two first-class matches – one against Queensland and the Test against New Zealand.

Inzamam-ul-Haq made Pakistan's only century in the Test series. But the true batting success was Basit Ali. He was new to international cricket, not having taken part in the earlier tours, yet from day one looked a mature batsman as well as an accomplished one. He was elegant and powerful in his attacking shots and possessed the skill to find gaps for ones and twos. Asif Mujtaba was consistent and resolute without being prolific. Waqar was Pakistan's most successful bowler, but was often expensive through being erratic in length. The fielding was indifferent. As for the captaincy, Wasim should have been given an easier first assignment. His own poor form diminished his authority.

For West Indies, the series came at the end of a busy winter. But the spirit cultivated in the side by their new captain, Richie Richardson, kept them buoyant. It must be said, however, that they were not fully tested. The facts that they suffered only one collective batting failure in the series and that they scored well over 300 runs on one day of every Test masked the brittleness of their batting. Brian Lara, Phil Simmons and Richardson all took turns to play innings of great brilliance, and Carl Hooper's 178 not out in Antigua was a masterpiece. But at the root of every other big West Indian total was Desmond Haynes, disciplined and responsible, but never dull.

There was not one bowler of the six West Indies called on who did not leave his mark on the series. If a tired Curtly Ambrose was not as explosive and devastating as he had been in Australia, he always struck vital blows. The main wicket-taker was Courtney Walsh, always willing and always a threat. Winston Benjamin, recalled after four years, also bowled fierily. Although the fast bowlers were all effective, Hooper, with his off-breaks, was an integral part of the West Indian attack, and in the Trinidad Test he was a match-winner with five for 40. Given ample runs to buy his wickets, Hooper bowled in attacking mode and, after Walsh, was the highest wicket-taker. In fact, had it not been for his contribution with the ball in the first two Tests, he might not have survived to play his memorable innings in Antigua; his scores in the first two Tests were 9, 0 and 15.

PAKISTANI TOURING PARTY

Wasim Akram (Lahore/PIA) (*captain*), Waqar Younis (Multan/United Bank) (*vice-captain*), Aamir Nazir (Income Tax), Aamir Sohail (Sargodha/Habib Bank), Aqib Javed (PACO), Asif Mujtaba (Karachi/PIA), Ata-ur-Rehman (Lahore/PACO), Basit Ali (Karachi/United Bank), Inzamam-ul-Haq (Multan/United Bank), Javed Miandad (Karachi/Habib Bank), Moin Khan (Karachi/PIA), Mushtaq Ahmed (Multan/United Bank), Nadeem Khan (Karachi/National Bank), Ramiz Raja (Lahore/PNSC), Rashid Latif (Karachi/United Bank), Shakeel Ahmed (Bahawalpur/Habib Bank), Zahid Fazal (PIA).

Aamir Sohail, Aqib Javed and Mushtaq Ahmed returned home early because of injuries. Kamran Khan and Nadeem Usmani played in Bermuda.

Tour manager: Khalid Mahmood.   *Cricket manager:* Mudassar Nazar.

PAKISTANI TOUR RESULTS

Test matches – Played 3: Lost 2, Drawn 1.
First-class matches – Played 6: Won 2, Lost 2, Drawn 2.
Wins – Jamaica, West Indian Under-23 XI.
Losses – West Indies (2).
Draws – West Indies, West Indies Board President's XI.
One-day internationals – Played 5: Won 2, Lost 2, Tied 1.
Other non first-class matches – Played 2: Won 2 v Bermuda.

TEST MATCH AVERAGES

WEST INDIES – BATTING

	T	I	NO	R	HS	100s	Avge	Ct/St
D. L. Haynes	3	6	3	402	143*	2	134.00	3
C. L. Hooper	3	5	2	231	178*	1	77.00	4
B. C. Lara...........	3	5	0	216	96	0	43.20	3
P. V. Simmons	3	6	1	189	87	0	37.80	2
R. B. Richardson	3	5	0	158	68	0	31.60	4
K. L. T. Arthurton....	3	5	0	90	56	0	18.00	2
A. C. Cummins	2	3	1	28	14*	0	14.00	0
J. R. Murray.........	3	4	0	39	35	0	9.75	8/1
C. A. Walsh	3	4	0	39	30	0	9.75	0
C. E. L. Ambrose.....	3	4	1	22	12*	0	7.33	1
I. R. Bishop	2	3	0	18	11	0	6.00	1

Played in two Tests: W. K. M. Benjamin 0, 12 (2 ct).

* *Signifies not out.*

BOWLING

	O	M	R	W	BB	5W/i	Avge
C. A. Walsh	80	19	207	12	4-56	0	17.25
W. K. M. Benjamin....	56	16	138	8	3-30	0	17.25
I. R. Bishop	46.5	14	127	7	5-43	1	18.14
A. C. Cummins	30	5	89	4	4-54	0	22.25
C. E. L. Ambrose......	95	33	208	9	4-34	0	23.11
C. L. Hooper	83.2	11	281	10	5-40	1	28.10

Also bowled: P. V. Simmons 6–0–22–0.

PAKISTAN – BATTING

	T	I	NO	R	HS	100s	Avge	Ct/St
Basit Ali	3	5	1	222	92*	0	55.50	0
Inzamam-ul-Haq...	3	5	0	172	123	1	34.40	1
Asif Mujtaba	3	5	0	143	59	0	28.60	2
Javed Miandad....	3	5	0	120	43	0	24.00	0
Aamir Sohail......	2	4	0	84	55	0	21.00	1
Ramiz Raja.......	3	5	0	82	37	0	16.40	0
Ata-ur-Rehman....	3	5	2	36	19	0	12.00	0
Waqar Younis	3	5	0	50	29	0	10.00	1
Wasim Akram	3	5	0	44	29	0	8.80	4
Moin Khan.......	2	4	0	35	18	0	8.75	7/1

Played in one Test: Aamir Nazir 1, 6*; Mushtaq Ahmed 3, 12*; Nadeem Khan 25; Rashid Latif 2 (1 ct, 1 st); Shakeel Ahmed 0.

* *Signifies not out.*

BOWLING

	O	M	R	W	BB	5W/i	Avge
Waqar Younis	98.5	13	384	19	5-104	1	20.21
Wasim Akram	108.1	17	358	9	4-75	0	39.77
Ata-ur-Rehman....	75	4	303	6	3-28	0	50.50

Also bowled: Aamir Nazir 22–1–90–2; Aamir Sohail 9–2–44–2; Asif Mujtaba 18–2–89–1; Basit Ali 1–0–6–0; Mushtaq Ahmed 21–2–66–1; Nadeem Khan 52–5–195–2.

PAKISTANI AVERAGES – FIRST-CLASS MATCHES

BATTING

	M	I	NO	R	HS	100s	Avge	Ct/St
Basit Ali	5	8	3	389	92*	0	77.80	0
Shakeel Ahmed.....	3	5	2	211	132*	1	70.33	1
Inzamam-ul-Haq....	5	7	0	362	123	2	51.71	1
Asif Mujtaba	6	11	2	425	102	1	47.22	4
Zahid Fazal........	3	5	0	165	80	0	33.00	1
Javed Miandad.....	4	6	1	152	43	0	30.40	0
Ramiz Raja........	5	7	0	203	75	0	29.00	2
Aamir Sohail.......	4	8	0	154	55	0	19.25	3
Moin Khan	4	6	0	75	32	0	12.50	12/3
Waqar Younis......	5	7	0	82	29	0	11.71	1
Ata-ur-Rehman....	6	8	4	45	19	0	11.25	2
Wasim Akram	5	7	0	64	29	0	9.14	6

Played in three matches: Mushtaq Ahmed 0, 3, 12*; Nadeem Khan 0, 25*, 25 (3 ct). Played in two matches: Aamir Nazir 1, 6*; Rashid Latif 19, 2 (2 ct, 2 st). Aqib Javed played in one match but did not bat.

* *Signifies not out.*

BOWLING

	O	M	R	W	BB	5W/i	Avge
Aamir Sohail	35	9	115	8	5-50	1	14.37
Mushtaq Ahmed	90	20	238	15	5-86	1	15.86
Waqar Younis	140.1	17	544	23	5-104	1	23.65
Wasim Akram	146.1	22	491	14	4-75	0	35.07
Nadeem Khan	112	17	421	9	4-21	0	46.77
Ata-ur-Rehman	129	6	551	11	3-28	0	50.09

Also bowled: Aamir Nazir 38–5–163–2; Aqib Javed 3.1–0–12–1; Asif Mujtaba 50–8–179–1; Basit Ali 2–0–11–0; Ramiz Raja 9–0–48–0; Zahid Fazal 9.1–1–35–0.

Note: Matches in this section which were not first-class are signified by a dagger.

JAMAICA v PAKISTANIS

At Kingston, March 18, 19, 20, 21. Pakistanis won by 144 runs. Toss: Pakistanis.

The tour's opening match was a gentler exercise for the Pakistanis because of the absence of Jamaica's two Test pace bowlers, Walsh and Patterson, and an uncharacteristically slow Sabina Park pitch. It played like one of their own at home. All the Pakistanis' four first-innings wickets were lost attempting to force the pace – though three chances dropped by Haynes added to the Pakistanis' prosperity. Inzamam-ul-Haq, dropped on 27, went on to 106. Wasim Akram declared midway through the second morning, and his bowlers were held up only by a fifth-wicket partnership of 171 between Davidson and Williams. But both were out immediately next morning. Despite the unhelpful pitch, Mushtaq Ahmed finished with five for 86. The match was thrown open when the Pakistanis, shuffling their batting order, lost three second-innings wickets for 58. But they recovered their poise and initiative thanks to Asif Mujtaba and Basit Ali. Hitherto unknown abroad, Basit drove and cut with power and used a lovely touch to find gaps. Jamaica, chasing 300 in 277 minutes, were never in the race. But Jeffrey Dujon, in his last first-class match, batted with a brief flourish and received a standing ovation.

Close of play: First day, Pakistanis 296-4 (Basit Ali 40*, Asif Mujtaba 0*); Second day, Jamaica 249-4 (C. A. Davidson 86*, L. R. Williams 65*); Third day, Pakistanis 213-5 (Basit Ali 53*, Waqar Younis 4*).

Pakistanis

Ramiz Raja c Andrews b Rose	46	
Aamir Sohail c Haynes b Rose	25	– (1) c Dujon b Rose 10
Inzamam-ul-Haq c Andrews b Haynes	106	
Zahid Fazal c Adams b Williams	62	– (2) c Gayle b Rose 2
Basit Ali not out	51	– (6) not out 84
Asif Mujtaba not out	7	– (3) c and b Williams 79
*Wasim Akram (did not bat)		– (4) b Williams 20
†Moin Khan (did not bat)		– (5) b Andrews 32
Waqar Younis (did not bat)		– (7) lbw b Williams 18
Mushtaq Ahmed (did not bat)		– (8) c Gayle b Rose 0
Ata-ur-Rehman (did not bat)		– (9) c Gayle b Williams 0
L-b 1, n-b 21	22	B 1, l-b 4, w 2, n-b 11 18

1/32 2/122 3/219 4/294   (4 wkts dec.) 319   1/15 2/23 3/58   (8 wkts dec.) 263
                                                      4/118 5/203 6/252
                                                      7/256 8/263

Bowling: *First Innings*—Rose 27.5–3–99–2; Andrews 11–1–36–0; Williams 19–0–61–1; Haynes 32–1–96–1; Adams 11–1–26–0. *Second Innings*—Andrews 15–1–44–1; Williams 21.4–6–66–4; Rose 19–4–79–3; Adams 10–2–24–0; Haynes 12–2–36–0; Morgan 3–0–9–0.

Jamaica

D. S. Morgan c Moin Khan b Wasim Akram	0	– c Ramiz Raja b Mushtaq Ahmed	29
R. G. Samuels run out	32	– b Wasim Akram	10
J. C. Adams st Moin Khan b Mushtaq Ahmed	27	– lbw b Ata-ur-Rehman	3
*P. J. L. Dujon lbw b Mushtaq Ahmed	7	– c Moin Khan b Ata-ur-Rehman	23
C. A. Davidson run out	86	– lbw b Aamir Sohail	10
L. R. Williams c Moin Khan b Mushtaq Ahmed	65	– b Wasim Akram	7
†P. A. Gayle b Waqar Younis	4	– (8) lbw b Mushtaq Ahmed	20
R. C. Haynes c Moin Khan b Waqar Younis	15	– (9) c Ramiz Raja b Mushtaq Ahmed	5
A. J. Andrews st Moin Khan b Mushtaq Ahmed	1	– (11) not out	0
F. A. Rose b Mushtaq Ahmed	5	– lbw b Waqar Younis	9
N. O. Perry not out	0	– (7) lbw b Wasim Akram	20
B 7, l-b 20, w 1, n-b 13	41	B 8, l-b 7, w 1, n-b 3	19

1/0 2/58 3/73 4/78 5/249   283   1/13 2/22 3/74 4/76 5/88   155
6/251 7/262 8/272 9/276   6/105 7/114 8/129 9/155

Bowling: First Innings—Wasim Akram 15–1–58–1; Waqar Younis 16–1–59–2; Mushtaq Ahmed 33–7–86–5; Aamir Sohail 3–0–15–0; Ata-ur-Rehman 14–2–38–0. *Second Innings*—Wasim Akram 11–2–25–3; Ata-ur-Rehman 9–0–43–2; Mushtaq Ahmed 21–7–43–3; Aamir Sohail 4–2–6–1; Waqar Younis 10.1–1–23–1.

Umpires: L. U. Bell and V. E. Harrison.

†WEST INDIES v PAKISTAN

First One-day International

At Kingston, March 23. West Indies won by four wickets. Toss: West Indies. International debut: Basit Ali.

An enthralling innings of 114, at a run a ball, from Lara crushed Pakistan. Haynes, Simmons and Richardson had contributed only 51 runs to the total of 180 when the little left-hander was out. If West Indies lost three more wickets getting the remaining 44 runs, it was because Lara's successors batted as if they did not want to suffer in comparison. Pakistan were asked to bat in testing conditions, a cloudy sky preserving dampness in the pitch. Their strategy was to conserve wickets against keen bowling by Ambrose and Walsh and mount a late offensive. The openers consumed 23 overs gathering 67 runs. Some loose bowling by Bishop and Inzamam-ul-Haq's assault on Adams gave Pakistan some momentum; Inzamam smashed 50 off 48 balls and added 118 in 21 overs with Aamir Sohail.

Man of the Match: B. C. Lara.

Pakistan

Aamir Sohail c sub (K. L. T. Arthurton) b Ambrose	87	Basit Ali st Murray b Hooper	17
Ramiz Raja b Simmons	22	†Rashid Latif not out	1
Inzamam-ul-Haq lbw b Bishop	50	B 4, l-b 7, w 11, n-b 8	30
*Wasim Akram c Hooper b Bishop	0		
Javed Miandad c Simmons b Hooper	16		

1/67 2/185 3/185   (6 wkts, 50 overs) 223
4/187 5/221 6/223

Asif Mujtaba, Waqar Younis, Mushtaq Ahmed and Aqib Javed did not bat.

Bowling: Ambrose 10–1–31–1; Walsh 10–2–40–0; Simmons 10–2–26–1; Bishop 9–1–54–2; Hooper 8–0–28–2; Adams 3–0–33–0.

West Indies

B. C. Lara b Aamir Sohail	114	J. C. Adams not out	11
D. L. Haynes c Ramiz Raja		†J. R. Murray not out	1
b Wasim Akram	7		
P. V. Simmons b Mushtaq Ahmed	28		
*R. B. Richardson b Wasim Akram	17	L-b 6, w 5, n-b 7	18
C. L. Hooper c and b Aamir Sohail	21		
A. L. Logie c Mushtaq Ahmed		1/21 2/101 3/180 (6 wkts, 44 overs) 224	
b Aamir Sohail	7	4/184 5/197 6/223	

I. R. Bishop, C. E. L. Ambrose and C. A. Walsh did not bat.

Bowling: Wasim Akram 9-0-47-2; Aqib Javed 6-0-18-0; Waqar Younis 10-1-46-0; Mushtaq Ahmed 10-0-64-1; Aamir Sohail 9-0-43-3.

Umpires: L. H. Barker and S. A. Bucknor.

†WEST INDIES v PAKISTAN

Second One-day International

At Port-of-Spain, March 26. West Indies won by five wickets. Toss: West Indies. International debut: Aamir Nazir.

Although Pakistan had lost the opening match for want of runs, they strengthened their attack, replacing Asif Mujtaba with Aamir Nazir. He proved the pick of their bowlers with three for 43. The toss again proved crucial. A heavy downpour before the start left behind a humid atmosphere and the ball moved about a lot. Further rain midway through Pakistan's innings deprived them of five overs in which to throw the bat. After another steady but cautious start a total of 194 was below par. But Pakistan really went out of the race when Inzamam-ul-Haq put down an easy slip chance from Lara off Wasim Akram's second ball. Thus reprieved, Lara piloted West Indies to victory with four overs to spare, though his unbeaten 95 from 106 balls seemed sedate compared with his century in Jamaica.

Man of the Match: B. C. Lara.

Pakistan

Aamir Sohail c Richardson b Simmons	47	Waqar Younis not out	4
Ramiz Raja c Richardson b Bishop	15	Mushtaq Ahmed not out	0
Inzamam-ul-Haq run out	11	B 1, l-b 6, w 20, n-b 5	32
Javed Miandad c Simmons b Hooper	41		
Basit Ali c Hooper b Walsh	34	1/56 2/85 3/108 (7 wkts, 45 overs) 194	
*Wasim Akram run out	0	4/170 5/170	
†Rashid Latif run out	10	6/187 7/188	

Ata-ur-Rehman and Aamir Nazir did not bat.

Bowling: Ambrose 10-0-40-0; Walsh 8-2-30-1; Bishop 7-0-42-1; Simmons 10-1-34-1; Hooper 10-0-41-1.

West Indies

B. C. Lara not out	95	A. L. Logie c Rashid Latif	
D. L. Haynes c sub (Asif Mujtaba)		b Wasim Akram	1
b Aamir Nazir	11	J. C. Adams not out	15
P. V. Simmons c Rashid Latif		L-b 11, w 9, n-b 9	29
b Waqar Younis	13		
*R. B. Richardson b Aamir Nazir	32	1/35 2/69 3/133 (5 wkts, 41 overs) 196	
C. L. Hooper lbw b Aamir Nazir	0	4/133 5/137	

†J. R. Murray, I. R. Bishop, C. E. L. Ambrose and C. A. Walsh did not bat.

Bowling: Wasim Akram 9-0-36-1; Waqar Younis 8-2-39-1; Aamir Nazir 9-0-43-3; Ata-ur-Rehman 10-0-42-0; Mushtaq Ahmed 5-0-25-0.

Umpires: S. A. Bucknor and C. E. Cumberbatch.

†WEST INDIES v PAKISTAN

Third One-day International

At Port-of-Spain, March 27. Pakistan won by seven wickets. Toss: West Indies. International debut: Nadeem Khan.

Much of the prize money for Pakistan's second win in their last 11 one-day games against West Indies went towards a fine for bowling only 45 overs in the time allotted for 50. Pakistan owed victory not to the shortfall, however, but to Inzamam-ul-Haq and Asif Mujtaba, who plundered West Indies' bowling for 131 from 18 overs. They also had to thank Aamir Sohail and Ramiz Raja, for a brisk start of 71 from 13 overs. For the first time in the series West Indies decided to bat, fearing that the pitch, the one used the day before, would be losing its bounce. Lara's first failure heralded West Indies' first defeat. Its impact was softened by a stand of 82 from Haynes and Simmons, but it was only in the last 15 overs that West Indies gathered momentum.

Man of the Match: Inzamam-ul-Haq.

West Indies

B. C. Lara c Rashid Latif			C. L. Hooper c Wasim Akram	
b Aamir Nazir .	5		b Waqar Younis .	34
D. L. Haynes c Basit Ali			A. L. Logie not out	1
b Aamir Nazir .	68		L-b 15, w 4, n-b 6	25
P. V. Simmons not out	80			
*R. B. Richardson c Inzamam-ul-Haq			1/33 2/115 (4 wkts, 45 overs) 259	
b Aamir Sohail .	46		3/182 4/249	

J. C. Adams, †J. R. Murray, I. R. Bishop, C. E. L. Ambrose and C. A. Walsh did not bat.

Bowling: Wasim Akram 10-0-62-0; Waqar Younis 10-3-50-1; Ata-ur-Rehman 10-0-31-0; Aamir Nazir 8-0-53-2; Nadeem Khan 6-0-38-0; Aamir Sohail 1-0-10-1.

Pakistan

Aamir Sohail c Ambrose b Bishop	42	Asif Mujtaba not out	45
Ramiz Raja run out	43	L-b 11, w 10, n-b 3	24
Inzamam-ul-Haq not out	90		
Basit Ali run out	17	1/71 2/100 3/130 (3 wkts, 43.1 overs) 261	

*Wasim Akram, †Rashid Latif, Waqar Younis, Nadeem Khan, Ata-ur-Rehman and Aamir Nazir did not bat.

Bowling: Ambrose 9-1-49-0; Walsh 10-0-63-0; Bishop 10-0-49-1; Simmons 7-0-44-0; Hooper 7.1-0-45-0.

Umpires: S. A. Bucknor and C. E. Cumberbatch.

†WEST INDIES v PAKISTAN

Fourth One-day International

At Kingstown, St Vincent, March 30. Pakistan won by 38 runs. Toss: West Indies.

Pakistan lost the toss for the fourth time and had to graft for runs on a slow, seaming pitch. For the first time, their openers failed to bring up 50, but Aamir Sohail survived and batted steadfastly, as did the other front-line batsmen, especially Basit Ali, though they were offered few bad balls. Pakistan's total of 186 looked inadequate only until they seized three West Indian wickets for 19 runs in their ten overs: Lara, who had been dropped before scoring, Haynes and Richardson. The bowling matched West Indies' for accuracy and surpassed it for incisiveness and hostility. Even Sohail and Asif Mujtaba, neither a specialist spinner, played their part. In five overs they dismissed Hooper and Logie, the last serious threats.

Man of the Match: Basit Ali.

Pakistan

Aamir Sohail c Richardson b Simmons	29	
Ramiz Raja lbw b Bishop	2	
Inzamam-ul-Haq c Murray b Hooper	17	
Javed Miandad b Ambrose	19	
Basit Ali b Walsh	60	
Asif Mujtaba c and b Hooper	23	
*Wasim Akram b Walsh	1	
†Rashid Latif not out	18	

Waqar Younis run out 1
Ata-ur-Rehman run out 2
Aamir Nazir not out 1
    L-b 4, w 5, n-b 5 13

1/9 2/52 3/54   (9 wkts, 50 overs) 186
4/111 5/159 6/161
7/166 8/169 9/180

Bowling: Bishop 10-0-44-1; Walsh 10-0-34-2; Ambrose 10-2-31-1; Hooper 10-1-35-2; Simmons 10-0-39-1.

West Indies

B. C. Lara c Rashid Latif b Waqar Younis	5	
D. L. Haynes lbw b Wasim Akram	6	
P. V. Simmons c Rashid Latif b Ata-ur-Rehman	20	
*R. B. Richardson c Rashid Latif b Ata-ur-Rehman	2	
C. L. Hooper b Aamir Sohail	16	
J. C. Adams c Javed Miandad b Wasim Akram	27	

A. L. Logie c Wasim Akram b Asif Mujtaba . 8
†J. R. Murray b Waqar Younis 14
I. R. Bishop not out 20
C. E. L. Ambrose b Wasim Akram 4
C. A. Walsh lbw b Wasim Akram 1
    B 3, l-b 3, w 9, n-b 10 25

1/14 2/14 3/19 4/48 5/75   (44.3 overs) 148
6/87 7/108 8/125 9/134

Bowling: Wasim Akram 7.3-2-18-4; Waqar Younis 8-0-27-2; Ata-ur-Rehman 10-0-38-2; Aamir Nazir 6-1-17-0; Aamir Sohail 6-1-23-1; Asif Mujtaba 7-0-19-1.

Umpires: L. H. Barker and G. T. Johnson.

†WEST INDIES v PAKISTAN

Fifth One-day International

At Georgetown, April 3. Tied. Toss: Pakistan.

The match finished with the scores level but the players left the field believing West Indies had won, having lost one less wicket. However, ICC referee Raman Subba Row intervened to declare a tie, because a crowd invasion impeded the fielding side while the last ball was still in play. With two runs needed to equal Pakistan's score, Bishop pushed the ball to deep mid-on. Even as he and Hooper ran the first, thousands of spectators swarmed on to the ground. Substitute Zahid Fazal returned the ball to the bowler, Wasim Akram, who dropped it, possibly distracted by the chaos. West Indies accepted Subba Row's decision as "absolutely fair". This result, after a see-sawing match, also left the series tied 2-2. Pakistan got the bulk of their 244 runs during the first seven overs and the last 17. In between, they lost momentum and wickets against keen bowling by Ambrose, Hooper and Cummins. Dismissing Lara early, they had a firm grip on the match until Richardson came in to blast 41. Even then all would have been over had Hooper not been missed on 27. Haynes helped him take West Indies within 22 runs of their target. Then two wickets went in successive overs, leaving 11 needed from the last.

Man of the Match: C. L. Hooper.

Pakistan

Aamir Sohail c and b Ambrose	33	
Ramiz Raja c and b Hooper	26	
Inzamam-ul-Haq lbw b Walsh	53	
Javed Miandad lbw b Cummins	2	
Basit Ali c Murray b Walsh	57	
*Wasim Akram not out	39	

†Rashid Latif c sub (K. L. T. Arthurton) b Bishop . 15
    B 1, l-b 6, w 6, n-b 6 19

1/66 2/76 3/85   (6 wkts, 50 overs) 244
4/188 5/189 6/244

Asif Mujtaba, Waqar Younis, Aamir Nazir and Ata-ur-Rehman did not bat.

Bowling: Bishop 10-0-62-1; Simmons 2-0-19-0; Walsh 10-0-48-2; Ambrose 10-1-44-1; Hooper 10-0-27-1; Cummins 8-0-37-1.

West Indies

D. L. Haynes lbw b Waqar Younis 82	A. L. Logie b Wasim Akram 1
B. C. Lara b Aamir Nazir 15	I. R. Bishop not out................ 3
P. V. Simmons run out 12	L-b 13, w 5, n-b 3........... 21
*R. B. Richardson st Rashid Latif	
b Aamir Sohail . 41	1/24 2/54 3/117 (5 wkts, 50 overs) 244
C. L. Hooper not out............... 69	4/223 5/228

†J. R. Murray, C. E. L. Ambrose, C. A. Walsh and A. C. Cummins did not bat.

Bowling: Wasim Akram 10-1-50-1; Waqar Younis 10-0-54-1; Ata-ur-Rehman 8-0-39-0; Aamir Nazir 8-0-28-1; Aamir Sohail 10-1-42-1; Asif Mujtaba 4-0-18-0.

Umpires: L. H. Barker and C. R. Duncan.

WEST INDIES BOARD PRESIDENT'S XI v PAKISTANIS

At Georgetown, April 5, 6, 7. Drawn. Toss: Pakistanis.

The tourists approached the first of their two remaining first-class matches before the Test series attempting to achieve a happy mix of practice and a decent contest. In this spirit they declared before the first day was out after three Test probables, Ramiz Raja, Basit Ali and Inzamam-ul-Haq, had spent time at the wicket. Four of the eight wickets lost went to the wrist-spin of an 18-year-old all-rounder, Shivnarine Chanderpaul, who later scored an unbeaten 140. The President's XI offered no positive response to the Pakistanis' challenge. They batted on long into the last day, piling up runs remorselessly but exasperating the crowd. Holder set out his claim for Test selection with a superb 144, while Arthurton scored an easy 74. Chanderpaul, a left-hander, started tentatively, but then drove with easy grace, hitting 22 fours in 265 minutes. Jacobs, who had kept wicket immaculately, made an aggressive unbeaten 100.

Close of play: First day, West Indies Board President's XI 23-2 (R. I. C. Holder 6*, K. L. T. Arthurton 0*); Second day, West Indies Board President's XI 276-4 (R. I. C. Holder 140*, S. Chanderpaul 24*).

Pakistanis

*Ramiz Raja c sub (N. E. F. Barry)	
b Chanderpaul . 75	
Shakeel Ahmed c Jacobs b Cummins 4	– (1) not out.................. 52
Asif Mujtaba c Adams b Chanderpaul 23	– not out...................... 67
Zahid Fazal c Jacobs b Cummins 8	– (2) c Cummins b Benjamin 13
Basit Ali c Jacobs b Chanderpaul 32	
Inzamam-ul-Haq st Jacobs b Chanderpaul 84	
†Moin Khan lbw b Benjamin 8	
Nadeem Khan b Benjamin 0	
Ata-ur-Rehman not out 0	
B 1, l-b 4, w 2, n-b 14 21	B 4, l-b 4, w 2, n-b 5 15

1/18 2/83 3/126 4/126 5/239	(8 wkts dec.) 255	1/36 (1 wkt) 147
6/252 7/252 8/255		

Aamir Nazir and Aqib Javed did not bat.

Bowling: *First Innings*—Benjamin 15-1-41-2; Cummins 15-2-48-2; Browne 6-2-28-0; Gibson 10-0-47-0; Chanderpaul 18.5-4-68-4; Adams 5-1-18-0. *Second Innings*—Cummins 7-1-26-0; Benjamin 5-0-22-1; Gibson 5-0-19-0; Browne 2-1-2-0; Chanderpaul 7-0-31-0; Adams 6-0-35-0; Arthurton 1-0-1-0; Joseph 1-0-3-0.

West Indies Board President's XI

D. A. Joseph b Aqib Javed	4	S. Chanderpaul not out	140
S. C. Williams c Ata-ur-Rehman		†R. D. Jacobs not out	100
b Nadeem Khan	11		
R. I. C. Holder c Asif Mujtaba			
b Ata-ur-Rehman	144	L-b 10, w 3, n-b 9	22
*K. L. T. Arthurton			
lbw b Ata-ur-Rehman	74	1/11 2/23	(5 wkts dec.) 508
J. C. Adams c Moin Khan		3/186 4/227	
b Nadeem Khan	13	5/284	

A. C. Cummins, B. St A. Browne, K. C. G. Benjamin and O. D. Gibson did not bat.

Bowling: Aqib Javed 3.1–0–12–1; Aamir Nazir 16–4–73–0; Nadeem Khan 37–8–129–2; Asif Mujtaba 32–6–90–0; Ata-ur-Rehman 20–0–106–2; Basit Ali 1–0–5–0; Zahid Fazal 9.1–1–35–0; Ramiz Raja 9–0–48–0.

Umpires: C. R. Duncan and R. W. Haynes.

WEST INDIAN UNDER-23 XI v PAKISTANIS

At St George's, Grenada, April 10, 11, 12. Pakistanis won by 111 runs. Toss: Pakistanis.

The match was nearly cancelled; 36 hours before it began, four of the touring team, including captain Wasim Akram, were arrested and charged with constructive possession of marijuana. They were on bail throughout the match, though the charges were dropped the night it finished. Three of the accused men played, but their indignation was not betrayed in their performance. The tourists' determination to win was clear when Wasim declared on the first day with only two wickets lost. The Under-23 attack made a hostile start, but Shakeel Ahmed and Asif Mujtaba profited from dropped chances to make centuries. After opening briskly and forcefully the Under-23s were undermined by the spin of Mushtaq Ahmed – carrying a back injury – and the slow left-armer Nadeem Khan. Rearranging their batting order, the Pakistanis increased their lead to 321 and gave themselves just under five hours to bowl out the Under-23s on a sound pitch. They demolished them with 75 minutes to spare, again relying on spin: Mushtaq took three wickets in just six overs and Aamir Sohail, with five for 50, finished the game.

Close of play: First day, West Indies Under-23 XI 22-0 (R. G. Samuels 7*, P. A. Wallace 14*); Second day, Pakistanis 178-6 (Asif Mujtaba 2*, Nadeem Khan 2*).

Pakistanis

Aamir Sohail c Eugene b Rose	10	– c Griffith b Cuffy	25
Shakeel Ahmed not out	132	– (5) c Eugene b Cuffy	23
Asif Mujtaba c Browne b Anthony	102	– (7) b Rose	4
Javed Miandad not out	32		
Zahid Fazal (did not bat)		– (2) run out	80
†Rashid Latif (did not bat)		– (3) lbw b Drakes	19
*Wasim Akram (did not bat)		– (4) lbw b Drakes	0
Waqar Younis (did not bat)		– (6) b Chanderpaul	14
Nadeem Khan (did not bat)		– (8) not out	25
Ata-ur-Rehman (did not bat)		– (9) not out	9
L-b 1, w 2, n-b 5	8	L-b 6, w 1, n-b 15	22

1/10 2/223	(2 wkts dec.) 284	1/29 2/67 3/68	(7 wkts dec.) 221
		4/118 5/166	
		6/176 7/186	

Mushtaq Ahmed did not bat.

Bowling: *First Innings*—Rose 12–5–46–1; Cuffy 13–3–43–0; Drakes 10–0–46–0; Anthony 15–5–41–1; Chanderpaul 18–2–73–0; Waldron 6–0–34–0. *Second Innings*—Rose 13–2–59–1; Drakes 11–0–44–2; Cuffy 10–0–23–2; Anthony 10–3–29–0; Chanderpaul 15–1–60–1.

West Indian Under-23 XI

P. A. Wallace c Asif Mujtaba b Ata-ur-Rehman	40	– lbw b Mushtaq Ahmed 23
R. G. Samuels c Wasim Akram		– c Ata-ur-Rehman
b Mushtaq Ahmed .	23	b Mushtaq Ahmed . 49
A. F. G. Griffith c Nadeem Khan		– (4) c Shakeel Ahmed
b Mushtaq Ahmed .	29	b Nadeem Khan . 20
*J. Eugene c Rashid Latif b Wasim Akram	13	– (3) b Mushtaq Ahmed 7
S. Chanderpaul st Rashid Latif		
b Mushtaq Ahmed .	0	– c Zahid Fazal b Aamir Sohail .. 1
H. R. Waldron c and b Nadeem Khan	44	– b Aamir Sohail 4
†C. O. Browne c and b Nadeem Khan	3	– b Aamir Sohail 44
H. A. G. Anthony c Wasim Akram		
b Nadeem Khan .	6	– b Aamir Sohail 11
V. C. Drakes c Aamir Sohail b Nadeem Khan	17	– run out 34
F. A. Rose lbw b Waqar Younis	0	– c and b Aamir Sohail 3
C. E. Cuffy not out	0	– not out 6
B 6, l-b 1, n-b 2	9	B 4, l-b 4 8

1/48 2/86 3/96 4/96 5/137		184	1/67 2/72 3/81 4/82 5/86	210
6/140 7/146 8/184 9/184			6/139 7/166 8/169 9/189	

Bowling: *First Innings*—Wasim Akram 8–1–30–1; Waqar Younis 8.2–1–53–1; Ata-ur-Rehman 7–0–37–1; Mushtaq Ahmed 9–2–36–3; Nadeem Khan 6–2–21–4. *Second Innings*—Wasim Akram 4–1–20–0; Ata-ur-Rehman 4–0–24–0; Mushtaq Ahmed 6–2–7–3; Aamir Sohail 19–5–50–5; Nadeem Khan 17–2–76–1; Waqar Younis 6.5–1–25–0.

Umpires: C. E. Cumberbatch and G. T. Johnson.

WEST INDIES v PAKISTAN

First Test Match

At Port-of-Spain, April 16, 17, 18. West Indies won by 204 runs. Toss: West Indies. Test debut: Basit Ali.

There was a fair amount of inept batting, but it was the poor pitch that had the match finished in three days. The main defect, its low bounce, was reflected in the 17 lbws in the match, eight against West Indies and nine against Pakistan. The previous record was 14 in the Pakistan–Sri Lanka Test at Faisalabad only 15 months earlier. This was all the more remarkable because one of the umpires was the Englishman Dickie Bird, who has always been regarded as harder to impress than most with lbw appeals.

The pitch was made more hazardous by being amenable to movement off the seam. Curiously, it became more regular in bounce on the second day and then reverted to its wretched behaviour on the third. It is customary in Tests at Queen's Park Oval to bowl first, because the pitch is generously watered to keep it bound. In this instance, it was bone dry, possibly because of the 24-hour delay to the game in the wake of the arrests in Grenada. In deciding to bat, Richardson must also have considered the perils Mushtaq Ahmed might pose in the fourth innings.

West Indies lasted less than two sessions, however. Almost half their meagre total of 127, their lowest on home soil against Pakistan, came from the opening partnership between Haynes and Simmons. But survival was not easy and would have been harder had Wasim Akram bowled more accurately. Mushtaq came on for the 11th over and had bowled Richardson, sweeping, by lunch. It took a superb ball from Ata-ur-Rehman, moving away late from a length, to dismiss Haynes, but his departure triggered the collapse. Lara played a loose shot at Waqar Younis who, in his next over, cut back two consecutive balls to claim Hooper and Murray lbw.

Pakistan's left-handed opener, Aamir Sohail, was the first batsman in the match to reach 50 and he was dropped when six. Sohail bided his time, punishing anything short to hit nine fours. He took Pakistan to 100 for two but after Hooper's spectacular low slip catch four more wickets fell for eight runs. Next day, when the last three wickets added 27, the pitch looked more benign.

In fact, it looked a committed ally of batsmen as West Indies raced to 333 for three from 76 overs. While Haynes secured one end, Richardson and then Lara audaciously attacked the wilting bowling. Richardson scored 68 off only 72 balls and Lara made an exhilarating 96 off 135 balls. He was out in the last over of the day, padding up to a ball well outside off stump and deflecting it on to his wicket. Armed with the new ball, Wasim and Waqar polished off the last seven batsmen for 49, but they could not subdue Haynes, who carried his bat for a record third time in Tests, after batting 459 minutes and, when 121, reaching 7,000 Test runs.

Pakistan, needing 370 to win, were 42 for four in just over an hour. The rot was halted by a partnership of 67 between Basit Ali, in his first Test, and Asif Mujtaba. As soon as they appeared comfortable against the tiring pace bowlers, Richardson called on Hooper's off-spin. His flight enticed Basit into lofting a catch and, bowling with guile, Hooper took four more wickets to complete the rout.

Man of the Match: D. L. Haynes.

Close of play: First day, Pakistan 113-7 (Asif Mujtaba 8*, Waqar Younis 1*); Second day, West Indies 333-3 (D. L. Haynes 115*, I. R. Bishop 1*).

West Indies

D. L. Haynes c Moin Khan b Ata-ur-Rehman	31	– not out..................................143
P. V. Simmons c Moin Khan b Ata-ur-Rehman	27	– c Asif Mujtaba b Aamir Sohail . 22
*R. B. Richardson b Mushtaq Ahmed	7	– c Wasim Akram b Waqar Younis 68
B. C. Lara c Aamir Sohail b Waqar Younis	6	– b Asif Mujtaba................... 96
K. L. T. Arthurton run out	3	– (6) lbw b Wasim Akram 1
C. L. Hooper lbw b Waqar Younis	9	– (7) lbw b Wasim Akram 0
†J. R. Murray lbw b Waqar Younis	0	– (8) lbw b Wasim Akram 0
I. R. Bishop c Inzamam-ul-Haq b Ata-ur-Rehman	4	– (5) c Moin Khan b Wasim Akram . 3
C. E. L. Ambrose lbw b Wasim Akram	4	– lbw b Wasim Akram 5
A. C. Cummins not out	14	– lbw b Wasim Akram 0
C. A. Walsh b Wasim Akram	0	– run out 6
B 6, l-b 3, w 2, n-b 11	22	B 1, l-b 18, w 2, n-b 17 .. 38
	127	**382**

1/63 (2) 2/76 (3) 3/85 (1) 4/85 (4) 5/95 (6) 6/95 (7) 7/102 (5) 8/102 (8) 9/127 (9) 10/127 (11)

1/57 (2) 2/160 (3) 3/329 (4) 4/342 (5) 5/356 (6) 6/358 (7) 7/358 (8) 8/371 (9) 9/371 (10) 10/382 (11)

Bowling: First Innings—Wasim Akram 10.2-2-32-2; Waqar Younis 11-3-37-3; Mushtaq Ahmed 8-1-21-1; Ata-ur-Rehman 9-1-28-3. *Second Innings*—Wasim Akram 27-6-75-4; Waqar Younis 23-2-88-3; Ata-ur-Rehman 19-0-82-0; Mushtaq Ahmed 13-1-45-0; Aamir Sohail 5-1-30-1; Asif Mujtaba 10-1-43-1.

Pakistan

Aamir Sohail c Hooper b Bishop	55	– lbw b Walsh 15
Ramiz Raja lbw b Bishop	9	– lbw b Ambrose 11
Inzamam-ul-Haq lbw b Walsh	10	– lbw b Walsh 6
Javed Miandad lbw b Ambrose	20	– c Murray b Bishop 4
Basit Ali lbw b Bishop	0	– c Richardson b Hooper 37
Asif Mujtaba c Lara b Bishop	10	– lbw b Hooper 20
*Wasim Akram c Richardson b Ambrose	2	– st Murray b Hooper 4
†Moin Khan c Murray b Ambrose	0	– c Bishop b Hooper 18
Waqar Younis c Lara b Ambrose	16	– lbw b Walsh 1
Mushtaq Ahmed c Hooper b Bishop	3	– not out 12
Ata-ur-Rehman not out	3	– c Ambrose b Hooper 19
L-b 6, n-b 6	12	L-b 10, n-b 8 18
	140	**165**

1/17 (2) 2/52 (3) 3/100 (1) 4/100 (5) 5/102 (4) 6/104 (7) 7/108 (8) 8/120 (6) 9/136 (9) 10/140 (10)

1/17 (2) 2/34 (3) 3/41 (1) 4/42 (4) 5/109 (5) 6/111 (6) 7/114 (7) 8/127 (9) 9/134 (8) 10/165 (11)

Bowling: *First Innings*—Ambrose 17–6–34–4; Bishop 15.5–6–43–5; Walsh 7–4–13–1; Cummins 5–0–19–0; Hooper 4–0–25–0. *Second Innings*—Ambrose 13–3–37–1; Bishop 11–2–28–1; Walsh 12–3–29–3; Cummins 5–1–16–0; Hooper 11.5–3–40–5; Simmons 1–0–5–0.

Umpires: H. D. Bird (England) and S. A. Bucknor. Referee: R. Subba Row (England).

WEST INDIES v PAKISTAN

Second Test Match

At Bridgetown, April 23, 24, 25, 27. West Indies won by ten wickets. Toss: Pakistan. Test debut: Aamir Nazir.

West Indies made one change, dropping Cummins for Winston Benjamin. Pakistan were forced to replace Mushtaq Ahmed, sent home because of his injured back, with the uncapped pace bowler, Aamir Nazir. Aamir Sohail played despite groin and hamstring injuries and Wasim Akram had barely recovered from flu.

The pitch was hard, with an island of green grass at each end on a fast bowler's length. Heavy rain before the start, and another shower after nine balls, were followed by hot sunshine, creating a degree of humidity ideal for bowling. Pakistan, in accordance with Kensington Oval tradition, chose to bowl first. But the move proved fruitless; wicket-keeper Moin Khan dropped Simmons twice in one over, denying Pakistan value for a fine opening spell by Waqar Younis, and Wasim again had little of his usual control. Simmons also edged and played and missed against Waqar but, having survived this ordeal, played a volatile innings of 87 off 90 balls. His belligerent tone was sustained in the afternoon by Richardson and Lara. Haynes batted in businesslike fashion to compile another century; if less adventurous than his partners, he severely punished the bad balls, which came regularly. At the end of the day, West Indies were 351 from 77 overs. Of the four batsmen dismissed, only Richardson, lbw, was genuinely beaten. Next day the new ball brought Pakistan just one success, Waqar having Hooper caught behind with a beautiful out-swinger. Wasim was bowling one of his better spells, and was unlucky to have Arthurton dropped at short leg in an over in which he passed his bat three times.

By the end of the day Pakistan had been reduced to 131 for five. Ambrose and Walsh had each produced one truly deadly ball, Haynes brought off a remarkable gully catch and Javed Miandad played a loose cut. However, Basit Ali survived and, on the third day, built the most heroic innings played for Pakistan in the series. In for 228 minutes, he was not out with 92, scored off 174 balls, with 11 fours and a six. Wasim, looking less than comfortable, supported him for most of the morning, but after he was caught at short leg the four remaining wickets went down for 32 runs, of which Basit scored 29, rejecting numerous singles to keep the strike.

Following on, Pakistan were 113 for three. Hopes of a recovery raised by a 66-run partnership between Asif Mujtaba and Miandad were shattered when Miandad wantonly chanced his arm seeking a second successive six off the penultimate ball of the day. West Indies resumed after the rest day without Bishop, who had an injured back, and dropped three chances. But Pakistan's scraps of good fortune were offset by an outrageous lbw decision against Mujtaba by umpire Barker and a dubious one against Inzamam-ul-Haq by Bird. Basit, eighth out, again strove valiantly, but it was the bravura of Waqar that forced West Indies to bat again. Nevertheless they won the Test, and thus the series, with more than a day to spare. Walsh took seven wickets in the match to become the seventh West Indian to pass the 200 mark in Test cricket.

Man of the Match: D. L. Haynes.

Close of play: First day, West Indies 351-4 (K. L. T. Arthurton 19*, C. L. Hooper 11*); Second day, Pakistan 131-5 (Basit Ali 33*, Wasim Akram 3*); Third day, Pakistan 113-3 (Asif Mujtaba 36*, Moin Khan 0*).

West Indies

D. L. Haynes b Aamir Nazir	125	– not out	16
P. V. Simmons c Moin Khan b Ata-ur-Rehman	87	– not out	8
*R. B. Richardson lbw b Waqar Younis	31		
B. C. Lara c Moin Khan b Ata-ur-Rehman	51		
K. L. T. Arthurton b Wasim Akram	56		
C. L. Hooper c Moin Khan b Waqar Younis	15		
†J. R. Murray st Moin Khan b Aamir Sohail	35		
I. R. Bishop c Moin Khan b Aamir Nazir	11		
C. E. L. Ambrose not out	12		
W. K. M. Benjamin b Waqar Younis	0		
C. A. Walsh c and b Waqar Younis	3		
B 1, l-b 1, w 2, n-b 25	29	W 3, n-b 2	5
	455	**(no wkt)**	**29**

1/122 (2) 2/200 (3) 3/303 (4) 4/337 (1)
5/363 (6) 6/426 (5) 7/440 (7)
8/440 (8) 9/445 (10) 10/455 (11)

Bowling: *First Innings*—Wasim Akram 32–2–95–1; Waqar Younis 25.5–3–132–4; Aamir Nazir 20–1–79–2; Ata-ur-Rehman 21–1–103–2; Asif Mujtaba 3–0–30–0; Aamir Sohail 4–1–14–1. *Second Innings*—Wasim Akram 2.3–0–18–0; Aamir Nazir 2–0–11–0.

Pakistan

Aamir Sohail c Murray b Ambrose	10	– c Benjamin b Ambrose	4
Ramiz Raja c Haynes b Ambrose	37	– lbw b Walsh	25
Asif Mujtaba c Richardson b Walsh	13	– lbw b Benjamin	41
Javed Miandad c Richardson b Benjamin	22	– c Arthurton b Hooper	43
Inzamam-ul-Haq lbw b Bishop	7	– (7) lbw b Benjamin	26
Basit Ali not out	92	– lbw b Walsh	37
*Wasim Akram c Simmons b Hooper	29	– (8) b Benjamin	0
†Moin Khan c Murray b Walsh	0	– (5) c Murray b Hooper	17
Waqar Younis c Murray b Walsh	0	– c Lara b Hooper	29
Ata-ur-Rehman c Benjamin b Walsh	0	– c Simmons b Walsh	13
Aamir Nazir c Arthurton b Benjamin	1	– not out	6
L-b 3, n-b 7	10	B 12, l-b 5, n-b 4	21
	221		**262**

1/12 (1) 2/31 (3) 3/62 (4) 4/79 (5)
5/109 (2) 6/189 (7) 7/190 (8)
8/190 (9) 9/200 (10) 10/221 (11)

1/4 (1) 2/47 (2) 3/113 (4)
4/133 (3) 5/141 (5) 6/207 (7)
7/207 (8) 8/215 (6)
9/238 (10) 10/262 (9)

Bowling: *First Innings*—Ambrose 16–5–42–2; Bishop 16–5–43–1; Walsh 18–2–56–4; Benjamin 19–5–55–2; Hooper 7–0–22–1. *Second Innings*—Ambrose 26–10–55–1; Bishop 4–1–13–0; Benjamin 17–7–30–3; Walsh 24–7–51–3; Hooper 32.3–6–96–3.

Umpires: L. H. Barker and H. D. Bird (England). Referee: R. Subba Row (England).

WEST INDIES v PAKISTAN

Third Test Match

At St John's, Antigua, May 1, 2, 4, 5, 6. Drawn. Toss: West Indies. Test debuts: Nadeem Khan, Shakeel Ahmed.

Wet weather on all but two days caused the game to be abandoned early on the final day, a mildly controversial decision as it was taken by the Englishmen, umpire Bird and referee Subba Row, without West Indian umpire Bucknor. There were stages of the match when Pakistan were in the ascendancy, yet but for the rain, West Indies would probably have won again. They had reinstated Cummins because Bishop was resting his back, and

Pakistan had two new caps. The injured Aamir Sohail having gone home, Shakeel Ahmed opened the batting, while Aamir Nazir was replaced by the left-arm spinner, Nadeem Khan. Rashid Latif had recovered from injury, to return as wicket-keeper.

Until the ball started to keep low on the fourth day the pitch was on the batsman's side. Entertainment was abundant on the opening day, with West Indies rattling up 344 while nine wickets fell. All their early batsmen established themselves, but got out trying to plunder runs, and the innings was in need of repair when Waqar Younis, who took five wickets for the first time in the series, had Arthurton lbw. Against this background Hooper played an innings of stirring virtuosity. He made 178 not out off 247 balls, with 19 fours and four sixes. He overwhelmed the bowling with strokes both majestically orthodox and cutely improvised. Walsh, his partner in a stand of 106 – West Indies' highest for the last wicket against all countries – needed to face only 30 balls in 23 overs.

Ambrose and Walsh removed Pakistan's openers for four runs. Asif Mujtaba, with a stolid fifty, and Javed Miandad rebuilt the innings. They were interrupted by rain and, when play resumed, Benjamin used the pitch's extra liveliness to make the breakthrough. Miandad was lbw and one ball later more rain ended play. Pakistan made little headway next morning; Mujtaba, so assured against pace, was completely tied up by Hooper. Basit Ali batted for 163 minutes but after he played across a full-length delivery Pakistan lost three more wickets for 31 runs, and needed another 12 to avoid the follow-on with only two wickets in hand. Inzamam-ul-Haq would have joined the procession but Benjamin dropped him at long leg. With Nadeem Khan he dug in to add 96, batting with authority and charm for his maiden Test century.

With Pakistan remaining until the end of the third day and the start of the fourth delayed, the draw was beyond doubt. But the match's embers were stoked by a thrilling eight-over spell from Waqar Younis. He did not come on until the 13th over, but almost at once bowled Simmons with a ball of full length and had Richardson lbw next delivery. Shortly after giving that verdict umpire Bird, suffering from a trapped nerve in the back, left the field. Within minutes, Waqar appealed to the reserve umpire, Clancy Mack, against Haynes for a close-call lbw and was denied. At 68, he claimed successfully against Lara and Arthurton. But Haynes and Hooper held out until the end of the day, and then the rain set in.

Man of the Match: C. L. Hooper.   *Man of the Series*: D. L. Haynes.

Close of play: First day, West Indies 344-9 (C. L. Hooper 116*, C. A. Walsh 0*); Second day, Pakistan 85-3 (Asif Mujtaba 50*, Basit Ali 0*); Third day, Pakistan 326; Fourth day, West Indies 153-4 (D. L. Haynes 64*, C. L. Hooper 29*).

West Indies

D. L. Haynes c Rashid Latif b Nadeem Khan	23	– not out 64
P. V. Simmons c Wasim Akram		
b Ata-ur-Rehman	28	– b Waqar Younis 17
*R. B. Richardson c Wasim Akram		
b Waqar Younis	52	– lbw b Waqar Younis 0
B. C. Lara st Rashid Latif b Nadeem Khan	44	– lbw b Waqar Younis 19
K. L. T. Arthurton lbw b Waqar Younis	30	– lbw b Waqar Younis 0
C. L. Hooper not out	178	– not out 29
†J. R. Murray lbw b Waqar Younis	4	
C. E. L. Ambrose lbw b Wasim Akram	1	
A. C. Cummins lbw b Waqar Younis	14	
W. K. M. Benjamin c Wasim Akram		
b Waqar Younis	12	
C. A. Walsh c Asif Mujtaba b Wasim Akram	30	
L-b 6, n-b 16	22	B 8, l-b 5, n-b 11 24

1/35 (2) 2/77 (1) 3/153 (4) 4/159 (3)   438   1/36 (2) 2/36 (3)   (4 wkts) 153
5/218 (5) 6/241 (7) 7/252 (8)   3/68 (4) 4/68 (5)
8/312 (9) 9/332 (10) 10/438 (11)

Bowling: *First Innings*—Wasim Akram 26.2–5–108–2; Waqar Younis 28–4–104–5; Ata-ur-Rehman 17–1–66–1; Nadeem Khan 38–5–147–2; Asif Mujtaba 1–0–7–0. *Second Innings*—Wasim Akram 10–2–30–0; Ata-ur-Rehman 9–1–24–0; Nadeem Khan 14–0–48–0; Waqar Younis 11–1–23–4; Asif Mujtaba 4–1–9–0; Basit Ali 1–0–6–0.

Pakistan

Ramiz Raja c Murray b Walsh	0	Waqar Younis c Hooper b Benjamin	4
Shakeel Ahmed lbw b Ambrose	0	Nadeem Khan c Murray b Cummins	25
Asif Mujtaba c Haynes b Hooper	59	Ata-ur-Rehman not out	1
Javed Miandad lbw b Benjamin	31	L-b 6, n-b 10	16
Basit Ali b Cummins	56		
Inzamam-ul-Haq c Haynes b Cummins	123	1/0 (2) 2/4 (1) 3/85 (4) 4/108 (3)	326
†Rashid Latif lbw b Cummins	2	5/196 (5) 6/206 (7) 7/221 (8)	
*Wasim Akram c Hooper b Benjamin	9	8/227 (9) 9/323 (6) 10/326 (10)	

Bowling: Ambrose 23–9–40–1; Walsh 19–3–58–1; Benjamin 20–4–53–3; Cummins 20–4–54–4; Hooper 28–2–98–1; Simmons 5–0–17–0.

Umpires: H. D. Bird (England) and S. A. Bucknor (C. Mack deputised for H. D. Bird on the 4th day). Referee: R. Subba Row (England).

†At St David's, Bermuda, May 8. Pakistanis won by five wickets. Bermuda 231 for nine (50 overs) (C. M. Marshall 49, S. Lightbourne 44; Nadeem Khan four for 34); Pakistanis 232 for five (46 overs) (Shakeel Ahmed 57, Ramiz Raja 54, Zahid Fazal 66, Moin Khan 30 not out).

†At Somerset Field, Bermuda, May 9. Pakistanis won by 139 runs. Pakistan 374 for seven (48 overs) (Shakeel Ahmed 70, Zahid Fazal 190, Moin Khan 50); Bermuda 235 for seven (48 overs) (A. C. Douglas 59, C. M. Marshall 60; Kamran Khan three for 54).

Kamran Khan, a member of a touring Philadelphian club, was one of two guest players to appear for the Pakistanis in Bermuda when their squad was reduced by injuries and contractual commitments. Nadeem Usmani, a waiter at the Southampton Princess Hotel on the island, played in the second match. Kamran was reported to have played with distinction; Nadeem, described as being more experienced as a spectator than a participant, was said to have fielded "somewhat tentatively".

BENSON AND HEDGES WORLD SERIES CUP, 1992-93

By TONY COZIER

Note: Matches in this section were not first-class.

PAKISTAN v WEST INDIES

At Perth, December 4 (day/night). Pakistan won by five wickets. Toss: West Indies. International debut: J. R. Murray.

Although Pakistan won with only four balls remaining, the target was always well within their grasp. Javed Miandad gathered his runs with characteristic innovation and scored 45 singles off his 82 balls. Then Inzamam-ul-Haq and Wasim Akram provided the necessary impetus to keep Pakistan on course towards the end, Wasim completing the victory with a square-leg boundary off Ambrose. West Indies started shakily when Haynes received a dubious decision in the second over. Even Lara, who scored 59, could never raise the rate above four an over.

Man of the Match: Wasim Akram.   *Attendance:* 7,950.

West Indies

D. L. Haynes c Rashid Latif	
b Waqar Younis . 1	†J. R. Murray b Waqar Younis 22
P. V. Simmons c Rashid Latif	I. R. Bishop c Rashid Latif
b Wasim Akram . 6	b Wasim Akram . 6
*R. B. Richardson c Wasim Akram	C. E. L. Ambrose not out 15
b Aamir Sohail . 23	A. C. Cummins c Javed Miandad
B. C. Lara c sub (Naved Anjum)	b Wasim Akram . 0
b Mushtaq Ahmed . 59	K. C. G. Benjamin not out 13
C. L. Hooper c Inzamam-ul-Haq	B 4, l-b 3, w 8, n-b 4 19
b Mushtaq Ahmed . 24	
K. L. T. Arthurton c Rashid Latif	1/1 2/12 3/64 (9 wkts, 50 overs) 197
b Wasim Akram . 9	4/119 5/138 6/140
	7/153 8/176 9/177

Bowling: Wasim Akram 9–1–46–4; Waqar Younis 7–2–26–2; Ata-ur-Rehman 10–0–29–0; Aamir Sohail 8–0–36–1; Mushtaq Ahmed 10–1–22–2; Asif Mujtaba 6–0–31–0.

Pakistan

Aamir Sohail c Haynes b Bishop 2	Wasim Akram not out 21
Ramiz Raja c Murray b Benjamin 34	
Salim Malik c Murray b Benjamin 35	L-b 4, w 3, n-b 10 17
*Javed Miandad not out 59	
Inzamam-ul-Haq c Lara b Hooper 28	1/6 2/62 3/102 (5 wkts, 49.2 overs) 199
Asif Mujtaba run out 3	4/157 5/163

†Rashid Latif, Mushtaq Ahmed, Waqar Younis and Ata-ur-Rehman did not bat.

Bowling: Ambrose 9.2–2–30–0; Bishop 10–1–34–1; Cummins 10–0–41–0; Benjamin 10–0–46–2; Hooper 10–0–44–1.

Umpires: R. J. Evans and L. J. King.

AUSTRALIA v WEST INDIES

At Perth, December 6. West Indies won by nine wickets. Toss: Australia.

Australia could not come to terms with accurate West Indies bowling and sharp fielding and laboured to 50 off 24.4 overs. Mark Waugh and Matthews added 58 off 14 overs before Waugh was stumped down the leg side off a delivery signalled wide by umpire Prue. Healy's unbeaten 21 off 23 balls came too late to provide a real challenge to West Indies. Haynes took 14 balls to get off the mark but gained momentum and was there at the end, hitting 11 fours to bring his team victory with nearly 12 overs to spare.

Man of the Match: P. V. Simmons.   *Attendance:* 17,149.

Australia

M. A. Taylor run out	0	†I. A. Healy not out 21
D. C. Boon c Murray b Bishop	6	P. R. Reiffel not out 9
D. M. Jones c Cummins b Simmons ...	14	
S. R. Waugh c Hooper b Simmons ...	4	L-b 9, w 11, n-b 3 23
M. E. Waugh st Murray b Hooper ..	36	
*A. R. Border run out	15	1/4 2/15 3/32 (7 wkts, 50 overs) 160
G. R. J. Matthews c Richardson		4/35 5/64
b Hooper .	32	6/122 7/137

C. J. McDermott and M. R. Whitney did not bat.

Bowling: Bishop 10-1-20-1; Cummins 10-1-35-0; Simmons 10-2-22-2; Ambrose 10-1-37-0; Hooper 10-0-37-2.

West Indies

D. L. Haynes not out	81
B. C. Lara c Border b Reiffel	29
P. V. Simmons not out	43
L-b 6, w 1, n-b 4	11
1/53 (1 wkt, 38.3 overs)	164

*R. B. Richardson, C. L. Hooper, K. L. T. Arthurton, A. L. Logie, †J. R. Murray, I. R. Bishop, C. E. L. Ambrose and A. C. Cummins did not bat.

Bowling: McDermott 7-2-32-0; Whitney 5-0-30-0; Reiffel 6-1-12-1; S. R. Waugh 8-2-31-0; Matthews 9-0-32-0; M. E. Waugh 3.3-0-21-0.

Umpires: R. J. Evans and T. A. Prue.

AUSTRALIA v WEST INDIES

At Sydney, December 8 (day/night). Australia won by 14 runs. Toss: West Indies.

Three days of rain had soaked the pitch and left it soft and treacherous. Both captains said it was unfit for play but the umpires ordered a match reduced to 30 overs that produced exciting, if unreal, cricket. The ball moved sharply off the pitch and batting was so difficult that Jones's 21 off 53 balls was the highest individual innings. As influential as the bowling was the catching of Taylor, who held four of high quality in the slips, for which he was named Man of the Match. It was a happy conclusion to his first game as captain in place of the injured Border.

Man of the Match: M. A. Taylor.   *Attendance:* 32,184.

Australia

D. C. Boon c Lara b Simmons	8	P. R. Reiffel not out 9
*M. A. Taylor b Simmons	9	C. J. McDermott lbw b Hooper 2
D. M. Jones c Murray b Ambrose	21	M. R. Whitney not out 1
S. R. Waugh c Murray b Simmons	1	
M. E. Waugh st Murray b Hooper ...	17	L-b 11, w 8 19
D. R. Martyn b Ambrose	0	
G. R. J. Matthews c Ambrose		1/31 2/32 3/34 (9 wkts, 30 overs) 101
b Cummins .	11	4/61 5/62 6/79
†I. A. Healy c Cummins b Ambrose ...	3	7/85 8/90 9/98

Bowling: Bishop 6-0-20-0; Simmons 6-2-11-3; Ambrose 6-0-18-3; Cummins 6-1-16-1; Hooper 6-0-25-2.

West Indies

D. L. Haynes c S. R. Waugh b Reiffel	5	I. R. Bishop c Healy b M. E. Waugh	11
B. C. Lara b Whitney	4	C. E. L. Ambrose not out	13
P. V. Simmons lbw b McDermott	0	A. C. Cummins run out	2
*R. B. Richardson c Healy b Whitney	6		
A. L. Logie c Taylor b Reiffel	20	L-b 13, w 2	15
K. L. T. Arthurton c Taylor			
b S. R. Waugh	3	1/6 2/7 3/18	(29.3 overs) 87
C. L. Hooper c Taylor b Reiffel	6	4/22 5/31 6/49	
†J. R. Murray c Taylor b S. R. Waugh	2	7/55 8/65 9/75	

Bowling: McDermott 6–1–11–1; Whitney 6–1–11–2; Reiffel 6–1–14–3; S. R. Waugh 5.3–0–25–2; M. E. Waugh 6–0–13–1.

Umpires: D. B. Hair and S. G. Randell.

AUSTRALIA v PAKISTAN

At Hobart, December 10. Tied. Toss: Australia.

Pakistan staged a remarkable late-order revival that culminated in the left-hander, Asif Mujtaba, hitting a slower ball from Steve Waugh for six over mid-wicket to tie the match. When Salim Malik was fifth out at 123 in the 36th over, Pakistan needed to score at 7.5 runs an over to reach their target. Mujtaba and Rashid Latif gave them hope with a stand of 68 but 17 were still required when Waugh started the final over. He dismissed Mushtaq with the first delivery. Mujtaba and Aqib Javed collected five each off the next four, leaving Pakistan seven short before Mujtaba let fly. Australia's innings had been handicapped by the run-outs of three key batsmen, Jones, Steve Waugh and Martyn, but it received an unexpected boost during tea when unofficial scorers in the press box convinced officials that a run had been missed. That apparent trifle proved crucial.

Man of the Match: Asif Mujtaba.   *Attendance:* 10,274.

Australia

*M. A. Taylor c Rashid Latif		P. R. Reiffel not out	23
b Aqib Javed	46	C. J. McDermott not out	2
D. C. Boon lbw b Aqib Javed	14		
D. M. Jones run out	53		
S. R. Waugh run out	26	B 3, l-b 15, w 1, n-b 3	22
M. E. Waugh b Mushtaq Ahmed	13		
D. R. Martyn run out		1/32 2/124 3/138	(7 wkts, 50 overs) 228
†I. A. Healy c Javed Miandad		4/164 5/172	
b Waqar Younis	24	6/179 7/218	

M. R. Whitney and T. B. A. May did not bat.

Bowling: Wasim Akram 10–3–34–0; Waqar Younis 9–1–43–1; Aqib Javed 10–0–35–2; Aamir Sohail 10–0–37–0; Mushtaq Ahmed 10–0–52–1; Asif Mujtaba 1–0–9–0.

Pakistan

Aamir Sohail c Martyn b McDermott	6	Waqar Younis b McDermott	8
Ramiz Raja c S. R. Waugh b Whitney	4	Mushtaq Ahmed c Reiffel	
Salim Malik c Healy b McDermott	64	b S. R. Waugh	0
*Javed Miandad lbw b Reiffel	14	Aqib Javed not out	5
Inzamam-ul-Haq c Martyn		L-b 6, w 1	7
b M. E. Waugh	22		
Asif Mujtaba not out	56	1/6 2/10 3/41	(9 wkts, 50 overs) 228
Wasim Akram c Healy b McDermott	3	4/91 5/123 6/129	
†Rashid Latif run out	39	7/197 8/207 9/212	

Bowling: McDermott 10–2–42–4; Whitney 10–3–29–1; Reiffel 8–2–29–1; S. R. Waugh 10–0–56–1; May 5–0–29–0; M. E. Waugh 7–0–37–1.

Umpires: S. G. Randell and C. D. Timmins.

PAKISTAN v WEST INDIES

At Adelaide, December 12. West Indies won by four runs. Toss: Pakistan.

After dropping five catches and missing several run-out chances, West Indies held their nerve while Pakistan panicked, losing their last seven wickets – four to run-outs – in 35 balls. West Indies had been 118 for five off 35 overs when rain intervened to reduce their allotted overs to 42. On resumption, they added 59 off their last seven overs, led by Richardson. But when Pakistan passed 100 in the 25th over, with only one wicket down, they seemed on course for victory before throwing the game away. Javed Miandad played his 200th limited-overs international, a mark passed only by A. R. Border and D. L. Haynes.

Man of the Match: C. L. Hooper.   *Attendance:* 6,254.

West Indies

D. L. Haynes b Wasim Akram	6	C. L. Hooper c Rashid Latif	
B. C. Lara b Aqib Javed	15	b Wasim Akram	24
P. V. Simmons c Aamir Sohail		I. R. Bishop c Asif Mujtaba	
b Wasim Akram	5	b Mushtaq Ahmed	17
*R. B. Richardson not out	76	A. C. Cummins not out	4
A. L. Logie c Ramiz Raja		B 1, l-b 13, w 8, n-b 4	26
b Aamir Sohail	1		
K. L. T. Arthurton c Inzamam-ul-Haq		1/16 2/27 3/56 4/61 (7 wkts, 42 overs) 177	
b Aamir Sohail	3	5/81 6/133 7/172	

†J. R. Murray and C. E. L. Ambrose did not bat.

Bowling: Wasim Akram 9-1-38-3; Waqar Younis 8-0-38-0; Aamir Sohail 10-1-26-2; Aqib Javed 5-2-30-1; Mushtaq Ahmed 8-1-23-1; Asif Mujtaba 2-0-8-0.

Pakistan

Aamir Sohail c Bishop b Simmons	41	Waqar Younis b Hooper	5
Ramiz Raja run out	52	Mushtaq Ahmed run out	3
Salim Malik c Simmons b Ambrose	22	Aqib Javed not out	7
*Javed Miandad c Simmons b Hooper	11	L-b 3, w 4, n-b 4	11
Inzamam-ul-Haq run out	18		
Asif Mujtaba run out	0	1/63 2/117 3/128 (41.5 overs) 173	
Wasim Akram b Hooper	2	4/148 5/148 6/151	
†Rashid Latif run out	1	7/153 8/162 9/162	

Bowling: Bishop 8-0-38-0; Ambrose 9-0-41-1; Cummins 9-1-31-0; Simmons 8-0-29-1; Hooper 7.5-0-31-3.

Umpires: S. J. Davis and T. A. Prue.

AUSTRALIA v PAKISTAN

At Adelaide, December 13. Australia won by eight wickets. Toss: Australia.

After a rain-delayed start, Pakistan were pinned down by the accuracy of Whitney and May before Inzamam-ul-Haq and Wasim Akram added 57 in seven overs. Wasim hit 36 off 15 balls, including two sixes, one off McDermott over the 110-metre straight boundary, and three fours. But it came too late to get Pakistan past the 200 mark and Australia achieved their victory comfortably. Taylor hit just one four in making 78 off 109 balls.

Man of the Match: M. A. Taylor.   *Attendance:* 18,179.

Pakistan

Aamir Sohail run out	8	Wasim Akram c Taylor b McDermott	36
Ramiz Raja b May	28	†Rashid Latif not out	0
Asif Mujtaba b S. R. Waugh	45	L-b 4, w 1, n-b 1	6
*Javed Miandad b May	6		
Inzamam-ul-Haq not out	60	1/10 2/60 3/68 (6 wkts, 47 overs) 195	
Saeed Anwar run out	6	4/120 5/137 6/194	

Waqar Younis, Mushtaq Ahmed and Aqib Javed did not bat.

Bowling: McDermott 9–0–56–1; Whitney 10–3–22–0; Reiffel 9–0–36–0; May 10–0–27–2;
S. R. Waugh 9–0–50–1.

Australia

D. C. Boon b Aamir Sohail	....	40
*M. A. Taylor run out	....	78
D. M. Jones not out	....	48
S. R. Waugh not out	....	15
L-b 6, w 5, n-b 4	....	15

1/70 2/171   (2 wkts, 45 overs) 196

M. E. Waugh, D. R. Martyn, †I. A. Healy, P. R. Reiffel, C. J. McDermott, M. R. Whitney
and T. B. A. May did not bat.

Bowling: Wasim Akram 9–0–39–0; Waqar Younis 10–2–32–0; Aqib Javed 9–0–36–0;
Aamir Sohail 9–0–36–1; Mushtaq Ahmed 7–0–36–0; Asif Mujtaba 1–0–11–0.

Umpires: I. S. Thomas and C. D. Timmins.

AUSTRALIA v WEST INDIES

At Melbourne, December 15 (day/night). Australia won by four runs. Toss: Australia.
A remarkable collapse in which they lost their last seven wickets for 21 off 31 balls
transformed what seemed certain West Indian victory into narrow defeat. The collapse was
set in motion by Mark Waugh, who took five for 16. With the outfield sluggish, Australia
had failed to muster an overall scoring-rate of four an over. Waugh made 57, which
included five of the innings' seven fours as well as three early chances. West Indies seemed
to be meeting their target comfortably as Lara and Richardson added 92 in 18 overs. When
12, Richardson reached 5,000 runs in one-day internationals. But once Lara was bowled, the
first of Waugh's five victims, the effort went into swift decline. Australia's acting-captain
Taylor had won three of his four matches in charge, the other being tied.
Man of the Match: M. E. Waugh.   *Attendance:* 74,450.

Australia

*M. A. Taylor c Hooper b Simmons ...	10		P. R. Reiffel run out	....	0
D. C. Boon c Haynes b Ambrose	.....	4	C. J. McDermott not out	....	0
D. M. Jones c Arthurton b Cummins ..	22				
S. R. Waugh run out	....	34	L-b 5, w 6, n-b 1	....	12
M. E. Waugh c Hooper b Ambrose	...	57			
D. R. Martyn c Murray b Ambrose	...	40	1/13 2/17 3/63	(8 wkts, 50 overs) 198
†I. A. Healy c Haynes b Hooper	......	13	4/86 5/160 6/186	
G. R. J. Matthews not out	....	6	7/192 8/197	

M. R. Whitney did not bat.

Bowling: Ambrose 10–3–25–3; Simmons 10–3–31–1; Walsh 10–1–42–0; Cummins
10–0–45–1; Hooper 10–0–50–1.

West Indies

B. C. Lara b M. E. Waugh	....	74	C. E. L. Ambrose run out	....	0
D. L. Haynes c Taylor b Whitney	.....	4	A. C. Cummins c McDermott		
P. V. Simmons c Healy b Reiffel	.....	24	b M. E. Waugh .	2
*R. B. Richardson c Taylor			C. A. Walsh not out	....	0
b M. E. Waugh .	61				
C. L. Hooper c Martyn b S. R. Waugh .	6		L-b 9	....	9
A. L. Logie run out	....	0			
K. L. T. Arthurton c Jones			1/18 2/66 3/158	(50 overs) 194
b M. E. Waugh .	9		4/173 5/178 6/178	
†J. R. Murray c and b M. E. Waugh ..	5		7/187 8/192 9/192	

Bowling: McDermott 7–1–27–0; Whitney 10–1–27–1; Reiffel 10–1–45–1; Matthews
7–0–24–0; S. R. Waugh 10–0–38–1; M. E. Waugh 6–0–24–5.

Umpires: L. J. King and T. A. Prue.

PAKISTAN v WEST INDIES

At Sydney, December 17 (day/night). West Indies won by 133 runs. Toss: West Indies.

Pakistan fell apart against Simmons's medium-pace swing, which earned him four wickets for three runs in ten overs, the most economical figures ever recorded from a full stint in a one-day international, bettering B. S. Bedi's 12-8-6-1 for India against East Africa in the 1975 World Cup. Only a relaxed West Indian approach towards the end and a ninth-wicket partnership of 24 between Waqar Younis and Mushtaq Ahmed carried Pakistan past their previous lowest total in one-day internationals, 74 against England in the World Cup a year earlier. West Indies' total was built around Haynes, who was eighth out four short of his 17th one-day international century. He faced 152 balls and hit six fours, but needed a runner after a knee injury when he was 92.

Man of the Match: P. V. Simmons.   *Attendance*: 12,635.

West Indies

B. C. Lara run out	3	K. C. G. Benjamin not out		9
D. L. Haynes b Wasim Akram	96	†J. R. Murray run out		0
P. V. Simmons c Salim Malik		C. E. L. Ambrose b Waqar Younis		0
b Aamir Sohail	10	B. P. Patterson not out		0
*R. B. Richardson c Wasim Akram		B 4, l-b 9, w 12, n-b 4		29
b Mushtaq Ahmed	33			
C. L. Hooper run out	17	1/10 2/40 3/107	(9 wkts, 50 overs)	214
A. L. Logie b Waqar Younis	0	4/151 5/156 6/195		
J. C. Adams lbw b Waqar Younis	17	7/209 8/210 9/213		

Bowling: Wasim Akram 10-0-37-1; Waqar Younis 10-1-29-3; Aamir Sohail 10-1-38-1; Ata-ur-Rehman 10-0-47-0; Mushtaq Ahmed 10-0-50-1.

Pakistan

Aamir Sohail c Benjamin b Simmons	6	Waqar Younis lbw b Hooper		17
Ramiz Raja c Lara b Patterson	0	Mushtaq Ahmed c Benjamin b Adams		15
Asif Mujtaba b Simmons	1	Ata-ur-Rehman not out		0
Salim Malik c Hooper b Simmons	0			
*Javed Miandad c Murray b Simmons	2	W 1, n-b 7		8
Inzamam-ul-Haq c Hooper b Benjamin	17			
Wasim Akram c Richardson		1/2 2/4 3/9	(48 overs)	81
b Benjamin	7	4/9 5/14 6/35		
†Rashid Latif c Murray b Patterson	8	7/35 8/54 9/78		

Bowling: Patterson 9-2-19-2; Simmons 10-8-3-4; Ambrose 10-4-19-0; Benjamin 9-1-28-2; Hooper 6-2-10-1; Adams 4-2-2-1.

Umpires: D. B. Hair and I. S. Thomas.

PAKISTAN v WEST INDIES

At Brisbane, January 9. West Indies won by nine wickets. Toss: Pakistan.

Pakistan returned from their short tour of New Zealand to continue where they had left off three weeks earlier, with a collapse. They capitulated to West Indies by lunch, the fastest finish in the tournament's history. On a pitch offering the fast bowlers some lift and movement they showed no fight, had lost half their wickets for 12 runs by the eighth over and were bowled out in 23.4 overs. This time they fell three short of their previous lowest limited-overs total. Bishop claimed three of his five wickets in his opening spell and returned to round off the innings. West Indies had no difficulty knocking off the runs; Richardson completed the formalities with a six over long-off Mushtaq Ahmed. But there were two casualties: Simmons and Murray collided as Simmons caught Wasim Akram. He had concussion, and Murray strained his back.

Man of the Match: I. R. Bishop.   *Attendance*: 9,535.

Pakistan

Saeed Anwar c Lara b Bishop	2	Waqar Younis c Lara b Ambrose		0
Shahid Saeed c Lara b Bishop	1	Mushtaq Ahmed c Richardson b Bishop		2
Inzamam-ul-Haq c Simmons b Benjamin	0	Aqib Javed c Benjamin b Bishop		4
*Javed Miandad c Murray b Bishop	0	L-b 3, w 8, n-b 1		12
Salim Malik b Ambrose	8			
Asif Mujtaba b Benjamin	1	1/2 2/7 3/7	(23.4 overs)	71
Wasim Akram c Simmons b Ambrose	19	4/11 5/12 6/31		
†Rashid Latif not out	22	7/54 8/55 9/58		

Bowling: Bishop 8.4-0-25-5; Benjamin 6-2-16-2; Ambrose 6-1-13-3; Hooper 3-0-14-0.

West Indies

B. C. Lara c Waqar Younis b Wasim Akram	10
D. L. Haynes not out	25
*R. B. Richardson not out	22
W 6, n-b 9	15
1/22 (1 wkt, 19.2 overs)	72

P. V. Simmons, K. L. T. Arthurton, J. C. Adams, C. L. Hooper, †J. R. Murray, I. R. Bishop, C. E. L. Ambrose and K. C. G. Benjamin did not bat.

Bowling: Wasim Akram 9-0-33-1; Waqar Younis 7-3-13-0; Aqib Javed 2-0-16-0; Mushtaq Ahmed 1.2-0-10-0.

Umpires: S. J. Davis and L. J. King.

AUSTRALIA v WEST INDIES

At Brisbane, January 10. West Indies won by seven runs. Toss: Australia.

Already qualified for the finals, West Indies made five changes from the previous day and their victory was a psychological fillip. Hooper's 65-ball 56 and his fifth-wicket partnership of 57 in 12.3 overs with Logie held the innings together after a shaky start, but their modest total required diligent defending. Patterson's sharp opening spell set back Australia, at ten for two, and slick fielding accounted for four run-outs as the last five wickets fell for 32. One of the victims was Mark Waugh, who scored his second successive fifty.

Man of the Match: C. L. Hooper.   *Attendance*: 19,877.

West Indies

D. L. Haynes c Healy b Reiffel	36	K. C. G. Benjamin c S. R. Waugh b May		17
B. C. Lara c Healy b Whitney	10	C. A. Walsh b S. R. Waugh		12
*R. B. Richardson c S. R. Waugh b Reiffel	1	B. P. Patterson not out		1
C. L. Hooper c Reiffel b M. E. Waugh	56	L-b 8, w 2		10
K. L. T. Arthurton c Taylor b Reiffel	2			
A. L. Logie c Reiffel b McDermott	26	1/26 2/38 3/65	(9 wkts, 50 overs)	197
†D. Williams not out	25	4/72 5/129 6/149		
A. C. Cummins run out	1	7/152 8/175 9/196		

Bowling: McDermott 10-2-25-1; Whitney 10-1-30-1; Reiffel 10-1-33-3; S. R. Waugh 7-1-30-1; May 8-0-48-1; M. E. Waugh 5-0-23-1.

Australia

D. C. Boon c Williams b Patterson	....	3	C. J. McDermott run out	7
M. A. Taylor c Richardson b Cummins		20	T. B. A. May not out	3
D. M. Jones c Williams b Patterson	...	0	M. R. Whitney run out	2
S. R. Waugh c Logie b Walsh	....	24	B 2, l-b 6, w 9, n-b 4	21
M. E. Waugh run out	....	54		
*A. R. Border b Hooper	....	11	1/5 2/10 3/51 (49 overs) 190	
†I. A. Healy lbw b Walsh	....	41	4/61 5/81 6/158	
P. R. Reiffel run out	....	4	7/173 8/176 9/187	

Bowling: Patterson 10-0-31-2; Benjamin 10-1-32-0; Cummins 10-1-27-1; Walsh 10-0-49-2; Hooper 9-0-43-1.

Umpires: I. S. Thomas and C. D. Timmins.

AUSTRALIA v PAKISTAN

At Melbourne, January 12 (day/night). Australia won by 32 runs. Toss: Australia.

Victory booked Australia's place in the finals and ended the last hopes of Pakistan, who again played without strategy or spirit. Jones survived a close lbw decision off Wasim Akram before he had scored and later sustained a hairline fracture of the right thumb when struck by a ball from the same bowler, but he provided the backbone of the total with a partnership of 124 with Boon. Then Border passed 6,000 runs in one-day internationals, the fourth player to do so, after D. L. Haynes, I. V. A. Richards and Javed Miandad. Pakistan never looked like coming to terms with their target; Inzamam-ul-Haq's robust, unbeaten 39 came too late to matter.

Man of the Match: D. M. Jones.   *Attendance*: 68,179.

Australia

M. A. Taylor c Rashid Latif			*A. R. Border not out	14
	b Aqib Javed .	4	†I. A. Healy run out	3
D. C. Boon c Shahid Saeed			A. I. C. Dodemaide not out	15
	b Asif Mujtaba	64	B 3, l-b 2, w 3, n-b 3	11
D. M. Jones b Waqar Younis	....	84		
S. R. Waugh c and b Asif Mujtaba	....	5	1/9 2/133 3/153 (6 wkts, 50 overs) 212	
M. E. Waugh b Waqar Younis	....	12	4/180 5/181 6/187	

P. R. Reiffel, C. J. McDermott and T. B. A. May did not bat.

Bowling: Wasim Akram 10-1-28-0; Aqib Javed 8-0-39-1; Waqar Younis 10-0-39-2; Aamir Sohail 5-0-27-0; Shahid Saeed 8-0-36-0; Asif Mujtaba 9-0-38-2.

Pakistan

Aamir Sohail c Healy b McDermott	...	3	†Rashid Latif c Healy b Reiffel	5
Ramiz Raja c Healy b S. R. Waugh	...	40	Asif Mujtaba not out	5
Shahid Saeed b Dodemaide	....	3		
Salim Malik b McDermott	....	37	B 1, l-b 4	5
*Javed Miandad c Border				
	b M. E. Waugh	40	1/10 2/28 3/69 (7 wkts, 50 overs) 180	
Inzamam-ul-Haq not out	....	39	4/97 5/142	
Wasim Akram c M. E. Waugh b Reiffel		3	6/154 7/171	

Waqar Younis and Aqib Javed did not bat.

Bowling: McDermott 10-2-26-2; Reiffel 10-1-37-2; S. R. Waugh 8-0-22-1; May 10-0-41-0; M. E. Waugh 4-0-24-1.

Umpires: D. B. Hair and C. D. Timmins.

AUSTRALIA v PAKISTAN

At Sydney, January 14 (day/night). Australia won by 23 runs. Toss: Australia.

Although the finalists were already settled, the match attracted Sydney's largest crowd of the season to date. Boon and Taylor shared the only century opening partnership of the tournament, and although Waqar Younis took three wickets in ten balls in his final spell, Australia scored 77 off the last ten overs. Pakistan were promisingly placed at 130 for two but then Ramiz Raja, Javed Miandad and Wasim Akram fell to spin in the space of three runs. Inzamam-ul-Haq and Asif Mujtaba added 71 but Australia were never seriously threatened again. It was Pakistan's sixth consecutive defeat in the competition.

Man of the Match: S. R. Waugh.   *Attendance*: 35,227.

Australia

D. C. Boon c sub (Saeed Anwar)	G. R. J. Matthews not out 10	
b Asif Mujtaba . 50	A. I. C. Dodemaide run out 5	
M. A. Taylor b Asif Mujtaba 58	P. R. Reiffel not out 2	
D. M. Jones b Mushtaq Ahmed 13		
S. R. Waugh c Asif Mujtaba	B 6, l-b 5, w 4, n-b 4 19	
b Waqar Younis . 64		
M. E. Waugh run out 11	1/112 2/124 3/144 (8 wkts, 50 overs) 260	
*A. R. Border b Waqar Younis 28	4/167 5/230 6/230	
†I. A. Healy lbw b Waqar Younis 0	7/245 8/257	

C. J. McDermott did not bat.

Bowling: Wasim Akram 10-0-39-0; Aqib Javed 9-0-52-0; Waqar Younis 9-1-55-3; Mushtaq Ahmed 10-0-39-1; Asif Mujtaba 9-0-47-2; Aamir Sohail 3-0-17-0.

Pakistan

Aamir Sohail b Dodemaide 7	Asif Mujtaba not out 47
Ramiz Raja c Border b Matthews 67	Waqar Younis not out 18
Salim Malik c Healy b Dodemaide 6	
*Javed Miandad c M. E. Waugh	B 1, l-b 6, w 4 11
b Border . 41	
Inzamam-ul-Haq b McDermott 40	1/24 2/46 3/130 (6 wkts, 50 overs) 237
Wasim Akram b Matthews 0	4/132 5/133 6/204

†Rashid Latif, Mushtaq Ahmed and Aqib Javed did not bat.

Bowling: McDermott 9-3-27-1; Dodemaide 8-2-30-2; Reiffel 10-0-53-0; S. R. Waugh 5-0-26-0; Matthews 10-0-54-2; Border 8-0-40-1.

Umpires: T. A. Prue and S. G. Randell.

QUALIFYING TABLE

	Played	Won	Lost	Tied	Points	Net run-rate
Australia	8	5	2	1	11	0.06
West Indies......	8	5	3	0	10	0.78
Pakistan	8	1	6	1	3	−0.85

Player of the Preliminaries: P. V. Simmons.

AUSTRALIA v WEST INDIES

First Final Match

At Sydney, January 16 (day/night). West Indies won by 25 runs. Toss: West Indies.

Haynes and Lara laid the foundations for West Indies' highest total in the competition by scoring 90 in 19.4 overs. The final momentum came from Hooper and Logie, whose partnership yielded 57 off as many balls; Logie's busy 38 needed only 36 deliveries. Ambrose dismissed both Australian openers in a fiery opening seven overs that became even hotter after Jones demanded that he remove his white wristbands. Australia were still in with a slight chance until Ambrose returned to take the last three wickets, bowling the dangerous Healy, who had hit 33 in 30 balls, with a slower ball.

Attendance: 37,581.

West Indies

B. C. Lara c Dodemaide b Border	67	K. C. G. Benjamin run out	0
D. L. Haynes c and b Matthews	38	I. R. Bishop b McDermott	1
P. V. Simmons c M. E. Waugh		C. E. L. Ambrose not out	5
b Matthews	5	B 2, l-b 8, n-b 2	12
*R. B. Richardson c Dodemaide			—
b Border	28	1/90 2/96 3/128 (8 wkts, 50 overs) 239
C. L. Hooper b S. R. Waugh	45	4/159 5/216 6/217
A. L. Logie b S. R. Waugh	38	7/220 8/239

†J. R. Murray and A. C. Cummins did not bat.

Bowling: McDermott 8-0-40-1; Dodemaide 7-0-23-0; Reiffel 5-1-30-0; Matthews 10-0-45-2; Border 10-0-46-2; S. R. Waugh 10-0-45-2.

Australia

M. A. Taylor c Simmons b Ambrose	28	A. I. C. Dodemaide c Lara b Ambrose	3
D. C. Boon c Murray b Ambrose	16	P. R. Reiffel not out	12
D. M. Jones c Simmons b Benjamin	13	C. J. McDermott c Simmons b Ambrose	0
S. R. Waugh c and b Hooper	15	L-b 3, n-b 2	5
M. E. Waugh run out	51		—
*A. R. Border c Ambrose b Hooper	27	1/41 2/48 3/69 (49.3 overs) 214
†I. A. Healy b Ambrose	33	4/91 5/147 6/160
G. R. J. Matthews c Lara b Benjamin	11	7/179 8/187 9/214

Bowling: Bishop 10-0-45-0; Simmons 2-0-14-0; Ambrose 9.3-2-32-5; Benjamin 10-0-35-2; Cummins 8-0-39-0; Hooper 10-0-46-2.

Umpires: T. A. Prue and S. G. Randell.

AUSTRALIA v WEST INDIES

Second Final Match

At Melbourne, January 18 (day/night). West Indies won by four wickets. Toss: Australia.

A tense, low-scoring match was closer than the deciding margin indicated. After Boon and Taylor scored 39 off the first ten overs West Indies choked the run supply with tight bowling backed by sharp fielding. Between the 20th and 30th overs Australia added only 13 while losing three batsmen. Ambrose made sure they did not prosper at the end, claiming three of the last four wickets. Boon and the Waugh brothers were all run out by direct hits, Mark Waugh for the fourth time in five one-day internationals following his run-out in the Third Test. West Indies started uncertainly, losing three for 23, until Lara and Hooper set them on course for their target of 148 with a partnership of 86. But Lara was caught in the gully in the 33rd over, off his 100th delivery, and two more wickets fell cheaply. When Bishop joined Hooper 22 more were needed and runs were hard to come by. The batsmen remained calm, however, to see West Indies to their sixth triumph in eight World Series competitions, and their fifth in five sets of finals against Australia.

Player of the Finals: C. E. L. Ambrose. *Attendance*: 72,492.

Australia

M. A. Taylor c Ambrose b Bishop	....	33
D. C. Boon run out	....	19
D. M. Jones c Murray b Bishop	......	5
S. R. Waugh run out	....	25
M. E. Waugh run out	....	8
*A. R. Border c and b Hooper	....	8
†I. A. Healy c and b Ambrose	....	16
G. R. J. Matthews c Logie		
b Ambrose	.	15

A. I. C. Dodemaide c Murray
                       b Ambrose .   1
P. R. Reiffel not out   7
C. J. McDermott b Hooper   0

L-b 3, n-b 7   10
                                    ——
1/54 2/63 3/65   (47.3 overs) 147
4/74 5/94 6/113
7/133 8/137 9/146

Bowling: Bishop 9-2-33-2; Benjamin 10-0-33-0; Ambrose 10-0-26-3; Cummins 10-1-24-0; Hooper 8.3-1-28-2.

West Indies

B. C. Lara c M. E. Waugh
                       b McDermott . 60
D. L. Haynes run out   0
P. V. Simmons c M. E. Waugh
                       b Dodemaide .   0
*R. B. Richardson c Reiffel
                       b McDermott .   5
C. L. Hooper not out 59

A. L. Logie c Healy b Reiffel   7
†J. R. Murray c Healy b Dodemaide ..   1
I. R. Bishop not out   4

L-b 7, w 2, n-b 3   12
                                    ——
1/7 2/8 3/23   (6 wkts, 47 overs) 148
4/109 5/125 6/126

K. C. G. Benjamin, C. E. L. Ambrose and A. C. Cummins did not bat.

Bowling: McDermott 10-4-35-2; Dodemaide 10-4-19-2; Reiffel 10-1-21-1; S. R. Waugh 10-1-30-0; M. E. Waugh 4-0-17-0; Matthews 3-0-19-0.

Umpires: D. B. Hair and C. D. Timmins.

PETER SMITH AWARD

The Peter Smith Award was instituted in 1992 by the Cricket Writers' Club in memory of the club's former chairman. The first winner, "for services to cricket", was David Gower. The citation now reads "for services to the presentation of cricket to the public" and the 1993 winner was John Woodcock, formerly both cricket correspondent of *The Times* and editor of *Wisden*.

WILLS TROPHY, 1992-93

In their first venture under the leadership of Wasim Akram, Pakistan claimed their sixth trophy in successive visits to Sharjah since March 1989. Playing only Test cricket's newest teams, Sri Lanka and Zimbabwe, they had a welcome opportunity to recover their self-confidence, after a poor showing in the World Series Cup in Australia. Pakistan won all three of their matches, and Wasim took four Sri Lankan wickets twice to be named the Player of the Series, but two notoriously weak attacks provided an insufficient challenge for Pakistan's top order. India refused to attend after their protest over what they considered to be biased umpiring in the previous tournament 16 months earlier. Former Pakistani Test bowler Sikander Bakht and opener Ramiz Raja both received benefit cheques of $US35,000 from the series. Pakistan won $20,000, beaten finalists Sri Lanka $12,500 and Zimbabwe $5,000.

Note: Matches in this section were not first-class.

PAKISTAN v ZIMBABWE

At Sharjah, February 1. Pakistan won by 49 runs. Toss: Zimbabwe. International debuts: Arshad Khan; G. A. Briant.

Zimbabwe's first appearance at Sharjah ended in defeat, but not disgrace. In reply to Pakistan's 262, the Flower brothers opened with 121 in 29 overs and took a heavy toll of the bowling of debutant Arshad Khan. But only their captain, Houghton, made significant runs after that and Waqar Younis dismissed him for his 100th wicket in 59 limited-overs internationals. Earlier, Shah had been the most successful of Zimbabwe's bowlers, removing Saeed Anwar, Javed Miandad and Salim Malik to reduce Pakistan to 88 for four. Inzamam-ul-Haq rallied the innings with a forceful 90, including 11 fours.

Man of the Match: Inzamam-ul-Haq.

Pakistan

Saeed Anwar c and b Shah	26	Mushtaq Ahmed not out		4
Ramiz Raja c A. Flower b Brandes	5	Arshad Khan not out		0
Inzamam-ul-Haq c Ranchod b Brandes	90			
Javed Miandad c A. Flower b Shah	14	B 4, l-b 6, w 10		20
Salim Malik c A. Flower b Shah	0			
†Rashid Latif c Dekker b Brain	39	1/18 2/47 3/88	(8 wkts, 50 overs)	262
*Wasim Akram c Shah b Brain	38	4/88 5/163 6/199		
Waqar Younis c G. W. Flower b Brain.	26	7/252 8/258		

Aqib Javed did not bat.

Bowling: Brandes 10-0-66-2; Brain 10-0-51-3; Ranchod 10-1-40-0; Shah 10-2-33-3; Peall 10-0-62-0.

Zimbabwe

†A. Flower run out	49	G. A. Briant not out		14
G. W. Flower c Waqar Younis		A. H. Shah b Waqar Younis		0
b Mushtaq Ahmed	57	S. G. Peall not out		12
K. J. Arnott c Rashid Latif		L-b 16, w 13, n-b 2		31
b Salim Malik	7			
*D. L. Houghton b Waqar Younis	36	1/121 2/127 3/138	(6 wkts, 50 overs)	213
M. H. Dekker run out	7	4/178 5/187 6/188		

E. A. Brandes, D. H. Brain and U. Ranchod did not bat.

Bowling: Wasim Akram 10–0–34–0; Aqib Javed 7–1–11–0; Arshad Khan 6–0–43–0; Waqar Younis 10–3–26–2; Mushtaq Ahmed 10–0–42–1; Salim Malik 7–0–41–1.

Umpires: R. V. Ramani and R. C. Sharma.

PAKISTAN v SRI LANKA

At Sharjah, February 2. Pakistan won by eight wickets. Toss: Pakistan.

Pakistan assured themselves of a place in the final by overtaking Sri Lanka's 180 with 5.4 overs to spare. Exactly half Sri Lanka's runs came from Gurusinha, who hit three sixes and five fours, but he could find little support after losing Hathurusinghe. Wasim Akram claimed three wickets, including Gurusinha, in his final spell, and figures of four for 24 were to earn him the match award. Against Pakistan's batsmen, only the occasional off-spinner of de Silva had much success, removing both openers in quick succession, but not until they had put on 132 for the first wicket.

Man of the Match: Wasim Akram.

Sri Lanka

R. S. Mahanama lbw b Wasim Akram .	1		†A. G. D. Wickremasinghe	
U. C. Hathurusinghe c Saeed Anwar			b Wasim Akram .	2
b Salim Malik .	36		C. P. H. Ramanayake	
A. P. Gurusinha c sub (Zahid Fazal)			b Waqar Younis .	15
b Wasim Akram .	90		G. P. Wickremasinghe not out	1
P. A. de Silva c Asif Mujtaba				
b Waqar Younis .	7			
*A. Ranatunga c Rashid Latif			L-b 7, w 3, n-b 2	12
b Aqib Javed .	8			
H. P. Tillekeratne lbw b Aqib Javed . . .	2		1/2 2/98 3/119	(9 wkts, 46 overs) 180
R. S. Kalpage c Asif Mujtaba			4/141 5/147 6/160	
b Wasim Akram .	6		7/160 8/164 9/180	

S. D. Anurasiri did not bat.

Bowling: Wasim Akram 10–1–24–4; Aqib Javed 10–1–31–2; Waqar Younis 10–0–37–2; Mushtaq Ahmed 10–1–41–0; Asif Mujtaba 2–0–16–0; Salim Malik 4–0–24–1.

Pakistan

Saeed Anwar c Tillekeratne b de Silva .	55
Ramiz Raja c Gurusinha b de Silva	73
Inzamam-ul-Haq not out	27
Asif Mujtaba not out	15
B 2, l-b 1, w 6, n-b 2	11

1/132 2/137   (2 wkts, 40.2 overs) 181

Javed Miandad, Salim Malik, †Rashid Latif, *Wasim Akram, Mushtaq Ahmed, Waqar Younis and Aqib Javed did not bat.

Bowling: Ramanayake 8.2–1–19–0; G. P. Wickremasinghe 7–0–30–0; Hathurusinghe 3–0–19–0; Kalpage 7–0–29–0; Ranatunga 3–0–18–0; Anurasiri 7–0–39–0; de Silva 5–0–24–2.

Umpires: R. V. Ramani and R. C. Sharma.

SRI LANKA v ZIMBABWE

At Sharjah, February 3. Sri Lanka won by 30 runs. Toss: Sri Lanka. International debut: N. Ranatunga.

If rain had not deprived Sri Lanka of their final seven overs, Zimbabwe would have been hard-pressed to keep their total under 300. Openers Mahanama and Hathurusinghe shared 112 in 84 minutes, and their middle order carried on the good work. Arjuna Ranatunga, whose brother Nishantha became the third of the family to represent Sri Lanka, passed

3,000 runs in his 115th limited-overs international. Faced with scoring 6.20 an over, Zimbabwe went down bravely. They lost Grant Flower and Arnott in Ramanayake's first spell, and Houghton and Briant were run out. The recovery from 85 for six was thanks largely to a maiden international fifty from Brandes, whose previous best was 23.

Man of the Match: E. A. Brandes.

Sri Lanka

R. S. Mahanama c Arnott b Crocker...	62	R. S. Kalpage not out	8
U. C. Hathurusinghe lbw b Brandes ...	66		
A. P. Gurusinha run out	20	L-b 3, w 8, n-b 1...........	12
P. A. de Silva b Brain	46		
*A. Ranatunga c Campbell b Brandes ..	39	1/112 2/154 3/165 (5 wkts, 43 overs) 266	
†H. P. Tillekeratne not out	13	4/243 5/246	

N. Ranatunga, C. P. H. Ramanayake, G. P. Wickremasinghe and S. D. Anurasiri did not bat.

Bowling: Brandes 9-1-57-2; Brain 7-0-41-1; Ranchod 9-1-46-0; Shah 6-0-37-0; G. W. Flower 7-0-45-0; Crocker 5-0-37-1.

Zimbabwe

†A. Flower b Gurusinha	26	A. H. Shah b Wickremasinghe........	26
G. W. Flower c Tillekeratne		G. J. Crocker not out	36
b Ramanayake .	0	D. H. Brain b Wickremasinghe	12
K. J. Arnott c Kalpage b Ramanayake .	8	U. Ranchod not out................	3
*D. L. Houghton run out	32		
G. A. Briant run out	3	L-b 15, w 11, n-b 1..........	27
A. D. R. Campbell c Mahanama			
b N. Ranatunga .	8	1/2 2/20 3/54 (9 wkts, 43 overs) 236	
E. A. Brandes c A. Ranatunga		4/65 5/85 6/85	
b Ramanayake .	55	7/154 8/194 9/219	

Bowling: Ramanayake 9-0-29-3; Wickremasinghe 9-0-51-2; de Silva 3-0-26-0; N. Ranatunga 9-0-33-1; Gurusinha 8-1-35-1; A. Ranatunga 3-0-23-0; Anurasiri 2-0-24-0.

Umpires: R. V. Ramani and R. C. Sharma.

QUALIFYING TABLE

	Played	Won	Lost	Points
Pakistan	2	2	0	4
Sri Lanka	2	1	1	2
Zimbabwe	2	0	2	0

FINAL

PAKISTAN v SRI LANKA

At Sharjah, February 4. Pakistan won by 114 runs. Toss: Sri Lanka.

Pakistan's batsmen outscored the Sri Lankans the previous day with 281 from just 41 overs, setting their opponents 6.87 an over to win. Sri Lanka were never in the hunt. Every match in the tournament had featured a century opening stand, but Saeed Anwar and Ramiz Raja did even better, putting on 204 in 34 overs to beat their own one-day record for Pakistan's first wicket: 202, also against Sri Lanka, at Adelaide in 1989-90. Anwar made his 110 from 105 balls and Ramiz his 109 from 115. Wasim Akram again quickly removed Sri Lankan opener Mahanama lbw for nought and trapped three more victims the same way to finish with an analysis of four for 24 for the second game running.

Man of the Match: Saeed Anwar.   *Man of the Series:* Wasim Akram.

Pakistan

Saeed Anwar c Ramanayake		
b Gurusinha .110	*Wasim Akram b Gurusinha	22
Ramiz Raja not out 109	Javed Miandad not out	12
Inzamam-ul-Haq c Wickremasinghe	L-b 6, w 2	8
b Ramanayake . 20	1/204 2/231 3/267 (3 wkts, 41 overs) 281

Salim Malik, Asif Mujtaba, †Rashid Latif, Waqar Younis, Mushtaq Ahmed and Aqib Javed did not bat.

Bowling: Ramanayake 10-1-62-1; Wickremasinghe 5-0-38-0; Gurusinha 7-1-63-2; N. Ranatunga 8-0-49-0; Warnaweera 7-0-39-0; Kalpage 4-0-24-0.

Sri Lanka

R. S. Mahanama lbw b Wasim Akram . 0	N. Ranatunga lbw b Wasim Akram . . .	0
U. C. Hathurusinghe	C. P. H. Ramanayake not out	1
c Mushtaq Ahmed b Aqib Javed . 42		
P. A. de Silva lbw b Aqib Javed 9	B 4, l-b 6, w 11, n-b 3	24
A. P. Gurusinha run out 36		
*A. Ranatunga lbw b Wasim Akram. . . 25	1/4 2/15 3/105 (7 wkts, 41 overs) 167
†H. P. Tillekeratne lbw b Wasim Akram 11	4/105 5/139
R. S. Kalpage not out 19	6/162 7/162

G. P. Wickremasinghe and K. P. J. Warnaweera did not bat.

Bowling: Wasim Akram 10-3-24-4; Aqib Javed 10-2-30-2; Mushtaq Ahmed 10-0-59-0; Waqar Younis 10-0-36-0; Salim Malik 1-0-8-0.

Umpires: R. V. Ramani and R. C. Sharma.

ONE HUNDRED YEARS AGO

From JOHN WISDEN'S CRICKETERS' ALMANACK FOR 1894

OXFORD v CAMBRIDGE: "Nine wickets were down for 95, and then on Wilson, the last man, joining Brain, an incident occurred which is likely to be talked about for a good many years to come. Three runs were added, making the score 98, or 84 short of Cambridge's total, and Oxford thus required only 5 runs to save the follow-on. The two batsmen were then seen to consult together between the wickets, and it was at once evident to those who had grasped the situation that the Dark Blues were going to throw away a wicket in order that their side might go in again. Had one of them acted on his own account, it is probable that the object would have been gained, but Wells, who was bowling from the Pavilion end, saw at once what was intended and promptly set to work to frustrate it. Going over the crease, he bowled a ball wide to the boundary, and then after an unsuccessful effort to bowl a wide all along the ground, sent another round-arm ball to the ropes, thus giving away another eight runs, but preventing Oxford going in a second time."

ETON v HARROW: "Uncertain weather and the strong counter-attraction of the meeting of Orme and La Flèche in the Eclipse Stakes at Sandown considerably affected the attendance on the opening day, the company scarcely numbering more than 12,000."

TOTAL INTERNATIONAL SERIES, 1992-93

By COLIN BRYDEN

Towards the end of the South African season, Pakistan and West Indies paid their first visits to South Africa to play a triangular series modelled on the World Series Cup. There was enormous local interest even after the home team failed to reach the final, which West Indies won comfortably. R. M. Cowper of Australia was the ICC referee for the whole series.

Note: Matches in this section were not first-class.

SOUTH AFRICA v PAKISTAN

At Durban, February 9. Pakistan won by ten runs. Toss: South Africa.

Pakistan, who lost Saeed Anwar in the first over, struggled in their innings and South Africa seemed well on the way to victory when Hudson and Wessels put on 101 for the first wicket. They started the last ten overs at 159 for one, needing only 50 to win. But Kirsten missed a cut against Asif Mujtaba off the first ball of the 41st over and in the next Hudson was bowled for 93 by a late in-swinger from Waqar Younis. Waqar went on to claim five wickets, all bowled, for ten runs and, with the bonus of three run-outs, ensured that South Africa suffered an astonishing collapse.

Man of the Match: Waqar Younis.

Pakistan

Saeed Anwar b Donald	0	†Rashid Latif c Richardson b McMillan.	15
Ramiz Raja c Richardson b Matthews	29	*Wasim Akram not out	20
Inzamam-ul-Haq run out	47	L-b 10, w 2	12
Javed Miandad c Richardson b McMillan	22	1/0 2/46 (6 wkts, 50 overs) 208	
Salim Malik c McMillan b Cronje	14	3/93 4/107	
Asif Mujtaba not out	49	5/132 6/166	

Waqar Younis, Mushtaq Ahmed and Aqib Javed did not bat.

Bowling: Donald 10-2-32-1; de Villiers 10-0-41-0; Matthews 10-0-54-1; McMillan 10-1-35-2; Cronje 10-0-36-1.

South Africa

A. C. Hudson b Waqar Younis	93	C. R. Matthews b Waqar Younis	3
*K. C. Wessels lbw b Wasim Akram	42	P. S. de Villiers b Waqar Younis	1
P. N. Kirsten b Asif Mujtaba	18	A. A. Donald not out	1
W. J. Cronje b Waqar Younis	11	L-b 7, w 1, n-b 3	11
D. J. Cullinan b Waqar Younis	0		
J. N. Rhodes run out	5	1/101 2/159 3/165 (50 overs) 198	
B. M. McMillan run out	2	4/165 5/180 6/181	
†D. J. Richardson run out	11	7/182 8/195 9/197	

Bowling: Wasim Akram 10-1-36-1; Aqib Javed 10-1-38-0; Mushtaq Ahmed 10-1-46-0; Waqar Younis 10-0-25-5; Asif Mujtaba 10-1-46-1.

Umpires: K. E. Liebenberg and C. J. Mitchley.

SOUTH AFRICA v WEST INDIES

At Port Elizabeth, February 11. South Africa won by six wickets. Toss: South Africa.

On a pitch of benign appearance but uneven bounce the West Indians suffered some early blows from Pringle and could not lift their scoring tempo much above three runs an over. Haynes took 104 balls over 43 runs, with a single boundary, one of only seven scored by his team. Patterson, the first change bowler, dismissed both South African openers in his first over, the 13th of the innings, and the host country laboured to 65 for four from 24 overs. However, an enterprising unbroken partnership of 85 between the 37-year-old Kirsten and Rhodes, 14 years his junior, saw South Africa home with more than three overs to spare.

Man of the Match: J. N. Rhodes.

West Indies

D. L. Haynes b de Villiers 43	C. E. L. Ambrose c Wessels b McMillan 9
B. C. Lara lbw b Pringle............. 13	C. A. Walsh c Cronje b Donald....... 12
P. V. Simmons lbw b Pringle 0	B. P. Patterson b Donald 1
*R. B. Richardson b McMillan 3	L-b 4, n-b 2 6
C. L. Hooper c Richardson b Callaghan 17	
A. L. Logie c Richardson b Donald.... 8	1/27 2/27 3/42 (49 overs) 149
†J. R. Murray not out 30	4/77 5/89 6/91
I. R. Bishop lbw b de Villiers........ 7	7/103 8/125 9/144

Bowling: Donald 10-1-27-3; de Villiers 9-2-21-2; Pringle 10-1-25-2; McMillan 10-0-32-2; Cronje 7-0-23-0; Callaghan 3-0-17-1.

South Africa

*K. C. Wessels c Murray b Patterson .. 8	J. N. Rhodes not out................ 46
A. C. Hudson c Murray b Patterson ... 10	L-b 4, w 10, n-b 16 30
W. J. Cronje c Simmons b Walsh 1	
P. N. Kirsten not out 45	1/29 2/32 (4 wkts, 46.5 overs) 150
D. J. Callaghan c Hooper b Bishop.... 10	3/33 4/65

B. M. McMillan, †D. J. Richardson, M. W. Pringle, P. S. de Villiers and A. A. Donald did not bat.

Bowling: Ambrose 10-3-17-0; Bishop 9-1-23-1; Patterson 8.5-0-46-2; Walsh 10-1-32-1; Hooper 7-1-21-0; Simmons 2-0-7-0.

Umpires: R. E. Koertzen and S. B. Lambson.

PAKISTAN v WEST INDIES

At Johannesburg, February 13. West Indies won by eight wickets, their target having been revised to 106 from 27 overs. Toss: Pakistan.

A capacity crowd of 30,000 watched the first international between two visiting teams in South Africa, enticed by the prospect of a contest between two outstanding pace attacks on the fastest, bounciest pitch in the country. The West Indians duly gave the Pakistan batsmen a torrid time, although Shoaib Mohammad, with his curious closed stance, hit eight boundaries in an uncharacteristically rapid 49 from 67 balls. Despite the loss of Simmons and Lara to successive balls from Waqar Younis, Haynes and Hooper batted aggressively to take West Indies to victory. Rain interrupted their innings at 73 for two from 18 overs, but it took little longer to reach a revised target of 106.

Man of the Match: D. L. Haynes.

Pakistan

Ramiz Raja c Logie b Patterson....... 13	Waqar Younis not out............... 3
Shoaib Mohammad c Lara b Bishop ... 49	Mushtaq Ahmed lbw b Bishop....... 5
Inzamam-ul-Haq c and b Simmons 23	Aqib Javed c Hooper b Bishop 0
Javed Miandad c Hooper b Ambrose .. 13	L-b 4, w 7, n-b 7............ 18
Salim Malik lbw b Walsh 1	
Asif Mujtaba c Richardson b Ambrose.. 5	1/21 2/74 3/100 (41.4 overs) 150
†Rashid Latif b Patterson............ 9	4/103 5/111 6/127
*Wasim Akram c Logie b Bishop 11	7/135 8/143 9/150

Bowling: Bishop 9.4-0-25-4; Patterson 8-1-33-2; Ambrose 8-0-31-2; Simmons 7-0-35-1; Walsh 9-2-22-1.

West Indies

D. L. Haynes not out		50
P. V. Simmons lbw b Waqar Younis		17
B. C. Lara b Waqar Younis		0
C. L. Hooper not out		22
	L-b 8, w 5, n-b 7	20

1/62 2/62 (2 wkts, 25.1 overs) 109

*R. B. Richardson, A. L. Logie, †J. R. Murray, I. R. Bishop, C. E. L. Ambrose, C. A. Walsh and B. P. Patterson did not bat.

Bowling: Wasim Akram 6–0–24–0; Aqib Javed 6–0–16–0; Waqar Younis 5–0–19–2; Mushtaq Ahmed 5–0–25–0; Salim Malik 1–0–8–0; Shoaib Mohammad 1.1–0–6–0; Asif Mujtaba 1–0–3–0.

Umpires: S. B. Lambson and C. J. Mitchley.

SOUTH AFRICA v PAKISTAN

At East London, February 15. Pakistan won by nine runs, South Africa's target having been revised to 172 from 31 overs. Toss: Pakistan. International debut: E. L. R. Stewart.

The visitors started badly against good bowling from Donald and de Villiers before a fourth-wicket partnership of 165, a record for Pakistan in limited-overs internationals, between Javed Miandad and Asif Mujtaba, swung the balance. Miandad started cautiously, needing 103 balls to reach 50. Thereafter he played with growing freedom. He brought up his century in the last over and then lofted a six off de Villiers before being run out off the final delivery, for 107 from 145 balls. Nevertheless, South Africa were on course for a target adjusted by rain, until a yorker from Wasim Akram ended a stand of 69 in nine overs between Cronje and Rhodes. He then wrecked the rest of the innings to return his best figures in one-day internationals.

Man of the Match: Javed Miandad.

Pakistan

Ramiz Raja c Callaghan b de Villiers		5
Shoaib Mohammad b de Villiers		0
Salim Malik c Callaghan b Pringle		13
Javed Miandad run out		107
Asif Mujtaba c Wessels b de Villiers		74
*Wasim Akram c Stewart b de Villiers		2
Saeed Anwar not out		1
L-b 4, w 6, n-b 2		12

1/0 2/7 3/29 (6 wkts, 50 overs) 214
4/194 5/206 6/214

†Rashid Latif, Waqar Younis, Mushtaq Ahmed and Aqib Javed did not bat.

Bowling: Donald 10–2–38–0; de Villiers 10–2–27–4; Pringle 10–1–41–1; McMillan 10–0–62–0; Cronje 8–0–30–0; Callaghan 2–0–12–0.

South Africa

A. C. Hudson b Wasim Akram		4
*K. C. Wessels run out		27
W. J. Cronje run out		81
P. N. Kirsten c Shoaib Mohammad b Salim Malik		1
J. N. Rhodes b Wasim Akram		35
D. J. Callaghan b Waqar Younis		0
†E. L. R. Stewart c Rashid Latif b Wasim Akram		1
B. M. McMillan lbw b Wasim Akram		1
M. W. Pringle run out		2
P. S. de Villiers not out		0
A. A. Donald b Wasim Akram		0
B 3, l-b 6, n-b 1		10

1/8 2/80 3/82 (30.1 overs) 162
4/151 5/154 6/155
7/157 8/160 9/162

Bowling: Wasim Akram 6.1–0–16–5; Aqib Javed 6–0–29–0; Mushtaq Ahmed 6–0–37–0; Waqar Younis 6–0–30–1; Shoaib Mohammad 1–0–11–0; Salim Malik 5–0–30–1.

Umpires: W. Diedricks and K. E. Liebenberg.

SOUTH AFRICA v WEST INDIES

At Cape Town, February 17. South Africa won by four runs. Toss: West Indies.

Neither side's batsmen could come to terms with good bowling on a pitch of uneven bounce that offered considerable sideways movement. Patterson immediately plunged South Africa into trouble, removing both openers with five on the board, and only Cullinan, in his second limited-overs international, looked comfortable, hitting 40 from 55 balls. A total of 140 seemed inadequate but superb fielding and accurate bowling kept West Indies under pressure. Haynes fell for nought to a direct hit by Rhodes from cover point, the first of three run-out victims.

Man of the Match: W. J. Cronje.

South Africa

A. C. Hudson c Simmons b Patterson	. .	0
*K. C. Wessels b Patterson		1
W. J. Cronje c Murray b Simmons		31
P. N. Kirsten c Logie b Walsh		30
D. J. Cullinan c Haynes b Simmons		40
J. N. Rhodes b Walsh		0
†E. L. R. Stewart c and b Bishop		1
C. R. Matthews c sub (J. C. Adams) b Hooper		9

M. W. Pringle not out	8
P. S. de Villiers c and b Hooper	0
A. A. Donald not out	0
L-b 5, w 6, n-b 9	20

1/2 2/5 3/66 (9 wkts, 50 overs) 140
4/99 5/100 6/110
7/130 8/139 9/140

Bowling: Patterson 9-0-20-2; Walsh 10-2-24-2; Ambrose 10-3-23-0; Bishop 10-1-31-1; Simmons 10-0-36-2; Hooper 1-0-1-2.

West Indies

D. L. Haynes run out		0
P. V. Simmons c Cronje b Pringle		20
*R. B. Richardson c de Villiers b Donald		2
B. C. Lara run out		14
C. L. Hooper lbw b Cronje		34
A. L. Logie c Hudson b Cronje		15
†J. R. Murray run out		1
I. R. Bishop c Rhodes b Pringle		6

C. E. L. Ambrose not out	19
C. A. Walsh c Stewart b Cronje	10
B. P. Patterson lbw b Pringle	1
L-b 9, w 4, n-b 1	14

1/15 2/17 3/30 (47 overs) 136
4/47 5/88 6/91
7/99 8/113 9/134

Bowling: Donald 10-2-20-1; de Villiers 10-3-28-0; Pringle 9-0-27-3; Matthews 10-1-25-0; Cronje 8-0-27-3.

Umpires: R. E. Koertzen and C. J. Mitchley.

PAKISTAN v WEST INDIES

At Durban, February 19. West Indies won by 124 runs. Toss: Pakistan.

For the first time in the series spectators were treated to a sustained display of commanding batsmanship. The left-hander Lara made his maiden limited-overs international century in glorious style, showing a consummate command of length as he flayed the Pakistan bowlers with a succession of crisp strokes off either foot. His 128 came off 126 balls, with 20 boundaries. He received splendid support from his fellow-Trinidadian Simmons in a second-wicket partnership of 197. Needing more than five an over, Pakistan were never in contention. For the second time in successive matches between the two teams Bishop took four wickets in an innings, as the last eight batsmen went for 49 runs.

Man of the Match: B. C. Lara.

West Indies

D. L. Haynes lbw b Wasim Akram	6	A. L. Logie c Rashid Latif	
B. C. Lara c Shoaib Mohammad		b Waqar Younis	5
b Waqar Younis	128	J. C. Adams not out	12
P. V. Simmons c Ramiz Raja			
b Aamir Sohail	70	L-b 8, w 6, n-b 6	20
*R. B. Richardson c Rashid Latif			
b Waqar Younis	7	1/12 2/209 3/229 (5 wkts, 50 overs)	268
C. L. Hooper not out	20	4/230 5/238	

†J. R. Murray, I. R. Bishop, C. E. L. Ambrose and C. A. Walsh did not bat.

Bowling: Wasim Akram 10-0-41-1; Aqib Javed 10-2-40-0; Ata-ur-Rehman 10-1-57-0; Waqar Younis 10-0-53-3; Aamir Sohail 4-0-27-1; Shoaib Mohammad 3-0-23-0; Asif Mujtaba 3-0-19-0.

Pakistan

Aamir Sohail c Hooper b Bishop	14	Waqar Younis c Simmons b Hooper	2
Ramiz Raja run out	34	Ata-ur-Rehman c Murray b Walsh	0
Shoaib Mohammad c Hooper b Bishop	0	Aqib Javed not out	3
Javed Miandad c and b Hooper	67	L-b 3, n-b 4	7
Zahid Fazal c Haynes b Ambrose	8		
Asif Mujtaba b Hooper	3	(46.5 overs)	144
†Rashid Latif c Hooper b Bishop	0	1/20 2/20 3/95	
*Wasim Akram c Ambrose b Bishop	6	4/108 5/113 6/114	
		7/125 8/133 9/133	

Bowling: Ambrose 8-2-18-1; Walsh 10-1-21-1; Simmons 9-0-43-0; Bishop 10-1-32-4; Hooper 9.5-1-27-3.

Umpires: W. Diedricks and S. B. Lambson.

SOUTH AFRICA v PAKISTAN

At Verwoerdburg, February 21. Pakistan won by 22 runs. Toss: Pakistan.

After the drama of their two previous encounters, in which South Africa had thrown away winning positions and collapsed before the pace attack, Pakistan achieved a routine, workmanlike victory in front of a capacity 20,000 crowd – which included a surprising number of flag-waving supporters from the local Moslem community. With Donald unusually wayward, openers Aamir Sohail and Ramiz Raja gave Pakistan an ideal start of 121. The South Africans could manage no substantial partnerships in reply, and were never able to achieve the required scoring-rate.

Man of the Match: Ramiz Raja.

Pakistan

Aamir Sohail c Wessels b Donald	62	Waqar Younis not out	20
Ramiz Raja c Wessels b de Villiers	53	Mushtaq Ahmed not out	1
Javed Miandad c Richardson b Pringle	16		
Zahid Fazal c Kirsten b Pringle	16	L-b 5, w 9, n-b 2	16
Salim Malik run out	9		
Asif Mujtaba b Pringle	8	(8 wkts, 50 overs)	220
†Rashid Latif c Richardson b Donald	3	1/121 2/131 3/147	
*Wasim Akram run out	16	4/167 5/169 6/174	
		7/192 8/218	

Aqib Javed did not bat.

Bowling: Donald 10-0-61-2; de Villiers 10-2-27-1; Pringle 10-0-52-3; Snell 10-0-31-0; Cronje 10-0-44-0.

South Africa

A. C. Hudson c Rashid Latif	
b Aqib Javed . 7	R. P. Snell lbw b Waqar Younis 19
*K. C. Wessels run out 39	†D. J. Richardson run out 10
W. J. Cronje c Waqar Younis	M. W. Pringle b Waqar Younis 10
b Mushtaq Ahmed . 17	P. S. de Villiers not out 6
P. N. Kirsten st Rashid Latif	A. A. Donald not out 5
b Mushtaq Ahmed . 35	L-b 2, w 2, n-b 6 10
D. J. Cullinan run out 15	—
J. N. Rhodes c Javed Miandad	1/18 2/52 3/84 (9 wkts, 50 overs) 198
b Wasim Akram . 25	4/117 5/130 6/163
	7/167 8/185 9/188

Bowling: Wasim Akram 10–0–34–1; Aqib Javed 10–0–31–1; Waqar Younis 10–0–50–2; Mushtaq Ahmed 10–0–29–2; Aamir Sohail 7–0–32–0; Asif Mujtaba 3–0–20–0.

Umpires: R. E. Koertzen and C. J. Mitchley.

SOUTH AFRICA v WEST INDIES

At Bloemfontein, February 23. West Indies won by nine wickets. Toss: South Africa.

South Africa needed victory to reach the final, but were unable to take advantage of an ideal batting pitch. They scored only 19 runs in the first ten overs and, although Wessels went on to 49 and Cullinan batted brightly, a total of 185 for six was nowhere near enough. Any thoughts of containing the West Indian batsmen, as they had done in their two previous matches, were quickly dispelled: Haynes and Lara shared an opening partnership that eventually yielded 152 runs and took their team to the brink of triumph. Lara again delighted spectators with his range of strokes, scoring an unbeaten 111, his second successive century, off 140 deliveries, with 12 fours and a six.

Man of the Match: B. C. Lara.

South Africa

A. C. Hudson lbw b Simmons 17	†E. L. R. Stewart not out 23
*K. C. Wessels b Simmons 49	R. P. Snell not out 0
W. J. Cronje b Bishop.............. 5	B 4, l-b 5, w 2, n-b 3 14
P. N. Kirsten b Ambrose 10	
D. J. Cullinan c Richardson b Bishop .. 45	1/52 2/60 3/84 (6 wkts, 50 overs) 185
J. N. Rhodes run out............... 22	4/92 5/138 6/183

M. W. Pringle, P. S. de Villiers and A. A. Donald did not bat.

Bowling: Ambrose 10–1–31–1; Walsh 10–2–26–0; Simmons 10–0–36–2; Bishop 10–0–52–2; Hooper 10–0–31–0.

West Indies

D. L. Haynes c Stewart b Snell 57	
B. C. Lara not out 111	
P. V. Simmons not out 6	
B 2, l-b 9, w 2, n-b 1 14	

1/152   (1 wkt, 44.3 overs) 188

*R. B. Richardson, A. L. Logie, C. L. Hooper, J. C. Adams, †J. R. Murray, I. R. Bishop, C. E. L. Ambrose and C. A. Walsh did not bat.

Bowling: Donald 10–1–24–0; de Villiers 10–0–38–0; Pringle 10–0–50–0; Snell 10–1–36–1; Cronje 4–0–25–0; Kirsten 0.3–0–4–0.

Umpires: S. B. Lambson and K. E. Liebenberg.

PAKISTAN v WEST INDIES

At Cape Town, February 25. West Indies won by seven wickets. Toss: West Indies. International debut: Ghulam Ali.

With both sides assured of playing in the final two days later there was nothing at stake, but a near-capacity crowd turned out to see two of the world's finest teams do battle. They witnessed an extraordinary anticlimax. Pakistan tumbled to 43 all out in 19.5 overs, the smallest total in the history of limited-overs internationals. The previous low was Canada's 45 in 40.3 overs, against England at Manchester in the 1979 World Cup. Pakistan's own worst performance had been 71 in 23.4 – then the shortest completed innings – also against West Indies, at Brisbane seven weeks earlier. The lack of incentive may have contributed to Pakistan's feeble effort, but on a pitch of unpredictable bounce and too much grass, which allowed excessive lateral movement, Walsh and Cummins – who both took three wickets in an over – and Patterson were all but unplayable. West Indies themselves lost three early wickets for 11 runs, but they needed only 12.3 overs and won before lunch. The groundsman was severely censured after an inquiry, and the Newlands ground's Test status was called into question by Krish Mackerdhuj, president of the UCBSA.

Man of the Match: C. A. Walsh.

Pakistan

Ramiz Raja c Lara b Patterson	0	Waqar Younis b Cummins		0
Ghulam Ali c Hooper b Patterson	2	Mushtaq Ahmed c Simmons b Cummins		0
Saeed Anwar c Murray b Walsh	5	Aqib Javed not out		4
Zahid Fazal c Lara b Simmons	21	B 1, l-b 1, w 2, n-b 6		10
Salim Malik c Haynes b Walsh	1			
Asif Mujtaba c Lara b Walsh	0	1/0 2/10 3/11	(19.5 overs)	43
*Wasim Akram c Hooper b Walsh	0	4/14 5/14 6/14		
†Rashid Latif c Logie b Cummins	0	7/25 8/25 9/26		

Bowling: Patterson 6–0–14–2; Walsh 9–2–17–4; Cummins 4–0–10–3; Simmons 0.5–0–0–1.

West Indies

D. L. Haynes lbw b Waqar Younis	0	*R. B. Richardson not out		7
B. C. Lara not out	26			
P. V. Simmons c Salim Malik		L-b 7, n-b 2		9
b Wasim Akram	2			
C. L. Hooper c Mushtaq Ahmed		1/0 2/9 3/11	(3 wkts, 12.3 overs)	45
b Wasim Akram	1			

A. L. Logie, J. C. Adams, †J. R. Murray, A. C. Cummins, B. P. Patterson and C. A. Walsh did not bat.

Bowling: Waqar Younis 5–1–7–1; Wasim Akram 6–0–22–2; Aqib Javed 1.3–0–9–0.

Umpires: W. Diedricks and K. E. Liebenberg.

QUALIFYING TABLE

	Played	Won	Lost	Points	Net run-rate
West Indies	6	4	2	8	1.05
Pakistan	6	3	3	6	−1.02
South Africa	6	2	4	4	−0.17

FINAL

PAKISTAN v WEST INDIES

At Johannesburg, February 27. West Indies won by five wickets. Toss: West Indies.

For the fourth time in as many matches in South Africa, West Indies outplayed the reigning World Cup champions. The result continued their ascendancy over Pakistan established in Australia, where they won the last three of their four meetings on their way to winning the World Series Cup. Despite a fine innings by the left-hander Aamir Sohail, Pakistan were unable to recover from the loss of their first five wickets while the total stuttered from 46 to 87. West Indies made another good start, with Haynes and Lara putting on 112 for the first wicket. A comfortable victory, with more than ten overs to spare, was sealed by some dazzling strokeplay from Logie. Lara, who had scored 341 runs at an average of 68.20, was named the outstanding player of the series; Haynes became the first batsman to score 8,000 runs in limited-overs internationals.

Man of the Match: Aamir Sohail.   *Man of the Series*: B. C. Lara.

Pakistan

Aamir Sohail c Hooper b Ambrose	 57	Waqar Younis b Ambrose	 37
Ramiz Raja lbw b Simmons	 11	Mushtaq Ahmed not out	 0
Shoaib Mohammad b Bishop	 0	Aqib Javed b Ambrose	 0
Javed Miandad lbw b Bishop	 0	L-b 7, w 5, n-b 3	 15
Zahid Fazal c Murray b Simmons	 7		
Asif Mujtaba run out	 25	1/46 2/48 3/55	(50 overs) 187
*Wasim Akram run out	 34	4/73 5/87 6/141	
†Rashid Latif run out	 1	7/142 8/187 9/187	

Bowling: Ambrose 10–2–33–3; Walsh 10–3–28–0; Simmons 10–1–23–2; Bishop 10–0–46–2; Hooper 10–0–50–0.

West Indies

D. L. Haynes b Waqar Younis	 59	A. L. Logie not out	 41
B. C. Lara b Aamir Sohail	 49	J. C. Adams not out	 5
P. V. Simmons b Waqar Younis	 5	L-b 4, w 1, n-b 3	 8
C. L. Hooper b Aqib Javed	 12		
*R. B. Richardson c Ramiz Raja		1/112 2/114 3/124	(5 wkts, 39.4 overs) 190
b Aamir Sohail . 11		4/142 5/158	

†J. R. Murray, I. R. Bishop, C. E. L. Ambrose and C. A. Walsh did not bat.

Bowling: Wasim Akram 8–0–32–0; Aqib Javed 7–0–32–1; Mushtaq Ahmed 5–0–27–0; Waqar Younis 9.4–1–63–2; Aamir Sohail 10–0–32–2.

Umpires: S. B. Lambson and K. E. Liebenberg.

SECRETARIES OF MCC

ENGLISH COUNTIES OVERSEAS, 1992-93

Scorecards of matches granted first-class status, played by English counties on pre-season tours to other countries.

WESTERN PROVINCE v YORKSHIRE

At Cape Town, South Africa, March 26, 27, 28. Drawn. Toss: Western Province. County debut: R. D. Stemp.

Western Province

K. C. Jackson c Chapman b Robinson	14	– lbw b Batty	22
F. B. Touzel c Byas b Robinson	37	– c Byas b Gough	2
H. H. Gibbs lbw b Stemp	34	– c Chapman b Batty	26
F. Davids lbw b Gough	17	– st Chapman b Batty	35
T. N. Lazard not out	63	– (6) not out	5
R. Koster lbw b Stemp	45	– (5) st Chapman b Stemp	26
D. B. Rundle not out	24	– c Byas b Batty	0
B 5, l-b 9, n-b 10	24	L-b 7, w 7, n-b 1	15

1/41 2/65 3/103   (5 wkts dec.) 258   1/11 2/62 3/75   (6 wkts dec.) 131
4/121 5/214   4/104 5/130 6/131

†R. J. Ryall, *C. R. Matthews, M. W. Pringle and A. Martyn did not bat.

Bowling: *First Innings*—Broadhurst 13-3-27-0; Gough 18-6-48-1; Robinson 19-4-44-2; Stemp 23-5-81-2; Batty 19.2-6-44-0. *Second Innings*—Gough 8-2-18-1; Broadhurst 6-1-15-0; Batty 15.3-3-54-4; Robinson 6-2-12-0; Stemp 8-1-25-1.

Yorkshire

*M. D. Moxon b Pringle	1	– b Martyn	97
A. A. Metcalfe lbw b Matthews	20	– c and b Davids	27
S. A. Kellett c Ryall b Pringle	11	– c Ryall b Koster	6
C. White b Koster	12	– c Ryall b Martyn	1
D. Byas c Pringle b Rundle	11	– not out	17
†C. A. Chapman c Jackson b Matthews	16	– c Ryall b Martyn	1
D. Gough run out	2	– not out	16
R. D. Stemp not out	21		
J. D. Batty c Ryall b Pringle	1		
M. Broadhurst c Ryall b Pringle	0		
M. A. Robinson b Pringle	0		
L-b 4, n-b 11	15	L-b 2, w 1, n-b 4	7

1/3 2/23 3/56 4/56 5/84   110   1/69 2/99 3/122   (5 wkts) 172
6/86 7/90 8/93 9/102   4/139 5/145

Bowling: *First Innings*—Pringle 11.3-0-31-5; Martyn 7-2-23-0; Koster 4-1-8-1; Matthews 10-3-12-2; Rundle 10-2-32-1. *Second Innings*—Pringle 7-1-17-0; Martyn 18-3-54-3; Matthews 2-1-7-0; Koster 7-1-19-1; Davids 6-1-27-1; Rundle 22-4-46-0.

Umpires: J. P. Lewis and P. Reypert.

ZIMBABWE B v KENT

At Harare, March 30, 31, April 1. Drawn. Toss: Kent. County debut: D. W. Headley. First-team debut: M. J. Walker.

Kent

T. R. Ward b Streak	62	– (7) not out	23
J. I. Longley c and b Strang	94	– (5) b Martin	4
M. A. Ealham b Streak	14	– (1) c Evans b Rennie	14
N. J. Llong st Campbell b Rennie	72	– (10) not out	11
*†S. A. Marsh c Burmester b Rennie	30	– (6) c Burmester b Martin	13
M. J. Walker not out	23	– (2) run out	16
M. V. Fleming not out	20	– (4) b Burmester	43
R. P. Davis (did not bat)		– (3) c Evans b Rennie	11
T. N. Wren (did not bat)		– (8) c Campbell b Martin	1
A. P. Igglesden (did not bat)		– (9) b Martin	2
B 1, l-b 4, w 3	8	B 4, l-b 8, n-b 1	13

1/108 2/142 3/191   (5 wkts dec.) 323   1/23 2/39 3/52   (8 wkts dec.) 151
4/262 5/285   4/86 5/114 6/116
                                                      7/119 8/125

D. W. Headley did not bat.

Bowling: *First Innings*—Burmester 10–1–50–0; Rennie 19–3–85–2; Streak 23–5–58–2; Peall 20–3–85–0; Strang 10–1–40–1. *Second Innings*—Burmester 14–1–50–1; Rennie 10–0–33–2; Streak 4–1–18–0; Martin 8–0–38–4.

Zimbabwe B

G. J. Whittal not out	10	– (4) c Igglesden b Davis	42
†D. J. R. Campbell c Walker b Igglesden	5	– (6) lbw b Davis	2
D. N. Erasmus b Igglesden	6	– (1) c Marsh b Davis	34
*G. C. Martin c Igglesden b Fleming	22	– (3) b Igglesden	0
C. N. Evans b Igglesden	0	– (2) b Igglesden	2
C. B. Wishart c Ward b Igglesden	65	– (5) not out	10
M. G. Burmester c Marsh b Igglesden	50	– not out	5
H. H. Streak b Igglesden	0		
P. A. Strang c Wren b Davis	6		
J. A. Rennie c Marsh b Ealham	6		
S. G. Peall c Ward b Igglesden	16		
B 1, l-b 4, n-b 3	8	L-b 6	6

1/15 2/32 3/38 4/59 5/164   194   1/5 2/5 3/65   (5 wkts) 101
6/164 7/167 8/177 9/188   4/82 5/84

In the first innings G. J. Whittal, when 10, retired hurt at 17 and resumed at 188.

Bowling: *First Innings*—Igglesden 18.1–6–37–7; Headley 11–4–27–0; Wren 6–1–23–0; Fleming 9–1–38–1; Davis 14–1–55–1; Llong 3–0–8–0; Ealham 1–0–1–1. *Second Innings*—Igglesden 7–1–13–2; Wren 8–2–15–0; Ealham 7–0–35–0; Davis 20–8–25–3; Fleming 3–0–5–0; Ward 5–3–2–0.

Umpires: G. Gilmour and R. Strang.

BOLAND v WARWICKSHIRE

At Brackenfell, South Africa, April 2, 3, 4. Drawn. Toss: Boland.

Boland

A. Wylie c Ostler b Munton	9	– c Piper b Small	7
*W. S. Truter c Ratcliffe b Reeve	16	– c Ostler b Asif Din	6
W. N. van As c Twose b Asif Din	12	– c Twose b Booth	50
N. M. Snyman c Munton b Booth	86	– c Piper b Munton	27
R. I. Dalrymple b Asif Din	15	– c Reeve b Booth	9
B. H. Richards c Reeve b Asif Din	6	– not out	50
M. Erasmus c Munton b Asif Din	38	– not out	3
B. A. S. Chedburn c Small b Reeve	12		
†A. J. Burger c Small b Asif Din	1		
C. W. Henderson c Penney b Booth	9		
S. Andrews not out	13		
B 5, l-b 3, n-b 1	9	B 4, l-b 5, w 1, n-b 1	11

1/18 2/26 3/69 4/93 5/121   226 1/13 2/13 3/74 (5 wkts) 163
6/183 7/189 8/200 9/208   4/85 5/146

Bowling: *First Innings*—Munton 13-4-28-1; Small 10-1-40-0; Reeve 15-6-26-2; Twose 4-1-16-0; Booth 20.3-7-41-2; Asif Din 27-9-61-5; Ratcliffe 2-1-6-0. *Second Innings*—Munton 7-4-10-1; Small 5-2-12-1; Asif Din 12-3-37-1; Booth 19-6-60-2; Twose 2-1-1-0; Reeve 6-3-8-0; Ratcliffe 6-0-23-0; Ostler 1.4-0-3-0.

Warwickshire

A. J. Moles b Henderson	59	Asif Din lbw b Chedburn	20
R. G. Twose c Burger b Richards	60	†K. J. Piper not out	15
J. D. Ratcliffe c Andrews b Henderson	40	L-b 13	13
D. P. Ostler b Andrews	56		
T. L. Penney not out	117	1/101 2/137 3/200	(6 wkts dec.) 393
*D. A. Reeve c van As b Chedburn	13	4/235 5/254 6/321	

P. A. Booth, G. C. Small and T. A. Munton did not bat.

Bowling: Chedburn 32-12-69-2; Erasmus 31-7-72-0; Henderson 42-10-92-2; Andrews 22-3-57-1; Richards 14-1-53-1; Truter 7-0-27-0; Dalrymple 2-0-10-0.

Umpires: W. Richard and B. van Wyk.

SRI LANKA BOARD OF CONTROL XI v GLOUCESTERSHIRE

At P. Saravanamuttu Stadium, Colombo, April 15, 16, 17. Sri Lanka Board of Control XI won by 177 runs. Toss: Sri Lanka Board of Control XI. County debut: K. E. Cooper.

Sri Lanka Board of Control XI

C. Mendis c Hinks b Cooper	0	– (2) b Cooper	5
D. P. Samaraweera c Wright b Davies	56	– (1) c Wright b Gerrard	20
M. S. Atapattu lbw b Davies	51	– c Alleyne b Cooper	5
R. S. Kaluwitharana not out	106	– c sub (J. M. de la Pena) b Gerrard	4
*†A. M. de Silva lbw b Ball	32	– c Davies b Ball	9
R. S. Kalpage c Gerrard b Davies	35	– not out	36
W. M. J. P. Weerasinghe c Hancock b Scott	5	– not out	7
G. P. Wickremasinghe st Williams b Davies	5		
P. K. Wijetunge c Gerrard b Davies	0		
K. R. Pushpakumara not out	5		
L-b 15, w 3, n-b 1	19	B 2, l-b 4	6

1/0 2/105 3/120 4/193 5/259 (8 wkts dec.) 314 1/11 2/31 3/31 (5 wkts dec.) 92
6/292 7/299 8/303   4/44 5/48

G. G. Ranga Yasalal did not bat.

Bowling: *First Innings*—Cooper 11-5-22-1; Gerrard 11-1-54-0; Ball 17-3-81-1; Scott 14-2-44-1; Davies 28-5-98-5. *Second Innings*—Cooper 9-2-18-2; Gerrard 10-4-13-2; Ball 10-1-22-1; Davies 9-1-33-0.

Gloucestershire

B. C. Broad st de Silva b Kalpage	77	– b Ranga Yasalal	11
S. G. Hinks c de Silva b Kalpage	20	– (7) b Kalpage	0
M. W. Alleyne lbw b Kalpage	13	– (2) c Samaraweera b Kalpage	13
T. H. C. Hancock c Weerasinghe b Kalpage	0	– (3) c de Silva b Pushpakumara	5
†R. C. J. Williams c de Silva b Wijetunge	0	– c Mendis b Kalpage	6
*A. J. Wright c Samaraweera b Wijetunge	0	– (4) c Atapattu b Pushpakumara	2
M. C. J. Ball st de Silva b Wijetunge	19	– (6) c Mendis b Kalpage	12
R. J. Scott c de Silva b Pushpakumara	24	– not out	0
M. Davies c Samaraweera b Kalpage	4	– lbw b Wijetunge	5
K. E. Cooper c Ranga Yasalal b Kalpage	0	– c Mendis b Wijetunge	0
M. J. Gerrard not out	0	– c Wijetunge b Kalpage	6
L-b 3, n-b 6	9	L-b 2, w 1	3

1/61 2/88 3/88 4/89 5/91 166 1/16 2/25 3/31 4/33 5/50 63
6/129 7/140 8/166 9/166 6/50 7/51 8/56 9/56

Bowling: *First Innings*—Pushpakumara 14–5–36–1; Ranga Yasalal 7–1–17–0; Kalpage 28.3–10–69–6; Wijetunge 15–0–41–3. *Second Innings*—Pushpakumara 9–4–19–2; Ranga Yasalal 3–0–19–1; Kalpage 11.5–8–12–5; Wijetunge 6–2–11–2.

Umpires: I. Anandappa and M. D. D. N. Guneratne.

DOUBLE INTERNATIONALS

Jeff Wilson, who was capped by the All Black rugby team in November 1993, was the 26th player to appear at senior international level in both cricket and rugby union, having represented the New Zealand cricket team in four one-day matches against Australia in March. The full list of double internationals follows. Where two countries are given, the player represented the first at cricket and the second at rugby.

J. H. Anderson (South Africa)
M. P. Donnelly (New Zealand and
 England)
M. K. Elgie (South Africa and Scotland)
R. H. M. Hands (South Africa and
 England)
T. A. Harris (South Africa)
A. N. Hornby (England)
P. S. T. Jones (South Africa)
G. MacGregor (England and Scotland)
*B. J. McKechnie (New Zealand)
W. H. Milton (South Africa and
 England)
§F. Mitchell (England/South Africa and
 England)
†O. E. Nothling (Australia)
H. G. Owen-Smith (South Africa
 and England)

A. W. Powell (South Africa)
A. R. Richards (South Africa)
R. O. Schwarz (South Africa and
 England)
J. H. Sinclair (South Africa)
M. J. K. Smith (England)
R. H. Spooner (England)
A. E. Stoddart (England)
E. W. T. Tindill (New Zealand)
M. J. Turnbull (England and Wales)
C. B. van Ryneveld (South Africa
 and England)
G. F. Vernon (England)
*J. W. Wilson (New Zealand)
§S. M. J. Woods (Australia/England
 and England)

 * *McKechnie and Wilson have appeared in limited-overs internationals for the New Zealand cricket team, but not in Tests.*

 † *The New Zealand authority disputes the status of the four international rugby matches in which Nothling represented Australia.*

 § *Mitchell and Woods played cricket for two countries.*

CRICKET IN AUSTRALIA, 1992-93

By JOHN MACKINNON

At their 61st attempt, Queensland once again failed to win the Sheffield Shield, a sequence that has taken its place in Australian folklore. This time they failed disastrously, reaching the final against New South Wales only to be bowled out for 75. New South Wales thus achieved their 41st victory in the Shield's 91 years and they also won the one-day Mercantile Mutual competition.

The season marked 100 years since the first Shield competition, but Australian domestic cricket was muted by the absence of the leading players. Most teams had about three matches at full strength and the stars even missed the final because they were finishing off a one-day series in New Zealand, leaving Allan Border unable to fulfil one of his remaining ambitions – helping Queensland end their extraordinary run. The system jeopardises the playing standards of Australian domestic cricket, but it does open the way for young players to get into the first-class game.

New South Wales had to cover for the Waugh brothers and Mark Taylor, all absent on higher duties. Mike Whitney might also have been called away, but a broken foot wrecked his season anyway. Michael Slater started the year as the state's reserve opener but, six months later, he was boarding the aircraft for England, more than 1,000 runs to the good and one of the brightest prospects in the country. Wayne Holdsworth had been bowling fast and abrasively for three years, but an inspired run over five matches earned him 39 wickets and a place on the tour – where his brittle-looking talent would be tested by the demands of slow English wickets. Not far behind these in ability and performance, Michael Bevan tightened up his batting. While still somewhat extravagant for a No. 4, he thrived on responsibility.

Two class all-rounders are bonuses to any side, and Brad McNamara and Greg Matthews rarely faltered with bat or ball. Matthews again achieved the double of 500 runs and 50 wickets; only in the Brisbane match did he fail to make a serious impact and New South Wales lost that easily. He also caught most that came his way at first slip. His spinning partner, David Freedman, a left-arm wrist-spinner who relies on the "chinaman," found the Sydney pitch less conducive but, as New South Wales won three matches away from home, the quality of their pace bowling was as important as their spin capability. Glen McGrath made the most of his opportunity when left-armers Whitney and Phil Alley succumbed to injury, and showed a useful turn of speed plus an effective late in-swinger. Masterminding the team effort, the wicket-keeper Phil Emery and his predecessor in the job, Steve Rixon, respectively captain and coach, deserved the highest praise. Emery took over the leadership in Taylor's absence, improved his batting and, more importantly, coped with the double stresses of keeping and captaining. Both he and Taylor were prepared to risk defeat in search of victory, a philosophy well taught by Geoff Lawson, the former captain. Rixon's four-year record of four finals, including two victories, speaks for itself.

Queensland this time did not use glamorous imports to try and break their duck, although Dirk Wellham, who was in Queensland teaching, walked straight into the team to take over the captaincy when Ian Healy was called up by Australia. Paul Jackson, the Victorian left-arm spinner, signed for the state but broke his arm in the nets and could not play until late February. Matthew Hayden confirmed all the good impressions of his first season, scoring over 1,000 runs again, though in playing 14 matches he had more cricket than anyone. The selectors picked him for the Australian XI against the West Indians in Hobart, but thereafter resisted all pressures to put him in the Test side. Hayden and Trevor Barsby were as good an opening combination as any but the rest of the batting was pretty fragile, exemplified by four feeble efforts against Tasmania and the hideous 75 in the final. Stuart Law certainly found some form late in the season, but his fine hundred in the first innings of the final only emphasised how much more he might have done earlier. Michael Kasprowicz dominated the fast bowling department so much that he was on most people's short list for the English tour and Greg Rowell never spared his somewhat sparse frame. Carl Rackemann was a late starter due to illness but by the end of the season was back to his best; Craig McDermott played only the first three matches. Spin was rarely a factor, though Border had a purple patch at St Kilda and Jackson bowled steadily when he made his belated appearance.

Tasmania leapt three places to finish third, and, with a more positive attitude, they could have reached the final. Having a settled team helped their cause and ten players appeared in eight or more games. The batting improved immeasurably, thanks largely to the emergence of 18-year-old Ricky Ponting, whose poise and fluency excited everyone who saw him. There was no lack of support, either: Dene Hills proved a staunch opening batsman and the middle order played its part. The bowling was dependable, if short of variety. Chris Matthews had another splendid season and the other medium-pacers, especially Peter McPhee and Shaun Young, were always steady, sometimes even threatening. Rod Tucker's first significant venture into captaincy should have provided him with valuable experience.

Western Australia were unpredictable and ultimately disappointing. Terry Alderman took on the coaching job and then lost it at the end of the season; Daryl Foster was due to return for 1993-94. The team got away to a fine start with a win in Brisbane, thanks to two brilliant hundreds by Damien Martyn and some excellent bowling by Bruce Reid. Martyn quickly added a couple more centuries and was lost to the Test team, while Reid sustained another injury, and that for him was almost that. The batting generally held up, with Geoff Marsh and Justin Langer outstanding, Tom Moody fighting valiantly to overcome the horrors of his tour to Sri Lanka, and Mike Veletta and Tim Zoehrer sharing the duties behind the stumps and making some useful scores. With Reid absent, the bowling resources were scant: Jo Angel and Brendon Julian were the only regular wicket-takers, but at a fair cost. Alderman struggled for form, though he overtook Lawson as the Shield's second leading wicket-taker in the first match, and finished the season on 384, still 129 behind Clarrie Grimmett. As usual for the West, there was barely a spinner in sight.

South Australia escaped bottom position thanks to a gift declaration by Western Australia in the last match. They had very little bowling to speak of and failed to dismiss their opposition (except England A) in the first innings of any match. Tim May managed to fight his way back to the Test team and his five for 42 against Tasmania at Adelaide earned South Australia their only other win. Peter Sleep, in his last year before moving to England, shouldered the spinning burden after May's departure but there was little else. The batting was altogether different. Jamie Siddons was absolutely dynamic, heading the averages with four superb hundreds, and fielded brilliantly as well. He was very unlucky not to be recognised by the selectors, but at least the umpires noticed, voting him Player of the Year; the players further endorsed his efforts with the Lord's Taverners Award for Australian Cricketer of the Year. Greg Blewett and Jamie Brayshaw both made significant progress and Tim Nielsen complemented his wicket-keeping with some useful innings. Peter Philpott ended his term as coach and moved to Rossall School in England.

Victoria finished bottom, their cause less than enhanced by the overt acrimony between the beleaguered captain Simon O'Donnell and cricket manager-cum-TV commentator Bill Lawry. The rift came to a head in mid-season and was never healed. When O'Donnell was widely criticised for his unimaginative leadership, Lawry – often at a distance because he was working for Channel Nine – conspicuously refused to support him. Meanwhile, Victoria's playing fortunes plummeted to final embarrassment at the MCG where they lost to New South Wales after being set a very reasonable target. Two of the better players packed their bags, Darren Lehmann returning to Adelaide and Neil Maxwell, a competitive all-rounder, to a job with the New South Wales Cricket Association. Victoria were well served by their opening batsmen, Paul Nobes and Wayne Phillips. Nobes, an unconventional but hefty striker, scored his runs at a good rate. Phillips put himself into Test match contention with 205 in Sydney but was overtaken soon afterwards by Hayden and Slater. Dean Jones found it hard to come to terms with being dropped from the Tests and barely played an innings of consequence. Both Lehmann and O'Donnell were capable of crushing any attack but often got out with the bowling at their mercy. The Test bowlers Merv Hughes and Shane Warne played only four matches for the state and were greatly missed. Damien Fleming, Tony Dodemaide and Maxwell were the best of the pace bowlers but Paul Reiffel appeared more committed to the international arena. Leg-spinner Craig Howard looked a promising substitute for Warne.

The ACB introduced an interesting experiment of using three umpires for Shield matches, standing in rotation to avoid fatigue. The umpires disliked the system. Their performances still attracted considerable criticism from players, officials and outsiders, notably because of the apparent disappearance of lbw as a means of dismissal. But the Board had a lot more on its plate: the executive was changing hands as David Richards departed to run the International Cricket Council, to be replaced by Graham Halbish, his deputy. The marketing contract with Kerry Packer's company, PBL, which had been responsible for setting so much of the tone of Australian cricket since the settlement with Packer in 1979, was also close to expiry. The Board was expected to set up its own marketing department. With the national ban on tobacco sponsorship due to expand to embrace cricket, thus ending the long-standing connection with Benson and Hedges, there would be plenty of problems for the new men if the so-called strongest domestic competition in world cricket was to survive.

FIRST-CLASS AVERAGES, 1992-93

BATTING

(Qualification: 500 runs)

	M	I	NO	R	HS	100s	Avge
J. D. Siddons (*SA*)	11	20	2	1,190	197	4	66.11
M. E. Waugh (*NSW*)	9	16	2	883	200*	3	63.07
D. R. Martyn (*WA*)	10	18	3	921	139	4	61.40
M. J. Slater (*NSW*)	10	19	2	1,019	143	3	59.94
M. L. Hayden (*Qld*)	14	26	2	1,249	161*	2	52.04
M. G. Bevan (*NSW*)	12	21	4	875	170	1	51.47
D. F. Hills (*Tas.*)	11	19	1	903	138	4	50.16
D. C. Boon (*Tas.*)	8	15	2	635	111	1	48.84
P. C. Nobes (*Vic.*)	9	16	2	682	146*	3	48.71
R. T. Ponting (*Tas.*)	11	18	1	782	125	3	46.00
D. J. Buckingham (*Tas.*)	9	14	3	501	161*	1	45.54
J. A. Brayshaw (*SA*)	11	22	2	908	110	1	45.40
S. P. O'Donnell (*Vic.*)	9	15	0	655	99	0	43.66
G. R. Marsh (*WA*)	11	21	0	905	138	5	43.09
A. R. Border (*Qld*)	9	16	1	616	116*	2	41.06
J. L. Langer (*WA*)	10	19	0	757	110	1	39.84
G. S. Blewett (*SA*)	11	22	1	834	119	2	39.71
D. S. Webber (*SA*)	8	15	1	553	135	1	39.50
S. G. Law (*Qld*)	12	21	0	823	142	2	39.19
J. Cox (*Tas.*)	10	17	1	606	137*	2	37.87
M. A. Taylor (*NSW*)	8	15	1	530	102	2	37.85
T. J. Barsby (*Qld*)	13	24	0	908	123	3	37.83
W. N. Phillips (*Vic.*)	11	20	0	752	205	2	37.60
D. S. Lehmann (*Vic.*)	11	20	1	704	112	1	37.05
G. R. J. Matthews (*NSW*) ...	13	20	3	625	79	0	36.76
M. R. J. Veletta (*WA*)	11	21	2	671	104*	2	35.31
S. R. Waugh (*NSW*)	9	16	1	523	100*	2	34.86
T. M. Moody (*WA*)	11	21	1	697	124	1	34.85
N. C. P. Courtney (*Tas.*)	11	19	1	568	88	0	31.55
T. J. Nielsen (*SA*)	11	20	2	541	109	1	30.05
T. J. Zoehrer (*WA*)	11	19	1	524	136	1	29.11
P. J. T. Goggin (*Qld*)	12	24	2	572	120	1	26.00

* Signifies not out.

BOWLING

(Qualification: 20 wickets)

	O	M	R	W	BB	5W/i	Avge
M. G. Hughes (*Vic.*)	347.2	77	954	43	6-83	2	22.18
C. G. Rackemann (*Qld*)	257.3	45	774	33	5-75	1	23.45
T. B. A. May (*SA*)	224.3	63	544	23	5-9	2	23.65
G. D. McGrath (*NSW*)	216	54	598	25	5-36	2	23.92
M. S. Kasprowicz (*Qld*)	435.1	100	1,231	51	6-59	3	24.13
N. D. Maxwell (*Vic.*)	272	68	756	30	5-46	1	25.20
D. Tazelaar (*Qld*)	224.2	68	564	22	4-39	0	25.63
D. W. Fleming (*Vic.*)	232.2	53	643	25	7-90	1	25.72
W. J. Holdsworth (*NSW*)	374.1	57	1,376	53	7-41	4	25.96
G. R. J. Matthews (*NSW*) ...	615	193	1,475	51	8-52	3	28.92
S. Young (*Tas.*)	341.3	98	984	34	5-56	2	28.94
B. E. McNamara (*NSW*)	237.4	57	673	23	4-68	0	29.26
C. D. Matthews (*Tas.*)	478.1	97	1,456	49	5-72	1	29.71

	O	M	R	W	BB	5W/i	Avge
G. J. Rowell (*Qld*)	290.1	71	842	28	5-31	2	30.07
B. P. Julian (*WA*)	382	72	1,342	43	5-72	3	31.20
C. J. McDermott (*Qld*)	339.5	70	1,102	32	4-35	0	34.43
J. Angel (*WA*)	338	86	1,112	32	6-71	2	34.75
M. R. Whitney (*NSW*)	281	66	818	23	5-43	1	35.56
T. M. Alderman (*WA*)	257.3	66	727	20	4-55	0	36.35
S. K. Warne (*Vic.*)	309.5	57	983	27	7-52	2	36.40
P. T. McPhee (*Tas.*)	368.4	97	1,020	28	5-48	1	36.42
A. I. C. Dodemaide (*Vic.*)	370	110	851	22	3-41	0	38.68
D. A. Freedman (*NSW*)	322.2	66	1,068	27	6-89	1	39.55
D. A. Reeves (*SA*)	215.2	33	877	22	4-57	0	39.86
P. R. Sleep (*SA*)	327.4	75	893	22	7-79	1	40.59

SHEFFIELD SHIELD, 1992-93

	Played	Won	Lost	Drawn	1st-inns Points	Points
New South Wales	10	5	1*	4	4	33.6†
Queensland	10	3	4*	3	8	26
Tasmania	10	2	1	7	10	22
Western Australia	10	3	3*	4	4	21‡
South Australia	10	2	4*	4	2	14
Victoria	10	0	2*	8	12	12

Final: New South Wales beat Queensland by eight wickets.

* *One outright loss after leading on first innings.*

† *0.4 points deducted for slow over-rates.* ‡ *1 point deducted for slow over-rates.*

Outright win = 6 pts; lead on first innings in a drawn or lost game = 2 pts.

Under Australian Cricket Board playing conditions, two extras are scored for every no-ball bowled whether scored off or not. Any runs scored off the bat are credited to the batsman, while byes and leg-byes are counted as no-balls, in accordance with Law 24.9, in addition to the initial penalty.

QUEENSLAND v WESTERN AUSTRALIA

At Brisbane, October 21, 22, 23, 24. Western Australia won by 50 runs. Western Australia 5.8 pts. Toss: Queensland. First-class debut: A. J. Bichel.

The emergence of Martyn brought him a century in each innings and gave Western Australia's fast bowlers the chance to engineer victory. On the first day, his 21st birthday, he joined Marsh, who defied a broken finger to score a typically courageous hundred, to see out a potential crisis after the new ball found out the middle order. Next morning Martyn hammered a sensational 78 in 97 minutes; even McDermott went for 19 in one hectic over. Queensland's batsmen played several attractive cameos but never quite came to terms with Reid and his colleagues: they escaped the follow-on by one run. On the third day, their bowlers restored the balance. But for Martyn Western Australia's batting would have been a shambles. His second hundred took only 162 minutes. He fell to the beguiling slow left-arm spin of Storey, who finished with splendid figures, though he owed much to McDermott and Tazelaar at the other end. Queensland needed 334 to win and looked to have a chance at 69 for one going into the final day. But the Western Australian pace bowlers held sway, though the six points earned were trimmed because of their slow over-rate.

Close of play: First day, Western Australia 260-7 (D. R. Martyn 55*); Second day, Queensland 221; Third day, Queensland 69-1 (M. L. Hayden 43*, P. J. T. Goggin 15*).

Western Australia

*G. R. Marsh lbw b Kasprowicz	121	– (2) c Healy b McDermott	1
M. R. J. Veletta c Healy b Bichel	26	– (1) lbw b Tazelaar	1
J. L. Langer run out	40	– c and b Storey	45
T. M. Moody c Goggin b Kasprowicz	4	– c Healy b Tazelaar	0
D. R. Martyn not out	133	– st Healy b Storey	112
W. S. Andrews c Law b Tazelaar	3	– run out	8
†T. J. Zoehrer c Healy b Tazelaar	0	– b Storey	0
B. P. Julian b Bichel	4	– lbw b Storey	4
J. Angel c Hayden b McDermott	16	– c Goggin b McDermott	0
T. M. Alderman c Healy b Tazelaar	11	– not out	1
B. A. Reid run out	3	– c Bichel b Storey	0
L-b 7, n-b 2	9	L-b 6, n-b 6	12

1/56 2/146 3/153 4/225 5/240   370   1/3 2/11 3/11 4/120 5/142   184
6/242 7/260 8/322 9/349   6/151 7/163 8/176 9/184

Bowling: *First Innings*—McDermott 34–6–115–1; Tazelaar 29–8–78–3; Kasprowicz 21.5–3–50–2; Bichel 18–3–67–2; Storey 16.5–5–53–0. *Second Innings*—McDermott 23–7–54–2; Tazelaar 7–2–23–2; Storey 22.5–6–55–5; Bichel 3–0–19–0; Kasprowicz 8–1–27–0.

Queensland

T. J. Barsby c Moody b Alderman	1	– lbw b Alderman	7
M. L. Hayden lbw b Reid	8	– c Veletta b Julian	63
P. J. T. Goggin c Alderman b Angel	46	– c Moody b Reid	15
S. G. Law c Zoehrer b Reid	28	– lbw b Reid	41
A. R. Border b Reid	23	– c Veletta b Angel	53
S. C. Storey c Langer b Julian	7	– b Angel	23
*†I. A. Healy run out	49	– lbw b Alderman	39
C. J. McDermott c Zoehrer b Reid	4	– c Veletta b Alderman	5
M. S. Kasprowicz b Julian	35	– c Langer b Julian	3
A. J. Bichel b Angel	0	– c Moody b Alderman	9
D. Tazelaar not out	3	– not out	3
L-b 7, n-b 10	17	B 4, l-b 10, n-b 8	22

1/5 2/13 3/75 4/106 5/113   221   1/17 2/74 3/109 4/141 5/209   283
6/156 7/166 8/201 9/201   6/216 7/248 8/271 9/273

Bowling: *First Innings*—Reid 16–3–58–4; Alderman 17–5–40–1; Angel 13–1–42–2; Julian 15.5–4–65–2; Martyn 1–0–9–0. *Second Innings*—Reid 25–8–70–2; Alderman 22.2–6–55–4; Angel 21–4–58–2; Julian 20–4–64–2; Zoehrer 7–1–22–0.

Umpires: A. J. McQuillan, P. D. Parker and C. D. Timmins.

NEW SOUTH WALES v VICTORIA

At Sydney, November 6, 7, 8, 9. Drawn. Victoria 2 pts. Toss: New South Wales.

Rain prevented play until mid-afternoon on the first day, when Taylor decided to bat. He watched with dismay as Hughes fired out Small and Steve Waugh with consecutive balls, but then he and Mark Waugh took command. They added 175 in 197 minutes before stumps, including four sixes off Warne's leg-spin. Hughes bowled superbly on the second morning and only some frenetic hitting by Bevan and Bayliss enabled Taylor to declare. Victoria were in no trouble against a varied attack and batted through the third day and on into the fourth for their highest total in Sydney. For nearly ten hours Phillips defied speed and spin and scored his maiden double-hundred. He was a tired man when he succumbed to a brilliant leg-side stumping. Warne reached fifty as night-watchman while Lehmann and O'Donnell hit out merrily. New South Wales struggled in their second innings and were not helped by Steve Waugh being given run out when clearly home. But Victoria's bid for victory was ended by bad light with 13 overs left. The time lost to rain had been made up on subsequent days through extending play by 30 minutes at either end, though O'Donnell regretted that the innovation did not cover bad light stoppages.

Close of play: First day, New South Wales 193-2 (M. A. Taylor 89*, M. E. Waugh 79*); Second day, Victoria 115-1 (W. N. Phillips 54*, S. K. Warne 1*); Third day, Victoria 495-7 (A. I. C. Dodemaide 29*, P. R. Reiffel 1*).

New South Wales

S. M. Small b Hughes	12	– b Hughes	1
*M. A. Taylor c Phillips b Reiffel	102	– c Berry b Warne	42
S. R. Waugh c Nobes b Hughes	0	– run out	36
M. E. Waugh c Warne b Hughes	88	– st Berry b Warne	2
M. G. Bevan c Phillips b Warne	68	– (8) not out	7
G. R. J. Matthews lbw b Hughes	6	– (5) c Berry b Dodemaide	54
T. H. Bayliss lbw b Hughes	64	– (6) b Reiffel	3
†P. A. Emery c O'Donnell b Hughes	7	– (7) c Lehmann b Reiffel	22
D. A. Freedman not out	11	– not out	5
B 5, l-b 8, n-b 6	19	L-b 3, n-b 4	7

1/18 2/18 3/208 4/223 5/247   (8 wkts dec.) 377
6/323 7/352 8/377

1/6 2/81 3/85 4/94   (7 wkts) 179
5/106 6/167 7/171

M. R. Whitney and W. J. Holdsworth did not bat.

Bowling: *First Innings*—Hughes 36.1–13–83–6; Dodemaide 35–9–85–0; Reiffel 25–5–71–1; Warne 18–1–94–1; O'Donnell 10–2–31–0. *Second Innings*—Hughes 17.3–6–42–1; Dodemaide 12–5–23–1; Warne 26–7–73–2; Jones 3–0–11–0; Reiffel 14–5–23–2; O'Donnell 1–0–4–0.

Victoria

W. N. Phillips st Emery b S. R. Waugh	205	
P. C. Nobes c Emery b S. R. Waugh	42	
S. K. Warne c M. E. Waugh b Whitney	52	
D. M. Jones b Whitney	9	
D. S. Lehmann c Emery b Whitney	49	
W. G. Ayres lbw b Matthews	16	
*S. P. O'Donnell st Emery b Freedman	67	
A. I. C. Dodemaide not out	53	
P. R. Reiffel c Emery b S. R. Waugh	18	
†D. S. Berry c sub b Whitney	1	
M. G. Hughes not out	2	
B 1, l-b 10, n-b 22	33	

1/112 2/202 3/214   (9 wkts dec.) 547
4/281 5/309 6/410
7/492 8/522 9/531

Bowling: Holdsworth 26–3–101–0; Whitney 37–5–122–4; M. E. Waugh 8–0–17–0; Freedman 32–8–81–1; Matthews 40–11–116–1; S. R. Waugh 27–7–90–3; Taylor 3–0–9–0.

Umpires: P. E. Dodd, D. B. Hair and I. S. Thomas.

QUEENSLAND v SOUTH AUSTRALIA

At Brisbane, November 6, 7, 8, 9. Queensland won by an innings and 61 runs. Queensland 6 pts. Toss: South Australia. First-class debut: N. R. Fielke.

South Australia were out of the game from the first day, when McDermott, Tazelaar and Rowell carried all before them and an inadequate first innings ended soon after tea. Tazelaar enjoyed a wonderful spell of four wickets for two runs in 19 balls. Hayden and Barsby got the Queensland innings off to a solid start and then Goggin scored his maiden century against a lightweight attack, which lost the services of Hutchison after he dislocated his shoulder in a fielding accident. Healy declared 307 ahead. With nearly two days left the South Australian batsmen put up slightly more resistance, but though most of the upper order got a start, only Blewett could reach 50 and, with McDermott producing the occasional thunderbolt, the innings folded before lunch on the last day.

Close of play: First day, Queensland 78-0 (M. L. Hayden 32*, T. J. Barsby 39*); Second day, Queensland 426-6 (I. A. Healy 26*, C. J. McDermott 14*); Third day, South Australia 201-6 (P. R. Sleep 10*).

South Australia

G. S. Blewett b Rowell	17	– lbw b Kasprowicz	50
N. R. Fielke c Rowell b McDermott	21	– c Goggin b Storey	23
J. A. Brayshaw c Kasprowicz b Tazelaar	49	– c Healy b Rowell	32
*J. D. Siddons b Rowell	30	– c Healy b McDermott	15
G. A. Bishop c Healy b Tazelaar	7	– c Border b Rowell	27
†T. J. Nielsen c Goggin b Tazelaar	2	– b McDermott	30
P. R. Sleep not out	18	– c Law b Tazelaar	11
T. B. A. May c Border b Tazelaar	0	– not out	18
P. J. Hutchison c Hayden b McDermott	5	– c Border b McDermott	2
P. W. Gladigau b Healy b McDermott	15	– b McDermott	5
D. J. Hickey b McDermott	4	– c and b Kasprowicz	12
B 4, l-b 6	10	B 5, l-b 12, n-b 4	21

1/37 2/41 3/102 4/124 5/126   178   1/75 2/93 3/129 4/134 5/185   246
6/133 7/133 8/146 9/174   6/201 7/203 8/214 9/230

Bowling: *First Innings*—McDermott 18.4–4–48–4; Rowell 14–6–28–2; Storey 10–3–24–0; Kasprowicz 7–1–29–0. *Second Innings*—McDermott 31–9–64–4; Tazelaar 23–6–49–1; Kasprowicz 17–7–40–2; Rowell 18–4–46–2; Storey 17–5–30–1.

Queensland

M. L. Hayden c Brayshaw b Sleep	77	C. J. McDermott c Bishop b May	25
T. J. Barsby c Sleep b Hutchison	49	M. S. Kasprowicz not out	20
P. J. T. Goggin c Brayshaw b Hickey	120	L-b 11, w 4, n-b 24	39
S. G. Law c Sleep b Hickey	69		
A. R. Border c Nielsen b Hickey	12	1/97 2/190 3/329 (7 wkts dec.) 485	
S. C. Storey c Fielke b Hickey	21	4/344 5/380	
*†I. A. Healy not out	53	6/383 7/446	

G. J. Rowell and D. Tazelaar did not bat.

Bowling: Hickey 27–4–120–4; Hutchison 11–3–40–1; May 33–7–106–1; Gladigau 33–9–116–0; Sleep 21–2–86–1; Blewett 1–0–6–0.

Umpires: A. J. McQuillan, M. D. Ralston and C. D. Timmins.

WESTERN AUSTRALIA v NEW SOUTH WALES

At Perth, November 14, 15, 16, 17. New South Wales won by five wickets. New South Wales 6 pts, Western Australia −0.8 pts. Toss: New South Wales.

Taylor won an important toss, opted to bowl on a green wicket and dictated the pattern of the game: his two left-arm fast bowlers, Whitney and Alley, had Western Australia struggling at 52 for five. The dogged Langer and more dashing Zoehrer put on 100 before there was another collapse, the last five wickets falling for seven runs. New South Wales also had to battle for runs until Bayliss and McNamara steered them towards a useful lead of 61. Marsh and Veletta knocked off the deficit but then wickets again began to tumble; Holdsworth received a warning after hitting Angel on the head twice. Western Australia left a target of 226, and their hopes soared when they reduced the visitors to 79 for four. But Matthews demonstrated concentration and responsibility and guided his team to a hard-fought victory. Alderman received a suspended fine of $A250 for showing dissent when called for a no-ball.

Close of play: First day, New South Wales 144-5 (T. H. Bayliss 19*, B. E. McNamara 14*); Second day, Western Australia 210-5 (W. S. Andrews 27*, T. J. Zoehrer 33*); Third day, New South Wales 189-5 (G. R. J. Matthews 51*, B. E. McNamara 26*).

Western Australia

M. R. J. Veletta c Emery b Whitney	12	– (2) c Emery b Alley	28
*G. R. Marsh c Taylor b Whitney	0	– (1) c and b Matthews	47
J. L. Langer c Small b Whitney	58	– lbw b Whitney	14
T. M. Moody c Emery b Whitney	0	– c Small b Holdsworth	34
M. P. Lavender c Small b Alley	9	– c Waugh b Holdsworth	4
W. S. Andrews c Taylor b Alley	6	– c Small b Whitney	40
†T. J. Zoehrer c McNamara b Alley	61	– c Emery b Alley	33
B. P. Julian b Alley	0	– c Emery b McNamara	35
J. Angel c Emery b Whitney	2	– not out	5
T. M. Alderman not out	2	– c Emery b McNamara	7
B. A. Reid b Alley	0	– c Emery b Whitney	7
L-b 5, n-b 4	9	L-b 5, n-b 27	32

1/0 2/25 3/25 4/46 5/52   159   1/83 2/85 3/117 4/130 5/139   286
6/152 7/152 8/154 9/158   6/211 7/245 8/259 9/275

Bowling: *First Innings*—Holdsworth 5-1-16-0; Whitney 19-3-43-5; Alley 17.4-4-43-5;
Matthews 10-0-44-0; McNamara 1-0-8-0. *Second Innings*—Holdsworth 16-2-55-2;
Whitney 27-9-72-3; McNamara 14-5-43-2; Alley 17-4-47-2; Matthews 15-6-34-1;
Waugh 5-0-30-0.

New South Wales

S. M. Small b Reid	0	– c Zoehrer b Alderman	10
*M. A. Taylor b Reid	12	– b Julian b Reid	2
M. E. Waugh run out	46	– c Zoehrer b Julian	35
M. G. Bevan c Langer b Alderman	11	– c Lavender b Julian	25
G. R. J. Matthews c Zoehrer b Julian	18	– not out	65
T. H. Bayliss c Zoehrer b Reid	52	– c Zoehrer b Reid	21
B. E. McNamara c Angel b Julian	35	– not out	45
†P. A. Emery b Angel	5		
P. J. S. Alley c Andrews b Julian	1		
W. J. Holdsworth not out	4		
M. R. Whitney c Langer b Julian	6		
L-b 2, n-b 28	30	L-b 10, n-b 16	26

1/2 2/25 3/54 4/105 5/111   220   1/5 2/12 3/76   (5 wkts) 229
6/195 7/207 8/209 9/210   4/79 5/138

Bowling: *First Innings*—Reid 19-1-89-3; Alderman 15-4-46-1; Angel 9-3-33-1; Julian
12.3-1-50-4. *Second Innings*—Reid 22-3-58-2; Alderman 26-10-40-1; Angel 18.3-8-63-0;
Julian 13-1-58-2.

Umpires: R. J. Evans, T. A. Prue and B. Rennie.

SOUTH AUSTRALIA v TASMANIA

At Adelaide, November 20, 21, 22, 23. South Australia won by 215 runs. South Australia
6 pts. Toss: South Australia. First-class debuts: D. A. Reeves; R. T. Ponting.
    Tasmania collapsed on the final day after a game of three declarations played mostly in
damp, grey weather. After a slow opening day, Nielsen and Scuderi improved the tempo,
putting on 133 in two and a half hours next day, and both reached centuries. Tasmania got
to the crease only on the third day: the highlight of their innings was a partnership of 127
between Boon and the 17-year-old debutant Ponting, who looked especially composed
against the pace bowlers. But Tasmania's greatest contributor was Extras, with 61: the off-
spinner May was called ten times which, under Shield rules, cost 20. Boon declared 70 runs
behind, to keep the game open, and was unimpressed when Siddons prolonged South
Australia's second innings to lunch on the fourth day. Equally upset, it seemed, were
Tasmania's batsmen, who capitulated without a whimper. May bowled superbly and
Reeves, on his debut, showed a useful turn of speed.
    Close of play: First day, South Australia 194-5 (T. J. Nielsen 39*, J. C. Scuderi 14*);
Second day, South Australia 368-7 (J. C. Scuderi 100*, T. B. A. May 3*); Third day, South
Australia 58-0 (G. S. Blewett 16*, N. R. Fielke 39*).

South Australia

G. S. Blewett c Tucker b Young	23	– c Courtney b Matthews	43
N. R. Fielke c Courtney b Matthews	6	– st Atkinson b Boon	74
J. A. Brayshaw b Hills b Young	23	– not out	73
*J. D. Siddons c Hills b Young	25	– not out	69
G. A. Bishop b Miller	50		
†T. J. Nielsen c McPhee b Tucker	109		
J. C. Scuderi not out	100		
P. R. Sleep c Matthews b Tucker	13		
T. B. A. May not out	3		
B 1, l-b 9, n-b 6	16	B 1, l-b 5, w 1, n-b 2	9

1/9 2/60 3/61 4/108 5/168   (7 wkts dec.) 368   1/120 2/124   (2 wkts dec.) 268
6/327 7/359

D. A. Reeves and D. J. Hickey did not bat.

Bowling: First Innings—Matthews 25-4-76-1; McPhee 28-5-87-0; Miller 32-8-90-1; Young 27-9-50-3; Tucker 17-1-54-2; Boon 1-0-1-0. *Second Innings*—Matthews 15-2-64-1; McPhee 14-2-60-0; Miller 9-1-46-0; Young 5-3-2-0; Boon 15-3-56-1; Courtney 7-0-34-0.

Tasmania

D. F. Hills lbw b Reeves	16	– lbw b May	20
N. C. P. Courtney c Bishop b Hickey	16	– b May	43
*D. C. Boon c Sleep b May	60	– c Nielsen b Reeves	8
R. T. Ponting c Nielsen b Hickey	56	– b Hickey	4
J. Cox c May b Hickey	11	– lbw b Scuderi	18
R. J. Tucker not out	49	– c Siddons b Reeves	6
S. Young c Siddons b May	0	– c and b May	7
C. D. Matthews not out	29	– b Sleep	4
†M. N. Atkinson (did not bat)		– c Siddons b May	1
C. R. Miller (did not bat)		– not out	0
P. T. McPhee (did not bat)		– c Fielke b May	0
L-b 6, w 10, n-b 45	61	L-b 3, w 3, n-b 6	12

1/31 2/50 3/177 4/195   (6 wkts dec.) 298   1/27 2/40 3/46 4/87 5/96   123
5/213 6/216   6/105 7/122 8/122 9/123

Bowling: First Innings—Hickey 18-4-75-3; Reeves 15-1-60-1; Scuderi 10-0-44-0; May 35-9-80-2; Blewett 1-1-0-0; Sleep 10-0-33-0. *Second Innings*—Hickey 14-1-37-1; Reeves 13-5-27-2; May 32.4-15-42-5; Sleep 8-5-3-1; Scuderi 9-5-11-1.

Umpires: S. J. Davis, D. J. Harper and R. G. Kinnear.

VICTORIA v QUEENSLAND

At St Kilda, November 20, 21, 22, 23. Drawn. Queensland 2 pts. Toss: Queensland.

The match saw almost more rain than cricket but Queensland came desperately close to an improbable victory. The first morning was wiped out and there was only 27 minutes' play on the second day. However, those 27 minutes belonged to Hughes, who exploited a gale at his back and a new ball to take three for two in 13 deliveries. Phillips and Nobes gave Victoria a rollicking start on the third day, with 60 off the first 12 overs. The advent of spin, from slow left-armers Border and Storey, scotched the scoring and then overcame the batsmen. Victoria lost the contest for first-innings points and with the wicket deteriorating Healy never forsook his aim of an outright win. Queensland grafted a lead of 171, and Healy then gave Victoria 32 overs to make the runs or survive; before they had decided which, Rowell and Kasprowicz were among the wickets. After 24 overs Victoria were 84 for nine but Warne and Hughes blocked to deny Queensland their victory.

Close of play: First day, Queensland 208-6 (A. R. Border 64*, C. J. McDermott 23*); Second day, Queensland 222-9 (G. J. Rowell 2*); Third day, Victoria 170-6 (A. I. C. Dodemaide 1*, P. R. Reiffel 8*).

Queensland

M. L. Hayden c Hughes b O'Donnell	51	– c Lehmann b Warne 28
T. J. Barsby c Ayres b Warne	35	– lbw b Dodemaide 0
P. J. T. Goggin b Dodemaide	25	– run out 45
S. G. Law c Ayres b O'Donnell	0	– not out 2
A. R. Border b Hughes	71	– c Reiffel b O'Donnell 21
S. C. Storey c Berry b Dodemaide	0	– c Berry b Dodemaide 20
*†H. A. Healy c Ayres b Reiffel	3	– c Reiffel b Hughes 16
C. J. McDermott c Jones b Hughes	26	– lbw b Dodemaide 10
M. S. Kasprowicz b Hughes	2	– b Hughes 0
G. J. Rowell not out	2	– not out 0
L-b 5, n-b 2	7	L-b 2 2

1/86 2/89 3/89 4/146 5/146   (9 wkts dec.) 222
6/160 7/218 8/219 9/222

1/4 2/50 3/55   (9 wkts dec.) 144
4/98 5/100 6/134
7/134 8/140 9/144

D. Tazelaar did not bat.

Bowling: *First Innings*—Hughes 22.2–4–51–3; Dodemaide 23–9–44–2; Reiffel 15–3–55–1; Warne 21–3–59–1; O'Donnell 8–4–8–2. *Second Innings*—Hughes 12–6–18–2; Dodemaide 14.5–3–41–3; Warne 13–0–48–1; Reiffel 15–5–24–0; O'Donnell 5–1–11–1.

Victoria

W. N. Phillips c Goggin b Border	28	– (2) c Goggin b Rowell 6
P. C. Nobes lbw b McDermott	70	– (1) lbw b Rowell 4
D. M. Jones c Goggin b Border	14	– lbw b Rowell 1
D. S. Lehmann c Goggin b Border	10	– c Hayden b Kasprowicz 3
W. G. Ayres c Hayden b Border	13	– (6) c Barsby b Kasprowicz 10
*S. P. O'Donnell c Law b Border	7	– (5) lbw b Kasprowicz 28
A. I. C. Dodemaide c Goggin b Rowell	8	– c Healy b Rowell 0
P. R. Reiffel c Healy b Rowell	22	– lbw b Kasprowicz 14
†D. S. Berry lbw b Storey	4	– c Storey b Rowell 2
S. K. Warne b Storey	0	– not out 3
M. G. Hughes not out	0	– not out 7
B 3, l-b 4, n-b 12	19	B 3, l-b 2, w 4, n-b 8 ... 17

1/76 2/100 3/116 4/146 5/158   195
6/162 7/182 8/191 9/195

1/7 2/12 3/15   (9 wkts) 95
4/22 5/46 6/48
7/64 8/71 9/84

Bowling: *First Innings*—McDermott 15–3–46–1; Tazelaar 6–1–33–0; Rowell 12–6–28–2; Storey 27.3–13–35–2; Border 21–6–46–5. *Second Innings*—McDermott 8–3–15–0; Rowell 10–2–31–5; Kasprowicz 11–0–42–4; Tazelaar 3–1–2–0.

Umpires: D. W. Holt, L. J. King and W. P. Sheahan.

TASMANIA v NEW SOUTH WALES

At Hobart, November 27, 28, 29, 30. Drawn. Tasmania 2 pts. Toss: New South Wales.

Phil Emery, in his first game as New South Wales captain, surrendered first use of a good pitch. However, Hills and Courtney clubbed 29 from the first few overs and Tasmania then made steady progress with Tucker, their stand-in captain, reaching a worthy century on the second day. Tasmania's bowlers then took the initiative. Chris Matthews and Miller proved constant problems, but not to the 22-year-old Slater. In only his third first-class game he struck 13 fours, none better than the slashing square drive off Miller to reach his maiden hundred. Buoyed up by a first-innings lead of 131, Tasmania's batsmen went for quick runs, and set New South Wales 343 at just above four an over. The visitors threw caution to the wind and, with Small in his element, they seemed well placed at 164 for two. However, after three quick wickets from Matthews and a run-out Emery, decided to end the heroics.

Close of play: First day, Tasmania 286-7 (R. J. Tucker 79*); Second day, New South Wales 83-2 (M. J. Slater 40*, M. G. Bevan 15*); Third day, Tasmania 113-1 (D. F. Hills 52*, J. Cox 55*).

Tasmania

D. F. Hills c Slater b Holdsworth	48	– c Small b McNamara	87
N. C. P. Courtney c McNamara b Whitney	60	– b Whitney	2
J. Cox lbw b Holdsworth	0	– c Emery b Whitney	73
R. T. Ponting c Small b Freedman	32	– (6) b Holdsworth	18
B. A. Cruse c Emery b Alley	7	– (7) not out	5
*R. J. Tucker run out	104	– (8) not out	2
S. Young b Holdsworth	43		
†M. N. Atkinson c Emery b Whitney	1		
M. G. Farrell not out	53		
C. D. Matthews c Holdsworth b McNamara	20	– (5) b McNamara	4
C. R. Miller c Bayliss b Holdsworth	11	– (4) b Whitney	3
B 3, l-b 5, w 2, n-b 14	24	L-b 5, n-b 12	17

1/84 2/84 3/131 4/145 5/181   403   1/8 2/150 3/156   (6 wkts dec.) 211
6/281 7/286 8/336 9/383   4/175 5/202 6/205

Bowling: *First Innings*—Holdsworth 23–2–108–4; Whitney 30–5–96–2; Alley 24–6–64–1; McNamara 17–4–43–1; Freedman 25–3–82–1; Bayliss 3–1–2–0. *Second Innings*—Holdsworth 9–1–41–1; Whitney 19–4–55–3; Alley 3–0–20–0; McNamara 22–4–80–2; Bayliss 11–5–10–0; Bevan 1–1–0–0.

New South Wales

S. M. Small c Hills b Miller	1	– b Matthews	88
M. J. Slater hit wkt b Matthews	138	– c Atkinson b Farrell	24
T. H. Bayliss c Atkinson b Miller	22	– run out	14
M. G. Bevan c Farrell b Matthews	21	– b Matthews	33
B. E. McNamara lbw b Miller	1	– (6) run out	9
M. T. Haywood c Tucker b Young	34	– (5) c Atkinson b Matthews	4
*†P. A. Emery c Young b Tucker	0	– not out	62
P. J. S. Alley lbw b Matthews	35	– lbw b Farrell	35
D. A. Freedman c Young b Miller	3	– not out	0
W. J. Holdsworth b Matthews	8		
M. R. Whitney not out	1		
L-b 7, w 1	8	B 1, l-b 12, w 1, n-b 4	18

1/1 2/52 3/95 4/96 5/202   272   1/70 2/101 3/164 4/170   (7 wkts) 287
6/203 7/231 8/238 9/263   5/175 6/184 7/281

Bowling: *First Innings*—Matthews 28.4–4–75–4; Miller 26–6–93–4; Young 19–3–51–1; Farrell 11–4–15–0; Tucker 15–4–31–1. *Second Innings*—Matthews 24–2–97–3; Miller 14–1–42–0; Farrell 23–6–53–2; Young 9–1–41–0; Tucker 11–3–41–0.

Umpires: R. P. Donaldson, T. R. Hogarth and B. T. Knight.

VICTORIA v WESTERN AUSTRALIA

At St Kilda, December 4, 5, 6, 7. Drawn. Victoria 2 pts. Toss: Western Australia.

The second game switched to the Junction Oval because of rebuilding work at the MCG was ruined by rain, just as the first had been. Marsh spent nearly three hours making 26 after winning the toss and when Western Australia tried to increase the tempo on the second day, Warne ran through the innings. Victoria's batsmen had little trouble securing first-innings points but, faced with the option of declaring and keeping the game open or pressing on for a big lead, O'Donnell characteristically chose the safer course. If he had hoped Western Australia would collapse on a deteriorating wicket, he was disappointed: Marsh and Martyn both scored centuries on a dead final day. Marsh enjoyed trouble-free practice over five and a half hours while Martyn, batting only two and a half hours, demonstrated both the variety and power of his strokeplay.

Close of play: First day, Western Australia 113-2 (J. L. Langer 51*, D. R. Martyn 15*); Second day, Victoria 2-0 (W. N. Phillips 0*, P. C. Nobes 0*); Third day, Victoria 352.

Western Australia

M. R. J. Veletta c Berry b Hughes	3	– (2) b Warne	20
*G. R. Marsh b Warne	26	– (1) c O'Donnell b Dodemaide	101
J. L. Langer c Berry b Warne	70	– b Warne	44
D. R. Martyn b Fleming	51	– not out	116
T. M. Moody c Berry b Hughes	2	– not out	35
W. S. Andrews lbw b Fleming	18		
†T. J. Zoehrer c Lehmann b Warne	0		
B. P. Julian b Fleming	3		
J. Angel c Dodemaide b Warne	0		
T. M. Alderman not out	1		
B. A. Reid c Allardice b Warne	4		
B 4, l-b 5, w 1, n-b 24	34	B 4, l-b 5, n-b 12	21

1/10 2/93 3/150 4/152 5/197   212   1/66 2/153 3/252   (3 wkts) 337
6/198 7/201 8/204 9/207

Bowling: *First Innings*—Hughes 20–3–52–2; Dodemaide 16–3–45–0; Fleming 18–4–45–3; O'Donnell 4–1–12–0; Warne 17.3–4–49–5. *Second Innings*—Hughes 13–2–44–0; Dodemaide 24–2–80–1; O'Donnell 14–3–34–0; Fleming 21–1–77–0; Warne 27–4–74–2; Lehmann 1–0–1–0; Ayres 2–0–11–0; Nobes 2–0–7–0.

Victoria

W. N. Phillips c Moody b Julian	27	S. K. Warne b Julian	69
P. C. Nobes c Martyn b Reid	8	M. G. Hughes b Andrews	1
G. J. Allardice c Veletta b Zoehrer	31	D. W. Fleming not out	3
D. S. Lehmann b Julian	60		
W. G. Ayres c Martyn b Julian	22	B 1, l-b 11, w 1, n-b 18	31
*S. P. O'Donnell c Marsh b Zoehrer	34		
A. I. C. Dodemaide c Zoehrer b Julian	50	1/15 2/80 3/90 4/170 5/205	352
†D. S. Berry st Veletta b Zoehrer	16	6/209 7/230 8/333 9/338	

Bowling: Reid 17–5–31–1; Alderman 21–4–67–0; Angel 14–3–53–0; Martyn 4–0–18–0; Zoehrer 24–4–66–3; Julian 25.2–5–84–5; Andrews 7–0–21–1.

Umpires: D. W. Holt, P. H. Jensen and K. A. P. Knott.

NEW SOUTH WALES v QUEENSLAND

At Sydney, December 11, 12, 13, 14. Drawn. Queensland 2 pts. Toss: Queensland.

Dirk Wellham came out of retirement to lead his third state team. Although his own contribution was insignificant, Queensland held the initiative from the opening day when wayward bowling helped their batsmen, most especially Storey, who caught the eye with a devastating hundred in 140 minutes, including 18 fours. The onslaught continued with a last-wicket stand of 69 between Kasprowicz and Tazelaar and, when Kasprowicz bowled Small with his second ball, Queensland were right on top. Slater and Bayliss restored the balance, putting on 129 in two hours. Bayliss went on to a splendid hundred and the gritty McNamara then held the fort, losing the chance of a maiden hundred only when the last man, Holdsworth, lashed out. Queensland struggled against the spinners in their second innings and were in some danger until the watchful Barsby took control and enabled Wellham to declare. Set 322 in a minimum 56 overs, New South Wales had a flying start but Emery called off the chase when wickets began falling.

Close of play: First day, Queensland 389-9 (M. S. Kasprowicz 5*, D. Tazelaar 8*); Second day, New South Wales 249-6 (B. E. McNamara 31*, D. A. Freedman 3*); Third day, Queensland 134-6 (T. J. Barsby 61*, B. N. J. Oxenford 12*).

Queensland

M. L. Hayden c Emery b Holdsworth	25	– (2) c Small b Robertson ... 30
T. J. Barsby lbw b McNamara	34	– (1) c Alley b Robertson ...123
P. J. T. Goggin c Bevan b Freedman	68	– c Holdsworth b Freedman ... 2
S. G. Law c Freedman b Bayliss	79	– c Small b Freedman ... 10
*D. M. Wellham c Bayliss b Robertson	12	– c Small b Freedman ... 0
S. C. Storey c Holdsworth b Alley	103	– c Alley b Robertson ... 8
†P. W. Anderson c Freedman b Holdsworth	2	– c Emery b Robertson ... 0
B. N. J. Oxenford b McNamara	23	– c Freedman b Robertson ... 37
M. S. Kasprowicz not out	27	– c sub b Robertson ... 22
G. J. Rowell b McNamara	0	– not out ... 4
D. Tazelaar lbw b McNamara	37	– not out ... 3
B 5, l-b 18, n-b 14	37	B 7, l-b 2, n-b 8 ... 17

1/32 2/93 3/189 4/220 5/292   447   1/62 2/69 3/86   (9 wkts dec.) 256
6/299 7/364 8/378 9/378   4/86 5/107 6/107
                                      7/173 8/241 9/249

Bowling: First Innings—Holdsworth 22–3–106–2; Alley 21–5–74–1; McNamara 22.5–4–68–4; Robertson 21–4–72–1; Freedman 16–1–69–1; Bayliss 8–2–25–1; Bevan 1–0–10–0. *Second Innings*—Holdsworth 3–0–11–0; Alley 2–0–6–0; Robertson 38–7–104–6; Bevan 3–1–32–0; Freedman 25–5–72–3; Bayliss 4–0–17–0; McNamara 2–0–5–0.

New South Wales

S. M. Small b Kasprowicz	0	– lbw b Tazelaar ... 45
M. J. Slater c Oxenford b Rowell	61	– c Hayden b Storey ... 72
T. H. Bayliss c Oxenford b Rowell	107	– c Wellham b Oxenford ... 3
M. G. Bevan b Tazelaar	8	– c and b Oxenford ... 19
B. E. McNamara not out	98	– (7) not out ... 55
M. T. Haywood c Anderson b Storey	0	– (5) c Anderson b Oxenford ... 5
*†P. A. Emery c Hayden b Kasprowicz	23	– (8) not out ... 36
D. A. Freedman b Kasprowicz	5	
G. R. Robertson c and b Tazelaar	48	
P. J. S. Alley c and b Rowell	1	– (6) c Rowell b Oxenford ... 3
W. J. Holdsworth c Anderson b Tazelaar	0	
L-b 5, n-b 26	31	B 2, l-b 3, n-b 4 ... 9

1/0 2/129 3/162 4/198 5/201   382   1/90 2/121 3/136   (6 wkts) 247
6/240 7/255 8/368 9/369   4/150 5/154 6/154

Bowling: First Innings—Kasprowicz 30–9–70–3; Rowell 30–3–101–3; Tazelaar 22.4–6–63–3; Oxenford 20–5–78–0; Storey 24–6–65–1. *Second Innings*—Kasprowicz 8–0–59–0; Rowell 7–0–31–0; Tazelaar 8–2–33–1; Storey 16–5–38–1; Oxenford 16–2–70–4; Law 2–0–11–0.

Umpires: K. I. Duffy, D. B. Hair and I. G. Jackson.

WESTERN AUSTRALIA v SOUTH AUSTRALIA

At Perth, December 11, 12, 13, 14. Western Australia won by three wickets. Western Australia 6 pts, South Australia 2 pts. Toss: South Australia. First-class debuts: M. P. Atkinson; D. J. Ritossa.

Marsh and Siddons deserved credit for their positive captaincy as well as for their memorable batting. First Siddons inspired South Australia with a gem-like 67. The pitch was so benign that even the last pair put on 71 and Western Australia's batsmen thrived as well. But, having reached 229 for one, they lost their direction. Marsh surprisingly declared 105 runs behind to go for the outright win. The ploy would have worked faster had not Siddons played the innings of a lifetime as his colleagues succumbed to the Western Australian pace attack. He batted for just over three and a half hours and scored 116 between lunch and tea on the third day. His declaration on the last morning set Western Australia 390 from 76 overs. If this was a stiffer target than expected, Marsh had no worries. He and Langer smote 203 in 162 minutes and, with Moody at last showing some form, the Western Australians were in command. Four run-outs shifted the balance again, and Western Australia still needed eight runs from the last over. Julian put Scuderi's first ball over mid-off for six and the second through mid-wicket for four.

Close of play: First day, South Australia 310-7 (P. R. Sleep 32*, D. A. Reeves 3*); Second day, Western Australia 211-1 (M. R. J. Veletta 59*, J. L. Langer 86*); Third day, South Australia 214-6 (J. D. Siddons 145*, P. R. Sleep 23*).

South Australia

G. S. Blewett c Langer b Atkinson	17	– c Atkinson b Julian	25
N. R. Fielke c Veletta b Julian	55	– b Alderman	0
J. A. Brayshaw c Langer b Angel	77	– b Alderman	2
*J. D. Siddons b Alderman	67	– not out	189
G. A. Bishop c Langer b Atkinson	20	– c Moody b Alderman	2
†T. J. Nielsen c Atkinson b Angel	28	– c Moody b Atkinson	8
J. C. Scuderi c Veletta b Alderman	0	– lbw b Atkinson	0
P. R. Sleep c Andrews b Alderman	47	– not out	44
D. A. Reeves c Zoehrer b Alderman	10		
D. J. Ritossa not out	37		
D. J. Hickey c Veletta b Atkinson	34		
L-b 9, n-b 8	17	B 9, l-b 4, w 1	14

1/41 2/104 3/193 5/250   409   1/8 2/14 3/66   (6 wkts. dec.) 284
6/250 7/296 8/327 9/338   4/90 5/130 6/136

Bowling: *First Innings*—Angel 26-11-60-2; Alderman 28-6-99-4; Atkinson 25-1-97-3; Julian 28-4-85-1; Zoehrer 9-4-34-0; Andrews 6-0-25-0. *Second Innings*—Angel 14-4-38-0; Alderman 14-4-61-2; Julian 9-3-28-2; Atkinson 10-2-45-2; Zoehrer 13-0-83-0; Andrews 2-0-16-0.

Western Australia

M. R. J. Veletta run out	68	– (2) c Nielsen b Reeves	10
*G. R. Marsh c Nielsen b Blewett	49	– (1) b Hickey	138
J. L. Langer c Scuderi b Sleep	96	– run out	110
T. M. Moody c Nielsen b Sleep	37	– run out	71
M. P. Lavender not out	20	– c Fielke b Hickey	24
W. S. Andrews c Nielsen b Sleep	0	– run out	3
†T. J. Zoehrer c Reeves b Sleep	1	– run out	1
B. P. Julian not out	4	– not out	11
M. P. Atkinson (did not bat)	–	– not out	0
L-b 8, w 1, n-b 20	29	L-b 13, w 1, n-b 10	24

1/77 2/229 3/238 4/297   (6 wkts. dec.) 304   1/22 2/225 3/307 4/365   (7 wkts) 392
5/297 6/299   5/370 6/380 7/382

J. Angel and T. M. Alderman did not bat.

Bowling: *First Innings*—Reeves 19-2-73-0; Scuderi 18-6-54-0; Hickey 26-6-68-0; Ritossa 5-1-14-0; Blewett 10-2-28-1; Sleep 32-13-59-4. *Second Innings*—Hickey 25-0-134-2; Reeves 6-1-28-1; Scuderi 17.2-0-99-0; Blewett 8-1-38-0; Sleep 14-1-62-0; Ritossa 5-0-18-0.

Umpires: R. J. Emerson, R. J. Evans and B. Rennie.

SOUTH AUSTRALIA v NEW SOUTH WALES

Centenary Match

At Adelaide, December 18, 19, 20, 21. New South Wales won by nine runs. New South Wales 6 pts. Toss: South Australia. First-class debut: D. S. Webber.

The centenary match of the Sheffield Shield, bringing together the states who played the inaugural game at Adelaide in December 1892, provided excitement to the last over. Put in on a greenish pitch, New South Wales launched a tremendous assault. Mark Waugh hit 20 fours all over the ground, plus a straight six off Sleep that carried 130 metres; between lunch and tea he scored 114. In between downpours Matthews then tied up South Australia and gave his team a lead of 184. Taylor elected not to enforce the follow-on and decided that 389 off 112 overs was the right last-day formula. But with Matthews putting down a couple of chances at slip, the South Australian batsmen launched a serious challenge.

Blewett and Fielke started splendidly and Nielsen and Scuderi put on 86 in 74 minutes for the sixth wicket, which could have tipped the scales, but Taylor courageously kept his spinners on. When Matthews began the final over, 12 were needed with the last pair together. Reeves hit the first ball for two, but found himself joined at the striker's end by Hickey, who was trying for a third. The ensuing run-out reversed the result of 1892, when South Australia won by 57 runs.

Close of play: First day, New South Wales 399-5 dec.; Second day, South Australia 114-5 (D. S. Webber 10*, J. C. Scuderi 1*); Third day, New South Wales 204-7 (M. E. Waugh 8*).

New South Wales

*M. A. Taylor lbw b Reeves	63	– (2) c Hickey b May	38
M. J. Slater c Siddons b Reeves	0	– (1) lbw b Sleep	82
S. R. Waugh c Fielke b May	38	– lbw b May	4
M. E. Waugh c Siddons b Scuderi	164	– (7) not out	8
G. R. J. Matthews c Nielsen b Scuderi	53	– c Webber b May	33
T. H. Bayliss not out	37	– (4) b Sleep	16
B. E. McNamara not out	23	– (6) b May	8
†P. A. Emery (did not bat)		– run out	7
L-b 4, w 1, n-b 16	21	L-b 1, w 1, n-b 6	8

1/16 2/82 3/165 4/319 5/344   (5 wkts dec.) 399   1/89 2/98 3/128   (7 wkts dec.) 204
                                                              4/162 5/188
                                                              6/192 7/204

D. A. Freedman, P. J. S. Alley and M. R. Whitney did not bat.

Bowling: First Innings—Hickey 8-1-60-0; Reeves 12-2-70-2; Scuderi 21-4-76-2; May 23-3-99-1; Blewett 5-2-6-0; Sleep 23-1-84-0. *Second Innings*—Reeves 8-0-36-0; Scuderi 5-2-12-0; May 24-5-66-4; Hickey 5-0-25-0; Sleep 16.4-1-64-2.

South Australia

G. S. Blewett c Matthews b Alley	39	– c Alley b Freedman	71
N. R. Fielke c Emery b Alley	12	– b Alley	48
J. A. Brayshaw c S. R. Waugh b McNamara	17	– c Emery b Alley	38
*J. D. Siddons lbw b McNamara	3	– c Whitney b Alley	21
D. S. Webber lbw b Matthews	36	– c and b Matthews	2
†T. J. Nielsen c Emery b Alley	1	– c Slater b Matthews	84
J. C. Scuderi c Slater b Freedman	44	– c Slater b Whitney	50
P. R. Sleep c Alley b Matthews	6	– c Whitney b Freedman	23
T. B. A. May c S. R. Waugh b Matthews	11	– run out	3
D. A. Reeves not out	12	– run out	14
D. J. Hickey c Taylor b Matthews	0	– not out	1
B 1, l-b 8, w 1, n-b 24	34	L-b 2, n-b 22	24

1/26 2/69 3/85 4/105 5/109   215   1/83 2/159 3/193 4/196 5/214   379
6/162 7/186 8/192 9/215   6/300 7/350 8/362 9/364

Bowling: First Innings—Whitney 22-8-46-0; Alley 19-4-68-3; S. R. Waugh 6-2-11-0; Matthews 32.5-19-25-4; McNamara 8-4-14-2; Freedman 15-5-42-1. *Second Innings*—Whitney 24-5-76-1; Alley 17-1-68-3; S. R. Waugh 8-3-30-0; Matthews 39.1-5-113-2; McNamara 5-0-19-0; Freedman 17-4-67-2; Bayliss 1-0-4-0.

Umpires: S. J. Davis, D. J. Harper and R. G. Kinnear.

WESTERN AUSTRALIA v TASMANIA

At Perth, December 18, 19, 20, 21. Drawn. Tasmania 2 pts. Toss: Tasmania.

Boon had no hesitation in fielding but was quite unprepared for the onslaught from Damien Martyn that followed. Martyn went to 52 in an hour with nine fours. His next 14 scoring shots were all boundaries. His 139, a career best, took 141 balls and occupied only three hours. Western Australia finished on 417, but Tasmania's reply benefited from some sloppy Western Australian catching and the absence of the injured Reid and Angel from their attack. Hills went to his century in 252 minutes, after half an hour on 99, and his opening partnership of 162 with Courtney was a record for Tasmania against Western Australia. The experienced Buckingham guided his team towards first-innings points, Boon declared with a lead of 40 and at tea on the last day there was a slim chance of wrapping up Western Australia's second innings in time for Tasmania to force victory. A hurricane partnership of 87 in 69 minutes between Julian and Atkinson ended these hopes.

Close of play: First day, Western Australia 325-5 (W. S. Andrews 18*, T. J. Zoehrer 43*); Second day, Tasmania 213-1 (D. F. Hills 103*, D. C. Boon 26*); Third day, Western Australia 19-0 (G. R. Marsh 7*, M. R. J. Veletta 10*).

Western Australia

M. R. J. Veletta run out	23	– (2) c Tucker b Young	26
*G. R. Marsh c Boon b Matthews	1	– (1) lbw b Young	40
J. L. Langer c Young b Matthews	43	– c Atkinson b Young	8
D. R. Martyn c sub b McPhee	139	– c and b McPhee	40
T. M. Moody b McPhee	41	– c Tucker b Young	2
W. S. Andrews c Young b McPhee	18	– lbw b Young	29
†T. J. Zoehrer c Buckingham b McPhee	52	– lbw b Matthews	3
B. P. Julian c Atkinson b Young	16	– c sub b Courtney	51
P. A. Capes lbw b Matthews	10	– lbw b Matthews	1
M. P. Atkinson c Courtney b Young	43	– not out	52
T. M. Alderman not out	9		
B 4, l-b 10, w 2, n-b 6	22	L-b 14, w 2	16

1/1 2/54 3/107 4/257 5/264	417	1/64 2/76 3/93 (9 wkts) 268
6/335 7/335 8/356 9/385		4/95 5/149 6/157
		7/167 8/181 9/268

Bowling: *First Innings*—Matthews 31-7-94-3; McPhee 32-9-96-4; Miller 13-2-64-0; Young 26.2-9-94-2; Tucker 12-0-48-0; Ponting 6-2-7-0. *Second Innings*—Matthews 23-5-70-2; McPhee 28-14-32-1; Young 28-10-88-5; Tucker 14-3-44-0; Ponting 1-0-3-0; Courtney 1.3-0-17-1.

Tasmania

D. F. Hills c Moody b Julian	138	C. D. Matthews c Moody b Alderman	3
N. C. P. Courtney c Zoehrer b Capes	58	C. R. Miller lbw b Alderman	0
*D. C. Boon c Langer b Capes	38		
R. T. Ponting lbw b Capes	25	B 3, l-b 23, w 2, n-b 18	46
D. J. Buckingham c Zoehrer b Julian	60		
R. J. Tucker c Martyn b Atkinson	32	1/162 2/231 3/287 (9 wkts dec.) 457
S. Young not out	29	4/303 5/366 6/398
†M. N. Atkinson c Veletta b Alderman	28	7/451 8/457 9/457

P. T. McPhee did not bat.

Bowling: Capes 36-5-105-3; Alderman 43.1-14-95-3; Julian 31-7-107-2; Atkinson 24-7-78-1; Martyn 6-2-24-0; Andrews 9-4-22-0.

Umpires: R. A. Emerson, R. J. Evans and T. A. Prue.

TASMANIA v VICTORIA

At Hobart, December 31, January 1, 2, 3. Drawn. Victoria 2 pts. Toss: Victoria.

Victoria dominated this match but chose not to enforce the follow-on and Tasmania, set 410 for an unlikely victory, succeeded in saving the match. From the start the Victorians set about a modest attack, which was further weakened by a knee injury to Matthews. The burly Nobes led the way with his highest score and Allardice went to his first century before the declaration. Tasmania's innings folded in four overs from Maxwell which yielded four wickets for one run. McPhee, the last man out, was so agitated when umpire Randell confirmed Maxwell's catch in the gully that he continued to complain during Victoria's second innings and was reported for breaching the code of behaviour. O'Donnell's decision not to enforce the follow-on surprised many, but after three hours of easy batting he declared, leaving his bowlers four sessions to force outright victory. The Tasmanians were uninterested in winning but their tail was obdurate enough to avoid defeat.

Close of play: First day, Victoria 342-4 (G. J. Allardice 94*, S. P. O'Donnell 25*); Second day, Tasmania 185-9 (C. D. Matthews 17*, P. T. McPhee 0*); Third day, Tasmania 80-1 (N. C. P. Courtney 33*, J. Cox 35*).

Victoria

W. N. Phillips c Farrell b Matthews	2 – (2) lbw b Tucker	31
P. C. Nobes c Buckingham b Young	145 – (1) c Atkinson b McPhee	35
D. M. Jones c Courtney b Tucker	56 – not out	72
D. S. Lehmann lbw b Tucker	1 – c Tucker b Young	52
G. J. Allardice b Farrell	116 – not out	0
*S. P. O'Donnell lbw b McPhee	59	
A. I. C. Dodemaide lbw b McPhee	14	
P. R. Reiffel not out	1	
B 2, l-b 14, w 3, n-b 4	23	L-b 6	6

1/4 2/108 3/110 4/294 5/391   (7 wkts dec.) 417   1/58 2/93 3/188   (3 wkts dec.) 196
6/409 7/417

N. D. Maxwell, †D. S. Berry and D. W. Fleming did not bat.

Bowling: *First Innings*—Matthews 10-3-34-1; McPhee 31.3-6-93-2; Young 24-2-111-1; Tucker 19-3-72-2; Farrell 25-5-76-1; Courtney 2-0-15-0. *Second Innings*—McPhee 15-1-54-1; Young 11-2-32-1; Farrell 12-0-57-0; Tucker 9-0-47-1.

Tasmania

D. F. Hills run out	5 – c Jones b Fleming	1
N. C. P. Courtney lbw b Dodemaide	32 – c and b Lehmann	88
J. Cox b Dodemaide	19 – c Jones b Maxwell	64
R. T. Ponting c Berry b Maxwell	6 – c Berry b Dodemaide	41
D. J. Buckingham lbw b Fleming	41 – c Berry b Maxwell	6
*R. J. Tucker c Jones b Maxwell	0 – c Jones b Maxwell	50
S. Young c Berry b Maxwell	0 – b Dodemaide	0
M. G. Farrell c and b Maxwell	4 – c O'Donnell b Maxwell . . .	26
†M. N. Atkinson c Berry b Maxwell	45 – not out	15
C. D. Matthews not out	29 – not out	1
P. T. McPhee c Maxwell b Dodemaide	4	
L-b 5, n-b 14	19	B 6, l-b 11, n-b 14	31

1/17 2/64 3/73 4/77 5/77   204   1/5 2/136 3/199 4/216   (8 wkts) 332
6/79 7/87 8/146 9/180   5/242 6/270 7/304 8/325

Bowling: *First Innings*—Dodemaide 21.5-8-51-3; Reiffel 19-7-44-0; Fleming 21-10-41-1; O'Donnell 4-1-17-0; Maxwell 23-7-46-5. *Second Innings*—Dodemaide 34-12-58-2; Fleming 18-3-52-1; Reiffel 24-7-71-0; Maxwell 32-4-107-4; O'Donnell 11-3-19-0; Lehmann 9-5-8-1.

Umpires: T. R. Hogarth, B. T. Knight and S. G. Randell.

SOUTH AUSTRALIA v QUEENSLAND

At Adelaide, January 8, 9, 10, 11. Drawn. Queensland 2 pts. Toss: South Australia. First-class debut: B. N. Wigney.

Matthew Hayden, the Queensland opener, spent the entire match on the field. Not many spectators would have stayed the course, however, and the game petered out after an academic third-innings declaration. Webber, in his second match, made 135 against some kindly spin bowling before the Queensland batsmen began a 500-minute occupation of the crease to secure first-innings points. Hayden batted throughout for 161 not out but his partners showed little enterprise against the leg-spinners, Sleep and McIntyre, and South Australia responded in kind, scoring 55 off 33 overs on the fourth morning.

Close of play: First day, South Australia 312-7 (D. S. Webber 119*, D. A. Reeves 0*); Second day, Queensland 213-3 (M. L. Hayden 103*, D. M. Wellham 24*); Third day, South Australia 142-3 (J. D. Siddons 49*).

South Australia

G. S. Blewett c Anderson b Rackemann	30	– c Anderson b Tazelaar	1
N. R. Fielke c Goggin b Kasprowicz	19	– run out	57
J. A. Brayshaw c Anderson b Tazelaar	7	– c Tazelaar b Storey	23
*J. D. Siddons c Anderson b Kasprowicz	75	– c Law b Kasprowicz	53
D. S. Webber c Rackemann b Tazelaar	135	– st Anderson b Storey	77
†T. J. Nielsen b Storey	10	– b Rackemann	0
J. C. Scuderi c Oxenford b Rackemann	4	– c Rackemann b Law	31
P. R. Sleep c Anderson b Tazelaar	17	– c Anderson b Kasprowicz	38
D. A. Reeves c Anderson b Kasprowicz	0	– c Anderson b Tazelaar	1
B. N. Wigney b Tazelaar	1	– not out	0
P. E. McIntyre not out	0		
L-b 4, n-b 31	35	B 6, l-b 5, n-b 18	29
	333	(9 wkts dec.)	310

1/23 2/57 3/77 4/218 5/235
6/246 7/308 8/313 9/333

1/3 2/38 3/142   (9 wkts dec.) 310
4/152 5/158 6/221
7/299 8/302 9/310

Bowling: *First Innings*—Kasprowicz 31–7–76–3; Tazelaar 31.4–7–89–4; Rackemann 19–5–55–2; Storey 19.2–2–77–1; Oxenford 5–0–32–0. *Second Innings*—Kasprowicz 20–7–44–1; Tazelaar 14–5–35–2; Rackemann 21–1–60–2; Storey 35–16–72–2; Oxenford 18–1–72–0; Law 6–1–16–1.

Queensland

T. J. Barsby c Nielsen b Scuderi	26	– (2) c Fielke b Reeves	1
M. L. Hayden not out	161	– (1) not out	35
P. J. T. Goggin c Siddons b Sleep	34	– not out	4
S. G. Law c Nielsen b Sleep	13		
*D. M. Wellham c Siddons b McIntyre	56		
S. C. Storey b Sleep	0		
B. N. J. Oxenford c Sleep b McIntyre	3		
†P. W. Anderson c Siddons b Sleep	2		
M. S. Kasprowicz not out	18		
B 7, l-b 7, w 3, n-b 5	22	L-b 1, n-b 2	3
	(7 wkts dec.) 335	(1 wkt)	43

1/48 2/126 3/144 4/281 5/286   (7 wkts dec.) 335
6/299 7/306

1/25   (1 wkt) 43

D. Tazelaar and C. G. Rackemann did not bat.

Bowling: *First Innings*—Reeves 8–0–38–0; Scuderi 21–4–59–1; Wigney 22–4–68–0; McIntyre 47.2–17–76–2; Sleep 40–10–80–4. *Second Innings*—Reeves 7–1–30–1; Wigney 6–3–7–0; Webber 1–0–2–0; Nielsen 1–0–3–0.

Umpires: D. J. Harper, R. G. Kinnear and R. B. Woods.

WESTERN AUSTRALIA v VICTORIA

At Perth, January 8, 9, 10, 11. Drawn. Western Australia 2 pts. Toss: Western Australia. First-class debut: L. D. Harper.

The Victorian middle order overcame extreme Perth heat and aggressive fast bowling to save the game after Western Australia had enforced the follow-on. Marsh had made the most of winning the toss, promoting Lavender to be his opening partner, and sharing a fine opening partnership of 223 in five hours. Victoria's batsmen could do little against Angel's spirited bowling, and despite a counter-attack by O'Donnell they trailed by 175. Following on, their upper order struggled and, entering the final day, Victoria led by just 19 with five wickets down. But then O'Donnell and Dodemaide shared a fighting stand of 100 in less than two hours. O'Donnell, on 99, steered a ball from Angel into the gully but Maxwell survived a caught-behind decision when Zoehrer sportingly indicated the ball had bounced, and was to remain unconquered after four hours of defiance. His partner Dodemaide fell only after reaching 123, his highest score.

Close of play: First day, Western Australia 265-2 (G. R. Marsh 122*, J. Angel 0*); Second day, Victoria 150-5 (S. P. O'Donnell 62*, A. I. C. Dodemaide 12*); Third day, Victoria 194-5 (S. P. O'Donnell 49*, A. I. C. Dodemaide 3*).

Western Australia

M. P. Lavender c Phillips b Lehmann . . 103	B. P. Julian c Harper b O'Donnell	3
*G. R. Marsh c Maxwell b O'Donnell . . 129	M. P. Atkinson not out	5
J. L. Langer lbw b Dodemaide 11	T. M. Alderman b Dodemaide	0
J. Angel c Berry b Hughes 11		
D. R. Martyn c Lehmann b Hughes . . . 29	B 8, l-b 1, n-b 32	41
T. M. Moody c Warne b Hughes 54		
M. R. J. Veletta b O'Donnell 6	1/223 2/263 3/280 4/311 5/320	440
†T. J. Zoehrer c Phillips b O'Donnell . . 48	6/336 7/393 8/431 9/439	

Bowling: Hughes 38–6–112–3; Dodemaide 30.2–9–81–2; O'Donnell 28–3–102–4; Maxwell 13–2–41–0; Warne 29–5–89–0; Lehmann 6–3–6–1.

Victoria

P. C. Nobes lbw b Atkinson	9 – (2) c Langer b Atkinson	0
W. N. Phillips c Moody b Atkinson	9 – (1) run out	42
G. J. Allardice c Langer b Julian	5 – c Zoehrer b Angel	3
D. S. Lehmann c Langer b Angel	13 – b Alderman	28
L. D. Harper c Moody b Angel	2 – c Veletta b Julian	58
*S. P. O'Donnell c Moody b Angel	62 – c Lavender b Angel	99
A. I. C. Dodemaide not out	31 – b Zoehrer	123
N. D. Maxwell c Zoehrer b Angel	6 – not out	64
†D. S. Berry c Martyn b Alderman	57 – not out	15
S. K. Warne c Veletta b Angel	0	
M. G. Hughes c and b Angel	24	
L-b 12, w 1, n-b 34	47	B 4, l-b 9, w 2, n-b 10 . . . 25
1/20 2/23 3/38 4/46 5/91	265	1/0 2/3 3/44 4/109 (7 wkts) 457
6/150 7/156 8/233 9/233		5/169 6/269 7/429

Bowling: *First Innings*—Angel 19.5–6–71–6; Atkinson 19–2–62–2; Alderman 10–0–40–1; Julian 13–0–76–1; Martyn 3–1–4–0. *Second Innings*—Angel 25–6–77–2; Atkinson 24–8–75–1; Alderman 22–6–64–1; Julian 24–6–69–1; Martyn 18–2–47–0; Zoehrer 48–8–112–1.

Umpires: R. A. Emerson, R. J. Evans and B. Rennie.

TASMANIA v SOUTH AUSTRALIA

At Hobart, January 15, 16, 17, 18. Drawn. Tasmania 2 pts. Toss: South Australia.

Tasmania's decision to use up nearly half the match making 454 for seven ensured a low level of entertainment. True, they were put in and lost Courtney and Cox in the third over. But after they recovered, the innings came to a virtual standstill, watched by a second-day crowd of 184. Buckingham deserved credit for his stay of seven and a half hours. With only first-innings points to play for, South Australia's batsmen fell well short of the follow-on, in spite of a 54-run contribution from Extras. Cooley was no-balled 19 times in the first innings and 14 times in the second, thus giving 66 runs away. He still achieved a fair turn of speed and looked the most penetrating of Tasmania's bowlers. But Bishop, Siddons and Webber had little trouble saving the game.

Close of play: First day, Tasmania 254-5 (D. J. Buckingham 81*, S. Young 42*); Second day, South Australia 77-1 (G. A. Bishop 25*, J. A. Brayshaw 17*); Third day, South Australia 41-1 (G. A. Bishop 3*, J. A. Brayshaw 32*).

Tasmania

D. F. Hills c Sleep b May	55	M. G. Farrell c Sleep b May		74
N. C. P. Courtney b Reeves	4	†M. N. Atkinson not out		23
J. Cox c Nielsen b Reeves	0	B 3, l-b 10, n-b 12		25
R. T. Ponting c Nielsen b Reeves	50			
D. J. Buckingham not out	161	1/5 2/5 3/117	(7 wkts dec.)	454
*R. J. Tucker b May	2	4/125 5/137		
S. Young c Sleep b Wigney	60	6/284 7/415		

C. D. Matthews and T. J. Cooley did not bat.

Bowling: Reeves 26-10-66-3; Wigney 27-4-77-1; Blewett 9-1-35-0; Scuderi 24-4-79-0; May 56-20-101-3; Sleep 29-5-83-0.

South Australia

G. S. Blewett c Atkinson b Tucker	19	- b Cooley	0
G. A. Bishop c Courtney b Matthews	41	- b Cooley	56
J. A. Brayshaw lbw b Tucker	42	- lbw b Matthews	36
*J. D. Siddons lbw b Young	16	- c Atkinson b Young	56
D. S. Webber c Buckingham b Cooley	43	- c Ponting b Cooley	89
†T. J. Nielsen hit wkt b Cooley	36	- run out	14
J. C. Scuderi c Atkinson b Cooley	0	- not out	14
P. R. Sleep c Atkinson b Farrell	6	- not out	3
D. A. Reeves not out	2		
T. B. A. May run out	9		
B. N. Wigney b Matthews	3		
B 1, l-b 7, w 8, n-b 38	54	L-b 12, w 1, n-b 32	45

1/40 2/126 3/126 4/146 5/219	271	1/0 2/70 3/158	(6 wkts) 314
6/223 7/242 8/246 9/259		4/200 5/275 6/305	

Bowling: *First Innings*—Matthews 25.5-5-75-2; Cooley 23-5-103-3; Tucker 15-5-16-2; Young 18-5-45-1; Farrell 16-4-24-1. *Second Innings*—Cooley 28-3-108-3; Matthews 16-4-48-1; Young 23-10-67-1; Tucker 11-7-7-0; Ponting 1-0-6-0; Farrell 15-4-35-0; Buckingham 6-2-18-0; Courtney 4-2-13-0.

Umpires: R. P. Donaldson, T. R. Hogarth and B. T. Knight.

QUEENSLAND v TASMANIA

At Brisbane, January 21, 22, 23. Tasmania won by an innings and five runs. Tasmania 6 pts. Toss: Tasmania. First-class debut: D. R. Kingdon.

Queensland's decision to prepare a "result" wicket backfired when Tasmania won the toss, put the home team in and had them out before tea on the first day. Tasmania struggled too, losing three early wickets, but Cox and Buckingham virtually settled the first-innings issue with a sterling partnership of 104. Cox remained unbeaten after 459 minutes, and brilliantly steered Tasmania to a 167-run lead. With the pitch easing, Barsby and Hayden knocked 53 off the deficit, but then Matthews broke through and McPhee finished the job. Queensland's humiliation was complete by mid-afternoon on the third day. It was a match of some irony, especially for Wellham, a former captain of Tasmania, and McPhee, a native Queenslander. It was also Tasmania's biggest win in Sheffield Shield cricket.

Close of play: First day, Tasmania 89-3 (J. Cox 31*, D. J. Buckingham 17*); Second day, Queensland 35-0 (T. J. Barsby 29*, M. L. Hayden 3*).

Queensland

T. J. Barsby c Cox b Cooley	8	– c Courtney b Matthews	39
M. L. Hayden c Atkinson b Young	46	– c sub b McPhee	46
P. J. T. Goggin c Atkinson b Cooley	0	– b Matthews	0
D. R. Kingdon c Cox b Matthews	0	– c Ponting b McPhee	1
*D. M. Wellham c Atkinson b Matthews	9	– c Atkinson b Young	4
S. C. Storey c Buckingham b Matthews	6	– c Atkinson b McPhee	19
†P. W. Anderson c Young b Cooley	16	– run out	3
M. S. Kasprowicz c Atkinson b Cooley	39	– lbw b McPhee	0
G. J. Rowell c Cox b McPhee	8	– c Atkinson b McPhee	10
D. Tazelaar c Tucker b Young	5	– not out	8
C. G. Rackemann not out	4	– b Tucker	1
L-b 3, w 2, n-b 16	21	B 1, l-b 3, w 1, n-b 26	31

1/10 2/17 3/18 4/44 5/64　　　　　　168　　1/53 2/55 3/62 4/78 5/132　　162
6/82 7/136 8/150 9/157　　　　　　　　　　6/133 7/133 8/149 9/155

Bowling: *First Innings*—Cooley 16–5–49–4; Matthews 16–2–66–3; McPhee 8.1–2–25–1; Young 10–3–25–2. *Second Innings*—Cooley 6–1–45–0; Matthews 21–6–56–2; McPhee 20–4–48–5; Young 5–2–8–1; Tucker 2.3–1–1–1.

Tasmania

D. F. Hills c Anderson b Kasprowicz	6	†M. N. Atkinson c and b Kasprowicz	9
N. C. P. Courtney c Kingdon b Kasprowicz	3	C. D. Matthews c Anderson b Rackemann	0
J. Cox not out	137	T. J. Cooley b Rowell	1
R. T. Ponting c Hayden b Rackemann	11	P. T. McPhee c Kingdon b Kasprowicz	15
D. J. Buckingham c Hayden b Rackemann	51	B 10, l-b 16, w 1, n-b 28	55
*R. J. Tucker c Hayden b Kasprowicz	27		335
S. Young b Kasprowicz	20	1/3 2/13 3/39 4/143 5/203	
		6/253 7/269 8/271 9/272	

Bowling: Kasprowicz 25.3–6–59–6; Tazelaar 29–12–62–0; Rackemann 23–4–82–3; Rowell 23–6–47–1; Storey 16–1–59–0.

Umpires: A. J. McQuillan, P. D. Parker and M. D. Ralston.

NEW SOUTH WALES v TASMANIA

At Sydney, January 27, 28, 29, 30. Drawn. New South Wales 2 pts. Toss: Tasmania. First-class debuts: A. C. Gilchrist, G. D. McGrath.

Ricky Ponting, at 18 years and 40 days, became the youngest Tasmanian to score a first-class hundred. Runs never came easily as McGrath, in his first game, and Greg Matthews bowled especially well, but Ponting did not give a chance. Three balls into their own innings, New South Wales were nought for two wickets. However, Bevan averted Chris Matthews's bid for a hat-trick and, with Slater, put on a sparkling 153, setting up first-innings points for New South Wales. Tasmania spent the next eight hours denying the bowlers. Again, Ponting played the best innings, while Hills reached a painstaking hundred. Greg Matthews bowled his off-spinners unchallenged but players and spectators alike were relieved when the umpires abandoned play half an hour early.

Close of play: First day, Tasmania 200-6 (R. T. Ponting 98*, S. Young 0*); Second day, New South Wales 213-5 (B. E. McNamara 13*, A. C. Gilchrist 16*); Third day, Tasmania 91-2 (D. F. Hills 56*, R. T. Ponting 24*).

Tasmania

D. F. Hills c Matthews b McGrath	3	– c Freedman b Matthews 101
N. C. P. Courtney c Bevan b McGrath	20	– c Small b Matthews 8
J. Cox lbw b Matthews	33	– c Slater b Freedman 1
R. T. Ponting c Small b Holdsworth	125	– c Small b Matthews 69
D. J. Buckingham c McNamara b Matthews	29	– lbw b McNamara 18
*R. J. Tucker c Emery b Holdsworth	3	– c Small b McNamara 3
C. D. Matthews c Emery b Matthews	0	– (10) not out 18
S. Young c McNamara b McGrath	23	– (7) run out 18
M. G. Farrell lbw b McGrath	17	– (8) c McNamara b Matthews ... 3
†M. N. Atkinson c Matthews b McGrath	23	– (9) lbw b Matthews 46
P. T. McPhee not out	1	– not out........................ 0
B 1, l-b 5, w 1, n-b 8	15	L-b 7, w 1, n-b 2........ 10

1/11 2/35 3/107 4/191 5/196   292   1/45 2/50 3/159   (9 wkts dec.) 295
6/197 7/246 8/257 9/287   4/192 5/204 6/205
                                        7/210 8/264 9/283

Bowling: *First Innings*—Holdsworth 23–5–74–2; McGrath 29.1–9–79–5; McNamara 9–3–14–0; Matthews 46–15–78–3; Freedman 14–5–41–0. *Second Innings*—Holdsworth 17–4–41–0; McGrath 13.3–6–29–0; Matthews 54–31–61–5; Freedman 22–3–80–1; Bayliss 10–4–29–0; Bevan 9–1–25–0; McNamara 13.3–4–23–2.

New South Wales

S. M. Small b Matthews	0	*†P. A. Emery not out 47
M. J. Slater c Atkinson b Matthews	79	D. A. Freedman c Atkinson b Farrell .. 12
T. H. Bayliss c Atkinson b Matthews	0	W. J. Holdsworth c Ponting b Tucker .. 17
M. G. Bevan c Tucker b McPhee	76	
G. R. J. Matthews c Atkinson		B 4, l-b 8, w 4, n-b 6 22
b Matthews	18	
B. E. McNamara c Buckingham		1/0 2/0 3/153 (9 wkts dec.) 338
b Farrell	51	4/176 5/188 6/213
A. C. Gilchrist lbw b Young	16	7/284 8/316 9/338

G. D. McGrath did not bat.

Bowling: Matthews 32–10–80–4; McPhee 25–7–83–1; Young 23–11–42–1; Tucker 18.2–5–53–1; Farrell 23–5–68–2.

Umpires: P. E. Dodd, I. G. Jackson and I. S. Thomas.

QUEENSLAND v VICTORIA

At Brisbane, January 28, 29, 30, 31. Queensland won by 211 runs. Queensland 6 pts. Toss: Victoria. First-class debuts: P. M. Anderson, S. H. Cook.

Victoria went down to their first outright defeat since February 1991, despite opting to bowl first and quickly racing through the Queensland first innings. The Victorians batted even more ineptly, and Rackemann bowled three devastating spells with all his old pace. The batsmen were so bemused that Law took three wickets with gentle seamers into the wind, raising his career total to five. Victoria were now ripe for the picking, and Hayden and Barsby made the most of their opportunity. They dominated the bowling in a match-winning stand of 198, Hayden scoring 112 in four and a half hours. Wellham declared an hour before stumps on the third day, leaving Victoria an unlikely target of 368. His initiative was rewarded as three wickets fell cheaply and on the final day Kasprowicz and Rackemann made short work of the remaining batsmen.

Close of play: First day, Victoria 27-0 (W. N. Phillips 4*, P. C. Nobes 20*); Second day, Queensland 77-0 (M. L. Hayden 43*, T. J. Barsby 29*); Third day, Victoria 46-3 (W. N. Phillips 9*, D. S. Lehmann 4*).

Queensland

T. J. Barsby c Anderson b Maxwell	20	– (2) c Reiffel b Lehmann	81
M. L. Hayden c Maxwell b Anderson	15	– (1) c Berry b Reiffel	112
P. J. T. Goggin lbw b O'Donnell	24	– c Reiffel b Maxwell	30
S. G. Law c Berry b Maxwell	37	– c sub b Cook	36
*D. M. Wellham c Berry b Reiffel	28	– (7) c Maxwell b Reiffel	2
D. R. Kingdon not out	27	– not out	12
S. C. Storey c Berry b O'Donnell	10	– (5) c Cook b Maxwell	12
†P. W. Anderson c Anderson b Reiffel	24	– c Maxwell b O'Donnell	17
M. S. Kasprowicz c Maxwell b Reiffel	4		
D. Tazelaar b Maxwell	1		
C. G. Rackemann c Jones b Cook	0		
L-b 7, w 2, n-b 2	11	L-b 15, n-b 4	19

1/32 2/49 3/72 4/129 5/135	201	1/198 2/216 3/264 (7 wkts dec.) 321
6/146 7/183 8/191 9/194		4/280 5/292
		6/298 7/321

Bowling: *First Innings*—Reiffel 22-7-46-3; Cook 10.5-4-25-1; Maxwell 18-8-31-3; Anderson 10-1-45-1; O'Donnell 13-3-36-2; Lehmann 3-0-11-0. *Second Innings*—Reiffel 25-8-68-2; Cook 12-1-50-1; Maxwell 22-4-73-2; Anderson 7-0-30-0; O'Donnell 9.2-3-23-1; Lehmann 15-2-38-1; Jones 7-3-24-0.

Victoria

W. N. Phillips c Goggin b Rackemann	9	– (2) c Barsby b Kasprowicz	27
P. C. Nobes c Anderson b Rackemann	24	– (1) lbw b Rackemann	0
D. M. Jones lbw b Law	12	– c Hayden b Kasprowicz	30
D. S. Lehmann c Tazelaar b Law	16	– (5) c Law b Kasprowicz	6
G. J. Allardice c Anderson b Rackemann	11	– (6) c Anderson b Rackemann	4
*S. P. O'Donnell c Barsby b Law	0	– (7) c Kingdon b Kasprowicz	5
N. D. Maxwell c Hayden b Kasprowicz	12	– (8) b Storey	36
P. R. Reiffel c Goggin b Rackemann	36	– (9) c Anderson b Tazelaar	10
†D. S. Berry c Kingdon b Kasprowicz	1	– (4) c Anderson b Kasprowicz	3
P. M. Anderson not out	19	– c Hayden b Rackemann	4
S. H. Cook c Storey b Tazelaar	2	– not out	7
B 1, l-b 6, n-b 6	13	L-b 1, n-b 23	24

1/35 2/36 3/69 4/76 5/76	155	1/0 2/37 3/41 4/51 5/58	156
6/86 7/111 8/115 9/146		6/63 7/100 8/135 9/139

Bowling: *First Innings*—Kasprowicz 21-6-41-2; Tazelaar 21-8-40-1; Rackemann 20-8-24-4; Law 16-4-25-3; Storey 6-1-17-0; Hayden 2-1-1-0. *Second Innings*—Rackemann 19.5-6-50-3; Kasprowicz 20-5-61-5; Storey 7-2-12-1; Tazelaar 11-3-18-1; Law 6-1-14-0.

Umpires: A. J. McQuillan, P. D. Parker and M. D. Ralston.

NEW SOUTH WALES v WESTERN AUSTRALIA

At Sydney, February 3, 4, 5, 6. New South Wales won by seven wickets. New South Wales 6 pts, Western Australia 2 pts. Toss: Western Australia. First-class debuts: S. Lee; R. C. Kelly, J. Stewart.

New South Wales surprised their most fervent supporters on the fourth day by converting what looked a certain draw into a comfortable victory. As so often before, Matthews produced some inspired off-spin: he reduced Western Australia from 68 for two to 168 all out on a wicket which took some slow turn but had been criticised as too easy for batsmen. Matthews achieved his best-ever figures, eight for 52, and was well supported by brilliant catching and Emery's aggressive field placing. Duly inspired, New South Wales's batsmen hit off the runs with ten overs to spare. In the first innings, Western Australia had advanced from 277 for eight to 467 as Julian, Herzberg and newcomer Stewart took toll of some dispirited and heat-exhausted bowling. Slater and Small put New South Wales back in the match, opening with a dynamic 163 in two and a half hours, and later Bevan helped

Slater to take the score to 264 for two. Slater fell to Julian, though he had been fortunate to escape on 96 when his foot apparently dislodged a bail, unseen by either umpire. New South Wales then lost their way, and even a stand of 88 for the ninth wicket could not give them a first-innings lead.

Close of play: First day, Western Australia 268-7 (T. J. Zoehrer 0*); Second day, New South Wales 163-0 (M. J. Slater 82*, S. M. Small 64*); Third day, Western Australia 68-2 (J. Angel 1*).

Western Australia

M. P. Lavender lbw b McNamara	40	– (2) c and b Matthews	46
*G. R. Marsh c Bayliss b Lee	31	– (1) c Emery b Matthews	13
R. C. Kelly b Matthews	34	– (4) c Gilchrist b Matthews	15
T. M. Moody c Bayliss b McNamara	78	– (5) c Bayliss b Matthews	30
M. R. J. Veletta c Holdsworth b Bayliss	45	– (6) run out	5
W. S. Andrews c Bayliss b Freedman	18	– (7) c Small b Matthews	9
J. Angel c Gilchrist b Bayliss	2	– (3) c Gilchrist b Freedman	5
†T. J. Zoehrer c Matthews b Bayliss	3	– c Bayliss b Matthews	0
B. P. Julian c Slater b McNamara	75	– c and b Matthews	18
S. Herzberg not out	57	– not out	12
J. Stewart c Gilchrist b Bayliss	51	– b Matthews	1
B 3, l-b 7, w 1, n-b 22	33	B 6, l-b 5, w 1, n-b 2	14

1/76 2/115 3/136 4/226 5/262　　　467　　1/49 2/68 3/84 4/97 5/107　　168
6/268 7/268 8/277 9/385　　　　　　　　　6/136 7/136 8/143 9/162

Bowling: *First Innings*—Holdsworth 22-4-80-0; Lee 15-3-66-1; McNamara 31-7-91-3; Bevan 4-2-17-0; Matthews 38-14-77-1; Freedman 15-4-62-1; Bayliss 22-7-64-4. *Second Innings*—Holdsworth 5-0-24-0; Lee 2-0-8-0; Matthews 26.2-10-52-8; Freedman 23-3-73-1.

New South Wales

M. J. Slater c Zoehrer b Julian	124	– c Veletta b Zoehrer	38
S. M. Small run out	64	– lbw b Stewart	41
T. H. Bayliss lbw b Julian	11	– c Zoehrer b Stewart	29
M. G. Bevan b Julian	103	– not out	44
G. R. J. Matthews c Lavender b Julian	7	– not out	28
B. E. McNamara lbw b Stewart	4		
A. C. Gilchrist c Herzberg b Stewart	75		
*†P. A. Emery c Lavender b Julian	0		
S. Lee b Herzberg	4		
D. A. Freedman not out	32		
W. J. Holdsworth b Stewart	4		
B 3, l-b 2, w 1, n-b 18	24	L-b 4, n-b 2	6

1/163 2/179 3/264 4/282 5/295　　452　　1/71 2/99 3/120　　(3 wkts) 186
6/337 7/345 8/360 9/448

Bowling: *First Innings*—Angel 15-1-72-0; Julian 33-7-132-4; Moody 6-2-16-0; Stewart 29.4-6-109-3; Herzberg 26-5-97-2; Zoehrer 8-0-21-0. *Second Innings*—Angel 2-0-12-0; Julian 7.2-1-23-0; Moody 1-0-5-0; Herzberg 6-1-24-0; Stewart 19-4-79-2; Zoehrer 10-0-39-1.

Umpires: D. B. Hair, I. G. Jackson and I. S. Thomas.

VICTORIA v SOUTH AUSTRALIA

At Melbourne, February 3, 4, 5, 6. Drawn. Victoria 2 pts. Toss: Victoria. First-class debuts: M. T. G. Elliott, C. Howard.

The two bottom teams met in 40°C heat and the toss was vital. Victoria won it and experienced few fears, as Siddons was forced to use six bowlers before lunch. Phillips worked hard for 91 and Lehmann returned to form with a sparkling century, enabling

O'Donnell to declare and then Reiffel to break through twice in successive overs. However, Siddons led a strong recovery, despite needing a runner after damaging a groin muscle, and eventually offered a challenging declaration, 128 behind. The Victorians responded positively, led by their new opener, Elliott. They exploited some ordinary bowling and attacking fields to score 201 in two and a half hours so that O'Donnell could declare 329 ahead with one day left. South Australia never quite came to terms with their task, with Siddons restricted by his injury. But though Dodemaide bowled well, the Victorians played as much to contain as to bowl the opposition out, leaving O'Donnell to rue another lost opportunity.

Close of play: First day, Victoria 258-4 (D. S. Lehmann 50*, S. P. O'Donnell 24*); Second day, South Australia 132-2 (G. S. Blewett 46*, J. D. Siddons 76*); Third day, Victoria 201-7 dec.

Victoria

W. N. Phillips c Wigney b McIntyre	91	– (2) b Wigney	4
M. T. G. Elliott c Sleep b McIntyre	24	– (1) c Siddons b Reeves	66
P. C. Nobes c Bishop b Wigney	45	– lbw b Reeves	35
D. M. Jones b McIntyre	4	– c McIntyre b Blewett	26
D. S. Lehmann run out	112	– c Sleep b Reeves	25
*S. P. O'Donnell b Scuderi	58	– c McIntyre b Blewett	5
A. I. C. Dodemaide c Nielsen b Reeves	24	– run out	20
N. D. Maxwell lbw b Scuderi	5	– not out	10
P. R. Reiffel not out	6		
†D. S. Berry not out	15		
L-b 5, w 3, n-b 14	22	L-b 2, w 6, n-b 2	10

1/69 2/155 3/176 4/191 5/321   (8 wkts dec.) 406   1/12 2/97 3/114   (7 wkts dec.) 201
6/376 7/381 8/385   4/164 5/170
                                                   6/170 7/201

C. Howard did not bat.

Bowling: *First Innings*—Wigney 22-2-78-1; Reeves 22-4-72-1; Scuderi 18-2-83-2; Blewett 4-0-8-0; McIntyre 36-10-100-3; Sleep 24-7-60-0. *Second Innings*—Wigney 10-0-43-1; Scuderi 9-0-44-0; Blewett 8-0-52-2; Reeves 7.4-0-60-3.

South Australia

G. S. Blewett b Maxwell	47	– c Maxwell b Dodemaide	69
G. A. Bishop c Berry b Reiffel	2	– lbw b Reiffel	10
J. A. Brayshaw c Berry b Reiffel	4	– b Maxwell	65
*J. D. Siddons lbw b Howard	100	– b O'Donnell	58
D. S. Webber b Dodemaide	7	– c Elliott b Reiffel	17
†T. J. Nielsen not out	63	– c O'Donnell b Dodemaide	34
J. C. Scuderi hit wkt b O'Donnell	19	– not out	24
P. R. Sleep lbw b Howard	17	– c Berry b Dodemaide	6
D. A. Reeves not out	10	– run out	3
B. N. Wigney (did not bat)		– not out	2
L-b 5, w 2, n-b 2	9	L-b 7, w 1, n-b 10	18

1/4 2/8 3/133 4/140 5/178   (7 wkts dec.) 278   1/21 2/136 3/174 4/213   (8 wkts) 306
6/218 7/256   5/243 6/269 7/287 8/296

P. E. McIntyre did not bat.

Bowling: *First Innings*—Reiffel 32-12-59-2; Dodemaide 36-9-72-1; O'Donnell 11-2-29-1; Maxwell 26-6-65-1; Howard 19-7-48-2. *Second Innings*—Reiffel 25-7-67-2; Dodemaide 23-8-53-3; Maxwell 14-0-51-1; O'Donnell 19-4-68-1; Howard 8-1-35-0; Lehmann 7-0-25-0.

Umpires: K. A. P. Knott, W. P. Sheahan and S. C. Walpole.

QUEENSLAND v NEW SOUTH WALES

At Brisbane, February 26, 27, 28, March 1. Queensland won by 200 runs. Queensland 6 pts, New South Wales 2 pts. Toss: New South Wales.

A century by Dirk Wellham in Queensland's second innings stood out in an otherwise low-scoring match. And he followed it with a disdainful declaration, setting New South Wales 348 to win in nine hours. His judgment was impeccable. After an opening stand of 80, the batsmen succumbed feebly to Rowell's pace and Jackson's left-arm spin and the match ended early on the fourth day. New South Wales had taken command on the first day when their seamers bowled out Queensland. But Rackemann and Kasprowicz were just as hostile and only stubborn batting by Emery gave his team a first-innings lead of two. Wellham, helped by Hayden and Law, who was dropped three times, then transformed the game.

Close of play: First day, New South Wales 79-1 (S. M. Small 50*, A. C. Gilchrist 2*); Second day, Queensland 186-3 (S. G. Law 73*, D. M. Wellham 30*); Third day, New South Wales 107-6 (B. E. McNamara 8*).

Queensland

M. L. Hayden b Holdsworth	4	– c Stobo b Matthews	67
T. J. Barsby c Emery b McNamara	14	– c Emery b Holdsworth	0
P. J. T. Goggin not out	11	– c Emery b Holdsworth	7
S. G. Law c and b Stobo	9	– c Emery b McGrath	84
*D. M. Wellham c McNamara b McGrath	7	– not out	111
D. R. Kingdon run out	47	– c Emery b McNamara	4
†P. W. Anderson c Bayliss b McNamara	6	– c Emery b Holdsworth	40
M. S. Kasprowicz c McNamara b McGrath	2	– c Bevan b Holdsworth	13
G. J. Rowell run out	40		
P. W. Jackson c Emery b Holdsworth	13		
C. G. Rackemann b McNamara	0		
B 4, l-b 3, n-b 12	19	B 4, l-b 3, n-b 16	23

1/10 2/29 3/40 4/50 5/62   172   1/1 2/23 3/127   (7 wkts dec.) 349
6/73 7/137 8/145 9/146   4/220 5/237
                                         6/313 7/349

In the first innings P. J. T. Goggin, when 2, retired hurt at 19 and resumed at 146.

Bowling: *First Innings*—Holdsworth 17.2–5–41–2; McGrath 19–6–50–2; Stobo 13–5–28–1; McNamara 21–9–46–3. *Second Innings*—Holdsworth 25.5–2–127–4; McGrath 19–3–82–1; Stobo 16–3–49–0; Matthews 16–3–42–1; McNamara 12–1–33–1; Bayliss 4–0–9–0.

New South Wales

M. J. Slater b Rackemann	22	– b Rowell	33
S. M. Small c Law b Rowell	51	– c Jackson b Rowell	47
A. C. Gilchrist c Hayden b Rackemann	19	– b Jackson	1
M. G. Bevan c Wellham b Kasprowicz	3	– b Rowell	10
T. H. Bayliss b Rackemann	10	– c Wellham b Kasprowicz	1
B. E. McNamara c Anderson b Law	2	– c Hayden b Rackemann	13
G. R. J. Matthews b Kasprowicz	23	– c Rowell b Jackson	1
*†P. A. Emery not out	26	– not out	19
W. J. Holdsworth b Kasprowicz	0	– lbw b Rowell	4
R. M. Stobo lbw b Kasprowicz	0	– lbw b Rowell	0
G. D. McGrath b Rackemann	0	– c Hayden b Jackson	8
L-b 3, w 1, n-b 8	12	B 1, l-b 9	10

1/52 2/88 3/93 4/115 5/116   174   1/80 2/81 3/91 4/97 5/100   147
6/126 7/158 8/158 9/174   6/107 7/129 8/136 9/136

Bowling: *First Innings*—Kasprowicz 17–3–41–3; Rackemann 15.3–0–75–5; Rowell 13–3–39–1; Jackson 8–3–9–0; Law 4–1–7–1. *Second Innings*—Kasprowicz 13–3–40–1; Rowell 17–6–39–5; Jackson 21.3–13–27–3; Rackemann 12–4–31–1.

Umpires: A. J. McQuillan, P. D. Parker and C. D. Timmins.

VICTORIA v TASMANIA

At Melbourne, February 26, 27, 28, March 1. Drawn. Tasmania 2 pts, Toss: Tasmania.

This match ended in a manner that might have been thrilling had it not been farcical. Tasmania, set 221 to win off 66 overs, had to be encouraged to chase them by the acting Victorian captain, Jones. In the second-last over, with eight wickets down, Fleming bowled five no-balls, under instructions, to concede ten runs and try to persuade the Tasmanians the game was still alive. Farrell took the bait and was stumped. With one ball left and the last pair together, Tasmania still needed eight. Jones decided nothing was impossible. He ordered Howard to bowl wide and the wicket-keeper to let it through, thus creating an extra ball and a tempting target of four. The ruse would have worked except that umpire King refused to rule the ball a wide. Tasmania were left with first-innings points, achieved through a measured hundred from Tucker and a good all-round performance by Young. Victoria were able to declare their second innings after a career-best 146 not out in six and a half hours by Nobes.

Close of play: First day, Tasmania 10-0 (D. F. Hills 2*, N. C. P. Courtney 7*); Second day, Tasmania 261-8 (R. J. Tucker 102*, C. D. Matthews 2*); Third day, Victoria 207-6 (P. C. Nobes 95*, D. S. Berry 16*).

Victoria

M. T. G. Elliott c Farrell b McPhee	0	(2) lbw b Young	12
W. N. Phillips c Atkinson b McPhee	8	(1) lbw b McPhee	5
P. C. Nobes b McPhee	4	not out	146
*D. M. Jones b Young	37	c Tucker b McPhee	9
D. S. Lehmann c Farrell b Young	69	c Hills b Matthews	46
A. I. C. Dodemaide c Buckingham b Young	35	c Buckingham b Young	3
N. D. Maxwell c Tucker b Matthews	6	lbw b Young	1
†D. S. Berry lbw b McPhee	13	c Atkinson b Matthews	35
J. A. Sutherland not out	18	b Matthews	0
D. W. Fleming c Matthews b Young	1	not out	14
C. Howard c Ponting b Young	7		
B 2, l-b 4, w 1, n-b 20	27	B 1, l-b 6, w 2, n-b 12	21

1/3 2/22 3/27 4/138 5/143   **225**   1/7 2/37 3/58   (8 wkts dec.) **292**
6/162 7/186 8/202 9/208   4/143 5/168 6/170
                                 7/245 8/245

Bowling: *First Innings*—Matthews 20-4-48-1; McPhee 26-3-71-4; Young 23.1-6-56-5; Tucker 7-0-29-0; Farrell 6-0-15-0. *Second Innings*—Matthews 27.5-4-79-3; McPhee 30-10-81-2; Young 29-7-75-3; Tucker 16-1-50-0.

Tasmania

D. F. Hills c Maxwell b Dodemaide	8	c Berry b Fleming	12
N. C. P. Courtney c Maxwell b Dodemaide	10	st Berry b Howard	14
J. Cox c Berry b Fleming	6	c Sutherland b Fleming	51
R. T. Ponting hit wkt b Sutherland	34	c Dodemaide b Howard	64
D. J. Buckingham c Jones b Dodemaide	2	c Berry b Fleming	6
*R. J. Tucker lbw b Fleming	120	c Berry b Maxwell	9
S. Young b Fleming	76	run out	11
†M. N. Atkinson c Elliott b Maxwell	6	(10) not out	7
M. G. Farrell c Berry b Maxwell	0	(9) st Berry b Howard	8
C. D. Matthews not out	19	(8) b Howard	0
P. T. McPhee c Maxwell b Fleming	0	not out	0
B 2, l-b 11, w 1, n-b 2	16	B 11, l-b 6, w 1, n-b 14	32

1/18 2/21 3/33 4/44 5/72   **297**   1/14 2/63 3/113   (9 wkts) **217**
6/234 7/259 8/259 9/297   4/119 5/150 6/177
                                 7/181 8/186 9/213

Bowling: *First Innings*—Fleming 23.4-6-47-4; Dodemaide 38-11-80-3; Maxwell 24-8-57-2; Sutherland 17-3-50-1; Howard 13-2-40-0; Lehmann 4-1-10-0. *Second Innings*—Dodemaide 13-4-21-0; Fleming 22-4-80-3; Howard 17-2-53-4; Maxwell 8-0-34-1; Sutherland 6-2-12-0.

Umpires: T. C. Chapman, D. W. Holt and L. J. King.

SOUTH AUSTRALIA v VICTORIA

At Adelaide, March 5, 6, 7, 8. Drawn. Victoria 2 pts. Toss: South Australia.

Blewett and Brayshaw set the scene for what looked like a big South Australian score with an impressive partnership of 198 in 227 minutes. But at 209 for one, Blewett was caught in the gully, and despite some good hitting by Nielsen, Victoria got back into the game. Phillips virtually assured them of first-innings points with a patient 122, while Jones played effortlessly before missing a high full toss. In the second innings Fleming bowled superbly, forcing South Australia's batsmen to defend rather than set up a declaration. His figures of seven for 90 were his best ever and his victims included Brayshaw, who played his second fine innings of the match. Victoria needed 272 to win off 47 overs and, while Nobes and Jones were adding 91 in an hour, had a fair chance. But Wigney and McIntyre, both originally from Victoria, pinned them back, bowling to deep-set fields, and earned the draw.

Close of play: First day, South Australia 302-6 (T. J. Nielsen 29*, D. A. Reeves 6*); Second day, Victoria 249-4 (W. N. Phillips 110*, S. P. O'Donnell 23*); Third day, South Australia 169-3 (J. A. Brayshaw 94*, T. J. Nielsen 16*).

South Australia

G. S. Blewett c O'Donnell b Maxwell	119	– c Dodemaide b Fleming	19
A. J. Hammond c Maxwell b Dodemaide	2	– (8) c Howard b Fleming	31
J. A. Brayshaw c Berry b Maxwell	91	– (2) lbw b Fleming	110
*J. D. Siddons st Berry b Howard	28	– (3) c Berry b Maxwell	6
D. S. Webber b Fleming	12	– (4) lbw b Fleming	29
†T. J. Nielsen run out	64	– (5) c Berry b Maxwell	20
P. R. Sleep c Berry b Fleming	4	– (6) run out	41
D. A. Reeves lbw b Maxwell	29	– (7) c Maxwell b Fleming	1
B. N. Wigney lbw b Howard	1	– b Fleming	4
D. J. Hickey not out	1	– lbw b Fleming	2
P. E. McIntyre c Berry b Howard	1	– not out	2
B 3, l-b 8	11	B 1, l-b 2, n-b 6	9
	362		**274**

1/11 2/209 3/232 4/252 5/273 6/291 7/356 8/357 9/361

1/27 2/57 3/105 4/179 5/197 6/207 7/247 8/259 9/261

Bowling: *First Innings*—Dodemaide 27–12–67–1; Fleming 28–10–72–2; Maxwell 29–7–81–3; Howard 29.3–8–71–3; O'Donnell 8–0–27–0; Lehmann 3–0–24–0; Jones 2–0–9–0. *Second Innings*—Dodemaide 22.6–6–50–0; Fleming 33.4–8–90–7; Howard 19–5–48–0; Maxwell 21–9–47–2; O'Donnell 6–1–16–0; Lehmann 2–1–4–0; Elliott 1–0–16–0.

Victoria

W. N. Phillips lbw b Wigney	122	– (2) st Nielsen b McIntyre	65
M. T. G. Elliott c Siddons b McIntyre	22	– (1) st Nielsen b McIntyre	19
P. C. Nobes b Hickey	13	– not out	102
D. M. Jones lbw b Reeves	67	– b Wigney	46
D. S. Lehmann lbw b Reeves	4	– b Wigney	19
*S. P. O'Donnell c Blewett b Wigney	86	– run out	1
A. I. C. Dodemaide c Nielsen b Wigney	19	– st Nielsen b McIntyre	0
N. D. Maxwell b Wigney	2	– b Wigney	3
†D. S. Berry not out	3	– not out	3
D. W. Fleming not out	0		
B 7, l-b 5, n-b 15	27	B 1, l-b 1, w 1	3
	365		**261**

1/64 2/97 3/219 4/223 5/301 6/357 7/362 8/362

(8 wkts dec.)

1/64 2/101 3/192 4/218 5/241 6/242 7/247

(7 wkts)

C. Howard did not bat.

Bowling: *First Innings*—Reeves 17–1–75–2; Wigney 27–7–73–4; Hickey 12–0–67–1; McIntyre 39.3–10–92–1; Brayshaw 1–0–1–0; Sleep 14–1–45–0. *Second Innings*—Reeves 4–0–21–0; Wigney 23–2–113–3; Hickey 4–0–23–0; McIntyre 16–0–102–3.

Umpires: S. J. Davis, D. J. Harper and R. B. Woods.

WESTERN AUSTRALIA v QUEENSLAND

At Perth, March 5, 6, 7, 8. Western Australia won by seven wickets. Western Australia 6 pts, Queensland 2 pts. Toss: Western Australia.

The two exiled Test batsmen, Marsh and Moody, made light work of a target of 317 from 88 overs. They shared a partnership of 231 in 221 minutes and Moody hit 13 fours in his only century of the season. Marsh carried on for nearly five hours and saw Western Australia almost to their victory, which came with more than ten overs to spare. Queensland had achieved a first-innings lead after being put in on a well-grassed pitch against an attack that looked less than forbidding, though Julian's persistence earned him five wickets. The Queensland bowlers achieved better control, but their batsmen surrendered the advantage with an inept second-innings display.

Close of play: First day, Queensland 343-8 (P. W. Anderson 38*, P. W. Jackson 1*); Second day, Western Australia 234-5 (M. R. J. Veletta 49*, T. J. Zoehrer 7*); Third day, Queensland 225-9 (D. R. Kingdon 56*, C. G. Rackemann 1*).

Queensland

M. L. Hayden c Lavender b Angel	49	– (2) c Zoehrer b Julian	30
T. J. Barsby c Zoehrer b Julian	13	– (1) c Marsh b Atkinson	28
P. J. T. Goggin c Marsh b Moody	24	– lbw b Moody	32
S. G. Law b Atkinson	116	– c Kelly b Angel	15
*D. M. Wellham c Zoehrer b Julian	36	– c Zoehrer b Julian	14
D. R. Kingdon c Zoehrer b Julian	9	– c Veletta b Angel	59
†P. W. Anderson b Julian	63	– b Julian	0
M. S. Kasprowicz c Julian b Moody	10	– c Zoehrer b Julian	0
G. J. Rowell b Atkinson	3	– c Zoehrer b Atkinson	30
P. W. Jackson not out	5	– lbw b Angel	5
C. G. Rackemann c Kelly b Julian	6	– not out	6
B 12, l-b 18, w 5, n-b 12	47	B 2, n-b 12	14

1/56 2/96 3/139 4/224 5/261   381   1/62 2/66 3/108 4/127 5/139   233
6/314 7/333 8/342 9/375   6/139 7/145 8/190 9/220

Bowling: *First Innings*—Angel 17-3-71-1; Atkinson 28-11-71-2; Julian 29-6-103-5; Moody 23-8-66-2; Stewart 12-2-40-0. *Second Innings*—Angel 19.5-53-3; Atkinson 18-3-73-2; Julian 24-4-82-4; Moody 14-10-18-1; Stewart 6-4-5-0.

Western Australia

M. W. McPhee st Anderson b Jackson	59	– retired hurt	11
*G. R. Marsh c Anderson b Rackemann	8	– b Kasprowicz	107
M. P. Lavender c Law b Rackemann	11	– c Barsby b Rackemann	4
T. M. Moody c Hayden b Kasprowicz	45	– c Rowell b Rackemann	124
M. R. J. Veletta c Kingdon b Rackemann	55	– not out	20
R. C. Kelly c Wellham b Kasprowicz	4	– not out	0
†T. J. Zoehrer c Law b Kasprowicz	35		
B. P. Julian c Hayden b Rackemann	7		
M. P. Atkinson c Anderson b Kasprowicz	14		
J. Angel c Hayden b Kasprowicz	2		
J. Stewart not out	2		
B 4, l-b 10, w 2, n-b 40	56	B 7, l-b 10, w 1, n-b 34	52

1/21 2/71 3/119 4/181 5/195   298   1/25 2/256 3/294   (3 wkts) 318
6/247 7/277 8/277 9/283

In the second innings M. W. McPhee retired hurt at 17.

Bowling: *First Innings*—Kasprowicz 24-7-64-5; Rowell 18-5-61-0; Rackemann 21-3-75-4; Law 16-9-35-0; Jackson 16-3-49-1. *Second Innings*—Kasprowicz 17-3-63-1; Rackemann 17-2-61-2; Rowell 14.1-2-66-0; Law 14-2-56-0; Jackson 15-1-55-0.

Umpires: R. A. Emerson, R. J. Evans and T. A. Prue.

NEW SOUTH WALES v SOUTH AUSTRALIA

At Sydney, March 11, 12, 13, 14. New South Wales won by nine wickets. New South Wales 6 pts. Toss: South Australia.

The New South Wales fast bowlers had a match to remember: Holdsworth returned career-best figures of seven for 81 on the first day, and ten in the match, while McGrath took a best-ever five for 36 on the third day. Unusually the New South Wales spinners did not take a single wicket. Siddons played on a different plane from his South Australian colleagues in the first innings after Holdsworth had them at 117 for six. After surviving a difficult chance to Matthews at slip when 18, Siddons dealt mercilessly with speed and spin alike, hitting 19 fours and a six in 290 minutes. New South Wales also started badly, losing three for 65. But Bevan, after a circumspect start, tore into the South Australian attack. New South Wales gained a lead of 76, whereupon Holdsworth and McGrath finished off South Australia's second innings in three and a half hours. Matthews made no mistake this time, catching Siddons first ball. It took only 50 minutes of the last day for New South Wales to complete a victory which put them back on top of the Shield table.

Close of play: First day, South Australia 317; Second day, New South Wales 338-6 (G. R. J. Matthews 40*, P. A. Emery 24*); Third day, New South Wales 43-0 (M. J. Slater 23*, S. M. Small 19*).

South Australia

G. S. Blewett b Holdsworth	6	– c Emery b McGrath	10
G. A. Bishop lbw b McGrath	11	– c Gilchrist b Holdsworth	7
J. A. Brayshaw c Slater b Holdsworth	19	– lbw b McNamara	15
*J. D. Siddons b Holdsworth	197	– c Matthews b Holdsworth	0
D. S. Webber lbw b Holdsworth	9	– b McNamara	30
†T. J. Nielsen c Chee Quee b Holdsworth	0	– b McGrath	0
J. C. Scuderi c Chee Quee b Holdsworth	6	– not out	57
P. R. Sleep c Matthews b McGrath	27	– c McNamara b McGrath	36
D. A. Reeves lbw b McGrath	24	– b McGrath	0
B. N. Wigney c Emery b Holdsworth	4	– b McGrath	0
P. E. McIntyre not out	0	– b McGrath	3
L-b 4, n-b 10	14	B 2, l-b 1, n-b 2	5

1/16 2/22 3/79 4/105 5/105   317   1/13 2/31 3/31 4/51 5/58   163
6/117 7/190 8/304 9/314   6/70 7/145 8/145 9/148

Bowling: *First Innings*—Holdsworth 25.2-3-81-7; McGrath 23.5-6-62-3; McNamara 17-2-58-0; Matthews 17-0-64-0; Freedman 7-1-48-0. *Second Innings*—Holdsworth 16-0-62-3; McGrath 17.3-4-36-5; Matthews 10-4-33-0; McNamara 9-1-29-2.

New South Wales

M. J. Slater c Siddons b Reeves	1	– not out	48
S. M. Small c Blewett b Reeves	12	– b McIntyre	26
A. C. Gilchrist c Nielsen b Wigney	36	– not out	13
M. G. Bevan c Siddons b Blewett	130		
R. Chee Quee c Nielsen b Scuderi	32		
B. E. McNamara c McIntyre b Blewett	49		
G. R. J. Matthews c Nielsen b Blewett	75		
*†P. A. Emery c Siddons b Wigney	29		
D. A. Freedman lbw b Blewett	9		
W. J. Holdsworth not out	4		
L-b 5, w 3, n-b 8	16	L-b 1	1

1/2 2/27 3/65 4/151 5/272   (9 wkts. dec.) 393   1/63   (1 wkt) 88
6/272 7/358 8/386 9/393

G. D. McGrath did not bat.

Bowling: *First Innings*—Wigney 30-1-96-2; Reeves 14-1-83-2; Blewett 15.2-2-45-4; Sleep 2-0-22-0; Scuderi 21-4-60-1; McIntyre 26-6-74-0; Brayshaw 4-1-8-0. *Second Innings*—Wigney 7-2-12-0; Reeves 5-1-27-0; Blewett 2-1-3-0; McIntyre 10.1-3-21-1; Sleep 10-2-24-0.

Umpires: P. E. Dodd, K. J. Duffy and D. B. Hair.

TASMANIA v WESTERN AUSTRALIA

At Hobart, March 11, 12, 13, 14. Drawn. Tasmania 2 pts. Toss: Tasmania.

With both sides anxious for outright points, Tucker gave Western Australia first use of a moist wicket. His bowlers had the visitors floundering at 75 for six before they were rescued by a dynamic partnership of 196 from Zoehrer and Julian. Zoehrer reached 136 before holing out to deep square leg. However, Ponting's superb strokeplay ensured first-innings points for Tasmania by lunch on the third day. To general surprise, Tucker delayed his declaration for 20 minutes. Initially he seemed to have made his point as Peter McPhee disposed of Marsh and Lavender with consecutive balls in his first over, Lavender thus failing to survive a ball in either innings. But a stand of 131 between Moody and Veletta baulked Tasmania's hopes. Tasmania eventually needed 251 off 50 overs. Three run-outs did not help their cause and Tucker abandoned the run-chase with 16 overs left, even though Ponting was in full flow. Another exotic innings made Ponting the youngest player to score two centuries in a Shield match at 18 years 85 days.

Close of play: First day, Western Australia 265-6 (T. J. Zoehrer 104*, B. P. Julian 84*); Second day, Tasmania 235-3 (R. T. Ponting 62*, C. R. Miller 1*); Third day, Western Australia 144-3 (T. M. Moody 71*, M. R. J. Veletta 60*).

Western Australia

M. W. McPhee c Buckingham b Matthews	14	– lbw b Matthews		12
*G. R. Marsh b Young	6	– b McPhee		0
M. P. Lavender lbw b Matthews	0	– b McPhee		0
T. M. Moody c Cox b Miller	8	– c Cox b McPhee		71
M. R. J. Veletta b Young	25	– c Tucker b Courtney		104
R. C. Kelly lbw b Miller	7	– c Ponting b Miller		34
†T. J. Zoehrer c Courtney b Miller	136	– c Miller b Young		52
B. P. Julian c Atkinson b Matthews	87	– c Ponting b Young		4
M. P. Atkinson c Buckingham b Matthews	4	– run out		7
J. Angel run out	8	– not out		5
J. Stewart not out	0	– run out		5
B 5, l-b 13, w 2, n-b 6	26	L-b 2, w 1, n-b 2		5
	321			299

1/22 2/22 3/22 4/39 5/61   1/1 2/1 3/13 4/144 5/210
6/75 7/271 8/277 9/307   6/271 7/276 8/288 9/289

Bowling: *First Innings*—McPhee 28-8-68-0; Matthews 39-14-77-4; Young 16-2-61-2; Miller 20.2-2-59-3; Tucker 9-1-32-0; Courtney 2-0-6-0. *Second Innings*—McPhee 24-8-45-3; Matthews 16-5-44-1; Young 17-3-46-1; Miller 19-7-54-2; Tucker 15-3-69-0; Courtney 10-2-38-1; Buckingham 2-1-1-0.

Tasmania

D. F. Hills c Zoehrer b Julian	57	– run out		0
N. C. P. Courtney c Atkinson b Julian	56	– c Angel b Moody		12
J. Cox st Zoehrer b Stewart	45	– c McPhee b Angel		22
R. T. Ponting c Zoehrer b Angel	107	– not out		100
C. R. Miller c Zoehrer b Angel	3			
D. J. Buckingham lbw b Angel	15	– (5) run out		18
*R. J. Tucker c Zoehrer b Atkinson	16	– (6) c Marsh b Stewart		21
S. Young not out	50	– (7) not out		0
†M. N. Atkinson not out	2	– (8) not out		7
L-b 11, w 2, n-b 6	19	B 3, l-b 2, w 1, n-b 4		10
	(7 wkts dec.) 370		(6 wkts)	190

1/84 2/147 3/223 4/238 5/293   1/1 2/18 3/67
6/300 7/354   4/101 5/145 6/146

C. D. Matthews and P. T. McPhee did not bat.

Bowling: *First Innings*—Angel 25-5-97-3; Atkinson 21-1-86-1; Julian 26-6-69-2; Moody 19-5-45-0; Stewart 18.1-4-62-1. *Second Innings*—Julian 10-0-32-0; Moody 10-1-40-1; Angel 6-1-35-1; Stewart 13-2-39-1; Atkinson 7-0-38-0; Marsh 1-0-1-0.

Umpires: T. R. Hogarth, B. T. Knight and S. G. Randell.

SOUTH AUSTRALIA v WESTERN AUSTRALIA

At Adelaide, March 18, 29, 20, 21. South Australia won by nine wickets. South Australia 6 pts. Toss: South Australia. First-class debut: G. J. Wright.

A recent Paul McCartney concert had left the Adelaide Oval seemingly under-prepared for cricket and Siddons gave Western Australia the first innings. Though Lavender promptly achieved his third consecutive nought the pitch held few terrors for the other batsmen and Veletta provided a solid back-up to the more aggressive McPhee and Zoehrer. Marsh's declaration, just after Veletta's hundred, was born of desperation for outright points. But in five hours on the second day, South Australia rattled up 313 for two. Siddons played another superb innings, but he was outshone by Blewett, who hooked and pulled the faster bowlers mercilessly to the short square boundaries. On the third morning, however, Moody bowled an inspired spell; South Australia lost six for 11, and only limped to a first-innings lead. As Western Australia pressed for quick runs, Sleep bowled his leg-spinners superbly to take seven for 79, his best-ever figures at the Adelaide Oval in his last match there. With the weather uncertain, Marsh declared overnight, setting South Australia 225 in a day. Thanks to a superb 112 from Blewett plus solid contributions from Faull and Brayshaw, they cruised to victory in under four hours. Reid, in his first game back for Western Australia after injury, failed to take a wicket in the match.

Close of play: First day, Western Australia 256-5 (M. R. J. Veletta 83*, T. J. Zoehrer 9*); Second day, South Australia 313-2 (J. A. Brayshaw 81*, J. D. Siddons 103*); Third day, Western Australia 235-9 (J. Angel 2*, B. A. Reid 10*).

Western Australia

M. P. Lavender b Wigney	0	– lbw b Scuderi	22
*G. R. Marsh run out	23	– b Sleep	50
J. L. Langer c George b Scuderi	38	– c Faull b Sleep	40
T. M. Moody lbw b Blewett	29	– c Siddons b Sleep	17
M. R. J. Veletta not out	104	– c Webber b Sleep	37
M. W. McPhee c Blewett b George	59	– (8) c Wigney b Sleep	7
†T. J. Zoehrer not out	51	– (6) lbw b Sleep	8
B. P. Julian (did not bat)	–	(7) b Wigney	22
J. Angel (did not bat)	–	not out	2
J. Stewart (did not bat)	–	st Nielsen b Sleep	9
B. A. Reid (did not bat)	–	not out	10
B 1, l-b 9, w 5, n-b 4	19	B 2, l-b 7, n-b 2	11

1/0 2/39 3/90 4/114 5/247 (5 wkts dec.) 323   1/52 2/106 3/130 (9 wkts dec.) 235
4/141 5/157 6/194
7/209 8/213 9/223

Bowling: *First Innings*—Wigney 29-4-98-1; George 30-6-76-1; Scuderi 18-5-34-1; Blewett 16-5-42-1; Sleep 11-2-37-0; Brayshaw 11-5-26-0. *Second Innings*—Wigney 21-8-44-1; George 20-3-63-0; Blewett 7-4-17-0; Scuderi 7-0-23-1; Sleep 22-5-79-7.

South Australia

G. S. Blewett lbw b Stewart	80	– not out	112
M. P. Faull b Angel	31	– lbw b Zoehrer	56
J. A. Brayshaw c Zoehrer b Angel	82	– not out	47
*J. D. Siddons run out	108		
D. S. Webber c Langer b Moody	0		
G. J. Wright not out	10		
†T. J. Nielsen lbw b Moody	2		
J. C. Scuderi c Julian b Moody	0		
P. R. Sleep c Stewart b Moody	3		
B. N. Wigney not out	0		
B 3, l-b 5, w 4, n-b 6	18	L-b 11	11

1/68 2/124 3/319 4/319 5/319 (8 wkts dec.) 334   1/126 (1 wkt) 226
6/322 7/322 8/330

S. P. George did not bat.

Bowling: *First Innings*—Reid 16–1–62–0; Julian 17–4–61–0; Moody 19–6–44–4; Angel 22–6–70–2; Stewart 14–4–64–1; Zoehrer 5–1–25–0. *Second Innings*—Angel 16–5–39–0; Reid 10–4–39–0; Moody 4–0–18–0; Julian 8–2–36–0; Stewart 14–3–48–0; Zoehrer 11–2–35–1.

Umpires: S. J. Davis, D. J. Harper and R. B. Woods.

TASMANIA v QUEENSLAND

At Hobart, March 18, 19, 20, 21. Tasmania won by six wickets. Tasmania 6 pts. Toss: Tasmania.

Tasmania secured their second outright win of the season over Queensland; it was all the sweeter because Wellham, their former captain, led their victims on both occasions. They began by asking Queensland to bat, but the visitors started well, Barsby and Hayden posting their fourth century opening stand of the season after Barsby survived a huge appeal for a catch at the wicket first ball. He then laid about him to great effect, making 100 out of 165 in 165 minutes until he hit a tame catch to mid-off. The Queensland innings folded to some steady bowling by McPhee and Young, and Tasmania's batsmen made short work of passing 290; Hills batted for more than a day and steered his side towards a lead of 49. Rain washed out most of the third day and Queensland, in desperate need of points, had to set up a fourth-day declaration to have any chance. But Wellham's dismissal, to a dubious catch behind off Matthews, precipitated another dreadful collapse. Thanks to the enterprise of Hills and Courtney, Tasmania easily reached a target of 162 off 37 overs.

Close of play: First day, Queensland 290; Second day, Tasmania 263-5 (D. F. Hills 105*, S. Young 49*); Third day, Tasmania 339.

Queensland

T. J. Barsby c Miller b Matthews	100	– c Hills b Young	12
M. L. Hayden c Cox b Young	82	– b Miller	34
P. J. T. Goggin c Ponting b Miller	14	– (6) lbw b Tucker	5
S. G. Law c Atkinson b Young	21	– c Miller b Matthews	37
*D. M. Wellham lbw b Young	4	– (3) c Atkinson b Matthews	74
D. R. Kingdon b McPhee	5	– (5) c Atkinson b Matthews	1
†P. W. Anderson c Ponting b Matthews	35	– c Atkinson b Matthews	6
M. S. Kasprowicz c Atkinson b McPhee	5	– c Tucker b Miller	21
G. J. Rowell lbw b McPhee	0	– c Ponting b Miller	6
P. W. Jackson c Courtney b McPhee	5	– not out	3
C. G. Rackemann not out	3	– c Atkinson b Matthews	3
L-b 7, w 1, n-b 8	16	L-b 6, w 2	8

1/178 2/207 3/207 4/222 5/237   290   1/24 2/92 3/156 4/165 5/170   210
6/245 7/255 8/255 9/284   6/170 7/197 8/197 9/207

Bowling: *First Innings*—Matthews 22.4–3–70–2; McPhee 22–8–77–4; Miller 23–4–75–1; Young 19–8–47–3; Tucker 3–1–13–0; Courtney 1–0–1–0. *Second Innings*—Matthews 23.1–6–72–5; McPhee 14–5–30–0; Young 9–2–43–1; Miller 15–5–33–3; Courtney 1–0–5–0; Tucker 10–4–21–1.

Tasmania

D. F. Hills run out	110	– c Wellham b Rackemann	50
N. C. P. Courtney c Barsby b Rowell	5	– c Anderson b Rackemann	37
J. Cox c Anderson b Rowell	0	– c Rowell b Rackemann	11
R. T. Ponting c Law b Rowell	12	– c Kasprowicz b Rowell	27
D. J. Buckingham c Wellham b Jackson	61	– not out	27
*R. J. Tucker c Law b Jackson	14	– not out	3
S. Young c Kasprowicz b Rackemann	53		
†M. N. Atkinson c Goggin b Rowell	16		
C. D. Matthews run out	35		
C. R. Miller not out	9		
P. T. McPhee c Anderson b Kasprowicz	0		
L-b 12, n-b 12	24	L-b 2, w 1, n-b 4	7

1/20 2/20 3/36 4/125 5/145   339   1/82 2/91 3/115 4/144   (4 wkts) 162
6/272 7/273 8/326 9/332

Bowling: *First Innings*—Kasprowicz 30.4–6–91–1; Rowell 27–7–95–4; Rackemann 26–5–67–1; Jackson 32–12–60–2; Law 5–0–14–0. *Second Innings*—Rowell 8.4–2–37–1; Kasprowicz 4–1–22–0; Rackemann 10–1–51–3; Jackson 13–1–50–0.

Umpires: R. P. Donaldson, T. R. Hogarth and S. G. Randell.

VICTORIA v NEW SOUTH WALES

At Melbourne, March 18, 19, 20, 21. New South Wales won by 58 runs. New South Wales 5.6 pts, Victoria 2 pts. Toss: New South Wales. First-class debut: A. J. Amalfi.

New South Wales came from behind to confirm their place at the top of the table and relegate Victoria to the dreaded wooden spoon. An old hand, Matthews, pulled the game back with six wickets in Victoria's first innings; then a century from the young opener, Slater, set up the declaration and pace bowler Holdsworth upgraded his career-best analysis for the second consecutive match. Impetuosity more than anything else had undone New South Wales's first innings. They reached 87 for one with Slater in full flow, then wickets tumbled to some extravagant strokes while leg-spinner Howard reinforced his reputation. Victoria made a steady reply, though Lehmann got out when well set. O'Donnell swung mightily and hit two sixes, the second ending up on the second tier of the Southern stand. But he was caught when Matthews lured him into attempting another. Slater's class quickly wiped out a first-innings deficit of 76 and established a useful lead for New South Wales. His 143 took just over six hours and a stand of 129 runs with the determined Emery seemed to deflate the Victorians. A generous declaration left Victoria a day plus half an hour to score 276. Two devastating spells by Holdsworth decided the match. Three wickets for six runs in 13 balls had Victoria reeling at 37 for four; then, after a defiant stand of 145 between Lehmann and O'Donnell, he took four wickets for three in 19 balls to conclude the contest.

Close of play: First day, Victoria 55-1 (M. T. G. Elliott 26*, W. N. Phillips 23*); Second day, New South Wales 86-2 (M. J. Slater 47*, P. A. Emery 0*); Third day, Victoria 10-1 (A. J. Amalfi 0*, D. W. Fleming 5*).

New South Wales

M. J. Slater c Cook b O'Donnell	53	– lbw b Fleming 143
S. M. Small c Fleming b Maxwell	21	– c Maxwell b Fleming........ 9
A. C. Gilchrist c Elliott b Cook	13	– b Lehmann 28
M. G. Bevan c Maxwell b Howard	14	– (5) c Amalfi b Fleming 65
R. Chee Quee b Howard	20	– (6) b Maxwell 18
B. E. McNamara c Elliott b Fleming	18	– (7) not out 15
G. R. J. Matthews c Maxwell b Howard	22	– (8) lbw b Maxwell 9
*†P. A. Emery c Fleming b Maxwell	0	– (4) c Berry b Maxwell 58
W. J. Holdsworth c Maxwell b Howard	6	– c Lehmann b Maxwell 0
M. R. Whitney b Cook	9	– not out 0
G. D. McGrath not out	6	
		B 1, l-b 1, w 2, n-b 2 6

1/35 2/87 3/87 4/116 5/121   182   1/14 2/85 3/214   (8 wkts dec.) 351
6/147 7/148 8/167 9/167   4/294 5/325 6/325
                           7/343 8/343

Bowling: *First Innings*—Cook 13.3–3–42–2; Fleming 16–3–39–1; Maxwell 15–4–44–2; O'Donnell 6–1–14–1; Howard 14–4–43–4. *Second Innings*—Cook 21–1–71–0; Fleming 31–4–100–3; Maxwell 27–9–79–4; Howard 21–2–82–0; O'Donnell 6–3–6–0; Lehmann 10–5–11–1.

Victoria

A. J. Amalfi b Holdsworth	4	– (2) c Emery b Holdsworth	6
M. T. G. Elliott c Emery b Matthews	52	– (1) lbw b McGrath	3
W. N. Phillips c Matthews b McGrath	23	– (4) c Emery b Holdsworth	7
D. S. Lehmann c Emery b Holdsworth	37	– (5) b Holdsworth	84
L. D. Harper c Gilchrist b Matthews	53	– (6) c McNamara b Holdsworth	2
*S. P. O'Donnell c Gilchrist b Matthews	58	– (7) c Emery b Whitney	86
N. D. Maxwell lbw b Matthews	14	– (8) lbw b Matthews	1
†D. S. Berry c and b Matthews	4	– (9) c Slater b Holdsworth	10
D. W. Fleming lbw b McNamara	6	– (3) b Holdsworth	7
C. Howard b Matthews	0	– not out	2
S. H. Cook not out	0	– lbw b Holdsworth	0
B 2, l-b 3, n-b 2	7	L-b 7, n-b 2	9

1/4 2/63 3/111 4/121 5/193   258   1/3 2/20 3/29 4/37 5/182   217
6/245 7/249 8/256 9/258   6/187 7/206 8/210 9/215

In the second innings D. W. Fleming, when 5, retired hurt at 10 and resumed at 206.

Bowling: *First Innings*—Holdsworth 12–1–48–2; McGrath 15–4–50–1; Whitney 15–4–58–0; McNamara 12.2–3–21–1; Matthews 31–11–76–6. *Second Innings*—Holdsworth 17.4–2–52–7; McGrath 16–3–59–1; McNamara 4–2–13–0; Whitney 15–4–41–1; Matthews 19–4–45–1.

Umpires: P. H. Jensen, L. J. King and S. C. Walpole.

FINAL

NEW SOUTH WALES v QUEENSLAND

At Sydney, March 26, 27, 28, 29, 30. New South Wales won by eight wickets. Toss: New South Wales. First-class debut: M. L. Love.

Queensland collapsed abjectly in two and threequarter hours in their second innings to just 75 all out, the lowest total in a Shield Final and the lowest of the season. This left New South Wales to claim victory – and their 41st Shield – early on the fifth morning. Emery had predictably given Queensland first use of a pitch whose location at one side of the square and mottled appearance dismayed the visitors. After Holdsworth fired out Hayden and Wellham in no time, the New South Wales fieldsmen dropped five catches. Law, who was not one of the beneficiaries, batted superbly, and, with Barsby, launched a calculated attack on the off-spinner Matthews. They plundered 41 runs off seven overs; next morning, however, Matthews helped McGrath finish off Queensland for a modest 311. Law was given out caught behind off Matthews and immediately went on radio to publicise his misfortune at being the victim of umpiring error. The next 13 hours were taken up by the New South Wales first innings: Slater and Small made a solid start but when Slater was stumped, swinging wildly at Jackson, Matthews took it upon himself not only to obstruct Queensland's challenge but virtually to bring the match to a standstill. For seven hours, he blocked and fiddled, and provoked as often as possible. New South Wales, needing only to avoid defeat to win the Shield, crawled to a lead of 30; more to the point, they left Queensland less than two days to build a lead and bowl them out again. It was never on. The batting bore an air of dejected surrender, which was all the encouragement Holdsworth needed. For the third match running, he took seven wickets in an innings and bettered his own best figures.

Close of play: First day, Queensland 226-4 (S. G. Law 124*, M. L. Love 12*); Second day, New South Wales 133-2 (A. C. Gilchrist 6*, M. G. Bevan 1*); Third day, New South Wales 291-6 (G. R. J. Matthews 64*, P. A. Emery 9*); Fourth day, New South Wales 9-1 (M. J. Slater 1*, A. C. Gilchrist 3*).

Queensland

T. J. Barsby c Emery b Whitney	51	– (2) lbw b Holdsworth	19
M. L. Hayden c Bevan b Holdsworth	4	– (1) c Matthews b Holdsworth	4
*D. M. Wellham c and b Holdsworth	0	– c Emery b Holdsworth	1
S. G. Law c Emery b Matthews	142	– c Holdsworth b McGrath	13
P. J. T. Goggin lbw b McGrath	19	– c Emery b Holdsworth	0
M. L. Love c Emery b McGrath	42	– c Emery b McGrath	9
†P. W. Anderson c Whitney b Matthews	2	– b Holdsworth	9
M. S. Kasprowicz c Slater b McGrath	7	– c Gilchrist b McGrath	0
G. J. Rowell b Matthews	26	– not out	6
P. W. Jackson not out	0	– c McNamara b Holdsworth	2
C. G. Rackemann b McGrath	0	– b Holdsworth	4
L-b 5, w 1, n-b 12	18	B 4, l-b 2, n-b 2	8

1/13 2/13 3/105 4/184 5/259   311   1/12 2/18 3/39 4/39 5/42   75
6/269 7/277 8/298 9/310   6/50 7/58 8/58 9/67

Bowling: *First Innings*—Holdsworth 18–5–43–2; McGrath 24.5–5–64–4; Whitney 22–7–55–1; Matthews 19–4–89–3; McNamara 11–1–55–0. *Second Innings*—Holdsworth 19–8–41–7; McGrath 18–5–28–3.

New South Wales

M. J. Slater st Anderson b Jackson	69	– c Rackemann b Kasprowicz	18
S. M. Small c Rackemann b Rowell	40	– c Hayden b Kasprowicz	0
A. C. Gilchrist c Anderson b Rowell	6	– not out	20
M. G. Bevan b Jackson	10	– not out	1
B. E. McNamara lbw b Rackemann	29		
G. R. J. Matthews c Hayden b Jackson	78		
T. H. Bayliss run out	26		
*†P. A. Emery c Barsby b Rackemann	17		
W. J. Holdsworth not out	10		
M. R. Whitney b Kasprowicz	7		
G. D. McGrath c Anderson b Kasprowicz	0		
B 5, l-b 12, n-b 32	49	W 3, n-b 4	7

1/119 2/124 3/134 4/146 5/195   341   1/0 2/45   (2 wkts) 46
6/261 7/320 8/322 9/341

Bowling: *First Innings*—Rackemann 37–5–92–2; Rowell 38–11–65–2; Kasprowicz 30.5–9–67–2; Jackson 69–34–91–3; Law 9–3–9–0. *Second Innings*—Rowell 6.2–1–23–0; Kasprowicz 6–1–23–2.

Umpires: D. B. Hair, T. A. Prue and S. G. Randell.

SHEFFIELD SHIELD WINNERS

1925-26	New South Wales	1962-63	Victoria
1926-27	South Australia	1963-64	South Australia
1927-28	Victoria	1964-65	New South Wales
1928-29	New South Wales	1965-66	New South Wales
1929-30	Victoria	1966-67	Victoria
1930-31	Victoria	1967-68	Western Australia
1931-32	New South Wales	1968-69	South Australia
1932-33	New South Wales	1969-70	Victoria
1933-34	Victoria	1970-71	South Australia
1934-35	Victoria	1971-72	Western Australia
1935-36	South Australia	1972-73	Western Australia
1936-37	Victoria	1973-74	Victoria
1937-38	New South Wales	1974-75	Western Australia
1938-39	South Australia	1975-76	South Australia
1939-40	New South Wales	1976-77	Western Australia
1940-46	No competition	1977-78	Western Australia
1946-47	Victoria	1978-79	Victoria
1947-48	Western Australia	1979-80	Victoria
1948-49	New South Wales	1980-81	Western Australia
1949-50	New South Wales	1981-82	South Australia
1950-51	Victoria	1982-83	New South Wales
1951-52	New South Wales	1983-84	Western Australia
1952-53	South Australia	1984-85	New South Wales
1953-54	New South Wales	1985-86	New South Wales
1954-55	New South Wales	1986-87	Western Australia
1955-56	New South Wales	1987-88	Western Australia
1956-57	New South Wales	1988-89	Western Australia
1957-58	New South Wales	1989-90	New South Wales
1958-59	New South Wales	1990-91	Victoria
1959-60	New South Wales	1991-92	Western Australia
1960-61	New South Wales	1992-93	New South Wales
1961-62	New South Wales		

New South Wales have won the Shield 41 times, Victoria 25, Western Australia 13, South Australia 12, Queensland 0, Tasmania 0.

MERCANTILE MUTUAL INSURANCE CUP

Note: Matches in this section were not first-class.

At Perth, October 9 (day/night). Western Australia won by ten wickets. Toss: Victoria. Victoria 132 (42.3 overs) (D. S. Lehmann 37; T. M. Moody three for 29, D. R. Martyn three for three); Western Australia 135 for no wkt (32.4 overs) (G. R. Marsh 51 not out, M. R. J. Veletta 72 not out).

At Brisbane, October 10. Queensland won by eight wickets. Toss: South Australia. South Australia 158 for eight (50 overs) (G. A. Bishop 63, T. J. Nielsen 34); Queensland 159 for two (43.4 overs) (M. L. Hayden 73 not out, P. J. T. Goggin 60).

At Perth, October 11. Western Australia won by eight wickets. Toss: Western Australia. New South Wales 206 for eight (50 overs) (S. M. Small 48, M. A. Taylor 84, M. G. Bevan 41; B. P. Julian three for 31, B. A. Reid three for 19); Western Australia 207 for two (47.5 overs) (M. R. J. Veletta 58, J. L. Langer 30, T. M. Moody 52 not out, D. R. Martyn 49 not out).

At Perth, October 17. Tasmania won by seven wickets. Toss: Tasmania. Western Australia 218 for eight (50 overs) (J. L. Langer 65, M. P. Lavender 51, W. S. Andrews 38 not out; P. T. McPhee three for 19, A. J. De Winter three for 39); Tasmania 219 for three (48.5 overs) (D. F. Hills 77 not out, N. C. P. Courtney 35, D. C. Boon 80).

At Adelaide, October 18. New South Wales won by 111 runs. Toss: South Australia. New South Wales 298 for three (50 overs) (S. M. Small 80, M. A. Taylor 67, S. R. Waugh 85 not out, M. E. Waugh 55); South Australia 187 (45.5 overs) (G. S. Blewett 31, J. A. Brayshaw 43).

At Adelaide, October 24. South Australia won by 36 runs. Toss: South Australia. South Australia 249 for six (50 overs) (J. A. Brayshaw 101 not out, J. D. Siddons 35); Tasmania 213 for seven (50 overs) (N. C. P. Courtney 40, R. J. Tucker 39, A. J. De Winter 34 not out).

At Brisbane, October 25. Queensland won by six wickets. Toss: Western Australia. Western Australia 221 for seven (50 overs) (J. L. Langer 87, W. S. Andrews 56, T. J. Zoehrer 34 not out); Queensland 222 for four (45.2 overs) (M. L. Hayden 121 not out, T. J. Barsby 76).

At Adelaide, October 31. Western Australia won by six wickets. Toss: South Australia. South Australia 173 for seven (47 overs) (N. R. Fielke 38, J. D. Siddons 32; J. Angel three for 37); Western Australia 176 for four (44.4 overs) (T. M. Moody 43, J. L. Langer 55 not out).

At Brisbane, November 1. New South Wales won by 11 runs. Toss: Queensland. New South Wales 252 for eight (50 overs) (S. R. Waugh 131); Queensland 241 for nine (50 overs) (T. J. Barsby 47, S. G. Law 34, A. R. Border 36, S. C. Storey 48, M. S. Kasprowicz 34; S. R. Waugh three for 50).

At Sydney, November 4. (day/night). No result. Toss: New South Wales. New South Wales 286 for five (50 overs) (M. A. Taylor 71, S. R. Waugh 48, M. E. Waugh 39, M. G. Bevan 77 not out); Victoria 40 for one (8.5 overs).

At Carlton, November 15. Victoria won by three wickets. Toss: Victoria. Queensland 210 for eight (50 overs) (T. J. Barsby 67, P. J. T. Goggin 44, A. R. Border 40 not out); Victoria 211 for seven (49.4 overs) (P. C. Nobes 86, D. M. Jones 41).

At Devonport, December 13. Victoria won by 58 runs. Toss: Tasmania. Victoria 222 (49 overs) (P. C. Nobes 52, D. S. Lehmann 76; N. C. P. Courtney four for 19); Tasmania 164 (46.5 overs) (D. F. Hills 35, D. J. Buckingham 30; A. I. C. Dodemaide three for 11, S. K. Warne three for 31).

At Sydney, January 31. New South Wales won by two wickets. Toss: Tasmania. Tasmania 219 (50 overs) (D. F. Hills 81, R. J. Tucker 50; W. J. Holdsworth three for 51); New South Wales 221 for eight (49.2 overs) (S. M. Small 31, B. E. McNamara 65 not out, P. A. Emery 47; R. J. Tucker three for 32).

At Hobart, February 6. Queensland won by 23 runs. Toss: Tasmania. Queensland 217 for six (50 overs) (M. L. Hayden 52, P. J. T. Goggin 51); Tasmania 194 (47.2 overs) (J. Cox 42, D. J. Buckingham 40; G. J. Rowell three for 35).

At Melbourne, February 7. Victoria won by seven wickets. Toss: Victoria. South Australia 135 for nine (50 overs) (J. C. Scuderi 31 not out; D. W. Fleming three for 25); Victoria 136 for three (26.2 overs) (M. T. G. Elliott 60, P. C. Nobes 37).

Qualifying Final

At Melbourne, February 13. Victoria won by 78 runs. Toss: Western Australia. Victoria 187 for nine (50 overs) (D. M. Jones 90 not out; B. P. Julian three for 41); Western Australia 109 (42.1 overs) (J. A. Sutherland three for 26, N. D. Maxwell four for 13).

FINAL

NEW SOUTH WALES v VICTORIA

At Sydney, February 20. New South Wales won by four wickets. Toss: Victoria.
Man of the Match: B. E. McNamara.

Victoria

M. T. G. Elliott st Emery b Robertson . 29	†D. S. Berry not out 21
P. C. Nobes c Emery b Robertson..... 41	J. A. Sutherland run out 0
D. M. Jones c Emery b McNamara.... 4	D. W. Fleming run out 1
D. S. Lehmann lbw McNamara....... 0	B 2, l-b 6, w 1, n-b 1 10
R. J. Herman c Robertson b Bayliss ... 20	
*S. P. O'Donnell lbw Bayliss 13	1/71 2/82 3/82 (50 overs) 186
A. I. C. Dodemaide c Emery b Stobo ... 13	4/82 5/114 6/115
N. D. Maxwell b McNamara......... 34	7/146 8/180 9/181

Bowling: McGrath 7-1-21-0; Stobo 10-2-49-1; McNamara 10-1-27-3; Robertson 10-3-35-2; Matthews 9-1-26-0; Bayliss 4-0-20-2.

New South Wales

M. J. Slater c Berry b Lehmann....... 54	A. C. Gilchrist b Fleming............ 0
S. M. Small c Elliott b Sutherland 31	G. R. Robertson not out 2
T. H. Bayliss c Lehmann b O'Donnell.. 4	B 1, l-b 3, w 2.............. 6
M. G. Bevan not out 64	
G. R. J. Matthews run out 0	1/39 2/56 3/120 (6 wkts, 49.4 overs) 187
B. E. McNamara run out 26	4/120 5/178 6/183

*†P. A. Emery, R. M. Stobo and G. D. McGrath did not bat.

Bowling: Dodemaide 10-2-38-0; Fleming 9.4-1-36-1; Sutherland 10-4-27-1; O'Donnell 7-2-28-1; Lehmann 8-1-26-1; Maxwell 5-0-28-0.

Umpires: D. B. Hair and C. D. Timmins.

SHEFFIELD SHIELD PLAYER OF THE YEAR

The Sheffield Shield Player of the Year Award for 1992-93 was won by J. D. Siddons of South Australia. The award, instituted in 1975-76, is adjudicated by the umpires over the course of the season. Each of the three umpires standing in each of the 30 Sheffield Shield matches during 1992-93 (excluding the final) allocated marks of 3, 2 and 1 to the three players who most impressed them during the game. Siddons earned 28 votes in his ten matches, four more than his nearest rival, G. R. J. Matthews of New South Wales.

CRICKET IN SOUTH AFRICA, 1992-93

By COLIN BRYDEN and FRANK HEYDENRYCH

For the first time since 1969-70, official international cricket was played in South Africa, with a full tour by India, who played four Tests and seven internationals, followed by a triangular one-day series between West Indies, Pakistan and South Africa.

The local domestic season was built around the major events, with the unfortunate consequence that there were gaps of up to 40 days in the programme for those players not in the national squad. The only first-class competition for the senior provinces, the Castle Cup, consisted of a single round of six four-day matches which were completed as early as January 12, effectively bringing to an end first-class cricket for the season. Although the limited-overs competitions remained to be decided, no domestic matches were scheduled during the triangular series which occupied most of February. For many players, therefore, it was a disjointed and unsatisfactory season. In particular there was widespread dissatisfaction at the paucity of first-class cricket, even for those who played in all four Tests.

Public interest in the game soared, however. A total of 793,317 spectators paid to watch cricket matches during the season, more than double the number that attended in 1991-92. Although the increase was mainly due to the international matches, attendance at domestic cricket was slightly up, the floodlit Benson and Hedges Series leading the way with 235,099 spectators. The Indian tour games were watched by 277,023 people while the ten matches in the Total Triangular series accounted for 168,728.

With South Africa winning the Test series against India to continue their moderately successful return to the international arena since readmission to ICC in 1991, there was cause for satisfaction at the general standard of the game in the country. This was reinforced by some good cricket in the Castle Cup. Particularly pleasing was the improvement in the standard of pitches, with provinces responding to a call from the United Cricket Board to produce pitches of near-Test quality. This followed several years of "doctored" pitches, designed to achieve results when domestic success was paramount. An exception to this satisfactory trend was Newlands in Cape Town, where the wickets seemed to be a problem throughout the season. Western Province have now brought in Andy Atkinson, the Edgbaston groundsman, from England to supervise the pitch preparation.

Despite a general acknowledgment that at international level South Africa's principal strengths were in seam bowling and fielding, batsmen prospered in these conditions; no fewer than ten of them averaged over 50 in the Castle Cup. Of these the only man not qualified to play for South Africa was Allan Lamb of England, who returned to his native Western Province after a ten-year absence and was the leading run-scorer with 636 (average 70.66). Lamb and Jimmy Cook of Transvaal each hit three centuries in the competition.

Three West Indians featured among the leading bowlers. The 34-year-old former Test star Malcolm Marshall, playing for Natal, topped the Castle Cup averages with 28 wickets at 16.10, Eldine Baptiste of Eastern Province was third with 25 wickets at 18.48 while the young Barbadian, Ottis Gibson, was named Castle Player of the Season after his efforts for Border.

Gibson was the leading wicket-taker with 33 at 24.15 and also played some stirring innings.

Orange Free State, with the fewest cricketers of any of the major provinces, won the first-class competition for the first time in their history in somewhat surprising circumstances. Transvaal led by four points from Free State and Western Province and by two from Eastern Province going into the last round of matches. After several twists of fortune in a remarkable home match against Natal, Transvaal recovered from a first-innings deficit and entered the final day with all second-innings wickets standing and only 145 runs required to win the match and the cup. They collapsed against the pace of Marshall and the off-spin of Patrick Symcox, the latter proving a potent threat on an increasingly helpful pitch.

Despite taking no points, Transvaal still had a faint hope of glory, depending on the other two matches in progress. Eastern Province could do no better than take two points for a first-innings lead in a rain-affected encounter with Northern Transvaal. Free State, meanwhile, produced a splendid performance against Western Province to take six points for an outright victory and leapfrog over their rivals.

Free State had developed a stable squad over a number of seasons and survived the loss of an inspirational coach in Eddie Barlow, who switched his allegiance to Transvaal, and the absence for half the season of Hansie Cronje, an outstanding young captain, who was playing for South Africa. Corrie van Zyl assumed the role of coach and, when Cronje was away, captain. Fast bowler Allan Donald and left-arm spinner Omar Henry also missed matches because of Test duty. Van Zyl, Henry and the West Indian Franklyn Stephenson were the main wicket-takers in a well-balanced attack, while Free State's batsmen seldom let the side down. Despite playing in only three matches, Cronje was a major contributor, scoring 395 runs at 98.75 including a crucial innings of 161 not out, his career-best, in the final victory.

Transvaal survived the trauma of effectively sacking their former captain, Clive Rice, who was told at the end of the previous season that his services were no longer required. Rice had decided to make himself unavailable for the closing matches of 1991-92 when he chose to work instead as a television commentator during the World Cup. The new management team – Cook as captain and Barlow as coach – could feel pleased by their efforts with a young and inexperienced squad. Cook, discarded by the national selectors after the first two Tests against India, found commanding form when he decided to move down the order after many years as an opening batsman. Mandy Yachad, who continued to open, was consistent, while the fast bowlers Richard Snell and Steven Jack and left-arm spinner Clive Eksteen performed well.

Eastern Province were unlucky to be affected by rain in two important matches. As well as their final game with Northern Transvaal they were robbed of victory in what turned out to be a crucial meeting with Orange Free State in Bloemfontein. Free State finished on 54 for seven in their second innings after being set 307 to win. Kepler Wessels and Mark Rushmere were the mainstays of Eastern Province's batting, while Baptiste had a magnificent season with the ball, ably backed up by the pace of Rudi Bryson. Natal's acquisition of two world-class players, Marshall and Rice, added much-needed experience to a young team led by Jonty Rhodes. But they paid dearly for a comprehensive defeat at home by the bottom team,

Northern Transvaal, for whom left-hander Mike Rindel hit two centuries in the match.

Western Province, still struggling to find consistency in their batting, started the competition with two outright wins and a first-innings win before losing their last three matches: their seam attack was weakened by Test calls for two of these. Lamb and the left-handed Gary Kirsten, younger brother of Peter, were the best batsmen while Eric Simons, primarily regarded as a seam bowler, was remarkably solid with the bat; he scored five fifties, usually after his more highly-rated team-mates had let the side down. Border and Northern Transvaal served mainly as a source of points for opponents, losing four matches each. Border escaped from the bottom of the table by beating their fellow-stragglers and pulling off a thrilling one-wicket win against Western Province. A dismal season for Northern Transvaal ended with the captain, Mike Haysman, resigning after a dispute over selection policy; a rare highlight for them was the splendid form of fast-medium bowler Fanie de Villiers which culminated in his selection for the one-day internationals.

Orange Free State followed up their triumph in the Castle Cup by winning the national 55-overs competition (renamed the Total Power Series after the withdrawal of previous sponsors Nissan) for the second successive season. Their victims in the final, as in 1991-92, were Eastern Province. But the UCB decided at the end of the season to discontinue the competition. Free State had hopes of a treble, which disintegrated when they failed to qualify for the semi-finals of the floodlit 45-overs Benson and Hedges Series after the round-robin stage. Transvaal went on to win a tense final in Durban by a single run, the third time in four seasons that Natal had failed in the final and the second time when victory had been possible with one ball to be bowled. In 1993-94, the Benson and Hedges Series was to be the only official limited-overs competition in South Africa, with matches lengthened from 45 to 50 overs a side.

Boland were convincing winners of the UCB Bowl for minor provinces, winning five of their six matches, usually by wide margins, and taking first-innings points in their final fixture. Alan Igglesden, the fast bowler from Kent, was a potent factor, particularly in the early matches: after Boland's first three wins he had already claimed 28 wickets at a cost of only 236 runs. The standard of cricket in the Bowl was generally disappointing, however, and was expected to be even lower in 1993-94 when Boland were promoted into the Castle Cup. There was some doubt about the wisdom of this decision but supporters of the move argued that Boland would be able to draw on the overflow of talent from neighbouring Western Province, in much the same way that Northern Transvaal have prospered from their proximity to Transvaal.

The first-class status of matches between B teams of major provinces was revoked in 1992-93. Instead, two competitions were introduced for Under-24 teams, divided into two sections and playing three-day matches, not regarded as first-class, followed by a limited-overs game. Fellow-ICC members Zimbabwe entered a team which won the limited-overs competition, while Eastern Province won the three-day contest. The B teams were due to regain their status in 1993-94 by being included in a revamped Bowl. A further incentive for younger players was an Under-24 international between South Africa and Sri Lanka. The South Africans, led by Test batsman Hansie Cronje, won a low-scoring contest by 36 runs on a Centurion Park pitch which helped the spin bowlers. Sri Lankan Test off-spinner Muttiah Muralitharan took ten wickets in the match and troubled all the South African batsmen with his unorthodox action and sharp turn. – C.B.

FIRST-CLASS AVERAGES, 1992-93

BATTING

(Qualification: 8 innings, average 35.00)

	M	I	NO	R	HS	100s	Avge
A. J. Lamb (*W. Province*).	5	10	1	636	206*	3	70.66
S. J. Cook (*Transvaal*)	9	16	3	864	228	4	66.46
K. C. Wessels (*E. Province*)	10	17	2	832	118	2	55.46
W. J. Cronje (*OFS*)	9	17	3	744	161*	2	53.14
P. G. Amm (*E. Province*)	5	8	2	311	114*	1	51.83
M. Yachad (*Transvaal*).	7	13	1	618	200	1	51.50
M. W. Rushmere (*E. Province*)	7	12	2	511	110	1	51.10
J. N. Rhodes (*Natal*)	10	17	2	761	135*	1	50.73
K. J. Bridgens (*Boland*)	7	10	5	244	41	0	48.80
E. O. Simons (*W. Province*)	6	10	2	380	93	0	47.50
A. J. van Deventer (*W. Transvaal*)	6	12	1	502	117*	1	45.63
I. A. Hoffmann (*N. Transvaal/E. Transvaal*). . . .	6	10	1	394	125*	1	43.77
A. C. Hudson (*Natal*).	8	16	2	609	159*	2	43.50
B. T. Player (*OFS*)	6	8	3	213	100*	1	42.60
F. J. C. Cronje (*Griqualand W.*)	9	16	1	635	138	3	42.33
M. J. R. Rindel (*N. Transvaal*)	7	14	1	549	111	2	42.23
O. Henry (*OFS*)	9	11	2	376	104*	1	41.77
D. J. Cullinan (*Transvaal*)	7	13	3	416	76*	0	41.60
W. S. Truter (*Boland*)	8	14	2	494	134	2	41.16
G. Kirsten (*W. Province*)	7	14	1	512	109	2	39.38
P. D. de Vaal (*E. Transvaal*)	7	11	6	195	37*	0	39.00
H. G. Prinsloo (*W. Transvaal*)	5	10	0	381	87	0	38.10
L. Seeff (*Transvaal*)	7	12	2	379	87	0	37.90
F. D. Stephenson (*OFS*)	6	10	0	377	141	2	37.70
V. F. du Preez (*N. Transvaal*)	7	14	1	486	161*	2	37.38
S. Jacobs (*Transvaal*)	6	8	4	148	83*	0	37.00
D. Jordaan (*Griqualand W.*)	9	16	0	581	123	2	36.31
M. J. Cann (*Griqualand W.*).	9	16	1	530	94	0	35.33

* *Signifies not out.*

BOWLING

(Qualification: 20 wickets)

	O	M	R	W	BB	5W/i	Avge
A. P. Igglesden (*Boland*)	209.2	49	460	39	7-28	3	11.79
H. Williams (*Boland*)	257.4	64	515	32	5-33	1	16.09
M. D. Marshall (*Natal*)	202.4	49	451	28	6-45	1	16.10
E. A. E. Baptiste (*E. Province*)	293.1	92	534	33	5-47	3	16.18
M. W. Pringle (*W. Province*).	256.1	66	534	30	6-60	3	17.80
P. W. E. Rawson (*Natal*).	217.3	70	498	27	5-43	1	18.44
S. D. Jack (*Transvaal*)	260.2	62	767	41	5-36	3	18.70

	O	M	R	W	BB	5W/i	Avge
L. C. R. Jordaan (*E. Transvaal*)	156.3	45	386	20	5-72	1	19.30
P. D. de Vaal (*E. Transvaal*)	187.1	52	464	24	6-41	1	19.33
R. E. Bryson (*E. Province*)	193.2	34	582	29	5-55	2	20.06
R. P. Snell (*Transvaal*)	254.5	56	657	31	6-33	1	21.19
C. R. Matthews (*W. Province*)	262.4	80	555	26	6-50	1	21.34
P. S. de Villiers (*N. Transvaal*)	225.3	47	665	31	6-62	3	21.45
C. W. Henderson (*Boland*)...........	275.4	82	666	31	7-82	1	21.48
L. D. Botha (*E. Transvaal*)	171.1	38	538	25	6-70	2	21.52
C. E. Eksteen (*Transvaal*)	334.4	118	777	36	5-48	3	21.58
C. J. P. G. van Zyl (*OFS*)	276.5	98	515	23	3-28	0	22.39
M. N. Angel (*Griqualand W.*)	283.3	78	713	31	5-44	1	23.00
A. J. Swanepoel (*Griqualand W.*)....	175.4	38	478	20	3-24	0	23.90
O. D. Gibson (*Border*)	257.5	39	797	33	7-104	1	24.15
B. N. Schultz (*E. Province*)	297.4	70	760	30	5-35	1	25.33
A. A. Donald (*OFS*)	307.1	87	696	26	7-84	2	26.76
B. M. McMillan (*W. Province*)	246	72	588	21	5-35	1	28.00
O. Henry (*OFS*)	355.5	96	865	30	6-72	2	28.83
A. Cilliers (*W. Transvaal*)	201.4	40	583	20	5-38	1	29.15
R. A. Lyle (*Natal*)	197.4	35	651	22	3-36	0	29.59
D. B. Rundle (*W. Province*)	319.5	80	746	22	6-74	2	33.90

CASTLE CUP, 1992-93

	Played	Won	Lost	Drawn	1st-inns Points	Points
Orange Free State	6	3	1	2	2	20
Transvaal	6	3	1	2	0	18
Natal	6	3	2	1	0	18
Eastern Province	6	2	1	3	6	18
Western Province	6	2	3	1	2	14
Border	6	2	4	0	0	12
Northern Transvaal	6	1	4	1	2	8

Outright win = 6 pts; lead on first innings in a drawn or lost game = 2 pts.

*In the following scores, * by the name of a team indicates that they won the toss.*

At Buffalo Park, East London, October 23, 24, 25, 26. Orange Free State won by seven wickets. Orange Free State* 422 for nine dec. (J. M. Arthur 46, W. J. Cronje 88, L. J. Wilkinson 115, C. J. P. G. van Zyl 81; B. M. Osborne three for 38) and 83 for three (W. J. Cronje 42 not out); Border 263 (A. G. Lawson 57, I. L. Howell 67, O. D. Gibson 41; O. Henry four for 73, C. J. P. G. van Zyl three for 28) and 239 (B. M. Osborne 92, P. C. Strydom 38; F. D. Stephenson three for 45, C. J. P. G. van Zyl three for 48, O. Henry three for 73). *Orange Free State 6 pts.*

At St George's Park, Port Elizabeth, October 23, 24, 25. Natal won by ten wickets. Eastern Province* 119 (M. W. Rushmere 37; P. W. E. Rawson four for 27, R. A. Lyle three for 46) and 312 (K. C. Wessels 108, D. J. Richardson 77; C. E. B. Rice six for 35, M. D. Marshall three for 55); Natal 418 (A. C. Hudson 100, N. E. Wright 88, J. N. Rhodes 85, P. L. Symcox 50; E. A. E. Baptiste five for 86) and 14 for no wkt. *Natal 6 pts.*

At Centurion Park, Verwoerdburg, October 23, 24, 25. Transvaal won by eight wickets. Northern Transvaal 126 (P. H. Barnard 39; S. D. Jack five for 36) and 205 (M. D. Haysman 42, M. J. R. Rindel 38, R. V. Jennings 47; S. D. Jack five for 78); Transvaal* 219 (M. Yachad 91, D. J. Cullinan 61; P. S. de Villiers five for 49) and 116 for two (M. Yachad 39, L. Seeff 49 not out). *Transvaal 6 pts.*

At Buffalo Park, East London, October 30, 31, November 1, 2. Eastern Province won by an innings and 42 runs. Border* 322 (P. N. Kirsten 158, P. C. Strydom 45, S. J. Palframan 36; R. E. Bryson three for 55, B. N. Schultz three for 84) and 150 (P. C. Strydom 46; T. G. Shaw five for 49, E. A. E. Baptiste three for 23); Eastern Province 514 (K. C. Wessels 93, M. W. Rushmere 110, L. J. Koen 54, T. G. Shaw 55, D. J. Callaghan 50, D. J. Richardson 42 not out, R. E. Bryson 57; R. J. McCurdy four for 119). *Eastern Province 6 pts.*

At Kingsmead, Durban, October 30, 31, November 1, 2. Drawn. Orange Free State* 280 (F. D. Stephenson 141, O. Henry 30; T. J. Packer four for 58, R. A. Lyle three for 72) and 321 (P. J. R. Steyn 36, J. M. Arthur 81, W. J. Cronje 80; R. A. Lyle three for 68, R. K. McGlashan three for 99); Natal 184 (A. C. Hudson 55, N. E. Wright 65; O. Henry six for 72) and 288 for eight (A. C. Hudson 159 not out, M. B. Logan 31). *Orange Free State 2 pts.*

At Newlands, Cape Town, October 30, 31, November 1, 2. Western Province won by 183 runs. Western Province* 248 (B. M. McMillan 34, A. P. Kuiper 35, E. O. Simons 55 not out, M. W. Pringle 43; P. S. de Villiers five for 83, P. J. Newport three for 54) and 341 for five dec. (A. J. Lamb 206 not out, A. P. Kuiper 79; P. S. de Villiers four for 64); Northern Transvaal 133 (M. D. Haysman 36, M. J. R. Rindel 38; M. W. Pringle three for 36) and 273 (M. D. Haysman 46, B. J. Sommerville 47, M. J. R. Rindel 79; M. W. Pringle three for 44, D. B. Rundle three for 83). *Western Province 6 pts.*

At Jan Smuts Ground, Pietermaritzburg, November 6, 7, 8, 9. Natal won by seven wickets. Border 199 (O. D. Gibson 79 not out; M. D. Marshall four for 36, P. W. E. Rawson three for 57) and 281 (P. N. Kirsten 66, P. J. Botha 42, P. C. Strydom 48, D. O. Nosworthy 35, O. D. Gibson 44; M. D. Marshall four for 61, T. J. Packer three for 70); Natal* 210 (J. N. Rhodes 67, C. E. B. Rice 33; R. J. McCurdy four for 54) and 272 for three (M. B. Logan 48, J. N. Rhodes 135 not out, C. E. B. Rice 59 not out). *Natal 6 pts.*

At Springbok Park, Bloemfontein, November 6, 7, 8, 9. Drawn. Eastern Province 337 (M. W. Rushmere 85, E. A. E. Baptiste 86, R. E. Bryson 33) and 199 for six dec. (K. C. Wessels 54, E. A. E. Baptiste 68 not out; B. T. Player three for 35); Orange Free State* 230 (G. F. J. Liebenberg 44, O. Henry 79; E. A. E. Baptiste five for 51, R. E. Bryson three for 50) and 54 for seven (E. A. E. Baptiste three for 19). *Eastern Province 2 pts.*

At Wanderers, Johannesburg, November 6, 7, 8, 9. Drawn. Western Province 410 for eight dec. (G. Kirsten 109, A. J. Lamb 134, A. P. Kuiper 33, E. O. Simons 50; S. Jacobs three for 48) and 46 for three (R. P. Snell three for 25, including a hat-trick); Transvaal* 333 (S. J. Cook 123, M. Yachad 42, D. J. Cullinan 72, R. P. Snell 44; C. R. Matthews six for 50). *Western Province 2 pts.*

At St George's Park, Port Elizabeth, November 20, 21, 22, 23. Drawn. Eastern Province* 466 for nine dec. (M. C. Venter 112, R. E. Veenstra 49, K. C. Wessels 44, D. J. Callaghan 124, R. E. Bryson 40 not out; C. E. Eksteen three for 126); Transvaal 202 (T. L. Seeff 72, D. R. Laing 33; E. A. E. Baptiste five for 47, R. E. Bryson three for 77) and 292 for four (S. J. Cook 107, B. M. White 98; R. E. Veenstra three for 48). *Eastern Province 2 pts.*

At Centurion Park, Verwoerdburg, November 20, 21, 22, 23. Border won by 165 runs. Border* 317 (B. M. Osborne 37, P. N. Kirsten 92, P. C. Strydom 60, D. O. Nosworthy 68; P. S. de Villiers three for 51) and 305 (P. N. Kirsten 33, P. J. Botha 65, B. M. Osborne 64, S. J. Palframan 73 not out); Northern Transvaal 247 (V. F. du Preez 82, M. J. Mitchley 47; O. D. Gibson three for 69, B. C. Fourie three for 26) and 210 (V. F. du Preez 117, M. D. Haysman 31; O. D. Gibson four for 59, I. L. Howell three for 51). *Border 6 pts.*

At Newlands, Cape Town, November 20, 21, 22, 23. Western Province won by five wickets. Natal 102 (B. M. McMillan five for 35, A. Martyn three for 22) and 294 (C. E. B. Rice 46, M. D. Marshall 35, P. L. Symcox 33, T. J. Packer 44, R. A. Lyle 35 not out; M. W. Pringle five for 92, A. Martyn three for 83); Western Province* 219 (G. Kirsten 32, A. J. Lamb 87; P. W. E. Rawson five for 43, M. D. Marshall three for 56) and 178 for five (G. Kirsten 66, A. J. Lamb 30, B. M. McMillan 43). *Western Province 6 pts.*

At Centurion Park, Verwoerdburg, December 19, 20, 21, 22. Orange Free State won by four wickets. Northern Transvaal* 388 (V. F. du Preez 37, J. J. Strydom 105, M. D. Haysman 82, M. J. R. Rindel 79, Extras 38; N. W. Pretorius four for 102) and 100 (D. J. van Zyl 36; F. D. Stephenson three for 24); Orange Free State 246 (P. J. K. Steyn 34, F. D. Stephenson 42, O. Henry 75 not out; S. Elworthy four for 42) and 243 for six (P. J. K. Steyn 82 not out, L. J. Wilkinson 50; P. J. Newport five for 79). *Orange Free State 6 pts, Northern Transvaal 2 pts.*

At Wanderers, Johannesburg, December 19, 20, 21, 22. Transvaal won by 196 runs. Transvaal* 299 (M. Yachad 61, S. Jacobs 83 not out; O. D. Gibson four for 94, B. C. Fourie three for 43) and 234 for six dec. (L. Seeff 38, D. J. Cullinan 38, S. J. Cook 97 not out); Border 160 (O. D. Gibson 83 not out; R. P. Snell six for 33) and 177 (M. P. Stonier 64, P. C. Strydom 31; R. P. Snell four for 54, S. D. Jack four for 47). *Transvaal 6 pts.*

At Newlands, Cape Town, December 19, 20, 21, 22. Eastern Province won by eight wickets. Western Province* 278 (G. Kirsten 65, A. J. Lamb 121; R. E. Bryson five for 66) and 202 (G. Kirsten 36, A. T. Holdstock 37, E. O. Simons 57; R. E. Bryson five for 55, B. N. Schultz three for 45); Eastern Province 350 (M. W. Rushmere 36, L. J. Koen 54, M. Michau 86, E. A. E. Baptiste 40, P. A. Tullis 33 not out, B. N. Schultz 31; D. MacHelm three for 58, E. O. Simons four for 83) and 134 for two (P. G. Amm 52, M. W. Rushmere 50 not out). *Eastern Province 6 pts.*

At Buffalo Park, East London, January 1, 2, 3, 4. Border won by one wicket. Western Province* 171 (T. N. Lazard 32, A. P. Kuiper 55; O. D. Gibson three for 47, B. C. Fourie three for 25) and 328 (A. J. Lamb 38, A. P. Kuiper 33, E. O. Simons 93, D. B. Rundle 47, R. J. Ryall 45 not out, Extras 42; O. D. Gibson seven for 104); Border 245 (S. J. Palframan 45, I. L. Howell 40 not out; D. B. Rundle five for 70) and 257 for nine (G. C. Victor 62, I. L. Howell 34 not out, Extras 37; D. B. Rundle six for 74). *Border 6 pts.*

At Kingsmead, Durban, January 1, 2, 3, 4. Northern Transvaal won by 124 runs. Northern Transvaal 209 (P. H. Barnard 39, M. J. R. Rindel 106; S. M. Pollock three for 28, P. L. Symcox three for 32) and 337 for eight dec. (V. F. du Preez 161 not out, M. J. R. Rindel 111); Natal* 137 (J. Payn 46, C. E. B. Rice 30; P. S. de Villiers six for 62, C. van Noordwyk three for 20) and 285 (M. B. Logan 100, M. D. Marshall 31, P. W. E. Rawson 60, Extras 32; P. S. de Villiers three for 83). *Northern Transvaal 6 pts.*

At Springbok Park, Bloemfontein, January 1, 2, 3, 4. Transvaal won by seven wickets. Orange Free State* 262 (F. D. Stephenson 34, C. J. P. G. van Zyl 67, C. F. Craven 71; C. E. Eksteen four for 78) and 374 (L. J. Wilkinson 94, F. D. Stephenson 108, J. F. Venter 33; S. D. Jack four for 87, C. E. Eksteen five for 134); Transvaal 517 for four dec. (M. Yachad 200, L. Seeff 71, R. F. Pienaar 57, S. J. Cook 128 not out, Extras 38; N. W. Pretorius three for 136) and 120 for three (B. M. White 46, R. F. Pienaar 32 not out). *Transvaal 6 pts.*

At St George's Park, Port Elizabeth, January 9, 10, 11, 12. Drawn. Northern Transvaal 236 (M. D. Haysman 35, S. Elworthy 52, P. S. de Villiers 42, C. van Noordwyk 41; R. E. Bryson three for 57, B. N. Schultz three for 62) and 92 for three (M. D. Haysman 35 not out, M. J. R. Rindel 36 not out); Eastern Province* 286 for seven dec. (P. G. Amm 50, K. C. Wessels 80, L. J. Koen 41, D. J. Callaghan 32; S. Elworthy four for 60). *Eastern Province 2 pts.*

At Springbok Park, Bloemfontein, January 9, 10, 11, 12. Orange Free State won by 114 runs. Orange Free State* 266 (L. J. Wilkinson 41, O. Henry 104 not out; M. W. Pringle six for 60) and 303 for one dec. (J. M. Arthur 71, W. J. Cronje 161 not out, P. J. K. Steyn 56 not out); Western Province 165 (E. O. Simons 40) and 290 (K. C. Jackson 34, G. Kirsten 105, E. O. Simons 50, Extras 35; O. Henry four for 68). *Orange Free State 6 pts.*

At Wanderers, Johannesburg, January 9, 10, 11, 12. Natal won by 49 runs. Natal 279 (N. E. Wright 65, E. L. R. Stewart 60, P. W. E. Rawson 33, P. L. Symcox 48 not out, Extras 32; C. E. Eksteen five for 48) and 71 (R. P. Snell three for 28, C. E. Eksteen four for 16); Transvaal* 154 (D. J. Cullinan 76 not out, S. D. Jack 31; M. D. Marshall six for 45) and 147 (M. Yachad 53, S. J. Cook 45; M. D. Marshall three for 30, P. W. E. Rawson three for 20, P. L. Symcox four for 40). *Natal 6 pts.*

CURRIE CUP AND CASTLE CUP WINNERS

The Currie Cup was replaced by the Castle Cup after the 1990-91 season.

1889-90	Transvaal	1959-60	Natal
1890-91	Kimberley	1960-61	Natal
1892-93	Western Province	1962-63	Natal
1893-94	Western Province	1963-64	Natal
1894-95	Transvaal	1965-66	Natal/Transvaal (Tied)
1896-97	Western Province	1966-67	Natal
1897-98	Western Province	1967-68	Natal
1902-03	Transvaal	1968-69	Transvaal
1903-04	Transvaal	1969-70	Transvaal/W. Province (Tied)
1904-05	Transvaal	1970-71	Transvaal
1906-07	Transvaal	1971-72	Transvaal
1908-09	Western Province	1972-73	Transvaal
1910-11	Natal	1973-74	Natal
1912-13	Natal	1974-75	Western Province
1920-21	Western Province	1975-76	Natal
1921-22	Transvaal/Natal/W. Prov. (Tied)	1976-77	Natal
1923-24	Transvaal	1977-78	Western Province
1925-26	Transvaal	1978-79	Transvaal
1926-27	Transvaal	1979-80	Transvaal
1929-30	Transvaal	1980-81	Natal
1931-32	Western Province	1981-82	Western Province
1933-34	Natal	1982-83	Transvaal
1934-35	Transvaal	1983-84	Transvaal
1936-37	Natal	1984-85	Transvaal
1937-38	Natal/Transvaal (Tied)	1985-86	Western Province
1946-47	Natal	1986-87	Transvaal
1947-48	Natal	1987-88	Transvaal
1950-51	Transvaal	1988-89	Eastern Province
1951-52	Natal	1989-90	E. Province/W. Province (Shared)
1952-53	Western Province		
1954-55	Natal	1990-91	Western Province
1955-56	Western Province	1991-92	Eastern Province
1958-59	Transvaal	1992-93	Orange Free State

UCB BOWL, 1992-93

	Played	Won	Lost	Drawn	1st-inns Points	Points
Boland	6	5	0	1	2	32
Griqualand West	6	3	2	1	0	18
Eastern Transvaal	6	1	3	2	4	10
Western Transvaal	6	0	4	2	2	2

Outright win = 6 pts ; lead on first innings in a drawn or lost game = 2 pts.

At Springs, November 13, 14, 15. Drawn. Western Transvaal 272 (J. D. Nel 104, A. J. van Deventer 43, G. P. Bouwer 30; L. C. R. Jordaan four for 74, P. D. de Vaal three for 45) and 183 (J. D. Nel 30, D. P. le Roux 35, A. J. van Deventer 64; L. D. Botha five for 22, P. D. de Vaal four for 49); Eastern Transvaal* 244 (C. R. Norris 31, T. A. Marsh 87, B. Randall 70; A. Cilliers four for 61, J. P. B. Mulder three for 65) and 120 for five (K. A. Moxham 30, C. R. Norris 37, P. J. Grobler 32; J. Peens three for 28). *Western Transvaal 2 pts.*

At Kimberley, November 13, 14, 15. Boland won by ten wickets. Griqualand West 201 (D. Jordaan 76, F. J. C. Cronje 50; A. P. Igglesden five for 38) and 78 (M. J. Cann 39; A. P. Igglesden seven for 28); Boland* 228 (R. I. Dalrymple 73, K. J. Bridgens 35, B. A. S. Chedburn 31; M. N. Angel three for 31, A. J. Swanepoel three for 46) and 52 for no wkt (N. M. Snyman 31 not out). *Boland 6 pts.*

At Potchefstroom, November 26, 27, 28. Griqualand West won by 126 runs. Griqualand West* 262 (F. J. C. Cronje 138, P. Kirsten 33, J. E. Johnson 37; A. Cilliers five for 38, J. P. B. Mulder three for 69) and 261 for three dec. (M. J. Cann 90, F. J. C. Cronje 121 not out); Western Transvaal 177 (C. P. J. Pienaar 33, H. G. Prinsloo 43, J. P. B. Mulder 41; M. N. Angel five for 44) and 220 (A. J. van Deventer 35, H. M. de Vos 43, H. M. Smith 34, A. Cilliers 42 not out; M. J. Cann four for 61, M. N. Angel three for 75). *Griqualand West 6 pts.*

At Brackenfell, November 27, 28, 29. Boland won by nine wickets. Eastern Transvaal* 244 (K. A. Moxham 41, C. R. Norris 71, I. A. Hoffmann 35; A. G. Elgar six for 44, A. P. Igglesden three for 53) and 64 (I. A. Hoffmann 33; A. P. Igglesden six for 11, H. Williams four for 21); Boland 215 (C. P. Dettmer 67, A. G. Elgar 33, K. J. Bridgens 31 not out; L. D. Botha six for 70) and 97 for one (C. P. Dettmer 40 not out, W. S. Truter 49 not out). *Boland 6 pts, Eastern Transvaal 2 pts.*

At Brackenfell, December 11, 12, 13. Boland won by eight wickets. Western Transvaal* 146 (H. G. Prinsloo 48; C. W. Henderson three for 26, H. Williams three for 35, A. P. Igglesden three for 39) and 213 (H. M. Smith 31, H. G. Prinsloo 70, A. Cilliers 31 not out; C. W. Henderson four for 62, A. P. Igglesden four for 67); Boland 257 for eight dec. (N. M. Snyman 54, W. S. Truter 107; A. Cilliers four for 88) and 105 for two (J. S. Roos 32 not out, R. I. Dalrymple 59 not out). *Boland 6 pts.*

At Springs, December 11, 12, 13. Griqualand West won by two wickets. Eastern Transvaal 225 for six dec. (C. R. Norris 45, P. J. Grobler 33, I. A. Hoffmann 92; F. J. C. Cronje three for 44) and forfeited second innings; Griqualand West* forfeited first innings and 226 for eight (D. Jordaan 44, M. J. Cann 76, G. F. Venter 39; L. D. Botha four for 50). *Griqualand West 6 pts.*

At Potchefstroom, January 7, 8, 9. Boland won by ten wickets. Western Transvaal 167 (C. P. J. Pienaar 48, H. G. Prinsloo 30; M. Erasmus three for 26) and 193 (A. J. van Deventer 48, D. P. le Roux 47 not out; C. W. Henderson three for 46); Boland* 310 for eight dec. (W. S. Truter 134, J. S. Roos 56, R. I. Dalrymple 31) and 53 for no wkt (W. S. Truter 43 not out). *Boland 6 pts.*

At Kimberley, January 8, 9, 10. Eastern Transvaal won by 46 runs. Eastern Transvaal* 260 (C. R. Norris 43, P. J. Grobler 61, L. D. Botha 34, G. Radford 40 not out; A. J. Swanepoel three for 51, M. N. Angel three for 102) and 210 for seven dec. (I. A. Hoffmann 125 not out; M. J. Cann four for 44); Griqualand West 232 for eight dec. (W. E. Schonegevel 39, D. Jordaan 45, F. C. Brooker 43, P. Kirsten 50; L. C. R. Jordaan five for 72) and 192 (D. Jordaan 112, M. J. Cann 31; P. D. de Vaal six for 41, L. C. R. Jordaan three for 23). *Eastern Transvaal 6 pts.*

At Springs, January 29, 30, 31. Boland won by three wickets. Eastern Transvaal 155 (H. Williams four for 32) and 194 (K. A. Moxham 40, H. M. Human 40; C. W. Henderson seven for 82); Boland* 223 (J. S. Roos 30, R. I. Dalrymple 65, K. J. Bridgens 41; P. D. de Vaal four for 44, L. D. Botha three for 54) and 130 for seven (W. N. van As 36; L. C. R. Jordaan four for 50). *Boland 6 pts.*

At Kimberley, January 29, 30, 31. Griqualand West won by 87 runs. Griqualand West* 320 for seven dec. (W. E. Schonegevel 37, M. J. Cann 37, F. J. C. Cronje 123, P. Kirsten 60 not out; D. J. van Schalkwyk three for 102) and 156 for six dec. (D. Jordaan 35, F. C. Brooker 45, P. Kirsten 39; J. C. Gous three for 28); Western Transvaal 188 (A. J. van Deventer 32, Extras 31; M. N. Angel four for 48) and 201 (H. M. de Vos 42, H. G. Prinsloo 39, A. J. van Deventer 45; M. J. Cann three for 56, M. N. Angel three for 65). *Griqualand West 6 pts.*

At Brackenfell, February 19, 20, 21. Drawn. Boland 295 (C. P. Dettmer 107, B. H. Richards 48, B. A. S. Chedburn 34; A. J. Swanepoel three for 24, J. E. Johnson three for 60, M. N. Angel three for 61) and 191 for six dec. (W. S. Truter 74, J. S. Roos 34, K. J. Bridgens 30 not out; M. J. Cann three for 15, M. N. Angel three for 72); Griqualand West* 224 (D. Jordaan 49, M. N. Angel 52 not out, J. E. Johnson 30, J. A. Carse 36; A. P. Igglesden three for 39) and 92 for three (F. C. Brooker 33 not out). *Boland 2 pts.*

At Potchefstroom, February 19, 20, 21. Drawn. Western Transvaal* 259 for seven dec. (H. P. Roesch 41, A. J. van Deventer 117 not out, Extras 38) and 279 for seven (H. M. de Vos 30, H. G. Prinsloo 87, A. J. van Deventer 68; P. D. de Vaal three for 81); Eastern Transvaal 339 for five dec. (K. A. Moxham 117, H. M. Human 114, P. J. Grobler 53 not out). *Eastern Transvaal 2 pts.*

OTHER FIRST-CLASS MATCHES

At Bredasdorp, September 14, 15, 16. Boland won by 25 runs. Boland* 261 for seven dec. (W. N. van As 109, J. S. Roos 33, M. S. van der Merwe 49, J. G. de Villiers 34 not out; M. R. Hobson three for 47) and 138 (M. Erasmus 34); Border 214 (G. C. Victor 41, K. Brown 59, M. Krug 50; H. Williams five for 33, H. Barnard three for 36) and 160 (A. G. Lawson 48, G. C. Victor 53; A. G. Elgar five for 50, H. Williams three for 31).

At Durban, September 14, 15, 16. Drawn. Western Province 249 (T. N. Lazard 57, G. Kirsten 35, F. Davids 33; P. W. E. Rawson four for 57, D. J. Pryke three for 45) and 106 for three (M. F. Voss 45 not out); Natal* 333 (N. E. Wright 69, J. N. Rhodes 77, E. L. R. Stewart 42, P. W. E. Rawson 43; C. R. Matthews three for 54, M. W. Pringle three for 60).

At Kimberley, September 18, 19, 20. Eastern Province won by three wickets. Griqualand West 269 (D. Jordaan 123, F. J. C. Cronje 59; E. A. E. Baptiste four for 43) and 168 (P. Kirsten 73; E. A. E. Baptiste four for 29); Eastern Province* 272 for four (P. G. Amm 114 retired hurt, R. E. Veenstra 32, K. C. Wessels 63, L. J. Koen 31 not out) and 166 for seven (D. J. Callaghan 41, K. C. Wessels 74 not out; A. J. Swanepoel three for 37).

At Pretoria, September 18, 19, 20. Transvaal won by 77 runs. Transvaal* 396 for three dec. (S. J. Cook 228, L. Seeff 87) and 173 for four dec. (R. F. Pienaar 40; L. Botes three for 63); Northern Transvaal 303 (P. H. Barnard 38, M. D. Haysman 55, L. P. Vorster 129 not out, M. J. Davis 30; S. D. Jack three for 59, C. E. Eksteen five for 73) and 189 (V. F. du Preez 51, G. C. Abbott 37, M. J. Davis 34; S. D. Jack five for 45, C. E. Eksteen three for 58).

At Kimberley, October 10, 11, 12. Drawn. Griqualand West 210 (M. J. Cann 69, F. J. C. Cronje 55; C. F. Craven four for 21); Orange Free State* 261 for eight (J. M. Arthur 67, J. F. Venter 31, B. T. Player 100 not out; M. N. Angel three for 66).

At Verwoerdburg, February 2, 3, 4. South Africa Under-24 won by 36 runs. South Africa Under-24 219 (P. H. Barnard 56, D. Jordaan 33, J. N. Rhodes 39; M. Muralitharan four for 60) and 158 (P. H. Barnard 41; M. Muralitharan six for 62, P. K. Wijetunge three for 32); Sri Lanka Under-24* 228 (P. K. Wijetunge 36, R. S. Kaluwitharana 31, S. Ranatunga 51 not out, D. K. Liyanage 56; S. D. Jack three for 32, B. N. Schultz three for 63) and 113 (S. D. Jack three for 42).

Western Province v Yorkshire (March 26, 27, 28) and Boland v Warwickshire (April 2, 3, 4) may be found in English Counties Overseas, 1992-93.

TOTAL POWER SERIES

(55 overs a side, not first-class.)

First round

At Brackenfell, October 3. Boland won by five runs. Boland* 230 (C. P. Dettmer 64, W. S. Truter 45, W. N. van As 59); Eastern Transvaal 225 for nine (S. E. Mitchley 63, T. A. Marsh 39; W. A. Bird four for 62).

At Queenstown, October 3. Western Province won by 127 runs. Western Province* 277 for four (G. Kirsten 103, B. M. McMillan 58 not out, F. Davids 35 not out); Border Country Districts 150 (M. W. Pringle three for 33).

At Witbank, October 3. Transvaal won by 204 runs. Transvaal* 309 for five (L. Seeff 36, M. Yachad 55, R. F. Pienaar 105, G. A. Pollock 77); Eastern Transvaal Country Districts 105 (D. R. Laing three for 13, C. E. Eksteen three for 19).

At Kimberley, October 3. Border won by eight wickets. Griqualand West* 155 (D. Jordaan 53; O. D. Gibson five for 19); Border 156 for two (A. G. Lawson 76 not out, B. M. Osborne 48).

At Empangeni, October 3. Orange Free State won by 176 runs. Orange Free State 270 for eight (J. M. Arthur 43, W. J. Cronje 117, C. J. P. G. van Zyl 32; G. Ecclestone four for 43); Natal Country Districts* 94 (P. Botha 45; A. A. Donald four for eight, O. Henry three for 14).

At Pietersburg, October 3. Eastern Province won by 226 runs. Eastern Province 286 for three (M. W. Rushmere 56, K. C. Wessels 127 not out, L. J. Koen 69 not out); Northern Transvaal Country Districts* 60 (E. A. E. Baptiste six for 13).

At Virginia, October 3. Northern Transvaal won by eight wickets. Orange Free State Country Districts 171 for six (R. van Rooyen 31, F. Viljoen 46; M. J. R. Rindel three for 16, S. Elworthy three for 44); Northern Transvaal* 173 for two (P. H. Barnard 85, J. J. Strydom 73).

At Potchefstroom, October 3. Natal won by 199 runs. Natal 307 for five (N. E. Wright 116 not out, E. L. R. Stewart 90); Western Transvaal* 108 (H. M. de Vos 34; M. D. Marshall four for 21).

Quarter-finals

At East London, January 16. Western Province won by 66 runs. Western Province* 228 for five (A. P. Plantema 32, G. Kirsten 88, B. M. McMillan 46); Border 162 (B. M. Osborne 30, G. C. Victor 31; E. O. Simons four for 22).

At Johannesburg, January 16. Orange Free State won by seven wickets. Transvaal* 132 (D. R. Laing 51 not out, R. P. Snell 31); Orange Free State 135 for three (W. J. Cronje 61, J. M. Arthur 36).

At Port Elizabeth, January 17. Eastern Province won by six wickets. Boland* 172 for nine (C. P. Dettmer 55; B. N. Schultz three for 33); Eastern Province 174 for four (K. C. Wessels 46, D. J. Callaghan 32 not out, D. J. Richardson 36 not out).

At Durban, January 17. Natal won by 43 runs. Natal 228 (A. C. Hudson 45, M. B. Logan 40, J. N. Rhodes 32; P. S. de Villiers five for 30); Northern Transvaal* 185 (J. J. Strydom 54, K. J. Rule 39; T. J. Packer four for 42, S. M. Pollock three for 39).

Semi-finals

At Cape Town, January 23. Western Province won by five wickets. Orange Free State 153 for seven (G. F. J. Liebenberg 37, O. Henry 34); Western Province* 154 for five (G. Kirsten 33).

At Bloemfontein, January 30. Orange Free State won by one run. Orange Free State 224 for nine (G. F. J. Liebenberg 37, L. J. Wilkinson 52, O. Henry 48); Western Province* 223 for eight (A. J. Lamb 42, B. M. McMillan 56, E. O. Simons 36 not out; B. T. Player three for 35).

At Bloemfontein, January 31. Orange Free State won by seven wickets. Western Province 224 for eight (K. C. Jackson 45, G. Kirsten 41, A. J. Lamb 53); Orange Free State* 225 for three (J. M. Arthur 56, G. F. J. Liebenberg 35, W. J. Cronje 72, L. J. Wilkinson 57 not out).

Orange Free State won 2-1.

At Port Elizabeth, January 24. Eastern Province won by six wickets. Natal 184 for nine (N. E. Wright 41, C. E. B. Rice 76 not out; R. E. Bryson four for 29); Eastern Province* 187 for four (K. C. Wessels 101 not out, L. J. Koen 32).

At Durban, January 30. Eastern Province won by 26 runs. Eastern Province 184 for eight (D. J. Callaghan 40); Natal* 158 (J. N. Rhodes 45, C. E. B. Rice 32, M. D. Marshall 30).

Eastern Province won 2-0.

Final

At Bloemfontein, February 6. Orange Free State won by six wickets. Eastern Province 202 for six (D. J. Richardson 57, E. A. E. Baptiste 61 not out; B. T. Player three for 37); Orange Free State* 205 for four (W. J. Cronje 75, P. J. R. Steyn 75 not out).

BENSON AND HEDGES NIGHT SERIES

(Day/night matches of 45 overs a side, not first-class.)

At Springs, October 8. Western Province won by 56 runs in a match reduced by rain to 32 overs a side. Western Province 173 for three (T. N. Lazard 41, G. Kirsten 42, Extras 32); Impalas* 117 (N. M. Snyman 41, S. E. Mitchley 32 not out; C. R. Matthews four for 24).

At Verwoerdburg, October 9. Northern Transvaal won by five wickets after rain revised their target to 108 from 23 overs. Eastern Province* 131 for two off 34.1 overs (K. C. Wessels 67 not out, M. W. Rushmere 30); Northern Transvaal 108 for five (G. C. Abbott 38 not out).

At Verwoerdburg, October 14. Transvaal won by 65 runs. Transvaal* 225 for seven (S. J. Cook 74, M. Yachad 81); Northern Transvaal 160 for eight (C. E. Eksteen three for 15).

At Bloemfontein, October 16. Orange Free State won by 15 runs. Orange Free State* 198 for seven (J. M. Arthur 30, W. J. Cronje 59, F. D. Stephenson 39); Northern Transvaal 183 (P. H. Barnard 65, M. J. R. Rindel 56; F. D. Stephenson four for 26).

At Johannesburg, October 16. Natal won by five wickets. Transvaal* 201 for five (S. J. Cook 63, D. J. Cullinan 63 not out); Natal 203 for five (M. B. Logan 43, J. N. Rhodes 60 not out, C. E. B. Rice 42).

At Springs, October 20. Eastern Province won by 87 runs. Eastern Province 192 for five (M. W. Rushmere 68, L. J. Koen 34, D. J. Richardson 30; A. P. Igglesden three for 26); Impalas* 105 (T. N. Marsh 51 not out; R. E. Bryson four for 27).

At Durban, October 21. Natal won by four wickets. Western Province 186 for five (A. P. Kuiper 62 not out, E. O. Simons 43); Natal* 188 for six (M. B. Logan 38, C. E. B. Rice 46 not out).

At Springs, March 2. Border won by seven wickets after rain had revised their target to 176 from 35 overs. Impalas 192 for seven (D. Jordaan 49, M. J. Cann 32, I. A. Hoffmann 31; B. C. Fourie four for 40); Border* 176 for three (M. P. Stonier 52, P. V. Simmons 41, B. M. Osborne 37).

At Port Elizabeth, March 3. Eastern Province won by six wickets. Orange Free State* 155 for five (G. F. J. Liebenberg 42, L. J. Wilkinson 49 not out); Eastern Province 156 for four (K. C. Wessels 82 not out, D. J. Callaghan 32 not out).

At Cape Town, March 3. Western Province won by three wickets. Northern Transvaal* 187 for eight (P. H. Barnard 32, B. C. Lara 38, J. J. Strydom 38; D. B. Rundle three for 44); Western Province 191 for seven (E. O. Simons 59 not out).

At Verwoerdburg, March 5. Northern Transvaal won by six wickets. Border 158 (P. V. Simmons 44, P. J. Botha 44; C. van Noordwyk three for 35); Northern Transvaal* 162 for four (J. J. Strydom 55, K. J. Rule 50 not out; P. V. Simmons three for 32).

At Bloemfontein, March 5. Orange Free State won by 140 runs. Orange Free State* 265 for six (J. M. Arthur 50, P. J. R. Steyn 117; L. D. Botha three for 42); Impalas 125 for six (D. Jordaan 50, F. J. C. Cronje 36).

At Springs, March 10. Transvaal won by nine wickets. Impalas* 140 for seven (D. Jordaan 34; C. E. Eksteen three for 23); Transvaal 141 for one (M. Yachad 48, B. M. White 47 not out, S. J. Cook 31 not out).

At Durban, March 10. Natal won by two wickets. Northern Transvaal* 178 for nine (B. C. Lara 48); Natal 181 for eight (P. L. Symcox 53 not out; M. J. R. Rindel four for 28).

At Cape Town, March 10. Western Province won by five wickets. Border* 149 (G. C. Victor 30, P. C. Strydom 37; E. O. Simons three for 39); Western Province 151 for five (A. J. Lamb 51, Extras 32).

At East London, March 12. Orange Free State won by nine wickets. Border* 145 (O. D. Gibson 41); Orange Free State 146 for one (P. J. R. Steyn 63 not out, W. J. Cronje 51 not out).

At Durban, March 12. Natal won by 79 runs after rain had revised Impalas's target to 128 from 20 overs. Natal* 204 for eight (M. B. Logan 55, N. E. Wright 37, P. L. Symcox 36; C. W. Henderson three for 33, A. P. Igglesden three for 50); Impalas 49 for six (M. D. Marshall four for 15).

At Johannesburg, March 12. Transvaal won by 68 runs. Transvaal 204 for four (S. J. Cook 65, D. J. Cullinan 78); Eastern Province* 136 for seven (T. G. Shaw 36 not out, R. E. Veenstra 33 not out).

At Port Elizabeth, March 17. Eastern Province won by six runs after rain had revised Border's target to 192 from 37 overs. Eastern Province 226 for four (P. G. Amm 74, K. C. Wessels 98); Border* 186 for five (M. P. Stonier 35, O. D. Gibson 35, P. C. Strydom 52 not out).

At Bloemfontein, March 17. Natal won by one wicket. Orange Free State* 195 for eight (F. D. Stephenson 68 not out, C. J. P. G. van Zyl 34); Natal 196 for nine (C. E. B. Rice 33, E. L. R. Stewart 52; C. J. P. G. van Zyl four for 35).

At Johannesburg, March 17. Transvaal won by four runs. Transvaal 188 for five (M. Yachad 47, S. J. Cook 53, R. P. Snell 39 not out); Western Province* 184 for six (F. B. Touzel 66, A. J. Lamb 35, B. M. McMillan 32).

At Port Elizabeth, March 19. Eastern Province won by six wickets. Western Province* 207 for seven (F. B. Touzel 40, A. J. Lamb 62, B. M. McMillan 44); Eastern Province 211 for four (D. J. Callaghan 82 not out, M. C. Venter 65 not out).

At Verwoerdburg, March 19. Northern Transvaal won by nine wickets. Impalas 148 for six (A. J. van Deventer 63 not out, B. Randall 45); Northern Transvaal* 149 for one (P. H. Barnard 59 not out, M. J. Mitchley 50 not out).

At East London, March 24. Transvaal won by 26 runs. Transvaal* 217 for eight (B. M. White 40, S. J. Cook 48, D. J. Cullinan 49, R. F. Pienaar 49); Border 191 for seven (M. P. Stonier 46, S. J. Palframan 31 not out; C. E. Eksteen three for 42).

At Cape Town, March 24. Western Province won by 20 runs. Western Province* 107 (F. D. Stephenson four for 10); Orange Free State 87 (D. B. Rundle three for ten, E. O. Simons three for 16).

At Durban, March 26. Eastern Province won by 29 runs. Eastern Province 133 (P. G. Amm 45; P. L. Symcox three for 27, S. M. Pollock three for 27); Natal* 104 (E. A. E. Baptiste three for 18).

At Bloemfontein, March 26. Orange Free State won by eight wickets. Transvaal* 224 for four (S. J. Cook 105 not out, D. J. Cullinan 45, R. P. Snell 32); Orange Free State 227 for two (J. M. Arthur 30, P. J. R. Steyn 114 not out, L. J. Wilkinson 56).

Semi-finals

At Cape Town, March 30. Natal won by 39 runs. Natal* 173 for five (A. C. Hudson 38, M. B. Logan 37, J. N. Rhodes 47 not out); Western Province 134 (A. J. Lamb 34; M. D. Marshall four for 15).

At Durban, April 2. Natal won by four wickets. Western Province* 164 for nine (G. Kirsten 38; D. N. Crookes four for 37); Natal 165 for six (M. B. Logan 40).

Natal won 2-0.

At Port Elizabeth, March 31. Transvaal won by eight wickets. Eastern Province* 165 for eight (D. J. Richardson 30, D. J. Callaghan 60; S. Jacobs three for 42); Transvaal 167 for two (B. M. White 67, S. J. Cook 47 not out).

At Johannesburg, April 2. Eastern Province won by eight wickets. Transvaal* 173 for eight (M. Yachad 32); Eastern Province 176 for two (P. G. Amm 43, K. C. Wessels 56, M. W. Rushmere 40 not out).

At Johannesburg, April 3. Transvaal won by five runs. Transvaal 218 for eight (M. Yachad 63, B. M. White 34, D. J. Cullinan 33, D. R. Laing 33; T. G. Shaw three for 38); Eastern Province* 213 for eight (K. C. Wessels 122 not out, M. W. Rushmere 39; S. Jacobs three for 37).

Transvaal won 2-1.

Final

At Durban, April 7. Transvaal won by one run. Transvaal 193 for seven (M. Yachad 86, S. J. Cook 50); Natal 192* for eight (A. C. Hudson 85, N. E. Wright 65; S. D. Jack three for 42).

FIFTY YEARS AGO

From WISDEN CRICKETERS' ALMANACK 1944

HEDLEY VERITY By R. C. Robertson-Glasgow: "Hedley Verity, Captain, The Green Howards, died of wounds a prisoner of war in Italy on July 31, 1943, some two months after his thirty-eighth birthday . . . Verity had the look and carriage of a man likely to do supremely well something that would need time and trouble. His dignity was not assumed; it was the natural reflection of mind and body harmonised and controlled. He was solid, conscientious, disciplined; and something far more. In all that he did, till his most gallant end, he showed the vital fire, and warmed others in its flame . . . There was no 'breaking-point' with Verity; and his last reported words: 'Keep going' were but a text on his short and splendid life."

NOTES BY THE EDITOR: "Far more than in the similar period of four summers over which the last war extended, cricket has proceeded alike for the recreation of all men in the various Services both as players and spectators, while the general public in their thousands flocked regularly to the grounds where any men of known fame were expected . . . there has not been any relaxation of this stimulus, Mr Ernest Bevin, Minister of Labour, last summer asking that cricket should be encouraged in every way."

MISCELLANEA: "Joe Hardstaff, the Nottinghamshire and England batsman, a Battery Sergt.-Major in India, in two games for the Maharajah of Cooch Behar's XI scored 80 not out and 103. He wrote, 'As I had not touched a bat for over 14 months I was very pleased.'"

CRICKET IN THE WEST INDIES, 1992-93

By TONY COZIER

The absence of the leading players on the full tour of Australia and the one-day series in South Africa diminished the standard of, and interest in, the 1992-93 domestic West Indian season. A year earlier the brief hiatus between the World Series Cup and the World Cup had at least allowed the international cricketers to take in a few domestic matches; this time the final round of the Red Stripe Cup was in progress by the time they returned to the Caribbean. The appeal of the premier regional tournament was further reduced by the simultaneous live television coverage of the West Indies team overseas. The circumstances offered an opportunity for new, young players to present their cases. But few did so and the most prominent individuals were already well known. Experience underpinned Guyana's Cup triumph, the fifth time they had won the first-class championship since its inception in 1965-66 as the Shell Shield, but their first since it became the Red Stripe Cup in 1987-88. Guyana also qualified for the final of the limited-overs Geddes Grant Shield against the Leeward Islands, but rain forced them to share that title.

Inspired by the shrewd captaincy and all-round capabilities of Roger Harper, Guyana won four of their five Red Stripe matches outright, two by an innings. While their batting totalled more than 350 three times, their varied bowling dismissed opponents for under 200 eight times. So often thwarted by their own unreliable equatorial weather, they played without interruption and were unquestionably the best led, most balanced and most confident team.

Thirteen years after his first-class debut, Harper scored 257 runs at an average of 42.83, took 18 wickets at 13.50 each with his off-spin and, as always, was a dynamo in the field. His main wicket-taking support came from fellow off-spinner Clyde Butts, aged 35 and playing in his 13th season. Butts's 34 wickets at 15.44 each were just two short of Courtney Walsh's tournament record, set the previous season, and carried him past 250 wickets in the competition, a standard previously reached only by another off-spinner, Ranjie Nanan of Trinidad & Tobago. Guyana did not rely on spin alone. Barrington Browne had 26 wickets in the tournament at 12.69 with his persistent fast-medium bowling, easily the best performance of his six-year career and second only to Butts.

Their batting was led by the forthright left-handed opener Clayton Lambert, who returned from Australian club cricket to make his case for reinstatement in the Test team. He started with 263 not out against the Windward Islands, hitting five sixes and 16 fours and passing the tournament's previous individual record, 250 by another left-handed Guyanan opener, Roy Fredericks, against Barbados in 1974-75. Lambert finished with 441 runs at 73.50 but, at 31, got no call-up during the subsequent series against Pakistan. His right-handed partner, Sudesh Dhaniram, made 304 runs at 43.42, his best aggregate since 1988-89. While Guyana's strength lay in their seasoned players, the youngest and most promising, 18-year-old Shivnarine Chanderpaul, confirmed first impressions. He had announced himself a year earlier with 90 on debut and continued his progress with his cultured left-hand batting and quick, low-trajectory leg-spin. His statistics were solid rather than formidable, but a maiden century and four wickets for the Board President's XI against the touring Pakistanis followed.

Guyana benefited from having only one player, Carl Hooper, absent on Test duty. The Leeward Islands had four – captain Richie Richardson, Curtly Ambrose, Keith Arthurton and Kenneth Benjamin – yet finished second in the Red Stripe Cup and qualified for the Geddes Grant final. Their position contrasted sharply with Trinidad & Tobago who, without Ian Bishop, Brian Lara, Gus Logie, Phil Simmons and David Williams, had a disastrous season, losing four of their five main matches to finish last. It was further proof that the Leewards, particularly Antigua (birthplace of Viv Richards, Andy Roberts, Richardson, Ambrose, the two Benjamins and Eldine Baptiste), continue to produce a depth of talent of which only Barbados could boast.

Barbados's stock has fallen of late and, defeated by Guyana at home for the first time since 1974-75, they finished joint third with Jamaica. Yet in their captain, Roland Holder, they possessed the batsman of the year. His 510 runs at 72.86, with hundreds against Jamaica, the Leewards and Trinidad & Tobago, moved him closer to the Test selection he had been seeking since his debut aged 18 in 1985-86. A well-organised right-hander, he further advertised himself with a fourth hundred for the Board President's XI against the tourists, and was later named captain of a West Indies Board team to play a series of one-day matches in Bermuda in June. Ridley Jacobs, a 25-year-old left-hander from Antigua, also took a century off the Pakistanis to complement his 423 runs (at 52.87) for the Leeward Islands in the Red Stripe Cup. Allied to his wicket-keeping, his record offered the Test selectors another possible successor to Jeffrey Dujon. A further candidate was Courtney Browne of Barbados, who set a tournament record of 27 dismissals in his third season. Dujon had announced his retirement a year earlier but changed his mind and returned, as captain of Jamaica for one last season. He made a memorable exit, starting with successive centuries against Barbados and Trinidad & Tobago, the second – 163 not out – a career-best, and ending with a Cup average of 106.25. But the statistics revealed a worrying overall level of batting. Dujon was one of only seven players to score hundreds in the 15 Red Stripe Cup matches. There were 22 all-out totals under 200, and only four over 400. Sub-standard pitches could be blamed in some cases; sub-standard batting was the more obvious reason.

In contrast to the absence of young batsmen, several new fast bowlers announced themselves. Franklyn Rose, 21, generated lively pace from a high action and spearheaded a Jamaican attack lacking Walsh and Patrick Patterson. He claimed 20 wickets at 17.45 runs each. Barbados, with its proud tradition of fast bowling, presented Ottis Gibson and Vasbert Drakes as its two newest aspirants to Test honours. Gibson broke off a season with Border in South Africa, where he had been named Castle Cup Player of the Year, and both he and Drakes performed impressively.

The extension of the format of the Geddes Grant Shield to a round-robin, leading to a final, more than doubled the number of one-day matches. Guyana recovered from defeat in their first two matches to qualify for the aborted final by winning their last three. The Leeward and Windward Islands also won three and lost two each, but Windwards were eliminated on net run-rate despite beginning with three consecutive victories. The success of Guyana's senior team followed that of their juniors, who won the annual Northern Telecom Youth Championships, which they hosted, in August. It was an important fillip since the country had lost most of its outstanding players of the past 25 years or so – Lance Gibbs, Rohan Kanhai, Clive Lloyd, Joe Solomon and Alvin Kallicharran – through emigration, depriving younger cricketers of role models.

FIRST-CLASS AVERAGES, 1992-93

BATTING

(Qualification: 200 runs)

	M	I	NO	R	HS	100s	Avge
D. L. Haynes (*West Indies*)	3	6	3	402	143*	2	134.00
R. I. C. Holder (*Barbados*)	6	9	1	654	162*	4	81.75
C. L. Hooper (*West Indies*)	3	5	2	231	178*	1	77.00
P. J. L. Dujon (*Jamaica*)	6	9	3	454	163*	2	75.66
C. B. Lambert (*Guyana*)	5	7	1	441	263*	1	73.50
R. D. Jacobs (*Leeward I.*)	6	11	3	523	119*	3	65.37
A. C. H. Walsh (*Leeward I.*)	5	10	1	408	92	0	45.33
S. Chanderpaul (*Guyana*)	7	10	2	356	140*	1	44.50
L. L. Lawrence (*Leeward I.*)	5	9	1	348	74	0	43.50
Sudesh Dhaniram (*Guyana*)	5	7	0	304	131	1	43.42
B. C. Lara (*West Indies*)	3	5	0	216	96	0	43.20
R. A. Harper (*Guyana*)	5	7	1	257	94	0	42.83
P. A. Wallace (*Barbados*)	6	10	0	428	96	0	42.80
D. A. Joseph (*Windward I.*)	6	10	1	317	98	0	35.22
C. A. Davidson (*Jamaica*)	4	7	0	242	86	0	34.57
S. C. Williams (*Leeward I.*)	6	11	0	378	99	0	34.36
A. F. G. Griffith (*Barbados*)	4	7	1	200	63	0	33.33
R. G. Samuels (*Jamaica*)	7	13	1	399	60	0	33.25
D. S. Morgan (*Jamaica*)	6	11	1	291	85	0	29.10
K. A. Williams (*T & T*)	5	10	0	276	113	2	27.60
H. R. Waldron (*Barbados*)	6	10	0	256	67	0	25.60
C. O. Browne (*Barbados*)	6	10	1	214	71	0	23.77
L. A. Harrigan (*Leeward I.*)	5	10	0	224	57	0	22.40
W. K. M. Benjamin (*Leeward I.*)	7	11	1	204	37*	0	20.40

BOWLING

(Qualification: 15 wickets)

	O	M	R	W	BB	5W/i	Avge
R. A. Harper (*Guyana*)	144.2	39	243	18	6-24	1	13.50
B. St A. Browne (*Guyana*)	135.4	40	360	26	6-51	2	13.84
N. O. Perry (*Jamaica*)	146.3	49	262	17	5-54	1	15.41
C. G. Butts (*Guyana*)	228	61	525	34	7-40	2	15.44
W. K. M. Benjamin (*Leeward I.*)	209	51	494	28	7-64	1	17.64
F. A. Rose (*Jamaica*)	198.3	38	632	27	5-65	1	23.40
W. D. Phillip (*Leeward I.*)	176.2	51	402	17	5-54	2	23.64
L. R. Williams (*Jamaica*)	137.4	26	410	17	4-66	0	24.11
V. deC. Walcott (*Barbados*)	136.5	36	368	15	3-35	0	24.53
O. D. Gibson (*Barbados*)	120.4	17	381	15	5-48	1	25.40
H. A. G. Anthony (*Leeward I.*)	166.1	37	449	17	6-22	1	26.41
C. E. Cuffy (*Windward I.*)	159.4	31	464	17	5-35	1	27.29
E. C. Antoine (*T & T*)	180.1	26	554	19	5-85	1	29.15
C. A. Davis (*Windward I.*)	134.5	23	460	15	4-71	0	30.66
V. A. Walsh (*Leeward I.*)	163.3	30	469	15	3-31	0	31.26
R. Dhanraj (*T & T*)	257.2	51	648	17	4-19	0	38.11

RED STRIPE CUP, 1992-93

	Played	Won	Lost	Drawn	1st-inns Points	Points
Guyana	5	4	0	1	4	72
Leeward Islands	5	2	0	3	0	44
Barbados	5	1	1	3	13	41
Jamaica	5	1	1	3	13	41
Windward Islands	5	1	3	1	0	20
Trinidad & Tobago	5	0	4	1	5	9

Win = 16 pts ; draw = 4 pts ; 1st-innings lead in drawn match = 4 pts ; 1st-innings lead in lost match = 5 pts.

In the following scores, * by the name of a team indicates that they won the toss.

At Guaracara Park, Pointe-à-Pierre (Trinidad), January 29, 30, 31, February 1. Windward Islands won by nine wickets. Trinidad & Tobago* 220 (K. A. Williams 113, K. Mason 30; R. A. Marshall six for 41) and 193 (K. Mason 34, H. Gangapersad 50; C. A. Davis four for 71, R. A. Marshall three for 34); Windward Islands 315 (D. A. Joseph 56, J. Eugene 40, R. A. Marshall 79, U. Pope 62; A. H. Gray four for 78, E. C. Antoine three for 85) and 99 for one (D. A. Joseph 52 not out, J. Eugene 44 not out). *Windward Islands 16 pts.*

At Skeldon, Berbice (Guyana), February 5, 6, 7. Guyana won by an innings and 226 runs. Windward Islands 128 (C. A. Davis 42, R. N. Lewis 38 not out; C. G. Belgrave three for 23, C. G. Butts three for 43) and 117 (R. A. Marshall 36; C. G. Butts six for 31); Guyana* 471 for four dec. (C. B. Lambert 263 not out, highest individual tournament score, Sudesh Dhaniram 74, K. F. Semple 50 not out). *Guyana 16 pts.*

At Sabina Park, Kingston, February 5, 6, 7, 8. Drawn. Barbados* 456 for nine dec. (C. A. Best 42, P. A. Wallace 96, R. I. C. Holder 162 not out, H. R. Waldron 62; F. A. Rose three for 84, A. Givance three for 97); Jamaica 287 for nine (R. G. Samuels 41, T. O. Powell 32, P. J. L. Dujon 107, Extras 33; S. M. Skeete three for 38). *Jamaica 4 pts, Barbados 4 pts.*

At Queen's Park Oval, Port-of-Spain, February 5, 6, 7, 8. Leeward Islands won by 90 runs. Leeward Islands 285 (L. A. Harrigan 39, L. L. Harris 35, L. L. Lawrence 74, H. A. G. Anthony 32; A. H. Gray three for 66, R. Mahabir four for 52) and 237 for eight dec. (S. C. Williams 41, R. D. Jacobs 119 not out; R. J. Bishop three for 38); Trinidad & Tobago* 200 (S. Ragoonath 36, R. A. M. Smith 44, R. Mahabir 40; V. A. Walsh three for 31, W. D. Phillip five for 54) and 232 (R. A. M. Smith 46, A. H. Gray 69; V. A. Walsh three for 42, W. D. Phillip five for 81). *Leeward Islands 16 pts.*

At Sabina Park, Kingston, February 12, 13, 14, 15. Drawn. Jamaica 400 (R. G. Samuels 57, P. J. L. Dujon 163 not out, T. O. Powell 36, Extras 32; E. C. Antoine three for 92, R. Dhanraj three for 67) and 187 for four (D. S. Morgan 85, R. G. Samuels 60); Trinidad & Tobago* 331 (K. A. Williams 103, K. Mason 31, R. A. M. Smith 58, D. Williams 36, A. H. Gray 44, Extras 30; F. A. Rose five for 65). *Jamaica 8 pts, Trinidad & Tobago 4 pts.*

At Warner Park, Basseterre (St Kitts), February 12, 13, 14, 15. Drawn. Guyana 380 (Sudesh Dhaniram 131, R. A. Harper 73, Sunil Dhaniram 43, C. G. Butts 34, Extras 33; H. A. G. Anthony three for 51, W. D. Phillip three for 104); Leeward Islands* 156 (A. C. H. Walsh 32, L. L. Lawrence 41; L. A. Joseph three for 38, S. Chanderpaul four for 48) and 375 (S. C. Williams 91, A. C. H. Walsh 88, L. L. Lawrence 70; B. St A. Browne three for 79, C. G. Butts four for 106, R. A. Harper three for 57). *Leeward Islands 4 pts, Guyana 8 pts.*

At Queen's Park, St George's (Grenada), February 12, 13, 14, 15. Drawn. Barbados 193 (P. A. Wallace 49, V. C. Drakes 49; R. N. Lewis three for 42) and 170 for five (P. A. Wallace 67, R. I. C. Holder 36); Windward Islands* 183 (D. A. Joseph 98; O. D. Gibson four for 50, V. C. Drakes four for 60). *Windward Islands 4 pts, Barbados 8 pts.*

At Kensington Oval, Bridgetown, February 19, 20, 21, 22. Guyana won by four wickets. Barbados 117 (R. I. C. Holder 49; C. G. Butts three for 54, R. A. Harper six for 24) and 213 (P. A. Wallace 85, A. F. G. Griffith 40; B. St A. Browne four for 46, C. G. Butts three for 70, R. A. Harper three for 56); Guyana* 113 (S. Chanderpaul 35; V. deC. Walcott three for 39, V. C. Drakes three for 13, S. M. Skeete four for 19) and 218 for six (Sudesh Dhaniram 47, S. Chanderpaul 56; V. deC. Walcott three for 63). *Guyana 16 pts, Barbados 5 pts.*

At Antigua Recreation Ground, St John's, February 19, 20, 21, 22. Drawn. Leeward Islands* 159 (A. C. H. Walsh 30, W. Davis 40, L. L. Lawrence 34; N. O. Perry five for 54) and 359 (L. A. Harrigan 57, S. C. Williams 99, R. D. Jacobs 115; N. O. Perry four for 90, L. R. Williams three for 90, R. C. Haynes three for 113); Jamaica 228 (D. S. Morgan 70, R. C. Haynes 32, F. A. Rose 46 not out; W. K. M. Benjamin seven for 64, H. A. G. Anthony three for 54) and 196 for three (C. A. Davidson 62, P. J. L. Dujon 77 not out). *Leeward Islands 4 pts, Jamaica 8 pts.*

At Bourda, Georgetown, February 26, 27, 28. Guyana won by an innings and 145 runs. Guyana 362 (C. B. Lambert 56, P. D. Persaud 40, R. A. Harper 94, K. F. Semple 30, Sunil Dhaniram 42); E. C. Antoine three for 66, R. Dhanraj three for 114); Trinidad & Tobago* 132 (B. St A. Browne six for 51) and 85 (C. G. Butts seven for 40). *Guyana 16 pts.*

At Grove Park, Charlestown (Nevis), February 26, 27, 28, March 1. Drawn. Leeward Islands 341 (S. C. Williams 40, A. C. H. Walsh 92, R. D. Jacobs 65, L. L. Lawrence 39; W. E. Reid three for 149, H. W. daC. Springer three for 54) and 345 for seven (S. C. Williams 43, L. A. Harrigan 51, A. C. H. Walsh 59, R. D. Jacobs 56, L. L. Harris 51, W. K. M. Benjamin 37 not out; W. E. Reid three for 124, H. W. daC. Springer three for 128); Barbados* 445 (P. A. Wallace 41, A. F. G. Griffith 63, R. I. C. Holder 125, C. O. Browne 71, S. M. Skeete 39; V. A. Walsh three for 107, L. C. Lake four for 99). *Leeward Islands 4 pts, Barbados 8 pts.*

At Arnos Vale, Kingstown (St Vincent), February 26, 27, 28. Jamaica won by ten wickets. Windward Islands* 159 (S. L. Mahon 31, U. Pope 45; F. A. Rose four for 31) and 145 (J. A. R. Sylvester 34, S. L. Mahon 42; F. R. Redwood three for 36, R. C. Haynes four for 33); Jamaica 302 (D. S. Morgan 45, L. R. Williams 64, N. O. Perry 75; C. E. Cuffy three for 53, C. A. Davis four for 76) and five for no wkt. *Jamaica 16 pts.*

At Kensington Oval, Bridgetown, March 4, 5, 7, 8. Barbados won by 197 runs. Barbados 79 (A. F. G. Griffith 37 not out, carrying his bat; R. Dhanraj four for 19) and 418 for eight dec. (S. L. Campbell 113, R. I. C. Holder 124, H. R. Waldron 67, C. O. Browne 36, M. J. Lavine 42; E. C. Antoine five for 85); Trinidad & Tobago* 178 (C. G. Yorke 51, K. Mason 43, D. Williams 35; O. D. Gibson four for 48, V. deC. Walcott three for 52) and 122 (V. deC. Walcott three for 35). *Barbados 16 pts, Trinidad & Tobago 5 pts.*

At Bourda, Georgetown, March 5, 6, 7, 8. Guyana won by six wickets. Jamaica 181 (R. G. Samuels 46, C. A. Davidson 52; B. St A. Browne four for 33, C. G. Belgrave three for 39) and 165 (R. G. Samuels 31, P. J. L. Dujon 49 not out, Extras 31; B. St A. Browne five for 44, C. G. Belgrave three for 48); Guyana* 159 (C. B. Lambert 61, S. Chanderpaul 31; F. A. Rose four for 35, N. O. Perry four for 20) and 188 for four (S. Chanderpaul 48 not out, R. A. Harper 34 not out). *Guyana 16 pts, Jamaica 5 pts.*

At Mindoo Phillip Park, Castries (St Lucia), March 5, 6, 7, 8. No play on first day, owing to rain. Leeward Islands won by seven wickets. Windward Islands 131 (D. A. Joseph 45; W. K. M. Benjamin four for 30) and 116 (K. K. Sylvester 35; H. A. G. Anthony six for 22); Leeward Islands* 137 (L. L. Lawrence 41 not out; C. E. Cuffy five for 35) and 111 for three (A. C. H. Walsh 62 not out, R. D. Jacobs 35 not out). *Leeward Islands 16 pts.*

SHELL SHIELD AND RED STRIPE CUP WINNERS

The Shell Shield was replaced by the Red Stripe Cup after the 1986-87 season.

1965-66	Barbados	1979-80	Barbados
1966-67	Barbados	1980-81	Combined Islands
1968-69	Jamaica	1981-82	Barbados
1969-70	Trinidad	1982-83	Guyana
1970-71	Trinidad	1983-84	Barbados
1971-72	Barbados	1984-85	Trinidad & Tobago
1972-73	Guyana	1985-86	Barbados
1973-74	Barbados	1986-87	Guyana
1974-75	Guyana	1987-88	Jamaica
1975-76 {	Trinidad	1988-89	Jamaica
	Barbados	1989-90	Leeward Islands
1976-77	Barbados	1990-91	Barbados
1977-78	Barbados	1991-92	Jamaica
1978-79	Barbados	1992-93	Guyana

GEDDES GRANT SHIELD, 1992-93

Note: Matches in this section were not first-class.

At Guaracara Park, Pointe-à-Pierre (Trinidad), January 27. Windward Islands won by eight wickets, their target having been revised by rain to 145 from 43 overs. Trinidad & Tobago 154 for nine (46 overs) (R. A. M. Smith 77; C. E. Cuffy three for 18, C. A. Davis three for 29); Windward Islands* 147 for two (38.2 overs) (D. A. Joseph 83 not out, J. Eugene 39).

At Albion, Berbice (Guyana), February 3. Windward Islands won by virtue of losing fewer wickets. Windward Islands 186 for six (46 overs) (D. A. Joseph 71, R. A. Marshall 34 not out); Guyana* 186 for nine (46 overs) (K. F. Semple 35, R. A. Harper 44, S. Chanderpaul 34, C. G. Butts 35 not out; D. A. Joseph four for 55).

At Sabina Park, Kingston, February 3. Barbados won by 80 runs. Barbados 191 for six (50 overs) (C. A. Best 46, R. I. C. Holder 42, H. R. Waldron 35); Jamaica* 111 (36.4 overs) (A. J. Andrews 42 not out; V. C. Drakes three for 15).

At Queen's Park Oval, Port-of-Spain, February 3. Trinidad & Tobago won by five wickets. Leeward Islands 144 (41.5 overs) (L. A. Harrigan 30, A. C. H. Walsh 38; E. C. Antoine three for 15, R. J. Bishop three for 33); Trinidad & Tobago* 148 for five (45 overs) (K. A. Williams 62 not out, R. Mahabir 34 not out).

At Sabina Park, Kingston, February 10. Trinidad & Tobago won by four wickets. Jamaica 181 for nine (49 overs) (F. R. Redwood 70, L. R. Williams 30); Trinidad & Tobago* 185 for six (49 overs) (C. G. Yorke 45, D. Williams 47 not out, R. Mahabir 32).

At Warner Park, Basseterre (St Kitts), February 10. Leeward Islands won by four wickets. Guyana 195 (49.4 overs) (R. A. Harper 35, S. Chanderpaul 44; J. C. Maynard three for 27); Leeward Islands* 197 for six (46.4 overs) (A. C. H. Walsh 32, R. D. Jacobs 52, L. L. Lawrence 43).

At Queen's Park, St George's (Grenada), February 10. Windward Islands won by six wickets. Barbados 133 (48 overs) (H. R. Waldron 41; C. E. Cuffy three for 25, C. A. Davis three for 30); Windward Islands* 137 for four (39.5 overs) (D. A. Joseph 30, R. A. Marshall 41).

At Kensington Oval, Bridgetown, February 17. Guyana won by six wickets. Barbados* 201 for six (50 overs) (A. F. G. Griffith 38, H. R. Waldron 54 not out, O. D. Gibson 34 not out); Guyana 204 for four (48.3 overs) (K. F. Semple 58 not out, R. A. Harper 31, S. Chanderpaul 34 not out, Extras 33).

At Antigua Recreation Ground, St John's, February 18. Jamaica won by one wicket. Leeward Islands* 238 for seven (50 overs) (S. C. Williams 105, R. D. Jacobs 45; R. C. Haynes three for 35); Jamaica 241 for nine (49.3 overs) (D. S. Morgan 65, T. O. Powell 76; V. A. Walsh three for 32).

At Enmore, Demerara (Guyana), February 24. Guyana won by six wickets. Trinidad & Tobago 176 (49.2 overs) (R. J. Bishop 33, K. A. Williams 32; R. A. Harper five for 37); Guyana* 180 for four (47.3 overs) (C. B. Lambert 67, K. F. Semple 38, R. A. Harper 32 not out).

At Arnos Vale, Kingstown (St Vincent), February 24. Jamaica won by 106 runs. Jamaica 256 for nine (48 overs) (D. S. Morgan 40, R. G. Samuels 75, C. A. Davidson 42 not out, L. R. Williams 36; W. L. Thomas three for 55); Windward Islands* 150 (44 overs) (S. L. Mahon 33; L. R. Williams three for 30, F. R. Redwood three for 40).

At Sturge Park, Plymouth (Montserrat), February 24. Leeward Islands won by one wicket. Barbados 155 (40.4 overs) (F. L. Reifer 33, M. J. Lavine 53; V. A. Walsh three for 22, W. K. M. Benjamin four for 21); Leeward Islands* 159 for nine (39.2 overs) (L. L. Lawrence 32 not out; O. D. Gibson four for 32).

At Kensington Oval, Bridgetown, March 3. Barbados won by seven wickets. Trinidad & Tobago 183 (47.3 overs) (K. A. Williams 44; O. D. Gibson three for 34, H. R. Waldron three for seven); Barbados* 185 for three (46 overs) (P. A. Wallace 63, R. I. C. Holder 79 not out).

At Bourda, Georgetown, March 3. Guyana won by 29 runs, the match having been reduced by rain to 40 overs an innings. Guyana 144 for nine (40 overs) (Sudesh Dhaniram 34; F. A. Rose three for 35, L. R. Williams three for 28); Jamaica* 115 for nine (40 overs) (R. A. Harper four for 27).

At Mindoo Phillip Park, Castries (St Lucia), March 3. Leeward Islands won by eight wickets, their target having been reduced by rain to 148 from 38 overs. Windward Islands 194 (47.3 overs) (K. K. Sylvester 33, J. Eugene 44, U. Pope 54; H. A. G. Anthony three for 35, J. C. Maynard three for 21); Leeward Islands* 151 for two (25.2 overs) (S. C. Williams 68 not out, R. D. Jacobs 67 not out).

Leeward Islands 6 pts, Guyana 6 pts, Windward Islands 6 pts, Jamaica 4 pts, Barbados 4 pts, Trinidad & Tobago 4 pts. Leeward Islands and Guyana qualified for the final on net run-rate.

Final

At Albion, Berbice, March 13-14. Guyana v Leeward Islands. Abandoned without a ball bowled, owing to rain.

CRICKET IN NEW ZEALAND, 1992-93

By TERRY POWER

Northern Districts won the Shell Trophy outright for only the third time, after sharing the title with Central Districts in 1991-92. A mixture of three and four-day matches evidently suited them, though in one-day cricket they extended their pointless streak to 13 Shell Cup matches and lost both fixtures in the experimental "action cricket". In contrast, Canterbury won the 50-overs Shell Cup and the 20-overs action cricket competition, but launched an internal enquiry after finishing bottom of the championship.

The Shell Trophy, played as a straight league with three-day matches since 1979-80, reverted to something closer to its earlier two-part format. Four-day games, used for finals in the first four seasons after the abolition of the old Plunket Shield in 1975-76, were reintroduced to prepare players for five-day Test cricket. First, the teams played each other once over three days: rain and inadequate covering meant that all but two of these 15 matches were drawn. Next, the top three – Northern Districts, Otago and Wellington – played the bottom three – Canterbury, Central Districts and Auckland – over four days. Northern Districts headed the final table by 22 points, then played second-placed Otago, in a four-day game which Otago had to win outright to take the Trophy. After an engrossing first three days, in which Northern Districts took a first-innings lead of 76 and Otago fought back to 309 for nine, rain made it easy for Northern Districts to bat out time.

The champions had no overseas player but benefited from the national selectors' lack of interest in their players, which was especially strange in the case of Richard de Groen and Shane Thomson. Simon Doull returned early from Zimbabwe with a back injury and only off-spinner Grant Bradburn was called away after that; both were available for the final. De Groen, a medium-fast right-armer of admirable control and stamina, took 46 wickets, easily the season's best. Thomson was a beautiful timer of the ball, but despite his all-out assault on Canterbury's Chris Cairns and Stu Roberts, who had reduced his team to 16 for five, and a Test average over 40, he was neglected by New Zealand. Opening batsman Blair Pocock had more success; like de Groen, he had switched to Northern Districts, having played only spasmodically for Auckland. After one season with his new team, he was picked to tour Australia. In his benefit year, captain David White earned the Trophy and two centuries to go with what is known locally as his very own "White House" – rather than just collecting cash, he had a new home in Hamilton built through donations. At 20, left-armer Matthew Hart was the most successful spinner in the country, headed the list of catchers in the field and was far from a negligible batsman. His brother Robert took over as wicket-keeper when Bryan Young decided to concentrate on his batting.

In the spring Otago had only two nationally known players: Ken Rutherford, who took the Redpath Cup as batsman of the year but, until the final, scored for country rather than province; and acting-captain Neil Mallender, who became the first overseas professional to have a benefit in New Zealand – his persistence and hostility made him the outstanding bowler until he missed the final matches through injury. But Otago had a new coach, Lance Cairns, under whom the younger pace bowlers made rapid progress and swept through to both Shell finals. Second only to Mallender in the national averages was Aaron Gale, who improved almost unrecognisably. Nineteen-year-old Jeff Wilson earned a place in the one-day squad to play Australia, and hit New Zealand to victory at Hamilton; he hurled the ball down with as much vigour as he threw himself around in the field. Shane Robinson exploited nicks off the pace bowlers to take 29 catches in the season, second only to Canterbury captain Lee Germon's 28 catches and two stumpings. Their batsmen had less success.

Central Districts briefly hauled themselves into second place in the table, until they met the leaders at Napier and were smashed by an innings and 163 runs. Tony Blain was an outstanding wicket-keeper-batsman and deserved his Test recall. In his second full season, 30-year-old Dean Askew was Central Districts' leading bowler. Tall, quickish and bouncy, he underlined Northern Districts' folly in persistently omitting him. New captain Mark Greatbatch was available only for three first-class matches.

The teams based in New Zealand's biggest cities – Auckland, Wellington and Canterbury – were prominent in the one-day matches but looked also-rans in the championship. Auckland failed to glean a single point in the three-day games, though they had successive four-day wins over both finalists. Their most reliable batsmen were John Wright, in his last season, and the all-rounder Steve Brown. Spectacular (some say flashy) wicket-keeper Adam Parore was the national choice until injured, and scored an unbeaten century against Wellington. Danny Morrison and Willie Watson gave glimpses of the form they showed against Australia, but Dipak Patel, who took over the captaincy, was disappointing. Wellington depended heavily on Martin Crowe, who re-emphasised his world class with twin hundreds against Canterbury, though their captain, Gavin Larsen, batted conscientiously. Heath Davis was very fast at variable length and even more unpredictable direction, but was hard to stop when straight. Canterbury had several handy all-rounders. The least well-known, Nathan Astle, was Man of the Match on their best day, the victory in the Shell Cup final, but their talented internationals were in bad form. Cairns was limited by his slow recovery from kidney surgery, Mark Priest seemed to lose interest and Chris Harris's batting average dropped from 44.77 in 1991-92 to 8.88. On the credit side, Rod Latham scored a vigorous 440 runs, opening bat Darrin Murray had a fine debut season, and left-hander Steve Fleming, who led New Zealand to a 1-0 series victory in three Under-19 "Tests" against Australia, blossomed in his second.

An experiment to counter the problem of limited-overs matches losing meaning when the team batting first has collapsed was played in November and December. In "action cricket" teams played two "sets" of 20 overs a side; if they won one each there was a "shoot-out" of two overs apiece, a team losing four wickets in the shoot-out was out. The outcome was the Sunday slog to end all Sunday slogs. At Wanganui, Greatbatch hit 92 from 44 balls, with nine fours and six sixes, in Central Districts' innings of 107 in 12.2 overs; of Otago's bowlers, so effective later in the season, Evan Marshall conceded 33 in 2.2 overs and Wilson 48 in four. Canterbury beat Auckland in the final and looked likely to retain their title in perpetuity; the New Zealand Board decided not to persevere. Northern Districts coach Geoff Howarth said that those who introduced "action cricket" should be locked up: "We've got too many who can bat for only 20 overs as it is."

FIRST-CLASS AVERAGES, 1992-93

BATTING

(Qualification: 5 completed innings, average 30.00)

	M	I	NO	R	HS	100s	Avge
M. D. Crowe (*Wellington*)....	7	14	1	803	163	3	61.76
J. G. Wright (*Auckland*).....	7	13	1	580	118	1	48.33
S. A. Thomson (*N. Districts*)..	9	13	2	515	167	2	46.81
D. J. Murray (*Canterbury*) ...	8	14	2	548	106*	1	45.66
B. A. Young (*N. Districts*) ...	9	12	2	406	138*	1	40.60
R. T. Latham (*Canterbury*)...	7	12	1	440	134	2	40.00
G. R. Larsen (*Wellington*)...	7	11	2	352	93*	0	39.11
S. P. Fleming (*Canterbury*)...	8	13	2	425	118	1	38.63
S. W. Brown (*Auckland*).....	4	8	2	231	65*	0	38.50
D. J. White (*N. Districts*) ...	9	14	2	459	155	2	38.25
B. A. Pocock (*N. Districts*) ...	8	12	1	414	130	1	37.63
A. H. Jones (*Wellington*).....	8	16	1	542	104	1	36.13
M. H. Austen (*Wellington*) ...	6	10	0	352	85	0	35.20
K. R. Rutherford (*Otago*)....	8	16	1	492	102	1	32.80
T. E. Blain (*C. Districts*)....	10	19	3	522	111	1	32.62
L. K. Germon (*Canterbury*) ..	8	12	1	334	60	0	30.36

  * Signifies not out.

BOWLING

(Qualification: 20 wickets)

	O	M	R	W	BB	5W/i	Avge
N. A. Mallender (*Otago*)	156.4	49	280	26	5-30	2	10.76
A. J. Gale (*Otago*)	216.5	79	408	30	4-12	0	13.60
D. K. Morrison (*Auckland*)	263.2	66	598	38	7-89	4	15.73
R. P. de Groen (*N. Districts*)	380.4	139	775	46	7-50	3	16.84
W. Watson (*Auckland*)	289.3	99	579	34	5-40	1	17.02
J. W. Wilson (*Otago*)	270	84	587	33	5-71	1	17.78
M. N. Hart (*N. Districts*)	310	89	622	34	5-37	1	18.29
G. E. Bradburn (*N. Districts*)...	199	70	383	20	5-56	1	19.15
D. N. Askew (*C. Districts*)	189.3	42	529	27	4-40	0	19.59
C. Pringle (*Auckland*)...........	175	50	406	20	5-52	1	20.30
H. T. Davis (*Wellington*)	170.5	40	493	23	4-40	0	21.43
S. J. Roberts (*Canterbury*)	216.2	44	597	27	5-59	2	22.11
M. J. Sears (*Wellington*)	187	40	488	20	4-88	0	24.40
M. L. Su'a (*Auckland*)	219.4	51	600	24	5-35	2	25.00
C. L. Cairns (*Canterbury*).......	247	73	540	20	3-34	0	27.00
D. N. Patel (*Auckland*)	276.5	73	743	23	5-93	1	32.30

SHELL TROPHY, 1992-93

	Played	Won	Lost	Drawn	1st-inns Points	Points
Northern Districts....	8	3	2	3	26*	62
Otago	8	2	2	4	16	40
Wellington	8	1	0	7	22*	34
Auckland	8	2	1	5	8	32
Central Districts	8	1	2	5	12	24
Canterbury	8	0	2	6	12	12

  Final: Northern Districts drew with Otago, but took the Shell Trophy by virtue of heading the Championship table.

Win = 12 pts; lead on first innings = 4 pts.

  * First-innings points shared in one match.

In the following scores, * by the name of a team indicates that they won the toss.

At Smallbone Park, Rotorua, November 26, 27, 28. Drawn. Central Districts* 177 (R. G. Twose 85; R. P. de Groen three for 45, S. A. Thomson three for 34, M. N. Hart four for 20) and 152 for five (T. E. Blain 46 not out, R. K. Brown 51 not out); Northern Districts 256 for eight dec. (B. S. Oxenham 50, D. J. White 110; S. W. Duff three for 46). *Northern Districts 4 pts.*

At Sunnyvale, Dunedin, November 26, 27, 28. Drawn. Otago* 193 (I. S. Billcliff 51, J. W. Wilson 34; D. K. Morrison four for 62) and 33 for no wkt; Auckland 105 (N. A. Mallender four for 21, E. J. Marshall three for 34). *Otago 4 pts.*

At Basin Reserve, Wellington, November 26, 27, 28. Drawn. Canterbury 288 for six dec. (D. J. Murray 47, R. T. Latham 134, N. J. Astle 34; M. J. Sears three for 58) and 52 for no wkt dec. (D. J. Murray 30 not out); Wellington* 78 for three dec. (G. P. Burnett 34 not out) and 261 for nine (M. H. Austen 85, R. T. Hart 33, G. P. Burnett 79; N. J. Astle three for 45). *Canterbury 4 pts.*

At Eden Park, Auckland, December 3, 4, 5. Drawn. Auckland* 136 (P. W. O'Rourke three for 35, G. R. Larsen three for 30) and 247 for six dec. (T. J. Franklin 38, M. J. Clark 64, D. N. Patel 38, A. P. O'Dowd 38); Wellington 153 (M. H. Austen 33, G. R. Larsen 33; R. J. Drown three for 55, W. Watson five for 40) and 145 for six (M. H. Austen 41, R. T. Hart 49; R. J. Drown three for 33). *Wellington 4 pts.*

At Lancaster Park, Christchurch, December 3, 4, 5. Drawn. Northern Districts 250 (B. A. Pocock 130, B. A. Young 58; S. J. Roberts four for 62, R. M. Ford four for 65) and 155 (S. A. Thomson 80 not out; S. J. Roberts four for 30, M. F. Sharpe three for 27); Canterbury* 249 (B. Z. Harris 30, D. J. Murray 38, R. T. Latham 88; R. P. de Groen four for 51) and 132 for seven (R. T. Latham 52, L. K. Germon 32; S. A. Thomson three for one). *Northern Districts 4 pts.*

At Queen Elizabeth Park, Masterton, December 3, 4, 5. Drawn. Otago 106 (D. N. Askew four for 40) and 86 for eight (S. A. Robinson 39; D. N. Askew three for 25, R. G. Twose three for 18); Central Districts* 125 (N. A. Mallender five for 41, A. J. Gale three for nine). *Central Districts 4 pts.*

At Eden Park, Auckland, December 10, 11, 12. Drawn. Central Districts 177 (C. D. Ingham 36, S. W. J. Wilson 42, R. G. Twose 35; D. K. Morrison five for 40) and 113 for six (C. D. Ingham 42 not out, M. J. Greatbatch 33; W. Watson three for 44); Auckland* 168 (A. P. O'Dowd 85, A. J. Hunt 34; D. J. Leonard six for 68). *Central Districts 4 pts.*

At Trust Bank Park, Hamilton, December 10, 11, 12. Drawn. Wellington 296 (G. P. Burnett 53, J. D. Wells 52, G. R. Larsen 43, E. B. McSweeney 45; M. N. Hart three for 68, S. A. Thomson three for 36); Northern Districts* 72 for one. *Northern Districts 2 pts, Wellington 2 pts.*

At Lancaster Park, Christchurch, December 11, 12, 13. Drawn. Otago 131 (P. W. Dobbs 45; S. J. Roberts four for 51, M. W. Priest three for eight) and 318 for nine (R. A. Lawson 31, R. N. Hoskin 65, J. W. Wilson 78, N. A. Mallender 62 not out; S. J. Roberts five for 75); Canterbury* 319 (D. J. Murray 80, S. P. Fleming 94, L. K. Germon 37; J. W. Wilson three for 80, E. J. Marshall four for 80). *Canterbury 4 pts.*

At Lancaster Park, Christchurch, December 29, 30, 31. Drawn. Canterbury 300 for seven dec. (B. R. Hartland 54, B. Z. Harris 82, L. K. Germon 60); Auckland* 293 (T. J. Franklin 46, J. G. Wright 118, Extras 44; S. J. Roberts three for 73, R. G. Petrie three for 69, M. W. Priest three for 37). *Canterbury 4 pts.*

At Molyneux Park, Alexandra, December 29, 30, 31. Otago won by 85 runs. Otago 124 (R. P. de Groen seven for 50, D. F. Potter three for 35) and 205 (P. W. Dobbs 77, D. S. McHardy 37, D. J. Nash 40; R. P. de Groen six for 49); Northern Districts* 139 (G. E. Bradburn 48; N. A. Mallender three for 44, A. J. Gale four for 12) and 105 (N. A. Mallender five for 30, A. J. Gale three for 13). *Otago 12 pts, Northern Districts 4 pts.*

At Basin Reserve, Wellington, December 29, 30, 31. Drawn. Central Districts 143 (P. W. O'Rourke four for 26) and 275 (C. D. Ingham 32, S. W. J. Wilson 45, S. W. Duff 34, D. J. Leonard 61; H. T. Davis three for 88); Wellington* 219 for six dec. (M. H. Austen 79, E. B. McSweeney 33 not out; D. J. Leonard three for 64) and 127 for six (M. P. Speight 39; S. W. Duff three for 50). *Wellington 4 pts.*

At Eden Park, Auckland, January 5, 6, 7. Northern Districts won by an innings and 19 runs. Northern Districts 367 for seven dec. (D. J. White 155, B. A. Young 138 not out); Auckland* 170 (S. J. Peterson 35, M. J. Horne 36; R. P. de Groen five for 39) and 178 (T. J. Franklin 56; G. E. Bradburn four for 59, M. N. Hart five for 37). *Northern Districts 16 pts.*

At Horton Park, Blenheim, January 5, 6, 7. Drawn. Central Districts* 277 (R. G. Twose 56, T. E. Blain 47, S. W. Duff 62, R. K. Brown 37 not out; C. L. Cairns three for 40, B. Z. Harris three for 13) and 237 for three dec. (M. W. Douglas 102 not out, T. E. Blain 63 not out); Canterbury 236 (N. J. Astle 34, S. P. Fleming 32, C. L. Cairns 79; A. J. Alcock three for 43) and 209 for eight (D. J. Murray 65, S. P. Fleming 31; S. W. Duff three for 86, P. D. Unwin three for 73). *Central Districts 4 pts.*

At Carisbrook, Dunedin, January 5, 6, 7. Drawn. Wellington* 283 (M. P. Speight 48, G. R. Larsen 93 not out, E. B. McSweeney 84; N. A. Mallender four for 22, J. W. Wilson four for 60) and 66 for two dec. (M. P. Speight 49); Otago 114 for eight dec. (H. T. Davis four for 45) and 152 for eight (P. W. Dobbs 59). *Wellington 4 pts.*

At Fitzherbert Park, Palmerston North, January 25, 26, 27, 28. Central Districts won by 40 runs. Central Districts* 327 (C. D. Ingham 31, R. G. Twose 154, S. W. J. Wilson 44, S. W. Duff 38; N. A. Mallender three for 46, J. W. Wilson five for 71) and 243 for six dec. (P. D. Unwin 38, T. E. Blain 111, S. W. Duff 41 not out); Otago 328 for eight dec. (D. S. McHardy 66, S. A. Robinson 30, K. R. Rutherford 33, R. A. Lawson 55, D. J. Nash 45; R. P. Wixon four for 83) and 202 (J. W. Wilson 37; P. D. Unwin four for 47). *Central Districts 12 pts, Otago 4 pts.*

At Trust Bank Park, Hamilton, January 25, 26, 27, 28. Northern Districts won by 69 runs. Northern Districts* 318 (B. A. Pocock 74, B. A. Young 43, G. E. Bradburn 80, S. B. Doull 30; C. L. Cairns three for 59) and 230 for nine dec. (S. A. Thomson 101, M. N. Hart 83; C. L. Cairns three for 34, S. J. Roberts five for 59); Canterbury 233 (D. J. Murray 106 not out, carrying his bat, L. K. Germon 57; G. E. Bradburn three for 63, M. N. Hart four for 42) and 246 (S. P. Fleming 73, L. K. Germon 45, S. J. Roberts 55; M. N. Hart three for 73). *Northern Districts 16 pts.*

At Basin Reserve, Wellington, January 25, 26, 27, 28. Drawn. Auckland 423 for seven dec. (T. J. Franklin 81, J. T. C. Vaughan 95, A. C. Parore 102 not out, Extras 52; M. J. Sears four for 88) and 180 for five dec. (S. W. Brown 65 not out, D. N. Patel 31); Wellington* 256 (A. H. Jones 104, M. D. Crowe 32, G. R. Larsen 91; C. Pringle five for 52, J. T. C. Vaughan three for 15) and 307 for nine (R. T. Hart 30, G. P. Burnett 33, A. H. Jones 38, M. D. Crowe 95, E. B. McSweeney 56). *Auckland 4 pts.*

At Eden Park, Auckland, January 30, 31, February 1, 2. Auckland won by 40 runs. Auckland 155 (S. W. Brown 39; J. W. Wilson three for 49, A. J. Gale four for 44) and 201 (J. G. Wright 44, J. T. C. Vaughan 50, S. W. Brown 42, D. N. Patel 30; J. W. Wilson four for 71, E. J. Marshall four for 46); Otago* 181 (P. W. Dobbs 72, D. S. McHardy 44; M. L. Su'a five for 35) and 135 (K. R. Rutherford 36, D. J. Nash 33; C. Pringle three for 19, W. Watson three for 25, D. N. Patel four for 52). *Auckland 12 pts, Otago 4 pts.*

At Lancaster Park, Christchurch, January 30, 31, February 1, 2. Drawn. Wellington* 381 (G. P. Burnett 32, A. H. Jones 77, M. D. Crowe 152, J. D. Wells 30; M. F. Sharpe three for 71) and 284 for one dec. (R. T. Hart 32, A. H. Jones 86 not out, M. D. Crowe 137 not out); Canterbury 342 for five dec. (D. J. Murray 42, S. P. Fleming 118, R. T. Latham 102 not out, L. K. Germon 30 not out, Extras 41; H. T. Davis four for 79) and 182 for four (L. G. Howell 63, D. J. Murray 49, S. P. Fleming 30). *Wellington 4 pts.*

At McLean Park, Napier, January 30, 31, February 1, 2. Northern Districts won by an innings and 163 runs. Northern Districts* 498 for six dec. (B. A. Pocock 75, D. J. White 91, S. A. Thomson 167, B. A. Young 69, S. B. Doull 48 not out); Central Districts 194 (R. G. Twose 30, S. W. J. Wilson 30, S. W. Duff 40; R. P. de Groen three for 49, M. N. Hart four for 44) and 141 (M. W. Douglas 42, T. E. Blain 40; S. B. Doull four for 15, M. N. Hart three for 39). *Northern Districts 16 pts.*

At Trust Bank Park, Hamilton, February 4, 5, 6. Auckland won by seven wickets. Northern Districts* 102 (M. L. Su'a four for 35, W. Watson three for 23) and 147 (S. A. Thomson 47; M. L. Su'a three for 47, W. Watson four for 14); Auckland 166 (J. G. Wright 84; R. P. de Groen four for 49, R. L. Hayes three for 25) and 85 for three (J. G. Wright 37; M. N. Hart three for 25). *Auckland 16 pts.*

At Carisbrook, Dunedin, February 4, 5, 6. Otago won by three wickets. Canterbury 42 (J. W. Wilson four for 15, A. J. Gale four for 17) and 153 (D. J. Murray 31, C. L. Cairns 58; J. W. Wilson three for 25, A. J. Gale four for 50, including a hat-trick); Otago* 104 (E. J. Marshall 32; M. B. Owens three for 18, M. A. Hastings four for 30) and 95 for seven. *Otago 16 pts.*

At Basin Reserve, Wellington, February 4, 5, 6. Wellington won by three wickets. Central Districts 117 (M. W. Douglas 62; G. J. Mackenzie five for 41, G. R. Larsen three for 23) and 162 (C. D. Ingham 40, T. E. Blain 33; H. T. Davis four for 40, P. W. O'Rourke three for 33, G. R. Larsen three for 28); Wellington* 122 (M. H. Austen 31; R. G. Twose four for 42, D. N. Askew three for 30) and 160 for seven (M. H. Austen 38, A. H. Jones 30, L. J. Doull 30 not out; D. N. Askew four for 54). *Wellington 16 pts.*

Final

At Trust Bank Park, Hamilton, February 12, 13, 14, 15. Drawn. Northern Districts won the Shell Trophy by virtue of heading the Championship table. Otago 139 (D. S. McHardy 50; S. B. Doull five for 46) and 309 for nine dec. (P. W. Dobbs 52, A. J. Gale 37, K. R. Rutherford 60, D. J. Nash 42; G. E. Bradburn five for 56); Northern Districts* 215 (B. A. Pocock 36, B. S. Oxenham 49; J. W. Wilson three for 46, A. J. Gale three for 42, D. J. Nash three for 31) and 81 for one (B. S. Oxenham 30, B. A. Pocock 40 not out).

PLUNKET SHIELD AND SHELL TROPHY WINNERS

The Plunket Shield was replaced by the Shell Trophy after the 1974-75 season.

1921-22	Auckland	1946-47	Auckland
1922-23	Canterbury	1947-48	Otago
1923-24	Wellington	1948-49	Canterbury
1924-25	Otago	1949-50	Wellington
1925-26	Wellington	1950-51	Otago
1926-27	Auckland	1951-52	Canterbury
1927-28	Wellington	1952-53	Otago
1928-29	Auckland	1953-54	Central Districts
1929-30	Wellington	1954-55	Wellington
1930-31	Canterbury	1955-56	Canterbury
1931-32	Wellington	1956-57	Wellington
1932-33	Otago	1957-58	Otago
1933-34	Auckland	1958-59	Auckland
1934-35	Canterbury	1959-60	Canterbury
1935-36	Wellington	1960-61	Wellington
1936-37	Auckland	1961-62	Wellington
1937-38	Auckland	1962-63	Northern Districts
1938-39	Auckland	1963-64	Auckland
1939-40	Auckland	1964-65	Canterbury
1940-45	No competition	1965-66	Wellington
1945-46	Canterbury	1966-67	Central Districts

1967-68	Central Districts	1981-82	Wellington
1968-69	Auckland	1982-83	Wellington
1969-70	Otago	1983-84	Canterbury
1970-71	Central Districts	1984-85	Wellington
1971-72	Otago	1985-86	Otago
1972-73	Wellington	1986-87	Central Districts
1973-74	Wellington	1987-88	Otago
1974-75	Otago	1988-89	Auckland
1975-76	Canterbury	1989-90	Wellington
1976-77	Otago	1990-91	Auckland
1977-78	Auckland	1991-92 {	Central Districts
1978-79	Otago		Northern Districts
1979-80	Northern Districts	1992-93	Northern Districts
1980-81	Auckland		

SHELL CUP, 1992-93

Note: Matches in this section were not first-class.

At Lancaster Park, Christchurch, January 1. Auckland won by four wickets. Canterbury 142 for nine (50 overs) (S. P. Fleming 38, L. K. Germon 47; A. J. Hunt four for 22); Auckland* 145 for six (46.1 overs) (R. G. Petrie three for 29).

At Molyneux Park, Alexandra, January 1. Otago won by 62 runs. Otago 214 (49.5 overs) (R. N. Hoskin 70, D. J. Nash 34, N. A. Mallender 37; R. P. de Groen four for 33); Northern Districts* 152 (42.5 overs) (S. A. Thomson 41; J. W. Wilson three for 34).

At Basin Reserve, Wellington, January 1. Wellington won by 66 runs. Wellington* 174 for nine (50 overs) (M. P. Speight 70, G. R. Larsen 39; D. N. Askew four for 27); Central Districts 108 (44.1 overs) (L. J. Doull three for 20).

At Eden Park No. 1, Auckland, January 3. Auckland won by 12 runs. Auckland 210 for eight (50 overs) (M. J. Horne 43, A. J. Hunt 44); Northern Districts* 198 (49.4 overs) (B. A. Pocock 65, G. E. Bradburn 40, M. D. Bailey 37 not out; C. Pringle four for 30, J. T. C. Vaughan three for 34).

At Levin Domain, Levin, January 3. Canterbury won on scoring-rate after rain ended play. Canterbury* 179 for nine (50 overs) (D. J. Murray 57, C. L. Cairns 50; D. N. Askew three for 33, R. G. Twose four for 33); Central Districts 89 for seven (36 overs) (C. D. Ingham 42).

At Molyneux Park, Alexandra, January 3. Wellington won by one wicket. Otago* 136 (49.5 overs); Wellington 137 for nine (49.4 overs) (D. A. Stirling 44; N. A. Mallender four for 16).

At Eden Park Outer Oval, Auckland, January 9. Auckland won by 73 runs. Auckland 199 for eight (50 overs) (J. T. C. Vaughan 37, M. J. Horne 67; D. J. Nash three for 41); Otago* 126 (47.1 overs) (J. T. C. Vaughan three for 18).

At Lancaster Park, Christchurch, January 9. Wellington won by six wickets. Canterbury* 239 for seven (50 overs) (C. L. Cairns 115, L. K. Germon 71; H. T. Davis three for 44, M. J. Sears three for 47); Wellington 240 for four (48 overs) (M. D. Crowe 110, M. P. Speight 96).

At Smallbone Park, Rotorua, January 9. Central Districts won by seven wickets. Northern Districts* 158 (49.4 overs) (B. A. Pocock 35; R. G. Twose four for 36); Central Districts 164 for three (47.4 overs) (G. P. McRae 31, S. W. J. Wilson 30 not out, M. W. Douglas 37 not out).

At Dannevirke Domain, Dannevirke, January 11. Otago won by 16 runs. Otago* 258 for six (50 overs) (J. W. Wilson 99, K. R. Rutherford 48, D. J. Nash 35; R. G. Twose three for 45); Central Districts 242 (49 overs) (C. D. Ingham 32, R. G. Twose 68, M. W. Douglas 41, T. E. Blain 37; A. J. Gale three for 49).

At Blake Park, Mount Maunganui, January 11. Canterbury won by four wickets. Northern Districts* 158 for nine (50 overs) (S. A. Thomson 40, M. N. Hart 62 not out; R. G. Petrie four for 32); Canterbury 161 for six (46 overs) (R. T. Latham 39; R. P. de Groen three for 26).

At Basin Reserve, Wellington, January 11. Wellington won by 50 runs. Wellington 202 for eight (50 overs) (M. D. Crowe 79, A. H. Jones 55; W. Watson four for 41); Auckland* 152 (45.5 overs) (A. J. Hunt 68; D. A. Stirling three for 22, M. D. Crowe three for 16).

At Lancaster Park, Christchurch, January 13. Otago won by nine runs. Otago* 223 for eight (50 overs) (P. W. Dobbs 58, K. R. Rutherford 62); Canterbury 214 for eight (50 overs) (C. Z. Harris 74; J. W. Wilson three for 37).

At Pukekura Park, New Plymouth, January 13. Central Districts won by five wickets. Auckland* 133 (48.1 overs) (A. C. Parore 37, J. T. C. Vaughan 39; A. J. Alcock three for 12, S. W. Duff three for 23); Central Districts 137 for five (17.2 overs) (T. E. Blain 36 not out).

At Trust Bank Park, Hamilton, January 13. Wellington won by 17 runs. Wellington* 212 for six (50 overs) (G. P. Burnett 102 not out; R. L. Hayes three for 51); Northern Districts 195 (49.2 overs) (M. Parlane 70; M. D. Crowe three for 47).

Wellington 10 pts, Otago 6 pts, Auckland 6 pts, Canterbury 4 pts, Central Districts 4 pts, Northern Districts 0 pts. Canterbury qualified for the semi-finals on net run-rate.

Semi-finals

At Carisbrook, Dunedin, January 17. Otago won by 48 runs. Otago 191 for seven (50 overs) (J. W. Wilson 37, K. R. Rutherford 53); Auckland* 143 (44.1 overs) (A. C. Parore 38; A. J. Gale three for 20).

At Basin Reserve, Wellington, January 17. Canterbury won by seven wickets. Wellington* 181 (50 overs) (G. P. Burnett 36, A. H. Jones 33, M. P. Speight 43; M. B. Owens four for 31); Canterbury 183 for three (40.2 overs) (B. R. Hartland 34, R. T. Latham 73, C. L. Cairns 30 not out).

Final

At Carisbrook, Dunedin, January 23. Canterbury won by 14 runs. Canterbury* 183 for eight (50 overs) (C. Z. Harris 40; A. J. Gale three for 38); Otago 169 for nine (50 overs) (P. W. Dobbs 36, R. N. Hoskin 45; M. B. Owens three for 30, C. L. Cairns four for 41).

CRICKET IN INDIA, 1992-93

By R. MOHAN and SUDHIR VAIDYA

The Ranji Trophy, a glittering silver cup of handsome proportions crowned by the figure of Father Time, returned to its state of origin when Punjab became champions for the first time. The Maharaj of Patiala, Bhupendra Singh, donated the trophy in 1934. In 58 years since the inception of the tournament neither Patiala (Southern Punjab) nor Northern Punjab had reached the final. It was in the 25th year since their merger into a unified Punjab that the championship arrived, when Punjab beat Maharashtra by 120 runs at Ludhiana on a pitch assisting bowlers of all types. Maharashtra, who had not won the trophy for 52 years, were crestfallen in defeat. Pre-final expectations had been whipped up in a year in which the grand old man of Maharashtra cricket, Professor D. B. Deodhar, celebrated his 101st birthday. The heroes of the Punjab camp were the 18-year-old batsman Amit Sharma, who dominated the first innings with a fine 161 in only his second first-class match, and Bharati Vij, the 26-year-old left-arm spinner, who captured nine wickets for 94, taking him to 49 at 17.55 in all.

In an extraordinarily busy season, with the national team absent touring South Africa and then playing England at home with unprecedented success, it was predictable that unfancied teams would have a better chance than usual. While the stars were busy with their international engagements, the second-string players had the opportunity to show their skills. This was also the year in which the knockout section of the Ranji Trophy was expanded to include the third-placed teams from each zone of the regional league, allowing 15 teams to stay in contention for the title rather than ten. This may have robbed the league of some excitement, since there was little chance of teams with any ability being eliminated in the first stage. However, the expanded format enabled the national selectors to scrutinise more players in five-day matches. But they saw no reason to make many changes to the squad which won four Tests in a row at home, beating England 3-0 and winning the one-off Test against Zimbabwe.

Well drilled by the former Test left-arm spinner Bishen Bedi, Punjab proved to be the best fielding side in the tournament. The close catching actively supported the successful bowlers – spinner Vij and seamers Bhupinder Singh senior, who took 36 wickets, and Arun Bedi, who had 32. The team enjoyed the services of the Test opener, Navjot Sidhu, for three of their eight matches, though he failed in both innings after rushing to Punjab for the final at the conclusion of the Zimbabwe series. Punjab exploited their home advantage by preparing a spiteful pitch, noting that Maharashtra's huge totals had all been made on the typical batting wickets of the country. Such heavy scorers as Santosh Jedhe, Surendra Bhave and Hemant Kinikar, who made a combined total of 2,361 runs during the tournament, managed only 119 between them in the final.

The Duleep Trophy championship, held before the Indian team left for South Africa, served as a trial for finalising the touring party. Played in the earliest part of the season, in August and September, the competition provided under-prepared pitches on which seamers and spinners flourished. The success of pace bowlers was accentuated so much that, for the first time in the history of Indian cricket, as many as five were picked in the squad of 16. Kapil Dev's North Zone triumphed, thanks to his own incisive bowling and that of his protégé Chetan Sharma. The champions had a tough time in the semi-final against South Zone, who took first-innings lead thanks to a brilliant century by Mohammad Azharuddin but then collapsed, aiming for a fourth-innings target of 307 against Maninder Singh and his fellow-spinners.

The other semi-final was a showcase for Central Zone's off-spinners, Rajesh Chauhan, later to play a role in India's triumph over England, and Pritam Gandhe, as they helped dismiss West Zone. But in a rain-affected final on a searing track they had no answer to the thrust of North Zone's seamers, who routed Central Zone for 97. So much time was lost that the first-innings lead had to settle the issue in a five-day match.

A bizarre decision by the previous season's Ranji champions, Delhi, to field first in the Irani Cup led to a one-sided match in which the Rest of India XI ran up a total in keeping with the traditional image of Indian cricket: 638. On a pitch wearing slowly, Anil Kumble shot back into prominence with a match haul of 13 wickets, ensuring his berth for the tour of South Africa at the expense of Maninder Singh, the left-arm spinner who had a successful Duleep Trophy season.

A strange over-rate rule penalising offenders by adding runs to their opponents' total changed the result of one match. In the final of the limited-overs Deodhar Trophy, North Zone just managed to hold the challenge of East Zone but surrendered the game because of their tardy over-rate. Nine runs – the average scoring-rate per over multiplied by the two overs short – were added to East Zone's total, so that their defeat by six runs became victory by three.

Overall, the season was notable for the restoration of the balance between bat and ball through some sporting pitches, at least at the higher level of domestic cricket, such as the Duleep Trophy and the Ranji knockout section. Punjab's outright wins, three of which came at the same venue, Ludhiana, were made possible by bowlers who had much going for them. This made for a refreshing change from the monotony of batting-oriented pitch preparation, which produces runs in meaningless multiples of hundreds. The new names in the first-class averages were ample evidence of the spread of talent in the country; so too was the crowning of a new set of champions in the country's oldest first-class tournament. – R.M.

FIRST-CLASS AVERAGES, 1992-93

BATTING

(Qualification: 500 runs)

	M	I	NO	R	HS	100s	Avge
V. G. Kambli (*Bombay*)	11	16	5	1,237	227	4	112.45
Rizwan Shamshad (*Uttar Pradesh*). . . .	7	12	2	732	145*	3	73.20
J. V. Paranjpe (*Bombay*)	8	11	2	611	218	1	67.88
S. S. Karim (*Bihar*)	6	10	2	538	180	2	67.25
S. V. Jedhe (*Maharashtra*)	8	15	2	867	168	4	66.69
V. S. Yadav (*Haryana*)	6	8	0	528	191	1	66.00
Bantoo Singh (*Delhi*)	7	11	2	559	141*	2	62.11
R. S. Dravid (*Karnataka*)	9	14	3	670	200*	1	60.90

	M	I	NO	R	HS	100s	Avge
T. B. Arothe (*Baroda*)	5	9	0	548	171	2	60.88
Ajay Sharma (*Delhi*)	8	14	2	684	150	2	57.00
Abdul Azeem (*Hyderabad*)	7	11	2	507	158	2	56.33
A. R. Khurasia (*Madhya Pradesh*)	8	12	0	661	238	3	55.08
S. S. Bhave (*Maharashtra*)	8	16	1	821	220	1	54.73
H. A. Kinikar (*Maharashtra*)	8	16	2	754	205*	3	53.85
Robin Singh (*Tamil Nadu*)	9	14	3	590	108	2	53.63
R. A. Swarup (*Hyderabad*)	7	11	1	519	140	2	51.90
P. K. Dwevedi (*Madhya Pradesh*)	7	12	0	588	174	1	49.00
A. S. Kaypee (*Haryana*)	7	12	1	528	122	3	48.00
Abhay Sharma (*Railways*)	7	11	0	509	170	3	46.27
Gursharan Singh (*Punjab*)	8	13	1	553	101	1	46.08
N. S. Sidhu (*Punjab*)	11	17	1	736	147	2	46.00
S. S. Sugwekar (*Maharashtra*)	7	12	0	547	143	2	45.58
Yusuf Ali Khan (*Railways*)	7	12	0	522	203	2	43.50
Vikram Rathore (*Punjab*)	8	14	1	560	169*	2	43.07

* *Signifies not out.*

BOWLING

(Qualification: 20 wickets, average 30)

	O	M	R	W	BB	5W/i	Avge
A. R. Bhat (*Karnataka*)	181.5	70	304	24	5-27	2	12.66
S. Subramaniam (*Tamil Nadu*)	235.2	71	520	39	7-57	4	13.33
U. Chatterjee (*Bengal*)	273.5	75	621	42	7-63	4	14.78
A. S. Bedi (*Punjab*)	206.3	52	514	32	5-53	2	16.06
F. Ghayas (*Delhi*)	114	23	359	22	7-53	2	16.31
B. Vij (*Punjab*)	377.2	106	860	49	7-67	3	17.55
R. Rathore (*Rajasthan*)	144.4	31	440	25	7-110	3	17.60
A. Kumble (*Karnataka*)	380.2	112	834	45	7-64	4	18.53
Maninder Singh (*Delhi*)	396.3	120	880	47	7-54	3	18.72
M. Venkataramana (*Tamil Nadu*)	238.1	59	682	35	6-73	3	19.48
Obaid Kamal (*Uttar Pradesh*)	308.4	80	854	43	6-21	3	19.86
Bhupinder Singh, sen. (*Punjab*)	325.4	98	719	36	5-43	1	19.97
Avinash Kumar (*Bihar*)	375.5	110	872	43	7-43	5	20.27
H. S. Sodhi (*Madhya Pradesh*)	157.1	30	428	21	6-24	1	20.38
P. Jain (*Haryana*)	269.5	68	592	28	7-119	3	21.14
N. D. Hirwani (*Madhya Pradesh*)	452.3	110	1,113	51	6-34	6	21.82
S. L. V. Raju (*Hyderabad*)	334	98	756	33	6-46	2	22.90
T. B. Arothe (*Baroda*)	196.5	28	581	25	6-75	3	23.24
S. V. Jedhe (*Maharashtra*)	330.1	91	861	37	6-119	2	23.27
S. A. Ankola (*Bombay*)	206.2	44	592	25	5-67	1	23.68
S. J. Jadhav (*Maharashtra*)	202.1	50	489	20	5-55	2	24.45
P. S. Vaidya (*Bengal*)	182.5	37	499	20	4-48	0	24.95
R. C. Thakkar (*Assam*)	204.5	57	499	20	4-35	0	24.95
S. S. Patil (*Bombay*)	276.4	99	650	26	5-94	1	25.00
Arshad Ayub (*Hyderabad*)	521	171	1,206	48	6-90	3	25.12
P. V. Gandhe (*Vidarbha*)	268	56	773	30	6-65	2	25.76
R. Ananth (*Karnataka*)	234.2	68	596	23	5-53	1	25.91
D. K. Nilosey (*Madhya Pradesh*)	121.5	15	553	21	5-101	1	26.33
M. S. Narula (*Baroda*)	157.2	30	532	20	6-92	1	26.60
K. Bharathan (*Railways*)	253.3	77	706	26	7-39	2	27.15
R. K. Chauhan (*Madhya Pradesh*) . . .	404	126	876	31	6-62	1	28.25
M. Majithia (*Railways*)	228.3	59	711	24	6-57	1	29.62

In the following scores, * by the name of a team indicates that they won the toss. When the fielding side failed to meet the required rate of 15 overs an hour, penalty runs (calculated at twice the batting side's run-rate) were added to the innings total for every over short.

DULEEP TROPHY, 1992-93

At S. E. Railway Stadium, Vishakhapatnam, August 21, 22, 23, 24, 25. South Zone won by 172 runs. South Zone* 226 (K. Srikkanth 49, W. V. Raman 91; Avinash Kumar four for 94, S. P. Mukherjee six for 77) and 341 (W. V. Raman 85, Robin Singh 65, A. Kumble 67; Avinash Kumar five for 108, R. B. Biswal five for 76); East Zone 254 (Sunil Kumar 90, S. S. Karim 79; S. L. V. Raju six for 71, Arshad Ayub three for 62) and 141 (C. S. Pandit 34; S. L. V. Raju six for 46, Arshad Ayub three for 52).

Semi-finals

At M. A. Chidambaram Stadium, Madras, August 28, 29, 30, 31, September 1. Central Zone won by 179 runs. Central Zone* 347 (K. K. Patel 37, A. Gautam 40, P. K. Amre 83, G. K. Pandey 30, Extras 30, Penalty 47; S. A. Ankola five for 67) and 256 (K. K. Patel 49, P. K. Amre 44, Sanjeeva Sharma 37; S. A. Ankola four for 41, B. M. Radia three for 72); West Zone 261 for eight dec. (R. J. Shastri 61, S. S. Bhave 40, S. V. Manjrekar 48; R. K. Chauhan six for 62) and 163 (A. Kuruvilla 38 not out; P. V. Gandhe six for 65).

At M. Chinnaswamy Stadium, Bangalore, August 28, 29, 30, 31. September 1. North Zone won by 200 runs. North Zone* 317 (A. D. Jadeja 39, M. Prabhakar 55, Ajay Sharma 61, A. S. Kaypee 38, V. S. Yadav 56; V. Prasad three for 68, A. Kumble three for 13) and 356 for nine dec. (M. Prabhakar 33, Ajay Sharma 32, K. Bhaskar Pillai 101, V. S. Yadav 66, Maninder Singh 66 not out; S. L. V. Raju four for 110); South Zone 367 (K. Srikkanth 38, D. Vasu 45, M. Azharuddin 153; Chetan Sharma five for 87) and 106 (D. Vasu 42; Maninder Singh six for 23).

Final

At Lal Bahadur Shastri Stadium, Hyderabad, September 9, 10, 11, 12, 13. Drawn. North Zone were declared winners by virtue of their first-innings lead. North Zone 268 (Ajay Sharma 50, Chetan Sharma 37 not out, Maninder Singh 31; Sanjeeva Sharma five for 66) and 147 for five (A. D. Jadeja 40; Sanjeeva Sharma three for 33); Central Zone* 97 (M. Prabhakar three for 31, Chetan Sharma three for 24).

IRANI CUP, 1992-93

Ranji Trophy Champions (Delhi) v Rest of India

At Feroz Shah Kotla Ground, Delhi, September 27, 28, 29, 30, October 1. Rest of India won by an innings and 122 runs. Rest of India 638 (W. V. Raman 184, N. S. Sidhu 59, V. G. Kambli 94, P. K. Amre 86, V. S. Yadav 82, Extras 34, Penalty 40; Maninder Singh three for 218, K. Azad three for 26); Delhi* 229 (M. Nayyar 42, R. Lamba 89; A. Kumble seven for 64) and 287 (M. Nayyar 33, R. Lamba 39, Bantoo Singh 69, M. Prabhakar 62; R. K. Chauhan three for 118, A. Kumble six for 74).

RANJI TROPHY, 1992-93

Central Zone

At VCA Ground, Nagpur, November 18, 19, 20, 21. Drawn. Vidarbha 160 (S. G. Gujar 42; Obaid Kamal six for 51) and 230 for seven dec. (M. G. Gogte 88, S. G. Gujar 35, U. I. Ghani 51 not out; Obaid Kamal three for 44); Uttar Pradesh* 276 (R. V. Sapru 38, Rizwan Shamshad 102; P. V. Gandhe three for 72, H. R. Wasu three for 58) and 23 for one. *Vidarbha 8 pts, Uttar Pradesh 12 pts.*

At Jayanti Stadium, Bhilai, November 21, 22, 23, 24. Madhya Pradesh won by an innings and 69 runs. Rajasthan* 144 (H. Joshi 65; N. D. Hirwani six for 34) and 106 (V. Yadav 46; N. D. Hirwani five for 40); Madhya Pradesh 319 (A. R. Khurasia 55, P. K. Dwevedi 63, M. S. Sahni 74; R. Rathore seven for 110). *Madhya Pradesh 21 pts, Rajasthan 4 pts.*

At NTPC Ground, Korba, November 28, 29, 30, December 1. Drawn. Madhya Pradesh* 563 (A. V. Vijayvargiya 142, K. K. Patel 31, A. R. Khurasia 238, P. K. Dwevedi 45, S. Agarwal 35 not out; T. Gonsalves three for 77, P. V. Gandhe four for 124) and 234 (K. K. Patel 50, P. K. Dwevedi 37, S. M. Patil 58; H. R. Wasu three for 32); Vidarbha 194 (P. B. Hingnikar 37, S. K. Kulkarni 43, Extras 33; H. S. Sodhi six for 24) and 317 for five (S. G. Gujar 87, Y. T. Ghare 121, U. I. Ghani 37 not out). *Madhya Pradesh 18 pts, Vidarbha 9 pts.*

At Mansarovar, Jaipur, November 28, 29, 30, December 1. Railways won by an innings and 29 runs. Railways* 410 (Yusuf Ali Khan 52, R. Adatrao 35, K. Bharathan 107, Manvinder Singh 38, K. K. Sharma 83; R. Rathore five for 79, Shamsher Singh three for 79); Rajasthan 158 (R. Rathore 39 not out; K. Bharathan seven for 39) and 223 (V. Yadav 58, A. Sinha 49, Extras 35; K. Bharathan four for 58, M. Majithia four for 46). *Railways 20 pts, Rajasthan 4 pts.*

At Palam, Delhi, December 5, 6, 7, 8. Drawn. Railways* 194 (R. Chanda 34, Manvinder Singh 40 not out; D. K. Nilosey four for 60) and 582 (Yusuf Ali Khan 203, P. Shepherd 47, Yashpal Sharma 56, Abhay Sharma 106, K. Bharathan 65, S. Sawant 50 not out; N. D. Hirwani five for 156, S. S. Lahore three for 114); Madhya Pradesh 407 (A. R. Khurasia 110, P. K. Dwevedi 91, S. M. Patil 82, M. S. Sahni 37, Extras 36; M. Majithia three for 96, K. Bharathan three for 123) and 300 for five (K. K. Patel 101, S. M. Patil 47, M. S. Sahni 75 not out, N. D. Nilosey 31). *Railways 14 pts, Madhya Pradesh 20 pts.*

At M. B. College Ground, Udaipur, December 5, 6, 7, 8. Uttar Pradesh won by 56 runs. Uttar Pradesh* 193 (R. P. Singh 40, S. Kesarwani 33; R. Rathore six for 69, Mohammad Aslam three for 42) and 271 (A. Gautam 55, R. V. Sapru 144; Mohammad Aslam five for 94); Rajasthan 255 (Parvinder Singh 40, A. Sinha 100; Obaid Kamal three for 52, S. Kesarwani four for 76) and 153 (V. Yadav 61; Obaid Kamal six for 21). *Uttar Pradesh 17 pts, Rajasthan 7 pts.*

At Karnail Singh Stadium, Delhi, December 20, 21, 22, 23. Vidarbha won by 165 runs. Vidarbha* 352 (P. B. Hingnikar 52, S. K. Kulkarni 91, P. V. Gandhe 46; Iqbal Thakur five for 113, K. K. Sharma three for 104) and 180 (P. B. Hingnikar 43, S. K. Kulkarni 67; M. Majithia six for 57); Railways 297 (Manvinder Singh 53, K. K. Sharma 61, Penalty 61; T. Gonsalves four for 67, H. R. Wasu three for 45) and 90 (R. Chanda 31; P. B. Hingnikar five for 25, P. V. Gandhe four for 27). *Vidarbha 20 pts, Railways 9 pts.*

At Nehru Stadium, Ghaziabad, December 28, 29, 30, 31. Uttar Pradesh won by three wickets. Railways* 298 (Manvinder Singh 39, Abhay Sharma 100, S. Sawant 62, Penalty 32; Obaid Kamal six for 69) and 432 (Yusuf Ali Khan 110, P. Shepherd 36, Manvinder Singh 51, Abhay Sharma 53, Penalty 106; Jasbir Singh three for 65, S. Kesarwani three for 84); Uttar Pradesh 416 (M. Mudgal 90, G. K. Pandey 152, R. V. Sapru 67, Rizwan Shamshad 54 not out; K. Bharathan six for 126, M. Majithia three for 111) and 318 for seven (S. S. Khandkar 100, A. Gautam 87, R. V. Sapru 34 not out, Rizwan Shamshad 52; A. Srivastava three for 62). *Uttar Pradesh 25 pts, Railways 13 pts.*

At VCA Ground, Nagpur, December 28, 29, 30, 31. Vidarbha won by 45 runs. Vidarbha* 338 (U. I. Ghani 94, H. R. Wasu 79, Penalty 42; R. Rathore four for 61, Shamsher Singh five for 72) and 204 (M. G. Gogte 45, Y. T. Ghare 74; P. Krishnakumar three for 40, L. Chaturvedi three for 35); Rajasthan 266 (V. Yadav 62, Parvinder Singh 40, V. Joshi 86; P. V. Gandhe three for 100) and 231 (V. Yadav 31, Parvinder Singh 108, A. Sinha 37; P. V. Gandhe five for 74, H. R. Wasu four for 72). *Vidarbha 17 pts, Rajasthan 10 pts.*

At K. D. Singh "Babu" Stadium, Lucknow, January 18, 19, 20, 21. Madhya Pradesh won by 66 runs. Madhya Pradesh 257 (Rajgopalan 34, P. K. Dwevedi 40, Zuber Khan 43, S. S. Lahore 36; Obaid Kamal three for 46, S. Shukla three for 62) and 309 (A. R. Khurasia 37, K. K. Patel 69, D. K. Nilosey 91, Penalty 43; R. P. Singh three for 60, Obaid Kamal three for 76); Uttar Pradesh* 307 (R. V. Sapru 56, Rizwan Shamshad 109, Obaid Kamal 41 not out, Extras 32; D. K. Nilosey five for 101) and 193 (S. S. Khandkar 48, M. Mudgal 36; N. D. Hirwani five for 60). *Madhya Pradesh 17 pts, Uttar Pradesh 10 pts.*

Madhya Pradesh 76 pts, Uttar Pradesh 64 pts, Railways 56 pts, Vidarbha 54 pts, Rajasthan 25 pts. Madhya Pradesh, Uttar Pradesh and Railways qualified for the knockout stage.

East Zone

At Tinsukhia Stadium, Tinsukhia, November 21, 22, 23, 24. Drawn. Assam* 295 (L. S. Rajput 92, D. Chakraborty 47, C. S. Pandit 58; Avinash Kumar five for 69, S. R. Sinha three for 58); Bihar 120 (S. S. Karim 31; R. C. Thakkar three for 39, S. Chakraborty three for 23) and 146 for three. *Assam 11 pts, Bihar 6 pts.*

At Polytechnic Ground, Agartala, November 21, 22, 23, 24. Bengal won by an innings and 203 runs. Bengal 432 (R. Moitra 31, Saurav Ganguly 64, Snehashish Ganguly 39, A. Malhotra 89, S. J. Kalyani 81, S. P. Mukherjee 36, Extras 41; A. Saha five for 69); Tripura* 88 (U. Chatterjee six for 24, S. P. Mukherjee four for 28) and 141 (H. Bhattacharya 35, C. Dey 38; U. Chatterjee seven for 63, Arun Lal three for 44). *Bengal 23 pts, Tripura 3 pts.*

At Eden Gardens, Calcutta, November 27, 28, 29, 30. Bengal won by 286 runs. Bengal* 293 (Saurav Ganguly 80, A. Malhotra 51, S. P. Mukherjee 56; Avinash Kumar seven for 60) and 305 for six dec. (R. Moitra 67, U. Chatterjee 48, A. Malhotra 100 not out, S. J. Kalyani 44; Avinash Kumar three for 106); Bihar 163 (P. Khanna 41; S. Sensharma three for 40, U. Chatterjee four for 36) and 149 (S. R. Sinha 51; U. Chatterjee four for 36, S. P. Mukherjee three for 62). *Bengal 22 pts, Bihar 7 pts.*

At Barabati Stadium, Cuttack, November 27, 28, 29, 30. Orissa won by an innings and 126 runs. Orissa 491 for nine dec. (P. Mohapatra 59, M. Roy 45, R. B. Biswal 84, Rajesh Singh 45, A. Khatua 71, B. D. Mohanty 100 not out; Pawan Kumar three for 112, C. Dey four for 89); Tripura* 110 (S. Mohapatra six for 38, R. B. Biswal four for 40) and 255 (R. Deb-Burman 72, Arup Deb-Burman 43, S. Dasgupta 33, Pawan Kumar 42; R. B. Biswal three for 58). *Orissa 20 pts, Tripura 2 pts.*

At Mecon, Ranchi, December 4, 5, 6, 7. Bihar won by an innings and 105 runs. Tripura* 102 (S. Paul 30, A. Podar 30; Avinash Kumar seven for 43) and 159 (R. Deb-Burman 33, S. Dasgupta 48; Avinash Kumar six for 73); Bihar 366 (S. S. Karim 180, S. Chatterjee 38, S. R. Sinha 51; A. Saha four for 91, Pawan Kumar four for 63). *Bihar 24 pts, Tripura 4 pts.*

At Nehru Stadium, Gauhati, December 4, 5, 6, 7. Drawn. Orissa 176 (A. Roy 67, A. Khatua 35; Rajinder Singh three for 46, R. C. Thakkar four for 53) and 219 for five dec. (P. Mohapatra 42, Rajesh Singh 32, A. Roy 61 not out, P. Sushil Kumar 36; R. C. Thakkar three for 84); Assam* 358 for eight dec. (L. S. Rajput 125, D. Chakraborty 31, C. S. Pandit 54, Javed Khan 30, Extras 30; P. Sushil Kumar five for 98) and one for no wkt. *Assam 14 pts, Orissa 6 pts.*

At Nehru Stadium, Gauhati, December 19, 20, 21, 22. Bengal won by nine wickets. Assam* 322 (D. Chakraborty 34, L. S. Rajput 30, R. C. Thakkar 92, Javed Khan 73; S. Sensharma three for 73, U. Chatterjee five for 84) and 148 (R. Bora 35; S. Sensharma five for 84); Bengal 429 (S. J. Kalyani 140, A. Malhotra 109, Snehashish Ganguly 42, P. S. Vaidya 38; Rajinder Singh five for 81) and 42 for one. *Bengal 21 pts, Assam 7 pts.*

At Nehru Stadium, Gauhati, December 25, 26, 27, 28. Assam won by an innings and 56 runs. Tripura* 80 (S. Roy 33; Rajinder Singh three for 23, S. Chakraborty three for eight) and 127 (S. Dasgupta 48; Izaz Hussain three for 20, R. C. Thakkar four for 35); Assam 263 (L. S. Rajput 50, Rajinder Singh 34, N. Das 30, R. C. Thakkar 41; A. Saha four for 45, Pawan Kumar four for 88). *Assam 22 pts, Tripura 4 pts.*

At Eden Gardens, Calcutta, December 25, 26, 27, 28. Bengal won by an innings and 338 runs. Bengal 636 for seven dec. (I. B. Roy 73, Arun Lal 169, S. J. Kalyani 143, A. Malhotra 100 not out, A. Sheikh 33, U. Chatterjee 54, Extras 38; R. B. Biswal five for 164); Orissa* 86 (P. S. Vaidya four for 31, U. Chatterjee three for five) and 212 (A. Roy 35; U. Chatterjee five for 91). *Bengal 25 pts, Orissa 4 pts.*

At Digwadih Stadium, Dhanbad, December 31, January 1, 2, 3. Drawn. Orissa 384 (M. Roy 42, R. B. Biswal 35, A. Roy 107, A. Khatua 93 not out, B. D. Mohanty 40; Hilalali Khan five for 67) and 340 for five dec. (M. Roy 112, P. Mohapatra 72, R. B. Biswal 97); Bihar* 519 (Indranil Bose 80, S. Arfi 31, B. S. Gosain 41, S. S. Karim 169 not out, Avinash Kumar 50, Hilalali Khan 46, Extras 39; S. Mohapatra four for 170, P. Sushil Kumar three for 140) and one for no wkt. *Bihar 13 pts, Orissa 10 pts.*

Bengal 91 pts, Assam 54 pts, Bihar 50 pts, Orissa 40 pts, Tripura 13 pts. Bengal, Assam and Bihar qualified for the knockout stage.

North Zone

At Services Sports Complex, Palam, Delhi, November 20, 21, 22, 23. Drawn. Services 111 for seven dec. (Shakti Singh six for 30); Himachal Pradesh* 114 for eight (Shakti Singh 36; M. V. Rao five for 52). *Services 6 pts, Himachal Pradesh 8 pts.*

At Feroz Shah Kotla Ground, Delhi, November 25, 26, 27, 28. Delhi won by an innings and 124 runs. Delhi* 495 for seven dec. (M. Nayyar 68, Bantoo Singh 103, Ajay Sharma 150, Sanjay Sharma 40 not out, V. Razdan 48; A. Sen four for 128); Himachal Pradesh 243 (R. Bittu 39, Sharath Kumar 41, R. Nayyar 72, Raj Kumar 32; Maninder Singh four for 45, Ajay Sharma four for 43) and 128 (Maninder Singh five for 38, K. Azad three for 46). *Delhi 25 pts, Himachal Pradesh 2 pts.*

At Services Sports Complex, Palam, Delhi, November 25, 26, 27, 28. Haryana won by an innings and 152 runs. Services 156 (G. S. Thapa 42, S. Subramaniam 33; K. Batra four for 53, P. Jain three for 24) and 207 (K. M. Roshan 37, S. Bhatnagar 48; K. Batra three for 70, Y. Bhandari three for 72); Haryana* 515 (Dhanraj Singh 86, Deepak Sharma 30, R. Puri 150, Y. Bhandari 48, Extras 41, Penalty 60; P. Maitreya three for 58). *Haryana 23 pts, Services 3 pts.*

At Indira Gandhi Stadium, Una, December 1, 2, 3, 4. Punjab won by an innings and 45 runs. Punjab* 415 (Vikram Rathore 159, Bhupinder Singh, jun. 116, K. Mohan 48, Extras 30; Shakti Singh three for 98, Brijinder Sharma three for 62); Himachal Pradesh 205 (R. Bittu 45, Jaswant Rai 37, Shambhu Singh 31; K. Mohan six for 39) and 165 (R. Nayyar 46, Shambhu Singh 39; B. Vij seven for 67). *Punjab 23 pts, Himachal Pradesh 2 pts.*

At Feroz Shah Kotla Ground, Delhi, December 7, 8, 9, 10. Delhi won by an innings and 42 runs. Services* 198 (K. M. Roshan 71; F. Ghayas seven for 53) and 210 (H. Bhaskar 34, G. S. Thapa 48, S. Bhatnagar 36; F. Ghayas six for 57); Delhi 450 (M. Nayyar 88, Sanjay Sharma 103, G. Vadhera 95, K. Azad 40, F. Ghayas 40; M. V. Rao three for 106, P. Maitreya four for 67). *Delhi 22 pts, Services 4 pts.*

At Burlton Park, Jalandhar, December 7, 8, 9, 10. Drawn. Punjab* 346 (R. Kalsi 35, S. Chopra 44, K. Mohan 129 not out, Arun Sharma 80; P. Jain seven for 119) and 119 for four dec. (R. Chopra 63); Haryana 427 (N. R. Goel 76, A. S. Kaypee 122, R. Puri 115, Sukhdev Singh 48; B. Vij three for 123, J. D. Singh five for 89) and two for no wkt. *Punjab 6 pts, Haryana 11 pts.*

At Paddal Ground, Mandi, December 13, 14, 15, 16. Haryana won by 114 runs. Haryana* 320 (Dhanraj Singh 32, N. R. Goel 102, A. S. Kaypee 101; Shakti Singh four for 39, Brijinder Sharma three for 62) and 203 for nine dec. (N. R. Goel 45, Sukhdev Singh 60, Y. Bhandari 33; Shakti Singh five for 82); Himachal Pradesh 237 (R. Nayyar 78; P. Jain six for 74, Deepak Sharma three for 73) and 172 (R. Bittu 37, Brijinder Sharma 46; P. Jain five for 80, Deepak Sharma five for 54). *Haryana 20 pts, Himachal Pradesh 9 pts.*

At Services Sports Complex, Palam, Delhi, December 13, 14, 15, 17, Punjab won by an innings and 123 runs. Services 132 (Bhupinder Singh, sen. five for 43, B. Vij four for 34) and 192 (S. Bhatnagar 46, Penalty 47; A. S. Bedi five for 53, K. Mohan three for 13); Punjab* 447 for five dec. (S. Chopra 114, N. S. Sidhu 147, Gursharan Singh 101, Bhupinder Singh, jun. 63 not out; S. Dhavan three for 110). *Punjab 25 pts, Services 3 pts.*

At Feroz Shah Kotla Ground, Delhi, December 19, 20, 21, 22. Drawn. Punjab* 390 (N. S. Sidhu 39, Gursharan Singh 95, K. Mohan 51, Bhupinder Singh, sen. 53, B. Vij 39, Extras 50; V. Razdan three for 59, F. Ghayas three for 87, Maninder Singh three for 67) and 65 for three (N. S. Sidhu 30); Delhi 235 (M. Nayyar 41, Bantoo Singh 68, Penalty 41; Bhupinder Singh sen. four for 51, B. Vij four for 61) and 289 for five dec. (Sanjay Sharma 41, Ajay Sharma 149 not out, K. Azad 50). *Delhi 9 pts, Punjab 14 pts.*

At Nehru Stadium, Gurgaon, December 24, 25, 26, 27. Drawn. Delhi* 250 (Ajay Sharma 57, Maninder Singh 102 not out; P. Thakur three for 60) and 266 for five dec. (Bantoo Singh 60, Ajay Sharma 74, K. Bhaskar Pillai 56); Haryana 226 (N. R. Goel 58, Ashok Singh 52; Maninder Singh seven for 54) and 137 for seven (P. Kaushik 41; V. Razdan three for 28, Maninder Singh three for 22). *Haryana 9 pts, Delhi 14 pts.*

Delhi 70 pts, Punjab 68 pts, Haryana 63 pts, Himachal Pradesh 21 pts, Services 16 pts. (Jammu and Kashmir did not take part because of political disturbances in the region.) Delhi, Punjab and Haryana qualified for the knockout stage.

South Zone

At MCV Stadium, Vishakhapatnam, November 6, 7, 8, 9. Drawn. Kerala* 227 for five (V. Narayan Kutty 36, B. Ramaprakash 71 not out, F. V. Rashid 50 not out; G. V. V. Gopalraju three for 91) v Andhra. *Andhra 4 pts, Kerala 2 pts.*

At Lal Bahadur Shastri Stadium, Hyderabad, November 6, 7, 8, 9. Hyderabad won by an innings and 56 runs. Hyderabad* 395 (R. A. Swarup 39, V. Jaisimha 35, V. Pratap 86, M. V. Ramanamurthy 64, N. R. Yadav 61; S. Harmalkar three for 90, N. Kambli three for 81); Goa 182 (P. Rivonkar 57, S. Mahadevan 43; M. V. Ramanamurthy three for 22, R. Sridhar three for 40) and 157 (A. Mishra 41, S. Mahadevan 42; Arshad Ayub four for 26). *Hyderabad 23 pts, Goa 3 pts.*

At Thapar Stadium, AOC Centre Ground, Secunderabad, November 12, 13, 14, 15. Drawn. Hyderabad* 448 (M. V. Sridhar 176, V. Jaisimha 67, M. V. Ramanamurthy 61, N. R. Yadav 30, R. Sridhar 30; K. G. Jayakumar three for 126, K. N. A. Padmanabhan three for 106) and 229 for eight dec. (Abdul Azeem 51, V. Jaisimha 72 not out, Abbas Ali Khan 33 not out; B. Ramaprakash four for 107); Kerala 409 (V. Narayan Kutty 125, I. Cherian 44, B. Ramaprakash 56, F. V. Rashid 31, K. N. A. Padmanabhan 39; Arshad Ayub four for 116, R. Sridhar three for 80) and 111 for three (P. T. Subramaniam 34 not out). *Hyderabad 17 pts, Kerala 13 pts.*

At Mahatma Gandhi Stadium, Salem, November 12, 13, 14, 15. Drawn. Andhra* 128 (S. Subramaniam three for 22, M. Venkataramana five for 24); Tamil Nadu 115 for two (K. Srikkanth 36, M. Senthilnathan 31 not out). *Tamil Nadu 6 pts, Andhra 2 pts.*

At Panji Gymkhana, Panjim, November 13, 14, 15, 16. Karnataka won by an innings and 73 runs. Karnataka* 362 (C. Saldanha 71, K. Srinath 43, R. S. Dravid 54, K. A. Jeshwant 33, S. M. H. Kirmani 63; N. Kambli four for 88, A. Shetty four for 81); Goa 102 (A. Mishra 55; A. R. Bhat four for 38, K. A. Jeshwant six for 24) and 187 (M. Sawkar 37, J. Cordozo 41; R. Ananth three for 57). *Karnataka 23 pts, Goa 4 pts.*

At Panji Gymkhana, Panjim, November 20, 21, 22, 23. Tamil Nadu won by an innings and 146 runs. Goa 108 (D. Vasu three for 20, M. Venkataramana three for 21) and 150 (A. Shetty 43; S. Subramaniam four for 24, M. Venkataramana four for 40); Tamil Nadu* 404 for nine dec. (V. B. Chandrasekhar 52, K. Srikkanth 104, M. Senthilnathan 35, D. Vasu 54, A. R. Kapoor 73 not out; A. Shetty three for 113, R. Kambli three for 95). *Tamil Nadu 25 pts, Goa 4 pts.*

At REC Ground, Kozhikode, November 20, 21, 22, 23. Karnataka won by an innings and 74 runs. Karnataka* 329 (P. V. Shashikanth 48, A. Vaidya 49, R. S. Dravid 37, K. A. Jeshwant 45, S. M. H. Kirmani 53; K. G. Jayakumar three for 53, B. Ramaprakash five for 96); Kerala 103 (A. R. Bhat five for 27) and 152 (M. A. Satish 31; V. Prasad three for 28, A. R. Bhat four for 24). *Karnataka 22 pts, Kerala 3 pts.*

At Railway Recreation Ground, Secunderabad, November 27, 28, 29, 30. Drawn. Tamil Nadu* 290 (Robin Singh 51, D. Vasu 78, S. Subramaniam 52; N. R. Yadav three for 71, R. Sridhar three for 43) and 322 for nine dec. (V. B. Chandrasekhar 40, K. Srikkanth 45, N. Gautam 30, Robin Singh 101 not out, M. Venkataramana 43; Arshad Ayub six for 90); Hyderabad 414 for nine dec. (R. A. Swarup 72, M. V. Sridhar 42, V. Pratap 33, Arshad Ayub 63, N. R. Yadav 52, Extras 34; D. Vasu four for 125) and 113 for one (Abdul Azeem 71 not out). *Hyderabad 15 pts, Tamil Nadu 9 pts.*

At M. Chinnaswamy Stadium, Bangalore, November 27, 28, 29, 30. Drawn. Karnataka* 531 for six dec. (P. V. Shashikanth 47, K. Srinath 51, R. S. Dravid 200 not out, K. A. Jeshwant 53, S. M. H. Kirmani 77, A. Vaidya 65) and 259 for two dec. (C. Saldanha 66, P. V. Shashikanth 102 not out, R. S. Dravid 56 not out); Andhra 356 (K. V. S. D. Kamaraju 112, V. Vijyasarathy 47, P. Prakash 40, V. Vinay Kumar 45; D. Johnson four for 115) and 216 for six (A. Pathak 38, R. Vivekanand 30 not out, K. Veerbrahman 90 not out; R. Ananth four for 53). *Karnataka 20 pts, Andhra 12 pts.*

At CAL Ground, Kochi, November 27, 28, 29, 30. Kerala won by five wickets. Goa* 177 (S. Mahadevan 69, A. Shetty 40; P. Jayaraj four for 42, B. Ramaprakash four for 41) and 99 (B. Ramaprakash three for 18, K. N. A. Padmanabhan three for 36); Kerala 163 (B. Ramaprakash 43, F. V. Rashid 36 not out, F. A. Aslam 37; A. Shetty three for 40) and 114 for five (P. T. Subramaniam 42; A. Shetty three for 45). *Kerala 17 pts, Goa 7 pts.*

At Nehru Stadium, Hubli, December 5, 6, 7, 8. Drawn. Karnataka* 503 (K. Srinath 125, R. S. Dravid 55, S. M. H. Kirmani 81, K. A. Jeshwant 61, S. Joshi 83 not out; N. R. Yadav three for 57, Arshad Ayub four for 191); Hyderabad five for no wkt. *Karnataka 4 pts, Hyderabad 3 pts.*

At Public Stadium, Tiruvalla, December 5, 6, 7, 8. Tamil Nadu won by an innings and nine runs. Kerala* 116 (S. Subramaniam five for 49, including a hat-trick, M. Venkataramana five for 43) and 228 (V. Narayan Kutty 35, P. T. Subramaniam 48, B. Ramaprakash 32, F. V. Rashid 41; M. Venkataramana six for 73); Tamil Nadu 353 for eight dec. (V. B. Chandrasekhar 58, Robin Singh 108, S. Sharath 38, A. R. Kapoor 34 not out, S. Subramaniam 50 not out; K. N. A. Padmanabhan five for 120). *Tamil Nadu 23 pts, Kerala 4 pts.*

At Dr Rajendra Prasad Stadium, Margao, December 12, 13, 14, 15. Andhra won by ten wickets. Goa 247 (M. Sawkar 77, S. Mahadevan 43, Extras 31; G. V. V. Gopalraju four for 45, P. Prakash three for 47) and 222 (M. Sawkar 60, S. Mahadevan 41, A. Shetty 60, N. A. Vernekar 32; D. Sudhakar Reddy three for 22); Andhra* 462 (A. Pathak 145, M. F. Rehman 79, K. V. S. D. Kamaraju 40, K. Veerbrahman 80, Extras 33; J. A. Fernandes three for 115, S. Mahadevan three for 91) and eight for no wkt. *Andhra 19 pts, Goa 3 pts.*

At M. A. Chidambaram Stadium, Madras, December 17, 18, 19, 20. Tamil Nadu won by six wickets. Karnataka* 295 (P. V. Shashikanth 76, K. Srinath 64, R. S. Dravid 79; S. Subramaniam four for 67, M. Venkataramana four for 61) and 291 (C. Saldanha 45, P. V. Shashikanth 74, K. A. Jeshwant 101; S. Subramaniam six for 50, A. R. Kapoor three for 83); Tamil Nadu 358 (K. Srikkanth 104, Robin Singh 45, M. Senthilnathan 45, A. R. Kapoor 37) and 259 for four (K. Srikkanth 38, Robin Singh 77 not out, M. Senthilnathan 68, Penalty 30). *Tamil Nadu 21 pts, Karnataka 10 pts.*

At Municipal Stadium, Vishakhapatnam, December 19, 20, 21, 22. Hyderabad won by an innings and 134 runs. Andhra* 130 (K. V. S. D. Kamaraju 41, K. Veerbrahman 37; N. R. Yadav four for 43, Arshad Ayub three for 37) and 291 (M. F. Rehman 46, K. V. S. D. Kamaraju 98, V. Vinay Kumar 62, P. Prakash 57 not out; M. V. Ramanamurthy four for 62, R. Sridhar three for 74); Hyderabad 555 (Abdul Azeem 120, R. A. Swarup 140, V. Jaisimha 68, V. Pratap 122 not out, Arshad Ayub 30, M. V. Ramanamurthy 35; G. V. V. Gopalraju three for 108, P. Prakash five for 170). *Hyderabad 22 pts, Andhra 2 pts.*

Tamil Nadu 84 pts, Hyderabad 80 pts, Karnataka 79 pts, Andhra 39 pts, Kerala 39 pts, Goa 21 pts. Tamil Nadu, Hyderabad and Karnataka qualified for the knockout stage.

West Zone

At Wankhede Stadium, Bombay, November 20, 21, 22, 23. Drawn. Baroda 347 (R. B. Parikh 31, T. B. Arothe 52, A. C. Bedade 62, J. J. Martin 64 not out; V. A. Shahane three for 71, S. S. Patil three for 69, S. V. Bahutule three for 39) and 385 for five dec. (R. B. Parikh 35, T. B. Arothe 73, A. C. Bedade 102, N. R. Mongia 78, J. J. Martin 53 not out); Bombay* 510 (Z. Bharucha 100, J. V. Paranjpe 69, V. G. Kambli 168, Penalty 42; T. B. Arothe six for 122) and 81 for two (V. G. Kambli 50 not out). *Bombay 15 pts, Baroda 9 pts.*

At Sardar Patel Stadium, Valsad, November 20, 21, 22, 23. Drawn. Gujarat* 159 (N. Modi 56; R. R. Garsondia four for 37, H. Joshi three for 30) and 278 (H. Thakkar 60, Maqbul Malam 87, D. T. Patel 37, N. Parikh 47 not out; R. R. Garsondia three for 72, B. M. Radia four for 73); Saurashtra 290 (N. R. Odedra 33, B. Dutta 107, M. Parmar 34; D. T. Patel four for 84, V. Sharma five for 87) and 118 for five (D. T. Patel three for 46). *Gujarat 10 pts, Saurashtra 11 pts.*

At Pithawala Stadium, Bhimpore, Surat, November 27, 28, 29, 30. Baroda won by 195 runs. Baroda* 214 (N. R. Mongia 30, J. J. Martin 37; D. T. Patel three for 66) and 425 for eight dec. (K. S. Chavan 43, T. B. Arothe 154, N. R. Mongia 63, J. J. Martin 86 not out; D. T. Patel three for 76); Gujarat 196 (M. H. Parmar 102; T. B. Arothe six for 75) and 248 (H. Thakkar 31, Maqbul Malam 35, M. H. Parmar 52, B. H. Mistry 51; T. B. Arothe five for 102, D. Soni four for 55). *Baroda 16 pts, Gujarat 6 pts.*

At University Ground, Bhavnagar, November 27, 28, 29, 30. Drawn. Maharashtra* 591 for five dec. (S. S. Bhave 220, H. A. Kinikar 110, S. S. Sugwekar 131, M. D. Gunjal 81 not out; B. M. Radia three for 177) and 234 for eight dec. (H. A. Kinikar 47, S. S. Sugwekar 42, M. D. Gunjal 62); Saurashtra 325 (S. S. Tanna 34, B. M. Jadeja 55, A. N. Pandya 75, M. Parmar 52, D. Chudasama 32; M. Kulkarni three for 90, S. J. Jadhav five for 83) and 41 for two. *Saurashtra 9 pts, Maharashtra 17 pts.*

At GSFC Ground, Baroda, December 4, 5, 6, 7. Maharashtra won by eight wickets. Baroda 265 (T. B. Arothe 51, A. C. Bedade 111 not out; M. Kulkarni three for 91) and 180 (J. J. Martin 33, A. H. Palkar 51; M. Kulkarni five for 85); Maharashtra* 187 (M. D. Gunjal 37, Penalty 30; M. S. Narula four for 51) and 259 for two (H. A. Kinikar 69, J. Narse 42, S. V. Jedhe 105 not out, R. Manohar 33 not out). *Maharashtra 19 pts, Baroda 7 pts.*

At Municipal Ground, Rajkot, December 19, 20, 21, 22. Drawn. Saurashtra* 294 (S. Kotak 76, B. M. Radia 52 not out, H. Joshi 34; S. A. Ankola three for 69, S. S. Patil four for 84) and 204 for four dec. (N. R. Odedra 104, B. M. Jadeja 65; S. V. Bahutule three for 71); Bombay 426 (S. S. Dighe 71, J. V. Paranjpe 88, S. More 80, Iqbal Khan 59, M. Karanjkar 46, S. V. Bahutule 35; D. Chudasama six for 125) and 40 for no wkt. *Saurashtra 4 pts, Bombay 11 pts.*

At IPCL Sports Complex Ground, Baroda, December 26, 27, 28, 29. Drawn. Saurashtra 341 (S. S. Tanna 161, S. Kotak 34, B. M. Radia 35, Penalty 33; M. S. Narula six for 92) and 221 for three dec. (S. S. Tanna 35, A. N. Pandya 53 not out, S. Kotak 60 not out, Penalty 31; K. D. Amin three for 51); Baroda* 495 for six dec. (R. B. Parikh 101, R. Naik 87, A. C. Bedade 69, N. R. Mongia 111 not out, M. S. Narula 58 not out; D. Chudasama three for 127). *Baroda 13 pts, Saurashtra 8 pts.*

At Poona Club, Pune, December 26, 27, 28, 29. Drawn. Bombay* 408 (Z. Bharucha 49, S. S. Dighe 100, J. V. Paranjpe 66, S. V. Bahutule 41, S. S. Patil 35; S. V. Jedhe three for 63) and 399 for four dec. (Z. Bharucha 96, J. V. Paranjpe 33, V. G. Kambli 202 not out, S. V. Bahutule 49 not out); Maharashtra 373 (S. S. Bhave 44, S. V. Jedhe 106, S. S. Sugwekar 58, S. J. Jadhav 74 not out; S. A. Ankola four for 61, S. S. Patil five for 94) and 116 for five (S. S. Bhave 34, H. A. Kinikar 36; S. S. Patil three for 19). *Maharashtra 10 pts, Bombay 18 pts.*

At Wankhede Stadium, Bombay, January 2, 3, 4, 5. Bombay won by an innings and 116 runs. Gujarat 331 (Maqbul Malam 52, Parashar Patel 123, N. Modi 46; S. A. Ankola three for 66, S. S. Patil three for 58) and 188 (M. H. Parmar 61, B. H. Mistry 55; A. Kuruvilla six for 61); Bombay* 635 for nine dec. (Z. Bharucha 79, J. V. Paranjpe 218, S. More 71, S. V. Bahutule 123 not out, S. S. Patil 38). *Bombay 24 pts, Gujarat 4 pts.*

At Railway Stadium, Bhusawal, January 8, 9, 10, 11. Maharashtra won by five wickets. Gujarat* 277 (M. H. Parmar 127 not out, Parashar Patel 38, N. Parikh 33; S. V. Jedhe three for 57, S. J. Jadhav three for 49) and 219 (Maqbul Malam 32, M. H. Parmar 73, B. H. Mistry 38, T. N. Varsania 46 not out: M. Kulkarni four for 83, S. V. Inamdar three for 31); Maharashtra 284 (H. A. Kinikar 114, S. V. Jedhe 58, S. D. Lande 58; T. N. Varsania six for 96) and 216 for five (J. Narse 57, R. Manohar 48 not out, M. M. More 30; T. N. Varsania three for 65). *Maharashtra 17 pts, Gujarat 7 pts.*

Bombay 68 pts, Maharashtra 63 pts, Baroda 45 pts, Saurashtra 32 pts, Gujarat 27 pts. Bombay, Maharashtra and Baroda qualified for the knockout stage.

Pre-quarter-finals

At M. Chinnaswamy Stadium, Bangalore, February 5, 6, 7, 8, 9. Madhya Pradesh won by five runs. Madhya Pradesh* 406 (P. K. Dwevedi 174, S. M. Patil 95, M. S. Sahni 47; A. R. Bhat four for 116, S. Joshi three for 92) and 173 (S. M. Patil 31, Zuber Khan 40, D. K. Nilosey 69 not out; R. Ananth four for 50, A. R. Bhat five for 57); Karnataka 342 (K. Srinath 144 not out, R. S. Dravid 89; N. D. Hirwani six for 123) and 232 (K. A. Jeshwant 87, S. Somasunder 59, A. Vaidya 43 not out; S. S. Lahore six for 95).

At Railway Stadium, Madras, February 6, 7, 8, 9, 10. Tamil Nadu won by an innings and 72 runs. Tamil Nadu* 547 (V. B. Chandrasekhar 37, M. Senthilnathan 189, S. Sharath 102, D. Vasu 55, S. Subramaniam 68, M. Sanjay 51 not out; Ijaz Hussain three for 66, R. C. Thakkar three for 157); Assam 251 (L. S. Rajput 60, Rajinder Singh 91, Javed Khan 35; M. Venkataramana three for 66, S. Subramaniam seven for 61) and 224 (L. S. Rajput 105, Z. Zuffri 49; M. Venkataramana three for 96, S. Subramaniam seven for 57).

At IPCL Sports Complex Ground, Baroda, February 12, 13, 14, 15, 16. Hyderabad won by 51 runs. Hyderabad* 416 (Abdul Azeem 158, V. Pratap 72, Penalty 48; K. D. Amin three for 59, M. S. Narula four for 82) and 320 (R. A. Swarup 125, V. Jaisimha 73; M. S. Narula four for 77, T. B. Arothe three for 89); Baroda 431 for nine dec. (K. S. Chavan 65, T. B. Arothe 171, J. Martin 82, Penalty 36; Arshad Ayub six for 147) and 254 (R. B. Parikh 36, A. C. Bedade 36, N. R. Mongia 91; R. A. Swarup five for 91).

At Brabourne Stadium, Bombay, February 12, 13, 14, 15, 16. Bombay won by an innings and 41 runs. Bihar* 182 (Tarun Kumar 50, S. S. Karim 40, S. Chatterjee 32; S. A. Ankola three for 29, M. Karanjkar four for 39) and 235 (Indranil Bose 30, Sunil Kumar 43, Tarun Kumar 100 not out; S. S. Patil four for 77, S. V. Bahutule four for 71); Bombay 458 (Z. Bharucha 101, M. Karanjkar 84, S. More 112, Iqbal Khan 69; Avinash Kumar four for 131, S. Arfi four for 53).

At Nehru Stadium, Pune, February 12, 13, 14, 15, 16. Drawn. Maharashtra were declared winners by virtue of their first-innings lead. Maharashtra* 405 (S. S. Bhave 93, S. V. Jedhe 31, S. D. Lande 56, Iqbal Siddiqui 51, S. V. Inamdar 55; Jaswinder Singh three for 75) and 393 for one dec. (S. S. Bhave 66, H. A. Kinikar 205 not out, S. V. Jedhe 121 not out); Railways 399 (Yusuf Ali Khan 54, P. Shepherd 50, Manvinder Singh 34, Abhay Sharma 170; S. V. Jedhe six for 119) and 124 for two (P. Shepherd 39 not out).

At Punjab Agricultural University Ground, Ludhiana, February 12, 13, 14, 15, 16. Punjab won by six wickets. Bengal* 209 (Arun Lal 60, Saurav Ganguly 32, Penalty 44; A. S. Bedi four for 31, B. Vij four for 62) and 327 (I. B. Roy 119, S. J. Kalyani 63, A. Malhotra 45, Snehashish Ganguly 49 not out; Bhupinder Singh, sen. four for 82, B. Vij five for 95); Punjab 196 (Vikram Rathore 48, Bhupinder Singh, sen. 30; P. S. Vaidya four for 64, U. Chatterjee four for 74) and 344 for four (Vikram Rathore 169 not out, Gursharan Singh 82, K. Mohan 42 not out).

At Nehru Stadium, Ghaziabad, February 12, 13, 14, 15, 16. Drawn. Uttar Pradesh were declared winners by virtue of their first-innings lead. Haryana* 278 (Deepak Sharma 31, A. S. Kaypee 64, V. S. Yadav 86, Chetan Sharma 36; Obaid Kamal four for 72, A. W. Zaidi five for 92) and 505 for six dec. (Deepak Sharma 62, N. R. Goel 56, A. S. Kaypee 109, V. S. Yadav 191, Penalty 30; S. Shukla three for 86); Uttar Pradesh 454 (M. Mudgal 107, R. Pal 31, S. S. Khandkar 137, Rizwan Shamshad 83; Chetan Sharma five for 137) and 263 for six (R. V. Sapru 31, Rizwan Shamshad 61, A. Gautam 63 not out, S. Shukla 30 not out; Chetan Sharma three for 73).

Quarter-finals

At BHEL Sports Ground, Bhopal, February 26, 27, 28, March 1, 2. Drawn. Madhya Pradesh were declared winners by virtue of their first-innings lead. Madhya Pradesh* 347 (A. R. Khurasia 31, P. K. Dwevedi 46, S. M. Patil 40, M. S. Sahni 47, Zuber Khan 72 not out, R. K. Chauhan 33; A. S. Wassan three for 70) and 263 for four (K. K. Patel 100, P. K. Dwevedi 45, M. S. Sahni 64); Delhi 330 (Bantoo Singh 141 not out, A. S. Wassan 30, F. Ghayas 45; N. D. Hirwani three for 112).

At Railway Stadium, Bhusawal, February 26, 27, 28, March 1, 2. Maharashtra won by ten wickets. Tamil Nadu* 267 (Robin Singh 38, D. Vasu 78, A. R. Kapoor 61; S. V. Inamdar four for seven, Iqbal Siddiqui six for 59) and 215 (S. Sharath 55, D. Vasu 39, M. Venkataramana 46; Iqbal Siddiqui four for 71, S. V. Jedhe five for 72); Maharashtra 384 (S. S. Bhave 99, S. V. Jedhe 168, S. S. Sugwekar 34, Extras 33; D. Vasu five for 81) and 102 for no wkt (S. S. Bhave 64 not out).

At Punjab Agricultural University Ground, Ludhiana, February 26, 27, 28, March 1, 2. Punjab won by nine wickets. Hyderabad 82 (Bhupinder Singh, sen. four for 37, A. S. Bedi three for 23, B. Vij three for five) and 180 (R. A. Swarup 58, V. Jaisimha 56; Bhupinder Singh, sen. four for 59, A. S. Bedi five for 77); Punjab* 198 (Vikram Rathore 47, Bhupinder Singh, sen. 30; Arshad Ayub five for 70) and 65 for one (R. Kalsi 32 not out).

At Green Park, Kanpur, February 26, 27, 28, March 1, 2. Drawn. Uttar Pradesh were declared winners on the toss of the coin, after rain. Bombay 133 for two dec. (S. S. Dighe 62 not out); Uttar Pradesh* 33 for no wkt.

Semi-finals

At Poona Club, Pune, March 12, 13, 14, 15, 16. Maharashtra won by 99 runs. Maharashtra* 378 (S. S. Bhave 72, H. A. Kinikar 30, S. V. Jedhe 61, S. S. Sugwekar 49, Extras 31; Obaid Kamal three for 108, A. W. Zaidi five for 115) and 317 (S. V. Jedhe 62, S. S. Sugwekar 143, S. Kondhalkar 31; Obaid Kamal four for 89, A. W. Zaidi four for 118); Uttar Pradesh 314 (G. K. Pandey 39, Rizwan Shamshad 145 not out, Obaid Kamal three for 88, S. V. Jedhe four for 88) and 282 (Rizwan Shamshad 93, R. V. Sapru 38, A. Gautam 62; Iqbal Siddiqui four for 77, S. V. Jedhe four for 109).

At Nehru Stadium, Indore, March 13, 14, 15, 16, 17. Punjab won by 80 runs. Punjab* 217 (R. Kalsi 38, Gursharan Singh 81, Amit Sharma 31, S. Chopra 30; N. D. Hirwani five for 47) and 216 (Gursharan Singh 44, Amit Sharma 30, K. Mohan 44, Arun Sharma 30; H. S. Sodhi three for 33, N. D. Hirwani four for 75); Madhya Pradesh 154 (S. M. Patil 31, Extras 34; A. S. Bedi four for 52, B. Vij three for 25, K. Mohan three for 19) and 199 (A. V. Vijayvargiya 41, P. K. Dwevedi 32; D. K. Nilosey 30; B. Vij four for 63).

Final

At Punjab Agricultural University Ground, Ludhiana, March 27, 28, 29, 30, 31. Punjab won by 120 runs. Punjab* 318 (Amit Sharma 161; S. V. Jedhe four for 111) and 146 (Gursharan Singh 44; S. V. Jedhe four for 40, S. J. Jadhav five for 55); Maharashtra 212 (S. V. Jedhe 42; Bhupinder Singh, sen. three for 85, B. Vij six for 61) and 132 (Bhupinder Singh, sen. three for 47, A. S. Bedi three for 35, B. Vij three for 33).

RANJI TROPHY WINNERS

1934-35	Bombay	1954-55	Madras	1974-75	Bombay
1935-36	Bombay	1955-56	Bombay	1975-76	Bombay
1936-37	Nawanagar	1956-57	Bombay	1976-77	Bombay
1937-38	Hyderabad	1957-58	Baroda	1977-78	Karnataka
1938-39	Bengal	1958-59	Bombay	1978-79	Delhi
1939-40	Maharashtra	1959-60	Bombay	1979-80	Delhi
1940-41	Maharashtra	1960-61	Bombay	1980-81	Bombay
1941-42	Bombay	1961-62	Bombay	1981-82	Delhi
1942-43	Baroda	1962-63	Bombay	1982-83	Karnataka
1943-44	Western India	1963-64	Bombay	1983-84	Bombay
1944-45	Bombay	1964-65	Bombay	1984-85	Bombay
1945-46	Holkar	1965-66	Bombay	1985-86	Delhi
1946-47	Baroda	1966-67	Bombay	1986-87	Hyderabad
1947-48	Holkar	1967-68	Bombay	1987-88	Tamil Nadu
1948-49	Bombay	1968-69	Bombay	1988-89	Delhi
1949-50	Baroda	1969-70	Bombay	1989-90	Bengal
1950-51	Holkar	1970-71	Bombay	1990-91	Haryana
1951-52	Bombay	1971-72	Bombay	1991-92	Delhi
1952-53	Holkar	1972-73	Bombay	1992-93	Punjab
1953-54	Bombay	1973-74	Karnataka		

FUTURE TOURS

1994	New Zealanders to England	1994-95	Sri Lankans to India
	South Africans to England		Sri Lankans to Zimbabwe
			West Indians to India
			West Indians to New Zealand
1994-95	Australians to New Zealand*		Zimbabweans to Australia
	Australians to West Indies		
	Australians to Sri Lanka*	1995	West Indians to England
	Australians to Pakistan*		
	England to Australia	1995-96	England to South Africa
	New Zealanders to South Africa		Pakistanis to Australia
	Pakistanis to Sri Lanka*		Sri Lankans to Australia
	Pakistanis to India*		West Indians to New Zealand
	South Africans to New Zealand		West Indians to Australia
	South Africans to India*		World Cup (*in India, Pakistan*
	South Africans to Pakistan*		*and Sri Lanka, February/March*
	South Africans to Zimbabwe*		*1996*)

* Signifies unconfirmed.

Note: The following tours were scheduled for 1993-94: Indians to Sri Lanka, South Africans to Sri Lanka, New Zealanders to Australia, South Africans to Australia, West Indians to Sri Lanka, Zimbabweans to Pakistan, Sri Lankans to India, England to West Indies, Pakistanis to New Zealand, Australians to South Africa, Indians to New Zealand.

CRICKET IN PAKISTAN, 1992-93

By ABID ALI KAZI

Domestic cricket in 1992-93 was an anticlimax after Pakistan's triumph in the World Cup the previous season. No international matches were staged on home soil; instead the national team toured England, Australia, New Zealand, Sharjah, South Africa, Zimbabwe and the West Indies. Between the Fifth Test in England in August and the First in the West Indies eight months later they played 30 limited-overs internationals, one Test and five other first-class matches; crushing defeat in an unexpectedly one-sided Test series with West Indies followed.

Meanwhile, the national first-class championship, the Quaid-e-Azam Trophy, was contested in December to February with most of the international players elsewhere. Karachi Whites, unusually the city's only first-class representatives, completed a hat-trick of titles, beating Sargodha in the final by an innings and 174 runs. Three of their batsmen scored centuries in their total of 593, and a rapid 145 from Basit Ali propelled him into the West Indian tour. After a bad start to the tournament – bowled out for 50 to lose their opening match – Karachi Whites topped the group table and beat third-placed Lahore City on first-innings lead in the semi-finals, while Sargodha won through in similar circumstances against group runners-up Bahawalpur. Multan were relegated, to be replaced by Karachi Blues, who regained first-class status after beating Karachi Greens in the Grade II final. Karachi Whites also won both the Quaid-e-Azam Friday League – Pakistan's equivalent to the English Sunday League, taking place concurrently with the first-class competition – and the national Under-19 championship. The latter, contested by ten teams divided into two groups, has grown in importance since its introduction in 1970-71 because of its usefulness in highlighting grassroots talent.

During the first half of the season, the country's other first-class tournament, the BCCP Patron's Trophy, introduced an experimental bonus points system. In addition to 12 points awarded for a win, batting and bowling points were awarded on the performance of teams during the first 85 overs of each first innings – confusingly, at the same time the 85-overs limit on the first innings was abolished. Bowling points were particularly easy to obtain, as the maximum four points were awarded for taking only six wickets. The new system was not carried over to the Quaid-e-Azam Trophy, which retained the 85-overs limit on the first innings and awarded ten points for an outright win and four points for a first-innings lead in a drawn match. Habib Bank retained the Patron's Trophy after leading on first innings in the final against ADBP. They were placed third after the group matches but defeated United Bank, who were top of the table, in the semi-finals. ADBP had their consolation when they won the final of the Patron's Trophy 40-overs Friday League. Grade II of the Championship was won by Pakistan Railways, who defeated Allied Bank despite a major reshuffle of the bank line-up, which brought in several Test stars. Railways were promoted at the expense of National Bank, though the latter protested that their performance in the closing stages had been adversely affected by the loss of their leading player Nadeem Khan to the national team.

The 12th Wills Cup, the national 50-overs tournament, was contested by a record 16 teams, those playing in both the Quaid-e-Azam and the Patron's Trophies, divided into four groups, whose leaders – all from the commercial teams – proceeded to the semi-finals. In the final National Bank ended Habib Bank's three-year reign as one-day champions.

Sajid Ali, of Karachi and National Bank, had the highest aggregate of runs, 1,232, and also headed the batting averages with 68.44. He and Shakeel Ahmed, who scored 1,198 for Islamabad and Habib Bank, made five centuries each; one other batsman, Aamer Hanif (Karachi and PACO), passed 1,000 runs. Waqar Younis topped the bowling averages with 21 wickets at 9.90 for United Bank before international duties claimed him; the leading wicket-taker was Akram Raza, of Sargodha and Habib Bank, with 71 at 24.28. Akram Raza was the season's leading all-rounder; in 17 matches he made 508 runs and took 13 catches, only one fewer than the top fielder, Shahid Javed, who took 14 catches in 14 matches for Rawalpindi and Habib Bank. Five other bowlers – Mohammad Zahid, Manzoor Elahi, Sajjad Akbar, Murtaza Hussain and Nadeem Khan – reached 50 wickets, but the best return was Zakir Khan's nine for 45 in an innings for ADBP against Habib Bank.

The outstanding individual performance of the season, however, was by Tahir Rashid, Habib Bank's wicket-keeper. His 40 dismissals in nine matches included a world record of nine in an innings – eight batsmen caught and one stumped in the match against PACO at Gujranwala. The previous record was eight, held jointly by three players and equalled six months later by the Australian Tim Zoehrer.

FIRST-CLASS AVERAGES, 1992-93

BATTING

(Qualification: 500 runs, average 25.00)

	M	I	NO	R	HS	100s	Avge
Sajid Ali (*National Bank/Karachi*)	11	19	1	1,232	203*	5	68.44
Ijaz Ahmed (*Habib Bank/Islamabad*)	10	12	1	655	143	3	59.54
Aamer Hanif (*PACO/Karachi*)	14	22	3	1,042	129	3	54.84
Shakeel Ahmed (*Habib Bank/Islamabad*)	15	24	2	1,198	184	5	54.45
Basit Ali (*United Bank/Karachi*)	14	19	2	865	145	4	50.88
Shahid Javed (*Habib Bank/Rawalpindi*)	14	20	1	884	111*	2	46.52
Mahmood Hamid (*PNSC/Karachi*)	16	23	4	863	107	2	45.42
Mansoor Rana (*ADBP/Lahore City*)	15	21	2	837	95	0	44.05
Shahid Nawaz (*PACO/Faisalabad*)	14	23	1	957	139	4	43.50
Shahid Anwar (*National Bank/Lahore City*)	14	24	3	905	117	3	43.09
Ghulam Ali (*PACO/Karachi*)	11	16	2	594	135*	2	42.42
Atif Rauf (*ADBP/Islamabad*)	15	23	1	919	119*	1	41.77
Sher Ali (*PACO/Bahawalpur*)	10	16	2	557	201*	2	39.78
Munir-ul-Haq (*HBFC/Karachi*)	15	21	1	794	135	2	39.70
Sohail Jaffer (*PNSC*)	8	14	1	514	160	2	39.53
Mujahid Jamshed (*PACO/Lahore City*)	14	20	1	747	119	3	39.31
Saleem Taj (*HBFC/Rawalpindi*)	11	19	3	604	105*	1	37.75
Aamer Bashir (*United Bank/Multan*)	11	17	0	583	67	0	34.29
Mohammad Nawaz (*Sargodha*)	9	17	0	579	146	1	34.05
Mohammad Hasnain (*Habib Bank/Sargodha*)	15	26	2	812	120	2	33.83
Zahoor Elahi (*ADBP/Multan*)	16	25	1	779	110	1	32.45

	M	I	NO	R	HS	100s	Avge
Akram Raza (*Habib Bank/Sargodha*)	17	23	5	508	80*	0	28.22
Saifullah (*United Bank/Bahawalpur*)	16	26	3	637	59	0	27.69
Manzoor Elahi (*ADBP/Multan*)	15	22	1	559	87	0	26.61
Pervez Shah (*United Bank/Sargodha*)	13	24	1	588	108	1	25.56

* *Signifies not out.*

BOWLING

(Qualification: 20 wickets)

	O	M	R	W	BB	5W/i	Avge
Waqar Younis (*United Bank*)	75.5	16	208	21	7-76	3	9.90
Mohammad Altaf (*Bahawalpur*)	135.4	30	342	22	7-30	1	15.54
Haaris Khan (*Karachi*)	328.1	78	776	42	6-52	3	18.47
Zakir Khan (*ADBP*)	301.3	72	789	41	9-45	2	19.24
Ijaz Ahmed (*Faisalabad*)	180.1	35	459	23	6-62	3	19.95
Mohammad Zahid (*PACO/Bahawalpur*)	486.1	105	1,328	64	7-198	7	20.75
Asadullah Butt (*Habib Bank/Islamabad*)	276.4	47	972	45	7-93	4	21.60
Mohammad Riaz (*Rawalpindi*)	246.3	46	633	29	7-115	4	21.82
Asif Siddiq (*Multan*)	263.4	35	710	32	5-50	1	22.18
Manzoor Elahi (*ADBP/Multan*)	424.5	80	1,237	55	6-60	2	22.49
Amin Lakhani (*PNSC*)	371.1	103	855	38	8-60	2	22.50
Masood Anwar (*United Bank*)	252.1	74	644	27	6-60	2	23.85
Humayun Hussain (*Karachi*)	176	24	630	26	6-44	1	24.23
Nadeem Afzal (*PNSC/Faisalabad*)	215	24	801	33	7-51	2	24.27
Akram Raza (*Habib Bank/Sargodha*)	615.5	115	1,724	71	7-91	5	24.28
Sajjad Akbar (*PNSC/Sargodha*)	565.3	128	1,351	53	7-44	4	25.49
Rashid Khan (*PIA*)	196.3	39	596	23	5-76	2	25.91
Athar Laeeq (*Karachi*)	172	22	630	24	4-55	0	26.25
Murtaza Hussain (*PACO/Bahawalpur*)	505.5	92	1,350	50	5-27	3	27.00
Azeem Hafeez (*PIA*)	193.3	37	706	26	7-54	3	27.15
Nadeem Khan (*National Bank/Karachi*)	538	111	1,454	53	7-84	4	27.43
Nadeem Ghauri (*Habib Bank*)	274	69	671	23	4-89	0	29.17
Shahid Hussain (*Islamabad*)	233.2	46	726	24	5-103	1	30.25
Tanvir Mehdi (*United Bank/Lahore City*) . . .	225.2	31	840	27	5-81	2	31.11
Mohammad Asif (*ADBP/Lahore City*)	334.5	54	923	27	4-33	0	34.18
Raja Afaq (*ADBP/Rawalpindi*)	319.3	64	873	25	5-89	1	34.92

QUAID-E-AZAM TROPHY, 1992-93

	Played	Won	Lost	Drawn	1st-inns Points	Points
Karachi Whites	7	4	1	2	4	44
Bahawalpur	7	4	1	2	4	44
Lahore City	7	2	2	3	4	24
Sargodha	7	2	3	2	4	24
Rawalpindi	7	1	1	5	12	22
Faisalabad	7	1	1	5	4	14
Islamabad	7	0	2	5	12	12
Multan	7	0	3	4	8	8

Semi-finals: Karachi Whites beat Lahore City by virtue of their first-innings lead; Sargodha beat Bahawalpur by virtue of their first-innings lead.

Final: Karachi Whites beat Sargodha by an innings and 174 runs.

Outright win = 10 pts; 1st-innings lead in drawn match = 4 pts.

*In the following scores, * by the name of a team indicates that they won the toss.*

Note: First innings closed at 85 overs in the group matches and semi-finals.

At Bahawal Stadium, Bahawalpur, December 26, 27, 28, 29. Bahawalpur won by six wickets. Sargodha 210 (Mohammad Hasnain 46, Mohammad Nawaz 54; Mohammad Zahid three for 50, Mohammad Altaf three for 46) and 127 (Murtaza Hussain four for 40); Bahawalpur* 215 for eight (Aamir Sohail 33, Shahzad Arshad 33, Saifullah 51, Mohammad Zahid 36 not out; Sajjad Akbar five for 62) and 123 for four (Shahzad Arshad 33, Saifullah 43 not out). *Bahawalpur 10 pts.*

At National Stadium, Karachi, December 26, 27, 28, 29. Faisalabad won by 267 runs. Faisalabad 260 for nine (Ijaz Ahmed 53, Saadat Gul 51 not out, Wasim Haider 48, Extras 31; Athar Laeeq three for 78, Aamer Hanif three for 73) and 193 (Wasim Haider 37; Athar Laeeq three for 80, Humayun Hussain four for 54, Aamer Hanif three for 46); Karachi Whites* 136 (Nadeem Afzal four for 41, Wasim Haider four for 37) and 50 (Nadeem Afzal five for 22, Naseer Shaukat five for 27). *Faisalabad 10 pts.*

At LCCA Ground, Lahore, December 26, 27, 28, 29. Lahore City won by 56 runs. Lahore City* 215 (Mujahid Jamshed 37, Zahid Fazal 39, Riffaqat Ali 66; Asadullah Butt four for 53, Arshad Khan four for 59) and 267 (Mujahid Jamshed 38, Shahid Anwar 52, Tariq Javed 71, Extras 34; Asadullah Butt five for 126, Arshad Khan three for 39); Islamabad 184 (Shakeel Ahmed 51; Tanvir Mehdi five for 87, Shahid Ali Khan five for 67) and 242 (Gulrez Shahid 38, Shakeel Ahmed 30, Atif Rauf 74; Tanvir Mehdi five for 81, Shahid Ali Khan three for 53). *Lahore City 10 pts.*

At Montgomery Biscuit Factory Ground, Sahiwal, December 26, 27, 28, 29. Drawn. Multan 286 (Zahoor Elahi 81, Tariq Mahboob 69, Raja Arshad 37, Mohammad Shafiq 51; Mohammad Riaz five for 86, Zahir Shah four for 100) and 206 (Tariq Mahboob 68; Naeem Akhtar seven for 98, Zahir Shah three for 75); Rawalpindi* 217 (Saleem Taj 48, Mujahid Hamid 36, Extras 33; Manzoor Elahi four for 62, Asif Siddiq five for 50) and 139 for eight (Naseer Ahmed 39 not out, Nadeem Abbasi 39; Manzoor Elahi three for 27). *Multan 4 pts.*

At Bahawal Stadium, Bahawalpur, January 2, 3, 4. Bahawalpur won by nine wickets. Faisalabad* 145 (Ijaz Ahmed 30; Murtaza Hussain four for 45) and 155 (Mohammad Ramzan 33, Sami-ul-Haq 49, Extras 34; Murtaza Hussain five for 48, Bilal Rana five for 35); Bahawalpur 288 for seven (Aamir Sohail 51, Sher Ali 101, Saifullah 32, Extras 31; Ijaz Ahmed four for 63) and 14 for one. *Bahawalpur 10 pts.*

At Marghzar Cricket Ground, Islamabad, January 2, 3, 4, 5. Drawn. Islamabad 300 for seven (Gulrez Shahid 41, Shakeel Ahmed 47, Atif Rauf 85; Ijaz Ahmed 69; Nadeem Iqbal four for 77); Multan* 156 for three (Zahoor Elahi 60 not out). *Islamabad 4 pts.*

At KRL Cricket Ground, Rawalpindi, January 2, 3, 4, 5. Drawn. Lahore City* 226 (Mujahid Jamshed 106 not out; Naeem Akhtar three for 38, Raja Afaq five for 89); Rawalpindi 229 for nine (Sabih Azhar 57, Shahid Javed 61; Kazim Hussain three for 51, Iqbal Zahoor three for 66, Shahid Ali Khan three for 73). *Rawalpindi 4 pts.*

At Sargodha Stadium, Sargodha, January 2, 3, 4, 5. Karachi Whites won by ten wickets. Sargodha 233 for eight (Mohammad Hasnain 33, Pervez Shah 108; Humayun Hussain three for 43, Haaris Khan three for 63) and 97 (Arshad Pervez 50 not out; Humayun Hussain six for 44); Karachi Whites* 286 for eight (Munir-ul-Haq 57, Aamer Hanif 127 not out, Aziz-ur-Rehman three for 51) and 46 for no wkt (Ghulam Ali 32 not out). *Karachi Whites 10 pts.*

At Iqbal Stadium, Faisalabad, January 9, 10, 11, 12. Drawn. Rawalpindi 217 (Saleem Taj 42, Shahid Javed 61; Nadeem Afzal three for 74, Wasim Haider three for 29) and 191 for five (Nadeem Younis 33, Tariq Javed 44, Saleem Taj 80 not out; Rashid Wali four for 40); Faisalabad* 258 (Nadeem Arshad 44, Shahid Nawaz 108, Saadat Gul 42; Sabih Azhar five for 72). *Faisalabad 4 pts.*

At Marghzar Cricket Ground, Islamabad, January 9, 10, 11, 12. Drawn. Bahawalpur 361 for six (Sher Ali 201 not out, Shahzad Arshad 49, Saifullah 34, Extras 40); Islamabad* 247 (Mufeez Murtaza 52, Atif Rauf 77; Murtaza Hussain three for 84, Mohammad Zahid four for 63). *Bahawalpur 4 pts.*

At LCCA Ground, Lahore, January 9, 10, 11, 12. Drawn. Lahore City 32 for one v Karachi Whites*.

At Sargodha Stadium, Sargodha, January 9, 10, 11, 12. Sargodha won by five wickets. Multan 248 (Zahoor Elahi 53, Raja Arshad 35, Aamer Bashir 47, Tariq Mahboob 32; Akram Raza six for 80) and 141 (Manzoor Elahi 61; Pervez Shah three for 27, Akram Raza four for 47); Sargodha* 223 (Mohammad Nawaz 69, Zameer-ul-Hasan 56, Arshad Pervez 38; Nadeem Nazar three for 89, Asif Siddiq four for 63) and 167 for five (Mohammad Nawaz 70, Mohammad Hasnain 35, Arshad Pervez 33 not out; Asif Siddiq three for 50). *Sargodha 10 pts.*

At LCCA Ground, Lahore, January 16, 17, 18, 19. Drawn. Lahore City 246 for nine (Tariq Javed 65, Mansoor Rana 45, Riffaqat Ali 34; Ijaz Ahmed three for 35); Faisalabad* 218 (Mohammad Ramzan 96, Sami-ul-Haq 36; Shahid Ali Khan six for 72, Iqbal Zahoor three for 75). *Lahore City 4 pts.*

At Montgomery Biscuit Factory Ground, Sahiwal, January 16, 17, 18, 19. Drawn. Multan 335 for six (Aamer Bashir 51, Tariq Mahboob 150 not out, Manzoor Elahi 87; Haaris Khan three for 124); Karachi Whites* 338 for eight (Ghulam Ali 123, Aamer Hanif 60, Mahmood Hamid 52; Nadeem Nazar five for 108). *Karachi Whites 4 pts.*

At Rawalpindi Cricket Stadium, Rawalpindi, January 16, 17, 18, 19. Drawn. Bahawalpur 107 (Bilal Rana 31; Raja Afaq three for 23); Rawalpindi* 111 for one (Nadeem Younis 53 not out). *Rawalpindi 4 pts.*

At Sargodha Stadium, Sargodha, January 16, 17, 18, 19. Drawn. Islamabad 240 for six (Mufeez Murtaza 89, Atif Rauf 56, Masood Mirza 38 not out; Akram Raza four for 89); Sargodha* 223 (Zameer-ul-Hasan 50, Akram Raza 80 not out; Shahid Hussain three for 68). *Islamabad 4 pts.*

At Bahawal Stadium, Bahawalpur, January 23, 24, 25, 26. Bahawalpur won by 266 runs. Bahawalpur 317 for nine (Aamir Sohail 61, Sher Ali 84, Shahzad Arshad 51, Tanvir Razzaq 34; Iqbal Zahoor three for 76) and 265 (Saifullah 43, Mohammad Tayyab 38, Tanvir Razzaq 72, Bilal Rana 47; Kazim Hussain three for 29, Iqbal Zahoor four for 57, Mansoor Rana three for 31); Lahore City* 197 (Shahid Anwar 55; Murtaza Hussain five for 55, Mohammad Zahid five for 50) and 119 (Ehsan Butt 31; Imran Adil three for 48, Murtaza Hussain five for 27). *Bahawalpur 10 pts.*

At Iqbal Stadium, Faisalabad, January 23, 24, 25, 26. Drawn. Faisalabad 292 (Mohammad Ramzan 30, Sami-ul-Haq 58, Shahid Nawaz 75; Asif Siddiq four for 99, Zahoor Elahi five for 55) and 330 for nine (Mohammad Ramzan 58, Saadat Gul 47, Bilal Ahmed 54, Naseer Shaukat 57, Extras 38; Asif Siddiq three for 59, Mohammad Afzal four for 81); Multan* 331 (Masroor Hussain 38, Zahoor Elahi 110, Aamer Bashir 67, Manzoor Elahi 39, Raja Arshad 32; Naved Nazir five for 85, Ijaz Ahmed three for 97). *Multan 4 pts.*

At Marghzar Cricket Ground, Islamabad, January 23, 24, 25, 26. Karachi Whites won by two wickets. Islamabad* 202 (Mufeez Murtaza 31, Gulrez Shahid 42, Atif Rauf 36; Nadeem Khan four for 60, Haaris Khan four for 67) and 248 (Shahid Hussain 60; Nadeem Khan four for 88, Haaris Khan five for 101); Karachi Whites 277 (Ameer-ud-din 38, Basit Ali 37, Aamer Hanif 104; Raja Sarfraz three for 86, Shahid Hussain three for 84) and 175 for eight (Ghulam Ali 51, Mahmood Hamid 39 not out; Asadullah Butt three for 64, Arshad Khan three for 36). *Karachi Whites 10 pts.*

At KRL Cricket Ground, Rawalpindi, January 23, 24, 25, 26. Rawalpindi won by ten wickets. Sargodha* 191 (Mohammad Nawaz 71, Pervez Shah 37; Mohammad Riaz five for 53, Azhar Hussain three for 54) and 122 (Mohammad Riaz five for 48); Rawalpindi 275 (Nadeem Younis 87, Saleem Taj 71, Shahid Javed 41; Akram Raza seven for 91, Aziz-ur-Rehman three for 55) and 39 for no wkt. *Rawalpindi 10 pts.*

At Bahawal Stadium, Bahawalpur, January 30, 31, February 1, 2. Bahawalpur won by five wickets. Multan 117 (Mohammad Altaf seven for 30, Mohammad Zahid three for 14) and 179 (Aamer Bashir 38, Raja Arshad 49; Murtaza Hussain three for 45, Mohammad Zahid three for 27); Bahawalpur* 137 (Tanvir Razzaq 33, Bilal Rana 30, Murtaza Hussain 33 not out; Asif Siddiq four for 30) and 163 for five (Saifullah 53 not out, Shahzad Arshad 30; Asif Siddiq three for 57). *Bahawalpur 10 pts.*

At Marghzar Cricket Ground, Islamabad, January 30, 31, February 1, 2. Drawn. Islamabad 352 for seven (Shakeel Ahmed 184, Mufeez Murtaza 40, Kashif Khan 35; Ijaz Ahmed five for 80) and 274 for six dec. (Shakeel Ahmed 51, Kashif Khan 91 not out, Aamer Nazir 37 not out); Faisalabad* 281 (Mohammad Ramzan 84, Mohammad Akram 48, Sami-ul-Haq 52, Ijaz Ahmed 59; Shahid Hussain five for 103) and 222 for four (Sami-ul-Haq 86, Ijaz Ahmed 30 not out, Mohammad Ashraf 51 not out). *Islamabad 4 pts.*

At National Stadium, Karachi, January 30, 31, February 1, 2. Karachi Whites won by 155 runs. Karachi Whites 348 for six (Sajid Ali 130, Moin Khan 46, Aamer Hanif 96) and 323 for seven dec. (Sajid Ali 83, Azam Khan 60, Aamer Hanif 54, Mahmood Hamid 32; Naeem Akhtar three for 95, Zahir Shah four for 92); Rawalpindi* 300 for nine (Saleem Taj 105 not out, Shahid Javed 48, Extras 34; Athar Laeeq three for 73, Nadeem Khan three for 75, Haaris Khan three for 62) and 216 (Naved Ashraf 44, Sabih Azhar 43, Shahid Javed 42; Humayun Hussain three for 62, Nadeem Khan five for 60). *Karachi Whites 10 pts.*

At Sargodha Stadium, Sargodha, January 30, 31, February 1, 2. Sargodha won by nine wickets. Lahore City 170 (Shahid Anwar 32, Mansoor Rana 36; Sajjad Akbar six for 57, Akram Raza three for 62) and 138 (Mujahid Jamshed 37; Sajjad Akbar four for 22, Akram Raza four for 29); Sargodha* 226 (Zameer-ul-Hasan 79, Akram Raza 37, Extras 44; Tanvir Mehdi three for 62, Tariq Rashid four for 21) and 85 for one (Mohammad Hasnain 52 not out). *Sargodha 10 pts.*

At Iqbal Stadium, Faisalabad, February 6, 7, 8, 9. Drawn. Sargodha 276 (Mohammad Hasnain 39, Mohammad Nawaz 61, Pervez Shah 54, Zameer-ul-Hasan 40; Naved Nazir three for 99, Ijaz Ahmed six for 62) and 267 (Anis-ur-Rehman 98 not out, Akram Raza 32; Nadeem Afzal four for 76, Rashid Wali four for 90); Faisalabad* 203 for nine (Mohammad Ramzan 75, Sami-ul-Haq 54; Akram Raza six for 71) and 211 for seven (Mohammad Ramzan 71 not out, Shahid Nawaz 65; Sajjad Akbar four for 64). *Sargodha 4 pts.*

At National Stadium, Karachi, February 6, 7, 8, 9. Karachi Whites won by eight wickets. Bahawalpur* 222 (Tanvir Razzaq 33, Saifullah 50, Shahzad Arshad 39, Murtaza Hussain 47 not out; Nadeem Khan five for 96, Haaris Khan three for 50) and 196 (Tanvir Razzaq 43, Mohammad Tayyab 40; Humayun Hussain three for 74, Athar Laeeq four for 55); Karachi Whites 248 for seven (Sajid Ali 55, Azam Khan 31, Munir-ul-Haq 50, Moin Khan 36; Bilal Rana three for 52) and 174 for two (Azam Khan 57 not out, Aamer Hanif 80 not out). *Karachi Whites 10 pts.*

At Montgomery Biscuit Factory Ground, Sahiwal, February 6, 7, 8, 9. Lahore City won by eight wickets. Multan 220 (Manzoor Elahi 75, Mohammad Shafiq 30; Mohammad Suleman three for 50) and 283 (Mohammad Siddiq 64, Aamer Bashir 51, Manzoor Elahi 53; Shahid Anwar three for 73); Lahore City* 251 (Shahid Anwar 57, Mansoor Rana 74, Mujahid Jamshed 36; Mujahid Khan three for 26) and 253 for two (Tahir Gulzar 55, Tariq Javed 42, Shahid Anwar 75 not out, Mansoor Rana 74 not out). *Lahore City 10 pts.*

At KRL Cricket Ground, Rawalpindi, February 6, 7, 8, 9. Drawn. Islamabad* 296 for seven (Mufeez Murtaza 48, Shakeel Ahmed 120, Aamer Nazir 46 not out; Azhar Hussain three for 95) and 274 (Kashif Khan 45, Atif Rauf 69, Aamer Nazir 73; Mohammad Riaz seven for 115, Azhar Hussain three for 74); Rawalpindi 313 for eight (Nadeem Younis 43, Shahid Javed 79, Mohammad Riaz 65, Mujahid Hamid 38 not out; Shahid Hussain four for 129, Ayaz Jilani three for 87) and 116 for six (Naseer Ahmed 32). *Rawalpindi 4 pts.*

Semi-finals

At National Stadium, Karachi, February 13, 14, 15, 16. Drawn. Karachi Whites were declared winners by virtue of their first-innings lead. Karachi Whites 322 for four (Sajid Ali 67, Basit Ali 121, Aamer Hanif 82 not out) and 371 for three dec. (Sajid Ali 203 not out Azam Khan 80, Mahmood Hamid 62); Lahore City* 225 for eight (Mansoor Rana 58; Nadeem Khan five for 103, Haaris Khan three for 85) and 157 for seven (Shahid Anwar 39 Tariq Javed 39; Haaris Khan six for 52).

At Gaddafi Stadium, Lahore, February 13, 14, 15, 16. Drawn. Sargodha were declared winners by virtue of their first-innings lead. Sargodha 224 (Aziz-ur-Rehman 64, Mohammad Nawaz 92; Mohammad Altaf four for 48, Mohammad Zahid three for 25) and 366 for five dec. (Mohammad Nawaz 146, Anis-ur-Rehman 70, Aziz-ur-Rehman 51 not out); Bahawalpur* 104 (Amanullah five for 32, Naeem Khan five for 49) and 101 for four (Aamir Sohail 38, Sher Ali 50 not out).

Final

At National Stadium, Karachi, February 19, 20, 21, 22, 23. Karachi Whites won by an innings and 174 runs. Karachi Whites* 593 (Sajid Ali 131, Basit Ali 145, Aamer Hanif 38, Munir-ul-Haq 135, Moin Khan 61; Akram Raza six for 164); Sargodha 209 (Mohammad Hasnain 54, Akram Raza 34, Naeem Khan 32; Athar Laeeq three for 85, Haaris Khan three for 36) and 210 (Aziz-ur-Rehman 67, Mohammad Hasnain 39; Haaris Khan five for 67, Nadeem Khan four for 68).

QUAID-E-AZAM TROPHY WINNERS

1953-54	Bahawalpur	1976-77	United Bank
1954-55	Karachi	1977-78	Habib Bank
1956-57	Punjab	1978-79	National Bank
1957-58	Bahawalpur	1979-80	PIA
1958-59	Karachi	1980-81	United Bank
1959-60	Karachi	1981-82	National Bank
1961-62	Karachi Blues	1982-83	United Bank
1962-63	Karachi A	1983-84	National Bank
1963-64	Karachi Blues	1984-85	United Bank
1964-65	Karachi Blues	1985-86	Karachi
1966-67	Karachi	1986-87	National Bank
1968-69	Lahore	1987-88	PIA
1969-70	PIA	1988-89	ADBP
1970-71	Karachi Blues	1989-90	PIA
1972-73	Railways	1990-91	Karachi Whites
1973-74	Railways	1991-92	Karachi Whites
1974-75	Punjab A	1992-93	Karachi Whites
1975-76	National Bank		

BCCP PATRON'S TROPHY, 1992-93

	Played	Won	Lost	Drawn	Bonus points	Points
United Bank	7	3	1	3	46	82
ADBP	7	3	1	3	44	80
Habib Bank	7	2	2	3	44	68
PNSC.	7	1	2	4	47	59
PACO	7	1	0	6	45	57
HBFC	7	1	2	4	43	55
PIA	7	1	3	3	42	54
National Bank	7	0	1	6	45	45†

Semi-finals: ADBP beat PNSC by 70 runs; Habib Bank beat United Bank by four wickets.

Final: Habib Bank beat ADBP by virtue of their first-innings lead.

† National Bank had 2 points deducted because of their slow over-rate.

Win = 12 pts; batting points (first 85 overs): 150 to 199 runs = 1 pt; 200 to 249 runs = 2 pts; 250 to 299 runs = 3 pts; 300 runs or over = 4 pts; bowling points (first 85 overs) 2 wkts = 1 pt; 3 or 4 wkts = 2 pts; 5 wkts = 3 pts; 6 or more wkts = 4 pts.

Note: In the following matches there was no overs-limit on the first innings.

At Multan Cricket Club Stadium, Multan, October 17, 18, 19, 20. United Bank won by eight wickets. PIA* 228 (Asif Mohammad 55, Moin Khan 40; Waqar Younis five for 52) and 225 (Nasir Khan 31, Aamer Malik 40, Asif Mohammad 38, Moin Khan 35 not out; Waqar Younis four for 51, Mushtaq Ahmed four for 91); United Bank 392 (Raees Ahmed 83, Aamer Bashir 57, Basit Ali 124 not out, Waqar Younis 36; Zahid Ahmed three for 119, Asif Mohammad five for 86) and 63 for two. *United Bank 20 pts, PIA 6 pts.*

At Montgomery Biscuit Factory Ground, Sahiwal, October 17, 18, 19, 20. Drawn. PNSC* 402 (Aamer Ishaq 37, Sohail Miandad 91, Sohail Jaffer 32, Sajjad Akbar 63, Zafar Iqbal 87; Murtaza Hussain three for 122, Mohammad Zahid six for 152); PACO 146 (Mujahid Jamshed 39; Amin Lakhani eight for 60) and 389 for eight (Ghulam Ali 35, Shahid Saeed 74, Mujahid Jamshed 75, Aamer Hanif 52, Umar Rasheed 90, Murtaza Hussain 33 not out; Sajjad Akbar three for 132, Amin Lakhani four for 116). *PNSC 7 pts, PACO 4 pts.*

At Sargodha Stadium, Sargodha, October, 17, 18, 19, 20. Habib Bank won by ten wickets. HBFC 187 (Naved Anjum three for 33, Nadeem Ghauri three for 28) and 266 (Aamer Khurshid 100, Riffat Alam 59; Nadeem Ghauri three for 33); Habib Bank* 420 for seven dec. (Shakeel Ahmed 142, Moin-ul-Atiq 45, Ijaz Ahmed 134; Zulfiqar Butt four for 105, Kazim Mehdi three for 138) and 34 for no wkt. *Habib Bank 20 pts, HBFC 5 pts.*

At Arbab Niaz Cricket Stadium, Peshawar, October 17, 18, 19, 20. Drawn. National Bank 348 for eight dec. (Shahid Anwar 101, Sajid Ali 121, Ameer Akbar 39; Javed Hayat three for 96) and 310 for eight (Sajid Ali 42, Hafeez-ur-Rehman 76, Naeem Ashraf 62 not out; Mohammad Asif four for 72); ADBP* 390 (Saeed Anwar 101, Atif Rauf 75, Mansoor Rana 95, Ghaffar Kazmi 39; Maqsood Rana three for 99, Nadeem Khan three for 106). *National Bank 8 pts, ADBP 8 pts.*

At Multan Cricket Club Stadium, Multan, October 24, 25, 26, 27. Drawn. PNSC* 275 (Sohail Miandad 42, Mohammad Javed 50, Mahmood Hamid 89; Wasim Akram four for 90, Zahid Ahmed three for 80) and 245 (Aamer Ishaq 43, Sohail Miandad 80, Mohammad Javed 32; Wasim Akram six for 53); PIA 290 (Rizwan-uz-Zaman 35, Asif Mohammad 35, Zahid Fazal 117, Zahid Ahmed 34; Amin Lakhani three for 105, Sohail Farooqi four for 72) and 183 for eight (Asif Mohammad 37, Nasir Khan 40, Babar Zaman 34; Amin Lakhani four for 69). *PNSC 7 pts, PIA 6 pts.*

At Montgomery Biscuit Factory Ground, Sahiwal, October 24, 25, 26, 27. Drawn. PACO* 274 (Mujahid Jamshed 36, Aamer Hanif 85, Umar Rasheed 68; Raees Ahmed four for 37) and 227 for nine (Shahid Nawaz 45, Umar Rasheed 39, Zulqarnain 52 not out; Masood Anwar three for 25, Mushtaq Ahmed five for 118); United Bank 428 (Saifullah 38, Raees Ahmed 48, Basit Ali 33, Aamer Bashir 61, Iqbal Imam 113, Rashid Latif 66, Extras 35; Mohammad Zahid seven for 198). *United Bank 6 pts, PACO 5 pts.*

At Rawalpindi Cricket Stadium, Rawalpindi, October 24, 25, 26, 27. ADBP won by 188 runs. ADBP 253 (Bilal Ahmed 71, Javed Hayat 60; Ali Ahmed three for 39, Shahzad Ilyas six for 69) and 342 for five dec. (Saeed Anwar 100, Zahoor Elahi 58, Mansoor Rana 34, Manzoor Elahi 53 not out, Bilal Ahmed 34 not out; Saleem Taj three for 49); HBFC* 269 (Munir-ul-Haq 53, Wasim Ali 48, Tariq Alam 52, Extras 32; Zakir Khan four for 84) and 138 (Munir-ul-Haq 49, Zulfiqar Butt 32 not out; Zakir Khan four for 49, Ghayyur Qureshi four for 50). *ADBP 19 pts, HBFC 7 pts.*

At Arbab Niaz Cricket Stadium, Peshawar, October 24, 25, 26, 27. Drawn. Habib Bank* 276 (Shakeel Ahmed 50, Shaukat Mirza 52, Ijaz Ahmed 35, Anwar Miandad 35, Tahir Rashid 55; Nadeem Khan seven for 84) and 366 for four (Moin-ul-Atiq 35, Shaukat Mirza 34, Ijaz Ahmed 109 not out, Shahid Javed 111 not out; Hafeez-ur-Rehman four for 72); National Bank 448 for nine dec. (Shahid Anwar 117, Wasim Arif 53, Saeed Azad 133, Naeem Ashraf 46; Nadeem Ghauri four for 89). *National Bank 7 pts, Habib Bank 4 pts.*

At Multan Cricket Club Stadium, Multan, October 31, November 1, 2, 3. PACO won by 142 runs. PACO* 224 (Ghulam Ali 135 not out, Shahid Saeed 45; Zahid Ahmed five for 74, Iqbal Sikandar four for 93) and 264 for eight dec. (Ghulam Ali 68, Shahid Nawaz 110, Umar Rasheed 56; Asif Mohammad three for 54, Zahid Ahmed three for 78); PIA 163 (Rizwan-uz-Zaman 42, Zahid Ahmed 36; Mohammad Zahid five for 52, Yahya Toor three for 20) and 183 (Rizwan-uz-Zaman 43; Murtaza Hussain three for 40, Mohammad Zahid four for 56). *PACO 18 pts, PIA 5 pts.*

At Montgomery Biscuit Factory Ground, Sahiwal, October 31, November 1, 2, 3. United Bank won by an innings and 19 runs. PNSC* 277 (Sohail Miandad 44, Farrukh Bari 54, Sajjad Akbar 51; Waqar Younis seven for 76) and 222 (Sohail Miandad 35, Mahmood Hamid 81; Waqar Younis five for 29, Masood Anwar three for 58); United Bank 518 (Mansoor Akhtar 99, Raees Ahmed 45, Inzamam-ul-Haq 178, Basit Ali 73, Masood Anwar 49). *United Bank 20 pts, PNSC 7 pts.*

At Rawalpindi Cricket Stadium, Rawalpindi, October 31, November 1, 2, 3. Drawn. HBFC 156 (Sohail Taqi 36, Munir-ul-Haq 34; Barkatullah three for 48, Maqsood Rana seven for 70) and 405 (Faisal Qureshi 36, Munir-ul-Haq 120, Wasim Ali 119, Zulfiqar Butt 30 not out, Extras 52; Ameer Akbar three for 29, Nadeem Khan three for 51); National Bank* 270 (Shahid Anwar 35, Ameer Akbar 73, Extras 32; Sohail Khan five for 100) and 41 for one (Sajid Ali 33). *National Bank 7 pts, HBFC 5 pts.*

At Arbab Niaz Cricket Stadium, Peshawar, October 31, November 1, 2, 3. ADBP won by 359 runs. ADBP 152 (Atif Rauf 63; Naved Anjum five for 59) and 457 (Saeed Anwar 151, Zahoor Elahi 39, Atif Rauf 44, Mansoor Rana 66, Ghaffar Kazmi 58, Manzoor Elahi 32, Javed Hayat 35; Nadeem Nazar three for 142, Akram Raza four for 149); Habib Bank* 123 (Tahir Rashid 30, Naved Anjum 35; Zakir Khan nine for 45) and 127 (Shahid Javed 46; Manzoor Elahi five for 39, Mohammad Asif four for 33). *ADBP 17 pts, Habib Bank 4 pts.*

At LCCA Ground, Lahore, November 7, 8, 9, 10. PNSC won by six wickets. Habib Bank 213 (Mohammad Hasnain 120; Amin Lakhani three for 63, Sajjad Akbar seven for 44) and 171 (Shahid Javed 57, Tahir Rashid 40; Mohammad Javed three for 12, Sajjad Akbar four for 30); PNSC* 270 (Sohail Jaffer 61, Mahmood Hamid 78, Mohammad Javed 33; Amin Lakhani four for 64) and 115 for four (Zafar Iqbal 59). *PNSC 19 pts, Habib Bank 6 pts.*

At Sargodha Stadium, Sargodha, November 7, 8, 9, 10. Drawn. United Bank* 362 (Raees Ahmed 108, Mansoor Akhtar 44, Pervez Shah 75 not out; Mohammad Asif three for 52) and 182 for three (Basit Ali 76, Pervez Shah 56); ADBP 310 (Zahoor Elahi 83, Mansoor Rana 92 not out, Extras 34; Tauseef Ahmed seven for 83). *United Bank 7 pts, ADBP 7 pts.*

At Bagh-e-Jinnah Ground, Lahore, November 8, 9, 10, 11. Drawn. National Bank 467 (Shahid Anwar 110, Sajid Ali 107, Shahid Tanvir 113, Tahir Shah 64 not out; Mohammad Zahid five for 158) and 290 for seven (Shahid Anwar 68, Shahid Tanvir 142; Ashfaq Ahmed three for 63); PACO* 353 (Abdullah Khan 38, Mujahid Jamshed 119, Shahid Nawaz 92; Barkatullah three for 67, Habib Baloch three for 55, Hafeez-ur-Rehman three for 126). *National Bank 8 pts, PACO 8 pts.*

At Rawalpindi Cricket Stadium, Rawalpindi, November 8, 9, 10, 11. HBFC won by seven wickets. PIA 202 (Aamer Malik 43, Extras 33; Kabir Khan five for 92, Ali Ahmed four for 64) and 204 (Babar Zaman 74; Shahzad Ilyas four for 93, Ali Ahmed five for 76); HBFC* 272 (Faisal Qureshi 43, Wasim Ali 62, Wasim Yousufi 54, Tariq Alam 38, Extras 31; Rashid Khan five for 93) and 135 for three (Munir-ul-Haq 51 not out; Rashid Khan three for 47). *HBFC 19 pts, PIA 6 pts.*

At Iqbal Stadium, Faisalabad, November 14, 15, 16, 17. Drawn. HBFC* 267 (Aamer Khurshid 82, Saleem Taj 32, Wasim Yousufi 36; Amin Lakhani five for 104) and 204 for six (Aamer Khurshid 74, Wasim Yousufi 50); PNSC 300 (Aamer Ishaq 31, Sohail Jaffer 48, Mahmood Hamid 107, Farrukh Bari 35; Zulfiqar Butt five for 90). *PNSC 7 pts, HBFC 5 pts.*

At Sargodha Stadium, Sargodha, November 14, 15, 16, 17. Drawn. PACO* 233 (Kamran Khan 67, Shahid Nawaz 45, Zulqarnain 31; Raja Afaq three for 57, Javed Hayat three for 34) and 232 for six (Ghulam Ali 52, Kamran Khan 65, Umar Rasheed 31 not out; Mohammad Asif four for 58); ADBP 238 (Zahoor Elahi 43; Mohammad Zahid five for 107, Murtaza Hussain three for 85). *PACO 6 pts, ADBP 6 pts.*

At National Stadium, Karachi, November 15, 16, 17, 18. Drawn. PIA 435 (Rizwan-uz-Zaman 58, Babar Zaman 39, Zahid Fazal 109, Aamer Malik 55, Asif Mohammad 32, Zahid Ahmed 85; Ijaz Ahmed five for 95); Habib Bank* 576 for nine (Agha Zahid 38, Mohammad Hasnain 50, Shakeel Ahmed 60, Shahid Javed 107, Tahir Rashid 182, Akram Raza 79; Rashid Khan three for 98, Iqbal Sikandar three for 82). *Habib Bank 6 pts, PIA 6 pts.*

At Rawalpindi Cricket Stadium, Rawalpindi, November 15, 16, 17, 18. United Bank won by 51 runs. United Bank 168 (Mansoor Akhtar 33; Barkatullah three for 28, Naeem Ashraf three for 30, Ameer Akbar four for 34) and 284 (Mansoor Akhtar 60, Saifullah 38, Aamer Bashir 38, Iqbal Imam 35; Barkatullah three for 75, Maqsood Rana three for 74); National Bank* 271 (Shahid Tanvir 68, Naeem Ashraf 114; Sajjad Ali three for 70) and 130 (Saeed Azad 33, Naeem Ashraf 36; Saleem Jaffer three for 25, Tanvir Mehdi four for 22). *United Bank 17 pts, National Bank 7 pts.*

At Gaddafi Stadium, Lahore, November 21, 22, 23, 24. Drawn. National Bank 296 (Sajid Ali 40, Saeed Azad 39, Ameer Akbar 121; Azeem Hafeez six for 114) and 216 (Shahid Anwar 37, Sajid Ali 66, Mohammad Jamil 31 not out; Rashid Khan three for 71, Azeem Hafeez five for 77); PIA* 325 for seven dec. (Rizwan-uz-Zaman 52, Moin Khan 100 not out, Asif Mohammad 39, Extras 35; Naeem Ashraf four for 117) and 158 for five (Shoaib Mohammad 39, Zahid Ahmed 36). *PIA 7 pts, National Bank 4 pts.*

At Iqbal Stadium, Faisalabad, November 22, 23, 24, 25. ADBP won by six wickets. PNSC 110 (Manzoor Elahi six for 60) and 263 (Mahmood Hamid 107, Mohammad Javed 71; Manzoor Elahi four for 48, Raja Afaq three for 35); ADBP* 254 (Mansoor Rana 50, Mohammad Asif 70, Raja Afaq 31 not out; Zafar Iqbal five for 64) and 120 for four (Zahoor Elahi 59, Ghaffar Kazmi 49 not out; Nadeem Afzal four for 35). *ADBP 18 pts, PNSC 4 pts.*

At National Stadium, Karachi, November 22, 23, 24, 25. Habib Bank won by ten wickets. United Bank* 216 (Saifullah 59, Basit Ali 37, Mansoor Akhtar 38; Ijaz Ahmed four for 61) and 223 (Basit Ali 121 not out, Iqbal Imam 43; Asadullah Butt seven for 93, Nadeem Ghauri three for 58); Habib Bank 439 for six dec. (Anwar Miandad 77, Ijaz Ahmed 143, Shahid Javed 74, Tahir Rashid 45 not out, Extras 34; Tanvir Mehdi three for 120) and one for no wkt. *Habib Bank 20 pts, United Bank 4 pts.*

At Bagh-e-Jinnah Ground, Lahore, November 22, 23, 24, 25. Drawn. HBFC* 308 (Faisal Qureshi 96, Munir-ul-Haq 62, Shahzad Ilyas 78; Mohammad Zahid five for 143); PACO 506 for seven (Mujahid Jamshed 116, Aamer Hanif 129, Shahid Nawaz 127 not out, Umar Rasheed 65 not out). *HBFC 8 pts, PACO 8 pts.*

At National Stadium, Karachi, November 28, 29, 30, December 1. Drawn. HBFC 318 (Saleem Taj 72, Wasim Ali 30, Tariq Alam 32, Raffat Alam 43, Zulfiqar Butt 32; Masood Anwar six for 98) and 197 for one (Aamer Khurshid 101 not out, Saleem Taj 49); United Bank* 507 (Saifullah 40, Raees Ahmed 131, Ali Zia 33, Mansoor Akhtar 34, Iqbal Imam 95, Pervez Shah 41, Raja Arshad 48, Masood Anwar 30, Extras 42; Zulfiqar Butt four for 160, Munir-ul-Haq three for 85). *United Bank 8 pts, HBFC 6 pts.*

At Montgomery Biscuit Factory Ground, Sahiwal, November 28, 29, 30, December 1. Drawn. PNSC* 501 (Aamer Ishaq 39, Sohail Miandad 48, Sohail Jaffer 160, Sajjad Akbar 46, Mohammad Javed 47, Farrukh Bari 41, Mutahir Shah 35; Hafeez-ur-Rehman three for 118) and 156 for two (Aamer Ishaq 39, Sohail Jaffer 102 not out); National Bank 314 (Wasim Arif 65, Sajid Ali 73, Tahir Shah 61, Barkatullah 31 not out; Amin Lakhani four for 77). *PNSC 8 pts, National Bank 4 pts.*

At Municipal Stadium, Gujranwala, November 28, 29, 30, December 1. Drawn. PACO* 376 (Abdullah Khan 50, Mujahid Jamshed 43, Shahid Nawaz 139, Umar Rasheed 54, Zulqarnain 47; Asadullah Butt six for 107); Habib Bank 302 for six (Mohammad Hasnain 49, Shakeel Ahmed 125, Shaukat Mirza 53, Sohail Fazal 34 not out). *PACO 8 pts, Habib Bank 8 pts. (Habib Bank wicket-keeper Tahir Rashid created a world record by dismissing nine batsmen in PACO's innings)*

At LCCA Ground, Lahore, November 28, 29, 30, December 1. PIA won by five wickets. ADBP 182 (Zahoor Elahi 54; Rashid Khan five for 76) and 112 (Mansoor Rana 32; Rashid Khan three for 52, Azeem Hafeez seven for 54); PIA* 210 (Shoaib Mohammad 57, Aamer Malik 103; Zakir Khan three for 51, Manzoor Elahi five for 90) and 89 for five (Zakir Khan four for 38). *PIA 18 pts, ADBP 5 pts.*

Semi-finals

At Gaddafi Stadium, Lahore, December 4, 5, 6, 7. ADBP won by 70 runs. ADBP 106 (Nadeem Afzal seven for 51, Zafar Iqbal three for 34) and 262 for eight dec. (Mansoor Rana 57, Ghaffar Kazmi 100 not out; Mohsin Kamal four for 111); PNSC* 176 (Aamer Ishaq 52; Zakir Khan for 63, Manzoor Elahi six for 94) and 122 (Aamer Ishaq 38, Sohail Jaffer 34; Zakir Khan four for 43, Manzoor Elahi six for 71).

At National Stadium, Karachi, December 4, 5, 6, 7. Habib Bank won by four wickets. United Bank* 203 (Mansoor Akhtar 54, Pervez Shah 42; Asadullah Butt three for 39, Nadeem Ghauri three for 58, Akram Raza three for 70) and 188 (Saifullah 40, Mansoor Akhtar 52; Asadullah Butt five for 31, Akram Raza four for 60); Habib Bank 170 (Akram Raza 34; Masood Anwar six for 60) and 224 for six (Agha Zahid 82, Shaukat Mirza 72; Tauseef Ahmed four for 113).

Final

At Gaddafi Stadium, Lahore, December 12, 13, 14, 15, 16, 17. Drawn. Habib Bank were declared winners by virtue of their first-innings lead. Habib Bank* 683 (Mohammad Hasnain 118, Shakeel Ahmed 161, Shaukat Mirza 114, Ijaz Ahmed 94, Akram Raza 71, Nadeem Ghauri 38, Extras 41; Zakir Khan five for 146); ADBP 367 (Bilal Ahmed 86, Atif Rauf 119 not out, Javed Hayat 108; Asadullah Butt four for 114, Qasim Jamal four for 106).

BCCP PATRON'S TROPHY WINNERS

1970-71	PIA	1978-79	National Bank	1986-87	National Bank
1971-72	PIA	†1979-80	IDBP	1987-88	Habib Bank
1972-73	Karachi Blues	†1980-81	Rawalpindi	1988-89	Karachi
1973-74	Railways	†1981-82	Allied Bank	1989-90	Karachi Whites
1974-75	National Bank	†1982-83	PACO	1990-91	ADBP
1975-76	National Bank	1983-84	Karachi Blues	1991-92	Habib Bank
1976-77	Habib Bank	1984-85	Karachi Whites	1992-93	Habib Bank
1977-78	Habib Bank	1985-86	Karachi Whites		

† *The competition was not first-class between 1979-80 and 1982-83, when it served as a qualifying competition for the Quaid-e-Azam Trophy.*

Note: Matches in the following section were not first-class.

NATIONAL UNDER-19 CHAMPIONSHIP

Final

At National Stadium, Karachi, March 30, 31, April 1, 2. Karachi Whites won by 145 runs. Karachi Whites* 303 (Abdullah Khan, jun. 104, Mohammad Masroor 43; Mohammad Nadeem three for 77) and 160 (Aaley Haider 40, Mohammad Hasnain 43 not out; Mohammad Nadeem three for 34, Mohammad Nawaz three for 56); Faisalabad 184 (Mohammad Nawaz 57, Ahmed Siddiq 38; Ali Hasan Rizvi six for 61) and 134 (Ahmed Siddiq 69 not out; Mohammad Hasnain three for 54, Ali Hasan Rizvi three for 43).

WILLS CUP

Semi-finals

At National Stadium, Karachi, October 2. National Bank won by 101 runs. National Bank 248 for seven (50 overs) (Sajid Ali 39, Wasim Arif 56, Saeed Azad 36, Ameer Akbar 43 not out, Tahir Shah 38); PACO* 147 (45.2 overs) (Shahid Saeed 42, Mujahid Jamshed 32; Nadeem Khan six for 28).

At Rawalpindi Cricket Stadium, Rawalpindi, October 2. Habib Bank won by four wickets. PIA 205 (48.2 overs) (Shoaib Mohammad 68, Zahid Ahmed 30; Nadeem Ghauri four for 42); Habib Bank* 208 for six (47.2 overs) (Salim Malik 33, Shahid Javed 30, Shaukat Mirza 41 not out).

Final

At Gaddafi Stadium, Lahore, October 9. National Bank won by five wickets. Habib Bank 269 for six (50 overs) (Shakeel Ahmed 62, Tahir Rashid 115, Salim Malik 30 not out; Nadeem Khan three for 52); National Bank* 272 for five (48 overs) (Shahid Anwar 46, Saeed Azad 112 not out, Tahir Shah 63).

BCCP PATRON'S TROPHY FRIDAY LEAGUE

Final

At Gaddafi Stadium, Lahore, December 3. ADBP won by five wickets. PNSC 176 for nine (40 overs) (Mahmood Hamid 37, Mohammad Javed 64; Manzoor Elahi three for 27); ADBP* 180 for five (37.2 overs) (Ghaffar Kazmi 59, Bilal Ahmed 37 not out).

QUAID-E-AZAM TROPHY FRIDAY LEAGUE

Final

At National Stadium, Karachi, February 10. Karachi Whites won by six wickets. Bahawalpur 170 for nine (40 overs) (Tanvir Razzaq 33, Mohammad Tayyab 39 not out); Karachi Whites* 171 for four (38.3 overs) (Basit Ali 55, Aamer Hanif 43).

CRICKET IN SRI LANKA, 1992-93

By GERRY VAIDYASEKERA

Domestic cricket took second place to Sri Lanka's busiest international season, which featured visits from Australia, New Zealand and England, while junior teams toured Bangladesh and South Africa.

The P. Saravanamuttu Trophy final did not take place until May. It was won by Sinhalese Sports Club, who defeated old rivals Nondescripts after a fluctuating game. Nondescripts had high hopes when Sinhalese SC, chasing 196, were 67 for five. But Nisal Fernando and Hemantha Wickremaratne put on 114 for the sixth wicket, and Fernando remained to secure victory and the Man of the Match award. On the first day Nondescripts captain Aravinda de Silva made a rapid 84, though he had little support apart from a half-century from Ruchira Palliyaguru. Sinhalese also leant heavily on two batsmen, Test captain Arjuna Ranatunga and Fernando. Nondescripts failed to exploit a lead of 41; only de Silva managed fifty as slow left-armer Piyal Wijetunge took his match haul to ten wickets. But Nondescripts' spinners set up the exciting finish.

Fourteen teams, divided into two groups, competed in the first-class stages of the tournament. Eight qualified from two Colombo regions and three each from the Southern and Central. Nondescripts headed their group with five wins and a draw; Sinhalese led theirs with four wins and a draw, and a points margin superior to Moratuwa's. The second group was reduced to six when title-holders Colts were disqualified. They refused to resume with Moratuwa in what they said were unsuitable conditions; the four games they had played were discounted from tournament calculations.

Sinhalese recorded the highest total of the season, a mammoth 497 for six, against Sebastianites. Ranatunga scored a swashbuckling double-hundred in just two sessions and 181 balls, hitting four sixes and 20 fours. He put on 291 for the third wicket with Asanka Gurusinha. On the same day, Burgher Recreation Club scored 452 for five, including three centuries, the first such instance in Sri Lankan domestic cricket. This was enough to ensure one of five innings defeats for their opponents, Ambalangoda Rio. It was against Rio that Thushara Kodikara of Wattala Antonians hit 236 not out off 209 balls, including two sixes and 29 fours. He and Priyantha Perera set a Sri Lankan record with 289 for the second wicket.

The 1992-93 season began in July, with a Super Tournament arranged to give players four-day match practice before the tour by Australia. Six teams took part, the top four from the previous P. Saravanamuttu Trophy plus two sides selected by the Board. Tamil Union, led by Test bowler Champaka Ramanayake, won the inaugural Coca Cola Bottlers' Trophy. De Silva and Hashan Tillekeratne shared a national record third-wicket stand of 293 for the Board President's XI against the Board Under-23 XI; de Silva hit 231 in 308 balls, with five sixes and 25 fours, and Tillekeratne 104. Another unbeaten century by de Silva enabled him to total 531 runs at 88.50. Jayananda Warnaweera took 26 wickets and off-spinner Ruwan Kalpage was man of the tournament with 286 runs and 18 wickets.

Tamil Union also won the Premadasa Trophy in the day-night competition at the Khettarama Stadium, beating Nondescripts by 21 runs. Sri Lanka Blues beat Sri Lanka Reds by one run in the final of the inaugural South Asia Double-wicket Tournament at the Tyronne Fernando Stadium; India and Pakistan also entered two teams each. Ranatunga led a Mercantile Cricket Association side to victory in the Royal Bangkok Cricket Association International Six-a-side Tournament, beating the Volvo-Singha Scribblers from Pakistan. A total of 32 teams took part. In the final of the Minor District Cricket Championship, carried over from 1991-92, Anuradhapura District defeated Monaragala, who were competing for the first time. Moratuwa University won the limited-overs inter-university tournament, with Peradeniya University as runners-up. In the Mercantile competition, Saman Fonseka made 214, the highest individual score in Sri Lankan limited-overs cricket, including three sixes and 35 fours, for Associated Motorways against Metropolitan Agencies.

In schools cricket, 96 teams competed for the Coca Cola Bottlers' Schools Trophy. Ananda College retained the trophy for the sixth successive year after defeating D. S. Senanayake Maha Vidyalala by four runs at Moratuwa. Peter Hamer, vice-captain of St Joseph's College in Colombo, hit an epic 280 against Wesley in February. He batted for six and a half hours, reaching 200 off 216 deliveries. Within a fortnight, 18-year-old Indika de Saram, from St Thomas's College, an outstation school in Matara, out-stripped both him and Jack Anderson's 1917 record of 291 for St Anthony's, Kandy. De Saram scored a grand 304 in two sessions, with 25 sixes and 19 fours. He aggregated 1,010 runs in 12 innings at 84.16. Malintha Perera of De Mazenod College, Kandana, created a wicket-keeper's double record, with 1,005 runs and 57 dismissals during the season. Perera's school-mate, pace bowler Chaminda Boteju, passed 100 wickets.

*In the following scores, * by the name of a team indicates that they won the toss.*

SUPER TOURNAMENT

At Maitland Place, Colombo (SSC), July 9, 10, 11, 12. Drawn. Board President's XI* 239 (N. Devarajan 125 not out, P. Munasinghe 32, Extras 35; C. P. H. Ramanayake four for 61); Tamil Union and AC 86 (A. P. Weerakkody four for 48, K. P. J. Warnaweera six for 19) and 12 for two.

At P. Saravanamuttu Stadium, Colombo, July 9, 10, 11, 12. Drawn. Colts CC 211 (H. H. Devapriya 49, D. K. Liyanage 31; S. Silva four for 53, S. Jayawardene three for 50) and 254 for six dec. (A. A. D. S. Perera 36, S. Ranatunga 65, D. Samarasekera 42, N. Ranatunga 63; R. S. Kalpage three for 55); Board Under-23 XI* 273 (R. Wimalasiri 47, H. D. P. K. Dharmasena 49, R. S. Kalpage 47, P. B. Dassanayake 30; D. K. Liyanage three for 95, N. Ranatunga three for 31) and 89 for two (R. Wimalasiri 32 not out).

At Tyronne Fernando Stadium, Moratuwa, July 9, 10, 11, 12. Drawn. Colombo CC 309 (N. de Silva 89, S. T. Jayasuriya 70, G. F. Labrooy 36, Extras 34; A. P. Gurusinha four for 51, P. K. Wijetunge four for 82); Sinhalese SC* 418 for six (M. S. Atapattu 163, A. Ranatunga 36, M. Munasinghe 40, A. H. Wickremaratne 44 not out, Extras 48; B. R. Jurangpathy three for 78).

At Tyronne Fernando Stadium, Moratuwa, July 16, 17, 18, 19. Colts CC won by five wickets. Board President's XI 133 (N. Ranatunga four for 43, J. C. Gamage four for 44) and 329 (S. Weerasinghe 36, W. M. J. Kumudu 110, A. G. D. Wickremasinghe 41, Extras 48; N. Ranatunga three for 66); Colts CC* 331 (C. Mendis 102, S. Ranatunga 61, E. Upashantha 63, Extras 39; A. P. Weerakkody three for 50, K. P. J. Warnaweera four for 129) and 135 for five (A. A. D. S. Perera 66 not out; S. D. Anurasiri three for 39).

At P. Saravanamuttu Stadium, Colombo, July 16, 17, 18, 19. Board Under-23 XI won by nine wickets. Board Under-23 XI* 459 (R. S. Kaluwitharana 156, R. S. Kalpage 69, P. B. Dassanayake 84, S. Silva 86; G. P. Wickremasinghe six for 71) and ten for one; Sinhalese SC 305 (U. N. K. Fernando 48, M. S. Atapattu 73, C. Ranasinghe 52 not out; R. S. Kalpage four for 77) and 163 (C. Ranasinghe 58; W. Labrooy four for 72, S. Silva four for 35).

At Maitland Place, Colombo (SSC), July 16, 17, 18, 19. Tamil Union C and AC won by 314 runs. Tamil Union C and AC 246 (R. Peiris 33, W. M. J. P. Weerasinghe 34, D. N. Nadarajah 43, Extras 41; G. F. Labrooy three for 65, B. R. Jurangpathy three for 37) and 270 (T. de Silva 94, U. C. Hathurusinghe 70, U. D. U. Chandana 32; K. I. W. Wijegunawardene three for 58); Colombo CC* 97 for eight dec. (C. P. H. Ramanayake three for 28, U. C. Hathurusinghe five for 35) and 105 (M. Muralitharan three for 12, R. K. B. Amunugama three for 30).

At P. Saravanamuttu Stadium, Colombo, July 23, 24, 25, 26. Colombo CC won by 223 runs. Colombo CC* 307 (S. T. Jayasuriya 72, A. Seneviratne 96; K. P. J. Warnaweera five for 103, S. D. Anurasiri three for 72) and 321 (R. S. Mahanama 82, N. de Silva 35, J. Bandara 38, B. R. Jurangpathy 42, Extras 30; K. P. J. Warnaweera five for 81, A. W. R. Madurasinghe three for 44); Board President's XI 294 (H. P. Tillekeratne 44, P. A. de Silva 198 not out; K. I. W. Wijegunawardene three for 89, B. R. Jurangpathy three for 46) and 111 (W. M. J. Kumudu 46, A. G. D. Wickremasinghe 31; C. R. Thenuwara four for 26).

At Tyronne Fernando Stadium, Moratuwa, July 23, 24, 25, 26. Drawn. Tamil Union C and AC 366 (U. C. Hathurusinghe 60, R. Peiris 42, S. Dharmasena 105, W. M. J. P. Weerasinghe 95; P. Perera three for 57) and 116 (S. Silva three for 35, R. S. Kalpage three for six); Board Under-23 XI* 188 (P. Perera 54, R. S. Kaluwitharana 33, R. S. Kalpage 42; C. P. H. Ramanayake five for 40) and nought for no wkt.

At Khettarama Stadium, Colombo, July 23, 24, 25, 26. Drawn. Colts CC 314 (D. P. Samaraweera 43, N. Ranatunga 101, D. K. Liyanage 43) and 232 (S. Ranatunga 40, N. Ranatunga 41, E. Upashantha 59, C. Mendis 33; M. Munasinghe four for 64); Sinhalese SC* 323 (U. N. K. Fernando 99, C. Ranasinghe 43, G. P. Wickremasinghe 55 not out, P. K. Wijetunge 46, Extras 39; D. K. Liyanage five for 114, N. Ranatunga four for 104) and 92 for three (M. S. Atapattu 31 not out).

At Khettarama Stadium, Colombo, July 30, 31, August 1, 2. Drawn. Sinhalese SC 312 (A. P. Gurusinha 123, U. N. K. Fernando 69, M. B. Halangoda 42; P. Rodrigo three for 61); Board President's XI* 388 (W. M. J. Kumudu 161, H. P. Tillekeratne 69, P. A. de Silva 74, Extras 38).

At P. Saravanamuttu Stadium, Colombo, July 30, 31, August 1, 2. Colombo CC won by 40 runs. Colombo CC 134 (B. R. Jurangpathy 31 not out; W. Labrooy four for 49) and 306 (N. de Silva 44, B. R. Jurangpathy 104, K. I. W. Wijegunawardene 34; D. Ekanayake seven for 129); Board Under-23 XI* 200 (R. J. Jaymon 34, R. S. Kalpage 45; G. F. Labrooy three for 53, K. I. W. Wijegunawardene five for 78) and 200 (R. S. Kaluwitharana 79; K. I. W. Wijegunawardene seven for 39).

At Maitland Place, Colombo (NCC), July 30, 31. Tamil Union C and AC won by eight wickets. Colts CC 137 (C. Mendis 30, D. P. Samaraweera 48, A. A. D. S. Perera 30; R. K. B. Amunugama four for 44, U. C. Hathurusinghe three for 36) and 83 (C. P. H. Ramanayake six for 36); Tamil Union C and AC* 130 (U. C. Hathurusinghe 33; D. K. Liyanage three for 23, E. Upashantha four for 28) and 92 for two (R. Peiris 64 not out).

At Maitland Place, Colombo (NCC), August 4, 5, 6. Board President's XI won by an innings and 114 runs. Board Under-23 XI 237 (R. J. Jaymon 41, R. S. Kaluwitharana 51, R. S. Kalpage 71 not out; S. D. Anurasiri three for 71) and 99 (R. S. Kaluwitharana 56; A. P. Weerakkody five for 46, K. P. J. Warnaweera three for 28); Board President's XI* 450 (H. P. Tillekeratne 104, P. A. de Silva 231; R. S. Kalpage four for 103, A. W. Ekanayake four for 114).

At P. Saravanamuttu Stadium, Colombo, August 4, 5. Colts CC won by an innings and 75 runs. Colombo CC 113 (A. Seneviratne 47; N. Ranatunga five for 54) and 160 (B. R. Jurangpathy 44, G. F. Labrooy 42; G. R. M. A. Perera three for 11); Colts CC 348 for eight dec. (A. A. D. S. Perera 102, S. Ranatunga 147 not out, D. K. Liyanage 33).

At Tyronne Fernando Stadium, Moratuwa, August 4, 5, 6, 7. Drawn. Sinhalese SC* 275 (A. P. Gurusinha 55, A. Ranatunga 86, C. Ranasinghe 40; R. K. B. Amunugama three for 49, M. Muralitharan four for 81) and 111 for three (M. S. Atapattu 55 not out); Tamil Union C and AC 364 (U. C. Hathurusinghe 48, R. Peiris 34, S. Dharmasena 74, W. M. J. P. Weerasinghe 64, C. P. H. Ramanayake 42, U. D. U. Chandana 32; M. Munasinghe three for 80).

P. SARAVANAMUTTU TROPHY, 1992-93

Group A

At Havelock Park, Colombo (BRC), January 8, 9, 10. Drawn. Burgher RC 258 (A. A. D. S. Perera 89, R. J. Jaymon 89; K. Dharmasena three for 57) and 263 (J. Perera 59, D. Madurapperuma 30, R. J. Jaymon 32, S. Jayasuriya 64 not out; P. Perera four for 65, A. M. J. G. Amerasinghe three for 68); Antonians SC* 240 (K. Dharmasena 41, P. Milton 64; A. A. D. S. Perera five for 77) and 169 for nine (V. S. Sittamige 63 not out; K. G. Priyantha three for 50, A. A. D. S. Perera three for 53).

At Panadura Esplanade, Panadura, January 8, 9, 10. Panadura SC won by an innings and 187 runs. Panadura SC* 382 (S. Jayawardene 52, A. K. D. S. Kumara 34, R. Soysa 63, M. V. Deshapriya 121 not out; H. L. Champika four for 88); Rio SC 92 (D. S. P. Tedlal 49; S. D. Anurasiri six for 16) and 103 (M. Jayasena six for 23).

At P. Saravanamuttu Stadium, Colombo, January 8, 9, 10. Tamil Union C and AC won by eight wickets. Kandy 180 (M. Wijesinghe 40, S. Dissanayake 43; C. P. H. Ramanayake six for 40, U. C. Hathurusinghe three for 49) and 233 (T. Guneratne 43, M. Wijesinghe 99; C. P. H. Ramanayake four for 39, C. D. Hathurusinghe three for 36); Tamil Union C and AC 388 for three dec. (U. C. Hathurusinghe 39, R. Peiris 135, T. M. Wijesinghe 100 retired hurt, S. Dharmasena 55 not out, W. M. J. P. Weerasinghe 39) and 26 for two.

At P. Saravanamuttu Stadium, Colombo, January 15, 16, 17. Antonians SC won by an innings and 116 runs. Rio SC 178 (C. Jayanath 34, G. W. Chandralal 30, S. Mahesh 30; K. Dharmasena six for 72, N. Devarajan three for 39) and 91 (S. Mahesh 39; P. Milton seven for 31); Antonians SC* 385 for two dec. (W. A. M. P. Perera 87, T. P. Kodikara 236 not out, V. S. Sittamige 33 not out).

At Havelock Park, Colombo (BRC), January 15, 16, 17. Drawn. Burgher RC* 139 (D. Madurapperuma 51, S. Jayasuriya 30; C. D. Hathurusinghe three for 55, U. C. Hathurusinghe three for 25) and 253 for five (U. Hettiarachchi 79 not out, R. J. Jaymon 37, D. Madurapperuma 36); Tamil Union C and AC 355 for nine dec. (D. N. Nadarajah 72, S. Karunasekera 51, C. P. H. Ramanayake 67, Extras 34; L. Sagara four for 98).

At Maitland Place, Colombo (NCC), January 15, 16, 17. Nondescripts CC won by 178 runs. Nondescripts CC 141 (R. V. Hewage 33, H. P. Tillekeratne 56 not out; P. Weragoda five for 42) and 307 for nine dec. (R. V. Hewage 39, P. A. de Silva 93, A. G. D. Wickremasinghe 43; I. Dissanayake five for 110, P. Weragoda three for 90); Kandy CC* 149 (N. Nanayakkara 35; M. J. H. Rushdie six for 30) and 121 (A. Ellepola 46; W. Labrooy five for 43, M. J. H. Rushdie three for 40).

At Havelock Park, Colombo (BRC), January 22, 23, 24. Burgher RC won by an innings and 187 runs. Burgher RC 452 for five dec. (P. de Souza 54, J. Perera 112, A. A. D. S. Perera 112, U. Hettiarachchi 118 not out); Rio SC* 150 (K. B. Chandana 51; K. G. Priyantha four for 42, A. A. D. S. Perera three for 19) and 115 (L. Sagara three for 26, A. A. D. S. Perera six for 44).

At Maitland Place, Colombo (NCC), January 22, 23, 24. Nondescripts CC won by ten wickets. Antonians SC 280 (V. S. Sittamige 82, N. Devarajan 74, Extras 40; M. J. H. Rushdie three for 57, H. P. Tillekeratne four for 37) and 144 (M. Hemantha 30; P. A. de Silva five for 35, H. P. Tillekeratne three for 38); Nondescripts CC* 377 (P. A. de Silva 143, H. P. Tillekeratne 72, W. Labrooy 55, R. Palliyaguru 42; A. M. J. G. Amerasinghe three for 69) and 48 for no wkt (R. V. Hewage 31 not out).

At Panadura Esplanade, Panadura, January 22, 23, 24. Drawn. Panadura SC* 145 (S. Jayawardene 73, M. V. Deshapriya 30; C. D. Hathurusinghe four for 17) and 129 for four (S. Jayawardene 52, S. Sooriyarachchi 32 not out); Tamil Union C and AC 204 (D. N. Nadarajah 56, U. D. U. Chandana 50; S. D. Anurasiri six for 71).

At Bloomfield Grounds, Colombo, January 29, 30, 31. Antonians SC won by 81 runs. Antonians SC 192 (P. Perera 35, K. Dharmasena 37; P. Weragoda six for 61) and 245 for nine dec. (P. Perera 52, N. Devarajan 36, K. Dharmasena 35, P. Milton 53 not out; P. Weragoda four for 85); Kandy SC* 235 (M. Wijesinghe 42, S. Peiris 75, T. Guneratne 47; P. Milton three for 61, K. Dharmasena four for 61) and 121 (S. Peiris 49; K. Dharmasena three for 18, N. Devarajan three for 19).

At Maitland Place, Colombo (NCC), January 29, 30, 31. Nondescripts CC won by 204 runs. Nondescripts CC* 301 (R. David 33, C. Handunettige 81, C. P. Mapatuna 110, R. Palliyaguru 30; S. Jayawardene four for 103, M. V. Deshapriya three for 42) and 227 (R. J. Ratnayake 86, W. Labrooy 44; M. de Mel five for 80, M. Jayasena three for 58); Panadura SC 164 (S. Thenuwara 34; B. Perera four for 52) and 160 (A. K. D. S. Kumara 88 not out; M. J. H. Rushdie three for 38, R. Palliyaguru four for 63).

At P. Saravanamuttu Stadium, Colombo, January 29, 30, 31. Tamil Union C and AC won by an innings and 145 runs. Rio SC* 99 (H. L. Champika 33; C. D. Hathurusinghe eight for 40) and 72 (R. K. B. Amunugama four for 35, C. D. Hathurusinghe five for 37); Tamil Union C and AC 316 for nine dec. (T. M. Wijesinghe 54, S. Karunasekera 105, Extras 34; A. M. C. V. Kumara four for 70).

At Havelock Park, Colombo (BRC), February 5, 6. Nondescripts CC won by ten wickets. Burgher RC 137 (Extras 35; P. Dabare five for 21, B. Perera three for 11) and 172 (P. de Souza 47, J. Perera 31; P. Dabare three for 24, B. Perera four for 61); Nondescripts CC* 309 (S. Weerasinghe 39, C. Handunettige 55, W. Labrooy 34, R. Palliyaguru 74, Extras 36; L. Sagara six for 84) and one for no wkt.

At Panadura Esplanade, Panadura, February 5, 6, 7. Panadura SC won by an innings and 39 runs. Panadura SC 453 for nine dec. (S. Jayawardene 53, S. Kumara 60, R. Soysa 166, A. K. D. S. Kumara 54, M. V. Deshapriya 45, M. Jayasena 41; P. Weragoda three for 146, S. Dissanayake three for 131); Kandy CC* 206 (S. Dissanayake 32, T. Guneratne 34, A. Ellepola 48, I. Dissanayake 34 not out; M. de Mel four for 65, M. Jayasena four for 45) and 208 (S. Herathge 31, S. Dissanayake 51, T. Guneratne 52; S. Jayawardene three for 40, M. Jayasena four for 35).

At P. Saravanamuttu Stadium, Colombo, February 5, 6, 7. Antonians SC won by eight wickets. Tamil Union C and AC 308 (T. M. Wijesinghe 38, D. N. Nadarajah 37, W. M. J. P. Weerasinghe 68, U. D. U. Chandana 60, Extras 33; P. Milton three for 88, A. M. J. G. Amerasinghe three for 69, K. Dharmasena three for 46) and 192 (T. M. Wijesinghe 31, S. Karunasekera 82 not out; P. Perera three for 44, A. M. J. G. Amerasinghe four for 46); Antonians SC* 413 (W. A. M. P. Perera 116, V. S. Sittamige 30, N. Devarajan 65, T. P. Kodikara 113; C. D. Hathurusinghe five for 114) and 91 for two (W. A. M. P. Perera 38).

At Havelock Park, Colombo (BRC), February 12, 13, 14. Panadura SC won by 12 runs. Panadura SC 248 (R. Soysa 32, A. K. D. S. Kumara 92, M. V. Deshapriya 43; K. G. Priyantha three for 49, D. Madurapperuma three for 44) and 160 (S. Kumara 31, R. Soysa 51, Extras 30; D. Madurapperuma five for 33); Burgher RC* 164 (L. Sagara 36 not out; M. de Mel three for 65, K. Silva three for 13) and 232 (P. de Souza 45, P. Polonowita 33, D. Madurapperuma 52, S. Jayasuriya 35; M. Jayasena four for 74, M. V. Deshapriya three for 50).

At Havelock Park, Colombo (Colts), February 12, 13, 14. Kandy CC won by 146 runs. Kandy CC* 306 (S. Dissanayake 146, S. Peiris 39, N. Nanayakkara 41; A. M. C. V. Kumara four for 90) and 259 for four dec. (M. Wijesinghe 56, S. Herathge 81, S. Dissanayake 55; M. W. Chaminda four for 66); Rio SC 185 (S. Mahesh 33, H. L. Champika 30; I. Dissanayake three for 59, D. Kolugala five for 65) and 234 (S. Mahesh 32, A. M. C. V. Kumara 40, H. L. Champika 62, S. Sanjeewa 52; D. Kolugala three for 62, S. Dissanayake three for 35).

At Maitland Place, Colombo (NCC), February 12, 13, 14. Drawn. Nondescripts CC* 327 (S. Weerasinghe 30, A. G. D. Wickremasinghe 33, P. A. de Silva 38, H. P. Tillekeratne 103, W. Labrooy 43, Extras 42; C. P. H. Ramanayake four for 74, C. D. Hathurusinghe five for 98) and 150 for six (C. Handunettige 61, R. S. Kalpage 41; U. C. Hathurusinghe three for 43, M. Muralitharan three for 32); Tamil Union C and AC 340 (R. Peiris 32, D. N. Nadarajah 159 not out, S. Karunasekera 50, Extras 45; R. Palliyaguru four for 80).

At Havelock Park, Colombo (BRC), February 19, 20, 21. Burgher RC won by 66 runs. Burgher RC* 244 (J. Perera 32, R. J. Jaymon 58, R. Weerakoon 30 not out, K. G. Priyantha 32; I. Dissanayake three for 67, P. Weragoda four for 84) and 211 (J. Perera 49, U. Hettiarachchi 48; P. Weragoda four for 83, S. Dissanayake six for 89); Kandy CC 172 (S. Peiris 62 not out; C. Rajkumara Perera four for 37) and 217 (M. Wijesinghe 59, S. Peiris 44; A. A. D. S. Perera four for 69, S. Jayasuriya four for 18).

At Maitland Place, Colombo (NCC), February 19, 20, 21. Nondescripts CC won by an innings and 214 runs. Nondescripts 418 for one dec. (S. Weerasinghe 84, R. David 201 not out, C. Handunettige 100 not out, Extras 33); Rio SC* 115 (U. W. Priyanthalal 47; A. P. Weerakkody seven for 39) and 89 (P. A. de Silva five for 31, H. P. Tillekeratne three for 34).

At Panadura Esplanade, Panadura, February 19, 20, 21. Panadura SC won by 159 runs. Panadura SC 268 (S. Jayawardene 47, S. Sooriyarachchi 38, A. K. D. S. Kumara 36, M. V. Deshapriya 61, M. de Mel 30; A. M. J. G. Amerasinghe three for 77, K. Dharmasena four for 108) and 186 (S. Jayawardene 30, S. Sooriyarachchi 62; P. Perera seven for 46, K. Dharmasena three for 33); Antonians SC* 151 (V. S. Sittamige 48, N. Devarajan 37; S. Jayawardene five for 57, S. D. Anurasiri three for 25) and 144 (V. S. Sittamige 52, W. A. M. P. Perera 49; S. D. Anurasiri five for 26, M. Jayasena five for 50).

Group B

At Braybrook Place, Colombo, January 8, 9, 10. Moors SC won by four wickets. Singha SC 240 (G. Sanjeewa 42, W. M. J. Kumudu 31, S. Jayantha 81; M. R. Farouk four for 57, S. Dharmasena four for 40) and 161 (S. Jayantha 48; M. R. Farouk four for 57, S. H. U. Karnain five for 17); Moors SC* 271 (I. Anthony 48, Y. Tillekeratne 70, S. H. U. Karnain 45; L. Ranasinghe four for 81, K. R. Pushpakumara three for 84) and 131 for six (M. R. D. Hameen 53 not out; S. Jayantha three for 32).

At Tyronne Fernando Stadium, Moratuwa, January 8, 9, 10. Moratuwa SC won by 31 runs. Moratuwa SC 174 (W. Fernando 43, M. P. A. Cooray 33; S. C. de Silva five for 50, A. Jabbar three for 34) and 143 (L. R. P. de Silva 31; S. C. de Silva four for 28, A. Jabbar four for 40); Sebastianites C and AC* 130 (K. Anton 30; M. P. A. Cooray three for 60, N. Dabare three for 32) and 156 (C. Mahesh 31, R. Wickremaratne 54; M. P. A. Cooray five for 52, N. Dabare four for 48).

At Braybrook Place, Colombo, January 15, 16, 17. Moratuwa SC won by ten wickets. Moors SC 80 (M. P. A. Cooray six for 22) and 227 (H. Wimalasekera 54, M. R. D. Hameen 47, I. Anthony 47; M. P. A. Cooray three for 54, N. Dabare four for 82); Moratuwa SC* 259 (R. Mapalagama 35, W. D. A. S. Perera 46, L. R. P. de Silva 32, W. Fernando 58 not out, Extras 31; Y. Tillekeratne five for 57) and 52 for no wkt.

At Maitland Place, Colombo (SSC), January 15, 16, 17. Sinhalese SC won by six wickets. Singha SC 220 (I. Peiris 33, N. Danasinghe 113; C. Fernando three for 65, A. Ranatunga three for 53) and 145 (G. Sanjeewa 42; A. Ranatunga five for 45); Sinhalese SC* 235 (C. Fernando 53, C. Ranasinghe 68; R. Priyantha three for 69, T. A. de Silva three for 81) and 133 for four (D. Ranatunga 33, A. H. Wickremaratne 59 not out).

At Tyronne Fernando Stadium, Moratuwa, January 22, 23, 24. Moratuwa SC won by an innings and 52 runs. Kurunegala SC 144 (A. H. Bandaranayake 43, M. Jayaratne 40; M. P. A. Cooray three for 43, N. Dabare four for 65) and 104 (J. Kaluhandiwala 36, P. Liyanage 30; M. P. A. Cooray four for 26, N. Dabare five for 21); Moratuwa SC* 300 for eight dec. (S. Soysa 138, W. D. A. S. Perera 60; A. H. Bandaranayake five for 108).

At Maitland Place, Colombo (SSC), January 22, 23, 24. Sinhalese SC won by an innings and 161 runs. Sinhalese SC 497 for six dec. (A. P. Gurusinha 162, A. Ranatunga 238 not out, U. N. K. Fernando 33; S. C. de Silva four for 115); Sebastianites C and AC* 142 (F. Aponsu 31, P. Salgado 35; M. Munasinghe five for 25, M. B. Halangoda three for 33) and 194 (A. Silva 105; M. Munasinghe six for 27).

At Havelock Park, Colombo (BRC), January 29, 30, 31. Sebastianites C and AC won by 139 runs. Sebastianites C and AC* 204 (S. K. Silva 32, F. Aponsu 64; A. H. Bandaranayake four for 66, V. Peiris five for 47) and 206 for six dec. (A. Silva 48, S. K. Silva 50, N. Abeyratne 61 not out; A. H. Bandaranayake three for 73, V. Peiris three for 56); Kurunegala SC 121 (S. C. de Silva five for 53, A. Jabbar three for 28) and 150 (C. Liyanage 34, A. H. Bandaranayake 30, J. Kaluhandiwala 33; A. Jabbar four for 28).

At Tyronne Fernando Stadium, Moratuwa, February 5, 6, 7. Drawn. Sebastianites C and AC 307 (F. Aponsu 62, C. Mahesh 47, A. Fernando 46, D. Dias 47 not out, M. Perera 43; N. Danasinghe three for 73) and 430 (A. Silva 59, S. K. Silva 87, F. Aponsu 39, C. Mahesh 131, A. Fernando 42; L. Ranasinghe five for 153, K. R. Pushpakumara five for 124); Singha SC* 268 (H. Premasiri 77, S. Jayantha 48; S. C. de Silva four for 91) and 27 for one.

At Maitland Place, Colombo (SSC), February 5, 6, 7. Drawn. Moratuwa SC 139 for nine dec. (S. A. R. Silva 47; C. Fernando three for 38) and 421 for six (A. Martis 92, S. A. R. Silva 116, W. D. A. S. Perera 63, S. Soysa 50 not out); Sinhalese SC* 391 for eight dec. (D. Ranatunga 121, E. F. M. U. Fernando 99, U. N. K. Fernando 57, C. Ranasinghe 39, Extras 31; M. Dissanayake three for 98).

At Braybrook Place, Colombo, February 12, 13, 14. Moors SC won by six wickets. Sebastianites C and AC 101 (P. Salgado 49; S. H. U. Karnain six for 33) and 219 (A. Silva 75, F. Aponsu 31, Extras 30; M. R. Farouk four for 55, Y. Tillekeratne six for 47); Moors SC* 256 (K. T. de Silva 44, H. Wimalasekera 50, I. Anthony 40, S. H. U. Karnain 65; S. C. de Silva three for 49, M. Perera six for 61) and 65 for four.

At Tyronne Fernando Stadium, Moratuwa, February 19, 20, 21. Moratuwa SC won by seven wickets. Singha SC 162 (N. Dabare three for 38, C. de Silva five for 45) and 220 (G. Sanjeewa 44, W. M. J. Kumudu 83, I. Peiris 40; M. Dissanayake four for 39, N. Dabare four for 98); Moratuwa SC* 319 for nine dec. (R. Mapalagama 49, A. Martis 37, L. R. P. de Silva 53, S. A. R. Silva 58, W. D. A. S. Perera 66; K. R. Pushpakumara four for 105, L. Karunaratne three for 31) and 65 for three.

At Bloomfield Grounds, Colombo, March 5, 6, 7. Sinhalese SC won by nine wickets. Kurunegala SC 89 (G. P. Wickremasinghe three for 27, M. Munasinghe three for 19) and 164 (C. Ratnayake 33, D. K. Bandara 42, P. Liyanage 36; M. Munasinghe three for 37, P. K. Wijetunge four for 50); Sinhalese SC* 201 for two dec. (D. Ranatunga 76 not out, U. N. K. Fernando 64, M. S. Atapattu 44 not out) and 55 for one (G. P. Wickremasinghe 42 not out).

At Braybrook Place, Colombo, March 26, 27, 28. Moors SC won by nine wickets. Kurunegala SC 125 (C. Ratnayake 46; Y. Tillekeratne three for 34) and 117 (C. Ratnayake 37; I. Thahir six for 40, H. Wimalasekera three for 15); Moors SC* 225 for eight dec. (I. Thahir 38, I. Anthony 51, A. Hettiarachchi 40 not out, Y. Tillekeratne 30, Extras 31; G. Subasinghe three for 65, J. Bakmeewewa three for 36) and 18 for one.

At Panadura Esplanade, Panadura, April 1, 2, 3. Singha SC won by nine wickets. Kurunegala SC* 222 (D. K. Bandara 68, C. Fernando 30, P. Liyanage 41) and 126 (P. Liyanage 57; R. Priyantha three for 19, L. Ranasinghe four for 25); Singha SC 300 (W. M. J. Kumudu 33, S. Jayantha 106, D. Amendra 47, Extras 31; P. Liyanage three for 74, G. Subasinghe three for 53) and 50 for one.

At Braybrook Place, Colombo, April 2, 3, 4. Sinhalese SC won by 418 runs. Sinhalese SC 405 (A. P. Gurusinha 82, M. S. Atapattu 133, A. H. Wickremaratne 31) and 195 for two dec. (D. Ranatunga 66, A. A. W. Gunawardene 88); Moors SC* 182 (S. H. U. Karnain 34, M. R. D. Hameen 68; G. P. Wickremasinghe three for 53) and forfeited second innings.

Scores for Colts CC's matches before they were disqualified were not available when Wisden *went to press.*

Final

At Tyronne Fernando Stadium, Moratuwa, May 13, 14, 15, 16. Sinhalese SC won by four wickets. Nondescripts CC* 263 (P. A. de Silva 84, R. Palliyaguru 67 not out; G. P. Wickremasinghe three for 66, P. K. Wijetunge four for 82) and 154 (P. A. de Silva 55; A. P. Gurusinha three for 25, P. K. Wijetunge six for 62); Sinhalese SC 222 (A. Ranatunga 47, U. N. K. Fernando 63, A. H. Wickremaratne 30; A. P. Weerakkody six for 59, P. A. de Silva three for 51) and 196 for six (U. N. K. Fernando 63 not out, A. H. Wickremaratne 43).

SINGER INTER-PROVINCIAL TOURNAMENT, 1991-92

At Asgiriya Stadium, Kandy, May 28, 29, 30, 31. Central Province won by seven wickets. Central Province* 334 (S. Fernando 36, T. P. Kodikara 107, R. S. Kalpage 50, U. H. Kodituwakku 60; W. Labrooy four for 88, S. D. Anurasiri three for 48) and 121 for three (T. P. Kodikara 33); Western Province (Suburbs) 137 (P. Perera 40, N. Devarajan 52; M. Muralitharan five for 36) and 317 (P. Perera 36, N. Devarajan 41, R. Soysa 43, A. K. D. S. Kumara 31, W. Labrooy 56, P. Munasinghe 39 not out; M. Muralitharan three for 83, P. K. Wijetunge four for 92).

At Welagedera Stadium, Kurunegala, May 28, 29, 30, 31. Western Province (South) won by seven wickets. Western Province (South) 352 (A. A. D. S. Perera 73, A. Ranatunga 126, C. N. Fernando 52; A. H. Bandaranayake three for 107, A. W. Ekanayake five for 89) and 14 for three; North-Western Province* 119 (N. Munasinghe 38; A. A. D. S. Perera three for 24, S. Ranatunga three for 24) and 246 (S. Gunawardene 43, J. Jaymon 62, P. Liyanage 30; A. A. D. S. Perera three for 73, M. S. Atapattu three for 27).

At Maitland Place, Colombo (SSC), May 28, 29, 30, 31. Drawn. Southern Province 201 (H. H. Devapriya 64, A. P. R. Shaman 32; U. C. Hathurusinghe four for 32) and 50 for one; Western Province (North)* 440 for eight dec. (U. C. Hathurusinghe 55, H. P. Tillekeratne 95, P. A. de Silva 87, A. G. D. Wickremasinghe 93, G. F. Labrooy 51 not out; S. M. Faumi three for 46).

At Asgiriya Stadium, Kandy, June 4, 5, 6, 7. Drawn. Southern Province* 146 for six (S. M. Faumi 34; T. P. Kodikara four for 30) v Central Province.

At P. Saravanamuttu Stadium, Colombo, June 4, 5, 6, 7. Drawn. North-Western Province 26 for one v Western Province (North)*.

At Tyronne Fernando Stadium, Moratuwa, June 4, 5, 6, 7. Drawn. Western Province (Suburbs)* 33 for one v Western Province (South).

At Uyanwatte Stadium, Matara, June 11, 12, 13, 14. Drawn. Southern Province 126 (K. Ratnaweera 31); Western Province (South)* 130 for three (M. S. Atapattu 41 not out, R. S. Kaluwitharana 35 not out).

At Maitland Place, Colombo (SSC), June 11, 12, 13, 14. Drawn. Central Province 194 (R. S. Kalpage 38, P. B. Dassanayake 47, U. H. Kodituwakku 36, Extras 32; C. P. H. Ramanayake three for 25); Western Province (North)* 459 for six (U. C. Hathurusinghe 120, K. Dharmasena 35, H. P. Tillekeratne 151, P. A. de Silva 73, Extras 31).

At P. Saravanamuttu Stadium, Colombo, June 11, 12, 13, 14. Western Province (Suburbs) won by three wickets. North-Western Province* 139 (S. D. Anurasiri five for 43) and 116 (S. D. Anurasiri five for 49, N. Devarajan three for 22); Western Province (Suburbs) 111 (S. Jayawardene 33, S. Sooriyarachchi 32; A. W. Ekanayake six for 26, A. W. R. Madurasinghe four for 38) and 145 for seven (N. Devarajan 57; A. H. Bandaranayake three for 30).

At Welagedera Stadium, Kurunegala, June 18, 19, 20, 21. Drawn. Southern Province* 191 (J. Nanda Kumara 39, U. D. U. Chandana 49, K. Ratnaweera 30; A. W. Ekanayake three for 58, A. W. R. Madurasinghe five for 48) and 143 for two (W. M. J. Kumudu 66 not out, S. M. Faumi 56 not out); North-Western Province 92 (J. C. Gamage four for 26, K. P. J. Warnaweera three for 24).

At Tyronne Fernando Stadium, Moratuwa, June 18, 19, 20, 21. Western Province (South) won by an innings and 28 runs. Central Province 114 (S. Ranatunga four for 33) and 179 (U. H. Koditwakku 44, D. N. Nadarajah 64 not out; G. P. Wickremasinghe six for 53); Western Province (South)* 321 (A. A. D. S. Perera 62, C. Mendis 32, M. S. Atapattu 98, N. Ranatunga 72; M. Muralitharan six for 116).

At P. Saravanamuttu Stadium, Colombo, June 18, 19, 20, 21. Western Province (North) won by an innings and 82 runs. Western Province (Suburbs)* 236 (N. Devarajan 81, P. Munasinghe 35, Extras 40; E. A. R. de Silva three for 62, B. R. Jurangpathy three for 45) and 101 (K. I. W. Wijegunawardene three for 23, E. A. R. de Silva four for 36); Western Province (North) 419 (K. Dharmasena 76, P. A. de Silva 36, S. T. Jayasuriya 132, E. A. R. de Silva 48; S. D. Anurasiri six for 120).

At Welagedera Stadium, Kurunegala, June 25, 26, 27, 28. Drawn. Central Province* 197 (R. S. Kalpage 85, J. Bandara 45; A. W. Ekanayake seven for 73) and 200 (D. N. Nadarajah 53, R. S. Kalpage 47; A. W. Ekanayake five for 78, A. H. Bandaranayake three for 35); North-Western Province 108 (H. N. T. Gamage three for 16, R. Boruppa three for 41) and 102 for six (J. Kalatunga 32; R. S. Kalpage three for 25).

At Maitland Place, Colombo (SSC), June 25, 26, 27, 28. Western Province (North) won by 342 runs. Western Province (North) 432 (U. C. Hathurusinghe 66, H. P. Tillekeratne 67, P. A. de Silva 185 not out, Extras 30; A. P. Gurusinha three for 55); Western Province (South)* 90 for two dec. (A. P. Gurusinha 39) and forfeited second innings.

Western Province (North) won the tournament when Western Province (South) conceded the match, because the pitch was judged too dangerous for play to continue.

At Panadura Esplanade, Panadura, June 25, 26, 27, 28. Western Province (Suburbs) won by seven wickets. Southern Province* 201 (S. Jayawardene four for 85, P. Perera four for 35) and 225 (W. M. J. Kumudu 49, A. P. R. Shaman 45; W. Labrooy three for 72); Western Province (Suburbs) 223 (S. Jayawardene 38, P. Munasinghe 66 not out; J. C. Gamage four for 62, K. P. J. Warnaweera three for 47) and 204 for three (N. Devarajan 98 not out, S. Sooriyarachchi 33 not out).

CRICKET IN ZIMBABWE, 1992-93

By TERRY YATES-ROUND

The advent of Test cricket gave the Zimbabwean game a new lease of life. Had it not been for the granting of Test status, cricket could easily have dwindled to a third-rate sport. Players who had been thinking of retirement or emigration because of the lack of first-class matches in Zimbabwe turned back to the game with enthusiasm and the Zimbabwe Cricket Union announced the first domestic first-class tournament, to begin in 1993-94. Meanwhile, it was developing its programme to extend cricket facilities and coaching to schools across the country and to discover fresh talent, especially among the black majority.

The inaugural Test match with India was the turning point. On October 18, 1992, a full Indian team graced the field at Harare Sports Club, the headquarters of Zimbabwean cricket. Though the crowd was disappointingly small, the home players in no way disgraced themselves: their first-innings total of 456 was much the highest by any country on Test debut, and their captain, David Houghton, celebrated his long-awaited first Test with a century. Zimbabwe even entertained hopes of becoming the first country to win their maiden Test since Australia in 1876-77 when John Traicos, the 45-year-old off-spinner, claimed three wickets to reduce India to 101 for five. But though he went on to take five for 86, the follow-on was saved and the match fizzled out into a draw.

It was Zimbabwe's most experienced cricketers who starred in the Test but, in the one-day international that followed, the younger players acquitted themselves well enough to show that the country had strength in depth as well. However, the subsequent visit from New Zealand displayed the weakness in Zimbabwe's attack, which lacked international-class seamers. The Second Test against New Zealand was lost, as were all the one-day internationals played during the season – one to India, two to New Zealand and one to Pakistan. Tours to Sharjah and India provided useful experience but no wins. A visit from Kent in late March and early April offered further practice to Zimbabwe's younger players.

From 1993-94 these will have the opportunity to compete in first-class matches for the Lonrho Logan Cup, to be contested by Mashonaland, Mashonaland Country Districts, Mashonaland Under-24 and Matabeleland. A series of three-day matches will culminate in a final between the two leading teams. Previous Zimbabwean competitions were staged over two days. In the 1992-93 league Old Georgians swept the board again: they took the Rothmans National League and Knockout trophies, the Vigne Cup for the winners of the Mashonaland league matches and the BP/Shell Shield. They possessed the most successful batsmen in the Flower brothers – Andy averaged 92 and Grant 62 – with Gavin Briant not far behind. The leading bowler was Mark Vickery, who took 17 wickets at a cost of 14 apiece.

Old Georgians and other clubs in the Harare district – Old Hararians, Harare Sports Club, Alexandra and the two Asian clubs, Universals and Sunrise – dominate Zimbabwean cricket, thanks to the superior facilities and the larger reservoir of players created by the concentration of population around the capital. The leading Bulawayo clubs, Queens and Bulawayo Athletic Club, lack their strength in depth. Harare's players also have the edge in selection for the national team because they can practise together regularly; the journey from Bulawayo takes up to five hours by road. When Gary Crocker was summoned to Harare as a late replacement for Ali Shah in the Inaugural Test, he drove through the night and arrived at 4 a.m. on the day of the match to make his first-class debut.

The ZCU's most important task is to encourage the steady progress of grass-roots cricket, on which its survival depends. Coaching is in the hands of John Lashbrook, chairman of the ZCU's coaching committee, Test player Andy Flower, Dave Levy, who is responsible for the mainly black "high density" schools, and Ian Tinker who is in charge of "low density" schools. With 900 teachers, student teachers and pupils from all schools having completed basic coaching courses, the principal obstacle to progress is the lack of equipment. Efforts have been concentrated on the "high density" areas inhabited chiefly by underprivileged blacks; Levy introduced "jumbo" cricket, using a soft ball and simple pine bats, to these areas back in 1982, but proper facilities such as those enjoyed by most of the low density schools have been in short supply. Concrete strips laid in the high density areas have proved successful: in Mashonaland, High Glen has four, catering for 28 schools and up to 360 boys; Chitungwiza has two concrete pitches, and four coaches, for 30 schools and 600 boys. The ZCU plans to extend the programme to the other provinces. The establishment of the Zimbabwe Cricket Coaching Academy, employing 12 coaches in Harare and nine in Bulawayo, with 16 nets, four of them concrete, is another significant step forward.

Bursaries from the ZCU have enabled promising black cricketers to take up places at leading schools, with proper cricketing facilities. Under this scheme, 14 boys are currently at Prince Edward School in Harare, once attended by England Test cricketer Graeme Hick, and one at Falcon College in Bulawayo. Past scholarship boys include George Thandi, who played for Zimbabwe Schools, and Stephen Mangongo, who appeared for Zimbabwe Under-23 in January. Mangongo, like Walter Chawaguta, who took A levels at Prince Edward, has become a full-time ZCU coach. The success of black youngsters like these has helped popularise cricket in their communities. In December two teams drawn from high density areas, High Glen (representing Highfield, Glen Norah and Glen View) and Chitungwiza (St Mary's, Zengeza and Seke) joined 35 other schools – including Harrow, Huntingdon Foundation and St Dunstan's from England – in the annual schoolboy festival organised by Clive Barnes. Under the supervision of Barnes, headmaster of Prince Edward School, this has become the pipe-opener to the Zimbabwean cricket season. Playing on turf for the first time, High Glen and Chitungwiza both achieved highly commendable results of two wins, two draws and one defeat.

The chance of touring has made Zimbabwean youngsters take the game seriously; in junior cricket, teams at Under-13, Under-15, Under-19 and Under-24 levels have represented Zimbabwe with success in countries as distant as Australia. Sponsorship is essential, and has been forthcoming, though it has been hampered by the severe economic problems caused by the long drought. The lack of foreign currency for importing cricket equipment has also made the game in Zimbabwe heavily reliant on gifts from former players and overseas sources. The Zimbabwean national team has also made its contribution, through the £150,000 which it brought back to the ZCU from the World Cup. Though £80,000 was needed to fund the visits from India and New Zealand, television rights from those tours also generated income to be put back into the cause of spreading the game.

CRICKET IN DENMARK, 1993

By PETER S. HARGREAVES

Danish cricket broke new ground in March when the senior national team undertook a brief tour of Natal to get practice against stronger opposition on turf wickets. The Danish team won two matches, against Country Districts and a Zenith XI, out of six. In July, this was followed by a tour of the English Home Counties. All this was part of the preparation for the 1994 ICC Trophy in Kenya.

The only match against another country played all year, however, was the second of the two planned against Holland over a wet weekend in Copenhagen. The first game was cancelled; in the second, held at the KB ground on August 1, the heavy conditions held down the imported batsmen in the Dutch team and they scored only 154 for nine. However, as at Utrecht the previous year, the Danish batsmen failed badly, this time in a match that was there for the winning, and were bowled out for 91.

About the only home player to impress against the Dutch was Søren Westergaard, who took four for 18 and continued to advance as an opening bowler all season. With Søren Henriksen, the country's best all-rounder, he ensured that the Svanholm club won their third Danish championship in succession. Svanholm also won the national knockout cup, beating Esbjerg in the final. In the league, however, they had to cope with a powerful challenge from the all-Pakistani club Nørrebro, who led the table at the summer break in early July.

Nørrebro's success was due mainly to Aftab Ahmed, who was responsible for Svanholm's only defeat of the season, scoring a century against them in the very first round of matches. Aftab finished the season with 924 runs and an average of 50.83. His nearest rival was Allan From Hansen with 887. Westergaard was the leading wicket-taker with 54 at 13.94 each; Morten Hedergaard had 53.

Glostrup came third in the table, ahead of Esbjerg, Chang, Skanderborg, KB and Nykøbing Mors. In 1994 the last two will change places with Herning and Husum, the top two in the second division, KB after losing narrowly in the challenge match against Husum, who come from Schleswig on the German side of the Danish-German border and thereby created history by reaching the First Division.

One of the three Pakistani clubs in Copenhagen, Ishøj, did remarkably well in youth cricket, winning five of the six championships on offer: Junior (under-18), Boys (under-15) and Lilliput (under-13) both indoor and outdoor. Their only failure was in the outdoor under-15s.

CRICKET IN THE NETHERLANDS, 1993

By DAVID HARDY

These days the Dutch national team creates a sensation every other year by winning against a professional team. In 1993 a second victory in four encounters with an England XI, this one containing five players with Test experience, followed the 1991 win against West Indies and the initial success against an England XI in 1989.

The first of the two one-day matches in Haarlem against the England team was, however, an emphatic win for the visitors by 128 runs, a result forgotten by the English press at the time. In this match half-centuries by captain Mark Benson, Nasser Hussain and Trevor Ward, followed by extremely tight bowling all round, were the foundations of a comprehensive victory. In the second match the Dutch turned the tables. Heroes of this last-over victory were New Zealander Roger Bradley, who made 88 not out in only his third match for the Dutch team, and Australian Peter Cantrell, who had not played the day before; they shared a third-wicket partnership of 138. The only Dutchman to make runs was Tim de Leede, whose ten not out sealed the match in the last over; the first four batsmen were all foreigners.

This revived discussion about the composition of the Dutch team. In 1993 the selectors leaned heavily on the expertise of the so-called "residents", particularly in the batting department. In addition to Cantrell and Bradley, others to appear regularly for Holland during 1993 were West Indians Nolan Clarke and Rupert Gomes, Sri Lankan Flavian Aponso and New Zealander Phil Keukelaar. The short-term benefits of such a policy are obvious, but the long-term value to Dutch cricket is dubious, particularly as three of these six are in their forties.

Two of Holland's rivals, Denmark and Ireland, were also soundly beaten during the season, the win in Copenhagen against Denmark in July being emphatic (the home side was bowled out for 91); the two wins against Ireland in The Hague followed defeats in the first four matches between the countries. The only disappointment of the season was the defeat by Leicestershire in July, the county team winning by seven wickets in a one-day game at The Hague.

In the domestic premier league (Hoofdklasse), Excelsior of Schiedam, the home club of the Somerset bowler Andre van Troost, won the title for the second time in three years, just pipping Voorburg CC on average points per match. The Excelsior player-coach, Western Australian Wayne Andrews, substituting for Tim Zoehrer who was on tour in England, played a significant role in his club's success with 865 runs at 66.53, as did van Troost's brother Luuk, who was the best all-rounder with 505 runs and 30 wickets.

In a glorious season for batsmen no fewer than ten averaged over 50, with Kampong Utrecht's Cantrell once again the top man at 74.13. Surprise of the season was the relegation from the premier league of The Hague's HCC, in the club's 110th year, for the first time in its history. Taking their place in 1994 will be neighbouring Quick, who won all their 17 completed matches in the first division (Eerste Klasse) under the astute leadership of former Hampshire professional Paul-Jan Bakker.

THE NETHERLANDS v ENGLAND XI

At Rood en Wit CC, Haarlem, July 9. England XI won by 128 runs. Toss: The Netherlands.

England XI

T. R. Ward c Gomes b Lefebvre 53	J. A. Daley not out 3
*M. R. Benson c Bradley b Lubbers . . . 61	
P. J. Prichard c Gomes b Lubbers 10	L-b 9, w 1, n-b 6 16
N. Hussain c Clarke b Jansen 52	
†R. J. Blakey b Jansen 32	1/84 2/123 3/138 (5 wkts, 40 overs) 238
J. P. Stephenson not out 11	4/217 5/230

D. Gough, R. D. Stemp, M. C. Ilott and M. A. Robinson did not bat.

Bowling: Jansen 8–1–33–2; Leemhuis 8–0–51–0; Keukelaar 6–0–42–0; Lefebvre 8–0–31–1; Lubbers 8–0–51–2; de Leede 2–0–21–0.

The Netherlands

N. E. Clarke b Stephenson 15	†R. H. Scholte not out 9
R. Vos c Blakey b Ilott 2	F. Jansen not out 4
R. R. A. Bradley c Hussain	
b Stephenson . 16	L-b 4, w 2, n-b 3 9
R. E. Gomes c Gough b Robinson 29	
T. B. M. de Leede b Stemp 10	1/15 2/21 3/62 (7 wkts, 40 overs) 110
R. P. Lefebvre c Ilott b Stemp 7	4/75 5/85
*S. W. Lubbers b Gough 9	6/86 7/105

P. P. Keukelaar and J. Leemhuis did not bat.

Bowling: Ilott 8–3–19–1; Gough 8–1–19–1; Robinson 8–2–16–1; Stephenson 8–1–28–2; Stemp 8–1–24–2.

Umpires: H. Huising and D. Ohm.

THE NETHERLANDS v ENGLAND XI

At Rood en Wit CC, Haarlem, July 10. The Netherlands won by seven wickets. Toss: The Netherlands.

England XI

T. R. Ward b Cantrell 14	D. Gough c Gomes b Visee 4
*M. R. Benson c Jansen b Lubbers 58	R. D. Stemp not out 4
P. J. Prichard c and b Jansen 26	L-b 7, w 3, n-b 1 11
N. Hussain lbw b Cantrell 4	
†R. J. Blakey c Scholte b Jansen 4	1/24 2/76 3/81 (7 wkts, 55 overs) 188
J. P. Stephenson c Gomes b Visee 41	4/90 5/140
J. A. Daley not out 22	6/168 7/178

M. J. McCague and M. A. Robinson did not bat.

Bowling: Lefebvre 11–2–32–0; Visee 11–2–18–2; Cantrell 11–0–40–2; Jansen 11–1–34–2; Lubbers 8–0–41–1; de Leede 3–0–16–0.

The Netherlands

N. E. Clarke lbw b Gough 13	T. B. M. de Leede not out 10
P. E. Cantrell run out 64	L-b 4, w 2, n-b 4 10
R. E. Gomes b Stephenson b Gough . . . 4	
R. R. A. Bradley not out 88	1/23 2/29 3/167 (3 wkts, 54.3 overs) 189

R. P. Lefebvre, *S. W. Lubbers, †R. H. Scholte, R. Vos, H. F. Visee and F. Jansen did not bat.

Bowling: McCague 10.3–0–42–0; Gough 11–2–28–2; Stephenson 11–1–51–0; Robinson 11–2–22–0; Stemp 11–1–42–0.

Umpires: W. Molenaar and E. van der Vegt.

CRICKET ROUND THE WORLD

ARGENTINA

Andy Moles, the Warwickshire professional, guided St Alban's to their first-ever First Division title in 1992-93. Moles scored 571 runs over the season, averaging 71.37. He was one of four English players who played and coached during the season, the others being Dean Hodgson of Gloucestershire and Monte Lynch and Tony Murphy of Surrey. Excluding the professionals, the Argentine captain, Leonardo Alonso of Belgrano Athletic Club, was both the leading scorer, with 514, and wicket-taker, with 29. The 94th North v South match, which dates back to 1891, was played over three days in March 1993, resulting in a 144-run win for South. The Brazilian Cricket Association staged a three-match tour in December 1992, losing their final match by 13 runs to Argentina, who thus retained the Bing Norris Cup.

BANGLADESH

The first-ever tournament under the auspices of the South Asian Association for Regional Co-operation (SAARC) was organised in Dhaka in December 1992, including strong B teams from India, Pakistan and Sri Lanka and the Bangladesh national team. The Bangladeshis began the tournament by bowling out the Sri Lankans for 85 and winning by seven wickets. Unfortunately, the match between Bangladesh and the Indians was called off after 35 minutes because crowds had gathered outside the Dhaka Stadium protesting against the demolition of the mosque in the Indian town of Ayodhya, and the organisers eventually called off the tournament. Club cricket remains very popular in Bangladesh and crowds of 30-35,000 watched games between leading club sides on four or five occasions in 1992-93.

BELGIUM

The 1993 League was the most competitive so far but was unfortunately decided by rain on the final day. Two of the contending teams, Antwerp and the Brussels side Twelve Stars, had to win to have a chance of overhauling Antwerp Indians, who then surprisingly lost to Mechelen Eagles by 66 runs. But both their rivals had their games abandoned, leaving Antwerp Indians with the title. Overall, they were a strong all-round side, with Amit Bhansali, who scored 343 runs and averaged 49, and Hemang Shah, who took 22 wickets at 11.50 each, their most consistent players. Royal Brussels, the pre-season favourites, had a miserable season and finished sixth out of the nine participants. – Ken Farmiloe.

BERMUDA

The 1993 season was almost exclusively devoted to preparing the national team for the 1994 ICC Trophy in Kenya. Bermuda played five matches in Barbados in March – the outstanding performance was 112 not out by Jeff Richardson against St Catherine's. Then Derbyshire toured Bermuda for six matches in April and Pakistan played two games in May. Although Bermuda's representative teams fared less than favourably against these first-class professionals, there were benefits in exposure. Michael Holding was engaged in the post-season period to fine-tune the Bermuda XI. The domestic programme was dominated by the success of St George's, who won all 15 league matches to be champions of the premier division as well as capturing the knockout cup. St George's also retained the famous Cup Match trophy by drawing the traditional two-day, two-innings fixture with Somerset CC. A final accolade for St George's came with the awards of Cricketer of the Year and Most Valuable Player to Clay Smith, who scored over a thousand runs and was prominently placed in both the bowling averages and fielding statistics. The team's solitary defeat came in the Camel Cup play-offs, between the top four league teams of 1992, when they were beaten by the eventual winners, Western Stars. – Maurice F. Hankey.

CANADA

The Canadian Cricket Association celebrated its centenary in March 1992. There are now 350 senior teams across the nation playing in 17 leagues, press coverage has increased and one radio station in Toronto has a weekly programme on the game. As in the United States, Canada's cricket has benefited in recent years because an estimated 35 per cent of immigrants are coming from Test-playing countries. One official claims there are more state schools playing cricket in Toronto than in Greater London. In the largest league in the country, the Toronto and District, Victoria Park won the premier division, defeating Grace Church by six wickets. In the west, Brockton Point of Vancouver – whose ground was once described by Sir Donald Bradman as the most beautiful in the world – won the British Columbia mainland league. In the Victoria League, Colts were the winners, with their batsman M. Brooks achieving the rare feat of a thousand runs in a Canadian season: 1,003 at 59.00. The *Canadian Cricketer* (561, Melita Crescent, Toronto MG6 3Y7) is an important vehicle of communication. – Gerald Howat.

EAST AND CENTRAL AFRICA

Malawi, captained by Vali Tarmahomed, captured the Sir Robert Menzies Trophy at the Quadrangular Regional tournament in Kampala in September 1993, beating the other three members of the Conference: Tanzania, Uganda and Zambia. This was Malawi's first victory since they became a member in 1981.

EUROPEAN NATIONS CHAMPIONSHIP

France beat Germany in a thrilling final in the inaugural European Nations Cup, organised by the European Cricket Federation, which was held in Berlin from July 13 to 17. Germany had France at 43 for five, chasing their total of 155. But the French recovered to win by four wickets with 11 balls of the 50 overs remaining. Twenty-year-old Franck Wassermann, from Chauny in Picardy, showed great promise as an all-rounder, scored the winning runs and took a crucial catch. This avenged France's defeat by a fully expatriate German side in the European Cricketer Cup in England in 1992. France, coached by the former Essex wicket-keeper David East, played Belgium, Italy and Austria in their group and dismissed them all for under 100. Germany were also unbeaten until the final, scoring wins over Greece, Sweden and Switzerland. The game against Switzerland produced the only century of the competition, scored by Jamal Mirza of Hamburg CC, a German passport holder. Under the rules of the competition, there must be seven nationals in each team, of whom at least three must be native-born. – Brian Fell and Simon Hewitt.

FIJI

The 1992-93 season was plagued by wet weather and the Crompton Cup, which has been played every Easter since 1951, had to be abandoned for the first time. Cricket in Fiji is played from late October to Easter. It could be played all year round if facilities were available but, as cricket has to share grounds with rugby, soccer and hockey, the sport is restricted to the hot, rainy summer months. Plans are afoot to obtain a ground in Suva, Fiji's capital, but, as always, lack of finance is a constraint. There are 13 district associations affiliated to the national body. However, since a journey to Suva from the distant islands of Rotuma or Ono-i-Lau takes two days by boat, it is not always easy to get everyone together for competition. Ten districts did get to Lautoka for the 50-over Inter-Association Competition, sponsored by Colonial Mutual. It was blessed by blazing sunshine and Tubou, from the island of Lakeba, beat Suva by four wickets in a low-scoring final. – Peter Knight.

FRANCE

Outside the European Nations Championship, which France won, the highlight of the French international season was a drawn three-day "Test" against Belgium at Château de Thoiry, near Versailles. In a rain-affected game Belgium scored 172 for nine declared in reply to France's paltry 109 all out. France batted out the last two sessions to reach 187 for three. Annual games between the two countries were first staged from 1906 to 1913 and revived in 1991. In the national league Château de Thoiry, champions in 1991 and 1992, failed to make it three in a row when they lost a high-scoring final to the Paris Université team led by the Guadeloupean brothers Guy and Valentin Brumant. In the last decade about 30 clubs have sprung up in every corner of the country from Boulogne to Monte Carlo.

The standard is highest in the Ile-de-France. A separate league exists in the south-west, won by Eymet in 1993. The south-west champions used to play off against the northern winners but this was discontinued when Périgueux were dismissed for five in 1991. Despite the indifferent standard in the south-west, where Damazan and Perpignan are the only clubs to rely more on local talent than on ageing expatriates, the league's first division remains open to clubs on a national basis. The national federation subsidises travel costs, which can be hefty when, say, Lyon meet Chauny, some 350 miles away. Another problem is finding the right balance between immigrants – mainly English and Asian – and Frenchmen. In 1993 all first division sides had to include three Frenchmen, a figure that will increase gradually in the years to come. The other major development in 1993 was the laying of France's first grass square, at Saumur, in the Loire Valley. – Simon Hewitt.

GERMANY

The choice of the British Army Sportsground near the Olympic Stadium in Berlin for the final of the European Nations Championship drew attention to the threat to the three excellent cricket grounds in the city, which are due to return to the German civilian authorities as British troops withdraw. There are about 17 other grounds in the country, mainly in north Germany, that could also be lost to cricket because of the pull-out. As well as the disappointment of losing the European final, a German selection lost by one wicket to a Dutch selection in Nijmegen in June with just three balls to go; Aamir bin Jung of Frankfurt CC hit 102 not out. In domestic cricket both the championship and the cup, which is reserved for German passport holders, were won by Hassloch Cosmopolitans. There were signs in 1992 that cricket is making inroads into the educational system. A handful of schools now encourage the sport, while at university level Passau, Göttingen, Darmstadt and Eichstadt all have cricket as an official part of their sports programme. – Brian Fell.

GIBRALTAR

The 1993 cricket season in Gibraltar was the longest in living memory, beginning in early April (instead of early May) and going on until October 16, instead of late September. The highlight was the visit of an MCC XI, which included Mushtaq Mohammad. They were far too strong for the local opposition, winning all three of their matches, but they were good enough to conduct some coaching clinics for the national squad. In the domestic competitions, Combined Services proved to be the best-organised and disciplined and they carried off the three major trophies: the BSG League, the Wiggins Shield and the Murto Cup. Once again teams from the Costa del Sol participated in these competitions. It was good to see a number of young players breaking through into the senior clubs. The mid-week evening 20-over league increased in popularity and several new teams joined in. – T. J. Finlayson.

HONG KONG

Hong Kong cricket had an enjoyable and eventful year in 1992-93. The Kowloon team Templars won both the Sunday League and the Rothmans Cup. In the Saturday competitions Little Sai Wan narrowly beat Nomads to the league although Nomads had the consolation of winning the Butani Cup. St George's won the Butani Plate. There are a number of new teams emerging but they are playing mainly social cricket because there are not enough grounds available to fit them into the league programme. There has been improvement to the ground at DBS, the only Chinese school that now has cricket facilities, and the Hong Kong Cricket Association is still hoping to retain the three British Forces grounds even after China takes over in 1997. However, the Association has to consider the acquisition of another ground; this will be difficult given the high land prices in Hong Kong. An alternative is to try and find funding for floodlighting of existing grounds to allow cricket to be played in the evenings as well as weekends. – John Cribbin.

HUNGARY

In May, the *Hungarian Times* reported the formation of the Magyar Cricket Club, which intended to play three other teams of expatriates, with kit provided by the British Embassy, on a matting wicket at Obudai Island. Two months later, however, it was reported that the kit had been stolen.

ISRAEL

The highlight of the 1993 season was the 14th Maccabiah Games in July. Cricket, as usual, was among the events and Jewish teams from Australia, England, South Africa, Ireland and India took part alongside Israel. Australia won the gold medal, South Africa silver and Ireland bronze. Local cricket went very smoothly. The league competition was won by Ashdod, whose star was a West Indian-born all-rounder, Louis Hall, with Nave Yonathan second. In the knockout competition, Hapoel Netanya easily beat the Lions' Club of Lod. – Noah Davidson.

ITALY

In contrast with 1992, 1993 was the happiest year in the brief history of Italian cricket and fittingly marked the bicentenary of the first recorded game in the peninsula. The celebrations included a tour by MCC, who won all their games except the two-day match against the national side when they struggled to earn a draw. Cesena retained the championship and also triumphed in the European Club Championship on their home ground, the Ippodromo del Sevio. Having beaten the Greek champions Phaeax and the Austrian champions Vienna, the home team then beat the holders, Château de Thoiry, by eight wickets thanks to a century by Sunandra Pearis. Italy's ambition in 1994 is to become the first ICC affiliate to be upgraded to Associate Membership. – Simone Gambino.

KENYA

Cricket in Kenya is nearly 80 years old. For the first 70 or so the game was played by the Europeans and Asians on matting wickets. It has been revolutionised both by the change to grass wickets and the emergence of indigenous Kenyans who now play a very important role. There are about 40 club teams, mainly in Nairobi and Mombasa. The season lasts from July to March, all games being played on an overs-limit basis on Sundays. In the 1993-94 league was won by Swamibapa with Aga Khan as runners-up. Swamibapa has seven national players in the line-up and is dominated by the three Tikolo brothers, Tom, David and Steve. Steve Tikolo scored 1,132 league runs in the season. – Jasmer Singh.

MALAYSIA

The decision to include cricket in the 1998 Commonwealth Games in Kuala Lumpur means the sport now has backing from the government, which is obliged to ensure that the sport has the best possible facilities for the Games. Cricket in Malaysia has a sizable following but cannot be compared to soccer or badminton. These sports have created millionaires here and parents would like to guide their children towards them rather than cricket, where they will only end up with a tan and no money. However, the Ministry of Education has included cricket as a curriculum sport and new eight-a-side formats have been introduced into schools to encourage involvement; Richie Robinson, the former Australian Test player, is coaching the national team. There are probably only five turf wickets left in the country but Malaysia has a major programme of installing artificial wickets over the next five years. After that, the next step in our vision of achieving Test status by 2020 is to introduce turf wickets gradually. Cricket is played throughout the year, except over Christmas. Johore won both the National Inter-State League and the Carlsberg Cup. The Benson and Hedges Carnival held in July was won by the Indian Sports Club of Dubai, who overcame a field including Singapore and seven Malaysian teams. In the final Dubai beat Johore by 49 runs, Mohammed Saqaqat taking four for 13. – Charlie Chelliah.

MALTA

Limited-overs league cricket was introduced to Malta for the first time in 1993 with four teams competing: Balzan Taverners won one competition and Marsaxlokk Ramblers the second. This continues the revival of cricket which began in 1989 with the formation of the Malta Cricket Association; the game had struggled for almost two decades after the withdrawal of British forces. The game is played year-round and in 1993 there were seven touring teams from England, one each from Guernsey, Italy and Switzerland, and visits from HMS *London*, HMS *Ark Royal* and the Royal Yacht *Britannia*. Five batsmen passed 1,500 runs, one of whom, Mike Caruana, also took 50 wickets. – Dennis Bradley.

NAMIBIA

United won the First National Bank Super League, ending many years of supremacy by Wanderers. However, Wanderers won both the Senior League and the Harry's Betting Services Sunday League, which provided experience for junior players as some seniors could not play on Sundays.

PAPUA NEW GUINEA

For the first time in the history of the Port Moresby competition the title was shared in 1993. In the 50-over A-grade grand final Steamships Mobil and Elcom both bowled each other out for 201 and so became Joint Premiers. Tau Ao scored 92 for Steamships Mobil while Elcom's Tani Amini took five for 42. A new development was the Mobil Country Cup, which brought 32 teams into Port Moresby for a week-long competition. However, there were complaints that not much work was done in town during the week because of the interest that was generated. Cricket in Papua New Guinea dates back to the arrival of missionaries along the Papuan coast in the 19th century. Many of the PNG representatives chosen for the ICC Trophy in 1994 learned their cricket in village and beach competitions, played much as they are in the West Indies. The Board is anxious to maximise the junior cricket programme, known as Liklik Cricket. – Wayne Satchell.

THE PHILIPPINES

A third team, the Good Men Cricket Club, has now been founded in The Philippines to join the Manila Nomads (founded 1912) and the Manila Anzacs (founded 1980). All three teams are made up largely of expatriates and most matches are against clubs from elsewhere in East Asia; The Philippines, as a former US colony, plays baseball. However, there are some signs of local interest and a game between GMCC and Nomads was recently televised. All matches are at the Nomads ground, which doubles up as a rugby pitch during the rainy season. The wicket is matting. Scores tend to be high as the boundaries are rather short and the outfield is fast as the grass is kept to a minimum by the goats that graze on it during lunch and tea breaks. However, the matting itself is worn and the bounce somewhat irregular. For that reason, there is normally a rule that batsmen cannot be out first ball. – Peter Foster.

RUSSIA

In July, an English touring team, the Explorers, played what was reported to be the first formal match in Moscow since the Bolshevik Revolution. Their opponents were the MCC: the newly formed Moscow Cricket Club. Owing to a misunderstanding, the pitch was originally laid out for a croquet match. Broomhandles had to be used in place of stumps: the man bringing some of the kit was stopped at Heathrow because he had forgotten to get a visa.

SWITZERLAND

Bern Cricket Club won the Swiss League in 1993 after an exciting final with the Nomads and thus qualified for the European Champion Clubs Competition to be held in Greece in 1994. This was Bern's first victory in the competition although they were among six founder members of the Swiss Cricket Association in 1980. There are now 16 clubs and about 350 playing members. The latest club to join is the St Moritz Winter Cricket Club, most famous for its ice cricket usually played on the frozen lake in February. This year's final, played between an English side, including Simon Hughes of Durham, Mark Nicholas of Hampshire and Nick Cook of Northamptonshire, and a mixed Swiss side resulted in a two-wicket win for the Swiss team. Most cricketers in Switzerland are expatriates, though a few Swiss have learned the game. One of the major problems is getting young people interested; cricket has to compete with baseball and American football, both of which are seen on prime-time TV. – Peter Nixon.

UNITED ARAB EMIRATES

The Union National Bank replaced New Medical Centre as the top team in 1992-93, winning the Ramadan Floodlit Gold Cup and the Panasonic Gold Cup. The bankers' hopes of winning a third trophy were lost when the Abu Dhabi Duty Free Trophy final was called off due to the start of summer holidays and the oppressive heat. An Emirates Cricket Board XI lost to Surrey by 129 runs at the Sharjah Cricket Stadium but beat a touring MCC team by eight wickets after Akbar Rana scored an unbeaten 64. The Wills Trophy matches between Pakistan, Sri Lanka and Zimbabwe are in the relevant section of *Wisden*.

UNITED STATES

Some 700 clubs, with an average membership of between 20 and 30, currently play in the US, an increase of about a quarter in the last four years. Most play limited-overs cricket on matting wickets. Outfields can be slow, especially in states where legislation requires grass in public places to be at least two and a half inches long to avoid liability insurance claims for injury. Cricket covers almost every major city: for instance, in Atlanta where Tropical were the champions; Houston, where Memorial won the League; and Phoenix, where the winners were the University of Arizona. Pakistan CC were the champions in the Colorado State League. In the Brooklyn League, Caribbean and Caricou were the principal clubs, the former winning the league competition and the latter the knockout. The Metropolitan League, of New York, again won the inter-league competition and celebrated their success with a tour of Jamaica. In the west, where some of the cricket is played on grass, United won the North Califorinan League with Marin coming second. Leading players included A. Reddy of United and O. Nana of Marin, each with more than 600 runs. In Southern

California, Corinthians and Pasadena were joint champions. R. Iranpur of Hollywood has been the most prolific scorer on the West Coast for some years and he again passed 500 runs. Once again, Southern California beat the North in the Raisinland Trophy. – Gerald Howat.

WEST AFRICA

Nigeria won the ninth West Africa quadrangular tournament held in Freetown, Sierra Leone, in April and May 1993, defeating all their opponents in the round, robin-tournament. They beat Ghana by 213 runs after bowling out the opposition for just 21, with Idowu taking three for four and Ntinu three for two; S. Elliott scored 101 not out for Nigeria. Ghana withdrew from their match against The Gambia the following day because six of their players were injured and there was no possibility of a rest day. Nigeria, who had beaten The Gambia by 56 runs in the opening match, then completed their success with a 43-run win over Sierra Leone. At its meeting following the tournament, the West Africa Cricket Conference formally noted that: "1. The general arrangement on the part of the host association left much to be desired. 2. The general standard exhibited by most of the players was below expectation. 3. The cost of living in Freetown was so high that much could not be done from our meagre resources to augment the feeding of the players." The *Daily Observer*, published in the Gambian capital, Banjul, carried an interview with the national coach J. B. Jarra, 75, described as "The Gambia's greatest cricket bowler of all time" and known as "Teacher". Jarra, a leg-break and googly bowler, was selected for the national team in 1955, when The Gambia was still a British colony, after an expatriate gave up his place in the team to him. Jarra said he remained dedicated to promoting the game among young Gambians because he loved it and did not wish to see it fade away.

PART FIVE:
ADMINISTRATION AND LAWS

INTERNATIONAL CRICKET COUNCIL

On June 15, 1909, representatives of cricket in England, Australia and South Africa met at Lord's and founded the Imperial Cricket Conference. Membership was confined to the governing bodies of cricket in countries within the British Commonwealth where Test cricket was played. India, New Zealand and West Indies were elected as members on May 31, 1926, Pakistan on July 28, 1952, Sri Lanka on July 21, 1981, and Zimbabwe on July 8, 1992. South Africa ceased to be a member of ICC on leaving the British Commonwealth in May, 1961, but was elected as a Full Member on July 10, 1991.

On July 15, 1965, the Conference was renamed the International Cricket Conference and new rules were adopted to permit the election of countries from outside the British Commonwealth. This led to the growth of the Conference, with the admission of Associate Members, who were each entitled to one vote, while the Foundation and Full Members were each entitled to two votes, on ICC resolutions. On July 12, 13, 1989, the Conference was renamed the International Cricket Council and revised rules were adopted.

On July 7, 1993, ICC ceased to be administered by MCC and became an independent organisation with its own chief executive, the headquarters remaining at Lord's. The category of Foundation Member, with its special rights, was abolished. On October 1, 1993, Sir Clyde Walcott became the first non-British chairman of ICC.

Officers

Chairman: Sir Clyde Walcott.

Chief Executive: D. L. Richards.

Constitution

Chairman: The nominee of the President of MCC, with the confirmation of the members at the annual conference. Prior to making his nomination, the President of MCC shall have appropriate consultations, to include all Full Members. The term of office is for one year, commencing October 1, but subject to the proviso that no Chairman shall remain continuously in office for more than four years, the Chairman may offer himself for re-nomination.

Chief Executive: Appointed by the Council. D. L. Richards has been given a contract until 1998.

Membership

Full Members: Australia, England, India, New Zealand, Pakistan, South Africa, Sri Lanka, West Indies and Zimbabwe.

Associate Members*: Argentina (1974), Bangladesh (1977), Bermuda (1966), Canada (1968), Denmark (1966), East and Central Africa (1966), Fiji (1965), Gibraltar (1969), Hong Kong (1969), Ireland (1993), Israel (1974), Kenya (1981), Malaysia (1967), Namibia (1992), Netherlands (1966), Papua New Guinea (1973), Singapore (1974), United Arab Emirates (1990), USA (1965) and West Africa (1976).

Affiliate Members*: Austria (1992), Bahamas (1987), Belgium (1991), Brunei (1992), France (1987), Germany (1991), Italy (1984), Japan (1989), Nepal (1988), Spain (1992) and Switzerland (1985).

* *Year of election shown in parentheses.*

The following governing bodies for cricket shall be eligible for election.

Full Members: The governing body for cricket recognised by ICC of a country, or countries associated for cricket purposes, or a geographical area, from which representative teams are qualified to play official Test matches.

Associate Members: The governing body for cricket recognised by ICC of a country, or countries associated for cricket purposes, or a geographical area, which does not qualify as a Full Member but where cricket is firmly established and organised.

Affiliate Members: The governing body for cricket recognised by ICC of a country, or countries associated for cricket purposes, or a geographical area (which is not part of one of those already constituted as a Full or Associate Member) where ICC recognises that cricket is played in accordance with the Laws of Cricket. Affiliate Members have no right to vote or to propose or second resolutions at ICC meetings.

THE CRICKET COUNCIL

The Cricket Council, which was set up in 1968 and reconstituted in 1974 and 1983, acts as the governing body for cricket in Great Britain. It comprises the following.

Chairman: W. R. F. Chamberlain.
Vice-Chairman: J. D. Robson.
8 Representatives of the Test and County Cricket Board: J. R. T. Barclay, Sir Lawrence Byford, W. R. F. Chamberlain, D. J. Insole, M. P. Murray, H. J. Pocock, D. Rich, F. M. Turner.
5 Representatives of the National Cricket Association: F. H. Elliott, E. K. Ingman, J. G. Overy, J. D. Robson, M. J. K. Smith.
3 Representatives of the Marylebone Cricket Club: Field Marshal The Rt Hon. The Lord Bramall, M. E. L. Melluish, D. R. W. Silk.
1 Representative (non-voting) of the Minor Counties Cricket Association: J. E. O. Smith.

Secretary: A. C. Smith.

Ireland and Scotland resigned from the Cricket Council in 1992 to join ICC; Scotland, however, has not yet been elected.

THE TEST AND COUNTY CRICKET BOARD

The TCCB was set up in 1968 to be responsible for Test matches, official tours, and first-class and minor county competitions. It is composed of representatives of the 18 first-class counties, Marylebone Cricket Club and Minor Counties Cricket Association (voting members); as well as Oxford University Cricket Club, Cambridge University Cricket Club, the Irish Cricket Union and the Scottish Cricket Union (non-voting members).

Officers

Chairman: W. R. F. Chamberlain.

Chairmen of Committees: W. R. F. Chamberlain (Executive); D. B. Carr (Pitches); O. S. Wheatley (Cricket); D. J. Insole (International); P. R. Bromage (Discipline); M. P. Murray (Finance); B. G. K. Downing (Marketing); D. R. W. Silk (Registration); A. C. Smith (Appointment of Umpires); Rev. M. D. Vockins (Second XI Competitions). Chairmen of new England selection and development committees to be elected.

Chief Executive: A. C. Smith. *Cricket Secretary:* T. M. Lamb. *Administration Secretary:* A. S. Brown. *Accountant:* C. A. Barker. *Marketing Manager:* T. D. M. Blake. *England Team Manager:* K. W. R. Fletcher.

THE NATIONAL CRICKET ASSOCIATION

With the setting up of the Cricket Council in 1968 it was necessary to form a separate organisation to represent the interests of all cricket below the first-class game, and it is the National Cricket Association that carries out this function. It comprises representatives from 51 county cricket associations and 18 national cricketing organisations. The following were in office in 1993-94:

Officers

President: M. J. K. Smith.
Chairman: J. D. Robson.
Vice-Chairman: F. H. Elliott.
Chief Executive: K. V. Andrew.
Director of Coaching: M. J. Stewart.

Cricket Development and Administration Manager: T. N. Bates.
Marketing Executive: D. A. Clarke.
Hon. Treasurer: D. W. Carter.

THE MARYLEBONE CRICKET CLUB

Patron: HER MAJESTY THE QUEEN

Officers

President: 1993-94 – D. R. W. Silk.

Treasurer: 1993-94 – M. E. L. Melluish.

Chairman of Finance: D. L. Hudd.

Trustees: J. J. Warr, D. J. Insole, Sir Oliver Popplewell.

Hon. Life Vice-Presidents: Sir Donald Bradman, D. G. Clark, G. H. G. Doggart, D. J. Insole, F. G. Mann, P. B. H. May, C. H. Palmer, C. G. A. Paris, E. W. Swanton, R. E. S. Wyatt.

Secretary: R. D. V. Knight.

Assistant Secretaries: M. R. Blow (Finance), J. A. Jameson (Cricket), J. R. Smith (Administration).

Personal Assistant to Secretary: Miss S. A. Lawrence.

Curator: S. E. A. Green.

Ground Administrator: A. W. P. Fleming.

MCC Committee, 1993-94: D. R. W. Silk (President), Field Marshal The Rt Hon. The Lord Bramall, C. A. Fry, R. G. Gibbs, The Rt Hon. The Lord Griffiths, D. L. Hudd, A. R. Lewis, N. E. J. Pocock, T. M. B. Rice, T. M. B. Sissons, B. M. Thornton, G. J. Toogood, J. A. F. Vallance, J. C. Woodcock.

Chairmen of main sub-committees: Sir Colin Cowdrey (Cricket); D. R. Male (Estates); R. V. C. Robins (General Purposes).

Chairmen of specialist sub-committees: J. R. T. Barclay (Indoor School Management); R. P. Hodson (Players and Fixtures); A. J. B. Mason (Tennis and Squash); H. M. Wyndham (Arts and Libraries).

ADDRESSES

INTERNATIONAL CRICKET COUNCIL

D. L. Richards, The Clock Tower, Lord's Cricket Ground, London NW8 8QN (Telephone 071-266 1818; fax 071-266 1777).

Full Members

AUSTRALIA: Australian Cricket Board, G. W. Halbish, 90 Jolimont Street, Jolimont, Victoria 3002.

ENGLAND: Cricket Council, A. C. Smith, Lord's Ground, London NW8 8QZ.

INDIA: Board of Control for Cricket in India, C. Nagaraj, Chinnaswamy Stadium, Mahatma Gandhi Road, Bangalore 560 001.

NEW ZEALAND: New Zealand Cricket Inc., G. T. Dowling, OBE, PO Box 958, 109 Cambridge Terrace, Christchurch.

PAKISTAN: Board of Control for Cricket in Pakistan, Shahid Rafi, Gaddafi Stadium, Lahore 54600.

SOUTH AFRICA: United Cricket Board of South Africa, Dr A. Bacher, PO Box 55009, Northlands 2116, Transvaal.

SRI LANKA: Board of Control for Cricket in Sri Lanka, N. Perera, 35 Maitland Place, Colombo 7.

WEST INDIES: West Indies Cricket Board of Control, G. S. Camacho, Kensington Oval, Fontabelle, St Michael, Barbados.

ZIMBABWE: Zimbabwe Cricket Union, P. Chingoka, PO Box 2739, Harare.

Associate and Affiliate Members

ARGENTINA: Argentine Cricket Association, C. M. Gibson, c/o The English Club, 25 de Mayo 586, 1002 Buenos Aires.

AUSTRIA: Austrian Cricket Association, W. Tesar, Brunner Strasse 34-38/17/16, A-1210 Vienna.

BAHAMAS: Bahamas Cricket Association, Mrs J. M. Forbes, PO Box N-10101, Nassau.

BANGLADESH: Bangladesh Cricket Control Board, M. Aminul Huq Moni, National Stadium, Dhaka 1000.

BELGIUM: Belgian Cricket Federation, C. Wolfe, Rue de l'Eglise St Martin 12, B-1390 BIEZ.

BERMUDA: Bermuda Cricket Board of Control, W. Smith, PO Box HM992, Hamilton HM DX.

BRUNEI: Brunei National Cricket Association, D. L. Gardiner (FAC/51), c/o Brunei Shell Petroleum Sdn Bhd, Seria 7082, Brunei via Singapore.

CANADA: Canadian Cricket Association, J. Kyle, 6700 No. 7 Road, Richmond, B C, V6W 1E9.

DENMARK: Danish Cricket Association, J. Holmen, Idraettens Hus, Brøndby, DK 2605.

EAST AND CENTRAL AFRICA: East and Central African Cricket Conference, R. A. Patel, PO Box 34321, Lusaka 1010, Zambia.

FIJI: Fiji Cricket Association, P. I. Knight, PO Box 300, Suva.

FRANCE: Fédération Française du Cricket, S. Hewitt, 32 Rue Molitor, 75016 Paris.

GERMANY: Deutscher Cricket Bund, R. Schwiete, Adalbert-Stifter-Strasse 6d, 6450 Hanau.

GIBRALTAR: Gibraltar Cricket Association, T. J. Finlayson, 21 Sandpits House, Withams Road.

HONG KONG: Hong Kong Cricket Association, J. A. Cribbin, University of Hong Kong, School of Professional and Continuing Education, Pokfulam Road.

IRELAND: Irish Cricket Union, D. Scott, 45 Foxrock Park, Foxrock, Dublin 18.

ISRAEL: Israel Cricket Association, N. Davidson, 31/24 Mintz Street, Petah Tiqwa 49481.

ITALY: Associazione Italiana Cricket, S. Gambino, Via S. Ignazio 9, 00186 Roma.

JAPAN: Japan Cricket Association, R. G. Martineau, Shizuoka City, Chiyoda 736, Yamadai Corp. 305, Japan 420.

KENYA: Kenya Cricket Association, B. Mauladad, PO Box 45870, Nairobi.

MALAYSIA: Malaysian Cricket Association, C. Chelliah, 1st Floor, Wisma OCM, Jalan Hang Jebat, 50150 Kuala Lumpur.

NAMIBIA: Namibia Cricket Board, L. Pieters, PO Box 457, Windhoek 9000.

NEPAL: Cricket Association of Nepal, Jaikumar N. Shah, PO Box 925, Kathmandu.

NETHERLANDS: Royal Netherlands Cricket Board, A. de la Mar, Neuiwe Kalfjeslaan 21-B, 1182 AA Amstelveen.

PAPUA NEW GUINEA: Papua New Guinea Cricket Board of Control, W. Satchell, PO Box 83, Konedobu.

SINGAPORE: Singapore Cricket Association, H. Singh, No. 7 Jalan Mahir, Singapore 1953.

SPAIN: Asociacion Española de Cricket, C. E. Woodbridge, Villa Valor A14 Hacienda Guadalupe, 29692 Sabinillas, Manilva (Malaga).

SWITZERLAND: Swiss Cricket Association, P. Nixon, Spitzackerstrasse 32, 4103 Bottmingen.

UNITED ARAB EMIRATES: Emirates Cricket Board, Abdul Rahman Bukhatir, Sharjah Cricket Stadium, PO Box 88, Sharjah.

USA: United States of America Cricket Association, Naseeruddin Khan, 2361 Hickory Road, Plymouth Meeting, Pennsylvania 19462.

WEST AFRICA: West Africa Cricket Conference, Mrs Tayo Oreweme, Tafawa Balewa Square, Surulere, Lagos, Nigeria.

UK ADDRESSES

TEST AND COUNTY CRICKET BOARD: A. C. Smith, Lord's Ground, London NW8 8QZ (Telephone 071-286 4405; fax 071-289 5619).

MARYLEBONE CRICKET CLUB: R. D. V. Knight, Lord's Ground, London NW8 8QN (Telephone 071-289 1611; fax 071-289 9100. Club office 071-289 8979; fax 071-266 3459).

First-class Counties

DERBYSHIRE: County Ground, Nottingham Road, Derby DE21 6DA (Telephone 0332-383211; fax 0332-290251).

DURHAM: County Ground, Riverside, Chester-le-Street, County Durham DH3 3QR (Telephone 091-387 1717; fax 091-387 1616).

ESSEX: County Ground, New Writtle Street, Chelmsford CM2 0PG (Telephone 0245-252420; fax 0245-491607).

GLAMORGAN: Sophia Gardens, Cardiff CF1 9XR (Telephone 0222-343478; fax 0222-377044).

GLOUCESTERSHIRE: Phoenix County Ground, Nevil Road, Bristol BS7 9EJ (Telephone 0272-245216; fax 0272-241193).

HAMPSHIRE: Northlands Road, Southampton SO9 2TY (Telephone 0703-333788; fax 0703-330121).

KENT: St Lawrence Ground, Old Dover Road, Canterbury CT1 3NZ (Telephone 0227-456886; fax 0227-762168).

LANCASHIRE: County Cricket Ground, Old Trafford, Manchester M16 0PX (Telephone 061-848 7021; fax 061-848 9021).

LEICESTERSHIRE: County Cricket Ground, Grace Road, Leicester LE2 8AD (Telephone 0533-831880/832128; fax 0533-440363).

MIDDLESEX: Lord's Cricket Ground, St John's Wood, London NW8 8QN (Telephone 071-289 1300; fax 071-289 5831).

NORTHAMPTONSHIRE: County Ground, Wantage Road, Northampton NN1 4TJ (Telephone 0604-32917; fax 0604-232855).

NOTTINGHAMSHIRE: County Cricket Ground, Trent Bridge, Nottingham NG2 6AG (Telephone 0602-821525; fax 0602-455730).

SOMERSET: The County Ground, St James's Street, Taunton TA1 1JT (Telephone 0823-272946; fax 0823-332395).

SURREY: The Oval, London SE11 5SS (Telephone 071-582 6660; fax 071-735 7769).

SUSSEX: County Ground, Eaton Road, Hove BN3 3AN (Telephone 0273-732161; fax 0273-771549).

WARWICKSHIRE: County Ground, Edgbaston, Birmingham B5 7QU (Telephone 021-446 4422; fax 021-446 4544).

WORCESTERSHIRE: County Ground, New Road, Worcester WR2 4QQ (Telephone 0905-748474; fax 0905-748005).

YORKSHIRE: Headingley Cricket Ground, Leeds LS6 3BU (Telephone 0532-787394; fax 0532-784099).

Minor Counties

MINOR COUNTIES CRICKET ASSOCIATION: D. J. M. Armstrong, Thorpe Cottage, Mill Common, Ridlington, North Walsham NR28 9TY.

BEDFORDSHIRE: D. J. F. Hoare, 5 Brecon Way, Bedford MK41 8DF (Telephone 0234-266648).

BERKSHIRE: C. M. S. Crombie, Orchard Cottage, Waltham St Lawrence, Reading, Berkshire RG10 0JH (Telephone 0734-343387 home, 0491-578555 business).

BUCKINGHAMSHIRE: S. J. Tomlin, Orchardleigh Cottage, Bigfrith Lane, Cookham Dean, Berkshire SL6 9PH (Telephone 0628-482202 home, 06285-24922 business).

CAMBRIDGESHIRE: P. W. Gooden, The Redlands, Oakington Road, Cottenham, Cambridge CB4 4TW (Telephone 0954-50429).

CHESHIRE: J. B. Pickup, 2 Castle Street, Northwich, Cheshire CW8 1AB (Telephone 0606-74970 home, 0606-74301 business; fax 0606-871034).

CORNWALL: The Rev. Canon Kenneth Rogers, The Rectory, Priory Road, Bodmin, Cornwall PL31 2AB (Telephone 0208-73867).

CUMBERLAND: D. Lamb, 42 Croft Road, Carlisle, Cumbria CA3 9AG (Tel 0228-23017).

DEVON: G. R. Evans, Blueberry Haven, 20 Boucher Road, Budleigh Salterton, Devon EX9 6JF (Telephone 0395-445216 home, 0392-58406 business; fax 0392-411697).

DORSET: K. H. House, The Barn, Higher Farm, Bagber Common, Sturminster Newton, Dorset DT10 2HB (Telephone 0258-473394).

HEREFORDSHIRE: P. Sykes, 5 Dale Drive, Holmer Grange, Hereford HR4 9RF (Telephone 0432-264703 home, 0432-382684 business).

HERTFORDSHIRE: D. S. Dredge, "Trevellis", 38 Santers Lane, Potters Bar, Hertfordshire EN6 2BX (Telephone 0707-58377 home, 071-359 3579 business).

LINCOLNSHIRE: C. J. White, "Lyndonholme", Castle Terrace Road, Sleaford, Lincolnshire NG34 7QF (Telephone 0529-302341 home, 0529-302181 business).

NORFOLK: S. J. Skinner, 27 Colkett Drive, Old Catton, Norwich NR6 7ND (Telephone 0603-485940 home, 0603-660255 ext 5542 business).

NORTHUMBERLAND: A. B. Stephenson, Northumberland County Cricket Club, Osborne Avenue, Jesmond, Newcastle-upon-Tyne NE2 1JS (Telephone 091-281 2738).

OXFORDSHIRE: A. W. Moss, 14 Croft Avenue, Kidlington, Oxford OX5 2HU (Telephone 08675-2399 home, 0865-226733/742277 business; fax 0865-226886).

SHROPSHIRE: N. H. Birch, 8 Port Hill Close, Shrewsbury, Shropshire SY3 8RR (Telephone 0743-233650).

STAFFORDSHIRE: W. S. Bourne, 10 The Pavement, Brewood, Staffordshire ST19 9BZ (Telephone 0902-850325 home, 0902-23038 business).

SUFFOLK: Toby Pound, 94 Henley Road, Ipswich IP1 4NJ (Telephone 0473-213288 home, 0473-232121 business).

WALES MINOR COUNTIES: Bill Edwards, 59a King Edward Road, Swansea SA1 4LN (Telephone 0792-462233).

WILTSHIRE: C. R. Sheppard, 45 Ipswich Street, Swindon SN2 1DB (Telephone 0793-511811 home, 0793-530784 business, 0831-565866 mobile).

Other Bodies

ASSOCIATION OF CRICKET UMPIRES: L. J. Cheeseman, 16 Ruden Way, Epsom Downs, Surrey KT17 3LN.

CLUB CRICKET CONFERENCE: A. E. F. Stevens, 361 West Barnes Lane, New Malden, Surrey KT3 6JF.

COMBINED SERVICES: Lt-Col. K. Hitchcock, c/o Army Sport Control Board, Clayton Barracks, Aldershot, Hampshire GU11 2BG.

ENGLISH SCHOOLS' CRICKET ASSOCIATION: K. S. Lake, 38 Mill House, Woods Lane, Cottingham, Hull HU16 4HQ.

LEAGUE CRICKET CONFERENCE: N. Edwards, 1 Longfield, Freshfield, Formby, Merseyside.

NATIONAL CRICKET ASSOCIATION: K. V. Andrew, Lord's Ground, London NW8 8QZ.

SCARBOROUGH CRICKET FESTIVAL: Colin T. Adamson, Cricket Ground, North Marine Road, Scarborough, North Yorkshire YO12 7TJ.

SCOTTISH CRICKET UNION: R. W. Barclay, Caledonia House, South Gyle, Edinburgh EH12 9DQ.

UNIVERSITIES ATHLETIC UNION: Suite 36, London Fruit Exchange, Brushfield Street, London E1 6EU.

WOMEN'S CRICKET ASSOCIATION: 41 St Michael's Lane, Headingley, Leeds LS6 3BR.

THE LAWS OF CRICKET

(1980 CODE)

As updated in 1992. World copyright of MCC and reprinted by permission of MCC. Copies of the "Laws of Cricket" may be obtained from Lord's Cricket Ground.

INDEX TO THE LAWS

LAW 1. THE PLAYERS

1. Number of Players and Captain

A match is played between two sides each of 11 players, one of whom shall be captain. In the event of the captain not being available at any time, a deputy shall act for him.

2. Nomination of Players

Before the toss for innings, the captain shall nominate his players, who may not thereafter be changed without the consent of the opposing captain.

Note

(a) **More or Less than 11 Players a Side**
A match may be played by agreement between sides of more or less than 11 players, but not more than 11 players may field.

LAW 2. SUBSTITUTES AND RUNNERS: BATSMAN OR FIELDSMAN LEAVING THE FIELD: BATSMAN RETIRING: BATSMAN COMMENCING INNINGS

1. Substitutes

In normal circumstances, a substitute shall be allowed to field only for a player who satisfies the umpires that he has become injured or become ill during the match. However, in very exceptional circumstances, the umpires may use their discretion to allow a substitute for a player who has to leave the field for other wholly acceptable reasons, subject to consent being given by the opposing captain. If a player wishes to change his shirt, boots, etc., he may leave the field to do so (no changing on the field), but no substitute will be allowed.

2. Objection to Substitutes

The opposing captain shall have no right of objection to any player acting as substitute in the field, nor as to where he shall field; however, no substitute shall act as wicket-keeper.

3. Substitute not to Bat or Bowl

A substitute shall not be allowed to bat or bowl.

4. A Player for whom a Substitute has Acted

A player may bat, bowl or field even though a substitute has acted for him.

5. Runner

A runner shall be allowed for a batsman who, during the match, is incapacitated by illness or injury. The person acting as runner shall be a member of the batting side and shall, if possible, have already batted in that innings.

6. Runner's Equipment

The player acting as runner for an injured batsman shall wear the same external protective equipment as the injured batsman.

7. Transgression of the Laws by an Injured Batsman or Runner

An injured batsman may be out should his runner break any one of Laws 33 (Handled the Ball), 37 (Obstructing the Field) or 38 (Run Out). As striker he remains himself subject to the Laws. Furthermore, should he be out of his ground for any purpose and the wicket at the wicket-keeper's end be put down he shall be out under Law 38 (Run Out) or Law 39 (Stumped), irrespective of the position of the other batsman or the runner, and no runs shall be scored.

When not the striker, the injured batsman is out of the game and shall stand where he does not interfere with the play. Should he bring himself into the game in any way, then he shall suffer the penalties that any transgression of the Laws demands.

8. Fieldsman Leaving the Field

No fieldsman shall leave the field or return during a session of play without the consent of the umpire at the bowler's end. The umpire's consent is also necessary if a substitute is required for a fieldsman, when his side returns to the field after an interval. If a member of the fielding side leaves the field or fails to return after an interval and is absent from the field for longer than 15 minutes, he shall not be permitted to bowl after his return until he has been on the field for at least that length of playing time for which he was absent. This restriction shall not apply at the start of a new day's play.

9. Batsman Leaving the Field or Retiring

A batsman may leave the field or retire at any time owing to illness, injury or other unavoidable cause, having previously notified the umpire at the bowler's end. He may resume his innings at the fall of a wicket, which for the purposes of this Law shall include the retirement of another batsman.

If he leaves the field or retires for any other reason he may resume his innings only with the consent of the opposing captain.

When a batsman has left the field or retired and is unable to return owing to illness, injury or other unavoidable cause, his innings is to be recorded as "retired, not out". Otherwise it is to be recorded as "retired, out".

10. Commencement of a Batsman's Innings

A batsman shall be considered to have commenced his innings once he has stepped on to the field of play.

Note

(a) Substitutes and Runners
For the purpose of these Laws, allowable illnesses or injuries are those which occur at any time after the nomination by the captains of their teams.

LAW 3.   THE UMPIRES

1. Appointment

Before the toss for innings, two umpires shall be appointed, one for each end, to control the game with absolute impartiality as required by the Laws.

2. Change of Umpires

No umpire shall be changed during a match without the consent of both captains.

3. Special Conditions

Before the toss for innings, the umpires shall agree with both captains on any special conditions affecting the conduct of the match.

4. The Wickets

The umpires shall satisfy themselves before the start of the match that the wickets are properly pitched.

5. Clock or Watch

The umpires shall agree between themselves and inform both captains before the start of the match on the watch or clock to be followed during the match.

6. Conduct and Implements

Before and during a match the umpires shall ensure that the conduct of the game and the implements used are strictly in accordance with the Laws.

7. Fair and Unfair Play

The umpires shall be the sole judges of fair and unfair play.

8. Fitness of Ground, Weather and Light

(a) The umpires shall be the sole judges of the fitness of the ground, weather and light for play.

   (i) However, before deciding to suspend play, or not to start play, or not to resume play after an interval or stoppage, the umpires shall establish whether both captains (the batsmen at the wicket may deputise for their captain) wish to commence or to continue in the prevailing conditions; if so, their wishes shall be met.

   (ii) In addition, if during play the umpires decide that the light is unfit, only the batting side shall have the option of continuing play. After agreeing to continue to play in unfit light conditions, the captain of the batting side (or a batsman at the wicket) may appeal against the light to the umpires, who shall uphold the appeal only if, in their opinion, the light has deteriorated since the agreement to continue was made.

(b) After any suspension of play, the umpires, unaccompanied by any of the players or officials, shall, on their own initiative, carry out an inspection immediately the conditions improve and shall continue to inspect at intervals. Immediately the umpires decide that play is possible they shall call upon the players to resume the game.

9. Exceptional Circumstances

In exceptional circumstances, other than those of weather, ground or light, the umpires may decide to suspend or abandon play. Before making such a decision the umpires shall establish, if the circumstances allow, whether both captains (the batsmen at the wicket may deputise for their captain) wish to continue in the prevailing conditions; if so, their wishes shall be met.

10. Position of Umpires

The umpires shall stand where they can best see any act upon which their decision may be required.

Subject to this over-riding consideration, the umpire at the bowler's end shall stand where he does not interfere with either the bowler's run-up or the striker's view.

The umpire at the striker's end may elect to stand on the off instead of the leg side of the pitch, provided he informs the captain of the fielding side and the striker of his intention to do so.

11. Umpires Changing Ends

The umpires shall change ends after each side has had one innings.

12. Disputes

All disputes shall be determined by the umpires, and if they disagree the actual state of things shall continue.

13. Signals

The following code of signals shall be used by umpires who will wait until a signal has been answered by a scorer before allowing the game to proceed.

Boundary	– by waving the arm from side to side.
Boundary 6	– by raising both arms above the head.
Bye	– by raising an open hand above the head.
Dead Ball	– by crossing and re-crossing the wrists below the waist.
Leg-bye	– by touching a raised knee with the hand.
No-ball	– by extending one arm horizontally.
Out	– by raising the index finger above the head. If not out, the umpire shall call "not out".
Short Run	– by bending the arm upwards and by touching the nearer shoulder with the tips of the fingers.
Wide	– by extending both arms horizontally.

14. Correctness of Scores

The umpires shall be responsible for satisfying themselves on the correctness of the scores throughout and at the conclusion of the match. See Law 21.6 (Correctness of Result).

Notes

(a) Attendance of Umpires
The umpires should be present on the ground and report to the ground executive or the equivalent at least 30 minutes before the start of a day's play.

(b) Consultation between Umpires and Scorers
Consultation between umpires and scorers over doubtful points is essential.

(c) Fitness of Ground
The umpires shall consider the ground as unfit for play when it is so wet or slippery as to deprive the bowlers of a reasonable foothold, the fieldsmen, other than the deep-fielders, of the power of free movement, or the batsmen of the ability to play their strokes or to run between the wickets. Play should not be suspended merely because the grass and the ball are wet and slippery.

(d) Fitness of Weather and Light
The umpires should suspend play only when they consider that the conditions are so bad that it is unreasonable or dangerous to continue.

LAW 4. THE SCORERS

1. Recording Runs

All runs scored shall be recorded by scorers appointed for the purpose. Where there are two scorers they shall frequently check to ensure that the score-sheets agree.

2. Acknowledging Signals

The scorers shall accept and immediately acknowledge all instructions and signals given to them by the umpires.

LAW 5. THE BALL

1. Weight and Size

The ball, when new, shall weigh not less than $5\frac{1}{2}$ ounces/155.9g, nor more than $5\frac{3}{4}$ ounces/163g; and shall measure not less than $8\frac{13}{16}$ inches/22.4cm, nor more than 9 inches/22.9cm in circumference.

2. Approval of Balls

All balls used in matches shall be approved by the umpires and captains before the start of the match.

3. New Ball

Subject to agreement to the contrary, having been made before the toss, either captain may demand a new ball at the start of each innings.

4. New Ball in Match of Three or More Days' Duration

In a match of three or more days' duration, the captain of the fielding side may demand a new ball after the prescribed number of overs has been bowled with the old one. The governing body for cricket in the country concerned shall decide the number of overs applicable in that country, which shall be not less than 75 six-ball overs (55 eight-ball overs).

5. Ball Lost or Becoming Unfit for Play

In the event of a ball during play being lost or, in the opinion of the umpires, becoming unfit for play, the umpires shall allow it to be replaced by one that in their opinion has had a similar amount of wear. If a ball is to be replaced, the umpires shall inform the batsman.

Note

(a) Specifications
The specifications, as described in 1 above, shall apply to top-grade balls only. The following degrees of tolerance will be acceptable for other grades of ball.

(i) *Men's Grades 2–4*
  Weight: $5\frac{5}{16}$ ounces/150g to $5\frac{13}{16}$ ounces/165g.
  Size: $8\frac{11}{16}$ inches/22.0cm to $9\frac{1}{16}$ inches/23.0cm.

(ii) *Women's*
  Weight: $4\frac{15}{16}$ ounces/140g to $5\frac{5}{16}$ ounces/150g.
  Size: $8\frac{1}{4}$ inches/21.0cm to $8\frac{7}{8}$ inches/22.5cm.

(iii) *Junior*
  Weight: $4\frac{11}{16}$ ounces/133g to $5\frac{1}{16}$ ounces/143g.
  Size: $8\frac{1}{16}$ inches/20.5cm to $8\frac{11}{16}$ inches/22.0cm.

LAW 6. THE BAT

1. Width and Length

The bat overall shall not be more than 38 inches/96.5cm in length; the blade of the bat shall be made of wood and shall not exceed $4\frac{1}{4}$ inches/10.8cm at the widest part.

Note

(a) The blade of the bat may be covered with material for protection, strengthening or repair. Such material shall not exceed $\frac{1}{16}$ inch/1.56mm in thickness.

LAW 7. THE PITCH

1. Area of Pitch

The pitch is the area between the bowling creases – see Law 9 (The Bowling and Popping Creases). It shall measure 5 feet/1.52m in width on either side of a line joining the centre of the middle stumps of the wickets – see Law 8 (The Wickets).

2. Selection and Preparation

Before the toss for innings, the executive of the ground shall be responsible for the selection and preparation of the pitch; thereafter the umpires shall control its use and maintenance.

3. Changing Pitch

The pitch shall not be changed during a match unless it becomes unfit for play, and then only with the consent of both captains.

4. Non-Turf Pitches

In the event of a non-turf pitch being used, the following shall apply:

(a) Length: That of the playing surface to a minimum of 58 feet/17.68m.

(b) Width: That of the playing surface to a minimum of 6 feet/1.83m.

See Law 10 (Rolling, Sweeping, Mowing, Watering the Pitch and Re-marking of Creases) Note (a).

LAW 8. THE WICKETS

1. Width and Pitching

Two sets of wickets, each 9 inches/22.86cm wide, and consisting of three wooden stumps with two wooden bails upon the top, shall be pitched opposite and parallel to each other at a distance of 22 yards/20.12m between the centres of the two middle stumps.

2. Size of Stumps

The stumps shall be of equal and sufficient size to prevent the ball from passing between them. Their tops shall be 28 inches/71.1cm above the ground, and shall be dome-shaped except for the bail grooves.

3. Size of Bails

The bails shall be each $4\frac{3}{8}$ inches/11.1cm in length and when in position on the top of the stumps shall not project more than $\frac{1}{2}$ inch/1.3cm above them.

Notes

(a) Dispensing with Bails

In a high wind the umpires may decide to dispense with the use of bails.

(b) Junior Cricket

For junior cricket, as defined by the local governing body, the following measurements for the wickets shall apply:

Width – 8 inches/20.32cm.

Pitched – 21 yards/19.20m.

Height – 27 inches/68.58cm.

Bails – each $3\frac{7}{8}$ inches/9.84cm in length and should not project more than $\frac{1}{2}$ inch/1.3cm above the stumps.

LAW 9. THE BOWLING, POPPING AND RETURN CREASES

1. The Bowling Crease

The bowling crease shall be marked in line with the stumps at each end and shall be 8 feet 8 inches/2.64m in length, with the stumps in the centre.

2. The Popping Crease

The popping crease, which is the back edge of the crease marking, shall be in front of and parallel with the bowling crease. It shall have the back edge of the crease marking 4 feet/1.22m from the centre of the stumps and shall extend to a minimum of 6 feet/1.83m on either side of the line of the wicket.

The popping crease shall be considered to be unlimited in length.

3. The Return Crease

The return crease marking, of which the inside edge is the crease, shall be at each end of the bowling crease and at right angles to it. The return crease shall be marked to a minimum of 4 feet/1.22m behind the wicket and shall be considered to be unlimited in length. A forward extension shall be marked to the popping crease.

LAW 10. ROLLING, SWEEPING, MOWING, WATERING THE PITCH AND RE-MARKING OF CREASES

1. Rolling

During the match the pitch may be rolled at the request of the captain of the batting side, for a period of not more than seven minutes before the start of each innings, other than the first innings of the match, and before the start of each day's play. In addition, if, after the toss and before the first innings of the match, the start is delayed, the captain of the batting side may request to have the pitch rolled for not more than seven minutes. However, if in the opinion of the umpires the delay has had no significant effect upon the state of the pitch, they shall refuse any request for the rolling of the pitch.

The pitch shall not otherwise be rolled during the match.

The seven minutes' rolling permitted before the start of a day's play shall take place not earlier than half an hour before the start of play and the captain of the batting side may delay such rolling until ten minutes before the start of play should he so desire.

If a captain declares an innings closed less than 15 minutes before the resumption of play, and the other captain is thereby prevented from exercising his option of seven minutes' rolling or if he is so prevented for any other reason, the time for rolling shall be taken out of the normal playing time.

2. Sweeping

Such sweeping of the pitch as is necessary during the match shall be done so that the seven minutes allowed for rolling the pitch, provided for in 1 above, is not affected.

3. Mowing

(a) Responsibilities of Ground Authority and of Umpires

All mowings which are carried out before the toss for innings shall be the responsibility of the ground authority; thereafter they shall be carried out under the supervision of the umpires. See Law 7.2 (Selection and Preparation).

(b) Initial Mowing

The pitch shall be mown before play begins on the day the match is scheduled to start, or in the case of a delayed start on the day the match is expected to start. See 3(a) above (Responsibilities of Ground Authority and of Umpires).

(c) Subsequent Mowings in a Match of Two or More Days' Duration

In a match of two or more days' duration, the pitch shall be mown daily before play begins. Should this mowing not take place because of weather conditions, rest days or other reasons, the pitch shall be mown on the first day on which the match is resumed.

(d) Mowing of the Outfield in a Match of Two or More Days' Duration

In order to ensure that conditions are as similar as possible for both sides, the outfield shall normally be mown before the commencement of play on each day of the match, if ground and weather conditions allow. See Note (b) to this Law.

4. Watering

The pitch shall not be watered during a match.

5. Re-marking Creases

Whenever possible the creases shall be re-marked.

6. Maintenance of Foot-holes

In wet weather, the umpires shall ensure that the holes made by the bowlers and batsmen are cleaned out and dried whenever necessary to facilitate play. In matches of two or more days' duration, the umpires shall allow, if necessary, the re-turfing of foot-holes made by the bowler in his delivery stride, or the use of quick-setting fillings for the same purpose, before the start of each day's play.

7. Securing of Footholds and Maintenance of Pitch

During play, the umpires shall allow either batsman to beat the pitch with his bat and players to secure their footholds by the use of sawdust, provided that no damage to the pitch is so caused, and Law 42 (Unfair Play) is not contravened.

Notes

(a) Non-turf Pitches
The above Law 10 applies to turf pitches.

The game is played on non-turf pitches in many countries at various levels. Whilst the conduct of the game on these surfaces should always be in accordance with the Laws of Cricket, it is recognised that it may sometimes be necessary for governing bodies to lay down special playing conditions to suit the type of non-turf pitch used in their country.

In matches played against touring teams, any special playing conditions should be agreed in advance by both parties.

(b) Mowing of the Outfield in a Match of Two or More Days' Duration
If, for reasons other than ground and weather conditions, daily and complete mowing is not possible, the ground authority shall notify the captains and umpires, before the toss for innings, of the procedure to be adopted for such mowing during the match.

(c) Choice of Roller
If there is more than one roller available, the captain of the batting side shall have a choice.

LAW 11.   COVERING THE PITCH

1. Before the Start of a Match

Before the start of a match, complete covering of the pitch shall be allowed.

2. During a Match

The pitch shall not be completely covered during a match unless prior arrangement or regulations so provide.

3. Covering Bowlers' Run-up

Whenever possible, the bowlers' run-up shall be covered, but the covers so used shall not extend further than 4 feet/1.22m in front of the popping crease.

Note

(a) Removal of Covers
The covers should be removed as promptly as possible whenever the weather permits.

LAW 12.   INNINGS

1. Number of Innings

A match shall be of one or two innings of each side according to agreement reached before the start of play.

2. Alternate Innings

In a two-innings match each side shall take their innings alternately except in the case provided for in Law 13 (The Follow-on).

3. The Toss

The captains shall toss for the choice of innings on the field of play not later than 15 minutes before the time scheduled for the match to start, or before the time agreed upon for play to start.

4. Choice of Innings

The winner of the toss shall notify his decision to bat or to field to the opposing captain not later than ten minutes before the time scheduled for the match to start, or before the time agreed upon for play to start. The decision shall not thereafter be altered.

5. Continuation after One Innings of Each Side

Despite the terms of 1 above, in a one-innings match, when a result has been reached on the first innings, the captains may agree to the continuation of play if, in their opinion, there is a prospect of carrying the game to a further issue in the time left. See Law 21 (Result).

Notes

(a) Limited Innings – One-innings Match
In a one-innings match, each innings may, by agreement, be limited by a number of overs or by a period of time.

(b) Limited Innings – Two-innings Match
In a two-innings match, the first innings of each side may, by agreement, be limited to a number of overs or by a period of time.

LAW 13. THE FOLLOW-ON

1. Lead on First Innings

In a two-innings match the side which bats first and leads by 200 runs in a match of five days or more, by 150 runs in a three-day or four-day match, by 100 runs in a two-day match, or by 75 runs in a one-day match, shall have the option of requiring the other side to follow their innings.

2. Day's Play Lost

If no play takes place on the first day of a match of two or more days' duration, 1 above shall apply in accordance with the number of days' play remaining from the actual start of the match.

LAW 14. DECLARATIONS

1. Time of Declaration

The captain of the batting side may declare an innings closed at any time during a match, irrespective of its duration.

2. Forfeiture of Second Innings

A captain may forfeit his second innings, provided his decision to do so is notified to the opposing captain and umpires in sufficient time to allow seven minutes' rolling of the pitch. See Law 10 (Rolling, Sweeping, Mowing, Watering the Pitch and Re-marking of Creases). The normal ten-minute interval between innings shall be applied.

LAW 15. START OF PLAY

1. Call of Play

At the start of each innings and of each day's play, and on the resumption of play after any interval or interruption, the umpire at the bowler's end shall call "play".

2. Practice on the Field

At no time on any day of the match shall there be any bowling or batting practice on the pitch.

No practice may take place on the field if, in the opinion of the umpires, it could result in a waste of time.

3. Trial Run-up

No bowler shall have a trial run-up after "play" has been called in any session of play, except at the fall of a wicket when an umpire may allow such a trial run-up if he is satisfied that it will not cause any waste of time.

LAW 16.   INTERVALS

1. Length

The umpire shall allow such intervals as have been agreed upon for meals, and ten minutes between each innings.

2. Luncheon Interval – Innings Ending or Stoppage within Ten Minutes of Interval

If an innings ends or there is a stoppage caused by weather or bad light within ten minutes of the agreed time for the luncheon interval, the interval shall be taken immediately.

The time remaining in the session of play shall be added to the agreed length of the interval but no extra allowance shall be made for the ten-minute interval between innings.

3. Tea Interval – Innings Ending or Stoppage within 30 Minutes of Interval

If an innings ends or there is a stoppage caused by weather or bad light within 30 minutes of the agreed time for the tea interval, the interval shall be taken immediately.

The interval shall be of the agreed length and, if applicable, shall include the ten-minute interval between innings.

4. Tea Interval – Continuation of Play

If, at the agreed time for the tea interval, nine wickets are down, play shall continue for a period not exceeding 30 minutes or until the innings is concluded.

5. Tea Interval – Agreement to Forgo

At any time during the match, the captains may agree to forgo a tea interval.

6. Intervals for Drinks

If both captains agree before the start of a match that intervals for drinks may be taken, the option to take such intervals shall be available to either side. These intervals shall be restricted to one per session, shall be kept as short as possible, shall not be taken in the last hour of the match, and in any case shall not exceed five minutes.

The agreed times for these intervals shall be strictly adhered to, except that if a wicket falls within five minutes of the agreed time then drinks shall be taken out immediately.

If an innings ends or there is a stoppage caused by weather or bad light within 30 minutes of the agreed time for a drinks interval, there will be no interval for drinks in that session.

At any time during the match the captains may agree to forgo any such drinks interval.

Notes

(a) **Tea Interval – One-day Match**
In a one-day match, a specific time for the tea interval need not necessarily be arranged, and it may be agreed to take this interval between the innings of a one-innings match.

(b) **Changing the Agreed Time of Intervals**
In the event of the ground, weather or light conditions causing a suspension of play, the umpires, after consultation with the captains, may decide in the interests of time-saving to bring forward the time of the luncheon or tea interval.

LAW 17. CESSATION OF PLAY

1. Call of Time

The umpire at the bowler's end shall call "time" on the cessation of play before any interval or interruption of play, at the end of each day's play, and at the conclusion of the match. See Law 27 (Appeals).

2. Removal of Bails

After the call of "time", the umpires shall remove the bails from both wickets.

3. Starting a Last Over

The last over before an interval or the close of play shall be started provided the umpire, after walking at his normal pace, has arrived at his position behind the stumps at the bowler's end before time has been reached.

4. Completion of the Last Over of a Session

The last over before an interval or the close of play shall be completed unless a batsman is out or retires during that over within two minutes of the interval or the close of play or unless the players have occasion to leave the field.

5. Completion of the Last Over of a Match

An over in progress at the close of play on the final day of a match shall be completed at the request of either captain, even if a wicket falls after time has been reached.

If, during the last over, the players have occasion to leave the field, the umpires shall call "time" and there shall be no resumption of play and the match shall be at an end.

6. Last Hour of Match – Number of Overs

The umpires shall indicate when one hour of playing time of the match remains according to the agreed hours of play. The next over after that moment shall be the first of a minimum of 20 six-ball overs (15 eight-ball overs), provided a result is not reached earlier or there is no interval or interruption of play.

7. Last Hour of Match – Intervals between Innings and Interruptions of Play

If, at the commencement of the last hour of the match, an interval or interruption of play is in progress or if, during the last hour, there is an interval between innings or an interruption of play, the minimum number of overs to be bowled on the resumption of play shall be reduced in proportion to the duration, within the last hour of the match, of any such interval or interruption.

The minimum number of overs to be bowled after the resumption of play shall be calculated as follows:

(a) In the case of an interval or interruption of play being in progress at the commencement of the last hour of the match, or in the case of a first interval or interruption, a deduction shall be made from the minimum of 20 six-ball overs (or 15 eight-ball overs).

(b) If there is a later interval or interruption, a further deduction shall be made from the minimum number of overs which should have been bowled following the last resumption of play.

(c) These deductions shall be based on the following factors:

(i) The number of overs already bowled in the last hour of the match or, in the case of a later interval or interruption, in the last session of play.

(ii) The number of overs lost as a result of the interval or interruption allowing one six-ball over for every full three minutes (or one eight-ball over for every full four minutes) of interval or interruption.

(iii) Any over left uncompleted at the end of an innings to be excluded from these calculations.

(iv) Any over of the minimum number to be played which is left uncompleted at the start of an interruption of play to be completed when play is resumed and to count as one over bowled.

(v) An interval to start with the end of an innings and to end ten minutes later; an interruption to start on the call of "time" and to end on the call of "play".

(d) In the event of an innings being completed and a new innings commencing during the last hour of the match, the number of overs to be bowled in the new innings shall be calculated on the basis of one six-ball over for every three minutes or part thereof remaining for play (or one eight-ball over for every four minutes or part thereof remaining for play); or alternatively on the basis that sufficient overs be bowled to enable the full minimum quota of overs to be completed under circumstances governed by (a), (b) and (c) above. In all such cases the alternative which allows the greater number of overs shall be employed.

8. Bowler Unable to Complete an Over during Last Hour of the Match

If, for any reason, a bowler is unable to complete an over during the period of play referred to in 6 above, Law 22.7 (Bowler Incapacitated or Suspended during an Over) shall apply.

LAW 18.   SCORING

1. A Run

The score shall be reckoned by runs. A run is scored:

(a) So often as the batsmen, after a hit or at any time while the ball is in play, shall have crossed and made good their ground from end to end.

(b) When a boundary is scored. See Law 19 (Boundaries).

(c) When penalty runs are awarded. See 6 below.

2. Short Runs

(a) If either batsman runs a short run, the umpire shall call and signal "one short" as soon as the ball becomes dead and that run shall not be scored. A run is short if a batsman fails to make good his ground on turning for a further run.

(b) Although a short run shortens the succeeding one, the latter, if completed, shall count.

(c) If either or both batsmen deliberately run short the umpire shall, as soon as he sees that the fielding side have no chance of dismissing either batsman, call and signal "dead ball" and disallow any runs attempted or previously scored. The batsmen shall return to their original ends.

(d) If both batsmen run short in one and the same run, only one run shall be deducted.

(e) Only if three or more runs are attempted can more than one be short and then, subject to (c) and (d) above, all runs so called shall be disallowed. If there has been more than one short run the umpires shall instruct the scorers as to the number of runs disallowed.

3. Striker Caught

If the striker is caught, no run shall be scored.

4. Batsman Run Out

If a batsman is run out, only that run which was being attempted shall not be scored. If, however, an injured striker himself is run out, no runs shall be scored. See Law 2.7 (Transgression of the Laws by an Injured Batsman or Runner).

5. Batsman Obstructing the Field

If a batsman is out Obstructing the Field, any runs completed before the obstruction occurs shall be scored unless such obstruction prevents a catch being made, in which case no runs shall be scored.

6. Runs Scored for Penalties

Runs shall be scored for penalties under Laws 20 (Lost Ball), 24 (No-ball), 25 (Wide-ball), 41.1 (Fielding the Ball) and for boundary allowances under Law 19 (Boundaries).

7. Batsman Returning to Wicket he has Left

If, while the ball is in play, the batsmen have crossed in running, neither shall return to the wicket he has left, even though a short run has been called or no run has been scored as in the case of a catch. Batsmen, however, shall return to the wickets they originally left in the cases of a boundary and of any disallowance of runs and of an injured batsman being, himself, run out. See Law 2.7 (Transgression by an Injured Batsman or Runner).

Note

> **(a) Short Run**
> A striker taking stance in front of his popping crease may run from that point without penalty.

LAW 19. BOUNDARIES

1. The Boundary of the Playing Area

Before the toss for innings, the umpires shall agree with both captains on the boundary of the playing area. The boundary shall, if possible, be marked by a white line, a rope laid on the ground, or a fence. If flags or posts only are used to mark a boundary, the imaginary line joining such points shall be regarded as the boundary. An obstacle, or person, within the playing area shall not be regarded as a boundary unless so decided by the umpires before the toss for innings. Sightscreens within, or partially within, the playing area shall be regarded as the boundary and when the ball strikes or passes within or under or directly over any part of the screen, a boundary shall be scored.

2. Runs Scored for Boundaries

Before the toss for innings, the umpires shall agree with both captains the runs to be allowed for boundaries, and in deciding the allowance for them, the umpires and captains shall be guided by the prevailing custom of the ground. The allowance for a boundary shall normally be four runs, and six runs for all hits pitching over and clear of the boundary line or fence, even though the ball has been previously touched by a fieldsman. Six runs shall also be scored if a fieldsman, after catching a ball, carries it over the boundary. See Law 32 (Caught) Note (a). Six runs shall not be scored when a ball struck by the striker hits a sightscreen full pitch if the screen is within, or partially within, the playing area, but if the ball is struck directly over a sightscreen so situated, six runs shall be scored.

3. A Boundary

A boundary shall be scored and signalled by the umpire at the bowler's end whenever, in his opinion:

> (a) A ball in play touches or crosses the boundary, however marked.
>
> (b) A fieldsman with ball in hand touches or grounds any part of his person on or over a boundary line.
>
> (c) A fieldsman with ball in hand grounds any part of his person over a boundary fence or board. This allows the fieldsman to touch or lean on or over a boundary fence or board in preventing a boundary.

4. Runs Exceeding Boundary Allowance

The runs completed at the instant the ball reaches the boundary shall count if they exceed the boundary allowance.

5. Overthrows or Wilful Act of a Fieldsman

If the boundary results from an overthrow or from the wilful act of a fieldsman, any runs already completed and the allowance shall be added to the score. The run in progress shall count provided that the batsmen have crossed at the instant of the throw or act.

Note

(a) Position of Sightscreens

Sightscreens should, if possible, be positioned wholly outside the playing area, as near as possible to the boundary line.

LAW 20.   LOST BALL

1. Runs Scored

If a ball in play cannot be found or recovered, any fieldsman may call "lost ball" when six runs shall be added to the score; but if more than six have been run before "lost ball" is called, as many runs as have been completed shall be scored. The run in progress shall count provided that the batsmen have crossed at the instant of the call of "lost ball".

2. How Scored

The runs shall be added to the score of the striker if the ball has been struck, but otherwise to the score of byes, leg-byes, no-balls or wides as the case may be.

LAW 21.   THE RESULT

1. A Win – Two-innings Matches

The side which has scored a total of runs in excess of that scored by the opposing side in its two completed innings shall be the winner.

2. A Win – One-innings Matches

(a) One-innings matches, unless played out as in 1 above, shall be decided on the first innings, but see Law 12.5 (Continuation after One Innings of Each Side).

(b) If the captains agree to continue play after the completion of one innings of each side in accordance with Law 12.5 (Continuation after One Innings of Each Side) and a result is not achieved on the second innings, the first innings result shall stand.

3. Umpires Awarding a Match

(a) A match shall be lost by a side which, during the match, (i) refuses to play, or (ii) concedes defeat, and the umpires shall award the match to the other side.

(b) Should both batsmen at the wickets or the fielding side leave the field at any time without the agreement of the umpires, this shall constitute a refusal to play and, on appeal, the umpires shall award the match to the other side in accordance with (a) above.

4. A Tie

The result of a match shall be a tie when the scores are equal at the conclusion of play, but only if the side batting last has completed its innings.

If the scores of the completed first innings of a one-day match are equal, it shall be a tie but only if the match has not been played out to a further conclusion.

5. A Draw

A match not determined in any of the ways as in 1, 2, 3 and 4 above shall count as a draw.

6. Correctness of Result

Any decision as to the correctness of the scores shall be the responsibility of the umpires. See Law 3.14 (Correctness of Scores).

If, after the umpires and players have left the field in the belief that the match has been concluded, the umpires decide that a mistake in scoring has occurred, which affects the result, and provided time has not been reached, they shall order play to resume and to continue until the agreed finishing time unless a result is reached earlier.

If the umpires decide that a mistake has occurred and time has been reached, the umpires shall immediately inform both captains of the necessary corrections to the scores and, if applicable, to the result.

7. Acceptance of Result

In accepting the scores as notified by the scorers and agreed by the umpires, the captains of both sides thereby accept the result.

Notes

> **(a) Statement of Results**
> The result of a finished match is stated as a win by runs, except in the case of a win by the side batting last when it is by the number of wickets still then to fall.
>
> **(b) Winning Hit or Extras**
> As soon as the side has won, see 1 and 2 above, the umpire shall call "time", the match is finished, and nothing that happens thereafter other than as a result of a mistake in scoring (see 6 above) shall be regarded as part of the match.
>
> However, if a boundary constitutes the winning hit – or extras – and the boundary allowance exceeds the number of runs required to win the match, such runs scored shall be credited to the side's total and, in the case of a hit, to the striker's score.

LAW 22.   THE OVER

1. Number of Balls

The ball shall be bowled from each wicket alternately in overs of either six or eight balls according to agreement before the match.

2. Call of "Over"

When the agreed number of balls has been bowled, and as the ball becomes dead or when it becomes clear to the umpire at the bowler's end that both the fielding side and the batsmen at the wicket have ceased to regard the ball as in play, the umpire shall call "over" before leaving the wicket.

3. No-ball or Wide-ball

Neither a no-ball nor a wide-ball shall be reckoned as one of the over.

4. Umpire Miscounting

If an umpire miscounts the number of balls, the over as counted by the umpire shall stand.

5. Bowler Changing Ends

A bowler shall be allowed to change ends as often as desired, provided only that he does not bowl two overs consecutively in an innings.

6. The Bowler Finishing an Over

A bowler shall finish an over in progress unless he be incapacitated or be suspended under Law 42.8 (The Bowling of Fast Short-pitched Balls), 9 (The Bowling of Fast High Full Pitches), 10 (Time Wasting) and 11 (Players Damaging the Pitch). If an over is left incomplete for any reason at the start of an interval or interruption of play, it shall be finished on the resumption of play.

7. Bowler Incapacitated or Suspended during an Over

If, for any reason, a bowler is incapacitated while running up to bowl the first ball of an over, or is incapacitated or suspended during an over, the umpire shall call and signal "dead ball" and another bowler shall be allowed to bowl or complete the over from the same end, provided only that he shall not bowl two overs, or part thereof, consecutively in one innings.

8. Position of Non-striker

The batsman at the bowler's end shall normally stand on the opposite side of the wicket to that from which the ball is being delivered, unless a request to do otherwise is granted by the umpire.

LAW 23. DEAD BALL

1. The Ball Becomes Dead

When:

    (a) It is finally settled in the hands of the wicket-keeper or the bowler.

    (b) It reaches or pitches over the boundary.

    (c) A batsman is out.

    (d) Whether played or not, it lodges in the clothing or equipment of a batsman or the clothing of an umpire.

    (e) A ball lodges in a protective helmet worn by a member of the fielding side.

    (f) A penalty is awarded under Law 20 (Lost Ball) or Law 41.1 (Fielding the Ball).

    (g) The umpire calls "over" or "time".

2. Either Umpire Shall Call and Signal "Dead Ball"

When:

    (a) He intervenes in a case of unfair play.

    (b) A serious injury to a player or umpire occurs.

    (c) He is satisfied that, for an adequate reason, the striker is not ready to receive the ball and makes no attempt to play it.

    (d) The bowler drops the ball accidentally before delivery, or the ball does not leave his hand for any reason other than in an attempt to run out the non-striker (See Law 24.5 – Bowler Attempting to Run Out Non-striker before Delivery).

    (e) One or both bails fall from the striker's wicket before he receives delivery.

    (f) He leaves his normal position for consultation.

    (g) He is required to do so under Law 26.3 (Disallowance of Leg-byes), etc.

3. The Ball Ceases to be Dead

When:

    (a) The bowler starts his run-up or bowling action.

4. The Ball is Not Dead

When:

    (a) It strikes an umpire (unless it lodges in his dress).

    (b) The wicket is broken or struck down (unless a batsman is out thereby).

    (c) An unsuccessful appeal is made.

    (d) The wicket is broken accidentally either by the bowler during his delivery or by a batsman in running.

    (e) The umpire has called "no-ball" or "wide".

Notes

(a) **Ball Finally Settled**

Whether the ball is finally settled or not – see 1(a) above – must be a question for the umpires alone to decide.

(b) **Action on Call of "Dead Ball"**

(i) If "dead ball" is called prior to the striker receiving a delivery, the bowler shall be allowed an additional ball.

(ii) If "dead ball" is called after the striker receives a delivery, the bowler shall not be allowed an additional ball, unless a "no-ball" or "wide" has been called.

LAW 24. NO-BALL

1. Mode of Delivery

The umpire shall indicate to the striker whether the bowler intends to bowl over or round the wicket, overarm or underarm, right or left-handed. Failure on the part of the bowler to indicate in advance a change in his mode of delivery is unfair and the umpire shall call and signal "no-ball".

2. Fair Delivery – The Arm

For a delivery to be fair the ball must be bowled, not thrown – see Note (a) below. If either umpire is not entirely satisfied with the absolute fairness of a delivery in this respect he shall call and signal "no-ball" instantly upon delivery.

3. Fair Delivery – The Feet

The umpire at the bowler's wicket shall call and signal "no-ball" if he is not satisfied that in the delivery stride:

(a) The bowler's back foot has landed within and not touching the return crease or its forward extension; or

(b) Some part of the front foot whether grounded or raised was behind the popping crease.

4. Bowler Throwing at Striker's Wicket before Delivery

If the bowler, before delivering the ball, throws it at the striker's wicket in an attempt to run him out, the umpire shall call and signal "no-ball". See Law 42.12 (Batsman Unfairly Stealing a Run) and Law 38 (Run Out).

5. Bowler Attempting to Run Out Non-striker before Delivery

If the bowler, before delivering the ball, attempts to run out the non-striker, any runs which result shall be allowed and shall be scored as no-balls. Such an attempt shall not count as a ball in the over. The umpire shall not call "no-ball". See Law 42.12 (Batsman Unfairly Stealing a Run).

6. Infringement of Laws by a Wicket-keeper or a Fieldsman

The umpire shall call and signal "no-ball" in the event of the wicket-keeper infringing Law 40.1 (Position of Wicket-keeper) or a fieldsman infringing Law 41.2 (Limitation of On-side Fieldsmen) or Law 41.3 (Position of Fieldsmen).

7. Revoking a Call

An umpire shall revoke the call "no-ball" if the ball does not leave the bowler's hand for any reason. See Law 23.2 (Either Umpire Shall Call and Signal "Dead Ball").

8. Penalty

A penalty of one run for a no-ball shall be scored if no runs are made otherwise.

9. Runs from a No-ball

The striker may hit a no-ball and whatever runs result shall be added to his score. Runs made otherwise from a no-ball shall be scored no-balls.

10. Out from a No-ball

The striker shall be out from a no-ball if he breaks Law 34 (Hit the Ball Twice) and either batsman may be run out or shall be given out if either breaks Law 33 (Handled the Ball) or Law 37 (Obstructing the Field).

11. Batsman Given Out off a No-ball

Should a batsman be given out off a no-ball the penalty for bowling it shall stand unless runs are otherwise scored.

Notes

    (a) Definition of a Throw
    A ball shall be deemed to have been thrown if, in the opinion of either umpire, the process of straightening the bowling arm, whether it be partial or complete, takes place during that part of the delivery swing which directly precedes the ball leaving the hand. This definition shall not debar a bowler from the use of the wrist in the delivery swing.

    (b) No-ball Not Counting in Over
    A no-ball shall not be reckoned as one of the over. See Law 22.3 (No-ball or Wide-ball).

LAW 25.   WIDE-BALL

1. Judging a Wide

If the bowler bowls the ball so high over or so wide of the wicket that, in the opinion of the umpire, it passes out of reach of the striker, standing in a normal guard position, the umpire shall call and signal "wide-ball" as soon as it has passed the line of the striker's wicket.
    The umpire shall not adjudge a ball as being wide if:

    (a) The striker, by moving from his guard position, causes the ball to pass out of his reach.

    (b) The striker moves and thus brings the ball within his reach.

2. Penalty

A penalty of one run for a wide shall be scored if no runs are made otherwise.

3. Ball Coming to Rest in Front of the Striker

If a ball which the umpire considers to have been delivered comes to rest in front of the line of the striker's wicket, "wide" shall not be called. The striker has a right, without interference from the fielding side, to make one attempt to hit the ball. If the fielding side interfere, the umpire shall replace the ball where it came to rest and shall order the fieldsmen to resume the places they occupied in the field before the ball was delivered.
    The umpire shall call and signal "dead ball" as soon as it is clear that the striker does not intend to hit the ball, or after the striker has made an unsuccessful attempt to hit the ball.

4. Revoking a Call

The umpire shall revoke the call if the striker hits a ball which has been called "wide".

5. Ball Not Dead

The ball does not become dead on the call of "wide-ball" – see Law 23.4 (The Ball is Not Dead).

6. Runs Resulting from a Wide

All runs which are run or result from a wide-ball which is not a no-ball shall be scored wide-balls, or if no runs are made one shall be scored.

7. Out from a Wide

The striker shall be out from a wide-ball if he breaks Law 35 (Hit Wicket), or Law 39 (Stumped). Either batsman may be run out and shall be out if he breaks Law 33 (Handled the Ball), or Law 37 (Obstructing the Field).

8. Batsman Given Out off a Wide

Should a batsman be given out off a wide, the penalty for bowling it shall stand unless runs are otherwise made.

Note

(a) Wide-ball Not Counting in Over
A wide-ball shall not be reckoned as one of the over – see Law 22.3 (No-ball or Wide-ball).

LAW 26. BYE AND LEG-BYE

1. Byes

If the ball, not having been called "wide" or "no-ball", passes the striker without touching his bat or person, and any runs are obtained, the umpire shall signal "bye" and the run or runs shall be credited as such to the batting side.

2. Leg-byes

If the ball, not having been called "wide" or "no-ball", is unintentionally deflected by the striker's dress or person, except a hand holding the bat, and any runs are obtained the umpire shall signal "leg-bye" and the run or runs so scored shall be credited as such to the batting side.

Such leg-byes shall be scored only if, in the opinion of the umpire, the striker has:

    (a) Attempted to play the ball with his bat; or

    (b) Tried to avoid being hit by the ball.

3. Disallowance of Leg-byes

In the case of a deflection by the striker's person, other than in 2(a) and (b) above, the umpire shall call and signal "dead ball" as soon as one run has been completed or when it is clear that a run is not being attempted, or the ball has reached the boundary.

On the call and signal of "dead ball" the batsmen shall return to their original ends and no runs shall be allowed.

LAW 27. APPEALS

1. Time of Appeals

The umpires shall not give a batsman out unless appealed to by the other side which shall be done prior to the bowler beginning his run-up or bowling action to deliver the next ball. Under Law 23.1 (g) (The Ball Becomes Dead), the ball is dead on "over" being called; this does not, however, invalidate an appeal made prior to the first ball of the following over provided "time" has not been called – see Law 17.1 (Call of Time).

2. An Appeal "How's That?"

An appeal "How's That?" shall cover all ways of being out.

3. Answering Appeals

The umpire at the bowler's wicket shall answer appeals before the other umpire in all cases except those arising out of Law 35 (Hit Wicket) or Law 39 (Stumped) or Law 38 (Run Out) when this occurs at the striker's wicket.

When either umpire has given a batsman not out, the other umpire shall, within his jurisdiction, answer the appeal or a further appeal, provided it is made in time in accordance with 1 above (Time of Appeals).

4. Consultation by Umpires

An umpire may consult with the other umpire on a point of fact which the latter may have been in a better position to see and shall then give his decision. If, after consultation, there is still doubt remaining the decision shall be in favour of the batsman.

5. Batsman Leaving his Wicket under a Misapprehension

The umpires shall intervene if satisfied that a batsman, not having been given out, has left his wicket under a misapprehension that he has been dismissed.

6. Umpire's Decision

The umpire's decision is final. He may alter his decision, provided that such alteration is made promptly.

7. Withdrawal of an Appeal

In exceptional circumstances the captain of the fielding side may seek permission of the umpire to withdraw an appeal provided the outgoing batsman has not left the playing area. If this is allowed, the umpire shall cancel his decision.

LAW 28.   THE WICKET IS DOWN

1. Wicket Down

The wicket is down if:

(a) Either the ball or the striker's bat or person completely removes either bail from the top of the stumps. A disturbance of a bail, whether temporary or not, shall not constitute a complete removal, but the wicket is down if a bail in falling lodges between two of the stumps.

(b) Any player completely removes with his hand or arm a bail from the top of the stumps, provided that the ball is held in that hand or in the hand of the arm so used.

(c) When both bails are off, a stump is struck out of the ground by the ball, or a player strikes or pulls a stump out of the ground, providing that the ball is held in the hand(s) or in the hand of the arm so used.

2. One Bail Off

If one bail is off, it shall be sufficient for the purpose of putting the wicket down to remove the remaining bail, or to strike or pull any of the three stumps out of the ground in any of the ways stated in 1 above.

3. All the Stumps Out of the Ground

If all the stumps are out of the ground, the fielding side shall be allowed to put back one or more stumps in order to have an opportunity of putting the wicket down.

4. Dispensing with Bails

If, owing to the strength of the wind, it has been agreed to dispense with the bails in accordance with Law 8, Note (a) (Dispensing with Bails), the decision as to when the wicket is down is one for the umpires to decide on the facts before them. In such circumstances and if the umpires so decide, the wicket shall be held to be down even though a stump has not been struck out of the ground.

Note

(a) Remaking the Wicket
If the wicket is broken while the ball is in play, it is not the umpire's duty to remake the wicket until the ball has become dead – see Law 23 (Dead Ball). A member of the fielding side, however, may remake the wicket in such circumstances.

LAW 29. BATSMAN OUT OF HIS GROUND

1. When out of his Ground

A batsman shall be considered to be out of his ground unless some part of his bat in his hand or of his person is grounded behind the line of the popping crease.

LAW 30. BOWLED

1. Out Bowled

The striker shall be out *Bowled* if:

(a) His wicket is bowled down, even if the ball first touches his bat or person.

(b) He breaks his wicket by hitting or kicking the ball on to it before the completion of a stroke, or as a result of attempting to guard his wicket. See Law 34.1 (Out Hit the Ball Twice).

Note

(a) Out Bowled – Not lbw
The striker is out bowled if the ball is deflected on to his wicket even though a decision against him would be justified under Law 36 (lbw).

LAW 31. TIMED OUT

1. Out Timed Out

An incoming batsman shall be out *Timed Out* if he wilfully takes more than two minutes to come in – the two minutes being timed from the moment a wicket falls until the new batsman steps on to the field of play.

If this is not complied with and if the umpire is satisfied that the delay was wilful and if an appeal is made, the new batsman shall be given out by the umpire at the bowler's end.

2. Time to be Added

The time taken by the umpires to investigate the cause of the delay shall be added at the normal close of play.

Notes

(a) Entry in Scorebook
The correct entry in the scorebook when a batsman is given out under this Law is "timed out", and the bowler does not get credit for the wicket.

(b) Batsmen Crossing on the Field of Play
It is an essential duty of the captains to ensure that the in-going batsman passes the out-going one before the latter leaves the field of play.

LAW 32. CAUGHT

1. Out Caught

The striker shall be out *Caught* if the ball touches his bat or if it touches below the wrist his hand or glove, holding the bat, and is subsequently held by a fieldsman before it touches the ground.

2. A Fair Catch

A catch shall be considered to have been fairly made if:

(a) The fieldsman is within the field of play throughout the act of making the catch.

  (i) The act of making the catch shall start from the time when the fieldsman first handles the ball and shall end when he both retains complete control over the further disposal of the ball and remains within the field of play.

  (ii) In order to be within the field of play, the fieldsman may not touch or ground any part of his person on or over a boundary line. When the boundary is marked by a fence or board the fieldsman may not ground any part of his person over the boundary fence or board, but may touch or lean over the boundary fence or board in completing the catch.

(b) The ball is hugged to the body of the catcher or accidentally lodges in his dress or, in the case of the wicket-keeper, in his pads. However, a striker may not be caught if a ball lodges in a protective helmet worn by a fieldsman, in which case the umpire shall call and signal "dead ball". See Law 23 (Dead Ball).

(c) The ball does not touch the ground even though a hand holding it does so in effecting the catch.

(d) A fieldsman catches the ball, after it has been lawfully played a second time by the striker, but only if the ball has not touched the ground since being first struck.

(e) A fieldsman catches the ball after it has touched an umpire, another fieldsman or the other batsman. However, a striker may not be caught if a ball has touched a protective helmet worn by a fieldsman.

(f) The ball is caught off an obstruction within the boundary provided it has not previously been agreed to regard the obstruction as a boundary.

3. Scoring of Runs

If a striker is caught, no run shall be scored.

Notes

(a) Scoring from an Attempted Catch
When a fieldsman carrying the ball touches or grounds any part of his person on or over a boundary marked by a line, six runs shall be scored.

(b) Ball Still in Play
If a fieldsman releases the ball before he crosses the boundary, the ball will be considered to be still in play and it may be caught by another fieldsman. However, if the original fieldsman returns to the field of play and handles the ball, a catch may not be made.

LAW 33. HANDLED THE BALL

1. Out Handled the Ball

Either batsman on appeal shall be out *Handled the Ball* if he wilfully touches the ball while in play with the hand not holding the bat unless he does so with the consent of the opposite side.

Note

(a) Entry in Scorebook
The correct entry in the scorebook when a batsman is given out under this Law is "handled the ball", and the bowler does not get credit for the wicket.

LAW 34.   HIT THE BALL TWICE

1. Out Hit the Ball Twice

The striker, on appeal, shall be out *Hit the Ball Twice* if, after the ball is struck or is stopped by any part of his person, he wilfully strikes it again with his bat or person except for the sole purpose of guarding his wicket: this he may do with his bat or any part of his person other than his hands, but see Law 37.2 (Obstructing a Ball From Being Caught).

For the purpose of this Law, a hand holding the bat shall be regarded as part of the bat.

2. Returning the Ball to a Fieldsman

The striker, on appeal, shall be out under this Law if, without the consent of the opposite side, he uses his bat or person to return the ball to any of the fielding side.

3. Runs from Ball Lawfully Struck Twice

No runs except those which result from an overthrow or penalty – see Law 41 (The Fieldsman) – shall be scored from a ball lawfully struck twice.

Notes

(a) Entry in Scorebook
The correct entry in the scorebook when the striker is given out under this Law is "hit the ball twice", and the bowler does not get credit for the wicket.

(b) Runs Credited to the Batsman
Any runs awarded under 3 above as a result of an overthrow or penalty shall be credited to the striker, provided the ball in the first instance has touched the bat, or, if otherwise, as extras.

LAW 35.   HIT WICKET

1. Out Hit Wicket

The striker shall be out *Hit Wicket* if, while the ball is in play:

(a) His wicket is broken with any part of his person, dress, or equipment as a result of any action taken by him in preparing to receive or in receiving a delivery, or in setting off for his first run, immediately after playing, or playing at, the ball.

(b) He hits down his wicket whilst lawfully making a second stroke for the purpose of guarding his wicket within the provisions of Law 34.1 (Out Hit the Ball Twice).

Notes

(a) Not Out Hit Wicket
A batsman is not out under this Law should his wicket be broken in any of the ways referred to in 1(a) above if:

(i) It occurs while he is in the act of running, other than in setting off for his first run immediately after playing at the ball, or while he is avoiding being run out or stumped.

(ii) The bowler after starting his run-up or bowling action does not deliver the ball; in which case the umpire shall immediately call and signal "dead ball".

(iii) It occurs whilst he is avoiding a throw-in at any time.

LAW 36.   LEG BEFORE WICKET

1. Out lbw

The striker shall be out *lbw* in the circumstances set out below:

(a) Striker Attempting to Play the Ball
The striker shall be out lbw if he first intercepts with any part of his person, dress or equipment a fair ball which would have hit the wicket and which has not previously touched his bat or a hand holding the bat, provided that:

(i) The ball pitched in a straight line between wicket and wicket or on the off side of the striker's wicket, or was intercepted full pitch; and

(ii) The point of impact is in a straight line between wicket and wicket, even if above the level of the bails.

(b) Striker Making No Attempt to Play the Ball

The striker shall be out lbw even if the ball is intercepted outside the line of the off stump if, in the opinion of the umpire, he has made no genuine attempt to play the ball with his bat, but has intercepted the ball with some part of his person and if the other circumstances set out in (a) above apply.

LAW 37.   OBSTRUCTING THE FIELD

1. Wilful Obstruction

Either batsman, on appeal, shall be out *Obstructing the Field* if he wilfully obstructs the opposite side by word or action.

2. Obstructing a Ball From Being Caught

The striker, on appeal, shall be out should wilful obstruction by either batsman prevent a catch being made.

This shall apply even though the striker causes the obstruction in lawfully guarding his wicket under the provisions of Law 34. See Law 34.1 (Out Hit the Ball Twice).

Notes

(a) **Accidental Obstruction**
The umpires must decide whether the obstruction was wilful or not. The accidental interception of a throw-in by a batsman while running does not break this Law.

(b) **Entry in Scorebook**
The correct entry in the scorebook when a batsman is given out under this Law is "obstructing the field", and the bowler does not get credit for the wicket.

LAW 38.   RUN OUT

1. Out Run Out

Either batsman shall be out *Run Out* if in running or at any time while the ball is in play – except in the circumstances described in Law 39 (Stumped) – he is out of his ground and his wicket is put down by the opposite side. If, however, a batsman in running makes good his ground he shall not be out run out if he subsequently leaves his ground, in order to avoid injury, and the wicket is put down.

2. "No-ball" Called

If a no-ball has been called, the striker shall not be given run out unless he attempts to run.

3. Which Batsman Is Out

If the batsmen have crossed in running, he who runs for the wicket which is put down shall be out; if they have not crossed, he who has left the wicket which is put down shall be out. If a batsman remains in his ground or returns to his ground and the other batsman joins him there, the latter shall be out if his wicket is put down.

4. Scoring of Runs

If a batsman is run out, only that run which is being attempted shall not be scored. If, however, an injured striker himself is run out, no runs shall be scored. See Law 2.7 (Transgression of the Laws by an Injured Batsman or Runner).

Notes

(a) **Ball Played on to Opposite Wicket**
If the ball is played on to the opposite wicket, neither batsman is liable to be run out unless the ball has been touched by a fieldsman before the wicket is broken.

(b) Entry in Scorebook

The correct entry in the scorebook when a batsman is given out under this Law is "run out", and the bowler does not get credit for the wicket.

(c) Run Out off a Fieldsman's Helmet

If, having been played by a batsman, or having come off his person, the ball rebounds directly from a fieldsman's helmet on to the stumps, with either batsman out of his ground, the batsman shall be "not out".

LAW 39. STUMPED

1. Out Stumped

The striker shall be out *Stumped* if, in receiving the ball, not being a no-ball, he is out of his ground otherwise than in attempting a run and the wicket is put down by the wicket-keeper without the intervention of another fieldsman.

2. Action by the Wicket-keeper

The wicket-keeper may take the ball in front of the wicket in an attempt to stump the striker only if the ball has touched the bat or person of the striker.

Note

(a) Ball Rebounding from Wicket-keeper's Person

The striker may be out stumped if, in the circumstances stated in 1 above, the wicket is broken by a ball rebounding from the wicket-keeper's person or equipment other than a protective helmet or is kicked or thrown by the wicket-keeper on to the wicket.

LAW 40. THE WICKET-KEEPER

1. Position of Wicket-keeper

The wicket-keeper shall remain wholly behind the wicket until a ball delivered by the bowler touches the bat or person of the striker, or passes the wicket, or until the striker attempts a run.

In the event of the wicket-keeper contravening this Law, the umpire at the striker's end shall call and signal "no-ball" at the instant of delivery or as soon as possible thereafter.

2. Restriction on Actions of the Wicket-keeper

If the wicket-keeper interferes with the striker's right to play the ball and to guard his wicket, the striker shall not be out except under Laws 33 (Handled the Ball), 34 (Hit the Ball Twice), 37 (Obstructing the Field) and 38 (Run Out).

3. Interference with the Wicket-keeper by the Striker

If, in the legitimate defence of his wicket, the striker interferes with the wicket-keeper, he shall not be out, except as provided for in Law 37.2 (Obstructing a Ball From Being Caught).

LAW 41. THE FIELDSMAN

1. Fielding the Ball

The fieldsman may stop the ball with any part of his person, but if he wilfully stops it otherwise, five runs shall be added to the run or runs already scored; if no run has been scored five penalty runs shall be awarded. The run in progress shall count provided that the batsmen have crossed at the instant of the act. If the ball has been struck, the penalty shall be added to the score of the striker, but otherwise to the score of byes, leg-byes, no-balls or wides as the case may be.

2. Limitation of On-side Fieldsmen

The number of on-side fieldsmen behind the popping crease at the instant of the bowler's delivery shall not exceed two. In the event of infringement by the fielding side the umpire at the striker's end shall call and signal "no-ball" at the instant of delivery or as soon as possible thereafter.

3. Position of Fieldsmen

Whilst the ball is in play and until the ball has made contact with the bat or the striker's person or has passed his bat, no fieldsman, other than the bowler, may stand on or have any part of his person extended over the pitch (measuring 22 yards/20.12m × 10 feet/3.05m). In the event of a fieldsman contravening this Law, the umpire at the bowler's end shall call and signal "no-ball" at the instant of delivery or as soon as possible thereafter. See Law 40.1 (Position of Wicket-keeper).

4. Fieldsmen's Protective Helmets

Protective helmets, when not in use by members of the fielding side, shall be placed, if above the surface, only on the ground behind the wicket-keeper. In the event of the ball, when in play, striking a helmet whilst in this position, five penalty runs shall be awarded as laid down in Law 41.1 and Note (a).

Note

(a) Batsmen Changing Ends
The five runs referred to in 1 and 4 above are a penalty and the batsmen do not change ends solely by reason of this penalty.

LAW 42.   UNFAIR PLAY

1. Responsibility of Captains

The captains are responsible at all times for ensuring that play is conducted within the spirit of the game as well as within the Laws.

2. Responsibility of Umpires

The umpires are the sole judges of fair and unfair play.

3. Intervention by the Umpire

The umpires shall intervene without appeal by calling and signalling "dead ball" in the case of unfair play, but should not otherwise interfere with the progress of the game except as required to do so by the Laws.

4. Lifting the Seam

A player shall not lift the seam of the ball for any reason. Should this be done, the umpires shall change the ball for one of similar condition to that in use prior to the contravention. See Note (a).

5. Changing the Condition of the Ball

Any member of the fielding side may polish the ball provided that such polishing wastes no time and that no artificial substance is used. No-one shall rub the ball on the ground or use any artificial substance or take any other action to alter the condition of the ball.

In the event of a contravention of this Law, the umpires, after consultation, shall change the ball for one of similar condition to that in use prior to the contravention.

This Law does not prevent a member of the fielding side from drying a wet ball, or removing mud from the ball. See Note (b).

6. Incommoding the Striker

An umpire is justified in intervening under this Law and shall call and signal "dead ball" if, in his opinion, any player of the fielding side incommodes the striker by any noise or action while he is receiving a ball.

7. Obstruction of a Batsman in Running

It shall be considered unfair if any fieldsman wilfully obstructs a batsman in running. In these circumstances the umpire shall call and signal "dead ball" and allow any completed runs and the run in progress, or alternatively any boundary scored.

8. The Bowling of Fast Short-pitched Balls

The bowling of fast short-pitched balls is unfair if, in the opinion of the umpire at the bowler's end, it constitutes an attempt to intimidate the striker. See Note (d).

Umpires shall consider intimidation to be the deliberate bowling of fast short-pitched balls which by their length, height and direction are intended or likely to inflict physical injury on the striker. The relative skill of the striker shall also be taken into consideration.

In the event of such unfair bowling, the umpire at the bowler's end shall adopt the following procedure:

(a) In the first instance the umpire shall call and signal "no-ball", caution the bowler and inform the other umpire, the captain of the fielding side and the batsmen of what has occurred.

(b) If this caution is ineffective, he shall repeat the above procedure and indicate to the bowler that this is a final warning.

(c) Both the above caution and final warning shall continue to apply even though the bowler may later change ends.

(d) Should the above warnings prove ineffective the umpire at the bowler's end shall:

    (i) At the first repetition call and signal "no-ball" and when the ball is dead direct the captain to take the bowler off forthwith and to complete the over with another bowler, provided that the bowler does not bowl two overs or part thereof consecutively. See Law 22.7 (Bowler Incapacitated or Suspended during an Over).

    (ii) Not allow the bowler, thus taken off, to bowl again in the same innings.

    (iii) Report the occurrence to the captain of the batting side as soon as the players leave the field for an interval.

    (iv) Report the occurrence to the executive of the fielding side and to any governing body responsible for the match, who shall take any further action which is considered to be appropriate against the bowler concerned.

9. The Bowling of Fast High Full Pitches

The bowling of fast high full pitches is unfair.

A fast high full-pitched ball is defined as a ball that passes, or would have passed, on the full above waist height of a batsman standing upright at the crease. Should a bowler bowl a fast high full-pitched ball, either umpire shall call and signal "no-ball" and adopt the procedure of caution, final warning, action against the bowler and reporting as set out in Law 42.8.

10. Time Wasting

Any form of time wasting is unfair.

(a) In the event of the captain of the fielding side wasting time or allowing any member of his side to waste time, the umpire at the bowler's end shall adopt the following procedure:

    (i) In the first instance he shall caution the captain of the fielding side and inform the other umpire of what has occurred.

    (ii) If this caution is ineffective he shall repeat the above procedure and indicate to the captain that this is a final warning.

    (iii) The umpire shall report the occurrence to the captain of the batting side as soon as the players leave the field for an interval.

    (iv) Should the above procedure prove ineffective the umpire shall report the occurrence to the executive of the fielding side and to any governing body responsible for that match, who shall take appropriate action against the captain and the players concerned.

(b) In the event of a bowler taking unnecessarily long to bowl an over the umpire at the bowler's end shall adopt the procedures, other than the calling of "no-ball", of caution, final warning, action against the bowler and reporting as set out in 8 above.

(c) In the event of a batsman wasting time (See Note (e)) other than in the manner described in Law 31 (Timed Out), the umpire at the bowler's end shall adopt the following procedure:

(i) In the first instance he shall caution the batsman and inform the other umpire at once, and the captain of the batting side, as soon as the players leave the field for an interval, of what has occurred.

(ii) If this proves ineffective, he shall repeat the caution, indicate to the batsman that this is a final warning and inform the other umpire.

(iii) The umpire shall report the occurrence to both captains as soon as the players leave the field for an interval.

(iv) Should the above procedure prove ineffective, the umpire shall report the occurrence to the executive of the batting side and to any governing body responsible for that match, who shall take appropriate action against the player concerned.

11. Players Damaging the Pitch

The umpires shall intervene and prevent players from causing damage to the pitch which may assist the bowlers of either side. See Note (c).

(a) In the event of any member of the fielding side damaging the pitch, the umpire shall follow the procedure of caution, final warning and reporting as set out in 10(a) above.

(b) In the event of a bowler contravening this Law by running down the pitch after delivering the ball, the umpire at the bowler's end shall first caution the bowler. If this caution is ineffective the umpire shall adopt the procedures, other than the calling of "no-ball", as set out in 8 above.

(c) In the event of a batsman damaging the pitch the umpire at the bowler's end shall follow the procedures of caution, final warning and reporting as set out in 10(c) above.

12. Batsman Unfairly Stealing a Run

Any attempt by the batsman to steal a run during the bowler's run-up is unfair. Unless the bowler attempts to run out either batsman – see Law 24.4 (Bowler Throwing at Striker's Wicket before Delivery) and Law 24.5 (Bowler Attempting to Run Out Non-striker before Delivery) – the umpire shall call and signal "dead ball" as soon as the batsmen cross in any such attempt to run. The batsmen shall then return to their original wickets.

13. Player's Conduct

In the event of a player failing to comply with the instructions of an umpire, criticising his decisions by word or action, or showing dissent, or generally behaving in a manner which might bring the game into disrepute, the umpire concerned shall, in the first place, report the matter to the other umpire and to the player's captain, requesting the latter to take action. If this proves ineffective, the umpire shall report the incident as soon as possible to the executive of the player's team and to any governing body responsible for the match, who shall take any further action which is considered appropriate against the player or players concerned.

Notes

(a) **The Condition of the Ball**
Umpires shall make frequent and irregular inspections of the condition of the ball.

(b) **Drying of a Wet Ball**
A wet ball may be dried on a towel or with sawdust.

(c) **Danger Area**
The danger area on the pitch, which must be protected from damage by a bowler, shall be regarded by the umpires as the area contained by an imaginary line 4 feet/1.22m from the popping crease, and parallel to it, and within two imaginary and parallel lines drawn down the pitch from points on that line 1 foot/30.48cm on either side of the middle stump.

(d) Fast Short-pitched Balls

As a guide, a fast short-pitched ball is one which pitches short and passes, or would have passed, above the shoulder height of the striker standing in a normal batting stance at the crease.

(e) Time Wasting by Batsmen

Other than in exceptional circumstances, the batsman should always be ready to take strike when the bowler is ready to start his run-up.

CHANGE IN THE LAWS

The following change in the Laws of Cricket has been made since the publication of *Wisden* in 1993.

Law 42.9 (Unfair Play) Previously a fast high full-pitched ball was defined as one that passed, or would have passed, above shoulder height of the striker in a normal batting stance. The umpire at the bowler's end adopted the procedure of caution, final warning, action against the bowler and reporting as in 42.8 if satisfied that such a ball was bowled at the striker deliberately, but did not call or signal "no-ball".

REGULATIONS OF THE INTERNATIONAL CRICKET COUNCIL

Extracts

1. Playing Conditions

The official Laws of Cricket shall be followed on all tours unless an agreement to meet special cases is arrived at between the Members concerned before the visiting team commences the first match of any tour.

2. Classification of First-class Matches

1. Definitions

A match of three or more days' duration between two sides of 11 players officially adjudged first-class shall be regarded as a first-class fixture.

2. Rules

(a) Full Members of ICC shall decide the status of matches of three or more days' duration played in their countries.

(b) In matches of three or more days' duration played in countries which are not Full Members of ICC:

    (i) If the visiting team comes from a country which is a Full Member of ICC, that country shall decide the status of matches.

    (ii) If the visiting team does not come from a country which is a Full Member of ICC, or is a Commonwealth team composed of players from different countries, ICC shall decide the status of matches.

Notes

(a) Governing bodies agree that the interest of first-class cricket will be served by ensuring that first-class status is *not* accorded to any match in which one or other of the teams taking part cannot on a strict interpretation of the definition be adjudged first-class.

(b) In case of any disputes arising from these Rules, the Secretary of ICC shall refer the matter for decision to the Council, failing unanimous agreement by postal communication being reached.

3. First-class Status

The following matches shall be regarded as first-class, subject to the provisions of 1(a) being completely complied with:

(a) **In the British Isles:** (i) County Championship matches. (ii) Official representative tourist matches from Full Member countries unless specifically excluded. (iii) MCC v any first-class county. (iv) Oxford v Cambridge and either University against first-class counties. (v) Scotland v Ireland.

(b) **In Australia:** (i) Sheffield Shield matches. (ii) Matches played by teams representing states of the Commonwealth of Australia between each other or against opponents adjudged first-class.

(c) **In India:** (i) Ranji Trophy matches. (ii) Duleep Trophy matches. (iii) Irani Trophy matches. (iv) Matches played by teams representing state or regional associations affiliated to the Board of Control between each other or against opponents adjudged first-class. (v) All three-day matches played against representative visiting sides.

(d) **In New Zealand:** (i) Shell Trophy matches. (ii) Matches played by teams representing major associations of the North and South Islands, between each other or against opponents adjudged first-class.

(e) **In Pakistan:** (i) Matches played by teams representing divisional associations affiliated to the Board of Control, between each other or against teams adjudged first-class. (ii) Matches between the divisional associations and the Universities Past and Present XI. (iii) Quaid-e-Azam Trophy matches. (iv) BCCP Patron's Trophy matches.

(f) **In South Africa:** (i) Castle Cup competition four-day matches between Transvaal, Northern Transvaal, OFS, Western Province, Eastern Province, Border and Natal. Boland joined the competition in 1993-94. (ii) The United Cricket Board Bowl competition three-day cricket between Eastern Transvaal, Western Transvaal, Griqualand West and Boland. Boland left the competition in 1993-94.

(g) **In Sri Lanka:** (i) Matches of three days or more against touring sides adjudged first-class. (ii) Singer Inter-Provincial Cricket tournament matches played over three days for the President's Trophy. (iii) Inter-Club Division I tournament matches played over three days for the P. Saravanamuttu Trophy. (iv) Super Tournament matches played over four days for the Coca Cola Bottlers' Trophy.

(h) **In West Indies:** Matches played by teams representing Barbados, Guyana, Jamaica, Trinidad & Tobago, the Windward Islands and the Leeward Islands, either for the Red Stripe Cup or against other opponents adjudged first-class.

(i) **In all Full Member countries represented on the Council:** (i) Test matches and matches against teams adjudged first-class played by official touring teams. (ii) Official Test Trial matches. (iii) Special matches between teams adjudged first-class by the governing body or bodies concerned.

3. Classification of Limited-overs International Matches

The following should be classified as limited-overs internationals:

(a) All matches played between the Full Member countries of ICC as part of an official tour itinerary.

(b) All matches played as part of an official tournament by Full Member countries. These need not necessarily be held in a Full Member country.

(c) All matches played in the official World Cup competition, including matches involving Associate Member countries.

(d) All matches played in the Asia Cup competition.

4. Qualification Rules for Test Matches and Limited-overs International Matches

Qualification by Birth

A cricketer is qualified to play cricket for the country of his birth provided he has not played cricket for any other Member country during the two immediately preceding years.

Qualification by Residence

A cricketer is qualified to play cricket for any Full or Associate Member country in which he has resided for at least 183 days in each of the four immediately preceding years provided that in each such case he has not played cricket for any other Member country during that period of four years.

Member Countries May Impose More Stringent Rules

The governing body for cricket of any Member country may impose more stringent qualification rules for that country.

REGULATIONS OF ICC FULL MEMBERS

Extracts

Duration of Test Matches

Within a maximum of 30 hours' playing time, the duration of Test matches shall be a matter for negotiation and agreement between the two countries in any particular series of Test matches.

When agreeing the Playing Conditions prior to the commencement of a Test series, the participating countries may:

(a) Extend the playing hours of the last Test beyond the limit of 30 hours, in a series in which, at the conclusion of the penultimate match, one side does not hold a lead of more than one match.

(b) In the event of play being suspended for any reason other than normal intervals, extend the playing time on that day by the amount of time lost up to a maximum of one hour, except in the last hour of the match.

(c) Play on the rest day, conditions and circumstances permitting, should a full day's play be lost on either the second or third scheduled days of play.

(d) Make up time lost in excess of five minutes in each day's play owing to circumstances outside the game, other than acts of God.

Note: The umpires shall determine when such time shall be made up. This could, if conditions and circumstances permit, include the following day.

Minimum Overs in the Day in Test Matches

Regulation for Test matches only.

(a) Play shall continue on each day until the completion of a minimum number of overs or until the scheduled cessation time, whichever is the later. The minimum number of overs to be completed, unless an innings ends or an interruption occurs, shall be:

(i) on days other than the last day – a minimum of 90 overs.

(ii) on the last day – a minimum of 75 overs (or 15 overs per hour) for playing time other than the last hour when a minimum of 15 six-ball overs shall be bowled. All calculations with regard to suspensions of play or the start of a new innings shall be based on one over for each full four minutes. If, however, at any time after 30 minutes of the last hour have elapsed both captains (the batsmen at the wicket may act for their captain) accept that there is no prospect of a result to the match, they may agree to cease play at that time.

Penalties for Slow Over-rates

(i) Test Matches

Over-rates shall be assessed on 15 overs per hour, i.e. a minimum of 90 overs in a six-hour day, subject to the following deductions:

Two minutes per wicket taken;
Actual time where treatment by authorised medical personnel is required on the ground, and also for a player leaving the field owing to serious injury;
Four minutes for one drinks break per session, except in the West Indies, where it is accepted that an additional drinks break should be permitted.

Overs will be calculated at the end of the match. For each over short of the target number, five per cent of each player's match fee in the fielding side is to be deducted.

(ii) Limited-overs International Matches

The target over-rate is to be 15 overs per hour. In the event of the target over-rate not being reached, for each over short of the number required to be bowled in the scheduled time, the fielding side will be fined an amount equal to five per cent of each player's match fee.

For touring teams where a tour fee is paid, the match fee will be taken to be the match fee paid by the touring team's country in its previous domestic season.

A penalty may be reviewed by the match referee if, after consultation with the umpires, he is of the opinion that events beyond the control of the fielding side, including time-wasting by the batting side, prevented that team from bowling the required number of overs. The batting side may be fined at the same rate as the fielding side if, in the opinion of the match referee, the batting side is guilty of slowing down the over-rate.

If the team fielding first fails to bowl the required number of overs by the scheduled time for cessation of the first session, play shall continue until the required number of overs has been bowled.

Unless otherwise determined by the referee, the innings of the team batting second shall be limited to the same number of overs bowled by it, at the scheduled time for cessation of the first session. The over in progress at the scheduled cessation time shall count as a completed over.

The interval shall not be extended and the second session shall commence at the scheduled time.

The referee may increase the number of overs to be bowled by the team bowling second if, after consultation with the umpires, he is of the opinion that events beyond the control of the bowling team prevented that team from bowling the required number of overs by the scheduled time for the cessation of the innings of the team batting first.

THE BOWLING OF FAST, SHORT-PITCHED BALLS: LAW 42.8

Experimental Regulation for Test matches only for three years
with effect from October 1, 1991

A bowler shall be limited to one fast, short-pitched ball per over per batsman. If this limit is exceeded, the following procedure shall be applied:

(a) If a bowler delivers a second fast, short-pitched ball in an over to the same batsman, the umpire shall call and signal "no-ball" and indicate the reason to the bowler, to the captain of the fielding side and to the other umpire.

(b) If a bowler is no-balled a second time in the innings for the same offence, the umpire shall warn the bowler, indicate to him that this is a final warning, and inform the captain of the fielding side and the other umpire of what has occurred.

(c) If the bowler is no-balled a third time in the same innings for the same offence, the umpire shall:

(i) As soon as the ball is dead, direct the captain of the fielding side to take the bowler off forthwith and to complete the over with another bowler, provided that the bowler does not bowl two overs, or part thereof, consecutively;

(ii) Not allow the bowler, thus taken off, to bowl in the same innings;

(iii) Report the occurrence to the captain of the batting side as soon as the players leave the field for an interval;

(iv) Report the occurrence immediately after the day's play to the management of the fielding side and to the governing body responsible for the match, who shall take any further action which is considered to be appropriate against the bowler concerned.

Definition

A fast, short-pitched ball shall be defined as a ball which passes, or would have passed, above the shoulder of the batsman standing upright at the crease.

BALL LOST OR BECOMING UNFIT FOR PLAY: LAW 5.5

Experimental Law

In the event of a ball during play being lost or, in the opinion of the umpires, being unfit for play through normal use, the umpires shall allow it to be replaced by one that in their opinion has had a similar amount of wear. If the ball is to be replaced, the umpires shall inform the batsmen.

PRACTICE ON THE FIELD: LAW 15.2

Experimental Law

At no time on any day of the match shall there be any bowling or batting practice on the pitch. In addition there shall be no bowling or batting practice on any part of the square or the area immediately adjacent to the match pitch after the commencement of play on any day. Any fielder contravening this Law may not bowl the next over.

No practice may take place on the field if, in the opinion of the umpires, it could result in a waste of time.

ICC CODE OF CONDUCT

1. The captains are responsible at all times for ensuring that play is conducted within the spirit of the game as well as within the Laws.

2. Players and team officials shall not at any time engage in conduct unbecoming to an international player or team official which could bring them or the game into disrepute.

3. Players and team officials must at all times accept the umpire's decision. Players must not show dissent at the umpire's decision.

4. Players and team officials shall not intimidate, assault or attempt to intimidate or assault an umpire, another player or a spectator.

5. Players and team officials shall not use crude or abusive language (known as "sledging") nor make offensive gestures.

6. Players and team officials shall not use or in any way be concerned in the use or distribution of illegal drugs.

7. Players and team officials shall not disclose or comment upon any alleged breach of the Code or upon any hearing, report or decision arising from such breach.

8. Players and team officials shall not make any public pronouncement or media comment which is detrimental either to the game in general; or to a particular tour in which they are involved; or about any tour between other countries which is taking place; or to relations between the Boards of the competing teams.

Application, Interpretation and Enforcement of the Code

1. The Code shall apply:

    (a) To players and, where applicable, to team officials of both teams for all Test matches and limited-overs international matches;

    (b) To players and, where applicable, to team officials of official touring teams for all matches, other than Test matches and limited-overs internationals ("other matches") with such modifications as ICC shall consider necessary in the absence of a match referee for other matches.

2. Breaches of the Code shall be deemed also to include a breach of any ICC Regulation in force from time to time, including (without limitation) those relating to advertising on cricket clothing and equipment, and, in Test matches, those relating to minimum over-rates.

3. The Code, breach of which may render a player or team official liable to disciplinary action, shall be enforced:

    (a) In the case of Test matches and limited-overs internationals in accordance with procedures and guidelines laid down for the match referee; and

    (b) In the case of other matches, in such manner as ICC shall consider appropriate at the time when the incident occurs. This shall, so far as is practicable, follow the procedures and guidelines laid down for the match referee.

Note: In 1992 ICC decided that the Code should also apply to Associate and Affiliate members of ICC but ruled that "application, interpretation and enforcement shall be determined in the way deemed most suitable by those concerned with the running of the game at these levels".

    ICC also ruled that breaches of Clause 8 of the Code of Conduct (public pronouncements) should be dealt with by match referees during a tour (except where related to a non-international match) and the home board of the player or official concerned in other circumstances.

ICC MATCH REFEREE

Extracts

1. Objective

To act on behalf of ICC to:

    (a) see that the full implications of Law 42.1 are properly understood and upheld; and

    (b) to ensure that the spirit of the game is observed and the conduct of the game maintained during Test matches and limited-overs internationals by players, umpires and team officials, either on or off the field, his responsibility being confined to the precincts of the ground.

2. Terms of Reference

    (a) To be the independent representative of ICC (appointed by the Chairman or, in his absence, the Secretary, after consultation with the Boards concerned), at all Test matches and limited-overs internationals, the latter being part of a Test match tour, respecting the authority of the host country which is promoting a series, or the ground authority which is administering a match or series of matches.

(b) To liaise with the appointed umpires, but not in any way to interfere with their traditional role.

(c) To carry out the following duties:

(i) Observe and adjudicate upon breaches of the Code of Conduct.

(ii) Impose penalties for failure to maintain the minimum over-rate as set by ICC (presently 15 overs per hour).

(iii) Impose penalties for deliberate acts of unfair play, e.g. the deliberate slowing-down of over-rates and the deliberate speeding-up of overs to make up for any shortfall during a day's play.

(iv) Impose penalties for infringements of the ICC Regulation relating to advertising on cricket clothing and equipment.

(v) Impose penalties incurred under any other ICC Regulation which may be passed from time to time and which falls within the Terms of Reference.

(vi) Ensure the conduct of the game is upheld by the umpires in accordance with the Laws of Cricket and the Playing Conditions as agreed by the two Boards concerned in a series, and to give support to the umpires in this regard if required.

3. Method of Operation

The match referee must be present on all days of the match or matches assigned to him from the time the players arrive within the precincts of the ground until a reasonable time after close of play, bearing in mind that reports can be submitted up to one hour after the end of the day's play. He must ensure, in conjunction with the ground authority, that he has a good view of the match and has access to a television monitor and video equipment.

The match referee must lay down the standards expected from the players, making it clear that the captains are responsible for their teams and for the good conduct of the game. The match referee must make it clear that *no* public criticism of the umpires will be tolerated.

The match referee must not interfere with the traditional role of umpires but should urge umpires to be decisive in upholding the Law.

4. Disciplinary Procedures

Should an umpire decide to report a player for an alleged breach of the Code of Conduct or other offence, he must inform the player's captain or manager and the match referee of his intention at the earliest opportunity and complete a report and hand it to the match referee not later than one hour after the close of the day's play . . . the match referee's decision is final.

5. Penalties

The referee may in his absolute discretion impose any penalty by way of reprimand and/or fine and/or suspension.

(a) Maximum fine to be imposed for breaches of the Code of Conduct and other ICC Regulations (excluding over-rates) – 75 per cent of a player's match fee.

When a player is on tour, the fine shall be calculated on the last match fee paid to that player in his previous domestic season. If a player did not participate in an international match during his previous domestic season, that player shall be fined on the basis which would have applied had he played in an international match in his previous domestic season.

(b) Maximum suspension to be imposed for breaches of the Code of Conduct and other ICC Regulations – three Test matches.

If any matches of international standard take place between Test matches, the ban will also include these. This ban may well carry over into a future series. In a series of one-day internationals, the maximum suspension will be three internationals but may not be carried over. A player's participation in his own domestic cricket during the period of any ban imposed by the ICC match referee will be up to his own Board to determine.

6. Payment of Fines

Fines must be paid within one calendar month by the player(s) to his (their) Board who will, in turn, forward such fine(s) to the Secretary of ICC. Any player(s) failing to meet this requirement will be rendered unavailable for selection in any fixture under the control of his (their) own Board.

INTERNATIONAL UMPIRES' PANEL

On December 21, the International Cricket Council announced the formation of an international umpires' panel, backed by £1.1 million sponsorship over three years from National Grid. Each Full Member of ICC was to nominate two officials – apart from England, who named four, because of their large number of professional umpires and the fact that most Tests take place during the English winter. A third-country member of the panel was to stand with a "home" umpire, not necessarily from the panel, in every Test staged from February 1994. Teams would have no right of objection to appointments.

The following umpires were appointed to serve on the panel until the end of September: B. L. Aldridge (New Zealand), L. H. Barker (West Indies), H. D. Bird (England), S. A. Bucknor (West Indies), B. C. Cooray (Sri Lanka), R. S. Dunne (New Zealand), K. T. Francis (Sri Lanka), D. B. Hair (Australia), K. Kanjee (Zimbabwe), Khizar Hayat (Pakistan), S. B. Lambson (South Africa), K. E. Liebenberg (South Africa), Mahboob Shah (Pakistan), K. E. Palmer (England), N. T. Plews (England), V. K. Ramaswamy (India), S. G. Randell (Australia), I. D. Robinson (Zimbabwe), D. R. Shepherd (England), S. Venkataraghavan (India).

REGULATIONS FOR FIRST-CLASS MATCHES IN BRITAIN, 1993

Hours of Play

1st, 2nd, 3rd days.... 11.00 a.m. to 6.30 p.m. or after 110 overs, whichever is the later.
4th day .... 11.00 a.m. to 6.00 p.m. or after 102 overs, whichever is the later.

Non-Championship matches:

1st, 2nd days....... 11.30 a.m. to 6.30 p.m. (11.00 a.m. to 6.30 p.m. or after 104 overs, whichever is the later, in tourist matches)
3rd day .... 11.00 a.m. to 6.00 p.m. (or after 96 overs in tourist matches)

Note: The hours of play, including intervals, are brought forward by half an hour for matches in September.

(a) If play is suspended (including any interval between innings) the minimum number of overs to be bowled in a day is reduced by one over for each $3\frac{1}{2}$ minutes or part thereof of such suspension or suspensions in aggregate (including the last hour).

(b) If at 5.00 p.m. on the final day, 19 overs or less remain to be bowled, the umpires shall indicate that play shall continue until a minimum of a further 20 overs has been bowled, or until 6.00 p.m., whichever is the later (a minimum of 16 overs must be bowled in tourist matches). Play may cease on the final day at any time between 5.30 p.m. and 6.00 p.m. by mutual agreement of the captains. Should an innings end between 4.50 p.m. and 5.00 p.m., the time at the end of the ten-minute interval to replace 5.00 p.m. (all timings brought forward by half an hour for matches in September).

(c) The captains may agree or, in the event of disagreement, the umpires may decide to play 30 minutes (a minimum ten overs, or eight in tourist matches) extra time at the end of the first and/or second day's play (and/or the third day of four) if, in their opinion, it would bring about a definite result on that day. In the event of the possibility of a finish disappearing before the full period has expired, the whole period must be played out. Any time so claimed does not affect the timing for cessation of play on the final day.

(d) The minimum number of overs remaining to be bowled in the day shall be shown on the scoreboard.

(*e*) If an innings ends during the course of an over, that part shall count as a full over so far as the minimum number of overs per day is concerned.

(*f*) Notwithstanding any other provision, there shall be no further play on any day, other than the last day, if a wicket falls during the last minimum over within two minutes of the scheduled cessation time or thereafter.

(*g*) If play is suspended for the day in the middle of an over, that over must be completed next day in addition to the minimum overs required that day.

Intervals

Lunch: 1.15 p.m. to 1.55 p.m. (1st, 2nd [3rd] days) in Championship and tourist matches, 1.30 p.m. to 2.10 p.m. in others
1.00 p.m. to 1.40 p.m. (final day)
In the event of lunch being taken early because of a stoppage caused by weather or bad light (Law 16.2), the interval shall be limited to 40 minutes.

Tea: 4.10 p.m. to 4.30 p.m. (1st, 2nd [3rd] days); or when 40 overs remain to be bowled, whichever is the later. 3.40 p.m. to 4.00 p.m. (final day), or when 40 overs remain to be bowled, whichever is the later. If an innings ends or there is a stoppage caused by weather within 30 minutes of the scheduled time, the tea interval shall be taken immediately. There will be no tea interval if the scheduled timing for the cessation of play is earlier than 5.30 p.m.

Substitutes

(Domestic matches only) Law 2.1 will apply, but in addition:

No substitute may take the field until the player for whom he is to substitute has been absent from the field for five consecutive complete overs, with the exception that if a fieldsman sustains an obvious, serious injury or is taken ill, a substitute shall be allowed immediately. In the event of any disagreement between the two sides as to the seriousness of an injury or illness, the umpires shall adjudicate. If a player leaves the field during an over, the remainder of that over shall not count in the calculation of the five complete overs.

A substitute shall be allowed by right immediately in the event of a cricketer currently playing in a Championship match being required to join the England team for a Test match (or one-day international). Such a substitute may be permitted to bat or bowl in that match, subject to the approval of the TCCB. The player who is substituted may not take further part in the match, even though he might not be required by England. If batting at the time, the player substituted shall be retired "not out" and his substitute may be permitted to bat later in that innings subject to the approval of the TCCB.

Fieldsman Leaving the Field

(Domestic matches only) No fieldsman shall leave the field or return during a session of play without the consent of the umpire at the bowler's end. The umpire's consent is also necessary if a substitute is required for a fieldsman at the start of play or when his side returns to the field after an interval.

If a member of the fielding side does not take the field at the start of play, leaves the field, or fails to return after an interval and is absent from the field longer than 15 minutes, he shall not bowl in that innings after his return until he has been on the field for at least the length of playing time for which he was absent; nor shall he be permitted to bat unless or until, in the aggregate, he has returned to the field and/or his side's innings has been in progress for at least the length of playing time for which he was absent or, if earlier, when his side has lost five wickets. The restrictions shall not apply if he has been absent for exceptional and acceptable reasons (other than injury or illness) and consent for a substitute has been granted by the opposing captain.

New ball

The captain of the fielding side shall have the choice of taking the new ball after 100 overs (85 in tourist matches) have been bowled with the old one.

Covering of Pitches and Bowler's Run-up

The whole pitch shall be covered:

    (a) The night before a match and, if necessary, until the first ball is bowled; and whenever necessary and possible at any time prior to that during the preparation of the pitch.

    (b) On each night of a match and, if necessary, throughout any rest days.

    (c) In the event of play being suspended because of bad light or rain, during the hours of play.

The bowler's run-up shall be covered to a distance of at least ten yards, with a width of four yards.

Declarations

Law 14 will apply, but, in addition, a captain may also forfeit his first innings, subject to the provisions set out in Law 14.2. If, owing to weather conditions, a County Championship match has not started when fewer than eight hours of playing time remain, the first innings of each side shall automatically be forfeited and a one-innings match played.

MEETINGS IN 1993

MCC SPECIAL GENERAL MEETING

The Marylebone Cricket Club, at a meeting in Central Hall, Westminster, on January 27, rejected a vote of no confidence in the England Test selectors over the choice of players for the tour of India and Sri Lanka. Dennis Silk, the MCC president, announced that the motion had been defeated by 6,135 votes (57.1 per cent) to 4,600 with 40 spoiled ballots, one forgery and a donation of £1.50 towards the cost of the meeting. However, most members had voted by post; those attending the meeting supported the motion by 715 to 412. The meeting had been called by the signatures of more than 200 members opposed to the omission of David Gower, in particular, and also Jack Russell and Ian Salisbury from the original touring party. Dennis Oliver, a businessman from Kent, began the revolt. He was supported by Lord Bonham Carter and Lord Gilmour, a former Cabinet minister, who attacked the selectors' refusal to justify their decisions: "We all know the cry My Country Right or Wrong. Now we have My Selectors Right or Wrong." The main speakers against the motion were Hubert Doggart, the former MCC treasurer, Field Marshal Lord Bramall and the previous MCC president, Lord Griffiths. Lord Bramall defended the omissions and the role of the England captain Graham Gooch: "What commander worth his salt does not want to have some right to decide the men he wants to take with him into the fray?"

ICC SPECIAL MEETING

The International Cricket Council special meeting at Lord's on February 2 awarded the sixth World Cup, scheduled for 1995, to India, Pakistan and Sri Lanka, who submitted a joint bid. However, the decision came late at night after the Test and County Cricket Board withdrew their bid to break a deadlock. Only one of the other six Test-playing countries, Zimbabwe, supported the sub-continent's bid but it was believed that a majority of Associate Members were in favour. Under ICC rules this meant neither of the rivals could get sufficient votes. A. C. Smith, chief executive of the TCCB, called the meeting "a shambles" and said: "We endured a fractious and unpleasant meeting beset by procedural wrangling. There was no talk of anything like cricket. It was, by a long way, the worst meeting I have ever attended." The TCCB withdrew its bid on condition England staged the seventh World Cup in 1998. It was agreed that in future there would be a rota, with the Cup being held every three years, and it was understood that South Africa would stage the eighth, in 2001. David Richards, the chief executive of the Australian Cricket Board, was elected as chief executive of ICC. The Council also voted that the rebel tours of South Africa between 1982 and 1990 should not be regarded as first-class. This decision was greeted with virtually unanimous opposition by statisticians.

TCCB SPRING MEETING

At its spring meeting, on March 9, 10, the Test and County Cricket Board discussed England's defeat in the Test series in India with Ted Dexter, the chairman of the England committee. There had been advance press reports that Dexter might face strong condemnation from the counties. A. C. Smith, the TCCB's chief executive, said the positions of Dexter, Keith Fletcher, the manager, and Graham Gooch, the captain, were not discussed. There had been two areas of disquiet: the "personal appearance" of some of the players and shortcomings in skill. The Board decided that the square-leg umpire should inspect the ball after every over in county cricket to prevent ball-tampering; the batsman would have the right to choose from six balls, including a new one, if there was evidence of tampering. The Board said £62,500 had been refunded to about 4,000 ticket-holders dissatisfied at seeing only two balls' play on the second day of the Edgbaston Test in 1992. In the Sunday League, teams would not be allowed more than two fielders outside the circle for the first 15 overs. Ireland were invited to join the Benson and Hedges Cup in 1994. Dennis Amiss was re-elected a Test selector for 1993.

MCC ANNUAL GENERAL MEETING

The president of the Marylebone Cricket Club, Dennis Silk, told the 206th annual general meeting, at Lord's on May 5, that, following the special meeting in January, MCC had decided to appoint a working party, under the chairmanship of Lord Griffiths, to consolidate the club's point of view on the question of England selection. He said this had the full support of the TCCB, which recognised the degree of unease among cricket followers on the subject. The chairman of finance, David Hudd, presenting the accounts, said income from commercial activities, particularly perimeter advertising, had suffered because of the economic recession and that the committee therefore proposed a five per cent increase in annual subscriptions. Hudd said it was important to keep adding to the club's investments to improve facilities, particularly to keep open the possibility of further development of the Nursery End. The annual surplus was £717,000 before tax, of which £199,000 had been paid in grants and assistance to the Cricket Foundation, the National Coaching Scheme and ICC amongst others. The president did not name a successor as he was serving a two-year term. Membership of the club on December 31, 1992, was 19,277, made up of 16,834 full members, 1,873 associate members, 490 honorary members and 80 senior members. There were 9,511 candidates awaiting election. In 1992, 512 vacancies arose, 290 caused by death, 118 by resignation and 104 by lapsing. At a special general meeting immediately after the AGM, members approved a revised Law of Cricket, in relation to the bowling of fast high full pitches, to replace the existing Law 42.9.

ICC ANNUAL MEETING

The International Cricket Council's annual meeting, at Lord's on July 6, 7, elected the former West Indian batsman Clyde Walcott, aged 67, as the first non-British chairman of ICC, to succeed Sir Colin Cowdrey on October 1. He was to work closely with ICC's new chief executive, David Richards, who took office after the meeting. England (formerly known as United Kingdom within ICC) and Australia relinquished their status and vetoes as Foundation Members, but it was agreed that issues designated as "important" would in future need the support of threequarters of the Full Members, i.e. seven out of nine, rather than two-thirds. The principle of electronic umpiring was extended to all countries, if the facilities were available. It was agreed to consider the rules for qualification of Test players, in the wake of the controversy of Martin McCague's selection for England, though no steps were taken. Ireland were accepted as Associate Members but applications by Scotland, Thailand and Nepal were deferred for a year. The ICC re-affirmed its decision in February that it considered rebel tours of South Africa were not first-class. It was decided to implement the principle that one umpire from a non-participating country should stand in each Test match, subject to the funding being available. National Grid, who sponsored the experiments with this system in 1992-93, were to fund the first-ever meeting of Test umpires, to be held in Coventry in August. An ICC cricket committee was appointed to comprise Walcott as chairman, Cowdrey and Doug Insole from England, Ali Bacher of South Africa, Steve Camacho of West Indies, Bob Cowper of Australia, Sunil Gavaskar of

India, Imran Khan of Pakistan, Joe Buzaglo of Gibraltar representing the Associate Members, and Richards. It was decided to continue the experimental law permitting only one bouncer per batsman per over for another year, until the end of its planned three-year period.

TCCB SUMMER MEETING

The Test and County Cricket Board's summer meeting, held at Lord's on August 17, was dominated by the crisis caused by England's succession of Test match defeats. Ted Dexter, who had announced his resignation as chairman of the England committee eight days earlier, made what he called "a plea from the heart" and said the TCCB should ask itself "whether the counties represent the 18 centres of excellence they should be ... if we are to succeed, money needs investing and energy devoted – and trust given – to the England committee". Dexter's resignation averted what was expected to be an attack on his position following a campaign led by Chris Middleton, chairman of Derbyshire. The Board made no decision on Dexter's replacement. "Today's meeting hasn't resolved to do nothing, it's resolved to do plenty," said A. C. Smith, the Board's chief executive. "But getting it right is more important than hasty decisions."

COMMONWEALTH GAMES FEDERATION

The Commonwealth Games Federation, meeting in Victoria, British Columbia, on October 2, accepted in principle a proposal from the Malaysian hosts to include cricket for the first time in the Games to be held in Kuala Lumpur in September 1998. The plan is subject to final approval of ICC. The Federation said teams would compete as Commonwealth Games entities rather than as ICC members. They would thus include the major Test-playing countries except West Indies, who would be replaced by individual islands, and South Africa, who are not in the Commonwealth. Other entrants might also include Jersey and the Isle of Man. The possibility of restricting participation to players under a certain age was to be discussed between Games and ICC officials.

MCC PRESS CONFERENCE

At a press conference at Lord's on November 18, Dennis Silk, the president of MCC, announced a new scheme to help boys on the MCC cricket staff further their education. Future MCC Young Cricketers will be offered a choice between a "summer only" cricket contract and one offering three summers of cricket and two winters of education. In the winters, the players would study towards the General National Vocational Qualification at advanced level in Leisure and Tourism at the City of Westminster College. Players without the appropriate GCSE grades could take other courses. The new scheme is intended to protect the future of those Young Cricketers who do not go on to a career in county cricket.

TCCB WINTER MEETING

The Test and County Cricket Board's winter meeting, held at Lord's on December 8, 9, decided to split the duties of the England committee, established when Ted Dexter took over as chairman in 1989. The selection committee is to revert to something like its pre-Dexter format, comprising a chairman, the manager, two members elected by the Board, and the captain. A working party led by Frank Chamberlain and A. C. Smith, the Board chairman and chief executive, was set up to choose the new chairman before the March meeting. The England committee's other functions are to be undertaken by a development committee, with similar personnel to the old England committee. The Board decided to veer away from two of the changes to domestic cricket introduced in the Murray report. As expected, the Sunday League is to revert to a 40-over format in 1994 after only one season at 50, instead of the three proposed in the Murray Report, following constant complaints by players and others. The Benson and Hedges Cup is to return to some form of zonal system, to ensure each county at least one home tie, in 1995.

CRICKET ASSOCIATIONS AND SOCIETIES

AUCKLAND, CRICKET SOCIETY OF: J. H. Palmer, Eden Park, PO Box 2860, Auckland 1, New Zealand.

AUSTRALIAN CRICKET SOCIETY: D. Manning, Ravenstone, 240-246 Oban Road, North Ringwood, Victoria 3134, Australia.

BLACKLEY CRICKET SOCIETY: D. N. Butterfield, 7 Bayswater Terrace, Halifax, West Yorkshire HX3 0NB.

CAMBRIDGE UNIVERSITY CRICKET SOCIETY: R. Hayes, Downing College, Cambridge CB2 1DQ.

CHELTENHAM CRICKET SOCIETY: P. Murphy, 1 Colesbourne Road, Benhall, Cheltenham, Gloucestershire GL51 6DJ.

CHESTERFIELD CRICKET SOCIETY: J. S. Cook, 44 Morris Avenue, Newbold, Chesterfield, Derbyshire S41 7BA.

COUNCIL OF CRICKET SOCIETIES, THE: B. Rickson, 31 Grange Avenue, Cheadle Hulme, Cheshire SK8 5EN.

COUNTY SUPPORTERS ASSOCIATION: W. Horsley, 10 Delamere Road, Northampton NN4 9QG.

CRICKET MEMORABILIA SOCIETY: A. Sheldon, 29 Highclere Road, Crumpsall, Manchester M8 6WS.

CRICKET SOCIETY, THE: E. R. Budd, 16 Storey Court, 39 St John's Wood Road, London NW8 8QX.

CRICKET SOCIETY, THE (Midlands Branch): Dr A. A. Walker, "Sarnia", Hernes Nest, Bewdley, Worcester, Worcestershire DY12 2ET.

CRICKET STATISTICIANS AND HISTORIANS, ASSOCIATION OF: P. Wynne-Thomas, 3 Radcliffe Road, West Bridgford, Nottingham NG2 5FF.

CRICKET STATISTICIANS AND SCORERS OF INDIA, ASSOCIATION OF: Dr Vasant Naik, 102 B. Madhav Wadi, M.M.G. Road, Dadar, Bombay 400 014, India.

DERBYSHIRE CRICKET SOCIETY: P. J. Peek, 78 Suffolk Avenue, Chaddesden, Derby DE21 6ER.

DUKINFIELD CRICKET LOVERS' SOCIETY: F. Stafford, 17 Clarence Road, Wallasey, Wirral.

EAST RIDING CRICKET SOCIETY: S. J. Clarke, 12 Meadow Lane, Newport, North Humberside HU15 2QN.

ESSEX CRICKET SOCIETY: M. K. Smith, 321 Westbourne Grove, Westcliff-on-Sea, Essex SS0 0PU.

GLOUCESTERSHIRE CRICKET LOVERS' SOCIETY: M. Simpson, 318 Canford Lane, Westbury-on-Trym, Bristol BS9 3PL.

GOOD EGG CRICKET SOCIETY: R. Whitaker, c/o 15 Sunnyfield Avenue, Cliviger, Burnley, Lancashire.

HAMPSHIRE CRICKET SOCIETY: J. Moore, 85 Kingsway, Chandlers Ford, Eastleigh, Hampshire.

HEAVY WOOLLEN CRICKET SOCIETY: G. S. Cooper, 27 Milford Grove, Gomersal, Cleckheaton, West Yorkshire BO19 4BB.

INDIA, THE CRICKET SOCIETY OF: Sander Nakai, 1047 Pocket-B, Sector-A, Vasant Kunj, New Delhi 1120 030 India.

LANCASHIRE AND CHESHIRE CRICKET SOCIETY: H. W. Pardoe, "Crantock", 117a Barlow Moor Road, Didsbury, Manchester M20 2TS.

LINCOLNSHIRE CRICKET LOVERS' SOCIETY: C. Kennedy, 26 Eastwood Avenue, Great Grimsby, South Humberside DN34 5BE.

MERSEYSIDE CRICKET SOCIETY: W. T. Robins, 11 Yew Tree Road, Hunts Cross, Liverpool L25 9QN.

NEEDWOOD CRICKET LOVERS' SOCIETY: A. D. Campion, 45 Fallowfield Drive, Barton-under-Needwood, Staffordshire DE13 8DH.

NORFOLK CRICKET SOCIETY: D. Lester King, 3 Buckling Court, Recorder Road, Norwich, Norfolk NR1 1NW.

NORTHERN CRICKET SOCIETY: K. Harvey, 5 St Margaret's Drive, Gledhow Lane, Roundhay, Leeds, Yorkshire LS8 1RU.

NOTTINGHAM CRICKET LOVERS' SOCIETY: G. Blagdurn, 2 Inham Circus, Chilwell, Beeston, Nottingham NG9 4FN.

PAKISTAN ASSOCIATION OF CRICKET STATISTICIANS: Abid Ali Kazi, 5-A, II/I Sunset Lane, Phase II, Defence Housing Authority, Karachi 75500, Pakistan.

ROTHERHAM CRICKET SOCIETY: J. A. R. Atkin, 15 Gallow Tree Road, Rotherham, South Yorkshire S65 3FE.

SCOTLAND, CRICKET SOCIETY OF: A. J. Robertson, 5 Riverside Road, Eaglesham, Glasgow G76 0DQ.

SOMERSET WYVERNS: R. Keeley, 62 Schubert Road, Putney, London SW15 2QS.

SOUTH AFRICA, CRICKET SOCIETY OF: Mrs J. Gleason, PO Box 78040, Sandton, Transvaal 2146, South Africa.

STOURBRIDGE AND DISTRICT CRICKET SOCIETY: R. Barber, 6 Carlton Avenue, Pedmore, Stourbridge, West Midlands DY9 9ED.

SUSSEX CRICKET SOCIETY: Mrs P. Brabyn, 4 Wolstonbury Walk, Shoreham-by-Sea, West Sussex BN43 5GU.

SWISS CRICKET ASSOCIATION: Dr B. Pattison, 9 Ch. du Bois Contens, 1291 Commugny, Switzerland.

WEST LANCASHIRE CRICKET SOCIETY: G. O. Shipton, 9 Breeze Road, Southport, Lancashire PR8 2HG.

WOMBWELL CRICKET LOVERS' SOCIETY: J. Sokell, 42 Woodstock Road, Barnsley, South Yorkshire S75 1DX.

YORKSHIRE CCC SUPPORTERS' ASSOCIATION: R. C. Johnson, 38 Micklebring Lane, Braithwell, Rotherham, South Yorkshire S66 7AS.

ZIMBABWE, CRICKET SOCIETY OF: J. B. Stockwell, 6 Howard Close, Mount Pleasant, Harare, Zimbabwe.

ERRATA

WISDEN, 1938

Page 455   The match between Northamptonshire and Sussex was played at Kettering, not Northampton.

WISDEN, 1982

Page 921   In the Third Test between West Indies and England at Bridgetown, West Indies lost the first wicket of their second innings at 0, not 10.

WISDEN, 1989

Pages 578 and 579   Nottinghamshire's bowling figures in their match against Warwickshire at Birmingham on June 4, 6, 7, 1988 were as follows:

First Innings—Cooper 32–10–59–3; Cairns 25–2–89–4; Saxelby 22–5–92–0; Birch 10–3–34–0; Hemmings 9.2–4–12–1. *Second Innings*—Cooper 10–2–25–3; Cairns 5–1–20–0; Hemmings 10–0–45–1; Newell 1–0–11–0.

WISDEN, 1993

Page 25   Rev. M. D. Vockins, secretary of Worcestershire, was a member of the committee that produced the Murray Report.

Page 28   The England captain in *A Bit of a Test*, by Ben Travers, was Gilbert Augustus Pogson.

Page 865   The Under-19 County Festivals were not sponsored in 1992.

PART SIX: MISCELLANEOUS

CHRONICLE OF 1993

JANUARY

3 Allan Border becomes the second player to score 10,000 runs in Tests. **5** Brian Lara scores 277 in the Sydney Test, the fourth-highest Test score by a West Indian; in Hamilton, Waqar Younis and Wasim Akram bowl New Zealand out for 93 to give Pakistan victory in the one-off Test. **23** In Cuttack, Graham Gooch becomes the 23rd player to score 100 hundreds. **25** Javed Miandad replaced as Pakistan captain by Wasim Akram. **26** West Indies beat Australia in Adelaide by one run, the narrowest-ever victory in Test cricket. **27** MCC members reject a motion of no confidence in the England Test selectors, by 6,135 to 4,600.

FEBRUARY

1 Curtly Ambrose has spell of seven wickets for one in Perth Test to give West Indies 2-1 win in series. **2** India, Pakistan and Sri Lanka awarded the 1995 World Cup after acrimonious ICC meeting at Lord's; ICC decide that "rebel" tours of South Africa are not first-class and that Gooch has thus scored only 99 centuries. **20** Graeme Hick scores his maiden Test century in his 22nd innings. **23** India beat England by an innings and 15 runs in Bombay to complete a 3-0 whitewash. **26** In Christchurch, Border becomes the leading run-scorer in Test cricket, overtaking Sunil Gavaskar's 10,122.

MARCH

16 New Zealand batsman John Wright announces retirement after scoring 5,334 runs in 82 Tests. **18** Sri Lanka beat England for the first time in a Test match, by five wickets in Colombo. **25** Roger Knight named as the new secretary of MCC. **30** New South Wales win the Sheffield Shield for the 41st time.

APRIL

9 Four Pakistani Test players arrested on drug charges (later dropped) in Grenada. **14** Computerised scoring introduced to England, at The Parks and Fenner's.

MAY

1 Gooch reaches his 100th hundred on ICC reckoning, by hitting a six against Cambridge University. **9** The new AXA Equity & Law League in England begins with coloured clothes, white ball and umpires in blue coats;

umpire Don Oslear walks on to the field at Leicester with a crate of empty bottles shouting "Milko". **11** The first experiment in England using TV replays for line decisions takes place at The Oval. **14** Andrew Caddick of Somerset takes nine for 32 against Lancashire at Taunton, the best first-class bowling figures in England for 18 years.

JUNE

7 Gooch becomes the fifth Test player to be given out "handled the ball". **11** Harold Larwood, aged 88, made an MBE, more than 60 years after his last Test match. **12** Hick, aged 27 years 20 days, becomes the youngest player to complete 20,000 first-class runs. **16** Death of former Australian captain Lindsay Hassett, aged 79. **19** In the Lord's Test, Robin Smith becomes the first player given out by TV replay in England. **21** Australia extend their 59-year-old sequence of never losing a Lord's Test, winning to go 2-0 up in the Ashes series.

JULY

2 Viv Richards and Adrian Dale put on 425 for Glamorgan against Middlesex, the seventh-highest fourth-wicket stand ever, though Glamorgan eventually lose the match. **3** Australians given an official warning for their on-field behaviour during the Trent Bridge Test by referee Clive Lloyd. **6** Graham Thorpe becomes the first England player since 1973 to score a century in his first Test. **7** Clyde Walcott elected as the first non-British chairman of ICC and David Richards takes office as first non-British chief executive. **9** In a Second XI match against Yorkshire at Todmorden, Mark Harvey of Lancashire bowls 18 consecutive no-balls, all of which go to the boundary, in an attempt to expedite a declaration. **11** Sunday game between Leicestershire and Surrey at Grace Road abandoned because of a "dangerous" pitch. **19** Ian Botham bowls 11 overs of slow medium pace for Durham against the Australians and retires from first-class cricket; Glen Chapple of Lancashire scores a century in 21 minutes against helpful Glamorgan bowling at Old Trafford, 14 minutes faster than the genuine world record. **26** Australia beat England by an innings and 148 at Headingley to retain the Ashes; Gooch resigns as England captain; England bowler Neil Foster announces retirement, five weeks after playing in the Lord's Test. **28** Mike Atherton appointed to succeed Gooch.

AUGUST

1 England win the women's World Cup, beating New Zealand in the final at Lord's by 67 runs. **2** First-ever international seminar of Test match umpires. **9** England go 4-0 down in the Ashes series at Edgbaston; Ted Dexter announces resignation as chairman of the selectors. **23** England win the Sixth Test at The Oval, their first win over Australia since December 1986, to cut the final margin to 4-1.

SEPTEMBER

4 Warwickshire win the NatWest Trophy by five wickets, passing Sussex's 321 for six, which had been the highest total scored in a Lord's final, off the last ball. **19** Viv Richards is at the crease, the day before retiring from first-class cricket, as Glamorgan win the AXA Equity & Law League, their first trophy in 24 years; Derek Randall plays his last match for Nottinghamshire; Terence Lazard scores 307 for Boland against Western Province, beating Eric Rowan's 53-year-old record for the highest first-class score in South Africa.

OCTOBER

2 The Commonwealth Games Federation agrees in principle to include one-day cricket in the 1998 Games to be held in Kuala Lumpur. **6** The sale of Stuart Surridge, a family batmaking business for more than a century, is announced, along with closure of the factory at Witham, Essex. **18** England bowler Phil DeFreitas signs for Derbyshire, his third county in six years. **25** Lazard's South African record falls after only 36 days when Daryll Cullinan scores 337 not out for Transvaal against Northern Transvaal.

NOVEMBER

4 Border becomes the second Australian, after Sir Donald Bradman, to score 25,000 first-class runs. **13** David Gower announces his retirement from first-class cricket. **14** Peter Short of Barbados elected as president of the West Indies Cricket Board in succession to Clyde Walcott. **18** After four days and an estimated £100,000 costs, Sarfraz Nawaz drops his High Court libel action against his former Northamptonshire team-mate Allan Lamb. **20** In Edinburgh, Jeff Wilson, who made his one-day debut for New Zealand in March, becomes the first man this century to score three tries on his international rugby debut. **29** In Hobart, New Zealand lose to Australia by an innings and 222, their heaviest-ever Test defeat.

DECEMBER

21 ICC announce formation of international panel of umpires to stand as neutral-country representatives in every Test. **31** Lt-Col. John Stephenson retires as secretary of MCC and is awarded CBE.

The following were also among the cricketing items reported in the newspapers during 1993:

After researching the careers of 10,000 first-class cricketers, John Aggleton, a psychologist at the University of Durham, said that left-arm bowlers were likely to die two years earlier than right-armers. The former England left-arm spinner Phil Edmonds described the news as "depressing". (*Daily Telegraph*, February 17)

In keeping with a tradition dating back to Bradman's time, the Australian captain Allan Border was presented with a whortleberry pie by the Castle Hotel, Taunton. Unfortunately, the whortleberry was out of season on the Quantocks and the tradition was maintained only when a local man came up with a supply from his freezer. (*The Times*, May 8)

Railway enthusiasts paid £1 to buy an 81-year-old carriage which has recently been used as the pavilion at the Initial Laundry ground at Borrowash, Derbyshire. They aim to restore the carriage and run it on the private Keighley and Worth Valley Railway. (*Daily Telegraph*, May 11)

Eddie Bancroft, a seam bowler with size 16 feet who plays for Churchtown, Lancashire, received a £260 grant from the Foundation for Sport and the Arts to buy hand-made boots. (*Daily Telegraph*, May 13)

NEACO, a team from an aluminium fencing works, were bowled out for four by the Railway Tavern in the Malton Pub and Works Evening League. However, NEACO won the game because their opponents had broken the League's registration rules. (*The Guardian*, May 14)

Lord Griffiths, the former president of MCC, was elected captain of the Royal & Ancient Golf Club, to become the first person ever to hold both offices. (*Daily Telegraph*, May 20)

An elderly woman pushing her bicycle past the ground at Burghill, Herefordshire, was taken to hospital after being hit by a six in a game against Hay-on-Wye. "It was certainly very unlucky," said the Burghill club chairman Len Sparrow, "especially as the lad who hit it normally can't play leg-side." (*Hereford Times*, May 27)

A stray cockerel, thought to have escaped from nearby South Park Aviary, evaded the groundstaff and took up residence at Feethams, Darlington. (*Daily Telegraph*, May 31)

Ian Harris, of the Veryan club near Truro, who continued playing after losing a leg in a farm accident in 1987, was told by the Cornwall Umpires' Association that he could not bat with a runner under Law 2.5, which only covers injuries received during the match. MCC said their interpretation was over-zealous and the umpires relented. (*The Guardian*, June 15)

Rob Kelly, 24, a sausage factory worker from Chard, hit 11 sixes off consecutive balls for Buckland St Mary against Taunton Casuals in Division Three of the West Somerset League. (*Daily Express*, June 19)

Phil Bradford hit 216 off 60 balls, with 26 sixes, playing for Torquay Fire Brigade against ICI in the South Devon Cup. (*Daily Express*, June 19)

Andrew Flintoff, 15, a pupil at Ribbleton Hall High School, Preston, hit 234 not out in only 20 overs with 20 sixes and 20 fours, for St Anne's against Fulwood and Broughton. (*Daily Mirror*, June 19)

A lorry driver drove off the A1 and parked on the pitch at Wansford, Cambridgeshire, to protest after 16-year-old Shaz Aftab had smashed his windscreen with a six. "He was very uptight and wouldn't move until we had exchanged insurance particulars," said umpire John Ingham. (*The Guardian*, June 22)

Dave Cutting, 36, was bitten by an adder as he went out to bat at Hastings, Sussex. (*The Sun*, July 6)

John Jordison of Trent College took ten for seven, nine bowled and one lbw, including the hat-trick, in an Under-12 match against Oakham. (*The Times*, July 10)

More than 60 people offered to give a home to a stray mongrel who ran on to the pitch at Trent Bridge as Merv Hughes was about to deliver the first ball of the Third Test. Graham and Sally Bosnall from Derby, who adopted him, followed the example of the staff at the RSPCA shelter and called him Merv. (*Daily Telegraph*, July 12)

Les Kempster, 70, took ten for 34 (13–3–34–10), playing for an XI put together by the former Sussex player John Denman against Worth Abbey School at Crawley. Kempster is a part-time cleaner at the school. (*Daily Telegraph*, July 17)

Hayley Rose, 13, was top scorer for Isis Middle School, Oxford, who won the final of the Wrigley softball cricket tournament at Edgbaston. (*Observer*, July 18)

Two players from Flackwell Heath Cricket Club, Buckinghamshire, both took five wickets in five balls during the season: Leigh Atkinson and Matthew Ward, for the Under-15s. Ward went on to take seven wickets in eight balls. (*The Times*, August 7)

After ten years of legal arguments with residents, Jordans Cricket Club, Buckinghamshire, moved away from the village green to play on a nearby college ground. (*Daily Telegraph*, August 7)

A 20-stone man streaked across the pitch during a match between Cockerton and Durham for a £15 bet. (*The Sun*, August 15)

Shaheed Ramzan, 25, hit 113 not out in 25 minutes at Maidenhead, Berkshire, then apologised to opponents and drove off to a family wedding. (*The Sun*, August 16)

Ernie Jones, 46, set up house in the scorebox at Crewe and Nantwich CC, moving in a bed and wiring up lights to a car battery. (*Daily Mirror*, August 16)

Simon Penny, ten, took eight wickets in 11 overs for Stogumber, Somerset, against Roadwater. He normally plays for the club Under-13s but was called into the first team at the last minute. He missed the after-match celebrations because it was past his bedtime. (*Daily Telegraph*, August 18)

Four players from Fowey were banned by the Cornwall League after a fracas during a Division Five game at Tideford. Among them was the Fowey captain Vince Hathaway who came on to the pitch and allegedly frog-marched umpire David Martin to the pavilion after a run-out decision. An official said it was perhaps the worst incident in the League's 90 years; the Fowey secretary, Edward Leverton, said Hathaway had only propelled the umpire backwards for about ten yards. (*Cornish Guardian*, September 16)

Despite many protests, the name of the Bat and Ball pub at Broadhalf-penny Down, traditional resort of the Hambledon players, was changed by the landlord to Natterjacks. (*Daily Telegraph*, December 2)

CRICKET BOOKS, 1993

By GEOFFREY MOORHOUSE

The publishing recession has once again reduced the number of titles submitted for review, with a notably higher proportion than before coming out of Sydney and surrounding district. What hasn't changed much is the ratio of excellent to unremarkable to utterly disposable books on cricket, a statistic that has rarely figured in anyone's assessment of the game and its attendant culture. Too often, too many of us have been over-impressed by the vast amount of writing cricket has generated, mistaking sheer bulk for guaranteed quality.

The one genre that seems to be holding its own in hard times is the biography of someone still playing or very recently retired, which is not my favourite form of cricket literature on several counts. Such books seldom tell much worth knowing about the man's life outside his profession or about his attitudes to anything except the game; they are so dense with match descriptions and statistics I've already read not long ago in newsprint, that I soon begin to skip page after page; and I'm usually left with a feeling that what would interest me most about this fellow is his next forty years rather than his cricketing career. They are, in short, discouragingly limited by their subject matter, when my only reason for reading any narrative is in hope of revelation, insight, imagination, wit, and a way with words that goes some distance beyond mere literacy. I wouldn't, myself, dream of trying to write more than an essay about a current sportsman: I'm impressed by the self-confidence of those who do.

Like Rob Steen, whose **Desmond Haynes: Lion of Barbados** is a cut above most texts of its kind, though he sometimes tries too hard to enliven an old tale. Thus, Michael Holding "took careful aim with his right boot and divorced the batsman's stumps from their moorings" during the 1980 Dunedin Test. I think not. More importantly, however, Steen never forgets the wider world in which Haynes's batting has entertained us all these past fifteen years. Inter-Caribbean tensions throb in the background of Desi's Test career and the issue of race is permanently there. It is at its most unpleasant whenever the West Indians are playing the Australians and scarcely an over seems to pass without dirty abuse or malicious bowling, the bullies on both sides encouraged by inferior captaincy. The superb series between Benaud's and Worrell's teams might never have been, for all that more recent combatants appear to understand the meaning of fierce but colour-blind rivalry. The West Indians believe that the white cricketing lands have lately ganged up against them on the subject of intimidation. As Haynes himself puts it: "One of my greatest sources of pride is to have been part of a side that kept winning while the world tried to change the rules to stop us." Still, he comes across as a likeable man, without Richards's mean streak or Lloyd's fundamental ambivalence: I doubt if he has ambitions to become an English Tory councillor. But even the good boys conform to the spirit of the times occasionally. Haynes makes his first entrance just after he has "promptly popped off a lawyer's letter to [David] Frith". That's another reason why I wouldn't try to emulate Rob Steen. Lawyers are what the rich or powerful reach for when they're not getting their own way; and Test cricketers now earn enough to become dangerously petulant under criticism.

Michael Holding has produced his own Life and Times ("with", as they coyly say, Tony Cozier) in **Whispering Death**. He tells us that every foreign Test captain became a special target of the West Indian quickies after Tony Greig made his infamous "grovel" remark, and he glides effortlessly and unrepentantly past the assault and battery of Old Trafford in 1976. He rather likes to have things both ways, bleakly noting that "Test cricket is a rugged business and captains need to be mentally strong" when Kim Hughes has been reduced to tears, but complaining about "unnecessary antagonism" when Allan Border subsequently starts playing it tough. Of his own last unhappy tour Down Under, when the West Indies were losing and bickering among themselves, he remarks that "even though I was now in a position of authority as vice-captain, I felt powerless to do anything to change it". Pelham Warner couldn't have put things more limply. If only one knew which attitudes and postures are pure Michael Holding, and which have been insinuated by his interpreter.

Four new paperbacks about some Australians are also aimed at contemporary hero-worshippers, but one of them is in a different class from the others. **Boon: In the Firing Line**, by A. Mark Thomas, makes the early assertion that "Boon's cricket career and achievements will be forever linked with Tasmanian cricket . . ." and doesn't get any better. **McDermott: Strike Bowler** is typified by the following observation towards the end: "Not many people seem to understand why fitness is vital in a sport like cricket." Not many people will take kindly to being patronised by Craig McDermott or his ghost writer. **Waugh Declared: The Story of Australia's Famous Cricketing Twins**, by Mark Gately, is remarkable for its nineteen photographs of the boys taken before they were eleven years old, which surely won't have been surpassed in all of cricket's (or any other) hagiography. By the time they're both successful Test players, we read that "No story about the Waugh twins can be written without taking time to take a peek at their eating habits . . ." And after that, their bowel movements, perhaps? **Henry: The Geoff Lawson Story** is the odd book out in this company; partly because it appears to be genuine autobiography, rather well written by Lawson himself. It is also the work of a man with strong but never offensive views on many things, including cricket administrators and journalists. He explains why he trained to become an optometrist because he assumes his readers might be interested (and this one was); and he is himself *interested* in the peculiarities of India and Pakistan, Heywood and Haslingden. Too many top cricketers give the impression that they couldn't care less about such things. The fact that Geoff Lawson's nose twitched when he first stepped from a plane in Bombay, and noticed that its scent was different from Sydney's, tells us something as important about this Australian as his fast bowling figures.

Robin Smith: Quest for Number One is a worthy attempt to break through the biographical conventions, by focusing on the psychology of the game and illustrating different aspects from the experience of one cricketer. The journalist John Crace writes in turn on Confidence, Preparation, Motivation, Concentration, Anxiety and so on, followed each time by Robin Smith's own three ha'p'orth. Quite a lot of biography is squeezed in – the domineering Dad in South Africa, who had young Robin up at 4.30 a.m. *every day between the ages of nine and seventeen* (critic's sceptical italics) for sports training, the adored wife and child waiting at home for the international tourist, the emetic paragraph about religious belief, the merely five-word reference to apartheid. Then there are the professional revelations: the fact that bowlers

often don't bowl properly in the nets and are therefore of limited value to the batsman; that Smith does a lot of skipping exercises before playing on a fast pitch from which he can expect many bouncers; that Graeme Hick spends hours practising his cover-drive when he might more profitably learn how and what to hook or pull. Smith is another pleasant man who has survived in a form of the game that, he admits, has become nastier since he first made it. Oh, and there's this, which we may as well have on the record: "A top Test player can earn over £100,000 per year, which is a good living and a great incentive to play Test cricket."

T. E. Bailey (as the scorecards put it in his day) earned £1,000 for touring Australia in 1958 as an amateur, whereas Jim Laker collected only £800 for playing in the same MCC side as a professional; a form of hypocrisy no longer practised in any sport but rugby. The great all-rounder's emolument is mentioned in **Trevor Bailey: A Life in Cricket**, by Jack Bailey, once an accomplished Essex fast bowler himself, and sometime MCC secretary. This is a thoughtful, sharp but always generous appraisal of a career that has been remembered most of all for two defensive innings against the Aussies: Bailey's 71 in a partnership with Willie Watson that saved the 1953 Lord's Test, and his 68 in seven hours 38 minutes at the 'Gabba five years later. Everyone has always recognised the first knock as magnificent; Jack Bailey thinks his namesake carried the can for unenterprising play by both sides in the hullabaloo that followed the second.

Ed Jaggard, too, is thoughtful and warm in **Garth: The Story of Graham McKenzie**. Here was a great fast bowler with "no histrionics, no mid-pitch glares", who was the backbone of the Australian Test attack throughout the sixties, and who thrilled home crowds in both Western Australia and Leicestershire, the county he joined because it offered him a better package than Middlesex. What else? Exemplary county cricketer, "notoriously careful with his money", so curious about "abroad" that he went to Stuttgart to buy a yellow Mercedes and drive it home to the English Midlands. I could have done with more about his larger life.

E. W. Swanton's **Arabs in Aspic 1935-1993** comes with a different pedigree from everything above, having little in common with the Test circuit apart from two XIs playing with twelve pieces of wood and a leather ball. It's about a very old-fashioned form of the game which might have disappeared when the distinction between first-class gents and players was abandoned a generation ago. When invitation teams like the Arabs still flourish, however, we have all the proof we need that the old boy network is still in great shape, no less than in Sir Julien Cahn's day; also that cricket can even now be played competitively, without any wish to humiliate or terrify. The Arabs are Jim Swanton's creation and this is his log from the start up to date. And yes, he's a tiresome old name-dropper as well as a tireless propagandist, and this is a society in which patently well-bred chaps play the game while their little women make all the right noises-off and don't get in the way, and ... It's easy to mock a great deal of Arab tribal behaviour judging by the Founder's account, and this is not by a long chalk my world because it is first and foremost an exclusive world. But it is also – and this is more than one can say of international cricket nowadays – a world in which people play the game (whatever they may do in the rest of their lives) according to a code of decency accepted without question by all hands. If anyone is tempted to sneer at that sentiment, let him consult the wisest of all West Indians, the polymathic C. L. R. James, and feel small. I have a quibble, though. I'm sure annual fixtures against Lord Porchester's XI, Yellowhammers, Band of Brothers, Hampshire Hogs and the like are tremendous fun for everyone concerned, and I hope they go on forever. But why, in all their sixty years, have the Arabs never played a side from the Lancashire League? Or any other such bunch of cricketers? I'd much like to know; but not if the answer comes coated with humbug.

There's not a trace of that in **The History of Northamptonshire County Cricket Club**, by Matthew Engel and Andrew Radd. This is an enormously affectionate but utterly realistic account of cricket in "a small area predisposed to apathy", whose people also suffer from a "fatalistic pessimism"; characteristics which the authors relate to the frustrating (and too often frustrated) story of the first-class game in Northants. They do this with great wit, as when they note that while the club was enduring a particularly barren spell (without a single win between May 1935 and May 1939), the British got through three kings and three prime ministers. They lament the effect of the motor car on Northants, depriving it periodically of star players like V. W. C. Jupp, Fred Bakewell and, above all, Colin Milburn: the pages on the tragedy of Milburn and his lack of self-pity are heartbreaking. But although the Northamptonshire story has too often been one of dogged application against various odds, there are some wonderfully lighter moments as well. That quintessential home-grown pro, Percy Davis, used to strip naked before play began each day, then dress for cricket starting with his county cap. I also like the story of the normally irascible Ken Turner, running round like a coolie to settle in the newly arrived Bishen Bedi and his family, "while Bedi, who was merely obeying the custom of the Indian middle-class, stood and watched". Turner turned down the MBE because he didn't think his contribution to society as county secretary was worth that much. He's part of a very large cast, on and off the field at Wantage Road, who help to make this such a richly satisfying history, its many virtues including a long and eloquent foreword by Frank Tyson. I think it may be one of a dozen books I shall henceforth urge non-cricketers to read if, puzzled, they wonder why this game has gripped my imagination for half a century now. Cricket is about character as much as athletic skills, tactical subtlety and headlong drama, and Engel and Radd demonstrate this vividly.

So does David Foot in **Beyond Bat & Ball: Eleven Intimate Portraits**, which starts with that mellowing old pug Wilf Wooller and ends with worn-out gypsy Tom Richardson. The team is completed by Siegfried Sassoon, Jack Fingleton, Bill Andrews, Andy Ducat, Bill Greswell, Big Jim Smith, Bev Lyon, Bertie Poore and Jack Mercer; all but Sassoon fine cricketers, every man rich in his humanity and chosen for that above all. Dennis Silk in a foreword suggests that Foot is as good as Robertson-Glasgow at his best, and I agree. At least as good; not only because he can describe Ducat handling his bat "with the respect that a professional musician shows for his violin", but also for other literary virtues. This is a sensitive, compassionate writer of originality, of a different order from the tone-deaf hirelings who churn out most of the cricket biographies these days, for quick profit rather than lasting value.

As well as character, cricket is about behaviour, starting with what is codified in its forty-two Laws. Don Oslear (Don Mosey in attendance) has come up with a truly novel idea in **The Wisden Book of Cricket Laws**. There have been books on this topic before, but never from a Test umpire who analyses each Law in turn and then illustrates it out of his own experience in

the middle. The result is fascinating. We learn that Ray Illingworth knew the
Laws better than any of his contemporaries (and, in Oslear's view, was one of
the fairest captains); that an Indian keeper was once fatally speared by an
uprooted and airborne stump; that the top umpires don't reckon to have a
problem with lbw, whatever the rest of us may think; and that the most
important Law of all is No. 23 (Dead Ball). Humour is allowed to intrude,
hilariously in the tale of the wicket-keeper who saw *four* batsmen bearing
down on him just as a throw arrived from the outfield, whereupon he tripped
up and flattened the stumps, but not with the hand holding the ball. You
could run a decent quiz from items in this book, as doubtless many soon will.
And although Oslear is as exercised as anyone about ball-tampering, here
he's only saying that in seasons 1991 and 1992 he submitted five reports to
Lord's, three of them involving the same team within 35 days. He implies
that he will tell all when his contract ends. A very correct man ("I had
complied fully with the Laws of Cricket, as I hope I always will"), he reminds
me a little of Arnold Bennett totting up his wordage and income at the end of
each year; only in Oslear's case it is, "I stood on 25 days, officiating for 2,496
overs, and I gave 86 lectures" during a trip to New Zealand in 1980-81. In
Zimbabwe his figures were 54 days, 4,435 overs, 150 lectures. Or am I
thinking of Leporello's inventory?

The Bombay umpire M. V. Gothoskar (with A. G. Bhagwat acting as his
bearer) challenges the notion that his English colleagues are superior to all
others. Reminiscing in **The Burning Finger** on his fifteen Tests and
considerable other experience of the game, he argues that technology has
proved the Englishmen to be as fallible as anyone. He also thinks match
referees are superfluous, disapproves of neutral officials "because the English
umpires stand to gain most", and believes he knows how to curb bad
behaviour from players: by appointing one female umpire per match. Should
women be so exposed to earfuls of Merv Hughes? Should anyone?

Jonathan Rice has overlooked Oslear's impaled Indian, but seems to have
scavenged every other bizarre incident from the annals of the game in his
Curiosities of Cricket, even though some of them are curiously imprecise.
Like the one about the MCC member who, at a Lord's Test "in the early
80s", died on one of the pavilion balconies before lunch and was joined after
tea by a member of the groundstaff, who chatted to the corpse till close of
play so that none of the other members should notice anything amiss. True,
this does tend to support four separate myths about MCC, but on the whole I
prefer Rice's note on the man who retired with measles on 99 in the Varsity
Match.

Durham CCC: Past, Present and Future is for the longer haul, a timely
salute to the eighteenth contender for the County Championship. The first
half of the book, by Jack Bannister, is a painstaking history of Durham from
1882 to 1991: it is followed by David Graveney's sometimes moving account
of Durham's entry into the first-class competition. A photo of the match at
Sunderland against the 1926 Australians, played before a crowd that
wouldn't have disgraced Roker Park (20,678 paid up on the first day alone),
isn't the only thing to make you wonder why Durham waited so long for
promotion. Graveney's reflection, after his side's first fixture at Canterbury,
that much of the old camaraderie between county cricket teams has vanished
during his time as a player, is not only sad and regrettable; it's ominous.

That and other ills of the first-class game are the subject of Graeme
Wright's **Betrayal: The Struggle for Cricket's Soul**. I'm content to find myself

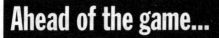

in approximately the same trench as *Wisden*'s former editor, and I applaud much of his general analysis; that the rot began *circa* 1962, that most people concerned with the administration of cricket (and not a few players) are responsible for its deterioration at the top level, and that commercialisation has become a curse instead of the blessing it might have been. This is doubtless one of those few books that everyone connected with the game ought to read and ponder. But I longed for something to make me smile occasionally, instead of yet another solemnity; not only from the ineffable Lord Harris (who is at least quoted in context), but also from Lucretius, Seneca, Martial, Machiavelli, Rousseau, Montaigne, Disraeli, Bagehot, Adam Smith, Edmund Burke, Goethe, Joyce, Wilde, Gibbon, Joshua Reynolds, Graves, Orwell, Edmund Wilson, Wesker, Wittgenstein and a Swiss philosopher I hadn't even heard of. I just hope I never have to read Mr Wright on the decline of Western civilisation.

A History of Australian Cricket is also unusual because its author, Chris Harte, has a taste for disclosures that cricket writers generally omit from their chronicles. He reveals, for instance, that A. E. R. Gilligan belonged to the British Union of Fascists when he captained the 1924 MCC tourists, and has discovered from file N4673 in the Australian PRO that the local secret service agency was warned about this by its London counterpart. Phew! Harte elsewhere implies more than he actually delivers: for example, on the saga of Packer versus the Australian Cricket Board, "a small group of diligent cricket historians have pieced together a sensational train of events which culminated in two intimate dinners and the announcement of a rapprochement ... Unfortunately it is still not possible to publish details." This is not a respectable way to write history. Yet this is a readable book of immense scope and Richie Benaud, who will be a better judge of it than I am, vouches in an introduction for its accuracy.

Harte once wrote the story of Sheffield Shield cricket, a topic that Geoff Armstrong also turns to in **A Century of Summers**. Someone should have told him that a history book without an index is less than useful; but this is an absorbing account, extremely well illustrated with material from local archives. It includes a justifiably withering view of W. G. Grace's "boorish and arrogant behaviour" during his captaincy of Lord Sheffield's touring party in 1891-92, and a graceful tribute to Tony Lock, who is seen as chiefly responsible for transforming Western Australia from a traditional chopping block to a side which has dominated Shield cricket as often as not in the past twenty years. Armstrong enthusiastically emphasises the recent feats of David Hookes, but the batting records at the end are a corrective. Hookes, 9,364 runs at 47.77 in 120 matches across 16 seasons: Bradman, 8,926 runs at 110.19 in 62 matches during 21 years interrupted by the war.

Jack Pollard, who has written doorstoppers of his own on both cricket and rugby in Australia, has now come up with **The Glovemen: The World's Best Wicket-keepers**. He starts with the Victorian Blackham, who almost always kept standing up (in both senses) with a sort of gardening mitten on his hands, and finishes with "a bewildering array" of men picked for England in recent years. His book is heavily weighted in favour of Australians, and Rod Marsh is nominated as the finest catcher of all time behind the stumps; though that depends on how you arrange the statistics. Pollard is another historian with an eye for odd detail, claiming that both Paul Gibb and Syed Kirmani wore wigs (surely not when wicket-keeping?), and that Stan Sismey often had to leave the field in the first post-war season for the removal of shrapnel from his back, legacy of being shot down in the RAAF three years earlier.

Pollard's is essentially a volume of anecdote and so, more obviously, is **More Views from the Boundary**, another compilation of Brian Johnston's lunch-time chats with celebrities on Test Match Special. Johnston himself will be missed, but I have to say that not all of his guests are interesting. Leslie Thomas clearly sees the slot as prime time for plugging his latest book, and the showbiz personalities generally tend to be tedious; but Bernard Lovell is good value on his installation of the light meters at Old Trafford, and even better is Michael Charlton on his memories of the tied Test at Brisbane in 1960. Best short take is Robert Runcie's story of his encounter with Isaiah Berlin, when the undergraduate Runcie was carrying a cricket bag in one hand and a copy of Plato in the other. "Ah! What we all stand for," he was informed in that Oxford quadrangle, "What we all stand for!"

Many good yarns also appear in David Lemmon's **For the Love of the Game: An Oral History of Cricket**. This begins with Cowden Clarke's reminiscences of Nyren and gradually works its way to conversations Lemmon himself has had with contemporary players. In spite of a confusing typography, this is a splendid account of the game's evolution across two centuries, told fondly by those who have played it best. N. S. Mitchell-Innes recalls Rowan and Mitchell scoring 330 for South Africa's first wicket against Surrey in 1935, with E. R. T. Holmes at his wits' end to get rid of them. When a lorry backfired in the road outside, his keeper, Brooks, remarked encouragingly: "There you are, skipper, number three's gone and shot himself."

Lemmon has notably avoided canvassing the greatest stars for his own material, and I think this is a strength of his book. Jack Bannister has inevitably taken the other tack in **The Innings of My Life**, which comes garlanded with a foreword by Ian Botham. Forty-three Test cricketers have been asked to choose and describe their greatest batting feats, with expert asides by Bannister. Bradman picks his 254 in the 1930 Lord's Test, Boycott his 146 in the Gillette Final of 1965, but not all the selections are centuries. Viv Richards prefers his 61 on the fifth day of West Indies v India at Kingston in 1983; and Botham *doesn't* go for Headingley or Old Trafford in 1981 ... Graham Gooch, too, is represented in Bannister and he has a similar book, **For Essex and England**, all to himself. He ("and Michael Down") has commented, in a handsome limited edition, on each of those hundred hundreds. During his first one (114 against Leicestershire at Chelmsford in 1974) he hit Graham McKenzie for six and then said: "Sorry, Mr McKenzie." Wouldn't happen today, would it?

Another old stand-by of cricket publishing, the tour book, makes its appearance as **Summer of Swing**, Khadim Hussain Baloch's account of the 1992 Pakistan campaign through England. This is a man who knows his cricket well and obviously cares deeply about its principles. When he's describing the play he is excellent, but far too often he descends to polemic, about the English umpires, about the English sledging, about the English journalists, about the English legislators. At the bottom of it all, I fear, is a familiar resentment. Admitting Imran's indictment of nepotism, favouritism and corruption in Pakistan's cricket establishment, he adds that this is "a heritage from the past, bestowed upon the country by their past Colonial masters". If Dr Baloch will send a stamped addressed envelope, I'll gladly provide him with a good reading list on the Mughals.

Colin Bateman's **If the Cap Fits** looks superficially like a potboiler for non-readers. It reviews each of the 267 men who have played for England since the war. The lesser lights (Coxon, Cranston, Crapp, several Smiths, Spooner, Tremlett and others) rate only thumbnail sketches, the biggest names a page apiece, but all are uncommonly well done. Someone with imagination has chosen the illustrations, too.

Tom Melville lives in Green Bay Packers country, but has chosen eccentrically to write **Cricket for Americans: Playing and Understanding the Game**. He is very knowledgeable and he offers many a perspective that may not often have occurred to blokes who once festooned the Tavern or barracked from the Hill. "Like a sprawling Russian novel, cricket just happens to be one of those expressions of humanity whose intricacies of plot and variety of characters need an extended period of time to unfold." This makes an agreeable change from, "Y'mean, they play for five days and they don't get a *result?!!?*"

Torrey Pilgrim has edited another collector's piece, **The Sir Frank Worrell Pictorial**, whose words and illustrations have been chosen and arranged from many sources out of the deepest possible affection. I first saw Frank when he was the Radcliffe pro, a man of infinite courtesy to spellbound youngsters like me, and I have cherished his memory ever since for much, much more than his cricketing genius; just as I shall treasure this small but perfect souvenir.

Lastly, the two most important books to be published in 1993, both of them expensive, both worth every penny of the asking price. I marvel at the research done by Philip Bailey, Philip Thorn and Peter Wynne-Thomas to produce the enlarged second edition of the **Who's Who of Cricketers**, a comprehensive record of every man who has played first-class cricket in the British Isles (including Samuel Beckett, his Nobel Prize, and his batting average of 8.75; and, of course, every overseas player who has simply toured here). I marvel no less at the indefatigable Bill Frindall's third edition of **The Wisden Book of Cricket Records**, which he has revised to the end of the home season in 1992. Together with Padwick (vols I and II) these should be the corner stones of any cricket library.

Geoffrey Moorhouse is a Fellow of the Royal Society of Literature and author of sixteen books, most of them histories or travel writings. An exception is The Best-Loved Game, *which won the Cricket Society's Award for 1979.*

THE CRICKET SOCIETY LITERARY AWARD

The Cricket Society Literary Award has been presented since 1970 to the author of the cricket book judged as best of the year. The 1993 award, worth £750 and sponsored by the *Daily Telegraph*, went to David Foot for **Beyond Bat & Ball: Eleven Intimate Portraits**.

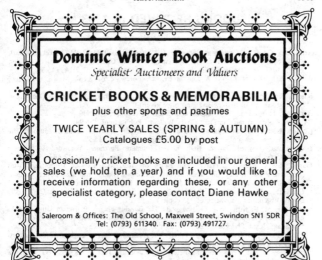

BOOKS RECEIVED IN 1993

GENERAL

Armstrong, Geoff **A Century of Summers**: 100 Years of Sheffield Shield Cricket (Ironbark Press, Sydney; obtainable from Sportspages, 94-96 Charing Cross Road, London WC2H 0JG, and Barton Square, St Ann's Square, Manchester M2 7HA, £16.50)

Bailey, Jack **Trevor Bailey: A Life in Cricket**. Foreword by Keith Miller (Methuen, £14.99)

Baloch, Khadim Hussain **Summer of Swing** (from the author, Little Court, Long Road East, Dedham, Colchester, Essex, no price given)

Bannister, Jack, comp. **The Innings of My Life** (Headline, £16.99)

Bateman, Colin **If the Cap Fits** (Tony Williams Publications, £16.99)

Craven, Nico **May to September** Foreword by Henry Blofeld (from the author, The Coach House, Ponsonby, Seascale, Cumberland CA20 1BX, £5.55)

Foot, David **Beyond Bat & Ball: Eleven Intimate Portraits**. Foreword by Dennis Silk (Good Books, Lagard Farm, Whitley, Nr Melksham, Wilts. SN12 8RL, £13.99)

Gately, Mark **Waugh Declared: The Story of Australia's Famous Cricketing Twins** (Ironbark Press, Sydney; obtainable from Sportspages, London and Manchester, £16.50)

Gooch, Graham and Down, Michael **For Essex and England**: Graham Gooch's Century of Centuries (Boundary Books, Southlands, Sandy Lane, Goostrey, Cheshire CW4 8NT, £48 + £3 p&p, limited edition of 333 copies)

Gothoskar, M. V. with Dr A. G. Bhagwat **The Burning Finger**: an Indian Umpire looks back (Marine Sports, Bombay; obtainable from Martin Wood, 2 St John's Road, Sevenoaks, Kent TN13 3LW, £6)

Griffiths, Peter and Wynne-Thomas, Peter **The Australian Tour to England 1953** (Limlow Books, St Peter's Hill, Litlington, Royston, Herts. SG8 0QF, £7.50 + 50p p&p)

Griffiths, Peter and Wynne-Thomas, Peter **The Australian Tour to England 1993** (Limlow Books, address as above, £7.50 + 50p p&p)

Harte, Chris **A History of Australian Cricket** (Andre Deutsch, £25)

Holding, Michael with Tony Cozier **Whispering Death: The Life and Times of Michael Holding** (Andre Deutsch, £14.99)

Howat, Gerald **Cricket Medley**: Collected Writings (Sports History Publishing; obtainable from North Moreton Press, OX11 8BA, £5.99)

Jaggard, Ed **Garth: The Story of Graham McKenzie** (Fremantle Arts Centre Press; obtainable from Sportspages, London and Manchester, £9.95)

James, Alfred **Ratu Kadavu's Fijian Cricket XI in Australia, 1907-08** (from the author, 65 Billyard Avenue, Wahroonga, New South Wales, Australia, £15 inc. airmail)

James, Alfred **The 2nd Australian Cricket XI, 1880** (from the author, address as above, £45 inc. airmail)

Jenkinson, Neil **C. P. Mead**: Hampshire's Greatest Run-maker (Paul Cave Publications, 74 Bedford Place, Southampton, £13.95)

Johnston, Brian **More Views from the Boundary** (Methuen, £12.99)

Lawson, Geoff **Henry: The Geoff Lawson Story** (Ironbark Press, Sydney; obtainable from Sportspages, London and Manchester, £9.95)

Lemmon, David **For the Love of the Game: An Oral History of Cricket** (Pelham Books, £16.99)

McDermott, Craig and Derriman, Philip **McDermott: Strike Bowler** (ABC Books, Sydney; obtainable from Sportspages, London and Manchester, £13.50)

Meher-Homji, Kersi **Out for a Duck** Foreword by Stephen Waugh (Kangaroo Press, 3 Whitehall Road, Kenthurst, NSW 2156, $A12.95)

Melville, Tom **Cricket for Americans: Playing and Understanding the Game**. Preface by Ian Chappell (Bowling Green University Popular Press, Bowling Green, Ohio 43403, $US25.95)

Oslear, Don, with Don Mosey **The Wisden Book of Cricket Laws** (Stanley Paul, £9.99)

Pervez Qaiser, S. **England Tour of India 1992-93**. Foreword by Sir Colin Cowdrey (Al Faisel Publications, 1433 Qasimjan Street, Ballimaran, Delhi 110006, India, £6 inc. registered airmail)

Pilgrim, Torrey **The Sir Frank Worrell Pictorial** (Creativity/Innovation, Barbados, obtainable from Martin Wood, address as above, £4.75)

Pollard, Jack **The Glovemen: The World's Best Wicket-keepers** (Kangaroo Press, address as above, no price given)

Rhys, Chris **The Cricketer Book of Cricket Days** (Lennard, £7.99)

Rice, Jonathan **Curiosities of Cricket** (Pavilion, £12.99)

Smith, Robin and Crace, John **Robin Smith: Quest for Number One** (Boxtree, £15.99)

Steen, Rob **Desmond Haynes: Lion of Barbados** (Witherby, £16.99)

Streeton, Richard **Twenty-One Years of the ACS** (Association of Cricket Statisticians, 3 Radcliffe Road, West Bridgford, Nottingham NG2 5FF, £3)

Thomas, A. Mark **Boon: In the Firing Line** (Pan Macmillan Australia; obtainable from Sportspages, London and Manchester, £11.95)

West, G. Derek **Guide to James Lillywhite's Cricketers' Annual** (signed copies from the author, 59 Blenheim Road, Caversham, Reading, Berks. RG4 7RT, £10 inc. postage in UK)

Wright, Graeme **Betrayal: The Struggle for Cricket's Soul** (Witherby, £16.99)

COUNTIES

Bannister, Jack and Graveney, David **Durham CCC: Past, Present and Future** (Lennard/Queen Anne Press, £16.95)

Engel, Matthew and Radd, Andrew **The History of Northamptonshire CCC** (Christopher Helm, £18.99)

Foot, David and Ponting, Ivan **Somerset Cricket:** A Post-War Who's Who (Redcliffe, £7.99)

Hayes, Dean **Famous Cricketers of Hampshire** (Spellmount, £15.95)

STATISTICAL

Bailey, Philip and Thorn, Philip **Cambridge University Cricketers 1820-92** (ACS, 3 Radcliffe Road, West Bridgford, Nottingham NG2 5FF, £3)

Bailey, Philip, Thorn, Philip and Wynne-Thomas, Peter **Who's Who of Cricketers:** A complete record of all cricketers who have played first-class cricket in the British Isles (Hamlyn, £40 inc. postage)

Bartlett, C. J., King, L., Thorn, P. R. and Trushell, K. S. C. **Lincolnshire Cricketers 1828-1993** (ACS, address as above, £3)

Collis, Anthony D. **Graeme Pollock:** His Record Innings-by-Innings (Famous Cricketers Series – no. 14) (ACS, address as above, £3)

Finlay, Ric **Alan Kippax:** His Record Innings-by-Innings (Famous Cricketers Series – no. 17) (ACS, address as above, £4.50)

Frindall, Bill ed. **The Wisden Book of Cricket Records:** Third Edition (Headline, £35)

Hatton, Les comp. **Sunday League Record Book 1969 to 1992** (ACS, address as above, £7.50)

Isaacs, Victor H **Hampshire County Cricket Club: First-Class Records 1864-1992** (Limlow Books, St Peter's Hill, Litlington, Royston, Herts. SG8 0QF, £7.50 + 50p p&p)

Ledbetter, Jim ed. **First-Class Cricket: A Complete Record 1937** (Limlow Books, address as above, £14.95 + £1.50 p&p)

Lodge, Derek **W. G. Grace:** His Record Innings-by-Innings (Famous Cricketers Series – no. 15) (ACS, address as above, £6.50)

Roberts, Rex and Wilde, Simon **Duleepsinhji:** His Record Innings-by-Innings (Famous Cricketers Series – no. 16) (ACS, address as above, £3.50)

West, William **Irish International Women Cricketers 1982 to 1992** (Lindis, Roundhay Road, Bridlington YO15 3JZ, £1.10)

Wilde, Geoffrey S. **Brian Statham:** His Record Innings-by-Innings (Famous Cricketers Series – no. 18) (ACS, address as above, £6.50)

TECHNICAL

Crowe, Martin **Winning Cricket:** a guide for aspiring cricketers (Moa, Auckland, obtainable from Martin Wood, 2 St John's Road, Sevenoaks, Kent TN13 3LW, £6.75)
Woolmer, Bob **Skilful Cricket** Foreword by Sir Colin Cowdrey (A & C Black, £8.99)

REPRINTS AND UPDATES

The Australians in England 1902 Contemporary account with new foreword by Sir Donald Bradman, and signed by him (J. W. McKenzie, 12 Stoneleigh Park Road, Ewell, Epsom, Surrey KT19 0QT, £45)
Crace, John **Wasim and Waqar:** Imran's Inheritors. Paperback edition (Boxtree, £5.99)
Frith, David **England versus Australia:** A Pictorial History of every Test match. Eighth revised edition (BBC, £12.99)
James Lillywhite's Cricketers' Annual 1894 (reprint from Cricket Lore, 22 Grazebrook Road, London N16 0HS, £10.95)
John Wisden's Cricketers' Almanack for 1894 (reprint from Willows Publishing, 17 The Willows, Stone, Staffs. ST15 0DE, £40 inc. postage UK, £42 inc. postage overseas).
John Wisden's Cricketers' Almanack for 1895 (reprint from Willows Publishing, address as above, £41 inc. postage UK, £43 inc. postage overseas).

HANDBOOKS AND ANNUALS

Armstrong, David ed. **Minor Counties Cricket Annual and Official Handbook** (ACS, 3 Radcliffe Road, West Bridgford, Nottingham NG2 5FF, £3.75)
Bailey, Philip comp. **ACS International Cricket Year Book 1993** (ACS, address as above, £7.50)

Benaud, Richie ed. **Cricket Yearbook 1993** including Ashes '93 report (Hamlyn Australia, 22 Salmon St, Port Melbourne, Victoria 3207, no price given)

Club Cricket Conference Official Handbook (77th edition, 1993) (361 West Barnes Lane, New Malden, Surrey KT3 6JF, £5 to affiliates)

English Schools Cricket Association Handbook 1993 (ESCA, no price given)

Frindall, Bill ed. **Playfair Cricket Annual 1993** (Headline, paperback £3.99; hardback £6.99)

Hatton, Les comp. **ACS First Class Counties Second Eleven Annual** (ACS, address as above, £3.75)

Lemmon, David ed. **Benson and Hedges Cricket Year**, Twelfth Edition (Headline, £19.99)

Miller, Allan ed. **Allan's Australian Cricket Annual 1992-93** (from Allan Miller, PO Box 974, Busselton, WA 6280, $A30 inc. postage or from Sport in Print, 3 Radcliffe Road, West Bridgford, Nottingham NG2 5FF, £14 inc. postage)

Munster Cricket Union Yearbook 1993 (C. T. Murphy, Cillmorna, Lacabawn, Donoughmore, Co. Cork, Ireland, £2.50 inc. postage)

Pike, Jeffery ed. **The Ashes 93:** The official BBC sports magazine (BBC, £2.95)

Sproat, Iain ed. **The Cricketers' Who's Who 1993** (Lennard/Queen Anne Press, £10.95)

Steen, Rob, ed. **Britannic Assurance 1993 Guide to County Cricket.** Foreword by Mike Atherton (Boxtree, £5.99)

TCCB **Official Test and County Cricket Board Cricket Review 1993** (TCCB, £3.50)

COUNTY YEARBOOKS

Durham (£6); **Glamorgan** (£4.50); **Hampshire** (£5); **Kent** (£4.50); **Lancashire** (£5.50); **Leicestershire** (£3); **Northamptonshire** (£6); **Warwickshire** (£4); **Worcestershire** (£2); **Yorkshire** – Centenary Edition (no price given)

SOUVENIRS AND BROCHURES

Rob Bailey 1993 Benefit Brochure (Northamptonshire CCC, no price given)

Gehan Mendis 1993 Benefit Brochure (Lancashire CCC, £2.50)

New Zealand Cricket Tour of Sri Lanka – November/December 1992 (Board of Control for Cricket in Sri Lanka, 35 Maitland Place, Colombo 7, Sri Lanka)

World Cup 1993: Official brochure for the Fifth International Women's Cricket Tournament (Women's Cricket Association, 41 St Michael's Lane, Leeds LS6 3BR, £1.50)

PERIODICALS

The Cricketer International (monthly) editorial director Richard Hutton (Beech Hanger, Ashurst, Tunbridge Wells, Kent TN3 9ST, £2.20)

Cricket Lore (10 per volume, frequency variable) ed. Richard Hill (Cricket Lore, 22 Grazebrook Road, London N16 0HS, £35 per volume)

Cricket World (monthly) managing ed. Michael Blumberg (The Club Cricketer, 2a Chelverton Road, London SW15 1RH, £1.95)

The Googly (fanzine, frequency uncertain) (29b Meteor Street, London SW11 5NZ, 70p, four issues £2.69)

JM 96 (fanzine, frequency uncertain) (1 Wellington Crescent, Bristol BS7 8SZ, £1)

The Journal of the Cricket Society (twice yearly) ed. Clive W. Porter (from Mr P. Ellis, 63 Groveland Road, Beckenham, Kent BR3 3PX, £3)

Red Stripe Caribbean Quarterly ed. Tony Cozier (Cozier Publishing, PO Box 40W, Worthing, Christ Church, Barbados, annual rate £12 Europe, BDS$22 Barbados, BDS$28/US$14 rest of the West Indies, US$18 US, Can$24 Canada, US$24 elsewhere)

The White Rose Magazine (quarterly) (Yorkshire CCC, 50p, free to members)

Wisden Cricket Monthly ed. David Frith (25 Down Road, Merrow, Guildford, Surrey GU1 2PY, £1.90)

MISCELLANEOUS

Hinneburg-Murphy, Colm **Catalogue of Cricket Philately** (C. T. Murphy, Cillmorna, Lacabawn, Donoughmore, Co. Cork, Ireland, £4 inc. postage)

CLUB HISTORIES

Barns Green Cricket Club: Illustrated Souvenir History (available from Tom Keeley, Clews, 7 Merryfield Drive, Horsham, West Sussex RH12 2AA, £3 + 65p p&p)

Hayward, John **Sixty Not Out!** Hollywood Cricket Club Diamond Anniversary 1932-1992 (Jimmy Colabavala, 900 E. Lomita Ave 201, Glendale, CA 91205, USA)

Hayward, Richard and Phelps, Anthony **A History of Civil Service Cricket** (Civil Service Sports Council, 708 Buckingham Place, High Wycombe, Bucks. HP13 5HW, £7.50 inc. postage)

Samara-Wickrama, Percy ed. **Twenty Seasons On:** Celebrating Twenty Years of Cricket in Weston Creek 1972-1992 (Weston Creek Cricket Club, PO Box 3047, Weston Creek, ACT 2611, Australia, $A28)

Swanton, E. W. **Arabs in Aspic 1935-1993** (Boundary Books, Southlands, Sandy Lane, Goostrey, Cheshire CW4 8NT, £17.95, also limited edition of 50 signed by E. W. Swanton and Tony Lewis, £65, both inc. postage)

Advertisement

DIRECTORY OF BOOK DEALERS

TIM BEDDOW CRICKET BOOKS, 62a Stanmore Road, Edgbaston, Birmingham B16 9TB. Tel: 021-420 3466 (24-hour answerphone). Require antiquarian, modern and remainders. Highest price paid. Catalogues also available. (Send 1st/2nd class stamp.)

K. V. BISHOP, 263 Long Riding, Basildon SS14 1QS. Cricket books, autographed material and memorabilia (especially caps and clothing) purchased and sold. Other sports also stocked and required.

BOUNDARY BOOKS, Southlands, Sandy Lane, Goostrey, Cheshire CW4 8NT. Tel: 0477 533106. Second-hand and antiquarian cricket books, autographs and memorabilia bought and sold. Deluxe limited editions published. Catalogues issued.

PETER BRIGHT, 11 Ravens Court, Ely, Cambs. CB6 3ED. Tel: 0353 661727. Send stamp for sample catalogue of Wisdens, general cricket books and printed ephemera. Books bought and 'wants' serviced.

CRICKET LIBRARIES, Gracelands, Lakeside, Littleborough OL15 0DD. Tel: 0706 374379. Specialists in new, second-hand and antiquarian cricket books and all types of cricketing memorabilia.

IAN DYER, 29 High Street, Gilling West, Richmond, North Yorkshire DL10 5JG. Tel: 0748 822786. Ian Dyer specialises in cricket books, Wisdens and year books. Collections purchased and collected. Send stamp for catalogue.

J. E. EMERY, 13 Long Street, Great Gonerby, Grantham, Lincs. NG31 8LN. Tel: 0476 74520. Specialists in cricket and all sports books. Monthly and cumulative catalogues available. Free booksearch service.

INVICTA BOOKSEARCH, 63 Weald View Road, Tonbridge, Kent TN9 2NQ. Tel: 0732 352684; fax: 0732 358300. Booksearch service: out-of-print books found, any subject, no obligation, no time limit.

C. P. W. JONKERS, 4 Field Lane, Stourbridge DY8 2JQ. Tel: 0384 393976. Antiquarian and second-hand cricket book specialist. Send large SAE for catalogue. Books bought, any quantity, better return than auction. Professional booksearch available.

E. O. KIRWAN, 3 Pine Tree Garden, Oadby, Leics. LE2 5UT. Tel: 0533 714267 (evenings and weekends only). Second-hand and antiquarian cricket books, Wisdens, autograph material and cricket ephemera of all kinds.

J. W. McKENZIE, 12 Stoneleigh Park Road, Ewell, Epsom, Surrey KT19 0QT. Tel: 081-393 7700; fax: 081-393 1694. Specialists in antiquarian, second-hand cricket books, particularly Wisdens. Books and collections bought. Catalogues sent on request.

ROGER PAGE, 10 Ekari Court, Yallambie, Victoria 3085, Australia. Tel: (03) 435 6332; fax: (03) 432 2050. Dealer in new and second-hand cricket books. Distributor of overseas cricket annuals and magazines. Agent for Cricket Statisticians and Cricket Memorabilia Society.

RED ROSE BOOKS (BOLTON), 196 Belmont Road, Astley Bridge, Bolton BL1 7AR. Tel: 0204 598080. Antiquarian and second-hand cricket books. Please send stamp for latest catalogue.

ROTHWELL & DUNWORTH, 14 Paul Street, Taunton, Somerset. Tel: 0823 282476. Open 11.00–5.15 daily. "The Best Cricket Bookshop in England" – Simon Heffer, *Spectator* Diary. General antiquarian, Wisdens and old cricket books.

CHRISTOPHER SAUNDERS, Orchard Books, Kingston House, High Street, Newnham-on-Severn, Gloucestershire GL14 1BB. Tel: 0594 516030; fax: 0594 517273. Visitors by appointment only. See advertisement on page 1302.

SPORTING VIEW, 53 Hockliffe Street, Leighton Buzzard, Beds. LU7 8EZ. Tel: 0525 851371. Purchase and sale of cricket books, Wisdens and cricketana. Send SAE for catalogue. Browsers are welcome.

SPORTSPAGES, Caxton Walk, 94–96 Charing Cross Road, London WC2H 0JG. Tel: 071-240 9604. Barton Square, St Ann's Square, Manchester M2 7HA. Tel: 061-832 8530. New cricket books, audio and videotapes, including imports, especially from Australasia; retail and mail order service.

DOMINIC WINTER, The Old School, Maxwell Street, Swindon SN1 5DR. Tel: 0793 611340; fax: 0793 491727. Book auctions, specialist auctioneers and valuers. Saleroom and offices at the above address. Specialist sales twice yearly. Valuations undertaken.

WISTERIA BOOKS, Wisteria Cottage, Birt Street, Birtsmorton, Malvern WR13 6AW. Tel: 0684 833578. Visit our family-run stall at county grounds for new, second-hand, antiquarian cricket books and ephemera, or contact Grenville Simons at the address above.

MARTIN WOOD, 2 St John's Road, Sevenoaks, Kent TM13 3LW. Tel: 0732 457205. Martin Wood has been dealing in cricket books since 1970, and has now posted 20,000 parcels. For a copy of his 1994 catalogue listing 2,600 items, send 25p stamp to the address above.

CRICKET AND THE LAW IN 1993

NAWAZ v LAMB

Sarfraz Nawaz, the Pakistani Test bowler, dropped an action for libel against his former Northamptonshire team-mate Allan Lamb halfway through the fourth day of the case at the High Court in London on November 18, 1993. Sarfraz withdrew from the case just before Ian Botham was due to give evidence for Lamb.

The case was brought over an article in the *Daily Mirror* in August 1992, in which Lamb accused the 1992 Pakistani touring team of cheating and said Sarfraz had taught him years ago how to doctor the ball by gouging it and smearing the surface with sweat to fool the umpires; this information, he alleged, had been passed down to the current Pakistani Test players.

Sarfraz's counsel, Jonathan Crystal, told Mr Justice Otton and the jury of nine women and three men that there had been an "appalling" libel, and accused Lamb of having double-standards: "If you play on the same side as Allan Lamb, you can cheat because he isn't going to complain about it. He never did in all the years they were colleagues . . . These allegations were false and without foundation as far as Sarfraz Nawaz was concerned."

Sarfraz said: "I never cheated in all my 15-year career in cricket. I never knew the word. I hate those people who cheat in any area of life." He said he had no trick, but had developed an entirely legal technique of making the old ball swing, which he showed to colleagues like Imran Khan and which became widely used in Pakistan in the 1970s.

Questioned by his counsel, David Eady QC, Lamb said he did not retract one word of the article; he had mentioned Sarfraz merely as an after-thought, but the point was that the Pakistani bowlers were doing what Sarfraz had described to him many years before.

A number of cricketers gave evidence for Lamb, including three past and present Northamptonshire players: Alan Hodgson said he had seen Sarfraz scratch the ball at a charity match; Wayne Larkins said Sarfraz had told him over a drink how to rough up an old ball; David Capel said he had heard Sarfraz speak "proudly" of having invented the technique.

The England player Robin Smith said he had seen the ball being "improperly" treated up to three times an over during the 1992 Test series against Pakistan. The one-time England captain Christopher Cowdrey said he had spotted 54 incidents of "irregular" Pakistani handling of the ball during the 1992 series; the jury were shown video clips.

Mirror Group Newspapers agreed to share the estimated £100,000 costs with Sarfraz, who would otherwise have been liable for them all. "It appears he isn't a rich man," said a spokesman.

THE CRICKET PRESS IN 1993

By MURRAY HEDGCOCK

President of MCC Dennis Silk was in modified headmasterly mode at the annual dinner of the Cricket Writers' Club in 1993. Silk, the retired Warden of Radley College, delivered an amiable but heart-felt message: today's cricket correspondents were too quick to find fault rather than enjoyment in the game. When England scored their Oval Test victory, many seemed more concerned with Australia's problems than the victors' achievement. Cricket, argued Silk, was meant to be enjoyed and he hoped the press would share and express that fun.

The Silk theme tied in with an early-season meeting at Lord's, when TCCB officials met cricket writers to explain the board's disciplinary committee procedures. The committee chairman Peter Bromage insisted they could not give more information on such topics as the ball-tampering allegations of 1992, and the drugs charges (rejected) against Yorkshire spinner Richard Stemp. The game would suffer if confidential information were made public, Bromage asserted: it was possible to investigate problems thoroughly only if those giving evidence were assured of secrecy. Not so, said the correspondents: the cricket public deserved the fullest information.

There was an echo of this conflict a week later when Bob Simpson, the coach of the Australian tourists, expressed regret that Australian journalists had followed the Fleet Street tabloids (as he saw it) in making a good deal of Allan Border's action in knocking down his stumps when dismissed by Middlesex. These episodes emphasise how officialdom wishes to present the best possible face on the game, and how the media will eagerly publicise the blemishes – partly in a proper search for truth, but also because controversy sells papers and the flawed idol is more newsworthy than the clean-cut hero.

Cricket coverage in 1993 was dominated by England's failure on the field and the English media's customary search for scapegoats. *The Independent* decided not to leave the verdict totally to its specialists. In its series Candid Caller, in which appropriate names from the telephone book comment on pertinent issues, W. G. Grace of Bournemouth declared: "I fear the best cricket days are behind us" – a view more or less supported by Mr Dexter of Tyneside, Mr Laker of Southampton, Mr Trueman of Rossendale, and Mrs Botham of Camberley, who described cricket as "very boring".

The Ashes failure came just as the England soccer team was heading out of the World Cup and John Major's Government was going through a period of unprecedented unpopularity and the three became linked in the public mind. After conducting its own *vox pop* exercise, the *Daily Telegraph* summed up the responses: "Cricket's a disaster, football's even worse and the Prime Minister's absolute rubbish."

By midsummer, the *Daily Mirror* was reaching back into history and quoting Cromwell: "In the name of God, go", marring its dignity with a sub-heading: "The *Mirror* speaks its mind about the Three Stooges", lumping together the chairman of selectors Ted Dexter, the manager Keith Fletcher and the captain Graham Gooch.

But most of the criticism focused on Dexter, whose patrician manner did not suit the mass-circulation tabloids. And he made it worse when he tried to lighten the gloom with the odd quip, such as his idea that England lost the Lord's Test because "we may be under the wrong star sign. Venus may be in juxtaposition with the wrong planet." Whimsy does not register with cricket writers, still less with tabloid sports editors. In the *Mirror* Chris Lander thundered: "Ted Dexter last night dared to stay on as England's cricket supremo. For bared-faced sporting cheek, this act of unbelievable complacency has been matched only by soccer chief Graham Taylor."

The Sun, with its gift for popular-culture headlines which may puzzle future cricket researchers, led its sports section with the call: "Drop the Ted Donkey" (a reference to the TV comedy series, "Drop the Dead Donkey"). The line was to haunt Dexter for the rest of his stay.

James Lawton, the *Daily Express* sports columnist, argued: "Dexter represents everything wrong with English cricket – complacency, obscurity, a thought process that hurtles from A to B: most of all, a total failure to grasp that what is happening to English cricket has become a matter of real shame." By July 27, when the papers recorded Gooch's resignation, they made much of the point that Dexter was out on the golf course at the time. In its headline *The Sun* grabbed the angle: "Tee off, Ted". The barrage was unending.

In the *Financial Times* Dominic Lawson saw it more coolly: "The pundits paid to tell us what we think about English cricket seem unable to believe that the team might possibly be less talented, simply worse, than any other nation. Their writings are based on the false premise that England are the premier cricketing nation, and that it is only the stupidity of selectors and managers which prevents us from demonstrating this to upstart colonials."

When Dexter did resign, after the Edgbaston Test, the broadsheet papers tended to suggest he was as much sinned against as sinning and that presiding over the rickety structure of English cricket was a hopeless task for anyone – but *The Sun* relentlessly listed the less perceptive comments of the chairman over four and a half years in charge, under the headline: "His Lordship was good for a laugh." Australian skipper Border was recorded in *The Times*: "We were puzzled when the crowd started cheering and clapping. We thought the players had passed some sort of milestone. The resignations of Goochie and Dexter take the gloss off our victories. All the headlines will be about Dexter, and not our win." No wonder Mike Selvey wrote in *The Guardian* how Mrs Susan Dexter burst into tears at her local supermarket that day, on seeing the newspaper rack full of pictures and headlines, in Ted's phrase, "lampooning and harpooning" her husband.

A much more anonymous administrator, Australian manager Des Rundle, also fell foul of his country's cricket writers. This led to the correspondent of the Melbourne paper *The Age*, Greg Baum, writing a brave column (in mid-July, rather than waiting for end-of-tour safety), saying the manager "appears to believe that the entire Ashes tour should happen in secret", had refused to answer legitimate questions, and was "the most superfluous member of this touring party". Baum added: "If he were a player, he would be sent home immediately." Relations were chilly for some time.

Mark Nicholas of Hampshire, one of an increasing number of players moving towards journalism, was also daring with an end-of-season attack in the *Daily Teledgh* – on his new colleagues. He believed the media contributed to the erosion of confidence in the England team because "each word in a bar, each whisper in a lift, each phrase at a press conference, each indiscriminate stroke on the pitch, is whacked on the back page, replayed on the screen, and tut-tutted on the wireless.

"They are there to be shot at, I suppose, these public and salaried figures, but what a shame they are shot at so vigorously, with such relish, and so often by people who know so little. What a shame that so much of the glow of the cricket essay has been replaced by the scowl of the tabloid."

But while Britain waded through the variable opinions of an army of cricket writers, Australian enthusiasts (enthused as long as the Aussies win) had to make do with the most limited print cover of any modern tour, thanks to the concentration of press ownership. Just four newspapermen accompanied Border's team, plus one agency reporter, with occasional contributions from London-based correspondents – and the Sydney press, astonishingly, was unrepresented. That proud city's News Limited papers (owned by Rupert Murdoch) had to use copy from the Brisbane journalist Robert Craddock, and the *Sydney Morning Herald* took reports from *The Age* man. It was a reminder that British cricket-lovers may not always think highly of their newspaper's view of the game – but they do have an incomparable choice.

CRICKETANA IN 1993

By DAVID FRITH

We shall never know exactly how many full sets of *Wisden Cricketers' Almanack* there are. Sets housed in institutions might, with some effort, be counted but, with private collectors often coy about revealing the true extent of their libraries, there can never be an accurate register. Those who do boast a full run invariably regard it as a great source of pride, a mark of aristocracy among collectors, with those who have resorted to facsimile editions of the early issues perhaps considering themselves as members of the baronetcy.

It is indisputable that *Wisdens* continue to hold their value and, in some years at least, to swell in price faster than the retail price index, with the ongoing clamour for the first 20 issues, 1864 onwards, as feverish as ever. At Phillips' London sale last October, a copy of the 1864 edition went under the hammer for £2,700 and an 1875, somewhat distressed, for the same figure. An 1869 sold for £2,500, 1865 for £2,200, 1866 for £1,900, and 1867 for £1,600. Even allowing for well over a century of inflation, the founder would have stood dumbfounded at the furore his shilling creations were causing.

These 1993 prices for old *Wisdens* (issues from the 1890s are still selling for well under £200) were merely the hammer prices. Buyers were obliged to pay a punitive tariff of 15 per cent at Phillips' (still 10 per cent at Christie's) termed "buyer's premium", on which VAT is charged. Time may show that alternative means of disposal and acquisition may be found or that provincial auction-houses such as Trevor Vennett-Smith of Nottingham and Dominic Winter of Swindon (both 10 per cent), with their more intimate atmosphere, contrasting with that of their monolithic metropolitan competitors, may attract a greater proportion of business.

The most active participants at the sales are dealers, many of whom have greater bulk-buying power than the collectors. It may safely be assumed that the saleroom alone enables the dealers to keep their shelves adequately stocked. If so, then unless their profit margins are reduced, demand may simply drop, though the formidable quantity of books and memorabilia which changed hands in 1993 suggests that such a process would be slow.

In the autumn, it seemed doubtful that a full set of *Wisdens* would ever again be offered on the open market, for it is now generally understood that a greater price is almost certain to be realised by separating the whole into single lots for the 19th century editions and into tens thereafter. When they were offered as a set at Phillips' last year, bidding for the 130 volumes trailed off at £21,000 net and the lot was passed in. Sold piecemeal immediately afterwards, the consequent 39 separate lots aggregated £25,450 (a shade short of £30,000 with the premium). Of course, they went to a variety of new owners: another set broken up, but conceivably with a number of collectors completing or closing in on their hearts' desire, a full set.

However, at Christie's in November a full set based on Sir Pelham Warner's collection remained unsold when bidding stopped at £22,000. The vendors decided the set should not be broken up.

By way of complication to the trading in *Wisdens*, challenges have been raised to certain descriptions of binding in the auction-houses' listings. Although certain *Wisdens*, even pre-1896, are to be found in hard covers, it seems certain that these are not properly described as "original hardback publisher's cloth" since they – and certain subsequent editions – were bound, sometimes many years later, either belatedly by John Wisden & Co. or by another bindery. This matters to the purist.

There is still a growing body of opinion that the facsimiles are completely satisfying. Modest in price and robust, they may be read without fear of costly accidental damage. Indeed, they are taking on such a collectability of their own that a buyer recently paid a total of £518 for the strongly bound and boxed facsimiles 1864–1878 which were still available from John Wisden (who produced them in 1991) at £450. The 1916 issue, rarest of this century's, has steadied in price (£541 gross at the last sighting) following Willows' facsimile release, and with the 1941 edition – one of only 800 hardbacks published in that dark year – selling for £336, a further facsimile might well be justified, for many people would enjoy reading it, a reality easily overlooked midst all the commercial calculations.

Elsewhere, postcards and caps and scorecards and prints continue to sell for prices that have older collectors gasping with relief and semi-disbelief. Letters, too, if not commanding such sums as the 76 Greta Garbo letters which fetched £26,450 in London last June, appear to be a good investment – and certainly remain unique in the full and intimate personal sense, as opposed to signatures, where authenticity is sometimes questionable.

But it is *Wisdens* which remain the banker. As Phillips' consultant Angus Gull has said, "They are the perfect collector's item. There is a finite number available, and a full set *can* be acquired." Not cheaply, he might have added.

CRICKET EQUIPMENT IN 1993

By NORMAN HARRIS

Whatever else may have been said about the revamped Sunday League – and the written media's response on the opening day was almost uniformly negative – by the end of the season, the white ball was judged a success. That was certainly true for spectators, and it was a view also held by some players. It therefore raises what traditionalists may regard as an heretical question: why not a white ball for all cricket? Football, rugby, hockey and tennis all now prefer a ball of the most visible colour – in most cases white. So does cricket's cousin, baseball.

Evidence from the Sunday League is supported by local teams who use a white ball for evening matches, or whose ground is surrounded by trees and has no sightscreens. Such teams may play in normal cricket gear, yet they have found that the ball does not get lost against white clothing, mainly thanks to its black seam. So worries about sightscreens may be a red (or white) herring. When white balls were first considered for the Sunday League they were used in experimental play at Lord's, during which the sightscreens were removed. To general surprise, this made very little difference to the batsmen – even with a background of white seats.

White balls are more difficult to make, in terms of dyeing and stitching. The red ball is not exposed to quite the same demands: after its light varnish wears off, the leather and its natural oils are exposed to grease, water, grass and dirt. The ball polishes up well and takes on a range of hues often much closer to dark brown than to red. In the same circumstances, a white ball would soon look very far from white. Indeed, on Sundays last summer, some turned rather grey after a short while. Others retained their whiteness thanks to the addition of polyurethane, which seals the surface but gives an almost permanent dull sheen. This can make it harder for bowlers to get the favoured contrast between a dull side and a polished side.

Even so, the makers were pleased – and perhaps a little surprised – at how their products performed. To go further would involve a technological drive that the tiny market does not at present justify. But the possibility that all cricket might one day use a white ball is an intriguing one.

There are other innovatory murmurings. It is 14 years since Dennis Lillee infamously hurled down the aluminium bat he was prevented from using in the Perth Test against England, thus ushering in the law specifying that all bats must be made of wood. But last summer a leading Australian sports merchant, Swan Richards, asked MCC (unsuccessfully) to consider allowing synthetic materials at club level, arguing that the shortage of best quality willow was pricing bats beyond the reach of average club cricketers. This manufacturer is developing graphite bats, which he says could easily be taken for willow. Elsewhere, research has been undertaken to see if poplar – which would be legal – could provide a useful substitute. Poplar is not as strong as willow, which has the added merit of elasticity, so 20 thin sections of poplar were bonded together to make a laminate as strong as those in wooden propellers and wings. The prototype was "rock hard", according to one user. That reaction echoed Slazenger's description of the graphite handles they tried some years ago: "They sounded bad and felt bad."

The most expensive bats in the shops are around £150, as they were a year ago. However, the top model of a less celebrated but well-respected batmaker, Warsop Stebbing, can be bought for a quarter of that price. The cost of willow would, therefore, appear to be a comparatively minor factor – hardly lending support to the idea that a substitute needs to be found. Certainly, batmaking is far from a gold mine, even in the country that invented cricket. That seemed to be underlined by the announcements that Stuart Surridge had been bought out by Dunlop Slazenger, while Duncan Fearnley had joined up with UK Patrick.

Finally, a postscript to last year's discussion of various prototype handguards. At least one model went into the shops last year, and was taken around the counties. Fitted to the handle, it could be used with or without gloves, and almost guaranteed the lower hand against damage. But first-class players seemed to resist the idea, much to the frustration of the manufacturer who thought that professionals would at any rate use one in the nets. The point was reinforced when Graham Thorpe broke his thumb batting in the nets within an hour of the start of the Oval Test.

CRICKET GROUNDS IN 1993

One new ground staged first-class cricket in 1993 when the Gloucester Festival was moved from its traditional home at the Wagon Works ground, which was ruled unfit for first-class cricket, to Archdeacon Meadow, the playing fields of King's School. Play began a day late because of rain which seeped under the covers and thus on May 28 – the day Charles Barnett died a few miles away – Gloucestershire found themselves on an old-fashioned sticky wicket and were bowled out by Worcestershire for 101 by three o'clock.

This nostalgic piece of cricket helped create enthusiasm for the Festival's new setting. The school will again stage the Gloucester fixtures in 1994, against Surrey, and are anxious to carry on. However, the City Council are keen to attract county cricket back to the Wagon Works. One way or another, the future of the Festival seemed more secure than for many years.

Archdeacon Meadow is built on the site of an old rubbish tip, within which are buried two double-decker buses and parts of several tanks. It was filled in and turned into a playing field in the late 1970s and in the mid-1980s was made into a proper square. Owing to a typing error, three inches of Surrey loam was poured on to the square as a top dressing instead of threequarters of an inch. When the mistake was discovered, the loam was mixed up with a foot of the top soil. The effect, by complete accident, was very successful.

The ground, ringed by poplars, is next to the Gloucester–Cardiff railway line. As is traditional in such settings, a member of staff is said to have hit a six that carried all the way to Cardiff in an open wagon.

No new grounds are scheduled to stage county matches in 1994. Uxbridge and Worksop both stage fixtures after missing out in 1993 while Chesterfield, relegated to one Derbyshire Championship fixture last season, gets three. The allocation of games to Chesterfield causes protest and counter-protest in Derbyshire between supporters from the north of the county and members of the Derby Executive Club who dislike missing their lunches. The deal with Staffordshire Moorlands Council, which meant Sunday League matches being allocated to various Staffordshire club grounds, has ended, resulting in the disappearance from the list of such venues as Cheadle, Checkley, Knypersley and Leek.

Glamorgan's fixture against the touring South Africans has been allocated to Ynysangharad Park, Pontypridd, where the 1929 South Africans played. Glamorgan lost this match, even though Jack Mercer took 14 wickets for 119. Taff Ely Borough Council, who have taken over control of the ground from the town council, are spending £300,000 on a new pavilion, which they hope will be ready for the South Africans. A high percentage of the games at Pontypridd have been ruined by rain. "On a nice day it's a very attractive setting for cricket," said a local official. "Unfortunately, no one can remember a nice day."

UMPIRING IN 1993

By JACK BAILEY

The 1993 season was a difficult one for umpires. When I was secretary of MCC and had to write the introduction to the 1980 Code of the Laws of Cricket, which, it should constantly be remembered, are framed to apply to all grades of cricket, I could come up with nothing better than: "The basic laws of cricket have stood remarkably well the test of well over 200 years of playing the game: and it is thought that the real reason for this is that cricketers have traditionally been prepared to play in the spirit of the game, as well as in accordance with the Laws. The unique character and enjoyment of cricket depends upon all cricketers, at whatever level, continuing to preserve this spirit."

In 1993 one could be pardoned for wondering whether those words were still remotely applicable. There was only one experimental law in operation – the one bouncer per over rule, designed to cut down on intimidatory bowling and make the task of umpires easier. But it was not an easier time for umpires at first-class level, and reports from all quarters lead one to believe that this applied to other levels of the game where doing it "as seen on TV" was, naturally enough, the order of the day.

We saw umpires under continuous fire. We saw appeals for all sorts of catches, especially of the bat-pad variety, which seemed to be not so much a request for a decision as part of a gradual build-up so that, by sheer weight of numbers, one appeal in ten would succeed. We saw appeals for all kinds of dismissal from the most unlikely corners of the field. We saw batsmen failing to walk when obviously out. The old camaraderie between player and umpire seemed at a low ebb.

Nor was the perception of the first-class umpire's lot helped by a BBC TV programme (*On the Line*) which showed that captains were given out lbw 17 per cent less often than other batsmen. The point at issue here was the long-standing system of captains reporting on umpires and the intrusion of bias into the system. Current umpires were unable to voice an opinion; their contracts saw to that. Those not thus inhibited, having left the list, came through as having an axe to grind. The question begged was whether the modern professional captain was capable of giving an objective assessment. Certainly, at this level, the attitude of so many players to the spirit of the game has not helped.

It is doubtful whether the authority taken from umpires in the middle by recourse to television umpires and the appointment of Test match referees has helped either. Once confidence is eroded it is not easily restored.

Whether the system of referees for Test matches upholding, or not, as the case may be, a code of conduct will eventually have the desired effect is something on which the jury is sure to be out for a considerable time. Certainly there were times when the necessary support for the umpires seemed not to be forthcoming.

The fallibility of the third umpire was demonstrated the first time one was used in England. The view of the "man in the box" during the Surrey v Lancashire Benson and Hedges match was infinitely worse than that of the man in the middle who asked for his opinion. More than likely, Wasim Akram, who appeared to lose contact with his bat at the vital moment, would have been given run out by the square-leg umpire in normal circumstances. Having called for a second opinion which proved inconclusive, he could hardly give against the batsman second time around.

Then there was the case of Lancashire (again) against Derbyshire in the Benson and Hedges Cup final. This time adjudication from the man in the box was called for to determine whether Neil Fairbrother had been run out. "Not out" came the answer. A still photograph later showed that the Derbyshire wicket-keeper had removed the bails legitimately before Fairbrother had gained his ground. In neither of these two examples could you really blame the square-leg umpire for covering his tracks. But . . .

In one case at least in 1993, the fielding side thought dissent had been positively rewarded. Against Northamptonshire at Canterbury, a caught-behind decision went against Graham Cowdrey of Kent. As he trudged back to the pavilion, he rubbed his arm, plainly disgruntled. He had almost reached the point of no return, the boundary's edge, when the umpire, Dickie Bird, changed his mind and called him back. He went on to make a century. There are those who would say that by expressing himself as he did, Cowdrey ruled himself out of all consideration of being recalled.

The Laws are there to assist the players who are expected to play within a spirit which, in the long term at least, will work to the advantage of all who play and are connected with the game. More and more in 1993 cricket appeared to confirm that it reflects the age in which it is played. Most of us hope and expect better than that. Just one final thought. If, as has been reported, those revolving signs on Test grounds – which appear behind the batsman receiving the bowling, and are chiefly coloured red – made the task of the umpire asked to give a difficult caught-behind decision virtually impossible, will they be removed and replaced by white sightscreens? The answer will tell us much about the way the game is going.

CHARITIES IN 1993

The Lord's Taverners raised slightly more than £1 million in 1993 to give away in 1994. The overall aim is "to give youngsters, especially the disadvantaged and disabled, a sporting chance" and at least half the money goes back into cricket. In 1993 this meant that about £500,000 went to the National Cricket Association, English Schools Cricket Association and other bodies. Another £500,000 went to help disabled people play or watch sport, largely through the New Horizons minibus campaign, which put 20 new buses on the road.

The major fund-raising events of 1993 included the Tim Rice Golf Classic, at St Pierre, Chepstow, sponsored by Avasta Steel, which raised £70,000; Prince Edward's real tennis marathon, when he played at Windsor for 12 solid hours and raised £30,000; and a cricket match against Lavinia,

Duchess of Norfolk's XI on August Bank Holiday, sponsored by Guinness, which produced £25,000.

Patrick Shervington, The Lord's Taverners, 22 Queen Anne's Gate, London SW1H 9AA. Telephone: 071-222 0707.

The Primary Club, one of the favourite charities of the late Brian Johnston, started at Beckenham Cricket Club in 1955. It now raises £60,000 a year for cricket and other sports for the blind. Most of the money goes to Dorton House School, Sevenoaks, but equipment has been provided for schools for the blind throughout the country. Membership is nominally restricted to players who have been dismissed first ball in any form of cricket.

Mike Thomas, PO Box 111, Bromley, Kent. Telephone: 081-467 5665.

The John Arlott Memorial Trust was launched in June 1993 to help provide affordable housing and improve recreational facilities in rural areas, by raising funds for the Rural Housing Trust and the National Playing Fields Association. In 1994 the Trust is planning a Village Cricket Challenge, culminating in a match between a village XI and a celebrity XI. Teams are invited to take part by designating any of their fixtures as a fund-raising match.

Janet Hart, John Arlott Memorial Trust, Hobart House, 40 Grosvenor Place, London SW1X 7AN. Telephone: 071-235 6318.

OBITUARY

ABBOTT, GLEN CHARLES, who was killed in a car accident on May 9, 1993, aged 23, was a very promising South African cricketer. He was a left-handed batsman whose form for Griqualand West in 1991-92 was sensational: in 11 innings in the UCB Bowl he hit three hundreds, and his aggregate for the season of 754 runs was second only to Kepler Wessels. He moved to Northern Transvaal to play Castle Cup cricket in 1992-93 but was not immediately successful. He was enthusiastically involved in township coaching. Ali Bacher, chief executive of the United Cricket Board, described him as "a very warm and sensitive young man".

ACHARYA, MAHIPAT, who died at Rajkot on January 7, 1993, aged 69, represented the states of Kathiawar and Saurashtra in the Ranji Trophy. Later he acted for many years as a selector, adviser and coach to the Saurashtra Cricket Association.

AGGARWAL, VIVEK, was killed on April 26, 1993, when an Indian Airlines plane crashed just after take-off from Aurangabad. He was 31 and a flight purser with the airline. He played in one first-class match, in the Ranji Trophy for Haryana against Bengal at Faridabad in 1982-83.

AHMED, HABEEB, died on July 10, 1993, aged 52, after a long illness. He was a right-hand batsman and off-spinner who played for Hyderabad, Railways and Madras in the Ranji Trophy and represented South Zone in the Duleep Trophy. In the 1958-59 season he scored 400 runs, averaging 80, and in 1962-63 took six for 12 for Madras against Mysore.

ALEXANDER, HARRY HOUSTON, died in Melbourne on April 15, 1993, aged 87. He was Australia's oldest living Test cricketer, a distinction which passed to Keith Rigg. "Bull" Alexander (the nickname was well-earned) was a strong, broad-chested man and a pacy and combative right-arm bowler. He played only one Test, at the end of the Bodyline series in 1932-33, but his appearance was eventful. Alexander had first encountered Douglas Jardine when he played his second match for Victoria four years earlier. He took four for 98 against MCC but Jardine complained that he was running on the pitch and forced him to bowl round the wicket; Jardine scored 115. No one had forgotten the incident when Alexander came to play for Australia. In the second innings, with England needing just 164 to win, Jardine again accused him of roughing up the pitch whereupon he bowled bouncer after bouncer, scoring several direct hits. "A disgraceful exhibition," said *Wisden*. It was not Bodyline bowling, as he did not have a packed leg-side field, but it was the nearest Australia had come to retaliation and the Hill roared with delight. It did not last long: England won easily and Alexander's match figures were one for 129 and nought for 25. Earlier in his career, Alexander had furthered his reputation by dismissing Bradman twice. He served in Crete, the Middle East and the Pacific in the war before settling in Euroa, the birthplace of Merv Hughes. In later years, he admitted that Jardine had "a ton of guts". But he insisted: "It's part of a fast bowler's trade to give 'em a few in the ribs occasionally. Keeps 'em honest."

ALI, SYED MUBARACK, who died on February 3, 1993, aged 79, was an off-spinner who was no-balled for throwing 29 times in an innings by umpire Eddie Ward, while playing for Trinidad against Barbados at Bridgetown in 1942. He took a wicket after being forced to switch to bowling underarm. When he bowled from the other end, umpire Herman Griffith had no complaint. This was the only time in his five first-class matches he was no-balled, though questions were raised on other occasions. He took 16 wickets at 32.25.

ALLSOPP, ARTHUR HENRY, who died on February 6, 1993, aged 84, played for New South Wales and Victoria after a deprived childhood, spent partly in a home for delinquents. He made an immediate impact in his first important match, for a Southern Districts XIII against Percy Chapman's MCC team in 1928-29, when he drove and pulled powerfully and made 79 not out. A year later he made 117 on first-class debut for New South Wales against MCC and 136 in his fourth Shield game, against South Australia. That season in the Shield he averaged 64.57, second only to Bradman. However, he had failed in a Test trial and could not recapture his best form the next season. Three years later, he played for Victoria and, against Tasmania, became the first man to make a hundred on debut for two states. His career finished when he caught enteric fever on Frank Tarrant's tour of India in 1935-36. Contemporaries believed he was top-class – his career average was 45.90 – and could have been chosen to tour England in 1930, but the Australian authorities were wary of his lack of social grace; there were "bad reports". However, his team-mates liked him and he was virtually adopted by Archie Jackson's family.

ANAND RAU, PADMANUR, who died at Madras in November 1991, was an Indian radio commentator sometimes described as South India's John Arlott. He worked from 1943 until the 1970s.

ASHENDEN, JACK GILBERT, who died on November 14, 1992, aged 81, was a right-arm medium-pacer. He played in 16 first-class matches in New Zealand, nearly all for Wellington between 1935 and 1945. He took 53 wickets at a cost of 28.27, his best return being six for 44 against Otago.

AYRES, RYALL SYDNEY, died on November 24, 1991, aged 60. "Tim" Ayres was a batsman and occasional leg-spinner who played in four games for Queensland in the 1950s. His father, S. W. Ayres, also played for the state.

BARLING, HENRY THOMAS, died at Hastings on January 2, 1993, aged 86. Tom Barling was a stalwart Surrey batsman from 1927 to 1948. He made a highly successful start but lost form for four seasons until 1933, when he began a six-year sequence of scoring 1,000 runs every season. The 1934 *Wisden* said that for several years he had been instructed not to play his natural game of driving half-volleys even when he had just come in; he almost left to join Middlesex. Returning to his own style, he scored 1,915 runs in the season, including 269 in just over five hours against Hampshire. He continued to score prolifically in a style which E. M. Wellings said was as correct and pleasing as anyone's in the game. But his strokeplay was far less assured against the fastest bowling and, since he was on the plumpish side, he was not the greatest of fielders. But in 1946, when he had turned 40, he was still good enough to pass 2,000 for the only time, including an unbeaten 233 against Nottinghamshire on the August Bank Holiday weekend, with The Oval packed. He made 19,209 runs at 34.61 in 391 first-class matches, with 34 centuries. He coached at Harrow from 1948 to 1966. Alf Gover, who shared a benefit with him in 1946, said: "Tom was a very fine strokemaker. He could hit the ball through the covers like anything. He was a very pleasant man too, full of fun."

BARNETT, CHARLES JOHN, who died in a nursing home at Stroud on May 28, 1993, aged 82, was one of the very best batsmen of the 1930s, an era of great batsmanship. He was a punishing right-hander who opened for Gloucestershire once he became established and played in 20 Tests for England before and after the war. He came from a well-known Gloucestershire cricketing family – his father (C. S.) and two uncles all played for the county, as amateurs – and after going to Wycliffe College he began as an amateur (against Cambridge in 1927, when he was 16). Although he turned professional in 1929, Barnett retained a certain amateur hauteur in his cricket and his life; the supporters knew him as Charlie, but he always regarded himself as Charles. In the dressing-room he became known as "The Guv'nor".

In the early days Barnett made a lot of runs in the middle order, often at great speed. But for several years there was more talk of his promise than his achievements. However, when the solid opener A. E. Dipper retired in 1932, Barnett was promoted in his place. It was the making of him – it was in his nature to get on with the business. But he also acquired more defence. In May 1933 he scored his first century in county cricket; in August he made 111 and 93 against Somerset "with an assurance and dash he had not quite previously approached". A week later he was playing for England against West Indies at The Oval. He made 52 even though he had to bat No. 8. By the end of the season he had scored 2,280 runs.

Barnett's attacking style was based on driving and a scorching square cut if given room; it was his ability to drive on the up on the sandy Bristol wickets which particularly astonished his team-mates. He was not a consistent player but between 1933 and 1948 he hit 48 centuries, averaged over 36, passed the 2,000 mark four times, and only twice scored less than 1,500 runs in an English season. A feature of Barnett's career was that he lacked a regular opening partner for either Gloucestershire or England. On the first of his two tours, to India in 1933-34, he was obliged to bat down the order; in Australia in 1936-37, when he was the leading run-scorer, he opened with Worthington, Fagg and Verity; in 1938 it looked as though Barnett and Hutton might become the successors to Hobbs and Sutcliffe, but he was dropped before The Oval, missed out on the tour to South Africa and did not play a Test match for nine years.

Yet in the First Test at Trent Bridge he came nearer than anyone had done to scoring a first-morning hundred before lunch; he got there the first ball he received afterwards, with a four past extra cover. And by tea-time he had a telegram from his mother in Cirencester: "Heartiest congratulations," it said, "everyone round about is delighted." It was the second and last of his Test centuries; the first, at Adelaide in 1936-37, was described by Neville Cardus as involving "severe discipline for him". Yet there were several near-misses. Robertson-Glasgow said Barnett was a player who made "colossal blunders". "He cuts the ball in the first over of a Test match, and the ball flies past the head of an outraged gully, who was dreaming of stalemates and composing himself to eternity. Or it doesn't fly past, but sticks in some hand . . . genius has turned to folly."

But in his mature years the genius often had the upper hand, with huge and dominating scores in county cricket: he hit 11 sixes in his 194 against Somerset in 1934, that same year he "simply flogged the bowling" for 170 against Worcestershire at Dudley. As the years went by, he also became an ever more effective bowler with a stock in-swinger above medium pace varied with a leg-cutter. In 1947 he was ninth in the bowling averages, with 50 wickets. In his career, he took 394 wickets at 30.98 to go with the 25,389 runs at 32.71, an average that suggests his style rather than his greatness.

He failed to make runs in his four Tests after the war, though he continued making big scores in county cricket. In 1948, he retired abruptly to play League cricket for Rochdale, to the chagrin of Gloucestershire supporters, who had recently lost Hammond as well. Though his batting was cheerful, he was a serious-minded man. On the SS *Orion* to Australia, Barnett shared a cabin with Verity and they read *The Seven Pillars of Wisdom* to each other. In retirement, he ran a business in Cirencester. A journalist called him "a fishmonger". He wrote an indignant letter, saying he supplied "high-class poultry and game", not least to the Duke of Beaufort. He maintained his amateur mien: he lived like a squire and hunted with the Beaufort and the Berkeley Vale, always, so it is said, with the uncomplicated verve he displayed at the crease.

BASS, JOHN GEORGE, who died on October 16, 1992, aged 89, played two Championship matches for Northamptonshire in 1935.

BAXTER, AUSTIN GODFREY, who died on January 17, 1993, aged 61, was an amateur batsman of whom Nottinghamshire had high hopes in the early 1950s. He scored 98, with strong driving, against Essex at Southend in 1953; it was said that he had the look of Joe Hardstaff. But he played only 13 matches before devoting himself to business.

BENNETT, FREDERICK ONSLOW ALEXANDER GODWYN, died on March 17, 1993, aged 79. Alex Bennett was chief executive of Whitbread Brewery from 1967 to 1975 and initiated the scholarship scheme whereby young cricketers were sent out to Australia each winter. Of the 27 chosen between 1976 and 1984, 16 played for England and one (Dipak Patel) for New Zealand. He opened the bowling for Winchester in 1931 and was a keen club cricketer.

BRAY, CHARLES, who died on September 12, 1993, aged 95, spent ten years playing as an amateur batsman for Essex, between 1927 and 1937, and 30 as the highly professional cricket correspondent of the *Daily Herald*, from 1935 until the paper's closure in 1964. Bray's playing record was unspectacular but he was a steady, handy, performer in a weak side and often had to deputise as captain. He was sometimes known as the Ranji of Leyton, though that was more a matter of his complexion and manner of keeping his shirts buttoned at the wrist than his batting. In 1931 he scored three centuries. In 1932 he was in charge on the famous day Holmes and Sutcliffe broke the record with 555 for the first wicket. It was his goodwill in agreeing to a missing no-ball that enabled the record to stand; Sutcliffe had given his wicket away with the scorebooks not backing up the board's assertion that they had passed the record. It was said Bray was not always so good-humoured about it and once accused a motor salesman of insulting him, after he tried to sell him a car with 555 on the number plate. The salesman knew nothing of cricket and was baffled. Bray was mentioned in dispatches as a war correspondent. As a cricket writer he had an easy style, strong opinions and operated in a spirit of popular-paper inquiry, though the questions were gentler than would become the norm in the *Herald*'s successor paper *The Sun*. His personal style was such that he was frequently presumed to be the gentleman from *The Times*.

BROADBENT, ROBERT GILLESPIE, who died on April 26, 1993, aged 68, was one of the mainstays of the Worcestershire side of the 1950s. Joining the club via Caterham School and five years' service as an RAF navigator, he played between 1950 and 1963, and established a reputation as an adaptable middle-order batsman and, above all, as an excellent close fielder, who took 297 catches in his

307 games. Before joining Worcestershire he played for Middlesex Second XI as an amateur and often reserved his best form for matches against his old county, including a match-winning 155 in 1951. He hit Keith Miller out of the ground at New Road at the start of the 1953 Australian tour, though his county's position often meant he had to be more obdurate. He also played first-class hockey for Worcestershire.

BROWN, EDWARD K., died on August 15, 1993, aged 82. Ted Brown gave up school-teaching in 1968 to become a full-time bookseller, specialising in cricket material. He was based in Liskeard, Cornwall, an address that became famous among collectors.

BRYAN, REGINALD CHARLES PETER, MBE, who died on May 9, 1993, aged 77, took six for 54 in his only first-class match, Europeans v Indians at Madras in 1937. After a career in the Army and naval intelligence, he became bursar of Worcester College, Oxford.

BURNETT, ANTHONY COMPTON, died on May 31, 1993, aged 69. "Tolly" Burnett was a middle-order batsman in the strong and successful Cambridge side of 1949, averaging 37.66 in the season, though he was out for a duck at Lord's. He failed to get a Blue in 1950 and then became a science master at Eton. However, he was regularly considered as a possible amateur captain for one of the smaller counties. Northamptonshire enquired about him in 1954 but were told he had become "rather portly". In 1958 Glamorgan went so far as to give him a run of eight matches to test him as a possible successor to Wilf Wooller as captain; he averaged 6.20 in ten Championship innings amid some internal dissent and the experiment was deemed to have failed.

BURNS, ROBERT CROSBIE, died in August 1993, aged 93. Bob Burns kept wicket for Canterbury in 14 matches between 1928 and 1934 and once effected five stumpings in a match off W. E. Merritt. He was New Zealand's oldest first-class player when he died.

CADOGAN, Col. EDWARD HENRY, CBE, who died on February 7, 1993, aged 84, was a fast-medium right-arm bowler whose Championship experience was confined to four matches for Hampshire in 1933 and 1934, but he finished top of the county's bowling averages in each season. He took five for 52 against Middlesex in 1934. Cadogan had captained Sandhurst and also played for the Army and, in India, the Europeans. He was wounded in Normandy during the war.

CASTLE, DENNIS, who died in February 1993, aged 78, counted cricket high among a variety of interests. He was member No. 111 of the Lord's Taverners and captained the charity's team. Of his two novels, one, *Run Out the Raj*, featured a fictional cricket team in India. He was the first editor of the comic *Radio Fun*.

CHAKRAPANY, V. M., who died on June 26, 1993, aged 69, was a broadcaster who covered numerous Tests for All India Radio and Radio Australia. He was based in Australia between 1968 and 1988.

CLARKE, Dr CARLOS BERTRAM, OBE, died in Putney on October 14, 1993, aged 75. "Bertie" Clarke was a Barbadian who came to England with the 1939 West Indian team and did unexpectedly well with his fast leg-breaks, taking 87 wickets, though only six of them came in the three Tests. He then decided to study medicine at Guy's Hospital and became a GP in Pimlico, London. He was a regular in the wartime British Empire XI. After the war, he played 49 times for

Northamptonshire and, after Freddie Brown's arrival cost him his place there, 18 times for Essex. He took 333 first-class wickets at 26.37. His later cricket was for the BBC – having been an early contributor to the Caribbean Service – but Clarke was such an enthusiast that even when playing county cricket he would catch a train to play in a BBC Sunday match. He played on for them until he was 70, taking an estimated 3,000 wickets, and still won the First XI Bowling Cup in his final season. He was awarded the OBE in 1983 for his community work amongst West Indians in London.

CLUGSTON, DAVID LINDSAY, died on September 27, 1993, aged 85. Lin Clugston was a left-handed batsman and spin bowler who played three games for Warwickshire in 1928 and three more in 1946. He later became familiar, until 1988, as the stentorian-voiced ground announcer at Edgbaston who would upbraid small boys for the slightest mischief in an echoing basso profundo. His successor is still sometimes called "the Cluggie".

COCK, DAVID FREDERICK, who died on September 26, 1992, aged 77, was an amateur batsman who was awarded his Essex cap after only 11 matches in 1939, when he scored 98 against Somerset at Westcliff. He reappeared briefly in 1946 but played only 14 matches in all. He was a long-serving and highly-regarded club cricketer for Bishop's Stortford.

COLE, Major-General ERIC STUART, CB, CBE, who died in December 1992, aged 86, played three matches for Kent in 1938 and on his county debut took four for 78 against Lancashire, bowling highly effective medium-fast out-swingers. He also played first-class cricket for the Army and the Free Foresters. Cole had a distinguished career in the Royal Corps of Signals and eventually became Director of Telecommunications at the War Office. In his youth he was Army light-heavyweight boxing champion.

COMFORT, Professor HOWARD, who died in Philadelphia on September 20, 1993, aged 89, spent almost the whole of his life at Haverford College, Pennsylvania, the last cricket-playing college in the US. As a student he made 124 against Merion and in 1925 captained Haverford on a tour of England. He stayed on to become Professor of Classics and founded the C. C. Morris Cricket Library at the college. He was a world authority on Roman pottery and, in the 1960s, was briefly US cultural attaché in Italy.

COSGRAVE, BRYAN, who died on November 26, 1992, aged 89, scored exactly 100 for Victoria against Tasmania in 1931-32, in one of his four first-class matches.

CRANFIELD, LIONEL MONTAGUE, died on November 18, 1993, aged 84. Monty Cranfield was an off-spinner who played for Gloucestershire 162 times between 1934 and 1951, his appearances being restricted by the presence of Tom Goddard, who played on until he was past 50. Cranfield was a big spinner of the ball and a popular, good-natured man. He took 233 first-class wickets at 32.91. Before joining Gloucestershire, he spent a year on the Lancashire staff. He was the Gloucestershire scorer from 1950 to 1952.

CRAWLEY, AIDAN MERIVALE, MBE, who died on November 3, 1993, aged 85, was one of seven members of his family, Harrovians all, to play first-class cricket, and perhaps the most brilliant. His 87 against Eton at Lord's in 1926 was widely regarded as the best innings in the match for many years. In *Wisden*, H. S. Altham called him "a beautiful player". In 1928 he broke the Oxford scoring record, with 1,137 runs (average 54.14) and five hundreds, including 167 against Essex and 162 against Surrey. In 1929, he made 204 against Northamptonshire at Wellingborough with ten sixes and 22 fours, apparently having driven to the ground straight from an Oxford ball. For the Gentlemen at Lord's he hit A. P. Freeman over the old free seats on to the Nursery End. He played 33 matches for Kent, mostly in 1931 and 1932, but his subsequent career took him off in many different directions, most of them distinguished, some contradictory: he was Labour MP for Buckingham (rising to be Under-Secretary of State for Air in 1951) and, having grown disillusioned with nationalisation, Conservative MP for West Derbyshire. He was also a pioneering documentary film-maker, a fighter pilot, a PoW who staged a spectacular if brief escape, the biographer of de Gaulle and an early TV personality, as presenter of the 1950s series *Viewfinder*. In 1955 he became the first head of Independent Television News, where he encouraged the then novel idea of probing questions, and he was later the first chairman of London Weekend Television. He retained his cricketing connections, was president of MCC in 1972-73, chairman of the National Cricket Association for its first seven years and one of the begetters of the National Village Championship. His perseverance did not always match his versatility and panache. The last years of this handsome, gilded figure were clouded with tragedy: his wife was killed in a car crash and his two sons in a plane crash.

CUTHBERTSON, GEOFFREY BOURKE, who died on August 9, 1993, aged 92, was captain of Northamptonshire in 1936 and 1937, two of the desperate seasons during the county's four-year sequence without a win. He played 43 matches for the county, of which none were won and 27 lost. Not surprisingly, he was remembered by team-mates as a genial optimist, as well as a bold batsman. Earlier, he had been a member of the Malvern XI, played for Cambridge (though he failed to get a Blue), Sussex (once) and Middlesex. When he died he was joint-senior member of MCC, having been elected in 1919.

DAVIES, HAYDN GEORGE, who died at Haverfordwest on September 4, 1993, aged 81, was Glamorgan's wicket-keeper from 1939 to 1958. He was thick-set, stocky – winner of two Welsh schoolboy rugby caps – but nimble enough to be a born Glamorgan wicket-keeper. In 1946 he was chosen for a Test trial; it was unfortunate for him that Godfrey Evans emerged at the same time. He settled to become a stalwart professional, and often captained the team before his retirement in 1958. He had 789 career dismissals (82 of them in 1955 alone). His batting was often effective and sometimes very bold, but not up to Evans's standard.

DEODHAR, Professor DINAKAR BALWANT, who died at Pune on August 24, 1993, aged 101, was the world's oldest living first-class cricketer. He not merely became a real-life centurion, he was the first Indian to score a hundred for a representative side against a visiting team: 148 for All India against A. E. R. Gilligan's MCC team in 1926-27. This confirmed his reputation as one of the best batsmen in India, secured over several seasons playing for the Hindus in the Bombay Quadrangular. India's Test status came too late for him, since he was already 42 by 1932, but he remained a successful batsman for Maharashtra in the Ranji Trophy until 1946. He led them to the trophy in 1939-40 and 1940-41, having effectively founded the team as a breakaway from Bombay and recruited V. S. Hazare to play for him. Deodhar was still scoring first-class centuries long after he was 50: two in a match against Nawanagar in 1944-45, the last in a charity match in 1946. He was almost 56 when he played his final first-class match in 1947-48. In 81 first-class matches he scored 4,522 runs, averaging 39.22 and hitting 12 centuries. He was a Professor of Sanskrit. He was also an Indian selector, first-class umpire, radio commentator and the author of three books in English and Marathi. When he was 97 he wrote an introduction to a book about C. K. Nayudu. The tribute included a rebuke about Nayudu's chain-smoking which, he said, led to "his early death at the age of 72".

DURLEY, ANTHONY WILLIAM, who died on January 1, 1993, aged 59, was a lower-order batsman and wicket-keeper who played five matches for Essex in 1957. Between 1960 and 1976 he played for Bedfordshire and later became chairman.

EDRICH, ERIC HARRY, who died at his home in Cambridgeshire on July 9, 1993, aged 79, was a member of the famous Norfolk cricketing family: the oldest of four brothers who all played first-class cricket. Bill Edrich was one of his younger brothers, along with Brian of Kent and Glamorgan and Geoff of Lancashire; John Edrich is their cousin. Eric was a wicket-keeper who played for Lancashire in 33 games between 1946 and 1948, having played for Norfolk before the war. In May 1948 he scored two consecutive centuries, the second in the Roses match at Headingley, then stumped Bradman off Malcolm Hilton. From this peak, he rapidly lost form and his place. He coached at Stowe School, briefly emigrated to New Zealand, then returned to Norfolk and chicken-farming.

FOLLEY, IAN, the former Lancashire left-arm spin bowler, died in hospital on August 30, 1993, aged 30. He had been struck under the eye trying to hook a short ball, while captaining Whitehaven in a North Lancashire League match against Workington. He jogged off the field and it was assumed he would only need a few stitches but, while under anaesthetic, apparently suffered a heart attack. Folley played for Lancashire from 1982 until 1990 and was regarded as a promising medium-pace bowler before the manager Jack Bond encouraged him to switch to spin. At first the change worked magnificently, and he took 68 Championship wickets in 1987, including seven for 15 against Warwickshire at Southport. He took 57 wickets in 1988 but then began to suffer "the yips" and found bowling almost impossible. In 1991 Folley moved to Derbyshire, but played in only four matches. In 140 first-class games he took 287 wickets. At the time of his death he was managing a night club.

GARLAND-WELLS, HERBERT MONTANDON, died on May 28, 1993, aged 85. Monty Garland-Wells was one of the leading amateur characters of the immediate pre-war period. Educated at St Paul's, he scored 64 not out and 70 for Oxford in the Varsity match in 1928, the year he made his debut for Surrey. He was a sporting all-rounder – he kept goal for the England amateur team – and a cricketing one. As a middle-order batsman, his batting never again touched the heights it did at University; nevertheless he, Errol Holmes and Freddie Brown were referred to at Surrey as the "Biff-Bang Boys". He also bowled medium-pace cutters good enough to bowl Bradman for 32 in May 1930 when he was striving for his 1,000. Garland-Wells took over the Surrey captaincy in 1939 and captained the team as he played, with a touch of unorthodoxy in the tradition of Percy Fender; he was also very popular with the professionals, without a hint of amateur aloofness. It promised to be a successful as well as a happy reign; however, the war came and commitments as a solicitor prevented him carrying on in 1946. Thereafter, he concentrated on golf and bowls. In the war his name was informally used as a code word in North Africa: Garland-Wells = Monty = Montgomery. This was more impenetrable to the Germans than the most complicated cipher.

GHOSH, WILLIAM, died on June 26, 1993, in Delhi, aged 64. "Willy" Ghosh was a left-arm spin bowler who took 207 first-class wickets at 17.07, playing for East Punjab, Railways and North Zone, and twice appeared in Test trials. He was unfortunate to be a contemporary of such players as Vinoo Mankad, Durani and Nadkarni.

GOBEY, STANLEY CLARKE, who died at his home at Harpole, Northamptonshire, on November 20, 1992, aged 76, played twice for Warwickshire in 1946 as a left-hand bat and right-arm medium-pace bowler.

GREENIDGE, WITNEY TYRONE, died of leukaemia on November 19, 1993, aged 28. Tyrone Greenidge was a 6ft 5in Barbadian fast bowler who played five games for Barbados between 1985 and 1987 and also league cricket in Lancashire, Sussex and Holland. He was a particularly considerate coach of young players.

GRIFFITH, STEWART CATHIE, CBE, DFC, TD, died aged 78 in a nursing home at Felpham in Sussex on April 7, 1993, after a long and trying illness. Batting as a makeshift opener in the Port-of-Spain Test of 1947-48, "Billy" Griffith became the first man to score his maiden first-class century for England and the only man to do so on debut. Later, he became secretary of MCC and guided the club from 1962 to 1974, during which time the club's role and the game itself changed profoundly.

At Dulwich, in spite of making more than 1,200 runs during four years in the XI, Griffith lived in the shadow of his friend Hugh Bartlett, whose scoring was phenomenal. However, when he took up wicket-keeping, he found an identity of his own. He won his Blue in his second year at Cambridge, 1935. "It is a long time since Cambridge had a better wicket-keeper," said *Wisden*. He toured Australia and New Zealand with a young MCC team under Errol Holmes in 1935-36, but lost his Cambridge place the following year to Paul Gibb. Griffith returned to Dulwich as cricket master, moved from Surrey (for whom he had played once) to Sussex and became first-choice keeper in 1939. He had a heroic war as an officer in the Glider Pilot Regiment, along with Bartlett. As second-in-command he carried the commander of the 6th Airborne Division, Major-General "Windy" Gale, into Normandy, crash-landing after being caught in a storm. He also took part at Arnhem and won the DFC. His exploits make his subsequent heroism on the cricket field easier to comprehend. After the war Griffith became captain and secretary of Sussex. Though he rapidly stood down as captain, he maintained his wicket-keeping form to be chosen for the 1947-48 tour of the West Indies. Called in as opener because three leading batsmen were unfit, he played an epic innings in the Second Test, battling for six hours and scoring 140. He would say later that he had to stay out there because he had run out his opening partner Jack Robertson for two and dared not face his captain's wrath. He toured South Africa in 1948-49 and played in the last two Tests before retiring to become cricket correspondent of the *Sunday Times* for two years and then one of two MCC assistant secretaries to Ronnie Aird. Ten years later he became secretary. Immediately afterwards, amateur status was abolished and one-day cricket began. In 1968, MCC surrendered its controlling role to the TCCB and cricket became embroiled in the D'Oliveira affair. Griffith was a man of enormous natural charm who never liked to say an unkind word to anyone, however acute the crisis; this sometimes meant that other people at MCC had to take the more unpleasant decisions.

HAMER, ARNOLD, who died on November 3, 1993, aged 76, played twice for Yorkshire in 1938 and was breaking records for Pudsey St Lawrence 11 years later when the Yorkshire president recommended him to Derbyshire. He was already

[*Patrick Eagar*

BILLY GRIFFITH

33 but became a county stalwart throughout the 1950s, playing in the phlegmatic Derbyshire manner but sometimes producing innings of great quality and elan, often on bad wickets: his 112 not out, carrying his bat, on a green pitch at The Oval in 1957 was one of the great innings of the season.

HANCOCK, LAURANCE WILLIAM, who died on January 2, 1993, aged 94, was almost synonymous with Minor Counties cricket in general and Staffordshire cricket in particular, with a record of service that is quite extraordinary. He became Staffordshire's assistant secretary in 1927 and seven years later followed his father as secretary. His father had done the job for 25 years; he did it for 53 and never missed a Staffordshire match until 1992 when he was taken ill. From 1970 to 1983 he also served as Hon. Secretary to the Minor Counties Cricket Association. He was awarded the Queen's Jubilee Medal in 1977, and in 1992 was made an Honorary Life Member of MCC. He nurtured Staffordshire-born players like David Steele and Bob Taylor and they revered him for it. "He was like a father to us," said Taylor.

HARRIS, TERENCE ANTHONY, died on March 7, 1993, aged 76. Tony Harris, only 5ft 6in tall, was one of those magnificently brave and athletic all-round sportsmen in which South Africa has long specialised; he may have been the greatest of them all. He excelled in half-a-dozen sports. While still a schoolboy in Kimberley he was playing Currie Cup cricket, scoring an unbeaten 114 on his debut for Griqualand West; before he was 21 he was the Springbok fly-half, partnering Danie Craven against the All Blacks in the only South African side to win a series in New Zealand; soon after that he found himself flying Spitfires until he was shot down off Italy in January 1945 and captured. As a cricketer, he was an attacking batsman and an athletic fielder. He played in three Tests after the war, scoring 60 in the First Test at Nottingham on the 1947 tour. He played again at Lord's and at Johannesburg on England's 1948-49 tour but without further success.

HASSETT, ARTHUR LINDSAY, MBE, died on June 16, 1993, aged 79. Lindsay Hassett followed Bradman both as captain of Australia and as the embodiment of the national tradition of pocket-sized batting geniuses. He was of course nowhere near Bradman's class as a batsman, but the two men differed most in their approach to life: Hassett was far more light-hearted and puckish. In 1953 he surrendered the Ashes to England but his team won many friends.

Hassett was born at Geelong and was a brilliant sportsman at Geelong College. His name first got noticed when he was a 17-year-old, scoring 147 not out for Combined Victoria Country XI against the West Indians in 1930-31 (it was not noticed everywhere: *Wisden* called him Bassett), but it took him several more years to establish himself in Victoria's first team. In the early 1930s he had a spell of seven ducks for South Melbourne – and he reckoned he was plumb lbw and dropped twice when he was still in line for his eighth. He made 150 and never looked back. He was chosen to tour England in 1938 and had the chance of 1,000 in May. The runs dried up but none the less he played in every Test of the series, the first four of his 43 Tests.

In 1945 he was chosen to lead the Australian Services to Britain for the Victory Tests. He declined a commission and did it all on a sergeant-major's pay of 12 shillings a day. The tour was hugely popular and re-established cricket's role in public life. He began the 1946-47 series against England with a stand of 276 with Bradman, though it was a grinding performance compared to the batting styles of the 1930s. Hassett, like the game itself, had changed. Before the war he was a quick-footed attacking player, reliant on the cut and pull, as one would expect

[*Popperfoto*

LINDSAY HASSETT

from someone of 5ft 6in, but he was also famous for his ability to take on Bill O'Reilly and hit him over the top. Now he was much more patient and cautious. In 1948 he became Bradman's vice-captain and his 137 played an important role in the victory at Nottingham that set the tone for the series. It was said he was chosen as Bradman's successor by only one vote. It may have been remembered that, among other pranks, he had once tied a goat to Bradman's bed. But he was highly successful against South Africa, West Indies and England and his batting remained absolutely staunch. He was 40 at the end of the 1953 tour of England but had scored centuries at Trent Bridge and Lord's. When he finally lost the Ashes, he made a gracious and humorous speech, having been introduced as "The Happy Warrior". It was his fourth defeat in 24 Tests as captain, against 14 wins and six draws. In retirement, he ran a sports goods business and commentated until 1981 when, he said, he could stand modern players' behaviour no more. In 216 matches he hit 16,890 at 58.24, an average bettered (amongst players with 10,000 runs or more) only by Bradman, Merchant, Ponsford and Woodfull. He scored 59 centuries in his 290 completed innings, 27 of them overseas. His Test record was 3,073 runs in 43 matches, at 46.56. He was a quick, smart fielder. Cardus described his century at Lord's in 1953 as "four and a half hours of cricket so nicely fashioned that the watchmaker's eye was required to detect a loose screw or loose end here or there". He once remarked in a press box during a boring passage: "I'm glad I wasn't up here when I was down there." "There are others who have made more runs and taken more wickets, but very few have ever got more out of a lifetime," wrote Richie Benaud. As an epitaph, "Happy Warrior" will do nicely.

HENDY, WILLIAM JAMES, was New Zealand's oldest first-class cricketer when he died on September 23, 1992, aged 92. Hendy played two first-class matches for Auckland in 1927-28. He is best remembered for a sensational innings for the Auckland Suburban Association against Christchurch HS OB, who had two future Test bowlers, Cromb and Merritt, in their attack. Hendy was 200 not out at lunch and finished on 300 not out.

HEWETSON, General Sir REGINALD HACKETT, GCB, CBE, DSO, died on January 19, 1993, aged 84. Reggie Hewetson played in six first-class matches, for the Europeans in India in 1929-30 and for the Army in 1935-37. He commanded field regiments of the Royal Artillery in Italy in the war, when he was awarded the DSO. He rose to be the Adjutant-General at the Ministry of Defence.

HIGSON, THOMAS ATKINSON, jun., who died on January 15, 1993, aged 81, followed his father by playing for both Derbyshire and Lancashire. He was a left-handed batsman who scored 101 in 95 minutes for Cheltenham against Haileybury at Lord's in 1930. After leaving school he played six times for Derbyshire then moved to captain Lancashire Second XI. He took over as first-team captain in 1939 when W. H. L. Lister was absent. Higson was earmarked for the captaincy at Old Trafford in 1946, but could not spare the time from his law firm. He was Lancashire president in 1977-78.

HOWARD, ALAN RAYMOND, who died in March 1993, aged 83, played for Glamorgan 59 times between 1928 and 1933, occasionally keeping wicket. His father and brother both played for Leicestershire.

JEFFREY, WILLIAM, who died on September 2, 1993, aged 43, was Guyana's highest-qualified coach. He played seven matches for Berbice and Guyana in 1969-70 and 1970-71.

JOHNSTON, BRIAN ALEXANDER, CBE, MC, who died on January 5, 1994, aged 81, was among the best-known and best-loved of all cricket broadcasters. Along with John Arlott, who died in 1991, he was the central figure of BBC's *Test Match Special* and responsible for its unique style. Brian Johnston's major contribution to the game was to maintain that it was wholly fun, like life itself; cricketers were never incompetent, they were always unlucky ("He's just dropped three catches, poor chap"). This could only be a partial view of cricket and his broadcasting thus never had the richness or depth of Arlott's. But he was a tremendous all-round professional – among the greatest ad-lib outside broadcasters – who upheld his standards and his enthusiasm until his heart attack a month before he died. Even then, he was on his way to another edition of his one-man touring show, *An Evening with Johnners*. He was mourned by many millions.

Johnston was born in Hertfordshire on June 24, 1912, and was only ten when his childhood was touched by tragedy with the death of his father in a drowning accident. He went to Eton and Oxford; at both he spent his summers keeping wicket, with more zest than brilliance. Johnston served in the Grenadier Guards, won the Military Cross and made the contacts that enabled him to join the BBC after the war. It was an example of the Old Boy network at its best: it rapidly became obvious that he was a heaven-sent radio personality with the gift of sounding fascinated by everything and everyone. He brought this, with immense success, to such programmes as *In Town Tonight* and *On The Job*. He interviewed music hall artistes, a task he loved, and, for *Down Your Way*, thousands of local worthies. If any of them failed to interest him, he never let on. With immense gusto, he performed such stunts as spending a night in the Chamber of Horrors, lying between railway tracks while an express thundered overhead and reporting from inside a pillar box, snatching letters from bemused members of the public.

His cricket commentaries began when Test cricket resumed on television in 1946 and he remained on TV until he was abruptly sacked – without a word of thanks – in 1970, when executives decided they wanted ex-players instead. At once, he switched to radio and, aged 58, began his stint of almost a quarter of a century on *Test Match Special*, during which he reached the height of his fame. The prep school japes, puns and nicknames and the chocolate cakes sent in to him by adoring women listeners became his trademarks. His double entendre ("Neil Harvey, standing at leg slip with his legs wide apart, waiting for a tickle") became legendary enough to attract their own Apocrypha: there is no record of him or anyone else ever saying live "the bowler's Holding, the batsman's Willey". After Arlott retired in 1980, some people felt that the frivolity had taken over the programme too much; indeed all Johnston's professionalism may not be remembered as much as the minute and a half of bizarre radio history created in 1991, when he broke down laughing after Jonathan Agnew had described a dismissal by noting that "Botham didn't quite get his leg over". Only very, very rarely did the humour drain away: he made an extraordinarily vehement speech against the boycott of South Africa at a special meeting of MCC in 1983. However, he will be remembered by friends, acquaintances and listeners alike for his sunny disposition. Even people who only heard him felt for certain he had a twinkle in his eye. It takes a superb performer to convey that on radio.

KAPLAN, JACK MAURICE, who died at Durban on October 13, 1991, aged 66, played eight first-class matches for Combined Universities and Natal in South Africa in the late 1940s and early 1950s. Later, he worked hard for the Natal Cricket Union.

KILBURN, JAMES MAURICE, died on August 28, 1993, aged 84. J. M. Kilburn was the extraordinarily durable cricket correspondent of the *Yorkshire Post* from 1934 to 1976. He was the representative of an important tradition of

[*Bob Thomas*

BRIAN JOHNSTON

cricket writing, quite different to that of Neville Cardus across the Pennines: harder, less flashy, more punctilious. He was originally a schoolmaster who was given a job on the paper because his name was familiar to the editor from the Bradford League columns – he bowled medium-paced off-breaks. Kilburn then developed his own method of writing: with a fountain pen on press telegram forms at 60 or 80 words a shilling. At the close of play he immediately concluded his essay; he hardly ever crossed anything out. His cricketing judgments were assured and rigorous, his style exact but sometimes elegant: "Leyland's bowling is a joke but it is an extremely practical joke." He was a tall, austere man who had little truck with press-box banter. He also refused to write anything about events off the field, though these became more and more important in Yorkshire cricket and his editors would send him plaintive notes about the need to compete with the *Daily Mail*. However, he had made his reputation, with seven books as well as his daily work, and was unsackable. Long before his retirement, he had started to cut an old-fashioned figure. That never worried his readers. Yorkshire cricket was losing its authority and hauteur; its most important chronicler never lost his. Though he became blind, Jim Kilburn remained an upright, dignified man until he died.

LAMB, HENRY JOHN HEY, died on February 5, 1993, aged 80. John Lamb was working as an articled clerk in his father's law firm when he was called out to captain Northamptonshire in 1936. He had played 15 county matches and established a reputation as a resolute batsman, but many years later he agreed he was not best equipped for the task of transforming what was then an entirely chaotic county. "All these people were so frightfully kind," he said. "They made no attempt to take advantage." He scored 91 not out against Essex and returned to lead the team six times in 1937. Thereafter, he was president of Kettering Town CC for 27 years.

LEWIS, CLAUDE, BEM, who died on April 26, 1993, aged 84, was a man of Kent through and through. Born at Sittingbourne, he joined the county in 1928 as a player, became the coach and retired as scorer in 1988. He was a slow left-arm bowler who did not get a first-team match until 1933 but thereafter continued until 1953, taking 301 wickets at 27.23 in 128 matches. In the damp summer of 1939 he came eighth in the bowling averages. On his retirement, he helped bring on some of Kent's finest players. As a scorer, he was efficient, humorous and much loved. He was awarded the British Empire Medal in 1989.

LINNEY, CHARLES KEITH, who died at Tunbridge Wells in September 1992, aged 80, was a vigorous left-handed batsman who played in 32 matches for Somerset between 1931 and 1937.

MACLAGAN, MYRTLE ETHEL, MBE, who died at Farnham on March 11, 1993, aged 81, was one of the best-known women cricketers of her day. She was in the cricket team at the Royal School, Bath, for six years and, having been coached by Tich Freeman, took five wickets in five balls with her off-breaks against Cheltenham Ladies College. She became a national personality after being chosen for the pioneering tour of Australia in 1934-35. In the first Test at Brisbane she made 72 and took seven for ten; in the second game at Sydney she made 119, the first hundred in a women's Test. England's men had just lost the Ashes but soon Maclagan's opening partnership with Betty Snowball was being compared to Hobbs and Sutcliffe and the *Morning Post* published the following quatrain:

> What matter that we lost, mere nervy men
> Since England's women now play England's game,
> Wherefore Immortal *Wisden*, take your pen
> And write MACLAGAN on the scroll of fame.

Maclagan made another century against Australia in 1937, toured again in 1948-49 and captained England in two Tests at home in 1951. She was an officer in the ATS during the war and rejoined the Army in 1951, becoming Inspector, PT for the WRAC. Her last major match was against the Australian touring team for the Combined Services in 1963, when she scored 81 not out. She was 52. In 1966 she was appointed MBE. At various times in her life she won prizes for squash, tennis, badminton and knitting. It was reported that so many people turned up for her 80th birthday she had to make a speech from the top of a step-ladder and got attention by a blast on her whistle.

MITRA, SUHRID, who died on February 24, 1993, aged 75, played in the Ranji Trophy, making his debut for Bengal in 1939-40. Later he became a successful coach. Among his protégés was the Test batsman Pranab Roy.

MUTTON, HOWARD JAMES CHARLES, who died on November 20, 1992, aged 68, played in five Sheffield Shield matches for South Australia in 1959-60. He captained the side in the last of these, at Adelaide against Western Australia. He later managed the South Australian team and coached at Pembroke School, Adelaide, and Tonbridge in England.

OVERTON, GUY WILLIAM FITZROY, who died on September 7, 1993, aged 74, was one of New Zealand's best-liked cricketers. He was a fast-medium right-arm swing bowler and a regular member of the Otago team from 1945 to 1956. He was also a particularly good-natured and hard-working player. Overton appeared in three Tests in South Africa in 1953-54, but his finest hour came when he took seven for 52 against Western Australia on the way home. He took 169 first-class wickets but scored only 137 runs.

PATEL, JASUBHAI MOTIBHAI, the Indian off-spinner, died on December 12, 1992, aged 68. Jasu Patel will always be remembered as the man who bowled India to their first-ever victory over Australia at Kanpur in 1959-60. He was already 35 with tinges of grey hair, but he was unexpectedly included at the insistence of Lala Amarnath, the chairman of selectors. Patel was known as a matting specialist but Amarnath thought the newly laid turf wicket might suit his unclassical whippy action. Patel responded by taking the best-ever analysis for India, nine for 69 in the first innings – McDonald, Harvey, Davidson, Benaud and Kline were all bowled – and five for 55 in the second. India won by 119 runs. He took 15 wickets in six other Tests, before and afterwards. Patel was the first cricketer to be awarded the Padma Shri, India's second-highest civilian award.

PEPPER, CECIL GEORGE, who died on March 24, 1993, aged 74, was a leg-spinner often described as the best Australian player never to win a Test cap. He was, without any doubt, one of the greatest characters ever to come near the game, to whom anecdotes clung, as with Fred Trueman, some of them actually true. He played 16 matches for New South Wales before the Sheffield Shield closed down for the war, building a reputation as a big spinner of the ball, a great exponent of the "flipper", and a hitter of devastating power. Next to Keith Miller he was the big attraction of the 1945 Australian Services team in England and he emulated C. I. Thornton's 1886 hit by smashing Eric Hollies over the houses at Scarborough and into Trafalgar Square. It was assumed he would soon play for Australia but a few months later at Adelaide he exchanged words with umpire Jack Scott, after Scott had turned down three appeals against Bradman. He left Australia to play League cricket for seven different clubs in Lancashire, Cheshire and Stafford-shire. He never did learn to keep quiet and it made him one of League cricket's great drawcards. A *Manchester Evening News* correspondent said he could not imagine any match involving Pepper pursuing a peaceful course. Usually there was more humour than anger, though when he went to India with the 1949-50 Commonwealth side he had to leave early because the umpiring annoyed him so much. It was thus gloriously ironic that in 1964 he became a first-class umpire. For 16 seasons he mixed an irreverent manner with a fearless if occasionally idiosyncratic approach to his job. He wrote to MCC warning them about the West Indian Charlie Griffith's action. "Three kicks and yer out," he would sometimes tell batsmen before the lbw law changed. The fearlessness may have been among the reasons he was never chosen for the Test panel, something that made him increasingly bitter; he never gave captains or top batsmen any special benefit of the doubt: "I used to shoot 'em out, no matter who." Lord's were also wary of the extent to which he fraternised with players. Among the great Pepper stories is the one (which has many variations) about the mild-mannered League umpire who finally lost patience with his swearing appeals and shouted back: "Not out, you fat Australian bastard." He ended his own umpiring career just as helmets were coming in. Dennis Amiss suggested Pepper might hold his. "You hold it, mate, and use it as a pisspot." Many of the stories concern his generosity. On his death, one friend said Cec was the only man he knew who could talk, spit, chew, belch and pass wind simultaneously. Peter Wight, who umpired with him, said he listened as well as talked.

POPE, GEORGE HENRY, who died at Chesterfield on October 29, 1993, aged 82, played 169 matches for Derbyshire and somehow came to seem the embodiment of the county's professionals: hard, rough-hewn, under-appreciated. As a bowler, he could move the ball sharply both ways and took 677 wickets at 19.92; as a batsman he was good enough to have a career average of 28.05 and tough enough to take Larwood and Voce on the chest. He missed most of Derbyshire's Championship season in 1936 through injury, but improved steadily as both batsman and bowler before the war and came close to a Test place (he was in the party for Trent Bridge in 1938 and was chosen for the abortive tour of India in 1939-40). He missed 1946 because he was committed to League cricket but in 1947 he received his one cap, against South Africa at Lord's. In 1948 he did the double for the second time – hitting 207 not out at Portsmouth – but promptly decided to retire to Jersey because of his wife's health. He came back to play more League cricket and stand as a first-class umpire between 1966 and 1974. He was mellower by then. The writer Michael Parkinson recalled playing a League game against Sheffield, when they were effectively Mr Pope's XI. "He would rap you on the pads, look ruefully down the wicket and say to himself: 'Nice little leg-cutter that, George. Just a little bit too much, perhaps. What do you think, Mr Umpire?' And the poor besotted creature was bound to agree, as he invariably did the next time Mr Pope struck the pads and this time bellowed a demand for lbw."

RAIKES, DOUGLAS CHARLES GORDON, who died on March 27, 1993, aged 83, played 12 first-class matches as a wicket-keeper for Oxford University (winning a Blue in 1931), his native Gloucestershire and Kent, where he briefly deputised for Godfrey Evans in 1948.

RANGACHARI, COMMANDUR RAJAGOPALACHARI, who died on October 9, 1993, aged 77, was a fast bowler who played four Tests for India against Australia and West Indies. He took four for 141 in unpromising circumstances (at one stage Australia were 503 for three) on his debut at Adelaide in 1947-48. But his real moment of glory came at Delhi ten months later, in India's first home Test for 15 years: with the game hardly started, he dismissed Rae, Stollmeyer and Headley to leave the score 27 for three. However, West Indies went on to make 631, though Rangachari's final figures were still five for 107. He took no other Test wickets and the nine eventually cost him 54.77 each. After the Bombay Test that followed he was dropped, but played on for Madras for another five seasons. He was a police officer.

RICHARDS, MALCOLM R., who died on August 8, 1993, played cricket for Antigua between 1944 and 1952 without appearing in a first-class match. He had four sons, three of whom were first-class cricketers and one of whom, Vivian, captained West Indies. Viv wrote of his father: "He was a proud man, and a disciplinarian, and it was the sheer power of his presence that initially shaped my approach towards life."

ROWAN, ERIC ALFRED BURCHELL, the South African Test player and elder brother of Athol, died on April 30, 1993, in Johannesburg, aged 83. Eric Rowan ranked with Dudley Nourse and Bruce Mitchell in the very forefront of Test batsmen from South Africa in the years before and after the Second World War. His long career (1929-30 to 1953-54) was spiced by controversy. He was always fearless – he sometimes batted without gloves and, so it was said, box – and not only as a batsman. He was small and wiry and cocky and feisty and contemptuous of authority. Having been left out of the 1947 tour of England because of personality clashes, he was chosen in 1951, as vice-captain, when he often had to lead the team because Nourse was injured, and dominated the tour.

Rowan, who played all his first-class cricket in South Africa for Transvaal, except for one season with Eastern Province, was a regular opener, occasionally going in at No. 3. He was a right-handed bat without much elegance, but with all the strokes. His maiden century came a year after his debut and by 1935 he was a natural choice to tour England. He made his Test debut at Trent Bridge and played throughout South Africa's successful series, though he did better outside the Tests, scoring 1,948 on the tour. *Wisden* was a little surprised: "He did not bat either with dignity or precision; he regarded his cricket in most light-hearted style, but his confidence was amazing." Rowan lost some of that confidence against the Australians in 1935-36, when Grimmett took his wicket five times out of six until he was dropped. And he struggled for form in some of the seasons before the war until he scored 306 not out against Natal in a first-class friendly in 1939-40, which stood as the highest score made in South Africa until 1993-94. As soon as non-competitive first-class cricket was resumed, he almost scored another triple-century, hitting 284 for Eastern Province against Griqualand West in 1945-46.

His non-selection for the 1947 tour was baffling, except in terms of character. But he was recalled when Nourse took over the captaincy from Melville and scored 156 not out to save the Test at Ellis Park in 1948-49, after the selectors had announced that he was dropped for the next Test. He batted six hours and reputedly found time to give the selectors a V-sign. He said he was giving the V for Victory; told that it was the wrong way round he supposedly replied: "That depends what part of the ground you're sitting." He was soon restored, though it was said his relations with Nourse were strained, and he got better and better. He made 277 not out for Transvaal against Griqualand West in 1950-51, then the highest Currie Cup score, and scored 176 before lunch against Rhodesia. He averaged 109 that season. But even in triumph he found trouble. He was one of *Wisden's* Five for his achievement in England in 1951. But, early on the tour, he and John Waite were slow handclapped by the crowd at Old Trafford during the Lancashire match. They sat down until there was quiet and later Rowan was involved in a scuffle in the pavilion. He was not picked for Australia in 1952-53 though, at 43, he was still in prime form; that, however, applied both to his batting and his effing and blinding at officialdom. In his 26 Tests he scored 1,965 runs and averaged 43.66; he scored 11,710 first-class runs at 48.58, including 30 centuries. He played for Jeppe Old Boys until he was 51 and continued working for schools cricket, though his later years were blighted by great pain after an accident when he fell in a hot bath. He bore that bravely too.

SALE, WILLIAM FRECKLETON, who died suddenly on October 5, 1993, aged 60, was the headmaster of Wellesley House School – the prep school where Sir Colin Cowdrey's three sons went – and the chairman of Kent. E. W. Swanton described him as "a man of tremendous tact and discernment who did a great deal behind the scenes".

SCOTT, COLIN JOHN, who died on November 22, 1992, aged 73, went straight from club cricket into the Gloucestershire team and made a tremendous impact as a fast bowler in the two seasons before the war. In 1938 he emerged straight from Downend and made an impression with his fine, flowing action and his youthful energy. In 1939 he took 121 wickets and, with George Lambert, formed one of Gloucestershire's most formidable new-ball partnerships. Anything seemed possible. But when he returned after the war he had lost his zip and in 1949 he switched to bowling off-breaks before reverting to medium pace and taking 100 wickets again in 1952. He played 235 matches for the county before finally retiring in 1954 and took 531 wickets at 31.57. His batting was uninhibited and occasionally effective and he caught beautifully, both in the slips and the deep.

SHARMA, HAR PRASAD, who died on November 12, 1992, aged 69, was an Indian Test umpire who gave a batsman out to the first ball of his first match: Sudhir Naik, caught behind off Andy Roberts in the Calcutta Test against West Indies in 1974-75. Sharma umpired two other Tests in India, both against England in 1976-77.

SHARPE, CLOUDESLEY BRERETON, who died on April 11, 1993, aged 89, was a slow-medium left-arm bowler from Sherborne School who played three matches for Middlesex in 1923, and also appeared for Dorset.

SMITH, KATH, who died in August 1993, aged 77, was one of the pioneers of Australian women's cricket. She represented Australia in the inaugural home Tests against England in 1934-35 and was a great success when Australia toured England in 1937, with scores of 88, 63 and 45 in the three Tests and four for 50 in the First Test at Northampton. She served with the WRAAF during the Second World War.

SOHONI, SRIRANGA WASUDEV, died on May 19, 1993, aged 75. "Ranga" Sohoni was a fast-medium bowler who toured both England and Australia and played four Tests for India just after the war without making much impact. In domestic cricket he was more successful and regarded as an all-rounder. He opened the batting for Maharashtra and scored three centuries, including 218 not out against Western India, in 1940-41, when he had an average of 131. He played on until 1959-60 and also represented Baroda, Bombay and the Hindus. He took 232 first-class wickets at 32.96 and scored 4,307 runs at 28.71.

SRIRAMAN, S., who died on June 11, 1993, aged 76, was President of the Board of Control for Cricket in India between 1985 and 1988 and was in office when the World Cup was held in India and Pakistan. He had earlier been the Board secretary for five years (1965-70) and was secretary of the Tamil Nadu CA for 31 years. He was a sensitive official, popular even among the players.

STACKPOLE, KEITH WILLIAM, who died on September 19, 1992, aged 76, played 20 matches for Victoria in the five years after the war and was a top Australian Rules footballer. His son Keith, the Australian Test batsman, maintained his father was the better player. They played together for the Collingwood club just once: the father's last match was the son's first.

STEELE, RAYMOND CHARLES, OBE, died on November 22, 1993, aged 76. Ray Steele was a lawyer and one of Australia's leading cricket administrators, as president of the Victorian Cricket Association from 1973 to 1992 and treasurer of the Australian Board for 16 years, a period that included the Kerry Packer crisis. He was manager of the Australian touring teams to England in 1964 and 1972. However, he never became chairman of the Australian Board; he admitted himself that his outspoken nature would have made him an improbable choice. David Richards, the chief executive of ICC, said: "His keen sense of humour and generous hospitality coupled with his forthright approach endeared him to many, although he was a tough, outspoken but fair negotiator who fought hard for cricket."

STEYN, STEPHEN SEBASTIAN LOUIS, who died on October 14, 1993, aged 88, was a member of South Africa's touring party to Australia in 1931-32, though he never played in a Test. "Stodgy" Steyn – despite his nickname – was an enterprising middle-order left-handed batsman who represented Western Province from 1924-25 to 1937-38. He scored 261 not out against Border in 1929-30.

TAYLOR, JAMES ALEXANDER SIMSON, who died on May 16, 1993, aged 75, was an amateur who did not play any first-class cricket while at Cambridge but appeared in three matches for Leicestershire in 1937. Later he taught at Loretto and played for Scotland, scoring 78 against Yorkshire in 1952.

TEBBITT, GILBERT GEORGE, died on December 29, 1993, aged 85. Gil Tebbitt played 11 matches for Northamptonshire between 1934 and 1938 as an amateur batsman and captained the team twice. He led Rugby Town for ten years after the war and was for many years a Northamptonshire committee member. He also played rugby for Northampton and became president of the East Midlands RFU.

TEW, JOHN EDWARD, who died on December 28, 1992, aged 87, hit the headlines with his batting for Eton against Harrow at Lord's in 1924. He scored 58 and 54 not out. H. S. Altham wrote in *Wisden* that he was "a most dangerous man, full of power, untroubled by nerves". But he played only once for Oxford and a few times for the Europeans in India.

THOMPSON, ERIC RICHARD, who died of cancer on September 4, 1992, aged 53, was perhaps Scotland's greatest fast bowler. Born in Orkney, he played 41 times for the national team, taking more than 100 wickets at a brisk but exceptionally accurate fast-medium. He played for his school old boys' team, Melville College Former Pupils, and then for Heriot's FP until he was 47. Thompson's finest hour came when he took six for 55 against the 1966 West Indies, his victims including Hunte and Kanhai.

TOMLINSON, DENIS STANLEY, who died on July 11, 1993, aged 82, was the first Rhodesian to represent South Africa abroad. Tomlinson was a leg-spinner picked to tour England in 1935 and unexpectedly included for the First Test at Trent Bridge, but he bowled only ten overs and failed to take a wicket. He had plenty of opportunities on the tour when his fellow leg-spinner Xenophon Balaskas was injured, but was unable to find the right length; the South African cricket writer Louis Duffus speculated that Tomlinson's action, dependent more on the arm than the body, made him inaccurate. On the way home, like Jock Cameron, he caught enteric fever: Cameron died; Tomlinson missed the next season and was affected for several years. Born at Umtali, he played one friendly match for Border in 1928-29 but otherwise played for Rhodesia from 1927-28 until after the war, taking 156 first-class wickets in all and batting in every position. He scored a century, as opener, against Eastern Province in 1931-32. His death left Balaskas, Bob Crisp and Bruce Mitchell as the only survivors of the victorious 1935 party.

TOWNSEND, LESLIE FLETCHER, who died in New Zealand on February 17, 1993, aged 89, was one of the finest inter-war all-rounders and a vital component of the strong Derbyshire team of the 1930s. Born at Long Eaton in Derbyshire, he played as a professional for the county from 1922 until 1939. He was a hard-hitting middle-order batsman who bowled fastish, very accurate off-breaks. He did not play cricket at his council school but paid regular visits to Trent Bridge, watched George Gunn and resolved to copy his methods. He took some time to develop but from then on every year produced a stride forward: he began to get runs in 1926 and wickets in 1927, when he was chosen for North v South; in 1928 he achieved the first of his three doubles; in 1929 he was chosen for the Players at Lord's and for the tour of the West Indies; in 1930 he made his maiden century; in 1931 he came eighth in the bowling averages; in 1932 he achieved the double in the Championship; in 1933 he passed 2,000 runs, took 100 wickets and was one of *Wisden's* Five. The editor noted that he was a teetotaller and non-smoker and concluded: "An admirable type of the present-day professional." He played in four Tests – one in the West Indies and three under Jardine in India in 1933-34 – but he was never picked for a home Test or a front-line tour, though some thought he might have gone to Australia ahead of the leg-spinner Mitchell in 1932-33. He never did himself justice in his Tests and caught salmonella poisoning at the end of the Indian tour. He convalesced in New Zealand and thereafter spent more and more time there, playing a few games for Auckland, though he stayed with Derbyshire until 1939 and was an important member of the Championship-winning team of 1936. He played 493 first-class matches, getting 19,555 runs at 27.50 and 1,088 wickets at 21.12. After the war, he settled in New Zealand, working as a joiner and cabinet-maker until a group of enthusiasts in Nelson asked him to go there as coach in 1954. Nelson has since gained a reputation as one of the most thriving cricketing cities in New Zealand, producing a disproportionate number of Test players. According to one of them, Tony Blain, "Les Townsend is the reason Nelson's been so strong." He was remembered there as a strict coach, who dressed in MCC sweater and beautifully pressed flannels and expected equally high standards from his pupils. He was especially keen on youngsters driving through the V, with their left elbow high, which is how spectators may best remember him.

TRESTRAIL, KENNETH BASIL, who died in Toronto on December 24, 1992, aged 65, was a Trinidadian who appeared in first-class cricket as a 16-year-old in 1943-44 and was regarded for the rest of the decade as one of the most promising young batsmen in the Caribbean. After scoring 161 not out against Jamaica, he was picked for the tour of England in 1950 but, on that triumphant trip, had a thin time. In 1953 he emigrated to Canada and returned to first-class cricket on the Canadians' 1954 tour of England, when he was both their most prolific and most entertaining batsman. He was also Trinidad's tennis champion.

VAN DER GUCHT, PAUL IAN, who died on December 15, 1993, aged 82, was a Radley-educated amateur who kept wicket for Gloucestershire in 1933 and, in an emergency, captained the side. He played little more first-class cricket in England because his work as an engineer took him to India, where he represented the Europeans and Bengal. He opened the batting for Bengal when they won the Ranji Trophy in 1938-39 and scored 115 for them against Central India. During the war he was taken prisoner in the Western Desert.

WALKER, CLIFFORD, who died on December 3, 1992, aged 73, played four games for Yorkshire in 1947 and 1948 before joining Hampshire, getting a regular first-team place, and passing 1,000 runs four times. Walker was a solid batsman who could and, at Hampshire, did bat almost anywhere in the order, fielded at slip and bowled occasional but economical medium pace. He left county cricket abruptly in 1954 and went into the Bradford League.

WATTS, HUGH EDMUND, who died on December 27, 1993, aged 71, won a Cambridge Blue in 1947 and played for Somerset 61 times between 1939 and 1952, often captaining the county. He was a left-handed batsman who made a century against Glamorgan in 1949, and was an effective bowler until he was injured in the war. He taught games and history at Downside until he left to found a new prep school, Moor Park, in Ludlow. After retiring to Cornwall, he became secretary and then captain of St Enodoc Golf Club.

WHARTON, ALAN, who died on August 26, 1993, aged 70, was an attacking left-handed batsman who spent 15 years with Lancashire, three with Leicestershire and played a solitary Test for England. After hitting three centuries, plus 73 not out in the Roses match, he was picked against New Zealand at Headingley in 1949. He made seven and 13, missed the next Test through injury and was never picked again. But he remained a successful Lancashire player until 1960, when he moved to Leicestershire. He passed 1,000 runs 11 times and 2,000 in 1959. In 1956 he scored the first century for Lancashire against the Australians since Ernest Tyldesley in 1934. His darkest hour came during his benefit match in 1958 when Lancashire were bowled out by Surrey for 27. In 482 matches he scored 21,796 runs at 32.24. He was also a useful partnership-breaking medium-pace bowler. In 1965, after briefly playing for Cumberland, Wharton returned to teaching, in Colne. He was a long-serving JP and played rugby league for Salford.

WHITE, ALLAN FREDERICK TINSDALE, who died on March 16, 1993, at the age of 77, captained Worcestershire for three seasons after the war. After playing for Uppingham and the successful Cambridge side of 1936 (he missed a Blue the following year), he played nine games for his native Warwickshire before joining Worcestershire in 1939. He had no immediate success but he returned after the war and emerged as a competent enough batsman to pass 1,000 runs, though he never scored a first-class century. He was made captain in 1947 and quickly established himself as a popular and enterprising leader. However, his mushroom-growing business made increasing demands. He retired after 1949, when he shared the captaincy with Bob Wyatt, and Worcestershire came close to their first-ever Championship.

WYETH, EZRA ROBERT, died in the United States on October 15, 1992, aged 82. "Boxer" Wyeth played for Queensland in 25 matches as a left-arm medium-pace bowler between 1933-34 and 1937-38. He was reportedly selected for the Australian tour to South Africa in 1935-36 but left out when the Board ordered the selectors to take one player less. A foot injury forced his retirement two years later. His nickname came from his prowess with his fists at school in Toowoomba.

He later became Professor of Education at California State University. He regularly took part in Hollywood cricket and also captained the American team at the first World Bowls Championship in 1966.

YOUNG, DOUGLAS MARTIN, died suddenly in Cape Town on June 18, 1993, aged 69. Martin Young played briefly for Worcestershire, before becoming a pillar of the Gloucestershire batting for 16 years from 1949 to 1964. He was an opening batsman with a sound technique, a pleasant style and good concentration: a fair share of his 40 hundreds were substantial ones. When he was almost 40, he was good enough to score 127 on a difficult pitch against Sobers and Griffith in full cry for the 1963 West Indians; it was easily the highest score of the match. Most of the time, he scored quietly and consistently, passing 1,000 in a season 13 times and 2,000 twice. But he was a little rotund – his team-mates called him "The Admiral" – and often vulnerable against the very quickest bowling. He tried to compensate for this by being extra courteous to the fastest bowlers; "I'll give him wife and kids," Peter Loader was once heard to mutter after one exchange of morning pleasantries. He played in 475 first-class matches, scored 24,555 runs and averaged 30.69. He emigrated to South Africa on retirement and became a sports commentator for SABC.

YOUNG, JOHN ALBERT, the Middlesex and England slow left-arm bowler, died at his home in St John's Wood on February 5, 1993, aged 80. Jack Young was 33 before his cricket career took off. He had played a few times for Middlesex in the 1930s. But in 1946 he established himself as a vital, if not the most obvious, member of what became one of the great Championship sides the following year. He was a short man who bowled from a gentle approach and a low trajectory. The whole effect was deceptive and he spent hours in the nets working on his tricks. In 1947 his success in completing the Middlesex wins that Denis Compton and Bill Edrich habitually started earned him the first of his eight Test caps. At Trent Bridge the following year he contained Bradman and Hassett, helped by a negative field, and finished with figures of 60–28–79–1. He was never a match-winner in Test cricket but he continued bowling successfully in county cricket until 1956, though he had considerable knee trouble in the last few years. He took 1,361 wickets in 341 first-class matches at an average of only 19.68. "He was a very under-rated bowler," said Denis Compton, "who bowled very well against the best batsmen. He was a model of accuracy and very difficult to get away."

SUPPLEMENTARY OBITUARY

ADAMS, SIDNEY CLARKE, was killed while crossing the Rhine with Allied forces on March 24, 1945, aged 40. He was a council clerk and leg-spinner who took wickets with his first two balls in first-class cricket, playing for Northamptonshire against Dublin University in 1926. Adams had scored 87 earlier in the game and finished with figures of six for 32. His first wicket was that of Samuel Beckett, later winner of the Nobel Prize for Literature. Adams's later career was less illustrious than his victim's, though he played nine more games for the county.

ANDERSON, JOHN HENRY, who died on March 11, 1926, aged 51, captained South Africa in his only Test, against Australia at Johannesburg in 1902-03. "Biddy" Anderson made 32 but South Africa were heavily beaten; he was the only member of the side left out of the next Test. He played regularly for Western Province between 1894 and 1907; his only century, 109 against Border in 1903-04, exceeded the combined total of both Border innings (55 and 52).

ATTEWELL, WALTER, who died on February 3, 1919, aged 54, played one match for Nottinghamshire in 1891 but was better known as a wandering coach who worked in Philadelphia in the 1890s and, from 1906 to 1912, at Shrewsbury School where he was assisted by Neville Cardus. However, in his *Autobiography* Cardus appears to confuse Attewell with his more famous cousin William.

BAGGULEY, ROBERT, who died on October 8, 1946, aged 73, was only 17 and 5ft 3in tall when he made an outstanding debut for Nottinghamshire in 1891. On a good wicket against Sussex at Hove, he took six for 74 bowling left-arm slow-medium. He also scored one brilliant century, 110 against Sussex at Trent Bridge in 1895, which included 102 on the second morning. Otherwise, his form was patchy.

BENSKIN, WILLIAM EWART, who died in Leicester on June 1, 1956, aged 76, was a fast-medium bowler whose first wickets in first-class cricket were a hat-trick: he finished off the Essex first innings on his debut for Leicestershire at Southend in 1906. He played 105 games in all up to 1924 for Leicestershire and, briefly, Scotland.

BESTWICK, ROBERT SAXTON, who died on July 3, 1980, aged 80, played five matches for Derbyshire in the early 1920s, two of them in the same team as his father, the fast bowler Bill Bestwick. For six overs against Warwickshire at Derby in 1922, Bestwick father and son bowled together against W. G. Quaife and his son, a unique occurrence in first-class cricket.

BROMLEY, ERNEST HARVEY, died at Clayton, Victoria, aged 54, on February 1, 1967. "Slogger" Bromley was a Western Australian who moved to Victoria and played twice in Ashes Tests: at Brisbane during the "Bodyline" series of 1932-33 when Australian cricket was in disarray, and again at Lord's in 1934. He ensured selection for that tour by scoring a superb 161 for Victoria against South Australia in 1933-34. His nickname was not ironic: he was an attacking bat with a weakness outside off stump. However, it was his fielding, and his throwing arm in particular, that was outstanding. In his four Test innings he scored only 38 but he continued playing for Victoria until the war, scoring 2,055 runs in 52 matches, averaging 28.54. He bowled occasional left-arm spin.

BROWN, EDWARD, who died on April 14, 1978, aged 66, was a right-arm fast-medium bowler from Darlington who played 28 matches for Warwickshire between 1932 and 1934. He was successful early on and, after taking eight for 35 against Surrey in 1933, was awarded his cap. He also played cricket for Durham and Northumberland and professional soccer for the Swiss club Servette.

BURTON, FREDERICK JOHN, died on August 25, 1929. It is now thought he was born in Collingwood, Victoria, on November 2, 1865, and was thus 63. He was chosen to keep wicket for Australia in the Second Test of the 1886-87 series when Jack Blackham was unavailable. Blackham returned for the only Test of the following season but Burton was retained as a batsman even though his career average was only 15 – he was out for one in each innings. His best score was 47 for New South Wales against Victoria in 1887-88 when he batted three hours and helped Harry Moses in a stand of 185; Moses went on to make 297. Burton later settled in New Zealand and died in Wanganui.

CAREW, GEORGE McDONALD, who died on December 9, 1974, aged 64, was a right-hand batsman from Barbados who scored a brilliant 107 for West Indies against England at Port-of-Spain in 1947-48. Chewing gum and wearing a felt hat, he put on 173 for the first wicket with Andy Ganteaume. He did little in his other three Tests but scored consistently for Barbados, where he was a well-known character and ran a taxi business.

CHOWDHURY, NIRODE RANJAN, died on December 14, 1979, aged 56, at Durgapur, where he was coach at the local steel plant. Chowdhury, the first Test cricketer from the state of Bihar, was a slightly-built but lively medium-paced off-spinner who played one Test for India in 1948-49 and another one three years later. He was picked to tour England in 1952 but hardly figured. His best analysis came in his first game in the Ranji Trophy, in 1941-42, when he took seven for 79 for Bihar against Bengal.

CLODE, HARRY PILE, who died on October 19, 1964, aged 87, appeared 40 times for Surrey between 1899 and 1903 as a right-arm slow bowler and later became professional with Wearmouth and played Minor Counties cricket for Durham. His son, H. P. Clode jun., followed him into the Durham side.

COTTAM, JOHN THOMAS, who died from typhoid, aged 29, in Western Australia on January 30, 1897, was one of five men drafted in to the Australian Test team at Sydney in 1886-87 because several established players had demanded, and been refused, payment for loss of earnings from their regular jobs. Cottam was 19 and had played only one first-class game – for New South Wales against England, and even for that he was a last-minute choice. In the Test he was out for one and three and never played for Australia again. He never even played Sheffield Shield cricket though he did tour New Zealand with a state team in 1889-90, batting well on bad wickets. He was reported to be a powerfully-built man, a stylish bat and a popular performer; his drift away from cricket in the eight years before his death remains a mystery.

DARTMOUTH, WILLIAM HENEAGE LEGGE, the 6th EARL OF, who died at his home in Staffordshire, Patshull House, on March 11, 1936, aged 84, was President of MCC in 1893. Under his courtesy title, Lord Lewisham, he played a first-class match for an indifferent MCC team against Hampshire at Lord's in 1877. He also played for Shropshire and Staffordshire and was MP for West Kent and then Lewisham. His grandson married Raine McCorquodale, who later married Earl Spencer and became the Princess of Wales's stepmother.

DENTON, ARTHUR DONALD, died on January 23, 1961, aged 64. Don Denton was a middle-order batsman for Northamptonshire who showed great promise in four matches in 1914 but lost part of a leg during the First World War. He also played three matches after the war, batting with a runner. The Lancashire captain, approached for special permission, wrote: "If any fellow has been to the war and has had his leg off and wants to play, he is good enough for me and can have 20 runners." His two elder brothers, the twins Jack and Billy Denton, also played for the county either side of the war.

DONNAN, HENRY, was one of Australia's longest-lived Test cricketers and was three months short of his 92nd birthday when he died near Sydney on August 13, 1956. He was also connected to one of Australian cricket's greatest families: he married Syd Gregory's sister. Harry Donnan was a slightly-built man who relied on timing rather than power in his batting. Initially he was regarded as a bowler but an innings of 87 not out for New South Wales against an Australian XI established his credentials. He did not make his Test debut until January 1892 and was unsuccessful in that game and again at Adelaide, where he was a late replacement. However, he had a magnificent season in 1895-96 and was an automatic choice for the 1896 tour of England, where he played in all three Tests, though again not with much success – the highest score in any of his five Tests was 15 at Old Trafford. However, he made 167, his best-ever score, against Derbyshire, where his family originated. Donnan worked for the Colonial Sugar Refining Company for 42 years until he retired in 1923. His pension cost the firm dear, since he lived for another 33 years.

DUCKFIELD, RICHARD GEORGE, died on December 30, 1959, aged 52. Dick Duckfield was a right-handed batsman from Maesteg who scored an "excellent" – *Wisden*'s word – century for the Players against the Gentlemen at The Oval in 1934, reaching 106 in only two hours, five minutes against a substandard attack. On the same ground two years later he scored 280 not out against Surrey, the highest score then made for Glamorgan. Otherwise, his form was ordinary; he retired in 1938 having scored exactly 7,000 runs, average 26.61.

DUNELL, OWEN ROBERT, who died at Lyons, France on October 21, 1929, aged 73, was South Africa's first captain, leading the team in the match of dubious standard against England at Port Elizabeth in 1888-89 that is now accepted as South Africa's first Test. Dunell played only one other first-class game outside the two Tests on this tour, when he led a Port Elizabeth team against Natal in December 1889. He was born in Port Elizabeth, and later went into business there but was educated at Eton and Oxford, where he played no cricket but excelled at tennis.

ELLIOTT, HAROLD, who died on April 15, 1969, aged 64, played only one first-class match, in 1930 for Lancashire as a wicket-keeper. Since he was third choice behind Duckworth and Farrimond, he had little chance of a playing career. However, in 1939 Elliott joined the first-class umpires' list, and stood in 245 Championship matches, and seven Tests between 1950 and 1953. He was a small, bespectacled man who habitually umpired in a trilby hat.

FARGUS, Rev. ARCHIBALD HUGH CONWAY, who died on October 6, 1963, aged 84, has been obituarised before in *Wisden*. However, this was 48 years before his death. The 1915 edition said Fargus had gone down with the *Monmouth*, the ship on which he was acting-chaplain, in action in the Pacific. But he had missed a train and failed to rejoin the ship. Fargus, whose father Hugh Conway was a well-known Victorian author, won a Cambridge Blue in 1900 and 1901 and played 15 games for Gloucestershire. His actual death was not reported in the Almanack.

FENLEY, STANLEY, who died on September 2, 1976, aged 76, was a leg-spinner who played as an amateur for Surrey in 1924 while on leave from work in the Gold Coast and was so successful that he stayed on as a professional. He played 116 matches in the 1920s and made a brief comeback for Hampshire, aged 39. He took 346 wickets in all.

FOTHERGILL, ARNOLD JAMES, who died on August 1, 1932, aged 77, played twice for England in South Africa in 1888-89 in the games that were later designated as the first Tests between the two countries, though they were arguably not even first-class. Born in Northumberland, he was a left-arm fast bowler who migrated to the emerging Somerset club, which engaged Fothergill and Alfred Brooks of Nottinghamshire as its first professionals. Technically, he was not qualified: in 1881 Kent objected to his presence and he had to drop out of the side even though he was the club's best bowler. Somerset were accepted as first-class in 1882 and Fothergill, safely qualified, was their most productive bowler for the next two seasons. He was also taken on to the Lord's staff and played much of his cricket for MCC before Major Gardner Warton took him on his pioneering tour of South Africa. In the two Tests, he scored 33, average 16.50, and took eight wickets for 90. He is then believed to have returned to Tyneside.

GAUKRODGER, GEORGE WARRINGTON, who died on January 4, 1938, aged 60, was a Yorkshireman who came to county cricket after living for some years in Belfast. He succeeded Tom Straw as Worcestershire wicket-keeper and appeared in 114 matches between 1900 and 1910. He also played international football for Northern Ireland, against Wales in 1894-95.

GLADSTONE, GEORGE, who died on May 19, 1978, aged 77, was a left-arm spinner who played once for West Indies, against England at Kingston in 1929-30. He was called up after only one match for Jamaica, in which he had match figures of nine for 252 against MCC. However, he took one for 189 in the Test and never played first-class cricket again. He remained a stalwart of the Railways Cricket Club for more than 30 years. His birth certificate says his name was George Gladstone Morais.

HARTKOPF, Dr ALBERT ERNST VICTOR, died at Kew, Victoria on May 20, 1968, aged 78. He played one Test for Australia, against England at Melbourne in 1924-25. Batting at No. 8, he made 80. However, Australia were not short of runs and Hartkopf had been chosen to bowl leg-breaks: his match figures of one for 134 were not what they wanted and he was never picked again. He was a successful all-rounder for Victoria over many seasons, scoring 1,758 runs (average 34.47) and taking 121 wickets at 30.79. He was a general practitioner in Melbourne.

HAWKWOOD, CLIFFORD, died on May 15, 1960, aged 50. "Chick" Hawkwood was a stalwart for the Lancashire League club Nelson and played 24 games for Lancashire, one of them the Roses match at Headingley in 1933. After three star Lancashire batsmen had fallen cheaply, Hawkwood put on 200 in 175 minutes with J. L. Hopwood, despite needing a runner because of sciatica. Hawkwood made 113 and Neville Cardus said in the *Manchester Guardian* that it was "one of the most courageous innings played for Lancashire by a young cricketer for ages". In his *Autobiography*, Cardus claimed that the Yorkshire bowler Emmott Robinson spent the day muttering "Hey, dear, dear, dear, what's t'matter, what's t'matter?" It was Hawkwood's only century.

HEARNE, THOMAS JOHN, who died on May 25, 1947, aged 59, was called late to take part in his only first-class match, for Middlesex against the Gentlemen of Philadelphia at Lord's in 1908, as a replacement for his cousin J. T. Hearne. However, the game was played on a treacherous pitch and finished in a day; Hearne, arriving late afternoon, never took the field. Many of his relatives were better-known cricketers; he did play usefully for Berkshire.

HONE, LELAND, who was born in Dublin and died there, aged 43, on December 31, 1896, was an old Rugbeian and a member of a well-known Irish cricketing family. He became the first player from outside the first-class counties to represent England when he was taken to Australia as a member of Lord Harris's largely amateur and quite unrepresentative party in 1878-79. Hone was obliged to keep wicket, and played in the only Test of the tour, scoring seven and six and taking two catches. He played only three first-class matches outside the tour, for MCC.

HULME, JOHN JOSEPH, who died on July 11, 1940, aged 78, was a left-arm fast-medium bowler who played 133 first-class matches for Derbyshire in a career that lasted between 1887 and 1903. He took nine for 27 in the second innings against Yorkshire at Sheffield in 1894.

KNUTTON, HERBERT JOHN, died at Bradford on December 12, 1946, aged 79. Jack Knutton had one day of cricketing glory when he came out of the Bradford League to skittle the 1902 Australians. No Australian game had been arranged for the date of King Edward VII's Coronation but when the King developed appendicitis and the festivities were postponed, the tourists hastily organised a match at Bradford against "an England XI". It included not a single Test player and Knutton was the only fast bowler. He clean bowled Noble, Hill and Darling in his second over, and though the Australians recovered and won by seven wickets, Knutton had first-innings figures of nine for 100 and dismissed Darling a second time to finish the game with ten for 117. Knutton, from Coventry, played just one other first-class match, for Warwickshire in 1894. But he took a thousand wickets in the Bradford League at high pace with an action sometimes regarded as suspect.

LILFORD, John Powys, 5th BARON, who died on December 17, 1945, aged 82, played one first-class match, for Northamptonshire against the Indians in 1911. He was a moderate but enthusiastic player who carried a ball round with him in the hope of some catching practice. He was also president of Northamptonshire for 18 years and its benefactor for almost half a century; without his support the club would undoubtedly have ceased to exist.

MAJOR, JOHN, who died at Wakefield, Yorkshire on December 31, 1930, aged 69, came to public attention as a professional right-handed batsman with an excellent style while playing Sussex Colts matches in 1888. However, he would have been a very elderly colt. Contemporary references said he was born in 1865; his birth certificate shows that he was actually four years older. Major played 11 first-class games for Sussex, averaging 17.28, scoring 106 against Gloucestershire in 1889. He played soccer for West Bromwich Albion and later joined the Warwickshire staff. On his death certificate, he was described as a "former general labourer".

MARX, WALDEMAR FREDERICK ERIC, died at Durban on June 2, 1974, aged 78. Eric Marx, educated at Malvern, was a right-hand batsman who made the highest score on a first-class debut, 240 for Transvaal against

Griqualand West at Johannesburg in 1920-21. He made another Currie Cup century that season and played all three Tests against Australia in 1921-22 before disappearing from the first-class game, as suddenly as he had arrived.

MEINTJES, DOUGLAS JAMES, who died on July 17, 1979, aged 89, played two Tests for South Africa against England in 1922-23 as a fast-medium bowler who could bat. He took six wickets for 115 and all the wickets were top-order batsmen. Meintjes was picked for the South African tour of England in 1924 but was never close to the Test team. Later, he became secretary to the Wanderers Cricket Club and was South African manager in 1948-49.

MINNETT, Dr ROY BALDWIN, died at Manly, New South Wales, on October 21, 1955, aged 67. He had given up cricket aged 26 to devote himself to his career as a doctor. Before that he had established himself as a spirited batsman and lively fast-medium bowler, regarded as more talented than his two elder brothers who also played for New South Wales. He played the first of his nine Tests against England at Sydney in 1911-12 and raced to 90 in 111 minutes, overshadowing even Victor Trumper. He struggled on the slow, damp wickets in England in 1912 and when he came home played less often. However, he took ten wickets for 84 in his final first-class match, against Victoria in December 1914, including eight for 50 in the first innings.

MOLONY, TREVOR JAMES, who died at Cannes on September 3, 1962, aged 65, is thought to have been the last cricketer selected for a county as an underarm bowler. Molony appears to have taken only one wicket when he was in the Repton XI in 1915 and he did not bowl in the Cambridge Freshmen's Trial in 1920. However, Surrey chose him, apparently at the instigation of their captain P. G. H. Fender, against Nottinghamshire at Trent Bridge in May 1921. According to a contemporary report, Molony bowled leg theory with only a mid-off on the off side. He bowled accurately, varied his flight and his "exceedingly good full tosses at an awkward height" caused the batsmen consternation. Payton and Barratt were caught on the boundary from wild leg-side heaves and Whysall took guard outside leg stump, and struck the ball over his head, tennis-smash style, straight to the only man on the off side. Molony was given only seven overs but he finished with three for 11. However, Surrey's enthusiasm for the experiment dimmed very rapidly. He bowled even less in his two other first-class matches and "the last of the lobsters" quickly disappeared from the first-class game though he did play for the Incogniti and Repton Pilgrims.

MORRIS, SAMUEL, who died on September 20, 1931, aged 76, was the first black Test cricketer and the only one to play for Australia. He was born in Tasmania, according to some reports the son of West Indian parents attracted by the gold-rush, became recognised as a wicket-keeper there and moved into first-class cricket as a batsman and medium-paced bowler after becoming appointed curator at the St Kilda ground in Melbourne. He played his only Test, at Melbourne in 1884-85, after the entire team from the previous Test had pulled out after a row about their share of the gate money. The team was predictably beaten but Morris dismissed two of England's top three and opened the batting in the first innings, when he was out for four. He remained a regular player for Victoria for the next eight years. He was curator at South Melbourne for 30 years from 1887, giving up only when he lost his sight.

MOSS, Rev. REGINALD HEBER, who died on March 19, 1956, aged 88, played for Oxford, winning his Blue in 1889, and had one further first-class game for Liverpool and District in 1893. He then played one Championship match for Worcestershire, against Gloucestershire at Worcester, as a 57-year-old in 1925 and took a wicket and two catches. He was then rector of Icomb, near Stow-on-the-Wold. The gap of 32 years between first-class appearances is a record.

NEWSTEAD, JOHN THOMAS, who died on March 25, 1952, aged 74, is the only *Wisden* Cricketer of the Year known to have died and not obituarised in the Almanack. Jack Newstead was chosen in 1909 after a spectacular season in 1908, when he took 140 wickets, at 16.50 each, and scored 927 runs. He played a major role in Yorkshire's return to the top of the County Championship and, had there been a Test series, would probably have played for England. However, this was the extent of his success. He had only just broken into the Yorkshire team after playing twice in 1903 and then joining the MCC staff. The following year, he quickly declined and in 1910 lost his place. Contemporaries described him as having a high and relaxed bowling action just above medium pace; he was regarded as a "talented but careless" batsman.

PARKER, GEORGE MACDONALD, who died in Thredbo, New South Wales on May 1, 1969, aged 69, was plucked from the Bradford League to play two Test matches for the outclassed 1924 South Africans in England. Born in Cape Town, he had been in England four years but had never played a first-class match before he was given a trial against Oxford. He took four wickets and had four catches dropped, though there was barely four hours play. The South Africans, desperately short of bowling, put him in the team for the First Test at Edgbaston. He took six for 152, including five on the opening day. "He bowled himself to a standstill," said *Wisden*, "and became so exhausted that he had to leave the field." In Lord's Test, when England scored 531 for two, he took the only two wickets to fall – Hobbs and Sutcliffe – for 121. But he never played first-class cricket again and eventually settled in Australia.

RAVILIOUS, ERIC WILLIAM, was presumed dead after a Coastal Command plane in which he was travelling disappeared on a flight from Iceland in September 1942. He was 39, and famous as a water-colour landscape artist and wood-engraver. Amongst his work is the colophon that has appeared on the front cover of *Wisden* since 1938.

ROBINSON, RAYFORD HAROLD, who died in his home town of Stockton, New South Wales on August 10, 1965, aged 51, led a shadowed life working as a labourer after playing just one Test in 1936-37. By making heavy scores with style and panache, Ray Robinson forced his way into the team for the Brisbane match but was dismissed for two and three (out hooking as Australia collapsed to defeat), was demoted to 12th man for the next game and then disappeared from the Test scene. He played later for South Australia, moved back to New South Wales and then went to Otago, but never recovered either the form or the style of his youth.

ST HILL, WILTON H., is believed to have died around 1957, when he would have been 64, but there is no firm evidence of his death – his later years remain mysterious. However, his cricket was immortalised in C. L. R. James's masterwork, *Beyond A Boundary*, in which he is the subject of a whole chapter. St Hill played in only three Test matches and was a great disappointment when he played in England in 1928. But he was a hero in Trinidad, where both his insouciance and his strokemaking were regarded with awe: he would habitually walk out to bat smoking a cigarette and would throw it away only after the bowler set his field. James wrote that he saw the ball very early and played it very late, even against bowlers as fast as George John:

"He never appeared to be flurried, never caught in two minds ... I do not remember any more frightening sight at cricket than John running, jumping and letting loose at his terrific pace, and St Hill playing back as if he had known he would have to do so long before the ball was bowled and was somewhat bored by the whole business." Learie Constantine, after watching one of St Hill's early innings, said he had perfect timing.

SMITH, DAVID BERTRAM MILLER, who died at Hawthorn, Victoria on July 29, 1963, aged 78, played in two Tests during the Triangular Tournament in 1912 when Australia played both England and South Africa with a weakened team. He scored only 30 Test runs, averaging 15. He was reported to have been "undisciplined" on a tour on which there were several incidents of drunken brawling and rudeness towards the public and English amateurs. He was summoned by the Board on his return home to explain himself but failed to turn up, pleading illness. He never played first-class cricket again.

SNOOKE, SIBLEY JOHN, died in Port Elizabeth on August 14, 1966, aged 85. "Tip" Snooke played in 26 Tests for South Africa as a stylish right-handed batsman and right-arm fast-medium bowler. He was a regular member of the side before the First World War, captaining the team in the five-Test series with England in 1909-10. He was recalled and opened the attack against England as a 42-year-old in 1922-23. Snooke scored 1,008 Test runs, making a century against Australia at Adelaide in 1910-11, and took 35 Test wickets. And he had a long first-class career, beginning as a 17-year-old for Border, going on to play for Western Province and Transvaal: 124 matches in all – a huge number for a South African in that era – in which he scored 4,821 runs (average: 25.91) and took 120 wickets at 25.14. He managed the successful 1935 South African side to England. His brother, S. D. Snooke, also played for South Africa and his grandsons, S. J. and W. J. McAdam, both appeared in the Currie Cup.

STEPHENS, ERIC JAMES, died in Gloucester, where he was born, on April 3, 1983, aged 74. "Dick" Stephens played for Gloucestershire as a professional in 216 matches between 1927 and 1937. He was a left-handed bat, occasional medium-paced bowler and an outstanding outfielder. He also played rugby for Gloucester (as fly-half), Southern League soccer and, later, bowls.

STEPHENS, GEORGE WILLIAM, who died on March 17, 1950, aged 60, was an attractive right-hand amateur batsman who played 123 times for Warwickshire between 1907 and 1925, scored four centuries, and captained the side in 1919. His twin brother, Frank, also played for the county.

STRAW, THOMAS, who died at Hucknall Torkard, Nottinghamshire, where he was born, on September 8, 1959, aged 89, was the Worcestershire wicket-keeper and the only man in cricket history to have been dismissed twice for obstructing the field. Both dismissals occurred when he was playing against Warwickshire. The first time, at Worcester in 1899, Straw lofted a ball towards the middle of the pitch and began to run while a fielder, A. C. S. Glover, ran in to try and catch it. They collided and Straw was given out by umpire Mycroft, to the loud disgust of the home crowd who complained that it was accidental. Two years later, at Edgbaston, Straw barged into the wicket-keeper, "Dick" Lilley, as he emerged from behind the stumps to take a simple pop-up catch.

This appears to have been a far more flagrant piece of obstruction; it is possible that Straw, after his earlier dismissal, was taking the mickey. This was his last full season: a hand injury virtually finished his career after he had been Worcestershire's first-choice keeper since 1895, four years before they joined the Championship, though he did play four more games in 1907 before returning to Nottinghamshire and his old job as a miner.

TRAVERS, JOSEPH PATRICK FRANCIS, died in Adelaide, where he was born, on September 15, 1942, aged 71. "Ike" Travers was a lower-order left-hand bat and left-arm spinner who hit a dramatic run of form in the 1900-01 Sheffield Shield, taking 21 wickets in two games for South Australia which included an analysis of nine for 30 when he rolled over Victoria for 76. The following year he was picked for the Fifth Test against England as a late replacement for the injured J. V. Saunders. He bowled only eight overs, taking one for 14, and never played for Australia again. He did continue in the Sheffield Shield: thereafter his bowling declined but his batting improved. In retirement he became a well-known coach and was reportedly instrumental in bringing Don Bradman to South Australia in 1935. Travers thought Bradman's presence would help counteract the growing popularity of tennis and suggested that his salary should be subsidised by up to £750 a year.

VINCENT, CYRIL LEVERTON, who died on August 24, 1968, aged 66, was a left-arm spinner and capable lower-order batsman who played 25 Tests for South Africa between 1927-28 and 1935. However, he only ever played in two Currie Cup matches, apparently because he could not get time off work. He was renowned for bowling long spells tirelessly. At Durban in 1930-31 he took six for 51 against England to secure the rubber for South Africa and he had match figures of eight for 149 in the Headingley Test of 1935. He was later chairman of the South African selectors.

WEBB, ARTHUR STUART, who died on December 3, 1952, aged 84, was a right-handed batsman relying on powerful forearms who was a regular member of the Hampshire team for ten years round the turn of the century. He appeared in 151 matches and scored 5,515 runs, averaging 21.54. His finest innings came in his benefit match, against Surrey, in 1904 when he scored an unbeaten 162 in 270 minutes. Unfortunately, the match was badly affected by rain and Webb's share of the takings was only £150. He later moved to Wales, where he was professional and groundsman at Briton Ferry Steelworks and then coach at Christ College, Brecon.

WHITEHEAD, RALPH, who died on August 23, 1956, aged 72, had one of the most sensational of all first-class debuts. He was 24 and showing progress as a middle-order batsman and medium-fast bowler when Lancashire put him in the first team against Nottinghamshire at Old Trafford in June 1908. Whitehead took three first-innings wickets then came in to bat with Lancashire on 117 for six. He put on 188 with his captain A. H. Hornby and, when the last wicket fell at 352, was left unbeaten on 131 after only three hours batting. Hornby gave him his county cap between innings and, perhaps assuming he was on infallible form, brought him on to bowl very soon. Then everything went wrong. Whitehead was called for throwing four times in his first five balls by the bowler's umpire, Tom Brown. After an exchange of words with the umpire, Hornby withdrew him from the attack and bowled him from the other end next day: Brown called him twice more from square leg. Whitehead survived in cricket; however, he never again made a comparable impact. He went on to play 106 more matches for Lancashire up to 1914, scoring 2,571 runs and taking 300 wickets, apparently without his action being challenged again.

WHITTLE, ALBERT EDWARD MARK, who died in the Dorset County Asylum on March 18, 1917, aged 39, was a successful all-rounder for Warwickshire and Somerset between 1900 and 1911 before he became ill. He was a well-built man, aggressive in his batting, who bowled medium-fast and had an unusually long, though sometimes erratic, throw.

WOOD, REGINALD, who died in poverty in Manly, Sydney on January 6, 1915, aged 54, was in the Charterhouse XI of 1876, played six games for Lancashire as an amateur between 1880 and 1884 and played a Test match for England on the 1886-87 tour of Australia. Wood had emigrated to Melbourne and reappeared in first-class cricket for Victoria against Alfred Shaw's English team. Shaw had brought only 11 players, and the First Test at Sydney was marked by a fight between the England player, William Barnes, and the Australian captain, Percy McDonnell. Barnes injured his hand, apparently after missing McDonnell's face and punching a wall. Wood was then co-opted into the Test team: batting No. 10 he scored six and nought, did not bowl and took no catches. He played for Shaw's team against Victoria then disappeared from first-class cricket. He became professional at both East Melbourne and Sydney Albert but was later reported to be working "in a lowly capacity, with sheep". A correspondent in Australia said that at his death he had little more than the clothes he wore and his tuckerbag.

INDEX TO CRICKETERS

Note: For reasons of space, certain entries which appear in alphabetical order in sections of the Almanack are not included in this index. These include names that appear in Test Cricketers, Births and Deaths of Cricketers and individual batting and bowling performances in the 1993 first-class season.

c. = catches; d. = dismissals; p'ship = partnership; r. = runs; w. = wickets.
* Signifies not out or an unbroken partnership.

I

Ibadulla, Khalid (Pak.):– Hundred on Test debut, *148, 216;* Obstructing the field, *126;* 402 for 4th wkt, *124;* Test p'ship record, *217.*

Iddon, J. (Eng.):– 46 hundreds, *112.*

Igglesden, A. P. (Eng.):– 12 w. in match, *958.*

Ijaz Ahmed (Lahore Greens):– Obstructing the field, *126.*

Ijaz Ahmed (Pak.):– 2 Test hundreds, *216;* 3 c. in W. Cup innings, *255;* Test p'ship record, *203.*

Ijaz Butt (Pak.):– Slow batting in Test, *158.*

Ijaz Faqih (Pak.):– 1 Test hundred, *238;* 107 w. in Pakistan season, *133;* Test p'ship record, *238.*

Illingworth, R. (Eng.):– Test captain (31), *175, 177, 191, 195, 198, 201;* All-round, *137;* All-round in Tests, *166;* 2 Test hundreds, *192, 199;* 2,072 w., *134;* Most w. in English season, *132;* 122 w. in Tests, *162;* 100 w. (10), *133;* 228 for 10th wkt, *125;* Test p'ship record, *200.*

Illingworth, R. K. (Eng.):– Wkt with 1st ball on Test debut, *154.*

Imran Adil (Bahawalpur):– 10 w. in innings, *128.*

Imran Khan (Pak.):– Test captain (48), *175, 201, 205, 228, 232, 235, 242;* 175 one-day ints, *253;* 28 W. Cup appearances, *256;* 3,807 r. in Tests, *153;* 6 Test hundreds, *202, 216, 229, 238;* Best bowling avge in English season, *132;* 362 w. in Tests, *164;* 182 w. in one-day ints, *250;* 40 w. in series, *161;* 34 w. in W. Cup, *255;* 14 w. in Test, *161, 243;* 10 w. or more in Test (6), *203, 217, 230, 238, 243;* 8 w. in Test innings (2), *160, 238, 243;* All-round in one-day ints, *252;* All-round in Tests, *166, 167;* Test p'ship records, *217, 238, 243;* W. Cup p'ship record, *254.*

Imran Zia (Bahawalpur):– 10 d. in match, *139;* 7 d. in innings, *138.*

Imtiaz Ahmed (Pak.):– Test captain, *201, 215;* 2,079 r. in Tests, *154;* 3 Test hundreds, *229, 233, 237;* 300* v Commonwealth XI, *107;* 308 for 7th wkt v New Zealand, *125, 159, 234;* Test p'ship records, *234, 238.*

Inman, C. C. (Leics.):– Fifty in 8 min., *119;* 32 r. in over, *121.*

Insole, D. J. (Eng.):– 25,241 r., *117;* Highest aggregate in English season, *115;* 54 hundreds, *112;* 1 Test hundred, *188.*

Intikhab Alam (Pak.):– Test captain, *201, 215, 228, 232;* Test debut at 17, *174;* 1 Test hundred, *202;* 1,571 w., *134;* 125 w. in Tests, *164;* 100 w. since 1969 (1), *132;* 10 w. or more in Test (2), *234;* Wkt with 1st ball on Test debut, *164;* All-round in

Tests, *166;* 190 for 9th wkt v England, *158, 203;* Test p'ship records, *203, 217, 234.*

Inzamam-ul-Haq (Pak.):– 1 Test hundred, *229;* Test p'ship records, *229, 230.*

Iqbal Qasim (Pak.):– 171 w. in Tests, *164;* 10 w. or more in Test (2), *217, 238;* Test p'ship records, *217, 234, 238, 243.*

Iqtidar Ali (Allied Bank):– Hit the ball twice, *127.*

Iredale, F. A. (Aust.):– 2 Test hundreds, *181.*

Ironmonger, H. (Aust.):– Oldest Australian Test player, *175;* Test debut at 46, *174;* 10 w. or more in Test (2), *207, 210;* 5 w. for 6 r. in Test innings, *161.*

Irvine, B. L. (SA):– 1 Test hundred, *206.*

Israr Ali (B'pur):– 6 w. for 1 r., *129.*

J

Jackman, R. D. (Eng.):– Most w. in English season, *132;* 234 w. in Sunday League, *791;* 100 w. since 1969 (1), *132;* 3 hat-tricks, *131.*

Jackson, A. A. (Aust.):– Hundred v England on Test debut, *148, 181.*

Jackson, Hon. Sir F. S. (Eng.):– Test captain, *177;* 5 Test hundreds, *179.*

Jackson, H. L. (Eng.):– 1,733 w., *134;* Best bowling avge in English season, *131;* 100 w. (10), *133.*

Jadeja, A. D. (Ind.):– 254* in 1992-93, *957;* 415 for 2nd wkt, *123, 958;* 405 for 3rd wkt, *124.*

Jaisimha, M. L. (Ind.):– 2,056 r. in Tests, *153;* 3 Test hundreds, *199, 214;* Slow batting in Test, *158.*

Jalal-ud-Din (Pak.):– Handled the ball, *126;* Hat-trick in one-day int., *251.*

Jameson, J. A. (Eng.):– 465* for 2nd wkt, *123.*

Jamshedji, R. J. D. (Ind.):– Oldest Indian Test debut, *174.*

Jardine, D. R. (Eng.):– Test captain, *177, 191, 195, 198;* 35 hundreds, *112;* 1 Test hundred, *192;* Test p'ship record, *182.*

Jarman, B. N. (Aust.):– Test captain, *177;* 10 d. in match, *139;* Test p'ship record, *214.*

Jarvis, M. P. (Zimb.):– Oldest Zimbabwean Test debut, *173.*

Jarvis, P. W. (Eng.):– Test p'ship record, *205.*

Jarvis, T. W. (NZ):– 1 Test hundred, *224;* Slow batting in Test, *157;* 387 for 1st wkt v West Indies, *159, 225.*

Javed Miandad (Pak.):– Test captain (34), *175, 201, 215, 228, 232, 240;* 121 Tests, *174;* 222 one-day ints, *253;* 28 W. Cup appearances, *256;* 28,504 r. (avge 53.67), *117, 118;* 8,689 r. (avge 53.30) in Tests,

L

P

Page, M. L. (NZ):– Test captain, *197, 219;* 1 Test hundred, *197.*

Pairaudeau, B. H. (WI):– Hundred on Test debut, *148, 226;* Test p'ship record, *227.*

Palmer, G. E. (Aust.):– 10 w. or more in Test (2), *184.*

Pandya, A. N. (S'tra):– Handled the ball, *126.*

Paranjpe, J. V. (Bombay):– 218 in 1992-93, *957.*

Parfitt, P. H. (Eng.):– 26,924 r., *117;* 1,000 r. (15), *114;* 58 hundreds, *112;* 7 Test hundreds, *188, 196, 199, 202;* 2 hundreds in match (2), *110;* Test p'ship records, *197, 203.*

Parkar, G. A. (Ind.):– 421 for 1st wkt, *123.*

Parkar, Z. (Bombay):– 10 d. in match, *139.*

Parker, C. W. L. (Glos.):– 3,278 w., *133;* 100 w. (16), *133;* 100 w. by June 12, *131;* 17 w. in match, *129;* 10 w. in innings, *127;* 6 hat-tricks, *131;* Double hat-trick, *130.*

Parker, J. M. (NZ):– Test captain, *232;* 3 Test hundreds, *197, 212, 231.*

Parker, P. W. G. (Eng.):– 47 hundreds, *112;* 32 r. in over, *121;* Highest for Durham, *107.*

Parkhouse, W. G. A. (Eng.):– 1,000 r. (15), *114.*

Parks, H. W. (Sussex):– 42 hundreds, *112.*

Parks, J. H. (Eng.):– 3,003 r. in season, *113;* 41 hundreds, *112;* All-round, *136.*

Parks, J. M. (Eng.):– 36,673 r., *116;* 1,000 r. (20), *114;* 51 hundreds, *112;* 2 Test hundreds, *188, 192;* 1,181 d., *140;* 114 d. in Tests, *169;* 8 d. in Test, *168;* Test p'ship records, *189, 194.*

Parks, R. J. (Hants):– 714 d., *140;* 10 d. in match, *139.*

Parsons, Rev. J. H. (Warwicks.):– 38 hundreds, *112.*

Passailaigue, C. C. (WI):– 487* for 6th wkt, *123, 124.*

Pataudi (sen.), Nawab of (Eng. and Ind.):– Test captain, *198;* 4 successive hundreds, *110;* Hundred on Test debut, *148, 179.*

Pataudi (jun.), Nawab of (Ind.):– Test captain (40), *175, 198, 213, 225, 230;* 2,793 r. in Tests, *153;* 6 Test hundreds, *200, 214, 231;* 2 hundreds in match (2), *110;* Slow batting in Test, *157.*

Patel, B. P. (Ind.):– 37 hundreds, *112;* 1 Test hundred, *227;* Test p'ship records, *227, 231.*

Patel, D. N. (NZ):– 12 sixes in innings, *122;* Best bowling v Zimbabwe, *237;* Test p'ship records, *197, 236.*

Patel, J. M. (Ind.):– 14 w. in Test, *161, 215;* 9 w. in Test innings, *159, 220.*

Patel, M. M. (Kent):– 12 w. in match, *313.*

Patel, Parashar (Gujarat):– Hundred on debut, *957.*

Patil, S. M. (Ind.):– 4 Test hundreds, *200, 214, 237;* Test p'ship record, *238, 239.*

Patterson, B. M. W. (Scotland):– Hundred on debut, *108.*

Paynter, E. (Eng.):– Highest against Sussex, *107;* 653 r. in series, *190;* 45 hundreds, *112;* 4 Test hundreds, *179, 188;* 2 hundreds in match (2), *110;* 2 hundreds in same Test, *149, 188;* 322 v Sussex, *106;* Test avge of 59.23, *154;* Test p'ship records, *182.*

Payton, W. R. D. (Notts.):– 39 hundreds, *112.*

Peach, H. A. (Surrey):– Fast scoring, *120;* 4 w. with consecutive balls, *130.*

Pearse, D. K. (Natal):– Handled the ball, *126.*

Pearson, A. J. G. (CUCC and Som.):– 10 w. in innings, *128.*

Peate, E. (Eng.):– 8 w. for 5 r., *128.*

Peel, R. (Eng.):– 1,752 w., *134;* 101 w. in Tests, *162;* 100 w. (8), *133;* 10 w. or more in Test, *183;* 292 for 8th wkt, *125.*

Pegler, S. J. (SA):– Fifty in 14 min., *119;* Test p'ship record, *207.*

Pellew, C. E. (Aust.):– 2 Test hundreds, *181.*

Perera, W. A. M. P. (Antonians):– 289 for 2nd wkt, *958.*

Perrin, P. A. (Essex):– Highest v Derbyshire, *107;* Highest for Essex, *107;* 29,709 r., *117;* 1,000 r. (18), *114;* 66 hundreds, *111;* 2 hundreds in match (4), *109;* 343* v Derbyshire, *105, 107;* 68 boundaries in innings, *106.*

Pervez Akhtar (Pak. Rlwys and Multan):– 337* v Dera Ismail Khan, *106;* Handled the ball, *126.*

Pervez Sajjad (Pak.):– 4 w. for 5 r. in Test innings, *161.*

Petherick, P. J. (NZ):– Hat-trick v Pakistan, *165.*

Phadkar, D. G. (Ind.):– 2 Test hundreds, *200, 214.*

Philip, I. L. (Scotland):– Hundred on debut, *108.*

Philipson, H. (OUCC):– 340 for 7th wkt, *125.*

Phillips, H. (Sussex):– 10 d. in match, *138.*

Phillips, R. B. (Qld):– 7 d. in innings, *138.*

Phillips, W. B. (Aust.):– Hundred on Test debut, *148, 216;* 2 Test hundreds, *209, 216;* 462* for 4th wkt, *124;* Test p'ship records, *212, 217.*

Phillips, W. N. (Aust.):– 205 in 1992-93, *957.*

Pickett, H. (Essex):– 10 w. in innings, *127.*

Q

R

INDEX OF FILLERS

INDEX TO TEST MATCHES

TEST MATCHES, 1993-94

Full details of these Tests, and others too late for inclusion, will appear in the 1995 edition of *Wisden*.

SRI LANKA v INDIA

First Test: At Kandy, July 17, 18, 19, 21, 22. Drawn. Toss: India. Sri Lanka 24 for three v India.

Rain washed out all play apart from 12 overs on the second day.

Second Test: At Sinhalese Sports Club, Colombo, July 27, 28, 29, 31, August 1. India won by 235 runs. Toss: India. India 366 (N. S. Sidhu 82, V. G. Kambli 125, Kapil Dev 35, Extras 38; G. P. Wickremasinghe three for 83, K. P. J. Warnaweera three for 76) and 359 for four dec. (M. Prabhakar 95, N. S. Sidhu 104, S. R. Tendulkar 104 not out); Sri Lanka 254 (U. C. Hathurusinghe 37, A. Ranatunga 88; M. Prabhakar three for 43, A. Kumble five for 87) and 236 (U. C. Hathurusinghe 43, A. P. Gurusinha 39, P. A. de Silva 93; M. Prabhakar three for 49, A. Kumble three for 85).

India won an overseas Test after ten defeats and 16 draws since beating England in the Second Test at Leeds in 1986. Kambli scored his third century in successive Test innings (following 224 against England and 227 against Zimbabwe). P. A. de Silva became the second Sri Lankan to reach 2,000 Test runs.

Third Test: At P. Saravanamuttu Stadium, Colombo, August 4, 5, 7, 8, 9. Drawn. Toss: Sri Lanka. Sri Lanka 351 (A. P. Gurusinha 56, P. A. de Silva 148, H. P. Tillekeratne 51, R. S. Kaluwitharana 40; R. K. Chauhan three for 59) and 352 for six (R. S. Mahanama 151, A. P. Gurusinha 35, H. P. Tillekeratne 86, S. T. Jayasuriya 31 not out; A. Kumble three for 108); India 446 (M. Prabhakar 55, N. S. Sidhu 39, V. G. Kambli 120, S. R. Tendulkar 71, M. Azharuddin 50, Extras 34; G. P. Wickremasinghe three for 95, M. Muralitharan four for 136).

Kambli scored his fourth century in his seventh Test as India took the series 1-0.

SRI LANKA v SOUTH AFRICA

First Test: At Moratuwa, August 25, 26, 28, 29, 30. Drawn. Toss: Sri Lanka. Sri Lanka 331 (R. S. Mahanama 53, A. Ranatunga 44, H. P. Tillekeratne 92, R. S. Kalpage 42; A. A. Donald five for 69, B. N. Schultz four for 75) and 300 for six dec. (P. A. de Silva 68, A. Ranatunga 131, H. P. Tillekeratne 33 not out; P. L. Symcox three for 75); South Africa 267 (K. C. Wessels 47, A. C. Hudson 90, D. J. Cullinan 33, P. L. Symcox 48; M. Muralitharan five for 104) and 251 for seven (D. J. Cullinan 46, J. N. Rhodes 101 not out, Extras 30).

Ranatunga became the first Sri Lankan to score 2,500 Test runs. South Africa were 138 for six chasing 365 to win before Rhodes scored his maiden Test century. New Zealander Brian Aldridge stood as umpire in this and the next two Tests.

Second Test: At Sinhalese Sports Club, Colombo, September 6, 7, 8, 10. South Africa won by an innings and 208 runs. Toss: Sri Lanka. Sri Lanka 168 (U. C. Hathurusinghe 34, P. A. de Silva 34, S. T. Jayasuriya 44; B. N. Schultz five for 48) and 119 (B. N. Schultz four for 58, R. P. Snell three for 32); South Africa 495 (K. C. Wessels 92, A. C. Hudson 58, W. J. Cronje 122, D. J. Cullinan 52, P. L. Symcox 50, R. P. Snell 48, Extras 42; M. Muralitharan five for 101, P. A. de Silva three for 39).

South Africa won their biggest-ever victory and their first overseas since they beat England in the Second Test at Leeds in 1965.

Third Test: At P. Saravanamuttu Stadium, Colombo, September 14, 15, 16, 18, 19. Drawn. Toss: South Africa. South Africa 316 (D. J. Cullinan 102, D. J. Richardson 62, P. L. Symcox 30; C. P. H. Ramanayake three for 75, M. Muralitharan four for 64) and 159 (W. J. Cronje 73 not out); Sri Lanka 296 for nine dec. (P. A. de Silva 82, A. Ranatunga 50, H. P. Tillekeratne 37, S. T. Jayasuriya 65; B. N. Schultz five for 63).

Final day lost to rain; South Africa took the series 1-0. Cullinan scored his maiden Test century in his fourth Test. Sri Lanka took 139.5 overs to score 296 runs.

AUSTRALIA v NEW ZEALAND

First Test: At Perth, November 12, 13, 14, 15, 16. Drawn. Toss: New Zealand. Australia 398 (M. A. Taylor 64, M. E. Waugh 36, S. R. Waugh 44, I. A. Healy 113 not out, P. R. Reiffel 51, C. J. McDermott 35; C. L. Cairns four for 113) and 323 for one dec. (M. J. Slater 99, M. A. Taylor 142 not out, D. C. Boon 67 not out); New Zealand 419 for nine dec. (B. A. Pocock 34, A. H. Jones 143, M. D. Crowe 42, C. L. Cairns 78, T. E. Blain 36; C. J. McDermott three for 127) and 166 for four (A. H. Jones 45, M. D. Crowe 31 not out, K. R. Rutherford 39).

McDermott took his 200th wicket in his 50th Test. Taylor scored his 11th Test century – all on different grounds. Boon reached 1,000 Test runs in 1993. Chasing 303 in 65 overs to win, New Zealand were 85 for three; Crowe batted nearly four hours to save the match, aggravating an old knee injury, which forced him to return home; Rutherford assumed the captaincy for the rest of the series.

Second Test: At Hobart, November 26, 27, 28, 29. Australia won by an innings and 222 runs. Toss: Australia. Australia 544 for six dec. (M. J. Slater 168, D. C. Boon 106, M. E. Waugh 111, A. R. Border 60); New Zealand 161 (A. H. Jones 47, T. E. Blain 40; T. B. A. May five for 65, S. K. Warne three for 36) and 161 (K. R. Rutherford 55; S. K. Warne six for 31).

Boon became the fifth Australian to reach 6,000 Test runs, during his 18th Test century in his 82nd Test. Warne ensured New Zealand's heaviest-ever defeat by finishing off their innings with four wickets for three runs in 14 balls.

Third Test: At Brisbane, December 3, 4, 5, 6, 7. Australia won by an innings and 96 runs. Toss: New Zealand. New Zealand 233 (B. A. Young 38, A. H. Jones 56, K. R. Rutherford 36, M. J. Greatbatch 35, T. E. Blain 42 not out; C. J. McDermott four for 39, S. K. Warne four for 66) and 278 (B. A. Young 53, K. R. Rutherford 86; G. D. McGrath three for 66, S. K. Warne four for 59); Australia 607 for six dec. (M. A. Taylor 53, D. C. Boon 89, M. E. Waugh 68, A. R. Border 105, S. R. Waugh 147 not out, S. K. Warne 74 not out).

Border became the first player to appear in 150 Tests and the first to take 150 Test catches; he also scored his 27th Test century. S. R. Waugh reached 3,000 Test runs. I. A. Healy was the first player to be given out by TV replay in a Test in Australia. Australia took the series 2-0 with their second consecutive innings victory.

PAKISTAN v ZIMBABWE

First Test: At Defence Stadium, Karachi, December 1, 2, 3, 5, 6. Pakistan won by 131 runs. Toss: Pakistan. Pakistan 423 for eight dec. (Aamir Sohail 63, Shoaib Mohammad 81, Javed Miandad 70, Basit Ali 36, Rashid Latif 68 not out; E. A. Brandes three for 106) and 131 for three dec. (Inzamam-ul-Haq 57 not out); Zimbabwe 289 (A. D. R. Campbell 53, D. L. Houghton 46, A. Flower 63, G. J. Whittal 33, G. K. Bruk-Jackson 31, Extras 31; Waqar Younis seven for 91) and 134 (Waqar Younis six for 44).

Defence Stadium became Test cricket's 70th ground and Karachi's second. Both captains were leading their country for the first time in Tests – Waqar Younis because of Wasim Akram's hand injury and A. Flower as Houghton's successor. Waqar Younis took 13 wickets for 135 – five bowled and seven lbw.

Second Test: At Rawalpindi, December 9, 10, 11, 13, 14. Pakistan won by 52 runs. Toss: Zimbabwe. Pakistan 245 (Inzamam-ul-Haq 38, Asif Mujtaba 54 not out, Rashid Latif 33; E. A. Brandes three for 82, D. H. Brain four for 41, H. H. Streak three for 58) and 248 (Basit Ali 40, Asif Mujtaba 51, Rashid Latif 61; E. A. Brandes three for 71, H. H. Streak five for 56); Zimbabwe 254 (M. H. Dekker 68, A. D. R. Campbell 63, Extras 30; Waqar Younis five for 88) and 187 (M. H. Dekker 68 not out, A. D. R. Campbell 75; Wasim Akram five for 65, Waqar Younis four for 50).

Rawalpindi Cricket Stadium became Test cricket's 71st ground and Rawalpindi's second. Zimbabwe needed 240 from 65 overs to win and reached 135 for one before losing nine wickets for 52; Dekker became the first Zimbabwean to carry his bat in a Test.

Third Test: At Lahore, December 16, 17, 18, 20, 21. Drawn. Toss: Zimbabwe. Pakistan 147 (Inzamam-ul-Haq 33, Javed Miandad 31; E. A. Brandes three for 45, D. H. Brain five for 42) and 174 for one (Aamir Sohail 32, Shoaib Mohammad 53 not out, Asif Mujtaba 65 not out); Zimbabwe 230 (G. W. Flower 30, D. L. Houghton 50, A. Flower 62 not out, Extras 31; Wasim Akram four for 70, Waqar Younis five for 100).

Play was severely disrupted by fog. Zimbabwe took an 83-run lead, but Shoaib Mohammad batted six hours and 15 minutes for 53 not out. Pakistan won the series 2-0.

SRI LANKA v WEST INDIES

Only Test: At Moratuwa, December 9, 10, 11, 12, 13. Drawn. Toss: Sri Lanka. Sri Lanka 190 (P. A. de Silva 53, A. Ranatunga 31, R. S. Kalpage 39; C. E. L. Ambrose three for 14, W. K. M. Benjamin four for 46) and 43 for two; West Indies 204 (R. B. Richardson 51, C. L. Hooper 62; S. D. Anurasiri three for 77, M. Muralitharan four for 47).

The first Test between West Indies and Sri Lanka, 12 years after Sri Lanka gained Test status. Rain and poor drainage prevented play on the first scheduled day, December 8, and the final two days after the teams agreed to begin on December 9 and to play on the rest day.

AUSTRALIA v SOUTH AFRICA

First Test: At Melbourne, December 26, 27, 28, 29, 30. Drawn. Toss: Australia. Australia 342 for seven dec. (M. A. Taylor 170, M. J. Slater 32, M. E. Waugh 84; C. R. Matthews three for 68); South Africa 258 for three (A. C. Hudson 64 retired hurt, W. J. Cronje 71, J. N. Rhodes 35 not out, K. C. Wessels 63 not out).

Rain permitted only 59 overs during the first three days of South Africa's first Test with Australia since March 1970. Wessels (Australia 1982-85) was the first player to appear for and against Australia since W. E. Midwinter (Australia 1877-87, England 1881-82). D. C. Boon passed R. N. Harvey (6,149) to become Australia's fourth-highest run-scorer. Taylor reached 4,000 runs in his 50th Test, including 1,000 in 1993; he is the second player (after M. D. Crowe) to score hundreds against seven Test countries and the first to do so on Test debut against four countries.

Second Test: At Sydney, January 2, 3, 4, 5, 6. South Africa won by five runs. Toss: South Africa. South Africa 169 (G. Kirsten 67, W. J. Cronje 41; S. K. Warne seven for 56) and 239 (G. Kirsten 41, W. J. Cronje 38, J. N. Rhodes 76 not out; C. J. McDermott four for 62, S. K. Warne five for 72); Australia 292 (M. J. Slater 92, A. R. Border 49, D. R. Martyn 59; A. A. Donald four for 83, P. S. de Villiers four for 80) and 111 (A. A. Donald three for 34, P. S. de Villiers six for 43).

The fourth-closest Test victory ever; Australia needed only 117 to win with more than a day left. K. C. Wessels fractured a finger fielding in Australia's first innings; he batted, but returned home after the match; Cronje captained in the field and in the following Test.

Third Test: At Adelaide, January 28, 29, 30, 31, February 1. Australia won by 191 runs. Toss: Australia. Australia 469 for seven dec. (M. A. Taylor 62, M. J. Slater 53, D. C. Boon 50, A. R. Border 84, S. R. Waugh 164, P. R. Reiffel 32 not out; A. A. Donald three for 122, B. M. McMillan three for 89) and 124 for six dec. (M. A. Taylor 38, D. C. Boon 38); South Africa 273 (A. C. Hudson 90, G. Kirsten 43, P. N. Kirsten 79; C. J. McDermott three for 49, S. R. Waugh four for 26) and 129 (P. N. Kirsten 42, P. S. de Villiers 30; C. J. McDermott four for 33, S. K. Warne four for 31).

Series drawn 1-1. Border became the first player to reach 11,000 Test runs, in his 153rd Test; I. A. Healy became the sixth wicket-keeper to make 200 dismissals, in his 59th. Warne reached 100 wickets in his 23rd Test, despite a shoulder injury, and Donald took his 50th in 11. Referee J. L. Hendriks fined P. N. Kirsten 25 per cent of his match fee for dissent after three of his batting partners were given out lbw by umpire D. B. Hair in the first innings.

FIXTURES, 1994

* Indicates Sunday play.   *† Not first-class.*

All County Championship matches are of four days' duration. Other first-class matches are of three days' duration unless stated.

Wednesday, April 13

Cambridge	Cambridge U. v Notts.
Oxford	Oxford U. v Durham

Saturday, April 16

Cambridge*	Cambridge U. v Northants
Oxford	Oxford U. v Hants

Tuesday, April 19

Uxbridge	†Middx 2nd XI v England Under-19 (4 days)

Wednesday, April 20

Cambridge	Cambridge U. v Kent
Oxford	Oxford U. v Glam.

Thursday, April 21

Lord's*	Middx v England A (4 days)

Saturday, April 23

Oxford	†Combined Universities v Glos. (1 day)

Sunday, April 24

Oxford (Christ Church)	†Combined Universities v Kent (1 day)

Tuesday, April 26

†Benson and Hedges Cup – First Round
(1 day)

Oxford	Combined Universities v Lancs.
Leicester	Leics. v Ireland
Lord's	Middx v Northants
Nottingham	Notts. v Minor Counties
The Oval	Surrey v Somerset
Hove	Sussex v Scotland

Thursday, April 28

Chesterfield*	Derbys. v Durham
Bristol*	Glos. v Somerset
Southampton*	Hants v Essex
Leicester*	Leics. v Northants
The Oval*	Surrey v Worcs.
Birmingham*	Warwicks. v Glam.
Manchester	Lancs. v Yorks. (friendly match, 4 days)
Oxford	Oxford U. v Notts.

Friday, April 29

Southgate	†England Amateur XI v New Zealanders (1 day)

Saturday, April 30

Cambridge*	Cambridge U. v Middx

Sunday, May 1

Arundel	†Lavinia, Duchess of Norfolk's XI v New Zealanders (1 day)
Manchester	†Lancs. v Yorks. (1 day)

Monday, May 2

The Oval	†Surrey v New Zealanders (1 day)

Wednesday, May 4

Worcester	Worcs. v New Zealanders
Lord's	†MCC v MCC Young Cricketers (1 day)

Thursday, May 5

Stockton-on-Tees	Durham v Essex
Bristol	Glos. v Sussex
Southampton	Hants v Derbys.
Canterbury	Kent v Notts.
Manchester	Lancs. v Surrey
Lord's	Middx v Yorks.
Northampton	Northants v Glam.
Birmingham	Warwicks. v Leics.

Saturday, May 7

Taunton*	Somerset v New Zealanders
Cambridge*	Cambridge U. v Worcs.

Tuesday, May 10

†Benson and Hedges Cup – Second Round
(1 day)

Derby	Derbys. v Combined Universities or Lancs.
Stockton-on-Tees	Durham v Worcs.
Chelmsford	Essex v Leics. or Ireland
Southampton	Hants v Yorks.
Canterbury	Kent v Glos.
Lord's or Northampton	Middx or Northants v Warwicks.
Nottingham or Oxford (Christ Church)	Notts. or Minor Counties v Sussex or Scotland
The Oval or Taunton	Surrey or Somerset v Glam.

Thursday, May 12

Lord's	Middx v New Zealanders
Chelmsford	Essex v Kent
Cardiff	Glam. v Yorks.
Leicester	Leics. v Somerset
Nottingham	Notts. v Durham
The Oval	Surrey v Derbys.
Hove	Sussex v Hants
Worcester	Worcs. v Glos.

Saturday, May 14

Cambridge*	Cambridge U. v Lancs.
Oxford	Oxford U. v Warwicks.

Sunday, May 15

Northampton	†Northants v New Zealanders (1 day)

Tuesday, May 17

Leicester	†Leics. v New Zealanders (1 day)

Wednesday, May 18

Oxford	Oxford U. v Leics.

Thursday, May 19

Birmingham	†ENGLAND v NEW ZEALAND (1st 1-day Texaco Trophy)
Derby	Derbys. v Worcs.
Gateshead Fell	Durham v Glos.
Southampton	Hants v Middx
Canterbury	Kent v Lancs.
Nottingham	Notts. v Sussex
Taunton	Somerset v Warwicks.
The Oval	Surrey v Northants
Leeds	Yorks. v Essex

Saturday, May 21

Lord's	†ENGLAND v NEW ZEALAND (2nd 1-day Texaco Trophy)

Tuesday, May 24

†Benson and Hedges Cup – Quarter-finals
(1 day)

Southampton or Leeds	Hants or Yorks. v New Zealanders

Thursday, May 26

Ilkeston	Derbys. v Notts.
Gloucester	Glos. v Surrey
Southport	Lancs. v Somerset
Leicester	Leics. v Kent
Lord's	Middx v Warwicks.
Hove	Sussex v Glam.
Worcester	Worcs. v Northants

Saturday, May 28

Chelmsford*	Essex v New Zealanders
Oxford	Oxford U. v Yorks.

Thursday, June 2

Nottingham*	ENGLAND v NEW ZEALAND (1st Cornhill Test, 5 days)
Chelmsford	Essex v Glos.
Swansea	Glam. v Surrey
Tunbridge Wells	Kent v Sussex
Lord's	Middx v Worcs.
Northampton	Northants v Lancs.
Taunton	Somerset v Hants
Birmingham	Warwicks. v Durham
Middlesbrough	Yorks. v Notts.

Tuesday, June 7

†**Benson and Hedges Cup – Semi-finals** (1 day)

Wednesday, June 8

| Birmingham or | Warwicks. or Surrey v |
| The Oval‡ | New Zealanders |

‡ *Or Glam. at Swansea if both Warwicks.*
and Surrey in B&H Cup semi-finals.

Thursday, June 9

Derby	Derbys. v Leics.
Hartlepool	Durham v Northants
Basingstoke	Hants v Notts.
Canterbury	Kent v Middx
Horsham	Sussex v Lancs.
Worcester	Worcs. v Essex
Bradford	Yorks. v Somerset

Saturday, June 11

Bristol*	Glos. v New
	Zealanders
Cambridge*	Cambridge U. v Glam.
The Oval*	Surrey v Oxford U.
Glasgow	Scotland v Ireland
(Hamilton	
Crescent)*	

Wednesday, June 15

| Cambridge | Cambridge U. v Essex |

Thursday, June 16

Lord's*	ENGLAND v NEW
	ZEALAND (2nd
	Cornhill Test,
	5 days)
Cardiff	Glam. v Derbys.
Manchester	Lancs. v Hants
Leicester	Leics. v Middx
Luton	Northants v Yorks.
Nottingham	Notts. v Glos.
Bath	Somerset v Surrey
Hove	Sussex v Durham
Birmingham	Warwicks. v Kent

Friday, June 17

| Worcester* | Worcs. v Oxford U. |

Tuesday, June 21

†**NatWest Bank Trophy – First Round**
(1 day)

Finchampstead	Berks. v Kent
March	Cambs. v Hants
Bowdon	Cheshire v Durham
Netherfield	Cumb. v Leics.
Exmouth	Devon v Yorks.

Swansea	Glam. v Lincs.
Bristol	Glos. v Derbys.
Manchester	Lancs. v Scotland
Northop Hall	Wales v Middx
Lakenham	Norfolk v Worcs.
Northampton	Northants v Ireland
Jesmond	Northumb. v Notts.
Aston Rowant	Oxon. v Somerset
The Oval	Surrey v Staffs.
Hove	Sussex v Essex
Birmingham	Warwicks. v Beds.

Wednesday, June 22

| Cambridge | Combined Universities |
| | v New Zealanders |

Thursday, June 23

Highclere	†Earl of Carnarvon's
	Invitation XI v
	South Africans
	(1 day)
Ilford	Essex v Notts.
Colwyn Bay	Glam. v Lancs.
Lord's	Middx v Durham
Northampton	Northants v
	Warwicks.
The Oval	Surrey v Leics.
Worcester	Worcs. v Sussex
Leeds	Yorks. v Hants

Saturday, June 25

Derby*	Derbys. v New
	Zealanders
Canterbury*	Kent v South Africans
Bristol*	Glos. v Cambridge U.

Tuesday, June 28

| Lord's | †Eton v Harrow |
| | (1 day) |

Wednesday, June 29

Hove	Sussex v South
	Africans
Lord's	Oxford U. v
	Cambridge U.

Thursday, June 30

Manchester	ENGLAND v NEW
	ZEALAND (3rd
	Cornhill Test,
	5 days)
Derby	Derbys. v Middx
Darlington	Durham v Surrey
Bristol	Glos. v Glam.
Maidstone	Kent v Yorks.
Leicester	Leics. v Essex
Nottingham	Notts. v Northants
Taunton	Somerset v Worcs.
Birmingham	Warwicks. v Lancs.

Saturday, July 2

Southampton*	Hants v South Africans

Wednesday, July 6

Derby or Bristol	Derbys. or Glos. v South Africans

†NatWest Bank Trophy – Second Round
(1 day)

March or Southampton	Cambs. or Hants v Berks. or Kent
Bowdon or Darlington	Cheshire or Durham v Glos. or Derbys.
Netherfield or Leicester	Cumb. or Leics. v Warwicks. or Beds.
Exmouth or Leeds	Devon or Yorks. v Oxon. or Somerset
Cardiff or Sleaford	Glam. or Lincs. v Sussex or Essex
Colwyn Bay or Uxbridge	Wales or Middx v Northants or Ireland
Lakenham or Worcester	Norfolk or Worcs. v Northumb. or Notts.
The Oval or Stone	Surrey or Staffs. v Lancs. or Scotland

Friday, July 8

Comber	†Ireland v New Zealanders (1 day)

Saturday, July 9

Lord's	†BENSON AND HEDGES CUP FINAL (1 day)

Sunday, July 10

Dublin (Malahide)	†Ireland v New Zealanders (1 day)
Glasgow (Titwood)	†Scotland v South Africans (1 day)

Monday, July 11

Harrogate	†Costcutter Cup (3 days)

Tuesday, July 12

Chester-le-Street	Durham v South Africans
Lord's	†MCC v MCC Schools (1 day)

Wednesday, July 13

Lord's	†MCC Schools v NAYC (1 day)

Thursday, July 14

Southend	Essex v Glam.
Portsmouth	Hants v Glos.
Canterbury	Kent v Worcs.
Blackpool	Lancs. v Derbys.
Taunton	Somerset v Notts.
Guildford	Surrey v Warwicks.
Arundel	Sussex v Middx
Harrogate	Yorks. v Leics.
Lord's	†NCA Young Cricketers v Combined Services (1 day)

Saturday, July 16

Northampton*	Northants v South Africans

Wednesday, July 20

Edinburgh and Glasgow	†Triple Crown Tournament (3 days)

Thursday, July 21

Lord's*	ENGLAND v SOUTH AFRICA (1st Cornhill Test, 5 days)
Durham Univ.	Durham v Leics.
Abergavenny	Glam. v Kent
Cheltenham	Glos. v Yorks.
Manchester	Lancs. v Middx
Northampton	Northants v Derbys.
Nottingham	Notts. v Surrey
Hove	Sussex v Somerset
Birmingham	Warwicks. v Essex
Worcester	Worcs. v Hants

Tuesday, July 26

†NatWest Bank Trophy – Quarter-finals
(1 day)

Wednesday, July 27

Nottingham or Manchester‡	Notts. or Lancs. v South Africans

‡ *Or Worcs. if both Notts. and Lancs. in NatWest quarter-finals.*

Thursday, July 28

Chesterfield	Derbys. v Warwicks.
Durham Univ.	Durham v Yorks.
Swansea	Glam. v Somerset
Cheltenham	Glos. v Kent
Southampton	Hants v Northants
Uxbridge	Middx v Essex
The Oval	Surrey v Sussex

Saturday, July 30

Leicester*	Leics. v South Africans

Thursday, August 4

Leeds*	ENGLAND v SOUTH AFRICA (2nd Cornhill Test, 5 days)
Chesterfield	Derbys. v Glos.
Chelmsford	Essex v Lancs.
Canterbury	Kent v Hants
Lord's	Middx v Glam.
Northampton	Northants v Sussex
Nottingham	Notts. v Leics.
Taunton	Somerset v Durham
Worcester	Worcs. v Warwicks.
Cardiff	†England Under-19 v India Under-19 (1st 1-day)

Saturday, August 6

Bristol	†England Under-19 v India Under-19 (2nd 1-day)

Tuesday, August 9

†NatWest Bank Trophy – Semi-finals (1 day)

Jesmond	England XI v Rest of the World XI (1 day)

Wednesday, August 10

Torquay	Minor Counties v South Africans
Jesmond	†England XI v Rest of the World XI (1 day)

Thursday, August 11

Colchester	Essex v Surrey
Bristol	Glos. v Northants
Canterbury	Kent v Durham
Leicester	Leics. v Worcs.
Lord's	Middx v Somerset
Eastbourne	Sussex v Derbys.
Birmingham	Warwicks. v Notts.
Leeds	Yorks. v Lancs.
Taunton*	†England Under-19 v India Under-19 (1st "Test", 4 days)

Saturday, August 13

Pontypridd*	Glam. v South Africans

Wednesday, August 17

Lord's	†MCC v Scotland (2 days)

Thursday, August 18

The Oval*	ENGLAND v SOUTH AFRICA (3rd Cornhill Test, 5 days)
Derby	Derbys. v Kent
Hartlepool	Durham v Glam.
Southampton	Hants v Surrey
Manchester	Lancs. v Glos.
Leicester	Leics. v Sussex
Northampton	Northants v Middx
Weston-super-Mare	Somerset v Essex
Kidderminster	Worcs. v Notts.
Scarborough	Yorks. v Warwicks.

†Bain Clarkson Trophy Semi-finals (1 day)

Friday, August 19

†Bain Clarkson Trophy Semi-finals (1 day) (if not played on August 18)

Wednesday, August 24

†Minor Counties Knockout Final (1 day)

Thursday, August 25

Birmingham	†ENGLAND v SOUTH AFRICA (1st 1-day Texaco Trophy)
Cardiff	Glam. v Leics.
Portsmouth	Hants v Durham
Northampton	Northants v Kent
Nottingham	Notts. v Lancs.
The Oval	Surrey v Middx
Hove	Sussex v Warwicks.
Worcester	Worcs. v Yorks.
Leeds*	†England Under-19 v India Under-19 (2nd "Test", 4 days)

Thursday, August 26

Lord's	†National Club Championship Final (1 day)

Saturday, August 27

Manchester	†ENGLAND v SOUTH AFRICA (2nd 1-day Texaco Trophy)

Sunday, August 28

Lord's	†National Village Championship Final (1 day)

Monday, August 29

Scarborough	†President's XI v South Africans (1 day)

Tuesday, August 30

Chelmsford	Essex v Sussex
Bristol	Glos. v Leics.
Manchester	Lancs. v Worcs.
Worksop	Notts. v Glam.
Taunton	Somerset v Northants
Birmingham	Warwicks. v Hants
Sheffield	Yorks. v Derbys.

Wednesday, August 31

Scarborough	President's XI v South Africans

Saturday, September 3

Lord's	†NATWEST BANK TROPHY FINAL (1 day)
Scarborough	†Yorks. v Durham (Northern Electric Trophy, 1 day)

Monday, September 5

	†Bain Clarkson Trophy Final (1 day)
Scarborough	†Tetley Bitter Festival Trophy (3 days)

Tuesday, September 6

Lord's	†MCC v Holders Hill CC, Barbados (1 day)

Thursday, September 8

Derby	Derbys. v Essex
Stockton-on-Tees	Durham v Lancs.
Cardiff	Glam. v Worcs.
Canterbury	Kent v Somerset
Leicester	Leics. v Hants
Lord's	Middx v Glos.
Scarborough	Yorks. v Surrey
Birmingham*	†England Under-19 v India Under-19 (3rd "Test", 4 days)

Thursday, September 15

Chelmsford	Essex v Northants
Bristol	Glos. v Warwicks.
Southampton	Hants v Glam.
Manchester	Lancs. v Leics.
Nottingham	Notts. v Middx
Taunton	Somerset v Derbys.
The Oval	Surrey v Kent
Hove	Sussex v Yorks.
Worcester	Worcs. v Durham

NEW ZEALAND TOUR, 1994

APRIL

29 Southgate	†v England Amateur XI (1 day)

MAY

1 Arundel	†v Lavinia, Duchess of Norfolk's XI (1 day)
2 The Oval	†v Surrey (1 day)
4 Worcester	v Worcs.
7 Taunton*	v Somerset
12 Lord's	v Middx
15 Northampton	†v Northants (1 day)
17 Leicester	†v Leics. (1 day)
19 Birmingham	†v ENGLAND (1st 1-day Texaco Trophy)
21 Lord's	†v ENGLAND (2nd 1-day Texaco Trophy)
24 Southampton or Leeds	v Hants or Yorks.
28 Chelmsford*	v Essex

JUNE

2 Nottingham*	v ENGLAND (1st Cornhill Test, 5 days)
8 Birmingham or The Oval‡	v Warwicks. or Surrey

‡ *Or Glam. at Swansea if both Warwicks. and Surrey in B&H Cup semi-finals.*

11 Bristol*	v Glos.
16 Lord's*	v ENGLAND (2nd Cornhill Test, 5 days)
22 Cambridge	v Combined Universities
25 Derby*	v Derbys.
30 Manchester	v ENGLAND (3rd Cornhill Test, 5 days)

JULY

8 Comber	†v Ireland (1 day)
10 Dublin (Malahide)	†v Ireland (1 day)

SOUTH AFRICAN TOUR, 1994

JUNE

23	Highclere	†v Earl of Carnarvon's Invitation XI (1 day)
25	Canterbury*	v Kent
29	Hove	v Sussex

JULY

2	Southampton*	v Hants
6	Derby or Bristol	v Derbys. or Glos.
10	Glasgow (Titwood)	†v Scotland (1 day)
12	Chester-le-Street	v Durham
16	Northampton*	v Northants
21	Lord's	v ENGLAND (1st Cornhill Test, 5 days)

27	Nottingham or Manchester‡	v Notts. or Lancs.

‡ *Or Worcs. if both Notts. and Lancs. in NatWest quarter-finals.*

30	Leicester*	v Leics.

AUGUST

4	Leeds*	v ENGLAND (2nd Cornhill Test, 5 days)
10	Torquay	v Minor Counties
13	Pontypridd*	v Glam.
18	The Oval*	v ENGLAND (3rd Cornhill Test, 5 days)
25	Birmingham	†v ENGLAND (1st 1-day Texaco Trophy)
27	Manchester	†v ENGLAND (2nd 1-day Texaco Trophy)
29	Scarborough	†v President's XI (1 day)
31	Scarborough	v President's XI

†AXA EQUITY & LAW LEAGUE, 1994

All matches are of one day's duration.

MAY

8–Durham v Essex (Stockton-on-Tees); Glos. v Sussex (Bristol); Hants v Derbys. (Southampton); Kent v Notts. (Canterbury); Lancs. v Surrey (Manchester); Middx v Yorks. (Lord's); Northants v Glam. (Northampton); Warwicks. v Leics. (Birmingham).

15–Essex v Kent (Chelmsford); Glam. v Yorks. (Cardiff); Leics. v Somerset (Leicester); Notts. v Durham (Nottingham); Surrey v Derbys. (The Oval); Sussex v Hants (Hove); Worcs. v Glos. (Worcester).

22–Derbys. v Worcs. (Derby); Durham v Glos. (Gateshead Fell); Hants v Middx (Southampton); Kent v Lancs. (Canterbury); Notts. v Sussex (Nottingham); Somerset v Warwicks. (Taunton); Surrey v Northants (The Oval); Yorks. v Essex (Leeds).

29–Derbys. v Notts. (Ilkeston); Glos. v Surrey (Gloucester); Lancs. v Somerset (Manchester); Leics. v Kent (Leicester); Middx v Warwicks. (Lord's); Sussex v Glam. (Hove); Worcs. v Northants (Worcester).

JUNE

5–Essex v Glos. (Chelmsford); Glam. v Surrey (Swansea); Kent v Sussex (Tunbridge Wells); Middx v Worcs. (Lord's); Northants v Lancs. (Northampton); Somerset v Hants (Taunton); Warwicks. v Durham (Birmingham); Yorks. v Notts. (Leeds).

12–Derbys. v Leics. (Derby); Durham v Northants (Hartlepool); Hants v Notts. (Basingstoke); Kent v Middx (Canterbury); Sussex v Lancs. (Horsham); Worcs. v Essex (Worcester); Yorks. v Somerset (Leeds).

19–Glam. v Derbys. (Swansea); Lancs. v Hants (Manchester); Leics. v Middx (Leicester); Northants v Yorks. (Luton); Notts. v Glos. (Nottingham); Somerset v Surrey (Bath); Sussex v Durham (Hove); Warwicks. v Kent (Birmingham).

26–Essex v Notts. (Ilford); Glam. v Lancs. (Colwyn Bay); Middx v Durham (Lord's); Northants v Warwicks. (Northampton); Surrey v Leics. (The Oval); Worcs. v Sussex (Worcester); Yorks. v Hants (Leeds).

JULY

3–Derbys. v Middx (Derby); Durham v Surrey (Darlington); Glos. v Glam. (Bristol); Kent v Yorks. (Maidstone); Leics. v Essex (Leicester); Notts. v Northants (Nottingham); Somerset v Worcs. (Taunton); Warwicks. v Lancs. (Birmingham).

10–Derbys. v Durham (Derby); Glos. v Somerset (Bristol); Hants v Essex (Southampton); Leics. v Northants (Leicester); Surrey v Worcs. (The Oval); Warwicks. v Glam. (Birmingham). *Note: Matches involving B&H Cup finalists to be played on July 12.*

17–Essex v Glam. (Southend); Hants v Glos. (Portsmouth); Kent v Worcs. (Canterbury); Lancs. v Derbys. (Manchester); Somerset v Notts. (Taunton); Surrey v Warwicks. (Guildford); Sussex v Middx (Arundel); Yorks. v Leics. (Scarborough).

24–Durham v Leics. (Durham Univ.); Glam. v Kent (Ebbw Vale); Glos. v Yorks. (Cheltenham); Lancs. v Middx (Manchester); Northants v Derbys. (Northampton); Notts. v Surrey (Nottingham); Sussex v Somerset (Hove); Warwicks. v Essex (Birmingham); Worcs. v Hants (Worcester).

31–Derbys. v Warwicks. (Chesterfield); Durham v Yorks. (Durham Univ.); Glam. v Somerset (Swansea); Glos. v Kent (Cheltenham); Hants v Northants (Southampton); Middx v Essex (Uxbridge); Surrey v Sussex (The Oval).

AUGUST

7–Derbys. v Glos. (Chesterfield); Essex v Lancs. (Chelmsford); Kent v Hants (Canterbury); Middx v Glam. (Lord's); Northants v Sussex (Northampton); Notts. v Leics. (Nottingham); Somerset v Durham (Taunton); Warwicks. v Worcs. (Birmingham).

14–Essex v Surrey (Colchester); Glos. v Northants (Bristol); Kent v Durham (Canterbury); Leics. v Worcs. (Leicester); Middx v Somerset (Lord's); Sussex v Derbys. (Eastbourne); Warwicks. v Notts. (Birmingham); Yorks. v Lancs. (Leeds).

21–Derbys. v Kent (Derby); Durham v Glam. (Hartlepool); Hants v Surrey (Southampton); Lancs. v Glos. (Manchester); Leics. v Sussex (Leicester); Northants v Middx (Northampton); Somerset v Essex (Weston-super-Mare); Worcs. v Notts. (Worcester); Yorks. v Warwicks. (Scarborough).

28–Glam. v Leics. (Neath); Hants v Durham (Portsmouth); Northants v Kent (Northampton); Notts. v Lancs. (Nottingham); Surrey v Middx (The Oval); Sussex v Warwicks. (Hove); Worcs. v Yorks. (Worcester).

SEPTEMBER

4–Essex v Sussex (Chelmsford); Glos. v Leics. (Moreton-in-Marsh); Lancs. v Worcs. (Manchester); Notts. v Glam. (Nottingham); Somerset v Northants (Taunton); Warwicks. v Hants (Birmingham); Yorks. v Derbys. (Leeds). *Note: Matches involving NatWest Trophy finalists to be played on September 6.*

11–Derbys. v Essex (Derby); Durham v Lancs. (Stockton-on-Tees); Glam. v Worcs. (Cardiff); Kent v Somerset (Canterbury); Leics. v Hants (Leicester); Middx v Glos. (Lord's); Yorks. v Surrey (Scarborough).

18–Essex v Northants (Chelmsford); Glos. v Warwicks. (Bristol); Hants v Glam. (Southampton); Lancs. v Leics. (Manchester); Notts. v Middx (Nottingham); Somerset v Derbys. (Taunton); Surrey v Kent (The Oval); Sussex v Yorks. (Hove); Worcs. v Durham (Worcester).

†MINOR COUNTIES CHAMPIONSHIP, 1994

All matches are of two days' duration.

MAY

22–Herts. v Bucks. (Shenley Park).

29–Berks. v Oxon. (Maidenhead & Bray); Devon v Wilts. (Sidmouth); Dorset v Salop (Weymouth); Herefords. v Wales (Colwall); Lincs. v Cambs. (Sleaford); Northumb. v Herts. (Jesmond).

31–Cumb. v Suffolk (Penrith).

JUNE

2–Staffs. v Suffolk (Longton).

12–Beds. v Cambs. (Henlow); Berks. v Wales (Falkland CC); Cumb. v Norfolk (Barrow); Dorset v Oxon. (Canford School); Northumb. v Bucks. (Jesmond); Salop v Wilts. (Ellesmere College); Suffolk v Lincs. (Bury St Edmunds).

13-Cornwall v Cheshire (Helston).

14-Cumb. v Bucks. (Netherfield); Staffs. v Norfolk (Wolverhampton).

15-Devon v Cheshire (Bovey Tracey).

26-Cheshire v Wales (Toft); Cumb. v Herts. (Millom); Lincs. v Northumb. (Grimsby Town); Oxon. v Cornwall (Challow & Childrey); Salop v Herefords. (Bridgnorth).

28-Berks. v Cornwall (Kidmore End); Cambs. v Northumb. (Wisbech); Staffs. v Herts. (Brewood).

JULY

3-Suffolk v Beds. (Ransome's, Ipswich). *Note: To be rearranged if either Suffolk or Beds. in MCC Trophy semi-finals.*

6-Cambs. v Staffs. (Cambridge).

10-Beds. v Norfolk (Bedford Town); Cornwall v Dorset (Truro); Herefords. v Devon (Brockhampton); Herts. v Lincs. (Hertford); Wilts. v Wales (Trowbridge).

12-Staffs. v Bucks. (Leek).

13-Cambs. v Suffolk (March).

17-Beds. v Northumb. (Dunstable Town); Cheshire v Salop (New Brighton); Dorset v Berks. (Dorchester); Lincs. v Cumb. (Bourne); Wales v Cornwall (Marchwiel); Wilts. v Oxon. (Westbury).

19-Beds. v Herts. (Luton); Cambs. v Cumb. (Peterborough); Herefords. v Cornwall (Brockhampton).

24-Berks. v Devon (Finchampstead); Cornwall v Wilts. (Falmouth); Herefords. v Dorset (Hereford City); Herts. v Cambs. (Bishop's Stortford); Norfolk v Lincs. (Lakenham); Wales v Salop (Pontarddulais).

25-Northumb. v Staffs. (Jesmond).

26-Oxon. v Devon (Pressed Steel, Oxford).

27-Cumb. v Staffs. (Carlisle).

28-Norfolk v Herts. (Lakenham).

31-Beds. v Cumb. (Leighton Buzzard); Bucks. v Lincs. (Slough); Dorset v Cheshire (Dean Park, Bournemouth); Oxon. v Herefords. (Banbury CC); Suffolk v Northumb. (Bury St Edmunds).

AUGUST

1-Cornwall v Salop (Camborne).

2-Norfolk v Northumb. (Lakenham); Wilts. v Cheshire (Trowbridge).

3-Devon v Salop (Torquay).

4-Norfolk v Cambs. (Lakenham).

7-Berks. v Herefords. (Reading); Cornwall v Devon (St Austell); Lincs. v Staffs. (Boston); Oxon. v Wales (Aston Rowant); Wilts. v Dorset (Marlborough CC).

14-Bucks. v Norfolk (Marlow); Cheshire v Oxon. (Bowdon); Lincs. v Beds. (Lincoln Lindum); Northumb. v Cumb. (Jesmond); Wales v Dorset (Colwyn Bay); Wilts. v Berks. (Swindon).

16-Salop v Oxon. (Wellington); Staffs. v Beds. (Stone).

17-Cambs. v Bucks. (Cambridge).

21-Cheshire v Herefords. (Neston); Devon v Dorset (Exmouth); Herts. v Suffolk (Long Marston).

23-Bucks. v Suffolk (Beaconsfield). *Note: To be rearranged if either Bucks. or Suffolk in MCC Trophy final.*

28-Bucks. v Beds. (Amersham); Salop v Berks. (Shrewsbury); Suffolk v Norfolk (Copdock CC); Wales v Devon (Swansea).

30-Cheshire v Berks. (Warrington); Herefords. v Wilts. (Dales, Leominster).

SEPTEMBER

11-Final at Worcester.

†HOLT CUP KNOCKOUT COMPETITION, 1994

All matches are of one day's duration.

Preliminary Round

May 22 Cumb. v Lincs. (Askham CC); Cheshire v Northumb. (Boughton Hall); Salop v Herefords. (Wellington); Wales v Staffs. (Usk).

First Round

June 5 Bucks. v Herts. (Aylesbury); Cambs. v Norfolk (The Leys School); Cornwall v Dorset (Truro); Cumb. or Lincs. v Cheshire or Northumb. (Kendal or Grantham); Oxon. v Berks. (Christ

Church); Salop. or Herefords. v Wales or Staffs. (Shrewsbury or Brockhampton); Suffolk v Beds. (Framlingham); Wilts. v Devon (Trowbridge).

Quarter-finals to be played on June 19.

Semi-finals to be played on July 3.

Final to be played on August 24 at Lord's.

†RAPID CRICKETLINE SECOND ELEVEN CHAMPIONSHIP, 1994

All matches are of three days' duration.

APRIL

25 – Derbys. v Notts. (Derby); Kent v Durham (Canterbury); Lancs. v Warwicks. (Manchester); Somerset v Surrey (Taunton); Worcs. v Glos. (Worcester).

28 – Sussex v Notts. (Hove).

MAY

2 – Derbys. v Glos. (Derby); Essex v Northants (Chelmsford); Leics. v Warwicks. (Leicester); Notts. v Durham (Nottingham); Somerset v Kent (Taunton).

3 – Glam. v Middx (Cardiff).

9 – Derbys. v Essex (Chesterfield); Kent v Glos. (Ashfield); Lancs. v Middx (Haslingden); Leics. v Durham (Hinckley); Sussex v Somerset (Haywards Heath); Worcs. v Hants (Kidderminster); Yorks. v Glam. (Leeds).

16 – Glam. v Leics. (Swansea); Glos. v Durham (Bristol); Kent v Surrey (Maidstone); Lancs. v Notts. (Manchester); Middx v Yorks. (Uxbridge); Northants v Sussex (Northampton).

17 – Hants v Somerset (Finchampstead).

23 – Durham v Sussex (Felling); Essex v Kent (Colchester); Lancs. v Derbys. (Lytham); Leics. v Worcs. (Oakham); Middx v Warwicks. (Uxbridge); Northants v Glam. (Oundle School); Surrey v Hants (Banstead); Yorks. v Glos. (Bradford).

30 – Derbys. v Kent (Derby); Durham v Warwicks. (South Shields CC); Somerset v Worcs. (Taunton); Surrey v Glos. (The Oval); Sussex v Essex (Eastbourne); Yorks. v Notts. (Leeds).

JUNE

1 – Hants v Glam. (Southampton).

6 – Derbys. v Worcs. (Abbotsholme School, Rocester); Glam. v Lancs. (Usk); Glos. v Leics. (Bristol); Hants v Sussex (Southampton); Middx v Kent (Southgate); Northants v Warwicks. (Old Northamptonians); Somerset v Yorks. (North Perrott); Surrey v Notts. (Oxted).

13 – Derbys. v Yorks. (Chesterfield); Hants v Lancs. (Southampton); Leics. v Essex (Leicester); Northants v Durham (Oundle School); Notts. v Glam. (Worksop CC); Sussex v Worcs. (Hove); Warwicks. v Kent (Knowle & Dorridge).

20 – Durham v Derbys. (Boldon CC); Essex v Surrey (Chelmsford); Kent v Lancs. (Canterbury); Middx v Somerset (Harrow); Worcs. v Notts. (Worcester); Yorks. v Hants (Harrogate).

27 – Glam. v Warwicks. (Swansea); Hants v Derbys. (Southampton); Lancs. v Essex (Liverpool); Leics. v Sussex (Egerton Park); Somerset v Notts. (Glastonbury); Worcs. v Hants (Barnt Green); Yorks. v Kent (Todmorden).

28 – Northants v Middx (Northampton).

30 – Surrey v Leics. (The Oval).

JULY

4 – Essex v Worcs. (Chelmsford); Glam. v Durham (Swansea); Glos. v Warwicks. (Dowty Arle Court, Cheltenham); Kent v Notts. (Dartford); Middx v Surrey (Harrow); Northants v Hants (Northampton); Yorks. v Leics. (Bingley).

11 – Glam. v Derbys. (Ammanford); Glos. v Middx (Bristol); Lancs. v Yorks. (Manchester); Northants v Leics. (Northampton); Notts. v Hants (Collingham); Surrey v Durham (The Oval); Sussex v Kent (Horsham); Warwicks. v Somerset (Leamington Spa).

18–Derbys. v Surrey (Derby); Durham v Yorks. (Seaton Carew); Glos. v Hants (Bristol); Leics. v Somerset (Uppingham); Northants v Lancs. (Wellingborough School); Notts. v Middx (Southwell CC); Warwicks. v Essex (Nuneaton); Worcs. v Kent (Kidderminster).

25–Durham v Lancs. (Shildon CC); Essex v Hants (Colchester); Glam. v Somerset (Cardiff); Kent v Leics. (Folkestone); Middx v Worcs. (Harrow); Northants v Glos. (Bedford School); Surrey v Sussex (Banstead); Warwicks. v Derbys. (Moseley).

AUGUST

1–Essex v Yorks. (Southend); Kent v Hants (Maidstone); Lancs. v Sussex (Manchester); Notts. v Glos. (Nottingham High School); Somerset v Northants (Clevedon); Warwicks. v Worcs. (Birmingham).

2–Durham v Middx (Riverside Ground, Chester-le-Street); Surrey v Glam. (The Oval).

8–Durham v Somerset (Riverside Ground, Chester-le-Street); Glam. v Lancs. (Cardiff); Lancs. v Worcs. (Blackpool); Leics. v Derbys. (Kibworth); Middx v Essex (Uxbridge); Notts. v Warwicks. (Worksop College); Yorks. v Northants (Marske-by-Sea).

15–Glos. v Glam. (King's School, Gloucester); Hants v Durham (Southampton); Notts. v Leics. (Nottingham); Somerset v Essex (Taunton); Sussex v Middx (Hove); Warwicks. v Yorks. (Walmley); Worcs. v Northants (Worcester).

22–Essex v Glos. (Chelmsford); Kent v Glam. (Gore Court, Sittingbourne); Leics. v Lancs. (Hinckley); Somerset v Derbys. (Taunton); Surrey v Northants (Cheam); Warwicks. v Sussex (Studley); Worcs. v Yorks. (Old Hill).

23–Hants v Middx (Southampton).

29–Lancs. v Somerset (Northern, Crosby); Leics. v Middx (Leicester).

30–Derbys. v Northants (Derby); Durham v Worcs. (Sunderland CC); Glam. v Essex (Pontymister); Glos. v Sussex (Cheltenham CC); Hants v Warwicks. (Portsmouth); Yorks. v Surrey (Elland).

SEPTEMBER

7–Durham v Essex (Benwell Hill CC); Glos. v Lancs. (Bristol); Hants v Leics. (Southampton); Notts. v Northants (Nottingham); Sussex v Derbys. (Horsham); Warwicks. v Surrey (Stratford-upon-Avon); Worcs. v Glam. (Worcester).

12–Essex v Notts. (Ilford); Glos. v Somerset (Bristol); Kent v Northants (British Gas, Eltham); Middx v Derbys. (RAF Vine Lane, Uxbridge); Surrey v Lancs. (The Oval); Sussex v Yorks. (Hove).

†BAIN CLARKSON TROPHY, 1994

All matches are of one day's duration.

APRIL

21–Derbys. v Lancs. (Derby).

22–Derbys. v Leics. (Derby).

MAY

5–Essex v Northants (Newbury Park); Notts. v Durham (Nottingham).

6–Kent v Northants (Maidstone); Leics. v Yorks. (Leicester).

12–Leics. v Durham (Barwell); Somerset v Warwicks. (Taunton); Worcs. v Hants (Bromsgrove School); Yorks. v Lancs. (Bradford).

13–Essex v Middx (Wickford); MCC Young Cricketers v Kent (Southgate); Somerset v Glos. (Taunton); Yorks. v Durham (Leeds).

16–Hants v Somerset (Southampton).

19–Kent v Surrey (Maidstone); Lancs. v Notts. (Manchester); Leics. v Derbys. (Leicester); Northants v Essex (Northampton); Warwicks. v Glam. (Old Edwardians CC).

20–Lancs. v Leics. (Manchester); Sussex v Middx (Hove); Worcs. v Glam. (Worcester).

26–Essex v Kent (Colchester); Hants v Warwicks. (Portsmouth); Lancs. v Derbys. (Blackpool); Somerset v Worcs. (Taunton).

Glos. v Glam. (Bristol); Northants v Kent (Northampton); Surrey v MCC Young Cricketers (The Oval).

Hants v Glam. (Portsmouth).

JUNE

Glos. v Somerset (Bristol); Sussex v Essex (Hove); Yorks. v Notts. (Scarborough).

Kent v Sussex (Canterbury); MCC Young Cricketers v Northants (Slough); Surrey v Middx (The Oval); Worcs. v Somerset (Worcester).

MCC Young Cricketers v Essex (Slough); Middx v Kent (Uxbridge); Notts. v Yorks. (Worksop College).

Derbys. v Durham (Chesterfield); Glam. v Hants (Bridgend); Leics. v Notts. (Leicester); Sussex v MCC Young Cricketers (Haywards Heath).

Middx v MCC Young Cricketers (Uxbridge).

Derbys. v Yorks. (Chesterfield); Lancs. v Durham (Liverpool); Surrey v Northants (The Oval); Worcs. v Glos. (Worcester).

7–Essex v Sussex (Chelmsford); Hants v Glos. (Southampton); Surrey v Kent (The Oval).

1–Warwicks. v Glos. (Coventry & N. Warwicks.).

13–Durham v Derbys. (Philadelphia CC); Essex v Surrey (Wickford); Glos. v Worcs. (Bristol); Kent v Middx (Canterbury); Notts. v Lancs. (Nottingham); Somerset v Glam. (Taunton).

24–Durham v Notts. (Durham City CC); Glam. v Glos. (Swansea); Somerset v Hants (Taunton); Sussex v Surrey (Hove); Warwicks. v Worcs. (Leamington Spa); Yorks. v Derbys. (Castleford).

27–MCC Young Cricketers v Middx (Southgate).

30–Glam. v Warwicks. (Cardiff).

JULY

1–Essex v MCC Young Cricketers (Newbury Park); Northants v Middx (Old Northamptonians).

7–Derbys. v Notts. (Ilkeston); Glos. v Warwicks. (Dowty Arle Court, Cheltenham); MCC Young Cricketers v Sussex (Slough); Middx v Surrey (Harrow); Yorks. v Leics. (York).

8–Kent v Essex (Canterbury); Middx v Sussex (Harrow); Northants v Surrey (Tring); Worcs. v Warwicks. (Worcester).

14–Lancs. v Yorks. (Wigan); Notts. v Leics. (Sleaford CC); Sussex v Kent (Horsham); Warwicks. v Somerset (Aston Unity CC).

15–Hants v Worcs. (Southampton); Middx v Essex (Southgate); Northants v MCC Young Cricketers (Bedford Modern School).

21–Durham v Yorks. (Bishop Auckland); Glos. v Hants (Bristol); Leics. v Lancs. (Leicester); Northants v Sussex (Banbury CC); Notts. v Derbys. (Farnsfield CC).

22–Glam. v Worcs. (Bridgend); Surrey v Essex (The Oval); Warwicks. v Hants (Stratford-upon-Avon).

28–Durham v Lancs. (Norton CC); Glam. v Somerset (Panteg); Kent v MCC Young Cricketers (Gillingham); Middx v Northants (Harrow); Surrey v Sussex (Guildford).

29–Durham v Leics. (Durham School); MCC Young Cricketers v Surrey (Southgate); Sussex v Northants (Hove).

Semi-finals to be played on August 18 or 19.

Final to be played on September 5 (reserve day September 6).

ENGLAND IN AUSTRALIA, 1994-95

OCTOBER

25 Lilac Hill, Perth	†v ACB Chairman's XI	(1 day)
27 Perth	†v Western Australia	(1 day, d/n)
29 Perth	v Western Australia	(4 days)

NOVEMBER

4 Adelaide	v South Australia	(4 days)
9 Canberra	†v Prime Minister's XI	(1 day)
12 Hobart	v Australian XI (4 days)	

| 18 | Sydney | v New South Wales (4 days) |
| 25 | Brisbane | v AUSTRALIA (1st Test, 5 days) |

DECEMBER

2	Perth	†v Zimbabwe (WSC, 1 day, d/n)
4	Perth	†v Australia (WSC, 1 day)
6	Sydney	†v Australia (WSC, 1 day, d/n)
10	Adelaide	†v Zimbabwe (WSC, 1 day)
13	Melbourne	†v Australia (WSC, 1 day, d/n)
15	Sydney	†v Zimbabwe (WSC, 1 day, d/n)
17	Brisbane	v Queensland (4 days)
24	Melbourne	v AUSTRALIA (2nd Test, 5 days)

JANUARY

1	Sydney	v AUSTRALIA (3rd Test, 5 days)
7	Brisbane	†v Zimbabwe (WSC, 1 day)
8	Brisbane	†v Australia (WSC, 1 day)
10	TBA	†v Australian Cricket Academy (1 day)
13	Bowral	†v Sir Donald Bradman's Invitation XI (1 day)
15	Sydney	†World Series Cup 1st final (1 day, d/n)
17	Melbourne	†World Series Cup 2nd final (1 day, d/n)
19	Melbourne	†World Series Cup 3rd final (1 day, d/n)
21	TBA	v Victoria (3 days)
26	Adelaide	v AUSTRALIA (4th Test, 5 days)

FEBRUARY

| 3 | Perth | v AUSTRALIA (5th Test, 5 days) |

ANNIVERSARIES IN 1994

250 YEARS AGO

1744   Laws of Cricket codified by the London Club.
JUNE 18 First great match of which full scores have survived: Kent beat All England by one wicket at the Artillery Ground, Finsbury.

200 YEARS AGO

1794   Charterhouse v Winchester at Lord's, the first properly recorded schools match.

150 YEARS AGO

1844   First match between Canada and the United States.

100 YEARS AGO

1894   MAY 22 Start of first South African tour of England.
JUNE 18 Tom Richardson of Surrey took ten for 45 against Essex at The Oval.
SEPTEMBER 7 Birth of Vic Richardson at Unley, South Australia.
NOVEMBER 24 Birth of Herbert Sutcliffe at Summerbridge near Harrogate.

50 YEARS AGO

1944   APRIL 17 Death of J. T. Hearne at Chalfont St Giles, Buckinghamshire.
AUGUST 5 Maurice Turnbull killed in action near Montchamp, Normandy.
NOVEMBER 17 Death of A. C. MacLaren at Warfield Park, Berkshire.

27–Glos. v Glam. (Bristol); Northants v Kent (Northampton); Surrey v MCC Young Cricketers (The Oval).

31–Hants v Glam. (Portsmouth).

JUNE

2–Glos. v Somerset (Bristol); Sussex v Essex (Hove); Yorks. v Notts. (Scarborough).

3–Kent v Sussex (Canterbury); MCC Young Cricketers v Northants (Slough); Surrey v Middx (The Oval); Worcs. v Somerset (Worcester).

9–MCC Young Cricketers v Essex (Slough); Middx v Kent (Uxbridge); Notts. v Derbys. (Worksop College).

10–Derbys. v Durham (Chesterfield); Glam. v Hants (Bridgend); Leics. v Notts. (Leicester); Sussex v MCC Young Cricketers (Haywards Heath).

13–Middx v MCC Young Cricketers (Uxbridge).

16–Derbys. v Yorks. (Chesterfield); Lancs. v Durham (Liverpool); Surrey v Northants (The Oval); Worcs. v Glos. (Worcester).

17–Essex v Sussex (Chelmsford); Hants v Glos. (Southampton); Surrey v Kent (The Oval).

21–Warwicks. v Glos. (Coventry & N. Warwicks.).

23–Durham v Derbys. (Philadelphia CC); Essex v Surrey (Wickford); Glos. v Worcs. (Bristol); Kent v Middx (Canterbury); Notts. v Lancs. (Nottingham); Somerset v Glam. (Taunton).

24–Durham v Notts. (Durham City CC); Glam. v Glos. (Swansea); Somerset v Hants (Taunton); Sussex v Surrey (Hove); Warwicks. v Worcs. (Leamington Spa); Yorks. v Derbys. (Castleford).

27–MCC Young Cricketers v Middx (Southgate).

30–Glam. v Warwicks. (Cardiff).

JULY

1–Essex v MCC Young Cricketers (Newbury Park); Northants v Middx (Old Northamptonians).

7–Derbys. v Notts. (Ilkeston); Glos. v Warwicks. (Dowty Arle Court, Cheltenham); MCC Young Cricketers v Sussex (Slough); Middx v Surrey (Harrow); Yorks. v Leics. (York).

8–Kent v Essex (Canterbury); Middx v Sussex (Harrow); Northants v Surrey (Tring); Worcs. v Warwicks. (Worcester).

14–Lancs. v Yorks. (Wigan); Notts. v Leics. (Sleaford CC); Sussex v Kent (Horsham); Warwicks. v Somerset (Aston Unity CC).

15–Hants v Worcs. (Southampton); Middx v Essex (Southgate); Northants v MCC Young Cricketers (Bedford Modern School).

21–Durham v Yorks. (Bishop Auckland); Glos. v Hants (Bristol); Leics. v Lancs. (Leicester); Northants v Sussex (Banbury CC); Notts. v Derbys. (Farnsfield CC).

22–Glam. v Worcs. (Bridgend); Surrey v Essex (The Oval); Warwicks. v Hants (Stratford-upon-Avon).

28–Durham v Lancs. (Norton CC); Glam. v Somerset (Panteg); Kent v MCC Young Cricketers (Gillingham); Middx v Northants (Harrow); Surrey v Sussex (Guildford).

29–Durham v Leics. (Durham School); MCC Young Cricketers v Surrey (Southgate); Sussex v Northants (Hove).

Semi-finals to be played on August 18 or 19.

Final to be played on September 5 (reserve day September 6).

ENGLAND IN AUSTRALIA, 1994-95

OCTOBER		NOVEMBER	
25 Lilac Hill, Perth	†v ACB Chairman's XI (1 day)	4 Adelaide	v South Australia (4 days)
27 Perth	†v Western Australia (1 day, d/n)	9 Canberra	†v Prime Minister's XI (1 day)
29 Perth	v Western Australia (4 days)	12 Hobart	v Australian XI (4 days)

| 18 | Sydney | v New South Wales (4 days) |
| 25 | Brisbane | v AUSTRALIA (1st Test, 5 days) |

DECEMBER

2	Perth	†v Zimbabwe (WSC, 1 day, d/n)
4	Perth	†v Australia (WSC, 1 day)
6	Sydney	†v Australia (WSC, 1 day, d/n)
10	Adelaide	†v Zimbabwe (WSC, 1 day)
13	Melbourne	†v Australia (WSC, 1 day, d/n)
15	Sydney	†v Zimbabwe (WSC, 1 day, d/n)
17	Brisbane	v Queensland (4 days)
24	Melbourne	v AUSTRALIA (2nd Test, 5 days)

JANUARY

1	Sydney	v AUSTRALIA (3rd Test, 5 days)
7	Brisbane	†v Zimbabwe (WSC, 1 day)
8	Brisbane	†v Australia (WSC, 1 day)
10	TBA	†v Australian Cricket Academy (1 day)
13	Bowral	†v Sir Donald Bradman's Invitation XI (1 day)
15	Sydney	†World Series Cup 1st final (1 day, d/n)
17	Melbourne	†World Series Cup 2nd final (1 day, d/n)
19	Melbourne	†World Series Cup 3rd final (1 day, d/n)
21	TBA	v Victoria (3 days)
26	Adelaide	v AUSTRALIA (4th Test, 5 days)

FEBRUARY

| 3 | Perth | v AUSTRALIA (5th Test, 5 days) |

ANNIVERSARIES IN 1994

250 YEARS AGO

1744　Laws of Cricket codified by the London Club.
JUNE 18 First great match of which full scores have survived: Kent beat All England by one wicket at the Artillery Ground, Finsbury.

200 YEARS AGO

1794　Charterhouse v Winchester at Lord's, the first properly recorded schools match.

150 YEARS AGO

1844　First match between Canada and the United States.

100 YEARS AGO

1894　MAY 22 Start of first South African tour of England.
JUNE 18 Tom Richardson of Surrey took ten for 45 against Essex at The Oval.
SEPTEMBER 7 Birth of Vic Richardson at Unley, South Australia.
NOVEMBER 24 Birth of Herbert Sutcliffe at Summerbridge near Harrogate.

50 YEARS AGO

1944　APRIL 17 Death of J. T. Hearne at Chalfont St Giles, Buckinghamshire.
AUGUST 5 Maurice Turnbull killed in action near Montchamp, Normandy.
NOVEMBER 17 Death of A. C. MacLaren at Warfield Park, Berkshire.